lonely planet

Great Britain

Isabel Albiston, Oliver Berry, Joe Bindloss, Fionn Davenport, Belinda Dixon, Peter Dragicevich, Anthony Ham, Damian Harper, Anna Kaminski, Catherine Le Nevez, Andy Symington, Tasmin Waby, Kerry Walker, Luke Waterson, Neil Wilson, Barbara Woolsey

PLAN YOUR TRIP

KAMIRA/SHUTTERSTOCK ©

BOROUGH MARKET P144

SAM SPICER/SHUTTERSTOCK ©

ARRAN P870

ON THE ROAD

Contents

ON THE ROAD

HELEN HOTSON/SHUTTERSTOCK ©
PEMBROKESHIRE P675

Contents

COVID-19

We have re-checked every business in this book before publication to ensure that it is still open after the COVID-19 outbreak. However, the economic and social impacts of COVID-19 will continue to be felt long after the outbreak has been contained, and many businesses, services and events referenced in this guide may experience ongoing restrictions. Some businesses may be temporarily closed, have changed their opening hours and services, or require bookings; some unfortunately could have closed permanently. We suggest you check with venues before visiting for the latest information.

Right: View from Caerphilly Castle (p663)

WELCOME TO

Great Britain

As a born-and-bred Brit, I've explored more of Britain's footpaths, back lanes, byways and bridleways than anywhere else, and yet every new journey I take reveals something new and unexpected: a beach I've never walked, a view I've never photographed, a hill I've never climbed, a castle I've not explored, a legend I've not heard (more often than not, it's a pub where I've never drunk a pint). I've been exploring this little island for half a lifetime, and still only uncovered a handful of its secrets.

By Oliver Berry, Writer
@olivertomberry olivertomberry
For more about our writers, see p1056

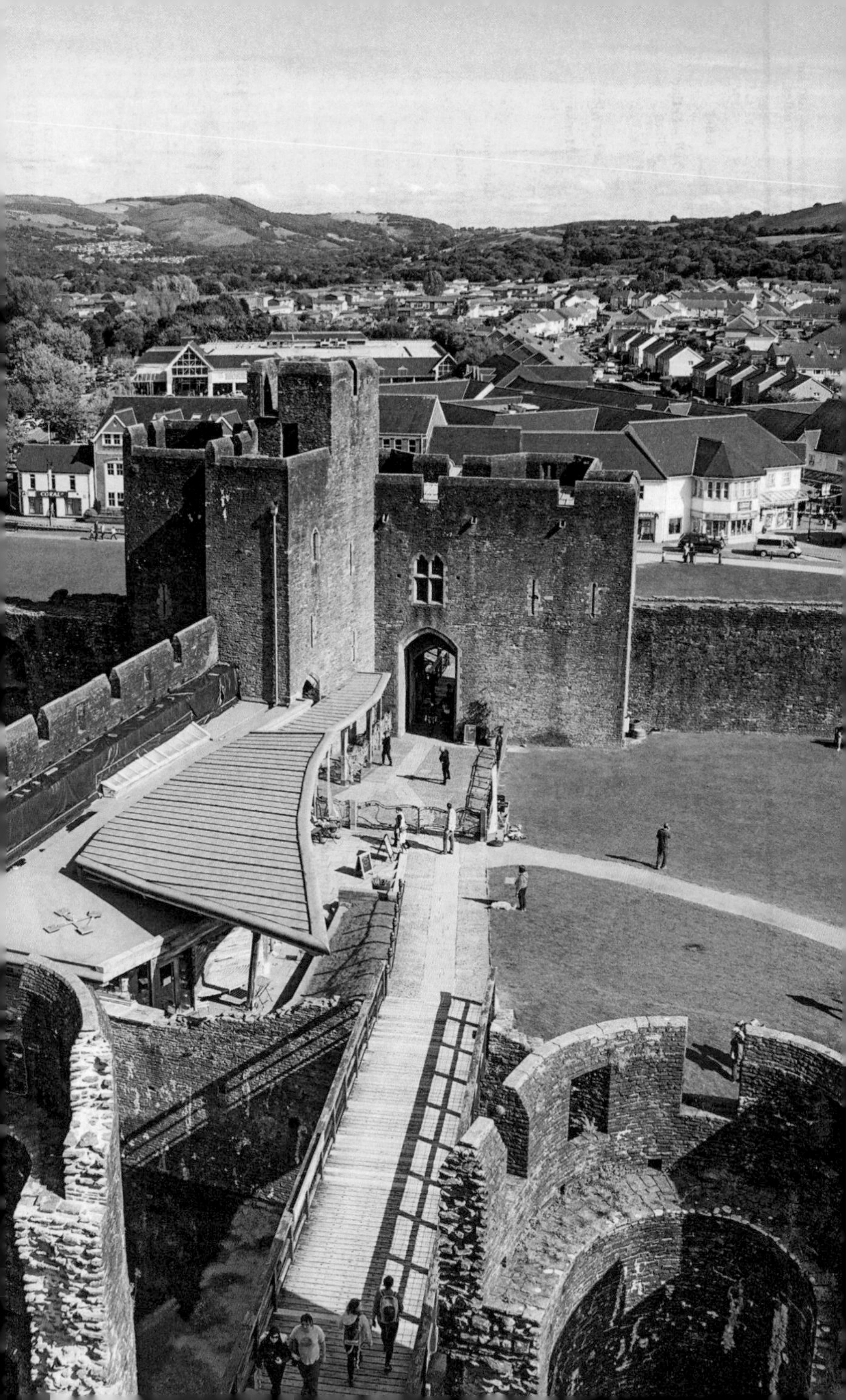

Great Britain

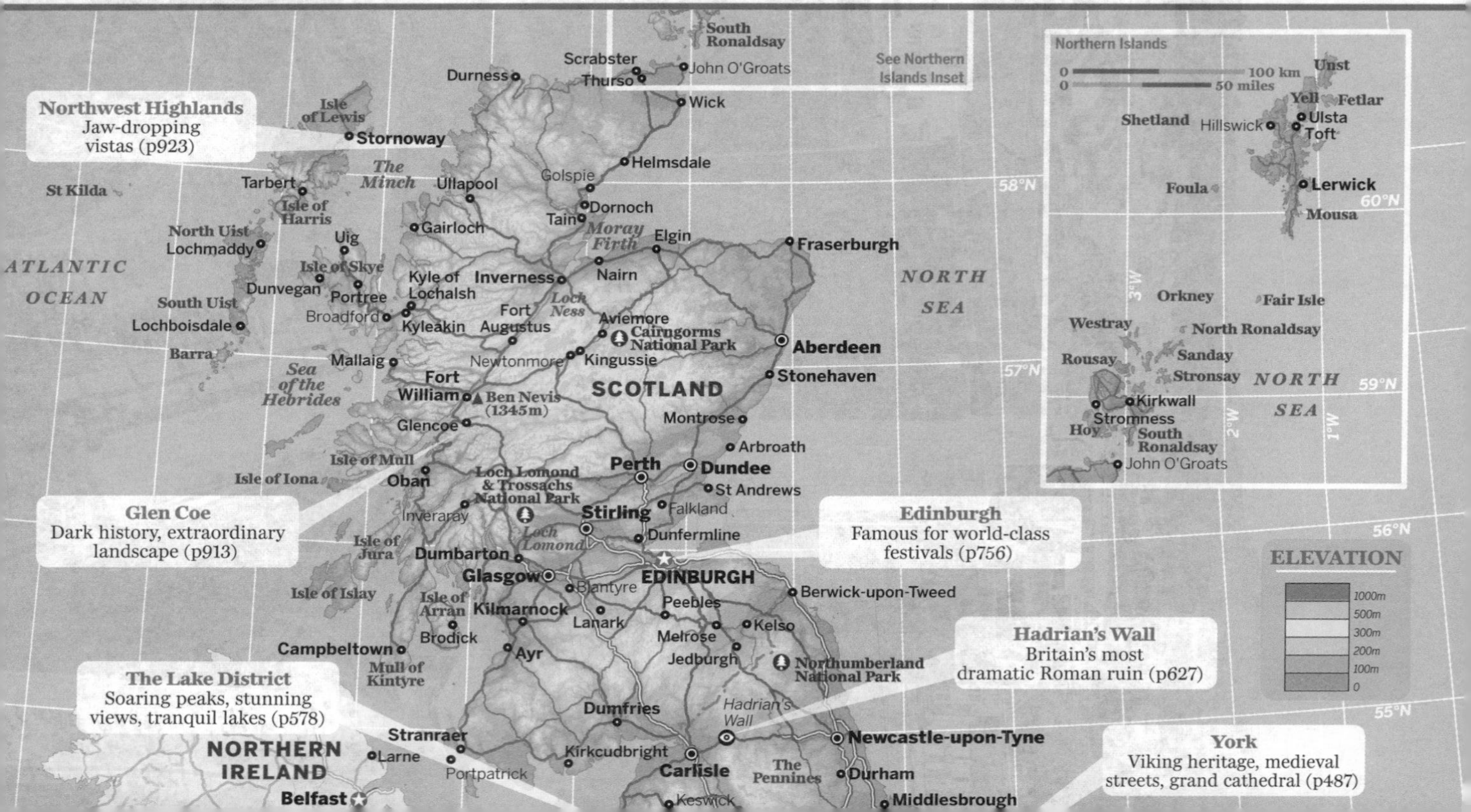

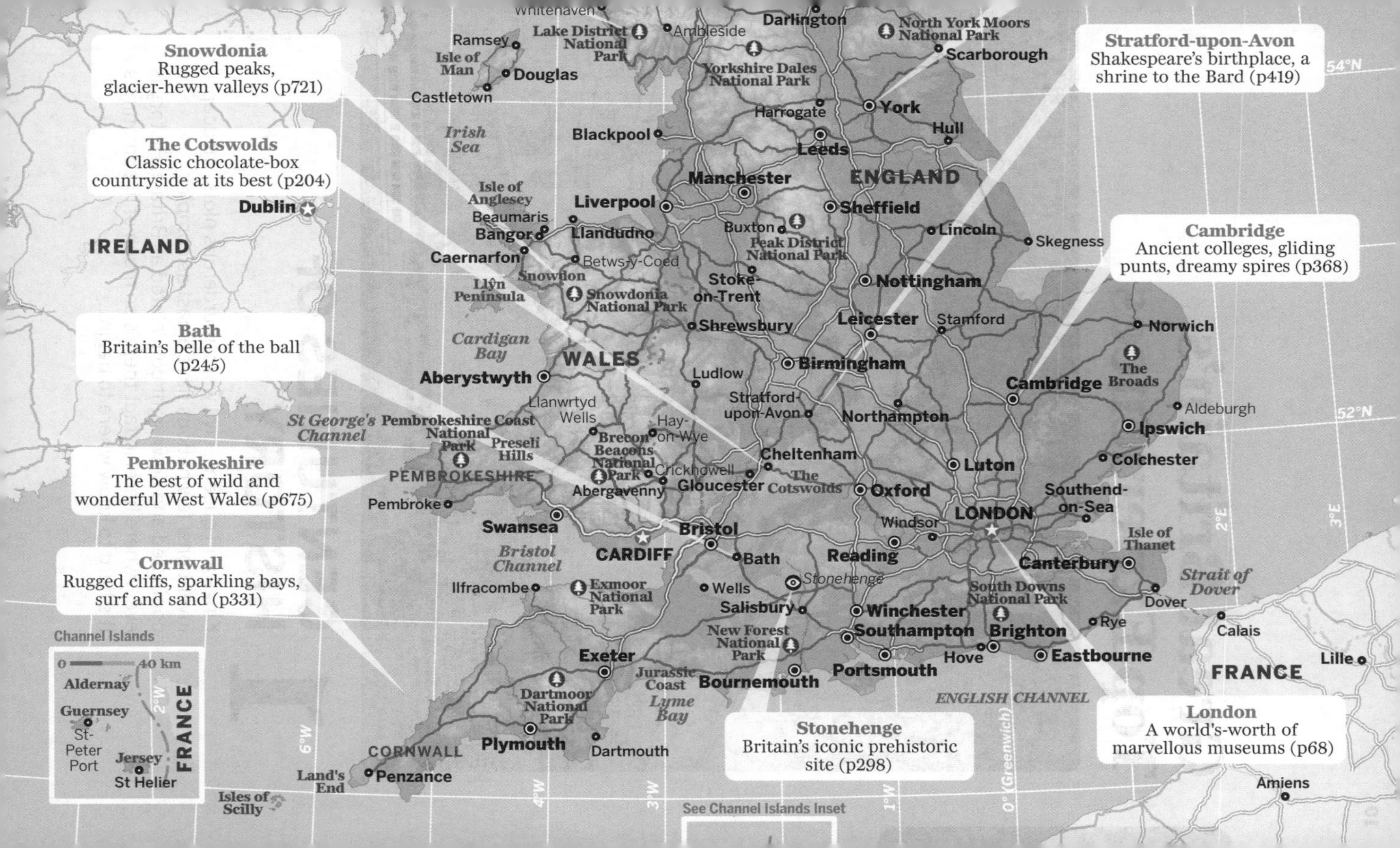
Snowdonia
Rugged peaks, glacier-hewn valleys (p721)
The Cotswolds
Classic chocolate-box countryside at its best (p204)
Bath
Britain's belle of the ball (p245)
Pembrokeshire
The best of wild and wonderful West Wales (p675)
Cornwall
Rugged cliffs, sparkling bays, surf and sand (p331)
Stratford-upon-Avon
Shakespeare's birthplace, a shrine to the Bard (p419)
Cambridge
Ancient colleges, gliding punts, dreamy spires (p368)
Stonehenge
Britain's iconic prehistoric site (p298)
London
A world's-worth of marvellous museums (p68)
IRELAND
Dublin
ENGLAND
WALES
FRANCE
LONDON
CARDIFF
Irish Sea
Cardigan Bay
St George's Channel
Bristol Channel
Lyme Bay
ENGLISH CHANNEL
Strait of Dover
Isle of Man
Ramsey
Douglas
Castletown
Whitehaven
Lake District National Park
Ambleside
Darlington
Yorkshire Dales National Park
North York Moors National Park
Scarborough
York
Harrogate
Hull
Leeds
Blackpool
Manchester
Liverpool
Sheffield
Isle of Anglesey
Beaumaris
Bangor
Llandudno
Caernarfon
Betws-y-Coed
Snowdon
Llŷn Peninsula
Snowdonia National Park
Buxton
Peak District National Park
Lincoln
Skegness
Stoke-on-Trent
Nottingham
Shrewsbury
Leicester
Stamford
Norwich
The Broads
Birmingham
Aberystwyth
Ludlow
Cambridge
Stratford-upon-Avon
Northampton
Aldeburgh
Ipswich
Llanwrtyd Wells
Hay-on-Wye
Pembrokeshire Coast National Park
Preseli Hills
Brecon Beacons National Park
Crickhowell
Abergavenny
Cheltenham
The Cotswolds
Gloucester
Oxford
Luton
Colchester
PEMBROKESHIRE
Pembroke
Swansea
Bristol
Bath
Windsor
Reading
Southend-on-Sea
Isle of Thanet
Canterbury
Dover
Ilfracombe
Exmoor National Park
Wells
Stonehenge
Salisbury
Winchester
South Downs National Park
Brighton
Rye
Calais
New Forest National Park
Southampton
Hove
Eastbourne
Lille
Exeter
Jurassic Coast
Bournemouth
Portsmouth
Dartmoor National Park
Plymouth
Dartmouth
CORNWALL
Penzance
Land's End
Isles of Scilly
Amiens
Channel Islands
0 40 km
Alderney
Guernsey
St-Peter Port
Jersey
St Helier
See Channel Islands Inset
54°N
52°N
2°E
3°E
6°W
4°W
3°W
2°W
1°W
0° (Greenwich)

Great Britain's Top Experiences

SAMOT/SHUTTERSTOCK ©

1 CENTURIES OF HISTORY

Kings and queens, civil wars, murderous plots, madcap inventions: few nations have a past as complex, conflicted and downright convoluted as Britain. History is everywhere here: in fact there's so much of it, sometimes it's hard to know where to begin...

KAMIRA/SHUTTERSTOCK ©

British Museum

For an overview of Britain's storied past, there's nowhere better than the British Museum – the nation's greatest repository of art, antiquities and artefacts (including plenty plundered from nations who'd quite like them back). The Rosetta Stone, the Sutton Hoo relics, the Parthenon sculptures – you'll find them all here, and so much more besides. p82

ROB BRUGGEMAN/SHUTTERSTOCK ©

CLAUDIO DIVIZIA/SHUTTERSTOCK ©

Canterbury Cathedral

The spiritual home of the Anglican Church and a place of worship for 15 centuries, Canterbury Cathedral dominates the local skyline. At its heart lies a 12th-century crime scene, the spot where Archbishop Thomas Becket was put to the sword. p156

Tower of London

Founded by William the Conqueror, the Tower of London has been standing watch over the capital for nearly 1000 years. It's been a fortress, a royal residence, a treasury, a mint, an arsenal and a prison. Today it's home to the Crown Jewels, protected by the red-coated Yeoman Warders (popularly known as Beefeaters) and a flock of fabled ravens. p90

PICMELODY/SHUTTERSTOCK ©

2 ANCIENT PAST

From stone circles to sprawling hill forts, Britain is littered with reminders of its ancient past. Stone Age tribes, Celts, Vikings, Romans, Angles and Saxons have all left their mark on the landscape; really, it's astonishing just how many of these remnants have survived.

OKSANA PERKINS/SHUTTERSTOCK ©

JENNYT/SHUTTERSTOCK ©

Stonehenge & Avebury

Britain's stone circles are a mysterious echo of its ancient past. Most famous, of course, is Stonehenge – the myth-laden ring on Salisbury Plain that's been drawing people to it for 5000 years – but there are many more, including the much larger one at nearby Avebury. p298

Hadrian's Wall

This magnificent barrier along the Anglo-Scottish border marked the outer edge of the Roman Empire. It's studded with forts, garrisons, towers and milecastles, many impressively preserved. p627

Skara Brae

Predating Stonehenge and the pyramids of Giza, Europe's best-preserved neolithic village gives a fascinating glimpse into the lives of ancient Britons. Amazingly, it was hidden under the sand until 1850. p954

3 WILD BRITAIN

Britain might be small, but it still has some surprisingly wild corners if you know where to look (and are willing to do a little bit of walking to discover them). The best places to experience Britain's wilder side are its national parks: a 15-strong collection of specially protected landscapes that encompass mountains, moors, valleys, coast, countryside and chalk downs. They offer a glimpse of a much older Britain where nature still holds sway.

Lake District National Park

William Wordsworth and his Romantic chums were the first to champion the charms of the Lake District, and it's easy to see what inspired them. This is England's hiking heartland: a place to walk the fells, soak up the scenery, then settle in for a post-hike pint in a centuries-old inn. p578

PAJOR PAWEL/SHUTTERSTOCK ©

ALEXEY FEDORENKO/SHUTTERSTOCK ©

The Cairngorms

For the classic Scottish vista – lochs, glens and lonely hills – the Cairngorms are hard to top. The UK's largest national park, it's also home to five of the six highest summits, and is a fantastic location for wildlife-spotting. p903

Snowdonia

Snowdonia is the essence of wild Wales: spiky mountains, glacier-gouged valleys, shining lakes. Mt Snowdon, the highest peak in Wales, is the main draw, but there's a wealth of lesser-known peaks where the crowds rarely venture. p721

4 CITY STYLE

FOTOKON/SHUTTERSTOCK ©

London to Liverpool, Bristol to Birmingham, Cardiff to Cambridge: Britain is primed for urban adventures. Every city has its own charms: historic architecture, buzzing nightlife, world-class museums, Michelin-starred restaurants. See as many as you can.

Bath

Founded by the Romans, Bath reached its heyday during the 18th century, when the cream of high society (including Jane Austen) turned it into a fashionable resort. The city's Georgian architecture is unparalleled, encompassing grand town houses and sweeping Palladian crescents. p245

Oxford

A seat of learning for nearly a millennium, Oxford is celebrated for its cloistered college quads and cobbled lanes. And while it's certainly still a place where archaic academic traditions endure, it's a lively, vibrant, modern city, too. p186

Edinburgh

Famous for its annual arts festival, Edinburgh (pictured) is worth visiting in any season. Wander the winding alleyways of the Old Town, delve into the history of the Scottish monarchy at Edinburgh Castle, or climb to the top of Arthur's Seat for the ultimate skyline view. p756

5 EPIC COASTLINE

With 18,000 nonstop kilometres of coastline, Britain boasts more beaches, bays, coves and clifftops than anywhere else in Europe (and that's not even including the islands). You could spend a lifetime exploring and still not see all of it.

TANIA SCOTT/SHUTTERSTOCK ©

PAOLO TROVO/SHUTTERSTOCK ©

TONY BAGGETT/SHUTTERSTOCK ©

Cornwall

Jutting out into the Atlantic, Britain's most southwesterly county is surrounded on three sides by sea. Awash with glorious beaches, it's the spiritual home of British surfing, and a perennially popular place. p331

Northwest Scotland

Highland drama unfurls as you drive the stunning coast road between Durness and Kyle of Lochalsh: deserted beaches, remote glens and the wild cliffs of Cape Wrath. p923

Pembrokeshire Coast

In the far west of Wales, Pembrokeshire's coastline forms part of a national park with natural arches, blowholes and sea stacks, as well as a hinterland of tranquil villages and secret waterways. p675

6 A GREEN & PLEASANT LAND

GORDON BELL/SHUTTERSTOCK ©

The Cotswolds

The Cotswolds is a postcard come to life: creeper-clad cottages, quaint churches and, of course, plenty of proper, old-fashioned pubs where you can sit down for a pint of ale and a ploughman's lunch. p204

COLIN WARD/SHUTTERSTOCK ©

The Yorkshire Dales

God's Own Country, the locals call it – and there's no doubt the hills and dales of Yorkshire are unfairly blessed in terms of scenery. Sometimes gentle, sometimes grand, they're made for road-tripping. p511

Britain's towns are captivating, but it's in the countryside that you'll find the nation's heart and soul. Patchwork fields, rolling valleys, sleepy villages: this is the Britain of your imagination.

Norfolk Broads

Many people overlook the east of England, but the Broads are worth a detour. A web of waterways winding through misty fens, this landscape has been inhabited since ancient times, and is best explored with a punt and a paddle. p396

7 CULTURE GALORE

Britain has always punched above its weight in the creative stakes. From the Bard to the Beatles, this imaginative island has left a lasting impression on the worlds of music, literature, theatre and art.

Shakespeare's Globe

For a sense of how Shakespeare's plays might have appeared to his own audience, this reconstruction of the Globe Theatre (the original burned down in 1613) is a must-visit. It's a cross between a working theatre and a living museum: you'll never hear the Bard the same way again. p97

COWARDLION/SHUTTERSTOCK ©

Dove Cottage

Wander round the tiny Lakeland cottage where William Wordsworth penned some of his most famous poems – then explore the landscape that inspired him. p586

Tate Modern

Housed inside a former power station, Tate Modern is the UK's leading venue to experience modern art. Look out for special commissions in the gargantuan Turbine Hall. p93

CHRISGHINDA/SHUTTERSTOCK ©

8 THE GREAT BRITISH MENU

KIT LEONG/SHUTTERSTOCK ©

Whether it's a Scottish haggis, a Cornish pasty, a Lancashire hotpot or a Welsh rarebit, every corner of the British Isles has its own unique tastes and flavours to experience – but there are a few classics you simply have to try.

A Pint in a Pub

What could be more British than settling down in the corner of a cosy old pub, pint in hand (just don't be surprised when the ale arrives warm – it's supposed to be that way). p135

Fish & Chips

It might not be wrapped up in yesterday's newspaper any more, but fish and chips remains Britain's favourite takeaway supper. Served plain or with lashings of salt, vinegar, ketchup or brown sauce – the choice is yours. p510

Whisky Tasting

There are distilleries dotted all over Scotland, but Speyside is the spot for connoisseurs. Some of the biggest names in whisky-making are found here, many of which offer guided tasting tours. p865

9 A CLASS ACT

Britain's magnificent collection of stately homes sum up all the pomp and pageantry of the nation's past. The sheer scale and luxury of these fabulous houses – and the unimaginable wealth required to build them – is quite something to behold.

FULCANELLI/SHUTTERSTOCK ©

LEONID ANDRONOV/SHUTTERSTOCK ©

LIANG MI/SHUTTERSTOCK ©

Blenheim Palace

The architectural audacity of the Duke of Marlborough's ancestral seat really has to be seen to be believed. Fittingly, Winston Churchill, that most British of heroes, was born here. p201

Castle Howard

Stately homes don't get more stately than Castle Howard, 15 miles northeast of York. This is the ancestral seat of the Earls of Carlisle. Highlights include a baroque great hall, a whimsical temple and vast, peacock-filled grounds. p495

Chatsworth

The Palace of the Peak, as it's often known, has been the home of the Earls and Dukes of Devonshire since the mid-16th century. The house is stunning, but it's the sprawling grounds (landscaped by Lancelot 'Capability' Brown) that steal the show. p472

10 LAND OF ISLANDS

LUCA QUADRIO/SHUTTERSTOCK ©

ANDREW ROLAND/SHUTTERSTOCK ©

Britain isn't really an island: it's an island of islands (more than 6000 of them, in fact). From accessible ones such as the Isle of Wight and the Isle of Man to the faraway shores of Shetland and Orkney, you could spend a lifetime island-hopping, and still never see them all.

Outer Hebrides

There aren't many regions of Britain that feel quite as far away from everything as the Outer Hebrides – a chain of 120-odd islands (five inhabited) where the wildlife outnumbers the people by a considerable margin. The ferry journey alone is worth the trip. p939

Isles of Scilly

Twenty-eight miles southwest of Land's End, this archipelago feels like stepping back 50 years into the past. Open-topped boats putter between the five inhabited islands, renowned for their golden beaches and tropical-blue waters. p359

Isle of Anglesey

Wales' largest island, Anglesey was once the home of the Druids, the high priests of ancient Britain, and it remains a stronghold of Celtic culture. Spot seabirds, visit ancient monuments or just stalk the coast. p749

Need to Know

For more information, see Survival Guide (p1021)

Currency

Pound sterling (£)

Language

English; also Welsh and Scottish Gaelic

Visas

Generally not needed for stays of up to six months. Britain is not a member of the Schengen Zone, so you will need to show your passport when arriving and leaving from a UK border point.

Money

ATMs and change bureaux are widely available, especially in cities and major towns.

Mobile Phones

Most modern mobiles/cellphones can operate on the UK's GSM 900/1800 network. 4G coverage is good in major towns and cities, but can be patchy in more rural areas. Local SIM cards are cheap and easily available.

Time

Greenwich Mean Time (UTC/GMT +00:00)

When to Go

High Season (Jun–Aug)

➡ Weather (usually) at its best. Accommodation rates peak – especially for August school holidays.

➡ Roads are busy, especially in seaside areas, national parks, and popular cities such as Oxford, Bath, Edinburgh and York.

Shoulder (Mar–May, Sep & Oct)

➡ Fewer crowds in popular areas.

➡ Weather often good. March to May has both sunny spells and sudden showers; September and October can be balmy.

➡ For outdoor activities in much of Scotland, May and September are the best months.

Low Season (Nov–Feb)

➡ Wet and cold. Snow falls in mountain areas, especially up north.

➡ Opening hours reduced October to Easter; some places shut for winter. Big-city sights (particularly in London) operate all year.

Useful Websites

BBC (www.bbc.co.uk) News and entertainment from the national broadcaster.

Visit Britain (www.visitbritain.com) Comprehensive official tourism website.

Lonely Planet (www.lonelyplanet.com/great-britain) Destination information, hotel bookings, traveller forum and more.

Traveline (www.traveline.info) Great portal site for public transport in all parts of Britain.

British Arts Festivals (www.artsfestivals.co.uk) Lists hundreds of festivals – art, literature, dance, folk and more.

Important Numbers

Area codes vary in length (eg 020 for London, 01225 for Bath). Omit the code if you're inside that area. Drop the initial 0 if you're calling from abroad.

Britain (& UK) country code	☎44
International access code	☎00
Emergency (police, fire, ambulance, mountain rescue, coastguard)	☎112 or ☎999

Exchange Rates

Australia	A$1	£0.55
Canada	C$1	£0.58
Europe	€1	£0.89
Japan	¥100	£0.66
New Zealand	NZ$1	£0.51
US	US$1	£0.72

For current exchange rates, see www.xe.com.

Daily Costs

Budget: Less than £55

- Dorm beds: £15–30
- Cheap meals in cafes and pubs: £8–12
- Long-distance coach: £15–40 (200 miles)

Midrange: £55–120

- Double room in midrange hotel or B&B: £65–130 (London £100–200)
- Main course in midrange restaurant: £10–20
- Long-distance train: £20–80 (200 miles)

Top end: More than £120

- Four-star hotel room: from £130 (London from £200)
- Three-course meal in a good restaurant: around £40
- Car rental per day: from £35

Opening Hours

Opening hours may vary throughout the year, especially in rural areas where many places have shorter hours or close completely from October or November to March or April.

Banks 9.30am–4pm or 5pm Monday to Friday; some open 9.30am–1pm Saturday

Pubs and bars Noon–11pm Monday to Saturday (many till midnight or 1am Friday and Saturday, especially in Scotland) and 12.30–11pm Sunday

Restaurants Lunch noon–3pm, dinner 6–9pm or 10pm (or later in cities)

Shops 9am–5.30pm (or to 6pm in cities) Monday to Saturday, and often 11am–5pm Sunday; big-city convenience stores open 24/7

Arriving in Great Britain

Heathrow Airport (London) Trains, the Tube and buses run to central London from around 5am to midnight. The Heathrow Express is fastest (£25, 15 minutes to London Paddington). Standard TfL trains (£10.90, 28 minutes) are only marginally slower; the Tube is cheapest (£6, 45 to 60 minutes). Taxis cost from £50 to £100 (more at peak hours).

Gatwick Airport (London) Gatwick Express trains (£17.80 to £19.90) run to London Victoria; standard services (around £12) are slower and run less frequently. Hourly buses run 24 hours (from £9). Taxis cost from £100 (more during peak times).

St Pancras International Station (Central London) Eurostar trains from Paris or Brussels arrive here, with connections to many Underground lines.

Victoria Coach Station (Central London) Intercity coaches and buses from Europe arrive here.

Getting Around

Transport in Britain can be expensive compared to continental Europe; bus and rail services are sparse in the more remote parts of the country. For timetables, check out www.traveline.info. Tourist offices can provide maps and information.

Car Useful for travelling at your own pace, or for visiting regions with minimal public transport. Cars can be hired in every town.

Train Relatively expensive, with extensive coverage and frequent departures throughout most of the country.

Bus Cheaper and slower than trains, but useful in more remote regions.

For much more on **getting around**, see p1029

First Time Great Britain

For more information, see Survival Guide (p1021)

Checklist

➡ Check the validity of your passport

➡ Check visa or entry requirements which may have changed post-Brexit

➡ Make advance bookings (sights, accommodation, theatre tickets, travel)

➡ Inform your credit-/debit-card company of your trip

➡ Organise travel insurance

➡ Check mobile (cell) phone compatibility

➡ Check rental car requirements

➡ Check airline baggage restrictions

➡ If carrying restricted items (eg liquids) in hold luggage, put them in a clear plastic bag

What to Pack

➡ Electrical plug adaptor

➡ Umbrella – because the rumours about the weather are true

➡ Lightweight waterproof jacket – because sometimes the umbrella is not enough

➡ Comfortable walking shoes – Britain's towns and countryside are best explored on foot

Top Tips for Your Trip

➡ At London airports, tickets for express trains into central London are available in the baggage arrivals hall – but there are often standard services that are much cheaper and only marginally slower. Buying tickets online in advance secures the cheapest fares.

➡ The easiest way to get currency is from an ATM (cash machine), but be aware that your bank may charge a transaction fee, and exchange rates are generally quite poor.

➡ If staying more than a few days in London, get an Oyster Card, which offers the cheapest fares on public transport.

➡ Pickpockets and hustlers lurk in crowded tourist areas, especially in London. No need to be paranoid, but do be on your guard.

➡ Britain's electrical plugs are unlike those in the rest of Europe (they have three rectangular pins rather than two round ones), so bring a UK-specific plug adaptor, or buy one when you arrive.

What to Wear

A rain jacket is essential, as is a small backpack to carry it in when the sun comes out. In summer you'll need sunscreen and an umbrella; you're bound to use both – possibly on the same day.

For sightseeing, comfortable shoes can make or break a trip. If you plan to enjoy Britain's great outdoors, suitable hiking gear is required in higher or wilder areas, but not for casual strolls in the countryside.

Casual clothes are fine for most pubs, bars and restaurants, although smarter dress is encouraged for more upmarket establishments.

Sleeping

Book accommodation in advance, especially in holiday areas and on islands. Easter, summer and school holidays are particularly busy. Book at least two months ahead for July and August.

B&Bs These small, family-run houses generally provide good value. More luxurious versions are more like boutique hotels.

Hotels British hotels range from several rooms above a pub to restored country houses, with a commensurate range in rates.

Hostels There are plenty of institutional and independent hostels, many housed in rustic or historic buildings.

Money

ATMs and change bureaux are widely available, especially in cities and major towns. Many foreign bank cards can be used to withdraw cash, but there's usually a transaction fee and exchange rates can be poor. Most ATMs only dispense £10 and £20 notes.

Bargaining

A bit of mild haggling is acceptable at flea markets and antique shops, but everywhere else you're expected to pay the advertised price.

Tipping

Restaurants Not obligatory, but around 10% in restaurants and cafes is the norm. Tips may be added to your bill as a 'service charge'.

Pubs and bars Unless you're eating and receive table service, you don't usually need to tip staff in bars or pubs.

Taxis Around 10%, or round up to the nearest pound, especially in London.

TUPUNGATO/SHUTTERSTOCK ©

A pub in Notting Hill, London (p68)

Etiquette

Manners The British have a reputation for being polite, and good manners are important in most situations. When asking directions, 'Excuse me, can you tell me the way to...' is a better tactic than 'Hey, where's...'

Queues In Britain, queuing ('standing in line' to Americans) is sacrosanct. Any attempt to 'jump the queue' will result in an outburst of tutting, hard stares and occasionally confrontation.

Escalators If you take an escalator or a moving walkway (especially at Tube stations in London), be sure to stand on the right, so folks in a hurry can pass on the left.

Eating

Booking restaurant tables in advance is usually advisable, especially in cities and popular tourist areas. You might not have to book in pubs and cafes, but it's always worth calling ahead to make sure.

Restaurants Britain has a wide range of restaurants, from top-end fine-dining temples to ubiquitous national chains. Small, independent places tend to have the most character.

Pubs Many pubs serve meals these days, especially 'gastropubs', which are as renowned for their food as for their beer.

Cafes For light lunches, all-day breakfasts and afternoon tea and cake, seek out the nearest cafe.

What's New

This has been a tumultuous few years for Britain: the epoch-changing decision to leave the European Union (EU), coupled with seismic political shifts, a global pandemic and a slowly fracturing Union has left Great Britain pondering its future. Are there sunlit uplands ahead – or storm clouds? Only time will tell.

A Greener Britain

Several recent reports have showed that Britain's wildlife and natural environment is suffering, and there has been widespread disquiet about the felling of ancient woodland during the construction of Britain's controversial high-speed train line, HS2. But it's not all doom and gloom – there's a growing movement to 'rewild' areas of landscape, returning cultivated or industrial land to its natural state to help encourage wildlife to return (in some cases, even reintroducing lost species such as beavers). Green issues are gradually moving up the agenda – bike lanes are springing up everywhere, habitats are being restored, and the world's largest wind farms are rising off the coast of Scotland and northern England to help the UK transition towards a cleaner, greener future.

Trail Finding

When the **England Coast Path** (www.nationaltrail.co.uk) is officially opened in 2021, it will offer walkers a nonstop route around England's edge – and will also become the world's longest continuous coastal trail. The new **Great Trossachs Path** (www.lochlomond-trossachs.org) runs for 30 miles between Callander and Loch Lomond, while **Loch Ness 360º** (www.lochness360.com) covers 80 miles around the circumference of Loch Ness, and Wales' **Coastal Way** opens up 180 spectacular miles of the Pembrokeshire coastline.

The Legacy of Empire

In the wake of the Black Lives Matter movement, many big British institutions have been asking themselves uncomfortable questions. Some of the nation's most prized

LOCAL KNOWLEDGE

WHAT'S HAPPENING IN GREAT BRITAIN

Oliver Berry, Lonely Planet writer

Britain finds itself a nation divided. Arguments over Brexit, trade deals, the fallout from Covid-19 and the diverging political directions of the devolved nations have raised questions about whether the centuries-old Union – which has glued the nation together since 1707 – may be in the process of breaking up.

However, big issues like these have encouraged the nation to take a long, hard look at itself: about the legacy of its colonial past, its place in the world, and most importantly the kind of country it wants to be in the years ahead. There's a growing sense of green consciousness, for example: offshore wind farms are springing up around the coast, rewilding programs are restoring areas of landscape, and the nationwide lockdown in early 2020 encouraged a spike in interest in outdoor activities and the natural world.

One thing's for sure – as Britain exits the EU after 47 years, this is a nation headed in a new (and uncertain) direction. There may be bumps in the road ahead, but in the meantime, Brits will simply do what they know best: keep calm and carry on.

exhibits, from the Elgin Marbles to ancient Egyptian artefacts, were acquired long before terms like cultural appropriation and white privilege were even dreamt of – but does this justify the forceful removal of such ancient treasures, especially when the nations from whence they came might now want them back? Accordingly, you may well encounter rejigged exhibits at museums and galleries – the Wellcome Collection (p112) is a great example.

Drink Up

Britain's long love affair with booze shows no sign of slowing down. Craft distilleries and brewers are popping up all over the place. At Plymouth Gin (p321) you can mix up your own boutique gin; at the Lakes Distillery (p594) you can taste one of England's only whiskies; while the Macallan Distillery (p865) in Dufftown holds up the best of Scotland's distilling traditions.

Wild Swimming

Britain's rivers, lochs, lakes and beaches are awash with swimmers these days, no matter the season or weather. If you prefer something less wild, there are lidos galore to explore – from Bristol to Brighton and Bath. Buxton's bubbling thermal springs (p478) have a flashy new heritage centre and spa incorporating the original Victorian baths, while Penzance's Jubilee Pool (p348) now has a geothermally heated section.

Windermere Jetty Museum

After years of delay, Windermere's vintage boat museum (p578) is finally open. A delightful collection of vintage steam yachts and lake boats is on display, two of which offer cruises onto Windermere. Toot-toot!

New Sutton Hoo

England's most precious Anglo-Saxon hoard (p386) has been revamped, with a full-sized sculpture of the burial ship, new interactive exhibits and a striking viewing tower.

Britain's First Vegan Hotel

There are now thought to be some two million vegans and plant-based eaters in Britain these days. They'll be glad to hear about the opening of Britain's very first vegan hotel, the lovely Saorsa 1875 (p911) in Pitlochry. More adventurous omnivores might like to try Grub Kitchen (p677) – the UK's only restaurant devoted to edible insects.

Sheep Trekking in the Brecon Beacons

For the ultimate Welsh walk, how about taking a sheep for a stroll? Jacob Sheep Trekking (p700) makes it possible, and there are few more authentic ways to experience the Brecon Beacons.

In the Footsteps of Peter Pan

A new childhood literacy centre has opened in Moat Brae (p829) in Dumfries – the house and garden that inspired JM Barrie to write *Peter Pan*.

LISTEN, WATCH & FOLLOW

For inspiration and up-to-date news, visit www.lonelyplanet.com/great-britain/articles.

BBC (www.bbc.co.uk) The national broadcaster has an amazing archive of TV, radio and podcasts (follow @BBCBreaking for news).

Ordnance Survey (www.ordnancesurvey.co.uk) Maps and routes from the UK's official cartographer.

Today in Focus A well-rounded current affairs podcast courtesy of *The Guardian* newspaper.

@ThisisPartridge (Twitter) Alan Partridge (aka comedian Steve Coogan) is a British institution – for all the wrong reasons.

@Banksy (Instagram) Britain's beloved artist-provocateur posts his latest work on Insta.

FAST FACTS

Food trend Local sourcing

Miles of coastline 11,073

Number of pubs Approx 39,000

Population 66.8 million

population per sq km

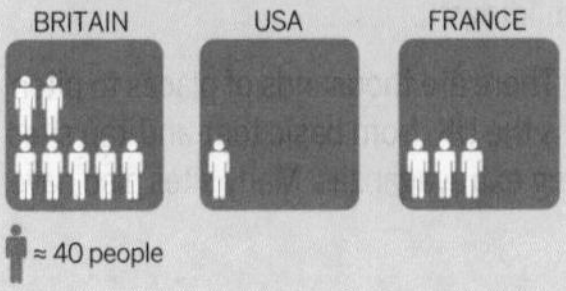

Accommodation

Find more accommodation reviews throughout the On the Road chapters (from p63)

Accommodation Types

B&Bs These small guesthouses range from basic family-run affairs to luxurious places that feel more like boutique hotels. Most have en-suite bathrooms and breakfast is nearly always included.

Hotels British hotels range from half a dozen rooms above a pub to restored country houses and castles, with a commensurate range in rates. Breakfast is often extra.

Pubs and inns Many pubs offer lodging, either above the pub or in a separate annexe. Rooms can be small, and sometimes noisy. Breakfast is generally included in rates.

Hostels There's a good choice of both institutional and independent hostels, many in rustic and/or historic buildings.

Camping There are thousands of places to pitch a tent across the UK, from basic tent-and-tap sites to glamping extravaganzas. Many sites also have separate areas for caravans, camper vans and motorhomes.

Cottages and self-catering For extended stays, there is a huge range of cottages and holiday homes; prices are at a premium during the summer and holiday periods.

University accommodation In many cities, universities rent out rooms at halls of residence during the holidays.

PRICE RANGES

The following price ranges refer to a double room with private bathroom in high season. Hotels in London are more expensive than the rest of the country, so have different price ranges. Prices in shoulder and low seasons are sometimes cheaper. Booking online often secures a discount.

Category	London	Elsewhere
£	less than £100	less than £65
££	£100–£200	£65–£130
£££	more than £200	more than £130

Best Places to Stay

Best on a Budget

Sticking to a budget while travelling round Britain can be a challenge. Local B&Bs, private rooms in hostels and the occasional carefully chosen hotel can all be part of the mix. The big cities – in particular London – can be especially tough for budgeteers, but with pre-planning you should be able to dig up somewhere to stay on the cheap(ish).

➡ Qbic (p122), London

➡ Tune Hotel (p560), Liverpool

➡ NQ1 Manchester (p546), Manchester

➡ Igloo Hybrid Hostel (p447), Nottinghamshire

➡ Deepdale Backpackers & Camping (p399), Burnham Deepdale

➡ Hop Garden (p661), Monmouthshire

Best for Families

There's a huge range of family-friendly accommodation to choose from, from vintage caravans to campsites. For the best value, self-catering cottages are a tempting option, especially if you don't mind staying in one area. Glamping is a big trend, with many sites specially geared towards families, with kids' activities and outdoor pursuits on hand.

- Vintage Vardos (p329), North Devon
- Teddy's Farm (p277), New Forest
- Warwick Castle Accommodation (p417), Warwick
- Vintage Vacations (p281), Isle of Wight
- Living Room Treehouses (p707), Machynlleth
- Eco Bells Glamping (p937), Skye

Best for Solo Travellers

The best option for solo travellers is nearly always the local hostel, where you can choose a dorm bed or a private room, and get to know other travellers. Some B&Bs offer single rooms, while others offer double rooms at a reduced rate. Hotels (apart from chains) rarely offer solo discounts.

- Kipps Brighton (p180), Brighton
- Generator London (p120), London
- Cambridge YHA (p376), Cambridge
- Keswick YHA (p594), Keswick
- Iona Hostel (p882), Iona
- Glasgow SYHA (p814), Glasgow

Best British Pubs & Inns

Britain's pubs, coaching inns and rural hostelries have provided shelter for weary travellers for centuries, and staying in one is a quintessentially British experience – so long as you don't mind awkward room shapes and low-hanging beams. Breakfast is usually included too.

- Drunken Duck (p589), Lake District
- Swan at Lavenham (p386), Suffolk
- Sign of the Angel (p301), Wiltshire
- Lord Crewe Arms (p629), Hadrian's Wall
- Bear (p696), Crickhowell
- Applecross Inn (p931), Northwest Scotland

Booking

Booking accommodation in advance is recommended, especially in popular holiday areas and on islands (where options are

ANDY GLENN/SHUTTERSTOCK ©

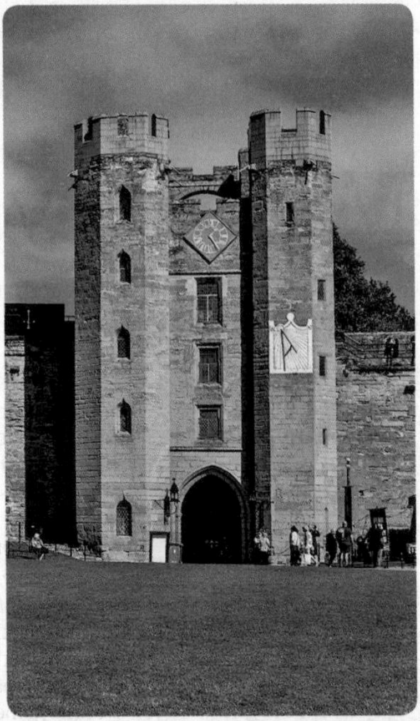

Warwick Castle (p417)

often limited). Easter, summer and school holidays (including half-terms) are particularly busy. Book several months ahead for July and August.

Lonely Planet (www.lonelyplanet.com/great-britain/hotels) Find independent reviews, as well as recommendations on the best places to stay – and then book them online.

Canopy & Stars (www.canopyandstars.co.uk) A huge selection of quirky camping and glamping locations, from shepherd's huts to treetop cabins.

Landmark Trust (www.landmarktrust.org.uk) Unusual heritage properties, many of which are notable for their architectural importance.

Stilwell's (www.cottagesdirect.co.uk) A good resource if you're looking for a self-catering cottage.

Sugar & Loaf (www.sugarandloaf.com) An enticing selection of luxurious self-catering picks across Wales.

Cottages & Castles (www.cottages-and-castles.co.uk) Intriguing places to stay in all corners of Scotland.

Month by Month

TOP EVENTS

Glastonbury Festival, June

Trooping the Colour, June

Edinburgh International Festival and Fringe, August

Braemar Gathering, September

Guy Fawkes Night, November

January

January is midwinter in Britain. Festivals and events to brighten the mood are thin on the ground, but luckily some include fire – lots of it.

London Parade

A ray of light in the gloom, the New Year's Day Parade in London (www.londonparade.co.uk) is one of the biggest events of its kind in the world, featuring marching bands, street performers, classic cars, floats and displays winding their way through the streets.

Up Helly Aa

Half of Shetland dresses up with horned helmets and battleaxes in this spectacular re-enactment of a Viking fire festival, with a torchlit procession leading the burning of a full-size Viking longship. (p959)

Celtic Connections

Glasgow plays host to a celebration of Celtic music, dance and culture (www.celticconnections.com), with participants from all over the globe.

February

Britain can be scenic under snow and sunshine, or more likely grey and gloomy under dark skies. Hang in there...

Jorvik Viking Festival

The ancient Viking capital of York becomes home once again to invaders and horned helmets galore, with the intriguing addition of longship races. (p491)

Fort William Mountain Festival

Britain's capital of the outdoors celebrates the peak of the winter season with ski workshops, mountaineering films and talks by famous climbers (www.mountainfestival.co.uk).

March

Spring finally arrives. There's a hint of better weather, and some classic sporting fixtures grace the calendar. Many locals stay hunkered down at home, though, so hotels offer special rates.

Six Nations Rugby Championship

The highlight of the rugby calendar (www.sixnationsrugby.com) runs from late January to March, with the home nations playing at London's Twickenham, Edinburgh's Murrayfield and Cardiff's Principality stadiums.

University Boat Race

Annual race down the River Thames in London between the rowing teams from Cambridge and Oxford universities; an institution since 1829 that still enthrals the country. (p119)

April

The weather slowly improves, with warmer and drier days bringing out spring blossoms. Attractions that close

for the low season open around the middle of the month or at Easter.

Grand National

On the first Saturday of the month half the country has a flutter on the highlight of the three-day horse race meeting at Aintree (http://aintree.thejockeyclub.co.uk) – a steeplechase with a testing course and notoriously high jumps.

London Marathon

More than 35,000 runners take to the streets; superfit athletes cover the 26.2 miles in just over two hours, while others dress up in daft costumes and take considerably longer (www.virginmoneylondonmarathon.com).

Beltane

Thousands of revellers climb Edinburgh's Calton Hill for this modern revival of a pagan fire festival (www.beltane.org) marking the end of winter.

Spirit of Speyside

Based in Dufftown, a Scottish festival of whisky, food and music, with five days of art, cooking, distillery tours and outdoor activities. (p866)

May

The weather is usually good, with more events to enjoy. There are two public holidays this month (the first and last Mondays) so traffic is very busy over the corresponding long weekends.

FA Cup Final

Grand finale of the football (soccer) season for over a century. Teams from across England battle it out over the winter months, culminating in this heady spectacle at Wembley Stadium – the home of English football.

Chelsea Flower Show

The Royal Horticultural Society flower show at Chelsea is the highlight of the British gardener's year. (p119)

Hay Festival

The ever-expanding 'Woodstock of the mind' brings an intellectual influx to booktown Hay-on-Wye. (p690)

Glyndebourne

Famous festival of world-class opera in the pastoral surroundings of East Sussex, running until the end of summer (www.glyndebourne.com).

June

Now it's almost summer. You can tell because this month sees the music-festival season kick off properly, while sporting events fill the calendar.

Derby Week

Horse racing, people watching and clothes spotting are on the agenda at this week-long meeting in Epsom, Surrey (www.epsomderby.co.uk).

Cotswolds Olimpicks

Welly-wanging, pole-climbing and shin-kicking are the key disciplines at this traditional Gloucestershire sports day, held every year since 1612. (p214)

Trooping the Colour

Military bands and bear-skinned grenadiers march down London's Whitehall in this martial pageant to mark the monarch's birthday. (p119)

Royal Ascot

It's hard to tell which matters more, the fashion or the fillies, at this highlight of the horse-racing year in Berkshire. (p229)

Wimbledon Tennis

The world's best-known tennis tournament, attracting all the big names, while crowds cheer and eat tonnes of strawberries and cream. (p143)

Glastonbury

One of Britain's favourite pop and rock gatherings is invariably muddy, and still a rite of passage for every self-respecting British music fan. (p260)

Pride

Highlight of the gay and lesbian calendar, this technicolour street parade heads through London's West End. (p119)

July

Proper summer. Festivals every week. School summer breaks begin, so there's a holiday tingle in the air, dulled only by busy roads on Fridays, because everyone's going somewhere for the weekend.

Henley Royal Regatta

Boats of every description take to the water for Henley's upper-crust river jamboree. (p230)

TRNSMT

This new Glasgow music festival, the spiritual successor to the long-running T in the Park, has booked major names including Radiohead, London Grammar and The Killers. (p810)

Great Yorkshire Show

Harrogate plays host to one of Britain's largest county shows. This is the place for Yorkshire grit, Yorkshire tykes, Yorkshire puddings, Yorkshire beef… (p498)

Latitude

Relaxed, family-friendly festival in the seaside town of Southwold, with theatre, cabaret, art and literature, plus top names from the alternative-music scene. (p390)

International Musical Eisteddfod

Festival of international folk music at Llangollen, with eclectic fringe and big-name evening concerts. (p719)

Royal Welsh Show

Prize bullocks and local produce at this national farm and livestock event in Builth Wells. (p704)

Cowes Week

Britain's biggest yachting spectacular on the choppy seas around the Isle of Wight. (p279)

Womad

Roots and world music take centre stage at this festival (www.womad.org) in a country park in the south Cotswolds.

All Points East

Held in Victoria Park, this young music festival (www.allpointseastfestival.com) has become one of the capital's key summer parties, attracting Tame Impala, Massive Attack, Thom Yorke, The Strokes and the Chemical Brothers in recent years.

August

Schools and colleges are closed, parliament is in recess, the sun is shining (hopefully), most people go away for a week or two, and the nation is in holiday mood.

Edinburgh Festivals

Edinburgh's most famous August happenings are the International Festival and Fringe, but this month the city also has an event for anything you care to name – books, art, theatre, music, comedy, marching bands…(www.edinburghfestivals.co.uk).

Camp Bestival

Quirky music festival (www.campbestival.net) on Dorset's Lulworth estate, with a different fancy-dress theme every year.

National Eisteddfod of Wales

The largest celebration of native Welsh culture, steeped in history, pageantry and pomp (www.eisteddfod.cymru); held at various venues around the country.

Brecon Fringe Festival

All musical tastes are catered for at this arts festival in the charming Mid-Wales town of Brecon. (p698)

World Bog Snorkelling Championships

Only in Britain – competitors, many in fancy dress, don snorkels and flippers for a swimming race along a muddy ditch in the middle of a peat bog (www.green-events.co.uk; check out some of their other madcap events).

Green Man Festival

One of Wales' best music festivals, held in the shadow of the beautiful Black Mountains, Green Man favours a more alternative line-up, with offbeat folk, country, world and Americana often taking centre stage. (p696)

Notting Hill Carnival

London's famous multicultural Caribbean-style street carnival in the district of Notting Hill. Steel drums, dancers, outrageous costumes. (p119)

September

The first week of September is still holiday time, but then schools reopen, traffic returns to

normal, and the summer party's over for another year. Ironically, the weather's often better than in August, now everyone's back at work.

Braemar Gathering

The biggest Highland Games in the Scottish calendar, traditionally attended by members of the Royal Family. Highland dancing, caber tossing and bagpipe playing – and a brand-new Highland Games Centre to visit too. (p909)

Ludlow Food Festival

A great foodie festival in a great foodie town. (p443)

Great North Run

Tyneside plays host to one of the biggest half marathons in the world (www.greatrun.org/great-north-run), with the greatest number of runners in any race at this distance.

Abergavenny Food Festival

The mother of all epicurean festivals and the champion of Wales' burgeoning food scene. (p662)

October

October means autumn. The leaves on the trees are changing colour, attractions start to shut down for the low season, and accommodation rates drop as hoteliers try to entice a final few guests before winter.

Falmouth Oyster Festival

The quaint Cornish harbour town of Falmouth marks the start of the traditional oyster-catching season (www.falmouthoysterfestival.co.uk) with a celebration of local food from the sea and fields of Cornwall.

Dylan Thomas Festival

A celebration of the Welsh laureate's work with readings, events and talks in Swansea.

November

Winter's here, and November is a dull month. The weather is often cold and damp, summer is a distant memory and Christmas is still too far away.

Guy Fawkes Night

Also called Bonfire Night (www.bonfirenight.net); on 5 November fireworks fill Britain's skies in commemoration of a failed attempt to blow up parliament, way back in 1605.

Remembrance Day

Red poppies are worn and wreaths are laid in towns and cities around the country on 11 November in commemoration of fallen military personnel (www.poppy.org.uk).

December

Schools break up earlier, but shops and businesses keep going until Christmas Eve; the last weekend before Christmas Day is busy on the roads as people visit friends and family, or head for the airport.

Stonehaven Fireball Festival

The Scottish fishing town of Stonehaven celebrates Hogmanay with a spectacular procession of fireball-swinging locals (www.stonehavenfireballs.co.uk).

New Year Celebrations

The last night of December sees fireworks and street parties in town squares across the country. London's Trafalgar Sq is where the city's largest crowds gather to welcome the New Year.

Itineraries

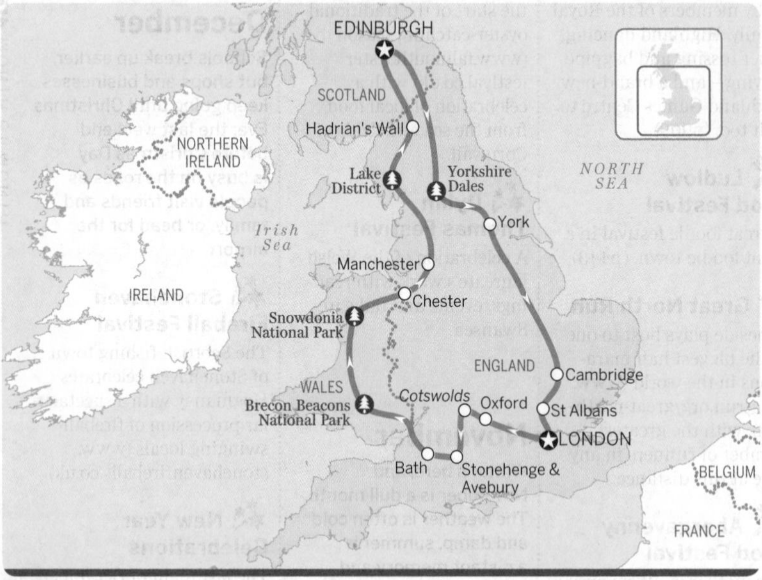

2 WEEKS Best of Britain

This circular whistle-stop tour ticks off Britain's greatest hits in an action-packed fortnight.

Start with at least three days exploring Britain's greatest city, **London**, seeing the world-famous sights: Buckingham Palace, Tower Bridge, Trafalgar Sq, the British Museum and more. From the capital, head west for the dreaming spires of England's oldest university city, **Oxford**, before touring the lovely villages of the **Cotswolds**.

Detour south to see **Stonehenge**, the nation's most celebrated stone circle, and its lesser-known counterpart **Avebury**, then head onwards to the Georgian city of **Bath**. From here, skip across the border through two Welsh national parks: the **Brecon Beacons** and **Snowdonia**. Stop in **Chester** to see the Roman walls, spend a day or two in lively **Manchester**, then walk the fells of the **Lake District**.

From here, it's easy to explore Roman Britain's most ambitious engineering project, the 73-mile **Hadrian's Wall**, before the drive to Scotland's capital, **Edinburgh**. On the long journey back south, drive through the rolling hills and valleys of the **Yorkshire Dales** and visit the handsome city of **York** and its medieval minster. Then it's a wander around the colleges and punt along the Backs of **Cambridge** before a visit to the cathedral in **St Albans**.

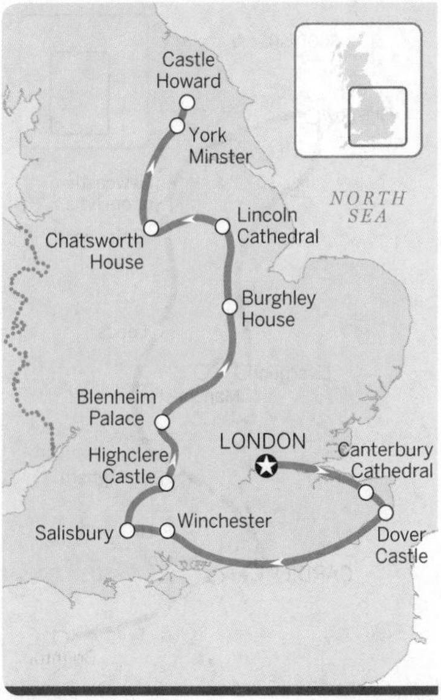

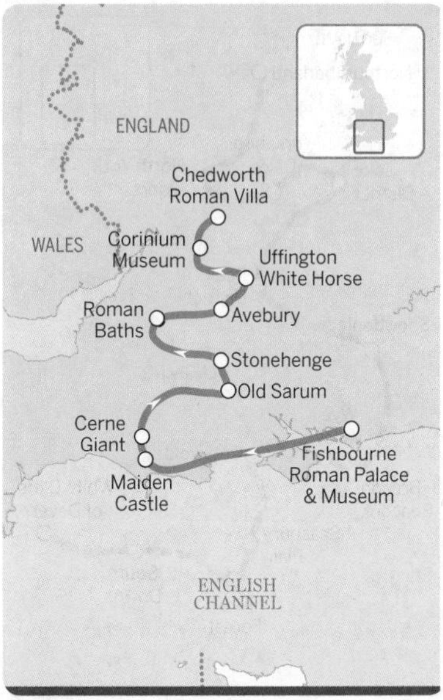

2 WEEKS Castles, Cathedrals & Country Houses

History is everywhere in England, not least in its incredible architecture. This itinerary takes in a selection of England's finest castles, cathedrals and stately homes.

London, of course, is awash with wonderful buildings. Pay homage at Westminster Cathedral, spot the monarch at Buckingham Palace and Windsor Castle, and get lost in the maze of Hampton Court.

Then comes **Canterbury Cathedral**, the seat of the Anglican church, and perhaps the finest ecclesiastical work in all of England. After soaking up the history here, head out to **Dover Castle**, then loop back along the south coast to see two more incredible cathedrals at **Winchester** and **Salisbury**.

Continue north to visit the home of Downton Abbey, **Highclere Castle**, then visit Churchill's birthplace at **Blenheim Palace** and walk through the glorious gardens of **Burghley House**.

If time allows, it's well worth continuing north to see the medieval marvel of **Lincoln Cathedral** and experience the eye-popping pomp of **Chatsworth House** and **York Minster**, ending with an unforgettable afternoon at **Castle Howard**.

2 WEEKS Ancient England

This loop takes you on a tour into Britain's ancient past, from the neolithic through the Iron Age into Roman Britain.

Begin with a visit to **Fishbourne Roman Palace**, the largest and most luxurious Roman villa ever discovered in Britain, then travel back in time to Dorset at **Maiden Castle** – Britain's largest Iron Age fort. Next comes ancient Britain's rudest monument, the upstanding **Cerne Giant** of somewhat uncertain age (he may be Celtic, may be not). A spin northeast brings you to **Old Sarum**, another huge Iron Age hill fort, before reaching the centrepiece attraction – **Stonehenge**, Britain's most celebrated stone circle, actually just a small part of what was once a gigantic sacred site.

After a detour to see Bath's **Roman Baths** (sadly no swimming allowed), swing over to **Avebury** to see Britain's largest stone circle – so large it has a village in the middle of it. Northeast gallops the **Uffington White Horse**, at c 3000 years old it's by far the oldest chalk figure in Britain. Further north, it's forward in time again to the Roman era in a visit to the **Corinium Museum** in Cirencester, and ending at another magnificent Roman villa in **Chedworth**.

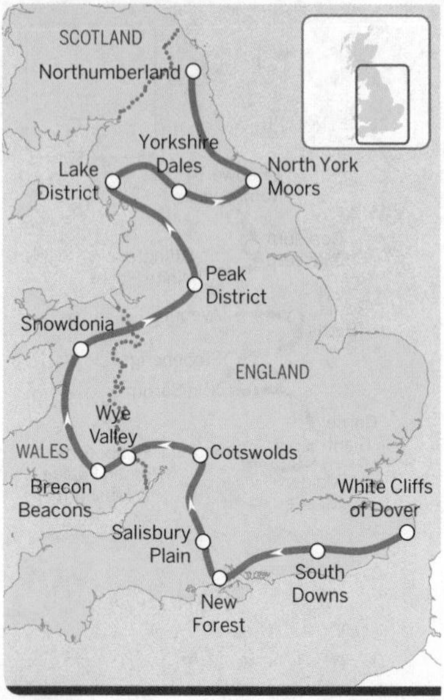

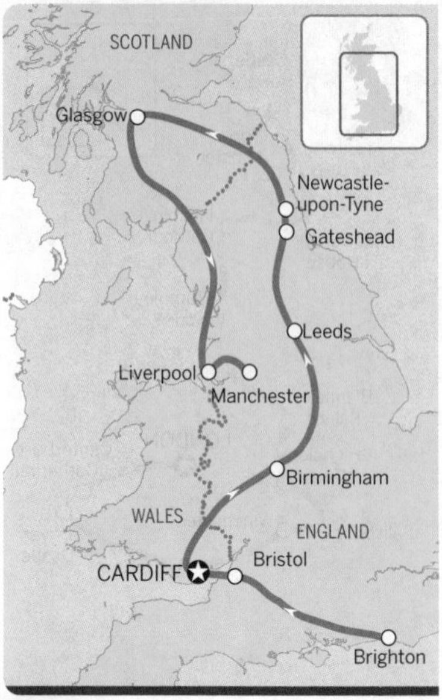

3 WEEKS Postcard Britain

This itinerary takes in a variety of British landscapes: hills, valleys, downs, mountains and wind-whipped coast.

From London, head southwards to stroll along Dover's famous **white cliffs**. From here, Britain's newest national park, the **South Downs**, sprawls over 600 sq miles of chalk downs, and makes for brilliant hiking and cycling. Further west is the patchwork of copses, heaths and scrubland that makes up the **New Forest**.

After **Salisbury Plain** comes the **Cotswolds**: thatched houses, quaint villages and cosy pubs. Across the Welsh border winds the **Wye Valley**, the home of Tintern Abbey, and the nearby **Brecon Beacons**, a stark region famous for its hiking. Wilder still is **Snowdonia**, home to Wales' highest mountain.

Back in England, there's more world-class walking in the **Peak District** and the **Lake District**. Then comes the **Yorkshire Dales**, whose green valleys and hills were immortalised by the novels of James Herriot and the Brontës. Starker, but just as scenic, are the **North York Moors**, while the **Northumberland coast** guards the wild border of England and Scotland.

3 WEEKS Urban Odyssey

To dig a little under Britain's skin, take this ride through some of its less-well-known and revitalised cities.

Kick off in **Brighton**, a south-coast city known for its alternative character, cool cafes and quirky shops, then head to **Bristol**, another proudly independent, slightly offbeat city centred around a historic harbour.

Cross over to **Cardiff**, the lively Welsh capital. Next stop is **Birmingham**, with a renovated waterside, museums and a space-age shopping centre. Onwards to **Leeds**, where run-down factories and warehouses have been turned into loft apartments, ritzy boutiques and stylish department stores.

Shopping not your thing? Head for **Newcastle-upon-Tyne** and twin city **Gateshead**; both have given up on heavy industries in favour of art and architecture, and are famous for to-the-hilt partying.

Scotland's **Glasgow** boasts fabulous galleries and welcoming pubs, then it's south to **Liverpool**, which has reinvented itself as a cultural hot spot thanks to its musical heritage and lively nightlife. Finish up in **Manchester**, another northern town that lives and breathes music, culture and – above all – football.

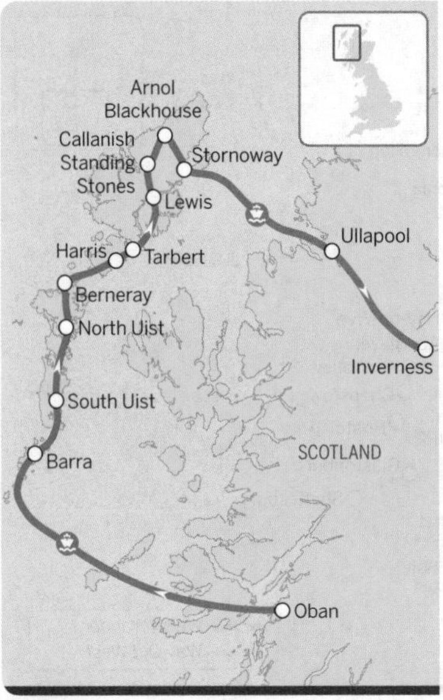

10 DAYS Island Hopscotch

This route is usually done by car, but it also makes a brilliant cycling tour (270 miles, including the 60 miles from Ullapool to Inverness train station, making both start and finish accessible by rail).

From **Oban** it's a five-hour ferry crossing to **Barra**; plan to spend the night here (book ahead). On day two, after a visit to Kisimul Castle and a tour around the island, take the ferry to **South Uist**. Walk the wild beaches of the west coast and sample the local seafood. Continue through Benbecula and **North Uist**, prime birdwatching country.

Overnight at Lochmaddy on North Uist (if you're camping or hostelling, a night at **Berneray** is a must) before taking the ferry to **Harris**, whose west coast has some of the most spectacular beaches in Scotland. The road continues north from **Tarbert** (good hotels) through rugged hills to **Lewis**.

Don't go directly to Stornoway, but loop west via the **Callanish Standing Stones** and **Arnol Blackhouse museum**. Spend your final night in **Stornoway**, then take the ferry to **Ullapool** for a scenic drive to **Inverness**.

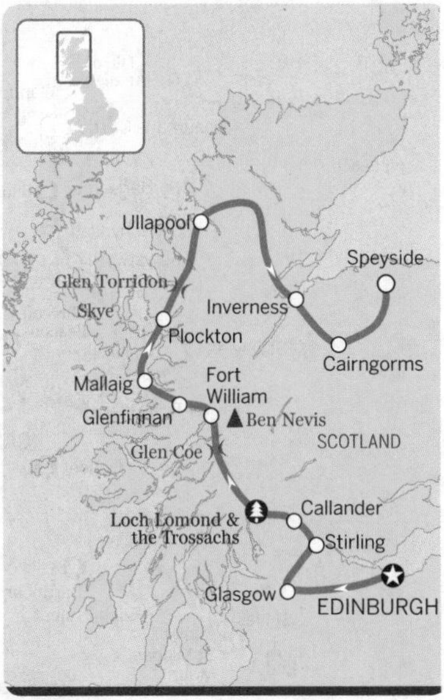

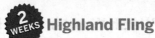

2 WEEKS Highland Fling

This itinerary is a tour of Scotland's finest and most famous sights.

It starts in **Edinburgh**, where highlights include the renowned castle, as well as the Royal Mile and the haunts of the Old Town. For a change of pace, hop over to **Glasgow** for a day or two. Then head northeast to see Scotland's other great castle at **Stirling**. Next stop is **Callander**, a good base for exploring the hills and lochs of the **Trossachs**.

Continue north and the landscape becomes ever more impressive, culminating in the grandeur of **Glen Coe**. Keen hill walkers will pause for a day at **Fort William** to trek to the top of **Ben Nevis** (and another day to recover!) before taking the 'Road to the Isles' past glorious **Glenfinnan** to the fishing harbour of **Mallaig**.

Take the ferry to the **Isle of Skye**, then head back to the mainland via the Skye Bridge to reach pretty **Plockton** and magnificent **Glen Torridon**. Travelling onwards, via **Ullapool**, takes you to the remote mountain landscape of Scotland's far northwest, then continue to Highland capital **Inverness**. Conclude with a drive through the **Cairngorms** and a tasting tour of the **Speyside whisky distilleries**.

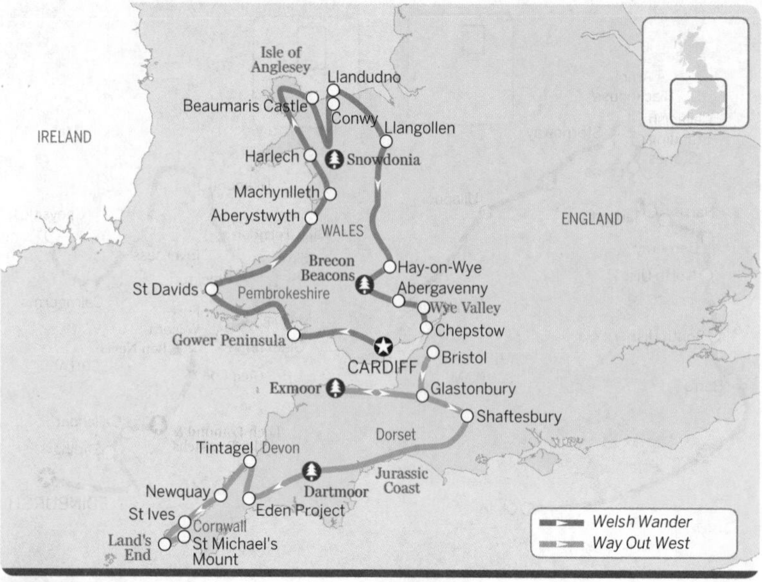

1 WEEK Welsh Wander

The coast and countryside of Wales has long been a favourite with visitors, and this tour includes most of the hot spots. Continue along England's southwest coast for a longer jaunt along Britain's Celtic fringe.

Start in **Cardiff**, with its fantastical castle, gigantic rugby stadium, revitalised waterfront and stunning Millennium Centre. Head west via the beautiful **Gower Peninsula** to reach the clear waters and sandy beaches of Pembrokeshire. Don't miss the ancient cathedral at **St Davids** – Britain's smallest city. Continue up the coast to **Aberystwyth**, then through 'alternative' **Machynlleth** to reach **Harlech** and its ancient castle. Divert to the tranquil Isle of Anglesey and historic **Beaumaris Castle**, then strike through the mountains of Snowdonia to reach **Conwy** (for another stunning castle) and the seaside resort of **Llandudno**.

Southwards takes you through **Llangollen**, with its steam trains and vertiginous aqueduct, then along the borderlands to book-mad **Hay-on-Wye**. Loop inland via **Brecon Beacons** to the foodie capital of **Abergavenny**, then saunter down the **Wye Valley** to finish at the frontier town of **Chepstow** – and yet another amazing castle.

2 WEEKS Way Out West

The southwest of England takes effort to reach but repays in full with a rich green landscape surrounded by glistening seas.

Start in **Bristol**, the capital of the West Country, then saunter south to reach **Glastonbury** – famous for its annual music festival and the best place to stock up on candles or crystals at any time of year.

West leads to the walking trails of heathery **Exmoor**, then it's south to Dorset, where highlights include picturesque **Shaftesbury** and the fossil-strewn Jurassic Coast. Onwards into Devon, and there's a choice of coasts, as well as **Dartmoor**, the highest and wildest hills in southern Britain.

Cross into Cornwall to explore the space-age biodomes of the **Eden Project**. Nearby is the legendary birthplace of King Arthur, the castle at **Tintagel**. Depending on your tastes, you can hang ten in surf-flavoured **Newquay** or browse the galleries at **St Ives**.

The natural finish to this wild west tour is **Land's End**, where the British mainland comes to a final full stop – but it's well worth visiting the nearby old port of Penzance and the amazing island abbey at **St Michael's Mount**.

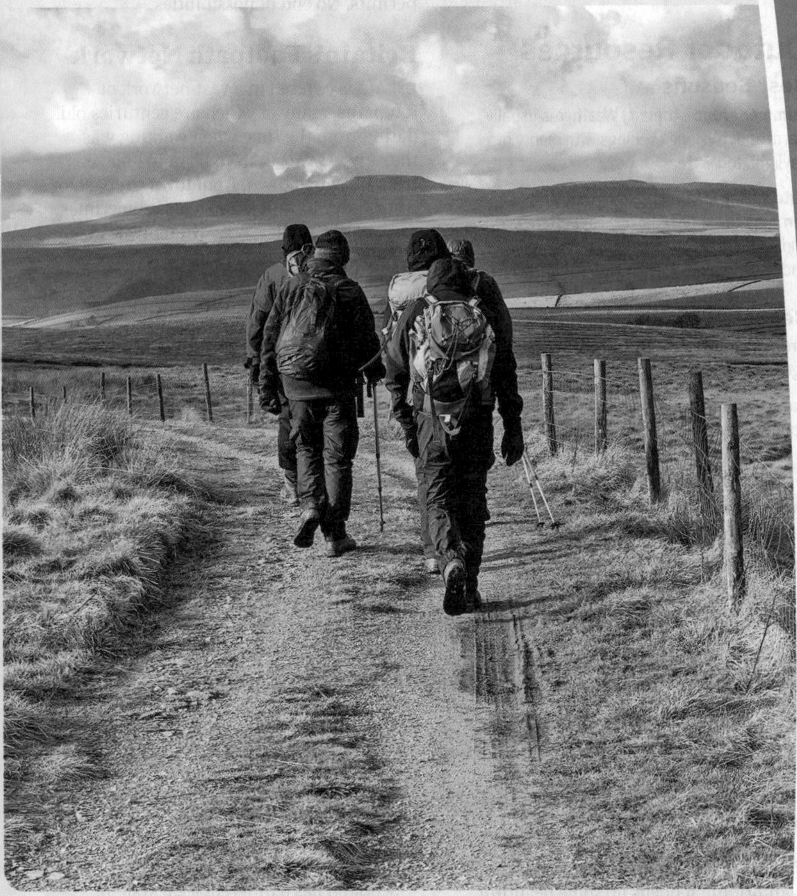

Walking the Pennine Way in the Peak District (p471)

Plan Your Trip

The Great Outdoors

What's the best way to slow down, meet the locals and get off the beaten track as you travel around Britain? Simple: go for a walk, or get on a bike. From the wild Highlands in the north to the salt-crusted coastal cliffs of the south, Britain offers an extraordinary diversity of terrain that begs to be explored.

Outdoor Resources

Best Seasons

Summer (June–August) Weather is usually warm and dry; long evenings with plenty of daylight, too.

Late spring (May) and early autumn (September) Fewer crowds; days are often mild and sunny. In Scotland, there's drier weather and fewer midges than in high summer.

Best Maps

Ordnance Survey UK's national mapping agency; Explorer series 1:25,000 scale.

Harvey Maps Specially designed for walkers; Superwalker series 1:25,000 scale.

Best Websites

www.walkhighlands.co.uk Superb database for walks of all lengths in Scotland.

www.walkingenglishman.com Short walks in England and Wales.

www.nationaltrail.co.uk Great for specifics on long-distance trails in England and Wales.

www.scotlandsgreattrails.com Long-distance trails in Scotland.

Walking

Walking is the most popular outdoor activity in Britain: it opens up some beautiful corners of the country, and can be done virtually on a whim. In fact, compared to hiking and trekking in some other parts of the world, it doesn't take much planning at all.

Getting Started

An established infrastructure for walkers already exists in Britain, so everything is easy for visitors or first-timers. Most villages and country towns in areas where walking is popular have shops selling maps and local guidebooks, while the local tourist office can provide leaflets and other information. In the national parks, suggested routes or guided walks are often available. This all means you can arrive in a place for the first time, pick up some info, and within an hour you'll be walking through some of Britain's finest landscapes. No fees. No permits. No end of possibilities.

Britain's Footpath Network

Britain is covered in a vast network of footpaths, many of which are centuries old, dating from the time when walking was the only way to get from farm to village, from village to town, from town to coast, or from valley to valley. You'll also sometimes walk along 'bridleways', originally used for horse transport, and old unsurfaced roads called 'byways'.

Recently, the **Slow Ways** (www.slowways.uk) campaign has gained a rapid following in its quest to reestablish the old network of footpaths that once connected all of the UK's towns and cities.

Rights of Way

The absolute pleasure of walking in Britain is mostly thanks to the 'right of way' network – public paths and tracks across private property, especially in England and Wales. In Britain, nearly all land (including in national parks) is privately owned, but if there's a right of way you can follow it through fields, pastures, woods, even farmhouse yards, as long as you keep to the route and do no damage. In some mountain and moorland areas, walkers can move freely beyond the rights of way and explore at will. Known as 'freedom to roam', where permitted it's clearly advertised with markers on gates and signposts. For more information see the Access pages on www.naturalengland.org.uk.

Scotland has a different legal system, where the Scottish Outdoor Access Code (www.outdooraccess-scotland.com) allows walkers to cross most private land providing they act responsibly. There are restrictions during lambing time, bird-nesting periods and the grouse- and deer-hunting seasons.

Britain's Best Walking Areas

Although you can walk just about anywhere in Britain, some areas are better than others. Here's a rundown of favourite places, suitable for short walks of a couple of hours, or longer all-day and multi-day outings.

Britain's Coast Paths

Thanks to Britain's long-standing tradition of open access to the countryside (coupled with recent 'right to roam' laws), much of Britain's spectacular coastline is open to walkers. Several areas have dedicated long-distance trails encompassing practically the entire coastline; these include the 870-mile Wales Coast Path (www.walescoastpath.gov.uk) and the 630-mile South West Coast Path (www.southwestcoastpath.org.uk), which forms part of the much larger 2795-mile England Coast Path (www.nationaltrail.co.uk/england-coast-path).

Much – but sadly not yet all – of Scotland's coastline is also accessible; Scotland's Great Trails (www.scotlandsgreattrails.com) has advice on coastal walks, including the Ayrshire Coastal Path, Berwickshire Coastal Path, Fife Coastal Path and Moray Coast Trail.

Southern England

The chalky hills of the South Downs stride across the counties of West Sussex and East Sussex, while the New Forest in Hampshire is great for easy strolls and the nearby Isle of Wight has excellent walking options. The highest and wildest area in southern England is Dartmoor, dotted with Bronze Age remains and granite outcrops called 'tors' – looking for all the world like abstract sculptures. Exmoor has heather-covered hills cut by deep valleys and a lovely stretch of coastline, while the entire coast of the southwest peninsula from Dorset to Somerset offers dramatic walking conditions – especially along the beautiful cliff-lined shore of Cornwall.

Central England

The gem of central England is the Cotswolds, classic English countryside with gentle paths through neat fields, mature woodland and pretty villages of honey-coloured stone. The Marches, where England borders Wales, are similarly bucolic with more good walking options. For something higher, aim for the Peak District, divided into two distinct areas: the White Peak, characterised by limestone, farmland and verdant dales, ideal for gentle strolls; and the Dark Peak, with high

THE NATIONAL TRAILS

Britain's most high-profile routes are its 15 National Trails (www.nationaltrail.co.uk). Traversing the nation's finest countryside, the routes are very well marked on the ground and well defined on maps, so there's little chance of getting lost (although just because they're easy to follow, it doesn't mean they're necessarily easy underfoot). The website also has good route tips, planning resources and suggestions for accommodation along the way.

Among the best-known:

The Pennine Way (431km; 19 days) England's first national trail traverses the stark, beautiful ridges of the Pennines.

The Ridgeway (139km; six days) Possibly the oldest path in England, trodden since neolithic times.

Hadrian's Wall Path (135km; seven days) Trace the course of the Roman wall from Cumbria's coast to Newcastle-upon-Tyne.

Offa's Dyke Path (285km; 14 days) Spectacular route on the Anglo-Welsh border, following an ancient earthwork.

Cotswold Way (164km; 10 days) Bucolic England at its best; chocolate-box countryside.

South Downs Way (160km; nine days) Walk across chalk downs to the English Channel and the famous Seven Sisters cliffs.

Pembrokeshire Coast Path (300km; 12 days) Cliffs, coves, beaches, hill forts, fishing villages: Wales' most glorious coastline.

South West Coast Path (1014km; 52 days) A coastal epic, encompassing the southwest peninsula from Minehead to Poole.

Thames Path (294km; 14 days) A capital walk along the course of the Thames, from the Cotswolds all the way to the city of London.

Windsurfing, Devon (p308)

peaty moorlands, heather and gritstone outcrops, for more serious hikes.

Northern England

The Lake District is the heart and soul of walking in England, a wonderful area of soaring peaks, endless views, deep valleys and, of course, beautiful lakes. On the other side of the country, the rolling hills of the Yorkshire Dales make it another very popular walking area. Further north, keen walkers love the starkly beautiful hills of Northumberland National Park, while the nearby coast is less daunting but just as dramatic – perfect for wild seaside strolls.

South & Mid-Wales

The Brecon Beacons is a large range of gigantic rolling whaleback hills with broad ridges and tabletop summits, while out in the west is Pembrokeshire, a wonderful array of beaches, cliffs, islands, coves and harbours, with a hinterland of tranquil farmland and secret waterways, and a relatively mild climate year-round.

North Wales

For walkers, North Wales *is* Snowdonia, where the remains of ancient volcanoes bequeath a striking landscape of jagged peaks, sharp ridges and steep cliffs. There are challenging walks on Snowdon itself – at 1085m, the highest peak in Wales – and many more on the nearby Glyderau and Carneddau ranges, or further south around Cader Idris.

Southern & Central Scotland

This extensive region embraces several areas just perfect for keen walkers, including Ben Lomond, the best-known peak in the area, and the nearby hills of the Trossachs, lying within the Loch Lomond and the Trossachs National Park. Also here is the splendid Isle of Arran, with a great choice of coastal rambles and high-mountain hikes.

Northern & Western Scotland

For serious walkers, heaven is the northern and western parts of Scotland, where the forces of nature have created a mountainous landscape of utter grandeur, including two of Scotland's most famous place names, Glen Coe and Ben Nevis (Britain's

Cycling, Perthshire (p909)

highest mountain at 1345m). Off the west coast lie the dramatic mountains of the Isle of Skye. Keep going north along the western coast, and things just keep getting better: it's a remote and beautiful area, sparsely populated, with scenic glens and lochs, and some of the largest, wildest and finest mountains in Britain.

Cycling & Mountain Biking

A bike is the perfect mode of transport for exploring back-road Britain. Once you escape the busy main highways, a vast network of quiet country lanes winds through fields and peaceful villages, ideal for cycle-touring. You can cruise through gently rolling landscapes, taking it easy and stopping for cream teas, or you can thrash all day through hilly areas, revelling in steep ascents and swooping downhill sections. You can cycle from place to place, camping or staying in B&Bs (many of which are cyclist-friendly), or you can base yourself in one area for a few days and go out on rides in different directions. All you need is a map and a sense of adventure.

Mountain bikers can go further into the wilds on the tracks and bridleways that criss-cross Britain's hills and high moors, or head for one of the many dedicated mountain-bike trail centres where specially built single-tracks wind through the forests. Options at these centres vary from delightful dirt roads ideal for families to gnarly rock gardens and precipitous drop-offs for hardcore riders, all classified from green to black in ski-resort style.

www.sustrans.org.uk Details of Britain's national network of cycling trails.

www.forestry.gov.uk/england-cycling Guide to forest cycling trails in England.

www.dmbins.com Guide to mountain-biking trails in Scotland.

Surfing, SUP & Windsurfing

Britain may not seem an obvious destination for surfing, but conditions are surprisingly good and the large tidal range often means a completely different set of breaks at low and high tides. If you've come from the other side of the world, you'll be delighted to learn that summer water temperatures in southern England are roughly equivalent to winter temperatures in southern Australia (ie you'll still need a wetsuit). At the main spots, it's easy enough to hire boards and wetsuits.

Top of the list are the Atlantic-facing coasts of Cornwall and Devon (Newquay is surf central, with all the trappings from VW vans to bleached hair), and there are

COASTEERING

If sometimes a simple clifftop walk doesn't cut the mustard, then coasteering might appeal. It's like mountaineering, but instead of going up a mountain, you go sideways along a coast – a steep and rocky coast – with waves breaking around your feet. And if the rock gets too steep, no problem – you jump in and start swimming. Coasteering centres provide wetsuits, helmets and buoyancy aids; you provide an old pair of training shoes and a sense of adventure. The sport is available all around Britain, but the mix of sheer cliffs, sandy beaches and warmer water make Cornwall and Devon prime spots.

www.coasteering.org Info on coasteering in Devon and Cornwall.

RAWDMC/SHUTTERSTOCK ©

Top: Rock climbing, Peak District (p469)

Bottom: Kayaking, Loch Lomond & the Trossachs National Park (p867)

WEATHER WATCH

While enjoying the outdoors, it's always worth remembering the fickle nature of the British weather. The countryside can appear gentle and welcoming, and often is, but sometimes conditions can turn nasty – especially on the higher ground. At any time of year, if you're walking on the hills or open moors, it's vital to be well equipped. You should carry warm and waterproof clothing (even in summer); a map and compass (that you know how to use); and drink and food, including high-energy stuff such as chocolate. If you're really going off the beaten track, leave details of your route with someone.

smaller surf scenes elsewhere, notably Pembrokeshire and the Gower in Wales, and Norfolk and Yorkshire in eastern England. Hardier souls can head for northern Scotland and the Outer Hebrides, which have some of the best and most consistent surf in Europe.

Windsurfing is hugely popular all around the coast. Top areas include Norfolk, Suffolk, Devon and Cornwall, the Isle of Wight, and the islands of Tiree, Orkney and the Outer Hebrides.

Another watersport that's growing in popularity is stand-up paddleboarding (SUP). You'll find it on offer in many coastal areas these days, as well as at a number of bays, estuaries and rivers.

www.surfinggb.com Listings of approved surf schools, courses, competitions and so on.

www.ukwindsurfing.com A good source of info.

Canoeing, Kayaking & Rafting

Britain's west coast, with its sheltered inlets, indented shoreline and countless islands, is ideal for sea kayaking, while its inland lakes and canals are great for Canadian canoeing. In addition, the turbulent spate rivers of Scotland and Wales offer some of Britain's best white-water kayaking and rafting.

Equipment rental and instruction are readily available in major centres such as Cornwall, Anglesey, the Lake District, Loch Lomond and the Isle of Skye.

www.gocanoeing.org.uk Lists approved canoeing centres in England.

www.canoescotland.org Canoe trails in Scotland.

www.ukrafting.co.uk White-water rafting in Wales.

Sailing & Boating

Scotland's west coast, with its myriad islands, superb scenery and challenging winds and tides, is widely acknowledged to be one of the finest yachting areas in the world, while the canals of England and Wales offer a classic narrow-boating experience.

Beginners can take a Royal Yachting Association (www.rya.org.uk) training course in yachting or dinghy sailing at many sailing schools around the coast. Narrowboaters only need a quick introductory lesson at the start of their trip – for more info see www.canalholidays.com.

Skiing & Snowboarding

Britain's ski centres are all in the Scottish Highlands:

Cairngorm Mountain (www.cairngormmountain.org) 1097m; has almost 30 runs spread over an extensive area.

Glencoe (www.glencoemountain.com) 1108m; has five tows and two chairlifts.

Glenshee (www.ski-glenshee.co.uk) 920m; situated on the A93 road between Perth and Braemar; offers the largest network of lifts and the widest range of runs in Britain.

Lecht (www.lecht.co.uk) 793m; the smallest and most remote centre, on the A939 between Ballater and Grantown-on-Spey.

Nevis Range (www.nevisrange.co.uk) 1221m; near Fort William; offers the highest ski runs, the grandest setting and some of the best off-piste potential.

The high season is from January to April, but it's sometimes possible to ski from as early as November to as late as May. Turn up at the slopes, hire some kit, buy a day pass and off you go.

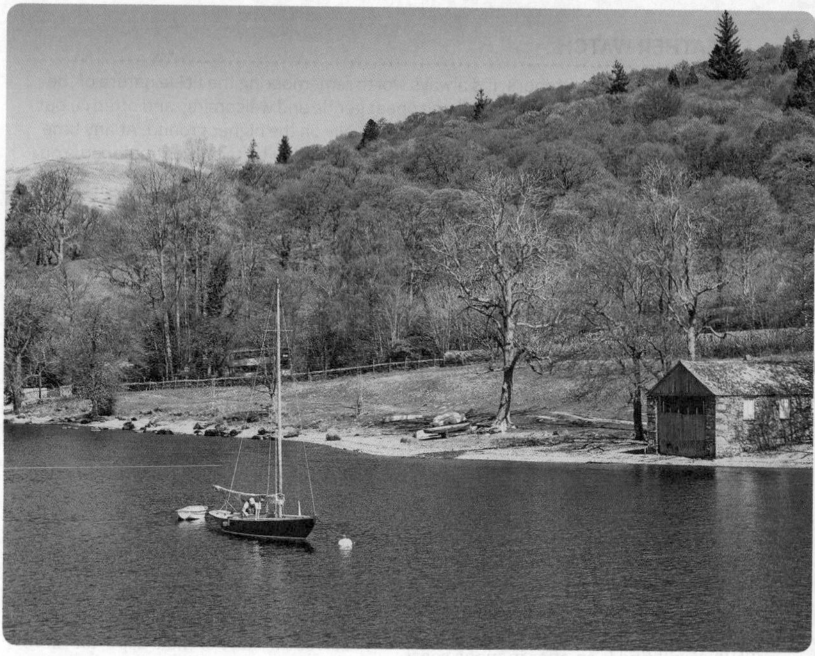

Sailing, Windermere (p578)

Weather and snow reports can be obtained from:

Ski Scotland (www.ski-scotland.com)

WinterHighland (www.winterhighland.info)

Rock Climbing

Britain has a long history of rock climbing and mountaineering, with many of the classic routes having been pioneered in the 19th century. The main rock-climbing areas include the Scottish Highlands, the Lake District, the Peak District and North Wales, plus the sea cliffs of South Wales, Devon and Cornwall, but there are also hundreds of smaller crags situated all over the country.

Comprehensive climbing guidebooks are published by the Scottish Mountaineering Club (www.smc.org.uk), the Fell & Rock Climbing Club (www.frcc.co.uk) and the Climbers Club (www.climbers-club.co.uk).

www.ukclimbing.com Full of useful information.

Horse Riding

If you want to explore the hills and moors but walking or cycling is too much of a sweat, seeing the wilder parts of Britain from horseback is highly recommended. In rural areas and national parks like Dartmoor and Northumberland, riding centres cater to all levels of proficiency, with ponies for kids and beginners, and horses for the more experienced.

www.bhs.org.uk The British Horse Society lists approved riding centres that offer day rides or longer holidays on horseback.

Plan Your Trip

Family Travel

Britain is ideal for travelling with children because of its compact size, packing a lot of attractions into a small area. So when the kids in the back of the car ask 'Are we there yet?', your answer can often be 'Yes, we are'.

Children Will Love...

All-Round Family Fun

Legoland Windsor (p229) Huge Lego models and thrilling rides galore – but be prepared to queue.

Alton Towers, Staffordshire (p424) Arguably the UK's best – and certainly most popular – theme park, with a riot of roller coasters and other rides to try.

Warner Bros Studio Tour: The Making of Harry Potter, Leavesden (p225) Step behind the scenes at the Leavesden studio where the films were shot.

Warwick Castle (p417) Jousting tournaments, trebuchet launches and waxworks bring medieval times to life.

Eden Project, Cornwall (p354) Learn about all manner of environmental matters in Cornwall's spectacular space-age greenhouse.

Jacobite Steam Train (p914) Catch the heritage train across the historic Glenfinnan Viaduct, as seen (yet again) in the Harry Potter films.

Outdoor Adventures

Surfing in Cornwall (p338) Pick up a board and hit the waves in the UK's surfing central.

Puzzlewood, Forest of Dean (p222) Wonderful woodland playground with mazy paths, weird rock formations and eerie passageways.

Bewilderwood, Norfolk (p397) Zip wires, jungle bridges, treehouses, marsh walks, boat trips, mazes and all sorts of old-fashioned outdoor adventure.

Keeping Costs Down

Accommodation

Camping is the cheapest option – there are some great ones to choose from. Alternatively, rent a self-catering property, or book a dorm in one of Britain's excellent youth hostels, which have several beds and often private ensuites.

Family Tickets

Many visitor attractions offer family tickets that cost less than if you all paid individually – sometimes the savings can be significant. Major British museums and galleries are free.

Transport

Family tickets are often available on buses, and if you're travelling by train, the Family & Friends Railcard (£30) gets big discounts for up to four adults and four children travelling together.

Eating Out

Eating at cafes and restaurants all the time will be expensive – pack picnics for lunch, and consider staying somewhere with its own kitchen facilities.

The Great Outdoors

All of Britain's national parks, and the majority of its countryside (including most of the bits owned by the National Trust) are free to enter. Houses, castles and monuments usually charge an entry fee.

Zip World, Bangor (☎01248-601444; www.zipworld.co.uk; Penrhyn Quarry, Bethesda; single ride £85; ⏰8am-6.30pm) Brave Europe's longest (and fastest) zip wire in a disused slate quarry.

Rothiemurchus Estate, Aviemore (p905) Tons of family-friendly activities including cycling, pony trekking and more.

Stealth Learning

Science Museum, London (p103) Seven floors of educational exhibits at the mother of all science museums.

Kielder Observatory, Northumberland National Park (p633) Stargaze at this Northumbrian astronomy centre.

Enginuity, Ironbridge (p437) Endless hands-on displays at the birthplace of the Industrial Revolution.

National Space Centre, Leicester (p459) Spacesuits, zero-gravity toilets and mini-astronaut training – guaranteed to boost little brains.

We the Curious, Bristol (p239) One of England's best interactive science museums, covering space, technology and the human brain.

Living History

Jorvik Viking Centre, York (p490) Excellent smells-and-all Viking settlement reconstruction.

Underground Passages, Exeter (p310) Explore the city's spooky medieval catacombs.

Ezekial Bone Tours, Nottingham (p447) Take a Robin Hood–themed tour in the sheriff's backyard. Bows and arrows not provided.

Scottish Crannog Centre, Kenmore (p913) Step into Scotland's prehistoric past on Loch Tay.

Lyme Regis, Dorset (p292) Scan the cliffs to find your own prehistoric fossil.

Animal Encounters

London Zoo (p111) The capital's century-old zoo is still a must-see for many kids.

Longleat, Wiltshire (p300) Pretend you're driving across the savannah at this Wiltshire country estate, surrounded by rhinos, giraffes, elephants and lions.

National Marine Aquarium, Plymouth (p321) Gaze into the shark tank at the UK's biggest aquarium.

Wildlife Cruises, Scotland's west coast (p918) Boat trips to see seals, porpoises and dolphins, and maybe even a whale.

Highland Wildlife Park, Kincraig (p906) See wolves, lynx, wild boar, beavers and bison at this Highland safari park.

Best Regions for Kids

England

London The capital has children's attractions galore: world-class museums, historic parks, incredible castles and palaces and loads of family-fun activities. The Tower of London (p90), the Natural History Museum (p99) and Hampton Court (p115) are essentials.

Canterbury & Southeast England Wandering the coastline around Beachy Head (p175), visiting the mighty castles of Leeds (p161) and Dover (p167) and picnicking on the beach in Brighton are all top fun. Chichester's Roman remains are interesting too.

Oxford & the Cotswolds Unleash your inner wizard at The Making of Harry Potter (p215), then dream away a day or two in elegant Oxford. The Cotswolds might be a little twee for kids, but they'll love Windsor Castle (p228).

Bristol, Bath & Somerset Bristol is a great city for kids, from historic steamships (p237) to science museums. Further afield, they could hike up Glastonbury Tor (p258), explore the Somerset Levels or go on a deer-spotting safari on Exmoor.

Hampshire, Wiltshire & Dorset This is a region of ancient stones and animal parks: ponder Stonehenge (p298), go wild at Longleat (p300), then do your level best to explain the Cerne Giant (p287). Good luck with that.

Devon, Cornwall & the Isles of Scilly Seaside superbia. Home to England's loveliest beaches, this is the land of bucket and spades, surfing, sailing and all kinds of other watery adventures – but don't miss the many castles, like Tintagel (p334) and Pendennis (p352), and the amazing Eden Project (p354).

Cambridge & East Anglia Your kids will love punting in the Norfolk Broads (p396), the Anglo-Saxon hoard of Sutton Hoo (p386) will fire the imagination, and the vintage aircraft at the Imperial War Museum (p378) will bring out their inner plane-spotter.

GOOD TO KNOW

Look out for the icon for family-friendly suggestions throughout this guide.

Prices Prices for accommodation and travel skyrocket during the school holidays and at half-terms. Be prepared for attractions to be busy, and book tickets online if you can.

Pubs Children under 18 are usually not allowed in pubs serving just alcohol. Pubs also serving meals generally allow children of any age (with their parents) in England and Wales, but in Scotland they must be over 14 and must leave by 8pm. If in doubt, simply ask bar staff.

Take the train If you're going by public transport, trains are great for families: intercity services have plenty of room for luggage and extra stuff like buggies (strollers). Many train companies offer family train tickets on certain routes.

Car hire Nearly all rental firms can provide child seats, which are required by law – but you may need to request one in advance.

Toilets & baby-changing Public loos can be hard to find in the UK these days – if you're stuck, head for the nearest supermarket or museum, where there will be public toilets and a room for baby-changing.

Breastfeeding Britain is still slightly buttoned up about breastfeeding. Older folks may tut-tut a bit if you give junior a top-up in public, but if done modestly it's usually considered OK.

Birmingham & the Midlands England's industrial heritage lives on in the Midlands, not least at the Unesco-listed Ironbridge Gorge (p437), but history is everywhere: you can visit Lincoln Castle (p453) and see the remains of Richard III (p459).

Yorkshire Hiking and biking in the beautiful Yorkshire Dales, industrial heritage at Magna (p531) and the National Coal Mining Museum (p525), and hunting for fossils (and Dracula) in Whitby (p506) – Yorkshire is maybe northern England's most child-friendly region.

Manchester, Liverpool & Northwest England Home of the Beatles (p560), the bright lights of Blackpool Tower (p565), the world's largest working waterwheel (p570) on the Isle of Man, and football heritage galore will provide plenty to keep the kids entertained here.

The Lake District & Cumbria Hiking's the thing here: there are 214 fells to tackle, and plenty of other outdoor pursuits too. It's also the home of Beatrix Potter and Arthur Ransome: you can see Potter's house at Hill Top (p588), and take a Swallows and Amazons cruise on Coniston Water (p590).

Newcastle & Northeast England Hadrian's Wall (p627) is the big attraction, but the Northumberland coastline is full of excitement and drama: Dunstanburgh (p637), Bamburgh (p639) and Alnwick (p635) have super castles.

Wales

Cardiff, Pembrokeshire & South Wales Pembrokeshire offers coastal potential: beaches, cliffs, coasteering, kayaking and more. Cardiff has a great castle, dinosaurs at the National Museum (p648) and science wizardry at **Techniquest** (Map p658; 029-2047 5475; www.techniquest.org; Stuart St, Cardiff Bay; adult/child/under 4 £9.59/7.73/free; 10am-1pm & 2-5pm Wed-Sun; P).

Brecon Beacons & Mid-Wales Caves to explore, castles to clamber, mountains to walk, cycle and stargaze. Highlights include the Brecon Beacons National Park (p690), the Big Pit National Coal Museum (p663) and medieval Powis Castle (p705).

Snowdonia & North Wales Wild Wales: race down zip lines, hike up mountains, ride railways, visit Harlech Castle (p728) and get in some beach time on Llŷn Peninsula. The north coast has a trio of World Heritage castles.

Scotland

Edinburgh Scotland's fairy-tale city. There's an incredible castle (p758), of course, as well as underground catacombs (p761), a great zoo (p775), a historic palace (p768) and some cracking museums too.

Glasgow & Southern Scotland The Scottish Borders are good for hiking and cycling, and there are some great abbeys and castles to visit, Culzean (p834) and Hermitage (p827) among them. Big-city Glasgow has loads of entertainment: the Kelvingrove Art Gallery & Museum (p809) is a must.

Stirling & Central Scotland Scottish history is everywhere here: especially at Scone Palace (p856), where Scotland's kings were crowned, and Stirling Castle (p840), a fortress straight out of *Braveheart*.

Inverness & the Highlands & Islands This is where Scotland gets really wild: a land of moody glens, misty lochs, snowy mountains and faraway islands. Wildlife spotting on the northwest coast is a definite highlight.

Useful Resources

Lonely Planet Kids (www.lonelyplanetkids.com) Loads of activities and great family-travel blog content.

Book: City Trails London (shop.lonelyplanet.com) Discover London's best-kept secrets, amazing stories and loads of other cool stuff.

MumsNet (www.mumsnet.com) No-nonsense advice from a vast network of UK mums.

Baby Goes 2 (www.babygoes2.com) Advice, tips and information for families on tour.

Kids Rule! (www.english-heritage.org.uk/members-area/kids) Engaging historical facts for UK sites.

Geocaching UK (www.geocaching.co.uk) Treasure hunting for the digital age.

Kids' Corner

Say What?

Chuffed	Pleased
Knackered	Tired
Miffed	Displeased

Did You Know?

- Medieval London's residents (human and animal) produced 50,000kg of poo a day – more than six double decker buses!

Have You Tried?

Jellied Eels
Boiled eels cooled to jelly.

Scotch egg, Borough Market (p144)

Plan Your Trip

Eat & Drink Like a Local

From the cosiest pubs to the buzziest bistros, it always pays to follow a local's tip on where to eat and drink in Britain. Nearly always, the best idea is to give the major chains a wide berth and seek out the smaller, independent venues that specialise in locally sourced ingredients and best-of-British provenance.

The Year in Food

March–May

Season of springtime veg (onions, garlic, asparagus, new potatoes) and tender lamb.

June–August

Salads, veg and summer fruits; fish and seafood is in season; food festivals abound.

Cheltenham Food & Drink Festival (www.cheltenhamfooddrinkfestival.co.uk) Gourmet gastronomy in Gloucestershire.

Taste of London (https://london.tastefestivals.com) The capital's longest-running (and largest) food fair.

Whitstable Oyster Festival (www.whitstableoysterfestival.co.uk) The bivalve takes centre stage.

The Big Feastival (www.thebigfeastival.com) Food meets music on Alex James' farm.

September–November

A second flush of food festivals, along with autumn fruits, game and shellfish.

Ludlow Food Festival (www.ludlowfoodfestival.co.uk) One of England's biggest food fairs.

Abergavenny Food Festival (www.abergavennyfoodfestival.com) The big event for Welsh producers.

Falmouth Oyster Festival (www.falmouthoysterfestival.co.uk) Cornish town celebrates its oyster haul.

December–February

Chestnuts, root veg, winter greens and roast turkey – the classic Christmas dinner.

Food Experiences

Meals of a Lifetime

Fat Duck (p230) Run by madcap chef Heston Blumenthal, this temple to modern gastronomy holds three Michelin stars.

City Social (p126) Jason Atherton's high-rise restaurant serves incredible food with cross-London views to match.

Le Manoir aux Quat'Saisons (p195) Raymond Blanc's legendary Oxfordshire restaurant is a hymn to classic French cookery.

Ynyshir Restaurant & Rooms (p707) Molecular gastronomy at this former royal retreat near Machynlleth.

Raby Hunt (p627) James Close works wonders at his double-Michelin-starred restaurant in Barnard Castle.

L'Enclume (p604) Cumbrian chef Simon Rogan experiments with tastes, textures, flavours and foraged ingredients.

Loch Bay (p938) The apotheosis of Scottish seafood, complete with a Michelin star.

Outlaw's New Road (p335) Britain's best seafood chef, Nathan Outlaw, has a new Cornish concept.

Cheap Treats

Bacon sandwich The breakfast of champions. Debate rages over the sauce – red (tomato ketchup) or brown (spicy pickled fruit sauce).

Fish and chips The nation's favourite takeaway meal, served in chip shops all over the country.

Cornish pasty A pastry-wrapped parcel of vegetables and steak, this must only be eaten in Cornwall. Absolutely nowhere else.

Cockles A classic seaside snack that has been enjoyed by generations of British holidaymakers, sprinkled with vinegar and eaten with a wooden fork.

Scotch egg This masterpiece of culinary engineering consists of a hardboiled egg wrapped in sausage meat, coated in breadcrumbs and deep-fried.

Dare to Try

Haggis Scotland's national dish is made from the chopped heart, liver and lungs of a sheep, mixed with oatmeal and onion, and wrapped in the sheep's stomach (or often an artificial casing).

Tripe Cow's stomach lining, traditionally poached in milk with onions. A wartime staple, but hard to find in restaurants today – though it's making a comeback.

Stinking Bishop Britain's most pungent cheese, made in Gloucestershire and redolent of old socks. Available from Harrods in London, and many specialist cheese shops.

Jellied eels Traditional London side dish that can still be found in the capital's pie-and-mash shops.

Black pudding Large sausage made from ground meat, offal, fat and blood, served for breakfast.

Local Specialities

London & Southeast England

Two old-school London specialities are worth trying, if only for bragging rights – pie and mash, and jellied eels. The staple menu of working-class Londoners since the 19th century, the former consists of a small pie filled with minced beef served with mashed potato and 'liquor' – a parsley-rich gravy made from the stock in which eels have been cooked. The eels are cooled and set in the jellied stock, and served as a side dish with malt vinegar – Poppie's (p128) is a good place to try them.

Oysters today have an expensive reputation, but in the 19th century they were a cheap and plentiful foodstuff, eaten by all. Whitstable oysters, from Kent – the native British species – have been harvested since Roman times.

London is also home to a huge (and growing) number of microbreweries (check out www.craftbeerlondon.com), distilleries and craft-spirit sellers.

Haggis

Northern England

The northeast is known for its kippers (smoked herring), traditionally grilled with butter and served for breakfast. The northwest's best-known dish is Lancashire hotpot (slow-cooked stew of lamb and onion topped with sliced potatoes), while in Cumbria you'll come across Cumberland sausage (a spiral-shaped pork sausage flavoured with herbs). And then of course there's Yorkshire pudding – not a pudding at all, but actually a crispy, puffed batter dish, traditionally served with roast beef and gravy. You might also want to try an Eccles cake – a traditional flaky pastry filled with currants.

The north is also known for its taste for 'real ale' – traditional ales that mature in the cask, and are served warm and flat. The north (and particularly Yorkshire) is home to a number of iconic breweries. The **Lakes Distillery** (www.lakesdistillery.com) produces England's only whisky.

Southwest England

Devon and Cornwall are famous for their dairy produce: particularly cheeses, milk, ice cream and the area's classic treat, clotted cream (a very thick cream made by heating full-cream milk).

Less refined but equally tasty are Cornish pasties (crimped pastry parcels containing a mix of beef and vegetables), once the lunchtime staple of miners and farm workers. They're protected by their own regional indicator, so Cornwall is the only place to try the real thing.

Fish and shellfish are also highlights here: there are sizeable fishing fleets at Newlyn (in west Cornwall) and Brixham (in Devon), and southwest-caught fish graces many of the country's top tables.

The southwest is cider country, a boozy drink made with fermented apple juice. Plymouth Gin Distillery is also one of the oldest in Britain, appropriately enough for a naval town.

Midlands

The Leicestershire town of Melton Mowbray is famed for its pork pies, always eaten cold, ideally with pickle. Only pies handmade in the eponymous town can carry the Melton Mowbray moniker – in the same way that only fizzy wine from the Champagne region of France can carry that name.

Another Midlands speciality is Stilton – a strong, marbled cheese that gets very smelly

Top: Caerphilly cheese, Borough Market (p144)

Bottom: Craft beer, Bermondsey

as it ripens. Only five dairies (four of which are in Derbyshire) are allowed to make Stilton. Bizarrely, the cheese cannot be made in the village of Stilton in Cambridgeshire, although this is where it originates from.

Bakewell pudding or tart features often on dessert menus. It's named after the Derbyshire town where it originated in 1860, and consists of a pastry base topped with jam, egg custard and almond paste.

Wales

Tender and tasty Welsh lamb is sought after, and is a key ingredient of the rustic dish called cawl (pronounced cowl) – a one-pot stew of lamb, bacon, cabbage, potato and swede. Laverbread, which is not bread but seaweed, is cooked with oatmeal and often served for breakfast with toast and bacon. Sweet-toothed visitors should look out for Welsh cakes (fruity griddle scones) and bara brith (a dense and spicy fruit cake flavoured with tea and marmalade).

Felinfoel is Wales' oldest brewery, founded in 1878, but as elsewhere, there's a huge number of craft breweries and distilleries these days. There's also a Welsh whisky, produced by Penderyn Distillery (p700).

Scotland

Scotland may be most famous for haggis, but seafood is where it excels. Fresh lobster, langoustine, salmon and scallops are the favourites of restaurant menus, but look out for traditional dishes such as Arbroath smokies (hot-smoked haddock) and Cullen skink (soup made with smoked haddock, onion, butter and milk). Oats have been a mainstay of the Scottish diet for centuries, appearing in the form of porridge and oatcakes, but also as a coating for fried trout or herring, and in the classic Scottish dessert known as cranachan (whipped cream flavoured with whisky and mixed with raspberries and toasted oatmeal).

Whisky (always spelt without an 'e' – whiskey with an 'e' is Irish or American) has been distilled in Scotland at least since the 15th century. Traditionally, Scots drink their whisky neat, or with a little water added. To appreciate the aroma and flavour to the utmost, a measure of malt whisky should be cut (diluted) with one-third to two-thirds as much spring water. At a bar, older Scots may order a 'half' or 'nip' of whisky as a chaser to a pint or half-pint of beer (called a 'hauf and a hauf').

SIX GREAT BRITISH CHEESES

Cheddar Sharp and savoury, Britain's favourite cheese originates in a little village in Somerset.

Stilton A pungent blue cheese, traditionally eaten after dinner with a glass of port.

Wensleydale Crumbly white cheese from Yorkshire, with a mild, honeyed flavour.

Caerphilly From the Welsh town of the same name, this hard, salty cheese has an annual festival dedicated to it.

Cornish Yarg A rich, creamy cheese wrapped in nettle leaves.

Caboc A Highland Scottish cream cheese rolled in oatmeal, whose recipe is more than 500 years old.

One tip: when ordering a dram, ask simply for a 'whisky' – only the English (and other foreigners) say 'Scotch'.

How to Eat & Drink

When to Eat

Breakfast Served in most hotels and B&Bs between 7am and 9am, or perhaps 8am to 10am on weekends. In cafes, the breakfast menu might extend to 11am through the week. Most places will serve a 'full English breakfast' – aka full Welsh, Scottish, Yorkshire etc – a plateful of fried food that might shock if you're just used to cereal.

Lunch Generally taken between noon and 2pm, and can range from a sandwich and a bag of crisps to a three-course meal with wine. Many restaurants offer a set menu two-course lunch at competitive prices on weekdays, while cafes often have a daily lunch special, or offer soup and a sandwich.

Afternoon tea A tradition inherited from the British aristocracy, afternoon tea is enjoying a revival in country hotels and upmarket tearooms. It consists of dainty sandwiches, cakes and pastries, plus, of course, a cup of tea, poured from a silver teapot and sipped politely from fine china cups.

Dinner Sometimes called supper, the main meal of the day is usually served in restaurants between 6pm and 9pm, and consists of two or three

Sunday roast

courses: starter, main and dessert. Upmarket restaurants might serve a tasting menu of even more courses.

Sunday lunch Another great British tradition. Sunday is the one day of the week when the British make lunch the main event. It's normally served between noon and 4pm. Many pubs and restaurants offer Sunday lunch, where the main course usually consists of roast beef, lamb or pork, accompanied by roast and mashed potatoes, gravy, and boiled vegetables such as carrots and peas.

Where to Eat & Drink

There's a huge range of places to eat in Britain these days, from formal fine dining to casual cafes and relaxed gastropubs.

Vegetarian, vegan and plant-based dining is becoming increasingly popular. Almost all restaurants have a decent choice of veggie or vegan dishes, and most towns and cities (and many rural areas too) have at least one or two exclusively veggie or vegan-specific places to eat out.

Cafes Traditional 'greasy spoon' cafes serve classic British staples – cooked breakfasts, sandwiches, pies, sausage and chips – but there's a huge range of cafe types these days, from urban eateries to vegan-friendly hangouts.

Tearooms The tearoom is another British institution, serving cakes, scones and sandwiches accompanied by pots of tea (though coffee is usually available, too). Upmarket tearooms may also serve afternoon tea.

Coffee shops In most cities and towns you'll also find coffee shops – both independents and international chains – serving lattes, cappuccinos and espressos, and continental-style snacks such as bagels, panini and ciabattas.

Restaurants London has scores of excellent restaurants that could hold their own in major cities worldwide, while eating places in other British cities can give the capital a run for its money (often for rather less money).

Pubs Many British pubs serve food, and it's often a good-value option whether you want a toasted sandwich between museum visits in London, or a three-course meal in the evening after touring the castles of Wales.

Gastropubs The modern phenomenon of the gastropub has reinvented British dining. The very best places serve food that rivals restaurant quality (a few have been awarded Michelin stars). The vibe is generally relaxed: no need to dress up. Some places offer table service, at others you'll be ordering at the bar.

Regions at a Glance

With three constituent nations and a smorgasbord of regional identities (many with their own accent and dialect to boot), in many ways Britain is really a country of many countries. The south presents perhaps the most classic vision of England: rolling countryside, patchwork fields, thatched cottages, chalk downs and village greens. Things get wilder out west: Devon, Cornwall and the west of Wales are known for their beaches and cliffs, while Wiltshire is home to the country's most important prehistoric monuments. The northern English cities of Manchester, Liverpool and Newcastle are worth visiting for their industrial heritage and nightlife, while mountain lovers will love the Lake District, the Peak District, North Wales and Yorkshire. Perhaps the grandest scenery of all can be found in Scotland's highlands and islands, where you can really leave the world behind.

London

History
Entertainment
Culture

The Thames

The mighty Thames is the river on which Britain's fortunes have been founded. Cruise past the House of Parliament and Tower Bridge, and ponder the many tales the river might tell: of empire, invasion, intrigue and enlightenment.

Showtime

From the theatreland of the West End to the buzzy clubs of East End, from Camden's music venues to Covent Garden's stately opera house, London offers the prospect of nonstop entertainment.

Museums & Galleries

While the British Museum is the crowd-puller, the capital has museums and galleries of every shape and size – from big hitters such as the V&A and Natural History Museum to little gems like the Sir John Soane's Museum.

p68

Canterbury & Southeast England

Architecture
History
Coast

Canterbury Cathedral

Canterbury Cathedral is one of the holiest places in Christendom. Write your own Canterbury tale as you explore its atmospheric chapels, cloisters and crypts.

Invasion Heritage

The southeast coast has long served as Britain's frontier. Castles and fortresses, the 1066 battlefield and Dover's secret wartime tunnels tell the region's story of invasion and defence.

Brighton & the South Coast

Brighton is a fun-filled south-coast city known for its offbeat, alternative character. Further afield, Hastings, Rye, Whitstable and Margate all have their own salty seaside charm.

p152

Oxford & the Cotswolds

Architecture
Stately Homes
Villages

Oxford Colleges

Oxford's incredible architecture can't fail to impress, whether you're gazing across the 'dreaming spires' from the top of Carfax Tower or tramping the medieval streets on foot.

Blenheim Palace

Favoured by the rich and powerful for centuries, this region is scattered with fabulous country houses. Top of the pile is the baroque masterpiece of Blenheim Palace, birthplace of Sir Winston Churchill.

The Cotswolds

The Cotswolds provide an idyllic snapshot of rural England: thatched cottages, neat greens, medieval churches and charm aplenty.

p186

Bristol, Bath & Somerset

History
Architecture
Scenery

Bristol Harbour

Once among the busiest in Britain, Bristol's harbour has been reinvented as a cultural hub, surrounded by museums, galleries, bars and restaurants. Pride of place is occupied by the monumental SS *Great Britain*.

Bath's Royal Crescent

Is there a grander street in all of England than this? Comprising a horseshoe of neo-Palladian mansions overlooking a broad green park, it's like a scene from a Jane Austen novel brought to life.

Glastonbury Tor

Surrounded by a swirl of myths and legends, this mythical green hill affords an incredible view over the surrounding Somerset Levels.

p232

Hampshire, Wiltshire & Dorset

Ancient History
Ships
Castles

Ancient Sites

From the stone circles of Stonehenge and Avebury to hillside monuments like the Uffington White Horse and the Cerne Giant, this part of England is awash with ancient interest.

Portsmouth's Historic Dockyard

The nation's finest collection of ships can be seen here, including Nelson's flagship, HMS *Victory*, and the wreck of the *Mary Rose*, a Tudor warship raised from the depths.

Castle Country

Fortresses abound here: Iron Age hill forts like Maiden Castle and Cadbury Castle, castellated beauties like Dunster, Portland and Sherborne, and romantic ruins like Corfe Castle.

p268

Devon, Cornwall & the Isles of Scilly

Beaches
Outdoors
Gardens

Beach Time

Devon and Cornwall are home to some of Britain's finest stretches of sand: bucket-and-spade beaches, surfing breaks and wild, secluded coves where the tourists never go.

Hiking & Surfing

A trio of moors (Exmoor, Dartmoor and Bodmin Moor) make for fantastic hiking, while the north coasts of Cornwall and Devon are surf central.

Gardens Galore

Thanks to a balmy climate, horticulture goes haywire in Devon & Cornwall. Tropical trees flourish in gardens like Heligan and Glendurgan, while even more outlandish specimens sprout in the space-age Eden Project.

p304

Cambridge & East Anglia

Architecture
Coastline
Waterways

Churches & Colleges

This corner of England is known for its spectacular cathedrals – Ely, Norwich and Peterborough chief among them – as well as the academic architecture of Cambridge's many colleges.

Seaside Resorts

The coast of East Anglia is a delight. Classic seaside resorts like Southwold and Cromer provide a breath of bracing sea air, while quaint villages and cosy pubs reward inland explorers.

The Broads

The Norfolk and Suffolk Broads is a tranquil area of lakes and meandering rivers, and an ideal spot for boating, birding, canoeing, cycling or walking.

p364

Birmingham & the Midlands

Activities
Stately Homes
Food & Drink

Hiking & Biking

The Peak District, the Malvern Hills and Offa's Dyke Path call out to hikers, while the Tissington Trail and the Pennine Cycleway are a magnet for bikers.

Aristocratic Architecture

Grand houses like Haddon Hall, Burghley House and Chatsworth promise sprawling deer-filled grounds, grand interiors full of priceless heirlooms and walls festooned with oil paintings.

Curry Capital

Birmingham is the curry capital of the country (and, increasingly, a magnet for Michelin-starred chefs), while the tiny town of Ludlow is an epicentre of gastronomic exploration.

p402

Yorkshire

Scenery
Food & Drink
History

National Parks

Yorkshire's landscapes encompass rolling hills, lonely crags and wild moorland. Two national parks – the Yorkshire Dales and the North York Moors – offer epic hiking, rock climbing and cycling.

Real Ale

Yorkshire's breweries turn out some of Britain's best beer, not to mention some of the country's cosiest pubs. Just don't be surprised when the ale's served warm!

Abbeys & Industry

Several strands of history run through Yorkshire: Viking heritage in York, the ancient abbeys of Rievaulx, Fountains and Whitby, and the Industrial Revolution in Leeds, Bradford and Sheffield.

p482

Manchester, Liverpool & Northwest England

History
Sport
Seaside Resorts

Museums

Inspiring places like the People's History Museum in Manchester and the International Slavery Museum in Liverpool bring the region's rich history to vivid life.

Football

Football's a religion in this part of Britain. Two cities, Liverpool and Manchester, give the world four famous clubs, including the two most successful in English history.

Blackpool

The epitome of the classic English seaside resort. Buy yourself some candy floss, and enjoy the bright lights and fairground atmosphere of the Pleasure Beach amusement park.

p536

The Lake District & Cumbria

Scenery
Activities
Literature

Lakes & Mountains

The Lake District is home to England's loftiest hills, including the grandaddy, Scafell Pike. Lakes abound too, some huge – Windermere, Coniston, Ullswater – others small and little-known.

Fell Walking

If anywhere is the heart and soul of walking in England, it's the Lake District. Casual strollers find gentle routes through foothills and valleys, while serious hikers tackle the higher fells.

Literary Lakeland

Countless writers and artists have been inspired by the Lakeland scenery – most famously Romantic poet William Wordsworth and children's writer Beatrix Potter.

p572

Newcastle & Northeast England

History
Landscape
Castles

Hadrian's Wall

Striding for over 70 miles across the neck of England, this massive barrier is one of the greatest Roman structures in the world – and an unforgettable sight.

Northumberland

The broad moors, stone villages and wild coastline of England's most northerly national park make for a stirring road-trip.

Alnwick Castle

Northumberland has lots of castles, including the coastal fortresses of Bamburgh and Dunstanburgh, but Alnwick – setting for the Harry Potter movies – is the most famous.

p610

Cardiff, Pembrokeshire & South Wales

Architecture
Coastline
Castles

Victorian Revival

The Welsh capital is a city with an elegant Victorian past, best glimpsed in the handsome shopping arcades and the whimsical, fairy-tale structures of Cardiff Castle and Castell Coch.

Pembrokeshire Coast

The Gower Peninsula and the Pembrokeshire Coast offer inspirational clifftop views, as well as family-friendly beaches, surfing spots and watery adventures.

Carreg Cennen

Castles are two-a-penny in this part of Wales. Chepstow and Pembroke are must-sees, but remote Carreg Cennen in the Brecon Beacons is the most dramatic of them all.

p646

Brecon Beacons & Mid-Wales

Wildlife
Local Culture
Food & Drink

Red Kites

In the mountains and moors of the Brecon Beacons and many other parts of the region you can spot birds of prey – most famously the once-rare red kites, most easily spotted at feeding stations such as Gigrin Farm in Rhayader.

Market Towns

From book-obsessed Hay-on-Wye to quirky Llanwrtyd Wells and quaint Llandrindod Wells, the market towns of Mid-Wales are full of charm.

Abergavenny

Restaurants, inns and gastropubs throughout the region are at the forefront of a new Welsh gastronomy, all focused on the nation's foodie capital at Abergavenny.

p688

Snowdonia & North Wales

Mountains
Coastline
Environment

Snowdonia

The mountains of Snowdonia stay snow-capped well into spring. A key target is Snowdon, Wales' highest mountain, but there are countless other (quieter) peaks to seek out, too.

Seaside Resorts

From the north coast's popular resort towns to the quiet bays of Anglesey and the Llŷn Peninsula, North Wales has plenty of beach to go round. Don't miss Portmeirion, a fantasyland of whimsical architecture.

Future Power

As the world searches for greener and cleaner energy, the pioneering Centre for Alternative Technology near Machynlleth shows the way.

p714

Edinburgh

Culture
History
Food & Drink

Festival City

The Scottish capital is a city of art and literature. Outside festival time, there's plenty to enjoy in the city's many theatres and world-class art galleries and museums.

Edinburgh Castle

Perched on a brooding black crag overlooking the city centre, Edinburgh Castle has played a pivotal role in Scottish history, the focus of the nation's capital city since medieval times.

Scottish Cuisine

Edinburgh has more restaurants per head of population than any city in the UK, while Scottish cuisine has been given a makeover by inventive chefs using top-quality local produce.

p756

Glasgow & Southern Scotland

Museums
Historic Buildings
Stately Homes

Kelvingrove Art Gallery & Museum

Glasgow's mercantile and industrial history has left the city with a legacy of museums and art galleries, dominated by the grand Victorian cathedral of culture that is Kelvingrove.

The Border Abbeys

Ruined abbeys are the big draws of the Borders: don't miss the Gothic ruins of Melrose, Jedburgh and Dryburgh.

Dumfries House

The Adam brothers designed many lavish mansions, like Culzean Castle and Floors Castle, but Dumfries House takes top prize: an almost perfectly preserved Chippendale time capsule.

p800

Stirling & Central Scotland

Castles
Islands
Whisky

Stirling Castle

Central and north-east Scotland are home to the greatest concentration of castles in the country, from the turreted exuberance of Craigievar to the more restrained elegance of Balmoral, but topped by the regal splendour of Stirling.

Island Hopping

Island-hopping is a great way to explore Scotland's western seaboard, and the islands of this region – wild Jura, scenic Mull and the jewel of Iona – provide a brilliant introduction.

Whisky Distilleries

No trip to Scotland is complete without a visit to a whisky distillery – the Speyside region and the isle of Islay are epicentres of the industry.

p836

Inverness & the Highlands & Islands

Activities
Scenery
Ancient History

Hill Walking

The ski resort of Aviemore and Fort William, self-styled outdoor capital of the UK, offers enough outdoor adventures to keep you busy year-round.

Lochs & Glens

Landscape photographers are spoilt for choice, with classic views ranging from the mountain beauty of Glen Coe and the snow-patched summits of the Cairngorms to the rock pinnacles of the Cuillin Hills.

Prehistoric Sites

The region is rich in prehistoric remains, including the standing stones of Callanish, the neolithic tomb of Maeshowe, and Skara Brae – Europe's best-preserved prehistoric village.

p890

On the Road

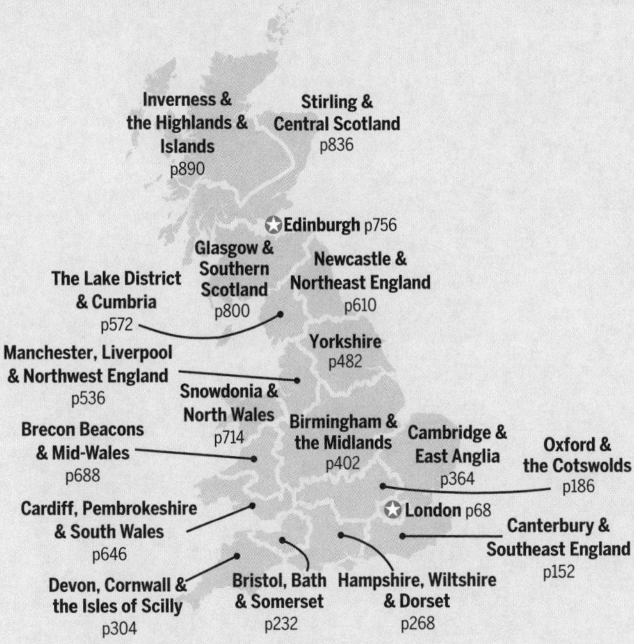

Inverness & the Highlands & Islands p890
Stirling & Central Scotland p836
Edinburgh p756
Glasgow & Southern Scotland p800
Newcastle & Northeast England p610
The Lake District & Cumbria p572
Yorkshire p482
Manchester, Liverpool & Northwest England p536
Snowdonia & North Wales p714
Brecon Beacons & Mid-Wales p688
Birmingham & the Midlands p402
Cambridge & East Anglia p364
Oxford & the Cotswolds p186
London p68
Cardiff, Pembrokeshire & South Wales p646
Canterbury & Southeast England p152
Devon, Cornwall & the Isles of Scilly p304
Bristol, Bath & Somerset p232
Hampshire, Wiltshire & Dorset p268

England

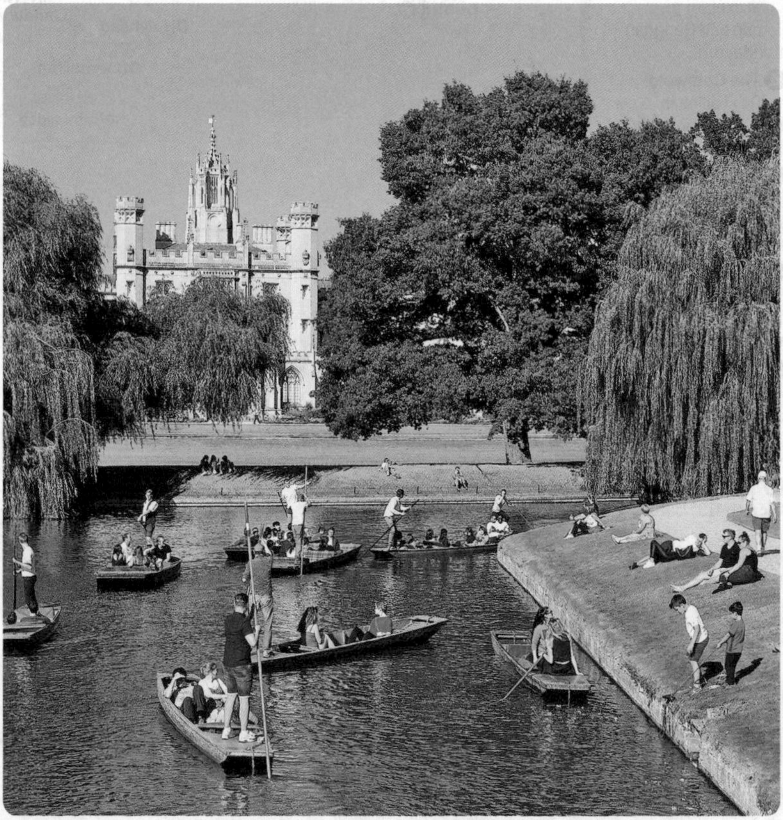

PUNTING BY CAMBRIDGE UNIVERSITY, CAMBRIDGESHIRE (P368); RON ELLIS/SHUTTERSTOCK ©

England Highlights

1 Stonehenge (p298) Marvelling at Britain's most iconic archaeological site.

2 Oxford (p188) Getting some higher education among the dreaming spires of this university town.

3 The Lake District (p578) Wandering lonely as a cloud in idyllic Lakeland.

4 York (p487) Exploring medieval walls, Viking sights and the soaring Gothic minster.

5 Bath (p245) Being a Jane Austen character for a day while exploring Roman and Georgian architecture.

6 The Cotswolds (p204) Falling in love with impossibly quaint villages.

7 Hadrian's Wall (p627) Seeing wild scenery and ancient engineering.

8 Cambridge (p368) Punting past historic colleges along the River Cam.

9 Liverpool (p555) Visiting the iconic Beatles sites and top museums along the waterfront.

10 Stratford-upon-Avon (p419) Catching a Shakespeare play or visiting the Bard's grave.

0 100 km
0 50 miles
Berwick-upon-Tweed
Kelso
Melrose
Northumberland National Park
Alnwick
Hadrian's Wall
7
Newcastle-upon-Tyne
Tynemouth
Durham
Penrith
Darlington
Whitby
North York Moors National Park
Scarborough
Yorkshire Dales National Park
Lancaster
Forest of Bowland
4 York
Leeds
Grimsby
Manchester
Peak District National Park
Sheffield
Chester
Buxton
Chesterfield
Lincoln
Skegness
Boston
The Wash
Holkam
Stoke-on-Trent
Derby
Nottingham
The Fens
King's Lynn
Norwich
Shrewsbury
Leicester
Stamford
The Broads
Birmingham
Ludlow
8 Cambridge
Worcester
10 Stratford-upon-Avon
Hereford
Cheltenham
The Cotswolds
6
Colchester
Gloucester
Forest of Dean
2 Oxford
St Albans
River Thames
Southend-on-Sea
Bristol
LONDON
Windsor
Isle of Thanet
Ostend
5 Bath
Newbury
Canterbury
BELGIUM
Leeds
1 Stonehenge
Dover
Veurne
Salisbury
Winchester
South Downs National Park
Calais
Rye
Strait of Dover
New Forest National Park
Worthing
Brighton
St-Omer
Bournemouth
Portsmouth
Eastbourne
Boulogne-sur-Mer
Isle of Wight
Lyme Bay
Weymouth
English Channel
FRANCE
Lens
Arras
Mers-les-Bains
Abbeville
Dieppe
Amiens
NORTH SEA
0° (Greenwich)
1°W
1°E
2°E
3°E
2°W

AT A GLANCE

POPULATION
8.8 million

OLDEST CHURCH
St Bartholomew-the-Great (founded in 1123; p93)

BEST FOOD MARKET
Borough Market (p144)

BEST COCKTAIL BAR
Connaught Bar (p133)

BEST TRADITIONAL PUB
Holly Bush (p137)

WHEN TO GO

Mar–May
Colour returns with daffodils, cherry blossoms and wisteria in bloom.

Jun–Sep
Parks fill with sunbathers and picnics, and the city is busy with summer festivals.

Oct–Dec
Halloween, Guy Fawkes Night and Christmas promise parties, decorations, fireworks, ice-skating, and possibly a whisper of snow.

The Shard (p87) and London skyline

London

Immersed in history, London's rich seams of eye-opening antiquity are everywhere, with landmarks like the Tower of London, Westminster Abbey and the Palace of Westminster. These are juxtaposed with modern icons like the Shard, the Gherkin and Tate Modern. London is also a city of ideas and the imagination – whether it's theatrical innovation, contemporary art, music, writing, cutting-edge design or culinary adventure. Throw in charming parks, historic neighbourhoods, leafy suburbs and tranquil riverbanks and you have, quite simply, one of the world's great metropolises.

INCLUDES

History

London first came into being as a Celtic village near a ford across the River Thames, but the city only really took off after the Roman conquest in 43 CE. The invaders enclosed their 'Londinium' in walls that still find refrain in the shape of the City (with a capital 'C') of London today.

By the end of the 3rd century CE, Londinium was home to some 30,000 people. Internal strife and relentless barbarian attacks wore the Romans down, however, and they abandoned Britain in the 5th century, reducing the settlement to a sparsely populated backwater. The Saxons moved in next, their 'Lundenwic' prospering and becoming a large, well-organised town.

As the city grew in importance, it caught the eye of Danish Vikings who launched numerous invasions. In 1016 the Saxons, finally beaten down, were forced to accept the Danish leader Knut (Canute) as King of England, after which London replaced Winchester as capital. In 1042, the throne reverted to the Saxon Edward the Confessor, who built Westminster Abbey.

The Norman Conquest of 1066 saw William the Conqueror march into London, where he was crowned king. He built the White Tower (the core of the Tower of London), negotiated taxes with the merchants, and affirmed the city's right to self-government. From then until the late 15th century, London politics were largely taken up by a three-way power struggle between the monarchy, the Church and city guilds.

An uneasy political compromise was reached between the factions, and the city expanded rapidly in the 16th century under the House of Tudor. In a rerun of the disease that wiped out half of London's population between 1348 and 1350, the Great Plague struck in 1665, and by the time the winter cold arrested the epidemic, 100,000 Londoners had perished.

The cataclysm was followed by further devastation when the Great Fire of 1666 sent the city skywards. One upshot of the conflagration was a blank canvas for master architect Sir Christopher Wren to build his magnificent churches. Despite these setbacks, London continued to grow, and by 1700 it was Europe's largest city, with 600,000 people. An influx of foreign workers brought expansion to the east and south, while those who could afford it headed to the more salubrious environs of the north and west.

Georgian London saw a surge in artistic creativity, with the likes of Dr Johnson, Handel, Gainsborough and Reynolds enriching the city's culture, while architects fashioned an elegant new metropolis. In 1837, 18-year-old Victoria began her epic reign, as London became the fulcrum of the British Empire. The Industrial Revolution saw the building of new docks and railways (including the first underground line in 1863), while the Great Exhibition of 1851 showcased London to the world. During the Victorian era, the city's population mushroomed from just over two million to 6.6 million.

Although London suffered a relatively minor bruising during WWI, it was devastated by the Luftwaffe in WWII, when huge swaths of the centre and East End were flattened and 32,000 people were killed. Ugly housing and low-cost developments followed, but prosperity gradually returned to the city, and creative energy bottled up in the postwar years was suddenly unleashed. In the 'Swinging Sixties', London became the capital of cool in fashion and music – a party followed morosely by the austere 1970s.

Since then the city has surfed up and down the waves of global fortunes, hanging on to its position as the world's leading financial centre. In 2000, the modern metropolis won its first mayor of London, an elected role covering the City and all 32 urban boroughs. Bicycle-riding Boris Johnson was elected in 2008, and retained his post in the 2012 mayoral election. In August 2011, numerous London boroughs were rocked by riots characterised by looting and arson, triggered by the controversial shooting of a man by police in Tottenham.

Both the Olympics and the Queen's Diamond Jubilee concocted a splendid display of pageantry for London in 2012. New overground train lines opened, a cable car was flung across the Thames and a once run-down and polluted area of East London was regenerated for the Olympic Park.

Since the Olympics, the city has changed leadership, with Labour politician Sadiq Khan taking over as mayor from Boris Johnson. Scores of new high-rise buildings transformed the London skyline, most notably on the South Bank. Another key development has been the Crossrail, the capital's large and costly construction project, which will

LONDON IN...

Two Days

Begin with the West End's big-draw sights: Westminster Abbey, then Buckingham Palace (p86) for the Changing of the Guard. Walk up the Mall to Trafalgar Square (p83) for its architectural grandeur and photo-op views down Whitehall, then take a spin round the National Gallery (p83). In the afternoon, hop over to the South Bank for a ride on the London Eye (p97) and a visit to the Tate Modern (p93), followed by an evening performance at Shakespeare's Globe (p97).

On day two, spend the day wandering around the marvellous British Museum (p82), followed by a spot of shopping around Covent Garden and Oxford St, then dining and bar hopping in Chinatown and Soho.

Four Days

On day three, head for London's finance-driven heart in the City, home to the sprawling and ancient Tower of London (p90). Spend the morning watching the Beefeaters and resident ravens preen and strut, and then marvel at the Crown Jewels. When you're finished, admire the iconic Tower Bridge (p92) from the banks of the Thames or through the glass floors of the walkways connecting the two towers. While away the rest of the day exploring the street art and shopping of the East End, with visits to Brick Lane and Spitalfields Market (p144).

On day four, hop on a boat from any central London pier and make your way down to Greenwich with its world-renowned architecture and links to time, the stars and space. Start your visit at the legendary Cutty Sark (p114), a star clipper during the tea-trade years, and have a look into the National Maritime Museum (p113). Stroll up through Greenwich Park all the way to the Royal Observatory (p113). Head back to South Bank and Southwark by ferry for a show or a film at one of its iconic theatres (p139).

Seven Days

With a few extra days, you'll have time to explore some of London's other neighbourhoods. On day five, head for North London, with a morning at Camden Market (p144), a visit to Highgate Cemetery (p112) and a walk over Hampstead Heath (p111). On day six, explore the famous Portobello Road Market (p114) in Notting Hill, then spend the rest of the day with chic shopping in Knightsbridge, or visiting the museums of South Kensington, such as the Natural History Museum (p99) and the Science Museum (p103). On day seven, head out to West London, where you'll discover the delightful green spaces of Kew Gardens and Richmond Park and the grand palace of Hampton Court (p115).

add a new east–west train line that promises to ease travel time and congestion for city commuters. But what lasting impact the Covid-19 pandemic coupled with Brexit will have on this great city's future remains to be seen.

Sights

West End

★Westminster Abbey CHURCH

(Map p78; ☎020-7222 5152; www.westminster-abbey.org; 20 Dean's Yard, SW1; adult/child £24/10, half-price Wed 4.30pm; ⏲9.30am-3.30pm Mon, Tue, Thu & Fri, to 6pm Wed, to 3pm Sat May-Aug, to 1pm Sat Sep-Apr; Ⓤ Westminster) A splendid mixture of architectural styles, Westminster Abbey is considered the finest example of Early English Gothic. It's not merely a beautiful place of worship – the Abbey is still a working church and the stage on which history unfolds. For centuries, the country's greatest have been interred here, including 17 monarchs from King Henry III (1272) to King George II (1760). Much of the Abbey's architecture is from the 13th century, but it was founded much earlier, in 960 CE.

Every monarch since William the Conqueror has been crowned here, with the exception of a couple of Eds who were either murdered (Edward V) or abdicated (Edward VIII) before the magic moment. Never a cathedral (the seat of a bishop), Westminster Abbey is what is called a 'royal peculiar', administered by the Crown.

At the heart of the Abbey is the beautifully tiled **sanctuary**, the stage for coronations,

London Highlights

❶ **British Museum** (p82) Marvelling at the epoch-spanning collections of the nation's flagship museum.

❷ **Tower of London** (p90) Viewing the dazzling Crown Jewels in this thousand year-old fortress.

❸ **St Paul's Cathedral** (p89) Reaching for the heavens inside and outside on that iconic dome.

❹ **Tate Modern** (p93) Exploring London's architecturally distinctive art museum.

❺ **Hampstead Heath** (p111) Wandering the paths and

woodlands of North London's green space.

6 Kew Gardens (p115) Stepping into a miniature rainforest inside the subtropical Palm House.

7 East London (p129) Snapping street art, vintage shopping and indulging in innovative dining.

8 Shakespeare's Globe (p97) Seeing one of the Bard's plays or taking a guided tour of the replica theatre.

9 Regent's Park (p112) Watching the world pass by in one of London's loveliest parks.

NEIGHBOURHOODS AT A GLANCE

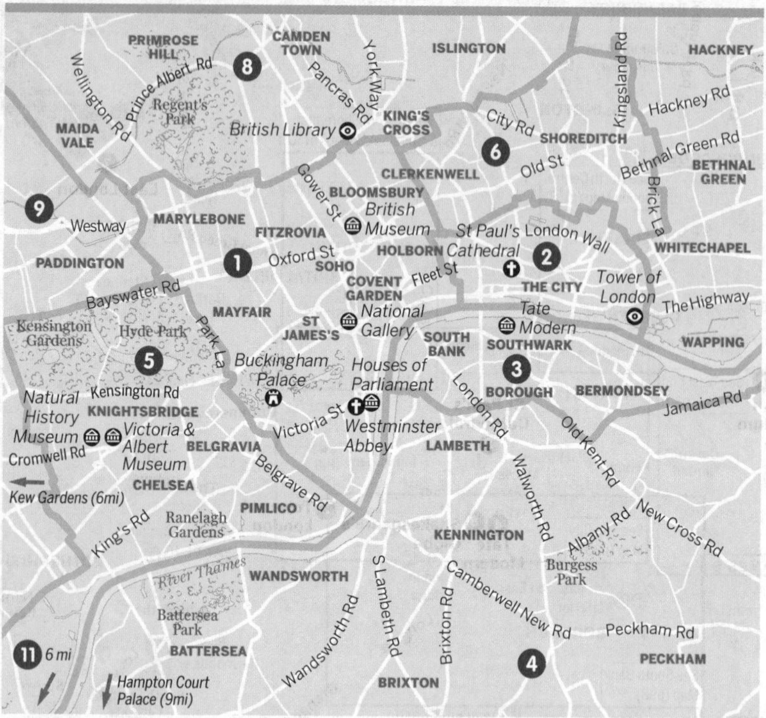

❶ West End (p71)

The West End encompasses many of London's most iconic locations, buildings and museums, notably Trafalgar Square, Piccadilly Circus, Buckingham Palace, Westminster Abbey and the British Museum – not to mention theatres, parks, shopping and nightlife.

❷ City of London (p89)

London's historic core is usually packed with office workers on weekdays but eerily quiet at weekends. The current millennium has seen a profusion of daring skyscrapers sprout, a visual contrast to famous sites such as Tower of London and St Paul's Cathedral.

❸ South Bank (p93)

South Bank is a must-visit area for art lovers, theatre-goers and architecture buffs, with the creative Tate Modern and iconic brutalist buildings to explore.

❹ Brixton, Peckham & South London (p114)

In Brixton and Peckham, Afro-Caribbean haunts bump up against pocket-sized eating and drinking venues. Sample suburban Clapham and Battersea for local life, and Dulwich Village for a country-hamlet vibe.

❺ Kensington & Hyde Park (p99)

Well-groomed Kensington is among London's handsomest neighbourhoods. It has three fine museums – the V&A, Natural History Museum and Science Museum – plus excellent dining and shopping, graceful parklands and grand period architecture.

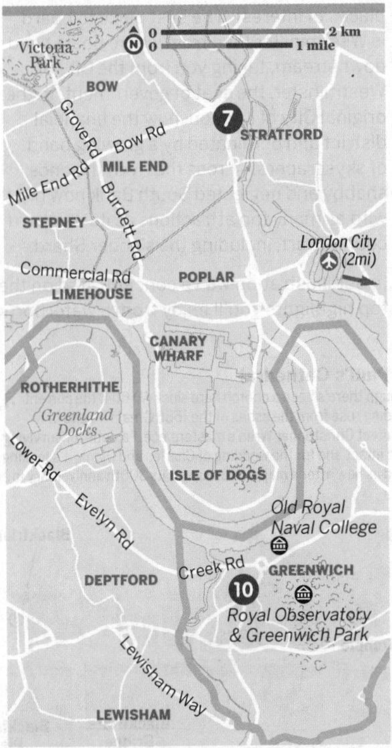

❻ Clerkenwell, Shoreditch & Spitalfields (p107)

Historic city-fringe neighbourhoods best known for culture and nightlife. Shoreditch and Hoxton long ago replaced Soho and Camden as London's hippest party spots.

❼ East London (p108)

Interesting museums and galleries, excellent pubs, canal-side dining, punctuated by street art and vintage stores.

❽ North London (p109)

Head east from Camden's famous market and unrivalled music scene to check out the transformed King's Cross Station area. Then take in the green spaces at Hampstead Heath and Regent's Park.

❾ West London (p114)

Come for Portobello Road Market, the Design Museum, historic cinemas, lush parkland, grand mansions and imposing churches. Stay for the superb pubs and clubs, diverse shopping and global eats.

❿ Greenwich (p113)

Regal historic Greenwich complements its riverside village feel with grand architecture, bustling weekend markets, grassy parklands and cosy riverside pubs.

⓫ Richmond, Kew & Hampton Court (p115)

Visit London's leafy, riverside region to get lost in Kew Gardens, deer-spot in Richmond Park, traipse around Wimbledon Common and down a pint waterside as the sun sets on the Thames.

The River Thames

A FLOATING TOUR

London's history has always been determined by the Thames. The city was founded as a Roman port nearly 2000 years ago and over the centuries since then many of the capital's landmarks have lined the river's banks. A boat trip is a great way to experience the attractions.

There are piers dotted along both banks at regular intervals where you can hop on and hop off the regular services to visit places of interest. The best place to board is Westminster Pier, from where boats head downstream, taking you from the City of Westminster, the seat of government, to the original City of London, now the financial district and dominated by a growing band of skyscrapers. Across the river, the once shabby and neglected South Bank now bristles with as many top attractions as its northern counterpart, including the slender Shard.

In our illustration we've concentrated on the top highlights you'll enjoy from a waterborne

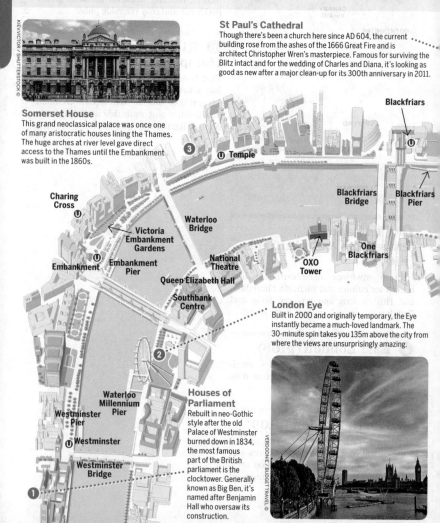

KIEV.VICTOR / SHUTTERSTOCK ©

Somerset House

This grand neoclassical palace was once one of many aristocratic houses lining the Thames. The huge arches at river level gave direct access to the Thames until the Embankment was built in the 1860s.

St Paul's Cathedral

Though there's been a church here since AD 604, the current building rose from the ashes of the 1666 Great Fire and is architect Christopher Wren's masterpiece. Famous for surviving the Blitz intact and for the wedding of Charles and Diana, it's looking as good as new after a major clean-up for its 300th anniversary in 2011.

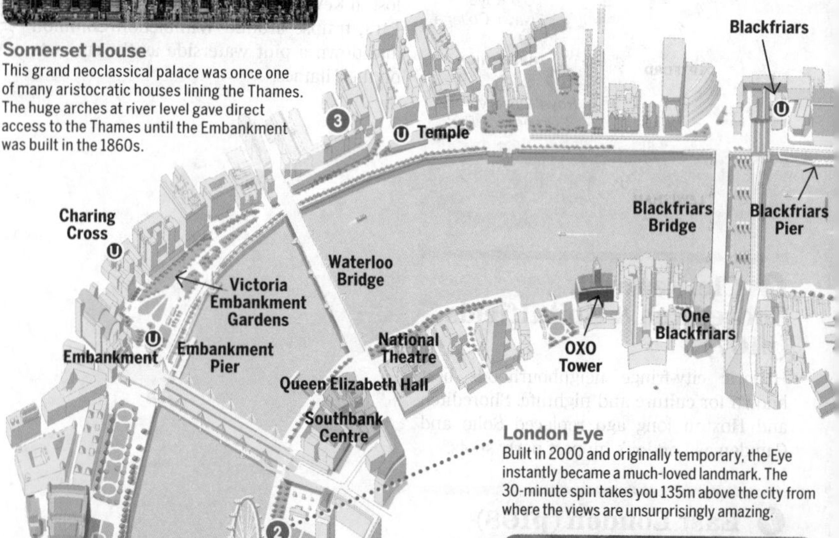

London Eye

Built in 2000 and originally temporary, the Eye instantly became a much-loved landmark. The 30-minute spin takes you 135m above the city from where the views are unsurprisingly amazing.

Houses of Parliament

Rebuilt in neo-Gothic style after the old Palace of Westminster burned down in 1834, the most famous part of the British parliament is the clocktower. Generally known as Big Ben, it's named after Benjamin Hall who oversaw its construction.

VERDOONIE / BUDGET TRAVEL ©

vessel. These are, from west to east, the **1 Houses of Parliament**, the **2 London Eye**, **3 Somerset House**, **4 St Paul's Cathedral**, the **5 Tate Modern**, **6 Shakespeare's Globe**, the **7 Tower of London** and **8 Tower Bridge**.

In addition to covering this central section of the Thames, boats can also be taken upstream as far as Kew Gardens and Hampton Court Palace, and downstream as far as Greenwich and the Thames Barrier.

BOAT HOPPING

Thames Clippers hop-on/hop-off services are aimed at commuters but are equally useful for visitors, operating every 15 minutes on a loop from piers at Westminster, Embankment, Waterloo, Blackfriars, Bankside, London Bridge and the Tower. Oyster cardholders get a discount off the boat ticket price.

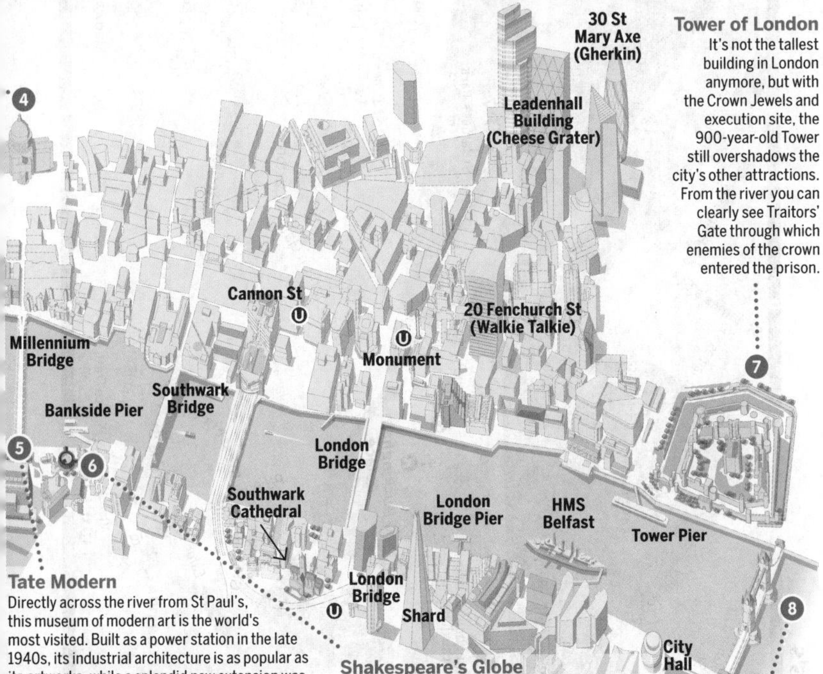

Tower of London
It's not the tallest building in London anymore, but with the Crown Jewels and execution site, the 900-year-old Tower still overshadows the city's other attractions. From the river you can clearly see Traitors' Gate through which enemies of the crown entered the prison.

Tate Modern
Directly across the river from St Paul's, this museum of modern art is the world's most visited. Built as a power station in the late 1940s, its industrial architecture is as popular as its artworks, while a splendid new extension was completed in 2016.

Shakespeare's Globe
The reconstructed Globe stands on the river a few hundred metres from where the original stood (and burnt down in 1613 during a performance). The life's work of American actor Sam Wanamaker, the theatre runs a hugely popular season from April to October each year.

Tower Bridge
It might look as old as its namesake neighbour but one of the world's most iconic bridges was only completed in 1894. Not to be confused with London Bridge upstream, this one's famous raising bascules allowed tall ships to dock at the old wharves to the west and are still lifted up to 1000 times a year.

Westminster & St James's

0 — 500 m
0 — 0.25 miles

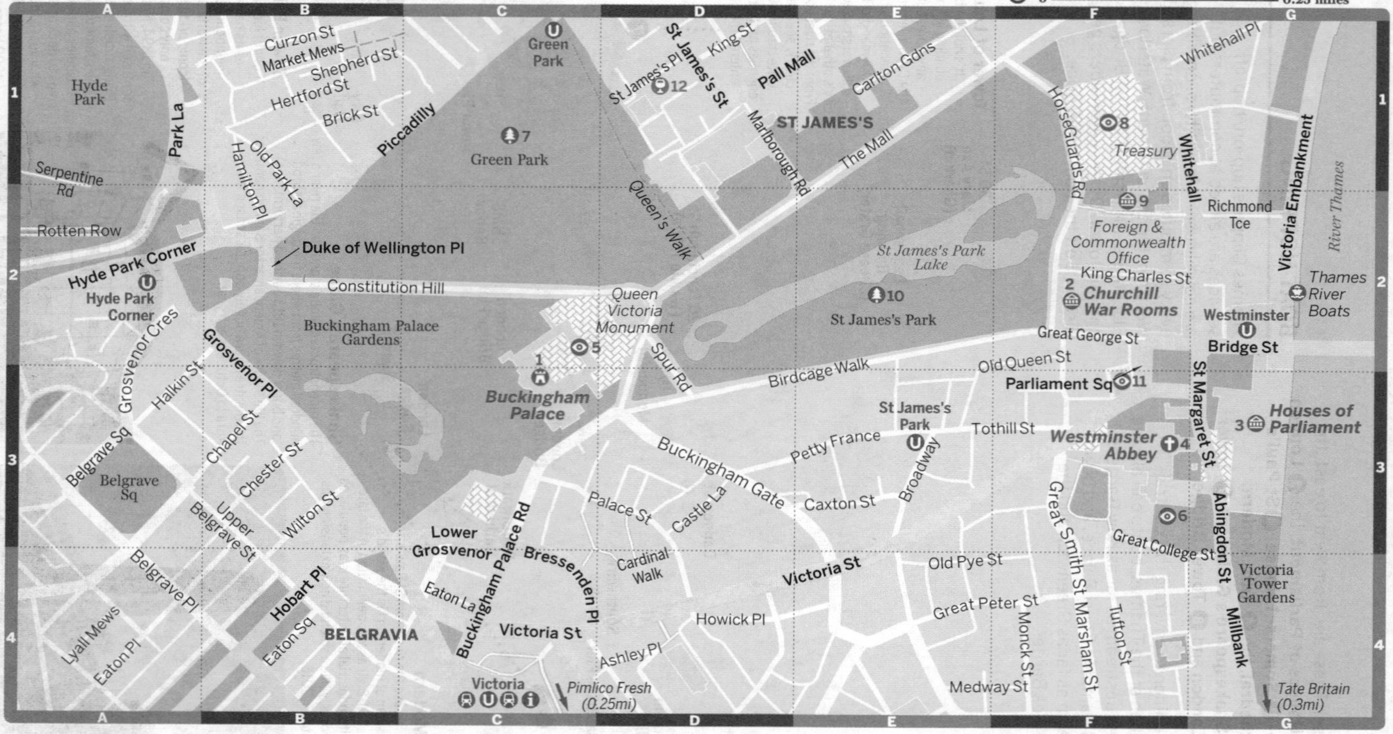
A
B
C
D
E
F
G
1
2
3
4
Hyde Park
Park La
Serpentine Rd
Rotten Row
Hyde Park Corner
Hyde Park Corner
Curzon St
Market Mews
Shepherd St
Hertford St
Brick St
Old Park La
Hamilton Pl
Piccadilly
Green Park
7
Green Park
Duke of Wellington Pl
Constitution Hill
Buckingham Palace Gardens
Grosvenor Cres
Halkin St
Grosvenor Pl
Belgrave Sq
Belgrave Sq
Chapel St
Chester St
Wilton St
Upper Belgrave St
Belgrave Pl
Lyall Mews
Eaton Pl
Hobart Pl
Eaton Sq
BELGRAVIA
St James's Pl
12
St James's St
King St
Pall Mall
Carlton Gdns
ST JAMES'S
Marlborough Rd
The Mall
Queen's Walk
Queen Victoria Monument
5
1
Buckingham Palace
Spur Rd
Lower Grosvenor
Buckingham Palace Rd
Bressenden Pl
Eaton La
Victoria St
Victoria
Pimlico Fresh (0.25mi)
Ashley Pl
Howick Pl
Cardinal Walk
Palace St
Castle La
Buckingham Gate
Petty France
Caxton St
Broadway
St James's Park
St James's Park Lake
10
St James's Park
Birdcage Walk
Great George St
Old Queen St
Parliament Sq
11
Tothill St
Victoria St
Old Pye St
Great Peter St
Monck St
Medway St
Great Smith St
Marsham St
Tufton St
Great College St
6
Westminster Abbey
4
St Margaret St
Abingdon St
Millbank
Victoria Tower Gardens
Tate Britain (0.3mi)
HorseGuards Rd
8
Treasury
9
Foreign & Commonwealth Office
King Charles St
2
Churchill War Rooms
Whitehall Pl
Whitehall
Richmond Tce
Victoria Embankment
River Thames
Thames River Boats
Westminster
Bridge St
3
Houses of Parliament

Westminster & St James's

Top Sights
1 Buckingham Palace ... C3
2 Churchill War Rooms ... F2
3 Houses of Parliament ... G3
4 Westminster Abbey ... F3

Sights
5 Changing the Guard ... C2
6 College Garden ... F3
7 Green Park ... C1
8 Horse Guards Parade ... F1
9 No 10 Downing Street ... F2
10 St James's Park ... E2
11 Supreme Court ... F3

Drinking & Nightlife
12 Dukes London ... D1

royal weddings and funerals. Architect George Gilbert Scott designed the ornate **High Altar** in 1873. In front of the altar is the **Cosmati Pavement**, dating to 1268. It has intricate designs of small pieces of stone and glass inlaid into plain marble, which symbolise the universe at the end of time (an inscription claims the world will end after 19,683 years). At the entrance to the lovely **Chapel of St John the Baptist** is a sublime translucent alabaster *Virgin and Child*, placed here in 1971.

The most sacred spot in the Abbey is the **shrine of St Edward the Confessor**, which lies behind the High Altar; access is restricted to guided tours to protect the fragile 13th-century flooring. King Edward, long considered a saint before he was canonised, was the founder of the Abbey, and the original building was consecrated a few weeks before his death in 1066. Henry III added a new shrine with Cosmati mosaics in the mid-12th century where the sick prayed for healing – and also chipped off a few souvenirs to take home.

The **Quire** (choir), a stunning space of gold, blue and red Victorian Gothic decoration above a black-and-white chequerboard tiled floor, dates to the mid-19th century. It sits where the original choir for the monks' worship would have been but bears little resemblance to the original. Nowadays, the Quire is still used for singing, but its regular occupants are the Choir of Westminster Abbey – about 30 boys and 12 'lay vicars' (men) who sing the daily services and evensong (5pm on weekdays except Wednesday and 3pm on weekends).

Henry III began work on the new Abbey building in 1245 but didn't complete it; the Gothic nave was finished under Richard II in 1388. Henry VII's magnificent Perpendicular Gothic–style **Lady Chapel**, with an impressive fan-vaulted ceiling and tall stained-glass windows, was completed after 13 years of construction in 1516.

Opened in 2018, the **Queen's Diamond Jubilee Galleries** (timed tickets, an additional £5) are a new museum and gallery space located in the medieval triforium, the arched gallery above the nave. Among its exhibits are the death masks and wax effigies of generations of royalty, armour and stained glass. Highlights are the graffiti-inscribed chair used for the coronation of Mary II, the beautifully illustrated manuscripts of the *Litlyngton Missal* from 1380 and the 13th-century Westminster Retable, England's oldest surviving altarpiece.

At the western end of the nave near the **Tomb of the Unknown Warrior**, killed in France during WWI and laid to rest here in 1920, is St George's Chapel, which contains the rather ordinary-looking **Coronation Chair**, upon which every monarch since the early 14th century has been crowned (apart from joint monarchs Mary II and William III, who had their own chairs fashioned for the event in 1689).

Apart from the royal graves, keep an eye out for the many famous commoners interred here, especially in **Poets' Corner**, where you'll find the resting places of Geoffrey Chaucer, Charles Dickens, Thomas Hardy, Alfred Tennyson, Samuel Johnson and Rudyard Kipling, as well as memorials to the other greats (William Shakespeare, Jane Austen, the Brontë sisters etc). Another set of illustrious stones is in **Scientists' Corner** near the north aisle of the nave, including the final resting places of Sir Isaac Newton, Charles Darwin and the ashes of Stephen Hawking.

Downloadable audio guides are included in the ticket price, but to get more out of your visit, join a 90-minute **verger-led tour** (an additional £7), which includes some 'VIP access', such as Edward's shrine and getting to sit in the Quire stalls.

Parts of the Abbey complex are free to visitors, including the Cloisters, Chapter

West End

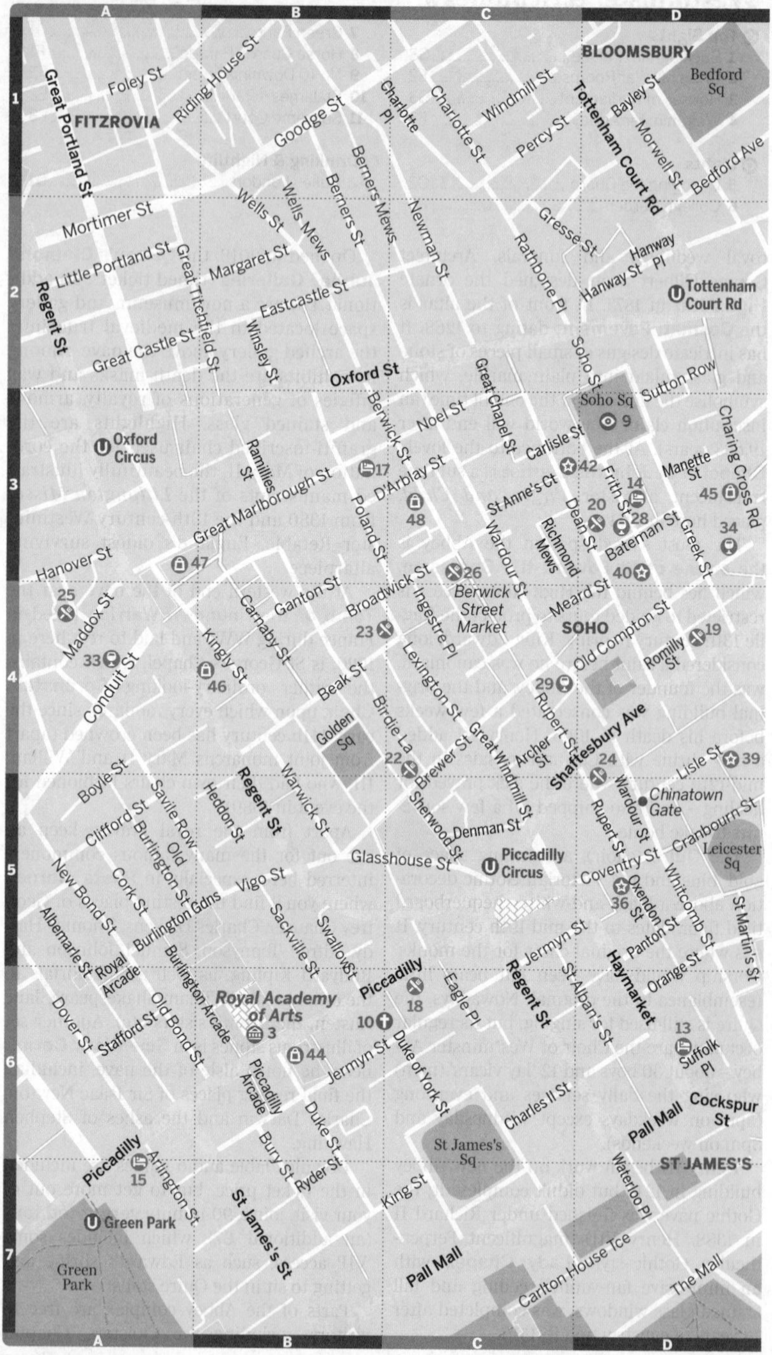

A
B
C
D
1
2
3
4
5
6
7
BLOOMSBURY
Bedford Sq
FITZROVIA
Great Portland St
Foley St
Riding House St
Goodge St
Charlotte Pl
Charlotte St
Windmill St
Tottenham Court Rd
Bayley St
Morwell St
Bedford Ave
Percy St
Berners Mews
Berners St
Wells Mews
Wells St
Newman St
Mortimer St
Little Portland St
Great Titchfield St
Margaret St
Eastcastle St
Rathbone Pl
Gresse St
Hanway St
Hanway Pl
Tottenham Court Rd
Regent St
Great Castle St
Winsley St
Oxford St
Great Chapel St
Soho St
Soho Sq
Sutton Row
9
Charing Cross Rd
Oxford Circus
Berwick St
Noel St
Carlisle St
Ramillies St
17
D'Arblay St
Manette St
42
Frith St
14
Great Marlborough St
St Anne's Ct
45
48
20
28
Poland St
Dean St
Richmond Mews
Wardour St
Bateman St
Greek St
34
Hanover St
47
26
40
Berwick Street Market
Broadwick St
Ingestre Pl
Meard St
25
Maddox St
Ganton St
Carnaby St
SOHO
Old Compton St
23
Romilly St
19
33
Kingly St
Lexington St
Conduit St
46
Beak St
29
Rupert St
Golden Sq
Birdie La
Brewer St
Great Windmill St
Archer St
Shaftesbury Ave
24
Lisle St
39
22
Chinatown Gate
Boyle St
Clifford St
Savile Row
Heddon St
Regent St
Warwick St
Sherwood St
Wardour St
Rupert St
Cranbourn St
Old Burlington St
Denman St
Leicester Sq
New Bond St
Cork St
Glasshouse St
Piccadilly Circus
Coventry St
Whitcomb St
Vigo St
Oxendon St
36
St Martin's St
Burlington Gdns
Sackville St
Albemarle St
Royal Arcade
Burlington Arcade
Swallow St
Jermyn St
Panton St
Piccadilly
Regent St
St Alban's St
Haymarket
Orange St
Dover St
Stafford St
Old Bond St
Royal Academy of Arts
18
Eagle Pl
3
10
13
44
Jermyn St
Duke of York St
Suffolk Pl
Piccadilly Arcade
Charles II St
Cockspur St
Duke St
Bury St
St James's Sq
Pall Mall
Piccadilly
Arlington St
Ryder St
Waterloo Pl
ST JAMES'S
15
King St
Green Park
St James's St
Pall Mall
Carlton House Tce
Green Park
The Mall

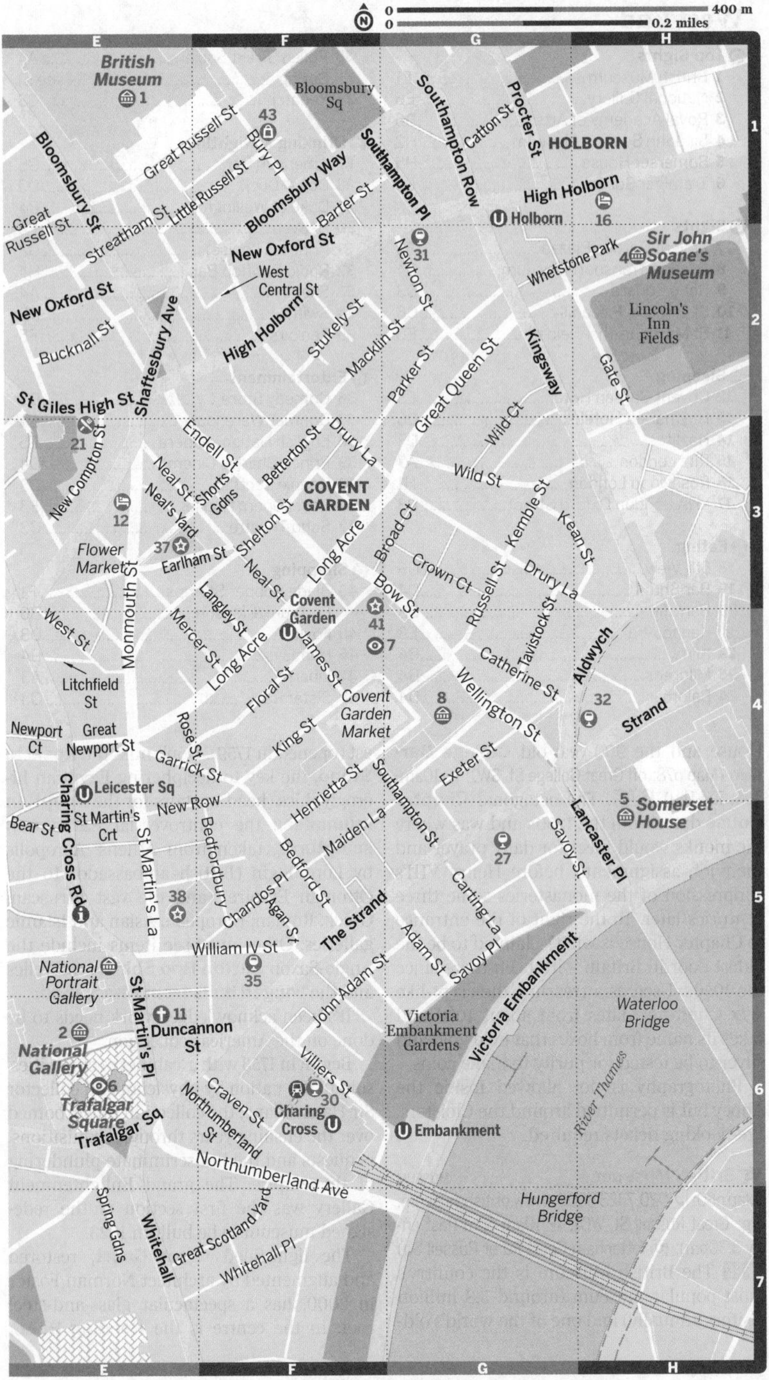
0 400 m
0 0.2 miles
E
F
G
H
1
2
3
4
5
6
7
British Museum
1
Bloomsbury Sq
43
Southampton Row
Procter St
Catton St
HOLBORN
High Holborn
16
Holborn
Great Russell St
Bury Pl
Bloomsbury Way
Southampton Pl
Bloomsbury St
Little Russell St
Barter St
Great Russell St
Streatham St
31
New Oxford St
Newton St
Whetstone Park
Sir John Soane's Museum
4
West Central St
New Oxford St
Lincoln's Inn Fields
Shaftesbury Ave
Bucknall St
High Holborn
Stukely St
Macklin St
Kingsway
Parker St
Great Queen St
Gate St
St Giles High St
21
New Compton St
Endell St
Drury La
Betterton St
Wild Ct
Wild St
Neal St
Shorts Gdns
Neal's Yard
COVENT GARDEN
12
Shelton St
Broad Ct
Kemble St
Kean St
37
Flower Market
Earlham St
Long Acre
Crown Ct
Russell St
Drury La
Neal St
Covent Garden
Bow St
41
Tavistock St
Monmouth St
Langley St
Mercer St
West St
Long Acre
James St
7
Aldwych
Catherine St
Litchfield St
Floral St
Covent Garden Market
8
Wellington St
32
Strand
Newport Ct
Great Newport St
Rose St
King St
Exeter St
Garrick St
Leicester Sq
Henrietta St
Southampton St
New Row
Lancaster Pl
5
Somerset House
Charing Cross Rd
Bear St
St Martin's Crt
St Martin's La
Bedfordbury
Maiden La
Savoy St
Bedford St
27
38
Chandos Pl
Carting La
Agan St
The Strand
Adam St
Savoy Pl
William IV St
Victoria Embankment
35
National Portrait Gallery
John Adam St
Waterloo Bridge
St Martin's Pl
11
Victoria Embankment Gardens
2
National Gallery
Duncannon St
Villiers St
River Thames
6
Trafalgar Square
Craven St
30
Trafalgar Sq
Northumberland St
Charing Cross
Embankment
Northumberland Ave
Hungerford Bridge
Spring Gdns
Whitehall
Great Scotland Yard
Whitehall Pl

West End

Top Sights
1 British Museum ... E1
2 National Gallery ... E6
3 Royal Academy of Arts ... B6
4 Sir John Soane's Museum ... H2
5 Somerset House ... H5
6 Trafalgar Square ... E6

Sights
7 Covent Garden Piazza ... F4
8 London Transport Museum ... G4
9 Soho Square ... D3
10 St James's Piccadilly ... C6
11 St Martin-in-the-Fields ... E6

Sleeping
12 Covent Garden Hotel ... E3
13 Haymarket Hotel ... D6
14 Hazlitt's ... D3
15 Ritz London ... A7
16 Rosewood London ... H1
17 YHA London Oxford Street ... B3

Eating
18 5th View ... C6
19 Bar Shu ... D4
20 Barrafina ... D3
21 Kanada-Ya ... E3
22 Kiln ... C4
23 Mildreds ... B4
24 Palomar ... D4
25 Pollen Street Social ... A4
Spring ... (see 5)
26 Yauatcha ... C3

Drinking & Nightlife
27 American Bar ... G5
28 Dog & Duck ... D3
29 Duke of Wellington ... C4
30 Heaven ... F6
31 Princess Louise ... G2
32 Radio Rooftop Bar ... H4
33 Sketch ... A4
34 Swift ... D3
35 Terroirs ... F5

Entertainment
36 Comedy Store ... D5
37 Donmar Warehouse ... E3
38 English National Opera ... E5
39 Prince Charles Cinema ... D4
40 Ronnie Scott's ... D3
41 Royal Opera House ... F3
42 Soho Theatre ... C3

Shopping
43 Blade Rubber Stamps ... F1
44 Fortnum & Mason ... B6
45 Foyles ... D3
46 Hamleys ... B4
47 Liberty ... A3
48 Sister Ray ... C3

House and the 900-year-old **College Garden** (Map p78; off Great College St, SW1; 10am-4pm Tue-Thu) FREE. The octagonal **Chapter House** dates from the 1250s and was where the monks would meet for daily prayer and their job assignments, before Henry VIII's suppression of the monasteries some three centuries later. To the right of the entrance to Chapter House is what's claimed to be the oldest door in Britain – it's been there since the 1050s. Used as a treasury, the crypt-like **Pyx Chamber** dates from about 1070 and takes its name from boxes that held gold and silver to be tested for purity to make coins.

Photography is not allowed inside the Abbey but is permitted around the Cloisters. Pre-booking tickets required.

★British Museum — MUSEUM

(Map p80; 020-7323 8000; www.britishmuseum.org; Great Russell St, WC1; 10am-5pm (last entry 3.30pm); U Tottenham Court Rd or Russell Sq) FREE The British Museum is the country's most popular museum (around 5.8 million visitors annually) and one of the world's oldest (opened in 1759). Don't miss the **Rosetta Stone**, the key to deciphering Egyptian hieroglyphics (head upstairs for the **Egyptian mummies**); the controversial **Parthenon sculptures**, taken from Athens' Acropolis by Lord Elgin (British ambassador to the Ottoman Empire); and the vast Etruscan, Greek, Roman, European, Asian and Islamic galleries. Other must-see items include the Anglo-Saxon **Sutton Hoo Ship Burial** relics and the **winged bulls from Khorsabad.**

It's been acknowledged work needs to be done on the Americas collection.

Begun in 1753 with a 'cabinet of curiosities' sold to the nation by physician and collector Sir Hans Sloane, the collection mushroomed over the ensuing years through acquisitions, bequests and the indiscriminate plundering of the empire. The grand Enlightenment Gallery was the first section of the redesigned museum to be built in 1823.

The light-filled **Great Court**, restored and augmented by architect Norman Foster in 2000, has a spectacular glass-and-steel roof. In the centre is the **Reading Room** (currently closed while the museum reworks this room since its books went to the British Library), where Karl Marx researched and wrote *Das Kapital;* Virginia Woolf and Mahatma Gandhi were also cardholders. See more on p74.

Due to Covid-19 restrictions on numbers at the time of research, it's imperative that you book your visit ahead of time. Audio guides aren't available, so pre-download the audio introductions to each of the galleries and listen on your own device via iTunes or Google Play. There's also a one-hour Highlights tour map of the blockbusters of the collection.

★Trafalgar Square SQUARE

(Map p80; Ⓤ Charing Cross or Embankment) Opened to the public in 1844, Trafalgar Sq is the true centre of London, where rallies and marches take place, tens of thousands of revellers usher in the New Year and locals congregate for anything from communal open-air cinema and Christmas celebrations to political protests. It is dominated by the 52m-high **Nelson's Column**, guarded by four **bronze lion statues**, and ringed by many splendid buildings, including the National Gallery (p83) and the church of **St Martin-in-the-Fields** (Map p80; ☎020-7766 1100; www.stmartin-in-the-fields.org; ⏲8.30am-6pm Mon-Fri, from 9am Sat & Sun).

★National Gallery GALLERY

(Map p80; ☎020-7747 2885; www.nationalgallery.org.uk; Trafalgar Sq, WC2; ⏲11am-6pm Sat-Thu, to 9pm Fri; Ⓤ Charing Cross) FREE With more than 2300 European masterpieces in its collection, this is one of the world's great galleries, with seminal works from the 13th to the mid-20th centuries, including masterpieces by Leonardo da Vinci, Michelangelo, Titian, Vincent van Gogh and Auguste Renoir. Many visitors flock to the eastern rooms on the main floor (1700–1930), where works by British artists such as Thomas Gainsborough, John Constable and JMW Turner, and Impressionist and post-Impressionist masterpieces by Van Gogh, Renoir and Claude Monet await. Pre-booking required.

★Houses of Parliament HISTORIC BUILDING

(Map p78; Palace of Westminster; ☎tours 020-7219 4114; www.parliament.uk; Parliament Sq, SW1; Ⓤ Westminster) A visit here is a journey to the heart of UK democracy. The Houses of Parliament are officially called the Palace of Westminster, and its oldest part is 11th-century **Westminster Hall**, one of only a few sections that survived a catastrophic 1834 fire. The rest is mostly a neo-Gothic confection built over 36 years from 1840. Tours inside were suspended at the time of research and online tours were the only option.

The palace's most famous feature is its clock tower, Elizabeth Tower (better known as **Big Ben**), covered in scaffolding until restoration works are finished in 2021.

Parliament is split into two houses. The green-hued **House of Commons** is the lower house, where the 650 elected Members of Parliament (MPs) sit. Traditionally the home of hereditary blue bloods, the scarlet-decorated **House of Lords**, with around 800 members, now has peers appointed through various means. Both houses debate and vote on legislation, which is then presented to the Queen for her Royal Assent (in practice, this is a formality; the last time Royal Assent was denied was in 1707). At the annual State Opening of Parliament in May or June, the Queen takes her throne in the House of Lords, having arrived in the gold-trimmed Irish State Coach from Buckingham Palace (her crown travels alone with equerries in Queen Alexandra's State Coach).

Visitors are welcome on Saturdays year-round and on some weekdays during parliamentary recesses (which includes Easter, summer and Christmas). If tours are running again, choose either a **self-guided audio tour** in one of nine languages lasting about 75 minutes or a much more comprehensive 90-minute **guided tour** of both chambers, Westminster Hall and other historic buildings (in English only). Tack on **afternoon tea** (an additional £30) in a riverside room in the House of Commons. It's best to book online far in advance (check the changing schedules), which also shaves a few pounds off the price. Otherwise, buy tickets from the office in front of Portcullis House on Victoria Embankment. UK residents can approach their MPs to arrange a free tour.

Residents and visitors can watch debates, Prime Minister's Question Time and Ministerial Question Time from the public galleries for free. Check the schedule online and book in advance when possible; queues can be long. Public access to the Houses of Parliament is via the Cromwell Green entrance on the southwestern side of the building. Expect airport-style security; bags larger than carry-on size are not allowed in.

The British Museum

A HALF-DAY TOUR

The British Museum, with almost eight million items in its permanent collection, is so vast and comprehensive that it can be daunting for the first-time visitor. To avoid a frustrating trip – and getting lost on the way to the Egyptian mummies – set out on this half-day exploration, which takes in some of the museum's most important sights. If you want to see and learn more, download the British Museum audio guide app to your phone pre-arrival.

A good starting point is the ❶ **Rosetta Stone**, the key that cracked the code to ancient Egypt's writing system. Nearby treasures from Assyria – an ancient civilisation centred in Mesopotamia between the Tigris and Euphrates Rivers – including the colossal ❷ **Winged Bulls from Khorsabad**, give way to the ❸ **Parthenon Sculptures**, high points of classical Greek art that continue to influence us today. Be sure to see both the sculptures and the

Winged Bulls from Khorsabad
This awesome pair of alabaster winged bulls with human heads once guarded the entrance to the palace of Assyrian King Sargon II at Khorsabad in Mesopotamia, a cradle of civilisation in present-day Iraq.

Parthenon Sculptures
The Parthenon, a white marble temple dedicated to Athena, was part of a fortified citadel on the Acropolis in Athens. There are dozens of sculptures and friezes with models and interactive displays explaining how they all once fitted together.

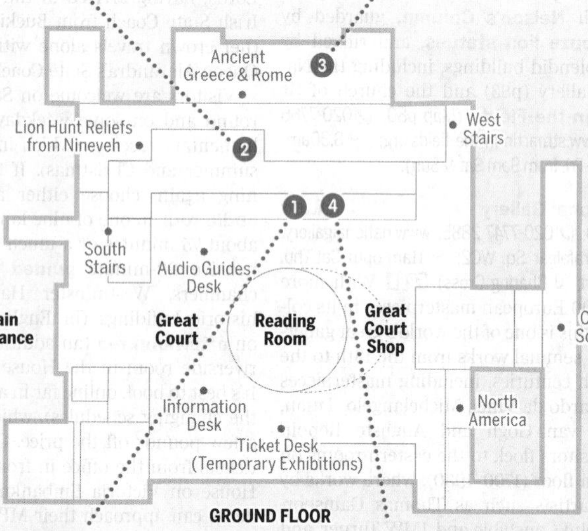

GROUND FLOOR

Bust of Pharaoh Ramesses II
The most impressive sculpture in the Egyptian galleries, this 725kg bust portrays Ramesses the Great, scourge of the Israelites in the Book of Exodus, as great benefactor.

PHOTOS.COM / GETTY IMAGES ©

Rosetta Stone
Written in hieroglyphic, demotic (cursive ancient Egyptian script used for everyday) and Greek, the 762kg stone contains a decree exempting priests from tax on the first anniversary of young Ptolemy V's coronation.

NATALYA OKOROKOVA / SHUTTERSTOCK ©

monumental frieze celebrating the birth of Athena. En route to the West Stairs is a huge ❹ **Bust of Pharaoh Ramesses II**, just a hint of the large collection of ❺ **Egyptian mummies** upstairs. (The earliest, affectionately called Ginger because of wispy reddish hair, was preserved simply by hot sand.) The Romans introduce visitors to the early Britain galleries via the rich ❻ **Mildenhall Treasure**. The Anglo-Saxon ❼ **Sutton Hoo Ship Burial** and the medieval ❽ **Lewis Chessmen** follow.

EATING OPTIONS

Court Cafe At the northern end of the Great Court; takeaway counters with salads and sandwiches; communal tables.

Gallery Pizzeria Out of the way off Room 12; quieter; children's menu available.

Great Court Restaurant Upstairs overlooking the former Reading Room; sit-down meals.

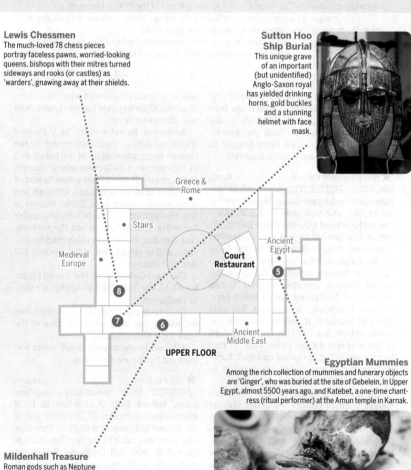

Lewis Chessmen
The much-loved 78 chess pieces portray faceless pawns, worried-looking queens, bishops with their mitres turned sideways and rooks (or castles) as 'warders', gnawing away at their shields.

Sutton Hoo Ship Burial
This unique grave of an important (but unidentified) Anglo-Saxon royal has yielded drinking horns, gold buckles and a stunning helmet with face mask.

MAVRITSINA IRINA/SHUTTERSTOCK ©

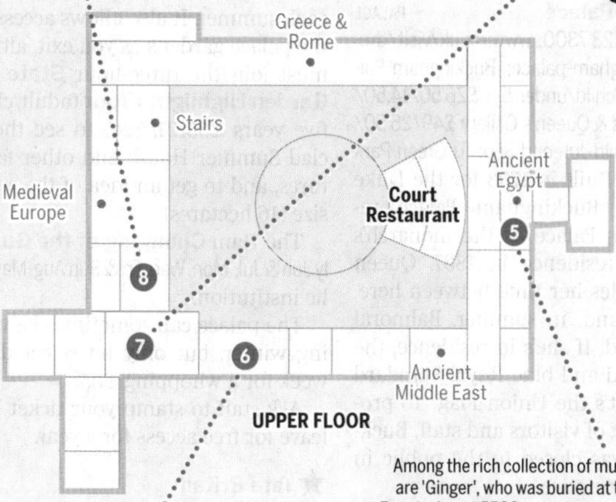

Egyptian Mummies
Among the rich collection of mummies and funerary objects are 'Ginger', who was buried at the site of Gebelein, in Upper Egypt, almost 5500 years ago, and Katebet, a one-time chantress (ritual performer) at the Amun temple in Karnak.

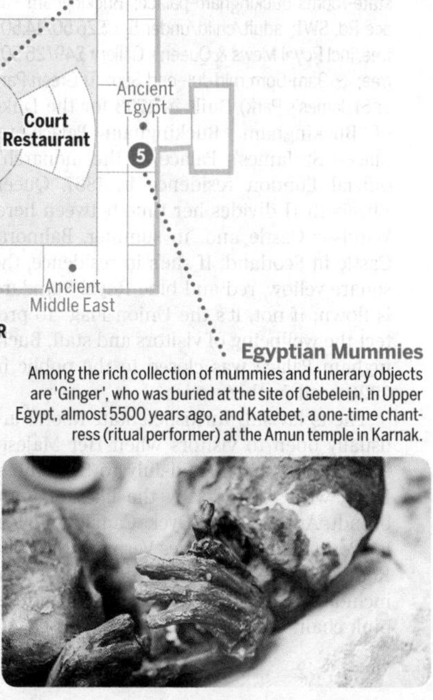
ILEANA_BT / SHUTTERSTOCK ©

Mildenhall Treasure
Roman gods such as Neptune and Bacchus share space with early Christian symbols like the *chi-rho* (short for 'Christ') on the find's almost three dozen silver bowls, plates and spoons.

LOCAL KNOWLEDGE

SOHO

London's most bohemian neighbourhood was once pastureland; the name Soho is thought to have evolved from a hunting cry. While the centre of London nightlife has shifted east, and Soho has recently seen landmark clubs and music venues shut down, the neighbourhood still comes into its own in the evenings and remains a proudly LGBT+ friendly district. During the day you'll be charmed by the area's sheer vitality.

At Soho's northern end, leafy **Soho Sq** (Map p80; Ⓤ Tottenham Court Rd or Leicester Sq) is the area's back garden. It was laid out in 1681 and originally called King's Sq; a statue of Charles II stands in its northern half. In the centre is a tiny half-timbered mock-Tudor cottage built as a gardener's shed in the 1870s. The space below it was used as an underground bomb shelter during WWII.

South of the square is **Dean St**, lined with bars and restaurants. No 28 was the home of Karl Marx and his family from 1851 to 1856; they lived here in extreme poverty as Marx researched and wrote *Das Kapital* in the Reading Room of the British Museum.

Old Compton St is the epicentre of Soho's gay village. It's a street loved by all, gay or other, for its great bars, risqué shops and general good vibes.

Seducer and heart-breaker Casanova and opium-addicted writer Thomas de Quincey lived on nearby **Greek St**, while the parallel **Frith St** housed Mozart at No 20 for a year from 1764.

The **House of Commons Members' Dining Room** is sometimes open to the public for set meals of seasonal British cuisine (lunch/dinner £45/55). Check the website for dates; bookings open three months in advance. Smart casual dress is required.

★ Buckingham Palace — PALACE

(Map p78; ☎ 0303 123 7300; www.rct.uk/visit/the-state-rooms-buckingham-palace; Buckingham Palace Rd, SW1; adult/child/under 5yr £26.50/14.50/free, incl Royal Mews & Queen's Gallery £49/26.50/free; ⏲ 9am-6pm mid-Jul–end Sep; Ⓤ Green Park or St James's Park) Built in 1703 for the Duke of Buckingham, Buckingham Palace replaced St James's Palace as the monarch's official London residence in 1837. Queen Elizabeth II divides her time between here, Windsor Castle and, in summer, Balmoral Castle in Scotland. If she's in residence, the square yellow, red and blue Royal Standard is flown; if not, it's the Union Flag. To protect the wellbeing of visitors and staff, Buckingham Palace was closed to the public in 2020 until further notice.

The 19 lavishly furnished State Rooms are usually open to visitors when Her Majesty is on holiday from mid-July to September. Hung with artworks by the likes of Rembrandt, Anthony van Dyck, Canaletto, Nicolas Poussin and Johannes Vermeer, the State Rooms are open for self-guided tours that include the **Throne Room**, with his-and-her pink chairs monogrammed 'ER' and 'P'. Access is by timed tickets with admission every 15 minutes (audio guide included) and visits take about two hours.

Admission includes entry to a themed special exhibition (royal couture during the Queen's reign, growing up at the palace etc) in the enormous **Ballroom**, which changes each summer. It also allows access to part of the palace gardens as you exit, although you must join the three-hour **State Rooms & Garden Highlights Tour** (adult/child/under five years £35/21/free) to see the wisteria-clad Summer House and other famous features, and to get an idea of the garden's full size (16 hectares).

The 11am **Changing of the Guard** (⏲ daily Jun & Jul, Mon, Wed, Fri & Sun Aug-May) is a public institution.

The palace can sometimes be visited during winter, but only on select days of the week for a whopping £85.

Ask staff to stamp your ticket before you leave for free access for a year.

★ Tate Britain — GALLERY

(☎ 020-7887 8888; www.tate.org.uk/visit/tate-britain; Millbank, SW1; ⏲ 10am-6pm, 1st Fri of month to 9pm; Ⓤ Pimlico) **FREE** On the site of the former Millbank Penitentiary, the older and more venerable of the two Tate siblings opened in 1892 and celebrates British art from 1500 to the present, including pieces from William Blake, William Hogarth, Thomas Gainsborough, John Constable and Joshua Reynolds, as well as vibrant modern and contemporary pieces from Lucian Freud, Barbara Hepworth, Gillian Ayres, Francis Bacon and Henry Moore. The stars of the show are, undoubtedly, the light-infused visions of JMW Turner in the **Clore Gallery**.

After Turner died in 1851, his estate was settled by a decree declaring that whatever had been found in his studio – 300 oil paintings and about 30,000 watercolours and sketches – would be bequeathed to the nation. The collection here constitutes a grand and sweeping display of his work, including classics such as *The Field of Waterloo* and *Norham Castle, Sunrise*.

Tate Britain is also home to seminal works from the Pre-Raphaelites, including William Holman Hunt's *Strayed Sheep*, John William Waterhouse's sculpture *Hylas Surprised by the Naiades*, *Christ in the House of His Parents* by John Everett Millais and Edward Burne-Jones' *The Golden Stairs*. Look out also for Francis Bacon's *Three Studies for Figures at the Base of a Crucifixion*.

The gallery hosts the prestigious and often controversial **Turner Prize** from October to early January every year (adult/child £13/free), plus a programme of ticketed exhibitions that changes every few months; consult the website for what's on.

Quick 15-minute **Art in Focus talks** on a selected work take place every Tuesday, Thursday and Saturday at 1.15pm; the piece under the microscope changes monthly, so check online or ask at the visitor information desk. Free 45-minute **themed guided tours** are held four times a day, and the 3pm slot is invariably on the work of JMW Turner. Both tours are free; booking is not required.

On the first Friday of each month, **Late at Tate Britain** means the gallery stays open until 9.30pm.

★Wallace Collection — GALLERY

(Map p124; ☎020-7563 9500; www.wallacecollection.org; Hertford House, Manchester Sq, W1; ⏲10am-4pm; Ⓤ Bond St) **FREE** Arguably London's finest smaller gallery, the Wallace Collection is an enthralling glimpse into 18th-century aristocratic life. The sumptuously restored Italianate mansion houses a treasure trove of 17th- and 18th-century paintings, porcelain, artefacts and furniture collected by generations of the same family and bequeathed to the nation by the widow of Sir Richard Wallace (1818–90) on the condition it remain displayed in the same fashion.

★Churchill War Rooms — MUSEUM

(Map p78; ☎020-7416 5000; www.iwm.org.uk/visits/churchill-war-rooms; Clive Steps, King Charles St, SW1; adult/child £23/11.50; ⏲9.30am-6pm; Ⓤ Westminster) Former Prime Minister Winston Churchill helped coordinate the Allied resistance against Nazi Germany on a Bakelite telephone from this underground complex during WWII. The **Cabinet War Rooms** remain much as they were when the lights were switched off in 1945, capturing the drama and dogged spirit of the time, while the modern multimedia **Churchill Museum** affords intriguing insights into the life and times of the resolute, cigar-smoking wartime leader.

Tickets are slightly cheaper if booked online and come with priority entry to beat the ever-present queue.

★Royal Academy of Arts — GALLERY

(Map p80; ☎020-7300 8000; www.royalacademy.org.uk; Burlington House, Piccadilly, W1; ⏲10am-6pm; Ⓤ Green Park) **FREE** Britain's oldest society devoted to fine arts was founded in 1768 and moved here to Burlington House a century later. For its 250th birthday in 2018, the RA gave itself a £56-million makeover. Its collection of drawings, paintings, architectural designs, photographs and sculptures by past and present Royal Academicians, such as Sir Joshua Reynolds, John Constable, Thomas Gainsborough, JMW Turner, David Hockney and Tracey Emin, has historically been male-dominated, but this is slowly changing.

★Sir John Soane's Museum — MUSEUM

(Map p80; ☎020-7405 2107; www.soane.org; 13 Lincoln's Inn Fields, WC2; ⏲10am-5pm Thu-Sat; Ⓤ Holborn) **FREE** This museum is one of the most atmospheric and fascinating in London. The Georgian building was the beautiful, bewitching home of architect Sir John Soane (1753–1837), which he bequeathed to the nation through an Act of Parliament on condition that it remain untouched after his death and free to visit. It's brimming with Soane's vast collection of art and archaeological purchases, as well as intriguing personal effects and curiosities. The house-museum represents his exquisite and eccentric tastes, persuasions and proclivities.

GETTING HIGH IN LONDON

Not so long ago, getting a good view of London was a near-impossible endeavour. Beyond joining the tourists on the London Eye (p97), dining at City Social (p126) involved a lot of forward planning. Things are a lot more democratic these days and, well, the sky's the limit.

The 72nd-floor open-air platform of the Shard (p99) is as high as you'll get in Europe. The lush interior Sky Garden (p93) is free with a forward booking. For all-night dining head for the 40th-floor location of Duck & Waffle (p126). For drinks we love **Radio Rooftop Bar** (Map p80; 020-7395 3440; https://radiorooftop.com/london; 10th fl, ME London, 336-337 The Strand, WC2; 7am-1am Mon-Wed, to 2am Thu-Sat, to midnight Sun; Temple or Covent Garden), Frank's at Peckham Levels (p127) or Seabird at Hoxton Southwark (p121). And the **5th View** (Map p80; 020-7851 2433; www.5thview.com; 5th fl, Waterstones Piccadilly, 203-206 Piccadilly, W1; mains £10-12; 9am-9.30pm Mon-Sat, noon-5pm Sun; ; Piccadilly Circus) atop Waterstones bookshop in Piccadilly is an option for afternoon tea.

London Transport Museum MUSEUM
(Map p80; 020-7379 6344; www.ltmuseum.co.uk; Covent Garden Piazza, WC2; adult/child £18.50/free; 10am-6pm; ; Covent Garden) Housed in Covent Garden's former flower-market building, this captivating museum looks at how London developed as a result of better transport. It's stuffed full of horse-drawn omnibuses, vintage Underground carriages with heritage maps, and old double-decker buses (some of which you can clamber through, making this something of a kids' playground). The **gift shop** also sells great London souvenirs such as retro Tube posters and pillows made from the same fabric as the train seats.

Madame Tussauds MUSEUM
(Map p124; 0870 400 3000; www.madametussauds.com/london; Marylebone Rd, NW1; adult/child 4-15yr £35/30; 10am-6pm; Baker St) It may be kitschy and pricey, but Madame Tussauds makes for a fun-filled day. There are photo ops with your dream celebrity (be it Daniel Craig, Lady Gaga, Benedict Cumberbatch, or Audrey Hepburn), the Bollywood gathering (starring studs Hrithik Roshan and Salman Khan) and the Royal Appointment (the Queen, Harry and Meghan, William and Kate). Book online for much cheaper rates and check the website for seasonal opening hours.

★**Somerset House** HISTORIC BUILDING
(Map p80; 020-7845 4600; www.somersethouse.org.uk; The Strand, WC2; 10am-7pm; Temple) Designed in 1775 for government departments and royal societies – perhaps the world's first office block – Somerset House now contains galleries, restaurants and cafes that encircle a lovely open courtyard and extend to an elevated sun-trap terrace. The **Embankment Galleries** are devoted to temporary exhibitions (usually related to photography, design or fashion). In summer, the grand courtyard hosts open-air live performances, dancing fountains for kids to cool off in and the Film4 Summer Screen (p119); there's an atmospheric ice-skating rink in winter.

No 10 Downing Street HISTORIC BUILDING
(Map p78; www.number10.gov.uk; 10 Downing St, SW1; Westminster) The official office of British leaders since 1735, when King George II presented No 10 to 'First Lord of the Treasury' Robert Walpole, this has also been the prime minister's London residence since the late 19th century. For such a famous address, No 10 is a small-looking Georgian building on a plain-looking street, hardly warranting comparison with the White House, for example. Yet it is actually three houses joined into one and boasts roughly 100 rooms plus a 2000-sq-metre garden.

Charles Dickens Museum MUSEUM
(Map p110; 020-7405 2127; www.dickensmuseum.com; 48-49 Doughty St, WC1; adult/child £9.50/4.50; 10am-5pm Fri-Sun; Russell Sq or Chancery Lane) The prolific writer Charles Dickens lived with his growing family in this handsome four-storey Georgian terraced house for a mere 2½ years (1837–39), but this is where his work really flourished, as he completed *The Pickwick Papers*, *Nicholas Nickleby* and *Oliver Twist* here. Each of the dozen rooms, some restored to their

original condition, contains various memorabilia, including the study where you'll find the desk at which Dickens wrote *Great Expectations*.

St James's Park PARK

(Map p78; www.royalparks.org.uk/parks/st-jamess-park; The Mall, SW1; 5am-midnight; St James's Park, Green Park) At 23 hectares, St James's is the second-smallest of the eight royal parks after **Green Park** (Map p78; www.royalparks.org.uk/parks/green-park; 5am-midnight; Green Park). But what it lacks in size it makes up for in grooming, as it is the most manicured green space in London. It has brilliant views of the London Eye, Westminster, St James's Palace, Carlton House Terrace and Horse Guards Parade; the picture-perfect sight of Buckingham Palace from the **Blue Bridge** spanning the central lake is the best you'll find.

City of London

★ **St Paul's Cathedral** CATHEDRAL

(Map p90; 020-7246 8357; www.stpauls.co.uk; St Paul's Churchyard, EC4; adult/child £17/7.20; 8.30am-4.30pm Mon-Sat; St Paul's) Towering over diminutive Ludgate Hill in a superb position that's been a place of Christian worship for more than 1400 years (and pagan before that), St Paul's Cathedral is one of London's most magnificent buildings. For Londoners, the vast dome is a symbol of resilience and pride, standing tall for more than 300 years. Viewing architect Sir Christopher Wren's masterpiece from the inside and climbing to the top for sweeping views of the capital is a celestial experience.

Following the destructive Great Fire of London in 1666, which burned 80% of the city, Wren designed St Paul's to replace the old church, and it was built between 1675 and 1710. The site is ancient hallowed ground, with four other cathedrals preceding Wren's English baroque masterpiece, the first dating from 604 CE.

The cathedral dome, inspired by St Peter's Basilica in the Vatican, is famed for surviving Luftwaffe incendiary bombs in the 'Second Great Fire of London' of December 1940, becoming an icon of London resilience during the Blitz. North of the church is the simple **People of London Memorial**, honouring the 32,000 civilians killed.

Inside, rising more than 85m above the floor, the dome is supported by eight huge columns. It actually consists of three parts: a plastered brick inner dome, a nonstructural lead outer dome visible on the skyline and a brick cone between them holding it all together. The walkway around its base, accessed via 257 steps from a staircase on the western side of the southern transept, is called the **Whispering Gallery**. A further 119 steps brings you to the exterior **Stone Gallery**, your first taste of the city vistas, and 152 iron steps more bring you to the **Golden Gallery** at the very top, with unforgettable views of London.

The **crypt** has memorials to around 300 of Britain's great and the good, including the Duke of Wellington and Vice Admiral Horatio Nelson, whose body lies directly below the dome. But the most poignant is to Wren himself. On a simple tomb slab bearing his name, part of a Latin inscription translates as: 'If you seek his monument, look around you'.

There's no charge to attend a service, but not all areas of the cathedral are accessible. To hear the cathedral choir, attend the 11.30am Sunday Eucharist or Evensong (5pm Monday to Saturday and 3.15pm Sunday),

LONDON TOP TIPS

➡ London is huge – organise your visit by neighbourhood to avoid wasting time (and money) on transport.

➡ An Oyster Card is a cheaper and convenient way to use public transport, but you can also pay by contactless bank cards and smart phones.

➡ Note that a large number of places are now cashless.

➡ Walk – it's free and the best way to discover central London.

➡ For last minute West End performances check out standby ticket options, which you buy on the day at the venue or from the booth on Leicester Sq.

➡ To treat yourself to fine dining without breaking the bank, opt for lunch rather than dinner, or try for pre- or post-theatre dinner deals.

➡ Book online for ticketed attractions to save money and skip queues.

➡ Download local apps for taxis (Gett), public transport (CityMapper) and theatre tickets (TodayTix).

The City

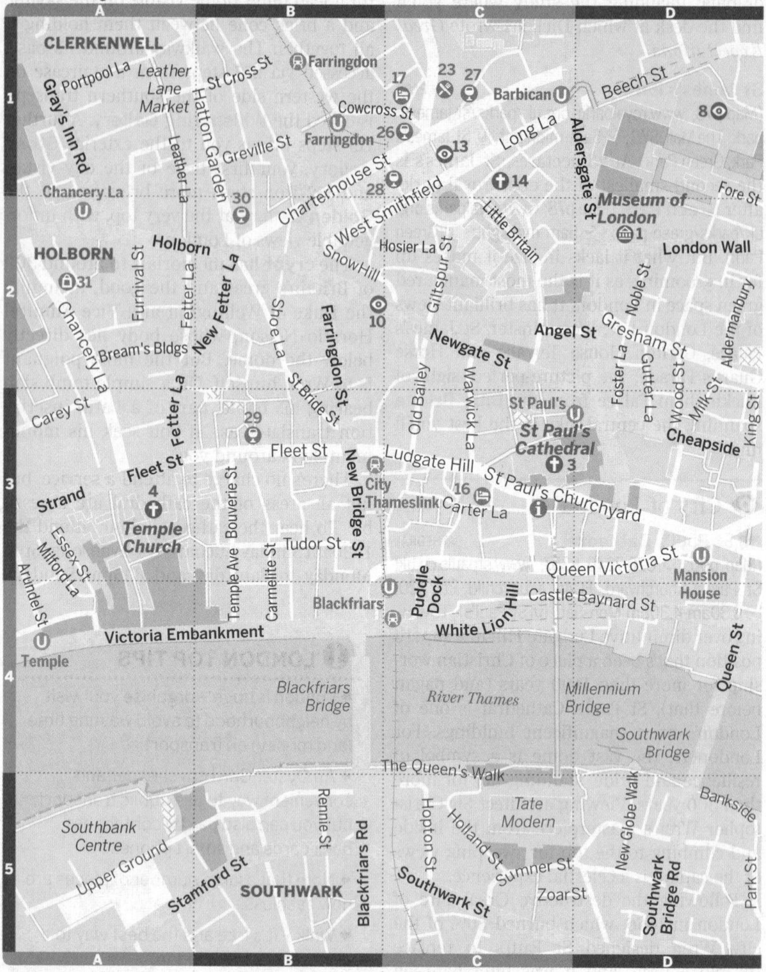

but check the website as a visiting choir may appear for the latter.

Book tickets online in advance for a slight discount and faster entry. Admission includes an audio guide. Free 1½-hour guided tours depart four times a day (10am, 11am, 1pm and 2pm); reserve a place at the tour desk, just past the entrance. About three times a month, one-hour tours (£8) visit the Geometric Staircase, Great Model and astonishing library (closed for renovations until at least spring 2021), and include impressive views down the nave from above the Great West Doors; check online for timings.

★ **Tower of London** HISTORIC SITE

(Map p90; ☎020-3166 6000; www.hrp.org.uk/tower-of-london; Petty Wales, EC3; adult/child £25/12.50; ⏰9am-4.30pm, from 10am Sun & Mon; Ⓤ Tower Hill) The unmissable Tower of London offers a window into 1000 years of gruesome and compelling history. A former royal residence, treasury, mint, armoury and zoo, it's perhaps most remembered as the prison where a king, three queens and many nobles met their deaths. The immaculately dressed Yeomen Warders (better known as the Beefeaters), who live on site, protect the spectacular Crown Jewels, containing the biggest diamonds in the world, and lead

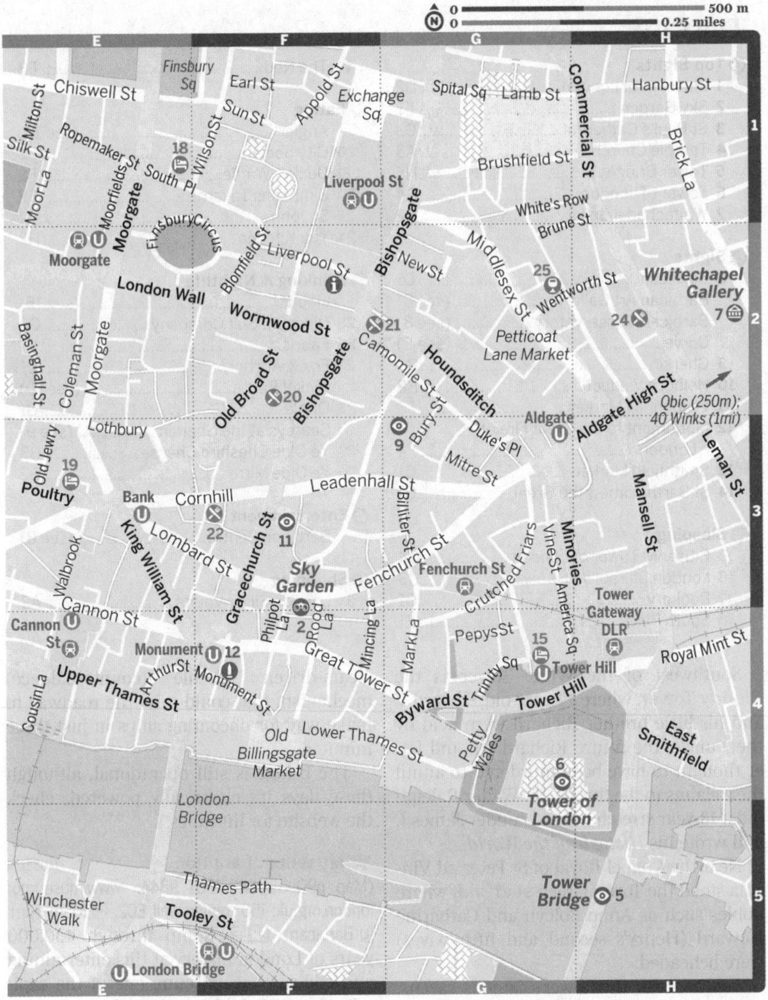

tours of the Tower, as soothsaying resident ravens flit overhead.

The Tower of London is a densely packed history-laden site, so expect to spend at least half a day. To get your bearings, take one of the entertaining (and free) **guided tours** with the Yeomen Warders; the 45-minute-long tours leave every 30 minutes from the bridge near the main entrance until 3.30pm (2.30pm in winter). For a quick visual overview, see p85.

Most visitors head straight to the Waterloo Barracks, which contains the **Crown Jewels**, including the platinum crown of the late Queen Mother, set with the 106-carat Koh-i-Nûr (Persian for 'Mountain of Light') diamond, and the Imperial State Crown, worn by the monarch at the State Opening of Parliament. Slow-moving walkways slide wide-eyed visitors past the collection.

Started in the 1070s by William the Conqueror, the striking **White Tower** is London's oldest building, with solid Norman architecture and four turrets. On the entrance floor is a collection from the **Royal Armouries**, including Henry VIII's commodious suit of armour. One floor up is the impressive but unadorned 11th-century **Chapel of St John the Evangelist**, which was once used as the national record office.

The City

Top Sights

1	Museum of London	D2
2	Sky Garden	F3
3	St Paul's Cathedral	C3
4	Temple Church	A3
5	Tower Bridge	H5
6	Tower of London	G4
7	Whitechapel Gallery	H2

Sights

8	Barbican	D1
	Barbican Art Gallery	(see 8)
	Barbican Conservatory	(see 8)
	Curve	(see 8)
9	Gherkin	G3
10	Holborn Viaduct	B2
11	Leadenhall Market	F3
12	Monument to the Great Fire of London	F4
13	Smithfield Market	C1
14	St Bartholomew the Great	C1

Sleeping

15	CitizenM Tower of London	G4
16	London St Paul's YHA	C3
17	Rookery	C1
18	South Place	E1
19	The Ned	E3

Eating

	Angler	(see 18)
20	City Social	F2
21	Duck & Waffle	F2
22	Simpsons Tavern	F3
23	St John	C1
24	Yuu Kitchen	H2

Drinking & Nightlife

	cloudM	(see 15)
25	Discount Suit Company	G2
26	Fabric	C1
27	Fox & Anchor	C1
	Nickel Bar	(see 19)
28	Oriole	C1
	Searcys at the Gherkin	(see 9)
29	Ye Olde Cheshire Cheese	B3
30	Ye Olde Mitre	B2

Entertainment

	Barbican Centre	(see 8)

Shopping

31	London Silver Vaults	A2

Southwest of the White Tower is the **Bloody Tower**, where 12-year-old Edward V and his little brother Richard were held by their uncle, the future Richard III, and later thought to have been murdered to annul their claims to the throne. Sir Walter Raleigh did a 13-year stretch here too under James I, and wrote his *Historie of the World*.

Near the Chapel Royal of St Peter ad Vincula stood the Tower Green **scaffold**, where nobles such as Anne Boleyn and Catherine Howard (Henry's second and fifth wives) were beheaded.

Look out for the Tower's famous ravens, which legend says could cause the Tower, and therefore the kingdom, to collapse should they leave (a spare bird is kept in the aviary, and their wing feathers are clipped in case they get any ideas). See feature p94.

Book online in advance for cheaper rates.

★ Tower Bridge — BRIDGE

(Map p90; ☎020-7403 3761; www.towerbridge.org.uk; Tower Bridge, SE1; Ⓤ Tower Hill) With its neo-Gothic towers and sky-blue suspension struts, Tower Bridge is one of London's most recognisable sights. London was a thriving port in 1894 when it was built as a much-needed crossing point in the east, equipped with a then-revolutionary steam-driven bascule (counterbalance) mechanism that could raise the roadway to make way for oncoming ships in just three minutes.

The bridge is still operational, although these days it's electrically powered; check the website for lift times.

★ Museum of London — MUSEUM

(Map p90; ☎020-7001 9844; www.museumoflondon.org.uk; 150 London Wall, EC2; ⏲10am-6pm; Ⓤ Barbican) FREE Romp through 450,000 years of London history at this entertaining and educational museum, one of the capital's finest. Exhibiting everything from a mammoth's jaw circa 200,000 BCE to Oliver Cromwell's death mask and the desperate scrawls of convicts on a cell from Wellclose Prison, interactive displays and reconstructed scenes transport visitors from Roman Londinium and Saxon Lundenwic right up to the 21st-century metropolis. Free themed tours are offered daily; check at reception for timings and topics.

★ Sky Garden — VIEWPOINT

(Map p90; ☎020-7337 2344; https://skygarden.london; 20 Fenchurch St, EC3; ⏲10am-6pm Mon-Fri, 11am-9pm Sat & Sun; Ⓤ Monument) FREE The ferns, fig trees and purple African lilies that clamber up the final three storeys of the 'Walkie Talkie' skyscraper are mere wallflowers at this 155m-high rooftop garden – it's the extraordinary 360-degree views of London that make this vast, airport-terminal-like space so popular. The Sky Garden has front-row seats overlooking the Shard (p99) and vistas that gallop for miles east and west. Visits must be booked online in advance, and tickets run out quickly.

The garden space includes a restaurant, a brasserie and three bars with varying opening times. If tickets have sold out, you can reserve a table at one of them to gain access, though you will have to order something.

Monument to the Great Fire of London MONUMENT

(Map p90; ☎020-7403 3761; www.themonument.org.uk; Fish St Hill, EC3; adult/child £5/2.50, incl Tower Bridge Exhibition £12/5.50; ⏰9.30am-5.30pm; Ⓤ Monument) Designed by Christopher Wren, this immense Doric column of Portland stone is a reminder of the Great Fire of London in 1666, which destroyed 80% of the city. It stands 62m high, the distance from the bakery in Pudding Lane where the fire is thought to have started. Although Lilliputian by today's standards, the Monument towered over London when it was built. Climbing up the column's 311 spiral steps still provides great views thanks to its central location.

Barbican ARCHITECTURE

(Map p90; ☎020-7638 4141; www.barbican.org.uk; Silk St, EC2; Ⓤ Barbican) The architectural value of this sprawling post-WWII brutalist housing estate divides Londoners, but the Barbican remains a sought-after living space as well as the City's preeminent cultural centre. Public spaces include a quirky **conservatory** (☎0845 120 7500; Level 3; ⏰noon-5pm Sun) FREE and the Barbican Centre theatres, cinema and two art galleries: **Barbican Art Gallery** (☎020-7638 8891; Level 3; ⏰noon-6pm Mon & Tue, to 9pm Wed-Fri, 10am-9pm Sat, to 6pm Sun) and **The Curve** (☎020-7638 8891; Level 1; ⏰11am-8pm Sat-Wed, to 9pm Thu & Fri) FREE. Navigating the Barbican, designed to be a car-free urban neighbourhood, requires reliance on a network of elevated paths that didn't quite come to fruition. Find your bearings on an **architecture tour** (adult/child £12.50/10).

St Bartholomew the Great CHURCH

(Map p90; ☎020-7600 0440; www.greatstbarts.com; W Smithfield, EC1; ⏰10am-4pm Mon-Wed, Fri & Sat, 10am-1pm Thu, 1-6pm Sun; Ⓤ Barbican) FREE Dating from 1123, St Bartholomew the Great is one of London's oldest churches. The Norman arches and profound sense of history lend this holy space an ancient calm, and it's even more atmospheric when entered through the restored 13th-century half-timbered gatehouse. The church was originally part of an Augustinian priory but became the parish church of Smithfield in 1539 when Henry VIII dissolved the monasteries.

Gherkin NOTABLE BUILDING

(Map p90; www.thegherkinlondon.com; 30 St Mary Axe, EC3; Ⓤ Aldgate) Nicknamed 'the Gherkin' for its distinctive shape, 30 St Mary Axe remains the City's most intriguing skyscraper, despite the best efforts of the engineering individualism that now surrounds it. It was built in 2003 by architect Norman Foster, with a futuristic exterior that has become an emblem of modern London. The top floors of the building, once a private members' club, are now open to the public as a **bar-restaurant** (Map p90; ☎0330 107 0816; https://searcysatthegherkin.co.uk; ⏰11am-10pm Mon-Sat, 10am-4pm Sun).

South Bank

★Tate Modern GALLERY

(Map p98; ☎020-7887 8888; www.tate.org.uk; Bankside, SE1; ⏰10am-6pm Sun-Thu, to 10pm Fri & Sat; Ⓤ Southwark) FREE One of London's most amazing attractions, this outstanding modern- and contemporary-art gallery is housed in the creatively revamped Bankside Power Station. A spellbinding synthesis of modern art and capacious industrial brick design, Tate Modern has been extraordinarily successful in bringing challenging work to the masses, both through its free permanent collection and fee-charged big-name temporary exhibitions. The stunning **Blavatnik Building**, with a panoramic 10th-floor viewing terrace, opened in 2016, increasing the available exhibition space by 60%.

The 200m-long building, made of 4.2 million bricks, is an imposing sight, and was designed by Swiss architects Herzog and de Meuron, who scooped the prestigious Pritzker Architecture Prize in 2001 for their

Tower of London

TACKLING THE TOWER

Although it's usually less busy in the late afternoon, don't leave your assault on the Tower until too late in the day. You could easily spend hours here and not see it all. Start by getting your bearings on one of the Yeoman Warder (beefeater) tours; they are included in the cost of admission, entertaining and the easiest way to access the **1 Chapel Royal of St Peter ad Vincula**, which is where they finish up.

When you leave the chapel, the **2 Scaffold Site** is directly in front. The building immediately to your left is Waterloo Barracks, where the **3 Crown Jewels** are housed. These are the absolute highlight of a Tower visit, so keep an eye on the entrance and pick a time to visit when it looks relatively quiet. Once inside, take things at your own pace. Slow-moving travelators shunt you past the dozen or so crowns that are the treasury's centrepieces, but feel free to double-back for a second or even third pass.

Allow plenty of time for the **4 White Tower**, the core of the whole complex, starting with the exhibition of royal armour. As you continue onto the 1st floor, keep an eye out for **5 St John's Chapel**.

The famous **6 ravens** can be seen in the courtyard south of the White Tower. Next, visit the **7 Bloody Tower** and the torture displays in the dungeon of the Wakefield Tower. Head next through the towers that formed the **8 Medieval Palace**, then take the **9 East Wall Walk** to get a feel for the castle's mighty battlements. Spend the rest of your time poking around the many other fascinating nooks and crannies of the Tower complex.

BEAT THE QUEUES

➡ Buy tickets online, avoid weekends and aim to be at the Tower first thing in the morning, when queues are shortest.

➡ The London Pass (www.londonpass.com) allows you to jump the queues and visit the Tower (plus some other 80 attractions) as often as you like.

FLIK47 / GETTY IMAGES ©

EXECUTION SITE MEMORIAL, BY BRIAN CATLING

Chapel Royal of St Peter ad Vincula
This chapel serves as the resting place for the royals and other members of the aristocracy who were executed on the small green out front. Several other historical figures are buried here too, including St Thomas More.

Scaffold Site
Seven people, including three queens (Anne Boleyn, Catherine Howard and Jane Grey), lost their heads here during Tudor times, saving the monarch the embarrassment of public executions on Tower Hill. The site features a rather odd 'pillow' sculpture by Brian Catling.

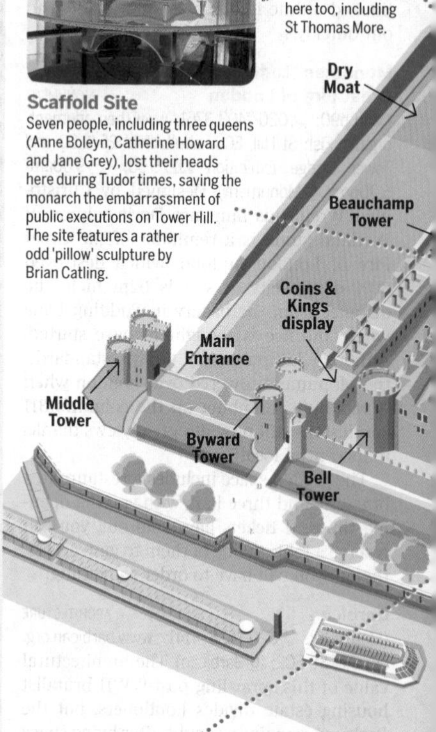

White Tower
Much of the White Tower is taken up with an exhibition on 500 years of royal armour. Look for the virtually cuboid suit made to match Henry VIII's bloated 49-year-old body, complete with an oversized armoured codpiece to protect, ahem, the crown jewels.

CHRISDORNEY / SHUTTERSTOCK ©

St John's Chapel

The White Tower's unadorned chapel dates from 1080, making it the oldest surviving Christian place of worship in London.

Crown Jewels

When it's not being worn for ceremonies of state, Her Majesty's bling is kept here. Among the 23,578 gems, look out for the 530-carat Great Star of Africa diamond at the top of the Sovereign's Sceptre with Cross, the largest part of what was then the largest diamond ever found.

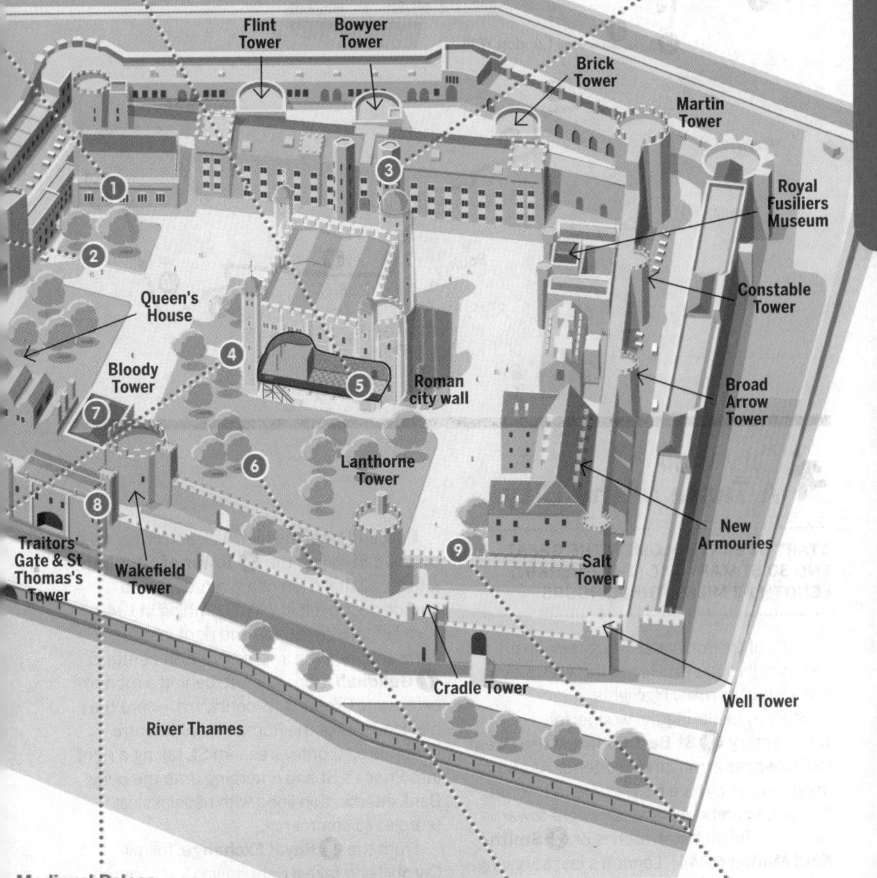

Medieval Palace

This part of the Tower complex was begun around 1220 and was home to England's medieval monarchs. Look for the recreations of the bedchamber of Edward I (1272–1307) in St Thomas's Tower and the throne room of his father, Henry III (1216–72) in the Wakefield Tower.

Ravens

This stretch of green is where the Tower's half-dozen ravens are kept, fed on raw meat and blood-soaked biscuits. According to legend, if the ravens depart the fortress, the Tower and the kingdom will fall.

Wall Walk

Follow the inner ramparts along the Tower's eastern and northern fortifications. Each of the seven towers along the way has themed displays, covering everything from the royal menagerie to the Tower during WWI.

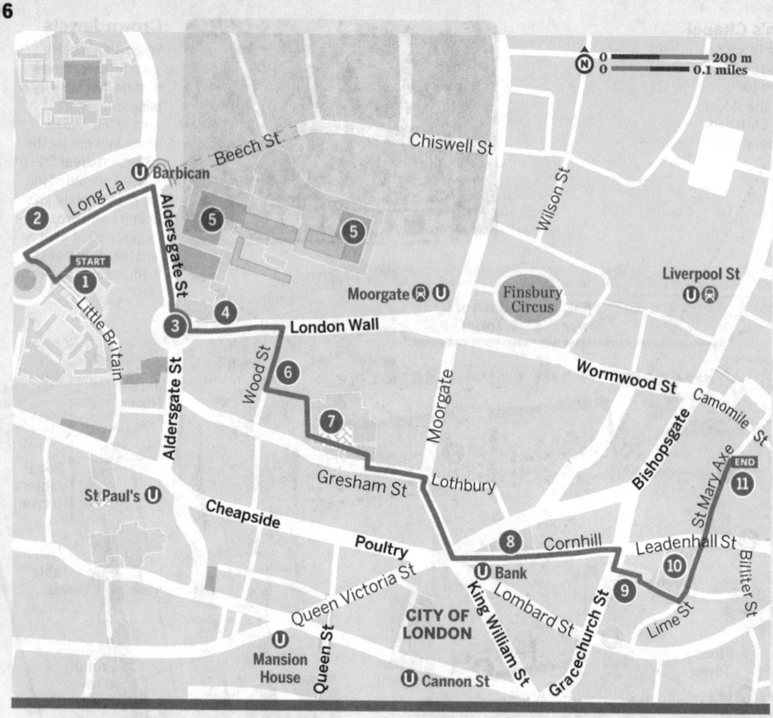

City Walk
A Taste of the City

START ST BARTHOLOMEW THE GREAT
END 30 ST MARY AXE (THE GHERKIN)
LENGTH 1.2 MILES; THREE HOURS

The City of London has as a huge wealth of history in its square mile, and this walk picks out just a few of its many highlights.

Start by exploring the wonderful 12th-century **1 St Bartholomew the Great** (p93), whose atmospheric interior has been used frequently as a film set. Head through the Tudor gatehouse and turn right towards the colourful Victorian arches of **2 Smithfield Market** (p144), London's last surviving meat market.

Head northeast along Long Lane and take a right at Aldersgate St. Follow the roundabout to the right and nip up the stairs (or take the lift) to the **3 Museum of London** (p92). After exploring the museum's excellent free galleries turn left onto the highwalk and pause to examine the ruins of the **4 Roman city walls** and behind them the distinctive towers of the **5 Barbican** (p93).

Descend from the highwalk and cross over to Wood St to find the **6 Tower of St Alban** (1698), all that's left of a Wren-designed church destroyed in WWII bombing in 1940. Turn left into Love Lane and right into Aldermanbury – the impressive 15th-century **7 Guildhall** is on your left, behind a modern extension. Crossing its courtyard – note the black outline of the Roman amphitheatre – continue east onto Gresham St, taking a right into Prince's St and emerging onto the busy Bank intersection lined with neoclassical temples to commerce.

From the **8 Royal Exchange**, follow Cornhill and take a right down Gracechurch St. Turn left into wonderful **9 Leadenhall Market** (p144), roughly where the Roman forum once stood. As you leave the market's far end, **10 Lloyd's of London** displays its innards for all to see. Turn left onto Lime St for **11 30 St Mary Axe** (the Gherkin; p93). Built nearly 900 years after St Bartholomew the Great, it's a tangible testimony to the city's ability to constantly reinvent itself.

transformation of the former power station. Significant achievements include leaving the building's central 99m-high chimney, adding a two-storey glass box onto the roof and turning the cavernous **Turbine Hall** into a dramatic exhibition space. Herzog and de Meuron also designed the later 10-storey Blavatnik Building extension.

Tate Modern's permanent collection is free to visit and is arranged by both theme and chronology on levels 2 and 4 of the riverside **Natalie Bell Building** and on levels 0, 3 and 4 of the Blavatnik Building. More than 60,000 works of the permanent collection are on constant rotation, and the curators have at their disposal paintings by Georges Braque, Henri Matisse, Piet Mondrian, Andy Warhol, Mark Rothko and Jackson Pollock, as well as pieces by Joseph Beuys, Barbara Hepworth, Damien Hirst, Rebecca Horn and Claes Oldenburg.

Don't miss sublime city views from the 10th-floor **Viewing Level** of the Blavatnik Building and the view of the River Thames and St Paul's Cathedral from the 6th-floor **cafe** in the Natalie Bell Building. Head to the level 4 bridge connecting the two buildings to get a lofty view of Turbine Hall.

Free guided tours of sections of the permanent collection depart at noon, 1pm and 2pm daily. To visit the sister museum Tate Britain (p86), hop on the RB2 riverboat service from **Bankside Pier** (Map p98; www.thamesclippers.com; one way adult/child £8.70/4.35).

★Shakespeare's Globe THEATRE

(Map p98; ☎020-7401 9919; www.shakespearesglobe.com; 21 New Globe Walk, SE1; tour adult/child £17/10; ⏲box office 10am-6pm; Ⓤ Blackfriars or London Bridge) The reconstructed Shakespeare's Globe was designed to resemble the 16th-century original as closely as possible, constructed with 600 oak pegs (there's not a nail or screw in the house), specially fired Tudor-style bricks and a circular thatch roof that leaves the theatre's centre – and the groundlings watching the performance – vulnerable to the elements. Guided tours take in the architecture and give access to the exhibition space, with displays on Shakespeare, life in Bankside and theatre in the 17th century.

Shakespeare wrote for both outdoor and indoor theatre, and outside the Globe's April to October season, the **Sam Wanamaker Playhouse** – an indoor Jacobean-style theatre – puts on year-round performances.

★London Eye VIEWPOINT

(Map p98; www.londoneye.com; near County Hall, SE1; adult/child from £24.50/22; ⏲10am-8.30pm, reduced hours in low season; Ⓤ Waterloo or Westminster) Standing 135m high in a fairly flat city, the London Eye is the world's largest cantilevered observation wheel and affords views 25 miles in every direction (as far as Windsor Castle), weather permitting. Each ride – or 'flight' – takes a gracefully slow 30 minutes. The London Eye is the focal point of the capital's midnight New Year's Eve fireworks display and one of the UK's most popular tourist attractions; book tickets online in advance for a slight discount or fast-track entry to jump the queue.

★Southbank Centre ARTS CENTRE

(Map p98; ☎020-3879 9555; www.southbankcentre.co.uk; Belvedere Rd, SE1; ⏲10am-11pm; 👪; Ⓤ Waterloo) Southbank Centre, Europe's largest space for performing and visual arts, is made up of three brutalist buildings that stretch across seven riverside hectares: Royal Festival Hall (p142), Queen Elizabeth Hall (p142) and **Hayward Gallery** (⏲11am-7pm Mon-Sat 10am-6pm Sun). With cafes, restaurants, shops and bars, this complex is always a hub of activity, from the singing lift up to the 6th floor to teenage skateboarders doing tricks in the Undercroft. In summer, the **fountains** and **artificial beach** on the waterfront are a hit with youngsters.

★Southwark Cathedral CATHEDRAL

(Map p98; ☎020-7367 6700; www.cathedral.southwark.anglican.org; Montague Cl, SE1; ⏲9am-5pm Mon-Fri, 9.30am-3.45pm & 5-6pm Sat, 12.30-3pm & 4-6pm Sun; Ⓤ London Bridge) Southwark Cathedral, a mostly Victorian construction but with a history dating back many centuries earlier, was the nearest church to what was once the only entry point into the city, London Bridge. The cathedral is relatively small, but the Gothic arched nave is impressive, as is the 16th-century saint-filled High Altar Screen. Tombs and memorials are scattered throughout (follow the one-way system), including the tomb of John Gower and an alabaster Shakespeare Memorial. Evensong takes place at 5.30pm on weekdays, 4pm on Saturdays and 3pm on Sundays.

London Dungeon AMUSEMENT PARK

(Map p98; ☎0333 321 2001; www.thedungeons.com/london; County Hall, Westminster Bridge Rd, SE1; adult/child £30/24; ⏲10am-4pm; Ⓤ Waterloo or Westminster) A scary tour of London's

South Bank

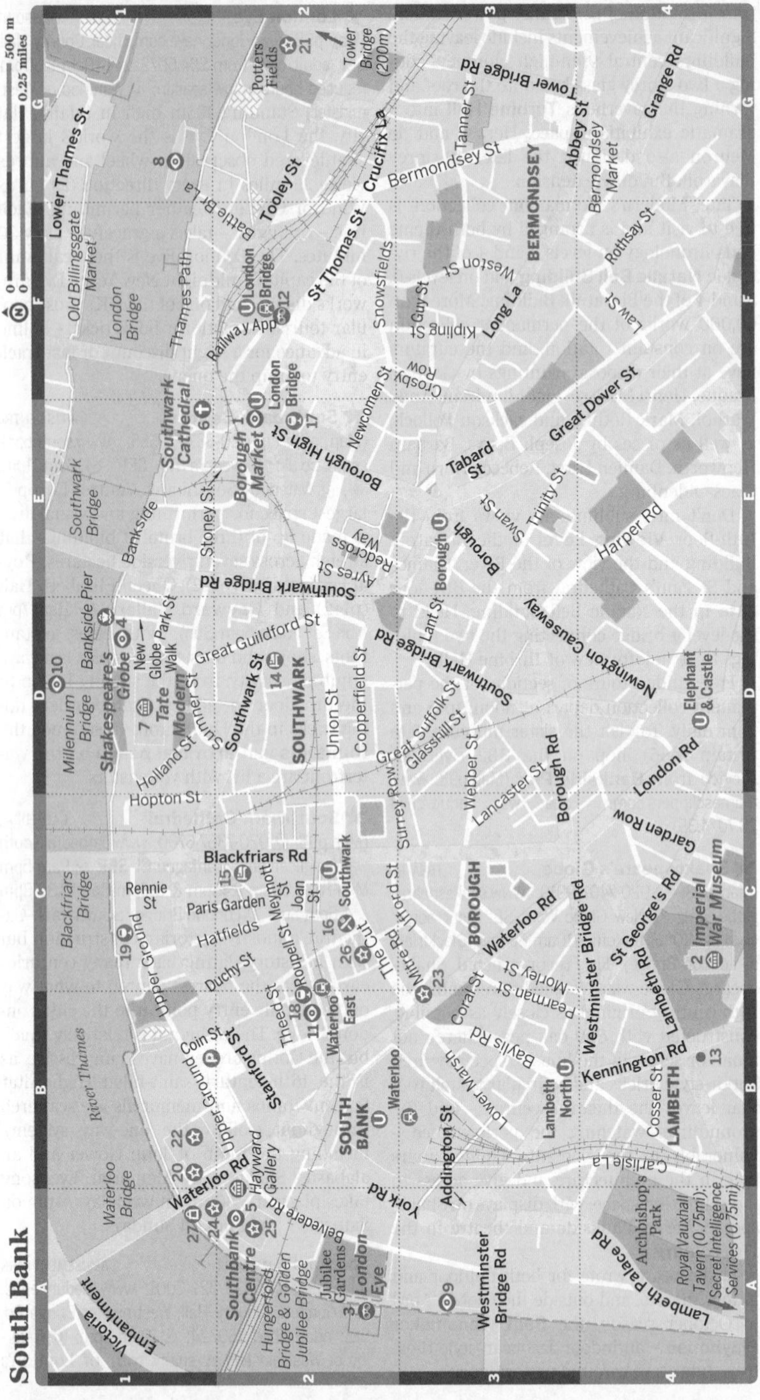
0 500 m
0 0.25 miles
Victoria Embankment
Waterloo Bridge
River Thames
Blackfriars Bridge
Millennium Bridge
Southwark Bridge
London Bridge
Old Billingsgate Market
Lower Thames St
Thames Path
Potters Fields
Tower Bridge (200m)
Hungerford Bridge & Golden Jubilee Bridge
Jubilee Gardens
London Eye
Southbank Centre
Hayward Gallery
Waterloo Rd
Belvedere Rd
Upper Ground
Coin St
Stamford St
Theed St
Roupell St
Duchy St
Hatfields
Paris Garden
Meymott St
Joan St
Rennie St
Blackfriars Rd
Southwark
Hopton St
Holland St
Sumner St
Shakespeare's Globe
Tate Modern
New Globe Walk
Park St
Bankside Pier
Bankside
Great Guildford St
Southwark St
SOUTHWARK
Union St
Copperfield St
Southwark Bridge Rd
Stoney St
Borough Market
Southwark Cathedral
London Bridge
Railway App
Battle Br La
Tooley St
St Thomas St
Crucifix La
Bermondsey St
Tower Bridge Rd
Tanner St
Abbey St
Grange Rd
BERMONDSEY
Bermondsey Market
Rothsay St
Weston St
Law St
Snowsfields
Guy St
Kipling St
Long La
Crosby Row
Newcomen St
Borough High St
Tabard St
Great Dover St
Trinity St
Swan St
Harper Rd
Borough
Redcross Way
Ayres St
Lant St
Newington Causeway
Elephant & Castle
London Rd
Great Suffolk St
Glasshill St
Surrey Row
Webber St
Lancaster St
Borough Rd
Garden Row
BOROUGH
Waterloo Rd
Westminster Bridge Rd
St George's Rd
Imperial War Museum
Lambeth Rd
Kennington Rd
Lambeth North
LAMBETH
Cosser St
Carlisle La
Archbishop's Park
Lambeth Palace Rd
Royal Vauxhall Tavern (0.75mi); Secret Intelligence Services (0.75mi)
Westminster Bridge Rd
Addington St
York Rd
SOUTH BANK
Waterloo
Waterloo East
The Cut
Mitre Rd
Ufford St
Coral St
Pearman St
Morley St
Baylis Rd
Lower Marsh
1 2 3 4 5 6 7 8 9 10 11 12 13 14 15 16 17 18 19 20 21 22 23 24 25 26 27
A B C D E F G

South Bank

Top Sights
1 Borough Market E2
2 Imperial War Museum C4
3 London Eye A2
4 Shakespeare's Globe D1
5 Southbank Centre A2
6 Southwark Cathedral E1
7 Tate Modern D1

Sights
8 HMS Belfast G1
9 London Dungeon A3
10 Millennium Bridge D1
11 Roupell St B2
12 Shard F2

Activities, Courses & Tours
13 London Bicycle Tour B4

Sleeping
14 CitizenM London Bankside D2
15 Hoxton Southwark C2
Shangri-La Hotel at the Shard ......(see 12)

Eating
16 Anchor & Hope C2
Padella ....(see 1)
Skylon ....(see 25)

Drinking & Nightlife
17 George Inn E2
18 Kings Arms B2
19 Lyaness C1
Queen Elizabeth Hall Roof Garden ....(see 24)
Seabird .... (see 15)

Entertainment
20 BFI Southbank B1
21 Bridge Theatre G2
22 National Theatre B1
23 Old Vic B3
24 Queen Elizabeth Hall A1
25 Royal Festival Hall A2
26 Young Vic C2

Shopping
27 Southbank Centre Book Market A1

gruesome history awaits. Expect darkness, sudden loud noises, flashing lights, squirts of unspecified liquid and unpleasant smells as you shuffle through themed rooms where actors, often covered in fake blood, tell creepy stories and goad visitors. It's spooky, interactive and fun if you like jumping out of your skin. Pre-booking tickets online is essential. It takes around 90 minutes to work your way through. Not suitable for young children.

Shard VIEWPOINT
(Map p98; ☎0844 499 7111; www.theviewfromtheshard.com; Joiner St, SE1; adult/child from £25/20; Ⓤ London Bridge) Puncturing the skies above London, the dramatic splinter-like form of the Shard has become an icon of the city and is one of the tallest buildings in Europe. The scene from the 244m-high viewing platforms on floors 69 and 72 is like none other in town, but it comes at an equally lofty price; book online in advance for a potential discount. Premium tickets come with a good-weather guarantee, meaning you might be able to return for free. Check online for opening hours, which vary depending on events.

HMS Belfast SHIP
(Map p98; www.iwm.org.uk/visits/hms-belfast; Queen's Walk, SE1; adult/child £19/9.50; ⏰10am-4pm; Ⓤ London Bridge) HMS *Belfast* is a magnet for kids of all ages. This large, light cruiser – launched in 1938 – served in WWII, helping to sink the Nazi battleship *Sand* shelling the Normandy coast on D-Day, and in the Korean War. Its 6in guns could bombard a target 12 miles distant. Displays offer great insight into what life on board was like, in peacetime and during military engagements. Excellent audio guides, included in the admission fee, feature anecdotes from former crew members.

Kensington & Hyde Park

★ **Natural History Museum** MUSEUM
(Map p100; www.nhm.ac.uk; Cromwell Rd, SW7; ⏰10am-5.50pm; 👪; Ⓤ South Kensington) FREE On a vast 5.7 hectare plot and housing 80 million specimens, this colossal and magnificent building is infused with the irrepressible Victorian spirit of collecting, cataloguing and interpreting the natural world. The **Dinosaurs Gallery** (Blue Zone) is a must for children, who gawp at the animatronic T-rex. Adults will love the intriguing Treasures exhibition in the **Cadogan Gallery** (Green Zone), which displays a host of unrelated objects, each telling its own unique story, from a chunk of moon rock to a dodo skeleton.

Also in the Green Zone, the **Mineral Gallery** is a breathtaking display of architectural perspective leading to the **Vault**,

Knightsbridge, South Kensington & Chelsea

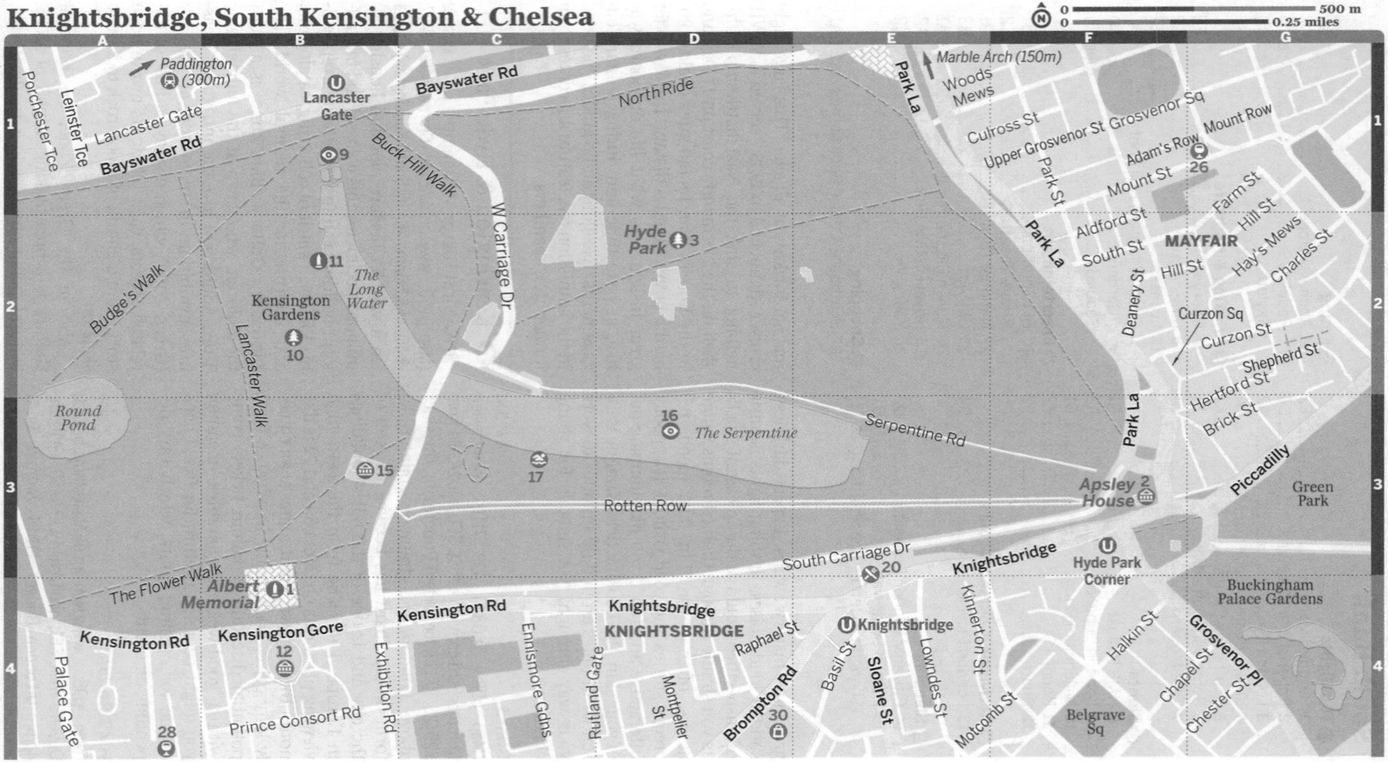

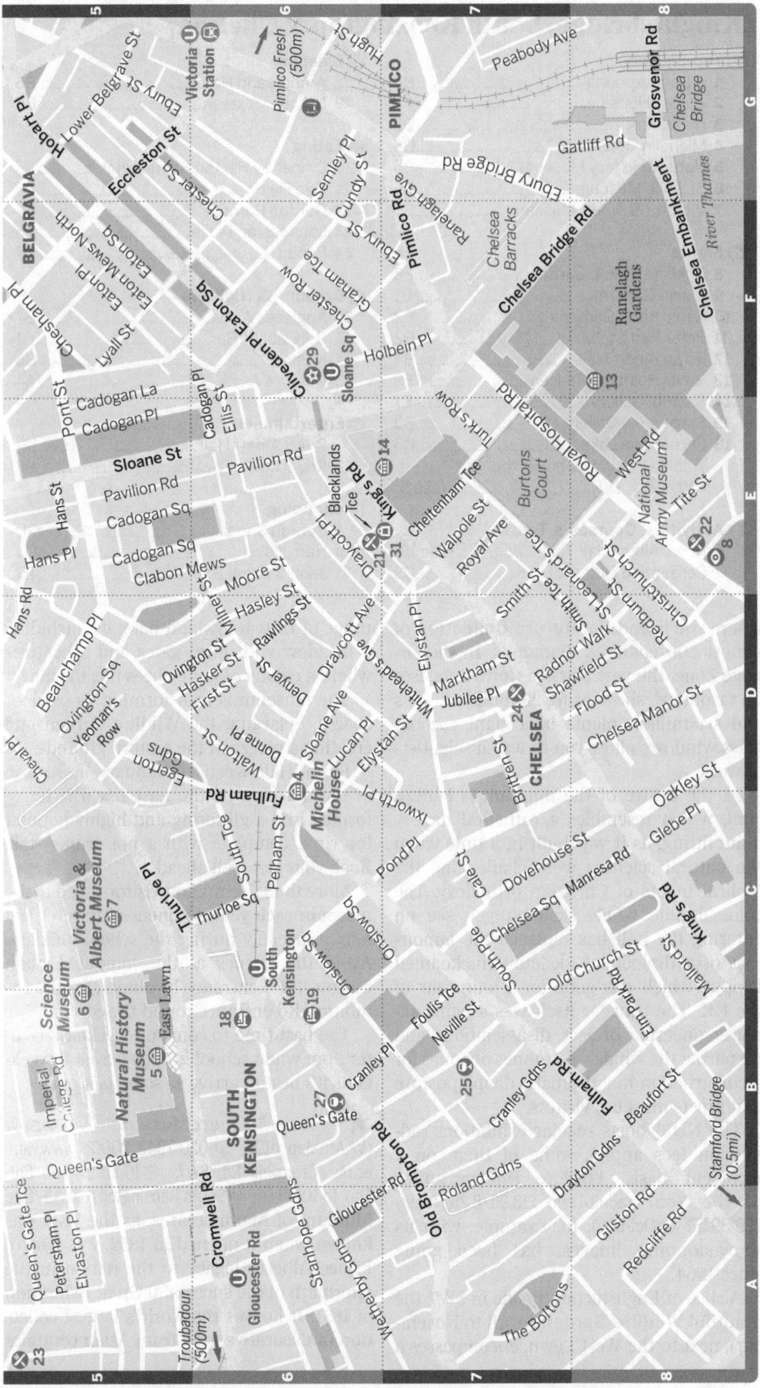
BELGRAVIA
Hobart Pl
Lower Belgrave St
Ebury St
Victoria Station
Pimlico Fresh (500m)
Hugh St
PIMLICO
Peabody Ave
Grosvenor Rd
Chelsea Bridge
Eccleston St
Chester Sq
Semley Pl
Cundy St
Gatliff Rd
Ebury Bridge Rd
Ranelagh Gve
Pimlico Rd
Ebury St
Graham Tce
Chester Row
Eaton Sq
Eaton Pl
Eaton Mews North
Chesham Pl
Lyall St
Cliveden Pl
Eaton Sq
29
Sloane Sq
Holbein Pl
Chelsea Barracks
Chelsea Bridge Rd
Ranelagh Gardens
Chelsea Embankment
River Thames
13
Royal Hospital Rd
Turk's Row
Pont St
Cadogan La
Cadogan Pl
Cadogan Pl
Ellis St
Sloane St
Pavilion Rd
Pavilion Rd
Blacklands Tce
14
King's Rd
Cheltenham Tce
Burtons Court
West Rd
National Army Museum
Hans St
Cadogan Sq
Cadogan Sq
Clabon Mews
Draycott Pl
21
31
Walpole St
Royal Ave
St Leonard's Tce
Tite St
22
8
Hans Pl
Moore St
Milner St
Hasley St
Rawlings St
Elystan Pl
Smith St
Smith Tce
Christchurch St
Redburn St
Hans Rd
Beauchamp Pl
Ovington Sq
Ovington St
Hasker St
First St
Denyer St
Draycott Ave
Whitehead's Gve
Markham St
Jubilee Pl
Radnor Walk
Shawfield St
24
Flood St
Chelsea Manor St
Yeoman's Row
Cheval Pl
Egerton Gdns
Walton St
Donne Pl
Sloane Ave
Lucan Pl
Elystan St
CHELSEA
Britten St
Fulham Rd
4
Michelin House
Ixworth Pl
Oakley St
Glebe Pl
Victoria & Albert Museum
7
Thurloe Pl
South Tce
Thurloe Sq
Pelham St
Pond Pl
Cale St
Dovehouse St
Manresa Rd
King's Rd
Science Museum
6
Natural History Museum
5
East Lawn
18
South Kensington
19
Onslow Sq
Onslow Sq
Chelsea Sq
South Pde
Old Church St
Mallord St
Foulis Tce
Neville St
Elm Park Rd
Imperial College Rd
SOUTH KENSINGTON
Queen's Gate
27
Queen's Gate
Cranley Pl
25
Cranley Gdns
Fulham Rd
Beaufort St
Queen's Gate Tce
Petersham Pl
Elvaston Pl
Cromwell Rd
Gloucester Rd
Stanhope Gdns
Gloucester Rd
Old Brompton Rd
Roland Gdns
Drayton Gdns
Stamford Bridge (0.5mi)
Gilston Rd
Redcliffe Rd
Wetherby Gdns
The Boltons
23
Troubadour (500m)
LONDON

Knightsbridge, South Kensington & Chelsea

Top Sights
1 Albert Memorial B4
2 Apsley House F3
3 Hyde Park D2
4 Michelin House D6
5 Natural History Museum B5
6 Science Museum B5
7 Victoria & Albert Museum C5

Sights
8 Chelsea Physic Garden E8
9 Italian Gardens B1
10 Kensington Gardens B2
11 Peter Pan Statue B2
12 Royal Albert Hall B4
13 Royal Hospital Chelsea F8
14 Saatchi Gallery E7
15 Serpentine Gallery B3
16 Serpentine Lake D3
Wildlife Photographer of the Year .... (see 5)

Activities, Courses & Tours
Royal Albert Hall Tour .... (see 12)
17 Serpentine Lido C3

Sleeping
18 Ampersand Hotel B6
19 Number Sixteen B6

Eating
20 Dinner by Heston Blumenthal E3
21 Five Fields E6
22 Gordon Ramsay E8
23 Launceston Place A5
24 Rabbit D7

Drinking & Nightlife
25 Anglesea Arms B7
26 Connaught Bar G1
27 K Bar B6
28 Queen's Arms A4

Entertainment
Royal Albert Hall .... (see 12)
29 Royal Court Theatre F6

Shopping
Conran Shop .... (see 4)
30 Harrods D4
31 John Sandoe Books E7

where you'll find the **Aurora Collection** of almost 300 coloured diamonds. In the Orange Zone, the vast **Darwin Centre** focuses on taxonomy, showcasing 28 million insects and six million plants in a giant cocoon; glass windows allow you to watch scientists at work.

At the centre of the museum is **Hintze Hall**, which resembles a cathedral nave – quite fitting, as it was built in a time when the natural sciences were challenging the biblical tenets of Christian orthodoxy. The colossal blue whale skeleton you see on entering the hall has replaced the famous cast of a diplodocus skeleton (nicknamed Dippy), which has gone on a long tour of the UK. The transfer itself was a painstaking engineering project, disassembling and preparing the whale's 4.5 tonnes of bones for reconstruction in a dramatic diving posture that greets museum visitors.

The NHM hosts regular exhibitions (admission fees apply), some of them on a recurrent basis. **Wildlife Photographer of the Year** (adult/child £13.95/8.25, family £29-39.50; Oct-Dec), for example, with its show-stopping images, has been going since 1964.

A slice of English countryside in SW7, the beautiful **Wildlife Garden** (April to November), next to the West Lawn, encompasses a range of British lowland habitats, including a meadow with farm gates and a bee tree where a colony of honey bees fills the air.

The museum is transforming its outdoor spaces, enlarging the Wildlife Garden and creating a piazza in the eastern grounds.

From Halloween to January, a section of the museum by the East Lawn is transformed into a glittering and highly popular **ice rink**, complete with a hot-drinks stall. Book your slot well ahead.

More than five million visitors head to the museum each year, so queues can often get long, especially during the school holidays. Avoid the queues at the congested main Cromwell Rd entrance by aiming for the Exhibition Rd entrance round the corner.

The best time to come on weekdays is after 2pm when school groups leave; at weekends it's best to arrive as soon as it opens.

★Victoria & Albert Museum MUSEUM
(V&A; Map p100; 020-7942 2000; www.vam.ac.uk; Cromwell Rd, SW7; 10am-5.45pm Sat-Thu, to 10pm Fri; South Kensington) FREE The Museum of Manufactures, as the V&A was known when it opened in 1852, was part of Prince Albert's legacy to the nation in the aftermath of the successful Great Exhibition of 1851. It houses the world's largest collection of decorative arts, from Asian ceramics

to Middle Eastern rugs, Chinese paintings, Western furniture, fashion from all ages and modern-day domestic appliances. The (ticketed) temporary exhibitions are another highlight, covering anything from David Bowie to Mary Quant retrospectives, car design, special materials and trends. See more on p104.

★ Science Museum MUSEUM

(Map p100; ☎0333 241 4000, 020-7942 4000; www.sciencemuseum.org.uk; Exhibition Rd, SW7; ⏲10am-6pm, last entry 5.15pm; 🚻; Ⓤ South Kensington) FREE This scientifically spellbinding museum will mesmerise adults and children alike, with its interactive and educational exhibits covering everything from early technology to space travel. On the ground floor, a perennial favourite is **Exploring Space**, a gallery featuring genuine rockets and satellites and a full-size replica of the *Eagle*, the lander that took Neil Armstrong and Buzz Aldrin to the moon in 1969. The **Making the Modern World Gallery** next door is a visual feast of locomotives, planes, cars and other revolutionary inventions.

★ Hyde Park PARK

(Map p100; www.royalparks.org.uk/parks/hyde-park; ⏲5am-midnight; Ⓤ Marble Arch, Hyde Park Corner, Knightsbridge, Queensway) Hyde Park is central London's largest green space, expropriated from the church in 1536 by Henry VIII and turned into a hunting ground and later a venue for duels, executions and horse racing. The 1851 Great Exhibition was held here, and during WWII the park became a vast potato field. These days, it's a place to stroll and picnic, boat on the **Serpentine lake** (Map p100; ☎020-7262 1330; Ⓤ Lancaster Gate, Knightsbridge), or catch a summer concert or outdoor film during the warmer months.

★ Kensington Palace PALACE

(Map p106; www.hrp.org.uk/kensington-palace; Kensington Gardens, W8; adult/child £21.50/10.70, cheaper weekdays after 2pm; ⏲10am-6pm, to 4pm Nov-Feb; Ⓤ High St Kensington) Built in 1605, Kensington Palace became the favourite royal residence under William and Mary of Orange in 1689, and remained so until George III became king and relocated to Buckingham Palace. Today, it remains a residence for high-ranking royals, including the Duke and Duchess of Cambridge (Prince William and his wife Kate). A large part of the palace is open to the public, however, including the King's and Queen's State Apartments.

Royal Albert Hall HISTORIC BUILDING

(Map p100; ☎0845 401 5034, box office 020-7589 8212; www.royalalberthall.com; Kensington Gore, SW7; tours adult/child from £14.25/7.25; ⏲tours from 10am; Ⓤ South Kensington) Built in 1871, thanks in part to the proceeds of the 1851 Great Exhibition organised by Prince Albert (Queen Victoria's husband), this huge, domed, red-brick amphitheatre, adorned with a frieze of Minton tiles, is Britain's most famous concert venue and home to the BBC's Promenade Concerts (the Proms) every summer. To find out about the hall's intriguing history and royal connections, and to gaze out from the Gallery, book an informative one-hour front-of-house **grand tour** (Map p100; ☎020-7589 8212; adult/child £14.25/7.25; ⏲hourly 9.30am-4.30pm Apr-Oct, 10am-4pm Nov-Mar), operating most days.

★ Apsley House HISTORIC BUILDING

(Map p100; ☎020-7499 5676; www.english-heritage.org.uk/visit/places/apsley-house; 149 Piccadilly, Hyde Park Corner, W1; adult/child £10.50/6.30, with Wellington Arch £13.60/8.20; ⏲11am-5pm Wed-Sun Apr-Oct, 10am-4pm Sat & Sun Nov-Mar; Ⓤ Hyde Park Corner) This stunning house, containing exhibits about the Duke of Wellington, who defeated Napoleon Bonaparte at Waterloo, was once the first building to appear when entering London from the west and was therefore known as 'No 1 London'. Wellington memorabilia, including the Duke's death mask, fills the **basement gallery**, while an astonishing collection of china and silver, and paintings by Velasquez, Rubens, Van Dyck, Brueghel, Murillo and Goya awaits in the 1st-floor **Waterloo Gallery**, which runs the length of the building's west flank.

Kensington Gardens PARK

(Map p100; ☎0300 061 2000; www.royalparks.org.uk/parks/kensington-gardens; ⏲6am-dusk; Ⓤ Queensway or Lancaster Gate) A delightful collection of manicured lawns, tree-shaded avenues and basins immediately west of Hyde Park, the picturesque expanse of Kensington Gardens is technically part of Kensington Palace, located in the far west of the gardens. The large **Round Pond** in front of the palace is enjoyable to amble around.

Also worth a look are the lovely fountains in the **Italian Gardens** (Ⓤ Lancaster Gate), believed to be a gift from Prince Albert to

Victoria & Albert Museum

HALF-DAY HIGHLIGHTS TOUR

The art- and design-packed V&A is vast: we have devised an easy-to-follow tour of the museum highlights to help cover some signature pieces while also allowing you to appreciate some of the grandeur of the museum architecture.

Enter the V&A by the main entrance off Cromwell Rd and immediately turn left to explore the Islamic Middle East Gallery and to discover the sumptuous silk-and-wool **1 Ardabil Carpet**. Among the pieces from South Asia in the adjacent gallery is the terrifying automated **2 Tipu's Tiger**. Continue to the outstanding **3 Fashion Gallery** with its displays of clothing styles through the ages. The magnificent gallery opposite houses the **4 Raphael Cartoons**, large paintings by Raphael used to weave tapestries for the Vatican. Take the stairs to level 2 and the Britain 1500–1760 Gallery; turn

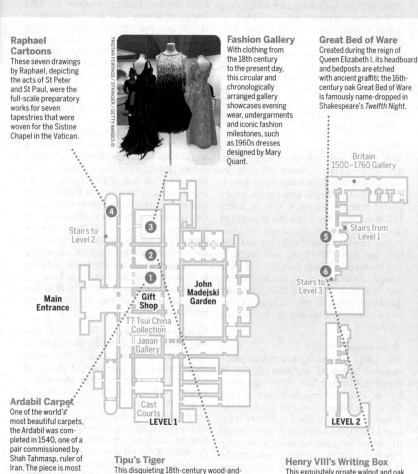

Raphael Cartoons
These seven drawings by Raphael, depicting the acts of St Peter and St Paul, were the full-scale preparatory works for seven tapestries that were woven for the Sistine Chapel in the Vatican.

TRISTAN FEWINGS / STRINGER / GETTY IMAGES ©

Fashion Gallery
With clothing from the 18th century to the present day, this circular and chronologically arranged gallery showcases evening wear, undergarments and iconic fashion milestones, such as 1960s dresses designed by Mary Quant.

Great Bed of Ware
Created during the reign of Queen Elizabeth I, its headboard and bedposts are etched with ancient graffiti; the 16th-century oak Great Bed of Ware is famously name-dropped in Shakespeare's *Twelfth Night*.

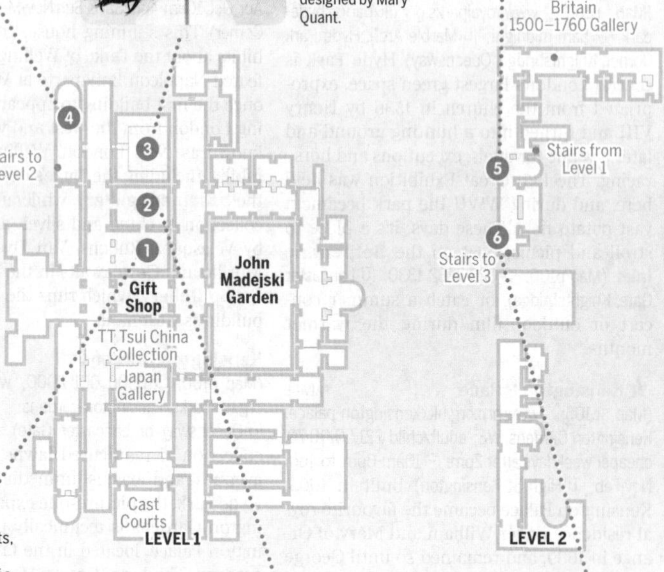

Ardabil Carpet
One of the world's most beautiful carpets, the Ardabil was completed in 1540, one of a pair commissioned by Shah Tahmasp, ruler of Iran. The piece is most astonishing for the artistry of the detailing and the subtlety of design.

Tipu's Tiger
This disquieting 18th-century wood-and-metal mechanical automaton depicts a European being savaged by a tiger. When a handle is turned, an organ hidden within the feline mimics the cries of the dying man, whose arm also rises.

Henry VIII's Writing Box
This exquisitely ornate walnut and oak 16th-century writing box has been added to over the centuries, but the original decorative motifs are superb, including Henry's coat of arms, flanked by Venus (holding Cupid) and Mars.

left in the gallery to find the 5 **Great Bed of Ware**, beyond which rests the exquisitely crafted artistry of 6 **Henry VIII's Writing Box**. Head up the stairs into the Ironwork Gallery on level 3 for the 7 **Hereford Screen**. Continue through the Ironwork and Sculpture Galleries and through the Leighton Corridor to the glittering 8 **Jewellery Gallery**. Exit through the Stained Glass Gallery, at the end of which you'll find stairs back down to level 1.

LAPAS77 / SHUTTERSTOCK ©

TRISTAN FEWINGS / STRINGER / GETTY IMAGES ©

TOP TIPS

- ➡ Museum attendants are always at hand along the route for information.
- ➡ Photography is allowed in most galleries, except the Jewellery Gallery, the Raphael Cartoons and in exhibitions.
- ➡ Avoid daytime crowds: visit the V&A in the evening, till 10pm on Fridays.

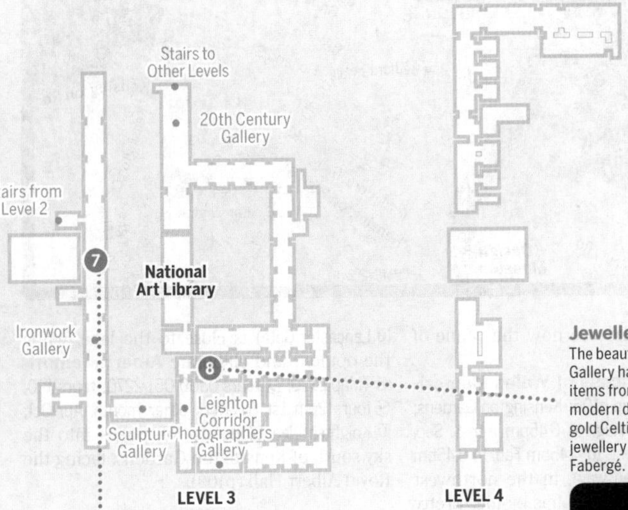

Jewellery Gallery

The beautifully illuminated Jewellery Gallery has a stunning collection of items from ancient Greece to the modern day, including a dazzling gold Celtic breastplate, art-nouveau jewellery and animals fashioned by Fabergé.

GAID KORNSILAPA / SHUTTERSTOCK ©

Hereford Screen

Designed by George Gilbert Scott, this awe-inspiring choir screen is a labour of love, originally fashioned for Hereford Cathedral. It's an almighty conception of wood, iron, copper, brass and hardstone, and there were few parts of the V&A that could support its great mass.

Notting Hill & Bayswater

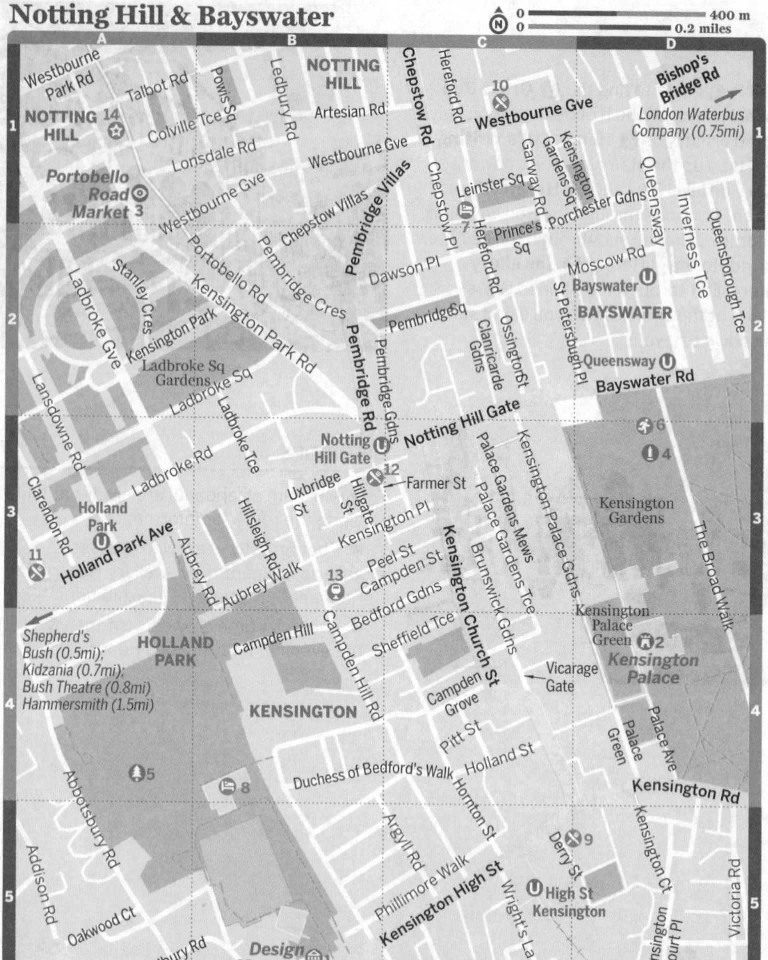

Queen Victoria; they are now the venue of a cafe.

The **Diana, Princess of Wales Memorial Playground** (Map p106; Kensington Gardens; 10am-7.45pm May-Aug, to 6.45pm Apr & Sep, to 5.45pm March & Oct, to 4.45pm Feb, to 3.45pm Nov-Jan; ; Queensway), in the northwest corner of the gardens, has some pretty ambitious attractions for children. Next to the playground stands the delightful **Elfin Oak** (Map p106), a 900-year-old tree stump carved with elves, gnomes, witches and small creatures. To the east, George Frampton's celebrated **Peter Pan statue** (Map p100; Lancaster Gate) is close to the lake, while the opulent and elaborate **Albert Memorial** (Map p100; tours 0300 061 2270; tours £10; tours 2pm 1st Fri every other month, Apr-Oct; Knightsbridge, Gloucester Rd) pokes into the sky south of Kensington Gardens, facing the Royal Albert Hall (p103).

Chelsea Physic Garden GARDENS
(Map p100; 020-7352 5646; www.chelseaphysicgarden.co.uk; 66 Royal Hospital Rd, SW3; adult/child under 15/family £9.50/8.50/37; Mon-Fri & Sun 11am-5pm, to 4pm Nov-Feb; Sloane Sq) You may bump into a wandering duck or two as

Notting Hill & Bayswater

Top Sights
1 Design Museum B5
2 Kensington Palace D4
3 Portobello Road Market A1

Sights
4 Elfin Oak D3
5 Holland Park A4

Activities, Courses & Tours
6 Diana, Princess of Wales Memorial Playground D3

Sleeping
7 New Linden Hotel C1
8 Safestay Holland Park B4

Eating
9 Dishoom D5
10 Farmacy C1
11 Flat Three A3
12 Geales B3

Drinking & Nightlife
13 Windsor Castle B3

Entertainment
14 Electric Cinema A1

you enter this walled pocket of botanical enchantment, established by the Apothecaries' Society in 1673 for students working on medicinal plants and healing. One of Europe's oldest of its kind, the small grounds are a compendium of botany, from carnivorous pitcher plants to rich yellow flag irises, a cork oak from Portugal, the largest outdoor fruiting olive tree in the British Isles and rare trees and shrubs.

Royal Hospital Chelsea MUSEUM
(Map p100; tours 020-7881 5493; www.chelsea-pensioners.co.uk; Royal Hospital Rd, SW3; grounds 10am-5pm, Great Hall 10am-noon & 2-4pm, museum 10am-4pm Mon-Fri; U Sloane Sq) FREE Designed by Christopher Wren, this superb structure was built in 1692 to provide shelter for ex-servicemen. Since the reign of Charles II, it has housed hundreds of war veterans, known as Chelsea Pensioners. They're fondly regarded as national treasures, and cut striking figures in the dark-blue greatcoats (in winter) or scarlet frock coats (in summer) that they wear on ceremonial occasions.

Serpentine Gallery GALLERY
(Map p100; 020-7402 6075; www.serpentinegalleries.org; Kensington Gardens, W2; 10am-6pm Tue-Sun; U Lancaster Gate or Knightsbridge) FREE This gallery is one of London's most important contemporary-art galleries. Damien Hirst, Andreas Gursky, Louise Bourgeois, Gabriel Orozco, Tomoko Takahashi and Jeff Koons have all exhibited here. A leading architect (who has never built in the UK) is annually commissioned to build a new 'Summer Pavilion' nearby, open from June to October. The galleries run a full program of readings, talks and workshops. Sister space the Serpentine Sackler Gallery, designed by Zaha Hadid, is a few minutes away over the bridge.

Clerkenwell, Shoreditch & Spitalfields

★ **Whitechapel Gallery** GALLERY
(Map p90; 020-7522 7888; www.whitechapelgallery.org; 77-82 Whitechapel High St, E1; 11am-6pm Tue, Wed & Fri-Sun, to 9pm Thu; U Aldgate East) FREE A firm favourite of art students and the avant-garde cognoscenti, this ground-breaking gallery doesn't have a permanent collection but is devoted to hosting edgy exhibitions of contemporary art. It made its name by staging exhibitions by both established and emerging artists, including the first UK shows by Pablo Picasso, Jackson Pollock, Mark Rothko and Frida Kahlo. The gallery's ambitiously themed shows change every couple of months (check online) and there's also often live music, talks and films on Thursday evenings.

Museum of the Home MUSEUM
(Map p130; 020-7739 9893; www.museumofthehome.org.uk; 136 Kingsland Rd, E2; 10am-5pm Tue-Sun; U Hoxton) FREE These beautiful ivy-clad brick almshouses (closed until 2021 for renovations at the time of research), were built in 1714 as a home for poor pensioners. Two rooms have been furnished to show how residents lived in the 1770s and 1880s, atmospherically lit by candles and the original gas lamps. The attention to detail is impressive, down to the vintage newspaper left open on the breakfast table.

★ **Dennis Severs' House** HISTORIC BUILDING
(Map p130; 020-7247 4013; www.dennissevershouse.co.uk; 18 Folgate St, E1; day/night £10/15; noon-2pm & 5-9pm Mon, 5-9pm Wed & Fri, noon-4pm Sun; U Liverpool St) This extraordinary Georgian house is set up as if its occupants – a family of Huguenot silk weavers – have just walked out the door. Each of the 10

rooms is stuffed with the minutiae of everyday life from centuries past: half-drunk cups of tea, emptied but gleaming wet oyster shells and, in perhaps unnecessary attention to detail, a used chamber pot by the bed. It's more an immersive experience than a traditional museum; explorations of the house are conducted in silence.

Old Truman Brewery HISTORIC BUILDING
(Map p130; ☎020-7770 6000; www.trumanbrewery.com; Brick Lane, E1; Ⓤ Shoreditch High St) Founded here in the 17th century, Truman's Black Eagle Brewery was, by the 1850s, the largest brewery in the world. Spread over a series of brick buildings and yards straddling both sides of Brick Lane, the complex is now completely given over to edgy markets, pop-up fashion stores, vintage clothes shops, cafes and bars – it's at its busy best when market stalls are set up on Sundays. Beer may not be brewed here any more, but it certainly is consumed.

East London

★**Museum of London Docklands** MUSEUM
(☎020-7001 9844; www.museumoflondon.org.uk/docklands; West India Quay, E14; ⊙10am-6pm; Ⓤ DLR West India Quay) FREE Housed in an 1802 warehouse, this educational museum combines artefacts and multimedia displays to chart the history of the city through its river and docks. The best strategy is to begin on the 3rd floor and work your way down through the ages. Perhaps the most illuminating and certainly the most disturbing gallery is **London, Sugar and Slavery**, which examines the capital's role in the transatlantic slave trade.

★**Columbia Road Flower Market** MARKET
(Map p130; www.columbiaroad.info; Columbia Rd, E2; ⊙8am-3pm Sun; Ⓤ Hoxton) A wonderful explosion of colour and life, this weekly market sells a beautiful array of flowers, pot plants, bulbs, seeds and everything you might need for the garden. It's a lot of fun and the best place to hear proper Cockney barrow-boy banter ('We got flowers cheap enough for ya muvver-in-law's grave' etc). It's popular, so

LONDON FOR (ALMOST) FREE

Sights It usually costs nothing to visit the Houses of Parliament (p83) if you're going to watch debates. Another institution of public life, the Changing of the Guard at Buckingham Palace (p76), is free to watch. For one weekend in September, Open House London (p119) opens the doors to some 850 buildings for free.

Museums & Galleries The permanent collections of all state-funded museums and galleries are open to the public free of charge. They include the V&A (p102), Tate Modern (p93), British Museum (p82) and National Gallery (p83). The **Saatchi Gallery** (Map p100; www.saatchigallery.com; Duke of York's HQ, King's Rd, SW3; ⊙10am-6pm; Ⓤ Sloane Sq) FREE is also free.

Views Why pay good money when some of the finest viewpoints in London are free? Head up to Level 10 of Switch House at Tate Modern (p93) or the Sky Gardens atop the Walkie Talkie (p92).

Concerts A number of churches usually offer free lunchtime classical music concerts. Try St Martin-in-the-Fields (p83). **St James's Piccadilly** (Map p80; ☎020-7734 4511; www.sjp.org.uk; 197 Piccadilly, W1; ⊙8am-8pm; Ⓤ Piccadilly Circus), **Temple Church** (Map p90; ☎020-7353 3470; www.templechurch.com; King's Bench Walk, EC4; adult/child £5/3; ⊙10am-4pm Mon, Tue, Thu & Fri, 2-4pm Wed, hours & days vary; Ⓤ Temple) and **St Alfege Church** (☎020-8853 0687; www.st-alfege.org; Greenwich Church St, SE10; ⊙11am-4pm Mon-Sat, from noon Sun; Ⓤ Cutty Sark).

Walks Walking around town is possibly the best way to get a sense of the city and its history. Roam through Hampstead Heath (p111) in North London, follow the Thames along the South Bank, or just walk from A to B in the compact West End.

Low-Cost Transport Bike-share your way around through Santander Cycles (p149) – the access fee is £2 for 24 hours; bike hire is then free for the first 30 minutes. Travel as much as you like on London Transport with a one-day Travelcard or an Oyster Card.

OFF THE BEATEN TRACK

REGENT'S CANAL

The towpath of the tranquil **Regent's Canal** (Map p128; https://canalrivertrust.org.uk/enjoy-the-waterways/canal-and-river-network/regents-canal) makes an excellent shortcut across North London, either on foot or by bike. In full, the ribbon of water runs 9 miles from Little Venice (where it connects with the Grand Union Canal) to the Thames at Limehouse.

You can make do with walking from Little Venice to Camden Town in less than an hour, passing Regent's Park and London Zoo, as well as beautiful villas designed by architect John Nash and redevelopments of old industrial buildings. Allow 25 to 30 minutes between Little Venice and Regent's Park, and 15 to 20 minutes between Regent's Park and Camden Town. There are plenty of well-signed exits along the way.

If you decide to continue on, it's worth stopping at the **London Canal Museum** (020-7713 0836; www.canalmuseum.org.uk; 12-13 New Wharf Rd, N1; adult/child £5/2.50; 10am-4.30pm Fri-Sun; King's Cross St Pancras) in King's Cross to learn more about the canal's history. Shortly afterwards you'll hit the 878m-long Islington Tunnel and have to take to the roads for a spell. After joining the path again near Colebrooke Row, you can follow the water all the way to the Thames at Limehouse Basin, or divert on to the Hertford Union Canal at Victoria Park and head to Queen Elizabeth Olympic Park (p109).

go as early as you can, or later on when the vendors sell off cut flowers cheaply.

★Queen Elizabeth Olympic Park PARK
(www.queenelizabetholympicpark.co.uk; E20; Stratford) The glittering centrepiece of London's 2012 Olympic Games, this vast 227-hectare expanse includes the main Olympic venues as well as playgrounds, walking and cycling trails, gardens and a diverse mix of wetland, woodland, meadow and other wildlife habitats – an environmentally fertile legacy for the future. The main focal point is London Stadium (p142), now the home ground for West Ham United FC.

ArcelorMittal Orbit TOWER
(0333 800 8099; www.arcelormittalorbit.com; 3 Thornton St, E20; adult/child £12.50/7.50, with slide £17.50/12.50; 11am-3pm Mon-Fri, 10am-7pm Sat & Sun; Stratford) Turner Prize–winner Anish Kapoor's 115m-high, twisted-steel sculpture towers strikingly over the southern end of Queen Elizabeth Olympic Park. In essence it's an artwork, but at the 80m mark it also offers an impressive panorama from a mirrored viewing platform, which is accessed by a lift from the base of the sculpture (the tallest in the UK). A dramatic tunnel slide running down the tower is the world's highest and longest, coiling 178m down to ground level.

Victoria Park PARK
(www.towerhamlets.gov.uk/victoriapark; Grove Rd, E3; 7am-dusk; Hackney Wick) The 'Regent's Park of the East End', this 86-hectare leafy expanse of ornamental lakes, monuments, tennis courts, flower beds and lawns was opened in 1845. It was the first public park in the East End, given the go-ahead after a local MP presented Queen Victoria with a petition of 30,000 signatures. It quickly gained a reputation as the 'People's Park' when many rallies were held here.

Viktor Wynd Museum of Curiosities, Fine Art & Natural History MUSEUM
(020-7998 3617; www.thelasttuesdaysociety.org; 11 Mare St, E8; £8; noon-11pm Wed-Sat, to 10pm Sun; Bethnal Green) Museum? Art project? Cocktail bar? This is not a venue that's easily classifiable. Inspired by Victorian-era cabinets of curiosities, Wynd's wilfully eccentric collection includes stuffed birds, pickled genitals, two-headed lambs, shrunken heads, a key to the Garden of Eden, dodo bones, celebrity excrement and a gilded hippo skull that belonged to Pablo Escobar. A self-confessed 'incoherent vision of the world displayed through wonder'; make of it what you will. Or stop by for a cocktail at the bar upstairs.

North London

★British Library LIBRARY
(Map p110; 0330-333 1144; www.bl.uk; 96 Euston Rd, NW1; 9.30am-8pm Mon-Thu, to 6pm Fri, to 5pm Sat, 11am-5pm Sun; King's Cross St Pancras) FREE Consisting of low-slung red-brick terraces and fronted by a large piazza with an oversized statue of Sir Isaac Newton, Colin St John Wilson's British

North Central London

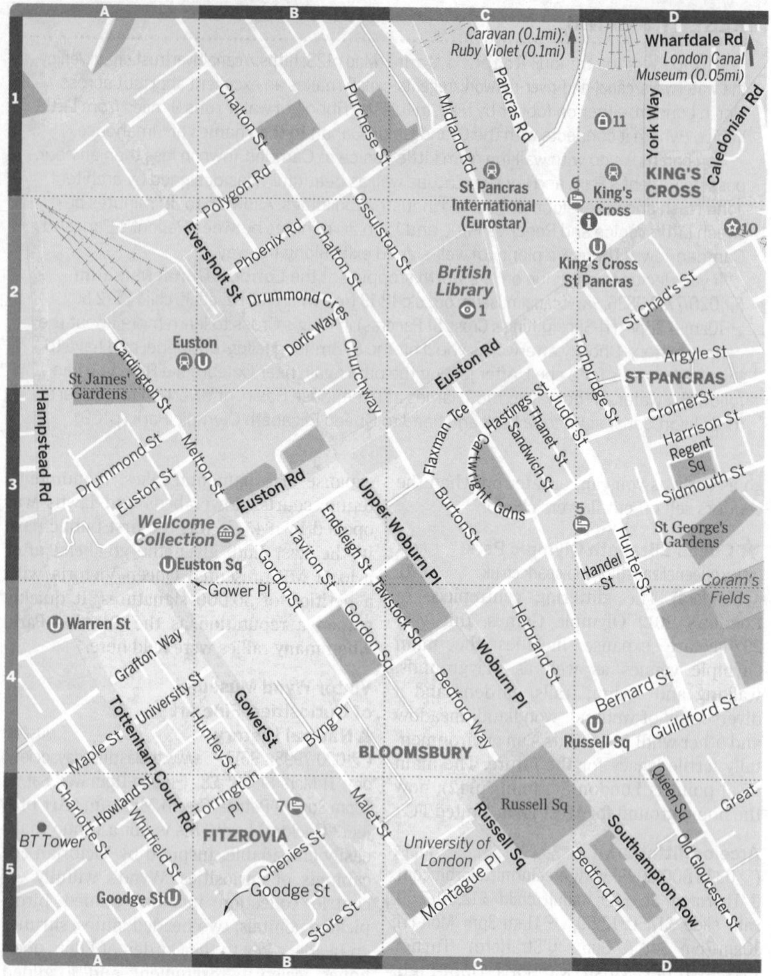

North Central London

Top Sights
1 British Library C2
2 Wellcome Collection B3

Sights
3 Charles Dickens Museum E4

Sleeping
4 Clink78 .... E2
5 Generator London D3
6 Great Northern Hotel C1
7 Jesmond Hotel B5
8 Zetter Hotel H4

Entertainment
9 Sadler's Wells G2
10 Scala D2

Shopping
11 Harry Potter Shop at Platform 9¾ D1

Library building is an architectural wonder. Completed in 1998, it's home to some of the greatest treasures of the written word, including the *Codex Sinaiticus* (the first complete text of the New Testament),

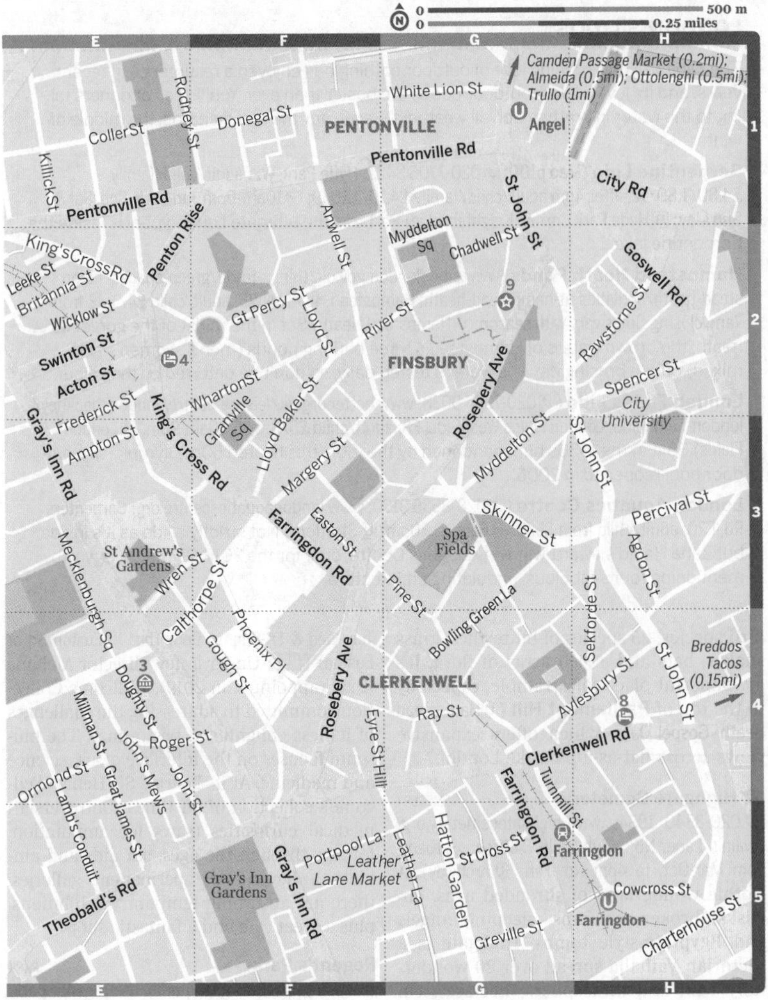

Leonardo da Vinci's notebooks and two copies of the Magna Carta (1215).

★ZSL London Zoo ZOO

(Map p128; ☎0344-225 1826; www.zsl.org/zsl-london-zoo; Outer Circle, Regent's Park, NW1; depending on date, adult £25-32.50, child £16-20.50; ⊙10am-6pm Apr-Aug, to 5pm mid-Feb–Mar, Sep & Oct, to 4pm Nov–mid-Feb; 👪; 🚌88, 274) Opened in 1828, London Zoo is the oldest in the world. The emphasis nowadays is firmly on conservation, breeding and education, with fewer animals and bigger enclosures. Highlights include Land of the Lions, Gorilla Kingdom, Night Life, Penguin Beach and the walk-through In with the Lemurs. There are regular feeding sessions and talks; various experiences are available, such as Keeper for a Day; and you can even spend the night in one of nine Gir Lion Lodge cabins.

★Hampstead Heath PARK

(www.cityoflondon.gov.uk/things-to-do/green-spaces/hampstead-heath; Ⓤ Hampstead Heath or Gospel Oak) Sprawling Hampstead Heath, with its rolling woodlands and meadows, feels a million miles away – despite being about 3.5 miles from Trafalgar Sq. It covers 320 hectares and is home to about 180

LONDON'S LIDOS

The capital's long-running love of outdoor bathing has enjoyed a resurgence in recent years, and its lovely lidos (outdoor pools) are busier than ever. You'll see Londoners taking to the water in pretty much all weathers – even, for the real diehards, the middle of winter.

Serpentine Lido (Map p100; ☎020-7706 3422; Hyde Park, W2; adult/child/family £4.80/1.80/12, after 4pm adult/child/family £4.10/1.10/9; ⊙10am-6pm Jun-early Sep, Sat & Sun May; Ⓤ Hyde Park Corner, Knightsbridge) Perhaps the ultimate London pool is inside the Serpentine lake.

Hampstead Heath Ponds (www.cityoflondon.gov.uk/things-to-do/green-spaces/hampstead-heath/activities-at-hampstead-heath; Hampstead Heath, NW5; adult/child £4/1; ⊙from 7am, closing times vary with season; Ⓤ Hampstead Heath) Set in the midst of the gorgeous heath, the brown waters of Hampstead's three bathing ponds (men's, women's and mixed) offer a bracing dip. The water's tested daily, so don't be deterred by the colour.

London Fields Lido (☎020-7254 9038; www.better.org.uk/leisure-centre/london/hackney/london-fields-lido; London Fields West Side, E8; adult/child £5/3; ⊙6.30am-9pm; Ⓤ London Fields) Built in the 1930s but abandoned by the '80s, this heated 50m Olympic-size outdoor pool reopened in 2006.

London Aquatics Centre (☎020-8536 3150; www.londonaquaticscentre.org; Carpenters Rd, E20; adult/child from £5/3; ⊙6am-10.30pm; Ⓤ Stratford) Not strictly a lido as it's inside, but Zaha Hadid's award-winning Aquatics Centre, built for the 2012 Olympics, is worth mentioning for its fabulous, undulating architecture.

bird species, 25 species of butterflies, grass snakes, bats and a rich array of flora. It's a wonderful place for a ramble, especially to the top of **Parliament Hill** (Ⓤ Hampstead Heath, Gospel Oak), which offers expansive views across flat-as-a-pancake London.

★Highgate Cemetery — CEMETERY

(☎020-8340 1834; www.highgatecemetery.org; Swain's Lane, N6; adult/child £4/free; ⊙10am-5pm Mar-Oct, to 4pm Nov-Feb; Ⓤ Archway) A Gothic wonderland of shrouded urns, obelisks, broken columns, sleeping angels and Egyptian-style tombs, Highgate is a Victorian Valhalla spread over 20 wonderfully wild and atmospheric hectares. On the eastern side, you can pay your respects to the graves of Karl Marx and Mary Ann Evans (better known as novelist George Eliot). The real highlight, however, is the overgrown **West Cemetery**, which can only be visited on a **guided tour** (☎020-8340 1834; www.highgatecemetery.org; Swain's Lane, N6; adult/child £12/6; ⊙1.45pm Mon-Fri, every 30min 10.30am-3pm Sat & Sun Nov-Feb, to 4pm Sat & Sun Mar-Oct; Ⓤ Archway). Tours of the East Cemetery (adult/child £8/4) depart at 2pm some Saturdays.

★Wellcome Collection — MUSEUM

(Map p110; ☎020-7611 2222; www.wellcomecollection.org; 183 Euston Rd, NW1; ⊙10am-6pm Tue, Wed & Fri-Sun, to 9pm Thu; Ⓤ Euston Sq or Euston) FREE Under a new director Melanie Keen (appointed in 2019), Wellcome Collection committed to addressing the challenges of its less enlightened beginnings. The museum focuses on the interface of art, science and medicine. At its heart is Sir Henry Wellcome's collection of (at times controversial) medical curiosities (saws for amputation, forceps through the ages, sex aids and amulets...). Beyond the permanent galleries, there are absorbing temporary exhibitions, plus a great cafe and a fantastic shop.

Regent's Park — PARK

(www.royalparks.org.uk/parks/the-regents-park; ⊙5am-dusk; Ⓤ Regent's Park or Baker St) The largest and most elaborate of central London's many Royal Parks, Regent's Park is one of the capital's loveliest green spaces. Among its many attractions are London Zoo (p111), Regent's Canal (p109), an ornamental lake, and sports pitches where locals meet to play football, rugby and volleyball. **Queen Mary's Gardens**, towards the south of the park, are particularly pretty, especially in June when the roses are in bloom. Performances take place here in an **open-air theatre** (☎0333 400 3562; www.openairtheatre.org; ⊙May-Sep; 👪; Ⓤ Baker St) during summer.

Abbey Road Studios HISTORIC BUILDING
(020-7266 7000; www.abbeyroad.com; 3 Abbey Rd, NW8; St John's Wood) Beatles aficionados can't possibly visit London without making a pilgrimage to this famous recording studio in St John's Wood. The studios themselves are off-limits, so you'll have to content yourself with examining the decades of fan graffiti on the fence outside. Stop-start local traffic is long accustomed to groups of tourists lining up on the zebra crossing to re-enact the cover of the fab four's 1969 masterpiece *Abbey Road*. In 2010 the crossing was rewarded with Grade II heritage status.

For a strangely engrossing real-time view of the crossing, hit the 'Visit' tab for the webcam on the studio's website; you can even find your own crossing shot by punching in your time. To reach Abbey Road Studios, take the tube to St John's Wood, cross the road, follow Grove End Rd to its end and turn right. Don't do what some disappointed fans do and head to Abbey Rd Station in West Ham in London's distant East End – it's no relation to the true site and miles off course. There are at least 10 Abbey Rds in London, adding to confusion.

Primrose Hill PARK
(Map p128; Chalk Farm) On summer weekends, Primrose Hill park is absolutely packed with locals enjoying a picnic and the extraordinary views over the city skyline. Come weekdays, however, and there are mostly just dog walkers and nannies. It's a lovely place to enjoy a quiet stroll or an alfresco lunch.

Greenwich

★National Maritime Museum MUSEUM
(020-8312 6565; www.rmg.co.uk/national-maritime-museum; Romney Rd, SE10; 10am-5pm; ; Cutty Sark) FREE Narrating the long, briny and eventful history of seafaring Britain, this excellent museum has three floors of engrossing exhibits. Highlights include JMW Turner's huge oil painting *Battle of Trafalgar* (1824), the 19m-long gilded state barge built in 1732 for the prince of Wales, and the colourful figureheads installed on the ground floor. Families will love the children's galleries, as well as the Great Map splayed out near the upper-floor cafe.

On the 1st floor, **Atlantic Worlds** and **Traders** look back on Britain's role in the transatlantic slave trade and commerce with the East in the 19th century. One floor up, **Nelson, Navy, Nation** focuses on the history of the Royal Navy during the conflict-ridden 17th century and even includes the coat in which Nelson was fatally wounded during the Battle of Trafalgar, with a musket-ball hole in the left shoulder. The **Exploration Wing**, opened in 2018, contains four galleries: Pacific Encounters, Polar Worlds, Tudor and Stuart Seafarers, and Sea Things, devoted to indigenous maritime civilisations, European exploration and human endeavour.

★Royal Observatory MUSEUM
(020-8312 6565; www.rmg.co.uk/royal-observatory; Greenwich Park, Blackheath Ave, SE10; adult/child £16/8; 10am-5pm Sep-Jun, to 6pm Jul & Aug; Greenwich or Cutty Sark) Rising like a beacon of time atop **Greenwich Park** (www.royalparks.org.uk/parks/greenwich-park; 6am-sunset; Greenwich, Maze Hill or Cutty Sark), the Royal Observatory is home to the prime meridian (longitude 0° 0' 0"). Tickets include access to the Christopher Wren–designed **Flamsteed House** (named after the first Royal Astronomer) and the **Meridian Courtyard**, where you can stand with your feet straddling the eastern and western hemispheres. You can also see the Great Equatorial Telescope (1893) inside the onion-domed **observatory** and explore space and time in the **Weller Astronomy Galleries**.

In a small brick structure next to the Meridian Courtyard, the astonishing **camera obscura** projects a live image of Queen's House – as well as the people moving around it and the boats on the Thames behind – onto a table. Enter through the thick, light-dimming curtains and close them behind you to keep the room as dark as possible.

Night-sky shows are projected daily on the inside of the roof of the **Peter Harrison Planetarium** (020-8858 4422; www.rmg.co.uk/whats-on/planetarium-shows; adult/child £10/5;).

The Royal Observatory was built by order of Charles II in 1675 to help solve the riddle of longitude. In 1884, Greenwich was designated as the prime meridian of the world, and Greenwich Mean Time (GMT) became the universal measurement of standard time.

★Old Royal Naval College HISTORIC BUILDING
(https://ornc.org; SE10; ⏲8am-11pm; Ⓤ Cutty Sark) **FREE** Home to the University of Greenwich and Trinity Laban Conservatoire of Music and Dance, the Christopher Wren-designed Old Royal Naval College is a masterpiece of baroque architecture. The sprawling grounds are open to the public, as well as the recently restored **Painted Hall** (☎020-8269 4799; www.ornc.org; adult/child £12/free; ⏲10am-5pm), nicknamed the 'Sistine Chapel of the UK' and covered from floor to ceiling with extraordinary 18th-century art, and the neoclassical **Chapel of St Peter and St Paul** (☎020-8269 4788; ⏲10am-5pm) **FREE**. Tours of the grounds are included in the price of the Painted Hall ticket.

Queen's House GALLERY
(☎020-8312 6565; www.rmg.co.uk/queens-house; Romney Rd, SE10; ⏲10am-5pm; Ⓤ Cutty Sark) **FREE** Designed by architect Inigo Jones, Queen's House was the UK's first classical building, and it's as enticing for its form as for its art collection. Many pieces on display are portraits and have an unsurprising maritime bent; don't miss the iconic *Armada Portrait of Elizabeth I*, which depicts the queen in a vibrantly coloured lace and jewelled gown and commemorates the failed invasion of England by the Spanish in 1588. It's in the immaculately restored **Queen's Presence Chamber** on the 1st floor.

Cutty Sark SHIP
(☎020-8312 6565; www.rmg.co.uk/cuttysark; King William Walk, SE10; adult/child £15/7.50; ⏲10am-5pm; Ⓤ Cutty Sark) The last of the great clipper ships to sail between China and England in the 19th century, the *Cutty Sark* was launched in 1869 and carried almost 4.5 million kg of tea in just seven years of service. Nearly a century later, it was dry-docked in Greenwich and opened to the public. Films, interactive maps, illustrations and props give an idea of what life on board was like. Book online.

Brixton, Peckham & South London

★Imperial War Museum MUSEUM
(Map p98; ☎020-7416 5000; www.iwm.org.uk; Lambeth Rd, SE1; ⏲10am-6pm; Ⓤ Lambeth North) **FREE** Fronted by an intimidating pair of 15in naval guns and a piece of the Berlin Wall, this riveting museum is housed in what was the Bethlem Royal Hospital, a psychiatric facility also known as Bedlam. Although the museum's focus is on military action involving British or Commonwealth troops, largely during the 20th century, it also covers war in the wider sense. Must-see exhibits include the state-of-the-art **First World War** galleries and **Witnesses to War** in the forecourt and atrium.

In Witnesses to War, you'll find huge remnants of war, from a Battle of Britain Spitfire and a towering German V-2 rocket to a Reuters Land Rover damaged by rocket attack in Gaza in 2006.

The 1st-floor exhibition **Turning Points: 1934–1945** takes a look at WWII through a series of poignant objects, including the casing made for the 'Little Boy' atomic bomb and a trunk sent by Jewish parents to their children who had already escaped from Nazi persecution to the UK. **Peace and Security: 1945–2014** on the 2nd floor dives into more recent events. The 3rd floor is given over to **Curiosities of War**, a mix of unexpected creations and artefacts from times of conflict, and temporary exhibitions.

One of the most challenging sections is the extensive and harrowing **The Holocaust** exhibition (not recommended for children under 14); its entrance is on the 4th floor.

West London

★Portobello Road Market MARKET
(Map p106; www.portobellomarket.org; Portobello Rd, W10; ⏲9am-6pm Mon-Wed, to 7pm Fri & Sat, to 1pm Thu; Ⓤ Notting Hill Gate or Ladbroke Grove) Lovely on a warm summer's day, Portobello Road Market is an iconic London attraction with an eclectic mix of street food, fruit and veg, antiques, curios, collectables, fashion and trinkets. The shops along Portobello Rd open daily and the fruit-and-veg stalls (from Elgin Cres to Talbot Rd) only close on Sunday. But while some antique stalls operate on Friday, the busiest day by far is Saturday, when antique dealers set up shop (from Chepstow Villas to Elgin Cres).

★Design Museum MUSEUM
(Map p106; ☎020-3862 5900; www.designmuseum.org; 224-238 Kensington High St, W8; ⏲10am-6pm, to 8pm or 9pm 1st Fri of month;

Ⓤ High St Kensington) FREE Relocated from its former Thames location to a stunning new £83-million home by Holland Park in 2016, this slick museum is dedicated to design's role in everyday life. Its permanent collection is complemented by a revolving program of special exhibitions, and it's a crucial pit stop for anyone with an eye for recent technology or contemporary aesthetics. Splendidly housed in the refitted former Commonwealth Institute (which opened in 1962), the lavish interior – all smooth Douglas fir and marble – is itself a design triumph.

Richmond, Kew & Hampton Court

★ Kew Gardens GARDENS

(Royal Botanic Gardens, Kew; www.kew.org; Kew Rd, TW9; adult/child £17.50/5.50; 10am-7pm Apr-Sep, to 6pm Mar & Oct, closes earlier rest of year; Kew Pier, Kew Bridge, Ⓤ Kew Gardens) In 1759 botanists began rummaging around the world for specimens to plant in the 3-hectare Royal Botanic Gardens at Kew. They never stopped collecting, and the gardens, which have bloomed to 121 hectares, provide the most comprehensive botanical collection on earth (including the world's largest collection of orchids). A Unesco World Heritage Site, the gardens can easily devour a day's exploration; for those pressed for time, the **Kew Explorer** (020-8332 5648; www.kew.org/kew-gardens/whats-on/kew-explorer-land-train; tours adult/child £5/2; 10.30am-3.30pm) hop-on/hop-off road train takes in the main sights.

Don't worry if you don't know your golden slipper orchid from your fengoky; a visit to Kew is a journey of discovery for everyone. Highlights include the enormous, steamy early Victorian **Palm House** (face covering required), a hothouse of metal and curved sheets of glass; the impressive **Princess of Wales Conservatory**; the red-brick 1631 **Kew Palace** (www.hrp.org.uk/kewpalace; 10.30am-5.30pm Apr-Sep), formerly King George III's country retreat; the celebrated **Chinese Pagoda**, designed by William Chambers in 1762; the **Temperate House**, the world's largest ornamental glasshouse; and the very enjoyable **Treetop Walkway**, where you can survey the tree canopy from 18m up in the air.

A lattice fashioned from thousands of pieces of aluminium illuminated with hundreds of LED lights, the 17m-high **Hive** mimics activity within a real beehive. Opened in 2016, the 320m-long **Great Broad Walk Borders** is the longest double herbaceous border in the UK. The idyllic, thatched **Queen Charlotte's Cottage** (11am-4pm Sat & Sun Apr-Sep) in the southwest of the gardens was popular with 'mad' George III and his wife; the beautiful carpets of bluebells around here are a draw in spring. Several long vistas (Cedar Vista, Syon Vista and Pagoda Vista) are channelled by trees from vantage points within Kew Gardens. An interactive **Children's Garden** the span of 40 tennis courts was added in 2019.

Check the website for a full list of activities at Kew, including free one-hour walking tours (daily), photography walks, theatre performances, outside cinema as well as a host of seasonal events and things to do.

Kew Gardens is easily reached by tube, but you might prefer to take a cruise on a riverboat with **Thames River Boats** (Map p78; 020-7930 2062; www.wpsa.co.uk; Westminster Pier, Victoria Embankment, SW1; adult/child Kew 1-way £15/7.50, return £22/11, Hampton Court 1-way £19/9.50, return £27/13.50; 10am-4pm Apr-Oct; Ⓤ Westminster).

★ Hampton Court Palace PALACE

(www.hrp.org.uk/hamptoncourtpalace; Hampton Court Palace, KT8; adult/child £24.50/12.20; 10am-6pm Apr-Oct, to 4.30pm Nov-Mar; Hampton Court Palace, Hampton Court) Built by Cardinal Thomas Wolsey in 1515 but coaxed from him by Henry VIII just before Wolsey (as chancellor) fell from favour, Hampton Court Palace is England's largest and grandest Tudor structure. It was already one of Europe's most sophisticated palaces when, in the 17th century, Christopher Wren designed an extension. The result is a beautiful blend of Tudor and 'restrained baroque' architecture. You could easily spend a day exploring the palace and its 24 hectares of riverside gardens, including a 300-year-old **maze**. See more on p116.

Richmond Park PARK

(0300 061 2200; www.royalparks.org.uk/parks/richmond-park; 7am-dusk; Ⓤ Richmond) At almost 1000 hectares (the largest urban parkland in Europe), this park offers everything

Hampton Court Palace

A DAY AT THE PALACE

With so much to explore in the palace and seemingly infinite gardens, it can be tricky knowing where to begin. It helps to understand how the palace has grown over the centuries and how successive royal occupants embellished Hampton Court to suit their purposes and to reflect the style of the time.

As soon as he had his royal hands upon the palace from Cardinal Thomas Wolsey, Henry VIII began expanding the ❶ **Tudor architecture**, adding the ❷ **Great Hall**, the exquisite ❸ **Chapel Royal**, the opulent Great Watching Chamber and the gigantic ❹ **Tudor kitchens**. By 1540 it had become one of the grandest and most sophisticated palaces in Europe. James I kept things ticking over, while Charles I added a new tennis court and did some serious art-collecting, including pieces that can be seen in the ❺ **Cumberland Art Gallery**.

PETER FIELDS / ALAMY STOCK PHOTO ©

OPEN FOR INSPECTION

The palace was opened to the public by Queen Victoria in 1838.

Tudor Kitchens

These vast kitchens were the engine room of the palace, and had a staff of 200 people. Six spit-rack-equipped fireplaces ensured roast meat was always on the menu (to the tune of 8200 sheep and 1240 oxen per year).

❼ The Maze

Around 150m north of the main building

Created from hornbeam and yew and planted in around 1700, the maze covers a third of an acre within the famous palace gardens. A must-see conclusion to Hampton Court, it takes the average visitor about 20 minutes to reach the centre.

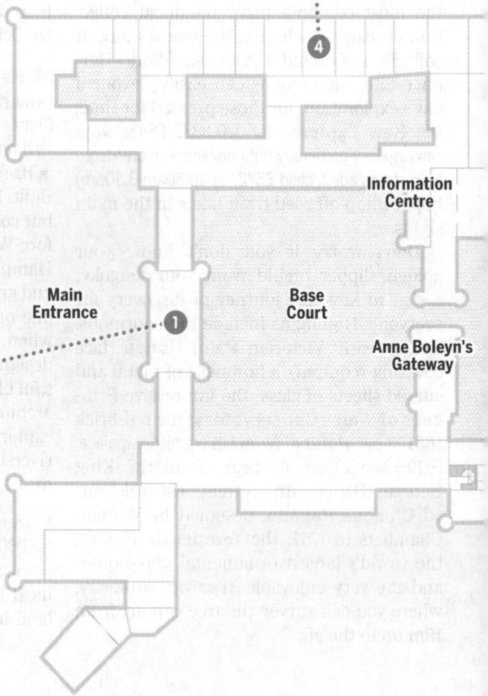

Tudor Architecture

Dating to 1515, the palace serves as one of the finest examples of Tudor architecture in the nation. Cardinal Thomas Wolsey was responsible for transforming what was originally a grand medieval manor house into a stunning Tudor palace.

KIEV.VICTOR / SHUTTERSTOCK ©

After the Civil War, puritanical Oliver Cromwell warmed to his own regal proclivities, spending weekends in the comfort of the former Queen's bedroom and selling off Charles I's art collection. In the late 17th century, William and Mary employed Christopher Wren for baroque extensions, chiefly the William III Apartments, reached by the 6 **King's Staircase**. William III also commissioned the world-famous 7 **maze**.

TOP TIPS

- Ask one of the red-tunic-garbed warders for anecdotes and information.
- Tag along with a themed tour led by costumed historians or do a dusk-till-dawn sleepover at the palace.
- Grab one of the audio tours from the Information Centre.

The Great Hall
This grand dining hall is the defining room of the palace, displaying what is considered England's finest hammer-beam roof, 16th-century Flemish tapestries that depict the story of Abraham, and some exquisite stained-glass windows.

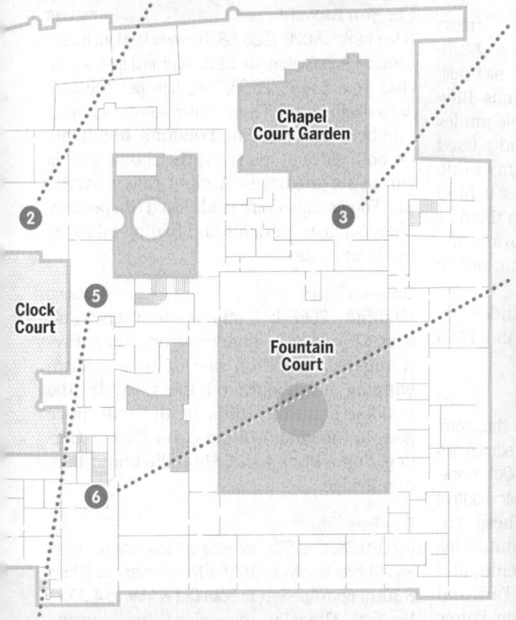

Chapel Royal
The blue-and-gold vaulted ceiling was originally intended for Christ Church, Oxford, but was installed here instead; the 18th-century oak reredos was carved by Grinling Gibbons. Books on display include a 1611 first edition of the King James Bible, printed by Robert Barker.

The King's Staircase
One of five rooms at the palace painted by Antonio Verrio and a suitably bombastic prelude to the King's Apartments, the overblown King's Staircase adulates William III by elevating him above a cohort of Roman emperors.

Cumberland Art Gallery
The former Cumberland Suite, designed by William Kent, has been restored to accommodate a choice selection of some of the finest works from the Royal Collection.

from formal gardens and ancient oaks to unsurpassed views of central London 12 miles away. It's easy to flee the several roads slicing up the rambling wilderness, making the park perfect for a quiet walk or a picnic, even in summer when Richmond's riverside heaves. Coming from Richmond, it's easiest to enter via Richmond Gate or from Petersham Rd.

Strawberry Hill HISTORIC BUILDING

(☎020-8744 1241; www.strawberryhillhouse.org.uk; 268 Waldegrave Rd, TW1; adult/child £12.50/free; ⊙house 11am-4pm Sun-Thu, garden 10am-4pm Sun-Thu; Ⓡ Strawberry Hill, Ⓤ Richmond Station) With its snow-white walls and Gothic turrets, this fantastical and totally restored 18th-century creation in Twickenham is the work of art historian, author and politician Horace Walpole. Studded with elaborate stained glass, the building reaches its astonishing apogee in the gallery, with its magnificent papier-mâché ceiling. For the full magic, join a twilight tour (£25). Last admission to the house is one hour before closing time.

Tours

★Guide London TOURS

(Association of Professional Tourist Guides; ☎020-7611 2545; www.guidelondon.org.uk; half-/full-day tours £176/288) Hire a prestigious Blue Badge Tourist Guide, knowledgeable guides who have studied for two years and passed a dozen written and practical exams to do their job. They can tell you stories behind the sights that you'd only hear from them or whisk you on a themed tour (eg Royalty, the Beatles, museums, parks). Go by car, public transport, bike or on foot.

For private tours by car, driver guides typically charge £405 for a half day and £585 for a full day.

★London Waterbus Company CRUISE

(☎07917 265114; www.londonwaterbus.com; Browning's Pool, Warwick Cres W2; tours adult/child 1-way £12/9; ⊙hourly 10am-5pm Apr-Oct, weekends only & less frequent departures other months; Ⓤ Warwick Avenue, Camden Town) These enclosed barges take enjoyable 50-minute trips on Regent's Canal between Little Venice and Camden Lock, passing by Regent's Park and stopping at London Zoo. Fewer departures go outside high season; check the website for schedules. One-way tickets (adult/child £32/25 from Little Venice or £30/22 from Camden Lock) include zoo entry and allow passengers to disembark within the zoo grounds. Buy tickets on board.

Look Up London CULTURAL

(https://lookup.london; per person £15-30) Walking tours include secrets of Bermondsey, Soho, Greenwich and the City plus a Feminist Jack the Ripper tour that tells the stories of the women involved in this bloody chapter of London's history. Group sizes are kept small. Tours go for one to two hours. Also does online tours.

Black History Walks HISTORY

(www.blackhistorywalks.co.uk; 2hr tours £10) Learn a little of London's 2000 years of black history in Soho, St Paul's and Notting Hill, to name a few locations where these informative, paradigm-shifting tours are run. Also runs online seminars.

Alternative London CULTURAL

(www.alternativeldn.com; per person from £18) Avoiding the obvious headline London sites, these small-group cycling and walking tours cover themes such as street art, culinary experiences and craft-beer spots, mainly around East London.

London Bicycle Tour CYCLING

(Map p98; ☎020-7928 6838; www.londonbicycle.com; 74 Kennington Rd, SE11; tour incl bike adult/child from £34.95/28.95, bike hire per day £24; Ⓤ Lambeth North) Three-hour tours begin in Lambeth and take in London's highlights on both sides of the river; the classic tour is run in six languages. A night ride is available. You can also hire traditional or specialty bikes, such as tandems and folding bikes, by the hour or day.

Unseen Tours WALKING

(☎07514 266774; https://unseentours.org.uk; tours £15) See London from an entirely different angle on one of these award-winning neighbourhood tours led by the London homeless (60% of the tour price goes to the guide). Tours cover Covent Garden, Soho, Brick Lane, Shoreditch and London Bridge.

Big Bus Tours BUS

(☎020-7808 6753; www.bigbustours.com; tours adult/child/family £39/29/107; ⊙every 5-20min 8.30am-6pm Apr-Sep, to 5pm Oct & Mar, to 4.30pm Nov-Feb) Globally recognised bus touring group with informative commentaries in 12 languages. Hop-on hop-off along four bus routes. The ticket includes a free river cruise with City Cruises and three thematic walking tours. The ticket is valid for 24 hours; for a small additional charge you can upgrade to the 48-hour 'premium' ticket.

London Mystery Walks WALKING
(☎07957 388280; www.tourguides.org.uk; per person from £15) Get spooked with London's ghost stories or serial killer Jack the Ripper-themed walking tours. For something more nourishing, try VIP chocolate or gelato tours (£40). Book in advance.

Festivals & Events

The Boat Race ROWING
(www.theboatrace.org; ⌚late Mar/early Apr) A grudge match held annually since 1829 between the rowing crews of Oxford and Cambridge universities. Surging upstream between Putney and Mortlake, the event (which included a female crew boat race for the first time in 2015) draws huge crowds along the river.

Chelsea Flower Show HORTICULTURE
(☎020-3176 5800; www.rhs.org.uk/chelsea; Royal Hospital Chelsea, Royal Hospital Rd, SW3; tickets £39.75-92.75; ⌚May; U Sloane Sq) Held at the lovely Royal Hospital Chelsea, this is arguably the world's most renowned horticultural show, attracting green fingers from all four corners of the globe.

Trooping the Colour PARADE
(www.householddivision.org.uk/trooping-the-colour; Horse Guards Parade, SW1; ⌚Jun; U Westminster or Charing Cross) Celebrating the Queen's official birthday (her actual birthday is in April), this ceremonial procession of troops, marching along the Mall for their sovereign's inspection, is pageantry overload, featuring 1400 officers and personnel on parade, plus 200 horses and 400 musicians from 10 bands.

The parade can be watched from the street, but to get closer to the action, enter an online draw to sit in the stands in **Horse Guards Parade** (Map p78). The ballot opens in January (£40 per person if you're successful). Smart casual dress is required.

Pride LGBT+
(www.prideinlondon.org; ⌚late Jun/early Jul) The LGBT+ community paints the town pink in this annual extravaganza, featuring a smorgasbord of experiences, from talks to live events, and culminating in a huge parade across London.

OFF THE BEATEN TRACK

LONDON WETLAND CENTRE

One of Europe's largest inland wetland projects, this 42-hectare **centre** (☎020-8409 4400; www.wwt.org.uk/wetland-centres/london; Queen Elizabeth's Walk, SW13; adult/child/family £13/8/36; ⌚9.30am-5.30pm, to 4.30pm Nov-Feb; R Barnes, U Hammersmith) run by the Wildfowl & Wetlands Trust was transformed from four Victorian reservoirs in 2000 and attracts some 140 species of birds, as well as frogs, butterflies, dragonflies and lizards, plus a thriving colony of watervoles. The glass-fronted observatory affords panoramic views over the lakes, while meandering paths and boardwalks lead visitors through the watery habitats of black swans, Bewick's swans, geese, red-crested pochards, sand martins, coots, bitterns, herons and kingfishers.

Film4 Summer Screen FILM
(☎0333 320 2836; www.somersethouse.org.uk; Somerset House, Strand, WC2; tickets from £19; ⌚Aug; U Temple) For two weeks every summer, Somerset House (p88) turns its stunning courtyard into an open-air cinema and screens an eclectic mix of film premieres, cult classics and popular requests. Pack a picnic and blankets or cushions to cover the hard ground (or pre-order them with your entry tickets for an extra fee).

Notting Hill Carnival CARNIVAL
(www.nhcarnival.org; ⌚Aug) Every year, August ends with a long bank-holiday weekend, and West London echoes to the ska, reggae, R&B, dancehall and soca sounds of the Notting Hill Carnival. Launched in 1964 by an Afro-Caribbean community keen to celebrate its culture and traditions, it has grown to become Europe's largest street festival (over two million people) and a highlight of London's calendar.

Open House London CULTURAL
(☎020-7383 2131; https://openhouselondon.open-city.org.uk; ⌚Sep) The annual two-day Open House London event during the third weekend of September sees over 800 buildings open to the public. Open House London is run by Open City, a charity promoting cities with a year-round programme of events and initiatives, including talks and architectural

tours on foot, by boat and bike to various parts of London.

London Film Festival FILM
(www.bfi.org.uk/lff; Oct) The city's premier film event attracts big overseas names and you can catch as many as 350 British and international films in venues across the city before their cinema release.

Sleeping

West End

YHA London Oxford Street HOSTEL £
(Map p80; 020-7734 1618; www.yha.org.uk/hostel/yha-london-oxford-street; 14 Noel St, W1; dm £18-36, tw £50-90; ; Oxford Circus) The most central of London's seven YHA hostels is also one of the most intimate with just 104 beds in 36 rooms. The excellent shared facilities include a fuchsia-coloured kitchen and a bright, funky lounge. Dormitories have two solid bunk beds, and there are doubles and twins. The in-house shop sells coffee and beer. Free wi-fi in common areas.

Generator London HOSTEL £
(Map p110; 020-7388 7666; https://staygenerator.com/hostels/london; 37 Tavistock Pl, WC1; dm/r from £11/61; ; Russell Sq) With its industrial lines and hip decor, the huge Generator (it has more than 870 beds) is one of central London's grooviest budget spots. The bar, complete with pool tables, stays open until 3am and there are frequent themed parties. Dorm rooms have between four and 13 beds; backing it up are twins and triples.

Jesmond Hotel B&B ££
(Map p110; 020-7636 3199; www.jesmondhotel.org.uk; 63 Gower St, WC1; s/d/tr/q from £80/105/140/160; ; Goodge St) The 15 guestrooms at this popular, family run Georgian-era B&B in Bloomsbury are basic but clean and cheerful (four are with shared bathroom); there's a small, pretty garden out back, and the prices are very attractive indeed. There's also laundry service and good breakfasts for kicking off your London day. Location is highly central.

★**Haymarket Hotel** HOTEL £££
(Map p80; 020-7470 4000; www.firmdalehotels.com/hotels/london/haymarket-hotel; 1 Suffolk Pl, off Haymarket, SW1; r/ste £350/550; ; Piccadilly Circus) With the trademark colours and lines of hotelier/designer duo Tim and Kit Kemp, in a converted building designed by John Nash, the Haymarket is scrumptious, with hand-painted Gournay wallpaper, signature fuchsia and green designs in the 50 different guest rooms – 206 has windows on two sides – a sensational 18m pool, an exquisite library lounge, and original artwork.

★**Ritz London** LUXURY HOTEL £££
(Map p80; 020-7493 8181; www.theritzlondon.com; 150 Piccadilly, W1; r/ste from £650/1500; ; Green Park) What can you say about a place that has lent its name to the English lexicon? This 136-room hotel, opened by the eponymous César in 1906, has a spectacular position overlooking Green Park and is supposedly the Royal Family's home away from home. (It is very close to the palace.) All rooms have Louis XVI–style interiors and antique furniture.

Covent Garden Hotel BOUTIQUE HOTEL £££
(Map p80; 020-7806 1000; www.firmdalehotels.com/hotels/london/covent-garden-hotel; 10 Monmouth St, WC2; d/ste from £360/550; ; Covent Garden) This gorgeous and discreet 58-room boutique hotel housed in a former French hospital features antiques; sumptuous bright fabrics; and quirky bric-a-brac to mark its individuality. There's an excellent bar-restaurant off the lobby and two stunning guest lounges with fireplaces (note the beautiful marquetry desk) on the 1st floor, which come into their own in the winter.

Rooms on the ground floor (such as rooms 3, 5 and 8) are larger and have higher ceilings. The Asian touches in room 4 are fetching.

Rosewood London HOTEL £££
(Map p80; 020-7781 8888; www.rosewoodhotels.com/en/london; 252 High Holborn, WC1; d/ste from £440/1100; ; Holborn) What was once the grand Pearl Assurance building (dating from 1914) now houses the stunning Rosewood hotel, where an artful marriage of period and modern styles, thanks to designer Tony Chi, can be found in its 262 rooms and 45 suites. British heritage is carefully woven throughout the bar, restaurant, lobby and even the housekeepers' uniforms.

Hazlitt's HERITAGE HOTEL £££
(Map p80; 020-7434 1771; www.hazlittshotel.com; 6 Frith St, W1; s/d/ste from £200/230/600; ; Tottenham Court Rd) Built in 1718 and comprising four original Georgian houses,

this Soho gem was the one-time home of essayist William Hazlitt (1778–1830). The 30 guest rooms are furnished with original antiques from the appropriate era and boast a profusion of seductive details, including panelled walls, mahogany four-poster beds, antique desks, Oriental carpets, sumptuous fabrics and fireplaces in every room.

City of London

London St Paul's YHA HOSTEL £
(Map p90; 020-7236 4965; www.yha.org.uk; 36 Carter Lane, EC4; dm/d from £20/70; ; St Paul's) Housed in the former boarding school for St Paul's Cathedral choir boys, this 213-bed hostel has notable period features, including Latin script in a band around the exterior. There's no kitchen, no lift and no en-suite rooms, but there is a comfortable lounge, a licensed cafe and all new beds with USB ports.

★**CitizenM Tower of London** DESIGN HOTEL ££
(Map p90; 020-3519 4830; www.citizenm.com/destinations/london/tower-of-london-hotel; 40 Trinity Sq, EC3; r from £170; ; Tower Hill) Downstairs it looks like a rich hipster's living room, with well-stocked bookshelves, kooky art like Warhol's *Reigning Queens* and Beefeater bric-a-brac. The 370 rooms are compact but well-designed, with an iPad controlling curtains, the TV and even the shower lighting. It's worth paying an extra £20 for the extraordinary Tower views, although they're even better from the two-level 7th floor bar.

★**The Ned** HERITAGE HOTEL £££
(Map p90; 020-3828 2100; www.thened.com; 27 Poultry, London, EC2; r £230-400; ; Bank) What was until recently the Midland Bank, designed by Sir Edwin 'Ned' Lutyens in 1924, has metamorphosed into a splendid butterfly with 250 rooms over nine floors. Choose a 'Cosy' room (there are a dozen different types) facing Queen Victoria St. The Ned counts a full seven restaurants in the erstwhile Grand Banking Hall, where there is daily live music.

The spa with enormous swimming pool, sauna and hammam in the basement is a delight. Beg, borrow or steal to get into the Vaults lounge and its adjacent bar with 3000 original safe-deposit boxes.

South Place HOTEL £££
(Map p90; 020-3503 0000; www.southplacehotel.com; 3 South Pl, EC2; d/ste from £232/740; ; Moorgate) A hip, design-led hotel, South Place impresses at every turn. From the art-filled lobby and espionage-inspired theme (a Russian spy ring was once located in this area) to the Michelin-starred **Angler** (Map p90; 020-3215 1260; www.anglerrestaurant.com; mains £32-38; noon-2.30pm & 6-10pm Mon-Sat, 6-10pm Sun) seafood restaurant and 80 beautifully laid-out rooms – every detail has been carefully considered. There are even cheeky hangover cures and sex kits alongside the British products in the luxurious minibar.

South Bank

★**Hoxton Southwark** HOTEL ££
(Map p98; 020-7903 3000; https://thehoxton.com/london/southwark; Blackfriars Rd, SE1; r £140-300; ; Southwark) This latest feather in the now three-plumed Hoxton cap counts 192 retro-styled rooms (antique radios, rotary telephones) and fabulous artwork displayed in every nook and cranny. Like its sisters the Hoxton Southwark offers stylish yet affordable accommodation in rooms that vary enormously in size and comfort; try Cosy room 419 or the bigger Roomy 408 looking onto a churchyard.

The lobby bar is always buzzy but the destination outlet here is the rooftop Seabird bar and restaurant, with unmatchable views.

CitizenM London Bankside BOUTIQUE HOTEL ££
(Map p98; 020-3519 1680; www.citizenm.com/destinations/london/london-bankside-hotel; 20 Lavington St, SE1; r £109-325; ; South-wark) If citizenM had a motto, it would be 'Less fuss, more comfort'. The hotel has done away with things it considers superfluous like room service and reception and instead has gone all out on mattresses and bedding, and state-of-the-art technology (everything from mood lighting to TV is controlled through a tablet computer and you unlock the door with your phone).

Shangri-La Hotel at the Shard HOTEL £££
(Map p98; 020-7234 8000; www.shangri-la.com/london/shangrila; 31 St Thomas St, SE1; d/ste from £500/1000; ; London Bridge) Unsurprisingly for a hotel occupying levels 34 to 52 of the Shard, there are breathtaking

views everywhere you look in the 202-room Shangri-La: be it the floor-to-ceiling windows in the bedrooms, the panoramic bathrooms (you've never had such a good view while having a bath), the Skypool, the bar or the restaurant. The decor is a stylish blend of Chinese influence and modern.

The Shard's tapering shape puts the suites on lower floors, and each guest room is slightly different in design. Rooms are the latest in comfort and technology, with Nespresso coffee machines, a pillow menu and imported Japanese toilets (with a mind-boggling array of options).

Kensington & Hyde Park

★Number Sixteen HOTEL £££

(Map p100; ☎020-7589 5232; www.firmdalehotels.com/hotels/london/number-sixteen; 16 Sumner Pl, SW7; s/d from £200/£300; ❄@📶🐾; Ⓤ South Kensington) With uplifting splashes of colour, choice art and a sophisticated-but-fun design ethos, Number Sixteen is simply ravishing. There are 41 individually designed rooms, a cosy drawing room, library and honesty bar. And wait till you see the idyllic, long back garden set around a pond stocked with koi or sit down for breakfast in the light-filled conservatory.

Great amenities for families, too. Lovely room 209 looks down to Sumner Pl.

Ampersand Hotel DESIGN HOTEL £££

(Map p100; ☎020-7589 5895; https://ampersandhotel.com; 10 Harrington Rd, SW7; s/d from £170/£216; ❄@📶🐾; Ⓤ South Kensington) It feels light, fresh and bubbly in the Ampersand, where smiling staff wear denims, waistcoats and ties rather than impersonal dark suits. The common rooms are colourful and airy, and the 111 stylish guest rooms are decorated with wallpaper designs celebrating the nearby arts and sciences of South Kensington's museums.

Deluxe studio 117 has two large windows looking to the street and a separate shower and toilet.

Clerkenwell, Shoreditch & Spitalfields

★Hoxton Shoreditch HOTEL ££

(Map p130; ☎020-7550 1000; www.thehoxton.com/london/shoreditch/hotels; 81 Great Eastern St, EC2; r £109-260; ❄📶; Ⓤ Old St) In the heart of hip Shoreditch, this sleek hotel takes the low-cost airline approach to selling its rooms – book long enough ahead and you might pay just £109. The 210 renovated rooms are small but stylish, with TVs, desks, fridges with complimentary bottled water and milk, and breakfast (orange juice, granola, yoghurt and banana) in a bag delivered to your door.

CitizenM London Shoreditch DESIGN HOTEL ££

(Map p130; www.citizenm.com/destinations/london/london-shoreditch-hotel; 6 Holywell Lane, EC2; r £119-300; ❄@📶; Ⓤ Shoreditch High St) CitizenM's winning combination of awesome interior design and a no-nonsense approach to luxury (yes to king-sized beds and high-tech pod rooms; no to pillow chocolates and room service) is right at home in Shoreditch. Rates at the 216 rooms are just right, and the convivial 24hr lounge/bar/reception on the ground floor always seems to be on the right side of busy.

★Rookery HERITAGE HOTEL £££

(Map p90; ☎020-7336 0931; www.rookeryhotel.com; 12 Peter's Lane, Cowcross St, EC1; d/ste from £249/650; ❄📶; Ⓤ Farringdon) This charming warren of 33 rooms has been built within a row of 18th-century Georgian townhouses and fitted out with period furniture (including a museum-piece collection of Victorian baths, showers and toilets), original wood panelling shipped over from Ireland and artwork selected by the owner. Highlights include the small courtyard garden and the library with its honesty bar and working fireplace.

Zetter Hotel BOUTIQUE HOTEL £££

(Map p110; ☎020-7324 4444; www.thezetter.com; St John's Sq, 86-88 Clerkenwell Rd, EC1; d from £210, studio £300-438; ❄📶; Ⓤ Farringdon) 🍃 The Zetter Hotel is a temple of cool minimalism with an overlay of colourful kitsch on Clerkenwell's main thoroughfare. Built using sustainable materials on the site of a derelict office block, its 59 rooms are spacious for this area. The rooftop studios are the real treat, with terraces commanding superb views. There is a hot-drink station on every floor for guests' use.

East London

Qbic DESIGN HOTEL £

(☎020-30213300; https://qbichotels.com/london-city; 42 Adler St, E1; r £54-100; Ⓟ❄📶🐾; Ⓤ Aldgate East) 🍃 There's a modern feel to this snappy hotel, with white tiling, neon signs, vibrant art and textiles and a pool table in the lobby. Its 171 rooms are sound-insulated, mattresses are excellent and rainforest showers powerful. Prices vary widely depending on when you book, and the cheapest rooms are windowless.

★**40 Winks** B&B ££
(☎020-7790 0259; www.40winks.org; 109 Mile End Rd, E1; s/d/ste £115/185/280; 📶; Ⓤ Stepney Green) Short on space but not on style, this 300-year-old townhouse in Stepney Green oozes quirky charm. There are just two bedrooms (a double and a compact single) that share a bathroom – or you can book both as a spacious suite. Owned by a successful designer, the rooms are uniquely and extravagantly decorated with an expert's eye.

North London

★**Clink78** HOSTEL £
(Map p110; ☎020-7183 9400; www.clinkhostels.com/london/clink78; 78 King's Cross Rd, WC1; dm/r from £16/65; @📶; Ⓤ King's Cross St Pancras) This fantastic 630-bed hostel is housed in a 19th-century magistrates' courthouse where Charles Dickens once worked as a scribe and members of the Clash stood trial in 1978. It features pod beds (including overhead storage space) in four- to 16-bed dormitories. There's a top kitchen with a huge dining area and a busy bar – Clash – in the basement.

Great Northern Hotel HISTORIC HOTEL £££
(Map p110; ☎020-3388 0800; www.gnhlondon.com; King's Cross Station, Pancras Rd, N1; r from £180; ❄@📶; Ⓤ King's Cross St Pancras) Built as the world's first railway hotel in 1854, the GNH is now an 88-room boutique hotel in a classic style reminiscent of luxury sleeper trains. Exquisite artisanship is in evidence everywhere. And in addition to the two lively bars and a restaurant, there's a 'pantry' on every floor, from which you can help yourself to hot or cold drinks and snacks.

Rooms come in three categories. Guests have access to a nearby gym with large swimming pool.

West London

Safestay Holland Park HOSTEL £
(Map p106; ☎020-7870 9626; www.safestay.com/london-kensington-holland-park; Holland Walk, W8; dm/r from £12.50/70; 📶; Ⓤ High St Kensington, Holland Park) This upbeat and well-run place has taken over a long-serving YHA hostel with over 300 beds. With a bright (fuchsia) and bold design, the hostel has dorm rooms with four to 21 bunk beds and twins with a single bunk, free wi-fi in the lobby and a fabulous location in the Jacobean east wing of Holland House in Holland Park.

There's a large and very comfortable bar and restaurant downstairs with mains from £6, a pool room and garden.

New Linden Hotel BOUTIQUE HOTEL ££
(Map p106; ☎020-7221 4321; www.newlinden.co.uk; 59 Leinster Sq, W2; s/d from £90/128; 📶; Ⓤ Bayswater) The Buddha bust in the lobby sets the zen tone for this light, airy and beautifully designed option located between Westbourne Grove and Notting Hill. Some of the 50 rooms (eg room 108 with a small balcony) are on the small side due to the Georgian building's quirky layout, but they feel cosy rather than cramped. Staff are charming, too.

Check out the gorgeous wooden door leading to the lounge. There's a lift, too.

Eating

West End

★**Kanada-Ya** RAMEN £
(Map p80; ☎020-7240 0232; www.kanada-ya.com; 64 St Giles High St, WC2; mains £11-13; ⏲noon-3pm & 5-10.30pm Mon-Sat, to 8.30pm Sun; Ⓤ Tottenham Court Rd) In the debate over London's best ramen, we're still voting for this one. With no reservations taken, queues can get impressive outside this tiny and enormously popular canteen, where ramen cooked in *tonkotsu* (pork-bone broth) draws in diners from near and far. The noodles arrive at just the right temperature and hardness, steeped in a delectable broth and rich flavours.

Mildreds VEGETARIAN £
(Map p80; ☎020-7494 1634; www.mildreds.co.uk; 45 Lexington St, W1; mains £12-13; ⏲11am-11pm Mon-Sat, to 10pm Sun; 📶🌱; Ⓤ Oxford Circus or Piccadilly Circus) One of the West End's most enduringly popular vegetarian restaurants, Mildreds is crammed at lunchtime: you can't be shy about sharing a table in the skylit dining room. Expect the likes of pumpkin gnocchi (boiled and fried) with pumpkin sauce and *pangrattato* (fried breadcrumbs), halloumi and harissa burgers and Levantine

Marylebone

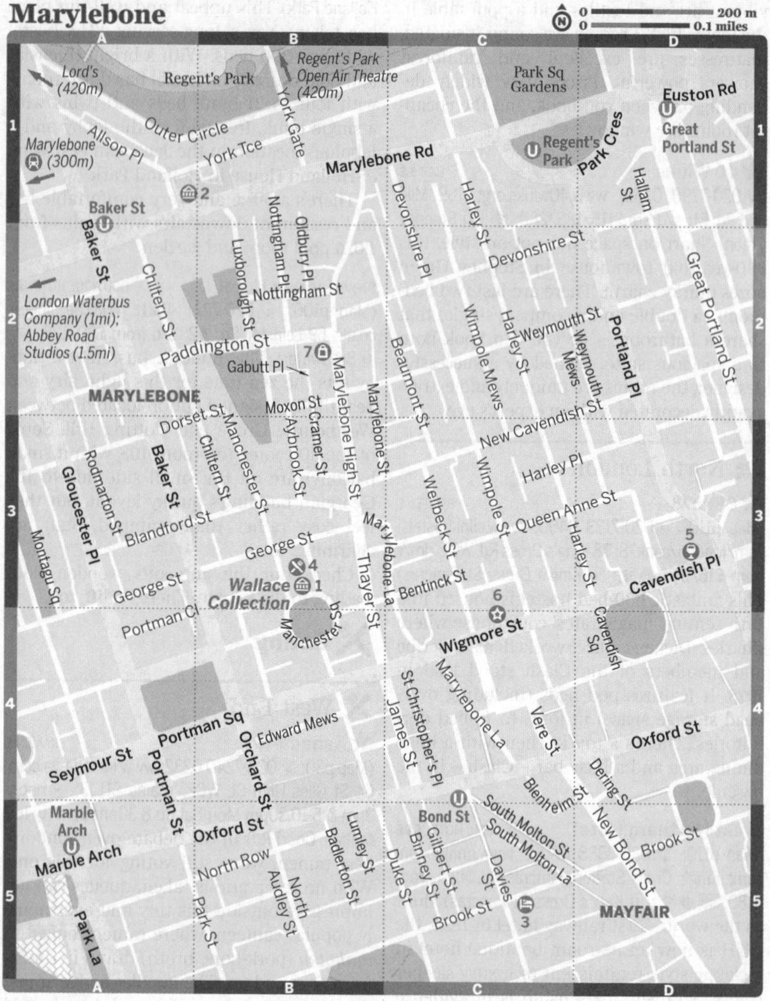

Chick'n kebabs. There are also vegan and gluten-free options.

So popular has Mildred's become, there are now branches in Dalston, Camden and King's Cross.

★Palomar ISRAELI **££**

(Map p80; ☎020-7439 8777; www.thepalomar.co.uk; 34 Rupert St, W1; mains £14-16; ⏰6-10pm Mon-Wed, 12.30-2.30pm & 6-10pm Thu-Sun; 📶; Ⓤ Piccadilly Circus) Packed and praised from the day it opened, Palomar is a wonderful Israeli/Levantine restaurant with the look of a 1930s diner and the constant theatre of expert chefs whipping up magic behind the central zinc bar. Unusual dishes such as date-glazed octopus with harissa will blow you away, as will slow-cooked Tel Aviv seafood and beetroot labneh with parsley vinaigrette.

It's usually possible to get one or two of the 16 bar stools at shortish notice for lunch, but book further ahead for a table in the 40-seat dining room, or for dinner.

★Kiln THAI **££**

(Map p80; www.kilnsoho.com; 58 Brewer St, W1; dishes £4.50-14; ⏰noon-3pm & 5-11pm Mon-Thu, noon-11pm Fri & Sat, to 10pm Sun; Ⓤ Piccadilly Circus) Crowned the UK's best restaurant

Marylebone

Top Sights
1 Wallace Collection ... B3

Sights
2 Madame Tussauds ... A1

Sleeping
3 Claridge's ... C5

Eating
Foyer & Reading Room at Claridge's ... (see 3)
4 Wallace Restaurant ... B3

Drinking & Nightlife
5 Artesian ... D3

Entertainment
6 Wigmore Hall ... C4

Shopping
7 Daunt Books ... B2

in 2018, this tiny Thai grill cooks up a storm in its long, narrow kitchen, overseen by diners on their stools. The short menu rides the small-plates wave and works best with a few friends so you can taste a greater variety. The beef-neck curry is phenomenal, as are the claypot-baked glass noodles.

Bar Shu SICHUAN ££
(Map p80; 020-7287 6688; http://barshurestaurant.co.uk; 28 Frith St, W1; mains £11-23; noon-10pm Sun-Thu, to 11.30pm Fri & Sat; Piccadilly Circus or Leicester Sq) You might think Bar Shu – adorned with slatted blinds, latticed woodwork and tasselled lanterns – was a sweet-and-sour honeytrap for Soho tourists; but you'd be missing out on possibly the best Sichuan food in London. The *ma-po* tofu ('pockmarked grandmother's tofu', reputedly Chairman Mao's favourite) is the best we've ever had: all funky fermented beans, chilli oil, pork and fresh beancurd.

There's a wide disparity in dish pricing: while simple choices such as the *ma-po* or 'ants climbing trees' (a classic stir-fried cellophane-noodle dish) come in at around £10, you'll be in for a shock if you order sea cucumber, abalone or crab without checking the prices first.

Barrafina TAPAS ££
(Map p80; 020-7440 1456; www.barrafina.co.uk; 26-27 Dean St, W1; basic tapas £4-7, larger plates £9-20; noon-3pm & 5-10pm Mon-Sat, 1-8pm Sun; Tottenham Court Rd) Tapas are always better value in Spain than in London (even more so when complimentary with drinks, as is traditional), but the exceptional quality at Barrafina justifies the extra expense. Along with *gambas al ajillo* (prawns in garlic), there are more unusual items, such as tuna tartare and grilled quail with alioli, plus a wonderful changing menu of specials.

Customers sit along the bar facing the busy chefs, so it's not a good choice for groups (and the maximum party size is four).

Yauatcha DIM SUM ££
(Map p80; 020-7494 8888; www.yauatcha.com; 15-17 Broadwick St, W1; mains £15-30, dim sum £8-10; noon-1am Mon-Sat, to midnight Sun; Tottenham Court Rd or Oxford Circus) London's glamorous Michelin-starred dim sum restaurant has a ground-floor dining room that's a blue-bathed oasis of calm amid the chaos of Berwick Street Market; downstairs is smarter, with constellations of 'star' lights. Lobster dumplings with *tobiko* (flying-fish roe) exemplify the refined dim sum, while spicy steamed bass with pickled chilli is just one of the more substantial options.

The Soho Lunch (£28 per person for at least two) is a great-value introduction to its divine dim sum. Unusually, Yauatcha also produces delicate cakes, macarons and other sweet delights.

★ Foyer & Reading Room at Claridge's BRITISH £££
(Map p124; 020-7107 8886; www.claridges.co.uk; Brook St, W1; afternoon tea £70, with champagne £80-90; 7am-10pm Mon-Sat, from 8am Sun, afternoon tea 2.45-5.30pm; ; Bond St) Refreshing the better sort of West End shopper since 1856, the jaw-dropping Foyer and Reading Room at **Claridge's** (Map p124; 020-7629 8860; www.claridges.co.uk; Brook St, W1; r/ste from £450/780; ; Bond St), refulgent with art-deco mirrors and a Dale Chihuly glass sculpture, really is a memorable dining space. Refined food is served at all mealtimes, but many choose to nibble in best aristocratic fashion on the finger sandwiches and pastries of a classic afternoon tea.

Smart attire is always required.

★Spring BRITISH £££
(Map p80; ☎020-3011 0115; www.springrestaurant.co.uk; New Wing, Somerset House, Lancaster Pl, WC2; mains £29-33, 2-/3-course lunch £29/32; ⊙noon-2.30pm & 5.30-10pm Mon-Sat; Ⓤ Temple) White walls, ball chandeliers and columns are offset by the odd blossom in this restored Victorian drawing room in Somerset House (p88). Award-winning Australian chef Skye Gyngell leads a team dedicated to sustainability – no single-use plastic – and an early-evening scratch menu (£25 for three courses) using food that would otherwise be wasted. Desserts are legendary.

Pollen Street Social EUROPEAN £££
(Map p80; ☎020-7290 7600; www.pollenstreetsocial.com; 8-10 Pollen St, W1; mains £41-44; ⊙noon-2.30pm & 6-10pm Mon-Sat; Ⓤ Oxford Circus) Chef Jason Atherton's cathedral to haute cuisine (Michelin-starred within six months of opening) is a worthy splurge, especially for those in search of the best produce in these islands. It's expensive, but if you fancy trying Braehead pheasant with chestnut gnocchi or roasted Cornish cod with salt-baked vegetables without overspending, the three-course lunch menu (£40) is excellent value.

City of London

Simpsons Tavern BRITISH £
(Map p90; ☎020-7626 9985; www.simpsonstavern.co.uk; Ball Ct, 38½ Cornhill, EC3; mains £9.75-15.80; ⊙8.30-10.30am Tue-Fri & noon-3.30pm Mon-Fri; Ⓤ Bank) 'Old school' doesn't even come close to describing Simpsons, a City institution since 1757. Huge portions of traditional British grub are served to diners in dark-wood and olive-green booths. Save space for the tavern's famous stewed-cheese dessert.

★Duck & Waffle BRITISH ££
(Map p90; ☎020-3640 7310; www.duckandwaffle.com; Heron Tower, 110 Bishopsgate, EC2; mains £14-44; ⊙24hr; 📶; Ⓤ Liverpool St) London tends to have an early bedtime, but Duck and Waffle is the best restaurant that's ready to party all night. Survey the kingdom from the highest restaurant in town (on the 40th floor) over a helping of the namesake dish: a fluffy waffle topped with a crispy leg of duck confit and a fried duck egg, drenched in mustard-seed maple syrup.

City Social BRITISH £££
(Map p90; ☎020-7877 7703; www.citysociallondon.com; Tower 42, 25 Old Broad St, EC2; mains £26-37; ⊙noon-2.30pm & 6-10.30pm Mon-Fri, 5-10.30pm Sat; Ⓤ Bank) City Social pairs sublime skyscraper views from its 24th-floor digs with delicate Michelin-starred cuisine. The interior is all art-deco inspired low-lit glamour. If you don't want to splash out on the full menu, opt for the bar, **Social 24**, which has longer hours and a compelling menu of nibbles (don't miss the goats'-cheese churros with locally sourced truffle-infused honey).

Bookings are essential; expect airport-style security before you can get in the lift.

South Bank

★Padella ITALIAN £
(Map p98; www.padella.co; 6 Southwark St, SE1; dishes £4-12.50; ⊙noon-3.45pm & 5-10pm Mon-Sat, to 9pm Sun; 🌶; Ⓤ London Bridge) Come hungry for the best pasta this side of Italy. Padella is a small, energetic bistro specialising in handmade noodles, inspired by the owners' extensive culinary adventures. The portions are small, which means that you can (and should!) have more than one dish. Download the WalkIn app to join the queue virtually to dine here then head to the market or pub.

Anchor & Hope GASTROPUB ££
(Map p98; ☎020-7928 9898; www.anchorandhopepub.co.uk; 36 The Cut, SE1; mains £12.40-19.40; ⊙5-10pm Mon, from 11am Tue-Sat, 12.30-3.15pm Sun; Ⓤ Southwark) Started by former chefs from nose-to-tail pioneer St John (p128), the Anchor & Hope is a quintessential gastropub: elegant but not formal, serving utterly delicious European fare with a British twist. The menu changes daily, but it could include grilled sole served with spinach, or roast rabbit with green beans in a mustard-and-bacon sauce. Bookings taken for Sunday lunch only.

Skylon EUROPEAN £££
(Map p98; ☎020-7654 7800; www.skylon-restaurant.co.uk; 3rd fl, Royal Festival Hall, Southbank Centre, Belvedere Rd, SE1; mains £16.50-34; ⊙noon-10pm Mon-Fri, 11.30am-3pm & 5-10pm Sat, 11.30am-10pm Sun; 📶👪; Ⓤ Waterloo) Named after the original structure in this location for the 1951 Festival of Britain, Skylon brings the 1950s into the modern era, with retro-futuristic decor (cool then, cooler now)

and a season-driven menu of contemporary British cuisine. But its biggest selling point might be the floor-to-ceiling windows that bathe you in magnificent views of the Thames and the city.

Brixton, Peckham & South London

Peckham Levels FOOD HALL £
(https://peckhamlevels.org; 95a Rye Lane, SE15; ⏲10am-11pm Mon-Wed, to 1am Thu-Sat, to midnight Sun; Peckham Rye) A few floors below famous **Frank's** (http://boldtendencies.com/franks-cafe; 10th fl, 95a Rye Lane, SE15; ⏲5-11pm Tue & Wed, from 2pm Thu & Fri, 11am-11pm Sat & Sun mid-May–mid-Sep), Peckham Levels is the place to go if you want to drink in a former car park year-round. The first five floors are filled with small business coworking spaces, so head straight to the 6th floor for a delightful mix of street-food stalls and bars with enclosed weather-proof views toward London's skyscrapers.

Kudu SOUTH AFRICAN ££
(020-3950 0226; www.kuducollective.com; 119 Queen's Rd, SE15; dishes £8.50-18; ⏲6-10pm Wed-Sun; Queens Rd Peckham) Northeast of Peckham's core, this family run neighbourhood restaurant is worth the venture. Decorated with dusky pink and exposed-brick walls and blue velvet banquettes, Kudu presents South African flavours with inventive ingredients on delicate sharing plates. The menu can do no wrong, so order as much as you can: pig's-head tortellini, Parmesan churros with brown crab mayo and the signature pot-baked kudu bread.

★**Chez Bruce** FRENCH £££
(020-8672 0114; www.chezbruce.co.uk; 2 Bellevue Rd, SW17; 3-course lunch/dinner from £39.50/60; ⏲noon-2.30pm & 6-9.30pm Mon-Thu, noon-2.30pm & 6-10pm Fri & Sat, 12.30-3.30pm Sun; Wandsworth Common) Far off the usual tourist track, the phenomenal Chez Bruce, opposite leafy Wandsworth Common, has been in business for more than two decades. Despite its Michelin star, the atmosphere remains less pretentious than at other fine-dining establishments, and tables are filled with well-heeled locals. Dishes rotate frequently, but duck is often the star of the menu.

Kensington & Hyde Park

Pimlico Fresh CAFE £
(020-7932 0030; 86 Wilton Rd, SW1; mains from £3.50; ⏲7.30am-7.30pm Mon-Fri, 9am-6pm Sat & Sun; Victoria) This chirpy two-room cafe will see you right, whether you need breakfast (French toast, bowls of porridge laced with honey, banana, maple syrup or yoghurt; £3.50), lunch (home-made quiches and soups, 'things' on toast) or just a good old latte and cake.

Rabbit MODERN BRITISH ££
(Map p100; 020-3750 0172; www.rabbit-restaurant.com; 172 King's Rd, SW3; mains £6-20; ⏲noon-9pm Tue-Sat, noon-8pm Sun; ; Sloane Sq) Three brothers grew up on a farm. One became a farmer, another a butcher, while the third worked in hospitality. So they pooled their skills and came up with Rabbit, a breath of fresh air in upmarket Chelsea. The restaurant rocks the agri-chic look, and the creative, seasonal and oft-changing Modern British menu is fabulous.

★**Dinner by Heston Blumenthal** MODERN BRITISH £££
(Map p100; 020-7201 3833; www.dinnerbyheston.com; Mandarin Oriental Hyde Park, 66 Knightsbridge, SW1; 3-course set lunch £48, mains £44-52; ⏲noon-2.15pm & 6-9.30pm Sun-Wed, noon-2.30pm & 6-10pm Thu-Sat; ; Knightsbridge) With two Michelin stars, sumptuously presented Dinner is a gastronomic tour de force, taking diners on a journey through British culinary history (with inventive modern inflections). Dishes carry historical dates to convey context, while the restaurant interior is a design triumph, from the glass-walled kitchen and its overhead clock mechanism to the large windows looking onto the park. Book ahead.

★**Gordon Ramsay** FRENCH £££
(Map p100; 020-7352 4441; www.gordonramsayrestaurants.com/restaurant-gordon-ramsay; 68 Royal Hospital Rd, SW3; 3-course lunch/dinner £70/130; ⏲noon-2.15pm & 6.30-9.45pm Mon-Fri; ; Sloane Sq) One of Britain's finest restaurants and London's longest-running with three Michelin stars (held since 2001), this is hallowed turf for those who worship at the altar of the stove. The blowout Menu Prestige (£160) is seven courses of perfection, also available in vegetarian form (£160); a three-course vegetarian menu

(£130) is also at hand. Smart dress code (enquire); reserve early.

For unstoppable enthusiasts, masterclasses with Chef de Cuisine Matt Abé are also available.

★Five Fields MODERN BRITISH £££

(Map p100; ☎020-7838 1082; www.fivefieldsrestaurant.com; 8-9 Blacklands Tce, SW3; tasting menus £90-110; ⊙noon-2pm Thu-Sat, 6.30-10pm Tue-Sat; 📶; Ⓤ Sloane Sq) The inventive British prix fixe cuisine, consummate service and enticingly light and inviting decor are hard to resist at this triumphant Chelsea restaurant – now with a Michelin star – but you'll need to plan early and book way up front. No children under 12.

Launceston Place MODERN BRITISH £££

(Map p100; ☎020-7937 6912; www.launcestonplace-restaurant.co.uk; 1a Launceston Pl, W8; mains £22-34, tasting menus £79, 'early dinner' 3-course set menu £40; ⊙noon-2.30pm & 5-10pm Wed-Sat, noon-3.30pm & 6.30-9pm Sun; 📶🖉; Ⓤ Gloucester Rd or High St Kensington) This exceptionally handsome, superchic Michelin-starred restaurant is almost anonymous on a picture-postcard Kensington street of Edwardian houses. Prepared by London chef Ben Murphy, dishes occupy the acme of gastronomic pleasures and are accompanied by an award-winning wine list. The adventurous will aim for the eight-course tasting menu (£85; vegetarian and vegan versions available).

Clerkenwell, Shoreditch & Spitalfields

★Breddos Tacos TACOS £

(☎020-3535 8301; www.breddostacos.com; 82 Goswell Rd, EC1; tacos from £5, mains £7.50-17; ⊙noon-3pm & 5-11pm Mon-Fri, noon-11.30pm Sat; 🖉; Ⓤ Old St or Farringdon) Started in an East London car park in 2011, Breddos found its first permanent home in Clerkenwell, dishing out some of London's best Mexican grub. Grab some friends and order each of the eight or so tacos, served in pairs, on the menu: fillings vary, but past favourites include confit pork belly, and veggie-friendly mole, queso fresco and egg.

Boiler House Food Hall MARKET £

(Map p130; https://theboilerhouse.org/conscious-market; Old Truman Brewery, 152 Brick Lane, E1; dishes £5-12; ⊙11am-6pm Sat & Sun; 🖉; Ⓤ Shoreditch High St) More than 50 plant-based food stalls and ethical retail brands pitch up in the Old Truman Brewery's high-ceilinged boiler room at the weekend. Munch on the likes of cauliflower 'wings', vegan hot dogs, barbecue seitan brisket sandwiches, and 'tofish' and chips.

★Smoking Goat THAI ££

(Map p130; www.smokinggoatbar.com; 64 Shoreditch High St, E1; dishes £4-29; ⊙noon-9pm Mon-Sun; Ⓤ Shoreditch High St) Trotting in on one of London's fleeting flavours of the week, Smoking Goat's modern Thai menu is top notch. The industrial-chic look of exposed brick, huge factory windows and original parquet floors surround the open kitchen. It's a tough place for the spice-shy; cool down with a cold one from the exquisite cocktail list. Don't miss the smoked five-spice chicken.

St John BRITISH ££

(Map p90; ☎020-7251 0848; www.stjohnrestaurant.com; 26 St John St, EC1; mains £17-26.50; ⊙noon-3pm & 6-11pm Mon-Fri, 6-11pm Sat, 12.30-4pm Sun; Ⓤ Farringdon) Around the corner from London's last remaining meat market, St John is the standard-bearer for nose-to-tail cuisine. With whitewashed brick walls, high ceilings and simple wooden furniture, it's surely one of the most humble Michelin-starred restaurants anywhere. The menu changes daily but is likely to include the signature roast bone marrow and parsley salad.

Yuu Kitchen ASIAN ££

(Map p90; ☎020-7377 0411; www.yuukitchen.com; 29 Commercial St, E1; dishes £5-10; ⊙6-10pm Tue-Fri, noon-10pm Sat, noon-5pm Sun; 🖉; Ⓤ Aldgate East) Manga images pout on the walls and birdcages dangle from the ceiling at this fun, relaxed place. Dishes are either bite-sized or designed to be shared, and while the focus is mainly Asian, some dishes from further along the Pacific Rim pop up, too. Hence Filipino *lechon kawali* (slow-braised pork belly) sits alongside Vietnamese rolls and show-stopping *bao* (Taiwanese steamed buns).

Poppie's FISH & CHIPS ££

(Map p130; ☎020-7247 0892; www.poppiesfishandchips.co.uk; 6-8 Hanbury St, E1; mains £12-17; ⊙11am-11pm Mon-Sat, to 10.30pm Sun; Ⓤ Liverpool St) This glorious recreation of a 1950s East End chippy comes complete with wait-staff in pinnies and hairnets, and Blitz memorabilia. As well as the usual fishy suspects, it does old-time London staples – jellied eels and mushy peas – plus kid-pleasing, sweet-tooth desserts (sticky toffee pudding or apple pie with ice cream), and there's a wine list.

★Hawksmoor Spitalfields STEAK £££

(Map p130; 020-7426 4850; www.thehawksmoor.com; 157a Commercial St, E1; mains £15-60; noon-3pm & 5-10.30pm Mon-Fri, noon-10.30pm Sat, noon-9pm Sun; ; Shoreditch High St) You could easily miss Hawksmoor, discreetly signed and clad in black brick, but dedicated carnivores will find it worth seeking out. The dark wood and velvet curtains make for a handsome setting in which to gorge yourself on the best of British beef. The Sunday roasts (£22) are legendary, but it's *the* place in London to order a steak.

East London

★Barge East BRITISH ££

(020-3026 2807; www.bargeeast.com; River Lee, Sweetwater Mooring, White Post Ln, E9; small plates £7-8.50, mains £14-19; 5-11pm Mon-Thu, noon-11.30pm Fri, 10am-10.30pm Sat, 11am-10.30pm Sun; Hackney Wick) Moored along the River Lee in Hackney Wick is the *De Hoop*, a 100-tonne barge that sailed from Holland to offer seasonal fare and delicious drinks with waterside views. Small plates like nduja scotch eggs with black garlic or large dishes of Szechuan aubergine with cashew cream wash down splendidly with cocktails like the Earl Grey–based East London iced tea.

Berber & Q NORTH AFRICAN ££

(020-7923 0829; www.berberandq.com; 338 Acton Mews, E8; mains £13-18; 6-11pm Tue-Fri, 11am-3pm & 6-11pm Sat & Sun; Haggerston) A mouth-watering barbecue smell greets you as you enter under the railway arches into this very cool Berber-style grill house. Lamb shawarma (kebab) is meltingly tender, while piquant treats include dukkah-crusted lamb nuggets, wood-roasted prawns with garlic confit, spiced beef *kofte*, and vegetarian-friendly shiitake- and oyster-mushroom kebab with porcini tahini.

Corner Room MODERN BRITISH ££

(020-7871 0460; www.townhallhotel.com; Patriot Sq, E2; mains £14-26, 5-course dinner £39; noon-2.30pm & 6-9.45pm; Bethnal Green) Tucked away on the 1st floor of the Town Hall Hotel, this relaxed industrial-chic restaurant serves expertly crafted dishes with complex yet delicate flavours, highlighting the best of British seasonal produce, with a French touch.

Bistrotheque MODERN BRITISH ££

(020-8983 7900; www.bistrotheque.com; 23-27 Wadeson St, E2; mains £14-31, 3-course early dinner £25; 6-10.30pm Mon-Fri, 11am-4pm & 6-10.30pm Sat & Sun; Bethnal Green) This unmarked warehouse conversion ticks all the boxes of a contemporary upmarket London bistro (the name made more sense when there was a club-like cabaret space downstairs). The food and service are uniformly excellent. One of the best weekend brunch spots in Hackney.

★Silo BRITISH £££

(020-7993 8155; https://silolondon.com; Unit 7, Queen's Yard, E9; 6-course tasting menu £50, brunch dishes £7.50-11.50; 6-10pm Tue-Fri, 11am-3pm & 6-10pm Sat, 11am-3pm Sun; Hackney Wick) Brighton's Silo, the world's first zero-waste restaurant, has moved to Hackney Wick. Here, trailblazing chef Doug McMaster fashions lesser-loved ingredients and wonky produce into the likes of beetroot prune with egg yolk fudge or Jerusalem artichoke in brown butter. The canalside space – where everything down to the lampshades is upcycled – is as gorgeous as the dishes on the ever-changing menu.

North London

★Ruby Violet ICE CREAM £

(020-7609 0444; www.rubyviolet.co.uk; Midlands Goods Shed, 3 Wharf Rd, N1; 1 scoop £3; 11am-7pm Mon & Tue, to 10pm Wed-Sun; King's Cross St Pancras) Ruby Violet takes ice cream to the next level: flavours are wonderfully original (masala chai, raspberry and sweet potato) and toppings and hot sauces are shop-made. Plus, there's Pudding Club on Friday and Saturday nights, when you can dive into a mini baked Alaska or hot chocolate fondant. Eat in or sit by the fountain on Granary Sq.

Chin Chin Labs ICE CREAM £

(Map p128; 07885 604284; www.chinchinlabs.com; 49-50 Camden Lock Pl, NW1; ice cream from £4.95; noon-7pm; Camden Town) This is

Hoxton, Shoreditch & Spitalfields

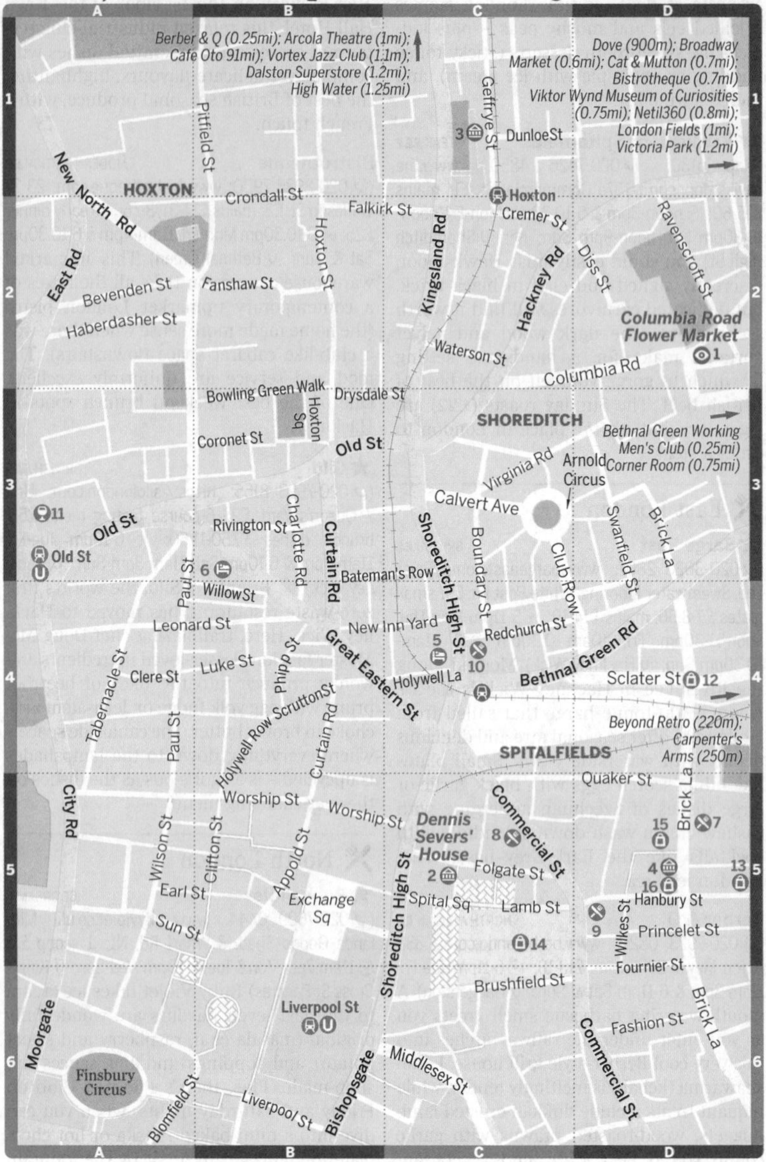

food chemistry at its absolute best. Chefs prepare the ice-cream mixture and freeze it on the spot by adding liquid nitrogen. Flavours change regularly and match the seasons (tonka bean, Valrhona chocolate, burnt-butter caramel or pandan leaf, for instance). The dozen toppings and sauces are equally creative. Try the ice-cream sandwich (£5.65): ice cream wedged inside gorgeous brownies or cookies.

Hook Camden Town FISH & CHIPS £

(Map p128; ☎020-74820475; www.hookrestaurants.com; 63-65 Parkway, NW1; mains £11-17; ⊙noon-

Hoxton, Shoreditch & Spitalfields

Top Sights
1 Columbia Road Flower Market.............D2
2 Dennis Severs' House.............C5

Sights
3 Museum of the Home.............C1
4 Old Truman Brewery.............D5

Sleeping
5 CitizenM London Shoreditch.............C4
6 Hoxton Shoreditch.............B3

Eating
7 Boiler House Food Hall.............D5
8 Hawksmoor Spitalfields.............C5
9 Poppie's.............D5
10 Smoking Goat.............C4

Drinking & Nightlife
11 Nightjar.............A3

Shopping
12 Brick Lane Market.............D4
13 Libreria.............D5
14 Old Spitalfields Market.............C5
15 Rough Trade East.............D5
16 Sunday Upmarket.............D5

3pm & 5.30-9pm Mon, to 10pm Tue-Thu, to 10.30pm Fri & Sat, to 9pm Sun; ; Camden Town) In addition to working entirely with sustainable small fisheries and local suppliers, Hook makes all its sauces on-site and wraps its fish in recycled materials, supplying diners with extraordinarily fine-tasting morsels. Totally fresh, the fish arrives in panko breadcrumbs or tempura batter, with seaweed salted chips. Wash it down with craft beer, wines and cocktails. There's also a great kids' menu.

★Ottolenghi MEDITERRANEAN ££
(020-7288 1454; www.ottolenghi.co.uk; 287 Upper St, N1; breakfast £5.90-12.50, mains lunch/dinner from £16.50/10; 8am-10.30pm Mon-Sat, 9am-7pm Sun; ; Highbury & Islington) Mountains of meringues tempt you through the door of this deli-restaurant, where a sumptuous array of baked goods and fresh salads greets you. Meals are as light and bright as the brilliantly white interior design, with a strong influence from the eastern Mediterranean. Mains at lunch are full platters and include two salads.

Trullo ITALIAN ££
(020-7226 2733; www.trullorestaurant.com; 300-302 St Paul's Rd, N1; mains £16.50-24; 12.30-2.45pm & 6-10.15pm Mon-Sat, to 9.15pm Sun; Highbury & Islington) Trullo's daily homemade pasta is delicious (pappardelle, fettuccine), but the main attraction here is the charcoal grill, which churns out the likes of succulent Italian-style pork chops, lamb rump and fish. The all-Italian wine list is brief but well chosen. Service is excellent, although dinner time can get packed. Book well in advance.

Caravan INTERNATIONAL ££
(020-7101 7661; www.caravanrestaurants.co.uk; 1 Granary Sq, N1; small plates £7.50-9, mains £17.50-19; 8am-10.30pm Mon-Fri, 10am-10.30pm Sat, to 4pm Sun; ; King's Cross St Pancras) Housed in the lofty Granary Building, the King's Cross redevelopment's first tenant is a vast industrial-chic destination for tasty fusion bites from around the world. You can opt for several small plates to share tapas-style, or stick to main-sized dishes. The outdoor seating area on Granary Sq is especially popular on warm days, and cocktails are popular regardless of the weather.

Greenwich

Marcella ITALIAN ££
(020-3903 6561; https://marcella.london; 165a Deptford High St, SE8; mains £12-16; noon-2.30pm & 6-10pm Wed-Thu, to 10.30pm Fri & Sat, noon-4pm Sun; ; Deptford) If you avoid pasta restaurants because you think you can make it just as easily at home, Marcella is here to prove you wrong. Perfect house-made pasta comes with seasonally changing sauces in simple but delicious combinations. Starters are equally tasty (the house ricotta is creamy heaven), as are the generously large fish- and meat-based mains, made to share.

West London

Potli INDIAN £
(020-8741 4328; www.potli.co.uk; 319-321 King St, W6; weekday 1-/2-course set lunch £7.95/10.95, weekend 3-course set lunch £14.95, mains £8-15; noon-2.30pm & 6-10.15pm Mon-Thu, noon-3pm & 5.30-10.30pm Fri & Sat, noon-10pm Sun; ; Stamford Brook or Ravenscourt Park) With its scattered pieces from Mumbai's Thieves

Market, Indian-market-kitchen/bazaar cuisine, homemade pickles and spice mixes, plus an accent on genuine flavour, tantalising Potli deftly captures the aromas of its culinary home. Downstairs there's an open kitchen, and service is friendly. But it's the alluring menu – where flavours are teased into a rich and authentic Indian culinary experience – that's the real crowd-pleaser.

Dishoom INDIAN ££

(Map p106; ☎020-7420 9325; www.dishoom.com/kensington; 4 Derry St, W8; ⏲8am-11pm Mon-Fri, from 9am Sat & Sun; 📶; Ⓤ High St Kensington) Dishy Dishoom is not only a delightful art-deco-style treat and a delicious picture to behold, but also serves some of the finest Indian food in London. Staff at this new Kensington branch of the famous restaurant are also first rate, though you may have to wait in the evening (no reservations for groups of less than six after 6pm).

Wallace Restaurant EUROPEAN ££

(Map p124; ☎020-7563 9505; www.peytonandbyrne.co.uk/venues/wallace-restaurant; Hertford House, Manchester Sq, W1; mains £20-24; 3-course set menu £35; ⏲10am-5pm Sun-Thu, to 11pm Fri & Sat; Ⓤ Bond St) Run by an outfit with broader catering experience, the Wallace Collection's (p87) cafe-restaurant is a notch above what you'd expect from a museum. Equally good for a daytime coffee and pastry, an evening drink, or a more substantial French-inspired meal, it's in the covered, candy-pink-and-white central courtyard. Even potted plastic bay and Japanese maple trees don't detract from the civilised atmosphere.

Afternoon tea is served daily between 2.30pm and 4.30pm. It's £19 per person, or £27 if you'd like a glass of bubbles with your Coronation chicken sandwiches.

★Flat Three INTERNATIONAL ££

(Map p106; ☎020-7792 8987; www.flatthree.london; 120-122 Holland Park Ave, W11; mains £18-36; ⏲noon-2.30pm Fri & Sat, 6-9.30pm Tue-Sat; 📶✍; Ⓤ Holland Park) With pronounced Japanese, Korean and Scandinavian inflections, this lovely downstairs Holland Park restaurant is full of surprises and creative discoveries. Juliana and her team have crafted something delectable in the kitchen, matched by a natural, simple and appealing dining space. Vegans will find themselves well looked after, too. The five-course menu is excellent, while superb cocktails add the final touch.

Geales SEAFOOD ££

(Map p106; ☎020-7727 7528; www.geales.com; 2 Farmer St, W8; mains £10-14, set meal from £22; ⏲noon-3pm Fri, 6-11pm Mon-Fri, noon-11pm Sat & Sun; 📶; Ⓤ Notting Hill Gate) Frying on Farmer St since 1939 – a bad year for the European restaurant trade – Geales has endured, despite its quiet location tucked away on a street corner behind Notting Hill Gate. The succulent fish in crispy batter is a fine catch, but the fish pie and rich mushy peas are also worth angling for, with jam roly poly and custard for pudding.

Farmacy VEGAN ££

(Map p106; ☎020-7221 0705; www.farmacylondon.com; 74 Westbourne Grove, W2; £15-16.50; ⏲9am-5pm & 6-10pm Mon-Fri, 9am-4pm & 6-10pm Sat, 9am-4pm & 6-9.30pm Sun; 📶✍; Ⓤ Bayswater) 🌿 Pricey and well in step with dining trends, Farmacy aims squarely at wholesome, organic, gluten-free, vegan detoxing. For breakfast (Monday to Friday, brunch at weekends), size up a healthy choice of chickpea pancake 'omelettes', avocado on sourdough toast and buckwheat granola with fruit and almond milk. Walnut, beetroot and mushroom burgers or meat-free lasagne are on the lunch menu.

Richmond, Kew & Hampton Court

★Gelateria Danieli GELATO £

(☎020-8439 9807; www.gelateriadanieli.com; 16 Brewers Lane, TW9; ice cream from £3; ⏲10am-6pm, from 11am Sun, open later in summer; 🚆Richmond, Ⓤ Richmond) Stuffed away down delightful narrow, pinched and flagstone-paved Brewer's Lane off Richmond Green, this tiny gelateria is a joy, and often busy. The handmade ice cream arrives in some two dozen lip-smacking flavours, from Bakewell Tart pudding to pistachio, walnut and tiramisu to pinenut and chocolate, scooped into small tubs or chocolate and hazelnut cones. There are milkshakes (£5) and coffee too.

★Petersham Nurseries Cafe MODERN EUROPEAN £££

(☎020-8332 8665; www.petershamnurseries.com; Church Lane, off Petersham Rd, TW10; mains £24-30; ⏲cafe noon-5pm Tue-Sun; Ⓤ Richmond) 🌿 In a greenhouse at the back of the fabulously located Petersham Nurseries is this award-winning cafe straight out of the pages of *The Secret Garden*. The confidently executed cuisine includes organic ingredients harvested from the nursery gardens and produce adhering to Slow Food principles. Seasonal dishes include chargrilled monkfish, sage pork chops and veggie tagine. Booking in advance is essential.

Glasshouse MODERN EUROPEAN £££
(020-8940 6777; www.glasshouserestaurant.co.uk; 14 Station Pde, TW9; 3-course lunch/dinner from £40/57.50; noon-12.30pm & 6.30-9.30pm Tue-Thu, noon-2.30pm & 6.30-10.30pm Fri & Sat, 12.30-4pm Sun; ; Kew Gardens, Kew Gardens) A day at Kew Gardens finds a perfect conclusion at this Michelin-starred gastronomic highlight. The glass-fronted exterior envelops a delicately lit, low-key interior, where the focus remains on divinely cooked food. Diners are rewarded with a seasonal, consistently accomplished menu from chef Gregory Wellman that combines English mainstays with modern European innovation.

Drinking & Nightlife

West End

★Connaught Bar COCKTAIL BAR
(Map p100; 020-7499 7070; www.the-connaught.co.uk/mayfair-bars/connaught-bar; Connaught Hotel, Carlos Pl, W1; 11am-1am Mon-Sat, to midnight Sun; ; Bond St) Drinkers who know their stuff single out the travelling martini trolley for particular praise, but almost everything mixed at the silver-and-platinum-toned bar at this iconic Mayfair hotel, built as the Coburg in 1815, gets the nod. You'll enjoy lavish art-deco design, faultless service, and some of the best drinks in town. Classic and reimagined cocktails range from £12 to £21.

★American Bar COCKTAIL BAR
(Map p80; 020-7836 4343; www.fairmont.com/savoy-london/dining/americanbar; Savoy Hotel, Strand, WC2; 11.30am-midnight Mon-Sat, from noon Sun; ; Temple, Charing Cross or Embankment) Home of the Lonely Street, Concrete Jungle and other house cocktails named after iconic songs collected in the 'Savoy Songbook', this seriously dishy American Bar is a London icon, with soft blue furniture, gleaming art-deco lines and live piano jazz from 6.30pm nightly. Cocktails start at £20 and peak at a stupefying £5000 (for the Sazerac, containing cognac from 1858).

Artesian COCKTAIL BAR
(Map p124; 020-7636 1000; www.artesian-bar.co.uk; Langham Hotel, 1c Portland Pl, W1; 11am-1am Mon-Wed, to 2am Thu-Sat, to midnight Sun; ; Oxford Circus) For a dose of colonial glamour with a touch of Oriental elegance, the sumptuous (often crowded) bar at the Langham hits many marks. Its cocktails (from £20) have won multiple awards, and the bar itself has been acclaimed the world's best. Its name acknowledges the 360ft-deep well beneath the hotel and, metaphorically, the immaculately designed 'source of indulgence' to be found within.

Sketch COCKTAIL BAR
(Map p80; 020-7659 4500; www.sketch.london; 9 Conduit St, W1; 7am-2am Mon-Fri, 8am-2am Sat, 8am-midnight Sun; Oxford Circus) Merrily undefinable, Sketch has all at once a two-Michelin-starred restaurant, a millennial-pink dining room lined with nonsensical cartoons by British artist David Shrigley, a mystical-forest-themed bar with a self-playing piano, and toilets hidden inside gleaming white egg-shaped pods. We don't know what's happening either, but we're here for it.

Dukes London COCKTAIL BAR
(Map p78; 020-7491 4840; www.dukeshotel.com/dukes-bar; Dukes Hotel, 35 St James's Pl, SW1; 2-11pm Mon-Sat, 4-10.30pm Sun; ; Green Park) Superb martinis and a gentlemen's-club-like ambience are the ingredients of this classic bar, where white-jacketed masters mix up perfect preparations. James Bond fans should make a pilgrimage here: author Ian Fleming used to frequent the place, where he undoubtedly ordered his drinks 'shaken, not stirred'. Smokers can ease into the secluded **Cognac and Cigar Garden** to enjoy cigars purchased here.

Swift COCKTAIL BAR
(Map p80; 020-7437 7820; www.barswift.com; 12 Old Compton St, W1; 3pm-midnight Mon-Sat, to 10.30pm Sun; Leicester Sq or Tottenham Court Rd) A favourite Soho drinking spot, Swift has a sleek, candlelit upstairs bar for walk-ins seeking a superior cocktail before dinner or the theatre, and a bookings-only downstairs bar (open from 5pm) offering more than 250 whiskies, art-deco-inspired sofas, and live blues and jazz from 9pm on Fridays and Saturdays. Bar snacks include oysters and olives.

LGBT+ LONDON

The West End, particularly Soho, is the visible centre of LGBT+ London, with venues clustered around Old Compton St and its surrounds, but there are queer-friendly venues scattered all over the capital.

Heaven (Map p80; 020-7930 2020; www.heavennightclub-london.com; Villiers St, WC2; 11pm-5am Mon, to 4am Thu & Fri, 10.30pm-5am Sat; Embankment or Charing Cross) Encouraging hedonism since 1979, when it opened on the site of a former roller disco, this perennially popular mixed/gay bar under the Charing Cross arches hosts excellent gigs and club nights, and has hosted New Order, The Birthday Party, Killing Joke and many a legendary act. Monday's mixed party Popcorn offers one of the best weeknight's clubbing in the capital.

The celebrated G-A-Y takes place here on Thursday (G-A-Y Porn Idol), Friday (G-A-Y Camp Attack) and Saturday (plain ol' G-A-Y).

Duke of Wellington (Map p80; 020-7439 1274; www.dukeofwellingtonsoho.co.uk/london; 77 Wardour St, W1; noon-midnight Mon-Sat, to 11.30pm Sun; ; Leicester Sq) This twin-floored pub off Old Compton St attracts a bearded, fun-loving gay crowd, welcoming friendly comers of all persuasions. A classic jumping-off point for wilder Soho nights, it spills onto the pavement in the warmer months, hosting free DJ after-parties when 'divas' such as Mariah Carey and Celine Dion are performing in town.

Royal Vauxhall Tavern (020-7820 1222; www.vauxhalltavern.com; 372 Kennington Lane, SE11; 7pm-midnight Mon-Thu, to 4am Fri, 9pm-4am Sat, 4-10.30pm Sun; Vauxhall) A gay landmark, the welcoming Royal Vauxhall Tavern is one of the city's most loved cabaret and performance venues, and there's something on every night of the week. Saturday's Duckie, dubbed a rock-and-roll honky tonk, is the club's signature queer performance.

Bethnal Green Working Men's Club (020-7739 7170; www.workersplaytime.net; 42-44 Pollard Row, E2; pub 6pm-late Wed-Sat, club hours vary; Bethnal Green) As it says on the tin, this is a true working men's club. Except that this one has opened its doors and let in all kinds of off-the-wall club nights, including trashy burlesque, LGBT+ shindigs, retro nights, beach parties and bake-offs. Expect sticky carpets, a shimmery stage set and a space akin to a school-hall disco.

Two Brewers (020-7819 9539; www.the2brewers.com; 114 Clapham High St, SW4; 5pm-2am Sun-Wed, to 3am Thu, to 4am Fri & Sat; Clapham Common) Two Brewers endures as one of the best London gay bars outside the LGBT+ villages of Soho and Vauxhall. There's cabaret, bingo or karaoke most nights of the week, and the venue is a full-on dancing madhouse on weekends. ID is required for entry, and there's often a cover charge.

Dalston Superstore (020-7254 2273; www.dalstonsuperstore.com; 117 Kingsland High St, E8; 5pm-2am Mon, noon-2am Tue-Fri, noon-3am Sat, 10am-2am Sun; Dalston Kingsland) Bar, club or diner? Gay, lesbian or straight? Dalston Superstore is hard to pigeonhole, which we suspect is the point. This two-level industrial space is open all day but really comes into its own after dark when there are club nights in the basement.

Princess Louise PUB

(Map p80; 020-7405 8816; 208 High Holborn, WC1; 11am-11pm Mon-Fri, from noon Sat, noon-6.45pm Sun; Holborn) The gorgeous ground-floor saloon of this Sam Smith's pub, dating from 1872, boasts pressed-tin ceilings, handsome tiling, etched mirrors and 'snob screens', and a stunning central horseshoe bar. The original Victorian wood partitions provide plenty of private nooks, and typical pub food is served from noon to 2.30pm Monday to Friday, and 6pm to 8.30pm Monday to Thursday (mains £8 to £12).

Terroirs WINE BAR

(Map p80; 020-7036 0660; www.terroirswinebar.com; 5 William IV St, WC2; noon-11pm Mon-Sat; ; Charing Cross) This food-friendly wine bar near Charing Cross has a fantastic selection of Old and New World wines, with plenty by the glass and available for take-away. Food isn't an afterthought either, with small plates such as burrata with clementine, radicchio and pine nuts augmented by a couple of mains (perhaps lamb rump with black-cabbage pesto and aubergine) and charcuterie platters.

Dog & Duck PUB

(Map p80; ☎020-7494 0697; www.nicholsonspubs.co.uk; 18 Bateman St, W1; ⏲11.30am-11pm Mon-Wed, to 1am Thu-Sat, noon-10.30pm Sun; Ⓤ Tottenham Court Rd) With a fine array of real ales and some stunning Victorian glazed tiling and pressed-tin ceilings adorning its intimate interior, the Dog & Duck has attracted an eclectic crowd since opening its doors around 1734 – including John Constable, Dante Gabrielle Rossetti, George Orwell and Madonna. Intriguing pies such as boar and chorizo and wild game reward the curious.

City of London

★Nickel Bar COCKTAIL BAR

(Map p90; ☎020-3828 2000; www.thened.com/restaurants/the-nickel-bar; 27 Poultry, EC2; ⏲8am-2am Mon-Fri, 9am-3am Sat, to midnight Sun; 📶; Ⓤ Bank) There's something *Great Gatsby*–ish about the Ned (p121) hotel: the elevated jazz pianists, the vast verdite columns, the classy American-inspired cocktails. Of all the public bars inside this magnificent former banking hall, the Nickel Bar soaks up the atmosphere best. Inspired by the glamorous art-deco saloons and the ocean-liner-era elegance, this is timeless nightcap territory.

★Oriole COCKTAIL BAR

(Map p90; ☎020-3457 8099; www.oriolebar.com; E Poultry Ave, EC1; ⏲6pm-2am Tue-Sun, to 11pm Mon; Ⓤ Farringdon) Down a darkened alley through the eerie evening quiet of Smithfield Market is an unlikely spot for one of London's best cocktail bars, but the journey of discovery is the theme at speakeasy-style Oriole. The cocktail menu, divided into Old World, New World and the Orient, traverses the globe, with out-of-this-world ingredients including clarified octopus milk, strawberry tree curd and slow-cooked chai palm.

cloudM ROOFTOP BAR

(Map p90; ☎020-3519 4830; www.citizenm.com/cloudm-tower-of-london; 40 Trinity Sq, citizenM Tower of London, EC3; ⏲7am-1am Mon-Fri, 3pm-1am Sat, to midnight Sun; 📶; Ⓤ Tower Hill) Settle into the sleek mod furniture at this hotel bar (p121), where floor-to-double-height-ceiling bookcases and pop-art portraits of the Queen overlook the Tower of London just across the street. The standard drinks menu doesn't stray into groundbreaking territory, but the wrap-around outdoor balcony provides unforgettable sundowner views.

Ye Olde Cheshire Cheese PUB

(Map p90; ☎020-7353 6170; Wine Office Ct, 145 Fleet St, EC4; ⏲noon-11pm Mon-Sat; 🚆City Thameslink, Ⓤ Blackfriars) Rebuilt in 1667 after the Great Fire, this is one of London's most famous – and most crowded – pubs. It has strong literary connections, with Mark Twain, Sir Arthur Conan Doyle and Charles Dickens on the list of regulars. The gloomy interior, narrow passageways and convoluted layout add to its appeal, but surly staff and tight quarters will force you to move on quickly.

South Bank

★Seabird ROOFTOP BAR

(Map p98; ☎020-7903 3050; https://seabirdlondon.com; Hoxton Southwark, 40 Blackfriars Rd, SE1; ⏲noon-midnight Mon-Thu, to 1am Fri, 11am-1am Sat, to midnight Sun; Ⓤ Southwark) South Bank's latest rooftop bar might also be its best. Atop the new Hoxton Southwark (p121) hotel, sleek Seabird has palm-filled indoor and outdoor spaces where you can spy St Paul's from the comfort of your wicker seat. If you're hungry, seafood is the speciality, and the restaurant claims London's longest oyster list.

★Kings Arms PUB

(Map p98; ☎020-7207 0784; www.thekingsarmslondon.co.uk; 25 Roupell St, SE1; ⏲11am-11pm Mon-Sat, noon-10.30pm Sun; Ⓤ Waterloo) Set on old-school **Roupell St** (Map p98; Roupell St, SE1; Ⓤ Waterloo), this charming backstreet neighbourhood boozer serves up a rotating selection of traditional ales and bottled beers. The after-work crowd often makes a pit stop here before heading to Waterloo station, spilling out onto the street at peak hours. The farmhouse-style room at the back of the pub serves decent Thai food.

George Inn PUB

(Map p98; ☎020-7407 2056; www.nationaltrust.org.uk/george-inn; 77 Borough High St, SE1; ⏲11am-11pm Mon-Thu, to midnight Fri & Sat, noon-10.30pm Sun; Ⓤ London Bridge) This magnificent galleried coaching inn is the last of its kind in London. The building, owned by the National Trust, dates from 1677 and is mentioned in Charles Dickens' *Little Dorrit*. In the evenings, the picnic benches in the huge cobbled courtyard fill up (no reservations); otherwise, find a spot in the labyrinth of dark rooms and corridors inside.

Lyaness COCKTAIL BAR
(Map p98; ☎020-3747 1063; https://lyaness.com; Sea Containers, 20 Upper Ground, SE1; ⏲4pm-1am Mon-Wed, noon-2am Thu-Sat, to 12.30am Sun; ; Ⓤ Southwark) Six months after Dandelyan was named the best bar in the world, renowned mixologist Ryan Chetiyawardana closed it down. Reincarnated in that space with much the same atmosphere and modus operandi is Lyaness. The bar prides itself on unusual ingredients; look out for vegan honey, whey liqueur and onyx, a completely new type of alcohol.

Kensington & Hyde Park

Anglesea Arms PUB
(Map p100; ☎020-7373 7960; www.angleseaarms.com; 15 Selwood Tce, SW7; ⏲11am-11pm Mon-Sat, to 10.30pm Sun; Ⓤ South Kensington) Seasoned with age and decades of ale-quaffing patrons (including Charles Dickens, who lived on the same road, and DH Lawrence), this old-school pub boasts considerable character and a strong showing of beers and gins (over two dozen), while the terrace out front swarms with punters in warmer months. Arch-criminal Bruce Reynolds masterminded the 1963 Great Train Robbery over drinks here.

K Bar COCKTAIL BAR
(Map p100; ☎020-7589 6300; www.townhousekensington.com/k-bar; Town House, 109-113 Queen's Gate, SW7; cocktails £10; ⏲4pm-midnight Mon-Thu, to 1am Fri, noon-1am Sat, to 11pm Sun; ; Ⓤ South Kensington) In a part of town traditionally bereft of choice, the K Bar is a reassuring presence. A hotel bar maybe, but don't let that stop you – the place exudes panache with its leather-panelled and green-marble counter bar, smoothly glinting brass, oak walls and chandeliers, drawing a cashed-up crowd who enjoy themselves. Cocktails are prepared with as much class as the ambience.

Queen's Arms PUB
(Map p100; www.thequeensarmskensington.co.uk; 30 Queen's Gate Mews, SW7; ⏲noon-11pm; Ⓤ Gloucester Rd) Just around the corner from the Royal Albert Hall is this blue-grey-painted godsend. Located in an adorable cobbled-mews setting off bustling Queen's Gate, the pub beckons with a cosy interior, welcoming staff and a right royal selection of ales – including selections from small, local cask brewers – and ciders on tap. In warm weather, drinkers stand outside in the mews (only permitted on one side).

Clerkenwell, Shoreditch & Spitalfields

★Nightjar COCKTAIL BAR
(Map p130; ☎020-7253 4101; https://barnightjar.com; 129 City Rd, EC1V; music cover £5-8; ⏲6pm-1am, to 2am Thu, to 3am Fri & Sat; Ⓤ Old St) Behind a nondescript, gold-knobbed door just north of the Old Street roundabout is this bona fide speakeasy, pouring award-winning libations from a four-section menu that delineates the evolution of the cocktail. Leather banquettes, brick-walled booths and art-deco liquor cabinets stocked with vintage spirits set the perfect scene for jazz and blues acts that take the stage nightly at 9.30pm.

★Discount Suit Company COCKTAIL BAR
(Map p90; ☎020-7247 8755; www.discountsuitcompany.co.uk; 29a Wentworth St, E1; ⏲5pm-midnight Mon-Thu, 2pm-1am Fri & Sat, 5-11pm Sun; Ⓤ Aldgate East) Tucked away like a hidden seam, Discount Suit Company is one of the city's finest speakeasies – though on weekends you'll see that this closet-sized space is no secret. Superb, reasonably priced concoctions (a rarity in this area) are created behind the bar, originally a storeroom for the suit company above. Superfriendly staff and mixologists who'll happily go off-piste seal the deal.

★Fabric CLUB
(Map p90; ☎020-7336 8898; www.fabriclondon.com; 77a Charterhouse St, EC1; ⏲11pm-7am Fri, to 8am Sat, to 5.30am Sun; Ⓤ Farringdon) The monarch of London's after-hours scene, Fabric is a huge subterranean rave cave housed in a converted meat cold store. Each room has its own sound system, which you'll really feel in Room One – it has a 'bodysonic' vibrating dance floor that's attached to 450 bass shakers, which emit low-end frequencies so the music radiates into your muscles just by standing there.

★Fox & Anchor PUB
(Map p90; ☎020-7250 1300; www.foxandanchor.com; 115 Charterhouse St, EC1; ⏲7am-11pm, from

8.30am Sat, from 11am Sun; 📶; Ⓤ Barbican) Behind the Fox & Anchor's wonderful 1898 art-nouveau facade is a stunning traditional Victorian boozer, one of the last remaining market pubs in London that's permitted to serve alcohol before 11am. Fully celebrating its proximity to Smithfield Market, the grub is gloriously meaty. Only the most voracious of carnivores should opt for the City Boy Breakfast (£19.50).

Ye Olde Mitre PUB

(Map p90; www.yeoldemitreholborn.co.uk; 1 Ely Ct, EC1; ⏲ 11am-11pm Mon-Fri; 📶; Ⓤ Farringdon) A delightfully cosy historic pub with an extensive beer selection, tucked away in a backstreet off Hatton Garden, Ye Olde Mitre was originally built in 1546 for the servants of Ely Palace. There's no music, so rooms echo only with amiable chit-chat. Queen Elizabeth I danced around the cherry tree by the bar, or so they say.

East London

Dove PUB

(☎ 020-7275 7617; www.dovepubs.com; 24-28 Broadway Market, E8; ⏲ noon-11pm, from 11am Sat; 📶; Ⓤ London Fields) The Dove has a rambling series of wooden floorboard rooms and a wide range of Belgian Trappist, wheat and fruit-flavoured beers. Drinkers spill on to the street in warmer weather, or hunker down in the low-lit back room with board games when it's chilly. Pub meals with good vegetarian options are available, too.

Cat & Mutton PUB

(☎ 020-7249 6555; www.catandmutton.com; 76 Broadway Market, E8; ⏲ noon-11pm Mon, to midnight Tue-Thu, to 1am Fri, 10am-1am Sat, noon-11.30pm Sun; Ⓤ London Fields) At this fabulous Georgian pub, Hackney locals sup pints under the watchful eyes of hunting trophies, B&W photos of old-time boxers and a large portrait of Karl Marx. If it's crammed downstairs, head up the spiral staircase to the comfy couches. Weekends get rowdy, with DJs spinning their best tunes until late.

Netil360 ROOFTOP BAR

(www.netil360.com; 1 Westgate St, E8; ⏲ noon-8.30pm Wed & Sun, to 10.30pm Thu-Sat Apr-Dec; 📶; Ⓤ London Fields) Perched atop Netil House, this uberhip rooftop cafe-bar offers incredible views over London, with brass telescopes enabling you to get better acquainted with workers in 'the Gherkin' building. In between drinks you can knock out a game of croquet on the Astroturf, or perhaps book a hot tub for you and your mates to stew in.

High Water COCKTAIL BAR

(☎ 020-7241 1984; www.highwaterlondon.com; 23 Stoke Newington Rd, N16; ⏲ 4.30pm-2am Mon-Thu, 3.30pm-3am Fri & Sat, 3.30pm-2am Sun; Ⓡ Dalston Kingsland) Table service is offered at this narrow, brick-walled bar – but if you like to indulge in conversations with complete strangers, we suggest grabbing a seat at the bar. That way you can interrogate the charming staff about what corners of their largely self-devised cocktail list will best cater to your taste, and then watch them concoct it.

Carpenter's Arms PUB

(☎ 020-7739 6342; www.carpentersarmsfreehouse.com; 73 Cheshire St, E2; ⏲ 4-11.30pm Mon-Thu, noon-midnight Fri & Sat, noon-10.30pm Sun; 📶; Ⓤ Shoreditch High St) Once owned by infamous gangsters the Kray brothers (who bought it for their old ma to run), this chic yet cosy pub has been beautifully restored and its many wooden surfaces positively gleam. A back room and small yard provide a little more space for the convivial drinkers. There's a huge range of draught and bottled beers and ciders.

North London

★Holly Bush PUB

(☎ 020-7435 2892; www.hollybushhampstead.co.uk; 22 Holly Mount, NW3; ⏲ noon-11pm Mon-Sat, to 10.30pm Sun; 📶👪🐾; Ⓤ Hampstead) This beautiful Grade II–listed Georgian pub boasts a splendid antique interior, with open fires in winter. It has a knack for making you stay longer than you planned. Set above Heath St, in a secluded hilltop location, it's reached via the Holly Bush Steps.

Edinboro Castle PUB

(Map p128; ☎ 020-7255 9651; www.edinborocastlepub.co.uk; 57 Mornington Tce, NW1; ⏲ noon-11pm Mon-Sat, to 10.30pm Sun; 📶; Ⓤ Camden Town) Large and relaxed, the Edinboro offers a fun atmosphere, a fine bar and a full menu. The highlight, however, is the huge beer garden, complete with warm-weather barbecues and decorated with coloured lights on long summer evenings. Patio heaters appear in winter.

Camden Town

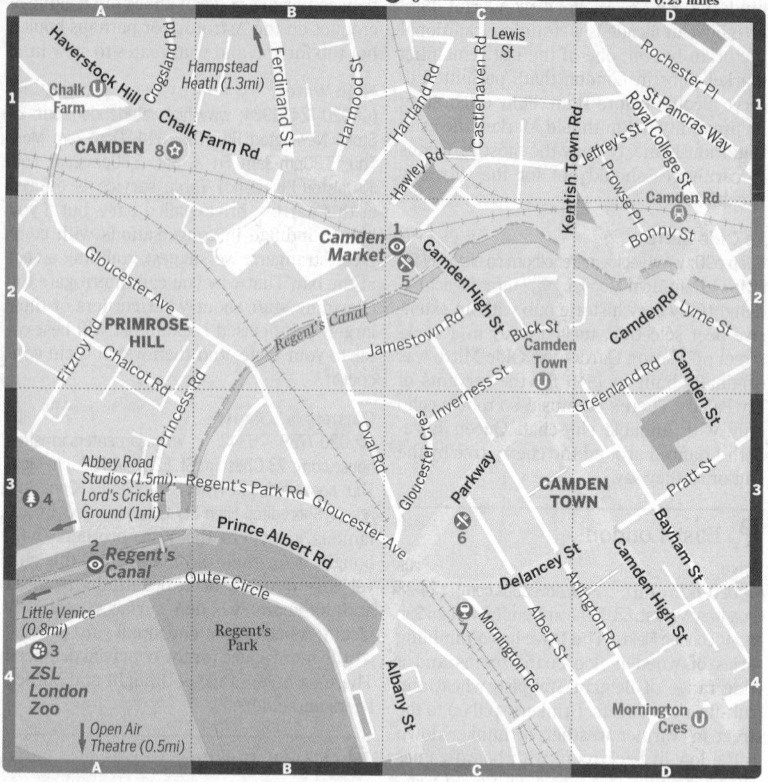

Camden Town

Top Sights

1 Camden Market C2
2 Regent's Canal A3
3 ZSL London Zoo A4

Sights

4 Primrose Hill A3

Eating

5 Chin Chin Labs C2
6 Hook Camden Town C3

Drinking & Nightlife

7 Edinboro Castle C4

Entertainment

8 Roundhouse A1

Greenwich

Old Brewery PUB

(020-3437 2222; www.oldbrewerygreenwich.com; Pepys House, Old Royal Naval College, SE10; 10am-11pm Mon-Sat, to 10.30pm Sun; ; Cutty Sark) On the grounds of the Old Royal Naval College (p114), the Old Brewery once housed Greenwich Meantime, one of London's earliest craft breweries. Now owned by Young's pub company, it serves decent pub food and a range of beers, best enjoyed in the huge beer garden.

Cutty Sark Tavern PUB

(020-8858 3146; www.cuttysarkse10.co.uk; 4-6 Ballast Quay, SE10; 11.30am-11pm Mon-Sat, noon-10.30pm Sun; ; Cutty Sark) Housed in a delightful bow-windowed, wood-beamed Georgian building directly on the Thames, this 200-year-old tavern is one of the few independent pubs left in Greenwich. Half a dozen cask-conditioned ales on tap line the bar, there's an inviting riverside seating area opposite and an upstairs dining room looking out on to glorious views.

Greenwich Union PUB
(☎020-8692 6258; www.greenwichunion.com; 56 Royal Hill, SE10; ⏰noon-11pm Mon-Thu, from 11.30am Fri & Sat, 11.30am-10.30pm Sun; 📶; Ⓤ Greenwich) The award-winning Union plies a handful of local microbrewery beers (it used to be owned by Greenwich-based Meantime Brewery) and a strong list of ales, plus bottled international brews. It's a handsome place with a welcoming long, narrow bar leading to a conservatory and beer garden at the back.

Trafalgar Tavern PUB
(☎020-3887 9886; www.trafalgartavern.co.uk; Park Row, SE10; ⏰noon-11pm Mon-Thu, to 1am Fri, 9am-1am Sat, to 11pm Sun; Ⓤ Cutty Sark) This elegant tavern, with crystal chandeliers, nautical decor and big windows overlooking the Thames, is steeped in history. Dickens apparently knocked back a few here – and used it as the setting for the wedding-breakfast scene in *Our Mutual Friend* – and Prime Ministers William Gladstone and Benjamin Disraeli used to dine on the pub's celebrated whitebait.

West London

★**Troubadour** BAR
(☎020-7341 6333; www.troubadourlondon.com; 263-267 Old Brompton Rd, SW5; ⏰cafe 9am-midnight, club 8pm-12.30am or 2am Mon-Sat, to 11.30pm Sun; 📶; Ⓤ Earl's Court) On a comparable spiritual plane to Paris' Shakespeare and Company bookshop, this eccentric, time-warped and convivial boho bar-cafe has been serenading drinkers since 1954. Adele, Ed Sheeran, Joni Mitchell, Jimi Hendrix and Bob Dylan have performed here, and there's still live music (largely jazz and folk) most nights downstairs. A wide-ranging wine list, Sunday roasts and a pleasant rear garden complete the picture.

Windsor Castle PUB
(Map p106; ☎020-7243 8797; www.thewindsorcastlekensington.co.uk; 114 Campden Hill Rd, W11; ⏰noon-11pm Mon-Sat, to 10.30pm Sun; 📶; Ⓤ Notting Hill Gate) This classic tavern on the brow of Campden Hill Rd has history, nooks and charm on tap. Alongside a decent beer selection and a solid gastropub-style menu, it has a historic compartmentalised interior, a roaring fire (in winter), a delightful beer garden (in summer) and affable regulars (all seasons). In the old days, Windsor Castle was visible from the pub, hence the name.

Richmond, Kew & Hampton Court

City Barge PUB
(☎020-8994 2148; www.metropolitanpubcompany.com/our-pubs/the-city-barge; 27 Strand on the Green, W4; ⏰noon-11pm Mon-Thu, to midnight Fri, 10am-midnight Sat, 10am-10.30pm Sun; 📶; Ⓤ Gunnersbury) In a line of small riverside cottages facing wooded Oliver's Island (where Cromwell is alleged to have taken refuge), this excellent pub looks straight onto the muddy Thames. Its lineage to the 14th century would make it one of London's most ancient pubs. There are three open fires, drinkers spill outside in clement weather and a fine gastropub menu has taken hold.

White Cross PUB
(☎020-8940 6844; www.thewhitecrossrichmond.com; Water Lane, TW9; ⏰10am-11pm, to 10.30pm Sun; 📶; Ⓤ Richmond) The riverside location and fine food and ales make this bay-windowed pub – on the site of a former friary – a winner. There are entrances for low and high tides, but when the river is at its highest, Cholmondeley Walk along the Thames floods and the pub is out of bounds to those not willing to wade. Wellies are provided.

☆ Entertainment

Theatre

Donmar Warehouse THEATRE
(Map p80; ☎020-3282 3808; www.donmarwarehouse.com; 41 Earlham St, WC2; Ⓤ Covent Garden) The 250-seat Donmar Warehouse is London's 'thinking person's theatre'. With new artistic director Michael Longhurst, works in progress are more provocative and less celebrity-driven than traditional West End theatre.

Almeida THEATRE
(☎020-7359 4404; www.almeida.co.uk; Almeida St, N1; tickets £10-42.50; Ⓤ Highbury & Islington) Housed in a Grade II–listed Victorian building, this plush 325-seat theatre can be relied on for imaginative programming. Its emphasis is on new, up-and-coming talent. For theatre-goers aged 25 and under, £5 tickets (two per person) are available for select performances.

★**Bush Theatre** THEATRE
(☎020-8743 5050; www.bushtheatre.co.uk; 7 Uxbridge Rd, W12; ⊙10am-11pm Mon-Sat; Ⓤ Shepherd's Bush) Located in the former Passmore Edwards Public Library building, this West London theatre is renowned for encouraging new writing. Its success since 1972 is down to strong plays from the likes of Jonathan Harvey, Conor McPherson, Stephen Poliakoff, Caroline Horton and Tanya Ronder. The Holloway Theatre is the main space; the Studio is the smaller, 70-seat venue. There's an excellent **cafe and bar** (⊙10am-11pm Mon-Sat; 📶).

National Theatre THEATRE
(Map p98; ☎020-7452 3000; www.nationaltheatre.org.uk; Upper Ground, SE1; Ⓤ Waterloo) The nation's flagship theatre delivers up to 25 shows every year across its three venues inside this brutalist block. Even if you're not here for a show, you can explore the foyers, which contain a bookshop, restaurants, bars and exhibition spaces. Get behind the scenes on a tour, including going backstage, a deep-dive into the building's architecture and an experience with the costume team.

Royal Court Theatre THEATRE
(Map p100; ☎020-7565 5000; www.royalcourttheatre.com; Sloane Sq, SW1; tickets £12-38; Ⓤ Sloane Sq) Equally renowned for staging innovative new plays and old classics, the Royal Court is among London's most progressive theatres and has continued to foster major writing talent across the UK for over 60 years. There are two auditoriums: the main Jerwood Theatre Downstairs and the much-smaller studio Jerwood Theatre Upstairs.

Old Vic THEATRE
(Map p98; ☎0344 871 7628; www.oldvictheatre.com; The Cut, SE1; Ⓤ Waterloo) This 1000-seater nonprofit theatre celebrated its 200th season in 2018 and continues to bring eclectic programming occasionally bolstered by big-name actors, such as Daniel Radcliffe.

Young Vic THEATRE
(Map p98; ☎020-7922 2922; www.youngvic.org; 66 The Cut, SE1; ⊙box office 10am-6pm Mon-Sat; Ⓤ Southwark) This groundbreaking theatre is as much about showcasing and discovering new talent as it is about people discovering theatre. The Young Vic features actors, directors and plays from across the world, many tackling contemporary political and cultural issues, such as the death penalty, racism or corruption, and often blending dance and music with acting.

Bridge Theatre THEATRE
(Map p98; ☎0333 320 0051; https://bridgetheatre.co.uk; 3 Potters Fields Park, SE1; Ⓤ London Bridge) Opened in 2017 and London's first new major theatre in 80 years, Bridge Theatre seats 900 in a cool, modern space and focuses on new productions, with the occasional classic thrown in.

Arcola Theatre THEATRE
(☎020-7503 1646; www.arcolatheatre.com; 24 Ashwin St, E8; Ⓤ Dalston Junction) Dalston's a fair schlep from the West End, but drama buffs still flock to this innovative theatre for its adventurous and eclectic productions. A unique annual feature is **Grimeborn**, an opera festival focusing on lesser-known or new works – it's Dalston's answer to East Sussex's world-famous Glyndebourne opera festival, taking place around the same time (August).

Live Music

★**Royal Albert Hall** CONCERT VENUE
(Map p100; ☎0845 401 5034; 020-7589 8212; www.royalalberthall.com; Kensington Gore, SW7; Ⓤ South Kensington) This splendid Victorian concert hall hosts classical music, rock and other performances, but is famously the venue for the BBC-sponsored Proms. Booking is possible, but from mid-July to mid-September Promenaders queue for £5 standing tickets that go on sale one hour before curtain-up. Otherwise, the box office and prepaid-ticket collection counter are through door 12 (south side of the hall).

★**Scala** LIVE MUSIC
(Map p110; ☎020-7833 2022; www.scala.co.uk; 275 Pentonville Rd, N1; cover £10-35; Ⓤ King's Cross St Pancras) Opened in 1920 as a cutting-edge golden-age cinema, Scala slipped into porn-movie territory in the 1970s, only to be reborn as a club and live-music venue in the early 2000s. It's one of the top places in London to catch an intimate gig and is a great dance space, too, hosting a diverse range of club nights.

★**Ronnie Scott's** JAZZ
(Map p80; ☎020-7439 0747; www.ronniescotts.co.uk; 47 Frith St, W1; ⊙6pm-3am Mon-Sat, noon-4pm & 6.30pm-midnight Sun; Ⓤ Leicester Sq or Tottenham Court Rd) Ronnie Scott's jazz club opened in 1959 and became widely known

as Britain's best, hosting such luminaries as Miles Davis, Charlie Parker, Ella Fitzgerald, Count Basie and Sarah Vaughan. The club continues to build upon its formidable reputation by presenting a range of big names and new talent. Book in advance, or come for a more informal gig at **Upstairs @ Ronnie's**.

Roundhouse CONCERT VENUE
(Map p128; ☎0300 678 9222; www.roundhouse.org.uk; Chalk Farm Rd, NW1; Ⓤ Chalk Farm) Built as a railway repair shed in 1847, this unusual Grade II–listed round building became an arts centre in the 1960s and hosted legendary bands before falling into near-dereliction in 1983. Its 21st-century resurrection as a creative hub has been a great success and it now hosts everything from big-name concerts to dance, circuses, stand-up comedy, poetry slams and improvisation.

O2 Academy Brixton LIVE MUSIC
(☎020-7771 3000; https://academymusicgroup.com/o2academybrixton; 211 Stockwell Rd, SW9; ⓊBrixton) The O2 hosts club nights and gigs galore inside a 1920s art-deco theatre with a nearly 5000-person capacity. The sloped floor guarantees good views, though if you aren't dancing enough, the ground, sticky with beer spills, may glue you into place.

Cafe Oto LIVE MUSIC
(www.cafeoto.co.uk; 18-22 Ashwin St, E8; ⌚9.30am-late; 📶; Ⓤ Dalston Junction) Dedicating itself to promoting experimental and alternative musicians, this is Dalston's premier venue for music nerds to stroke their proverbial beards while listening to electronic bleeps, Japanese psychedelica or avant-folk. Set in a converted print warehouse, it's one of London's most idiosyncratic live-music venues. When there are no gigs on, it's open as a cafe-bar.

Vortex Jazz Club JAZZ
(☎020-7254 4097; www.vortexjazz.co.uk; 11 Gillett Sq, N16; ⌚8pm-midnight; Ⓡ Dalston Kingsland) With a fantastically varied menu of jazz, the Vortex hosts an outstanding line-up of musicians, singers and songwriters from the UK, the US, Europe, Africa and beyond. It's a small venue so make sure you book if there's an act you particularly fancy.

Cinemas

★Prince Charles Cinema CINEMA
(Map p80; ☎020-7494 3654; www.princecharlescinema.com; 7 Leicester Pl, WC2; Ⓤ Leicester Sq) The last independent theatre in the West End, Prince Charles Cinema is universally loved for its show-anything attitude. Singalongs and quote-a-longs (*Frozen*, *Elf* and *The Rocky Horror Picture Show* are perennial faves), all-nighter movie marathons (including PJ parties), and anniversary and special-format screenings regularly grace its listings. Arriving in costumed character is encouraged.

Electric Cinema CINEMA
(Map p106; ☎020-7908 9696; www.electriccinema.co.uk; 191 Portobello Rd, W11; adult £17.50-45, child £10; Ⓤ Ladbroke Grove) Having notched up its centenary in 2011, the Electric is one of the UK's oldest cinemas, now updated. Avail yourself of the luxurious leather armchairs, sofas, footstools and tables for food and drink in the auditorium, or select one of the six front-row double beds! Tickets are cheapest on Mondays.

BFI Southbank CINEMA
(Map p98; ☎020-7928 3232; https://whatson.bfi.org.uk; Belvedere Rd, SE1; ⌚9.45am-11pm; Ⓤ Waterloo) Tucked almost out of sight under the arches of Waterloo Bridge, the British Film Institute contains four cinemas that screen thousands of films each year (many art-house), a gallery devoted to the moving image, and a mediatheque where you can watch movie and TV highlights from the BFI National Archive.

Comedy

Comedy Store COMEDY
(Map p80; ☎0844 871 7699; www.thecomedystore.co.uk; 1a Oxendon St, SW1; Ⓤ Piccadilly Circus) This is one of the first (and some say one of the best) comedy clubs in London. The Comedy Store Players take the stage on Wednesday and Sunday nights, with the wonderful Josie Lawrence, a veteran of the scene, plus special guest comedians. On Thursdays, Fridays and Saturdays, Best in Stand Up features the best of London's comedy circuit.

Soho Theatre COMEDY
(Map p80; ☎020-7478 0100; https://sohotheatre.com; 21 Dean St, W1; tickets £8-25; Ⓤ Tottenham Court Rd) The Soho Theatre has developed a superb reputation for showcasing new comedy-writing talent as well as drama. It hosts top stand-up and sketch-based comedians, plus cabaret. At the time of research you could watch previous shows online.

SPORTING LONDON

You're very unlikely to land tickets to the FA Cup Final at Wembley Stadium or front-row seats for the Wimbledon finals, but there are plenty of ways to enjoy sport in London. You could find yourself watching the Oxford–Cambridge boat race (p119), cheering runners at the London Marathon or catching some park cricket in summer – there's lots on offer. Why not check out the impressive facilities in the Queen Elizabeth Olympic Park (p109), which hosts the (former Olympic) London Stadium, the stunning Aquatics Centre and the cutting-edge Velodrome.

Alternatively, take a tour of one of the capital's great sporting stadia:

Lord's (020-7616 8500; https://apps.lords.org/lords/tours-and-museum; St John's Wood Rd, NW8; tours adult/child £25/16; 4-6 tours daily; St John's Wood) The hallowed 'home of cricket', with a fascinating museum.

Wimbledon Lawn Tennis Museum (020-8946 6131; www.wimbledon.com/museum; Gate 4, Church Rd, SW19; adult/child £13/8, museum & tour £25/15; 10am-5pm, last admission 4.30pm; Wimbledon, Wimbledon, Wimbledon, Southfields) Chart the history of lawn tennis, and see Centre Court from the 360-degree viewing box.

Wembley Stadium (0800 169 9933; www.wembleystadium.com; tours adult/child £19/12; Wembley Park) The city's landmark national stadium, used for football test matches and mega concerts.

Twickenham Stadium (020-8892 8877; www.englandrugby.com/twickenham; 200 Whitton Rd, Twickenham, TW2; tours adult/child £25/15; Twickenham, Hounslow East) London's famous rugby union stadium, used for international test matches.

London Stadium (020-8522 6157; www.london-stadium.com; Queen Elizabeth Olympic Park, E20; tours adult/child £19/11; tours 10am-4.15pm, to 4.45pm Sat; Pudding Mill Lane) Built as the centrepiece stadium for the 2012 Olympics and now home to West Ham United FC.

Arsenal Emirates Stadium (020-7619 5003; www.arsenal.com/tours; Hornsey Rd, N7; self-guided tours adult/child £25/16, guided tours £40/20; 10am-5pm Mon-Fri, 9.30am-6pm Sat, 10am-4pm Sun; Holloway Rd) Offers both self-guided tours or tours led by former Arsenal players.

Stamford Bridge (0371 811 1955; www.chelseafc.com; Stamford Bridge, Fulham Rd, SW6; tours adult/child £24/15; museum 9.30am-6.30pm Jul & Aug, to 5.30pm Apr-Jun, to 5pm Sep-Mar; tours 10am-5pm Jul & Aug, to 4pm Apr-Jun, to 3pm Sep-Mar; Fulham Broadway) Home of Chelsea FC.

Classical Music

★Wigmore Hall CLASSICAL MUSIC

(Map p124; 020-7935 2141; www.wigmore-hall.org.uk; 36 Wigmore St, W1; Bond St) Wigmore Hall, built in 1901 as a piano showroom, is one of the best and most active classical-music venues in town, with more than 460 concerts a year. This isn't just because of its fantastic acoustics, beautiful Arts and Crafts–style cupola over the stage and great variety of concerts, but also because of the sheer quality of the performances.

Royal Festival Hall CONCERT VENUE

(Map p98; 020-3879 9555; www.southbankcentre.co.uk/venues/royal-festival-hall; Southbank Centre, Belvedere Rd, SE1; ; Waterloo) The 2700-capacity Royal Festival Hall is one of the best places in London to hear modern and classical music, poetry and spoken-word performances. The hall has four resident orchestras, including the **London Philharmonic Orchestra** and the **London Sinfonietta**.

Queen Elizabeth Hall LIVE PERFORMANCE

(Map p98; 020-3879 9555; www.southbankcentre.co.uk/venues/queen-elizabeth-hall; Southbank Centre, Belvedere Rd, SE1; Waterloo) Queen Elizabeth Hall has a full programme of gigs, chamber orchestras, dance performances and opera throughout the year, on a smaller scale than the nearby Royal Festival Hall that's also part of Southbank Centre (p97).

The space reopened in 2018 after a three-year refurb. In summer, don't miss the plant-strewn cafe-bar on the **roof** (noon-9pm Apr–mid-Jun & Sep-Oct, 10am-10.30pm mid-Jun–Aug).

Sport

Wimbledon Championships SPECTATOR SPORT
(020-8944 1066; www.wimbledon.com; Church Rd, SW19; grounds £8-25, tickets £33-225; 493, Southfields) For a few weeks each June and July, the sporting world's attention is fixed on the quiet southern suburb of Wimbledon, as it has been since 1877. Most show-court tickets for the Wimbledon Championships are allocated through public ballot, applications for which begin in early August of the preceding year and close at the end of December.

Opera & Dance

Royal Opera House OPERA
(Map p80; 020-7304 4000; www.roh.org.uk; Bow St, WC2; gift shop & cafe from 10am; Covent Garden) Opera and ballet have a fantastic setting on Covent Garden Piazza, and a night here is a sumptuous affair. Although the programme has modern influences, the main attractions are still the classic productions with their world-class performers. A three-year, £50-million revamp finished in October 2018, with new areas open to the non-ticketed public for the first time, including the cafe and bar.

Sadler's Wells DANCE
(Map p110; 020-7863 8000; www.sadlerswells.com; Rosebery Ave, EC1; Angel) A glittering modern venue that was first established in 1683, Sadler's Wells is the most eclectic modern-dance and ballet venue in town, with experimental dance shows of all genres and from all corners of the globe. The Lilian Baylis Studio stages smaller productions.

English National Opera OPERA
(ENO; Map p80; 020-7845 9300; www.eno.org; St Martin's Lane, WC2; Leicester Sq) The English National Opera is celebrated for making opera modern and more accessible, as all productions are sung in English. It's based at the impressive London Coliseum, built in 1904 and lovingly restored a century later. The **English National Ballet** also holds regular performances at the Coliseum. Tickets range from £12 to £125.

Barbican Centre PERFORMING ARTS
(Map p90; 020-7638 8891; www.barbican.org.uk; Silk St, EC2; box office 10am-9pm Mon-Sat, noon-8pm Sun; Barbican) You'll get as lost in the astounding programme as you will in the labyrinthine brutalist building. Home to the **London Symphony Orchestra**, the **BBC Symphony Orchestra** and the **Royal Shakespeare Company**, the Barbican Centre is the City's premier cultural venue. It hosts concerts, theatre and dance performances, and screens indie films and Hollywood blockbusters at the cinema on Beech St.

Shopping

West End

★**Fortnum & Mason** DEPARTMENT STORE
(Map p80; 020-7734 8040; www.fortnumandmason.com; 181 Piccadilly, W1; 10am-9pm Mon-Sat, 11.30am-6pm Sun; Green Park or Piccadilly Circus) With its classic eau-de-Nil (pale green) colour scheme, the 'Queen's grocery store' (established in 1707) refuses to yield to modern times. Its staff – both men and women – still wear old-fashioned tailcoats, and its glamorous food hall is supplied with hampers, marmalade and speciality teas. Stop for a spot of afternoon tea at the **Diamond Jubilee Tea Salon**, visited by Queen Elizabeth II in 2012.

★**Foyles** BOOKS
(Map p80; 020-7434 1574; www.foyles.co.uk; 107 Charing Cross Rd, WC2; 9.30am-9pm Mon-Sat, noon-6pm Sun; Tottenham Court Rd) London's most legendary bookshop, where you can find even the most obscure titles. Once synonymous with chaos, Foyles got its act together and now this carefully designed store is a joy to explore. The cafe is on the 5th floor, plus a small gallery for art exhibitions. Grant & Cutler, the UK's largest foreign-language bookseller, is on the 4th floor.

Hamleys TOYS
(Map p80; 0371 704 1977; www.hamleys.com; 188-196 Regent St, W1; 10am-9pm Mon-Fri, from 9.30am Sat, noon-6pm Sun; ; Oxford Circus) The biggest and oldest toy emporium in the world, Hamleys houses six floors of fun for kids of all ages, from the basement's Star Wars and Harry Potter collections up to Lego World, a sweet shop and tiny cafe

LOCAL KNOWLEDGE

LONDON'S MARKETS

Perhaps the biggest shopping draw for visitors is the capital's famed markets. A treasure trove of small designers, unique jewellery pieces, original framed photographs and posters, colourful vintage pieces and bric-a-brac, they are the antidote to impersonal, carbon-copy shopping centres.

Camden Market (Map p138; www.camdenmarket.com; Camden High St, NW1; ⏲10am-late; Ⓤ Camden Town, Chalk Farm) London's busiest and best-known market may have stopped being cutting-edge several thousand cheap leather jackets ago, but it remains one of London's most popular attractions. There are three main market areas – Buck Street Market, Camden Lock Market and Stables Market – extending most of the way from Camden Town tube station to Chalk Farm tube station. You'll find a bit of everything: clothes (of varying quality) in profusion, bags, jewellery, arts and crafts, candles, incense and myriad decorative bits and pieces.

Sunday Upmarket (Map p130; ☎020-7770 6028; www.sundayupmarket.co.uk; Old Truman Brewery, 91 Brick Lane, E1; ⏲11am-5.30pm Sat, 10am-6pm Sun; Ⓤ Shoreditch High St) Open all weekend, this lively market in the Old Truman Brewery offers a mix of young designers, food stalls in the Boiler House, antiques and bric-a-brac, and a huge range of vintage clothes in the basement across the street.

Old Spitalfields Market (Map p130; www.oldspitalfieldsmarket.com; Commercial St, E1; ⏲10am-8pm, to 6pm Sat, to 5pm Sun; Ⓤ Liverpool St, Shoreditch High St, Aldgate East) Traders have been hawking their wares here since 1638 and it's still one of London's best markets. Sundays are the biggest and best days, but Thursdays are good for antiques and Fridays for independent fashion. There are plenty of food stalls too.

Smithfield Market (Map p90; ☎020-7248 3151; www.smithfieldmarket.com; Charterhouse St, EC1; ⏲2-10am Mon-Fri; Ⓤ Farringdon) This is central London's last surviving meat market, and though most of the transactions today are wholesale, visitors are invited to shop too; arrive before 7am to see it in full swing. The market has been at this location since the 12th century, but the current colourful building was designed in 1868 by Horace Jones.

Leadenhall Market (Map p90; www.leadenhallmarket.co.uk; Gracechurch St, EC3; ⏲public areas 24hr; Ⓤ Bank) The ancient Romans had their forum on this site, but this covered shopping arcade harks back to the Victorian era, with cobblestones underfoot and 19th-century ironwork linking its shops, restaurants and pubs. The market appears as Diagon Alley in *Harry Potter and the Philosopher's Stone*.

Borough Market (Map p98; https://boroughmarket.org.uk; 8 Southwark St, SE1; ⏲full market 10am-5pm Wed & Thu, to 6pm Fri, 8am-5pm Sat, limited market 10am-5pm Mon & Tue; Ⓤ London Bridge) Located in this spot since the 13th century (possibly since 1014), 'London's Larder' is always overflowing with food lovers, gastronomes and Londoners in search of dinner inspiration. The full market runs from Wednesday to Saturday, but some traders and takeaway stalls also open Mondays and Tuesdays.

Brick Lane Market (Map p130; ☎020-7364 1717; www.visitbricklane.org; Brick Lane, E1; ⏲10am-5pm Sun; Ⓤ Shoreditch High St) Spilling out into its surrounding streets, this irrepressibly vibrant market fills a vast area with household goods, bric-a-brac, secondhand clothes, cheap fashion and ethnic food.

Greenwich Market (www.greenwichmarket.london; College Approach, SE10; ⏲10am-5.30pm; Ⓤ Cutty Sark) This small market has a different theme every day. On Tuesdays, Thursdays and Fridays, you'll find vintage, antiques and collectables. Wednesdays, Fridays and weekends are the best days for artists, indie designers and crafts.

South Bank Book Market (Map p98; Queen's Walk, SE1; ⏲11am-7pm, shorter hours in winter; Ⓤ Waterloo) Prints and secondhand books under the arches of Waterloo Bridge.

on the 5th floor. Staff on each level have opened the packaging and are playing with everything from boomerangs to bubbles. Kids will happily spend hours here planning their Santa letters.

Liberty DEPARTMENT STORE
(Map p80; 020-7734 1234; www.libertylondon.com; Regent St, entrance on Great Marlborough St, W1; 10am-8pm Mon-Sat, 11.30am-6pm Sun; ; Oxford Circus) One of London's most recognisable shops, Liberty department store has a white-and-wood-beam Tudor Revival facade that lures shoppers in to browse luxury contemporary fashion, homewares, cosmetics and accessories, all at sky-high prices. Liberty is known for its fabrics and has a full haberdashery department; a classic London gift or souvenir is a Liberty fabric print, especially in the form of a scarf.

★**Daunt Books** BOOKS
(Map p124; 020-7224 2295; www.dauntbooks.co.uk; 83 Marylebone High St, W1; 9am-7.30pm Mon-Sat, 11am-6pm Sun; Baker St) An original Edwardian bookshop, with oak panels, galleries and gorgeous skylights, Daunt is one of London's loveliest bookshops. There are several Daunt outlets but none as gorgeous as this. Browse its travel, general fiction and nonfiction titles over two floors.

Blade Rubber Stamps ARTS & CRAFTS
(Map p80; 020-7831 4242; www.bladerubberstamps.co.uk; 12 Bury Pl, WC1; 10.30am-6pm Mon-Sat, 11.30am-4.30pm Sun; Holborn) This specialist stationary shop stocks just about every wooden-handled rubber stamp you care to imagine: from London icons like phone boxes and the Houses of Parliament to landscapes, planets, rockets and Christmas stamps. You can have one made to your design or DIY with a stamp-making kit. They make excellent lightweight gifts!

Sister Ray MUSIC
(Map p80; 020-7734 3297; www.sisterray.co.uk; 75 Berwick St, W1; 10am-8pm Mon-Sat, noon-6pm Sun; Oxford Circus or Tottenham Court Rd) A stalwart of the Soho record-shop scene, specialising in a collection that BBC 1's John Peel would be proud of: innovative, experimental and indie music. Staff are knowledgeable, and the tunes are banging (that means good, not painful).

City of London

London Silver Vaults ANTIQUES
(Map p90; 020-7242 3844; https://silvervaultslondon.com; 53-64 Chancery Lane, WC2; 9am-5.30pm Mon-Fri, to 1pm Sat; Chancery Lane) For one of London's oddest shopping experiences, pass through security and descend 12m into the windowless subterranean depths of the London Silver Vaults, which house the largest collection of silver for sale in the world. The 30-odd independently owned shops, each entered through thick bank-safe-style doors, offer vintage Victorian and Georgian silver, cufflinks, candleholders, goblets and much more.

Kensington & Hyde Park

★**John Sandoe Books** BOOKS
(Map p100; 020-7589 9473; www.johnsandoe.com; 10 Blacklands Tce, SW3; 9.30am-6.30pm Mon-Sat, 11am-5pm Sun; Sloane Sq) Steeped in literary charm and a perfect antidote to impersonal book superstores, this three-storey bookshop in an 18th-century premises inhabits its own universe. A treasure trove of literary gems and hidden surprises, it's been in business for over six decades. Loyal customers swear by it, and knowledgeable booksellers spill forth with well-read pointers and helpful advice.

Illustrated books that are hard to find elsewhere are a particular strong point, as are privately published works that larger bookshops would pass on. Should you have the money and the inclination, staff can even help you create your own personal home library.

★**Harrods** DEPARTMENT STORE
(Map p100; 020-7730 1234; www.harrods.com; 87-135 Brompton Rd, SW1; 10am-9pm Mon-Sat, 11.30am-6pm Sun; Knightsbridge) Garish and stylish in equal measure, perennially crowded Harrods is an obligatory stop for visitors, from the cash-strapped to the big spenders. The stock is astonishing, as are many of the price tags. Many visitors don't make it past the ground floor where designer bags, myriad scents from the perfume hall and the mouthwatering counters of the food hall provide plenty of entertainment.

Conran Shop DESIGN
(Map p100; 020-7589 7401; www.conranshop.co.uk; Michelin House, 81 Fulham Rd, SW3; 10am-6pm Mon, Tue & Fri, to 7pm Wed & Thu, to 6.30pm

Sat, noon-6pm Sun; Ⓤ South Kensington) The original design store (going strong since 1987), the Conran Shop is a treasure trove of beautiful things – from radios to sunglasses, kitchenware to children's toys and books, bathroom accessories to greeting cards. Browsing bliss. Spare some time to peruse the magnificent art nouveau/deco **Michelin House** the shop is housed in.

Clerkenwell, Shoreditch & Spitalfields

Libreria BOOKS
(Map p130; https://libreria.io; 65 Hanbury St, E1; ⊙10am-6pm Tue & Wed, to 8pm Thu-Sat, 11am-6pm Sun; Ⓤ Aldgate East) Mismatched vintage reading lamps spotlight the floor-to-ceiling canary-yellow shelves at this delightful indie bookshop, where titles are arranged according to themes like 'wanderlust', 'enchantment for the disenchanted', and 'mothers, madonnas and whores'. Cleverly placed mirrors add to the labyrinthine wonder of the space, which is punctuated with mid-century furniture that invites repose and quiet contemplation.

Rough Trade East MUSIC
(Map p130; ☎020-7392 7788; www.roughtrade.com; Old Truman Brewery, 91 Brick Lane, E1; ⊙9am-9pm Mon-Thu, to 8pm Fri, 10am-8pm Sat, 11am-7pm Sun; Ⓤ Shoreditch High St) It's no longer directly associated with the legendary record label (home to the Smiths, the Libertines and the Strokes, among others), but this huge record shop is still tops for picking up indie, soul, electronica and alternative music. In addition to an impressive selection of CDs and vinyl, it also dispenses coffee and stages gigs and artist signings.

East London

★Broadway Market MARKET
(www.broadwaymarket.co.uk; Broadway Market, E8; ⊙9am-5pm Sat; 394) There's been a market down here since the late 19th century, but the focus these days is artisanal food, handmade gifts and unique clothing. Boutique shops along both sides of the street (open seven days a week) do a roaring trade with coffee-drinking shoppers. Stock up on edible treats then head to **London Fields** (Richmond Rd, E8; Ⓤ London Fields) for a picnic.

Beyond Retro VINTAGE
(☎020-7729 9001; www.beyondretro.com; 110-112 Cheshire St, E2; ⊙11am-7pm Mon-Sat, 11.30am-6pm Sun; Ⓤ Shoreditch High St) A huge selection of vintage clothes, including wigs, shoes, jackets and sunglasses, expertly slung together in a lofty warehouse.

North London

★Camden Passage Market ANTIQUES
(www.camdenpassageislington.co.uk; Camden Passage, N1; ⊙9am-6pm Wed & Sat; Ⓤ Angel) Not to be confused with Camden Market (p144), Camden Passage is a pretty cobbled lane in Islington lined with antique stores, vintage-clothing boutiques and cafes. Scattered along the lane are three not-so-separate market areas. The main market days are Wednesday and Saturday, though some open on Thursday, Friday and Sunday as well, and the shops are open all week.

Harry Potter Shop at Platform 9¾ GIFTS & SOUVENIRS
(Map p110; ☎020-3427 4200; www.harrypotterplatform934.com; King's Cross Station, N1; ⊙8am-10pm Mon-Sat, 9am-10pm Sun; Ⓤ King's Cross St Pancras) Pottermania refuses to die down and Diagon Alley remains impossible to find, but if you have junior witches and wizards seeking a wand of their own, take the family directly to King's Cross Station. This little wood-panelled store also stocks jumpers sporting the colours of Hogwarts' four houses (Gryffindor having pride of place) and assorted merchandise, including, of course, the books.

Information

DANGERS & ANNOYANCES

London is a fairly safe city for its size, but exercise common sense.

- Occasional terror attacks have afflicted London over the last few decades, but risks to individual visitors are remote.
- Keep a hand on your handbag/wallet, especially in bars and nightclubs, and in crowded areas such as the Underground.
- Be discreet with your tablet/smartphone – snatch-and-run happens all too often.
- When crossing the road look out for silent high-speed cyclists.
- Victims of rape and sexual abuse can contact **Rape Crisis England & Wales** (☎0808 802 9999, www.rapecrisis.org.uk); anyone in emotional distress contact **Samaritans** (☎116 123 toll-free, 24 hours; www.samaritans.org).

EMERGENCY

London area code	020
International access code	00
Police, fire or ambulance emergency	999
Non-emergency police	101

INTERNET ACCESS

- Virtually every London hotel provides free wi-fi now.
- Numerous cafes and restaurants offer free wi-fi to customers, as do cultural venues such as the Barbican or the Southbank Centre.
- Street level wi-fi access is available in some areas, look for signs.
- Major train stations, airport terminals and some of the 270 Underground stations and 79 Overground stations offer free wi-fi (though signals are often weak).

MEDICAL SERVICES

A number of London hospitals have 24-hour accident and emergency departments. However, in an emergency just call an ambulance.

Charing Cross Hospital (020-3311 1234; www.imperial.nhs.uk/charingcross; Fulham Palace Rd, W6; U Hammersmith) Hammersmith

Chelsea & Westminster Hospital (020-3315 8000; www.chelwest.nhs.uk; 369 Fulham Rd, SW10; 14 or 414, U South Kensington, Fulham Broadway) Fulham

Guy's & St Thomas' Hospital (020-7188 7188; www.guysandstthomas.nhs.uk; Westminster Bridge Rd, SE1; U Waterloo or Westminster) Waterloo

Royal Free Hospital (020-7794 0500; www.royalfree.nhs.uk; Pond St, NW3; U Belsize Park, Hampstead Heath) Hampstead

Royal London Hospital (020-7377 7000; www.bartshealth.nhs.uk; Whitechapel Rd, E1; U Whitechapel) Whitechapel (includes children's hospital)

University College London Hospital (020-3456 7890; www.uclh.nhs.uk; 235 Euston Rd, NW1; U Warren St or Euston Sq) Euston

TOURIST INFORMATION

Visit London (www.visitlondon.com) has info on special events, tours, accommodation, eating, theatre, shopping etc.

Getting There & Away

AIR

The city has six airports: Heathrow, which is the largest, to the west; Gatwick to the south; Stansted to the northeast; Luton to the northwest; London City in the Docklands and London Southend.

BUS

Victoria Coach Station (Map p100; 164 Buckingham Palace Rd, SW1; U Victoria) Long-distance and international buses arrive and depart from Victoria Coach Station, close to the Victoria Tube and rail stations.

TRAIN

Main national rail routes are served by a variety of private train-operating companies. Tickets are not cheap, but if you book ahead you can get better deals. If you're planning to do a lot of train travel, look into the cost of a Rail Card and how much you may save, especially if travelling in a family group. Check the website of **National Rail** (www.nationalrail.co.uk) for timetables, fares and Rail Cards.

Eurostar (www.eurostar.com) High-speed passenger rail service linking London St Pancras International with Paris, Brussels, Amsterdam and Marseilles, with up to 19 daily departures. Fares vary greatly, from £29 for a one-way standard-class ticket to around £245 each way for a fully flexible business premier ticket (prices based on return journeys). Sign up to Eurostar social media channels or email to get notifications of special deals and sales.

Getting Around

TO/FROM THE AIRPORTS

Heathrow

The Underground, commonly referred to as 'the Tube', is the cheapest way of getting anywhere from Heathrow (approximately one hour) and trains depart every three to nine minutes. It runs from just after 5am to 11.45pm (11.28pm Sunday); to the airport it runs from 5.47am to 12.32am (11.38pm Sunday). The Tube runs all night Friday and Saturday on this line, with reduced frequency. Buy a local Oyster card (reusable charge card) at Heathrow Tube station. The ticket machines are fairly simple to use and issue cards for £5 (refundable when you return them on departure).

Heathrow Express (www.heathrowexpress.com; one way/return £25/37, children free;), every 15 minutes, and **Heathrow Connect** (0343 222 1234; www.tfl.gov.uk; adult single/open return £10.20/12.50), every 30 minutes, trains link Heathrow with Paddington train station. Heathrow Express trains take a mere 15 minutes to reach Paddington. Trains on each service run from around 5am to between 11pm and midnight.

National Express (www.nationalexpress.com) coaches (one way from £6, 40 to 90 minutes, every 30 minutes to one hour) link Heathrow

OYSTER CARD

The cheapest way to get around London is with an **Oyster Card**, a smart card on which you store credit as well as Travelcards valid for periods from a day to a year. Oyster Cards are valid across the entire public transport network in London, and fares are lower than standard ones. If you make several journeys in a day, the total is capped at the appropriate Travelcard rate (peak or off-peak).

Oyster Cards can be bought (£5 refundable deposit required) and topped up at any Underground station, travel information centre or shop displaying the Oyster logo. To get your deposit back along with any remaining credit, simply return your Oyster Card at a ticket booth.

All you need to do when entering a station is touch your card on a reader (which has a yellow circle with the image of an Oyster Card on it) and then touch again on your way out. For bus journeys, you only need to touch once upon boarding. Note that some train stations don't have exit turnstiles, so you will need to tap out on the reader before leaving the station; if you forget, you will be hugely overcharged.

Contactless payment cards (which do not require chip and pin or a signature) are subject to the same Oyster fares, but foreign visitors should bear in mind the cost of card transactions.

Central bus station with Victoria coach station. The first bus leaves Heathrow Central bus station (at Terminals 2 and 3) at 4.20am, with the last departure at 10.05pm. The first bus leaves Victoria at 1am, the last at around midnight.

If you arrive very late, the **N9 bus** (£1.50, 1¼ hours, every 20 minutes) connects Heathrow Central bus station (and Heathrow Terminal 5) with central London, terminating at Aldwych.

A metered black-cab trip to/from central London will cost between £50 and £100 and take 45 minutes to an hour, depending on traffic.

Ride-share services, such as Uber, require organising a meeting point near the airport exit directly with your driver; problematic if you're relying on airport wi-fi.

Gatwick

National Rail (www.nationalrail.co.uk) Regular train services to/from London Bridge (30 to 45 minutes, every 15 to 30 minutes), London King's Cross (55 minutes, every 15 to 30 minutes) and Victoria (30 to 50 minutes, every 10 to 15 minutes) run almost all night. Fares vary depending on the time, route, company (Southern or Thameslink) and class you take. Ticket machines are near the airport exit to the train station or pay with an Oyster Card, or contactless payment card.

Gatwick Express (www.gatwickexpress.com; one-way/return adult £19.90/36.70, child £9.95/18.35, under 5yrs free) Trains run every 15 minutes from the station near the Gatwick South Terminal to Victoria. From the airport, there are services between 6am and 11pm. From Victoria, they leave between 5am and 10.44pm. The journey takes 30 minutes; book online for the slightly cheaper fares.

National Express (www.nationalexpress.com) Coaches run throughout the day from Gatwick to Victoria coach station (one way from £10). Services depart hourly around the clock. Journey time is between 80 minutes and two hours, depending on traffic.

EasyBus (www.easybus.com) Runs 13-seater minibuses to Gatwick every 15 to 20 minutes on several routes, including from Earl's Court/West Brompton and Victoria coach station (one way from £2 if you book ahead online). The service runs around the clock. The journey time averages 75 minutes; it must be booked in advance.

Taxi A metered black-cab trip to/from central London costs around £100 and takes just over an hour. Minicabs or ride-share taxis are usually, but not always, cheaper.

Stansted

Stansted Express (☎ 0345 600 7245; www.stanstedexpress.com; one-way/return £19.40/30.70) Rail service (45 minutes, every 15 to 30 minutes) linking the airport with Liverpool St station via Tottenham Hale (which also has good Tube connections). From the airport, the first train leaves at 5.30am, the last at 12.30am. Trains depart Liverpool St station from 4.40am (on some days at 3.40am) to 11.25pm.

National Express (www.nationalexpress.com) Coaches run around the clock, offering 200 services per day.

Airbus A6 (☎ 0871 781 8181; www.nationalexpress.com; one way from £10) Runs to Westminster (around one hour to 1½ hours, every 20 minutes) via Marble Arch, Paddington, Baker St and Golders Green. **Airbus A7** (☎ 0871 781 8181; www.nationalexpress.com; one way from

£10) also runs to Victoria coach station (around one hour to 1½ hours, every 20 minutes), via Waterloo and Southwark. **Airbus A8** (☎ 0871 781 8181; www.nationalexpress.com; one way from £7) runs to Liverpool St station (60 to 80 minutes, every 30 minutes), via Bethnal Green and Shoreditch High St. **Airbus A9** (one-way from £7, 50 minutes) goes to London Stratford.

Airport Bus Express (www.airportbusexpress.co.uk; one-way from £8) Runs every 30 minutes to Victoria coach station, Baker Street, Liverpool St and London Stratford.

EasyBus (www.easybus.com) Runs services to Victoria coach station via Waterloo station every 15 minutes, or Liverpool St station via London Stratford. The total journey to central London (one-way from £2) takes 1¾ hours.

Terravision (www.terravision.eu) Coaches link Stansted to Liverpool St station (one-way from £7, 75 minutes) and Victoria coach station (from £7, two hours) every 20 to 40 minutes between 6am and 1am.

London City

Docklands Light Railway (DLR; www.tfl.gov.uk/dlr) stops at the London City Airport station (zone 3). Trains depart every eight to 10 minutes from just after 5.30am to 12.15am Monday to Saturday, and 7am to 11.15pm Sunday. The journey to Bank takes just over 20 minutes.

Luton

National Rail (www.nationalrail.co.uk) Has 24-hour services (one-way from £16.70, 35 to 50 minutes, regular departures during peak times) from London St Pancras International to Luton Airport Parkway station, from where an airport shuttle bus (one-way/return £2.40/3.80, half-price for five- to 15-year-olds, kids under five ride for free) will take you to the airport in 10 minutes. Cash or contactless payment cards are accepted on the shuttle bus.

Airbus A1 (www.nationalexpress.com; one way if booked online from £7) Runs over 60 times daily around the clock to Victoria coach station, via Portman Sq, Baker St, St John's Wood, Finchley Rd and Golders Green. It takes around one to 1½ hours.

Green Line Bus 757 (Map p100; ☎ 0344 800 4411; www.greenline.co.uk; one way/return £11.50/17.50) Runs to Luton Airport from Victoria coach station every 30 minutes on a 24-hour service via Marble Arch, Baker St, Finchley Rd and Brent Cross. The journey takes 75 to 90 minutes.

London Southend

Trains run to/from a purpose-built station at the airport (adult/child £17.80/8.90), making connecting to London Liverpool St or Stratford station an easy one-hour journey. Six trains run per hour during peak times, fewer off-peak. The first train from Liverpool St leaves at 4.30am to meet early-morning flight departures, and the last train leaves at 11.59pm.

Flight delays or any procrastinating will mean you're in a fix after midnight. It's either an expensive taxi ride (£110, but can be split with others, of course) or an airport hotel. Phone **Andrews Taxis** (01702 200 000), currently the only option at this hour.

BICYCLE

London's main cycle-hire scheme is called **Santander Cycles** (☎ 0343 222 6666; www.tfl.gov.uk/modes/cycling/santander-cycles). The bikes have proven as popular with visitors as with Londoners.

The idea is simple: pick up a bike from one of the 750 (and counting) docking stations dotted around the capital; cycle; drop it off at another docking station.

The access fee is £2 for 24 hours. All you need is a credit or debit card. The first 30 minutes are free; it's £2 for any additional period of 30 minutes, to keep you regularly docking the bikes.

You can take as many bikes as you like during your access period (24 hours), leaving five minutes between each trip.

The pricing structure is designed to encourage short journeys rather than longer rentals; for those, go to a hire company. You'll also find that although easy to ride, the bikes only have three gears and are quite heavy. You must be aged 18 to buy access and at least 14 to ride a bike.

Alternatively, Uber's bike-share scheme **Jump** (www.jump.com) has been superseded by **Beryl Bikes** (https://beryl.cc/bikeshare/london) and **Lime Scooters** (www.li.me/en-us/home). There's likely to be an even newer option for cycling, scootering, e-biking or hovercrafting by the time you visit.

CAR

London has a congestion charge in place to reduce the traffic and pollution in the city centre. The charge zone begins at Euston and Pentonville Rds to the north, Park Lane to the west, Tower Bridge to the east, and Elephant and Castle and Vauxhall Bridge Rd to the south. As you enter the zone, you will see a large white 'C' in a red circle on signs and painted on the road.

If you enter the zone between 7am and 6pm Monday to Friday (excluding public holidays), you must pay the £11.50 charge (payable in advance or on the day) or £14 on the first charging day after travel to avoid receiving a fine (£160, or £80 if paid within 14 days).

In addition, if your car is not a new cleaner greener model, the Ultra Low Emission Zone (ULEZ) charge needs to be paid in the same zone 24/7. You can pay online or over the phone. For full details, see the TFL website (www.tfl.gov.uk).

PUBLIC TRANSPORT

Boat

Several companies operate along the River Thames; only **Thames Clippers** (www.thamesclippers.com; one way adult/child £8.70/4.35) really offers commuter services, however. It's fast, pleasant and you're almost always guaranteed a seat and a view. All boats are fully wheelchair-accessible and all piers are wheelchair-accessible apart from Cadogan Pier, Wandsworth Riverside Quarter Pier and London Bridge City Pier.

Thames Clippers boats run regular services between Embankment, Waterloo (London Eye), Blackfriars, Bankside (Shakespeare's Globe), London Bridge, Tower Bridge, Canary Wharf, Greenwich, North Greenwich and Woolwich piers from 6.28am to 11.38pm (from 8.10am to 11.20pm on weekends).

Thames Clippers River Roamer tickets (adult/child £17.80/8.90) give the freedom to hop on and off boats on most routes all day. Book online for the discounted fare; only piers with a ticket booth accept cash payments.

You can also get a discount if you're a pay-as-you-go Oyster Card holder or Travelcard holder (paper ticket or on Oyster Card). Children under five travel free on most boats.

Between April and October, Hampton Court Palace can be reached by boat on the 22-mile route along the Thames from Westminster Pier in central London (via Kew and Richmond). The trip can take up to four hours, depending on the tide. Boats are run by **Westminster Passenger Services Association** (www.wpsa.co.uk; one-way/return adult £19/27, child £9.50/13.50).

The London Waterbus Company (p118) runs canal boats between Camden Lock and Little Venice.

Bus

London's ubiquitous red double-decker buses afford great views of the city, but be aware that the going can be slow, thanks to traffic jams and dozens of commuters getting on and off at every stop.

There are excellent bus maps at every stop detailing all routes and destinations served from that particular area (generally a few bus stops within a two- to three-minute walk, shown on a local map).

Bus services normally operate from 5am to 11.30pm. Many bus stops have LED displays listing bus arrival times, but downloading an app such as Citymapper to your smartphone is the most effective way to keep track of when your next bus is due.

Almost all buses are now wheelchair- and pram-accessible, lowering to the pavement with an automated ramp facility – you'll need to board at the middle doors and touch on with your Oyster Card when you can. Other passengers are mostly patient and courteous when assisting people on and off the bus with items like prams or large suitcases.

Cash cannot be used on London's buses. You must pay with an Oyster Card, Travelcard or a contactless payment card. Bus fares are a flat £1.50, no matter the distance travelled. If you don't have enough credit on your Oyster Card for a £1.50 bus fare, you can make the journey (and go into the black) but must top up your credit before your Oyster Card will work again.

Children aged under 11 travel free; 11- to 15-year-olds travel half-price if registered on an accompanying adult's Oyster Card on the Young Visitor Discount (register at Zone 1 or Heathrow Tube stations).

- More than 50 night-bus routes (prefixed with the letter 'N') run from around 11.30pm to 5am.
- There are also another 60 bus routes operating 24 hours; the frequency decreases between 11pm and 5am.
- Oxford Circus, Tottenham Court Rd and Trafalgar Sq are the main hubs for night routes.
- Night buses can be infrequent and stop only on request, so remember to ring for your stop.

Underground, DLR & Overground

The London Underground ('the Tube'; 11 colour-coded lines) is part of an integrated-transport system that also includes the Docklands Light Railway (DLR; www.tfl.gov.uk/dlr; a driverless train operating in the eastern part of the city) and Overground network (mostly outside of Zone 1 and sometimes underground). Despite the never-ending upgrades and 'engineering works' requiring weekend closures and escalators out of action, it is overall the quickest and easiest way of getting around the city.

The Tube runs roughly 5am to 1am, but when your last train departs varies by line and the day of the week. Apps like TfL Go (www.tfl.gov.uk/maps_/tfl-go) and CityMapper (www.citymapper.com) will give you the most up-to-date information. Several lines (the Victoria and Jubilee lines, plus most of the Piccadilly, Central and Northern lines) run all night on Friday and Saturday to get revellers home (on what is called the 'Night Tube'), with trains every 10 minutes or so. Fares are off-peak.

During weekend closures, schedules, maps and alternative route suggestions are posted in every station, and staff are at hand to help redirect you.

Some stations, most famously Leicester Sq and Covent Garden, are much closer in reality than they appear on the map.

Not all Tube stations are fully step-free and are therefore inaccessible to travellers with prams, wheelchairs and even heavy luggage. Stops that have lifts are marked on the Tube map with a wheelchair symbol so you can plan your journey accordingly. Station staff will assist with a portable ramp to enable wheelchair users to board trains safely.

TAXI

Black Cabs

The black cab is as much a feature of the London cityscape as the red double-decker bus. Licensed black-cab drivers have The Knowledge, acquired over three to five years of rigorous training and a series of exams. They are supposed to know 25,000 streets within a 6-mile radius of Charing Cross/Trafalgar Sq and the 100 most-visited spots of the moment, including clubs and restaurants.

➡ Cabs are available for hire when the yellow sign above the windscreen is lit; just stick your arm out to signal one.

➡ All are supposed to be wheelchair-accessible but experiences reported on the ground belie this claim.

➡ Fares are metered, with the flagfall charge of £2.60 (covering the first 235m during a weekday), rising by increments of 20p for each subsequent 117m.

➡ Fares are more expensive in the evening and overnight.

➡ You can tip taxi drivers up to 10%, but most Londoners simply round up to the nearest pound.

➡ Apps such as **Gett** (https://gett.com) use your smartphone's GPS to locate the nearest black cab. You only pay the metered fare.

➡ **ComCab** (☎ 020-7908 0271; www.comcab-london.co.uk) operates one of the largest fleets of black cabs in town.

Minicabs

➡ Minicabs, which are licensed, are (usually) cheaper competitors to black cabs.

➡ Unlike black cabs, minicabs cannot legally be hailed on the street; they must be hired by phone or directly from one of the minicab offices (every high street has at least one).

➡ Minicabs don't have meters; there's usually a fare set by the dispatcher. Make sure you ask before setting off.

➡ Your hotel or host will be able to recommend a reputable minicab company in the neighbourhood. Alternatively, phone a large 24-hour operator such as **Addison Lee** (www.addisonlee.com).

➡ Ride-share apps such as **Uber** (www.uber.com) allow you to book a ride easily

AT A GLANCE

POPULATION
Kent: 1,846,000

OLDEST CASTLES
Pevensey Castle, Leeds Castle, Dover Castle, Arundel Castle

BEST VIEWS
Box Hill (p183)

BEST SEAFOOD
Angela's (p162)

BEST PUB
Fordwich Arms (p159)

WHEN TO GO

Apr & May
The hiking season commences for tackling the South Downs Way.

Jun
Visitors revel in frilly Victoriana at the Dickens Festival in Broadstairs.

Jul & Aug
Perfect weather for hitting the glorious beaches of Thanet in East Kent.

Christ Church Gate, Canterbury Cathedral (p148)
ROBERT MULLAN/SHUTTERSTOCK ©

Canterbury & Southeast England

Rolling chalk hills, venerable Victorian resorts, fields of hops and grapes: welcome to England's sunny southeast, four soothing counties' worth of country houses and fairy-tale castles, accompanied by lots of fine food and drink. That fruit-ripening sun also warms a string of seaside towns and beaches wedged between formidable chalk cliffs. There's something for everyone here, from the medieval quaintness of Sandwich to the bohemian spirit of hedonistic Brighton.

England's spiritual heart is Canterbury; its cathedral and ancient World Heritage–listed attractions are essential viewing, while the southeast is also pockmarked with reminders of darker days: the region's position as the front line against Continental invaders has left a wealth of relics of more turbulent times.

INCLUDES

Canterbury & Southeast England Highlights

1 **Brighton & Hove** (p177) Shopping, tanning and partying in the hedonist capital of the southeast.

2 **Canterbury Cathedral** (p156) Making a pilgrimage to one of England's most important religious sites.

3 **Dover Castle** (p167) Delving into the atmospheric WWII tunnels beneath this sprawling castle.

4 **Rye** (p169) Ambling around the lanes of one of England's prettiest towns.

5 **RHS Garden Wisley** (p175) Wandering among flowers, bushes, trees and superb horticultural vistas.

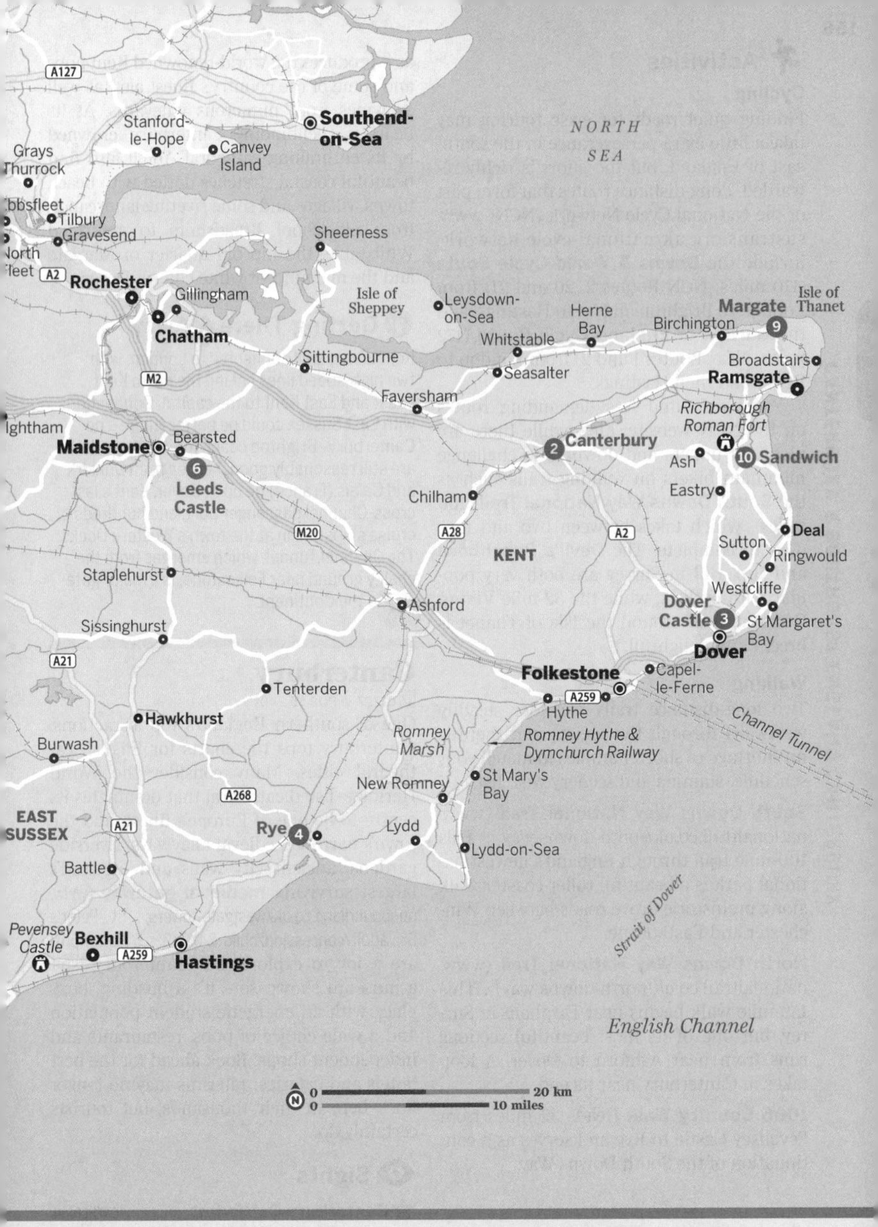

6 Leeds Castle (p161) Getting into exploration mode at this moated marvel.

7 Beachy Head (p175) Scrambling up this spectacular headland with its icing-sugar-white chalk cliffs.

8 Chichester (p184) Discovering Roman remains and an excellent art gallery in this historic cathedral city.

9 Margate (p161) Getting down with the hipsters in the art capital of the southeast.

10 Sandwich (p166) Becoming hopelessly lost in a maze of crooked medieval streets.

Activities

Cycling

Finding quiet roads for cycle touring may take a little extra perseverance in the south-east of England, but the effort is richly rewarded. Long-distance routes that form part of the National Cycle Network (NCN; www.sustrans.org.uk/national-cycle-network) include the **Downs & Weald Cycle Route** (110 miles; NCN Routes 2, 20 and 21) from London to Brighton and on to Hastings, and the **Garden of England Cycle Route** (172 miles; NCN Routes 1 and 2) from London to Dover and then Hastings.

You'll also find less demanding routes on the NCN website. Meanwhile there are plenty of uppers and downers to challenge mountain bikers on walking trails such as the **South Downs Way National Trail** (100 miles), which takes between two and four days to complete. The **Devil's Punchbowl** and **Box Hill** in Surrey are both very popular with cyclists, while the 32-mile **Viking Coastal Trail** around the Isle of Thanet is breezy and delightful.

Walking

Two long-distance trails meander steadily westward through the region, and there is no shortage of shorter ambles to match your schedule, stamina and scenery wish list.

South Downs Way National Trail (www.nationaltrail.co.uk/south-downs-way) This 100-mile trail through England's newest national park is a beautiful roller-coaster walk along prehistoric drove roads between Winchester and Eastbourne.

North Downs Way National Trail (www.nationaltrail.co.uk/north-downs-way) This 153-mile walk begins near Farnham in Surrey, but one of its most beautiful sections runs from near Ashford to Dover. A loop takes in Canterbury near its end.

1066 Country Walk Heads 32 miles from Pevensey Castle to Rye and serves as a continuation of the South Downs Way.

KENT

Kent isn't known as the Garden of England for nothing. Within its largely sea-lined borders extends a fragrant landscape of gentle hills, fertile farmland, cultivated country estates and fruit-laden orchards. It could also be described as the beer garden of England as it produces the world-renowned Kent hops and some of the country's finest ales, as well as wines from numerous vineyards. At its heart is spellbinding Canterbury, crowned by its enthralling cathedral. You'll also find beautiful coastal stretches dotted with beach towns, villages and some riveting landscapes, from old-school Broadstairs to gentrified Whitstable, the hip old quarter of Margate and the magnificent white cliffs of Dover.

Getting There & Away

Kent is very well connected to London, with two high-speed lines linking the north Kent coast and East Kent to the capital. Connections with East Sussex could be better (there's no Canterbury–Brighton coach for instance), but are still reasonably good. Ferries from Dunkirk and Calais (France) tie up at Dover, Kent's last cross-Channel passenger port, and hundreds of cruise ships call in at the town's Western Docks. The Channel Tunnel, which emerges from the chalky ground near Folkestone, is a major gateway to the Continent.

Canterbury

01227 / POP 55,240

One of southern England's top attractions, Canterbury tops the charts for English cathedral cities. Many consider the World Heritage–listed cathedral that dominates its centre to be one of Europe's finest, and the town's narrow medieval alleyways, riverside gardens, ancient city walls and England's largest surviving **medieval gateway** (www.onepoundlane.co.uk/westgate-towers; St Peter's St; adult/concession/child £4/3/2; 11am-4pm) are a joy to explore. But Canterbury isn't a museum showcase – it's a bustling, busy place with an energetic student population and a wide choice of pubs, restaurants and independent shops. Book ahead for the best hotels and eateries: pilgrims may no longer flock here in their thousands, but tourists certainly do.

Sights

★**Canterbury Cathedral** CATHEDRAL
(www.canterbury-cathedral.org; adult/concession/child £12.50/10.50/8.50, tours adult/child £5/4, audio guide £4/3; 10am-4.30pm Mon-Sat, 12.30-4.30pm Sun) A rich repository of more than 1400 years of Christian history, the Church of England's crown jewel is a truly extraordinary place and an astonishing spectacle. This Gothic cathedral, the highlight of the

Canterbury

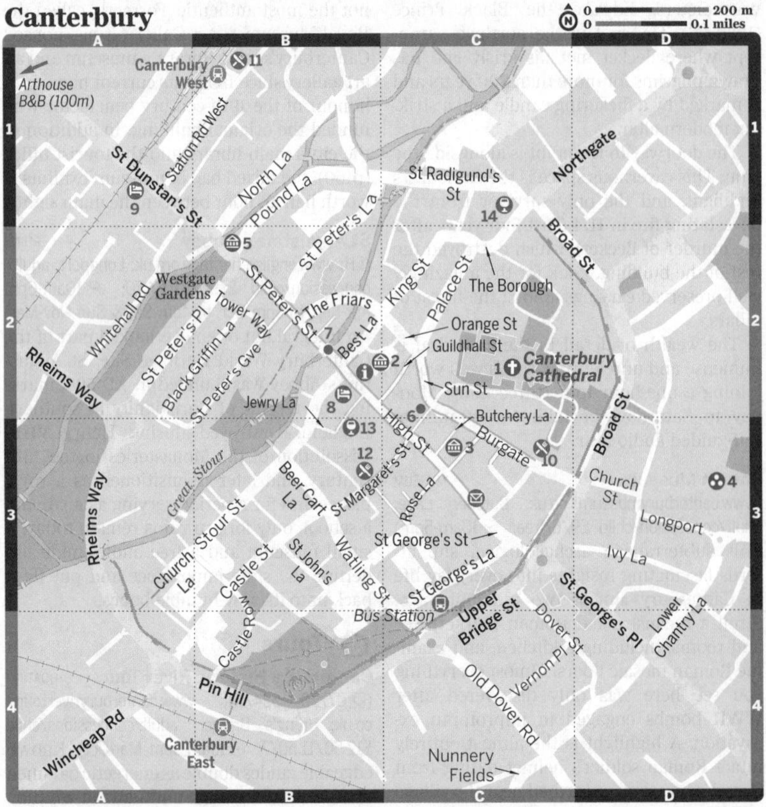

Canterbury

Top Sights
1 Canterbury Cathedral C2

Sights
2 Beaney House of Art & Knowledge B2
3 Roman Museum C3
4 St Augustine's Abbey D3
5 West Gate Towers B2

Activities, Courses & Tours
6 Canterbury Guided Tours C2
7 Canterbury Historic River Tours B2

Sleeping
8 ABode Canterbury B2
9 House of Agnes A1

Eating
10 Chapter C3
11 Goods Shed B1
12 Tiny Tim's Tearoom B3

Drinking & Nightlife
13 Foundry Brewpub B3
14 Parrot C1

city's World Heritage sites, is southeast England's top tourist attraction and a holy place of worship. It's also the site of one of English history's most notorious murders: Archbishop Thomas Becket met his maker here in 1170. Allow at least two hours to do the cathedral justice.

The cathedral is an overwhelming edifice crammed with enthralling stories, arresting architecture and a very real and enduring sense of spirituality – although visitors can't help but pick up on ominous undertones of violence and bloodshed that whisper from its walls.

This ancient structure is packed with monuments commemorating the nation's battles. Also here are the grave and heraldic tunic of one of the nation's most famous warmongers, Edward the Black Prince (1330–76). The spot in the northwest transept where Becket met his grisly end has drawn pilgrims for more than 800 years and is marked by a flickering candle and a striking modern altar.

The doorway to the crypt is alongside the altar. This cavernous space is the cathedral's highlight, and the only survivor from the devastating fire in 1174 (just four years after the murder of Becket), which destroyed the rest of the building. Look for the amazingly well-preserved carvings among the forest of pillars.

The wealth of detail in the cathedral is immense and unrelenting, so it's well worth joining a one-hour tour (three daily, Monday to Saturday) or taking a 40-minute self-guided audio tour.

Roman Museum MUSEUM
(www.canterburymuseums.co.uk; Butchery Lane; adult/concession/child £9/6/free; ⏲10am-5pm) This subterranean archaeological site affords fascinating insights into everyday life in Canterbury almost two millennia ago. Stroll a reconstructed Roman marketplace and rooms, including a kitchen, and examine Roman mosaic floors. Almost everything you see here was only discovered after WWII bombs engaged in impromptu excavation. A highlight is the almost entirely intact Roman soldier's helmet dating from Caesar's invasion, unearthed near the village of Bridge in 2012. It's the most complete example ever found in the UK.

Beaney House of Art & Knowledge MUSEUM
(www.canterburymuseums.co.uk; 18 High St; ⏲museum 10am-5pm Tue-Sat, 11am-4pm Sun; 🚻) FREE This mock-Tudor edifice is the grandest on the main shopping thoroughfare, if not the most authentic. Formerly called the Royal Museum & Art Gallery, it has housed Canterbury's main library, a museum and an art gallery since 1899 – its current name is in honour of the 19th-century benefactor who funded the original building. In addition to the city's main library and the tourist office (p160), the mixed bag of museum exhibits is worth half an hour between the main sights.

St Augustine's Abbey RUINS
(EH; www.english-heritage.org.uk; Longport; adult/concession/child £7.90/7.10/4.70; ⏲10am-6pm Apr-Sep, to 5pm Oct, to 4pm Sat & Sun Nov-Mar) An integral but often overlooked part of the Canterbury World Heritage Site, St Augustine's Abbey was founded in AD 598, marking the rebirth of Christianity in southern England. Destroyed during Henry VIII's Dissolution of the Monasteries in the 16th century, and later requisitioned as a royal palace and for a period serving as a jail and a school, only forlorn ruins remain today. A small museum and a free audio guide underline the site's importance and put flesh back onto its now-humble bones.

☞ Tours

Canterbury Historic River Tours BOATING
(☎07790 534744; www.canterburyrivertours.co.uk; King's Bridge; adult/concessions/child £12.50/11.50/7; ⏲10am-5pm Mar-Oct) Knowledgeable guides double as energetic oarsmen on these fascinating, multi-award-winning River Stour minicruises, which depart from King's Bridge.

Canterbury Guided Tours WALKING
(☎01227-459779; www.canterburyguidedtours.com; adult/concession/child from £8/7.50/6.50; ⏲11am Feb-Oct, plus 2pm Jul-Sep) Ninety-minute walking tours led by professional green-badge guides leave from opposite the Canterbury

THE CANTERBURY TALES

If English literature has a father figure, then it is Geoffrey Chaucer (1342–1400), the first English writer to introduce characters – rather than 'types' – into fiction, doing so to greatest effect in his best-known work, *The Canterbury Tales*.

Written between 1387 and his death, in the hard-to-decipher Middle English of the day, Chaucer's Tales is an unfinished series of 24 vivid stories told by a party of pilgrims journeying between London and Canterbury. Chaucer successfully created the illusion that the pilgrims, not Chaucer (though he appears in the tales as himself), are narrating the stories, which gave him unprecedented freedom as an author. *The Canterbury Tales* remains one of the pillars of the literary canon, but more than that, it's a collection of rollicking good yarns of adultery, debauchery, crime and edgy romance, stuffed with Chaucer's perceptive and witty observations about human nature.

Cathedral entrance. Tickets can be purchased from the tourist office and online.

Sleeping

★ ABode Canterbury BOUTIQUE HOTEL ££
(☎01227-766266; www.abodecanterbury.co.uk; 30-33 High St; r from £74; 📶) The 72 rooms at this super-central hotel, the only boutique hotel in town, are graded from 'comfortable' to 'fabulous' (via 'enviable'), and for the most part live up to their names. They come with features such as handmade beds, chesterfield sofas, tweed cushions and beautiful modern bathrooms. There's a splendid champagne bar, restaurant and tavern, too.

★ Pig at Bridge Place HOTEL ££
(☎01227-830208; www.thepighotel.com/at-bridge-place; Bourne Park Rd, Bridge; d/lodge from £109/305; 📶) Oozing character and charmingly nestled in the Nailbourne Valley, 4 miles southeast of Canterbury, this delightfully restored period house (and former rock venue – Led Zeppelin played here) is one of a litter of seven Pig hotels across the UK. Rooms range from titchy with an imposing four-poster bed to fully equipped lodges for families. Expect much wood panelling, fireplaces and a superb restaurant.

Each room comes with a stocked larder. Prices rise at weekends.

House of Agnes HOTEL ££
(☎01227-472185; www.houseofagnes.co.uk; 71 St Dunstan's St; r incl breakfast £70-145; 📶) This rather wonky 13th-century beamed inn, mentioned in Dickens' *David Copperfield*, has eight themed rooms bearing names such as 'Marrakesh' (Moorish), 'Venice' (carnival masks), 'Boston' (light and airy) and 'Canterbury' (antiques, four-poster, heavy fabrics). If you prefer your room to have straight lines and right angles, there are eight less exciting, but no less comfortable, 'stable' rooms in the garden annexe.

Arthouse B&B B&B ££
(☎07976 725457; www.arthousebandb.com; 24 London Rd; r from £75; P📶) Housed in a 19th-century fire station, the stylishly designed and quirky ambience at this light and bright choice is a welcome relief. The whole effect is good-looking and distinctive, with contemporary and comfortable double rooms. There's also a two-bedroom red-brick fireman's cottage that sleeps four.

Eating

Tiny Tim's Tearoom CAFE £
(www.tinytimstearoom.com; 34 St Margaret's St; mains £6-10.50, afternoon tea £18.95; ⏰9.30am-5.30pm Mon-Sat, 10.30am-4.30pm Sun) It's no mean feat to be declared 'Kent Tearoom of the Year', an accolade awarded to this swish 1930s cafe in 2015. It offers hungry shoppers big breakfasts packed with Kentish ingredients, and tiers of cakes, crumpets, cucumber sandwiches and scones plastered in clotted cream. On busy shopping days you're guaranteed to queue for a table.

Chapter ITALIAN £
(☎01227-809198; www.chaptercanterbury.co.uk; 11-12 Burgate; mains around £8, 2/3-course brunch menu £35/39; ⏰noon-3pm & 5-10pm Mon-Wed, noon-10pm Thu & Fri, 11am-10pm Sat, 11am-8pm Sun; 📶) You literally seem to eat your dinner off the floor in this place – the tables are made of what looks like squares of reclaimed parquet flooring. Thankfully there's a plate between that and the very authentic Italian fare – a brief menu of simple, flavour-packed sourdough pizzas. The bottomless Saturday brunch is a popular blowout, with limitless drink.

★ Goods Shed MARKET ££
(☎01227-459153; www.thegoodsshed.co.uk; Station Rd West; mains £17.50-20; ⏰market 9am-7pm Tue-Sat, to 4pm Sun, restaurant noon-2.30pm & 6pm-midnight Tue-Fri, 8am-9.30pm Sat, 9am-3pm Sun) Aromatic farmers market, food hall and fabulous restaurant rolled into one, this converted warehouse by Canterbury West train station is a hit with everyone from itinerant self-caterers to sit-down gourmands. The chunky wooden tables sit slightly above the market hubbub, but in full view of its appetite-whetting stalls. Daily specials exploit the freshest farm goodies the Garden of England offers.

★ Fordwich Arms BRITISH £££
(☎01227-710444; www.fordwicharms.co.uk; King St, Fordwich; mains £30-32, tasting menu £75, set lunch/dinner £35/50; ⏰noon-2.30pm & 6-9pm Tue-Sat, noon-4pm Sun; 📶) By the River Stour in England's smallest town (population 400), this pub is elevated by both views from the riverside terrace and a twinkling Michelin star. With its 1930s bar, the restaurant, under the leadership of head chef Daniel Smith, has caused a Kentish stir. Each dish is a work of art, employing fresh creativity and locally sourced ingredients.

Expect such delightful choices as rock oysters and mignonette dressing; line-caught turbot, mussels, cabbage, smoked bacon and *vin jaune;* or roast duck with parsnip, pickled walnut and quince. Vegetarian menus are also available. The home-baked bread with home-churned butter is very moreish. Fordwich is 3.5km east of Canterbury, south of the A28.

Drinking & Nightlife

Foundry Brewpub MICROBREWERY
(www.thefoundrycanterbury.co.uk; White Horse Lane; noon-midnight Mon-Sat, to 6pm Sun) Canterbury's brewpub pumps out award-winning craft beers in the industrial setting of the former foundry where New York's first streetlights were made. It also stocks a wide range of local and national ales and ciders, serves light snacks and meals, and distils its own gin and rum.

Parrot PUB
(www.parrotcanterbury.co.uk; 1-9 Church Lane; noon-11pm Mon-Sat, to 10.30pm Sun;) Flung up in 1370 on Roman foundations, Canterbury's oldest boozer has a snug, beam-rich, slightly upmarket pub downstairs and a much-lauded dining room (with vegetarian and vegan choices) upstairs, beneath yet more ageing oak. Many a local ale is pulled in both spaces.

Information

Tourist Office (01227-862162; www.canterbury.co.uk; 18 High St; 9am-6pm Mon-Wed & Fri, to 8pm Thu, to 5pm Sat, 10am-5pm Sun;) Located in the Beaney House of Art & Knowledge (p158). Staff can help book accommodation, excursions and theatre tickets.

Getting There & Away

BUS

The city's **bus station** (St George's Lane) is just within the city walls. Canterbury connections:

Dover (£5.70, 34 minutes, three hourly)

London Victoria (National Express; £11, two hours, hourly)

Margate (£5.70, one hour, two hourly)

Ramsgate (£5.70, 45 minutes, hourly)

Sandwich (£4.40, 40 minutes, three hourly)

Whitstable (£5.20, 30 minutes, every 10 minutes)

TRAIN

There are two train stations: Canterbury East for London Victoria, and Canterbury West for London's Charing Cross and St Pancras stations. Canterbury connections:

Broadstairs (£6.20, 25 minutes, half-hourly) Runs mainly from Canterbury West train station, with some from Canterbury East.

Dover Priory (£8.90, 28 minutes, half-hourly) Runs from Canterbury East train station.

London St Pancras (£34.70, one hour, hourly) High-speed service.

London Victoria and Charing Cross (£5.80, 1¾ hours, two hourly)

Whitstable

01227 / POP 32,100

Perhaps it's the oysters harvested since Roman times? Maybe it's the weatherboard houses and shingle beach? Or perhaps it's the pleasingly old-fashioned main street with petite boutiques, art galleries, been-there-forever outfitters and emporia of vintage frillies? Most likely it's for all of these reasons that Whitstable has become a bit of a weekend magnet for metropolitan types seeking refuge from the city hassle. It's also a simple day trip from Canterbury, to which it is linked by regular local bus.

For a week in late July, the town hosts the **Whitstable Oyster Festival** (www.whitstableoysterfestival.co.uk; late Jul), a seafood, arts and music extravaganza offering a packed schedule of events, from history walks, crab catching and oyster-eating competitions to a beer festival and traditional 'blessing of the waters'.

Eating

Wheelers Oyster Bar SEAFOOD ££
(01227-273311; www.wheelersoysterbar.com; 8 High St; dozen oysters from £12, mains from £7.50; 10am-4pm Thu-Sun) Squeeze onto a stool by the bar, or into the four-table Victorian dining room of this baby-blue and pink restaurant, then choose from the seasonal menu and enjoy the best seafood in Whitstable. This place knows its stuff, as it's been serving oysters since 1856. Bookings are crucial unless you're travelling solo. Cash only.

Samphire MODERN BRITISH ££
(01227-770075; www.samphirewhitstable.co.uk; 4 High St; mains £9-20; 8am-9.30pm Sun-Tue & Thu, 9am-9.30pm Wed, 8am-10pm Fri & Sat) The shabby-chic jumble of tables and chairs, big-print wallpaper and blackboard menus create the perfect stage for meticulously crafted mains containing East Kent's most flavour-packed ingredients. An interesting

DON'T MISS

LEEDS CASTLE

An immense moated pile just east of Maidstone, **Leeds Castle** (www.leeds-castle.com; adult/concession/child £27/25/18.50; ⏲10am-6pm Apr-Sep, to 5pm Oct-Mar; 👪) is, for many, the world's most romantic castle, and it's certainly one of the most visited in Britain. Positioned stoutly on two islands, the formidable and hefty bastion is known as something of a 'ladies castle', because – during its 1000 years of history – it has been home to a who's who of medieval queens, most famously Henry VIII's first wife, Catherine of Aragon.

The castle was transformed from fortress to lavish palace over the centuries, and its last owner, the high-society hostess Lady Baillie, used it as a princely family home and party pad to entertain the likes of Errol Flynn, Douglas Fairbanks and John F Kennedy.

The castle's vast estate offers enough attractions of its own to justify a day trip: peaceful walks, a duckery, aviary, and falconry displays. You'll also find possibly the world's sole dog-collar museum, plenty of kids' attractions and a hedge maze, overseen by a grassy bank from where fellow travellers can shout encouragement or misdirections.

Since Lady Baillie's death in 1974, a private trust has managed the property. This means that some parts of the castle are periodically closed for private events.

Trains run from London Victoria to Bearsted, where you catch a special shuttle coach to the castle.

side dish is its namesake samphire, an asparagus-like plant that grows on sea-sprayed rocks and cliffs, often found on menus in these parts.

★**Sportsman Pub** BRITISH £££
(www.thesportsmanseasalter.co.uk; Faversham Rd, Seasalter; five-course tasting menu £60; ⏲restaurant noon-2pm & 7-9pm Tue-Sat, 12.30-2.45pm Sun) The anonymous village of Seasalter, 4 miles west of Whitstable, would barely deserve mention without the deceivingly ramshackle Sportsman Pub, decorated with a Michelin star (held for 12 years). Local ingredients from sea, marsh and woods are crafted by Whitstable-born chef Stephen Harris into taste-packed Kentish creations that have food critics drooling.

Shopping

Chappell Contemporary ART
(☎01227-637329; www.chappellcontemporary.com; 30 Oxford St) This cool art gallery primarily displays bold, colourful, edgy and exciting silk screen prints, lithographs and etchings from established and up-and-coming British artists.

Information

There is no tourist information office in Whitstable, though you can glean info from the **Whitstable Community Museum & Gallery** (☎01227-264742; www.whitstablemuseum.org; 5 Oxford St; adult/concession/child £3/2/free; ⏲10.30am-4.30pm Thu-Sat, 10.30am-4.30pm Wed-Sat during school holidays).

Getting There & Away

BUS

Whitstable has connections to Canterbury (£5.20, 30 minutes, every 10 minutes) and London Victoria (£12.60, two hours, daily).

TRAIN

Whitstable has the following connections:

London St Pancras (£32.10, 80 minutes, hourly)
London Victoria (£25.30, 80 minutes, hourly)
Margate (£7.90, 20 minutes, twice hourly)
Ramsgate (£10.30, 36 minutes, twice hourly)

Margate

☎01843 / POP 65,000

A popular resort for more than two centuries, Margate's late-20th-century slump was long and bleak as British holidaymakers ditched Victorian frump for the carefree *costas* of Spain. But this grand old seaside resort, with fine-sand beaches, artistic associations and the famous **Dreamland** (www.dreamland.co.uk; Marine Tce; entry £5, rides £1.50-5; ⏲10am-6pm, days vary throughout the year; 👪) amusement park, has bounced off the bottom, re-emerging with a new and fashionable nickname: Shoreditch-on-Sea, in honour of the London hipster ghetto. Major cultural regeneration projects, including the

WORTH A TRIP

CHATHAM HISTORIC DOCKYARD

On the riverfront in Chatham, **Chatham Historic Dockyard** (01634-823800; https://thedockyard.co.uk; Dock Rd; adult/concession/child £25/22.50/15; 10am-6pm Apr-Oct, to 4pm mid-Feb–Mar & Nov), a candidate for Unesco World Heritage status, occupies a third of what was once the Royal Navy's main dock facility. It is possibly the most complete 18th-century dock in the world and has been transformed into a maritime museum examining the Age of Sail. Exhibits include well-restored ships, exhibitions on a variety of shipbuilding themes and a working steam railway.

spectacular Turner Contemporary art gallery, are reversing the town's fortunes, and a bevy of superb restaurants adds to the boho cafes and carefully curated junk emporia of the rejuvenated old town.

Sights

★Turner Contemporary GALLERY
(01843-233000; www.turnercontemporary.org; Rendezvous; 10am-5pm Wed-Sun) FREE This blockbuster contemporary art gallery, bolted together on the site of the seafront guesthouse where master painter JMW Turner used to stay, is one of East Kent's top attractions. The opinion-cleaving architecture – 'alien, brutal and bleak' was one assessment – may leave you cold, but the artwork is riveting, while the sea view from the floor-to-ceiling windows allows you to fully fathom the very thing Turner loved so much about Margate – the sea, sky and refracted light of the north Kent coast.

The gallery attracts top-notch contemporary installations by high-calibre artists such as Tracey Emin (who grew up in Margate) and Alex Katz. When you're finished with the art, culinary creations await in the cafe, and the gift shop is excellent. At the time of writing, the gallery was closed for refurbishment and was due to reopen in 2021, in time to mark its 10th anniversary with a special programme of exhibitions and events.

Shell Grotto CAVE
(www.shellgrotto.co.uk; Grotto Hill; adult/child £4.50/2; 10am-5pm Apr-Oct, 11am-4pm Sat & Sun Nov-Mar) Margate's unique attraction is a mysterious subterranean grotto, discovered in 1835. It's a claustrophobic collection of rooms and passageways embedded with 4.6 million shells arranged in symbol-rich mosaics. It has inspired feverish speculation over the years – some think it a 2000-year-old pagan temple or a secret meeting place for cultists, while others see an elaborate 19th-century hoax. Either way, it's a one-of-a-kind spot.

Sleeping

★Reading Rooms B&B £££
(01843-225166; www.thereadingroomsmargate.co.uk; 31 Hawley Sq; r incl breakfast £190;) Occupying an unmarked 18th-century Georgian town house on a tranquil square just five minutes' walk from the sea, this luxury two-bedroom boutique B&B is an elegant treat. Antique white-painted rooms with waxed wooden floors and beautiful French antique reproduction furniture contrast with the 21st-century bathrooms fragrant with luxury cosmetics. Breakfast is served in your room. Bookings essential.

No children or pets. There is no bell, just a door knocker.

Eating

★Peter's Fish Factory FISH & CHIPS £
(12 The Parade; fish & chips from £4.75; 11am-11pm) The queues for this super-popular place – frying up for decades – go round the block, so get in line and wait for some first-rate and very fresh fish and moreish chips. If there's space, grab one of the outside tables, or take away and munch on the move around Margate.

★Angela's SEAFOOD ££
(01843-319978; www.angelasofmargate.com; 21 The Parade; mains £12-21; noon-2.30pm & 5.45-10pm Tue-Sat) Simple white-fronted Angela's casts its net wide over local and visiting diners seeking top-notch seafood. Built on a sustainable ethic and run by lovely staff, the restaurant serves delightful goodies from the brine. The menu changes daily but expect options like smoked haddock chowder, Whitstable rock oysters, mussels with cider and garlic, or ray wing with leek, rosemary and smoked paprika.

Sit outside in the sea breeze or fold in your elbows and squeeze inside.

Hantverk & Found JAPANESE ££
(☎01843-280454; www.hantverk-found.co.uk; 18 King St; set menu from £20; ⏲noon-4pm & 6.30-9.30pm Thu, to 11pm Fri, noon-11pm Sat, noon-4pm Sun) Hantverk & Found serves up seafood with imagination, flair and a Japanese focus, whether as bento or kaiseki menus or takeaway sushi. With a titchy bar, the dining space is simple and understated, the ingredients Kent-sourced wherever possible, and it doubles as a commissioning gallery with regularly changing shows of top-quality art.

Shopping

Margate Bookshop BOOKS
(☎01843-639660; www.themargatebookshop.com; 2 Market Pl; ⏲10am-5pm Tue-Sat, to 4pm Sun) This mint-coloured cutesy bookshop is a small and intimate book-lined space, with cups of coffee brewed up behind the till, bookish staff, a browse-worthy selection of titles – many from independent publishers – and a writer's room upstairs (day pass £5) if you feel those sudden and irrepressible literary urges.

Information

Tourist Office (☎01843-577637; www.visitthanet.co.uk; Droit House, Stone Pier; ⏲10am-5pm daily Easter-Oct, Tue-Sat Nov-Easter) In the building with the clock tower obliquely opposite the Turner Contemporary by the harbour, the helpful tourist office hands out *Isle*, a glossy magazine crammed with Thanet listings, published twice a year, and a free quarterly newspaper called the *Mercury*, containing all the latest happenings.

Getting There & Away

BUS

Departure and arrival points for local buses are Queen St and adjacent Cecil St. Margate connections:

Broadstairs (Thanet Loop Bus; £2.30, 22 minutes, up to every 10 minutes)

Canterbury (£5.70, one hour, two hourly)

London Victoria (National Express; from £8.60, three hours, seven daily)

Ramsgate (Thanet Loop Bus; £2.90, 30 minutes, up to every 10 minutes)

TRAIN

The train station is just a few steps from the beach. There are hourly services to London Victoria (£25.80, 110 minutes) and a high-speed service to London St Pancras (£28.20, 1½ hours) that runs twice hourly.

Getting Around

The 32-mile Viking Coastal Trail cycling route loops around the Isle of Thanet (p163), embracing Ramsgate, Broadstairs and Margate, as well as dramatic scenery, bays, beaches, coves, churches and sleepy rural villages. The **Bike Shed** (☎01843-423193; www.thebikeshedkent.co.uk; 71 Canterbury Rd; 1/5 hours £5/20; ⏲9am-5pm Tue-Sat) hires out good-looking, powder-blue, British-built Pashley parabikes. Kid's bikes also available. The bike collection point is at Margate train station.

Broadstairs

☎01843 / POP 25,000

While its bigger, brasher neighbours seek to revive and regenerate themselves, quaint little Broadstairs quietly gets on with what it's done best for the past 150 years – wowing visitors with its tight sickle of coarse sand (Viking Bay) and shallow, sun-warmed sea. Charles Dickens certainly thought it an agreeable spot, spending most summers here between 1837 and 1859. The resort now plays the Victorian nostalgia card at every opportunity, but this is a minor distraction for the fine-weather crowds that descend from London in search of sun, sand and surf.

OFF THE BEATEN TRACK

ISLE OF THANET

You won't need a wetsuit, a ferry or snorkel to reach the Isle of Thanet and its towns of Margate, Ramsgate and Broadstairs: the 2-mile-wide Wantsum Channel, which divides the island from the mainland, silted up in the 16th century, transforming the East Kent landscape forever. In its island days, Thanet was the springboard for several epochal episodes in English history. It was here that the Romans kicked off their invasion in the 1st century BC, landing at Pegwell Bay south of present-day Ramsgate (a large Roman fort from 55 to 50 BC has been recently excavated here) and where St Augustine landed in AD 597 to launch his conversion of the pagans. If global warming forecasts are right, Thanet could once again be an island by the end of the century.

Sights

Dickens House Museum MUSEUM
(www.dickensfellowship.org; 2 Victoria Pde; adult/child £3.75/2.10; 1-4.30pm Easter–mid-Jun & mid-Sep–Oct, 10am-4.30pm mid-Jun–mid-Sep, 1-4.30pm Sat & Sun Nov) This quaint museum is Broadstairs' top indoor attraction and the former home of Mary Pearson Strong – Dickens' inspiration for the character of Betsey Trotwood in *David Copperfield*. Diverse Dickensiana on display includes letters from the author.

Festivals & Events

Dickens Festival CULTURAL
(www.broadstairsdickensfestival.co.uk; mid-Jun) Broadstairs' biggest bash, this week-long festival culminates in a banquet and ball in Victorian fancy dress.

Sleeping & Eating

Bay Tree Hotel HOTEL ££
(01843-862502; www.baytreebroadstairs.co.uk; 12 Eastern Esplanade; s/d from £70/130) Whichever way you turn, you bump into a framed Harry Potter poster at this lovingly refurbished 10-room hotel overlooking Stone Bay, run by friendly staff. Most of the tastefully furnished rooms have sea views and one has a balcony; there's a cosy library and bar downstairs and a comfortable living room. The restaurant serves all meals, including afternoon tea.

Morelli's GELATO £
(01843-862500; www.facebook.com/morellisgelatouk; 14 Victoria Pde; gelato from £2; 8am-5.30pm Mon-Fri, to 8pm Sat & Sun) When the sun is radiant, head here. Facing straight onto Viking Bay, Morelli's is a Broadstairs gelato institution. With its pronounced retro look, it has been serving tubs, cones and glasses of ice cream to families clustered around Formica tabletops since 1932, or for takeaway to tots and adults alike.

★**Wyatt & Jones** BRITISH ££
(01843-865126; www.wyattandjones.co.uk; 23-27 Harbour St; mains £6-21; 9am-8.30pm Wed & Thu, to 9.30pm Fri & Sat, to 4pm Sun) Broadstairs' best gastronomical offering is this contemporary British restaurant just a few steps off the beach. Savour unashamedly local dishes such as Whitstable oysters, local sea trout, mussels and chips, or a day-launching breakfast in an uncluttered interior of gun-metal blue and scratched timber floors. Then admire your expanding waistline in the retro mirror wall.

Drinking & Nightlife

Chapel Bar & Bookshop BAR
(www.chapelbroadstairs.com; 44-46 Albion St; 4pm-1am Mon-Wed, noon-2am Thu-Sat, noon-1am Sun;) Bar. Bookshop. Chapel. Cafe. Books for hymn and her: booze as your browse through this endearing two-floor space – stuffed to its holy rafters with literature – meditate on God, or just sit for a coffee and unwind amid all the literary charm.

LOCAL KNOWLEDGE

HOPS & VINES

Both Kent and Sussex produce some of the most delicious ales in the UK, and the southeast's wines are even outgunning some traditional continental vintners.

Kent's **Shepherd Neame Brewery** (01795-542016; www.shepherdneame.co.uk; 10 Court St, Faversham; tours £14; tours 2pm daily) is Britain's oldest and cooks up aromatic ales brewed from Kent-grown premium hops. Sussex's reply is **Harveys Brewery** (01273-480209; www.harveys.org.uk; Bridge Wharf; 9am-5pm), which perfumes Lewes' town centre with a hop-laden scent. Book well in advance for tours of either brewery.

Thanks to warmer temperatures and determined winemakers, English wine, particularly of the sparkling variety, is also developing a strong fan base all of its own. Award-winning vineyards exist in both Sussex and Kent, where the chalky soils are likened to France's Champagne region. Many vineyards now offer tours and wine tastings. Two of the most popular are **Biddenden Vineyards** (01580-291726; www.biddendenvineyards.com; Gribble Bridge Lane; £1 donation to charity, tours £10; 10am-5pm Mon-Sat, 11am-5pm Sun, tours Sat Apr-Sep), 1 mile due south along the A262 from the village of Biddenden, and **Chapel Down Vinery** (01580-766111; www.chapeldown.com; Small Hythe, Tenterden; tours £20; tours daily Mar-Nov), located 2.5 miles south of Tenterden on the B2082.

Located in the former St Mary's Chapel (1601), with an excellent range of craft beer at hand.

Getting There & Away

BUS

Broadstairs connections include the following:

Canterbury (£5.70, 1½ hours, twice hourly)

London Victoria (National Express; from £9, 3¼ hours, seven daily)

Margate (Thanet Loop Bus; £2.30, 22 minutes, up to every 10 minutes)

Ramsgate (Thanet Loop Bus; £1.80, 14 minutes, up to every 10 minutes)

TRAIN

Broadstairs is connected to London Victoria (£25.80, two hours, hourly) and by high-speed service to London St Pancras (£34.70, 80 minutes to two hours, twice hourly).

Ramsgate

☎01843 / POP 40,400

The most varied of Thanet's towns, Ramsgate has a friendlier feel than rival Margate and is more vibrant than quaint little Broadstairs. A forest of masts whistles serenely in the breeze below the handsomely curved walls of Britain's only royal harbour, and the seafront is surrounded by bars and cosmopolitan street cafes. Just one celebrity chef away from being labelled 'up and coming', Ramsgate retains a shabbily undiscovered charm, with its sweeping, environmentally sanctioned Blue Flag beaches and some spectacular Victorian architecture making it well worth the visit. August sees experimental music bands performing in the two-day (and free) Contra Pop Festival on Ramsgate Beach.

Sights

Spitfire & Hurricane Memorial Museum MUSEUM

(www.spitfiremuseum.org.uk; Manston Rd; 10am-5pm Mar-Oct, to 4pm Nov-Feb) FREE Around 4 miles northwest of Ramsgate's town centre, at Manston Airport, this purpose-built museum stores two WWII planes: a Spitfire and a Hurricane. Both look factory-fresh but are surprisingly delicate and so, sadly, there's no clambering aboard, though you can have a go in a rather amateurishly built simulator (£30 for 30 minutes). Gathered around the planes are myriad flight-associated exhibits, many relating to Manston's role as an airfield during the Battle of Britain, when many Spitfires were based here.

The museum has a decent cafe with views of the airstrip. Take bus 38 or 11 from King St and ask the driver to drop you as near as possible.

> **WORTH A TRIP**
>
> **DOWN HOUSE**
>
> Charles Darwin's home from 1842 until his death in 1882, **Down House** (EH; www.english-heritage.org.uk; Luxted Rd, Downe; adult/concession/child £14.50/13.10/8.70; 10am-6pm Apr-Sep, to 5pm Oct, 10am-5pm Sat & Sun Nov-Mar) witnessed the development of Darwin's theory of evolution by natural selection. The house and gardens have been restored to look much as they would have in Darwin's time, including the study where he undertook much of his reading and writing, the drawing room where he tried out some of his indoor experiments, and the gardens and greenhouse where some of his outdoor experiments are recreated.
>
> There are three self-guided trails in the area, where you can follow in the great man's footsteps. Take bus 146 from Bromley North or Bromley South railway station, or service R8 from Orpington.

Sleeping & Eating

Glendevon Guesthouse B&B ££

(☎01843-570909; www.glendevonguesthouse.co.uk; 8 Truro Rd; s/d from £52.50/70; P) Run by energetic and knowledgeable hosts, this comfy guesthouse takes the whole eco-friendly thing seriously, with guest recycling facilities, eco-showers and energy-saving hairdryers. The hallways of the grand Victorian house, a block back from the seafront, are decorated with works by local artists. All six rooms and apartments have kitchenettes, and breakfast (£12.50) is convivially taken around a communal table.

Royal Harbour Hotel BOUTIQUE HOTEL ££

(☎01843-591514; www.royalharbourhotel.co.uk; 10-12 Nelson Cres; s/d from £70/110;) Occupying two Regency town houses on a glorious seafront crescent, this boutique hotel feels enveloped in warmth and quirkiness – an eclectic collection of books, magazines, games and artwork line the hotel. Rooms

DON'T MISS

CHARTWELL

The home of Sir Winston Churchill from 1924 until his death in 1965, **Chartwell** (NT; www.nationaltrust.org.uk; Westerham; adult/child £17.25/8.60; ⌚11.30am-5pm Mar-Oct) offers a breathtakingly intimate insight into the life of England's famous cigar-chomping bombast. This 19th-century house and its rambling grounds have been preserved much as Winnie left them, full of books, pictures, maps and personal mementos. Churchill was also a prolific painter and his now extremely valuable daubings are scattered throughout the house and fill the garden studio. Chartwell is 6 miles west of Sevenoaks.

Transport options are very limited without a car; it's best to have your own set of wheels. Take a taxi from the nearest train station Edenbridge (4 miles), accessible from London Victoria (£10).

range from tiny singles to country-house-style four-poster suites, most with postcard views over the forest of masts below. All are perfectly appointed with bags of character.

★**Royal Victoria Pavilion** PUB FOOD £
(www.jdwetherspoon.com; Harbour Pde; mains £5-11; ⌚8am-midnight Sun-Thu, to 1am Fri & Sat; 📶) The old pavilion has sat on Ramsgate seafront like an upturned boat since 1904, its grand architecture, based on the Little Theatre at Versailles, a vacant symbol of the British seaside's bygone glory days. The hall was brought spectacularly back to life by Wetherspoons (it's the chain's biggest) and is now a place to eat that packs a wow factor.

Information

Tourist Office (☎01843-598750; www.ramsgatetown.org; Customs House, Harbour Pde; ⌚10am-4pm) A small, staffed visitor centre with out-of-hours brochure stands.

Getting There & Away

BUS

Ramsgate has the following bus connections:

Broadstairs (Thanet Loop Bus; £1.80, up to every 10 minutes)

London Victoria (National Express; from £9.20, three hours, six daily)

Margate (Thanet Loop Bus; £2.30, 29 minutes, up to every 10 minutes)

Sandwich (£3.40, 28 minutes, hourly)

TRAIN

Ramsgate has many services to London Victoria (£25.80), London St Pancras (£34.70) and London Charing Cross (£34.70). Journey times range from 1¼ to two hours. There are also services to Sandwich (£5.40, 12 minutes, hourly) and Dover (£10.60, 35 minutes, two hourly).

Sandwich

☎01304 / POP 5000

As close as you'll get to a living museum, Sandwich was once England's fourth city (after London, Norwich and Ipswich). It can be hard to grasp this as you wander its drowsy medieval lanes, discovering its ancient churches, Dutch gables, crooked peg-tiled roofs and overhanging timber-framed houses. Once a port to rival London, Sandwich began its decline when the entrance to the harbour silted up in the 16th century, and this once-vital gateway to and from the Continent spent the next 400 years retreating into quaint rural obscurity. Preservation is big here today, with huge local interest in period authenticity. In the town's historic core, unlisted buildings are few and far between.

Sights

Sandwich's web of medieval and Elizabethan streets is perfect for ambling through and getting pleasantly lost (as many do). Strand St in particular has one of the country's highest concentrations of half-timbered buildings. Ornate brickwork on some houses betrays the strong influence of 350 Protestant Flemish refugees (referred to as 'the Strangers') who settled in the town in the 16th century at the invitation of Elizabeth I. The tiny **Empire Cinema** (☎01304-620480; www.empiresandwich.co.uk; Delf St) is preserved as an art deco museum piece and the 1920s garage deals more in classic cars than modern vehicles.

Sandwich Quay WATERFRONT
Several attractions line the River Stour. The cute little flint-chequered Barbican tollgate was built by Henry VIII and controls traffic flow over the river's only road bridge. Nearby rises Fishergate, built in 1384 and once the main entrance to the town, through which goods from the Con-

tinent and beyond passed. On fair-weather days, hop aboard the **Sandwich River Bus** (☎07958-376183; www.theriverbus.co.uk; The Quay; adult/child 30min trip £7/5, seal spotting £20/14; ⏲11am-6pm Thu-Sun Apr-Sep, Sat & Sun Oct-Mar) beside the toll bridge for seal-spotting trips along the River Stour and out into Pegwell Bay.

Guildhall Museum MUSEUM
(www.sandwichguildhallmuseum.co.uk; Guildhall, Cattle Market; ⏲10am-4pm Wed-Sun) FREE Sandwich's small but thorough museum is a good place to start exploring the town. The exhibition space was fully renovated in 2017 to house a copy of the Magna Carta, accidentally discovered in Sandwich's archives in 2015. Other exhibitions examine the town's rich past as a Cinque Port (p172), its role in various wars, and the gruesome punishments meted out to felons, fornicators and phoney fishers.

Sleeping

★**Bell Hotel** HOTEL ££
(☎01304-613388; www.bellhotelsandwich.co.uk; Sandwich Quay; d/f from £75/85; P 📶) Today the haunt of celebrity golfers, the Bell Hotel has been sitting on the town's quay since Tudor times, though much of the remaining building is from the 19th century. A splendid sweeping staircase leads to luxurious rooms, some with pretty quay views. The Old Dining Room restaurant is one of East Kent's poshest nosh spots.

Information

Tourist Office (www.open-sandwich.co.uk; Guildhall, Cattle Market; ⏲10am-5pm) Located in the historic Guildhall.

Getting There & Away

BUS

Buses go to Ramsgate (£3.40, 25 minutes, hourly), Dover (£4.20, 80 minutes, two hourly) and Canterbury (£4.40, 40 minutes, three hourly).

TRAIN

Trains run to Dover Priory train station (£7.80, 22 minutes, hourly), Ramsgate (£5.40, 12 minutes, hourly) and London St Pancras (£34.70, 1½ hours, hourly).

Dover

☎01304 / POP 31,000

One of the Cinque Ports (p172), Dover has certainly seen better days. Its derelict postwar architecture and shabby town centre is a rather uninspiring introduction to England for travellers arriving on cross-Channel ferries and cruise ships, most of whom breeze through speedily. But the town has a couple of redeeming, stellar attractions. The port's vital strategic position so close to mainland Europe gave rise to an important and sprawling hilltop castle, embedded with some 2000 years of history. The spectacular white cliffs, as much a symbol of English wartime resilience as Winston Churchill or the Battle of Britain, rear in chalky magnificence to the east and west.

Sights

★**Dover Castle** CASTLE
(EH; ☎03703-331181; www.english-heritage.org.uk; adult/concession/child £17/15.30/10.20; ⏲10am-6pm Apr-Jul & Sep, 9.30am-6pm Aug, to 5pm Oct, 10am-4pm Sat & Sun Nov-Mar; P) Occupying top spot, literally and figuratively,

THE WHITE CLIFFS OF DOVER

Immortalised in song, film and literature, the iconic white cliffs of Dover are embedded in the national consciousness, forming a big 'Welcome Home' sign to generations of travellers and soldiers. The cliffs rise to 100m in height and extend either side of Dover, but the best bit is the 6-mile stretch that starts about 2 miles east of town, properly known as the **Langdon Cliffs** and now managed by the National Trust.

From the **White Cliffs of Dover Visitor Centre** (☎01304-202756; www.nationaltrust.org.uk; Upper Rd; ⏲10am-5pm Mar-Oct, 11am-4pm Nov-Feb), follow the stony path east along the clifftops for a bracing 2-mile walk to the stout Victorian **South Foreland Lighthouse** (NT; www.nationaltrust.org.uk; adult/child £6/3; ⏲guided tours 11am-5.30pm Fri-Mon mid-Mar–Oct). This was the first lighthouse to be powered by electricity, and was the site of the first international radio transmissions, in 1898.

A trail runs along the cliffs as far as **St Margaret's Bay**, a popular spot among locals. Bus 81 shuttles back to Dover or onto Deal every hour from St Margaret's Bay.

Dover

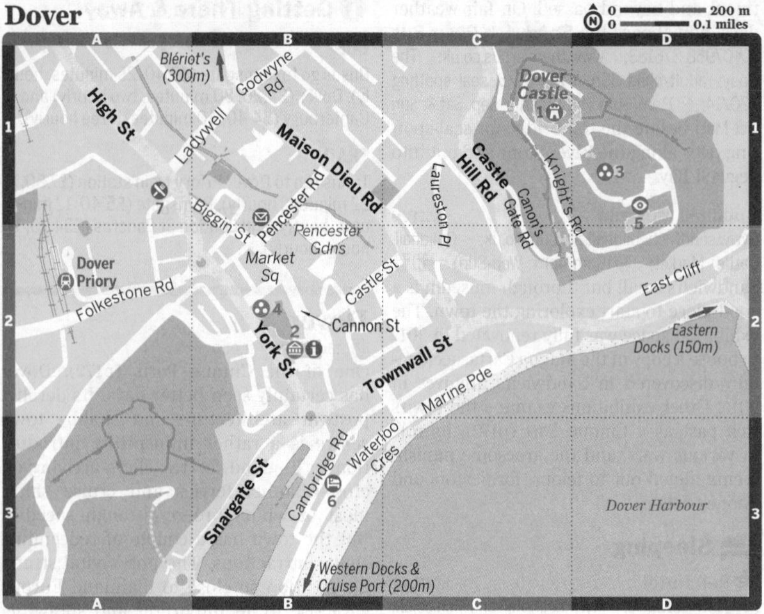

Dover

Top Sights

1 Dover Castle C1

Sights

2 Dover Museum B2
3 Roman Lighthouse D1
4 Roman Painted House B2
5 Secret Wartime Tunnels D1

Sleeping

6 Dover Marina Hotel B3

Eating

7 Allotment A1

in Dover's townscape, this most impressive of castles was built to bolster the country's weakest point at the shortest sea crossing to mainland Europe. The highlights here are the unmissable secret wartime tunnels and the Great Tower, but the huge area across which it sprawls has a lot of other interesting sights, so allow at least three hours for your visit – more if you stand to admire the views across the Channel to France.

The site has been in use for as much as 2000 years. On the vast grounds are the remains of a **Roman lighthouse**, which dates from AD 50 and may be the oldest standing building in Britain. Beside it is the restored Saxon **Church of St Mary in Castro**.

The robust 12th-century **Great Tower**, with walls up to 7m thick, is a medieval warren filled with interactive exhibits and light-and-sound shows that take visitors back to the times of Henry II.

The biggest draw of all, however, is the network of **secret wartime tunnels**. The claustrophobic chalk-hewn passageways were first excavated during the Napoleonic Wars and then expanded to house a command post and hospital in WWII. The highly enjoyable 50-minute guided tour (every 20 minutes, included in the ticket price) tells the story of one of Britain's most famous wartime operations, code-named Dynamo, which was directed from here in 1940 and saw hundreds of thousands of soldiers evacuated from the beaches at Dunkirk.

The story here is told in a very effective way, with video projected sharply onto the tunnel walls and sounds rumbling through the rock. At one point, the entire passageway is consumed in flames, and at others, visitors are plunged into complete darkness.

Roman Painted House RUINS
(https://karu.org.uk/roman_painted_house; 25 New St; adult/child £4/3; ⏲10am-5pm Tue-Sun Apr-Sep; P) A crumbling 1960s bunker is the unlikely setting for some of the most extensive, if stunted, Roman wall paintings north of the Alps. Several scenes depict Bacchus (Roman god of wine and revelry), which makes perfect sense as this large villa was built around AD 200 as a *mansio* (hotel) for travellers needing a little lubrication to unwind.

Sleeping & Eating

Blériot's GUESTHOUSE £
(☎01304-211394; www.bleriotsguesthouse.co.uk; 47 Park Ave; s/d/tr/f from £40/62/82/96; P) This spacious eight-room guesthouse in a quiet residential location is within walking distance of all the sights. Some of the light-filled rooms have original Victorian fireplaces, there's a cosy lounge and the hosts are super friendly. Breakfast is £8 (£5 for kids) extra.

Dover Marina Hotel HOTEL ££
(☎01304-203633; www.dovermarinahotel.co.uk; Waterloo Cres; s/d from £59/69;) Just a few steps from Dover's beach, this seafront hotel crams 81 rooms of varying dimensions into a gently curving 1870s edifice. The undulating corridors show the building's age, but there's nothing wonky about the rooms with their colourful cushions, big-print wallpaper and contemporary artwork. Half the rooms have unrivalled sea views and 10 boast much-sought-after balconies.

★**Allotment** BRITISH ££
(☎01304-214467; www.theallotmentrestaurant.com; 9 High St; mains £13.50-18; ⏲noon-9pm Tue-Sat, 12.30-4pm Sun) Dover's best dining spot sources fish and meat from around Canterbury, to be seasoned with herbs from the tranquil garden out back. Cleanse your palate with a Kentish wine in a relaxed, understated setting as you admire the view of the Maison Dieu (13th-century pilgrims' hospital) directly opposite through the exquisite stained-glass frontage.

Information

Tourist Office (☎01304-201066; www.whitecliffscountry.org.uk; Market Sq; ⏲9.30am-5pm Mon-Sat) Located in the **Dover Museum** (www.dovermuseum.co.uk).

Getting There & Away

BOAT

Ferries depart for France from the Eastern Docks below the castle. Fares vary according to season and advance purchase. Services seem to be in a constant state of flux, with companies rising and falling as often as the Channel's swell.

DFDS (☎0871-574 7235; www.dfdsseaways.co.uk) Services to Dunkirk (two hours, every two hours) and Calais (1½ hours, at least hourly).

P&O Ferries (☎01304-448888; www.poferries.com) Runs to Calais (1½ hours, every 40 to 60 minutes).

BUS

Dover has bus connections to the following:

Canterbury (£5.70, 30 minutes, three hourly)

London Victoria (National Express 007; from £7.10, three to 3½ hours, every two hours)

Rye (bus 102; £6.70, 2¼ hours)

Sandwich (£4.20, 70 minutes, two hourly)

TRAIN

Dover is connected by train to Canterbury (£8.90, 28 minutes, two hourly), London St Pancras, Victoria and Charing Cross (£34.70, one to 2½ hours, up to five hourly), and Ramsgate (£10.60, 35 minutes, two hourly) via Sandwich.

EAST SUSSEX

Home to rolling countryside, medieval villages and a gorgeous coastline, this inspiring corner of England is besieged by weekending Londoners whenever the sun pops out. And it's not hard to see why as you explore the cobbled medieval streets of Rye, wander around historic Battle (where William the Conqueror first engaged the Saxons in 1066) and peer over the edge of Beachy Head or admire the sublimely undulating length of of the breathtaking Seven Sisters chalk cliffs near genteel Eastbourne. Brighton, a highlight of any visit, offers some kicking nightlife, offbeat shopping and British seaside fun. Off the beaten track, you can stretch your legs on the South Downs Way, which traverses England's newest national park, the South Downs National Park.

Rye

☎01797 / POP 9041

Possibly southeast England's quaintest town, Rye is a precious little nugget of the past, a medieval settlement that looks like someone hit the temporal pause button.

Even the most jaded sightseer can't fail to be wooed by Rye's cobbled lanes, mysterious passageways and crooked half-timbered Tudor buildings. Tales of resident smugglers, ghosts, writers and artists add to the mystique.

Rye was once one of the Cinque Ports (p172), occupying a high promontory above the sea. Today the town rises 2 miles from the briny depths and sheep graze where the Channel's strong tides once swelled (and could swell again: apocalyptic predictions see Rye under water again by the year 2050, due to rising sea levels).

Sights

Mermaid Street AREA

Most start their exploration of Rye on famous Mermaid St, a short walk from the Rye Heritage Centre (p172). It bristles with 15th-century timber-framed houses with quirky names such as 'The House with Two Front Doors' and 'The House Opposite'.

Lamb House MUSEUM

(NT; www.nationaltrust.org.uk; West St; adult/concession £7.90/3.95; ⌚11am-5pm Fri-Mon late Mar-Oct) This Georgian town house is a favourite stomping ground for local apparitions, but its most famous resident was American writer Henry James, who lived here from 1898 to 1916, during which time he wrote *The Wings of the Dove*. Until 2017 this was a private house, but with the tenants gone, the National Trust has opened up more rooms to the public and created a more hands-on experience. For budding writers there are writing spaces and courses on offer.

Ypres Tower MUSEUM

(Rye Castle; www.ryemuseum.co.uk; Church Sq; adult/concession/child £4/3/free; ⌚10.30am-5pm Apr-Oct, to 3.30pm Nov-Mar) Just off Church Sq stands the sandcastle-esque Ypres Tower (pronounced 'wipers'). You can scramble through the 13th-century building to learn about its long history as a fort, prison, mortuary and museum (the last two at overlapping times), and an annexe contains one of the last surviving Victorian women's prisons in the country. From here, there are widescreen views of Rye Bay and even France on very clear days.

Driving Tour
Dover to Rye

START DOVER EASTERN DOCKS
END RYE
LENGTH 35.5 MILES; AT LEAST FOUR HOURS

If you've just rolled off a cross-Channel ferry or have a day away from a cruise ship docked in Dover, instead of heading north to London, why not explore this fascinating route along the white cliffs and across the flat marshes of the Kent–Sussex border to find some of the southeast's hidden corners? Buses 100, 101 and 102 (The Wave) follow this route between Dover, Lydd and Hastings.

Starting at the exit to Dover's frantic ❶ **Eastern Docks**, where all cross-Channel ferries tie up, take the A20 along the seafront. After a few minutes, this dual carriageway begins to climb onto the famous white cliffs west of Dover. Your first stop is just outside town – take the turning for ❷ **Samphire Hoe** country park, a ledge of parkland created between the white cliffs and the sea, using 5 million cu metres of chalk excavated during the construction of the Channel Tunnel. It's a fine spot for a picnic as you watch the 30 local species of butterfly flutter by.

On the A20 again, it's a mere 1.75 miles to the exit for the village of Capel-Le-Ferne (on the B2011). Well signposted at the end of the village is the ❸ **Battle of Britain Memorial**, a striking monument to the pilots who took part in the decisive struggle with the Luftwaffe in the skies above Kent and Sussex. An airman seated at the centre of a huge Spitfire propeller looks out serenely across the Channel and there's a multimedia visitor centre and museum experience to enjoy. Returning to the B2011, a few gear changes will have you on the outskirts of ❹ **Folkestone**. Take a left at the first roundabout then the sixth right onto Dover Rd. This will take you into the centre of this formerly grand old resort, once a favourite stomping ground of royal bon viveur King Edward VII and a forgotten piece of England's seaside past. Take a stroll through the seafront Leas Coastal Park with its subtropical flora, then halt

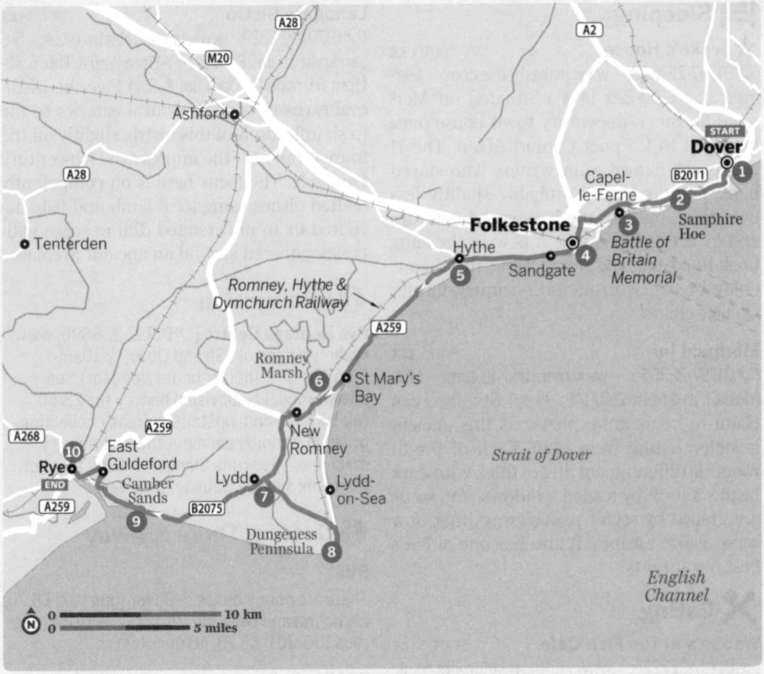

for fish and chips at the old fish market before ambling up through the Creative Quarter, Folkestone's old town, now occupied by artists' studios and craft shops.

Rolling out of Folkestone to the west on the A259 Sandgate Rd, you pass through Sandgate with its antique shops and shingle beach. From there it's another 2.5 miles to fascinating little 5 **Hythe**. You could spend a full day in this original Cinque Port (p172). Not only is it the eastern terminus of the fascinating narrow-gauge Romney, Hythe and Dymchurch Railway (RH&D Railway), but the Royal Military Canal also flows through the town and there's a quaint high street and beach to explore.

Heading further west, a series of not-so-attractive shingle resorts, including Dymchurch and St Mary's, are strung along the A259, cowering below their huge dykes, which keep the high tides from turning this stretch of coast into sea bottom. You've now left the white cliffs behind and are entering the 6 **Romney Marsh**, a flat, sparsely populated landscape of reed beds and sheep-dotted fields. There's a visitor centre (www.kentwildlifetrust.org.uk) between St Mary's Bay and New Romney (on the A259) for those with time.

Having negotiated New Romney, another of the original five Cinque Ports, take the turning to the left onto the B2075, which leads to 7 **Lydd**, a quaint former corporate member of the Cinque Ports. From here detour along the lonely Dungeness Rd, which heads across the flats of the eerie 8 **Dungeness Peninsula**, a low shingle spit dominated by its brooding nuclear power station. As well as boasting the southeast's largest seabird colony, it's also the western terminus of the RH&D Railway.

Back in Lydd, stick with the B2075 heading west for 6 miles until you reach Camber. Thought the entire south coast had just shingle beaches? Well, the main attraction here is 9 **Camber Sands**, a wide expanse of golden grains and dunes, ideal for picnicking and strolling.

The B2075 winds through shingly, scrubby wetlands until it rejoins the A259 at the hamlet of East Guldeford, where you should turn left towards Rye. Along the roads around here you will see the main source of revenue from the Romney Marsh – thousands of sheep grazing on the verdant flats. The A259 barrels across the marshes, eventually depositing you in 10 **Rye** (p169), one of the southeast's quaintest towns.

Sleeping

★Jeake's House HOTEL ££

(☎01797-222828; www.jeakeshouse.com; Mermaid St; r £100-225; P 📶) Situated on Mermaid St, this 17th-century town house once belonged to US poet Conrad Aiken. The 11 rooms are named after writers who stayed here. The decor was probably slightly less bold then, missing the beeswaxed antiques and lavish drapery. Take a pew in the snug book-lined bar and, continuing the theme, enjoy breakfast in an 18th-century former Quaker chapel.

Mermaid Inn HOTEL £££

(☎01797-223065; www.mermaidinn.com; Mermaid St; s/d from £90/140; P 📶) Few inns can claim to be as atmospheric as this ancient hostelry, dating from 1420. Each of the 31 rooms is different, but all are thick with dark beams and lit by leaded windows, and some are graced by secret passageways that now serve as fire escapes. It also has one of Rye's best restaurants.

Eating

Webbe's at the Fish Cafe SEAFOOD ££

(☎01797-222226; www.webbesrestaurants.co.uk; 17 Tower St; mains £13-18; ⊙noon-2pm daily & 6-9.30pm Mon-Thu, 5.30-9.30pm Fri-Sun) Rye's best fish restaurant is a simple dining room flooded with natural light from large arched windows. The menu features local fish such as Rye Bay flounder in cider sauce and Rye cod in beer batter. The restaurant doubles as a cookery school and is the venue for the annual Scallop Week in March.

Landgate Bistro BRITISH ££

(☎01797-222829; www.landgatebistro.co.uk; 5-6 Landgate; mains £17-21; ⊙7-11pm Wed & Thu, 6.30-11pm Fri, noon-2.30pm Sat & Sat) Flee the medieval excesses of Rye's central eateries to the fresh inflections of this bistro, slightly off the tourist trail near the impressive 14th-century Landgate. The focus here is on competently crafted dishes using local lamb and fish, devoured in an understated dining space with tables gathered around an ancient fireplace.

Information

Rye Heritage Centre (☎01797-226696; www.ryeheritage.co.uk; Strand Quay; ⊙10am-5pm Apr-Oct, shorter hours Nov-Mar) See a town-model audiovisual history for £3.50 (kids £1.50) and, upstairs, a freaky collection of still-functional penny-in-the-slot novelty machines. Also runs themed walking tours of the town; see the website for details.

Getting There & Away

BUS

There are hourly buses to Dover (bus 102; £6.70, 2¼ hours) and twice-hourly services to Hastings (bus 100/101; £5.70, 40 minutes).

TRAIN

There are hourly trains to Hastings (£5.90, 19 minutes). For London St Pancras (£36.70, one hour, hourly), change in Ashford.

Hastings

☎01424 / POP 92,855

Forever associated with the Norman invasion of 1066 (even though the decisive events unfolded 6 miles away), Hastings prospered

CINQUE PORTS

Due to their proximity to Europe, southeast England's coastal towns were the frontline against raids and invasion during Anglo-Saxon times. In the absence of a professional army and navy, these ports were frequently called upon to defend themselves, and the kingdom, on land and at sea.

In 1278 King Edward I formalised this ancient arrangement by legally defining the Confederation of Cinque Ports (pronounced 'sink ports'). The five original ports – Sandwich, Dover, Hythe, Romney and Hastings – were awarded numerous perks and privileges in exchange for providing the king with ships and men. At their peak, the ports were considered England's most powerful institution after Crown and Church.

The importance of the ports eventually evaporated when the shifting coastlines silted up several Cinque Port harbours and a professional navy was based at Portsmouth. But still the pomp and ceremony remain. The Lord Warden of the Cinque Ports is a prestigious post now bestowed on faithful servants of the Crown. The Queen Mother was warden until she passed away, succeeded by Admiral Lord Boyce. Previous incumbents include the Duke of Wellington and Sir Winston Churchill.

WORTH A TRIP

BATTLE

'If there'd been no battle, there'd be no Battle', goes the saying in this unassuming village, which grew up around the hillside where invading French duke William of Normandy, aka William the Conqueror, scored a decisive victory over local king Harold in 1066. Visitors flock to this epicentre of 1066 country to see the spot where Harold got it in the eye, with the biggest crowd turning up mid-October to witness the annual re-enactment on the original battlefield.

The aptly named **Battle Abbey** (EH; www.english-heritage.org.uk; High St; adult/concession/child £13.60/12.20/8.20; ⏲10am-6pm Apr-Sep, to 4pm Sat & Sun Oct-Mar) marks the site of the pivotal event, which had an unparalleled impact on the country's subsequent social structure, language and, well, pretty much everything. Four years after, the Normans began constructing an abbey here, a penance ordered by the pope for the loss of life incurred. Only the foundations of the original church remain; the altar's position is supposedly the spot where Harold took an arrow in his eye.

There are train connections to Hastings (£4.50, 15 minutes, twice hourly) and London Charing Cross (£25.60, 80 minutes, twice hourly). Buses 304 and 305 (£3.40, 30 minutes) travel between Battle and Hastings.

as one of the Cinque Ports and, in its Victorian heyday, was one of Britain's most fashionable resorts. After a period of steady postwar decline, the town, with its restored **pier** (1-10 White Rock; ⏲10am-9pm) FREE and ruined **castle** (www.discoverhastings.co.uk; Castle Hill Rd; adult/concession/child £5.25/4.65/4.25; ⏲10.30am-3.30pm Thu-Sun), has enjoyed a mini-renaissance, and these days is an intriguing mix of family seaside resort, working fishing port and arty hang-out.

Sights

Stade AREA
(Rock-A-Nore Rd) The seafront area called the Stade (below East Hill) is home to distinctive black clapboard structures known as Net Shops. These were built to store fishing gear back in the 17th century, but some now house fishmongers who sell off the catch of Europe's largest beach-launched fishing fleet, usually hauled up on the shingle behind. All these fishy goings-on keep the Stade very much a working place, with the combined pong of diesel and guts scenting the air.

Hastings Contemporary GALLERY
(www.hastingscontemporary.org; Rock-A-Nore Rd; adult/concession £8/6; ⏲11am-4pm Fri-Sun) This large, purpose-built exhibition venue at the end of the Stade is used for temporary shows of contemporary British art as well as themed installations from the Jerwood collection. The building has a great cafe with sunny Channel views. The black-tiled building was designed to blend in with the adjacent Net Shops.

Hastings Museum & Art Gallery MUSEUM
(www.hmag.org.uk; Johns Pl, Bohemia Rd; ⏲10am-5pm Tue-Sat, noon-5pm Sun Apr-Oct, shorter hours Nov-Mar) FREE A short walk west of the train station, this marvellous little museum is housed in a red-brick mansion. Highlights include the intricately Moorish Durbar Hall and a section on John Logie Baird, who invented television while recuperating from an illness in Hastings between February 1923 and November 1924.

Sleeping

★**Swan House** B&B £££
(☎01424-430014; www.swanhousehastings.co.uk; 1 Hill St; s/d incl breakfast from £110/130; @📶) Inside its 15th-century timbered shell, this four-room place blends contemporary and vintage chic to perfection. Rooms feature organic toiletries, fresh flowers, hand-painted walls and huge beds. The guest lounge, where pale sofas, painted floorboards and striking modern sculptures rub shoulders with beams and a huge stone fireplace, is a stunner. Minimum two-night stay at weekends.

Eating & Drinking

St Mary in the Castle Cafe & Bar CAFE £
(www.stmaryinthecastle.co.uk/cafe; Pelham Pl; mains £4.50-10; ⏲10am-6pm Sun-Thu, to 10pm Fri & Sat; 📶🌶) Amid the greasy cafes that line the seafront, it's a relief to find this laid-back oasis of decent food offering nutritious

WORTH A TRIP

DE LA WARR PAVILION

This restored Grade I–listed modernist **marvel** (www.dlwp.com) FREE on the seafront at Bexhill-on-Sea is a must for fans of art deco architecture. With its curvilinear and straight-edged, machine-age styling, the building, designed in 1935, today serves as a contemporary arts centre and hosts – in a quite intimate space – performances from such names as Goldfrapp, Saint Etienne and Jack Dee.

A cafe/bar serves cakes, pastries and drinks. Bexhill-on-Sea is 8km west of Hastings.

titbits such as tofu on toast, halloumi kebabs and a range of tempting specials. The cafe and bar is part of a larger arts centre and gallery; the latter is in the crypt of the church above and free to enter.

Hanushka Coffee House CAFE
(28 George St; ⏲9.30am-6pm) Hastings' best caffeine stop resembles a very well-stocked secondhand bookshop, with every inch of wall space packed with browsable titles. The low-lit and tightly packed space in between provokes inter-table interaction, or you can seek sanctuary on the sofas and perches in the window.

Information

Tourist Office (☎01424-451111; www.visit1066country.com; Muriel Matters House, Pelham Pl; ⏲9am-5pm Mon-Fri, 10am-3pm Sat & Sun)

Getting There & Away

BUS

Hastings has the following bus connections:

Battle (£3.40, 28 minutes, hourly)

Eastbourne (bus 99; £5.20, 1¼ hours, three hourly)

Rye (bus 100/101; £5.70, 40 minutes, twice hourly)

TRAIN

Hastings has connections with Brighton (£14.70, one to 1¾ hours, two hourly), via Eastbourne, as well as London Charing Cross (£25.80, two hours, at least hourly), Battle (£4.50, 17 minutes, twice hourly) and Rye (£5.90, 20 minutes, hourly).

Getting Around

Hastings has two delightful old Victorian funiculars, the East Hill Cliff and West Hill Cliff Railways, useful if you need to get up onto the cliffs and don't fancy the walk. The **East Hill Cliff Railway** (Rock-A-Nore Rd; adult/child return £2.70/1.70; ⏲10am-5.30pm Apr-Sep, 11am-4pm Sat & Sun Oct-Mar) funicular ascends from the Stade to Hastings Country Park, while the **West Hill Cliff Railway** (George St; adult/child return £2.70/1.70; ⏲10am-5.30pm Mar-Sep, 11am-4pm Oct-Mar) funicular saves visitors' legs when climbing up to Hastings Castle. Otherwise the town can be easily tackled on foot.

Eastbourne

☎01323 / POP 103,745

With its whitewashed late-Victorian hotels, Eastbourne's 3.5-mile sweeping, palm-tree-lined seafront is one of the UK's grandest, with one of the nation's finest Victorian **piers** (www.eastbournepier.com; ⏲24hr).

Holding the semi-official title as 'Britain's sunniest town', Eastbourne was also long known for its snoozing pensioners in deckchairs and fusty guesthouses. But while these perceptions endure, the town was long ago invigorated by an influx of students, the arrival of the southeast's largest Portuguese and Polish communities and the opening, over a decade ago, of the Towner Art Gallery, which energised Eastbourne's artistic persona.

Add to this the South Downs National Park that nudges its western suburbs, and the wind-lashed beauty of Beachy Head, and Eastbourne makes an enjoyable day trip from London or Brighton. It's also the start or end point for a hike along the 100-mile South Downs Way.

Sights

★**Towner Art Gallery** GALLERY
(☎01323-434670; www.townereastbourne.org.uk; Devonshire Park, College Rd; ⏲10am-5pm Tue-Sun) FREE One of the southeast's most exciting exhibition spaces, this purpose-built structure has temporary shows of contemporary work on the ground and 2nd floors, while the 1st floor is given over to rotating themed shows created from the gallery's 5000-piece collection. Events take place in the auditorium, and the free tour focuses on the climate-controlled art store; see the website for details of both. At the time of writing, the gallery's exterior had been

transformed into a stunning maze of colours by German artist Lothar Götz.

Sleeping & Eating

Albert & Victoria B&B ££

(01323-730948; www.albertandvictoria.com; 19 St Aubyns Rd; s/d from £45/80;) Book ahead to stay at this delightful Victorian terraced house, whose fragrant rooms, canopied beds, crystal chandeliers and secluded walled garden for summer breakfasts are mere paces from the seafront promenade. The four rooms are named after four of Queen Victoria's offspring.

Lamb Inn PUB FOOD ££

(01323-720545; www.thelambeastbourne.co.uk; 36 High St; mains £7-20; noon-7pm Mon-Sat, to 5pm Sun) This ancient Eastbourne institution, less than a mile northwest of the train station in the under-visited Old Town, has been plonking Sussex ales on the bar for eight centuries, and now serves gourmet British pub grub and some token vegan platters. A holidaying Charles Dickens left a few smudged napkins here when he stayed across the road.

Shopping

★**Camilla's Bookshop** BOOKS

(01323-736001; www.camillasbookshop.com; 57 Grove Rd; 10am-5pm Mon-Sat) Literally packed to the rafters with over half a million musty volumes, this incredible second-hand-book repository, an interesting amble from the train station, fills three floors of a crumbling Victorian town house. It's the best place to source preloved reading matter on the south coast, if not the entire southeast.

Information

Tourist Office (01323-415415; www.visiteastbourne.com; Compton St, Welcome Building; 9.30am-5pm) Tourist information plus tickets to anything happening in Eastbourne.

Getting There & Away

BUS

There are buses to Brighton (bus 12; £4.80, 1¼ hours, up to every 10 minutes) and Hastings (bus 99; £5.20, 1¼ hours, three hourly).

TRAIN

Twice-hourly trains service Brighton (£11.60, 30 to 40 minutes) and London Victoria (£19.80, 1½ hours).

South Downs National Park

The South Downs National Park (www.southdowns.gov.uk), England's newest national park, is more than 600 sq miles of rolling chalk downs stretching west from Eastbourne to Winchester, a distance of about 100 miles. The South Downs Way extends its entire length. The park is all about rolling English countryside and views down to the coast. It's a delight at any time of year, though May to October is the best time for exploration.

Sights & Activities

Beachy Head LANDMARK

(www.beachyhead.org.uk) The famous cliffs of Beachy Head are the highest point of the chalky rock faces that slice across the rugged coastline at the southern end of the South Downs. It's off the B2103, from the A259 between Eastbourne and Newhaven. From here the stunning **Seven Sisters Cliffs** undulate their way west. A clifftop path (a branch of the South Downs Way) rides the waves of chalk as far as picturesque **Cuckmere Haven**.

Beachy Head is a spot of thrilling beauty, the brilliant white chalk rising high into the blue Sussex sky. But on a darker note, it is also known as one of Europe's most frequented suicide spots.

Along the clifftop path, you'll stumble upon the tiny seaside hamlet of **Birling Gap**.

DON'T MISS

RHS GARDEN WISLEY

These fabulous horticultural **gardens** (01483-224234; www.rhs.org.uk/gardens/wisley; off the A3, Woking; adult/child £14.95/7.45; 9.30am-5pm Mon-Fri, 9am-5pm Sat & Sun; P) are the UK's second-most-visited ticketed gardens after the Royal Botanic Gardens in Kew, London. Explore at your own leisure a wonderland of blooms, bushes and trees, admiring the Wisteria Walk, Oakwood, Orchard, Alpine Meadow, Bonsai Walk, Water Lily Pavilion, Exotic Garden and grass-verged Jellicoe Canal while keeping an eye out for riveting pieces of sculpture (including an astonishing metal head en route to the Pinetum) that pop out of the blue.

There is a handy National Trust cafe here and a lovely, secluded sun-trap of a beach that is popular with locals and walkers taking a breather.

Stupendous views of the Seven Sisters can be had from **Hope Gap** to the west, where parking is available.

Pevensey Castle RUINS

(EH; www.english-heritage.org.uk; Castle Rd, Pevensey; adult/concession/child £6.90/6.20/4.10; ⏲10am-5pm Apr-Oct, to 4pm Sat & Sun only Nov-Mar) The dramatic ruins of William the Conqueror's first stronghold sit 5 miles east of Eastbourne, just off the A259. Regular train services between London Victoria and Hastings via Eastbourne stop at Westham, half a mile from Pevensey. Picturesquely dissolving into its own moat, the castle marks the point where William the Conqueror landed in 1066, just two weeks before the Battle of Hastings. He wasted no time after his landing, building upon sturdy Roman walls to fashion this castle.

The castle was gainfully employed time and again through the centuries, right up to WWII, when it bristled with machine-gun nests while serving as a command and observation post in preparation for a Nazi invasion. You have to pay to enter the Inner Bailey of the castle itself, but not to wander around within the outer walls.

Sleeping

★ Belle Tout Lighthouse B&B £££

(☎01323-423185; www.belletout.co.uk; South Downs Way, Beachy Head; d from £175) Perched precariously close to the edge of the white cliffs, this early 18th-century decommissioned lighthouse somehow manages to contain six rooms, all imaginatively done out and all rather restricted space-wise. The highlight must be the Lantern Room, a circular guest seating area in the glass top of the building, the perfect place to enjoy a truly memorable Sussex sunset.

Getting There & Away

Bus 12 (up to every 10 minutes) heads through some of the South Downs National Park on the way to Brighton. A good place to alight is Cuckmere Haven, from where you can walk back to Eastbourne across the Seven Sisters. Bus 99 (every 20 minutes) runs from Eastbourne to Pevensey.

Lewes

☎01273 / POP 17,300

Strung out along an undulating high street flanked by elegant Georgian buildings, a part-ruined **castle** (www.sussexpast.co.uk; 169 High St; adult/concession/child £8.50/8/4.60; ⏲10am-5.30pm Tue-Sat, 11am-5.30pm Sun & Mon Mar-Oct, to 3.45pm Nov-Feb; P) and a traditional brewery, Lewes (pronounced 'Lewis') is

THE CHANNEL ISLANDS

Just off the coast of France, Jersey, Guernsey, Sark, Herm and Alderney beckon with exquisite coastlines, shaded lanes and old-world charm. Not quite Britain and not quite France, the islands are proudly independent, self-governing British Crown dependencies that straddle the gap between the two. Their citizens owe their allegiance to Her Majesty and some still speak local dialects that stem from medieval Norman French, including Guernésiais (Dgèrnésiais) on Guernsey, Jèrriais on Jersey and Sercquiais on Sark. Other Norman languages, such as Auregnais (which was spoken on Alderney), are now extinct.

The warm Gulf of St Malo ensures subtropical plants and an incredible array of birdlife. The Channel Islands enjoy sunnier days and milder winters than the UK, attracting walkers and outdoorsy types for surfing, kayaking, coasteering and diving. Watch out for rip tides, especially around Jersey. Superb local seafood graces the tables of local restaurants in the culture hubs of St Helier (Guernsey) and St Peter Port (Jersey).

Numerous forts and castles dot the coastlines, while poignant museums – some housed in old war tunnels and bunkers – provide an insight into the islanders' fortitude during WWII.

There are daily flights to Guernsey from London Gatwick, as well as from Jersey, Manchester, Birmingham, Southampton and Bristol, and seasonal departures to other airports in the UK. Jersey receives daily flights from London Heathrow and London Gatwick, as well as from Liverpool, Manchester, Southampton, Bristol, Birmingham, Exeter and Guernsey, as well as several flights from Europe.

a charmingly affluent hillside town with a turbulent past and fiery traditions. Off the main drag, however, there's a more intimate atmosphere as you descend into twisting narrow streets called 'twittens' – the remainder of the town's original medieval street plan.

One of Lewes' claims to fame is that it straddles the 0 degrees line of longitude. An inconspicuous plaque on Western Rd marks the meridian, though modern measuring methods have actually placed the line around 100m to the east.

Lewes also holds what it claims is the biggest Bonfire Night bash in the world with tens of thousands of people descending on the town on 5 November to watch a carnival, fireworks display and effigies of villains of the day going up in flames.

Sleeping

Shelleys HOTEL **£££**
(☎01273-472361; www.the-shelleys.co.uk; 135-136 High St; r from £130; 📶) Lewes' top address is this 16th-century manor house on the high street, brimful of grand old-fashioned charm and once home to the earl of Dorset and owned by the Shelley family (of Percy Bysshe fame). The stylish, country rooms are the best in Lewes, while an elegant restaurant overlooks the lovely walled garden.

Information

Tourist Office (☎01273-483448; www.visitlewes.co.uk; 187 High St; ⏲9.30am-4.30pm Mon-Fri, to 2pm Sat, 10am-2pm Sun Apr-Sep, shorter hours Sat & closed Sun Oct-Mar)

Getting There & Away

Lewes has the following rail connections:
Brighton (£4.60, 15 minutes, four hourly)
Eastbourne (£8.40, 20 to 25 minutes, four hourly)
London Victoria (£19.80, 70 minutes, two hourly)

Brighton & Hove

☎01273 / POP 290,000

Raves on the beach, Graham Greene novels, mods and rockers in bank-holiday fisticuffs, naughty weekends for Mr and Mrs Smith, and the UK's biggest gay scene – this coastal city evokes many images for the British. But one thing is certain: with its bohemian, hedonistic vibe, Brighton is where England's seaside experience goes from cold to cool.

Brighton is Britain's most colourful and outrageous city. Here burlesque meets contemporary design, microbrewed ales share bar space with 'sex on the beach' and stags watch drag.

The highlight for sightseers is the Royal Pavilion, a 19th-century party palace built by the Prince Regent, who kicked off Brighton's love of the outlandish.

The huge wind farm visible far off in the channel is the Rampion Offshore Wind Farm; learn all about it at the **Rampion Offshore Wind Farm Visitor Centre** (www.rampionoffshore.com/visitor-centre; 76-81 Kings Rd Arches; ⏲10am-6pm Tue-Sun May-Sep, to 4pm Oct-Apr) FREE.

Sights

★**Royal Pavilion** PALACE
(☎03000-290900; http://brightonmuseums.org.uk/royalpavilion; Royal Pavilion Gardens; adult/child £15.50/9.50; ⏲9.30am-5.45pm Apr-Sep, 10am-5.15pm Oct-Mar) The Royal Pavilion is the city's must-see attraction. The glittering party pad and palace of Prince George, later Prince Regent and then King George IV, it's one of the most opulent buildings in England, and certainly the finest example of early 19th-century chinoiserie anywhere in Europe. It's an apt symbol of Brighton's reputation for decadence. An unimpressed Queen Victoria called the Royal Pavilion 'a strange, odd Chinese place', but for visitors to Brighton it's an unmissable chunk of Sussex history.

The entire palace is an eye-popping spectacle, but some interiors stand out even amid the riot of decoration. The dragon-themed banqueting hall must be the most incredible in all of England. More dragons and snakes writhe in the music room, with its ceiling of 26,000 gold scales, and the then-state-of-the-art kitchen must have wowed Georgians with its automatic spits and hot tables. Prince Albert carted away all of the furniture, some of which has been loaned back by the present queen.

Brighton Museum & Art Gallery MUSEUM
(www.brightonmuseums.org.uk; Royal Pavilion Gardens; adult/child £6.20/3.60; ⏲10am-5pm Tue-Sun) Set in the Royal Pavilion's renovated stable block, this museum and art gallery has a glittering collection of 20th-century art and design, including a crimson Salvador Dalí sofa modelled on Mae West's lips. There's also an enthralling gallery of world art, an impressive collection of Egyptian

Brighton & Hove

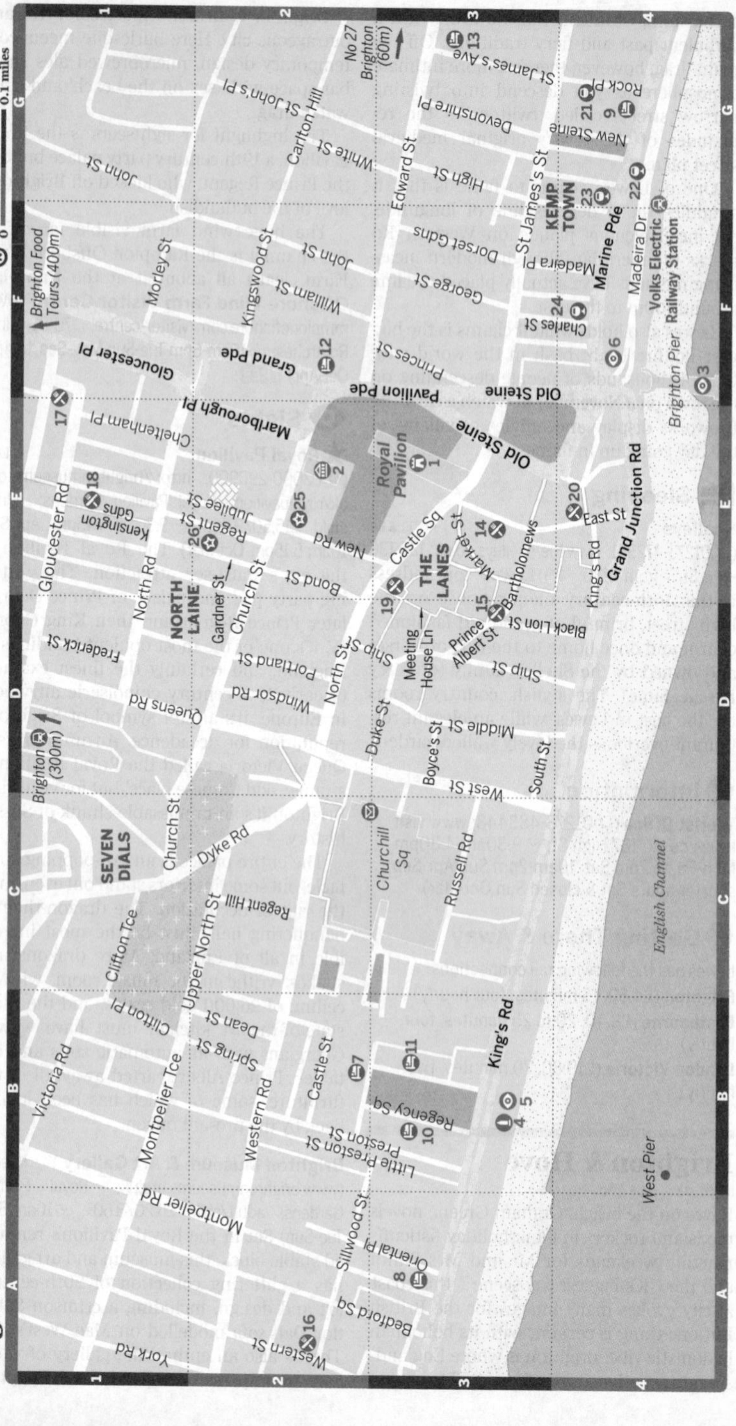

Brighton & Hove

Top Sights
1 Royal Pavilion....E3

Sights
2 Brighton Museum & Art Gallery....E2
3 Brighton Pier....F4
4 i360 Tower....B3
5 Rampion Offshore Wind Farm Visitor Centre....B3
6 SEA LIFE Brighton....F4

Sleeping
7 Artist Residence....B2
8 Baggies Backpackers....A3
9 Drakes....G4
10 Hotel Pelirocco....B3
11 Hotel Una....B3
12 Kipps Brighton....F2
13 No 27 Brighton....G3

Eating
14 English's of Brighton....E3
15 Food for Friends....D3
16 Gingerman....A2
17 Isaac At....F1
18 Iydea....E1
19 Riddle & Finns....E3
20 Terre à Terre....E4

Drinking & Nightlife
21 Brighton Rocks....G4
22 Concorde 2....G4
23 Legends Club....G4
24 Patterns....F4

Entertainment
25 Brighton Dome....E2
26 Komedia Theatre....E2

artefacts, and an 'Images of Brighton' multimedia exhibit containing a series of oral histories and a model of the defunct West Pier.

Brighton Pier LANDMARK
(www.brightonpier.co.uk; Madeira Dr; ⊙11am-9pm Mon-Fri, 10am-10pm Sat, 10am-9pm Sun) Superb fun for the little people, this grand old Edwardian pier is the place to experience Brighton's full-on and shameless seaside kitsch. There are plenty of stomach-churning fairground rides and noisy amusement arcades to keep you entertained, and candyfloss and Brighton rock are on tap to ruin your teeth. Just west are the desolate remains of the **West Pier** (www.westpier.co.uk), a skeletal iron hulk that attracts flocks of starlings at sunset.

i360 Tower TOWER
(☎03337-720360; www.britishairwaysi360.com; Lower King's Rd; adult/16-24 years/child £16.50/11.10/8.25; ⊙10am-7.30pm Sun-Thu, to 9.30pm Fri & Sat) This sci-fi column rises above the Brighton surf at the point where the now-defunct West Pier used to make landfall. The world's most slender tower is an uncompromising, 162m-tall column of reinforced steel and concrete, poking like a space-age cheese-stick from the seafront, with a huge, impaled, glass doughnut taking 'passengers' 138m above the city for gobsmacking views of the Sussex coast.

SEA LIFE Brighton AQUARIUM
(☎01273-604234; www.visitsealife.com/brighton; Marine Pde; adult/child £21.50/13.50; ⊙9am-5.30pm, 10am-4pm in winter; 👪) Not just for children, this aquarium is an underground exhibition of nature's fascinating water creatures. Walking around the church-like interior, visitors can get up close to eels, tropical fish and other sea life. For those who are keen, there are opportunities to feed the animals, touch starfish and ride a glass-bottomed boat over a pool of sharks, rays and turtles.

Tours

Brighton Food Tours FOOD & DRINK
(☎07904 346603; www.brightonfoodtours.com; St Bartholomew's Church, Ann St; per person £55-70; ⊙Fri & Sat) Two enthusiastic local ladies show off the best of Brighton via a trail of tasters and tales. The walking tours highlight culinary treats and street-food secrets, in keeping with the town's creative vibe. Options include the VIB (Very Independent Brighton) tour, Brighton Food & Beer tour, Brighton Wine Rebellion tour and Kemptown tour. Bring comfy shoes and an empty stomach.

Tours leave from several locations – at the time or writing, the main VIB tour left from St Bartholomew's Church on Ann St.

Festivals & Events

Brighton Festival PERFORMING ARTS
(www.brightonfestival.org; ⊙May) England's largest curated annual multi-arts festival, drawing star performers from around the globe for three weeks by the sea.

Brighton Fringe PERFORMING ARTS
(www.brightonfringe.org; May) As with the famous Edinburgh Festival, the Brighton Festival has its fringe – a month of irreverent comedy, art and theatre around the city.

Brighton Pride LGBT
(www.brighton-pride.org; early Aug) The UK's biggest gay bash, with a rainbow-hued parade and concerts in Preston Park.

Sleeping

Kipps Brighton HOSTEL £
(01273-604182; www.kipps-brighton.com; 76 Grand Pde; dm £18-35, s/d from £28/36;) These commendable budget digs have a real cafe vibe around reception, and facilities include a communal kitchen, while free movies plus pizza and pub nights aim to disconnect guests from their wi-fi-enabled devices.

Baggies Backpackers HOSTEL £
(01273-733740; www.baggiesbackpackers.com; 33 Oriental Pl; dm/q from £16/60;) With a warm, familial atmosphere, worn-in charm, attentive service and clean, snug dorms, this long-established hostel is a Brighton institution. There's a cosy basement music and chill-out room, and a TV lounge. The hostel has a single four-person room.

★**No 27 Brighton** B&B ££
(01273-694951; www.brighton-bed-and-breakfast.co.uk; 27 Upper Rock Gardens; r £100-160;) Brighton's favourite B&B has five sumptuous rooms, perfectly presented with antique-style, but fresh, charm. All the fabrics, furniture and decoration have been painstakingly selected to fit a subtle and understated theme, based on people related to King George IV. Some rooms have sea views, but the superb decor is just as diverting. Breakfast (£7.50) is served on crisp linen and fine English china.

★**Hotel Pelirocco** HOTEL ££
(01273-327055; www.hotelpelirocco.co.uk; 10 Regency Sq; s/tw £59/84, d £99-155, tr/ste £165/249;) One of Brighton's sexiest and nuttiest places to stay, the Pelirocco is the ultimate venue for a flirty rock-and-roll weekend. Flamboyant rooms, some designed by artists, include the 'Lord Vader's Quarters', paying homage to *Star Wars;* the 'Do Knit Disturb' room, a knitted room with even a knitted telephone; the Rockabilly room, a shrine to 1950s nostalgia; a 'Modrophenia' room and a Bowie boudoir.

The room everyone wants, or wishes they could have, is the 'Lovers Lair' suite with 3m circular bed, mirrored ceiling and pole-dancing area.

Blanch House BOUTIQUE HOTEL ££
(01273-603504; www.blanchhouse.co.uk; 17 Atlingworth St; s/d incl breakfast from £79/89;) Themed rooms are the name of the game at this boutique hotel, but there's nothing tacky about them – swish art deco styling rules in the Legacia Room, while the Snowstorm is a frosty vision in white and tinkling ice. The magnificently stylish fine-dining restaurant is all white leather banquettes and space-age swivel chairs, and there's a snazzy cocktail bar.

GAY & LESBIAN BRIGHTON

Brighton has the most vibrant LGBT community in the country outside London, with Brighton Pride the highlight of the annual calendar. Kemptown (aka Camptown) on and off St James's St is where it's all at. The old Brunswick Town area of Hove is a quieter alternative to the traditionally cruisy (and sometimes seedy) scene in Kemptown.

For up-to-date information on the LGBT scene in Brighton, check out www.realbrighton.com, or pick up the free monthly magazine *Gscene* (www.gscene.com) from LGBT venues.

Brighton Rocks (01273-600550; www.brightonrocksbar.co.uk; 6 Rock Pl; 4-11pm Mon-Thu, noon-1am Fri & Sat, noon-9pm Sun;) Incongruously located in an alley of garages and used-car lots, this cocktail bar is firmly established on the Kemptown gay scene, but welcomes all comers with Sussex martinis and Bloody Marys, well-executed plates of food and theme parties.

Legends Club (www.legendsbrighton.com; 31-34 Marine Pde; bar 11am-5am, club 10pm-5am Wed & Fri-Sun;) Located beneath the Legends Hotel, this is arguably the best gay bar and club in town.

★Hotel Una BOUTIQUE HOTEL **£££**
(01273-820464; www.hotel-una.co.uk; 55-56 Regency Sq; d £155-210, ste from £165, spa room from £295, all incl breakfast;) All of the 19 generous rooms here wow guests with their bold-patterned fabrics, supersized leather sofas, free-standing baths and vegan, veggie or carnivorous breakfast in bed. Some, such as the two-level suite with its home cinema and private bar, and the under-pavement chambers with their own spa, are truly showstopping and not as expensive as you might expect.

All this plus a cool cocktail bar and lots of time-warp period features make the Una our *numero uno*. Most rooms are two-night minimum stay at weekends.

★Artist Residence BOUTIQUE HOTEL **£££**
(01273-324302; www.artistresidencebrighton.co.uk; 34 Regency Sq; d £120-290;) Eclectic doesn't quite describe the rooms at this wonderful 24-room town-house hotel, set amid the splendour of Regency Sq. As befits the name, every bedroom is a hip blend of bold wall murals, bespoke and vintage furniture, rough wood cladding and in-room roll-top baths. The Set Restaurant downstairs enjoys a glowing reputation.

Drakes BOUTIQUE HOTEL **£££**
(01273-696934; www.drakesofbrighton.com; 43-44 Marine Pde; r £110-300;) This stylishly minimalist boutique hotel oozes understated class. So understated is the entrance, in fact, you could easily miss it. All rooms have similar decor in bold fabrics and European elm panelling, but it's the feature rooms everyone wants – their giant free-standing tubs are set in front of full-length bay windows with widescreen Channel views. The basement restaurant is superb.

Eating

★Iydea VEGETARIAN **£**
(www.iydea.co.uk; 17 Kensington Gardens; mains £5-8; 9.30am-5.30pm;) Even by Brighton's high standards, the food at this multi-award-winning vegetarian cafe is a treat. The daily-changing choices of curries, lasagnes, felafel, enchiladas and quiches are full of flavour and can be washed down with a selection of vegan wines, organic ales and homemade lemonades. If you're on the hop, you can get any dish to take away in plastic-free packaging.

DON'T MISS

THE LANES

In the market for a pair of vegan shoes, a striking portrait of a Lego man, or a letter opener in the shape of a...? Well, whatever item you yearn for, old or new, you'll probably find it in Brighton.

The tightly packed Lanes is the most popular shopping district, its every twist and turn jam-packed with jewellers and gift shops, coffee shops and boutiques selling everything from antique firearms to hard-to-find vinyl.

There's another, less-claustrophobic shopping district in North Laine, a series of partially pedestrian thoroughfares north of the Lanes, including Bond, Gardner, Kensington and Sydney Sts, lined with retro-cool boutiques and bohemian cafes.

★Terre à Terre VEGETARIAN **££**
(01273-729051; www.terreaterre.co.uk; 71 East St; mains from £16.95; noon-10pm Tue-Sun;) Take your taste buds around a meat-free world in this vegetarian restaurant, where inventive and flavourful dishes are meticulously plated in a casual and friendly ambience. The range is breathtaking, from wasabi-crusted cashews to fondue soufflé and steamed Szechuan buns, rounded off with salt caramel truffles. A daily afternoon-tea service includes a vegan option.

English's of Brighton SEAFOOD **££**
(01273-327980; www.englishs.co.uk; 29-31 East St; mains £16-40; noon-10pm) A 75-year-old institution and celebrity haunt, this local seafood paradise dishes up everything from Essex oysters to locally caught lobster and Dover sole. It's converted from fishers' cottages, with shades of the elegant style of the Edwardian era inside, and has al fresco dining on the pedestrian square outside.

Riddle & Finns SEAFOOD **££**
(01273-721667; www.riddleandfinns.co.uk; 12b Meeting House Lane; mains £14.50-22.50; noon-10pm Sun-Fri, 11.30am-11pm Sat) Regarded as the town's most refined seafood spot, R&F is light on gimmicky interiors (think white butcher-shop tiles, marble tables and candles) but heavy on taste. With the kitchen open to the street outside, chefs put on a public cooking class with every dish as they prepare your smoked haddock in champagne sauce or some wild sea bass.

WORTH A TRIP

THE DEVIL'S PUNCHBOWL

A delightfully scenic valley scooped out of the verdant Surrey hills, the **Devil's Punchbowl** (NT; www.nationaltrust.org.uk; London Rd, Hindhead; dawn-dusk, cafe 10am-4pm; P) is a beautiful diversion that can swallow up an entire day of walking or cycling through heather-strewn landscape, dense woodland and across fields and crystal-clear streams. Five scenic hiking trails are marked out, from a 1.6km stroll to a more energetic 5km steeper-gradient walk. Legend attests that the depression was the result of Thor throwing a huge handful of earth into the Devil's face, leaving the hollow.

In geological terms, the Devil's Punchbowl is actually the result of a process called 'spring sapping', involving rainwater hitting an impermeable layer of clay and emerging as spring water, eroding the local sandstone and, over millennia, creating the vast bowl-like shape.

Food for Friends VEGETARIAN ££

(01273-202310; www.foodforfriends.com; 17-18 Prince Albert St; mains £6-16; 9am-10pm Sun-Thu, to 10.30pm Fri & Sat;) An ever-inventive choice of vegetarian and vegan food keeps loyal diners returning here to see and be seen – literally, by every passerby through the huge street-side windows. Kept fresh-looking, zestful and as popular as the day it opened in 1981, it also serves breakfast and brunch daily. Be prepared to wait for a table on busy shopping days.

Gingerman MODERN EUROPEAN £££

(01273-326688; www.gingermanrestaurants.com; 21a Norfolk Sq; 2-/3-course menu £40/50, Sunday lunch 1/2/3 courses £23/30/35; 12.30-2pm & 6-10pm Tue-Sun) Hastings seafood, Sussex beef, Romney Marsh lamb, local sparkling wines and countless other seasonal, local and British treats go into the adroitly flash-fried and slow-cooked dishes served at this snug 32-cover eatery. Reservations are advised. Norfolk Sq is a short walk west along Western Rd from the Churchill Sq shopping centre.

The tasting menu and vegetarian tasting menu are both £65.

Isaac At BRITISH £££

(07765-934740; www.isaac-at.com; 2 Gloucester St; 3-course set menu £30, tasting menu £60; 12.30-2.30pm Sat & 6-10.30pm Wed-Sat) Tucked on a street corner, this intimate fine-dining restaurant is run by a small team of culinary talent, all aged under 30. Every ingredient is locally sourced, including the wines, with food miles for each ingredient noted on the menu. It's probably the homeliest high-end dining experience in the area. First-class, fresh and thoughtful food.

The three-course menu is available on Wednesday and Thursday evenings and Saturday lunch. Gluten-free and vegan menus are also provided.

Drinking & Nightlife

Concorde 2 CLUB

(01273-673311; www.concorde2.co.uk; Madeira Dr; live shows 7.30-11pm Sun-Thu, 7-10pm Fri & Sat, club 11pm-4am Fri & Sat;) Brighton's best-known and best-loved club is a disarmingly unpretentious den. Each month there's a huge variety of club nights, live bands and emerging singers and concerts by international names.

Patterns CLUB

(01273-894777; www.patternsbrighton.com; 10 Marine Pde; Wed-Sat, hours vary;) Some of the city's top club nights are held downstairs at this ear-numbing venue in a former 1920s hotel. The music is top priority, attracting big-name acts and a young crowd. There's a fine terrace with superb views out to sea.

Entertainment

Komedia Theatre COMEDY

(01273-647100; www.komedia.co.uk; 44-47 Gardner St) The UK's top comedy venue attracts the best stand-up acts from the English-speaking world. Book well in advance.

Brighton Dome THEATRE

(01273-709709; www.brightondome.org; Church St) Once the stables for King George IV's horses, this art deco complex within the Royal Pavilion estate houses three theatre venues. ABBA famously won the 1974 Eurovision Song Contest here. Restoration work was ongoing at the time of writing.

Information

Incredibly, Brighton closed its busy tourist office several years ago, replacing it with 13 visitor information points (VIPs) across the city – mostly racks of brochures in hotels, shops and museums; one is in Brighton train station.

Contact **Visit Brighton** (☎01273-290337; www.visitbrighton.com) for information.

Getting There & Away

BUS

Services run between Brighton and London Victoria (from £11, 2½ hours) at least every two hours.

TRAIN

There are three trains hourly to London Victoria (£19.80, one hour), and half-hourly trains to London St Pancras (£19.10, 1¼ hours). London-bound services pass through Gatwick Airport (£9.30, 25 to 35 minutes, up to five hourly).

Getting Around

Day citySaver bus tickets (£5) are available from the drivers of all Brighton and Hove buses. Alternatively, a £3.90 PlusBus ticket on top of your rail fare gives unlimited bus travel for the day.

The city operates a pricey pay-and-display parking scheme. In the town centre, it costs between £1 and £3.60 per hour for a maximum stay of two hours. Alternatively there's a Park & Ride 2.5 miles northwest of the centre at Withdean, from where bus 27 (return £5) zips into town.

Cab companies include **Brighton Streamline Taxis** (☎01273-202020; www.streamlinetaxis.org) and **Brighton & Hove Radio Cabs** (☎01273-204060; www.brightontaxis.com) and there's a taxi rank at the junction of East and Market Sts.

WEST SUSSEX

West Sussex offers pastoral escapes into a charming and historic corner of England. The serene hills and valleys of the South Downs ripple across this green county, fringed by a sheltered coastline. Time-warped Arundel and cultured, ancient Chichester make superb bases from which to explore the county's winding country lanes and remarkable Roman ruins.

Arundel

☎01903 / POP 3500

Arguably the prettiest town in West Sussex, Arundel is clustered around a vast fairy-tale castle, its hillside streets overflowing with antique emporiums, creaking bookshops, teashops, inviting eateries and intriguing art galleries. While much of the town appears medieval – the whimsical castle has been home to the dukes of Norfolk for centuries – most of it dates back to Victorian times. The ostentatious 19th-century Catholic **cathedral** (www.arundelcathedral.org; London Rd; 9am-6pm Apr-Oct, to dusk Nov-Mar) FREE is another of Arundel's dominating features.

Sights

Arundel Castle CASTLE

(www.arundelcastle.org; adult/child/family £15/5/35; 10am-5pm Tue-Sun Easter-Oct) An imposing bastion rising above Arundel, the castle was first built in the 11th century – the motte dates to 1068, the gatehouse dates from 1070 and the restored keep (which you can climb up to and explore) atop the motte was originally built of wood around the same time. Ransacked during the English Civil War, the rest of the castle is the result of reconstruction by the various dukes of Norfolk between 1718 and 1900. Don't miss the colossal Baron's Hall and the stunning library.

The current duke still lives in part of the castle, with eight bedrooms at his disposal, and only uses the halls and rooms that visitors can see for select functions. The formal gardens are also quite spectacular and worth exploration, while the magnificent tulip displays are a sight to behold in April. A recently opened feature is the water gardens – originally the 'stew ponds' where fish were kept – with its swans, ducks, roundhouse and charming thatched boathouse. Consult the website for information on family-friendly activities, such as jousting demonstrations in summer.

DON'T MISS

BOX HILL

The famous setting of the picnic in Jane Austen's *Emma*, **Box Hill** (☎01306-885502; www.nationaltrust.org.uk/box-hill; Zig Zag Rd, Box Hill; dawn-dusk; P) is pure bliss. A vast chunk of the chalk expanse of the North Downs, Box Hill offers some sublimely photogenic, entrancing and ranging views over the Surrey countryside. Popular with cyclists and family day trippers, Box Hill is home to almost infinite walking opportunities (check out the downloadable walks on the National Trust website) as well as a dense profusion of wildlife, trees and plants.

Sleeping & Eating

Arden Guest House B&B ££
(01903-884184; www.ardenhousearundel.com; 4 Queens Lane; d £99, without bathroom £89; P) For the classic British B&B experience, head to this seven-room guesthouse just over the river from the historical centre. Rooms are kept very pleasant, fresh and airy, the hosts are amiable and inviting, and breakfasts are cooked.

★**Motte & Bailey Cafe** CAFE £
(01903-883813; www.motteandbaileycafe.com; 49 High St; mains £6.95-9.95; 8.30am-4pm Mon & Tue, 8.30am-5pm & 6pm-late Wed-Sat, 8.30am-5pm Sun;) A modish interior of white, dark blue, varnished floorboards and glimpses of exposed brick, this airy and bright space is a welcome recuperation spot after castle explorations. There's ample vegetarian choice on the brief menu, which ranges from poached eggs and smashed avocado to delectable salmon, cod and prawn fishcakes, or just a bowl of its exceedingly tasty chips.

Shopping

★**Arundel Contemporary** ART
(www.arundelcontemporary.com; 53 High St; 10am-4pm Sun-Tue & Thu, to 5pm Fri & Sat) This excellent art gallery eschews the mundane for some simply riveting pieces, carefully selected and curated. The ceramic works from South Korea–born Jin Eui Kim are exquisite in their patterns and fragile beauty, while a profusion of thought-provoking and engaging art hangs from the walls. The helpful owner is loquacious about each and every piece.

Getting There & Away

Arundel has the following train connections:

Brighton (£11.40, 1¼ hours, half-hourly) Change at Barnham or Ford.

Chichester (£4.90, 25 minutes, twice hourly) Change at Ford or Barnham.

London Victoria (£19.80, 1½ hours, twice hourly)

Chichester

01243 / POP 26,795

A lively Georgian market town still almost encircled by its ancient Roman and medieval town walls, the administrative capital of West Sussex keeps watch over the plains between the South Downs and the sea. Visitors flock to Chichester's splendid cathedral, streets of handsome 18th-century town houses, its famous theatre and its pedestrianised shopping streets packed with big-name and independent shops. A Roman port garrison in its early days, the town is also a gateway to nearby Roman remains of immense archaeological value, as well as to Arundel and a popular stretch of attractive coast.

Sights

Chichester Cathedral CATHEDRAL
(www.chichestercathedral.org.uk; West St; 7.15am-6.30pm, free tours 11.15am & 2.30pm Mon-Sat) This understated cathedral was begun in 1075 and largely rebuilt in the 13th century. The free-standing church tower went up in the 15th century – the spire dates from the 19th century, after its predecessor famously toppled over without warning in 1861. Inside, three storeys of beautiful arches sweep upwards and Romanesque carvings are dotted around. Interesting features to track down include a smudgy stained-glass window added by artist Marc Chagall in 1978 and a glassed-over section of Roman mosaic flooring.

Pallant House Gallery GALLERY
(01243-774557; www.pallant.org.uk; 9 North Pallant; adult/child £11/free; 10am-4pm Tue-Sat, 11am-4pm Sun) A Queen Anne mansion, handsome Pallant House, and a 21st-century wing host this superb gallery. The focus is on mostly 20th-century British art. Show-stoppers Patrick Caulfield, Lucian Freud, Graham Sutherland, Frank Auerbach and Henry Moore are interspersed with international names such as Emil Filla, Le Corbusier and RB Kitaj. Most older works are in the mansion, while the newer wing is packed with pop art, contemporary work and a huge, colourful geometric mural from Lothar Götz on the staircase walls.

Chichester City Walls ARCHITECTURE
(www.chichesterwalls.org/chichester-city-walls) Chichester's almost complete ring of Roman defensive walls are around 1.5 miles in length, and provide a pleasant escape from the retail bustle they now contain. Pick up a leaflet and booklet from the tourist office and head out along the route, much of which leads through parkland. Built to defend the town of Noviomagus Reginorum 1800 years ago, they are just about the most intact set of Roman city walls in Britain. Best accessed from West or East Sts.

Novium Museum MUSEUM
(☎01243-775888; www.thenovium.org; Tower St; ⏰10am-3pm Tue-Fri, to 4pm Sat) FREE Chichester's purpose-built museum provides a home for the eclectic collections of the erstwhile District Museum, as well as some artefacts from Fishbourne Palace and a huge mosaic from Chilgrove Roman villa. The highlight is the set of Roman *thermae* (baths) discovered in the 1970s, around which this £6-million wedge of architecture was designed.

Sleeping & Eating

Trents B&B ££
(☎01243-773714; 50 South St; d from £64;) Neat and tidy Trents is one of very few places in which to hit the sack in the thick of the city-centre action, with five snazzy rooms above a trendy bar-restaurant. Guests heap praise on the helpful staff and big breakfast.

Chichester Harbour Hotel BOUTIQUE HOTEL £££
(☎01243-778000; www.chichester-harbour-hotel.co.uk; North St; s/d from £105/125;) An enticing option that boasts a stylish restaurant, this Georgian hotel has comfortable, period rooms spiced up with bold colours. Book well ahead.

Purchases BRITISH ££
(☎01243-771444; www.purchasesrestaurant.co.uk; 31 North St; mains £15-30, set menu 2/3 courses £22.95/25.95; ⏰8am-10pm Mon-Sat, to 5pm Sun;) Aptly named for Chichester's shopping streets, this crisply done-out, slightly upmarket restaurant plates up modern takes on British classics such as beef Wellington, beer-battered fish of the day and roast lamb rump. The pre-theatre menu is much better value than selecting from the main menu. Very attractive and colourful accommodation is also provided.

Information

Tourist Office (☎01243-775888; www.visitchichester.org; Tower St; ⏰10am-5pm Mon-Sat, to 4pm Sun summer, 10am-5pm Wed-Sat, to 4pm Sun winter) Located in the Novium Museum.

DON'T MISS

FISHBOURNE ROMAN PALACE

The largest-known Roman residence in Britain, **Fishbourne Roman Palace** (☎01243-785859; www.sussexpast.co.uk; Roman Way; adult/concession/child £10/9.60/5.20; ⏰10.30am-4pm Mar-Oct, reduced hours & days Nov-Feb) has an area larger than Buckingham Palace. Lying just off the A259 1.5 miles west of Chichester, and chanced upon by labourers laying a water main in the 1960s, this once-luxurious mansion was probably built around AD 75 for a Romanised local king, though debate still swarms around the owner's identity. Housed in a modern pavilion are its foundations, hypocaust and painstakingly relaid mosaics. Take bus 700 from outside Chichester Cathedral.

The centrepiece is a spectacular mosaic floor depicting Cupid riding a dolphin, flanked by sea horses and panthers. There's also a fascinating little museum and replanted Roman gardens.

Getting There & Away

BUS

Chichester has bus connections to the following:

Brighton (bus 700; £5.20, three hours, twice hourly)

Portsmouth (bus 700; £4.90, 70 minutes, twice hourly)

TRAIN

Chichester has train connections to the following:

Arundel (£4.90, 24 minutes, twice hourly) Change at Ford or Barnham.

Brighton (£14.40, 50 minutes, half-hourly)

London Victoria (£19.80, 1½ hours, half-hourly)

Portsmouth (£8.30, 30 to 40 minutes, three hourly)

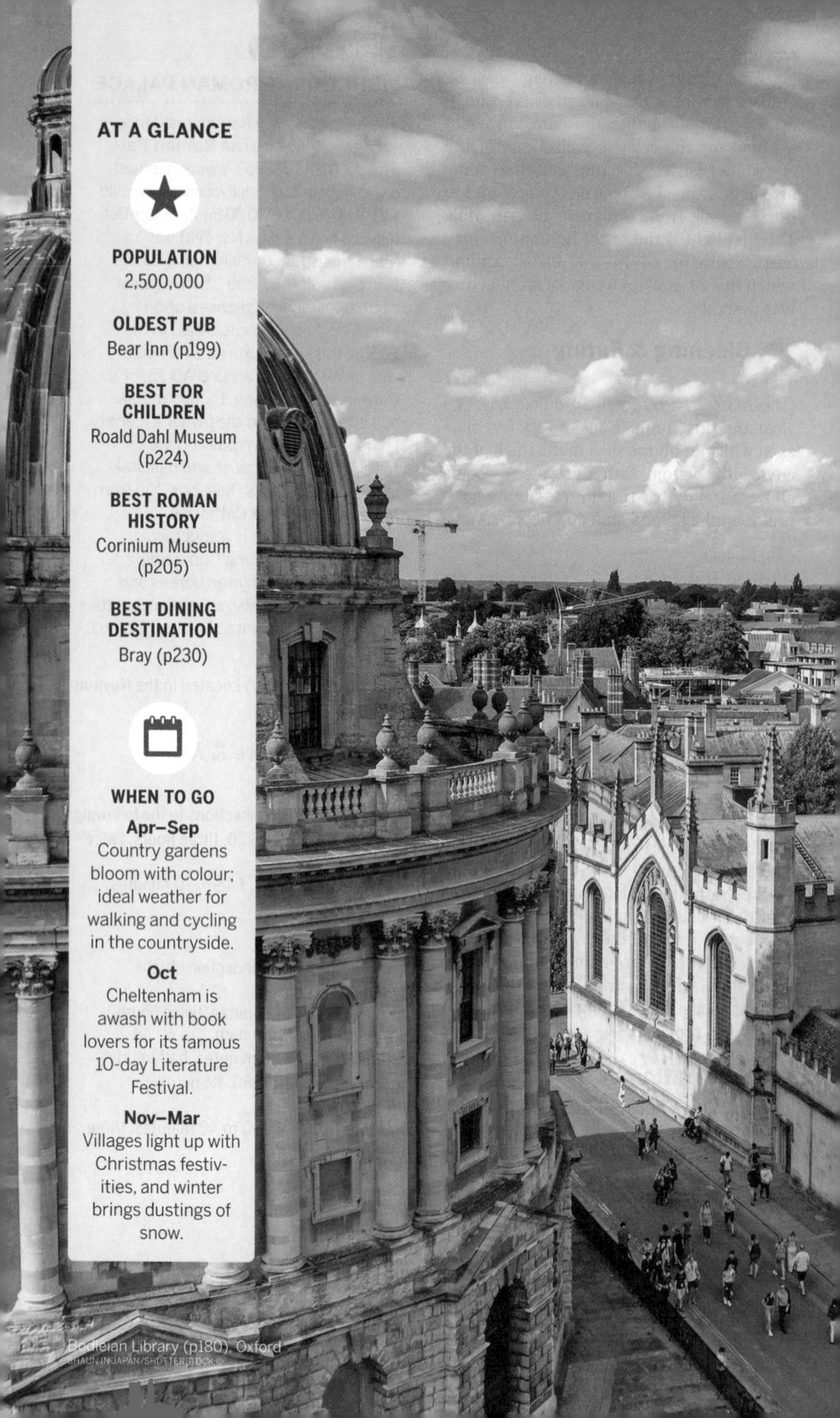

AT A GLANCE

POPULATION
2,500,000

OLDEST PUB
Bear Inn (p199)

BEST FOR CHILDREN
Roald Dahl Museum (p224)

BEST ROMAN HISTORY
Corinium Museum (p205)

BEST DINING DESTINATION
Bray (p230)

WHEN TO GO

Apr–Sep
Country gardens bloom with colour; ideal weather for walking and cycling in the countryside.

Oct
Cheltenham is awash with book lovers for its famous 10-day Literature Festival.

Nov–Mar
Villages light up with Christmas festivities, and winter brings dustings of snow.

Bodleian Library (p180), Oxford

Oxford & the Cotswolds

Sprinkled with picture-perfect villages and historic sites, this section of England that stretches westwards from London to the border with Wales comes as close to a fairytale version of England as you'll ever find. Green-cloaked hills, rose-clad stone cottages, graceful churches and thatched roofed houses abound. Add the university city of Oxford, with its majestic architecture, and you can see why the region draws visitors in droves.

The Cotswolds work their finest magic when you find your own romantic hideaway. Splendid country houses lie tucked away throughout Buckinghamshire, Bedfordshire and Hertfordshire. Further west, the Forest of Dean offers the promise of outdoorsy adventures.

This region deserves at least a week to be properly enjoyed.

INCLUDES

Getting There & Around

A car will give you the greatest freedom, especially if you want to explore the scattered villages of the Cotswolds.

Local buses, run by various operators, link larger towns to each other and surrounding villages. For timetables, use the journey planner tool on Traveline (www.traveline.info).

Oxford, Moreton-in-Marsh, Stroud, Cheltenham, Gloucester, Bletchley, Hatfield, St Albans, Henley-on-Thames and Windsor are all serviced by trains, most with direct lines to London. Other direct trains go as far as Birmingham, Manchester and Newcastle (from Oxford), and Cardiff, Edinburgh and Exeter (from Cheltenham).

OXFORD

☎01865 / POP 161,300

A glorious ensemble of golden-hued architecture and lush water meadows, Oxford ranks among England's most beautiful cities. In fact, as you stroll through its university college campuses, it can be hard to believe you're in modern England at all. Certain buildings stand out, like the domed and glowing Radcliffe Camera, or admire others built by famous English architects, Sir Christopher Wren and Nicholas Hawksmoor. One of the main joys of visiting Oxford lies in the sense of intellectual history being forged in the centuries-old colleges, each with its own permutations of Gothic chapels, secluded cloisters and tranquil quadrangles.

History

Strategically placed at the confluence of the Rivers Cherwell and Thames (called the Isis here, from the Latin Tamesis, because, well, this is Oxford after all), this was once a key Saxon town, heavily fortified by Alfred the Great during the war against the Danes. It continued to grow under the Normans, who founded its castle in 1071.

By the 11th century, the Augustinian abbey in Oxford had begun training clerics, and when Anglo-Norman clerical scholars were expelled from the Sorbonne in 1167, the abbey began to attract students in droves. The first three colleges – University, Balliol and Merton – were founded in the mid-13th century. Alongside Oxford's growing prosperity grew the enmity between local townspeople and new students ('town and gown'), culminating in the St Scholastica's Day Massacre in 1355, which started as an argument over beer but resulted in 90 deaths. Thereafter, the king ordered that the university be broken up into colleges, each of which developed its own traditions.

The university, largely a religious entity at the time, was rocked in the 16th century by the Reformation; the public trials and burning at the stake of Protestant heretics under Mary I; and by the subsequent hanging, drawing and quartering of Catholics under her successor Elizabeth I. As the Royalist headquarters, Oxford backed the losing side during the Civil War, but flourished after the restoration of the monarchy, with some of its most notable buildings constructed in the late 17th and early 18th centuries.

The arrival of the canal system in 1790 had a profound effect on Oxford. By creating a link with the Midlands' industrial centres, work and trade suddenly expanded beyond the academic core. This was further strengthened by the construction of the railways in the 19th century.

The city's real industrial boom came, however, when William Morris began producing cars here in 1913. With the success of his Bullnose Morris and Morris Minor, his Cowley factory went on to become one of the largest motor plants in the world. Although works have been scaled down since, Minis still run off BMW's Cowley production line today, although the Covid-19 pandemic had cast a shadow over its future.

Sights

Oxford is a compact city, with its major sights largely congregated in the centre. Almost all, including the Bodleian Library and the Ashmolean Museum, are connected with the university, while several of the university colleges themselves are favourite visitor attractions. Plans to pedestrianise some city streets gained traction during the Covid-19 pandemic, promising to make outdoor dining and social distancing more achievable.

City Centre

★Bodleian Library LIBRARY

(☎01865-287400; www.bodleian.ox.ac.uk/bodley; Catte St; ⏲9am-5pm Mon-Sat, 11am-5pm Sun) At least five kings, dozens of prime ministers and Nobel laureates, and luminaries such as Oscar Wilde, CS Lewis and JRR Tolkien have studied in Oxford's Bodleian Library, a

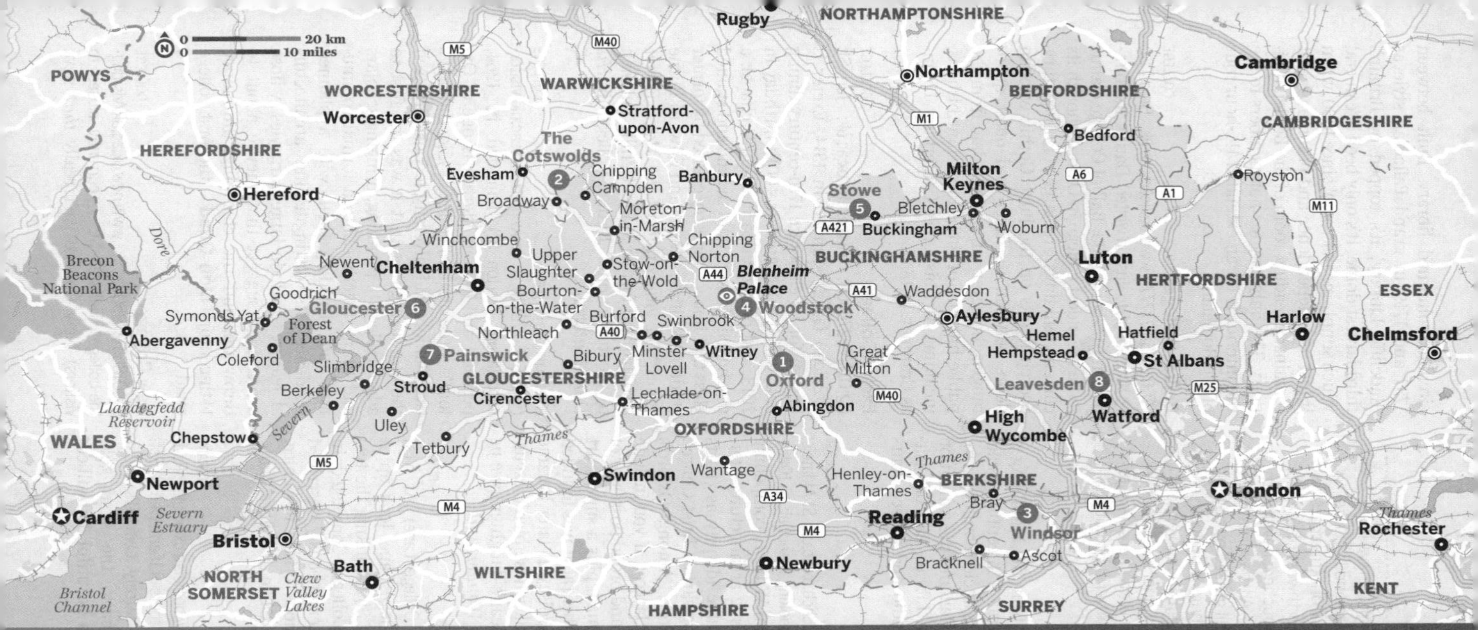

Oxford & the Cotswolds Highlights

1 **Oxford** (p188) Following in the inspirational footsteps of JRR Tolkien, CS Lewis and Lewis Carroll as you explore magical colleges.

2 **The Cotswolds** (p204) Strolling through gold-tinged Cotswolds villages, such as Chipping Campden or Broadway.

3 **Windsor** (p227) Catching a glimpse of how royalty relaxes at the Queen's weekend hideaway.

4 **Blenheim Palace** (p201) Lording it up at one of Britain's greatest stately homes, in Woodstock.

5 **Stowe Gardens** (p226) Getting lost in a serene world of spectacular 18th-century landscaped gardens.

6 **Gloucester Cathedral** (p223) Strolling the elegant cloisters of this exquisite Perpendicular Gothic creation.

7 **Painswick** (p218) Enjoying one of the most beautiful towns in the Cotswolds.

8 **The Making of Harry Potter** (p225) Unleashing your inner wizard at this working studio tour.

PORT MEADOW

Although archaeologists have identified traces of Bronze and Iron Age settlements bulging from this marshy Thames meadow, northwest of Jericho, it has remained untouched, never even ploughed, ever since. A treasure trove of rare plants, it's still grazed by cows and horses, and it's hugely popular with walkers (stopping off at riverside pub, the Trout) and runners. In winter it gets so waterlogged that hikers have to go round the edge rather than cutting straight across!

magnificent survivor from the Middle Ages. Wander into its central 17th-century quad, and you can admire its ancient buildings for free. Both Blackwell Hall and the exhibition rooms in the Weston Library can be visited free of charge. Audio and guided tours available.

★Christ Church COLLEGE
(☎01865-276492; www.chch.ox.ac.uk; St Aldate's; adult/child £15/14, pre-booking essential; ⌚10am-5pm Mon-Sat, 2-5pm Sun) With its compelling combination of majestic architecture, literary heritage and double identity as (parts of) Harry Potter's Hogwarts, Christ Church attracts tourists galore. Among Oxford's largest colleges – *the* largest, if you include its bucolic meadow – and proud possessor of its most impressive quad, plus a superb art gallery and even a cathedral, it was founded in 1525 by Cardinal Wolsey. It later became home to Lewis Carroll, whose picnic excursions with the then-dean's daughter gave us *Alice's Adventures in Wonderland*.

Bridge of Sighs BRIDGE
(Hertford Bridge; New College Lane) As you stroll along New College Lane, look up at the steeped Bridge of Sighs linking the two halves of Hertford College. Completed in 1914, it's sometimes erroneously described as a copy of the famous bridge in Venice, but it looks much more like that city's Rialto Bridge.

Radcliffe Camera LIBRARY
(☎01865-287400; www.bodleian.ox.ac.uk; Radcliffe Sq; tours £15; ⌚tours 9.15am Wed & Sat, 11.15am & 1.15pm Sun) Surely Oxford's most photographed landmark, the sandy-gold Radcliffe Camera is a beautiful, light-filled, circular, columned library. Built between 1737 and 1749 in grand Palladian style as 'Radcliffe Library', it's topped by Britain's third-largest dome. It's only been a 'camera', which simply means 'room', since 1860, when it lost its independence and became what it remains: a reading room of the Bodleian Library. The only way for nonmembers to see the interior is on an extended 1½-hour tour of the Bodleian.

Balliol College COLLEGE
(☎01865-277777; www.balliol.ox.ac.uk; Broad St; ⌚10am-5pm, to dusk in winter) Dating its foundation to 'about' 1263, Balliol College claims to be the oldest college in Oxford, though its current buildings are largely 19th-century. Scorch marks on the huge Gothic wooden doors between its inner and outer quadrangles, however, supposedly date from the public burning of three Protestant bishops, including Archbishop of Canterbury Thomas Cranmer, in 1556.

Exeter College COLLEGE
(☎01865-279600; www.exeter.ox.ac.uk; Turl St; ⌚2-5pm) FREE Founded in 1314, Exeter is known for its elaborate 17th-century dining hall, which celebrated its 400th birthday in 2018, and ornate Victorian Gothic chapel, a psychedelic blast of gold mosaic and stained glass that holds a tapestry created by former students William Morris and Edward Burne Jones, *The Adoration of the Magi*. Exeter also inspired former student Philip Pullman to create fictional Jordan College in *His Dark Materials*.

Merton College COLLEGE
(☎01865-276310; www.merton.ox.ac.uk/visitor-information; Merton St) Founded in 1264, peaceful and elegant Merton is one of Oxford's three original colleges. Like the other two, Balliol and University, it considers itself the oldest, arguing that it was the first to adopt collegiate planning, bringing scholars and tutors together into a formal community and providing them with a planned residence. Its distinguishing architectural features include large gargoyles, whose expressions suggest that they're about to throw up, and the charming, diminutive 14th-century **Mob Quad** – the first college quad.

New College COLLEGE
(☎01865-279500; www.new.ox.ac.uk/visiting-the-college; Holywell St; ⌚currently closed to visitors) New College isn't really *that* new.

Established in 1379 as Oxford's first undergraduate college, it's a glorious Perpendicular Gothic ensemble. Treasures in the chapel include superb medieval stained glass and Sir Jacob Epstein's disturbing 1951 statue of Lazarus, wrapped in his shroud; in term time, visitors can attend the beautiful choral Evensong service (6.15pm nightly). The 15th-century cloisters and evergreen oak featured in *Harry Potter and the Goblet of Fire*, while the dining hall is the oldest in Oxbridge.

Trinity College COLLEGE
(☎01865-279900; www.trinity.ox.ac.uk; Broad St; adult/child £3/2; ⊙9.30am-noon & 2pm-dusk) Founded in 1555, this small college boasts a lovely 17th-century garden quad, designed by Sir Christopher Wren. Its exquisite chapel, a masterpiece of English baroque, contains a limewood altar screen adorned with flowers and fruit carved by master craftsman Grinling Gibbons in 1694, and is looking fabulous after recent restoration work. Famous students have included Cardinal Newman, William Pitt the Elder, two British prime ministers, and the fictional Jay Gatsby, the Great Gatsby himself.

Museum of the History of Science MUSEUM
(☎01865-277293; www.mhs.ox.ac.uk; Broad St; ⊙noon-5pm Tue-Sun) FREE Students of science will swoon at this fascinating museum, stuffed to the ceilings with awesome astrolabes, astonishing orreries and early electrical apparatus. Housed in the lovely 17th-century building that held the original Ashmolean Museum, it displays everything from cameras that belonged to Lewis Carroll and Lawrence of Arabia, to a wireless receiver used by Marconi in 1896 and a blackboard that was covered with equations by Einstein in 1931, when he was invited to give three lectures on relativity.

University Church of St Mary the Virgin CHURCH
(☎01865-279111; www.university-church.ox.ac.uk; High St; church free, tower £5; ⊙10am-6pm Mon-Sat, noon-6pm Sun) The ornate 14th-century spire of Oxford's university church is arguably the dreamiest of the city's legendary 'dreaming spires'. The church is famous as the site where three Anglican bishops, including the first Protestant archbishop of Canterbury, Thomas Cranmer, were tried for heresy in 1556, during the reign of Mary I. All three were later burned at the stake on Broad St. Visitors can climb the church's 1280 tower for excellent views of the adjacent Radcliffe Camera.

Jericho & Science Area

★Ashmolean Museum MUSEUM
(☎01865-278000; www.ashmolean.org; Beaumont St; ⊙10am-5pm Tue-Sun, to 8pm last Fri of month; 👪) FREE Britain's oldest public museum, Oxford's wonderful Ashmolean Museum is surpassed only by the British Museum in London. It was established in 1683, when Elias Ashmole presented Oxford University with a collection of 'rarities' amassed by the well-travelled John Tradescant, gardener to Charles I. You could easily spend a day exploring this magnificent neoclassical building, and family-friendly pamphlets draw kids into select exhibits. Pre-booking required.

★Pitt Rivers Museum MUSEUM
(☎01865-270927; www.prm.ox.ac.uk; South Parks Rd; ⊙10am-5pm; 👪) FREE If exploring an enormous room full of eccentric and unexpected artefacts sounds like your idea of the perfect afternoon, welcome to the amulets-to-zithers extravaganza that is the Pitt Rivers museum. Tucked behind Oxford's natural history museum, and dimly lit to protect its myriad treasures, it's centred on an anthropological collection amassed by a Victorian general, and revels in exploring how differing cultures have tackled topics like 'Smoking and Stimulants' and 'Treatment of Dead Enemies'.

Oxford University Museum of Natural History MUSEUM
(☎01865-272950; www.oum.ox.ac.uk; Parks Rd; ⊙10am-5pm; 👪) FREE Housed in a glorious

TOLKIEN'S RESTING PLACE

Lord of the Rings author JRR Tolkien (1892–1973) is buried with his wife Edith at **Wolvercote Cemetery** (Banbury Rd, Wolvercote; ⊙7am-8pm Mon-Fri, 8am-8pm Sat & Sun Apr-Sep, to 5pm Oct-Mar), 2.5 miles north of Oxford city centre. Their gravestone bears the names Beren (for him) and Lúthien (for her), referencing the love between a mortal man and an elf maiden who gave up her immortality to be with him.

Oxford

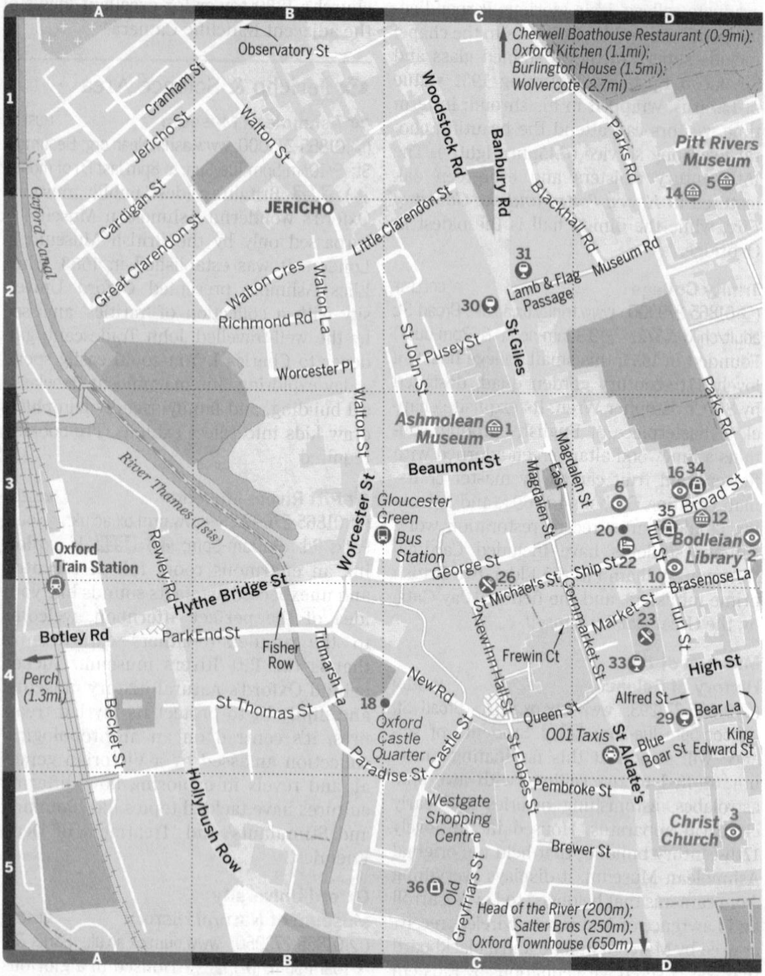

Victorian Gothic building, with cast-iron columns, flower-carved capitals and a soaring glass roof, this museum makes a superb showcase for some extraordinary exhibits. Specimens from all over the world include a 150-year-old Japanese spider crab, but it's the dinosaurs that really wow the crowds. As well as a towering T-rex skeleton – 'Stan', the second most complete ever found – you'll see pieces of Megalosaurus, which was in 1677 the first dinosaur ever mentioned in a written text.

Southeast Oxford

★**Magdalen College** COLLEGE

(☎01865-276000; www.magd.ox.ac.uk; High St; adult/child £7/6, pre-booking required; ⌚10am-7pm late Jun-late Sep, 1pm-dusk rest of year) Guarding access to a breathtaking expanse of private lawns, woodlands, river walks and even its own deer park, Magdalen ('mawd-lin'), founded in 1458, is one of Oxford's wealthiest and most beautiful colleges. Beyond its elegant Victorian gateway, you come to its medieval chapel and glorious 15th-century tower. From here,

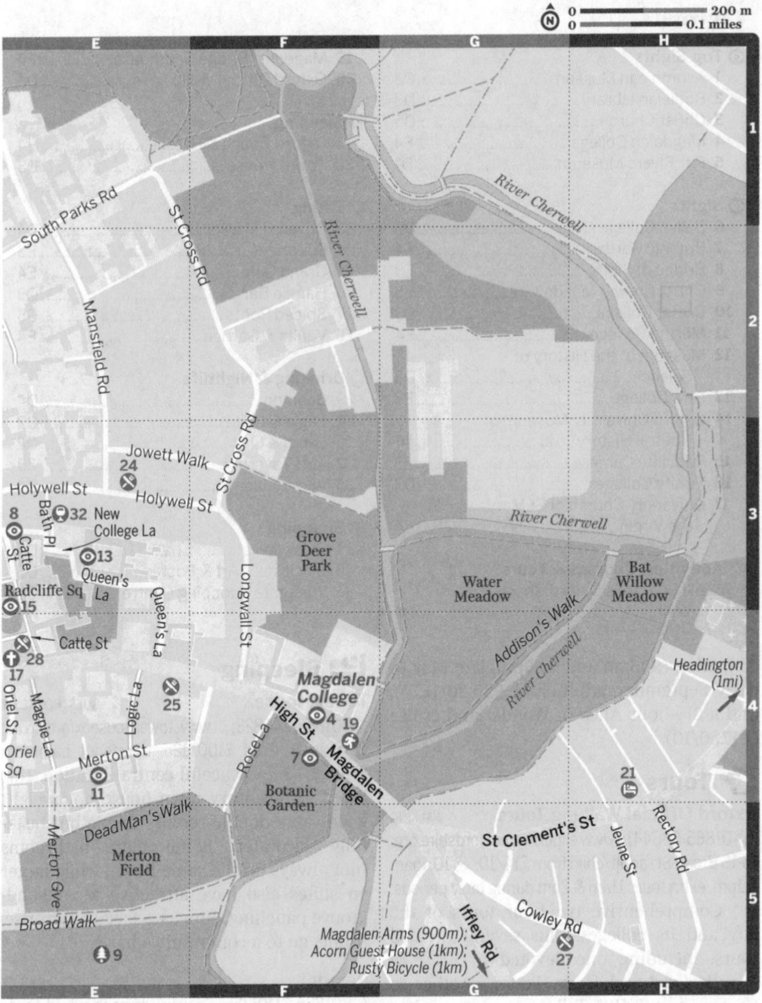

move on to the remarkable 15th-century **cloisters**, where the fantastic grotesques (carved figures) may have inspired CS Lewis' stone statues in *The Chronicles of Narnia*.

Activities

Magdalen Bridge Boathouse BOATING

(☎01865-202643; www.oxfordpunting.co.uk; High St; chauffeured 4-person punts per 30min £30, punt rental per hour £22; ⏲9.30am-dusk Feb-Nov) Right beside Magdalen Bridge, this boathouse is the most central location to hire a punt, chauffeured or otherwise. From here you can either head downstream around the Botanic Garden and Christ Church Meadow, or upstream around Magdalen Deer Park. You can also hire rowboats and pedalos.

Salter Bros BOATING

(☎01865-243421; www.salterssteamers.co.uk; Folly Bridge; punt/rowboat/motorboat per hour £20/20/45; ⏲10am-6pm Easter-Oct) As well as renting out punts, rowing boats and motorboats for private hire, Salter Bros usually offers scenic cruises along the Thames, passing college boathouses and busy riverside pubs. Options include the 8-mile, two-hour trip to the historic market town of

Oxford

Top Sights
1 Ashmolean Museum C3
2 Bodleian Library D3
3 Christ Church D5
4 Magdalen College F4
5 Pitt Rivers Museum D1

Sights
6 Balliol College D3
7 Botanic Garden F4
8 Bridge of Sighs E3
9 Christ Church Meadow E5
10 Exeter College D3
11 Merton College E4
12 Museum of the History of Science D3
13 New College E3
14 Oxford University Museum of Natural History D1
15 Radcliffe Camera E3
16 Trinity College D3
17 University Church of St Mary the Virgin E4

Activities, Courses & Tours
18 Bill Spectre's Oxford Ghost Trail C4
19 Magdalen Bridge Boathouse F4
20 Oxford Official Walking Tours D3

Sleeping
21 Oxford Coach & Horses H4
22 Tower House D3

Eating
23 Covered Market D4
24 Edamamé E3
25 Grand Café E4
26 Handle Bar C3
27 Spiced Roots G5
28 Vaults & Garden E4

Drinking & Nightlife
29 Bear Inn D4
30 Eagle & Child C2
31 Lamb & Flag C2
32 Turf Tavern E3
33 Varsity Club D4

Shopping
34 Blackwell's D3
35 Blackwell's Art & Poster D3
36 Westgate Shopping Centre C5

Abingdon (9.15am and 2.30pm, late May to early September, adult/child £20.80/11.70), and a 2½-hour Alice in Wonderland cruise (£17.50/10).

Tours

Oxford Official Walking Tours WALKING

(01865-686441; www.experienceoxfordshire.org; 15-16 Broad St; adult/child from £14/10; 10.45am & 1pm, extra tours 11am & 2pm during busy periods;) Comprehensive two-hour tours of the city and its colleges, plus several themed tours, including one devoted to *Alice in Wonderland* and Harry Potter, another to CS Lewis and JRR Tolkien, and a third to Inspector Morse. Check online for details, or book at the tourist office.

Bill Spectre's Oxford Ghost Trail WALKING

(07941-041811; www.ghosttrail.org; Oxford Castle; adult/child £10/7; 6.30pm Fri & Sat;) For a theatrical and entertaining voyage through Oxford's uncanny underbelly, plus the occasional magic trick, take a 1¾-hour tour with Victorian undertaker Bill Spectre. No bookings needed, audience participation more than likely.

Sleeping

Tower House GUESTHOUSE ££

(01865-246828; www.towerhouseoxford.co.uk; 15 Ship St; s/d £100/125, d without bathroom £110;) In a peaceful central location, this listed 17th-century town house holds eight good-value double rooms, simple but tastefully decorated. Some share bathrooms (not always on the same floor), while larger en suites also have attractive tongue-and-groove panelling. Run as a social enterprise, profits go to a community charity.

Remont B&B ££

(01865-311020; www.remont-oxford.co.uk; 367 Banbury Rd, Summertown; d/q £125/180; P@) All modern style, subtle lighting and ultracolourful furnishings, this boutique family-run guesthouse holds 25 varying rooms decked out in cool neutrals with silky bedspreads, abstract art, vibrant bedheads, writing desks and huge TVs. There's a sunny garden and roomy breakfast hall out back. It's 2.5 miles north of the centre, in an inconspicuous residential setting, but there's good public transport.

Acorn Guest House B&B ££

(01865-247998; www.oxford-acorn.co.uk; 260 Iffley Rd; s/d £50/75; P) Spread through two adjoining houses, Acorn offers eight comfortable rooms at very reasonable prices, close to great pubs and restaurants and a short bus ride from the centre. Single rooms and 'budget' doubles share bathrooms; en suite facilities cost just £5 more. Everything has the feel of a family home, but key safes allow for a contactless check-in.

★**Oxford Coach & Horses** B&B £££
(01865-200017; www.oxfordcoachandhorses.co.uk; 62 St Clement's St; s/d £130/150; P) A former 18th-century coaching inn, this fabulous English-Mexican-owned boutique B&B hides behind a fresh powder-blue exterior, just a few metres from the Cowley Rd action. The eight light-filled rooms are cosy, spacious and individually styled in soothing pastels with exposed beams and splashes of turquoise and mauve. The converted ground floor houses an airy, attractive breakfast room.

★**Head of the River** HOTEL £££
(01865-721600; www.headoftheriveroxford.co.uk; Folly Bridge, St Aldate's; r incl breakfast £189;) One of the more central Oxford hotels, this large and characterful place at Folly Bridge, immediately south of Christ Church, was originally a Thames-side warehouse. Each of its 20 good-sized rooms is individually decorated with contemporary flair, featuring exposed brickwork and/or tongue-and-groove panelling plus modern fittings. Rates include breakfast cooked to order in the (excellent) pub (p198) downstairs.

Burlington House HOTEL £££
(01865-513513; www.burlington-hotel-oxford.co.uk; 374 Banbury Rd, Summertown; s/d incl breakfast £102/139; P) This small, well-managed hotel, in a beautifully refreshed Victorian home 2 miles north of central Oxford, offers 12 elegant contemporary rooms – some in a courtyard annex – with patterned wallpaper, immaculate bathrooms and luxury touches. Personal service is as sensational as the delicious breakfast, with organic eggs, homemade bread, yoghurt, granola and fresh juice. Public transport links are good.

Oxford Townhouse BOUTIQUE HOTEL £££
(01865-722500; www.theoxfordtownhouse.co.uk; 90 Abingdon Rd; s/d incl breakfast £136/166; P) Fifteen comfortable, subtly chic, minimalist-modern rooms, with white-and-navy striped blankets, varnished-wood desks and blue flourishes, in a gorgeously restyled pair of red-brick Victorian town houses, half a mile south of the centre. Some are quite small for the price, though. Colourful paintings of Oxford adorn the walls, and the breakfasts are classy.

Eating

★**Edamamé** JAPANESE £
(01865-246916; www.edamame.co.uk; 15 Holywell St; mains £7-10.50; 11.30am-2.30pm Wed & Thu, 11.30am-2.30pm & 5-8.30pm Fri & Sat, noon-3.30pm Sun;) No wonder a constant stream of students squeeze in and out of this tiny diner – it's Oxford's top spot for delicious, gracefully simple Japanese cuisine. Changing noodle and curry specials include fragrant chicken miso ramen, tofu stir-fries, or mackerel with soba noodles; at the time of writing, it served sushi or sashimi on Thursday evenings only. No bookings; arrive early and be prepared to wait.

★**Vaults & Garden** CAFE £
(01865-279112; www.thevaultsandgarden.com; University Church of St Mary the Virgin, Radcliffe Sq; mains £9-10.50; 9am-5pm;) This beautiful lunch venue spreads from the vaulted 14th-century Old Congregation House of the University Church into a garden facing the Radcliffe Camera. Come early and queue at the counter to choose from wholesome organic specials such as carrot and nutmeg soup, chicken panang

WORTH A TRIP

LE MANOIR AUX QUAT'SAISONS

Oxford food lovers make the 9-mile pilgrimage east to **Le Manoir aux Quat'Saisons** (01844-278881; www.belmond.com/le-manoir-aux-quat-saisons-oxfordshire; Church Rd, Great Milton; 5-course lunch/7-course dinner £105/190; 6.30-9.30pm Mon, 11.45am-2.15pm & 6.30-9.30pm Tue-Sun), an impressive manor house that has enjoyed two Michelin stars since chef Raymond Blanc has been working his magic here for the past 35 years. Imaginative and complex dishes use ingredients from the amazing on-site kitchen garden. Book ahead and dress smartly.

It also has 32 hotel rooms, and a cookery school. It's truly a gastronomic destination hotel.

curry, or slow-roasted lamb shoulder with red currant. Breakfast and afternoon tea (those scones!) are equally good.

Covered Market MARKET £
(www.oxford-coveredmarket.co.uk; Market St; prices vary; 8am-5.30pm Mon-Sat, 10am-5pm Sun;) A haven for impecunious students, this indoor marketplace holds 20 restaurants, cafes and takeaways. Let anyone loose here, and something's sure to catch their fancy. Brown's no-frills cafe, famous for its apple pies, is the longest-standing veteran. Look out too for Georgina's upstairs; two excellent pie shops; and good Thai and Chinese options. Traders keep their own varied hours.

Handle Bar CAFE £
(01865-251315; www.handlebaroxford.co.uk; Bike Zone, 28-31 St Michael's St; mains £8-13; 8am-6pm Mon & Tue, 8am-11pm Wed-Fri, 9am-11pm Sat, 9am-5pm Sun;) Upstairs above a bike shop, this chatty, friendly cafe has bikes galore, including penny-farthings, dangling from its ceiling and white-painted brick walls. It's usually packed with students, professionals and lucky tourists, all here for luscious, health-focused bites, like avocado and beetroot hummus toast, pan-fried tofu salad and granola breakfast 'pots', plus tasty cakes, smoothies, teas and coffees. Across from the bike shop downstairs is a coffee and cocktail bar serving the same menu.

Grand Café TEAHOUSE £
(01865-204463; www.thegrandcafe.co.uk; 84 High St; patisserie items £5-7, mains £9-13; 9am-6.30pm Mon-Thu, to 7pm Fri-Sun;) Boasting of being England's first-ever coffee house – though not, unlike its rival opposite, open ever since – the Grand looks very much the part, with its columns and gold leaf. While it serves sandwiches, bagels and a towering afternoon tea (from £18), it's the patisserie counter that's the real attraction: fresh, sweet pastry tarts and feather-light *mille-feuilles* pair brilliantly with tea.

Rusty Bicycle GASTROPUB £
(01865-435298; www.therustybicycle.com; 28 Magdalen Rd; mains £6.50-12; 9am-11pm Sun-Thu, to midnight Fri & Sat;) This funky neighbourhood pub, tucked off Iffley Rd a mile out of town and brought to you by the people responsible for Jericho's Rickety Press, serves top-notch burgers and pizzas, along with excellent local beers in a popular beer garden.

Walking Tour
A Riverside Stroll in Central Oxford

START CHRIST CHURCH
END MAGDALEN COLLEGE
LENGTH 2.5 MILES; TWO HOURS

Few cities can match Oxford for retaining such glorious countryside so close to its centre. Oxford's secret lies in the fact that the riverside meadows just outside the medieval city walls belonged then, and still belong today, to hugely wealthy colleges that have never felt the urge to build on them, let alone sell them. Modern visitors can therefore simply step away from the busy city streets to enjoy an idyllic stroll along delightful rural footpaths.

Start by approaching **1 Christ Church** (p190) via the gates on St Aldate's. Follow Broad Walk straight ahead for 140m, until the college's visitor entrance is on your left, then turn right onto Poplar Walk. This broad avenue heads directly south, to reach the Thames after 410m. Turning right at the river would bring you to Folly Bridge, spanning the original 'oxen ford' for which Oxford is named, but turn left, downstream, and follow the waterfront footpath known as the Meadow Walk. You'll probably see rowing eights out on the Thames. Looking back the way you've come, you're now separated from Christ Church, a shimmering vision of splendour, by the broad expanse of **2 Christ Church Meadow** (www.chch.ox.ac.uk; St Aldate's; dawn-dusk) FREE, where you may see longhorn cattle grazing. After 180m, the path leaves the river, curving beside a cut-off channel that brings you in 360m to the River Cherwell. Once there, keep following the curve, and after another 450m you meet Broad Walk at its eastern end.

Across Merton Field, straight ahead, the long, high wall of **3 Merton College** (p190) traces the route of Oxford's medieval city wall. During the Middle Ages, the local Jewish community had to bury their dead outside the walls. Their funerals followed this footpath, which became known as Dead Man's Walk. The trees that tower over it stand within Merton's enclosed Fellows' Garden. JRR Tolkien's rooms overlooked this spot when he was writing *The Lord of the Rings*.

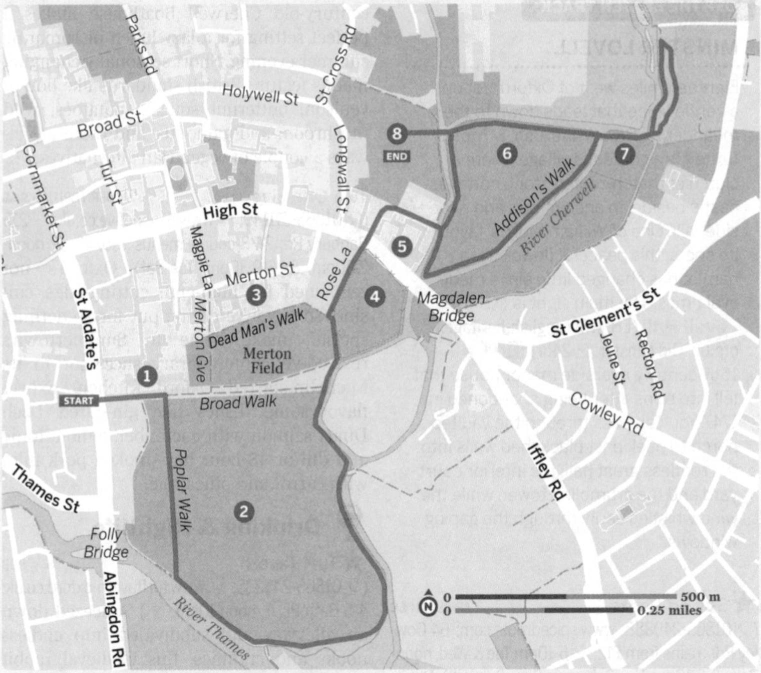

Ninety metres north of Broad Walk, fork right along Rose Lane, which leads up to High St along Merton's eastern boundary. The former Jewish cemetery now lies on your right, though for the past four centuries it's served instead as Oxford's 4 **Botanic Garden** (☎01865-610305; www.botanic-garden.ox.ac.uk; High St; adult/child £5.45/free; ⊙9am-5pm Mar-Oct, to 4pm Nov-Feb, last entry an hour before closing). If you've time, add an extra half-mile to this walk by dropping in to admire its greenhouses of rare plants, and relax in its tranquil spaces.

The visitors' entrance to 5 **Magdalen College** (p192) is directly across High St from the north end of Rose Lane. To continue your walk, pay for admission and head through the stunning 15th-century cloisters (during the university year, visitors can only enter in the afternoon). Tolkien's contemporary, CS Lewis, lived in Magdalen, and the grotesque carvings here reappeared in his *Chronicles of Narnia*.

Turn right beyond the cloisters, and you're swiftly back on the banks of the Cherwell. Get ready for the absolute highlight of the walk. Magdalen took over these riverside lands almost six centuries ago, and has left them to be enjoyed as open countryside ever since. Cross the footbridge straight ahead of you to reach the 6 **Water Meadow**, a triangular islet in the river. The gloriously bucolic footpath known as Addison's Walk takes just under a mile to loop around its perimeter. At its southern tip, you get a head-on view of punts and rowing boats setting off below Magdalen Bridge. The Water Meadow is one of just a half-dozen places where the snakeshead fritillary still grows; you may spot its purple or white flowers in late April.

Leave the Water Meadow by its northeastern end to enter smaller 7 **Bat Willow Meadow**, where Mark Wallinger's sculpture *Y*, resembling a two-dimensional tree, was installed amid genuine willows in 2008 to mark Magdalen's 550th anniversary. Immediately south, Angel and Greyhound Meadow was named for two long-vanished coaching inns that pastured their horses here. The secluded Fellows' Garden, across another bridge beyond, was laid out in 1866.

When you're ready to re-emerge into city life, retrace your footsteps back to the high street. Spare a glance, though, for the 8 **Grove Deer Park**, north of the college buildings. If you're here between July and early December, you may have encountered the college's own herd of deer browsing in the riverside meadows; before that, to spare the fritillaries, they're here in the Grove.

OFF THE BEATEN TRACK

MINSTER LOVELL

Eighteen miles west of Oxford, set on a gentle slope that leads down to the meandering River Windrush, **Minster Lovell** is a gorgeous village where a clutch of thatch-roofed stone cottages nestle beside an ancient pub and riverside mill. One of William Morris' favourite spots, this peaceful flower-filled hamlet has changed little since medieval times. The main sight is **Minster Lovell Hall** (EH; www.english-heritage.org.uk; Old Minster; 24hr) FREE, a 15th-century riverside manor house that fell into ruins after being abandoned in 1747. You can pass through the vaulted porch to peek past blackened walls into the roofless great hall, the interior courtyard and the crumbling tower, while the wind whistles eerily through the gaping windows.

★Spiced Roots CARIBBEAN ££
(01865-249888; www.spicedroots.com; 64 Cowley Rd; mains from £12; 6-10pm Tue & Wed, noon-3pm & 6-10pm Thu-Sat, noon-8pm Sun;) From black rice with pomegranates to oxtail with mac cheese and plantains – and, of course, spicy jerk chicken – everything is just perfection at this flawless Caribbean restaurant. There are plenty of vegetarian options, as well as curried fish or goat. And adding a cocktail or two from the thatched rum bar is pretty much irresistible. Look out for tasting classes.

★Magdalen Arms BRITISH ££
(01865-243159; www.magdalenarms.co.uk; 243 Iffley Rd; mains £14-26; 11am-10pm Tue-Sat, to 9pm Sun;) A mile beyond Magdalen Bridge, this extra-special neighbourhood gastropub has won plaudits from the national press. A friendly, informal spot, it offers indoor and outdoor space for drinkers, and dining tables further back. From vegetarian specials such as broad-bean tagliatelle to the fabulous sharing-size steak-and-ale pie (well, it's a stew with a suet-crust lid, really) everything is delicious, with gutsy flavours.

Cherwell Boathouse Restaurant BRITISH ££
(01865-552746; www.cherwellboathouse.co.uk; Bardwell Rd; mains £18-22; noon-2.30pm & 6-9.30pm;) With its lovely riverside setting, 1.5 miles north of central Oxford, the century-old Cherwell Boathouse makes a perfect setting for a lazy lunch or romantic summer evening. Short seasonally changing menus feature British standards like lion of venison, butternut squash, potatoes, wild mushroom and game jus, and there are always a couple of vegetarian alternatives.

Two One Five MODERN BRITISH £££
(01865-511149; www.twoonefive.co.uk; 215 Banbury Rd; 2-/3-course menus £35/40; noon-2.30pm & 6-9.30pm Tue-Sat) Oxford's not renowned for high-end, cutting-edge cuisine, so if you're crying out for something special, make haste to Summertown's relaxed-yet-contemporary successor to its Michelin-starred Oxford Kitchen. Expect flavoursome dishes like gin-cured Loch Duart salmon with cucumber, lemon, tonic and dill or 48-hour hay-smoked pork fillet with carrot and pineapple.

Drinking & Nightlife

★Turf Tavern PUB
(01865-243235; www.turftavern-oxford.co.uk; 4-5 Bath Pl; noon-10pm;) Squeezed down an alleyway and subdivided into endless nooks and crannies, this medieval rabbit warren dates from around 1381. The definitive Oxford pub, it's where Bill Clinton famously 'did not inhale'. Other patrons have included Oscar Wilde, Stephen Hawking and Margaret Thatcher. Home to a fabulous array of real ales and ciders, it's always pretty crowded, but there's outdoor seating, too.

★Perch PUB
(01865-728891; www.the-perch.co.uk; Binsey Lane, Binsey; 10.30am-11pm Mon-Sat, to 10.30pm Sun;) This thatched and wonderfully rural 800-year-old inn can be reached by road, but it's more enjoyable to walk half an hour upstream along the Thames Path, then follow an enchanting footpath punctuated by floral pergolas. Its huge willow-draped garden is an idyllic spot for a pint or two of Fullers, but summer crowds can mean a long wait for food.

Head of the River PUB
(01865-721600; www.headoftheriveroxford.co.uk; Folly Bridge, St Aldate's; 8am-10.30pm Sun-Thu, to 11.30pm Fri & Sat) For a summer-evening riverside drink, central Oxford holds no finer setting than the Thames-facing terrace of this imposing former warehouse – hence the hand-cranked crane, still outside – and later a boatyard. The beer's good, courtesy of

Fullers brewery. There's plenty of room indoors – as well as decent food, and a stylish hotel upstairs – but the lure of the river is irresistible.

Lamb & Flag PUB

(12 St Giles; noon-11pm Mon-Sat, to 10.30pm Sun;) This relaxed 17th-century tavern remains one of Oxford's nicest pubs for a sturdy pint or glass of wine. Thomas Hardy wrote (and set) parts of *Jude the Obscure* at these very tables, while CS Lewis and JRR Tolkien shifted their custom here in later years. The food's nothing special, but buying a pint helps fund scholarships at St John's College.

Bear Inn PUB

(01865-728164; www.bearoxford.co.uk; 6 Alfred St; 11am-11pm Mon-Thu, 11am-midnight Fri & Sat, 11.30am-10.30pm Sun) Oxford's oldest pub – there's been a pub here since 1242 – the creaky old Bear requires almost everyone to stoop while passing from room to room. An ever-expanding collection of ties, framed and fading behind glass, covers walls and ceilings alike. Affiliated with Fuller's chain, it usually offers interesting guest ales, plus basic pub grub.

Eagle & Child PUB

(01865-302925; www.nicholsonspubs.co.uk/theeagleandchildoxford; 49 St Giles; 11am-10pm Mon-Sat, noon-10pm Sun) Affectionately nicknamed the 'Bird & Baby', and a favourite haunt of JRR Tolkien, CS Lewis and their fellow Inklings, this quirky, rambling pub dates from 1650. Its narrow wood-panelled rooms still look great, and it's still serving decent real ales with a generic pub menu.

Varsity Club COCKTAIL BAR

(01865-248777; www.tvcoxford.co.uk; 9 High St; noon-midnight;) At this sleekly minimalist rooftop cocktail bar, spectacularly located in the town centre, cocktails and small dishes are served with sensational views across Oxford's dreaming spires. Heaters, blankets and canopies keep things cosy in colder weather, while lounges and dance spaces sprawl across three floors below.

Trout PUB

(01865-510930; www.thetroutoxford.co.uk; 195 Godstow Rd, Wolvercote; noon-10pm;) Three miles northwest along the Thames from Oxford – a wonderful walk– this old-world pub has been drawing drinkers for around four centuries, and was popularised by TV detective Inspector Morse. Its expansive riverside terrace is usually packed, and there are peckish ducks patrolling the parapet wall. If you fancy sampling its modern British cuisine, book a table in advance.

Shopping

★Blackwell's BOOKS

(01865-792792; www.blackwells.co.uk; 48-51 Broad St; 9am-6.30pm Mon & Wed-Sat, 9.30am-6.30pm Tue, 11am-5pm Sun) The most famous bookshop in the most studenty of cities, Blackwell's is, with its vast range of literature, treatises and guilty pleasures, a book-lover's dream. Be sure to visit the basement Norrington Room, an immense inverted step pyramid, lined with 3 miles of shelves and hailed in the Guinness Book of Records as the largest book-selling room in the world.

Blackwell's Art & Poster ART

(01865-333641; www.blackwell.co.uk; 27 Broad St; 10am-6.30pm Mon-Sat, 11am-5pm Sun) Blackwell's split-level sibling store, all but opposite the main bookshop, specialises in reference books, coffee-table tomes, posters, cards and stationery, ranging across art forms from Expressionism to origami, and film stills to anime. Browsing is welcome, and leaving without a purchase near impossible.

Westgate Shopping Centre MALL

(01865-263600; www.westgateoxford.co.uk; Castle St; shops 10am-8pm Mon-Fri, 9am-8pm Sat, 11am-5pm Sun, restaurants open longer hours;

WORTH A TRIP

THE REAL DOWNTON ABBEY

A 19th-century Victorian structure, **Highclere Castle** (01635-253210; www.highclerecastle.co.uk; Newbury RG20 9RN; adult/child £24/14; open on selected dates across the year) was used to film all six seasons of the hugely successful ITV/PBS TV series *Downtown Abbey*. Visitors can relive memories of the show (as if the Crawleys were once inhabitants) while gathering some insights into the private lives of the castle's real inhabitants, the Earl and Countess of Carnarvon. The castle itself covers 100,000 sq ft and has a total of 300 rooms, but only a limited number are open to the public.

WORTH A TRIP

VALE OF THE WHITE HORSE

Lying around 20 miles southwest of Oxford, this verdant valley is home to the historic market town of Wantage, birthplace of Alfred the Great (AD 849–899). Its most interesting attractions, however, are much older even than that. **White Horse Hill**, 7.5 miles west of Wantage, is decorated with Britain's most ancient chalk figure, the 3000-year-old Uffington White Horse, while the nearby hill fort known as Uffington Castle dates from 700 BC, and Wayland's Smithy is a neolithic long barrow.

The 10m-high, flat-topped mound known as **Dragon Hill** was believed by locals to be the site where St George slew the dragon. Archaeologists prefer to think that it's a natural formation, the summit of which was scraped level during the Iron Age and used for rituals.

) Originally built in 1972 on the site of Oxford's medieval West Gate, this enormous mall expanded in 2017. Like Alice it seems just to keep on growing, with around 100 big-name shops including a large John Lewis department store, plus indoor golf and a cinema. Several of the smart, contemporary chain restaurants on the top floor have outdoor roof-terrace seating with views over the city.

Information

The Oxford tourist office website (www.experienceoxfordshire.org) covers the whole of Oxfordshire and sells local Oxford guidebooks, makes reservations for local accommodation and walking tours, and sells tickets for events and attractions.

Getting There & Away

BUS

Oxford's chaotic outdoor **bus station** (Gloucester Green) is in the centre, on Gloucester Green near the corner of Worcester and George Sts. The main bus companies are **Oxford Bus Company** (01865-785400; www.oxfordbus.co.uk), **Stagecoach** (01865-772250; www.stagecoachbus.com) and **Swanbrook** (01452-712386; www.swanbrook.co.uk).

CAR & MOTORCYCLE

Driving and parking in central Oxford is a nightmare; consider booking accommodation that offers parking. There are five Park & Ride car parks along the major routes leading into town, all at least 2 miles out. Parking costs £2 to £4 per day, with a total charge of £6.80 if you use the buses that run to/from the centre every 15 to 30 minutes, and take 12 to 25 minutes for the journey.

TRAIN

Oxford's main train station is conveniently located just west of the city centre, roughly 10 minutes' walk from the main shopping area. Fares vary enormously according to what time you travel and how far in advance you book. Destinations include:

Birmingham (£20, 1¼ hours)
London Marylebone (£28, 1¼ hours)
London Paddington (£28, 1¼ hours)
Manchester (£40, 2¾ hours)
Moreton-in-Marsh (£12, 35 minutes)
Newcastle (£70, 4½ hours)
Winchester (£20, 1¼ hours)

Getting Around

BICYCLE

There's a real cycling culture in Oxford, and it's a popular way to get around the city for students and visitors alike. **Cyclo Analysts** (01865-424444; www.cycloanalysts.com; 150 Cowley Rd; per day/week from £10/36; 9am-6pm Mon-Sat) and **Summertown Cycles** (01865-316885; www.summertowncycles.co.uk; 200-202 Banbury Rd, Summertown; per day/week £18/35; 9am-5.30pm Mon-Sat, 10.30am-4pm Sun) sell, repair and rent out bikes, including hybrids.

BUS

Oxford Bus Company and Stagecoach serve an extensive local network with regular buses on major routes. Single journeys cost around £2.50 (return £4). Pay when you board the bus with a contactless card.

An unlimited bus travel ticket (per day) is available (adult/child £10/7). Buy tickets in advance on the Stagecoach Bus app.

TAXI

There are taxi ranks at the train and bus stations, as well as on St Giles and at Carfax. Alternatively, contact **001 Taxis** (01865-240000; www.001taxis.com) or **Oxford Cars** (01865-406070; www.oxfordcars.co.uk).

AROUND OXFORD

The Oxfordshire countryside abounds in rustic charm. To the northwest, Witney has a pretty town centre, but the major highlight is magnificent Blenheim Palace, birthplace of Sir Winston Churchill, adjoining attractive Woodstock. Southwest of Oxford, the Vale of the White Horse offers some intriguing prehistoric attractions.

Woodstock

01993 / POP 2730

Woodstock, 8 miles northwest of Oxford, is a beautiful old town that has long had close links to royalty. Fine stone houses, venerable inns and pubs, and antique shops jostle shoulder to shoulder in its well-heeled centre, but what really draws the crowds here is Blenheim Palace, a majestic baroque extravaganza that was the birthplace of Sir Winston Churchill.

Sights

★ **Blenheim Palace** PALACE

(01993-810530; www.blenheimpalace.com; Woodstock; adult/child £28.50/16.50, park & gardens only £18.50/8.60; palace 10.30am-4.30pm, park & gardens 9.30am-6.30pm or dusk; P) One of Britain's greatest stately homes, and a Unesco World Heritage Site, Blenheim Palace is a monumental baroque fantasy, designed by Sir John Vanbrugh and Nicholas Hawksmoor, and built between 1705 and 1722. Queen Anne gave the land, and the necessary funds, to John Churchill, Duke of Marlborough, as thanks for defeating the French at the 1704 Battle of Blenheim. Sir Winston Churchill was born here in 1874, and Blenheim (blen-num) remains home to the 12th duke.

Inside, beyond majestic oak doors, the palace is stuffed with statues, tapestries, sumptuous furniture, priceless china and giant oil paintings in elaborate gilt frames. Visits start in the **Great Hall**, a soaring space that's adorned with images of the first duke and topped by a 20m-high ceiling. From here, you can either wander through the various grand state rooms independently, or join one of the free 45-minute guided tours, which depart every 30 minutes (except on Sunday, when guides are stationed in all rooms). Highlights include the famous **Blenheim Tapestries**, a set of 10 large wall hangings commemorating the first duke's triumphs; the **State Dining Room**, with its painted walls and trompe l'lœil ceilings; and the magnificent **Long Library**, overlooked by an elaborate 1738 statue of Queen Anne, where the 56m ceiling was decorated by Nicholas Hawksmoor.

Upstairs is the **Untold Story tour**, where a phantom chambermaid leads you on a half-hour audiovisual tour of tableaux that recreate important scenes from Blenheim's history. Between February and September you can also join additional tours (adult/child £5/4.50) of the duke's private apartments, the palace bedrooms or the household staff areas.

A separate sequence of rooms downstairs holds the **Churchill Exhibition**, included in the ticket price and dedicated to the life, work, paintings and writings of Winston Churchill. Official history has it that the future prime minister, grandson of the 7th duke and cousin of the 9th, was born by chance at the palace, after his mother went into premature labour. It's widely believed, however, that the tale was concocted to conceal that she was already pregnant when she married his father, seven months earlier. Winston Churchill is buried in the local parish church in Bladon, 1.5 miles south, just outside the grounds.

Ensure you have enough time to visit the vast, lavish **gardens and parklands**, parts of which were landscaped by the great

DON'T MISS

KELMSCOTT MANOR

A gorgeous garden-fringed Tudor pile, **Kelmscott Manor** (01367-252486; www.sal.org.uk/kelmscott-manor; Kelmscott; adult/child £10/5; 11am-5pm Wed & Sat Apr-Oct), nestling near the Thames 20 miles west of Oxford (northwest of Faringdon), was bought in 1871 by a prestigious pair of artist-poets: Dante Gabriel Rossetti and William Morris, founder of the Arts and Crafts movement. The interior is true to Morris' philosophy that one should own nothing that is neither beautiful nor useful, and displays his personal effects along with fabrics and furniture designed by Morris and his associates. Closed for renovations, it will hopefully be ready for visitors again by the time you're reading this.

Literary Britain

Britain's literary heritage is astoundingly rich and globally renowned. As the English language spread around the world in the colonial era, so too did its literature, with novelists such as Charles Dickens and George Eliot and poets including Samuel Taylor Coleridge and Robert Burns being read far from home in the late 18th and 19th centuries.

1

S-F/SHUTTERSTOCK ©

ULMUS MEDIA/SHUTTERSTOCK ©

1. Radcliffe Camera (p190), Oxford
One of the most photographed landmarks in Oxford, it stores part of the Bodleian Library's collection.

2. Shakespeare's Birthplace (p419), Stratford-upon-Avon
Shakespeare was born in this house in 1564 and lived here at the beginning of his marriage to Anne Hathaway.

3. Charles Dickens Museum (p88), London
This museum is housed in Dickens' only surviving London home.

4. Statue of Robert Burns, Stirling (p836)
Burns is Scotland's most famous poet.

PXL.STORE/SHUTTERSTOCK ©

Lancelot 'Capability' Brown. Immediately outside, two large water terraces hold fountains and sphinxes, while a mini train (£1) takes visitors to the **Pleasure Gardens**, where features include a yew maze, adventure playground, lavender garden and butterfly house.

For quieter and longer strolls, there are glorious walks of up to 4.5 miles, leading past lakes to an arboretum, rose garden, cascade and Vanbrugh's Grand Bridge. Look out for the Temple of Diana, where Winston Churchill proposed to his future bride, Lady Clementine, on 10 August 1908.

Sleeping

Feathers HOTEL ££

(☎01993-812291; www.feathers.co.uk; Market St; r incl breakfast from £109; 📶) Oozing contemporary chic, this handsome 17th-century town house – previously a sanatorium, a draper's and a butcher's – offers stylish, comfortable rooms adorned with patterned wallpaper, modern art, fuzzy throws and rich-coloured fabrics. The smart bar downstairs stocks 401 types of gin.

★ **Glove House** B&B £££

(☎01993-813475; www.theglovehouse.co.uk; 24 Oxford St; d/ste from £175/200; 📶) Luxuriously renovated but proudly displaying evidence of its venerable age, this elegant 400-year-old town house conceals three sumptuous rooms, all with the added bonus of a glorious rear garden. The Charlbury suite has a freestanding copper bathtub in its wonderful lounge-equipped bathroom.

Getting There & Away

Stagecoach buses (p200) head to/from Oxford (30 minutes), Burford (45 minutes), Chipping Norton (20 minutes) and Witney (30 minutes). Buses S3 and 233 stop outside Blenheim Palace. See www.traveline.info for fares and timetables.

An unlimited bus travel ticket (per day) is available (adult/child £10/7). Buy tickets in advance on the Stagecoach Bus app.

THE COTSWOLDS

Undulating gracefully across six counties, the Cotswolds region is a delightful tangle of golden villages, thatched cottages, evocative churches and honey-coloured mansions. In 1966 it was designated an Area of Outstanding Natural Beauty, surpassed for size in England by the Lake District alone.

No one's sure what the name means, but 'wolds' are rolling hills, while 'cots' might be 'cotes', or sheep pens. Certainly the region owes its wealth, and exquisite architecture, to the medieval wool trade, when 'Cotswold Lion' sheep were prized across Europe. Attentions later turned towards textiles instead, but the Industrial Revolution passed the Cotswolds by. Hailed by William Morris in the 19th century as encapsulating a timeless English rural idyll, it remains both a moneyed residential area and a treasured tourist destination.

Criss-crossed by long-distance trails including the 102-mile Cotswold Way, these gentle yet dramatic hills are perfect for walking, cycling and horse riding.

Activities

Cycling

Gentle gradients and wonderfully scenic panoramas make the Cotswolds ideal for cycling. Quiet country lanes and byways criss-cross the countryside, and only the steep western escarpment poses a significant challenge to the legs. You can also follow the signposted **Thames Valley Cycle Way** (NCN Routes 4 and 5) between Oxford and Windsor (and on to London).

Companies such as **Cotswold Country Cycles** (☎01386-438706; www.cotswoldcountrycycles.com; Longlands Farm Cottage; 3-day/2-night tours from £285) organise maps, luggage transfers and B&B stays for a range of self-guided cycling tours.

Walking

The 102-mile **Cotswold Way** (www.nationaltrail.co.uk/cotswold-way) gives walkers a wonderful overview of the region. Meandering from Chipping Campden in the northeast to Bath in the southwest, it passes through some lovely countryside, linking ancient sites and tiny villages, with no major climbs or difficult stretches. It's also easily accessible from many points en route, if you fancy tackling a shorter section or a circular walk from your village of choice.

Other long-distance trails that pass through the Cotswolds include the 100-mile **Gloucestershire Way**, which runs from Chepstow to Tewkesbury via Stow-on-the-Wold; the 55-mile **St Kenelm's Way** into Worcestershire; and the 184-mile **Thames Path** (www.nationaltrail.co.uk/thames-path), which tracks from just southwest of Cirencester all the way to London.

Local tourist offices can advise on routes and usually sell walking maps.

Cirencester

01285 / POP 19,100

Charming Cirencester (siren-sester), the most significant town in the southern Cotswolds, is just 15 miles south of Cheltenham. Amazingly, under the Romans – who knew it as Corinium – Cirencester ranked second only to London in terms of size and importance, but little now survives from that era. The medieval wool trade brought further prosperity, with wealthy merchants funding the construction of a superb church.

Cirencester today is both elegant and affluent, but refreshingly unpretentious. Upmarket boutiques and fashionable delis now line its narrow streets, but its Monday and Friday markets remain at the core of its identity. Beautiful Victorian buildings flank the busy central square, while the surrounding streets showcase a harmonious medley of historic architecture.

Sights

★Corinium Museum MUSEUM

(01285-655611; www.coriniummuseum.org; Park St; adult/child £5.60/2.70; 10am-5pm Mon-Sat, 2-5pm Sun Apr-Oct, 10am-4pm Mon-Sat, 2-4pm Sun Nov-Mar;) Most of this wonderful modern museum is dedicated to Cirencester's Roman past; reconstructed rooms, videos and interactive displays bring the era to life. Among the highlights are some beautiful floor mosaics, unearthed locally and including a 4th-century mosaic depicting the mythical lyre-player Orpheus charming animals, and the 2nd-century 'Jupiter column', a carved capital depicting Bacchus and his drunken mates. There's also an excellent Stone Age room, an Anglo-Saxon section, and exhibits covering medieval Cirencester through to its prosperous wool trade.

St John the Baptist's Church CHURCH

(01285-659317; www.cirenparish.co.uk; Market Sq; 10am-4pm) One of England's largest parish churches, the cathedral-like St John's boasts an outstanding Perpendicular Gothic tower with flying buttresses (c 1400), plus a majestic three-storey south porch, built as an office in the late 15th century but subsequently used as Cirencester's town hall. Soaring arches, magnificent fan vaulting and a Tudor nave adorn the light-filled interior, where a wall safe holds the Boleyn Cup, made for Anne Boleyn in 1535.

On some Wednesdays and summer Saturdays, it's possible to climb the tower (adult/child £3/1.50).

> **COTSWOLDS DISCOVERER**
>
> The Cotswolds Discoverer, a great-value car-free one-day travel pass that gives unlimited travel on bus or train routes throughout the region (adult/child £10.50/5.25), can be bought at all UK mainline train stations, and aboard participating buses within the Cotswolds.

Sleeping

★No 12 B&B ££

(01285-640232; www.no12cirencester.co.uk; 12 Park St; d/ste £130/150;) This welcoming and very central Georgian town house offers four gloriously unfussy, very private rooms kitted out with a tasteful mix of antiques and modern furnishings. Romantic room 1 has an in-room bath, while the suite has two bathrooms and overlooks the lovely garden, with extra-long beds, piles of feather pillows and splashes of red throughout. The included breakfasts are superb.

Kings Head LUXURY HOTEL ££

(01285-700900; www.kingshead-hotel.co.uk; 24 Market Pl; d/ste from £119/199;) A coaching inn since the 14th century, this plush spot facing the church offers slick boudoirs and super-polished service. Exposed beams, red-brick walls and wood panelling pop up between Nespresso machines and Apple TVs. Enjoy the tucked-away spa, cosy bar and smart restaurant.

Eating

New Brewery Arts Cafe CAFE £

(01285-657181; www.newbreweryarts.org.uk; Brewery Ct; mains £6-8.50; 9am-5pm Mon-Sat;) Drop into this friendly day-time-only cafe, on the upper level of Cirencester's lively arts centre, for breakfast eggs, toast or pancakes, or for wholesome, good-value lunchtime sandwiches, salads and wraps. It also serves tasty cakes and fresh smoothies.

The Cotswolds

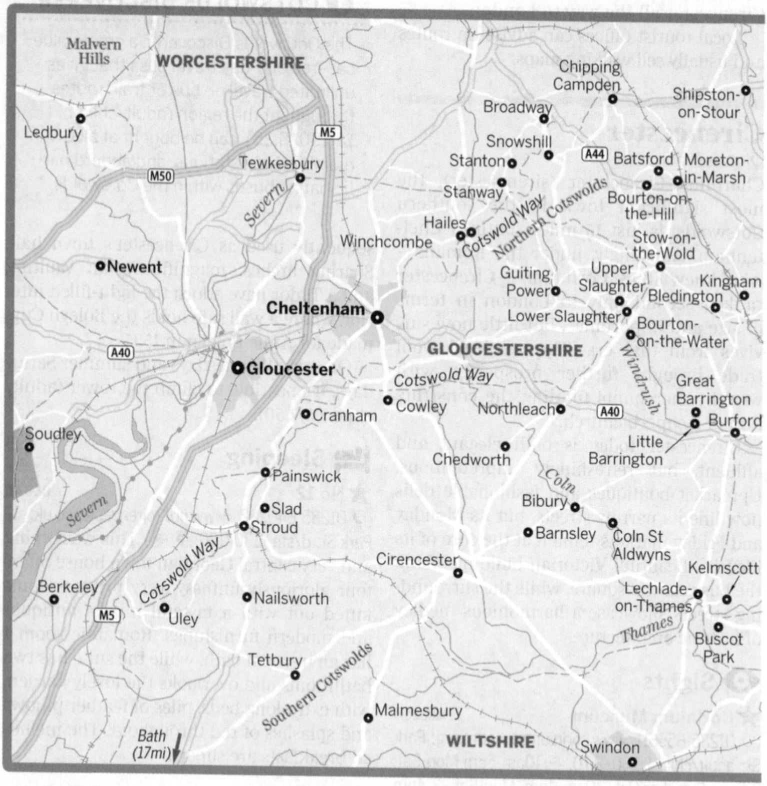

Made by Bob MODERN BRITISH ££

(☎01285-641818; www.mbbbrasserie.co.uk; Corn Hall, 26 Market Pl; mains £8.50-22.50; ⊙8am-10pm Mon-Sat, noon-8.30pm Sun; ✎) Filling a substantial light-filled space inside a central mall, and focused around an enormous open-plan kitchen, Bob's is part deli, part brasserie, and popular for its casual atmosphere. The breakfast selection is excellent – granola, smashed avocado, full English – while lunch bites include salads, soups, pastas, risottos and charcuterie platters.

ℹ Information

Tourist Office (☎01285-654180; www.cotswolds.com; Corinium Museum, Park St; ⊙10am-5pm Mon-Sat, 2-5pm Sun Apr-Oct, 10am-4pm Mon-Sat, 2-4pm Sun Nov-Mar) Doubling as the museum gift store, this helpful office can arrange accommodation and sells a leaflet detailing a self-guided walk around Cirencester.

ℹ Getting There & Away

The closest station to Cirencester, at Kemble 4.5 miles south, is connected by train with London Paddington (£28, 1¼ hours).

Stagecoach (p200) serves Cirencester. Buses stop outside the Corn Hall on Market Pl. Buses run to/from Cheltenham (40 minutes), Gloucester (50 minutes), Northleach (20 minutes) and Tetbury (30 minutes). See www.traveline.info for fares and timetables.

An unlimited bus travel ticket (per day) is available (adult/child £10/7). Buy tickets in advance on the Stagecoach Bus app.

National Express (www.nationalexpress.com) coach destinations include Birmingham (£18, 2½ hours) and London Victoria (£25, 2½ hours).

Bibury

☎01285 / POP 630

Memorably described as 'England's most beautiful village' by no less an authority than

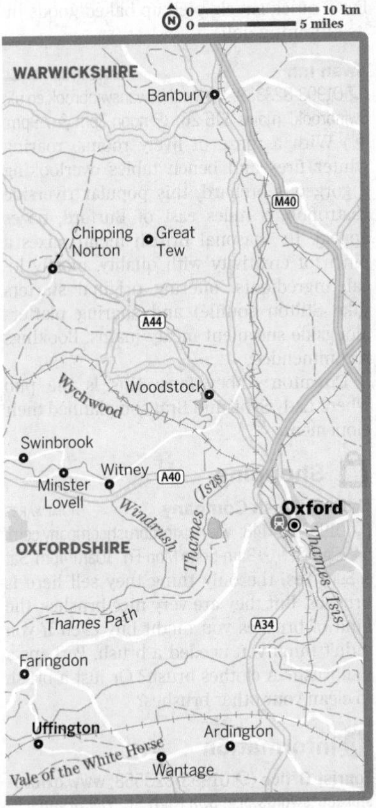

William Morris, Bibury, 8 miles northeast of Cirencester, epitomises the Cotswolds at its most picturesque. With a cluster of perfect cottages beside the River Coln, and a tangle of narrow streets flanked by attractive stone buildings, small wonder that it's a major halt on large-group Cotswold tours.

Sights

★Arlington Row STREET

Bibury's most famous attraction, this ravishing row of rustic cottages – as seen in movies such as *Stardust* – was originally a 14th-century wool store, before being converted into workers' lodgings. They overlook Rack Isle, a low-lying, marshy area once used to dry cloth and graze cattle, and now a wildlife refuge. Visitors are reminded to admire the cottages but respect the residents' privacy as you stroll the flower-lined lane alongside.

Church of St Mary the Virgin CHURCH

(Church Rd; 10am-dusk) Bibury's Saxon-built church has been much altered since its original construction, but many 8th-century features are still visible among the 12th-, 13th- and 15th-century additions. It's just off the B4425 in the village centre.

Sleeping

New Inn PUB ££

(01285-750651; www.new-inn.co.uk; Main St, Coln St Aldwyns; r incl breakfast £119-149; P) The jasmine-clad 16th-century New Inn, 2.5 miles southeast of Bibury, offers 14 spacious and atmospheric bedrooms divided between the main pub building and a neighbouring cottage. Idiosyncratic contemporary stylings include bold colours, fluffy throws, smart furnishings and the odd freestanding bathtub, while the pub itself, with its exposed beams, is the place for a burger and beer.

★Barnsley House LUXURY HOTEL £££

(01285-740000; www.barnsleyhouse.com; B4425, Barnsley; r incl breakfast from £319; P) For pure indulgence and romance, this 1697 country house and its famously beautiful garden take some beating. Each of its 18 rooms is individually styled; some have lavish oriental touches or in-room baths, most are elegantly understated. Facilities include a spa, a pool, a private cinema, the Potager restaurant and the knowingly re-named Village Pub. Guests must be aged 14 or over.

Getting There & Away

Most drivers approach Bibury along the B4425, which passes through the village centre halfway between Burford (9 miles northeast) and Cirencester (8 miles southwest).

Pulhams Coaches bus 855 heads to/from Cirencester (15 minutes) and Northleach (20 minutes); there's no Sunday service.

See www.traveline.info for fares and timetables.

Burford

01993 / POP 1410

Gliding down a steep hillside to an ancient (and still single-lane) crossing point on the River Windrush, 20 miles west of Oxford, Burford has hardly changed since its medieval glory days. Locals insist it's a town not a village, having received its charter in 1090, but it's a very small town, and a very picturesque one too, home to an appealing mix of stone cottages, gold-tinged Cotswold town houses, and the odd Elizabethan or Georgian treasure.

Throw in a wonderfully preserved, centuries-old church and an array of delightful hotels and restaurants, and Burford makes an attractive stop. Antique shops, chintzy tearooms and specialist boutiques peddle nostalgia to the many summer visitors, but it's easy to escape the crowds and wander along quiet side streets, seemingly lost in time.

Sleeping & Eating

★ Star Cottage B&B ££

(☎01993-822032; www.burfordbedandbreakfast.co.uk; Meadow Lane, Fulbrook; r £125, apt £150; 📶) A mile northeast of Burford, this wonderful old Cotswold cottage holds two comfortable and character-filled en-suite rooms done up in tastefully creative blues, whites and greys, with gorgeous quilted curtains. The smaller room holds a grand canopied bed; the larger has a beautiful bathroom; and the back barn hosts a separate four-person apartment. The home-cooked, locally sourced breakfasts are fantastic.

Lamb Inn PUB £££

(☎01993-823155; www.cotswold-inns-hotels.co.uk/the-lamb-inn; Sheep St; s/d incl breakfast from £150/160; P📶🐾) A rambling 15th-century inn, off the main street, where the flagstone floors, exposed beams and creaking stairs are complemented by 17 opulent antique-furnished rooms. A few have four-poster beds, and one even has its own private garden, while modern touches include Nespresso machines and slick bathrooms.

Modern British cuisine is served in both the romantic restaurant and the bar.

Huffkins CAFE £

(☎01993-824694; www.huffkins.com; 98 High St; mains £6-15; ⊙9am-4.30pm Mon-Fri, 9am-5pm Sat, 10am-5pm Sun; 👪) The original outlet of a Cotswolds chain that's been baking and serving delicious scones, cakes and pies since 1890, this lively, friendly cafe is usually busy with locals enjoying quiches, soups, macaroni cheese or burgers. It also offers all-day cooked breakfasts and full-blown afternoon teas. For a quick snack, pick up baked goods in its adjoining deli.

Swan Inn MODERN BRITISH ££

(☎01993-823339; www.theswanswinbrook.co.uk; Swinbrook; mains £16-26; ⊙noon-2pm & 7-9pm; P) With a maze of lively rooms, roaring winter fires and bench tables overlooking a gorgeous orchard, this popular riverside gastropub, 3 miles east of Burford, oozes appeal. Its seasonal British menu mixes a pinch of creativity with quality, mostly local, ingredients, offering original starters (like Stilton soufflé) and sharing platters alongside succulent meaty mains. Bookings recommended.

Downton Abbey fans: this is the pub where Lady Sybil and Branson planned their elopement.

Shopping

Oxford Brush Company HOMEWARES

(☎01993-824148; www.oxfordbrushcompany.com; 54 High St; ⊙9am-5pm Mon-Fri, 10am-4pm Sat & Sun) Yes, the only thing they sell here is brushes. But they are very nice brushes, the kind of brushes you might buy even if you didn't think you needed a brush. Perhaps a nailbrush? A clothes brush? Or just a brush to clean your other brushes?

Information

Tourist Office (☎01993-823558; www.oxfordshirecotswolds.org; 33a High St; ⊙9.30am-5pm Mon-Sat, 10am-4pm Sun) Information on local walks.

Getting There & Away

Stagecoach and Swanbrook buses run to/from Burford. Local buses stop on High or Sheep Sts, but express services stop at the A40 roundabout, five minutes' walk south of the centre. Bus destinations include Cheltenham (45 minutes), Gloucester (1¼ hours), Oxford (45 minutes to 1¼ hours), Minster Lovell (15 minutes), Witney (20 minutes) and Woodstock (45 minutes).

See www.traveline.info for fares and timetables. An unlimited bus travel ticket (per day) is available (adult/child £10/7). Buy tickets in advance on the Stagecoach Bus app.

Northleach

☎01451 / POP 1840

Oddly under-visited, and refreshingly uncommercialised despite holding some interesting attractions, Northleach, 14 miles southeast of Cheltenham, has been a small market town since 1227. Late-medieval cottages, imposing merchants' stores and half-timbered Tudor houses jostle for position in a wonderful melange of styles around Market Sq and the narrow laneways that lead off it.

Sights

Chedworth Roman Villa ARCHAEOLOGICAL SITE
(NT; 01242-890256; www.nationaltrust.org.uk; Yanworth; adult/child £10.50/5.25; 10am-5pm Apr-Oct, to 4pm mid-Feb–Mar & Nov; P) This large and luxurious Roman villa was rediscovered by a gamekeeper in 1864. Though the earliest section dates to around 175 CE, it was at its most magnificent around 362 CE, equipped with two sets of bathhouses, a water shrine and a dining room with underfloor heating. A fine modern gallery preserves several exquisite mosaics, though yet more, unearthed recently, had to be re-buried due to lack of resources.

It's at the far end of a dead-end rural road, 4.5 miles west of Northleach and signposted from the A429.

Church of St Peter & St Paul CHURCH
(www.northleach.org; Church Walk) The grandeur and complexity of this masterpiece of the Cotswold Perpendicular style testifies to its wool-era wealth. Although the chancel and 30m tower date from the 14th century, it was extensively reworked during the 15th-century wool boom. A modern highlight is the 1964 stained-glass window depicting Christ in Glory, behind the altar, while earlier treasures include an unusual 14th-century font.

Sleeping & Eating

★**Wheatsheaf** BOUTIQUE HOTEL £££
(01451-860244; www.cotswoldswheatsheaf.com; West End; r incl breakfast £123-255; P) The 14 different rooms at this former coaching inn, very popular with an exclusive London set, blend atmospheric period touches, such as freestanding bathtubs, with modern comforts including power showers, organic toiletries and country-chic decor. Downstairs, an outrageously popular **restaurant** (01451-860244; www.cotswoldswheatsheaf.com; West End; mains £14.50-24; 8-10am, noon-3pm & 6-9pm Mon-Thu & Sun, to 10pm Fri & Sat; P) adds a contemporary twist to delightful seasonal British dishes.

Getting There & Away

Stagecoach buses head to/from Burford (15 minutes), Cheltenham (45 minutes), Cirencester (20 minutes), Gloucester (one hour) and Oxford (one hour). See www.traveline.info for fares and timetables.

An unlimited bus travel ticket (per day) is available (adult/child £10/7). Buy tickets in advance on the Stagecoach Bus app.

The Slaughters

01451 / POP 400

The picture-postcard villages of Upper and Lower Slaughter, roughly a mile apart and around 3.5 miles southwest of Stow-on-the-Wold, have somehow managed to maintain their unhurried medieval charm, despite receiving a multitude of visitors. Their names have nothing to do with abattoirs; they come from the Old English 'sloughtre', meaning slough or muddy place.

Meandering sleepily through the two villages, the River Eye passes a succession of classic gold-tinged Cotswolds houses. It's Lower Slaughter that's the real gem, with the river canalised between limestone banks to flow just a few inches below road level, and with flowery footpaths to either side. If you've time for a stroll, you can follow the Eye from one village to the other – the central stretch is away from the traffic – for a round trip that typically takes around two hours.

Old Mill NOTABLE BUILDING
(01451-820052;www.oldmill-lowerslaughter.com; Lower Slaughter; 10am-6pm Mar-Oct, to dusk Nov-Feb) Right on the River Eye, the Old Mill houses a cafe and crafts shop as well as a small museum, where you can find out all about the building's former life as a water-powered flour mill. A watermill is recorded as operating in this location as far back as the Domesday Book (1086).

Lords of the Manor HISTORIC HOTEL £££
(01451-820243; www.lordsofthemanor.com; Upper Slaughter; r incl breakfast £240-465; P) Although from the outside this 17th-century mansion appears to embody traditional rural splendour, its spacious, supremely tasteful rooms are surprisingly up to date. Expect fresh, white styling, floral-print

spreads and exposed beams, along with gorgeous countryside panoramas, superb service and a fantastic Michelin-starred **restaurant** (☎01451-820243; www.lordsofthemanor.com; Upper Slaughter; 3-/7-course dinner £72.50/£90; ⏲6.45-9pm daily & noon-1.30pm Sat & Sun; P).

Getting There & Away

Buses are not permitted in the Slaughters, so unless you're hiking or cycling, a car is your best option. To reach Lower Slaughter, detour half a mile west from the A429, 2.5 miles southwest of Stow-on-the-Wold or 6 miles northeast of Northleach. Upper Slaughter is another mile further west.

Stow-on-the-Wold

☎01451 / POP 2040

The highest town in the Cotswolds (244m), Stow-on-the-Wold centres on a large square surrounded by handsome buildings. The high-walled alleyways that lead into it originally served to funnel sheep into the fair, and it also witnessed a bloody massacre at the end of the English Civil War, when Roundhead soldiers dispatched defeated Royalists in 1646.

Standing on the Roman Fosse Way (now the A429), at the junction of six roads 4.5 miles south of Moreton-in-Marsh, Stow is still an important market town. It's also a major tourist destination, usually crowded with visitors in summer, and famous for hosting the twice-yearly (May and October) Stow Horse Fair.

Sights

Cotswold Farm Park ZOO
(☎01451-850307; www.cotswoldfarmpark.co.uk; Guiting Power; adult/child £10/9.50; ⏲10.30am-5pm mid-Feb–late Dec; P)
Owned by TV presenter Adam Henson, Cotswold Farm Park sets out to introduce little ones to the world of farm animals, while also preserving rare breeds, such as Exmoor ponies and Cotswold Lion sheep. There are milking demonstrations, lamb-feeding sessions, an adventure playground, a 2-mile wildlife walk and pedal tractors to ride on. It's 6 miles west of Stow-on-the-Wold, signposted from the B4077 and B4068.

Driving Tour
Classic Cotswolds

START BURFORD
END WINCHCOMBE
LENGTH 54 MILES; ONE TO THREE DAYS

Given the Cotswolds' intricate spider's-web of winding country lanes that connect its market towns, villages and stately homes, it's impossible to cover every highlight in a single day. This tour, though, spans three counties and takes in some of the most picturesque spots in the northern half of the range. You could drive it in a day, but you'll enjoy it more if you stretch it into two or three, with plentiful stop-offs along the way.

Begin in Oxfordshire at the gorgeous hillside market town of 1 **Burford** (p207), then head 10 miles west on the A40 into Gloucestershire, following signs to classic Cotswolds town 2 **Northleach** (p208). The Cotswolds Discovery Centre here has excellent displays covering the history, geography, flora and fauna of the Cotswolds Area of Outstanding Natural Beauty (AONB). There's a fine church in town, and a fascinating Roman villa nearby.

From Northleach, spin 7 miles northeast on the A429 to 3 **Lower Slaughter**, a serene riverside village lined with houses made of that irresistible Cotswolds golden stone. Spare the time if you can to stroll a mile northwest, along the river, to 4 **Upper Slaughter**, less visited than its sibling but no less attractive. Book ahead, and you can have lunch in an exquisite Jacobean mansion, at Lords of the Manor.

Continue 3 miles north on the A429 to 5 **Stow-on-the-Wold**, the highest Cotswold village at 244m. Explore the market square, then follow the A429 north, along the route of the ancient Roman Fosse Way. After 4.5 miles you'll reach 6 **Moreton-in-Marsh** (p216), known for its weekly Tuesday market and excellent shops.

Next, zip 3 miles west on the A44 to tiny 7 **Bourton-on-the-Hill**, filled with attractive 17th- and 18th-century cottages. It's famous for two things: the gibbeting cage in which the bodies of dead highwaymen were hung in the 19th century, and horse training – there are several stud farms in the vicinity. The Horse & Groom here is a good lunch option.

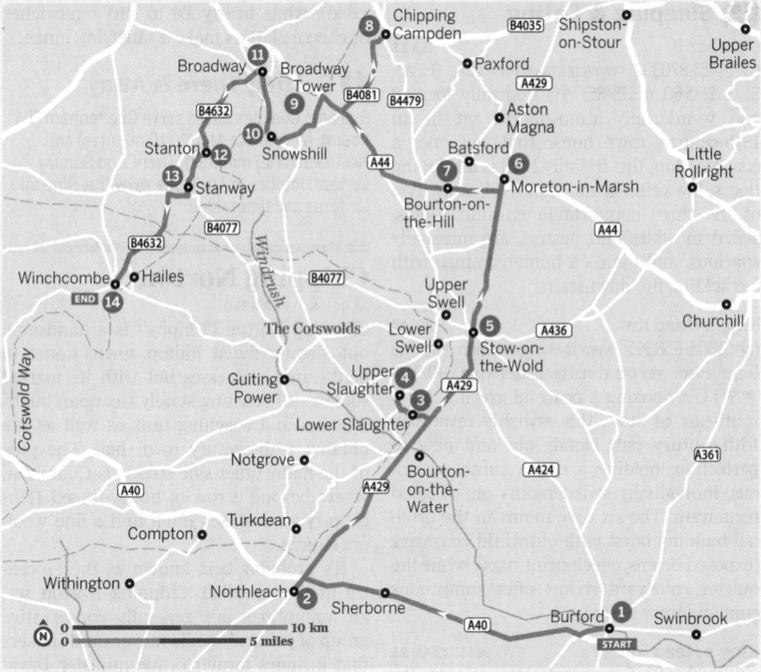

Head 3 miles west on the A44, then turn right (northeast) onto the B4081 to **8 Chipping Campden** (p213), one of the Cotswold's most bucolic towns. After admiring 15th-century St James' Church and the honey-toned buildings along High St, backtrack to the A44. Drive a mile northwest, crossing into the Worcestershire corner of the Cotswolds, and turn off at signposted **9 Broadway Tower** (p215), an 18th-century Gothic folly perched atop the escarpment.

Leaving Broadway Tower, continue 1 mile south and turn right (southwest) at the crossing. You'll soon see signs to pretty little **10 Snowshill**, a mile further on and one-time film set for *Bridget Jones's Diary*. If you're visiting in June or July, you'll swing by spectacularly purple fields of flowering lavender. From Snowshill, whizz 2.5 miles north to **11 Broadway** (p214), home to an excellent museum and gallery. After cruising along broad High St, hop on the B4632 southwest towards Cheltenham.

After 3 miles, take the left (east) turn-off to **12 Stanton**, a tiny stunner of a village. Its houses are crafted out of gold-tinged Cotswolds stone, with not a shop or quaint tearoom in sight. The buildings most likely to catch your eye are Jacobean Stanton Court and St Michael & All Angels' Church, the latter with its fine Perpendicular tower and beguiling medieval interior. Stanton Court once belonged to civil architect Sir Philip Stott (1858–1937), who restored many other Stanton houses.

You're sure to see walkers passing through Stanton, heading along the Cotswold Way to **13 Stanway**, a mile south; follow the narrow road that runs parallel to the trail. There's little more to idyllic Stanway than a few thatched-roofed cottages, a church and Stanway House, a magnificent Jacobean manor house concealed behind a triple-gabled gatehouse. Its beautiful baroque water gardens feature Britain's tallest fountain. The private home of the Earls of Wemyss for 500 years, the manor has a delightful, lived-in charm, with much of its original furniture and character intact.

Traverse Stanway, turn right (west) onto the B4077 and then left (southwest) back onto the B4632. After 3.5 miles, you'll reach **14 Winchcombe** (p217), an ancient Anglo-Saxon town and walkers' favourite with good sleeping and eating options, including 5 North St. You'll probably want to stay overnight to explore wonderful Sudeley Castle in the morning.

Sleeping & Eating

Number 9 B&B ££

(01451-870333; www.number-nine.info; 9 Park St; s £50-60, d £75-85;) Centrally located and wonderfully atmospheric, set in an 18th-century town house that was once a coaching inn, this friendly B&B is all sloping floors, low ceilings and exposed beams. Two of the three comfortable en-suite rooms, styled in white and pastels, are unusually spacious, and there's a homely lounge with a crackling fire downstairs.

King's Head Inn INN ££

(01608-658365; www.thekingsheadinn.net; The Green, Bledington; s/d incl breakfast from £90/110; P) Overlooking a peaceful green 4 miles southeast of Stow, this stylishly revamped 16th-century pub blends old and new to perfection, holding a dozen subtly luxurious, individually styled rooms plus a good restaurant. The six cosy rooms in the original building burst with old-world character (exposed beams, check-print rugs), while the quieter courtyard rooms offer sumptuous contemporary design.

King's Head Inn GASTROPUB ££

(01608-658365; www.thekingsheadinn.net; The Green, Bledington; mains £14-26; noon-2pm & 6.30-9pm Mon-Sat, noon-3pm & 6.30-9pm Sun; P) 'National Inn of the Year' in 2020, and set in a 16th-century cider house with a lovely garden 4 miles southeast of Stow, the King's Head is ideal for eating, drinking or both. Seasonal menus draw on local produce such as Cotswold lamb, adding Mediterranean flavours (mozzarella and pomegranate salad), while hearty £8 to £10 sandwiches or cheese platters make a satisfying lunch.

> **DAYLESFORD ORGANIC**
>
> A country-chic temple to the Cotswolds' organic movement, 4 miles east of Stow, the sprawling **Daylesford Organic** (01608-731700; www.daylesford.com; Daylesford; 8am-8pm Mon-Sat, 10am-4pm Sun) operation was kickstarted 40 years ago when a family farm turned sustainable. Centred on a gleaming food hall, crammed with Daylesford-brand produce, it also holds an excellent cafe-restaurant serving organic-fuelled treats (£13 to £19), plus an upmarket boutique, rental cottages, and a luxury spa.

Getting There & Away

Pulhams Coaches buses serve Cheltenham (1¼ hours), Moreton-in-Marsh (10 minutes) and Northleach (30 minutes). There's no Sunday service October to April. See www.traveline.info for fares and timetables.

Chipping Norton

01608 / POP 6300

Chipping Norton ('Chippy') is a handsome but slightly faded hilltop town, home to banks and businesses but with its market square still boasting stately Georgian buildings and old coaching inns as well as the pillared 19th-century town hall. The pick of the many quiet side streets is Church St, where beyond a row of honey-tinged 17th-century almshouses you'll find a fine wool-era church.

It's probably best known as the epicentre of the so-called 'Chipping Norton set', an amorphous but generally conservative group of political/media movers and shakers that includes former prime minister David Cameron, and Rebecca Brooks, former CEO of News International.

Sights

Rollright Stones ARCHAEOLOGICAL SITE

(www.rollrightstones.co.uk; off A3400, Great Rollright; suggested adult/child £1/50p; 24hr) Linked by a footpath through open fields, the ancient Rollright Stones stand to either side of an unnamed road 4 miles north of Chipping Norton. The most remarkable, the King's Men, consist of the weathered remnants of a stone circle that surrounded a Neolithic ceremonial centre in around 2500 BC, while the taller King Stone probably marked a Bronze Age cemetery, a millennium later. Payment made online.

Cotswolds Distillery DISTILLERY

(01608-238533; www.cotswoldsdistillery.com; Phillip's Field, Whichford Rd, Stourton; tours £15; tours 11am, 1pm & 3pm, shop & cafe 10am-5pm) This ambitious, ecofriendly gin and whisky distillery sits tucked into the northern Cotswolds, 8 miles north of Chipping Norton. Join a tour of the facilities to learn how its delicious Cotswolds-flavoured liquors are produced, then wrap things up with a tasting session. Reservations essential.

Sleeping & Eating

★ Falkland Arms PUB ££

(www.falklandarms.co.uk; 19-21 The Green, Great Tew; s/d incl breakfast £85/90; ⌚3-9pm Mon & Tue, noon-10pm Wed-Sat, noon-6pm Sun; P 📶) For its blissful bucolic setting and historic charm, there's no beating the thatched, 16th-century Falkland Arms, in the picture-postcard village of Great Tew, 6 miles east of Chipping Norton. The half-dozen freshly restored and upgraded rooms are great value, the pub downstairs serves fine ales and decent pub grub (mains £13 to £20), and there's lovely walking in every direction.

Wild Thyme MODERN BRITISH ££

(☎01608-645060; www.wildthymerestaurant.co.uk; 10 New St; ⌚set menu supper clubs) This little 'restaurant with rooms' thrills palates with top-notch creative dishes packed with flavour, such as asparagus and goat's cheese risotto or steamed Cornish turbot with Japanese pickles. The desserts – from apple crumble to chocolate fondant – are nothing short of sublime.

Jaffé & Neale Bookshop Cafe CAFE

(☎01608-641033; www.jaffeandneale.co.uk; 1 Middle Row; ⌚9.30am-4pm Mon-Sat; 📶) The cosy little cafe in this busy independent bookshop on the main square serves delicious cakes and coffees at tables squeezed between the bookshelves, or in the cosy upstairs reading lounge with sofas.

Getting There & Away

Stagecoach and/or Pulhams buses head to Oxford (one hour), Witney (45 minutes), and Woodstock (20 minutes). See www.traveline.info for fares and timetables.

Chipping Campden

☎01386 / POP 2310

A standout gem, even for an area of such pretty towns, Chipping Campden is a glorious reminder of Cotswolds life in medieval times. While 'Chipping' derives from the Old English 'ceapen', meaning 'market', it owes its conspicuous prosperity to its success in the wool trade. Its gracefully curving main street is flanked by a picturesque array of stone cottages, fine terraced houses, ancient inns and historic homes, most made of that beautiful honey-coloured Cotswolds stone. Westington, southwest of the centre, holds some especially striking thatch-roofed cottages.

As the northeastern end of the Cotswold Way, which rambles 102 miles southwest from here to Bath, Chipping Campden is a popular way station for walkers and cyclists, and welcomes crowds of visitors year-round. Despite its obvious allure, though, it remains surprisingly unspoiled.

Sights

Hidcote GARDENS

(NT; www.nationaltrust.org.uk; Hidcote Bartrim; adult/child £8/4; ⌚10am-6pm Apr-Sep, to 5pm Oct, shorter hours rest of year, closed Jan; P) Hidcote, 4 miles northeast of Chipping Campden, ranks among the finest Arts and Crafts gardens in Britain. Laid out from 1907 onwards by American horticulturalist Lawrence Johnston, and acquired by the National Trust in 1948, it consists of a series of outdoor 'rooms' filled with flowers and rare plants from across the globe. There's also a cafe and garden centre.

Grevel House HISTORIC BUILDING

(High St; ⌚closed to the public) Built around 1380 for the supremely prosperous wool merchant William Grevel, complete with gargoyles and mullioned windows, Grevel

WORTH A TRIP

BATSFORD ARBORETUM

Created from 1880 onwards by Bertie Mitford (Lord Redesdale), and later briefly home to his famous granddaughters, the Mitford sisters, **Batsford Arboretum** (☎01386-701441; www.batsarb.co.uk; Batsford Park; adult/child £8.95/3.50; ⌚9am-4pm; P 🐕) is 1.5 miles west of Moreton. These exotic 22-hectare woodlands hold around 1600 species of labelled trees, bamboos and shrubs. Drawn especially from Nepal, China and Japan, many are rare or endangered, or were planted pre-WWI. Highlights include flowering Japanese cherries (at their best in spring), some vast North American redwoods and an enormous davidia, and the strangely churchlike 'cathedral' lime.

A 1.7-mile footpath from Moreton leads direct to the arboretum itself; motorists have to drive a mile north up the approach road from the entrance on the A44.

SHIN KICKING & CHEESE-ROLLING

The medieval sport of shin kicking lives on in the extraordinary **Cotswold Olimpicks** (www.olimpickgames.co.uk; Dover's Hill, Chipping Campden; late May/early Jun), first celebrated in 1612. One of England's most bizarre and entertaining traditional sports days, it still features many of the original events, such as tug o' war.

Equally odd is the age-old (and surprisingly hazardous) pastime of **cheese-rolling** (Cooper's Hill; admission free; last May bank holiday). Following a 200-year-old tradition, crowds run, tumble and slide down Cooper's Hill, 4.5 miles northeast of Painswick, pursuing an 8lb round of Double Gloucester cheese. The prize? The cheese itself – and the glory of catching it.

House is Chipping Campden's oldest building. It's still a private home, but you can admire its splendid Perpendicular Gothic–style gabled window and sundial from the street.

Court Barn Museum MUSEUM
(01386-841951; www.courtbarn.org.uk; Church St; adult/child £5/free; 10am-5pm Wed-Sun Apr-Oct, to 4pm Nov-Mar) Ever since architect and designer Charles Robert Ashbee (1863–1942) moved his Guild of Handicraft here from East London in 1902, Chipping Campden has been linked with the Arts and Crafts movement. This small but interesting museum displays work by nine luminaries of the movement, which celebrated traditional artisans in an age of industrialisation. Sadly, robberies in 2011 and 2017 removed its prize jewellery collection, but surviving artefacts include sculpture, book-binding and ceramics. It also stages two selling exhibitions each year.

Sleeping & Eating

Eight Bells Inn PUB ££
(01386-840371; www.eightbellsinn.co.uk; Church St; r incl breakfast £99-143;) This friendly and atmospheric 14th-century inn offers six bright, modern rooms with iron bedsteads, soothing neutral decor, flowery wallpaper and warm accents. Room 7 – there's no number 4 – with its chunky old-world beams, is especially striking. The cosy pub downstairs serves contemporary country cooking.

★**Badgers Hall** BAKERY £
(01386-840839; www.badgershall.com; High St; afternoon tea per person £7.50-24.50; 8am-5.30pm Thu-Sat;) Set in a glorious old mansion facing the market hall, this definitive Cotswold tearoom is renowned for its no-holds-barred afternoon teas, served from 2.30pm onwards. Lunch is also a treat, starring the most wonderful cheese scones you've ever tasted. Guests staying in the cosy B&B rooms upstairs (£140) get to sample its baking all week; nonguests are welcome Thursday to Saturday only.

Information

Tourist Office (01386-841206; www.campdenonline.org; Old Police Station, High St; 9.30am-5pm mid-Mar–Oct, 9.30am-1pm Mon-Thu, to 4pm Fri-Sun Nov–mid-Mar) Pick up a town guide (£1.50) for a self-guided walk around Chipping Campden's most significant buildings. Between May and September, the Cotswold Voluntary Wardens run guided tours (suggested donation £3).

Getting There & Away

From Monday to Saturday, Johnsons Excelbus services head to/from Moreton-in-Marsh (50 minutes), Broadway (20 minutes) and Stratford-upon-Avon (50 minutes). See www.traveline.info for the latest fares and timetables.

Broadway

01386 / POP 2540

The graceful, golden-hued cottages of the quintessentially English village of Broadway, set at the foot of a steep escarpment, now hold antique shops, tearooms and art galleries, interspersed with luxurious hotels. One of the Cotswolds' most popular destinations, just 5 miles west of Chipping Campden, the village attracted the likes of writer-designer William Morris and artist John Singer Sargent during the Victorian era.

The village of Snowshill, 2.5 miles south, may look familiar; a local house starred in the hit film *Bridget Jones's Diary* as Bridget's parents' home.

Sights

Snowshill Manor & Garden HOUSE
(NT; www.nationaltrust.org.uk; Snowshill; adult/child £8/4; noon-5pm daily mid-Mar–Oct, 11am-

2.30pm Sat & Sun Nov, closed Dec–mid-March) Once home to eccentric poet and architect Charles Paget Wade (1883–1956), this wonderful medieval mansion stands just over 2 miles south of Broadway. It now displays Wade's extraordinary collection of crafts and design, ranging from musical instruments to Southeast Asian masks and Japanese samurai armour.

Broadway Tower TOWER
(☎01386-852390; www.broadwaytower.co.uk; Middle Hill; adult/child £8/4, with separate Nuclear Bunker tours; ⏲10am-5pm; P) Built in 1798 to resemble an imaginary Saxon fort, this turreted Gothic folly looks down on Broadway from atop the escarpment, 1 mile southeast. William Morris spent a summer here, so exhibitions on its successive levels focus on the Arts and Crafts movement. The main reason to visit, though, is for the stunning all-round views from its rooftop platform.

Broadway Museum & Art Gallery MUSEUM
(☎01386-859047; www.ashmoleanbroadway.org; Tudor House, 65 High St; adult/child £5/2; ⏲10am-5pm Tue-Sun Feb-Oct, to 4pm Tue-Sun Nov & Dec, closed Jan) Set in a magnificent 17th-century coaching inn, Broadway's town museum has close links with Oxford's prestigious Ashmolean Museum. Its fascinating displays of local crafts, art and antiques, and its stimulating temporary exhibitions draw exclusively on the Ashmolean collection, so the quality is consistently high. Paintings in the sumptuous upstairs galleries include 18th-century works by Joshua Reynolds and Thomas Gainsborough.

Sleeping & Eating

Olive Branch B&B ££
(☎01386-853440; www.theolivebranch-broadway.com; 78 High St; s/d from £95/120; ☎) At the quiet upper end of the high street, this snug B&B offers eight homey rooms cheerfully done up in pinks, creams and whites. Number 4 has its own four-poster bed, while the two top-floor rooms accommodate families. All hold umbrellas, tea and coffee, and walking information. The hospitable owners prepare good home-cooked breakfasts.

Foxhill Manor DESIGN HOTEL £££
(☎01386-898164; www.foxhillmanor.com; Farmcombe Estate; r incl breakfast from £439; P) Occupying a 1904 Arts and Crafts mansion on a sprawling hillside estate, 2.5 miles northeast of Broadway, this ultra-luxurious hideaway epitomises Cotswolds chic. From dazzlingly bold decor – rich oranges, grey metro tiles, twin window-facing baths – to period stucco-work, each of its five sleek rooms and three suites has an individual flair. An in-house chef prepares whatever you fancy eating.

Russell's HOTEL £££
(☎01386-853555; www.russellsofbroadway.co.uk; The Green, 20 High St; r incl breakfast from £130; ⏲restaurant noon-2.15pm & 6-9.15pm Mon-Sat, noon-2.30pm Sun; P) Housed in the former workshop of furniture designer Gordon Russell, this Arts and Crafts–influenced hotel offers seven sizeable rooms, some with exposed beams, four-poster beds and armchairs, and all with contemporary bathrooms and fresh white styling. Choose from the á la carte or two-/three-course set menu (£30/£35) in the restaurant.

★**Mount Inn** PUB FOOD ££
(☎01386-584316; www.themountinn.co.uk; Stanton; mains £13-22; ⏲noon-2pm & 6-9pm Mon-Sat, to 8pm Sun; P) Revelling in glorious hilltop views above pretty honey-washed Stanton, just off the Cotswolds Way 3.5 miles southwest of Broadway, this pub is not just idyllically located, it serves great food too: hearty country favourites, prepared with contemporary flair. Menus range over breaded local St Eadburgha cheese, beer-battered haddock, gammon steaks, mushroom-halloumi burgers and seasonal specials.

Getting There & Away

BUS

Marchants and Johnsons ExcelBus services head to Cheltenham (40 minutes), Chipping Campden (20 minutes), Moreton-in-Marsh (30 minutes), Stratford-upon-Avon (45 minutes) and Winchcombe (30 minutes). See www.traveline.info for the latest fares and timetables.

TRAIN

A limited rail service returned to Broadway in 2018 after a 58-year hiatus, with the reopening of the long-defunct Broadway Station. Most days in summer, following an intricate schedule, the volunteer-run Gloucestershire Warwickshire Railway (p218) runs excursion trains between Cheltenham racecourse and Broadway, via Winchcombe, for a return fare from £18.

WORTH A TRIP

HIGHGROVE

The private residence of Prince Charles and the Duchess of Cornwall, a mile southwest of Tetbury, **Highgrove** (☎0303-123 7310; www.highgrovegardens.com; Doughton; tours £27.50; ⊙Apr-Sep; Ⓟ) is famous for its exquisite, sustainable, organic gardens, which include rows of shape-clipped yews and a 'carpet garden' modelled on an oriental rug. Two-hour garden tours run on select summer days, detailed on the website and varying from 17 days in a month to just one. They usually sell out far in advance, but last-minute tickets are sometimes available through **Highgrove Shop** (☎01666-505666; www.highgroveshop.com; 10 Long St; ⊙9.30am-5pm Mon-Sat, 10.30am-4.30pm Sun).

Moreton-in-Marsh

☎01608 / POP 3820

Graced by an ultrabroad High St that follows the die-straight line of the Roman Fosse Way (now the A429) and is lined with beautiful 17th- and 18th-century buildings, Moreton-in-Marsh is a historic Cotswolds town that's sadly rather marred by the constant heavy traffic that hurtles right through the centre. Take the time to wander around, though – ideally on a Tuesday, when the weekly market bursts into life – and you'll find plenty of tearooms, cafes and pubs, along with intriguing shops. It's 4.5 miles north of Stow-on-the-Wold.

Sights

★Cotswold Falconry Centre BIRD SANCTUARY

(☎01386-701043; www.cotswold-falconry.co.uk; Batsford Park; adult/child £12/6; ⊙10.30am-5pm mid-Feb–mid-Nov; Ⓟ) Home to over 150 birds of prey (owl, vulture, eagle and, of course, falcon), this exciting spot stages displays of the ancient practice of falconry at 11.30am, 1.30pm and 3pm daily (plus 4.30pm April to October). The birds fly best on windy days. Hands-on experiences (from £40) include a one-hour 'Flying Start' during which visitors get to fly hawks.

Chastleton House HISTORIC BUILDING

(NT; ☎01608-674355; www.nationaltrust.org.uk; Chastleton; adult/child £10.50/6; ⊙1-5pm Wed-Sun Mar-Oct; Ⓟ) Four miles southeast of Moreton-in-Marsh, signposted off the A44 halfway to Chipping Norton, Chastleton is one of England's finest and most complete Jacobean houses. Built between 1607 and 1612 and barely altered since, it's bursting with rare tapestries, family portraits and antique furniture; the Long Gallery is particularly resplendent. Outside, there's a wonderful topiary garden. Free garden tours run most afternoons.

Sleeping & Eating

White Hart Royal Hotel HOTEL ££

(☎01608-650731; www.whitehartroyal.co.uk; High St; s/d £100/110; Ⓟ) 'Royal' refers to the fact that Charles I stayed in this low-slung honey-coloured inn during the Civil War. He may not have used the iPod docks and flat-screen TVs, but he certainly walked down the atmospheric half-timbered corridors. Standard rooms these days are comfy and well-equipped, even if they lack character.

Martha's Coffee House CAFE £

(☎01608-651999; Gavel Cottage, High St; mains £7-9; ⊙9am-5pm Mon-Sat, to 4pm Sun;) In an appealing historic cottage on the main road, Martha's is a local mainstay, dependable from the moment it serves the first of its all-day pancake-and-eggs breakfasts to the last of its £7.50-per-person cream teas. Lunchtime sees good-value sandwiches and toasties, but the real highlights are the £4.50 savoury scones, featuring flavours like beetroot and basil.

Horse & Groom PUB FOOD ££

(☎01386-700413; www.horseandgroom.info; A44, Bourton-on-the-Hill; mains £12-23; ⊙noon-3pm & 6.30-9.30pm Mon-Sat, to 8.30pm Sun; Ⓟ) This laid-back but welcoming pub, in a tiny hamlet 2 miles west of Moreton-in-Marsh, is a firm favourite with well-heeled horsey types who appreciate its extravagant array of gins. As well as serving good food, with a menu that showcases local lamb, beef and fresh produce in general, it also has five swish rooms upstairs (£130 to £170).

Getting There & Away

BUS

Pulhams, Stagecoach and/or Johnsons Excelbus buses head to/from Broadway (30 minutes), Cheltenham (1½ hours), Chipping Campden (50 minutes), Northleach (40 minutes) and Stow-on-the-Wold (10 minutes). See www.traveline.info for the latest fares and timetables.

TRAIN

The station is towards the northern end of town, just off High St. Trains head to/from Hereford (£20, 1¾ hours), Ledbury (£18, 1½ hours), London Paddington (£18, 1½ hours), Oxford (£12, 35 minutes) and Worcester (£14, 40 minutes). See www.thetrainline.com for the latest fares and timetables.

Winchcombe

☎01242 / POP 5020

Winchcombe, 8 miles northeast of Cheltenham, is very much a living, working town, where butchers, bakers and independent shops line the main streets. Capital of the Anglo-Saxon kingdom of Mercia, it remained a major trading town until the Middle Ages, and was a centre for (illegally) growing tobacco in the 17th century. Reminders of that illustrious past can still be seen in Winchcombe's dramatic stone and half-timbered buildings. Keep an eye out for the picturesque cottages on Vineyard St and Dents Tce. As Winchcombe is on the Cotswold Way and other trails, it's especially popular with walkers.

Sights

Sudeley Castle CASTLE

(☎01242-604244; www.sudeleycastle.co.uk; adult/child £12/5; ⏲10.45am-5pm mid-Mar–Oct; P 🚻) During its thousand-year history, this magnificent castle has welcomed many a monarch, including Richard III, Henry VIII and Charles I. Half a mile southeast of Winchcombe, it's most famous as the home and final resting place of Catherine Parr (Henry VIII's widow), who lived here with her fourth husband, Thomas Seymour. In fact it's the only private house in England where a queen is buried – Catherine lies in its Perpendicular Gothic St Mary's Church. It also boasts 10 splendid gardens.

Belas Knap Long Barrow ARCHAEOLOGICAL SITE

(EH; www.english-heritage.org.uk; near Charlton Abbots; ⏲dawn-dusk) FREE Dating from around 3000 BC, Belas Knap is one of the country's best-preserved neolithic burial chambers, complete with 'false' portal leading nowhere. The remains of 31 people were found when its four chambers were excavated. At 290m, views across Sudeley Castle and the surrounding countryside are breathtaking. The barrow can be accessed from Winchcombe by a 2½-mile hike south along the Cotswold Way. Alternatively, park on Corndean Lane and take a steep half-mile walk up across fields.

Hailes Abbey RUINS

(EH; www.english-heritage.org.uk; Hailes; adult/child £6.90/4.10; ⏲10am-6pm Jul & Aug, to 5pm Easter-Jun, Sep & Oct; P) Now lying in ruins 3 miles northeast of Winchcombe, this 13th-century Cistercian abbey was once, thanks to a long-running medieval scam, one of England's main pilgrimage centres. The abbey was said – by Geoffrey Chaucer in *The Canterbury Tales*, among others – to possess a vial of Christ's blood. Until that was denounced during the Reformation as containing no more than coloured water, thousands of pilgrims contributed to the abbey's wealth. At the time of writing, the abbey was only open Friday to Sunday.

Sleeping & Eating

Wesley House B&B ££

(☎01242-602366; www.wesleyhouse.co.uk; High St; s £75-85, d £95-110; ⏲restaurant noon-2pm & 7-9pm Tue-Sat, noon-2pm Sun; 📶🐾) Methodist founder John Wesley once stayed in this ravishing 15th-century half-timbered town house, which offers five pleasant rooms plus a warm welcome. 'Mumble Meadow', splashed with reds, overlooks the street, while 'Almsbury' has its own terrace gazing out across the countryside. Rates rise on Saturdays. Downstairs, the restaurant serves fabulous modern-British cuisine.

★5 North St MODERN EUROPEAN £££

(☎01242-604566; www.5northstreetrestaurant.co.uk; 5 North St; 2-/3-course lunch £26/32, 3-/7-course dinner £54/74; ⏲12.30-1.30pm Tue-Sun & 7-9pm Wed-Sat; ✍) This veteran gourmet restaurant is a treat from start to finish, from its splendid 400-year-old timbered exterior to the elegant, inventive creations you eventually find on your plate. Marcus Ashenford's cooking is rooted in traditional seasonal ingredients, but the odd playful experiment (think duck-egg pasta or malt ice cream) adds that extra magic. Vegetarians can enjoy a separate £45 menu.

Information

Tourist Office (☎01242-602925; www.winchcombe.co.uk; Town Hall, High St; ⏲10am-4pm daily Apr-Oct, to 3pm Sat & Sun Nov-Mar) Has maps of local walks and runs free guided town tours at 11am and 2.30pm on Sunday, from Easter to October.

Getting There & Away

BUS

Marchants buses travel to/from Broadway (30 minutes) and Cheltenham (20 minutes). See www.traveline.info for the latest fares and timetables.

TRAIN

Several days each week in summer, to a convoluted schedule, the **Gloucestershire Warwickshire Railway** (GWR; ☎01242-621405; www.gwsr.com; day pass adult/child £18/8; ⏱Mar-Dec; ♿) runs around five trains that stop at Winchcombe en route between Cheltenham (£5, 25 minutes) and Broadway (£9, 20 minutes).

Painswick

☎01452 / POP 1740

Among the Cotswolds' most beautiful and unspoiled villages, hilltop Painswick sits 10 miles southwest of Cheltenham. Cars stream through, along its single-lane main road, but other than walkers on the Cotswold Way, few visitors allow themselves the pleasure of wandering its narrow winding streets to admire picture-perfect cottages, handsome stone houses and medieval inns. Keep an eye out for Bisley St, the original main drag, which was superseded by the now ancient-looking New St in medieval times.

Bucolic little Slad, 2 miles south towards Stroud in the Slad Valley, was the much-loved home of writer Laurie Lee (1914–97), who immortalised its beauty in *Cider with Rosie*.

Sights

Painswick Rococo Garden GARDENS

(☎01452-813204; www.rococogarden.org.uk; off B4073; adult/child £10/4.90; ⏱10.30am-5pm mid-Jan–Oct; P♿) England's only surviving rococo garden, half a mile north of Painswick, was laid out by Benjamin Hyett in the 1740s as a vast 'outdoor room'. Restored to its original glory thanks to a contemporary painting, it's absolutely stunning. Winding paths soften its geometrical precision, leading visitors to scattered Gothic follies that include the eccentric Red House, which has Latin quotes from the Song of Solomon etched into its stained-glass windows. There's also a children's nature trail and maze.

St Mary's Church CHURCH

(www.beaconbenefice.org.uk/painswick; New St; ⏱9.30am-dusk) Painswick centres on this fine 14th-century, Perpendicular Gothic wool church, surrounded by 18th-century tabletop tombs and clipped yew trees sculpted to resemble giant ice lollies. Legend has it that only 99 trees could ever grow here, as the devil would shrivel the 100th. To celebrate the millennium, they planted one anyway, and – lo and behold! – another one toppled. At the foot of the churchyard there's a rare set of iron stocks.

Sleeping & Eating

Troy House B&B ££

(☎01452-812339; www.troyguesthouse.co.uk; Gloucester St; d/tr £85/115; 📶) This great little B&B sleeps guests in four sweet, spacious rooms, two of which occupy a separate rear cottage accessed across an attractive courtyard. They're prettily decked out with soothing cream decor, comfy beds and baskets of toiletries, and the freshly cooked breakfasts are excellent.

★**Painswick** LUXURY HOTEL £££

(☎01452-813688; www.thepainswick.co.uk; Kemps Lane; r/ste from £201/404; ⏱restaurant noon-2.30pm & 7-10pm; P📶) Focused on an imposing 18th-century house somehow squeezed into the heart of the village, and seriously chic within its stern stone walls, the Painswick offers 16 luxurious, individually decorated, pastel-painted rooms, some with four-poster beds, that spread through assorted outbuildings. As well as massage/treatment rooms, there's a futuristic bar, a colour-popping lounge and a good modern restaurant (mains £21 to £28).

Woolpack Inn PUB FOOD ££

(☎01452-813429; www.thewoolpackslad.com; Slad; mains £19; ⏱noon-11pm Sun & Mon, to midnight Tue-Thu, to 1am Fri & Sat, food served 6-9pm Mon, noon-3pm & 6-9pm Tue-Sat, noon-4pm Sun; 🐾) This lively little rural pub in Slad, 2 miles south of Painswick, was a favourite watering hole of local author Laurie Lee, whose portrait and books adorn its walls. Perfect for a pint, stocking excellent local beers including Uley Bitter, it also serves a daily-changing menu of classics such as gammon or fish and chips alongside pasta, burgers and curries.

Information

Tourist Office (☎01452-812278; www.painswicktouristinfo.co.uk; Gravedigger's Hut, St Mary's Church, New St; ⏱10am-4pm Mon-Fri, to 1pm Sat Mar-Oct) Beside the main road, but accessed from within the church grounds.

Getting There & Away

Stagecoach bus 66 heads to/from Cheltenham (40 minutes) and Stroud (10 minutes). See www.traveline.info for the latest fares and timetables.

WESTERN GLOUCESTERSHIRE

West of the Cotswolds, Gloucestershire's greatest asset is the elegant Regency town of Cheltenham, home to tree-lined terraces, upmarket boutiques and a tempting assortment of hotels and restaurants. The county capital, Gloucester, is also worth visiting, to see its magnificent Perpendicular Gothic cathedral, while Berkeley, not far southwest, has a historic Norman castle. Further west, the Forest of Dean is a leafy backwater that's perfect for walking, cycling, kayaking and other adventurous activities.

Cheltenham

01242 / POP 117,500

Cheltenham, on the western edge of the Cotswolds and the region's major town, owes its air of gracious refinement to its heyday as a spa resort during the 18th century. At that time, it rivalled Bath as *the* place for ailing aristocrats to recuperate, and it stills boast many graceful Regency buildings and manicured squares. These days, however, it's better known for its racecourse, where the upper classes still arrive in droves for the mid-March Cheltenham Cup.

Cheltenham's excellent hotel and restaurant offerings make it a much more appealing base than Gloucester (12 miles west), but in the end this mid-tier town is unlikely to be the highlight of your trip.

Central Cheltenham extends around the grand tree-lined Promenade, with the fashionable Montpellier neighbourhood at its southern end.

Sights

The Promenade STREET

Famed as one of the most beautiful streets in England, this broad, tree-lined boulevard leads down from the high street to Montpellier, and is flanked by imposing period buildings that are now filled with fancy shops. The striking **Municipal Offices**, behind the flower-filled Long Gardens on its western side, were built in 1825 as private residences. A statue in front commemorates Cheltenham-born explorer Edward Wilson (1872–1912), who perished on Captain Scott's ill-fated second expedition to the Antarctic.

Montpellier AREA

As well as plenty of handsome architecture, the village-y Montpellier district hosts a lively assortment of bars, restaurants, hotels, independent shops and boutiques. Along **Montpellier Walk**, 32 caryatids (draped female figures based on those of Athens' Acropolis), each balancing an elaborately carved cornice on her head, function as structural supports between the 1840s edifices that now serve as shops. The attractive Montpellier Gardens, directly opposite, were laid out in 1809, and are the focus of major local festivals.

Pittville Pump Room NOTABLE BUILDING

(0844-576 2210; www.pittvillepumproom.org.uk; Pittville Park;) FREE The Pittville Pump Room is Cheltenham's finest Regency building. Modelled on an ancient Athenian temple, it was built in 1830 as the centrepiece of a large new residential area a quarter of a mile north of the town centre. Admire its beautiful columned exterior, then wander into the main auditorium, where, if the pump is operating, you can sample the pungent spa waters from the ornate fountain. The lovely surrounding ornamental park is home to a lake, lawns and an aviary.

WORTH A TRIP

BERKELEY CASTLE

A superb red-stone structure, **Berkeley Castle** (01453-810303; www.berkeley-castle.com; adult/child £14/7; 11am-5pm Sun-Wed Apr-Oct; P) has been home to the Berkeleys for nearly 900 years, and little has changed since it was built as a sturdy Norman fortress. Edward II was imprisoned here in 1327 and swiftly died, probably murdered on the orders of his wife and her lover. Highlights include its central 12th-century keep, the King's Gallery, complete with Edward's cell and dungeon, and the spectacular medieval Great Hall, lined with tapestries. Free 45-minute guided tours run every 30 minutes.

Cheltenham

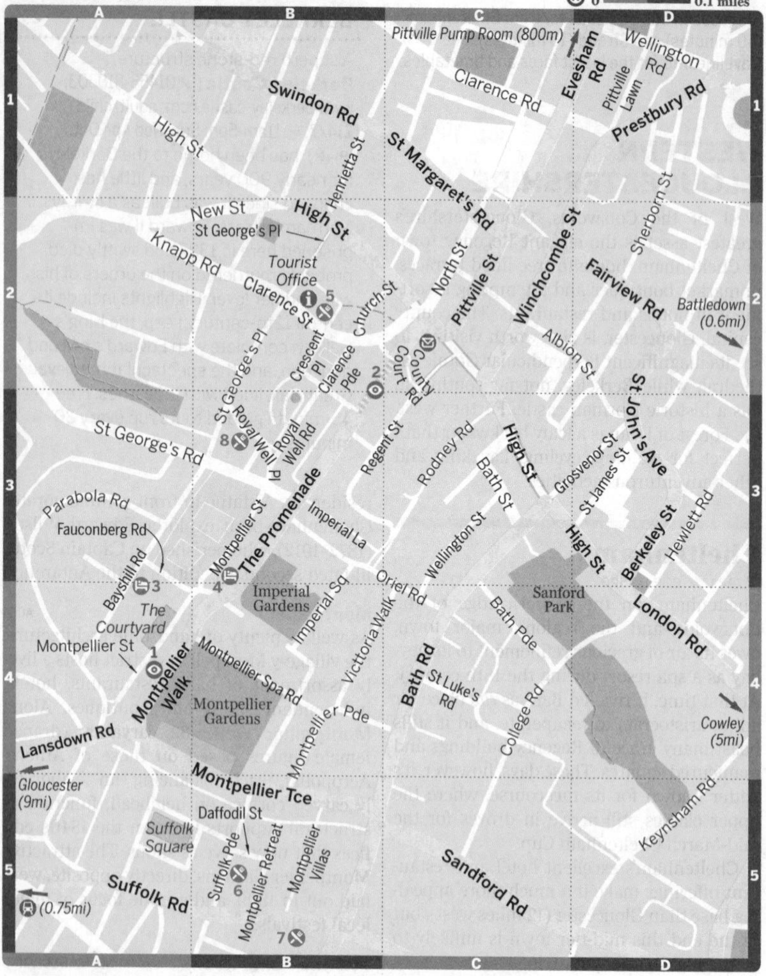

Cheltenham

Sights

1 Montpellier	A4
2 The Promenade	B2

Sleeping

3 Bradley	A4
4 No 131	B3

Eating

5 Boston Tea Party	B2
6 Daffodil	B5
7 Le Champignon Sauvage	B5
8 Tavern	B3

Festivals

Cheltenham Literature Festival LITERATURE

(☎01242-850270; www.cheltenhamfestivals.com; ⊙early Oct) One of the world's oldest book-focused festivals kicks off over 10 days in autumn, hosting an astounding array of talks, workshops, interviews and debates by 600 top writers, actors, scholars and other literary figures. Its headquarters is in Montpellier Gardens.

Sleeping

★Bradley B&B ££

(☎01242-519077; www.thebradleyhotel.co.uk; 19 Bayshill Rd; s/d from £115/120;) This splendidly preserved Regency house in Montpellier has lost none of its original flair in its transition into a fabulous, wonderfully comfortable, luxury B&B. Each of the eight recently redecorated rooms has its own style, blending antique furniture, vintage trinkets and original artwork with modern amenities.

★No 131 BOUTIQUE HOTEL £££

(☎01242-822939; www.no131.com; 131 The Promenade; r incl breakfast from £199;) Set in a stunning Georgian town house, this exquisite luxury hotel holds 11 chic, supremely comfortable rooms that combine original artwork with antique touches such as 19th-century roll-top baths and contemporary comforts (Nespresso machines, iPod docks). Some have in-room baths, others step-down walk-in showers. Scented candles dot the corridors, the Crazy Eights bar buzzes (DJs Thursday to Saturday), and there's a luxe, laid-back vibe.

Eating

Boston Tea Party CAFE £

(☎01242-573935; www.bostonteaparty.co.uk; 45-49 Clarence St; mains £7.50-12; ⌚8am-5pm;) A spacious, friendly, vintage-chic cafe chain, where relaxed decor – all blue faux-leather booths and rough wood tables, fresh flowers and colourful cans – makes the perfect setting for a contemporary British-international menu focused on ethically sourced ingredients. All-day breakfasts and brunches and tasty vegan and gluten-free choices keep it buzzing. Options include halloumi- or spiced-lamb-stuffed flatbreads, grain bowls and Vietnamese Banh-Mi sandwiches.

Tavern GASTROPUB ££

(☎01242-221212; www.thetaverncheltenham.com; 5 Royal Well Pl; mains £13-26; ⌚11.30am-10pm Mon-Fri, 10am-10pm Sat, to 5pm Sun;) Behind its bare-bones exterior, this stylish gastropub serves Modern British food with a punch, amid exposed brick, bare wooden tables, blue-velvet booths and tile-covered floors. Classy mains – ricotta dumplings with chanterelle mushrooms, wild garlic and pine nuts; cod cheeks with Puy lentils and pancetta – plus steaks, and pub classics from mac-cheese to burgers. The warm, welcoming service is spot on.

Daffodil BRASSERIE ££

(☎01242-700055; www.thedaffodil.com; 18-20 Suffolk Pde; mains £23-33; ⌚5-11pm Mon, Wed & Thu, noon-midnight Fri & Sat, noon-7pm Sun;) This breathtaking brasserie conjures its retro setting, in a 1920s cinema, into fabulous art deco glamour, with a delightful daffodil theme from its tiled floor to the plaster cornices. Charcoal-grilled offerings range from halloumi or lobster to calves' liver and, especially, steaks, but it also has veggie options such as aubergine, coconut and lemongrass curry and open goat's-cheese ravioli.

★Le Champignon Sauvage FRENCH £££

(☎01242-573449; www.lechampignonsauvage.co.uk; 24-28 Suffolk Rd; set menus £33-90; ⌚12.30-1.30pm & 7.30-8.45pm Tue-Sat) For over 30 years, chef David Everitt-Matthias has been thrilling visitors and locals alike in this Michelin-starred Cheltenham favourite. Imaginative flavour combinations in his finely executed dishes include the likes of lamb loin with wild garlic pesto, sheep's curd and anchovy emulsion. We're not alone in thinking it's Gloucestershire's best restaurant. The set lunch and dinner menus are good value.

Information

Tourist Office (☎01242-387492; www.visitcheltenham.com; The Wilson, Clarence St; ⌚9.30am-5.15pm Mon-Wed, to 7.45pm Thu, to 5.30pm Fri & Sat, 10.30am-4pm Sun) A desk inside the Wilson Museum.

Getting There & Away

BUS

Stagecoach, Pulhams, Marchants and Swanbrook operate local buses from Cheltenham. Most buses depart from the bus station; some use stops along the Promenade.

Bus destinations include Broadway (40 minutes), Cirencester (40 minutes), Gloucester (45 minutes), Oxford (1½ hours), Stow-on-the-Wold (1¼ hours), Stratford-upon-Avon (1½ hours), Stroud (45 minutes) and Winchcombe (20 minutes). See www.traveline.info for the latest fares and timetables.

National Express coach destinations include Birmingham (£10, 1½ hours), Bristol (£9, 1½ hours), Leeds (£40, six hours), London Victoria (£23, three hours), Newcastle-upon-Tyne (£40, eight hours) and Nottingham (£28, 4¼ hours).

OFF THE BEATEN TRACK

SLIMBRIDGE WETLAND CENTRE

A pioneer in wetlands conservation, **Slimbridge Wetland Centre** (WWT; ☎01453-891900; www.wwt.org.uk/slimbridge; Bowditch, Slimbridge; adult/child £14.50/8.40; ⏲9.30am-5.30pm Apr-Oct, to 5pm Nov-Mar; P), a 325-hectare reserve beside the River Severn 5 miles northeast of Berkeley, is a haven for migratory and resident birds. Hides are scattered throughout, and an observation tower affords spectacular 360-degree views for potential sightings of 200-plus feathered species, ranging from visiting swallows, peregrine falcons, white-fronted geese and Bewick's swans to hot-pink resident flamingos. Migratory birds visit in winter, while spring brings plenty of chicks.

Activities include guided walks, otter talks, and self-guided 'canoe safaris' (£7).

TRAIN

Cheltenham Spa train station is a mile west of the centre. The pleasant 'Honeybourne Line' footpath leads through parkland to the heart of town in around 20 minutes, while buses (D/E; £2) run every 10 minutes. Train connections include:

Bath (£11.90, 1¼ hours)
Bristol (£9.10, 40 minutes)
Cardiff (£19.10, 1½ hours)
Edinburgh (£159.50, six hours)
Exeter (£31.30, 1¾ hours)
Gloucester (£4.80, 10 minutes)
London Paddington (£34.30, two hours)

Forest of Dean

POP 85,400

England's oldest oak forest is a wonderfully scenic place for outdoor adventures. Designated England's first National Forest Park in 1938, this 42-sq-mile woodland had previously been a royal hunting ground and a centre of iron and coal mining. Its mysterious depths supposedly inspired the forests of JRR Tolkien's Middle Earth, while key scenes in *Harry Potter & the Deathly Hallows* were filmed here.

There's no 'Dean' in the Forest of Dean – no one knows what it means – but it also gives its name to a Gloucestershire district that includes the towns of Newent and Coleford, north and west of the forest. To the northwest, the forest spills over into Herefordshire, while the River Wye skirts its western edge, offering glorious views to canoeists who paddle from the village of Symonds Yat.

The Dean Heritage Centre, outside Soudley within the forest's eastern fringe, is a good place to begin exploring.

Sights & Activities

★International Centre for Birds of Prey BIRD SANCTUARY
(☎01531-820286; www.icbp.org; Boulsdon House, Newent; adult/child £12.50/7; ⏲10.30am-5.30pm Feb-Nov; P) Watch raptors swoop and dive at this large, long-standing countryside complex, 2 miles southwest of Newent (follow signs). There are three flyings per day (11.30am, 2pm and 4.15pm in summer; 11.30am, 1.30pm and 3.30pm in winter), along with aviaries housing 70 species of owls, falcons, kestrels, eagles, buzzards, hawks, kites and other birds of prey from all over the world. For the hands-on feel, choose from various 'experience days', devoted to specific birds (from £70).

Symonds Yat VILLAGE
On the northwest edge of the Forest of Dean, squeezed between the River Wye and the towering limestone outcrop known as **Symonds Yat Rock** (Symonds Yat East; ⏲24hr; P), Symonds Yat is a tiny, endearing tangle of pubs, guesthouses and campsites, with great walks and a couple of canoeing centres. The river splits it into two halves, one in Gloucestershire and one in Herefordshire. They're connected by an ancient hand-hauled ferry (adult/child/bicycle £1.20/60p/60p; dawn to dusk).

Puzzlewood FOREST
(☎01594-833187; www.puzzlewood.net; Perrygrove Rd, Coleford; adult/child £7/6; ⏲10am-5pm Apr-Oct, to 3.30pm Wed, Sat & Sun mid-Feb–Mar, Nov & Dec; P 👪) A pre-Roman open-cast iron mine, overgrown with eerie moss-covered trees, Puzzlewood is a 6-hectare woodland web of paths, weird rock formations, tangled vines, rickety bridges, uneven steps and dark passageways, all seemingly designed to disorientate. Parts of hit TV shows *Doctor Who* and *Merlin*, as well as *Star Wars The Force Awakens*, were shot here. There's a mile of pathways to explore and kids will love the farm animals.

Clearwell Caves CAVE
(☎01594-832535; www.clearwellcaves.com; Clearwell; adult/child £8/6.50; ⏲10am-5pm Apr-Aug, to 4pm mid-Feb–Mar & Sep-Dec; P 🚸) Descend into the damp subterranean world of a 4500-year-old iron and ochre mine, comprising a warren of dimly lit passageways, caverns and pools, and home to several species of bats. 'Deep Level Caving' sessions (adult/child £25/18) take you even further in. From November, the caves are transformed into a hugely popular Christmas grotto.

Dean Forest Railway RAIL
(☎01594-845840; www.deanforestrailway.co.uk; Forest Rd, Lydney; day ticket adult/child £14/6; ⏲Wed, Sat & Sun mid-Mar–Oct; 🚸) Three days a week for most of the year, classic steam engines ply this 4.5-mile line between Lydney and Parkend. Occasionally, though, it operates diesel trains instead (check online). The standard ride is 30 minutes, but special events range from Sunday lunch in 1st-class carriages to 'drive your own steam engine' experiences. Thomas the Tank Engine makes the occasional appearance. Book ahead.

Wyedean Canoe & Adventure Centre ADVENTURE SPORTS
(☎01600-890238; www.wyedean.co.uk; Symonds Yat East; half-day hire from £30) Hires out canoes and kayaks, and organises white-water trips, archery, high ropes, abseiling, caving, rock climbing and stand-up paddle-boarding (SUP). Hours depend on conditions.

DON'T MISS

GLOUCESTER CATHEDRAL

Gloucester's spectacular **cathedral** (☎01452-528095; www.gloucestercathedral.org.uk; 12 College Green; ⏲10am-5pm) is among the first and finest examples of the English Perpendicular Gothic style. Benedictine monks built a Norman church here in the 12th century, on the site of a Saxon abbey. After Edward II died mysteriously at nearby Berkeley Castle (p219) in 1327, he was buried here, and his tomb became a place of pilgrimage. Further elements, including the present-day tower, were added to the church during the 15th century.

Inside, the finest features of Norman Romanesque and Gothic design are skilfully combined, with stout columns creating a sense of gracious solidity. The **Cloister**, which featured in the first, second and sixth Harry Potter films, is a real highlight. Completed in 1367, this airy space contains the earliest example of fan vaulting in England and is matched in beauty only by Henry VII's chapel at Westminster Abbey. When the sun shines through, the light-dappled Cotswold stone glows with a rosy light.

From the breathtaking 14th-century wooden choir stalls, you'll get a good view of the imposing 22m-high **Great East Window**. The size of a tennis court, it was the largest in Europe when it was installed in the 1350s, and around 85% of the glass you see today is still original.

Edward II's elaborate alabaster tomb, originally gilded and bejewelled, stands beneath the window in the northern ambulatory. Behind the altar, the glorious 15th-century **Lady Chapel** was largely destroyed during the Reformation, but following restoration work, completed in 2018, it's looking wonderful once more. In addition to its soaring vaulted roof and astonishingly delicate stone arches, its Arts and Crafts stained-glass windows rank among the cathedral's greatest treasures, featuring Adam and Eve, scenes from the life of Mary, and various English saints.

Alongside the crypt, **St Andrew's Chapel** is emblazoned from floor to ceiling with colourful 19th-century frescoes that hint at how vibrant and dazzling the medieval Abbey must have been.

Tours (from £3) give access to otherwise inaccessible areas including the 15th-century library and its illuminated manuscripts (weekly, 30 minutes); the 69m tower, with its amazing views (three weekly, one hour); and the Norman crypt (daily, 30 minutes). Unexpected treasures in the five simple chapels in the crypt, the oldest part of the cathedral, range from a pillar carving of a mysterious moustachioed figure to a hefty granite font built by George Gilbert Scott in 1878.

Sleeping

Garth Cottage B&B ££
(☎01600-890364; www.symondsyatbandb.co.uk; Symonds Yat East; per person £42.50; ⊙mid-Mar–Oct; P 📶) An exceedingly friendly and efficiently run family-owned B&B, right by the River Wye and alongside the ferry crossing. Comfy, chintzy, spotlessly maintained rooms have floral fabrics, tea and coffee kits, and gorgeous river views. Home-cooked breakfasts are excellent. Rates drop for longer stays.

Saracens Head Inn INN ££
(☎01600-890435; www.saracensheadinn.co.uk; Symonds Yat East; r incl breakfast from £129; P 📶) Honey-toned woods, fresh cream decor and understated modern style make this revamped 16th-century riverside inn, overlooking Symond Yat's ferry crossing, a wonderful choice. Eight of its 10 bright, comfortable rooms have river views; the spacious lounge-equipped Upper Boathouse room is especially popular. The downstairs pub-restaurant is excellent.

★ **Tudor Farmhouse** BOUTIQUE HOTEL £££
(☎01594-833046; www.tudorfarmhousehotel.co.uk; High St, Clearwell; r incl breakfast from £189; P 📶) Sleep in a chic, contemporary world of whites, creams and spiralling Tudor-era staircases, inside a beautifully updated farmhouse. Stylish rooms, most with exposed beams, check-print blankets and Nespresso machines, are scattered through the main house. The spacious 'Roost' suite, with its claw-foot bath, is particularly romantic. More rooms sit in adjacent buildings. There's also an exceptional Modern British restaurant.

> **WORTH A TRIP**
>
> **THE ROALD DAHL STORY**
>
> Housed in an old coaching inn, in the village where children's and short story writer Roald Dahl lived until his death in 1990, this delightful small **museum** (www.roalddahl.com/museum; 81 High St, Great Missenden; adult/child £7.40/4.90; ⊙10am-4pm Thu-Sun, plus school holidays; 👪) is perfectly pitched to children and adults. A guided tour introduces you to Roald Dahl's favourite characters, the writer's original backyard shed where he did much of his writing, and other behind-the-scenes insights into the man via interactive displays. It's a 45-minute train ride from London.

Information

Dean Heritage Centre (☎01594-822170; www.deanheritagecentre.com; Camp Mill, Soudley; adult/child £8/6; ⊙10am-5pm Apr-Oct, to 4pm Nov-Mar; P 👪) The Forest's heritage museum doubles as its main information office.

Getting There & Away

BUS

Stagecoach is the main bus operator in the region, while National Express coaches run to Newent from cities further afield. See www.traveline.info for the latest fares and timetables.

TRAIN

Trains from Gloucester serve Lydney (£8.20, 20 minutes), on the southern side of the forest.

BUCKINGHAMSHIRE, BEDFORDSHIRE & HERTFORDSHIRE

Now poised at the edge of London's commuter belt, these three green-clad counties once served as rural boltholes for the city's rich and titled, especially when the stench and grime of the industrial age was at its peak. The sweeping valleys and forested hills remain scattered with majestic stately homes and splendid gardens, many of which are open to the public.

The 324-sq-mile Chilterns Area of Outstanding Natural Beauty (AONB; www.visitchilterns.co.uk) extends southwest from Hitchin (Hertfordshire), through Bedfordshire and Buckinghamshire, and into Oxfordshire.

St Albans

☎01727 / POP 151,000

As Verulamium, encircled by a 2-mile wall and 26 miles from Londinium (London), St Albans was the third-biggest city in Roman Britain. Its current name derives from Alban, a Christian Roman soldier who was beheaded here around AD 250, becoming

WORTH A TRIP

THE HOME OF HARRY POTTER

Whether you're a fair-weather fan or a full-on Potterhead, the magical **Warner Bros Studio Tour: The Making of Harry Potter** (☎0345 084 0900; www.wbstudiotour.co.uk; Studio Tour Dr, WD25; adult/child £47/38; ⊙8.30am-10pm, hours vary Oct-May; P 👪) is well worth the admittedly hefty admission price. All visitors have to book tickets online, in advance, for a specific time slot, and arrive 20 minutes beforehand; allow three hours or more to do the complex full justice. Visits begin with a short film, before you're ushered through giant doors, though we won't say to where – it's just the first of many 'wow' moments.

You can then explore the rest of the complex at your own pace. One large hangar contains the most familiar interior sets – Dumbledore's office, the Gryffindor common room, Hagrid's hut – while another holds Platform 9¾, complete with the Hogwarts Express. An outdoor section features the exterior of Privet Drive, the purple triple-decker Knight Bus, Sirius Black's motorbike and a shop selling snacks and (sickly sweet) butterbeer. Video screens along the way burst into life to discuss elements of the production.

Other highlights include the animatronic workshop (say 'Hi' to the Hippogriff) and a stroll down Diagon Alley. All your favourite Harry Potter creatures are on display, from an enormous Aragog to Dobby the House-Elf, as well as props such as Harry's Invisibility Cloak. The most magical treat is saved for last – a shimmering, gasp-inducing 1:24 scale model of Hogwarts, used for exterior shots.

Then comes the biggest challenge for true fans and parents: a quite extraordinary gift shop stocked with all your wizardry accessories, including uniforms for each of the Hogwarts houses and replicas of the individually designed wands used by pretty much any character you can think of.

The Studio Tour is 20 miles northwest of London, not far off the M1 and M25 motorways. By rail, catch a train from London Euston to Watford Junction (approximately £10, 20 minutes), then a shuttle bus or taxi for the last 15-minute hop to the studios. There's also a Golden Tours tickets-and-transfer bus package direct from London and Birmingham.

the first English martyr. Now a bustling and prosperous market town, just beyond London's northwestern fringes, it's home to a huge and historic cathedral, amid a host of crooked Tudor buildings and elegant Georgian town houses.

Sights

★**St Albans Cathedral** CATHEDRAL
(☎01727-890210; www.stalbanscathedral.org; off High St & Holywell Hill; ⊙8.30am-5.45pm, free tours 11.30am & 2.30pm Mon-Fri, 11.30am & 2pm Sat, 2.30pm Sun) FREE Vast out of all proportion to the modern town, St Albans' majestic cathedral was founded as a Benedictine monastery by King Offa of Mercia in AD 793, around a shrine to St Alban, martyred five centuries earlier. It's now a glorious mashup of Norman Romanesque and Gothic architecture, with rounded arches built using bricks salvaged from Roman Verulamium, and the country's longest medieval nave, adorned with 13th-century murals. A stone reredos screens off the restored tomb of St Alban.

Verulamium Museum MUSEUM
(☎01727-751810; www.stalbansmuseums.org.uk; St Michael's St; adult/child £5/2.50, combined ticket with Roman Theatre £6.50/3.50; ⊙10am-5.30pm Mon-Sat, 2-5.30pm Sun) Based in what looks outside like a suburban house, this modern and highly engaging museum celebrates everyday life in Roman Verulamium. Assorted galleries cover themes like death, crafts and trade, with exhibits including farming utensils, armour, coins and pottery. Best of all are the five superb mosaic floors discovered locally, including a beautiful shell-shaped mosaic from AD 130.

Sleeping & Eating

St Michael's Manor Hotel HOTEL £££
(☎01727-864444; www.stmichaelsmanor.com; Fishpool St; d incl breakfast £155-200; P 📶) In a lovely location, with its own lake, this 500-year-old manor offers 30 opulent rooms

hidden down hushed carpeted corridors. Those in the manor itself are unshowy but comfortable, with historic charm, while the eight more contemporary 'luxury garden' rooms, named for plants and trees, are sumptuously sleek, with rich colours and patterned wallpaper; two have four-poster beds.

Lussmanns Fish & Grill MODERN BRITISH ££
(☎01727-851941; www.lussmanns.com; Waxhouse Gate, off High St; mains £14-28; ⊙noon-9pm Sun-Tue, to 9.30pm Wed & Thu, to 10.30pm Fri & Sat;) This bright, modern restaurant, steps from the cathedral, serves a changing, season-focused, ethically sourced menu of creative British dishes with Mediterranean touches, such as pomegranate-infused salad or chicken with pancetta. The set lunches (two/three courses £15.50/18.50) offer great value.

Information

Tourist Office (☎01727-864511; www.enjoystalbans.com; St Peter's St; ⊙10am-4pm Mon-Sat) In the St Albans Museum and Gallery.

Getting There & Away

Regular trains connect St Albans City, a mile east of the centre, with London King's Cross/St Pancras (£12.20, 20 minutes) and London Blackfriars (£12.20, 30 minutes).

> **WORTH A TRIP**
>
> **HATFIELD HOUSE**
>
> For over 400 years, **Hatfield House** (☎01707-287010; www.hatfield-house.co.uk; Hatfield; adult/child £9/4, house & gardens £19/9; ⊙garden 10am-5pm Thu-Sun Apr-Sep, house currently closed) has been home to the Cecils, one of England's most influential political families. This magnificent Jacobean mansion was built between 1607 and 1611 for Robert Cecil, first earl of Salisbury and secretary of state to both Elizabeth I and James I. Elizabeth spent much of her childhood in the 'Old Palace' here, and the house, which is awash with tapestries, furnishings and armour, proudly displays the Rainbow Portrait, depicting her holding a rainbow. Hatfield train station has trains to London King's Cross/St Pancras (20 minutes). Tickets must be pre-purchased.

Stowe

Located 3 miles northwest of the market town of Buckingham, and 14 miles west of Milton Keynes, Stowe has had a manor since before the Norman conquest. While the house itself is now a private school, the extraordinary Georgian gardens that surround it remain intact, and are definitely worth visiting. The most spectacular approach is via the 1.5-mile-long tree-lined Stowe Ave.

★Stowe Gardens GARDENS
(NT; ☎01280-817156; www.nationaltrust.org.uk; New Inn Farm; adult/child £10/5; ⊙10am-5pm mid-Feb–Oct, to 4pm Nov–mid-Feb; P) The glorious Stowe Gardens were shaped in the 18th century by Britain's greatest landscape gardeners. Among them was master landscape architect Lancelot 'Capability' Brown, who kick-started his career here as head gardener from 1741 until 1751. The gardens are famous for the temples and follies commissioned by the super-wealthy Richard Temple (1st Viscount Cobham), whose family motto was *Templa Quam Dilecta* (How Delightful are Your Temples). Paths meander past lakes, bridges, fountains and cascades, and through Capability Brown's Grecian Valley.

Getting There & Away

You'll need a car to get to Stowe House and Gardens, which are well signposted 3 miles northwest of Buckingham.

Woburn

☎01525 / POP 930

The peaceful village of Woburn has been nestling blissfully in the Bedfordshire countryside since the 10th century. One of its best draws, Woburn Abbey, is closed for renovations until 2022, but the Woburn Safari Park is a popular destination for families.

Woburn Safari Park ZOO
(www.woburnsafari.co.uk; Woburn Park; adult/child £24/19; ⊙10am-6pm, check online for dates) Sprawling across 150 hectares, the country's largest drive-through animal reserve

WORTH A TRIP

BLETCHLEY PARK

During WWII, the very existence of **Bletchley Park** (☎01908-640404; www.bletchleypark.org.uk; Bletchley; adult/12-17yr £18.25/10.75; ⏲9.30am-5pm Mar-Oct, to 4pm Nov-Feb; Ⓟ) was England's best-kept secret. By breaking German and Japanese codes, as dramatised in the 2014 film *The Imitation Game*, Bletchley's team of almost 8500 scientists and technicians made a huge contribution to winning the war itself. Up to 20,000 enemy messages were intercepted each day, then decrypted, translated and interpreted. Inside Hut 11A, you can see the Bombe machine itself, crucial to cracking the famous Enigma code; volunteers explain its inner workings.

Entry includes an optional hour-long guided tour of the grounds – dress warm – and a multimedia guide. Both provide a real insight into the complex, frustrating and ultimately rewarding code-breaking process. The machines built here, by pioneers including Alan Turing, are now regarded as major steps in development of programmable computers. In fact, Facebook made a substantial donation to the site during the Covid-19 economic slowdown as homage.

Regular trains connect Bletchley station, close to the park, with London Euston (£16, 40 minutes).

can only be visited in your own car (so long as it's not a convertible!). Animals such as rhinos, tigers, lions, elephants and giraffes – grouped into separate enclosures, for obvious reasons – will approach your car, or, if they're monkeys, climb on top of it. The 'foot safari' area holds sea lions, penguins, meerkats and wallabies.

★ **Paris House** MODERN BRITISH £££

(☎01525-290692; www.parishouse.co.uk; Woburn Park, London Rd; tasting menu £75; ⏲noon-1.30pm & 6.45-8.30pm Thu-Sun) On the Woburn Estate, Paris House is a handsome, black-and-white, half-timbered structure to which the 9th duke of Bedford took a shine while visiting the French capital. He shipped it back here, and it now holds Bedfordshire's top fine-dining restaurant, serving an exquisite tasting menu of beautifully presented contemporary cuisine. Phone bookings only.

ℹ Getting There & Away

Woburn is 8 miles southeast of Milton Keynes, 7 miles southeast of Bletchley Park, and 22 miles northwest of St Albans. Woburn itself does not have a train station so a car is a must.

THE THAMES VALLEY

The prosperous valley of the River Thames, west of London, has long served as a country getaway for the English elite, from royalty on down. Within easy reach of the capital, but utterly different in character, its pastoral landscape is peppered with handsome villages and historic houses.

It's Windsor Castle, favoured residence of the Queen, that really draws the crowds here, but Ascot, with its royal race-meet in June, and Henley-on-Thames, with its rowing regatta a month later, both boast their days in the sun. Meanwhile, the riverside village Bray has a genuine claim to be the country's gastronomic capital.

Windsor & Eton

☎01753 / POP 32,200

Facing each other across the Thames, with the massive bulk of Windsor Castle looming above, the twin riverside towns of Windsor and Eton have a rather surreal atmosphere. Windsor on the south bank sees the daily pomp and ritual of the changing of the guards, while schoolboys dressed in formal tailcoats wander the streets of tiny Eton to the north.

Thanks to its tourist trade, Windsor is filled with expensive boutiques, grand cafes and buzzing restaurants. Eton is far quieter, its single commercial street flanked by antique shops and art galleries. Both are easily accessible on a day trip from London.

Windsor & Eton

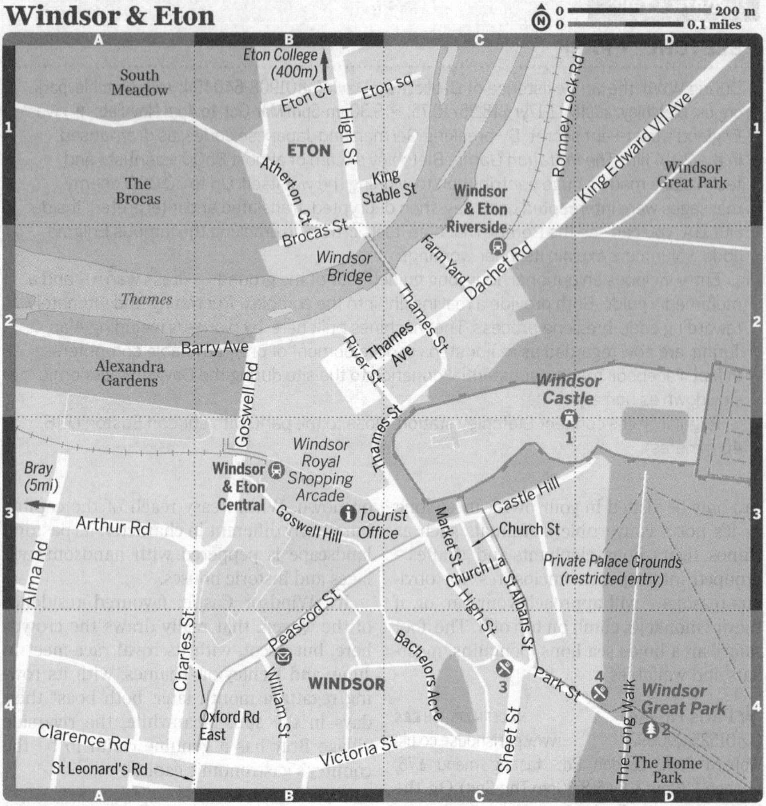

Windsor & Eton

Top Sights

1 Windsor Castle C3
2 Windsor Great Park D4

Eating

3 A la Russe C4
4 Two Brewers D4

Sights

★Windsor Castle — CASTLE

(☎03031-237304; www.royalcollection.org.uk; Castle Hill; adult/child £23.50/13.50; ⏰10am-5.15pm Mar-Oct, to 4.15pm Nov-Feb; 👪; 🚌702 from London Victoria, 🚆London Waterloo-Windsor & Eton Riverside, 🚆London Paddington-Windsor & Eton Central via Slough) The world's largest and oldest continuously occupied fortress, Windsor Castle is a majestic vision of battlements and towers. Used for state occasions, it's one of the Queen's principal residences – when she's at home, the Royal Standard flies from the Round Tower.

Frequent, free guided tours introduce visitors to the castle precincts, divided into the Lower, Middle and Upper Wards. Free audio tours guide everyone through its lavish State Apartments and beautiful chapels; certain areas may be off limits if in use.

★Windsor Great Park — PARK

(☎01753-860222; www.windsorgreatpark.co.uk; Windsor; ⏰dawn-dusk) FREE Windsor Great Park stretches south from Windsor Castle almost all the way to Ascot, 7 miles southwest. Accessed via Park St, it covers just under 8 sq miles and holds a lake, walking tracks, woods, gardens and a deer park where red deer roam free. Its 2.7-mile Long Walk leads from King George IV Gate to the 1831 Copper Horse statue (of George III) on Snow

Hill, the park's highest point. Paid parking by card only.

Runnymede HISTORIC SITE

(NT; ☎01784-432891; www.nationaltrust.org.uk; Windsor Rd, Old Windsor; ⏲site dawn-dusk, car park 8.30am-7pm Apr-Sep, to 5pm Feb, Mar, Oct & Nov, to 4pm Dec & Jan; 🅿) FREE Over 800 years ago, in June 1215, King John met his barons in this unassuming field, 3 miles southeast of Windsor. Together they hammered out an agreement on a basic charter of rights that guaranteed the liberties of the king's subjects, and restricted the monarch's absolute power. The document they signed, the Magna Carta, was the world's first constitution. The field remains much as it was, plus a few modern memorials and two 1929 lodges, designed by Edwin Lutyens.

Eton College NOTABLE BUILDING

(☎01753-370600; www.etoncollege.com; High St, Eton; adult/child £10/free; ⏲tours 2pm & 4pm Fri Apr-Aug) Eton College is England's most famous public – as in, private and fee-paying – boys' school, and arguably the most enduring symbol of the British class system. High-profile alumni include 20 British prime ministers, countless princes, kings and maharajas, Princes William and Harry, George Orwell, John Maynard Keynes, Bear Grylls and Eddie Redmayne. It can only be visited on guided tours, on summer Fridays, which take in the school yard, chapel and the Museum of Eton Life. To visit, book online.

Activities

Legoland Windsor AMUSEMENT PARK

(www.legoland.co.uk; Winkfield Rd, Windsor; £47-60; ⏲10am-6pm Jul & Aug, reduced hours rest of year) The child-oriented Legoland theme park, 3 miles southwest of Windsor, is more about white-knuckle thrills than building Lego-brick castles, though its many rides, from submarines to roller coasters, do zoom past vast Lego-built models. Adults and children pay the same prices, while 'Q-Bots', enabling you to avoid long queues for popular rides, cost up to £80 extra per person.

Shuttle buses connect Legoland with Windsor's Theatre Royal (return adult/child £5/2.50, 20 minutes; www.courtneybuses.com), from around 9.30am until 30 minutes after park closure.

Eating

Two Brewers PUB FOOD ££

(☎01753-855426; www.twobrewerswindsor.co.uk; 34 Park St, Windsor; mains £15-26; ⏲11.30am-10pm Mon-Sat, noon-10pm Sun) This atmospheric 18th-century inn, at the gateway to Windsor Great Park, serves tasty, well-prepped food ranging from soups, salads and fishcakes to steak, cod loin and cheeseboards. Sunny benches front the flower-covered exterior; inside are low-beamed ceilings, dim lighting and a roaring winter fire.

A la Russe FRENCH, MEDITERRANEAN ££

(☎01753-833009; www.alarusse.co.uk; 6 High St, Windsor; mains £13-23, 2-/3-course lunch menus £12.50/16.50; ⏲6-9.30pm Mon, noon-2.30pm & 6-9.30pm Tue-Sat) A fine array of set-price lunch and dinner menus and warm, friendly service make this Continental-style bistro excellent value. As well as French classics such as rabbit with mustard and chicken supreme, it also serves pasta dishes, chilli pork and assorted steaks. It's a quick walk down High St from the castle, towards the Great Park.

Information

Tourist Office (☎01753-743900; www.windsor.gov.uk; Old Booking Hall, Windsor Royal Shopping Arcade, Thames St, Windsor; ⏲10am-5pm Apr-Sep, to 4pm Oct-Mar) Tickets for attractions and events, plus guidebooks and walking maps.

ROYAL ASCOT

Don your finest duds and join the glitterati at **Royal Ascot** (☎08443-463000; www.ascot.co.uk; Ascot; Windsor Enclosure per day from £37, Queen Anne Enclosure per day from £75; ⏲mid-Jun), the biggest racing meet of the year, going strong since 1711. The royal family, A-list celebrities and other rich and famous folk gather for this five-day festival, 7 miles southwest of Windsor, to show off their Jimmy Choos and place the odd bet. It's essential to book tickets well in advance.

ROCK AND MORE AT READING FESTIVAL

Each August Bank Holiday weekend since 1989 (well except in 2020 when it was cancelled due to Covid-19), around 80,000 revellers descend on the industrial town of Reading for the **Reading Festival** (☎02070-093001; www.readingfestival.com; tickets day/weekend £80/250; ⏲late Aug), one of the UK's biggest and most accessible music festivals. The three-day extravaganza draws headliners across genres, although rock dominates. One-day tickets are available as well as multi-day camping.

Reading has regular trains to/from London Paddington (£20.20, 25 minutes to one hour).

Getting There & Away

BUS

Green Line buses (www.greenline.co.uk) connect Windsor and Eton with London Victoria (1½ hours) and Heathrow terminal 5 (40 minutes). Courtney Buses (www.courtneybuses.com) offers services between Windsor and Bray (30 minutes). See www.traveline.info for the latest fares and timetables.

TRAIN

The quickest rail route from London connects London Paddington with Windsor & Eton Central, opposite the castle, but you have to change at Slough (£10.50, 30 to 45 minutes). London Waterloo has slower but direct services to Windsor & Eton Riverside, on Dachet Rd (£10.50, 45 minutes to one hour).

Bray

☎01628 / POP 4650

This tiny village of flint, brick and half-timbered cottages, strung along the Thames between Windsor and Maidenhead, is also considered by many to be the gastronomic capital of Britain. Bray is home to two of the four UK restaurants to be awarded the highest possible rating of three stars by foodie bible, the Michelin guide. There's little more to do here than to dine fabulously, the river is tucked away behind the mansions.

Eating

★Fat Duck MODERN BRITISH £££

(☎01628-580333; www.thefatduck.co.uk; High St; degustation menu per person £250-325; ⏲noon-1.15pm & 7-8.15pm Tue-Sat) Arguably Britain's most famous restaurant, the Fat Duck is the flagship property of Heston Blumenthal. A pioneer of 'molecular' cuisine, he transformed the place from a run-down pub into a three-starred restaurant that was once voted the world's best. Reserve your 'ticket' in advance and enjoy a journey-themed, seasonally changing set menu. Drinks and service are charged in addition to the dining price.

★Waterside Inn FRENCH £££

(☎01628-620691; www.waterside-inn.co.uk; Ferry Rd; mains £55-68, 2-/3-course lunch Wed-Fri £52/63.50; ⏲noon-2pm & 7-10pm Wed-Sun, closed late Dec-end Jan) From the moment the uniformed valet greets you until the last tray of petit fours is served, this three-Michelin-starred riverfront restaurant is something special. For more than 40 years, chef Alain Roux has worked his magic, constructing exceptional dishes for a small army of staff to serve, in a room overlooking the Thames. It also has rooms (from £275).

Hind's Head GASTROPUB £££

(☎01628-626151; www.hindsheadbray.com; High St; mains £20-40, 5-course tasting menu £62; ⏲noon-2pm & 6-9pm Mon-Sat, noon-3.30pm Sun; 🅿) Oozing atmosphere, this sumptuous 15th-century pub offers diners the chance to experience Heston Blumenthal's highly creative cuisine in a relatively affordable, and more informal setting. The dishes are less adventurous than you might expect, but still have plenty of whimsical touches.

Getting There & Away

Bray is a short drive from Windsor but there are limited parking options in town. Courtney Buses (www.courtneybuses.com) offers a service between Windsor and Bray (30 minutes).

Henley-on-Thames

☎01491 / POP 11,494

The attractive commuter town of Henley, 15 miles northwest of Windsor, is synonymous with its annual rowing tournament, the **Henley Royal Regatta** (www.hrr.co.uk; tickets

£25-32, on-site parking £34; ⏲ early Jul). For the rest of the year, it remains a pretty riverside town that's a delight to stroll around, particularly along the Thames.

★River & Rowing Museum MUSEUM
(☎01491-415600; www.rrm.co.uk; Mill Meadows; adult/child £12.50/10; ⏲10am-4pm Thu-Mon; P 🚸) This excellent modern museum examines why Henley is so crazy for rowing. The airy 1st-floor galleries tell the story of rowing as an Olympic sport, with striking displays that include the early-19th-century Royal Oak, Britain's oldest racing boat. Downstairs, a sweet 3D exhibition pays homage to Kenneth Grahame's *The Wind in the Willows*. The romanticised river that book so lovingly depicts was inspired by the Thames around Henley.

ℹ Getting There & Away

Trains run to/from London Paddington (£16.70, one hour), but you have to change at Slough and/or Twyford.

AT A GLANCE

POPULATION
1.1 million

BIGGEST CITY
Bristol: 428,234

BEST BUILDING
Royal Crescent (p248)

BEST BRIDGE
Clifton Suspension Bridge (p239)

BEST HARBOUR
Porlock Weir (p264)

WHEN TO GO

May & Jun
Upfest celebrates street art in Bristol; music-festival fever takes hold at Glastonbury.

Sep
Warm weather, with seasonal attractions still open. Bath's accommodation prices begin to descend from August highs.

Oct
Exmoor's deer rut sees huge stags battle for supremacy.

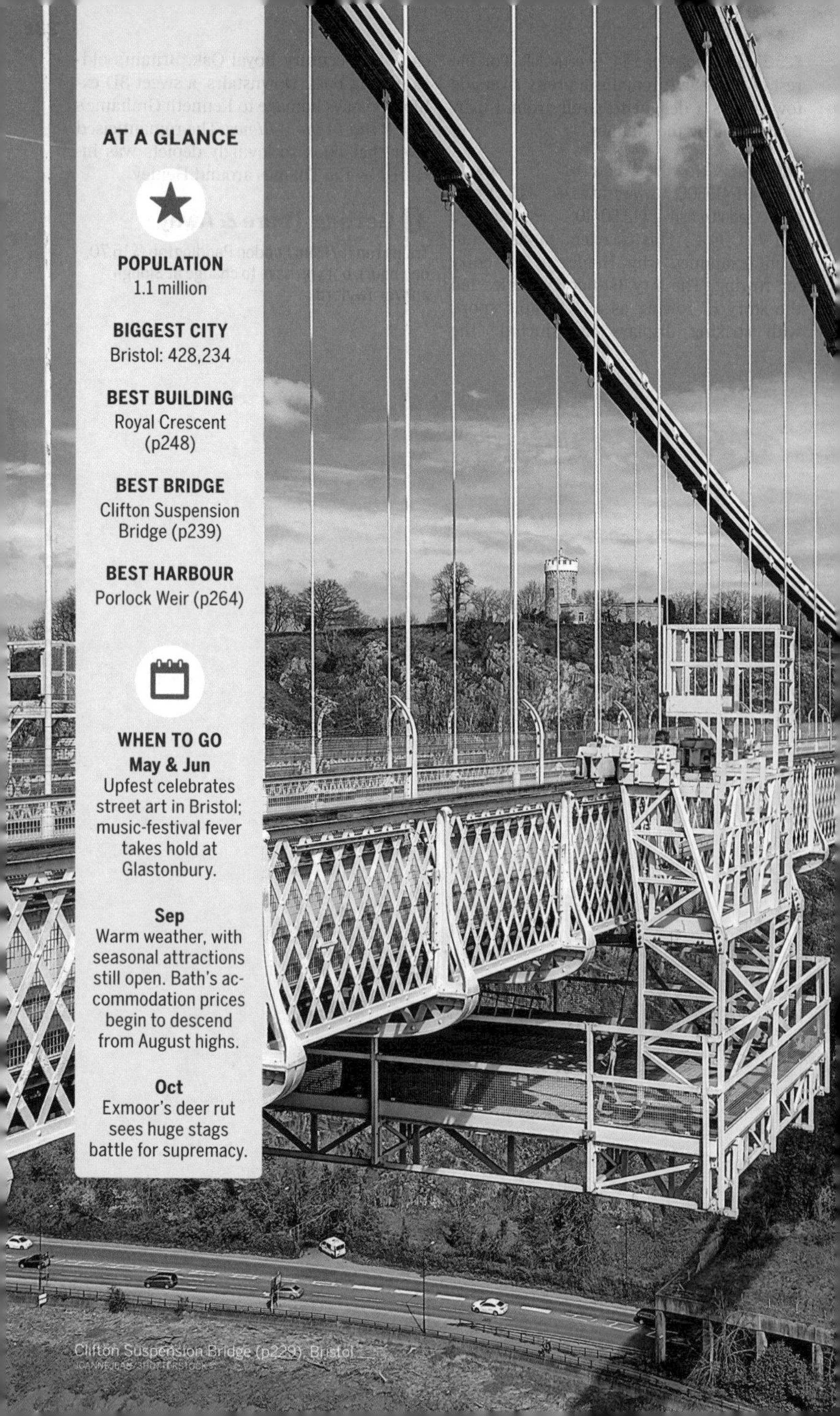

Clifton Suspension Bridge (p229), Bristol
JOANNE JEAN/SHUTTERSTOCK ©

Bristol, Bath & Somerset

Historic city, edgy urban hub, jagged coasts and forgotten moors – this region is as richly rewarding as it is diverse. Bath delivers dazzling Georgian architecture; some of the gems in England's crown. In dynamic Bristol creative types hang out in cool cafes surrounded by famous street art. Nearby sit hippy haven Glastonbury, and Wells, a delightful, diminutive cathedral city. In beguiling Exmoor wild ponies roam, russet moors surge towards sheer cliffs, and red deer hide in densely wooded coombes. Add empty beaches, geothermal pools, snazzy spas, stately homes, rural backroads and plenty of rustic pubs and you're faced with the best kind of travelling dilemma: what to do first?

INCLUDES

Activities

Cycling

Routes here range from disused railway lines to rural lanes. The 14-mile **Bristol and Bath Railway Path** (www.bristolbathrailwaypath.org.uk) is a flat, largely traffic-free trail that's dotted with public art.

Exmoor's rollercoaster roads see you powering up 500m at Dunkery, while the National Park's bridleways offer superb, challenging off-road mountain biking.

Sweeping from Bristol to the west of Cornwall, the **National Cycle Network (NCN Route 3)** is a 328-mile trail that takes in Wells, Glastonbury and the southern edge of Exmoor.

Sustrans (www.sustrans.org.uk) and local tourist offices can advise further.

Walking

Sometimes called the 630-mile adventure, the **South West Coast Path** (www.southwestcoastpath.org.uk) stretches from Minehead in Somerset via Land's End to Poole in Dorset. You can pick it up along the coast for short and spectacular day hikes or tackle longer stretches.

Exmoor National Park offers a tempting blend of open moorland and 34 miles of precipitous cliffs, while the 51-mile **Coleridge Way** (www.coleridgeway.co.uk) cuts from Nether Stowey in the Quantock Hills to Lynmouth, in the footsteps of the eponymous Romantic poet.

Other Activities

Local firms offer guided caving, coasteering, and climbing sessions. In Bristol you can take kayaking and stand-up paddleboarding lessons in the central **harbour** (☎0117-422 5858; www.supbristol.com; Baltic Wharf, Cumberland Rd; 1½hr £25, 2½hr £40).

Climbers enjoy higher-grade sport and trad routes at limestone Cheddar Gorge (p257). The Avon Gorge also offers memorable climbs. Check with the BMC (www.thebmc.co.uk) for updates on local restrictions.

Getting Around

BUS

Bus provision in Bristol and Bath is good; inevitably services become more patchy the further into the countryside you go. National Express (www.nationalexpress.com) can provide the quickest bus link between cities and larger towns.

PlusBus (www.plusbus.info) adds local bus travel to your train ticket (£2 to £4 per day). Participating cities include Bath and Bristol. Buy tickets at train stations.

First (www.firstgroup.com) runs buses in and around Bath, Bristol, Glastonbury and Wells. Smaller operators provide services around Exmoor National Park.

First offers subregional tickets, such as the Freedom Travelpass (one day/week £13.50/59). This gives unlimited bus and train travel in Bath, Bristol and northeast Somerset, although it doesn't cover Glastonbury, Wells or Exmoor. Day Rover and Ranger tickets are available for specific areas.

CAR & MOTORCYCLE

The main car-hire firms have offices at Bristol Airport, and in and around Bath and Bristol; rates reflect those elsewhere in the UK.

Bath and Bristol have efficient Park & Ride services, helping avoid traffic congestion and pricy parking. Having your own wheels gives you more freedom as you head into rural areas.

TRAIN

Bristol is a main train hub with links including those to Bath, London Paddington, Scotland and Birmingham, plus services to Exeter, Swindon, Weymouth and Portsmouth.

Key regional rail firms are GWR (www.gwr.com), CrossCountry (www.crosscountrytrains.co.uk) and South Western Railway (www.southwesternrailway.com). For timetables and fares see National Rail (www.nationalrail.co.uk).

The Freedom of the South West Rover offers either three days' train travel in seven days (adult/child £106/53) or eight days' travel in 15 days (£148/74). Journeys are unlimited in an area west of, and including, Bath, Bristol, Salisbury, Portsmouth and Weymouth.

BRISTOL

☎0117 / POP 428,234

Bristol is a city that's on the rise. Derelict docks are becoming leisure venues, heritage attractions ooze imagination and a world-class street-art scene adds colour and spice.

History

Bristol began as a Saxon village and developed into the medieval river port of Brigstow, an important trading centre for cloth and wine. In 1497 'local hero' John Cabot (actually a Genoese sailor called Giovanni Caboto) sailed from Bristol to discover Newfoundland. By the 18th century Bristol's docks were the second largest in the country.

Bristol, Bath & Somerset Highlights

1. **Bath** (p245) Exploring atmospheric Roman baths then swimming in a stylish modern-day spa.
2. **Bristol** (p234) Striding around the deck of Brunel's groundbreaking steamship, the SS *Great Britain*.
3. **Lynmouth** (p265) Rattling up steep-sided cliffs in a water-powered, Victorian railway.
4. **Exmoor National Park** (p261) Watching out for red deer amid deep valleys and open moors.
5. **Dunster** (p264) Discovering a charismatic russet castle set high on a wooded hill.
6. **Glastonbury** (p258) Touching base with your inner hippy in the UK's counter-culture hub.
7. **Wells** (p256) Marvelling at exquisite architecture in a pocket-sized cathedral city.

Bristol

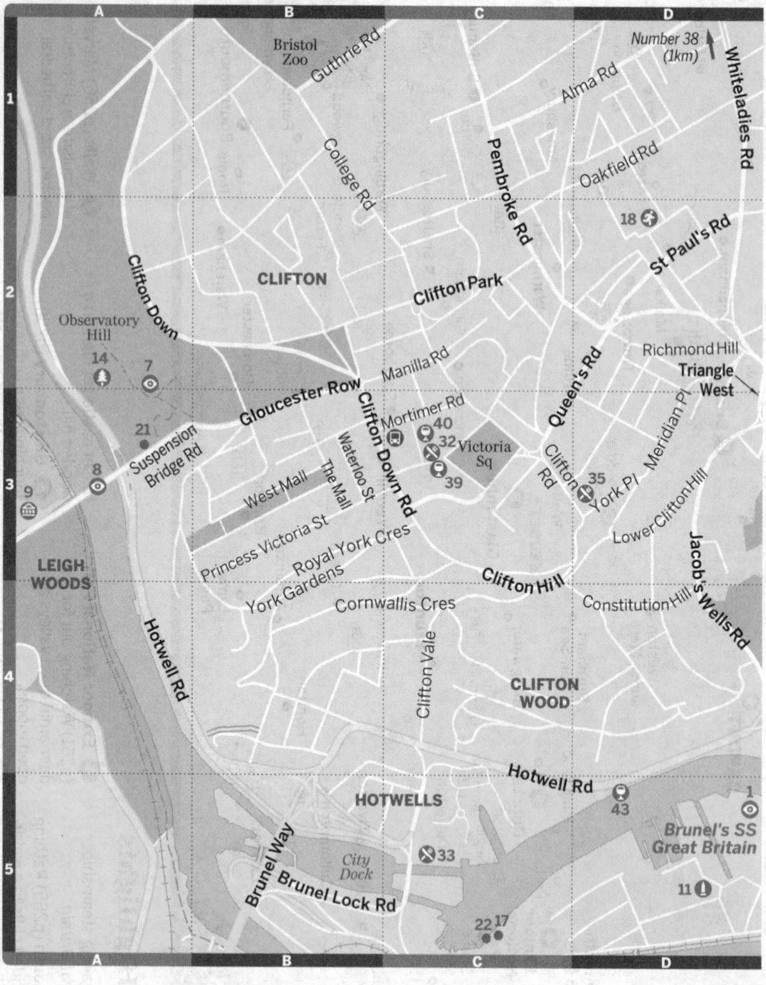

They enabled the city to play a major part in the so-called Triangular Slave Trade, in which Africans were enslaved, shipped to New World colonies and bartered for sugar, tobacco, cotton and rum. Bristol traders transported more than 500,000 enslaved people and much of the city's 18th-century splendour – including Clifton's grand terraces – were partly financed on the profits. The M Shed Museum (p238) takes an honest look at the story, referencing also the local campaigners who fought for abolition.

After being usurped by rival ports, Bristol repositioned itself as an industrial and shipbuilding centre, and in 1840 became the western terminus for the newly built Great Western Railway line from London. Its audacious chief engineer was Isambard Kingdom Brunel, whose Bristol legacy includes the Clifton Suspension Bridge (p239) and SS Great Britain.

Bristol's industrial importance made it a target for German bombing during WWII, and much of the city centre and harbourside was reduced to rubble. Fast-forward 40 years and parts of Bristol, including Stokes

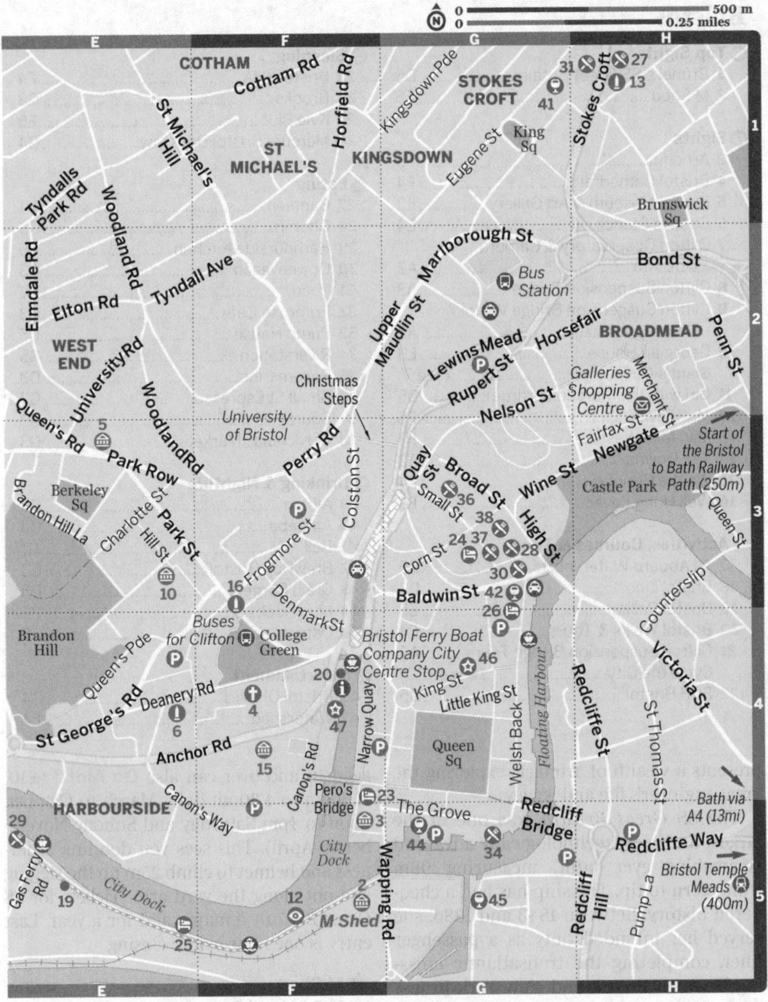

Croft, became known for a counterculture tradition, occasional neighbourhood riots and a burgeoning street-art scene. One of those leaving his creative mark on city walls was Banksy – an anonymous artist whose works sell for millions of pounds. The city is also home to Oscar-winning Aardman Animations, creators of *Wallace and Gromit*.

In July 2020, Bristol's historic links with slavery made the national headlines when, during the Black Lives Matter protests, a crowd toppled a statue of 17th-century slave-trader Edward Colston and threw it in the harbour.

Sights

★Brunel's SS Great Britain HISTORIC SHIP

(☎0117-926 0680; www.ssgreatbritain.org; Great Western Dock, Gas Ferry Rd; adult/child/family £18/10/48; ⏲10am-6pm Apr-Oct, to 4.30pm Nov-Mar) This mighty, innovative steamship was designed by engineering genius Isambard Kingdom Brunel in 1843. You get to wander the galley, surgeon's quarters and dining saloon and see a massive replica steam engine at work. Highlights are going below the 'glass sea' on which the ship sits to view the screw propeller and climbing up the rigging in Go Aloft!. The **Being Brunel** exhibit

Bristol

Top Sights

1 Brunel's SS Great Britain D5
2 M Shed F5

Sights

3 Arnolfini F5
4 Bristol Cathedral F4
5 Bristol Museum & Art Gallery E3
6 Castles Stencil E4
7 Clifton Observatory & Camera Obscura A2
8 Clifton Suspension Bridge A3
9 Clifton Suspension Bridge Visitor Centre A3
10 Georgian House E3
Giant's Cave .... (see 7)
11 Girl with the Pierced Eardrum D5
12 Matthew F5
13 Mild Mild West H1
14 The Downs A2
15 We the Curious F4
16 Well Hung Lover F3

Activities, Courses & Tours

17 All Aboard Watersports C5
18 Bristol Lido D2
19 Bristol Packet E5
20 Bristol Walks & Tours F4
21 Clifton Suspension Bridge Tours A3
Cycle the City .... (see 20)
22 SUP Bristol C5

Sleeping

23 Bristol YHA F4
24 Brooks G3
25 Kyle Blue E5
26 Mercure Bristol Brigstow G4

Eating

27 Canteen H1
28 Chomp G3
29 Harbourside Kitchen E5
30 Ooweevegan G3
31 Poco H1
32 Primrose Cafe C3
33 Pump House C5
34 Riverstation G5
35 Rosemarino D3
36 Small St Espresso G3
37 Source G3
38 St Nicholas Market G3

Drinking & Nightlife

39 Albion C3
40 Amoeba C3
41 Bell G1
42 BrewDog Bristol G3
43 Grain Barge D5
44 Mud Dock G5
45 Ostrich G5

Entertainment

46 Bristol Old Vic G4
47 Watershed F4

presents a wealth of artefacts exploring the great engineer's life and legacy.

The SS *Great Britain* was one of the largest and most technologically advanced steamships ever built, measuring 98m from stern to tip. The ship has had a chequered history. Between 1843 and 1886, she served her intended duty as a passenger liner, completing the transatlantic crossing between Bristol and New York in just 14 days. Unfortunately, enormous running costs and mounting debts led her towards an ignominious fate: she was eventually sold off and subsequently served as a troop vessel, quarantine ship, emigration transport and coal hulk, before finally being scuttled near Port Stanley in the Falklands in the 1930s.

Happily, that wasn't the end. The ship was towed back to Bristol in 1970, and has since undergone an impressive 30-year restoration. It's resulted in a multisensory experience: prepare to stroll the deck, peep into luxury cabins, listen to passengers' stories and catch a whiff of life on board. Those aged 10 and over can also **Go Aloft!** (£10; 11.30am to 4.30pm daily March to October, noon to 4pm Saturday and Sunday November to April). This sees you donning a harness and helmet to climb 25m up the rigging and out along the yard arm. Tickets for SS *Great Britain* remain valid for a year. Last entry is one hour before closing.

★M Shed MUSEUM

(☎0117-352 6600; www.bristolmuseums.org.uk; Princes Wharf; ⊙10am-5pm Tue-Sun; 📶) FREE Set amid the iconic cranes of Bristol's dockside, this impressive museum is a treasure trove of memorabilia. It's divided into four main sections: People, Place, Life and the vast Working Exhibits outside. They provide an absorbing overview of Bristol's history – from slaves' possessions and *Wallace and Gromit* figurines to a Banksy artwork. There are regular guided walks and trips on the museum's boats, trains and cranes (free to £6); see the website for details.

It's all highly interactive and child-friendly, especially the rides on the steam and electric cranes (tickets £3), steam trains (single/return £2.50/3.50) and tug and fire boats (adult/child £6/4). Another highlight is Banksy's unsettling *Grim Reaper* stencil, which used to sit on the waterline of the nightclub boat *Thekla*. It was removed amid much controversy and can now be found on the 1st floor.

The museum's imaginatively themed guided tours help bring the city's past to life.

Clifton Suspension Bridge BRIDGE

(☎0117-974 4664; www.cliftonbridge.org.uk; Suspension Bridge Rd) The 76m-high Clifton Suspension Bridge that spans the Avon Gorge was designed by master engineer Isambard Kingdom Brunel, with construction beginning in 1836. It's free to walk or cycle across; car drivers pay a £1 toll. The **visitor centre** (⏲10am-5pm; 📶) FREE at the bridge's western end is worth exploring.

The free **bridge tours** (⏲3pm Sat & Sun Easter-Oct) are excellent, as are the two-hour **Hard Hat Tours**, which go inside one of the massive supporting towers (£14; book ahead).

We the Curious MUSEUM

(☎0117-915 1000; www.wethecurious.org; Anchor Rd; adult/child £15/10; ⏲10am-5pm Mon-Fri, to 6pm Sat & Sun) Bristol's interactive science museum is a playful, hands-on space where 300 'exhibits' fly the flag for curiosity, scientific collaboration and creativity. Meet Aardman characters, become an animator, discover cosmic rays, walk through a tornado and explore subjects ranging from anatomy to flight. There are also performances from the Live Science Team, immersive **planetarium shows** (£2.50 to £3.50) and weekly stargazing sessions (£10) for those aged over 15.

Matthew HISTORIC SHIP

(☎0117-927 6868; www.matthew.co.uk; Princes Wharf; ⏲10am-4pm Tue-Sun Mar-Oct, Sat & Sun Nov-Feb) FREE The most striking thing about this replica of the vessel in which John Cabot made his landmark voyage from Bristol to Newfoundland in 1497 is its size. At 24m it looks tiny but it would have carried an 18-strong crew. Step aboard to climb below into their quarters, walk the deck and gaze up at the rigging.

Bristol Museum & Art Gallery MUSEUM

(☎0117-922 3571; www.bristolmuseums.org.uk; Queen's Rd; ⏲10am-5pm Tue-Sun; 📶) FREE This classic Edwardian museum delivers some surprises. Look out for the *Paint-Pot Angel* by street artist Banksy in the entrance hall. A funerary statue with an upturned pot of pink paint on her head, she's designed to challenge our expectations of museum exhibits and the value of art. Just above sits the Bristol Boxkite, a prototype propeller-powered biplane, which dangles from the ceiling.

Georgian House HISTORIC BUILDING

(☎0117-921 1362; www.bristolmuseums.org.uk; 7 Great George St; ⏲11am-4pm Sat-Tue Apr-Dec) FREE You'll find insights into two sides of the Georgian trade in enslaved Africans in this ornate 18th century house. It was the home of both the wealthy slave plantation owner and sugar merchant John Pinney, and his enslaved valet Pedro Jones. A small display outlines their stories, alongside a huge kitchen, book-lined library and basement plunge-pool.

The Downs PARK

The grassy parks of Clifton Down and Durdham Down (often called just the Downs) fan out from the Clifton Suspension Bridge, making a fine picnic spot. Nearby, the **Clifton Observatory** (☎0117-974 1242; www.cliftonobservatory.com; Litfield Rd, Clifton Down; adult/child £5/2.50; ⏲10am-5pm Mar-Sep, to 4pm Oct-Feb) houses a **camera obscura** and a tunnel leading down to the **Giant's Cave**, a natural cavern that emerges halfway down the cliff with dizzying views across the Avon Gorge.

Activities

★Bristol Street Art Tours WALKING

(Where the Wall; ☎07748 632663; www.wherethewall.com; adult/child £11/6; ⏲2-6 per week) Some serious spray-paint skills (including Banksy's) are on show in two-hour tours starting in the city centre and ending in counter-culture Stokes Croft. Or join an hour-long **Stencil Art Spray Session** (£15, Saturday, 2pm) to 'get your hands on the cans'.

★Bristol Lido BATHHOUSE

(☎0117-933 9530; www.lidobristol.com; Oakfield Pl; nonmembers £25; ⏲nonmembers 1-4pm Mon-Fri)

BANKSY – STREET ARTIST

If there's one Bristolian nearly everyone has heard of, it's Banksy (www.banksy.co.uk) – the guerrilla street artist whose distinctive stencilled style and provocative artworks have earned him worldwide notoriety.

It's thought Banksy was born in 1974 in the Bristol area and honed his skills in a local graffiti outfit. His works take a wry view of 21st-century culture – especially capitalism, consumerism and the cult of celebrity. Among his best-known pieces are the production of spoof banknotes (featuring Princess Diana's head instead of the Queen's), a series of murals on Israel's West Bank barrier (depicting people digging holes under and climbing ladders over the wall) and a painting of a caveman pushing a shopping trolley at the British Museum (which the museum promptly claimed for its permanent collection). His documentary *Exit Through the Gift Shop*, about an LA street artist, was nominated for an Oscar in 2011.

Once despised by the authorities, Banksy's artworks have become a tourist magnet. Highlights include those in our Art & History Waking Tour (p243). It's also worth hunting out these pieces:

Paint-Pot Angel (Bristol Museum & Art Gallery, p239) Pink paint meets funerary monument.

Mild Mild West (Canteen Bar, Stokes Croft) A Molotov cocktail–wielding teddy bear facing three riot police.

Valentine's Day mural (Barton Hill) A girl catapulting red flowers onto the side of a house.

The tourist office (p244) can advise on locations, while the Bristol Street Art Tours (p239) take in the main Banksy sites.

Bristol's public hot tub dates back to 1849 – a naturally heated, 24m pool with a water temperature of a balmy 24°C. Admission includes three hours' use of the pool, sauna, steam room and outdoor hot tub.

If you want to visit outside the times listed, consider one of their Spa packages (from £95).

Cycle the City CYCLING
(☎07873 387167; www.cyclethecity.org; 1 Harbourside) These guided bike tours are an ideal way to discover off-the-beaten track Bristol. Opt for a two-hour highlights trip (£18), a Food Tour (£40) or a tour focused around cheese and wine. You can pre-book bike hire too (per day £18).

Bristol Walks & Tours WALKING
(☎0333-321 0101; www.bristolwalks.co.uk; adult/child £8/3; Mar-Nov) The Highlights tour takes in the old town, city centre and Harbourside and runs on Saturday at 11am. A walk looking at Bristol's links with the Slave Trade and its abolition starts at noon on Sunday. Both leave from the tourist office (p244), there's no need to book.

Festivals & Events

★Upfest ART
(www.upfest.co.uk; May/Jun) FREE Where better for a street-art festival than the city that brought us Banksy? Upfest sees 250 artists descending on the city to paint live, in front of audiences, at scores of venues. There are music gigs and affordable art sales too.

International Balloon Fiesta AIR SHOW
(www.bristolballoonfiesta.co.uk; Aug) More than 100 brightly coloured hot-air balloons, often of mind-boggling shapes, fill the skies at Ashton Court in what is the largest event of its type in Europe. The highlights are the fireworks and Nightglow flights.

Sleeping

★Kyle Blue HOSTEL £
(☎0117-929 0609; www.kylebluebristol.co.uk; Wapping Wharf; dm/s/d £29/60/70;) What a boon for budget travellers: a boutique hostel set on a boat that's moored in easy reach of the central sights. Cabins are compact but supremely comfy, the showers and kitchen gleam and the smart lounge is the ideal spot to watch the river traffic float by.

Bristol YHA HOSTEL £

(☎0345 371 9726; www.yha.org.uk; 14 Narrow Quay; dm £18-35, s/d/tr 59/69/79; @ 📶) Few hostels can boast a position as good as this one, right beside the river in the centre of town. Facilities in the converted red-brick warehouse include kitchens, a cycle store, a games room and the excellent Grainshed cafe-bar.

★**Brooks** B&B ££

(☎0117-930 0066; www.brooksguesthousebristol.com; Exchange Ave; d £93-120, tr £99-133, trailers £111-129; 📶) Welcome to urban glamping – four vintage Airstream trailers sit in a bijou AstroTurf roof garden slap bang in the heart of Bristol. They're predictably tiny (ranging from 16ft to 20ft) but still have sleek seating areas, pocket-sized bathrooms and rooftop views. Guesthouse bedrooms are compact but smart, featuring subtle tones and checked throws.

Mercure Bristol Brigstow HOTEL ££

(☎0117-929 1030; www.mercure.com; 5 Welsh Back; r £85-133; ❄ 📶) A harbourside location and attractive modern design make the Mercure a sound, central option. Bedrooms are made less corporate by hardwood floors, big circular rugs and gently curving walls.

★**Number 38** B&B £££

(☎0117-946 6905; www.number38clifton.com; 38 Upper Belgrave Rd; s £115, d £125-180, ste £220; P 📶) Set on the edge of the Downs, this upmarket B&B is *the* choice for style-conscious travellers. Rooms are huge and contemporary in soft grey and blue tones. Waffle bathrobes and designer bath goodies ramp up the luxury, while sweeping city views unfold from most bedrooms and the roof terrace.

Eating

★**Primrose Cafe** CAFE £

(☎0117-946 6577; www.primrosecafe.co.uk; 1 Boyce's Ave; dishes £7-12; ⊙9am-5pm Mon-Sat Apr-Oct, 9am-4pm Mon-Sat Nov-Mar, 9.30am-4pm Sun year-round; 🖉) 🍃 The Primrose richly deserves its status as a Clifton institution, thanks to decades of serving towering homemade cakes and imaginative lunches, such as halloumi and courgette burgers, and slow-cooked pheasant. Pavement tables and a secluded roof garden add to the appeal, as do belt-busting brunches that are served impressively late (to 3.30pm); the eggs Benedict and Belgian waffles are legendary.

★**Canteen** CAFE £

(☎0117-923 2017; www.canteenbristol.co.uk; 80 Stokes Croft; mains £5-10; ⊙noon-3pm & 5-9pm Mon-Sat, noon-4pm Sun; 📶) 🍃 Occupying the ground floor of an old office block, this community-run cafe-bar sums up Bristol's alternative character: it's all about slow food, local suppliers and fair prices, whether you pop in for breakfast, veggie chilli, sit-down supper or nightly live music. The bar stays open until 11pm (1am Friday and Saturday).

The Banksy mural **Mild Mild West** is on the wall outside.

Ooweevegan VEGAN £

(☎0117-280 0152; www.ooweevegan.com; 65 Baldwin St; mains £8; ⊙11.30am-10.30pm Sun-Thu, to 11pm Fri & Sat; 🖉) Looking every inch a fast-food outlet, Oowee turns that meat-heavy genre on its head. Here plant-based versions include crispy, fried not-chicken burgers, beyond meat quarter pounders and dirty fries.

Source CAFE £

(☎0117-927 2998; www.source-food.co.uk; 1 Exchange Ave; mains £7-15; ⊙8am-4pm Mon & Sat,

EXPLORING BRISTOL'S WATERWAYS

Bristol has grown up around its harbour and docks. Exploring by water takes you to the heart of the city.

Bristol Ferry Boat Company (p245) A 16-stop waterbus linking Bristol Temple Meads train station, the city centre and the SS *Great Britain*.

SUP Bristol (p234) Discover the city's waterways while mastering stand-up paddleboard techniques.

All Aboard Watersports (☎0117-929 0801; www.allaboardwatersports.co.uk; Underfall Yard, Cumberland Rd; per 2½hr £15) Kayak activity sessions in the city's iconic harbour.

Matthew (p239) Set sail aboard a replica of a 15th-century transatlantic explorer's ship.

Bristol Packet (☎0117-926 8157; www.bristolpacket.co.uk; Wapping Wharf, Gas Ferry Rd; cruises from adult/child £7/5) Classic boat trips ranging from 45-minute harbour tours to cruises up the Avon Gorge.

to 4.30pm Tue-Fri) Local, seasonal produce is piled high at the deli counters of this market cafe, from sourdough bread and artisan cheese to charcuterie and smoked salmon and eels. Breakfast (8am to 11.45am) includes pancakes and kippers with capers; lunch might feature shellfish bisque or lamb sausage and chickpea stew.

Small St Espresso CAFE £
(www.smallstreetespresso.co.uk; 23 Small St; snacks £4-6; ⏲7.30am-4.30pm Mon-Fri, 9.30am-4.30pm Sat) A gleaming pale-blue espresso machine sits at the heart of this artisan coffee house where caffeine connoisseurs sit at tiny clumps of tables munching on banana bread and sourdough toast. Opt for a house blend or the guest single origin; for cold-brewed or Aeropressed – this is coffee as craft.

St Nicholas Market MARKET £
(St Nicks Market; ☎0117-922 4014; www.bristol.gov.uk/web/st-nicholas-markets; Corn St; ⏲9.30am-6pm Mon-Sat, 10am-5pm Sun) The city's lively covered market includes a bevy of food stalls selling everything from local gourmet Pieminister pies and mezze platters to cuts from the Low & Slow Smokehouse. Lines can be long at lunchtime, but it's worth the wait. Look out, too, for the Wednesday **Farmers Market** (9.30am to 2.30pm).

★**Poco** TAPAS ££
(☎0117-923 2233; www.pocotapasbar.com; 45 Jamaica St; tapas £5-9; ⏲9am-midnight Mon-Fri, 10am-midnight Sat, 10am-11pm Sun; 🖉) Having started life as a food truck touring the UK's festivals, Poco has now set up shop in a chilled-out Stokes Croft tapas bar. Vast jars of candied lemons and chilli oil line the shelves, while the open-plan kitchen creates generously sized dishes such as spicy charred broccoli, crunchy potatoes and soft wood pigeon with lentils and pear.

★**Rosemarino** ITALIAN ££
(☎0117-973 6677; www.rosemarino.co.uk; 1 York Pl; mains £8-16; ⏲9am-3pm & 6-10pm Tue-Sat, 9am-3pm Sun; 🖉) A firm favourite among Bristol's cognoscenti, Rosemarino brings a warm, home-cooked Italian foodie hug to Clifton's streets. Pesto, anchovies, taleggio and sage infuse dishes with Mediterranean flavours; the truffle-laced slow-cooked ox-cheek lasagna is a delight.

Chomp BURGERS ££
(☎07872 354375; www.chompgrill.co.uk; 10 St Nicholas St; mains £11-35; ⏲6-10pm Mon-Fri, 5-10pm Sat, 6-9pm Sun) In this dimly lit shrine to the three Bs (beef, burgers and bourbon), specials might see succulent patties slathered with Gorgonzola, while steaks are West Country raised and aged for around 25 days. Wine is on offer, but the smart money is on a pint of the punchy Chomp House Brew.

Riverstation BRITISH ££
(☎0117-914 4434; www.riverstation.co.uk; The Grove; bar/restaurant mains £14/17; ⏲10am-10pm Mon-Sat, to 6pm Sun) Riverstation's waterfront views are hard to beat, but it's the food that truly shines. Rich, classical flavours define dishes served up in the restaurant and less-formal bar. Expect truffle-fragranced wild mushrooms for breakfast, seasonal risotto for lunch, and stone bass and samphire for dinner.

Pump House GASTROPUB ££
(☎0117-927 2229; www.the-pumphouse.com; Merchants Rd; mains £17-22; ⏲noon-3pm & 6-9pm Mon-Sat, noon-5pm Sun; 📶🖉) A big, mirror-backed bar, red tile floors, retro signage and tall ceilings complete the transformation of this Victorian pumping station into warmly welcoming waterside gastropub. Innovative takes on pub grub classics dot the menu: truffle cauliflower cheese, beef with black garlic butter, and salt-baked veg. Or just sip a Butcombe beer on the harbourside terrace.

Drinking & Nightlife

★**Grain Barge** PUB
(☎0117-929 9347; www.grainbarge.com; Mardyke Wharf, Hotwell Rd; ⏲noon-11pm Sun-Wed, to 11.30pm Thu-Sat) Even in a city awash with harbourside bars this former 1930s cargo vessel is a special spot. Bristol Beer Factory ales grace the pumps, floor to ceiling windows frame wide water views and the top deck terrace allows you to watch the boats drift by.

Bell PUB
(☎0117-909 6612; www.butcombe.com; 18 Hillgrove St; ⏲4pm-midnight Mon, 2pm-midnight Tue-Thu, 3pm-1am Fri & Sat, 3pm-midnight Sun) Tucked away in a side road lined with street art, the Bell is a mellow favourite meeting point for Stokes Croft locals, with scuffed floorboards, well-worn tables, newspapers on the bar and Bristol's Butcombe brews on tap.

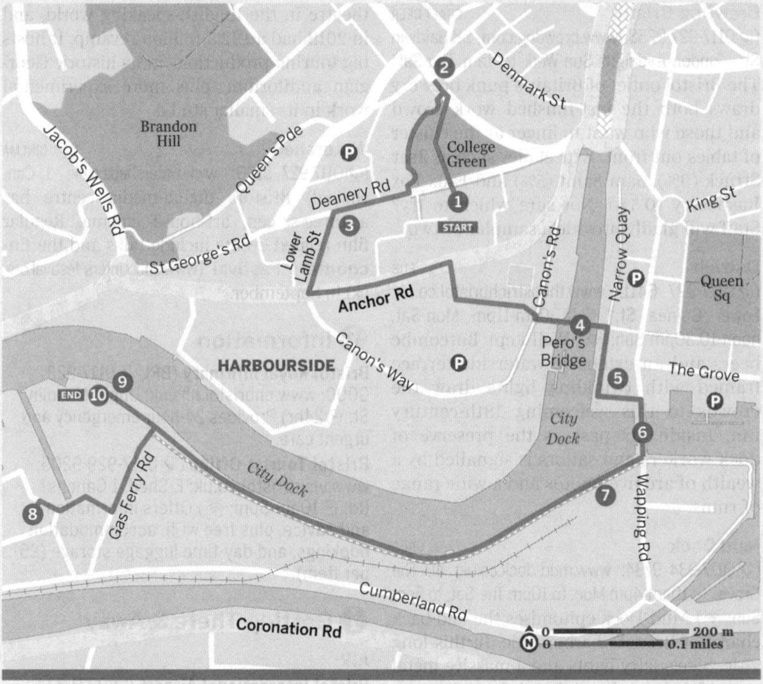

Walking Tour Bristol: Art & History

START BRISTOL CATHEDRAL
END SS GREAT BRITAIN
LENGTH 1.7 MILES; THREE HOURS

Hunt out the medieval choir and Saxon carvings in 1 **Bristol Cathedral** (☎0117-926 4879; www.bristol-cathedral.co.uk; College Green; ⊙8am-5pm Mon-Fri, to 3.15pm Sat & Sun) FREE then cross College Green to find the 2 **Well Hung Lover** (Frogmore St), a saucy Banksy depicting a cheating spouse. Re-cross College Green to the right, passing Bristol Library. Go down the steps immediately after it to see your second Banksy – the 3 **Castles Stencil** (Lower Lamb St) beside the delivery dock proclaims 'you don't need planning permission to build castles in the sky'. Continue on Lower Lamb St, then turn left along busy Anchor Rd, turning right at We the Curious. Edge the square to emerge onto the harbour side. Cross padlock-studded 4 **Pero's Bridge** and turn right to feel cobbles under your feet.

Drop by the 5 **Arnolfini** (☎0117-917 2300; www.arnolfini.org.uk; 16 Narrow Quay; ⊙11am-6pm Tue-Sun; 📶) FREE to check out its exhibitions, art bookshop and cafe. Then cross the 6 **Prince Street Swing Bridge** to pass under four mighty cranes. Head into the 7 **M Shed** (p238) museum and upstairs to see slavery and *Wallace and Gromit* exhibits and your third Banksy: the *Grim Reaper*, which the artist originally painted on the side of a nightclub boat. Then continue along the waterside path, coveting houseboats and reading plaques until you see the masts of Brunel's mighty SS *Great Britain*. Go left up Gas Ferry Rd, then right through an alleyway (signed Harbourside Walk). Duck around the front of the clock tower of the white building to see your fourth Banksy: 8 **Girl With A Pierced Eardrum**, a street-art twist on that famous Vermeer portrait. Retrace your steps – the water-view 9 **Harbourside Kitchen** (☎0117-926 0680; www.ssgreatbritain.org; Great Western Dockyard; mains £6-10; ⊙9am-6pm Easter-Oct, to 4.30pm Nov-Easter; 📶), right outside the 10 **SS Great Britain** (p237), is a prime place to refuel.

BrewDog Bristol CRAFT BEER
(☎0117-927 9258; www.brewdog.com; 58 Baldwin St; ⊙noon-midnight Sun-Wed, to 1am Thu-Sat) The Bristol outlet of Britain's punk brewery draws both the just-finished work crowd and those who want to linger at the cluster of tables out front. Expect ales such as Tsar Struck (9%), 5am Saint (5%) and Faux Fox Raspberry (0.5%). Not sure which to try? Staff will gladly provide a sampler or two.

Ostrich PUB
(☎0117-927 6411; www.theostrichbristol.co.uk; Lower Guinea St; ⊙11.30am-11pm Mon-Sat, noon-10.30pm Sun; 🐾) Well-kept Butcombe beers and an extensive waterside terrace framed with twinkling lights draw the crowds to this welcoming 18th-century inn. Inside, its past as the preserve of dock workers and sailors is signalled by a wealth of archive photos and a wide range of rums.

Mud Dock PUB
(☎0117-934 9734; www.mud-dock.co.uk; 40 The Grove; ⊙10am-4pm Mon, to 10pm Tue-Sat, to 5pm Sun; 📶) Mud Dock epitomises the laid-back charm of Bristol's harbourside. In this long attic, bikes, fairy lights and a massive metal swordfish hang from the girders. Summer sees people packing the mellow waterside terrace, enjoying craft ales and cracking views.

Amoeba CRAFT BEER
(☎0117-946 6461; www.amoebaclifton.co.uk; 10 Kings Rd; ⊙4pm-midnight Mon-Thu, 1pm-1am Fri & Sat, 1pm-midnight Sun) Some 70 craft beers, 60 cocktails (£9 to £14) and a hundred-and-something (who's counting?) spirits draw style-conscious drinkers to this chilled-out wine bar, where patrons sit on bench seats smothered in cushions and nibble on platters of charcoal crackers and artisan cheese (£8).

Albion PUB
(☎0117-973 3522; www.thealbionclifton.co.uk; Boyce's Ave; ⊙noon-11pm Sun-Wed, to midnight Thu-Sat) Cliftonites make a beeline for this village local for a post-work pint, drawn by the sofas, log burner, a beer terrace framed by fairy lights and Bath Ales on tap.

☆ Entertainment

★Bristol Old Vic THEATRE
(☎0117-987 7877; www.bristololdvic.org.uk; 16 King St) Established in 1766, the much-respected Old Vic is the longest continuously running theatre in the English-speaking world, and in 2018 had a £12.5-million revamp. It hosts big touring productions in its historic Georgian auditorium, plus more experimental work in its smaller studio.

Watershed CINEMA
(☎0117-927 5100; www.watershed.co.uk; 1 Canon's Rd) Bristol's digital-media centre has a three-screen, art-house cinema. Regular film-related events include talks and the **Encounters Festival** (www.encounters-festival.org.uk) in September.

ℹ Information

Bristol Royal Infirmary (BRI; ☎0117-923 0000; www.uhbristol.nhs.uk; Upper Maudlin St; ⊙24hr) Provides 24-hour emergency and urgent care.

Bristol Tourist Office (☎0117-929 9205; www.visitbristol.co.uk; E-Shed, 1 Canons Rd; ⊙10am-5pm; 📶) Offers information and advice, plus free wi-fi, accommodation bookings, and day-time luggage storage (£5 per item).

ℹ Getting There & Away

AIR

Bristol International Airport (☎0371 334 4444; www.bristolairport.co.uk) Bristol's airport is 8 miles southwest of the city. Destinations in the UK and Ireland include Aberdeen, Belfast, Edinburgh, Cork, Glasgow and Newcastle (mainly handled by easyJet). Direct links with cities in mainland Europe include those to Barcelona, Berlin, Milan and Paris.

Bristol Airport Flyer (http://flyer.bristolairport.co.uk) Runs shuttle buses (one way/return £8/13, 30 minutes, every 10 minutes at peak times) from the bus station and Bristol Temple Meads train station.

Arrow (☎01275-475000; www.arrowprivatehire.co.uk) Bristol Airport's official taxi service. Prices start from £33 (one way) from the city centre.

BUS

Bristol's **bus station** (Marlborough St; ⊙ticket office 8am-6pm) is 500m north of the city centre. From there buses shuttle into central areas and fan out around the city. There's a taxi rank nearby.

National Express (www.nationalexpress.com) coaches include those running direct to the following:

Bath (£5, 50 minutes, one a day).

Exeter (£6, two hours, five daily).

London Victoria (£11, three hours, hourly).

TRAIN

Bristol's main train station, Bristol Temple Meads, is just over a mile east of the city centre.

Direct services include the following:

Destination	Cost (£)	Duration (hr)	Frequency
Bath Spa	8	15min	4 per hour
Birmingham	35	2	hourly
Edinburgh	95	7	hourly
Exeter	19	1½	half-hourly
Glasgow	96	8½	2 daily
London Paddington	36	2	half-hourly

Getting Around

BICYCLE

Bristol Cycle Shack (0117-955 1017; www.bristolcycleshack.co.uk; 25 Oxford St; per 24hr from £15; 11am-6pm Mon, 9am-6pm Tue-Fri, 10am-5pm Sat) Hires out bikes from its base just east of Bristol Temple Meads train station.

Cycle the City (p240) Rents out bikes (if pre-booked) and runs cycling tours from the central harbour area.

BOAT

Bristol Ferry Boat Company (0117-927 3416; www.bristolferry.com; 4 stops adult/child £2/1/50) boats leave roughly hourly from the dock at Cannon's Rd near the tourist office. Its Hotwells service runs west, with stops including the SS *Great Britain*, while the Temple Meads service runs east, with stops including Welsh Back, Castle Park (for Cabot Circus) and Temple Meads (for the train station). Fares depend on distance travelled; an all-day pass is adult/child £7/6.

BUS

Bus journeys in Bristol's city centre cost £1.20 for up to three stops; longer trips cost £2.50. A day pass (£5) provides unlimited travel.

Bus 8 Runs every 15 minutes from Bristol Temple Meads train station, via College Green in the city centre, to Clifton and on to Bristol Zoo Gardens.

MetroBus The M2 service (www.metrobusbristol.co.uk; single £2.25) links Bristol Temple Meads train station with Long Ashton Park & Ride via the city centre and SS *Great Britain*. Buy tickets (no cash) before boarding.

CAR & MOTORCYCLE

Heavy traffic and pricey parking make driving in Bristol a headache.

Park & Ride Buses (0345-602 0121; www.travelwest.info/park-ride/bristol; peak/off-peak return £5/3.50; 6am-9pm Mon-Sat, 9.30am-6pm Sun;) include those running into central Bristol from Portway to the north-west (off Junction 18 of the M5) daily, and Brislington to the southeast (from near the A4), Monday to Saturday only.

TAXI

You can usually find a cab at the taxi ranks at the train and bus stations and on **St Augustine's Pde** (Narrow Quay).

To phone for a cab, try **V Cars** (0117-925 2626; www.v-cars.com) or **Bristol Taxis** (0117-944 4666; www.bristol-taxis.com; 24hr). If you're taking a nonmetered cab, agree on the fare in advance.

BATH

01225 / POP 88,850

Bath is one of Britain's most appealing cities. Exquisite Roman and Georgian architecture, counter-culture hang-outs and swish spas make it hard to resist.

History

Legend has it King Bladud, a Trojan refugee and father of King Lear, founded Bath some 2800 years ago when his pigs were cured of leprosy by a dip in the muddy swamps. The Romans established the town of Aquae Sulis in 44 CE and built the extensive baths complex and a temple to the goddess Sulis-Minerva.

In 944 a monastery was founded on the site of the present abbey, helping Bath's development as an ecclesiastical centre and wool-trading town. But it wasn't until the early 18th century that Ralph Allen and the celebrated dandy Richard 'Beau' Nash made Bath the centre of fashionable society. Allen developed the quarries at Coombe Down, constructed Prior Park and employed the two John Woods (father and son) to create Bath's signature buildings.

During WWII, Bath was hit by the Luftwaffe during the so-called Baedeker raids, which targeted historic cities in an effort to sap British morale. In 1987 Bath became the only city in Britain to be declared a Unesco World Heritage Site in its entirety.

Sights

★Roman Baths HISTORIC BUILDING
(01225-477785; www.romanbaths.co.uk; Abbey Church Yard; adult £16-23, child £8.50-15.50; 9am-9pm mid-Jun–Aug, to 5pm Mar–mid-Jun,

Bath

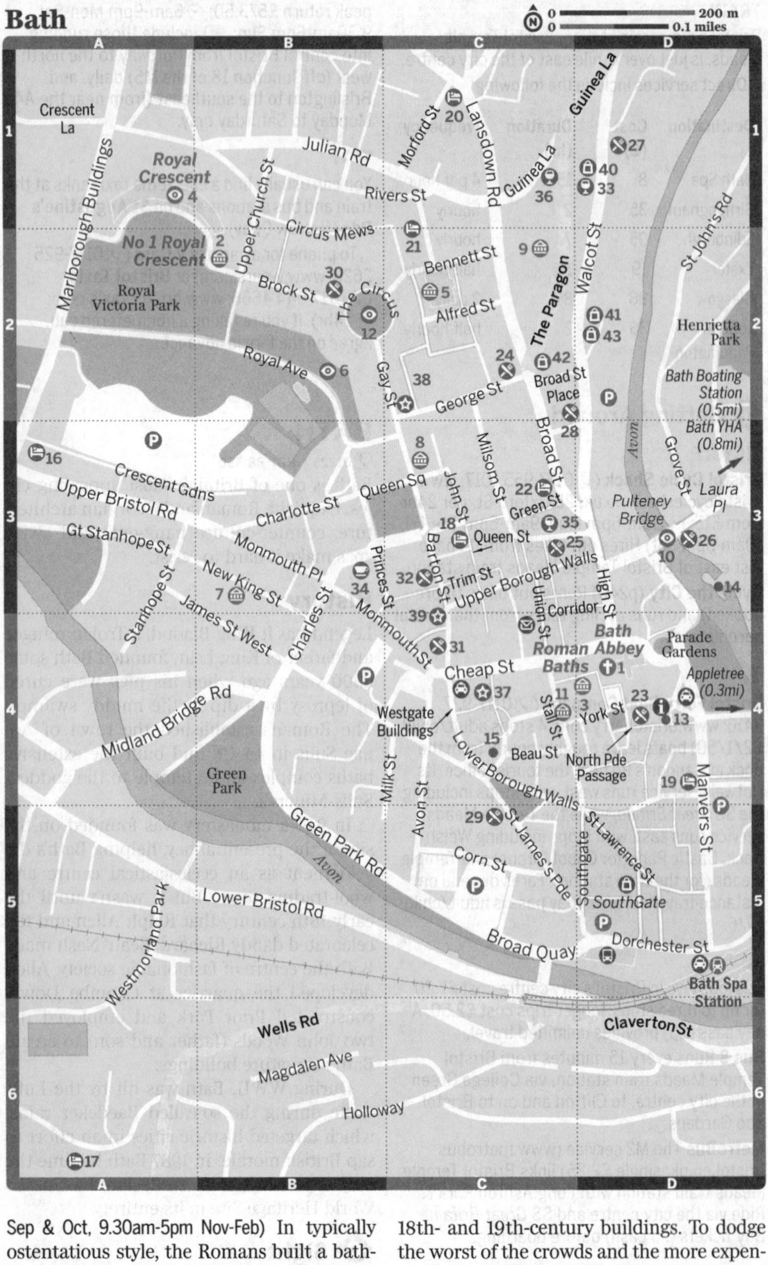

Sep & Oct, 9.30am-5pm Nov-Feb) In typically ostentatious style, the Romans built a bath-house complex above Bath's 46°C (115°F) hot springs. Set alongside a temple dedicated to the healing goddess Sulis-Minerva, the baths now form one of the world's best-preserved ancient Roman spas, and are encircled by 18th- and 19th-century buildings. To dodge the worst of the crowds and the more expensive tickets, avoid weekends and July and August. Fast-track online tickets bypass the queues.

The heart of the complex is the **Great Bath**, a lead-lined pool filled with steaming,

Bath

Top Sights
1 Bath Abbey ... D4
2 No 1 Royal Crescent ... B2
3 Roman Baths ... D4
4 Royal Crescent ... A1

Sights
5 Bath Assembly Rooms ... C2
6 Georgian Garden ... B2
7 Herschel Museum of Astronomy ... B3
8 Jane Austen Centre ... C3
9 Museum of Bath Architecture ... C2
10 Pulteney Bridge ... D3
11 Pump Room ... C4
12 The Circus ... B2

Activities, Courses & Tours
13 Bizarre Bath Comedy Walk ... D4
Mayor's Guide Tours ... (see 11)
14 Pulteney Cruisers ... D3
15 Thermae Bath Spa ... C4

Sleeping
16 Brooks ... A3
17 Grays Bath ... A6
18 Haringtons ... C3
19 Henry ... D4
20 Hill House Bath ... C1
21 Queensberry ... C2
22 St Christopher's Inn ... C3

Eating
23 Acorn ... D4
24 Adventure ... C2
25 Bertinet Bakery ... C3
26 Chez Dominique ... D3
27 Corkage ... D1
28 Fine Cheese Co ... C2
29 Noya's Kitchen ... C5
Pump Room Restaurant ... (see 11)
Sally Lunn's ... (see 23)
30 The Circus ... B2
31 The Oven ... C4
32 Thoughtful Bread Company ... C3

Drinking & Nightlife
33 Bell ... D1
34 Colonna & Smalls ... B3
35 Old Green Tree ... C3
36 Star ... C1

Entertainment
37 Little Theatre Cinema ... C4
38 Moles ... C2
39 Theatre Royal ... C4

Shopping
40 Bath Aqua Glass Workshop ... D1
41 Katherine Fraser ... D2
42 Topping & Company ... C2
43 Yellowshop ... D2

geothermally heated water from the so-called 'Sacred Spring' to a depth of 1.6m. Though now open-air, the bath would originally have been covered by a 45m-high barrel-vaulted roof.

More bathing pools and changing rooms are to the east and west, with excavated sections revealing the **hypocaust system** that heated the bathing rooms. After luxuriating in the baths, Romans would have reinvigorated themselves with a dip in the circular **cold-water pool**.

The **King's Bath** was added sometime during the 12th century around the site of the original Sacred Spring. Every day, 1.5 million litres of hot water still pour into the pool. Beneath the Pump Room are the remains of the **Temple of Sulis-Minerva**.

Digital reconstructions pop up in some sections of the complex, especially in the Temple Courtyard and the West and East Baths, which feature projections of bathers. There is also a **museum** displaying artefacts discovered on the site. Look out for the famous gilded bronze head of Minerva and a striking carved gorgon's head, as well as some of the 12,000-odd Roman coins thrown into the spring as votive offerings to the goddess.

The complex of buildings around the baths was built in stages during the 18th and 19th centuries. John Wood the Elder and his son, John Wood the Younger, designed the buildings around the Sacred Spring, while the famous **Pump Room** (Stall St; 9.30am-5pm) FREE was built by their contemporaries, Thomas Baldwin and John Palmer, in neoclassical style, complete with soaring Ionic and Corinthian columns. The building now houses a **restaurant** (snacks £5-9, 1/2/3 courses £16/22/28; 9.30am-4pm), where offerings include magnificent afternoon teas (from £20, or £36 with champagne). You can also taste samples of the spring waters (50p), which were believed in Victorian times to have curative properties. If you're lucky, you might even have music provided by the Pump Room's string trio.

Admission to the Roman Baths includes an audio guide, featuring commentary in 12 languages – there's also one especially for children and a guide in sign language. One of the English guides is read by bestselling author Bill Bryson. Free hourly **guided**

LOCAL KNOWLEDGE

ORIENTATION

Bath's blockbuster sights are concentrated in two key, fairly small areas: in the city centre around the Roman Baths where you'll also find Bath Abbey and the Victoria Art Gallery, and in northern Bath around the Royal Crescent – the Circus, Jane Austen Centre and Fashion Museum are nearby.

The two neighbourhoods are around half a mile apart and walking between the two is a pleasant way to soak up the city's atmosphere and see the architecture. Many people spend the first day sightseeing in the city centre, and the second in northern Bath.

tours start at the Great Bath on the hour. The last entry to the complex is an hour before closing.

★Bath Abbey CHURCH

(☎01225-422462; www.bathabbey.org; Abbey Church Yard; suggested donation adult/child £5/2.50; ⏲9.30am-5.30pm Mon, 9am-5.30pm Tue-Fri, to 6pm Sat, 12.15-1.45pm & 4-6.30pm Sun) Looming above the city centre, Bath's huge abbey church was built between 1499 and 1616, making it the last great medieval church raised in England. Its most striking feature is the west facade, where angels climb up and down stone ladders, commemorating a dream of the founder, Bishop Oliver King.

★Royal Crescent ARCHITECTURE

Bath is famous for its glorious Georgian architecture, and it doesn't get any grander than this semicircular terrace of majestic town houses overlooking the green sweep of Royal Victoria Park. Designed by John Wood the Younger (1728–82) and built between 1767 and 1775, the houses appear perfectly symmetrical from the outside, but the owners were allowed to tweak the interiors, so no two houses are quite the same. **No 1 Royal Crescent** (☎01225-428126; www.no1royal crescent.org.uk; 1 Royal Cres; adult/child/family £11/5.40/27; ⏲10am-5pm) offers an intriguing insight into life inside.

A walk east along Brock St from the Royal Crescent leads to the **Circus**, a ring of 33 houses divided into three semicircular terraces. Plaques on the houses commemorate famous residents such as Thomas Gainsborough, Clive of India and David Livingstone. The terrace was designed by John Wood the Elder, but he died in 1754, and it was completed by his son in 1768.

To the south along Gravel Walk is the **Georgian Garden** (☎01225-394041; off Royal Ave; ⏲9am-7pm) FREE, restored to resemble a typical 18th-century town-house garden.

Jane Austen Centre MUSEUM

(☎01225-443000; www.janeausten.co.uk; 40 Gay St; adult/child £12/6.20; ⏲9.45am-5.30pm Apr-Oct, 10am-4pm Sun-Fri, 9.45am-5.30pm Sat Nov-Mar) Bath is known to many as a location in Jane Austen's novels, including *Persuasion* and *Northanger Abbey*. Although Austen lived in Bath for only five years, from 1801 to 1806, she remained a regular visitor and a keen student of the city's social scene. Here, guides in Regency costumes regale you with Austen-esque tales as you tour memorabilia relating to the writer's life in Bath.

Pulteney Bridge BRIDGE

Elegant Pulteney Bridge has spanned the River Avon since the late 18th century and is a much-loved, much-photographed landmark (the view from Grand Parade, southwest of the bridge, is the best). It's also one of only four bridges in the world with shops lining both sides.

Museum of Bath Architecture MUSEUM

(☎01225-333895; www.museumofbatharchitec ture.org.uk; The Countess of Huntingdon's Chapel, off the Paragon; adult/child £7/3.50; ⏲1-5pm Mon-Fri, 10am-5pm Sat & Sun mid-Feb–Nov) The intriguing stories behind the building of Bath's most striking structures are explored here, using maps, drawings, antique tools, displays on Georgian construction methods and a 1:500 scale model of the city. On weekdays in July and August, it opens at 11am.

A joint ticket covering the Museum of Bath Architecture, No 1 Royal Crescent, the **Herschel Museum of Astronomy** (☎01225-446865; www.herschelmuseum.org.uk; 19 New King St; adult/child £7/3.50; ⏲1-5pm Mon-Fri, 10am-5pm Sat & Sun) and Beckford's Tower costs adult/child/family £16/8/40.

Activities

★Thermae Bath Spa SPA

(☎01225-331234; www.thermaebathspa.com; Hot Bath St; spa £37-42; treatments from £72; ⏲9am-9.30pm, last entry 7pm) Taking a dip in the Roman Baths might be off limits, but you can still sample the city's curative waters at this fantastic modern spa complex, housed in a shell of local stone and plate glass. The showpiece is the open-air rooftop pool, where you can bathe in naturally heated, mineral-rich waters with a backdrop of Bath's cityscape – a don't-miss experience, best enjoyed at dusk.

Bath Boating Station BOATING
(☎01225-312900; www.bathboating.co.uk; Forester Rd; adult/child per hour £8/4, per day £20/10; ⏲10am-5.30pm Wed-Sun Easter-Sep) You can pilot your own vessel down the Avon from this Victorian-era boathouse, which rents out traditional rowing boats, punts, kayaks and Canadian canoes. It's in the suburb of Bathwick, a 20-minute walk northeast from the city centre.

Pulteney Cruisers BOATING
(☎01225-863600; www.bathboating.com; Pulteney Bridge; adult/child £10/5; ⏲mid-Mar–Oct) Pulteney Cruisers offers frequent, hour-long cruises up and down the River Avon from the Pulteney Bridge area.

Tours

★Bizarre Bath Comedy Walk WALKING
(www.bizarrebath.co.uk; adult/student £10/7; ⏲8pm Apr-Oct) A multi-award-winning stroll that's billed as 'hysterical rather than historical'. That it actually has little to do with Bath doesn't matter a bit. Leaves nightly from outside the Huntsman Inn. There's no need to book.

Mayor's Guide Tours WALKING
(www.bathguides.org.uk; ⏲10.30am & 2pm Sun-Fri, 10.30am Sat) FREE The excellent historical two-hour tours provided free by the Mayor's Corp of Honorary Guides leave from within the Abbey Churchyard, outside the Pump Room. There are extra tours at 6pm on Tuesdays and Thursdays May to August. Booking isn't required.

Festivals & Events

Bath Festival CULTURAL
(☎01225-614180; www.bathfestivals.org.uk; ⏲May) A multi-arts festival that features classical, jazz, world and folk music with fiction, debate, science, history, politics and poetry.

Bath Fringe Festival THEATRE
(www.bathfringe.co.uk; ⏲mid-May–early Jun) Theatre-focused festival that also includes folk and world music gigs, dance and performance walks.

Sleeping

Bath YHA HOSTEL £
(☎0345 371 9303; www.yha.org.uk; Bathwick Hill; dm £21-30, d/q from £69/99; P@📶) Split across an Italianate mansion and modern annexes, this impressive hostel is a steep climb (or a short hop on bus U1/U18) from the city. The listed building means the rooms are huge, and some have period features such as cornicing and bay windows.

St Christopher's Inn HOSTEL £
(☎01225-481444; www.st-christophers.co.uk; 9 Green St; dm £26-30, d £59; 📶) The Bath outpost of this European hostel chain has cheerful staff, clean if small rooms, a central location and a party vibe, thanks to the drinks and food deals in the popular in-house bar. If you're not a night owl you might like to look elsewhere.

Haringtons HOTEL ££
(☎01225-461728; www.haringtonshotel.co.uk; 8 Queen St; r £120-200; P📶🐾) If Bath's classical trappings aren't to your taste, head for this strictly modern city-centre crash pad, with vivid colour schemes, clashing wallpapers and a fun, young vibe. The location is fantastic, with the central sights just a few minutes' walk away.

Hill House Bath B&B ££
(☎01225-920520; www.hillhousebath.co.uk; 25 Belvedere; r £95-135; P📶) When you walk through the door of this four-storey Georgian townhouse it almost feels like you're staying with friends. The decor is quietly quirky: moustache-themed cushions, retro pictures and objets d'art abound.

MUSEUM DISCOUNTS

Saver tickets covering the Roman Baths and the Fashion Museum cost adult/child/family £26/16/70.

There is also a joint ticket (adult/child/family £16/8/40) that includes entry into No 1 Royal Crescent, the Museum of Bath Architecture and the Herschel Museum of Astronomy.

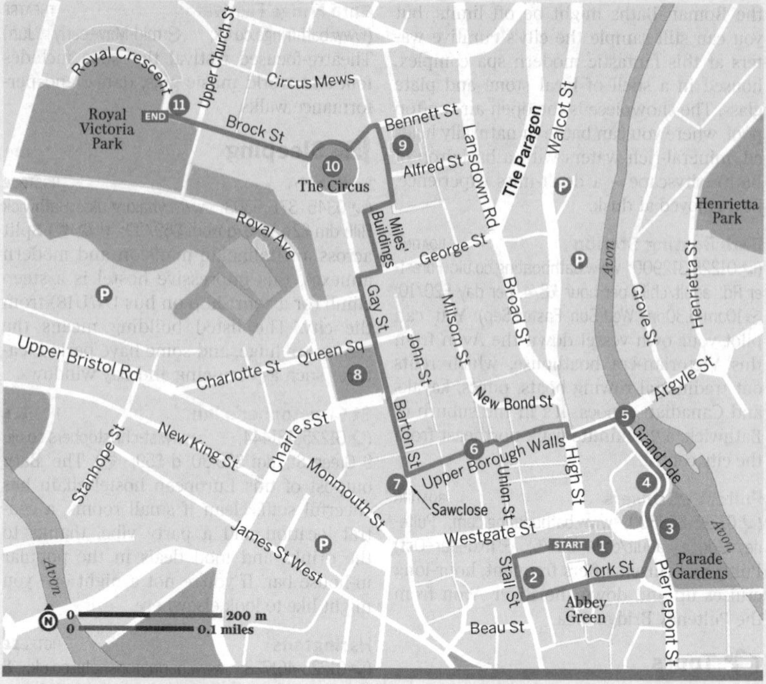

Walking Tour Historic Bath

START BATH ABBEY
END ROYAL CRESCENT
LENGTH 1.5 MILES; TWO HOURS

Explore **1 Bath Abbey** (p248), an iconic edifice built on the site of an 8th-century chapel. Next, head south along Stall St for views of the 19th-century **2 Pump Room** (p247). Turn left onto York St, following it east to **3 Parade Gardens**, a landscaped Victorian park beside the River Avon.

Grand Parade leads north. Look out for the **4 Empire**, built as a luxurious hotel in 1901, on the corner. Next comes **5 Pulteney Bridge**, designed by Robert Adams in 1773, one of only a handful in the world to be lined with shops (the most famous other example is Florence's Ponte Vecchio). West of the bridge, **6 Upper Borough Walls** marks the northern extent of medieval Bath; look out for sections of the medieval wall that remain.

At Sawclose spot the elaborate facade of Bath's **7 Theatre Royal** (p255); it's been staging productions since 1805. Then follow Barton St on to **8 Queen Sq**. The oldest of Bath's Georgian squares, it was built to demonstrate the talents of its architect, John Wood the Elder.

Head north on to Gay St, and right on to George St. Next to Clayton's Kitchen restaurant, Miles' Buildings (an alley) leads north, emerging at the **9 Assembly Rooms** (NT; ☎01225-477789; www.nationaltrust.org.uk; 19 Bennett St; ⊙10.30am-6pm Mar-Oct, to 5pm Nov-Feb) FREE, the heart of Georgian Bath's social life. After Bennett St turn left to reach the **10 Circus** (p248), designed to echo the Colosseum in Rome. The three-tiered pillars feature classical architectural styles (Doric, Ionic and Corinthian), while the facades are studded with masonic symbols.

Brock St leads west to Bath's Georgian glory, the Royal Crescent. Constructed by John Wood the Younger in 1774, the terrace is now Grade I listed, making it as architecturally significant as Buckingham Palace. **11 No 1 Royal Crescent** (p248) is open to the public.

Appletree B&B ££

(☎01225-337642; www.appletreebath.com; 7 Pulteney Gardens; r £95-160; P) Owner, Ling, ran a city-centre hotel for 15 years, and those skills shine throughout this classy B&B. Bedrooms are named after the eponymous fruit. The best is Royal Gala, which features a sleigh bed and sofa, but even the cheaper rooms are bright and fresh and dotted with Asian art.

Brooks B&B ££

(☎01225-425543; www.brooksguesthouse.com; 1 Crescent Gardens, Upper Bristol Rd; s from £62, d £85-125;) In the smoothly comfy rooms at Brooks, a scattering of antiques meet plush modern furnishings, smart bathrooms and top-notch toiletries. Add eggs Benedict for breakfast, and an honesty bar and you have a stylish, fairly central bolthole.

Henry B&B ££

(☎01225-424052; www.thehenry.com; 6 Henry St; s £85-105, d £105-150, f £150-210;) This tall terrace is just a few steps from the centre of Bath. The seven simple, small rooms are jazzed up with striped cushions and mints on the pillows.

★Queensberry HOTEL £££

(☎01225-985086; www.thequeensberry.co.uk; 4 Russell St; r £235-323, ste £460-510; P) Stylish but unstuffy Queensberry is Bath's best luxury spoil. In these Georgian town houses heritage roots meet snazzy gingham checks, bright upholstery, original fireplaces and free-standing tubs. It's witty (see The Rules on the website), independent (and proud of it), and service is first-rate.

★Grays Bath B&B £££

(☎01225-403020; www.graysbath.co.uk; 9 Upper Oldfield Park; r £125-185; P) Boutique treat Grays is a beautiful blend of modern, pared-down design and family treasures, many picked up from the owners' travels. All the rooms are individual: choose from floral, polka dot or maritime stripes. Perhaps the pick is the curving, six-sided room in the attic, with partial city views.

Eating

★Thoughtful Bread Company BAKERY £

(☎01225-471747; www.thethoughtfulbreadcompany.com; 19 Barton St; baked goods £2-5; 8am-5pm Tue-Sat, 9am-4pm Sun) Come lunchtime they could well be queuing out the door of this snug artisan bakery, where chunky loaves sit alongside delicate macaroons and salted-caramel bombs. Its vegan donuts are fruit-dotted, multi-coloured works of art.

Bertinet Bakery BAKERY £

(☎01225-313296; www.bertinetbakery.com; 1 New Bond St Pl; baked goods £2.50-5; 8am-5pm Mon-Fri, 8.30am-5.30pm Sat, 10am-4pm Sun) Temptation is all around at Richard Bertinet's take-out bakery, be it in the shape of rich quiches, cheese-studded croissants, *viennoiserie*, fresh-baked bread or irresistible pistachio swirls.

Adventure CAFE £

(☎01225-462038; www.adventurecafebar.co.uk; 5 Princes Bldgs, George St; mains £6-11; 8am-1am Mon-Fri, 9am-1am Sat & Sun;) This cool cafe-bar offers something for everyone at most times of the day: breakfast bagels, lunchtime burgers and late-night pizza, cocktails and beer. There's great outdoor seating at the back.

Sally Lunn's CAFE £

(☎01225-461634; www.sallylunns.co.uk; 4 North Pde Passage; mains £7-13, afternoon tea £8-40; 10am-8pm) Eating a Bath Bunn (a bit like brioche) at Sally Lunn's is a Bath tradition. It's all about proper English tea here, brewed in bone-china teapots, with finger sandwiches and dainty cakes.

Noya's Kitchen VIETNAMESE £

(☎01225-684439; www.noyaskitchen.co.uk; 7 St James's Pde; mains £7-12; 11.45am-3pm Tue-Sat, plus 6-9pm Wed & Thu, 7-10pm Fri & Sat) Let the fragrances wafting from this intimate Vietnamese restaurant draw you in for fresh, aromatic, delicately flavoured dishes. Lunch menus are admirably short, evenings bring *pho* (noodle soup) on Wednesday, zingy curries on Thursday and the immensely popular, five-course Supper Club (£45) on Friday and Saturday – book well in advance.

The Oven PIZZA ££

(☎01225-311181; www.theovenpizzeria.co.uk; 3 Sawclose; pizzas £9-15; noon-10.30pm Sun-Thu, to 11pm Fri & Sat;) Bath's best pizzeria is a little slice of Italy with a warm atmosphere, cool tunes and basil-scented air. The wood-fired pizzas are authentic; thin, crisp and piled with prime ingredients such

BILLY STOCK/SHUTTERSTOCK ©

1. Dunster (p264)
One of the oldest villages in Exmoor features a castle on a wooded hill.

2. Royal Crescent (p248), Bath
This semicircular terrace of town houses is a stunning example of Georgian architecture.

3. Red deer (p263), Exmoor National Park
Autumn rutting season is a popular time to visit this large wild red deer population.

4. Brunel's SS Great Britain (p237), Bristol
You can explore this groundbreaking steamship designed in 1843.

as smoked mozzarella, grilled asparagus and toasted hazelnuts. The tiramisu is gorgeous and vast.

The Circus MODERN BRITISH ££
(☎01225-466020; www.thecircusrestaurant.co.uk; 34 Brock St; mains lunch £14-20, dinner £18-25; ⏲10am-11pm Mon-Sat;) Chef Ali Golden has turned this bistro into one of Bath's destination addresses. The menu mixes traditional British fare with global influences – here slow-cooked lamb and caramelised cauliflower meet harissa-infused aubergine, and rabbit in velouté cream sauce.

Acorn VEGETARIAN ££
(☎01225-446059; www.acornvegetariankitchen.co.uk; 2 North Pde Passage; lunch 2/3 courses £20/25, dinner 2/3 courses £30/39; ⏲noon-3pm & 5.30-9.30pm;) Revelling in an ethical and eco ethos, Bath's premier vegetarian restaurant brings vegetables and grains to a whole new level of deliciousness. Contemporary fine dining using imaginative cookery methods and global flavours result in beautiful plates of food. The six-course taster menu (£50) is worth the outlay – it's a true celebration of plant-based food.

Chez Dominique FRENCH ££
(☎01225-463482; www.chezdominique.co.uk; 15 Argyle St; mains £18-24; ⏲11.30am-3pm & 5-11pm Mon-Sat, 11.30am-3.30pm & 6-9pm Sun) The unfussy decor here prepares you for classic French bistro cooking, with time-honoured methods and ingredients delivering punchy flavours. From the chalked-up *soupe du jour* and steak with *pommes frites* to the salted-caramel ice cream, it's a gorgeous dollop of France.

Corkage BISTRO ££
(☎01225-422577; www.corkagebath.com; 132a Walcot St; ⏲5-11pm Tue, 5-11.30pm Wed & Thu, noon-11.30pm Fri & Sat) At this intimate, friendly neighbourhood bistro the aromas of imaginative dishes fill the air and regiments of bottles fill the shelves. It offers scaled-down versions of main courses (£6 to £13) and an extensive international wine list.

★Menu Gordon Jones MODERN BRITISH £££
(☎01225-480871; www.menugordonjones.co.uk; 2 Wellsway; 7 courses £65, with wines £120; ⏲12.30-2pm & 7-9pm Tue-Sat;) Gordon Jones delights in delivering dining laced with surprise. Menus are dreamt up daily and showcase the chef's taste for experimental ingredients such as wild New Forest mushrooms and Dorset snails. The presentation is eye-catching (perhaps featuring test tubes or paper bags) and Gordon himself often pops out to explain the dishes. Reservations essential.

Drinking & Nightlife

★Bell PUB
(www.thebellinnbath.co.uk; 103 Walcot St; ⏲11.30am-11pm Mon-Thu, to midnight Fri & Sat, noon-10.30pm Sun;) The locals loved

BATH'S ARTISAN QUARTER

Bath is rightly famous for its rich past. But hidden among the heritage is a cool, contemporary city. It's in evidence in the self-styled Artisan Quarter around Walcot St. You won't be knee-deep in craftspeople, but independent shops, bistros and a classic live-music pub make it worth a visit.

Fine Cheese Co (☎01225-448748; www.finecheese.co.uk; 31 Walcot St; dishes £7-16; ⏲9am-5pm Mon-Sat) Exquisite pastries, punchy coffee, a vast cheese selection and creative specials.

Yellowshop (www.yellowshop.co.uk; 72 Walcot St; ⏲10.30am-5.30pm Mon-Sat, noon-4pm Sun) Pre-loved clothing heaven crammed with cowboy boots, chunky sweaters and faded jeans.

Katherine Fraser (☎01225-461341; www.katherinefraser.co.uk; 74 Walcot St; ⏲10am-5pm Mon-Sat) An artisan weaver works amid beautiful, bold designs.

Bath Aqua Glass Workshop (☎01225-428146; www.bathaquaglass.com; 105 Walcot St; ⏲9.30am-4pm Mon-Fri, 11.15am-2.15pm Sat) Look through the open doors to see craftspeople at work, or head inside for a demo.

Topping & Company (☎01225-428111; www.toppingbooks.co.uk; The Paragon; ⏲8.30am-8pm) Some 50,000 books, rolling library ladders, free tea and proper coffee.

the Bell so much they bought it; the pub is a co-operative, owned by more than 500 customers and staff. Get chatting to some of them over table football, bar billiards, backgammon and chess, while sipping one of nine real ales. Or enjoy the DJ sets and live music spanning folk and jazz to the blues.

★Colonna & Smalls CAFE
(☎07766 808067; www.colonnaandsmalls.co.uk; 6 Chapel Row; ⏰8am-5.30pm Mon-Fri, 8.30am-5.30pm Sat, 10am-4pm Sun; 📶) If you're keen on caffeinated beans, this is a cafe not to miss. A mission to explore coffee means there are three guest espresso varieties, and smiling staff are on hand to share their expertise. They'll even tell you that black filter coffee – yes, filter coffee – is actually the best way to judge high-grade beans.

Star PUB
(☎01225-425072; www.abbeyales.co.uk; 23 The Vineyards, The Paragon; ⏰noon-midnight Sun-Wed, to 12.30am Thu, to 1am Fri & Sat) Few pubs are registered relics, but the Star is just that. First licensed in 1760, historic features include 19th-century bar fittings, wooden benches and four drinking snugs. It's the brewery tap for Bath-based Abbey Ales; some beers are served in traditional jugs, and you can even ask for a pinch of snuff in the 'smaller bar'.

Old Green Tree PUB
(☎01225-448259; 12 Green St; ⏰11am-11pm Mon-Sat, noon-6.30pm Sun) In this tiny, traditional, entirely wood-panelled pub you'll be welcomed warmly to a fuss-free atmosphere, a minuscule lounge bar and a good range of real ales.

☆ Entertainment

Moles LIVE MUSIC
(☎01225-437537; www.moles.co.uk; 14 George St; ⏰5pm-3am Mon-Thu, to 4am Fri & Sat) Bath's main music venue keeps the crowds happy with indie, alternative, house and hip-hop, club classics, DJ sets and cheesy pop hits (Tuesdays) spanning five decades.

Little Theatre Cinema CINEMA
(☎0871 9025735; www.picturehouses.com; St Michael's Pl) An excellent art-house cinema screening fringe films and foreign-language flicks in art-deco surrounds.

LOCAL KNOWLEDGE

SHOPPING IN BATH

Bath's shops are some of the best in the west. The city's main shopping centre is **SouthGate** (www.southgatebath.com; ⏰shops 9am-6pm Mon-Wed, Fri & Sat, 9am-7pm Thu, 11am-5pm Sun), where you'll find all the major chain stores.

High-quality, independent shops line the narrow lanes just north of Bath Abbey and Pulteney Bridge. Milsom St is good for upmarket fashion, while Walcot St has food shops, design stores, vintage-clothing retailers and artisans' workshops.

Theatre Royal THEATRE
(☎01225-448844; www.theatreroyal.org.uk; Sawclose) Bath's historic theatre dates back more than 200 years. Major touring productions appear in the main auditorium and smaller shows take place in the **Ustinov Studio**.

ℹ Information

Bath Tourist Office (☎01225-614420; www.visitbath.co.uk; 2 Terrace Walk; ⏰9.30am-5.30pm Mon-Sat, 10am-4pm Sun, closed Sun Nov-Jan) Offers advice and information. Also runs an accommodation booking service and sells a wide range of local books and maps.

Royal United Hospital (☎01225-428331; www.ruh.nhs.uk; Combe Park; ⏰24hr) Offers 24-hour emergency and urgent care.

ℹ Getting There & Away

BUS

Bath's **bus and coach station** (Dorchester St) is near the train station.

National Express (www.nationalexpress.com) coaches include those running direct to:

Bristol (£5, 50 minutes, daily)
London Heathrow (£27, 2½ hours, two-hourly)
London Victoria (£15, three hours, hourly)

Services to many other destinations change at Bristol.

First Bus (www.firstgroup.com) is the biggest local bus company. Services to:

Bristol (bus 38/39/X39; £6.60, one hour, four per hour Monday to Saturday, half-hourly on Sunday)
Wells (bus 172/173/174; £6.60, 1½ hours, two per hour Monday to Saturday, hourly Sunday)

TRAIN

Bath's train station, Bath Spa, is at the south end of Manvers St. Some services connect through Bristol, including many to the southwest and north of England. Direct services include the following:

Destination	Cost (£)	Duration (hr)	Frequency
Bristol	8	15min	4 per hour
Cardiff Central	12	1¼	hourly
London Paddington	35	1½	hourly
Salisbury	12	1	half-hourly

Getting Around

BICYCLE

Bath is hilly. The canal paths along the Kennet and Avon Canal and the 13-mile **Bristol & Bath Railway Path** (www.bristolbathrailwaypath.org.uk) are great to explore by bike.

Bath Bike Hire (01225-447276; www.bath-narrowboats.co.uk; Sydney Wharf, Bathwick Hill; adult/child per day £18/15; 9am-5pm) A 10-minute walk from the centre. Handy for the canal and railway paths.

BUS

BathRider (adult/child £4.50/3.50) A multi-operator, all-day ticket covering a 3-mile radius of central Bath. It's valid until 3am the next day. A seven-day ticket costs adult/child £20/15.

Bus U1 Runs from the bus station, via High St and Great Pulteney St, up Bathwick Hill, past the YHA to the university every 20 minutes (£2.50).

Bus 11 Goes to Bathampton (£2.50, 10 minutes, hourly) from the bus station.

CAR & MOTORCYCLE

Bath has serious traffic problems, especially at rush hour. **Park & Ride services** (0871 200 22 33; www.firstgroup.com; return Mon-Fri £3.60, Sat & Sun £3.10; 6.15am-8.30pm Mon-Sat, 9.30am-6pm Sun) operate from Lansdown to the north, Newbridge to the west and Odd Down to the south. It takes about 10 minutes to the centre; buses leave every 10 to 15 minutes.

There's a central car park underneath the SouthGate shopping centre (two/eight hours £3.50/11).

TAXI

There's a taxi rank at Bath Spa train station, or call **V Cars Bath** (01225-464646; www.v-cars.com; 24hr).

SOMERSET

With its pastoral landscape of hedgerows, fields and hummocked hills, sleepy Somerset is the very picture of the rural English countryside, and makes the perfect escape from the bustle of Bath and the hustle of Bristol. Things certainly move at a drowsier pace around these parts – it's a place to drink in the sights at your own pace.

The cathedral city of Wells is an atmospheric base for exploring the limestone caves and gorges around Cheddar, while the hippie haven of Glastonbury is handy for venturing on to the high hills of the Quantocks. To the west sits Exmoor National Park, where sheer cliffs meet open moors roamed by red deer.

Information

The Taunton **tourist office** (01823-340470; www.visitsomerset.co.uk/taunton; Market House, Fore St; 9.30am-4.30pm Mon-Sat) has info about Somerset as a whole.

The website www.visitsomerset.co.uk is a useful source of information.

Getting There & Around

The M5 heads south past Bristol to Bridgwater and Taunton, while the A39 leads west across the Quantocks to Exmoor.

Key train services link Bath, Bristol, Bridgwater, Taunton and Weston-super-Mare.

First (www.firstgroup.com) is a key local bus operator.

For timetables and general information, contact **Traveline South West** (www.travelinesw.com).

Wells & Around

01749 / POP 10,530

In Wells, small is beautiful. This is England's smallest city, and only qualifies for the title thanks to a magnificent medieval cathedral, which sits beside the grand Bishop's Palace – the official residence of the Bishop of Bath and Wells since the 12th century. Medieval buildings and cobbled streets radiate out from the cathedral green to a marketplace that has been the bustling heart of Wells for nine centuries (Wednesday and Saturday are market days).

WORTH A TRIP

CHEDDAR GORGE

Carved out by glacial meltwater during the last ice age, **Cheddar Gorge** (☎01934-742343; www.cheddargorge.co.uk; adult/child £20/15; ⏰10am-5pm, to 5.30pm late July-Aug) is England's deepest natural canyon, in places towering 138m above the twisting B3135. The gorge is riddled with subterranean caverns with impressive displays of stalactites and stalagmites. Highlights are Gough's Cave and the multimedia Dreamhunters exhibit in Cox's Cave; deeper caves can be explored on caving trips with **Rocksport** (☎01934-742343; www.cheddargorge.co.uk/rocksport; Cheddar Gorge; adult/child £25/19).

Cheddar is also famous as the home of one of the nation's favourite cheeses, produced here since the 12th century. At the **Cheddar Gorge Cheese Company** (☎01934-742810; www.cheddargorgecheeseco.co.uk; The Cliffs, Cheddar; adult/child £2/free; ⏰10am-5pm Easter-Oct, winter hours vary), you can watch the cheesemaking process, sample the produce, then buy some whiffy souvenirs.

Cheddar Gorge is 10 miles northwest of Wells on the A371.

Sights

★Wells Cathedral — CATHEDRAL

(Cathedral Church of St Andrew; ☎01749-674483; www.wellscathedral.org.uk; Cathedral Green; requested donation adult/child £6/5; ⏰7am-7pm Apr-Sep, to 6pm Oct-Mar) Wells' gargantuan Gothic cathedral sits plumb in the centre of the city, surrounded by one of the largest cathedral closes in England. It was built in stages between 1180 and 1508, and showcases several Gothic styles. Among its notable features are the **West Front**, decorated with more than 300 carved figures, and the famous **scissor arches**, an ingenious architectural solution to counter the subsidence of the central tower. Don't miss the **High Parts Tour** (adult/child £13/10; ⏰Mon-Sat May-Oct) that heads up into the roof.

Bishop's Palace — HISTORIC BUILDING

(☎01749-988111; www.bishopspalace.org.uk; Market Pl; adult/child £9/4.50; ⏰10am-6pm Apr-Oct, to 4pm Nov-Mar) Built for the bishop in the 13th century, this moat-ringed palace is purportedly the oldest inhabited building in England. Inside, the palace's state rooms and ruined great hall are worth a look, especially on one of the free tours, but it's the shady gardens that are the real draw. The natural springs after which Wells is named bubble up in the palace's grounds.

Wookey Hole — CAVE

(☎01749-672243; www.wookey.co.uk; Wookey Hole; adult/child £20/16; ⏰10am-5pm Apr-Oct, to 4pm Nov-Mar, closed Mon-Fri Dec–mid-Feb; P) The River Axe has gouged out this network of deep limestone caverns, which are famous for striking stalagmites and stalactites, one of which is the legendary Witch of Wookey Hole who, it's said, was turned to stone by a local priest. Admission to the caves is by guided tour. Up on top you'll find 20 beyond-kitsch attractions ranging from animatronic dinosaurs to pirate adventure golf. Wookey Hole is 2 miles northwest of Wells; look out for brown tourist signs on the A371.

Sleeping

Ancient Gate House Hotel — HOTEL ££

(☎01749-672029; www.ancientgatehouse.co.uk; 20 Sadler St; s £80-113, d £88-166;) This old hostelry is built right into the cathedral's west gate. Rooms are decorated in regal reds and duck-egg blues. The best have four-poster beds and knockout cathedral views through latticed windows; they're £15 extra, and worth it. Prices rise significantly at weekends.

No 23 — B&B ££

(☎01749-677648; www.bedandbreakfastinwells.co.uk; 23 Glastonbury Rd; s/d £103/110; P) It's a 15-minute walk from the centre of Wells to this sweet, redbrick B&B. Inside, smart, contemporary rooms have all the home comforts, your breakfast has quality ingredients and owner Liz has a dry sense of humour.

Beryl — B&B £££

(☎01749-678738; www.beryl-wells.co.uk; Hawkers Lane; s £75-100, d £120-170, tr from £165; P) This grand gabled mansion offers a beautiful blast of English eccentricity. Every inch of the house is crammed with antique atmosphere, and the rooms boast grandfather clocks, chaise longues and four-posters galore. It's about a mile from Wells.

Eating

Strangers with Coffee CAFE £
(☎07729 226200; www.facebook.com/StrangersWithCoffee; 31 St Cuthbert St; cakes from £2.50, mains from £6; ⏰7.30am-4pm Tue-Sat) The motto 'life is too short to drink bad coffee' is something they've taken to heart here as staff work caffeinated magic with the best beans in town. There's a tempting selection of multi-storey cakes to match.

Good Earth CAFE £
(☎01749-678600; www.thegoodearthwells.co.uk; 4 Priory Rd; mains £7-11; ⏰9am-4.30pm Mon-Sat;) They've been running this cafe, wholefood store and homeware shop for 40 years now. Plenty of time to perfect serving up towering quiches, colourful salads and filling-packed jacket potatoes in a light-filled, cheerful, relaxed space.

Goodfellows EUROPEAN ££
(☎01749-673866; www.goodfellowswells.co.uk; 5 Sadler St; dinner mains £14-24; ⏰noon-3pm Sun & Mon, 10am-3pm Tue-Sat & 6-9pm Wed-Sat) There's a choice of eating options in Goodfellows' three vibrant rooms: the continental cafe menu offers cakes, pastries and light lunches (from £6), or book for an evening fine-dining experience – £33 gets you three classy courses, while the five-course seafood tasting menu (£50) is an absolute treat.

Information

Tourist Office (☎01749-671770; www.wellssomerset.com; Town Hall, Market Pl; ⏰10am-4pm)

Getting There & Away

The bus station is south of Cuthbert St, on Princes St. Useful services include:

Bath (bus 172/173/174; £6.60, 1½ hours, two per hour Monday to Saturday, hourly Sunday)

Bristol (bus 376; £6.60, 1¼ hours, half-hourly)

Cheddar (bus 126; £3.85, 25 minutes, hourly Monday to Saturday) Continues to Weston-super-Mare (£4, 1½ hours)

Glastonbury (bus 376; £2.40, 15 minutes, half-hourly)

Glastonbury

☎01458 / POP 8930

Ley lines converge, white witches convene and shops are filled with the aroma of smouldering joss sticks in good old Glastonbury, the southwest's undisputed capital of alternative culture. Now famous for the musical mudfest of a festival, held on Michael Eavis' farm in nearby Pilton, Glastonbury has a much more ancient past: the town's iconic tor was an important pagan site and is often linked to King Arthur. Some also believe the area is a hub of positive otherworldly energy. Whatever the truth of the legends swirling round Glastonbury, one thing's for certain – watching the sunrise from the top of the tor is an experience you won't forget in a hurry.

Sights

★Glastonbury Tor LANDMARK
(NT; ☎01278-751874; www.nationaltrust.org.uk; ⏰24hr) FREE Topped by the ruined, 15th-century Chapel of St Michael, the iconic hump of Glastonbury Tor is visible for miles around, and provides Somerset with one of its most unmistakable landmarks. It takes half an hour to walk up from the start of the trail on Wellhouse Lane; the steepest sections are stepped. Between April and September the Tor Bus (adult/child return £3.30/1.50) runs every half-hour from St Dunstan's car park near Glastonbury Abbey to the trailhead.

The tor is the focal point for a wealth of local lore. According to Celtic legend, the tor is the home of Arawn or Gwyn ap Nudd, king of the underworld and lord of the faeries. A more famous legend identifies the tor as the mythic Isle of Avalon, where King Arthur was taken after being mortally wounded in battle, and where Britain's 'once and future king' sleeps until his country calls again. Others believe that the tor marks an ancient mystical node where invisible lines of energy, known as ley lines, converge.

It's easy to see why the tor has inspired so many myths. It's a strange presence in an otherwise pan-flat landscape, and in ancient times (when the area around Glastonbury was covered by water for much of the year) the tor would indeed have appeared as an island, wreathed in mist and cut off by rivers, marshes and bogs.

Glastonbury

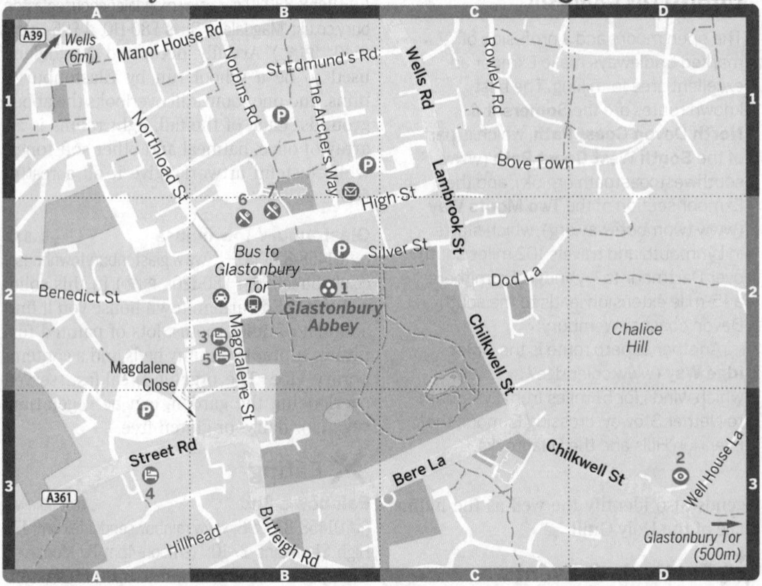

Glastonbury

Top Sights
1 Glastonbury Abbey B2

Sights
2 Chalice Well & Gardens D3

Sleeping
3 Covenstead B2
4 Glastonbury Townhouse A3
5 Magdalene House B2

Eating
6 George & Pilgrim B2
7 Rainbow's End B2

★ Glastonbury Abbey RUINS

(☎01458-832267; www.glastonburyabbey.com; Magdalene St; adult/child £8.60/4.70; ⏲9am-8pm Jun-Aug, to 6pm Mar-May, Sep & Oct, to 4pm Nov-Feb) The scattered ruins of Glastonbury Abbey give little hint that this was once one of England's great seats of ecclesiastical power. It was torn down following Henry VIII's dissolution of the monasteries in 1539, and the last abbot, Richard Whiting, was hung, drawn and quartered on the tor. Today's striking ruins include some of the nave walls, the remains of St Mary's chapel, and the crossing arches, which may have been scissor-shaped like those in Wells Cathedral.

The grounds also contain a museum, a cider orchard and a herb garden. According to legend, the abbey's famous holy thorn tree sprang from the staff of Joseph of Arimathea, Jesus' great-uncle, who is said to have visited the abbey following Christ's death. It blooms at Christmas and Easter.

The abbey even has an Arthurian connection. In the 12th century, monks supposedly uncovered a tomb in the abbey grounds inscribed *Hic iacet sepultus inclitus rex arturius in insula avalonia,* or 'Here lies buried the renowned King Arthur in the Isle of Avalon'. Inside the tomb were two entwined skeletons, purportedly those of Arthur and his wife Guinevere. The bones were reburied beneath the altar in 1278, but were lost following the abbey's destruction.

Chalice Well & Gardens GARDENS

(☎01458-831154; www.chalicewell.org.uk; Chilkwell St; adult/child £4.60/2.30; ⏲10am-6pm Apr-Oct, to 4.30pm Nov-Mar) Shaded by yew trees and criss-crossed by quiet paths, the Chalice Well and Gardens have been sites of pilgrimage since the days of the Celts. The iron-red waters from the 800-year-old well are rumoured to have healing properties, good for everything from eczema to smelly feet. Some

HIKING ON EXMOOR

The open moors and a profusion of marked bridleways make Exmoor an excellent area for hiking. The best-known routes are the **Somerset & North Devon Coast Path**, which is part of the **South West Coast Path** (www.southwestcoastpath.org.uk), and the Exmoor section of the **Two Moors Way** (www.twomoorsway.org), which starts in Lynmouth and travels 102 miles south over Dartmoor to Ivybridge. From there a 15-mile extension leads to the south Devon coast at Wembury.

Another superb route is the **Coleridge Way** (www.coleridgeway.co.uk), which winds for 51 miles from Lynmouth to Nether Stowey, crossing Exmoor, the Brendon Hills and the Quantocks.

legends also identify the well as the hiding place of the Holy Grail.

Festivals & Events

Glastonbury Festival of Contemporary Performing Arts MUSIC
(www.glastonburyfestivals.co.uk; Pilton; tickets £270; Jun or Jul) A majestic (and frequently mud-soaked) extravaganza of music, theatre, dance, cabaret, carnival, spirituality and general all-round weirdness that's been held on farmland in Pilton, just outside Glastonbury, since 1970 (bar periodic 'fallow' years to let the farm recover). Tickets usually go on sale in the autumn, and always sell out within a matter of minutes.

Sleeping

Check whether nearby **Street YHA** (0345 371 9143; www.yha.org.uk; Ivythorn Hill, Street; P), which switched to exclusive hire in 2020, has resumed taking individual bookings.

★**Covenstead** B&B ££
(01458-830278; www.covenstead.co.uk; Magdalene St; s £75, d £80-120; P 📶) It's as if they've distilled the wacky essence of Glastonbury and poured it all over this weirdly wonderful B&B. The downstairs is a riot of oddities: mock skeletons, witches hats, upcycled antlers and draped python skins. Bedroom themes range from fairy via green man and Gothic to Halloween honeymoon. A tad crazy, yes, but also delightfully done.

Magdalene House B&B ££
(01458-830202; www.magdalenehouseglastonbury.co.uk; Magdalene St; s £80-110, d £95-110, tr £140; P 📶) Artfully decorated Magdalene used to be a school run by Glastonbury's nuns, and one room still overlooks the abbey grounds. Each of the tall, light rooms is an array of olive, oatmeal and other soft tones, while tasteful artworks give it all a restful feel.

Glastonbury Townhouse B&B ££
(01458-831040; www.glastonburytownhouse.co.uk; Street Rd; r £80-120; P 📶) In this solid, red-brick, Edwardian town house you'll find a clutch of quiet rooms, lots of painted furniture, supremely comfy beds and a contemporary vibe. The organic breakfast, served overlooking the garden, can be vegetarian, vegan, or dairy- or gluten-free.

Eating

Rainbow's End VEGETARIAN £
(01458-833896; www.rainbowsendcafe.com; 17b High St; mains £7-10; noon-4pm Fri-Mon;) This psychedelic cafe sums up the Glastonbury spirit, with its all-veggie food, potted plants and mix-and-match furniture. Head out back into the pretty garden to tuck into homity pie, a hot quiche, and scrumptious homemade cake.

George & Pilgrim PUB FOOD ££
(01458-831146; www.historicinnz.co.uk; 1 High St; mains £7-22; food noon-3pm & 6-9pm) In hippy-chic Glastonbury a rarity: an ancient inn with one of the town's most authentically historic interiors – timbers, flagstones and all. Tuck into everything from homemade scotch eggs with dill mayonnaise to its signature slow-braised Somerset lamb.

Information

Tourist Office (01458-832954; www.glastonburytic.co.uk; Magdalene St; 10am-4pm Mon-Sat, 11am-3pm Sun) In the town hall.

Getting There & Away

There is no train station in Glastonbury. Useful bus routes include:

Taunton (bus 29; £5, 1¼ hours, four to seven daily Monday to Saturday)

Wells (bus 376; £2.40, 15 minutes, every half hour)

EXMOOR NATIONAL PARK

Exmoor is more than a little addictive, and chances are you won't want to leave its broad, russet views. In the middle sits the higher moor, an empty, expansive, otherworldly landscape of tawny grasses and huge skies. In the north, sheer, rock-strewn river valleys cut into the plateau and coal-black cliffs lurch towards the sea.

Amid these towering headlands, charismatic Porlock and the twin villages of Lynton and Lynmouth are atmospheric places to stay. Relaxed Dulverton delivers a country-town vibe, while appealing Dunster has cobbled streets and a russet-red castle. Everywhere on Exmoor life is attuned to the rhythms and colours of the seasons – newborn livestock in spring, purple heather in late summer, gold-bronze leaves in autumn, and crisp days and log fires in winter. It all ensures Exmoor delivers insights into an elemental and traditional world.

Activities

★Exmoor Adventures OUTDOORS
(☎07976 208279; www.exmooradventures.co.uk; Old Bus Garage, Porlock Weir) Sessions covering all skill levels for couples, families and small groups in kayaking, canoeing and SUP (per person £35/65 per half-/full day), mountain biking (from £30 per half day), coasteering (£30) and rock climbing (£65).

Cycling

Cycling is hugely popular on Exmoor's formidable hills. The 328-mile **West Country Way** (NCN Route 3) from Bristol to Padstow crosses the park, as does the **Devon Coast to Coast** (NCN Route 27), between Ilfracombe and Plymouth.

Exmoor is also an exhilarating off-road cycling destination, with a wealth of accessible bridleways and tracks. National Park visitor centres can advise.

The mountain bike sessions run by Exmoor Adventures include day-long trips down red and black trails (£80) and night rides (£40). It also rents mountain bikes (£25 per day).

Pompys CYCLING
(☎01643-704077; www.pompyscycles.co.uk; Mart Rd, Minehead; per day £18; ⏰9am-4pm Mon-Sat) Bike sales and hire.

Walking

Open moors and a profusion of marked bridleways make Exmoor an excellent hiking area. Good routes include:

➡ **Somerset & North Devon Coast Path** Part of the **South West Coast Path** (www.southwestcoastpath.org.uk).

➡ **Two Moors Way** (www.twomoorsway.org) Tracking 117 miles south from Lynmouth, over Dartmoor and onto the south Devon coast at Wembury.

➡ **Coleridge Way** (www.coleridgeway.co.uk) Winds for 51 miles from Lynmouth to Nether Stowey, crossing Exmoor, the Brendon Hills and the Quantocks.

➡ **Tarka Trail** (www.tarkatrail.org.uk) A coastal section sweeps from Lynton to Bideford, before heading down into north Devon.

Exmoor National Park

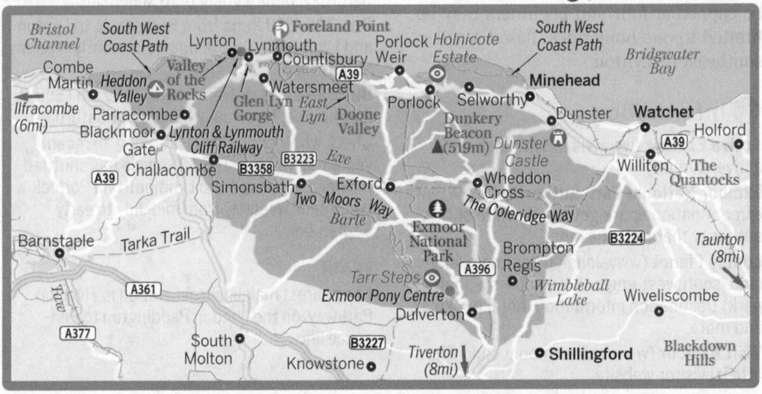

STARGAZING ON EXMOOR

Exmoor holds the distinction of being named Europe's first International Dark Sky Reserve, in recognition of the night-time inky blackness overhead. But what does that mean in practice? Namely, a whole host of local organisations striving to limit light pollution, plus, for visitors, some simply spectacular star displays.

The Exmoor National Park Authority (ENPA; www.exmoor-nationalpark.gov.uk) has produced the excellent, free *Dark Skies Guide,* which includes star charts, tips and maps pinpointing the best local light-free spots. Download it from the website, or pick one up at visitor centres.

It's worth seeing if the ENPA is staging any guided moonlit strolls, and whether the Exmoor Dark Skies Festival is running – it tends to be held over two weeks from late October.

Or just look upwards on your own. For optimum stargazing, central, higher Exmoor is best – try Brendon Two Gates (on the B3223) or Webber's Post (just north of Dunkery Beacon).

See if walks run by the Exmoor National Park Authority (p262) are running. Past events include deer safaris, nightjar birdwatching walks and dark-sky strolls.

Exmoor National Park Authority (ENPA) tourist offices also sell a great range of day walk leaflets (£1).

Pony Trekking & Horse Riding

Exmoor is prime riding country, with stables offering pony and horse treks from around £50 for a two-hour ride.

Check if local stables **Outovercott Stables** (www.outovercott.co.uk) and **Burrowhayes Farm** (www.burrowhayes.co.uk) have resumed riding sessions.

Brendon Manor HORSE RIDING
(☎01598-741246; www.brendonmanor.com; Brendon Manor; per 1hr/2hr £30/50) Runs a full range of horse-riding trips, from one to three hours, that head onto the open moor and down into the valleys. Depending on distancing regulations, groups may be capped at four and beginners may be limited to one-hour rides. Based 4 miles southeast of Lynton.

ℹ Information

Active Exmoor (www.visit-exmoor.co.uk/active-exmoor)

Exmoor National Park Authority (ENPA; www.exmoor-nationalpark.gov.uk) Website of the authority that runs the moor.

Lonely Planet (www.lonelyplanet.com/england/southwest-england/exmoor-national-park) Destination information, hotel bookings and more.

Visit Exmoor (www.visit-exmoor.co.uk) The official visitor website.

The Exmoor National Park Authority runs three tourist offices:

Dulverton (☎01398-323841; www.visit-exmoor.co.uk; 7 Fore St; ⏰10am-4pm Apr-Oct, reduced hours Nov-Mar)

Dunster (☎01643-821835; www.visit-exmoor.co.uk; Dunster Steep; ⏰10am-4pm Apr-Oct, reduced hours Nov-Mar)

Lynmouth (☎01598-752509; www.visit-exmoor.co.uk; The Esplanade, Lynmouth; ⏰10am-4pm)

There's also a council-run tourist office in **Porlock** (☎01643-863150; www.porlock.co.uk; West End, Porlock; ⏰10am-2pm Mon-Sat Easter-Oct, to 12.30pm Mon-Sat Nov-Easter).

ℹ Getting Around

BUS

Exmoor isn't that easy to navigate without your own vehicle, but if you plan ahead you can get around by bus. Key routes include:

Bus 198 Links Dulverton with Dunster (£4.20, 1¼ hours) two to three times daily, Monday to Saturday, before going onto Minehead.

Bus 309/310 Runs from Barnstaple to Lynton and Lynmouth (£3.60, one hour, hourly Monday to Saturday).

Bus 398 Links Dulverton with Tiverton (£5.50, 45 minutes, three daily Monday to Saturday).

Check whether bus 300 is running. In recent years this vintage (1950s) vehicle has shuttled between Minehead and Lynmouth via Porlock twice each weekday from mid-July to early September.

TRAIN

The nearest mainline train station is Tiverton Parkway, on the London Paddington to Penzance line.

Bus 1 (£2.40, 25 minutes, hourly Monday to Saturday, five on Sunday) links the station with Tiverton town, 13 miles away.

Dulverton

01398 / POP 2490

The southern gateway to Exmoor National Park, Dulverton sits at the base of the Barle Valley near the confluence of two key rivers: the Exe and Barle. A traditional country town, it's home to a collection of gun sellers, fishing-tackle stores and gift shops, and makes an attractive edge-of-moor base.

Sights

★Tarr Steps LANDMARK

(P) Exmoor's most famous landmark is an ancient stone clapper bridge shaded by gnarled old trees. Its huge slabs are propped up on stone columns embedded in the River Barle. Local folklore aside (which declares it was used by the Devil for sunbathing), it first pops into the historical record in the 1600s, and has had to be rebuilt after 21st-century floods. The steps are signed off the B3223 Dulverton–Simonsbath road, 5 miles northwest of Dulverton.

It's a 450m walk from the car park to the bridge itself. You can also hike there from Dulverton along the banks of the River Barle (12 miles return).

Exmoor Pony Centre WILDLIFE RESERVE

(01398-323093; www.exmoorponycentre.org.uk; Ashwick, near Dulverton; donations requested; 10am-4pm Mon, Wed-Fri & Sun early Feb-Oct; P) You'll see them cantering across the open moor, but this is a great way to get up close to Exmoor's stubby ponies. Originally bred as beasts of burden, they're famously hardy despite their diminutive size.

Sleeping & Eating

Town Mills B&B ££

(01398-323124; www.townmillsdulverton.co.uk; 1 High St; s/d/ste £95/105/125; P) The top choice in Dulverton town itself is a thoroughly contemporary riverside mill with creamy carpets, magnolia-coloured walls and bursts of floral art.

Tarr Farm HOTEL £££

(01643-851507; www.tarrfarm.co.uk; Tarr Steps, TA22 9QA; s/d £90/160; P) This is the place to really lose yourself: a charming farmhouse nestled among the woods near the Tarr Steps bridge, 7 miles from Dulverton. The nine contemporary bedrooms are spacious and luxurious, with spoil-yourself extras such as organic bath goodies and homemade biscuits. The farm is also renowned for its food.

Exclusive Cake Co BAKERY £

(01398-324131; www.exclusivecakecompany.co.uk; Northmoor Rd; snacks from £3; 7am-2pm Mon-Fri, 9am-2pm Sat) Real rarities stack the shelves here: bread made with Exmoor ale, cheese and wholegrain mustard; Somerset cider cake; venison and port pie. Note the typically Exmoor warning: 'Game pies may contain lead shot'.

Tantivy DELI £

(01398-323465; www.tantivyexmoor.co.uk; 12 Fore St; snacks from £3; 9am-5pm;) Alongside maps, books and gift shop trinkets you'll also find a good little deli, packed with cured meats, cheese, locally smoked fish, ice cream, wine and beer. Or be tempted by the punchy takeaway espressos and gorgeous, gooey cakes.

★Woods BISTRO ££

(01398-324007; www.woodsdulverton.co.uk; 4 Bank Sq; mains £13-19; bar noon-3pm & 7-11pm, food noon-2pm & 7-9.30pm) With its deer antlers, hunting prints and big wood-burning stove, multi-award-winning Woods is Exmoor to its core. No surprise then to find menus with full-bodied ingredients: expect

> LOCAL KNOWLEDGE
>
> **EXMOOR RED DEER**
>
> Exmoor supports one of England's largest wild red deer populations, best experienced in autumn when the annual 'rutting' season sees stags bellowing, charging at each other and clashing antlers in an attempt to impress prospective mates.
>
> Check the Exmoor National Park Authority (ENPA) website to see if their deer-spotting hikes are running. Also check whether the following firms have resumed off-road jeep **safaris** (per half-day £25).
>
> **Red Stag Safari** (www.redstagsafari.co.uk)
>
> **Barle Valley Safaris** (www.exmoorwildlifesafaris.co.uk)
>
> **Discovery Safaris** (www.discoverysafaris.com)

confit leg of guinea fowl, slow-roast lamb shoulder, and asparagus and wild garlic risotto. The clutch of tables outside and in the flower-framed courtyard garden are first-come, first-served.

Dunster

01643 / POP 1220

Centred on a scarlet-walled castle and a medieval yarn market, Dunster is one of Exmoor's oldest villages, a tempting tangle of cobbled streets, bubbling brooks and packhorse bridges.

Sights

★Dunster Castle CASTLE

(NT; 01643-821314; www.nationaltrust.org.uk; Castle Hill; gardens adult/child £8/4; 11am-5pm Mar-Oct; P) Rosy-hued Dunster Castle crowns a densely wooded hill. Built by the Luttrell family, which once owned much of northern Exmoor, the oldest sections are 13th century, while the turrets and exterior walls are 19th-century additions. The parkland and colourful terraced gardens feature riverside walks, a working watermill, a pop-up cafe and views across Exmoor's shores.

Sleeping & Eating

Dunster Castle Hotel HOTEL ££

(01643-823030; www.thedunstercastlehotel.co.uk; 5 High St; d £110-195;) Everything feels rich in this former coaching inn, from the ruby-red furnishings and puffed-up quilts, to the burnished trunks and gilt-framed mirrors. The best rooms overlook Dunster's cobbled High St.

Millstream Cottage B&B ££

(01643-822413; www.millstreamcottagedunster.co.uk; 2 Mill Lane; s £65, d £80-90) In the 1600s this was Dunster's workhouse. Now it's a sweet-as-pie guesthouse with country-cottage-style rooms with beams, pine doors and stone fireplaces. Breakfast treats include porridge, toast with Exmoor jams and smoked haddock and poached eggs.

Luttrell Arms HISTORIC HOTEL £££

(01643-821555; www.luttrellarms.co.uk; High St; r £210-260; P) In medieval times, the baronial Luttrell Arms was the guesthouse of the Abbots of Cleeve. The grander rooms have private terraces and garden access. But even the standard digs are gorgeous; expect a plethora of four-poster beds, brass plates, beams and a plaster fireplace or two.

The acclaimed food (noon to 3pm and 6.30pm to 9.30pm; mains £12 to £29) ranges from sumptuous cream teas to classic, locally sourced à la carte.

★Reeve's BRITISH £££

(01643-821414; www.reevesrestaurantdunster.co.uk; 20 High St; mains £16-28; 6-9pm Tue-Sat, noon-2pm Sun) The leafy, parasol-dotted garden at Reeve's sets the scene for some seriously stylish, award-winning cuisine. The complex creations showcase Exmoor produce. Opt for venison wellington steeped in red wine sauce, or meltingly tender lamb roasted with rosemary and garlic. To finish? Some toasted walnut bread with local hard and soft cheeses.

Porlock & Porlock Weir

01643

The coastal village of Porlock is one of the prettiest on the Exmoor coast; the huddle of thatched cottages lining its main street is framed on one side by the sea and on the other by steeply sloping hills. Winding lanes lead to the charismatic breakwater of Porlock Weir, 2 miles to the west, with an arching pebble beach and striking coastal views.

Sights & Activities

★Porlock Weir HARBOUR

(P) Porlock Weir's stout granite quay curves around a shingly beach, which is backed by pubs, fisherfolks' storehouses and a scattering of seasonal shops. The weir has been around for almost a thousand years (it's named in the Domesday Book as 'Portloc'). It makes a glorious place for a picnic lunch and a stroll, with stirring views across the Vale of Porlock and easy access to the South West Coast Path.

The shingle beach to the west of the weir forms part of the Porlock Ridge and Saltmarsh SSSI (Site of Special Scientific Interest), a popular spot for local birdwatchers.

Holnicote Estate ARCHITECTURE

(NT; 01643-862452; www.nationaltrust.org.uk; near Porlock; P) FREE The 50-sq-km Holnicote Estate sweeps southeast out of Porlock, taking in a string of impossibly pretty villages. Picturesque **Bossington** leads to charming **Allerford** and its 15th-century packhorse bridge. The biggest village,

Selworthy, offers eye-catching Exmoor views and cob-and-thatch cottages clustering around the village green.

Porlock's Hills SCENIC DRIVE

If you're driving (or cycling) into Porlock, choose from several picturesque routes. On the main road (the A39) Porlock Hill is a snaking, brake-burning 25% gradient descent. The New Rd toll road (cars £3) peels off the A39 some 3 miles west of Porlock to sweep into the village through pine forests and around U-bends. Another toll road, the Porlock Scenic (Worthy) Toll Rd (cars £2), provides an alternative, bouncing, route in and out of Porlock Weir.

Sleeping

Burrowhayes Farm CAMPGROUND £

(01643-862463; www.burrowhayes.co.uk; West Luccombe; sites per 2 adults £17-19; mid-Mar–Oct; P) The large sweep of grass at the centre of this peaceful, well-run site is reserved for tents. Pitches are spacious, but arrive early to avoid the slopes. It's 1 mile east of Porlock.

Sea View B&B ££

(01643-863456; www.seaviewporlock.co.uk; High Bank, Porlock; s from £40, d £75-78; P) Value-for-money Sea View has tiny rooms that are pleasantly packed with painted furniture, trinkets and oil paintings. Thoughtful extras include blister plasters and muscle soak for hikers tackling Porlock's precipitous hills.

Cottage B&B ££

(01643-862996; www.cottageporlock.co.uk; High St, Porlock; s/d/tr £50/75/90; P) Evidence of the Cottage's 18th-century origins remains – a big fireplace in the guest lounge, duck-your-head lintels and quirkily shaped bedrooms. The decor though is stylishly modern, with light-coloured furniture in rooms of earthy or aquamarine tones.

Eating & Drinking

Porlock Weir Hotel PIZZA ££

(01643-800400; www.porlockweirhotel.co.uk; Porlock Weir; pizzas £10-13; pizzas noon-9pm) Grandstand views of Porlock's sweeping pebble beach, a sea-view terrace bar and crispy wood-fired pizzas (eat there or takeaway). Bliss.

Ship Inn PUB FOOD ££

(Top Ship; 01643-862507; www.shipinnporlock.co.uk; High St, Porlock; snacks £6, mains £11-17; noon-2.30pm & 6-8.30pm; P) Romantic poet Samuel Taylor Coleridge and pal Robert Southey both downed pints in this 13th-century thatched Porlock inn – there's even a snug still dubbed 'Southey's Corner'. Substantial pub food – mainly steaks, local fish, roasts and stews – is served in the beer gardens or the roomy restaurant.

Locanda On The Weir ITALIAN £££

(01643-863300; www.locandaontheweir.co.uk; Porlock Weir; mains £20-26; 7-9pm Wed-Sun, longer summer hours; P) The chef-proprietor hails from Italy so the dishes at this smart inn are a happy fusion of Exmoor produce and flavours of the Med. Your gnocchi could come with gorgonzola and truffle, the local lamb might be roasted in fragrant spices, while the fish might be *baccala' alla Livornese* (cod with capers, potatoes and olives).

Ship Inn PUB

(Bottom Ship; 01643-863288; www.shipinnporlockweir.co.uk; Porlock Weir; 11am-11pm, winter hours vary) The Bottom Ship (so called because – yep – it's at the bottom of the hill onto Porlock Weir) is loved by locals for its huge terrace, flagstone floors, wood burner, real ales (including Exmoor Stag) and ciders (including Cheddar Valley).

Lynton & Lynmouth

01598

Tucked in amid precipitous cliffs and steep, tree-lined slopes, these twin coastal towns are a landscape-painter's dream. Bustling Lynmouth sits beside the shore, a busy harbour lined with pubs and souvenir shops. On the clifftop, Lynton feels much more genteel and well-to-do. A cliffside railway links the two: it's powered by the rushing West Lyn River, which feeds numerous cascades and waterfalls nearby.

Sights

★**Cliff Railway** HERITAGE RAILWAY

(01598-753486; www.cliffrailwaylynton.co.uk; The Esplanade, Lynmouth; one way adult/child £3/2; 11am-4pm) This extraordinary piece of Victorian engineering involves two cars with tiny balconies, that are linked by a steel cable, descending and ascending the steeply sloping cliff face according to the weight of water in the cars' tanks. All burnished wood and polished brass, it's been running since 1890 and makes for an unmissable ride.

HIKES AROUND LYNTON & LYNMOUTH

The plunging cliffs and densely wooded valleys around Lynton and Lynmouth make for memorable day hikes. Some paths are particularly popular so ask at local tourist offices about the less-trod trails. A good map helps, such as Ordnance Survey's *Explorer OL9*.

Valley of the Rocks Spot formations dubbed the Devil's Cheesewring and Ragged Jack, and feral goats wandering cliff-side paths. Quieter routes to the valley are the inland ones snaking south and west from Lynton.

Countisbury Common Open, hilly terrain, leading north to the lighthouse at Foreland Point.

Watersmeet A quieter route into this popular, waterfall-dotted valley is to hike in from Leeford village to the east, or Coombe Park Wood to the south.

Lyn Cleave After the Glen Lyn Gorge, head up to a ridge-top hike across fields towards Higher and Lower East Lyn.

Trentishoe Down Some 8 miles west of Lynmouth, four separate car parks are gateways to the coast path and the wooded Heddon Valley far below.

Flood Memorial MUSEUM
(The Esplanade, Lynmouth; 10am-5pm Easter-Oct) FREE On 16 August 1952 a huge wave of water swept through Lynmouth following torrential rain. The devastation was immense: 34 people lost their lives, and four bridges and countless houses were washed away. This exhibition features photos of the aftermath and personal testimonies of those involved. It's volunteer run – hours may vary.

Sleeping

Heddon Valley CAMPGROUND £
(01643-863905; www.nationaltrust.org.uk; Heddon Valley, near Parracombe; sites per 2 adults £20; mid-Jul–Aug; P) It's kept deliberately bare-bones in this unmanicured, pop-up campsite, so prepare to collect your own water and sit on a compost toilet while you listen to the surf hitting the shore far below.

★ **Bath Hotel** HOTEL ££
(01598-752238; www.bathhotellynmouth.co.uk; The Harbour, Lynmouth; d £90-145, ste £155; P) The Bath Hotel has been a feature of the town since Victorian times. These days it's a swish affair with premium rooms featuring gorgeously nautical styling, Victorian curios, supremely comfortable beds and expansive harbour and headland views. The 'Austerity' rooms are much less snazzy – but they're also £50 cheaper.

Lynn Valley B&B ££
(01598-753300; www.lynvalleyguesthouse.com; Riverside Rd, Lynmouth; s from £60, d £80-110, q £150; P) Walkers love this smart little guesthouse thanks to baths to soak in and a setting right on the coast path. Even if you're not hiking you'll like the crisp, bright decor, harbour views and mini-decanters of sherry in the rooms.

North Walk House B&B £££
(01598-753372; www.northwalkhouse.co.uk; North Walk, Lynton; s from £93, d £150-190; P) Polished wooden floors, colourful rugs, sparkling bathrooms and a cliff-side terrace give North Walk House a boutique, hideaway feel. The sweeping views over the sea and rugged headlands are fantastic, while the all-organic breakfasts feature Exmoor bacon and sausages, and Aga-baked eggs.

Rising Sun INN £££
(01598-753223; www.risingsunlynmouth.co.uk; Harbourside, Lynmouth; d £145-170) A former 14th-century smugglers' haunt has been transformed into an intimate hideaway with a sleek designer feel. Elegant flourishes are all around, from the subtle lighting to the local art. Ask for a sea-view room to watch the tide rise and fall in the harbour just outside.

Eating

Esplanade Fish Bar FISH & CHIPS £
(01598-753798; 2 The Esplanade, Lynmouth; mains from £8; noon-8pm) An award-winning chippy set a few steps from the rough-sand beach.

★Ancient Mariner PUB FOOD ££
(☎01598-752238; www.bathhotellynmouth.co.uk; The Harbour, Lynmouth; mains £12-19; ⏲10-11.30am, noon-4pm & 5.30-9pm; 📶) The Mariner brings a burst of shipwreck chic to Lynmouth, thanks to a copper bar top, curved ship's decking, covered outdoor seating and a figurehead that isn't entirely clothed. Drink it all in while tucking into a stacked-high Mariner Burger, complete with Exmoor ale and black-treacle-braised brisket, onion jam and blue-cheese mousse.

Vanilla Pod BISTRO ££
(☎01598-753706; www.thevanillapodlynton.co.uk; 10 Queen St, Lynton; snacks from £5, mains £13-18; ⏲10am-4pm & 6-9pm, closed Feb; 📶) They've got all meal times covered here: it might be bacon butties for breakfast, mezze for lunch or grilled sea bass for supper. Plus afternoon cream teas.

ℹ Getting There & Away

Bus 309/310 Runs year-round from Barnstaple via Parracombe to Lynton and Lynmouth (£3.60, one hour, hourly Monday to Saturday).

Bus 300 A seasonal, vintage (1950s) bus that shuttles between Minehead and Lynmouth (£10, 55 minutes), via Porlock (£6, 15 minutes). Services run twice daily Monday to Friday, from mid-July to early September only.

AT A GLANCE

POPULATION
3 million

BIGGEST CITY
Southampton: 236,882

BEST BEACH
Chesil Beach (p291)

BEST CHALK FIGURE
Cerne Giant (p287)

BEST HILL FORT
Maiden Castle (p288)

WHEN TO GO

Apr & May
Campsites, B&Bs and beachside cafes reopen ahead of summer crowds.

Jun–Aug
School holidays bring busier beaches and attractions – and higher accommodation costs.

Sep & Oct
Quieter and still warm – an ideal time to hike in Dorset, the New Forest and the Isle of Wight.

Beach near Durdle Door (p286)
OCTUS_PHOTOGRAPHY/SHUTTERSTOCK ©

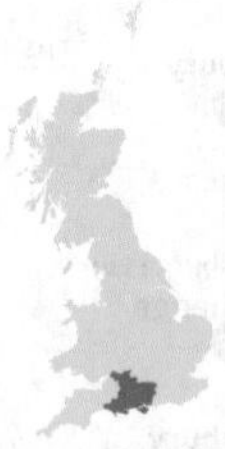

Hampshire, Wiltshire & Dorset

For holidays amid the best of ancient England, head to three counties with a checklist of charms. Wiltshire offers mighty, mysterious Stonehenge, plus – in lesser-known Avebury – the largest stone circle in the world. Dorset tempts you to swim in picturesque coves before sipping cider beside thatched pubs. The Jurassic Coast sees you foraging for fossils and discovering wave-carved sea stacks and bays. On the Isle of Wight, chalky white cliffs frame campsites dotted with vintage camper vans. Portsmouth excels at maritime history, the New Forest delivers tranquil woods, and everywhere hilltop castles litter landscapes studded with stately homes. Bewitching and engaging, these three counties offer endless delights to explore.

INCLUDES

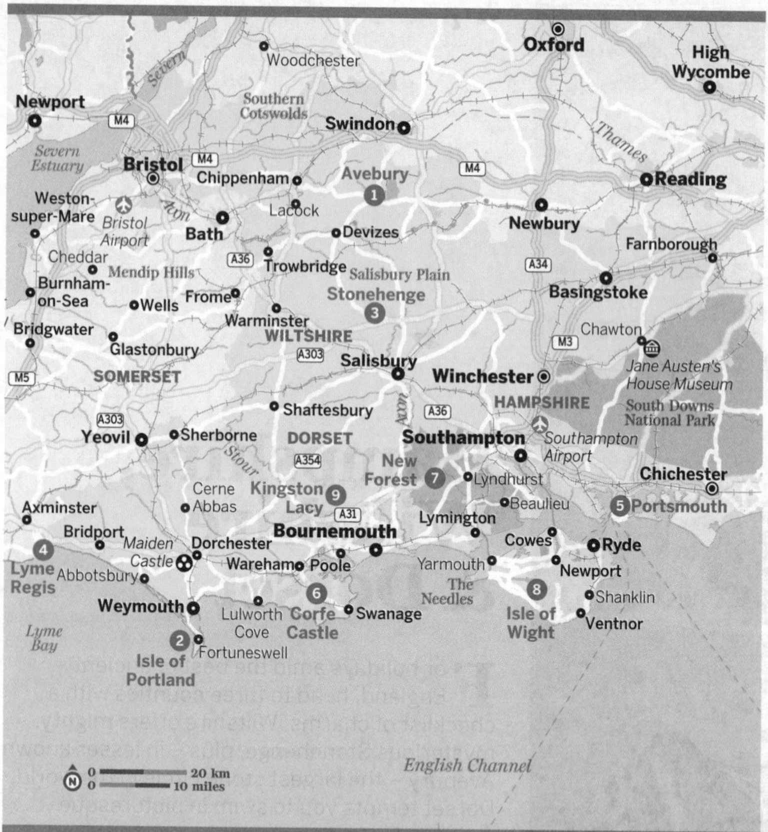

Hampshire, Wiltshire & Dorset Highlights

1 Avebury (p301) Wandering around the largest stone circle in the world.

2 Portland (p290) Discovering world-class statues carved into the rock at Tout Quarry.

3 Stonehenge (p298) Embarking on a magical dawn walk inside the massive sarsen ring.

4 Lyme Regis (p292) Foraging for fossils that pop out from crumbling cliffs.

5 Portsmouth Historic Dockyard (p274) Staring at the ancient timbers of Henry VIII's salvaged warship.

6 Corfe Castle (p285) Roaming the towering, shattered ruins of a mighty fortress.

7 New Forest (p274) Spotting deer and wild ponies as you cycle amid woods.

8 Isle of Wight (p278) Exploring a fortress set on the chalk cliffs of a holiday isle.

9 Kingston Lacy (p286) Revelling in the ornate interiors of Dorset's finest stately home.

Activities

Walking

Connecting Poole in Dorset with Minehead in Somerset, the legendary **South West Coast Path** (www.southwestcoastpath.org.uk) stretches for 630 miles around the end of England. The Dorset section includes the World Heritage Site Jurassic Coast – a 95-mile strip of shore where rock formations, beaches and cliffs span 185 million years of geology.

On the Isle of Wight, a testing 67-mile coast path encircles a network of rural and family-friendly trails. The New Forest

National Park offers gentle, picturesque walking along hundreds of miles of paths through heathland and ancient woods.

Other hiking highlights are Wiltshire's 87-mile **Ridgeway National Trail** (www.nationaltrail.co.uk/ridgeway), which starts near Avebury and winds through chalk downland and the wooded Chiltern hills.

Cycling

The New Forest has more than 140 miles of car-free trails that snake through wildlife-rich heaths and woods. Routes range from short, family-friendly rides to 20-mile jaunts.

Just offshore, the Isle of Wight boasts 200 miles of bike-friendly trails and a hilly, but hugely popular 65-mile **Round Island Route**.

Launched in 2020, the 220-mile, circular **King Alfred's Way** connects four national trails. It starts in Winchester and takes in Salisbury, Stonehenge and Avebury.

Mountain-biking highlights include the largely off-road **South Downs Way**, which traces a chalk ridge for 100 miles from Winchester to Eastbourne on the coast.

Good information sources are **Sustrans** (www.sustrans.org.uk) and local tourist offices.

Watersports

World-class sailing hubs include the vast, 890-hectare Portland Harbour near Weymouth, and the yachting havens of the Isle of Wight and Poole. Stand-up paddleboarding (SUP) and sit-on-top kayaks can be hired out by the hour in sheltered coastal spots. Firms offering windsurfing lessons, coasteering and guided sea-kayaking tours pepper the coasts.

Weymouth and Portland offer top-class diving, with a wide range of depths, environments and wrecks. Local firms hire out gear and run dive trips.

Climbing

Dorset draws climbers with its creamy white coastal crags. The Isle of Portland has a wealth of prime limestone sport routes for all grades, plus some bouldering and deep-water solo options.

Getting There & Around

BUS

The region's bus links are good. As ever in England, connections reduce and service frequency falls the further you go from main urban areas.

National Express (www.nationalexpress.com) Often provides the quickest bus link between cities and larger towns.

First (www.firstgroup.com) Key provider in Dorset and Portsmouth.

More (www.wdbus.co.uk) Useful service across Wiltshire and Dorset and into the New Forest. Day tickets (adult/child £9/6) for the biggest zone (ABC) are good value. An unlimited weekend ticket costs £16.

Stagecoach (www.stagecoachbus.com) Key bus provider in Hampshire.

PlusBus (www.plusbus.info) Adds local bus travel to your train ticket (£2 to £4 per day) in towns including Portsmouth, Salisbury and Weymouth. Buy tickets at train stations.

CAR & MOTORCYCLE

Routes range from motorways in the east, via A roads and busy streets, to winding country lanes. In the New Forest some are unfenced – prepare for animals on the roads.

Some of the coastal routes, especially in Dorset and on the isles of Wight and Portland, offer spectacular views.

TRAIN

South Western Railway (www.southwesternrailway.com) is the main operator. It runs trains from London and the southeast to destinations including Winchester, Portsmouth, Southampton, Salisbury and Weymouth. It also provides services to the New Forest, and links the region with Exeter and Bristol.

The Freedom of the South West Rover pass takes in much of the region. It offers three days of train travel in seven days (adult/child £106/53) or eight days travel in 15 days (£148/74). Journeys are unlimited in an area west of, and including, Portsmouth, Salisbury, Bath and Bristol.

HAMPSHIRE

Hampshire's history is regal and rich. Kings Alfred the Great, Knut and William the Conqueror all based their reigns in its ancient cathedral city of Winchester, whose jumble of historic buildings sits in the centre of undulating chalk downs. The county's coast is awash with heritage, too – in rejuvenated Portsmouth you can clamber aboard the pride of Nelson's navy, HMS *Victory,* and wonder at the *Mary Rose* (Henry VIII's flagship), before wandering wharfs buzzing with restaurants, shops and bars. Hampshire's southwestern corner claims the open heath and woods of the New Forest National Park.

Winchester

☎01962 / POP 116,600

Calm, collegiate Winchester is a mellow must-see. The past still echoes strongly around the flint-flecked walls of this ancient cathedral city. It was the capital of Saxon kings and a power base of bishops, and its statues and sights evoke two of England's mightiest myth makers: Alfred the Great and King Arthur (he of the round table). Winchester's architecture is exquisite, from the handsome Elizabethan and Regency buildings in the narrow streets to the wondrous cathedral at its core, while its river valley location means there are charming waterside trails to explore.

Sights

Check whether tours of prestigious **Winchester College** (☎01962-621209; www.winchestercollege.org; College St), suspended in 2020, have resumed.

★Winchester Cathedral — CATHEDRAL

(☎01962-857200; www.winchester-cathedral.org.uk; The Close; adult/child £10/free; ⏲10am-4pm) One of southern England's most awe-inspiring buildings, 11th-century Winchester Cathedral boasts a fine Gothic facade, one of the longest medieval naves in Europe (164m) and a fascinating jumble of features from all eras. Other highlights include the intricately carved medieval choir stalls, which sport everything from mythical beasts to a mischievous green man. Look out too for Jane Austen's grave (near the entrance) – there's a brass plaque and a window commemorating the celebrated writer alongside.

Today's cathedral sits beside foundations that mark Winchester's original 7th-century minster church. The cathedral was begun in 1070 and completed in 1093, and was subsequently entrusted with the bones of its patron saint, St Swithin (Bishop of Winchester from 852 to 862). He is best known for the proverb stating that if it rains on St Swithin's Day (15 July), it will rain for a further 40 days and 40 nights.

Soggy ground and poor construction spelled disaster for the early church. The original tower collapsed in 1107 and major restructuring continued until the mid-15th century. Look out for the monument at the far end of the building to diver William Walker, who saved the cathedral from collapse by delving repeatedly into its waterlogged underbelly from 1906 to 1912 to bolster rotting wooden foundations with vast quantities of concrete and brick.

Distancing regulations at the time of research may affect what you can see and do. Check the cathedral website for details of whether the **Winchester Bible** is on display. As the biggest, brightest and best-surviving 12th-century English Bible, the dazzling, four-volume tome has vivid illuminated pages. It was commissioned in 1160, possibly by the grandson of William the Conqueror. If the crypt is open it offers views of *Sound II*, an enigmatic life-size depiction of a contemplative man by Anthony Gormley.

If the Tower and Roof Tours (£6.50) are running they'll lead through narrow stairwells, up 213 steps, across an interior gallery high above the nave, through the bell chamber and out onto the roof. When operating, the highly informative, one-hour Cathedral Body Tours and the atmospheric Crypt Tours are included in the admission price.

Regular services include those on Sunday at 10am and Wednesday at noon.

The cathedral's tree-fringed lawns make for tranquil spots to take time out, especially on the quieter south side beyond the cloisters.

★Wolvesey Castle — CASTLE

(EH; ☎0370 333 1181; www.english-heritage.org.uk; College St; ⏲10am-5pm Apr-Oct, to 4pm Sat & Sun Nov-Mar) FREE The fantastical, crumbling remains of early-12th-century Wolvesey Castle huddle in the protective embrace of the city's walls. Completed by Henry de Blois, it served as the Bishop of Winchester's residence throughout the medieval era, with Queen Mary I and Philip II of Spain celebrating their wedding feast here in 1554.

Round Table & Great Hall — HISTORIC BUILDING

(☎01962-846476; www.hants.gov.uk/greathall; Castle Ave; adult/child £3/free; ⏲10am-5pm) Winchester's cavernous Great Hall is the only part of 11th-century Winchester Castle that Oliver Cromwell spared from destruction. Crowning the wall like a giant-sized dartboard of green and cream spokes is what centuries of mythology have dubbed King Arthur's Round Table. It's actually a 700-year-old copy, but is fascinating nonetheless. It's thought to have been constructed in the late 13th century and then painted in the reign of Henry VIII (King Arthur's image is unsurprisingly reminiscent of Henry's youthful face).

Winchester

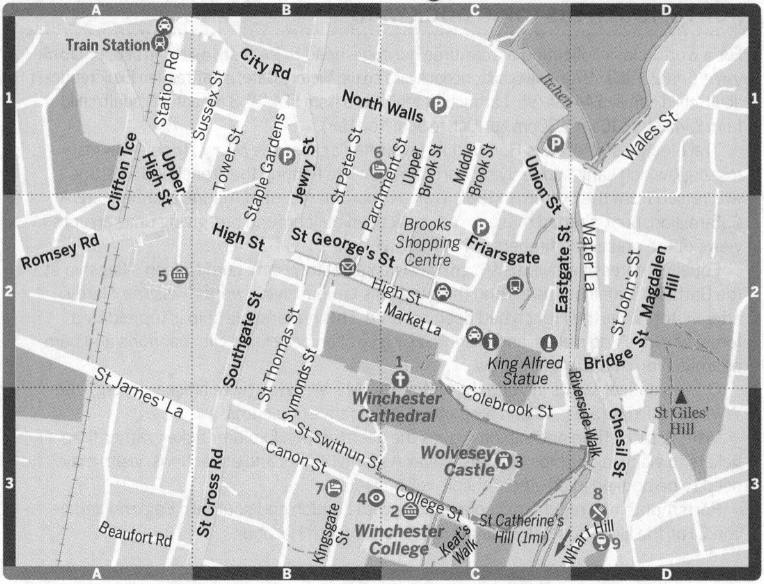

Winchester

Top Sights
1 Winchester Cathedral C2
2 Winchester College C3
3 Wolvesey Castle C3

Sights
4 Jane Austen's House B3
5 Round Table & Great Hall A2

Sleeping
6 16a B1
7 Wykeham Arms B3

Eating
8 Black Rat D3

Drinking & Nightlife
9 Black Boy D3

Activities

Winchester's tempting walks include the 1-mile **Keats' Walk** through the water meadows to the Hospital of St Cross. Its beauty is said to have prompted the poet to pen the ode *To Autumn;* pick up the trail near Wolvesey Castle. Alternatively, head down Wharf Hill, through the water meadows to St Catherine's Hill (1 mile), or take the tranquil **Riverside Walk** from Wolvesey Castle along the River Itchen's banks to High St.

Sleeping

★16a B&B £££

(☎07730 510663; www.16a-winchester.co.uk; 16a Parchment St; r £145-185; 📶) The word 'boutique' gets bandied around freely, but here it fits. The sumptuous conversion of this old dance hall sees an antique piano and honesty bar frame a wood-burning stove. Gorgeous bedrooms feature exposed brick, lofty ceilings, vast beds and baths on the mezzanines with views of the stars.

★Wykeham Arms INN £££

(☎01962-853834; www.wykehamarmswinchester.co.uk; 75 Kingsgate St; s £84, d £144-194; P📶) At 250-odd years of age, the Wykeham bursts with history – it used to be a brothel and also put Nelson up for a night (some say the events coincided). Creaking stairs lead to plush bedrooms that manage to be both deeply established and on-trend – sleigh beds meet jazzy fabrics, oak dressers sport stylish lights. Simply smashing.

Eating & Drinking

★Black Rat MODERN BRITISH £££

(☎01962-844465; www.theblackrat.co.uk; 88 Chesil St; mains £18-29; ⏱6-9.15pm Wed-Sun, noon-2.15pm Sat & Sun) The aromas are irresistible, the food frankly fabulous, the

DON'T MISS

PORTSMOUTH HISTORIC DOCKYARD

For a world-class collection of maritime heritage, head to **Portsmouth Historic Dockyard** (☎023-9283 9766; www.historicdockyard.co.uk; Victory Gate; all-attraction Explorer ticket adult/child/family £44/34/95, 1 attraction adult/child from £24/19, 3 attractions adult/child from £34/24; ⏲10am-5.30pm Apr-Oct, to 5pm Nov-Mar).

The blockbuster draw is Henry VIII's favourite flagship, the **Mary Rose** (www.maryrose.org), which sank suddenly off Portsmouth while fighting the French in 1545. She was raised from the bottom in 1982 in an extraordinary feat of marine archaeology. A £35-million, boat-shaped museum has now been built around her, giving uninterrupted views of the preserved timbers of her massive hull.

Equally impressive is **HMS Victory** (www.hms-victory.com), Lord Nelson's flagship at the Battle of Trafalgar (1805) and the site of his famous dying words 'Kiss me, Hardy', after victory over the French had been secured. This remarkable ship is topped by a forest of ropes and masts, and weighted by a swollen belly filled with cannons and paraphernalia for an 850-strong crew.

Other nautical sights include the Victorian **HMS Warrior** (www.hmswarrior.org), the WWI warship **HMS M.33** and a wealth of imaginative museums.

Visiting more than one exhibit makes the all-attraction Explorer ticker, rather than tickets to visit single ships, the best value. As for all sights and attractions, visits may need to be booked in advance; check well ahead.

Portsmouth has regular rail connections with London and southern England and beyond. For the Historic Dockyard, get off at Portsmouth Harbour.

cooking highly technical and the ingredients dare to surprise – expect chalk stream trout to be joined by wasabi and beetroot ice cream, and meats to be smoked with hay. That'll be why the Black Rat deserves its Michelin star.

The decor is vaguely bohemian, the garden features heated huts and the extensive drinks menu lists 45 gins.

Black Boy PUB
(☎01962-861754; www.theblackboypub.com; 1 Wharf Hill; ⏲noon-2.30pm & 5-11pm Mon-Fri, noon-midnight Sat, noon-10.30pm Sun) Two open fires, a random array of dented antiques, a clutch of draught ciders and five real ales make this a legendary local. There's also a spacious, heated, sheltered garden out back.

ℹ Information

Tourist Office (☎01962-840500; www.visitwinchester.co.uk; Guildhall, High St) Set in Winchester's Victorian Guildhall – check it's reopened to visitors.

ℹ Getting There & Away

Winchester is 65 miles west of London. Trains leave half-hourly to hourly for London Waterloo (£19, 1¼ hours) and hourly for Portsmouth (£13, one hour).

ℹ Getting Around

Bicycle Bikes can be hired from **Bespoke Biking** (www.bespokebiking.com; 4 Middle Brook St; per half-/full day £15/25; ⏲9am-5pm Mon-Sat, 10am-4pm Sun). It's best to book.

Car Park & Ride car parks (per day £3) are signed off junctions 10 and 11 of the M3. Services run roughly from 6.30am to 6.30pm, Monday to Saturday.

Taxi There are taxi ranks on the High St, and outside the train station and tourist office, or call **Wintax** (☎01962-250250; www.wintaxcars.com).

New Forest

With typical, accidental, English irony the New Forest is anything but new – it was first proclaimed a royal hunting preserve in 1079. It's also not much of a forest, being mostly heathland ('forest' is from the Old French for 'hunting ground'). Designated a national park in 2005, the forest's combined charms make it a joy to explore. Wild ponies mooch around pretty scrubland, deer flicker in the distance and rare birds flit among the foliage. Genteel villages dot the landscape, connected by a web of walking and cycling trails.

Activities

★New Forest Activities ADVENTURE SPORTS
(☎01590-612377; www.newforestactivities.co.uk; High St, Beaulieu) Runs a wide range of sessions including canoeing (adult/child per 90 minutes from £29/16), kayaking (per two hours from £40/37) and archery (adult/child per 90 minutes £24/13).

Walking

The forest is gentle, largely level hiking territory. Ordnance Survey (OS) produces a detailed 1:25,000 Explorer map (New Forest; *OL22*, £9); *Pathfinder New Forest Short Walks* (£8) features 20 circular day hikes of 2 to 6 miles.

The New Forest Centre (p276) in Lyndhurst stocks maps and guides.

Check whether Forestry England's programme of guided **walks** (☎0300 068 0400; www.forestry.gov.uk/newforestevents), suspended in 2020, have resumed.

Cycling

The New Forest makes for superb cycling, with 100 miles of routes linking the main villages and the key railway station at Brockenhurst. *The New Forest By Bike* map (£4.50) features 12 routes ranging from 8 to 32 miles. The *New Forest Cycling Guide* (£4) features six day-cycle routes of between 4 and 22 miles on a 1:25,000 OS map. Maps and guides can be bought from an information point in Lyndhurst's New Forest Centre.

To rent bikes, you'll need to pay a deposit (usually £20 to £25) and provide identification.

AA Bike Hire CYCLING
(☎02380-283349; www.aabikehirenewforest.co.uk; Fernglen, Gosport Lane, Lyndhurst; per day adult/child £10/5; ⏲9am-5.30pm Apr-Oct) Based in Lyndhurst's main car park.

Woods Cyclery CYCLING
(New Forest Cycle Hire; ☎02380-282028; www.thewoodscyclery.co.uk; 56 High St, Lyndhurst; per day adult/child £20/10; ⏲9am-5pm Tue-Sun) Also rents out electric bikes and kids' bike seats.

Cyclexperience CYCLING
(New Forest Cyclehire; ☎01590-624808; www.cyclex.co.uk; Train Station, Brockenhurst; per day adult/child from £18.50/9; ⏲10am-5pm) Based in a vintage railway carriage. They also deliver bikes across the national park and rent out electric bikes (per half-day £30 to £35).

Horse Riding

Social distancing measures at the time of research may mean stables can only take experienced riders, and that you need to bring your own riding hat. Expect to pay from £33 per hour. Check online for updates.

Local stables include **Arniss Equestrian Centre** (☎01425-654114; www.arnissequestrian.co.uk; Godshill, Fordingbridge) and **Burley Villa** (Western Riding; ☎01425-610278; www.burleyvilla.co.uk; Bashley Common Rd, near New Milton).

Sleeping

Campers can ask whether **Forestry England** (www.campingintheforest.co.uk) has reopened its 10 or so relatively rural New Forest sites.

Information

New Forest (www.thenewforest.co.uk) The area's official visitor website.

New Forest Centre (☎01425-880020; www.thenewforest.co.uk; main car park, Lyndhurst; ⏲10.30am-4.30pm) Has a Visitor Information Point stocked with maps, leaflets and books.

Getting There & Around

BUS

National Express (www.nationalexpress.com) Buses stop at Ringwood and Southampton.

Bus 6 (hourly Monday to Saturday, five on Sunday) Runs from Southampton to Lyndhurst (£5, 40 minutes), Brockenhurst (£6.70, 50 minutes) and Lymington (£6.70, 1¼ hours).

Bus X1/X2 Links Bournemouth with Lymington (£6.50, 1½ hours, half-hourly Monday to Saturday, four on Sunday).

New Forest Tour (☎01202-338420; www.thenewforesttour.info; per 1/2/5 days adult £17/23/34, child £9/11/16; ⏲9am-6pm early Jul-Aug) Three connecting routes of hop-on, hop-off buses, stopping at Lyndhurst's main car park, Brockenhurst train station, Lymington, Ringwood, Beaulieu and Exbury.

TRAIN

Two trains an hour run to Brockenhurst from London Waterloo (£26, two hours) via Winchester (£16, 30 minutes) and on to Bournemouth (£8, 20 minutes).

Local trains shuttle twice an hour between Brockenhurst and Lymington (£4, 11 minutes).

Lyndhurst & Brockenhurst

The quaint country villages of Lyndhurst and Brockenhurst are separated by just 4 miles. Their picturesque accommodation and superb eating options ensure they're atmospheric bases from which to explore the New Forest.

Sights

New Forest Centre MUSEUM
(02380-283444; www.newforestcentre.org.uk; main car park, Lyndhurst; 10.30am-4.30pm;) FREE Features a local labourer's cottage (complete with socks drying beside the fire), potato dibbles and a cider press. The mini-film makes for an accessible introduction to the park – listen, too, for recordings of the autumn pony sales, which take place after the annual drifts (round-ups).

The centre also houses a Visitor Information Point, with leaflets, maps and books.

Beaulieu HISTORIC BUILDING
(01590-612345; www.beaulieu.co.uk; adult/child £25/10; 10am-5pm) Petrolheads, historians and ghost-hunters gravitate to Beaulieu (*bew*-lee) – a vintage car museum, stately home and tourist complex centred on a 13th-century Cistercian monastery. Motor-maniacs will be in raptures at Lord Montague's **National Motor Museum**. Tickets are valid for a year; Beaulieu is served by the New Forest Tour (p275).

Sleeping & Eating

★Pig BOUTIQUE HOTEL £££
(01590-622354; www.thepighotel.com/brockenhurst; Beaulieu Rd, Brockenhurst; r £189-350; P) One of the New Forest's classiest hotels remains an utter delight: log baskets, croquet mallets and ranks of guest gumboots give things a country-house air; espresso machines and mini-larders lend bedrooms a luxury touch. The effortless elegance makes it feel like you've just dropped by a friend's (very stylish) rural retreat.

The Pig's 25-mile-radius menus change hourly depending on what's been found foraging or in the hotel's kitchen garden. Look out for lovage and potato soup, chalk stream trout and Beaulieu venison. Or plump for veg- and meat-topped flat breads (£13) from the wood-fired oven. Food (mains £15 to £21) is served between noon and 9.30pm.

Daisybank Cottage B&B £££
(01590-622086; www.bedandbreakfast-newforest.co.uk; Sway Rd, Brockenhurst; s £130-140, d £140-150; P) The seven gorgeous themed bedrooms here are mini pamper palaces. Enjoy aromatic smellies in gleaming bathrooms, stylish luxurious furnishings and lots of little extras: handmade chocolates, smartphone docks, digital radios, and breakfasts, packed with New Forest produce, delivered to your room.

Snakecatcher PUB ££
(01590-622348; www.thesnakecatcher.co.uk; Lyndhurst Rd, Brockenhurst; mains £9-15; noon-11pm Mon-Wed, to 11.30pm Thu-Sat, to 10.30pm Sun;) In this handsome red-brick pub near Brockenhurst station you'll find local real ales, craft beers, ciders and a wide range of tasty burgers. Eat inside or go alfresco in the vast astroturfed garden beside the pop-up bar.

Getting There & Away

Bus 6 Shuttles between Lyndhurst and Lymington (£4.40, hourly Monday to Saturday, five on Sunday), via Brockenhurst; as does the New Forest Tour (p275).

Trains Run twice an hour between Brockenhurst and Lymington (£4, 11 minutes).

Buckler's Hard

For such a tiny place, this picturesque huddle of 18th-century cottages, near the mouth of the River Beaulieu, has a big history. It started in 1722, when a duke of Montague built a port to finance a Caribbean expedition. His dream faltered, but when war with France came, this embryonic village and sheltered gravel waterfront became a secret boatyard where several of Nelson's triumphant Battle of Trafalgar warships were built. In the 20th century it played its part in the preparations for the D-Day landings.

Sights

Buckler's Hard Story MUSEUM
(01590-616203; www.bucklershard.co.uk; adult/child £7.50/5.20; 10am-5pm Apr-Sep, to 4pm Oct-Mar) The hamlet's fascinating Maritime Museum and heritage centre chart the inlet's shipbuilding history and role in WWII, and feature immaculately preserved 18th-century workshops and labourers' cottages.

Sleeping & Eating

★Master Builder's House HOTEL £££
(01590-616253; www.hillbrookehotels.co.uk; d £135-180; P) In this beautifully restored 18th-century hotel, room styles range from

stately to crisp with hints of nauticalia. Soft lighting, burnished trunks and plush fabrics abound.

Your dining options range from classy restaurant fare to family-friendly grub in the cool hotel **bar** (mains £14-27; ⌚noon-9pm).

Lymington

☎01590 / POP 15,400

Yachting haven, New Forest base and jumping-off point to the Isle of Wight – the appealing Georgian harbour town of Lymington has several strings to its tourism bow. This former smuggler's port offers nautical shops, prime eating and sleeping spots and, in **Quay St**, an utterly quaint cobbled lane.

Activities

Puffin Cruises BOATING

(☎07850 947618; www.puffincruiseslymington.com; Lymington Quay; adult/child from £8.50/4.50; ⌚10am-4pm Apr-Oct) Runs 30-minute cruises on the *Puffin Billi* that meander down the winding Lymington River to saltmarshes packed with birds. Smaller swashbucklers love the half-hour pirate-themed *Black Puffin* trips that set off to search for lost treasure.

Sleeping

★**Teddy's Farm** CAMPGROUND £

(Battramsley Farm; ☎07815 189767; www.teddysfarm.co.uk; Shirley Holms Rd, Boldre; campsite per pitch £24, bell tent per 2 nights £350; ⌚mid-Jul–early Sep) The affable Teddy presides over a chilled-out site where undulating fields are home to firepits for hire, compost loos and alfresco showers. The glamping field has four-person, pre-pitched bell tents, complete with bunting and tealight chandeliers. It's 2 miles north of Lymington.

Mill at Gordleton HOTEL ££

(☎01590-682219; www.themillatgordleton.co.uk; Silver St, Hordle; d £105-150, ste £180-299; P 🛜) Step inside here and know, instantly, you're going to be looked after beautifully. Velvet and gingham dot the gorgeous rooms (each one comes with a sweet soft toy duck), while the garden is a magical mix of rushing water, fairy lights and modern sculpture. The Mill is 4 miles west of Lymington.

Stanwell House BOUTIQUE HOTEL £££

(☎01590-677123; www.stanwellhouse.com; 14 High St; d £145, ste £255-295; @🛜🐾) There are boutique tweaks everywhere at Stanwell. Swish Georgian rooms manage to be both period and modern: the four-poster ones sport reproduction furniture and subtle colours, while the suites are simply irresistible – two even have their own roof terrace for sunny days and moonlit nights.

Eating

Deep Blue FISH & CHIPS £

(☎01590-679491; www.deepbluerestaurants.com; 130 High St; fish & chips £10; ⌚11.30am-3pm daily, plus 5-7.30pm Sun-Thu, 5-8pm Fri & Sat) They're often queuing out the door at this classic British chippy, which dishes up sustainable fish, freshly cut chips, mushy peas and pickled eggs. Eat in or take away.

Ship PUB FOOD ££

(☎01590-676903; www.theshiplymington.co.uk; The Quay; mains £12-26; ⌚kitchen noon-10pm Mon-Sat, to 9pm Sun;) A pub for all seasons: knock back summertime drinks on the waterside terrace; in winter, a toasty log burner gets you warm. Well-judged food ranges from plant-based dirty burgers and crispy pizzas to juicy fillet steaks.

★**Elderflower** MODERN BRITISH £££

(☎01590-676908; www.elderflowerrestaurant.co.uk; 5 Quay St; mains £17-37, 4/5/7 courses £50/60/70; ⌚noon-2.30pm & 6.30-9.30pm Wed-Fri, 9.30am-2.30pm & 6.30-10pm Sat, 9.30am-4pm Sun) An Anglo-French feel infuses Elderflower – from the garlic-laced snails to the black treacle cured bacon. Innovative puddings are a real treat – where else can you get a squid-ink doughnut with blackcurrant gel? Ask if the classy takeaway menu, which features oysters, lobster and chateaubriand, is still running.

Getting There & Away

Lymington has two train stations: Lymington Town and Lymington Pier. Isle of Wight ferries connect with Lymington Pier. Trains run to Southampton (£11, 50 minutes), with a change at Brockenhurst, twice an hour.

Wightlink Ferries (☎0333 999 7333; www.wightlink.co.uk) has car and passenger ferries that run hourly to Yarmouth on the Isle of Wight (40 minutes). An adult/child foot-passenger single costs £13.60/6.80; day returns cost £17.60/8.80. Summer-time fares for a car and two passengers start at around £67 for a short-break return.

Isle of Wight

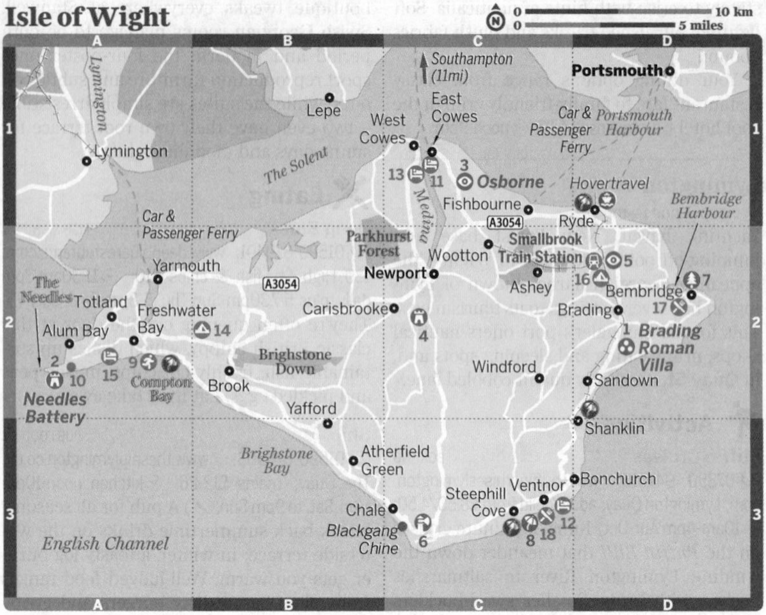

Isle of Wight

Top Sights

1 Brading Roman Villa ... D2
2 Needles Battery ... A2
3 Osborne ... C1

Sights

4 Carisbrooke Castle ... C2
5 Isle of Wight Steam Railway ... D2
6 St Catherine's Oratory ... C3
7 St Helens Duver ... D2
8 Steephill Cove ... C3

Activities, Courses & Tours

9 Isle of Wight Adventure Activities ... A2
10 Needles Pleasure Cruises ... A2

Sleeping

11 Fountain ... C1
Hambrough ... (see 12)
12 Harbour View ... C3
13 onefiftycowes ... C1
14 Tom's Eco Lodge ... B2
15 Totland Bay YHA ... A2
16 Vintage Vacations ... D2

Eating

17 Best Dressed Crab ... D2
Crab Shed ... (see 8)
18 Spyglass Inn ... C3

ISLE OF WIGHT

These days the Isle of Wight has the air of a holiday destination busy reinventing itself. For decades this slab of rock anchored off Portsmouth was a magnet for vacationing families, and it still has seaside kitsch by the bucket and spade. But now the proms and amusement arcades are framed by pockets of cool. Just-caught seafood is served in kooky fishers' cafes, and glamorous camping rules – here sites are dotted with yurts and vintage camper vans. Yet still the isle's principal appeal remains: a mild climate, myriad outdoorsy activities and a 67-mile shore lined with beaches, dramatic white cliffs and tranquil sand dunes.

Activities

Cycling

With 200 miles of cycle routes, the Isle of Wight makes pedal pushers smile. The island's official visitor website (www.visitisleofwight.co.uk) lists suggested trips (complete with maps), ranging from family-friendly tootles along former railway lines to the 65-mile **Round the Island Cycle Route**.

Bike rentals start at around £18/65 per day/week. Many firms deliver and collect on orders over £30.

The IW Cycle Festival is usually held in late August; see online for updates.

Walking

This is one of the best spots in southern England for rambling, with 500 miles of well-marked walking paths, including 67 miles of coastal routes.

Look on the isle's visitor website to see if the walking festival, held over two weeks in May or October, is running.

Watersports

Watersports are serious business on the Isle of Wight. Cowes is the sailing centre; surfers, windsurfers and kitesurfers flock to the southwest, especially around Compton Bay, while powerboats run trips out to the Needles rocks.

Isle of Wight Adventure Activities ADVENTURE SPORTS
(www.adventureactivitiesisleofwight.co.uk; Gate La, Freshwater) Delivers two-hour activity sessions, including kayaking (adult/child £40/25) and coasteering (adult/child £45/30).

Festivals

Isle of Wight Festival MUSIC
(www.isleofwightfestival.com; mid-Jun) The isle's festival tradition kicked off in 1968, when an estimated 200,000 hippies came to see The Doors, The Who, Joni Mitchell and rock icon Jimi Hendrix's last performance. Generations on, its gatherings are still some of England's top musical events. The festival was cancelled in 2020 because of Covid-19, but will hopefully be back in 2021.

Cowes Week SAILING
(www.aamcowesweek.co.uk; early Aug) Cowes Week, first held in 1826, is one of the biggest and longest-running sailing regattas in the world. It's due to resume in 2021.

Information

www.visitisleofwight.co.uk The island's official visitor website.

Information Points Collections of leaflets and maps include those at Yarmouth Harbour Office, Newport bus station and the bus staton on Ryde Esplanade.

Getting There & Away

Hovertravel (01983-717717; www.hovertravel.co.uk; Quay Rd, Ryde; day-return adult/child £24/12) Shuttles foot passengers between Southsea (a Portsmouth suburb) and Ryde, half-hourly to hourly.

Red Funnel (02380-248500; www.redfunnel.co.uk) Runs car-and-passenger ferries between Southampton and East Cowes (same-day return adult/child £19/9.50, from £60 with car, 60 minutes, hourly), and high-speed passenger ferries between Southampton and West Cowes (same-day return adult/child £27.20/13.60, 25 minutes, one to two per hour).

Wightlink Ferries (0333 999 7333; www.wightlink.co.uk) Operates passenger ferries at least every hour from Portsmouth to Ryde (day-return adult/child £20.60/10.30, single adult/child £16.10/8.05, 22 minutes). It also runs hourly car-and-passenger ferries from Portsmouth to Fishbourne (45 minutes) and from Lymington to Yarmouth (40 minutes). For both, an adult/child foot-passenger single is £13.60/6.80; day returns cost £17.60/8.80. Car fares start at around £67 for a short-break return.

Getting Around

BUS

Southern Vectis (www.islandbuses.info) runs buses between the eastern towns roughly every 30 minutes. Regular services to the remoter southwest, especially between Blackgang Chine and Brook, are less frequent.

Check whether the **Island Coaster** service, suspended in 2020, has resumed. Between April and September it normally runs along the southern shore from Ryde in the east to Yarmouth in the west.

CAR

Enterprise (01983-559357; www.enterprise.co.uk; 50 Crocker St, Newport; per day from £25) Hires out cars from its offices in the island's capital, Newport.

TRAIN

South Western Railway (www.southwesternrailway.com) runs Island Line trains twice hourly from Ryde to Shanklin (same-day return £4.80, 25 minutes), via Smallbrook Junction, Brading and Sandown.

Cowes

01983 / POP 14,200

Pack your yachting cap – the hilly Georgian harbour town of Cowes is famous for the Cowes Week annual yachting regatta. Fibreglass playthings and vintage sailing boats line Cowes' waterfronts, which are lopped

CAR FERRY COSTS

The cost of car ferries to the Isle of Wight can vary enormously. Save by booking ahead, asking about special offers and travelling off-peak (midweek and later in the day). Long stays tend to be cheaper and some deals include admission to island attractions. Booking online can mean paying around £20 less.

into East and West Cowes by the picturesque River Medina.

The island's capital, Newport, is 5 miles south.

Sights

★Osborne HISTORIC SITE
(EH; ☎0370 333 1181; www.english-heritage.org.uk; York Ave, East Cowes; adult/child £19/11.40; ⏲10am-5pm Apr-Oct, to 4pm Sat & Sun Nov-Mar; P) Lemon-frosted and Italianate, Osborne House is pure Victorian pomp. Built in the 1840s at the behest of Queen Victoria, the monarch grieved here for many years after her husband's death. Extravagant rooms include the opulent Royal Apartments and Durbar Room; other highlights are horse and carriage rides, the Swiss Cottage – where the royal ankle-biters would play – and the stroll down Rhododendron Walk to Her Majesty's private beach.

Carisbrooke Castle CASTLE
(EH; ☎01983-522107; www.english-heritage.org.uk; Castle Hill, Newport; adult/child £11.30/6.80; ⏲10am-5pm Apr-Oct, 10am-4pm Sat & Sun Nov-Mar; P) Charles I was imprisoned here before his execution in 1649. Today you can clamber the sturdy ramparts and stroll around the bowling green the doomed monarch used.

Sleeping

★onefiftycowes B&B ££
(☎07795 296399; www.onefiftycowes.co.uk; 150 Park Rd, West Cowes; s £70-75, d £90-110; P 📶) All the trappings of a luxury hotel, all the individuality of a B&B – at onefiftycowes, wicker chairs sit beside stand-alone sinks; feature fireplaces are stacked with sea-smoothed pebbles. The best room is Solent, where a pair of binoculars is waiting to help you gaze at the partial sea views.

Fountain HOTEL ££
(☎01983-292397; www.oldenglishinns.co.uk; High St, West Cowes; s £55-80, d 77-115; 📶) Georgian-repro style rules at this appealing harbourside inn, where mock-flock wallpaper and old, wooden furniture define comfy rooms; number 21 has slanting ceilings and prime views of the ferry quay. The snug bar and sunny terrace are good places to sample pints and pub-grub classics (mains from £12; food served 11am to 10pm).

Ryde to Bembridge

The nippiest foot-passenger ferries between Wight and Portsmouth alight in Ryde, a workaday but appealing Victorian town rich in the trappings of the British seaside. Next come the cutesy village of Brading, with its fine Roman villa, and photogenic Bembridge Harbour, which is fringed by sandy beaches.

Further south lie the twin resort towns of Sandown and Shanklin, with promenades and hordes of families wielding buckets and spades.

Sights

★Brading Roman Villa RUINS
(☎01983-406223; www.bradingromanvilla.org.uk; Morton Old Rd, Brading; adult/child £9.50/4.75; ⏲hours vary) The exquisitely preserved mosaics here (including a famous cockerel-headed man) make this one of the finest Romano-British sites in the UK. Wooden walkways lead over rubble walls and brightly painted tiles, allowing you to gaze right down onto the ruins below.

St Helens Duver NATURE RESERVE
(NT; ☎01983-741020; www.nationaltrust.org.uk; near St Helens; ⏲24hr; P) At this idyllic sand-and-shingle spit bordering the mouth of the River Yar, trails snake past swathes of sea pink, marram grass and rare clovers. It's signed from the village of St Helens, near Bembridge Harbour.

Isle of Wight Steam Railway HERITAGE RAILWAY
(☎01983-882204; www.iwsteamrailway.co.uk; Smallbrook Junction; adult/child return from £13/6.50; ⏲4-9 trains daily mid-Apr–Sep) Chugs along for the one-hour return journey from Smallbrook Junction to Wootton.

Sleeping & Eating

★ Vintage Vacations CAMPSITE ££
(☎07802 758113; www.vintagevacations.co.uk; Hazelgrove Farm, Ashey Rd; 2-/4-/6-person caravans per week £630/720/780; ⏲Apr-Oct; P) The bevy of 1960s Airstream trailers on this farm is vintage chic personified. The gleaming aluminium shells shelter retro radios and lovingly selected mismatched crockery. Alternatively, opt for a beach-shack retreat, a 1930s scout hut, or the Mission: a late-Victorian tin chapel.

Best Dressed Crab SEAFOOD ££
(☎01983-874758; www.thebestdressedcrabintown.co.uk; Fisherman's Wharf, Bembridge Harbour; mains £9-28; ⏲10am-4pm daily Mar-Dec, Sat & Sun Jan & Feb) Welcome to an idyllic spot to munch your lunch. At this bijou cafe tacked on to a pontoon, the day's crab and lobster harvest is turned into supremely tasty sandwiches, salads and soups. Best eaten at one of the tables perched beside the water as local fishing boats unload their catch.

Ventnor & Steephill Cove

The Victorian town of Ventnor slaloms so steeply down the island's southern coast that it feels more like the south of France. The shops in the town's winding streets are worth browsing, the seafront is worth a stroll, and nearby atmospheric Steephill Cove is well worth a detour.

Sights

Steephill Cove BEACH
(www.steephillcove-isleofwight.co.uk) A 1-mile walk west along the coast path from Ventnor leads to Steephill Cove – a tiny, sandy bay fringed by stone cottages and rickety-looking shacks. Beach finds festoon porches dotted with driftwood furniture and draped with fishing nets; a tiny clapboard lighthouse presides over the scene. It's all studiedly nautical, but still very nice.

Steephill Cove is off-limits to cars but you can park at the nearby Botanical Gardens (£5) and walk down.

St Catherine's Oratory LIGHTHOUSE
(near Niton) FREE Known locally as the Pepperpot, this 34ft, octagonal, 14th-century tower constitutes England's only surviving medieval lighthouse.

Sleeping & Eating

Harbour View GUESTHOUSE ££
(St Augustine Villa; ☎01983-852285; www.harbourviewhotel.co.uk; The Esplanade, Ventnor; s £77-93, d £86-102; P 📶) Country-house collectables dot this Italianate Victorian villa, where wing-backed chairs sit in stately bedrooms and rich red fabrics frame superb sea views. They'll have you watching the sun set from your sofa or the waves roll from your four-poster bed. The window-seated Tower Room has light pouring in from three sides. At the time of research the rates didn't include breakfast; look for updates online.

Hambrough B&B £££
(☎01983-856333; www.thehambrough.com; Hambrough Rd, Ventnor; d £140-230; 📶) What you see from the pick of the rooms at the Hambrough is truly fabulous – the suites have balconies with wrap-around sea views, while you can watch the waves from the bathtub in room 4. The furnishings are smooth and smart, rather than stunning; comfort comes courtesy of mini-fridges, underfloor heating and espresso machines.

Crab Shed CAFE £
(☎01983-855819; www.steephillcove-isleofwight.co.uk; Steephill Cove; snacks from £5; ⏲noon-3pm Apr-Sep) Lobster pots and fishing boats line the slipway outside a shack that's a riot of sea-smoothed spars, cork floats and faded buoys. Irresistible takeaway treats include meaty crab salads, mackerel ciabatta and crumbly crab pasties.

Spyglass Inn PUB FOOD ££
(☎01983-855338; www.thespyglass.com; The Esplanade, Ventnor; mains £10-27; ⏲noon-9pm) When a beachfront pub is this bedecked with pirate paraphernalia, ships' lanterns and lifebelts, you tend to be wary of the meals. No need. The seafood platters and salads here are renowned, especially the grilled, garlic-butter-laced lobster – book these, they tend to sell out. There are lots of wave-side tables at which to down a pint.

West Wight

Rural and remote, Wight's westerly corner is where the island really comes into its own. Sheer white cliffs rear from a surging sea as the stunning coastline peels west to Alum Bay and the most famous chunks of chalk in the region: the **Needles**. These jagged rocks rise, shardlike, out of the sea, like the backbone of a prehistoric sea monster. West Wight is also home to arguably the isle's best beach: sandy, windswept **Compton Bay**.

Sights & Activities

★Needles Battery FORT
(NT; ☎01983-754772; www.nationaltrust.org.uk; The Needles; adult/child £5/2.50; ⏱10am-5.30 mid-Mar–Oct) The Victorian fort complex at Wight's western tip was built in 1862 to prepare for a French invasion that never came. The site went on to serve in two world wars and then became a secret Cold War rocket-testing base. Walk to the battery along the cliffs from Alum Bay (1 mile) or hop on the summer-only, open-top **Needles Breezer tourist bus** (www.islandbuses.info; per 24hr adult/child £10/5; ⏱10am-5pm mid-Mar–Oct) that runs regularly between battery and bay.

Needles Pleasure Cruises BOATING
(☎01983-761587; www.needlespleasurecruises.co.uk; Alum Bay; adult/child £7/4; ⏱10.30am-4.30pm Apr-Oct) Twenty-minute voyages run half-hourly from Alum Bay beach to the towering Needles chalk stacks, providing cracking views of those soaring white cliffs.

Sleeping

Ask if **Totland Bay YHA** (☎03452 602912; www.yha.org.uk; Hirst Hill, Totland Bay; P @ ᯤ) has reopened for individual bookings.

★Tom's Eco Lodge CAMPSITE ££
(☎01983-758729; www.tomsecolodge.com; Tapnell Farm, Yarmouth; 2-person pod per night from £155, 4-person log cabin per 4 nights from £665; P ᯤ) Eco pods, log cabins, safari tents – the full gamut of comfy camping options sit happily on this spacious, sea-view site. They're beautifully decked out with their own showers and loos; some even have log-burning stoves.

DORSET

Holiday hotspot Dorset has one of Britain's best shorelines. It boasts the Jurassic Coast – a World Heritage Site flecked with sea-carved bays, crumbly cliffs and beaches loaded with fossilised souvenirs. Swimming, kayaking and hiking here are memorable. Inland, Thomas Hardy's lyrical landscape serves up vast Iron Age hill forts, rude chalk figures, fairy-tale castles and must-see stately homes. Then there's the Isle of Portland's rugged, bleak appeal and sailing waters that have hosted Olympic events. It's true the county's charms can make some places over-busy in peak season, but if you avoid the honeypots in the height of summer, and seek out the lesser-trod trails, Dorset still delights.

Information

Visit Dorset (www.visit-dorset.com) The county's official tourism website.

Lonely Planet (www.lonelyplanet.com) Destination information, hotel bookings, traveller forum and more.

Getting There & Around

BUS

First (www.firstgroup.com/wessex-dorset-south-somerset) Runs services linking the main towns. A useful route is bus X53, which links Weymouth with Axminster, running along the shore.

More (www.morebus.co.uk) Key bus operator in Bournemouth, Poole and surrounding rural areas.

TRAIN

Cross Country (www.crosscountrytrains.co.uk) Runs regular direct trains from Manchester to Bournemouth (£96, five hours) via Birmingham.

GWR (www.gwr.com) Provides direct services from Bristol, via Bath and Dorchester West, to Weymouth (£21, 2½ hours, at least two daily).

South Western Railway (www.southwesternrailway.com) Links London Waterloo with Weymouth (£35, three hours), via Southampton, Bournemouth, Poole and Dorchester South. Also runs services between Waterloo and Exeter St David's, which call at Sherborne and Gillingham.

Bournemouth

☎01202 / POP 183,490

If one thing has shaped Bournemouth, it's the beach. This glorious, 7-mile strip of soft sand first drew holidaymakers in the Victorian days. More than 150 years later, it's still drawing sun-loving crowds. Sometimes a few too many – when restrictions were first eased immediately after England's 2020 Covid-19 lockdown, the resort became a byword for temporarily overcrowded beaches and gridlocked roads. But Bournemouth is more than just a full-on party town. If you're savvy about avoiding the crowds, you'll find some hip hideaways, fine restaurants and colourful gardens.

Sights

Bournemouth Beach BEACH

Bournemouth's long sandy shore regularly clocks up seaside awards. It stretches from Southbourne in the far east to Alum Chine in the west – an immense promenade backed by some 3000 deckchairs, ornamental gardens, kids' playgrounds, cafes and 200 beach huts. The resort also has two piers: **Bournemouth Pier** and **Boscombe Pier**.

Conscious that in 2020 Bournemouth's beaches were at times too crowded, the local council produced the **BCP Beach Check app**. It allows you to spot and avoid congested areas.

Russell-Cotes MUSEUM

(01202-451858; www.russellcotes.com; East Cliff Promenade; adult/child £7.50/4; 10am-5pm Tue, Wed, Sat & Sun) Ostentation oozes from almost every inch of this arresting structure – a mash-up of Italianate villa and Scottish baronial pile. It was built at the end of the 1800s for Merton and Annie Russell-Cotes as somewhere to showcase the remarkable range of souvenirs gathered on their world travels.

Alum Chine GARDENS

(Mountbatten Rd; 24hr) FREE Bournemouth's 1920s heyday is beautifully evoked at a subtropical enclave containing plants from the Canary Islands, New Zealand, Mexico and the Himalaya; their bright-red bracts, silver thistles and purple flowers are set against the glittering sea. It's 1.5 miles west of Bournemouth Pier.

Sleeping

★ **Mory House** B&B ££

(01202-433553; www.moryhouse.co.uk; 31 Grand Ave, Southbourne; s/d/f £105/125/175; P) In this serene, pristine B&B, stained glass and an elegant stairwell hint at the house's Edwardian age. Contemporary bedrooms are styled in muted colours; the pick is number 3, where the pint-sized balcony is an ideal spot to nibble on a home-baked cookie. Mory House is in the beach-backed suburb of Southbourne, 3 miles east of central Bournemouth.

Amarillo B&B ££

(01202-553884; www.amarillohotel.co.uk; 52 Frances Rd; s £50, d £80-115; P) At great-value Amarillo smart bedrooms feature jazzy wallpaper, white wooden furniture and subtle lighting. The two single loft rooms have shared bathrooms.

Urban Beach HOTEL £££

(01202-301509; www.urbanbeach.co.uk; 23 Argyll Rd; s £72, d £130-145; P@) Stylish Urban Beach revels in a 'no worries' air that sees free loans of wellingtons, umbrellas and DVDs. Soft brown, dark grey and flashes of terracotta define bedrooms – some have bay windows, others sport velvet chairs and there's even a chandelier or two.

WORTH A TRIP

MONKEY SANCTUARY

Monkey World (01929-462537; www.monkeyworld.co.uk; Longthorns, BH20 6HH; adult/child/family £16/11/32; 10am-5pm; P) overflows with the 'aah' factor. The sanctuary's 26 hectares are home to bounding, noisy colonies of chimpanzees, orangutans, gibbons, marmosets and some ridiculously cute ring-tailed lemurs. Most have been rescued from primate smuggling rings, circuses, laboratories, working on beaches or being mistreated as pets. Monkey World is near Wool, 5 miles west of Wareham.

Eating & Drinking

★ **Urban Reef** BISTRO ££

(01202-443960; www.urbanreef.com; Undercliff Dr, Boscombe; snacks from £6, mains £10-25; 8am-10pm, winter times vary;) On sunny weekends a cool crowd queues out the door at Urban Reef. They're drawn by a waterfront deck and balcony, punchy coffee, top-notch snacks and quality, sustainable, imaginative fare. On stormy days head for the spacious, 1st-floor à la carte bistro for sweeping sea views. On fine days their takeaway menu appeals.

James & White BISTRO ££

(01202-280656; www.jamesandwhitebarandkitchen.com; 42 Sea Rd, Boscombe; mains £9-21; 11am-11pm Mon-Fri, 9am-11pm Sat & Sun;) A mellow soundtrack and a sea-view terrace give this chilled-out grill a surf-bar vibe. Brunch ranges from healthy vegan cooked breakfasts to French toast laced with maple syrup and topped with berries. The grill menu takes in vodka-spiked cheese fondue, hot-stone-cooked steaks and spiced lamb skewers – best enjoyed while sipping a craft beer, watching the waves.

West Beach SEAFOOD ££

(☎01202-587785; https://west-beach.co.uk; Pier Approach; mains £15-30; ⏰9-11am & noon-9.30pm) The seafood and setting are hard to beat – book a table on the decking beside the sand, watch the waves lap Bournemouth Pier and tuck into perfectly cooked, perfectly fresh fish: perhaps turbot with chorizo and capers, or a full-flavoured lobster thermidor.

★**Sixty Million Postcards** PUB

(www.sixtymillionpostcards.com; 19 Exeter Rd; ⏰noon-11pm Mon-Sat, to 10.30pm Sun) An oasis of hipster grunginess amid pound-a-pint Bournemouth, Sixty Million draws a decidedly beatnik crowd. Worn wooden floors, fringed lampshades and a sun terrace dotted with brightly coloured chairs set the scene for craft beers, unusual ciders, classic nachos and towering burgers (mains £6 to £11).

ℹ Information

Tourist Office (☎01202-451781; www.bournemouth.co.uk; Pier Approach; ⏰9.30am-5pm) Set right beside Bournemouth Pier.

ℹ Getting There & Around

BUS

Direct National Express (www.nationalexpress.com) buses departing from Bournemouth's coach station, which is near the train station, include:

Bristol (£18, three hours, daily)
London Victoria (£15, 2½ hours, hourly)
Southampton (£7, 50 minutes, four per day)

Useful local buses include:

Poole (M1/M2, £2.80, 35 minutes, every 5 minutes)
Salisbury (X3, £7, 1¼ hours, at least hourly)

Morebus Zone A Dayrider (adult/child £4.30/2.80) gives a day's unlimited travel in much of Poole, Bournemouth and neighbouring Christchurch.

TRAIN

Direct services include those to:

Dorchester South (£12, 45 minutes, half-hourly to hourly)
London Waterloo (£25, 2½ hours, half-hourly)
Poole (£4, 10 minutes, half-hourly)
Weymouth (£14, one hour, hourly)

Poole

☎01202 / POP 147,640

In the quaint old port of Poole there's a whiff of money in the air: the town borders Sandbanks, a sandy beach backed by some of the world's most expensive chunks of real estate. Big bucks aside, Poole also boasts excellent restaurants and is the springboard for a raft of watersports and some irresistible boat trips.

Sights & Activities

Brownsea Island ISLAND

(NT; ☎01202-707744; www.nationaltrust.org.uk; Poole Harbour; ferry & admission adult/child £17.50/9.50; ⏰9am-5.30pm late Mar-Oct) On this small, wooded island in the middle of Poole Harbour, trails weave through heath and woods, past peacocks, red squirrels, red deer and a wealth of birdlife – the water-framed views to the Isle of Purbeck are stunning. Free guided walks focus on the wartime island, birdlife, smugglers and pirates. Ferries to the island leave from Poole Quay at least hourly.

Poole Museum MUSEUM

(☎01202-262600; www.boroughofpoole.com/museums; 4 High St; ⏰10am-1pm & 2-5pm Apr-Oct) FREE The building alone is worth seeing – a beautifully restored 15th-century warehouse. The star exhibit is a 2300-year-old **Iron Age logboat** dredged up from Poole Harbour. At almost 10m long and weighing some 14 tonnes, it's the largest to be found in southern Britain and probably carried 18 people.

Sandbanks BEACH

A 2-mile, wafer-thin peninsula of land that curls around the expanse of Poole Harbour, Sandbanks is studded with some of the most expensive houses in the world. But the white-sand beaches that border them are free, have some of the best UK water-quality standards and are home to a host of watersports operators.

Poole Harbour Watersports WATER SPORTS

(☎01202-700503; www.pooleharbour.co.uk; 284 Sandbanks Rd) Delivers lessons for small groups in stand-up paddleboarding (SUP; per 1½ hours £25), windsurfing (per six hours £78) and kitesurfing (per day £99), plus memorable kayak and SUP tours (per three hours £45).

WORTH A TRIP

CORFE CASTLE

The startling, fractured battlements of **Corfe Castle** (NT; 01929-481294; www.national trust.org.uk; The Square; adult/child £10/5; 10am-6pm Apr-Sep, to 5pm Mar & Oct, to 4pm Nov-Feb) were once home to Sir John Bankes, Charles I's right-hand man. The Civil War saw the castle besieged by Cromwellian forces; in 1646 the plucky Lady Bankes directed a six-week defence and the castle fell only after being betrayed from within. The Roundheads then gunpowdered Corfe Castle apart; turrets and soaring walls still sheer off at precarious angles – the splayed-out gatehouse looks like it's just been blown up.

The **Swanage Steam Railway** (01929-425800; www.swanagerailway.co.uk; per person single/return £8/12.50; daily Apr-Oct, Sat & Sun Nov, Dec & Mar) stops at Corfe Castle as it shuttles between Swanage and Norden. You may have to pre-book a table to board the train; look online for updates.

Sleeping

Loch Fyne HOTEL ££
(01202-609000; www.greenekinginns.co.uk; 47 Haven Rd, Canford Cliffs; s/d from £75/90; P) There's a touch of the colonial tea plantation about the exterior of this smart hotel, set above the eponymous seafood restaurant. Small but cheerful bedrooms feature bursts of tartan in earthy or maritime tones. It's also just a 1.5-mile stroll to Sandbanks beach.

Blue Shutters B&B ££
(01202-748129; www.blueshutters.co.uk; 109 North Rd; s/d from £80/103; P) It's a little way out (2 miles from Poole Quay and 4 miles from Sandbanks) but bay windows and neutral colour schemes here keep the bedrooms light and bright. Other pluses include a quiet garden, a sunny patio and parking (at a real premium in Poole town).

Merchant House B&B £££
(01202-661474; www.themerchanthouse.org.uk; 10 Strand St; s £110, d £140-160) Tucked one street back from Poole Quay, tall, red-brick Merchant House is boutiquery at its best. Hefty wooden sculptures, wicker rocking chairs and crisp linen ensure it's stylish; the odd teddy bear keeps it cheery, too.

Eating

Rockfish SEAFOOD ££
(01202-836255; www.therockfish.co.uk; 9 The Quay; mains £10-18; noon-3.30pm & 4-9pm) Restaurateur Mitch Tonks has bagged a prime spot on the quay for the Poole outpost of his eight-strong West Country restaurant chain. Set in a high-ceilinged converted pottery, it delivers his trademark sustainable, beautifully cooked, super-fresh local fish with the usual friendly flair.

Storm SEAFOOD ££
(01202-674970; www.stormfish.co.uk; 16 High St; mains £14-19; noon-8pm Mon-Wed) How rare is this? The dish you're eating could well have been caught by the chef. At chilled-out Storm, fisher Pete also rattles the pots 'n' pans, delighting in dishing up intense Goan fish curry, seafood ramen, and a classic Poole Bay Dover sole *à la meunière*.

Check the website to see if longer opening hours have resumed.

Poole Arms PUB FOOD ££
(01202-673450; www.poolearms.co.uk; 19 Poole Quay; mains £8-19; 11am-11pm Mon-Sat, noon-11pm Sun) The grub at this ancient, green-tiled pub is strong on locally landed seafood – try the homemade fish pie, local crab or Poole rock oysters (£2.25 each). Order some New Forest beer, then settle down on the terrace overlooking the quay.

★ **Guildhall Tavern** FRENCH £££
(01202-671717; www.guildhalltavern.co.uk; 15 Market St; mains £18-23; 11.30am-3.30pm & 6-9.30pm Tue-Sat) Poole's top table consistently delights, combining local ingredients with lashings of French elan. Fish features strongly – the rope-grown mussels poached in Muscadet are superb as is the sea bass flambéed with Pernod – but the boeuf bourguignon also makes carnivores smile.

Information

Tourist Office (01202-262600.; www.poole tourism.com; 4 High St; 10am-1pm & 2-5pm Apr-Oct) Set inside Poole Museum.

WORTH A TRIP

KINGSTON LACY

Set some 2 miles west of Wimborne, Dorset's must-see stately **home** (NT; 01202-883402; www.nationaltrust.org.uk; Wimborne Minster; adult/child £10/5; house hours vary, grounds 9am-6pm Mar-Oct, 10am-4pm Nov-Feb; P) looks every inch the setting for a period drama. Highlights include the gold- and gilt-smothered Spanish Room, the hieroglyphics in the Egyptian Room and the elegant marble staircase and loggia. The opening hours and days for the house vary – see the website for updates. In the extensive landscaped grounds, hunt out the restored Japanese Tea Garden and the Iron Age hill fort of Badbury Rings.

Getting There & Around

BOAT

Brittany Ferries (0330 159 7000; www.brittany-ferries.com) Services between Poole and Cherbourg in France were suspended in 2020; check the website to see if they've resumed.

Sandbanks Ferry (01929-450203; www.sandbanksferry.co.uk; per pedestrian/car £1/4.50; 7am-11pm) Makes the four-minute trip from Sandbanks to Studland every 20 minutes. It's a shortcut from Poole to Swanage, Wareham and the Isle of Purbeck, but the summer queues can be a pain.

BUS

A Morebus Zone A Dayrider (adult/child £4.30/2.80) gives a day's unlimited travel in much of Poole and Bournemouth.

Bournemouth Bus M1/M2, £2.80, 35 minutes, every 5 minutes

London Victoria National Express, £18, 3½ hours, every two hours

Sandbanks Bus 60, £3.80, 25 minutes, half-hourly or hourly, from mid-July to early September

TAXI

Dial-a-Cab (01202-666822; www.pooletaxis.co.uk)

TRAIN

Direct services include:

Bournemouth £4, 10 minutes, half-hourly

Dorchester South £10, 30 minutes, hourly

London Waterloo £30, 2¼ hours, half-hourly to hourly

Weymouth £13, 45 minutes, hourly

Lulworth Cove

POP 740

In this stretch of southeast Dorset the coast steals the show. For millions of years the elements have been creating an intricate shoreline of curved bays, caves, stacks and weirdly wonderful rock formations – most notably the massive natural arch at Durdle Door.

The charismatic hamlet of Lulworth Cove is a pleasing jumble of thatched cottages and fishing gear, which winds down to a perfect crescent of white cliffs. Inevitably it all gets very busy in summer; avoid peak season if you can.

Sights & Activities

Check whether **Jurassic Coast Activities** (01305-835301; www.jurassiccoastactivities.co.uk), which suspended kayaking tours in 2020, is up and running again.

★Durdle Door LANDMARK

(www.lulworth.com; near Lulworth Cove, BH20 5PU; parking half-/full day £5/10) The poster child of Dorset's Jurassic Coast, this immense, 150-million-year-old Portland stone arch was created by a combination of massive earth movements and erosion. Today it's framed by shimmering bays; bring a swimsuit and head down the hundreds of steps for an unforgettable dip.

The beach and car park can get very busy in summer. You can pre-book a parking space, or join the throngs hiking the coast path from Lulworth Cove (2.5 miles return). A quieter and much more rewarding (if testing) walk is east along the coast from Ringstead, or from the car park 0.5 miles northeast of that village (7.4 miles return).

Lulworth Cove Visitor Centre MUSEUM

(01929-400587; www.lulworth.com; main car park; 10am-5pm Easter-Sep, to 4pm Oct-Easter) FREE Excellent displays outline how geology and erosion have combined to shape the area's remarkable shoreline. Staff can advise about walks, too.

A money-saving tip: if you're heading onto Durdle Door, your Lulworth Cove parking ticket (per half-/full day £5/10) is also valid at the two, non-premium-rate Durdle Door car parks.

Stair Hole Bay BAY

Stair Hole Bay sits just a few hundred metres west of Lulworth Cove. This diminutive semicircle is almost enclosed by cliffs that feature tiny rock arches – a route in that's popular with kayakers. On the landward side is the delightfully named Lulworth Crumple, where layers of rock form dramatically zigzagging folds.

Lulworth Castle CASTLE

(EH; ☎01929-400352; www.lulworth.com; adult/child £6/4, parking £3; ⏲10.30am-5pm Sun-Fri Apr-Dec) A confection in creamy, dreamy white, this baronial pile looks more like a French chateau than a traditional English castle. Built in 1608 as a hunting lodge, it's survived extravagant owners, extensive remodelling and a disastrous fire in 1929. It has been extensively restored, especially the kitchen and cellars. Ask whether the tower has reopened – it offers sweeping coastal views.

Sleeping

Check whether **Lulworth YHA** (☎0345 371 9331; www.yha.org.uk; School Lane, West Lulworth; P), which switched to exclusive hire for 2020, has reopened to individual bookings.

Durdle Door Holiday Park CAMPSITE £

(☎01929-400200; www.lulworth.com; West Lulworth, BH20 5PU; sites £28-44; ⏲Mar-Oct; P wifi) An attractive, spacious site, just minutes from the creamy cliffs, and 1.5 miles west of the hamlet of Lulworth Cove. Opt for a good old tent, or a four-person wooden pod (£85).

★**Lulworth Cove Inn** INN £££

(☎01929-400333; www.lulworth-coveinn.co.uk; Main Rd; d £135-150; P wifi) One to delight your inner beachcomber. In this veritable vision of driftwood-chic, whitewashed floorboards and aquamarine panels frame painted wicker chairs and roll-top baths. Add cracking sea views, a mini roof terrace and top-quality gastropub grub (mains £13 to £17, food served from noon to 9pm) and you have an irresistible inn.

Rudds of Lulworth B&B £££

(☎01929-400552; www.ruddslulworth.co.uk; Main Rd; d £85-185, ste £160-200; wifi pool) An idyllic setting, pared-down designs, top-notch linen and pamper-yourself toiletries combine to make this a memorable place to stay, especially if you opt for a room with Lulworth Cove views. Or just lounge beside the pool, which also overlooks that circle of bay.

Eating & Drinking

Boat Shed CAFE ££

(☎01929-400810; www.lulworth.com; Main Rd; snacks from £3, mains £7-17; ⏲9.30am-5pm Apr-Sep, to 4pm Oct-Mar) Views don't come much better than from the terrace of this converted fishers' storage shack set right beside Lulworth's glittering circular cove. The food spans fine brunches, Dorset cream teas, meze platters and – of course – fish.

Castle PUB

(☎01929-400311; www.butcombe.com/the-castle-inn-dorset; 8 Main Rd, West Lulworth; ⏲noon-9pm; wifi dogs) A picture-perfect, rambling thatched inn with a swish new interior, large terrace and regularly changing selection of prime Dorset ciders.

WORTH A TRIP

THE CERNE GIANT

Nude, full frontal and notoriously well endowed, the **Cerne Giant** (NT; ☎01297-489481; www.nationaltrust.org.uk; Cerne Abbas; ⏲24hr; P) FREE chalk figure, on the hillside above the village of Cerne Abbas, is revealed in all his glory – and he's in a state of excitement that wouldn't be allowed in most magazines. The giant is around 60m high and 51m wide and his age remains a mystery; some claim he's Roman, but the first historical reference comes in 1694, when three shillings were set aside for his repair. These days a car park provides grandstand views.

The Victorians found it all deeply embarrassing and allowed grass to grow over his most outstanding feature. Today the hill is grazed by sheep and cattle, though only the sheep are allowed to do their nibbling over the giant – the cows would do too much damage to his lines.

Down in the village, the **New Inn** (☎01300-341274; www.thenewinncerneabbas.co.uk; 14 Long St; d £100-140, ste £160-190; P wifi) – which is more than 400 years old – makes a quaint place to stay.

The village is eight miles north of Dorchester.

JURASSIC COAST

The kind of massive, hands-on geology lesson you wish you'd had at school, the Jurassic Coast is England's first natural World Heritage Site, putting it on a par with the Great Barrier Reef and the Grand Canyon. This striking shoreline stretches from Exmouth in East Devon to Swanage in Dorset, encompassing 185 million years of the earth's history in just 95 miles. It means you can walk, in just a few hours, many millions of years in geological time.

It began when layers of rocks formed, their varying compositions determined by different climates: desertlike conditions gave way to higher, then lower, sea levels. Massive earth movements then tilted all the rock layers, forcing most of the oldest formations to the west, and the youngest to the east. Next, erosion exposed the different strata.

The differences are very tangible. Devon's rusty-red Triassic rocks are 200–250 million years old. Lyme Regis' fossil-rich, dark-clay Jurassic cliffs are 190 million years old. Pockets of much younger, creamy-coloured Cretaceous rocks (a mere 65–140 million years old) pop up, notably around Lulworth Cove, where erosion has sculpted a stunning display of bays, stacks and rock arches.

The coast's website (www.jurassiccoast.org) is a great information source; also look out locally for the highly readable *Official Guide to the Jurassic Coast* (£4.95).

Upstairs sit 12 cosy bedrooms (doubles £155 to £175), which team mod cons (such as digital radios) with modern, country-cottage styling.

Getting There & Away

Bus X54 (two to five daily, Monday to Saturday) stops at Lulworth Cove en route between Weymouth and Wareham and Poole.

Dorchester

01305 / POP 19,060

With Dorchester you get two towns in one: a real-life, bustling county town and Thomas Hardy's fictional Casterbridge. The Victorian writer was born nearby and his literary locations can still be found among Dorchester's Georgian terraces. Add cracking archaeological sites and attractive places to eat and sleep and you have an appealing base for a night or two.

Sights

After a multi-million-pound refurbishment, **Dorset County Museum** (01305-262735; www.dorsetcountymuseum.org; High West St) is due to open in 2021; see the website for updates.

Access to the two main Thomas Hardy sites near Dorchester was suspended in 2020. Check online to see if you can now visit his thatched birthplace, **Hardy's Cottage** (NT; 01305-262366; www.nationaltrust.org.uk; Higher Bockhampton), and his home in later life, **Max Gate** (NT; 01305-262538; www.nationaltrust.org.uk; Alington Ave).

Hardy fans can also hunt down the Casterbridge literary locations tucked away in modern Dorchester's streets. They include **Lucetta's House** (Trinity St), a grand Georgian affair with ornate doorposts, while a nearby red-brick, mid-18th-century building (now a bank) is named as the inspiration for the **House of the Mayor of Casterbridge** (South St). Check whether the **tourist office** (01305-267992; www.visit-dorset.com; Dorchester Library, Charles St) has reopened; it sells book location guides.

★ Maiden Castle ARCHAEOLOGICAL SITE
(EH; www.english-heritage.org.uk; Winterborne Monkton; dawn-dusk; P) FREE Occupying a massive slab of horizon on the southern fringes of Dorchester, imposing Maiden Castle is the largest and most complex Iron Age hill fort in Britain. The first defences were built on the site around 500 BCE – in its heyday it was densely populated with clusters of roundhouses and a network of roads. The Romans besieged and captured Maiden Castle in 43 CE – an ancient Briton skeleton with a Roman crossbow bolt in the spine was found at the fort.

Roman Town House HISTORIC BUILDING
(www.dorsetcouncil.gov.uk; Northern Hay; 24hr) FREE The knee-high flint walls and beautifully preserved mosaics here powerfully conjure up the Roman occupation of Dorchester (then Durnovaria). Peek into the summer dining room to see the

underfloor heating system (hypocaust), where charcoal-warmed air circulated around pillars to produce a toasty room temperature of 18°C (64°F). Search for 'Roman Town House' on the Dorset Council website for more information.

Sleeping

★Beggars Knap B&B ££
(☎07768 690691; www.beggarsknap.co.uk; 2 Weymouth Ave; s £80-90, d £100-115, f from £125; P 📶) Despite the name, this altogether fabulous, vaguely decadent guesthouse is far from impoverished. Opulent rooms drip with chandeliers and gold brocades; beds draped in fine cottons range from French sleigh to four-poster. You could pay much, much more and get something half as nice.

Westwood B&B ££
(☎01305-268018; www.westwoodhouse.co.uk; 29 High West St; s/d/f from £90/107/127; 📶 👪) A skilled designer's been at work in this 18th-century town house, producing a contemporary-meets-Georgian style: muted greens, brass lamps, subtle checks and mini-sofas. The modern bathrooms glint, while tiny fridges harbour fresh milk for your tea.

Yalbury Cottage HOTEL ££
(☎01305-262382; www.yalburycottage.com; Lower Bockhampton; s/d £85/125; P 📶) Yalbury is almost your archetypal English cottage, framed by flowers and crowned by moss-studded thatch. Inside fresh, simple, gently rustic bedrooms overlook the garden or fields. It's in Lower Bockhampton, 3 miles east of Dorchester.

Eating

★Taste BRASSERIE ££
(☎01305-257776; www.facebook.com/pg/tasterestaurant; Trinity St; mains £10-18; ⏲9am-2pm Mon-Wed, Fri & Sat) 🍃 One of Dorchester's best, buzziest brunch and lunch spots has fleets of fans thanks to a buy-local ethos and emphasis on super-fresh sustainable ingredients. They crop up in everything from platters, tapas and melts to classy bistro dishes: grilled steak, confit duck and garlicky linguine.

Cow & Apple BURGERS ££
(☎01305-266286; www.cowandapple.co.uk; 30 Trinity St; burgers £9-16; ⏲5-9pm Tue-Fri, noon-5pm Sat) Piled high and oozing all the trimmings, the dirty burgers here are decidedly good – spice things up with jalapeños, brie or a seriously sticky BBQ sauce. The cider list – more than 50 types – could take a while to work through.

Brewers Arms PUB FOOD ££
(☎01305-889361; www.thebrewersarms.com; Burnside, Martinstown; mains £10-14; ⏲noon-3pm & 6-11pm Tue-Sat, noon-3pm Sun) Dorset produce and homemade dishes pack the menu of this charming village pub – from the steak and Stilton pie to the homemade rhubarb crumble. Or just head to the sunny beer garden and chill out with a pint of golden ale.

It's set in the pretty village of Martinstown, 3 miles west of Dorchester.

Getting There & Away

BUS

London Victoria (National Express, £18, 3¾ hours, one daily)
Lyme Regis (Bus X51, £5, 1¼ hours, hourly Monday to Saturday, three on Sunday)
Sherborne (Bus X11, £4.90, 1¼ hours, four daily Monday to Friday)
Weymouth (Bus 10, £2.20, 20 minutes, half-hourly)

TRAIN

Dorchester has two train stations.

Trains leave Dorchester West for Bath and Bristol (£21, two to 2½ hours, at least two daily).

Services from Dorchester South, running at least hourly, include:
Bournemouth (£12, 45 minutes)
London Waterloo (£30, three hours)
Southampton (£26, 1¾ hours)
Weymouth (£5, 10 minutes)

Weymouth

☎01305../ POP 52,200

At just over 225 years old, Weymouth is a weather-worn resort with a couple of tricks up its faded sleeve. Candy-striped kiosks and deckchairs line a golden, 3-mile beach; chuck in cockles and chippies and prepare to promenade down seaside memory lane. But Weymouth is about more than just that sandy shore; the town boasts a historic harbour, some fine seafood restaurants and easy access to the watersports centres of the neighbouring Isle of Portland.

Sights & Activities

Check whether **Coastline Cruises** (☎01305-785000; www.coastlinecruises.com; Trinity Rd) has resumed its 90-minute sailings, suspended in 2020, to Portland.

Sandworld SCULPTURE
(☎07411 387529; www.sandworld.co.uk; Lodmoor Country Park, Preston Beach Rd; adult/child £7.75/5.75; ⏲10am-3.30pm) Set up by a third-generation Weymouth sand sculptor, the intricate creations here include lifelike representations of fairy-tale castles, sly dragons and scenes from films spanning *Finding Nemo* and *Star Wars* to Disney favourites.

Nothe Fort FORT
(☎01305-766626; www.nothefort.org.uk; Barrack Rd; adult/child £8/2; ⏲11am-4pm Apr-Oct) Weymouth's photogenic 19th-century defences are studded with cannons, searchlights and 30cm coastal guns. Exhibits detail Dorset's Roman invasion, a Victorian soldier's drill and Weymouth in WWII.

Sleeping & Eating

★**Roundhouse** B&B ££
(☎01305-761010; www.roundhouse-weymouth.com; 1 The Esplanade; d £105-125; 📶) The decor here is as gently eccentric as the owner – interiors combine snazzy modern art with comfy sofas and bursts of purple and bright blue. But the big draw is the view – you can see both the beach out front and the harbour behind from all bedrooms.

Old Harbour View B&B £££
(☎01305-774633; www.oldharbourviewweymouth.co.uk; 12 Trinity Rd; s/d £90/130; P📶) In this pristine Georgian terrace you get boating themes in the fresh, white bedrooms, and boats right outside the front door. One room overlooks the busy quay, the other faces the back.

Marlboro FISH & CHIPS £
(☎01305-785700; www.marlbororestaurant.co.uk; 46 St Thomas St; mains £9-14; ⏲11.30am-9.45pm) 🍃 A sustainable slant and a 40-year history help lift this traditional chippy, just metres from Weymouth's quay, above its rivals. Mackerel features among the long list of super-fresh fish. Take it away and duck the seagulls or get munching in the bay-windowed, licensed cafe (open till 8pm).

★**Crustacean** SEAFOOD ££
(☎01305-777222; www.crustaceanrestaurant.co.uk; 59 St Mary St; mains £15-37; ⏲noon-9pm Mon-Thu, to 9.30pm Fri & Sat) At Crustacean you'll find an imaginative chef with a passion for the finest, freshest fish and seafood. Get cracking on a whole lobster, slurp some oysters, lunch on a robust chowder or dine on pan-fried sea bass with a creamy saffron sauce.

Getting There & Away

BUS

Dorchester Bus 10 (£2.20, 20 minutes, half-hourly)
Fortuneswell Bus 1 (£2.20, 20 minutes, four per hour to hourly)
London Victoria National Express (£12, four hours, one direct daily)
Portland Bill Bus 501 (£2.60, 50 minutes, seven daily, runs from late July to August)

The Jurassic Coaster/Bus X53 (four to five daily, no service winter Sundays) travels west from Weymouth to Axminster (2½ hours), via Abbotsbury (20 minutes) and Lyme Regis (1¼ hours).

TRAIN

Trains running at least hourly include the following direct services:
Bournemouth (£14, one hour)
Dorchester South (£5, 10 minutes)
London Waterloo (£29, 3½ hours)

Direct services every two hours:
Bath (£20, two hours)
Bristol (£20, 2¾ hours)

Isle of Portland

The 'Isle' of Portland is a hard, high comma of rock fused to the rest of Dorset by the ridge of Chesil Beach. On its 150m central plateau, a quarrying past still holds sway, evidenced by huge craters and large slabs of limestone. Portland offers jaw-dropping views down on to 18-mile Chesil Beach and the neighbouring Fleet – Britain's biggest tidal lagoon.

Proud, and at times bleak and rough around the edges, Portland is decidedly different from the rest of Dorset, and is all the more compelling because of it. The Isle's industrial heritage, watersport facilities, rich birdlife and starkly beautiful cliffs make it worth at least a day trip.

The isle's biggest settlement is Fortuneswell, at the northern end; beachside Chiswell sits alongside.

Sights

★Tout Quarry SCULPTURE
(near Fortuneswell; dawn-dusk; P) FREE Portland's white limestone has been quarried for centuries and has been used in some of the world's finest buildings, such as the British Museum and St Paul's Cathedral. Tout Quarry's disused workings now house more than 50 sculptures that have been carved into the rock in situ, resulting in a fascinating combination of the raw material, the detritus of the quarrying process and the beauty of chiselled works.

Tout Quarry is signed off the main road, just south of Fortuneswell.

★Portland Lighthouse LIGHTHOUSE
(01305-821050; www.trinityhouse.co.uk; Portland Bill; adult/child £7.50/5.50; hours vary; P) For a real sense of Portland's remote nature, head to its southern tip, Portland Bill, to climb the 41m-high, candy-striped lighthouse. It offers breathtaking views of rugged cliffs and the Race, a surging vortex of conflicting tides. The interactive displays in the former lighthouse-keepers' cottages include *Into the Dark*, a recreation of sailing into stormy seas.

Tours run on varying days (often Sunday, Tuesday and Thursday); see the website for dates and pre-booking requirements.

Portland Castle CASTLE
(EH; 01305-820539; www.english-heritage.org.uk; Liberty Rd, Castletown; adult/child £6.90/4.10; 10am-4pm Apr-Oct) A particularly fine product of Henry VIII's castle-building spree, with expansive views over Portland Harbour.

Activities

Andrew Simpson Centre BOATING
(01305-457400; www.aswc.co.uk; Osprey Quay, Portland Harbour) Activities include Royal Yachting Association (RYA) sailing lessons (adult/child per two days £199/180). Look out for their £20 taster sessions.

OTC WATER SPORTS
(Official Test Centre; 01305-230296; www.otc-windsurf.com; Osprey Quay, Portland Harbour) Offers lessons in stand-up paddleboarding (SUP; one/two hours £25/40) and windsurfing (two hours/one day/two days £59/139/225). It also rents out SUP boards (per hour £10).

Sleeping & Eating

Portland YHA (03453 719339; www.yha.org.uk; Castle Rd, Castletown; P) suspended individual bookings in 2020; see the website for updates.

★Queen Anne House B&B ££
(01305-820028; www.queenannehouse.co.uk; 2 Fortuneswell; s/d £70/95;) It's impossible to know which room to pick: White, with skylight, beams and a hobbit-esque door; Lotus, with its grand furniture; ornate Oyster with its half-tester bed; or Garden, a suite with a French bath and mini-conservatory. It doesn't matter, though – they're all great value and gorgeous.

★Crab House Cafe SEAFOOD ££
(01305-788867; www.crabhousecafe.co.uk; Ferrymans Way, Wyke Regis; mains £14-30; noon-2.30pm & 6-9pm Wed-Sat, noon-3.30pm Sun) This is where the locals head on hot summer days, to sit beside Fleet Lagoon in beach-shack-chic, tucking into fresh-as-it-gets seafood. Fish is enlivened by chilli, curry, lemon and herbs, crab comes spicy Chinese-style or whole for you to crack, and the oysters are served with either pesto and parmesan or bacon and cream. Opening hours can vary.

Cove House PUB
(01305-820895; www.thecovehouseinn.co.uk; 91 Chiswell Seafront; 11.30am-9pm) Head to this history-rich fishers' inn for a Chesil Beach-side beer terrace with expansive views, memorable sunsets and great pub grub (mains £9 to £12).

Getting There & Away

Bus 1 runs from Weymouth to Fortuneswell (£2.20, 20 minutes, four per hour to hourly).

Bus 501 operates between Weymouth and Portland Bill from late July to August (£2.60, 50 minutes, seven daily).

Chesil Beach

One of the most breathtaking beaches in Britain, Chesil is 18 miles long, 15m high and moving inland at the rate of 5m a century. This mind-boggling, 100-million-tonne pebble ridge is the baby of the Jurassic Coast. A mere 6000 years old, its stones range from pea-sized in the west to hand-sized in the east.

Sights

Chesil Beach Centre NATURE CENTRE
(Fine Foundation; 01305-206191; www.dorsetwildlifetrust.org.uk; Ferrybridge; parking per hour £1; 10am-5pm Easter-Sep, to 4pm Oct-Easter; P) FREE This centre at the start of the bridge to Portland is a great gateway to Chesil Beach. The pebble ridge is at its highest here – 15m compared to 7m at Abbotsbury. From the car park an energy-sapping hike up sliding pebbles leads to the constant surge and rattle of waves on stones and dazzling views of the sea, with the thin pebble line and the expanse of the Fleet Lagoon behind.

★**Abbotsbury Swannery** WILDLIFE RESERVE
(01305-871858; www.abbotsbury-tourism.co.uk; New Barn Rd, Abbotsbury; adult/child £10/5; 10am-5pm late Mar-Oct) Every May some 600 free-flying swans choose to nest at this swannery, which shelters in the Fleet Lagoon, protected by the ridge of Chesil Beach. Wandering the network of trails that wind between the swans' nests is an awe-inspiring experience that's punctuated by occasional territorial displays (snuffling coughs and stand-up flapping), ensuring that even the liveliest children are stilled.

The swannery is near the picturesque village of Abbotsbury, 10 miles from Weymouth, off the B3157.

Lyme Regis

01297 / POP 3670

Fantastically fossil-packed Lyme Regis packs a heavyweight historical punch. Rock-hard relics of the past pop out repeatedly from the surrounding cliffs – exposed by the landslides of a retreating shoreline. Lyme is now a pivot point of the Unesco-listed Jurassic Coast: fossil fever is definitely in the air and everyone, from proper palaeontologists to those out for a bit of fun, can engage in a spot of coastal rummaging. Add sandy beaches and some delightful places to sleep and eat, and you get a charming base for explorations.

Sights & Activities

Lyme Regis Museum MUSEUM
(01297-443370; www.lymeregismuseum.co.uk; Bridge St; up to 2 people £12, family £15; 10am-4pm Wed-Sat) In 1814 local teenager Mary Anning found the first full ichthyosaur skeleton near Lyme Regis, propelling the town onto the world stage. An incredibly famous fossilist in her day, Miss Anning did much to pioneer the science of modern-day palaeontology. This museum, on the site of her former home, tells her story and exhibits its spectacular fossils and other prehistoric finds.

Cobb LANDMARK
First built in the 13th century, Lyme's iconic, curling sea defences have been strengthened and extended over the years, and hence don't present the elegant line they once did, but it's still hard to resist wandering their length to the tip.

Dinosaurland MUSEUM
(01297-443541; www.dinosaurland.co.uk; Coombe St; adult/child £5/4; 10am-5pm mid-Feb–mid-Oct, winter hours vary;) This joyful, mini, indoor Jurassic Park overflows with fossilised remains; look out for belemnites, a plesiosaurus and an impressive locally found ichthyosaur. Lifelike dinosaur models will thrill youngsters – the rock-hard tyrannosaur eggs and 73kg dinosaur dung will have them in raptures.

★**Undercliff** WALKING
This wildly undulating, 304-hectare nature reserve just west of Lyme was formed by massive landslides. They've left a challenging hiking landscape of slipped cliffs, fissures and ridges, where paths snake between dense vegetation, exposed tree roots and tangles of brambles. The Undercliff starts a mile west of central Lyme Regis; follow footpath signs from Holmbush Car Park.

Sleeping & Eating

Lyme Townhouse B&B ££
(01929-400252; www.lyme-townhouse.co.uk; 8 Pound St; d £105-135;) With stylish decor and luxury flourishes this good-value guesthouse is hard to resist. Most of the seven rooms are on the small size (as signalled by the categories Super-Snug and Snug), but the central location, sea glimpses and views onto the town make it hard to beat.

Alexandra HERITAGE HOTEL £££
(01297-442010; www.hotelalexandra.co.uk; Pound St; d £180-£285; P) It's like the setting for an Agatha Christie mystery, minus the murder. Wicker chairs dot manicured lawns, glittering Lyme Bay sweeps out behind. The best bedrooms boast bay windows and sea views; the (much cheaper) back-facing ones are charming too.

FOSSIL HUNTING

On Dorset's Jurassic Coast, fossil fever is catching. Lyme Regis sits in one of the most unstable sections of Britain's shore, and regular landslips mean nuggets of prehistory keep tumbling from the cliffs.

Joining a guided walk aids explorations. Three miles east of Lyme, the **Charmouth Heritage Coast Centre** (01297-560772; www.charmouth.org; Lower Sea Lane, Charmouth; 11am-4pm daily Easter-Oct, Fri-Mon Nov-Easter) FREE runs between one and 10 small-group fossil-hunting walks (adult/child £8/4) per week in the summer and school holidays.

Or, in Lyme itself, Lyme Regis Museum runs three to seven small-group fossil-hunting walks per week (up to six people £125), with times dictated by the tides. Also in Lyme, check whether local expert **Brandon Lennon** (07854 377519; www.lymeregisfossilwalks.com) has resumed his walks. All fossil-hunting trips are popular – book well ahead.

For the best chances of a find, visit within two hours of low water. If you do hunt by yourself, official advice is to check tide times and collect on a falling tide, observe warning signs, keep away from cliffs, only pick up from the beach and always leave some behind for others. Oh, and tell the experts if you find a stunner.

It's also the perfect spot for a proper English **afternoon tea** (£10 to £31), complete with scones, jam and dainty sandwiches.

★Oyster & Fish House SEAFOOD ££
(01297-446910; www.theoysterandfishhouse.co.uk; Cobb Rd; mains £16-26; noon-10pm;) Expect sweeping views of the Cobb and dazzling food at this super-stylish, open-plan cabin. Dishes depend on the day's catch, but the crab might be wok-fried, the lobster soup might be laced with Somerset cider and the bacon chops might come with cockles.

Harbour Inn PUB FOOD ££
(01297-442299; www.harbourinnlymeregis.co.uk; 23 Marine Pde; mains £13-19; noon-2.30pm & 5-9pm, closed Sun eve Oct-Mar) A flower-framed, beachside veranda, smart but snug interior and some of the best bistro/pub grub in town – the bouillabaisse is suitably intense.

Information

At the time of research Lyme's tourist office had closed. Check for updates at www.visit-dorset.com/visitor-information.

Getting There & Away

Bus X51 (£5, 1¼ hours, hourly Monday to Saturday, three on Sunday) Shuttles to Dorchester.

Jurassic Coaster/Bus X53 (four to five daily, no service winter Sunday) Goes east to Weymouth (£7.80) via Chesil Beach, and west to Axminster (£6.20), with regular connections on to Exeter from there.

Sherborne

01935 / POP 9520

Sherborne gleams with a mellow, orangey-yellow stone – it's been used to build a cluster of 15th-century buildings and the impressive abbey church. This serene town exudes wealth, thanks partly to a batch of exclusive private schools.

Sights

Sherborne Abbey CHURCH
(01935-812452; www.sherborneabbey.com; Abbey Cl; suggested donation £4; check website for hours) At the height of its influence, the magnificent Abbey Church of St Mary the Virgin was the central cathedral of 26 succeeding Saxon bishops. Established early in the 8th century, it became a Benedictine abbey in 998 and functioned as a cathedral until 1075. The church has mesmerising fan vaulting that's the oldest in the country, a central tower supported by Saxon Norman piers and an 1180 Norman porch.

Sherborne Old Castle CASTLE
(EH; 01935-812730; www.english-heritage.org.uk; Castleton; adult/child £5.90/3.50; 10am-5pm Wed-Sun Apr-Oct; P) These days the epitome of a picturesque ruin, Sherborne's Old Castle was built by Roger, Bishop of Salisbury, in 1120 – Elizabeth I gave it to her one-time favourite Sir Walter Raleigh in the late 16th century. It became a Royalist stronghold during the English Civil War, but Cromwell reduced it to rubble after a 16-day siege

in 1645, leaving just the fractured southwest gatehouse, great tower and north range.

Sherborne New Castle GARDENS
(☎01935-812072; www.sherbornecastle.com; New Rd; adult/child £9/free; ⊙10am-5pm Apr-Sep; P) Sir Walter Raleigh began building the impressive Sherborne New Castle in 1594, but only got as far as the central block before being imprisoned by James I. James promptly sold the castle to Sir John Digby, who added the splendid wings you see today. In 1753 the grounds received a mega-makeover at the hands of landscape-gardener extraordinaire Capability Brown, who added a massive lake and the 12-hectare waterside gardens.

Sleeping & Eating

★**Cumberland House** B&B ££
(☎01935-817554; www.bandbdorset.co.uk; Greenhill; d £80-85; P) Artistry emanates from these history-rich rooms – bright scatter rugs sit on flagstone floors, and lemon and oatmeal walls undulate between wonderfully wonky beams. Gourmet breakfasts include freshly squeezed orange juice, fresh-fruit compote and homemade granola.

Stoneleigh Barn B&B ££
(☎01935-817258; www.stoneleighbarn.co.uk; North Wootton; d/f £100/120; P) Warm, weathered stone and extensive gardens ensure this 18th-century barn delights on the outside. Inside, exposed trusses frame spacious rooms named after their attractive colour schemes – choose from Red or Blue.

George PUB £
(☎01925-812785; www.thegeorgesherborne.co.uk; 4 Higher Cheap St; mains £8-11; ⊙noon-5pm daily, plus 6-9pm Mon & Tue;) It's five centuries since Sherborne's oldest, cosiest inn pulled its first pint; today it signals its age with wooden settles polished smooth by countless behinds. Pub-grub fare includes ham and egg and a 'roast of the day'; there's a compact terrace out front.

★**Green** MODERN BRITISH ££
(☎01935-813821; www.greenrestaurant.co.uk; 3 The Green; mains £13-22; ⊙noon-2.30pm & 6.30-9.30pm Tue-Sat) In this affable, elegant spot, the food is pure West Country elan. Goodies might include Dorset crab with chargrilled hake, or a confit Devon duck terrine. For a great-value feed, plump for the cracking *menu du jour* (three-course lunch £23; dinner £27).

Information

Sherborne's **tourist office** (☎01935-815341; www.visit-dorset.com; Digby Rd) suspended in-person visits in 2020. Call for updates.

Getting There & Away

BUS

Dorchester, via Cerne Abbas (Bus X11, £4.90, 1¼ hours, four daily Monday to Friday)

Yeovil (Bus 58, £2.70, 30 minutes, every one to two hours)

TRAIN

Exeter (£20, 1¼ hours, every one to two hours)

London Waterloo (£44, 2¼ hours, hourly)

Salisbury (£14, 45 minutes, hourly)

WILTSHIRE

Wiltshire is rich in the reminders of ritual and packed with not-to-be-missed sights. Its verdant landscape is littered with more mysterious stone circles, processional avenues and ancient barrows than anywhere else in Britain. It's a place that teases and tantalises the imagination – here you'll experience the prehistoric majesty of Stonehenge and the atmospheric stone ring at Avebury. Add the serene 800-year-old cathedral at Salisbury, the supremely stately homes at Stourhead and Longleat and the impossibly pretty village of Lacock, and you have a county crammed full of English charm waiting to be explored.

Getting There & Around

BUS

Wiltshire's bus coverage can be patchy, especially in the northwest.

First (www.firstgroup.com) Runs services to Weymouth, Portland, Dorchester and the X53 Jurassic Coaster between Weymouth and Axminster.

Salisbury Reds (www.salisburyreds.co.uk) Covers Salisbury and many rural areas; offers network-wide, one-day Rover Tickets (adult/child £9.20/6) and seven-day passes (Salisbury area £15, network-wide £26).

TRAIN

Trains run at least hourly east from Salisbury to London Waterloo (£25, 1½ hours) and west to Exeter (£21, 2¾ hours). Another line runs north to Bath (£11, one hour, hourly) and Bristol (£13, 1¼ hours, hourly).

Salisbury

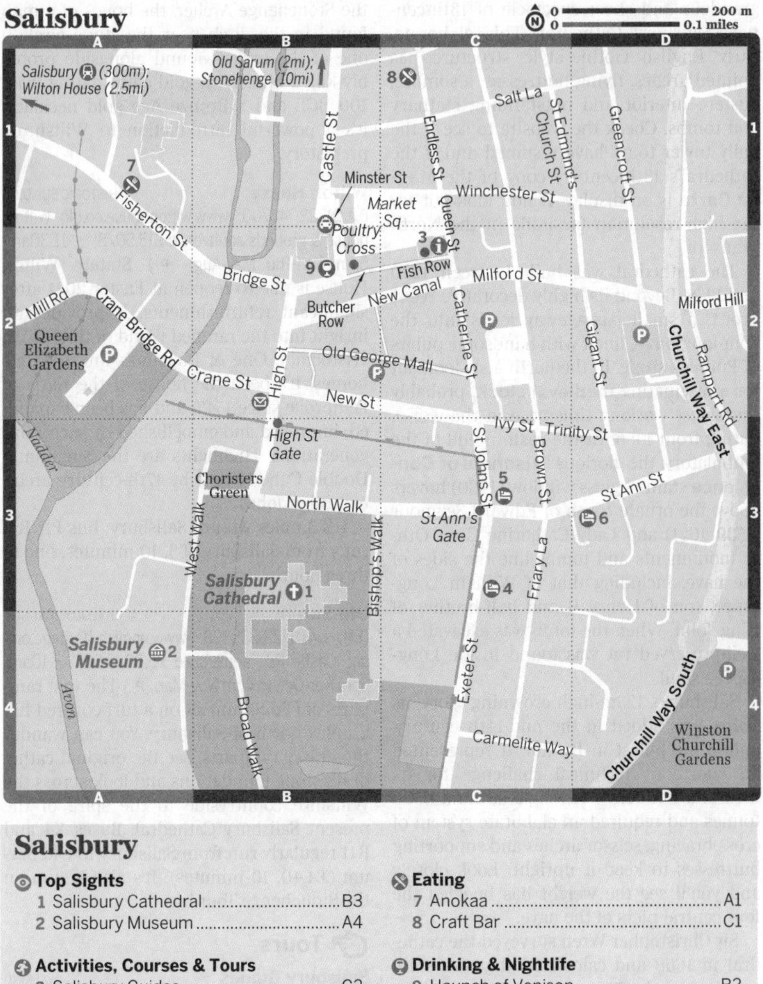

Salisbury

Top Sights
1 Salisbury Cathedral B3
2 Salisbury Museum A4

Activities, Courses & Tours
3 Salisbury Guides C2

Sleeping
4 Cathedral View C3
5 Chapter House C3
6 St Ann's House D3

Eating
7 Anokaa A1
8 Craft Bar C1

Drinking & Nightlife
9 Haunch of Venison B2

Salisbury

01722 / POP 40,300

Centred on a majestic cathedral that's topped by the tallest spire in England, Salisbury has been an important provincial city for more than a thousand years. Its streets form an architectural timeline ranging from medieval walls and half-timbered Tudor town houses to Georgian mansions and Victorian villas.

Sights

★Salisbury Cathedral CATHEDRAL

(01722-555150; www.salisburycathedral.org.uk; The Close; requested donation adult/child £7.50/3; 9am-4pm Mon-Sat) Few of England's stunning churches can hold a candle to the grandeur and sheer spectacle of 13th-century Salisbury Cathedral. This elaborate, early English Gothic-style structure has pointed arches, flying buttresses, a sombre, austere interior and outstanding statuary and tombs. Check the website to see if the daily tower tours have resumed and if the cathedral's 13th-century copy of the **Magna Carta** is on display. If not, look out for the high-resolution facsimile in the North Transept.

The cathedral was built between 1220 and 1258. Beyond its highly decorative **West Front**, a small passageway leads into the 70m-long **nave**, lined with handsome pillars of Purbeck stone. In the north aisle look out for a fascinating **medieval clock**, probably the oldest working timepiece in the world, dating from 1386. At the eastern end of the ambulatory, the glorious **Prisoners of Conscience** stained-glass window (1980) hovers above the ornate **tomb** of Edward Seymour (1539–1621) and Lady Catherine Grey. Other monuments and tombs line the sides of the nave, including that of William Longespée, son of Henry II and half-brother of King John. When the tomb was excavated a well-preserved rat was found inside Longespée's skull.

Salisbury's 123m-high crowning glory, its **spire**, was added in the mid-14th century, and is the tallest in Britain. It represented an enormous technical challenge for its medieval builders – it weighs around 6500 tonnes and required an elaborate system of cross-bracing, scissor arches and supporting buttresses to keep it upright. Look closely and you'll see the weight has buckled the four central piers of the nave.

Sir Christopher Wren surveyed the cathedral in 1668 and calculated that the spire was leaning by 75cm. A brass plate in the floor of the nave is used to measure any shift, but no further lean was recorded in 1951 or 1970. Despite this, reinforcement of the notoriously 'wonky spire' continues to this day.

If distancing regulations mean the one-way system is still in operation, you may be lucky enough to be routed through the normally out-of-bounds stonemasonry yard, one of only nine in the country.

★Salisbury Museum MUSEUM
(☎01722-332151; www.salisburymuseum.org.uk; 65 The Close; adult/child £8/4; ⏲11am-4pm Thu-Sun) The hugely important archaeological finds in the Wessex Gallery include the Stonehenge Archer, the bones of a man found in the ditch near the stone circle – one of the arrows found alongside probably killed him. With gold coins dating from 100 BCE and a Bronze Age gold necklace, it's a powerful introduction to Wiltshire's prehistory.

Wilton House HISTORIC BUILDING
(☎01722-746700; www.wiltonhouse.co.uk; Wilton; house & grounds adult/child £15.50/8; ⏲11.30am-5pm Sun-Thu May-Aug; P) Stately Wilton House is due to reopen at Easter 2021 after significant refurbishments. It provides an insight into the rarefied world of the British aristocracy. One of England's finest stately homes, it's been the house of the Earls of Pembroke since 1542, and has been expanded, improved and embellished by successive generations. Highlights are the Single and Double Cube Rooms by 17th-century architect Inigo Jones.

It's 3 miles west of Salisbury; bus PR/R 3 runs from Salisbury (£3, 10 minutes, one to three hourly).

Old Sarum ARCHAEOLOGICAL SITE
(EH; ☎01722-335398; www.english-heritage.org.uk; Castle Rd; adult/child £5.90/3.50; ⏲10am-5pm Apr-Oct, to 4pm Nov-Mar; P) The vast ramparts of Old Sarum sit on a turf-covered hill 2 miles north of Salisbury. You can wander the grassy ramparts, see the original cathedral's stone foundations and look across the Wiltshire countryside to the spire of the present Salisbury Cathedral. Buses X4 and R11 regularly run from Salisbury to Old Sarum (£4.40, 10 minutes). It's also a stop on the Stonehenge Tour bus.

Tours

Salisbury Guides WALKING
(☎07873-212941; www.salisburycityguides.co.uk; adult/child £7/4; ⏲11am daily Apr-Oct, 11am Sat & Sun Nov-Mar) These 90-minute trips leave from the tourist office.

Sleeping

St Ann's House B&B ££
(☎01722-335657; www.stannshouse.co.uk; 32 St Ann St; d £65-90; ☜) Utter elegance reigns at 18th-century St Ann's, where cast-iron fireplaces, mini-chandeliers and sash windows cosy up to warm colours and well-chosen antiques. Breakfast goodies include locally baked bread and homemade orange and star anise marmalade.

WORTH A TRIP

SHAFTESBURY: HISTORIC HILLTOP TOWN

Crowning a ridge of hogbacked hills and overlooking pastoral meadows, the agreeable market town of Shaftesbury circles around its medieval **abbey ruins** (☎01747-852910; www.shaftesburyabbey.org.uk; Park Walk; donation requested; ⏲10am-4pm Sat & Sun Apr-Oct). Once England's largest and richest nunnery, it was founded in 888 by King Alfred the Great; his daughter, Aethelgifu, was its first abbess. St Edward is thought to have been buried here, and King Knut died at the abbey in 1035. Most of the buildings were dismantled by Henry VIII, but you can still spot the foundations amid swathes of grass and wildflowers, and hunt out the medieval-inspired herb and fruit-tree collections. A few minutes' walk away you'll find **Gold Hill** – an often-photographed, painfully steep, cobbled slope lined by chocolate-box cottages.

The imposing ruins of **Old Wardour Castle** (EH; ☎01747-870487; www.english-heritage.org.uk; near Tisbury; adult/child £5.90/3.50; ⏲10am-5pm Wed-Sun; Ⓟ) sit some 4 miles east of Shaftesbury. Built around 1393, it suffered severe damage during the English Civil War. The views from the upper levels are fabulous, while its grassy lawns make a fine spot for a picnic.

Bus 29 links Shaftesbury with Salisbury (£5.20, one hour) every one to two hours, Monday to Saturday.

Cathedral View B&B ££

(☎01722-502254; www.cathedral-viewbandb.co.uk; 83 Exeter St; s £90, d £100-140; Ⓟ📶) Admirable attention to detail defines this Georgian town house, where miniature flower displays and home-baked biscuits sit in quietly elegant rooms. Breakfasts include prime Wiltshire sausages and the B&B's own bread and jam, while homemade lemon drizzle cake will be waiting for your afternoon tea.

★ **Chapter House** INN £££

(☎01722-341277; www.thechapterhouseuk.com; 9 St Johns St; s £95-145, d £115-155; 📶) In this 800-year-old boutique beauty, wood panels and wildly wonky stairs sit beside duck-your-head beams. The cheaper bedrooms are swish but the posher ones are stunning, starring slipper baths and the odd heraldic crest. The pick is room 6, where King Charles is reputed to have stayed. Lucky him.

They're also renowned for perfectly cooked, top-quality steaks, ribs and roasts (mains £13 to £23).

Eating & Drinking

Craft Bar BURGERS £

(Salisbury Arms; ☎01722-41170; www.thecraftbar.wordpress.com; 31 Endless St; meals £11; ⏲6-9.30pm Wed-Sat) It's a winning combo: towering burgers, hand-cut fries, creative cocktails and craft beer and cider. All set in a pub with a relaxed vibe.

★ **Anokaa** INDIAN ££

(☎01722-414142; www.anokaa.com; 60 Fisherton St; mains £16-19; ⏲5-9pm Sun-Fri, noon-9pm Sat; 🌶) The neon and ultra-modern decor signals what's in store here: a contemporary, multilayered take on high-class Indian cuisine. The spice and flavour combos make the ingredients sing, the meat-free menu makes vegetarians gleeful, and the early evening deal (two courses with wine for £16) makes everyone smile.

Haunch of Venison PUB

(☎01722-411313; www.haunchpub.co.uk; 1 Minster St; ⏲11am-11pm Mon-Sat, to 6pm Sun) Featuring wood-panelled snugs, spiral staircases and crooked ceilings, this 14th-century drinking den is packed with atmosphere – and ghosts. One is a cheating whist player whose hand was severed in a game – look out for his mummified bones on display inside.

Entertainment

Live performances at the renowned **Salisbury Playhouse** and **Salisbury Arts Centre** were suspended in 2020. Check **Wiltshire Creative** (www.wiltshirecreative.co.uk) for updates on all cultural events.

Information

Tourist Office (☎01722-342860; www.visitwiltshire.co.uk/salisbury; Fish Row; ⏲9am-5pm Mon-Fri, 10am-4pm Sat; 📶)

Getting There & Away

BUS

National Express (www.nationalexpress.com) services stop at Millstream Approach, near the train station. Direct services include:

Bath (£11, 1½ hours, one daily)
Bristol (£6, two hours, one daily)
London Victoria via Heathrow (£12, three hours, two daily)

Local services leave from stops around the town; they include:

Devizes (bus 2, £5.70, 1¼ hours, hourly Monday to Saturday)
Shaftesbury (bus 29, £5.20, one hour, every one to two hours Monday to Saturday)
Stonehenge (☎01202-338420; www.thestonehengetour.info; incl admissions adult/child/ £32/21, bus-only adult/child £16/10) Tour buses leave Salisbury train station regularly.

TRAIN

Salisbury's train station is half a mile northwest of the cathedral. Half-hourly connections include:

Bath (£12, one hour)
Bristol (£20, 1¼ hours)
London Waterloo (£25, 1½ hours)
Southampton (£10, 40 minutes)

Hourly connections:

Exeter (£20, two hours)
Portsmouth (£20, 1¼ hours)

Stonehenge

Welcome to Britain's most iconic archaeological site. This compelling ring of monolithic stones has been attracting a steady stream of pilgrims, poets and philosophers for the last 5000 years and is still a mystical, ethereal place – a haunting echo from Britain's forgotten past, and a reminder of those who once walked the ceremonial avenues across Salisbury Plain.

Sights

★Stonehenge ARCHAEOLOGICAL SITE
(EH; ☎0370 333 1181; www.english-heritage.org.uk; near Amesbury; adult/child £21/13; ⏲9.30am-5pm, hours may vary; P) An ultra-modern makeover at ancient Stonehenge has brought an impressive visitor centre and the closure of an intrusive road (now restored to grassland). The result is a strong sense of historical context, with dignity and mystery returned to an archaeological gem.

Stonehenge operates by pre-booked, timed tickets – secure yours well in advance. At the time of research, opening hours were reduced; check whether summertime early evening visits have resumed. The VIP Stone Circle Experience (p300), where you walk within the stone circle itself, is highly recommended.

Stonehenge is one of Britain's great archaeological mysteries: despite countless theories about the site's purpose, from a sacrificial centre to a celestial timepiece, no one knows for sure what drove prehistoric Britons to expend so much time and effort on its construction, although recent archaeological findings show the surrounding area was sacred for hundreds of years before work began.

The first phase of building started around 3000 BCE, when the outer circular bank and ditch were erected. Within this were 56 pits called **Aubrey Holes**, named after John Aubrey, who discovered them in the 1600s. Cremations were buried around these pits; it's thought they may also have held timber posts or stones.

About 500 years later, Stonehenge's main stones were dragged to the site, erected in a circle and crowned by massive lintels to make the trilithons (two vertical stones topped by a horizontal one). The 30 huge slabs of stone were worked carefully to ensure they locked together. The sarsen stones were cut from an extremely hard rock found on the Marlborough Downs, 20 miles from the site. It's estimated that dragging one of the 50-tonne stones across the countryside would have required about 600 people.

Two curving rows of smaller 'bluestones' were also added. The four Station stones were probably set up at around the same time. Then in around 2300 BCE the central bluestones were rearranged forming inner circles and ovals, which were later rearranged to form a **bluestone horseshoe**.

It's thought some of the mammoth 4-tonne bluestone blocks were hauled from the Preseli Mountains in South Wales, some 250 miles away – an extraordinary feat for Stone Age people equipped with only the simplest of tools. Although no one is entirely sure how the builders transported the stones so far, it's thought they probably used

Stonehenge

0 — 50 m
0 — 0.025 miles

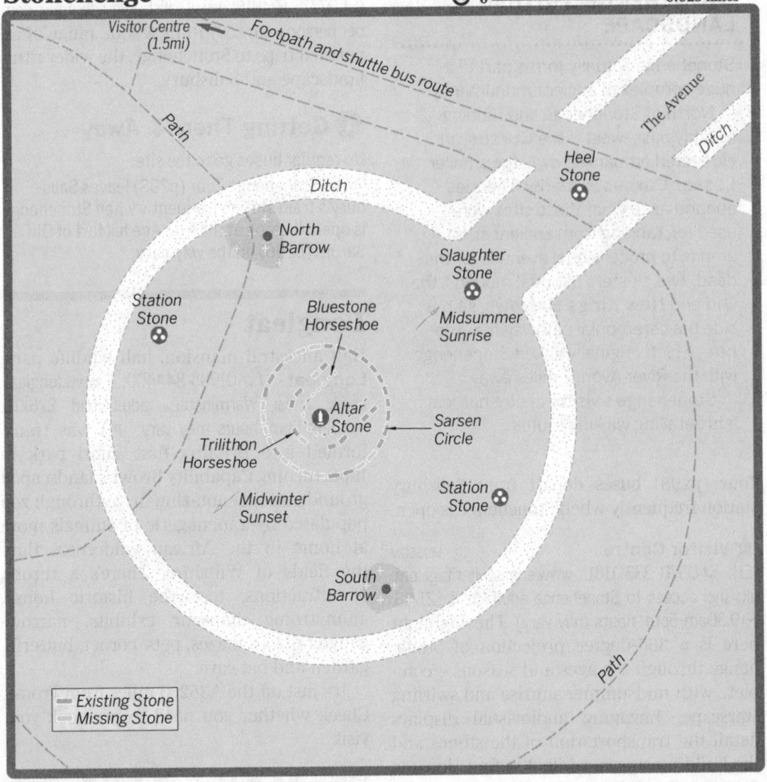

a system of ropes, sledges and rollers fashioned from tree trunks – Salisbury Plain was still covered by forest during Stonehenge's construction.

Today, three of the five sets of stones in the **trilithon horseshoe** are intact; the other two have just a single upright. Of the major **sarsen circle** of 30 massive vertical stones, 17 uprights and six lintels remain.

Just inside this circle are the **South** and **North Barrows**, each originally topped by a stone. Like many stone circles in Britain (including Avebury, 22 miles away), the stones are aligned to coincide with sunrise at the midsummer solstice, which some claim supports the theory that the site was some kind of astronomical calendar.

Prehistoric pilgrims would have entered the site via the **Avenue**, whose entrance to the circle is marked by the **Slaughter Stone** and the **Heel Stone**, located slightly further out on one side.

A decision on long-standing plans to turn parts of the main A303 road, which runs close to the site, into a tunnel has been repeatedly delayed. The proposed tunnel aims to reduce traffic around Stonehenge, although opponents fear it could damage other monuments in the area.

Stonehenge's visitor centre (p300) is some 1.5 miles from the stones. A fleet of trolley buses makes the 10-minute trip, although it's more atmospheric to walk, via a 2.6-mile circular trail through the ancient landscape.

Visiting the site is free for English Heritage and National Trust members, but they still have to secure a timed ticket. If social-distancing measures are in place, visitor numbers and hours will be reduced, making it harder to secure a time slot – book well ahead.

Trains run from London Waterloo to Salisbury station (£27, 1½ hours, every half hour), nine miles from Stonehenge. Stonehenge

STONEHENGE'S RITUAL LANDSCAPE

Stonehenge actually forms part of a huge complex of ancient monuments.

North of Stonehenge and running roughly east–west is the **Cursus**, an elongated embanked oval; the smaller **Lesser Cursus** is nearby. Theories abound as to what these sites were used for, ranging from ancient sporting arenas to processional avenues for the dead. Two clusters of burial mounds, the **Old** and **New Kings Barrows**, sit beside the ceremonial pathway the **Avenue**, which originally linked Stonehenge with the River Avon, 2 miles away.

Stonehenge's visitor centre has leaflets detailing walking routes.

Tour (p298) buses depart from Salisbury station frequently when Stonehenge is open.

★**Visitor Centre** MUSEUM
(EH; ☎0370 333 1181; www.english-heritage.org.uk; incl access to Stonehenge adult/child £21/13; ⊙9.30am-5pm, hours may vary) The highlight here is a 360-degree projection of Stonehenge through the ages and seasons – complete with midsummer sunrise and swirling starscape. Engaging audiovisual displays detail the transportation of the stones and the building stages, while 300 finds include flint chippings, bone pins and arrowheads. There's also a strikingly lifelike model of the face of a Neolithic man whose body was found nearby. Outside you can step into recreations of Stone Age houses and watch rope-making and flint-knapping demonstrations.

Tours

★**Stone Circle Experience** WALKING
(☎0370 333 0605; www.english-heritage.org.uk; adult/child £47/28) Visitors normally have to stay outside the stone circle, but on these hour-long, self-guided walks, you get to wander around the heart of the archaeological site, getting up-close views of the iconic bluestones and trilithons. Tours occur in the evening or early morning, when the quieter atmosphere and slanting sunlight add to the effect. Each visit only takes 15 people; book at least three months in advance.

Salisbury Guided Tours HISTORY
(☎07775 674816; www.salisburyguidedtours.com; per person from £59) Runs a wide range of expert-led trips to Stonehenge, the wider ritual landscape and Salisbury.

Getting There & Away

No regular buses go to the site.

The Stonehenge Tour (p298) leaves Salisbury's train station frequently when Stonehenge is open. It stops at the Iron Age hill fort of Old Sarum (p296) on the way back.

Longleat

Half ancestral mansion, half wildlife park, **Longleat** (☎01985-844400; www.longleat.co.uk; near Warminster; adult/child £26/19; ⊙10am-5pm, hours may vary; P) was transformed into Britain's first safari park in 1966, turning Capability Brown's landscaped grounds into an amazing drive-through zoo populated by a menagerie of animals more at home in the African wilderness than the fields of Wiltshire. There's a throng of attractions, too: the historic house, animatronic dinosaur exhibits, narrow-gauge railway, mazes, pets' corner, butterfly garden and bat cave.

It's just off the A362, 3 miles from Frome. Check whether you need to pre-book your visit.

Lacock

POP 1160

With its geranium-covered cottages and higgledy-piggledy rooftops, pockets of the medieval village of Lacock seem to have been preserved in mid-19th-century aspic. The village has been in the hands of the National Trust since 1944, and in many places is remarkably free of modern development – there are no telephone poles or electric street lights and the main car park on the outskirts keeps visitors' cars away. Unsurprisingly, it's a popular location for costume dramas and feature films – the village and its abbey pop up in the *Harry Potter* films, *Downton Abbey, The Other Boleyn Girl* and BBC adaptations of *Wolf Hall, Moll Flanders* and *Pride and Prejudice*.

Sights

Lacock Abbey ABBEY
(NT; ☎01249-730459; www.nationaltrust.org.uk; Hither Way; adult/child £10/5; ⊙10.30am-5pm

Mar-Oct, 11am-4pm Nov-Feb) Lacock Abbey is a window into a medieval world. It was founded in 1232 by Ela, Countess of Salisbury, and some of the original structure is evident in the cloisters; there are traces of medieval wall paintings, too. Check whether the abbey's deeply atmospheric rooms, temporarily closed in 2020, have reopened. Highlights include the stunning Gothic entrance hall and the bizarre terracotta figures; hunt out the scapegoat with a lump of sugar on its nose.

Admission to the abbey includes entry into the **Fox Talbot Museum**. It profiles William Henry Fox Talbot (1800–77), who pioneered the photographic negative. A prolific inventor, he began developing the system in 1834 while working at Lacock Abbey. The museum details his groundbreaking processes and displays a superb collection of his images.

Sleeping & Eating

★Sign of the Angel INN ££
(01249-730230; www.signoftheangel.co.uk; 6 Church St; s £85-115, d £115-145; P) Every inch of this gorgeous, 15th-century restaurant-with-rooms is rich in heritage pizzazz. Burnished beams, slanting floors and open fires meet duck-down duvets, upcycled furniture and neutral tones, delivering a fresh provincial rustic feel. Treats include luxury toiletries and chef-baked cookies.

Pear Tree INN ££
(01225-704966; www.peartreewhitley.co.uk; Top Lane, Whitley; d £95-135, q £150; P) It takes a lot of skill to make rooms look so beautifully casual and yet so smart – the bedrooms here are a mash-up of mullioned windows, worn wooden chairs, waterfall showers and framed cartoons. Rooms in the ancient inn have more heritage features; those in the converted barn have a sleeker feel. It's 4 miles southwest of Lacock.

The **restaurant** (mains £16 to £20) is famous for its terrace, beamed sunroom and inventive dishes crammed with kitchen garden produce. Food is served from noon to 2.30pm and 6pm to 9pm.

Red Lion INN ££
(01249-730456; www.redlionlacock.co.uk; 1 High St; d £99-130; P) In historic Lacock, where better to sleep than a Georgian coaching inn that oozes ambience. Step on flagstone floors past open fires, up a grand staircase to sweet rooms where padded cushions line stone window frames with picture-postcard views. The kitchen does the pub classics well (mains £13, served 11.30am to 8.30pm).

Avebury

POP 530

While the tour buses head straight for Stonehenge, prehistoric purists make for the massive stone circle at Avebury. Though it lacks the dramatic trilithons of its sister site across Salisbury Plain, Avebury is just as rewarding to visit. It's bigger and older, and a large section of the village is actually inside the stones – footpaths wind around them, allowing you to really soak up the extraordinary atmosphere. Avebury also boasts an encircling landscape that's rich in prehistoric sites.

Sights

Visits to the National Trust's imaginatively restored **Avebury Manor** were suspended in 2020; it's worth checking to see whether they've resumed.

★Avebury Stone Circle ARCHAEOLOGICAL SITE
(NT; 01672-539250; www.nationaltrust.org.uk; parking per day £7; dawn-dusk; P) FREE With a diameter of 348m, Avebury is the largest stone circle in the world. It's also one of the oldest, dating from 2500 to 2200 BCE. Today, more than 30 stones are in place; pillars show where missing stones would have been. Wandering between them emphasises the site's sheer scale, evidenced also by the massive bank and ditch that line the circle;

DON'T MISS

STOURHEAD

Overflowing with vistas, temples and exotic trees, **Stourhead** (NT; 01747-841152; www.nationaltrust.org.uk; Mere; gardens adult/child £13/6.50; gardens 9am-5pm; P) is landscape gardening at its finest. The magnificent 18th-century gardens spread across the valley, with a picturesque 2-mile garden circuit taking you past ornate follies, around a centrepiece lake and to the Georgian Temple of Apollo. A 3.5-mile side trip can be made from near the Pantheon to a 50m-high folly called King Alfred's Tower. Stourhead is off the B3092, 10 miles south of Frome.

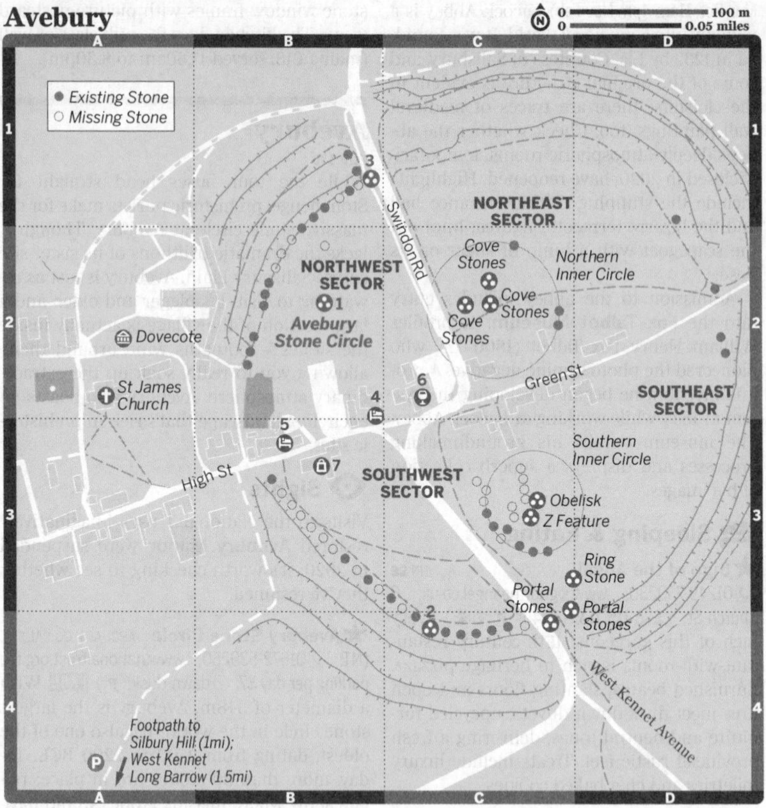

Avebury

Top Sights
1 Avebury Stone Circle B2

Sights
2 Barber Surgeon Stone C4
3 Swindon Stone B1

Sleeping
4 Avebury Lodge B2
5 Manor Farm B3

Drinking & Nightlife
6 Red Lion C2

Shopping
7 Henge Shop B3

the quieter northwest sector is particularly atmospheric.

Avebury henge originally consisted of an outer circle of 98 standing stones of up to 6m in length, many weighing 20 tonnes. The stones were surrounded by another circle delineated by a 5m-high earth bank and a ditch up to 9m deep. Inside were smaller stone circles to the north (27 stones) and south (29 stones).

In the Middle Ages, when Britain's pagan past was an embarrassment to the Church, many of the stones were buried, removed or broken up. In 1934 wealthy businessman and archaeologist Alexander Keiller supervised the re-erection of the stones; he later bought the site for posterity using funds from his family's marmalade fortune.

Modern roads into Avebury neatly dissect the circle into four sectors. Starting at High St near the **Henge Shop** (☎01672-539229; www.hengeshop.com; High St; ⊙9.30am-5pm) and walking round the circle in an anticlockwise direction, you'll encounter 11 standing stones in the southwest sector. They include the **Barber Surgeon Stone**, named after the skeleton of a man found under it – the equipment buried with him suggests he was a barber and surgeon.

The southeast sector starts with huge **portal stones** marking the entry to the circle from **West Kennet Avenue**. The **southern inner circle** stood in this sector and within this ring was the **obelisk** and a group of stones known as the **Z Feature**. Just outside this smaller circle, only the base of the **Ring Stone** survives.

In the **northern inner circle** in the northeast sector, three sarsens remain of what would have been a rectangular **cove**. The northwest sector has the most complete collection of standing stones, including the massive 65-tonne **Swindon Stone**, one of the few never to have been toppled.

Check whether the National Trust–run guided walks of the site (£3), which were suspended in 2020, have resumed.

Silbury Hill ARCHAEOLOGICAL SITE

(EH; www.english-heritage.org.uk; near Avebury; P) FREE Rising abruptly from the fields just south of Avebury, 40m-high Silbury Hill is the largest artificial earthwork in Europe, comparable in height and volume to the Egyptian pyramids. It was built in stages from around 2500 BCE, but the precise reason for its construction remains unclear. Direct access to the hill isn't allowed, but you can view it from footpaths on the north side and a lay-by on the A4.

For the most atmospheric views, walk from Avebury village – head through the main National Trust car park, cross the main road, then pick up the footpath just to the west that cuts south across the fields (2 miles return) to the hill's north side.

West Kennet Long Barrow ARCHAEOLOGICAL SITE

(EH; www.english-heritage.org.uk; near Marlborough; dawn-dusk) FREE England's finest burial mound dates from around 3500 BCE. Its entrance is guarded by huge sarsens and its roof is made out of gigantic overlapping capstones. About 50 skeletons were found when it was excavated. The barrow is a half-mile walk across fields from a parking lay-by beside the A4.

A footpath leads from Avebury Stone Circle to West Kennet (3 miles return), passing the vast earthwork of Silbury Hill en route.

Sleeping

Avebury Lodge B&B £££

(01672-539023; www.aveburylodge.co.uk; High St; s/d/tr £155/200/255; P) It's as if gentlemanly archaeologists are still in situ: antiquarian prints of stone circles smother the walls, pelmets and chandeliers are dotted around, and whenever you glance from a window, a bit of Avebury henge appears. It's lovely, but arguably not good value for money – it's the location that pushes the room rates up here.

Drinking & Nightlife

Red Lion PUB

(01672-539266; www.oldenglishinns.co.uk; High St; 11am-10pm Sun-Thu, to 11pm Fri & Sat) Having a pint here means downing a drink at the only pub in the world inside a stone circle. The best table is the Well Seat, where the glass tabletop covers a 26m-deep, 17th-century well – believed to be the last resting place of at least one unfortunate villager.

The kitchen rustles up hearty pub-food standards (mains £8 to £12, served 11am to 9pm).

Getting There & Away

Bus 49 runs hourly to Swindon (£3.20, 30 minutes) and Devizes (£3.20, 20 minutes), Monday to Saturday. There are six services on Sunday.

AT A GLANCE

POPULATION
1.6 million

BIGGEST CITY
Plymouth: 256,384

BEST BEACH
Perranporth (p340)

BEST CAMPSITE
Kudhva (p335)

BEST SEAFOOD CAFE
S&P (p331)

WHEN TO GO

Apr & May
Cliffs, hillsides and gardens burst into bloom; attractions reopen; boat trips start.

Sep
The busy school holidays end, ushering in cheaper sleep spots, quieter beaches and warmer seas.

Oct
Bigger waves draw surfers to the north coasts; the winter storm-watching season begins.

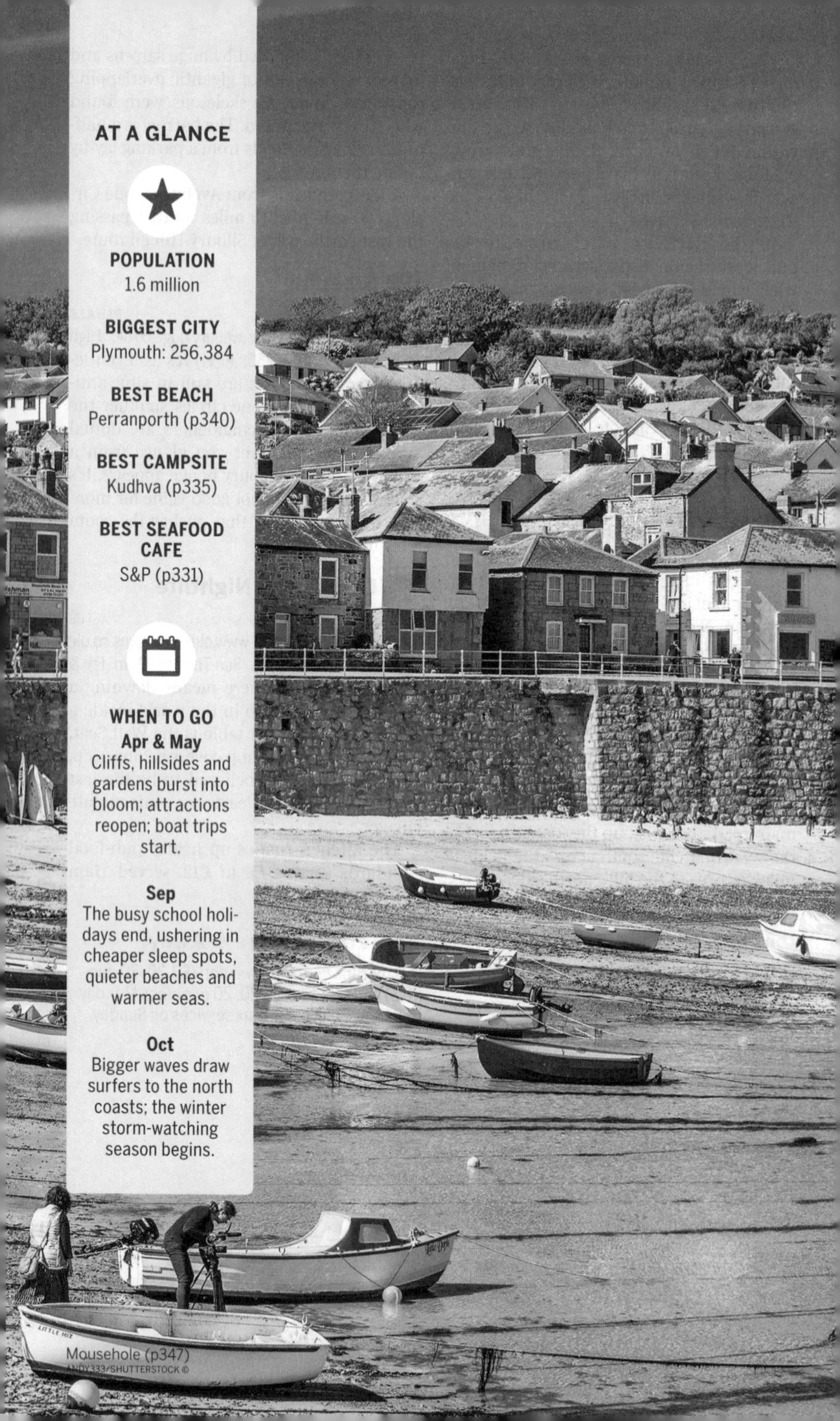

Mousehole (p347)
ANDY333/SHUTTERSTOCK ©

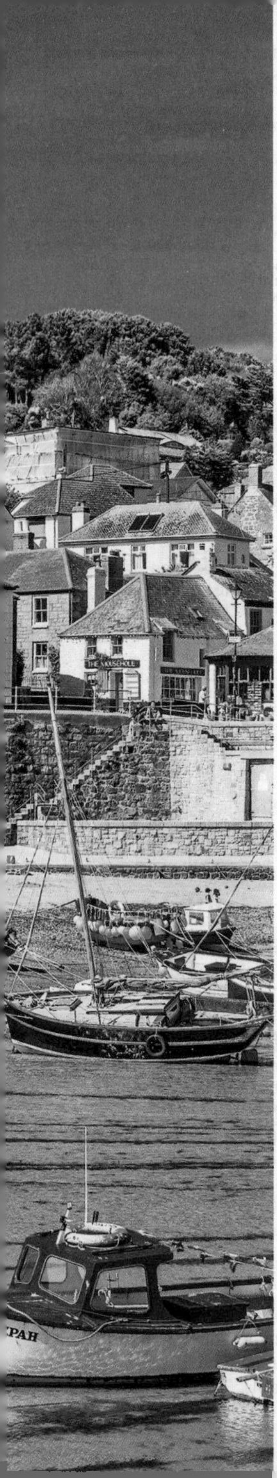

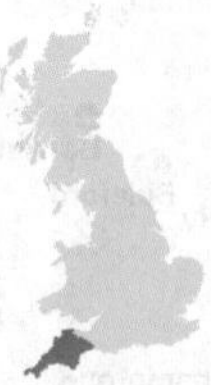

Devon, Cornwall & the Isles of Scilly

Welcome to England's wild, wild west – a land of gorse-clad cliffs, booming surf, white sand and widescreen skies. Flung out on a finger of land, Devon and Cornwall are packed with potential and made for making memories. Here you can hike roller-coaster clifftop trails, kayak sleepy creeks and go wild swimming on deserted moors. Foodie fans delight in cracking fresh crab, sampling just-caught fish and sipping wines in vineyard cafes. The past is ever present in neolithic monuments, medieval castles and ruined mine stacks clinging to cliffs. Hang out on surfer beaches or stargaze under inky skies – whatever you do, Devon and Cornwall help you breathe deeply, rediscover, reinvent and revive.

INCLUDES

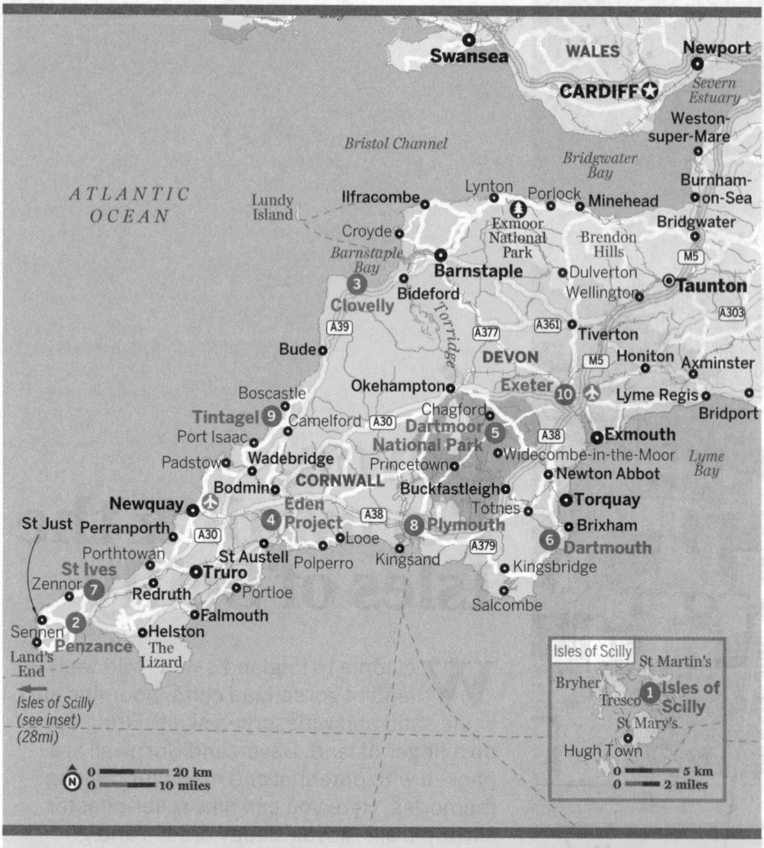

Devon, Cornwall & the Isles of Scilly Highlights

1. **Isles of Scilly** (p359) Ferry-hopping around an idyllic archipelago.
2. **Penzance** (p348) Discovering a geothermally heated lido and a medieval island abbey.
3. **Clovelly** (p330) Strolling the cobbled streets of a pretty fishing village.
4. **Eden Project** (p354) Marvelling at space-age biomes in a disused Cornish claypit.
5. **Dartmoor National Park** (p323) Wild swimming in streams and moorland pools.
6. **Dartmouth** (p315) Touring the pretty grounds of Agatha Christie's home.
7. **Tate St Ives** (p341) Getting inspired by art in this Cornish port.
8. **Plymouth** (p319) Exploring colonial history then sampling gin on a distillery tour.
9. **Tintagel** (p334) Pondering Arthurian legends at a fairytale clifftop fortress.
10. **Exeter** (p308) Clambering up to the roof of a gloriously gothic cathedral.

Activities

Walking

The sheer diversity of landscapes in Devon and Cornwall gives walkers itchy feet. Some of the most dramatic sections of the **South West Coast Path** are to be found here. The epic route sweeps for 630 miles from Minehead in Somerset via Land's End in Cornwall to Poole in Dorset. Along the way are countless memorable day hikes, which can often be teamed with inland sections to make circular trails. The South West Coast Path Association (www.southwestcoastpath.

org.uk) has a detailed website and publishes an annual guide.

For wilderness hikes, Dartmoor National Park has 368 sq miles to explore. Longer self-guided hikes include the 117-mile, coast-to-coast **Two Moors Way** (www.twomoorsway.org) and the 18-mile **Templer Way**.

On Bodmin Moor the 60-mile **Copper Trail** starts in the village of Minions and takes in a wealth of photogenic ruined mines. In both moors, rounded hills, or tors, pepper a rolling, primitive landscape studded with stone rows and prehistoric remains.

Cycling

The cycling in Devon and Cornwall is superb, if strenuous. The 328-mile **West Country Way** (NCN Route 3) connects the far west of Cornwall with Bristol, taking in Mevagissey, the Eden Project, Bude, north Devon and the fringes of Exmoor en route.

The 99-mile **Devon Coast to Coast** powers from North Devon's beaches, alongside the Taw and Torridge estuaries, around the western edge of Dartmoor to Plymouth's seafront.

Dartmoor National Park's unfenced, undulating roads offer steep hill climbs and are popular for touring. The moor's picturesque mountain-bike routes include those ranging from 6 to 18 miles along disused granite quarry tramways around Princetown.

Many cycle trails trace the routes of former railway lines, including Cornwall's popular 18-mile **Camel Trail** linking Padstow with Bodmin Moor, and Devon's 11-mile **Granite Way** between Okehampton and Lydford.

Sustrans (www.sustrans.org.uk) and local tourist offices can provide more information.

Surfing & Boating

North Cornwall, and to a slightly lesser extent north Devon, have the best surf in England. Party-town Newquay is the epicentre; other top spots are Bude in Cornwall and Croyde in Devon. Region-wide surf conditions can be found at www.magicseaweed.com.

For sailing, key ports include Falmouth, Fowey, Plymouth and Dartmouth.

Other Activities

Devon and Cornwall are prime places for lessons in kitesurfing, windsurfing, diving, sea kayaking, white-water kayaking, wakeboarding and climbing. Stand-up paddleboarding (SUP) continues to grow in popularity, as does wild swimming – in everything from moorland pools to secret coves.

Climbers of all abilities head to Dartmoor's granite crags and bouldering spots. In Torquay, Anstey's Cove has limestone sport and trad routes, while in north Cornwall Bosigran offers legendary granite, single- and multi-pitch sea-cliff routes.

Check out www.visitsouthwest.co.uk for links to activity operators.

Getting Around

BUS

The region's bus services are generally reliable, providing a safe, cost-effective way to travel. Services are better in urban areas, but can dwindle to one a day, a week or even none, in rural areas.

National Express (www.nationalexpress.com) runs frequent services between the region's cities, major towns and resorts. Example direct services include Penzance to Torquay (£21, four hours, one daily) and Plymouth to Torquay (£10, one hour, two daily).

The following are key local bus firms.

First Kernow (www.firstgroup.com/cornwall) Major operator in Cornwall.

Stagecoach (www.stagecoachbus.com) Devon's main cross-county operator.

Stagecoach offers a range of weekly Megarider passes covering individual towns (eg Exeter, adult £15) and wider areas (eg North Devon £16; the South West £30).

PlusBus (www.plusbus.info) adds local bus travel to your train ticket (£2 to £4 per day). Participating towns and cities include Exeter, Torquay, Plymouth, Totnes, Truro, Newquay, Penzance and Falmouth. Buy tickets at train stations.

CAR & MOTORCYCLE

National car-hire firms have offices at Exeter and Newquay airports and the region's cities and bigger towns.

There are no motorways west of Exeter and while many stretches of key A roads are dual carriageway, some aren't; the lesser A roads are rarely so. They can become severely congested at peak holiday times.

Petrol stations are fairly plentiful, but it's still worth filling up before heading into rural areas and onto the moors.

TRAIN

Major companies operating in Devon and Cornwall include **GWR** (www.gwr.com),

CrossCountry (www.crosscountrytrains.co.uk) and **South Western Railway** (www.southwesternrailway.com).

Stops on GWR's London Paddington–Penzance service include Exeter, Plymouth, Liskeard, St Austell and Truro. Spur lines run to Barnstaple, Paignton, Gunnislake, Looe, Falmouth, St Ives and Newquay.

CrossCountry trains run from Penzance to Scotland, via Exeter, Bristol, the Midlands and the North.

South Western Railway provides links between Exeter and London and the southeast. Other destinations include Bournemouth, Portsmouth, Salisbury and Bristol.

The Freedom of Devon and Cornwall Rover pass offers three days train travel in seven days (adult/child £53/26) or eight days travel in 15 days (£85/42). It allows unlimited travel across the two counties.

DEVON

Devon's rippling, beach-fringed landscape is studded with historic homes, vibrant cities and wild, wild moors. Here you can hike rugged coast paths, take scenic boat trips, or get lost in hedge-lined lanes that aren't even on your map. Discover collegiate Exeter, touristy Torquay, yachting-haven Dartmouth, bewitching Salcombe and alternative Totnes. Or escape to wilderness Dartmoor and the remote, surf-dashed north coast. In Devon you can sample wines made from the vines beside you and food that's fresh from field, furrow or sea. However you decide to explore – surfing, cycling, kayaking, horse riding, sea swimming or barefoot beachcombing – visiting Devon might feel like coming home.

Information

Visit Devon (www.visitdevon.co.uk) The official tourism website.

Getting Around

BUS

Most bus services between larger towns and villages are run by Stagecoach (www.stagecoachbus.com), with a number of smaller coach companies offering buses to other areas. Inevitably Dartmoor has fewer services.

Bus passes include the Devon Day Ticket (adult/child/family £9.60/6.40/19.20) which covers all companies. The Stagecoach South West Explorer (adult/child/family £8.30/5.50/16.60) and South West Megarider Gold tickets (one week £30) only cover Stagecoach buses. Day Rider tickets, covering different parts of Devon, may be cheaper than standard return fares. Check the Stagecoach website for details.

Travel Devon (www.traveldevon.info) features a useful interactive bus-route map.

TRAIN

Devon's main line links Exeter with Plymouth and Cornwall. Branch lines include the 39-mile Exeter–Barnstaple Tarka Line, the 15-mile Plymouth–Gunnislake Tamar Valley Line and the scenic Exeter–Torquay Paignton line. The Dartmouth Steam Railway (p316) provides views of the lush River Dart.

The Freedom of Devon & Cornwall Rover ticket (three days off-peak travel in seven days adult/child £52/26, eight days travel in 15 days £85/43) is good value if you're using the train extensively.

Exeter

☎01392 / POP 117,770

Well-heeled and comfortable, Exeter exudes evidence of its centuries-old role as the spiritual and administrative heart of Devon. The city's Gothic cathedral presides over pockets of cobbled streets; medieval and Georgian buildings and fragments of the Roman city wall stretch out all around. A snazzy contemporary shopping centre brings bursts of the modern, thousands of university students ensure a buzzing nightlife, and the vibrant quayside acts as a launch pad for cycling or kayaking trips. Throw in some stylish places to stay and eat, and you have a relaxed but lively base for explorations.

History

Exeter's past can be read in its buildings. The Romans marched in around AD 55; their 17-hectare fortress included a 2-mile defensive wall, crumbling sections of which remain, especially in Rougemont and Northernhay Gardens. Saxon and Norman times saw growth: a castle went up in 1068, the cathedral 40 years later. The Tudor wool boom brought Exeter an export trade, riches and half-timbered houses. Prosperity continued into the Georgian era, when hundreds of merchants built genteel homes. The Blitz of WWII brought devastation; in just one night in 1942, 156 people died and 12 hectares of the city were

Exeter

Exeter

Top Sights

1	Exeter Cathedral	C3
2	RAMM	C2
3	Underground Passages	D2

Activities, Courses & Tours

	Exeter Cathedral Roof Tours	(see 1)
4	Redcoat Tours	C2
5	Saddles & Paddles	C4

Sleeping

6	Globe Backpackers	C4
7	Hotel du Vin Exeter	D3
8	Silversprings	B1
9	Telstar	A1

Eating

10	Dinosaur Cafe	B1
11	Exploding Bakery	B1
12	Herbies	B2
13	Hourglass	D4
14	Lloyd's Kitchen	C2

Drinking & Nightlife

15	Old Firehouse	D1

Entertainment

16	Exeter Phoenix	C2
17	Exeter Picturehouse	B3

flattened. In the 21st century, the £220 million Princesshay Shopping Centre added shimmering glass and steel lines. But 2016 saw a serious fire at the Royal Clarence Hotel, a much-loved 18th-century building in the heart of Cathedral Yard.

Sights & Activities

★ **Exeter Cathedral** CATHEDRAL
(Cathedral Church of St Peter; ☎01392-285983; www.exeter-cathedral.org.uk; The Close; adult/child £5/free; ⏲10am-4pm Mon-Sat) Magnificent in warm, honey-coloured stone,

UPDATES: EXETER'S SIGHTS

Some of Exeter's key attractions suspended operations in 2020 due to Covid-19 regulations. Check their websites to see whether they've opened up again.

Royal Albert Memorial Museum & Art Gallery (RAMM; 01392-265858; www.rammuseum.org.uk; Queen St;) FREE Imaginative, insightful displays on the city's Roman history, world cultures, echinoderms and fine art.

Exeter's Underground Passages (01392-665887; www.exeter.gov.uk/passages; 2 Paris St) Hard hat tours of the city's medieval vaulted passages.

Bill Douglas Cinema Museum (01392-724321; www.bdcmuseum.org.uk; Old Library, Prince of Wales Rd; 10am-5pm; P) FREE Superb collection of movie-themed artefacts and memorabilia.

Redcoat Tours (01392-265203; www.exeter.gov.uk/leisure-and-culture) FREE Wide range of free, engaging guided walks around the city's historic streets.

Exeter's cathedral is one of Devon's most impressive ecclesiastical sights and dates largely from the 12th and 13th centuries. Outside, the **Great West Front** features scores of weather-worn figures. They line a once brightly painted screen and now form England's largest collection of 14th-century sculpture. Inside, the ceiling soars upwards to the longest span of unbroken Gothic vaulting in the world, dotted with ornate ceiling bosses in gilt and vibrant colours.

The site has been a religious one since at least the 5th century, but the Normans started the current building in 1114; the towers of today's cathedral date from that period. In 1270, a 90-year remodelling process began, introducing a mix of Early English and Decorated Gothic styles.

The cathedral's exquisitely symmetrical ceiling soars up and along, towards the north transept and the 15th-century **Exeter Clock**: in keeping with medieval astronomy, the clock shows Earth as a golden ball at the centre of the universe with the sun, a fleur-de-lis, travelling around it. Still ticking and whirring, it chimes on the hour.

The huge oak canopy over the **Bishop's Throne** was carved in 1312. The 1350 **minstrels' gallery** is decorated with 12 angels playing musical instruments. Cathedral staff will point out the famous sculpture of the lady with two left feet and the tiny **St James Chapel**, built to repair the one destroyed in the Blitz. Look out for the chapel's unusual carvings: a cat, a mouse and, oddly, a rugby player.

The cathedral offers **brass rubbing** and activity trails for children. You can also borrow free **audio guides**, or book a **guided tour** (adult/child £10/5). These include trips around the cathedral precincts and cloisters, but the highlight is the **Exeter Cathedral Roof Tour** (01392-285983; www.exeter-cathedral.org.uk; per 5 people £40; times vary), which sees you clambering way up into the towers for panoramic views over the city's rooftops. Scaling some 251 steps takes you into the roof void above the Nave, through the bell's Ringing Chamber and onto the North Tower. Tours are currently only available to family groups of up to five people but check the website for changes.

Check online for updates on times of services, and to see if choral evensong, suspended in 2020, has resumed.

Powderham Castle HISTORIC BUILDING
(01626-890243; www.powderham.co.uk; adult/child £10/8; gardens 10am-5pm, house 11.30am-3.30pm Fri-Sun; P) The historic home of the Earl of Devon, Powderham is a stately but still friendly place built in 1391 and remodelled in the Victorian era. A visit takes in a fine wood-panelled Great Hall, parkland with 650 deer and glimpses of life 'below stairs' in the kitchen. Powderham is on the River Exe near Kenton, 8 miles south of Exeter.

Saddles & Paddles OUTDOORS
(01392-424241; www.sadpad.com; Exeter Quay; 9am-6pm Thu-Tue) This hire shop beside the quay rents out bikes (adult per hour/day £7/18), SUP boards (£15/45), single and double kayaks (£12/45) and Canadian canoes (£18/60). It also offers advice on suggested routes featuring the canal and River Exe (p312).

Sleeping

Globe Backpackers HOSTEL £
(01392-215521; www.exeterbackpackers.co.uk; 71 Holloway St; dm/d £18.50/45; P) A firm favourite among budget travellers, this spot-

lessly clean, rambling former town house boasts three doubles and roomy dorms. Current measures include limited numbers, reduced occupancy of dorms and allocated showers but this may change in future.

★Telstar B&B ££
(☎01392-272466; www.telstar-hotel.co.uk; 77 St David's Hill; s £40-50, d £60-85, f £85-105; P 📶) 'Victoriana with a twist' best defines this excellent B&B, where stately fireplaces meet mock-flock wallpaper and stag heads wear aviator goggles. Rooms team a heritage feel with modern comforts; bathrooms feature 19th-century-style tiles. If you like outdoors space, request the double with its own roomy deck.

Silversprings APARTMENT ££
(☎01392-494040; www.silversprings.co.uk; 12 Richmond Rd; 1 bedroom apt £85-99, 2 bedroom apt £110-140; P 📶) There are so many reasons to make these sleek, serviced apartments your Exeter pied-à-terre. Tucked away off a square a short walk from the city centre, each has a lounge and mini-kitchen, plus home comforts such as a DVD player and satellite TV.

★Hotel du Vin Exeter BOUTIQUE HOTEL £££
(☎01392-790120; www.hotelduvin.com/locations/exeter; Magdalen St; s from £112, d £136-171; @📶) This grand red-brick edifice (once Exeter's eye hospital) is now part of the plush Hotel du Vin chain. Quietly stylish rooms combine Victorian architecture (bay windows, cornicing, wood floors) with bold colours, offbeat wallpapers and Scandi-style sofas. There's a smart octagon-shaped restaurant, an excellent bar and a swish spa.

Eating

★Exploding Bakery CAFE £
(☎01392-427900; www.explodingbakery.com; 1 The Crescent, Queen St; snacks from £3; ⏰8am-4pm Mon-Fri, 9am-4pm Sat; 📶) 🌿 One of Exeter's hippest little bakeries flies the flag for ethical ingredients, delivers superb flat whites and makes gorgeous cakes with imaginative flavours – the lemon, polenta and pistachio is a hit.

Dinosaur Cafe MIDDLE EASTERN £
(☎01392-490951; 5 New North Rd; mains £8-10; ⏰noon-9pm Mon-Sat) At this cheery mezze bar a clutch of pavement tables and chunky wooden furniture set the scene for tasty couscous, kofta and spicy *mücver* fritters. The Turkish breakfasts (eggs, pepperoni and feta) are a welcome change from the norm.

Herbies VEGETARIAN £
(☎01392-258473; www.herbiesrestaurant.co.uk; 15 North St; mains £8-14; ⏰11am-2.30pm & 6-9pm Tue-Fri, 11.30am-3.30pm & 6-9.30pm Sat; 🌱) Herbies has been cheerfully feeding Exeter's plant-based food aficionados since 1990. Expect classics such as pea and courgette risotto, in various vegetarian, vegan and gluten-free versions.

Hourglass PUB FOOD ££
(☎01392-258722; www.hourglassexeter.co.uk; 21 Melbourne St; dishes £7-15, roasts £16; ⏰5-9.30pm Wed-Sat, noon-2.30pm Sun) Exeter's foodies love the Hourglass thanks to a convivial atmosphere, historic feel (they pulled the first pint in 1848), small plates such as homemade pappardelle with rabbit ragu, and legendary Sunday roasts.

Lloyd's Kitchen BISTRO ££
(☎01392-499333; www.lloydskitchen.co.uk; 16 Catherine St; mains £9-24; ⏰noon-3pm Mon-Thu, 9am-3pm & 6-10pm Fri & Sat, 10am-3pm Sun) White-tiled walls and bare lightbulbs welcome you to a bistro where Devon ingredients – from honey to chicken and beef – pepper the menu. Dishes range from Thai cod and prawn fishcakes for lunch, to pan-fried scallops and steak for dinner.

Or opt for a great-value three-course evening meal (£25).

WORTH A TRIP

RIVER COTTAGE RESTAURANTS

Known for his media campaigns on sustainability and organic food, TV chef Hugh Fearnley-Whittingstall launched his culinary career back in 1999 as he learned how to run a smallholding. These days his idyllic farm and kitchen garden host dining events ranging from pizza lunches (per person £15) and picnics (£25) to slap-up multi-course feasts (£80). They're very popular, so book well ahead. The farm runs cooking and foraging courses, and you can also eat at his **canteen** (☎01297-631715; www.rivercottage.net; Trinity Sq, Axminster; mains £8-16; ⏰10am-4pm Tue-Sat; 🌱) in nearby Axminster.

LOCAL KNOWLEDGE

EXETER'S FOOT & CYCLE PATHS

Foot and cycle paths head southeast from Exeter Quay to join the **Exe Valley Way**, a trail shadowing both the Exeter Canal and the ever-broadening River Exe, which meets the sea around 10 miles away. The paths and waterways make for good biking, hiking and kayaking trips: the first 3 miles are a blend of heritage city, countryside and light industrial landscape; the later sections are more rural.

About 1.5 miles downstream from Exeter Quay the route reaches the laid-back **Double Locks pub**, which features real ale and a waterside terrace. The **Exminster Marshes Nature Reserve** starts about 2 miles further on. Around 2 miles inside the reserve, the waterside Turf pub clings to a slither of land – an idyllic setting for good grub and summer barbecues. You can also navigate this route on the canal by kayak, making for an enjoyable, non-tidal paddle past pubs.

After the Turf pub, a rougher trail connects with a path to appealing Powderham Castle (p310).

Hire bikes, kayaks, SUPs and canoes from Exeter's Saddles & Paddles (p310).

Drinking & Nightlife

Old Firehouse PUB

(☎01392-277279; www.oldfirehouseexeter.co.uk; 50 New North Rd; ⏲4-11pm Sun, Wed & Thu, to 1am Fri & Sat) Step into the snug, candlelit interior of this Exeter institution and instantly feel at home. Dried hops hang from rafters above flagstone floors and walls of exposed stone. The range of draught ciders and cask ales is truly impressive, while the pizzas (served from 4pm) have kept countless students fed.

Turf PUB

(☎01392-833128; www.turfpub.net; near Exminister; ⏲10am-9pm Easter-Oct, hours vary Nov-Easter) The location of this former lock-keeper's house is simply superb: bookending a slither of land snaking between mudflats and the Exeter Canal. The views are expansive, the welcome is warm, and the BBQs (mains £8 to £14) and alfresco bar add a holiday vibe. Walk from the Exminster Marshes Nature Reserve (1 mile), or cycle from Exeter Quay (allow 2½ hours each way).

Entertainment

Exeter Phoenix ARTS CENTRE

(☎01392-667080; www.exeterphoenix.org.uk; Gandy St; ⏲10am-11pm Tue-Sat; 📶) The Phoenix Arts Centre has a cool cafe-bar. Check online for the latest on its indie cinema, galleries and performance space.

Exeter Picturehouse CINEMA

(☎0871 902 5730; www.picturehouses.co.uk; 51 Bartholomew St W) An independent cinema, screening mainstream and art-house movies.

Information

Ask if **Exeter Tourist Office** (☎01392-665700; www.visitexeter.com; Dix's Field), closed due to distancing measures in 2020, has reopened.

Getting There & Away

AIR

Exeter International Airport (☎01392-367433; www.exeter-airport.co.uk) is 6 miles east of the city. Flights connect with UK cities including Manchester, Newcastle, Edinburgh and Glasgow, and with the Isles of Scilly and the Channel Islands.

Bus 56 links the airport with Exeter St David's train station (£4, 30 minutes) hourly between 6am and 11pm Monday to Saturday, and between 8am and 7pm on Sunday.

BUS

Exeter's **bus station** (Paris St) is at the heart of a multimillion-pound revamp; services may be relocated to other city centre stops.

Lyme Regis Bus 9A (£7.70, at least hourly, six on Sunday). No Sunday service in winter.

Plymouth Bus X38 (£7.70, 1¼ hours, six daily Monday to Saturday, two on Sunday).

TRAIN

Main-line services stopping at St David's train station include:

Bristol £30, 1¼ hours, half-hourly

London Paddington £60, 2½ hours, half-hourly to hourly

Penzance £30, three hours, half-hourly to hourly

Plymouth £10, one hour, half-hourly to hourly

Torquay £8, 45 minutes, half-hourly to hourly

Totnes £8, 45 minutes, half-hourly

Getting Around

BICYCLE

Saddles & Paddles (p310) Rents out bikes.

BUS

Bus H (two to four per hour) links Exeter St David's train station with Exeter Central train station (£1) and the High St, passing near the bus station.

TAXI

There are taxi ranks at Exeter St David's and **Exeter Central** (Queen St) train stations.

Apple Central Taxis (01392-666666; www.appletaxisexeter.co.uk)

Z Cars (01392-595959)

Torquay

01803 / POP 65,245

A seaside resort since Victorian times Torquay remains a classic destination for the good, old-fashioned British summer getaway. It bills itself as the heart of the 'English Riviera' thanks to a palm-lined seafront and russet-red cliffs. Its visitors are a curious mix of elderly tourists, sun-seeking families and stag and hen parties. But with a smattering of fine-dining restaurants and boutique B&Bs, Torquay also has something a bit more classy. The closure in 2020 of one of the resort's key attractions – the Living Coasts zoo – has been a blow, but Torquay's unique model village, a cliff railway, Agatha Christie connections and a bevy of fine beaches still have plenty of appeal.

Sights & Activities

Torquay boasts no fewer than 20 beaches and an impressive 22 miles of coast. Tidal **Torre Abbey Sands** (Torbay Rd) is central, locals head for the sand-and-shingle beaches beside the 73m red-clay cliffs at **Oddicombe Beach**, and sea swimmers love picturesque **Anstey's Cove**.

★ **Babbacombe Model Village** MUSEUM
(01803-315315; www.model-village.co.uk; Hampton Ave, Babbacombe; adult/child £12.50/10.50; 10am-6pm Fri-Mon, to 6.30pm Tue-Thu Apr-Aug, to 5.30pm Sep, to 5pm Oct, to 4pm Nov-Mar; P) There are 425 tiny buildings, inhabited by 13,160 even tinier people, on display at this Lilliputian attraction. The epitome of English eccentricity, settings include a small-scale Stonehenge, a football stadium, a beach (complete with nude sunbathers), an animated circus, a castle (under attack from a fire-breathing dragon) and a thatched village where firefighters are tackling a blaze. It's bizarre but brilliant.

★ **Paignton Zoo** ZOO
(01803-697500; www.paigntonzoo.org.uk; Totnes Rd, Paignton; adult/child £18.55/15.30; 10am-5pm Apr-Oct, to 4.30pm Nov-Mar; P) In this innovative, 32-hectare zoo spacious enclosures recreate habitats from savannah and wetland to tropical forest and desert. Highlights include the orangutan island, a glass-walled big-cat enclosure and a lemur wood. Then there's the crocodile swamp with pathways winding over and beside Nile, Cuban and saltwater crocs.

WORTH A TRIP

BRIXHAM

An appealing, pastel-painted tumbling of fisher cottages leads down to Brixham's horseshoe harbour, where arcades and gift shops coexist with winding streets, brightly coloured boats and one of England's busiest fishing ports.

Life in Brixham revolves around the fish market. It sells more than £40 million worth of fish a year, making it England's biggest by value of fish sold. Check with the tourist office (p315) to see whether early-morning tours have resumed. At the harbour look out for a replica of the **Golden Hind** (01803-856223; www.goldenhind.co.uk; The Quay; adult/child £7/5; 10am-4.30pm Mar-Oct), Francis Drake's famous globetrotting ship. Don't miss gorgeous art-deco, open-air **Shoalstone Pool** (07799 414702; www.shoalstonepool.com; Berry Head Rd; requested donation adult/family £2/5; 10am-6pm May-Sep), built into natural rock to the east of the breakwater.

The most enjoyable way to arrive in Brixham is aboard the venerable Western Lady (p315), which runs along the coast between Brixham Harbour and Torquay.

AGATHA CHRISTIE

Torquay is the birthplace of one-woman publishing phenomenon Dame Agatha Mary Clarissa Christie (1890–1976), a writer of murder mysteries who is beaten only by the Bible and William Shakespeare in terms of sales. Her characters are world famous: Hercule Poirot, the moustachioed, conceited Belgian detective; and Miss Marple, a surprisingly perceptive busybody.

Born Agatha Miller in Torquay's Barton Rd, the young writer had her first piece published by the age of 11. By WWI she'd married Lieutenant Archie Christie and was working at the Red Cross Hospital in Torquay Town Hall, acquiring a knowledge of poisons that would lace countless plot lines, including that of her first novel, *The Mysterious Affair at Styles* (1920). Christie made her name with *The Murder of Roger Ackroyd* six years later with the use of what was then an innovative and cunning plot twist.

Then came 1926: in one year her mother died, Archie asked for a divorce and the writer mysteriously disappeared for 10 days, her abandoned car prompting a massive search. She was eventually discovered in a hotel in Harrogate, where she'd checked in under the name of the woman her husband wanted to marry. Christie always maintained she'd suffered amnesia; some critics saw it as a publicity stunt.

Christie later married archaeologist Sir Max Mallowan, and their trips to the Middle East provided masses of material for her work. By the time she died in 1976, Christie had written 75 novels and 33 plays.

Torquay's harbourside tourist office stocks the free *Agatha Christie Literary Trail* leaflet, which guides you around significant local sites. **Torquay Museum** (☎01803-293975; www.torquaymuseum.org; 529 Babbacombe Rd; adult/child £7.10/4.40; ⏲10am-4pm Mon-Sat) has a fine collection of photos and handwritten notes relating to Christie's famous detectives, as well as a recreation of Hercule Poirot's art-deco study, featuring furniture and props from the ITV adaptation *Agatha Christie's Poirot*.

The highlight, though, is Greenway, the author's bewitching summer home and gardens near Dartmouth. To get there, take the ferry from Dartmouth, hike from Kingswear (4 miles) or check whether the steam train from Paignton (p316) is once again stopping at nearby Greenway Halt.

Babbacombe Cliff Railway RAIL
(☎01803-328750; www.babbacombecliffrailway.co.uk; Babbacombe Downs Rd; adult/child return £2.90/2.10; ⏲9.30am-4.30pm Feb-Oct, hours may vary) A marvel of engineering, Babbacombe's glorious 1920s funicular railway sees you climbing into a tiny carriage and rattling up and down rails set into the cliff on a journey down to picturesque Oddicombe Beach. At the very least, it saves you the steep walk back up.

Sleeping

★The 25 B&B ££
(☎01803-297517; www.the25.uk; 25 Avenue Rd; r £119-225; P 📶) 'We banished magnolia,' says the owner proudly. And how: the playful bedrooms here team zebra print with acid yellow, or burgundy with peacock blue. Pop-art flourishes, and great gadgets abound; play with the mood lighting via the iPad or watch TV in the shower. Great value, great fun.

Hillcroft B&B ££
(☎01803-297247; www.thehillcroft.co.uk; 9 St Lukes Rd; d £75-95 ste £120-130; P 📶) One of the better B&B options in Torquay town, with bedrooms styled after Morocco, Bali, Lombok and Tuscany. The spacious suites include Provençal, with an ormolu bed and sitting room, and India, with Indian art and a four-poster bed.

★Cary Arms BOUTIQUE HOTEL £££
(☎01803-327110; www.caryarms.co.uk; Babbacombe Beach; d £125-365, ste £355-470; P 📶 👪) In a dreamy spot beside Babbacombe's sands, this heritage hotel has more than a hint of a New England beach retreat. Bright, light-filled rooms with white furniture shimmer with style, but for the best view book a stylish beach 'hut', complete with Smeg fridge, mezzanine bedroom and knockout beach-view patio.

Eating

Number 7 SEAFOOD ££

(☎01803-295055; www.no7-fish.com; 7 Beacon Tce; mains £14-22; ⏲noon-1.45pm Wed-Sat & 7-9pm Mon-Sat) Excellent, no-fuss fish is the order of the day at this small family-run bistro. Super-fresh crab, lobster, scallops and cod steaks can be seared, grilled or roasted, and laced with garlic butter or dusted with Moroccan spices.

On the Rocks BISTRO ££

(☎01803-203666; www.ontherocks-torquay.co.uk; 1 Abbey Cres; mains lunch 2/3 courses £20/25, dinner 2/3 courses £25/30; ⏲1-3pm & 6-9pm) Sliding doors and pavement tables make the most of the seaside view at this relaxed, informal cafe-bistro – it's just a shame the main beach road gets in the way. Still, it's a pleasant spot to tuck into Brixham scallops, juicy West Country steaks or spicy bean burgers.

★ **Elephant** MODERN BRITISH £££

(☎01803-200044; www.elephantrestaurant.co.uk; 3 Beacon Tce; mains £15-27, 8-course tasting menu £80; ⏲noon-2pm & 6-10pm Tue-Sat; 👪) The jumbo on Torquay's fine-dining scene: Michelin-starred and critically lauded, Elephant belongs to chef Simon Hulstone, whose taste for seasonal food (much of it grown on his own farm) and delicate presentation takes centre stage. The food is modern with classical underpinnings – though expect surprising flavour combos – and every plate looks as pretty as a painting.

The set lunch (two/three courses £25/28) is a steal.

Information

Torquay Tourist Office (☎01803-211211; www.theenglishriviera.co.uk; 5 Vaughan Pde; ⏲9.30am-1pm, hours may vary) By the central harbour.

Getting There & Away

BUS

Brixham Stagecoach Bus 12 (£4.50, 30 minutes, half-hourly) runs via Paignton.

Totnes Stagecoach Gold (£3.50, 35 minutes, half-hourly to hourly). From Totnes bus 92 goes on to Dartmouth.

FERRY

Between April and September the **Western Lady** (☎01803-293797; www.westernladyferry.com; single/return £2/3) shuttles between Torquay and Brixham – a 30-minute ride. Buy tickets at the **kiosk** (6 Vaughn Pde) before boarding.

TRAIN

Trains run directly from Exeter Central to Torquay (£8, 45 minutes, half-hourly to hourly) and on to Paignton (52 minutes), for the same fare.

Dartmouth

☎ 01803/ POP 5,060

Home to the nation's most prestigious naval college, the riverside town of Dartmouth is one of Devon's prettiest. It's awash with pastel-coloured 17th- and 18th-century buildings that lean at all angles, and is edged by yachts and clanking boat masts. It may be distinctly chic, but it's still a working port, and the triple draw of river-boat cruises, the art-deco estate of Coleton Fishacre and Greenway, the former home of Agatha Christie, make Dartmouth all but irresistible.

Dartmouth is on the west side of the Dart estuary. It's linked to the village of Kingswear on the east bank by fleets of car and foot ferries, also providing key transport links to Torquay. It makes a picturesque base for exploring Devon's south coast.

Sights & Activities

★ **Greenway** HISTORIC BUILDING

(NT; ☎01803-842382; www.nationaltrust.org.uk; Greenway Rd, Galmpton; gardens adult/child £8/4; ⏲10.30am-5pm mid-Feb–Oct, 11am-4pm Sat & Sun Nov & Dec) High on Devon's must-see list, the captivating summer home of crime-writer Agatha Christie sits beside the placid River Dart. Here the bewitching waterside gardens include features that pop up in Christie's mysteries. If distancing measures mean you can go inside, you'll see a series of rooms where the furnishings and knick-knacks are much as the author left them. The most atmospheric way to arrive is by **Greenway Ferry** (☎01803-882811; www.greenwayferry.co.uk; adult/child return £9.50/7; ⏲5-8 ferries daily mid-Mar–Oct).

The gardens feature woods speckled with magnolias, while daffodils and hydrangeas frame the water. The planting creates intimate, secret spaces – the boathouse and the views over the river are sublime. In Christie's book *Dead Man's Folly*, Greenway doubles as Nasse House, with the boathouse making an appearance as a murder scene.

Christie owned Greenway between 1938 and 1959, and the house feels frozen in time – if it's reopened (extra charges will apply) you'll see piles of hats in the lobby, her books in the library and her clothes in the wardrobe.

Check whether the Dartmouth Steam Railway, which runs from Paignton, is once again stopping at nearby Greenway Halt. You can also hike to Greenway along the picturesque **Dart Valley Trail** from Kingswear (4 miles).

★Coleton Fishacre HISTORIC BUILDING

(NT; ☎01803-842382; www.nationaltrust.org.uk; Brownstone Rd, near Kingswear; adult/child £8/4; ⏲10.30am-5pm mid-Feb–Oct, 11am-4pm Sat & Sun Nov & Dec; P) For an evocative glimpse of Jazz Age glamour, visit the former seaside retreat of the D'Oyly Carte family of theatre impresarios. Built in the Arts and Crafts style in the 1920s, the house has a croquet terrace that leads to deeply shelved subtropical gardens and suddenly revealed vistas of the sea. Check whether the house's interior has reopened. Its faultless art-deco embellishments include original Lalique tulip uplighters, comic bathroom tiles and a stunning saloon.

You can get here by car, but the most dramatic way to arrive is to hike 4 miles along the cliffs from Kingswear.

Dartmouth Castle CASTLE

(EH; ☎01803-833588; www.english-heritage.org.uk; Castle Rd; adult/child £8/4.70; ⏲10am-6pm Wed-Sun Apr-Sep, to 5pm Oct, to 4pm Sat & Sun Nov-Mar; P) Discover maze-like passages, atmospheric guardrooms and great views from the battlements of this picturesque castle. The best way to arrive is via the tiny, open-top **Castle Ferry** (www.dartmouthcastleferry.co.uk; adult/child single £2.50/1.50; ⏲10am-4.45pm Easter-Sep, to 3.45pm Oct), or walk or drive along the coast road from Dartmouth (1.5 miles).

★Dartmouth Steam Railway RAIL

(☎01803-555872; www.dartmouthrailriver.co.uk; Torbay Rd, Paignton; adult/child return £19/11.50; ⏲4-9 trains daily mid-Feb–Oct) Chugging from seaside Paignton to the beautiful banks of the River Dart, these vintage trains roll back the years to the age of steam. The 7-mile, 30-minute journey puffs past Goodrington Sands to the village of Kingswear, where ferries shuttle across to picturesque Dartmouth.

The service is run by the **Dartmouth Steam Railway & Riverboat Company**. It operates a wealth of other trips, including coastal cruises and excursions on a paddle steamer; see the website for a full round-up.

Sleeping

Alf Resco B&B ££

(☎01803-835880; www.cafealfresco.co.uk; Lower St; d from £99-115, apt £135; 📶) Not content with providing some of the town's yummiest food, Alf's also offers a batch of characterful rooms, including bunk beds in the 'Crew's Quarters' and the self-contained 'Captain's Cabin', squeezed in under the rafters with plenty of nautical trappings (lanterns, panelled walls and watery views.

★Bayard's Cove B&B £££

(☎01803-839278; www.bayardscoveinn.co.uk; 27 Lower St; d £114-190, f £165-320; 📶) Crammed with character and bursting with beams, Bayard's Cove's seven rooms have you sleeping within whitewashed stone walls and beside huge church candles. The lavish family suites feature grand double beds and kids' cabins, complete with bunk beds and tiny TVs. There are even estuary glimpses from the rooms.

Eating

★Alf Resco CAFE £

(☎01803-835880; www.cafealfresco.co.uk; Lower St; dishes from £7; ⏲7am-2pm; 📶) This indie cafe is the preferred hang-out for a variety of discerning Dartmouthians, from yachties and families to riverboat crews, all tucking into cracking coffee, copious all-day breakfasts, granola pots, smoked fish platters, healthy salads and gooey cakes.

Crab Shell SANDWICHES £

(☎01803-839036; 1 Raleigh St; sandwiches £5.50; ⏲10.30am-2.30pm, winter hours vary) Sometimes all you want is a classic crab sarnie, and this little kiosk will happily oblige: the shellfish is landed on the quay a few steps away. Salmon, lobster and mackerel butties are also available.

Rockfish SEAFOOD ££

(☎01803-832800; www.therockfish.co.uk; 8 South Embankment; mains £9-17; ⏲noon-3.30pm & 4-9pm) At the Dartmouth outpost of award-winning chef Mitch Tonks' eight-strong West Country bistro chain, seafood is firmly the speciality, and the weathered boarding and maritime decor fit right in along Dartmouth's streets. The fish and chips are delicious.

★ **Seahorse** SEAFOOD £££

(☎01803-835147; www.seahorserestaurant.co.uk; 5 South Embankment; mains £23-34; ⊙noon-2.30pm & 6-9.30pm Tue-Sat) What celebrity chef Rick Stein is to Cornwall, Mitch Tonks is to Devon – a seafood supremo with a clutch of restaurants. The Seahorse is the original and the best: a classic fish restaurant where the just-landed produce is roasted over open charcoals.

Check whether the seasonal pop-up **Seahorse al Mare**, in a nearby quayside marquee with adjustable sides, has opened up again.

Information

Dartmouth Tourist Office (☎01803-834224; www.discoverdartmouth.com; Mayor's Ave; ⊙10.30am-12.30pm & 1.30-4pm Mon-Sat)

Getting There & Away

BUS

Plymouth Bus 3 (£7.60, 2¼ hours, hourly Monday to Saturday) travels via Kingsbridge. On Sunday two buses travel only as far as Kingsbridge (£7, one hour).

Totnes Bus 92 (£3.90, 45 minutes, every two hours Monday to Saturday, two Sunday).

FERRY

Two appealing car and foot-passenger ferries regularly shuttle across the River Dart, providing shortcuts to Torquay.

Dartmouth–Kingswear Higher Ferry (☎07866 531687; www.dartmouthhigherferry.com; per car/pedestrian one-way £6.70/70p; ⊙6.30am-10.50pm Mon-Sat, from 8am Sun) Avoids narrow streets.

Dartmouth–Kingswear Lower Ferry (www.southhams.gov.uk; per car/pedestrian £6/1.50; ⊙7.10am-10.45pm)

TRAIN

The Dartmouth Steam Railway links Kingswear and Paignton. The nearest mainline connections are from Totnes.

Totnes

☎01803/ POP 8070

Totnes has such a reputation for being alternative that local jokers wrote 'twinned with Narnia' under the town sign. For decades famous as Devon's hippie haven, ecoconscious Totnes also became Britain's first 'transition town' in 2005, when it began to reduce its dependence on oil. Sustainability aside, Totnes boasts a sturdy Norman castle and a mass of fine Tudor buildings, and is the springboard for a range of outdoor activities.

Sights & Activities

Totnes Castle CASTLE

(EH; ☎01803-864406; www.english-heritage.org.uk; Castle St; adult/child £6/3.50; ⊙10am-4pm daily Apr-Oct, to 3pm Sat & Sun Nov-Mar) High on a hilltop above town, Totnes' castle is a fine example of a Norman 'motte and bailey' castle (a round keep sitting on a raised earthwork). Although the interior is largely empty, the views over Totnes' rooftops are captivating.

Dartington Estate HISTORIC SITE

(☎01803-847000; www.dartington.org; ⊙dawn-dusk; P) FREE Henry VIII gave this pastoral 324-hectare estate to two of his wives (Catherines Howard and Parr). The 14th-century manor house is surrounded by a deer park, walking trails and riverbanks from which you can kayak and swim. There's also a heritage B&B (p318), cool campsite and good cafe (p318). It's about 2 miles northwest of Totnes, a peaceful riverside walk from the town.

★ **Dynamic Adventures** ADVENTURE SPORTS

(☎01803-862725; www.dynamicadventurescic.co.uk; Park Rd, Dartington Estate) On summer weekends this superb activity centre offers kayak and SUP hire on a tranquil stretch of the River Dart (10am to 5pm, per hour £10). There are also plenty of **wild swimming** spots nearby.

Check to see whether it has resumed lessons in sea kayaking, caving, rock climbing and archery.

Totnes Kayaks KAYAKING

(☎07799 403788; www.totneskayaks.co.uk; The Quay, Stoke Gabriel; single kayak half/full day £33/40; ⊙10am-5pm Jul & Aug, 10am-5pm Fri-Sun Apr-Jun, Sep & Oct) Five miles southeast of Totnes in Stoke Gabriel, this friendly outdoors company rents out single and double sit-on-top kayaks.

Sleeping

Camp Dartington CAMPGROUND £

(☎01803-847077; www.dartington.org; Upper Dr, Dartington Estate; adult/child £12/8) Hip tent-only campsite with ancient woods to walk in, a river to swim in and views onto Dartmoor. Bring your own off-ground firepit.

★Dartington Hall B&B ££
(☎01803-847150; www.dartington.org; Dartington Estate; s/d from £55/90; P 📶) The wings of this idyllic ancient manor house have been carefully converted into rooms that range from heritage themed to deluxe modern. Ask for one overlooking the grassy, cobble-fringed courtyard, and settle back for a truly tranquil night's sleep.

★Cott Inn PUB ££
(☎01803-863777; www.cottinn.co.uk; Cott Lane, Dartington; s/d £110/135; P) The 14th-century Cott is pretty much the perfect English inn: rambling, thatched and lined with beams. Rooms blend undulating walls with artfully distressed furniture and crisp eco-linens. Ingredients for the classy gastro pub fare are sourced locally – lamb from Dartington, potatoes from Kingsbridge and crab from Salcombe.

Eating & Drinking

Green Table BISTRO £
(www.dartington.org; Dartington Estate; dishes £5-9; ⏲10am-4pm; 📶 ✍) It's the ethos and ingredients that make this stylish, light-filled bistro stand out – dishes brim with locally sourced, seasonal, often organic food. Check whether it's still operating as takeaway only. If it is, the wide terrace provides plenty of outdoor seating.

Rumour PUB FOOD ££
(☎01803-864682; www.rumourtotnes.com; 30 High St; mains £7-20; ⏲noon-9.30pm; ✍) Rumour is a local institution – a narrow, cosy pub-restaurant with low lighting and local art. It's famous for its pizzas (£9 to £14), but you'll also find risottos, steaks, stews and fish of the day. The bar is open from 11am to 11pm.

★Riverford Field Kitchen MODERN BRITISH £££
(☎01803-227391; https://fieldkitchen.riverford.co.uk; Wash Farm; 3-course brunch/lunch/dinner £20/28/32; ⏲sittings 12.30pm & 7pm Wed-Fri, 10am, 12.30pm & 7pm Sat, noon & 3.30pm Sun; ✍) This ecofriendly, organic, plough-to-plate farm is where everyone wants to eat. What began as a food-box scheme has now branched out into a delightful barn bistro serving mammoth set-course meals. Dishes are packed with rustic flavours: expect delicious salads, roast meats, imaginative veggie options and irresistible desserts.

★Totnes Brewing Co MICROBREWERY
(☎01803-849290; www.thetotnesbrewingco.co.uk; 59 High St; ⏲5pm-midnight Mon-Thu, from noon Fri-Sun) There are scores of craft beers to choose from at this trendy town hang-out, from its own brews to Trappist-style wheat beers and imperial stouts. It's no dark old dive – expect stripped wood and big glass windows looking out on to the high street.

Getting There & Away

BUS

Dartmouth Bus 92 (£3.90, 45 minutes, every two hours Monday to Saturday, two Sunday).

Exeter Bus 7 (£6.30, 1¼ hours, two to seven daily).

Plymouth Stagecoach Gold (£3.70, one hour, half-hourly Monday to Saturday, hourly Sunday).

Torquay Stagecoach Gold (£3.50, 35 minutes, half-hourly Monday to Saturday, hourly Sunday).

TRAIN

Trains run at least hourly to Exeter (£8, 45 minutes) and Plymouth (£8, 30 minutes).

Salcombe

☎01548 / POP 3350

Oh-so-chic Salcombe sits charmingly at the mouth of the Kingsbridge estuary, its network of ancient, winding streets bordered by sparkling waters and sandy coves. Its beauty has pushed many properties here above the £1 million mark, and a significant number of houses are second homes. Out of season, Salcombe can have a ghost-town feel, but the pretty port's undoubted appeal remains, offering tempting opportunities to catch a ferry to a beach, head out kayaking and savour local seafood.

Sights & Activities

Check whether the excellent **Sea Kayak Salcombe** (☎01548-843451; www.southsandssailing.co.uk; South Sands), which suspended guided trips in 2020, is up and running again.

★South Sands BEACH
(P) Although it gets busy in the summer holidays, South Sands has immense charm. It's something to do with the broad beach (at low tide), the cool cafe and the impossibly cute **South Sands Ferry** (☎07831 568684; www.southsandsferry.co.uk; Whitestrand Quay; adult/child one-way £4.50/3.50; ⏲9.45am-5.30pm Apr-Oct), which delivers you onto an improbable motorised platform.

To avoid the ferry queues, head up Fore St then continue south for around 2 miles on Cliff Rd, sticking to the waterfront.

★Mill Bay BEACH
(P) Salcombe's best high-tide beach, sand-filled Mill Bay sits across the water on the east side of the estuary. Get there by taking the East Portlemouth passenger **ferry** (Salcombe Ferry; ☎01548-842061; return adult/child £3/2; ⏲9am-6pm). You can then either walk the lane south from East Portlemouth's ferry dock, or – at low tide – stroll along the sandy shore.

Between April and October the East Portlemouth Ferry departs from Jubilee Pier (off Fore St); from November to March it leaves from Whitestrand Quay.

Salcombe Kayaks KAYAKING
(☎07834 893191; www.salcombekayaks.co.uk; per week from £90) Rents out sit-on-top kayaks by the week and will deliver to your accommodation. It may have resumed daily hire; check online for updates.

Whitestrand BOATING
(☎01548-843818; www.whitestrandboathire.co.uk; Whitestrand Quay; per half/full day from £100/135; ⏲9am-5pm) Will hire you a motorboat so you can explore the Salcombe estuary at your own pace. Fuel is extra.

Sleeping

Waverley B&B ££
(☎01548-842633; www.waverleybandb.co.uk; Devon Rd; s/d £60/95; P ᯤ) Opt for a top-floor room at this sweet edge-of-town B&B where you'll sleep among candy stripes and sea hues. Window seats give glimpses of the estuary. It's great value for Salcombe.

Fortescue PUB £££
(☎01548-842868; www.thefortsalcombe.co.uk; Union St; d incl breakfast £135-160; P ᯤ) The bedrooms may be above a busy town-centre locals' pub, but they're a treat. The exposed stone speaks of the building's 300-year history; chunky wooden headboards and pristine bathrooms bring things bang up to date.

Eating & Drinking

Salcombe Yawl DELI £
(☎01548-288380; 10 Clifton Pl; snacks from £3; ⏲9am-5pm) The wide-ranging goodies on offer here span sourdough toasties, Scotch eggs and huge Cornish pasties.

★Crab Shed SEAFOOD ££
(☎01548-844280; www.crabshed.com; Fish Quay, Gould Rd; mains £11-21; ⏲noon-2.30pm & 6-9pm) With a terrace set plumb on the water's edge, this smart shack has you eating fish and shellfish just metres from its landing spot. Homemade stock ensures bisques and bouillabaisse are intensely flavoured, the pan-seared scallops melt in your mouth and the sweet Salcombe crab is superb.

Ferry Inn PUB
(☎01548-844000; www.theferryinnsalcombe.com; Fore St; ⏲11am-11pm Sun-Thu, to midnight Fri & Sat; ᯤ) If the sun is shining, this is an unbeatable location: the big beer terrace clings to the waterfront, providing cracking harbour views.

Bo's Beach Cafe CAFE
(☎01548-843451; www.southsandssailing.co.uk; South Sands; ⏲9am-5pm Apr-Oct) Caffeine-laden espressos, tempting cakes, tasty pizzas, a chilled vibe, a waterside terrace and sandy feet. Perfect.

Getting There & Away

Bus 606 runs to Kingsbridge (£4, 30 minutes, hourly Monday to Saturday).

Plymouth

☎01752 / POP 256,380

For decades, some have dismissed Plymouth as sprawling and ugly, pointing to its architectural eyesores and sometimes palpable poverty. But the arrival of a multimillion-pound museum and ongoing waterfront regeneration beg a rethink. Yes the city, an important Royal Naval port, suffered heavy WWII bomb damage, and even today it can appear more gritty than pretty, but Plymouth is also packed with possibilities: swim in an art-deco lido, tour a gin distillery, learn to SUP, kayak and sail, roam an aquarium, then take a harbour boat trip. And the aces

Plymouth

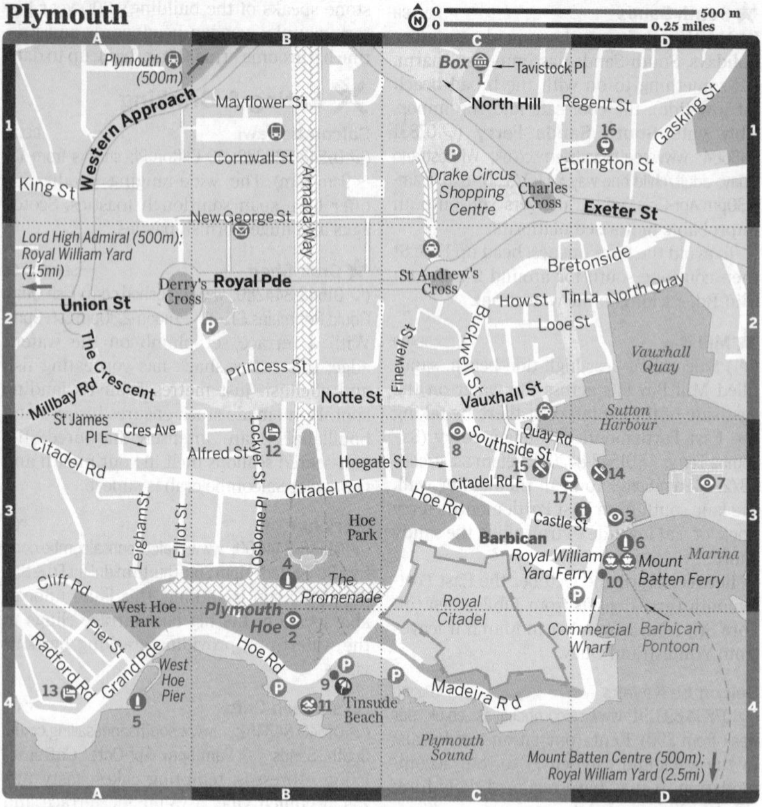

Plymouth

Top Sights
- 1 Box C1
- 2 Plymouth Hoe B4

Sights
- 3 Barbican D3
- 4 Drake Statue B3
- 5 LOOK II A4
- 6 Mayflower Steps D3
- 7 National Marine Aquarium D3
- 8 Plymouth Gin Distillery C3

Activities, Courses & Tours
- 9 Ocean City Kayaking B4
- 10 Plymouth Boat Trips D3
- 11 Tinside Lido B4

Sleeping
- 12 Imperial B3
- 13 Sea Breezes A4

Eating
- 14 Harbour D3
- 15 Jacka Bakery C3

Drinking & Nightlife
- 16 Bread & Roses D1
- 17 Dolphin C3

in the pack? The history-rich Barbican district and Plymouth Hoe – a cafe-dotted, wide, grassy headland offering captivating views of a boat-studded bay.

History

Plymouth's history is dominated by the sea. The first recorded cargo left in 1211 and by the late 16th century it was the port of choice for explorers and adventurers. It has waved off Sir Francis Drake, Sir Walter Raleigh, the fleet that defeated the Spanish Armada, the pilgrims who founded America, Charles Darwin, Captain Cook and countless boats carrying emigrants to Australia and New Zealand.

During WWII Plymouth suffered horrendously at the hands of the German Luftwaffe; more than 1000 civilians died in the Blitz, which reduced the city centre to rubble. The 21st century has brought both regeneration to waterfront areas, and the Box – a museum that is a significant heritage draw.

Sights

★Box MUSEUM
(☎01752-304774; www.theboxplymouth.com; Tavistock Pl; ⏱10am-5pm Tue-Sun) FREE Looking as if it's been deposited by a giant hand, the shimmering, £46 million block that is the Box is impossible to ignore. Inside the museum and archive hub, galleries feature 14 massive, suspended ships' figureheads, a full-sized woolly mammoth, artfully arranged natural-history specimens and the kind of map, film and photography archives that'll keep you absorbed for hours.

The *Mayflower 400 Legend & Legacy* exhibition (non-residents £5, due to finish in September 2021) marks the Pilgrim Fathers' 1620 voyage from Plymouth, England to what is now Plymouth, Massachusetts. It's been created in partnership with the indigenous Wampanoag community and uses objects and images to explore the impact and legacy of colonialism and of the *Mayflower*'s voyage.

★Plymouth Hoe LANDMARK
Francis Drake supposedly spied the Spanish fleet from this memorial-backed grassy headland overlooking Plymouth Sound (the city's wide bay); the bowling green on which he continued to finish his game after the sighting is reputed to have been where his **statue** now stands.

Barbican AREA
(www.barbicanwaterfront.com) Plymouth's historic harbour features part-cobbled streets lined with Tudor and Jacobean buildings, and old dockside warehouses that have been turned into bars and restaurants. It's also famous as the point from which the Pilgrim Fathers set sail for the New World in 1620: the **Mayflower Steps** (Sutton Harbour) mark the approximate spot.

Plymouth Gin Distillery DISTILLERY
(☎01752-665292; www.plymouthdistillery.com; 60 Southside St; tours £11; ⏱tour times vary) This heavily beamed distillery has been concocting gin since 1793, making it the oldest working producer of the spirit in England. Regular tours thread past the stills and take in a tutored tasting before retiring to the beautiful Grade II–listed cocktail bar for a complimentary G&T.

National Marine Aquarium AQUARIUM
(☎0844 893 7938; www.national-aquarium.co.uk; Rope Walk; adult/child £19.50/14.40; ⏱10am-5pm) The UK's biggest aquarium boasts an impressive Atlantic Ocean tank where 2.5 million litres of water are home to sand tiger sharks, lemon sharks, barracuda, rays and Friday, a green turtle. Other highlights are the vibrant fish of the Great Barrier Reef tank.

LOOK II STATUE
(West Hoe Pier) When seen from certain angles Antony Gormley's twice-life-size figure made out of 22 hollow iron blocks takes on a human form. Gazing out to sea, it invites us to consider the yearning to set sail.

Activities

★Tinside Lido SWIMMING
(☎01752-261915; www.everyoneactive.com/centre/tinside-lido; Hoe Rd; adult/child £5/4; ⏱noon-5.30pm Mon-Fri, 10am-5.30pm Sat, Sun & school holidays late May-early Sep) This glorious open-air, unheated, saltwater swimming pool is one of Plymouth's best-loved sights. Nestled beneath the Hoe with views onto Plymouth Sound, it's a gem of the Jazz Age, built in 1935 with gracious white curves and strips of light- and dark-blue tiles. Like something straight out of an F Scott Fitzgerald novel, it makes for a gorgeous dip.

★Ocean City Kayaking KAYAKING
(☎07376 954991; www.oceancityseakayaking.com; Tinside Beach; half/full day from £60/110) Be guided by the effortlessly cool Tom (who has been known to transport his sea kayak by skateboard) on trips heading along Plymouth's striking shoreline, around Drake's Island, or out to the breakwater more than 2 miles away.

Mount Batten Centre WATER SPORTS
(01752-404567; www.mount-batten-centre.com; 70 Lawrence Rd) An excellent centre where watersports tuition includes two-hour taster sessions on sit-on-top kayaks and stand-up paddleboarding (£27).

It's on the Mount Batten peninsula and is linked to Plymouth's Barbican by a **passenger ferry** (07930 838614; www.mountbattenferry.co.uk; Barbican Pontoon; adult/child single £2/1).

Plymouth Boat Trips BOATING
(01752-253153; www.plymouthboattrips.co.uk; Barbican Pontoon) The pick of this firm's trips is the **Cawsand Ferry**, a 30-minute blast across the bay to the quaint, pub-packed Cornish fishing villages of Kingsand and Cawsand (adult/child single £5/2.50, six daily, Easter to October). Year-round, one-hour excursions head around Plymouth's dockyard and naval base (adult/child £8.50/5).

Sleeping

Residence One B&B ££
(01752-262318; www.bistrotpierre.co.uk; 7 Royal William Yard; d £105-140, ste £165) Your chance to sleep in the former digs of an admiral. The exquisite rooms in this listed building team fluffy duvets and sea-chic styling with original shutters and cast-iron radiators. And all just a few steps from the shore.

Sea Breezes B&B ££
(01752-667205; www.plymouth-bedandbreakfast.co.uk; 28 Grand Pde; s £55-75, d £74-95, f £95-125;) With its sea-themed colours and pristine rooms Sea Breezes is a supremely comfortable place to stay. Add a charming owner, cast-iron bedsteads, old-fashioned alarm clocks and sea views, and you have a winner.

Imperial HOTEL ££
(01752-227311; www.imperialplymouth.co.uk; Lockyer St; s £61-91, d £82-125, f £112-141, incl breakfast; P) The pick of the small hotels on Plymouth Hoe is this 1840s town house. A few heritage features remain but its revamp has made it quite modern, with beige carpets, wooden furniture and the odd bit of candy-striped wallpaper.

★ **St Elizabeth's House** BOUTIQUE HOTEL £££
(01752-344840; www.stelizabeths.co.uk; Longbrook St, Plympton St Maurice; d £140-160; P) In this 17th-century manor house turned boutique bolthole, free-standing slipper baths, oak furniture and Egyptian cotton grace the rooms; the suites feature palatial bathrooms and private terraces. It's in the suburb-village of Plympton St Maurice, 5 miles east of Plymouth.

SHOPPING IN PLYMOUTH

The £200m **Drake Circus** centre (www.drakecircus.com; 1 Charles St; 9am-6pm Mon-Wed, Fri & Sat, to 8pm Thu, 10.30am-4.30pm Sun) draws shoppers to the city centre; other well-known names line the nearby pedestrianised streets.

The independent stores of the Barbican cater to a less mainstream market, featuring galleries, gift shops and antiques markets.

Eating & Drinking

★ **Jacka Bakery** BAKERY £
(01752-262187; 38 Southside St; snacks £4-9; 9am-2.30pm Wed-Mon) Quietly groovy, fantastically friendly and extremely good at baking things, Jacka is much loved by locals. It excels at vast sausage rolls, immense croissants, cinnamon swirls, and irresistible sourdough loaves.

Lord High Admiral PUB FOOD £
(The LHA; 01752-256881; www.the-lha.co.uk; 33 Stonehouse St; dishes £4-7, pizza £5-10) The 2020 COVID lockdown saw this old drinking den morph into a community lifeline, sporting the tagline 'it's now a hub, not a pub'. Its cosy rooms and bijou beer garden are home to the **Hutong Cafe** (8am to 2pm), a collection point for **Tilt** burgers (Thursday, Friday and Saturday nights), a craft beer **bar** (4pm to 9pm) and **Kneed Pizza** (4pm to 9pm). They're all excellent.

Harbour SEAFOOD ££
(01752-228556; www.harbourbarbican.co.uk; 21 Sutton Harbour; mains £12-22; 11am-9pm) With harbour-view picture windows in an airy, open-plan dining room, and a takeaway hatch, Harbour is a sound seafood choice whatever the weather. And it's not just fish and chips – expect monkfish curry, clam chowder and scallop burgers.

★ **Dolphin** PUB
(01752-660876; 14 The Barbican; 10am-10pm) This gloriously unreconstructed Barbican boozer is all scuffed tables, padded bench seats and an authentic, no-nonsense atmosphere. Feeling peckish? Get a fish-and-

LOCAL KNOWLEDGE

ROYAL WILLIAM YARD

In the 1840s this stately complex of waterfront warehouses supplied stores for countless Royal Navy vessels. Roaming past a former slaughterhouse, bakery, brewery and cooperage underlines just how big the supplies operation was. Today it's home to sleek apartments and a cluster of B&Bs, restaurants, galleries, cafes and pubs, including the **Vignoble** (01752-222892; www.levignoble.co.uk; Royal William Yard; noon-9pm Sun-Thu, to 10pm Fri & Sat) wine bar.

The yard is 2 miles west of the city centre. Hop on bus 34 (£1.40, nine minutes, half-hourly) or, better still, catch the hourly **ferry** (07979 152008; www.royalwilliamyard.com/getting-here/by-waterbus; Barbican Pontoon; one-way adult/child £3.50/2.50; 10am-5pm May-Sep).

chip takeaway from Harbour, just over the road, then settle in with your pint.

Bread & Roses PUB
(01752-659861; www.breadandrosesplymouth.co.uk; 62 Ebrington St; 4-10pm Mon-Fri, noon-10pm Sat & Sun;) Plymouth's arty crowd loves this characterful combo of hip boozer and social-enterprise cultural hub. Amid its Edwardian-meets-modern decor you'll find a good pint, occasional appearances by cool local bands and lots of people hatching creative plans.

Information

Tourist Office (01752-306330; www.visitplymouth.co.uk; 3 The Barbican; 9am-5pm Mon-Sat, 10am-4pm Sun Apr-Oct, 10am-4pm Mon-Sat Nov-Mar)

Getting There & Away

BUS

National Express services call at Plymouth's **bus station** (Mayflower St).

Bristol £23, three hours, four to six daily
London Victoria £28, 5½ hours, six daily
Penzance £7, 2¾ hours, five daily

Local services include the following.

Exeter Bus X38 (£7.70, 1¼ hours, six daily Monday to Saturday, two on Sunday).
Totnes Stagecoach Gold (£3.70, one hour, half-hourly Monday to Saturday, hourly Sunday).

TRAIN

Direct services include the following.

Bristol Temple Meads £37, two hours, hourly
Exeter £10, one hour, half-hourly to hourly
London Paddington £60, 3¼ hours, hourly
Penzance £11, two hours, half-hourly
Totnes £8, 30 minutes, half-hourly to hourly

Dartmoor National Park

Dartmoor (01822-890414; www.visitdartmoor.co.uk) is Devon's wild heart. Covering 368 sq miles, the national park feels like it has tumbled out of a Tolkien tome, with its honey-coloured heaths, moss-smothered boulders, tinkling streams and eerie granite hills (known locally as tors).

On sunny days, Dartmoor is idyllic: ponies wander at will and sheep graze beside the road. It makes for a cinematic location, used to memorable effect in Steven Spielberg's WWI epic *War Horse*. But when sleeting rain and swirling mists arrive, you'll understand why Dartmoor is also the setting for Sir Arthur Conan Doyle's *The Hound of the Baskervilles:* the moor morphs into a bleak wilderness where tales of a phantom hound can seem very real indeed.

Dartmoor is an outdoor activities hotspot for hiking, cycling, riding, climbing and white-water kayaking, and has plenty of rustic pubs and country-house hotels where you can hunker down when the fog rolls in.

Activities

Dartmoor is a fantastic place to get out and be active, whether that means an afternoon hike or a horseback hack. For a broad-based overview, multiactivity providers such as **Adventure Okehampton** (01837-53916; www.adventureokehampton.com; YHA Bracken Tor, Klondyke Rd; per half/full day £25/50; school holidays only) and **CRS Adventures** (01364-653444; www.crsadventures.co.uk; Holne Park; per person per day from £35) offer a range of ways to get your pulse racing.

Walking

Some 730 miles of public footpaths snake across Dartmoor's open heaths and rocky

Dartmoor National Park

tors. The Ordnance Survey (OS) Pathfinder *Dartmoor Walks* (£13) guide includes 28 hikes of 4 to 11 miles, while its *Dartmoor Short Walks* (£8) features 20 family-friendly treks of up to 5.5 miles.

Templer Way An 18-mile two- to three-day stretch from Haytor to Teignmouth.

West Devon Way A 37-mile trek linking Okehampton and Plymouth.

Dartmoor Way (www.dartmoorway.co.uk) A 100-mile loop circling from Buckfastleigh in the south, through Moretonhampstead, northwest to Okehampton and south through Lydford to Tavistock.

Two Moors Way (www.twomoorsway.org) An epic, 117-mile trek from Wembury on the south Devon coast, across Dartmoor and Exmoor to Lynmouth, on the north coast.

Be prepared for Dartmoor's notoriously fickle weather and carry a map and a compass – many trails are not waymarked. The Ordnance Survey (OS) Explorer 1:25,000 map *Dartmoor, OL28* (£9), is the most comprehensive and shows park boundaries and Ministry of Defence firing-range areas.

★ Moorland Guides HIKING
(www.moorlandguides.co.uk; adult/child from £5/free) A superb range of walks, from one-hour rambles to strenuous all-day hikes, on themes spanning heritage, geology, wildlife, myths and navigation. The hikes leave from various locations – you'll be told where at the time of booking.

Cycling

Visits from the Tour of Britain have helped ensure powering up Dartmoor's hill climbs is increasingly popular. Good off road routes include:

Granite Way Part of NCN Route 27, running for 11 miles off-road along a former railway line between Okehampton and Lydford.

Princetown Railway Opt for 6-mile or 18-mile loops from Princetown along disused tramways to Burrator Reservoir.

Princetown to Burrator A 12-mile trail taking in permitted bridleways and open moorland.

Tourist offices sell the *Dartmoor for Cyclists* map (£15).

Devon Cycle Hire CYCLING
(☎01837-861141; www.devoncyclehire.co.uk; Sourton Down, near Okehampton; per day adult/child £17/11; ⏲9am-5pm Thu-Tue Apr-Sep, plus Wed school holidays) Located right on the Granite Way (part of NCN Route 27). Will deliver bikes for a small charge.

Fox Tor Cafe Cycle Hire CYCLING
(☎01822-890238; www.foxtorcafe.com/cycles; Fox Tor Cafe, Two Bridges Rd; per day adult/child £18.50/10; ⏲9am-5pm) Handy for the Princetown and Burrator mountain-bike routes.

Outdoor Swimming

Wild swimmers love Dartmoor's rivers, natural pools and cascades.

Trinnaman's Pool A deep pool with tumbling cascades. A 20-minute riverside walk north from Ivybridge.

Salmon Leaps Cascades and a decent pool. Near Chagford; hike there from the Castle Drogo (p329) car park.

Crazywell Pool A large pool in open moorland, 1 mile northeast of Burrator Reservoir.

Red Lake A remote, former china clay pit. An 8-mile hike north from Ivybridge up the Two Moors Way.

The book *Wild Swimming Walks; Dartmoor and South Devon* (£15) by Sophie Pierce and Matt Newbury features 28 hikes and dips.

Be aware the water can be fast flowing and dangerously cold; seek safety advice from tourist offices and www.devonandcornwallwildswimming.co.uk – the website also has a wild swimming map.

Moretonhampstead, Chagford, Bovey Tracey, Buckfastleigh and Ashburton also have small, elegant, seasonal, unheated outdoor pools. Times vary; local tourist offices can advise.

Horse Riding

Cholwell HORSE RIDING
(☎01822-810526; www.cholwellridingstables.co.uk; near Mary Tavy; 1/2hr rides £25/46) A family-run stables that leads small groups of novices and experts. It's near an old silver mine on the edge of the moor near the village of Mary Tavy, about halfway between Okehampton and Tavistock.

ℹ Information

Dartmoor National Park Authority (DNPA; www.dartmoor.gov.uk) The DNPA is the main administrative body for Dartmoor. It runs a number of visitor centres.

DNPA Haytor (☎01364-661520; TQ13 9XT, off B3387; ⏲10am-4pm Apr-Oct) Four miles west of Bovey Tracey.

DNPA Postbridge (☎01822-880272; PL20 6TH, beside B3212; ⏲10am-4pm Apr-Oct) New, state-of-the-art visitor centre and displays.

DNPA Princetown (☎01822-890414; Tavistock Rd; ⏲10am-4pm Apr-Oct, winter hours vary) Also home to the National Park Tourist Office, Princetown (p326).

Visit Dartmoor (www.visitdartmoor.co.uk) Official tourism site, has information on accommodation, activities, sights and events.

ℹ Getting There & Around

Key Dartmoor bus services reach in from Tavistock and Yelverton in the south west, Newton Abbot in the south and Exeter in the east. DNPA tourist offices can advise.

Bus 1 (four per hour Monday to Saturday, hourly Sunday) Shuttles from Plymouth to Tavistock

> **ℹ WARNING**
>
> The military uses three adjoining areas of Dartmoor as training ranges where live ammunition is used. Tourist offices can outline these locations; they're also marked on Ordnance Survey (OS) maps. You're advised to check if the hiking route you're planning falls within a range; if it does, find out if firing is taking place when you're planning to walk via the **Firing Information Service** (☎0800 458 4868; www.mod.uk/access). During the day, red flags fly at the edges of in-use ranges; red flares burn at night. Even when there's no firing, beware of unidentified metal objects lying in the grass. Don't touch anything you find: note its position and report it to the **authorities** (☎01837-657210).

(£5.20, one hour) via Yelverton (£4.70, 30 minutes).

Bus 98 (one daily Monday to Saturday) Runs from Tavistock to Princetown, Two Bridges and Postbridge, then circles back to Yelverton.

Bus 173 (two daily Monday to Saturday) Links Exeter with Chagford and Moretonhampstead.

Bus 672 Runs once a week (Wednesday) between Widecombe-in-the-Moor, Buckfastleigh, Ashburton and Newton Abbot.

Check whether the summer-only Haytor Hoppa Bus 271 (suspended in 2020) has resumed services linking Newton Abbot, Haytor and Widecombe-in-the-Moor.

Princetown

☎01822/ POP 1366

Set in the heart of the remote higher moor, Princetown is dominated by the grey, foreboding bulk of Dartmoor Prison, and on bad-weather days the town can have a remote, even bleak, feel. But it's also an evocative reminder of the harsh realities of moorland life and, thanks to some good places to eat and stay, makes an atmospheric base for archaeological explorations, walks and bike rides.

Sights

Check whether the absorbing **Dartmoor Prison Museum** (☎01822-322130; www.dartmoor-prison.co.uk; P), which suspended visits in 2020, has reopened.

National Park Tourist Office MUSEUM

(DNPA; ☎01822-890414; www.dartmoor.gov.uk; Tavistock Rd; ⊙10am-4pm Apr-Oct, winter hours vary) FREE At the tourist office–visitor centre, displays include those on the moor's archaeology and wildlife, as well as a children's discovery zone.

The building used to be the Duchy Hotel; one former guest was Sir Arthur Conan Doyle, who went on to write *The Hound of the Baskervilles*. Dartmoor lore recounts that local man Henry Baskerville took the novelist on a carriage tour, and the brooding landscape he encountered, coupled with legends of huge phantom dogs, inspired the thriller.

Merrivale Stone Rows ARCHAEOLOGICAL SITE

FREE These two parallel stone rows are up to 260m long, with large stone slabs, or 'terminal stones' at the eastern end. In the centre, hunt out the circular remains of a tiny stone burial chamber. Some 100m south of the rows' west end you'll find a stone circle of 11 small stones; 40m southwest again is a slanting, 3m standing stone or menhir.

The site is beside the B3357, 3 miles west of Princetown, near the Eversfield Organic cafe.

Sleeping & Eating

Tor Royal Farm B&B ££

(☎01822-890189; www.torroyal.co.uk; Tor Royal Lane, near Princetown; s £70, d £85-115, tr £130; P 📶) An easygoing, country-cottage-styled farmhouse packed with lived-in charm. Heritage-style rooms feature cream-and-white furniture, puffy bedspreads and easy chairs. They'll even rustle up an evening meal, probably featuring the farm's own reared beef or lamb.

Two Bridges HOTEL £££

(☎01822-892300; www.twobridges.co.uk; Two Bridges; r incl breakfast £99-200; P 📶) The definitive Dartmoor heritage hotel rejoices in polished wood panels, huge inglenook fireplaces, and a guest list that includes Wallis Simpson, Winston Churchill and Vivien Leigh. The Premier and Historic rooms have massive wooden four-poster beds and antique furniture aplenty; cheaper rooms are heavy on the florals. It's 1.5 miles northeast of Princetown.

★ **Fox Tor Cafe** CAFE £

(☎01822-890238; www.foxtorcafe.com; Two Bridges Rd; mains £6-13; ⊙9am-4pm Mon-Fri, to 5pm Sat & Sun; 📶 🐾) Known as FTC to locals, this friendly little cafe is a favourite for hearty breakfasts, doorstep sandwiches and massive chunks of cake, but it does more filling fare, too, such as spicy chilli and mushroom stroganoff. On cold, wet Dartmoor days the two wood-burning stoves are particularly welcoming.

Fox Tor also hires out bikes (p325).

Eversfield Organic CAFE £

(Dartmoor Inn; ☎01837-871400; www.eversfieldorganic.co.uk; Merrivale; snacks £3-6; ⊙10am-6pm; 🐾) An organic Dartmoor farm has set up shop in this old moorland pub, offering tor-view alfresco tables, covered seating and an all-organic menu of homemade pasties, barbecued burgers, ice cream, lager and wine.

It's just over the road from the Merrivale Stone Rows (p326), 3 miles west of Princetown.

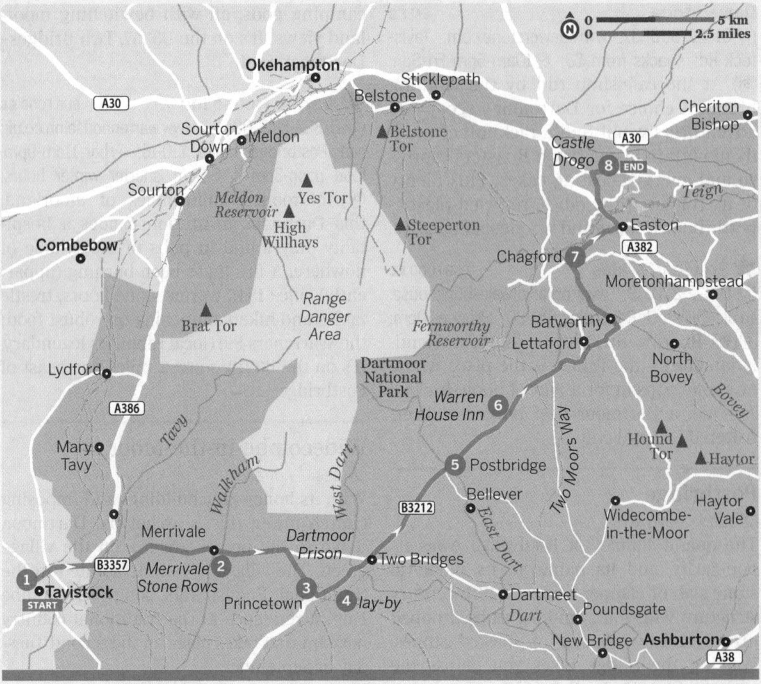

Driving Tour
A Dartmoor Road Trip

START TAVISTOCK
END CASTLE DROGO
LENGTH 20 MILES; ONE DAY

Driving on Dartmoor is like being inside a feature film: compelling 360-degree views are screened all around. This scenic, west-to-east trans-moor traverse sweeps up and through this wilderness, taking in a bleak prison, prehistoric remains, a rustic pub and a unique castle.

Start by strolling among the fine 19th-century architecture of **1 Tavistock**, perhaps dropping by its Pannier Market to rummage for antiques. Next take the B3357 towards Princetown. It climbs steeply (expect ears to pop), crosses a cattle grid (a sign you're on the unfenced moor) and crests a hill to reveal swaths of honey-coloured tors.

Just after the Eversfield Organic Cafe at the Dartmoor Inn, park on the right and stroll over the rise (due south) to explore the **2 Merrivale Stone Rows**. Back in the car, after a short climb, turn right towards Princetown, glimpsing the brooding bulk of Dartmoor Prison (signs warn you can't stop here; there's a better vantage point later). In the heart of rugged **3 Princetown**, turn left onto the B3212 towards Two Bridges; the **4 lay-by** immediately after you leave Princetown provides prime Dartmoor Prison views.

Follow signs for Moretonhampstead; soon an expansive landscape unfurls. At **5 Postbridge**, stroll over the 700-year-old bridge, then dangle hot feet in the cold River Dart. Next, the **6 Warren House Inn** (p328) makes an atmospheric spot for lunch. After the sign to Manaton, at Batworthy, take the easy-to-miss lane left, signed **7 Chagford**, to visit its thatch-dotted square and time-warp shops. Finally head to **8 Castle Drogo** (p329) to explore the gardens of a unique modern castle, and maybe have a bracing dip in the nearby River Teign.

Dewerstone CAFE £

(01822-890037; www.dewerstone.com; Tavistock Rd; snacks from £3; 10am-5pm Fri-Sun;) At the cafe-shop run by the clothing brand of choice for Dartmoor's eco-aware adventurers you'll find a rack full of muddy mountain bikes, Dawn Roasters espresso and energy-boosting cakes. Plus plenty of its trademark hoodies, recycled-plastic-bottle board shorts and wooden sunglasses.

★ **Prince of Wales** PUB FOOD ££

(01822-890219; www.princeofwalesbunkhouse.co.uk; Tavistock Rd; mains £10-20; noon-10pm; P) Roaring fires, low ceilings, a friendly landlord – the Prince is the place where everyone pops in for a pint of home-brewed Jail Ale, a Dartmoor beef burger or beer-battered cod and chips.

Postbridge

01822/ POP 170

The quaint hamlet of Postbridge owes its popularity, and its name, to its medieval stone slab or clapper bridge: a 13th-century structure with four, 3m-long slabs propped up on sturdy columns of stacked stones. Walking the bridge takes you across the rushing East Dart; it's a picturesque spot to whip off your boots and plunge your feet into the icy stream.

Check whether **Dartmoor YHA** (Bellever; 0845 371 9622; www.yha.org.uk; P), which switched to exclusive hire in 2020, has resumed individual bookings.

Brimpts Farm CAMPGROUND £

(0845 034 5968; www.brimptsfarm.co.uk; Dartmeet; sites per tent £8, 4-person pods from £40; P) A beauty of a Dartmoor farm, as traditional as afternoon tea, and all the better for it. Choose from the basic camping fields or timber-and-aluminium camping pods, all with bewitching moorland views. It's on the B3357, Two Bridges–Dartmeet road.

★ **Warren House Inn** PUB FOOD ££

(01822-880208; www.warrenhouseinn.co.uk; near Postbridge; mains £10-16; bar 11am-9pm, food noon-3pm & 6-8pm, shorter winter hours; P) Marooned amid miles of moorland, this Dartmoor institution exudes a hospitality only found in pubs in the middle of nowhere. A fire that's been burning (apparently) since 1845 warms stone floors, trestle tables and hikers munching on robust food; the Warreners Pie (local rabbit) is legendary. It's on the B3212, some 2 miles northeast of Postbridge.

DRIVING ON DARTMOOR

Dartmoor's roads are gorgeous to drive, but large stretches have unfenced grazing, so you'll come across Dartmoor ponies, sheep and even cows in the middle of the road. Many sections have a 40mph speed limit. Car parks on the moor can be little more than lay-bys; their surface can be rough to very rough. Break-ins at isolated car parks are not unknown – keep valuables stashed out of sight.

Widecombe-in-the-Moor

01364/ POP 570

With its honey-grey buildings and imposing church tower, this is archetypal Dartmoor, down to the ponies grazing on the village green. The village is commemorated in the traditional English folk song 'Widecombe Fair', a reference to the traditional country pageant that takes place on the second Tuesday of September.

St Pancras Church CHURCH

(01364-621334; The Green) St Pancras' immense 40m tower has seen it dubbed the Cathedral of the Moor. In 1638 a violent storm knocked a pinnacle from the roof, killing several parishioners. As ever on Dartmoor, the Devil was blamed, said to be in search of souls.

★ **Rugglestone Inn** PUB FOOD £

(01364-621327; www.rugglestoneinn.co.uk; mains £11; food noon-2pm & 6-8pm) Just one pint at this wisteria-clad pub is enough to make you want to drop everything and move to Dartmoor. It's a classic wood-beamed, low-ceilinged, old-fashioned history-packed village boozer. There's a picturesque beer garden, a strong range of real ales on tap, and a menu featuring lasagne, curries, quiches and homemade pies.

Chagford & Moretonhampstead

01647 / POP 3150

One of the prettiest of Dartmoor's villages, Chagford's stone-walled cottages, whitewashed buildings and thatched roofs are backed by views of tors and set around a quintessential village square. The market town of Moretonhampstead sits 5 miles to the southeast.

Sights

★Castle Drogo HISTORIC BUILDING

(NT; ☎01647-433306; www.nationaltrust.org.uk; near Drewsteignton; gardens adult/child £5/2.50; ⊙11am-5pm mid-Mar–Oct; P) Three miles northeast of Chagford sits an outlandish architectural flight of fancy. Designed by Sir Edwin Lutyens for self-made food-millionaire Julius Drewe, it was built between 1911 and 1931 and was intended to be a medieval-style castle but with modern comforts. Although currently the focus of a massive six-year restoration project, the gardens remain open.

The castle car park is also a starting point for spectacular hikes in the plunging, densely wooded Teign Gorge. Bring your swimsuit for a bracing dip at Salmon Leaps (p325).

Sleeping & Eating

Moretonhampstead's backpacker hostel, **Sparrowhawk** (☎01647-440318; www.sparrowhawkbackpackers.co.uk; 45 Ford St; dm/d/f £19/45/55;) suspended individual bookings in 2020; ask if they've reopened the dorms.

★Gidleigh Park HOTEL £££

(☎01647-432367; www.gidleigh.co.uk; Gidleigh, near Chagford; r £240-500, ste from £750, mains £14-32, 3-course dinner £115; ⊙restaurant 12.30-9pm Tue-Sat; P) Without doubt Devon's grandest, fanciest and priciest hotel. At the end of a long private drive, the mock-Tudor house is an unashamedly opulent pamper pad: vast suites with wet-room showers, luxurious lounges with crackling fires and a restaurant overseen by multiple-award-winning Chris Eden. It's 2 miles west of Chagford.

★Horse PIZZA £

(☎01647-440242; www.thehorsedartmoor.co.uk; 7 George St, Moretonhampstead; pizza £7-14; ⊙12.30-2.30pm Tue-Sat & 6.30-8.30pm Wed-Sat) One of Dartmoor's coolest gastropubs dishes up simple but superb pizzas (made from twice-risen, focaccia dough, no less), plus platters of fennel salami, buffalo mozzarella and memorable Dartmoor beef bresaola.

WORTH A TRIP

COOL CAMPING

There's every chance you'll fall utterly in love with **Vintage Vardos** (☎07977 535233; www.fishertonfarm.com; Higher Fisherton Farm, near Atherington; campsite per night £260-330; ⊙Easter-Oct; P), an enchanting encampment of restored Romany caravans 15 miles southeast of Croyde. The three brightly painted, two-person wagons boast log burners, funky fabrics and snug sleeping platforms. Night lights in jam jars lead to a firepit fringed by log benches, a hamper full of crockery and ranks of cast-iron pans.

There's even a bailer-twine-sprung outdoor bed, so you can slumber under the stars. It's all done with love and humour, and is impossible to resist.

Blacks DELI £

(☎01647-433545; www.blacks-deli.com; 28 The Sq, Chagford; snacks £4-7; ⊙7.30am-2pm Mon-Sat) Tempting breads, cheeses, olives, pies and pasties are stacked high. Homemade quiches might include leek and Stilton or spicy pepper with chorizo.

Croyde & Braunton

☎01271 / POP 8911

Croyde has the kind of cheerful, chilled vibe you'd expect from its role as North Devon's surf central. The old world meets a new surfing wave here: thatched roofs peep out over racks of wetsuits; crowds of hip wave-riders sip beers outside 17th-century inns; and powerful waves line up to roll in towards acres of sand. The traffic-thronged village of Braunton sits 2 miles inland.

Sights & Activities

The water's hard to resist in Croyde. **Ralph's** (☎01271-890147; Hobb's Hill; surfboard & wetsuit hire per 4/24hr £12/18, bodyboard & wetsuit £10/15; ⊙9am-dusk mid-Mar–Dec) is among those hiring out wetsuits and surfboards. Lessons are provided by **Surf South West** (☎01271-890400; www.surfsouthwest.com; Croyde Burrows car park; half/full day £35/65; ⊙mid-Mar–mid-Nov) and **Surfing Croyde Bay** (☎0800 188 4860; www.surfingcroydebay.co.uk; Freshwell Camping; half/full day £35/70). They also run coasteering and SUP lessons (per day £40 to £60).

★Museum of British Surfing MUSEUM
(☎01271-815155; www.museumofbritishsurfing.org.uk; Caen St, Braunton; adult/child £2/free; ⊙11am-3pm Fri-Sun Easter-Dec) Few museums are this cool. Vibrant surfboards and vintage wetsuits line the walls; sepia images catch your eye. The stories are compelling: 18th-century British sailors riding Hawaiian waves – England's 1920s homegrown surf pioneers. Here, heritage meets hanging ten.

Braunton Burrows WILDLIFE RESERVE
(www.explorebraunton.org; near Braunton; P) FREE The vast network of dunes here is the UK's largest. Paths wind past sandy hummocks, salt marshes, purple thyme, yellow hawkweed and pyramidal orchids. The burrows fringe an immense sweep of sandy beach, and were the main training area for American troops before D-Day. Mock landing craft are still hidden in the tufted dunes near the car park at its southern tip.

Sleeping & Eating

Cherry Tree Farm CAMPGROUND £
(☎01271-890495; www.cherrytreecampingcroyde.co.uk; off Moor Lane, Croyde; sites per 2 adults £26; P) Large grassy pitches, a no-caravans policy and broad ocean views make this chilled-out campsite a sought-after choice. You can also often put up a tent in unpitched fields. The 10-minute walk into the village means it's away from Croyde's crowds.

Ocean Pitch CAMPSITE £
(☎07581 024348; www.oceanpitch.co.uk; Moor Lane, Croyde; sites per 2 adults £30; ⊙mid-Jun–early Sep; P) A surfers' favourite, with brilliant views of the breakers, luxury sleeping pods (£99 per night) and classic VW campers (£99 per night).

★Baggy's HOSTEL, B&B ££
(☎01271-890078; www.baggys.co.uk; Baggy Point, Croyde; dm/d from £33/110; P) Baggy's is light, bright and inviting with lots of wood, minimal clutter and stylish double rooms. The surfy cafe has an outside deck where you can eat breakfast while watching the waves.

Dorms may be limited to three guests from the same household.

★Biffen's Kitchen STREET FOOD £
(www.biffenskitchen.com; Ocean Pitch Campsite, Moor Lane; dishes £4.50-7; ⊙8.30-10.30am Tue-Sun & 5-8pm Wed-Sat mid-Apr–Sep;) Inspired by surf-themed street food, the eponymous Biff set up this snack shack in 2019 after ditching a London marketing job to ride north Devon's waves. Expect chipotle jackfruit tacos, jerk chicken curry and plenty of beach-bum flair.

Information

Braunton Tourist Office (☎01271-816688; www.visitbraunton.co.uk; Caen St, Braunton; ⊙10am-3pm Mon-Fri year-round, plus to 1pm Sat Jun-Dec) Inside the town's (free) museum. It's volunteer run, so hours may vary.

Getting There & Away

Bus 21/21A links Braunton with Croyde (£2, 15 minutes, hourly Monday to Saturday), Ilfracombe (£2.10, 30 minutes, half-hourly daily) and Barnstaple (£2.90, 20 minutes, half-hourly daily).

DON'T MISS

CLOVELLY

Clovelly (☎01237-431781; www.clovelly.co.uk; adult/child £8/4.60; ⊙9am-5pm, book visits in advance; P) is the quintessential picture-postcard Devon village. Its cottages cascade down cliffs to meet a curving crab claw of a harbour that's lined with lobster pots and backed by a deep-blue sea.

Clovelly is privately owned, and admission is charged at the hilltop visitor centre. The village's cobbled streets are so steep that cars can't cope, so supplies are brought in by sledge; you'll see these big bread baskets on runners leaning outside homes. Charles Kingsley, author of the children's classic *The Water Babies*, spent much of his early life in Clovelly – don't miss his former house, or the highly atmospheric fishers' cottage and the village's twin chapels.

The village website outlines places to stay, including the smart harbourside hotel and local B&Bs.

Ilfracombe

☎01271/ POP 11,180

If there's anywhere that sums up the faded grandeur of the British seaside, it's surely Ilfracombe. Parts look decidedly tired, but it's also framed by precipitous cliffs, golf greens and a promenade strung with twinkling lights. The resort also springs a mighty surprise in the form of *Verity*; a towering, startling statue by the provocative artist Damien Hirst.

Sights & Activities

Check whether **Tunnelsbeaches** (www.tunnelsbeaches.co.uk), Ilfracombe's atmospheric, tidal, Victorian bathing pools have reopened.

★Verity LANDMARK

(The Pier) Pregnant, naked and holding aloft a huge spear, Damien Hirst's 20m-high statue *Verity* towers above Ilfracombe's harbour mouth. On the seaward side her skin is peeled back, revealing sinew, fat and foetus. Critics say she detracts from the scenery; the artist says she's an allegory for truth and justice. Either way, she's drawing the crowds.

Ilfracombe Aquarium AQUARIUM

(☎01271-864533; www.ilfracombeaquarium.co.uk; The Pier; adult/child £6.25/5.25; ⏰10am-4pm or 5pm late May–Sep, to 3pm early Feb–late May & Oct) Recreates aquatic environments from Exmoor to the Atlantic, via estuary, rock pool and harbour.

Ilfracombe Princess BOATING

(☎01271-879727; www.ilfracombeprincess.co.uk; The Pier; adult/child £12/6; ⏰1-4 trips daily Easter-Oct) Hop aboard this cute little yellow boat for a one-hour cruise along a dramatic shore to see seals and smuggler's caves.

Sleeping & Eating

Ocean Backpackers HOSTEL £

(☎01271-867835; www.oceanbackpackers.co.uk; 29 St James Pl; s/d/tr/q £38/50/66/80; P@Ⓦ) Brightly painted en-suite rooms, low prices and a cheerful, backpacker vibe make this convivial hostel an appealing option.

At the time of writing, dorms (beds from £20) and bedrooms were only available to household groups.

★Norbury House B&B ££

(☎01271-863888; www.norburyhouse.co.uk; Torrs Park; d £110-130, tr £135; PⓌ) Each of the rooms in this gorgeous guesthouse is done up in a different style: choose from pop art, art deco or contemporary chic. Fabulous furnishings, light-filled interiors, charming hosts and cracking sea-and-town views seal the deal.

★S&P SEAFOOD ££

(☎01271-865923; www.sandpfish.co.uk; 1 The Cove; dishes £6-15, seafood platters £64; ⏰10am-4pm Mon-Sat, 11am-4pm Sun) Seafood doesn't get much fresher than S&P's cafe and fishmongers – its trawlers land catches just metres away. The covered outdoor tables on the harbourside are prime places to tuck into lobster sandwiches, Devon oysters and shellfish platters crammed with cockles, mussels, lobster and crab. And perhaps sip a Prosecco or chilled white wine.

Information

Tourist Office (☎01271-863001; www.visitilfracombe.co.uk; The Seafront; ⏰11am-3pm Mon-Sat) Inside the seafront Landmark Theatre building.

Getting There & Away

Bus 21/21A Runs to Barnstaple (£2.90, one hour, half-hourly) via Braunton (£2.10, 30 minutes).

> OFF THE BEATEN TRACK
>
> **A REMOTE SLEEP SPOT**
>
> For a tucked-away North Devon hideaway, try **Peppercombe Bothy** (NT; ☎0344-335 1296; www.nationaltrust.org.uk; Peppercombe; hut per night £28; P), a four-person stone hut 7 miles east along the coast from Clovelly. The definition of bare-bones, it has two sleeping platforms, a sink with running water and a terrace with its own firepit. Arguably the best bit is the outdoor loo with unforgettable sea views.

CORNWALL

You can't get further west than the ancient Celtic kingdom of Cornwall (or Kernow, as it's known to Cornish speakers). Blessed with the southwest's wildest coastline and most breathtakingly beautiful beaches, this proudly independent peninsula has always marched to its own tune.

While the staple industries of old – mining, fishing and farming – have all but disappeared, Cornwall has since reinvented itself as one of the nation's creative corners. Whether it's exploring the space-age domes of the Eden Project, sampling the culinary creations of a celebrity chef or basking on a deserted beach, you're guaranteed to feel the itch of inspiration. Time to let a little Kernow into your soul.

Getting There & Away

The county's main airport (p340) is just outside Newquay, with regular links to London Heathrow, Leeds Bradford, Dublin and Cork. **First Kernow** (www.firstgroup.com/cornwall) bus 56 (£4, 30 minutes) shuttles to the airport from Newquay every one or two hours.

The main train line from London Paddington runs through the centre of the county before ending at Penzance, stopping at major towns in between. Trains also link Cornwall with the Midlands, the north of England and Scotland.

The major road into Cornwall, the A30, is prone to summer traffic jams. The A38 from Plymouth over the Tamar Bridge into Cornwall is an alternative, but can be a more circuitous route. You only pay the Tamar Bridge toll (cars £2) when leaving Cornwall.

Getting Around

Bus, train and ferry timetables can be found on the Traveline South West (www.travelinesw.com) website.

Great Scenic Railways (www.greatscenicrailways.com) links to timetables for Cornwall's picturesque railway branch lines.

BUS

Cornwall's main provider, **First Kernow** (☎0345 646 0707; www.firstgroup.com/cornwall), runs most buses between major towns. Around 20 smaller companies also provide services.

A one-day ticket covering all First Kernow buses costs adult/child/family £15/7/30. The Ride Cornwall Ranger covers both bus and train travel.

You can buy a series of day and multi-day tickets through the First app; prices can be several pounds cheaper than buying on board.

TRAIN

Cornwall's main railway line follows the coast as far as Penzance, with branch lines to Gunnislake, Looe, Newquay, Falmouth and St Ives.

Most trains are provided by **GWR** (Great Western Railway; ☎0345 7000 125; www.gwr.com), although **CrossCountry Trains** (☎03447 369 123; www.crosscountrytrains.co.uk) also run through major stations.

Both companies have useful apps featuring timetable queries and e-ticket purchases.

TRANSPORT PASSES

Several passes cover public transport in Cornwall.

Ride Cornwall Ranger (adult/child/family £18/9/36) is the best all-round value covering a day's bus and train travel across Cornwall, and between Cornwall and Plymouth. The ticket can be purchased from train and bus stations, and from bus drivers, and is valid after 9am Monday to Friday and weekends.

The **Freedom of Devon & Cornwall Rover** (three days off-peak travel in seven days adult/child £52/26, eight days travel in 15 days £85/43) is good value if you're using the train extensively through Devon and Cornwall.

Off-peak day-return tickets offer good value on Cornwall's branch railway lines; Truro to Falmouth costs £4.80.

If you have a permanent address in Cornwall (eg a holiday home), you can also buy a **Devon & Cornwall Railcard** (£12), which gives a 30% discount on off-peak train travel within Devon and Cornwall, including all the branch lines.

Bude

☎01288 / POP 9220

A scant few miles from the Devon border, Bude is a breezy seaside town with a batch of impressive beaches and a 1930s seawater lido that seems to sprout from the rock. The town is also a springboard for hikes on the stunning coastline that stretches out to either side.

Sights & Activities

Bude's beaches include popular, sandy **Summerleaze**, just off the town centre. Three miles south of town is **Widemouth Bay** (pronounced *wid*-muth), a broad, sandy beach great for both families and surfers. Two miles further is the shingly beach of **Millook**, followed by the dramatic cliffs around **Crackington Haven**, 10 miles south of Bude.

Three miles north of town are the National Trust–owned **Northcott Mouth** and **Sandymouth**.

A mile further on is pebbly **Duckpool**, often quiet even in summer.

★Bude Castle MUSEUM
(☎01288-357300; www.thecastlebude.org.uk; The Wharf; ⏲10am-4pm; 📶) FREE Housed in a striking folly behind Summerleaze beach,

the modern, bright, engaging displays here take in shipwrecks, life-saving and Bude's story as a holiday resort.

Bude Sea Pool SWIMMING
(www.budeseapool.org; Summerleaze Beach; 24hr) FREE The walls of Bude's handsome saltwater lido were integrated into an existing rock bowl, creating a sheltered pool were you can swim in the sea but are protected from its force. Built in the 1930s and measuring an impressive 90m by 45m, it's perfect for kids – it also warms up fast on sunny days.

Big Blue Surf School SURFING
(01288-331764; www.bigbluesurfschool.co.uk; Summerleaze Beach; per lesson £30) A well-established school offering lessons mainly to beginner and intermediate surfers. Also runs women-only sessions and those for surfers with disabilities.

Sleeping & Eating

Elements HOTEL ££
(01288-352386; www.elements-life.co.uk; Marine Dr; incl breakfast s £65, d £100-160, f £160; P) Despite a boxy exterior, this clifftop hotel sports soothing sea colours, bold fabrics, big coastal views and thoughtful mod cons including DVD library, Bluetooth speakers and Playstation 2 in the family rooms.

Edgcumbe B&B ££
(01288-353846; www.edgcumbe-hotel.co.uk; Summerleaze Cres; s/d/f from £65/130/135; P) There's a friendly, laid-back feel to this bright, modern B&B – helped by a location just a few minutes' walk from Summerleaze Beach. Some bedrooms offer lounge area, luxury bathroom and sea views. Its Deck bistro (4pm to 8pm, mains from £9) rustles up tasty surf 'n' turf focused food.

★**Beach at Bude** HOTEL £££
(01288-389800; www.thebeachatbude.co.uk; Summerleaze Cres; incl breakfast d £125-215, ste £195-355; P) Space, style and broad views steal the show at the Beach at Bude. Pale wood furniture, Lloyd Loom chairs and peach-and-taupe colours conjure the feel of a New England beach cabin. The suites sleep four.

Life's a Beach CAFE £
(01288-355222; www.lifesabeach.info; 16 Summerleaze Cres; mains £7-12; food 10am-7pm, bar to 9pm) Beloved of locals, Life's a Beach (or LAB as it's known) is a top spot for a baguette, burger, salt and pepper squid or some grilled fish. It's at its best as the sun goes down over the best view in town.

Information

Bude Tourist Office (01288-354240; www.visitbude.info; The Crescent; 10am-5pm Mon-Sat, plus to 4pm Sun summer) Beside the main long-stay car park.

Getting There & Away

First Kernow bus 95 (£4 to £6.50, one to four daily) runs between Bude and Boscastle (30 minutes), Tintagel (one hour) and Camelford (1½ hours).

Bus 10 (two to three daily) connects Camelford with Port Isaac (£3.50, 30 minutes) and Polzeath (£6, one hour).

Boscastle

01840 / POP 640

Tucked into the crook of a steep coombe (valley) at the confluence of three rivers, Boscastle's seafaring heritage stretches back to Elizabethan times. With its quaint cottages, flower-clad cliffs, tinkling streams and a sturdy quay, it's almost impossibly photogenic. But the peaceful setting belies a stormy incident: in 2004 Boscastle was hit by one of Britain's largest-ever flash floods, which carried away cars, bridges and buildings. Happily, the village has been rebuilt to its picturesque best.

Sights

Boscastle Harbour HARBOUR
(NT; 01840-250010; www.nationaltrust.org.uk) Dramatic to hike, Cornwall's north shore is highly hazardous for ships. Boscastle sprung up because it was the only spot for 40 miles where a harbour could be built. Strolling from the village beside the narrow channel towards the sea reveals a compact, curving harbour wall, a sharply curling promontory and the Meachard, a tiny island. Look out for the blowhole at Penally Point. If conditions are right, it spouts water across the harbour entrance an hour either side of low tide.

Sleeping & Eating

Pint-sized **Boscastle YHA** (0345 371 9006; www.yha.org.uk; Palace Stables, The Harbour) suspended bookings from individual travellers in 2020 – ask if they've resumed.

Pencuke Farm CAMPING £
(☎01840-230360; www.pencukefarm.co.uk; Pencuke La, St Gennys; sites per 4 adults £18, hut £150; P @ 🐾) This organic farm, roughly halfway between Boscastle and Bude, is a great place to pitch a tent. They've limited camping to just nine pitches in the spacious sea-view meadow; campfires seal the deal. Or opt for an Atlantic-view shepherd's hut (sleeps four), with hot tub, wood burner and sea views.

Boscastle House B&B ££
(☎01840-250654; www.boscastlehouse.co.uk; Doctors Hill; d £128; P 📶) The best of Boscastle's B&Bs occupies a Victorian house overlooking the valley. Five classy rooms have a bright, contemporary feel that mixes neutral colours with bold print wallpapers. Charlotte has bay-window views; Nine Maidens has twin sinks and a free-standing bath; and Trelawney has its own sofa.

★**Boscastle Farm Shop** CAFE £
(☎01840-250827; www.boscastlefarmshop.co.uk; Hillsborough Farm, near Boscastle; dishes £6-11; ⏰9am-5pm; P) In the spacious cafe of this excellent farm shop, tall windows look out onto green fields and the coast. It's the perfect setting for breakfasts of dry-cured local bacon, sandwiches packed with Tregida smoked salmon, or Ruby Red burgers with Cornish blue cheese. The drinks menu features prime Cornish lager, cider and wine.

Information

Boscastle Tourist Office (☎01840-250010; www.visitboscastleandtintagel.com; The Harbour; ⏰10am-5pm Mar-Oct, 10.30am-4pm Nov-Feb) Near the quay.

Getting There & Away

Coastal bus 95 (£4 to £6.50, one to four daily) stops in Boscastle on its way from Bude (30 minutes), then continues on to Tintagel (25 minutes) and Camelford (45 minutes).

From Camelford, catch connecting bus 10 to Port Isaac (£3.50, 30 minutes, two to three daily).

Tintagel

☎01840 / POP 1720

The spectre of legendary King Arthur looms large over Tintagel and its dramatic clifftop castle. Though the present-day ruins mostly date from the 13th century, archaeological digs have revealed the foundations of a much earlier fortress, fuelling speculation that Arthur may indeed have been born at the castle, as locals like to claim. It's a stunningly romantic sight, with crumbling walls teetering precariously above the sheer cliffs, and is well worth exploring for half a day.

Sights

★**Tintagel Castle** CASTLE
(EH; ☎01840-770328; www.english-heritage.org.uk; Castle Rd; adult/child £14.50/8.70; ⏰10am-5pm) Famous as the supposed birthplace of King Arthur, Tintagel's epic clifftop castle has been occupied since Roman times and once served as a residence for Cornwall's Celtic kings. The present castle is largely the work of Richard, Earl of Cornwall, who built a base here during the 1230s. An elegant new footbridge now spans a plunging 60m gully, linking the two sides of the medieval castle and recreating a land bridge that existed 500 years ago.

Although the Arthurian links might be tenuous, it's hard to think of a more soul-stirring spot for a stronghold. Though much of the castle has long since crumbled, it's still possible to make out the footprint of the Great Hall and several other rooms. There's also a curious tunnel that's still puzzling archaeologists; it may have been used as a larder or cold store.

Trails lead along the headland to the atmospheric medieval chapel of **St Materiana**, and on the beach below the castle the rocky mouth of **Merlin's Cave** is exposed at low tide – local legend claims it's where the wizard once cast his spells.

★**St Nectan's Glen** WATERFALL
(☎01840-779538; www.st-nectansglen.co.uk; near Trethevy; adult/child £6/4.70; ⏰10am-4pm) Hidden away in a secret valley a mile east of Tintagel, this little glen feels like something from a fairy tale. Fringed by climbing ivy and shrubs, a 60ft waterfall tumbles across the slate into a kieve (plunge pool). It's a mystical spot, supposedly frequented by Cornish *piskies* (pixies), and legendarily associated with King Arthur – you'll see ribbons and offerings dangling from the trees around the pool. It's also a bracing spot for a dip, although the water's icy-cold.

Getting There & Away

First Kernow bus 95/96 (£4 to £6.50, one to four daily) stops in Tintagel en route from Camelford (15 minutes) to Bude (50 minutes).

DON'T MISS

TREEHOUSE HIDEOUT

Meaning hideout in Cornish, **Kudhva** (www.kudhva.com; Sanding Rd, Trebarwith Strand; 2-person tent/pod £58/120, 6-person cabin £360; Apr-Oct) combines a cluster of ubermodern sleeping pods on stilts with a wooden cabin, and tents suspended in trees. It's an irresistible, off-grid retreat and a magical reimagining of a former slate quarry, complete with firepits, wild swimming spots, a wood-fired hot tub and corking coastal views.

It's tucked away 2 miles southeast of Tintagel, near the gorgeous low-tide beach of Trebarwith Strand.

Port Isaac

01208 / POP 720

Port Isaac is a classic Cornish fishing town, where cobbled alleyways, slender *opes* (lanes) and cob-walled cottages collect around a medieval harbour and slipway. The picturesque setting draws the cameras – the hit TV series *Doc Martin* is filmed here – and some top restaurants.

A short walk east along the coast leads to the harbour of Port Gaverne. Hiking 2.5 miles west along the shore leads to the sheltered inlet of Port Quin, now owned by the National Trust.

Sleeping & Eating

Old School Hotel HOTEL ££
(01208-880721; www.theoldschoolhotel.co.uk; Fore St; incl breakfast s £67-101, d £119-185, tr from £200;) A small hotel that was originally Port Isaac's schoolhouse. Eagle-eyed fans of the *Doc Martin* TV series might recognise it as the show's village school. Appropriately, rooms are named after school subjects: the best are Latin, with its sleigh bed and cupboard bathroom; Biology, with its sofa and church-style windows; and split-level Mathematics, with bunk beds and a shared terrace.

★**Fresh from the Sea** SEAFOOD ££
(01208-880849; www.freshfromthesea.co.uk; 18 New Rd; sandwiches £6.50-12, mains £8.50-30; 9am-4pm Mon-Sat) Local man Callum Greenhalgh takes his boat *Mary D* out daily in search of crab and lobster, then sells the catch at his tiny Port Isaac shop. Seafood doesn't get any fresher; a crab salad costs £15 and a whole lobster is £30. If in season, oysters from nearby Porthilly cost £2.25 each.

★**Outlaw's New Road** SEAFOOD £££
(01208-880896; www.nathan-outlaw.com; 6 New Rd; mains £22-60; noon-2pm & 6-9pm Tue-Sat;) Top chef Nathan Outlaw has reimagined his double-Michelin-starred Restaurant Nathan Outlaw into a more accessible, fun-loving place. Dishes are pared down and cheaper, but the winning emphasis on fresh ingredients and the skill and simplicity of the cooking remains.

Outlaw's Fish Kitchen SEAFOOD £££
(01208-881183; www.nathan-outlaw.com; 1 Middle St; per person £80; noon-3pm & 6-9pm Tue-Sat;) Nathan Outlaw's tiny, Michelin-starred, harbourside restaurant has only three tables and specialises in a set, seven-dish seafood menu for the whole table to share. It's dictated by whatever's landed on the day by local fishers; it might feature raw scallops, cured brill and Dover sole.

Getting There & Away

First Kernow bus 96/55 stops in Port Isaac two to five times daily en route between Camelford (£4.50, 30 minutes) and Wadebridge (£3.50, 50 minutes).

Padstow & Rock

01841 / POP 4196

If anywhere symbolises Cornwall's increasingly chic credentials, it's Padstow. This old fishing port has become the county's most cosmopolitan corner thanks to the arrival of a bevy of celebrity chefs, and restaurants and boutiques now sit alongside pubs and pasty shops. Whether the town's held onto its soul in the gentrification process is debatable, but it's hard not to be charmed by the seaside setting.

Across the Camel Estuary from Padstow lies Rock, a small village turned uberexclusive getaway. Nearby, the sandy sweep of Daymer Bay unfurls along the estuary, a lifelong favourite of poet John Betjeman.

WORTH A TRIP

CORNISH VINEYARDS

Cornwall might not seem an obvious place for winemaking, but they've been producing award-winning vintages at the **Camel Valley Vineyard** (☎01208-77959; www.camelvalley.com; Nanstallon; tours £5-12; ⊙shop 10am-5pm Mon-Fri, tours 2.30pm Mon-Fri Apr-Sep; P), on the north side of Bodmin Moor, since 1989. The range includes award-winning whites and rosés, and a bubbly that's Champagne in all but name. The wines have a fresh, light quality that comes from the mild climate and pure sea air. Book for a tour and to sip wines by the glass on the sun terrace, or just drop by the shop.

Around 5 miles south of Padstow, Trevibban Mill offers pre-booked tours, tastings and classy bar snacks best enjoyed on a picture-perfect, flower-framed patio.

Sights & Activities

Padstow is surrounded by fine beaches, including the so-called Seven Bays: Trevone, Harlyn, Mother Ivey's, Booby's, Constantine, Treyarnon and Porthcothan.

In the middle of the Camel estuary runs a treacherous sandbank known as the Doom Bar, which has claimed many ships over the years, and also gave its name to a popular local ale.

★Trevibban Mill VINEYARD
(☎01841-541413; www.trevibbanmill.com; Dark Lane, St Issey; ⊙noon-5pm Wed-Sun, tours Wed, Thu & Sat) Trevibban is a fine place to sample vintages in a dreamy Cornish setting. Book for a tour (£15), which leads you around the vineyard and winery before finishing with a tutored tasting of five wines. Or just turn up for a tasting of seven wines (£15). Allow time to sit on the bewitching patio framed by wildflower meadows and sip a crisp, chilled white wine.

Trevibban's **Winery Bar** (snacks £1.50 to £3, platters £11 to £19) offers elegant nibbles and light meals. Here hummus might come with beetroot and pomegranate, the charcuterie plate includes English salami, and platters feature irresistible Cornish cheeses.

National Lobster Hatchery HATCHERY
(☎01841-533877; www.nationallobsterhatchery.co.uk; South Quay; adult/child £4/2; ⊙hours vary) In an effort to combat falling lobster stocks, this harbourside hatchery rears baby lobsters in tanks before returning them to the wild. Displays detail the crustaceans' life cycle, and there are tanks where you can watch the residents in action. Check the website for updates on opening hours.

★Camel Trail CYCLING
(☎0300 1234 202; www.cornwall.gov.uk/cameltrail) The old Padstow–Bodmin railway was closed in the 1950s, but reemerged decades later as the Camel Trail, now Cornwall's most popular cycle route. The main section starts in Padstow and heads east through Wadebridge (5.75 miles). The trail then runs on all the way to Poley Bridge on Bodmin Moor (18 miles).

Bikes can be hired from **Trail Bike Hire** (☎01841-532594; www.trailbikehire.co.uk; unit 6, South Quay; per day adult/child from £15/10; ⊙9am-5pm) in Padstow, or from **Bridge Bike Hire** (☎01208-813050; www.bridgebikehire.co.uk; off Commissioners Rd; per day adult/child from £14/10; ⊙10am-5pm) in Wadebridge.

Most people do the route from Padstow and back, so it's quieter (and much, much easier to find parking) if you start from the Wadebridge side.

Padstow Sealife Safaris BOATING
(☎07754 822404; www.padstowsealifesafaris.co.uk; North Quay; 2hr cruises adult/child £39/25) Scenic trips to see the local seabird colonies and offshore islands around Padstow. A shorter one-hour tour (adult/child £22.50/15) heads to a seal cave.

Festivals & Events

May Day CULTURAL
(⊙1 May) Also known as Obby Oss Day, Padstow's biggest party is said to have its roots in an ancient pagan fertility rite, and sees two coloured *'osses* (red and blue) twirl through the streets before meeting up beneath the maypole. It attracts thousands of visitors, so plan well ahead.

Sleeping

Treyarnon Bay YHA HOSTEL £
(☎0845 371 9664; www.yha.org.uk; Treyarnon Bay; sites £15, d £29, 4-person bell tent £99; ⊙reception 7-10am & 5-10pm; P) Set in a super 1930s beach hostel on the bluffs above Treyarnon Bay, the sleeping options here range from

bring-your-own tents to camping pods, bell tents and private rooms. The sunsets are spectacular. It's 4.5 miles east of Padstow.

Dorm beds were made temporarily unavailable in 2020; see online for updates.

Woodlands B&B £££
(☎01841-532426; www.woodlands-padstow.co.uk; Treator; s/d £126/146; P 📶 🐾) Offering green fields and distant flashes of sea, this is a great B&B base for Padstow. Cosy rooms feature creams and frills, and the breakfasts are prodigious. It's a mile or so from Padstow's harbourside, beside the A389.

Althea House APARTMENT £££
(☎07980 017113; www.altheahouse-padstow.co.uk; 64 Church St; per night/week from £300/750; P 📶) If you want to stay in Padstow proper, this charming ivy-clad house is hard to beat. There are two stylish self-catering suites: Rafters is accessed via a private staircase, while Driftwood has a pine four-poster bed. Both suites have sofas, Nespresso coffee machine, bath and small studio kitchen.

Treverbyn House B&B £££
(☎07534 095961; www.treverbynhouse.com; Station Rd; d £135-140; P 📶) The sweeping views of Padstow's sandy estuary from this gorgeous guesthouse linger long in the memory. Choose from yellow- or green-themed rooms or a romantic turret hideaway. Either way you get oriental rugs, brass bedsteads and a table on the terrace at which to enjoy breakfasts of homemade jams and smoked kippers.

Eating

Check whether the popular seafood bar **Prawn on the Lawn** (☎01841-532223; www.prawnonthelawn.com; 11 Duke St; mains £7.50-45), which relocated to a farm a mile outside Padstow for the summer of 2020, has moved back to town.

★**Chough Bakery** BAKERY £
(☎01841-533361; www.thechoughbakery.co.uk; 1-3 The Strand; pasties £3-5; ⏲9am-5pm Mon-Sat) A family-run bakery right in the heart of town, renowned for traditionally made pasties – it regularly scoops top honours in the World Pasty Championships.

Rojano's in the Square ITALIAN ££
(☎01841-532796; www.paul-ainsworth.co.uk; 9 Mill Sq; pizza & pasta £8.50-20; ⏲8.30am-10pm) Under the stewardship of Michelin-starred chef Paul Ainsworth, this excellent little Italian bistro turns out fantastic wood-fired pizza, spicy pasta and antipasti. It's a fun and laid-back place to dine, and prices are very reasonable.

Cornish Arms GASTROPUB ££
(☎01841-532700; www.rickstein.com; St Merryn; mains £13-23; ⏲noon-10pm) This country pub near the village of St Merryn is owned by Rick Stein's foodie empire, and offers everything from scampi in a basket to 10oz rump steak – all with creative twists and firm local provenance, naturally. It's a 3-mile drive from Padstow.

Look online to see if they're still rustling up takeaway wood-fired pizzas (£10 to £14, served 4pm to 9pm).

★**Paul Ainsworth at No 6** BRITISH £££
(☎01841-532093; www.paul-ainsworth.co.uk; 6 Middle St; 4-course lunch/dinner £75/85; ⏲noon-2.30pm & 6-9.30pm Tue-Sat) Rick Stein might be the household name, but Paul Ainsworth is often touted as Padstow's pretender to the throne. His food combines surprising flavours and impeccable presentation with a refreshingly unpretentious approach, and the town-house setting is a relaxed, unfussy place to dine. Now Michelin-starred, this is Padstow's most sought-after table and gets booked up months in advance.

★**Seafood Restaurant** SEAFOOD £££
(☎01841-532700; www.rickstein.com; Riverside; 3-course lunch £40, mains £20-58; ⏲noon-10pm) The restaurant that started the Stein dynasty, and still one of Cornwall's top places to eat. Stein senior rarely puts in any hours these days – Rick's son Jack runs the show. As ever, fish is the raison d'être: from fresh lobster to turbot, John Dory and *fruits de mer*, all served in an elegant, light-filled dining room.

Information

Padstow Tourist Office (☎01841-533449; www.padstowlive.com; South Quay; ⏲10am-2pm Mon, Tue, Thu & Fri, hours may vary) At the Padstow Harbour Commissioners.

Getting There & Away

BOAT

Black Tor Ferry (☎01841-532239; www.padstow-harbour.co.uk; adult/child single £3/1.50, bikes £4) Departure points for the

LOCAL KNOWLEDGE

CARNEWAS AT BEDRUTHAN

The stately rock stacks of **Carnewas at Bedruthan** (Bedruthan Steps; NT; www.nationaltrust.org.uk) loom from the landscape roughly halfway between Newquay and Padstow. These mighty granite pillars have been carved out by relentless wind and waves. Those same natural forces caused a rockfall in early 2020, prompting the closure of the steps onto the beach (check the website for updates). The clifftop footpaths remain open and deliver dramatic views; walking options include a 4.5-mile loop.

ferry that links Padstow with Rock vary; look for notices at the harbour. The first ferry from Padstow is at 8am year-round. The last ferry back from Padstow is at 7pm from June to mid-September, at 6pm from April to May and from mid-September to mid-October, and at 5pm from mid-October to March.

The last ferry leaves Rock 15 minutes before the final Padstow ferry.

CAR

There are a couple of car parks beside the harbour in Padstow, but they fill up quickly, so it's usually better to park at one of the large car parks at the top of town and walk down.

BUS

First Kernow bus A5 runs along the coast to Newquay (£5.40, one hour, four to five times daily) taking in Harlyn Bay, Porthcothan Bay, Carnewas at Bedruthan (Bedruthan Steps), Mawgan Porth and Watergate Bay.

Newquay

01637 / POP 20,340

Despite a genuinely gorgeous coast, for many years surf-central Newquay has been better known for its boisterous nightlife, trashy clubs, rowdy pubs and blinking amusement arcades. But if you know where to look, the town also has trendy bistros, clifftop cafes, gourmet bakeries and health-food shops. And along the coast, a bevy of boutique hotels are attracting a more discerning clientele. Yes, Newquay's bargain-basement vibe is still there, but it's not the whole story.

Sights

Newquay has a truly knockout location among some of North Cornwall's finest beaches. The trio close to town – **Towan**, **Great Western** and **Tolcarne** – are guaranteed to be packed in the middle of summer. Most surfers head for **Fistral**, on Newquay's western edge, but the very best beaches such as **Crantock**, **Holywell Bay** and **Watergate Bay** lie a couple of miles out of town.

Trerice HISTORIC BUILDING
(NT; 01637-875404; www.nationaltrust.org.uk; Kestle Mill; gardens adult/child £5/2.50; gardens 10am-5pm) Built in 1751, the grounds of this Elizabethan manor are home to an allium-filled knot garden, bright borders and a turf maze. Visits inside the house were suspended in 2020. It features an elaborate barrel-roofed ceiling in the Great Chamber, and 576 panes of 16th-century stained glass in the great window. It's around 3 miles southeast of Newquay.

Blue Reef Aquarium AQUARIUM
(01637-878134; www.bluereefaquarium.co.uk/newquay; Towan Promenade; adult/child £11.80/9; 10am-6pm;) The deep-sea denizens at this small aquarium include reef sharks, loggerhead turtles and a giant Pacific octopus. If they're operating limited visitor numbers, prepare for long queues. There's a discount for online bookings.

Newquay Zoo ZOO
(01637-873342; www.newquayzoo.org.uk; Trenance Gardens; adult/child £14.85/11.15; 10am-5pm;) Pint-sized Newquay Zoo's population of penguins, lemurs, meerkats and zebras will keep the kids happy.

Check to see whether set feeding times have resumed.

Activities

Newquay is brimming with surf schools, but quality is variable. Choose one that offers small-group sessions with a no-stag-party policy. Ask about teachers' accreditation and experience, and whether they travel to beaches other than Fistral – good schools follow the best waves.

Extreme Academy WATER SPORTS
(01637-860840; www.extremeacademy.co.uk; Watergate Bay) Owned by the nearby Watergate Bay Hotel, this watersports provider offers lessons in surfing, stand-up paddleboarding (SUP) and hand-planing (which involves catching a wave with a miniature surfboard attached to your wrist). A 2½-hour beginners' surf lesson costs £35, bodyboarding £25 and SUP £40. Or opt for a

three-hour SUP tour (£45), where you snorkel, stop for a cup of tea and look out for spider crabs.

The Academy also hires out wetsuits (per three hours £8) and boards (per three hours from £8).

Rip Curl English Surf School SURFING
(Newquay Activity Centre; ☎01637-879571; www.englishsurfschool.com; Towan Promenade; lessons from £35) Based on Towan Beach, this is one of the most experienced and efficient large schools, linked with Rip Curl and staffed by English Surfing Federation–approved instructors (including the British team coach). Taster lessons cost £35; a set of four lessons is £150.

The surf school is part of the **Newquay Activity Centre** (www.newquayactivitycentre.co.uk). It offers bodyboarding lessons (two hours £38), as well as coasteering sessions (two hours £45) and kayak and SUP tours (two hours £45). Or just hire kit including wetsuits (two hours/day £10/14), surfboards (£12/15), SUP boards (£15/25) and kayaks (£15/25).

EboAdventure OUTDOORS
(Newquay Water Sports Centre; ☎01637-498200; www.eboadventure.co.uk; South Quay Hill; per 3hr session/tour from £35/45) As well as surfing, Ebo offers kayak tours, stand-up paddleboarding and coasteering from its base at Newquay Harbour.

Sleeping

St Bernard's B&B ££
(☎01637-872932; www.stbernardsguesthouse.com; 9 Berry Rd; d from £75; P 📶 🐾) Bright, modern bedrooms, a central location, off-site parking (£2.50) and accommodating hosts make this family-run B&B a good-value choice. They'll even offer you breakfast in bed.

★**Scarlet** HOTEL £££
(☎01637-861800; www.scarlethotel.co.uk; Tredragon Rd, Mawgan Porth; r £250-370; P 📶 🏊 🐾) 🍃 For out-and-out luxury, Cornwall's fabulously chic adults-only eco-hotel takes the crown. In a regal location above Mawgan Porth, 5 miles from Newquay, it screams designer style, from the huge sea-view rooms with their sleek furniture and minimalist decor to the outdoor pool and cliff-side alfresco hot tubs. The restaurant's a beauty, too.

★**Watergate Bay Hotel** HOTEL £££
(☎01637-860543; www.watergatebay.co.uk; Watergate Bay; d incl breakfast from £330; P 📶 🏊 🐾) At beach-side Watergate Bay you can watch the surfers from your bath. Rooms are decked out in coastal colours and slatted wood, and the glorious indoor pool overlooks the bay. It's posh but reassuringly unpretentious: wet feet and sandy footprints are not a problem here. Prices plummet off-peak.

Eating

The summer of 2020 saw Emily Scott, of the remowned St Tudy Inn (p359), set up a pop-up bistro at Watergate Bay; see if she's returned.

★**Pavilion Bakery** BAKERY £
(www.pavilionbakery.com; 37 Fore St; breads £3.50, pizza £8-10; ⏰8am-8pm Tue-Sat, to 4pm Sun, to 3pm Mon) To hip Pavilion's stunning sourdoughs, artisan breads and melt-in-your-mouth croissants you can now add irresistible takeaway wood-fired pizzas topped with seasonal ingredients (served noon to 8pm Tuesday to Saturday). Also look out for culinary collaborations that turn the place into a pop-up bistro.

Sprout VEGETARIAN £
(☎01637-875845; www.sprouthealth.co.uk; Crescent Lane; mains £4-6; ⏰10am-4.30pm Mon-Sat; 🌶) At this excellent wholefood shop the one-pot veggie meals (such as vegan African peanut stew) are delicious and sell out fast – almost as fast as the delectable gluten-free cakes.

Fern Pit CAFE ££
(☎01637-873181; www.fernpit.co.uk; Riverside Cres, Pentire; mains £5-17; ⏰10am-6pm; P) Locals love this legendary clifftop hang-out because of the breathtaking views, terraced garden and sandwiches crammed with crab that's been caught by the cafe's own boat. You can walk or drive here from Fistral Beach's southern end. Or check if the ferry and footbridge access from the Crantock Beach side of the Gannel estuary, suspended in 2020, has resumed.

You can even pre-order cooked lobster (per pound £11) to take away.

★**Fish House Fistral** SEAFOOD ££
(☎01637-872085; www.thefishhousefistral.com; Fistral Beach; mains lunch £9-20, dinner £19-25; ⏰noon-9.30pm) This beachside seafooderie has become a firm favourite for local diners

and Fistral visitors alike, and it's thoroughly deserved. Filling fishy dishes are the catch of the day, underscored by French, Italian and Asian flavours, and the beach-shack vibe is bang-on.

Beach Hut BISTRO ££

(☎01637-860543; www.watergatebay.co.uk; Watergate Bay; mains £12-23; ⊙9am-9pm) After a beach walk or a quick surf at Watergate, this is where everyone heads for a coffee, cake or something more filling. With big picture windows filled with wide sea views, it's a lovely spot to eat easygoing dishes such as burgers, meze, mussels, pad Thai and seafood curry.

Lewinnick Lodge BISTRO ££

(☎01637-878117; www.lewinnicklodge.co.uk; Pentire Head; mains £8-18; ⊙8am-10pm) There's a knock-out perspective of Newquay's coastline from the long terrace of this restaurant, perched on the cliffs of Pentire Head. The decor is modern – lots of wood and plate glass – and the food is decent: steamed Cornish mussels, slow-cooked pork burgers and seaweed- and sesame-crusted tofu.

Drinking & Nightlife

Brash bars abound and the town centre gets notoriously rowdy on Friday and Saturday nights, especially in summer.

Tom Thumb BAR

(☎01637-498180; www.tom-thumb.co.uk; 27a East St; ⊙3-11.30pm) Newquay's classiest cocktail bar has reclaimed wood furniture, a cool spiral staircase and a fine selection of home-mixed drinks, ranging from originals and classics to Driving Juice (aka alcohol free).

Information

Newquay Tourist Office (☎01637-838516; www.visitnewquay.org; Marcus Hill; ⊙9am-5pm Mon-Fri, 10am-4pm Sat & Sun Apr-Sep, 10am-4pm Mon-Fri, to 3pm Sat & Sun Oct-Mar) Distancing measures may mean you can't go in, but you'll be able to talk to staff by phone, or through a hatch.

Getting There & Away

AIR

Cornwall Airport Newquay (NQY; ☎01637-860600; www.cornwallairportnewquay.com; St Mawgan) Cornwall's main airport is 5 miles northeast of Newquay. It has regular connections to London Heathrow with British Airways (www.britishairways.com); Leeds Bradford with Eastern Airways (www.easternairways.com); Dublin and Cork with Aer Lingus (www.aerlingus.com) and the Isles of Scilly with IoS Skybus.

First Kernow (www.firstgroup.com/cornwall) bus 56 (£4, 30 minutes) runs to the airport from Newquay every one or two hours.

Taxis cost around £18 from the town centre.

BUS

Newquay's bus station is on Manor Rd. The following services are operated by First Kernow.

Padstow Bus A5 (£5.40, one hour, four to five times daily) heads up the coast via Watergate Bay, Mawgan Porth, Carnewas at Bedruthan (Bedruthan Steps), Porthcothan and Harlyn Bay.

St Agnes Bus 87 (£5.40, 50 minutes, hourly in summer) stops at Perranporth en route to St Agnes and continues to Truro.

Truro Bus 91 (£5.40, one hour, hourly Monday to Saturday, five on Sunday).

TRAIN

Newquay is at the end of a branch line that runs to Par (£5.20, 50 minutes, five to seven daily) on the main London Paddington–Penzance line.

Perranporth to Porthtowan

Southwest of Newquay, Cornwall's craggy northern coastline dips and curves through a stunning panorama of wild, sea-smacked cliffs and golden bays. Tempting stops include the family-friendly beach of Perranporth, the old mining town of St Agnes and the surfy hang-out of Porthtowan.

Sights & Activities

★Perranporth Beach BEACH

(P 👪) Perranporth's huge, flat, sandy beach is a favourite for everyone: dog-walkers, families, kite-buggiers and surfers alike. Its main draw is its sheer size – more than a mile long, backed by dunes and rocky cliffs – meaning there's usually space even on the busiest days.

★Chapel Porth BAY

(NT; ☎01872-552412; www.nationaltrust.org.uk; parking per day £4; P) Two miles southwest of St Agnes sits one of Cornwall's most beautiful coves. Chapel Porth is a wild, rocky beach framed by steep, gorse-covered cliffs. Above the cove is the ruined engine stack of **Wheal Coates**, and from here the coast path winds all the way to the blustery outcrop of **St Agnes Head**. It's a panorama that graces many a postcard – don't forget your camera.

Blue Hills Tin Streams WORKSHOP
(01872-553341; www.cornishtin.com; Trevellas Coombe; adult/child £7/3; 10am-2pm Tue-Sat mid-Apr–mid-Oct) A mile east of St Agnes (signed to Wheal Kitty) is the rocky valley of **Trevellas Porth**, home to one of Cornwall's last tin manufacturers. You can watch the whole tinning process, from mining and smelting through to casting and finishing. It sells handmade jewellery too.

Eating & Drinking

Chapel Porth Cafe CAFE £
(01872-552487; Chapel Porth; sandwiches & cakes £3-6; 10am-5pm, shorter winter hours) This cafe down on the edge of Chapel Porth beach is a local institution, serving hot chocolate, cheesy baguettes, sausage butties, flapjacks and the house speciality: hedgehog ice cream (vanilla ice cream topped with clotted cream and hazelnuts).

★ **Blue Bar** BAR
(01209-890329; www.bluebarporthtowan.com; Beach Rd, Porthtowan; mains £8-18; 10am-11pm;) For a seaside sundowner the Blue Bar, with its casual surf vibe, is hard to beat. If the tables overlooking the sand are full, you can take away everything from draught Korev lager to plant-based burgers, stone-baked pizzas and dirty chips. Brunch (served 10am to 11.45am) brings maple-syrup-laced waffles with bacon and toasted banana bread.

Watering Hole BAR
(01872-572888; www.the-wateringhole.co.uk; 19 St Pirans Rd, Perranporth Beach; 10am-11pm) Generations of Cornish youth have passed through this venerable beach bar, which is set right on Perranporth's expanse of golden sand. With a sweep of outdoor tables it's a prime spot for a post-surf coffee or a beer as the sun goes down. It also has regular alfresco live music ranging from Ibiza classics to funk and soul.

Getting There & Away

Bus 87 (hourly in summer) runs between Newquay and Truro, taking in Perranporth and St Agnes en route.

St Ives

01736 / POP 9960

If there was a prize for the prettiest of Cornish ports, St Ives would be a clear contender. A tightly packed cluster of slate roofs, fishers' cottages and church towers spread out around turquoise bays – it's an unfailingly dazzling sight. Once a busy pilchard harbour, St Ives later became the centre of Cornwall's arts scene in the 1920s and '30s, when luminary figures such as Barbara Hepworth, Terry Frost, Ben Nicholson and Naum Gabo migrated here in search of artistic freedom.

St Ives remains an artistic centre, with numerous galleries lining its cobbled streets, as well as the renowned Tate St Ives. The town is also one of Cornwall's holiday home hot spots, and is packed with tourists in summer - visit in spring or autumn if you can.

Sights

Ask if **Leach Pottery** (01736-799703; www.leachpottery.com; Higher Stennack), a museum in the studio of ground-breaking potter Bernard Leach, has reopened. At the time of writing, only the shop was open. It sells works by contemporary potters, but by appointment only.

★ **Tate St Ives** GALLERY
(01736-796226; www.tate.org.uk/stives; Porthmeor Beach; adult/child £9.50/free, joint ticket with Barbara Hepworth Museum £12/free; 10am-5.20pm, last admission 4pm) St Ives' most illustrious gallery boasts a new monumental exhibition space that's been added to the museum's original, spiral-shaped core. Focusing on the

PARKING IN ST IVES

Parking is one of the main headaches for anyone planning on visiting St Ives: traffic can be very bad in summer, and attempting to drive through the town centre is a recipe for holiday nightmares.

The largest car park by far is Trenwith, a brisk uphill walk from town; it's usually the likeliest to have spaces in summer.

Another useful alternative worth considering is to use the park-and-ride system by leaving your car at St Erth or Lelant stations, and then catching the scenic St Ives train line into town.

West Cornwall

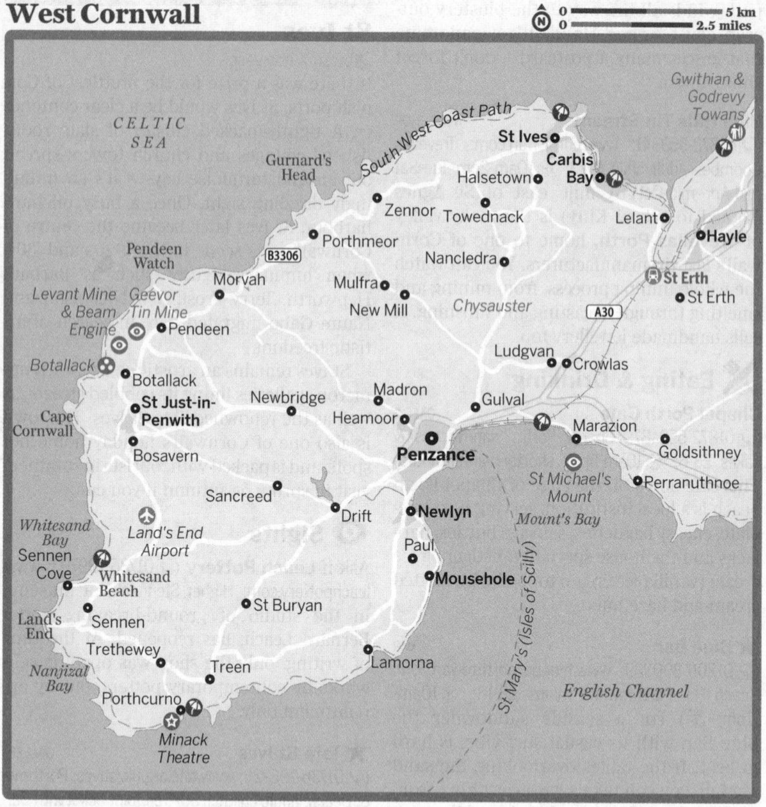

coterie of experimental artists who congregated at St Ives after WWII and turned the little seaside town into a magnet for modern artists, the museum showcases the work of Barbara Hepworth, Terry Frost, Peter Lanyon and Patrick Heron in luminous, white-walled surroundings.

Barbara Hepworth Museum MUSEUM
(☎01736-796226; www.tate.org.uk/stives; Barnoon Hill; joint ticket with Tate St Ives adult/child £12/free; ⏲10am-5.20pm Mar-Oct, to 4pm Nov-Feb) Barbara Hepworth (1903–75) was one of the leading abstract sculptors of the 20th century and a key figure in the St Ives art scene. Her studio on Barnoon Hill has remained almost untouched since her death and the adjoining garden contains several of her most notable sculptures, many of which were inspired by the elemental forces she discovered in her adopted Cornish home: rock, sea, sand, wind, sky.

Hepworth's work is scattered throughout St Ives; look for works outside the Guildhall and inside the 15th-century St Ia parish church.

Activities

The largest town beaches are **Porthmeor** and **Porthminster**, both of which have sand and space aplenty. Between them juts the grassy promontory known as the Island, topped by the tiny pre-14th-century **Chapel of St Nicholas**. On the peninsula's east side is the little cove of **Porthgwidden**, a smaller beach that can be a good place to escape the crowds.

St Ives Boats BOATING
(☎0777 300 8000; www.stivesboats.co.uk; The Wharf; adult/child from £20/10; 🐾) St Ives Boats runs daily, one-hour trips along the scenic shore, including seal-spotting cruises and trips out to the stubby Godrevy Lighthouse.

It's an accredited wildlife-safe operator, and the crew features a marine mammal medic, specialising in the rescue of dolphins and seals.

Sleeping

Parking in summer is scarce; check if your accommodation has its own or a deal with a car park.

Saltwater B&B ££
(07391 086299; www.saltwaterstivesbb.co.uk; 3 Belmont Tce; d £110-150, tr £130-180;) It's driftwood-chic all the way at Saltwater, where bright blue and yellow bedrooms have USB charging points; most also have sea views. It's a few minutes' walk from Porthmeor, and offers surfboard hire and breakfast in bed.

Mustard Tree B&B ££
(01736-795677; www.mustard-tree.co.uk; St Ives Rd, Carbis Bay; s/d/t £100/124/170; P) If bagging a bedroom amid St Ives' picture-postcard-pretty streets is proving a problem, try this friendly B&B in nearby Carbis Bay. The contemporary rooms may be simple, but there's free parking and St Ives is just a three-minute train ride away.

★Primrose House B&B £££
(01736-794939; www.primroseonline.co.uk; Primrose Valley; s/d from £165/185; P) Chic Primrose Valley has one massive selling point – it's a one-minute walk from Porthminster's sands. Other pluses include light rooms, wicker lamps, Scandi-style dressers, wooden cladding and model ships. Some rooms also boast balconies with sea views.

Trevose Harbour House B&B £££
(01736-793267; www.trevosehouse.co.uk; 22 The Warren; d £210-295;) In this stylish six-room town house you'll find a sea-themed combo of fresh whites and stripy blues. It's been beautifully finished, with Neal's Yard bath goods, iPod docks and retro design pieces in the rooms; there's also a book-lined lounge and minimalist courtyard patio.

Channings APARTMENT £££
(01736-799500; www.channingsstives.co.uk; 3 Talland Rd; 10 people per week from £1100; P) The panoramic sea views from the slanting windows of this five-bedroom Victorian terrace are hard to leave – unless perhaps you're heading to its patio overlooking St Ives Bay. Decor is modern and there's parking for three cars.

Eating

Moomaid of Zennor ICE CREAM £
(www.moomaidofzennor.com; The Wharf; ice cream from £2.50; 9.30am-10pm Apr-Sep, to 5pm Oct-Mar) Moomaid's ice cream is legendary locally. It makes its many flavours on the home farm just outside Zennor, using only its own milk and Rodda's clotted cream. Exotic concoctions include Prosecco sorbet and salted almond.

Searoom BISTRO £
(01736-794325; www.stivesliquor.co/searoom; 1 Wharf House, The Wharf; dishes £3.50-10; noon-9pm Mon-Sat) Run by the St Ives Liquor Company (makers of the town's premium craft gin), this wharf-side restaurant specialises in Cornish-tinged small plates ranging from sushi to chips with crab meat, and glazed mackerel rolls. It's great for cocktails and has a cracking harbour view.

★Porthminster Beach Café BISTRO ££
(01736-795352; www.porthminstercafe.co.uk; Porthminster Beach; mains £15-22; 9am-10pm) Less a beach cafe, more a full-blown bistro with a gorgeous sun-trap terrace and superb Mediterranean-influenced menu, specialising in seafood. Tuck into rich bouillabaisse, seafood curry or Provençal fish soup, and settle back to enjoy the breezy beach vistas.

Porthminster Kitchen BISTRO ££
(01736-799874; www.porthminster.kitchen; The Wharf; mains £15-19; 9am-10pm) This relaxed place rustles up beachy dishes like seafood linguine, Goan fish curry and pan-fried scallops. The most sought-after seats are on the 1st-floor harbour-front terrace.

Porthgwidden Beach Cafe CAFE ££
(01736-796791; www.porthgwiddencafe.co.uk; Porthgwidden; mains £10-16; 9am-10pm) Head to the dreamy terrace beside Porthgwidden's beach huts to savour classy dishes like smoked-haddock chowder or spicy dressed crab.

Blas Burgerworks BURGERS ££
(01736-797272; www.blasburgerworks.co.uk; The Warren; meals £13-15; 5-9.30pm;) Check whether St Ives' boutique burger joint has reopened its dining room after closing it due to distancing measures. If it hasn't you can still pre-order its succulent patties to take away. For full-blooded flavour try a beef or bean burger topped with Cornish Blue cheese, with a side of chips and truffle aioli.

St Ives

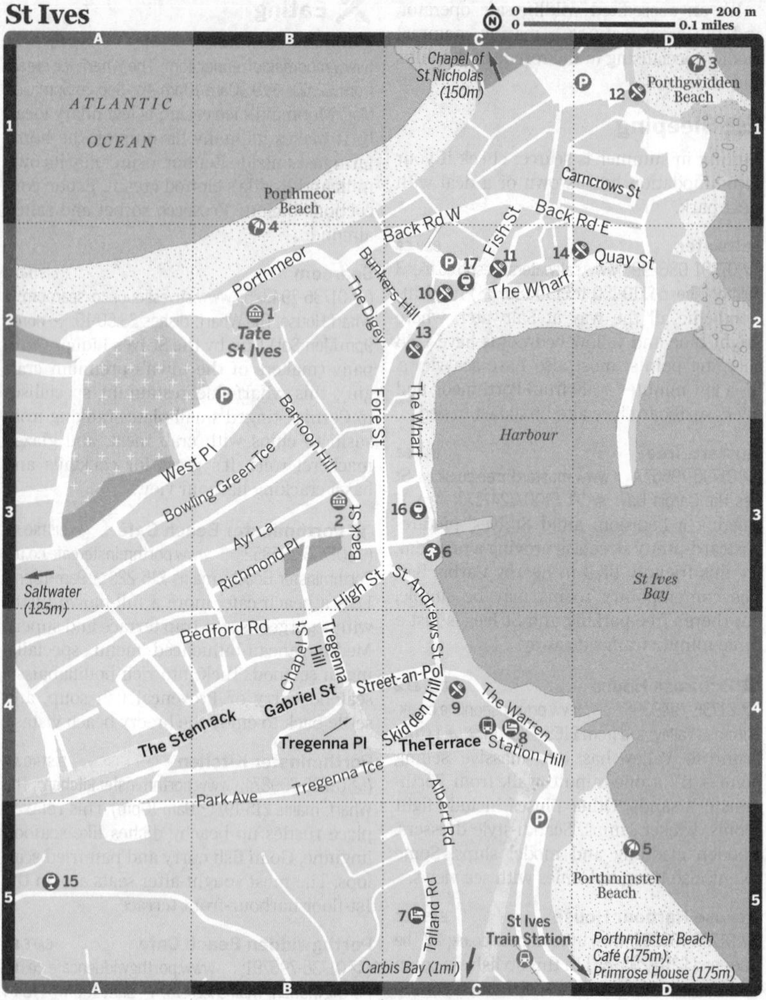

St Ives

Top Sights
1 Tate St Ives B2

Sights
2 Barbara Hepworth Museum B3
3 Porthgwidden Beach D1
4 Porthmeor Beach B2
5 Porthminster Beach D5

Activities, Courses & Tours
6 St Ives Boats C3

Sleeping
7 Channings C5
8 Trevose Harbour House C4

Eating
9 Blas Burgerworks C4
10 Moomaid of Zennor C2
11 One Fish Street C2
12 Porthgwidden Beach Cafe D1
13 Porthminster Kitchen C2
14 Searoom D2

Drinking & Nightlife
15 Brewhouse A5
16 Hub C3
17 Sloop Inn C2

One Fish Street SEAFOOD **£££**
(07521 295047; www.onefishstreet.co.uk; 1 Fish St; 3/6 courses £30/45; 5-9.30pm Tue-Sat) The six-course tasting menu here depends on what's been landed just yards away on the day. It might include white crab with heritage-tomato gazpacho, oysters with wasabi and seaweed, and Thai cod and coconut curry. Or opt for the early-evening three-course menu to get a sense of the chef's skills.

Drinking & Nightlife

Brewhouse CAFE-BAR
(01736-793467; www.stives-brewery.co.uk; Trewidden Rd; cakes from £3; 9am-5pm Mon-Sat) A terrace with superb views down onto the bay and an awesome array of cakes make this cafe-bar a memorable spot to tuck into vegan banana loaf, freshly baked doughnuts and punchy coffee. It's run by St Ives Brewery so you can also sample its flagship brews – Boilers, a golden session ale, and the hoppy IPA-style Knill By Mouth.

Hub BAR
(01736-799099; www.hub-stives.co.uk; The Wharf; 11.30am-9pm, to 10pm Fri & Sat) The open-plan Hub is the heart of St Ives' (admittedly limited) nightlife: coffee and burgers by day, cocktails after dark, and a harbour-front balcony and terrace.

Sloop Inn PUB
(01736-796584; www.sloop-inn.co.uk; The Wharf; 11am-11pm) On sunny days, the picnic tables of this whitewashed, beam-lined boozer are one of the most popular spots for a harbourside pint in town.

Information

Check whether the **Tourist Office** (www.stives-cornwall.co.uk; 01736-796297), in the town's Library in Gabriel St, has reopened.

Getting There & Away

BUS

Bus 17 (£5.40, 30 minutes, half-hourly Monday to Saturday, hourly Sunday) Runs to Penzance, via Lelant.

Bus A3 (four daily) Heads along the north coast via Zennor, the Gurnard's Head pub, Geevor Tin Mine and St Just to Land's End (£5.40, 1¼ hours). At Land's End the bus becomes the A1 and continues onto Porthcurno and Penzance.

Bus A2 (6 daily) Goes via St Erth train station to Penzance (£5.40, one hour) via Marazion (for St Michael's Mount).

TRAIN

The branch train line from St Ives is worth taking just for the coastal views. Trains shuttle between St Ives train station via Carbis Bay to St Erth (£3, 11 minutes, half-hourly) where you can catch connections along the Penzance–London Paddington main line.

Zennor & St Just-in-Penwith

01736 / POP: 5000

The superbly scenic B3306 coast road between St Ives and Zennor ventures into a wild, remote landscape of ancient farmland, windswept moors and ruined mine stacks. The industrial heritage here makes it well worth a visit, and it feels a far cry from Cornwall's over-touristed harbour towns.

Tiny Zennor is set around the medieval Church of St Senara, while 9 miles further west, sits the old granite village of St Just-in-Penwith. It's been linked with mining and quarrying for centuries, but these days its mainly known as a hub for artists, sculptors and creative types.

Sights

Church of St Senara CHURCH
This little church in the hamlet of Zennor dates from at least 1150. Inside, a famous carved chair depicts the legendary Mermaid of Zennor, who is said to have fallen in love with the singing voice of local lad Matthew Trewhella. Locals say you can still sometimes hear them singing down at nearby Pendour Cove – and even if you don't, the views along the coast path are reward enough.

★**Geevor Tin Mine** MINE
(01736-788662; www.geevor.com; Pendeen; adult/child £16.10/9; 9am-5pm Sun-Thu, hours may vary) Just north of St Just near Pendeen, this historic mine closed in 1990 and now provides a powerful insight into the dark, dingy and dangerous conditions in which Cornwall's miners worked. Above ground, you can view the dressing floors and the original machinery used to sort the minerals and ores, before taking a guided tour into some of the underground shafts.

WORTH A TRIP

MINACK THEATRE & PORTHCURNO

Teetering right out on Cornwall's far-western tip, the sandy wedge of Porthcurno is one of the best beaches in west Cornwall for swimming and sunbathing. Around the headland, the lesser-known beach of **Pednvounder** is good if you like to sunbathe *au naturel* – it's one of Cornwall's few naturist beaches.

But the area is best known for its spectacular clifftop theatre, the **Minack** (☎01736-810181; www.minack.com; performance tickets £10-40, admission adult/child £6/3), carved out of the granite rock with sweeping views of the Atlantic waves below. Created between the 1930s and 1970s by theatre-lover Rowena Cade, there are few finer places to watch a play than this. You can also book daytime visits to explore the terraces and subtropical gardens and take in the ocean views.

Porthcurno was also once a crucial hub for transatlantic telecommunications; it's well worth seeing if the **Porthcurno Telegraph Museum** (☎01736-810966; www.telegraphmuseum.org), which tells the compelling story, has reopened.

★Botallack RUINS

(NT; Crowns Engine House; ☎01736-786934; www.nationaltrust.org.uk) Clinging to the cliffs near Levant, this dramatic complex of mine workings is one of the most atmospheric sights from Cornwall's industrial past. The main mine stack, properly known as the Crowns, teeters picturesquely on the cliff edge above a cauldron of boiling surf. It's famously photogenic and a frequent filming location, most recently used by the BBC in *Poldark*. The National Trust website has a 1-mile looped walking trail taking in Botallack.

During its 19th-century heyday, the mine was one of the county's richest and deepest, producing 14,500 tonnes of tin and 20,000 tonnes of copper ore from shafts that snaked nearly half a mile out to sea. Look out for the Count House, which was once home to the captain of the mine.

Levant Mine & Beam Engine HISTORIC SITE

(NT; ☎01736-786156; www.nationaltrust.org.uk; Trewellard, Pendeen) It's worth checking if visits to this clifftop site have resumed after being suspended in 2020. Levant is one of the world's only working beam engines. Built in 1840, these great machines were the driving forces behind the Cornish mining boom, powering mineral trains, running lifts down into mine shafts and pumping water from underground tunnels. Closed in 1930, it's since been lovingly restored by a team of enthusiasts, and is a sight to behold when it's in full steam.

Levant was also the site of one of Cornwall's worst mining disasters: in 1919 a link between the rod and engine broke, sending 31 men to their deaths. More recently it was also used as a location in the BBC's recent *Poldark* adaptation.

Cape Cornwall LANDMARK

(P) Jutting out from the cliffs near St Just is Cornwall's only cape, a craggy outcrop of land topped by an abandoned mine stack. Below the cape is the rocky beach of **Priest's Cove**, while nearby are the ruins of **St Helen's Oratory**, supposedly one of the first Christian chapels built in West Cornwall.

Sleeping & Eating

See if the **Zennor Chapel Guesthouse** (☎01736-798307; www.zennorchapelguesthouse.com; Wayside St; P), which suspended bookings in the summer of 2020, has reopened.

★Gurnard's Head BRITISH ££

(☎01736-796928; www.gurnardshead.co.uk; B3306, near Zennor; mains £11.50-24, d £135-200; P) On the rolling coast road between Zennor and St Just, you can't miss the Gurnard's – its name is emblazoned on the roof. It's earned a reputation as one of west Cornwall's top dining pubs, known for classic, traditionally inspired British dishes, and a top Sunday roast. Wooden furniture, book-lined shelves and sepia prints conjure a cosy, lived-in feel.

The bedrooms are delightful, with their warm colours, country-cottage styling, Roberts radios and fresh flowers.

Land's End & Sennen

Beyond St Ives, the coastline gets wilder and emptier as you near Cornwall's tip at Land's End, the westernmost point of mainland England, where the coal-black cliffs plunge into the pounding surf, and the views can stretch all the way to the Isles of Scilly.

You don't have to head into the **Legendary Land's End** (☎01736-871501; www.landsend-landmark.co.uk; day ticket adult/child £12.60/9; ⊙10am-5pm Mar-Oct; ♿) theme park itself, instead you can just pay for parking (£6) and go for an exhilarating clifftop stroll, looking out for the historic Longships Lighthouse on a reef 1.25 miles out to sea. Consider booking parking to guarantee a space.

From Land's End, follow the coast path west to the secluded cove of **Nanjizal Bay**, or east to the old harbour of Sennen, which overlooks the glorious beach of **Whitesand Bay**, the area's most impressive stretch of sand.

Mousehole

☎01736 / POP 697

With a tight tangle of cottages and alleyways gathered behind the granite breakwater, Mousehole (pronounced *mowzle*) looks like something from a children's storybook (a fact not unnoticed by author Antonia Barber, who set her much-loved fairy tale *The Mousehole Cat* here). In centuries past this was Cornwall's busiest pilchard port, but the fish dried up in the late 19th century, and the village now survives mostly on tourist traffic. Packed in summer and deserted in winter (Mousehole is renowned for its high proportion of second homes), it's ripe for a wander, with a maze of slips, net lofts and courtyards.

Sleeping & Eating

★Old Coastguard HOTEL £££

(☎01736-731222; www.oldcoastguardhotel.co.uk; The Parade; d incl breakfast £135-200; ⊙food noon-3pm & 5.30-9.30pm; P 📶 🐾) Run by the owners of the Gurnard's Head, this coastal beauty ranks as one of Cornwall's top shoreside hotels. Stylish rooms team gingham with painted wood; the best have sea views. The day's catch takes prominence in the excellent **restaurant** (mains £15 to £25) and sunny days bring meals on the gently sloping lawns.

2 Fore St FRENCH ££

(☎01736-731164; www.2forestreet.co.uk; Fore St; mains £8-17; ⊙noon-9pm) This laid-back harbour-side bistro majors in French-inspired classics – unsurprising, given the head chef trained under Raymond Blanc. There's a small dining room, a sweet garden and a locally focused menu strong on the very freshest seafood.

Getting There & Away

Bus M6 makes the 20-minute journey along the seafront to Penzance (£3.40, half-hourly to hourly), stopping in Newlyn en route.

ST MICHAEL'S MOUNT

Looming up in the middle of Mount's Bay and connected to the mainland at Marazion via a cobbled causeway, **St Michael's Mount** (NT; ☎01736-710507; www.stmichaelsmount.co.uk; Marazion; castle adult/child £11.50/5.50, gardens adult/child £8.50/4; ⊙hours vary) is an unforgettable sight, and one of Cornwall's most iconic images.

There's been a monastery here since at least the 5th century, but the present abbey was mostly built by Benedictine monks during the 12th century (the same religious order also constructed the island's sister abbey at Mont St-Michel in France). Highlights of the main house include the rococo drawing room, the armoury and the 14th-century church, but it's the amazing clifftop gardens that really steal the show. Thanks to the local subclimate, many exotic flowers and shrubs flourish here, and it's all a riot of colour in summer.

Recent excavations found an axe head, a dagger and a metal clasp, proving the island has been inhabited since at least the Bronze Age, but it was almost certainly used by prehistoric people long before. According to some scholars, the island may have been a trading post for locally mined copper and tin for several thousand years.

Distancing regulations could mean you have to book a timed slot in which to start your visit to the island. If restrictions are in force you might have to walk to the island at low tide via the causeway from Marazion. If no restrictions are in place you can probably either stroll along the causeway (the most atmospheric way to arrive) or, in summer, hop on a boat (adult/child £2/1). Check online to see whether cheaper joint tickets to the castle and gardens have been reinstated.

Penzance

☎01736 / POP 21,040

Overlooking the majestic sweep of Mount's Bay, the old harbour of Penzance has a salty, sea-blown charm that feels altogether more authentic than many of Cornwall's polished-up ports. Its streets and shopping arcades still feel real and a touch ramshackle, and there's nowhere better for a windy-day walk than the town's seafront Victorian promenade. The town also has a superb array of places to eat, and a significant tourist draw in the now geothermally heated 1930s Jubilee Pool.

Sights & Activities

★Tremenheere Sculpture Garden GARDENS
(☎01736-448089; www.tremenheere.co.uk; near Gulval; adult/child £9/4.50; ⏲10.30am-5.30pm; 🚸) In this magical, tropical-plant-filled valley you get to hunt out site-specific works of art. Highlights include *Black Mound*, a pile of tree stumps by David Nash; *Camera Obscura* by Billy Wynter, which offers a unique panorama of the gardens and Mount's Bay; Amy Cooper's *Se Bryck*, a sea-view brick armchair; and, in a dig at Cornwall's tricky second homes issue, Richard Wood's *Holiday Homes*. The gardens are just over 2 miles northeast of Penzance.

The garden's super takeaway cafe, **TK Hut** (10am to 3pm, snacks from £4) rustles up brunches, salad boxes, coffee and home-made cakes to eat on the sloping lawns.

Penlee House Gallery & Museum GALLERY
(☎01736-363625; www.penleehouse.org.uk; Morrab Rd; adult/child £6/3; ⏲10am-5pm Mon-Sat Apr-Oct, to 4pm Nov-Mar) This small museum is ideal for a primer on the artistic heritage of West Cornwall. It showcases a fine collection of paintings by artists of the Newlyn School (including Stanhope and Elizabeth Forbes, Walter Langley and Lamorna Birch) inside a handsome 19th-century building.

★Jubilee Pool SWIMMING
(☎01736-369224; www.jubileepool.co.uk; Western Promenade Rd; main pool adult/child £4.25/3, geothermal pool £11.75/8; ⏲10am-5pm Tue-Sun early Jun-Nov, winter hours vary) In a triumph of engineering and imagination, a £1.8-million upgrade has turned Penzance's art-deco sea-water pool into the UK's first geothermally heated lido. Sections of the gorgeous 1930s open-air pool are now heated to a toasty 35°C. The rest – sleek, sharp and white-washed – is still beautiful but the water undeniably more bracing.

As elsewhere, distancing measures may mean pool sessions have to be booked. Demand for the geothermal section is very high, so reserve well in advance.

The project has also brought new changing rooms and a cafe. The aim is to be able to open year-round; check online for updates.

Sleeping

Check to see if individual bookings at **Penzance YHA** (☎0345 371 9653; www.yha.org.uk; Castle Horneck, Alverton; P 📶) have resumed.

★Venton Vean B&B ££
(☎01736-351294; www.ventonvean.co.uk; Trewithen Rd; d £98-105, tr £142; 📶) The picture of a modern B&B, finished in stylish greys and blues, with stripped wood floors, bay windows and a keen eye for design. The sumptuous breakfast choice includes pancakes, smoked Newlyn fish and avocado on sourdough toast.

Boswarthen Farm CAMPSITE ££
(☎07731 776767; www.boswarthenfarm.co.uk; near Madron; 3 nights glamping tent £390, lodge/caravan £405/235) There are three glamping choices at this rustic dairy farm near Madron: safari-style tents, a two-storey lodge-tent and a vintage caravan. The safari tents are spacious, with kitchen units and dining areas, a wood-burning stove and two bedroom areas, while the lodge adds a mezzanine floor.

★Artist Residence Penzance B&B £££
(☎01736-365664; www.artistresidence.co.uk; 20 Chapel St; d £95-250, tr/ste from £135/209; 📶🚸🐾) Hands down Penzance's most entertaining hotel, this converted town house on Chapel St has been impeccably renovated to team period architecture with modern style. Details abound: Robert's radios, roll-top baths, antique furniture, old tea chests and the odd wall mural or two.

Eating & Drinking

★Tolcarne Inn PUB FOOD ££
(☎01736-363074; www.tolcarneinn.co.uk; Tolcarne Pl; mains lunch £6.50-12, dinner £19-24; ⏲noon-2.30pm & 6.30-9.30pm) The ethos at this Newlyn inn is refreshingly honest – top-quality fish, seafood and locally sourced

Penzance

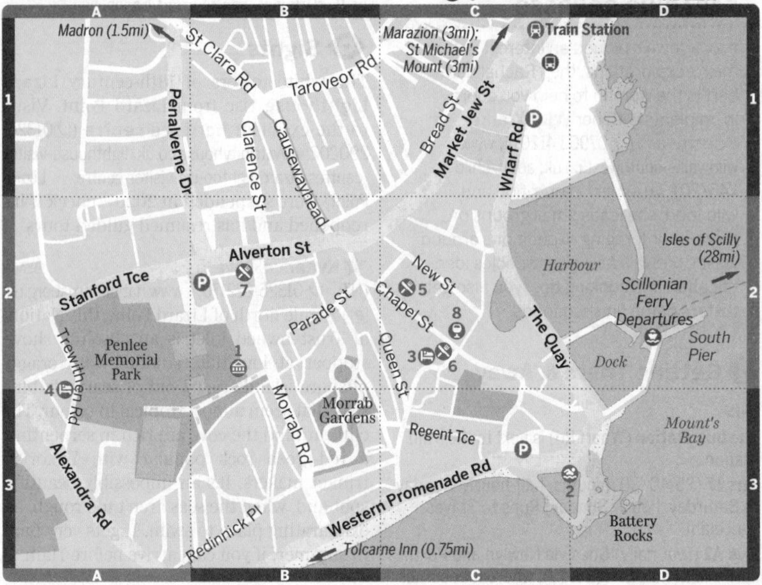

meat, served with minimal fuss. It's a snug space, full of smuggler's pub charm, with blackboard menus, whitewashed walls and a cluster of outdoor tables tucked in beside the harbour wall.

Clubhouse BISTRO ££
(☎01736-365664; www.artistresidence.co.uk; 20 Chapel St; mains £12-21; ⏲8-10.30am & 6-9pm daily, plus noon-2.30pm Fri-Sun) With its exposed brick, scuffed timber, bare bulbs and blazing wood-burner, the bistro on the ground floor of the Artist Residence Penzance nails the gourmet hipster vibe. Tuck into everything from garlicky squid and charred seabass to beer-can smoked chicken with house slaw.

Bakehouse MEDITERRANEAN ££
(☎01736-331331; www.bakehouserestaurant.co.uk; Chapel St; mains £14-20, steaks £11-25; ⏲noon-2pm & 6-9pm Tue-Sat) Laid-back double-floored diner down an alley off Chapel St with it's own palm-fringed, fairy-light-festooned dining courtyard. Steaks take the honours here: choose your cut and match it with your choice of sauce or spicy rub. You'll also find a couple of seafood and veggie options.

★ Shore MODERN BRITISH £££
(☎01736-362444; www.theshorerestaurant.uk; 14 Alverton St; 5 courses £60; ⏲1 sitting at 7pm Tue-Sat) This brilliant seafood bistro is all about precisely cooked, classic fish and shellfish, sourced from the Newlyn day boats and served with a strong French-Italian influence and lashing of creative flair.

Admiral Benbow PUB
(☎01736-363448; 46 Chapel St; ⏲4-11pm) On historic Chapel St, the salty old Benbow looks as if it's dropped from the pages of *Treasure Island,* with nautical decor mostly reclaimed from shipwrecks: anchors, lanterns, figureheads and all.

Penzance

Sights
1 Penlee House Gallery & Museum....... B2

Activities, Courses & Tours
2 Jubilee Pool....... D3

Sleeping
3 Artist Residence Penzance....... C2
4 Venton Vean....... A3

Eating
5 Bakehouse....... C2
6 Clubhouse....... C2
7 Shore....... B2

Drinking & Nightlife
8 Admiral Benbow....... C2

LOCAL KNOWLEDGE

FORAGING COURSES

If lockdown's piqued an interest in micro-explorations, then Rachel Lambert is the woman to help you zoom in on plants with her **Wild Walks Southwest** (☎07903 412014; www.wildwalks-southwest.co.uk; adult/child £45/20). An expert in nutrition and wild food, she leads small groups on three-hour foraging expeditions around west Cornwall. As well as species identification and cooking tips, you also get tasters of the finished foods.

Getting There & Away

BUS

The **bus station** (Wharf Rd) is next to the train station.

Bus 17 (£5.40, 30 minutes, half-hourly Monday to Saturday, hourly Sunday) Runs to St Ives, via Lelant.

Bus A1 (four daily) Goes via Newlyn and Porthcurno to Land's End (£5.40), where it becomes the A3 and continues along the north coast to St Ives via St Just, Geevor Tin Mine, the Gurnard's Head pub and Zennor.

Bus A2 Shuttles to St Ives (£5.40, one hour, six daily) via Marazion (for St Michael's Mount).

Bus U4 Runs to Falmouth (£7.40, 1½ hours, hourly Monday to Saturday, six on Sunday) via Marazion and Helston.

TRAIN

Penzance is the last stop on the line from London Paddington. Regular daily services include the following.

Exeter £30, three hours

London Paddington £63, five hours

St Ives £4.70, 50 minutes, change at St Erth

Truro £7.40, 40 minutes

The Lizard

Cornwall's coast takes a wild turn around the Lizard Peninsula, where fields and heaths plunge into a melee of black cliffs, churning surf and sawtooth rocks. Bordered by the River Helford and framed by treacherous seas, the Lizard was once an ill-famed graveyard for ships, and the peninsula still has a raw, untamed edge. Wind-lashed in winter, in summer its clifftops blaze with wildflowers, and its beaches and coves are perfect for a bracing wild swim. Remote Lizard village and the increasingly foodie port of Porthleven, make good bases.

Sights

The white towers of 18th-century **Lizard Lighthouse** rise from Lizard Point. Visits to the excellent **heritage centre** (☎01326-290202; www.trinityhouse.co.uk/lighthouse-visitor-centres/lizard-lighthouse-visitor-centre; Lizard Point) were suspended in 2020 – check if it's reopened and has resumed guided tours.

★**Kynance Cove** BEACH
(NT; ☎01326-222170; www.nationaltrust.org.uk; P) A mile north of Lizard Point, this National Trust–owned inlet is an absolute showstopper at low tide, studded with craggy offshore islands rising out of searingly blue seas that seem almost tropical in colour. The cliffs around the cove are rich in serpentine, a red-green rock popular with Victorian trinket makers. It's an impossibly beautiful spot and, when the seas aren't too rough, an exhilarating place to swim. It gets very busy in summer; if you can, arrive before 11am.

★**Cornish Seal Sanctuary** ANIMAL SANCTUARY
(☎01326-221361; www.visitsealife.com/gweek; Gweek; adult/child £15.50/12.50; ⏲10am-5pm) The 'ah' factor goes into overdrive at this sea-life centre some 5 miles east of Helston. It cares for sick and orphaned seals washed up along the Cornish coastline before returning them to the wild. The website outlines whether talks and feeding sessions have resumed.

Sleeping & Eating

Check whether **Lizard YHA** (☎0845 371 9550; www.yha.org.uk; Lizard Point), which is set right beside the lighthouse, has resumed individual bookings.

★**Henry's Campsite** CAMPSITE £
(☎01326-290596; www.henryscampsite.co.uk; Caerthillian Farm, Lizard village; adult/child £12/6; 🐾) In this endearingly eccentric campsite, sites are private and the garden is dotted with flotsam and jetsam – hand-painted signs, old buoys and fishing tackle. It's a prime place to rent a firepit and settle back to gaze at sunsets and sea views.

Kynance Cove Cafe CAFE £
(☎01326-290436; www.kynancecovecafe.co.uk; Kynance Cove; mains £5-14; ⏲9am-5.30pm) There can be few beachside cafes in Cornwall with a finer location than this, huddled

among the rocks on the edge of Kynance Cove. Sample pasties, crab sandwiches and burgers, chased down with classic cream teas and yummy cakes, all best savoured at one of the picnic tables.

★Kota INTERNATIONAL ££

(☎01326-562407; www.kotarestaurant.co.uk; Harbour Head; 2/3 courses £25/30, mains £16-28; ⏲6-9.30pm Mon-Sat) Porthleven's top restaurant is run by half Maori, half Chinese-Malay chef Jude Kereama. Set in an old harbourside mill, the menu is spiced with Far Eastern and fusion flavours, underpinned by classic French credentials. The dishes look beautiful, with edible flowers and other flourishes.

Kota also offers three smart double bedrooms (from £80).

Halzephron Inn PUB FOOD ££

(☎01326-240406; www.halzephron-inn.co.uk; mains £10-15; ⏲bar 11am-11pm; food noon-2pm & 6-9pm) The Halzephron sits high on the hills above the cove of Gunwalloe. It's a classic Cornish local – whitewashed and slate-topped, with brassy trinkets and stout beams. Picnic tables either overlook rolling fields or a sweep of Mounts Bay, making it just the spot to tuck into seabass with samphire, moules marinière or steak and ale pie.

Falmouth

☎01326 / POP 21,790

Few seaside towns in Cornwall boast such an arresting location as Falmouth, overlooking the broad Fal River as it empties into the English Channel. Surrounded by green hills and blue sea, Falmouth is an appealing jumble of lanes, old pubs, slate roofs and trendy cafes. With its wealth of bars and bistros, trio of beaches and excellent maritime museum, it's an ideal base for exploring Cornwall's fine gardens and south coast.

Though it now derives much of its revenue from nearby Falmouth University, the town made its fortune during the 18th and 19th centuries thanks to lucrative maritime trade. Falmouth has the world's third-deepest natural harbour, and the town grew rich when tea clippers, trading vessels and mail packets stopped here to unload their cargoes. The port is still an important centre for ship repairs – spot the dockyard cranes as you head to Pendennis Point.

Sights

Falmouth's trio of beaches – **Gyllyngvase**, **Swanpool** and **Maenporth** – aren't quite up to north-coast standards, but they're nice enough. The beaches have car parks, but they fill up quickly in summer.

★National Maritime Museum MUSEUM

(☎01326-313388; www.nmmc.co.uk; Discovery Quay; adult/child £14/7; ⏲10am-5pm) Falmouth's big museum is the sister outpost of the National Maritime Museum in Greenwich, London. Imaginative displays focus on Falmouth's history as a port, and on the broader impact of the sea on history and culture. The centrepiece is the five-storey **Flotilla Gallery**, where an array of small vessels, ranging from rowboats to rescue craft, are suspended from the ceiling.

From the top floor of the Lookout tower, there's a 360-degree panorama across Falmouth Bay. Regular nautically themed exhibitions cover subjects ranging from the Titanic and Captain Bligh to the tradition of tattooing. Check to see whether the hour-long heritage boat tours have resumed. Admission tickets are valid for one year.

★Potager Garden GARDENS

(☎01326-341258; www.potagergarden.org; High Cross, Constantine; suggested donation £3; ⏲10am-5pm Thu-Sun) Rescued from dilapidation by its current owners, this gorgeous garden has been renovated by volunteers into a delightful working garden modelled on the French 'potager'. Highlights include the 30m greenhouse, and the super veggie **cafe** (mains £6 to £10), popular with lunching locals at weekends. The garden is 6 miles southwest of Falmouth.

Glendurgan GARDENS

(NT; ☎01326-250906; www.nationaltrust.org.uk; Mawnan Smith; adult/child £5/2.50; ⏲10.30am-5pm Tue-Sun) Glendurgan was established by Alfred Fox in the 1820s to show off the weird and wonderful plants brought back from the far corners of the empire, from Himalayan rhododendrons to Canadian maples and New Zealand tree ferns. Tumbling down a stunning subtropical valley, the garden offers breathtaking views of the Helford and leads to a secluded beach near Durgan village. Glendurgan is 7 miles southwest of Falmouth.

Trebah Garden GARDENS

(☎01326-252200; www.trebahgarden.co.uk; Mawnan Smith; adult/child £11/5.50; ⏲10.30am-4.30pm, last entry 2.30pm) Trebah Garden was planted in 1840 by Charles Fox, younger brother of Alfred, who established neighbouring Glendurgan Garden. It's less formal, with gigantic rhododendrons, gunnera and jungle ferns lining the sides of a steep ravine leading down to the quay and shingle beach. There's also a great takeaway cafe.

Pendennis Castle CASTLE

(EH; ☎01326-316594; www.english-heritage.org.uk; Castle Dr; adult/child £12/7.30; ⏲10am-5pm; P) Designed in tandem with its sister castle in St Mawes across the estuary, this Tudor castle sits proudly on Pendennis Point, and was built as part of Henry VIII's massive coastal castle-building program. You can wander around the central keep and the Tudor gun deck, as well as the governor's bedroom, a WWI guardhouse and the WWII-era Half-Moon Battery.

Activities

★AK Wildlife Cruises WILDLIFE WATCHING

(☎01326-753389; www.akwildlifecruises.co.uk; Premier Marina; adult/child from £50/40) Run by the amiable and unfailingly enthusiastic 'Captain Keith', this specialist wildlife cruise sets out from Falmouth Harbour in search of local marine life. Depending on the season, there's a good chance of spotting dolphins, porpoises, basking sharks, puffins and seals – it's not unheard of to spy minke whales.

Fal River Boat Trips BOATING

(Enterprise Boats; ☎01326-741194; www.falriver.co.uk/ferries/enterprise-boats; Prince of Wales Pier; return adult/child £14/7; ⏲2 sailings daily, Sun-Fri Apr-Sep) Falmouth's main pier is the departure point for a range of boat trips. One of the best is the regular two-hour round trip from Falmouth to Trelissick Gardens (p354), via St Mawes.

Gylly Adventures KAYAKING

(☎07341 890495; www.gyllyadventures.co.uk; Gyllyngvase Beach, Cliff Rd; tours per person £45) 'Gylly' Beach's watersports company hires the usual kit: stand-up paddleboards (per hour £15), kayaks (per hour £12), wetsuits (per hour £6) and bodyboards (per hour £5). It also offers great, small-group guided kayaking trips. Options include a tour of Falmouth harbour, a paddle into local caves, and (best of all) a night kayak trip illuminated by LED head torches.

Sleeping

★Highcliffe B&B ££

(☎01326-314466; www.highcliffefalmouth.com; 22 Melvill Rd; s £65, d £105-150, ste £145-160; P 📶) Vintage furniture and upcycled design pieces give each of the soothing rooms here an individual feel. The pick of the bunch is the light-filled Attic Penthouse, with skylight windows overlooking Falmouth Bay. Room-service breakfasts in picnic baskets might feature toasted muffins, pancakes with bacon, or homemade granola with compote.

Bosanneth B&B ££

(☎01326-314649; www.bosanneth.co.uk; 1 Stracey Rd; d £90-130; P 📶) There's a mix-and-match decorative vibe running through this eight-room B&B. Some of the rooms feel vintage, with old mirrors, reclaimed furniture and classic colours, while others go for a more up-to-date look. The 'oasis' garden, with a sea-view sun deck, is a particular delight.

★Greenbank HOTEL £££

(☎01326-312440; www.greenbank-hotel.co.uk; harbourside; s/d/tr incl breakfast from £160/220/250; P 📶) Greenbank is the queen of Falmouth's hotels, with a knockout position right beside the boat-filled estuary. It feels like the setting for an Agatha Christie novel – nautical knick-knacks and ships in cabinets dot public areas, while tall windows look out on to the water. Modern rooms are done out in cream with bursts of aquamarine; the best boast edge-of-the-water views.

Eating

★Espressini CAFE £

(39 Killigrew St; snacks from £4; ⏲9am-3pm Thu-Sat; 📶) Cornwall's best coffee house, bar none, is run by committed coffee aficionado Rupert Ellis. The choice of blends, roasts and coffees fills a 2m blackboard. Exquisitely crafted edibles might encompass beetroot and goats-cheese tart, towering breakfast baps and squidgy dark-chocolate brownies.

★Stone's Bakery BAKERY £

(☎07791 003183; www.stonesbakery.co.uk; 35 High St; breads £2-3.50; ⏲8.30am-1.30pm

Wed-Sat;) Freshly baked loaves line the window like pieces of art at this gorgeous bakery, which focuses on traditional hand-shaped rustic loaves – the tangy maltster and the organic sourdough are as delicious as you'll taste.

Harbour Lights FISH & CHIPS £
(01326-316934; www.harbourlights.co.uk; Arwenack St; fish & chips from £8; noon-9pm Sun-Thu, to 9.30pm Fri & Sat) Falmouth's classic – and best – chippy keeps notching up awards (it was voted one of Britain's top 10 in 2019). All the fish is responsibly sourced; the day's catch might mean you tuck into lemon sole, pollock or hake. Check online to see if the restaurant, with Fal River views, has reopened.

Meat Counter BURGERS £
(01326-312220; www.facebook.com/themeatcounterfalmouth; 25 Arwenack St; burgers £7-13; noon-9pm;) Perennially popular with Falmouth's hungry students, this specialist burger joint turns out the best patties in town. The teetering stacks feature beef, chicken or falafel topped by garlic mayo, wild rocket and dirty American cheese. The side order might be Cornish sea-salt skin-on fries. If distancing is in force, it's likely to be takeaway and delivery only.

Ferryboat Inn GASTROPUB ££
(01326-250625; www.ferryboatcornwall.co.uk; Helford Passage; mains £8-14; food noon-3pm & 4.30-8pm) This age-old riverside pub is a Cornish classic. The picnic tables have dreamy views over the Helford River; inside, it's all wood, slate and open plan. Dishes might include seafood chowder, Thai fish curry, brioche lobster rolls and truffle fries. Visit the website to see if you need to order food online in advance.

Drinking & Nightlife

A tip for ale-loving bookworms: check whether the fabulous combo of bookshop and pub that is **Beerwolf Books** (01326-618474; www.beerwolfbooks.com; 3 Bells Ct) has reopened.

Chintz Symposium BAR
(07538 006495; www.thechintzbar.com; Old Brewery Yard; 3-11.30pm Mon-Fri, 1-11.30pm Sat & Sun;) Wine, charcuterie, cheese and cocktails take centre stage at this uber-trendy, slightly surreal hang-out. Junk-shop furniture, wooden toys, no parking signs and glowing lanterns fill the sunny courtyard and A-framed attic space. The wine list is copious.

Chain Locker PUB
(01326-311085; www.chainlockerfalmouth.co.uk; Quay St; 10am-11pm) One of Falmouth's oldest pubs, and also one of the town's best-loved waterside drinking dens. Old signs, ships' ephemera and black-and-white photos dot the bar; the dockside tables are perfect on a sunny day.

Working Boat PUB
(01326-314283; www.theworkingboat.co.uk; Greenbank Quay; 11am-midnight) With its quayside tables, alfresco pop-up bar, sea-themed styling and wide harbour views, you can't get much more nautical than the Working Boat. Rustic pizzas and beer-battered fish and chips (mains from £10) seal the deal.

Information

The **Fal River Information Centre** (01326-741194; www.falriver.co.uk; 11 Market Strand, Prince of Wales Pier; 10am-5pm Mon-Sat, hours may vary) advises on ferries and books accommodation.

Getting There & Away

Falmouth is at the end of the railway branch line from Truro (£4.70, 30 minutes, one to two per hour). Truro is on the main Penzance to London Paddington line.

Bus coverage is also fairly good, with regular links between the big towns in the area, and at least one bus service serving most of the local villages. Falmouth has several services that head to the Lizard and Helston.

Falmouth's Moor Bus Station is central. First Kernow (www.firstgroup.com/cornwall) routes include the following.

Helston (£5.80, one hour, hourly Monday to Saturday) Bus 35/35A, stops at Glendurgan and Trebah gardens en route.

Penzance (£7.40, 1½ hours, hourly Monday to Saturday, six on Sunday) Bus U4, via Helston and Marazion.

Redruth (£5.80, 40 minutes, hourly Monday to Friday, every two hours Sunday) Bus U2, via Penryn.

Truro (£5.80, 1¼ hours, half-hourly Monday to Saturday, hourly Sunday) Bus U1, via Penryn.

Buses 65 and 67 regularly shuttle from Falmouth to Gyllyngvase and Swanpool beaches.

Truro

01872 / POP 18,700

Dominated by the three mighty spires of its 19th-century cathedral, which rises above town like a neo-Gothic supertanker, Truro is

THE EDEN PROJECT & THE LOST GARDENS OF HELIGAN

Five miles from St Austell, at the bottom of a china clay pit, the giant biomes of the **Eden Project** (01726-811911; www.edenproject.com; Bodelva; adult/child £28.50/15; 9.30am-6pm; P) – the world's largest greenhouses – have become Cornwall's most famous landmark, and an absolutely essential visit. Looking rather like a lunar landing station, Eden's bubble-shaped biomes maintain miniature ecosystems that enable all kinds of weird and wonderful plants to flourish – from stinky rafflesia flowers and banana trees in the Rainforest Biome to cacti and soaring palms in the Mediterranean Biome. The Eden site is 3 miles northeast of St Austell.

The Eden Project is the brainchild of former record producer turned entrepreneur Tim Smit, who also rescued the **Lost Gardens of Heligan** (01726-845100; www.heligan.com; Pentewan; adult/child £16/8; 10am-6pm Mar-Oct, to 5pm Nov-Feb; P) from ruin. Formerly the family estate of the Tremaynes, Heligan's magnificent 19th-century gardens fell into disrepair following WWI, but have been splendidly restored by an army of gardeners and volunteers. In this horticultural wonderland you'll encounter formal lawns, working kitchen gardens, fruit-filled greenhouses, a secret grotto and 25m-high rhododendron, plus a lost-world Jungle Valley of ferns, palms and tropical blooms. Heligan is 10 miles southwest of the Eden Project.

Cornwall's capital and its only city. It's the county's main centre for shopping and commerce: the streets here are lined with high-street chains and independent shops, while the twice-weekly farmers market brings field-fresh produce to town.

Sights

★Trelissick GARDENS
(NT; 01872-862090; www.nationaltrust.org.uk; grounds £4; grounds 10.30am-5pm) Grandly located at the head of the Fal estuary, 4 miles south of Truro, Trelissick is one of Cornwall's most beautiful aristocratic estates. Its formal garden, which is filled with magnolias and hydrangeas, is surrounded by fields and parkland that is criss-crossed by walking trails. The prettiest route is to head to the estate's pebble beach and then wander upriver along the Fal's wooded banks.

Truro Cathedral CATHEDRAL
(01872-276782; www.trurocathedral.org.uk; High Cross; suggested donation £5; 10am-3pm Mon-Sat, 1-3pm Sun) Built on the site of a 16th-century parish church in soaring Gothic Revival style, Truro Cathedral was completed in 1910, making it the first cathedral built in England since St Paul's. Inside, the vast nave contains some fine Victorian stained glass and the impressive Father Willis Organ.

Royal Cornwall Museum MUSEUM
(01872-272205; www.royalcornwallmuseum.org.uk; River St; 10am-3pm Tue-Thu & Sat, noon-6pm Fri) FREE Collections at the county's main museum encompass everything from geological specimens to a ceremonial carriage and Bronze Age lunalae (ornate collars shaped like crescent moons). Upstairs the ancient civilisations section features Egyptian, Greek and Roman artefacts. Artworks change frequently and might include pieces by Turner, van Dyck and the Newlyn artist Stanhope Forbes.

Sleeping

Mannings Hotel HOTEL ££
(01872-270345; www.manningshotels.co.uk; Lemon St; r £95-125, apt £135-145; P) At the best place to stay in the city centre, a part-Georgian building has been tastefully modernised, with bright colours and functional furniture. The nine self-contained apartments come with small kitchen and spiral staircase. Its Secret Garden pop-up cafe-bistro is a fun spot for an alfresco drink.

Merchant House HOTEL ££
(01872-272450; www.merchant-house.co.uk; 49 Falmouth Rd; s/d/f incl breakfast from £75/110/150; P) This Victorian house with a cheery sea-blue colour scheme is handy for town. Some bedrooms have skylights, others overlook the garden.

Eating & Drinking

Farmers Market MARKET £
(www.trurofarmers.co.uk; Lemon Quay; snacks from £3; 9am-3pm Wed & Sat) The green and white stalls that pop up twice a week here

are piled high with locally produced bread, cheese, fruit, veg, eggs, smoked fish, cakes and preserves. You'll also find street food that might span curries, slow-smoked brisket and churros.

Bustopher Jones BISTRO ££
(☎01872-430000; www.bustopher-jones.co.uk; 62 Lemon St; mains £13-21; ⏱5-10pm Mon-Wed, to 3am Fri, to 2am Sat, noon-4pm Sun) Head to the covered, heated garden lounge at impeccably designed Bustopher Jones to indulge in a little downtown dining on burgers, steaks and grilled fish. Or sip on something from their extensive drinks list – the cocktails are mini works of art.

★108 Coffee CAFE
(☎07582 339636; 109 Kenwyn St; ⏱8am-2pm Mon-Sat) Set up by unapologetic coffee nuts Paul and Michelle, this is Truro's premier place for a caffeine fix. The beans come courtesy of Cornish coffee roasters Origin, and the flat whites and espressos are among the county's best.

Old Ale House PUB
(☎01872-271122; www.old-ale-house.co.uk; 7 Quay St; ⏱noon-11pm) A proper ale-drinker's pub, with sawdust on the floor, beer mats on the ceiling and a menu of guest ales. Most of the beers come from Skinner's Brewery, rejoicing under names like Betty Stogs (4%, bitter), Penny Come Quick (4.5%, milk stout) and the fabled Cornish Knocker (4%, golden ale).

ℹ Information

Truro Tourist Office (☎01872-274555; www.visittruro.org.uk; 30 Boscawen St; ⏱9am-5.30pm Mon-Fri, to 5pm Sat)

ℹ Getting There & Away

BUS

Truro's bus station is beside Lemon Quay.

Falmouth (£5.80, 1¼ hours, half-hourly Monday to Saturday, hourly Sunday) Bus U1, via Penryn.

Penzance (£5.80, 1½ hours, hourly) Bus T1.

St Ives (£5.80, 1½ hours, hourly) Bus T2.

TRAIN

Truro is on the main London Paddington–Penzance line and the branch line to Falmouth. Frequent connections include the following.

Bristol £51, 3½ hours

Exeter £19.60, 2¼ hours

Falmouth £45, 30 minutes

London Paddington £70, 4½ hours

Penzance £8, 40 minutes

Fowey

☎01726 / POP 2130

Fowey makes a bewitching south-coast base. In this working port turned well-heeled holiday town, pastel-coloured houses, portside pubs and tiered terraces overlook the wooded banks of the River Fowey. The town has been an important port since Elizabethan times, and later became the adopted home of the writer Daphne du Maurier, who used the nearby house at Menabilly Barton as the inspiration for *Rebecca*.

A passenger ferry (p357) shuttles to the impossibly pretty village of **Polruan**, on the east side of Fowey harbour. A few miles north along the creek, the riverside hamlet of **Golant** is also well worth a detour, with a waterfront pub for lunch and excellent kayaking opportunities.

Sights & Activities

Polkerris Beach BEACH
(☎01726-813306; www.polkerrisbeach.com) Some 3 miles west of Fowey, this is the area's largest and busiest beach. Sailing lessons, windsurfing and stand-up paddleboarding are all available.

Fowey River Expeditions KAYAKING
(☎01726-833627; www.foweyexpeditions.co.uk; Albert Quay; adult/child £30/15; ⏱Apr-Oct) On these guided, two-hour, entry-level tours in single and double open cockpit canoes you'll either head up river towards Golant or explore Fowey harbour.

More experienced kayakers can also hire boats for self-guided trips (single/double kayak per day £30/45).

★Encounter Cornwall KAYAKING
(☎07976 466123; www.encountercornwall.com; The Boatshed, Golant; adult/child £30/20) These three-hour guided kayaking trips might form some of the most memorable moments of your Cornish stay. Setting off from Golant, just north of Fowey, tours see you gliding up creeks and backwaters, spotting egrets, kingfishers and seals. Encounter also offers two-hour early-morning and 'sundowner' expeditions (adult/child £25/15).

WORTH A TRIP

POLPERRO & MEVAGISSEY

Even in a county where picturesque fishing harbours seem to fill every cove, it's hard not to fall for Polperro – a warren of cottages, boat stores and alleyways, all set around a stout granite harbour. Unsurprisingly, this was once a smugglers' hideout, and it's still a place with a salty, sea-dog atmosphere, despite the inevitable summer crowds. The coast path between Polperro and Looe is particularly scenic. The main car park is 750m uphill from the village, from there it's a 15-minute stroll down to the quayside.

Just along the coast, the little village of Mevagissey hasn't been gentrified to quite the same degree as other ports along the coast, and feels all the better for it. There are alleys to wander, great pubs, secondhand bookshops and galleries to browse, and the harbour is one of the best places on the south coast for crabbing. In summer, ferries run along the coast from Mevagissey Harbour to Fowey.

Sleeping

Old Embassy House B&B ££
(01726-834939; www.oldembassyhouse.co.uk; Lostwithiel St; s £95-125, d £105-125; P) At friendly Old Embassy House design themes range from four poster, via geometric to seaside. The best bedroom is nautically themed, 1st-floor Lantic, which has a window seat with views down onto the tree-framed, boat-dotted river below.

★ **Coriander Cottages** APARTMENT £££
(01726-834998; www.foweyaccommodation.co.uk; Penventinue Lane; 1-bed cottages £130-150; P) A delightfully rural cottage complex on the outskirts of Fowey, with ecofriendly accommodation in open-plan, self-catering barns, all with quiet country views. The stone barns have been beautifully modernised, and use a combination of solar panels, ground-source heating and rainwater harvesting to reduce environmental impact. Handily, cottages are available per night, so you're not restricted to weekly stays.

Old Quay House HOTEL £££
(01726-833302; www.theoldquayhouse.com; 28 Fore St; incl breakfast d £250-360, ste from £400;) The epitome of Fowey's upmarket trend, this exclusive quayside hotel is all natural fabrics, rattan chairs and tasteful monochrome tones, and the rooms are a mix of estuary-view suites and attic penthouses. It's right in the centre of town, in a handsome riverside building. The restaurant specialises in upmarket seafood.

Eating & Drinking

Kittows DELI £
(01726-832639; www.kittowsfowey.co.uk; 3 South St; 8.30am-5.30pm Mon-Sat, 9am-4pm Sun) The deli at Fowey's fifth-generation butcher sells perfect picnic goodies: fish and meat kebabs, cooked crab and lobster, Fowey Valley Cider and Cornish Blue cheese.

Sam's BISTRO ££
(01726-832273; www.samscornwall.co.uk; 20 Fore St; mains £12-18; noon-9.30pm) Sam's has been a stalwart in Fowey for years. Alfresco, river-view tables, booth seats, Day-Glo menus and a lively local vibe keep the feel laid-back, and the menu of flash-cooked fish, salads, steaks and gourmet burgers proves perennially popular.

Sam's on the Beach BISTRO ££
(01726-812255; www.samscornwall.co.uk; Polkerris; mains £15-24, pizza £8-16; noon-10pm Sun-Fri, 9am-10pm Sat) Lodged in the old lifeboat house on Polkerris, this beachside outpost of the mini Sam's empire dishes up pan-seared sardines, mussels cooked in Cornish cider and sourdough pizza fresh from the wood-fired oven. All made memorable thanks to tables beside the sands and cracking bay views.

King of Prussia PUB
(01726-833694; www.kingofprussiafowey.co.uk; 3 Town Quay; 11am-11pm) Fowey has lots of pubs, but you might as well go for the one with the best harbour view, named after notorious 'free trader' (aka smuggler) John Carter – the eponymous Prussia refers to Cornwall's Prussia Cove.

Pub-grub meals (mains £13 to £20) include mussels steamed with chorizo, coq au vin and blue-cheese gnocchi.

Information

Fowey's Website (www.fowey.co.uk) has tourist information.

Getting There & Away

Bus 24 (hourly Monday to Saturday, six on Sunday) runs to St Austell, Heligan and Mevagissey. It also stops at Par train station, where you can catch trains on the main London–Penzance line.

Polruan Ferry (www.ctomsandson.co.uk/polruan-ferry; Whitehouse Pier; adult/child £2.30/1, bicycle £1.70, dog 40p; ⏲7am-11pm Mon-Sat, 10am-11pm Sun mid-Jul–Sep, 8am-9pm Mon-Sat, 10am-5pm Sun Oct–mid-Jul) Passenger ferry to Polruan. In winter and on summer evenings, it runs from Town Quay; in summer during the day, it runs from Whitehouse Pier on the Esplanade.

Bodinnick Ferry (Fowey slipway; www.ctomsandson.co.uk/bodinnick-ferry; car & 2 passengers £5, pedestrian/bicycle £2/free; ⏲7am-8pm Mon-Fri, 9am-8pm Sat & Sun May-Sep, last ferry 7pm Oct-Apr) Car ferry crossing the river to Bodinnick.

Looe

☎01503 / POP 5110

Nestled in the crook of a steep-sided valley, the twin settlements of East and West Looe stand on either side of a broad river estuary, connected by an arched Victorian bridge built in 1853. There's been a settlement here since the days of the Domesday Book, and the town thrived as a medieval port before reinventing itself as a holiday resort for well-to-do Victorians – famously, the town installed one of the county's first 'bathing machines' beside **Banjo Pier** (named for its circular shape) in around 1800, and it's been a popular beach retreat ever since.

In contrast to Fowey, Looe feels a little behind-the-times – chip shops, souvenir sellers and chintzy B&Bs still very much rule the roost here – but if it's a classic seaside town you're looking for, you've definitely found it in Looe.

Sights

Looe Island ISLAND

(www.cornwallwildlifetrust.org.uk/looeisland; guided walks £25) A mile offshore from Hannafore Point is densely wooded Looe Island (officially known as St George's Island), a 9-hectare nature reserve and haven for marine wildlife. You can explore on foot, or take a guided walk with the island ranger, who can help spot local wildlife including grey seals, cormorants, shags and oystercatchers. Book well in advance.

Between April and September, the **Moonraker** (☎07814 264514; Buller Quay; return adult/child £10/5, plus landing fee £4/1) putters over from Looe's Buller Quay. Trips are dependent on weather and tides; booking essential.

Sleeping

Penvith Barns B&B ££

(☎01503-240772; www.penvithbarns.co.uk; St-Martin-by-Looe; r £95-119; P 📶 🐾) Escape the Looe crowds at this rural barn conversion in the nearby hamlet of St-Martin-by-Looe. Rooms range from small to spacious: the Piggery is tiny and tucked under the eaves, while the Dairy has enough space for a spare bed and sofa. Each room has its own private entrance. Two-night minimum in summer.

Commonwood Manor B&B ££

(☎01503-262929; www.commonwoodmanor.com; St Martins Rd; d £90-130; P 📶 🐾) In a prime position on the East Looe hillside, this elegant villa with a long river-view terrace is a cut above your average B&B. Room design spans cream to floral, and if you bag one of the bay-window bedrooms, you'll have the

DON'T MISS

COTEHELE

At the head of the Tamar Valley sits the Tudor manor of **Cotehele** (NT; ☎01579-351346; www.nationaltrust.org.uk; St Dominick; gardens adult/child £8/4; ⏲gardens 10am-5pm), one of the Edgcumbe dynasty's modest country retreats. The gardens sweep down past the 18th-century Prospect Folly to Cotehele Quay, where there's a discovery centre exploring the history of the Tamar Valley and a vintage sailing barge, the **Shamrock**.

If the interior has reopened you'll see a cavernous great hall and an unparalleled collection of Tudor tapestries, armour and furniture.

A short walk inland leads to the restored **Cotehele Mill**. If it's operating, you'll be able to watch the original waterwheel grinding corn several days a week, and see a miller and baker at work. The house is famous for its Christmas wreath, a massive ornamental ring of foliage made from materials gathered on the estate.

best views in town. There's usually a two-night minimum.

Information

Check to see whether the **Looe Tourist Office** (☎01503-262072; www.looeguide.co.uk; Guildhall, Fore St) is back up and running.

Getting There & Away

Looe sits at the end of a railway branch line that links to the main London Paddington to Penzance service at Liskeard. The journey (adult/child return £4.60/3.30, 30 minutes, hourly) tracks through wooded valleys out to the seaside; a day out in itself.

Bodmin Moor

It can't quite boast the wild majesty of Dartmoor, but Bodmin Moor has a bleak beauty all of its own. With its heaths and granite hills, including Rough Tor ('rowtor', 400m) and Cornwall's highest point, Brown Willy (420m), it's a desolate place that works on the imagination, with prehistoric remains and legends of mysterious beasts.

The northern and central parts of the Moor are largely barren and treeless, while the southern section is greener. Apart from the hills, the moor's main landmark is Jamaica Inn, made famous by Daphne du Maurier's novel of the same name.

Sights & Activities

For an intriguing insight into life for the British aristocracy, check whether the interior of the magnificent manor house of **Lanhydrock** (NT; ☎01208-265950; www.nationaltrust.org.uk) has reopened.

It's also worth seeing whether the **Bodmin & Wenford Railway** (☎01208-73555; www.bodminrailway.co.uk) is up and running again.

★Golitha Falls WATERFALL

(near Redgate) FREE With water cascading down a 90m drop, these crashing falls are one of the most renowned beauty spots on the moor. The site is surrounded by the remains of an ancient oak wood that once covered much of the moor. The falls are just over a mile west of St Cleer. There's a car park half a mile's walk from the reserve, near Draynes Bridge.

Carnglaze Caverns CAVE

(☎01579-320251; www.carnglaze.com; near St Neot; adult/child £8/5; ⏲10am-5pm, to 8pm Aug; 👪🐾) Slate was once an important local export on Bodmin Moor, and these deep caverns were cut out by hand by miners, leaving behind an atmospheric network of caves and a glittering underground pool. The site is just outside St Neot and well-signed.

Cheesewring ARCHAEOLOGICAL SITE

(near Minions) Looking like a gigantic game of granite Jenga, this stack of rocks on the edge of the small village of Minions is said to have been the work of giants – but the truth is even stranger. A combination of wind, rain and natural erosion has carved out the outcrop's peculiar disc-like shapes. The name refers to the formation's similarity to the bags of apple pulp (or cheeses) that are used in cider presses.

PREHISTORIC SITES OF BODMIN MOOR

The highest concentration of prehistoric sites is found in the southern moor. Near the small village of Minions, about 2 miles east of Siblyback Lake, the curious triple stone circles known as the **Hurlers** are said to be the remains of men turned to stone for daring to play the Cornish sport of hurling on a Sunday. Nearby is the **Cheesewring**, a weird stack of granite stones that's said to be the work of local giants, but is actually the result of natural erosion. Three miles south near Darite is **Trethevy Quoit** – sometimes known as King Arthur's Quoit or the Giant's House – another example of Cornwall's distinctive Neolithic burial chambers, standing almost 4.5m high.

But the most impressive monument is the structure known as **King Arthur's Hall**, a huge rectangle of standing stones measuring 20m across and 50m long. It's an archaeological conundrum; nothing of its size exists anywhere else in Cornwall, and so far experts are stumped as to what it was used for. The current explanation is that it may have been a ceremonial pool, but it's really anyone's guess. It's reached via a muddy trail from St Breward.

Eating

★Woods Cafe CAFE £

(☎01208-78111; www.woodscafe.co.uk; Cardinham Woods; mains £6-12; ⏲10.30am-3pm Mon-Fri, to 4pm Sat & Sun) In an old forester's cottage lost among the trees of Cardinham, this cracking cafe has become a locals' favourite thanks to home-baked cakes, cockle-warming soups and sausage sandwiches. Perfect for post-walk sustenance.

★St Tudy Inn MODERN BRITISH ££

(☎01208-850656; www.sttudyinn.com; St Tudy; mains £14-25; ⏲hours vary) Locally lauded chef Emily Scott temporarily relocated to a pop-up cafe at Watergate Bay for the summer of 2020. Check whether she's back at this smart moorland village pub, to deliver imaginative food combining traditional British flavours with a modern, season-driven style.

There is also a selection of elegant **rooms** (doubles from £140) in attached barns.

ISLES OF SCILLY

While only 28 miles west of the mainland, in many ways the Isles of Scilly feels like a different world. Life on this archipelago of around 140 tiny islands seems hardly to have changed in decades: there are no traffic jams, no supermarkets, no multinational hotels, and the only noise pollution comes from breaking waves and cawing gulls. That's not to say that Scilly is behind the times – you'll find a mobile-phone signal and broadband internet on the main islands – but life ticks along at its own island pace. Renowned for glorious beaches, there are few places better to escape.

Only five islands are inhabited: St Mary's is the largest, followed by Tresco, while only a few hardy souls live on Bryher, St Martin's and St Agnes. Regular ferry boats run between all five islands.

Unsurprisingly, summer is by far the busiest time. Many businesses shut down completely in winter.

Information

Isles of Scilly Tourist Information Centre (☎01720-620600; www.visitislesofscilly.com; Porthcressa Beach; ⏲9am-1pm & 4-5pm) The islands' only tourist office.

Simply Scilly (www.simplyscilly.co.uk) Unofficial tourist site.

Getting There & Away

Isles of Scilly Travel (☎01736-334220; www.islesofscilly-travel.co.uk) There are frequent flights year-round from Land's End Airport, near St Just (adult/child £90/71, 20 minutes) and from Newquay Airport (£115/88, 30 minutes). Between mid-March and October flights also run from Exeter (£169/124, one hour). Planes only fly Monday to Saturday.

Scillonian III (☎01736-334220; www.islesofscilly-travel.co.uk; ⏲mid Mar–Oct) Scilly's ferry plies the notoriously choppy waters between Penzance and St Mary's (one-way adult/child £55/29). There's at least one daily crossing in summer, but there are no ferries in winter. It sails in most weathers, but seasickness is a distinct possibility: be prepared.

Penzance Helicopters (☎01736-780828; www.penzancehelicopters.co.uk; Penzance Heliport, Jelbert Way; single £130; ⏲Mon-Sat) These 15-minute flights link Penzance Heliport with St Mary's and Tresco.

Getting Around

Inter-island ferries between St Mary's and the other islands are provided by the **St Mary's Boatmen's Association** (☎01720-423999; www.scillyboating.co.uk; adult/child return to any island £10/5). If you're staying at one of the hotels on Tresco, there's also a separate transfer service.

The only bus and taxi services are on St Mary's.

St Mary's

☎01720 / POP 1650

First stop for every visitor to Scilly (unless you're arriving aboard your own private yacht) is St Mary's, the largest and busiest of the islands, and home to the vast majority of hotels, shops, restaurants and B&Bs. Just over 3 miles at its widest point, St Mary's is shaped like a crooked circle, with a claw-shaped peninsula at its southwestern edge – home to the island's capital, Hugh Town, and the docking point for the Scillonian ferry. The main airport is a mile east near Old Town.

Sights & Activities

Isles of Scilly Museum MUSEUM

(☎01720-422337; www.iosmuseum.org; Church St, Hugh Town; adult/child £3.50/1) Check whether the excellent Isles of Scilly Museum, which suspended visits in 2020, has reopened. It provides an evocative introduction to the islands' history, with an eclectic mix of archaeological finds and artefacts from shipwrecks. Among the collection are Neolithic remains such as tools and jewellery, clay pipes left behind by generations of sailors, a couple of sailing boats and a small exhibition on Edward Heath, the British prime minister who loved Scilly so much he was buried here.

St Mary's Bike Hire CYCLING
(07552 994709; www.stmarysbikehire.co.uk; The Strand; half/full day £8.50/13.50, week £65; 9am-5pm Mon-Sat Mar-Oct, plus 9am-noon Sun Jun-Aug) Rents out bikes from a base in Hugh Town, but can also deliver island-wide (£2.50 per bike). It also hires out electric bikes (half/full day £16.50/25) and a tandem (£17.50/27).

Tours

Scilly Walks WALKING
(01720-423326; www.scillywalks.co.uk; adult/child £7/3.50) Three-hour archaeological and historical tours of St Mary's, plus regular guided walking trips to other islands, conducted by local historian and archaeologist Katherine Sawyer.

Island Wildlife Tours WALKING
(01720-422212; www.islandwildlifetours.co.uk; half/full day £7/14) Regular birdwatching and wildlife walks with local character and resident ornithologist Will Wagstaff, the undisputed authority on Scilly's natural history. Most tours start in the morning on St Mary's, but there are regular walks on other islands too. You need to add on the cost of the boat transfer.

Island Sea Safaris BOATING
(01720-422732; www.islandseasafaris.co.uk) Trips to see local seabird and seal colonies (adult/child £38/29), plus one-hour 'island taster' tours (£26 per person).

Sleeping

Garrison Campsite CAMPSITE £
(01720-422670; www.garrisonholidaysscilly.co.uk; Tower Cottage, Garrison; adult/child £14/7;) St Mary's main campsite sits in a lofty spot above Hugh Town, beside the Garrison fort. It's a big site, covering 3.5 hectares, with plenty of pitches (some with electrical hook-ups), plus wi-fi, a small shop and a laundry-shower block. It also offers pre-erected tents (two/four people per three nights £175/315).

Mincarlo B&B ££
(01720-422513; www.mincarloscilly.com; s £45-55, d £83-120;) There's no better location on St Mary's than this little guesthouse in a prime spot with views all the way to Hugh Town from the western end of Town Beach. Rooms are plain and cosy (the attic's a bargain), breakfast is great, and owners Nick and Bryony are full of local info.

Star Castle HOTEL £££
(01720-422317; www.star-castle.co.uk; Garrison; s/d from £130/145;) Shaped like an eight-pointed star, this former fort on Garrison Point is one of Scilly's top hotels, with heritage-style castle rooms and more-modern garden suites. It's fairly formal but the views are some of the best on the island, and the grassy gardens – set right into the ramparts – are a delight.

Atlantic INN £££
(01720-422417; www.atlanticinnscilly.co.uk; Hugh St; r £140-195;) The fresh, summery rooms in this age-old inn come complete with colourful prints, pastel colours and plush fabrics – the best have captivating edge-of-the-water views. The food (mains £13 to £18) takes in fish and chips, burgers and Thai curries, best enjoyed on the glass-framed, harbour-side terrace.

Eating

Dibble & Grub CAFE £
(01720-423719; www.dibbleandgrub.co.uk; Porthcressa; lights meals £6-9; 10am-10pm Apr-Sep;) At the terrace of Dibble & Grub you're just paces from the sands of Porthcressa beach. The menu gives island ingredients a Mediterranean twist; choose from Cornish pork souvlaki or breakfast ciabatta with Scilly free-range eggs, chased by a zingy raspberry smoothie.

Juliet's Garden BISTRO ££
(01720-422228; www.julietsgardenrestaurant.co.uk; Seaways/Porthlow; lunch mains £7-15; 10am-5pm;) St Mary's bistro has been in business for over three decades and is still the best place to eat. Set in a converted barn 15 minutes' walk from town, it's fringed by a glorious, sea-view garden. Gourmet sandwiches feature treacle-glazed salmon and hand-picked local crab, or opt for smoked cheese and spinach on toasted flatbread. They might open early evening too – check the website.

Getting Around

Public transport on the island might be affected by distancing regulations. Check with the tourist office (p359) whether the airport bus is running to Hugh Town, and whether the **Island Rover** (☎01720-422131; www.islandrover.co.uk) vintage bus tours are operating.

For taxis on St Mary's, try **Toots** (☎01720-422142; www.tootstaxi.co.uk). Or rent a bike from St Mary's Bike Hire.

Tresco

☎01720 / POP 167

A short boat hop across the channel from St Mary's brings you to Tresco, the second-largest island, once owned by the monks of Tavistock Abbey, and now privately leased by the Dorrien-Smith family from the Duchy of Cornwall.

The main attraction here is the fabulous subtropical garden, but the rest of the island is a lovely place just to explore by bike. The whole place is privately leased, so it feels a little more manicured than the other, more community-driven islands, especially since the focus here is very much on high-end visitors.

Sights

★Tresco Abbey Garden GARDENS

(☎01720-424108; www.tresco.co.uk/enjoying/abbey-garden; adult/child £15/5; ⊙10am-4pm) Tresco's key attraction – and one of Scilly's must-see gems – is this subtropical estate, laid out in 1834 on the site of a 12th-century Benedictine priory by the horticultural visionary Augustus Smith. The 7-hectare gardens are now home to more than 20,000 exotic species, from towering palms to desert cacti and crimson flame trees, all nurtured by the temperate Gulf Stream. Admission also covers the **Valhalla collection**, made up of figureheads and nameplates salvaged from ships wrecked off Tresco.

Sleeping & Eating

★New Inn PUB, HOTEL £££

(☎01720-423006; www.tresco.co.uk; r £175-300; ⊙food noon-2.30pm & 6.30-9pm; 📶🐕) By Tresco standards, the New Inn is a bargain. The rooms are soothingly finished in buttery yellows and pale blues, although inevitably you'll have to fork out for a view. The inn itself serves tasty food (mains £10 to £18), with dishes such as mackerel burgers, baked Tresco duck eggs and Bryher-crab mac and cheese.

Ruin Beach CAFE ££

(☎01720-424849; www.tresco.co.uk; mains £12-21, pizzas £13-16; ⊙noon-3pm & 6-9pm) With a beach-side terrace, a relaxed vibe and flavoursome food, the Ruin makes for a memorable place to feast on dishes fresh from the wood-fired oven. It's as equally adept at producing beetroot, scallops and peppers as it is crispy pizzas.

Bryher

Only around 80 people live on Bryher, Scilly's smallest and wildest inhabited island. Covered by rough bracken and heather, and fringed by white sand, this slender chunk of rock takes a fearsome battering from the Atlantic – Hell Bay hasn't earned its name for nothing. But on a bright sunny day, it's an island idyll par excellence, ideal for exploring on foot.

The island has a strong sense of community; you'll see little stalls selling freshly cut flowers, homegrown veg, jams and packets of fudge.

Sleeping & Eating

Bryher Campsite CAMPSITE £

(☎01720-422068; www.bryhercampsite.co.uk; per person £11.50; 👪) Bare-bones but beautiful, the island's campsite sits in a secluded spot surrounded by drystone walls and is just steps from the sea. Hot showers and tractor transport from the quay are included in the nightly rates. Its four-person bell tents (per week £500 to £565) come complete with kitted-out kitchen, picnic benches and deck chairs.

★Hell Bay HOTEL £££

(☎01720-422947; www.hellbay.co.uk; d incl breakfast £360-640; P📶👪) Pretty much the poshest place to stay in Scilly, and a true island getaway, Hell Bay blends New England–style furnishings with sunny golds, sea blues and pale wood beams. It has the feel of a luxurious beach villa, with lovingly tended gardens and an excellent restaurant (mains £14 to £25).

The prices here roughly halve in spring and autumn.

Bryher Shop DELI £
(01720-423601; www.bryhershop.co.uk; 9am-2pm Mon-Sat) Pick up all your essential supplies at the island's charming general store, which also has a post office. Opening hours may have increased – check the website.

Fraggle Rock CAFE ££
(01720-422222; www.bryher.co; mains £9-16; 9am-9pm;) This relaxed cafe also doubles as Bryher's pub. The menu is mainly quiches, salads and burgers, ideally served in the front garden, where chickens scratch around and there are views out to Hangman's Rock. It's a lively evening hang-out in season.

St Martin's

01720 / POP 113

The third-largest and furthest north of the islands, St Martin's (www.stmartinsscilly.co.uk) is the main centre for Scilly's flower-growing industry, and the island's fields are a riot of colourful blooms in season. It's also blessed with gin-clear waters and the kind of untouched sands you'd more usually associate with St Lucia than Cornwall.

Sights & Activities

Check whether **Scilly Seal Snorkelling** (01720-422848; www.scillysealsnorkelling.com) has resumed its guided swims.

St Martin's Vineyard WINERY
(01720-423418; www.stmartinsvineyard.co.uk; Higher Town) The UK's smallest and most southwesterly vineyard produces its own range of organic white, rosé and red wines. If guided tours aren't being held because of distancing measures, self-guided tours (adult/child £7.50/1) and tastings of four wines are available instead. See the website for the latest opening hours.

Sleeping

Accommodation here is limited apart from a super-expensive hotel and a handful of B&Bs.

St Martin's Campsite CAMPSITE £
(01720-422888; www.stmartinscampsite.co.uk; Oaklands Farm, Middletown; per person £11.50-12.50, dogs £3; Apr-Sep;) The second-largest campsite in Scilly, at the western end of Lawrence's Bay, has 50 pitches (maximum 100 people) spread across three fields. You'll find showers, stunning sunsets and views of a glittering Milky Way. Book well ahead.

Polreath B&B £££
(01720-422046; www.polreath.com; Higher Town; d £140-150;) This friendly granite cottage has small rooms and a sunny conservatory serving cream teas, homemade lemonade and evening meals. Weekly stays required May to October.

Eating & Drinking

Island Bakery BAKERY £
(01720-42211; www.theislandbakery-stmartins.com; Higher Town; bread & cakes £2-5, pizza £9-12.50; 9am-5pm Mon-Sat Easter-Oct) Gorgeous organic breads, Cornish pasties, pies and takeaway pizzas. Best followed up by homemade cakes.

Adam's Fish & Chips FISH & CHIPS £
(01720-423082; www.adamsfishandchips.co.uk; Higher Town; fish & chips takeaway adult/child £10/7; hours vary) The fish here is about as fresh as it gets – whatever's caught on the day is what ends up in your batter. At the time of writing opening hours and days varied, but orders had to be placed by 5pm. Check for updates at the village shop or call ahead.

Seven Stones PUB
(01720-423777; www.sevenstonesinn.com; Lower Town; 11am-3pm & 5-11pm Wed-Mon) St Martin's only boozer is a lively, welcoming place with cracking views over the islands from the terrace and a menu featuring gourmet Stones Burgers, Scilly produce and net-fresh seafood. Food (mains £8 to £14) is served from noon to 2pm and 6pm to 8pm.

St Agnes

01720 / POP 83

Scilly's southernmost island feels really remote, with a string of empty coves and a scattering of prehistoric sites. Visitors disembark at Porth Conger, near the old lighthouse, from where you wander along the coast path around the whole island.

At low tide, a narrow sandbar appears and provides a bridge to the neighbouring island of Gugh, where many ancient burial sites and a few chamber tombs can be found.

Sleeping & Eating

★Troytown Farm CAMPSITE £

(☎01720-422360; www.troytown.co.uk; adult/child £10.25/5.75, tents £2-8) The journey to St Agnes' beach-side campsite is quite an event – you're met at the quay and your luggage is trundled to the campsite by tractor trailer while you make the 15-minute walk. The camping field is small, but wonderfully located on the island's sunset coast, surrounded by drystone walls and a sea-blue, big-sky horizon.

Luggage transfer costs £4 per person. The campsite also rents pre-pitched, four-person bell tents (from £480 to £515 per week) and three two- to four-person self-catering cottages (£385 to £1045 per week). Bring a torch, as the island gets very, very dark.

★Turk's Head PUB FOOD ££

(☎01720-422434; The Quay; mains £14-16; ⏲10.30am-9pm) You can almost smell the history at Britain's most southerly alehouse. It's covered in maritime memorabilia – model ships in glass cabinets, vintage maps of the islands, black-and-white photos of seafarers. There are few finer places than the cove-side terrace in which to sup a pint.

Hearty food takes in everything from imaginative burgers and curries to mackerel caught on the pub's own boat.

AT A GLANCE

POPULATION
4.3 million

MILES OF COASTLINE
490

BEST VILLAGE
Cley-next-the-Sea
(p395)

BEST BEACH
Holkham National Nature Reserve
(p398)

BEST FIVE-STAR DINNER
Midsummer House
(p378)

WHEN TO GO

Apr, May, Sep & Oct
Mild weather and fewer crowds; Cambridge colleges close April to June for exams.

Jun–Aug
Warm weather and festivals, but prices peak and things get busy on the coast.

Nov & Dec
Music fills Cambridge's King's College Chapel in December; Christmas services at medieval churches everywhere.

Ely Cathedral (p380)
NASTYA ARSENTYEVA/SHUTTERSTOCK ©

Cambridge & East Anglia

Bulging gently eastwards towards the sea, the vast flatlands of East Anglia were once one of the wealthiest parts of the country, before reverting to backwater status during the Industrial Revolution. Farmers relied on working horses here as recently as the 1960s, and tales of witchcraft still permeate the folklore of this agreeably traditional corner of the country.

For visitors, East Anglia is best known for its rich Roman, Saxon, Viking and medieval history, its sweeping sandy beaches and bucolic rural landscapes that once inspired Constable and Gainsborough. Against this rustic backdrop, the dynamic university city of Cambridge rises out of the Fens like a beacon.

INCLUDES

Cambridge & East Anglia Highlights

❶ **Cambridge** (p368) Punting along the Granta before poking a nose into the historic colleges of Cambridge University.

❷ **Sandringham** (p399) Pulling back the curtain on royal life in the Queen's country estate.

❸ **Norfolk Broads** (p396) Canoeing or boating through tranquil waterways with swans and windmills for company.

❹ **Holkham** (p398) Admiring the lavish excess of the grand Palladian home, before tottering over to the endless sands of Holkham Beach.

❺ **Lavenham** (p386) Weaving between the leaning timbered houses of this museum-piece medieval market town.

❻ **Norwich** (p391) Mixing history and culture in this elegant, historic wool city, home to one of England's grandest cathedrals.

❼ **Aldeburgh** (p388) Dining on spray-fresh seafood and walking the prom in this agreeably gentle seaside town.

❽ **Imperial War Museum** (p378) Unleashing your inner plane-spotter in the aircraft-filled hangers of this remarkable military museum.

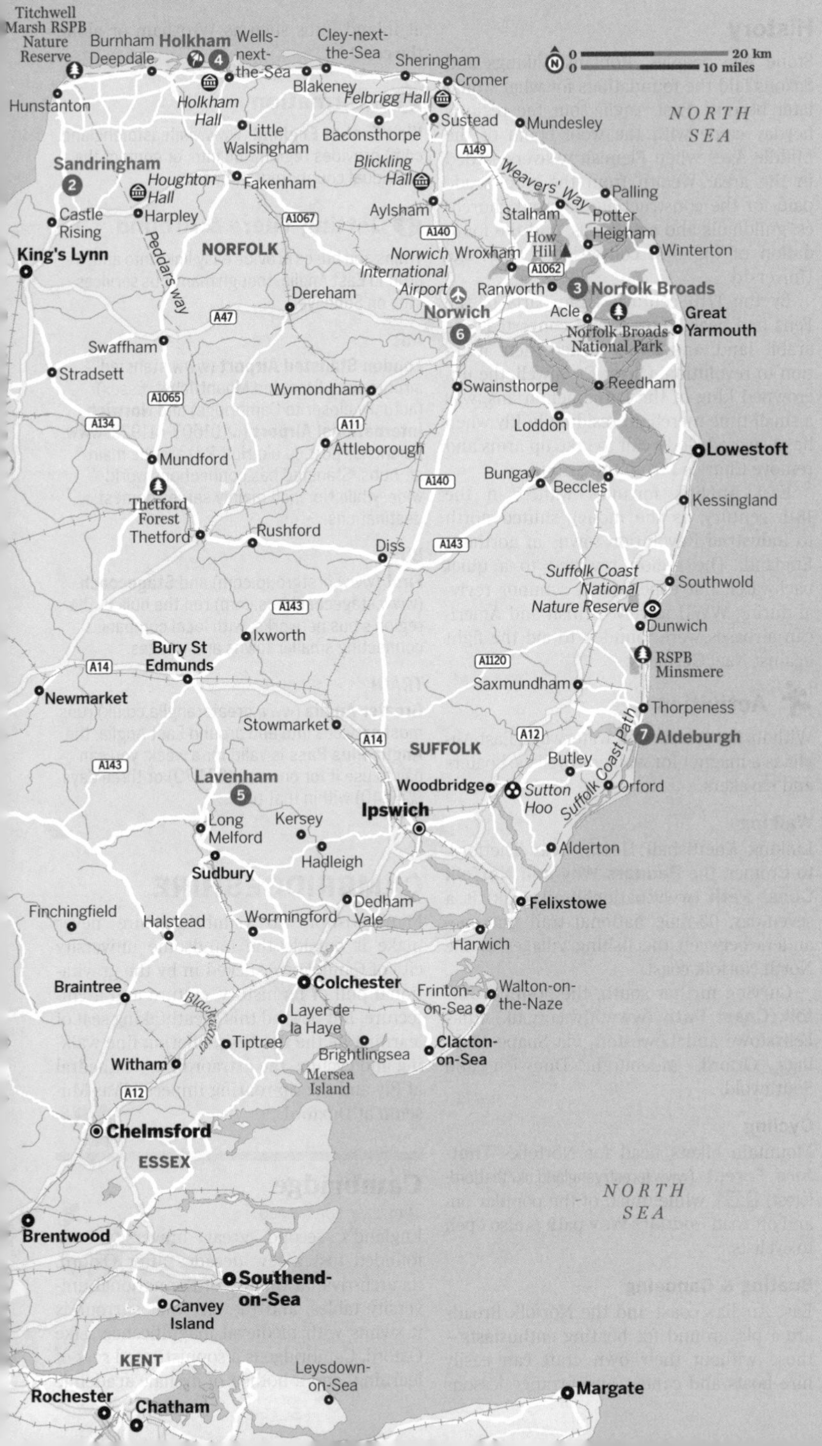

Titchwell Marsh RSPB Nature Reserve
Burnham Deepdale
Holkham
4
Wells-next-the-Sea
Cley-next-the-Sea
Sheringham
Cromer
0 20 km
0 10 miles
N
Hunstanton
Holkham Hall
Blakeney
Felbrigg Hall
Sustead
Mundesley
NORTH SEA
Little Walsingham
Baconsthorpe
A149
Sandringham
2
Houghton Hall
Fakenham
Blickling Hall
Weavers' Way
Palling
Castle Rising
Harpley
Aylsham
Stalham
Potter Heigham
A1067
A140
How Hill
Winterton
King's Lynn
Peddars Way
NORFOLK
Norwich International Airport
Wroxham
A1062
Ranworth
3
Norfolk Broads
Dereham
Norwich
Acle
Great Yarmouth
A47
6
Norfolk Broads National Park
Swaffham
Stradsett
Wymondham
Swainsthorpe
Reedham
A1065
A134
A11
Loddon
Attleborough
Lowestoft
Mundford
Bungay
A140
Beccles
Thetford Forest
Kessingland
Thetford
Rushford
Diss
A143
Suffolk Coast National Nature Reserve
Southwold
A143
Dunwich
Ixworth
RSPB Minsmere
Bury St Edmunds
A14
A1120
Saxmundham
Newmarket
Thorpeness
Suffolk Coast Path
Stowmarket
7
Aldeburgh
A14
A12
SUFFOLK
A143
Butley
Lavenham
5
Woodbridge
Sutton Hoo
Orford
Ipswich
Long Melford
Kersey
Hadleigh
Alderton
Sudbury
Dedham Vale
Felixstowe
Finchingfield
Halstead
Wormingford
Harwich
Colchester
Braintree
Blackwater
Frinton-on-Sea
Walton-on-the-Naze
Layer de la Haye
Tiptree
Brightlingsea
Clacton-on-Sea
Witham
Mersea Island
A12
Chelmsford
ESSEX
NORTH SEA
Brentwood
Southend-on-Sea
Canvey Island
KENT
Leysdown-on-Sea
Rochester
Chatham
Margate

History

Stone Age peoples, Romans, Vikings and Saxons laid the foundations for what would later become East Anglia, but the region's heyday came with the wool boom of the Middle Ages when Flemish weavers settled in the area. Wealth from the wool trade paid for the construction of grand churches, guildhalls and cathedrals, and the foundation of the first colleges of Cambridge University.

By the 17th century, large parts of the Fens had been drained and converted into arable land, and locals turned their attention to revolution. Oliver Cromwell, the uncrowned king of the Parliamentarians, was a small-time merchant residing in Ely when he answered God's call to take up arms and remove Charles I from the throne.

East Anglia's fortunes waned in the 18th century, as the money shifted north to Industrial Revolution towns in northern England. The region reverted to a quiet backwater, but experienced a minor revival during WWII as new British and American airbases were founded to aid the fight against Nazi Germany.

Activities

With its flat terrain and waterways, East Anglia is a magnet for walkers, cyclists, boaters and kayakers.

Walking

Linking Knettishall Heath, near Thetford, to Cromer, the **Peddars Way and Norfolk Coast Path** (www.nationaltrail.co.uk) is a seven-day, 93-mile national trail that meanders between the fishing villages of the North Norfolk coast.

Curving further south, the 50-mile **Suffolk Coast Path** (www.ldwa.org.uk) links Felixstowe and Lowestoft, via Snape Maltings, Orford, Aldeburgh, Dunwich and Southwold.

Cycling

Mountain bikers head for Norfolk's **Thetford Forest** (www.forestryengland.uk/thetford-forest) FREE, while much of the popular on- and off-road **Peddars Way** path is also open to cyclists.

Boating & Canoeing

East Anglia's coast and the Norfolk Broads are a playground for boating enthusiasts – those without their own craft can easily hire boats and canoes and arrange lessons at inland hubs such as Wroxham or along the coast.

Information

Visit East of England (www.visiteastofengland.com) provides regionwide info, or contact the individual county tourist boards.

Getting There & Around

Trains and buses provide easy links into and around East Anglia, though many bus services stop on Sundays.

AIR

London Stansted Airport (www.stanstedairport.com; Stansted Mountfichet, Essex) (actually closer to Cambridge) and **Norwich International Airport** (☎01603-411923; www.norwichairport.co.uk; Holt Rd) are the main air hubs. Stansted has connections worldwide, while Norwich mainly serves domestic destinations.

BUS

First (www.firstgroup.com) and **Stagecoach** (www.stagecoachbus.com) run the bulk of the region's bus networks, with local companies connecting smaller towns and villages.

TRAIN

Greater Anglia (www.greateranglia.co.uk) runs most services into and around East Anglia; the **Anglia Plus Pass** is valid for a week; you can pay to use it for one day (£24.70) or three days (£49.40) within that time.

CAMBRIDGESHIRE

Many visitors to Cambridgeshire never make it outside the handsome university city of Cambridge, sucked in by the gravitational pull of its history, culture and architecture. But beyond this breathtaking seat of learning lie the flat Fens, offering fine walking and cycling, the extraordinary cathedral at Ely and the rip-roaring Imperial War Museum at Duxford.

Cambridge

☎01223 / POP 136,800

England's second great university was founded just a few decades after Oxford, its arch-rival at the top of the national university tables, and the city that surrounds it swims with medieval magnificence. Like Oxford, Cambridge is a sophisticated seat of learning, and a hotbed of archaic academic traditions. Also like Oxford, the old centre is peppered with handsome historic buildings, and the streets are friendly to cyclists and pedestrians and unfriendly to cars – wise travellers come by bus or train.

Perhaps the most striking thing about Cambridge, once you get over the initial wow-factor of the colleges and historic buildings, is the way the countryside seems to spill into the city centre. The looping River Cam – known in the centre as the Granta – is lined with green parks and patches of common land, some still used for grazing livestock, lending the city a surprisingly rural mood.

History

Cambridge has been inhabited since at least the Iron Age, but its fortunes soared in the 11th century, when an Augustinian order of monks set up shop here, creating religious seats of learning that later morphed into the colleges of Cambridge University.

When the rival university town of Oxford exploded in a riot between town and gown in 1209, many scholars upped sticks to Cambridge, cementing the city's reputation and prestige. The first proper Cambridge college, Peterhouse (never Peterhouse *College*), was founded in 1284, and in 1318 Pope John XXII declared Cambridge to be an official university by papal bull.

By the 14th century, colleges had proliferated across the city, and the colleges continued to be a powerful patriarchy right up until 1869, when the first women-only college was established. By 1948, Cambridge minds had broadened sufficiently to allow women to actually graduate!

Sights

As well as the famous colleges and museums, look out for the golden **Corpus Clock** (Bene't St) just south of King's College, which displays the time through a series of concentric LED lights, while a hideous-looking insect 'time-eater' inches across the top of the dial.

If you need to catch your breath, take a picnic to **Jesus Green** (Park Parade), a lovely stretch of parkland tucked into a curve of the Granta.

★King's College Chapel — CHURCH

(☎01223-331100; www.kings.cam.ac.uk; King's Pde; adult/child £10/8; ⏲9.30am-3.15pm Mon-Sat, 1.15-2.30pm Sun term time, 9.30am-4.30pm rest of year) This grandiose, limestone-faced, 16th-century chapel is one of England's most extraordinary Gothic monuments. During services, the sound of the chapel's famous choir reverberates off the walls and rises to an almost impossibly intricate fan-vaulted ceiling – the world's largest. Think of it as a firework display, expressed as architecture. At the time of writing, the chapel was only open at set times – check ahead for the latest opening times.

Founded in 1446 as an act of piety by Henry VI, the chapel was only finished by Henry VIII around 1516, and lofty **stained-glass windows** flank the chapel's sides, filling the interior with light. The glass is original, reputedly spared from the excesses of England's 17th-century Civil War thanks to a personal order from Oliver Cromwell, himself a Cambridge graduate.

The antechapel and the choir are divided by a superbly carved **wooden screen**, designed and executed by Peter Stockton for Henry VIII. Look for the king's initials entwined with those of Anne Boleyn on the screen. Beyond, the high **altar** is framed by Rubens' masterpiece *Adoration of the Magi* (1634). To the left of the altar in the side chapels, an **exhibition** charts the construction of this landmark monument.

Under normal circumstances, visitors congregate here for **Evensong** (5.30pm Monday to Saturday, 10.30am and 3.30pm Sunday). Each Christmas Eve, King's College Chapel stages the **Festival of Nine Lessons & Carols**, broadcast globally by the BBC.

★Trinity College — COLLEGE

(☎01223-338400; www.trin.cam.ac.uk; Trinity St) The largest of Cambridge's colleges, Trinity grabs attention with an extraordinary

A VERY LEARNED BOOKSTORE

Facing the grand chapel of King's College, the **Cambridge University Press** (www.cambridge.org; 1-2 Trinity St; ⏲10am-5.30pm Mon Sat, 11am-5pm Sun) is the oldest university press in the world – founded by royal charter from Henry VIII in 1534. It's also the official printer of the British monarchy. With Cambridge being at the frontline of academic thinking and research, it's always worth popping in to read the latest on everything from gender rights to quantum field theory.

Cambridge

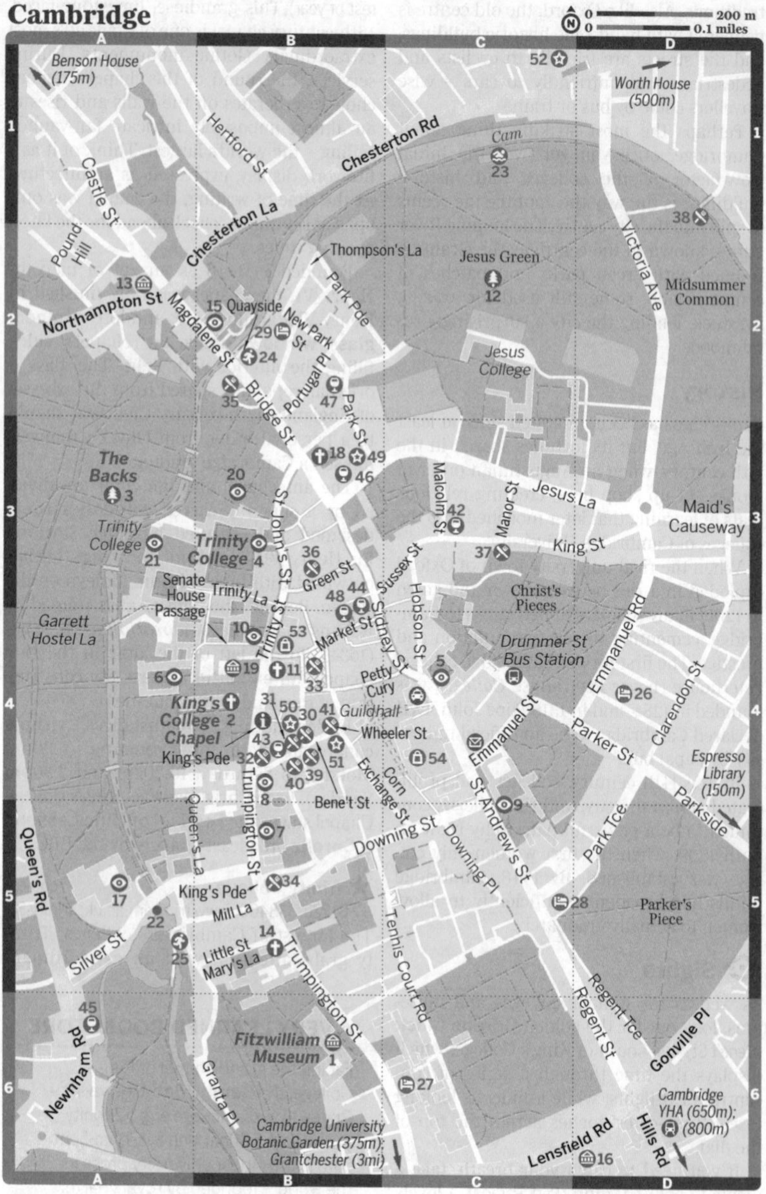

Tudor gateway, capped by a stern-looking statue of the college founder, Henry VIII. Beyond lies the vast Great Court flanked by cloisters and Gothic halls and spires. The famous, musty **Wren Library** contains more than 55,000 books published before 1820, including works by Shakespeare, St Jerome, Newton and Swift and an original *Winnie the Pooh* (both AA Milne and his son, Christopher Robin, were graduates).

Cambridge

As you enter Trinity through the part-gilded gate, take a closer look at the **statue** of the college's founder. The king holds a golden orb in his left hand, while his right grips not the original sceptre but a table leg, put there by student pranksters and never replaced.

The expansive **Great Court** is ringed by grand architecture. To the right of the entrance is a small tree, said to be a descendant of the apple tree made famous by Trinity alumnus Sir Isaac Newton. Other alumni include Francis Bacon, Lord Byron, Tennyson and HRH Prince Charles.

Across from the main gate is the college's Hogwarts-like **hall**, with its dramatic hammerbeam roof and lantern. Behind are the dignified cloisters of **Nevile's Court**, while to the right is the college's imposing 16th-century **chapel**.

★Fitzwilliam Museum MUSEUM
(www.fitzmuseum.cam.ac.uk; Trumpington St; by donation; ⏲10am-5pm Tue-Sat, from noon Sun) Fondly dubbed 'the Fitz' by locals, this colossal neoclassical treasure house was one of the first public art museums in Britain, built to house the fabulous collection that the seventh Viscount Fitzwilliam bequeathed to his old university. There are obvious parallels to the British Museum, and highlights include Roman, Egyptian and Cypriot grave goods, artworks by great masters and one of the country's finest collections of ancient, medieval and modern pottery.

The **lower galleries** are filled with priceless treasures spanning the ancient world; look for the Roman-era 'Swiss army knife', intricate suits of armour, and Roman coffins intricately carved with scenes of bacchanalian excess.

The **upper galleries** showcase works by Leonardo da Vinci, Titian, Rubens, the impressionists, Gainsborough, Constable, Rembrandt and Picasso.

Guided tours of the museum were suspended at the time of research – check ahead to see if they have resumed.

★The Backs PARK

The rear ends of the grand colleges along King's Pde spill onto the banks of the river in a long sweep of parks, gardens and even grazing pastures for livestock. Collectively known as the Backs, these genteel spaces are abuzz with student activity. While the colleges are closed, the Backs are best glimpsed from the pathways and bridges along the Granta or from the comfort of a rented or chauffeured punt. When the colleges reopen, visitors should be free to explore these spaces more fully.

If you're exploring from the water, check out the famous, fanciful **Bridge of Sighs** in the grounds of St John's College (p374), and the nearby **Kitchen Bridge**, designed by Christopher Wren. The oldest river crossing is at **Clare College** (01223-333200; www.clare.cam.ac.uk; Trinity Lane), built in 1639 and ornamented with decorative balls (one allegedly vandalised by its architect in protest at the measly fee he was paid).

Most curious of all is the flimsy-looking wooden **Mathematical Bridge** (visible from Silver St) that joins the two halves of Queens' College (p374). It was first built in 1749 using what were then world-leading engineering principles.

Gonville & Caius College COLLEGE

(01223-332400; www.cai.cam.ac.uk; Trinity St) Known locally as Caius (pronounced 'keys'), Gonville and Caius boasts three fascinating **gates** – known as Virtue, Humility and Honour – symbolising the progress of the good student. Down the alley beside the college, the **Porta Honoris** (an occult-looking, sundial-topped confection that pays a nod to the Treasury at Petra in Jordan) leads to the **Senate House** (Senate House Passage) and thus graduation.

The college was actually founded twice, first by a priest called Gonville, in 1348, and then again in 1557 by Dr Caius (a Latin-version of the name Keys), a brilliant physician who undermined his legacy by insisting in the statutes that the college admit no 'deaf, dumb, deformed, lame, chronic invalids, or Welshmen'.

Former students include Francis Crick (of DNA-discoverers Crick and Watson) and the late, great Stephen Hawking, who was a fellow here for more than 50 years.

Christ's College COLLEGE

(01223-334900; www.christs.cam.ac.uk; St Andrew's St) Christ's College has been educating the great and the good for 500 years and the gleaming **Great Gate** is emblazoned with heraldic carvings of Tudor roses, a portcullis and spotted Beaufort yale (mythical antelope-like creatures). Its founder, Lady Margaret Beaufort, mother of Henry VII, hovers above like a guiding spirit. A stout oak door leads into picturesque **First Court**, Cambridge's only circular front court.

Dedicated to alumnus Charles Darwin, the college gardens feature plant species brought back from his famous Galapagos voyage. The Second Court has a gate to the **Fellows' Garden** (open Monday to Friday only), which contains a mulberry tree under which 17th-century poet John Milton reputedly wrote *Lycidas*.

Magdalene College COLLEGE

(01223-332100; www.magd.cam.ac.uk; Magdalene St) A former Benedictine hostel, riverside Magdalene – properly pronounced 'Maud-lyn' – is home to the famous **Pepys Library** (01223-332115) FREE, housing 3000 books bequeathed by the mid-17th-century diarist to his old college. This idiosyncratic library covers everything from illuminated medieval manuscripts to the *Anthony Roll*, a 1540s depiction of the Royal Navy's ships.

Emmanuel College COLLEGE

(01223-334200; www.emma.cam.ac.uk; St Andrew's St) Looking rather unadorned from the outside, the 16th-century Emmanuel College ('Emma' to students) is famous for its exquisite **chapel** designed by Sir Christopher Wren. Seek out the plaque commemorating John Harvard, a scholar here in the 1630s, who later settled in New England and left his money to a certain Cambridge College in Massachusetts – now Harvard University.

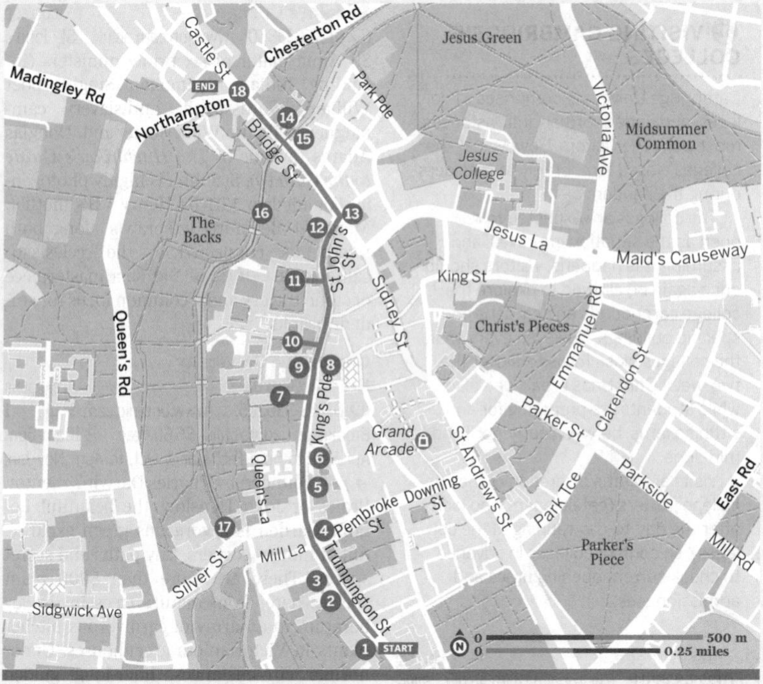

City Walk
The Colleges and the Backs

START FITZWILLIAM MUSEUM
END KETTLE'S YARD
LENGTH 3 MILES; FOUR HOURS

To start your exploration of this most learned of cities, brush up your knowledge at the ❶ **Fitzwilliam Museum** (p371) amid mummies and old masters. Follow Trumpington St north past ❷ **Peterhouse**, Cambridge's oldest college, and ❸ **Little St Mary's** (p375), one of the city's oldest churches. Pause for a Chelsea bun break at ❹ **Fitzbillies** (p377), the city's favourite bakery, then continue north past ❺ **Corpus Christi College** (p374), former stomping ground of Christopher Marlowe, and note the Harry Potter-esque ❻ **Corpus Clock** (p369) on the corner. Just beyond lies ❼ **King's College Chapel** (p369), arguably the crown and sceptre in Cambridge's architectural crown jewels.

Cross the road to ❽ **Great St Mary's Church** (p375), where a steep climb up the tower will deliver Cambridge's most spectacular views. Continue past the neoclassical ❾ **Senate House** and nip right into Senate House Passage to view the occult-looking Porta Honoris, the most impressive of the three gateways to ❿ **Gonville & Caius College**. Next comes ⓫ **Trinity College** (p369); if it's open, duck through the Tudor gateway to view the extraordinary collection of tomes in the Wren Library. Continue along St John's St past the arms-topped gatehouse of ⓬ **St John's College** (p374) to reach the ⓭ **Round Church** (p374), an enigmatic, Templar relic.

Follow Bridge St and Magdalene St towards ⓮ **Magdalene College** and rent a punt from ⓯ **Scudamore's** (p375) at Quayside for a behind-the-scenes tour of the college Backs (look out for the ecclesiastical-looking ⓰ **Bridge of Sighs** and the skeletal timbers of the ⓱ **Mathematical Bridge**). Return your punt to Quayside and end as you started, surrounded by artworks, in the light-filled spaces of ⓲ **Kettle's Yard** (p374).

VISITING CAMBRIDGE'S COLLEGES

Cambridge University comprises 31 colleges, and under normal circumstances, most welcome visitors. However, all the colleges closed temporarily to outsiders during the pandemic.

The colleges are expected to reopen as the situation improves, and assuming this happens, visitors should once again be allowed to explore the college compounds and gardens and specific buildings. However, every year, the colleges close to visitors over the two-week Christmas break, and also while students are preparing for and sitting exams, between early April and mid-June.

Visits are at the discretion of the college porters (gatekeepers who look after the day-to-day running of the colleges), so contact colleges in advance to check current opening times and admission fees.

Queens' College COLLEGE

(☎01223-335511; www.queens.cam.ac.uk; Silver St) Genteel 15th-century Queens' College sits elegantly astride the river; the two halves of the college are connected by the precarious-looking **Mathematical Bridge**, best viewed from the Backs (p372). Highlights include two elegant medieval courtyards and the beautiful half-timbered **President's Lodge.** Dutch scholar and reformer Desiderius Erasmus, whose name was later taken for the European student exchange program, studied here from 1510 to 1514.

Corpus Christi College COLLEGE

(☎01223-338000; www.corpus.cam.ac.uk; King's Pde) Graceful Corpus Christi was founded in 1352, a heritage reflected in its venerable buildings and monastic atmosphere. Within the medieval **Old Court**, note the fascinating sundial and plaque to past student Christopher Marlowe (1564–93), author of *Doctor Faustus* and *Tamburlaine*. The less dramatic **New Court** (a mere 200 years old) leads to the **Parker Library**, which holds the world's finest collection of Anglo-Saxon manuscripts (open only to visitors on guided city tours).

St John's College COLLEGE

(☎01223-33860; www.joh.cam.ac.uk; St John's St) Alma mater of six prime ministers (including India's Manmohan Singh), poet William Wordsworth, anti-slavery campaigner William Wilberforce and Douglas Adams (author of *The Hitchhiker's Guide to the Galaxy*), St John's is highly photogenic. Founded in 1511 by Henry VII's mother, Margaret Beaufort, it sprawls along both riverbanks, connected by the ecclesiastical-looking **Bridge of Sighs**, a masterpiece of stone tracery and a common focus for student pranks.

Cambridge University Botanic Garden GARDENS

(☎01223-336265; www.botanic.cam.ac.uk; 1 Brookside; adult/child £6.60/free; ⊙10am-6pm Apr-Sep, to 5pm Feb, Mar & Oct, to 4pm Nov-Jan;) Founded by Charles Darwin's mentor, Professor John Henslow, the beautiful Botanic Garden is a gorgeous green expanse, full of hidden corners, tiny paths and secret spaces. There are more than 8000 plant species here, from mature trees in the arboretum to an army of carnivorous pitcher plants in Victorian-era greenhouses. Under normal circumstances, hour-long guided tours (free) run from May through to September; check to see if they've resumed.

The gardens are 1200m south of the city centre, accessible from either Trumpington Rd or Hills Rd.

Kettle's Yard GALLERY

(☎01223-748100; www.kettlesyard.co.uk; Castle St; ⊙11am-5pm Wed-Sun) FREE If you've ever wondered what art gallery curators do at home, pop into Kettle's Yard, a living art gallery created by HS 'Jim' Ede, a former curator at the Tate Gallery in London. A lifetime's collection of artworks and found objects is displayed inside a line of elegantly converted cottages, including works by Miró, Henry Moore and lesser-known artists such as WWI-era sculptor Henri Gaudier-Brzeska and primitive nautical artist Alfred Wallis.

A modern annexe showcases some quirky contemporary exhibitions.

Round Church CHURCH

(☎01223-311602; www.roundchurchcambridge.org; Bridge St; £3.50; ⊙10am-4.30pm Fri & Sat, from 12.30pm Sun) Looking like a prime setting for a Dan Brown novel, Cambridge's atmospheric Round Church is one of only four round medieval churches in England. It was built by the mysterious Knights Templar in 1130, making it older than the university, and the unusual circular knave is ringed by chunky Norman pillars. Guided walks explore the church and local area, leaving on Saturday and Sunday at 2.15pm.

Great St Mary's Church CHURCH

(☎ 01223-747273; www.gsm.cam.ac.uk; Senate House Hill; tower per person/family £6/16; ⏱ 11am-5pm Tue-Sun) FREE The foundations of Cambridge's sublime university church date from 1010, but it burnt to the ground in the 1290s, so most of what you can see today comes from a 1351 reconstruction and a grand Gothic remodelling from 1478 to 1519. The melody of its chiming clock was copied for the chimes of Big Ben in London.

The tower was added in 1690; buy a ticket to climb it for truly awe-inspiring views over Cambridge's dreaming spires. Check out the 3D model outside before you head up so you know what you're looking at.

Little St Mary's Church CHURCH

(☎ 01223-366202; www.lsm.org.uk; Trumpington St; ⏱ 8am-6pm) FREE This small, modest-looking church was formerly St Peter's-without-Trumpington-Gate, giving nearby Peterhouse its name. Inside is a memorial to student Godfrey Washington, great-uncle of George. His family coat of arms was the stars and stripes, reputedly the inspiration for the US flag. Check ahead to see if it is admitting visitors.

Polar Museum MUSEUM

(☎ 01223-336540; www.spri.cam.ac.uk/museum; Lensfield Rd) FREE In this compelling university museum, the trials, victories and tragic mistakes of such great Polar explorers as Roald Amundsen, Ernest Shackleton and Captain Scott are powerfully evoked, using paintings, photographs, equipment, maps, journals and even last messages left for loved ones. The museum was temporarily closed in 2020 – check ahead for the latest opening times.

Activities

Scudamore's Punting BOATING

(☎ 01223-359750; www.scudamores.com; Mill Lane; chauffeured punt trips per bench/boat from £70/120, 6-person punt hire from £51; ⏱ 10am-7pm Mon-Fri, to 8pm Sat & Sun) At this long-established operator, you can hire punts to pole yourself along the Granta, or take chauffeured trips to Granchester and the Backs. Prices are flexible and staff cruise the jetty offering discounts. Note that you can hire just a row of seats to reduce rates.

It has a second hire station north of the centre at Quayside.

Cambridge Chauffeur Punts BOATING

(☎ 01223-354164; www.punting-in-cambridge.co.uk; Silver St Bridge; chauffeured punts from adult/child £20/12 per hour, 6-person self-punt per hour £30; ⏱ 9am-8pm Jun & Aug, 10am-dusk Apr, May, Sep & Oct) Runs regular chauffeured punting tours of the Backs and to Granchester; also offers self-hire.

Jesus Green Lido SWIMMING

(☎ 01223-302579; www.better.org.uk; Jesus Green; adult/child £5/2.50; ⏱ 7am-7pm Mon-Fri, 10am-6pm Sat & Sun May-Sep) This slender, 1920s open-air swimming pool near the river in Jesus Green is unheated, but hugely popular, with sunbathers as well as swimmers.

Tours

With the (hopefully temporary) closure of the tourist office, **walking tours** run by official Blue Badge and Green Badge guides run from beside the Guildhall on Peas Hill at 11am and 1.30pm (one hour tour adult/child £10/5), taking in the main sights.

GREAT GRADUATES

The honour roll of famous Cambridge students and academics is an international who's who of high achievers. This is the town where Newton refined his theory of gravity, where Whipple invented the jet engine, where Stephen Hawking wrote *A Brief History of Time*, where Crick and Watson (relying heavily on the work of Rosalind Franklin, also a scientist at Cambridge) discovered DNA.

Alongside Britain's favourite comedians – everyone from Rowan Atkinson to the Monty Python team found an audience thanks to the university's Footlights Dramatic Club – you'll find 98 Nobel Prize winners (more than any other institution in the world), 13 British prime ministers, nine archbishops of Canterbury, plus an immense number of scientists, poets and authors.

LOCAL KNOWLEDGE

PRANKSTERS & NIGHT CLIMBERS

In a city of intellectual high achievement, it shouldn't be entirely surprising to find students turning their great minds to pranks and mischief. The most impressive prank ever to take place in Cambridge – lifting an Austin Seven van on to the roof of the landmark Senate House (p372) in 1958 – involved a great deal of planning from four Mechanical Sciences students; copycats later suspended another Austin Seven from the ornate Bridge of Sighs (p374).

King's College has long been a target of 'night climbers'. A Trinity College student, Geoffrey Winthrop Young, wrote the definitive *Roof Climber's Guide to Trinity* back in 1900. Cast an eye upwards towards the nearby pinnacles of King's College Chapel (p369) and you'll often spot out-of-place objects – anything from traffic cones to Santa hats.

Finally, there's the Cubes (Cambridge University Breaking and Entering Society): its objective is to access places members shouldn't be and leave distinctive calling cards – the most famous being the wooden mallard in the rafters of Trinity's Great Hall.

Festivals & Events

Bumps SPORTS
(www.cucbc.org/bumps; Feb & Jun) Traditional rowing races along the Cam (or the Granta, as the Cambridge stretch is called), in which college boat clubs compete to 'bump' the crew in front.

Beer Festival BEER
(www.cambridgebeerfestival.com; May) Hugely popular five-day beer and cider extravaganza on Jesus Green, featuring brews from all over the country.

Folk Festival MUSIC
(www.cambridgefolkfestival.co.uk; late Jul-early Aug) This acclaimed four-day festival pushes the envelope of what is usually classified as folk music. It's hosted by Cherry Hinton Hall, 4 miles southeast of the city centre.

Sleeping

Cambridge YHA HOSTEL £
(0345-371 9728; www.yha.org.uk; 97 Tenison Rd; r £35-49; @ wi-fi) A smart, friendly and deservedly popular hostel with compact rooms (and dorms, but these were closed during the pandemic) and good facilities. Handily, it's very near the train station.

Rosa's B&B £
(01223-512596; www.rosasbedandbreakfast.co.uk; 53 Roseford Rd; s £65; P wi-fi; bus 8) Handy for solo travellers: a friendly, family-run B&B with three bright, snug singles, decorated in calming tones. It's 2 miles north of the city centre; bus 8 runs nearby.

Worth House B&B ££
(01223-316074; www.worth-house.co.uk; 152 Chesterton Rd; s/d/tr from £100/110/150; P wi-fi) The welcome is warm and the rooms are delightful at this friendly, upbeat B&B. In the rooms, cool greys and whites meet flashes of colour, bathrooms have a hint of glam and the breakfast is a feast.

Benson House B&B ££
(01223-311594; www.bensonhouse.co.uk; 24 Huntingdon Rd; s/d from £80/125; P wi-fi) Little things lift Benson a cut above the average B&B – think real feather pillows, tasteful textiles, tea served from Royal Doulton china and award-winning breakfasts.

★**University Arms Hotel** LUXURY HOTEL £££
(01223-606066; www.universityarms.com; Regent St; r from £240) This extravagant but refined hotel looks as old as the Cambridge colleges, but the grand frontage is actually a skilful reconstruction of a historic wing that was demolished to build a modern eyesore in the 1960s. Inside, the hotel oozes class, and the best rooms have fabulous bathrooms with free-standing bathtubs and views over Parker's Piece common.

★**Varsity Hotel** BOUTIQUE HOTEL £££
(01223-306030; www.thevarsityhotel.co.uk; Thompson's Lane; d £190-325; air-con @ wi-fi) Modernist Varsity soars above the old part of Cambridge, topped by a terrace (p378) with eye-popping views. The 44 sleek rooms come with designer flourishes such as parquet floors, roll-top baths and floor-to-ceiling windows, plus espresso machines, smartphone docks and other hip tech – an elegant experience all round.

★ Duke House B&B £££
(☎01223-314773; www.dukehousecambridge.co.uk; 1 Victoria St; apt from £110, r from £140; P 📶) Set in the house owned by the Duke of Gloucester when he was a student at Magdalene College, this beautifully styled B&B has gleaming white rooms with elegant armchairs and floral chandeliers, a gorgeous pale blue lounge and a roof terrace. It's just outside the hubbub near Christ's Pieces.

Hotel du Vin BOUTIQUE HOTEL £££
(☎01223-928991; www.hotelduvin.com; 15-19 Trumpington St; d/ste from £150/240; @ 📶) This maze-like luxe hotel near the 'Fitz' oozes history, as well it should – it's spread over five Georgian mansions formerly owned by the University of Cambridge. Reached via narrow corridors, the atmospheric rooms have free-standing roll-top baths, monsoon showers and floating-on-air beds. Other perks include a cosy cellar bar and a cool bistro (mains £16 to £23).

Eating

For cheap eats, join the students cruising the line of Asian and Middle Eastern restaurants east of the centre on **Mill Road**, or try the street food in the central **market** (Market Hill; ⏰10am-4pm Mon-Sat).

Fitzbillies CAFE £
(www.fitzbillies.com; 52 Trumpington St; mains £5-15; ⏰8.30am-5pm Mon-Fri, 9am-5.30pm Sat & Sun) Cambridge's oldest bakery has a soft, doughy place in the hearts of generations of students. Its stock-in-trade is sticky Chelsea buns and cream teas (available to eat in or beautifully boxed to take away), but it also serves upmarket sandwiches, bacon rolls, English breakfasts and salads.

There's a smaller **branch** (www.fitzbillies.com; 36 Bridge St; light mains £5-15; ⏰8.30am-5pm Mon-Fri, 9am-6pm Sat & Sun) on Bridge St.

Aromi ITALIAN £
(☎01223-300117; www.aromi.co.uk; 1 Bene't St; mains from £5; ⏰9am-7pm Sun-Thu, to 9pm Fri & Sat; 🖊) A pocket-sized bakery cafe with downstairs seating and a ground-floor counter stacked with delectable sourdough sandwiches and Sicilian pizzas, topped with parma ham, rucola and the like, and sold by the slice.

Aromi has another **cafe** (www.aromi.co.uk; Peas Hill; snacks from £5; ⏰11am-9pm) and gelateria (with great ice cream) just a few doors down on Peas Hill.

Espresso Library CAFE £
(☎01223-367333; www.espressolibrary.com; 210 East Rd; mains £6-15; ⏰8am-4pm; 📶🖊) Customers with laptops at almost every table send a signal that this industrial-chic cafe is a student favourite. Thank the coffee, the cyclist-friendly attitude, and the wholesome food – sourdough sandwiches, soups, frittata and shaksuka.

Locker CAFE £
(www.thelockercafe.co.uk; 54 King St; snacks £3.50-7.50; ⏰8.30am-5.30pm Mon-Fri, from 9.30am Sat, 10am-4pm Sun; 📶🖊) 🌿 Fair-trade coffee, salmon bagels, and avocados (and other things) smashed on sourdough toast lift this artsy, wholesome cafe above the herd. Its toasties have a faithful student following.

It's also home to occasional gigs and photography displays.

Pint Shop MODERN BRITISH ££
(☎01223-981070; www.pintshop.co.uk; 10 Peas Hill; 2/3 courses £22/26; ⏰noon-9pm Mon-Wed, to 10pm Thu-Sat, to 6pm Sun) Popular Pint Shop is part craft-beer sampling house, part hearty kitchen. Wash down tasty pub grub (charred salmon, burgers, flatbread kebabs) with artisan ciders, ales and fruit beers (including coconut, passionfruit and mango).

Smokeworks BARBECUE ££
(☎01223-365385; www.smokeworks.co.uk; 2 Free School Lane; mains £7.50-19.50; ⏰noon-8pm Mon & Tue, to 9pm Wed-Sat, to 5pm Sun; 📶) This dark, industrial-looking dining room draws a young, hip crowd of carnivores with melt-in-your-mouth rib racks, wings and wonderfully smoky pulled pork. For drinks, try the house beers or salted-caramel milkshakes in glasses the size of your head.

TIME FOR TEA

Packed afternoon teas – sandwiches, scones, pastries, buns, and a hint of the 1920s – are all the rage in Cambridge. Pick your park and grab a gorgeously boxed afternoon tea to go from **Harriet's Cafe Tearooms** (www.harrietscafetearooms.co.uk; 16-17 Green St; cakes & sandwiches from £3, afternoon tea from £12.95; ⏰10am-3.30pm Mon-Fri, 9.30am-4.30pm Sat, 10.30am-3.30pm Sun) or Fitzbillies, who also serve similarly packaged Chelsea buns.

WORTH A TRIP

IMPERIAL WAR MUSEUM

Plane-spotters will be in aviation heaven at the **Imperial War Museum** (01223-835000; www.iwm.org.uk; Duxford; adult/child including donation £19.80/9.90; 10am-6pm; P), Europe's biggest aircraft museum, with around 200 vintage aircraft – many veterans of WWI and WWII – spread across a series of enormous hangars. You'll see everything from dive bombers to biplanes, Hurricanes and the Concorde, which was moved here after ending service in 2003. The awe-inspiring **American Air Museum** hangar pays homage to US WWII servicemen and planes.

Cambridge Chop House BRITISH ££
(01223-359506; www.cambscuisine.com/cambridge-chop-house; 1 King's Pde; mains £17-27; 11.30am-8.30pm Mon-Fri, to 9pm Fri & Sat, to 5pm Sun) The window seats here look right onto King's College and the food is pure English establishment: hearty steaks, grilled chops, breaded coley, roast meats and grilled lobster. Schedule a long walk afterwards to burn off the calories.

Sticks'n'Sushi SUSHI ££
(01223-907900; www.sticksnsushi.com; 2 Wheeler St; mains £10-25; noon-9pm Mon-Thu, to 10pm Fri & Sat) Lovely soy-saucy smells linger around the entrance to this Asian restaurant. Although part of a Danish-Japanese chain, it's chic and vaguely New York-ey; the menu runs from sushi and sashimi bites to meaty skewers.

★**Midsummer House** MODERN BRITISH £££
(01223-369299; www.midsummerhouse.co.uk; Midsummer Common; set lunch/tasting menu £115/230; 10am-5pm Wed-Sat) A lone house in parkland beside the Granta, the region's top table shows off the culinary creativity of chef Daniel Clifford, recipient of two Michelin stars. Set menus, which include champagne and hot infusions or coffee, might include such delights as salted beetroot with venison tartare and buttermilk poached Cornish cod with champagne beurre blanc.

Drinking & Nightlife

★**Roof Terrace** BAR
(01223-306030; www.thevarsityhotel.co.uk; Varsity Hotel, Thompson's Lane; 2pm-10pm Mon-Thu, from noon Fri & Sat) The rooftop terrace at the Varsity Hotel (p376) is an achingly cool eyrie perched high above the old town, and people flood here every afternoon for sundowners looking out over the rooftops. Smart dress recommended.

★**Cambridge Brew House** MICROBREWERY
(01223-855185; www.thecambridgebrewhouse.com; 1 King St; 4-10pm Mon-Fri, noon-11pm Sat, noon-10pm Sun) Order a pint here and there's a good chance it'll have been brewed in the gleaming vats beside the bar. Add a buzzy vibe, eclectic upcycled decor, dirty burgers and British tapas (mains from £10) and you have the kind of pub you wish was just down your road.

Eagle PUB
(01223-505020; www.eagle-cambridge.co.uk; Bene't St; 11am-11pm Mon-Thu, to midnight Fri & Sat, to 10.30pm Sun;) Cambridge's most famous pub has loosened the tongues of many an illustrious academic, among them Nobel Prize–winning scientists Crick and Watson, who discussed their research into DNA here. The interior is 15th-century, wood-panelled and rambling; note the WWII airmen's signatures on the ceiling.

Hidden Rooms COCKTAIL BAR
(01223-514777; www.hiddenrooms.co.uk; 7b Jesus Lane; 6.30-10pm Fri & Sat) Hard to find – the name is no accident – this is a cocktail bar for aficionados of the craft. It's under Pizza Express, but the moody leather booths feel like stepping into a David Lynch movie. Reserve ahead.

Ta Bouche COCKTAIL BAR
(www.tabouche.co.uk; 10-15 Market Passage; 9.30am-1am Mon-Thu, to 2am Fri & Sat, 10am-midnight Sun) A carnival-coloured, fun-filled cocktail bar that pulls in a crowd on any going-out night, with good-value specials that appeal to student pocketbooks. It serves globe-trotting street food by day, cocktails by night.

Maypole PUB
(01223-352999; www.maypolefreehouse.co.uk; 20a Portugal Pl; noon-2pm & 5-11pm Tue-Thu, noon-11pm Fri & Sat, noon-3pm Sun) A dozen pumps dispensing real ale, artisan gin, a roomy beer garden and a friendly, unreconstructed vibe make this red-brick pub a student favourite. There's hearty, homemade Italian food.

Granta PUB
(☎01223-505016; 14 Newnham Rd; ⏰11am-11pm Sun-Thu, to 11.30pm Fri & Sat) The exterior of this picturesque waterside pub, overhanging a pretty mill pond, may look familiar from its cameos in TV dramas. With its snug deck, riverside terrace and punts moored up alongside, it's an atmospheric spot to sit and watch the world drift by.

Fez CLUB
(☎0203-475 2176; www.cambridgefez.com; 15 Market Passage; ⏰from 10pm Tue-Sun) Moroccan-themed Fez serves up an international menu of hip hop, dancehall, R&B, techno, funk, indie, house and garage; in normal circumstances, it hosts regular slots from top-name DJs.

☆ Entertainment

Live entertainment ground to a halt during the pandemic, but the following venues are expected to reopen in 2021.

ADC THEATRE
(☎01223-300085; www.adctheatre.com; Park St) This famous student-run theatre is home to the university's Footlights comedy troupe, whose past members include Emma Thompson, Rowan Atkinson and Stephen Fry.

Cambridge Arts Theatre THEATRE
(☎01223-503333; www.cambridgeartstheatre.com; 6 St Edward's Passage) Cambridge's biggest bona-fide theatre hosts everything from highbrow drama and dance, to panto and shows fresh from London's West End.

Corn Exchange PERFORMING ARTS
(☎01223-357851; www.cornex.co.uk; Wheeler St) Venue attracting the top names, from pop and rock to comedy.

Junction PERFORMING ARTS
(☎01223-511511; www.junction.co.uk; Clifton Way) Theatre, dance, comedy, club nights and an eclectic line-up of live bands; close to the railway station.

Portland Arms LIVE MUSIC
(☎01223-357268; www.theportlandarms.co.uk; 129 Chesterton Rd; ⏰noon-3pm & 4.30-10pm Tue-Thu, to 11pm Fri & Sat, noon-5pm Sun) A popular student haunt, the 200-capacity Portland is the best spot in town to catch a gig from up-and-coming Cambridge bands.

ℹ Information

Visit Cambridge (www.visitcambridge.org) closed during the pandemic, along with the tourist office in the Guildhall on Peas Hill. It's likely to reopen, but in the meantime, brochures on local attractions can be picked up at cafes, tourist sights and the train station.

If you need to leave a bag for the day, try **Campkins Cameras** (☎01223-368087; www.campkinscameras.com; 12a King's Parade; per bag £5; ⏰9am-5pm Mon-Sat, 11am-4pm Sun) opposite King's College.

ℹ Getting There & Away

BUS

National Express buses run from London Victoria (from £19, 12 daily, 2½ hours), dropping you at Parkside just east of Cambridge's city centre.

Take bus 9/9X from the Drummer St bus station for Ely (£5, hourly, one hour). All-day Dayrider tickets (£7) cover trips as far afield as Ely, King's Lynn and Bury St Edmunds.

CAR

Cambridge's centre is largely pedestrianised and savvy travellers park and walk (or cycle). All the car parks tend to fill up fast in the morning; the underground parking under the **Grand Arcade** (www.grandarcade.co.uk; Downing St;

OFF THE BEATEN TRACK

GRANTCHESTER

With its thatched cottages, flower-filled gardens, breezy meadows and classic cream teas, Grantchester is the picture-postcard image of England. Walk, punt or cycle here from central Cambridge, then flop into a deckchair under a leafy apple tree and wolf down cakes or light lunches at the lovely **Orchard Tea Garden** (☎01223-840230; www.theorchardteagarden.co.uk; 47 Mill Way; lunch mains £6-10; ⏰9am-6pm Apr-Oct, to 4pm Wed-Sun Nov-Mar), a favourite haunt of the Bloomsbury Group who came to camp, picnic, swim and push back social boundaries. If you don't feel up to the walk or punt, bus 18 runs here from Cambridge's Drummer St bus station (£2.80, 15 minutes, hourly Monday to Saturday).

⏲9am-7pm Mon-Sat, 10am-5pm Sun) mall is conveniently central.

Circling the city on major road routes are five **Park & Ride car parks** (www.cambridgepark andride.info). Parking is currently free for up to 18 hours but you'll pay £3 return for a bus to the centre (services run every 10 to 15 minutes – check the schedule on arrival).

TRAIN

The train station is 1.5 miles southeast of the centre (easily accessible by bus). Trains zip very regularly to London (from £19.90, one hour), Ely (£4.70, 15 minutes, half-hourly), King's Lynn (£10.70, one hour, hourly), Stansted Airport (£11.40, 30 minutes to one hour, every 20 minutes) and other local hubs.

Getting Around

BICYCLE

Cambridge is incredibly bike-friendly; recommended bicycle-hire outfits include:

S&G Cycles (☎01223-311134; 15 Laundress Lane; per hour/day from £7/18; ⏲9am-4pm Mon-Sat, from 11am Sun) A simple operation near the Silver St bridge.

Rutland Cycling (☎0330-555 0080; www.rutlandcycling.com; Corn Exchange St; per half-day/day from £12/18; ⏲8am-5pm Mon-Fri, 9am-5pm Sat, 10am-4pm Sun) In the heart of town at the Grand Arcade shopping centre. There's a branch (☎01223-352728; www.rutlandcycling.com; 156 Great Northern Rd) just off Station Rd by the train station.

BUS

Local buses zip around town from the main Drummer St bus station (or nearby roads). Most services operate from around 6am until around 11pm, but there are few buses on Sundays.

All-day Dayrider bus tickets (£4.50) cover 24 hours of unlimited bus travel around Cambridge. Take bus 18 for Granchester (£2.80, hourly, 15 minutes). Buses C1, C3 and C7 stop at the train station (£1 to £2.20, 30 minutes).

TAXI

If you don't Uber, call local firm **Panther Taxi** (☎01223-715715; www.panthertaxis.co.uk).

Ely

☎01353 / POP 20,100

Sleepy Ely (*ee-lee*) feels like a gentle backwater, but the city gave English history one of its greatest heroes – or villains, depending on who you speak to – Oliver Cromwell. Ely's once-powerful status is obvious from its imposing Georgian town houses and the soaring cathedral that dominates the city centre.

The name Ely comes from the eels that once inhabited the surrounding Fens, but the city built its fortunes on the production of opium, with high-class ladies holding 'poppy parties' and families calming their children with highly effective 'poppy tea'.

Sights

The engaging **Ely Museum** (www.elymuseum.org.uk), in the old town jail on Market St, is closed for renovations until 2021.

★Ely Cathedral CATHEDRAL

(☎01353-667735; www.elycathedral.org; The Gallery; adult/child £8/free; ⏲10am-4pm Mon-Sat, 1-3.30pm Sun) Ely's soaring Gothic Cathedral's was dubbed the 'Ship of the Fens' because its towering spire was visible for miles across the vast, flat sweep of Cambridgeshire. It's an eye-catching structure, best known for the fascinating 14th-century **Lady Chapel**, which has been preserved much as it was at the end of the English Civil War, after iconoclasts had hacked and defiled most of its delicate statues.

Inside, cast your eyes upwards to admire the striking **Octagon**, which transfers the weight of the tower onto eight monumental columns. There's some stunning stained glass (look out for the masons hard at work raising the Tower of Babel), and the attached **Stained Glass Museum** (☎01353-660347; www.stainedglassmuseum.com; adult/child £4.50/free; ⏲10.30am-5pm Mon-Sat, 12.30-4.30pm Sun) has panels collected from across Europe.

Tours of the cathedral and tower were suspended at the time of writing, but should resume, so check ahead. Evensong shows off the building's impressive acoustics; check to see if visitors are able to attend.

Oliver Cromwell's House MUSEUM

(☎01353-662062; www.olivercromwellshouse.co.uk; 29 St Mary's St; adult/child £5.20/3.50; ⏲10am-5pm Apr-Oct, 11am-4pm Nov-Mar) England's premier Puritan lived in this attractive, half-timbered house with his family from 1636 to 1647, when he was the local tithe collector, before embarking on his momentous campaign to separate the king from his throne (and head) and institute a parliamentary republic. Inside are thought-provoking audiovisual displays on Cromwell's life and times (pick up a handset as you enter).

Sleeping

★Peacocks B&B ££

(☎07900 666161; www.peacockstearoom.co.uk; 65 Waterside; s/d from £110/135; 📶) Walk into the roomy suites in this wisteria-covered house near the quay and you'll feel instantly at home. In the Cottage Suite, floral Laura Ashley wallpaper sets a late Victorian mood; in the Brewery Suite, vintage books, gilt mirrors and antiques conjure up a Victorian gentlemen's club.

Its award-winning **cafe** (☎01353-661100; snacks from £8, cream teas £9-19; ⏲10.30am-5pm Wed-Sun, plus Tue Jul-Aug) serves cream teas, soups, salads, sandwiches and more substantial mains.

Riverside B&B ££

(☎01353-661677; www.riversideinn-ely.co.uk; 8 Annesdale; s £59-79, d £80-169; P📶) This Georgian guesthouse on Ely's quay looks outwardly traditional, but inside, rooms are full of rich reds and golds and Regency stripes. It's all very grand, and the glam finish extends to the bathrooms. Rooms at the front look towards the houseboats bobbing about on the River Great Ouse.

Eating

★The Almonry CAFE £

(☎01353-666360; off High St; cream tea £6, light meals from £7; ⏲9am-4pm Mon-Sat, from 11am Sun) This elegant tearoom and restaurant sits in neatly pruned gardens at the back of the cathedral compound, serving cream teas, sandwiches and a few more ambitious mains – chicken breast stuffed with brie and asparagus, squash and chickpea burgers and the like. The cathedral views are sublime.

Old Fire Engine House BRITISH ££

(☎01353-662582; www.theoldfireenginehouse.co.uk; 25 St Mary's St; lunch 2/3 courses £18/24, mains £17; ⏲10.30am-8.30pm Mon-Sat, 12.15-2pm Sun; ✎) Eating in this elegant town house restaurant is like stepping into an East Anglian farmhouse kitchen. It's all about seasonal and local produce, so dishes might include local lamb shoulder with mint and lemon, plum crumble and mitoon of pork (a coarse local pâté).

Information

Tourist Office (☎01353-662062; www.visitely.org.uk; 29 St Mary's St; ⏲10am-5pm Apr-Oct, 11am-4pm Nov-Mar) In Oliver Cromwell's House; ask about local walks.

Getting There & Away

You can walk to Ely from Cambridge along the 17-mile riverside Fen Rivers Way. The 9/9X bus runs here from Cambridge (£5, hourly, one hour). Rail connections include:

Cambridge (£4.70, 20 minutes, up to four per hour)

King's Lynn (£7.50, 30 minutes, one or two per hour)

Norwich (£18.50, one hour, every 30 minutes)

ESSEX

The inhabitants of Essex have put up with years of jokes from the rest of England, but you'll see through the reality show stereotypes if you venture up here in person. The south of the county may feel like an extension of London's East End, but head into the countryside and you'll find charming villages, dripping with history, and landscapes that have changed little since Constable painted them in the early 19th century.

Colchester

☎01206 / POP 194,706

Dominated by a sturdy Norman castle and extensive Roman walls, Colchester is Britain's oldest recorded town, dating from the 5th century BCE. In 43 CE the Romans came, saw and conquered, and constructed Camulodunum, which was razed by Boudica just 17 years later. The thriving market town that emerged from the ruins later saw extensive action in the Norman Conquest, the Reformation and the English Civil War.

Sights

The best of the city's half-timbered houses are clustered together in the Tudor-era Dutch Quarter, just north of High St, founded by Flemish weavers in the 16th century. Along gorgeous **Maidenburgh Street**, you can see glimpses of a Roman theatre through the windows of houses built over the ruins.

★Colchester Castle CASTLE

(☎01206-282939; https://colchester.cimuseums.org.uk; Castle Park; adult/child £10/5.95; ⏲10am-5pm Mon-Sat, from 11am Sun) Built in 1076 on the foundations of the Roman Temple of Claudius, England's largest surviving Norman keep is bigger than the White Tower in London. Over the centuries it's been a royal residence, a prison and home to the Witchfinder General. Among the treasures inside, look out for the Roman-era Colchester Vase, decorated with scenes of hunting and gladiatorial combat, and the Fenwick Treasure, a horde of Roman jewels hidden during Boudica's siege.

firstsite ARTS CENTRE
(☎01206-713700; https://firstsite.uk; Lewis Gardens; ⏰10am-5pm; 🚻) FREE This shiny, curved, glass-and-copper arts centre rises above a section of the Roman Walls; inside are art spaces hosting cutting-edge shows by visiting big names, plus a cinema, a calm cafe, and a restored Roman mosaic visible through a glass floor.

Hollytrees Museum MUSEUM
(☎01206-282920; https://colchester.cimuseums.org.uk; Castle Park; ⏰10am-5pm Mon-Sat) FREE In this Georgian town house by the park, toys, costumes, ornaments and clocks conjure up the domestic life of the wealthy original owners and their servants. Look for the shipwright's baby carriage in the shape of a boat, and the intricate, envy-inducing doll's house.

Sleeping & Eating

For a gourmet picnic in Castle Park, pick up ingredients at **H Gunton Ltd** (www.guntons.co.uk; 81-83 Crouch St; ⏰9am-2pm Mon-Fri, to 4pm Sat), a gorgeous deli that has hardly changed since it opened in 1936.

Four Sevens B&B ££
(☎01206-546093; www.foursevens.co.uk; 28 Inglis Rd; r with/without bathroom from £75/65; 🅿📶) This far-from-frilly B&B is housed in a graceful Victorian house, a mile southwest of the centre (just off the B1022 to Maldon). It's set on a genteel residential street and the spacious, modern rooms get plenty of light.

North Hill HOTEL ££
(☎01206-574001; www.northhillhotel.com; 51 North Hill; s/d from £85/95; 📶) A sleek contemporary hotel with loads of calm common spaces, spread across three historic buildings on the hill leading down to North Station. Ask for a room in the cottage-style back building for wonky beams and exposed red brick alongside modern creature comforts.

The hotel's excellent **Green Room** restaurant (open noon to 2pm and 6pm to 9pm Monday to Saturday and noon to 5pm Sunday) serves tasty comfort-food with a contemporary twist – so treats such as confit duck leg with radish and kohlrabi (mains £11 to £21).

Information

Tourist Office (☎01206-282920; www.visitcolchester.com; Castle Park; ⏰10am-5pm Mon-Sat) Inside the Hollytrees Museum.

Getting There & Away

Trains run to London Liverpool St (£25, one hour, every 15 minutes); the station is a 20-minute walk north of the centre, or take bus 62 (£1.90, 10 minutes, every 15 minutes).

Direct National Express buses go to and from London Victoria (from £6.60, three hours, four daily). Regional buses leave from the stand on Osborne St.

Dedham Vale

John Constable's romantic visions of meandering hedgerows and babbling brooks were inspired by and painted in this serene corner of the country. The artist was born in East Bergholt in 1776 and painted his most famous work, *The Hay Wain,* nearby at Flatford Mill in 1821. Today, the pretty village of Dedham is the best base for exploring Constable Country – on foot, by bike, or by rowboat along the River Stour.

Sights & Activities

The best way to get from Dedham to Flatford is to follow the river through pretty water meadows fringed by weeping willows. It's a 1½-mile walk, or you can rent rowboats in Dedham at the **Boathouse Restaurant** (☎01206-323153; www.dedhamboathouse.com; Mill Lane; boats per hour £16; ⏰9.30am-4pm Tue-Sun).

Flatford HISTORIC SITE
(NT; ☎01206-298260; www.nationaltrust.org.uk; Bridge Cottage, near East Bergholt; parking £5; ⏰10am-6pm Apr-Oct, to 3.30pm Sat & Sun Nov-Mar; 🅿) FREE Preserved immaculately by the National Trust, the cluster of 16th- and 17th-century buildings at Flatford has changed little since Constable's time. At least five of the painter's greatest works were created here, and the view across the millpond from **Flatford Mill** (now an education centre) towards **Willy Lott's House** is like stepping into *The Hay Wain* in real life. There's an exhibition on the painter near the car park, and tiny **Bridge Cottage**, with its

knee-high windows, has been restored as it was in Constable's day.

Sleeping & Eating

★ Dedham Hall B&B ££
(☎ 01206-323027; www.dedhamhall.co.uk; Brook St, Dedham; s/d £75/120; P) An air of old England infuses Dedham Hall, a delightfully relaxed 15th-century farmhouse set in a gorgeous garden. Inside, candlesticks perch above red-brick fireplaces, beams poke through walls and ceilings and sunlight spills through windows over soft sofas and freshly made beds.

Sun Inn INN ££
(☎ 01206-323351; www.thesuninndedham.com; High St, Dedham; s/d £90/145; P) This mustard-yellow inn is the epitome of heritage-chic: the 15th-century atmosphere of the pub downstairs gives way to cool modern design when you get into the bedrooms. Each room is different, but all have have been designed with taste and sensitivity.

Milsoms HOTEL £££
(☎ 01206-322795; www.milsomhotels.com; Stratford Rd, Dedham; r £155-230; P) Vine-cloaked, yellow-brick Milsoms is where those who can come to stay, lured here by great food and cool design with a sense of fun – think zebra stripes, riveted tin and black leather upholstery. Bicycle and canoe hire means easy access to all of Dedham Vale.

★ Le Talbooth BRITISH £££
(☎ 01206-323150; www.milsomhotels.com; Gunn Hill; mains £21-42; ⊙ noon-2.15pm & 6-8pm Mon-Sat) Most of the menu at this swish restaurant overlooking the River Stour has been produced in the local area, from Dedham beef fillet to Thetford forest venison. Chefs elevate traditional British food into the realms of gastronomy; desserts are simply divine.

Getting There & Away

Manningtree train station, on the Colchester–Ipswich line, is a lovely 2-mile walk from Flatford Mill.

Bus links from Colchester:

Dedham Panther Travel (www.panther-travel.co.uk) Bus 81 (£4.60, 30 minutes, every two hours. Monday to Saturday)

East Bergholt Ipswich Bus (www.ipswichbuses.co.uk) Buses 93 and 94 (£8.50, 40 minutes, every two hours Monday to Saturday)

Saffron Walden

☎ 01799 / POP 15,504

The dainty 12th-century market town of Saffron Walden is a delightful knot of half-timbered houses, narrow lanes and ancient churches. It gets its name from the purple saffron crocus (the source of the world's most expensive spice), which was cultivated in the surrounding fields between the 15th and 18th centuries. Oliver Cromwell used the timbered **Old Sun Inn** on Church St as his HQ during the Civil War.

Sights

★ Audley End House & Gardens HISTORIC BUILDING
(EH; ☎ 01799-522842; www.english-heritage.org.uk; off London Rd; adult/child £19/11.40; ⊙ timed visits 10am-3pm; P) Palatial in scale, the fabulous early Jacobean Audley End House was clearly designed to place its creator, the first Earl of Suffolk, at the top table of the English gentry. The house eventually did become a royal palace when it was purchased by Charles II in 1668. The rooms inside are lavishly decorated with priceless furniture, oil paintings, woodcarvings and taxidermy. The elegant gardens, designed by Lancelot 'Capability' Brown, include a walled kitchen garden full of traditional varieties.

Saffron Walden Museum MUSEUM
(☎ 01799-510333; www.saffronwaldenmuseum.org; Museum St; adult/child £2.50/free; ⊙ 10am-5pm Tue-Sat, from 2pm Sun;) In this excellent museum dating back to 1835, you'll find eclectic collections covering everything from Essex history and 18th-century costumes to geology, Victorian toys and ancient Egyptian artefacts.

Bridge End Gardens GARDENS
(Bridge End; ⊙ 8am-4pm Mon-Thu, to noon Fri) FREE Careful restoration has returned these seven interlinked gardens to their former Victorian glory. An elegant sprawl of water features, gazebos and manicured hedges, it's a great place to play hide and seek; check to see if the maze has reopened.

Eating

Eight Bells PUB FOOD ££
(☎ 01799-522790; www.theeightbellssaffronwalden.com; 18 Bridge St; mains £15-26; ⊙ noon-3pm & 6-10pm Mon-Sat, noon-6pm Sun;) Medieval meets design mag at this historic 16th-century pub, where ancient timbers

collide above walls crammed with mismatched paintings. The menu is more traditional, with steaks, roasts (including nut) and posh burgers.

Information

Tourist Office (☎01799-524002; www.visitsaffronwalden.gov.uk; 1 Market Pl; ⊙9.30am-5pm Mon-Sat) Has a good leaflet on the town's historic buildings.

Getting There & Away

Bus 7 runs between Saffron Walden and Cambridge (£5, 1¼ hours), hourly between Monday and Saturday. Bus 132 makes the same journey every two hours on Sunday, passing the Duxford air museum.

The nearest train station is 2 miles west of Saffron Walden at Audley End, served by trains from Cambridge every 20 minutes (£8.20, 20 minutes). Bus 59 is one of several buses from Saffron Walden that pass close to the entrance to Audley End (£2.40, 15 minutes, every two hours Monday to Saturday).

Southend-on-Sea

☎01702 / POP 174,300

London's closest beach, Southend is the English seaside at its most uninhibited. Gambling machines beep and jangle, fairground rides gallop and nightlife bubbles out onto the seafront. But there's also another, gentler Southend, best experienced in the old fishing village of Leigh-on-Sea, a short train-ride west of the hubbub.

Sights

The seaside fun is centred on the pier and the flanking **Adventure Island** (☎01702-443400; www.adventureisland.co.uk; Western Esplanade; day passes £20-32; ⊙11am-8pm, but hours vary) theme park, but the best stretch of beach is east of the centre towards Shoeburyness.

For a more interesting take on the English seaside, take the local train west to **Leigh-on-Sea**, a pocket of cobbled lanes, historic seafront pubs and gelato stands, flanking a busy line of working cockle sheds.

Southend Pier LANDMARK
(www.southend.gov.uk/pier; Western Esplanade; adult/child £2/1; ⊙10.15am-8pm Jul-Sep, to 6pm Mar-Jun & Oct-Nov, to 6pm Wed-Sun Dec-Mar) Welcome to the world's longest pier – a staggering 1.341 miles long, to be precise – built in 1830 and still standing despite numerous mishaps, from boat crashes to fires. It's a long, windy stroll to the restored Pier Head, with its cafe and quirky **museum** (☎01702-611214; www.southendpiermuseum.co.uk; Western Esplanade; adult/child £1.50/50p; ⊙11am-5pm Sat, Sun, Tue & Wed May-Oct); hopping on the **Pier Railway** (one way adult/child £5/2.50) saves the long slog back.

Sleeping & Eating

The area around the pier is crammed with places serving so-so fish and chips. For more exciting food, head to Leigh-on-Sea.

★**Roslin Beach** HOTEL £££
(☎01702-586375; www.roslinhotel.com; Thorpe Esplanade; r from £179; ⊙food noon-9pm; P ❄ ⓦ 🐾) Seafront Roslin takes the classic seaside hotel and sprinkles some design-magazine stardust. Facing the best part of Southend beach, the interior is full of designer flourishes – candlelit lanterns, flower bouquets, palm-tree wallpaper – and rooms manage to feel both nostalgic and modern, thanks to an art-deco-green colour scheme and masses of soft upholstery.

Osborne Bros SEAFOOD £
(☎01702-477233; High St, Leigh-on-Sea; snacks/mains from £3/9; ⊙9am-4pm Mon-Fri, 8am-5pm Sat & Sun) Part fish stall, part bare-bones cafe, Osborne's is set right on Old Leigh's waterfront, so you can enjoy views of the boats on the Thames Estuary while tucking into cockles, crabs, smoked haddock, jellied eels and seafood platters, washed down with a pint from the pub next door.

Boatyard SEAFOOD ££
(☎01702-475588; www.theboatyardrestaurant.co.uk; 8/13 High St; mains £14-23; ⊙noon-8pm Thu-Sat, to 5pm Sun) A swanky alternative to the terrace restaurants along the waterfront, with its own wooden deck overlooking the water, a cruise-ship-like interior, and a quality menu of ale-battered cod, peppercorn steaks, antipasti, prawn and crayfish cocktails and the like.

Information

Tourist Office (☎01702-215620; www.visitsouthend.co.uk; Southend Pier, Western Esplanade; ⊙10.15am-8pm) At the pier.

Getting There & Away

Trains from London Liverpool St and Fenchurch St (£13, 1¼ hours, every 15 minutes) run to both Southend Victoria station and nearby Southend

Central, also the departure point for trains to Leigh-on-Sea (£3.10, 10 minutes, every 15 minutes).

SUFFOLK

While Essex is influenced by London's gravitational pull, sleepy Suffolk moves to its own rhythms. The county made its money on the back of the medieval wool trade, and magnificent churches and lavish timbered houses attest to this prosperous past. Then there's the coast, with lovely seaside resorts such as Aldeburgh and Southwold offering fresh seafood and gentle promenades in place of fairground rides and amusement arcades.

Long Melford

☎01787 / POP 3918

A thin strip of a village, pretty Long Melford sprawls south from a village green flanked by not one but two medieval mansions and a medieval church and hospital. Fine restaurants, tearooms and antique shops provide more reasons to meander through.

Sights

Kentwell Hall HISTORIC BUILDING

(☎01787-310207; www.kentwell.co.uk; adult/child £10.75/7.50; hours vary; P) Gorgeous, turreted, Tudor-era Kentwell Hall may date from the 1500s, but it's still used as a private home, lending it a wonderfully lived-in feel. The mansion is framed by a rectangular moat, lush gardens and a rare-breeds farm, and during Tudor re-enactment events, the whole estate bristles with bodices, codpieces and hose. Opening hours are erratic; call for the latest information.

Melford Hall HISTORIC BUILDING

(NT; ☎01787-379228; www.nationaltrust.org.uk; Hall St; P) From outside, the romantic Elizabethan mansion of Melford Hall has changed little since the days when Queen Elizabeth I was an honoured guest. Inside, there's a panelled banqueting hall, masses of Regency and Victorian finery, and a display on Beatrix Potter, a cousin of the Hyde Parkers, who owned the house from 1786 to 1960. Melford Hall is usually open Wednesday to Sunday in summer, but this may change – call for the latest hours and fees.

> **WORTH A TRIP**
>
> **IPSWICH**
>
> You may find yourself passing through Suffolk's county capital en route to the coast or countryside. If you have a few hours to kill, the Tudor-era **Christchurch Mansion** (☎01473-433554; https://ipswich.cimuseums.org.uk; Soane St, Ipswich; 10am-5pm Mon-Sat, 11am-5pm Sun, to 4pm Nov-Feb) FREE displays an impressive collection of paintings by Thomas Gainsborough and John Constable. The train station is a 15-minute walk south of the centre; county buses leave from the Old Cattle Market bus station on Turret Lane.

Holy Trinity CHURCH

(☎01787-310845; www.longmelfordchurch.com; Church Walk; donation requested; 10am-6pm) Surrounded by jellybean-shaped hedges, magnificent Holy Trinity looks more like a cathedral than a church. Inside, you can see a series of 15th-century stained glass panels that survived both the Reformation and the English Civil War. The red-brick mansion in front of the churchyard once served as a medieval hospital.

Sleeping & Eating

Black Lion HOTEL ££

(☎01787-312356; www.theblacklionlongmelford.com; The Green; r/ste from £90/130; P) At the Black Lion, you'll find a heritage-meets-design mag mash-up of old paintings, cast-iron fireplaces, luxe upholstery and fine fabrics. Colour schemes range from calm off-whites to vivid greens and the restaurant downstairs serves good steaks, fish and upmarket takes on pub classics (mains £15 to £23, served noon to 2.30pm and 6pm to around 9pm Wednesday to Sunday).

★ **Scutcher's** MODERN BRITISH £££

(☎01787-310200; www.scutchers.com; Westgate St; mains £24-29; noon-2pm & 7-9.30pm Thu-Sat) Beautiful reinventions of traditional recipes have made this unpretentious place renowned throughout the Stour Valley. Expect interesting riffs on classic dishes made with turbot, sea bass, lamb loin, calves' liver and farm-fresh local produce.

DON'T MISS

SUTTON HOO

Located 11 miles northeast of Ipswich off the B1083, the green hummocks of **Sutton Hoo** (NT; ☎01394-389700; www.nationaltrust.org.uk; near Woodbridge; adult/child £8/4; ⏲10.30am-3.30pm Sat-Wed; P) were just a topographical oddity until the local landowner, Edith Pretty, paid for one of the mounds to be excavated, uncovering the boat burial of an Anglo Saxon king and a hoard of exquisite gold and silver grave goods.

The king in question is believed to be Raedwald, who ruled from around 600 CE; his intricate, jewelled helmet, shield and sword are among the finest treasures housed in the British Museum in London (replicas of his boat and treasures are displayed at Sutton Hoo).

Paths encircle 18 unexcavated burial mounds surrounding the king's burial site, and a viewing tower offers dramatic views over the 'royal cemetery'. Check to see if access to the tower and tours of the site have resumed.

There's no public transport, but the site is a 1¼-mile walk from Melton station, on the Ipswich–Lowestoft line.

Getting There & Away

Chambers (www.chambersbus.co.uk) bus 753 runs to Bury St Edmunds (£4.60, one hour, hourly Monday to Saturday), Sudbury (£1.70, 10 minutes) and Lavenham (£4.10, 25 minutes).

Lavenham

☎01787 / POP 1722

One of England's most immaculately preserved medieval towns, tiny Lavenham built its fortunes on the wood trade, which paid for this atmospheric sprawl of wonky, leaning, timbered houses and pubs. Many buildings here feature original pargeting (ornamental plasterwork) from the 15th century. It's all very lovely and heavily touristed; come early in the morning if you want uninterrupted photographs.

Sights

Lavenham Guildhall HISTORIC BUILDING

(NT; ☎01787-247646; www.nationaltrust.org.uk; Market Pl; adult/child £9.30/4.65; ⏲10.30am-4pm Wed-Sun) Lavenham's triangular marketplace is dominated by the whitewashed guildhall, a superb example of close-studded, timber-framed, early-16th-century architecture. It's now a museum with displays on the wool trade and medieval guilds; in its tranquil garden you can see plants that produced typical medieval dyes.

Little Hall HISTORIC BUILDING

(☎01787-247019; www.littlehall.org.uk; Market Pl; adult/child £4/free; ⏲2-4pm Sat & Sun) The caramel-coloured, 14th-century Little Hall was once home to a successful wool merchant, and the interiors have been restored to their medieval splendour through the efforts of the Gayer-Anderson twins, who made it their home in the 1920s and 1930s.

St Peter & St Paul CHURCH

(www.lavenhamchurch.onesuffolk.net; Church St; ⏲10am-4pm) Built between 1485 and 1530, this soaring late-Perpendicular church was one of Suffolk's last great wool churches, with fine woodwork and stained glass, and a churchyard full of gravestones carved with skulls and cherubs.

Sleeping & Eating

Angel HOTEL ££

(☎01787-247388; www.theangellavenham.co.uk; Market Pl; r from £79; ⏲food noon-3pm & 6-9pm Mon-Fri, noon-9pm Sat, 6-8pm Sun; P) In Lavenham's oldest building, narrow corridors lead to gorgeously renovated, large, bright rooms with exposed timbers. Downstairs, it's English pub all the way, with Suffolk ales and good-quality pub grub, from pizzas and burgers to steaks, salads and sandwiches (mains £9 to £15), which you can eat at outdoor tables facing the square.

★ **Swan at Lavenham** HOTEL £££

(☎01787-247477; www.theswanatlavenham.co.uk; High St; r £110-180, ste from £210; P) Marvellously medieval, the stylish Swan is Lavenham's signature place to stay – a bent and leaning timbered coaching inn, with flawless service, fine modern British cuisine and rooms decorated in soothing colours and bound by a latticework of ancient beams.

The house spa offers a full range of relaxing treatments in rooms lit by candles and sunlight.

★ Great House MODERN BRITISH £££
(☎01787-247431; www.greathouse.co.uk; Market Pl; 3-course lunch/dinner from £23/28; ⏰noon-2.30pm Wed-Sun, 7-9.30pm Tue-Sat) Contrasting cultures combine at this elegant restaurant, so expect East Anglian ingredients and French and Italian gastronomy. Dining here could see you eating *pâté en croûte,* Gravlax salmon, roast Suffolk pork or handmade gnocchi.

Getting There & Away

Chambers bus 753 connects Lavenham to Bury St Edmunds (£4.50, 30 minutes, hourly Monday to Saturday), continuing to Long Melford (£4.10, 25 minutes) and Sudbury (£4.30, 35 minutes).

Bury St Edmunds

☎01284 / POP 41,113

A centre of pilgrimage for centuries, Suffolk's second city is rich in history and attractively decked out with handsome Georgian architecture. Named for the Anglo-Saxon king Edmund the Martyr, it rewards those who step off the tourist trail with fine food, and a pleasing fragrance of yeast and malt thanks to the enormous Greene King brewery.

Sights

Abbey Gardens RUINS
(Mustow St; ⏰dawn-dusk) FREE Now a picturesque, skeletal ruin, Bury's once-mighty abbey is still impressive, despite being plundered for building stone after the dissolution of the monasteries. Dotted around a pretty park behind the cathedral (once part of the abbey itself), sections of eroded masonry form fantastical shapes against the greenery, marking out an immense complex that was once one of Britain's largest religious buildings.

St Edmundsbury Cathedral CATHEDRAL
(☎01284-748720; www.stedscathedral.org; Angel Hill; by donation; ⏰10am-4pm Mon-Sat) Bury's cathedral was once a minor part of the abbey, but after the Reformation it became the focus of attention. Most of the building is early 16th century, but the 45m-high tower was only completed in 2005, using traditional stone-working techniques. Ask if tours of the tower have resumed. Next to the cathedral is the appealingly ancient **Norman Tower**, the original entrance to the great abbey church.

Moyse's Hall MUSEUM
(☎01284-706183; www.moyseshall.org; Cornhill; adult/child £5/3; ⏰10am-5pm Mon-Sat, noon-4pm Sun; 🚻) Set in an impressive 12th-century undercroft, Moyse's Hall museum displays a curious collection of artefacts, from a locket of Mary Tudor's hair to the death mask of 19th-century murderer William Corder (and, contentiously, a book bound in his skin!). Check out the fascinating displays on the town's ruined abbey and the chilling Bury witch trials.

Theatre Royal HISTORIC BUILDING
(NT; ☎01284-769505; www.theatreroyal.org; Westgate St; tours £7.50; ⏰tours 11am Wed, Thu & Sat) Britain's only working Regency playhouse features ornate gilding, an elegant round of boxes and a *trompe l'oeil* ceiling painted to resemble the open sky. Its secrets are revealed on fascinating guided front-of-house and backstage tours – call to check things are running as normal.

St Mary's Church CHURCH
(☎01284-754680; www.wearechurch.net; Honey Hill; donation requested; ⏰10am-4pm Mon-Sat, to 3pm Oct-Easter) Once part of the abbey, St Mary's is one of the largest parish churches in England, and it contains the tomb of Mary Tudor – Henry VIII's sister and a one-time queen of France. Built around 1430, it's famous for its hammer-beam roof, with a host of vampire-like angels swooping from the ceiling.

Sleeping

Fox Inn INN ££
(☎0845 6086040; www.greenekinginns.co.uk; 1 Eastgate St; r from £115; P 📶) Tied to the Greene King brewery, this historic pub offers rooms in converted animal barns, with bleached beams, weathered brick walls and even some of the old livestock tethering

THE APEX

Bury's cutting-edge arts' centre and music venue, the **Apex** (☎01284-758000; www.theapex.co.uk; 1 Charter Sq), boasts a lively program of live music, theatre, art shows and more.

rings. Posh wallpaper, leather sofas and the odd chandelier add extra class.

★Chantry HOTEL £££
(☎01284-767427; www.chantryhotel.com; 8 Sparhawk St; r £120-175; P@) This family-run town house B&B has the feel of a country hotel, with a gorgeous collection of four-poster, metal-framed and antique timber beds, set in inviting rooms with the odd original Georgian feature. There's a convivial lounge and tiny bar to help guests feel right at home.

Angel HOTEL £££
(☎01284-714000; www.theangel.co.uk; 3 Angel Hill; r from £135; P) Almost hidden behind a cloak of vines and climbers, Bury's grand dame hotel faces the abbey gates across Angel Hill, flanked by a string of stately Georgian mansions. Rooms feature designer fabrics and wallpapers and quirky design details (brass tubs, cowskin armchairs, antique beds), and higher categories come with ecclesiastical views.

Eating & Drinking

★Pea Porridge MODERN BRITISH ££
(☎01284-700200; www.peaporridge.co.uk; 29 Cannon St; mains £12-22; 6.30-8.30pm Thu, noon-1.30pm & 6.30-9.30pm Fri & Sat) Happy chatter and enticing aromas greet you at this intimate neighbourhood restaurant where local, seasonal produce is cooked up together with ingredients from the Med. Tickle your tastebuds with Moorish fish soup, rabbit *kibbeh* (Levantine meatballs) and grilled Galician octopus.

Maison Bleue FRENCH £££
(☎01284-760623; www.maisonbleue.co.uk; 31 Churchgate St; 3-course meals £32-55; noon-2pm & 7-9.30pm, closed Mon) You may want to dress up to eat in this elegant restaurant, serving modern French cuisine with real flair. Fabulous set meals take in such flavour sensations as halibut with chorizo butter, Aylesbury duck with beetroot and plum sauce, and sea trout with coconut and lime.

★Old Cannon PUB
(☎01284-768769; www.oldcannonbrewery.co.uk; 86 Cannon St; 11am-11pm;) In this microbrewery, gleaming mash tuns (malt mashing vats) sit alongside the bar, where you can quaff the end results – try the feisty Gunner's Daughter (ABV 5.5%) or Powder Monkey (4.75%), named in homage to naval gun traditions. Ask about brewery tours.

Nutshell PUB
(☎01284-764867; www.thenutshellpub.co.uk; The Traverse; 11am-11pm, to 10.30pm Sun) Beer tables, a handful of chairs, a ceiling smothered in international banknotes, a suspended pufferfish: it's amazing what they've squeezed into this thimble-sized, timber-framed pub, recognised by the *Guinness Book of Records* as Britain's smallest.

Information

Tourist Office (☎01284-764667; www.visit-burystedmunds.co.uk; The Apex, Charter Sq; 10.30am-4pm Mon-Sat) In the Arc Shopping Centre; ask about city tours.

Getting There & Away

BUS

The main bus station is on St Andrew's St North. Direct services include:

Cambridge Stagecoach bus 11 (£5, one hour, hourly Monday to Saturday)

Lavenham Chambers bus 753 (£4.50, 30 minutes, hourly Monday to Saturday)

TRAIN

The train station is a 10-minute walk north of the centre of town. Services include:

Cambridge (£11.40, 40 minutes, hourly)

Ipswich (£10, 40 minutes, two per hour)

Aldeburgh

☎01728 / POP 3225

The coastal town of Aldeburgh (pronounced *orld*-bruh) floats in a charming time warp. Along the pebble shore, wooden sheds sell ocean-fresh seafood hauled in by the boats perched on the beach, while sightseers stroll along the prom, with nary a slot machine in sight. The town follows the shoreline in a thin strip, dotted with interesting shops, galleries and cafes. Aldeburgh's two festivals and connections with composer Benjamin Britten are also a big draw.

Sights

The pebble beach runs north to **Thorpeness**, with its pretty windmill; it's a pleasant walk and on the way you'll pass Maggi Hambling's sculpture **Scallop**, a giant metal shell incised with quotes from the opera *Peter Grimes* by composer Benjamin Britten, who spent much of his life in Aldeburgh. In

OFF THE BEATEN TRACK

ORFORD NESS

Formerly owned by the Ministry of Defence, wind-whipped, remote **Orford Ness** (NT; ☎01394-450900; www.nationaltrust.org.uk) is the largest vegetated shingle spit in Europe. The lonely shoreline is dominated by a line of forbidding-looking **pagodas** that were used to test the explosive triggers for nuclear weapons (fortunately, without the radioactive parts). Today, you're more likely to spot wading birds, madcap hares and rare coastal plants. Ferries operate from Orford Quay.

The adjacent village of Orford is a gorgeous spot, full of historic houses and cute pubs and dominated by a striking 12th-century **castle** (EH; www.english-heritage.org.uk; adult/child £7.90/4.70; ⏲tours hourly 10am-noon, 2pm & 3pm Fri-Sun; P) formed from three conjoined towers. While you're here, don't miss the fresh Butley oysters, fish pie, potted crab and grilled lobster at the **Butley Orford Oysterage** (☎01394-450277; www.pinneysof orford.co.uk; Market Hill; mains £14-28; ⏲noon-2.15pm daily, plus 6.30-9pm Wed-Fri, 6-9pm Sat) on the market square; it also runs a **deli** (☎01394-459183; www.pinneysoforford.co.uk; Quay St; from £4; ⏲10am-4.30pm, to 4pm Sun) near the quay.

the distance, you'll spot the looming mass of Sizewell nuclear power station.

Moot Hall MUSEUM
(www.aldeburghmuseum.org.uk; Market Cross Pl; adult/child £3/1; ⏲1-4pm Apr-Oct, 1-4pm Sat & Sun Nov-Mar) The town museum is worth a visit as much for the gorgeous building – a 16th-century merchant's house constructed from oak timbers and herringbone brick – as for the displays inside, which cover fishing, shipbuilding, coastal defences and Regency-era tourism.

RSPB Minsmere NATURE RESERVE
(RSPB; www.rspb.org.uk; near Westleton; adult/child £9/5; ⏲reserve dawn-dusk, visitor centre 10am-4pm; P) About 8 miles north of Aldeburgh, the nature reserve at RSPB Minsmere is home to one of England's rarest birds, the bittern, along with dozens of other migratory bird species, best spotted in the autumn. Trails run across the marshes that line the foreshore to hides that offer prime spotting opportunities. The reserve borders the National Trust–administered **Dunwich Heath** (NT; www.nationaltrust.org.uk; Dunwich; parking £6; ⏲10am-5pm), another fine spot for coastal birdwatching.

Festivals & Events

Aldeburgh Festival MUSIC
(www.snapemaltings.co.uk/season/aldeburgh-festival; ⏲Jun) Founded by Benjamin Britten in 1948, this exploration of classical music takes in new and reinterpreted pieces, as well as the classics.

Sleeping & Eating

Wentworth Hotel HOTEL £££
(☎01728-452312; www.wentworth-aldeburgh.com; s/d from £127/230; P 📶) Aldeburgh's grandest hotel is an elegant old dame at the end of the promenade, with a lavish, Regency-style dining room, tasteful bedrooms with fine fabrics and little dabs of colour, and a healthy dose of nostalgia. Seaview rooms come at a premium, but you can watch the shore from the terrace.

Fish & Chip Shop FISH & CHIPS £
(☎01728-452250; www.aldeburghfishandchips.co.uk; 226 High St; mains £5-8; ⏲noon-2pm daily, plus 5-8pm Thu-Sat) Aldeburgh has a reputation for the finest fish and chips in the area, and this cheerful takeaway is the place to find out why. The same owners operate two sit-down restaurants along the strip, but it's more fun to perch on the seawall.

★**Lighthouse** MODERN BRITISH ££
(☎01728-453377; www.lighthouserestaurant.co.uk; 77 High St; mains £12-22.50; ⏲noon-3pm & 5-9.30pm; 👪) The owner of this interesting, unpretentious eatery was formerly a waiter here, and he's taken the place to new heights with a fine menu of modern British dishes, many featuring cod, sole and other seafood bought fresh from the boats on the beach.

Getting There & Away

Bus 64/65 links Aldeburgh with Ipswich (return £6.80, 1½ hours, hourly Monday to Saturday). From there you can connect to the rest of the region.

WORTH A TRIP

THOMAS GAINSBOROUGH'S HOUSE

The great English painter Thomas Gainsborough (1727–1788) made his fortune from portraits of the gentry and Suffolk landscapes, and many of his works are displayed in his atmospheric **birthplace** (☎01787-372958; www.gainsborough.org; 46 Gainsborough St) in the village of Sudbury. The museum closed for renovations in 2020; when it reopens look out for the exquisite *Portrait of Harriett, Viscountess Tracy,* celebrated for its delicate portrayal of drapery. Call for the latest opening hours and prices.

Buses run at least hourly (not Sundays) from Sudbury to Ipswich (£5.50, one hour) and Colchester (£4.70, 50 minutes). Bus 753 (hourly Monday to Saturday) runs through Long Melford (£1.70, 10 minutes) and Lavenham (£4.30, 25 minutes) to Bury St Edmunds (£4.70, one hour).

Southwold

☎01502 / POP 1098

Southwold's reputation as a holiday getaway for well-heeled Londoners earned it the nickname 'Kensington-on-Sea' – indeed, city-slickers have been escaping here since at least the Regency period. With its fine sand beach, beachfront bathing huts, and general absence of seaside kitsch, the resort has long been a favourite hangout for artists, including JMW Turner, Charles Rennie Mackintosh, Lucian Freud and Damien Hirst.

Sights

Southwold's shorefront promenade is its main attraction, but amble inland and you'll find pretty streets of Regency houses and a squat 19th-century **lighthouse**.

Southwold Pier AREA
(☎01502-722105; www.southwoldpier.co.uk; North Pde; ⊙pier 10am-7pm, to 5pm winter) FREE At the north end of the strip, the 190m-long pier, first built in 1899, is worth a visit for its eccentric **Under the Pier Show**, a kooky collection of handmade coin-operated amusement machines combining daft fun with political satire. The same maker built the Heath Robinson–esque water clock further along the pier.

Adnams BREWERY
(☎01502-727225; www.adnams.co.uk; Adnams Pl; tours £20; ⊙tours daily Mar-Sep) Southwold's huge brewery fills the streets with pleasant smells, and with advance booking you can tour the premises and be amazed at the high-tech kit inside these venerable Victorian buildings. Hour-long tours (for over-18s only) also include a tutored tasting of the house beers, including the ever-popular Ghost Ship (4.5%). Call for timings.

Festivals & Events

Latitude Festival ART
(www.latitudefestival.co.uk; Henham Park; ⊙Jul) An eclectic mix of music, literature, dance, drama and comedy set in a country estate.

Sleeping & Eating

★**Sutherland House** HOTEL £££
(☎01502-724544; www.sutherlandhouse.co.uk; 56 High St; r from £175; P 📶) Past guests at this former mayor's residence include the prince who later became James II, and the Earl of Sandwich. Modern-day travellers can enjoy a hint of the same extravagant lifestyle in sumptuous rooms with pargeted ceilings, exposed beams and free-standing baths.

Classy meals (mains £17 to £32, noon to 2pm and 6.30pm to 9pm, closed Monday) range from aged sirloin steaks to pan-seared halibut and whole lobster.

Swan HOTEL £££
(☎01502-722186; www.theswansouthwold.co.uk; Market Sq; s/d £155/200; P 📶 🐾) A super-stylish pub-hotel owned by the Adnams brewery, so you can be sure the beer in the bar has been expertly stored. The building is 17th-century, but rooms are anything but traditional – think four-poster beds with neon-pink posts, turquoise wine-bottle carpets and designer lamps.

Two Magpies BAKERY £
(www.twomagpiesbakery.co.uk; 88 High St; snacks from £3, pizzas from £8; ⊙8am-5pm Sun-Fri, to 8.30pm Sat) This enterprising bakery produces all manner of tasty buns, breads, pastries and savoury treats, including delicious sourdough pizzas on Saturday evenings. Ask about its speciality baking courses.

Getting There & Away

Bus 146 links Southwold with Norwich (£4.70, 1½ hours, hourly Monday to Saturday).

For services south, including those to and from Aldeburgh, catch bus 99A to Halesworth (£2.50, 30 minutes, every two hours Monday to Saturday) and continue on the 521 (£4.80, one hour, three daily).

NORFOLK

At the risk of sounding like Alan Partridge, there's more to Norfolk than Norwich and the Broads (though the historic county capital and the meandering waterways that surround it are both wonderful places to spend time). Continue north, and you'll hit some lavish stately homes and some of England's loveliest coastal resorts – all brick-edged, flint-stone houses, windswept, bird-filled marshes and endless strips of sand.

Norwich

☎01603 / POP 132,512

Norwich (norr-ich) – the affluent and easy-going home of TV's Alan Partridge – is one of East Anglia's most historic cities, and its winding, part-pedestrianised streets are crammed with ancient flint churches and venerable timbered buildings that speak volumes about the wealth that the wool trade brought to Norfolk in the medieval period. The castle and cathedral are obvious drawcards, but it's worth staying on to haggle for antiques in eclectic emporiums and feast at some of the county's finest restaurants.

Sights

The area known as **Tombland**, opposite Norwich Cathedral, is where the city's market was originally located ('tomb' is an old Norse word for empty, relating to the open market place). Enter through the archway of the precariously leaning **Augustine Steward House**, duck behind the church, and follow Princes St to cobbled **Elm Hill**, Norwich's most perfect medieval street, curving downhill towards the river. The thatched, timbered house containing the **Britons Arms** (www.britonsarms.co.uk; 9 Elm Hill; light mains from £5.50; ⏲10am-4pm Mon-Sat) coffee house has been here since 1347.

★Norwich Cathedral CATHEDRAL
(☎01603-218300; www.cathedral.org.uk; 65 The Close; donations requested; ⏲10am-4pm Mon-Fri, 10am-3pm Sat, 1-3pm Sun) Norwich's most impressive landmark is its magnificent, medieval Anglican cathedral (not to be confused with the Catholic cathedral, a Victorian copy on the north side of town). Its needle spire soars higher than any other church in England, apart from Salisbury, and its fan-vaulted ceiling is a masterpiece of medieval engineering. Be sure to check out the collection of ornate ceiling bosses in the medieval cloisters, featuring everything from pagan-inspired green men to devouring dragons.

★Norwich Castle MUSEUM
(☎01603-495897; www.museums.norfolk.gov.uk; Castle Hill) An imposing cube of masonry crowning a hilltop overlooking central Norwich, this massive 12th-century castle is one of England's best-preserved examples of Anglo-Norman military architecture. Inside, a superb **interactive museum** crams in lively exhibits on Boudica and the Iceni, the Anglo-Saxons, the Vikings and the gruesome medieval punishments once carried out here. Call ahead to check the latest opening times and prices.

★Museum of Norwich MUSEUM
(☎01603-629127; www.museums.norfolk.gov.uk; Bridewell Alley; adult/child £6.20/5.30; ⏲10am-4.30pm Tue-Sat) Be on your best behaviour: this engaging little museum is set in a 14th-century house of correction. Displays here explore Norwich's prominence as England's second city in the Middle Ages and its 19th-century industrial heritage.

★Blickling Hall HISTORIC BUILDING
(NT; ☎01263-738030; www.nationaltrust.org.uk; Blickling; adult/child £10/5; ⏲house noon-4pm, grounds 10am-4pm; P 👪) Gorgeous Blickling was remodelled in the 17th century for Sir Henry Hobart, James I's chief justice, but the house is best known for its previous owners, the Boleyn family, though the jury is out on whether Anne Boleyn actually lived here before her unfortunate marriage to Henry VIII. Impressive enough from the outside, Blickling is something else on the inside – many of the extravagant interiors date to the early 17th century, including some of the finest Jacobean moulded plaster ceilings still in existence.

Sainsbury Centre for Visual Arts GALLERY
(☎01603-593199; www.scva.ac.uk; University of East Anglia (UEA); ⏲9am-6pm Tue-Fri, 10am-5pm Sat & Sun; 🚌22, 25, 26) FREE The eclectic art collection of Sir Robert Sainsbury (of

Norwich

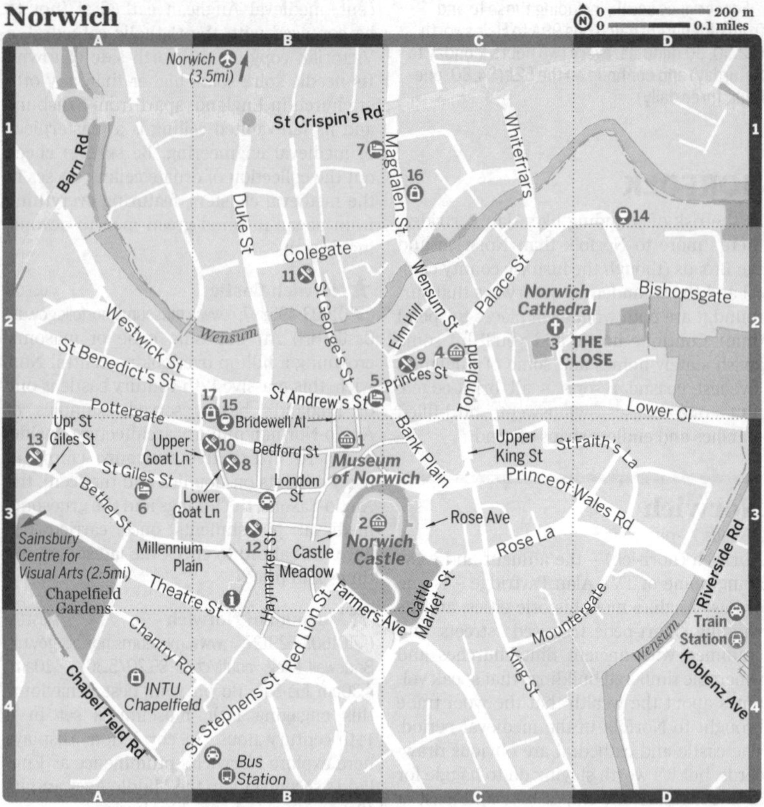

Norwich

Top Sights
1 Museum of Norwich B3
2 Norwich Castle B3
3 Norwich Cathedral C2

Sights
4 Augustine Steward's House C2

Sleeping
5 3 Princes B2
6 38 St Giles A3
7 Gothic House B1

Eating
8 Biddy's Tearoom B3
9 Britons Arms C2
10 Grosvenor Fish Bar B3
11 Last Wine Bar & Restaurant B2
12 Norwich Market B3
13 Roger Hickman's A3

Drinking & Nightlife
14 Adam & Eve D1
15 Birdcage B3

Shopping
16 Looses Emporium C1
17 St Gregory's Antiques Collectables B2

supermarket fame) is displayed in the first major public building by renowned architect Norman Foster. Displayed around the hangar-like space are striking sculptures and paintings (including many works by Francis Bacon, David Hockney, Henry Moore, Degas and Giacometti) mixed in with ethnological curiosities from dozens of tribal cultures.

The gallery is in the University of East Anglia's grounds, 2 miles west of the city centre. To get there take bus 22, 25 or 26 (£2.80, 15 minutes).

Sleeping

Gothic House B&B ££
(☎01603-631879; www.gothic-house-norwich.com; King's Head Yard, Magdalen St; s/d £75/105; P 📶) Tucked into a courtyard at the quiet end of town, this handsome town-house B&B will whisk you back to the Regency era. Wood panelling, columns and cornices border the swirling stairs that lead to striking floral rooms with intricate timber windows.

★**3 Princes** B&B £££
(☎01603-622699; www.3princes-norwich.co.uk; 3 Princes St; s/d from £89/185; 📶) A handsome old town house with a walled, tree-shaded courtyard garden, 3 Princes puts you in the medieval heart of the city, yards from lovely Elm Hill. Behind the historic exterior, the wood-floored rooms come in a modernist colour scheme of greys and whites, with small swatches of blue from cushions and bedspreads.

38 St Giles B&B £££
(☎01603-662944; www.38stgiles.co.uk; 38 St Giles St; s/d from £125/150; P 📶) Boutique 38 St Giles reinvents the English B&B with period glamour. The lavish rooms are all vintage furniture, fine fabrics, damask blinds, and floor rugs laid over polished floorboards. The excellent breakfasts feature all sorts of local and organic ingredients, and you can swap a full English for crème fraiche pancakes with bacon and fresh berries.

Eating

For cheap eats, try the globe-trotting food stands inside the town's partly covered **market** (Market Pl; snacks from £3; ⏰9am-3pm Mon-Sat).

★**Grosvenor Fish Bar** FISH & CHIPS £
(www.fshshop.com; 28 Lower Goat Lane; mains from £5; ⏰10.45am-7.30pm Mon-Sat) At this hip chippy, fish and chips comes as fresh cod goujons and chips fried in vegan-friendly oil, a 'Big Mack' is a crispy mackerel fillet in a roll, and the 'Six Quid Squid' (squid rings with garlic aioli) really is £6. Either eat in the basement, take away, or they'll deliver to the Birdcage pub opposite.

Biddy's Tearoom CAFE £
(www.biddystearoom.com; 15 Lower Goat Lane; cakes from £3; ⏰10.30am-4pm) Biddy's takes the traditional tearoom into design-magazine territory, with reclaimed furniture, leather armchairs, vintage sweet jars, premium teas and giant, rich sticky buns stuffed with cinnamon, raspberries and chocolate that could feed a family. The baking is top class; it also does breakfasts, finger sandwiches and afternoon teas.

★**Roger Hickman's** MODERN BRITISH £££
(☎01603-633522; www.rogerhickmansrestaurant.com; 79 Upper St Giles St; 2/3 courses lunch £22/27, dinner £40/50; ⏰noon-2.30pm & 7-10pm Wed-Sat) Understated elegance is the name of the game in this prestigious modern British establishment. The dining room is elegant and intimate, and the creations of chef Roger Hickman feature imaginative preparations of pigeon, lamb loin, halibut, cep mushrooms, parsnip gnocchi and fermented beetroot among other top-tier ingredients.

Last Wine Bar & Restaurant BRITISH £££
(☎01603-626626; www.lastwinebar.co.uk; 70 St George's St; mains £18-29; ⏰noon-2.30pm & 6-9.30pm Mon-Sat) The decor in this stylish bar and eatery reflects the building's past life as a shoe factory, with lasts (wooden shoe moulds) as light fittings and Singer sewing machine tables. Impressively, the food lives up to the setting – venison, duck, hake, steaks, posh burgers, and some above-average options for vegetarians.

Drinking & Nightlife

★**Birdcage** PUB
(www.thebirdcagenorwich.co.uk; 23 Pottergate; ⏰noon-9pm Fri & Sat; 📶) Footloose and fancy free, this beatnik public house is currently open just at weekends, but as things normalise, expect a revival of its regular program of poetry, cabaret, life-drawing and music events throughout the week. The ales are real, the cocktails cool, and you can ferry in fish and chips from the Grosvenor Fish Bar over the road.

Adam & Eve PUB
(☎01603-667423; Bishopsgate; ⏰11am-11pm Mon-Sat, noon-10.30pm Sun) Charming, Dutch-eaved Adam & Eve is Norwich's oldest surviving pub, founded way back in 1249, when medieval masons used to drop by while constructing Norwich cathedral. Tiny, with a sunken floor and part-panelled walls, it attracts a mixed band of regulars, choristers and ghost hunters. Check opening hours in advance.

ANTIQUE NORWICH

In Norwich's emporiums, you can find everything from bone china and Ormolu clocks to military uniforms, tin toys, salvaged shop signs and fibreglass Daleks from *Dr Who*. Start the rummaging in the sprawling **St Gregory's Antiques & Collectable** (01603-305372; www.facebook.com/stgregorysantiques; St Gregory's Church, Pottergate; 10am-5pm Mon-Fri, to 6pm Sat, 11am-4pm Sun), set inside the historic St Gregory's Church, or browse finds from more than 60 dealers in the Aladdin's Cave–like **Looses Emporium** (01603-665600; www.loosesemporium.co.uk; 23-35 Magdalen St; 10am-5pm Mon-Fri, 9am-6pm Sat, 10am-4pm Sun).

Information

Tourist Office (01603-989500; www.visitnorwich.co.uk; Millennium Plain; 10am-5.30pm Mon-Sat) Inside the Forum complex; ask about local walking tours.

Getting There & Around

AIR

Norwich International Airport (01603-411923; www.norwichairport.co.uk; Holt Rd) is 4 miles north of town. Get here on bus 501 from the centre (adult/child £3.80/1.10, every 10 to 15 minutes).

BUS

The **bus station** (Queen's Rd) is 400m south of the castle on Queens Rd. **National Express** (www.nationalexpress.com) covers longer routes; **First** (www.firstgroup.com), **Konect** (www.konectbus.co.uk) and others operate in and around the city:

Cromer Bus X44 (£4.20, one hour, hourly Monday to Saturday)

Wroxham Konect 5B (£3, one hour, hourly)

King's Lynn First Excel (£6.40, 1½ hours, hourly Monday to Saturday)

London Victoria (£13.30, three hours, every two hours)

TRAIN

The train station is off Thorpe Rd, 600m east of Norwich Castle. Destinations include:

Cambridge (£19.50, 1¼ hours, hourly)

Colchester (£13.50, one hour, every 30 minutes)

London Liverpool St (£10, two hours, every 30 minutes)

Cromer

01263 / POP 7683

The once-fashionable Victorian resort of Cromer still flourishes as a busy fishing port, famous for the sweet-tasting brown crabs which are hauled in daily during the March to October crabbing season. The long, cliff-edged seafront is lined with fishing boats and the tractors that pull them onto the pebbles, and the beach sees some impressive swell for surfers.

Sights & Activities

Cromer's historic **pier** (01263-512495; www.cromerpier.co.uk; Esplanade; 10am-dusk) FREE has existed in one shape or another since around 1391, and it hosts one of the country's last end-of-pier shows (think dancers, sing-alongs and nostalgia).

Surfers can rent boards and take lessons at **Glide Surf School** (01263-805005; www.glidesurfschool.co.uk; lessons adult/child £27/32, board hire per day from £17; 9.30am-5.30pm Mon-Sat, to 4pm Sun Apr-Oct, 10am-4pm Sat & Sun Nov-Mar), just east of the pier.

Felbrigg Hall HISTORIC BUILDING

(NT; 01263-837444; www.nationaltrust.org.uk; Felbrigg; adult/child £8/4; house noon-3pm, garden 10am-4pm; P) An elegant Jacobean mansion boasting a fine, painting-filled Georgian interior, Felbrigg is 2 miles south-west of Cromer, off the B1436. Topped by a curious parapet spelling out the family motto, the house sits amid attractive gardens that include a walled-kitchen garden and an 18th-century orangery. Call ahead to see if longer opening hours have resumed.

Henry Blogg Museum MUSEUM

(RNLI Lifeboat Museum; 01263-511294; www.rnli.org; The Gangway; 10am-5pm Tue-Sun Apr-Sep, to 4pm Oct, Nov, Feb & Mar) FREE Hands-on gizmos add to the appeal of this excellent museum housed in the local lifeboat station and named after highly decorated local coxswain Henry Blogg. Inside, you can learn to tap out a message in Morse and spell your name in semaphore flags, while learning tales of the brave sea rescues carried out by the station.

Sleeping & Eating

★Red Lion INN ££

(01263-514964; www.redlioncromer.co.uk; Brook St; s/d/ste from £68/125/145; P) Coloured floor tiles, wooden banisters and stained glass signal this seafront inn's 18th-century heritage, but stylish, sea-themed rooms bring the package bang up to date. All bedrooms come with bathtubs. You can see the sea from the dreamy deluxe suite (room 7), which also has its own sea-facing balcony.

★Davies SEAFOOD £
(☎01263-512727; 7 Garden St; crab £3.50-6; ⏲8.30am-5pm Mon-Sat, 10am-4pm Sun) At this Cromer institution, the crabs on sale were caught on the owner's boat, the *Richard William,* and boiled, cracked and dressed on the premises. Other treats include cockles, mussels and homemade fish pâté. Hours are often reduced in winter.

Rocket House CAFE £
(☎01263-519126; www.rockethousecafe.co.uk; The Gangway; mains £6.50-11; ⏲9am-4pm Mon-Fri, 10am-5pm Sat & Sun;) Upstairs in the same art-deco building as the lifeboat station and Henry Blogg Museum, this much-loved cafe has a balcony that almost perches you over the waves. The menu jumps from sandwiches. burgers and salads to fish and chips and dressed Cromer crab.

Getting There & Away

Trains link Cromer with Norwich (£8.20, 45 minutes, hourly). Bus X44 also runs to Norwich (£4.20, one hour, hourly Monday to Saturday), while the daily **Coasthopper CH1** (www.sanders coaches.com) runs west along the coast as far as Wells-next-the-Sea (£4.40, one hour, hourly), where there are frequent connections on to King's Lynn.

Cley-next-the-Sea

☎01263 / POP 437

A strong contender for the title of prettiest Norfolk village, sleepy Cley (pronounced 'cly' to rhyme with 'tie') is a dainty huddle of brick-edged flint houses spilling onto bird-filled marshes, centred on an *extremely* photogenic windmill.

Sights

Cley Marshes NATURE RESERVE
(☎01263-740008; www.norfolkwildlifetrust.org.uk; near Cley-next-the-Sea; adult/child £4.50/free; ⏲reserve dawn-dusk, visitor centre 10am-5pm Mar-Oct, to 4pm Nov-Feb; P) One of England's premier birdwatching sites, Cley Marshes hosts more than 300 resident bird species and numerous migratory visitors – all easily spotted from the visitor centre and a network of walking trails and bird hides tucked among the golden reeds. Marsh harriers, bitterns and bearded reedlings are top spots here.

Sleeping & Eating

★Cley Windmill B&B £££
(☎01263-740209; www.cleywindmill.co.uk; High St; d £159-295, apt per week from £495; P) If you've ever fancied staying in a windmill, you won't find one much lovelier than this fully intact, 19th-century gem. The curiously shaped but cosy rooms are named after their former working lives, and many look directly over reed-filled salt marshes. A cute four-person self-catering cottage sits just next door.

The windmill has a great kitchen too – satisfying Norfolk-themed taster menus cost £32.50 (6.30pm to 8pm, bookings required).

★Picnic Fayre DELI £
(☎01263-740587; www.picnic-fayre.co.uk; High St; snacks from £3; ⏲9am-4pm Mon-Sat, from 10am Sun) A deli to ditch the diet for, fully stocked with imaginative variations on English picnic classics – pork pies with chorizo, sausages smothered with sweet-chilli sauce, and home-baked lavender bread.

Blakeney

☎01263 / POP 801

The pretty village of Blakeney was once a busy fishing and trading port before its harbour silted up. It's since become a popular spot for day-trippers, who sit and admire the yachts on the creek, take seal-spotting boat

BUSING THE NORTH NORFOLK COAST

Though the villages on the north Norfolk coast feel agreeably isolated, it's easy to get between them thanks to excellent bus links. The daily **Coasthopper CH1** (www.sanderscoaches.com) runs from Cromer to Wells-next-the-Sea (£4.40, one hour, hourly), via Cley-next-the-Sea and Blakeney. At Wells, you can hop onto the **Coastliner 36** (www.lynxbus.co.uk) to King's Lynn (£5.80, 1¾ hours, hourly), via Holkham and Burnham Deepdale. A special all-day £10 ticket allows unlimited travel on both routes.

THE NORFOLK BROADS

Why Should I Visit a Swamp?

These vast wetlands were formed when the rivers Wensum, Bure, Waveney and Yare flooded gaping holes created by 12th-century crofters digging for peat. In the process, a vast and valuable wetland ecosystem was created – as well as a playground for leisure boating. Today, there are 125 miles of winding waterways to explore; pop into the **visitor centre** (01603-782281; www.visitthebroads.co.uk; Station Rd, Hoveton; 9am-5pm Easter-Nov) in Hoveton for local information.

If you prefer not to sleep on the water, **St Gregory's B&B** (01603-784319; www.stgregoryswroxham.co.uk; 11 Stalham Rd, Hoveton; s/d from £60/80; P) in Hoveton is a fine spot to regain your land legs, and there are plenty of cafes nearby and over the bridge in Wroxham.

Exploring by Boat

The main hubs for renting boats are Wroxham and Hoveton, just northeast of Norwich, and the villages along the A149 between Potter Heigham and Stalham, on the edge of Hickling Broad. Launches range from basic day-boats with outboard motors to comfortable live-aboard cruisers with cabins, kitchens and bathrooms; most operators rent by the half-day, day or week, and renters receive an introduction to inland navigation before setting off.

Broads Tours (01603-782207; www.broadstours.co.uk; The Bridge, Wroxham; boat hire per hour/day from £21/130, tours adult/child from £9.50/6; 8am-5.30pm Mar-Oct) Lets out boats by the day, as well as running popular one- to two-hour riverboat tours.

Barnes Brinkcraft (01603-782625; www.barnesbrinkcraft.co.uk; Riverside Rd, Wroxham; canoe hire per half-/full day £30/45, boat hire per hour/day £20/121, 4-berth boat per week from £600; Apr-Oct) Has day-boats, canoes and live-aboard cruisers.

Sutton Staithe Boatyard (01692-581653; www.dayboathire.com; Sutton Staithe; boat hire per half-/full day £80/120, canoe hire per half-/full day £25/40) Rents out boats and canoes at the quieter end of the Broads near Sutton.

For longer boating holidays, try **Blakes** (0345 498 6184; www.blakes.co.uk; 4-berth boat per week from £600) or **Richardson's** (01692-668981; www.richardsonsboatingholidays.co.uk; The Staithe, Stalham; boats per week from £550).

Exploring by Canoe

Canoes and kayaks can be rented for £35 to £40 per day at most of the big boating hubs. Hickling Broad offers lovely paddling, with fewer day boats competing for space.

Whispering Reeds (01692-598314; www.whisperingreeds.net; Staithe Rd, Hickling; canoe hire per 3/6hr £25/40; Easter-Oct) On the edge of Hickling Broad.

Waveney River Centre (01502-677343; www.waveneyrivercentre.co.uk; Burgh St Peter; kayak & canoe hire per day £35; Easter-Oct) On the River Waveney near Lowestoft.

trips from the quay, or walk into the **Blakeney National Nature Reserve** (NT; 01263-740241; www.nationaltrust.org.uk; dawn-dusk) FREE with long camera lenses in search of migratory birds. The spit on the far side of the reeds serves up a stunning, lonely sweep of sand.

Tours

At the end of the nature reserve, **Blakeney Point** is home to thousands of grey and common seals. who come to this secluded spot to pup, in winter and summer respectively. **Bishop's Boats** (01263-740753; www.bishopsboats.com; Blakeney Quay; adult/child £13/7; 1-4 boats daily Mar-Oct) runs here daily from Blakeney quay; **Beans Seal Trips** (01263-740505; www.beansboattrips.co.uk; Morston Quay; adult/child £13/7; 1-3 daily) runs from nearby Morston Quay, 1.5 miles east.

Sleeping & Eating

Kings Arms INN ££
(01263-740341; www.blakeneykingsarms.co.uk; Westgate St; r from £100; P) Simple, old-fashioned rooms (colourful carpets, bedspreads, pine furniture) in a pub that's been welcoming fishermen for centuries. Order

Mark the Canoe Man (☎07873-748408; www.thecanoeman.com; canoe hire 3/6hr £45/55, guided trips from £40; ⏱Apr-Oct) Arranges guided trips to areas the cruisers can't reach, as well as renting canoes and kayaks for self-paddling; you can put in at Wroxham, Horning, Beccles and other locations.

Exploring on Foot & by Bike

Despite its waterlogged reputation, the Broads are criss-crossed by a web of walking trails, including the 61-mile **Weavers' Way**, which links Cromer to Great Yarmouth.

The 15-mile section between Aylsham and Stalham is open to bicycles, and you can pick up wheels at **Broadland Cycle Hire** (☎07887 480331; www.norfolkbroadscycling.co.uk; Bewilderwood, Hoveton; bike hire adult/child per day £18/7, per week £70/30; ⏱10am-5pm Easter-Oct), based at the Bewilderwood adventure park near Hoveton.

Sights & Activities that Don't Involve Water?

Whether on foot, in a car, or in a boat, the following sights are well worth visiting.

Museum of the Broads (☎01692-581681; www.museumofthebroads.org.uk; The Staithe, Stalham; adult/child £6/2, boat trips £5/3; ⏱10am-4.30pm Sun-Fri Easter-Oct) Just off the A149 in Stalham, this folky museum features fine boats and some interesting displays on the life and history of the local marshmen. You can ride on a steam launch too.

Toad Hole Cottage (☎01692-678763; www.howhilltrust.org.uk; How Hill; ⏱10am-5pm Easter-Oct) FREE The life of Fen dwellers is revealed at this tiny cottage, a restored eel-catcher's home. You can also explore the gardens of attractive How Hill House, and follow a picturesque nature trail (adult/child £2.50/150) past some of the 'skeleton' windmills that were used to drain sections of the marshes.

Bewilderwood (☎01692-633033; www.bewilderwood.co.uk; Horning Rd, Hoveton; adult/child £17.50/15.50; ⏱10am-5.30pm Easter-Oct; 👪; 🚌5B) A forest fantasy playground for children and families, with zip wires, rope bridges, treehouses, boat trips, marsh walks, aerial mazes and more, to trigger young imaginations.

St Helen's Church (☎01603-270340; Ranworth; ⏱10.30am-5pm) The 'Cathedral of the Broads' is a handsome 14th-century structure, and inside you can see a magnificent painted medieval rood screen and a 15th-century *antiphoner* (illustrated book of prayers).

Bure Valley Steam Railway (☎01263-733858; www.bvrw.co.uk; Aylsham; adult/child return £14.50/7; ⏱2-7 trains daily Apr-Oct; P) Steam buffs will love this miniature loco, which puffs along 9 miles of narrow-gauge tracks between Aylsham and Wroxham.

Getting Around

Wroxham is the easiest place to reach by public transport; Konect bus 5B runs from Norwich (£3, 45 minutes, hourly Monday to Saturday), continuing to Stalham (£3.20, 35 minutes).

some substantial pub grub (mains from £10 to £15; meals served noon to 9pm), then, for great theatre gossip, ask landlady Marjorie about her career on the stage.

Moorings MODERN BRITISH ££
(☎01263-740054; www.blakeney-moorings.co.uk; High St; mains £17-27; ⏱11am-2.30pm & 6pm-9pm Tue-Sat) Perfectly pitched fish dishes have won this bright, friendly bistro a loyal following – try the spicy Norfolk crab cakes or about the most East Anglian dish you could imagine: sea trout, clams and samphire, with saffron jus.

Wells-next-the-Sea

☎01328 / POP 2165

After the marsh-fringed villages of Cley and Blakeney, Wells feels like a return to the classic English seaside. From the busy fishing quay a mile-long road runs out over former marshland to the vast, sandy Wells Beach, backed by a pastel sweep of elevated beach huts and a long bank of dunes. It's extremely family-friendly and gets very busy on sunny days – come early to bag a parking space.

Sights & Activities

Lovely **Wells Beach** is the main focus of attention. There's a good beach cafe, and a miniature train (per person £1.50) connects town and beach during the tourist season.

Wells Maltings ART CENTRE
(01328-710885; www.wellsmaltings.org.uk; Staithe St; exhibitions 10am-4pm) FREE Part music venue, part theatre, part cinema, part museum and part exhibition space, Wells Maltings is the town's cultural hub. Check the website to see what's happening.

Wells & Walsingham Railway RAIL
(01328-711630; www.wwlr.co.uk; Stiffkey Rd; adult/child return £9.50/7.50; 4-5 trains daily Mar-Nov) The longest 10.25in narrow-gauge railway in the world puffs for five picturesque miles from Wells to the village of Little Walsingham, a Catholic pilgrimage site since medieval times, centred on the ruins of Reformation-ravaged Walsingham Priory.

Sleeping & Eating

Check to see if the **Wells YHA hostel** (www.yha.org.uk) on Church Plain has reopened to guests.

★ **Old Custom House** B&B ££
(01328-711463; www.eastquay.co.uk; East Quay; s/d from £100/120, ste s/d £110/130; P) This stately but comfortable white house by the quay has worn timbers, alcoves full of books and gorgeous creek views. Choose from snug 'Captain's Quarters' rooms or the grand four-poster suite. It also has two cute self-catering cottages for longer stays.

Wells Beach Cafe CAFE £
(www.holkham.co.uk; Wells Beach; mains from £5; 10am-5pm Mon-Fri, from 9am Sat & Sun;) This pastel-blue weatherboard cafe keeps beachgoers stocked up with bacon baps, chips, homemade chilli and takeaway hot chocolates. Outside there's a corral of picnic tables; inside there's a wood-burning stove for when the wind whips round.

Wells Crab House SEAFOOD £££
(01328-710456; www.wellscrabhouse.co.uk; 38 Freeman St; mains £18-30; noon-2.30pm & 6-9pm Tue-Sat, noon-3pm Sun) This temple to seafood can be booked out weeks in advance, so plan ahead if you want to feast on Wells crab, buttered lobster, crayfish tails, smoked salmon, cockles and more. Look out for more ambitious seafood dishes such as plaice fillets stuffed with chorizo, peppers and preserved lemons.

Information

Tourist Office (01328-710885; www.north-norfolk.gov.uk; Wells Maltings, Staithe St; 10am-3pm Wed-Mon) Lots of local leaflets and maps.

Getting There & Away

Wells is a pivot point for coastal bus services. The daily Coasthopper CH1 runs east to Cromer (£4.40, one hour, hourly); the Coastliner 36 runs west to King's Lynn (£5.80, 1¾ hours, hourly).

Holkham

01328 / POP 220

The village of Holkham was the pet project of a single family. The Cokes, hereditary Earls of Leicester, constructed both lavish Holkham Hall, and the immaculate village of brick and flint houses that surrounds it.

Sights

★ **Holkham National Nature Reserve** NATURE RESERVE
(www.holkham.co.uk; parking per hour/day £2/9; car park 6am-6pm;) The shoreline in front of Holkham is a stunning sweep of dune-backed sand, divided from the village by a wide buffer of salt marshes, meadows and pine forest. It's arguably Norfolk's prettiest beach, but it's no secret, and visitors come in droves to paddle, sunbathe, picnic and scan the dunes for rare birds from hides on the edge of the woods. Access to the 14-sq-mile reserve is from the car park opposite Holkham village, but be ready for a 1-mile walk to the sand.

★ **Holkham Hall & Estate** HISTORIC BUILDING
(01328-713111; www.holkham.co.uk; adult/child £17/8.50, parking £4; noon-4pm Sun, Mon & Thu Mar-Oct, grounds daily 9am-5pm, till 4pm Nov-Mar; P) Holkham Hall was the ancestral seat of the Earls of Leicester and the present earl still lives in the palatial 18th-century Palladian mansion constructed by Earl Thomas Coke. The perfectly symmetrical, Italianate house was essentially constructed as a display case for the earl's astonishing collection of classical sculpture and painting, assembled during a grand tour of Europe from 1712 to 1718. Guided visits explore the guest rooms, with their original tapestry and *cafoy* (fabric) wall

THE QUEEN'S COUNTRY ESTATE

Both monarchists and republicans will find fuel for their respective positions at **Sandringham** (☎01485-545400; www.sandringhamestate.co.uk; adult/child £15.30/7.50 plus booking fee; ⊙10am-4pm selected dates Apr-Oct; P; 🚌35), the Queen's extravagant country estate.

No luxury was spared when this elegant stately home was built in 1870 by the then Prince and Princess of Wales (who later became King Edward VII and Queen Alexandra). Appropriately, the house is still decorated as it was in Edwardian times, and an army of gardeners still tends to the vast sea of gardens and grounds.

It's surreal to imagine generations of royals treating this grand house as just a family home. The stables today house a flag-waving museum filled with royal memorabilia. The superb vintage-car collection includes the very first royal motor from 1900.

Sandringham is 6 miles northeast of King's Lynn off the A149. Bus 35 runs from King's Lynn (£2.80, 20 minutes, every two hours).

coverings, and the warren of hidden passageways used by servants.

Sleeping

★Victoria INN £££
(☎01328-711008; www.holkham.co.uk; Park Rd; s/d from £125/150; P 🛜 🐾) In the village of staff houses constructed to service Holkham Hall, the graceful, flint-fronted Victoria is an elegant place to stay or dine after exploring the hall and beach. Spread over several buildings, rooms pay a subtle nod to Edwardian design, with gleaming bathrooms and soft upholstery. The kitchen cooks up a storm (mains £7 to £27), using produce sourced from Holkham Estate; check if it has reopened to nonguests.

Burnham Deepdale & Around

☎01485 / POP 877

The stretch of coast spanning the tiny villages of Burnham Deepdale, Brancaster Staithe, Titchwell and Thornham is a lovely span of marshes, creeks and distant dune-backed beaches. Just inland, the hamlet of **Burnham Thorpe** was the childhood home of Admiral Lord Nelson. A side lane from Brancaster provides the easiest access to the sand. Contact the **tourist office** (☎01485-210256; www.deepdalebackpackers.co.uk; Burnham Deepdale; ⊙9am-5pm Mon-Sat, 10am-4pm Sun) at Deepdale Farm for information on kitesurfing or windsurfing.

Sights

RSPB Titchwell Marsh NATURE RESERVE
(RSPB; ☎01485-210779; www.rspb.org.uk; Titchwell; adult/child £5/2.50; ⊙9.30am-5pm Mar-Oct, to 4pm Nov-Feb; P) About 3 miles west of Burnham Deepdale, the marshland, sandbars and lagoons of Titchwell Marsh nature reserve attract vast numbers of birds, and similar numbers of birders. In spring, listen out for the booming call of the bittern; summer brings marsh harriers, avocets, terns and nesting bearded tits. In winter you'll see more than 20 species of wading birds and countless ducks and geese.

Sleeping & Eating

★Deepdale Backpackers & Camping HOSTEL £
(☎01485-210256; www.deepdalebackpackers.co.uk; Burnham Deepdale; dm £13-21, r £40-110, sites £9-59; P @ 🛜) 🍃 For backpackers it doesn't get much better than this: you can camp in the grounds (in your own tent or motor home), stay in private rooms, or – in normal times – sleep in spick-and-span en-suite dorms in converted stables. There's a capacious and well-equipped kitchen, a barbecue area, hot showers, and a colourful lounge warmed by a wood-burning stove. Check to see if dorm beds are available again.

★Titchwell Manor HOTEL £££
(☎01485-210221; www.titchwellmanor.com; Titchwell, near Brancaster; r £150-290; P @ 🛜) Dreamy Titchwell Manor is a swish, contemporary reinvention of a grand Victorian house. Inside, you'll find a modern-meets-mid-century theme, with bold designer wallpaper, Regency curtains and eclectic furniture; rooms at the front gaze across the marshes to the sea.

HOUGHTON HALL

Built for Britain's first de-facto prime minister, Sir Robert Walpole, in 1730, Palladian-style **Houghton Hall** (01485-528569; www.houghtonhall.com; near King's Lynn; adult/child £16/free; 11am-5pm Wed, Thu & Sun May-late Sep; P) is famed for its lavish interiors, overflowing with gilt, tapestries, murals, woodcarving, statuary and heirloom furniture. The surrounding park and the 2-hectare walled garden are dotted with contemporary sculptures by Rachel Whiteread, Henry Moore and others. Houghton Hall is just off the A148, 13 miles east of King's Lynn. Hours vary; call for the latest information.

★**White Horse** MODERN BRITISH ££
(01485-210262; www.whitehorsebrancaster.co.uk; Main Rd, Brancaster Staithe; mains £14-26; noon-9pm; P) Backing onto a sweep of marshland, the White Horse celebrates Norfolk seafood in all its myriad forms: locally smoked salmon and prawns, saffron-pickled cockles, Brancaster oysters, dressed Cromer crab. It also serves plenty of local meats and poultry. Dine inside or under a marquee in the garden; the sharing seafood platter (£62) is a veritable feast.

King's Lynn

01553 / POP 42,800

Historically one of England's most important ports, King's Lynn was long known as 'the Warehouse on the Wash' after the nearby bay at the mouth of the River Great Ouse. In its heyday, it was said you could cross from one side of the river to the other by simply stepping from boat to boat. A certain nautical tang still remains, but most visitors come to admire the magnificent town houses built by medieval merchants along the cobbled streets, and enjoy the relaxed, unfussed pace of life.

Sights

Start your explorations at the 15th-century town hall, then follow a genteel row of town houses along Queen St to Purfleet Quay, where a statue of Charles II crowns the **Custom House**, built in 1683. Along the riverbank, note the sturdy flood defences, built to end centuries of inundation from the Great Ouse. Continue along King St past the 15th-century **St George's Guildhall** (www.shakespearesguildhalltrust.org.uk; 29 King St; 10am-2pm Mon-Sat), where Shakespeare reputedly performed, and a succession of courtyards crowded with medieval merchants' warehouses.

Stories of Lynn MUSEUM
(01553-774297; www.storiesoflynn.co.uk; Saturday Market Pl; adult/child £3.95/1.95; 10am-4.30pm) The lower levels of King's Lynn's town hall – a magnificent chequerboard flint structure that started life in 1421 as a guildhall – are given over to a highly entertaining interactive museum telling the stories of local seafarers, explorers, mayors and ne'er-do-wells. Don't miss local murderer Eugene Aram relating his sorry tale in the Georgian-era jail.

Lynn Museum MUSEUM
(01553-775001; www.museums.norfolk.gov.uk; Market St; adult/child £4.70/4, Oct-Mar free; 10am-5pm Tue-Sat) The town museum is worth a nosey for its fairground relics, gold Iceni coins and the **Seahenge Gallery**, which tells the fascnating story of the early Bronze Age timber circle that lay submerged off Holme-next-the-Sea for 4000 years, before being rediscovered in 1998.

True's Yard MUSEUM
(01553-770479; www.truesyard.co.uk; North St; adult/child £3/1.50; 10am-4pm Tue-Sat) Few of the fishermen's cottages that once sprawled inland from the quayside survived the decline of fishing at King's Lynn, but you can see two 18th-century homes restored to their lived-in state at this intriguing museum, alongside displays on shipbuilding and fishing culture. Spare a thought for the families who once lived squeezed like sardines into these tiny dwellings.

King's Lynn Minster CHURCH
(St Margaret's Church; 01553-772858; www.stmargaretskingslynn.org.uk; St Margaret's Pl; noon-2pm Tue & Thu) Built in a patchwork of styles, this great church includes Flemish brasses and a remarkable 17th-century moon dial, which informed residents of the tide, not the time. You'll find historic flood-level markings by the west door. Hours vary; call for the latest information.

Festivals & Events

King's Lynn Festival CULTURAL
(www.kingslynnfestival.org.uk; ⏲Jul) East Anglia's most important cultural gathering, with a diverse mix of music, from medieval ballads to opera, as well as literary talks.

Sleeping & Eating

★ **Bank House** BOUTIQUE HOTEL ££
(☎01553-660492; www.thebankhouse.co.uk; King's Staithe Sq; s £85-120, d £115-220; P 📶) A statue of Charles I casts an eye over arrivals to this handsome Georgian town house near the quay, but inside the rooms are modern and fun-filled, with lots of soft upholstery and eye-pleasing splashes of colour.

Set behind arched windows in a wood-floored annexe, the house brasserie (dishes £14 to £25, open noon to 8pm) serves seriously good modern British food.

Marriott's Warehouse BRITISH ££
(☎01583-818500; www.marriottswarehouse.co.uk; South Quay; mains £13-18; ⏲10am-2.30pm & 5-9pm Mon-Sat, 10am-3pm Sun) This restored 16th-century warehouse is a great place for a pint or a bite overlooking the River Great Ouse. Enjoy steaks, smoked salmon, mushroom burgers, fish and chips and more, either inside or outdoors next to a sculpture of drying fish fillets.

Information

Tourist Office (☎01553-763044; www.visitwestnorfolk.com; Town Hall, Saturday Market Pl; ⏲10am-5pm Mon-Sat, from noon Sun Apr-Sep, to 4pm Oct-Mar) At the town hall.

Getting There & Away

Bus From Monday to Saturday, the **Coastliner 36** (www.lynxbus.co.uk) bus runs from King's Lynn along the north Norfolk coast to Wells-next-the-Sea (£5.80, 1¾ hours), where you can swap to the **Coasthopper CH1** (www.sanderscoaches.com) to Cromer (£4.40, one hour, hourly). A special all-day £10 ticket allows unlimited travel on both routes.

Train There are hourly trains from Cambridge (£10.70, one hour) via Ely, and from London King's Cross (£38.60, 1¾ hours).

AT A GLANCE

POPULATION
7.7 million

LARGEST CITY
Birmingham

BEST HISTORIC PUB
Ye Olde Trip to Jerusalem (p448)

BEST GASTROPUB
Hammer & Pincers (p461)

BEST FARM SHOP
Ludlow Food Centre (p444)

WHEN TO GO

Jun–Sep
Typically warm and sunny; the best season for walking and cycling.

Oct–Feb
Chilly, often damp weather; some sights closed; festive lights, fairs and celebratory menus in the lead-up to Christmas.

Mar–May
Lengthening days; spring blossoms; flourishing cultural activities.

Ye Olde Trip to Jurasalem pub (p438), Nottingham
NIGEL JARVIS/SHUTTERSTOCK ©

Birmingham & the Midlands

If you're searching for quintessentially English countryside – green valleys, chocolate-box villages of wonky black-and-white houses, woodlands steeped in legend and magnificent stately homes – you'll find it here in the country's heart.

You'll also find the relics of centuries of industrial history, exemplified by the World Heritage–listed mills of Ironbridge and the Derwent Valley, and today's dynamic cities, including Britain's second-largest, Birmingham: a canal-woven industrial crucible reinvented as a cultural and creative hub. Beyond are tumbling hills where the air is so clean you can taste it and walkers and cyclists head to vanish into the vastness of the landscape.

INCLUDES

Birmingham & the Midlands Highlights

1 **Library of Birmingham** (p406) Surveying the buzzing city of Birmingham from its library's rooftop 'secret garden'.

2 **Peak District** (p469) Hiking, cycling or driving through England's first national park.

3 **Lincoln** (p453) Strolling the William the Conqueror–built castle walls overlooking the soaring cathedral in this historic city.

4 **Ironbridge Gorge** (p437) Museum-hopping in the birthplace of the Industrial Revolution.

5 **King Richard III: Dynasty, Death & Discovery** (p459) Learning about King Richard III's life and death and the discovery of his remains in Leicester.

6 **Stratford-upon-Avon** (p419) Visiting the Bard's schoolroom and reimagined town house before catching an RSC performance in his Tudor hometown.

7 **Morgan Motor Company** (p429) Touring Great Malvern's venerable car factory and taking a car for a spin through the surrounding hills.

8 **Burghley House** (p457) Wandering the halls and gardens of this stately Stamford home.

North Sea
Humber
Scunthorpe
M180
Grimsby
Doncaster
M1
Rotherham
SHEFFIELD
Sheffield
A57
Worksop
Gainsborough
Market Rasen
Louth
Trent
Eyam
Chatsworth House
Sherwood Forest National Nature Reserve
Tuxford
Lincoln
Chesterfield
Bakewell
Hardwick Hall
A1(M1)
Horncastle
Skegness
Waddington
Spilsby
Matlock Bath
Edwinstowe
Newstead Abbey
Clipstone
LINCOLNSHIRE
A16
Cromford
Newark-on-Trent
Southwell
Coningsby
NOTTINGHAMSHIRE
Witham
Belper
M1
A46
A17
Sleaford
Boston
The Wash
Ashbourne
DERBYSHIRE
Nottingham
Derby
Grantham
East Midlands Airport
A38
Woolsthorpe Manor
Wymeswold
Spalding
A17
Burton-upon-Trent
Loughborough
Melton Mowbray
A1
The Fens
A16
Packington
NORFOLK
Whitwell
Stamford
Oakham
Sutton Cheney
M1
Tamworth
Leicester
Rutland Water
Edith Weston
Peterborough
Drayton Manor
Bosworth Battlefield
LEICESTERSHIRE
A47
Lyddington
A5
Fotheringhay
Market Harborough
Birmingham Airport
Kettering
CAMBRIDGESHIRE
Coventry
Catthorpe
Rugby
NORTHAMPTONSHIRE
Kenilworth
Stoneleigh Abbey
Althorp House
M40
Warwick
Northampton
Cambridge
Charlecote Park
Sulgrave Manor
Stratford-upon-Avon
Stoke Bruerne
Towcester
BEDFORDSHIRE
M1
Silverstone
Banbury
Milton Keynes
Luton
HERTFORDSHIRE
BUCKINGHAMSHIRE
OXFORDSHIRE
3
5
6
8

Activities

Famous walking trails such as the **Pennine Way** and **Limestone Way** wind across the Peak District's hills, while challenging cycling routes include the **Pennine Cycleway**. The Marches, tracing the English–Welsh border, are also wonderful walking territory.

Watersports abound at Rutland Water; Hereford and Ironbridge Gorge offer canoeing and kayaking.

Getting There & Around

Birmingham Airport (p413) and East Midlands Airport (p466), near Derby, are the main air hubs.

There are excellent rail connections to towns across the Midlands. **National Express** (☎ 08717 818181; www.nationalexpress.com), at Birmingham Coach Station, and local bus companies connect larger towns and villages to each other and to destinations further afield, though services are reduced in the low season. For general route information, consult Traveline for the **East Midlands** (☎ 0871 200 2233; www.travelineeastmidlands.co.uk) or the **West Midlands** (☎ 0871 200 2233; www.traveline-midlands.co.uk). Ask locally about discounted all-day tickets.

BIRMINGHAM

☎ 0121 / POP 1,128,100

Regeneration, renewal and grand-scale construction continue apace in Britain's second-largest city. A state-of-the-art library, a gleaming shopping centre atop revitalised New St station and beautifully restored Victorian buildings are just some of the successful initiatives of its Big City Plan, following the striking Mailbox and Bullring shopping malls and the iconic Selfridges building's 'bubble-wrapped' facade. Work is underway on extensions to the Metro (light rail/tram) network, and on the centrepiece Paradise development's new hotels, public spaces, and glitzy residential and commercial buildings, with final completion due in 2025.

Alongside Birmingham's picturesque canals, waterside attractions, outstanding museums and galleries is an explosion of gastronomic restaurants, cool and/or secret cocktail bars and craft breweries. Thriving legacies of the city's industrial heritage include its Jewellery Quarter, Cadbury manufacturing plant and former custard factory turned cutting-edge creative hub.

And in 2022 – all things going well – Birmingham will host the Commonwealth Games. 'Brum', as it's locally dubbed, is buzzing.

Sights

City Centre

Birmingham's grandest civic buildings are clustered around pedestrianised **Victoria Square**, at the western end of New St, dominated by the stately facade of **Council House**, built between 1874 and 1879, and the 1834 **Town Hall** (☎ 0121-780 4949; www.thsh.co.uk/town-hall), styled after the Temple of Castor and Pollux in Rome. Public art here includes modernist sphinxes and a **fountain** topped by a naked female figure, dubbed 'the floozy in the Jacuzzi', overlooked by a disapproving **statue of Queen Victoria**.

To the west, **Centenary Square** is bookended by the art-deco Hall of Memory War Memorial, the **International Convention Centre** (ICC; ☎ 0121-200 2000; www.theicc.co.uk; 8 Centenary Sq) and the **Symphony Hall** (☎ 0121-289 6333; www.thsh.co.uk; 8 Centenary Sq). There's a gleaming golden **statue** of the leading lights from Birmingham's Industrial Revolution: Matthew Boulton, James Watt and William Murdoch. Centenary Sq's showpiece is the spiffing Library of Birmingham.

★ Library of Birmingham LIBRARY
(☎ 0121-242 4242; www.birmingham.gov.uk/libraries; Centenary Sq; ⌚ground fl 9am-9pm Mon & Tue, 11am-9pm Wed-Fri, to 5pm Sat, rest of bldg 11am-7pm Mon & Tue, to 5pm Wed-Sat) Resembling a glittering stack of gift-wrapped presents, the Francine Houben–designed Library of Birmingham is an architectural triumph. The 2013-opened building features a subterranean amphitheatre, spiralling interior, viewing decks and glass elevator to the 7th-floor 'secret garden' with panoramic views over the city. In addition to its archives, and photography and rare-book collections (including Britain's most important Shakespeare collection), there are gallery spaces, 160-plus computers and a cafe. The British Film Institute Mediatheque provides free access to the National Film Archive.

Birmingham Back to Backs HISTORIC BUILDING
(NT; ☎ 0121-666 7671; www.nationaltrust.org.uk; 55-63 Hurst St; 75min tour adult/child £8.65/5.25; ⌚tours by reservation Tue-Sun) Quirky tours of

this cluster of restored back-to-back terraced houses take you through four working-class homes, telling the stories of those who lived here between the 1840s and the 1970s. Book ahead by phone for the compulsory guided tour. For an even more vivid impression of what life was like here, you can book to stay in basic three-storey period cottages at 52 and 54 Inge St (doubles with wi-fi from £130). Guests receive a free Back to Backs tour.

Birmingham Museum & Art Gallery MUSEUM, GALLERY
(0121-348 8000; www.birminghammuseums.org.uk; Chamberlain Sq; 10am-5pm Sat-Thu, 10.30am-5pm Fri) FREE Major Pre-Raphaelite works by Rossetti, Edward Burne-Jones and others are among the highlights of the delightful Birmingham Museum & Art Gallery's impressive collection of ancient treasures and Victorian art. Excellent temporary exhibitions range from historical collections to emerging contemporary artists.

Its **Edwardian Tearooms** are an elegant spot for afternoon tea and have 'champagne buzzers' installed in its booths to order bubbles at the touch of a button. There's also a casual cafe.

Birmingham Cathedral CATHEDRAL
(0121-262 1840; www.birminghamcathedral.com; Colmore Row; by donation; 7.30am-6.30pm Mon-Fri, to 5pm Sat & Sun) Dedicated to St Philip, this small but perfectly formed cathedral was constructed in a neoclassical style between 1709 and 1715. Pre-Raphaelite artist Edward Burne-Jones was responsible for the magnificent stained-glass windows.

Times for free guided tours and concerts are posted on its website's What's On page.

Thinktank MUSEUM
(0121-348 8000; www.birminghammuseums.org.uk; Millennium Point, Curzon St; adult/child £14/10.25, planetarium show £2.50; 10am-5pm) Surrounded by the footprints of vanished factories, the Millennium Point development incorporates this entertaining and ambitious attempt to make science accessible to children. Highlights include galleries on the past (Birmingham's industrial breakthroughs), present (how stuff works) and future, as well as an outdoor science garden and a planetarium.

St Martin's Church CHURCH
(0121-600 6020; www.bullring.org; Egbaston St; 10am-4pm Mon-Sat, 9am-7pm Sun) Birmingham architect Alfred Chatwin designed this Victorian Gothic church in the Bullring. The 1873-completed structure occupies a site where a church has stood since 1290 and is thought to have been a place of worship as far back as Saxon times.

Birmingham Canals

During the industrial age, Birmingham was a major hub on the English canal network and today the city has more miles of canals than Venice. Narrow boats still float through the heart of the city, passing a string of glitzy wharf-side developments.

Ikon Gallery GALLERY
(0121-248 0708; www.ikon-gallery.org; 1 Oozells Sq; 11am-4pm Tue-Sun) FREE Within the glitzy Brindley Pl development of banking offices and designer restaurants, a converted Gothic schoolhouse contains the cutting-edge Ikon Gallery. Prepare to be thrilled, bemused or outraged, depending on your take on conceptual art.

National Sea Life Centre AQUARIUM
(0121-643 6777; www.visitsealife.com; 3a Brindley Pl; £18.30; 10am-5pm Mon-Fri, to 6pm Sat & Sun) Exotic marine creatures including otters, jellyfish, piranhas and razor-jawed hammerhead sharks swim in the Sir Norman Foster–designed National Sea Life Centre. Tickets must be pre-purchased online. Check for information about various talks, feeding times, tours and activities.

Jewellery Quarter

Birmingham has been a major jewellery player since Charles II acquired a taste for it in 17th-century France. The gentrifying Jewellery Quarter, three-quarters of a mile northwest of the city centre, still produces 40% of UK-manufactured jewellery. Dozens of workshops open to the public are listed online at www.jewelleryquarter.net.

Take the Metro from Snow Hill or the train from Moor St to the Jewellery Quarter station.

Museum of the Jewellery Quarter MUSEUM
(0121-348 8140; www.birminghammuseums.org.uk; 75 Vyse St; adult/child £7/3; 10.30am-4pm Tue-Sat) The Smith & Pepper jewellery factory is preserved as it was on its closing day in 1981 after 80 years of operation. Guided tours lasting around one hour explain the long history of the trade in Birmingham and let you watch master jewellers at work. Entry to the temporary exhibition space and shop is free.

Birmingham

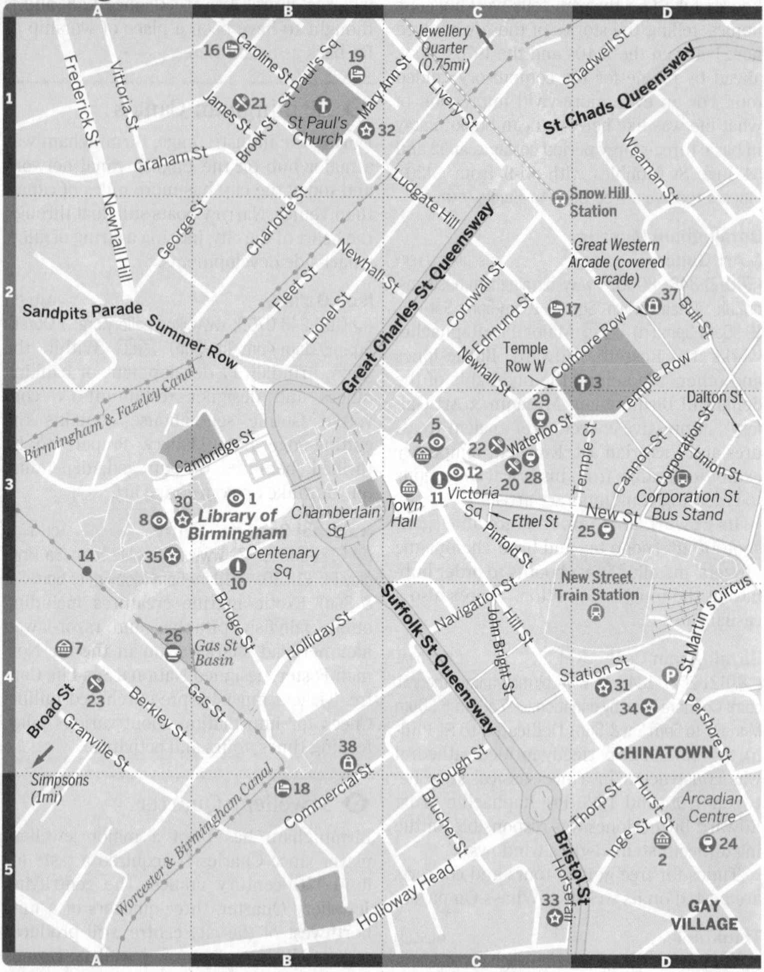

Outlying Areas

★Barber Institute of Fine Arts GALLERY

(☎0121-414 7333; www.barber.org.uk; University of Birmingham, Edgbaston; ⏰10am-5pm Mon-Fri, 11am-5pm Sat & Sun) **FREE** At the University of Birmingham, 3 miles south of the city centre, the Barber Institute of Fine Arts has an astonishing collection of Renaissance masterpieces; European masters, such as Rubens and Van Dyck; British greats, including Gainsborough, Reynolds and Turner; and classics from modern titans Picasso, Magritte and others. Trains run from Birmingham New St to University station (£2.80, seven minutes, every 10 minutes), from where it's a 10-minute walk.

Custard Factory ARTS CENTRE

(☎0121-224 7777; www.digbeth.com/spaces/custardfactory; Gibb St; ⏰shops 10am-6pm Tue-Sat, event times vary) Just over a mile south-east of the city centre, Digbeth's creative quarter centres on the Custard Factory, a hip art-and-design enclave set in the converted buildings of the factory that once churned out British favourite Bird's Custard. The open-plan space is now full of artists' galleries, quirky design boutiques,

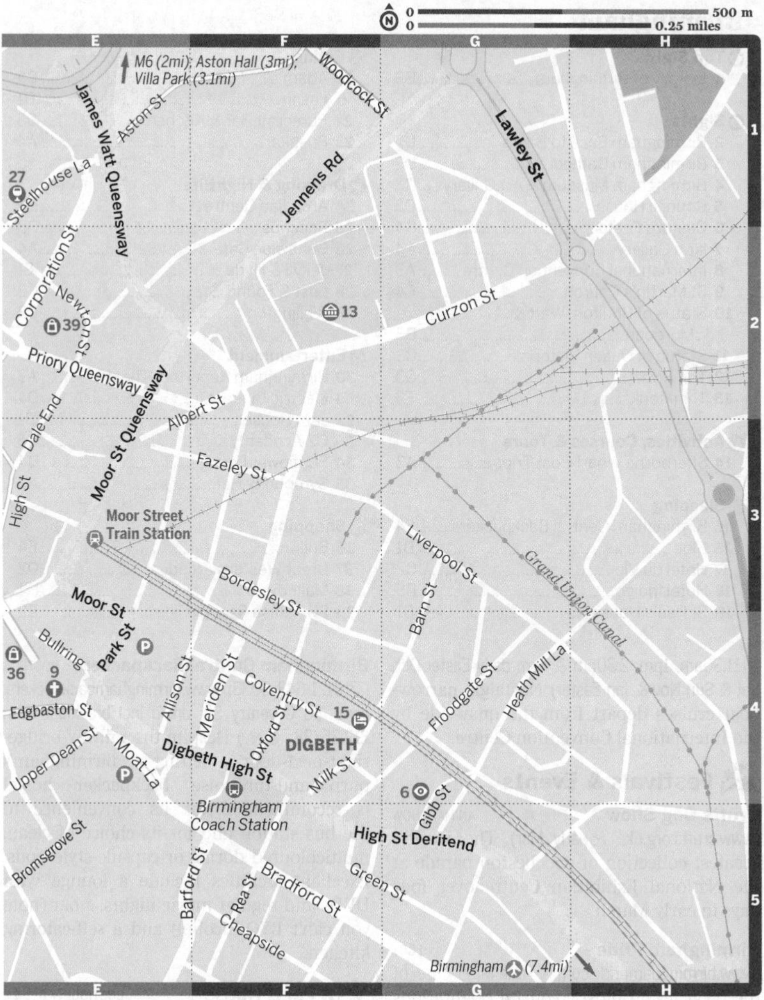

vintage-clothing outlets, one-off shops such as a skateboard specialist, and affordable, offbeat cafes and pop-up street-food stalls.

Cadbury World MUSEUM
(0121-393 6004; www.cadburyworld.co.uk; Linden Rd, Bournville; adult/child £18/13.25; 9am-4.30pm, hours vary) The next best thing to Willy Wonka's chocolate factory is Cadbury World, 4 miles south of Birmingham. It educates visitors about the history of cocoa and the Cadbury family, sweetening the deal with free samples, displays of chocolate-making machines and chocolate-themed attractions, including a 4D cinema with motion-sensor seats. Opening hours vary substantially; bookings are essential. Trains run from Birmingham New St to Bournville (£2.90, seven minutes, every 10 minutes), from where it's a signposted 10-minute walk.

Surrounding the aromatic chocolate works, pretty Bournville Village was built by the philanthropic Cadbury family to accommodate early-20th-century factory workers.

Tours

Sherborne Wharf Boat Trips CRUISE
(0121-455 6163; www.sherbornewharf.co.uk; Sherborne St; 65min cruise adult/child £8/6;

Birmingham

Top Sights	**Eating**
1 Library of Birmingham ... B3	20 Adam's ... C3
	21 Lasan ... B1
Sights	22 Purecraft Bar & Kitchen ... C3
2 Birmingham Back to Backs ... D5	23 Pushkar ... A4
3 Birmingham Cathedral ... D2	
4 Birmingham Museum & Art Gallery ... C3	**Drinking & Nightlife**
5 Council House ... C3	24 Arcadian Centre ... D5
6 Custard Factory ... G4	25 Bacchus ... D3
7 Ikon Gallery ... A4	26 Canalside Cafe ... A4
8 International Convention Centre ... A3	27 Jekyll & Hyde ... E1
9 St Martin's Church ... E4	28 Lost & Found ... C3
10 Statue of Boulton, Watt & Murdoch ... B3	29 Wellington ... C3
11 Statue of Queen Victoria ... C3	**Entertainment**
12 The River ... C3	30 Birmingham Repertory Theatre ... A3
13 Thinktank ... F2	31 Electric Cinema ... D4
	32 Jam House ... B1
Activities, Courses & Tours	33 O2 Academy ... C5
14 Sherborne Wharf Boat Trips ... A3	34 Sunflower Lounge ... D4
	35 Symphony Hall ... A3
Sleeping	
15 Birmingham Central Backpackers ... F4	**Shopping**
16 Bloc ... B1	36 Bullring ... E4
17 Hotel du Vin ... C2	37 Great Western Arcade ... D2
18 Hotel Indigo ... B5	38 Mailbox ... B4
19 St Pauls House ... B1	39 Swordfish Records ... E2

11.30am, 1pm, 2.30pm & 4pm daily Easter-Oct, Sat & Sun Nov & Jan-Easter) Nostalgic narrowboat cruises depart from the quay-side by the International Convention Centre.

Festivals & Events

Crufts Dog Show ANIMAL SHOW
(www.crufts.org.uk; early Mar) The world's greatest collection of pooches on parade at the National Exhibition Centre over four days in early March.

Birmingham Pride LGBT
(www.birminghampride.com; late May) One of the biggest and most colourful celebrations of LGBT+ culture in the country takes place over a weekend in late May.

Sleeping

Chains dominate Birmingham's hotel scene, which is aimed at business travellers, ensuring high weekday prices. Look out for cheap deals at weekends. Accommodation is often limited but several new hotels are set to open over the coming years.

B&Bs are concentrated outside the city centre in Acocks Green (to the southeast) or Edgbaston and Selly Oak (to the southwest).

Birmingham Central Backpackers HOSTEL £
(0121-643 0033; www.birminghambackpackers.com; 58 Coventry St; dm/d incl breakfast from £12.35/38;) Despite the railway-bridge-right-next-door setting, Birmingham's purple-and-turquoise backpacker hostel is recommended for its convenience to the bus station and for its choice of clean, multicoloured dorms or capsule-style pods. Excellent facilities include a lounge with DVDs and regular movie nights, a bar (note you can't BYO alcohol) and a self-catering kitchen.

★ **St Pauls House** BOUTIQUE HOTEL ££
(0121-272 0999; www.saintpaulshouse.com; 15-20 St Paul's Sq; d from £99;) Overlooking a park in the Jewellery Quarter, this independent hotel has 34 fresh, contemporary rooms with welcoming touches, such as hot-water bottles in woollen covers. Upcycled decor in its hip bar (with live music Saturday nights and Sunday afternoons) and restaurant includes industrial-style ropes (as wall hangings and in furnishings) referencing the building's original use as a rope factory.

Bloc HOTEL ££
(0121-212 1223; www.blochotels.com; 77 Caroline St; d/apt from £79/114;) Located in

the Jewellery Quarter, Bloc excels in sharp, contemporary pod design. Rooms are tiny but space is cleverly stretched: flatscreen TVs are built into walls; there's under-bed storage; and bathrooms are compact but with luxe shower heads. Apartments have a kitchenette. Book carefully: rooms come with window or without.

Hotel du Vin BOUTIQUE HOTEL £££
(☎0121-794 3005; www.hotelduvin.com; 25 Church St; d/ste from £179/249; ❄@📶) Housed in the Victorian red-brick former Birmingham Eye Hospital, this branch of the upmarket Hotel du Vin chain has real class, with wrought-iron balustrades and classical murals. Its 66 rooms have spectacular bathrooms; there's a spa and a gym, a bistro with worn floorboards and a stellar wine list, plus a pub and lounge bar with comfy leather furniture.

Hotel Indigo BOUTIQUE HOTEL £££
(☎0121-643 2010; www.ihg.com; The Cube, Wharfside St; d from £174; 📶) A stylish operation on the 23rd and 24th floors of the Mailbox's annexe, the Cube, Birmingham's branch of the high-end Hotel Indigo chain marries a handy location with snazzy amenities and great views from its 52 rooms (some with balcony). There's a spa and small pool in the same building.

Eating

Pushkar INDIAN ££
(☎0121-643 7978; www.pushkardining.com; 245 Broad St; mains £8.25-19, 5-course vegetarian/meat tasting menu £30/41; ⏰5-11pm Mon-Sat) Classy north Indian and Punjabi cuisine takes centre stage in this glass-fronted, white tableclothed, gold-trimmed dining room. The elegant presentation extends to boxed menus and serviette-wrapped naan bread as well as stunning cocktails. Its swanky spin-off, **Praza** (☎0121-456 4500; www.praza.co.uk; 94-96 Hagley Rd, Edgbaston; mains £8-19, Sun Indian afternoon tea £20; ⏰5-11pm Mon-Sat, 1-9pm Sun), in Edgbaston, is also superb.

Purecraft Bar & Kitchen GASTROPUB ££
(☎0121-237 5666; www.purecraftbars.com; 30 Waterloo St; mains £9-18.50; ⏰noon-10pm Tue-Sat) Fabulous dishes created in Purecraft's open kitchen come with suggested beer pairings. The regularly changing menu might include Lawless Lager–battered fish and chips (with Veltins Pilsener); Brewer's Grain asparagus and broad-bean risotto (with Odell St Lupulin American Pale Ale); or grilled plaice with beer-and-parsley butter and Jersey Royal new potatoes (with Purity Mad Goose). Cards only (no cash).

Lasan INDIAN ££
(☎0121-212 3664; www.lasan.co.uk; 3-4 Dakota Bldgs, James St; mains £14-25; ⏰noon-2.30pm & 5-10pm Tue-Fri, noon-11pm Sat, to 9pm Sun) Expletive-loving chef Gordon Ramsay famously proclaimed elegant, upmarket Lasan, in Birmingham's Jewellery Quarter, Britain's 'Best Local Restaurant'. Its changing menu of elevated Indian dishes are served in an intimate dining room, accompanied by cocktails (and mocktails).

★**Simpsons** BRITISH £££
(☎0121-454 3434; www.simpsonsrestaurant.co.uk; 20 Highfield Rd, Edgbaston; 2-/3-course lunch menu £40/50, 3-course dinner menu £75; ⏰12.30-2.30pm & 6-10pm Wed-Fri, 12.30-3.30pm & 6.30-9pm Sat, 1-5pm Sun; 🌿👪) It's worth the 2.5-mile journey southwest of the centre to this gorgeous Georgian mansion in leafy Edgbaston for sensational Michelin-starred menus (kids and vegetarians catered for) in its contemporary dining rooms. You can also stay in one of three luxurious bedrooms upstairs (from £150) or take an all-day cookery class (Wednesday and Saturday, £150) at its Eureka Kitchen. Book ahead.

Adam's BRITISH £££
(☎0121-643 3745; www.adamsrestaurant.co.uk; New Oxford House, 16 Waterloo St; 3-course midweek lunch menu £45, 3-course/tasting dinner menu £75/97; ⏰noon-2pm & 7-9pm Tue-Sat) Michelin-starred Adam's wows with intricately prepared and presented flavour combinations, such as lamb sweetbreads with goats curd, mint and radish, monkfish with wild mussels, champagne and caviar, and pear, toasted hay, caramel and praline. English vintages are represented on its excellent wine list, which has extensive by-the-glass options. Book well ahead.

Drinking & Nightlife

Independent pubs and bars proliferate throughout the city.

Nightlife hubs in Birmingham include Broad St (aka the 'golden mile' – some say for the prevalence of fake tan here) and Chinatown's **Arcadian Centre** (www.thearcadian.co.uk; Hurst St; ⏰individual venue hours vary).

Postindustrial Digbeth has alternative clubs and club events in and around the Custard Factory (p408).

★Jekyll & Hyde PUB
(☎0121-236 0345; www.thejekyllandhyde.co.uk; 28 Steelhouse Lane; ⊙noon-11pm Mon-Thu, to midnight Fri, to 1am Sat; 📶) Potent cocktails (or rather 'elixirs, concoctions and potions') at this trippy spot are served in sweets jars, watering cans, teapots and miniature bathtubs – even a top hat. Downstairs, Mr Hyde's emporium has a cosy drawing room and an *Alice in Wonderland*–themed courtyard; upstairs is Dr Jekyll's Gin Parlour with over 100 different gins.

Lost & Found BAR
(www.the-lostandfound.co.uk; 8 Bennett's Hill; ⊙11am-10pm Mon-Sat, noon-10pm Sun; 📶) Fictitious Victorian-era explorer/professor Hettie G Watson is the inspiration for the botanical-library theme of this bar in an 1869-built former bank. Inside the domed entrance, amid soaring columns and timber panelling, its elevated seating is surrounded by plants, books, globes and maps. Hettie's 'secret emporium' bar-within-a-bar has antique mirrors, brass and steel fixtures, and more plants.

Wellington PUB
(www.thewellingtonrealale.co.uk; 37 Bennett's Hill; ⊙10am-midnight) The pastel wallpaper, timber bar and polished brass give the impression the Welly is frozen in time, but this spruced-up pub sheltering a timber-decked roof terrace is the best in the city for real ale. Its 27 hand-pulled beers and ciders include favourites from Black Country and Wye Valley as well as rare brews.

Snacks are limited to pork scratchings, pretzels et al, but you can BYO food or have takeaway delivered.

Bacchus BAR
(☎0121-632 5445; www.nicholsonspubs.co.uk; Burlington Arcade, New St; ⊙noon-10pm Mon-Fri, 11am-10pm Sat & Sun; 📶) Buried beneath the Burlington Arcade, this darkened drinking den has the ambience of a decadent underworld. Down a faux-marble-encased staircase, crumbling pillars and giant Grecian murals give way to soaring medieval-style stone arches, swords, suits of armour and candelabras. There's a great range of cask ales, gins and whiskies.

Canalside Cafe CAFE
(☎0121-643 3170; 35 Worcester Bar, Gas St; ⊙9am-11pm Mon-Sat, to 10.30pm Sun) Narrow boats glide past the terrace of this 18th-century lock-keeper's cottage, where the low-ceilinged interior is strung with nautical paraphernalia and warmed by an open fire. Drop by for a cuppa, a real ale, or a steaming mulled cider in winter.

☆ Entertainment

Sunflower Lounge LIVE MUSIC
(☎0121-632 6756; www.thesunflowerlounge.com; 76 Smallbrook Queensway; ⊙bar noon-1am Mon-Thu, noon-2am Fri & Sat, 2pm-1am Sun) This quirky little indie bar pairs a magnificent alternative soundtrack with a packed program of live gigs and DJ nights.

Electric Cinema CINEMA
(☎0121-643 7879; www.theelectric.co.uk; 47-49 Station St; standard/sofa seats £11.50/12.80, sofa seats with waiter service £16.80) Topped by its art-deco sign, this is the UK's oldest working cinema, operating since 1909. It screens mainly art-house films. Be waited upon in plush two-seater sofas, or have a drink in the small bar, which has a traditional absinthe fountain, cocktails themed around films currently showing and 'poptails' (popcorn-flavoured cocktails, in lieu of popcorn being available).

Birmingham Repertory Theatre THEATRE
(The Rep; ☎0121-236 4455; www.birmingham-rep.co.uk; Centenary Sq) Founded in 1913, today theatre production company 'the Rep' has three performance spaces: the Main House; the more experimental Door; and a 300-seat studio theatre presenting edgy drama and musicals, with an emphasis on contemporary work.

Jam House LIVE MUSIC
(☎0121-200 3030; www.thejamhouse.com; 3-5 St Paul's Sq; ⊙6pm-midnight Tue & Wed, to 1am Thu, to 2am Fri & Sat) Pianist Jools Holland was the brains behind this moody, smart-casual music venue (dress accordingly). Acts range from jazz big bands to famous soul crooners. Over 21s only.

O2 Academy LIVE MUSIC
(☎07704 001028; www.academymusicgroup.com/o2academybirmingham; 16-18 Horsefair, Bristol St; ⊙box office noon-4pm Mon-Sat) Birmingham's leading venue for big-name rockers and tribute bands as well as up-and-coming talent.

Shopping

Great Western Arcade SHOPPING CENTRE
(www.greatwesternarcade.co.uk; btwn Colmore & Temple Rows; ⊙individual shop hours vary) Topped with a glass roof, this tile-floored

Victorian-era arcade is a jewel filled with mostly independent shops.

Swordfish Records MUSIC
(www.swordfishrecords.co.uk; 66 Dalton St; ⏰10am-5.30pm Mon-Sat) A Birmingham institution, this independent record shop down a tiny backstreet brims with new and secondhand vinyl (and some CDs), including its own label releases. Robert Plant, Duran Duran's John Taylor, Dave Grohl and Neil Diamond are among its past customers. It's a great place to find out about under-the-radar gigs and festivals.

Mailbox MALL
(www.mailboxlife.com; 7 Commercial St; ⏰mall 10am-7pm Mon-Sat, 11am-5pm Sun, individual shop hours vary) Birmingham's stylish canal-side shopping experience, the redevelopment of the former Royal Mail sorting office, comes complete with designer hotels, a fleet of upmarket restaurants, the luxury department store Harvey Nichols and designer boutiques. Its super-snazzy metallic extension, the **Cube** (www.thecube.co.uk), houses Marco Pierre White's panoramic Steakhouse Bar & Grill on the 25th floor.

Bullring MALL
(www.bullring.co.uk; St Martin's Circus; ⏰10am-8pm Mon-Fri, 9am-8pm Sat, 11am-5pm Sun, individual shop hours vary) Split into two vast retail spaces – the East Mall and West Mall – the Bullring has all the international brands and chain cafes you could ask for, plus the standout architectural wonder of Selfridges, which looks out over the city like the compound eye of a giant robot insect.

Information

Comprehensive tourist information is available at www.visitbirmingham.com.

The ground-floor reception of the Library of Birmingham (p406) can also provide information for tourists.

The city centre, especially south of the Bullring and on and around Broad St, can get very rowdy with revellers on weekend nights.

Digbeth bus station and its surrounds can be quite rough after dark.

Getting There & Away

AIR

Birmingham Airport (BHX; ☎0871 222 0072; www.birminghamairport.co.uk), 8 miles east of the city centre, has direct flights to destinations around the UK and Europe, as well as direct long-haul routes to Dubai, India and the USA.

Fast and convenient trains run regularly between Birmingham New St and Birmingham International stations (£3.90, 15 minutes, every 10 minutes). Birmingham International is linked to the terminal by the Air-Rail Link monorail (free, two minutes, frequent), which runs from 3.30am to 12.30am.

Alternatively, take bus X1 (£2.50, 35 minutes, up to two hourly) from Moor St Queensway, which run 24 hours.

A taxi from the airport to the city centre typically costs £30 to £45.

BUS

Most intercity buses run from **Birmingham Coach Station** (☎0871 781 8181; Mill Lane, Digbeth).

National Express (www.nationalexpress.com) coaches link Birmingham with major cities across the country, including the following.

London Victoria £3 to £14.40, 3¼ hours, hourly or better

Manchester £3 to £24, 2½ hours, every 90 minutes

Oxford £8 to £25, 1¾ hours, six daily

TRAIN

Most long-distance trains leave from Birmingham New St station, but Chiltern Railways runs to London Marylebone (£25, two hours, two per hour) from Birmingham Snow Hill, and West Midlands Railway runs to Stratford-upon-Avon (£8.60, 40 minutes, half-hourly) from Birmingham Moor St stations.

Construction on the High Speed Rail (HS2) line – connecting London with Birmingham in just 40 minutes – is set to commence in 2029 and to be completed by 2033.

Useful services from New St include the following.

Derby £20.40, 40 minutes, two per hour

Leicester £15.40, one hour, hourly

Lichfield £5.70, 30 minutes, up to three per hour

London Euston £92, 1½ hours, up to four per hour

Manchester £39.60, 1½ hours, three per hour

Nottingham £35.20, 1¼ hours, up to three per hour

Shrewsbury £16.20, one hour, two per hour

Getting Around

CAR

During central Birmingham's ongoing construction, traffic into and around the city is severely disrupted and parking is limited. Check with your accommodation about access (don't rely on your satnav, or assume hotels' car parks are operational). Updated details of road closures are posted at www.birmingham.gov.uk/roadworks.

A 'Clean Air Zone' levying fees on older vehicles to reduce pollution in Birmingham is set to come into effect in 2021; visit www.brumbreathes.co.uk for information.

PUBLIC TRANSPORT

Local buses run from a convenient hub located on Corporation St, just north of where it connects with New St. For routes, download a copy of the *Network Birmingham Map and Guide* from www.nxbus.co.uk. Single-trip tickets start from £1.50.

Be aware that bus stops may change during construction works in the city centre and journey times may be extended.

Birmingham's single tram line, the Metro (www.westmidlandsmetro.com), links Centenary Sq with Wolverhampton via Victoria Sq, New St station, the Jewellery Quarter, West Bromwich and Dudley.

An extension from Centenary Sq to Edgbaston is due to open in 2021.

Tickets start from £1.50. Various saver tickets covering buses and trains are available from the **Network West Midlands Travel Centre** (www.networkwestmidlands.com; ⏲8.30am-5.30pm Mon-Sat) at New St station.

WARWICKSHIRE

Warwickshire could have been just another picturesque county of rolling hills and market towns were it not for the English language's most famous wordsmith. William Shakespeare was born and died in Stratford-upon-Avon, and the sights linked to his life draw tourists from around the globe. Famous Warwick Castle attracts similar crowds. Elsewhere visitor numbers dwindle but Kenilworth has atmospheric castle ruins, Rugby celebrates the sport that takes its name at its World Rugby Hall of Fame, and Coventry, the UK City of Culture from mid-2021 to mid-2022, claims two extraordinary cathedrals and an unmissable motoring museum.

Getting There & Around

Coventry is the main transport hub, with frequent rail connections to London Euston and Birmingham New St.

Coventry

☎024 / POP 352,900

Coventry was once a bustling hub for the production of cloth, clocks, bicycles, automobiles and munitions. It was this last industry that drew the German Luftwaffe in WWII: on the night of 14 November 1940, the city was so badly blitzed that the Nazis coined a new verb, *coventrieren,* meaning 'to flatten'. A handful of medieval streets that escaped the bombers offer a glimpse of old Coventry.

The city faced a further setback with the collapse of the British motor industry in the 1980s, but is undergoing a resurgence today thanks to its redeveloped and expanded university, and its vibrant cultural scene, which saw it awarded the UK City of Culture 2021, bringing renewed investment and new openings.

Sights

★Coventry Transport Museum MUSEUM

(☎024-7623 4270; www.transport-museum.com; Hales St; adult/child £14/7, speed simulator adult/child £5/3.50; ⏲10am-5pm, last admission 3pm) This stupendous museum has hundreds of vehicles, from horseless carriages to jet-powered, land-speed-record breakers. There's a brushed-stainless-steel DeLorean DMC-12 (of *Back to the Future* fame) with gull-wing doors, alongside a gorgeous Jaguar E-type, a Daimler armoured car and, for 1970s British-design-oddity enthusiasts, a Triumph TR7 and an Austin Allegro 'Special'. View the Thrust SCC, the current holder of the World Land Speed Record and the Thrust 2, the previous record holder. Kids will love the 4D Thrust speed simulator.

Also on display are 300 bicycles and 120 motorcycles. Tickets are valid for multiple entries over one year.

★Coventry Cathedral CATHEDRAL

(☎024-7652 1210; www.coventrycathedral.org.uk; Priory Row; cathedral & ruins by donation, tower climb adult/child £5/2.50, Blitz Experience Museum £1; ⏲cathedral & tower 10.30am-3pm Mon-Sat, to 2.30pm Sun, ruins 9am-5pm daily, museum closed Nov–mid-Feb, hours can vary) The evocative ruins of **St Michael's Cathedral**, built around 1300 but destroyed by Nazi incendiary bombs in the Blitz, stand as a memorial to Coventry's darkest hour and as a symbol of peace and reconciliation. Climb the 180 steps of the **Gothic spire** for panoramic views.

WORTH A TRIP

RUGBY

Warwickshire's second-largest hub, Rugby is an attractive market town whose history dates to the Iron Age. But it's most famous for the sport that was invented here and now takes its name, and is a place of pilgrimage for fans.

The game was invented at a prestigious Rugby School in 1823 when William Webb Ellis is said to have caught the ball during a football match and broken the rules by running with it. Situated just across from the **Webb Ellis Rugby Football Museum** (☎01788-567777; 5-6 Matthews St; ⊙9.30am-5pm Mon-Sat) FREE, the school itself is closed to the public, but you can peek at the hallowed ground through the gates on Barby Rd. A **statue of William Webb Ellis** (cnr Lawrence Sheriff St & Dunchurch Rd) stands outside the main Rugby School gates.

The whizz-bang interactive **World Rugby Hall of Fame** is inside the **Rugby Art Gallery & Museum** (☎01788-533217; www.ragm.co.uk; Little Elborow St; ⊙gallery & museum 10am-4pm Tue-Fri, to 3pm Sat, World Rugby Hall of Fame 10.15am-4.15pm Tue-Fri, to 3.15pm Sat) FREE complex. You'll need to book separate timeslots for the Hall of Fame and for the Art Gallery & Museum.

The top place to stay is **Brownsover Hall** (☎01788-546100; www.brownsoverhall.co.uk; Brownsover Lane, Old Brownsover; d from £112; P 🛜), a Grade II–listed Gothic Revival manor (where Frank Whittle designed the turbo jet engine) with 47 rooms split between the creaking old house with a monumental central timber staircase and the more modern converted stables (dinner, bed and breakfast packages available). Set in 2.8 hectares of woodland and manicured gardens, it's 2.7 miles north of Rugby.

Rugby is 13 miles east of Coventry, served by regular trains (£6.30, 10 minutes, up to four per hour). Trains also link Rugby with Birmingham (£10.50, 40 minutes, up to four per hour).

Symbolically adjoining St Michael's Cathedral's sandstone walls is the Sir Basil Spence–designed modernist architectural masterpiece Coventry Cathedral, with a futuristic organ, stained glass, and Jacob Epstein statue of the devil and St Michael.

Volunteers at the **Blitz Experience Museum** provide a vivid overview of Coventry before the Blitz and in its aftermath. Children must be aged over eight to climb the tower.

Fargo Village CULTURAL CENTRE

(www.fargovillage.co.uk; Far Gosford St; ⊙hours vary) Markets, live-music gigs, moonlight cinema screenings and workshops (eg gardening or blacksmithing) are just some of the events that take place at this post-industrial cultural hub spread over a former car-radiator plant. Shops here sell everything from secondhand books to upcycled furniture; there are also art-and-craft studios, a barber shop and a brilliant microbrewery, the Twisted Barrel, along with cafes, bakeries and street-food stalls.

St Mary's Guildhall HISTORIC BUILDING

(☎024-7683 3328; www.stmarysguildhall.co.uk; Bayley Lane; ⊙10am-4pm Sun-Thu mid-Mar–Sep) FREE One of the most evocative insights into pre-WWII Coventry is this half-timbered and brick hall where the town's trades came together in the Middle Ages to discuss town affairs. As one of England's finest guildhalls, it was chosen to be a jail for Mary Queen of Scots. Stained-glass windows glorify the kings of England; further down the hall stands WC Marshall's statue of Lady Godiva. Look out for the Coventry Tapestry, dating from 1500, depicting the Virgin Mary's assumption. The vaulted stone undercroft houses an atmospheric cafe.

Herbert Art Gallery & Museum GALLERY, MUSEUM

(☎024-7623 7521; www.theherbert.org; Jordan Well; ⊙10am-4pm Mon-Sat, noon-4pm Sun) FREE Behind Coventry's twin cathedrals, the Herbert has an eclectic collection of paintings and sculptures (including work by TS Lowry, Stanley Spencer and David Hockney), and thought-provoking history galleries spanning natural history and archaeology to Coventry's social and industrial history. Poignant and uplifting exhibits focus on conflict, peace and reconciliation. There are lots of activities aimed at kids, creative workshops for adults (calligraphy, silversmithing etc) and a light-filled cafe.

Sleeping & Eating

★ Coombe Abbey Hotel HISTORIC HOTEL ££
(024-7645 0450; www.coombeabbey.com; Brinklow Rd, Binley; d incl breakfast from £129; P 📶) Queen Elizabeth I lived as a child at this 200-hectare estate, 5.5 miles east of Coventry. The 12th-century abbey was converted into a stately manor in 1581, with parkland, formal gardens and a lake. Many of its 121 uniquely decorated rooms have ornate four-poster beds; some have bathrooms hidden behind bookcases. There's a glass-paned conservatory restaurant and regular themed banquets.

Golden Cross PUB FOOD ££
(024-7655 1855; www.thegoldencrosscoventry.co.uk; 8 Hay Lane; mains £9.50-15; 11.30am-9.30pm Mon-Thu, to 10.30pm Fri & Sat, to 6pm Sun; 📶) Constructed in 1583, this beautiful Tudor building with beamed ceilings, original stained glass and a toasty wood-burning stove is an inviting place for a pint, but the food – entirely gluten-free – such as ale-battered cod with mushy peas, bavette with tarragon butter or jerk-spiced sweetcorn with lime mayo, merits a visit in its own right. Live music plays on Saturdays.

Information

Tourist Office (024-7623 4284; www.visitcoventryandwarwickshire.co.uk; Herbert Art Gallery & Museum, Jordan Well; 10am-4pm Mon-Sat, noon-4pm Sun) Located in the reception area of the Herbert Art Gallery & Museum (p415).

Getting There & Away

BUS

Buses X17 and X18 go to Kenilworth (£3,10, 40 minutes) and Warwick (£3.40, 45 minutes) five times daily Monday to Saturday.

TRAIN

Regular services include the following.

Birmingham (£4.90, 30 minutes, every 10 minutes)

London Euston (£56, 1¼ hours, every 10 to 20 minutes)

Rugby (£6.30, 10 minutes, up to four per hour)

Kenilworth

01926 / POP 22,413

An easy deviation off the A46 between Warwick and Coventry, the atmospheric ruin of Kenilworth Castle was the inspiration for Walter Scott's 1821 novel *Kenilworth*, and it still feels pretty inspiring today. The town is essentially split into two by Finham Brook: the historic village-like area, of most interest to visitors, is on the northern side, while the southern side is the commercial centre.

Sights

Kenilworth Castle CASTLE, RUINS
(EH; 01926-852078; www.english-heritage.org.uk; Castle Green; adult/child £12.60/7.60; 10am-6pm Apr-Sep, to 5pm Oct, to 4pm Sat & Sun Nov–mid-Feb, to 4pm Wed-Sun mid-Feb–Mar) This spine-tingling ruin sprawls among fields and hedges on Kenilworth's outskirts. Built in the 1120s, the castle survived the longest siege in English history in 1266, when the forces of Lord Edward (later Edward I) threw themselves at the moat and battlements for six solid months. The fortress was dramatically extended in Tudor times, but it fell in the English Civil War and its walls were breached and water defences drained. Don't miss the magnificent restored Elizabethan gardens.

Download a free audio guide to your phone from the website.

Stoneleigh Abbey HISTORIC BUILDING
(01926-858535; www.stoneleighabbey.org; B4115; adult/child grounds & tour £14/5, grounds only £7/1.50; tours hourly 10am-3pm, grounds to 5pm Sun-Thu Easter-Oct; P) The kind of stately home that makes film directors go weak at the knees, Stoneleigh name-drops Charles I and Jane Austen among its past visitors. Completed in 1726 and only viewable on tours (included in admission), the splendid Palladian west wing contains richly detailed plasterwork ceilings and wood-panelled rooms. A 'reflecting lake' effect is created by the widened stretch of the River Avon, which runs through the grounds. It's 2 miles east of Kenilworth.

The original abbey was founded by Cistercian monks in 1154, though little remains except the 14th-century gatehouse; the house was built on the site of the monastery by the wealthy Leigh family (distant cousins of the Austens) in the 16th century.

Sleeping & Eating

Old Bakery B&B ££
(01926-864111; www.theoldbakery.eu; 12 High St; s/d/tr from £75/80/90; bar 5.30-11pm Mon-Thu, 5-11pm Fri & Sat, 5-10.30pm Sun; P 📶) East of the castle, with restaurants nearby, this appealing 14-room B&B has attractively attired modern

rooms and a cosy, welcoming bar serving well-kept real ales on the ground floor.

★Cross GASTROPUB £££
(☎01926-853840; www.thecrosskenilworth.co.uk; 16 New St; 2-/3-course menus lunch £29/35, dinner £55/65; ⊙noon-2pm & 6.30-9.30pm Tue-Thu, noon-2pm & 6-9.30pm Fri, noon-2.30pm & 6-9.30pm Sat, noon-3.30pm Sun;) One of England's culinary jewels, this Michelin-starred gastropub occupies a romantic 19th-century inn. Prepare to be dazzled by exquisite creations like seared scallops with seaweed butter, duck breast with smoked beetroot and raspberry vinegar, and brioche pudding with apple-and-blackberry compote and bay-leaf ice cream.

Vegetarian menus are available; junior gourmands have their own three-course children's menu (£17).

Getting There & Away

From Monday to Saturday, buses X17 and X18 run five times daily between Coventry (£3.10, 40 minutes) and Kenilworth and on to Warwick (£4.40, 30 minutes). There are no buses on Sunday.

Warwick

☎01926 / POP 31,345

Regularly name-checked by Shakespeare, Warwick was the ancestral seat of the earls of Warwick, who played a pivotal role in the Wars of the Roses. Despite a devastating fire in 1694, Warwick remains a treasure house of medieval architecture, with rich veins of history and charming streets, dominated by the soaring turrets of Warwick Castle.

Sights

★Warwick Castle CASTLE
(☎01926-495421; www.warwick-castle.com; Castle Lane; castle adult/child £20/17, castle & dungeon £30/17; ⊙10am-5pm Apr-Sep, to 4pm Oct-Mar; P) Founded in 1068 by William the Conqueror, stunningly preserved Warwick Castle is the biggest show in town. The ancestral home of the earls of Warwick remains impressively intact, and the Tussauds Group has filled the interior with flamboyant, family-friendly attractions that bring the castle's rich history to life. Waxworks populate the private apartments; there are also jousting tournaments, daily trebuchet firings, themed evenings and a dungeon. Discounted online tickets provide fast-track entry. Great accommodation options are available on-site.

Collegiate Church of St Mary CHURCH
(☎01926-403940; www.stmaryswarwick.org.uk; Old Sq; church by donation, tower adult/child £3/1.50; ⊙10am-4.30pm Mon-Sat, 12.30-4.30pm Sun) This magnificent 1123-founded Norman church was badly damaged in the Great Fire of Warwick in 1694, but is packed with 16th- and 17th-century tombs. Highlights include the Norman crypt with a 14th-century extension; the impressive Beauchamp Chapel, built between 1442 and 1464 to enshrine the mortal remains of the earls of Warwick; and, up 134 steps, the tower, which provides supreme views over town (kids must be aged over eight).

Lord Leycester Hospital HISTORIC BUILDING
(☎01926-491422; www.lordleycester.com; 60 High St; adult/child £8.50/5, garden only £2; ⊙10am-5pm Tue-Sun Apr-Sep, to 4pm Oct-Mar) A survivor of the 1694 fire, the wonderfully wonky Lord Leycester Hospital has been used as a retirement home for soldiers (but never as a hospital) since 1571. Visitors can wander around the chapel, guildhall, regimental museum and restored walled garden, which includes a knot garden and a Norman arch.

Sleeping & Eating

Tilted Wig PUB ££
(☎01926-400110; www.tiltedwigwarwick.co.uk; 11 Market Pl; d £85;) Bang on the central Market Pl, this brilliantly named 17th-century Georgian inn has four snug but comfortable rooms overlooking the square and some of the better pub food in town, such as Warwickshire rare-breed sausages with creamy garlic mash or pork belly with apple and black-pudding croquettes (mains £10.50 to £20).

Rose & Crown PUB ££
(☎01926-411117; www.roseandcrownwarwick.co.uk; 30 Market Pl; d/f incl breakfast from £92/102;) Dating from the 17th century, this family-run inn on the town square has five lovely, spacious and tastefully decorated rooms upstairs from the pub and another eight in the building across the lane, as well as great ales and bottled beers, and an excellent Modern British menu (mains £13 to £20). Four of its rooms are set up for families.

★Warwick Castle Accommodation RESORT £££
(☎0871 097 1228; www.warwick-castle.com; Warwick Castle; glamping/lodge/tower ste per night from £145/172/588; ⊙tower ste & lodge year-round, glamping Easter-Sep; P) Atmospheric

Warwick

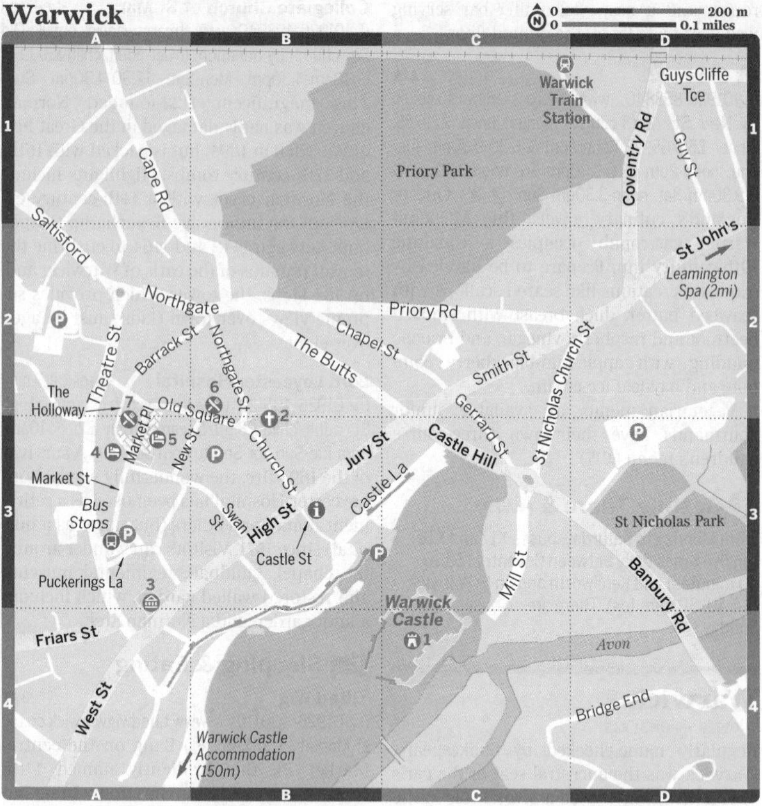

accommodation at Warwick Castle (p417) includes two days' castle admission. The castle itself contains two four-poster-bed Tower Suites (including a private tour, champagne and breakfast). The riverside Knight's Village has woodland and knight-themed lodges (all with terrace and some with kitchenette) and medieval entertainment. Themed tents (with shared bathrooms) make up the 'glamping' ground. All sleep up to five people.

Old Coffee Tavern BRITISH ££

(☎01926-679737; www.theoldcoffeetavern.co.uk; 16 Old Sq; mains £10.50-15.50; ⊙kitchen 7am-10pm Mon-Fri, noon-10pm Sat, to 8pm Sun, bar 7am-11pm Mon-Thu, to 12.30am Fri, 8am-12.30am Sat, to 10pm Sun; 📶) An 1880-built beauty with many of its Victorian features intact, this tavern was originally established as a teetotal alternative to Warwick's pubs. Today you can order real ales, craft ciders, wines and cocktails, along with elevated versions of British classics like toad-in-the-hole and chicken-and-ham-hock pie. Upstairs are 10 stylish oyster-toned guest rooms (doubles including breakfast from £125).

Tailors BRITISH £££

(☎01926-410590; www.tailorsrestaurant.co.uk; 22 Market Pl; 2-/3-course lunch menus £20/25,

3-/6-course dinner menus £35/59; ⏲6.30-8.30pm Tue, noon-1.30pm & 6.30-8.30pm Wed-Sat) Set in a former tailor's shop, this elegant restaurant, owned and run by two hotshot chefs, serves prime ingredients – guinea fowl, pork belly and lamb from named farms – complemented by intricate creations like brown-butter crumb and black truffle and fennel candy.

Information

Tourist Office (☎01926-492212; www.visitwarwick.co.uk; Court House, Jury St; ⏲9.30am-4.30pm Mon-Fri, 10am-4.30pm Sat year-round, plus 10am-4pm Sun Apr–mid-Dec) Within the flagstone-floored Court House (1725). A Heritage Walk map costs £1.

Getting There & Away

BUS

Buses depart from outside **Westgate House** (Market St).

Stagecoach X17 and X18 run to Coventry (£4.40, 40 minutes, five daily Monday to Saturday) via Kenilworth (£4.10, 30 minutes). Bus X18 also runs to Stratford-upon-Avon (£5.50, 40 minutes, two per hour Monday to Saturday, hourly Sunday).

TRAIN

The train station is half a mile northeast of the town centre on Station Rd.

Trains run to Birmingham (£7.50, 30 minutes, two per hour), Stratford-upon-Avon (£7.30, 25 minutes, every two hours) and London Marylebone (£48, 1½ hours, up to four per hour; some require a change in Leamington Spa).

Stratford-upon-Avon

☎01789 / POP 27,455

The author of some of the most quoted lines ever written in the English language, William Shakespeare was born in Stratford in 1564 and died here in 1616. Experiences linked to his life in this unmistakably Tudor town range from the touristy (medieval recreations and Bard-themed tearooms) to the humbling (Shakespeare's modest grave in Holy Trinity Church) and the sublime (taking in a play by the world-famous Royal Shakespeare Company).

Sights

★Shakespeare's Birthplace HISTORIC BUILDING

(☎01789-204016; www.shakespeare.org.uk; Henley St; adult/child £15/11; ⏲10am-4pm Mon-Fri, to 5pm Sat & Sun) Start your Shakespeare quest at the house where the renowned playwright was born in 1564 and spent his childhood days. John Shakespeare owned the house for a period of 50 years. William, as the eldest surviving son, inherited it upon his father's death in 1601 and spent his first five years of marriage here. Behind a modern facade, the house has restored Tudor rooms, live presentations from famous Shakespearean characters and an engaging exhibition on Stratford's favourite son.

★Shakespeare's New Place HISTORIC SITE

(☎01789-338536; www.shakespeare.org.uk; cnr Chapel St & Chapel Lane; adult/child £12.50/8; ⏲10am-5pm Apr-Aug, to 4.30pm Sep & Oct, to 3.30pm Nov-Mar) When Shakespeare retired, he swapped the bright lights of London for a comfortable town house at New Place, where he died of unknown causes in April 1616. The house was demolished in 1759, but an attractive Elizabethan knot garden occupies part of the grounds. A major restoration project has uncovered Shakespeare's kitchen and incorporated new exhibits in a reimagining of the house as it would have been. You can also explore the adjacent Nash's House, where Shakespeare's granddaughter Elizabeth lived.

Holy Trinity Church CHURCH

(☎01789-266316; www.stratford-upon-avon.org; Old Town; Shakespeare's grave adult/child £3/2; ⏲noon-2pm Mon-Thu, to 4pm Fri, 11am-4pm Sat) The final resting place of the Bard, where he was also baptised and where he worshipped, is said to be the most visited parish church in England. Inside are handsome 16th- and 17th-century tombs (particularly in the Clopton Chapel), some fabulous carvings on the choir stalls and, of course, the grave of William Shakespeare, with its ominous epitaph: 'cvrst be he yt moves my bones'.

MAD Museum MUSEUM

(☎01789-269356; www.themadmuseum.co.uk; 4-5 Henley St; adult/child £7.80/5.20, combination ticket with Shakespeare's School Room £13.10/8.60; ⏲10am-5.30pm) Fun, hands-on exhibits at Stratford's Mechanical Art & Design Museum (aka MAD) make physics accessible for kids, who can build their own gravity-propelled marble run, use their energy to light up electric panels, and pull levers and turn cranks to animate displays. Tickets are valid all day, so you can come and go as you please.

Stratford-upon-Avon

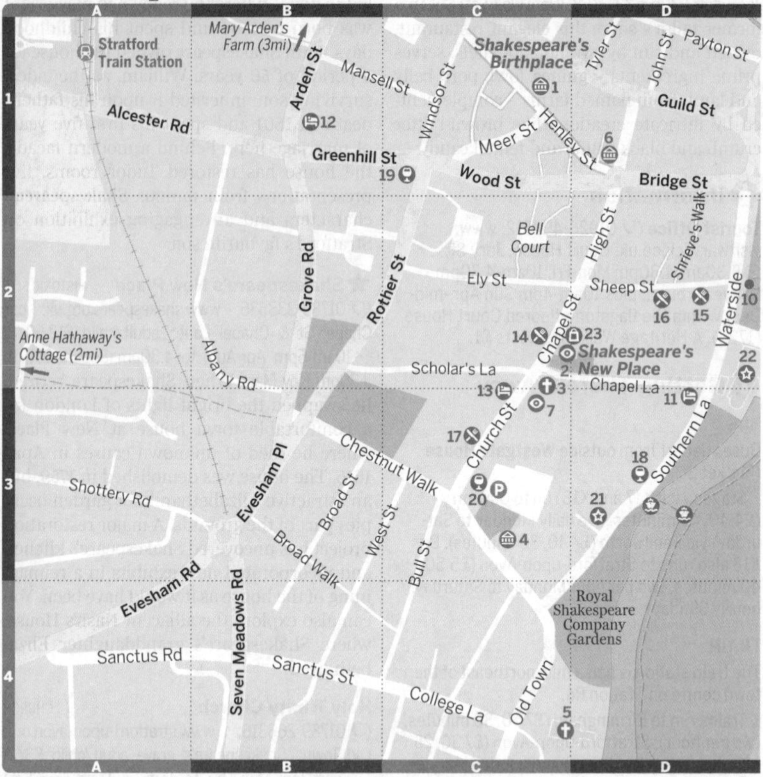

Mary Arden's Farm HISTORIC SITE, FARM

(☎01789-338535; www.shakespeare.org.uk; Station Rd, Wilmcote; adult/child £15/10; ⏱10am-5pm Apr-Aug, to 4.30pm Sep & Oct; 👪) Shakespeare genealogists can trace the family tree to the childhood home of the Bard's mother at Wilmcote, 3 miles west of Stratford. Aimed squarely at families, the working farm traces country life over the centuries, with nature trails, falconry displays and a collection of rare-breed farm animals. You can get here on the **City Sightseeing bus** (☎01789-299123; www.city-sightseeing.com; adult/child 24hr £15/7.50, 48hr £23/11.50; ⏱9.30am-5pm Apr-Oct), or cycle via Anne Hathaway's Cottage, following the Stratford-upon-Avon Canal towpath. Note that, unlike the other Shakespeare properties, it's closed from November to March.

Shakespeare's School Room HISTORIC SITE

(☎01789-203170; www.shakespearesschoolroom.org; King Edward VI School, Church St; adult/child £8.50/5.50, combination ticket with MAD Museum £13.10/8.60; ⏱11am-5pm) Shakespeare's alma mater, King Edward VI School (still a prestigious grammar school today), incorporates a vast black-and-white timbered building, dating from 1420, that was once the town's guildhall, where Shakespeare's father John served as bailiff (mayor). In the Bard's former classroom, you can sit in on mock-Tudor lessons, watch a short film and test yourself on Tudor-style homework.

It's adjacent to the 1269-built **Guild Chapel** (www.guildchapel.org.uk; cnr Chapel Lane & Church St; by donation; ⏱10am-4pm).

Anne Hathaway's Cottage HISTORIC BUILDING

(☎01789-338532; www.shakespeare.org.uk; Cottage Lane, Shottery; adult/child £12.50/8; ⏱9am-5pm Apr-Aug, to 4.30pm Sep & Oct, 10am-3.30pm Nov-Mar) Before tying the knot with Shakespeare, Anne Hathaway lived in Shottery, 1 mile west of the centre of Stratford, in this delightful thatched farmhouse. As well as

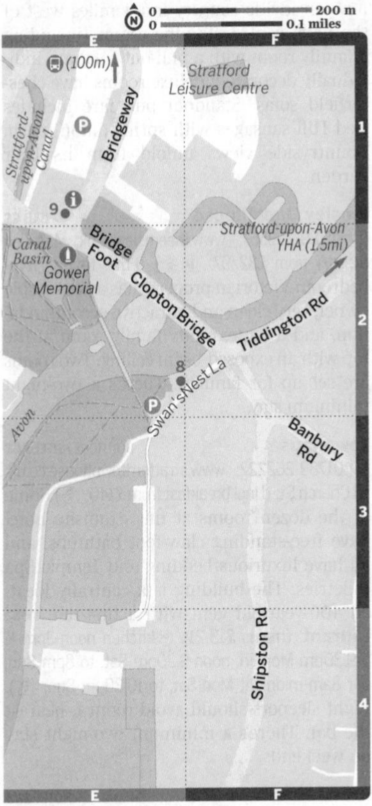

Stratford-upon-Avon

Top Sights
1 Shakespeare's Birthplace ... C1
2 Shakespeare's New Place ... C2

Sights
3 Guild Chapel ... C2
4 Hall's Croft ... C3
5 Holy Trinity Church ... C4
6 MAD Museum ... D1
7 Shakespeare's School Room ... C3

Activities, Courses & Tours
8 Avon Boating ... E2
9 City Sightseeing ... E1
10 Stratford Town Walk ... D2

Sleeping
11 Arden Hotel ... D3
12 Emsley Guesthouse ... B1
13 Townhouse ... C3

Eating
14 Edward Moon's ... C2
15 Fourteas ... D2
16 Lambs ... D2
Rooftop Restaurant ... (see 22)
17 Salt ... C3
Townhouse ... (see 13)

Drinking & Nightlife
18 Dirty Duck ... D3
19 Old Thatch Tavern ... C1
20 Windmill Inn ... C3

Entertainment
21 Other Place ... D3
22 Royal Shakespeare Company ... D2
Swan Theatre ... (see 22)

Shopping
23 Chaucer Head ... D2

period furniture, it has gorgeous gardens and an orchard and arboretum, with examples of all the trees mentioned in Shakespeare's plays. A footpath (no bikes allowed) leads to Shottery from Evesham Pl.

Hall's Croft HISTORIC BUILDING
(☎01789-338533; www.shakespeare.org.uk; Old Town; adult/child £8.50/5.50; ⏲10am-5pm Apr-Aug, to 4.30pm Sep & Oct, 11am-3.30pm Nov-Mar) The handsome Jacobean town house belonging to Shakespeare's daughter Susanna and her husband, respected doctor John Hall, stands south of Stratford's centre. The exhibition offers fascinating insights into medicine in the 16th and 17th centuries, and the lovely walled garden sprouts with aromatic herbs employed in medicinal preparations.

Tours

Avon Boating BOATING
(☎01789-267073; www.avon-boating.co.uk; The Boathouse, Swan's Nest Lane; river cruises adult/child £7/5; ⏲9am-dusk Easter-Oct) Avon Boating runs 40-minute river cruises that depart every 20 minutes from either side of the main bridge. It also hires rowboats, canoes and punts (per hour £7, minimum charge £12) and motorboats (per hour £50).

Stratford Town Walk WALKING
(☎07855 760377; www.stratfordtownwalk.co.uk; town walk adult/child £7/3, ghost walk £8/5; ⏲town walk 11am Sun-Fri, 11am & 2pm Sat, ghost walk by reservation 7.30pm Sat) Popular two-hour guided town walks depart from Waterside, opposite Sheep St (prebooking not necessary). Chilling ghost walks lasting 90 minutes leave from the same location but must be booked ahead.

WORTH A TRIP

CHARLECOTE PARK

A youthful Shakespeare allegedly poached deer in the grounds of **Charlecote Park** (NT; ☎01789-470277; www.nationaltrust.org.uk; Loxley Lane, Charlecote; house & garden adult/child £11.45/5.70, garden only £8/4; ⏲house 11am-4.30pm Thu-Tue mid-Mar–Oct, noon-3.30pm Thu-Tue mid-Feb–mid-Mar, noon-3.30pm Sat & Sun Nov & Dec, garden 9am-5pm Mar-Oct, to 4.30pm Nov-Feb), a lavish Elizabethan pile on the River Avon, 5 miles east of Stratford-upon-Avon. Fallow deer still roam the grounds today. The interiors were restored from Georgian chintz to Tudor splendour in 1823. Highlights include Victorian kitchens, filled with culinary moulds, and an original 1551 Tudor gatehouse.

Bus X17 runs to Charlecote hourly from Stratford (£5.50, 30 minutes, two per hour Monday to Friday, hourly Saturday and Sunday).

Festivals & Events

Stratford Literary Festival LITERATURE

(☎01789-470185; www.stratfordliteraryfestival.co.uk; ⏲late Apr/early May) A highlight of Stratford's cultural calendar is the week-long annual Stratford Literary Festival, which has attracted literary big-hitters of the calibre of Robert Harris, PD James and Simon Armitage.

Sleeping

Stratford-upon-Avon YHA HOSTEL £

(☎0345 371 9661; www.yha.org.uk; Wellesbourne Rd, Alveston; dm/d/glamping from £18/49/59; P ᯤ) Set in a large 200-year-old mansion 1.5 miles east of the town centre, this superior 134-bed hostel attracts travellers of all ages. Of its 32 rooms and dorms, 16 are en suite. There's a canteen, bar and kitchen. Buses 6 and 15 (£3.60, 12 minutes, up to two per hour) run here from Bridge St. Wi-fi is in common areas only.

Tepee-style glamping tents and hut-like camping pods with kitchenette are available from April to September.

Stag at Red Hill INN ££

(☎01789-764634; www.stagredhill.co.uk; Alcester Rd, Alcester; d/f incl breakfast from £78/128; P ᯤ) Stratford's formidable one-time courthouse and prison, dating back over 500 years, is now an idyllic country inn 4 miles west of the town centre. Its nine rooms (including a family room with a pull-out sofa) are individually decorated; deluxe rooms have chesterfield sofas. Standout pub fare includes Red Hill sausages with spring-onion mash. Countryside views unfold from its beer garden.

Emsley Guesthouse B&B ££

(☎01789-299557; www.theemsley.co.uk; 4 Arden St; d/f from £82/97; P ᯤ) This lovely five-bedroom Victorian property has a personable owner, very clean and attractive accommodation, and a large, pretty family room at the top with an exposed-beam ceiling. Two rooms are set up for families. There's a two-night minimum stay.

Townhouse BOUTIQUE HOTEL £££

(☎01789-262222; www.stratfordtownhouse.co.uk; 16 Church St; d incl breakfast from £140; ᯤ) Some of the dozen rooms at this exquisite hotel have free-standing claw-foot bathtubs, and all have luxurious bedding and Temple Spa toiletries. The building is a centrally located 400-year-old gem with a first-rate **restaurant** (mains £13-21; ⏲kitchen noon-3pm & 5-9.30pm Mon-Fri, noon-9.30pm Sat, to 8pm Sun, bar 8am-midnight Mon-Sat, to 10.30pm Sun; ᯤ). Light sleepers should avoid room 1, nearest the bar. There's a minimum two-night stay on weekends.

Arden Hotel HOTEL £££

(☎01789-298682; www.theardenhotelstratford.com; Waterside; s/d incl breakfast from £134/169; P ᯤ) Facing the Swan Theatre, this elegant property has a sleek brasserie and champagne bar. Its 45 rooms feature designer fabrics and its bathrooms are full of polished marble. Interconnecting rooms are ideal for families. Kids receive welcome bags with games.

Eating

Fourteas CAFE £

(☎01789-293908; www.thefourteas.co.uk; 24 Sheep St; dishes £4.50-9.50, afternoon tea with/without Prosecco £20/15; ⏲9.30am-5.30pm Mon-Sat, 10.30am-5.30pm Sun) Breaking with Stratford's Shakespearean theme, this tearoom takes the 1940s as its inspiration with beautiful old teapots, framed posters and staff in period costume. As well as premium loose-leaf teas and homemade cakes, there are all-day breakfasts, soups, sandwiches (including a chicken and bacon 'Churchill club') and lavish afternoon teas. Gluten-free scones, cakes and sandwiches are available.

Lambs MODERN EUROPEAN ££
(☎01789-292554; www.lambsrestaurant.co.uk; 12 Sheep St; mains £13-25; ⏲5-9pm Mon, noon-2pm & 5-9pm Tue-Sat, noon-2pm & 6-9pm Sun) Lambs swaps Shakespeare chintz in favour of modern elegance but throws in authentic 16th-century ceiling beams for good measure. The menu embraces Gressingham duck, Hereford steaks and, yes, lamb (a herb-crusted rack with dauphinoise potatoes, mustard green beans and rosemary jus), backed by a strong wine list.

Edward Moon's BRITISH ££
(☎01789-267069; www.edwardmoon.com; 9 Chapel St; mains £12-20; ⏲noon-2.30pm & 5-9pm Tue-Thu, noon-2.30pm & 5-9.30pm Fri & Sat, noon-3pm Sun; 👪) Named after a famous travelling chef who cooked up the flavours of home for the British colonial service, this snug independent restaurant serves hearty English dishes, such as steak-and-ale pie and meltingly tender lamb shank with redcurrant gravy. Kids get a two-course menu for £7.95.

Rooftop Restaurant INTERNATIONAL ££
(☎01789-403449; www.rsc.org.uk; 3rd fl, Royal Shakespeare Theatre, Waterside; mains £14-26; ⏲10.30am-9.30pm Mon-Thu, to 9.45pm Fri & Sat, to 3.30pm Sun; 📶👪) Glorious views of the River Avon extend from the dining room and outdoor terrace of this restaurant atop the Royal Shakespeare Theatre (p414). Global flavours range from crab linguine to Sri Lankan cauliflower, squash and cashew curry; there are various set menus, including for vegans and gluten-free diners, and for kids. Its bar mixes the best cocktails in town.

★Salt BRITISH £££
(☎01789-263566; www.salt-restaurant.co.uk; 8 Church St; 4-/6-course lunch menu £45/55, 8-course dinner menu £78; ⏲noon-2pm & 6.30-10pm Wed-Sat, noon-2pm Sun) Stratford's gastronomic (and Michelin) star is this intimate, beam-ceilinged bistro. In the semi-open kitchen, owner-chef Paul Foster produces stunning creations influenced by the seasons: spring might see glazed parsley root with chicory and black-truffle shavings, onglet of beef with malted artichoke, cured halibut with oyster and apple emulsion, and sea-buckthorn mille-feuille with fig and goat's-milk ice cream.

Recreate its magic at its cookery school (half-day courses from £95).

Drinking & Nightlife

★Old Thatch Tavern PUB
(www.oldthatchtavernstratford.co.uk; Greenhill St; ⏲11.30am-11pm Mon-Sat, noon-11pm Sun; 📶) To truly appreciate Stratford's olde-worlde atmosphere, join the locals for a pint at the town's oldest pub. Built in 1470, this thatch-roofed treasure has great real ales and a gorgeous summertime courtyard.

Dirty Duck PUB
(www.greeneking-pubs.co.uk; Waterside; ⏲noon-11.30pm Mon-Thu, to midnight Fri & Sat, to 11pm Sun; 📶) Also called the 'Black Swan', this enchanting riverside alehouse is the only pub in England to be licensed under two names. It's a favourite thespian watering hole, with a roll call of former regulars (Olivier, Attenborough et al) that reads like a who's who of actors.

Windmill Inn PUB
(www.greeneking-pubs.co.uk; Church St; ⏲11am-11pm Sun-Thu, to midnight Fri & Sat; 📶) Ale was already flowing at this low-ceilinged pub when rhyming couplets gushed from Shakespeare's quill. Flowers frame the white-washed facade; there's a shaded rear beer garden.

Entertainment

★Royal Shakespeare Company THEATRE
(RSC; ☎box office 01789-331111; www.rsc.org.uk; Waterside; ⏲tour times vary, tower 10am-5pm Sun-Fri, 10am-12.15pm & 2-5pm Sat mid-Mar–mid-Oct, 10am-4.30pm Sun-Fri, to 12.15pm Sat mid-Oct–

SHAKESPEARE HISTORIC HOMES

Five of the most important buildings associated with Shakespeare – Shakespeare's Birthplace (p419), Shakespeare's New Place (p419), Hall's Croft (p421), Anne Hathaway's Cottage (p420) and Mary Arden's Farm (p420) – contain museums that form the core of the visitor experience at Stratford. All are run by the Shakespeare Birthplace Trust (www.shakespeare.org.uk).

A Full Story ticket (adult/child £22/14.50) covering all five properties is available online or at the sites, and provides up to a 60% discount off individual admission prices.

mid-Mar) Stratford has two grand stages run by the world-renowned Royal Shakespeare Company – the **Royal Shakespeare Theatre** and the Swan Theatre on Waterside – as well as the smaller Other Place. The theatres have witnessed performances by such legends as Lawrence Olivier, Richard Burton, Judi Dench, Helen Mirren, Ian McKellan and Patrick Stewart. One-hour guided tours (on hold at the time of research) take you behind the scenes.

Zipping up the lift/elevator of the Royal Shakespeare Theatre's **tower** rewards with panoramic views over the town and River Avon. Spectacular views also unfold from its 3rd-floor Rooftop Restaurant (p423), which opens to a terrace.

Contact the RSC for performance times, and book well ahead as capacity is limited (though there are plans to stream performances as well).

There are often special deals for under-25-year-olds, students and seniors. A few tickets are held back for sale on the day of performances but get snapped up fast.

Other Place THEATRE
(☎ box office 01789-331111; www.rsc.org.uk; 22 Southern Lane) The smallest stage of the Royal Shakespeare Company (p423) has 200 seats.

ALTON TOWERS

Phenomenally popular **Alton Towers** (☎ 0871 222 3330; www.altontowers.com; Farley Lane, Alton; adult/child amusement park £53/44, water park £16.50/12.50; ⏰ hours vary), 4 miles east of Cheadle off the B5032, offers maximum G-force for your buck. Wild rides include the Th13teen, Nemesis, Oblivion, Galactica and Wickerman coasters. Gentler thrills span carousels and stage shows to a pirate-themed aquarium and splashtastic water park.

Check seasonal schedules online and pre-purchase tickets to skip ticket queues and take advantage of discounted entry deals. Five on-site hotels with themed rooms offer perks such as an hour's early park entry.

Your own transport is best (a monorail loops between the car park and the main entrance). In summer, one daily bus links Alton Towers with Stoke-on-Trent, Nottingham and Derby; schedules are available from Traveline (p406).

New work is presented here; it also hosts regular free live music and spoken word nights.

Swan Theatre THEATRE
(☎ 01789-331111; www.rsc.org.uk; Waterside) Hosting productions by the Royal Shakespeare Company (p423), this grand stage has a capacity of 426 people.

Shopping

Chaucer Head BOOKS
(www.chaucerhead.com; 21 Chapel St; ⏰ 11am-5.30pm Mon-Fri, 10am-5pm Sat) Bargain-priced paperbacks through to rare antiquarian books worth thousands of pounds are stocked at the Chaucer Head, which was originally founded in Birmingham in 1830 and relocated to literary-famed Stratford in 1960.

Information

Tourist Office (☎ 01789-264293; www.shakespeares-england.co.uk; Bridge Foot; ⏰ 9am-5.30pm Mon-Sat, 10am-4pm Sun) Just west of Clopton Bridge.

Getting There & Away

BUS

Buses run from Stratford's Riverside bus station (behind the Stratford Leisure Centre on Bridgeway).

National Express services run to London Victoria (£10.50, three hours, four direct services per day).

CAR

If you're driving, be warned that town car parks charge high fees, 24 hours a day.

TRAIN

From Stratford-upon-Avon train station, West Midlands Railway runs to Birmingham (£8.60, 40 minutes, half-hourly); Chiltern Railways serves London Marylebone (£38.20, 2¼ hours, up to two per hour), some with a change in Leamington Spa; and East Midlands runs to Warwick (£7.30, 25 minutes, every two hours).

The nostalgic **Shakespeare Express Steam Train** (☎ 0121-708 4960; www.vintagetrains.co.uk; return 1st/2nd class £45/35; ⏰ Sun Jul–mid-Sep) chugs twice every Sunday in summer between Stratford and Birmingham Moor St; the one-way journey time is one hour.

Getting Around

From 10am to 6pm April to October, a 1937-built, hand-wound chain ferry yo-yos across the Avon between the west bank and the east bank (one-way 20p).

A bicycle is handy for getting out to the outlying Shakespeare properties. **Stratford Bike Hire** (☎07711-776340; www.stratford-bikehire.com; The Stratford Greenway, Seven Meadows Rd; bike hire per half/full day from £10/15; ⏰9.30am-5pm) will deliver to your accommodation for free within a 6-mile radius of Stratford.

WORTH A TRIP

LORD LICHFIELD'S SHUGBOROUGH

A regal, neoclassical mansion, **Shugborough** (NT; ☎01889-880166; www.nationaltrust.org.uk; Great Haywood; adult/child house & grounds £13/6.50, grounds only £8/4; ⏰house 11am-4.30pm Mar-Oct, 10am-3pm Dec, grounds 9am-5pm Mar-Oct, to 4pm Nov & Dec) is the ancestral home of royal photographer Lord Lichfield. A good proportion of the wall space is devoted to his work; the highlight is the staterooms' collection of exquisite Louis XV and XVI furniture. One-hour guided tours (included in admission) run between 11am and 1pm. Shugborough is 6 miles east of Stafford on the A513; bus 825 linking Stafford and Lichfield stops 1 mile from the manor (£4.40, 30 minutes, hourly Monday to Saturday).

STAFFORDSHIRE

Wedged between the ever-expanding conurbations of Birmingham and Manchester, Staffordshire is surprisingly green, with the northern half of the county rising to meet the rugged hills of the Peak District.

Regular trains and buses serve Lichfield, Stafford and other major towns.

Lichfield

☎01543 / POP 32,219

Even without its magnificent Gothic cathedral – one of the most spectacular in the country – this charming cobbled market town would be worth a visit to tread in the footsteps of lexicographer and wit Samuel Johnson, and natural philosopher Erasmus Darwin, grandfather of Charles. Johnson once described Lichfield folk as 'the most sober, decent people in England', which was rather generous considering that this was the last place in the country to stop burning people at the stake.

Sights

★Lichfield Cathedral CATHEDRAL
(☎01543-306150; www.lichfield-cathedral.org; 19 Cathedral Close; adult/child £2/free; ⏰9.30am-4pm Mon-Sat, 12.30-4pm Sun) Crowned by three dramatic towers, Lichfield Cathedral is a Gothic fantasy, constructed in stages from 1200 to 1350. The enormous vaulted nave is set slightly off line from the choir, creating a bizarre perspective when viewed from the west door, and carvings inside the cathedral still bear signs of damage caused by Civil War soldiers sharpening their swords.

In the octagonal Chapter House, you can view the illuminated *Chad Gospels*, created around AD 730; an ornate Anglo-Saxon bas-relief known as the *Lichfield Angel*; and a faded but glorious medieval wall painting above the door.

The grand west facade positively bows under the weight of 113 statues of bishops, saints and kings of England. Be sure to stroll the delightful, once-fortified Cathedral Close, ringed with imposing 17th- and 18th-century houses.

Erasmus Darwin House HISTORIC BUILDING
(☎01543-306260; www.erasmusdarwin.org; Beacon St; house £5, garden free; ⏰house 10am-3.30pm Thu-Sun, garden 10am-3.30pm daily) After turning down the job of royal physician to King George III, Erasmus Darwin became a leading light in the Lunar Society, debating the origins of life with luminaries including Wedgwood, Boulton and Watt decades before his grandson Charles came up with the theory of evolution. The former house of the 'Grandfather of Evolution' contains intriguing exhibits, including his notebook containing drawings of his inventions. At the back, a fragrant culinary and medicinal herb garden leads to Cathedral Close.

Samuel Johnson Birthplace Museum MUSEUM
(☎01543-264972; www.samueljohnsonbirthplace.org.uk; Breadmarket St; ⏰10.30am-4.30pm Mar-Oct, 11am-3.30pm Nov-Feb) FREE This absorbing museum charts the life of the pioneering lexicographer, wit, poet and critic Samuel

THE POTTERIES – STOKE-ON-TRENT

Situated at the heart of the Potteries (the famous pottery-producing region of Staffordshire), Stoke-on-Trent is famed for its ceramics. Don't expect cute little artisanal producers: this was where pottery shifted to mass production during the Industrial Revolution, and Stoke today is a sprawl of industrial townships tied together by flyovers and bypasses. There are dozens of active potteries that you can visit in the greater area, including the famous Wedgwood factory.

The **tourist office** (01782-236000; www.visitstoke.co.uk; Bethesda St, Hanley; 10am-5pm Mon-Sat, 11am-4pm Sun) has information on all the potteries that are open to the public.

Potteries Museum & Art Gallery (01782-236000; www.stokemuseums.org.uk; Bethesda St, Hanley; 10am-5pm Mon-Sat, 11am-4pm Sun) Providing a thorough overview of the Potteries area's history, this museum and gallery houses an extensive ceramics display, from Toby jugs and jasperware to outrageous ornamental pieces. Other highlights include treasures from the 2009-discovered Staffordshire Hoard (the largest hoard of Anglo-Saxon gold and silver metalwork ever found, incorporating 5.1kg of gold, 1.4kg of silver and some 3500 pieces of jewellery); displays on the WWII Spitfire, created by the Stoke-born aviator Reginald Mitchell; and artworks by TS Lowry and Sir Henry Moore.

Some temporary exhibitions incur an extra charge.

World of Wedgwood (01782-282986; www.worldofwedgwood.com; Wedgwood Dr, Barlaston; factory tour & museum adult/child £10/8, museum only free; factory 10am-4pm Mon-Fri, museum to 5pm daily) Set in attractive parkland 8 miles south of Hanley, the modern production centre for Josiah Wedgwood's porcelain empire displays an extensive collection of historic pieces, including plenty of Wedgwood's delicate, neoclassical blue-and-white jasperware at its museum. On weekdays there are guided factory tours lasting 45 minutes (reserve in advance). Pot throwing (over-12s only) and design workshops take place at its Master Craft and Decorating studios.

Johnson, who moved to London from his native Lichfield and devoted nine years to producing the first major dictionary of the English language. Johnson's dictionary helped define the word 'dull' with this example: 'to make dictionaries is dull work'. On the 1st floor, a short dramatised film narrates Johnson's life story. It's a lovely property to explore.

Hub at St Mary's MUSEUM
(01543-414749; www.thehubstmarys.co.uk; Market Sq; 9.30am-1pm Tue-Thu, to 8pm Fri & Sat, 11am-3pm Sun) Dating from 1870, the revamped St Mary's Church contains the town's library and art gallery, along with a performance space for theatre, live music and events, and a cafe. Climb the tower's 120 steps for sweeping city views.

Sleeping & Eating

George Hotel HOTEL ££
(01543-414822; www.thegeorgelichfield.co.uk; 12-14 Bird St; s/d from £90/109; P) An old Georgian pub has been upgraded into a comfortable, midrange hotel with 45 rooms that scores points for location rather than atmosphere.

Swinfen Hall Hotel HISTORIC HOTEL £££
(01543-481494; www.swinfenhallhotel.co.uk; Swinfen; s/d/ste incl breakfast from £140/150/315; P) Georgian manor house Swinfen Hall, built in 1757, sits 3 miles southeast of Lichfield amid 40 wooded hectares with formal gardens, wild hay meadows and a deer park. Parkland views extend from its 17 rooms, which have either traditional or contemporary styling. Its fine-dining restaurant has multicourse tasting menus accompanied by wine flights.

Damn Fine Cafe CAFE £
(www.facebook.com/damnfinecafe; 16 Bird St; dishes £2.50-6.50; 9am-2pm Tue-Fri, to 3pm Sat & Sun) Teeming with locals, this cafe is a handy spot for all-day bacon-and-sausage or vegetarian toad-in-the-hole breakfasts, soup, mozzarella melts and sandwiches on a variety of breads.

Trooper GASTROPUB ££
(01543-480413; www.thetrooperwall.co.uk; Watling St, Wall; mains £13.50-28, steaks £18-45;

kitchen noon-9.15pm Mon-Wed, to 9.45pm Thu-Sat, to 8pm Sun, bar noon-midnight Mon-Sat, to 10pm Sun;) Idyllically situated 3 miles southwest of Lichfield in the tiny village of Wall, this gastropub prides itself on ingredients sourced from local suppliers and herbs from its gardens. Chargrilled wagyu steaks are the house speciality, alongside contemporary twists on pub classics, such as ham-and-cider pie. In fine weather, enjoy its fabulous real ales in the sunny beer garden.

Its three-course kids' menu (£10) has the option of a mini 4oz steak with fries.

Wine House BRITISH ££
(01543-419999; www.thewinehouselichfield.co.uk; 27 Bird St; mains £12.50-28; noon-10pm Mon-Sat, to 6pm Sun) Well-chosen wines complement the upmarket pub fare at these smart, red-brick premises. Choices range from slow-cooked pork belly with apple sauce to steaks and seafood, such as line-caught sea bass with white wine, shallots and clams.

Drinking & Nightlife

Beerbohm BAR
(http://beerbohm.co.uk; 19 Tamworth St; 11am-11pm Tue-Sat;) Behind a peppermint-painted traditional shopfront, Beerbohm's richly coloured lounge-style interior is filled with handmade furniture. Its discerning drinks list includes local ales and small-batch gins, English wines and artisan malt whiskies plus imported craft beers (some gluten-free). It doesn't serve food but provides plates and cutlery for you to bring your own.

Whippet Inn PUB
(21 Tamworth St; noon-2.30pm & 4.30-10pm Wed & Thu, noon-10pm Fri & Sat, to 5pm Sun) Ales and craft keg beers from independent British breweries are the hallmark of this adorable little one-room micropub, along with a wonderful selection of ciders and wines, but it resolutely doesn't serve lager or spirits. Artisan bar snacks include pork pies, Scotch eggs and sausage rolls.

Information

Tourist Office (01543-308924; www.visitlichfield.co.uk; Market Sq; 9.30am-4pm Mon-Sat) In the Hub at St Mary's.

Getting There & Away

The bus station is opposite the main Lichfield City train station on Birmingham Rd. Bus 825 serves Stafford (£4.60, 1¼ hours, hourly Monday to Saturday).

Lichfield has two train stations.

Lichfield City Trains to Birmingham (£5.70, 30 minutes, up to three per hour) leave from Lichfield City station in the town centre.

Lichfield Trent Valley Trains to London Euston (£56, 1¾ hours, up to two per hour) run from Lichfield Trent Valley station on the eastern side of town, 1.5 miles east of the centre, with a change in Birmingham.

WORCESTERSHIRE

Famed for its eponymous condiment, invented by two Worcester chemists in 1837, Worcestershire marks the transition from the industrial heart of the Midlands to the peaceful countryside of the Marches along

NATIONAL BREWERY CENTRE

Burton-upon-Trent grew up around its 7th-century abbey, which was famed for its healing spring waters. Brewing began here around 1700 and in the early 18th century, the River Trent was opened for navigation, allowing Burton to become a major brewing centre. Its fascinating history is brought to life through two-hour guided tours of the **National Brewery Centre** (01283-532880; www.nationalbrewerycentre.co.uk; Horninglow St, Burton-upon-Trent; adult/child £11.95/6.95; centre 10am-5pm, guided tours 11am & 2pm Thu-Sun), a vast complex that contains a museum and still has a microbrewery today. Staff can point you to Burton's other breweries and traditional ale houses.

During tours, you'll learn, for example, that Burton developed pale ale to export to colonial-era India: the origins of IPA (Indian Pale Ale) today; and also taste samples (there are soft drinks for kids).

Trains run from Derby (£8, 15 minutes, up to three per hour) and Birmingham (£17.80, 30 minutes, up to three per hour) to Burton's train station; a half-mile walk southwest of the National Brewery Centre.

the English–Welsh border. The southern and western fringes of the county burst with lush countryside and sleepy market towns, while the capital is a classic English county town, whose magnificent cathedral inspired the composer Edward Elgar to write some of his greatest works.

Activities

The 210-mile riverside **Severn Way** winds through Worcestershire en route from Plynlimon in Wales to the sea at Bristol. A shorter challenge is the 100-mile **Three Choirs Way**, linking Worcester to Hereford and Gloucester. The Malvern Hills are also prime country for walking and cycling; information is available at www.malvernhillsaonb.org.uk.

Getting There & Around

Worcester is a convenient rail hub. Kidderminster is the southern railhead of the quaint Severn Valley Railway (p440).

Buses and trains connect larger towns, but bus services to rural areas can be frustratingly infrequent. Search the transport pages at www.worcestershire.gov.uk or Traveline (p406) for bus companies and timetables.

Worcester

☎01905 / POP 101,328

Worcester (*woos*-ter) has enough historic treasures to forgive the architectural eyesores from the postwar love affair with all things concrete. The home of the famous Worcestershire sauce (an unlikely combination of fermented tamarinds and anchovies), this ancient cathedral city was the site of the last battle of the Civil War, the Battle of Worcester, which took place on 3 September 1651. The defeated Charles II only narrowly escaped the pursuing Roundheads by hiding in an oak tree, an event still celebrated in Worcester every 29 May, when government buildings are decked out with oak sprigs.

Sights

★**Worcester Cathedral** CATHEDRAL

(☎01905-732900; www.worcestercathedral.co.uk; 8 College Yard; cathedral by donation, tower adult/child £5/free, tours £7/free; ⏲cathedral 11am-3pm Mon-Sat, 1-3pm Sun, tower hours vary, tours 11am & 2.30pm Mon-Sat Mar-Nov, Sat Dec-Feb) Rising above the River Severn, Worcester's majestic cathedral is the final resting place of Magna Carta signatory King John. The strong-legged can scale 235 steps to the top of the **tower** (confirm times ahead), from where Charles II surveyed his troops during the disastrous Battle of Worcester. Hour-long **tours** run from the gift shop. Several works by local composer Edward Elgar had their first public outings here – to appreciate the acoustics, come for **evensong** (5.30pm Monday to Saturday, 4pm Sunday).

Royal Worcester Porcelain Works MUSEUM

(☎01905-21247; www.museumofroyalworcester.org; Severn St; adult/child incl audio guide £6.50/free; ⏲10am-5pm Thu-Sat, to 4pm Sun) Up there with the country's most famous potteries, the Royal Worcester porcelain factory gained an edge over its rivals by picking up the contract to provide fine crockery to the British monarchy. An entertaining audio tour reveals some quirkier sides to the Royal Worcester story, including its brief foray into porcelain dentures and 'portable fonts' designed for use during cholera outbreaks. The shop has some splendid pieces, from monk-shaped candle snuffers to decorated thimbles and pill boxes.

Greyfriars HISTORIC BUILDING

(NT; ☎01905-23571; www.nationaltrust.org.uk; Friar St; adult/child £5.45/2.70; ⏲11am-5pm Tue-Sat Mar-Oct, to 4pm Nov–mid-Dec) Friar St was largely chock-a-block with historic architecture until the iconoclastic 1960s when much was demolished, including the lovely medieval Lich Gate. Some creaky old almshouses survive and Greyfriars was saved in the nick of time by the National Trust, offering the chance to poke around a timber-framed merchant's house from 1480. It's full of atmospheric wood-panelled rooms and is backed by a pretty walled garden.

Sleeping

Diglis House Hotel HOTEL ££

(☎01905-353518; www.diglishousehotel.co.uk; Severn St; s/d/ste incl breakfast from £90/115/145; P 📶) Next to the boathouse in a gorgeous waterside setting, this rambling yet cosy 28-room Georgian house is a short stroll from the cathedral. The best rooms have four-poster beds, luxe bathrooms and river views. Its elegant restaurant (mains £12 to £18) opens to a terrace overlooking the river. Guests can work out at the nearby gym for free.

Eating & Drinking

★**Old Rectifying House** BRITISH ££

(☎01905-619622; www.theoldrec.co.uk; North Pde; mains £12-29; ⏲kitchen 6-9pm Tue-Thu, to 9.30pm

Fri & Sat, bar noon-11pm Tue-Thu & Sun, to midnight Fri & Sat;) Worcester's hippest dining space has a candlelit, painted-brick interior and umbrella-shaded terrace tables. Its switched-on menu features dishes such as braised pork cheek with a crispy ham bonbon. DJs often hit the decks in the lounge bar, which mixes craft cocktails including a 'Hedgerow Shire' with local gin and birch liqueur.

Kids, vegetarians and vegans are catered for; vegan dishes include a Sunday nut roast (advance orders essential).

★Cardinal's Hat PUB
(01905-724006; www.the-cardinals-hat.co.uk; 31 Friar St; 4-10pm Mon, noon-10pm Tue-Sun;) Dating from the 14th century, and claiming a resident ghost, Worcester's oldest and grandest pub retains original features, including timber panelling and log-burning stoves. English craft beers and ciders dominate the taps, while the kitchen specialises in pies (eg steak, red wine and Stilton, £11). Upstairs are six Georgian-style boutique guest rooms (doubles £82.50 to £125).

Information

Tourist Office (01905-726311; www.visitworcestershire.org; Guildhall, High St; 9.30am-5pm Mon-Fri, 10am-4pm Sat) Inside the Grade I–listed Guildhall, dating from 1721.

Getting There & Away

BUS

The **bus station** (Crowngate Centre, Friary Walk) is inside the Crowngate Centre on Friary Walk. National Express has services to London Victoria (£18.50, 3¾ hours, two daily Monday to Friday, one Saturday and Sunday).

TRAIN

Worcester Foregate is the main rail hub, but services also run from Worcester Shrub Hill.

Birmingham £9, one hour, up to three per hour
Great Malvern £5.90, 15 minutes, up to two per hour
Hereford £10.60, 50 minutes, hourly
Ledbury £7.70, 25 minutes, hourly
London Paddington £44.60, 2½ hours, up to three per hour

Great Malvern

01684 / POP 29,626

Tumbling down the side of a forested ridge about 7 miles southwest of Worcester, the picturesque spa town of Great Malvern is the gateway to the Malverns, a soaring 9-mile-long range of volcanic hills that rise unexpectedly from the surrounding meadows. In Victorian times, the medicinal waters were prescribed as a panacea for everything from gout to sore eyes – you can test the theory by sampling Malvern water straight from the ground at public wells dotted around the town.

THE FIRS – ELGAR'S BIRTHPLACE

England's most popular classical composer is celebrated at the humble country **cottage** (NT; www.nationaltrust.org.uk/the-firs; Crown East Lane, Lower Broadheath; adult/child £8/5.10) where Edward Elgar was born in 1857. A sculpture of Elgar, sitting on a bench looking out over the Malvern Hills, created by artist Jemma Pearson, is in the flower-filled garden.

The property is run by the National Trust; check the website for opening times as well as details of concerts here. It's 4 miles west of Worcester; you'll need your own transport.

Sights

★Morgan Motor Company FACTORY, MUSEUM
(01684-573104; www.morgan-motor.com; Pickersleigh Rd; museum free, tours adult/child £24/12; museum 8.30am-5pm Mon-Thu, to 2pm Fri, tours by reservation) Morgan has been handcrafting elegant sports cars since 1909. You can see the mechanics at work on two-hour guided tours of the unassuming shed-like buildings comprising the factory (pre-bookings essential), and view a fleet of vintage classics adjacent to the museum. If buying one of these beautiful machines is beyond your budget, it's possible to hire one (per day/weekend/week from £235/635/1095, including insurance) for a spin through the Malvern Hills.

Great Malvern Priory MONASTERY
(01684-561020; www.greatmalvernpriory.org.uk; Church St; 9am-5pm) FREE The 11th-century Great Malvern Priory is packed with remarkable features, from original Norman pillars to surreal modernist stained glass. The choir is enclosed by a screen of 15th-century tiles and the monks' stalls are decorated with delightfully irreverent 14th-century

LOCAL KNOWLEDGE

WALKING IN THE MALVERN HILLS

The jack-in-the-box Malvern Hills, which dramatically pop up out of the Severn plains on the boundary between Worcestershire and Herefordshire, rise to the lofty peak of the Worcester Beacon (419m), reached by a steep 3-mile climb above Great Malvern. More than 100 miles of trails traipse over the various summits, which are mostly capped by exposed grassland, offering the kind of views that inspire orchestral movements.

Great Malvern's tourist office has racks of pamphlets covering popular hikes, including a map of the mineral-water springs, wells and fountains of the town and surrounding hills. The enthusiast-run website www.malverntrail.co.uk is also a goldmine of useful walking information.

A single £4.40 parking ticket per day is valid at locations throughout the hills.

misericords, depicting everything from three rats hanging a cat to the mythological reptile, the basilisk. Charles Darwin's daughter Annie is buried here.

Sleeping & Eating

Abbey Hotel HOTEL £££
(01684-892332; www.sarova-abbeyhotel.com; Abbey Rd; d/f from £139/179; P) Tangled in vines like a Brothers Grimm fairy-tale castle, this stately property has 103 elegant rooms in a prime location by the local-history museum and priory.

Mac & Jac's CAFE £
(www.macandjacs.co.uk; 23 Abbey Rd; dishes £4-13; 9am-4pm Wed-Fri, to 5pm Sat, 10am-4pm Sun) Creative salads, flatbreads, sharing plates, spelt risotto and a savoury tart of the day are served at this light, bright cafe set in a chic white-painted shopfront near the priory.

St Ann's Well Cafe CAFE, VEGETARIAN £
(01684-560285; www.stannswell.co.uk; St Ann's Rd; mains £5.50, cakes £2.90; 11.30am-3.30pm Tue-Fri, 10am-4pm Sat & Sun;) A s-t-e-e-p climb above St Ann's Rd (so best to check opening times beforehand), this quaint cafe is set in an early-19th-century villa, with mountain-fresh spring water bubbling into a carved basin by the door. All-vegetarian food (including vegan options) spans soups to pies, filled baguettes, cakes, pastries and puddings.

Fig Tree MEDITERRANEAN ££
(01684-569909; www.thefigmalvern.co.uk; 99b Church St; breakfast dishes £6.50-9.50, mains lunch £8.50-13, dinner £16.50-24; 10am-2pm & 5.30-9.30pm Tue-Sat;) Tucked down an alleyway off Church St, this 19th-century former stable serves hearty breakfasts (including vegan options), and Mediterranean-inspired fare at lunch (focaccia, pastas and salads) and dinner (chorizo-stuffed squid, lamb souvlaki with tzatziki and saffron rice). Don't miss its signature almond-and-lemon polenta cake with fig ice cream.

Information

Tourist Office (01684-892289; www.visitthemalverns.org; 6 Church St; 10am-5pm Apr-Oct, 10am-5pm Mon-Sat, to 4pm Sun Nov-Mar) The tourist office is a mine of walking and cycling information.

Getting There & Away

Buses are limited, making trains your best bet. The train station is east of the town centre, off Avenue Rd.

Rail services include the following.

Hereford £9.70, 30 minutes, hourly
Ledbury £5.50, 10 minutes, up to two per hour
Worcester £5.90, 15 minutes, up to two per hour

HEREFORDSHIRE

Adjoining the Welsh border, Herefordshire is a patchwork of fields, hills and cute little black-and-white villages, many dating back to the Tudor era and beyond.

Activities

As well as the famous **Offa's Dyke Path**, which follows the English–Welsh border for 177 miles alongside the 8th-century Offa's Dyke, walkers can follow the **Herefordshire Trail** (www.herefordshiretrail.com) on a 150-mile circular loop through Leominster, Ledbury, Ross-on-Wye and Kington.

Only slightly less ambitious is the 136-mile **Wye Valley Walk** (www.wyevalleywalk.org), which runs from Chepstow in Wales through Herefordshire and back out again to Plynlimon.

The **Three Choirs Way** is a 100-mile route connecting the cathedrals of Hereford, Worcester and Gloucester.

Cyclists can trace the **Six Castles Cycleway** (NCN Route 44) from Hereford to Leominster and Shrewsbury, or NCN Route 68 to Great Malvern and Worcester.

Getting Around

Trains run frequently to destinations including Hereford and Ledbury, with bus connections on to the rest of the county. For bus timetables, contact Traveline (p406).

Hereford

01432 / POP 58,896

Surrounded by apple orchards and rolling pastures at the heart of the Marches, Hereford straddles the River Wye. This lively city's key draw for visitors is its magnificent cathedral.

Sights

★Hereford Cathedral CATHEDRAL

(01432-374200; www.herefordcathedral.org; 5 College Cloisters, Cathedral Close; cathedral entry by donation, Mappa Mundi £6; cathedral 10am-3pm Mon-Sat, noon-3pm Sun, Mappa Mundi 10am-3pm Mon-Sat) After Welsh marauders torched the original Saxon cathedral, the Norman rulers of Hereford erected a larger, grander cathedral on the same site. The building was subsequently remodelled in a succession of medieval architectural styles.

The signature highlight is the magnificent **Mappa Mundi**, a single piece of calfskin vellum intricately painted with some rather fantastical assumptions about the layout of the globe in around 1290. The same wing contains the world's largest surviving **chained library** of rare manuscripts manacled to the shelves.

Cider Museum Hereford MUSEUM

(01432-354207; www.cidermuseum.co.uk; Pomona Pl) Mills and presses, glassware, watercolours, photographs and films are among the displays at this former cider-making factory (Bulmer's original premises), along with costrels (minibarrels) used by agricultural workers to carry their wages, which were partially paid in cider. Download brochures outlining walks through Herefordshire's orchards from its website. It's half a mile west of the city centre; follow Eign St and turn south along Ryelands St.

The museum was closed at the time of research – check the website for updates.

Sleeping

Charades B&B ££

(01432-269444; www.charadeshereford.co.uk; 32 Southbank Rd; s/d from £75/85; P@) Handy for the bus station, this imposing Victorian house dating from 1877 has six inviting rooms with high ceilings, big and bright windows, and some with soothing countryside views. The house itself has character in spades – look for old service bells in the hall and the plentiful *Titanic* memorabilia. Traditional or vegetarian breakfasts are available.

★Castle House BOUTIQUE HOTEL £££

(01432-356321; www.castlehse.co.uk; Castle St; s/d/ste from £140/175/200; P) In a regal Georgian town house where the Bishop of Hereford once resided, this tranquil 16-room hotel has two sophisticated restaurants using ingredients sourced from its own nearby farm, a sunny garden spilling down to Hereford's former castle moat, and magnificent rooms and suites. Another eight newer rooms (some wheelchair accessible) are a short walk away at 25 Castle St.

Eating & Drinking

★Burger Shop BURGERS £

(01432-351764; www.aruleoftum.com; 32 Aubrey St; burgers £7.50-11.50; noon-9pm Sun-Wed, to 10pm Thu-Sat;) Exposed brick, elongated wooden benches and a courtyard garden are the backdrop for brilliant brioche-bun burgers such as the Hereford Hop (pulled beef shin, Hereford Hop cheese, dill pickles and mustard mayo). Vegan burgers are cooked on a separate grill; you can order gluten-free buns made from quinoa flour. Alongside local ciders, kickin' cocktails include a vodka-fuelled Marmalade Mule.

Hereford Deli DELI £

(01432-341283; www.theherefordeli.com; 4 The Mews, St Owen St; sandwiches £2-3; 8am-6pm Mon-Fri, 9am-4pm Sat) At this gourmet emporium with a clutch of tables, fantastic sandwiches are a steal. Combinations include curried free-range chicken with mango chutney, Scottish smoked salmon with lemon-and-dill butter, or local roast beef with Cropwell Bishop Stilton and rosehip jelly. It's hidden down a narrow laneway near a large public car park.

LOCAL KNOWLEDGE

HEREFORDSHIRE CIDER

The **Herefordshire Cider Route** (www.ciderroute.co.uk) drops in on numerous local cider producers, where you can try before you buy, and then totter off to the next cidery. Mindful of road safety, tourist offices have maps and guide booklets to help you explore by bus or bicycle.

If you only have time to visit one Herefordshire cider-maker, make it **Westons Cider Mills** (01531-660108; www.westons-cider.co.uk; The Bounds, Much Marcle; tours adult/child £12.50/5; 9am-5pm Mon-Fri, 10am-5pm Sat & Sun), whose house brew is even served in the Houses of Parliament. Informative tours (1½ hours) start at 11am, 12.30pm, 2pm and 3.30pm from Monday to Friday, with free cider and perry tastings for the grown-ups. There's also a fascinating bottle museum, and a restaurant that incorporates cider in its dishes. It's just under a mile west of the tiny village of Much Marcle.

★Beer in Hand PUB
(https://beer-in-hand.square.site; 136 Eign St; 5-10pm Thu-Sat) Ciders at this independent pub are sublime and most are locally sourced. It's also the tap room for its own Odyssey beers (such as Black Out, a dark-malt, full-bodied American black ale brewed with fresh oranges, which it brews on the nearby National Trust Brockhampton Estate). There are board games but no TVs.

Information

Tourist Office (01432-383837; www.facebook.com/tichereford; 8 St Owen's St; 10am-4pm Tue-Sat) Located inside Hereford's town hall.

Getting There & Away

BUS

The bus station is on Commercial Rd, 500m northeast of the city centre.

Bus 33 runs to Gloucester (£4.50, 1¾ hours, hourly Monday to Saturday) via Ross-on-Wye (£4, one hour).

TRAIN

The train station is 950m northeast of the city centre.

Regular services include the following:

Birmingham £18.90, 1½ hours, hourly

Ledbury £6.90, 15 minutes, hourly

London Paddington £61.20, three hours, up to two per hour – either direct or with a change in Newport, South Wales

Ludlow £10.90, 25 minutes, up to two per hour

Worcester £10.60, 50 minutes, hourly

Ledbury

01531 / POP 9290

Creaking with history and dotted with antique shops, Ledbury's crooked black-and-white streets zero in on a delightfully leggy medieval **Market House**. The timber-framed structure is precariously balanced atop a series of wooden posts supposedly taken from the wrecked ships of the Spanish Armada.

Almost impossibly cute Church Lane, crowded with tilting timber-framed buildings, runs its cobbled way from High St to the town church.

Sleeping & Eating

Feathers Hotel HOTEL ££
(01531-635266; www.feathersledbury.co.uk; 25 High St; d incl breakfast from £115; P) A Ledbury landmark, this black-and-white Tudor hotel built in 1564 looms over the main street. Of its 22 rooms, those in the oldest part of the building come with sloping floorboards, painted beams and much more character than rooms in the modern extension. There's an atmospheric wood-panelled restaurant (mains £14 to £29), and an indoor swimming pool.

Verzon House Hotel HOTEL ££
(01531-670381; www.verzonhouse.com; Hereford Rd, Trumpet; s/d/ste from £80/100/180; P) The ultimate country-chic retreat, this lovely Georgian farmhouse 3.8 miles northwest of Ledbury on the A438 has nine luxuriously appointed rooms with free-standing baths, goose-down pillows and deep-pile carpets. Locally sourced produce underpins the Modern British menu at its restaurant (mains £17 to £32).

Malthouse Cafe & Gallery CAFE ££
(01531-634443; Church Lane; mains lunch £5-7.50, dinner £14-19; 9am-5pm Tue-Thu, 9am-5pm & 6-11pm Fri & Sat, 10am-4pm Sun & Mon;) Set back from the street in a cobbled courtyard, this ivy-draped building is a delightful spot for breakfast (such as poached eggs with a thyme, leek and parsnip cake) or lunch

(black-pudding sausage rolls, goats cheese and rosemary filo parcels). On Friday and Saturday evenings, mains might include mustard-glazed pork belly or slow-cooked Herefordshire beef ribs.

Shopping

★Malvern Hills Vintage ANTIQUES
(☎01531-633608; www.malvernhillsvintage.com; Lower Mitchell Barns, Eastnor; shop & cafe 10am-5pm Wed-Sat, 11am-5pm Sun) A vast timber barn 1.5 miles northeast of Ledbury is packed to the rafters with retro, antique and industrial treasures – everything from Victorian lamps and brass cash registers to mahogany dressers, oak-framed mirrors, leather Chesterfields and even classic cars, such as a 1974 MG Midget RWA 1275 convertible. On the mezzanine, its tearoom serves scones, cakes and slices.

Getting There & Away

Buses are limited, but regular train services include the following.

Great Malvern £5.50, 10 minutes, up to two per hour

Hereford £6.90, 15 minutes, hourly

Worcester £7.70, 25 minutes, up to two per hour

Ross-on-Wye

☎01989 / POP 10,582

Set on a red sandstone bluff over a kink in the River Wye, hilly Ross-on-Wye was propelled to fame in the 18th century by Alexander Pope and Samuel Taylor Coleridge, who penned tributes to philanthropist John Kyrle, 'Man of Ross', who dedicated his life and fortune to the poor of the parish.

Sights

Market House GALLERY
(☎01989-769398; www.madeinross.co.uk; Market Pl; 11am-3pm) FREE The 17th-century Market House sits atop weathered sandstone columns in Market Pl. The salmon-pink building is now home to artist collective Made in Ross, whose members live and work in a 20-mile radius, and exhibit and sell their arts and crafts here. Regular markets take place on the square at the front.

Sleeping & Eating

King's Head INN ££
(☎01989-763174; www.kingshead.co.uk; 8 High St; d/f from £77/95; P) Dating from the 14th century, this half-timbered inn is a charmer. Some of its 15 sage- and oyster-toned rooms have four-poster beds, and there's a timber bar serving local ales and ciders, and a candlelit, book-lined library, as well as a conservatory restaurant. There is limited parking available for guests.

Pots & Pieces CAFE £
(www.potsandpieces.com; 40 High St; dishes £3-8.50; 9am-3pm Mon-Fri, 10am-4.45pm Sat, 11am-2.45pm Sun) Browse ceramics and crafts at this tearoom by the marketplace, and choose from cakes such as lemon drizzle, coffee, and walnut and carrot. Savoury options include quiches, sandwiches and a soup of the day.

Truffles Delicatessen DELI £
(www.trufflesdeli.co.uk; 46 High St; dishes £3.50-7.50; 10am-4pm Mon-Fri, 9am-5pm Sat) Packed to the rafters with local artisan products (cheeses, breads, chutneys et al), Truffles also has stellar sandwiches, soups and salad boxes to take away for a riverside picnic.

Getting There & Away

The bus stand is on Cantilupe Rd. Bus 33 runs to Hereford (£4, 50 minutes, hourly Monday to Saturday). In the opposite direction, it serves Gloucester (£4.50, 45 minutes, hourly Monday to Saturday).

BLACK & WHITE VILLAGES

A triangle of Tudor England survives almost untouched in northwest Herefordshire, where higgledy-piggledy black-and-white houses cluster around idyllic village greens, seemingly oblivious to the modern world. A delightful 40-mile circular drive follows the **Black and White Village Trail** (www.blackandwhitetrail.org), meandering past the most handsome timber-framed buildings. It starts at Leominster and loops round through Eardisland and Kington, the southern terminus of the 30-mile waymarked Mortimer Trail footpath from Ludlow.

Pick up guides to exploring the villages by car, bus or bicycle at tourist offices.

SHROPSHIRE

Sleepy Shropshire is a glorious scattering of hills, castles and timber-framed villages tucked against the Welsh border. Highlights include castle-crowned Ludlow, industrial Ironbridge and the beautiful Shropshire Hills, which offer the best walking and cycling in the Marches.

Activities

The rolling Shropshire Hills call out to walkers like a siren. Between Shrewsbury and Ludlow, the landscape rucks up into dramatic folds, with spectacular trails climbing the flanks of **Wenlock Edge** and the **Long Mynd** near Church Stretton. The county is also crossed by long-distance trails, including the famous **Offa's Dyke Path** and the popular **Shropshire Way**, which meanders around Ludlow and Church Stretton.

Mountain bikers head for the muddy tracks that scramble over the **Long Mynd** near Church Stretton, while road riders aim for the **Six Castles Cycleway** (NCN 44), which runs for 58 miles from Shrewsbury to Leominster.

Tourist offices sell copies of *Cycling for Pleasure in the Marches,* a pack of five maps and guides covering the entire county.

Getting There & Away

Shrewsbury is the local transport hub, with good bus and rail connections. Church Stretton and Ludlow also have handy rail services.

From May to September, **Shropshire Hills Shuttles** (www.shropshirehillsaonb.co.uk; single ticket £3, Day Rover ticket adult/child £10/4) runs an hourly bus service along popular hiking routes on weekends and bank holidays.

Shrewsbury

01743 / POP 71,715

A delightful jumble of winding medieval streets and timbered Tudor houses leaning at precarious angles, Shrewsbury was a crucial front in the conflict between the English and the Welsh in medieval days. Even today, the road bridge running east towards London is known as the English Bridge to mark it out from the Welsh Bridge leading northwest towards Holyhead. Shrewsbury is also the birthplace of Charles Darwin (1809–82).

The pronunciation of the town's name has long been a hot topic. A charity debate hosted by University Centre Shrewsbury in 2015 declared '*shroos*-bree' (rhyming with 'grew') the winner over the posher '*shrows*-bree' (rhyming with 'grow'), as did a survey by the *Shropshire Star,* though you'll still hear both pronunciations in the town and across British media.

Sights

Shrewsbury Castle CASTLE, MUSEUM
(01743-358516; www.soldiersofshropshire.co.uk; Castle St; castle adult/child £4.50/2, grounds free; 10.30am-5pm Mon-Wed, Fri & Sat, to 4pm Sun Apr–mid-Sep, to 4pm Mon-Wed, Fri & Sat mid-Feb–Mar & mid-Sep–mid-Dec) Hewn from flaking red Shropshire sandstone, the town castle contains the **Shropshire Regimental Museum**. There are fine views from **Laura's Tower** and the battlements. The lower level of the **Great Hall** dates from 1150.

Shrewsbury Abbey CHURCH
(01743-232723; www.shrewsburyabbey.com; Abbey Foregate; by donation; 10am-4pm Apr-Oct, 10.30am-3pm Nov-Mar) All that remains of a vast, cruciform Benedictine monastery founded in 1083 is the lovely red-sandstone Shrewsbury Abbey. Twice used for meetings of the English Parliament, the abbey church lost its spire and two wings when the monastery was dissolved in 1540. It sustained further damage in 1826 when engineer Thomas Telford ran the London–Holyhead road right through the grounds. Nevertheless, you can still see some impressive Norman, Early English and Victorian features, including an exceptional 14th-century west window.

St Mary's Church CHURCH
(www.visitchurches.org.uk; St Mary's St; by donation; 11am-3pm Mon-Fri) The fabulous interior of this tall-spired medieval church contains an impressive collection of stained glass, including a 1340 window depicting the Tree of Jesse (a biblical representation of the lineage of Jesus) and a magnificent oak ceiling in the nave, which largely collapsed in a huge gale in 1894 when the top of the spire blew off. Much of the glass in the church is sourced from Europe, including some outstanding Dutch glass from 1500.

Shrewsbury Prison HISTORIC BUILDING
(01743-343100; www.shrewsburyprison.com; The Dana; prison adult/child £15/9.50, ghost tour £20/15; prison tours 10am-5pm, ghost tours 7.30pm & 9.30pm) Built in 1793, this was a working prison as recently as 2013. Today

Shrewsbury

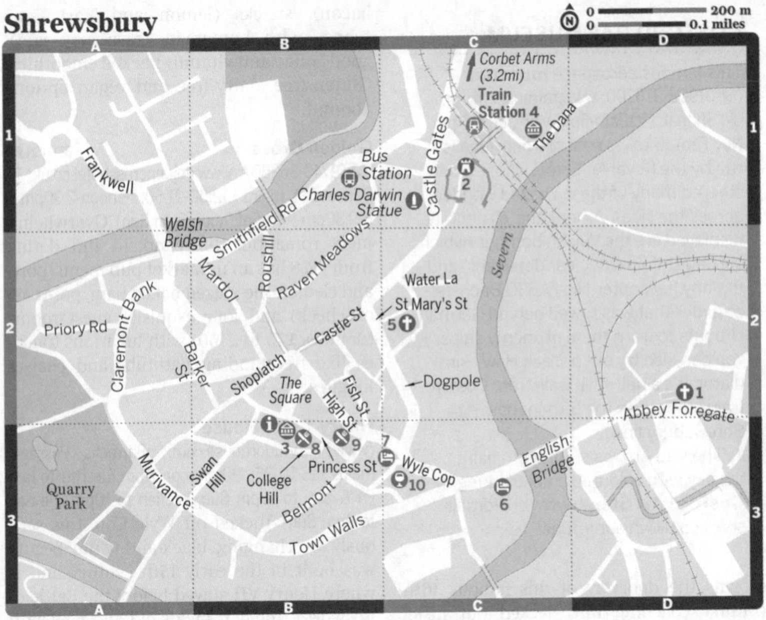

Shrewsbury

Sights

1 Shrewsbury Abbey D2
2 Shrewsbury Castle C1
3 Shrewsbury Museum & Art Gallery B3
4 Shrewsbury Prison C1
5 St Mary's Church C2

Sleeping

6 Lion & Pheasant C3
7 Lion Hotel C3

Eating

8 Ginger & Co B3
9 Golden Cross B3

Drinking & Nightlife

10 Henry Tudor House C3

tours are led by former prison guards: when you arrive, you're 'processed' as a prisoner and escorted into the general population wing, before having the opportunity to enter a cell, which is ominously locked behind you. Alternatively, you can take a self-guided tour. Chilling evening ghost tours (minimum age 12 years) include the prison's execution room where 11 inmates were hanged.

Shrewsbury Museum & Art Gallery MUSEUM
(☎01743-258885; www.shrewsburymuseum.org.uk; The Square; adult/child £5/3; ⊙10am-5pm Mon-Sat, 11am-4pm Sun) Diverse exhibits at Shrewsbury's town museum cover everything from Roman treasures to Shropshire gold, including the Bronze Age Perry Bracelet. Its Prehistory and Roman Gallery is free of charge.

Sleeping

Corbet Arms PUB ££
(☎01743-709232; www.thecorbetarms.com; Church Rd, Uffington; d/f incl breakfast from £80/105; P 📶) Peacefully situated 4 miles east of Shrewsbury in the pint-sized village of Uffington on the banks of the River Severn, this family-friendly pub has nine stylish en-suite rooms reached by a staircase. Try for top-floor room 10, which has exposed beams, a spacious sitting area and panoramic views of the surrounding countryside. High-quality pub food includes outstanding Sunday roasts.

Lion Hotel HOTEL ££
(☎01743-353107; www.thelionhotelshrewsbury.com; Wyle Cop; s/d/ste incl breakfast from £74/109/135; P 📶) A gilded wooden lion

COSFORD RAF MUSEUM

This famous aerospace **museum** (01902-376200; www.rafmuseum.org.uk; Shifnal; 10am-5pm Mar-Oct, to 4pm Nov-Feb) 13 miles east of Ironbridge is run by the Royal Air Force, whose pilots steered many of these winged wonders across the skies. Among the 70 aircraft displayed are the Vulcan bomber (which carried Britain's nuclear deterrent) and the tiny helicopter-like FA330 Bachstelze glider that was towed behind German U-boats to warn them of enemy ships. You can also try out a Black Hawk simulator. It's a half-mile walk from Cosford train station, on the Birmingham–Shrewsbury line.

The Red Arrows stunt team paint the sky with coloured smoke during the **Cosford Air Show** (www.cosfordairshow.co.uk) in early June.

crowns the doorway of this famous 16th-century coaching inn, decked out inside with portraits of lords and ladies in powdered wigs. Charles Dickens was a former guest, and the lounge is warmed by a grand stone fireplace. Its 59 rooms are lovely, right down to the period-pattern fabrics and ceramic water jugs.

Lion & Pheasant BOUTIQUE HOTEL £££
(01743-770345; www.lionandpheasant.co.uk; 50 Wyle Cop; s/d incl breakfast from £99/130; P) This former coaching inn is now a stylish town house offering 22 individually styled rooms with comfy goose- and duck-down pillows, and some with Severn views. Original features throughout the property include magnificent exposed timber beams. Classy Modern British fare is served in the whitewashed restaurant (mains £16 to £27). Parking for overnight guests is first come, first served.

Eating & Drinking

Ginger & Co CAFE £
(www.gingerandcocoffee.com; 30-31 Princess St; dishes £3.50-11.50; 8.30am-3pm Mon-Thu, to 4pm Fri & Sat, 10am-3pm Sun;) A successful crowd-funding campaign propelled the opening of this airy, L-shaped cafe filled with upcycled furniture. It's a great option for a light brunch or lunch (avocado on artisan toast with oak-smoked streaky bacon), snacks (lemon and Earl Grey scones with homemade raspberry jam), good coffee and vitamin-packed smoothies. Gluten-free, dairy-free and vegan options abound.

Golden Cross BRITISH ££
(01743-362507; www.goldencrosshotel.co.uk; 14 Princess St; mains £12.50-21.50; noon-2.30pm & 6-9.30pm Wed-Sat, noon-3pm Sun) Overwhelmingly romantic, this candlelit inn dating from 1428 has an upmarket pub menu (port- and clementine-glazed baked ham, pot-roast ox cheek) and four exquisite guest rooms (doubles £75 to £150) with luxurious touches like freestanding bathtubs and chaises longues.

Henry Tudor House PUB
(www.henrytudorhouse.com; Barracks Passage; mains £13.50-25; bar noon-11pm Tue-Thu, to 1am Fri & Sat, to 10pm Sun, kitchen to 10pm Tue-Sat, to 9pm Sun) Tucked off Wyle Cop, this seriously overhanging black-and-white beauty was built in the early 15th century and is where Henry VII stayed before the Battle of Bosworth. Today it melds old and new with a zinc bar, a light-filled conservatory and birdcage-encased chandeliers. Live gigs regularly take to the stage.

Food (mackerel with cucumber puree, Shropshire beef Wellington) is superb, too.

Information

The **tourist office** (01743-258888; www.originalshrewsbury.co.uk; The Square; 10am-5pm Mon-Sat, 11am-4pm Sun) shares space with the Shrewsbury Museum & Art Gallery.

Getting There & Away

BUS

The **bus station** (Smithfield Rd) is beside the river. Direct services include the following:

Church Stretton Bus 435, £3.90, 40 minutes, hourly Monday to Friday, every two hours Saturday

Ironbridge Bus 96, £4.90, 50 minutes, four daily

Ludlow Bus 435, £4.50, 1¼ hours, hourly Monday to Friday, every two hours Saturday

TRAIN

The train station is on the northeastern edge of the town centre at the bottom of Castle Foregate. Destinations include the following:

Birmingham £16.20, one hour, two per hour

Holyhead £46.40, 2½ hours, hourly

London Euston £106.50, 2¾ hours, every 20 minutes, change in Crewe or Birmingham
Ludlow £14.20, 30 minutes, hourly

Ironbridge Gorge

☎01952 / POP 2582

Strolling or cycling through the woods, hills and villages of this leafy river gorge, it's hard to believe such a peaceful enclave could really have been the birthplace of the Industrial Revolution. Nevertheless, it was here that Abraham Darby perfected the art of smelting iron ore with coke in 1709, making it possible to mass-produce cast iron for the first time.

Abraham Darby's son, Abraham Darby II, invented a new forging process for producing single beams of iron, allowing Abraham Darby III to astound the world with the first-ever iron bridge, constructed in 1779. The bridge remains the focal point of this World Heritage Site, and 10 very different museums tell the story of the Industrial Revolution in the buildings where it took place.

Sights

★Iron Bridge — BRIDGE

(www.ironbridge.org.uk; bridge 24hr, tollhouse 10am-5pm) FREE The arching Iron Bridge, which gives the area its name, was built to flaunt the new technology invented by the pioneering Darby family. At the time of its construction in 1779, nobody could believe that anything so large – it weighs 384 tonnes – could be built from cast iron without collapsing under its own weight. There's a small exhibition on the bridge's history at the former **toll house**. The bridge is dramatically illuminated at night.

★Museum of the Gorge — MUSEUM

(www.ironbridge.org.uk; The Wharfage; 10am-5pm) FREE An ideal place to kick off your Ironbridge Gorge visit is at the Museum of the Gorge. Occupying a Gothic riverside warehouse, it offers an overview of the World Heritage Sites using film, photos and exhibits, including a 12m-long 3D model of the town in 1796.

Enginuity — MUSEUM

(www.ironbridge.org.uk; Wellington Rd; adult/child £9.95/6.95; 10am-4pm mid-Mar–Sep, closed Mon Oct–mid-Mar) Kids will love this levers-and-pulleys science centre where they can control robots, move a steam locomotive with their bare hands (and a little engineering know-how) and power up a vacuum cleaner with self-generated electricity.

Blists Hill Victorian Town — MUSEUM

(☎01952-433424; www.ironbridge.org.uk; Legges Way; adult/child £20/12; 10am-5pm Wed-Sun) Set at the top of the Hay Inclined Plane (a cable lift that once transported coal barges uphill from the Shropshire Canal), Blists Hill is a lovingly restored Victorian village repopulated with townsfolk in period costume, busy with day-to-day chores. There's even a bank, where you can exchange your modern pounds for shillings to use at the village shops. In summer, a Victorian fair is an added attraction for young ones, as is the ice rink in November and December.

Darby Houses — MUSEUM

(☎01952-433424; www.ironbridge.org.uk; Darby Rd; adult/child £6.50/4.50, incl Museum of Iron £11.95/7.95; 11am-3pm mid-Mar–Sep) Just uphill from the Museum of Iron (p439), these beautifully restored 18th-century homes housed generations of the Darby family in gracious but modest Quaker comfort. In the Rosehill house, kids and adults can try on Victorian dress and view china displays. The highlight of the Darby family house is the study where Abraham Darby III designed the Iron Bridge.

Coalport China Museum — MUSEUM

(www.ironbridge.org.uk; Coalport High St; adult/child £9.95/6.95; 10am-4pm daily mid-Mar–Sep, closed Mon Oct–mid-Mar) As ironmaking fell into decline, Ironbridge diversified into manufacturing china pots, using the fine clay mined around Blists Hill. Dominated by a pair of towering bottle kilns, the atmospheric old china-works now contains an absorbing museum tracing the history of the industry, with demonstrations of traditional pottery techniques.

IRONBRIDGE GORGE PASSPORT

The 10 Ironbridge museums are administered by the Ironbridge Gorge Museum Trust (www.ironbridge.org.uk). You'll save considerably by buying a Passport ticket (adult/child £27.50/17.50) at any of the museums or from the tourist office (p440). Valid for 12 months, it allows unlimited entry to all of Ironbridge Gorge's sites.

Ironbridge Gorge

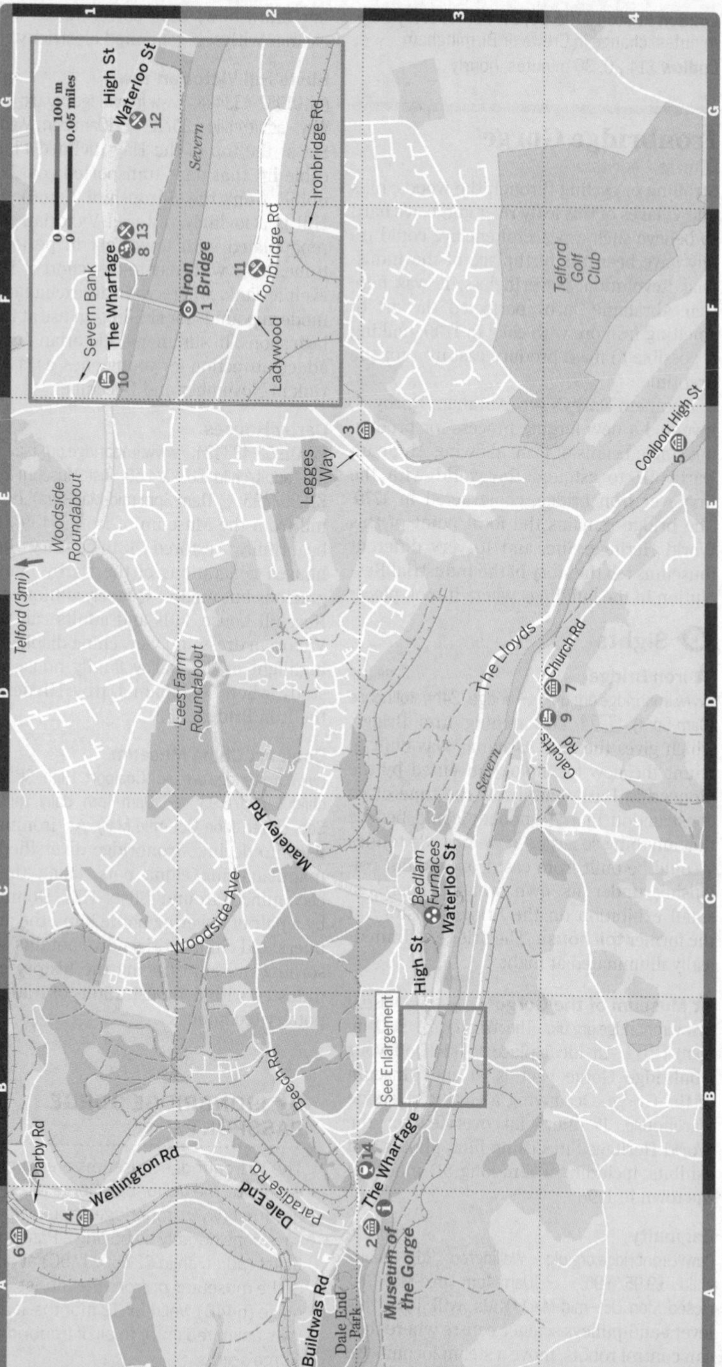

See Enlargement
Severn Bank
The Wharfage
Iron Bridge
High St
Waterloo St
Severn
Ironbridge Rd
Ladywood
100 m
0.05 miles
500 m
0.25 miles
Telford (5mi)
Woodside Roundabout
Lees Farm Roundabout
Legges Way
Telford Golf Club
Coalport High St
The Lloyds
Church Rd
Calcutts Rd
Madeley Rd
Woodside Ave
Bedlam Furnaces
Beech Rd
Darby Rd
Wellington Rd
Dale End
Paradise Rd
Buildwas Rd
Dale End Park
Museum of the Gorge

Ironbridge Gorge

On Wednesdays during summer, you can also view the **Tar Tunnel** (Coalport High St) accompanied by a guide.

Jackfield Tile Museum MUSEUM
(www.ironbridge.org.uk; Salthouse Rd; adult/child £9.95/6.95; 10am-5pm) Once the largest tile factory in the world, Jackfield was famous for its encaustic tiles, with ornate designs produced using layers of different coloured clay. Tiles are still produced here today for period restorations. Gas-lit galleries recreate ornately tiled rooms from past centuries, including Victorian public conveniences. The museum is on the south bank of the Severn – cross the footbridge at the bottom of the Hay Inclined Plane.

Coalbrookdale Museum of Iron MUSEUM
(www.ironbridge.org.uk; Wellington Rd; adult/child £9.95/6.95, incl Darby Houses £11.95/7.95; 10am-4pm Wed-Sun) Set in the brooding buildings of Abraham Darby's original iron foundry, the Coalbrookdale Museum of Iron contains some excellent interactive exhibits. As well as producing the girders for the Iron Bridge, the factory became famous for heavy machinery and extravagant ornamental castings, including the gates for London's Hyde Park.

Activities

Ironbridge Canoe & Kayak Hire CANOEING, KAYAKING
(07594 486356; www.ironbridgecanoeandkayakhire.co.uk; 31 High St; canoe/kayak rental per half/full day from £45/85; by appointment Mon-Fri, 9am-8pm Sat & Sun Easter-Oct) In summer, when the river is at a safe level, you can rent canoes and kayaks to explore the gorge and surrounding areas.

Shropshire Raft Tours RAFTING
(01952-427150; www.shropshirerafttours.co.uk; The Wharfage; rafting trips adult/child £14.95/6.95, canoe & kayak hire per hour/day £15/40, bike hire per half/full day from £19/29; equipment hire 9am-5pm Easter-Oct, tours by reservation 11.30am, 2pm & 4.30pm Easter-Oct, plus 7pm Jul & Aug) Ironbridge Gorge might not have any rapids but you can take a gentle, highly enjoyable 90-minute trip along a 1.2-mile stretch of the River Severn floating past stunning gorge scenery with this eco-conscious outfit. Life jackets are provided. It also hires canoes, kayaks and bikes, including electric bikes.

Sleeping

★ **Library House** B&B ££
(01952-432299; www.libraryhouse.com; 11 Severn Bank; s/d from £75/100; P) Up an alley off the main street, this lovingly restored Georgian library building built in 1730 is hugged by vines, backed by a beautiful garden and decked out with stacks of vintage books, curios, prints and lithographs. There are three charmingly well-preserved, individually decorated rooms, named Milton, Chaucer and Eliot. The affable dog whipping around is Millie.

Calcutts House B&B ££
(01952-882631; www.calcuttshouse.co.uk; Calcutts Rd; d from £80; P) This former ironmaster's pad dates from the 18th century. Traditionally decorated rooms have heaps of character, and one is furnished with an outsized 200-year-old four-poster bed. It's tucked away on the south bank around the corner from the Jackfield Tile Museum, a mile east of the bridge.

SEVERN VALLEY RAILWAY

The historic steam or diesel locomotives of the **Severn Valley Railway** (☎ 01299-403816; www.svr.co.uk; Hollybush Rd, Bridgnorth; adult/child one-way £14.50/9.50, day ticket £21/14; ⏲ daily May-Sep, Sat & Sun Oct-Apr) chug between Bridgnorth, 9 miles southwest of Ironbridge Gorge, and Kidderminster (one hour), starting from Bridgnorth's station on Hollybush Rd. Check the calendar for additional event dates, such as afternoon teas, gin and whisky tastings, 1940s re-enactments and evening ghost trains.

Cyclists can follow a beautiful 20-mile section of the Mercian Way (NCN Route 45) beside the railway line towards the Wyre Forest; bikes are free to bring on board the trains.

'Driving experiences', during which you can learn how to drive the steam or diesel trains, start from £160.

Eating & Drinking

Pondicherry INDIAN ££
(☎ 01952-433055; www.pondicherryrestaurant.co.uk; 57 Waterloo St; mains £11-17; ⏲ 5-10pm Wed-Sun) Original features of this 1862-built former police station and courtroom include four lock-up cells (one's now the takeaway waiting area), the magistrate's bench and blue-painted bars on the windows. Above-average contemporary Indian cuisine includes crowd-pleasers like tandoori platters and chicken tikka masala along with chef specialities, such as lamb *saag mamyam* (braised Staffordshire lamb with spinach and spices).

D'arcys at the Station MEDITERRANEAN ££
(☎ 01952-884499; www.darcysironbridge.co.uk; Ladywood; mains £11.50-15; ⏲ 6-9.30pm Wed-Sat) Just over the bridge by the river, the handsome old station building is the backdrop for flavoursome Mediterranean dishes, from Moroccan chicken to Cypriot kebabs and Tuscan bean casserole. Kids aged over 10 are welcome.

Restaurant Severn EUROPEAN £££
(☎ 01952-432233; www.restaurantsevern.co.uk; 33 High St; 2-/3-course menus £29/36; ⏲ 6-11pm Thu-Sat) The menu at this highly praised fine-dining restaurant changes frequently but might feature dishes such as Shropshire venison medallions with cognac and sun-dried-cranberry sauce. The setting is intimate, food is artistically presented and the riverside location beautiful.

Malthouse PUB
(☎ 01952-433712; www.themalthouseironbridge.co.uk; The Wharfage; ⏲ bar 11.30am-11pm Sun-Thu, to 12.30am Fri & Sat, kitchen to 9.30pm) This renovated inn on the Severn's riverbanks makes a great place to drink, eat and/or sleep. Local ales, craft gins and cocktails feature on the drinks list, the street-food-inspired menu spans fish tacos to southern fried chicken (mains £10 to £19) and ultra-contemporary rooms (doubles including breakfast from £75) are splashed with vibrant colours. Live music plays on weekends.

Information

Tourist Office (☎ 01952-433424; www.discovertelford.co.uk/visitironbridge; The Wharfage; ⏲ 10am-5pm) Located at the Museum of the Gorge (p437).

Getting There & Away

The nearest train station is 6 miles away at Telford, from where you can travel to Ironbridge by bus (£4.80, 15 minutes, four daily Monday to Friday, three Saturday). The same bus continues to Much Wenlock (£4.90, 30 minutes).

Buses also link Ironbridge with Shrewsbury (£4.90, 50 minutes, four daily Monday to Saturday).

Much Wenlock

☎ 01952 / POP 2877

With one of those quirky names that abound in the English countryside, Much Wenlock is as charming as it sounds. Surrounding the time-worn ruins of Wenlock Priory, the streets are studded with Tudor, Jacobean and Georgian houses, and locals say hello to everyone. This storybook English village also claims to have jump-started the modern Olympics.

Sights

Wenlock Priory RUINS
(EH; ☎ 01952-727466; www.english-heritage.org.uk; 5 Sheinton St; adult/child incl audio guide £6.90/4.10; ⏲ 10am-5pm) The maudlin Cluniac ruins of Wenlock Priory rise up from vivid green lawns, sprinkled with animal-shaped topiary. The priory was raised by Norman monks over the ruins of a Saxon monastery from AD 680, and its hallowed remains

include a finely decorated chapterhouse and an unusual carved lavabo, where monks came to ceremonially wash before eating.

Guildhall HISTORIC BUILDING

(01952-727509; www.muchwenlock-tc.gov.uk; Wilmore St; 11am-4pm Fri-Mon Apr-Oct) FREE Built in classic Tudor style in 1540, the wonky Guildhall features some splendidly ornate woodcarving. One of the pillars supporting it was used for public floggings in medieval times.

Sleeping & Eating

Wilderhope Manor YHA HOSTEL £

(0845 371 9149; www.yha.org.uk; Longville-in-the-Dale; dm/d/f from £13/39/69, camping per person £12; hostel year-round, camping Apr-Oct; P@) A gloriously atmospheric gabled greystone Elizabethan manor, with spiral staircases, wood-panelled walls, an impressive stone-floored dining hall and spacious, oak-beamed rooms – this is hostelling for royalty. Wi-fi is available in public areas. In the warmer months, the camping field has space for a handful of tents. It's 7.5 miles southwest of Much Wenlock, best reached by your own wheels.

Raven Hotel INN ££

(01952-727251; www.ravenhotel.com; 30 Barrow St; d/ste incl breakfast from £120/150; P) Much Wenlock's finest place to stay is this 17th-century coaching inn and converted stables with oodles of charm and country-chic styling in its spacious guest rooms. Overlooking a flower-filled courtyard, the excellent restaurant (lunch mains £13 to £22, two-/three-course dinner menus £29/39) serves Mediterranean and British fare.

Fox PUB FOOD ££

(01952-727292; www.foxinnmuchwenlock.co.uk; 46 High St; mains £9-22; kitchen 5-9pm Mon-Fri, noon-9pm Sat, to 8pm Sun, bar to 11pm;) Warm yourself by the massive fireplace, then settle down in the dining room to savour locally sourced venison, pheasant and beef, swished down with a pint of Shropshire ale, in this 16th-century inn. Candlelit dinners here are lovely. It also has five contemporary rooms (single/double/family from £65/85/100).

Information

Tourist Office (01952-727679; www.visitmuchwenlock.co.uk; The Square; 10.30am-1pm & 1.30-4pm daily Apr-Oct, Fri-Sun Nov-Mar) Has a modest museum of local history (adult/child £2.50/1).

Getting There & Away

Buses link Shrewsbury with Much Wenlock (£4.80, 35 minutes, hourly Monday to Saturday) and continue on to Bridgnorth (£4.50, 15 minutes).

Buses also serve Ironbridge (£4.90, 30 minutes, four daily Monday to Friday, three Saturday).

Church Stretton & Around

01694 / POP 2789

Tucked in a deep valley formed by the Long Mynd and the Caradoc Hills, Church Stretton is an ideal base for walks or cycling trips through the Shropshire Hills. Although black-and-white timbers are heavily in evidence, most of the buildings in town are 19th-century fakes, built by the Victorians who flocked here to take the country air.

Sights & Activities

Walking is the big draw here. The tourist office has maps and details of local mountain-biking circuits and horse-riding stables. Information on activities is also available at www.shropshiresgreatoutdoors.co.uk.

Acton Scott Estate FARM

(01694-781307; www.shropshire.gov.uk/acton-scott; Marshbrook; adult/child £9/5; farm 10am-4pm Fri-Sun, courses Apr-Dec) On the sprawling Acton Scott Estate, 4 miles south of Church Stretton, this historic working farm has traditional breeds of poultry and livestock, and daily demonstrations of Victorian farming techniques, such as barrel making, horseshoeing and cartwheel construction. Book ahead for courses including blacksmithing, beekeeping, plant identification and 19th-century cookery.

Snailbeach MINE

(07716 116732; www.shropshiremines.org.uk; Shop Lane, Snailbeach; site free, mine tours adult/child £15/5; site 24hr, tours by reservation Thu & Sun Apr-Oct) The former lead- and silver-mining village of Snailbeach, 11 miles northwest of Church Stretton, is littered with intriguing, rusting machinery relics. You can download a self-guided trail from the website of the **Bog Centre tourist office** (01743-792484; www.bogcentre.co.uk; The Bog, Stiperstones; noon-5pm Mon, 10am-5pm Tue-Sun Easter-Sep, noon-4pm Mon, 10am-4pm Tue-Sun Oct;) to explore the site, or reserve ahead for guided tours (waterproof footwear required) that take you into the mine.

★ Kerry Vale Vineyard WINERY
(☎01588-620627; www.kerryvalevineyard.co.uk; Pentreheyling; tours £20-40; ⊙tours by appointment Thu, Sat & Sun mid-Mar–Nov, shop & cafe 10am-4pm Tue-Sun mid-Mar–Oct, to 3pm Nov & Dec) More than 6000 vines are now planted over 2.4 hectares of the former Pentreheyling Roman Fort, where pottery and metalwork have been uncovered and are displayed at the winery shop. Tours range from an hour-long guided walk through the vines, with a talk on the site's Roman history and tastings, to two-hour guided visits with tastings, a tutorial and an afternoon tea including the vineyard's own sparkling wine. Or pop by the cafe for a wine tasting flight.

It's 19 miles southwest of Church Stretton.

Sleeping

Bridges Long Mynd YHA HOSTEL £
(☎03452-602569; www.yha.org.uk; Bridges; dm from £22, camping per person from £10; P) On the Long Mynd's western side, this wonderfully isolated hiker favourite, with 38 beds (plus garden tent sites), is housed in a former school in the tiny hamlet of Bridges. No wi-fi, no mobile-phone reception, no credit cards. Cross the Mynd to Ratlinghope, from where it's 1.1 miles southwest, or take buses run by Shropshire Hills Shuttles (p434) in season.

The Bridges pub is nearby, but the hostel also provides breakfast (£6), packed lunches (£5) and three-course evening meals (£12.50) incorporating ingredients from its own vegetable garden.

Mynd House B&B B&B ££
(☎01694-722212; www.myndhouse.co.uk; Ludlow Rd, Little Stretton; s/d from £62/87; P 📶) Just under 2 miles south of Church Stretton, this inviting guesthouse has splendid views across the valley and backs directly onto the Mynd. Its eight rooms are named after local landmarks. There's a small bar and lounge stocked with local books, as well as bike storage and a room for drying your boots.

Eating & Drinking

Van Doesburg's DELI £
(☎01694-722867; www.thegourmetfoodshop.com; 3 High St; dishes £1.85-5; ⊙9am-4pm Tue-Sat; ✎) A fantastic place to pick up picnic ingredients, Van Doesburg's has over 80 British cheeses and other deli items, such as chutneys. Ready-to-eat dishes to take away include chicken-and-mushroom pies, salads, quiches, soups and outstanding sandwiches (eg roast beef with pickles and mustard or farmhouse cheddar with plum-and-apple relish). Phone ahead to order customised hampers.

Bridges PUB FOOD ££
(☎01588-650260; www.thebridgespub.co.uk; Ratlinghope; mains £8-15.50; ⊙kitchen 12.30-8.30pm, bar noon-11pm; 📶) Some 5 miles northeast of Church Stretton, at the base of Long Mynd by the river, this is one of those secret country pubs revered for its Three Tuns ale, live music, riverside terrace, relaxed accommodation (dorm/double/family from £30/60/140) and impressive food (lamb shank and mint sauce, beef lasagne...). Mini burgers are among the choices on the kids' menu.

Three Tuns PUB
(www.thethreetunsinn.co.uk; Salop St, Bishop's Castle; ⊙noon-11pm Mon-Sat, to 10.30pm Sun; 📶) In the pretty village of Bishop's Castle, 13 miles southwest of Church Stretton, the tiny Three Tuns Brewery has been rolling barrels of nut-brown ale across the courtyard since 1642. It's a lively local, and the ales are delicious. Jazz, blues and brass bands perform regularly in summer.

Information

Tourist Office (☎01694-723133; www.churchstretton.co.uk; Church St; ⊙9.30am-1pm & 1.30-5pm Mon-Sat Apr-Sep, 9.30am-1pm & 1.30-3pm Mon-Sat Oct-Mar) Adjoining the library, Church Stretton's tourist office has abundant walking information.

Getting There & Away

BUS

Bus 435 runs from Church Stretton north to Shrewsbury (£4, 40 minutes, hourly Monday to Friday, every two hours Saturday) and south to Ludlow (£4, 30 minutes, hourly Monday to Friday, every two hours Saturday).

On summer weekends, Shropshire Hills Shuttles (p434) runs an hourly service from the Carding Mill Valley near Church Stretton to the villages atop the Long Mynd, passing the YHA at Bridges, and Stiperstones near the Snailbeach mine.

TRAIN

Trains between Ludlow (£8) and Shrewsbury (£6.90) stop in Church Stretton hourly, taking 15 minutes from either end.

Ludlow

01584 / POP 11,003

On the northern bank of the swirling River Teme, this genteel market town fans out from the rambling ruins of its fine Norman castle, with some magnificent black-and-white Tudor buildings lining its cobbled streets. Premium produce from the lush surrounding countryside has helped the town become a gastronomic beacon, with superb markets, delis, restaurants and food festivals.

Sights

Ludlow Castle CASTLE
(01584-873355; www.ludlowcastle.com; Castle Sq; adult/child £8/3.50; 10am-5pm mid-Mar–Oct, to 4pm Nov–early Jan & early Feb–mid-Mar, to 4pm Sat & Sun early Jan-early Feb) Perched in an ideal defensive location atop a cliff above a crook in the river, the town castle was built to ward off the marauding Welsh – or to enforce the English expansion into Wales, perspective depending. Founded after the Norman conquest, the castle was dramatically expanded in the 14th century.

The Norman chapel in the inner bailey is one of the few surviving round chapels in England, and the sturdy keep (built around 1090) offers wonderful views over the hills.

Ludlow Brewing Company BREWERY
(01584-873291; www.theludlowbrewingcompany.co.uk; The Railway Shed, Station Dr; tours £8; tours by reservation 3pm Mon-Fri, 2pm Sat, visitor centre & taproom 11am-5pm Sun-Thu, 10am-7pm Fri & Sat) Up an inconspicuous laneway, the Ludlow Brewing Company produces award-winning all-natural brews and sells directly from the brewery and its airy, post-industrial-style bar. Tours include six samples.

Church of St Laurence CHURCH
(www.stlaurences.org.uk; 2 College St; admission by donation; 10am-5pm) One of Britain's largest parish churches, the church of St Laurence contains grand Elizabethan alabaster tombs and delightfully cheeky medieval misericords carved into its medieval choir stalls, including a beer-swilling chap raiding his barrel. The Lady Chapel contains a marvellous **Jesse Window**, originally dating from 1330 (although the glass is mostly Victorian). Four windows in St John's Chapel date from the mid-15th century, including the honey-coloured **Golden Window**. Climb 200 steps up the **tower** (included in donation) for stunning views.

Festivals & Events

Ludlow Spring Festival CULTURAL
(www.ludlowspringestival.co.uk; mid-May) The two-day Ludlow Spring Festival uses the castle as its dramatic backdrop for beer, cider and food stalls, a vintage car show and live concerts.

Ludlow Food Festival FOOD & DRINK
(www.ludlowfoodfestival.co.uk; early Sep) At Ludlow Castle, the Ludlow Food Festival spans three days in early September, with over 180 exhibitors from the town and the Welsh Marches.

Sleeping

Feathers Hotel HISTORIC HOTEL ££
(01584-875261; www.feathersatludlow.co.uk; 21 Bull Ring; d from £109; P) Behind its impossibly ornate timbered Jacobean facade, this 1619-built treasure is all tapestries, creaky furniture, timber beams and stained glass: you can almost hear the cavaliers toasting the health of King Charles. The best rooms are in the old building; rooms in the newer wing lack character and romance. Dinner, bed and breakfast packages are available at its restaurant.

Clive Arms BOUTIQUE HOTEL ££
(01584-856565; www.theclive.co.uk; Bromfield Rd, Bromfield; d/f incl breakfast from £114/150; P) For foodies, this is Ludlow's ultimate place to stay. Located 4 miles northwest of town adjoining the Ludlow Food Centre (p444), it has its own top-end restaurant; breakfast is served at the Ludlow Kitchen. Many of its 18 spacious rooms are on ground level; family rooms have two sleeping areas separated by a bathroom, giving parents and kids their own space.

Charlton Arms INN ££
(01584-872813; www.thecharltonarms.co.uk; Ludford Bridge; d incl breakfast £100-195; P) The pick of the rooms at this landmark inn overlook the River Teme, and the pick of those have terraces (one with an outdoor hot tub as well as a four-poster bed). Its pub, also opening to a terrace, serves top-quality Modern British cuisine. Service is superb. There's a large free car park on-site.

Eating

Ludlow Kitchen CAFE £
(01584-856000; www.ludlowfarmshop.co.uk; Bromfield Rd, Bromfield; breakfast £3.50-9, lunch mains £6-13; 8am-4pm Mon-Sat, to 3.30pm

Sun; ☎) Produce from the Ludlow Food Centre artisanal farm shop is served at its sunlit cafe. Fantastic breakfasts (granola with homemade yoghurt; full English fry-ups with farmhouse eggs, artisan bacon and black pudding; eggs royale) are the precursor to lunch dishes such as Ludlow Brewing Company beer-battered fish with zingy tartare.

Fish House SEAFOOD ££
(☎01584-879790; www.thefishhouseludlow.co.uk; 51 Bull Ring; dishes £8-12, sharing platters £25-60; ⏰kitchen noon-3pm Wed-Sat, shop to 4pm Wed-Sat) Except on Saturdays when it's first come, first served, bookings are recommended for the barrel tables at this stylish fish and oyster bar. It sources Britain's best seafood – Whitby crab and lobster, Arbroath smokies, Bigbury Bay oysters – and serves it with organic bread, lemon and mayo, along with wines, local ales, ciders and champagne.

Bistro 7 BISTRO ££
(☎01584-877412; www.bistro7ofludlow.co.uk; 7 Corve St; mains £16-26; ⏰noon-3pm & 6-10pm Tue-Sat) Ludlow's red-brick former post office is the setting for creative bistro cooking. Knowledgeable staff can guide you through the regularly changing menu, which might feature dishes like wood-pigeon salad, black-pudding-stuffed pork loin and red-wine-poached plums with rosemary meringue. Or finish with a platter of local cheeses served with nettle and spiced-apple chutney.

Mortimers BRITISH £££
(☎01584-872325; www.mortimersludlow.co.uk; 17 Corve St; 2-/3-course lunch menu £26.50/29.50, 3-course dinner menu £55, 7-course tasting menu £65, with paired wines £105; ⏰6.30-8.30pm Wed, noon-2pm & 6.30-8.30pm Thu-Sat, noon-2pm Sun; ☎) For fine dining, this is Ludlow's top table. Dark timber panelling and cosy nooks create a romantic backdrop for intricate dishes such as scallops with truffled pumpkin puree or lacquered Ludlow duck with pastrami-wrapped celeriac. Vegetarians can pre-book a meat-free version of Saturday evening's seven-course tasting menu, featuring creations like asparagus with roast baby beetroot and sorrel panna cotta.

Shopping

★Ludlow Food Centre FOOD & DRINKS
(☎01584-856000; www.ludlowfarmshop.co.uk; Bromfield Rd, Bromfield; ⏰8.30am-5pm Mon-Sat, 9am-4pm Sun) More than 80% of the cheeses, meats, breads, fruit and vegetables are sourced from the surrounding region and tantalisingly displayed at this enormous farm shop, including many produced on the estate. Watch through viewing windows to see traditional preserves, pies, ice cream and more being made. It's signposted 2.8 miles northwest of Ludlow off Bromfield Rd (the A49).

Look out for regular events including tastings. There's a kids' playground and a picnic area. Produce is used by the adjoining cafe-restaurant, the Ludlow Kitchen (p443).

Ludlow Market MARKET
(www.ludlowmarket.co.uk; Castle Sq; ⏰9.30am-2pm Mon, Wed, Fri & Sat) Ludlow Market's stalls sell fresh produce, artisan food and drink, flowers, books, gifts and more. Various spin-off markets (farmers markets, flea markets, book markets and craft markets) take place on Thursdays and Sundays.

Information

Tourist Office (☎01584-875053; www.ludlow.org.uk/ludlowvisitorcentre.html; 1 Mill St; ⏰10am-4pm Mon-Sat Mar-Dec, to 2pm Mon-Sat Jan & Feb) On the 3rd floor of the **Ludlow Assembly Rooms** (☎01584-878141; www.ludlowassemblyrooms.co.uk; 1 Mill St; adult/child standard £8/6, balcony £9/7), which contains the town cinema and hosts live entertainment.

Getting There & Away

BUS

Bus 435 runs to Shrewsbury (£4.80, 1¼ hours, hourly Monday to Saturday) via Church Stretton (£4, 30 minutes).

TRAIN

Trains run frequently from the station located on the north edge of town to Hereford (£10.90, 25 minutes, hourly) and Shrewsbury (£14.20, 30 minutes, hourly), via Church Stretton (£8, 15 minutes).

NOTTINGHAMSHIRE

Say Nottinghamshire and people think of one thing – Robin Hood. Whether the hero woodsman existed is hotly debated, but the county plays up its connections to the outlaw. Storytelling seems to be in Nottinghamshire's blood – local wordsmiths include provocative writer DH Lawrence, of *Lady Chatterley's Lover* fame, and hedonistic poet Lord Byron. Designated a

Unesco City of Literature in 2015, the city of Nottingham is the bustling hub; venture into the surrounding countryside and you'll discover historic towns and stately homes surrounding the green bower of Sherwood Forest.

Getting There & Away

National Express and **Trent Barton** (☎01773-712265; www.trentbarton.co.uk) buses provide the majority of bus services. See Traveline (p406) for timetables. Trains run frequently to most large towns, and to many smaller villages in the Peak District.

Nottingham

☎0115 / POP 321,550

Forever associated with men in tights and a sheriff with anger-management issues (aka the Robin Hood legend), Nottingham is a dynamic county capital with big-city aspirations, evocative historical sights, and a buzzing music and club scene thanks to its spirited student population.

Sights

Nottingham Castle CASTLE, GALLERY

(www.nottinghamcastle.org.uk; Lenton Rd) Nottingham's castle crowns a sandstone outcrop worm-holed with caves and tunnels. Founded by William the Conqueror, the original castle was held by a succession of English kings before falling in the English Civil War.

Its 17th-century manor-house-like replacement is undergoing major renovations, and is closed until spring 2021. When it reopens, it will feature a new Robin Hood Gallery, a Rebellion Gallery, covering social unrest from medieval times, and displays on art and manufacturing, including salt-glazed stoneware and lacemaking.

Access to the cave system will be extended, parts of the castle grounds will be remodelled to reveal more of the medieval site, and a new visitor centre and cafe will open here. The 17th-century cottages comprising the **Museum of Nottingham Life at Brewhouse Yard** (www.nottinghamcity.gov.uk; Castle Blvd) will also reopen in mid-2021.

The much-snapped **statue of Robin Hood** (Castle Rd) stands in the former moat and remains accessible while works take place.

Wollaton Hall HISTORIC BUILDING

(☎0115-876 3100; www.wollatonhall.org.uk; Wollaton Park, Derby Rd; tours adult/child £10/free, grounds free; ⏲tours noon & 2pm, grounds 8am-dusk Mon-Fri, from 9am Sat & Sun) Built in 1588 for coal mogul Sir Francis Willoughby by avant-garde architect Robert Smythson, Wollaton Hall sits within 200 hectares of grounds roamed by fallow and red deer. Tours lasting one hour lead you through extravagant rooms from the Tudor, Regency and Victorian periods. There's also a natural-history museum here.

Wollaton Hall is 2.5 miles west of Nottingham city centre; take bus L2 or 30 from Victoria bus station (£4.20, 15 minutes, every 15 minutes Monday to Saturday, half-hourly Sunday).

The hall starred as Wayne Manor in 2012's Batman film *The Dark Knight Rises*.

City of Caves CAVE

(☎0115-952 0555; www.nationaljusticemuseum.org.uk/venue/city-of-caves; Garner's Hill; adult/child £8.75/7.65, incl National Justice Museum £17.60/15.10; ⏲tours 10am-4pm) Over the centuries, the sandstone underneath Nottingham has been carved into a honeycomb of caverns and passageways. Tours lead you through a WWII air-raid shelter, a medieval underground tannery, several pub cellars and a mock-up of a Victorian slum dwelling. Book ahead.

The entrance is adjacent to the Nottingham Contemporary gallery.

BYRON'S NEWSTEAD ABBEY

Founded as an Augustinian priory in around 1170, **Newstead Abbey** (☎01623-455900; www.newsteadabbey.org.uk; Newstead; house & gardens adult/child £10/6, park free; ⏲house & gardens noon-4pm Sat & Sun, park 10am-5pm daily) was converted into a residence in 1539. This evocative lakeside property inextricably associated with the original tortured romantic, Lord Byron (1788–1824), who inherited the house in 1798, selling it in 1818.

Newstead Abbey is 12 miles north of Nottingham, off the A60. Pronto buses (£3.80, 25 minutes, every 10 minutes Monday to Saturday, half-hourly Sunday) from Victoria bus station stop at the gates, a mile from the house and gardens.

Byron's old living quarters are full of suitably eccentric memorabilia, and the landscaped grounds include a monument to his yappy dog, Boatswain.

Nottingham

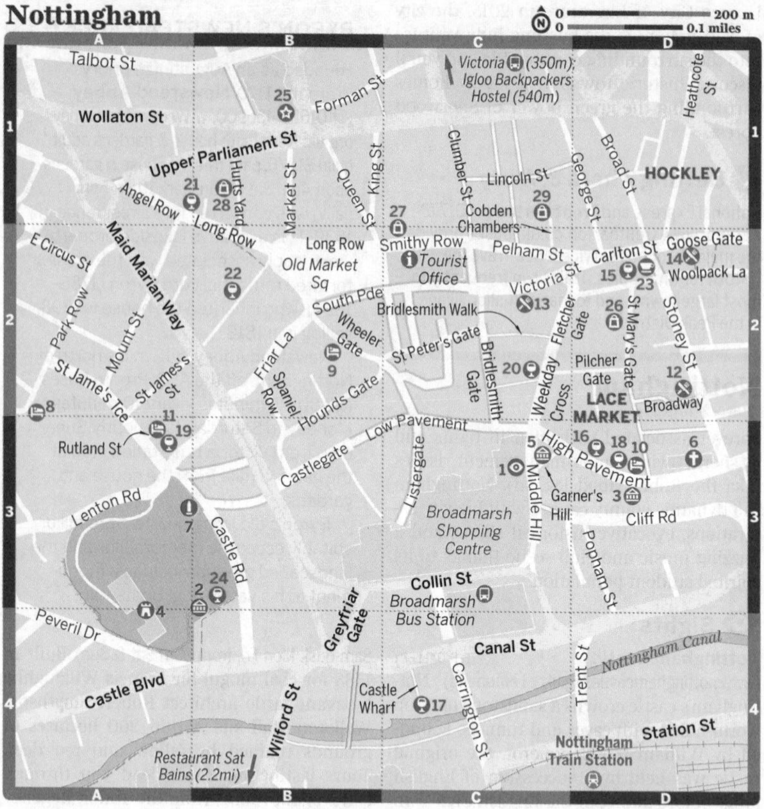

Nottingham

Sights

1 City of Caves C3
2 Museum of Nottingham Life at Brewhouse Yard B3
3 National Justice Museum D3
4 Nottingham Castle A4
5 Nottingham Contemporary C3
6 St Mary's Church D3
7 Statue of Robin Hood A3

Sleeping

8 Hart's A2
9 Igloo Hybrid Hostel B2
10 Lace Market Hotel D3
11 St James Hotel A3

Eating

12 Annie's Burger Shack D2
13 Delilah Fine Foods C2
Hart's Restaurant .... (see 8)
14 Larder on Goosegate D2

Drinking & Nightlife

15 Boilermaker D2
16 Brass Monkey D3
17 Canal House C4
18 Cock & Hoop D3
19 Crafty Crow A3
20 Cross Keys C2
21 Dragon A1
22 Malt Cross B2
23 Outpost Coffee Roasters D2
24 Ye Olde Trip to Jerusalem B3

Entertainment

25 Theatre Royal & Royal Concert Hall B1

Shopping

26 Debbie Bryan D2
27 Five Leaves Bookshop C2
28 Rob's Records B1
29 Studio Chocolate C1

National Justice Museum MUSEUM
(☎0115-952 0555; www.nationaljusticemuseum.org.uk; High Pavement; adult/child £12.05/8.75, incl City of Caves £17.60/15.10; ⊙9.30am-5pm Thu-Mon) In the grand Georgian Shire Hall, the National Justice Museum offers a ghoulish stroll through centuries of British justice, including medieval trials by fire and water. There are costumed characters representing historical figures, and activities, exhibitions and re-enacted courtroom performances regularly take place. Tickets are valid all day.

Nottingham Contemporary GALLERY
(☎0115-948 9750; www.nottinghamcontemporary.org; Weekday Cross; ⊙10am-6pm Tue-Sat, 11am-5pm Sun) FREE Behind its lace-patterned concrete facade, Nottingham Contemporary holds edgy, design-driven exhibitions of paintings, prints, photography and sculpture.

Its shop sells works by Nottingham and UK-based artists, designers and crafts people, and its cafe specialises in locally sourced food.

St Mary's Church CHURCH
(www.stmarysnottingham.org; 40 High Pavement; ⊙10am-3pm Mon-Sat, 9.30am-8pm Sun) The most atmospheric time to visit this beautiful stone church with a history stretching back to Saxon times is during evensong (6.15pm Wednesday during term time, 6.30pm Sunday year-round).

Tours

★Ezekial Bone Tours WALKING
(☎07941 210986; www.ezekialbone.com; Robin Hood Town Tour adult/child £14.50/8; ⊙Robin Hood Town Tour 2pm Sat Mar-Oct) Hugely entertaining, history-focused tours led by multi-award-winning 'modern-day Robin Hood' Ezekial Bone (aka historian/actor/writer/local legend Ade Andrews) are a highlight of visiting Nottingham. Robin Hood Town Tours lasting 2½ hours depart from the **Cross Keys pub** (www.crosskeysnottingham.co.uk; 15 Byard Lane; ⊙9am-11pm Sun-Thu, to midnight Fri, to 1am Sat).

Various other tours, including Lace Market tours, Magic Lantern backstage tours of the Theatre Royal and Robin Hood Sherwood Forest tours are also available by request.

Festivals & Events

Goose Fair FAIR
(⊙early Oct) The five-day Goose Fair has evolved from a medieval travelling market to a modern funfair with over 500 attractions and rides.

Robin Hood Beer & Cider Festival DRINK
(www.beerfestival.nottinghamcamra.org; ⊙mid-Oct) This four-day tasting festival features more than 1000 beers and 250 ciders and perries.

Robin Hood Live CULTURAL
(www.visit-nottinghamshire.co.uk/whats-on/robin-hood-live-p454861; ⊙varies) The family-friendly Robin Hood Live – a medieval celebration featuring costumed performances and activities – takes place over two days each year. Check with the tourist office (p451) for location information and dates.

Sleeping

Igloo Hybrid Hostel HOSTEL £
(☎0115-948 3822; www.igloohostel.co.uk; 4-6 Eldon Chambers, Wheeler Gate; dm from £20, s/d sleep box from £32/64, s with/without en suite from £39/34, d with/without en suite £84/72; 📶) The sister property of the much-loved **Igloo Backpackers Hostel** (☎0115-947 5250; 100 Mansfield Rd; dm/s/d/tr from £20/40/80/84; 📶) has a central location footsteps from the Old Market Sq. Cabin-style 'sleep boxes' incorporate USB ports and reading lights; there's a well-equipped self-catering kitchen and a sociable courtyard garden.

St James Hotel BOUTIQUE HOTEL ££
(☎0115-941 1114; www.stjames-hotel.com; 1 Rutland St; s/d/ste from £65/80/185; 📶) Patterned wallpaper, richly coloured textured fabrics and designer elements, such as stag heads made from stainless steel, set the striking St James apart. More than 500 books line its library shelves; there's a public car park next door.

★Lace Market Hotel BOUTIQUE HOTEL £££
(☎0115-948 4414; www.lacemarkethotel.co.uk; 29-31 High Pavement; s/d/ste incl breakfast from £76/140/194; P❄📶) In the heart of the gentrified Lace Market, this elegant Georgian town house has 42 sleek rooms with state-of-the-art furnishings and amenities, some with air-conditioning. Its adjoining pub, the **Cock & Hoop** (25 High Pavement; ⊙noon-11pm Sun-Thu, to midnight Fri & Sat), serves real ales and traditional pub food all day.

Hart's BOUTIQUE HOTEL £££
(0115-988 1900; www.hartsnottingham.co.uk; Standard Hill, Park Row; d/ste incl breakfast from £169/309; P) Within the former Nottingham General Hospital compound, this swish hotel has ultra-contemporary rooms (some with small terrace) in a striking modernist building. Its renowned **restaurant** (mains £16.50-25.50, 2-/3-course menus £22/28; 7am-2.30pm & 6-10pm Mon-Sat, 7.30am-2.30pm & 6-9pm Sun;) is housed in a historic redbrick wing. Work out in the small gym or unwind in the private garden.

Eating

★Delilah Fine Foods DELI, CAFE £
(0115-948 4461; www.delilahfinefoods.co.uk; 12 Victoria St; dishes £4-15, platters £19-26; 9am-5pm Wed-Mon;) Impeccably selected cheeses (more than 150 varieties), pâtés, meats and more from artisan producers are available to take away or eat on-site at this foodie's fantasy land, housed in a grand former bank with mezzanine seating. It doesn't take reservations but you can pre-order customised hampers for a gourmet picnic.

Annie's Burger Shack BURGERS, AMERICAN £
(0115-684 9920; www.anniesburgershack.com; 5 Broadway; burgers £9-13, breakfast £6-10; 8-10.30am daily plus noon-9.30pm Sun-Wed, 4-9.30pm Thu, noon-10pm Fri & Sat;) More than 30 different burgers (available in vegan, veggie or meat versions) are on the menu at Annie's, a wildly popular joint in the Lace Market that stays true to its owner's US roots (and adds real ales to its offerings). Midweek breakfast menus feature American classics (blueberry pancakes with maple syrup and bacon, Boston franks 'n' beans). Book ahead.

Larder on Goosegate BRITISH ££
(0115-950 0111; www.thelarderongoosegate.co.uk; 16-22 Goosegate; mains £15-24, afternoon tea from £16.50; 5.30-10pm Tue-Thu, noon-2.30pm & 5.30-11pm Fri & Sat) Floor-to-ceiling windows fill this 1st-floor restaurant with light and provide bird's-eye views of busy Goosegate below. Blue-goats-cheese and beetroot cheesecake, Shetland Queen scallops with wild-garlic butter and roast spring lamb with smoked aubergine are among its superbly executed British dishes. On Fridays and Saturdays, afternoon tea is served on antique bone china. Book ahead.

Restaurant Sat Bains GASTRONOMY £££
(0115-986 6566; www.restaurantsatbains.com; Lenton Lane; 7-/10-course tasting menus £125/155; 6-9pm Wed & Thu, to 9.45pm Fri & Sat;) Boundary-pushing chef Sat Bains has been awarded two Michelin stars for his wildly inventive tasting menus (no à la carte; dietary restrictions can be catered for with advance notice). Book *well* ahead and beware of hefty cancellation charges. It also has chic guest rooms (double £180 to £260, suite £375). It's 2 miles southwest of the city centre off the A52.

Drinking & Nightlife

★Ye Olde Trip to Jerusalem PUB
(0115-947 3171; www.triptojerusalem.com; Brewhouse Yard, Castle Rd; 11am-11pm Sun-Thu, to midnight Fri & Sat;) Carved into the cliff below the castle, this atmospheric alehouse claims to be England's oldest pub. Founded in 1189, it supposedly slaked the thirst of departing crusaders, and its warren of rooms and cobbled courtyards make it the most ambient place in Nottingham for a pint.

Call ahead to ask about tours of its cellars and caves.

★Crafty Crow PUB
(www.magpiebrewery.com/craftycrow; 102 Friar Lane; noon-11pm Sun-Thu, 11am-midnight Fri & Sat;) Rotating brews at this beer specialist include several from its own Nottingham-based Magpie Brewery, made from British hops and malts, plus handpulls from local microbreweries and craft beers and ciders on tap. Timber-planked walls line the TV-free split-level space; don't miss the bathrooms with sinks and taps made out of kegs. Gastropub food is locally sourced.

Outpost Coffee Roasters COFFEE
(www.outpost.coffee; 2 Stoney St; 8am-5pm Mon-Fri, 9am-5pm Sat, 10am-4pm Sun;) Outpost roasts sustainably sourced beans on the city-centre's northwestern edge and brews them up here at its espresso bar. Oat, almond and soy milk is available; you can also order turmeric lattes.

Dragon PUB
(0115-941 7080; www.the-dragon.co.uk; 67 Long Row; noon-11.30pm Sun-Wed, to midnight Thu, to 1am Fri & Sat;) The Dragon has a fabulous atmosphere any time, thanks to homemade food, a beer garden and DJs Thursday to

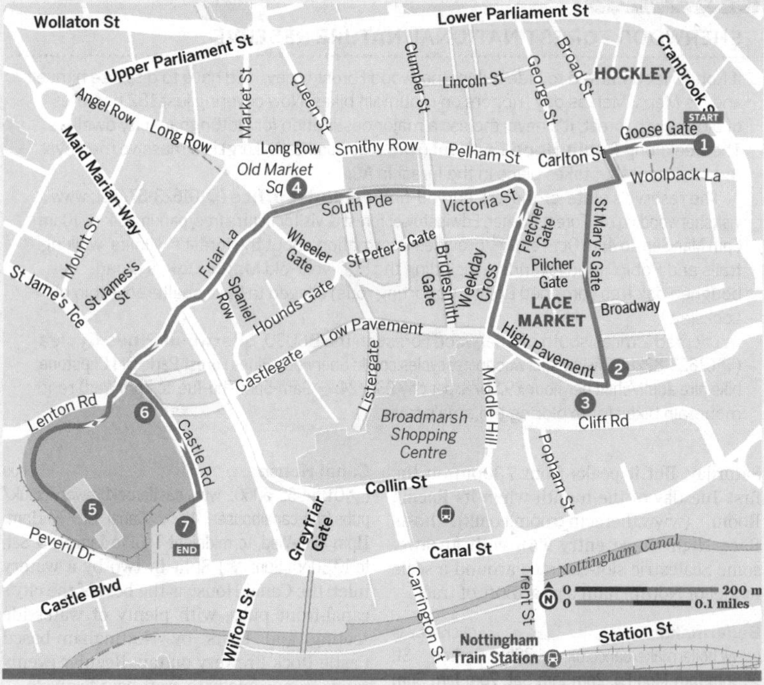

Walking Tour
On the Trail of Robin Hood

START GOOSE GATE
END YE OLDE TRIP TO JERUSALEM
LENGTH 1.2 MILES; TWO HOURS

While the origins of the Robin Hood legend are shrouded in mystery, on this walk you can discover more about the famous outlaw's connections to Nottingham as you take in some of the city's most historic sights.

Begin as Robin Hood likely did on arriving from Sherwood Forest at **1 Goose Gate**, once one of the entrances to the city (today no remains of the medieval walls are visible). Head southwest on St Mary's Gate to reach **2 St Mary's Church** (p447), mentioned in the 1450 *Ballad of Robin Hood and the Monk*. Robin Hood was allegedly recognised here by a monk he had previously robbed. The monk reported him to the Sherriff of Nottingham, who arrested him.

Just west of the church on High Pavement is the former Shire Hall and County Gaol, where the sheriff held office. There was a court on this site since 1375 or earlier, and a jail from 1449; today the **3 National Justice Museum** (p447) is located here.

Walk north along Weekday Cross and west on Victoria St to **4 Old Market Sq**. The square is mentioned in *Robin Hood and the Potter* (c 1500), in which Robin Hood disguises himself as a pot pedlar, and goes on to demonstrate his archery prowess.

Take Friar Lane southwest and cross Maid Marian Way to reach **5 Nottingham Castle** (p445). A Robin Hood gallery is the centrepiece of the castle's multimillion-pound renovations unveiled in 2021.

Just below the castle gates, on Castle Rd, you'll see Nottingham's iconic **6 statue of Robin Hood** (p445), along with smaller statues and bas-relief plaques depicting his Merry Men.

Continue downhill along Castle Rd to what's believed to be England's oldest pub, the 1189 **7 Ye Olde Trip to Jerusalem**, for a post-walk pint. Robin Hood is said to have escaped from the castle via underground caves and tunnels to the cliff-carved pub.

DON'T MISS

SHERWOOD FOREST NATIONAL NATURE RESERVE

If Robin Hood wanted to hide out in Sherwood Forest today, he'd have to disguise himself and his Merry Men as day trippers on mountain bikes. Now covering just 182 hectares of old-growth forest, it's nevertheless a major destination for Nottingham city dwellers. The week-long **Robin Hood Festival** (www.robinhoodfestival.org) is a massive medieval re-enactment that takes place in the forest in August.

The reserve's state-of-the-art, curved-timber **tourist office** (☎01623-677321; www.visitsherwood.co.uk; Forest Corner, Edwinstowe; forest & visitor centre free, parking £4; ⏲10am-6pm Mar-Sep, to 4pm Oct-Feb) provides information about the forest's wildlife, walking trails and Robin Hood legends – including the 800-year-old **Major Oak**, a broad-boughed oak tree (propped up by supporting rods) alleged to have sheltered Robin of Locksley.

Located 2 miles south of Sherwood Forest on the B6030, **Sherwood Pines Cycles** (☎01623-822855; www.sherwoodpinescycles.co.uk; Sherwood Pines Forest Park, Old Clipstone; bike hire adult/child per hour £9.50/8, per day £35/24; ⏲9am-5pm Thu-Tue, to 7pm Wed) rents mountain bikes for exploring the area's trails.

Saturday. But it peaks from 7.30pm on the first Tuesday of the month when its Racing Room (www.theracingroom.co.uk) hosts Race Night (race entry £5), with an awesome Scalextric slot-car race around a scale model of Nottingham along 180ft of track.

Boilermaker COCKTAIL BAR
(www.boilermakerbar.co.uk; 36b Carlton St; ⏲5pm-1am Mon-Fri, 2pm-1am Sat, 7pm-1am Sun) Entering what appears to be an industrial boilermaker's shop and navigating your way through two secret doors brings you into this cavernous, low-lit speakeasy spinning chilled lounge music. Out-there cocktail combinations (eg Figgy Stardust, with tequila, artichoke-based Cynar liqueur, figs, pomegranate shrub and black walnuts) add to the unique-and-then-some experience.

Malt Cross PUB
(www.maltcross.com; 16 St James's St; ⏲4-10pm Tue-Thu, 2-10pm Fri, 11am-10pm Sat, noon-10pm Sun) A fine place for a pint, the Malt Cross occupies a stately old Victorian music hall, where past performers included Charlie Chaplin. It's now a community space run by the Christian Charity Trust hosting art exhibitions and live music. Top-notch bar food includes towering burgers.

Brass Monkey COCKTAIL BAR
(www.brassmonkeybar.co.uk; 11 High Pavement; ⏲8pm-4am Mon-Sat) Nottingham's original cocktail bar rocks the Lace Market with DJ sets and quirky takes on favourites such as elderflower mojitos. The roof terrace gets packed on summer evenings. Happy hour runs to midnight.

Canal House PUB
(☎0115-955 5060; www.castlerockbrewery.co.uk/pubs/the-canalhouse; 48-52 Canal St; ⏲11am-11pm Mon-Wed, to midnight Thu, to 1am Fri & Sat, to 10.30pm Sun; 📶) Split in two by a watery inlet, the Canal House is the best of the city's canal-front pubs, with plenty of waterside seating and beers by Nottingham-based Castle Rock Brewery on tap. Regular events range from comedy to craft-beer festivals.

☆ Entertainment

Theatre Royal & Royal Concert Hall PERFORMING ARTS
(☎0115-989 5555; www.trch.co.uk; Theatre Sq, Upper Parliament St) Nottingham's 19th-century Theatre Royal and adjoining 20th-century Royal Concert Hall host musicals, touring theatre shows and veteran music acts.

Shopping

Five Leaves Bookshop BOOKS
(☎0115-837 3097; www.fiveleavesbookshop.co.uk; Swann's Yard, 14a Long Row; ⏲10am-5pm Mon-Sat) Opened as an extension of its own publishing imprint in 2013, this splendid independent bookshop is hidden down a passageway off Low Row. In addition to its own titles, it stocks fiction, poetry and non-fiction works (politics, poetry, counterculture, LGBT, cityscapes and landscapes) by other independent and commercial publishers. Readings, book launches and talks regularly take place.

Debbie Bryan FASHION & ACCESSORIES
(☎0115-950 7776; www.debbiebryan.co.uk; 18 St Mary's Gate; ⏲noon-4pm Fri & Sun, to 5pm

Sat) In Nottingham's historic Lace Market quarter, Debbie Bryan revives its traditions, designing and making lace creations spanning jewellery to clothing and homewares, such as lampshades and framed lace artworks. Scones, cakes and slices are served at the on-site tearoom. Ask about design workshops.

Updated details of opening times are posted online.

Studio Chocolate CHOCOLATE
(☎0115-947 4903; www.studio-chocolate.co.uk; 3 Cobden Chambers; ⏲10am-4pm Wed-Sun) Nottingham chocolatier Ellie Wharrad works with premium-grade chocolate to handcraft and hand paint pralines. Unique flavour combinations at her shop include gin and tonic, beer caramel and pear cider; ask about regular chocolate-making classes. Enter via Pelham St.

Rob's Records MUSIC
(www.facebook.com/robsrecordsnottingham; 3 Hurts Yard; ⏲11am-5.30pm Mon-Sat) Vinyl records, along with CDs, DVDs, videos and cassettes cram every conceivable floor, wall and ceiling space at this music lover's nirvana.

Information

Nottingham's **tourist office** (☎0844 477 5678; www.visit-nottinghamshire.co.uk; The Exchange, 1-4 Smithy Row; ⏲10am-3pm Wed-Sat) has racks of information along with Robin Hood merchandise.

Getting There & Away

AIR

East Midlands Airport (p466) is 13.5 miles southwest of central Nottingham; Skylink buses pass the airport (one-way/return £5.40/10.80, one hour, at least hourly, 24 hours).

BUS

Local services run from the Victoria bus station, behind the Victoria shopping centre on Milton St. Bus 26 runs to Southwell (£4.50, one hour, every 30 minutes) and bus 90 to Newark (£5.60, 55 minutes, five daily Monday to Saturday, every two hours Sunday).

Long-distance buses operate from the **Broadmarsh bus station** (Collin St).

Frequent National Express services:

Birmingham £12, 1½ hours, four daily
Leicester £5, 45 minutes, three daily
London Victoria £28, 3½ hours, hourly

TRAIN

The train station is on the southern edge of the city centre.

Derby £8, 30 minutes, three hourly
Grantham £11.60, 35 minutes, up to two per hour
Lincoln £12.60, 55 minutes, hourly
London King's Cross/St Pancras £61, 1¾ hours, up to three per hour
Manchester £29.20, 1¾ hours, hourly

Newark-on-Trent

☎01636 / POP 27,700

Newark-on-Trent paid the price for backing the wrong side in the English Civil War. After surviving four sieges by Oliver Cromwell's men, the town was ransacked by Roundheads when Charles I surrendered in 1646. Today, the riverside town is a peaceful place worth a stop to wander its castle ruins.

Sights

Newark Castle CASTLE
(www.newark-sherwooddc.gov.uk/newarkcastle; Castle Gate; grounds free, tours adult/child £5.50/2.75; ⏲grounds dawn-dusk, tours by reservation Wed & Fri-Sun) In a pretty park overlooking the River Trent, the ruins of Newark Castle include an impressive Norman gate and a series of underground passages and chambers. The real King John, portrayed as a villain in the Robin Hood legend, died here in 1216. Book tour tickets online at www.palacenewarktickets.com. Concerts, festivals and various cultural events regularly take place in the grounds.

Newark Air Museum MUSEUM
(☎01636-707170; www.newarkairmuseum.org; Drove Lane, Winthorpe; adult/child £9.50/5; ⏲10am-5pm Mar-Oct, to 4pm Nov-Feb) Situated 2 miles east of Newark by the Winthorpe Showground, this aviation museum has over 100 aircraft, including a fearsome Vulcan bomber, a Vampire T11, a Gloster Meteor and a de Havilland Tiger Moth, along with a small exhibition on the Royal Air Force.

Eating & Drinking

Old Bakery Tea Rooms CAFE £
(☎01636-611501; www.oldbakerytearooms.co.uk; 4 Queens Head Ct; pastries £2-5, mains £6-12; ⏲9.30am-5pm Mon-Sat; ☑) Everything, including heavenly sweet and savoury scones, is baked fresh on the premises at the Old Bakery Tea Rooms, housed in an enchanting

15th-century Tudor building. Lunch specials include soups, frittata, bruschetta and smoked-salmon brioche. Cash only.

Castle Barge BAR
(☎01636-677320; www.castlebarge.com; The Wharf; ⏱10.30am-midnight) Moored on the River Trent overlooking Newark Castle, this former grain barge, which once plied the waters between Hull and Gainsborough, is an idyllic spot for a local ale inside or up on deck, with additional picnic seating on the riverbanks. Its menu includes stone-baked pizzas.

Information

Tourist Office (☎01636-655765; www.newark-sherwooddc.gov.uk; 14 Appleton Gate; ⏱10am-4pm) On the northeastern edge of the historic centre.

Getting There & Away

Buses 28 and 29 serve Southwell (£4.70, 35 minutes, two per hour).

Newark has two train stations.

Newark Castle East Midlands trains serve Nottingham (£6.80, 30 minutes, up to two per hour) and Lincoln (£5.80, 30 minutes, up to two per hour).

Newark North Gate Trains on the East Coast Main Line serve London King's Cross (£46.80, 1½ hours, up to four per hour); destinations to the north require a change in Doncaster (£25.50, 30 minutes, hourly).

Southwell

☎01636 / POP 7297

A graceful scattering of grand, wisteria-draped country houses, pretty little Southwell is straight out of the pages of a novel from the English Romantic period.

Sights

★**Southwell Minster** CHURCH
(www.southwellminster.org; Church St; suggested donation £5; ⏱8am-7pm Mar-Oct, to 6.30pm Nov-Feb) Rising from the village centre, the awe-inspiring Southwell Minster, built over Saxon and Roman foundations, blends 12th- and 13th-century features, including zigzag door frames and curved arches. Its chapter-house features some unusual stained glass and detailed carvings of faces, animals and leaves of forest trees.

Southwell Workhouse MUSEUM
(NT; ☎01636-817260; www.nationaltrust.org.uk; Upton Rd; adult/child £8/4; ⏱noon-5pm Wed-Sun Marearly Nov) On the road to Newark, 1 mile east of the village centre, the Southwell Workhouse is a sobering reminder of the tough life faced by paupers in the 19th century. You can explore the factory floors and workers' chambers accompanied by an audio guide narrated by 'inmates' and 'officials'. One-hour guided tours of the exteriors take place at 11am.

Sleeping & Eating

Saracen's Head Hotel HISTORIC HOTEL ££
(☎01636-812701; www.saracensheadhotel.com; Market Pl; s/d/f/ste incl breakfast from £90/100/130/150; P 📶 🐾) Set around a flower-filled courtyard in the village heart, this rambling, black-and-white timbered coaching inn has 27 beautifully refurbished rooms (some with four-poster beds and claw-foot baths) across its old and new wings. Illustrious past guests included Charles I, Lord Byron and Dickens. Its oak-panelled restaurant serves traditional British fare (mains £10 to £21.50).

Family rooms sleep up to four; baby cots are available.

Old Theatre Deli CAFE, DELI £
(☎01636-815340; www.theoldtheatredeli.co.uk; 4 Market Pl; dishes £5.50-11.50; ⏱8.30am-4pm Mon-Fri, to 5pm Sat) Artisan breads from the Midlands' renowned Hambleton Bakery, gourmet sandwiches, quiches, pies, salads and hot specials, such as corn-and-bacon fritters, are among the treats to take away or eat inside or out on the pavement terrace. You can also order picnic hampers complete with blankets. It's housed inside a Georgian former theatre.

Getting There & Away

Bus 26 runs from Nottingham (£4.50, one hour, every 30 minutes). For Newark-on-Trent, take bus 28 or 29 (£4.70, 35 minutes, two per hour).

LINCOLNSHIRE

Lincolnshire unfolds over low hills and the sparsely populated, pancake-flat Fens where the farmland is strewn with windmills and, more recently, wind turbines. Surrounding the history-steeped county town of Lincoln you'll find seaside resorts, scenic waterways, serene nature reserves and stone-built towns tailor-made for English period dramas.

Two of the county's most famous 'yellow-bellies' (as Lincolnshire locals call themselves) were Sir Isaac Newton, whose home, Woolsthorpe Manor, can be visited, and the late former prime minister Margaret Thatcher, the daughter of a humble greengrocer from the market town of Grantham.

Activities

Traversing the area occupied by Norse invaders in the 9th century, the 147-mile **Viking Way** walking trail snakes across the gentle hills of the Lincolnshire Wolds from the banks of the River Humber to Oakham in Rutland.

Cyclists can find information on routes across the county in any of the local tourist offices. The 33-mile **Water Rail Way** is a flat, sculpture-lined on-road cycling route that follows the River Witham through classic Fens countryside along the former railway line between Lincoln and Boston.

Getting There & Around

East Midlands trains connect Lincoln, Newark Castle and Nottingham. Newark North Gate and Grantham lie on the East Coast Main Line between London King's Cross and Edinburgh.

Local buses link Lincolnshire's towns, but services are slow and infrequent. Check the transport pages at www.lincolnshire.gov.uk.

Comprehensive transport information is available from Traveline (p406).

Lincoln

01522 / POP 97,541

Ringed by historic city gates – including the Newport Arch on Bailgate, a relic from the original Roman settlement – this beautiful city's old centre is a tangle of cobbled medieval streets surrounding its 11th-century castle and colossal 12th-century cathedral. The lanes that topple over the edge of Lincoln Cliff are lined with Tudor town houses, ancient pubs and independent shops.

Flanking the River Witham at the base of the hill, the new town is less absorbing, but the revitalised Brayford Waterfront development by the university is a popular spot to watch the boats go by.

Sights

★Lincoln Cathedral CATHEDRAL

(01522-561600; www.lincolncathedral.com; Minster Yard; cathedral adult/child £8/4.80 Mon-Sat; 10am-4pm Mon-Sat, 11am-3.30pm Sun) Towering over the city like a medieval skyscraper, Lincoln's magnificent cathedral is a breathtaking representation of divine power on earth. The great tower rising above the crossing is the third-highest in England at 83m, but in medieval times, a lead-encased wooden spire added a further 79m, topping even the great pyramids of Giza. One-hour **guided tours** (included in admission) take place at least twice daily Monday to Saturday; there are also tours of the roof and tower (£5, book in advance).

The vast interior of the church is too large for modern congregations – services take place instead in **St Hugh's Choir**, a church within a church running east from the crossing. The choir stalls are accessed through a magnificent carved stone screen; look north to see the stunning rose window known as the Dean's Eye (c 1192), mirrored to the south by the floral flourishes of the Bishop's Eye (1330). There's more stained glass in the three Services Chapels in the north transept.

Beyond St Hugh's Choir, the **Angel Choir** is supported by 28 columns topped by carvings of angels and foliate scrollwork. Other interesting details include the 10-sided **chapterhouse** – where Edward I held his parliament and where the climax of *The Da Vinci Code* was filmed in 2005.

The best time to hear the organ resounding through the cathedral is during **evensong**; check times online.

★Lincoln Castle CASTLE

(01522-554559; www.lincolncastle.com; Castle Hill; castle day ticket adult/child £14/7.50, walls only £10/5.50, grounds free; 10am-5pm Apr-Sep, to 4pm Oct-Mar) One of the first castles erected by the victorious William the Conqueror, in 1068, to keep his new kingdom in line, Lincoln Castle offers awesome views over the city and miles of surrounding countryside. A major 2015-completed restoration program opened up the entire castle walls and gave the 1215 **Magna Carta** (one of only four copies) a swanky, subterranean new home. One-hour guided tours, included in the castle admission, depart from the eastern gate; check the blackboard for times.

Bishops' Palace RUINS

(EH; 01522-527468; www.english-heritage.org.uk; Minster Yard; adult/child £6.90/4.10; 10am-6pm Wed-Sun Apr-Sep, to 5pm Wed-Sun Oct, to 4pm Sat & Sun Nov-Mar) Beside Lincoln Cathedral lie the time-ravaged but still imposing

Lincoln

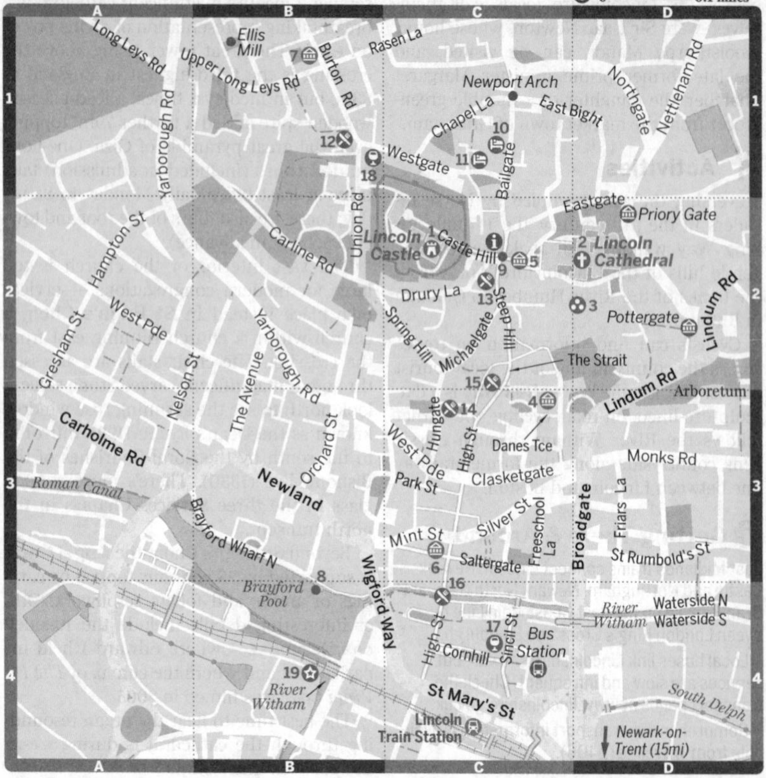

Lincoln

Top Sights
1 Lincoln Castle C2
2 Lincoln Cathedral D2

Sights
3 Bishops' Palace D2
4 Collection C3
5 Exchequergate C2
6 Lincoln Guildhall C3
7 Museum of Lincolnshire Life B1

Activities, Courses & Tours
8 Brayford Belle B4
9 Ghost Walks C2

Sleeping
10 Bail House C1
11 Castle Hotel C1

Eating
12 Bronze Pig B1
13 Brown's Pie Shop C2
14 Cheese Society C3
15 Jews House C2
Reform .... (see 11)
16 Stokes High Bridge Café C4

Drinking & Nightlife
17 Cosy Club C4
18 Strugglers Inn B1

Entertainment
19 Engine Shed B4

ruins of the 12th-century Bishops' Palace, gutted by parliamentary forces during the Civil War. From here, the local bishops once controlled a diocese stretching from the Humber to the Thames. Grapevines are planted in its hillside terraced garden.

Museum of Lincolnshire Life MUSEUM
(01522-782040; www.lincolnshire.gov.uk; Old Barracks, Burton Rd; 10am-4pm) FREE Displays at this charming community museum housed in an old Victorian barracks span everything from Victorian farm implements to the tin-can tank built in Lincoln for WWI.

Collection MUSEUM
(01522-782040; www.thecollectionmuseum.com; Danes Tce; 10am-4pm Wed-Mon) FREE Archaeology bursts into life at this museum, with loads of hands-on displays. Kids can handle artefacts and dress up in period costume. Check out the crushed skull of a 4000-year-old 'yellowbelly' (as locals are dubbed), pulled from a Neolithic burial site near Sleaford. Free one-hour tours run at 2pm on Saturdays. Look out for various evening events.

Exchequergate HISTORIC BUILDING
Located between the castle and the cathedral, the triple-arched, battlement-topped Exchequergate, where the church's tenants paid their rent, dates from the 14th century. A black-and-white chequered cloth was used to help count the payments, giving rise to the term exchequer.

Lincoln Guildhall HISTORIC BUILDING
(01522-873303; www.lincoln.gov.uk; Saltergate; tour free; by 90min guided tour 10am, noon & 2pm Mon, Wed & Fri) Arcing over Lincoln's High St, the guildhall has been home to the city council since its completion in 1520. Regalia here includes the sword of Richard II.

Tours

Ghost Walks WALKING
(01673-857574; www.lincolnghostwalks.co.uk; adult/child £6/4; 7pm Wed-Sat) Genuinely spooky 75-minute ghost walks depart adjacent to the tourist office year-round. Bookings aren't required; turn up 10 minutes before tours begin.

Brayford Belle CRUISE
(01522-708508; www.lincolnboattrips.co.uk; Brayford Wharf North; adult/child £7/4; tours 11am, 12.15pm, 1.30pm & 2.45pm Tue-Sun Easter-Sep, hours vary Oct) Boat trips lasting around 50 minutes aboard the *Brayford Belle* travel along the River Witham and Fossdyke Navigation, a canal system dating to Roman times. No credit cards.

Sleeping

Castle Hotel BOUTIQUE HOTEL ££
(01522-538801; www.castlehotel.net; Westgate; s/d/coach house incl breakfast from £90/120/220;) Each of the Castle Hotel's 18 rooms have been exquisitely refurbished in olive, truffle and oyster tones, as has its family-friendly four-person coach house. It was built on the site of Lincoln's Roman forum in 1852; the red-brick building's incarnations variously included a school and a WWII lookout station. Take advantage of great-value dinner, bed and breakfast deals with its award-winning restaurant **Reform** (01522-538801; www.reformrestaurant.co.uk; mains £15-25; noon-2.30pm & 7-9pm Wed-Sat, noon-3pm Sun).

Bail House B&B ££
(01522-541000; www.bailhouse.co.uk; 34 Bailgate; d/f from £65/125;) Stone walls, worn flagstones, secluded gardens and one room with an extraordinary timber-vaulted ceiling are just some of the charms of this lovingly restored Georgian town house in central Lincoln. There's limited on-site parking, a garden and a children's playground, and even a seasonal heated outdoor swimming pool. Family rooms sleep four.

Eating

Stokes High Bridge Café CAFE £
(01522-513825; www.stokescoffee.com; 207 High St; dishes £5.50-10.50; 8am-4pm Mon-Sat, 10am-4pm Sun;) A Lincoln landmark, this soaring 1540-built black-and-white Tudor building is England's only one atop a medieval bridge (1160). Within its preserved half-timbered interior, 1892-established, family-run roastery Stokes brews superb coffees made from speciality beans. Classic fare includes English breakfasts (served all day), traditional roasts and afternoon teas.

Cheese Society CHEESE £
(www.thecheesesociety.co.uk; 1 St Martin's Lane; dishes £5-10.50, cheese boards £10-22; kitchen 11am-3.30pm Mon-Fri, to 4pm Sat, shop 10am-4.30pm Mon-Fri, to 5pm Sat) Not only does this light, bright place stock over 90 mostly British cheeses, it also serves them at its 12-seat cafe. Try its elaborate cheese boards or dishes such as twice-baked Dorset Blue Vinney soufflé or Wensleydale and herb scones with smoked salmon.

DON'T MISS

THE HOME OF SIR ISAAC NEWTON

Sir Isaac Newton fans may feel the gravitational pull of **Woolsthorpe Manor** (NT; 01476-862823; www.nationaltrust.org.uk; Water Lane; house & grounds adult/child £9.20/4.60, grounds only £4.10/2.90; 11am-5pm Wed-Mon mid-Mar–Oct, Fri-Sun Nov–mid-Mar), the great man's birthplace, about 8 miles south of Grantham. The humble 17th-century house contains reconstructions of Newton's rooms; the apple that inspired his theory of gravity allegedly fell from the tree in the garden. There's a nifty kids' science room and a cafe. Take Centrebus 9 from Grantham (£3.80, 20 minutes, four per day Monday to Saturday).

Brown's Pie Shop PIES ££
(01522-527330; www.brownspieshop.co.uk; 33 Steep Hill; mains £9.75-26.50; noon-2.30pm & 5-9.30pm Mon-Fri, noon-9.30pm Sat, to 8pm Sun) Hearty 'pot pies' (no pastry bottoms) at this long-established, quintessentially British restaurant are stuffed with locally sourced beef, rabbit and game. Pies aside, traditional dishes include Lincolnshire sausages with caramelised onion gravy and slow-roasted pork belly.

★**Bronze Pig** BRITISH £££
(01522-524817; www.thebronzepig.co.uk; 4 Burton Rd; mains £18-27, 2-/3-course lunch menus £25/29; by reservation 6-9pm Tue, noon-1.30pm & 6-9pm Wed-Sat, noon-2pm Sun) BBC *MasterChef* finalist Irishman Eamonn Hunt and Sicilian chef Pompeo Siracusa have taken Lincoln's dining scene by storm since opening the Bronze Pig. Their exceptional Modern British cooking has an Italian accent and ingredients are locally sourced. Reserve well ahead and prepare to be wowed. It also has four deluxe guest rooms (doubles from £105).

Jews House EUROPEAN £££
(01522-524851; www.jewshouserestaurant.co.uk; 15 The Strait, Steep Hill; mains £16.50-27; 6-9.30pm Thu-Sat, 1-4pm Sun) This local favourite serves gourmet fare (roast wood pigeon, truffle custard and bacon foam; baked lemon sole with scallop mousse) in one of England's oldest houses, the 1160-built Romanesque Jews House.

Drinking & Entertainment

Cosy Club BAR
(www.cosyclub.co.uk; Sincil St; 9am-11pm Sun-Wed, to midnight Thu, to 1am Fri & Sat;) Spectacularly converted with soaring skylit ceilings, this 1848-built corn exchange now contains one of Lincoln's liveliest bars. Along with cocktails like English Rose (gin, rosewater, strawberries and sparkling wine) and the Earl's Breakfast (vodka, Earl Grey tea and lime juice), it serves breakfast, brunch, tapas and international dishes.

Strugglers Inn PUB
(www.facebook.com/thestrugglersinn; 83 Westgate; noon-midnight Tue-Sat, to 11pm Sun & Mon) A sunny walled-courtyard beer garden out the back, an interior warmed by an open fire and a superb selection of real ales on tap make this the pick of Lincoln's independent pubs.

Engine Shed LIVE MUSIC
(0871 220 0260; www.engineshed.co.uk; Brayford Pool) Lincoln's largest live-music venue occupies a former railway-container storage facility. Past acts have included Kings of Leon, Fat Boy Slim and Manic Street Preachers. Music aside, it also hosts sports events, comedy and pop-up markets.

Information

Tourist Office (01522-545458; www.visitlincoln.com; 9 Castle Hill; 10am-5pm Mon-Sat, 10.30am-4pm Sun) In a half-timbered, 16th-century building.

Getting There & Away

BUS

The **bus station** (Melville St) is just northeast of the train station in the new town.

Stagecoach buses include bus 1 to Grantham (£6.10, 1½ hours, hourly Monday to Saturday, five on Sunday).

TRAIN

The train station is 250m east of the Brayford Waterfront development in the new town.

Boston £15.30, 1¼ hours, hourly, change at Sleaford

London King's Cross £88.50, 2¼ hours, up to three per hour, some require a change in Newark or Peterborough

Newark-on-Trent Newark Castle, £5.80, 30 minutes, two per hour

Nottingham £12.60, one hour, hourly

Sheffield £21.60, 1¼ hours, hourly

Stamford

☎01780 / POP 19,704

One of England's prettiest towns, Stamford seems frozen in time, with elegant streets lined with honey-coloured limestone buildings and hidden alleyways dotted with alehouses, interesting restaurants and small independent boutiques. A forest of historic church spires rises overhead and the gently gurgling River Welland meanders through the town centre. It's a favourite with filmmakers seeking the postcard vision of England, and has appeared in everything from *Pride and Prejudice* to the *Da Vinci Code*.

Sights

★Burghley House HISTORIC BUILDING

(☎01780-752451; www.burghley.co.uk; Barnack Rd; house & garden adult/child £17/9, garden only £9.50/5.50, park free; ⏲house 10.30am-5pm Wed-Sun Apr-early Oct, garden 10.30am-1pm & 2-4.30pm daily Apr-Oct, park 7am-6pm daily year-round) Set in more than 810 hectares of grounds, landscaped by Lancelot 'Capability' Brown, opulent Burghley House (bur-lee) was built by Queen Elizabeth's chief adviser William Cecil, whose descendants still live here. It bristles with cupolas, pavilions, belvederes and chimneys; the lavish staterooms are a particular highlight. In early September the renowned Burghley Horse Trials take place here. The estate is 1.3 miles southeast of Stamford; follow the marked path for 15 minutes through the park by Stamford's train station.

St Mary's Church CHURCH

(www.stamfordbenefice.com; St Mary's St; ⏲8am-6pm, hours can vary) An endearingly wonky 13th-century broach spire tops the 12th-century St Mary's Church. Classical concerts are held here in summer; tickets (from £14) are sold at Stamford's tourist office.

Sleeping & Eating

William Cecil at Stamford HISTORIC HOTEL ££

(☎01780-750070; www.hillbrookehotels.co.uk; High St, St Martin's; d/f incl breakfast from £110/160, lunch mains £10.50-14.95, 2-/3-course dinner menus £29.50/35; P 🛜) Within the Burghley Estate, this stunningly renovated hotel has 27 rooms inspired by Burghley House, with period furnishings and luxuries such as Egyptian cotton linens and complimentary organic vodka. The smart **restaurant** turns out stylish British classics and opens to a wicker-chair-furnished patio.

Family rooms sleep four; interconnecting rooms are also available.

★George Hotel HISTORIC HOTEL £££

(☎01780-750750; www.georgehotelofstamford.com; 71 High St, St Martin's; s/d/ste/4-poster incl breakfast from £145/250/270/310, mains £24-42; P 🛜 🐾) Stamford's luxurious landmark inn opened its doors in 1597. Today its 45 individually sized and decorated rooms impeccably blend period charm and modern elegance. Superior Modern British cuisine is served at its oak-panelled **restaurant**, while its more informal garden-room restaurant hosts afternoon tea in its courtyard. Its two bars include a champagne bar.

Drinking & Nightlife

Tobie Norris PUB

(www.kneadpubs.co.uk; 12 St Paul's St; ⏲noon-11pm Mon-Thu, to midnight Fri & Sat, to 10.30pm Sun; 🛜) A wonderful stone-walled, flagstone-floored pub dating from 1280, the Tobie Norris has a warren of rooms with open fireplaces, a sunny, flower-filled courtyard and local ales. Wood-fired pizzas are a highlight of its wide-ranging menu (mains £14 to £18).

BELTON HOUSE

Amid 14.2 hectares of elegant formal gardens, **Belton House** (NT; ☎01476-566116; www.nationaltrust.org.uk; Belton; house & grounds adult/child £15.70/10, grounds only £8/4; ⏲house 12.30-5pm Wed-Sun Mar-Oct, grounds 10am-5pm Mar-Oct, to 4pm Nov-Feb) is a dream filming location for English period dramas, *Jane Eyre, Tom Jones* and the Colin Firth version of *Pride and Prejudice* among them. Built in 1688 in classic Restoration style, the house retains stunning original features, including ornate woodcarvings by master Dutch carver Grinling Gibbons. It's off the A607 2.5 miles northeast of Grantham, served by Stagecoach bus 1 (£2, 15 minutes, hourly Monday to Saturday, every two hours Sunday).

The surrounding 526-hectare grounds have been home to a fallow deer herd for more than 300 years. Also on the site are a farm shop, a restaurant, a cafe and an adventure playground.

LINCOLNSHIRE: BOMBER COUNTY

The Royal Air Force (RAF) was formed in 1918 following WWI and two years later its college was established in Lincolnshire. During WWII, England's 'Bomber County' was home to numerous squadrons and by 1945 had more airfields (49) than any other in the country. US Navy flying boats flew antisubmarine patrols from here and B-29 bombers were also based here.

Just south of Lincoln, the International Bomber Command Centre has a moving memorial and an attached museum. Lincoln's tourist office (p456) has details of other aviation legacies throughout the county.

International Bomber Command Centre (☎01778-421420; www.internationalbcc.co.uk; Kanwick Hill, LN4 2HQ; memorial free, museum adult/child £8.70/5.50; ⏲memorial 24hr, museum 9.30am-5pm Tue-Sun) This 4.5-hectare site 1.5 miles south of Lincoln centres on a 31m-high metallic spire (at 102ft, the exact length of the wingspan of a Lancaster Bomber) surrounded by rusted-metal walls inscribed with the names of the 57,861 men and women who served and supported Britain's Bomber Command. Next to the memorial, a state-of-the-art museum has high-tech interactive displays covering the history of Bomber Command, including poignant stories from those who witnessed WWII's bombings first-hand.

Battle of Britain Memorial Flight Visitor Centre (☎01522-782040; www.lincolnshire.gov.uk; Dogdyke Rd, Coningsby; museum free, hangar tours adult/child £9/5; ⏲hangar tours by reservation 10am-4pm Mon-Fri) See Spitfires and the four-engined *Lancaster City of Lincoln* on 90-minute hangar tours. Bus IC5 (£4.80, one hour, hourly Monday to Saturday) runs here from Lincoln.

Lincolnshire Aviation Heritage Centre (☎01790-763207; www.lincsaviation.co.uk; East Kirkby, near Spilsby PE23 4DE; adult/child £9/3; ⏲9.30am-5pm Tue, Thu & Sat Easter-Oct, 10am-4pm Tue, Thu & Sat Nov-Easter) An original WWII Bomber Command airfield complete with its original wartime control tower is now home to the Lincolnshire Aviation Heritage Centre, with wartime planes and automobiles on display. It's 30 miles southeast of Lincoln via the A153; there's no public transport.

The star attraction is an Avro Lancaster Bomber from 1941, one of only three still working (for £350, you can ride in it around the airfield, though not in the air, on Saturdays by reservation).

Paten & Co PUB
(www.kneadpubs.co.uk; 7 All Saints' Pl; ⏲noon-midnight Mon-Sat, to 6pm Sun; 📶) When the current owners stripped back this 18th-century building during renovations, they uncovered Paten & Co wine and spirits merchants' painted sign and got permission to use the original name. Twists on old-fashioned cocktails (eg raspberry and thyme Collins) are its speciality, along with charcoal-smoked street food. The top floor has breathtaking views of All Saints' church spires.

All Saints Brewery BREWERY
(www.allsaintsbrewery.co.uk; 22 All Saints' St; ⏲noon-11pm Mon-Sat, to 10.30pm Sun; 📶) Victorian-era steam-brewing equipment is used to make organic fruit beers at this operation, which has revived the site's original 1825 brewery after it was shuttered for several decades. Try its cherry, strawberry, raspberry and apricot brews at the attached pub or in the umbrella-shaded courtyard. Bar staff can advise on informal brewery tours.

Information

Tourist Office (☎01780-755611; www.stamfordartscentre.com; 27 St Mary's St; ⏲9.30am-5pm Mon-Sat; 📶) Inside the Stamford Arts Centre.

Getting There & Away

BUS

Centrebus 4 runs to Grantham (£4.70, 1¼ hours, three per day Monday to Saturday) and Centrebus 9 serves Oakham (£3.60, 30 minutes, five daily Monday to Friday, four Saturday).

TRAIN

Trains run to Birmingham (£41.50, 1¾ hours, hourly), Cambridge (£27.20, 1¼ hours, hourly),

Nottingham (£26.80, 1¾ hours, hourly) with a change in Leicester (£21.50, 40 minutes) and Stansted Airport (£43.50, 2½ hours, every two hours).

LEICESTERSHIRE

Leicestershire was a vital creative hub during the Industrial Revolution, but its factories were a major target for German air raids in WWII and most towns in the county still bear the scars of wartime bombing. Nevertheless, there are some impressive remains, from Roman ruins to Elizabethan castles and King Richard III's resting place at Leicester Cathedral following the 21st-century discovery of his unmarked grave in a car park in the busy, multicultural capital Leicester.

Getting There & Around

Leicester is well served by buses and trains. For bus routes and timetables, visit the 'Roads and Transport' pages at www.leicestershire.gov.uk.

Regular buses connect Rutland to Leicester, Stamford and other surrounding towns.

Leicester

0116 / POP 348,300

Built over the buried ruins of two millennia of history, Leicester (*les*-ter) suffered at the hands of the Luftwaffe and postwar planners but an influx of textile workers from India and Pakistan from the 1960s transformed the city into a bustling multicultural hub.

The astonishing 2012 discovery and 2013 identification of the remains of King Richard III in a Leicester car park sparked a flurry of developments, including a spiffing visitor centre on the site, and the restoration of the cathedral, where the king was reburied in 2015.

Sights

★King Richard III: Dynasty, Death & Discovery MUSEUM

(www.kriii.com; 4a St Martin's Pl; adult/child £9.25/4.75; 10am-4pm Sun-Fri, to 5pm Sat) Built following the incredible 2012 discovery and 2013 DNA testing of King Richard III's remains, Leicester's high-tech King Richard III visitor centre encompasses three fascinating sections. Dynasty explores his rise to become the final Plantagenet king. Death delves into the Battle of Bosworth, when Richard became the last English king to be killed in battle. Discovery details the University of Leicester's archaeological dig and identification, and lets you view the site of the grave in which he was found.

Its Murder, Mystery and Mayhem exhibition covers the key players, battles and milestones of the Wars of the Roses between the House of York (symbolised by a white rose) and the House of Lancaster (red rose).

★Leicester Cathedral CATHEDRAL

(0116-261 5357; www.leicestercathedral.org; Peacock Lane; by donation; 11am-3pm Wed-Sat, noon-3pm Sun) Pride of place at this substantial medieval cathedral goes to the contemporary limestone tomb atop the vault where the remains of King Richard III were reburied in 2015, following the discovery of his skeleton nearby. Look too for the striking carvings on the cathedral's roof supports.

Every day except Sunday, 30-minute King Richard III tours (adult/child £3.50/free) depart at 11am, noon, 2pm and 3pm. One-hour guided tours (adult/child £5/free) are available on request.

National Space Centre MUSEUM

(0116-261 0261; www.spacecentre.co.uk; Exploration Dr; adult/child £15.50/12.50; 10am-4pm Mon-Fri, to 5pm Sat & Sun) Although British space missions usually launch from French Guiana or Kazakhstan, Leicester's space museum is a fascinating introduction to the mysteries of the spheres. The ill-fated 2003 *Beagle 2* mission to Mars was controlled from here. Fun, kid-friendly displays cover

WORTH A TRIP

ALTHORP HOUSE

The ancestral home of the Spencer family, **Althorp House** (01604-770107; www.spencerofalthorp.com; A428, Althorp; adult/child £14/7; 11am-4pm Aug) – pronounced 'altrup' – is the final resting place of Diana, Princess of Wales, commemorated by a memorial. The outstanding art collection features works by Rubens, Gainsborough and van Dyck. Profits go to charities supported by the Princess Diana Memorial Fund.

Althorp is off the A428, 5.5 miles northwest of Northampton, and is not served by public transport.

Leicester

Leicester

Top Sights

1 King Richard III: Dynasty, Death & Discovery B3
2 Leicester Cathedral B2

Sights

Great Hall .... (see 5)
3 Guildhall B2
4 Jewry Wall Museum A2
5 Leicester Castle A3
6 Leicester Museum & Art Gallery D4
7 Magazine B3
8 Newarke Houses Museum A3
9 St Mary de Castro A3
10 St Nicholas Church A2

Sleeping

11 Belmont Hotel D4

Eating

12 Good Earth C2

Drinking & Nightlife

13 Bread & Honey C3
14 Globe B2

Entertainment

15 Cookie B2
16 Curve Theatre D2

everything from astronomy to the status of current space missions. It's 1.5 miles north of the city centre. Take bus 54 (£1.60, 15 minutes, every 10 minutes Monday to Saturday, every 20 minutes Sunday) from **Haymarket bus station** (Charles St).

Leicester Castle RUINS
(www.leicestercastle.co.uk; Castle View) Scattered around the **Newarke Houses Museum** (0116-225 4980; www.leicestermuseums.org; The Newarke; noon-4.30pm Thu-Sun) **FREE** are the ruins of Leicester's medieval castle,

where Richard III spent his final days before the Battle of Bosworth. The monumental gateway known as the **Magazine** (Newarke St) was once a storehouse for cannonballs and gunpowder. Dating from the 12th century and clad in Georgian brickwork, the **Great Hall** (Castle Yard) stands behind a 15th-century gate near the church of **St Mary de Castro** (www.facebook.com/pg/mdcleicester; 15 Castle View; ⏲noon-2pm, hours can vary), where Geoffrey Chaucer was married in 1366.

Leicester Museum & Art Gallery MUSEUM, GALLERY

(☎0116-225 4900; www.leicestermuseums.org; 53 New Walk; ⏲11am-4.30pm Mon-Fri, to 5pm Sat & Sun;) FREE Highlights of this grand Victorian museum include the dinosaur galleries (a reliable favourite with kids), the painting collection (with works by Turner and Degas), ceramics by Picasso, and the Egyptian gallery, where real mummies rub shoulders with displays on Boris Karloff's 1932 film *The Mummy*. Reserve a timeslot in advance.

Guildhall HISTORIC BUILDING

(☎0116-253 2569; www.leicestermuseums.org; Guildhall Lane; ⏲noon-4.30pm Thu-Sun) FREE Leicester's perfectly preserved 14th-century guildhall, one of England's finest, is reputed to be the city's most haunted building.

Jewry Wall Museum MUSEUM

(EH; www.english-heritage.co.uk; St Nicholas Circle; ⏲11am-4.30pm Feb-Oct) FREE This museum exploring the history of Leicester from Roman times to the modern day was undergoing renovations at the time of writing, and is expected to reopen to the public in spring 2021. In front of the museum is the **Jewry Wall**, part of Leicester's Roman baths. Tiles and masonry from the baths were incorporated in the walls of neighbouring **St Nicholas Church** (www.stnicholasleicester.com; St Nicholas Circle; by donation; ⏲2-4pm Sat, 6.30-8.30pm Sun, hours can vary).

Activities

Great Central Railway RAIL

(☎01509-632323; www.gcrailway.co.uk; return adult/child £18/9) Steam locomotives chug from Leicester North station on Redhill Circle to Loughborough Central, following the 8-mile route along which Thomas Cook ran the original package tour in 1841. The locos operate most weekends year-round and some summer weekdays; check timetables online.

For Leicester North station, take bus 25 (£1.60, 20 minutes, every 10 minutes) from Haymarket bus station.

Sleeping

Businesslike chain hotels are plentiful in Leicester's centre, with more bucolic options in the surrounding areas including Rutland.

Belmont Hotel HOTEL ££

(☎0116-254 4773; www.belmonthotel.co.uk; 20 De Montfort St; s/d/f/ste from £71/90/115/125; P❄@📶) Owned and run by the same family for four generations, the 19th-century Belmont has 74 stylish, contemporary, individually designed rooms and a fantastic location overlooking leafy New Walk. Family rooms have a double bed and bunks. Its restaurant is highly regarded; the two bars, Jamie's and Bowie's, open to a terrace and a conservatory respectively.

Eating

Bobby's INDIAN £

(☎0116-266 0106; www.bobbys-restaurant.co.uk; 154-156 Belgrave Rd; dishes £5-7.50; ⏲11am-9pm Mon, Wed & Thu, to 10pm Fri, 10am-10pm Sat & Sun;) The top pick along Leicester's Golden Mile – lined with sari stores, jewellery emporiums and curry houses – is Bobby's, a 1970s-established institution serving all-vegetarian classics.

LOCAL KNOWLEDGE

HAMMER & PINCERS

For a mind-blowing meal, head to **Hammer & Pincers** (☎01509-880735; www.hammerandpincers.co.uk; 5 East Rd, Wymeswold; mains £20-35, 3-course dinner menu £55, with wine £90; ⏲noon-2pm & 6-9.30pm Tue-Sat, to 4pm Sun;), an idyllic gastropub at the edge of the cute village of Wymeswold. Everything is homemade, down to the breads and condiments; seasonal specialities might include cider-cured sea trout, gin-marinated pheasant and rosemary rhubarb sorbet. Don't miss its signature twice-baked cheese soufflé. It's 16 miles north of Leicester via the A46.

Check the website for rates and availability of three luxury en-suite guest rooms built in 2020.

Belgrave Rd is about 1 mile northeast of Leicester's city centre. Follow Belgrave Gate and cross Burleys Flyover; alternatively, numerous buses (£1.60, seven minutes, every five minutes) run from St Margaret's bus station.

Good Earth VEGETARIAN £
(☎0116-262 6260; www.facebook.com/veggiegoodearth; 19 Free Lane; mains £3.50-7.50; ⊙noon-3pm Mon-Fri, to 4pm Sat; ✎) This venerable vegetarian cafe has a daily changing menu of wholesome veggie bakes, huge salads and homemade cakes, and hosts occasional evening events such as live-music gigs. Cash only.

★ **John's House** BRITISH £££
(☎01509-415569; www.johnshouse.co.uk; Stonehurst Farm, 139-141 Loughborough Rd, Mountsorrel; 2-/3-course lunch menus £26/30, 2-/3-/7-course dinner menus £48/55/79; ⊙noon-2pm & 7-9pm Tue-Sat) Chef John Duffin was born here on 16th-century Stonehurst Farm, 8 miles north of Leicester. After working in Michelin-starred restaurants, he returned in 2014 to open his restaurant, and has since gained a Michelin star of his own. Multicourse menus (no à la carte) showcase his imagination in dishes like creamed Porthilly oysters with smoked Mountsorrel eels and foraged lovage.

Still a working farm today, Stonehurst (www.stonehurstfarm.co.uk) also has a fabulous farm shop, a tearoom, a petting farm and a motor museum housing vintage vehicles.

Drinking & Nightlife

Bread & Honey COFFEE
(www.breadnhoneycoffee.com; 15 King St; ⊙7.45am-3pm Mon-Fri; 📶) Beans from single farm estates and co-ops sourced and roasted by London-based Monmouth are brewed at this little bare-boards hole in the wall; the flat whites are the best for miles around. Steaming soups, preservative-free bread, made-from-scratch hot dishes and fantastic cakes (chocolate fudge cake with white-chocolate icing, honey-glazed banana loaf...) are all available, too.

Globe PUB
(www.theglobeleicester.com; 43 Silver St; ⊙11am-10pm Mon-Thu, to 11pm Fri & Sat, to 8pm Sun) In the atmospheric Lanes – a tangle of alleys south of the High St – this old-fashioned pub has fine draught ales and a crowd that rates its drinks by quality rather than quantity.

Entertainment

Cookie LIVE MUSIC
(☎0116-253 1212; www.thecookieleicester.co.uk; 68 High St; ⊙bar 3-11pm Tue & Wed, noon-11pm Thu, to 1am Fri & Sat, to 5pm Sun, concert hours vary) With a capacity of 350 in its brick cellar, this indie venue is a brilliant place to catch live bands and comedy nights in an intimate setting.

Curve Theatre THEATRE
(☎0116-242 3595; www.curveonline.co.uk; 60 Rutland St; backstage tours adult/child £5/4) This sleek artistic space hosts big-name shows and some innovative modern

THE BATTLE OF BOSWORTH

Given a few hundred years, every battlefield ends up simply a field, but the site of the **Battle of Bosworth** (☎01455-290429; www.bosworthbattlefield.org.uk; Ambion Lane, Sutton Cheney; adult/child £8.95/5.75, guided walk £4.50/3; ⊙heritage centre 10.30am-4pm Sat-Wed, grounds dawn-dusk) – where Richard III met his maker in 1485 – is enlivened by an entertaining heritage centre full of skeletons and musket balls; guided walks around the site last 90 minutes. Enthusiasts in period costume re-enact the battle each August.

Although it lasted just a few hours, the Battle of Bosworth marked the end of the Plantagenet dynasty and the start of the Tudor era. This was where the mortally wounded Richard III famously proclaimed: 'A horse, a horse, my kingdom for a horse'. (Actually, he didn't: the quote was invented by that great Tudor propagandist William Shakespeare.)

After visiting the battlefield, head for lunch at the 17th-century coaching inn, **Hercules Revived** (☎01455-699336; www.herculesrevived.co.uk; Sutton Cheney; mains £11-23; ⊙kitchen noon-2.30pm & 6-9pm Mon-Sat, noon-4pm Sun, bar to 11.30pm daily), which serves top-tier gastropub food.

The battlefield is 16 miles southwest of Leicester at Sutton Cheney, off the A447; there's no public transport.

theatre, and has good accessibility for theatregoers who are aurally or visually impaired. Call the ticket office to book backstage tours.

De Montfort Hall LIVE MUSIC
(☎0116-233 3111; www.demontforthall.co.uk; Granville Rd) Orchestras, ballets, musicals and other big song-and-dance performances are all featured on the bill at this huge venue.

Information

Tourist Office (☎0116-299 4444; www.visitleicester.info; 51 Gallowtree Gate; ⏲10am-4pm) Helpful office with reams of city and county info.

Getting There & Away

BUS

Intercity buses operate from **St Margaret's bus station** (Gravel St), north of the city centre. The useful Skylink bus runs to East Midlands Airport (£7.40, 50 minutes, at least hourly, 24 hours) and continues on to Derby (£7.40, 1¼ hours).

National Express services:

Coventry £10, 45 minutes, three daily
London Victoria £18.90, 2¾ hours, every two hours
Nottingham £5, 45 minutes, three daily

TRAIN

East Midlands trains:

Birmingham £26.60, one hour, up to two per hour, some with a change in Derby
Derby £14.30, 20 minutes, three daily
London St Pancras £92, 1¼ hours, up to four per hour

Rutland

Tiny Rutland was merged with Leicestershire in 1974, but in 1997 regained its 'independence' as England's smallest county.

Rutland centres on Rutland Water, a vast artificial reservoir created by the damming of the Gwash Valley in 1976. Covering 4.19 sq miles, the reservoir attracts some 20,000 birds, including ospreys.

Sights & Activities

Rutland Water Nature Reserve NATURE RESERVE
(☎01572-770651; www.lrwt.org.uk/rutland-water; Egleton; adult/child incl parking £6/3.50; ⏲9am-5pm Mar-Oct, to 4pm Nov-Feb) Near Oakham, the Rutland Water Nature Reserve has 31 hides throughout the reserve and a viewing section upstairs in the **Anglian Water Birdwatching Centre**, which has an exhibition on the area's abundant birdlife, including ospreys, long-tailed tits, lesser whitethroats, bullfinches, garden warblers and jays. Look out too for water voles, which thrive here. The reserve's **Lyndon Visitor Centre** (☎01572-737378; Manton; adult/child incl parking £6/3.50; ⏲9am-5pm mid-Mar–early Sep), for which tickets are valid, opens in warmer months.

Rutland Watersports WATER SPORTS
(☎01780-460154; www.anglianwater.co.uk; Whitwell Leisure Park, Bull Brigg Lane, Whitwell; windsurf/kayak/SUP rental per hour from £26/10/12.50; ⏲9am-8pm Wed & Thu, to 7pm Fri-Tue Apr-Oct, shorter hours Nov-Mar) Aquatic activities offered by Rutland Watersports include windsurfing, kayaking and stand-up paddleboarding (SUP). You can hire gear or take lessons.

Rutland Belle CRUISE
(☎01572-787630; www.rutlandwatercruises.com; Bull Brigg Lane, Whitwell; adult/child £10/7; ⏲hourly noon-3pm Mon-Sat, 11am-3pm Sun mid-Jul–Aug, shorter hours Apr–mid-Jul, Sep & Oct) Take a 45-minute round-trip cruise from Whitwell to Normanton on the southern shore of the Rutland reservoir. On some afternoons, it also runs later birdwatching cruises lasting 90 minutes (adult/child £15/10).

WORTH A TRIP

GEORGE WASHINGTON'S ANCESTRAL HOME

An impressively preserved Tudor mansion, **Sulgrave Manor** (☎01295-760205; www.sulgravemanor.org.uk; Manor Rd, Sulgrave; adult/child £7.20/3.60; ⏲11am-5pm Thu, Fri & Sun Apr-Sep) was built by Lawrence Washington in 1539. The Washington family lived here for almost 120 years before Colonel John Washington, the great-grandfather of America's first president, George Washington, sailed to Virginia in 1656.

Sulgrave Manor is 20 miles southwest of Northampton, just off the B4525 near Banbury; you'll need your own wheels to get here.

OFF THE BEATEN TRACK

STOKE BRUERNE & THE GRAND UNION CANAL

Brightly painted barges frequent this charming little village 8.2 miles south of Northampton on the Grand Union Canal, the main thoroughfare of England's canal network. From here, you can follow the waterways all the way to Leicester, Birmingham or London.

A converted corn mill houses the entertaining **Canal Museum** (☎01604-862229; www.canalrivertrust.org.uk; 3 Bridge Rd; adult/child £4.75/3.10; ⏰10am-5pm Apr-Oct, shorter hours Nov-Mar), which charts the history of the canal network and its barge workers, lock-keepers and pit workers. Scale models abound; outside you can see the historic narrowboat *Sculptor*, listed on the National Historic Boat Register.

The **Boat Inn** (☎01604-862428; www.boatinn.co.uk; Bridge Rd; mains restaurant £19-26, bistro £8.50-11.50; ⏰restaurant noon-2pm & 7-9pm Tue-Sat, noon-2.30pm Sun, bar 9am-11pm Mon-Sat, to 10.30pm Sun) is a canal-side landmark. With picnic tables on the quay, this sociable local pub has a relaxed bistro serving pub classics until 9pm, a more formal restaurant with refined dishes such as steaks, and a great range of ales.

Sleeping & Eating

Hambleton Hall HISTORIC HOTEL £££
(☎01572-756991; www.hambletonhall.com; Ketton Rd, Hambleton; s/d/ste incl breakfast from £225/325/650; P 📶 ❄ 🐾) One of England's finest country hotels, rambling former hunting lodge Hambleton Hall, built in 1881, sits on a peninsula jutting out into Rutland Water, 3 miles east of Oakham. Its luxuriant floral rooms and Michelin-starred restaurant (two-course lunch menu £34.50, three-/four-course dinner menus £83/103) are surrounded by gorgeous gardens, which also shelter an outdoor heated swimming pool (May to September).

Otters Fine Foods DELI, CAFE £
(☎01572-756481; www.ottersfinefoods.co.uk; 44 High St, Oakham; dishes £6.50-11; ⏰9am-5.30pm Mon-Sat) A pretty brick terrace with a slate roof houses this Oakham deli. Pick up sandwiches, quiches, soups, salads, cheeses, meats, charcuterie and more for a lakeside picnic, or preorder a hamper. If it's not picnic weather, dine at its in-store cafe.

Getting There & Away

Bus 9 links Oakham with Stamford (£3.60, 30 minutes, hourly Monday to Friday, four services Saturday) via Rutland Water's north shore.

Trains link Oakham with Leicester (£16.20, 30 minutes, every two hours).

DERBYSHIRE

The Derbyshire countryside is painted in two distinct tones: the lush green of rolling valleys criss-crossed by dry-stone walls, and the barren mottled-brown hilltops of the high, wild moorlands. The biggest draw here is the Peak District National Park, which preserves some of England's most evocative scenery, attracting legions of hikers, climbers, cyclists and cave enthusiasts.

Getting There & Around

East Midlands Airport (p466) is the nearest air hub, and Derby is well served by trains, but connecting services to smaller towns are few. In the Peak District, the Derwent Valley Line runs from Derby to Matlock. Edale and Hope lie on the Hope Valley Line from Sheffield to Manchester.

For a comprehensive list of Derbyshire bus routes, visit the 'Transport and Roads' pages at www.derbyshire.gov.uk.

Derby

☎01332 / POP 248,752

Gloriously sited at the southeastern edge of the Derbyshire hills that roll towards the Peak District, Derby is one of the Midlands' most energetic, creative cities. This was one of the crucibles of the Industrial Revolution: almost overnight, a sleepy market town was transformed into a major manufacturing centre, producing everything from silk to bone china and, later, locomotives and Rolls-Royce aircraft engines. The city suffered the ravages of industrial decline in the 1980s, but bounced back with impressive cultural developments and a rejuvenated riverfront.

Sights

Royal Crown Derby Factory MUSEUM, FACTORY
(☎01332-712800; www.royalcrownderby.co.uk; 194 Osmaston Rd; museum & factory tour adult/

child £5/2.50, museum only £2/1; ⌚museum 10am-4pm Mon-Sat, factory tours 11am & 1.30pm Mon-Thu, 11am Fri) Derby's historic potteries still turn out some of the finest bone china in England, from edgy Asian-inspired designs to the kind of stuff your grandma collects. Reservations are essential for factory tours, which last 90 minutes and include a visit to the museum. Royal Crown Derby's china (including seconds and discontinued items) is sold at its on-site shop, and is used as tableware at its elegant tearoom.

Derby Cathedral CATHEDRAL
(☎01332-341201; www.derbycathedral.org; 18 Irongate; cathedral by donation, tower tours adult/child £8/4; ⌚cathedral 8.30am-5.30pm, tower tours vary) Founded in AD 943 and reconstructed in the 18th century, Derby Cathedral's vaulted ceiling towers above a fine collection of medieval tombs, including the opulent grave of the oft-married Bess of Hardwick, who at various times held court at Hardwick Hall, Chatsworth House and Bolsover Castle. Check the website for dates when historians lead tours up 189 steps into the Tudor tower, the second-highest bell tower in the UK.

Peregrine falcons nest in the tower; follow their progress at www.derbyperegrines.blogspot.com.

Derby Museum & Art Gallery MUSEUM
(☎01332-641901; www.derbymuseums.org; The Strand; ⌚10.30am-4.30pm Tue-Sat, noon-4pm Sun) FREE Local history and industry displays include fine ceramics produced by Royal Crown Derby and an archaeology gallery, along with paintings by renowned artist Joseph Wright of Derby (1734–97).

Quad GALLERY, CINEMA
(☎01332-290606; www.derbyquad.co.uk; Market Pl; gallery free, cinema tickets adult/child £9/7; ⌚gallery 11am-5pm Mon-Sat, noon-5pm Sun) A striking modernist cube on Market Pl, Quad contains a futuristic art gallery and an art-house cinema.

Sleeping

Coach House B&B ££
(☎01332-554423; www.coachhousederby.com; 185a Duffield Rd; s/d from £90/105; P W) Surrounded by a rambling cottage garden, this red-brick 1860-built property 1.7 miles north of Derby has four countrified rooms with richly patterned wallpapers in the main house, and three contemporary loft-style rooms in the superbly converted stables. Personalised touches include free homemade brownies. Vegan and gluten-free breakfasts are possible (reserve ahead). Off-street parking is first come, first served.

Farmhouse at Mackworth INN ££
(☎01332-824324; www.thefarmhouseatmackworth.com; 60 Ashbourne Rd; d/f incl breakfast from £90/110; P W) The Farmhouse at Mackworth is just 2.5 miles northwest of Derby in undulating countryside, with the bonus of plentiful free parking. The designer inn's 10 boutique rooms have checked fabrics, rustic timber cladding and chrome fittings, plus amenities including Nespresso machines and fluffy robes. There's a fabulous bar and a restaurant with a Josper charcoal oven (mains £12 to £32).

Cathedral Quarter Hotel HOTEL ££
(☎07710 982690; www.cathedralquarterhotel.com; 16 St Mary's Gate; d/ste incl breakfast from £95/145; W) A bell's peal from the cathedral, this grand Georgian edifice houses a 38-room hotel. The service is as polished as the grand marble staircase, and there's an on-site spa and a fine-dining restaurant (2-/3-course dinner menu £23/26).

★Cow INN £££
(☎01332-824297; www.cowdalbury.com; The Green, Dalbury Lees; d incl breakfast from £135; P W) This whitewashed 19th-century inn 6.5 miles west of Derby has solid oak floors, stone walls and timber-lined ceilings. Its 12 individually styled rooms range from Victorian and art deco to retro vintage, and feature locally handcrafted mattresses and Egyptian cotton sheets. The bar-restaurant's stools are fashioned from milk cans; food is sourced within a 30-mile radius (mains £10.50 to £17.50).

Dishes might include ham hock Scotch egg, pulled barbecue chicken with chestnut pesto, and rhubarb and custard fool with pink-peppercorn shortbread.

Eating

Wonky Table BISTRO ££
(☎01332-295000; www.wonkytable.co.uk; 32 Sadler Gate; small plates £4.50-9, mains £10-18; ⌚5-11pm Fri, noon-4pm & 5-11pm Sat, noon-6pm Sun;) Inside an inviting retro-vintage dining room with exposed-brick walls, Wonky Table has a variety of small tapas-style sharing dishes such as heritage beetroot, orange and goats-cheese terrine or black-pudding-stuffed chicken wings, along with mains like

OFF THE BEATEN TRACK

CONKERS & THE NATIONAL FOREST

The National Forest (www.nationalforest.org) is an ambitious project to generate new areas of sustainable woodland by planting 30 million trees in Leicestershire, Derbyshire and Staffordshire, covering a total area of 51,800 hectares or 200 sq miles. More than 9 million saplings have already taken root. Visitor attractions here include the kid-friendly nature centre, **Conkers** (01283-216633; www.visitconkers.com; Rawdon Rd, Moira; adult/child £7.30/6.30; 10am-6pm Easter-Sep, to 5pm Oct-Easter). There are also several bike trails; bikes can be hired from **Hicks Lodge** (01530-274533; Willesley Wood Side, Moira; bike hire per 3hr adult/child £17.50/15; trails 8am-dusk, bike hire & cafe 9am-5pm Fri-Wed, to 9pm Thu mid-Feb–Oct, 10am-4pm Mon-Wed & Fri, 9am-9pm Thu, to 5pm Sat & Sun Nov–mid-Feb).

If you fancy overnighting, the **National Forest YHA** (0845 371 9672; www.yha.org.uk; 48 Bath Lane, Moira; dm/d/f from £16/58/77;) has impressive eco features (such as rainwater harvesting and solar biomass boiler usage), 23 spotless en-suite rooms, bike storage, and a restaurant serving local produce and organic wines. It's 300m west of Conkers along Bath Lane.

halloumi, lentil and green-bean curry or pork loin with pickled plums.

Darleys BRITISH £££

(01332-364987; www.darleys.com; Waterfront, Darley Abbey Mill; 2-/3-course menus lunch £25/29.50, dinner £36/40; noon-2pm & 6-8.30pm Tue-Fri, 12.30-2.30pm & 7-9pm Sat, noon-4pm Sun;) Two miles north of the city centre, this upmarket restaurant has a gorgeous setting in a bright converted mill overlooking the river, with a beautiful waterside terrace. It serves classy fare such as sea trout with cockle cream, curry oil and a samphire pakora. Vegetarian and vegan menus are available at all times.

Drinking & Nightlife

★**Old Bell Hotel** PUB

(www.bellhotelderby.co.uk; 51 Sadler Gate; noon-11pm Sun-Thu, to 1.30am Fri & Sat) Dating from 1650 and hosting Bonnie Prince Charlie's soldiers in 1745, this history-steeped black-and-white inn was restored by local entrepreneur Paul Hurst, retaining original features, antiques and photographs. There's a central courtyard and, allegedly, several ghosts. Real-ale tasting flights, snacks and lunches are served in its Tavern and Tudor bars; the Belfry Bar has an upmarket steakhouse.

Tap PUB

(www.brewerytap-dbc.co.uk; 1 Derwent St; 5-11pm Tue & Wed, noon-11pm Thu & Sun, to midnight Fri & Sat) The Tap serves its own brews, guest ales and over 80 craft beers from around the world in elegant Victorian surrounds.

Shopping

Bennetts DEPARTMENT STORE

(www.bennettsofderby.co.uk; 8 Irongate) Founded as an ironmongers in 1734, Bennetts is the world's oldest department store. It was closed at the time of research while major renovations were carried out under new owners, and will showcase new brands, along with premium food and drinks at its two restaurants and bar – check the website for reopening details.

Information

Tourist Office (01332-643411; www.visitderby.co.uk; Market Pl; 9.30am-8pm Mon-Sat) Under the Assembly Rooms in the main square.

Getting There & Away

AIR

East Midlands Airport (EMA; 0808 169 7032; www.eastmidlandsairport.com), 11.5 miles southeast of Derby, is served by regular Skylink buses (£4.70, 40 minutes, at least hourly). Buses operate 24 hours.

BUS

Local and long-distance buses run from Derby's bus station, immediately east of the Westfield shopping mall. High Peak has buses every two hours between Derby and Buxton (£6.60, 1¾ hours), via Matlock (£4.60, 45 minutes) and Bakewell (£5.20, 1¼ hours). One bus continues to Manchester (£8, 2¼ hours).

Other services:

Leicester Skylink; £7.40, 1¼ hours, one to two hourly

Nottingham Red Arrow; £5.40, 35 minutes, at least three per hour

TRAIN

The train station is about half a mile southeast of the city centre on Railway Tce.

Birmingham £20.40, 40 minutes, two per hour

Leeds £42.70, 1½ hours, hourly

London St Pancras £68, 1½ hours, up to two hourly

Nottingham £8, 30 minutes, two per hour

Ashbourne

☎01335 / POP 8377

Perched at the southern edge of the Peak District National Park, Ashbourne is a pretty patchwork of steeply slanting stone streets lined with cafes, pubs and antique shops.

Activities

Ashbourne Cycle Hire Centre CYCLING
(☎01335-343156; www.peakdistrict.gov.uk; Mapleton Rd; per half/full day standard bike from £14/17, electric bike £32/36; ⏰9.30am-5pm Mar-Oct, shorter hours Nov-Feb) Situated 1km northwest of town, the Cycle Hire Centre is right on the Tissington Trail, at the end of a huge and atmospheric old railway tunnel leading under Ashbourne. Helmets, puncture-repair kits and maps are included. You can also rent mountain bikes, children's bikes, bikes with baby seats, trailers for buggies and tandems.

Sleeping & Eating

Compton House B&B ££
(☎01335-343100; www.comptonhouse.co.uk; 27-31 Compton St; s/d from £55/75; P 📶) Fresh, clean, frilly rooms, a warm welcome and a central location make this the pick of Ashbourne's B&Bs. There's a minimum two-night stay on weekends.

Flower Cafe CAFE £
(www.facebook.com/theflowercafeashbourne; 5 Market Pl; mains £5-12.50; ⏰8.30am-4pm Tue-Sun; 🌿) Soups such as parsnip, chorizo and chestnut, broccoli and Stilton, and spicy bean and lentil are a year-round speciality at this cute-as-a-button cafe where everything is homemade. In summer it also cooks delicious quiches (cheesy leek and mushroom; bacon, brie and cranberry...). Gluten-free and dairy-free dishes are plentiful.

Information

Tourist Office (☎01335-343666; www.visitpeakdistrict.com; Market Pl; ⏰10am-2pm Mon, Tue, Thu & Fri, 9am-1pm Wed) Inside the town hall.

Getting There & Away

Bus services include the following.

Buxton High Peak routes 441 and 442; £4.50, 1¼ hours, hourly Monday to Saturday

Derby Trent Barton Swift; £4.50, 40 minutes, hourly Monday to Saturday, five Sunday

Matlock Bath

☎01629 / POP 753

Matlock Bath (not to be confused with the larger, workaday town of Matlock, 2 miles north) looks like a British seaside resort that somehow lost its way and ended up at the foot of the Peak District National Park. Following the River Derwent through a sheer-walled gorge, the main promenade is lined with amusement arcades, tearooms, fish-and-chip shops, pubs and shops catering to the motorcyclists who congregate here on summer weekends. Outside summer, the town is considerably quieter. The area's industrial history is evident in the many surrounding mills, which can be visited.

Sights

Peak District Lead Mining Museum MUSEUM
(☎01629-583834; www.peakdistrictleadminingmuseum.co.uk; The Grand Pavilion, South Pde; museum adult/child £5.50/3.50, mine £6.50/4, combined ticket £10/6; ⏰11am-3.45pm Wed, Sat & Sun Apr-Oct, Sat & Sun Nov-Mar; 👪) An educational introduction to the mining history of Matlock is provided by this enthusiast-run museum set in an old Victorian dance hall. Kids can wriggle through its maze of tunnels and shafts while adults browse historical displays. After the mine tour, you can go into the workings of the **Temple Mine** and pan for 'gold' (well, shiny minerals). Reservations for mine tours are recommended, as are sturdy shoes, as the mine can be muddy.

Cromford Mill MUSEUM
(☎01629-823256; www.cromfordmills.org.uk; Mill Lane, Cromford; adult/child £10/free; ⏰10am-5pm) Founded in the 1770s by Richard Arkwright, the Cromford Mill was the first modern factory, producing cotton on automated machines powered by a series of waterwheels along the River Derwent. This prototype inspired a succession of mills, ushering in the industrial age. It's 1 mile south of Matlock Bath (a 20-minute walk), or you can take the train one stop to Cromford (£2.60, five minutes, hourly).

Caudwell's Mill MUSEUM

(☎01629-734374; www.caudwellsmill.co.uk; Rowsley; ⏰9am-5pm Mon-Sat, 10am-4pm Sun) FREE This chugging, grinding, water-powered mill still produces flour the old-fashioned way – 20 different types are for sale, along with six different oat products, and yeast and biscuits. Also here is a tearoom. You can get to Rowsley directly from Matlock Bath by bus (£3.60, 20 minutes, hourly) on the route to Bakewell.

At the time of research the upper floors were being restored, but it's free to walk around the lower levels.

Masson Mills MUSEUM

(☎01629-581001; www.massonmills.co.uk; Derby Rd; adult/child £5/free; ⏰10am-5.30pm Mon-Sat, to 5pm Sun Jan-Nov) A museum tells the story of the valley's textile mills at this large complex 1 mile south of Matlock Bath. The attached shopping village is full of outlet stores for big clothing brands.

Activities

Heights of Abraham AMUSEMENT PARK

(☎01629-582365; www.heightsofabraham.com; Dale Rd; adult/child £19/13; ⏰10am-5pm mid-Mar–early Nov; 👪) A spectacular cable-car ride (accessible with admission ticket only) from the bottom of the gorge brings you to this hilltop leisure park – its cave and mine tours and fossil exhibitions are a winner with kids. The cave is a constant 10°C, so bring a jacket.

Sleeping

Grouse & Claret INN ££

(☎01629-733233; www.grouseclaretpub.co.uk; Station Rd, Rowsley; d incl breakfast from £92; P📶) Located in the village of Rowsley, 6.2 miles northwest of Matlock Bath, this 18th-century stone inn has eight comfy, country-style wallpapered rooms, a restaurant specialising in spit-roasted chicken, and a huge, sunny beer garden with umbrella-shaded tables.

Hodgkinson's Hotel & Restaurant HOTEL ££

(☎01629-582170; www.hodgkinsons-hotel.co.uk; 150 South Pde; s/d/f incl breakfast from £60/110/155; P📶) The eight rooms at this central Grade II–listed Victorian beauty conjure up Matlock's golden age with antique furnishings, cast-iron fireplaces, flowery wallpaper, handmade soaps and goose-down duvets. The restaurant (open Tuesday to Saturday evenings; two-/three-course menus £28/32) has just 18 seats, so bookings are advised. From April to September there's a minimum two-night stay on weekends.

Shopping

Scarthin Books BOOKS

(www.scarthinbooks.com; The Promenade, Cromford; ⏰9am-6pm Mon-Sat, 10am-6pm Sun) More than 100,000 new and secondhand books cram into 12 rooms in this biblio-paradise, which hosts regular literary events and has a vegetarian cafe (dishes £3 to £6.50) serving organic pizza, soups, wraps, pies and burritos.

Information

Tourist Office (☎01629-583834; www.visitpeakdistrict.com; The Grand Pavilion, South Pde; ⏰10am-5pm Apr-Sep, 11am-3pm Oct-Mar) At the Peak District Lead Mining Museum (p467).

Getting There & Away

Matlock is a hub for buses around the Peak District.

Bakewell High Peak; £3.50, 35 minutes, every two hours

Derby High Peak; £4.60, 40 minutes, every two hours

Trains run hourly between Matlock Bath and Derby (£6.70, 35 minutes, every two hours).

Chesterfield

☎01246 / POP 103,800

The eastern gateway to the Peaks, Chesterfield is a busy service centre that's famed for the twisted spire atop its church.

Nearby is the magnificent Elizabethan mansion Hardwick Hall.

Sights

Hardwick Hall HISTORIC BUILDING

(NT; ☎01246-850430; www.nationaltrust.org.uk; Doe Lea; house & garden adult/child £13.95/7, garden only £8/4, incl Hardwick Old Hall £20.75/11.10; ⏰house 11am-5pm Wed-Sun mid-Feb–Oct, to 3pm Wed-Sun Nov–mid-Feb, garden 10am-5pm daily year-round) One of the most complete Elizabethan mansions in the country, Hardwick Hall was designed by eminent architect Robert Smythson. The building featured all the latest mod-cons of the time, including fully glazed windows. The atmospheric interiors are decked out with magnificent

DON'T MISS

KEDLESTON HALL

Sitting pretty in vast landscaped grounds, neoclassical **Kedleston Hall** (NT; ☎01332-842191; www.nationaltrust.org.uk; Kedleston Rd, Quarndon; house & gardens adult/child £13.60/6.80, garden only £10/5; ⊙house noon-5pm Sat-Thu Feb-Oct, garden 10am-5pm Feb-Oct, to 4pm Nov-Jan) is a must for fans of stately homes. Entering the house through a grand portico, you'll reach the breathtaking Marble Hall with massive alabaster columns and statues of Greek deities.

Kedleston Hall is 5 miles northwest of Derby, off the A52. Bus 114 between Derby and Ashbourne (£3.60, 25 minutes, six daily Monday to Saturday) stops at the gates when the hall is open.

The Curzon family has lived here since the 12th century, but the current wonder was built by Sir Nathaniel Curzon in 1758. Meanwhile, the poor old peasants in Kedleston village had their humble dwellings moved a mile down the road, as they interfered with the view. Ah, the good old days...

Highlights include Indian treasures amassed by Viceroy George Curzon, and a domed, circular saloon modelled on the Pantheon in Rome, as well as 18th-century-style pleasure gardens.

tapestries and oil paintings of forgotten dignitaries.

Hardwick Hall is 10 miles southeast of Chesterfield, just off the M1; it's best reached by your own wheels.

The hall was home to the 16th-century's second-most powerful woman, Elizabeth, Countess of Shrewsbury (known to all as Bess of Hardwick), who amassed a staggering fortune by marrying wealthy noblemen with one foot in the grave. Hardwick Hall was constructed using her inheritance from husband number four, who shuffled off this mortal coil in 1590.

Set aside time to explore the formal gardens or the longer walking trails of Hardwick Park.

Next door to the manor are the ruins of Bess' first house, **Hardwick Old Hall**, which is undergoing renovations until 2022.

St Mary & All Saints Church CHURCH
(☎01246-206506; www.crookedspire.org; Church Way; spire tours adult/child £6/4; ⊙church 9am-4pm Mon-Sat) Chesterfield is worth a visit to see the astonishing crooked spire that rises atop St Mary & All Saints Church. Dating from 1360, the 68m-high spire is twisted in a right-handed corkscrew that leans several metres southwest. It's the result of the lead casing on the south-facing side having buckled in the sun. Spire tours lasting 45 minutes take you up into the tower. Tours typically take place at 2.30pm on Saturdays; call to confirm.

ℹ Information

Tourist Office (☎01246-345777; www.visitpeakdistrict.com; Rykneld Sq; ⊙9.30am-5pm Mon-Fri) Directly opposite St Mary & All Saints Church.

ℹ Getting There & Away

BUS

From Chesterfield coach station on Beetwell St, buses 170 and X70 serve Bakewell (£3.60, 45 minutes, hourly Monday to Saturday).

TRAIN

Chesterfield lies on the main rail line between Nottingham (£11.70, 35 minutes, up to three hourly) and Derby (£12.70, 20 minutes, up to three hourly), which continues to Sheffield (£4.60, 20 minutes). The station is just east of the centre.

PEAK DISTRICT

Rolling across the Pennines' southernmost hills is the glorious Peak District National Park. Ancient stone villages are folded into creases in the landscape, and the hillsides are littered with stately homes and rocky outcrops. The Dark Peak is dominated by exposed moorland and gritstone 'edges', while to the south, the White Peak is made up of the limestone dales.

No one knows how the Peak District got its name – certainly not from the landscape, which has hills and valleys, gorges and lakes, wild moorland and gritstone escarpments,

Peak District National Park

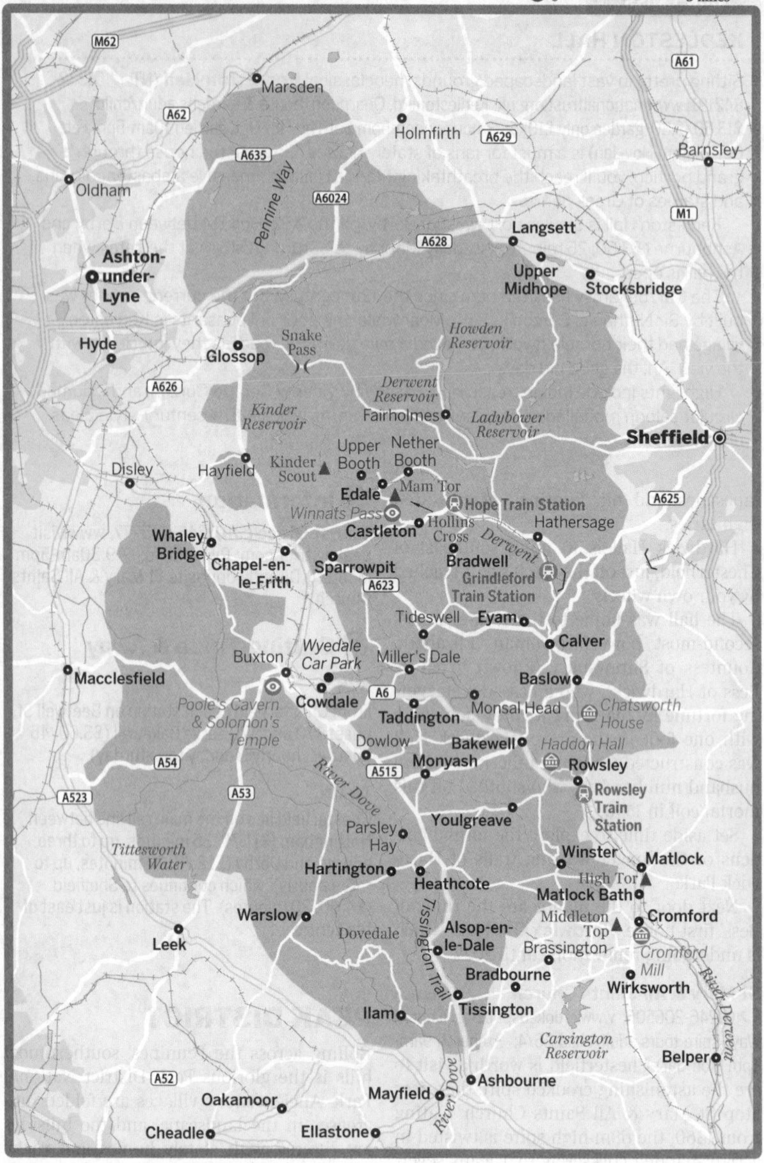

but no peaks. The most popular theory is that the region was named for the Pecsaetan, the Anglo-Saxon tribe who once populated this part of England.

Founded in 1951, the Peak District was England's first national park and is Europe's busiest. But even at peak times, there are 555 sq miles of open English countryside in which to find solitude.

Activities

Walking

The Peak District is one of the most popular walking areas in England, with awe-inspiring vistas of hills, dales and sky that attract legions of hikers in summer. The White Peak is perfect for leisurely strolls, which can start from pretty much anywhere. Be sure to close gates behind you as you go. When exploring the rugged territory of the Dark Peak, make sure your boots are waterproof and beware of slipping into rivulets and marshes.

The Peak's most famous walking trail is the **Pennine Way**, which runs north from Edale for 268 miles, finishing in the Scottish Borders. If you don't have three weeks to spare, you can reach the pretty town of Hebden Bridge in Yorkshire comfortably in three days.

The 46-mile **Limestone Way** winds through the Derbyshire countryside from Castleton to Rocester in Staffordshire, following footpaths, tracks and quiet lanes. Many people walk the 26-mile section between Castleton and Matlock in one long, tiring day, but two days is better. Tourist offices have a detailed leaflet.

Other popular routes include the **High Peak Trail**, the **Tissington Trail** and the **Monsal Trail & Tunnels**. Numerous short walks are available.

Cycling

Plunging dales and soaring scarps provide a perfect testing ground for cyclists, and local tourist offices are piled high with cycling maps and trail guides. For easy traffic-free riding, head for the 17-mile **High Peak Trail**, which follows the old railway line from Cromford, near Matlock Bath, to Dowlow near Buxton. The trail winds through beautiful hills and farmland to Parsley Hay, where the **Tissington Trail**, part of NCN Route 68, heads south for 13 miles to Ashbourne. Trails are off-road on dedicated cycle paths, suitable for road bikes.

Mirroring the Pennine Way, the **Pennine Bridleway** is another top spot to put your calves through their paces. Around 120 miles of trails have been created between Middleton Top and the South Pennines, and the route is suitable for horse riders, cyclists and walkers. You could also follow the **Pennine Cycleway** (NCN Route 68) from Derby to Buxton and beyond. Other popular routes include the **Limestone Way**, running south from Castleton to Staffordshire, and the **Monsal Trail & Tunnels** between Bakewall and Wyedale, near Buxton.

The **Peak District National Park Authority** (☎01629-816200; www.peakdistrict.gov.uk) operates cycle-hire centres at Ashbourne (p467), Derwent Reservoirs (p476) and **Parsley Hay** (☎01298-84493; www.peakdistrict.gov.uk; Parsley Hay; per half/full day standard bike £14/17, electric bike £32/36; ⏲10am-4.30pm mid-Feb–early Nov). You can hire a bike from one location and drop it off at another for no extra charge.

Caving & Climbing

The limestone sections of the Peak District are riddled with caves and caverns, including a series of 'showcaves' in Castleton, Buxton and Matlock Bath. The website www.peakdistrictcaving.info, run by the Derbyshire Caving Association, has comprehensive information. **Peaks & Paddles** (☎07896 912871; www.peaksandpaddles.org; canoeing & caving from £55, abseiling from £25; ⏲by reservation) runs caving trips, along with canoeing and abseiling expeditions.

England's top mountaineers train in this area, which offers rigorous technical climbing on a series of limestone gorges, exposed tors (crags) and gritstone 'edges' that extend south into the Staffordshire Moorlands. Gritstone climbing in the Peak District is predominantly on old-school trad routes, requiring a decent rack of friends, nuts and hexes. Bolted sport routes are found on several limestone crags in the Peak District, but many use ancient pieces of gear and most require additional protection. Contact the British Mountaineering Council (www.thebmc.co.uk) for advice and details of local resources.

ℹ Getting There & Away

Buses run from regional centres such as Sheffield and Derby to destinations across the Peak District. Be aware that many services close down completely in winter. Bakewell and Matlock (not Matlock Bath) are the two main hubs – from these you can get anywhere in the Peak District. Timetables are available from all tourist offices as well as Traveline (p406). Trains run to Matlock Bath, Buxton, Edale and several other towns and villages.

Bakewell

☎01629 / POP 3950

The second-largest town in the Peak District, charming Bakewell is a great base for exploring the limestone dales of the White Peak. Filled with storybook stone buildings, the town is ringed by famous walking trails and stately homes, but it's probably best known for its famous Bakewell pudding, a pastry shell filled with jam and a custard-like mixture of eggs, butter, sugar and almonds, invented here in 1820.

Sights

★Chatsworth House HISTORIC BUILDING
(☎01246-565300; www.chatsworth.org; house & gardens adult/child £23/12.50, gardens only £14/7.50, playground £7, park free; ⏰9.30am-5.30pm late May-early Sep, shorter hours mid-Mar-late May & early Sep-early Jan) Known as the 'Palace of the Peak', this vast edifice 3 miles northeast of Bakewell has been occupied by the earls and dukes of Devonshire for centuries. Inside, the lavish apartments and mural-painted staterooms are packed with priceless paintings and period furniture. The house sits in 25 sq miles of grounds and ornamental gardens, some landscaped by Lancelot 'Capability' Brown. Kids will love the farmyard adventure playground.

From Bakewell, take bus 218 (£2.70, 15 minutes, half-hourly).

The manor was founded in 1552 by the formidable Bess of Hardwick and her second husband, William Cavendish, who earned grace and favour by helping Henry VIII dissolve the English monasteries. Mary, Queen of Scots was imprisoned at Chatsworth on the orders of Elizabeth I in 1569.

Look out for the portraits of the current generation of Devonshires by Lucian Freud.

Also on the estate is one of the country's premier farm shops (p474) and an attached cafe.

Walkers can take footpaths through Chatsworth park via the mock-Venetian village of Edensor (en-sor), while cyclists can pedal via Pilsley.

Haddon Hall HISTORIC BUILDING
(☎01629-812855; www.haddonhall.co.uk; Haddon Rd; adult/child £18.50/free; ⏰10.30am-5pm daily late Mar-Sep, Fri-Mon Oct, to 4pm daily Dec) With stone turrets, time-worn timbers and walled gardens, Haddon Hall, 2 miles southeast of Bakewell on the A6, looks exactly like a medieval manor house should. Founded in the 12th century, it was expanded and remodelled throughout medieval times but lay dormant from 1700 until its restoration in the 1920s. Take the High Peak bus from Bakewell (£2.50, 10 minutes, every two hours) or walk along the footpath through the fields, mostly on the east side of the river.

Spared from the more florid excesses of the Victorian period, Haddon Hall has been used as the location for numerous period blockbusters (such as 2005's *Pride and Prejudice* and 1998's *Elizabeth*).

Thornbridge Brewery BREWERY
(☎01629-815994; www.thornbridgebrewery.com; Buxton Rd; tours £12.50; ⏰tours by reservation 3pm Wed, Thu & Fri, shop 9am-4.30pm Mon-Fri) Brews by this riverside brewery include bottled varieties (such as a fruity strawberry-blonde ale, I Love You Will You Marry Me), keg beers (Vienna-style lager Kill Your Darlings) and cask ales (including its hoppy Brother Rabbit). Tours lasting 1½ hours take you behind the scenes and include tastings in Thornbridge glasses, which you get to keep afterwards. Under-five-year-olds aren't permitted on tours. It's half a mile from the centre of Bakewell on the northwestern edge of town.

Old House Museum MUSEUM
(☎01629-813642; www.oldhousemuseum.org.uk; Cunningham Pl; adult/child £5/2.50; ⏰10.30am-4pm Wed-Sat late Mar-early Nov) Bakewell's local-history museum occupies a time-worn stone house that was built as a tax collector's premises during Henry VIII's rule and was expanded in the Elizabethan era, before being split into tiny mill workers' cottages during the Industrial Revolution. Check out the Tudor toilet and the displays on wattle and daub, a traditional technique for building walls using woven twigs and cow dung.

Activities

The scenic **Monsal Trail** follows the path of a disused railway line from Combs Viaduct on the outskirts of Bakewell to Topley Pike in Wye Dale (3 miles east of Buxton), including a number of reopened old railway tunnels, covering 8.5 miles in all.

For a rewarding shorter walk, follow the Monsal Trail for 3 miles to the dramatic viewpoint at Monsal Head, where you can pause for refreshment at the Monsal Head Hotel (p474), which serves real ales and excellent Modern British cuisine. With more time, continue to **Miller's Dale**, where viaducts give a spectacular vista across the steep-sided valley. The tourist offices at Bakewell and Buxton have full details.

Other walking routes go to the stately homes of Haddon Hall and Chatsworth House.

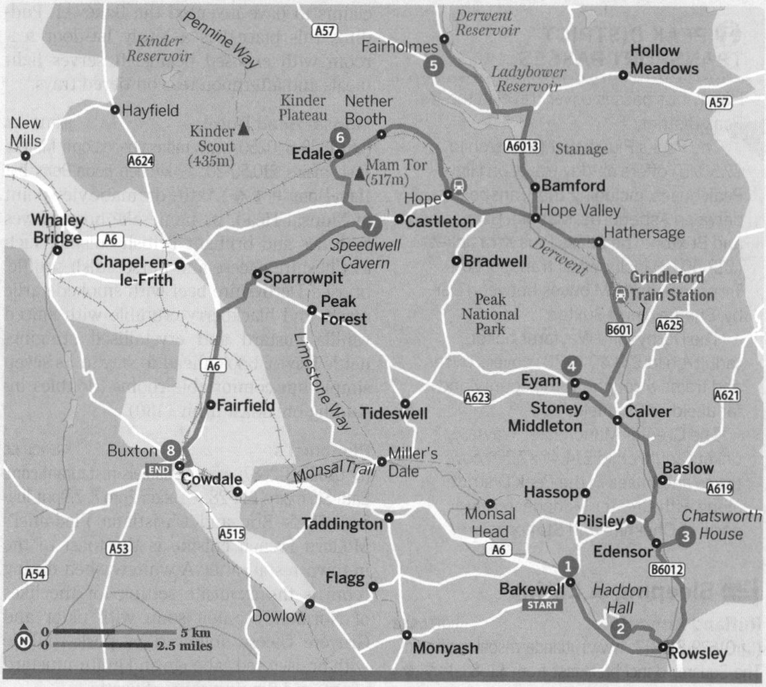

Driving Tour Peak District

START BAKEWELL
END BUXTON
LENGTH 52 MILES; ONE TO TWO DAYS

Although you can drive this route in just a few hours, there's a lot to see and even more to do, so pack your hiking boots and consider breaking your journey overnight.

Fuel up at pretty ① **Bakewell** (p471), famed for its distinctive pudding. Head south on the A6 for 3.5 miles to Rowsley. Turn left on winding Church Lane for 2 miles to visit medieval manor ② **Haddon Hall**.

Return to Rowsley, turn left on the A6 and left on the B6012 – follow it for 2.9 miles before turning right to reach the 'Palace of the Peak', ③ **Chatsworth House**.

Back on the B6012, turn right to join the A619. At Baslow, home to the country hotel and Michelin-starred restaurant Fischer's Baslow Hall, turn left at the roundabout and travel along the A623 for 3.4 miles to the turn-off for ④ **Eyam** (p475). Drive up the hill to its quaint museum, where you can learn about the town's plague history. There's fantastic walking here.

Continue up the hill. Turn right on Edge Rd, then right on Sir William Hill Rd and left on the B601 at Grindleford. Continue to Hathersage and turn left on the A6187 to Hope Valley. Turn right on the A6013, passing Ladybower Reservoir, to reach the ⑤ **Derwent Dam Museum** (p476). Learn about the Dambusters squadron's 'bouncing bombs' tests during WWII.

It's 5.8 miles back to the Hope Valley turn-off. Turn right onto Hathersage Rd, then right on Edale Rd. Follow the valley to stretch your legs at prime walking spot ⑥ **Edale** (p476). Scenery peaks as you climb the steep hill near 517m-high Mam Tor to Winnats Rd. Follow the spectacular former coral-reef canyon Winnats Pass to ⑦ **Speedwell Cavern** (p478), half a mile west of charming Castleton.

From Speedwell Cavern, head west along Arthurs Way onto Winnats Rd. Turning right on the A623 brings you to the riot of Victoriana in former spa town ⑧ **Buxton** (p478).

PEAK DISTRICT TRANSPORT PASSES

Handy bus passes cover travel in the Peak District.

The Peaks Plus ticket (adult/child £7.50/5) offers all-day travel on High Peak buses, including the Transpeak between Ashbourne, Matlock Bath and Buxton. The Peaks Plus Xtra ticket (£12.50/8) includes all transport on Transpeak and TM buses between Derby, Sheffield and Buxton.

The Derbyshire Wayfarer ticket (adult/child £13.40/6.70) covers buses and trains throughout the county and as far afield as Sheffield.

The Greater Manchester Wayfarer ticket (adult/child £14.40/7.20) covers trains and buses in the Peak District, along with Greater Manchester and parts of Cheshire and Staffordshire.

Sleeping & Eating

Rutland Arms Hotel HOTEL £££

(01629-812812; www.rutlandarmsbakewell.co.uk; The Square; d incl breakfast from £168; P) Jane Austen is said to have stayed in room 2 of this aristocratic, 1804-built stone coaching inn while working on *Pride and Prejudice*. Its 33 rooms are in the main house and adjacent courtyard building; higher-priced rooms have lots of Victorian flourishes. Upmarket British classics (£14 to £23) such as pheasant and parsnip pie are served at its restaurant.

★Chatsworth Estate Farm Shop Cafe CAFE, DELI £

(www.chatsworth.org; Pilsley; dishes £6.50-15.50; cafe 9am-5pm Mon-Sat, 10am-5pm Sun, shop 9am-6pm Mon-Sat, 11am-5pm Sun;) One of the finest places to eat in the Peak District, this bucolic cafe serves hearty breakfasts (eggs Benedict with Chatsworth-cured bacon or salmon, strawberry-and-honey Chatsworth yoghurt with muesli) until 11.30am, segueing to lunches (steak-and-kidney suet pudding, traditional roasts) until 3pm, and an afternoon menu. Over half the products at its adjacent farm shop are produced on the estate.

Old Original Bakewell Pudding Shop BAKERY, CAFE £

(www.bakewellpuddingshop.co.uk; The Square; dishes £8-13; 9am-5pm) One of those that claims to have invented the Bakewell Pudding, this place has a lovely 1st-floor tearoom with exposed beams. It serves light meals and afternoon teas on tiered trays.

Monsal Head Hotel BRITISH ££

(01629-640250; www.monsalhead.com; Monsal Trail; mains £10.50-20; kitchen noon-9pm, bar 11am-11pm; P) At the dramatic viewpoint of Monsal Head, its namesake hotel serves real ales and brilliant British cuisine, such as Cheshire cheese and horseradish soufflé, braised Derbyshire beef with smoked-garlic mash, and blackberry crumble with spiced vanilla custard and crystallised stinging-nettle leaves. Book ahead to stay in its seven simple but comfortable rooms (doubles including breakfast from £130).

Piedaniel's FRENCH ££

(01629-812687; www.piedaniels-restaurant.com; Bath St; mains £14-28; noon-2pm & 7-9pm Tue-Sat) Chefs Eric and Christiana Piedaniel's Modern French cuisine is the toast of the in-town restaurants. A whitewashed dining room is the exquisite setting for the likes of Normandy onion soup with cider and Gruyère cheese, followed by pork roulade with braised red cabbage and grain-mustard sauce, and flaming crêpes Suzette.

★Fischer's Baslow Hall GASTRONOMY £££

(01246-583259; www.fischers-baslowhall.co.uk; 259 Calver Rd, Baslow; 2-/3-course lunch menus £38/46.50, 3-course/tasting dinner menus £79.50/90; noon-1.30pm & 7-9pm;) This 1907-built manor house, 4 miles northeast of Bakewell, has a magnificent dining room showcasing British produce (Derbyshire lamb, Yorkshire game, Cornish crab...) along with vegetables from its kitchen garden. Six sumptuous floral bedrooms are in the main house, with another five in the adjacent garden house (doubles including breakfast from £287, including a three-course dinner menu from £444).

Shopping

Lambton Larder FOOD & DRINKS

(www.thelambtonlarder.com; Rutland Sq; 9am-2pm Mon-Thu, to 4pm Fri & Sat) Peak District–roasted Full Moon coffee, Matlock Bath honey, Bakewell puddings, and locally cured meats, chutneys, jams and pies fill the shelves of this enticing deli, along with over 50 British cheeses, including artisan varieties made nearby at the Hope Valley's Cow Close Farm. You can also pick up sandwiches, wraps and soups for a riverside picnic (hampers available too).

Bakewell Market MARKET
(Granby Rd; ⏲9am-2.30pm Mon) Local producers including Hope Valley Ice Cream, Peak Ales, Bittersweet Chocolates, Brock & Morten (cold-pressed oils) and Caudwell Mill (flour) are among the 160-plus regular stalls at Bakewell's lively Monday market.

Information

Tourist Office (☎01629-816558; www.visitpeakdistrict.com; Bridge St; ⏲10.30am-4pm) In the old Market Hall, with a photography gallery on the mezzanine.

Getting There & Away

Bakewell lies on the High Peak bus route. Buses run every two hours to Buxton (£5.10, 30 minutes), Derby (£6.60, 1¼ hours) and Matlock Bath (£3.50, 35 minutes). One service a day continues to Manchester (£8, 1¾ hours).

Other services:

Castleton Bus 173; £3.40, 50 minutes, four per day Monday to Saturday, via Tideswell (£3.10, 30 minutes)

Chesterfield Buses 170 and X70; £3.60, 45 minutes, hourly Monday to Saturday

Eyam

☎01433 / POP 969

Quaint little Eyam (ee-em), a former lead-mining village, has a poignant history that's all the more resonant in light of the global Covid-19 pandemic. In 1665 the town was infected by the dreaded Black Death plague, carried here by fleas on a consignment of cloth from London, and the village rector, William Mompesson, convinced villagers to quarantine themselves. Some 270 of Eyam's 800 inhabitants succumbed, while surrounding villages remained relatively unscathed. The village's heartbreaking yet uplifting story is beautifully told in the 2001 novel *Year of Wonders: A Novel of the Plague* by Geraldine Brooks.

Today, Eyam's sloping streets of old cottages backed by rows of green hills are delightful to wander.

Sights

Eyam Parish Church CHURCH
(St Lawrence's Church; www.eyamchurch.org; Church St; by donation; ⏲9am-6pm Easter-Sep, to 4pm Oct-Easter) Many victims of the village's 1665 Black Death plague outbreak were buried at Eyam's church, whose history dates back to Saxon times. You can view stained-glass panels and moving displays telling the story of the outbreak. The churchyard contains a cross carved in the 8th century.

Eyam Museum MUSEUM
(☎01433-631371; www.eyam-museum.org.uk; Hawkhill Rd; adult/child £3/2.50; ⏲10am-4pm Tue-Sun Easter-Oct) Vivid displays on the Eyam plague are the centrepiece of the engaging town museum, alongside exhibits on the village's history of lead mining and silk weaving.

Eyam Hall HISTORIC BUILDING
(☎01433-630080; www.eyamhall.net; Main Rd; craft centre free, house & garden adult/child £12/6; ⏲craft centre 10am-4.30pm Wed-Sun year-round, house & garden 11am-3pm Wed, Thu & Sun mid-Feb–late Apr) Surrounded by a traditional English walled garden, this solid-looking 17th-century manor house with stone windows and door frames has a craft centre, a bookshop, a craft-beer shop and a superb bistro (mains £12.50 to £18) in its grounds.

Sleeping & Eating

Miner's Arms PUB ££
(☎01433-630853; www.theminersarmseyam.co.uk; Water Lane; s/d from £45/70; 📶) Although

> **THE CATHEDRAL OF THE PEAK**
>
> Dominating the former lead-mining village of Tideswell, the massive parish church of St John the Baptist – aka the **Cathedral of the Peak** (☎01298-871317; www.tideswellchurch.org; Commercial Rd, Tideswell; ⏲8.30am-5.30pm) – has stood here virtually unchanged since the 14th century. Look out for the wooden panels inscribed with the Ten Commandments and the grand 14th-century tomb of local landowner Thurston de Bower, depicted in full medieval armour. It's 8 miles east of Buxton, linked by bus 65 (£4.10, 30 minutes, every two hours Monday to Saturday).
>
> Bus 173 links Tideswell with Bakewell (£3.10, 20 minutes, seven per day Monday to Saturday). Four services a day Monday to Saturday continue from Tideswell to Castleton (£3, 20 minutes).

its age isn't immediately obvious, this traditional village inn was built shortly before the Black Death hit Eyam in 1665. Inside you'll find beamed ceilings, affable staff, a blazing open fire, comfy en-suite rooms and good-value pub food (mains £11 to £15.50).

Village Green CAFE £
(☎01433-631293; www.cafevillagegreen.com; The Square; dishes £3-8; ⏰9am-4pm Thu-Mon; 📶) On the village square, with tables on the cobblestones outside, this sweet cafe has homemade soups, a mouthwatering array of cakes and slices (some gluten-free), and decent coffee.

Getting There & Away

Bus services include the following.

Bakewell Bus 275; £3.90, 25 minutes, five per day Monday to Saturday

Buxton Bus 65; £4.70, 40 minutes, every two hours Monday to Saturday, three Sunday

Sheffield Bus 65; £6.10, one hour, every two hours Monday to Saturday, three Sunday

Derwent Reservoirs

North of the Hope Valley, the upper reaches of the Derwent Valley were flooded between 1916 and 1935 to create three huge reservoirs – the Ladybower, Derwent and Howden Reservoirs – to supply Sheffield, Leicester, Nottingham and Derby with water. These constructed lakes soon proved their worth – the Dambusters (Royal Air Force Squadron No 617) carried out practice runs over Derwent Reservoir before unleashing their 'bouncing bombs' on the Ruhr Valley in Germany in WWII.

These days, the reservoirs are popular destinations for walkers, cyclists and mountain bikers – and lots of ducks, so drive slowly!

Sights & Activities

Derwent Dam Museum MUSEUM
(☎01433-650953; www.dambusters.org.uk; Fairholmes; ⏰10am-4.30pm Mon-Fri, 9.30am-5.30pm Sat & Sun Apr-Oct, shorter hours Nov-Mar) FREE The exploits of the Royal Air Force Squadron No 617, aka the Dambusters, are the focus of the Derwent Dam Museum in the lower car park just south of the dam where they tested their 'bouncing bombs'. The relocated museum, adjacent to the tourist office, is due to open sometime in 2021.

Derwent Cycle Hire Centre CYCLING
(☎01433-651261; www.peakdistrict.gov.uk; Fairholmes; per half/full day standard bike £14/17, electric bike £32/36; ⏰9.30am-4.30pm early Feb–early Nov) Fairholmes' cycle-hire centre rents wheels including mountain bikes, kids' bikes and electric bikes.

Information

Tourist Office (☎01433-650953; www.visitpeakdistrict.com; Fairholmes; ⏰10am-4.30pm Mon-Fri, 9.30am-5.30pm Sat & Sun Apr-Oct, shorter hours Nov-Mar) Provides walking and cycling advice.

Edale

☎01433 / POP 353

Surrounded by majestic Peak District countryside, this cluster of stone houses centred on a pretty parish church is an enchanting place to pass the time. Edale lies between the White and Dark Peak areas, and is the southern terminus of the Pennine Way. Despite the remote location, the Manchester–Sheffield train line passes through the village, bringing throngs of weekend visitors.

Sleeping & Eating

Fieldhead Campsite CAMPSITE £
(☎01433-670386; www.fieldhead-campsite.co.uk; Fieldhead; site per person/car £7/3.50; ⏰Feb-Dec; P📶) Next to the Moorland Tourist Office, this pretty and well-equipped campsite spreads over six fields, with some pitches right by the river. Showers cost 20p. No campervans are allowed; fires and barbecues are not permitted.

Edale YHA HOSTEL £
(☎0845 371 9514; www.yha.org.uk; Rowland Cote, Nether Booth; dm/d/f from £16/68/102; P📶) Spectacular views across to Back Tor unfold from this country-house hostel 1.5 miles east of Edale, signposted from the Hope road. All 157 beds are bunks; wi-fi in public areas only. Check availability ahead as it's often busy with school groups.

Stonecroft B&B ££
(☎01433-670262; www.stonecroftguesthouse.co.uk; Grindsbrook; s/d from £65/110; P📶) 🍃 This handsomely fitted-out 1900s stone house has three comfortable guest rooms (two doubles, one single). Host Julia's organic breakfasts are gluten-free, with vegetarian and vegan options; packed lunches (£7.50) and Friday- and Saturday-evening meals

(£35) available by request when booking. Bike rental costs £25 per half-day. Pick-up from the train station can be arranged. Kids aren't permitted.

Newfold Farm Cafe CAFE £

(01433-670401; www.facebook.com/newfoldfarmcafe; Grindsbrook; dishes £2-9.50; 8am-5pm daily Apr-Sep, Sat & Sun only Oct-Mar;) Fuel up on soups, jacket potatoes and pizzas, and choose from a tempting selection of cakes (gluten-free and vegan options available) at this cheerful cafe close to the village school.

Rambler Inn PUB FOOD ££

(01433-670268; www.theramblerinn.co.uk; Grindsbrook; mains £9-14; kitchen noon-9pm Mon-Sat, to 8pm Sun, bar to 11pm daily;) Opposite the train station, this stone pub warmed by open fires serves real ales and pub standards, such as stews and sausages and mash, plus veggie options like spiced lentil and coconut soup. There's a kids' menu, nine basic B&B rooms (double/triple from £100/120) and occasional live music.

Information

Moorland Tourist Office (01433-670207; www.peakdistrict.gov.uk; Fieldhead; 9.30am-5pm Apr-Sep, reduced hours Oct-Dec & Feb-Mar) Topped by a sedum-turf 'living roof', with a waterfall splashing across its glass panels, this eco-conscious visitor centre has maps, displays on the moors and an adjacent campsite.

Getting There & Away

Trains run from Edale to Manchester (£12.20, 45 minutes, hourly) and Sheffield (£7.80, 40 minutes, hourly).

Castleton

01433 / POP 742

Guarding the entrance to the forbidding Winnats Pass gorge, charming Castleton is a magnet for Midlands visitors on summer weekends – come midweek if you want to enjoy the sights in relative peace and quiet. Castleton village's streets are lined with leaning stone houses, with walking trails criss-crossing the surrounding hills. The atmospheric ruins of Peveril Castle crown the ridge above, while the bedrock below is riddled with fascinating caves.

Sights & Activities

Situated at the base of 517m-high Mam Tor, Castleton is the northern terminus of the **Limestone Way**, which follows narrow, rocky Cave Dale, far below the east wall of the castle. The tourist office (p478) has maps and leaflets, including details of numerous easier walks.

Peveril Castle CASTLE, RUINS

(EH; 01433-620613; www.english-heritage.org.uk; adult/child £7.60/4.60; 10am-5pm Wed-Sun Easter-Oct, to 4pm Sat & Sun Nov-Easter) Topping the ridge to the south of Castleton, a 350m walk from the town centre, this evocative castle has been so ravaged by the centuries that it almost looks like a crag itself. Constructed by William Peveril, William the Conqueror's son, the castle was used as a hunting lodge by Henry II, King John and Henry III, and the crumbling ruins offer swooping views over the Hope Valley. Before heading up here, check ahead to avoid closures for maintenance.

Castleton Museum MUSEUM

(01629-816572; www.peakdistrict.gov.uk; Buxton Rd; 9.30am-5pm Apr-Sep, 10am-5pm Mon-Fri, 9.30am-5pm Sat & Sun Oct-Mar) FREE Attached to the tourist office (p478), the cute town museum has displays on everything from mining and geology to rock climbing, hang-gliding and the curious Garland Festival (p478).

Treak Cliff Cavern CAVE

(01433-620571; www.bluejohnstone.com; Buxton Rd; adult/child £12.50/6; 9am-4.30pm Mar-Oct, to 3.30pm Nov-Feb) Captivating Treak Cliff has a forest of stalactites and exposed seams of colourful Blue John Stone, which is still mined to supply the jewellery trade. Audio tours (downloadable from the website) focus on the history of mining – prebook a timeslot online). Check too for details of workshops where you can polish your own Blue John Stone. It's just under a mile west of Castleton's village centre.

Blue John Cavern CAVE

(01433-620638; www.bluejohn-cavern.co.uk; Old Mam Tor Rd; adult/child £14/7; 9.30am-4pm Mon-Fri, to 5pm Sat & Sun Apr-Oct, to dusk Nov-Mar) Up the southeastern side of Mam Tor, 2 miles west of Castleton, Blue John is a maze of natural caverns with rich seams of Blue John Stone that are still mined every winter. Access is via a one-hour guided tour that departs every 20 minutes, and involves a climb of 245 steps. A walking trail leads here from Winnats Pass, just west of Castleton; the tourist office has maps.

Speedwell Cavern CAVE
(01433-623018; www.speedwellcavern.co.uk; Winnats Pass; tour £17; 10am-5pm daily Apr-Oct, Sat & Sun Nov-Mar) Just over half a mile west of Castleton at the mouth of Winnats Pass, this claustrophobe's nightmare is reached by descending 106 steps for an eerie boat ride through flooded tunnels, emerging by a huge subterranean lake called the Bottomless Pit. Tours last 45 minutes; tickets must be pre-purchased online. New chambers are discovered here all the time by potholing expeditions.

Peak Cavern CAVE
(01433-620285; www.peakcavern.co.uk; Peak Cavern Rd; adult/child £15/8; 10am-5pm daily Apr-Oct, Sat & Sun Nov-Mar) Castleton's most convenient cave is easily reached by a pretty 250m streamside walk south of the village centre. It has the largest natural cave entrance in England, known (not so prettily) as the Devil's Arse. Dramatic limestone formations are lit with fibre-optic cables. Buy tickets ahead online.

Festivals & Events

Garland Festival CULTURAL
(www.castleton-garland.com; 29 May) Castleton celebrates Oak Apple Day on 29 May (28 May if the 29th is a Sunday) as it has for centuries, with the Garland King (buried under an enormous floral headdress) and Queen parading through the village on horseback.

Sleeping & Eating

Ye Olde Nag's Head Hotel PUB ££
(01433-620248; www.yeoldenagshead.co.uk; Cross St; d £65-95;) The cosiest of the 'residential' pubs along the main road has nine comfortable, well-appointed rooms; top-category rooms have four-poster beds and spas. Ale tasting trays are available in its bar, which has regular live music and a popular restaurant serving pub classics (mains £9 to £19).

Three Roofs Cafe CAFE £
(www.threeroofscafe.com; The Island; dishes £6-11; 10am-4pm Mon-Fri, to 5pm Sat & Sun;) Castleton's most popular purveyor of cream teas also has filling sandwiches, pies, fish and chips, burgers and jacket potatoes. Opposite the turn-off to the tourist office.

★ **Samuel Fox** BRITISH £££
(01433-621562; www.samuelfox.co.uk; Stretfield Rd, Bradwell; 2-/3-/7-course menus £34/44/54; 6-9pm Wed-Sat Feb-Dec;) In the Hope Valley village of Bradwell, 2.5 miles southeast of Castleton, this enchanting inn owned by pedigreed chef James Duckett serves exceptional British cuisine: venison with pickled red cabbage; roast pheasant with braised sprouts, bacon and parsnips. Guests staying in its four pastel-shaded guest rooms upstairs (doubles including breakfast from £130) can dine on Monday and Tuesday evenings.

Vegetarian menus are available. Look out for dinner, bed and breakfast deals.

Information

Tourist Office (01629-816572; www.visitpeakdistrict.com; Buxton Rd; 9.30am-5pm Apr-Sep, 10am-5pm Mon-Fri, 9.30am-5pm Sat & Sun Oct-Mar) In the Castleton Museum (p477).

Getting There & Away

BUS

Bus 173 serves Bakewell (£3.40, 50 minutes, four daily Monday to Saturday), via Hope (£2, five minutes), and in the opposite direction from Castleton, Tideswell (£3.30, 30 minutes).

Buses 271 and 272 run to Sheffield (£4.20, one hour, four per day Monday to Friday, three Saturday).

TRAIN

The nearest train station is at Hope, an easy 2-mile walk east of Castleton, on the line between Sheffield (£6.20, 30 minutes, hourly) and Manchester (£12.50, 55 minutes, hourly).

Buxton

01298 / POP 22,115

The 'capital' of the Peak District National Park, albeit just outside the park boundary, Buxton is a confection of Georgian terraces, Victorian amusements and parks in the rolling hills of the Derbyshire dales. The town built its fortunes on its natural warm-water springs, which attracted health tourists in Buxton's turn-of-the-century heyday.

Today, visitors are drawn here by the flamboyant Regency architecture and the natural wonders of the surrounding countryside. Tuesdays and Saturdays are market days, bringing colour to the grey limestone marketplace.

Buxton

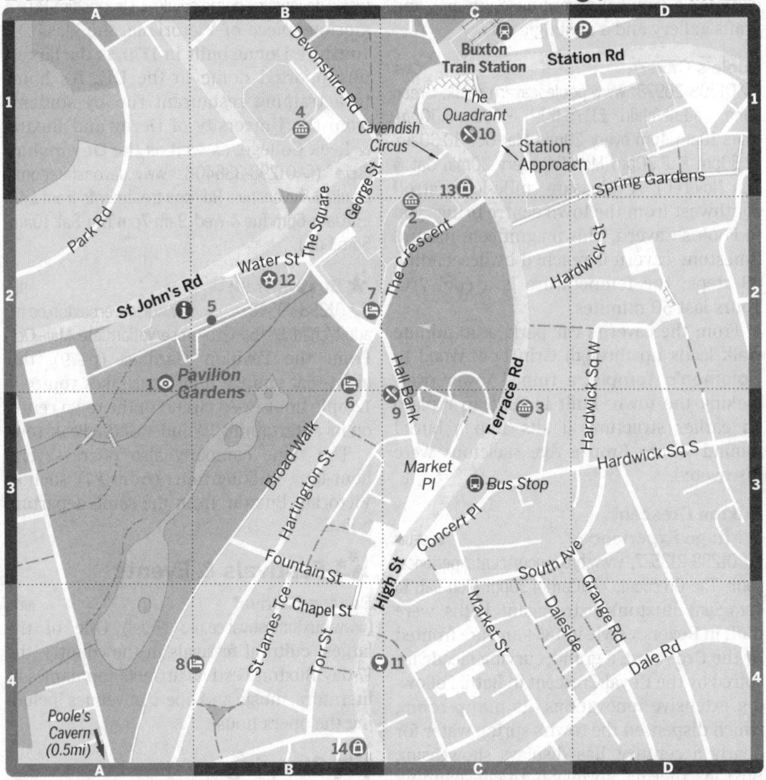

Buxton

Top Sights
1 Pavilion Gardens A2

Sights
2 Buxton Crescent Heritage Experience C2
3 Buxton Museum & Art Gallery C3
4 Devonshire Dome B1

Activities, Courses & Tours
5 Buxton Tram B2
Devonshire Spa .... (see 4)

Sleeping
6 Grosvenor House B2
7 Old Hall Hotel B2
8 Roseleigh Hotel B4

Eating
9 Columbine Restaurant C3
10 La Capri's C1

Drinking & Nightlife
11 Old Sun Inn B4

Entertainment
12 Opera House B2

Shopping
13 Cavendish Arcade C1
14 Scrivener's Books & Bookbinding B4

Sights & Activities

★Pavilion Gardens GARDENS
(www.paviliongardens.co.uk; St John's Rd; 9am-6pm Jul & Aug, shorter hours Sep-Jun) FREE Adjoining Buxton's opulent opera house are the equally flamboyant Pavilion Gardens. These 9.3 hectares are dotted with domed pavilions; concerts take place in the bandstand

throughout the year. The main building contains a tropical greenhouse, an arts and crafts gallery and a nostalgic cafe.

Poole's Cavern CAVE
(☎01298-26978; www.poolescavern.co.uk; Green Lane; adult/child £11/5.50; ⏲10am-4.30pm, tours 10am-4pm every 20min Mar-Oct, 10.30am, 12.30pm & 2.30pm Mon-Fri, every 20min Sat & Sun Nov-Feb) A pleasant mile-long stroll southwest from the town centre brings you to Poole's Cavern. This magnificent natural limestone cavern is reached by descending 28 steps; the temperature is a cool 7°C. Tours last 50 minutes.

From the cavern's car park, a 20-minute walk leads up through Grin Low Wood to **Solomon's Temple**, a ruined tower overlooking the town. Built in 1896 to replace an earlier structure, it sits atop a burial mound where Bronze Age skeletons were discovered.

Buxton Crescent Heritage Experience MUSEUM
(☎01298-213577; www.buxtoncrescentexperience.com; The Crescent; ⏲10am-4.30pm Mon-Sat, to 4pm Sun) Buxton's extravagant baths were built in Regency style in 1854 and are fronted by the **Crescent**, a grand, curving facade inspired by the Royal Crescent in Bath. Following extensive renovations, its **pump room**, which dispensed the town's spring water for nearly a century, has displays showcasing Buxton's thermal springs heritage spanning their Roman discovery to today.

Within the complex is a **five-star hotel** (double/suite from £155/195) and lavish **spa** including the original Victorian baths with naturally heated 28°C water.

The tourist office is located here.

Adjacent to the complex is **St Anne's Well**, where Buxton's restorative waters still flow freely; bring a bottle to fill up.

Buxton Museum & Art Gallery MUSEUM, GALLERY
(☎01629-533540; www.derbyshire.gov.uk/leisure/buxton-museum/buxton-museum-and-art-gallery.aspx; Terrace Rd; ⏲10am-5pm Tue-Sat year-round, plus noon-4pm Sun Easter-Sep) FREE In a handsome Victorian building, the town museum has records of fossils found in the Peak District, photographs, fine arts, bric-a-brac covering the town's social history and curiosities from Castleton's Victorian-era 'House of Wonders', including Harry Houdini's handcuffs.

Devonshire Dome HISTORIC BUILDING
(www.devonshiredome.co.uk; 1 Devonshire Rd) A glorious piece of Victoriana, the glass Devonshire Dome, built in 1779, is the largest unsupported dome in the UK. It's home to a training restaurant run by students from the University of Derby and Buxton & Leek College, as well as the **Devonshire Spa** (☎01298-338408; www.devonshiredome.co.uk; 1 Devonshire Rd; spa treatments from £40; ⏲10am-6pm Tue & Wed, 9am-7pm Thu-Sat, 10am-5pm Sun).

★**Buxton Tram** BUS
(☎01298-79648; www.discoverbuxton.co.uk; adult/child £8/5; ⏲by reservation late Mar–Oct) From the Pavilion Gardens (p479), this eight-seat vintage milk float takes you on a 12mph, hour-or-so circuit of the town centre on its entertaining 'Wonder of the Peak' tour.

The same company also offers several hour-long walking tours (from £7), such as Victorian Buxton, from the same departure point.

Festivals & Events

Buxton Festival ARTS
(www.buxtonfestival.co.uk; ⏲Jul) One of the largest cultural festivals in the country, the 17-day Buxton Festival attracts top names in literature, music and opera at venues including the opera house.

Sleeping

Buxton's grandest address to spend the night is the 2020-opened Buxton Crescent Hotel.

Old Hall Hotel HISTORIC HOTEL ££
(☎01298-22841; www.oldhallhotelbuxton.co.uk; The Square; s/d incl breakfast from £69/89; 📶🐾) There's a tale to go with every creak of the floorboards at this history-soaked establishment, supposedly the oldest hotel in England. Among other esteemed residents, Mary, Queen of Scots stayed here from 1576 to 1578, albeit against her will. The rooms still retain their grandeur (some have four-poster beds), and there are several bars, lounges and dining options.

Roseleigh Hotel B&B ££
(☎01298-24904; www.roseleighhotel.co.uk; 19 Broad Walk; d from £94; P📶) This gorgeous family-run B&B in a roomy old Victorian house has lovingly decorated rooms, many with fine views over the Pavilion Gardens. The owners are a welcoming couple, both seasoned travellers, with plenty of interest-

ing stories. There's a minimum three-night stay on summer weekends.

Grosvenor House B&B ££

(☎01298-72439; www.grosvenorbuxton.co.uk; 1 Broad Walk; s/d/f from £55/77/100; P) Overlooking the Pavilion Gardens, the Grosvenor is an old-school Victorian guesthouse with a huge parlour overlooking the park. Its eight rooms (including one family room sleeping three people plus space for a cot) have antique furniture and patterned wallpaper and drapes. At peak times, there's a minimum two-night stay and singles aren't available.

Eating & Drinking

La Capri's MEDITERRANEAN ££

(☎01298-71392; www.lacapris.co.uk; 7 The Quadrant; tapas £4-6, mains £9-16; 4-10.30pm Tue-Thu, noon-11pm Fri & Sat, to 10.30pm Sun;) Small tapas and *cicchetti* (Venetian small dishes), such as rosemary- and garlic-marinated prawns, grilled pork belly with balsamic fig glaze, and chorizo-stuffed mushrooms, are the speciality of this snazzy shop on the Quadrant (count on around three dishes per person). Larger mains include paella, pasta and stone-baked pizzas.

Columbine Restaurant MODERN BRITISH ££

(☎01298-78752; www.columbinerestaurant.co.uk; 7 Hall Bank; mains £14.50-24; 7-10pm Mon & Wed-Sat) On the lane leading down beside the town hall, this understated restaurant is the top choice among discerning Buxtonites. The chef conjures up imaginative dishes primarily made from local produce, such as High Peak lamb with mint butter. Two of its three dining areas are in the atmospheric stone cellar. Bookings are recommended.

Old Sun Inn PUB

(www.facebook.com/oldsuninnbuxton; 33 High St; 4-10pm Mon & Wed, noon-10pm Thu-Sun;) The cosiest of Buxton's pubs, this 17th-century coaching inn has a warren of rooms full of original features, proper cask ales and a lively crowd that spans the generations.

Entertainment

Opera House OPERA

(☎01298-72190; www.buxtonoperahouse.org.uk; Water St; tours £10; tours by reservation) Designed by theatre architect Frank Matcham in 1903 and restored in 2001, Buxton's gorgeous opera house hosts a full program of drama, dance, concerts and comedy. Guided backstage tours lasting 90 minutes can be booked via the website. Its neighbouring **Pavilion Arts Centre** also hosts performances and has a 360-seat cinema.

Shopping

Scrivener's Books & Bookbinding BOOKS

(☎01298-73100; www.scrivenersbooks.co.uk; 42 High St; 10am-4pm Tue-Sat, noon-4pm Sun) At this delightfully chaotic bookshop, sprawling over five floors, books are filed in piles and the Dewey system has yet to be discovered.

Cavendish Arcade SHOPPING CENTRE

(www.cavendisharcade.co.uk; Cavendish Circus; 9am-6pm Mon-Sat, 10am-5pm Sun, individual shop hours vary) Covered by a barrel-vaulted, stained-glass canopy, Cavendish Arcade houses boutiques selling upmarket gifts.

Glass floor panels reveal the thermal baths (on the site of earlier Roman baths) that were once here.

Information

Tourist Office (☎01298-214577; www.visitpeakdistrict.com; Pump House, The Crescent; 9.30am-4pm Apr-Oct, 10am-4pm Fri-Sun Nov-Mar;) At the Buxton Crescent Heritage Experience; can provide details of walks and activities in the area.

Getting There & Away

Buses stop on both sides of the road at Market Pl. A High Peak service runs to Derby (£6.60, 1¾ hours, every two hours), via Bakewell (£5.10, 30 minutes) and Matlock Bath (£6.60, one hour); five services daily continue to Manchester (£8, 1¼ hours). Buses also run to Ashbourne (£4.50, 1¼ hours, 10 daily Monday to Friday, eight Saturday).

Northern Rail has trains to/from Manchester (£12.50, one hour, hourly).

AT A GLANCE

POPULATION
5,288,200

HIGHEST LAKE
Malham Tarn (377m; p515)

BEST MICROBREWERY
Brass Castle (p497)

BEST FESTIVAL
Whitby Goth Weekends (p509)

BEST MEAL
Cochon Aveugle (p494)

WHEN TO GO

Apr–Jul
Daffodils bloom in Dales and North York Moors; Malton Food Lovers Festival; Great Yorkshire Show in Harrogate.

Aug & Sep
Perfect hiking weather in Dales; Walking Festival in Richmond; Harrogate Autumn Flower Show.

Oct–Mar
Goth Weekends in Whitby; week-long Jorvik Viking Festival in York.

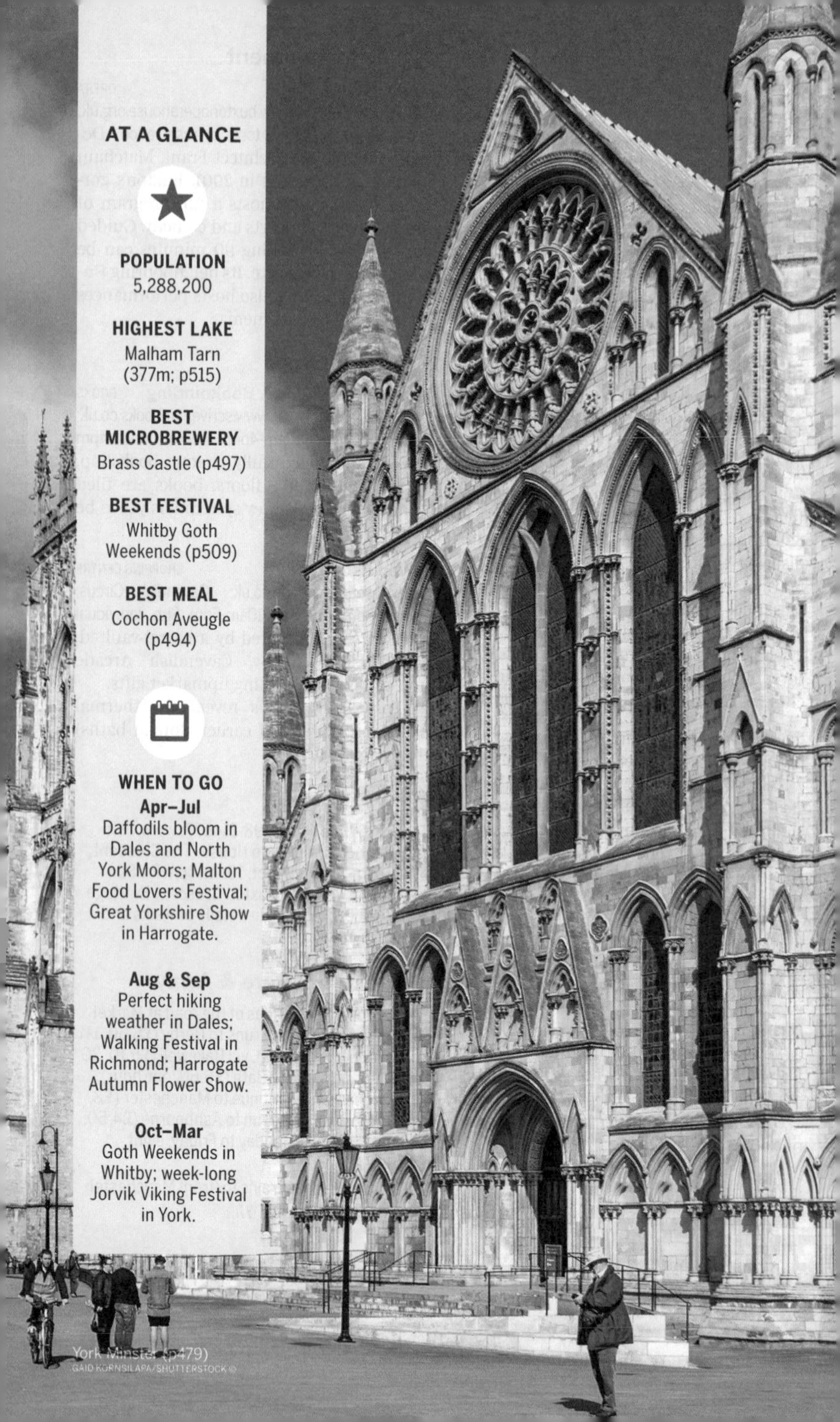

York Minster (p479)

Yorkshire

With a population as big as Scotland's and an area half the size of Belgium, Yorkshire – made up of four separate counties – is almost a country in itself. It has its own flag, dialect and celebration – Yorkshire Day. People have long been drawn here for walking and cycling, framed by some of Britain's finest scenery – brooding moors and green dales rolling down to a dramatic coast. Medieval York is the heart-throb, but there are countless other atmospheric towns and villages, abbey ruins, castles and gardens. But Yorkshire refuses to fade into the past – once-derelict urban areas are regenerating and modern Britishness is fusing with Yorkshire heritage.

INCLUDES

Yorkshire Highlights

1 York (p487) Exploring the medieval streets of the city and its awe-inspiring cathedral.

2 Yorkshire Dales National Park (p511) Getting off the beaten track and exploring lesser-known corners, like Swaledale.

3 Fountains Abbey (p498) Wandering among the atmospheric medieval ruins.

4 North Yorkshire Moors Railway (p506) Riding on one of England's most scenic train lines.

5 Whitby (p506) Sitting on the pier and munching the world's best fish and chips.

6 Castle Howard (p495) Reliving the story of *Brideshead Revisited*.

7 Malham Cove (p514) Pulling on your hiking boots and tackling the steep paths around this scenic cove.

8 Leeds (p519) Getting stuck into Yorkshire's craft-beer scene, hopping around innovative brewery taprooms.

9 Hull (p532) Exploring maritime heritage and the regenerated marina area of Yorkshire's biggest east-coast town.

10 Malton (p496) Touring artisan food and drink producers in a revitalised Georgian market town.

0 20 km
0 10 miles
NORTH SEA
Billingham
Middlesbrough
Stockton-on-Tees
A174
A171
Whitby
Stokesley
Danby
Esk
Hawsker
Robin Hood's Bay
Boggle Hole
Grosmont
Leven
A19
A171
North York Moors National Park
North Yorkshire Moors Railway
Seph
The Hambleton Hills
Hutton-le-Hole
Lastingham
Scarborough
Cayton Bay
Helmsley
Pickering
Thirsk
Derwent
Hertford
Filey
Seven
Bempton Cliffs Nature Reserve
Rye
A19
Cleveland Hills
Malton
Castle Howard
Flamborough Head
Bridlington
Boroughbridge
B1363
Kirkham Priory
A64
Great Driffield
A166
A59
York
EAST RIDING OF YORKSHIRE
Hull
A1079
Hornsea
Wetherby
South Dalton
A1
A19
Beverley
A164
Selby
Barlby
Hull
Hull Ferry Terminal
Monk Fryston
Howden
Patrington
Ouse
To Rotterdam & Zeebrugge
Humber
Trent
Easington
Kilnsea
NORTH LINCOLNSHIRE
A15
High Ackworth
Thorne
Scunthorpe
Grimsby
Spurn Head
Cleethorpes
Doncaster
NORTHEAST LINCOLNSHIRE
A15
Rotherham
Gainsborough
Market Rasen
Worksop
LINCOLNSHIRE
A158
NOTTINGHAMSHIRE
A57
Chesterfield
Lincoln
DERBYSHIRE

History

As you drive through Yorkshire on the main A1 road, you're following in the footsteps of the Roman legions who conquered northern Britain in the 1st century CE. In fact, many Yorkshire towns – including York, Catterick and Malton – were founded by the Romans, and many modern roads (including the A1, A59, A166 and A1079) follow the alignment of Roman roads.

When the Romans departed in the 5th century, native Britons battled for supremacy with the Angles, an invading Teutonic tribe, and, for a while, Yorkshire was part of the Kingdom of Northumbria. In the 9th century, the Vikings arrived and conquered most of northern Britain, an area that became known as the Danelaw. They divided the territory that is now Yorkshire into *thridings* (thirds), which met at Jorvik (York), their thriving commercial capital.

In 1066 Yorkshire was the scene of a pivotal showdown in the struggle for the English crown, when the Anglo-Saxon king, Harold II, rode north to defeat the forces of the Norwegian king, Harold Hardrada, in the Battle of Stamford Bridge, before returning south for his appointment with William the Conqueror – and a fatal arrow – in the Battle of Hastings.

The inhabitants of northern England did not take the subsequent Norman invasion lying down. In order to subdue them, the Norman nobles built a chain of formidable castles throughout Yorkshire, including those at York, Richmond, Scarborough, Skipton, Pickering and Helmsley. The Norman land grab formed the basis of the great estates that supported England's medieval aristocrats.

By the 15th century, the duchies of York and Lancaster had become so wealthy and powerful that they ended up battling for the English throne in the Wars of the Roses (1455–87). The dissolution of the monasteries by Henry VIII from 1536 to 1540 saw the wealth of the great abbeys of Rievaulx, Fountains and Whitby fall into the hands of noble families, and Yorkshire quietly prospered for 200 years, with fertile farms in the north and the Sheffield cutlery business in the south, until the big bang of the Industrial Revolution transformed the landscape.

South Yorkshire became a centre of coal mining and steel-making, while West Yorkshire nurtured a massive textile industry, and the cities of Leeds, Bradford, Sheffield and Rotherham flourished. By the late 20th century, another revolution was taking place. The heavy industries had died out, and the cities of Yorkshire were reinventing themselves as shiny, high-tech centres of finance, digital innovation and tourism.

Information

The Yorkshire Tourist Board (www.yorkshire.com) has plenty of general leaflets and brochures. For more specific information, try the excellent network of local tourist offices.

Activities

Yorkshire's varied landscape of wild hills, tranquil valleys, high moors and spectacular coastline offers plenty of opportunities for outdoor activities.

Cycling

Yorkshire is prime cycling country, with a vast network of cycle-friendly country lanes. Interest in cycling surged after the region hosted the start of the 2014 Tour de France, which also led to the establishment of the annual **Tour de Yorkshire** (www.letour.yorkshire.com) cycle race in 2015. Note that the national parks also attract lots of motorists so even minor roads can be busy at weekends.

Mountain bikers can avail themselves of the network of bridleways, former railways and disused mining tracks now converted for two-wheel use. **Dalby Forest** (Map p503; www.forestry.gov.uk/dalbyforest), near Pickering, sports purpose-built mountain-biking trails of all grades from green to black, and there are newly waymarked trails at the Sutton Bank National Park Centre (p503).

Walking

For shorter walks and rambles, the best area is the **Yorkshire Dales**, with a great selection of walks through scenic valleys or over wild hilltops, plus a few higher summits thrown in for good measure. The East Riding's **Yorkshire Wolds** hold hidden delights, while the quiet valleys and dramatic coast of the **North York Moors** are also home to some excellent trails. For longer walks, see p492.

Getting There & Around

BUS

Long-distance coaches operated by **National Express** (☎0871 781 8181; www.nationalexpress.com) serve most cities and large towns in Yorkshire from London, the south of England, the Midlands and Scotland.

Bus transport around Yorkshire is frequent and efficient, especially between major towns. Services are more sporadic in the national parks, but are still adequate for reaching most places if you're not in a rush, particularly in summer (June to September).

CAR

The major north–south road transport routes – the M1 and A1 motorways – run through the middle of Yorkshire, serving the key cities of Sheffield, Leeds and York. If you're arriving by sea from northern Europe, Hull in the East Riding district is the region's main port.

Traveline Yorkshire (☎ 0871 200 2233; www.traveline.info) Provides public-transport information for all of Yorkshire.

TRAIN

The main rail line between London and Edinburgh runs through Yorkshire, with at least 10 trains calling each day at York and Doncaster, where you can change trains for other Yorkshire destinations. There are also direct links to northern cities such as Manchester and Newcastle. For timetable information, contact **National Rail Enquiries** (☎ 03457 48 49 50; www.nationalrail.co.uk).

NORTH YORKSHIRE

History has been kind to the rolling hills of England's largest county. Unlike the rest of northern England, North Yorkshire was left untouched by the dirty paw of the Industrial Revolution, leaving it alone to do what it's being doing since the Middle Ages – living off the sheep's back.

Rather than closed-down factories, mills and mines, the manmade monuments dotting the landscape in these parts are of the stately variety – the great houses and wealthy abbeys that sit, ruined or restored, as a reminder that sheep's woolly wealth went a long way.

All the same, North Yorkshire's biggest attraction is an urban one. While the genteel spa town of Harrogate and the storied seaside resort of Whitby have many fans, nothing compares to the unparalleled splendour of medieval York, England's most-visited city outside London.

York

☎ 01904 / POP 153,717

No other city in northern England says 'medieval' quite like York – minus the smells, open slaughterhouses and ridiculously low life expectancy. Instead, what you get is an enchanting spider's web of narrow streets and alleyways enclosed within a magnificent circuit of 13th-century walls. At its heart is the immense, awe-inspiring York Minster, one of the most beautiful Gothic cathedrals in the world. York's long history and rich heritage is woven into virtually every brick and beam, and the modern, tourist-oriented city – with its myriad museums, restaurants, cafes and traditional pubs – is a carefully maintained heir to that heritage.

Try to avoid the inevitable confusion by remembering that around these parts, *gate* means street and *bar* means gate.

> **ℹ YORK PASS**
>
> If you plan on visiting a number of sights, the **YorkPass** (www.yorkpass.com) will save you some money. The one-day city pass (adult/child £48/30) gives you free access to city centre attractions including York Minster and Jorvik, while the multi-day York & Beyond pass (two/three/six days adult £65/80/130, child £35/40/70) also includes attractions throughout the North York Moors. You can buy it at the York Tourist Office (p495) or online.

Sights

★**York Minster** CATHEDRAL

(☎ 01904-557200; www.yorkminster.org; Deangate; adult/child £11.50/free; ⏲ 11am-4.30pm Mon-Thu, from 10am Fri & Sat, 12.30-2.30pm Sun) York Minster is the largest medieval cathedral in northern Europe, and one of the world's most beautiful Gothic buildings. Seat of the archbishop of York, primate of England, it is second in importance only to Canterbury, seat of the primate of *all* England – the separate titles were created to settle a debate over the true centre of the English Church. Note that the quire, east end and undercroft close in preparation for evening service around the time of last admission.

The first church on this site was a wooden chapel built for the baptism of King Edwin of Northumbria on Easter Day 627; its location is marked in the crypt. This was replaced with a stone church built on the site of a Roman basilica, parts of which can be seen in the foundations. The first Norman minster was built in the 11th century and, again, you can see surviving fragments in the foundations and crypt.

York

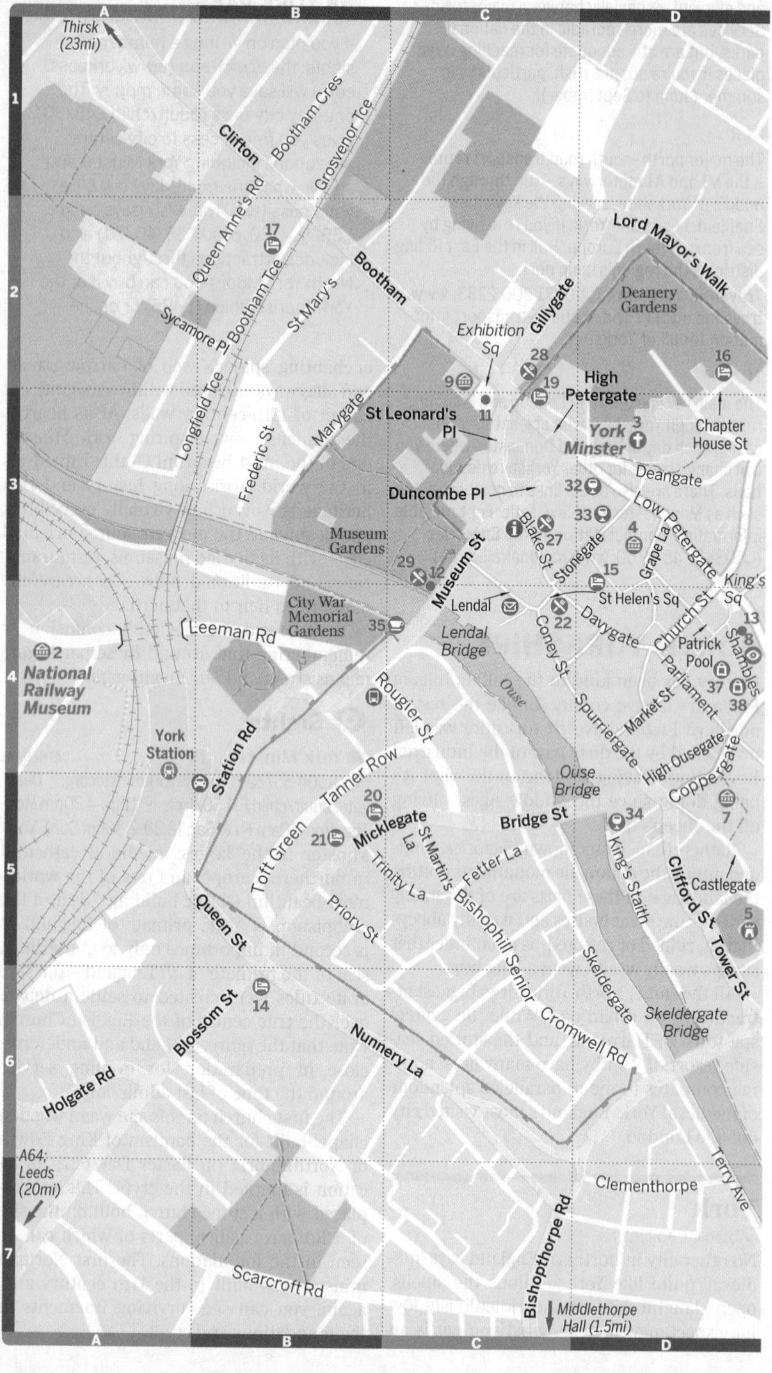
Thirsk (23mi)
Clifton
Bootham Cres
Grosvenor Tce
Queen Anne's Rd
Bootham Tce
Bootham
Lord Mayor's Walk
Deanery Gardens
Sycamore Pl
St Mary's
Gillygate
Exhibition Sq
High Petergate
Longfield Tce
Frederic St
Marygate
St Leonard's Pl
York Minster
Chapter House St
Deangate
Duncombe Pl
Low Petergate
Museum Gardens
Blake St
Stonegate
Grape La
Museum St
King's Sq
St Helen's Sq
Lendal
Davygate
Church St
City War Memorial Gardens
Lendal Bridge
Coney St
Leeman Rd
Patrick Pool
Shambles
National Railway Museum
Parliament
Ouse
Rougier St
Spurriergate
Market St
York Station
Station Rd
High Ousegate
Coppergate
Tanner Row
Ouse Bridge
Micklegate
Bridge St
King's Staith
Toft Green
St Martin's La
Trinity La
Fetter La
Clifford St
Castlegate
Priory St
Bishophill Senior
Queen St
Tower St
Skeldergate
Skeldergate Bridge
Blossom St
Cromwell Rd
Nunnery La
Holgate Rd
A64; Leeds (20mi)
Clementhorpe
Terry Ave
Bishopthorpe Rd
Scarcroft Rd
Middlethorpe Hall (1.5mi)
YORKSHIRE

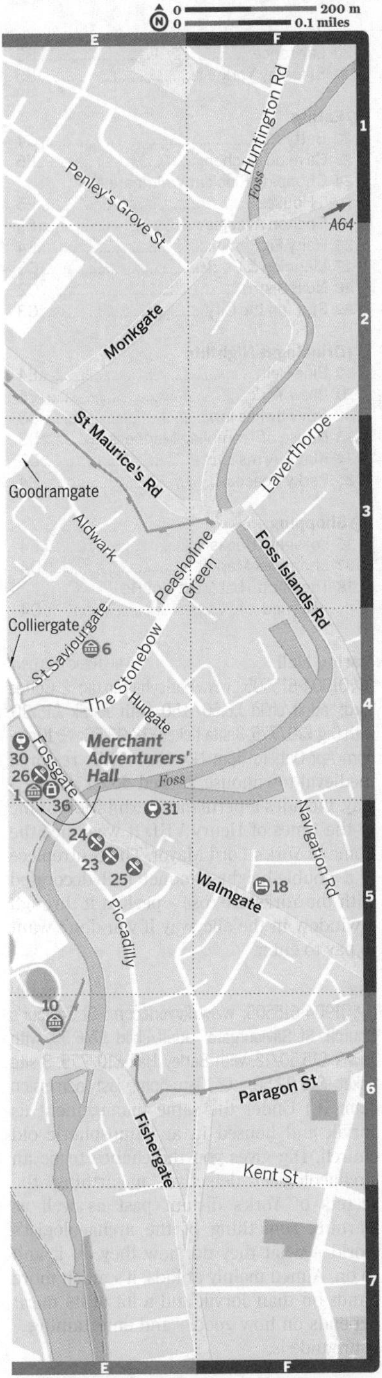

The present minster, built mainly between 1220 and 1480, manages to encompass all the major stages of Gothic architectural development. The transepts (1220–55) were built in Early English style; the octagonal chapter house (1260–90) and nave (1291–1340) in the Decorated style; and the west towers, west front and central (or lantern) tower (1470–72) in Perpendicular style.

Closed for the duration of the pandemic emergency are the massive **tower** – reached via a fairly claustrophobic climb of 275 steps – and the **undercroft.** When it reopens you can explore its excellent interactive exhibition, York Minster Revealed.

The cathedral is open longer hours for worshippers.

★National Railway Museum MUSEUM

(www.railwaymuseum.org.uk; Leeman Rd; ⏲10am-5pm Wed-Sun; P 🚻) FREE York's National Railway Museum – the biggest in the world, with more than 100 locomotives – is well presented and crammed with fascinating stuff. It is laid out on a vast scale and housed in a series of giant railway sheds – allow at least two hours to do it justice. The museum also now includes a high-tech simulator experience of riding on the **Mallard** (£3), which set the world speed record for a steam locomotive in 1938 (126mph). Pre-booking only.

Highlights for trainspotters include a replica of George Stephenson's **Rocket** (1829), the world's first 'modern' steam locomotive; a 1960s Japanese **Shinkansen bullet train**; and an exhibition dedicated to the world-famous **Flying Scotsman**, the first steam engine to break the 100mph barrier (now restored to full working order and touring the UK). There's also a massive 4-6-2 loco from 1949, which has been cut in half to demonstrate how it works (daily talk at 4pm).

Even if you're not a rail nerd, you'll enjoy looking through the gleaming, silk-lined carriages of the royal trains used by Queens Mary, Adelaide and Victoria, and King Edward VII.

The museum is about 400m west of the train station. A road train (adult/child £3/2) runs between the minster and museum every 30 minutes from 11am to 4pm, weather permitting.

★Merchant Adventurers' Hall HISTORIC BUILDING

(☎01904-654818; www.merchantshallyork.org; Fossgate; adult/child £6.50/free; ⏲10am-4.30pm

York

Top Sights

1 Merchant Adventurers' Hall E4
2 National Railway Museum A4
3 York Minster D3

Sights

4 Barley Hall D3
5 Clifford's Tower D5
6 Dig E4
7 Jorvik Viking Centre D5
8 The Shambles D4
9 York Art Gallery C2
10 York Castle Museum E6

Activities, Courses & Tours

11 Association of Voluntary Guides C3
12 City Cruises York C4
13 Ghost Hunt of York D4

Sleeping

14 Bar Convent B6
15 Fort D3
16 Grays Court D2
17 Hedley House Hotel B2
18 Hotel Indigo F5
19 Lamb & Lion Inn C3
20 Lawrance B5
21 Safestay York B5

Eating

22 Bettys C4
23 Cave du Cochon E5
24 Chopping Block at Walmgate Ale House E5
25 Cochon Aveugle E5
26 Hairy Fig E4
27 Mannion & Co C3
28 No 8 Bistro C2
29 Star Inn the City C3

Drinking & Nightlife

30 Blue Bell E4
31 Brew York E5
32 Guy Fawkes Inn D3
33 House of Trembling Madness D3
34 King's Arms D5
35 Perky Peacock C4

Shopping

36 Fossgate Books E4
37 Shambles Market D4
38 The Shop That Must Not Be Named D4

Sun-Fri, to 1.30pm Sat) York's most impressive semi-timbered building is still owned by the fraternity that built it almost 650 years ago and it is the oldest surviving guildhall of its kind in Britain. The owner was originally a religious fraternity and one of the hall's chambers is still a chapel, but the building's name refers to the pioneering business exploits that made the fraternity's fortunes while 'adventuring' their money in overseas markets at a time when York was an important international port.

Jorvik Viking Centre MUSEUM

(☎ticket reservations 01904-615505; www.jorvikvikingcentre.co.uk; Coppergate; adult/child £12.50/8.50, with Barley Hall £15/10, with Dig £15.50/12, 3-site ticket £18/12.50; ⏰10am-5pm Apr-Oct, to 4pm Nov-Mar) Interactive multimedia exhibits aimed at bringing history to life often achieve exactly the opposite, but the much-hyped Jorvik manages to pull it off with aplomb. It's a smells-and-all reconstruction of the Viking settlement unearthed here during excavations in the late 1970s, experienced via a 'time-car' monorail that transports you through 9th-century Jorvik (the Viking name for York). Book your timed-entry tickets online.

Barley Hall HISTORIC BUILDING

(☎01904-615505; www.barleyhall.co.uk; 2 Coffee Yard; adult/child £6.50/3.50, with Jorvik £15/10, with Dig £10/7.75, 3-site ticket £18/12.50; ⏰10am-5pm Apr-Oct, to 4pm Nov-Mar) This restored medieval townhouse, tucked down an alleyway, includes a permanent exhibition of life in the times of Henry VIII. It was once the home of York's Lord Mayor. The centrepiece is a double-height banquet hall decorated with the Yorkshire rose – peek at it through a window in the alleyway if you don't want to pay to enter.

Dig MUSEUM

(☎01904-615505; www.digyork.com; St Saviour's Church, St Saviourgate; adult/child £7/6.50, with Jorvik £15.50/12, with Barley Hall £10/7.75, 3-site ticket £18/12.50; ⏰10am-5pm, last admission 4pm; 👪) Under the same management as Jorvik and housed in an atmospheric old church, Dig gives you the chance to be an 'archaeological detective', unearthing the secrets of York's distant past as well as learning something of the archaeologist's world – what they do, how they do it and so on. Aimed mainly at kids, it's much more hands-on than Jorvik and a lot of its merit depends on how good – and entertaining – your guide is.

The Shambles STREET

The Shambles takes its name from the Saxon word *shamel*, meaning 'slaughterhouse' – in 1862 there were 26 butcher shops on this street. Today the butchers are long gone, but this narrow cobbled lane, lined with 15th-century Tudor buildings that overhang so much they seem to meet above your head, is the most picturesque in Britain, and one of the most visited in Europe, often filled with visitors wielding cameras.

York Castle Museum MUSEUM

(www.yorkcastlemuseum.org.uk; Tower St; adult/child £10/free; guided tour only, 10am-4pm Thu-Sun) This excellent museum has displays of everyday life through the centuries, with reconstructed domestic interiors, a Victorian street and a prison cell where you can try out a condemned man's bed – and it could be that of highwayman Dick Turpin (imprisoned here before being hanged in 1739). For the time being all visits are by pre-booked guided tour only.

York Art Gallery GALLERY

(01904-687687; www.yorkartgallery.org.uk; Exhibition Sq; adult/child £8/free; 11am-4pm Wed-Sun;) As well as an impressive collection of Old Masters, York Art Gallery possesses works by LS Lowry, Pablo Picasso, Grayson Perry, David Hockney, and the controversial York artist William Etty who, in the 1820s, was the first major British painter to specialise in nudes. A unique feature is the gallery's hands-on sculpture sessions (where you can handle the works), and its brilliant interactive ceramics centre (www.centreofceramicart.org.uk), housing more than 1000 pieces dating from Roman times to the present day.

Clifford's Tower CASTLE

(EH; www.english-heritage.org.uk; Tower St; adult/child £5.90/3.50; 10am-6pm Apr-Sep, to 5pm Oct, to 4pm Nov-Mar) There's precious little left of York Castle except for this evocative stone tower, a highly unusual four-lobed design built into the castle's keep after the original one was destroyed in 1190 during anti-Jewish riots. An angry mob forced 150 Jews to be locked inside the tower and the hapless victims took their own lives rather than be killed. There's not much to see inside, but the views over the city are excellent. Pre-booked tickets only.

Tours

Association of Voluntary Guides WALKING

(www.avgyork.co.uk; tours 10.15am & 1.15pm year-round, 6.15pm Jun-Aug) FREE Two-hour city walking tours, setting out from Exhibition Sq in front of York Art Gallery.

★ **Brewtown** BREWERY

(01904-636666; www.brewtowntours.co.uk; £70; 11.30am-5pm) These craft-brewery minivan tours are a fuss-free way to get behind the scenes at Yorkshire's smaller breweries, some of which only open to the public for these tours. Owner Mark runs different routes (around York, Malton or Leeds) depending on the day of the week; each tour visits three breweries with tastings along the way, and sometimes even beer-pairing nibbles.

City Cruises York BOATING

(www.citycruisesyork.com; Lendal Bridge; adult/child from £10.50/6; tours 10.30am, noon, 1.30pm & 3pm;) These hour-long cruises on the River Ouse depart from King's Staith and, 10 minutes later, Lendal Bridge. Special lunch, afternoon-tea and evening cruises are also offered. You can buy tickets on board or book at the office by Lendal Bridge.

Ghost Hunt of York WALKING

(01904-608700; www.ghosthunt.co.uk; adult/child £10/6.66; tours 6pm & 7.30pm) Kids will love this award-winning and highly entertaining 75-minute tour laced with authentic ghost stories. It begins on the Shambles, whatever the weather (it's never cancelled), and there's no need to book – just turn up and wait till you hear the handbell ringing...

Festivals & Events

Jorvik Viking Festival CULTURAL

(www.jorvik-viking-festival.co.uk; mid-Feb) For a week in mid-February, York is invaded by Vikings as part of this festival, which features battle re-enactments, themed walks, markets and other bits of Viking-related fun.

York Food Festival FOOD & DRINK

(www.yorkfoodfestival.com; late Sep) A 10-day celebration of all that's good to eat and drink in Yorkshire, with food stalls, tastings, a beer tent, cookery demonstrations and more. The main event is in late September, but there's a small taster festival in June and a chocolate festival on Easter weekend.

YORKSHIRE'S BEST WALKS

Cleveland Way (www.nationaltrail.co.uk/clevelandway) A venerable moor-and-coast classic that circles the North York Moors National Park on its 109-mile, nine-day route from Helmsley to Filey.

Coast to Coast Walk (www.wainwright.org.uk/coasttocoast.html) One of England's most popular walks: 190 miles across northern England from the Lake District through the Yorkshire Dales and North York Moors National Parks. The Yorkshire section takes a week to 10 days and offers some of the finest walking of its kind in England.

Dales Way (www.dalesway.org.uk) A charming and not-too-strenuous 80-mile amble from the Yorkshire Dales to the Lake District. It starts at Ilkley in West Yorkshire, follows the River Wharfe through the heart of the Dales and finishes at Bowness-on-Windermere.

Pennine Way (www.nationaltrail.co.uk/pennineway) The Yorkshire section of England's most famous walk runs for more than 100 miles via Hebden Bridge, Malham, Horton-in-Ribblesdale and Hawes, passing near Haworth and Skipton.

White Rose Way (www.nationaltrail.co.uk/yorkshirewoldsway) A beautiful but oft-overlooked 79-mile walk that winds through the most scenic part of Yorkshire's East Riding district. It starts at Hessle near the Humber Bridge and ends at the tip of Filey Brigg, a peninsula on the east coast just north of the town of Filey. Billed as 'Yorkshire's best-kept secret', it takes five days and is an excellent beginners' walk.

Sleeping

Safestay York
HOSTEL £

(01904-627720; www.safestay.com; 88-90 Micklegate, YO1 6JX; dm/tw/f from £14/65/80; @ wi-fi) Housed in a Grade I Georgian town house, this is a large boutique hostel with contemporary, colourful decor and good facilities including a bar with pool table. Rooms are mostly en suite and have a bit more character than you'd usually find in hostels, with the added intrigue of plaques outside doors describing the history of different rooms in the house.

It's popular with school groups and stag and hen parties – don't come here looking for peace and quiet. Family rooms are strategically positioned right at the top of the house.

York YHA
HOSTEL £

(0345 371 9051; www.yha.org.uk; 42 Water End, Clifton; s/d/tr from £39/49/69; P wi-fi) Originally the Rowntree (Quaker confectioners) mansion, this handsome Victorian house makes a spacious and child-friendly youth hostel, with more than 250 beds, a broad garden and on-site restaurant. It's often busy, so book early. It's about a mile northwest of the city centre; there's a riverside footpath from Lendal Bridge (poorly lit, so avoid after dark).

Alternatively, take bus 2 from the train station or Museum St, though be aware it doesn't run in the evenings.

Fort
HOSTEL £

(01904-620222; www.thefortyork.co.uk; 1 Little Stonegate; dm/d from £10/50; wi-fi) This boutique hostel showcases the interior design of young British talents, creating affordable accommodation with a dash of character and flair. There are six- and eight-bed dorms, along with five doubles, but don't expect a peaceful retreat – it's central and there's a lively club downstairs (earplugs are provided!). Towels are included, as well as free tea, coffee and laundry.

★Lawrance
APARTMENT ££

(01904-239988; www.thelawrance.com/york; 74 Micklegate; 1-/2-bed apt from £90/190; air-con wi-fi) Set back from the road in a huddle of old red-brick buildings that once formed a factory, the Lawrance is an excellent find: super-swish serviced apartments with all mod cons on the inside and heritage character on the outside. Some apartments are split-level and all are comfy and spacious, with leather sofas, flatscreen TV and luxurious fixtures and fittings.

Hotel Indigo
BOUTIQUE HOTEL ££

(01904-231333; www.hotelindigoyork.co.uk; 88-96 Walmgate; r from £60) One of the best midrange options in town is this hotel on Walmgate, which opened in 2019 and manages to be ignored by most visitors despite being inside the city walls and a short walk from the Shambles. The colourful rooms are well appointed and comfortable.

Lamb & Lion Inn INN ££
(☎01904-612078; www.lambandlioninnyork.com; 2-4 High Petergate; d from £70; 📶) Occupying a perfect spot in the shadow of Bootham Bar, the Lamb & Lion is a quaint 1756 Georgian pub with 12 simple period rooms, an AA Rosette gastropub, and possibly York's best beer garden out back. Even if you don't stay, it's a good place for a drink around the old city walls.

Bar Convent B&B ££
(☎01904-643238; www.bar-convent.org.uk; 17 Blossom St; s/d from £60/100; 📶) This mansion just outside Micklegate Bar is less than 10 minutes' walk from the train station. It houses England's oldest working convent, a cafe, meeting rooms and also offers good B&B accommodation. Open to visitors of all faiths and none. Charming bedrooms are modern and well-equipped, breakfasts are superb, and there's a garden and hidden chapel to enjoy.

Hedley House Hotel HOTEL ££
(☎01904-637404; www.hedleyhouse.com; 3 Bootham Tce; d/f from £75/100; P📶) 🍃 This large red-brick terrace-house hotel sports a variety of options including family-friendly rooms sleeping up to five and self-catering apartments. The designer lounge has the feel of a much bigger hotel, plus there's a yoga studio and Jacuzzi on the outdoor terrace at the back. It's five minutes' walk from the city centre through the Museum Gardens.

★Grays Court HISTORIC HOTEL £££
(☎01904-612613; www.grayscourtyork.com; Chapter House St; d £180-240, ste £265-300; P📶) This medieval mansion with just 11 rooms feels like a country-house hotel. It's set in lovely gardens with direct access to the city walls, and bedrooms combine antique furniture with modern comfort and design. The oldest part of the building was built in the 11th century, and King James I once dined in the Long Gallery.

Eating

★Mannion & Co CAFE, BISTRO £
(☎01904-631030; www.mannionandco.co.uk; 1 Blake St; mains £7-14; ⏰10am-4pm Sun-Mon & Wed-Thu, 9am-4pm Fri-Sat) Expect to queue for a table at this busy bistro (no reservations), with its convivial atmosphere and selection of delicious daily specials. Regulars on the menu include eggs Benedict for breakfast, a chunky Yorkshire rarebit (cheese on toast) made with home-baked bread, and lunch platters of cheese and charcuterie. Oh, and pavlova for pudding.

Cave du Cochon PIZZA £
(☎01904-633669; www.caveducochon.uk; 19 Walmgate; mains £7-10; ⏰5-10pm Wed-Fri, noon-10pm Sat-Sun) New York–style sourdough pizza is the mainstay at this elegant wine bar – the sister business to the Cochon Aveugle (p494). It also serves some locally sourced charcuterie (£22) and cheese (£15) from one of the UK's very best producers, the Courtyard Dairy near Settle.

★Hairy Fig CAFE £
(☎01904-677074; www.thehairyfig.co.uk; 39 Fossgate; mains £6-12; ⏰9am-4.30pm Mon-Sat) This cafe-deli is a standout in York. On the one side you have the best of Yorkshire tripping over the best of Europe, with Italian white anchovies and truffle-infused olive oil stacked alongside York honey mead and baked pies; on the other you have a Dickensian-style sweet shop and backroom cafe serving dishes crafted from the deli.

Star Inn the City BRITISH ££
(☎01904-619208; www.starinnthecity.co.uk; Lendal Engine House, Museum St; mains £16-25; ⏰9.30-11.30am, noon-9.30pm Mon-Sat, to 7.30pm Sun; 👪) Its riverside setting in a Grade II–listed engine house and quirky British menu make Andrew Pern's York outpost of the Star Inn (p505) an exceedingly pleasant place to while away the hours. Expect country-themed cosiness in winter, and dining out on the broad terrace in summer.

Chopping Block at Walmgate Ale House BRITISH ££
(www.thechoppingblock.co.uk; 25 Walmgate; mains £14-18; ⏰5-10pm Tue-Fri, noon-10pm Sat, to 9pm Sun; 🖉) This restaurant above a pub wears its Yorkshire credentials with pride. Local produce underpins the menu, which turns out mainly meat dishes (lamb shoulder, confit of duck leg, pork belly), given a French-flavoured gourmet twist, that are fine examples of contemporary British cuisine. Vegetarian options include tasty dishes like pea pancakes with spiced cauliflower.

No 8 Bistro BISTRO ££
(☎01904-653074; www.cafeno8.co.uk; 8 Gillygate; dinner mains £17; ⏰noon-10pm Mon-Fri,

9am-10pm Sat & Sun;) A cool little place with modern artwork mimicking the Edwardian stained glass at the front, No 8 offers a day-long menu of top-notch bistro dishes using fresh local produce, such as Jerusalem artichoke risotto with fresh herbs, and Yorkshire lamb slow-cooked in hay and lavender. Booking recommended.

Bettys CAFE ££

(01904-659142; www.bettys.co.uk; 6-8 St Helen's Sq; mains £6-14, afternoon tea £18.50; 9am-7pm;) Old-school afternoon tea, with white-aproned waiters, linen tablecloths and a teapot collection ranged along the walls. The house speciality is the Yorkshire Fat Rascal, a huge fruit scone smothered in melted butter, while breakfast and lunch dishes, like bacon and raclette rösti, and Yorkshire rarebit, show off Betty's Swiss-Yorkshire heritage. Book ahead, or be prepared to queue.

★Cochon Aveugle FRENCH £££

(01904-640222; www.lecochonaveugle.uk; 37 Walmgate; 4-course lunch £75, 8-course tasting menu £95; 6-9pm Wed-Sat, noon-1.30pm Sat) Black-pudding macaroon? Salt-baked gurnard with lardo? Warm hen's yolk with smoked taramasalata? Fussy eaters beware – this small restaurant with huge ambition serves an ever-changing tasting menu (no à la carte) of infinite imagination and invention. You never know what will come next, except that it will be delicious. Bookings are essential. Its wine bar, Cave du Cochon (p493), is a few doors away.

Drinking & Nightlife

★Blue Bell PUB

(01904-654904; 53 Fossgate; 11am-11pm Mon-Thu, to midnight Fri & Sat, noon-10.30pm Sun;) This is what a proper English pub looks like – a tiny, 200-year-old wood-panelled room with a smouldering fireplace, decor untouched since 1903, a pile of ancient board games in the corner, friendly and efficient bar staff, and weekly cask-ale specials chalked on a board. Bliss, with froth on top – if you can get in (it's often full).

House of Trembling Madness BAR

(01904-640009; www.tremblingmadness.co.uk; 48 Stonegate; 10am-midnight Mon-Sat, from 11am Sun) When a place describes itself as a 'medieval drinking hall', it clearly deserves investigation. The ground floor and basement host an impressive shop stacked with craft beers, gins, vodkas and even absinthes; but head upstairs to the 1st floor and you'll find the secret drinking den – an ancient timber-framed room with high ceilings, a bar and happy drinkers.

Guy Fawkes Inn PUB

(01904-466674; www.guyfawkesinnyork.com; 25 High Petergate; 11am-11pm Mon-Thu & Sun, to midnight Fri & Sat) The man who famously plotted to blow up the Houses of Parliament and inspired Bonfire Night in the UK was born on this site in 1570. Walk through the lovely Georgian wood-panelled pub to find Guy Fawkes' grandmother's cottage at the far end of the back patio, watched over by a giant wall mural.

Brew York MICROBREWERY

(01904-848448; www.brewyork.co.uk; Enterprise Complex, Walmgate; noon-11pm Tue-Sat, to 9pm Sun) Housed in a cavernous old warehouse, half the floor space in this craft brewery is occupied by giant brewing tanks while the rest is given over to simple wooden drinking benches and a bar with rotating keg and cask beers. At the far end of the brewery there's a small riverside terrace overlooking Rowntree Wharf.

Perky Peacock CAFE

(Lendal Bridge; 7am-5pm Mon-Fri, 9am-5pm Sat, to 4pm Sun) One of York's charms is finding teeny places like this cafe, shoe-horned into historic buildings. In this case the host is a 14th-century, rotund watchtower crouched by the riverbank. Sup an excellent coffee under the ancient wood beams, or grab a street-side table for a tasty pastry.

King's Arms PUB

(01904-659435; King's Staith; noon-11pm Mon-Sat, to 10.30pm Sun) York's best-known pub enjoys a fabulous riverside location, with tables spilling out onto the quayside. It's the perfect spot on a summer evening, but be prepared to share it with a few hundred other people.

Shopping

Fossgate Books BOOKS

(01904-641389; fossgatebooks@hotmail.co.uk; 36 Fossgate; 10am-5.30pm Mon-Sat) A classic, old-school secondhand bookshop, with towers of books on the floor and a maze of floor-to-ceiling shelves crammed with titles covering every subject under the sun, from crime fiction and popular paperbacks to arcane academic tomes and 1st editions.

The Shop That Must Not Be Named GIFTS & SOUVENIRS
(30 The Shambles; ⏲10am-6pm) This shop on the Shambles – the street said to be the inspiration for Diagon Alley – has everything to cast a spell over Harry Potter fans. Wands? Tick. Quidditch fan gear? Tick. Potions? Tick. Pure magic for muggles. There's now no less than three Potter shops on the Shambles, but this is the original and still the most convincing.

Shambles Market FOOD
(www.shamblesmarket.com; The Shambles; ⏲9am-5pm) Yorkshire cheeses, Whitby fish and local meat make good fodder for self-caterers at this anything-goes market behind the Shambles, which also touts arts, crafts and Yorkshire flat caps. The food-court section near where the Shambles joins Pavement is a good spot for cheap eats, coffee and ice-cream at picnic tables.

ℹ Information

York Tourist Office (☎01904-550099; www.visityork.org; 1 Museum St, YO1 7DT; ⏲9am-5pm Mon-Sat, 10am-4pm Sun) Visitor and transport info for all of Yorkshire, plus accommodation bookings (for a small fee) and ticket sales.

ℹ Getting There & Away

BUS

York does not have a bus station; intercity buses stop outside the train station, while local and regional buses stop here and also on **Rougier St** (Rougier St), about 200m northeast of the train station.

For timetable info call **Traveline Yorkshire** (☎0871 200 2233; www.yorkshiretravel.net) or check the computerised 24-hour information points at the train station and Rougier St. There's a bus information point (8am to 4pm Monday to Saturday) in the train station's Travel Centre.

Birmingham £34, four hours, three daily
Edinburgh £28, 5½ hours, three daily
London from £30, 5½ hours, three daily
Newcastle £10, 2¼ hours, two daily

CAR

A car is more hindrance than help in the city centre, so use one of the six Park & Ride (www.itravelyork.info/park-and-ride) car parks at the edge of the city. If you want to explore the surrounding area, rental options include **Europcar** (☎0371 384 3458; www.europcar.co.uk; Queen St; ⏲8am-6pm Mon-Fri, to 4pm Sat), located next to the long-stay car park at the train station.

TRAIN

York is a major railway hub, with frequent direct services to many British cities.

Birmingham £74, 2¼ hours, two per hour
Edinburgh £59, 2½ hours, two to three per hour
Leeds £7.70, 25 minutes, at least every 15 minutes
London King's Cross £57.50, two hours, every 30 minutes
Manchester £30.40, 1½ hours, four per hour
Newcastle £22.50, one hour, four to five per hour
Scarborough £9.20, 50 minutes, hourly

ℹ Getting Around

Central York is easy to get around on foot – you're never more than 20 minutes' walk from any of the major sights.

BICYCLE

The tourist office has a useful free map showing York's cycle routes, or visit iTravel-York (www.itravelyork.info/cycling). Castle Howard (15 miles northeast of York via Haxby and Strensall) is an interesting destination, and there's also a section of the **Trans-Pennine Trail cycle path** (www.transpenninetrail.org.uk) from Bishopthorpe in York to Selby (15 miles) along the old railway line.

BUS

Local bus services are operated by First York (www.firstgroup.com/york). Single fares range from £1.60 to £4, and a day pass valid for all local buses is £4.50 (available on the bus or at Park & Ride car parks).

Castle Howard

Stately homes may be two a penny in England, but you'll have to try pretty damn hard to find one as breathtakingly stately as **Castle Howard** (☎01653-648333; www.castlehoward.co.uk; YO60 7DA; adult/child house & grounds £22/12, grounds only £12.95/8.50; ⏲house 10am-2pm Wed, Fri & Sat, grounds to 5.30pm daily, pre-booked tickets only; Ⓟ), a work of theatrical grandeur and audacity set in the rolling Howardian Hills. This is one of the world's most beautiful buildings, instantly recognisable from its starring role as Sebastian Flyte's home in both screen versions of Evelyn Waugh's 1945 paean to the English aristocracy, *Brideshead Revisited*.

When the Earl of Carlisle hired his pal Sir John Vanbrugh to design his new home in 1699, he was hiring a man who had no formal training and was best known as a playwright. Luckily, Vanbrugh hired Nicholas Hawksmoor, who had worked as Christopher Wren's clerk of works on St Paul's Cathedral. Not only did Hawksmoor have a big part to play in the design, bestowing on the house a baroque cupola modelled after St Paul's – the first on a domestic building in England – but he and Vanbrugh would later work wonders with Blenheim Palace. Today the house is still home to the Hon Nicholas Howard and his family and he can often be seen around the place.

As you wander about the peacock-haunted grounds, views open up over Vanbrugh's playful Temple of the Four Winds, Hawksmoor's stately mausoleum and the distant hills. Inside, you'll find the house split into two distinct styles; the east wing, which includes the Great Hall, was built in the 1700s and is extravagantly baroque in style, whereas the west wing wasn't completed until the 1800s, by which time the fashion was for much more classical Palladian. The house is full of treasures – the breathtaking Great Hall with its soaring Corinthian pilasters, Pre-Raphaelite stained glass in the chapel, and corridors lined with classical antiquities.

The pandemic forced the estate to move to an exclusively online booking system so as to control the flow of visitors. The advantage of limited numbers is that you'll have plenty of space to appreciate this hedonistic marriage of art, architecture, landscaping and natural beauty, but the downside is that the talk and tours of the house and gardens were suspended for the duration of the crisis. There are also boat tours down at the lake, and the entrance courtyard has a good cafe, a gift shop and a farm shop filled with foodie delights from local producers – you could quite easily spend an entire day at the site.

Castle Howard is 15 miles northeast of York, off the A64. Bus 181 from York goes to Malton via Castle Howard (£11 return, one hour, four times daily Monday to Saturday year-round).

Malton

01653 / POP 4888

It was the legendary late Italian chef Antonio Carluccio who first gave Malton the moniker of 'Yorkshire's food capital', and this sweet market town has worked hard to make the title stick. With good reason, too – the food scene is fabulous for a town of its size, with overflowing delis championing produce from the moors, wolds and dales, pint-sized artisan food and drink businesses, food-focused tours and a monthly food market.

Although there are no specific sights to speak of, the town does have some lovely Georgian architecture and independent shops. And like York, Malton has a crooked Shambles, now crammed with vintage shops, where butchers would have once slaughtered the lambs brought in for the town's sheep markets.

The town also has connections to Charles Dickens, who regularly visited a friend here. He wrote *A Christmas Carol* here on one of his trips.

Festivals & Events

Malton Food Lovers Festival FOOD & DRINK
(www.visitmalton.com/food-festival-yorkshire; end May) The biggest event on the calendar is Malton's annual three-day Food Lovers Festival with cooking demos, street food and music, attracting celebrity chefs and more than 30,000 visitors each May.

Eating & Drinking

★Talbot Yard FOOD HALL £
(www.visitmalton.com/talbot-yard-food-court; Yorkersgate; dishes £4-7; hours vary) Across the road from the Talbot Hotel, this huddle of converted stables has been reimagined as an extraordinary food court housing the stuff of gourmands' dreams. Here you'll find the only UK shop from award-winning macaron master Florian Poirot, and the home base of artisan Yorkshire bakery Blue Bird, among others. Come for gelato, posh pork pies, freshly ground coffee, Chelsea buns and macarons.

Talbot Yard is the main focus of the **Malton Artisan Food Tour**, but it's also easy to browse independently, and is perfect for picnic fodder.

La Pizzeria PIZZA £
(01653-690768; www.fatchefcompany.co.uk; 51 Wheelgate; mains £7-10; 11.30am-3pm & 5-9pm Tue-Fri, 11.30am-9pm Sat & Sun) Delicious wood-fired pizza in a modern, casual setting with blackboard specials and cocktails. A simple, winning concept and welcome change from pies, roasts and fish and chips.

Malton Relish DELI £
(☎01653-699389; www.maltonrelish.co.uk; 58 Market Pl; dishes £4-9; ⏰9am-5.30pm Mon-Sat, 10am-4pm Sun) This lovely deli overlooking Malton's market square is a good place to shop for local produce or sit down and taste it. The menu includes sandwiches, cheese boards and light lunches such as broccoli, pancetta and Yorkshire blue-cheese quiche with salad. Its monthly supper-club evening is worth looking into (book ahead), and there's a cute antiques store upstairs.

★Brass Castle MICROBREWERY
(☎01653-698683; www.brasscastle.co.uk; 10 Yorkersgate; ⏰noon-7pm Fri-Sun) This microbrewery began life in a garage in 2011 and surprised even itself when its beer won a prestigious CAMRA Beer Festival award within the first two months of production. Fast forward six years and it finally opened this taproom in central Malton. Its beers are unfiltered, vegan and gluten-free, and the taproom always has experimental brews on rotation.

Getting There & Away

Malton is easily accessible by train from York (£11.70, 25 minutes, hourly), and the train station is less than a 10-minute walk south from Market Pl.

The town is also a stop on the Coastliner 840 bus route that runs from Leeds to Whitby via York and Pickering. Departures from/to Leeds and York are hourly; Whitby and Pickering buses are less frequent.

Harrogate

☎01423 / POP 75,070

Queen Victoria's favourite spot for a spa break, prim and pretty Harrogate has long been associated with a certain kind of old-fashioned Englishness – the kind that seems the preserve of retired army majors and formidable dowagers who always vote Tory and get all their news from the *Daily Telegraph*. They come to Harrogate to enjoy the flower shows and gardens that fill the town with magnificent displays of colour, especially in spring and autumn. It is here that Agatha Christie fled to, incognito, in 1926 to escape her broken marriage.

And yet, this picture of Victoriana redux is not quite complete. While it's undoubtedly true that Harrogate remains a firm favourite of visitors in their golden years, the town has plenty of smart hotels and trendy dining spots catering to the boom in Harrogate's latest trade – conferences. All those dynamic young sales-and-marketing guns have to eat and sleep somewhere.

Sights & Activities

Royal Pump Room Museum MUSEUM
(www.harrogate.gov.uk; Crown Pl; adult/child £3/1; ⏰10.30am-5pm Mon-Sat, 2-5pm Sun Apr-Oct, to 4pm Nov-Mar) You can learn all about Harrogate's history as a spa town in the ornate Royal Pump Room, built in 1842 over the most famous of the town's sulphurous springs. It gives an insight into how the phenomenon of visiting spas to 'take the waters' shaped the town, and records the illustrious visitors it attracted. Beside the stained-glass counter where tonics would have once been dispensed, you can sit down and watch old black-and-white film of patients taking treatments such as peat baths.

The ritual of visiting spa towns as a health cure became fashionable in the 19th century and peaked during the Edwardian era in the years before WWI.

Montpellier Quarter AREA
(www.montpellierharrogate.com) The most attractive part of town is the Montpellier Quarter, overlooking Prospect Gardens between Crescent Rd and Montpellier Hill. It's an area of pedestrianised streets lined with restored 19th-century buildings that are now home to art galleries, antique shops, fashion boutiques, cafes and restaurants – an upmarket annex to the main shopping area around Oxford and Cambridge Sts.

★Turkish Baths SPA
(☎01423-556746; www.turkishbathsharrogate.co.uk; Parliament St; Mon from 6pm & Tue-Thu £19, Mon & Fri £23, Sat & Sun £32, guided tour per person £5; ⏰guided tours 9-10am Wed) Plunge into Harrogate's past at the town's fabulously tiled Turkish Baths. This mock-Moorish facility is gloriously Victorian and offers a range of watery delights: hot rooms, steam rooms, a plunge pool and so on, plus use of the original wooden changing cubicles and historic Crapper toilets. There's a complicated schedule of opening hours that are by turns single sex or mixed, so call or check online for details. The weekly guided tour of the building is fascinating and cheap – book ahead.

DON'T MISS

FOUNTAINS ABBEY

The alluring and strangely obsessive water gardens of the Studley Royal estate were built in the 18th century to enhance the picturesque ruins of 12th-century **Fountains Abbey** (NT; www.fountainsabbey.org.uk; adult/child £13/6.50; ⊙10am-5pm Mar-Oct, to 4pm Sat-Thu Nov-Jan, 10am-4pm Feb; P). Together, they present a breathtaking picture of pastoral elegance and tranquillity that have made them a Unesco World Heritage site and the most visited of all the National Trust's pay-to-enter properties.

After falling out with the Benedictines of York in 1132, a band of rebel monks came here to establish their own monastery. Struggling to make it alone, they were formally adopted by the Cistercians in 1135. By the middle of the 13th century, the new abbey had grown wealthy from trading wool and had become the most successful Cistercian venture in the country. After the Dissolution, when Henry VIII confiscated Church property, the abbey's estate was sold into private hands, and between 1598 and 1611 Fountains Hall was partly built using stone from the abbey ruins. The hall and ruins were united with the Studley Royal estate in 1768.

Studley Royal was owned by John Aislabie, once Chancellor of the Exchequer, who dedicated his life to creating the park after a financial scandal saw him expelled from Parliament. The main house of Studley Royal burnt down in 1946, but the superb landscaping, with its serene artificial lakes, survives almost unchanged from the 18th century.

The remains of the abbey are impressively grandiose, gathered around the sunny Romanesque cloister, with a huge vaulted cellarium leading off the west end of the church. Here, the abbey's 200 lay brothers lived, and food and wool from the abbey's farms were stored. At the east end is the soaring Chapel of Nine Altars, and on the outside of its northeast window is a green man carving (a pre-Christian fertility symbol).

A choice of scenic walking trails leads for a mile from the abbey ruins to the famous water gardens, designed to enhance the romantic views of the ruined abbey. Don't miss **St Mary's Church** (⊙noon-4pm Easter-Sep) FREE above the gardens.

Fountains Abbey is 4 miles west of Ripon off the B6265. Bus 139 travels from Ripon to Fountains Abbey visitor centre year-round (£4.40 return, 15 minutes, four times daily on Monday, Thursday and Saturday).

Festivals & Events

Spring Flower Show FAIR
(www.flowershow.org.uk; £17.50; ⊙late Apr) The year's main event, held at the Great Yorkshire Show Ground. A colourful three-day extravaganza of blooms and blossoms, flower competitions, gardening demonstrations, market stalls, crafts and gardening shops.

Great Yorkshire Show FAIR
(www.greatyorkshireshow.co.uk; adult/child £25/12.50; ⊙mid-Jul) Staged over three days by the Yorkshire Agricultural Society. Expect all manner of primped and prettified farm animals competing for prizes, and entertainment ranging from showjumping and falconry to cookery demonstrations and hot-air-balloon rides.

Autumn Flower Show FAIR
(www.flowershow.org.uk; £17.50; ⊙late Sep) Fruit- and veg-growing championships, cookery demonstrations and kid's events.

Sleeping

Hotel du Vin BOUTIQUE HOTEL ££
(☎01423-856800; www.hotelduvin.com/locations/harrogate; Prospect Pl; r/ste from £140/250; P 📶) An extremely stylish boutique hotel with dapper lounge – the loft suites with exposed oak beams, hardwood floors and extravagant bathrooms featuring two claw-footed baths and dual showers are among the nicest rooms in town, but even the standard bedrooms are spacious and very comfortable (though they can be noisy). Rates can plummet at quiet times, so keep an eye online.

Ascot House Hotel BOUTIQUE HOTEL ££
(☎01423-531005; 53 King's Rd, HG1 5HJ; r from £50; 🚌2A & 2B from city centre) This traditional Victorian house is now a 19-room boutique hotel with comfy, modern rooms. Nothing too fancy, but the service is friendly, the wi-fi is strong and the breakfast (£12) is sensational.

Unbeatable at this price. It's less than a mile north of the centre.

Acorn Lodge B&B ££

(☎01423-525630; www.acornlodgeharrogate.co.uk; 1 Studley Rd; s/d from £48/69; P 📶) Attention to detail is spot on at Acorn Lodge: stylish decor, crisp cotton sheets, powerful showers and perfect poached eggs for breakfast. Rooms 5, 6 and 7 in the eaves at the top of the house are particularly lovely. The location is good too, just a 10-minute walk from the town centre.

★Inn at Cheltenham Parade BOUTIQUE HOTEL £££

(☎01423-505041; www.harrogatebrasserie.co.uk; 26-30 Cheltenham Pde; s/d £80/90, apt from £99; P 📶) The incredibly central location makes this one of Harrogate's most appealing places to stay. Rooms are all individual, with subtle colour combinations and the occasional leather armchair; number 5 has a huge bathroom, and there's a pair of sweet studios with little balconies tucked at the top of the house. Behind the main building, there are also two larger apartments that would suit families.

Eating

Baltzersen's CAFE £

(☎01423-202363; www.baltzersens.co.uk; 22 Oxford St; mains £8.95-11; ⏰8am-5pm Mon-Sat, 10am-4pm Sun; 📶👪) This simple Scandi-style cafe serves Nordic waffles and pastries, plus Norwegian stew and open-sided sandwiches such as curried herring with potato salad. It also has great coffee, courtesy of North Star in Leeds and Falcon in nearby Pannal.

Bettys CAFE £

(☎01423-814070; www.bettys.co.uk; 1 Parliament St; mains £5-13, afternoon tea £18.50; ⏰9am-9pm; 👪) Arguably the most famous tearoom in Britain, Bettys is a Yorkshire institution. It was established in 1919 by a Swiss immigrant confectioner who took the wrong train, ended up in Yorkshire and decided to stay. Everything's made in-house, and there is almost always a queue for a table for speciality tea and cake; book your table online.

Tannin Level BISTRO ££

(☎01423-560595; www.tanninlevel.co.uk; 5 Raglan St; mains £15.95-28.95; ⏰noon-2pm & 5.30-9pm Tue-Fri, to 9.30pm Sat, noon-5pm Sun) 🍃 Old terracotta floor tiles, polished mahogany tables and gilt-framed mirrors and paintings create a relaxed yet elegant atmosphere at this popular bistro. A competitively priced menu based on seasonal British produce – think Yorkshire lamb rump or heirloom courgette and Yorkshire Fettle cheese tart – makes this a popular choice. Book ahead.

Drinking & Nightlife

★Bean & Bud COFFEE

(☎01423-508200; www.beanandbud.co.uk; 14 Commercial St; ⏰8am-3pm Mon-Tue & Thu-Fri, to 4pm Sat, 10am-4pm Sun; 📶) Small and bohemian, this cafe takes its drinks seriously, with names of coffee growers and altitudes of their plantations displayed proudly on the walls. It's also the sort of place that serves single-origin hot chocolates and puts fair-trade unrefined sugar on the tables. There's a choice of two or three freshly ground blends every day, plus top-quality white, green, oolong and black teas.

★Major Tom's Social CRAFT BEER

(☎01423-566984; www.majortomssocial.co.uk; The Ginnel, off Montpellier Gardens; ⏰noon-11.30pm Sun-Thu, to 1am Fri & Sat) Grungy and effortlessly cool, this 1st-floor drinking den is the type of place where locals cram onto sociable wooden bench tables and talk rubbish all night, sampling far more of the interesting draught beers than they meant to. Mismatched retro sofas and walls lined with vintage film and music posters complete the picture. There's also a cheap pizza menu (£7.50 to £9.50).

Harrogate Tap CRAFT BEER

(☎01423-501644; www.harrogatetap.co.uk; Station Pde; ⏰11am-11pm Sun-Thu, to midnight Fri, from 10am Sat; 📶) Set in a restored red-brick railway-station building dating from 1862, the Tap does a grand job of conjuring up the ambience of a bustling Victorian pub, but with the added attractions of a dozen rotating hand-pulled cask ales, another dozen keg taps and a menu of around 120 bottled craft beers from all over the world.

Hales Bar PUB

(☎01423-725570; www.halesbar.co.uk; Crescent Rd; ⏰noon-11pm Sun-Thu, to 1am Fri & Sat) There's a touch of the gothic about this candlelit coaching house, which claims to be the oldest pub in Harrogate (c 1766). It is still partially illuminated by its original gas lighting (look behind the bar – apparently this is the place to come in a blackout), but far more impressive are the theatrical Victorian open-flame cigarette lighters that still line the bar.

Shopping

Spirit of Harrogate DRINKS

(www.wslingsby.co.uk/experience; 5-7 Montpellier Pde; 11am-5.30pm Mon-Sat) Craft gin is the raison d'être of this quaint shop, which local gin brand Slingsby runs as a bottle shop by day and as a convivial setting for gin-tasting sessions by night. On alternate Friday evenings and Saturday afternoons it holds a 'Spirit of Gin' experience, which includes a talk on the history of gin, tasters and nibbles for £30; book ahead.

Information

Harrogate Tourist Office (01423-537300; www.visitharrogate.co.uk; Crescent Rd; 10am-5pm Mon-Sat Aug-Oct, 9.30am-5pm Nov-Mar)

Getting There & Away

Bus Harrogate & District (www.harrogatebus.co.uk) bus 36 connects Harrogate with Leeds (£6.70, 45 minutes, two to four hourly) and Ripon (£6.70, 30 minutes).

Train There are trains to Harrogate from Leeds (£9.10, 35 minutes, every 30 minutes) and York (£9.40, 35 minutes, hourly).

Scarborough

01723 / POP 61,749

A redeveloped Victorian spa, grand water park and Edwardian gardens are the remaining vestiges of Scarborough's 18th- and 19th-century heyday, when its natural spa waters made it a popular seaside holiday town. Its two large beaches are still a draw, but the downbeat city centre feels like it's stuck in the past, and not in a fashionably retro sort of way.

Cliff-scaling tramways ferry visitors down to the South Bay promenade, lined with arcades and fish-and-chip shops, while sitting on the headland are the toothsome ruins of its medieval castle.

Sights & Activities

Scarborough Castle CASTLE

(EH; www.english-heritage.org.uk; Castle Rd; adult/child £7.90/4.70; 10am-6pm Apr-Sep, to 5pm Oct-Mar) The massive medieval keep of Scarborough Castle occupies a commanding position atop its headland. Legend has it that Richard I loved the views from here so much that his ghost just keeps coming back. Take a walk out to the edge of the cliffs, where you can see the 2000-year-old remains of a **Roman signal station**. There's also a cafe and picnic tables. Visits are by pre-booked time slots only.

Peasholm Park PARK

(www.peasholmpark.com; Columbus Ravine; 24hr) FREE Set back from North Bay, Scarborough's beautiful Edwardian pleasure gardens, complete with hilltop pagoda, are famous for their summer sessions of **Naval Warfare** (adult/child £4.50/2.50; 3pm Mon, Thu & Sat Jul & Aug), when large model ships re-enact famous naval battles on the boating lake (check the website for dates).

Rotunda Museum MUSEUM

(01723-353665; www.scarboroughmuseumstrust.com; Vernon Rd; adult/child £3/free; 10am-5pm Tue-Sun;) The Rotunda Museum is dedicated to the coastal geology of northeast Yorkshire, which has yielded many of Britain's most important dinosaur fossils. The strata in the local cliffs were also important in deciphering England's geological history. Founded by William Smith, 'the father of English geology', who lived in Scarborough in the 1820s, the museum has original Georgian exhibits as well as a hands-on gallery for kids. Admission by pre-booked time slot only.

Sea Life AQUARIUM

(www.sealife.co.uk; Scalby Mills; adult/child under 3 £15.60/free; 10am-4pm Mon-Fri, to 5pm Sat & Sun, last admission 1hr before closing; P) At this family-oriented attraction you can see coral reefs, turtles, octopuses, seahorses, otters and many other fascinating creatures. The biggest draws are the talks and feeding times at the seal pool and penguin enclosure. The centre is at the far north end of North Beach; the miniature North Bay Railway (p502) runs the 0.75-mile route. You need to pre-book your ticket online. A lot of the attractions are outdoors, so it's not an ideal rainy-day refuge.

Sleeping & Eating

★ **Windmill** B&B ££

(01723-372735; www.scarborough-windmill.co.uk; Mill St; d/f from £85/120, apt £100-130; P) Quirky doesn't begin to describe this place, a beautifully converted 18th-century windmill in the middle of town. There are two self-catering apartments in the windmill itself, along with cottages, a family room and four-poster doubles around a

Scarborough

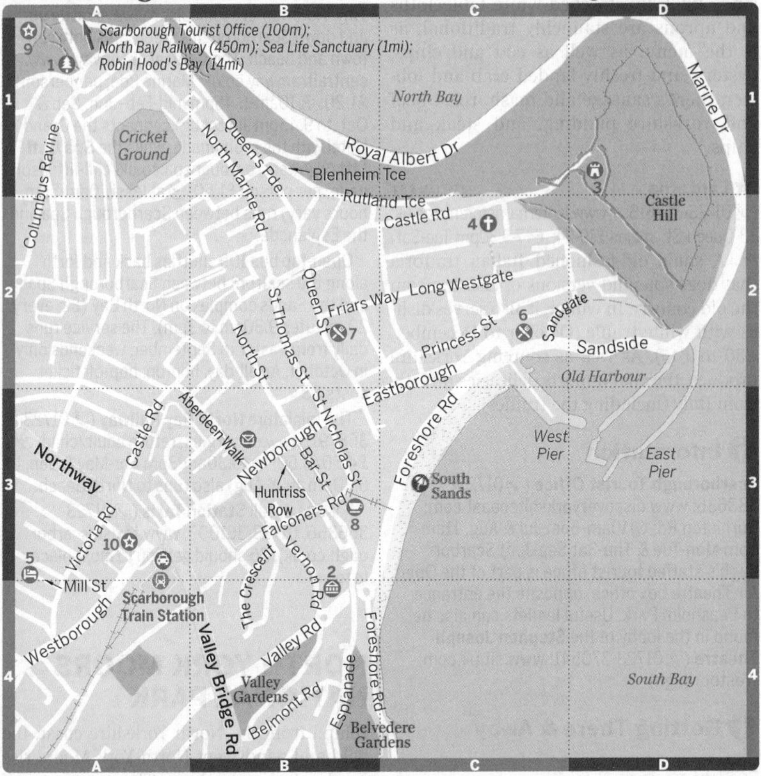

Scarborough

Sights
1 Peasholm Park A1
2 Rotunda Museum B4
3 Scarborough Castle D1
4 St Mary's Church C2

Sleeping
5 Windmill A3

Eating
6 Golden Grid C2
7 Lanterna B2

Drinking & Nightlife
8 Cat's Pyjamas B3

Entertainment
9 Naval Warfare A1
10 Stephen Joseph Theatre A3

cobbled courtyard. Try to secure the upper apartment (from £100 a night) in the windmill, which has great views from its wraparound balcony.

Cat's Pyjamas CAFE £
(☎01723-331721; www.thecatspyjamascafebars.co.uk; 2 St Nicholas Cliff; dishes £6-10; ⏰8am-5pm Sun-Thu, 9am-10pm Fri & Sat; 📶) Tucked inside the heritage Central Tramway shed and with sea views from its upstairs seating area, this 1920s-themed cafe and gin bar is a breath of fresh air in staid Scarborough. It serves simple brunches and lunches such as posh fish butties, plus coffee, cakes and G&Ts accompanied by jazz and swing music.

Golden Grid FISH & CHIPS ££
(☎01723-360922; www.goldengrid.co.uk; 4 Sandside; mains £10-20; ⏰11am-8.45pm Mon-Thu, 10.30am-9.30pm Fri-Sun; 👪) The Golden Grid is a sit-down fish restaurant that has

been serving the best cod in Scarborough since 1883. Its starched white tablecloths and aprons are staunchly traditional, as is the menu: as well as cod and chips, oysters, and freshly landed crab and lobster, there's sausage and mash, roast beef and Yorkshire pudding, and steak and chips.

★**Lanterna** ITALIAN **£££**
(☎01723-363616; www.lanterna-ristorante.co.uk; 33 Queen St; mains £19-24; ⏲7-9.30pm Tue-Sat) A snug, old-fashioned Italian trattoria that does splendid versions of classics from the old country. In winter, it also serves dishes with white truffle (October to December, £30 to £45). As well as sourcing Yorkshire produce, the chef imports delicacies directly from Italy (including the truffles).

Information

Scarborough Tourist Office (☎01723-383636; www.discoveryorkshirecoast.com; Burniston Rd; ⏲10am-6pm Jul & Aug, 11am-5pm Mon-Tue & Thu-Sat Sep-Jun) Scarborough's staffed tourist office is part of the Open Air Theatre box office, opposite the entrance to Peasholm Park. Useful leaflets can also be found in the lobby of the **Stephen Joseph Theatre** (☎01723-370541; www.sjt.uk.com; Westborough).

Getting There & Away

BUS

Bus 128 (www.eyms.co.uk) travels along the A170 from Helmsley to Scarborough via Pickering, while Arriva (www.arrivabus.co.uk) buses 93 and X93 come from Middlesborough and Whitby via Robin Hood's Bay. Coastliner (www.coastliner.co.uk) bus 843 runs to Scarborough from Leeds and York.

Helmsley £9.20, 1¾ hours, hourly Monday to Saturday, at least four daily on Sunday
Leeds £13.70, 2¾ hours, hourly
Whitby £7, one hour, once or twice hourly
York £14, 1¾ hours, hourly

TRAIN

Book in advance for cheaper tickets to York and Leeds.

Hull £16, 1½ hours, nine daily Monday to Saturday, six on Sunday
Leeds £33.60, 1¼ hours, hourly
Malton £9.60, 25 minutes, hourly
York £19.20, 45 minutes, hourly

Getting Around

Tiny Victorian-era funicular railways rattle up and down Scarborough's steep cliffs between town and beach. The **Central Tramway** (www.centraltramway.co.uk; Marine Pde; per person £1.20; ⏲10am-5.45pm mid-Feb–Jun, Sep & Oct, to 9.45pm Jul & Aug) connects the Grand Hotel with the promenade, while the **Spa Cliff Lift** (www.scarboroughspa.co.uk/cliff-lift; Esplanade; per person £1.50; ⏲at least 10am-5pm, hours vary) runs between Scarborough Spa and the Esplanade.

Open-top bus 109 shuttles back and forth along the seafront between Scarborough Spa and the Sands complex on North Bay (£2, every 20 minutes 9.30am to 3pm). The service runs daily from Easter to September, weekends only in October. An all-day, hop-on, hop-off ticket costs £3.

The miniature **North Bay Railway** (☎01723-368791; www.nbr.org.uk; return adult/child £4.50/3.50; ⏲10.30am-3pm Apr-May & Sep, to 5.30pm Jul & Aug) also runs to North Beach.

For a taxi, call **Station Taxis** (☎01723-366366, 01723-361009; www.taxisinscarborough.co.uk); £6 should get you to most places in town.

NORTH YORK MOORS NATIONAL PARK

Inland from the North Yorkshire coast, the wild and windswept North York Moors rise in desolate splendour. Three-quarters of all the world's heather moorland is found in Britain, and this is the largest expanse in England. Ridgetop roads climb up from lush green valleys to the bleak open moors, where weather-beaten stone crosses mark the lines of ancient roadways. In summer, heather blooms in billowing drifts of purple haze.

This is classic walking country. The moors are criss-crossed with footpaths old and new, and dotted with pretty, flower-bedecked villages. The national park is also home to one of England's most picturesque steam railways, and at its eastern edge lies historic Whitby – one of England's dreamiest and most haunting coastal towns.

The park produces the useful *Out & About* visitor guide, available from tourist offices and hotels, with information on things to see and do as well as a monthly events calendar. See also www.northyorkmoors.org.uk.

North York Moors National Park

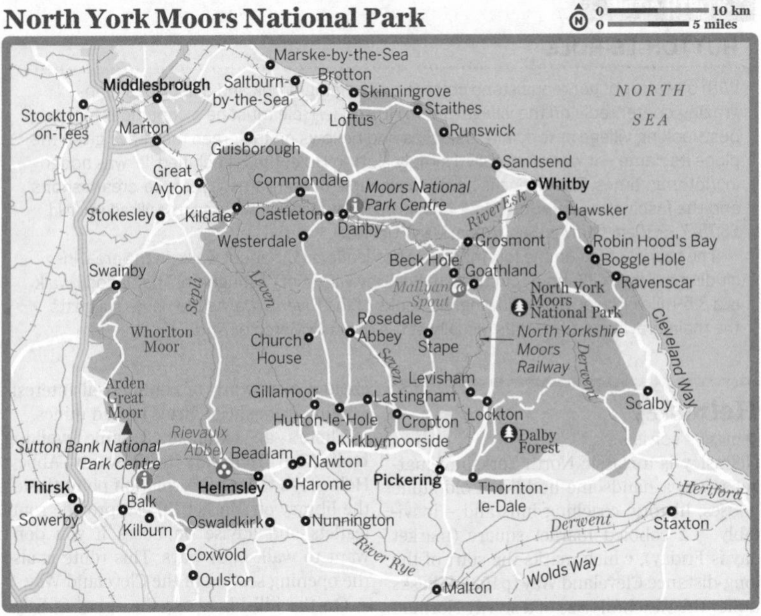

Activities

Yorkshire Cycle Hub CYCLING
(☎01287-669098; www.yorkshirecyclehub.co.uk; Fryup; ⊙9.30am-4.30pm Mon-Tue & Thu-Sun; 👪) Wedged in the middle of the North York Moors National Park, this centre is a great aid for local and visiting cycling enthusiasts. There's cycle hire (mountain bikes and e-bikes), a repairs shop, a simple bunkhouse (£35 per night; there are plans to add camping pods), bike wash and storage, and an excellent cafe with a log-burner and fabulous rural views.

North York Moors Guided Walks WALKING
(☎01439-772738; www.northyorkmoors.org.uk) FREE Each year the national park publishes a schedule of mostly free guided walks led by volunteers and specialists. Some skirt high moors along ancient paths to seek out medieval sites or ruined castles; others pass through bluebell woods, track birds, or delve into the myths and mysteries of the coastal villages. Places must be booked online or by phone.

Information

There are two national park visitor centres, providing information on walking, cycling, wildlife and public transport.

Moors National Park Centre (☎01439-772737; www.northyorkmoors.org.uk; Lodge Lane, Danby; parking 2/24hr £3/5.50; ⊙10am-5pm; 👪)

Sutton Bank National Park Centre (☎01845-597426; www.northyorkmoors.org.uk; Sutton Bank, by Thirsk; ⊙10am-5pm Apr-Oct, to 4pm Nov-Mar; 📶)

Getting Around

On Sundays and bank holiday Mondays from late May to September, a number of minibus services aimed at hikers shuttle around various locations within the national park; all are detailed on the Moorsbus (www.moorsbus.org) website.

For example, the **Moors Explorer** (☎01482-592929; www.eastyorkshirebuses.co.uk; all-day hop-on, hop-off ticket £12.50) service runs from Hull to the Moors National Park Centre in Danby with stops along the way, but only runs six or so times a year. An all-day hop-on, hop-off ticket costs £12.50. Download the EYMS app with timetables and track bus arrival times live.

The North Yorkshire Moors Railway (p506), running between Pickering and Whitby, is an excellent way of exploring the central moors in summer.

If you're planning to drive on the minor roads over the moors, beware of wandering sheep and lambs – hundreds are killed by careless drivers every year.

WORTH A TRIP

HUTTON-LE-HOLE

With a scatter of gorgeous stone cottages, a gurgling brook and a flock of sheep grazing contentedly on the village green, Hutton-le-Hole must be a contender for the best-looking village in Yorkshire. The dips and hollows on the green may have given the place its name – it was once called simply Hutton Hole; the Frenchified 'le' was added in Victorian times. The village is home to a couple of tearooms, a pub, ice-cream shops and the fascinating **Ryedale Folk Museum** (www.ryedalefolkmuseum.co.uk; adult/child £8.75/7; ⏲10am-5pm Apr-Sep, to 4pm Mar & Oct-Nov).

The tourist office (in the folk museum) has leaflets (£1) about walks in the area, including a 4-mile (2½-hour) circuit to the nearby village of Lastingham. The Daffodil Walk is a 3.5-mile circular walk following the banks of the River Dove. As the name suggests, the main drawcard is the daffs, usually at their best in March or April.

Helmsley

☎01439 / POP 1515

Helmsley is a classic North Yorkshire market town, a handsome huddle of old stone houses, historic coaching inns and – inevitably – a cobbled market square (market day is Friday), which marks the start of the long-distance Cleveland Way (p492). It basks under the watchful gaze of a sturdy Norman castle ruin and stately home surrounded by rolling fields. Nearby are the romantic ruins of Rievaulx Abbey, several excellent restaurants and a fistful of country walks.

Sights

★Rievaulx Abbey RUINS

(EH; www.english-heritage.org.uk; adult/child £11/6.60; ⏲10am-6pm Apr-Sep, to 5pm Oct, to 4pm Sat & Sun Nov–mid-Feb, daily Mar; Ⓟ) In the secluded valley of the River Rye about 3 miles west of Helmsley, amid fields and woods loud with birdsong, stand the magnificent ruins of Rievaulx Abbey (*ree*-voh). The extensive remains give a wonderful sense of the size and complexity of the community that once lived here, and their story is fleshed out in a series of fascinating exhibits in the attached museum. There's also a cafe with floor-to-ceiling windows and an outdoor terrace from which to gawp at the ruins.

This idyllic spot was chosen by Cistercian monks in 1132 as a base for their missionary activity in northern Britain. St Aelred, the third abbot, famously described the abbey's setting as 'everywhere peace, everywhere serenity, and a marvellous freedom from the tumult of the world'. But the monks of Rievaulx were far from unworldly and soon created a network of commercial interests ranging from sheep farms to lead mines.

There's an excellent 3.5-mile **walking trail** from Helmsley to Rievaulx Abbey; Helmsley's tourist information point (inside the library on Market Pl) can provide route leaflets and advise on buses if you don't want to walk both ways. This route is also the opening section of the Cleveland Way.

On the hillside above the abbey is **Rievaulx Terrace**, built in the 18th century by Thomas Duncombe II as a place to admire views of the abbey. Note that there's no direct access between the abbey and the terrace, and the two sites have separate admission fees. Their entrance gates are about a mile apart along a narrow road (a 20-minute walk steeply uphill if you're heading from the abbey to the terrace).

Helmsley Castle CASTLE

(EH; www.english-heritage.org.uk; Castlegate; adult/child £7.90/4.70; ⏲10am-6pm Apr-Sep, to 5pm Oct, to 4pm Fri-Sun Nov-Mar; Ⓟ) The impressive ruins of 12th-century Helmsley Castle are defended by a striking series of deep ditches and banks, to which later rulers added the thick stone walls and defensive towers. Only one tooth-shaped tower survives, following the dismantling of the fortress after the Civil War. The castle's tumultuous history is well explained in the 14-century West Range at the back of the site.

National Centre for Birds of Prey ANIMAL SANCTUARY

(☎01439-772080; www.ncbp.co.uk; Duncombe Park; adult/child £9/6.50; ⏲10am-5.30pm) Set in 300 acres of parkland that make up the Duncombe estate, this relatively new conservation centre has the north's largest collection of vultures, eagles, owls, hawks, falcons and other birds of prey. The aviaries are huge and the visitor interaction is terrific. The signposting is engaging – 'I'm a turkey vulture…to keep cool, I poo on my legs and feet' – and you can try your hand (literally) at falconry in the Raptor Experience (£65, over 10s only). There's also a good on-site cafe.

Duncombe Park GARDENS
(www.duncombepark.com; adult/child £5/3; 10.30am-5pm Sun-Fri Apr-Aug; P) On the outskirts of Helmsley lies the superb ornamental landscape of Duncombe Park estate, laid out in 1718 for Thomas Duncombe (whose son would later build Rievaulx Terrace), with the stately Georgian mansion of Duncombe Park House at its heart. From the house (not open to the public) and formal gardens, wide grassy walkways and terraces lead through woodland to mock-classical temples, while longer walking trails are set out in the landscaped parkland, now protected as a nature reserve.

Sleeping

Feathers Hotel INN ££
(01439-770275; www.feathershotelhelmsley.co.uk; Market Pl; s/d from £80/120; P) One of a number of old coaching inns on the market square that offer B&B, decent grub and a pint of hand-pumped real ale. The rooms have a contemporary touch, but there are historical trimmings throughout.

Canadian Fields CAMPGROUND ££
(01439-772409; www.canadianfields.co.uk; Gale Lane; safari tents £80-100; Feb–mid-Nov; P) This luxury campsite 3 miles east of Helmsley offers comfortable and unusual accommodation in spacious 'safari tent' cabins with kitchens, electricity and wood-burning stoves under canvas, alongside private outdoor showers. There are also sites where you can pitch your own tent (from £15 a night), and a bar-restaurant housed in a giant tepee provides a convivial social hub.

Feversham Arms HOTEL £££
(01439-772935; www.fevershamarmshotel.com; High St; d/ste from £160/230; P) Just behind Helmsley's church, the Feversham Arms has a snug and sophisticated atmosphere where country charm meets boutique chic. Service is excellent and rooms are comfy (the luxury pool suites with balcony are especially light and spacious), but it's the spa and lovely heated outdoor pool that brings guests from far and wide; the on-site restaurant is not worth the money.

Eating

Vine Cafe CAFE £
(01439-771194; www.vinehousecafehelmsley.co.uk; Helmsley Walled Garden, Cleveland Way; mains £7-11; 10am-5pm Apr-Oct;) Goodies plucked from the gardens take centre stage at this whimsical cafe housed in vine-draped Victorian greenhouses within creepers distance of Helmsley Walled Garden. Everything on the menu is fresh and simple, like the homemade hummus and chickpea curry, organic frittata and Helmsley butcher's ham sandwich. It's licensed, too, so you can take a Yorkshire G&T with lunch in the sun.

★Star Inn MODERN BRITISH £££
(01439-770397; www.thestaratharome.co.uk; Harome, YO62 5JE; mains £18-34; noon-2pm Tue-Sat, 4.30-8.30pm Mon-Sat, noon-6.30pm Sun; P) This thatch-roofed country pub is home to a Michelin-starred restaurant, with a menu specialising in top-quality produce from the surrounding countryside: Whitby crab with pickled cockles and avocado 'ice', or roast English quail with braised salsify and bergamot preserve. The tasting menu (£85, £175 with matching wines) is magnificent. Harome is about 2 miles southeast of Helmsley off the A170.

The Star is the sort of place you won't want to leave, and the good news is you don't have to – the adjacent lodge has nine magnificent bedrooms (£150 to £240), each decorated in classic but luxurious country style.

★Hare Inn MODERN BRITISH £££
(01845-597769; www.thehare-inn.com; Scawton; tasting menu £85, half-board package from £167; noon-2.30pm & 6-9pm Wed-Sat; P) Drowsing in a secluded hamlet 4 miles west of Helmsley, the Hare is a 21st-century restaurant in a 13th-century inn, where gourmet dining is relaxed, informal and even fun. There's no à la carte, just a seasonal tasting menu, and only seven tables; bookings must be made in advance. In 2019 they added a couple of guest rooms.

Getting There & Away

Buses stop in the main square. From Scarborough, bus 128 (£9.20, 1¾ hours, hourly Monday to Saturday) runs to Helmsley via Pickering, with an additional Sunday service April to October (six daily).

Pickering

01751 / POP 6830

Pickering is a lively market town with an imposing Norman castle that advertises itself as the 'gateway to the North York Moors'. That gateway is also the terminus of the wonderful North Yorkshire Moors Railway, a picturesque survivor from the great days of steam.

Two scenic drives head north across the moors: the A169 to Whitby leads past the **Hole of Horcum** beauty spot and the hiking trails of Goathland (p509); and the Blakey Ridge road (beginning 6 miles west of town) passes the pretty village of Hutton-le-Hole (p504) and the famous **Lion Inn** on the way to Danby.

Sights

★North Yorkshire Moors Railway HERITAGE RAILWAY
(NYMR; www.nymr.co.uk; Park St; Pickering–Whitby day-rover ticket adult/child £35/20; Easter-Oct, reduced service Nov-Easter) This privately owned railway runs for 18 miles through beautiful countryside from Pickering to Whitby. Lovingly restored steam locos pull period carriages with wooden booths, appealing to railway buffs and day trippers alike. For visitors without wheels, it's excellent for reaching out-of-the-way spots and devising walks between stations. You must book online.

Pickering Castle CASTLE
(EH; www.english-heritage.org.uk; Castlegate; adult/child £5.90/3.70; 10am-6pm Apr-Sep, to 5pm Oct) Pickering Castle is a lot like the castles we drew as kids: thick stone outer walls circle the keep, and the whole lot is perched atop a high motte (mound) with great views of the surrounding countryside. Founded by William the Conqueror around 1070, it was added to and altered by later kings, but there's not much of it left.

Sleeping

★White Swan Hotel HOTEL £££
(01751-472288; www.white-swan.co.uk; Market Pl; incl breakfast s from £140, d £170-220; P) The top spot in town successfully combines a smart pub, a superb restaurant serving a daily changing menu of local produce (mains £14 to £22) and a luxurious boutique hotel. Nine rooms lie within the converted coach house itself, but the best are in a quiet, hidden block out back, where guests get the added perks of underfloor heating and free robes.

Eating & Drinking

Black Swan PUB
(01751-798209; www.blackswan-pickering.co.uk; 18 Birdgate; mains £14-20; 11.30am-11pm Mon-Thu, to 11.30pm Fri & Sat, to 10.30pm Sun;) This 18th-century coaching inn has had an ambitious makeover to return it to its former glory. The food is recommended, the beers are brewed in-house (ask behind the bar and you might get a mini guided tour of the microbrewery), and there's also a 1920s-themed cocktail den that you enter around the back of the pub. Fresh, modern B&B rooms upstairs cost from £95.

Getting There & Away

Bus 128 between Helmsley (£5.70, 40 minutes) and Scarborough (£7, one hour) runs hourly via Pickering. Bus 840 between Leeds and Whitby also travels via Pickering (hourly).

Whitby

01947 / POP 13,213

Wonderful, a little weird and occasionally weather-beaten Whitby is a town with three distinct personalities. The huddle of 18th-century fisher's cottages along the East Cliff are testament to its longtime role as a busy commercial and fishing port – it was here that 18th-century explorer Captain James Cook earned his sea legs. The genteel Victorian suburb atop the West Cliff is a clue to Whitby's place as a traditional seaside resort complete with sandy beach, amusement arcades and promenading holidaymakers.

Keeping a watchful eye over the town and the River Esk that divides it is an atmospheric ruined abbey, the inspiration and setting for part of Bram Stoker's Gothic horror story *Dracula*. But tales of witchery and ghostly legends have haunted Whitby ever since Anglo-Saxon St Hilda landed here to found a monastic community in 657 CE. The town embraces its pseudo-sinister reputation, which culminates in two hugely successful Goth Weekends each year.

Sights

★Whitby Abbey RUINS
(EH; www.english-heritage.org.uk; East Cliff; adult/child £10/6; 10am-6pm Apr-Sep, to 5pm Oct, to 4pm Nov-Mar; P) There are ruined abbeys,

Whitby

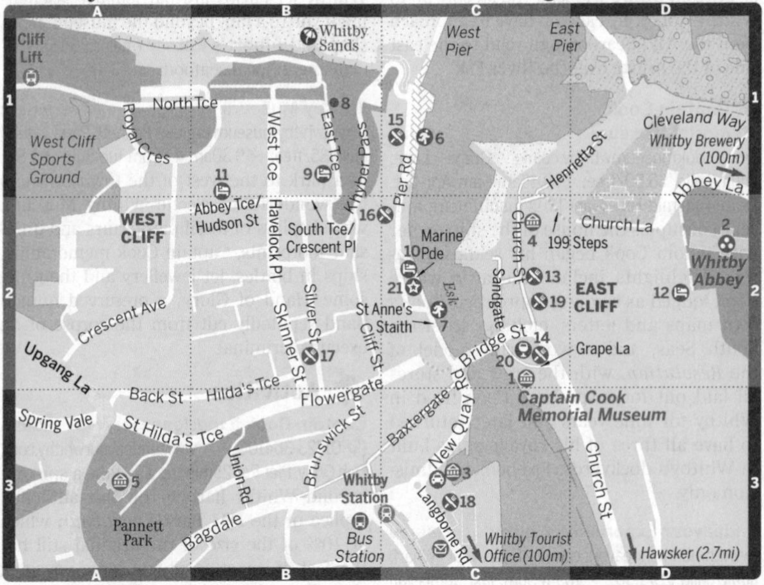

Whitby

Top Sights
1 Captain Cook Memorial Museum C2
2 Whitby Abbey D2

Sights
3 Endeavour Experience Whitby C3
4 Museum of Whitby Jet C2
5 Whitby Museum A3

Activities, Courses & Tours
6 Captain Cook Experience C1
7 Whitby Coastal Cruises C2
8 Whitby Ghost Walks B1

Sleeping
9 La Rosa Hotel B1
10 Marine Hotel C2
11 Rosslyn House B1
12 Whitby YHA D2

Eating
13 Cornish Bakery C2
14 Humble Pie 'n' Mash C2
15 Magpie Cafe C1
16 Quayside C2
17 Rusty Shears B2
18 Star Inn the Harbour C3
19 White Horse & Griffin C2

Drinking & Nightlife
20 Green Dragon C2

Entertainment
21 Dracula Experience C2

and there are picturesque ruined abbeys. And then there's Whitby Abbey, dominating the skyline above the East Cliff like a great Gothic tombstone silhouetted against the sky. Looking as though it was built as an atmospheric film set rather than a monastic establishment, it is hardly surprising that this medieval hulk inspired the Victorian novelist Bram Stoker (who holidayed in Whitby) to make it the setting for Count Dracula's dramatic landfall.

The stately mansion beside the abbey ruins was built by the Cholmley family, who leased the Whitby estate from Henry VIII after the dissolution of England's monasteries in the 1530s. Following a £1.5 million revamp in 2019, the abbey has dramatically improved its museum, added a small coffee shop with outdoor seating in the abbey grounds, and replaced its free audio guide with a more family-friendly 'ammonite quest' to explore the site with.

From the end of Church St, the 199 steps of **Church Stairs** will lead you steeply up to Whitby Abbey. By car, you have to approach from the A171 Scarborough road to the east side of the bridge over the River Esk.

★Captain Cook Memorial Museum MUSEUM
(www.cookmuseumwhitby.co.uk; Grape Lane; adult/child £6.50/free; ⏲9.45am-5pm Apr-Oct, 11am-4pm mid-Feb–Mar) This fascinating museum occupies the house of the ship owner with whom Cook began his seafaring career. Highlights include the attic where Cook lodged as a young apprentice, Cook's own maps and letters, etchings from the South Seas, and a wonderful model of the *Resolution,* with the crew and stores all laid out for inspection. Cook lived in Whitby for nine years and later returned to have all three of his voyage ships built in Whitby's dockyards. Pre-booked admission only.

Endeavour Experience Whitby MUSEUM
(www.hmbarkendeavour.co.uk; Endeavour Wharf; adult/child £5/1.50; ⏲10am-5pm, last admission 4pm; 👪) In the 18th century, Whitby was one of Britain's greatest shipbuilding centres, James Cook was apprenticed here and the original HM Bark *Endeavour* was built in the town. It was aboard this ship that Cook charted New Zealand and the east coast of Australia for the first time.

In 2018, a full-size replica of the *Endeavour* became a permanent fixture in Whitby harbour and opened to the public as a visitor attraction. On board, 11 cabins have been transformed into a cafe, mini galleries and interactive exhibits about life at sea and Cook's 1768 voyage of discovery aboard *Endeavour*. Highlights include the 'Sea Shanty' karaoke room, animated film projections in the Great Cabin and a display of Southern Hemisphere constellations the crew would have used for navigation.

Museum of Whitby Jet MUSEUM
(☎01947-667453; www.museumofwhitbyjet.com; Wesley Hall, Church St; ⏲9.30am-5.30pm) FREE Housed inside a 1901 chapel, this small museum has created a temple to Whitby jet – one of the town's most prized exports, a gothic icon, and a favourite gem of Queen Victoria. The exhibition explores how jet is formed over millions of years on the Yorkshire coast and has historically been turned into jewellery. The displays of 19th-century Whitby jet curios are particularly fascinating if you're a fan. Beyond the museum lies a shop and **Albert's Eatery** (mains £5-16), specialising in local seafood.

Whitby Museum MUSEUM
(www.whitbymuseum.org.uk; Pannett Park; adult/child £5/free; ⏲9.30am-4.30pm Tue-Sun; 👪) Set in a park to the west of the town centre is the wonderfully eclectic Whitby Museum, with displays of fossil plesiosaurs and dinosaur footprints, Captain Cook memorabilia, ships in bottles, jet jewellery and the gruesome 'Hand of Glory', a preserved human hand reputedly cut from the corpse of an executed criminal.

Activities

Captain Cook Experience BOATING
(☎01723-364100; www.endeavourwhitby.com; Fish Quay, Pier Rd; 25min trip £5) Take a spin out beyond Whitby harbour on this authentic replica of the HM Bark *Endeavour,* which at 40% of the size of the original still has the feel of an atmospheric large voyaging ship. The skipper will regale you with tales of Captain Cook's ordeals at sea and his long-standing associations with Whitby. Good fun for young and old.

Whitby Coastal Cruises BOATING
(☎07981 712419; www.whitbywhalewatching.net; Brewery Steps; 3½hr trip £15) Spot birds, seals, dolphins or even steam trains on a coastal or River Esk boat trip with this long-running family business. September is whale-watching season, during which time you can join its sister business Whitby Whale Watching on a trip (£40) where the chances of seeing minke whales (and more rarely humpbacks) are high.

Tours

★Whitby Ghost Walks WALKING
(☎01947-880485; www.whitbywalks.com; Whale Bone Arch, West Cliff; adult/child £5/3; ⏲7.30pm) Whitby wouldn't be Whitby without ghoulish tales and strange happenings, and nobody knows them better than Dr Crank, who manages to confidently keep to the right side of naff with his fascinating 75-minute tour around West Cliff's most haunted and storied alleyways. You'll learn of legends like the screaming tunnel, the hand of glory and the headless horseman, plus tidbits of local history.

Hidden Horizons OUTDOORS
(☎ 01723-817017; www.hiddenhorizons.co.uk; adult/child from £9/6) You can get down on the beaches around Whitby to hunt for fossils (and there's plenty to find), take a dinosaur-footprint walk, go rock-pooling, or join a star-gazing session with this local tour company. Sessions are entertaining but also educational. Check the online calendar for upcoming events, and book ahead.

Festivals & Events

Whitby Goth Weekends CULTURAL
(www.whitbygothweekend.co.uk; tickets 1/2 days £40/70; ⏲ late Apr/early May & late Oct/early Nov) Goth heaven attracting more than 8000 visitors biannually, with live-music gigs, events and the Bizarre Bazaar – dozens of traders selling Goth gear, jewellery, art and music. Held twice yearly in late April or early May and late October or early November (around Halloween).

Whitby Steampunk Weekend CULTURAL
(www.wsofficial.com; Whitby Pavilion; ⏲ late Jul) Science fiction meets Victoriana fantasy in Whitby on the last weekend in July, when fans of the steampunk genre descend for balls, costumed promenading, entertainment and shopping at the Steampunk Emporium. A little bit Gothic, a little bit geeky – very Whitby. Events are anchored on the Whitby Pavilion on West Cliff.

Sleeping

Whitby YHA HOSTEL £
(☎ 0845 371 9049; www.yha.org.uk; Church Lane; tw/f from £35/30; P 📶) With an unbeatable setting in an old mansion next to the abbey, this hostel is incredibly popular – you'll have to book well in advance to get your body into one of the bunks here. Hike up the 199 steps from the town, or take bus 97 from the train station to Whitby Abbey (twice hourly Monday to Saturday).

★ **La Rosa Hotel** HOTEL ££
(☎ 01947-606981; www.larosa.co.uk/hotel; 5 East Tce; d incl breakfast £90-145; P 📶) Weird, but wonderful. Lewis Carroll, author of *Alice in Wonderland,* once stayed in this house while holidaying in Whitby. Entering today is like stepping through the looking glass into a world of love-it-or-hate-it Victorian bric-a-brac and kitsch, peppered with vintage film props. Eight quirky and atmospheric bedrooms, great sea views, no TV, an in-house bar, and breakfast served in a basket in your room.

OFF THE BEATEN TRACK

GOATHLAND

This picture-postcard halt on the North Yorkshire Moors Railway stars as Hogsmeade train station in the Harry Potter films, while the village appeared as Aidensfield in the British TV series *Heartbeat*. It's also the starting point for lots of easy and enjoyable walks, often with the chuff-chuff-chuff of passing steam engines in the background.

The hamlet of Beck Hole is home to the wonderfully atmospheric **Birch Hall Inn** (www.beckhole.info; Beck Hole; ⏲ 11am-11pm May-Sep, 11am-3pm & 7.30-11pm Wed-Mon Oct-Apr; 👪 🐾), which is less 'hall' and more like two 18th-century cottages where you drink in a tiny sitting room (or outside by the beck). Drinks are served through a hole in the wall: order a pork pie and pint of ale brewed in the village. Cash only.

Rosslyn House B&B ££
(☎ 01947-604086; www.rosslynhousewhitby.co.uk; 11 Abbey Tce; s/d/f from £65/85/105; 📶) Lovely Victorian terrace house that stands out amid the sea of B&Bs on West Cliff, with a friendly welcome and bright, modern decor. The single room is snug; the family room large (though the hotel does not admit children under 12). There's a convenient drying room for walkers.

★ **Marine Hotel** INN £££
(☎ 01947-605022; www.the-marine-hotel.co.uk; 13 Marine Pde; r from £150; 📶) Feeling more like mini-suites than ordinary hotel accommodation, the four bedrooms at the Marine are quirky, stylish and comfortable; it's the sort of place that makes you want to stay in rather than go out. Ask for one of the two rooms with a balcony – they have great views across the harbour.

Eating

★ **Rusty Shears** BRITISH £
(☎ 01947-605383; 3 Silver St; brunch £4-8; ⏲ 9.30am-5pm; 📶) This vintage cafe covers many bases. There's an astounding drinks menu with more than 100 gins and gin flights (despite the fact it's closed evenings), a walled courtyard for alfresco light

WORTH A TRIP

ROBIN HOOD'S BAY

Picturesque Robin Hood's Bay has nothing to do with the hero of Sherwood Forest – the origin of its name is a mystery, and the locals call it Bay Town or just Bay – but it was once a major centre for smuggling. All that is in the past – well explored in the volunteer-led **Bay Museum** (http://museum.rhbay.co.uk; Fisherhead; ⏲ hours vary, school holidays only) – and the fishing village is now just one of the prettiest spots on the Yorkshire coast.

Leave your car at the parking area in the upper village (£4.40 for four hours), where 19th-century ships' captains built comfortable Victorian villas, and walk downhill to Old Bay, the oldest part of the village (don't even think about driving down). This maze of narrow lanes and passages is dotted with tearooms, pubs, craft shops and artists' studios (there's even a tiny cinema), and at low tide you can go down onto the beach and fossick around in the rock pools.

Robin Hood's Bay is 6 miles southeast of Whitby. Bus 93 runs hourly between Whitby and Scarborough via Robin Hood's Bay.

lunches, and a cluster of retro-styled rooms for cosy chats over excellent coffee and cakes like treacle tart or Yorkshire tea loaf. The brunches with Fortune's smoked bacon and creamy scrambled eggs deserve a medal.

Cornish Bakery BAKERY £
(92 Church St, YO22 4BH; mains £3.60-4.30; ⏲ 8am-5pm) It might be far from Cornwall, but this superb bakery serves freshly made Cornish pasties as well as delicious pastries including *pain au raisin* and Portuguese-style *pastel de nata*. Rinse them down with an expertly brewed coffee and you've fuelled up for the walk up the 199 steps to the abbey.

Humble Pie 'n' Mash BRITISH £
(☎ 01947-606444; www.humblepie.tccdev.com; 163 Church St; pie meal £9.99; ⏲ noon-8pm) Superb homemade gravy-laden pies with fillings ranging from haggis and neeps (turnips) to roast veg and goats cheese, served in a cosy timber-framed cottage with a 1940s nostalgia vibe. No bookings, cash only.

★ Magpie Cafe SEAFOOD ££
(☎ 01947-602058; www.magpiecafe.co.uk; 14 Pier Rd; mains £13-28; ⏲ 11.30am-9pm; 📶👪) The Magpie flaunts its reputation for serving the 'World's Best Fish and Chips'. Damn fine they are too, but the world and his dog knows about it and summertime queues can stretch along the street. Takeaway fish and chips cost £7.95; the sit-down restaurant is more expensive, but offers a wide range of seafood dishes, from grilled sea bass to paella.

★ White Horse & Griffin BRITISH ££
(☎ 01947-604857; www.whitehorseandgriffin.com; 87 Church St; mains £14-24; ⏲ 8-9.30am, noon-3pm & 5-9pm Mon-Sat, 12.30-4pm & 5.30-9pm Sun; 📶🐾) This splendid old coaching inn is as old as Captain Cook, and indeed the man himself used it as a meeting place to fix his crews in the 17th century. Squeeze into the narrow bar and the restaurant behind it is barely noticeable, but what a find: expect elegantly presented, top-quality British cooking that celebrates both local seafood and meat.

Quayside FISH & CHIPS ££
(☎ 01947-825346; www.quaysidewhitby.co.uk; 7 Pier Rd; mains £10-16; ⏲ 11am-8pm Mon-Sat, to 7pm Sun; 👪) Top-notch, award-winning fish and chips. The queues aren't nearly as long as at nearby competitor the Magpie Cafe, but that might be because they don't have 'world's best' on their tagline. Oh, the power of advertising.

Star Inn the Harbour BRITISH ££
(☎ 01947-821900; www.starinntheharbour.co.uk; Langborne Rd; mains £12-28; ⏲ 11.30am-9pm Mon-Fri, noon-9pm Sat, to 7pm Sun) Yorkshire food hero Andrew Pern, of Michelin-starred Star Inn (p505) fame, gutted the former tourist office to create this spin-off restaurant on the harbour front in his home town of Whitby. It's no surprise that the theme is nautical and the menu leans heavily on its fishy environs, though there are also playful dishes such as Yorkshire pudding and foie gras.

Drinking & Nightlife

★ Whitby Brewery MICROBREWERY
(☎ 01947-228871; www.whitby-brewery.com; Abbey Lane, East Cliff; ⏲ 11am-5pm; 🐾) Walkers are pleased as punch when they find this

place on the clifftop behind Whitby Abbey. There's just enough room inside the modern brew plant for three tables – half the space is taken up by a gloriously incongruous Edwardian bar counter, behind which the bartender is well and truly trapped. There's a short selection of craft ales, and extra seating out front.

Green Dragon CRAFT BEER
(www.thegreendragonwhitby.co.uk; Grape Lane; noon-7.30pm Mon-Sat, to 6pm Sun) In a quaint old house on Whitby's most crooked lane, Green Dragon has grabbed the bull by the horns and dragged Britain's progressive craft-beer scene into this traditional real-ale town. It's part bottle shop, part teeny-weeny beer bar with five rotating taps running Yorkshire breweries like Northern Monk, Abbeydale and Vocation. It also sells mead and absinthe.

☆ Entertainment

Dracula Experience THEATRE
(01947-601923; 9 Marine Pde; adult/child £3/2.50; 9.45am-5pm Easter-Oct, Sat & Sun Nov-Easter) There's definitely an element of Gothic geekdom about this theatrical walk-through of *Dracula*'s tale, with special effects, an occasional live actor appearing out of thin air and many a thing that goes bump in the night designed to spook you in the darkness. Wonderfully weird and very Whitby; not suitable for under eights.

Information

Whitby Tourist Office (01723-383636; www.visitwhitby.com; Harbour Master's Office, Langborne Rd; 9am-5pm May-Oct, to 4pm Thu-Sun Nov-Apr)

Getting There & Away

BUS

Two buses, 93 and X93, run south to Scarborough (£6.20, one hour, every 30 minutes), with every second bus going via Robin Hood's Bay (£5.20, 15 minutes, hourly); and north to Middlesborough (£7, one hour, hourly), with fewer services on Sunday. The **bus station** is next to Whitby's train station.

The Coastliner service 840 runs from Leeds to Whitby (£15.70, 3¼ hours, four times daily Monday to Saturday, twice on Sundays, though you'll need to change at Malton) via York and Pickering.

TRAIN

Coming from the north, you can get to Whitby by train along the Esk Valley Railway from Middlesbrough (£7.50, 1½ hours, four daily), with connections from Durham and Newcastle. From the south, it's easier to get a train from York to Scarborough, and then a bus from Scarborough to Whitby.

YORKSHIRE DALES NATIONAL PARK

The Yorkshire Dales – named from the old Norse word *dalr*, meaning 'valleys', and protected as a national park since the 1950s – are beloved as one of England's best hiking and cycling areas. The park's glacial valleys are characterised by a distinctive landscape of high heather moorland, stepped skylines and flat-topped hills, punctuated by delightful country pubs and windswept trails.

Down in the green valleys, patchworked with drystone dykes and little barns, are picture-postcard villages where sheep still graze on village greens. And in the limestone country of the southern Dales you'll find England's best examples of karst scenery (created by rainwater dissolving the underlying limestone bedrock).

The whole area is seriously scenic and easy to explore. Consequently it's popular with holidaying Britons – book accommodation ahead as there are no big hotels here. Beds get particularly scarce on public holiday weekends and during events such as the annual Tour de Yorkshire.

Getting There & Away

About 90% of visitors to the park arrive by car, and the narrow roads can become extremely crowded in summer. Parking can also be a serious problem.

We recommend that you use public transport where possible, but bus services are limited and many run in summer only – some on Sundays and bank holidays only. Pick up a DalesBus timetable from tourist offices, or consult the DalesBus (www.dalesbus.org) website.

By train, the best and most interesting access to the Dales is via the famous **Settle–Carlisle Line** (SCL; 01768-353200; www.settle-carlisle.co.uk). Trains run between Leeds and Carlisle, stopping at Skipton, Settle and numerous small villages, offering unrivalled access to the hills straight from the station platform.

Yorkshire Dales National Park

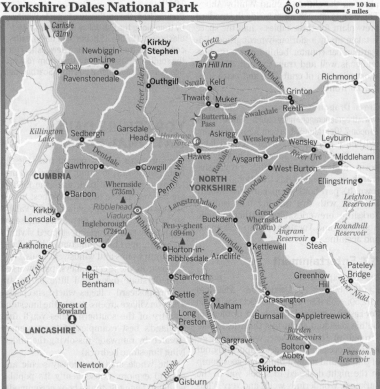

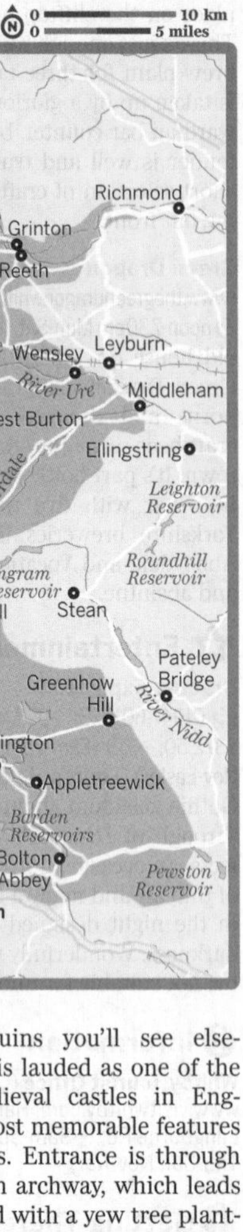

Skipton

☎01756 / POP 14,623

Home to one of England's best-preserved medieval castles and gateway to the southern Dales, this busy market town takes its name from the Anglo-Saxon *sceape ton* (sheep town). There are no prizes for guessing how it made its money. Monday, Wednesday, Friday and Saturday are market days, bringing crowds from all over and giving the town something of a festive atmosphere.

The Leeds–Liverpool Canal carves right through central Skipton, making the town a good jumping-off point for canal-boat trips.

Sights & Activities

★**Skipton Castle** CASTLE
(www.skiptoncastle.co.uk; High St; adult/child £8.70/5.50; ⏲10am-4pm) What makes Skipton Castle so fascinating is its splendid state of preservation, providing a striking contrast to the ruins you'll see elsewhere. Although it is lauded as one of the best-preserved medieval castles in England, many of its most memorable features date to Tudor times. Entrance is through the original Norman archway, which leads to a Tudor courtyard with a yew tree planted by Lady Anne Clifford in 1659, and beyond that is a warren of rooms to explore. Grab the informative free illustrated guide to the castle from the ticket office, available in several languages.

Pennine Cruisers BOATING
(☎01756-795478; www.penninecruisers.com; The Wharf, Coach St; per person £4; ⏲10.30am-dusk Mar-Oct) No trip to Skipton is complete without a cruise along the Leeds–Liverpool Canal, which runs through the middle of town. Pennine Cruisers runs half-hour trips along the canal and back, as well as canal-boat day hire, skippered trips and longer holiday rentals. Pre-booking essential.

Sleeping

★Pinfold GUESTHOUSE ££
(☎07510-175270; www.thepinfoldskipton.co.uk; Chapel Hill; r £60-80; P 📶) This petite, room-only guesthouse has three light and airy, oak-beamed rooms with a lovely fresh country feel. Forgive the tiny shower rooms, because the excellent location around the corner from Skipton Castle more than compensates. The Littondale room has its own entrance, parking and small grassy patio. The Little Pinfold Cottage, a one-room self-catering cottage across the street, has been added more recently.

Park Hill B&B ££
(☎01756-792772; www.parkhillskipton.co.uk; 17 Grassington Rd; d £95; P 📶) From the complimentary glass of sherry on arrival to the hearty breakfasts based on local produce, such as farm-fresh eggs and home-grown tomatoes, this B&B provides a real Yorkshire welcome. It enjoys an attractive semi-rural location half a mile north of the town centre, on the B6265 road towards Grassington. No children under 12.

Eating & Drinking

Bizzie Lizzies FISH & CHIPS £
(☎01756-701131; www.bizzielizzies.co.uk; 36 Swadford St; mains £10-13; ⏲11am-9pm; 👪) An award-winning, old-fashioned fish-and-chip restaurant overlooking the canal, with a busy takeaway counter offering fish and chips for £6.65 (counter open to 11.30pm). Gluten-intolerant? No problem – Bizzie Lizzies also dishes up gluten-free chips accredited by Coeliac UK.

★Le Caveau BRITISH £££
(☎01756-794274; www.lecaveau.co.uk; 86 High St; 2/3-course menu £22.50/28.50; ⏲noon-2.30pm & 7-9pm Tue-Fri, 5-9pm Sat) 🍃 Thanks to the stylish decoration there's no hint that this 16th-century cellar was once a prison for sheep rustlers. It's now one of Skipton's best bistros, offering a seasonal menu built lovingly around fresh local produce, with tempting dishes such as twice-baked smoked Ribblesdale goats-cheese soufflé and slow-roasted Nidderdale lamb shoulder.

Narrow Boat PUB
(www.markettowntaverns.co.uk; 38 Victoria St; ⏲noon-11pm; 📶👪🐾) Down a back alley beside Skipton's canal basin, this friendly pub is essentially a modern craft-beer bar but still manages to cultivate a traditional feel with wooden beams and old bar furniture. The beer selection is great; soak it up with interesting bar food such as halloumi chips, southern fried chicken burgers and a rotating range of flatbread pizzas.

Information

Tourist Office (☎01756-792809; www.welcometoskipton.com; Town Hall, High St; ⏲9.30am-4pm Mon-Sat)

Getting There & Away

Skipton is the last stop on the Metro rail network from Leeds (from £5.80, 45 minutes, frequent departures). Buses 580 to 582 link Skipton with Settle Monday to Saturday (£6.20, 40 minutes, hourly during the day), with many departures continuing on to Ingleton. There are also twice daily buses from Skipton to Malham (£4.70, 40 minutes) Monday to Saturday, and frequent departures from Skipton to Grassington.

Grassington

☎01756 / POP 1611

A good base for jaunts around the south Dales, Grassington's handsome Georgian centre teems with walkers and visitors throughout summer, soaking up an atmosphere that – despite the odd touch of faux rusticity – is as attractive and traditional as you'll find in these parts.

OFF THE BEATEN TRACK

FORBIDDEN CORNER

There can surely be no other place like **Forbidden Corner** (☎01969-640638; www.theforbiddencorner.co.uk; Tupgill Park Estate, near Leyburn; adult/child £13/11; ⏲noon-dusk Mon-Sat Easter-Oct, Sun only Nov & Dec; P 👪) in the world: a modern walled garden furnished with Victorian-style follies, some veering into Gothic horror, others merely surreal fantasy. There's no map, so it's a case of diving in to explore the many tunnels, twisted turns and dead-ends – an experience that may make you feel like you've fallen into David Bowie's *Labyrinth*. Small children are guaranteed to feel scared witless at some turns; adults may leave feeling a little rattled, too. Tickets must be pre-booked.

WORTH A TRIP

BRITAIN'S HIGHEST PUB

At an elevation of 528m (1732ft) **Tan Hill Inn** (☎01833-628246; www.tanhillinn.com; Tan Hill, Swaledale; ⏲8am-11.30pm Jul & Aug, 9am-9.30pm Sep-Jun;) is Britain's highest pub. Built to cater for 19th-century miners, it perches in the middle of nowhere about 11 miles northwest of Reeth. At times the howling wind can make it feel a bit wild up here, but inside it's unexpectedly comfortable and welcoming, with an ancient fireplace in the atmospheric, stone-flagged public bar and leather sofas in the lounge.

Festivals & Events

Grassington Festival ART
(www.grassington-festival.org.uk; ⏲mid-Jun–early Jul) Highlight of the cultural year in the Yorkshire Dales is the Grassington Festival, a two-week arts extravaganza that attracts many big names in music, theatre and comedy, and also includes offbeat events like drystone-walling workshops.

Grassington 1940s Weekend FAIR
(www.grassington1940sweekend.co.uk; ⏲Sep) This vintage celebration brings classic cars, planes and army vehicles to town, as well as WWII military re-enactment encampments, for a weekend in mid-September.

Sleeping & Eating

Ashfield House B&B ££
(☎01756-752584; www.ashfieldhouse.co.uk; Summers Fold; d/ste from £89/155;) A secluded 17th-century country house with a walled garden, open fireplaces, honesty bar and all-round cosy feel. It's just off the main square.

★ **Devonshire Fell** HOTEL ££
(☎01756-718111; www.devonshirefell.co.uk; Burnsall; r from £95;) This former gentleman's club for mill owners in the scenic village of Burnsall has a very contemporary feel and spacious rooms, many with beautiful valley views. The conservatory (used as a restaurant, breakfast room and for afternoon tea) has a stunning outlook. It's 3 miles southeast of Grassington, which can be reached via a walking path by the river.

Corner House Cafe CAFE £
(☎01756-752414; www.cornerhousegrassington.co.uk; 1 Garr's Lane; mains £7-10; ⏲10am-4pm;) This cute little white cottage, just uphill from the village square, serves good coffee and unusual homemade cakes (citrus and lavender-syrup sponge is unexpectedly delicious), as well as tasty made-to-order sandwiches and lunch specials such as Dales lamb hotpot or chicken and chorizo gratin. Breakfast, served till 11.30am, ranges from cinnamon toast to the full-English fry-up.

Information

Grassington National Park Centre (☎01756-751690; Hebden Rd; 2/24hr parking £3/6; ⏲10am-5pm Apr-Oct, to 3pm Sat & Sun Nov, Dec, Feb & Mar)

Getting There & Away

Grassington is 6 miles north of Skipton; take bus 72 from Skipton bus or train station (£5, 30 minutes, hourly Monday to Saturday), or X43 (hourly, Sunday and public holidays) from the bus station only. For onward travel, bus 72 continues up the valley to the villages of Kettlewell and Buckden.

Malham

POP 238

Even in the Dales, where competition is fierce, Malham is quite the looker. Stone cottages and inns huddle around a river that meanders through the village centre – which is always busy with walkers drawn to its world-famous hiking paths. If you're only visiting one village in the Dales, make it this one.

The village is set within the largest area of limestone country in England, stretching west from Grassington to Ingleton – a distinctive landscape pockmarked with potholes, dry valleys, limestone pavements and gorges. Two of the most spectacular features – Malham Cove and Gordale Scar – are within walking distance of Malham's centre.

Sights & Activities

★ **Malham Cove** NATURAL FEATURE
North of Malham village, a 0.75-mile field walk beside a lovely babbling stream leads to Malham Cove, a huge rock amphitheatre lined with 80m-high vertical cliffs. A large

glacial waterfall once tumbled over this cliff, but it dried up hundreds of years ago. You can hike up the steep steps on the left-hand side of the cove (follow Pennine Way signs) to see the extensive limestone pavement above the cliffs – a filming location in *Harry Potter and the Deathly Hallows*.

Peregrine falcons nest at the top in spring, when the Royal Society for the Protection of Birds (RSPB) sets up a birdwatching lookout with telescopes near the base of the cliff – call the national park centre (p516) for the schedule as it changes every year.

Malham Tarn LAKE

A glacial lake and nature reserve 3.5 miles north of Malham village, accessible via a 1.5-mile walk north from Malham Cove, or by car. There are two car parks: the one at the southern edge is bigger and picks up a trail that skirts the eastern side of the lake; the one to the north (follow signs to Arncliffe/Grassington) allows easy access to an extensive bog-skimming boardwalk that wends through fen and woodland scrub. Roe deer, heron and water voles can sometimes be spotted here.

Malham Landscape Trail WALKING

(www.malhamdale.com) This 5-mile circular trail is one of the best day hikes in Yorkshire, linking three impressive natural features: Malham Cove; spectacular **Gordale Scar**, a deep limestone canyon with scenic cascades; and the remains of an Iron Age settlement, and **Janet's Foss** waterfall. A leaflet describing the trail in detail can be downloaded from the website or picked up at pubs and hotels in the village.

Sleeping & Eating

★Lister Barn B&B £££

(☎01729-830444; www.listerarms.co.uk; Cove Rd; d £120-165; P 📶 🐾) The Lister Arms pub runs this chic barn conversion on the main road through the village, with eight modern rooms centred on a lovely open-plan communal area with free herbal teas and a log burner to huddle around after long walks. One room is suitable for wheelchair users and there are two family rooms with bunks and a separate bedroom.

Lister Arms PUB FOOD ££

(☎01729-830444; www.thwaites.co.uk; Cove Rd; mains £10-17; ⏰8am-11pm Mon-Sat, to 10.30pm Sun; P 📶 👶 🐾) This comfy coaching inn is the best spot in Malham to kick back after a walk, with open fires for chilly days, a beer garden out back and classic pub meals, plus chalkboard specials. In the busy summer months drinkers lounge out on the grass in front of the pub.

RIBBLESDALE & THE THREE PEAKS

Scenic Ribblesdale cuts through the southwestern corner of the Yorkshire Dales National Park, where the skyline is dominated by a trio of distinctive hills known as the Three Peaks: Whernside (735m), Ingleborough (724m) and Pen-y-ghent (694m). Easily accessible via the Settle–Carlisle railway line (p511), this is one of England's most popular areas for outdoor activities, attracting thousands of hikers, cyclists and cavers each weekend.

At the head of the valley, 5 miles north of Horton, is the spectacular 30m-high Ribblehead Viaduct, built in 1874 and, at 400m, the longest on the Settle–Carlisle Line. You can hike there along the Pennine Way and travel back by train from Ribblehead station.

In a huddle of old stone barns is the simply marvellous **Courtyard Dairy** (☎01729-823291; www.thecourtyarddairy.co.uk; Crows Nest Barn, Austwick, near Settle; ⏰9.30am-5.30pm Mon-Sat, 10am-5pm Sun), a cheesemongers and cafe that has arguably the best farmhouse cheeses in the Yorkshire Dales. Owners Andy and Kathy Swinscoe are passionate supporters of small-scale producers, and deli staff are eager to hand out tasters. The cafe upstairs in the eaves of the barn slathers the cheese all over its menu. Come here to try 'Raclette Anglaise' and inventive grilled-cheese-sandwich wedges such as Wensleydale and caramelised-carrot chutney. Don't miss the delicious rich fruit cake with a slab of local Dales cheese: a Yorkshire tradition. There's also a small, hugely informative museum about cheesemaking in Yorkshire, maturing rooms you can peer into, and Andy runs one-day cheesemaking courses (£120) on-site; check the website for dates.

WORTH A TRIP

GRANTLEY HALL

Just outside the boundary of the national park is the Palladian pile of **Grantley Hall** (☎01765-667970; www.grantleyhall.co.uk; B6265, Ripon; r from £385, with dinner from £485), built in the 17th century for Thomas Norton and now Yorkshire's most luxurious hotel.

Opulence and the highest aesthetic considerations permeate the 47 rooms (huge beds and Tielle linen, gorgeous Italian marble bathrooms) and sweeping public spaces, including the Michelin-starred restaurant, **Shaun Rankin at Grantley Hall**. It's a classic country-house hotel, but the overall look is enhanced by some graceful modern notes. The enormous **Three Graces Spa** has an 18-metre pool, two gyms and a snow room, as well as altitude training facilities, making this the kind of destination that would suit an Olympic athlete in training as it would Lord Grantham in repose. In a separate building, the pan-Asian restaurant **EightyEight** (mains £25) is also superb.

It's 4 miles west of Ripon, off the B6265.

Information

Malham National Park Centre (☎01729-833200; www.yorkshiredales.org.uk; parking 2/24hr £3.50/6; ⊙10am-5pm Apr-Oct, to 4pm Sat & Sun Nov, Dec, Feb & Mar) In the car park at the southern edge of Malham village; the walking leaflets it sells (£1.50) include more detail than the free leaflet given out around the village.

Getting There & Away

There are at least two buses a day Monday to Saturday year-round from Skipton to Malham (£4.70, 35 minutes). The scenic Malham Tarn Shuttle bus route links Settle with Malham (£4.30, 30 minutes), Malham Tarn and Ingleton six times daily on Sundays and bank holidays only, Easter to October. Check the DalesBus website (www.dalesbus.org) or ask at Malham National Park Centre for details.

Note that Malham is reached via narrow roads that can get very congested in summer, so leave your car at the national park centre and walk into the village.

Hawes

POP 1137

Right at the heart of Wensleydale, Hawes is a thriving, pretty market town (Tuesday is market day) surrounded by rolling hills and drystone walls that will be familiar to fans of the 1970s TV series, *All Creatures Great and Small,* based on James Herriot's books. It has several antique, art and craft shops, and the added attraction of its own waterfall in the village centre. The village can get pretty busy in summer, so leave the car in the parking area beside the national park centre at the eastern entrance to the village.

A mile northwest of Hawes, the pretty village of **Hardraw** has an even more impressive waterfall, a country church and an excellent old pub offering accommodation for those who prefer a quieter rural base. The whole area is also full of hiking trails.

Sights

Hardraw Force WATERFALL

(www.hardrawforce.com; Hardraw; adult/child £4/2; P) About 1.5 miles north of Hawes is 30m-high Hardraw Force, the highest unbroken waterfall in England, but by international standards not that impressive (except after heavy rain). Access is via a lovely landscaped walk (400m) from the car park behind the Green Dragon Inn. There's an admission fee (coins only) to access the walk, and a cafe selling local ice cream.

Wensleydale Creamery MUSEUM

(www.wensleydale.co.uk; Gayle Lane; adult/child £1.95/free; ⊙10am-4pm; P ♿) Wensleydale Creamery is devoted to the production of a crumbly white cheese that's the favourite of animation characters Wallace and Gromit. You can visit the cheese museum, watch cheesemakers in action in the viewing gallery (Monday to Friday), and then try-before-you-buy in the shop (which is free to enter). An interactive exhibit for kids explains the process from grass to cow to cheese.

Dales Countryside Museum MUSEUM

(☎01969-666210; www.dalescountrysidemuseum.org.uk; Station Yard; adult/child £4.80/free; ⊙10am-5pm Feb-Dec; P ♿) Sharing a building with the national park centre, the Dales Countryside Museum is a beautifully presented social history of the area that explains the forces shaping the landscape, from geology to lead mining to land enclosure and the railways.

Sleeping & Eating

★Green Dragon Inn INN ££
(☎01969-667392; www.thegreendragoninnhardraw.com; Hardraw; d/ste £90/110; P 📶 🐾) A lovely old pub with flagstone floors, low timber beams, ancient oak furniture and Theakston on draught, the Dragon serves up a tasty steak-and-ale pie and offers B&B in pleasant, simple rooms behind the pub, as well as a pair of fancy suites above the bar. It's 1 mile northwest of Hawes.

Information

Hawes National Park Centre (☎01969-666210; Station Yard; parking 2/24hr £2.50/5; ⏱10am-5pm Apr-Oct, closes early Nov, Dec, Feb & Mar, closed Jan)

Richmond

☎01748 / POP 8415

The handsome market town of Richmond perches on a rocky outcrop overlooking the River Swale and is guarded by the ruins of a massive castle, beneath which a small, frothy waterfall flows. It has been a garrison town for centuries and home to one of England's most decorated regiments, which now resides nearby at modern-day Catterick Garrison.

Elegant Georgian buildings and photogenic stone cottages line the streets that radiate from the broad cobbled market square (market day is Saturday), with glimpses of the surrounding hills and dales peeking through the gaps. There are plenty of local walks, and the town makes a pleasant base for exploring the northern Dales.

For themed walks, alongside talks, films and other events, visit the town during the **Richmond Walking & Book Festival** (☎01748-824243; www.booksandboots.org; ⏱Sep/Oct).

Sights

★Georgian Theatre Royal HISTORIC BUILDING
(www.georgiantheatreroyal.co.uk; Victoria Rd; adult/child £5/2; ⏱tours hourly 10am-4pm Mon-Sat mid-Feb–mid-Nov) Built in 1788, this is the most complete Georgian playhouse in Britain. It closed in 1848 and was used as an auction house into the early 20th century, reopening as a working theatre again in 1963 after a period of restoration. Fascinating tours (starting on the hour) include a look at the country's oldest surviving stage scenery, painted between 1818 and 1836.

Richmond Castle CASTLE
(EH; www.english-heritage.org.uk; Tower St; adult/child £6.90/4.10; ⏱10am-5pm Wed-Sun) The impressive heap that is Richmond Castle, founded in 1070, has had many uses through the years, including a stint as a prison for conscientious objectors during WWI (there's a small and fascinating exhibition about their part in the castle's history – enter through the shop). The best part of a visit is the view from the top of the remarkably well-preserved 30m-high keep, which dates to the late 12th century and towers over the town.

Sleeping & Eating

Frenchgate Hotel BOUTIQUE HOTEL ££
(☎01748-822087; www.thefrenchgate.co.uk; 59-61 Frenchgate; s/d incl breakfast from £98/148; P 📶) Nine elegant bedrooms occupy the upper floors of this converted Georgian town house, with flash touches such as memory-foam mattresses and heated marble floors in luxurious bathrooms. Parts of the house date to 1650, so we can forgive a crack here or peeling paint there. Downstairs there's an excellent restaurant (three-course dinner £39), an oasis of a garden and a private rear car park.

★George & Dragon PUB FOOD £
(☎01748-518373; www.georgeanddragonhudswell.co.uk; Hudswell; mains £9-11; ⏱food served noon-2pm & 5-8pm Mon-Sat, noon-4pm Sun; 📶 👶) A mile and a half west of Richmond, the George & Dragon is a genuine local pub,

BIKING IN THE DALES

The centre of mountain biking in the Yorkshire Dales, the **Dales Bike Centre** (☎01748-884908; www.dalesbikecentre.co.uk; Fremington; mountain bike/e-bike per day from £40/50; ⏱9am-5pm), 12 miles west of Richmond, provides quality rentals (mountain and road bikes, as well as e-bikes), a bike shop and repair service, advice and trail maps, guided rides (£199 per day for up to seven people), a cosy cafe with decent coffee and comfortable bunkhouse accommodation (two-bunk room £58 a night).

WORTH A TRIP

MASHAM BREWERIES

Located 9 miles northwest of Ripon, the little village of Masham is famous for producing some of Yorkshire's best beers. Yorkshire's best-known brewery, **Theakston's** (☎01765-680000; www.theakstons.co.uk; The Brewery, Masham; tour adult/child £8.50/4.95; ⏲10.30am-4.30pm Sep-Jul, to 5pm Aug), was founded way back in 1827, then taken over by global brewer Scottish & Newcastle in 1987, but since 2004 has been back in family hands. Old Peculier, its most famous ale, takes its name from the Peculier of Masham, a medieval parish court established to deal with offences such as drunkenness and brawling. There's a visitor centre that doubles as a bar, and four tours a day (five in August).

Across the village, **Black Sheep Brewery** (☎01765-680101; www.blacksheepbrewery.com; Wellgarth, Masham; tours adult/child £9.50/4.95; ⏲10am-5pm Sun-Wed, to 11pm Thu-Sat; P 👪) was founded in 1992 by the 'black sheep' of the Theakston family, Paul Theakston, who left to start his own brewery after the controversial Scottish & Newcastle takeover. It's now almost as famous as its near neighbour, with four entertaining tours a day, an excellent casual bistro, and a bar where you can sample most of the Black Sheep brews.

owned and managed by the community. It serves a small menu of freshly prepared pub grub, including roast beef and Yorkshire pudding on Sundays, and has won awards for its excellent rotating beer selection. The backyard terrace has gorgeous Dales views.

The Station BRITISH £
(☎01748-850123; www.thestation.co.uk; Station Yard; mains £7-11; ⏲10am-4pm Mon-Tue, to 7pm Thu-Sat, 9am-4pm Sun) Richmond's defunct Victorian railway station has been converted into a bold multipurpose space housing exhibition galleries, an independent cinema, craft brewery (offering tastings and sales) and ice-cream parlour. Locals come for takeaway lunch at Angel's Share Bakery, which bakes fresh breads, quiches and local specialities such as Yorkshire curd tart on-site. Take your goodies to the grassy picnic area outside.

ℹ Information

Richmond Tourist Office (☎01609-532980; www.richmond.org; Richmond Library, Queens Rd; ⏲10am-5pm Mon-Fri, to 1pm Sat) A tiny tourist office with less information than can be found at other outlets across Yorkshire.

ℹ Getting There & Away

From Darlington (on the railway between London and Edinburgh) it's easy to reach Richmond on bus X26 or X27 (£6.20, 30 minutes, every half-hour, hourly on Sunday). All buses stop in Trinity Church Sq.

On Sundays and bank-holiday Mondays only, from May to September, the Northern Dalesman bus 830 runs from Richmond to Hawes (£4.70, 1½ hours, twice daily) via Reeth, and the afternoon bus continues to Ribblehead.

WEST YORKSHIRE

It was the tough and unforgiving textile industry that drove West Yorkshire's economy from the 18th century onward. The woollen mills, factories and canals built to transport raw materials and finished products defined much of the county's landscape. The mills have long since closed, and recent decades have seen the hard-bitten landscape soften once more.

Leeds and Bradford, two adjoining cities so big they've virtually become one, are undergoing radical redevelopment and reinvention, prettifying their centres and tempting more adventurous tourists with new museums, galleries and restaurants. Beyond the cities lies a landscape of wild moorland dissected by deep valleys dotted with old mill towns and villages, scenes that were so vividly described by the Brontë sisters, West Yorkshire's most renowned literary export and biggest tourist draw.

ℹ Getting There & Around

The Metro is West Yorkshire's highly efficient train and bus network, centred on Leeds and Bradford, which are also the main gateways to the county. For transport information, contact **West Yorkshire Metro** (☎0113-245 7676; www.wymetro.com).

Day Saver tickets (£9) are good for one day's unlimited travel on Metro buses and trains from 9.30am to 4pm and after 6.30pm on weekdays, and all day at weekends. A range of additional Rover tickets covering buses and/or trains, plus heaps of useful Metro maps and timetables, are available from bus and train stations and most tourist offices in West Yorkshire.

Leeds

☎0113 / POP 474,632

Just an hour south of the southern Dales and one of the fastest-growing cities in the UK, Leeds is the glitzy embodiment of rediscovered northern self-confidence. A decade and a half of redevelopment has transformed the city centre from a near-derelict mill town into a vision of 21st-century urban chic, with architecturally eye-catching malls woven into the fabric of the city centre, a revitalised Victorian mill district and an innovative independent dining and drinking scene. The decision by national broadcaster Channel 4 to move its HQ north from London just adds an extra feather to Leeds' cap.

People come from all over the north to indulge in shopping weekends, concert trips and the lively nightlife, giving the town a decidedly confident Yorkshire swagger. Excellent transport links to the Dales, York, Harrogate, Manchester and Haworth (of Brontë literary fame) can make it a good base, without the touristy veneer of neighbouring York.

Sights

★Royal Armouries MUSEUM

(www.royalarmouries.org; Armouries Dr; 10am-5pm Wed-Sun, last admission 3.30pm; P ♿) FREE Leeds' most interesting museum was originally built in 1996 to house armour and weapons from the Tower of London, but subsequently expanded to cover 3000 years of combat and self-defence, becoming home to the national collections. The exhibits are as varied as they are fascinating, covering subjects such as jousting, fencing and Indian elephant armour. Walk east along the river from Centenary Footbridge (approx 10 minutes), or take the water taxi (p526) from Granary Wharf outside the train station's southern entrance.

Leeds Art Gallery GALLERY

(www.leeds.gov.uk/artgallery; The Headrow; 10am-4pm Tue-Sat) FREE This major gallery is packed with 19th- and 20th-century British heavyweights – Turner, Constable, Stanley Spencer, Wyndham Lewis et al – along with contemporary pieces by more recent arrivals such as Damien Hirst and Antony Gormley, sculptor of the *Angel of the North*. The stunning **Tiled Hall Cafe** – formerly a reading room and then a sculpture court – is the city's most elegant spot for a break.

Leeds Industrial Museum MUSEUM

(Armley Mills; ☎0113-378 3173; www.leeds.gov.uk/museumsandgalleries/armleymills; Canal Rd, Armley; adult/child £4.50/2.50; 10am-5pm Tue-Fri, 1-5pm Sat-Sun; P ♿; 🚌15 from city centre) One of the world's largest textile mills has been transformed into a museum telling the story of Leeds' industrial past, both glorious and ignominious. The city grew rich from the textile industry, but at some cost in human terms – working conditions were Dickensian. As well as a selection of mill machinery, there's an informative display about how cloth is made. The museum is 2 miles west of the city centre; take the bus from Vicar Lane near Kirkgate Market.

Kirkstall Abbey CHURCH

(www.leeds.gov.uk/kirkstallabbey; Abbey Rd, Kirkstall; 10am-4.30pm Tue-Sun Apr-Sep, to 4pm Oct-Mar; 🚌33, 33A or 757 from city centre) FREE Leeds' most impressive medieval structure is beautiful Kirkstall Abbey, founded in 1152 by Cistercian monks from Fountains Abbey in North Yorkshire. These days the city makes good use of it as an atmospheric backdrop for pop-up events and a monthly weekend food market (April to November; check online for dates). It's 3 miles northwest of the centre.

Across the road is the **Abbey House Museum** (www.leeds.gov.uk/museumsandgalleries; Abbey Walk, Kirkstall; adult/child £5.45/2.80; 10am-noon & 1-4pm Wed-Fri & Sun, noon-5pm Sat; P ♿), which was once the Great Gate House to the abbey. It contains meticulously reconstructed shops and houses that evoke Victorian Leeds, plus rotating exhibitions mostly aimed at kids.

Tetley GALLERY

(☎0113-320 2423; www.thetetley.org; Hunslet Rd; 11am-4pm Wed-Sun) Tetley Brewery's defunct 1930s offices have been converted into a contemporary-arts venue with a restaurant and pub on the ground floor, spilling out onto an outdoor terrace. Upstairs the old meeting rooms have been put to good use as quirky gallery spaces, housing rotating exhibitions from international and local artists and photographers. An immaculately preserved 1930s lift dominates the central stairwell shaft.

Henry Moore Institute GALLERY

(www.henry-moore.org/hmi; The Headrow; 10am-5pm Tue-Sun) FREE Housed in a converted Victorian warehouse in the city

Leeds

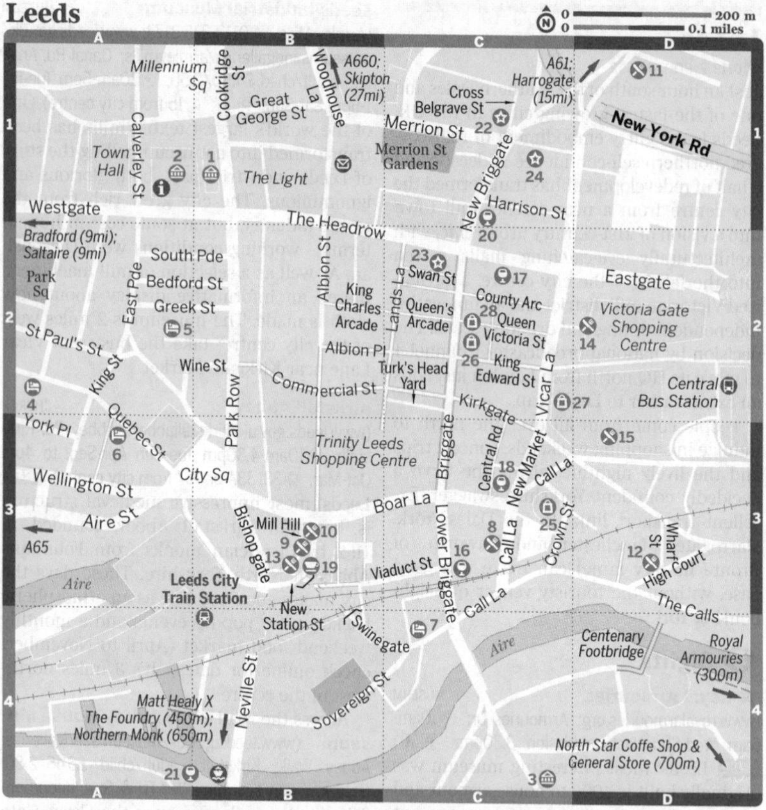

centre, this gallery showcases the work of 20th-century sculptors, but not, despite the name, anything by Henry Moore (1898–1986), who graduated from the Leeds School of Art. To see works by Moore, head to the Yorkshire Sculpture Park (p522) and Hepworth Wakefield (p522).

Festivals & Events

Leeds Indie Food FOOD & DRINK

(www.leedsindiefood.co.uk; mid-May;) This home-grown festival takes over Leeds' food scene for two weeks each May and has become one of the UK's most inventive celebrations of independent local producers, restaurants, cafes and boozers. There are dozens of quirky events around town, such as kitchen takeovers, wine- and beer-pairing dinners, film nights, food-photography workshops, foraging walks and brewery crawls.

Leeds Beer Week BEER

(www.leedsbeerweek.co.uk; late Aug) Tap takeovers, food- and beer-pairing evenings, new beer launches, beer cocktail menus – expect Leeds' city bars to be raining craft beer during this annual week of events, spread across independent venues all over town. Some events are drop-in but some need to be booked ahead (check online); it takes place the week running up to the August bank holiday.

Leeds Festival MUSIC

(www.leedsfestival.com; end Aug) The August bank holiday weekend sees 50,000-plus music fans converge on Bramham Park, 10 miles outside the city centre, for the Leeds Festival. Spread across several stages, it's one of England's biggest rock-music extravaganzas. There are various camping/glamping options on site, or you can buy day tickets.

Leeds

Sights

1 Henry Moore Institute B1
2 Leeds Art Gallery A1
3 Tetley C4

Sleeping

4 Chambers A2
5 Dakota A2
6 Quebecs A3
7 Roomzzz Leeds City C4

Eating

8 Art's Cafe Bar & Restaurant C3
Belgrave Music Hall & Canteen ......(see 22)
9 Bundobust B3
10 Friends of Ham B3
Ox Club ......(see 17)
11 Reliance D1
12 Shears Yard D3
13 Tharavadu B3
14 The Man Behind the Curtain D2
15 The Owl D3

Drinking & Nightlife

16 Bar Fibre C3
17 Headrow House C2
18 HiFi Club C3
19 Laynes Espresso B3
20 North Bar C1
21 Water Lane Boathouse A4

Entertainment

22 Belgrave Music Hall & Canteen C1
23 City Varieties C2
24 Domino C1

Shopping

25 Corn Exchange C3
26 Harvey Nichols C2
27 Kirkgate Market C2
28 Victoria Quarter C2

Sleeping

Roomzzz Leeds City APARTMENT ££
(0203-504 5555; www.roomzzz.com/aparthotels/leeds-city; 10 Swinegate; studio from £74, 2-person apt from £95; @) This outfit offers bright and modern luxury apartments complete with fitted kitchen, with the added advantage of 24-hour hotel reception and a great city-centre location. There are two other branches, both on Burley Rd, but this is by far the most central.

Quebecs BOUTIQUE HOTEL ££
(0113-244 8989; www.quebecshotel.co.uk; 9 Quebec St; d/ste from £89/189; P) Victorian grace at its opulent best is the theme of Quebecs, a conversion of the former Leeds & County Liberal Club. The elaborate wood panelling and heraldic stained-glass windows in the public areas are mirrored by the grand design flourishes in the bedrooms, but it's a listed building (which means no double glazing) so expect some street noise.

★**Chambers** APARTMENT £££
(0113-386 3300; www.morethanjustabed.com; 30 Park Pl; 2-person apt £120-190, parking per night £14; P) This grand Edwardian office building has been converted into 63 luxury serviced apartments, ranging from two-person studios to a two-bedroom penthouse (£350 a night) that will sleep up to four adults. Simple, fresh and spotlessly clean, there's also a 24-hour reception with great service, a gym, honesty bar and pretty little patio for aperitifs or night caps.

★**Dakota** HOTEL £££
(0113-322 6261; http://leeds.dakotahotels.co.uk; 8 Russell St; d/ste from £136/270;) Raising the bar for luxury sleeps in Leeds, this gleaming hotel has quickly become popular thanks to its central location close to shops and bars, swanky yet muted designer interior and five-star service. Rooms are plush, modern and classic, and the suites are like mini-apartments, with open-plan lounge area and dressing room with robes.

Eating

Belgrave Music Hall & Canteen STREET FOOD £
(www.belgravemusichall.com; 1 Cross Belgrave St; mains £6.95-12.95; food served 11am-10pm;) This bar and music venue has two great kitchens. Dough Boys serves artisan pizza (watch out for the napalm chilli sauce); Patty Smiths offers brunch and probably the best burgers in Yorkshire, all at great-value prices. Every second Saturday of the month the place hosts the **Belgrave Feast** (11am to 8pm), an art market and street-food festival.

Bundobust INDIAN £
(0113-243 1248; www.bundobust.com; 6 Mill Hill; dishes £4-6.75; kitchen noon-9.30pm Mon-Thu, to 10pm Fri & Sat, to 8pm Sun;) What could be more Yorkshire than craft beer and Indian street food rolled into one no-frills, brick-walled bar? The beers come from both local and international breweries, and food inspiration comes from vegetarian street-hawker

ART IN YORKSHIRE

Yorkshire Sculpture Park (☎01924-832631; www.ysp.co.uk; Bretton Park, near Wakefield; £6; ⊙10am-6pm; P) One of England's most impressive collections of national and international sculpture is scattered across the formidable 18th-century estate of Bretton Park, 200-odd hectares of lawns, fields and trees. The park is partly a homage to local heroes Barbara Hepworth (1903–75), who was born in Wakefield, and Henry Moore (1898–1986), though more of their works are on display at the Hepworth Wakefield. Advance booking is required.

The rural setting is especially fitting for Moore's work, as the artist was hugely influenced by the outdoors and preferred his art to be sited in the landscape rather than indoors. Other highlights include pieces by Andy Goldsworthy and Eduardo Paolozzi, and Roger Hiorns' famous work *Seizure 2008/2013*, an apartment coated in blue copper sulphate crystals (open weekends only). There's also a program of temporary exhibitions and installations by visiting artists, plus a bookshop and cafe.

The park is 12 miles south of Leeds and 18 miles north of Sheffield, just off Junction 38 on the M1 motorway. If you're on public transport, take a train from Leeds to Wakefield (£4.70, 15 to 30 minutes, frequent departures), or from Sheffield to Barnsley (£5.20, 25 minutes, four hourly), and then take bus 96, which runs between Wakefield and Barnsley via Bretton Park (£3.40 to £4, 30 minutes, hourly Monday to Saturday).

Hepworth Wakefield (☎01924-247360; www.hepworthwakefield.org; Gallery Walk, Wakefield; parking £5; ⊙10am-5pm Wed-Sun; P) West Yorkshire's standing in the international arts scene got a boost in 2011 when the Yorkshire Sculpture Park was joined by this award-winning gallery of modern art, housed in a stunningly angular building on the banks of the River Calder. The gallery has been built around the works of Wakefield-born sculptor Barbara Hepworth, perhaps best known for her work *Single Form*, which graces the UN Headquarters in New York.

The gallery is smaller than it looks from the outside, but showcases more than a dozen Hepworth originals, as well as works by other 20th-century British artists including Ivon Hitchens, Paul Nash, Victor Pasmore, John Piper and Henry Moore.

The gallery is near the centre of Wakefield, a 10-minute walk south of Wakefield Kirkgate train station, easily reached from Leeds by train (£3.90, 15 to 30 minutes, three to four hourly).

Salts Mill (☎01274-531163; www.saltsmill.org.uk; Victoria Rd, Saltaire; ⊙9am-4pm Fri, to 5pm Sat-Sun; P) Saltaire, a Victorian-era landmark and Unesco World Heritage Site, was an industrial village purpose-built in 1851 by philanthropic wool baron and teetotaller Titus Salt. The village's huge factory was once the largest in the world. It is now Salts Mill, a splendidly bright and airy cathedral-like building where the main draw is a permanent exhibition of works by Bradford-born artist David Hockney.

offerings across India. The okra fries are a favourite with drinkers; more substantial bites include paneer and mushroom tikka, and biryani bhaji balls.

Friends of Ham DELI ££

(☎0113-242 0275; www.friendsofham.co.uk; 4-8 New Station St; dishes £6-19; ⊙11am-11pm Mon-Wed, to midnight Thu-Sat, to 10pm Sun; 🛜) This stylish bar serves the finest charcuterie and cheeses – Spanish, French, British – accompanied by fine wines and craft beers. The food is carefully selected and prepared, and utterly delicious; you can order individual tapas-like portions, or huge sharing platters with olive-oil-drizzled bread. Brunch served 11am till 2pm.

Reliance BRITISH ££

(☎0113-295 6060; www.the-reliance.co.uk; 76-78 North St; mains £12.50-18; ⊙noon-10pm Mon-Wed, to 10.30pm Thu-Sat, to 8.30pm Sun; 🛜) The Reliance is a comfortable-as-old-slippers bar where you can happily while away an afternoon reading or chatting with a Yorkshire beer or good glass of natural wine in hand. Yet it's also one of Leeds' best gastropubs, serving Sunday roasts, seasonal Modern British dishes like pig cheeks with beetroot and smoked apple, and platters of homemade charcuterie.

Tharavadu SOUTH INDIAN ££

(☎0113-244 0500; www.tharavadurestaurants.com; 7-8 Mill Hill; mains £13-18; ⊙noon-2pm & 6-9.30pm Mon-Thu, noon-2pm & 5-10pm Fri & Sat) This Michelin-guide-recommended restaurant is the go-to for a classy South Indian meal in Leeds city centre, with a Keralan menu that's heavy on fish curries and regional specialities such as whole crab and spiced king prawns. The restaurant is snug and packs diners in like sardines, which guarantees a lively atmosphere. Book in advance, especially on weekends.

Matt Healy X The Foundry EUROPEAN ££

(☎0113-245 0390; www.mhfoundry.co.uk; 1 Saw Mill St; mains £13-27; ⊙5-9.30pm Thu, noon-9.30pm Fri-Sat, to 7pm Sun) Matt Healy, in case you're wondering, was a 2016 *MasterChef: The Professionals* finalist. In 2018 he took over The Foundry, a red-brick warehouse restaurant, and breathed new life into it with creative, high-end sharing plates such as harissa-spiced lamb with giant couscous and sous vide duck breast with baby beets. It's good but pricey; there's a two-course lunch deal with wine for £22.50.

Shears Yard MODERN BRITISH ££

(☎0113-244 4144; www.shearsyard.com; 11-15 Wharf St; mains £14-16; ⊙5.30-10pm Tue-Sat, 11am-3pm Sat, noon-4pm Sun;) Acres of exposed brick, concrete floors and a soaring roof provide an industrial-chic setting (it's a former rope-making yard) for painterly presentations of imaginative dishes such as ox-cheek fritter with roast-onion consommé, or squid with puffed potato and coriander emulsion. An eight-course tasting menu is available at lunch on Saturdays (£30) and dinner on Fridays and Saturdays (£40).

★The Man Behind the Curtain BRITISH £££

(☎0113-243 2376; www.themanbehindthecurtain.co.uk; 68-78 Vicar Lane; lunch/dinner tasting menu £85/120; ⊙6.30-8.15pm Tue-Thu, 12.15-2pm & 6-9.15pm Fri-Sun) You'll have to book a couple of months in advance to stick your cutlery into Michael O'Hare's Michelin-starred tasting menu. His inventive reinterpretations of classic British dishes are as masterful as they are whimsical (yellow-fin tuna flavoured with a Fisherman's Friend lozenge?), while the presentation is brilliantly theatrical.

★Ox Club GRILL £££

(☎07470 359961; www.oxclub.co.uk; Bramleys Yard, The Headrow; mains £22-32; ⊙5-10pm Tue-Sat, brunch 11am-3pm Sat & Sun) Arguably the best restaurant in Leeds (or at least, the best without a Michelin star), Ox Club occupies an intimate, minimalist space and champions local produce with a deceptively simple menu. Though it bills itself as a grill restaurant, the Modern British dishes are far more inventive than what you'll find in your average barbecue joint – venison tartare with smoked fat, for example.

★The Owl BRITISH £££

(www.theowlleeds.co.uk; Kirkgate Market; 2-/3-course lunch £24/27, 4-/5-course dinner £40/47; ⊙8.30am-5.30pm Mon-Thu, to 10pm Fri-Sat) Kirkgate Market's first new pub for 150 years is home to an exquisite dining experience. The menu – staunchly British, locally sourced and wonderfully inventive – is pub grub transformed by a gourmet wand. How about north sea trout with caviar sauce? The Tap Room menu is perfect if you just want to graze over a pint.

Drinking & Nightlife

★Laynes Espresso COFFEE

(☎07828 823189; www.laynesespresso.co.uk; 16 New Station St; ⊙7am-7pm Mon-Fri, 9am-6pm Sat & Sun;) Locals have Laynes to thank for the complete reinvention of the Leeds coffee scene; when it opened in 2011 there was nothing else like it in the city. Now expanded and serving excellent all-day brunch – buckwheat pancakes and smashed avocado on toast, naturally – and Yorkshire rarebit alongside strong coffee, it's still the best indie cafe in town for an espresso or flat white.

★Northern Monk BREWERY

(☎0113-243 0003; www.northernmonk.com; The Old Flax Store, Marshall St; ⊙3-8pm Wed, 3-10pm Thu, noon-10pm Fri-Sat, to 8pm Sun) So successful has this craft brewery become that its beers are now stocked in UK supermarkets. But it's best drunk at the source, in the brewery's Grade II–listed taproom just south of Leeds city centre in the regeneration 'hood of Holbeck. Draft options run the gamut from hoppy IPAs or rich porters to small-batch collaborations and guest beers; brewery tours also available.

North Star Coffee Shop & General Store COFFEE

(www.northstarroast.com; Unit 33, The Boulevard, Leeds Dock; ⊙7.30am-5.30pm Mon-Fri, 9am-5pm Sat, 10am-4pm Sun) This minimalist cafe and coffee emporium is attached to the production facility of Leeds' first independent roastery, near the Royal Armouries. Watch the daily grind through giant glass doors and inhale the aromas while sampling a flat white and cake (baked fresh onsite each day), or indulge in brunch – the slow-cooked scrambled eggs on a buttery four-cheese rye scone is small yet deliciously decadent.

Headrow House BAR

(☎0113-245 9370; www.headrowhouse.com; Bramleys Yard, The Headrow; ⏲noon-10pm) A former textile mill and one-time grotty dive pub, the historic building that now houses Headrow House was given a hefty makeover to transform it into the four-floor nightlife venue it is today. The ground-floor beer hall sells its own pilsner straight from tanks lining one wall. Upstairs there's a cocktail bar and Leeds' best roof-terrace drinking spot. It's also home to Ox Club (p523) restaurant.

North Bar CRAFT BEER

(www.northbar.com; 24 New Briggate; ⏲11am-1am Mon & Tue, to 2am Wed-Sat, noon-midnight Sun; 📶) This narrow bar has long been an institution in Leeds as a haven of international craft beers. It now brews its own under the banner North Brewing Co, and they're rather good. Drink them here, or visit the brewery taproom (Sheepscar Grove), which is BYO food and open Fridays 4pm to 10pm and Saturdays noon to 10pm, a 10-minute walk north of North Bar.

Water Lane Boathouse CRAFT BEER

(☎0113-246 0985; www.waterlaneboathouse.com; Water Lane; ⏲11am-11pm Sun-Thu, to 12.30am Fri & Sat) Watch canal boats chug into Granary Wharf from the floor-to-ceiling windows or generous outside seating area at this beer bar, occupying a prime historic spot on the water close enough to clink glasses with boaters. The top-quality global craft beers are pricey, but the setting is hard to beat. There's also tasty pizza available from £6.

Bar Fibre CLUB

(www.barfibre.com; 168 Lower Briggate; ⏲noon-1am Sun-Thu, to 3am Fri, to 4am Sat) In the heart of Leeds' LGBT+ area, spilling out onto the cheekily named Queen's Court, this is the city's most popular gay bar, although it's not just the gay crowd that loves its party atmosphere. This is where the beautiful people congregate; the dress code is…dressy, so look your best or you won't get in. Download the bar's app for deals such as buy one, get one free.

HiFi Club CLUB

(☎0113-242 7353; www.thehificlub.co.uk; 2 Central Rd; ⏲11pm-4am Tue-Sun) If it's Tamla Motown or the percussive beats of dance-floor jazz that shake your booty, this is the spot for you. Also has stand-up comedy sessions (£14) on Saturdays from 7pm, which can be combined with dinner at **Art's Cafe** (☎0113-243 8243; www.artscafebar.com; 42 Call Lane; mains £13-18; ⏲noon-11pm Mon-Sat, to 9pm Sun; 📶🖉) for £26.95 (book online).

☆ Entertainment

★Belgrave Music Hall & Canteen LIVE MUSIC

(☎0113-234 6160; www.belgravemusichall.com; 1 Cross Belgrave St; ⏲11am-midnight Sun-Thu, to 3am Fri & Sat) Belgrave is the city's best live-music venue, with a diverse roll call of acts from burlesque to comedy and folk to hip-hop. Its three floors also encompass a huge bar bristling with craft-beer taps, two kitchens (p521), loads of shared tables and sofa space, and a fantastic roof terrace with views across the city. Why would you ever leave?

Domino JAZZ

(www.thedomino.co.uk; 7 Grand Arcade; Fri & Sat night admission £5; ⏲6pm-3am Mon-Sun) A wooden door at the back of Lords' barbershop takes you down to this broody basement cocktail bar and live-jazz club. Shows are free and start around 9pm most nights. Grab a booth and enjoy the table service.

City Varieties LIVE MUSIC, COMEDY

(☎0113-243 0808; www.leedsheritagetheatres.com; Swan St) Founded in 1865, City Varieties is the world's longest-running music hall, where the likes of Harry Houdini, Charlie Chaplin and Lily Langtry once trod the boards. Its program features stand-up comedy, live music, pantomime and old-fashioned variety shows.

🛍 Shopping

Corn Exchange SHOPPING CENTRE

(www.leedscornexchange.co.uk; Call Lane; ⏲10am-6pm Mon-Wed, Fri & Sat, to 9pm Thu, 10.30am-4.30pm Sun; 📶) The dramatic Corn Exchange, built in 1863 to house grain-trade merchants, has a wonderful wrought-iron roof that today shelters a fine collection of independent shops and boutiques. It sells everything from vinyl and craft beer to fashion, jewellery and Yorkshire design.

WORTH A TRIP

YORKSHIRE'S BLACK GOLD

For close to three centuries, West and South Yorkshire were synonymous with coal production. The collieries shaped and scarred the landscape, and entire villages grew up around the pits. The industry came to a shuddering halt in the 1980s, but the imprint of coal is still very much in evidence, even if there's only a handful of collieries left. One of these, the former Caphouse Colliery, is now the **National Coal Mining Museum for England** (www.ncm.org.uk; Overton, near Wakefield; parking £2, tour £4, miniature train return £1.50; ⌚10am-5pm Wed-Sun, last tour 3.15pm; P 👪) FREE.

The highlight of a visit is the underground tour (departing every 10 to 15 minutes): equipped with helmet and head-torch, you descend almost 140m in the 'cage', then follow subterranean passages to the coal seam, where massive drilling machines now stand idle. Former miners work as guides and explain the detail – sometimes with a suitably authentic and almost impenetrable mix of local dialect and technical terminology.

The museum is 10 miles south of Leeds on the A642 between Wakefield and Huddersfield, reached via Junction 40 on the M1. By public transport, take a train from Leeds to Wakefield (£3.90, 15 to 30 minutes, three to four hourly), and then bus 232 or 128 towards Huddersfield (£3.10, 25 minutes, hourly).

Kirkgate Market MARKET
(www.leeds.gov.uk/leedsmarkets; Kirkgate; ⌚8am-5.30pm Mon-Sat) Britain's largest covered market sells fresh meat, fish, and fruit and vegetables, as well as household goods, and also has a popular street-food hall and the fabulous Owl (p523) pub. The best section is at the top near Vicar Lane, where the original Victorian stalls are still inhabited by traders – this was where UK retailing giant Marks & Spencer started out in 1884.

Victoria Quarter SHOPPING CENTRE
(www.victorialeeds.co.uk; Vicar Lane; 📶) The mosaic-paved, stained-glass-roofed Victoria Quarter shopping arcade, between Briggate and Vicar Lane, is well worth visiting for aesthetic reasons alone, as is **County Arcade**, which runs parallel. Dedicated shoppers can join the footballers' wives browsing boutiques such as Louis Vuitton and Vivienne Westwood. The flagship store here is **Harvey Nichols** (www.harveynichols.com; 107-111 Briggate; ⌚10am-7pm Mon-Sat, 11am-5pm Sun).

ℹ Information

Leeds Tourist Office (☎0113-378 6977; www.visitleeds.co.uk; Leeds Art Gallery, Headrow; ⌚10am-5pm Mon-Sat, 11am-3pm Sun; 📶) In the basement of the city art gallery.

ℹ Getting There & Away

AIR

Leeds Bradford International Airport (www.leedsbradfordairport.co.uk) is 11 miles northwest of the city via the A65, and has flights to a range of domestic and international destinations. The Flying Tiger 757 bus (£4, 40 minutes, every 20 to 30 minutes) runs between Leeds bus and train stations and the airport. A taxi costs about £22.

BUS

National Express (www.nationalexpress.com) serves most major cities, while Yorkshire Coastliner (www.coastliner.co.uk) buses run to York, Pickering, Malton, Scarborough and Whitby. A Daytripper Plus ticket (£16) gives unlimited travel on all Coastliner buses for a day. The **Central Bus Station** is near Victoria Gate Shopping Centre.

London £11.60 to £33, 4½ hours, hourly

Manchester £6, 1¼ hours, at least hourly

Scarborough £13.50, three hours, hourly

Whitby £19.30, 3½ hours, four daily Monday to Saturday, twice daily Sundays

York £7, 1¼ hours, at least hourly

TRAIN

Leeds train station has good rail connections with the rest of the country and Manchester's international airport. It's also the starting point for trains on the scenic Settle–Carlisle line (p511). Tickets for Manchester and York can be had for a song if you book ahead and can be flexible on times.

London King's Cross £59, 2¼ hours, at least hourly

Manchester £10.30, one to 1½ hours, every 10 to 20 minutes

Manchester Airport £24, 1½ hours, three hourly

Sheffield £9.40, one hour, six hourly

York £8.30, 25 minutes, at least every 15 minutes

Getting Around

Leeds has a compact city centre and it's quicker to walk everywhere than attempt to take a bus. CityBus 70 South Bank (£1 flat fare) links the train station with Leeds Dock (for the Royal Armouries), but a nicer way to travel between the two is the **water taxi** (www.leedsdock.com/whos-here/watertaxis; £1; every 15min 7am-7pm Mon-Fri, 10am-6pm Sat-Sun) that runs from Granary Wharf, at the train station's southern entrance.

Various WY Metro (www.wymetro.com) Day Rover passes covering trains and/or buses are good for reaching Bradford, Haworth and Hebden Bridge.

Bradford

01274 / POP 349,561

Their suburbs may have merged into one sprawling urban conurbation, but Bradford remains far removed from its much more glamorous neighbour, Leeds.

Thanks to its role as a major player in the wool trade, Bradford attracted large numbers of immigrants from Bangladesh and Pakistan during the 20th century. Despite occasional racial tensions, these new arrivals have helped reinvigorate the city and give it new energy, plus a reputation for superb curry restaurants – Bradford has been crowned Curry Capital of Britain six times in recent years. But the main reason to visit is still the National Science & Media Museum.

Sights

National Science & Media Museum MUSEUM
(www.scienceandmediamuseum.org.uk; off Little Horton Lane; 10am-6pm Wed-Sun) FREE Bradford's top attraction is housed in an impressive glass-fronted building and chronicles the story of photography, film, TV, radio and the web from 19th-century cameras and early animation to digital technology and the psychology of advertising. International visitors may find themselves a little lost with the British-focused TV exhibits, but there is lots of other hands-on stuff, including a trippy interactive image-and-sound tech gallery and a room crammed with 1980s video games (Pacman! Street Fighter!).

The museum looks out over **City Park**, Bradford's award-winning central square, which is home to the Mirror Pool, the country's largest urban water feature.

Eating

Bradford is famous for its curries, so don't miss out on trying one of the city's hundred or so restaurants. A great help is the Bradford Curry Guide (www.visitbradford.com/explore/bradford_curry_guide.aspx), which helps sort the rogan josh from the rubbish nosh.

Kashmir INDIAN £
(01274-726513; 27 Morley St; mains £5-8; 11am-1am Sun-Thu, to 4am Fri & Sat;) Don't be put off by the dodgy-looking facade: Bradford's oldest curry house has top tucker, served with no frills and no booze (although it is BYO). At quieter times you'll be seated in the windowless basement, with all the character of a 1950s factory canteen, but the food is still excellent. It's just around the corner from the National Science & Media Museum.

Zouk Tea Bar INDIAN, PAKISTANI £
(01274-258025; www.zoukteabar.co.uk; 1312 Leeds Rd; mains £9-13; noon-midnight;) This modern and stylish cafe-restaurant staffed by chefs from Lahore offers an upmarket menu and some unusual twists on traditional Indian and Pakistani food, such as delicious shawarma wraps and curried lamb shank slow-cooked in aromatic spices. It's in a Bradford suburb; the 72 bus that runs between Bradford Interchange and Leeds bus station will drop you outside.

Getting There & Away

Bradford is on the Metro train line from Leeds (£4.60, 20 minutes, three to five per hour) and also a stop on the line that links Leeds with Hebden Bridge.

Hebden Bridge

01422 / POP 4235

Tucked tightly into a fold of a steep-sided valley, Yorkshire's funkiest small town is a former mill centre that refused to go gently with the dying of industry's light. Instead, it raged a bit and then morphed into an attractive outdoorsy tourist trap with a distinctly bohemian atmosphere. The town is home to university academics, artists, diehard hippies and a substantial gay community. All of this explains the abundance of vintage shops, organic and vegan cafes, and second-hand bookstores. Walking trails leading from the centre of town and up into the hills are another attraction.

Sights & Activities

Gibson Mill HISTORIC BUILDING
(NT; 01422-846236; www.nationaltrust.org.uk; parking £5; 11am-4pm mid-Mar–Oct, to 3pm Sat & Sun Nov–mid-Mar; P) This renovated, sustainably powered 19th-century cotton mill is home to a visitor centre covering the industrial and social history of the mill and its workers. Although it is currently closed, you can visit the cafe (11am to 4pm) or wander amid the woods and waterfalls of local beauty spot **Hardcastle Crags** (open dawn to dusk, admission free), 1.5 miles north of town, reachable via a 45-minute walk from St George's Sq, partly following the river. Go to www.hbwalkersaction.org.uk for directions.

Hebden Bridge Mill HISTORIC BUILDING
(www.innovationhebdenbridge.co.uk; St George's Sq; hours vary) The spindly chimney of Hebden Bridge's old red-brick mill is a central landmark that predates the town itself, and was saved from demolition in 1974. It is now a home for vintage stores and small studios, anchored by the Innovation Shop & Cafe-Bar on the ground floor, where the mill's working water wheel and Archimedes' screw (water pump) are located. Heritage panels explain the history of the site, which is now run on sustainable water power. Shop opening hours vary; weekends are most reliable.

Heptonstall VILLAGE
(www.heptonstall.org) Above Hebden Bridge lies the much older village of Heptonstall, its narrow cobbled street lined with 500-year-old cottages and the ruins of a beautiful **13th-century church**. But it's the churchyard of the newer **St Thomas' Church** (1854) that draws literary pilgrims, for here is buried the poet Sylvia Plath (1932–63), whose husband, poet Ted Hughes (1930–98), was born in nearby Mytholmroyd. You'll have to hunt hard to find her grave, in the new cemetery beyond the church's far wall.

Hebden Bridge Cruises CRUISE
(07966 808717; www.hebdenbridgecruises.com; Stubbing Wharf, King St; adult/child from £10/7; 1pm & 2.15pm Sat) Join a colourful canal boat for a 40-minute guided cruise along the Rochdale Canal. There's also an afternoon-tea cruise (adult/child £18/12), a 50-minute fish-and-chip cruise (adult/child £23/15) where you feast on battered haddock and chips or a 90-minute Sunday-lunch cruise (adult/child £33/20). Departs from the Stubbing Wharf Pub, half a mile west of the town centre.

Sleeping

Hebden Bridge Hostel HOSTEL £
(01422-843183, 07786 987376; www.hebdenbridgehostel.co.uk; Birchcliffe Centre, Birchcliffe Rd; s/tw/q from £35/55/75; Easter–early Nov; P) Just a 10-minute walk uphill from the town centre, this eco-hostel is set in a peaceful stone building, complete with sunny patio, tucked behind a former Baptist chapel. There's a cosy library, comfy and clean en-suite rooms, and a vegetarian-food-only kitchen. An inconvenience is that the hostel locks guests out of their rooms from 10am to 5pm daily.

★ **Thorncliffe B&B** B&B ££
(01422-842163, 07949 729433; www.thorncliffe.uk.net; Alexandra Rd; s/d £55/75;) This delightful Victorian house is perched on the hill above town, and the guest accommodation is right at the top of the house – a spacious and peaceful attic double with private bathroom and lovely views across the valley, and a 1st-floor en-suite double room, but without the views. A healthy vegetarian continental breakfast is served in your room.

Eating & Drinking

Mooch CAFE £
(01422-846954; www.moochcafebar.wordpress.com; 24 Market St; mains £4-10; 9am-8pm Mon-Thu, to 10pm Fri-Sat, 10am-8pm Sun;) This chilled-out little cafe-bar exemplifies Hebden's alternative atmosphere, with a menu that includes a full-vegan breakfast, brie-and-grape ciabatta, and Mediterranean lunch platters of olives, hummus, stuffed vine leaves, tabbouleh and more. There are also bottled beers, wine, excellent espresso, and a petite enclosed outdoor terrace through the back.

Leila's Kitchen VEGETARIAN £
(01422-843587; www.leilaskitchen.co.uk; Old Oxford House, Albert St; mains £5-8; 9am-4pm Mon & Wed-Fri, to 9pm Sat, 10am-4pm Sun;) A lovely vegetarian cafe that serves primarily Persian-style cuisine, but also has a fine selection of vegan dishes and other veggie bits like Welsh rarebit and a particularly tasty chickpea burger.

★**Vocation & Co** CRAFT BEER
(☎01422-844838; www.vocationbrewery.com; 10 New Rd; ⏲noon-11pm; 📶) A goldmine for hopheads, the first taproom from local craft brewer Vocation Brewery is housed in an imposing Victorian building overlooking Hebden Bridge's marina. Inside it's quite a contrast: an ultramodern, minimalist set-up with 20 draught lines including beers from other top northern breweries such as Magic Rock and Cloudwater, plus a delicious taco menu (Tuesday to Sunday).

☆ Entertainment

Trades Club LIVE MUSIC
(☎01422-845265; www.thetradesclub.com; Holme St) Built in 1923 as a social club by the local trade unions, this place was revived in the 1980s and has since gone on to become one of the UK's coolest live-music venues, hosting names as big and diverse as the Buzzcocks, Patti Smith, the Fall and George Ezra in recent years, as well as a host of up-and-coming indie talent.

ℹ Information

Hebden Bridge Visitor Centre (☎01422-843831; www.hebdenbridge.co.uk; Butlers Wharf, New Rd; ⏲10am-5pm) Has a good stock of maps and leaflets on local walks and bicycle routes.

ℹ Getting There & Away

There's only one main road through town and it can become horribly congested on sunny days, so try to arrive by train. Hebden Bridge is on the line from Leeds (£6.20, 50 minutes, every 20 minutes Monday to Saturday, twice hourly on Sunday) to Manchester (£10.50, 35 minutes, three or four per hour).

Haworth

☎01535 / POP 6380

It seems that only Shakespeare himself is held in higher esteem than the Brontë sisters – Emily, Anne and Charlotte – judging by the thousands of visitors a year who come to pay their respects at Haworth's handsome parsonage where the literary classics *Jane Eyre* and *Wuthering Heights* were penned.

Not surprisingly, the village is the beating heart of a cottage industry that has grown up around Brontë-linked tourism, but even without the literary associations Haworth – the upper village rather than the workaday town below – is worth a visit. Its cobbled heritage high street has become a home for interesting independent vintage, craft and art shops selling work by local Yorkshire artisans, and it's possible to strike out onto the famed Brontë moors right from the parsonage's back door.

👁 Sights

Haworth Parish Church CHURCH
(www.haworthchurch.co.uk; Church St; ⏲12.30-3.30pm Sun & Wed) The Brontë family vault lies beneath a pillar in the southeast corner of this handsome parish church, which was built on the site of an older church where Patrick Brontë served as vicar between 1820 and 1861; it was demolished in 1879. A polished brass plaque on the floor commemorates Charlotte and Emily; Anne is buried at **St Mary's Church** (Castle Rd; ⏲10am-4pm Mon-Fri, 1-4pm Sun May-Sep) FREE in Scarborough.

Brontë Parsonage Museum MUSEUM
(☎01535-642323; www.bronte.org.uk; Church St; adult/child £9.50/4; ⏲10am-5pm Wed-Sun) Set in a pretty garden overlooking Haworth parish church and graveyard, the house where the Brontë family lived from 1820 to 1861 is now a museum. The rooms are meticulously furnished and decorated exactly as they were in the Brontë era, including Charlotte's bedroom, her clothes and her writing paraphernalia. There's also an informative exhibition, which includes the fascinating miniature books the Brontës wrote as children.

Keighley & Worth Valley Railway HERITAGE RAILWAY
(www.kwvr.co.uk; Station Rd; adult/child return £15/7) This vintage railway runs steam and classic diesel engines between Keighley and Oxenhope via Haworth. The classic 1970 movie *The Railway Children* was shot along this line: Mr Perks was stationmaster at Oakworth, where the Edwardian look has been meticulously maintained. Trains operate about hourly every day June to August but the timetable is sporadic in other months; check the website. Tickets to view the Haworth platform and incoming trains cost 50p, but you can get a good look from the nearby pedestrian bridge.

🛏 Sleeping

Apothecary Guest House B&B £
(☎01535-643642; www.theapothecaryguesthouse.co.uk; 86 Main St; s/d £40/60; 📶) A quaint and ancient building at the top end of Main St,

with narrow, slanted passageways that lead to simple rooms with cheerful modern decor; excellent value.

★Old Registry B&B ££
(☎01535-646503; www.theoldregistryhaworth.co.uk; 2-4 Main St; d £80-135; P 📶) This place is a bit special. It's an elegantly rustic guesthouse where each of the carefully themed rooms has either a four-poster bed, whirlpool bath or valley views. The Secret Garden room has a glorious view across parkland to the lower village with, if you're lucky, a steam train chuffing sedately by. Parking is £3 per night, at nearby Haworth Old Hall.

Eating & Drinking

Cobbles & Clay CAFE £
(www.cobblesandclay.co.uk; 60 Main St; mains £6-9; ⏲9am-5pm; 📶) This buzzy, child-friendly cafe not only offers fair-trade coffee and healthy salads and snacks – Tuscan bean stew, or hummus with pita bread and raw veggie sticks – but also provides the opportunity to indulge in a bit of pottery painting. Its ploughman's lunch comes with local Haworth cheese.

Hawthorn BRITISH ££
(☎01535-644477; www.thehawthornhaworth.co.uk; 103-109 Main St; mains £12-28; ⏲5-11pm Wed-Fri, noon-11pm Sat-Sun) The former home of a well-known Georgian clockmaker is now a classy, candlelit restaurant-bar serving Modern British dishes such as pea-and-ham soup with quails egg, Yorkshire Dales lamb and North Sea hake with foraged garlic. There's also a Josper grill for making delicious steaks.

Haworth Steam Brewery MICROBREWERY
(☎01535-646059; www.hawortsteambrewery.co.uk; 98 Main St; ⏲11am-11pm Thu-Sat, to 6pm Sun-Wed) This cosy bar must surely be one of Britain's smallest microbreweries, serving its own award-winning real ales and Haworth's Lamplighter gin, plus specials such as an IPA and gin created for Haworth's annual steampunk weekend in November. There's also a good pub-grub menu (mains £10 to £14) with brewhouse lamb shank, Whitby scampi and beef-brisket sandwiches.

Shopping

Cabinet of Curiosities GIFTS & SOUVENIRS
(www.the-curiosity-society.myshopify.com; 84 Main St; ⏲10am-5.30pm) It was to this apothecary that Branwell Brontë staggered for his laudanum drug hits in the 1840s, contributing to his untimely death in September 1848. The current owners have restored it to its Victorian glory and it's now a fancy shop selling Gothic curios and beautiful bath products. Well worth a look inside.

Information

The Brontë Parsonage Museum has information about the town.

Getting There & Away

From Leeds, the easiest approach is via Keighley, which is on the Metro rail network. The B1, B2 and B3 buses (www.keighleybus.co.uk) run from Keighley bus station to Haworth (£3.20, 20 minutes, every 20 minutes) and the hourly B3 continues to Hebden Bridge. However, the most interesting way to get from Keighley to Haworth is via the Keighley & Worth Valley Railway.

SOUTH YORKSHIRE

What wool was to West Yorkshire, so steel was to South Yorkshire. A confluence of natural resources – coal, iron ore and ample water – made this part of the country a crucible of the British iron and steel industries. From the 18th to the 20th centuries, the region was the industrial powerhouse of northern England.

Sheffield's and Rotherham's blast furnaces and the coal pits of Barnsley and Doncaster may have closed long ago, but the hulking reminders of that irrepressible Victorian dynamism remain, not only in the old steelworks and pit heads (some of which have been converted into museums and exhibition spaces), but also in the grand civic buildings that grace Sheffield's city centre, fitting testaments to the untrammelled ambitions of their 19th-century patrons.

Sheffield

☎0114 / POP 518,090

The steel industry that made Sheffield famous is long gone, but after many years of decline this industrious city is on the up again – like many of northern England's cities, it has grabbed the opportunities presented by urban renewal with both hands and, shored up by a thriving student population, is working hard to reinvent itself.

Some of its old foundries, mills and forges are now interesting museums celebrating

South Yorkshire's industrial heyday, and Kelham Island in particular is in the throes of a fascinating redevelopment. Sheffield isn't likely to win any prizes for its looks anytime soon, but its history is interesting enough to warrant a day's exploration.

Sights

★Kelham Island Museum MUSEUM
(www.simt.co.uk; Alma St; adult/child £7/free; ⏲11am-3pm Mon-Wed, to 4pm Sat-Sun; P 🚸) Sheffield's prodigious industrial heritage is the subject of this excellent museum, set on a human-made island in the city's oldest industrial district. Exhibits cover all aspects of industry, from steel-making to knife-sharpening. The most impressive display is the thundering 12,000-horsepower River Don steam engine (the size of a house), which gets powered up twice a day, at noon and 2pm. The museum is 800m north of the city centre; take the tram (£1.70) from Sheffield train station to the Shalesmoor stop.

Winter Gardens GARDENS
(Surrey St; ⏲8am-8pm Mon-Sat, to 5pm Sun) Pride of place in Sheffield's city centre goes to this wonderfully ambitious public space with a soaring glass roof supported by graceful arches of laminated timber. The 21st-century architecture contrasts sharply with the nearby Victorian **town hall** and the **Peace Gardens** – complete with fountains, sculptures, and lawns full of lunching office workers.

Millennium Gallery GALLERY
(www.museums-sheffield.org.uk; Arundel Gate; ⏲10am-4pm) FREE Sheffield's cultural revival is embodied in this collection of four galleries under one roof. Inside, the **Ruskin Collection** houses an eclectic display of paintings, manuscripts and interesting objects established and inspired by Victorian artist, writer, critic and philosopher John Ruskin, who saw Sheffield as the embodiment of Britain's industrial age. The **Sykes Gallery Metalwork Collection** charts the transformation of Sheffield's steel industry into craft and design, with 13,000 glinting objects – the 'Sheffield steel' stamp now has the cachet of designer chic.

Graves Gallery GALLERY
(www.museums-sheffield.org.uk; Surrey St; ⏲11am-4pm Tue-Sat) FREE This gallery has a neat and accessible display of British and European art from the 16th century to the present day, plus touring exhibitions; the big names represented include Turner, Sisley, Cézanne, Gauguin, Miró, Klee, LS Lowry and Damien Hirst.

Abbeydale Industrial Hamlet MUSEUM
(www.simt.co.uk; Abbeydale Rd S; adult/child £4/free; ⏲10am-4pm Mon-Thu & Sat, 11am-4.45pm Sun; P 🚸) In the days before steel mills, metalworking was carried out in hamlet communities like Abbeydale, situated by rivers and dams that were harnessed for water power. This industrial museum, now swallowed up by Sheffield's suburban sprawl, gives an excellent run-down of that innocent era, with restored 18th-century forges, workshops and machinery including the original, working waterwheel. It's 4 miles southwest of the centre on the A621 (towards the Peak District).

Sleeping

Leopold Hotel BOUTIQUE HOTEL ££
(☎0114-252 4000; www.leopoldhotels.com; 2 Leopold St; r/ste from £60/100; 📶) Housed in a Grade II–listed former grammar-school building, Sheffield's first boutique hotel offers style and sophistication at a reasonable rate. Rooms can suffer late-night noise from the bars on Leopold Sq – ask for a quiet room at the back.

Houseboat Hotels HOUSEBOAT ££
(☎07776 144693; www.houseboathotels.com; Victoria Quays, Wharfe St; r from £95; P) Here's something a bit different: kick off your shoes and relax on board your very own permanently moored houseboat, complete with self-catering kitchen and patio area. You can choose between the Laila Mai or Millie Grace, each a double bedroom (with flatscreen TV), decent-sized bathroom, a kitchenette and a dining area (where the bench folds out into another bed).

Eating

Street Food Chef MEXICAN £
(☎0114-275 2390; www.streetfoodchef.co.uk; 90 Arundel St; mains £3-6; ⏲5-9pm Wed-Thu, to 10pm Fri, noon-9pm Sat, to 7pm Sun) Local students flock to this down-to-earth, healthy Mexican canteen, which started life as a street-food truck and now has several outlets in Sheffield. It focuses on freshly prepared, great-value burritos, tacos and quesadillas, available to eat in or take away. Look for its brekky and lunch deals, and gluten- or dairy-free options.

WORTH A TRIP

THE AGE OF STEEL

At its peak, the Templeborough steelworks was the world's most productive steel smelter, with a 10,000-strong workforce manning six 3000°C furnaces that produced 1.8 million tonnes of metal a year. It has now been reborn as **Magna** (01709-720002; www.visitmagna.co.uk; Sheffield Rd, Templeborough, Rotherham; adult/child £12.95/10.95; 10am-5pm, last entry 4pm; P), an unashamed celebration of heavy industry, and a hands-on paradise for kids of all ages. Displays are based on the themes of earth, air, water and fire. The latter section is especially impressive, with a towering tornado of flame as a centrepiece and the chance to use a real electric arc to create your own tiny puddle of molten steel (if only for a moment or two). The hourly 'Big Melt' – a massive sound, light and fireworks show – memorably re-enacts the firing up of one of the original arc furnaces.

Magna is 4 miles northeast of Sheffield, just off the M1 near Rotherham; phone before visiting as it closes at 2pm some days.

Blue Moon Cafe VEGETARIAN £

(www.bluemooncafesheffield.com; 2 St James St; mains £8; 8.30am-4pm Mon-Sat;) A Sheffield institution offering tasty veggie and vegan creations, breakfasts till 11am and a rotation of single-price mains with a side of rice. It's famed for the magnificent heritage room within which it sits, with high blue ceilings and an atrium glass roof – perfect for a spot of Saturday afternoon lounging.

Marmaduke's CAFE £

(www.marmadukes.co; 22a Norfolk Row; mains £6-12; 9am-5pm Mon-Sat, 10am-4pm Sun;) This appealingly cramped and chaotic cafe, crammed with recycled furniture and fittings, and run by a young and enthusiastic crew, serves an all-day breakfast menu that highlights local and organic produce, and lunch dishes that range from deli sandwiches and quiches to vegetarian specials such as the halloumi and herb burger. They've opened a second cafe on **Cambridge St** (42 Cambridge St; mains £6-9.50; 8.30am-5pm Mon-Fri, 9am-5pm Sat, to 4pm Sun).

Vero Gusto ITALIAN ££

(0114-276 0004; www.verogusto.com; 12 Norfolk Row; mains £15-31; 5-11pm Tue-Sat;) Gusto is a *real* Italian restaurant, from the Italian waistcoated servers dishing out homemade Italian food to the genuine Italian coffee enjoyed by Italian customers reading Italian newspapers...you get the idea. Bookings essential.

Drinking & Nightlife

Fat Cat PUB

(0114-249 4801; www.thefatcat.co.uk; 23 Alma St; noon-11pm Sun-Thu, to midnight Fri & Sat) The 'Cat' is an old-fashioned independent boozer in a handy spot around the corner from Kelham Island Museum. It serves Kelham Island Brewery beers and ales made in the building next door, along with pork pies and pub grub. Its fans are an eclectic mix of students and local fixtures.

Sheffield Tap CRAFT BEER

(0114-273 7558; www.sheffieldtap.com; Sheffield Train Station; 11am-11pm Sun-Thu, 10am-midnight Fri & Sat;) This lovingly restored Edwardian railway bar is a reliable stalwart for Sheffield beer drinkers. It has several bar areas, and the aroma of hops and malts gets stronger as you approach the far room where the bar produces its own Two Tapped Brew Co beers, with working brewery kit towering above drinking tables. Dozens of other local and international beers are sold here, too.

Entertainment

Showroom CINEMA

(0114-275 7727; www.showroomworkstation.org.uk; 15 Paternoster Row) This is the largest independent cinema in England, set in a grand art-deco complex and screening a great mix of art-house, offbeat and not-quite-mainstream films.

Leadmill LIVE MUSIC

(0114-272 7040; www.leadmill.co.uk; 6 Leadmill Rd) Every touring band has played the dark and dingy Leadmill on the way up (or on the way down), and it remains the best place in town to hear live rock and alternative music. There are club nights too, but they tend to play cheesy 1970s and '80s disco classics.

Information

There's no tourist office, but www.welcometosheffield.co.uk is a good source of information.

Getting There & Away

For all travel-related info for Sheffield and South Yorkshire, contact **Travel South Yorkshire** (01709-515151; www.travelsouthyorkshire.com).

BUS

The bus station, called the Interchange, is just east of the centre, about 250m north of the train station. National Express coaches run from here to London (from £6, 4½ hours, eight daily).

TRAIN

Prices can double on the day of travel; book ahead.

Leeds £11.90, one hour, two to five hourly
London St Pancras £79, 2¼ hours, at least hourly
Manchester £9.40, one hour, twice hourly
York £6.70, 1¼ hours, twice hourly

EAST RIDING OF YORKSHIRE

The rolling farmland of the East Riding of Yorkshire meets the sea at Hull, a no-nonsense port that looks to the broad horizons of the Humber estuary and the North Sea for its livelihood. Just to its north, and in complete contrast to Hull's salt and grit, is Beverley, the East Riding's most attractive town, with lots of Georgian character and one of England's finest churches.

Hull

01482 / POP 284,321

The principal port town of England's east coast, Hull (properly known but rarely referred to as Kingston-upon-Hull) grew up around an economy focused on wool, wine trading, whaling and fishing.

A major program of refurbishment on the back of the city's title as UK City of Culture in 2017 improved the old waterfront but more importantly sparked a cultural flowering – especially in the Fruit Market district around Humber St, where derelict buildings have been reclaimed as artists' studios, and cool cafes and bars have flourished. Hard-bitten Hullensians may smirk, but their city has developed serious cool kudos.

The city centre isn't exactly pretty, but the old cobbled Georgian enclave is an under-the-radar delight. Other attractions include fascinating museums, Philip Larkin heritage (the poet lived here) and an excellent aquarium.

Sights

★The Deep — AQUARIUM

(01482-381000; www.thedeep.co.uk; Tower St; adult/child £13.50/11.50; 10am-6pm, last entry 5pm; P) Hull's biggest tourist attraction is The Deep, Britain's most spectacular aquarium, housed in a colossal angular building that appears to lunge above the muddy waters of the Humber like a giant shark's head. Inside, it's just as dramatic, with echoing commentaries and computer-generated interactive displays that guide you through the formation of the oceans, the evolution of sea life and global conservation issues.

The largest aquarium tank is 10m deep, filled with sharks, stingrays, moray eels and colourful coral fishes. A glass elevator plies up and down inside the tank, though you'll get a better view by taking the stairs. Don't miss the cafe on the top floor, which has a great view of the Humber estuary.

★Old Town — AREA

Hull's Old Town is where a grand minster and cobbled streets flush with Georgian town houses give a flashback to the prosperity the town once knew. It occupies the thumb of land between the River Hull to the east and Princes Quay to the west. Recent regeneration efforts have brought back to life the dockside **Fruit Market**, where vintage shops, art studios and independent bars and cafes are flourishing along Humber St; and the indoor **Trinity Market**, now housing street-food vendors.

★Wilberforce House — MUSEUM

(www.hullcc.gov.uk/museums; High St; 10am-4.30pm Mon-Sat, to 4pm Sun) FREE The wealth that Britain amassed as the world's first industrial nation was directly aided by the transatlantic slave trade, and this important museum ensures that the facts are told, detailing the part that Britain played in bringing millions of Africans to Europe between the 17th and 19th centuries. Wilberforce House (1639) was the birthplace in 1759 of politician and antislavery crusader William Wilberforce, whose campaigning efforts eventually led to the abolition of slavery in England in 1833.

Humber St Gallery GALLERY
(www.humberstreetgallery.co.uk; 64 Humber St; ⏲11am-3pm Thu-Sun, cafe to 4pm Thu-Fri, to 6pm Sat-Sun) FREE This slick three-storey contemporary gallery in a former banana-ripening warehouse anchors Hull's revamped Fruit Market. Rotating exhibitions celebrate international and local visual art, design, photography and film, but a permanent feature is a beloved piece of 1960s graffiti by Len 'Pongo' Rood saved from demolition by local campaigners. Behold *Dead Bod* – a rusty shed wall from Hull's docks that would have once signified home for returning sailors. The site was demolished in 2015, but *Dead Bod* lives on in Humber St Gallery's cafe.

Ferens Art Gallery GALLERY
(☎01482-300300; www.hullcc.gov.uk/ferens; Queen Victoria Sq; ⏲10am-4.30pm Mon-Sat, to 4pm Sun; 👪) FREE The permanent art collection at this fine gallery ranges from old masters like Frans Hals and Antonio Canaletto to modern works by Lucian Freud, Peter Nash, Peter Blake, David Hockney and Gillian Wearing.

Humber Bridge BRIDGE
(www.humberbridge.co.uk; P) Opened in 1981, the Humber Bridge swoops gracefully across the broad estuary of the River Humber. Its 1410m span made it the world's longest single-span suspension bridge – until 1998 when it lost the title to Japan's Akashi Kaikyo bridge, but it is still a Grade I–listed structure. The best way to appreciate the scale of the bridge, and the vastness of the estuary, is to walk or cycle out along the footway from the Humber Bridge tourist office at its north end on Ferriby Rd.

The bridge is a mile west of the small riverside town of Hessle, about 4 miles west of Hull. It links Yorkshire to Lincolnshire along the A15, opening up what was once an often-overlooked corner of the country.

Bus 350 runs from Hull Paragon Interchange to Ferriby Rd in Hessle (25 minutes, every 30 minutes), from where it's a 300m walk to the tourist office.

Hull Pier Toilets HISTORIC BUILDING
(Nelson St) There are not too many places where a public toilet counts as a tourist attraction, but coach parties regularly stop to take photos of these Edwardian lavatories. The building is interesting but inside they're not very special. Serviceable, but no tourist attraction, that's for sure.

Sleeping

Hull Trinity Backpackers HOSTEL £
(☎01482-223229; www.hulltrinitybackpackers.com; 51-52 Market Pl; s/tw from £32/45; 📶) This centrally located hostel with simple rooms is just the ticket for a cheap sleep in Hull. It's clean and friendly, and the owner is passionate about showing off the city's best sides. There's a lovingly designed common area, free laundry, fluffy bedding and bike storage. Plus handy USB and plug sockets by each bed.

★**Hideout** APARTMENT ££
(☎01482-212222; www.hideouthotel.co.uk; North Church Side; d from £90, 1-bed apt £110-130, 2-bed apt from £130; P📶) These luxury serviced apartments show just how far Hull has come since its City of Culture year. Slick and contemporary, it's the type of place where staff put retro radio on for you before check-in, and leave an easel in the living room for spontaneous creative scribbles. It's also incredibly central, in the shadow of the Old Town's minster.

Eating

★**Thieving Harry's** CAFE £
(www.thievingharrys.co.uk; 73 Humber St; mains £5-9; ⏲kitchen 10am-4pm Mon-Fri, 9am-4pm Sat, to 6pm Sun; 🖊) Thieving Harry's has all the trappings of a favourite local cafe: friendly faces, a breezy casual vibe, strong coffee and generous brunches, all wrapped up in a comfy warehouse conversion with mismatched retro furniture and lovely marina views of bobbing boats. The menu is interesting, with excellent dishes like fried eggs with chorizo, sourdough and coriander sour cream, plus good veggie options.

★**The Old House** BRITISH ££
(☎01482-210253; www.shootthebull.co.uk/the-old-house; 5 Scale Lane; mains £15-29; ⏲4-9.30pm Wed-Thu, from noon Fri-Sat, to 6pm Sun) Once an old pub, now the base of Hull street-food brand Shoot the Bull, this lovely restaurant does refined comfort food exceptionally well. Locally sourced meat and fish might translate into blow-torched mackerel followed by a rare-breed beef pie with smoked eel mash and parsley sauce. Its signature dish is on the street-food menu: a butter-lathered, rare-breed flat-iron steak sandwich in a posh bun.

A second outlet focusing solely on street food is inside Trinity Market in the Old Town.

Tapasya Marina INDIAN ££

(☎01482-242607; www.tapasyarestaurants.co.uk; 2-3 Humber Dock St; mains £14-20) Marrying old and new in a converted warehouse with giant windows onto Hull's marina and a projector showing old black-and-white films, this sharp modern restaurant specialises in fine-dining Indian fusion cuisine using the best seasonal, local produce. Savour dishes like roe deer biryani with Himalayan basmati rice, or Yorkshire lamb drenched in fragrant masala sauce with a side of indulgently buttery nan.

Hitchcock's Vegetarian Restaurant VEGETARIAN ££

(☎01482-320233; www.hitchcocksrestaurant.co.uk; 1 Bishop Lane, High St; per person £22; ⌚8-10.30pm Tue-Sat;) The word 'quirky' could have been invented to describe this place. It's an atmospheric maze of small rooms, with an all-you-can-eat vegetarian buffet whose theme – Mexican, Indian, Caribbean, whatever – is chosen by the first person to book that evening. But the food is excellent and the welcome is warm. Bookings necessary..

Drinking & Entertainment

★**Olde Black Boy** PUB

(☎01482-215040; 150 High St; ⌚5-11.30pm Mon & Tue, from noon Wed-Sun) A favourite watering hole of poet Philip Larkin, Hull's oldest pub has been serving ale since 1729. Oak floors and roof beams, dark-wood panelling and a snug log fire in winter make for a great atmosphere. There's live folk music on Wednesday afternoons.

Humber St Distillery COCKTAIL BAR

(☎01482-219886; www.hsdc.co.uk; 18 Humber St; ⌚noon-11pm Tue-Sun) This ambitious, gin-obsessed cocktail bar in the heart of Hull's Fruit Market area has dark-wood bar panelling offset by exposed-brick walls. The gin menu is a tome of around 150 world gins, including many local and limited-edition releases; you can take a gin flight (weeknights only); and the bar has even started producing its own gin.

Two Gingers COFFEE

(www.twogingerscoffee.co.uk; Paragon Arcade, Paragon St; ⌚8am-4pm Mon-Fri, 10am-4pm Sat & Sun) Inside pretty Paragon Arcade, this Australian-style speciality coffee house is bright, minimalist and focused firmly on the main event: excellent coffee.

Minerva PUB

(www.minerva-hull.co.uk; Nelson St; ⌚11.30am-11pm Mon-Sat, noon-11pm Sun;) Try a pint of Black Sheep at this lovely 200-year-old pub down by the waterfront. On a sunny day you can sit outdoors and watch the ships go by, while tucking into a plate of fish and chips (£9.50). A unique feature is its real-ale and gin flights.

Information

Hull Tourist Office (☎01482-300306; www.visithullandeastyorkshire.com; Paragon Interchange, Ferensway; ⌚8am-6.30pm Mon-Fri, from 9am Sat, 10am-5pm Sun) Inside Hull's Paragon Interchange, at the train station.

Getting There & Away

BOAT

The ferry port is 3 miles east of the centre at King George Dock; a bus connects the train station with the ferries. There are ferry services to Zeebrugge (Belgium) and Rotterdam (Netherlands).

BUS

Intercity buses depart from Hull Paragon Interchange. Mega Bus (https://uk.megabus.com) runs cheap buses to London. The X62 is a direct link to Leeds. During summer the X21 runs directly to Scarborough, but at other times of year you'll need to change at Bridlington. The X46/47 to York runs via Beverley.

London £20, 4½ hours, four daily
Leeds £6, two hours, three daily
York £13, 1¾ hours, hourly

TRAIN

The train station is part of Hull Paragon Interchange, an integrated rail and bus station.

Leeds £6.70, one hour, hourly
London King's Cross £47, 2¾ hours, every two hours
York £32, 1¼ hours, hourly

Beverley

☎01482 / POP 10,109

Handsome Beverley is one of the most attractive towns in Yorkshire, largely due to its magnificent minster – a rival to any cathedral in England – and the tangle of streets that lie beneath it, each brimming with Georgian and Victorian buildings.

All the sights are a short walk from either the train or bus station. There's a large market on Saturdays in the square called Saturday

Market, and a smaller one on Wednesdays in the square called...Wednesday Market.

Sights

Beverley Minster CHURCH

(www.beverleyminster.org; St John St; ⊙11am-3pm Wed-Sat, noon-3pm Sun) FREE One of the great glories of English religious architecture, Beverley Minster is the most impressive church in the country that is not a cathedral. The soaring lines of the exterior are imposing, but it is inside that the charm and beauty lie. The 14th-century north aisle is lined with original stone carvings, mostly of musicians; much of our knowledge of early musical instruments comes from these images. Look out for the bagpipe player. You'll also see goblins, devils and grotesque figures.

Construction began in 1220 – this was the third church to be built on this site, with the first dating from the 7th century – and continued for two centuries, spanning the Early English, Decorated and Perpendicular periods of the Gothic style.

Close to the altar, the elaborate and intricate **Percy Canopy** (1340), a decorative frill above the tomb of local aristocrat Lady Eleanor Percy, is a testament to the skill of the sculptor and the finest example of Gothic stone carving in England. In complete contrast, in the nearby chancel is the 10th-century Saxon **frith stool**, a plain and polished stone chair that once gave sanctuary to anyone escaping the law.

In the roof of the tower is a restored treadwheel crane, where workers ground around like hapless hamsters to lift the huge loads necessary to build a medieval church.

Beverley Westwood PARK

(Walkington Rd) The western edge of Beverley is bounded by this large area of common pasture studded with mature trees, which has been used as grazing for local livestock for centuries. The land, owned 'in common' by the community since 1380, is overseen by the Pasture Masters, a group of men elected from the Freemen of Beverley each March. Contented cows amble across the unfenced road, while walkers stroll and enjoy the gorgeous views of Beverley Minster.

Sleeping & Eating

Kings Head INN ££

(☎01482-868103; www.kingsheadpubbeverley.com; 38 Saturday Market; r/ste from £90/150; P 🛜) A Georgian coaching inn given a modern makeover, the Kings Head is a lively pub with 10 bright and stylish rooms above the bar. The pub opens late on weekend nights, but earplugs are supplied for those who don't want to join the revelry.

Vanessa Delicafe CAFE £

(☎01482-868190; www.vanessadelicafe.co.uk; 21-22 Saturday Market; mains £4.50-10; ⊙9.30am-5pm Mon-Thu, 9am-5pm Fri-Sat; 🛜) This popular cafe sits above a delicatessen, with sofas and bookshelves scattered among the tables, and window seats overlooking the market square. Settle down for cappuccino and cake with the Sunday papers, or tuck into hearty lunch specials such as venison burger or a Yorkshire platter of pork pie, roast ham, cheese and chutney.

★ **Pipe & Glass Inn** GASTROPUB £££

(☎01430-810246; www.pipeandglass.co.uk; West End, South Dalton; mains £16-35; ⊙noon-2pm & 6-9.30pm Tue-Sat, noon-4pm Sun; P 🛜) Set in a picturesque hamlet 4 miles northwest of Beverley, this charming Michelin-starred country pub has a delightfully informal setting, with weathered timber tables, stone hearths and leather sofas. Yet a great deal of care is lavished on the food – even seemingly simple dishes such as fish pie are unforgettable. After your meal, you can tour its herb gardens.

If you want to stay the night, there are five luxurious bedrooms to choose from (£200 to £245 per night, including breakfast), but the waiting list for a weekend night is several months long; weeknights can be booked about two months in advance.

Information

Beverley Tourist Office (☎01482-391672; www.visithullandeastyorkshire.com/beverley; Treasure House, Champney Rd; ⊙9.30am-5pm Mon, Wed & Fri, to 8pm Tue & Thu, 9am-4pm Sat) Beverley Tourist Office lives inside Treasure House, also home to the town's art gallery, next to the library.

Getting There & Away

There are frequent bus services from Hull, including numbers 121, 122, 246 and X46/X47 (£5.20, 30 minutes, hourly). Bus X46/X47 links Beverley with York (£7.90, 1¼ hours, hourly).

Trains run regularly to Scarborough (£14.90, 1¼ hours, every one to two hours) and Hull (£7.30, 15 minutes, twice hourly).

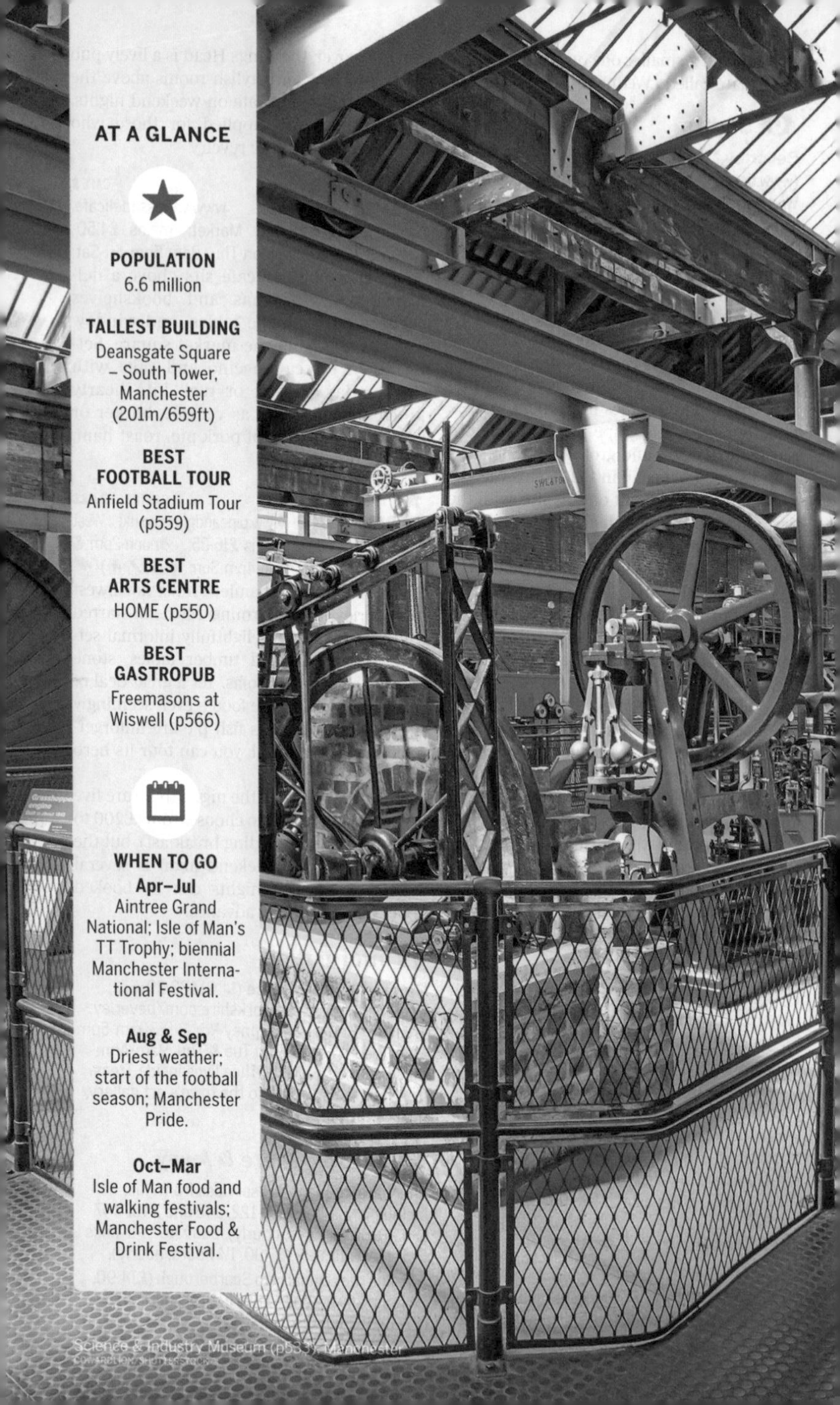

AT A GLANCE

POPULATION
6.6 million

TALLEST BUILDING
Deansgate Square – South Tower, Manchester (201m/659ft)

BEST FOOTBALL TOUR
Anfield Stadium Tour (p559)

BEST ARTS CENTRE
HOME (p550)

BEST GASTROPUB
Freemasons at Wiswell (p566)

WHEN TO GO

Apr–Jul
Aintree Grand National; Isle of Man's TT Trophy; biennial Manchester International Festival.

Aug & Sep
Driest weather; start of the football season; Manchester Pride.

Oct–Mar
Isle of Man food and walking festivals; Manchester Food & Drink Festival.

Science & Industry Museum (p533), Manchester

Manchester, Liverpool & Northwest England

Revolution, music and football: if you were to limit the story of the northwest to these three alone, it would still be a page-turner. Forged on the anvil of the Industrial Revolution, the region fomented social change, organised the first league of the world's most popular sport and produced some of the most enduring popular music. At the heart of it all is mighty Manchester, a city built on innovation and bursting with creativity. Nearby is its perennial rival Liverpool, fiercely proud of its ability to hold its own in most matters, from food to football. Between them is Chester, a Tudor gift enveloped by Roman walls. The bucolic charms of the Lancashire countryside lie to the north, while offshore is the Isle of Man, so pretty that Unesco gave it Biosphere Reserve status.

INCLUDES

Manchester, Liverpool & Northwest England Highlights

1. **Liverpool Cathedral** (p555) Being overwhelmed by Sir Giles Gilbert Scott's awesome neo-Gothic masterpiece.
2. **Beatles' Childhood Homes** (p560) Visiting the Liverpool houses where John and Paul grew up – and wrote their earliest hits.
3. **Rows** (p554) Exploring Chester's Tudor-era shopping district.
4. **Football** (p550) Taking a tour of your favourite team's ground or – better still – going to a match.

5 Blackpool Tower (p565) Visiting the ballroom and climbing to the top of Blackpool's iconic structure.

6 Great Laxey Wheel (p570) Viewing the world's largest working waterwheel.

7 People's History Museum (p540) Learning about social justice in Manchester.

8 Philharmonic Dining Rooms (p563) Enjoying a drink in this Liverpool pub, one of Britain's most beautiful.

Information

Visit North West (www.visitnorthwest.com) is the centralised tourist authority, but all cities and most towns have their own dedicated tourist authorities; for the Isle of Man check out **Isle of Man** (www.visitisleofman.com).

Getting There & Away

Both Manchester and Liverpool have international airports and are well served by trains from all over the UK, including London, only two hours away. The West Coast Line serves Preston, Lancaster and Blackpool. For Lancashire's smaller towns, there's an extensive bus service. The Isle of Man is accessible by ferry from Liverpool and Heysham, and there are regular flights from throughout the UK.

Getting Around

The towns and cities covered are all within easy reach of each other, and are well linked by public transport. The two main cities, Manchester and Liverpool, are only 34 miles apart and are linked by hourly bus and train services. Chester is 18 miles south of Liverpool, but is also easily accessible from Manchester by train or via the M56. Blackpool is 50 miles to the north of Manchester and Liverpool, and is also well connected on the M6.

MANCHESTER

0161 / POP 510,746

Manchester is a city on the move. Upwards and outwards, mostly: the skyline is getting taller and old neighbourhoods are getting a new lease of life. The one-time engine room of the Industrial Revolution is now spearheading a digital upheaval, with four universities feeding a tech cluster that is Britain's largest outside London.

The result – besides lots of construction and rising property prices – is a steady uptick in the city's choice of bars, hotels and restaurants, including Manchester's first Michelin star for four decades.

And while many locals aren't all that enthused about what they consider the gentrification of their beloved city – this is, after all, a radical burgh that incubated communism, suffragism, vegetarianism and a bunch of other 'isms' aimed at improving humanity's lot – Manchester doesn't look like it's slowing down any time soon.

History

Canals and steam-powered cotton mills were what transformed Manchester from a small, disease-infested provincial town into a big, disease-infested industrial city. It all happened in the 1760s, with the opening of the Bridgewater Canal between Manchester and the coal mines at Worsley in 1763, and with Richard Arkwright patenting his super cotton mill in 1769. Thereafter Manchester and the world would never be the same again. When the canal was extended to Liverpool and the open sea in 1776, Manchester – dubbed 'Cottonopolis' – kicked into high gear and took off on the coal-fuelled, steam-powered gravy train.

There was plenty of gravy to go around, but the good burghers of 19th-century Manchester made sure that the vast majority of the city's swollen citizenry (with a population of 90,000 in 1801, and two million 100 years later) never got their hands on any of it despite producing most of it. Their reward was life in a new kind of urban settlement: the industrial slum. Working conditions were dire, with impossibly long hours, child labour, work-related accidents and fatalities all commonplace. Mark Twain commented that he would like to live here because the 'transition between Manchester and Death would be unnoticeable'. So much for Victorian values.

The wheels started to come off towards the end of the 19th century. The USA had begun to flex its own industrial muscles and was taking over a sizeable chunk of the textile trade; production in Manchester's mills began to slow, and then it stopped altogether. By WWII there was hardly enough cotton produced in the city to make a tablecloth. The postwar years weren't much better: 150,000 manufacturing jobs were lost between 1961 and 1983, and the port – still the UK's third largest in 1963 – finally closed in 1982 due to declining traffic.

The 21st century has been much kinder to Manchester, with ongoing developments continuing to transform the city and its outlying suburbs into a powerhouse of development and innovation.

Sights

City Centre

★**People's History Museum** MUSEUM
(0161-838 9190; www.phm.org.uk; Left Bank, Bridge St, Spinningfields, M3 3ER; 10am-5pm Tue-Sun) FREE The story of Britain's 200-year march to democracy is told in all its pain and pathos at this superb museum, housed in a

MANCHESTER IN ONE DAY

Start your exploration in the light-filled galleries of the Manchester Art Gallery, home to one of the most important collections in the north. The Science & Industry Museum will take up at least a couple of hours – more if you've got kids or you're a science geek. Alternatively, the People's History Museum is a fascinating exploration of social history. Lunch at Rudy's (p547) or take your pick at Mackie Mayor (p548).

Hop on the tram to Salford Quays, where you can explore the Imperial War Museum North (p544) or take a guided tour of the BBC's northern headquarters at MediaCity-UK (p544); fans of Manchester United should take the tour of Old Trafford (p550), where you'll get to stand in the tunnel and pretend you're a player. Make dinner reservations (well in advance) for Mana (p548).

After dinner, there's drinks at the Refuge (p549) or at a choice of bars in the Northern Quarter. Alternatively, you can always head south towards Castlefield and take in a film or a play at the superb HOME (p550) arts centre.

refurbished Edwardian pumping station. You clock in on the 1st floor (literally: punch your card in an old mill clock, which managers would infamously fiddle with so as to make employees work longer) and plunge into the heart of Britain's struggle for basic democratic rights, labour reform and fair pay.

Amid artifacts like the (tiny) desk at which Thomas Paine (1737–1809) wrote *Rights of Man* (1791), and an array of beautifully made and colourful union banners, are compelling interactive displays, including a screen where you can trace the effects of all the events covered in the museum on five generations of the same family. The 2nd floor takes up the struggle for equal rights from WWII to the current day, touching on civil rights for gay people, anti-racism initiatives and the defining British sociopolitical landmarks of the last half-century, including the founding of the National Health Service (NHS), the Miners' Strike and the widespread protests against the Poll Tax.

★Science & Industry Museum MUSEUM

(MOSI; ☎0161-832 2244; www.scienceandindustrymuseum.org.uk; Liverpool Rd, M3 4FP; suggested donation £4, special exhibits £6-10; ⏲10am-5pm Wed-Sun; 👪; 🚌1 or 3, 🚊Deansgate-Castlefield) Manchester's rich industrial legacy is explored in this excellent museum set within the enormous grounds of the old Liverpool St station, the oldest rail terminus in the world. The large collection of steam engines, locomotives and original factory machinery tells the story of the city from the sewers up, while a host of new technology looks to the future.

It's an all-ages kind of museum, but the emphasis is on making sure the young 'uns don't get bored – they could easily spend a whole day poking about, testing an early electric-shock machine here and trying out a printing press there. You can get up close and personal with fighter jets and get to grips with all kinds of space-age technology; the museum also includes an astronaut virtual-reality experience called Space Descent VR with Tim Peake (£6). A unifying theme is that Manchester and Mancunians had a key role to play: this is the place to discover that Manchester was home to the world's first stored-program computer (a giant contraption nicknamed 'baby') in 1948 and that the world's first steam-powered submarine was built to the designs of local curate Reverend George Garrett in 1879.

Admission by pre-booked ticket only. A new exhibition space will open in spring 2021.

★Manchester Art Gallery GALLERY

(☎0161-235 8888; www.manchesterartgallery.org; Mosley St, M2 3JL; ⏲11am-4pm Thu-Sun; 🚊St Peter's Square) FREE A superb collection of British art and a hefty number of European masters are the highlights at the city's top art gallery. It's home to the best assemblage of Pre-Raphaelite art as well as a permanent collection of pre-17th-century art, mostly by Dutch and early Renaissance masters. It also hosts exciting exhibitions of contemporary art and the newish *What is Manchester Art Gallery?*, which tells the story of the gallery and its city connections. Tickets must be pre-booked online.

★Chetham's Library & School of Music LIBRARY

(☎0161-834 7861; www.chethamsschoolofmusic.com; Long Millgate; donation suggested £3; ⏲timed entry hourly 10am-noon & 1.30-3.30pm

Manchester

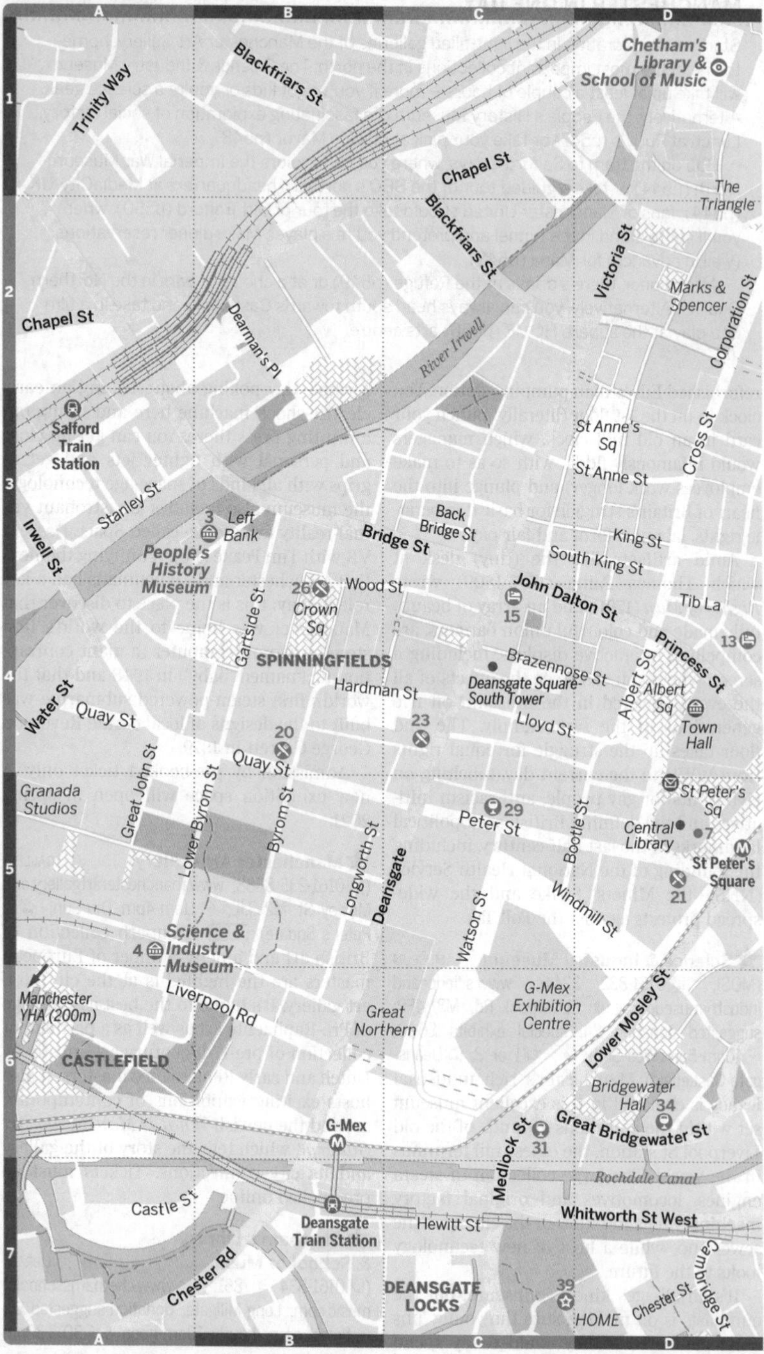
A
B
C
D
1
2
3
4
5
6
7
Chetham's Library & School of Music
1
Blackfriars St
Trinity Way
Chapel St
The Triangle
Blackfriars St
Victoria St
Marks & Spencer
Corporation St
Chapel St
Dearman's Pl
River Irwell
Salford Train Station
St Anne's Sq
Cross St
St Anne St
Stanley St
3
Left Bank
Back Bridge St
King St
Irwell St
People's History Museum
Bridge St
South King St
26
Wood St
John Dalton St
Tib La
Crown Sq
15
13
Gartside St
SPINNINGFIELDS
Brazennose St
Princess St
Albert Sq
Water St
Deansgate Square-South Tower
Hardman St
Albert Sq
Town Hall
Quay St
23
Lloyd St
20
Quay St
Great John St
St Peter's Sq
Granada Studios
Lower Byrom St
29
Peter St
Byrom St
Longworth St
Bootle St
Central Library
7
Deansgate
St Peter's Square
21
Windmill St
Science & Industry Museum
4
Watson St
Lower Mosley St
Manchester YHA (200m)
Liverpool Rd
G-Mex Exhibition Centre
Great Northern
CASTLEFIELD
Bridgewater Hall
34
G-Mex
Medlock St
Great Bridgewater St
31
Rochdale Canal
Castle St
Deansgate Train Station
Hewitt St
Whitworth St West
Chester Rd
DEANSGATE LOCKS
39
Chester St
Cambridge St
HOME

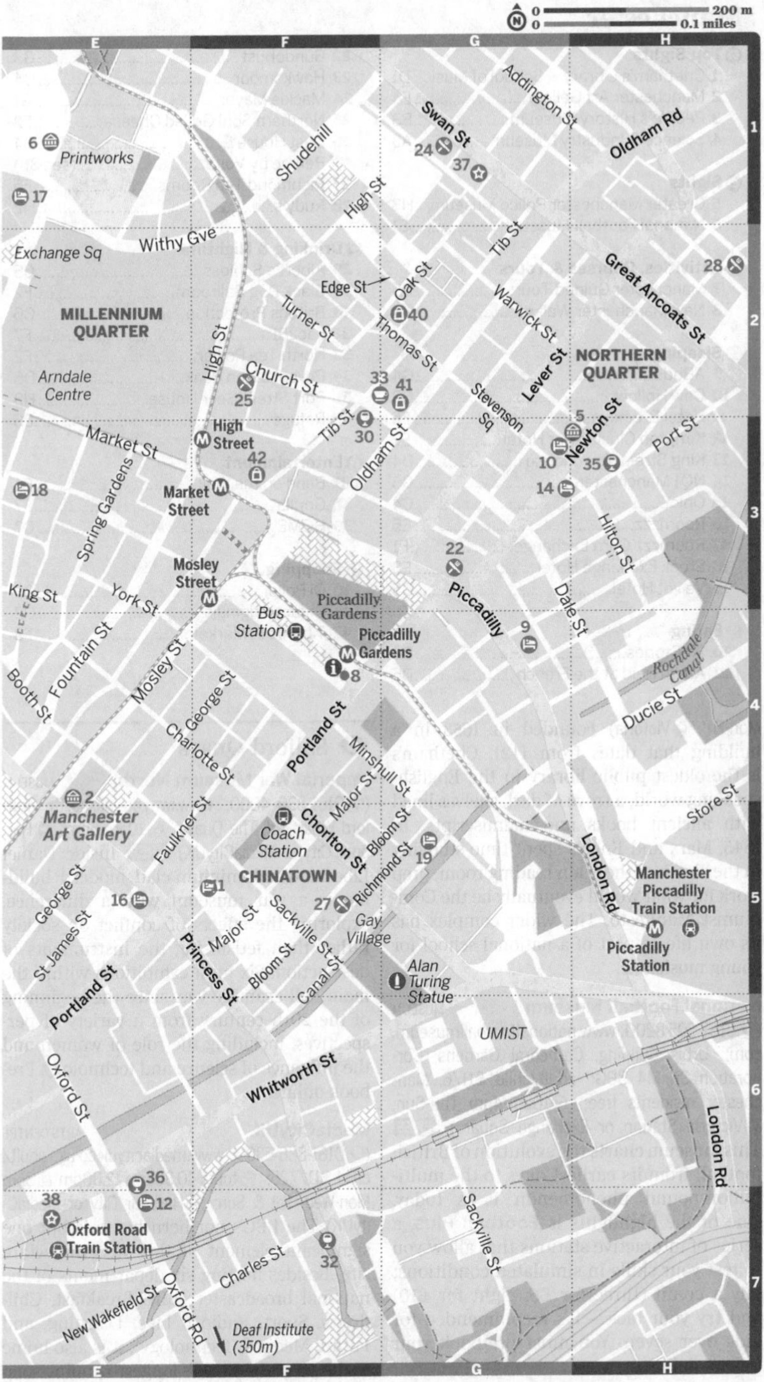

0 200 m
0 0.1 miles
E
F
G
H
1
2
3
4
5
6
7
Printworks
Exchange Sq
Withy Gve
MILLENNIUM QUARTER
Arndale Centre
Shudehill
High St
Swan St
Addington St
Oldham Rd
Tib St
Great Ancoats St
Edge St
Oak St
Turner St
Thomas St
Warwick St
Church St
Lever St
NORTHERN QUARTER
Stevenson Sq
Newton St
Port St
Tib St
Oldham St
Market St
High Street
Market Street
Spring Gardens
Hilton St
Mosley Street
King St
York St
Piccadilly
Piccadilly Gardens
Bus Station
Dale St
Fountain St
Mosley St
Rochdale Canal
Booth St
George St
Charlotte St
Portland St
Minshull St
Ducie St
Major St
Manchester Art Gallery
Faulkner St
Coach Station
Chorlton St
Bloom St
Richmond St
Store St
London Rd
CHINATOWN
Manchester Piccadilly Train Station
George St
St James St
Major St
Sackville St
Gay Village
Piccadilly Station
Princess St
Bloom St
Canal St
Alan Turing Statue
Portland St
UMIST
Oxford St
Whitworth St
London Rd
Sackville St
Oxford Road Train Station
Charles St
New Wakefield St
Oxford Rd
Deaf Institute (350m)
MANCHESTER, LIVERPOOL & NORTHWEST ENGLAND

Mon-Fri; Victoria) Founded in 1653 in a building that dates from 1421, Chetham's is the oldest public library in the English-speaking world, a trove of dark shelves lined with ancient books and manuscripts. In 1845, Marx and Engels spent time studying in the alcove of the main reading room, prep work for what would eventually be the Communist Manifesto. The wider complex has its own life as part of a national school for young musicians.

National Football Museum MUSEUM
(0161-605 8200; www.nationalfootballmuseum.com; Urbis Building, Cathedral Gardens, Corporation St, M4 3BG; adult/child £11/6, Manchester residents free; 10am-4pm Thu-Sun; Victoria Station or Exchange Square) FREE This museum charts the evolution of British football from its earliest days to the multi-billion-pound phenomenon it is today. One of the highlights is **Football Plus**, a series of interactive stations that allow you to test your skills in simulated conditions; buy a credit (three for £6, eight for £10) and try your luck – it's recommended for kids over seven. You must pre-book your tickets online.

Salford Quays

Imperial War Museum North MUSEUM
(0161-836 4000; www.iwm.org.uk/north; Trafford Wharf Rd, The Quays; 10am-5pm; Harbour City or MediaCityUK) FREE Inside Daniel Libeskind's aluminium-clad modern building is a war museum with a difference, exploring the effects of conflict on society rather than fetishising the instruments of destruction. Six mini exhibitions within the main hall examine war since the beginning of the 20th century from a variety of perspectives, including the role of women and the influence of science and technology. Pre-book online.

MediaCityUK ARTS CENTRE
(0161-886 5300; www.mediacityuk.co.uk; adult/child £11/7.25; tours 10.30am, 12.30pm & 3pm Mon-Wed, Sat & Sun; Harbour City or MediaCityUK) The BBC's northern home is but one significant element of this vast 81-hectare site. Besides hosting six departments of the national broadcaster (BBC Breakfast, Children's, Sport, Radio 5 Live, Learning, and Future Media & Technology), it is also home to the set of the world's longest-running soap

opera, ITV's perennially popular *Coronation Street,* which you can visit on a **tour** (www.itv.com/coronationstreettour; The Studios at dock10; adult/child £35/17.50; ⏲10am-4pm selected weekend days; 🚊MediaCityUK).

You can visit the BBC's set-up and see the sets of some of TV's most iconic programmes on a guided 90-minute tour that also includes a chance for kids to 'make' a programme in an interactive studio; see www.bbc.co.uk/showsandtours. There are plenty of cafes and restaurants in the area.

Lowry ARTS CENTRE
(☎box office 0843-208 6000; www.thelowry.com; Pier 8, Salford Quays; ⏲10am-6pm, later during performances; 🚊Harbour City or MediaCityUK) With multiple performance spaces, bars, restaurants and shops, this contemporary arts centre attracts more than a million visitors a year to its myriad functions, which include everything from big-name theatrical productions to comedy, kids' theatre and even weddings. The centre is also home to 300 beautifully humanistic depictions of urban landscapes by LS Lowry (1887–1976), who was born in nearby Stretford, and after whom the complex is named.

Activities

Three Rivers Gin GUIDED TOUR
(☎0161-839 2667; www.manchesterthreerivers.com; 21 Red Bank Parade, M4 4HF; £95; ⏲7.30pm Thu-Sat, plus 1pm Sat & Sun) This award-winning Manchester micro-distillery cranks back the shutters a few times a week to let visitors behind the scenes with the master distiller. Its three-hour 'Gin Experience' starts with a potted history of Manchester and the city's relationship with gin, throws in several gin cocktails and culminates in mixing botanicals to cook up your own 1L batch to take home.

Tours

Manchester Guided Tours WALKING
(☎07505 685942; www.manchesterguidedtours.com; £12; ⏲11am) A daily walking tour of the city's highlights (departing from the Central Library at 11am), including Manchester Cathedral and the Royal Exchange. There's also a huge range of other themed tours including music, Victorian heritage and a tasty food and drink tour.

New Manchester Walks WALKING
(☎07769 298068; www.newmanchesterwalks.com; £10-12) The complete menu of tours includes explorations of every aspect of Manchester's personality, from music to history and politics to pubs. There are a handful of football-related walks and an extensive list of 'weird and wonderful' walks, from Victorian eating habits to the history of Strangeways prison. Starting points differ.

Festivals & Events

Manchester Day PARADE
(www.manchesterday.co.uk; ⏲mid-Jun) A day to celebrate all things Manchester, inspired by New York's Thanksgiving Day parade: 50 performances across three city centre squares culminate in a colourful parade.

Manchester International Festival ART
(☎0161-238 7300; www.mif.co.uk; ⏲Jul) A three-week-long biennial arts festival of artist-led new work across visual arts, performance and popular culture. Recent performers included Damon Albarn, Marina Abramović, Björk and the Steve McQueen Band. 2022 will see the opening of the Factory, a new multimedia arts venue that will be a flagship host of the festival.

★**Manchester Pride Festival** LGBT
(☎0161-831 7700; www.manchesterpride.com; ⏲late Aug; 🚊Piccadilly Gardens) One of England's biggest celebrations of LGBT+ life, held over three days of the August bank holiday weekend at the end of the month. There's a big party in the Gay Village (£10 to £15), live gigs at nearby Mayfield (one

OFF THE BEATEN TRACK

MANCHESTER POLICE MUSEUM

One of the city's best-kept secrets is this superb **museum** (☎0161-856 4500; www.gmpmuseum.co.uk; 57a Newton St; ⏲10.30am-3.30pm Tue) FREE housed within a former Victorian police station. The original building has been magnificently – if a little creepily – brought back to life, and you can wander in and out of 19th-century cells where prisoners rested their heads on wooden pillows, visit a restored magistrates' court from 1895 and examine the case histories (complete with mugshots and photos of weapons) of some of the more notorious names to have passed through its doors.

WORTH A TRIP

WHITWORTH ART GALLERY

Manchester's second-most important **art gallery** (0161-275 7450; www.whitworth.manchester.ac.uk; University of Manchester, Oxford Rd, M15 6ER; 10am-5pm Fri-Wed, to 9pm Thu; 15, 41, 42, 43, 140, 143 or 147 from Piccadilly Gardens) FREE is arguably its most beautiful, following a restoration that saw the doubling of its exhibition space through the opening of its sides and back, and the construction of glass-screened promenades. Inside is a fine collection of British watercolours, the best selection of historic textiles outside London and galleries devoted to the work of artists from Dürer and Rembrandt to Lucian Freud and David Hockney.

All this high art aside, you may find that the most interesting part of the gallery is the group of rooms dedicated to wallpaper – proof that bland pastels and horrible flowery patterns are not the final word in home decoration. There's also a lovely cafe on the grounds.

night/weekend £35/65), debates, films, lectures and community projects (the Superbia Weekend), and a huge parade.

Manchester Food & Drink Festival FOOD & DRINK
(www.foodanddrinkfestival.com; Albert Sq; late Sep-early Oct) Manchester's superb foodie scene shows off its wares over 10 days between the end of September and the beginning of October. Farmers markets, pop-up restaurants and gourmet events are just part of the UK's biggest urban food fest. Much of the action takes place on Albert Sq, in front of the town hall.

Sleeping

★Qbic HOTEL £
(www.qbichotels.com/manchester; John Dalton House, Deansgate, M2 6JR; r from £60;) Qbic's eco-friendly hotel philosophy arrives in Manchester with aplomb in this brilliant budget option. The rooms are compact but cleverly designed, while the recycled furniture, refillable toiletries and glass carafes are just the most visible examples of its commitment to sustainability (there are also solar panels on the roof). Comfortable, convenient and eco-conscious – it's how all hotels should be.

NQ1 Manchester HOSTEL £
(0161-236 4414; www.selina.com; 50 Newton St; s/d from £48/54; ; all city centre) Newly refurbished and part of the Selina hostel group, at this former millinery the selection of rooms and co-working spaces make it one of the best budget options in town. The location is a boon: smack in the heart of the Northern Quarter, you won't have to go far to get the best of alternative Manchester.

Manchester YHA HOSTEL £
(0345 371 9647; www.yha.org.uk; Potato Wharf; d from £29; ; Deansgate-Castlefield) This purpose-built canalside hostel in the Castlefield area is one of the best in the country. It's a top-class option, with four- and six-bed dorms, all with bathroom, as well as three doubles and a host of good facilities. Potato Wharf is just left off Liverpool Rd.

Roomzzz APARTMENT ££
(0161-236 2121; www.roomzzz.com; 36 Princess St; r from £70; ; all city centre) The inelegant name belies the designer digs inside this beautifully restored Grade II-listed building, which features serviced apartments equipped with a kitchen and the latest connectivity gadgetry, including sleek iMac computers and free wi-fi throughout. There's a small pantry, with food for sale downstairs. Highly recommended if you're planning a longer stay. There's also a **branch** (Corn Exchange, Exchange Sq; r from £100; Exchange Square) in the Corn Exchange, with rooms ranging in size from snug to spacious.

Hotel Brooklyn HOTEL ££
(0161-518 2936; www.bespokehotels.com/hotelbrooklyn; 59 Portland St; r/ste from £60/120;) This New York City–themed hotel has 189 comfortable rooms kitted out in nu-retro style (Smeg fridges, rotary dial phones, old-style sound systems) spread across 10 floors of a new building. There's a bar on the 9th floor and Runyon's Restaurant on the ground floor, which serves upscale New York diner fare. A little gimmicky, sure, but it's a very good hotel nonetheless.

ABode HOTEL ££

(☎0161-247 7744; www.abodemanchester.co.uk; 107 Piccadilly; r from £90; ❄@☎; 🚌all city centre, 🚋Piccadilly Gardens) The original fittings at this converted textile factory have been combined successfully with 61 bedrooms divided into four categories of ever-increasing luxury: Comfortable, Desirable, Enviable and Fabulous on Fifth, the last being five seriously swanky top-floor suites.

Kimpton Clocktower Hotel HOTEL ££

(☎0161-288 2222; www.kimptonclocktowerhotel.com; Oxford St, M60 7HA; r from £90; @☎🐾; 🚋St Peter's Square) Beyond the triple-height lobby of this 19th-century beaut are 270 newly refurbished loft-style rooms that are incredibly popular with both leisure and business visitors alike. From the lobby you can access the wonderful Refuge (p549).

Cow Hollow BOUTIQUE HOTEL ££

(☎07727 159727; www.cowhollow.co.uk; 57 Newton St; r/ste from £90/120; ☎; 🚌all city centre) Set in a stick-thin 19th-century weavers' mill, Cow Hollow has 16 snug rooms graced with original beams, brick walls and flashy bathrooms; some have original machinery incorporated into the decor. Little luxury touches include Hypnos beds, goose-down duvets, and free Prosecco and tapas each evening. Reception is in the ground-floor bar.

Velvet Hotel BOUTIQUE HOTEL ££

(☎0161-236 9003; www.velvetmanchester.com; 2 Canal St; r from £80; ☎🍴; 🚌all city centre) Nineteen beautiful bespoke rooms here each ooze style: there's the sleigh bed in room 24, the double bath of room 34, and the saucy framed photographs of a stripped-down David Beckham (this is Gay Village, after all!). Despite the tantalising decor and location, this is not an exclusive hotel and is as popular with straight visitors as it is with the same-sex crowd.

★King Street Townhouse BOUTIQUE HOTEL £££

(☎0161-667 0707; www.eclectichotels.co.uk; 10 Booth St; r/ste from £180/£280; ❄@☎🍴; 🚌all city centre) This beautiful 1872 Italian Renaissance-style former bank is now an exquisite boutique hotel with 40 bedrooms ranging from snug to suite. Furnishings are the perfect combination of period elegance and contemporary style. On the top floor is a small spa with an infinity pool overlooking the town hall; downstairs is a nice bar and restaurant. Online rates are cheaper.

Stock Exchange Hotel HOTEL £££

(☎0161-470 3901; www.stockexchangehotel.co.uk; 4 Norfolk St, M2 1DW; d from £200; ❄@☎) The 1906 Stock Exchange building is now a modish 40-room hotel in the heart of the city. It's modern and luxurious, but you're never too far from the purpose of the Edwardian original: the Bull & Bear restaurant is where the trading floor used to be, while check-in (including tea and biscuits) is in the trader's lounge.

✕ Eating

Rudy's PIZZA £

(☎0161-820 8292; www.rudyspizza.co.uk; 9 Cotton St, Ancoats, M4 5BF; pizzas £4.90-8.40; ⏰noon-10pm Mon-Sat, to 9pm Sun; 🚋Piccadilly Gardens, bua 42, 42B, 142 from city centre) Makers of the best pizza in town, Rudy's can be a tough table to get (put your name down and wait), but it is oh, so worth it. It makes its own dough, and uses proper San Marzano tomatoes and *fior di latte* mozzarella to create pies that a Neapolitan would approve of. There's another branch on Peter St.

Grub STREET FOOD £

(www.grubmcr.com; 50 Redbank, M4 4HF; ⏰4-10pm Wed-Fri, from noon Sat, noon-6pm Sun) 🌿 A mix of ever-changing traders make this street-food collective one of the most exciting places in town to get a bite. There's a global slant and a heavy focus on plant-based cuisine (including vegan wine and spirits); there's even a dog bar that gives out free (vegan) doggie biscuits. On Sundays, everything is vegan.

Northern Soul Grilled Cheese SANDWICHES £

(www.northernsoulmcr.com; 10 Church St; mains £4.90-7.50; ⏰8.30am-3pm Mon-Fri, to 5.30pm Sat)

> **ℹ NEW IN 2021**
>
> After a major renovation, 2021 will see the long-awaited reopening of the excellent **Manchester Jewish Museum** (☎0161-834 9879; www.manchesterjewishmuseum.com; 190 Cheetham Hill Rd, M8 8LW). Across the Irwell in Salford, the historic grounds of Worsley New Hall – a Gothic-style mansion built in the 19th century for the Duke of Bridgewater – will be transformed into **RHS Garden Bridgewater**, a 62-hectare landscaped garden managed by the Royal Horticultural Society.

Carving out a niche for artery-clogging, gooey grilled-cheese delights in Manchester's grungy Northern Quarter, Northern Soul bills itself as 'gourmet' but there's nothing fancy about the makeshift shack it occupies, or its prices. The menu features cheese sandwiches in various guises, plus deliciously tangy mac 'n' cheese, and milkshakes. There's another branch on Tib St.

Richmond Tea Rooms CAFE £

(☎0161-237 9667; www.richmondtearooms.com; Richmond St; mains £5-11, afternoon teas £8.25-26.95; 🚌all city centre) If the Mad Hatter were to have a tea party in Manchester, it would be in this haphazard tearoom with a potpourri of period furniture and a counter painted to look like the icing on a cake. Sandwiches and light meals are the mainstay, but the real treat is the selection of afternoon teas, complete with finger sandwiches, scones and cakes.

Bundobust INDIAN £

(☎0161-359 6757; www.bundobust.com; 61 Piccadilly; dishes £3.75-6.75; ⏲noon-9.30pm Mon-Thu, to 10pm Fri & Sat, to 8pm Sun; 🖉; 🚌all city centre, 🚊Piccadilly Gardens) Enjoy Indian veggie street food and craft beer at this export from Leeds. The format's the same in Manchester, right down to the pallet wall-panelling at the entrance, but this basement venue is much bigger than the original. Bookings only.

★Refuge by Volta INTERNATIONAL ££

(☎0161-233 5151; www.refugemcr.co.uk; Oxford St; small plates £5.50-11; ⏲noon-2.45pm & 5-9pm Mon-Thu, to 9.30pm Fri, noon-9.30pm Sat, noon-9pm Sun; 🚌all city centre) Manchester's snazziest dining room occupies one half of the Refuge, one of the city's best bars. The menu is made up of *voltini*, sharing plates with global influences from the Middle East to Korea (think lamb shawarma and kimchi), inspired by the travels of restaurateurs and DJs Luke Cowdrey and Justin Crawford (aka the Unabombers). Superb.

★Mackie Mayor FOOD HALL ££

(www.mackiemayor.co.uk; 1 Eagle St; mains £9-15; ⏲10am-10pm Tue-Thu, to 11pm Fri, 9am-11pm Sat, 9am-8pm Sun; 🚌all city centre) This restored former meat market is now home to a superb food hall with a fine selection of 10 individual traders. The pizzas from Honest Crust are divine; the pork-belly bao from Baohouse is done just right; Nationale 7 does wonders with a basic sandwich; and Tender Cow serves really tasty steaks. Dining is communal, across two floors.

Oast House INTERNATIONAL ££

(☎0161-829 3830; www.theoasthouse.uk.com; The Avenue Courtyard, M3 3AY; mains £11.50-19.50; ⏲noon-midnight Mon-Wed & Sun, to 1am Thu-Sat; 🚌all city centre) Modelled on a Kentish oast house (a medieval kiln used to dry out hops), this is one of the most popular spots in Spinningfields. The broad-ranging menu has burgers, kebabs, steaks and rotisserie chickens cooked in the BBQ oven, but you can also get a delicious fondue and a fine selection of homemade pies.

★Mana BRITISH £££

(www.manarestaurant.co.uk; 42 Blossom St, M4 6BF; set lunch/dinner £65/140; ⏲noon-1.30pm & 7pm-late Thu-Sat, 7pm-late Wed; 🚌74, 76, 216, 217, 230, 231 from city centre) Manchester's first Michelin star since 1977 has come courtesy of ex-Noma chef Simon Martin, who takes dishes recognisable from a classic British menu (roast chicken, poached turbot, scallops) and delivers them with a host of new flavours (Daurenki caviar, grand fir and – for the chicken – sage tea). This is edible art.

20 Stories BRITISH £££

(☎0161-204 3333; www.20stories.co.uk; 1 Spinningfields, Hardman Sq; mains £19-35; ⏲noon-2.45pm & 5.30-10.15pm Mon-Thu, noon-3.45pm & 5.30-10.30pm Fri & Sat, noon-3.15pm & 5.30-8.45pm Sun; 🚌all city centre) The most anticipated opening of 2018 was this rooftop restaurant atop a 20-storey tower, marshalled by local star Aiden Byrne (formerly of Manchester House). Great views and great food, courtesy of Byrne's signature style of supremely elegant, unpretentious cuisine. There's an outdoor terrace with a firepit and a grill that serves good burgers and fish and chips.

Adam Reid at the French MODERN BRITISH £££

(☎0161-932 4198; http://the-french-manchester.co.uk; Midland Hotel, 16 Peter St; lunch/dinner tasting menu £75/99; ⏲6.30-8.30pm Tue-Thu, 5.30-9.30pm Fri, noon-1pm & 5.30-9.30pm Sat; 🚊St Peter's Square) 🍃 Adam Reid's exquisite Modern British cuisine is considered one of Manchester's culinary highlights, with each dish of the seven-course tasting menu exquisitely prepared and presented. The room is dark and moody, the soundtrack indie rock – an interesting counterpoint to the subtlety of the food. Reservations are very much recommended.

Hawksmoor STEAK £££

(☎0161-836 6980; www.thehawksmoor.com; 184-186 Deansgate, M3 2EQ; steaks £21-36; ⏲5-10pm

Mon-Fri, noon-3pm & 5-10pm Sat, noon-9pm Sun; St Peter's Square) Hawksmoor is the place to go for steak. Everything inside this Grade II–listed former courthouse is carefully put together to create a 1930s-style atmosphere, which is the perfect setting to indulge your most carnivorous instincts. The steaks – also available by weight – are prepared perfectly and the sides – including dripping fries, triple-cooked chips, mac 'n' cheese – are just divine.

Drinking & Nightlife

★Refuge BAR

(0161-233 5151; www.refugemcr.co.uk; Oxford St; 8am-midnight Mon-Wed, to 1am Thu, to 2am Fri & Sat, to 11.30pm Sun; all city centre) Occupying what was once the Victorian Gothic ground floor of the Refuge Assurance Building, this is not just Manchester's most beautiful bar, but arguably its coolest too – all thanks to the rep and aesthetic sensibilities of its creative director duo, DJs and restaurateurs Luke Cowdrey and Justin Crawford, aka the Unabombers, who run Homoelectric, the best club nights in the northwest.

Fac251 CLUB

(0161-272 7251; www.factorymanchester.com; 112-118 Princess St; £1-6; 11pm-4am Thu-Mon; all city centre) Located in Tony Wilson's former Factory Records HQ, Fac251 is one of the most popular venues in town. There are three rooms, all with a broad musical appeal, from drum and bass to Motown and indie rock. There's something for everybody, from Monday's Quids In (for students) to the Big Weekender on Saturday (commercial R & B).

Peveril of the Peak PUB

(0161-236 6364; 127 Great Bridgewater St; 11am-11pm; Deansgate-Castlefield) The best of Manchester's collection of beautiful Victorian pubs. Check out the gorgeous glazed tilework outside.

Britons Protection PUB

(0161-236 5895; 50 Great Bridgewater St; noon-midnight Mon-Thu, to 1am Fri & Sat, to 11pm Sun; Castlefield-Deansgate) Whisky – over 300 different kinds of it (the Cu Dhub 'black whisky' is a particular treat with its touch of coffee and honey) – is the beverage of choice at this liver-threatening, proper English pub that also does home-style meals (gammon, pies etc). An old-fashioned boozer with open fires in the back rooms and a cosy atmosphere, it's perfect on a cold evening.

NIGHTLIFE IN THE AGE OF COVID-19

Manchester's legendary nightlife took a proper kicking in 2020/1, with some of its best-known venues struggling to survive through the Covid-19 pandemic. Much-loved venues like the Deaf Institute (p550) and Gorilla (p550) nearly went under but were saved from closure by a coalition of promoters and The Charlatans' Tim Burgess. Nevertheless, most nightclubs and late-night venues were closed right through 2020, grimly holding on for the end of the crisis.

Albert's Schloss BEER HALL

(www.albertsschloss.co.uk; 27 Peter St; 8am-2am Mon-Fri, 9.30am-2am Sat & Sun; St Peter's Square) The strapline says 'Cook Haus and Bier Palace', and this big version of a night out in Central Europe is just that. The *bier* is unpasteurised Pilsner Urquell, shipped directly from the brewery near Prague. The food is more local, but still true to theme – you can get all kinds of wursts, sauerbraten and 'schweins in blankets'. *Wunderbar!*

North Tea Power CAFE

(0161-833 3073; www.northteapower.co.uk; 36 Tib St; 8am-7pm Mon-Fri, from 9am Sat, 10am-6pm Sun;) The name may say tea but the interior of this cafe screams coffee shop. North Tea Power is one of Manchester's early adopters of the artisanal coffee scene, with the requisite communal tables, industrial pillars and Macbook-wielding tribe. As well as flat whites, AeroPress and pour-overs, the menu features a load of loose-leaf teas, cakes and all-day breakfast options.

Port Street Beer House CRAFT BEER

(www.portstreetbeerhouse.co.uk; 39-41 Port St; noon-midnight Sun-Fri, to 1am Sat; Piccadilly Gardens) Fans of real ale love this Northern Quarter boozer, with its seven hand pulls, 18 draught lines and more than 100 beers from around the world, including gluten-free ales and some heavy hitters: Brewdog's Tactical Nuclear Penguin is a £45 stout, but at 32% alcohol you won't need more than one. It hosts regular tastings and tap takeovers.

Black Dog Ballroom BAR

(0161-839 0664; www.blackdogballroom.co.uk; 52 Church St; 4-10pm Mon-Fri, from noon Sat & Sun; ; all city centre) A basement bar with a speakeasy vibe, but there's nothing illicit

FOOTBALL TOURS

Manchester United Museum & Tour (0161-826 1326; www.manutd.com; Sir Matt Busby Way; tours adult/child £18/12; museum 9.30am-5pm Mon-Sat, 10am-4pm Sun, tours every 10 min 9.40am-4.30pm Mon-Sat, to 3.30pm Sun, closed match days; Old Trafford or Exchange Quay) You don't have to be a fan of the world's most famous football club to enjoy a visit to its impressive 75,000-plus-capacity Old Trafford stadium, but it helps. The museum tour includes a walk down the tunnel onto the edge of the playing surface, where Manchester United's superstar footballers ply their lucrative trade.

Other highlights of the excellent tour include a seat in the stands, a stop in the changing rooms and a peek at the players' lounge (from which the manager is banned unless invited by the players) – all ecstatic experiences for a Man United devotee. The museum has a comprehensive history of the club and a state-of-the-art call-up system that means you can view your favourite goals.

Manchester City Stadium Tour (0161-444 1894; www.mancity.com; Etihad Campus; tours adult/child £25/15; 9am-5pm Mon-Sat, 10am-4pm Sun except match days; Etihad Campus) On this 90-minute tour of Manchester City's stadium you'll visit both the home and away dressing rooms (note the huge difference between the two), the pitchside dugouts, the press room and the Tunnel Club, where VIP guests get to see the players walk through on match days. The tour also includes a visit to the trophy room, now full of trophies won under the tutelage of superstar manager Josep 'Pep' Guardiola.

Other tours combine the stadium with the nearby academy. Online bookings are cheaper.

about drinking here: the cocktails are terrific (it runs occasional mixology sessions), the atmosphere is always buzzing and the music always good and loud – the resident DJs spin some great tunes Thursday through Saturday nights.

☆ Entertainment

★HOME ARTS CENTRE
(0161-200 1500; www.homemcr.org; 2 Tony Wilson Pl, First St; tickets £5-25; box office noon-8pm, bar 10am-11pm Mon-Thu, to midnight Fri & Sat, 11am-10.30pm Sun; all city centre) One of Britain's best arts centres, HOME has two theatre spaces that host provocative new work in a variety of contexts, from proscenium sets to promenade pieces. The five cinema screens show the latest indie releases as well as classics. There's also a ground-floor bar and a cafe that serves good food on the 1st floor.

Band on the Wall LIVE MUSIC
(0161-834 1786; www.bandonthewall.org; 25 Swan St; 5pm-late; all city centre) A top-notch venue that hosts everything from rock to world music, with splashes of jazz, blues and folk thrown in.

Gorilla LIVE MUSIC
(0161-826 2998; www.thisisgorilla.com; 54-56 Whitworth St, M1 5WW; 11pm-late; all city centre) Brilliant mid-sized venue to see up-and-comers, alternative artists and big stars looking to enhance their alternative credentials. There's a bar and a restaurant too.

Deaf Institute LIVE MUSIC
(www.thedeafinstitute.co.uk; 135 Grosvenor St; 10am-midnight; all city centre) This is an excellent venue in a former institute for deaf people; it also includes a smaller venue in the basement and a cafe on the ground floor. It's where you'll hear alt rock and pop by dozens of local bands we guarantee you've never heard of (as well as some visiting bands you may have).

Shopping

Oi Polloi CLOTHING
(www.oipolloi.com; 63 Thomas St; 10am-6pm Mon-Sat; all city centre) Besides the impressive range of casual footwear, this hip boutique also stocks a huge range of designers including A Kind of Guise, LA Panoplie, Nudie Jeans Co and Maison Kitsuné.

Tib Street Market MARKET
(0161-234 7357; Tib St; 10am-5pm Sat; all city centre) Local designers get a chance to display their wares at this weekly market, where you can pick up everything from purses to lingerie and hats to jewellery.

Oxfam Originals VINTAGE
(Unit 8, Smithfield Bldg, Oldham St; 10am-6pm Mon-Sat, noon-5pm Sun; all city centre) If you're

into retro, this terrific store has high-quality gear from the 1960s and '70s. Shop in the knowledge that it's for a good cause.

Information

Tourist Office (www.visitmanchester.com; 1 Piccadilly Gardens; 9.30am-5pm Mon-Sat, 10.30am-4.30pm Sun; Piccadilly Gardens) This is mostly a self-service tourist office, with brochures and interactive maps to help guide visitors.

Getting There & Away

AIR

Manchester Airport (0808-169 7030; www.manchesterairport.co.uk) The airport is 12 miles south of the city.

Bus £4.20, 30 minutes, every 20 minutes to Piccadilly Gardens

Metrolink £4.20, 40 minutes, every 12 minutes; change at Cornbrook or Firswood for city centre

Taxi £20 to £30, 25 to 40 minutes

Train £5, 20 minutes, every 10 minutes to Piccadilly Station

BUS

National Express (08717 81 81 81; www.nationalexpress.com) serves most major cities from the **coach station** (Chorlton St), including the following:

Leeds £6, one hour, hourly

Liverpool £4, 1½ hours, hourly

London £8.40, 4¼ hours, hourly

TRAIN

Manchester Piccadilly (east of Piccadilly Gardens) is the main station for most mainline train services across Britain; Victoria Station (north of the National Football Museum) serves destinations in the northwest including Blackburn, Halifax and Huddersfield but also Leeds and Liverpool. The two stations are linked by Metrolink. Off-peak fares are considerably cheaper. Destinations include the following:

Blackpool £9.50, 1¼ hours, half-hourly

Liverpool Lime St £15.30, 45 minutes, half-hourly

London Euston £64, three hours, seven daily

Newcastle £76, three hours, six daily

Getting Around

BUS

The Metroshuttle is a free service with three separate routes around the heart of Manchester every 10 minutes. Pick up a map from the tourist office. Most local buses start from Piccadilly Gardens.

METROLINK

The **Metrolink** (www.metrolink.co.uk) light-rail network is the best way to get between Victoria and Piccadilly train stations, and further afield to Salford Quays, Didsbury and other suburbs, as well as the Trafford Centre. It also serves the airport, but you need to change at either Cornbrook or Firswood. Trams run every few minutes throughout the day from 6am to 11pm. Buy your tickets from the platform machine.

TRAIN

Castlefield is served by Deansgate station with suburban rail links to Piccadilly, Oxford Rd and Salford stations.

CHESTER

01244 / POP 118,200

Chester's Tudor-and-Victorian heart is justifiably famous as one of Britain's prettiest town centres. This collection of black-and-white timber-framed beauties and red-sandstone buildings surrounded by an original set of Roman-era walls is one of the northwest's biggest tourist attractions.

Beyond the cruciform-shaped historic centre, Chester is an ordinary, residential town; it's hard to believe today, but throughout the Middle Ages Chester made its money as the most important port in the northwest. However, the River Dee silted up over time and Chester fell behind Liverpool in importance.

Sights & Activities

★City Walls LANDMARK

A good way to get a sense of Chester's unique character is to walk the 2-mile circuit along the walls that surround the historic centre. Originally built by the Romans around 70 CE, the walls were altered substantially over the following centuries, but have retained their current position since around 1200. The tourist office's *Walk Around Chester Walls* leaflet is an excellent guide and you can also take a 90-minute guided walk.

Of the many features along the walls, the most eye-catching is the prominent **Eastgate**, where you can see the most famous clock in England after London's Big Ben, built for Queen Victoria's Diamond Jubilee in 1897.

At the southeastern corner of the walls are the **wishing steps**, added in 1785. Local legend claims that if you can run up and down these uneven steps while holding your breath your wish will come true.

Chester

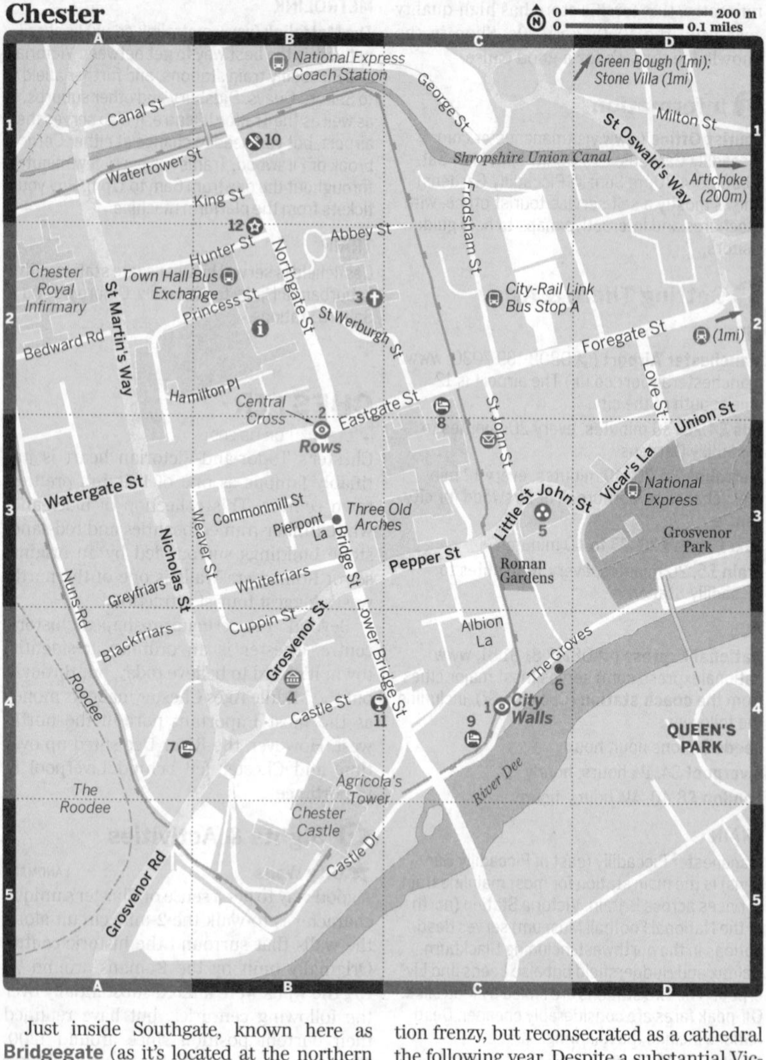

Just inside Southgate, known here as **Bridgegate** (as it's located at the northern end of the Old Dee Bridge), is the **Bear & Billet** pub, Chester's oldest timber-framed building, built in 1664, and once a toll gate into the city.

Chester Cathedral CATHEDRAL
(☎01244-324756; www.chestercathedral.com; 12 Abbey Sq; ⊙10am-4pm Mon-Sat, noon-4pm Sun) FREE Chester Cathedral was originally a Benedictine abbey built on the remains of an earlier Saxon church dedicated to St Werburgh (the city's patron saint); it was shut down in 1540 as part of Henry VIII's Dissolution frenzy, but reconsecrated as a cathedral the following year. Despite a substantial Victorian facelift, the cathedral retains much of its original 12th-century structure. You can amble about freely, but the **tours** (www.chestercathedral.com; adult/child 1hr tour £8/6, 30min tour £6; ⊙full tour 11am & 3pm daily, short tour 12.30pm & 1.15pm Mon & Tue, 2pm & 4pm Wed-Sat) are excellent, as they take you up to the top of the panoramic bell tower.

Roman Amphitheatre ARCHAEOLOGICAL SITE
(Little St John St) FREE Just outside the city walls is what was once an arena that seated 7000 spectators (making it the country's

Chester

Top Sights
1 City Walls ... C4
2 Rows ... B3

Sights
3 Chester Cathedral ... B2
4 Grosvenor Museum ... B4
5 Roman Amphitheatre ... C3

Activities, Courses & Tours
Cathedral Tours ... (see 3)
6 Chester Boat ... C4

Sleeping
7 ABode Chester ... A4
8 Chester Grosvenor Hotel & Spa ... C2
9 Edgar House ... C4

Eating
10 Joseph Benjamin ... B1
Simon Radley at the Grosvenor ... (see 8)
The Kitchen ... (see 12)

Drinking & Nightlife
11 Brewery Tap ... B4

Entertainment
12 Storyhouse ... B2

largest); some historians have suggested that it may have also been the site of King Arthur's Camelot and that his knights' 'round table' was really just this circular construction. Excavations continue; during summer months there are occasional shows held here.

Blue Planet Aquarium AQUARIUM
(www.blueplanetaquarium.com; Cheshire Oaks, CH65 9LF; adult/child £18/13; 10am-5pm; 1 or X1 from Bus Exchange) Things aren't done by halves around Chester, where you'll find Blue Planet, which was the country's largest aquarium when it opened in 1998. It's home to 10 different kinds of shark, which can be viewed from a 70m-long moving walkway that lets you eye them up close. The aquarium is at the Cheshire Oaks Outlet Centre (p554), 7 miles north of Chester at Junction 10 of the M53 to Liverpool. Pre-booking essential.

Grosvenor Museum MUSEUM
(01244-972197; www.grosvenormuseum.westcheshiremuseums.co.uk; 27 Grosvenor St; 10.30am-1pm & 2-4.30pm Tue-Sat, last admission 3.45pm) FREE This excellent museum has the country's most comprehensive collection of Roman tombstones. At the back of the museum is a preserved Georgian house, complete with kitchen, drawing room, bedroom and bathroom. Pre-booking only.

Chester Boat BOATING
(01244-325394; www.chesterboat.co.uk; Boating Station, Souters La, The Groves; 30min/2hr cruise £7/15; 11am-5pm) Runs hourly 30-minute and two-hour cruises (the latter at noon and 2.30pm Saturday and Sunday) up and down the Dee, including a foray into the gorgeous Eaton Estate, home of the Duke and Duchess of Westminster. All departures are from the riverside along the promenade known as the Groves.

Sleeping

Stone Villa B&B ££
(01244-345014; www.stonevillachester.co.uk; 3 Stone Pl, Hoole Rd; s/d from £65/95; P; 9 from city centre) This award-winning, beautiful 1850 villa has everything you need for a memorable stay. Elegant bedrooms, a fabulous breakfast and welcoming, friendly owners all add up to excellent lodgings. The property is about a mile from the city centre. You can even rent the whole house – which sleeps 22 – for £900 a night.

ABode Chester HOTEL ££
(01244-347000; www.abodechester.co.uk; Grosvenor Rd; r/ste from £74/249; P) Contemporary hotel with 84 rooms all equipped with handcrafted Vispring beds and handsome bathrooms complete with monsoon showers. Good toiletries, flat-screen TVs and cashmere throws on the beds give it a touch of elegance. Rooms come in categories: Comfortable, Desirable, Enviable, Most Enviable and Fabulous suites. South-facing rooms have great views of the Roodee racecourse.

★ **Edgar House** BOUTIQUE HOTEL £££
(01244-347007; www.edgarhouse.co.uk; 22 City Walls; r from £199) These award-winning digs are the ultimate in boutique luxury: a Georgian house with seven rooms, each decorated in its own individual style – some have free-standing claw-foot tubs and French doors that lead onto an elegant terrace. There's beautiful art on the walls and fabulous touches of the owners' gorgeous aesthetic throughout.

DON'T MISS

THE ROWS

Besides the City Walls, Chester's other great draw is the Rows, a series of two-level, half-timbered galleried arcades along the four streets that fan out in each direction from the Central Cross. Aside from the 13th-century **Three Old Arches** building, the architecture is a handsome mix of Victorian and Tudor (original and mock) buildings that house a fantastic collection of independently owned shops.

The origin of the Rows is a little unclear, but it is believed that as the Roman walls slowly crumbled, medieval traders built their shops against the resulting rubble banks, while later arrivals built theirs on top.

Chester Grosvenor Hotel & Spa HOTEL £££
(☎01244-324024; www.chestergrosvenor.com; 58 Eastgate St; r from £160; P @) The black-and-white timbered Grosvenor is the city's top hotel by location (right next to the Eastgate Clock) and quality, offering a five-star experience throughout. The lobby's main feature is the chandelier, with 28,000 pieces of crystal; move on from there to the huge rooms with exquisite period furniture. There's also a top spa (open to nonguests) and a Michelin-starred restaurant.

Eating

★**The Kitchen** LEBANESE £
(www.thekitchenstoryhouse.co.uk; Storyhouse, Hunter St; mains £7-10; 8am-9.30pm Mon-Sat, 9.30am-9pm Sun) Delicious meze and other small plates from the Levant are the mainstay at the ground-floor restaurant in Storyhouse, Chester's exciting award-winning arts centre. The brunch menu (available from 10am) is a treat – how about harissa sausage and streaky bacon roll or cumin-spiced rice with smoked haddock and kedgeree?

Joseph Benjamin MODERN BRITISH ££
(☎01244-344295; www.josephbenjamin.co.uk; 134-140 Northgate St; mains £14-17; noon-2.30pm & 5-10pm Wed-Sun) A bright star in Chester's culinary firmament is this combo restaurant, bar and deli that delivers carefully prepared local produce to take away or eat in. Excellent sandwiches and gorgeous salads are the mainstay of the takeaway menu, while the more formal dinner menu features fine examples of Modern British cuisine.

Artichoke MODERN BRITISH ££
(www.artichokechester.co.uk; The Steam Mill, Steam Mill St; mains £7-13; 3.30-9pm Mon-Fri, from 12.30pm Sat, 12.30-7pm Sun) One of a number of warehouse conversions along the Shropshire Union Canal (now known as the Canal Quarter), this cafe-bar serves sandwiches and smaller bites as well as tasty main courses, such as sea trout in a sweet pea wasabi velvet cream, and confit of duck legs with Jersey potatoes, pancetta and red cabbage. It's a popular drinking spot too.

Simon Radley at the Grosvenor MODERN BRITISH £££
(☎01244-324024; www.chestergrosvenor.com; 58 Eastgate St, Chester Grosvenor Hotel; tasting menu Tue-Thu £79, Fri & Sat £99; 6.30-7.30pm Tue-Sat) Simon Radley's formal restaurant has served near-perfect Modern British cuisine since 1990, when it was first awarded the Michelin star that it has kept ever since. The food is divine and the wine list extensive. It's one of Britain's best, but a little stuffy: smart attire only and no children under 12 allowed. Oh, and switch your mobile phone to silent.

Drinking & Entertainment

Brewery Tap PUB
(www.the-tap.co.uk; 52-54 Lower Bridge St; noon-11pm Mon-Sat, to 10.30pm Sun) If you're looking for the best pint in the city, the aficionados at the Campaign for Real Ale (Camra) reckon you'll get it at this boozer in a Grade II–listed Jacobean banqueting hall; its seven taps offer a rotating range of quality brews from all over England.

★**Storyhouse** ARTS CENTRE
(☎01244-409113; www.storyhouse.com; Hunter St) The 1930s art deco Odeon has been converted into an award-winning modern arts centre with two theatre spaces – a larger 800-seat arena and a 150-seat studio theatre – plus a cinema that screens indie and art movies. The Lebanese-inspired Kitchen restaurant on the ground floor is excellent.

Shopping

Cheshire Oaks Outlet Centre SHOPPING CENTRE
(www.mcarthurglen.com; Ellesmere Port; 10am-8pm Mon-Fri, 9am-8pm Sat, 10am-6pm Sun; 1 or X1 from Bus Exchange) Britain's largest shopping outlet, Cheshire Oaks has 145 stores

offering discounts of up to 60% on goods from previous seasons. The village layout means the shops are divided into helpful districts, dotted with restaurants and cafes along the way. It's 7 miles north of Chester.

Information

Tourist Office (☎01244-402111; www.visitchester.com; Town Hall, Northgate St; ⊙10am-5pm Mon-Sat, to 4pm Sun) Tourist information, accommodation-booking service and brochures.

Getting There & Away

BUS

Local buses leave from the **Town Hall Bus Exchange** (Princess St). **National Express** (☎08717 81 81 81; www.nationalexpress.com) coaches stop on Vicar's Lane, just opposite the tourist office by the Roman amphitheatre. Destinations include the following:

Birmingham £18.30, two hours, four daily
Liverpool £7, 45 minutes, four daily
London £34.60, 5½ hours, three daily
Manchester £6.50, 1¼ hours, three daily

TRAIN

The train station is about a mile from the city centre via Foregate St and City Rd, or Brook St. City-Rail Link buses are free for people with rail tickets, and operate between the station and **Bus Stop A** (Frodsham St). Destinations include the following:

Liverpool £7.70, 45 minutes, hourly
London Euston £64.40, 2½ hours, hourly
Manchester £18.60, one hour, hourly

Getting Around

A car's not much use in town, as much of the centre is closed to traffic from 10.30am to 4.30pm. The city is easy to walk around anyway, and most places of interest are close to the wall. There are regular buses to the aquarium.

LIVERPOOL

☎0151 / POP 552,267

It's hard not to be infected by a Liverpudlian's love for their own city. For decades this was a hardscrabble town beset by all manner of social ills, but still the love endured, finding its expression in a renowned gallows wit and an obsession with football.

With the worst of times now firmly behind them, it's much easier to feel the love. The city's impressive cultural heritage, dating back to when Liverpool was Britain's second-most important city, is a source of justifiable pride to Scousers – as the locals are named, after Scouse, a fish-and-biscuit stew popular with sailors – but what really excites them is the ongoing programme of urban regeneration that is transforming a once dilapidated city centre into one of the most pleasant cities in northern England.

History

Liverpool grew wealthy on the back of the triangular trading of slaves, raw materials and finished goods (the horrors of which are documented at the International Slavery Museum, p550). From 1700 ships carried cotton goods and hardware from Liverpool to West Africa, where they were exchanged for slaves, who in turn were carried to the West Indies and Virginia, where they were exchanged for sugar, rum, tobacco and raw cotton.

As a great port, the city drew thousands of Irish and Scottish immigrants, and its Celtic influences are still apparent. Between 1830 and 1930, however, nine million emigrants – mainly English, Scots and Irish, but also Swedes, Norwegians and Russian Jews – sailed from here to the New World.

The start of WWII led to a resurgence of Liverpool's importance. More than one million American GIs disembarked here before D-Day and the port was, once again, hugely important as the western gateway for transatlantic supplies. The GIs brought with them the latest American records, and Liverpool was thus the first European port of call for the new rhythm and blues that would eventually become rock and roll. Within 20 years, the Mersey Beat was *the* sound of British pop, and four mop-topped Scousers had formed a skiffle band...

Sights

The main attractions are Albert Dock (west of the city centre) and the trendy Ropewalks area (south of Hanover St and west of the two cathedrals). Lime St station, the bus station and the Cavern Quarter – a mecca for Beatles fans – lie just to the north.

City Centre

★**Liverpool Cathedral** CHURCH
(☎0151-709 6271; www.liverpoolcathedral.org.uk; Upper Duke St; Tower Experience adult/student £5.50/4.50; ⊙11am-2.45pm Mon-Fri, to 2.30pm Sat, 12.30-2.30pm Sun; 🚌82 & 86 from city

Liverpool

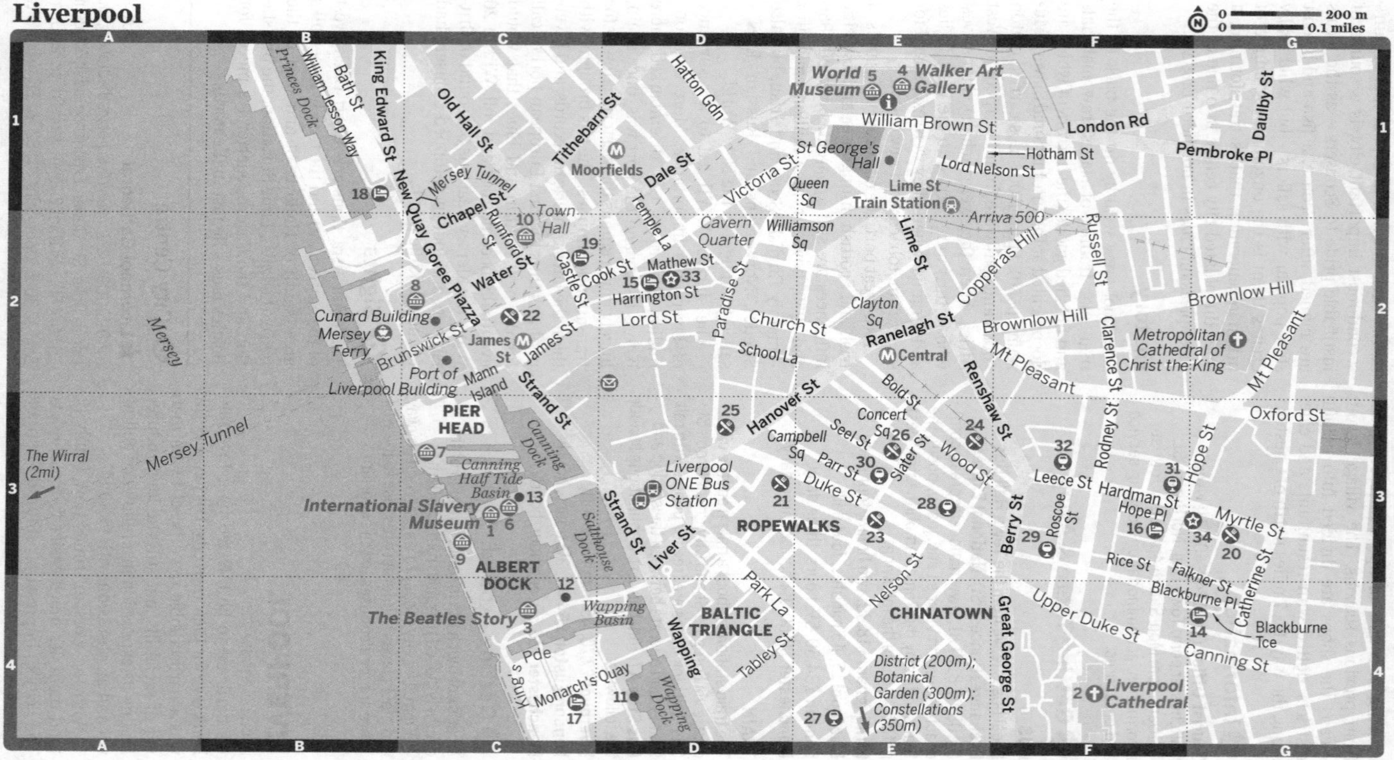
0 200 m
0 0.1 miles
World Museum 5
4 Walker Art Gallery
William Brown St
London Rd
Daulby St
Pembroke Pl
Hotham St
Lord Nelson St
St George's Hall
Lime St Train Station
Arriva 500
Queen Sq
Williamson Sq
Cavern Quarter
Victoria St
Dale St
Tithebarn St
Moorfields
Hatton Gdn
Old Hall St
King Edward St
Bath St
William Jessop Way
Princes Dock
18
New Quay
Goree Piazza
Mersey Tunnel
Chapel St
Rumford St
Town Hall
10
Water St
19
Castle St
Cook St
Mathew St
15
33
Harrington St
Temple La
Lime St
Copperas Hill
Russell St
Brownlow Hill
Clarence St
Metropolitan Cathedral of Christ the King
Mt Pleasant
8
Cunard Building
Mersey Ferry
Brunswick St
22
James St
Lord St
Paradise St
Church St
Clayton Sq
Ranelagh St
Central
School La
Port of Liverpool Building
Mann Island
Strand St
Mersey
Mersey Tunnel
The Wirral (2mi)
PIER HEAD
7
Canning Dock
Canning Half Tide Basin
13
International Slavery Museum
1
6
9
ALBERT DOCK
12
The Beatles Story
3
Wapping Basin
Salthouse Dock
King's Pde
Monarch's Quay
17
11
Wapping Dock
Wapping
Liver St
Liverpool ONE Bus Station
25
Hanover St
Bold St
Concert Sq
26
Seel St
Campbell Sq
Parr St
30
Slater St
Wood St
24
Renshaw St
Mt Pleasant
Duke St
21
ROPEWALKS
23
28
Park La
BALTIC TRIANGLE
Tabley St
Nelson St
CHINATOWN
District (200m); Botanical Garden (300m); Constellations (350m)
27
Great George St
Berry St
29
Roscoe St
Leece St
32
Rodney St
Oxford St
Hope St
31
Hardman St
Hope Pl
16
34
Myrtle St
20
Rice St
Falkner St
Blackburne Pl
Catherine St
14
Blackburne Tce
Upper Duke St
Canning St
2
Liverpool Cathedral

Liverpool

centre) Britain's largest church, this magnificent neo-Gothic building is also the world's largest Anglican cathedral. It was designed by Sir Giles Gilbert Scott (creator of the red telephone box) and is a stunning bit of architecture, managing at once to provoke awe at its size as well as a profound feeling of intimacy. Pre-booking is essential to climb the tower, which affords views as far as Blackpool (on a clear day).

The **Tower Experience** was closed at the time of writing, but once it reopens you can enjoy *Great Space,* a 10-minute, panoramic high-definition movie about the history of the cathedral, which was begun in 1904 but not completed until 1978; and a view of Great George, the world's heaviest set of bells. The vast interior is marked by a studied emptiness, but worth noting is the organ, split between two chambers on opposite sides of the Choir and comprising 10,268 pipes and 200 stops, making it most likely the world's largest operational model. The cathedral is also home to a collection of artworks, including a piece over the West Doors called *For You* by Tracey Emin: a pink neon sign that says 'I felt you and I knew you loved me'. Guides are on hand to offer tours; a donation of £3 is suggested.

★Walker Art Gallery GALLERY
(0151-478 4199; www.liverpoolmuseums.org.uk/walker; William Brown St; 10am-5pm Wed-Sun; all city centre) FREE The city's foremost art gallery is the national gallery for northern England, housing an outstanding collection of art from the 14th to the 21st centuries. Its strong suits are Pre-Raphaelite art, modern British art and sculpture – not to mention the rotating exhibits of contemporary expression. It's a family-friendly place too: the ground-floor Big Art for Little Artists gallery is designed for under-eights and features interactive exhibits and games that will (hopefully) result in a lifelong love affair with art.

★World Museum MUSEUM
(0151-478 4399; www.liverpoolmuseums.org.uk/wml; William Brown St; 10am-5pm Wed-Sun; all city centre) FREE Natural history, science and technology are the themes of the oldest museum in town, which opened in 1853. Its exhibits range from live bugs to human anthropology. This vastly entertaining and educational museum is spread across five themed floors, from the aquarium on the 1st floor to the planetarium on the 5th, where you'll also find exhibits dedicated to space (moon rocks, telescopes etc) and time (clocks and timepieces from the 1500s to 1960). Highly recommended.

Western Approaches Museum MUSEUM
(www.liverpoolwarmuseum.co.uk; 1-3 Rumford St; adult/child £13.50/8; 10am-4.15pm Wed-Sun; all city centre) Between 7 February 1941 and 15 August 1945 the secret command

LIVERPOOL IN ONE DAY

Start your day at the Beatles Story (p560) on the Albert Dock: it's an excellent intro to the Fab Four, but fans should make sure they've booked a morning tour (p560) to Mendips and 20 Forthlin Rd, the childhood homes of John Lennon and Paul McCartney respectively; the tour leaves from Albert Dock. If you're not a die-hard Beatles fan, then visit the International Slavery Museum and then head into town for a visit to the stunning cathedral (p555). For lunch, try the Salt House (p562).

If you've still got a cultural hunger, you can explore the Walker Art Gallery (p557) or the wonderful natural science exhibits of the World Museum (p557). Football fans should make the trip to Anfield and take the tour of Liverpool Football Club (p563). For dinner, go to Wreckfish (p561) or Art School (p562).

After dinner, be sure to get a drink at the Philharmonic Dining Rooms (p563), after which you can take in a gig across the street at the Philharmonic Hall (p564). If you're into something a little more adrenalised, the clubs of the Baltic Triangle are worth a punt: our favourite is Constellations (p564), which always has something interesting going on.

centre for the Battle of the Atlantic was in the basement rooms of Derby House. Known as Western Approaches because its main task was to monitor enemy approaches in the Atlantic west of the British Isles, the labyrinthine nerve centre of Allied operations is pretty much as it was at war's end. Highlights include the all-important map room, where you can imagine playing a real-life, full-scale version of Risk.

Albert Dock

Liverpool's biggest tourist attraction is Albert Dock, 2.75 hectares of water ringed by enormous cast-iron columns and impressive five-storey warehouses that make up the country's largest collection of protected buildings and are a World Heritage Site. A fabulous redevelopment programme has really brought the dock to life – here you'll find several outstanding museums and an extension of the Tate Gallery, as well as some good restaurants and bars.

★International Slavery Museum MUSEUM
(0151-478 4499; www.liverpoolmuseums.org.uk/ism; Albert Dock; 10am-5pm Wed-Sun) FREE Museums are, by their very nature, a document of the past, but the extraordinary International Slavery Museum resonates very much in the present. It reveals slavery's unimaginable horrors – and Liverpool's own role in the triangular slave trade – in a clear and uncompromising manner. It does this through a remarkable series of multimedia and other displays, and it doesn't baulk at confronting racism, slavery's shadowy ideological justification for this inhumane practice.

The history of slavery is made real through a series of personal experiences, including a carefully kept ship's log and captain's diary. These tell the story of one slaver's experience on a typical trip, departing Liverpool for West Africa. The ship then purchased or captured as many slaves as it could carry before embarking on the gruesome 'middle passage' across the Atlantic to the West Indies. The slaves that survived the torturous journey were sold for sugar, rum, tobacco and raw cotton, which were then brought back to England for profit. Exhibits include original shackles, chains and instruments used to punish rebellious slaves – each piece of metal is more horrendous than the next.

Royal Liver Building 360 MUSEUM
(0151-559 1950; www.rlb360.com; Pier Head; adult/child £15/10; 9am-6.30pm Mar-Sep, to 5.30pm Oct-Feb) One of Pier Head's trio of Edwardian buildings known as the 'Three Graces', the Royal Liver Building (pronounced lie-ver) opened to the public for the first time in 2019. The 70-minute tour takes you through the history of the building and some of its beautiful rooms right to the clock tower at the top, crowned by the famous 5.5m copper Liver Bird that is the city's symbol.

Merseyside Maritime Museum MUSEUM
(0151-478 4499; www.liverpoolmuseums.org.uk/maritime; Albert Dock; 10am-5pm Wed-Sun; all city centre) FREE The story of one of the world's great ports is the theme of this excellent museum and, believe us, it's a graphic and compelling page-turner. One of the many great exhibits is Emigration to

a New World (in the basement), which tells the story of nine million emigrants and their efforts to get to North America and Australia; the walk-through model of a typical ship shows just how tough conditions on board really were.

Museum of Liverpool MUSEUM
(0151-478 4545; www.liverpoolmuseums.org.uk/mol; Pier Head; 10am-5pm Wed-Sun; all city centre) FREE Liverpool's storied past is explored through an interactive exploration of the city's cultural and historical milestones: the railroad, poverty, wealth, *Brookside* (a popular '80s and '90s TV soap opera set in the city), the Beatles and football (the film on what the game means to the city is worth the 15 minutes). The desire to tell all of the city's rich story means there isn't a huge amount of depth, but the kids will love it.

The museum is constantly introducing new elements and temporary exhibitions, with a view towards ensuring that all visits are connected with a contemporary experience of the city. Recent exhibits include a retrospective of Linda McCartney's photographs, German expressionist prints and a show on artificial intelligence.

Tate Liverpool GALLERY
(0151-702 7400; www.tate.org.uk/liverpool; Albert Dock; special exhibitions adult/child from £6/5; 10am-5.50pm; all city centre) FREE Touted as the home of modern art in the north, this gallery features a substantial checklist of 20th-century artists across its four floors, as well as touring exhibitions from the mother ship on London's Bankside. But it's all a little sparse, with none of the energy we'd expect from the world-famous Tate.

Tours

★Anfield Stadium Tour TOUR
(www.liverpoolfc.com; Anfield Stadium; stadium tour adult/child £20/15; 9am-5pm except match days; 26 & 27 from Liverpool ONE Bus Station, 17 from Queens St Bus Station) For fans of Liverpool FC, Anfield is a special place, and this is reflected in the reverential tone of the hour-long self-guided audio tour that starts at the top of the new Main Stand (with a video greeting from manager Jürgen Klopp) and continues down to pitchside. Stops along the way include the home and away dressing rooms and the luxurious players' lounge.

You'll also see the press room and the home dugout, accessed via the 'walk of champions' tunnel, where you can touch the iconic 'This is Anfield' sign. Also included is the new 'Boom Room' exhibition, which tells the story of how Klopp and his charges won the league title in 2020 – after a 30-year wait. Staff positioned at various points throughout the tour are on hand to answer questions, generally with a touch of humour that makes the whole experience a memorable one for fans and especially kids. The ground is 2.5 miles northeast of the city centre.

Old Docks Tour TOURS
(0151-478 4499; www.liverpoolmuseums.org.uk/maritime; Merseyside Maritime Museum, Albert Dock; 10.30am, noon & 2.30pm Mon-Wed; all city centre) Free and a lot of fun, the guided tours of the Old Dock – the world's first commercial enclosed wet dock – offer an insight into the history of Liverpool as a powerful port city (and the source of all its wealth). You'll also get to see the bed of the Pool, the creek that gave the city its name.

Magical Mystery Tour CULTURAL
(0151-703 9100; www.cavernclub.org; per person £19.95; tours hourly 11am-4pm; all city centre) This two-hour tour takes in all the Beatles-related landmarks – their birthplaces, childhood homes, schools and places such as Penny Lane and Strawberry Field – before finishing up in the Cavern Club (which isn't the original). It departs from opposite the tourist office on Albert Dock.

THE THREE GRACES

The area to the north of Albert Dock is known as **Pier Head**, after a stone pier built in the 1760s. This is still the departure point for ferries across the River Mersey, and was for millions of migrants their final contact with European soil.

The Museum of Liverpool is an impressive architectural interloper, but pride of place in this part of the dock still goes to the trio of Edwardian buildings known as the 'Three Graces', dating from the days when Liverpool's star was still ascending: the **Port of Liverpool Building**, the **Cunard Building** and the **Royal Liver Building**, which is topped by Liverpool's symbol, the famous 5.5m copper Liver Bird, and recently opened as a museum.

DON'T MISS

BEATLEMANIA LIVES

They broke up more than 50 years ago and two of their members are dead, but the Beatles are bigger business than ever in Liverpool.

Most of it centres around tiny Mathew St, site of the original Cavern Club, which is now the main thoroughfare of the 'Cavern Quarter', an unashamedly commercial effort to cash in on the legacy of the Fab Four. Here you can shuck oysters in the Rubber Soul Oyster Bar, buy a George pillowcase in the From Me to You shop and put it on the pillows of the Hard Days Night Hotel. The **Beatles Story** (☎0151-709 1963; www.beatlesstory.com; Albert Dock; adult/child/student £16/9/12.50; ⊙10am-4.30pm; 🚌all city centre) in Albert Dock is the city's most visited museum, but if you really want to dig deep into Beatles lore, we strongly recommend a visit to the National Trust–owned **Mendips**, the home where John lived with his aunt from 1945 to 1963, and **20 Forthlin Rd**, the plain terraced home where Paul grew up, available only by prebooking a place on the **Beatles' Childhood Homes Tour** (☎0151-427 7231; www.nationaltrust.org.uk; Jury's Inn, 31 Keel Wharf, Wapping Dock; adult/child £23/7.25; ⊙10am, 11am, 2.10pm & 3pm Wed-Sun Mar-Nov). Just around the corner from Mendips is **Strawberry Field Forever** (☎0151-252 6130; www.strawberryfieldliverpool.com; Beaconsfield Rd, Woolton; £8.95; ⊙10am-5pm Tue-Sun; 🚌75 from Liverpool ONE Bus Station), a wonderful new museum on the grounds of the old Salvation Army home where John used to play as a child.

If you'd rather do it yourself, the tourist offices stock the *Discover Lennon's Liverpool* guide and map, and Ron Jones' *The Beatles' Liverpool*.

Festivals & Events

★Grand National SPORTS
(☎0151-523 2600; http://aintree.thejockeyclub.co.uk; Aintree Racecourse, Ormskirk Rd; ⊙Apr; 🚌300, 311, 345, 350 & 351 from Liverpool ONE Bus Station, 🚆Aintree from Liverpool Central) The world's most famous steeplechase takes place on the first Saturday in April and is run across 4.5 miles and over the most difficult fences in world racing. Book tickets well in advance. Aintree is 6 miles north of the city centre.

Liverpool Sound City MUSIC
(www.soundcity.uk.com; Baltic Triangle; ⊙May; 🚌all cross-city buses) The first weekend in May sees one of the biggest alternative-music festivals in town take over the Baltic Triangle and Cains Brewery.

Liverpool International Music Festival MUSIC
(☎0151-239 9091; www.limfestival.com; Sefton Park; ⊙late Jul; 🚌75 from Lime St Station) A festival showcasing local bands and international acts during the last weekend of July. There's even a VIP experience that gives you access to private bars.

International Beatleweek MUSIC
(www.internationalbeatleweek.com; ⊙late Aug; 🚌all main bus station services) Sing along to your favourite Beatles song with 70 tribute acts from 20 countries during the last week in August. Organised by the Cavern Club, there are some serious and talented acts on display; some are so good you'll wonder if they're even better than the real thing. They're not.

Sleeping

Tune Hotel HOTEL £
(☎0151-239 5070; www.tunehotels.com; 3-19 Queen Bldgs, Castle St; r from £25; ❄@📶; 🚌all city centre) A slightly upscale version of a pod hotel, Tune offers a comfortable night's sleep (courtesy of a superb mattress and good-quality linen) in a range of en-suite rooms. The cheapest of them have no windows and are quite small, but at this price and in this location, it's an easy sacrifice to make. Bathrooms have power showers.

★Hope Street Hotel BOUTIQUE HOTEL ££
(☎0151-709 3000; www.hopestreethotel.co.uk; 40 Hope St; r/ste from £110/175; @📶; 🚌all city centre) One of the best digs in town is this Scandi-chic hotel on the city's most elegant street. King-sized beds draped in Egyptian cotton, oak floors with underfloor heating and sleek modern bathrooms are the norm in the original hotel as well as its new extension, where there's also a huge spa. Breakfast, taken in the marvellous London Carriage Works (p562), is £18.50.

Titanic Liverpool HOTEL ££
(☎0151-559 1444; www.titanichotelliverpool.com; Stanley Dock, Regent Rd; r/ste from £100/200; P ❄ @ 📶; 🚌135 & 235 from Liverpool ONE Bus Station) The preferred choice of visiting football teams is this fabulous warehouse conversion on Stanley Dock, now a huge hotel with massive rooms decorated in Scandi-minimalist style – lots of space, leather and earth-tones. Downstairs is the Rum Bar – a tribute to the primary stock of the 19th-century warehouse – and the basement is home to a nice spa.

Hard Days Night Hotel HOTEL ££
(☎0151-236 1964; www.harddaysnighthotel.com; Central Bldgs, North John St; r £70-140, ste from £250; @ 📶; 🚌all city centre) You don't have to be a fan to stay here, but it helps: unquestionably luxurious, the 110 ultramodern rooms are decorated with specially commissioned drawings of the Beatles. And if you opt for one of the suites, named after Lennon and McCartney, you'll get a white baby grand piano in the style of 'Imagine' and a bottle of fancy bubbly.

Hotel Pullman HOTEL ££
(☎0151-945 1000; www.all.accor.com; King's Pde, L3 4FP; r/ste from £90/110; P ❄ @ 📶) Part of the French Accor group, the new Pullman is a contemporary, business-friendly hotel in the heart of the Liverpool docks. The 219 rooms are designed for maximum comfort but lack any real character, which may be irrelevant to its core demographic – business travellers and visitors on a weekend break.

Malmaison HOTEL ££
(☎0151-229 5000; www.malmaison.com; 7 William Jessop Way, Princes Dock; r/ste from £70/130; P @ 📶; 🚌135 or 235 from Liverpool ONE Bus Station) Malmaison's preferred colour scheme of plum and black is everywhere in this purpose-built hotel, which gives it an air of contemporary sophistication. Everything about the Liverpool Mal is plush, from the huge beds and the deep baths to the heavy velvet curtains and the excellent buffet breakfast. After a while you'll ignore the constantly piped music of the Beatles.

★2 Blackburne Terrace B&B £££
(www.2blackburneterrace.com; 2 Blackburne Tce; r £160-180; ❄ @ 📶; 🚌all city centre) This exquisite B&B, in a converted Grade II–listed Georgian town house from 1826, might just be the most elegant option in town. It only has four rooms, but each is impeccably appointed with a mix of period furniture and modern touches. Breakfast is fabulous and the lounge an absolute delight. Only Room 1 has a shower; all have free-standing baths.

Eating

Mowgli Street Food INDIAN £
(www.mowglistreetfood.com; 69 Bold St; mains £3.95-8.95; ⏰noon-9.30pm Mon-Sat, to 9pm Sun; 🚌all city centre) Nisha Katona's ambition to serve authentic Indian street food has been so successful that this is just the first of a handful of restaurants spread throughout the northwest and south as far as Oxford. You'll find no stodgy curries or bland kormas here, just flavoursome dishes that would pass muster with a resident of Delhi.

★Wreckfish MODERN BRITISH ££
(www.wreckfish.co; 60 Seel St; 2-/3-course menu £34/39; 🚌all city centre) Restaurateur Gary Usher's crowd-funded restaurant is a marvellous example of Modern British cuisine at its best: nothing overly fussy, but everything done just right. From the open kitchen come fine dishes such as a roast wing of skate in a brown butter dressing and a near-perfect ribeye with truffle and parmesan chips.

Duke Street Market FOOD HALL ££
(www.dukestreetmarket.com; 46 Duke St; mains £8-15; ⏰noon-10pm Wed, Thu & Sun, to 11pm Fri & Sat) 🌿 This food hall has become a huge hit in town, its six vendors – ranging from meaty Bone & Block to healthy Indigo Greens – granting a range of equally tasty options under one roof. Last orders are at 9pm (8pm on Sunday).

Monro GASTROPUB ££
(☎0151-707 9933; www.themonro.com; 92 Duke St; 2-/3-course lunch £19.95/24.95, mains £12-17; ⏰10am-10pm Thu-Sat, from 11am Sun; 🚌all city centre) 🌿 The Monro is one of the city's favourite spots for lunch, dinner and, especially, weekend brunch. The constantly changing menu of classic British dishes made with ingredients sourced as locally as possible has transformed this handsome old pub into a superb dining experience. It's tough to find pub grub this good elsewhere.

Belzan DELI ££
(☎0151-733 8595; www.belzan.co.uk; 371 Smithdown Rd, Toxteth; mains £10-12; ⏰11am-6.30pm Mon-Wed, to 11pm Thu-Sat; 🚌86 from Liverpool ONE Bus Station) By day, this is one of the city's best spots to pick up charcuterie, cheeses and other deli delicacies as well as lunch

WORTH A TRIP

SPEKE HALL

A marvellous example of an Elizabethan half-timbered hall, **Speke Hall** (NT; www.nationaltrust.org.uk; adult/child £12/6; ⏲12.30am-5pm Wed-Sun, also Tue Aug; 🚌500 from Liverpool ONE Bus Station) is filled with gorgeously timbered and plastered rooms. The house contains several 'priest's holes', where the hall's sympathetic owners hid Roman Catholic priests during the anti-Catholic 16th and 17th centuries.

This diagonally patterned Tudor house dates from 1490 to 1612 and was once surrounded by thousands of acres of land, but these days all that remains is the drive and an oasis of meticulously maintained gardens; the hall's Chapel Farm became the nucleus of nearby Liverpool Airport.

The afternoon tours to Paul McCartney's and John Lennon's childhood homes (p560) leave from Speke Hall.

Call ahead to check opening and tour times; pre-booking is recommended. Speke Hall is about 7.5 miles from central Liverpool; the bus will drop you about 0.6 miles from the entrance.

options like confit rabbit leg or celeriac *boulangère*. From Thursday through Saturday, the five-course evening tasting menu (£40) elevates things even further. Menus change monthly, but be ready for food that is both relaxed and occasionally challenging. Book ahead.

Etsu JAPANESE ££
(☎0151-236 7530; www.etsu-restaurant.co.uk; 25 The Strand, off Brunswick St; mains £13-17, 15-piece sashimi £15.50; ⏲noon-2.30pm & 5-9pm Tue, Thu & Fri, 5-9pm Wed & Sat, 4-9pm Sun; 🚌all city centre) The best Japanese food in town is in this contemporary spot on the ground floor of an office building. The speciality of the house is its fresh sushi and sashimi, but you'll find the usual selection of Japanese classics, from chicken *kara-age* (crispy fried chicken pieces marinated in soy, ginger and garlic) to *unagi don* (grilled eel over rice).

Salt House SPANISH ££
(www.salthousetapas.co.uk; Hanover Sq; tapas £6-9; ⏲noon-10.30pm; 🚌all city centre) Liverpool has grown fond of its Spanish tapas bars, and this gorgeous spot – half deli, half restaurant – is the best of them. The cooking is authentic, varied and delicious, from the choice of charcuterie to the wonderful fish dishes. The takeaway counter at the deli does fab sandwiches too.

Art School MODERN BRITISH ££
(☎0151-230 8600; www.theartschoolrestaurant.co.uk; 1 Sugnall St; 3-course prix fixe £34, tasting menu £95; ⏲noon-2pm & 6-9.15pm Thu-Sat, noon-4pm Sun; 🌿; 🚌all city centre) The old lantern room of a Victorian 'home for destitute children' is now one of the top spots in town for contemporary British cuisine, courtesy of chef Paul Askew (ex–London Carriage Works). Take your pick of expertly presented British classics from a series of menus, including two vegetarian and one vegan. The wine list is superb.

London Carriage Works MODERN BRITISH £££
(☎0151-705 2222; www.thelondoncarriageworks.co.uk; 40 Hope St; 2-/3-course meal £24.50/30, mains £12-30; ⏲7-10am, noon-3pm & 5-10pm Mon-Fri, 8-11am & noon-10pm Sat, to 9pm Sun; 🚌all city centre) This award-winning restaurant successfully blends ethnic influences from around the globe with staunch British favourites and serves up the result in a beautiful dining room – actually more of a bright glass box divided only by a series of sculpted glass shards. Reservations are recommended.

🍷 Drinking & Nightlife

Ropewalks is Liverpool's busiest bar district – with a lot of late-night spots that keep them drinking and dancing until the wee hours – but there's a fine selection of great bars spread throughout the city. If you're looking to hang with the city's creative crowd, you'll most likely find them in the Baltic Triangle.

★Botanical Garden BAR
(www.baltictriangle.co.uk/botanical-garden; 49 New Bird St; ⏲noon-11pm Mar-Sep; 🚌all city centre) A seasonal pop-up that specialises in gin cocktails, this is one of the city's coolest summer bars. There's a fine selection of beers if

you prefer, and a kitchen that serves excellent Mexican food; in rainy weather you can retreat to the indoor greenhouse, which has a bar made from a converted VW camper van. Weekends feature top-class DJs.

★Grapes PUB
(www.thegrapesliverpool.co.uk; 60 Roscoe St; ⌚3.30pm-1am Sun-Wed, to 2am Thu-Sat; 🚌all city centre) One of the friendliest boozers in town is this superb old pub that serves a fine range of local ales (Bier Head, from the Liverpool Organic Brewery, is our favourite). The Beatles would stop in here during their Cavern days, but that's well down the list of reasons to stop by this wonderful, higgledy-piggledy classic.

Roscoe Head PUB
(☎0151-709 4365; www.roscoehead.co.uk; 24 Roscoe St; ⌚11.30am-midnight Tue-Sat, noon-midnight Sun, 11.30am-11pm Mon; 🚌all city centre) This venerable old pub, which serves a good selection of ales to its ever-loyal clientele, is an institution among Liverpool boozers. It gets pretty crowded at weekends, but that just makes for an even better atmosphere.

24 Kitchen Street CLUB
(☎0780 1982583; www.facebook.com/24kitchenstreet; 24 Kitchen St; ⌚9pm-4am Fri & Sat; 🚌all city centre) This venue splits its focus between the arts and electronic music (tickets £8 to £12). The converted Victorian building is one of the best places in town to dance.

Philharmonic Dining Rooms PUB
(36 Hope St; ⌚10am-midnight; 🚌all city centre) This extraordinary bar, designed by the shipwrights who built the *Lusitania,* is one of the most beautiful in all of England. The interior is resplendent with etched and stained glass, wrought iron, mosaics and ceramic tiling – and if you think that's good, just wait until you see inside the marble men's toilets, the only heritage-listed lav' in the country.

As per the name, they also serve food (mains £10 to £15), such as fish and chips and a fine selection of pie dishes.

Arts Club CLUB
(☎0151-707 6171; www.academymusicgroup.com/artsclubliverpool; 90 Seel St; ⌚7pm-3am Mon-Sat; 🚌all city centre) This converted theatre is home to one of Liverpool's most beloved clubs, despite going through several name and management changes. It still hosts some fabulous nights (£5 to £13), with a mix of live music and DJs keeping everyone entertained with some of the best music in town.

Merchant BAR
(www.themerchantliverpool.co.uk; 40 Slater St; ⌚noon-midnight Mon-Thu & Sun, to 2am Fri, to 3am Sat; 🚌all city centre) In a converted merchant's house, Merchant has something of a Scandi feel to it (stripped-back walls, wooden bar tables), making it one of the coolest spots in town. The bar serves 50 different craft beers, gin by the goblet and – wait for it – Prosecco on tap. Good DJs provide the soundtrack.

☆ Entertainment

★Liverpool Football Club FOOTBALL
(☎0151-263 9199, ticket office 0151-220 2345; www.liverpoolfc.com; Anfield Rd; 🚌26 from Liverpool ONE Bus Station, 17 from Queen Square Bus Station or 917 from St Johns La) Led by their magnetic manager Jürgen Klopp, Liverpool FC won the domestic league in 2020 for the first time in 30 years, reaffirming their status as one of Britain's most successful teams. With a huge global following, Liverpool are also one of the world's most famous football clubs. They play their home games at the wonderful Anfield stadium, north of the city centre.

The experience of a live match – and especially the sound of the fans singing the club's anthem, 'You'll Never Walk Alone', is one of England's sporting highlights. If you can't get a ticket for a game, you can still visit the stadium as part of the Anfield Stadium Tour (p559), which brings fans to the home dressing room and down the tunnel into the pitchside dugout. On match days, the **Soccerbus** (www.merseyrail.org; Sandhills

THE BALTIC TRIANGLE

Forget Ropewalks – most of Liverpool's best nightlife is in the Baltic Triangle (www.baltictriangle.co.uk), a once-rundown area of warehouses, roughly between the city centre and the docks just north of Toxteth, that is now the city's self-styled creative hub. The best spots to check out include 24 Kitchen Street, pop-up gin bar Botanical Garden, the recycling-yard-turned-multipurpose-venue Constellations (p564) and District (p564), the first venue to open in the area.

Station; single/return adult £2/3.50, child £1/1.50; ⊙from 2hr before kick-off) runs from Sandhills Station on the Merseyrail Northern Line.

★Constellations LIVE PERFORMANCE
(☎0151-345 6302; www.constellations-liv.com; 35-39 Greenland St; ⊙9am-midnight Mon-Thu, to 2am Fri & Sat, 10am-midnight Sun; 🚌all city centre) Whether you're looking to join a drumming circle, take part in a martial-arts workshop or lose yourself at a rave, this terrific venue in a former recycling yard will have something worth checking out. In good weather DJs play in the garden – one of the best spots in town. It does Sunday meals in summer.

Philharmonic Hall CLASSICAL MUSIC
(☎0151-709 3789; www.liverpoolphil.com; Hope St; 🚌75, 80, 86 from city centre) One of Liverpool's most beautiful buildings, the art deco Phil is home to the city's main orchestras and is the place to go for classical concerts and opera – as well as a broad range of other genres, from synth pop to avant-garde.

District LIVE MUSIC
(☎07812 141936; 61 Jordan St; ⊙7pm-4am Fri & Sat) The first venue to open in the Baltic Triangle, District is an old-school club in a warehouse, hosting live music and cinema screenings as well as fabulous dance-floor nights. The sound system is reputed to be the best in Liverpool.

Cavern Club LIVE MUSIC
(☎0151-236 1965; www.cavernclub.org; 8-10 Mathew St; entry before/after 2pm free/£5; ⊙10am-midnight Mon-Wed & Sun, to 1.30am Thu, to 2am Fri & Sat; 🚌all city centre) The Cavern Club was where the Beatles played their early gigs. This is a reconstruction (albeit a faithful one), and not in the exact same location (the original was a few doors away), but the 'world's most famous club' is still a great spot to see local bands, including (invariably) Beatles cover bands.

ℹ Information

Tourist Office (www.visitliverpool.com; Liverpool Central Library, William Brown St; ⊙9.30am-5pm; 🚌all city centre) Leaflets, maps and information are provided in the small tourist office.

ℹ Getting There & Away

AIR

Liverpool John Lennon Airport (☎0870 750 8484; www.liverpoolairport.com; Speke Hall Ave; 🚌86 or 500 from city centre) serves 70 destinations across the UK, Europe and Africa.

The airport is 8 miles south of the centre. **Arriva 500** (www.arriva.co.uk; adult/child £4.50/2.50; ⊙4.30am-7pm) runs every 30 minutes to Liverpool ONE bus station and takes about 30 minutes. A taxi to the city centre should cost no more than £20.

BUS

All coaches arrive and depart from **Liverpool ONE Bus Station** (www.merseytravel.gov.uk; Canning Pl). There are services to/from most major towns, including the following:

Birmingham £5.90, 2½ hours, five daily
London £12.90, five to six hours, six daily
Manchester £4, one hour, hourly
Newcastle £26, 5½ hours, three daily

TRAIN

Liverpool's main station is Lime St. It has hourly services to almost everywhere, including the following:

Chester £7.70, 45 minutes
London Euston £37, 3¼ hours
Manchester £6.30, 45 minutes

ℹ Getting Around

If you plan on using a lot of public transport you should invest in a MetroCard, a contactless fare card available throughout the city for an initial cost of £1. You can then load up the following fare-saver passes on it:

Saveaway (adult/child £5.55/2.85) A single-day pass valid for off-peak travel on buses, trains and Mersey ferries.

Solo Ticket (1/3/5 days £4.90/13.80/21.50) For unlimited bus travel throughout Merseyside.

BOAT

The famous **Mersey ferry** (www.merseyferries.co.uk; one-way/return £2.80/3.70) crossing for Woodside and Seacombe departs from Pier Head Ferry Terminal, next to the Royal Liver Building (to the north of Albert Dock).

BUS

Liverpool ONE Bus Station is in the city centre. Local public transport is coordinated by **Merseytravel** (www.merseytravel.gov.uk).

CAR

You won't really have much use for a car in Liverpool, but there's plenty of car-parking space, either in sheltered or open monitored car parks. Costs range from around £5 to £13 per day, with the exception being the huge car park at Liverpool ONE, which costs £2.70 an hour and £17 for a day. Car break-ins are a significant problem, so leave absolutely nothing of value in your vehicle.

TRAIN

Merseyrail (www.merseyrail.org) is an extensive suburban rail service linking Liverpool with the Greater Merseyside area. There are four stops in the city centre: Lime St, Central (handy for Ropewalks), James St (close to Albert Dock) and Moorfields (for the Liverpool War Museum).

LANCASHIRE

As you travel north, past the concrete blanket that covers much of the southern half of the county, Lancashire's undulating landscape begins to reveal itself in all its bucolic glory. East of Blackpool – the faded queen of beachside holidays – the Ribble Valley is a gentle and beautiful appetiser for the Lake District that lies beyond the county's northern border. Lancaster is the county's handsome Georgian capital.

Blackpool

01253 / POP 150,331

Blackpool's enduring appeal – in the face of low-cost airlines transporting its natural constituents to sunnier coasts – is down to its defiant embrace of a more traditional kind of holiday, coupled with the high-tech adrenaline hit of its famed Pleasure Beach amusement park.

The town is also famous for its tower and its three piers. A successful ploy to extend the brief summer holiday season is the Illuminations, when – from early September to early November – 5 miles of the Promenade are illuminated with thousands of electric and neon lights.

Sights

★Blackpool Tower AMUSEMENT PARK

(0844 856 1000; www.theblackpooltower.com; 1/2/3 attractions adult £13.95/21.60/29.60, child £11.25/17.20/24.40; from 10am, closing hours vary) Built in 1894, this 154m-high tower is Blackpool's most recognisable landmark. Watch a 4D film on the town's history in the **Blackpool Tower Eye** before taking the lift up to the observation deck, which has great views and only a (thick) glass floor between you and the ant-sized people below.

Down at ground level, the **dungeon** exhibit sits alongside the old Moorish **circus** and the magnificent rococo **ballroom**, with its extraordinary sculptured and gilded plasterwork, murals, chandeliers and couples gliding across the beautifully polished wooden floor to the melodramatic tones of a huge Wurlitzer organ. There's also **Jungle Jim's** adventure playground for kids and **Dino Golf** on level 7 – a nine-hole mini-golf course.

You need to book online; you can buy tickets that include one, two or three attractions in the tower.

Blackpool Pleasure Beach AMUSEMENT PARK

(box office 0871 222 9090, enquiries 0871 222 1234; www.blackpoolpleasurebeach.com; Ocean Beach; 1-day Unlimited Ride e-ticket adult/child from £39/33; hours vary, usually 10am-8pm in summer) The lifeblood of Blackpool's commercial life is the Pleasure Beach, a 16-hectare collection of more than 145 rides that attracts some seven million visitors annually. As amusement parks go, it's Britain's most popular by far. You buy an e-ticket online that is downloaded to your phone.

North Pier LANDMARK

(Promenade) FREE Built in 1862 and opening a year later, the most famous of Blackpool's three Victorian piers once charged a penny for admission; its plethora of unexciting rides are now free.

Sleeping

Number One BOUTIQUE HOTEL ££

(01253-343901; www.numberoneblackpool.com; 1 St Lukes Rd; r from £135; P 📶) Far fancier than anything else around, this stunning boutique guesthouse is all luxury and contemporary style. Everything exudes a discreet elegance, from the dark-wood furniture and high-end mod cons to the top-notch breakfast. It's on a quiet road just set back from the South Promenade near the Pleasure Beach amusement park.

Big Blue Hotel HOTEL ££

(01253-400045; www.bigbluehotel.com; Blackpool Pleasure Beach; r from £105; P @ 📶) A handsome family hotel with smartly kitted-out rooms. Kids are looked after with DVD players and computer games, while its location at the southern entrance to Blackpool Pleasure Beach should ensure that everyone has something to do.

Information

Tourist Office (01253-478222; www.visitblackpool.com; Festival House, Promenade; 9am-5pm Mon-Sat, 10am-4pm Sun) The

GREAT LANCASHIRE GASTROPUBS

Freemasons at Wiswell (☎01254-822218; www.freemasonsatwiswell.com; 8 Vicarage Fold, Wiswell; mains £27-40, 5-course tasting menu £60; ⊙noon-2.30pm & 6-9pm Wed-Sat, noon-6pm Sun) Steven Smith's multi-award-winning restaurant in the lovely village of Wiswell serves a proper feast of the best of New British cuisine. The room is classic English pub, with plain wooden tables and a roaring fire, in contrast to the sophisticated menu. We recommend the suckling pig, slow cooked and served with black pudding, baked sweet potato and fermented-rhubarb sauce.

White Swan (www.whiteswanatfence.co.uk; 300 Wheatley Ln Rd, Fence, Burnley; 4-course tasting menu £45; ⊙noon-2pm & 5.30-8.30pm Tue-Thu, to 9.30pm Fri & Sat, noon-4pm Sun) It mightn't look like much from the outside, but this pub in the working village of Fence serves simply outstanding Modern British cuisine. It's all courtesy of chef Tom Parker, who cut his chops in the kitchen of Michelin-starred Northcote Hotel (p568). The tasting menu is divine; the award-winning Taylors ales heavenly.

Cartford Inn (☎01995-670166; www.thecartfordinn.co.uk; Cartford La, Little Eccleston; mains £18-28; ⊙5.30-9pm Mon, noon-2pm & 5.30-9pm Tue-Thu, to 10pm Fri & Sat, noon-8.30pm Sun) The decor at this higgledy-piggledy pub might be a touch eccentric, but the menu is anything but – with classic British pub grub exalted by classic French cooking techniques. You won't eat a nicer oxtail, beef skirt and real ale suet pudding, while the desserts are so good you won't feel bad for ordering two. You can also **stay** (☎01995-670166; www.thecartfordinn.co.uk; Cartford La, Little Eccleston; r £150, cabins £250) here.

tourist office is just south of the North Pier on the Promenade.

Getting There & Away

BUS

The central coach station is on Talbot Rd, near the town centre. Services include the following:

London £23.40, seven hours, four daily

Manchester £9.10, 1¾ hours, four daily

TRAIN

The main train station is Blackpool North, about five blocks east of the North Pier on Talbot Rd. Most arrivals change in Preston, but there's a direct service from the following:

Liverpool £9.20, 1½ hours, seven daily

Manchester £9.50, 1¼ hours, half-hourly

Preston £7.20, 30 minutes, half-hourly

Getting Around

With more than 14,000 car-parking spaces in Blackpool, you'll have no problem finding a spot. A host of travel-card options for trams and buses ranging from one day to a week are available at the tourist office and most newsagents. The **tramway** (1 stop £1.90, up to 16 stops £2.10; ⊙from 10.30am Apr-Oct) shuttles funsters for 11 miles, including along the pier and as far as the Fylde Coast (also serving the central-corridor car parks), every eight minutes or so throughout the day.

Lancaster

☎01524 / POP 143,500

Lancashire's handsome Georgian county town is a quiet enough burg these days, but its imposing castle and beautiful, honey-coloured architecture are evidence of its former power and wealth accrued in its 18th-century heyday, when it was an important trading port and a key player in the slave trade.

Sights

★Lancaster Castle CASTLE

(☎01524-64998; www.lancastercastle.com; Castle Park; adult/child £8.50/7; ⊙9.30am-5pm, guided tours hourly 10am-3pm Mon-Fri, every 30min Sat & Sun) Lancaster's most imposing building is its castle, built in 1150 but added to over the centuries: the **Well Tower** dates from 1325 and is also known as the Witches' Tower because its basement dungeon was used to imprison the accused in the infamous Pendle Witches Trial of 1612. Also dating from the early 14th century is the impressive twin-towered **gatehouse**. Also imprisoned here was George Fox (1624–91), founder of the Quaker movement. The castle was heavily restored in the 18th and 19th centuries to suit a new function as a prison, and it continued to house Category C prisoners until 2011 – the A wing of the prison is part of the guided tour.

Visits are by guided tour only as the castle is used as a Crown Court.

Williamson Park & Tropical Butterfly House GARDENS
(Tropical Butterfly House adult/child £4/3; ⌚9am-5pm Apr-Sep, to 4pm Oct-Mar; 🚌18 from bus station) Lancaster's highest point is the 22-hectare spread of this gorgeous park, the highlights of which (besides the views) are the **Tropical Butterfly House**, full of exotic and stunning species, and the **Ashton Memorial**, a 67m-high baroque folly built by Lord Ashton (the son of the park's founder, James Williamson) for his wife. The memorial stands on what was once Lancaster Moor, the spot where until 1800 those sentenced to death at the castle were brought to meet the hangman. Take the bus from the station, or else it's a steep, short walk up Moor Lane.

Lancaster Priory CHURCH
(☎01524-65338; www.lancasterpriory.org; Priory Cl; ⌚9.30am-5pm) Immediately next to Lancaster Castle is the equally fine priory church, founded in 1094 but extensively remodelled in the Middle Ages.

Sleeping

Sun Hotel & Bar HOTEL ££
(☎01524-66006; www.thesunhotelandbar.co.uk; 63-65 Church St; r from £75; P 📶) A fine hotel in a 300-year-old building with a rustic, old-world look that stops at the bedroom doors – beyond them are 16 stylish and contemporary rooms. The pub downstairs is one of the best in town and a top spot for a bit of grub; mains cost between £10 and £12.

The Borough BOUTIQUE HOTEL ££
(☎01524-64170; www.theboroughlancaster.co.uk; 3 Dalton Sq; r from £60; P @ 📶) The Borough has nine beautifully appointed rooms – each with an Italian-marble wet-room bathroom for added luxury – spread over two floors of this elegant Georgian building. The downstairs bar has a microbrewery attached, so you don't have to go far to get your fill of locally made cask ales.

Eating & Drinking

★Bay Horse Inn GASTROPUB ££
(☎01524-791204; www.bayhorseinn.com; Bay Horse La, Ellel; mains £14-32; ⌚5.30-8pm Wed-Sun; 🚌40, 41 & 42 from Lancaster Bus Station) One of Lancashire's best spots for exquisite local dishes is this handsome pub 6 miles south of town. Chef Craig Wilkinson displays his locavore links with a sign outside showing distances to the farms that supply his produce, which he then transforms into fabulous dishes such as slow-cooked, maize-fed duck legs with grilled figs or a perfectly grilled hake fillet.

★The Hall CAFE
(☎01524-65470; www.thecoffeehopper.com; 10 China St; ⌚10am-4pm Mon-Fri & Sun, to 5pm Sat) Nitro, Chemex, batch brew, siphon…whichever way you want it, this superb cafe in the old parish hall can satisfy even the most demanding coffee connoisseur with the perfect brew. It's part of Atkinsons Coffee Roasters, which has been roasting beans since 1840. It also does excellent sandwiches and cakes.

Shopping

★Charter Market MARKET
(www.lancaster.gov.uk; Market Sq; ⌚9am-4.30pm Wed & Sat Apr-Oct, to 4pm Nov-Mar) Lancaster's historic market is one of the best in the northwest, a gathering place for local producers. You'll find potted shrimp from Morecambe Bay, locally made hotpots and pies, as well as a range of more exotic dishes from around the world. It extends from Market Sq onto Market St and Cheapside.

★Atkinsons Coffee Roasters COFFEE
(☎01524-65470; www.thecoffeehopper.com; 12 China St; ⌚9am-5pm Mon-Sat, 11am-4pm Sun) Atkinsons is one of Britain's most prestigious coffee merchants, serving up all kinds of exotic beans and loose-leaf teas since 1840. It has been at this location since 1901: inside, the walls are covered in original tea and coffee urns, while original direct flame roasters from the 1930s give off a fabulous aroma. It's worth popping in just for the scent.

Information

Tourist Office (☎01524-582394; www.visitlancaster.org.uk; The Storey, Meeting House Lane; ⌚10am-4pm Mon-Sat) Books, maps, brochures and tickets for a variety of events and tours.

Getting There & Away

Lancaster Bus Station is the main hub for transport throughout Lancashire, with regular buses to all the main towns and villages.

Lancaster is on the main west-coast railway line and on the Cumbrian coast line. Destinations include the following:

Carlisle £22.80, one hour, hourly
Manchester £19.20, one hour, hourly

Ribble Valley

Known locally as 'Little Switzerland', Lancashire's most attractive landscapes lie east of brash Blackpool and north of the sprawling urban areas of Preston and Blackburn.

Clitheroe, the Ribble Valley's largest market town, is best known for its impressive Norman keep, built in the 12th century and now, sadly, standing empty; it offers great views of the river valley below.

The northern half of the valley is dominated by the sparsely populated moorland of the **Forest of Bowland**, an Area of Outstanding Natural Beauty since 1964 and a fantastic place for walks. The southern half features rolling hills, attractive market towns and ruins, with the River Ribble flowing between them.

Sights & Activities

Norman Keep & Castle Museum HISTORIC BUILDING
(www.lancashire.gov.uk; Castle Hill; museum adult/child £4.40/3.30; ⏲ keep dawn-dusk, museum 11am-4pm Mar-Oct, noon-4pm Mon, Tue & Fri-Sun Nov-Feb) Dominating the skyline for the last 800 years, this Norman keep is England's smallest and the only remaining castle in the country to have kept a royal garrison during the Civil War. It was built in 1186 and captured by Royalist troops in 1644, but managed to avoid destruction afterwards. The extensive grounds are home to a museum that explores 350 million years of local history.

★**Cycle Adventure** CYCLING
(☎07518 373007; www.cycle-adventure.co.uk) A bike-hire service that will deliver and collect a bike almost anywhere in the northwest of England. Day rates range from £25 for a mountain bike to £34 for a road bike. A child's mountain bike costs from £19 a day. Helmets and other gear are also available, and it has lots of information, trail maps and other guides.

Ribble Way WALKING
One of the most popular long-distance paths in northern England is the Ribble Way, a 70-mile footpath that follows the River Ribble from its source at Ribblehead (in the Yorkshire Dales), passing through Clitheroe to the estuary at Preston.

Lancashire Cycle Way CYCLING
(www.visitlancashire.com) The Ribble Valley is well covered by the northern loop of the Lancashire Cycle Way; for more information about routes, safety and more, check out Cycle Adventure.

Sleeping & Eating

★**Inn at Whitewell** INN £££
(☎01200-448222; www.innatwhitewell.com; Forest of Bowland; r from £140) Once the home of Bowland's forest keeper, this superb guesthouse with antique furniture, peat fires and Victorian claw-foot baths is one of the finest accommodations in northern England. Everything is top-notch, including the views: it's like being in the French countryside. Its restaurant is excellent too.

Parkers Arms GASTROPUB ££
(☎01200-446236; www.parkersarms.co.uk; Newton-in-Bowland; mains £19-28; ⏲noon-2pm & 6-8pm Thu-Sat, 12.30-5pm Sun) This unspoilt village pub is where you'll find the simply exceptional cooking of terroir chef Stosie Madi. She's best known for her superb pies, but her menus – which change up to twice daily depending on what's available – explore the very best of Lancashire cuisine, from Newton venison with local bramble and unpasteurised cheese to a superb Lancashire hotpot.

★**Northcote Hotel** MODERN BRITISH £££
(☎01254-240555; www.northcote.com; Northcote Rd, Langho; tasting menu £85; ⏲noon-2.30pm & 6-9.30pm Wed-Sun) One of the finest restaurants in northern England, Northcote's Michelin-starred menu is the unpretentious, delicious creation of chef Lisa Goodwin-Allen and sommelier Craig Bancroft. Duck, lamb, beef and chicken are given Modern British treatment and the result is fantastic. Upstairs are 26 beautifully styled bedrooms (£180 to £330), making this one of the northwest's top gourmet getaways.

ISLE OF MAN

The Isle of Man (Ellan Vannin in the local lingo, Manx) has beautiful scenery in its lush valleys, barren hills and rugged coastlines; in 2016 Unesco designated it a biosphere reserve (one of five in the UK), marking it out as one of the most beautiful spots in Britain to enjoy nature.

Forget what you may have heard on the mainland too: there's nothing odd about the Isle of Man. The island's reputation for oddity is entirely down to its persistent insistence that it do its own thing, rejecting England's warm embrace in favour of a semiautonomous status (it is home to the world's oldest continuous parliament, the Tynwald).

The island's bucolic charm is shattered during the world-famous **Tourist Trophy** (TT) motorbike racing season, which attracts 50,000 punters every May and June. Needless to say, if you want a slice of silence, avoid the high-rev bike fest.

Festivals & Events

Isle of Man Food & Drink Festival FOOD & DRINK
(www.gov.im; Villa Marina Gardens, Douglas; £3; mid-Sep) Over two days in mid-September more than 50 of the island's producers gather to showcase their wares. There's plenty of street food, baked goods, beer and cider, as well as music.

Isle of Man Walking Festival WALKING
(www.iomevents.com; Oct) A five-day walking festival held in early October; walks start in different parts of the island and are led by experienced walkers. In the evenings there are plenty of social events generally fuelled by the produce of a Manx brewery.

Getting There & Away

AIR

Ronaldsway Airport (www.iom-airport.com) is 10 miles south of Douglas near Castletown. The following airlines have services to the island:

Aer Lingus Regional (www.aerlingus.com; from £25)

British Airways (www.britishairways.com; from £75)

Easyjet (www.easyjet.com; from £25)

Loganair (www.loganair.co.uk; from £60)

BOAT

Isle of Man Steam Packet (www.steam-packet.com; foot passenger single/return from £20/37.50, car & 2 passengers return from £150) offers a car ferry and high-speed catamaran service from Liverpool and Heysham (10 miles west of Lancaster) to Douglas. From mid-April to mid-September there's also a service to Dublin and Belfast.

Getting Around

Buses link the airport with Douglas every 30 minutes between 7am and 11pm. Taxis have fixed fares to destinations throughout the island; a cab to Douglas costs from £14, to Peel from £16.

The island has a comprehensive bus service (www.gov.im); the tourist office in Douglas has timetables and sells tickets. It also sells the Go Explore ticket (one day adult/child £18/10, three day £40/18), which gives you unlimited public-transport use, including the tram to Snaefell and Douglas' horse-trams.

Bicycles can be hired from **Simpsons** (01624-842472; www.facebook.com/simpsonsiom; 27 Michael St, Peel; per day/week £15/80; 9am-5pm Mon-Sat) in Peel.

Petrolheads will love the scenic, sweeping bends that make for some exciting driving – and the fact that outside of Douglas town there's no speed limit. Naturally, the most popular drive is along the Tourist Trophy route. Car-hire operators have desks at the airport, and charge from £37 per day.

The 19th-century electric and steam **rail services** (01624-663366; www.iombusandrail.info; Mar-Oct) are a thoroughly satisfying way of getting from A to B:

Douglas–Castletown–Port Erin Steam Train
Return £13.40

Douglas–Laxey–Ramsey Electric Tramway
Return £12.40

Laxey–Summit Snaefell Mountain Railway
Return £12

MANX HERITAGE HOLIDAY PASS

The island's 11 major sights are managed by Manx Heritage (MH; www.manxnationalheritage.im), the island's version of the British National Trust. They include castles, historic homes, museums and the world's largest working waterwheel. Unless otherwise indicated, Manx Heritage sites are open 10am to 5pm daily, from Easter to October. The Manx Heritage Holiday Pass (www.manxheritageshop.com; adult/child £25/12) grants entry to all of the island's heritage attractions; it's available at tourist offices or online.

Douglas

01624 / POP 26,218

Douglas is the island's largest town and most important commercial centre. It's a little faded around the edges and a far cry from its Victorian heyday when it was, like Blackpool across the water, a favourite with British holidaymakers. The bulk of the island's hotels and restaurants are still here – as well as most of the finance houses that are frequented so regularly by tax-allergic Brits.

PEEL

Peel is the west coast's most appealing town, with a fine sandy beach. Its big attraction is the ruin of the 11th-century **Peel Castle** (MH; www.manxnationalheritage.im; adult/child £5.50/free; ⏲11am-3pm Thu-Sun Aug-Nov), stunningly positioned atop St Patrick's Island and joined to Peel by a causeway. There's an audio guide available to help you make sense of the ruins, and you're also advised to keep your eyes open for the castle's ghost – a black dog called Moddey Dhoo.

Sights

Manx Museum & National Art Gallery MUSEUM
(MH; www.manxnationalheritage.im; Kingswood Grove; ⏲10am-4pm) FREE This modern museum (Thie Tashtee Vannin in Manx) begins with an introductory film to the island's 10,000-year history and then races through it, making various stops including Viking gold and silver, the history of the Tynwald, the island's internment camps during WWII and the famous TT races. Also part of the museum is the National Art Gallery, which has works by the island's best-known artists including Archibald Knox and John Miller Nicholson. Overall a fine introduction to the island.

Sleeping

★Saba's Glen Yurt YURT ££
(www.sabasglenyurt.com; Close Ny Howin, Main Rd, Union Mills; 2-person yurt from £95) In the conservation area of Union Mills you can bed down in a solar-powered eco-yurt that comes equipped with a king-sized bed and a wood burner. Outside are hot tubs filled with steaming water that you can sink into up to your shoulders.

There's a two-night minimum weekend stay between April and September. It's 2.5 miles northwest of town on the road to Peel.

Inglewood BOUTIQUE HOTEL ££
(☎01624-674734; www.inglewood.im; 26 Palace Tce, Queens Promenade; s/d incl breakfast from £42.50/85; P@☎) Sea-view suites in this beautifully refurbished, friendly hotel have big wooden beds and leather sofas. The homemade breakfasts are superb, and the residents' bar specialises in whisky from all over the world.

Claremont Hotel HOTEL £££
(☎01624-617068; www.claremonthoteldouglas.com; 18-22 Loch Promenade; r from £130; P❄@☎) The island's fanciest hotel is this classic on the promenade, with huge rooms kitted out with handsome wooden floors, seaside colours and comfortable beds with crisp linen.

Eating

★Little Fish Cafe SEAFOOD ££
(www.littlefishcafe.com; 31 North Quay; mains £16-24; ⏲11am-9pm) Superb seafood presented in a variety of ways, from hake with mustard and lemon butter to Kerala-style fish curry. For brunch, the Queenie Po'Boy – battered Manx queenies (queen scallops), paprika mayo and avocado on sourdough brioche – is divine. It also does meat dishes, but the real focus is on the sea.

14North MODERN BRITISH ££
(☎01624-664414; www.14north.im; 14 North Quay; 2-/3-course menu £35/39; ⏲6-9.30pm Tue, noon-2.30pm & 6-9.30pm Wed-Fri, noon-5pm & 6-9.30pm Sat) An old timber merchant's house is home to this smart restaurant specialising in local dishes including pickled herring, lamb rump and, of course, queenies (queen scallops) – all sourced locally.

Information

Tourist Office (☎01624-686766; www.visitisleofman.com; Sea Terminal Bldg, Douglas; ⏲9.15am-7pm, closed Sun Oct-Apr)

Northern Isle of Man

North of the capital, the dominant feature is **Snaefell** (621m), the island's tallest mountain. You can follow the Tourist Trophy circuit up and over the mountain towards **Ramsey**, or take the alternate route along the coast, going through **Laxey**, where you can also take the electric tram to near the top of Snaefell, from where it's an easy walk to the summit.

Sights

★Great Laxey Wheel HISTORIC SITE
(MH; www.manxnationalheritage.im; Mines Rd, Laxey; adult/child £7/free; ⏲10am-4pm Sat-Wed) It's no exaggeration to describe the Lady Isabella Laxey Wheel (Queeyl Vooar Laksey in Manx), built in 1854 to pump water from a mine, as a 'great' wheel: it measures 22m across and can draw 1140L of water per

minute from a depth of 550m. The largest wheel of its kind in the world, it's named after the wife of the then lieutenant-governor.

Grove Museum of Victorian Life MUSEUM
(MH; www.manxnationalheritage.im; Andreas Rd, Ramsey; adult/child £5.50/free; ⌚11am-3pm Thu-Sun Aug-Nov) This imposing house (Thie Tashtee 'Yn Chell') was built in the mid-19th century by Liverpool shipping merchant Duncan Gibb as a summer retreat for himself and his family. It has been maintained pretty much as it was in its Victorian heyday, and you can wander through its period rooms – and even learn what it was like to be a scullery maid! The house was occupied by the Gibb family until the 1970s. It's on the edge of Ramsey.

ℹ Getting There & Away

Bus Vannin services travel the 15 miles between Ramsey and Douglas either via Laxey and the coast (bus 3, 3A) or more directly inland past Snaefell (bus X3). Alternatively, there's the electric tram, which trundles up the coast to Ramsey. Another tram serves Snaefell from Laxey.

Southern Isle of Man

The quiet harbour town of **Castletown**, at the southern end of the island, was the Isle of Man's original capital. It is home to a fabulous castle and the old parliament.

Port Erin is a smallish Victorian seaside resort that plays host to the small **Railway Museum** (www.iombusandrail.im; Station Rd; adult/child £2/1; ⌚9.30am-5pm). **Port St Mary** lies across the headland and is linked to by steam train. The Calf of Man bird sanctuary is accessed from Port St Mary.

Sights

★**Castle Rushen** CASTLE
(MH; www.manxnationalheritage.im; Castletown Sq, Castletown; adult/child £9/free; ⌚10am-4pm Thu-Mon May-Aug) Castletown is dominated by the impressive 13th-century Castle Rushen (Cashtal Rushen), one of the most complete medieval structures in Europe. You can visit the gatehouse, medieval kitchens, dungeons and the Great Hall. The flag tower affords fine views of the town and coast.

Cregneash Village Folk Museum MUSEUM
(MH; www.manxnationalheritage.im; adult/child £7/free; ⌚10am-2pm Wed, 11am-2.30pm Thu & Fri, open for tours only) Until the early part of the 20th century, most farmers on the island engaged in a practice known as crofting – a social system defined by small-scale communal food production. This folk museum on a raised plateau on the island's southern tip includes a traditional Manx cottage where you can see how crofters lived, while out in the fields you can see four-horned sheep and Manx cats, which you're encouraged to pat.

Old House of Keys MUSEUM
(MH; www.manxnationalheritage.im; Parliament Sq, Castletown; debate adult/child £6/3, other times free; ⌚10am-4pm Apr-Oct) The former home of the Manx Parliament (Tynwald's lower house; Shenn Thie yn Chiare as Feed in Manx) has been restored to its 1866 appearance – a key date in island history, when the parliament voted to have its members elected by popular mandate. At 11am and 2.45pm visitors can participate in a debate on the hot topics of the day – gaining an insight into how this parliamentary democracy went about its business. You can also learn about the island's struggle for self-determination.

Calf of Man BIRD SANCTUARY
(www.manxnationalheritage.im; ⌚Apr-Sep) This small island just off Cregneash is on one of western Britain's major bird migration routes, and 33 species breed annually here, including Manx shearwaters, kittiwakes, razorbills and shags. Other species normally observed on the island include peregrines, hen harriers, choughs and ravens. It's been an official bird sanctuary since 1939. **Gemini Charter** (☎01624-832761; www.geminicharter.co.uk; trips 1-4hr per person £20-35) runs birdwatching trips to the island from Port St Mary.

ℹ Getting There & Away

There is a regular Bus Vannin service between Castletown and Douglas (and the airport en route), and between Castletown, Port Erin and Port St Mary (£1.90). There's also the Douglas to Port Erin Steam Train (£13.40 return) which stops in Castletown. A taxi from the airport to Castletown costs around £9.

AT A GLANCE

POPULATION
499,800

NUMBER OF FELLS
214

BEST BOAT TRIP
Steam Yacht Gondola (p590)

BEST POST-HIKE PUB
Wasdale Head Inn (p593)

BEST LAKE VIEW
Crummock Water from Buttermere (p599)

WHEN TO GO

Mar–May
Spring in the Lakes brings green growth, decent weather and relatively few visitors; snow lingers on high fells.

Jun–Sep
Peak tourist season; warm weather, summer festivals, plentiful traffic, maximum crowds. Book everything well ahead.

Oct–Feb
Winter brings snow, bitter wind and icy temperatures: perfect for cosy pub dinners, but the fells are for hardcore hikers only.

Ashness Bridge (p588)
ROBCHIC/SHUTTERSTOCK

The Lake District & Cumbria

William Wordsworth mused, 'no part of the country is more distinguished by its sublimity', and two centuries later, his words still ring true. Nowhere in England can compare to the Lake District's natural splendour: poets, painters and perambulators alike have come here for inspiration, and it's still the nation's favourite place to revel in the delights of the landscape.

At 885 square miles, the Lake District is England's largest national park and, since 2017, a Unesco World Heritage Site. With its rugged fells, sheep-flocked valleys, glittering lakes and whitewashed inns, it's many people's idea of the quintessential English view, immortalised in the work of writers including Beatrix Potter, Arthur Ransome and the grandfather of Lakeland hiking, Alfred Wainwright. Don't forget to pack your walking boots.

INCLUDES

The Lake District & Cumbria

❶ **Helvellyn** (p600) Tackling the most thrilling high-wire ridge walk in England.

❷ **Windermere Jetty Museum** (p578) Tracing two centuries of boating history.

❸ **Rydal Mount** (p583) Visiting the family home of William Wordsworth.

❹ **Borrowdale and Buttermere** (p597) Taking a road trip through the loveliest Lakeland valleys.

❺ **Keswick Launch** (p594) Cruising around the wooded shores of Derwentwater.

❻ **Castlerigg Stone Circle** (p593) Pondering the mysteries of Lakeland's answer to Stonehenge.

❼ **Grizedale Forest** (p589) Cycling woodland trails surrounded by outdoor art.

❽ **Great Langdale** (p591) Exploring Lakeland's most dramatic valley – and its hikes.

❾ **Carlisle Castle** (p606) Patrolling the battlements of Carlisle's medieval fortress.

❿ **Lowther Castle & Gardens** (p608) Visiting a great Cumbrian estate that's slowly being brought back to life.

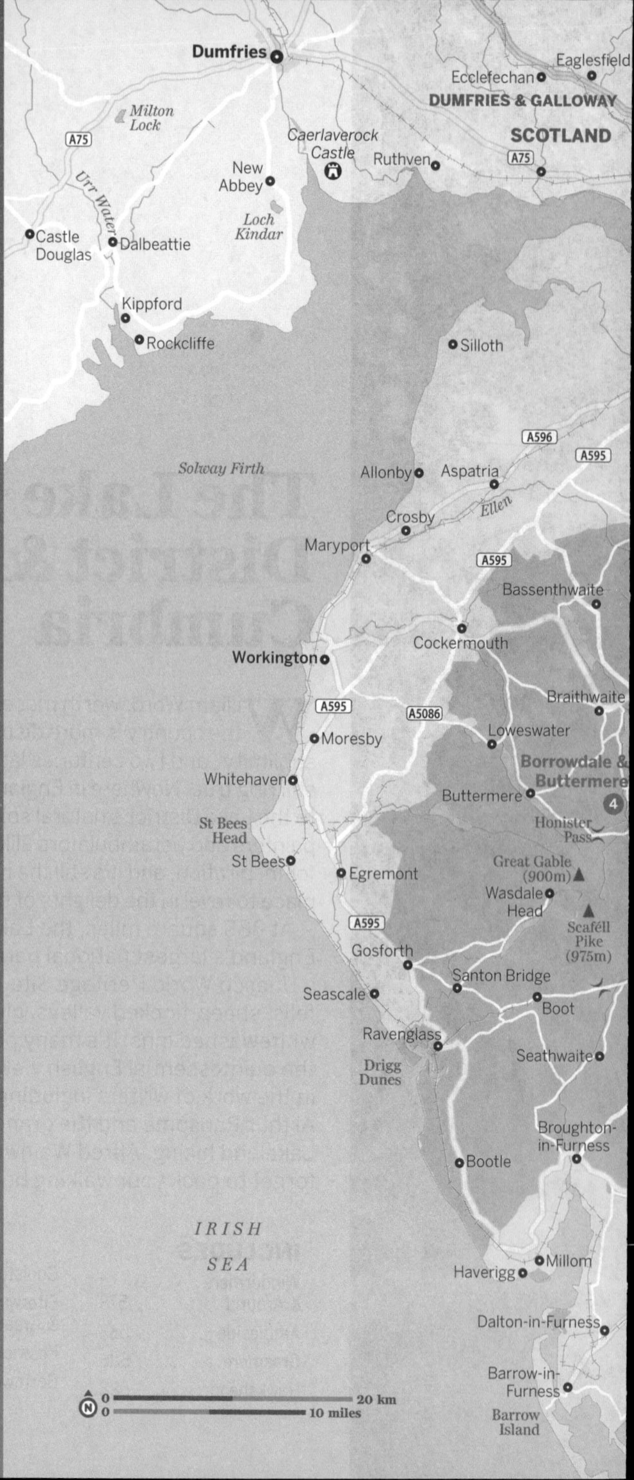

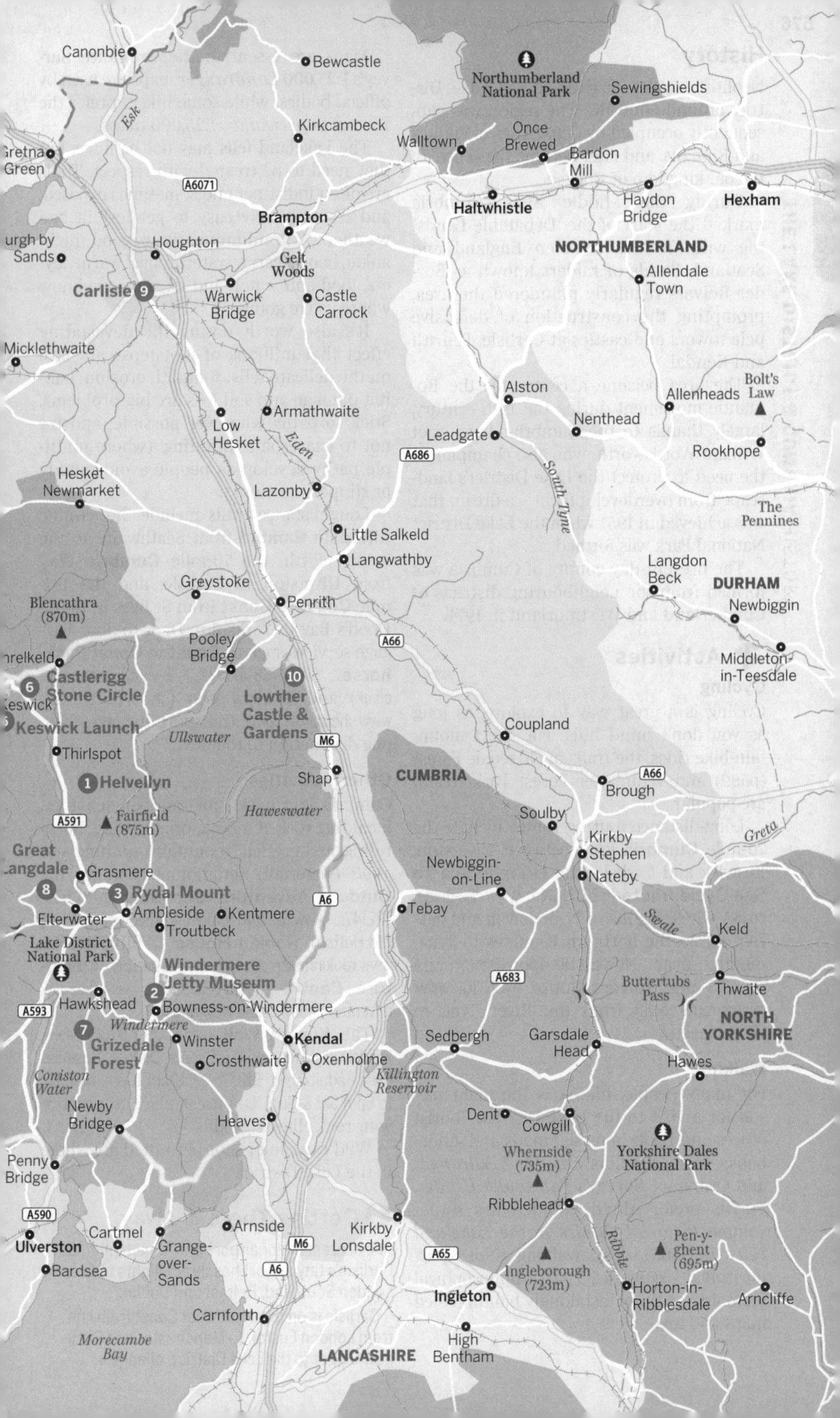
Canonbie
Bewcastle
Northumberland National Park
Sewingshields
Esk
Kirkcambeck
Walltown
Once Brewed
Gretna Green
Bardon Mill
A6071
Haydon Bridge
Hexham
Haltwhistle
Brampton
Burgh by Sands
Houghton
NORTHUMBERLAND
Gelt Woods
Allendale Town
Carlisle
9
Warwick Bridge
Castle Carrock
Micklethwaite
Bolt's Law
Alston
Allenheads
Armathwaite
Low Hesket
Nenthead
Leadgate
Eden
A686
Rookhope
Hesket Newmarket
South Tyne
Lazonby
The Pennines
Little Salkeld
Langwathby
Langdon Beck
DURHAM
Greystoke
Blencathra (870m)
Penrith
Newbiggin
Pooley Bridge
A66
Middleton-in-Teesdale
Threlkeld
6
Castlerigg Stone Circle
10
Lowther Castle & Gardens
Keswick
Keswick Launch
Coupland
Ullswater
M6
Thirlspot
Shap
CUMBRIA
A66
1
Helvellyn
Brough
Haweswater
Fairfield (875m)
A591
Soulby
Greta
Great Langdale
Kirkby Stephen
Newbiggin-on-Line
Grasmere
Nateby
8
3
Rydal Mount
A6
Elterwater
Ambleside
Kentmere
Tebay
Swale
Troutbeck
Keld
Lake District National Park
Windermere Jetty Museum
A683
Buttertubs Pass
Thwaite
2
Hawkshead
A593
Bowness-on-Windermere
NORTH YORKSHIRE
Windermere
7
Grizedale Forest
Winster
Kendal
Sedbergh
Garsdale Head
Crosthwaite
Oxenholme
Hawes
Coniston Water
Killington Reservoir
Newby Bridge
Dent
Cowgill
Heaves
Whernside (735m)
Yorkshire Dales National Park
Penny Bridge
Ribblehead
A590
Arnside
Kirkby Lonsdale
Cartmel
Ulverston
Grange-over-Sands
M6
Ribble
Pen-y-ghent (695m)
A65
A6
Bardsea
Ingleborough (723m)
Horton-in-Ribblesdale
Arncliffe
Ingleton
Carnforth
High Bentham
Morecambe Bay
LANCASHIRE

History

Neolithic settlers arrived in the Lake District around 5000 BC. The region was subsequently occupied by Celts, Angles, Vikings and Romans, and later became the centre of the old kingdom of Rheged.

During the Middle Ages, Cumbria marked the start of the 'Debatable Lands', the wild frontier between England and Scotland. Bands of raiders known as Border Reivers regularly plundered the area, prompting the construction of defensive pele towers and castles at Carlisle, Penrith and Kendal.

The area became a centre for the Romantic movement during the 19th century, largely thanks to the Cumbrian-born poet William Wordsworth, who also championed the need to protect the Lake District's landscape from overdevelopment – a dream that was achieved in 1951 when the Lake District National Park was formed.

The present-day county of Cumbria was formed from the neighbouring districts of Cumberland and Westmorland in 1974.

Activities

Cycling

Cycling is a great way to explore, as long as you don't mind hills. For short mountain-bike rides, the trails of Grizedale Forest (p589) and Whinlatter Forest Park (p595) are popular.

Long-distance touring routes include the 70-mile **Cumbria Way** between Ulverston, Keswick and Carlisle; the 140-mile **Sea To Sea Cycle Route** (C2C, NCN 7; www.c2c-guide.co.uk), which begins in Whitehaven and cuts east across the northern Pennines to Tynemouth, near Newcastle-upon-Tyne; and the 173-mile **Reivers Route** (NCN 10; www.reivers-route.co.uk) from the River Tyne to Whitehaven.

Walking

For many people, hiking is the main reason for a visit to the Lake District. Tourist offices and bookshops sell maps and guidebooks, such as Collins' *Lakeland Fellranger* and Ordnance Survey's *Pathfinder Guides*. Purists prefer Alfred Wainwright's seven-volume *Pictorial Guides to the Lakeland Fells* (1955–66) – part walking guides, part illustrated artworks, part philosophical memoirs – with painstakingly hand-penned maps and text.

Maps are essential: the Ordnance Survey's 1:25,000 *Landranger* maps are used by official bodies, while some hikers prefer the Harvey *Superwalker* 1:25,000 maps.

The Lakeland fells may not be huge, but they need to be treated with respect. Trails are often indistinct and sometimes exposed, and it's extremely easy to get lost in bad weather. At minimum, wear good high-ankle boots, carry waterproofs, warm layers, food and water, and let someone know where you're going.

It's also worth noting the devastating effect that millions of footsteps can have on the delicate fells: footpath erosion, habitat damage and soil loss are big problems. Stick to paths wherever possible, and try not to exacerbate 'braiding' (where multiple paths develop as people avoid muddy or slippery sections).

Long-distance trails include the 54-mile **Allerdale Ramble** from Seathwaite to the Solway Firth, the 70-mile **Cumbria Way** from Ulverston to Carlisle, and the 191-mile **Coast to Coast** from St Bees to Robin Hood's Bay in Yorkshire. Door-to-door baggage services such as **Coast to Coast Packhorse** (☎01768-371777; www.c2cpackhorse.co.uk) and **Sherpa Van** (☎0871-520 0124; www.sherpavan.com) transport luggage from one destination to the next.

Other Activities

Cumbria is a haven for outdoor activities, including rock climbing, orienteering, horse riding, archery, fell (mountain) running and *ghyll* (waterfall) scrambling. Contact the **Outdoor Adventure Company** (☎01539-722147; www.theoutdooradventurecompany.co.uk; Old Hutton), **Rookin House** (☎01768-483561; www.rookinhouse.co.uk) or **Keswick Adventure Centre** (☎01768-775687; www.keswickadventurecentre.co.uk; Newlands).

The **Kendal Wall** (☎01539-721766; www.kendalwall.co.uk; unit 27, Lake District Business Park; adult/child £12/7; ⏲10am-10pm Mon-Fri, to 6pm Sat & Sun) is a great place to practice your rock-climbing skills.

Wild camping is not permitted anywhere in the Lake District.

Getting There & Away

The nearest major airport is in Manchester, but Carlisle's tiny airport has direct flights to/from London Southend, Belfast and Dublin.

Carlisle is on the main West Coast train line from London Euston to Manchester and Glasgow. To get to the Lake District, change at

ALFRED WAINWRIGHT, THE FELL-WALKERS' FELL-WALKER

Hero to many a Lakeland hiker, Alfred Wainwright (1907–91) – AW to his fans – was an author, artist, cartographer and inveterate hill-walker whose classic seven-volume guidebook series, *The Pictorial Guides to the Lakeland Fells*, remain the choice for many walkers. Filled with hand-illustrated maps, painstaking route descriptions and quirky, sometimes poetic writing, they are the record of a lifelong love affair with the Lakeland landscape.

The first guide was published in 1955, and six decades later they've sold well over a million copies. Second revised editions were published in 2011 by author Chris Jesty, followed by the third updated editions in 2020 by Clive Hutchby.

There are many locations linked with AW: you can see some of his possessions in Kendal Museum (p601), view a plaque dedicated to him in the village church in Buttermere and, most poignantly of all, hike to the top of Haystacks, AW's favourite fell, where his ashes were scattered in 1991.

While nothing beats reading the great man's words, several of his routes have been recorded as podcasts, with AW's voice evocatively brought to life by actor Nik Wood Jones. They can be downloaded from the Visit Lake District website (www.visitlakedistrict.com).

Oxenholme for Kendal and Windermere. The lines around the Cumbrian coast, and between Settle and Carlisle, are particularly scenic.

National Express coaches run direct from London Victoria and Glasgow to Windermere, Carlisle and Kendal.

Getting Around

BOAT

There are round-the-lake ferry services on Windermere, Coniston Water, Ullswater and Derwentwater. Windermere also has cruises and a cross-lake ferry service.

BUS

The main bus operator is **Stagecoach** (www.stagecoachbus.com). Services are reduced in winter. You can download timetables from the Stagecoach website or the Cumbria County Council website (www.cumbria.gov.uk). Bus timetables are also available from tourist offices.

Useful services:

Bus 555 (Lakeslink) Lancaster to Keswick, stopping at all the main towns, including Windermere and Ambleside.

Bus 505 (Coniston Rambler) Kendal, Windermere, Ambleside and Coniston.

Bus X4/X5 Penrith to Workington via Troutbeck, Keswick and Cockermouth.

CAR

Traffic can be a nightmare during peak season and holiday weekends. Many Cumbrian towns use timed parking permits for on-street parking, which you can pick up free from local shops and tourist offices.

If you're driving to the Lake District, National Trust membership is a good idea, as it means you can park for free at all of the National Trust's car parks (which otherwise charge extortionately high rates).

TRAVEL PASSES

Several travel passes are available in Cumbria. Dayrider tickets can be bought on buses; Ranger tickets can be bought at any staffed train station.

Central Lakes Dayrider (adult/child/family £8.50/6.30/23.50) For bus-only travel, this good-value pass covers Stagecoach buses around Bowness, Ambleside, Grasmere, Langdale and Coniston; it includes buses 599, 505 and 516. You can also buy a combination ticket that includes a boat cruise on Windermere or Coniston.

Lakes Day Ranger (adult/child/family £25.20/12.60/49.40) The best-value one-day ticket, allowing travel on trains and buses in the Lake District. It also includes a boat cruise on Windermere, 10% discount on the Ravenglass & Eskdale and Lakeside & Haverthwaite railways and 20% discount on the Ullswater Steamers.

Cumbria Day Ranger (adult/child £47.20/23.60) This pass provides one day's train travel in Cumbria and parts of Lancashire, North Yorkshire, Northumberland and Dumfries and Galloway. It also includes the Settle to Carlisle line.

Keswick & Honister Dayrider (adult/child/family £8.50/6.30/23.50) Covers buses from Keswick through Borrowdale, Buttermere, Lorton and Whinlatter Forest Park.

North West Megarider Gold (per week £29) Covers seven days' travel on all Stagecoach buses operating in Lancashire, Merseyside, Cumbria, West Cheshire and Newcastle.

THE LAKE DISTRICT

POP 40,478

The Lake District (or Lakeland, as it's commonly known round these parts) is the UK's most popular national park. Every year, some 15 million people pitch up to explore the region's fells and countryside, and it's not hard to see why. Ever since the Romantic poets arrived in the 19th century, its postcard panorama of craggy hilltops, mountain tarns and glittering lakes has been stirring the imaginations of visitors. Since 2017 it has also been a Unesco World Heritage Site, in recognition of its unique hill-farming culture.

Information

The national park's main visitor centre is at Brockhole (p582), just outside Windermere, and there are tourist offices in Windermere (p582), Bowness (p582), Ambleside (p586), Keswick (p596), Coniston (p591) and Carlisle (p608).

Windermere & Around

☎01539 / POP 6180

Stretching for 10.5 glittering miles between Ambleside and Newby Bridge, Windermere is the undisputed queen of Lakeland lakes (and the largest in England, closer in stature to a Scottish loch). Framed by low fells and green fields, it's been a centre for tourism since the first trains chugged into town in 1847, and it's still one of the national park's busiest spots.

Most of the action is located on the eastern shore. Touristy, overdeveloped Bowness-on-Windermere (usually shortened just to Bowness) sits directly beside the lake, with a cluster of shops, restaurants and sights straggling haphazardly along the shoreline, along with cruise boats puttering out from the lake jetties. One and a half miles inland, at the top of the steep Lake Rd, lies Windermere Town, home to the Lake District's main train station and copious B&Bs.

Practically every visitor strays through Windermere at some point during their stay, and accommodation (and parking) can be hard to come by, so plan accordingly.

Sights & Activities

★**Windermere Jetty Museum** MUSEUM

(☎01539-637940; www.lakelandarts.org.uk/windermere-jetty-museum; Rayrigg Rd; adult/child £9/4.50; ⊙10am-5pm Mar-Oct, 10.30am-4.30pm Nov-Feb) Two centuries of boating are explored at Windermere's fabulous lakeside museum, opened in 2019 after a long £20 million redevelopment. Housed in a striking wooden structure that resembles a *Grand Designs* take on a traditional boat shed, it contains a collection of gorgeous vintage vessels from the lake's history, including steam launches, lug-sailed boats, racing boats and even a 1936 glider. You can also peek into the restoration workshop, pilot a radio-controlled boat or take a cruise in an Edwardian steam launch.

The centrepiece of the collection is the *Branksome*, an 1896 teak-hulled steam launch originally built for the owner of Langdale Chase; it also has the distinction of twice carrying royal visitors. Also of literary note is the *Esperance*, which provided the inspiration for Captain Flint's houseboat in Arthur Ransome's *Swallows and Amazons*.

WINDERMERE & THE ISLANDS

Windermere gets its name from the old Norse, Vinandr mere (Vinandr's lake; so Lake Windermere is actually tautologous). Encompassing 5.7 sq miles between Ambleside and Newby Bridge, the lake is a mile wide at its broadest point, with a maximum depth of about 220m.

The lake's shoreline is owned by a combination of private landholders, the National Park Authority and the National Trust, but the lakebed (and thus the lake itself) officially belongs to the people of Windermere (local philanthropist Henry Leigh Groves purchased it on their behalf in 1938).

There are 18 islands on Windermere: the largest is Belle Isle, encompassing 16 hectares and an 18th-century Italianate mansion, while the smallest is Maiden Holme, little more than a patch of soil and a solitary tree.

Windermere Lake Cruises (☎01539-443360; www.windermere-lakecruises.co.uk; cruises from £9.50) offers sightseeing cruises, departing from Bowness Pier.

Lake District

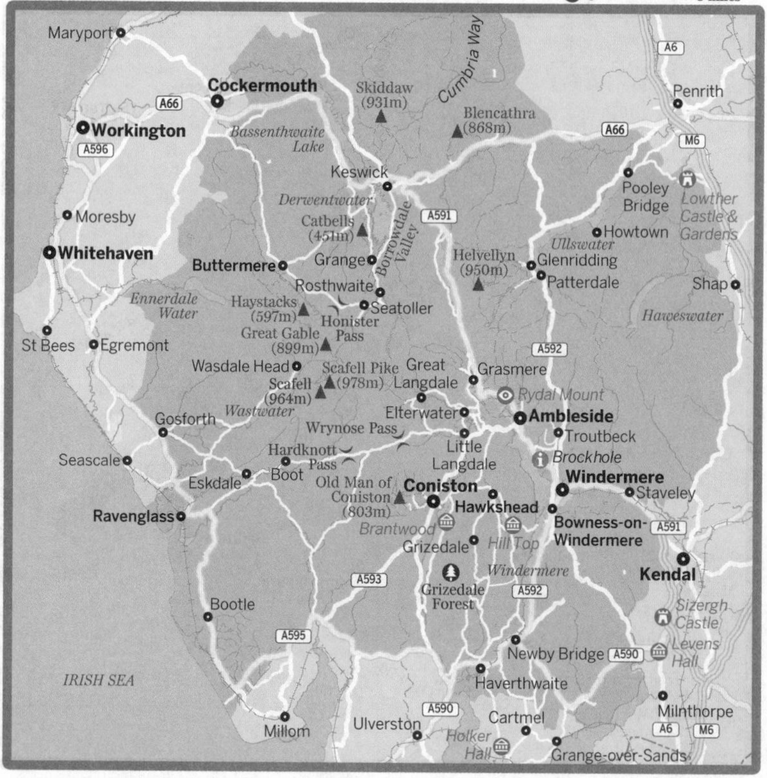

Cruises are provided by the 1902 *Osprey* and the 1930 *Penelope II*: there's no more stylish way to see Windermere.

★ Blackwell House — HISTORIC BUILDING

(01539-446139; www.lakelandarts.org.uk/blackwell; adult/child under 16yr £9/4.50; 10.30am-5pm Apr-Oct, to 4pm Nov-Mar) Two miles south of Bowness on the B5360, Blackwell House is a glorious example of the 19th-century Arts and Crafts movement, which championed handmade goods and craftsmanship over the mass-produced mentality of the Industrial Revolution. Designed by Mackay Hugh Baillie Scott for Sir Edward Holt, a wealthy brewer, the house shimmers with Arts and Crafts details: light, airy rooms, bespoke craftwork, wood panelling, stained glass and delft tiles. The mock-medieval Great Hall and serene White Drawing Room are particularly fine.

The cafe has brilliant views over Windermere.

Wray Castle — HISTORIC SITE

(NT; www.nationaltrust.org.uk/wray-castle; adult/child £10.40/5.20; 10am-6pm, cafe 10am-4pm) An impressive sight with its turrets and battlements, this mock-Gothic castle was built in 1840 for James Dawson, a retired doctor from Liverpool, but it has been owned by the National Trust since 1929. Though the interior is largely empty, the lakeside grounds are glorious. It was once used as a holiday home by Beatrix Potter's family. The best way to arrive is by boat from Bowness; there's limited parking and preference is given to non-driving visitors on busy days.

Fell Foot Park — GARDENS

(NT; www.nationaltrust.org.uk/fell-foot-park; 10am-6pm Apr-Sep, to 5pm Oct-Mar, cafe 10am-3pm) FREE Located at the southern end of Windermere, 7 miles south of Bowness, this 7-hectare lakeside estate originally belonged to a manor house. It's now owned by the National Trust and its shoreline paths and

Windermere Town

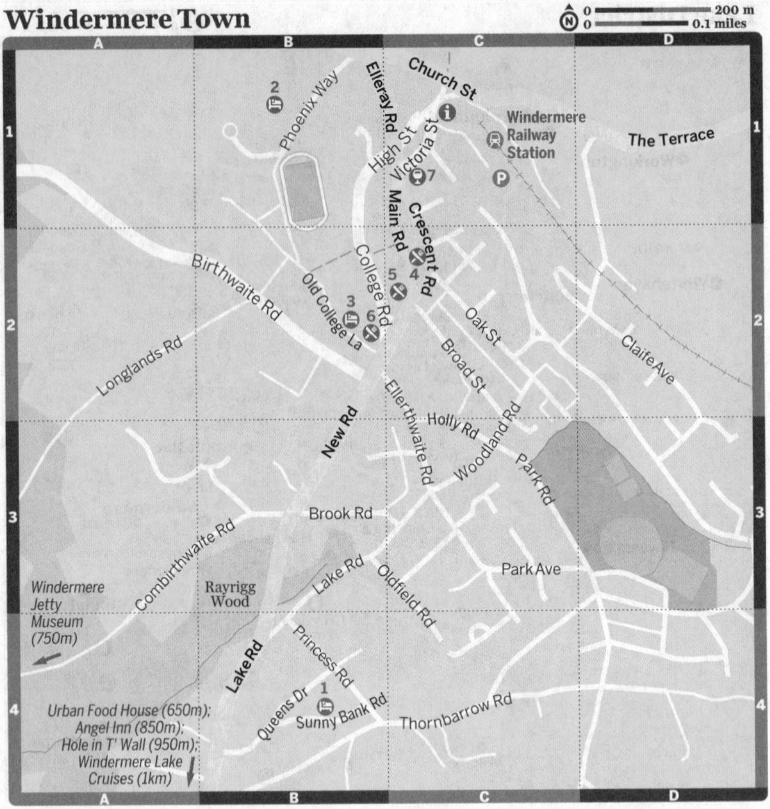

Windermere Town

Sleeping

Eating

Drinking & Nightlife

grassy lawns are ideal for a sunny-day picnic. There's a small cafe, and rowing boats are available for hire.

Lakeland Motor Museum MUSEUM
(☎01539-530400; www.lakelandmotormuseum.co.uk; Backbarrow; adult/child £9/5.40; ⏲9.30am-5.30pm Apr-Sep, to 4.30pm Oct-Mar) Two miles south of Newby Bridge on the A590, this museum is a must for petrolheads. Its vintage-car collection ranges from the classic (Minis, Austin Healeys, MGs) to the sporty (DeLoreans, Audi Quattros, Aston Martins) and downright odd (Scootacars, Amphicars). There are also quirky exhibits on the history of caravans and vintage bicycles. A separate building explores Donald and Malcolm Campbell's speed record attempts on Coniston Water, with replicas of the 1935 Bluebird car and 1967 *Bluebird K7* boat.

Lakes Aquarium AQUARIUM
(☎01539-530153; www.lakesaquarium.co.uk; Lakeside; adult/child £7.95/5.75; ⏲10am-5.30pm) At the southern end of the lake near Newby Bridge, this aquarium explores underwater habitats from tropical Africa through to Morecambe Bay. Windermere Lake Cruises (p578) and the Lakeside & Haverthwaite Railway stop beside the aquarium, as does bus 6/X6 from Bowness.

Lakeside & Haverthwaite Railway RAIL
(☎01539-531594; www.lakesiderailway.co.uk; adult/child return from Haverthwaite to Lakeside £7.20/3.60; ⏰mid-Mar–Oct) Built to carry ore and timber to the ports at Ulverston and Barrow, these dinky steam trains puff their way between Haverthwaite, near Ulverston, and Newby Bridge and Lakeside. There are five to seven trains a day, timed to correspond with the Windermere cruise boats – combo tickets include an onward lake cruise to Bowness or Ambleside.

Sleeping

Windermere YHA HOSTEL £
(☎0845-371 9352; www.yha.org.uk; Bridge Lane; d/tr/q/f from £49/79/99/119; ⏰reception 7.30-11.30am & 3-10pm; P @) Slightly misleadingly, the closest YHA to Windermere is actually about 1.5 miles from the lake, halfway between Troutbeck Bridge and Troutbeck village. Once a private mansion with grand lake views, the hostel is at present only open for exclusive hires, though camping and cabins are available in the grounds.

Inconveniently, buses from Windermere stop about a mile downhill at Troutbeck Bridge.

★**Rum Doodle** B&B ££
(☎01539-445967; www.rumdoodlewindermere.com; Sunny Bank Rd, Windermere Town; d £79-139; P 📶) Named after a classic travel novel about a fictional mountain in the Himalayas, this B&B zings with imagination. Its rooms are themed after places and characters in the book, with details such as book-effect wallpaper, vintage maps and old suitcases. Top of the heap is the Summit, snug under the eaves with a separate sitting room. Two-night minimum in summer.

The Hideaway B&B ££
(☎01539-443070; www.thehideawayatwindermere.co.uk; Phoenix Way; d £70-165; P 📶) There's a fine range of rooms available at this much-recommended B&B in a former schoolmaster's house. There's a choice for all budgets, from Mini Comfy (simple decor, not much space) all the way to Ultimate Comfy (claw-foot tub, split-level mezzanine, space galore). Regardless which you choose, you'll be treated to spoils such as homemade cakes and afternoon tea every day.

Wheatlands Lodge B&B ££
(☎01539-443789; www.wheatlandslodge-windermere.co.uk; Old College Lane; d £99-140; P 📶) Halfway between Windermere and Bowness, this elegant Victorian B&B is a fine choice. Rooms vary in size: largest are the four-poster room 5 (with its own bay window) and the two top-floor suites. Breakfast is a definite high point, with homemade bread and granola, locally sourced bacon, milk and sausages, and jams from Hawkshead Relish company.

Gilpin Hotel HOTEL £££
(☎01539-488818; https://thegilpin.co.uk; Crook Rd; r £275-465; P) If you really want to push the Windermere boat out, this famously posh country-house retreat offers the final word in lake luxury. The fancy rooms are named after fells, garden suites have their own decks and outdoor hot tubs, and the exclusive Lake House nearby comes with its own chauffeur.

A Michelin-starred restaurant, lovely spa and hectares of grounds complete the high-class package.

Eating

★**Homeground** CAFE £
(☎01539-444863; www.homegroundcafe.co.uk; 56 Main Rd, Windermere Town; mains £7-10; ⏰8.30am-5pm Mon-Fri, 9am-5pm Sat & Sun) Windermere gets its own artisan coffee house, serving flat whites and cappucinos garnished with impressive milk art. It's super for brunch too, with bang-on-trend options such as pressed tofu and hummus flatbreads, homemade kedgeree benny and tahini waffles. All in all, a thoroughly welcome new addition to town.

★**Hooked** SEAFOOD ££
(☎01539-448443; www.hookedwindermere.co.uk; Ellerthwaite Sq, Windermere Town; mains £16-20; ⏰5-9pm) Fresh fish comes every day direct from Hartlepool Dock in County Durham, and this first-class fish restaurant takes full advantage. From hake with pomme purée to Cajun swordfish and squid-ink ravioli, it's a pescatarian's perfect night out. It's small, so bookings are essential.

Urban Food House CAFE ££
(☎01539-454345; www.urbanfoodhouse.co.uk; Lake Rd, Bowness-on-Windermere; lunch mains £8-12, dinner mains £12-22; ⏰10am-10pm Mon-Sat, to 7pm Sun) A peculiar name for a Lakeland cafe, perhaps, but it makes sense given the hipsterish design: red-brick walls, rough-wood tables, bare lightbulbs, casual service. There's range of grub, from fish-finger

LOCAL KNOWLEDGE

CLASSIC PUBS AROUND WINDERMERE

Several super country pubs are within a few miles' drive of Windermere.

Mason's Arms (01539-568486; www.masonsarmsstrawberrybank.co.uk; Bowland Bridge; mains £12.95-19.95; noon-10pm) Three miles east of the lake, near Bowlands Bridge, this marvellous pub is a local secret – particularly for the gorgeous views over fields and fells from the terrace.

Brown Horse Inn (01539-443443; www.thebrownhorseinn.co.uk; Winster; mains £12.95-17.95; lunch noon-2pm, dinner 6-9pm) Also three miles from Windermere in Winster, the Brown Horse is known for its food – much of the produce (including meat and game) comes from its own estate.

Watermill Inn (01539-821309; www.watermillinn.co.uk; Ings; mains £11-20; 11am-11pm Mon-Sat, to 10.30pm Sun) Two miles from Windermere in Ings, this is a resolutely traditional Cumbrian inn – beamed ceilings, whitewashed walls, log fires, hand pumps and all. It's renowned for its home-brewed beer.

baps and flatbreads to mussel bowls and herb-crusted lamb (some good veggie options, too).

Francine's BISTRO ££
(01539-444088; www.francinesrestaurantwindermere.co.uk; 27 Main Rd, Windermere Town; mains £14-18; 10am-2.30pm & 6.30-11pm Tue-Sat) The definition of a neighbourhood bistro: it's a locals' favourite and if you come more than once you'll probably be greeted by name. It's a tiny space with crammed-in tables, so watch your elbows with your neighbours. Food is solid if not stellar, with tastes tending toward the hearty, such as roast guinea fowl, confit pork belly and chicken supreme.

Angel Inn PUB FOOD ££
(01539-444080; www.angelbowness.com; Helm Rd, Bowness-on-Windermere; mains £10.95-16.50; 11.30am-4pm & 5-9pm) A decent gastropub on a grassy knoll in Bowness. The menu is nothing fancy – burgers, beer-battered haddock, Cumberland sausage and mash – but the setting is fantastic, with Windermere views from the front lawn.

Drinking & Nightlife

★**Crafty Baa** CRAFT BEER
(01539-488002; https://thecraftybaa.business.site; 21 Victoria St, Windermere Town; 11am-11pm) Brilliant and slightly bonkers, festooned with a mishmash of upcycled materials, this much-loved Windermere craft bar has scooped numerous awards: choose from Czech pilsners, weissbiers, smoked lagers and fruit beers, chalked up on slates behind the bar and served with accompanying snack platters. It's so successful, it's opened a sister pub in Keswick (p596).

Hole in T' Wall PUB
(01539-443488; Fallbarrow Rd, Bowness-on-Windermere; 11am-11pm) Bowness' oldest boozer, dating back to 1612 and offering lashings of rough-beamed, low-ceilinged atmosphere.

Hawkshead Brewery BREWERY
(01539-822644; www.hawksheadbrewery.co.uk; Mill Yard, Staveley; noon-11pm) This renowned craft brewery has its own impressive beer hall in Staveley, 3 miles east of Windermere. Core beers include Hawkshead Bitter, dark Brodie's Prime and fruity Red.

Information

Brockhole National Park Visitor Centre (01539-446601; www.brockhole.co.uk; 10am-5pm) The lakes' main information centre in a former country house 3 miles north of Windermere along the A591.

Windermere Information Centre (01539-446499; www.windermereinfo.co.uk; Victoria St, Windermere Town; 8.30am-5.30pm) A small information point in Windermere Town, near the railway station, run by Mountain Goat. It also offers booking services and luggage storage.

Bowness Visitor Information Centre (0845-901 0845; bownesstic@lake-district.gov.uk; Glebe Rd, Bowness-on-Windermere; 10am-5pm Apr-Oct, to 4.30pm Nov-Mar;) Basic information point near the Bowness jetty, with a shop and cafe.

Getting There & Away

BOAT

To cross Windermere by car, bike or on foot, head south of Bowness to the **Windermere Ferry** (www.cumbria.gov.uk/roads-transport/highways-pavements/windermereferry.asp; car/bicycle/pedestrian £5/2/1; ⏲6.50am-9.50pm Mon-Sat, 8.50am-10pm Sun Apr-Oct, to 8.50pm Oct-Mar), which shuttles between Ferry Nab on the east bank to Ferry House on the west bank. Expect car queues in summer.

BUS

Note that if you're travelling any further than Grasmere – or if you're planning on returning from anywhere – you're best to buy a Central Lakes Dayrider (p577) ticket.

Bus 555/556 Lakeslink (£4.90 to £10, at least hourly every day) Starts at the train station, stopping at Troutbeck Bridge (five minutes), Brockhole Visitor Centre (seven minutes), Ambleside (£4.90, 15 minutes), Grasmere (£7.40, 30 minutes) and Keswick (£10, one hour). In the opposite direction it continues to Kendal (£6.50, 25 minutes).

Bus 505 Coniston Rambler (hourly every day) Travels from Bowness to Coniston (£12.60, 50 minutes) via Troutbeck, Brockhole, Ambleside, Skelwith Fold, Hawkshead and Hawkshead Hill. Two buses a day serve Kendal.

Bus 599 Lakes Rider (£4.00 to £7.40, three times hourly every day) Open-top bus between Bowness, Troutbeck, Brockhole, Rydal Church (for Rydal Mount), Dove Cottage and Grasmere. Some buses stop at Windermere train station.

TRAIN

Windermere is the only town inside the national park accessible by train. It's on the branch line to Kendal and Oxenholme, with onward connections to Edinburgh, Manchester and London Piccadilly.

DESTINATION	ONE-WAY FARE (£)	DURATION
Edinburgh	70.80	2½hr
Glasgow	58	2¼-2¾hr
Kendal	5.70	15min
Lancaster	15.50	45min
London Euston	80.90	3½hr
Manchester Piccadilly	25.80	1½hr

Ambleside

☎01539 / POP 2529

Once a busy mill and textile centre, Ambleside is an attractive little town at Windermere's northern tip, built from the same slate and stern grey stone so characteristic of Lakeland. Ringed by fells, it's a favourite base for hikers, with a cluster of outdoors shops and plenty of cosy pubs and cafes providing fuel for adventures.

The town's best-known landmark is **Bridge House**, a tiny cottage that spans the clattering brook of Stock Ghyll. Now occupied by a National Trust shop, it's thought to have originally been built as an apple store.

Sights & Activities

★**Rydal Mount** HISTORIC BUILDING
(☎01539-433002; www.rydalmount.co.uk; adult/child £7.50/4, grounds only £5; ⏲9.30am-5pm

WORTH A TRIP

TROUTBECK

This out-of-the-way hamlet on the way to Kirkstone Pass is worth a detour – the views of the fells and distant Windermere are fantastic. But it's also home to one of Lakeland's best (and oldest) inns, the **Mortal Man** (☎01539-433193; www.themortalman.co.uk; mains £13.95-24.85; P 🐾). Dating from 1689, with a gabled facade, traditional rooms and a cracking outlook from the beer garden, it's a real beauty of a boozer. And if you're wondering about the curious name, have a look at the pub sign on your way in – it's taken from an old Lakeland rhyme.

Troutbeck is also home to the National Trust–owned farmhouse of **Townend** (NT; ☎01539-432628; www.nationaltrust.org.uk/townend; adult/child £8.50/4.25; ⏲garden 10am-5pm Fri-Mon), which belonged to farmer Ben Browne and his family until 1943. The house is brimming with the family's possessions and memorabilia of their rural agricultural life, but its opening hours vary: when it isn't open, the delightful cottage garden is well worth a wander.

Bus 508 from Windermere (£4.90, 25 minutes, five daily) stops in Troutbeck, then continues over Kirkstone Pass to Ullswater and Penrith.

Apr-Oct, 11am-4pm Wed-Sun Nov, Dec, Feb & Mar) The poet William Wordsworth's most famous residence in the Lake District is undoubtedly Dove Cottage (p586), but he actually spent a great deal more time at Rydal Mount, 1.5 miles northwest of Ambleside, off the A591. This was the Wordsworth family's home from 1813 until the poet's death in 1850 and the house contains a treasure trove of Wordsworth memorabilia. Bus 555 (and bus 599 from April to October) stops at the end of the drive.

Downstairs you can wander around the library, dining room and drawing room; upstairs are the family bedrooms and Wordsworth's attic study, containing his encyclopedia and a sword belonging to his brother John, who was lost in a shipwreck in 1805.

There is a plethora of fascinating objects, including recently unveiled exhibits such as the Wordsworth's family Bible (which includes the christening dates of all the Wordsworth children in delicate copperplate) and William's beloved walking sticks (complete with his silver crest). Look closely and you'll also spy gems such as his pen, inkstand and picnic box in the cabinets.

The gardens are lovely, too – Wordsworth fancied himself as a landscape gardener and much of the grounds were laid out according to his designs. Below the house is Dora's Field, a peaceful meadow in which Wordsworth planted daffodils in memory of his eldest daughter, who died from tuberculosis in 1847.

Entry at the time of research was by online bookings only.

Stock Ghyll Force WALKING

Ambleside's most popular walk is the half-hour stroll up to the 18m-high waterfall of Stock Ghyll Force – the trail is signposted behind the old market hall at the bottom of Stock Ghyll Lane. If you feel energetic, you can follow the trail beyond the falls up **Wansfell Pike** (482m), a reasonably steep walk of about two hours.

Low Wood Watersports BOATING

(☎01539-439441; www.englishlakes.co.uk/low-wood-bay/watersports; Low Bay Marina) This water-sports centre offers waterskiing, sailing and kayaking and has rowboats and motorboats for hire. For two hours, kayaks cost £20, canoes £30 and stand-up paddleboards £25.

Sleeping

★Ambleside YHA HOSTEL £

(☎0345-371 9620; www.yha.org.uk; Lake Rd; d/f from £39/59; P wi-fi) This huge lakeside hostel is a fave for activity holidays (everything from kayaking to ghyll scrambling). At the time of research, bookings were for private rooms only (either en suite or with shared bathrooms), and the lounge and kitchen were closed due to Covid-19. It's between Ambleside and Windermere.

Low Wray CAMPSITE £

(NT; ☎bookings 01539-432733; www.nationaltrust.org.uk/features/lake-district-camping; campsite for 2 adults £18-44, ecopod £30-80; ⊙year-round) One of the most popular of the National Trust's four Lakeland campsites, in a fine spot along Windermere's shores, 3 miles from Ambleside along the B5286. There are 120 tent pitches and nine hard pitches for caravans, plus a handful of camping pods, safari tents and two wacky 'tree tents'. Choose from lake view, woodland, field or water's edge. Bus 505 stops nearby.

Rooms at the Apple Pie B&B £

(☎01539-433679; www.applepieambleside.co.uk; Rydal Rd; d £55-85; P wi-fi) Not content with making the best apple pie in town, the eponymous cafe has expanded its accommodation operations into a separate building next door. There are good-value rooms, plainly furnished and on the small side, but thoroughly comfy. The loft rooms share a landing, so are ideal for families. There's a small car park, too.

Waterwheel B&B ££

(☎01539-433286; www.waterwheelambleside.co.uk; 3 Bridge St; d £100-120; wi-fi) Fall asleep to the sound of the river at this tiny B&B, tucked off the main street. The three rooms are small but sweet: Rattleghyll is cosily Victorian, Loughrigg squeezes under the rafters and Stockghyll features a brass bed and claw-foot bath. The drawback? The only parking is in a public car park 250m away. Two-night minimum.

Gables B&B ££

(☎01539-433272; www.thegables-ambleside.co.uk; Church Walk; s £60-65, d £95-145; P wi-fi) One of Ambleside's best-value B&Bs, in a double-gabled house (hence the name) in a quiet spot overlooking the recreation ground. Spotty cushions and colourful prints keep things cheery, but room sizes are variable

FIVE CLASSIC FELL WALKS

The Lake District's most famous fell-walker, the accountant-turned-author Alfred Wainwright, recorded 214 official fells in his seven-volume *Pictorial Guides* (as if that weren't enough, he usually outlined at least two possible routes to the top or, in the case of Scafell Pike, five). If you only have limited time, here are five hikes that offer a flavour of what makes fell-walking in the Lake District so special.

Scafell Pike (p593) The daddy of Lakeland hikes, a six- to seven-hour slog to the top of England's highest peak. The classic route is from Wasdale Head.

Helvellyn (p600) Not for the faint hearted; a vertiginous scramble along the knife-edge ridge of Striding Edge. It takes at least six hours, starting from Glenridding or Patterdale.

Blencathra A mountain on its own, Blencathra (868m) offers a panoramic outlook on Keswick and the northern fells. Count on four hours from Threlkeld.

Haystacks Wainwright's favourite mountain and the place where his ashes were scattered. Haystacks (597m) is a steep, three-hour return hike from Buttermere village.

Catbells The fell for everyone, Catbells (451m) is accessible to six-year-olds and septuagenarians alike. It's on the west side of Derwentwater and takes a couple of hours to climb.

(in this instance, bigger is definitely better). Guests receive discounts at the owner's restaurant, **Sheila's Cottage** (☎01539-433079; The Slack; mains £12.50-18; ⏲noon-9pm). There's a tiny first-come, first-served car park.

Ambleside Townhouse B&B £££
(☎01539-433240; www.amblesidetownhouse.co.uk; Lake Rd; d £94-154; P ᯤ) Halfway between a B&B and a mini-hotel, this place is handily placed for the town centre. The rooms are simply but smartly decorated in neutral tones; some superior rooms have a full-size wall mural featuring a local beauty spot. Some are in the main building, others in an attached annexe. Breakfast is buffet-style, and there's plenty of parking.

Waterhead Hotel HOTEL £££
(☎08458 504503; www.englishlakes.co.uk; Lake Rd; r £145-360; P ᯤ 🐾) For a proper hotel stay in Ambleside (complete with the all-essential Windermere view, of course), the Waterhead is definitely the choice. Outside it's clad in traditional Lakeland stone; inside there are 40-something rooms that, while perfectly comfortable, feel a tad corporate in style. Lake views command a premium, but there are often good online deals.

Eating

★Great North Pie PIES £
(☎01625-522112; www.greatnorthpie.co; unit 2 The Courtyard, Rothay Rd; pies £4-8; ⏲9am-5pm) Based in Wilmslow, this much-garlanded pie maker has opened an Ambleside outlet, and it's rightly become a town favourite. Go for a classic such as Swaledale beef mince or Lancashire cheese and onion, or opt for something on the seasonal pie menu – they're all delicious, and served with lashings of mash and gravy (veggie, should you wish).

Apple Pie CAFE £
(☎01539-433679; www.applepieambleside.co.uk; Rydal Rd; lunches £5-10; ⏲9am-5.30pm) For a quick lunch stop, you won't go far wrong at this friendly caff, which serves stuffed sandwiches, hot pies, baked spuds, sausage rolls and yummy cakes (the apple pie is locally legendary). Everything is available either eat in or takeaway.

Zeffirelli's ITALIAN £
(☎01539-433845; www.zeffirellis.com; Compston Rd; pizzas & mains £10-15; ⏲11am-10pm) A beloved local landmark, Zeff's is generally packed out for its quality and good-value pizza and pasta. The £24.75 movie deal includes a ticket at **Zeffirelli's Cinema** (☎01539-433100; Compston Rd).

Kysty BISTRO ££
(☎01539-433647; www.kysty.co.uk; 3/4 Cheapside; lunch mains £14-19, dinner mains £18-26; ⏲noon-2pm Wed-Sat, 6-9pm Tue-Sat) Run by the same team behind the Old Stamp House (p586), this town bistro offers a simplified take on its sister restaurant's superb Cumbrian-sourced food. Simple and seasonal, the food is a treat, and the space is lovely, with old-fashioned mullion windows and wooden tables. In case you're

wondering, *kysty* is a Cumbrian word for a fussy eater.

Fellini's VEGETARIAN ££
(☎01539-432487; www.fellinisambleside.com; Church St; mains £14.95; ⏰5.30-10pm; ☑) Fear not, veggies: even in the land of the Cumberland sausage and the tattie hotpot, you won't go hungry thanks to Fellini's 'vegeterranean' food. The dishes are creative and beautifully presented – think delicate Moroccan filo parcels, stuffed portobello mushrooms and radicchio provolone ravioli.

★**Old Stamp House** BISTRO £££
(☎01539-432775; www.oldstamphouse.com; Church St; lunch/dinner menu £45/75; ⏰12.30-2pm Wed-Sat, 6.30-10pm Tue-Sat) In the cellar of the building where Wordsworth worked as a distributor of stamps, this fine-dining bistro run by Ryan Blackburn champions Cumbrian produce, much of it raised, caught, shot or cured within a few miles' radius (think Arctic char, Herdwick hogget and roe deer, partnered with foraged ingredients). Outstanding – and now Michelin-starred.

★**Lake Road Kitchen** BISTRO £££
(☎01539-422012; www.lakeroadkitchen.co.uk; Lake Rd; 5-/8-course tasting menu £65/90; ⏰6-9.30pm Wed-Sun) Quite simply one of the hottest places to dine in the Lakes. Its Noma-trained head chef, James Cross, explores 'cold climate' cooking (think Scandi-inspired, impeccably presented and laced with experimental ingredients aplenty). From shore-sourced seaweed to pickled vegetables and forest-picked mushrooms, the flavours are constantly surprising – and the stripped-back styling feels very appropriate.

ℹ Information

Hub (☎01539-432582; tic@thehubofambleside.com; Central Buildings, Market Cross; ⏰9am-5pm) Ambleside's info centre sells walking guides, local books and also houses the town's post office.

ℹ Getting There & Away

Bus 555 Runs at least hourly (including Sundays) to Grasmere (£4.90) and Keswick (£9), and to Bowness, Windermere (£4.90) and Kendal (£7.80) in the opposite direction.

Bus 599 Open-top service that leaves at least hourly (including weekends) to Grasmere, Bowness, Windermere and Brockhole Visitor Centre; four buses daily continue to Kendal. Prices as for bus 555.

Bus 505 To Hawkshead and Coniston (£6.10, hourly each day).

Bus 516 To Elterwater and Langdale (£4.60, six daily).

Grasmere

☎01539 / POP 1458

Few corners of the Lake District have such an illustrious literary heritage as little Grasmere. Huddled at the edge of an island-studded lake surrounded by woods, pastures and slate-coloured hills, this was the home of the grand old daddy of the Romantics himself, poet William Wordsworth, who set up home at nearby Dove Cottage in 1799 and spent most of the rest of his life in and around the village. Two of the poet's former homes can be visited, and there's an excellent museum that explores the area's Romantic connections. Most poignantly of all, you can pay your respects at the Wordsworth's family plot in the village churchyard.

Grasmere's literary cachet has its drawbacks: the village's streets are crammed to bursting throughout summer, and the modern-day rash of gift shops, tearooms and coach-tour hotels has done little to preserve the quiet country charm that drew Wordsworth here.

Sights & Activities

Popular hikes starting from Grasmere include **Helm Crag** (404m), often known as the 'Lion and the Lamb', thanks to its distinctive shape; **Silver Howe** (394m); **Loughrigg Fell** (335m); and the multi-peak circuit known as the **Easedale Round** (five to six hours, 8.5 to 9 miles).

A less taxing option is to follow the **Old Coffin Trail** (4 miles) between Grasmere and Rydal Mount, which was once used by pallbearers carrying coffins to St Oswald's Church. The trail begins near Dove Cottage.

★**Dove Cottage & Jerwood Museum** HISTORIC BUILDING
(☎01539-435544; www.wordsworth.org.uk; adult/child £9.50/4.50; ⏰9.30am-5.30pm Mar-Oct, 10am-4.30pm Nov, Dec & Feb) This tiny, creeper-clad cottage was famously inhabited by William Wordsworth between 1799 and 1808. On the edge of Grasmere, described by Wordsworth as 'the loveliest spot that man hath ever found', the cottage has cramped rooms full of artefacts, including the poet's passport, spectacles, dinner set and a por-

trait (given to him by Sir Walter Scott) of his dog, Pepper.

Wordsworth lived here happily – initially with his beloved sister Dorothy, and later his wife Mary and first three children, John, Dora and Thomas. Much of his early work was composed at the cottage, often with the help and support of Dorothy, who penned her *Grasmere Journal* while living at the cottage – a fascinating work in its own right for Wordsworth students. In 1808 when the family moved to a nearby house at Allen Bank, the cottage was subsequently rented by Thomas de Quincey (author of *Confessions of an English Opium Eater*).

Around the house is the delightful cottage garden, which Wordsworth described as his own 'little domestic slip of mountain'.

Entry is by prebooked group. Tickets also include admission to the excellent **Jerwood Museum** next door, which houses one of the nation's main collections relating to the Romantic movement, including many original manuscripts, Dorothy's original journal and a huge collection of letters and rare editions by leading Romantic figures.

Grasmere Lake & Rydal Water LAKE

Quiet paths lead along the shores of Grasmere's twin-set lakes. Rowboats can be hired at the northern end of Grasmere Lake from the **Grasmere Tea Gardens** (☎01539-435590; Stock Lane; ⊙9.30am-5pm), a five-minute walk from the village centre.

St Oswald's Church CHURCH

(Church Stile) Named after a Viking saint, Grasmere's medieval chapel is where Wordsworth and his family attended service every Sunday for many years. It's also their final resting place – in a corner of the churchyard, the Wordsworth's family graves are under the spreading bows of a great yew tree. A memorial garden to fund the church's restoration has recently been established next door – planted, of course, with daffodils.

Among the tombstones are those belonging to William, his wife Mary, his sister Dorothy and his children Dora, William, Thomas and Catherine. Samuel Taylor Coleridge's son Hartley is also buried here, along with several Quillinans – Edward Quillinan became Wordsworth's son-in-law in 1841, having married his beloved daughter Dora.

The church itself is worth a look. Inside you'll find Wordsworth's own prayer book and his favourite pew, marked by a plaque. The church is one of the oldest in the Lake District, mostly dating from the 13th century, but thought to have been founded sometime in the 7th century. It was restored and re-rendered in 2017.

Sleeping

Butharlyp How YHA HOSTEL £

(☎0845 371 9319; www.yha.org.uk; Easedale Rd; r £49-59; ⊙reception 7am-11pm; P 📶) Grasmere's YHA is in a large Victorian house set among grassy grounds within easy walking distance of the village. There's a licensed bar, and camping space in the grounds, plus waterproof 'landpods' for hire.

Thorney How HOSTEL £

(☎01539-435597; www.thorneyhow.co.uk; Easedale Rd; d from £55) Once a much-loved YHA hostel, this ancient farmhouse off Easedale Rd has been totally renovated since becoming independently run. Snug rooms are available on an en-suite B&B basis, and there's an attached bunkhouse (exclusive hire only at the time of research). Located down a rambling lane, it scores high on Lakeland charm.

Heidi's Grasmere Lodge B&B ££

(☎07568-333950; www.heidisgrasmerelodge.co.uk; Red Lion Sq; d £99-125; 📶) Not one for minimalists, this five-room B&B in the centre of the village is awash with frills, puffy cushions and Cath Kidston–style prints. The picks are room 1, with a private balcony offering mountain views, or room 6, reached via a spiral staircase and with its own roof terrace.

How Foot Lodge B&B ££

(☎01539-435366; www.howfootlodge.co.uk; Town End; d £85-95; P) Just a stroll from Dove Cottage in Town End, this stone house has six rooms finished in fawns and beiges. Nicest are the deluxe doubles, one with a sun terrace, the other with a private sitting room. Rates are a bargain for the location.

★ **Forest Side** BOUTIQUE HOTEL £££

(☎01539-435250; www.theforestside.com; Keswick Rd; r £189-369; P 📶) This boutique beauty – a former hunting lodge – is hard to top for luxury. Renovated at huge expense by hotelier Andrew Wildsmith, it's a design temple: crushed-velvet sofas, Zoffany fabrics, stag heads and 20 country-chic rooms from 'Cosy' to 'Master'. Its restaurant is Michelin-starred, and the grounds (including a working kitchen garden) are gorgeous.

Daffodil Hotel BOUTIQUE HOTEL £££
(☎01539-463550; www.daffodilhotel.co.uk; d £160-240, ste £200-320; P 📶) Opened in 2012 this upscale hotel occupies a Victorian building, but the 78 rooms zing with modern style: swirly carpets, art prints and bold shades of lime, purple and turquoise. There's a choice of lake or valley views and lovely bathrooms with pan-head showers and Molton Brown bath products. A restaurant and spa complete the package.

Eating

Heidi's Cafe CAFE £
(☎01539-435248; www.heidisgrasmerelodge.co.uk; Red Lion Sq; mains £4-8; ⊙9am-5.30pm) This cheery village cafe is the place for homemade soup or an indulgent slice of cake.

Baldry's Tea Room CAFE £
(☎01539-435301; Red Lion Sq; lunch £5-9; ⊙10am-5pm) This old-school tearoom serves a classic cream tea in a bone-china pot, accompanied by buttery scones, flapjacks or Victoria sponge.

Greens CAFE £
(☎01539-435790; www.greensgrasmere.com; College St; mains £4.75-10.50; ⊙9.30am-4pm) A popular little village cafe, good for everything from a Cumbrian fry-up to a lunch of stuffed baguettes, wraps and rarebits.

★**The Yan** BISTRO ££
(☎01539-435055; www.theyan.co.uk; Broadrayne Farm; mains £13.95-15.95; ⊙5-10pm Mon-Fri, 3-10pm Sat & Sun) Rustic-meets-refined at the Yan (from an old Cumbrian word for 'one'). Lodged in an ancient farmhouse a mile north of Grasmere, the design marries minimalism with chunky wooden tables, a futuristic fireplace and hefty wood beams, and the food offers a fun, modern spin on traditional classic like fish pie, chicken Kiev and bacon chop. Lovely bedrooms, too.

Jumble Room MODERN BRITISH ££
(☎01539-435188; www.thejumbleroom.co.uk; Langdale Rd; mains £14.50-23; ⊙5-9pm Mon-Wed, Fri & Sat) Grasmere's venerable dining landmark, run for many years by Andy and Crissy Hill. Crissy's eclectic, globetrotting menu spans everything from Malaysian noodles to Turkish lamb, cauliflower and chickpea curry and fish pie.

Shopping

★**Sarah Nelson's Gingerbread Shop** FOOD
(☎01539-435428; www.grasmeregingerbread.co.uk; Church Cottage; ⊙9.15am-5.30pm Mon-Sat, 12.30-5pm Sun) In business since 1854, this famous sweet shop next to the village church makes Grasmere's essential souvenir: traditional gingerbread with a half-biscuity, half-cakey texture (six/12 pieces for £3.95/7.50), cooked using the original top-secret recipe.

Getting There & Away

The regular 555 bus (at least hourly, including Sundays) runs from Windermere to Grasmere (15 minutes) via Ambleside, Rydal Church and Dove Cottage, then travels onwards to Keswick.

The open-top 599 (two or three per hour in summer) runs to Grasmere from Windermere and Bowness via Troutbeck Bridge and Ambleside.

Both buses charge the same fares: Grasmere to Ambleside is £4.90; to Bowness and Windermere is £7.40.

Hawkshead

☎01539 / POP 1640

Lakeland villages don't come more perfect than pint-sized Hawkshead, a jumble of whitewashed cottages, cobbled lanes and old pubs lost among bottle-green countryside between Ambleside and Coniston. The village has literary cachet, too – Wordsworth went to school here and Beatrix Potter's husband, William Heelis, worked here as a solicitor for many years (his old office is now a National Trust art gallery devoted to Beatrix Potter's work).

Cars are banned in the village centre.

Sights

A number of Hawkshead's sights, including the **Beatrix Potter Gallery** (www.nationaltrust.org.uk/beatrix-potter-gallery) and the **Hawkshead Grammar School** (www.hawksheadgrammar.org.uk), which Wordsworth attended, were closed at time of research due to Covid-19. Check their websites for opening times and booking details before you visit.

★**Hill Top** HISTORIC BUILDING
(NT; ☎01539-436269; www.nationaltrust.org.uk/hill-top; garden adult/child £5/2.50; ⊙10am-5.30pm Jun-Aug, to 4.30pm Sat-Thu Apr, May, Sep & Oct, weekends only Nov-Mar) Two miles south of Hawkshead, in the tiny village of

GRIZEDALE FOREST

Stretching for 2428 hectares across the hilltops between Coniston Water and Esthwaite Water is Grizedale Forest, a dense conifer forest whose name derives from the Old Norse 'griss-dale', meaning 'valley of the pigs'. Though it looks lush and unspoilt today, the forest has been largely replanted over the last 100 years – by the late 19th century the original woodland had practically disappeared thanks to the demands of the local logging, mining and charcoal industries.

The forest has nine walking trails and seven cycling trails to explore – some are easy and designed for families, while others are geared towards hardcore hikers and cyclists. Along the way you'll spot more than 40 outdoor sculptures hidden in the undergrowth, created by artists since 1977 (there's a useful online guide at www.grizedalesculpture.org). There's also a **Go Ape** (www.goape.co.uk/locations/grizedale; ⌚9-5pm daily Mar-Oct, Sat & Sun Nov-Feb; 👪) forest adventure centre.

Trail maps of the forest are sold at the **visitors centre** (☎0300 067 4495; www.forestry.gov.uk/grizedale; ⌚10am-1pm & 1.45-4pm), while bikes can be hired from **Grizedale Mountain Bikes** (☎01229-860335; www.grizedalemountainbikes.co.uk; adult/child half-day from £35/20; ⌚9am-5pm).

Near Sawrey, this idyllic farmhouse was purchased in 1905 by Beatrix Potter and inspired many of her tales: the house features in *Samuel Whiskers, Tom Kitten, Pigling Bland* and *Jemima Puddle-Duck*, among others, and you might recognise the kitchen garden from *Peter Rabbit*. Check the NT website for the latest opening times, and to prebook..

★Tarn Hows LAKE
(NT; www.nationaltrust.org.uk/coniston-and-tarn-hows) Two miles off the B5285 from Hawkshead, a winding country lane leads to this famously photogenic artificial lake, now owned by the National Trust. Trails wind their way around the lakeshore and surrounding woodland - keep your eyes peeled for red squirrels in the treetops.

There's a small National Trust car park, but it fills quickly. Several buses, including the 505, stop nearby.

Sleeping & Eating

Hawkshead YHA HOSTEL £
(☎0845 371 9321; www.yha.org.uk; r £29-49; P@📶) This impressive YHA is lodged in a Grade II–listed Regency house overlooking Esthwaite Water, a mile from Hawkshead along the Newby Bridge road. It's a fancy spot considering the bargain prices: the rooms are spacious, and there are camping pods outside, as well as bike rentals. The 505 bus stops at the end of the lane.

★Yewfield B&B ££
(☎01539-436765; www.yewfield.co.uk; Hawkshead Hill; s £90-115, d £100-145; P📶) 🍃 This rambling Victorian mansion is one of the best options around Hawkshead, in a tranquil rural spot near Tarn Hows. It's veggie-only and ecofriendly (all heating and hot water comes from a biomass boiler supplied from the hotel's own woodland), and the handsome rooms are stocked with antiques. The spacious landscaped grounds are a highlight.

★Drunken Duck PUB FOOD £££
(☎01539-436347; www.drunkenduckinn.co.uk; Barngates; mains £24; ⌚noon-2.30pm & 6-8.45pm; P📶) Long one of the Lakes' premier dining destinations, the Drunken Duck is a blend of historic pub and fine-dining restaurant. On a wooded crossroads on the top of Hawkshead Hill, it's renowned for its luxurious food and home-brewed ales, and the flagstones and sporting prints conjure a convincing country atmosphere. Book well ahead.

If you fancy staying, you'll find the rooms (£125 to £250) are as fancy as the food. The pub's tricky to find: drive along the B5286 from Hawkshead towards Ambleside and look for the brown signs.

Getting There & Away

Bus 505 (£4.90 to £6.10, hourly every day) links Hawkshead with Windermere, Ambleside and Coniston.

Coniston

☎01539 / POP 641

Hunkered beneath the pockmarked peak known as the **Old Man of Coniston** (803m), this lakeside village was originally established to support the local mining industry – the surrounding hilltops are littered with the remains of old copper workings. These days most people visit with two things in mind: to cruise on the lovely old Coniston Launch, or to tramp to the top of the Old Man, a steep but rewarding return hike of around 6 miles.

Coniston's other claim to fame is as the location for a string of world-record speed attempts made by Sir Malcolm Campbell and his son, Donald, between the 1930s and 1960s. Tragically, after beating the record several times, Donald was killed during an attempt in 1967 when his futuristic jetboat *Bluebird* flipped at around 320mph. The boat and its pilot were recovered in 2001, and Campbell was buried in the cemetery of St Andrew's church.

Sights

Coniston Water LAKE

Coniston's gleaming 5-mile-long lake – the third largest in the Lake District after Windermere and Ullswater – is a half-mile walk from town along Lake Rd. The best way to explore the lake is on one of the two cruise services or, better still, by paddling it yourself. Dinghies, rowing boats, canoes, kayaks and motorboats can be hired from the Coniston Boating Centre.

Along with its connections to the speed attempts made here by Malcolm and Donald Campbell, the lake is famous for inspiring Arthur Ransome's classic children's tale *Swallows and Amazons*. Peel Island, towards the southern end of Coniston Water, supposedly provided the model for Wild Cat Island in the book.

Brantwood HISTORIC BUILDING

(☎01539-441396; www.brantwood.org.uk; gardens only adult/child £6.20/free; ⏰10.30am-5pm) John Ruskin (1819–1900) was one of the great thinkers of 19th-century society. A polymath, philosopher, painter and critic, he expounded views on everything from Venetian architecture to lacemaking. In 1871 he purchased this grand house and spent two decades modifying it, championing traditional handmade crafts (he even designed the wallpaper). The house was closed at the time of research, but the cafe and gardens remained open, with fantastic cross-Coniston views. The best way to arrive is on a boat trip from Coniston.

Activities

★ **Steam Yacht Gondola** BOATING

(NT; ☎01539-0432733; www.nationaltrust.org.uk/steam-yacht-gondola; Coniston Jetty; cruises adult/child/family £17/8.50/38) Built in 1859 and restored in the 1980s by the National Trust, this wonderful steam yacht looks like a cross between a Venetian *vaporetto* and an English houseboat, complete with cushioned saloons and polished wood seats. It's a stately way to see the lake, especially if you're visiting Brantwood, and it's ecofriendly – since 2008 it's been powered by waste wood.

Old Man of Coniston HIKING

Hunkering above Coniston like a benevolent giant, the Old Man (803m) presents an irresistible challenge. The most popular route is up the east side along the Coppermines Valley – a leg-sappingly steep slog, but well worth it for the views at the top. Along the way you'll pass the remains of several slate and copper mines.

Coniston Launch BOATING

(☎01539-436216; www.conistonlaunch.co.uk; Coniston Jetty; Red Route adult/child return £12.50/6.25, Yellow Route £13.75/6.90, Green Route £18.25/9.15) Coniston's two modern launches have been solar-powered since 2005. The regular 45-minute **Northern Service (Red Route)** calls at the Waterhead Hotel, Torver and Brantwood. The 60-minute **Wild Cat Island Cruise (Yellow Route)** tours the lake's islands.

The 105-minute **Southern Service (Green Route)** is themed: it's *Swallows and Amazons* on Monday and Wednesday, and the Campbell story on Tuesday and Thursday.

Coniston Boating Centre BOATING

(☎01539-441366; www.conistonboatingcentre.co.uk; Coniston Jetty) Hires out rowing boats (£15 per hour), kayaks and stand-up paddleboards (£20 for two hours), Canadian canoes (£25 for two hours) and motorboats (£30 per hour). It also rents out bikes (adult/child £15/5 for two hours).

Sleeping

Hoathwaite Campsite CAMPSITE £

(NT; ☎bookings 01539-463862; www.nationaltrust.org.uk/holidays/hoathwaite-campsite-lake-district; adult, tent & car £9-15, extra adult/child £6/3; ⏰Easter-Nov) This back-to-basics National Trust–owned campsite is on the A593 between Coniston and Torver. There's a toilet block, water taps and not much else – but the views over Coniston Water are super.

Lakeland House B&B ££
(01539-441303; www.lakelandhouse.co.uk; Tilberthwaite Ave; s £45-85, d £60-114, ste £160-185) You're smack bang in the centre of Coniston at this good-value, basic B&B above Hollands cafe. The best rooms have views of the Old Man; the Lookout Suite has its own sitting room and in-room bathtub.

Bank Ground Farm B&B ££
(01539-441264; www.bankground.com; East of the Lake Rd; d from £110; P) This lakeside farmhouse has literary cachet: Arthur Ransome used it as the model for Holly Howe Farm in *Swallows and Amazons*. Parts of the house date back to the 15th century, so the rooms are snug. Some have sleigh beds, others exposed beams. The tearoom is a beauty, and there are cottages for longer stays. Two-night minimum.

Eating

Herdwicks CAFE £
(01539-441141; Yewdale Rd; mains £4-10; 10am-4pm) Run by a local family, this bright and cheery cafe makes the perfect stop for lunch, whether you're in the mood for homemade soup, a big chunky sandwich, or a slice of sinful cake. Everything is locally sourced where possible, and the light-filled, large-windowed space is inviting.

Bluebird Cafe CAFE £
(01539-441649; Lake Rd; mains £4-8; 9.30am-5.30pm) This lakeside cafe does a brisk trade from people waiting for the Coniston launches. The usual salads, jacket spuds and sandwiches are on offer and there are lots of tables outside where you can look out on the lake.

Steam Bistro BISTRO ££
(01539-441928; www.steambistro.co.uk; Tilberthwaite Ave; 2-/3-course menu £24.95/29.95; 6-11pm Wed-Sun) This swish new bistro has become the go-to address for Coniston dining. Its magpie menu borrows lots of global flavours – you'll find everything from Japanese dumplings to Cajun pulled pork and Greek-style *kleftiko* (slow-cooked lamb) on the specials board. Even better, everything is *prix fixe* (fixed price). At the time of writing, it was operating on a takeaway-only basis.

Drinking & Nightlife

Sun Hotel PUB
(01539-441248; www.thesunconiston.com; Sun Hill; 10am-11pm) Famously used as a headquarters by Donald Campbell during his fateful campaign, this trad boozer is a good place for a pint, with a fell-view beer garden and cosy crannies in which to hunker down – look out for Campbell memorabilia. Food (mains £12 to £22) is hit-and-miss at busy times.

Black Bull PUB
(01539-441335; www.conistonbrewery.com/black-bull-coniston.htm; Yewdale Rd; 10am-11pm) Coniston's main meeting spot, the old Black Bull offers a warren of rooms and a popular outside terrace. The pub grub's good (mains £8 to £18), but it's mainly known for its home-brewed ales: Bluebird Bitter and Old Man Ale are always on tap and there are seasonal ones, too.

Information

Coniston Tourist Office (01539-441533; www.conistontic.org; Ruskin Ave; 9.30am-4.30pm Mon-Sat, 10am-2pm Sun)

Getting There & Away

Bus 505 runs to Windermere (£9.80, hourly every day) via Hawkshead and Ambleside. A couple of buses a day go on to Kendal. Note that for most bus journeys, the best value is to buy a 24-hour Central Lakes Dayrider (p577) ticket.

The Coniston Bus-and-Boat ticket (adult/child £19/8.30) includes return bus travel on the 505, plus a trip on the launch and entry to Brantwood.

Elterwater & Great Langdale

01539

Travelling north from Coniston, the road passes into the wild, empty landscape of Great Langdale, one of Lakeland's iconic hiking valleys. As you pass the pretty village of Elterwater, imposing fells stack up like dominoes along the horizon, looming over a pastoral patchwork of tumbledown barns and lime-green fields.

The circuit around the line-up of fells known as the **Langdale Pikes** – Pike O' Stickle (709m), Loft Crag (682m), Harrison Stickle (736m) and Pavey Ark (700m) – is the valley's most popular hike, allowing you to tick off between three and five Wainwrights depending on your route, and covering around six steep, hard-going miles. Allow a good six hours.

Sleeping

Great Langdale Campsite CAMPSITE £
(NT; ☎01539-463862; www.nationaltrust.org.uk/features/great-langdale-campsite; Great Langdale; sites £12-26, extra adult £6, pods £30-85; ⏰year-round; P) Possibly the most spectacularly positioned campsite in the Lake District, spread over grassy meadows overlooked by Langdale's fells. It gets crowded in high season, so it's best to book in advance. Camping pods and yurts available.

Elterwater Hostel HOSTEL £
(☎01539-437245; www.elterwaterhostel.co.uk; Elterwater; s/tw/f £55/63/82.25; ⏰check-in 4.30-9pm; @) Formerly owned by the YHA, this indie hostel, which was once a farmhouse, is near Elterwater's grassy green. Rooms vary in size and scope, but they're attractively decorated. Breakfast is included, and dinner is available on a prebooked basis.

★**Old Dungeon Ghyll** HOTEL ££
(☎01539-437272; www.odg.co.uk; Great Langdale; s £62.50, d £116-135; P 🛜 🐾) Affectionately known as the ODG, this inn is awash with Lakeland heritage: many famous walkers have stayed here, including Prince Charles and mountaineer Chris Bonington. It's endearingly olde worlde (well-worn furniture, four-poster beds) and even if you're not staying, the slate-floored, fire-warmed **Hiker's Bar** is a must for a post-hike pint – it's been the hub of Langdale's social life for decades.

★**Eltermere Inn** HOTEL £££
(☎01539-437207; www.eltermere.co.uk; Elterwater; r £145-295; P 🛜) This charming inn is one of Lakeland's loveliest boltholes. Rooms are simple and classic, tastefully decorated in fawns and taupes with quirky features such as window seats and free-standing baths. The food's excellent, too, served in the inn's snug bar; afternoon tea is served on the lawn on sunny days.

Eating & Drinking

Sticklebarn PUB FOOD £
(☎01539-437356; Great Langdale; lunch mains £5-8, dinner mains £11-13.50; ⏰11am-9pm) Now run by the National Trust, this converted barn is a walkers' favourite, serving wholesome, hearty food and a good ale selection.

Chesters by the River CAFE ££
(☎01539-432553; www.chestersbytheriver.co.uk; Skelwith Bridge; lunch mains £8-15; ⏰8.30am-5pm) Beside a rattling brook at Skelwith Bridge, halfway between Ambleside and Elterwater, this smart cafe is more gourmet than greasy spoon, serving delicious salads, specials and cakes.

Britannia Inn PUB
(☎01539-437210; www.thebritanniainn.com; Elterwater; ⏰11am-11pm) On Elterwater's green, this classic whitewashed inn has been serving ale for five centuries: the current line-up includes brews from Coniston Brewery and the nearby Langdale Brewing Company (our pick is the superbly named Neddy Boggle Bitter). Arrive early to bag a table on the grassy lawn on sunny days.

Getting There & Away

Bus 516 (six daily) is the only bus, with stops at Ambleside, Skelwith Bridge, Elterwater and the Old Dungeon Ghyll hotel in Great Langdale.

WORTH A TRIP

THE STEEPEST ROAD IN ENGLAND

Zigzagging over the fells between the valleys of Little Langdale and Eskdale, an infamous mountain road traverses England's two highest road passes: **Wrynose** and **Hardknott**. In use since ancient times, the old packhorse route was substantially improved by the Romans: at the top of Hardknott Pass, there's a ruined **Roman fort** – you can still see the remains of the walls, parade ground and commandant's house. The views from here to the coast are stunning.

A favourite of TV motoring shows, motorbikers and hardcore cyclists, the road is perfectly drivable if you take things slow and steady, but probably best avoided if you're a hesitant reverser or don't like driving next to steep drops. This is not a road to rush; you'll need to be prepared for plenty of reversing when you meet vehicles coming the opposite way.

To get to the passes from Ambleside, follow road signs on the A593 to Skelwith Bridge, then turn off to Little Langdale. When you reach the Three Shires Inn, the road gets really steep. Alternatively, you can approach from the west: drive along the A595 coast road and turn off towards Eskdale, then follow the road past Boot to the passes.

The fare from Ambleside all the way into Great Langdale is £6.10.

Parking in Langdale can be a problem in summer. There are National Trust car parks at Stickle Ghyll and the Old Dungeon Ghyll hotel (free for NT members), plus one car park run by the National Park Authority opposite the New Dungeon Ghyll, but all are often full by 10am. Local farmers often open one of their fields to act as an overflow.

Wasdale

01946

Carving its way for 5 miles from the Cumbrian coast, the craggy, wind-lashed valley of Wasdale is where the Lake District scenery takes a turn for the wild. Ground out by a long-extinct glacier, the valley is home to the Lake District's highest and wildest peaks, as well as the steely grey expanse of Wastwater, England's deepest and coldest lake.

Wasdale's fells are an irresistible draw for hikers, especially those looking to conquer Scafell Pike.

Activities

★ Scafell Pike HIKING

At 978m, England's highest mountain features on every self-respecting hiker's bucket list. The classic route starts from Wasdale Head; it's hard going but achievable for moderately fit walkers, though it's steep and hard to navigate in bad weather. It's a return of around six to seven hours.

Proper gear is essential: raincoat, rucksack (backpack), map, food, water and hiking boots, as is a favourable weather forecast.

It's worth noting that the pressure of people on the top of Scafell Pike can be pretty intense in summer – save it for the shoulder season if you can to minimise damage.

Sleeping

Wasdale Head Campsite CAMPSITE £

(NT; bookings 01539-463862; www.nationaltrust.org.uk/holidays/wasdale-campsite-lake-district; sites £12-26, extra adult £6, pods £30-85) This National Trust campsite is in a fantastically wild spot, nestled beneath the Scafell range. Facilities are basic (laundry room, showers), but the views are out of this world. Camping pods (some with electric hook-ups) provide a bit more shelter in case Wasdale's notorious weather decides to make an appearance.

> **OFF THE BEATEN TRACK**
>
> **ENNERDALE**
>
> To the north of Wasdale, the remote valley of Ennerdale and its namesake lake were once home to slate mines and timber plantations, but these are slowly being removed and the valley is being returned to nature as part of the Wild Ennerdale (www.wildennerdale.co.uk) project.
>
> The valley is paradise if you prefer your trails quiet. Several popular routes head over the fells to Wasdale, while walking towards Buttermere takes you past the **Black Sail YHA** (0845-371 9680; www.yha.org.uk; dm from £15), a marvellously remote hostel inside a shepherd's bothy, much loved by mountaineers and hikers.

★ Wasdale Head Inn B&B ££

(01946-726229; www.wasdale.com; s/d/tr £60/120/180; P) A slice of hill-walking heritage here. Hunkering beneath the brooding bulk of Scafell Pike, this 19th-century hostelry is gloriously old-fashioned and covered in vintage photos and climbing memorabilia. The rooms are cosy, with roomier suites in a converted stable. There's masses of outside seating, and a choice of dining settings in the bar or dining room.

Camping costs £6 a night.

Keswick

01768 / POP 4821

The most northerly of the Lake District's major towns, Keswick (pronounced kezzick) has perhaps the most beautiful location of all: encircled by cloud-capped fells and nestled alongside the idyllic, island-studded lake of Derwentwater, a silvery curve criss-crossed by puttering cruise boats. It's also brilliantly positioned for further adventures into the nearby valleys of Borrowdale and Buttermere, and a great base for walking.

Sights

★ Castlerigg Stone Circle MONUMENT

FREE Set on a hilltop a mile east of town, this jaw-dropping stone circle consists of 48 stones that are between 3000 and 4000 years old, surrounded by a dramatic ring of mountain peaks.

WORTH A TRIP

WORDSWORTH'S BIRTHPLACE

Set at the confluence of the flood-prone Rivers Cocker and Derwent, the Georgian town of Cockermouth has a major claim to literary fame: it's the birthplace of William Wordsworth, who was born on 7 April 1770 in a handsome Georgian house at the end of Main St.

Now known as **Wordsworth House** (NT; 01900-824805; www.nationaltrust.org.uk/wordsworth-house; Main St; adult/child £8.80/4.40; 11am-5pm Sat-Thu Mar-Oct), and run by the National Trust, the house has been meticulously restored based on accounts from the Wordsworth family archive: the kitchen, drawing room, study and bedrooms look much as they would have to a young William. Costumed guides provide added period authenticity.

Bus X4/X5 (half-hourly Monday to Saturday, hourly Sunday) travels from Cockermouth to Keswick (£6.30) and Penrith (£8.20).

Keswick Museum MUSEUM
(01768-773263; www.keswickmuseum.org.uk; Station Rd; adult/child £4.95/3; noon-4pm) Keswick's excellent town museum explores the area's history, from ancient archaeology through to the arrival of industry in the Lakes. It's a diverse collection, taking in everything from Neolithic axe heads mined in the Langdale valley to a huge collection of taxidermied butterflies. Its best-known exhibits are a 700-year-old mummified cat and the Musical Stones of Skiddaw, a weird instrument made from hornsfel rock that was once played for Queen Victoria.

Lakes Distillery DISTILLERY
(01768-788850; www.lakesdistillery.com; tours £12.50; 11am-6pm) The first craft distillery in the Lake District has made a big splash since opening in 2014. It's located on a 'model farm' built during the 1850s and was founded by a team of master distillers. Its range includes several gins, vodkas, blended whiskies and a flagship single malt. Guided tours take you through the process and include a tasting of the three spirits.

The smart bistro (mains £12.50 to £16.50) is well worth a look for lunch, too.

Derwent Pencil Museum MUSEUM
(01768-773626; www.derwentart.com; Southy Works; adult/child £4.60/3.70; 9.30am-5pm) Only in Britain: a museum dedicated to the pencil, with exhibits including a pencil made for the Queen's Diamond Jubilee, wartime spy pencils that were hollowed out for secret maps, and the world's largest pencil (a mighty 8m long). It all stems from the discovery of graphite in the Borrowdale valley during the 17th century, after which Keswick became a major pencil manufacturer.

Phone ahead to reserve a ticket.

Activities

Hiking opportunities abound around Keswick. **Catbells** (451m) is a family-friendly favourite – a mini-mountain on the west shore of Derwentwater, easily reached via the Keswick Launch.

Further afield, the hefty fells of **Skiddaw** (931m) and **Blencathra** (868m) present sterner challenges.

Keswick Launch BOATING
(01768-772263; www.keswick-launch.co.uk; round-the-lake pass adult/child/family £11/5.70/27.50) Derwentwater is undoubtedly one of the prettiest of the Lakeland lakes, studded with wooded islands and ringed by craggy fells. The lovely Keswick Launch runs regular cross-lake excursions, and rowboats (£15 per hour) and motor boats (£33) can be hired next to the jetties.

Festivals & Events

Keswick Mountain Festival OUTDOORS
(www.keswickmountainfestival.co.uk; May) This May festival celebrates all things mountainous.

Keswick Beer Festival BEER
(www.keswickbeerfestival.co.uk; Jun) Lots and lots of beer is drunk during Keswick's real-ale fest in June.

Sleeping

Keswick YHA HOSTEL £
(0845 371 9746; www.yha.org.uk; Station Rd; r £49-69;) Keswick's riverside YHA is one of the best in the Lakes, with cracking views over Fitz Park and the rushing River Greta. The decor is standard YHA, but some rooms have private riverside balconies. What a treat! Food is available from the on-site cafe.

★Howe Keld B&B ££

(01768-772417; www.howekeld.co.uk; 5-7 The Heads; s £80-95, d £120-140; P 🛜) A cut above your usual cookie-cutter B&B: the spoils here are numerous, from feather-and-down duvets to glossy wooden floors to furniture made from local materials. The best rooms have views across Crow Park and the golf course, and the breakfast is a pick-and-mix delight. Free parking is available on The Heads if there's space.

Linnett Hill B&B ££

(01768-744518; www.linnetthillkeswick.co.uk; 4 Penrith Rd; s £53, d £90-100; 🛜) Much recommended by travellers, this lovingly run B&B has lots going for it: crisp white rooms, a great location near Fitz Park and keen prices that stay the same year-round. Breakfast is good, too – there's a blackboard of specials to choose from and the dining room has gingham-check tablecloths and a crackling wood burner.

The Mount B&B ££

(01768-773821; www.themountkeswick.co.uk; The Mount, Portinscale; r from £92.50) In the neighbouring hamlet of Portinscale, a mile from town, this super-friendly B&B puts nary a foot wrong, with crisply decorated rooms (some with fell views), an Aga-cooked breakfast (including owner Clive's home-baked bread) and even a shepherd's hut in the garden, should you prefer to sleep al fresco.

Eating

★Fellpack CAFE £

(01768-771177; www.fellpack.co.uk; 19 Lake Rd; mains £11-13; 5-11pm Tue-Sat) This on-trend cafe specialises in 'fell pots' – a Lakeland-style Buddha bowl, incorporating an all-in-one meal such as sweet potato and chickpea curry, chicken ham and leek crumble, or braised chilli beef. It's been a big hit, so the owners have also opened a burger joint, **The Round** (01768-773991; www.fellpack.co.uk; 21 Main St; burgers £8.50-10; 4-11pm Tue-Fri, noon-11pm Sat), off Main St.

★Lingholm Kitchen CAFE £

(01768-771206; www.thelingholmkitchen.co.uk; mains £6.50-13.50; 9am-5pm) What a setting this splendid cafe has: in a delightful walled garden on the Lingholme Estate, with a 30m glass wall that presents cinematic views of Skiddaw, plus a dainty old greenhouse. For lunch, expect modern brunch dishes such as poached eggs on sourdough, rarebit, a toasted reuben and (of course) avocado toast.

Jasper's Coffee House CAFE £

(01768-773366; www.jasperscoffeehouse.com; 20 Station St; mains £6.50-7.50; 10am-4pm Mon-Thu, 9am-5pm Fri-Sun; 🐾) A canine-themed cafe serving simple salads, wraps and sandwiches named after dogs of legend (the Pongo, the Hooch, the Huckleberry Hound).

Square Orange CAFE £

(01768-773888; www.thesquareorange.co.uk; 20 St John's St; pizzas £8.65-10.95; noon-10pm) This lively cafe-bar is an ever-popular hangout for its thin-crust pizzas, cheese platters and tapas. With its big wooden bar and packed-in tables, it all feels rather continental.

Morrel's BRITISH ££

(01768-772666; www.morrels.co.uk; Lake Rd; 2-/3-course menu £20/25; cafe 9.30am-3.30pm Tue-Sun, restaurant 6-9.30pm Thu-Sat) The best option in Keswick for a sit-down dinner, majoring in British bistro-style food. Glossy wood, spotlights and glass give it a refined feel.

Pheasant Inn PUB FOOD ££

(01768-776234; www.the-pheasant.co.uk; Bassenthwaite Lake; mains £15-22; 11am-11pm) A short drive along Bassenthwaite Lake is this fine-dining pub. Hunting prints and pewter tankards cover the old bar, which is stocked with vintage whiskies and Lakeland ales, and there's superior pub grub to fill your

WORTH A TRIP

WHINLATTER FOREST PARK

Encompassing 4.6 sq miles of pine, larch and spruce, **Whinlatter** (www.forestry.gov.uk/whinlatter) FREE is England's only true mountain forest, rising to 790m about 5 miles from Keswick. The forest is a red squirrel reserve; you can check out video feeds from squirrel cams at the visitor centre. It's also home to two mountain-bike trails and a tree-top assault course.

Entry to the forest is free, but parking isn't (£2 for one hour, £8 all day).

Bus 77 (four daily) runs from Keswick. If you're driving, head west on the A66 and follow the brown signs near Braithwaite.

belly. A bit old-school, perhaps, but big on the Lakeland vibes.

★Cottage in the Wood HOTEL £££
(☎01768-778409; www.thecottageinthewood.co.uk; Braithwaite; lunch/dinner menu £40/55; ⏰lunch 12.30-1.30pm, dinner 6.30-9.30pm; P 📶) Under chef Ben Wilkinson, this Michelin-starred coaching inn en route to Whinlatter Pass has become Keswick's premier dining destination. The food is seasonal, flavoursome and delicately presented – the Taste Cumbria menu (themed around Stream, Woodland, Coasts and Fells) is an inventive delight. If you fancy making a night of it, sleek rooms survey woods and countryside.

Drinking & Nightlife

Crafty Baa PUB
(☎01768-785405; https://thecraftybaa.business.site; 13 Bank St; ⏰11am-11pm) This tiny craft-beer bar is decorated with a mishmash of upcycled materials – the ceiling is festooned with Union Jacks, old traffic cones, chandeliers and upside-down lampshades – but it's the fantastic selection of beers and ales that's made it such a hit with Keswick drinkers.

Dog & Gun PUB
(☎01768-773463; 2 Lake Rd; ⏰11am-11pm) Benches, beams, hearths, rugs: the old Dog is the picture of a Lakeland pub. Order a pint of Thirst Rescue ale, which includes a donation to the Keswick Mountain Rescue Team.

Shopping

★George Fisher SPORTS & OUTDOORS
(☎01768-772178; www.georgefisher.co.uk; 2 Borrowdale Rd; ⏰9am-5.30pm Mon-Sat, 10am-4pm Sun) Quite possibly the most famous outdoors shop in the Lake District, founded in 1967 and still the place where discerning hikers go to buy their gear (even if it is a bit more expensive than the chains). There are three floors of boots, tents and gear, and the boot-fitting service is legendarily thorough.

On the top floor, **Abraham's Tea Rooms** (mains £6-10; ⏰10am-5pm Mon-Sat, 10.30am-4.30pm Sun) serves a filling lunch.

Information

Keswick Tourist Office (☎01768-772645; www.keswick.org; Moot Hall, Market Pl; ⏰9.30am-4.30pm; 📶) The town's tourist office is well run and the staff are very informed. It also sells discounted tickets for the Keswick Launch (p594), and has free wi-fi.

Getting There & Away

The Keswick & Honister Dayrider (p577) is the best-value ticket for buses to Borrowdale and Buttermere (bizarrely, it's cheaper than buying a return).

555/556 Lakeslink Hourly to Grasmere (£8.50, 40 minutes), Ambleside (£9, 45 minutes), Windermere (£10, one hour) and Kendal (£10.80, 1½ hours).

77/77A Circular route (five to seven daily) from Keswick via Portinscale, Catbells, Grange, Seatoller, Honister Pass, Buttermere, Lorton and Whinlatter.

78 (at least hourly Monday to Friday, half-hourly weekends) The main Borrowdale bus, with stops at Lodore, Grange, Rosthwaite and Seatoller.

Borrowdale

☎01768 / POP 417

With their patchwork of craggy hills, broad fields, tinkling streams and drystone walls, Borrowdale and its neighbouring valley of Buttermere are many people's idea of the quintessential Lakeland landscape. Once a centre for mineral mining (especially slate, coal and graphite), this is walkers' country these days and, apart from the odd rickety barn or puttering tractor, there's precious little to spoil the view.

South of Keswick, the B5289 tracks Derwentwater into the heart of Borrowdale, winding past the small farming villages of **Grange-in-Borrowdale**, **Rosthwaite** and **Stonethwaite**.

Sights & Activities

Watendlath Tarn LAKE
This National Trust–owned tarn is reached via a turn-off on the B5285 south of Keswick. On the way the road passes over one of the Lake District's most photographed packhorse crossings at **Ashness Bridge**. Parking at the tarn is free for NT members, but the road is narrow and has few passing places, so it's more pleasant to walk up in summer (2.3 miles from the B5285 turn-off).

Bowder Stone NATURAL FEATURE
A mile south of Grange, a turn-off leads up to the geological curiosity known as the Bowder Stone, a 1700-tonne lump of rock

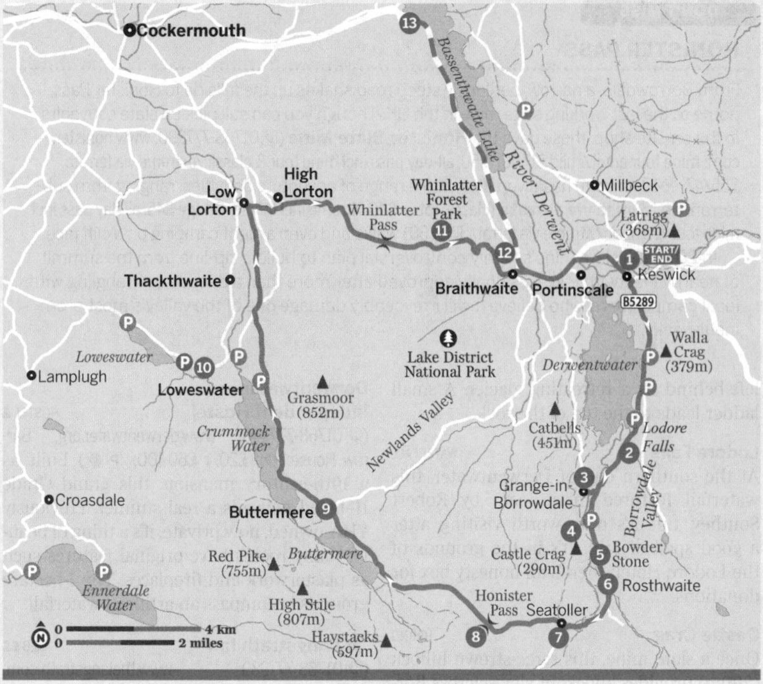

Driving Tour
Borrowdale & Buttermere

START KESWICK
END KESWICK
LENGTH 28 MILES; THREE TO FOUR HOURS

This is one of the Lakes' most beautiful road trips – a perfect day out of Keswick.

Begin with breakfast in 1 **Keswick**, (p593) then head along the B5289 into Borrowdale. First stop is 2 **Lodore Falls**, a pretty cascade at the southern end of Derwentwater. Next, detour to the little hamlet of 3 **Grange-in-Borrowdale**, where a trail leads up the slate-strewn sides of 4 **Castle Crag** (p598), a small fell with great views over Borrowdale.

From Grange carry on to the huge boulder known as the 5 **Bowder Stone**, shifted into position by the long-gone glacier that carved out the Borrowdale Valley. Pootle on to 6 **Rosthwaite** for tea and cake at the Flock In Tea-Room, or continue to 7 **Seatoller** for lunch.

In the afternoon tackle the steep crawl up to 8 **Honister Pass** (p598), where you can pick up some slate souvenirs, take a tour into the depths of the old slate mine, or venture out onto the hair-raising via ferrata.

From here the road drops into the beautiful valley of 9 **Buttermere** (p599). Spot the zigzag peaks of High Stile, Haystacks and Red Pike looming on your left-hand side over the lake, stop for a drink at the Fish Inn and remember to pay your respects to hiker and author Alfred Wainwright inside St James' Church.

Continue along the shore of Crummock Water past 10 **Loweswater**, where you could make an optional but very worthwhile detour to the excellent Kirkstile Inn. When you reach Low Lorton, a right-hand turn carries you over Whinlatter Pass to 11 **Whinlatter Forest Park** (p595).

There are a couple of great options for dinner on your way back to Keswick: the 12 **Cottage in the Wood** (p596) just before Braithwaite, or the traditional 13 **Pheasant Inn** (p595) on the shores of Bassenthwaite Lake.

DON'T MISS

HONISTER PASS

From Borrowdale, a narrow, perilously steep road snakes up the fellside to Honister Pass, home to the last working slate mine in the UK. Though you can still pick up slate souvenirs in the on-site shop, these days the **Honister Slate Mine** (☎01768-777230; www.honister.com; mine tour adult/child £17.50/9.50, all-day pass incl mine tour & classic/extreme via ferrata £55/47; ⏲10am-5pm) has diversified with a range of adventure activities, ranging from subterranean tours to **via ferrata** (classic route £40, Xtreme incl Infinity Bridge £45, all day pass incl mine tour & classic/Xtreme via ferrata £55/60) walks and even a night camping on a cliff face.

In 2019, the slate mine's highly controversial plan to build a zip-line from the summit of nearby Fleetwith Pike was finally approved after more than a decade of wrangling with local campaigners, who believe it will irrevocably damage one of the valley's most prominent peaks.

left behind by a retreating glacier. A small ladder leads to the top of the rock.

Lodore Falls WATERFALL

At the southern end of Derwentwater, this waterfall featured in a poem by Robert Southey, but it's only worth visiting after a good spell of rain. It's in the grounds of the Lodore Hotel; there's an honesty box for donations.

Castle Crag HIKING

Once a slate mine, this scree-strewn hillock (290m) provides knockout views across Borrowdale. It's reached along a mainly level trail from Grange, but it gets steep towards the end and the heaps of slate on the hillside make the going slippery in the wet. There are several side trails on the way; bring a map to avoid getting lost.

From the car park in Grange, it's a there-and-back hike of around an hour.

Platty+ BOATING

(☎01768-776572; www.plattyplus.co.uk; kayaks & canoes per hour £8.50-16) Based at the Lodore Boat Landings at the southern end of Derwentwater, this company hires out kayaks, canoes, rowing boats and sailing dinghies. It also runs instruction courses.

Sleeping & Eating

Seatoller Farm CAMPSITE £

(☎01768-777232; www.seatollerfarm.co.uk; adult/child £9/3; ⏲Easter-Oct) A lovely, tucked-away site on a 500-year-old farm near Seatoller, with a choice of riverside or woodland pitches. Applejacks, the farm's new on-site food barn, serves wood-fired pizzas and breakfasts.

Derwentwater Independent Hostel HOSTEL £

(☎01768-777246; www.derwentwater.org; Barrow House; dm £20, r £60-100; P@) Built as a 19th-century mansion, this grand Grade II–listed house is a real stunner. Previously YHA-owned, now private, it's a thing of beauty: many rooms have original features such as plasterwork and fireplaces. The 7-hectare grounds encompass an artificial waterfall.

★**Langstrath Inn** B&B ££

(☎01768-777239; www.thelangstrath.com; Stonethwaite; d £125-140; ⏲restaurant noon-2.30pm & 6-8.30pm Tue-Sun; P) This simple country inn makes one of the best little bases in Borrowdale. Its eight rooms are snug and simple, with crimson throws and the occasional roof beam to add character, but it's the views that really sell the place. Hearty, unpretentious food (dinner mains £14.25) and ales from Hawkshead Brewery are served in the restaurant.

Glaramara Hotel HOTEL ££

(☎01768-777222; www.glaramara.co.uk; Seatoller; s £64, d £79-128; P) If your budget won't stretch to Borrowdale's plush country hotels, this activity-focused hotel makes a good-value alternative. The decor is corporate (pine-effect furniture, no-frills furnishings), but the location can't be faulted: on the doorstep of Honister Pass, surrounded by fells and greenery. The hotel has its own outdoor-activities centre for ghyll scrambling, rock climbing, mine exploring and more.

Getting There & Away

Bus 77/77A (from £3.30, seven daily Monday to Saturday, five on Sunday) makes a circular route from Keswick via Portinscale, the trailhead for Catbells and all the Borrowdale villages, then heads over Honister Pass, through Buttermere and Lorton, over Whinlatter Pass and back to Keswick.

Bus 78 (£6.40 to £8.50, at least hourly, half-hourly on weekends from July to August) shuttles through Borrowdale as far as Seatoller, then heads back the same way to Keswick.

If you're planning on making a return journey the same day, it's nearly always cheaper to buy the Keswick & Honister Dayrider (p577) than a return fare.

Buttermere

☎ 01768 / POP 121

Stretching 1.5 miles northwest of Honister Pass, the deep bowl of Buttermere was gouged out by a steamroller glacier and is backed by a string of impressive peaks and emerald-green hills. The valley's twin lakes, **Buttermere** and **Crummock Water**, were once joined but became separated by glacial silt and rockfall.

The little village of Buttermere sits halfway between the two and provides a wonderfully cosy base for exploring the rest of the valley and the many nearby fells, including **Haystacks** (597m), the favourite mountain and the last resting place of the patron saint of Lakeland walkers, the author Alfred Wainwright.

Sleeping & Eating

Buttermere YHA HOSTEL £

(☎ 0845 371 9508; www.yha.org.uk; r £29-59; ⏲ mid-Mar–Nov; P 📶) Perched in a perfect position on the Honister–Buttermere road, this excellent slate-fronted hostel (once a hotel) has rooms looking out across the lake. The decor is smart, colourful and surprisingly modern, and there are landpods and tent pitches for al fresco stays.

★ **Syke Farm** CAMPSITE £

(☎ 01768-770222; www.sykefarmcampsite.com; adult/child £8/4; ⏲ Easter-Oct) Set on a bumpy riverside site, Syke Farm is back-to-basics camping, but you'll wake up to knockout views of Red Pike, High Stile and Haystacks. Check in at the farm shop in the village first and make sure to sample some of its homemade ice cream.

★ **Kirkstile Inn** PUB FOOD ££

(☎ 01900-85219; www.kirkstile.com; mains £13.50-24) A finer country pub you could not hope to find. Hidden away near the little lake of Loweswater, a mile or so north of Buttermere, the Kirkstile is a joy: crackling fires, oak beams, worn carpets, wooden bar and all. It's particularly known for its award-winning ales (try the Loweswater Gold).

Rooms (singles £66 to £95, doubles £121 to £171) are quaint; some have views across Lorton Vale.

Bridge Hotel PUB FOOD ££

(☎ 01768-770252; www.bridge-hotel.com; mains £10-16; P 📶) As the name suggests, this venerable hostelry is right beside Buttermere's village bridge. There's standard pub food in the walkers' bar, or more upmarket fare in the smart-casual restaurant.

Getting There & Away

Bus 77/77A (£6.40, five to seven daily) serves Buttermere and Honister Pass from Keswick. For same-day return journeys, the Keswick & Honister Dayrider (p577) is cheapest.

Ullswater & Around

☎ 01768

After Windermere, the second-largest lake in the Lake District is Ullswater, stretching for 7.5 miles between **Pooley Bridge** at the northern end and **Glenridding** and **Patterdale** at the southern end. Carved out by a long-gone glacier, the deep valley in which the lake sits is flanked by an impressive string of fells, most notably the razor ridge of **Helvellyn**, England's third-highest mountain at 950m.

The lake's eastern shore is where the three main villages are located. The remote west side is well off the beaten track, and great for crowd-free hiking around the village of **Howtown** and the picturesque valley of **Martindale**.

The area has been badly hit by floods in recent years: the 300-year-old bridge at Pooley Bridge was completely swept away by Storm Desmond in 2015, and was finally replaced by a modern structure in late 2020.

Sights & Activities

The signposted **Ullswater Way** (www.ullswaterway.co.uk) makes a complete 20-mile circuit of the Ullswater shoreline; it's possible to combine sections of the walk with Ullswater 'Steamers' (p600).

Gowbarrow Park & Aira Force PARK

(NT) FREE This rolling park stretches across the lakeshore between Pooley Bridge and Glenridding. Well-marked paths lead up to the impressive 20m-high waterfall of Aira

Force. Another waterfall, **High Force**, is further up the hillside. South of Gowbarrow Park is **Glencoyne Bay**, where the springtime daffodils inspired William Wordsworth to pen one of his most famous poems.

★Ullswater 'Steamers' BOATING
(☎01768-482229; www.ullswater-steamers.co.uk; cruise 'all piers' pass adult/child £16.80/10.10) Ullswater's historic steamers are a memorable way to explore the lake. The various vessels include the stately *Lady of the Lake,* launched in 1877 and supposedly the world's oldest working passenger boat. The boats run east–west from Pooley Bridge to Glenridding via Howtown; tickets should be prebooked online.

★Helvellyn HIKING
The Lake District's most famous ridge walk takes in the twin ridges of Striding and Swirral Edges, which are spectacular but very exposed and involve some scrambling and dizzyingly steep drops on either side – if you're at all nervous of heights, Helvellyn is not the fell for you.

The usual routes climb from Glenridding or Patterdale. Always check the weather forecast and take necessary supplies.

The mountain can get crowded in summer, especially at weekends, and queuing on an exposed ridge like this is definitely not ideal; save it for spring or autumn.

Hallin Fell HIKING
For a quick up-and-down jaunt, this little 388m-high fell on Ullswater's east side is hard to beat – the knockout views from the top are quite out of proportion to its diminutive size. The easiest way up is to catch an Ullswater Steamer to Howtown and follow the trail towards Martindale Church and the summit.

Sleeping

Quiet Site CAMPSITE £
(☎07768-727016; www.thequietsite.co.uk; sites £25-45, pods from £65, hobbit holes from £110; ⏲year-round; P 📶) Ecofriendly campsite on the fells above Ullswater, with pre-erected tents and ecopods available as well as fun 'hobbit holes' (timber-lined cabins built into the hillside). Camping is very pricey in summer, but there's plenty of space and the views are outstanding.

Old Water View B&B ££
(☎01768-482175; www.oldwaterview.co.uk; Patterdale; d £105; P 📶) Patterdale has several B&Bs, but this one's the pick. It's a simple place focusing on the essentials: friendly service, comfy rooms and value. There's also a little shepherd's hut in the garden (from £85 per night).

Lowthwaite B&B B&B ££
(☎01768-482343; www.lowthwaiteullswater.com; Matterdale; d £100; P 📶) This lovely farmhouse in Matterdale is owned by Jim and Tine, who have filled the place with souvenirs from their travels (they previously ran expeditions up Kilimanjaro). Rustic beams meet Tanzanian furniture in the rooms, and breakfast is copious. It's a couple of miles from the lake, off the A5091 to Dockray. Two-night minimum on weekends.

Howtown Hotel HISTORIC HOTEL ££
(☎01768-486514; www.howtown-hotel.co.uk; Howtown; r £110-210) On Ullswater's eastern shore, this creeper-clad, gabled hotel is a time capsule: charmingly chintzy rooms filled with old-fashioned furniture; a traditional resident's bar complete with ticking grandfather clocks and cosy armchairs; a cute tea room for lunch; and delightfully personal service. Bookings must be confirmed by letter; you'll receive a personal reply from owner Mrs Baldry.

★Another Place, The Lake BOUTIQUE HOTEL £££
(☎01768-486442; www.another.place; Watermillock; r £190-370; P 📶 🏊 🐾) Run by the owners of Cornwall's Watergate Bay Hotel, this lakeshore hotel is one of the national park's most luxurious, family-friendly getaways. A striking new wing has added a wonderful infinity pool and contemporary rooms onto the hotel's original part, which is more classic in feel. There's a restaurant, bar, well-stocked library, lakefront lawns and a wealth of outdoor activities, including SUP and wild swimming.

Eating

Granny Dowbekin's CAFE £
(☎01768-486453; www.grannydowbekins.co.uk; Pooley Bridge; mains £6-12; ⏲9am-5pm) For a filling all-day brekkie, a ploughman's lunch, chunky sandwich or a slice of something naughty and cake-shaped, this cafe in Pooley Bridge is a favourite. The homemade 'gingerbridge' makes a yummy souvenir.

Fellbites CAFE ££
(☎01768-482781; www.fellbitescafe.co.uk; Glenridding; lunch mains £4.25-11.50, dinner mains £12-21; ⏲11am-8pm Wed-Sun, to 5pm Mon & Tue) Beside

the main car park in Glenridding, this cafe is a good bet at any time of day: sandwiches, burgers and rarebits for lunch, rib-eye steaks, battered cod and a roast of the day for dinner.

1863 BISTRO ££
(☎01768-486334; www.1863ullswater.co.uk; High St, Pooley Bridge; 3-course dinner £45; ⏲dinner 6-9pm, bar 2-10pm, lunch 1-3pm Sat & Sun) A classy addition to Pooley Bridge's dining scene, overseen by head chef Phil Corrie, who has a fondness for the classics: think wood pigeon, saddleback pork and Cumbrian lamb, delicately served and deliciously flavoured. It's now open for lunch at weekends (mains £10 to £15).

There are rooms (doubles £95 to £150) upstairs, too, showcasing some adventurous wallpaper choices.

Information

Lake District National Park Ullswater Information Centre (☎01768-482414; ullswatertic@lake-district.gov.uk; Glenridding; ⏲10am-4pm Apr-Oct, to 3.30pm Sat & Sun Nov-Mar)

Getting There & Away

The A592 runs along Ullswater's west side. At the southern end, the road climbs up to **Kirkstone Pass** (which, at 453m, is the highest road pass in the Lake District) before descending via Troutbeck to Windermere.

Bus 508 travels from Penrith to Glenridding and Patterdale (£5.70, nine daily). Five buses continue to Windermere.

Kendal

☎01539 / POP 28,586

Often known as the 'Auld Grey Town' thanks to the sombre grey stone used for many of its buildings, Kendal is a historic town that sits just outside the eastern edge of the national park. It's worth visiting for its funky arts centre and intriguing museums, but it'll forever be synonymous in many people's minds with its eponymous mint cake, a teeth-grindingly sweet, calorific hiker's staple that was famously munched by Edmund Hillary and Tenzing Norgay during their ascent of Everest in 1953.

Sights

Kendal's fine-art gallery, **Abbot Hall** (☎01539-722464; www.lakelandarts.org.uk/abbot-hall), is currently undergoing major redevelopment, scheduled to reopen in 2022.

OFF THE BEATEN TRACK

KIRKBY LONSDALE BREWERY

Established in 2009 high up in the Pennines town of Kirkby Lonsdale, this **brewery** (☎01524-271918; www.klbrewery.com; New Rd; ⏲10am-9.30pm Mon-Wed, to 11pm Thu-Sat, 11am-10pm Sun) regularly scoops awards as the punters' favourite in Cumbria, and has now opened its own pub, **The Royal Barn**. The house specials are fruity, spicy Ruskin's and the malty, bitter-sweet Pennine Ambler, the official beer of the Pennine Way.

Kendal Museum MUSEUM
(☎01539-815597; www.kendalmuseum.org.uk; Station Rd; adult/child £5/2; ⏲9.30am-4.30pm Thu-Sat) Founded in 1796 by the inveterate Victorian collector William Todhunter, this mixed-bag museum features everything from stuffed beasts and transfixed butterflies to medieval coin hoards. There's also some interesting memorabilia relating to Alfred Wainwright, who served as honorary curator at the museum from 1945 to 1974: look out for his knapsack and well-chewed pipe.

Levens Hall HISTORIC BUILDING
(☎01539-560321; www.levenshall.co.uk; house & gardens adult/child £14.50/5, gardens only £10.50/4; ⏲house 10.30am-3.30pm, gardens 10am-5pm Sun-Thu Mar-Oct) This Elizabethan manor is built around a mid-13th-century fortified pele tower, and fine Jacobean furniture litters its interior, though the real draw is the 17th-century topiary garden – a surreal riot of pyramids, swirls, curls, pompoms and peacocks straight out of *Alice in Wonderland*. It's advisable to prebook tickets.

Sizergh Castle CASTLE
(NT; ☎01539-560070; www.nationaltrust.org.uk/sizergh; gardens only £8/4; ⏲gardens 10am-5pm) Three-and-a-half miles south of Kendal along the A591, this National Trust–owned castle is the feudal seat of the Strickland family. Set around a pele tower, it's worth visiting for its 650-hectare estate encompassing lakes, orchards, woods and pasture.

Sleeping

Kendal is low on quality sleeping options, and just as easily visited from Windermere.

Sonata Guest House B&B ££
(☎01539-732290; www.sonataguesthouse.co.uk; 19 Burneside Rd; d £65-90; 📶) A fairly standard

ANDY J BILLINGTON/SHUTTERSTOCK ©

1. Cyclists on Monsal Trail (p471), Peak District National Park 2. Haystacks (p599), Lake District 3. Horse riding, Dartmoor National Park (p323) 4. Surfer, Devon (p308)

2

DUNCAN ANDISON/SHUTTERSTOCK ©

4

England's Great Outdoors

The English love the great outdoors. Every weekend sees a mass exodus to the hills, moors and coastline. Walking and cycling are popular pursuits, but there's a huge range of activities. Getting wet and muddy in one of England's beautiful wild places might actually be a highlight of your trip.

Walking

England can seem crowded, but away from the cities there are many beautiful areas, perfect for walking. You can go for a short riverside stroll or a major hike over mountain ranges – or anything in between. The best places include the Cotswolds, Sussex, the Lake District and the Yorkshire Dales.

Cycling

A bike is ideal for getting to know England's countryside. Areas such as Suffolk, Yorkshire and Wiltshire offer a vast network of quiet country roads, disused train lines and marked cycle routes that are ideal for cycle touring. For off-road fun, mountain bikers can go further into the wilds: the Peak District, the North Yorkshire Moors and the South Downs. For the latest cycle adventure, look up King Alfred's Way, which passes Stonehenge.

Horse Riding

If you want to explore the hills and moors at a more leisurely pace, seeing the wilder parts of England from horseback is the way to go. In rural areas and national parks such as Dartmoor and Northumberland there are riding centres catering to all levels of proficiency.

Surfing

England may not be an obvious destination for surfers, but conditions can be surprisingly good at key locations. Top of the list are the west-facing coasts of Cornwall and Devon, while there are smaller scenes on the east coast, notably in Norfolk and Yorkshire.

DON'T MISS

CARTMEL

Tiny Cartmel is known for three things: its 12th-century **priory** (9am-5.30pm May-Oct, to 3.30pm Nov-Apr) FREE, its small **racecourse** and its world-famous sticky toffee pudding, sold at the **Cartmel Village Shop** (01539-536280; www.cartmelvillageshop.co.uk; 1 The Square; 9am-5pm Mon-Sat, 10am-4.30pm Sun). The small Cark and Cartmel train station is 2 miles southwest of the village and has regular connections to all stations along the Cumbrian Coast line.

More recently Cartmel has become known as a dining destination: some of Cumbria's top chefs have their restaurants here, notably Simon Rogan (often dubbed Cumbria's answer to Heston Blumenthal) and Kevin Tickle, who has recently taken over the Crown Inn.

Rogan's flagship restaurant, **L'Enclume** (01539-536362; www.lenclume.co.uk; Cavendish St; set lunch £65, lunch & dinner menu £159; noon-1.30pm & 6-8.15pm Tue-Sun), showcases his boundary-pushing cuisine and madcap presentation, as well as his passion for foraged ingredients.

He also runs a more relaxed bistro just across the village, **Rogan & Company** (01539-535917; www.roganandcompany.co.uk; The Square; 2-/3-course set lunch £29/33, mains £24-28; noon-1.45pm & 6-9pm Mon & Wed-Sat, noon-2pm Sun), which is now Michelin-starred in its own right. Bookings are essential for both.

B&B in a Kendal-typical grey-stone terraced house, but it's cosy enough, with feminine rooms, floral wallpapers and nice little touches such as goose-down pillows and well-stocked tea trays. Parking is a pain.

★Lyth Valley Country Inn — HOTEL £££

(01539-568295; https://lythvalleycountryhouse.co.uk; Lyth; r from £125; P) It's seven miles west of Kendal, but there's a reason to head out so far – this hotel sits in a gorgeous spot overlooking the little-visited Lyth Valley, famous locally for its damson plums. Rooms are all named after animals, and they're attractively decorated with solid wooden furniture and patches of exposed brickwork.

Eating

Brew Brothers — CAFE £

(01539-722237; www.brew-brothers.co.uk; 69 Highgate; mains £6.50-9.25; 8.30am-5.30pm Mon-Sat) Hipster coffee culture comes to Kendal: with its scruffy wood furniture and black-aproned baristas, it's got the aesthetic down, but its owners are Lakeland through and through – they previously ran a cafe in Windermere. Smashed avocado, eggs benny in various forms and other on-trend dishes are all on offer if you're hungry.

★Yard 46 — CAFE £

(07585 320522; www.yard46.co.uk; Branthwaite Brow; lunches £3-8; 10am-3pm Tue-Sat) This little gem is well worth seeking out. It's down a blink-and-you'll-miss-it alleyway, with a little courtyard and an old whitewashed building with cruck-framed attic dining room. Serves delicious soups, imaginative salads and yummy cakes.

Baba Ganoush — DELI £

(01539-738210; www.facebook.com/pages/Baba-Ganoush-Canteen; 27 Berry's Yard, Finkle St; mains £5-9; 10.30am-3pm Tue-Sat) This Mediterranean-inspired cafe has two identities: it's a soup kitchen all week, with veggie cafe dishes served from Thursday onwards. The food is delicious and generous, from crispy falafels to bang-bang cauliflower.

★Punch Bowl Inn — PUB FOOD ££

(01539-568237; www.the-punchbowl.co.uk; Crosthwaite; mains £14.50-24.50; noon-4pm & 5.30-8.30pm; P) If you don't mind the 5-mile drive from Kendal, this renowned gastropub in the village of Crosthwaite has long been known for its top-notch food. Whitewashed outside, carefully modernised inside, it's a cosy, inviting space in which to dine. Guinea fowl, pork tenderloin, ham hock for mains; blackberry soufflé or elderflower fool for pudding.

The rooms (£135 to £320) are lovely, too: they're all different, but the nicest ones have reclaimed beams, sloping eaves, slate-floored bathrooms and his-and-hers claw-foot tubs.

★The Moon Highgate — BISTRO ££

(01539-729254; www.themoonhighgate.com; 129 Highgate; 2-/3-course Sunday lunch £20/25, dinner mains £16-21; 5-10pm Thu-Sat, noon-6pm Sun) Chef Leon Whitehead has made his bistro

Kendal's go-to address for dinner. Seasonal and creative, his food is full of rich, classic flavours, such as pan-roasted Cumbrian chicken with braised barley and chestnut mushrooms, or roast red leg partridge with celeriac and roast shallots. Sunday lunch is a cracker.

Drinking & Entertainment

Factory Tap CRAFT BEER
(01539-482541; www.thefactorytap.co.uk; 5 Aynam Rd; 4-9pm or 10pm) With nine hand pulls and four keg lines (mostly supplied from one of Cumbria's 40-odd breweries), the Factory Tap is the venue of choice for Kendal's craft-beer connoisseurs. Street food is served in the yard several nights a month.

Brewery Arts Centre THEATRE, CINEMA
(01539-725133; www.breweryarts.co.uk; Highgate) A cracking arts centre with a gallery, cafe, theatre and two cinemas, hosting the latest films as well as music, theatre, dance and much more.

Shopping

Low Sizergh Barn FOOD
(01539-560426; www.lowsizerghbarn.co.uk; A590; 9am-5.30pm) A prodigious selection of Lakeland goodies is available at this farm shop, just outside Kendal. Look for the raw-milk vending machine beside the shop entrance. Only in Cumbria!

Getting There & Away

The train line from Windermere runs to Kendal (£5.70, 15 minutes, hourly) en route to Oxenholme.

Bus 555/556 Regular bus (half-hourly Monday to Friday, hourly at weekends) to Windermere (£6.70, 30 minutes), Ambleside (£7.80, 40 minutes) and Grasmere (£10, 1¼ hours).

Bus 106 To Penrith (£11.50, one hour 20 minutes, one or two daily Monday to Friday).

CUMBRIAN COAST

01229

While the central lakes and fells pull in a never-ending stream of visitors, surprisingly few make the trek west to explore Cumbria's coastline – and that's a shame. While it might not compare to the wild grandeur of Northumberland, or the rugged splendour of Scotland's shores, Cumbria's coast is well worth exploring – a bleakly beautiful landscape of long sandy bays, grassy headlands, salt marshes and seaside villages stretching from Morecambe Bay to the shores of the Solway Coast. There's an important seabird reserve at St Bees Head, and the majestic grounds of Holker Hall are well worth a wander.

Historically, Cumbria's coast served the local mining, quarrying and shipping industries. Barrow-in-Furness remains a major shipbuilding centre, while the nuclear plant of Sellafield continues to divide local opinion more than half a century from its inception.

Sights & Activities

★**Holker Hall** HISTORIC BUILDING
(01539-558328; www.holker.co.uk; adult/child £18/free, gardens only £9; house 10.30am-4pm Wed-Sun) Three miles southwest of Cartmel on the B5278, Holker Hall has been the family seat of the Cavendish family for four centuries. The house was almost entirely rebuilt following a devastating fire in 1871. It's a typically ostentatious Victorian affair: mullioned windows, gables, copper-topped turrets and a warren of rooms. The showstopper is the **Long Gallery**, notable for its plasterwork ceiling and fine English furniture.

Other highlights are the **drawing room**, packed with Chippendale furniture and historic oil paintings, and the **library**, containing an antique microscope belonging to Henry Cavendish (discoverer of nitric acid) and more than 3500 antique books (some of which are fakes, designed to conceal light switches when the house was converted to electric power in 1911).

Holker's grounds sprawl for more than 10 hectares, encompassing a rose garden, woodland, ornamental fountains and a 22m-high lime tree.

There's also a food hall that stocks produce from the estate, including two renowned products: venison and salt marsh lamb.

St Bees Head WILDLIFE RESERVE
(RSPB; stbees.head@rspb.org.uk) Located 1½ miles north of the tiny town of St Bees, this wind-battered headland is an important reserve for seabirds. Depending on the season, species nesting here include fulmars, kittiwakes and razorbills, as well as Britain's only population of resident black guillemots. There are more than 2 miles of cliff paths to explore.

Muncaster Castle CASTLE
(01229-717614; www.muncaster.co.uk; adult/child £18/9; gardens & owl centre 10.30am-5pm, castle noon-4pm Sun-Fri) This crenellated

castle, 1.5 miles east of Ravenglass, was originally built around a 14th-century pele tower, constructed to resist Reiver raids. Home to the Pennington family for seven centuries, the castle is visitable on a guided tour. The architectural highlights are the great hall and octagonal library. Outside you'll find an ornamental maze and splendid grounds, as well as a hawk and owl centre, which stages several flying displays a day. Tickets can be prebooked online.

Muncaster is also known for its numerous ghosts: keep your eyes peeled for the Muncaster Boggle and a malevolent jester known as Tom Fool (hence 'tomfoolery').

Laurel & Hardy Museum MUSEUM
(☎01229-582292; www.laurel-and-hardy.co.uk; Brogden St, Ulverston; adult/child £6/3; ⊙10am-5pm Easter-Oct) Founded by avid Laurel and Hardy collector Bill Cubin back in 1983, this madcap museum in Ulverston (the birthplace of Stan Laurel) is located in the town's old Roxy cinema. It's crammed with cinematic memorabilia, from original posters to film props, and there's a shoebox-sized cinema showing back-to-back Laurel and Hardy classics. Now run by Bill's grandson, it's a must for movie buffs.

★**Ravenglass & Eskdale Railway** RAIL
(☎01229-717171; www.ravenglass-railway.co.uk; adult/child return £18/12; 🚻) Affectionately known as La'al Ratty, this pocket-sized railway was built to ferry iron ore from the Eskdale mines to the coast. It's now one of Cumbria's most beloved family attractions, with miniature steam trains that chug for 7 miles through the Eskdale valley between Ravenglass and the village of Dalegarth, stopping at stations in between.

Getting There & Away

The Furness and Cumbrian Coast railway lines loop 120 miles from Lancaster to Carlisle, stopping at the coastal towns of Grange, Ulverston, Ravenglass, Whitehaven and Workington. The **Cumbria Coast Day Ranger** (adult/child £20.20/10.10) covers a day's unlimited travel on the line and works out cheaper than a return journey from Carlisle or Lancaster.

NORTHERN & EASTERN CUMBRIA

Many visitors speed through the northern and eastern reaches of Cumbria in a headlong dash for the Lake District, but it's worth taking the time to venture inland from the national park. It might not have the big-name fells and chocolate-box villages, but it's full of interest, with traditional towns, crumbling castles, abandoned abbeys and sweeping moors set alongside the magnificent Roman engineering project of Hadrian's Wall.

Carlisle

☎01228 / POP 75,306

Carlisle isn't Britain's prettiest city, but it has history and heritage aplenty. Precariously perched on the frontier between England and Scotland, in the area once ominously dubbed the 'Debatable Lands', Cumbria's capital is a city with a notoriously stormy past: sacked by the Vikings, pillaged by the Scots and plundered by the Border Reivers, the city has been on the front line of England's defences for more than 1000 years.

Reminders of the past are evident in its great crimson castle and cathedral, built from the same rosy-red sandstone as most of the city's houses. On English St, you can also see two massive circular **towers** that once flanked the city's gateway.

The closest section of **Hadrian's Wall** begins at nearby Brampton.

Sights

★**Carlisle Castle** CASTLE
(EH; ☎01228-591922; www.english-heritage.org.uk/visit/places/carlisle-castle; Castle Way; adult/child £11.20/6.40; ⊙10am-5pm) Carlisle's brooding, rust-red castle guards the city's north side. Founded around a Celtic and Roman stronghold, the castle's Norman keep was added in 1092 by William Rufus and refortified by Henry II, Edward I and Henry VIII (who added the supposedly cannon-proof towers). From the battlements, the stirring views stretch as far as the Scottish borders. The castle also houses **Cumbria's Museum of Military Life**, which has military memorabilia associated with the region's regiments. At the time of research tickets had to be prebooked online.

Carlisle Cathedral CHURCH
(☎01228-548151; www.carlislecathedral.org.uk; 7 The Abbey; suggested donation £3; ⊙10am-3pm Mon-Sat, noon-3pm Sun) Built from the same red sandstone as Carlisle Castle, Carlisle's cathedral began life as a priory church in 1122 and became a cathedral when its first abbot, Athelwold, became the first bishop of

Carlisle. Among its notable features are the 15th-century choir stalls, the barrel-vaulted roof and the 14th-century East Window, one of the largest Gothic windows in England. Surrounding the cathedral are other priory relics, including the 16th-century **fratry** and the **prior's tower**.

A striking wing houses the cathedral's **cafe**, with views over the cathedral's grounds.

Tullie House Museum MUSEUM
(☎01228-618718; www.tulliehouse.co.uk; Castle St; adult/child £10/free; ⊙10am-3pm Tue-Sat) Carlisle's flagship museum covers 2000 years of the city's past. The **Roman Frontier Gallery** explores Carlisle's Roman foundations, while the **Border Galleries** explore the city's past, from prehistoric settlers through to the Vikings and Border Reivers. There are some fascinating artefacts on display, including finds from the Cumwhitton Viking cemetery, which revealed a haul of helmets, swords and grave goods. The top-floor Lookout has cracking views of the castle.

A separate part inside Old Tullie House displays decorative art, sculpture and porcelain.

Sleeping

Carlisle's accommodation leaves a lot to be desired. The B&Bs in the centre are uninspiring, so you're better off heading further out.

★**Willowbeck Lodge** B&B ££
(☎01228-513607; www.willowbeck-lodge.com; Lambley Bank, Scotby; d £115-165; P ☎) If staying in the city centre isn't important, then this palatial B&B is Carlisle's top choice. The four rooms are huge, contemporary and plush, with luxuries such as underfloor heating, Egyptian-cotton bedding and tasteful shades of beige and taupe. Some rooms have balconies overlooking the gardens and pond.

★**Halston Aparthotel** HOTEL £££
(☎01228-210240; www.thehalston.com; 20-34 Warwick Rd; 1-bed apt £140-165, 2-bed apt £240-280; P ☎) Housed in the former general post office, this complex of self-catering apartments is Carlisle's best place to stay. While not huge, the apartments are well appointed with small studio kitchens, and the decor combines parquet-style flooring, sleek furniture and neutral-toned fabrics. For dining, there's **Bartons Yard** for tapas and bistro dishes, and **Penny Blue** for light bites and cakes.

OFF THE BEATEN TRACK

HIDDEN RIVER CAFE & CABINS

A piece of Canada comes to Cumbria at this rustic **lodge complex** (☎01228-791318; www.hiddenrivercabins.co.uk; Longtown, Carlisle; cabins from £430), which offers timber-built log cabins that look like something out of *Jeremiah Johnson*. They're very private and quite luxurious, with slate floors, proper bathrooms and outdoor hot tubs. The excellent **cafe** (mains £10 to £15) is worth the trip even if you're not staying.

It's 11 miles north of Carlisle.

Warwick Hall B&B £££
(☎01228-561546; www.warwickhall.co.uk; Warwick-on-Eden; r £128-180) This country house, 2 miles from the centre along Warwick Rd, is a real retreat. With its huge rooms, high ceilings and old-fashioned decor, it feels like staying on an aristocratic friend's estate. There are hectares of grounds and even a private stretch of river for fishing.

Eating

★**David's** BRITISH ££
(☎01228-523578; www.davidsrestaurant.co.uk; 62 Warwick Rd; 2-/3-course menus lunch £17.95/22.95, dinner £22.95/27.95; ⊙noon-1.30pm & 6-9pm Tue-Sat) For many years this town-house restaurant has been the address for formal dining in Carlisle. It majors in rich, traditional dishes with a strong French influence: duo of venison, pan-fried turbot, roast chicken with champ mash. The feel is formal, so dress appropriately. À la carte only on Friday and Saturday evenings.

Coco Mill GASTROPUB ££
(☎01228-318559; www.cocomill.co.uk; 47-49 Lowther St; mains £12-20; ⊙noon-11pm) This shabby-stylish gastropub is a welcome addition to the city centre. Chunky wood, worn sofas and old bits of luggage characterise the decor. There's a good beer and wine selection, and plenty of easy-eating dishes (steaks, chicken katsu, honey salmon and generous platters). The veggie range is good, too.

Thin White Duke BISTRO ££
(☎01228-402334; www.thinwhiteduke.info; 1 Devonshire St; mains £8.95-14.95; ⊙11.45am-11pm) This central 'eating and drinking abode' is housed in a former monastery. The menu is mainly burgers, wraps and gastropub classics – chicken-in-a-basket, battered haddock, pork belly– and there are some inventively named cocktails (the Tom Hardy – 'slicker than Tom in Inception').

Information

Carlisle Tourist Office (☎01228-598596; www.discovercarlisle.co.uk; Greenmarket; ⊙9.30am-5pm Mon-Sat, 10.30am-4pm Sun)

Getting There & Away

AIR

From Carlisle's tiny **airport** (www.carlisleairport.co.uk), 8 miles northeast of the centre, **Loganair** (www.loganair.co.uk) operates flights to/from London Southend, Dublin and Belfast.

BUS

Bus 554 goes to Keswick (£9.40, one hour 10 minutes, four daily Monday to Saturday, three on Sunday) and bus 104 goes to Penrith (£6.50, 40 minutes, half-hourly Monday to Saturday, nine on Sunday).

TRAIN

Carlisle is on the west-coast line from London to Glasgow. It's also the terminus for the scenic Cumbrian Coast and Tyne Valley lines, as well as the historic **Settle to Carlisle Railway** (www.settle-carlisle.co.uk; adult return £26.90) across the Yorkshire Dales (check the website for steam train trip schedules).

Glasgow £19.10, 1¼ hours
Lancaster £13.40, 45 minutes
London Euston £84.50, 3½ hours
Manchester £43.60, two hours 10 minutes
Newcastle-upon-Tyne £17.50, 1½ hours

Penrith

☎01768 / POP 15,181

Just outside the Lake District National Park, red-brick Penrith perhaps has more in common with the stout market towns of the Yorkshire Dales. It's a solid, traditional place with plenty of cosy pubs and quaint tea-shops and a lively market on Tuesdays. It's also the main gateway for exploring the picturesque **Eden Valley** and the remote area around **Haweswater**, an artificial reservoir created in 1935.

The ruins of Penrith's 14th-century castle loom on the edge of town, opposite the train station.

Sights

★ **Lowther Castle & Gardens** HISTORIC SITE
(☎01931-712192; www.lowthercastle.org; adult/child £11/7; ⊙10am-5pm) Six miles south of Penrith, this sprawling country estate, once the ancestral home of the powerful Lowther dynasty, is undergoing a huge, multimillion-pound restoration project. Though the castle itself is to remain a ruin, restoration work is breathing life back into the gardens, which fell into disrepair following WWII. Among the areas to visit are the Iris Garden, the Great Yew Walk, a restored parterre and many hidden follies, lakes and woodland areas. Bikes are available for hire.

A fantasy land of turrets and mock battlements, the house itself was commissioned in 1806 by William, first Earl of Lonsdale, but a combination of chronic mismanagement, debts and death duties meant that in 1957, James Lonsdale, the seventh Earl, stripped it for parts. Practically everything, including all its furnishings and even the castle's roof, was sold. Now an empty shell, it's an atmospheric monument to the plummeting fortunes of one of Cumbria's oldest and most powerful families.

Sleeping

Lounge HOTEL ££
(☎01768-866395; www.theloungehotelandbar.co.uk; King St; d/f from £88/115; 📶) For a town-centre hotel at reasonable prices, you can't do any better than this chic little number. Pine furniture, laminate floors and tasteful tints of pistachio, cream and taupe feel a tad generic, but it's chintz-free and central. The three-bed apartment (£180) has its own mini-kitchen. Breakfast and dinner is served in the ground-floor bistro.

Brooklands B&B ££
(☎01768-863395; www.brooklandsguesthouse.com; 2 Portland Pl; s £50-85, d £95-105; 📶) An upmarket B&B in a terrace of red-brick houses. It's Victorian outside, but inside it has fancy furnishings and posh extras such as White Company toiletries, in-room fridges and chocolates on the tea tray. There's a four-poster room, too.

George Hotel HOTEL £££
(☎01768-862696; www.thegeorgehotelpenrith.co.uk; Devonshire St; d £119-159; P📶) Penrith's

venerable red-brick coaching inn offers rather old-fashioned rooms, plus a quaint bar and restaurant. It's not quite the heritage beauty it might appear to be at first glance – rooms are comfortable enough, but disappointingly bland.

Eating

Pick up picnic supplies at Penrith's lovely old grocer and victuals shop, **JJ Graham** (☎01768-862281; www.jjgraham.co.uk; 6-7 Market Sq; ⏲8.30am-5.30pm Mon-Sat).

★Four & Twenty BISTRO ££
(☎01768-210231; www.fourandtwentypenrith.co.uk; 14 King St; 2-/3-course lunch menu £18/23, dinner menu £20/25; ⏲noon-2.30pm & 6-9.30pm Tue-Sat) Penrith's top place to eat is this welcoming, surprisingly swish bistro. A spacious dining room filled with wooden furniture, big windows and banquette seats, and a flavoursome menu that goes big on country flavours – things such as slow-cooked lamb, potted wild boar terrine and ale-braised beef. À la carte only on Friday and Saturday night.

George & Dragon PUB FOOD ££
(☎01768-865381; www.georgeanddragonclifton.co.uk; Clifton; mains £14-21; ⏲food served noon-2.30pm & 5-8.15pm) If you don't mind a drive (3½ miles from Penrith), this pretty pub in the village of Clifton makes a super stop. It's situated on the Lowther Estate (p608) and sources much of its produce (including game) from there. Fires, benches and rafters make for a cosy setting and the food is extremely good.

For something more upmarket, the pub's sister restaurant, **Allium at Askham Hall** (☎01931-712350; www.askhamhall.co.uk; Askham; dinner menu £75; ⏲6-10pm Tue-Sat), is now Michelin starred.

Information

Penrith Tourist Office (☎01768-867466; pen.tic@eden.gov.uk; Middlegate; ⏲10am-4pm Mon & Thu-Sat) Also houses the town's small museum.

Getting There & Away

There are frequent train connections north to Carlisle (£6.30, 15 minutes) and south to Oxenholme (£7.50, 25 minutes), where you can change for branch trains to Windermere.

The bus station is northeast of the centre, off Sandgate. Bus 104 goes to Carlisle (£6.50, 40 minutes, half-hourly Monday to Saturday, nine on Sunday), and bus X4/X5 goes to the Cumbrian coast (£7 to £11.40, half-hourly Monday to Saturday, hourly Sunday) via Rheged, Keswick and Cockermouth.

AT A GLANCE

POPULATION
2.596 million

LARGEST CITY
Newcastle-upon-Tyne (p615)

BEST BEACH
Tynemouth (p621)

BEST CASTLE
Bamburgh Castle (p639)

BEST WILDERNESS AREA
Northumberland National Park (p633)

WHEN TO GO

Jun–Aug
The best time to discover the region's miles of wide, sandy beaches; can be crowded, so consider visiting at other times.

Sep & Oct
Great for losing yourself in the autumnal landscapes of Northumberland National Park.

Jan–May
The best months for surfing Tynemouth's world-class waves.

Bamburgh Castle (p639)

Newcastle & Northeast England

Irrepressible Newcastle-upon-Tyne anchors England's northeast. Handsome Victorian buildings adorn the steep hills of this former industrial powerhouse. Galleries, museums, bars and entertainment venues now occupy the city's former factories and warehouses; Newcastle's nightlife is legendary.

Newcastle is also an ideal gateway for exploring the northeast's wild, starkly beautiful countryside. Inland, seek out the Cheviot Hills in brooding Northumberland National Park and the remote North Pennines, or explore spectacular Hadrian's Wall, which cuts a lonely path through the landscape, dotted with dramatic fortress ruins. The stunning coastline is the north's greatest surprise, a little-known succession of long, desolate beaches, wind-worn castles and magical islands offshore.

INCLUDES

Newcastle & Northeast England Highlights

1 Hadrian's Wall (p627) Hiking along the remains of Britain's mightiest Roman legacy.

2 Durham (p622) Exploring the medieval core of one of the north's most atmospheric towns.

3 Newcastle-upon-Tyne (p615) Falling in love with this gutsy, artsy, style-conscious and vibrant city.

4 Holy Island (Lindisfarne) (p639) Crossing the causeway to reach this other-worldly pilgrimage site.

5 Northumberland National Park (p633) Exploring the wild back-country of

England's last great wilderness.

6 **Bamburgh Castle** (p639) Returning to the past at Northumberland's most spectacular castle.

7 **Berwick Walls** (p641) Circumnavigating the Elizabethan walls of England's northernmost city, Berwick-upon-Tweed.

8 **Bowes Museum** (p626) Viewing extraordinary objets d'art in the chateau-housed museum at Barnard Castle.

9 **Craster** (p637) Walking along the wild and beautiful coast to reach one of the north's most haunting ruins.

10 **Alnwick** (p635) Discovering the charming village of Alnwick with its storied bookshop and Harry Potter's Hogwarts, aka Alnwick Castle.

History

Violent history has shaped this region more than any other in England, primarily because of its frontier position. Hadrian's Wall marked the northern limit of Roman Britain and was the Empire's most heavily fortified line. Following the Romans' departure, the region became part of the Anglian kingdom of Bernicia, which united with the kingdom of Deira (encompassing much of modern-day Yorkshire) to form Northumbria in 604.

The kingdom changed hands and borders shifted several times over the next 500 years as Anglo-Saxons and Danes struggled to seize it. The land north of the River Tweed was finally ceded to Scotland in 1018, while the nascent kingdom of England kept everything below it.

The arrival of the Normans in 1066 saw William I eager to secure his northern borders against the Scots. He commissioned most of the castles you see along the coast, and cut deals with the prince bishops of Durham to ensure their loyalty. The new lords of Northumberland became very powerful because, as Marcher Lords (from 'march' as a synonym of 'border'), they kept the Scots at bay.

Northumberland's reputation as a hotbed of rebellion was well-earned during the Tudor years, when the largely Catholic north, led by the seventh duke of Northumberland, Thomas Percy, rose up against Elizabeth I in the defeated Rising of the North in 1569. The Border Reivers, raiders from both sides of the border in the 16th century, kept the region in a perpetual state of lawlessness that only subsided after the Act of Union between England and Scotland in 1707.

Coal mines were key to the 19th-century industrialisation of the northeast, powering steelworks, shipyards and armament works that rose along the Tyne and Tees. In 1825, the mines also spawned the world's first steam railway, the Stockton & Darlington, built by local engineer George Stephenson. Social strife emerged in the 20th century, however, with mines, shipbuilding, steel production and the railway industries all winding down during the Great Depression and postwar years. Reinventing the northeast has been a mammoth task, but regeneration continues.

Activities

Cycling

The northeast has some of England's most inspiring cycle routes.

Part of the National Cycle Network (NCN), a long-time favourite is the 200-mile **Coast & Castles Cycle Route** (www.coast-and-castles.co.uk), which runs south–north along the glorious Northumberland coast between Newcastle-upon-Tyne and Berwick-upon-Tweed and Edinburgh, Scotland.

The 140-mile **Sea to Sea Cycle Route** (www.c2c-guide.co.uk/route/C2C-Guide) runs across northern England between the Cumbrian coast (St Bees, Whitehaven or Workington) and Tynemouth or Sunderland via the northern Lake District and wild North Pennines' hills.

Another coast-to-coast option is **Hadrian's Cycleway** (www.hadrian-guide.co.uk), a 174-mile route between South Shields or Tynemouth and Ravenglass in Cumbria following the route of Hadrian's Wall.

Also running coast to coast is the 173-mile **Reivers Route** (www.reivers-route.co.uk) from Whitehaven to Tynemouth via Kielder Forest, the Scottish Borders and the Lake District.

Walking

The North Pennines – along with the Cheviots further north – are considered England's last wilderness. Northumberland National Park (p633) in particular has some fine trails.

Long routes through the hills include the famous **Pennine Way** (www.nationaltrail.co.uk/en_GB/trails/pennine-way), Britain's first national trail, established in 1965, which keeps mainly to the high ground between the Yorkshire Dales and the Scottish border, but also crosses sections of river valley and some tedious patches of plantation. The whole route is 268 miles, but the 70-mile section between Bowes and Hadrian's Wall is a fine four-day taster.

Hadrian's Wall has a huge range of easy loop walks taking in forts and other historical highlights. One of the finest walks along the windswept **Northumberland coast**, between the villages of Craster and Bamburgh via Dunstanburgh, includes two of the region's most spectacular castles. Another superb coastal trail is the 30-mile **Berwickshire Coastal Path** (www.walkhighlands.co.uk/borders/berwickshire-coastal-path.shtml) from Berwick-upon-Tweed to Cockburnspath in Scotland.

Getting There & Around

BUS

Bus transport around the region can be sporadic, particularly around the more remote reaches of western Northumberland. Contact **Traveline** (☎0871-200 2233; www.travelinenortheast.info; ⏲7am-10pm) for information on connections, timetables and prices.

TRAIN

The East Coast Main Line runs north from London King's Cross to Edinburgh via Durham, Newcastle and Berwick; Northern Rail operates local and interurban services in the north, including west to Carlisle.

There are numerous Rover tickets for single-day travel and longer periods; check www.networkonetickets.co.uk.

Newcastle-upon-Tyne

☎0191 / POP 293,200

Against a dramatic backdrop of Victorian elegance and industry, this fiercely independent city harbours a spirited mix of heritage and urban grit and sophistication in equal measure. It's a city with attitude yet filled with culture, excellent art galleries and a magnificent concert hall, along with boutique hotels, some exceptional restaurants and, of course, interesting bars: Newcastle is renowned throughout Britain for its thumping nightlife. The city retains deep-rooted traditions, embodied by the no-nonsense, likeable locals.

Allow at least a couple of days to explore the Victorian city centre and quayside areas along the Tyne and across the river in Gateshead, as well as the rejuvenated Ouseburn Valley to the east, gentrified Jesmond to the north, and, on the coast, the surf beaches of Tynemouth.

Sights

City Centre

Newcastle's grand Victorian centre, a compact area bordered roughly by Grainger St to the west and Pilgrim St to the east, is one of the most compelling examples of urban rejuvenation in England. Down by the quays are the city's most recognisable attractions, including the iconic bridges that span the Tyne and the striking buildings that flank it.

★Discovery Museum MUSEUM
(☎0191-232 6789; www.discoverymuseum.org.uk; Blandford Sq; ⏲10am-4pm Mon-Fri, 11am-4pm Sat & Sun) FREE Tyneside's rich history is explored at this unmissable museum. Exhibitions spread across three floors of the former Co-operative Wholesale Society building around the mightily impressive 30m-long *Turbinia*, the fastest ship in the world in 1897 and the first to be powered by steam turbine. Other highlights are a section on shipbuilding on the Tyne, with a scale model of the river in 1929, and the 'Story of Newcastle', spanning the city's history from Pons Aelius (Roman Newcastle) to Cheryl Cole.

★Life Science Centre MUSEUM
(☎0191-243 8210; www.life.org.uk; Times Sq; adult/child £15/8; ⏲10am-6pm Mon-Sat, 11am-6pm Sun) Part of a sober-minded institute devoted to the study of genetic science, this centre lets you discover the secrets of life through a fascinating series of hands-on exhibits. The highlight is the Motion Ride, a simulator that lets you 'experience' bungee jumping and the like (the 4D film changes every year). There are lots of thought-provoking arcade-style games, and if the information sometimes gets lost along the way, no-one seems to mind. Book ahead at busy times.

Mornings on school days see it filled with groups; visit after 2pm to avoid the crowds.

Great North Museum MUSEUM
(☎0191-208 6765; www.greatnorthmuseum.org.uk; Barras Bridge; general admission free, planetarium adult/child £3.75/2; ⏲10am-5pm Mon-Fri, 10am-4pm Sat, 11am-4pm Sun) FREE The contents of Newcastle University's museums and the prestigious Hancock Museum's natural-history exhibits come together in the latter's neoclassical building. The result is a fascinating jumble of dinosaurs, Roman altar stones, Egyptian mummies, samurai warriors and impressive taxidermy. Standout exhibits include a life-size Tyrannosaurus rex recreation and an interactive model of Hadrian's Wall showing every milecastle and fortress. There's also lots of hands-on stuff for kids and a planetarium with screenings throughout the day.

Newcastle Castle CASTLE
(☎0191-230 6300; www.newcastlecastle.co.uk; Castle Garth; adult/child £8.50/5; ⏲10am-5pm) The stronghold that put both the 'new' and 'castle' into Newcastle has been largely swallowed up by the train station, leaving only a few remaining fragments including the square Norman keep and the Black Gate. Exhibits inside the two restored buildings cover the history of the city, its castle and its residents from Roman times onwards. The 360-degree city views from the keep's rooftop are the best in town.

Newcastle-upon-Tyne

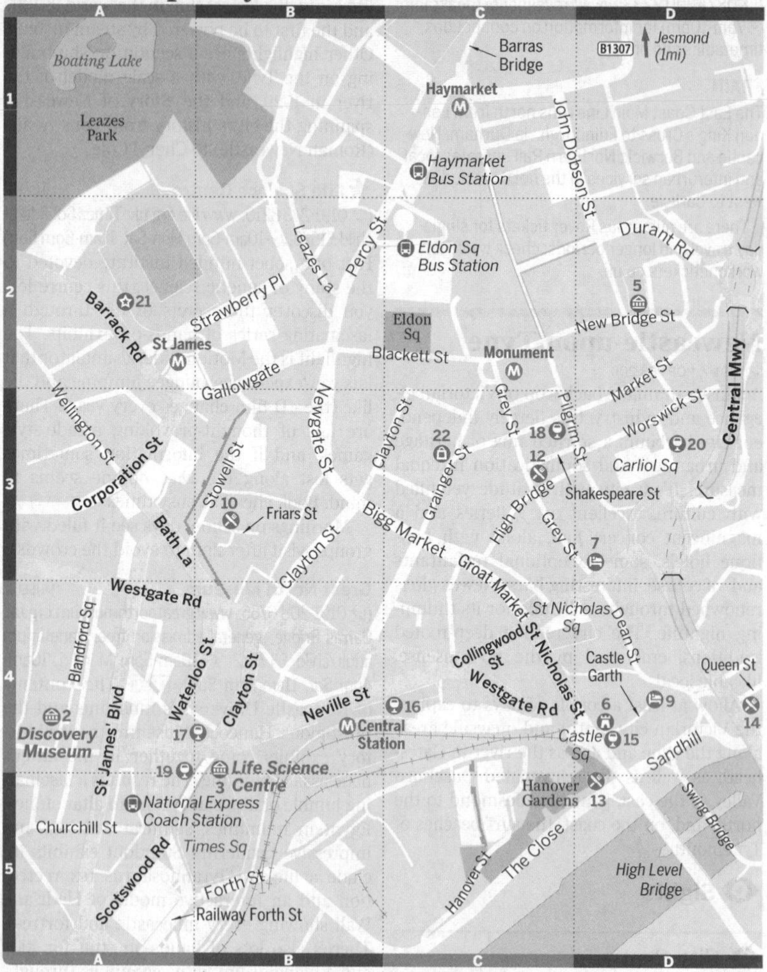

Laing Art Gallery GALLERY
(☎0191-278 1611; www.laingartgallery.org.uk; New Bridge St; ⏲10am-4.30pm Mon-Sat) FREE The exceptional collection at the Laing includes works by Gainsborough, Gauguin and Henry Moore, and an important collection of paintings by Northumberland-born artist John Martin (1789–1854). Check the 'What's On' section of the website for events including talks and tours. Temporary exhibitions may incur an extra charge.

Biscuit Factory GALLERY
(www.thebiscuitfactory.com; 16 Stoddart St; ⏲10am-5pm Mon-Fri, 10am-6pm Sat, 11am-5pm Sun) FREE No prizes for guessing what this commercial art gallery used to be. These days, it's the UK's biggest contemporary art, craft and design gallery/shop, where you can browse and/or buy works by more than 200 artists each season in a variety of mediums, including painting, sculpture, glassware and furniture, many with a northeast theme. There's an on-site cafe, the Factory Kitchen, and fine-dining restaurant, Artisan.

Ouseburn Valley

Now semi-regenerated, Newcastle's 19th-century industrial heartland, Ouseburn

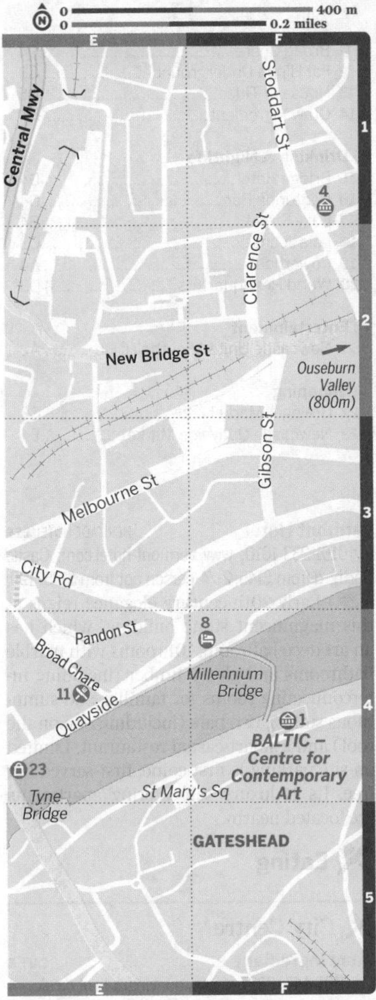

Valley, one mile east of the city centre, has potteries, glass-blowing studios and other creative workspaces, along with pubs, bars and entertainment venues.

★Victoria Tunnel HISTORIC SITE
(☎0191-230 4210; www.ouseburntrust.org.uk; Victoria Tunnel Visitor Centre, 55 Lime St; tours adult/child £8/4.50; ⏲by reservation) Walking Newcastle's streets, you'd never know this extraordinary tunnel runs for 2.5 miles beneath your feet. Built between 1839 and 1842 as a coal-wagon thoroughfare, it was used as an air-raid shelter during WWII. Volunteer-led two-hour tours take you through an atmospheric 700m-long level section of the tunnel. Book ahead as numbers are limited, and wear good shoes and a washable jacket for the limewashed walls; it's not suitable for kids under seven. Tours finish back at Victoria Visitor Centre.

Special one-hour family tours (including for under-sevens) operate during school holidays.

Seven Stories – The Centre for Children's Books MUSEUM
(www.sevenstories.org.uk; 30 Lime St; adult/child £7.70/6.60; ⏲10am-5pm Tue-Sat, to 4pm Sun) A marvellous conversion of a handsome Victorian mill has resulted in Seven Stories, a hands-on museum dedicated to the wondrous world of children's literature. Across the seven floors you'll find original manuscripts and artwork from the 1930s onwards, and a constantly changing program of child-oriented exhibitions, activities and events designed to encourage the AA Milnes of the new millennium. There's a bookshop, coffee shop and cafe.

Gateshead

★BALTIC – Centre for Contemporary Art GALLERY
(☎0191-478 1810; www.baltic.art; Gateshead Quays; ⏲10.30am-6pm) FREE Once a huge mustard-coloured grain store, Baltic is now a huge mustard-coloured art gallery rivalling London's Tate Modern. There are no permanent exhibitions; instead, rotating shows feature the work and installations of some of contemporary art's biggest show-stoppers. The complex has artists in residence, a performance space, a cinema, a bar, a spectacular rooftop restaurant (bookings essential) and a ground-floor restaurant with riverside tables. A 4th-floor outdoor platform and 5th-floor viewing box offer fabulous panoramas of the Tyne.

Sleeping

Newcastle Jesmond Hotel HOTEL £
(☎0191-239 9943; www.newcastlejesmondhotel.co.uk; 105 Osborne Rd; s/d from £38/45; P wifi) Rooms are smallish at this refurbished red-brick property footsteps from the bars and restaurants of Osborne Rd, but they're cosy, comfy and spotlessly clean, and come with the bonus of free parking (though spaces are limited, so reserve one when you book). Wi-fi can be patchy.

Newcastle-upon-Tyne

Top Sights
1 BALTIC – Centre for Contemporary Art ... F4
2 Discovery Museum ... A4
3 Life Science Centre ... B4

Sights
4 Biscuit Factory ... F1
5 Laing Art Gallery ... D2
6 Newcastle Castle ... D4

Activities, Courses & Tours
St James Park Tours ... (see 21)

Sleeping
7 Grey Street Hotel ... D3
8 Malmaison ... F4
9 Vermont Hotel ... D4

Eating
10 Blackfriars ... B3
11 Broad Chare ... E4
12 Fat Hippo Underground ... C3
13 House of Tides ... D5
14 Quay Ingredient ... D4

Drinking & Nightlife
15 Bridge Hotel ... D4
16 Centurion Bar ... C4
17 Eazy Street ... B4
18 Lola Jeans ... C3
19 Powerhouse ... A4
20 World Headquarters ... D3

Entertainment
21 Newcastle United Football Club ... A2

Shopping
22 Grainger Market ... C3
23 Newcastle Quayside Market ... E4

Grey Street Hotel BOUTIQUE HOTEL £
(☎0191-230 6777; www.greystreethotel.co.uk; 2-12 Grey St; d/ste from £49.50/67.50;) On the city centre's most elegant street, this beautiful Grade II–listed former bank has been adapted for contemporary needs, including triple glazing on the sash windows, wall-sized murals and splashes of colour. Its 49 individually designed rooms have big beds and stylish colour combinations; some have giant black-and-white photographs covering one wall.

★ **Jesmond Dene House** BOUTIQUE HOTEL ££
(☎0191-212 3000; www.jesmonddenehouse.co.uk; Jesmond Dene Rd; d from £125; P@) Large bedrooms at this exquisite 40-room property are furnished in a modern interpretation of the Arts and Crafts style and have stunning bathrooms complete with underfloor heating, as well as the latest tech; some have private terraces. The fine-dining restaurant is sublime; dinner, bed and breakfast packages are available.

Malmaison BOUTIQUE HOTEL ££
(☎0191-389 8627; www.malmaison.com; 104 Quayside; d/ste from £75/105; P) The affectedly stylish Malmaison touch has been applied to this former warehouse with considerable success, even down to the French-speaking lifts. Big beds, sleek lighting and designer furniture embellish the 122 plush rooms. The best rooms have views of the Millennium Bridge. There's a spa, gym and on-site brasserie.

Vermont Hotel HERITAGE HOTEL £££
(☎0191-233 1010; www.vermont-hotel.com; Castle Garth; d from £145, 2-/4-person apt from £175/199; P) Early 20th-century elegance reigns at this magnificent stone building, which has an art deco ballroom, 101 rooms with marble bathrooms and glossy timber (including interconnecting rooms for families and sumptuous suites), two bars (including one on the roof) and a smart-casual restaurant. Limited on-site parking is first-come, first-served but free. Its 11 luxury self-catering apartments are located nearby.

Eating

City Centre

Quay Ingredient CAFE £
(☎0191-447 2327; www.quayingredient.co.uk; 4 Queen St; sandwiches £3-8; ⊙8am-5pm;) Beneath the Tyne Bridge's soaring steel girders, this chic hole-in-the-wall has a devoted following for cooked breakfasts (scrambled eggs with white truffle oil and toasted brioche, Craster kippers with lemon parsley) served until 11.30am on weekdays and all day on weekends. At lunch there are soups and spectacular sandwiches (think hoisin confit duck wrap or Toulouse sausage with fried onions).

★ **Broad Chare** GASTROPUB ££
(☎0191-211 2144; www.thebroadchare.co.uk; 25 Broad Chare; mains £9-27, bar snacks from £4; ⊙kitchen noon-2.30pm & 5.30-10pm Mon-Sat,

noon-5pm Sun, bar 11am-11pm Mon-Sat, to 10pm Sun) Spiffing English classics and splendid cask ales are served in the dark-wood bar and mezzanine of this perfect gastropub. Starters, such as crispy pig ears, pork pies and venison terrine, are followed by mains that might include a divine grilled pork chop with black pudding and cider sauce.

Blackfriars BRITISH ££
(0191-261 5945; www.blackfriarsrestaurant.co.uk; Friars St; mains £15-32; noon-2.30pm & 5.30-8.30pm Mon-Thu, noon-2.30pm & 5-8.30pm Fri & Sat, noon-4pm Sun;) A 13th-century friary is the atmospheric setting for 'modern medieval' cuisine. Beautiful stained-glass windows frame the dining room; in summer, tables are set up in the cloister garden. Consult the table-mat map for the provenance of your cod, wood pigeon or rare-breed pork. Everything else is made from scratch on site, including breads, pastries, ice creams and sausages. Bookings recommended.

A 'little monk's menu' (mains from £5.50) is available for kids. Check the website for cookery courses.

★**House of Tides** GASTRONOMY £££
(0191-230 3720; www.houseoftides.co.uk; 28-30 The Close; tasting menus lunch £65, incl wines £130, dinner £80, incl wines £150; 6-8.30pm Wed, noon-1.15pm & 6-8.30pm Thu & Fri, noon-1.15pm & 5.30-8.45pm Sat) A 16th-century merchant's house is now the home of Newcastle's most celebrated restaurant, the Michelin-starred House of Tides. Established by acclaimed Newcastle-born chef Kenny Atkinson, it incorporates premium ingredients – Orkney scallops, Norfolk quail, wild blackberries, black truffles and nasturtiums – in regularly changing multicourse tasting menus. Some diners with dietary requirements, including vegetarians, can be catered for by prior arrangement.

Jesmond

Fat Hippo Jesmond BURGERS £
(0191-340 8949; www.fathippo.co.uk; 35a St Georges Tce; mains £11-16; noon-9.30pm Mon-Thu, noon-10pm Fri, 11am-10pm Sat, 11.30am-9.30pm Sun) Humongous burgers arrive on wooden planks with stainless-steel buckets of triple-fried, hand-cut chips at this local success story. Stinky Pete comes with blue cheese, jalapeño peppers and red-onion jam; 4x4 has a whopping four patties. Veggie burgers include spicy bean; sides span deep-fried gherkins to mac 'n' cheese balls and house-made slaw. There are craft beers, ciders and boozy shakes.

Its city-centre sibling, the **Fat Hippo Underground** (0191-447 1161; 2-6 Shakespeare St; burgers £11-16; noon-10pm Mon-Thu, 11am-10pm Fri & Sat, 11.30am-10pm Sun), occupies a vaulted cellar.

Patricia BISTRO ££
(0191-281 4443; www.the-patricia.com; 139 Jesmond Rd; mains £13-24, 6-course dinner menu £55; 5-10pm Wed-Fri, noon-2.30pm & 6-10pm Sat, noon-4pm Sun;) Named for owner-chef Nick Grieves' grandmother, the Patricia is perpetually busy; book ahead to feast on dishes like raw Orkney scallops with fermented red pepper, and roast quail with chocolate and fennel, all prepared in the semi-open kitchen. Excellent vegetarian choices might include roast leeks with aged feta foam. Many of its old- and new-world wines are available by the glass.

★**Jesmond Dene House** BRITISH £££
(0191-212 5555; www.jesmonddenehouse.co.uk; Jesmond Dene Rd; mains £17-33, 2-/3-course menus £23.50/27.50, afternoon tea £29.50; 7-10am, noon-5pm & 7-9pm Mon-Thu, to 9.30pm Fri, 7.30-10.30am, noon-5pm & 7-9.30pm Sat, 7.30-10.30am & noon-9pm Sun) Executive Head Chef Michael Penaluna is the architect of an exquisite regional menu – venison from County Durham, oysters from Lindisfarne and herbs plucked straight from the garden. The result is a gourmet extravaganza.

It's located at the historic hotel Jesmond Dene House.

Drinking & Nightlife

Central Newcastle can get seriously rowdy on Friday and Saturday nights, especially the areas around Bigg Market (just south of Newgate St) and Newcastle Central Station. Less raucous alternatives include Jesmond's bars and the Ouseburn Valley's pubs, which attract a mellower, arty crowd.

The Crack (www.thecrackmagazine.com) has comprehensive theatre, music, cinema and club listings for the entire northeast.

City Centre

Lola Jeans COCKTAIL BAR
(0191-230 1921; www.lolajeans.co.uk; 1-3 Market St; noon-midnight Mon-Thu, to 1am Fri-Sun) At this Jazz Age–styled bar with chandeliers, velveteen chairs and dazzling murals,

cocktails served in vintage glassware include concoctions such as the Stormy Daniels (Stolichnaya vanilla vodka, sour passion fruit, pineapple shrub and prosecco) or the Shikoku Fizz (hand-batched lychee gin, jasmine syrup, Yuzu puree and tonic water).

World Headquarters CLUB
(☎0191-281 3445; www.welovewhq.com; Curtis Mayfield House, Carliol Sq; ⊙11pm-5am Fri & Sat, weekday hours vary) Dedicated to the genius of black music – funk, rare groove, dance-floor jazz, northern soul, genuine R&B, lush disco, proper house, reggae and more – this brilliant club is one of the coolest spots in the city centre.

Bridge Hotel PUB
(☎0191-232 6400; www.sjf.co.uk/our-pubs/bridge-hotel; Castle Sq; ⊙11.30am-11pm Mon-Thu, 11.30am-midnight Fri & Sat, noon-10.30pm Sun) Dating from 1901, this traditional pub retains original features including Victorian snugs, carved woodwork, stained-glass windows and mosaic tiles. At least 10 hand-pulled ales are on tap; there's also a great whisky selection. Its panoramic beer garden overlooking the High Level and Tyne Bridges incorporates part of Newcastle's medieval city walls.

Centurion Bar BAR
(www.centurion-newcastle.com; Central Station; ⊙10am-11pm Mon-Thu, to midnight Fri-Sun) With floor-to-ceiling ornate Victorian tiling, Central Station's former 1st-class waiting room – a Grade I–listed treasure dating from 1893 – is ideal for a pre-club drink in style.

LGBT+ NEWCASTLE

Newcastle's vibrant gay scene centres on the 'Pink Triangle', formed by Waterloo, Neville and Collingwood Sts, though venues stretch south to Scotswood Rd.

Eazy Street (☎0191-222 0606; 8-10 Westmorland Rd; ⊙4pm-3am) Gay and all-welcoming Eazy Street draws a crowd for its nightly feast of cabaret drag shows, karaoke and DJs.

Powerhouse (www.facebook.com/PowerhouseClub; 9-19 Westmorland Rd; ⊙11pm-4am Sun, Mon & Thu, 11.30pm-4am Fri, 11.30pm-5am Sat) Mixed but mainly gay, this massive four-floor club has flashing lights, a pumping sound system and lots of suggestive posing.

Ouseburn Valley

★Tyne Bar PUB
(☎0191-265 2550; www.thetyne.com; 1 Maling St; ⊙noon-11pm Mon-Thu, to midnight Fri & Sat, to 10.30pm Sun; 📶) An outdoor stage hosting free gigs, a free jukebox, beer-garden-style seating under one of the brick arches of the Glasshouse Bridge and a sprawling expanse of grass with knockout river views make this tucked-away waterfront pub a magnet for locals. Free bar food is laid on between 7pm and 9pm on Tuesdays (you'll still need to pay for drinks).

Ship Inn PUB
(☎0191-2220878; www.facebook.com/shipouseburn; Stepney Bank; ⊙3-10pm Mon & Tue, noon-10pm Wed-Sat, noon-8pm Sun) Spilling onto a small green out front, this red-brick charmer in the Ouseburn Valley has been pouring pints since the early 1800s. Its current owners have breathed new life into its interior, with art on the walls and an excellent vegan kitchen.

Shopping

Grainger Market MARKET
(www.facebook.com/GraingerMarketNewcastle; btwn Grainger & Clayton Sts; ⊙9am-5.30pm Mon-Sat) Trading since 1835, Newcastle's gorgeous covered market has over 110 stalls selling everything from fish, farm produce, meat and vegetables to clothes, accessories and homewares. Between alleys 1 and 2, look out for the historic Weigh House, where goods were once weighed. There are some fantastic food stalls to pick up lunch on the run.

Newcastle Quayside Market MARKET
(under the Tyne Bridge; ⊙9.30am-4pm Sun) Stalls displaying jewellery, photographic prints, art, clothing, homewares and more set up along the quays around the Tyne Bridge every Sunday (except in adverse weather). Buskers and food stalls add to the street-party atmosphere.

Information

Information on the city is available at www.newcastlegateshead.com.

Getting There & Away

Two tollway vehicle tunnels (www.tt2.co.uk; one-way £1.80) travel beneath the Tyne.

AIR

Newcastle International Airport (NCL; ☎0871 882 1121; www.newcastleairport.com; Woolsington), 7 miles north of the city off the A696,

NEWCASTLE UNITED & THE GEORDIE NATION

Few football clubs in England arouse quite the same passions as **Newcastle United** (NUFC; ☎0844 372 1892; www.nufc.co.uk; St James Park, Strawberry Pl; ⏲box office 10am-5pm Mon-Fri, 9am-4pm Sat, 9am-half-time on match days). NUFC is more than just a football team – it's the collective expression of Geordie hope and pride.

Many NUFC supporters refer to themselves as Geordies, a widely used nickname for people from the Tyneside region. There is no agreement on where the name 'Geordie' comes from. Some sources date it to local support for George II during the 18th-century Jacobite Rebellion, or to miners' use of safety lamps designed by George Stephenson – no one knows for sure. The Geordie dialect is now considered the closest language to 1500-year-old Anglo-Saxon left in England.

Wherever the name comes from, the football club that Geordies traditionally support is an essential part of that identity. NUFC plays its football at the 52,305-seat St James Park and, despite fluctuating fortunes in recent years, the stadium is invariably full on match day. They are the ninth-most-successful club in the history of English football, with four league titles and six FA Cups among their successes. Recent successes have, however, been few. The excitement of finishing runners-up in the Premier League in 1995-96 and again in 1996-97 under manager Kevin Keegan and with local idol Alan Shearer leading the line, gave way to some difficult years: they were relegated from the Premier League in both 2009 and 2016.

Match tickets can be difficult to come by, but you can try online, by phone or at the box office in the Milburn Stand of St James Park. Various **stadium tours** (stadium tours adult/child £15/8, rooftop tours £20/15; ⏲tours by reservation) include rooftop tours.

has direct services to many UK and European cities as well as long-haul flights to Dubai. Tour operators fly charters to the USA, Middle East and Africa.

The airport is linked to town by the Metro (£3.15, 25 minutes, every 12 minutes).

A taxi to central Newcastle costs around £25.

BUS

Local and regional buses leave from **Haymarket** (Percy St) or Eldon Sq bus stations. National Express buses arrive and depart from the **coach station** (Churchill St). For local buses around the northeast, the excellent-value Explorer North East ticket (adult/child £10.90/5.70) is valid on most services.

Bus X15 runs north along the A1 to Berwick-upon-Tweed (£7.20, 2½ hours, hourly Monday to Saturday, every two hours Sunday). Bus X18 travels along the coast to Berwick (£7.20, four hours, three daily).

National Express operates services to Edinburgh (£14.30, 2¾ hours, three daily), London (£24.60, eight hours, three daily) and Manchester (£19.40, 4½ hours, four daily).

TRAIN

Newcastle is on the main rail line between London and Edinburgh and is the starting point of the scenic Tyne Valley Line west to Carlisle.

Alnmouth (for bus connections to Alnwick) from £2.50, 35 minutes, hourly

Berwick-upon-Tweed £12.70, 45 minutes, up to two per hour

Carlisle from £8.10, 1½ hours, hourly

Durham from £2, 18 minutes, five hourly

Edinburgh from £23.50, 1½ hours, up to two hourly

Hartlepool from £9.10, 50 minutes, hourly

London King's Cross from £49, 3¼ hours, up to four hourly

York from £18.90, 1¼ hours, up to four hourly

ℹ Getting Around

There's a large bus network, but the best means of getting around is the excellent Metro (www.nexus.org.uk).

Single fares for public transport start from £1.55.

The DaySaver pass (£3.20 to £5.30) gives unlimited Metro travel for one day for travel after 9am, and the DayRover (adult/child £7.80/3.90) gives unlimited travel on all modes of transport in the Tyne and Wear county for one day for travel any time.

Tynemouth

☎0191 / POP 67,520

At the mouth of the Tyne, 9 miles east of Newcastle, Tynemouth is a pretty seaside town with a lovely priory. It's also one of England's best surf spots, with great all-year breaks off the immense, crescent-shaped Blue Flag beach.

Sights & Activities

Tynemouth Priory & Castle RUINS

(EH; www.english-heritage.org.uk; Pier Rd; adult/child £6.90/4.10; 10am-5pm) Built by Benedictine monks on a strategic bluff above the mouth of the Tyne in the 11th-century ruins, Tynemouth Priory was ransacked during the Dissolution in 1539. The military took over for four centuries, only leaving in 1960, and today the haunting, ruined remains of the priory church sit alongside the castle's old military installations, their guns aimed out to sea at an enemy that never came.

Tynemouth Surf Company SURFING

(0191-258 2496; www.tynemouthsurf.co.uk; Grand Pde; group surf lesson per person £30; shop 10am-5pm, surf lesson 1pm Sat & Sun Mar-Nov) For all your surfing needs, call into this surf company, which also provides group lessons for beginners and classes for kids.

Sleeping & Eating

Grand Hotel HERITAGE HOTEL ££

(0191-293 6666; www.grandhoteltynemouth.co.uk; Grand Pde; d/f incl breakfast from £87/108; P@) Built in 1872, this was the one-time summer residence of the Duke and Duchess of Northumberland. Many of the rooms in the main building and neighbouring town house overlook the beach (sea views cost £10 extra); some have four-poster beds and spa baths. Its Victorian-style real-ale pub, drawing room serving high tea and brasserie are excellent. Book well ahead.

DON'T MISS

NORTHERN ANGEL

Nicknamed the Gateshead Flasher, the **Angel of the North** (www.gateshead.gov.uk; Durham Rd, Low Eighton), an extraordinary 200-tonne, rust-coloured, winged human frame, has loomed over the A1 motorway some 6 miles south of Newcastle since 1998. Sir Antony Gormley's iconic work (which saw him knighted in 2014) stands 20m high, with a wingspan wider than a Boeing 767. Bus 21 from Newcastle's Eldon Sq (£2.50, 20 minutes) stops here. There's a free car park by the base.

★**Riley's Fish Shack** SEAFOOD ££

(0191-257 1371; www.rileysfishshack.com; King Edward's Bay; mains £16-27; 9.30am-10pm Mon-Sat, to 5.30pm Sun, hours can vary) Steep timber stairs lead from East St to the beach and this rustic, tucked-away shack. Phenomenal local seafood underpins wood-fired dishes from mackerel wraps to empanadas and mains like cod on puy lentils with pancetta and parmesan crumb, served in environmentally friendly wooden boxes. There's a handful of stools outside and deckchairs spread on the sand.

Staith House GASTROPUB ££

(01912-708441; www.thestaithhouse.co.uk; 57 Low Lights; mains £12-27; kitchen noon-4pm & 5-8pm Wed & Thu, noon-4pm & 5.30-9pm Fri, noon-4pm & 6-9pm Sat, noon-5.30pm Sun, bar noon-1am Mon-Sat, noon-10.30pm Sun;) Opposite the fishing quay where catches are landed daily, gastropub Staith House has a sunny beer garden, a bar made from recycled timbers and an outstanding menu drawing on local, sustainable produce. Seafood is the star (South Shields crab, Lindisfarne oysters, North Sea hake...) but there are also meat dishes such as Northumberland lamb rump.

Reserve ahead for a nine-course seafood tasting menu (£70).

Getting There & Away

From Newcastle, the easiest way to reach Tynemouth is by Metro (£3.60, 25 minutes, every 12 minutes).

Durham

0191 / POP 48,070

England's most beautiful Romanesque cathedral, a huge castle, and, surrounding them both, a cobweb of hilly, cobbled streets – welcome to Durham, one of the most beautiful towns in England's north. Throw into the mix a big student population drawn to England's third university of choice (after Oxford and Cambridge) and you have one fine place to visit.

Sights

★**Durham Cathedral** CATHEDRAL

(0191-386 4266; www.durhamcathedral.co.uk; Palace Green; cathedral by donation, guided tours adult/child £5/4.50, tower adult/child £5/2.50; cathedral 10am-4pm Mon-Sat, 1-3pm Sun, cathedral tours 10.30am, 11am & 2pm Mon-Sat) Monumental Durham Cathedral is the

Durham

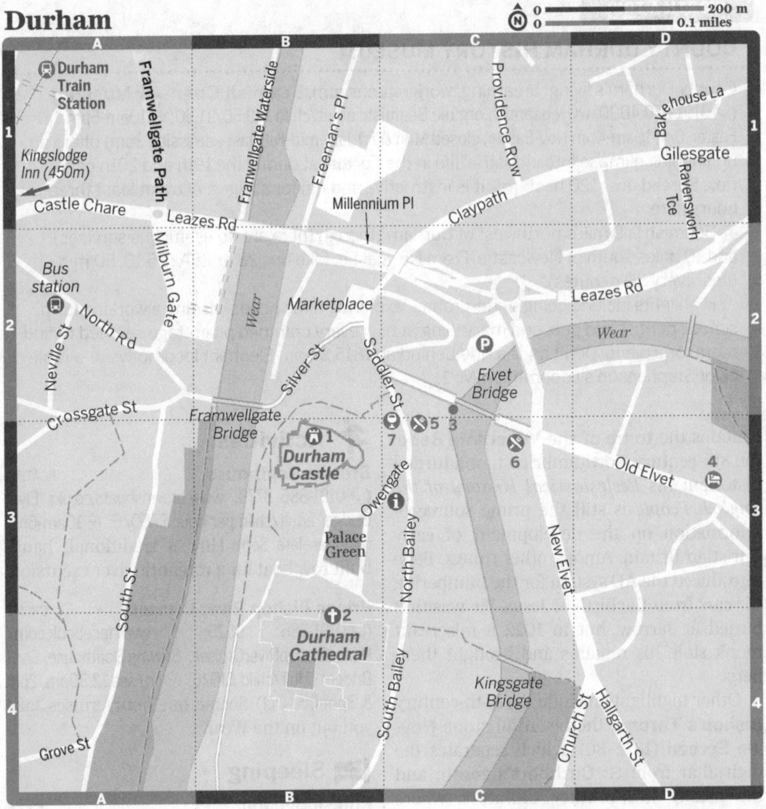

Durham

definitive Anglo-Norman Romanesque structure, a resplendent monument and, since 1986, a Unesco World Heritage Site. Beyond the main door – and the famous **Sanctuary Knocker**, which medieval felons would strike to gain 37 days asylum within the cathedral before standing trial or leaving the country – the interior is spectacular. Highly worthwhile guided tours last one hour. Climb the tower, restored in 2018 and reached by 325 steps, for extraordinary Durham views.

Durham was the first European cathedral to be roofed with stone-ribbed vaulting, which upheld the heavy stone roof and made it possible to build pointed transverse arches – a great architectural achievement. The central tower dates from 1262, but was damaged in a fire caused by lightning in 1429 and unsatisfactorily patched up until it was entirely rebuilt in 1470. The western towers were added in 1217–26.

The northern side of the beautiful, 1175-built **Galilee Chapel** features rare surviving examples of 12th-century wall painting (thought to feature portraits of Sts Cuthbert and Oswald). Galilee Chapel also

WORTH A TRIP

COUNTY DURHAM HISTORY MUSEUM

County Durham's living, breathing, working museum, **Beamish Open-Air Museum** (0191-370 4000; www.beamish.org.uk; Beamish; adult/child £19.50/11.50; 10am-5pm Easter-Oct, 10am-4pm Nov-Easter, closed Mon & Fri Jan–mid-Feb, last admission 3pm) offers an unflinching glimpse into industrial life in the northeast during the 19th and 20th centuries. Spread over 120 hectares, it is instructive and fun for all ages. Allow at least three hours here.

Beamish is 9 miles northwest of Durham (though there are no useful bus services), and 10 miles south of Newcastle. From Newcastle, take bus 28 or 28A (£5.10, 50 minutes, every 30 minutes).

Highlights include going underground, exploring mine heads, visiting a working farm, school, dentist and pub, and marvelling at how every cramped pit cottage seemed to find room for a piano. Don't miss a ride behind an 1815 Steam Elephant locomotive or a replica of Stephenson's *Locomotion No 1*.

contains the **tomb of the Venerable Bede**, the 8th-century Northumbrian monk turned historian: his *Ecclesiastical History of the English People* is still the prime source of information on the development of early Christian Britain. Among other things, Bede introduced the AD system for the numbering of years from the birth of Jesus. He was first buried at Jarrow, but in 1022 a miscreant monk stole his remains and brought them here.

Other highlights include the 14th-century **Bishop's Throne**; the beautiful stone **Neville Screen** (1372–80), which separates the high altar from **St Cuthbert's tomb**; and the mostly 19th-century **Cloisters** where you'll find the **Monk's Dormitory**, now a library of 30,000 books, with Anglo-Saxon carved stones. There are audiovisual displays on the building of the cathedral and the life of St Cuthbert, and a rolling program of exhibitions.

★**Durham Castle** CASTLE
(0191-334 2932; www.dur.ac.uk/durham.castle; Palace Green; adult/child £5/4; guided tours by reservation 1.15pm, 2.15pm, 3.15pm & 4.15pm) Built as a standard motte-and-bailey fort in 1072, Durham Castle was the prince bishops' home until 1837, when it became the University of Durham's first college. It remains a university hall today. Highlights of the 50-minute tour include the 17th-century Black Staircase and the beautifully preserved Norman chapel (1080). Book ahead by phone, or at the Palace Green Library or the World Heritage Site Visitor Centre.

Tours run most days, with additional tours during university holidays.

Activities

Browns Boathouse BOATING
(0191-386 3779; www.brownsboats.co.uk; Elvet Bridge; adult/child per hour £7.50/5; 10am-6pm mid-Mar–late Sep) Hire a traditional, hand-built row boat for a romantic river excursion.

Prince Bishop River Cruiser CRUISE
(0191-386 9525; www.facebook.com/PrinceBishopRiverCruiser; Browns Boathouse, Elvet Bridge; adult/child £10/6; cruises 12.30pm, 2pm & 3pm Mar-Oct) Scenic one-hour cruises take you out on the Wear.

Sleeping

Kingslodge Inn INN ££
(0191-370 9977; www.kingslodgeinn.co.uk; Waddington St, Flass Vale; d/f incl breakfast from £100/130; P) Handily positioned half-a-mile west of the city centre and a quarter of a mile west of the train station, with the bonus of free parking, this comfortable inn is surrounded by woodland woven with walking trails. Its 23 rooms have tartan carpets and furnishings; there's a pub-style restaurant and bar.

Family rooms have pull-out sofa beds; cots are on hand for babies.

★**Lumley Castle** CASTLE £££
(0191-389 1111; www.lumleycastle.com; Ropery Lane, Chester-le-Street; d £75-180, ste from £210; P) Spiralling stone tower steps and creaking corridors lead to richly decorated rooms with heavy drapes and patterned wallpapers, many with canopied four-poster beds, at this atmosphere-steeped 14th-century castle; there are also more modern courtyard rooms. Within the castle's walls are a fine-dining restaurant and antiquarian book-lined library

bar; regular events include Elizabethan banquets. It's 7 miles northeast of Durham.

The 'Castle State Room' is an extraordinary step back in time.

Guests can wander through the state rooms when they're not being used for private functions.

Townhouse BOUTIQUE HOTEL £££
(☎0191-384 1037; www.thetownhousedurham.co.uk; 34 Old Elvet; d from £135; 📶) Each of the Townhouse's 11 luxurious rooms has a theme, from French-styled Le Jardin to ocean-liner-like Cruise and the Edwardian Express, recreating a night in a yesteryear sleeper compartment. A couple of rooms have private outdoor hot tubs. Aged steaks are the speciality of the Modern British restaurant.

Eating

Tealicious CAFE £
(☎0191-340 1393; www.tealicioustearoom.co.uk; 88 Elvet Bridge; dishes £3-7, high tea per person £19.95; ⏲10am-4pm Wed-Sat; 👪) Inside this quaint pastel-blue and white building, homemade cakes (such as white-chocolate cheesecake or ginger and lime), soups and sandwiches are complemented by 24 blends of tea served from individual pots in fine bone china. High tea here is a treat for both adults and kids. It's tiny, so book ahead.

Garden House Inn BRITISH ££
(☎0191-386 3395; www.gardenhouseinn.com; Framwellgate; sandwiches £6-12, mains £11-18; ⏲5-10pm Mon-Thu, 4-11pm Fri, noon-11pm Sat, noon-10pm Sun; 📶👪) Dating from the 18th century, rustic country-style inn Garden House does great lunchtime sandwiches, such as lobster or crab, fennel and nduja (spicy pork salami) and locavore menus at both lunch and dinner (Lindisfarne oysters with wild garlic and smoked chilli, roast Northumberland lamb with hazelnut-crusted beetroot). Its six cosy rooms (four doubles, two for families; from £80/100) have vintage-inspired decor.

Cellar Door Durham BRITISH ££
(☎0191-383 1856; www.thecellardoordurham.co.uk; 41 Saddler St; mains £17-25, 2-/3-course lunch menus £14/16; ⏲noon-5pm) Accessed via an inconspicuous door on Saddler St, this 12th-century building has glorious river views, including from the terrace. The internationally influenced menu features starters such as smoked chicken mousse with torched gem lettuce followed by mains such as salt-aged striploin or sea bass with feta and mint croquettes (vegetarian and vegan options available). Service is spot on.

Drinking & Nightlife

Shakespeare Tavern PUB
(63 Saddler St; ⏲11am-11.30pm) Built in 1190, this authentic-as-it-gets locals' boozer is complete with dartboard, cosy snugs, a terrific selection of beers and spirits, and wise-cracking characters propping up the bar – as well as, allegedly, a resident ghost. Look out for folk-music jam sessions. There's a gin bar on the 1st floor.

Information

Durham's **World Heritage Site Visitor Centre** (☎0191-334 3805; www.durhamworldheritagesite.com/visit/whs-visitor-centre; 7 Owengate; ⏲9.30am-5pm Feb-Dec, to 4.30pm Jan) is in the shadow of the castle.

Comprehensive info on the city and county is available online at www.thisisdurham.com.

Getting There & Away

BUS

The bus station is on North Rd, on the western side of the river.

Destinations include:

Hartlepool Bus 57A; £7.80, one hour, two hourly
London National Express; £30, 6¾ hours, two daily
Newcastle Bus 21, X12 and X21; £4.80, 1¼ hours, at least four hourly

LOCAL KNOWLEDGE

A GOURMET FARM SHOP

It's worth stopping off 12 miles northwest of Durham en route to Northumberland National Park and Hadrian's Wall at **Knitsley Farm Shop & Cafe** (☎01207-592059; www.knitsleyfarmshop.co.uk; East Knitsley Grange Farm, Knitsley; dishes £5-14; ⏲shop 10am-5pm Tue-Sat, to 4pm Sun, cafe 10am-5pm Tue-Fri, 9.30am-5pm Sat, 9.30am-4pm Sun) to stock up on its incredible cheeses, meats, fruits, veggies, homemade sweets, biscuits, cakes and breads. It's even better if you can make time to dine at its wonderful cafe on fresh-as-it-gets soups, farmyard sausages, and pulled-pork and crackling baps.

TRAIN

The East Coast Main Line provides speedy connections to destinations including:

Edinburgh from £13.10, 1¾ hours, hourly

London King's Cross from £38.50, three hours, hourly

Newcastle from £2, 18 minutes, five hourly

York from £7.80, 50 minutes, four hourly

Barnard Castle

☎01833 / POP 5500

The charming market town of Barnard Castle, better known by locals as 'Barney', is a traditionalist's dream, full of antique and craft shops, and atmospheric old pubs. It's a wonderful setting for the town's twin draws: a daunting ruined castle that gives the town its name, and, improbably, an extraordinary French chateau.

Sights

★Bowes Museum MUSEUM

(☎01833-690606; www.thebowesmuseum.org.uk; Newgate; adult/child/family £14/5/30; ⏲10am-5pm) A monumental chateau half a mile east of the centre contains the lavishly furnished Bowes Museum. Funded by 19th-century industrialist John Bowes, and opened in 1892, this brainchild of his Parisian actress wife, Josephine, was built by French architect Jules Pellechet to display a collection the Bowes had travelled the world to assemble. Serious masterpieces share space with the marvellous 18th-century mechanical silver swan, which performs every day at 2pm. If you miss it, a film shows it in action.

Look for works by Canaletto, El Greco and Goya as well as 55 paintings by Josephine herself. Among the 15,000 other objets d'art are dresses from the 17th century through to the 1970s as part of an exhibit on textiles through the ages, and clocks, watches and tableware in gold and silver in the precious-metals section. It also houses finds unearthed from the nearby Binchester Roman Fort. Tickets are valid for a year, so you can come and go as you please.

Local suppliers provide ingredients for its outstanding cafe. Afterwards, stroll through its formal parterre garden and woodland; there are play areas for kids and events including markets and theatre performances.

Barnard Castle RUINS

(EH; ☎01833-638212; www.english-heritage.org.uk; Scar Top; adult/child £6.90/4.10; ⏲10am-6pm daily Easter-Sep, to 5pm daily Oct, 10am-4pm Sat & Sun Nov-Easter) Built on a cliff above the River Tees by Guy de Bailleul and rebuilt around 1150, Barnard Castle was partly dismantled some four centuries later, but its ruins still manage to cover two very impressive hectares, and there are wonderful river views. Inhale the sensory garden.

Raby Castle CASTLE

(☎01833-660202; www.rabycastle.com; Staindrop; castle, gardens & park adult/child £13/6.50, gardens & park only £8/4; ⏲11am-4pm Tue-Sun Jul & Aug, 11am-4pm Wed-Sun late Mar-Jun & Sep) Sprawling Raby Castle was a stronghold of the Catholic Neville family until it engaged in ill-judged plotting (the 'Rising of the North') against the Protestant Queen Elizabeth in 1569. Most of the interior dates from the 18th and 19th centuries, but the exterior remains true to the original design, built around a courtyard and surrounded by a moat. It's 6.8 miles northeast of Barnard Castle; take bus 85A (£3.30, 15 minutes, eight daily Monday to Friday, six Saturday and Sunday).

The stables now house tearooms. There are beautiful formal gardens and a deer park; you can hire bikes to explore.

Sleeping & Eating

Old Well Inn INN ££

(☎01833-690130; www.theoldwellinn.co.uk; 21 The Bank; s/d incl breakfast from £65/90; 📶) Built over a huge concealed well, this old coaching inn has 10 enormous rooms. No 9 is the most impressive with its own private entrance, flagstone floors and a bath. The pub has regional ales on tap that you can sip in the leafy beer garden in fine weather.

Cross Lanes Organic Farm Shop CAFE £

(☎01833-630619; www.crosslanesorganics.co.uk; Cross Lanes, Barnard Castle; sandwiches from £5, mains £10-14; ⏲9am-3.30pm Mon, Wed & Thu, 9am-4pm Fri & Sat, 10am-4pm Sun; 📶👪) 🌿 Sheep graze on the grass-covered roof of this award-winning farm shop and cafe 1.5 miles south of Barnard Castle, right by the A66. The cavernous interior brims with all-organic produce; breakfasts (home-cured bacon, homemade sausages, and eggs from the farm's chickens) segue into lunches including gourmet sandwiches, steak or veggie burgers and wood-fired pizzas, and 'rustic afternoon tea'.

★**Raby Hunt** GASTRONOMY £££

(☎01325-374237; www.rabyhuntrestaurant.co.uk; Summerhouse, Darlington; tasting menu £200, chef's table £240; ⊙6-9.30pm Wed-Sat, noon-2pm Sun; 📶) A two-century-old, ivy-clad drovers' inn 11 miles east of Barnard Castle is now the staging post for gastronomic expeditions by self-taught chef James Close, who received his first Michelin star in 2012 and second in 2017. Tasting menus (no à la carte) typically feature 16 or more intricate courses, such as in-the-shell razor clams with brown shrimp. Reserve weeks ahead.

In the former stables are three luxurious guest rooms (doubles including breakfast from £180).

★**Bay Horse** GASTROPUB £££

(☎01325-720663; www.thebayhorsehurworth.com; The Green, Hurworth-on-Tees; mains dinner £22-33, 2-/3-course set lunch menu from £17/21; ⊙kitchen noon-2.30pm & 6-9.30pm Mon-Sat, noon-4pm Sun, bar 11am-11pm Mon-Sat, noon-10.30pm Sun; 🖉) It's worth travelling 19 miles east of Barnard Castle to this 15th-century coaching inn in the pretty riverside village of Hurworth-on-Tees. Book ahead so you don't miss exceptional dishes such as monkfish wrapped in Parma ham, mint raita, prawn risotto, apple dressing, charred cucumber, sweet potato puree, and curried granola. Wild garlic, leeks, nettles and herbs are foraged nearby.

Getting There & Around

Barnard Castle is poorly served by public transport and several of its key draws are outside the town so you really need your own wheels to get here and explore.

Hadrian's Wall

Named in honour of the emperor who ordered it built, Hadrian's Wall was one of Rome's greatest engineering projects. This enormous 73-mile-long wall was built between 122 and 128 CE to separate Romans and Scottish Picts. Today, the sections that remain evoke Roman ambition and tenacity. When completed, the mammoth structure ran across the island's narrow neck, from the Solway Firth in the west almost to the mouth of the Tyne in the east.

Every Roman mile (0.95 miles) there was a gateway guarded by a small fort (milecastle) and between each milecastle were two observation turrets. Milecastles are numbered right across the country, starting with Milecastle 0 at Wallsend – where you can visit the wall's last stronghold, Segedunum – and ending with Milecastle 80 at Bowness-on-Solway.

A series of forts were developed as bases some distance south (and may predate the wall), and a further 16 lie astride it.

Preserved remains of forts and garrisons and intriguing museums punctuate the route, along with sections of the wall you can freely access.

Activities

The **Hadrian's Wall Path** (www.nationaltrail.co.uk/en_GB/trails/hadrians-wall-path) is an 84-mile national trail that runs the length of the wall from Wallsend in the east to Bowness-on-Solway in the west. The entire route should take about seven days on foot, giving plenty of time to explore the rich archaeological heritage along the way.

Information

There are tourist offices in **Hexham** (☎01670-620450; www.visitnorthumberland.com; Queen's Hall, Beaumont St, Hexham; ⊙9am-5pm Mon-Fri, 9.30am-5pm Sat), Haltwhistle (p633) and Corbridge (p629). The Walltown Visitor Centre (p634), aka the Northumberland National Park Visitor Centre, is located at Greenhead. Tourist information is also available from the **Sill** (☎01434-341200; www.thesill.org.uk; Military Rd, Once Brewed; ⊙10am-5pm Apr-early Nov), aka the National Landscape Discovery Centre, at Once Brewed.

Hadrian's Wall Country (www.hadrianswallcountry.co.uk) is the official portal for the entire area.

HEXHAM ABBEY

Bustling Hexham is a handsome if somewhat scuffed market town centred on its grand Augustinian **abbey** (☎01434-602031; www.hexhamabbey.org.uk; Beaumont St, Hexham; by donation; ⊙10am-4pm), a marvellous example of Early English architecture. It cleverly escaped the Dissolution of 1537 by rebranding as Hexham's parish church, a role it still has today. The highlight is the 7th-century Saxon crypt, the only surviving element of St Wilfrid's Church, built with inscribed stones from Corstopitum in 674.

Hadrian's Wall & Northumberland National Park

Getting There & Around

BUS

The AD122 Hadrian's Wall bus (five daily, Easter to September) is a hail-and-ride service that runs between Hexham and Carlisle, with one bus a day starting and ending at Newcastle's Central Station; not all services cover the entire route. Bikes can be taken aboard AD122 buses, but space is limited.

Bus 10 links Newcastle with Hexham (£5.50,1½ hours, every 30 minutes Monday to Saturday, hourly on Sunday).

West of Hexham, the wall runs parallel to the A69, which connects Carlisle and Newcastle. Buses X84 and X85 run along the A69 every 30 minutes, passing 2 to 3 miles south of the main sites.

All these services except the X84 and X85 can be used with the **Hadrian's Wall Rover Ticket** (one day adult/child £12.50/6.50, three days £25/13). Show your Rover Ticket to get 10% off admission to all museums and attractions.

The **Hadrian's Frontier Ticket** (one day adult/child £16/8, three day £32/16) provides unlimited transport on all buses throughout Northumberland.

Both tickets are available from bus drivers and tourist offices, where you can also get timetables.

CAR & MOTORCYCLE

Your own wheels are the easiest way to get around, with one fort or garrison usually just a short hop from the next. Parking costs £10 per day; tickets are valid at all sites along the wall.

The B6318 follows the course of the wall from the outskirts of Newcastle to Birdoswald. The main A69 road and the railway line follow 3 or 4 miles to the south.

TRAIN

The railway line between Newcastle and Carlisle (Tyne Valley Line; from £7.50, 1½ hours, hourly) has stations at Corbridge, Hexham, Haydon Bridge, Bardon Mill, Haltwhistle and Brampton, but be aware that not all services stop at all stations.

Corbridge

01434 / POP 3670

Above a green-banked curve in the Tyne, Corbridge's shady, cobbled streets are lined with old-fashioned shops and pubs. Inhabited since Saxon times when there was a substantial monastery here, many of the village's charming buildings feature stones nicked from nearby Corstopitum.

Sights

Corbridge Roman Site & Museum HISTORIC SITE
(EH; www.english-heritage.org.uk; Corchester Lane; adult/child £9/5.40; 10am-5pm) What's left of the Roman garrison town of Corstopitum lies about half a mile west of Market Pl on Dere St, once the main road from York to Scotland. It's the oldest fortified site in the area, predating the wall itself by some 40 years. Most of what you see here, though, dates from around 200 CE, when the fort had developed into a civilian settlement and was the main base along the wall.

You get a sense of the domestic heart of the town from the visible remains. Revamped in 2018, the superb museum here displays artefacts unearthed at the site, including Roman sculpture and carvings such as the amazing 3rd-century Corbridge Lion.

Sleeping & Eating

★Lord Crewe Arms INN £££
(01434-677100; www.lordcrewearmsblanchland.co.uk; The Square, Blanchland; d from £175; P) An 1165-built abbot's house in the honey-stone North Pennines village of Blanchland, 11 miles south of Corbridge, shelters some of this entrancing inn's 21 rooms, while others are located in former miners' cottages. Rates almost halve outside high season. Non-guests can dine on outstanding Modern British fare and drink in the vaulted bar, the Crypt, with a monumental medieval fireplace.

★Corbridge Larder DELI £
(01434-632948; www.corbridgelarder.co.uk; 18 Hill St; mains £4-10; 9am-5pm Mon-Sat, 10am-4pm Sun) Gourmet picnic fare at this fabulous deli includes bread, over 100 varieties of cheese, chutneys, cakes, chocolates and wine (you can get hampers made up) as well as made-to-order sandwiches, pies, quiches, tarts, and antipasti and meze delicacies. Upstairs from the wonderland of provisions there's a small sit-down cafe serving dishes such as Moroccan spiced chicken.

Information

Tourist Office (01434-632815; www.visitnorthumberland.com; Hill St; 10am-4.30pm Mon-Sat Apr-Sep, 11am-4pm Wed, Fri & Sat Oct-Mar) Occupies a corner of the library.

Getting There & Away

Buses X84 and X85 between Newcastle (£5.50, 45 minutes, hourly) and Carlisle (£8.10, 2¼ hours, hourly) come through Corbridge, as does bus 10 from Newcastle (£5.50, one hour, every 30 minutes Monday to Saturday, hourly Sunday) to Hexham (£2.40, 12 minutes, every 30 minutes Monday to Saturday, hourly Sunday). At Hexham you can connect with the Hadrian's Wall bus AD122 in summer or bus 185 year-round.

Corbridge is also on the railway line between Newcastle (£6.70, 45 minutes, hourly) and Carlisle (£15.80, 1½ hours, hourly).

Haltwhistle & Around

01434 / POP 3810

The village of Haltwhistle, little more than two intersecting streets, has more key Hadrian's Wall sights in its surrounds than anywhere else along the wall, but tourist infrastructure here is surprisingly (some would say refreshingly) underdeveloped.

Haltwhistle claims to be the geographic centre of the British mainland, although the jury is still out.

Sights

★Housesteads Roman Fort & Museum HISTORIC SITE
(EH; 01434-344363; www.english-heritage.org.uk; Haydon Bridge; adult/child £9/5.40; 10am-6pm Apr-Sep, to 5pm Oct, to 4pm Nov-Mar) The most dramatic site of Hadrian's Wall – and the best-preserved Roman fort in the whole country – is at Housesteads, 4 miles north of Bardon Mill on the B6318, and 6.5 miles northeast of Haltwhistle. Set high on a ridge and covering 2 hectares, from here you can survey the moors of Northumberland National Park and the snaking wall, with a sense of awe at the landscape and the aura of the Roman lookouts.

Up to 800 troops were based at Housesteads at any one time. Its remains include an impressive hospital, granaries with a carefully worked out ventilation system, and barrack blocks. Most memorable are the

Hadrian's Wall

ROME'S FINAL FRONTIER

Of all Britain's Roman ruins, Emperor Hadrian's 2nd-century wall, cutting across northern England from the Irish Sea to the North Sea, is by far the most spectacular; Unesco awarded it World Heritage status in 1987.

We've picked out the highlights, one of which is the prime remaining Roman fort on the wall, Housesteads, which we've reconstructed here.

GANNET77 / GETTY IMAGES ©

Housesteads' Granaries

Nothing like the clever underground ventilation system, which kept vital supplies of grain dry in Northumberland's damp and drizzly climate, would be seen again in these parts for 1500 years.

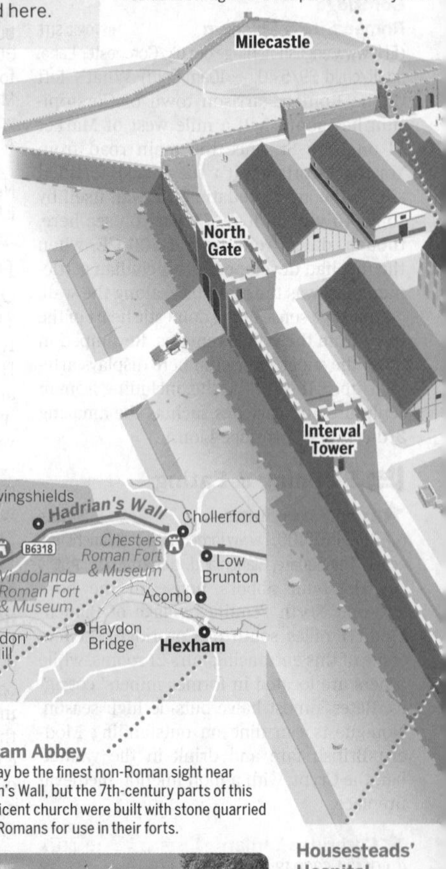

STEPHEN DOREY / GETTY IMAGES ©

Birdoswald Roman Fort

Explore the longest intact stretch of the wall, scramble over the remains of a large fort then head indoors to wonder at a full-scale model of the wall at its zenith. Great fun for the kids.

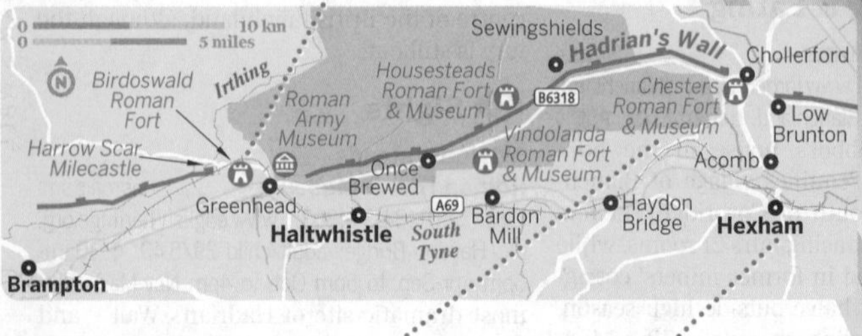

Chesters Roman Fort

Built to keep watch over a bridge spanning the River North Tyne, Britain's best-preserved Roman cavalry fort has a terrific bathhouse, essential if you have months of nippy northern winter ahead.

Hexham Abbey

This may be the finest non-Roman sight near Hadrian's Wall, but the 7th-century parts of this magnificent church were built with stone quarried by the Romans for use in their forts.

STEPHAN GOERLICH / GETTY IMAGES ©

VERITYJOHNSON / SHUTTERSTOCK ©

Housesteads' Hospital

Operations performed at the hospital would have been surprisingly effective, even without anaesthetics; religious rituals and prayers to Aesculapius, the Roman god of healing, were possibly less helpful for a hernia or appendicitis.

ALISON ROSCOE / GETTY IMAGES ©

Housesteads' Latrines
Communal toilets were the norm in Roman times and Housesteads' are remarkably well preserved – fortunately no traces remain of the vinegar-soaked sponges that were used instead of toilet paper.

QUICK WALL FACTS & FIGURES

Latin name Vallum Aelium

Length 73.5 miles (80 Roman miles)

Construction date AD 122–128

Manpower for construction
Three legions (around 16,000 men)

Features At least 16 forts, 80 milecastles, 160 turrets

Did you know Hadrian's wasn't the only Roman wall in Britain – the Antonine Wall was built across what is now central Scotland in the AD 140s, but it was abandoned soon after.

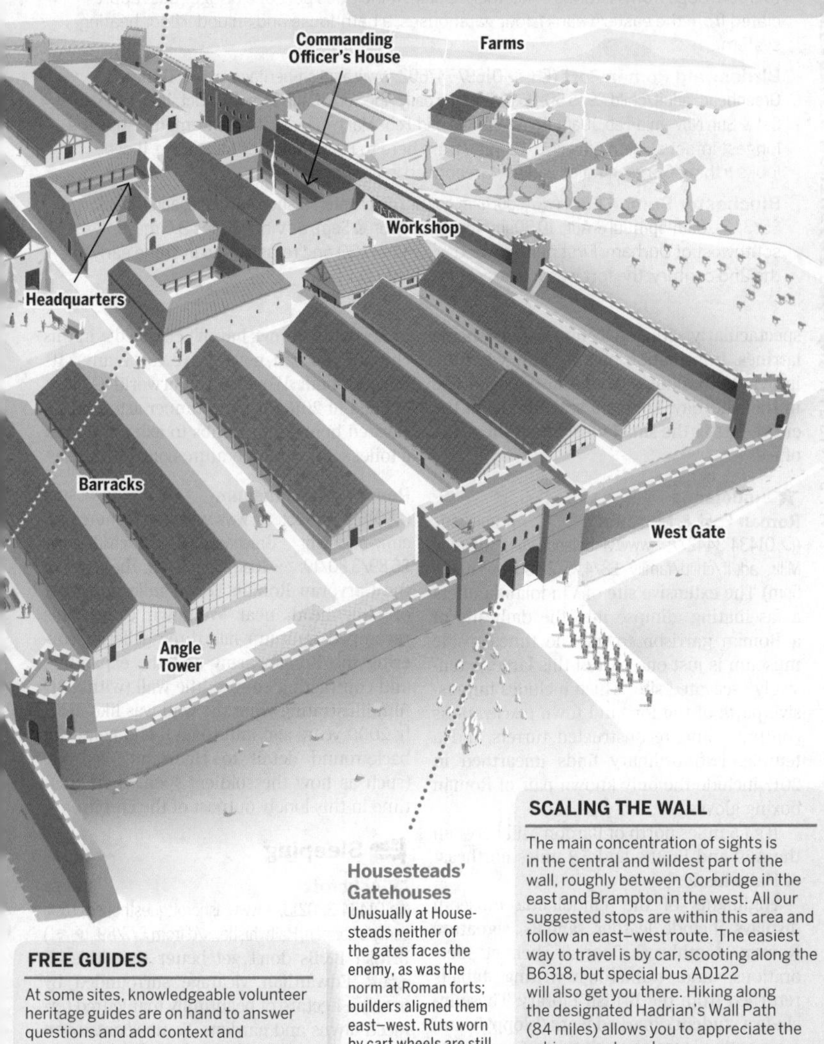

Housesteads' Gatehouses
Unusually at Housesteads neither of the gates faces the enemy, as was the norm at Roman forts; builders aligned them east–west. Ruts worn by cart wheels are still visible in the stone.

SCALING THE WALL

The main concentration of sights is in the central and wildest part of the wall, roughly between Corbridge in the east and Brampton in the west. All our suggested stops are within this area and follow an east–west route. The easiest way to travel is by car, scooting along the B6318, but special bus AD122 will also get you there. Hiking along the designated Hadrian's Wall Path (84 miles) allows you to appreciate the achievement up close.

FREE GUIDES

At some sites, knowledgeable volunteer heritage guides are on hand to answer questions and add context and interesting details to what you're seeing.

HADRIAN'S WALL SITES

Along with key sites such as Housesteads (p629) and Vindolanda, there are numerous other Roman remains stationed along Hadrian's Wall.

Segedunum (0191-278 4217; www.segedunumromanfort.org.uk; Buddle St, Wallsend; adult/child £4.95/free; 10am-4pm Jun–mid-Sep, to 3pm mid-Sep–early Dec & mid-Jan–May) was the last strong post of Hadrian's Wall, 5 miles east of Newcastle in the suburb of Wallsend. Beneath the 35m-high tower is an absorbing site that includes a reconstructed Roman bathhouse (with steaming pools and frescos) and a museum.

Chesters Roman Fort (EH; 01434-681379; www.english-heritage.org.uk; Chollerford; adult/child £9/5.40; 10am-6pm daily Apr-Sep, 10am-5pm daily Oct, 10am-4pm Sat & Sun Nov–mid-Feb, 10am-4pm Wed-Sun mid-Feb–Mar) near the village of Chollerford housed up to 500 troops from Asturias in northern Spain. It includes part of a bridge (best appreciated from the eastern bank), four gatehouses, a bathhouse and an underfloor heating system.

Birdoswald Roman Fort (EH; 01697-747602; www.english-heritage.org.uk; Gilsland, Greenhead; adult/child £9/5.50; 10am-6pm daily Apr-Sep, 10am-5pm daily Oct, 10am-4pm Sat & Sun Nov–mid-Feb, 10am-4pm Wed-Sun mid-Feb–Mar) – Banna to the Romans – has the longest intact stretch of wall, extending from here to Harrow's Scar Milecastle. It overlooks Irthing Gorge, 4 miles west of Greenhead in Cumbria.

Binchester Roman Fort (www.durham.gov.uk/binchester; Bishop Auckland; adult/child £5/3; 10am-5pm Jul & Aug, 10.30am-4pm Easter-Jun & Sep), or Vinovia, lies 9.6 miles southwest of Durham. First built in wood around AD 80 and refashioned in stone early in the 2nd century, the fort was the largest in County Durham.

spectacularly situated communal flushable latrines. Information boards show what the individual buildings would have looked like in their heyday. There's a scale model of the entire fort in the small museum at the ticket office.

★Vindolanda Roman Fort & Museum
HISTORIC SITE

(01434-344277; www.vindolanda.com; Bardon Mill; adult/child/family £8/4.75/22.80; 10am-5pm) The extensive site of Vindolanda offers a fascinating glimpse into the daily life of a Roman garrison town. The time-capsule museum is just one part of this large, extensively excavated site, which includes impressive parts of the fort and town (excavations continue) and reconstructed turrets and a temple. Extraordinary finds unearthed in 2017 include the only known pair of Roman boxing gloves.

It's 1.5 miles north of Bardon Mill between the A69 and B6318, and 5.8 miles northeast of Haltwhistle.

Highlights of the Vindolanda museum displays include leather sandals, signature Roman toothbrush-flourish helmet decorations, and numerous writing tablets returned from the British Library. These include a student's marked work ('sloppy'), and a parent's note with a present of socks and underpants (things haven't changed – in this climate you can never have too many). Its purpose-built Wooden Underworld Gallery, opened in 2018, displays timber artefacts excavated here (from combs to axles and even a toilet seat) in temperature-controlled cases.

Roman Army Museum
MUSEUM

(01697-747485; www.vindolanda.com/roman-army-museum; Greenhead; adult/child/family £6.89/3.80/19; 10am-5pm) On the site of the Carvoran Roman Fort a mile northeast of Greenhead, near Walltown Crags, this revamped museum has three galleries covering the Roman army and the expanding and contracting empire; the wall (with a 3D film illustrating what the wall was like nearly 2000 years ago and today); and colourful background detail to Hadrian's Wall life (such as how the soldiers spent their R&R time in this lonely outpost of the empire).

Sleeping

★Ashcroft
B&B ££

(01434-320213; www.ashcroftguesthouse.co.uk; Lanty's Lonnen, Haltwhistle; s/d from £77/89; P) British B&Bs don't get better than this elegant Edwardian vicarage surrounded by nearly a hectare of beautifully manicured terraced lawns and gardens. Some rooms open to private balconies and terraces and all have soaring ceilings and 21st-century gadgets. Breakfast (included) is cooked on a cast-iron Aga and served in a grand dining room.

Holmhead Guest House B&B ££
(☎01697-747402; www.bandb-hadrianswall.co.uk; Greenhead; campsites per 1/2 people £7.50/11, s/d from £70/80; ⊙guesthouse year-round, camping & bunk barn May-Sep; P 📶) Built using recycled bits of the wall on whose foundations it stands, this superb farmhouse half a mile north of Greenhead offers comfy rooms and five unpowered campsites. The Pennine Way and the Hadrian's Wall Path pass through the grounds and Thirwall Castle's jagged ruins loom above. Ask to see the 3rd-century Roman graffiti.

★**Langley Castle Hotel** CASTLE £££
(☎01434-688888; www.langleycastle.com; Langley; d castle view/castle from £175/270; P 📶 🐾) Soaring above 12 acres of gardens, this 1350-built castle is a beauty, with creaking hallways lined by suits of armour and an alleged resident ghost. Its nine castle rooms are appointed with antique furnishings (many have four-poster beds); there are another 18 'castle view' rooms in the grounds with access to castle facilities. Check for dinner, bed and breakfast packages.

Information

Tourist Office (☎01434-321863; www.visitnorthumberland.com; Mechanics Institute, Westgate; ⊙10am-4.30pm Mon-Fri, to 1pm Sat) On Haltwhistle's main street.

Getting There & Around

Bus 185 runs to the Roman Army Museum (£3, 10 minutes, three daily) and Birdoswald Roman Fort (£3.40, 25 minutes, three daily).

Haltwhistle is also linked by train to Hexham (£7.30, 20 minutes, hourly) and Newcastle (£14, one hour, hourly).

Northumberland National Park

England's last great wilderness is the 405 sq miles of natural wonderland that make up the country's least populated national park. The finest sections of Hadrian's Wall run along its southern edge and the landscape is dotted with prehistoric remains and fortified houses – the thick-walled peles were the only solid buildings built here until the mid-18th century.

Adjacent to the national park, the Kielder Water & Forest Park is home to the vast artificial lake Kielder Water, holding 200,000 million litres. Surrounding its 27-mile-long shoreline is England's largest plantation forest, with 150 million spruce and pine trees.

Sights

★**Kielder Observatory** OBSERVATORY
(☎0191-265 5510; www.kielderobservatory.org; Black Fell, off Shilling Pot; adult/child from £20/15; ⊙by reservation) In 2013, Northumberland National Park was awarded dark-sky status by the International Dark Skies Association (www.darksky.org). For the best views of the resulting Northumberland International Dark Sky Park, attend a stargazing session at this state-of-the-art observatory. Its program spans night-time observing sessions to family events and astrophotography. Book well ahead, and dress warmly: it's seriously chilly here at night. At the signs towards Kielder Observatory and Skyspace, turn left; it's a 2-mile drive up the track.

Chillingham Castle CASTLE
(☎01668-215359; www.chillingham-castle.com; Chillingham; castle adult/child £10.50/6.50, Chillingham Wild Cattle £8.50/4, castle & Chillingham Wild Cattle £17.50/6.50; ⊙castle noon-5pm Apr-Oct, Chillingham Wild Cattle tours 10am, 11.30am, 1.45pm & 3.15pm Apr-Oct) Steeped in history, warfare, torture and ghosts, 13th-century Chillingham is said to be one of the country's most haunted places, with spectres from a phantom funeral to Lady Mary Berkeley seeking her errant husband. Owner Sir Humphry Wakefield has passionately restored the castle's extravagant medieval staterooms, stone-flagged banquet halls and grisly torture chambers. Chillingham is 6 miles southeast of Wooler. Bus 470 (four daily Monday to Saturday) between Alnwick (£3.30, 25 minutes) and Wooler (£3.30, 20 minutes) stops at Chillingham.

Dates for two-hour evening ghost tours (per person £25), some family-friendly, are listed on the website. Committed ghost hunters can undertake a four-hour hunt (£50) overseen by the castle's dedicated paranormal team.

It's possible to stay at the medieval fortress in one of eight self-catering apartments (doubles from £100) where the likes of Henry III and Edward I once snoozed.

The grounds are home to some 100 Chillingham wild cattle, thought to be the last descendants of the aurochs that once roamed Britain until becoming all but extinct during the Bronze Age, making them one of the world's rarest breeds of any species. Tours lasting one hour are led by a park warden; wear sturdy shoes.

Cragside House, Garden & Woodland HISTORIC BUILDING
(NT; ☎01669-620333; www.nationaltrust.org.uk; adult/child £15/7.50; ⊙house 11am-5pm, gardens & woodland 10am-6pm mid-Mar–Oct, hours vary) One mile northeast of Rothbury just off the B6341 is the astonishing country retreat of the first Lord Armstrong. In the 1880s, the house had hot and cold running water, a telephone and alarm system, and was the world's first to be lit by electricity, generated through hydropower. The sprawling Victorian gardens feature lakes, moors and one of Europe's largest rock gardens. Visit late May to mid-June to see Cragside's famous rhododendrons in bloom.

Sleeping

Wooler YHA HOSTEL £
(☎01668-281365; www.yha.org.uk; 30 Cheviot St, Wooler; d/q from £46/84; ⊙Apr-Oct; P 📶) In a low, red-brick building above Wooler, this handy hostel contains beds in a variety of rooms (including handcrafted 'shepherds' huts' sleeping two to three people warmed by electric heating), a modern lounge and a small restaurant, as well as a self-catering kitchen, drying room and bike storage.

★Otterburn Castle Country House Hotel CASTLE £££
(☎01830-520620; www.otterburncastle.com; Main St, Otterburn; d incl breakfast £140-165, ste £220; P 📶 🐾) Founded by William the Conqueror's cousin Robert de Umfraville in 1086 and set in almost 13 hectares of grounds, this story-book castle has 17 classically furnished rooms; some of its suites have four-poster beds and fireplaces. Modern British fare is served in its wood-panelled Oak Room Restaurant (two-/three-course menus £24/30); open fires blaze in its bar.

WILDLIFE OF NORTHUMBERLAND NATIONAL PARK

Northumberland National Park is a wonderful place to go looking for wildlife as you explore on foot. The park has recorded 169 different bird species, including numerous waders (among them lapwing, snipe, redshank, oystercatcher, golden plover and curlew) and ground-dwellers such as red or black grouse. Mammals include red squirrels, roe deer, and the much-sought-after wild Cheviot goat, a primitive goat species with a long shaggy coat.

Information

For information, contact the **Northumberland National Park information service** (☎01434-605555; www.northumberlandnationalpark.org.uk).

As well as tourist offices in towns including **Wooler** (☎01668-282123; www.wooler.org.uk; Cheviot Centre, 12 Padgepool Pl, Wooler; ⊙10am-4.30pm Mon-Fri, to 1pm Sat) and **Rothbury** (☎01669-621979; www.visitnorthumberland.com; Rothbury Library, Front St, Rothbury; ⊙10am-4.30pm Mon-Fri, 10.30am-4pm Sat Apr-Oct, reduced hours Nov-Mar), there's a national park office, the **Walltown Visitor Centre** (Northumberland National Park Visitor Centre; ☎01434-344396; www.northumberlandnationalpark.org.uk; Greenhead; ⊙10am-6pm daily Apr-Sep, to 5pm daily Oct, 10am-4pm Sat & Sun Nov-Mar), near Haltwhistle. Inside Kielder Castle, a hunting lodge built in 1775, the **Forest Park Centre** (☎01434-250209; www.visitkielder.com; Forest Dr, Kielder; ⊙10am-4pm) has tourist information on the Northumberland National Park, including hiking, mountain biking and watersports in the Kielder area.

Getting There & Away

Public transport options are limited at best – to explore properly, you really need your own wheels.

Otterburn Bus 808 (£4, one hour, one daily Monday to Saturday) runs between Otterburn and Newcastle.

Wooler Buses 470 and 473 link Wooler and Alnwick (£3.30, 40 minutes, four daily Monday to Saturday). Buses 267 and 464 run between Wooler and Berwick-upon-Tweed (£4.90, one hour, every two hours Monday to Saturday).

DON'T MISS

NORTHUMBERLAND NATIONAL PARK'S BEST HIKES

Northumberland National Park is a wonderful place to walk and the park's website (www.northumberlandnationalpark.org.uk) details 35 hikes of between one and seven hours, from easy to strenuous. These include five with Hadrian's Wall as the focal point, with a further 17 taking you through the Cheviot Hills, frequently passing by prehistoric remnants. Local tourist offices can provide maps, guides and route information.

Our favourites, all of moderate difficulty, include:

Vindolanda & Hadrian's Wall (6 miles or 9.6km, 3½ hours) Among the wall's most rewarding sections with Vindolanda Roman Fort (p632) and stunning views. Begins and ends at the Sill (p627).

Steel Rigg & Crag Lough (4 miles or 6.4km, two hours) One of the prettiest sections of Hadrian's Wall that's especially good for families. The walk begins and ends at the Steel Rigg National Park car park.

Winshield Crags & Cawfields (6 miles or 9.6km, 3½ hours) Some of the loveliest sections of Hadrian's Wall. Starts at the Sill (p627) and ends at Crawfields car park.

Breamish Valley Hillfort Trail (4.5 miles or 7.2km, 3½ hours) Five hillforts and stunning views in the Cheviots.

Harthope Valley (4 miles or 6.4km, two hours) Climb to top of the Cheviots with views that go all the way to the sea. Starts and ends at the Carey Burn bridge southwest of Wooler.

Northumberland Coast

Northumberland's coast is one of the UK's most underrated shores. Instead of glitzy seaside resorts, it's strewn with charming, castle-crowned villages along miles of wide, sand. Like Northumberland's wild and remote interior, the coast is sparsely populated, meaning you might just have all of this beauty to yourself.

Alnwick

☎01665 / POP 8100

Northumberland's historic ducal town, Alnwick (pronounced 'annick') is an elegant maze of narrow cobbled streets around its colossal medieval castle. Alnwick is also home to a famous bookshop and the spectacular Alnwick Garden.

Sights

★Alnwick Castle CASTLE

(☎01665-511178; www.alnwickcastle.com; The Peth; adult/child £8/free; ⏲10am-5pm Apr-Sep, 10am-4pm Oct) Set in parklands designed by Lancelot 'Capability' Brown, the imposing ancestral home of the Duke of Northumberland has changed little since the 14th century. It's a favourite set for film-makers and starred as Hogwarts for the first couple of *Harry Potter* films. The interior is sumptuous and extravagant; the six rooms open to the public – staterooms, dining room, guard chamber and library – have an incredible display of Italian paintings, including Titian's *Ecce Homo* and many Canalettos.

Various free tours include several focusing on *Harry Potter* (check the website for broomstick training times on weekends) and other productions that have used the castle as a backdrop, including British comedy series *Blackadder* and period drama *Downton Abbey*.

For the best views of the castle's exterior, take The Peth to the River Aln's northern bank and follow the woodland trail east.

Alnwick Garden GARDENS

(www.alnwickgarden.com; Denwick Lane; adult/child £13/5; ⏲10am-6pm Apr-Oct, hours vary rest of year) This 4.8-hectare walled garden incorporates a series of magnificent green spaces surrounding the breathtaking Grand Cascade – 120 separate jets spurting some 30,000L of water down 21 weirs. Half a dozen other gardens include a Franco-Italian-influenced Ornamental Garden (with over 15,000 plants), a Rose Garden and a fascinating Poison Garden, home to some of the deadliest – and most illegal – plants in the world, including cannabis, magic mushrooms, belladonna

Driving Tour Northumberland Coast

START NEWBIGGIN-BY-THE-SEA
END BERWICK-UPON-TWEED
LENGTH 78 MILES; ONE DAY

It's possible to shadow the coast to the Scottish border from Tynemouth, but the scenery really picks up at **1 Newbiggin-by-the-Sea**. Newbiggin's beach was restored in 2007, when over 500,000 tonnes of Skegness' sand was relocated here to counteract erosion, and Sean Henry's gigantic bronze sculpture *The Couple* was installed offshore.

Continuing north along the A1068 coast road for 13 miles brings you to the fishing port of **2 Amble**, with a boardwalk along the seafront and puffin cruises (p640). Less than 2 miles north, biscuit-coloured **3 Warkworth** is a cluster of houses around a loop in the River Coquet, dominated by the craggy ruin of 14th-century Warkworth Castle (p631). The castle features in Shakespeare's *Henry IV* Parts I and II, and the 1998 film *Elizabeth* was shot here.

Some 5 miles north of Warkworth is **4 Alnmouth**, with brightly painted houses and pretty beaches. It's another 5 miles inland to the bustling town of **5 Alnwick** to see its imposing castle (p635) – which starred as Harry Potter's Hogwarts – and glorious Alnwick Garden. Turn back towards the coast and follow the B1339 for 4.7 miles before turning east on Windside Hill to **6 Craster**, famed for its smoked kippers, which you can buy direct from the smokery (p638) or taste at its restaurant. From Craster, there are spectacular views of brooding Dunstanburgh Castle. Around 5 miles north at **7 Low Newton-by-the-Sea**, on Embleton Bay, pause for a pint brewed at the Ship Inn (p638).

Past the village of Seahouses (the jumping-off point for the Farne Islands), quaint **8 Bamburgh** is home to the most dramatic castle (p639) yet. Another 17 miles on, via a tidal causeway (check tide times!), the sacred priory ruins (p640) of otherworldly **9 Holy Island (Lindisfarne; p639)** still attract spiritual pilgrims. Return to the mainland where, 14 miles north, you can walk almost the entire length of the Elizabethan walls (p641) encircling England's northernmost city, beautiful **10 Berwick-upon-Tweed** (p641).

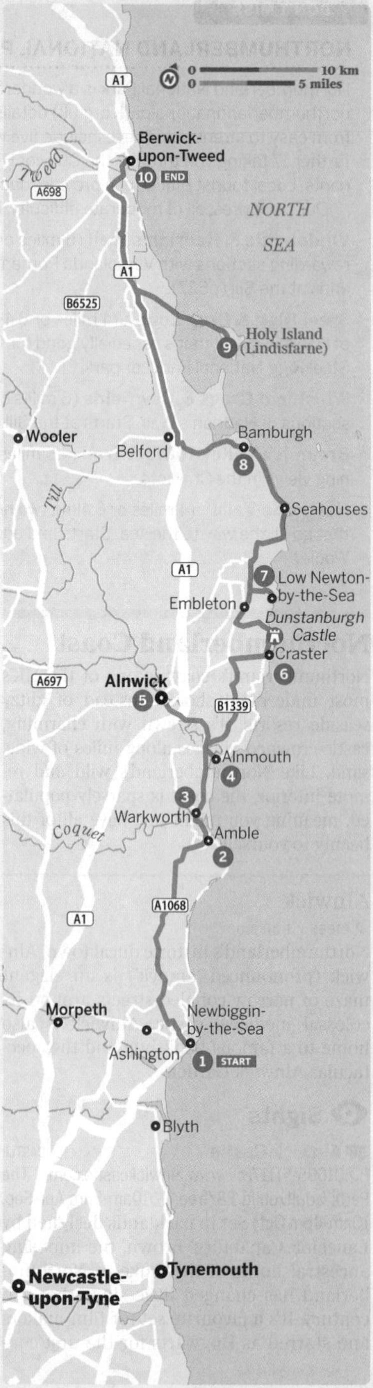

and tobacco. Check the website for opening times, which can change monthly.

Enveloped by – but not in – the treetops, the timber-lined restaurant Treehouse (p637) serves Modern British cuisine.

Sleeping & Eating

★ Alnwick Lodge B&B, CAMPGROUND ££
(☎01665-604363; www.alnwicklodge.com; West Cawledge Park, A1; tent sites from £15, glamping incl linen £45-60, B&B s £45-55, d & tw £62-130; P 📶 🐾) Three miles south of Alnwick's centre, this gorgeous Victorian farmstead has 15 antique-filled rooms with quirky touches like free-standing, lidded baths. Cooked breakfasts are served around a huge circular banqueting table. You can also go 'glamping' in restored gypsy caravans, wagons and shepherds' huts (with shared bathrooms), or pitch up on the sheltered meadow.

White Swan Hotel HOTEL ££
(☎01665-602109; www.classiclodges.co.uk; Bondgate Within; d/ste from £105/175; P 📶 🐾) In the heart of town, this 300-year-old coaching inn has 56 superbly appointed rooms, including family rooms that sleep up to four. Its architectural showpiece is the fine-dining **Olympic restaurant** (mains £13-23, 2-/3-course lunch menus £15/19, 3-course dinner menu £37; ⊙noon-3pm & 5-9pm).

Treehouse BRITISH ££
(☎01665-511852; www.alnwickgarden.com; Alnwick Garden, Denwick Lane; mains £11-18; ⊙noon-2.30pm Mon & Tue, noon-2.30pm & 6-8.30pm Wed-Sat, noon-4pm Sun) Surrounded by Alnwick Garden's treetops (but not perched up within them as its name would imply), this timber-lined restaurant serves contemporary fare: twice-baked wild garlic soufflé, beetroot- and British gin–cured salmon, and sticky toffee pudding with salted-caramel sauce and honeycomb ice cream. There is often live classical music in the evenings. Bookings are essential.

Shopping

★ Barter Books BOOKS
(☎01665-604888; www.barterbooks.co.uk; Alnwick Station, Wagon Way Rd; ⊙9am-6pm) Coal fires, velvet ottomans, reading rooms and a cafe make this secondhand bookshop in Alnwick's Victorian former railway station wonderfully atmospheric and one of Britain's great bookstores. As you browse the crammed bookshelves, the silence is interrupted only by the tiny toy train that runs along the track above your head.

Taste of Northumbria FOOD & DRINKS
(☎01665-602490; www.facebook.com/tasteofnorthumbria; 4-6 Market Pl; ⊙10am-5pm Mon-Sat, 11am-3pm Sun) Alnwick-distilled rum and Lindisfarne-made mead along with a range of boutique English gins and Scottish whiskies are sold at this locavore shop in the town centre. Alnwick rum is also used in seasonal Christmas puddings sold here.

Information

Tourist Office (☎01670-622152; www.visitalnwick.org.uk; 2 The Shambles; ⊙9am-6pm Mon-Sat) Alnwick's friendly tourist office is by Market Pl.

Getting There & Away

Bus X15 zips along the A1 to Berwick-upon-Tweed (£7.20, one hour, hourly Monday to Saturday, every two hours Sunday) and Newcastle (£7.20, 1½ hours, hourly Monday to Saturday, every two hours Sunday). Bus X18 follows the coast to Berwick-upon-Tweed (£7.20, two hours, three daily) and Newcastle (£7, two hours, hourly).

Craster

☎01665 / POP 300

Sandy, salty Craster is a small, sheltered fishing village about 6 miles northeast of Alnwick. It stands in the heart of some glorious coastal scenery, and there's a splendid castle nearby. Craster is also famous for its kippers. In the early 20th century, 2500 herring were smoked here daily. The kippers still produced today are said to often grace the Queen's breakfast table.

Dunstanburgh Castle CASTLE
(EH; www.english-heritage.org.uk; Dunstanburgh Rd; adult/child £5.90/3.50; ⊙10am-6pm daily Apr-Aug, to 5pm daily Sep, to 4pm daily Oct, 10am-4pm Sat & Sun Nov-Mar) The dramatic 1.5-mile walk along the coast from Craster (not accessible by car) is the most scenic path to this moody, weather-battered castle. Construction began in 1314 and it was strengthened during the Wars of the Roses, but left to crumble, becoming ruined by 1550. Parts of the original wall and gatehouse keep are still standing and it's a tribute to its builders that so much remains.

You can also reach the castle on foot from Embleton (1.5 miles), but access can be cut off at high tide.

Jolly Fisherman GASTROPUB ££

(☎016650-576461; www.thejollyfishermancraster.co.uk; Haven Hill; mains lunch £8-15, dinner £12-26; ⏲11am-8.30pm Mon-Sat, noon-7pm Sun Apr-Oct, to 5pm Sun Nov-Mar) Crab (in soup, sandwiches, fish platters and more) is the speciality of this gastropub, but it also has a variety of fish dishes, as well as a house burger and steaks served with beef-dripping chips. A strong wine list complements its wonderful real ales. There's a blazing fire in the bar and a beer garden overlooking Dunstanburgh Castle.

★**Robson & Sons** FOOD

(☎01665-576223; www.kipper.co.uk; Haven Hill; kippers per kg from £9; ⏲9am-4.30pm Mon-Fri, 9am-3.30pm Sat, 11am-3.30pm Sun) Four generations have operated this traditional fish smokers; loyal customers include the Royal Family. It's best known for its kippers, but it also smokes salmon and other fish.

ℹ Getting There & Away

Bus X18 runs to Alnwick (£5.90, 55 minutes, three daily), Berwick-upon-Tweed (£7.10, 1½ hours, three daily) and Newcastle (£7.10, 2½ hours, three daily). From Monday to Saturday, bus 418 also links Craster to Alnwick (£5.50, 30 minutes, four daily).

Embleton Bay

Beautiful Embleton Bay, a pale wide arc of sand, stretches from Dunstanburgh past the endearing village of Embleton and curves in a broad vanilla-coloured strand around to end at Low Newton-by-the-Sea, a tiny whitewashed, National Trust–preserved village.

Behind the bay is a path leading to the **Newton Pool Nature Reserve**, an important spot for breeding and migrating birds such as black-headed gulls and grasshopper warblers. There are a couple of hides where you can watch them. You can continue walking along the headland beyond Low Newton, where you'll find **Football Hole**, a delightful hidden beach between headlands.

Joiners Arms PUB £££

(☎01665-576112; www.joiners-arms.com; High Newton-by-the-Sea; d from £155; 🅿📶🐾) This is a fantastic place to stay: the five contemporary guest rooms here are individually and exquisitely decorated with details like exposed brick, free-standing baths and four-poster beds. Locals also love this gastropub (mains from £9) for its locally sourced ingredients; the seafood and steaks are excellent, and families are warmly welcomed.

Ship Inn PUB FOOD ££

(☎01665-576262; www.shipinnnewton.co.uk; Low Newton-by-the-Sea; mains lunch £6.50-9, dinner £13-29; ⏲11am-7pm Sun-Tue, to 9.30pm Wed-Sat) 🍃 Set around a village green, this idyllic pub brews over two dozen different beers – blond, wheat, rye, bitter, stout and seasonal – using local River Coquet water. The food is first-rate, too, from crab and lobster to regional farm-sourced meat. There is often live music on weekends.

ℹ Getting There & Away

Bus X18 to Newcastle (£7.20, 2¾ hours, three daily), Berwick-upon-Tweed (£6.10, 1¼ hours, three daily) and Alnwick (£5.90, 45 minutes, three daily) stops outside the Joiners Arms. From Monday to Saturday, bus 418 (£5.50, 35 minutes, four daily) links the village of Embleton with Alnwick.

KEEP CALM & CARRY ON

Alnwick's Barter Books (p637) is responsible for one of the most unlikely pop culture icons of the early 21st century. At the outbreak of WWII in 1939, the British government produced a series of propaganda posters designed to boost national morale during the difficult days that lay ahead. An estimated 2.5 million posters with the slogan 'Keep Calm and Carry On' were printed but never distributed. They disappeared from view until 2000 when the owners of Barter Books unearthed the poster in a box of books while converting the station. The owners liked it so much that they framed one and put it on the wall. A year later, responding to popular demand, they began to sell the posters, little knowing that the poster and its offshoots would become a successful industry in its own right. The slogan is at once quintessentially British and captures the nation's memories of war-time Britain; the posters are now seen all across the nation. The original is still on the wall behind the till.

Bamburgh

☎01668 / POP 410

High up on a basalt crag, Bamburgh's mighty castle looms over the quaint village – a clutch of houses around a pleasant green – which continues to commemorate the valiant achievements of local heroine Grace Darling. In a 2019 study of British seaside resort villages, Bamburgh ranked No.1 in the UK.

★**Bamburgh Castle** CASTLE
(☎01668-214515; www.bamburghcastle.com; Links Rd; adult/child £11.75/5.75; ⊙10am-5pm daily early Feb-early Nov, 11am-4.30pm Sat & Sun early Nov-early Feb) Northumberland's most dramatic castle was built around a powerful 11th-century Norman keep by Henry II. The castle played a key role in the border wars of the 13th and 14th centuries, and in 1464 was the first English castle to fall during the Wars of the Roses. It was restored in the 19th century by the great industrialist Lord Armstrong, and is still home to the Armstrong family.

Its name is a derivative of Bebbanburgh, after the wife of Anglo-Saxon ruler Aedelfrip, whose fortified home occupied this basalt outcrop 500 years earlier. Antique furniture, suits of armour, priceless ceramics and artworks cram the castle's rooms and chambers, but top billing goes to the neo-Gothic King's Hall with wood panelling, leaded windows and hefty beams supporting the roof.

RNLI Grace Darling Museum MUSEUM
(☎01668-214910; www.rnli.org; 1 Radcliffe Rd; ⊙10am-5pm Mon-Fri & Bank Holiday weekends, Easter-Sep, 10am-4pm Tue-Fri Oct-Easter) FREE Born in Bamburgh, Grace Darling was the lighthouse keeper's daughter on Outer Farne who rowed out to the grounded, flailing SS *Forfarshire* in 1838 and saved its crew in the middle of a dreadful storm. This refurbished museum even has her actual coble (row boat) as well as a film on the events of that stormy night. Grace was born just three houses down from the museum and is buried in the churchyard opposite.

Her ornate wrought-iron and sandstone tomb was built tall so as to be visible to passing ships.

Potted Lobster SEAFOOD ££
(☎01668-214088; www.thepottedlobster.co.uk; 3 Lucker Rd; mains £14-28, half-/full lobster £22/39, seafood platter for 2 £69; ⊙noon-9pm Jul & Aug, noon-3pm & 6-9pm Sep-Jun) Bamburgh lobster – served as a creamy egg and brandy thermidor stuffed in the shell, grilled with garlic and parsley butter, or poached and served cold with wild garlic mayo – is the star of this nautical-styled gem. Seafood platters for two, piled high with lobster, Lindisfarne oysters, Craster crab, pickled herring and more, come with hand-cut chips and crusty home-baked bread.

> DON'T MISS
>
> **WARKWORTH CASTLE**
>
> Looking like the ultimate sandcastle you'd see at the beach, **Warkworth Castle** (EH; www.english-heritage.org.uk; Castle Tce, Warkworth; adult/child £7.90/4.70, incl Hermitage £11.30/6.80; ⊙10am-5pm), a honey-stone edifice atop a hillock, was built around 1200. From the 14th to 17th centuries, it was home to the Percy family (whose descendants still live at Alnwick Castle), and was pivotal in the Wars of the Roses and the English Civil War. It became a national monument in 1915 but the Duke's Rooms remained under the family's control until 1987. Audio guides give a vivid account of its history.

ℹ Getting There & Away

Take bus X18 north to Berwick-upon-Tweed (£7.20, 50 minutes, three daily) or south to Newcastle (£7.20, 3¼ hours, three daily).

Holy Island (Lindisfarne)

There's something almost other-worldly about this tiny, 2-sq-mile island. Connected to the mainland by a narrow causeway that only appears at low tide, cutting the island off from the mainland for about five hours each day, it's fiercely desolate and isolated, scarcely different from when St Aidan arrived to found a monastery in 635.

As you cross the empty flats, it's easy to imagine the marauding Vikings who repeatedly sacked the settlement between 793 and 875, when the monks finally took the hint and left. They carried with them the illuminated *Lindisfarne Gospels* (now in the British Library in London) and the miraculously preserved body of St Cuthbert, who lived here for a couple of years but preferred the hermit's life on Inner Farne. A priory was re-established in the 11th century, but didn't survive the Dissolution in 1537.

Sights

Lindisfarne Priory RUINS

(EH; www.english-heritage.org.uk; adult/child £7.90/4.70; 10am-5pm, times vary with tides) The skeletal, red and grey ruins of the priory are an eerie sight and give a glimpse into the isolated life of the Lindisfarne monks. The later 13th-century St Mary the Virgin Church is built on the site of the first church between the Tees and the Firth of Forth, and the adjacent museum displays the remains of the first monastery and tells the story of the monastic community before and after the Dissolution.

Lindisfarne Castle CASTLE

(NT; www.nationaltrust.org.uk; adult/child £7.30/3.60; 11am-5pm Tue-Sun late May-Sep, 10am-4pm Easter-late May & Oct) Built atop a rocky bluff in 1550, this tiny, storybook castle was extended and converted by Sir Edwin Lutyens from 1902 to 1910 for Edward Hudson, the owner of *Country Life* magazine – you can imagine some of the glamorous parties that graced its alluring rooms. It's half a mile east of the village. Opening times can vary due to tide times.

Sleeping & Eating

Lindisfarne Inn INN ££

(01289-381223; www.lindisfarneinn.co.uk; Beal Rd, Beal; s/d/f incl breakfast from £71/89/120; P) This mainland inn on the A1 next to the turn-off to the causeway is a handy alternative to island accommodation and/or dining if you're cutting it fine with crossing times. Its 23 spotless, modern rooms with tartan carpets are set far back enough that road noise isn't a problem. Well-above-average pub food (such as suet pudding with Northumbrian game) changes seasonally.

Crown & Anchor INN ££

(01289-389215; www.holyislandcrown.co.uk; Market Pl; s/d from £60/70; P) A cornerstone of the island's social life, this venerable pub has brightly coloured guest rooms and solid pub food, but the biggest winner is the beer garden with a postcard panorama of the castle, priory and harbour.

Barn @ Beal PUB FOOD ££

(01289-540044; www.barnatbeal.com; Beal Farm, Beal; lunch £10-23; cafe 9am-6pm Mon-Sat, 9am-5pm Sun, bar hours vary seasonally;) You can watch the causeway tides on webcam at this sociable mainland pub 1 mile northeast of the A1 turn-off (2 miles west of the island). Lindisfarne seafood, including lobster, is a menu highlight, as are house-speciality burgers utilising farm produce. There's a kids' play area. It also has 12 tent pitches (from £10) and nine caravan sites (from £25).

Shopping

St Aidan's Winery FOOD, DRINK

(Lindisfarne Mead; 01289-389230; www.lindisfarne-mead.co.uk; Prior Lane; 11am-3.30pm Mon, to 4.30pm Tue, 11.30am-5pm Wed, noon-5pm Thu, 9.30am-5pm Fri & Sat, 10am-5pm Sun, may vary with tides) Mead is made here on Lindisfarne by St Aidan's Winery to a traditional Roman recipe using locally drawn water and honey. Free tastings let you try its three varieties – original, blood orange and spiced – as well as its fortified wines, such as ginger, wild strawberry, elderberry, blackberry and cherry. Other products include mead-based chocolate truffles and jams. Check ahead for opening hours.

Getting There & Away

When tides permit, the Holy Island Hopper (www.berwickupontweedtaxis.co.uk; £3, 15 minutes) links the island with the mainland on the corner of Beal Rd and the A1 to connect with buses X15 and X18, serving Berwick-upon-Tweed, Alnwick and Newcastle. If using the

THE PUFFINS OF COQUET ISLAND

For three days in late May to early June, the **Amble Puffin Festival** (www.amblepuffinfest.co.uk) celebrates the hatching of puffin chicks on nearby Coquet Island with events including local history talks, guided birdwatching walks, exhibitions, watersports, a craft fair, a food festival and live music. Festivities occur across town.

During the breeding season, you can also take a boat trip to see the birds with **Dave Gray's Puffin Cruises** (01665-711975; www.puffincruises.co.uk; Amble Harbour, Amble; adult/child £10/5; by reservation Apr-Oct).

OFF THE BEATEN TRACK

THE FARNE ISLANDS

During breeding season (roughly May to July), you can see feeding chicks of 20 seabird species (including puffin, kittiwake, Arctic tern, eider duck, cormorant and gull), and some 6000 grey seals, on this rocky **archipelago** (NT; ☎01289-389244; www.nationaltrust.org.uk; adult/child excl boat transport £34.80/17.40, cheaper outside breeding season; ⏰by reservation, season & conditions permitting Mar-Oct) 3 miles offshore from the fishing village of Seahouses. Boat operators, contactable through Seahouses' **tourist office** (☎01670-625593; www.visitnorthumberland.com; Seafield car park, Seahouses; ⏰9.30am-4pm Thu-Tue Apr, 9.30am-4pm daily May-Oct), depart from Seahouses' dock, including **Billy Shiel** (☎01665-720308; www.farne-islands.com; Harbour Rd, Seahouses; adult/child excl island landing fees 2½hr tour £20/15, 6hr tour £40/25; ⏰by reservation Apr-Oct).

Crossings can be rough (impossible in bad weather); wear warm, waterproof clothing and an old hat to guard against the birds!

causeway, drivers need to pay close attention to crossing-time information, posted at tourist offices and on notice boards throughout the area, and at www.holy-island.info. Alternatively, call ☎01289-330733. Every year drivers are caught midway by the incoming tide and have to abandon their cars.

Getting Around

Park in the signposted car park (£5.50 per day). A shuttle bus (£2 return) runs from the car park to the castle every 20 minutes from Easter to September; alternatively it's a level 300m walk to the village centre and 1 mile to the castle.

Berwick-upon-Tweed

☎01289 / POP 12,400

England's northernmost city is a picturesque fortress town, cleaved by the River Tweed. The Grade I–listed Berwick Bridge (aka Old Bridge), built from sandstone between 1611 and 1624, and the Royal Tweed (1925–28), both span the river.

Sights & Activities

★Berwick Walls HISTORIC SITE
(EH; www.english-heritage.org.uk; ⏰dawn-dusk) FREE You can walk almost the entire length of Berwick's hefty Elizabethan walls, begun in 1558 to reinforce an earlier set built during the reign of Edward II. The mile-long walk is a must, with wonderful, wide-open views. Only a small fragment remains of the once-mighty border castle, most of the building having been replaced by the train station.

Berwick Barracks MUSEUM, GALLERY
(EH; www.english-heritage.org.uk; The Parade; adult/child £5.90/3.50; ⏰10am-5pm Wed-Sun Apr-Oct) Designed by Nicholas Hawksmoor, Britain's oldest purpose-built barracks (1717) now house an assortment of museums and art galleries, covering a history of the town and British soldiery since the 17th century. The Gymnasium Gallery hosts big-name contemporary art exhibitions.

Berwick Boat Trips CRUISE
(☎07713 170845; www.berwickboattrips.co.uk; Berwick-upon-Tweed Quayside; 2hr North Sea wildlife tour adult/child £18/12, 1hr river tour £10/7; ⏰by reservation) Choose from a North Sea cruise spotting seals, dolphins and sea birds, a river cruise along the Tweed, or a scenic trip along the estuary at sunset. Schedules are posted online.

Sleeping & Eating

Berwick YHA HOSTEL £
(☎01629-592700; www.yha.org.uk; Dewars Lane; d from £39; P@🛜) A mid-18th-century granary has been converted into a state-of-the-art hostel with private rooms (all with en suite bathrooms). Contemporary facilities include a TV room, a laundry and wi-fi in common areas. Staff are terrifically helpful.

★Marshall Meadows Country House Hotel HERITAGE HOTEL ££
(☎01289-331133; www.marshallmeadowshotel.co.uk; Marshall Meadows; d/f incl breakfast from £99/119; P🛜🐾) England's most northerly hotel, just 600m from the Scottish border, sits amid 6 hectares of woodland and ornamental gardens. The Georgian manor's 19 rooms (including a ground-floor family room) have countrified checked and floral fabrics. There are two cosy bars with open fireplaces, a conservatory, and an

ENGLISH OR SCOTTISH?

As you might expect from a town perilously close to one of the continent's most contested borders, Berwick is the most fought-over settlement in European history: between 1174 and 1482 it changed hands 14 times between the Scots and the English. And it's not just about history. Although firmly English since the 15th century, Berwick retains its own identity, with locals south of the border speaking with a noticeable Scottish burr.

Less known (but just as important to many modern locals), the town's football team, Berwick Rangers, is the only English team to play in the Scottish Football League. In 2019, after 114 years in the top three or four tiers of Scottish football (without much success, it must be said), Berwick Rangers were relegated from Scottish League Two. Even so, at the time of writing, Berwick Rangers were still one of very few teams in world football to play in a national league other than that of the country in which they're located: they now play in Scotland's fifth-tier Lowland Football League.

oak-panelled restaurant serving breakfast (including kippers), and evening meals by candlelight.

Audela BRITISH **££**
(01289-308827; www.audela.co.uk; 64 Bridge St; mains £18-23, 2-/3-course Sunday lunch $20/24.50; noon-2.30pm & 5.30-9pm Thu-Mon) Named for the last vessel to be built at Berwick Shipyard (in 1979) and set in a former cockle shop, Audela is the town's top table.

Local suppliers provide the ingredients for dishes such as Borders venison loin with, among other ingredients, pickled brambles.

Getting There & Away

On the East Coast Main Line linking London and Edinburgh, Berwick-upon-Tweed is almost exactly halfway between Edinburgh (from £11.60, one hour, up to two per hour) and Newcastle (from £12.70, 45 minutes, up to two per hour).

Buses stop on Golden Sq (where it meets Marygate). National Express coaches between Edinburgh (£17, 1¼ hours, twice daily) and London (£43.50.10, eight hours, twice daily) stop here.

Newcastle is served by the X15 (via Alnwick; £7.20, 2½ hours, hourly Monday to Saturday, every two hours Sunday) and X18 (£7.20, four hours, three daily).

Wales

CONWY CASTLE, CONWY (P744): ABCBRITAIN/SHUTTERSTOCK ©

Wales Highlights

1 **Wales Coast Path** (p660) Swooning over staggeringly beautiful coastscapes on this 870-mile route.

2 **Snowdonia** (p721) Puffing up Wales' highest peak, 1085m Snowdon, for views over moor, lake and mountain.

3 **St Davids** (p675) Chilling in coastal St Davids, capped off by Wales' most impressive cathedral.

4 **Conwy Castle** (p744) Admiring the crown jewel of Edward I's 'Iron Ring' of castles.

5 **Pembrokeshire** (p675) Seeking out hidden bays,

prehistoric standing stones and puffin-filled islands.

6 Brecon Beacons (p690) Hoofing it up a mountain before relaxing with a pint in a medieval coaching inn.

7 Hay-on-Wye (p690) Getting lost in the second hand bookshops in this literary colossus of a town.

8 Cardiff (p648) Exploring the Welsh capital's fantasy castle, Victorian shopping arcades and pumping nightlife.

9 Portmeirion (p737) Experiencing a fanciful slice of baroque Italy clinging to the North Welsh coast.

AT A GLANCE

POPULATION
Cardiff: 335,000

HIGHEST MOUNTAIN
Pen y Fan (886m)

BEST CRAFT BEER BAR
Tiny Rebel (p656)

COOLEST COUNTRY RESTAURANT
Wright's Food Emporium (p674)

BEST COASTAL THRILL
Preseli Venture (p678)

WHEN TO GO

Jan–Mar
The coldest months, but Wales' home matches in the Six Nations Rugby Championship warm local spirits.

Jul
A big month for festivals in Cardiff.

Apr–May & Sep
Surf is great on the Gower and in Pembrokeshire in April; Pembrokeshire's best hiking weather is often September.

Cardiff Castle (p648)
LENISECALLEJA PHOTOGRAPHY/SHUTTERSTOCK ©

Cardiff, Pembrokeshire & South Wales

Stretching from castle-dominated Chepstow through to the jagged Pembrokeshire coast in the west, South Wales packs in the sights. Hugging the border, the Wye Valley is the birthplace of British tourism. For centuries, people have come to explore this tranquil waterway and its wooded vale, where the ruins of Tintern Abbey have inspired generations of poets and artists. The nation's capital, Cardiff, flies the flag for big-city sophistication. Just out of Swansea, Wales' second city, the Gower Peninsula revels in its coastal beauty. To the north, the fecund heartland of rural Carmarthenshire offers country comfort in abundance. Beyond Cardiff, the biggest draw in South Wales remains Pembrokeshire, where almost 200 miles of magical shoreline has been declared a national park, delineated by craggy cliffs, golden sands, villages and resorts.

INCLUDES

CARDIFF

☎029 / POP 335,000

Vacillating between gritty and glitzy, the Victorian and the voguish, Cardiff is master of reinvention. Wales' capital since just 1955, it has vigorously embraced the role and regularly transforms to nurture its increasingly interesting reputation.

The two top sights between which this chameleon-like city spreads embody its verve for innovation. An ancient fort forms Cardiff Castle's foundation but the flamboyant 19th-century rethinking of the fortress captivates most. Cardiff's creativity and confidence, embodied in the radical transformation of Cardiff Bay from unsightly mudflats to Europe's biggest, boldest waterfront development, are infectious. Come weekends it buzzes as shoppers hit the Hayes, rugby supporters' roars resound through the centre and revellers relish the thriving nightlife.

Cardiff makes an excellent base for day trips to surrounding valleys and coast, bombastic castles and intriguing industrial sites.

History

The name Cardiff probably derives from Caer Tâf (Fort on the River Taff). In AD 75 the Romans built a fort where Cardiff Castle now stands. In 1093 a Norman knight named Robert Fitzhamon (conqueror of Glamorgan and later earl of Gloucester) built himself a castle within the Roman walls and a small town grew up around it. Both were damaged in a Welsh revolt in 1183 and the town was sacked in 1404 by Owain Glyndŵr during his ill-fated rebellion against English domination.

The first of the Tudor Acts of Union in 1536 put the English stamp on Cardiff and brought stability. But despite its importance as a port, market town and bishopric, under 10,000 people were living here in 1801.

The city owes its present stature to iron and coal mining in the valleys to the north. Coal was first exported from Cardiff on a small scale as early as 1600. In 1794 the Bute family – which owned much of the land from which Welsh coal was mined – built the Glamorganshire Canal for the shipment of iron from Merthyr Tydfil down to Cardiff. Around the same time, the second marquess of Bute had completed the first docks at Butetown, just south of Cardiff, getting the jump on other South Wales ports. By the time it dawned on everyone what immense reserves of coal the valleys contained – precipitating a kind of black gold rush – the Butes were well-positioned to insist it be shipped from Butetown. Cardiff was off and running.

The docklands expanded rapidly, the Butes grew staggeringly rich and the city boomed. A large, multiracial workers' community known as Tiger Bay grew up in harbourside district Butetown. In 1905 Cardiff was officially designated a city and in 1913 the world's top coal port, exporting over 10 million tonnes of the stuff.

The post-WWI slump in the coal trade and the Great Depression of the 1930s slowed the expansion. Calamities accumulated as the city was badly damaged by WWII bombing, and the Butes left town in 1947, donating the castle and a large chunk of land to the city.

Wales had no official capital and the need for one was seen as an important focus for Welsh nationhood. Cardiff had the advantage of being Wales' biggest city and boasted significant architectural riches: it got proclaimed first-ever capital of Wales in 1955.

Reinvention has been the mantra for the city ever since, epitomised in the development of Europe's largest waterfront regeneration project, Cardiff Bay, during the 1990s and 2000s.

Sights

City Centre

★National Museum Cardiff MUSEUM

(Map p654; ☎0300 111 2333; www.museum.wales/cardiff; Gorsedd Gardens, CF10 3NP; ⏰10am-5pm Tue, Thu, Sat & Sun; P ♿) FREE Devoted mainly to art and natural history, this grand neoclassical building is the centrepiece of several institutions countrywide that together form the Welsh National Museum. It's among Britain's best museums; devote at least three hours to doing it justice. Boasting one of the world's most significant impressionist and post-impressionist collections, the **main gallery** rooms exhibit treasures such as Monet's *Water Lilies*, alongside his scenes of London, Rouen and Venice; a cast of Rodin's *The Kiss*; and Van Gogh's anguished *Rain, Auvers*.

★Cardiff Castle CASTLE

(Map p654; ☎029-2087 8100; www.cardiffcastle.com; Castle St; adult/child £14.50/10, incl guided tour £19.50/14; ⏰9am-6pm Mar-Oct, to 5pm Nov-Feb) There's a medieval keep at its

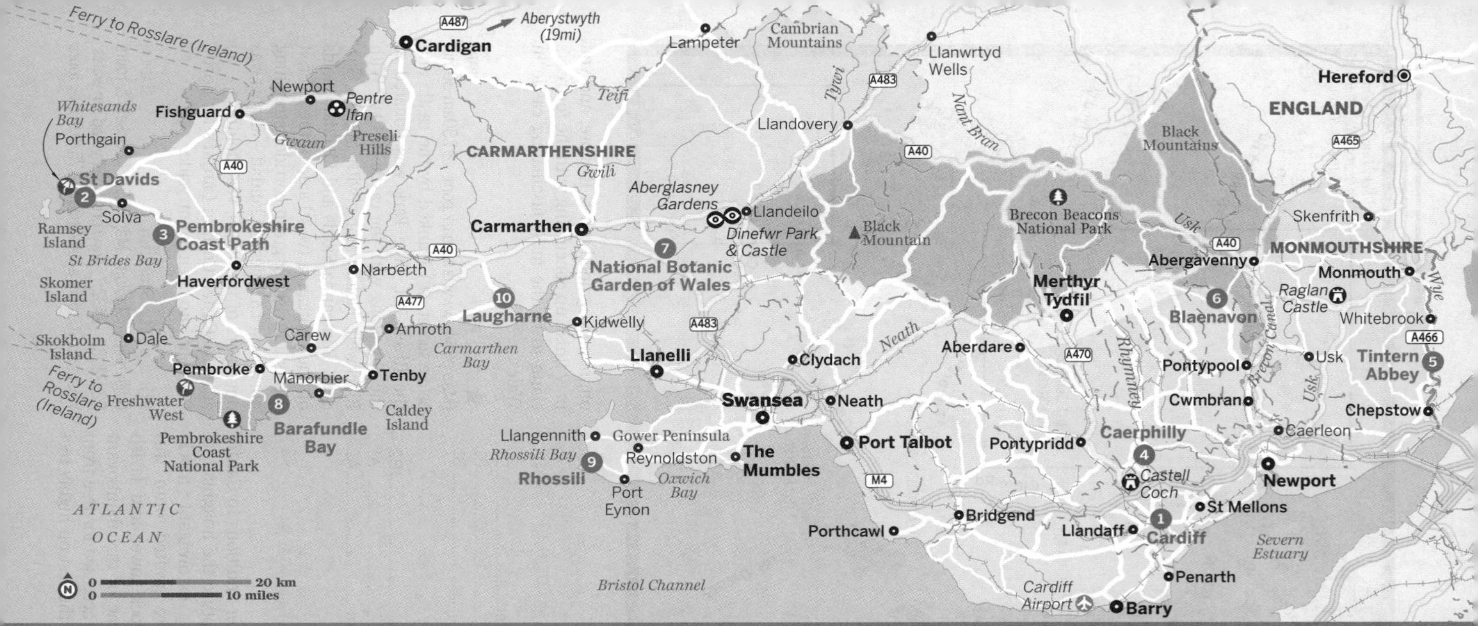

Cardiff Highlights

1. **Cardiff Castle** (p648) Marvelling at the Victorian extravagances grafted onto the city's citadel.
2. **St Davids** (p675) Exploring the little city with the spectacular cathedral.
3. **Pembrokeshire Coast Path** (p686) Tracing a collision of rock and sea along the county's coast.
4. **Caerphilly Castle** (p663) Crossing the moat and wandering into a fairy tale.
5. **Tintern Abbey** (p661) Strolling among romantic ruins in the glorious Wye Valley.
6. **Blaenavon** (p663) Feasting on World Heritage industrial sites and world-class cheese.
7. **National Botanic Garden of Wales** (p673) Admiring these glorious gardens.
8. **Barafundle Bay** (p683) Discovering which of Pembrokeshire's myriad majestic beaches is the finest.
9. **Rhossili** (p671) Watching the waves crash over Worms Head.
10. **Laugharne** (p673) Finding inspiration in the coastal town that stimulated Dylan Thomas.

Cardiff

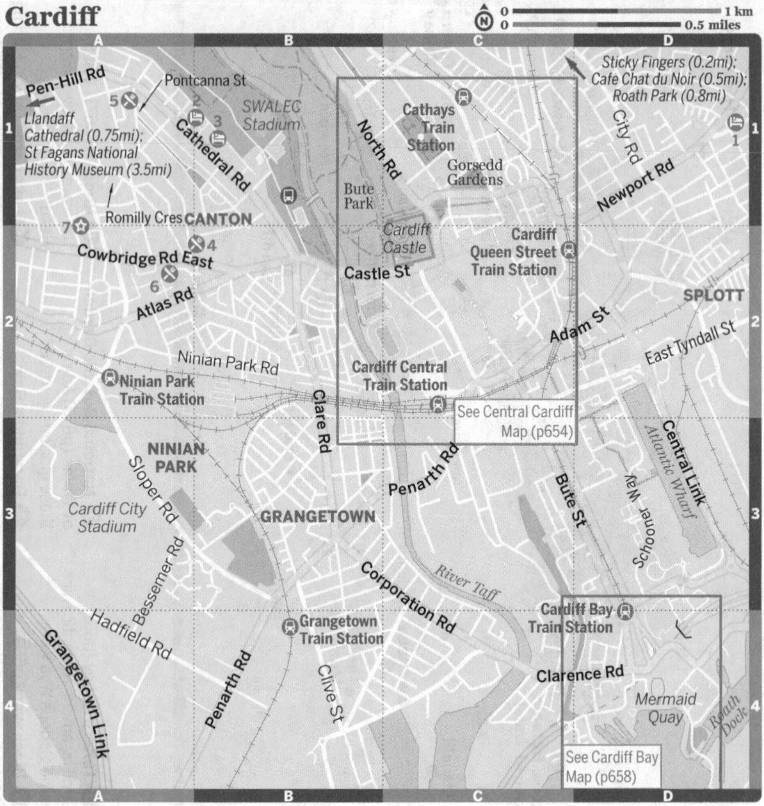

Cardiff

Sleeping

Eating

Entertainment

heart, but it's the later additions to Cardiff Castle that really capture the imagination. In Victorian times, extravagant mock-Gothic features were grafted onto this relic, including a clock tower and lavish banqueting hall. Some of this flamboyant fantasy world can be accessed for free from the castle courtyard; the rest on highly recommended guided tours. Explore, and you may finish up concurring with the fortress's claim to be the most fascinating castle in Wales.

★Bute Park PARK

(Map p654; www.bute-park.com; 7.30am-30min before sunset;) Flanked by the castle and the River Taff, Bute Park was donated to the city along with the castle in 1947. With Blackweir Fields, along with Sophia Gardens, Pontcanna Fields and Llandaff Fields on the Pontcanna (west) side of the river, it forms a ravishing green corridor stretching northwest 1.5 miles to Llandaff – all this was once part of the Butes' vast holdings – on again to Castell Coch in Cardiff's far north, then out into open countryside.

Principality Stadium STADIUM

(Millennium Stadium; Map p654; tickets & tours 029-2082 2432; www.principalitystadium.wales; Westgate St; tours adult/child £13.75/9.90; tours

10am-5pm Mon-Sat, 10.15am-4pm Sun) Also known as Millennium Stadium ('Principality' is the current naming-rights sponsor), this spectacular venue is Welsh rugby's heart and soul, squatting like a stranded spaceship on the River Taff's east bank. Seating 74,500 and built at a cost of £168 million, the three-tiered, retractable-roofed arena was completed in time to host 1999's Rugby World Cup. If you can't get match tickets, it's well worth taking a tour – book online for the best prices.

★St Fagans National History Museum MUSEUM

(☎0300 111 2333; https://museum.wales/stfagans; St Fagans; parking £6.50; ⌚10am-5pm Tue, Thu, Sat & Sun; P 🚸; 🚌32, 32A, 320) FREE Historic buildings from all over the country have been dismantled and re-erected in the semirural surrounds of St Fagans village, 5 miles west of central Cardiff. Almost 50 buildings are on show, including thatched farmhouses, barns, a watermill, a school, an 18th-century Unitarian chapel and shops selling period-appropriate goods. Buses 32, 32A and 320 (£2, 25 minutes) head here from Cardiff. By car it's reached from the continuation of Cathedral Rd (which becomes Pencisely Rd then St Fagans Rd).

Castell Coch CASTLE

(Cadw; ☎029-2081 0101; www.cadw.gov.wales; Castle Rd, Tongwynlais; adult/child £6.50/3.90; ⌚10am-1pm & 2-5pm Mar-Oct, 10am-4pm Wed-Sun Nov, Dec & Feb, closed Jan; P; 🚌26, 132) Cardiff Castle's fanciful little brother sits perched up a thickly wooded crag on the northern fringes of Cardiff. It was the summer retreat of the third marquess of Bute and, like Cardiff Castle, was designed by oddball architect William Burges in gaudy Gothic-revival style. Raised on the ruins of Gilbert de Clare's 13th-century Castell Coch (Red Castle), the Butes' Disneyesque holiday home is a monument to high camp. An excellent audio guide is included in the admission price.

⊙ Cardiff Bay

Lined with important national institutions, Cardiff Bay is where the modern Welsh nation is displayed in an architect's playground of interesting buildings, open spaces and public art.

It wasn't always thus. By 1913 more than 13 million tonnes of coal were being shipped from Cardiff's docks. Following the post-WWII slump, the docklands deteriorated into wasteland.

But the area has now been radically redeveloped. The real turning point came with the completion of state-of-the-art Cardiff Bay Barrage in 1999. Landmark buildings popped up in the early 2000s, and the area is ever-evolving even today.

Whilst there is astounding architecture here, most can be adequately appreciated from outside, or from further afield such as on the **Cardiff Bay Barrage** (www.cardiffharbour.com/barrage-story; 🚸) over which you can walk to Penarth.

Wales Millennium Centre ARTS CENTRE

(Map p658; ☎029-2063 6464; www.wmc.org.uk; Bute Pl, CF10 5AL; ⌚10am-6pm, later on show nights) FREE The centrepiece of Cardiff Bay's regeneration is this £106-million edifice, an architectural masterpiece of stacked Welsh slate in shades of purple, green and grey topped with an overarching bronzed steel shell. Designed by Welsh architect Jonathan Adams, it opened in 2004 as Wales' premier arts complex, housing major cultural organisations such as the Welsh National Opera and National Dance Company Wales.

Pierhead Building MUSEUM

(Map p658; ☎0300 200 6565; www.senedd.wales/en/visiting; Pierhead St, CF10 4PZ; ⌚9.30am-4.30pm Mon-Fri, from 10.30am Sat) FREE One of the waterfront's few Victorian remnants, Pierhead is a red-brick French Gothic confection, built in 1897 with Bute family money to impress the maritime traffic. Its ornate clock tower earned it the nickname 'Wales' Big Ben'. Once headquarters of Cardiff Railway, it is now shows a short film of what Cardiff Bay looked like pre-refurb, from the 1800s onwards, complemented by interactive displays and artefacts.

It's an offshoot of the **Senedd** (Map p658; www.assembly.wales; CF99 1SN; ⌚9.30am-4.30pm Mon-Fri, from 10.30am Sat & Sun) FREE, Wales' National Assembly, next door.

⊙ Northern Suburbs

Some of Cardiff's most intriguing areas lie in the suburbs immediately north of the city centre. East of Bute Park, proximity to the university makes the tightly packed Victorian terrace houses of up-and-coming Cathays and Maindy popular with students. It's fabulously multicultural and still gritty in parts.

For a broader (and very tourist-free!) taste of Cardiff life, stroll along the thoroughfares here. In the north, these areas become more well-heeled as they merge with more-affluent **Roath**, arranged around one of Cardiff's loveliest **parks** (www.outdoorcardiff.com/parks; Lake Rd, Roath; ⏲7.30am-sunset). Meanwhile, northwest of the centre, and backed by fetching fecund parkland, is **Pontcanna**. Come here to see upmarket Cardiff, ensconced among leafy streets, where some of the city's best places to brunch, lunch and dine await. To the north, Pontcanna bounds **Llandaff**, a handsome former village enfolding Cardiff's most eye-catching ecclesiastical sight, **Llandaff Cathedral** (☎029-2056 4554; www.llandaffcathedral.org.uk; Cathedral Close, CF5 2LA, Llandaff; ⏲2-4pm Mon-Fri, to 5pm Sat & Sun).

Festivals & Events

Six Nations SPORTS
(www.sixnationsrugby.com; ⏲Feb & Mar) The premier European rugby championship, with Wales taking on England, Scotland, Ireland, Italy and France. Cardiff normally hosts two or three home games at Principality Stadium (p650) – the atmosphere is supercharged, and accommodation should be booked well in advance.

Sŵn Festival MUSIC
(www.swnfest.com; ⏲Oct) New music from Wales and further afield is the thing here, backed by a little film and art, held in venues across Cardiff each October. Sŵn means 'noise' in English, by the way.

SEASIDE FUN

Cardiff's by the sea, right, so how about some rollicking good Welsh seaside fun, full of Victorian pleasure piers, ice cream licking on pretty beaches and even, should you dare to brave the temperatures, swimming? Such things happen not in the capital, but in the adjacent Vale of Glamorgan. **Penarth** is just across the River Ely from Cardiff and can supply the pier pleasure; less refined but certainly up-and-coming and with oodles of old-school sandy seaside charm is **Barry**, 7 miles west of Cardiff.

Sleeping

City Centre

Hotel One Hundred HOTEL $
(Map p650; ☎029-2010 5590; www.hotelonehundred.com; 100 Newport Rd, Adamsdown, CF24 1DG; r from £45; P 📶) Patterned metallic wallpaper and chandeliers add a touch of glam to the rooms of this small B&B-like hotel. It's on a busy arterial road, so expect some street noise in the front rooms. A continental breakfast is included in the rates. A minimum two-night stay applies, but one-night bookings are accepted for any unsold rooms three days prior to arrival.

It's self check-in with a code provided before arrival. Book in advance.

Sleeperz HOTEL $
(Map p654; ☎029-2047 8747; www.sleeperz.com/cardiff; Station Approach, Saunders Rd; r from £38.70; 📶) Some of the best budget private rooms in the city, small but clean, are provided in trademark style by the Sleeperz chain, which has four hotels across the UK. Cardiff's is right by (as in, alongside) Cardiff Central station in a large, five-floor contemporary building. Breakfast is £7.95 extra. Book online for cheapest rates.

★**Hotel Indigo** BOUTIQUE HOTEL $$
(Map p654; ☎0871 942 9104; www.ihg.com; Dominions Arcade, Queen St; r/ste from £62/103; 📶) The Indigo Hotel Group (IHG) has over a dozen hotels UK-wide, but only this one in Wales. Like other IHG offerings, it tailors itself uniquely to Cardiff and Welsh culture. Spacious rooms cleverly allude to aspects such as traditional Welsh fabrics above bed headboards, pictures of old industrial scenes and sheep decorating crockery. Insanely good value.

Park Plaza HOTEL $$
(Map p654; ☎029-2011 1111; www.parkplazacardiff.com; Greyfriars Rd; r £79-134, ste £149-169; ❄📶🏊) Luxurious without being stuffy, the Plaza has all the five-star facilities you'd expect from an upmarket business-oriented hotel, including a gym for guests, a spa, a restaurant/bar (open to all) and Egyptian cotton on the beds. The slick reception has a gas fire blazing along one wall, and rear rooms have leafy views over the Civic Centre.

Rates can be a smidgeon cheaper if you book online, in advance, and midweek. No parking, though – despite the name.

CARDIFF IN...

Two Days

Start with a stroll around the historic city centre, stopping to explore Cardiff Castle (p648) and National Museum Cardiff (p648) along the way. Lunch could be picnicking in Bute Park (p650) with treats acquired at Cardiff Market (p657) or, if the weather's not cooperating, a meal at any of the wondrous, dynamic, central-city eateries. On day two, either head back to the future at Cardiff Bay (p651), reconnoitring a remarkable mix of 19th-century and contemporary architecture backed by brilliant bayside vistas, or saunter through Wales' variegated past at the nation's foremost museum, St Fagans National History Museum (p651).

Four Days

Spend day three heading over to the Vale of Glamorgan, scouting out venerable seaside resorts Penarth (p652) and Barry Island (p652). On your last day, venture north to Llandaff Cathedral (p652), then continue on to Castell Coch (p651) and Caerphilly Castle (p663). For your last night, have a blast in one of the city's endlessly inventive bars (p656) or live-music venues (p656).

Pontcanna & Canton

Long, leafy Cathedral Rd is lined with B&Bs and small hotels, nearly all in restored Victorian town houses. It's only a 15- to 20-minute walk from the city centre, or a £10 taxi ride from the train and bus stations. Street parking is mostly unrestricted, but check signage carefully.

Lincoln House HOTEL $$

(Map p650; ☎029-2039 5558; www.lincolnhotel.co.uk; 118-120 Cathedral Rd, Pontcanna, CF11 9LQ; r £100-135, 2-4-person penthouse £190-290; P ☎) Walking a middle line between a large B&B and a small hotel, Lincoln House is a generously proportioned Victorian property with heraldic emblems in the stained-glass windows of its book-lined sitting room, and a separate bar. There are 21 rooms and a loft penthouse sleeping up to four. For added romance, book a four-poster room.

Saco Cardiff APARTMENT $$

(Map p650; ☎0845 122 0405; www.sacoapartments.co.uk; 76 Cathedral Rd, Pontcanna, CF11 9LN; 1-/2-bedroom apt from £105/129; P) This large town house has been given a contemporary makeover by Saco, which operates in several UK cities, converted into one- and two-bedroom serviced apartments with comfortable lounges and fitted kitchens. They're set up for longer visits: one-night stays are possible midweek, but rates can increase at weekends. The two-bedroom apartments are good value for families with kids.

Cardiff Bay

Voco St David's Hotel & Spa SPA HOTEL $$

(Map p658; ☎029-2045 4045; www.thestdavidshotel.com; Havannah St, CF10 5SD; d incl breakfast from £100; P @) One of the few five-star hotels in Cardiff, this high-end modern hotel favoured by corporate types and couples occupies the water's edge in Cardiff Bay. Its location offers panoramic views across Cardiff Bay, Penarth and over the Bristol Channel towards England. Rooms are plush and spacious, and the design, with its dramatic, futuristic central atrium, is a bit different.

The spa is one of Wales' best. Parking spaces go for a premium £20.

Eating

City Centre

Uncommon Ground Coffee Roastery CAFE $

(Map p654; www.uncommon-ground.co.uk; 10-12 Royal Arcade; sandwiches & snacks £3-7; 7.30am-6.30pm Mon-Sat, 10am-5pm Sun) Highly accomplished coffee roasters with a dark, debonair, bare-brick interior in one of Cardiff's classiest retail settings. The speciality teas and coffees are a welcome pick-me-up, the brownies are veritable slabs and a panini/salad selection completes the billing.

Pettigrew Tea Rooms CAFE $

(Map p654; ☎029-2023 5486; www.pettigrew-tearooms.com; West Lodge, Castle St; mains £6-12, afternoon tea for 1 person £17.50; 10am-6pm, closes 30min before dusk in winter) Cuppas and

Central Cardiff

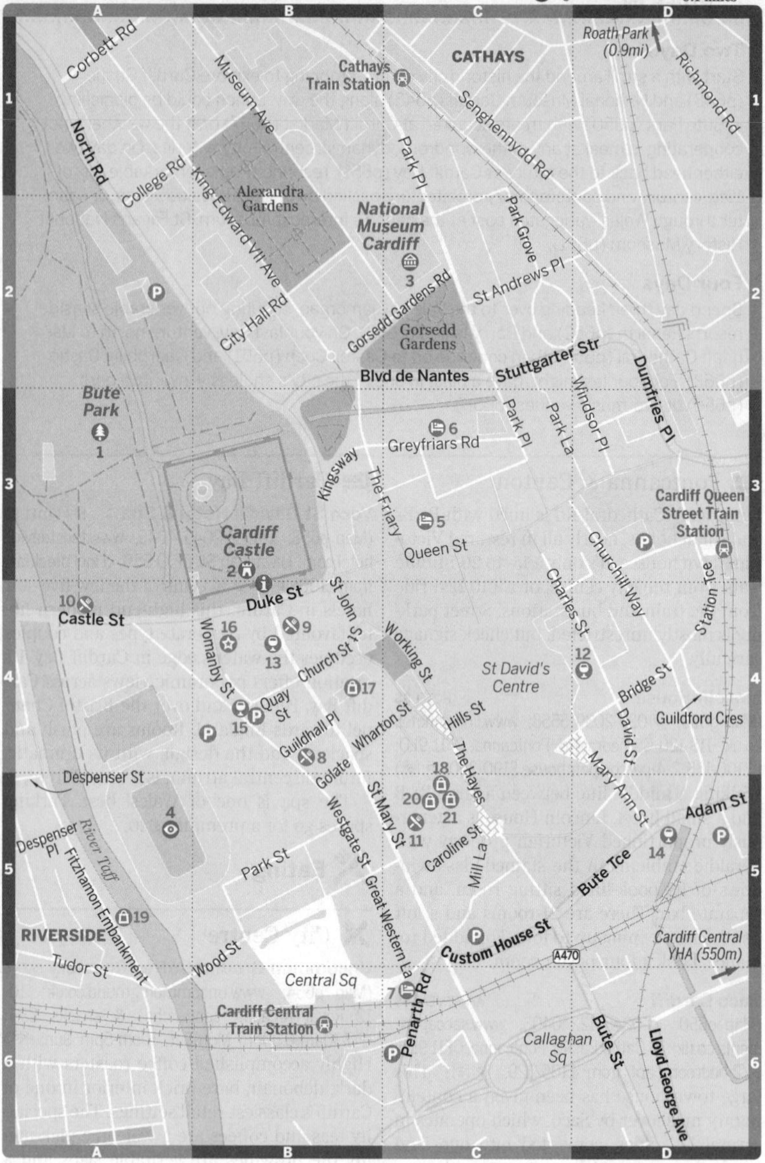

cakes are served on delicate china at this atmospheric little tearoom within the crenellated confines of Bute Park's 1863 gatehouse. Cucumber sandwiches, fabled afternoon teas, scuffed vintage furniture and crackly '20s tunes accompany the extensive range of beverages on offer – or try the ploughman's platter if you're after something more hearty.

★Curado SPANISH **$$**

(Map p654; ☎029-2034 4336; www.curadobar.com; Guildhall Pl; pintxos £3.50, other dishes £7-15; ⏲5-10pm Tue-Thu, noon-10pm Fri & Sat, to 6pm

Central Cardiff

Sun) This ranks among central Cardiff's best places to eat right now. Elegant Spanish food personally sourced by the owners is Wales' finest, served in the divine forms of *pintxos*, northern Spain's answer to tapas. Big glass windows and metro-tiled walls enclose two floors and a downstairs deli. We recommend *morcilla*, Spanish black pudding with goats cheese and peppers.

Staff are also incredibly knowledgeable, and the Spanish wine selection is eclectic. You need perhaps four small dishes for a filling meal, making this a brilliant midrange dining option.

Pasture STEAKHOUSE $$
(Map p654; ☎07511 217422; www.pasturerestaurant.com; 8-10 High St; mains £14-36; ⏲noon-10pm Mon-Sat, 11.45am-7pm Sun) The classy steakhouse that began in Bristol now has its second home in Cardiff – it was the Welsh capital's see-and-be-seen place as we went to press. Its glitzy presence on High St has dated most of its neighbours. Steak, steak, steak is the raison d'être, whether that's chateaubriand, tomahawk or porterhouse. Meats are dry-aged for 35 days minimum.

Pontcanna & Canton

Milkwood Bistro BISTRO $
(Map p650; ☎029-2023 2226; www.milkwoodcardiff.com; 83 Pontcanna St, Pontcanna, CF11 9HS; plates £4-11; ⏲5-10pm Wed, noon-10pm Thu-Sat) Brunch, lunch or dine here and feel the Pontcanna love. It advertises itself as modern Welsh, but while many ingredients fit the bill, the small plates, pizzas, burgers and sandwiches are pan-European, or even pan-world, encompassing buffalo wings, celeriac and schnitzel burgers, cod fritters and ox-cheek fries.

Purple Poppadom INDIAN $$
(Map p650; ☎029-2022 0026; www.purplepoppadom.com; 185a Cowbridge Rd E, Canton, CF1 9AJ; mains £11-20; ⏲5-10pm Tue-Sat, 1-9pm Sun; ✎) Trailblazing a path for 'nouvelle Indian' cuisine, chef and author Anand George adds his own twist to dishes from all over the subcontinent – from Kashmir to Kerala. The emphasis is on perfecting tried-and-tested regional delights rather than anything unnecessarily wacky. Plump for a *nadan kozhi* chicken thigh and coconut curry. Flavours are thought-provokingly rich.

La Cuina CATALAN $$
(Map p650; ☎029-2019 0265; www.lacuina.co.uk; 11 Kings Rd, Pontcanna, CF11 9BZ; mains £13-23; ⏲5.30-9.30pm Wed & Thu, to 10pm Fri & Sat) This cute Catalonian restaurant is *so* Pontcanna: a desirable, unpretentious place that passersby look longingly upon from the leafy streets, and which bursts with culinary love. Start with octopus, pea puree and paprika, then proceed with Aragón mountain lamb, washed back by vino from Catalan micro-producers. Chef-owner Montserrat has made this one of the neighbourhood's longest-running success stories. *Bravissimo.*

Cathays, Maindy & Roath

Sticky Fingers STREET FOOD $
(☎029-2047 0803; www.stickyfingersstreetfood.com; 199-201 Richmond Rd, Roath, CF24 3BT; ⏲5-10pm Mon-Fri, noon-10pm Sat & Sun) Based in

Roath, this permanent one-stop address for Cardiff street food has ever-changing stalls such as Cardiff classics **Dusty Knuckle** (07506 659306; www.dustyknuckle.co.uk; The Boneyard, Paper Mill Rd, Canton, CF11 8DH; pizza £8-15; 5-9pm Wed & Thu, noon-9pm Fri-Sun) and Tukka Tuk with its Indian fare from Anand George of Purple Poppadom (p655). At the bar, Cardiff breweries Pipes and Crafty Devil preside on the taps and there are good cocktails, too. Food Thursday to Sunday only.

Cafe Chat du Noir FRENCH $$
(029-2048 8993; 6 Wellfield Court Arcade, Wellfield Rd, Roath, CF24 3PB; mains £7-15; 4-9pm Wed & Thu, noon-9pm Fri & Sat, noon-4pm Sun) Eating out on trendy Wellfield Rd should start with this elegant French-Mediterranean-focused bistro that is forever making 'best in Cardiff' lists. You might opt for a croque – not just the standard monsieur, but also the likes of the Breton (with salmon) or *du Chat Noir* special (chicken and goats cheese), or plump for paella.

Drinking & Nightlife

Porter's BAR
(Map p654; www.porterscardiff.com; Harlech Ct, Bute Tce; 5-10pm Sun-Wed, 4-10pm Thu & Fri, noon-10pm Sat) Owned by a self-confessed 'failed actor', this friendly, attitude-free bar has something on most nights, whether it's a quiz, live music, comedy, theatre or movie screening (there's a little cinema attached). Local drama is showcased in the 'Other Room', the adjoining 44-seat theatre, while there's a wonderful beer garden out back.

Dead Canary COCKTAIL BAR
(Map p654; 029-2023 1263; www.thedeadcanary.co.uk; Barrack Lane; 5-10pm Tue-Sun) Inspired by Prohibition-era bars, this swanky speakeasy is hidden behind a narrow city-centre lane. Find the bell with a feather painted nearby (it's near a fire-exit sign). You'll then enter the dimly lit bar, with low seats, a jazz-club vibe and the best cocktails in town. Book ahead.

Tiny Rebel CRAFT BEER
(Map p654; 029-2039 9557; www.tinyrebel.co.uk; 25 Westgate St; 5-10pm Mon-Thu, noon-10pm Fri-Sun;) Slathered in graffiti art, this sprawling grunge-chic corner bar is the Cardiff outpost of an award-winning craft brewery from neighbouring Newport. Expect 15 craft beers on keg, 10 on cask and others by the bottle – both their own and guest brews (we love an Easy Livin' pale ourselves). Good whiskies and regular gigs (from punk to cabaret) in non-Covid-19 times.

Gin & Juice JUICE BAR
(Map p654; 029-2022 1556; www.ginandjuice.com; 2-6 Castle Arcade; 8.30am-10pm) In a seriously beautiful, tile-festooned, old-photograph-studded premises where historic Castle Arcade meets High St, and with tables spilling out onto the latter, Gin and Juice is an exuberant all-day affair. By day it's a juice, coffee, smoothie and bagel bar, and by night a gin den lovingly nursing some 400 varieties of gin.

Academy @ Platform CAFE
(Map p658; www.academycoffee.co.uk/academy-platform; Bute St, Cardiff Bay railway station, CF10 5LE; 9am-5pm Mon-Thu, to 10pm Fri & Sat, 10am-5pm Sun) Alighting from the train at Cardiff Bay, you won't find a better place for java than this swish platform new-build. Beans get sustainably sourced in Minas Gerais, Brazil, and consequent cuppas are pretty darned special (remember this as you invariably shun our advice and stray to the waterside vainly searching for nicer drinking spots). Come for craft beer and cocktails, too.

☆ Entertainment

It's really important, especially when much entertainment has been disrupted by Covid-19, to get an up-to-the-minute take on what's happening. Pick up a copy of *Buzz* (www.buzzmag.co.uk), a free monthly magazine with up-to-date entertainment listings, available from tourist offices, bars, theatres and the like. Staff at the tourist office (p657) at Cardiff Castle can also help out with recommendations.

★ Clwb Ifor Bach LIVE MUSIC
(Map p654; 029-2023 2199; www.clwb.net; 11 Womanby St; cover from £5; 7-10.30pm Sun-Wed, to 4am Thu-Sat) Named for 12th-century Welsh rebel Ifor Bach, the legendary Clwb ('Club') has broken many a Welsh band since it first opened its doors in 1983, building a reputation as Cardiff's most important indie-music venue. It now hosts bands performing in many tongues – from young upstarts to more established acts – along with regular club nights (Saturday is the big one).

Chapter ARTS CENTRE

(Map p650; 029-2031 1050; www.chapter.org; Market Rd, Canton, CF5 1QE; 9am-9pm;) Established in 1972 and still Cardiff's edgiest arts venue, Chapter masterminds a varied rota of art exhibitions (often free), art-house cinema (tickets £6), contemporary drama, workshops and dance performances. There's also a very popular cafe-bar, with a big range of international beers and real ale on tap.

Shopping

Cardiff Market MARKET

(Map p654; www.cardiffcouncilproperty.com/cardiff-market; St Mary St, CF10 1AU; 8am-4.30pm Mon-Sat) There's been a market here since the 18th century, but the current iron-framed covered market dates to 1891. Stalls sell everything from fresh fish to knitting supplies, and there's inspirational fare for a Bute Park picnic. Top stalls? Ashton's (fishmongers; supposedly trading on this spot 150-plus years), Noglu (delicious gluten-free treats), Hatts Emporium (vintage clothes and accessories) and upstairs, Kelly's Records (vinyl).

Riverside Market MARKET

(Map p654; www.riversidemarket.org.uk; Fitzhamon Embankment, Riverside, CF11 6AN; 10am-1.30pm Sun) Every Sunday, this street market takes over the embankment across the Taff from Principality Stadium. Independent producers flaunt their wares, from speciality cheeses, homemade sourdough bread and cured meats to fresh vegetables, jars of jam and hefty cronuts. Seating lets you watch the river go by while sipping great coffee and scoffing your goodies.

Morgan Quarter SHOPPING CENTRE

(Map p654; www.morganquarter.co.uk; btwn St Mary St & The Hayes) Cardiff's oldest arcade, the Royal (1858), connects with Morgan Arcade via a series of covered lanes, forming a ritzy shopping precinct called the Morgan Quarter, which is the most beautiful of the city's arcade experiences. Along with name-brand fashion, shops sell skateboards, vintage books and antiques. Look for **Spillers Records** (029-2022 4905; www.spillersrecords.co.uk; 27 Morgan Arcade; 10.30am-5pm Mon-Sat) and excellent **Wally's Delicatessen** (029-2022 9265; www.wallysdeli.co.uk; 38-46 Royal Arcade; 9am-5.30pm Mon-Sat, 11am-4pm Sun) for scoffable takeaway goodies or foodie souvenirs.

Information

Tourist Office (Map p654; 029-2087 2167; www.visitcardiff.com; Cardiff Castle; 9am-5pm Mar-Oct, to 4pm Nov-Feb) In the Cardiff Castle courtyard, this is Cardiff's key tourist information centre. Souvenir shop and eateries adjacent.

Getting There & Away

AIR

Cardiff Airport (01446-711111; www.cardiff-airport.com; Rhoose, CF62 3BD) is 12 miles southwest of Cardiff, past Barry. Airlines with regular scheduled flights into Cardiff:

Eastern Airways (www.easternairways.com) Belfast, Anglesey, Teeside.

KLM (www.klm.com) Amsterdam.

Loganair (www.loganair.co.uk) Edinburgh, Glasgow.

Ryanair (www.ryanair.com) Málaga, Faro.

TUI Airways (www.tui.co.uk; Mar-Oct only) Alicante, Gran Canaria, Lanzarote, Málaga, Tenerife, Rhodes, Antalya, Paphos, Dubrovnik, Corfu.

Vueling (www.vueling.com) Alicante, Málaga, Palma de Mallorca.

BUS

Cardiff's big new bus station is due to open in Wood St in 2023. In the meantime, buses call at stops scattered around the city; see www.traveline.cymru for details. Welsh destinations served include Caerphilly (£5.60, 45 minutes, half-hourly), Newport (£2.30, one hour, frequent) and Brecon (£7.20, two hours, five daily). Swansea (£5, 1¼ hours, every one to two hours) is best for points further west.

National Express (www.nationalexpress.com) coaches depart from **Cardiff Coach Station** (Map p650; Sophia Gardens). Destinations include Swansea (from £5.50, 1¼ hours, two daily), Bristol (£7.60, 1¼ hours, seven daily) and London (£15 to £25, 4½ hours, three daily).

If you're connecting between Cardiff and London Heathrow Airport, you don't need to go via central London but can take the direct bus (from £14, 3½ hours, three daily).

Megabus (www.megabus.com) coaches stop on Kingsway. Destinations include Swansea (from £5, one hour, one daily) and Newport (from £3, 30 minutes, five daily). Services to Bristol (from £5, 1¼ hours, every two hours) usually continue to Heathrow Airport (from £17.50, 3¾ hours, six daily) and London (from £15, 4½ hours, six daily).

Cardiff Bay

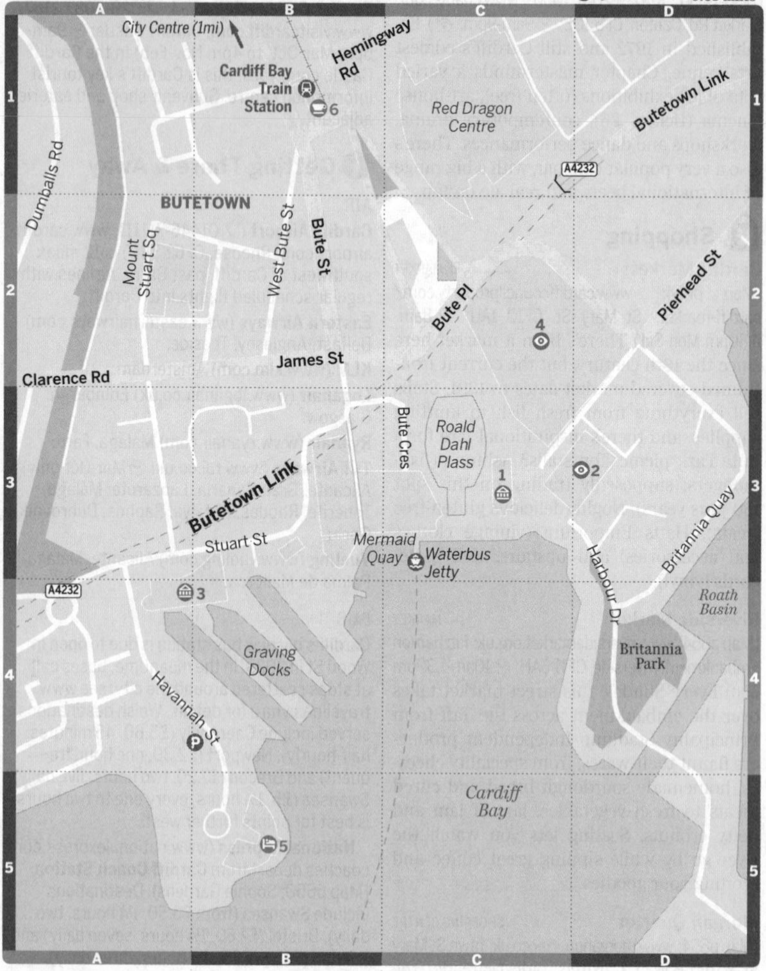

Cardiff Bay

Sights
1 Pierhead Building C3
2 Senedd D3
3 Techniquest A4
4 Wales Millennium Centre C2

Sleeping
5 Voco St David's Hotel & Spa B5

Drinking & Nightlife
6 Academy @ Platform B1

TRAIN

Trains from major British cities arrive at Cardiff Central station, on the southern edge of the city centre. Direct services to/from Cardiff include London Paddington (from £27.60, two hours, hourly), Abergavenny (£14.70, 40 minutes, at least hourly), Swansea (£12, one hour, at least hourly), where you can change for points further west such as Tenby and Fishguard Harbour, and Shrewsbury (£48.60, two hours, hourly), where you can change for points in North Wales. For the latest timetables and bookings, see www.thetrainline.com.

Getting Around

TO/FROM THE AIRPORT

The T9 Cardiff Airport Express bus (£5, 44 minutes, every 20 minutes) heads between the airport and Cardiff Bay via the city centre, though this was suspended at the time of writing due to Covid-19. The 304 Cardiff–Llantwit Major service (£2.65, one hour, hourly) stops at the airport, too.

The 905 shuttle bus (£1, nine minutes) links the airport terminal to nearby Rhoose Cardiff Airport railway station. Trains from Rhoose to Cardiff Central station (£4.80, 35 minutes) run hourly Monday to Saturday and every two hours on Sunday.

FlightLink Wales (☎01446-728 500; www.flightlinkwales.com) has the airport taxi concession, providing minibus shuttles to the city for £33.

BOAT

Aquabus (☎029-2034 5163; https://aquabus.co.uk; adult/child £4/2) and **Cardiff Boat** (☎07445 440874; www.cardiffboat.com; adult/child £5/2) run alternating waterbus services along the River Taff between Bute Park to Cardiff Bay's Mermaid Quay, departing every half-hour from 10am to 5pm. The journey takes about 25 minutes.

BUS

Most local buses are operated by **Cardiff Bus** (☎029-2066 6444; www.cardiffbus.com; single trip/day pass £2/4); buy your ticket from the driver (cash or contactless; no change given). Useful routes from the city centre:

- **6** ('The Baycar') and **8/8S/9** to Cardiff Bay (from Customhouse St)
- **28** to Cathays and Roath Park (from the Fitzalan Pl stop on the A4161 just north of Queen St train station)
- **61** and **63** via Cathedral Rd to Llandaff (from Westgate St)
- **32A** (operated by Easyway) and **320** (operated by New Adventure Travel) to St Fagans (from Westgate St)

TRAIN

Trains can (sometimes) be as convenient as buses for some cross-Cardiff trips. Useful routes:

- Cardiff Queen St–Cardiff Bay (£2.30)
- Cardiff Queen St–Llandaff (£3.20)
- Cardiff Central–Penarth (£3.20)

Journey time is about seven minutes for any of these.

MONMOUTHSHIRE (SIR FYNWY)

You need only ponder the preponderance of castles to realise that this pleasantly rural county was once a wild frontier. The Norman marcher lords kept stonemasons extremely busy, erecting mighty fortifications to keep the Welsh at bay. Despite this stone line marking out a very clear border along the Rivers Monnow and Wye, the 1543 second Act of Union left Monmouthshire in a kind of jurisdictional limbo between England and Wales. This legal ambiguity wasn't put to rest until 1974, when Monmouthshire was definitively confirmed as part of Wales. In some ways, towns such as Chepstow and Monmouth are among Wales' most English-looking today.

The River Wye, Britain's fifth longest, flows from the mountains of Mid-Wales, tootles its way into England and then returns to the middle ground – forming the border of the two countries – before emptying into the River Severn below Chepstow. Much of it is designated an Area of Outstanding Natural Beauty (AONB; www.wyevalleyaonb.org.uk), famous for its limestone gorges, dense broadleaved woodland and epic medieval ruins.

Chepstow

☎01291 / POP 12,400

Stick to the several remaining unspoilt historic thoroughfares snaking about its bulky castle battlements and you will find Chepstow clinging on to some of its century-old good looks. Its main attraction is its magnificent 11th-century fortress: the town was first developed as a base for Norman conquest of southeast Wales (and was only narrowly 'Welsh', with the Wye cutting its eastern edge made the Wales–England boundary by kingdom-forming King Athelstan, in 982). Chepstow later prospered as a timber and wine port, but as river-borne commerce gave way to the railways, its importance diminished to reflect its name, which means 'market place' in Old English. Its status as a major hiking centre, however, means it's well worth staying the night.

Sights

★Chepstow Castle CASTLE
(Cadw; ☎01291-624065; www.cadw.gov.wales; Bridge St; adult/child £6.50/3.90; ⏲10am-1pm & 2-5pm Wed-Sun Mar-Oct, to 4pm Nov-Feb; 👪)

Imposing Chepstow Castle perches atop limestone cliffs overhanging the river, guarding the main river crossing from England into South Wales. It is among Britain's oldest castles – building started in 1067, under a year after William the Conqueror invaded England – and the nation's oldest post-Roman stone-built structure. The impressive Great Tower dates from the 1060s and includes bricks plundered from Caerwent, a nearby Roman town. It was extended over the centuries, resulting in a long, narrow complex snaking along the hill.

Activities

Chepstow teems with walking possibilities (the same applies to upstream Tintern), with the winding Wye offering scenic strolls close to town along its verdant banks.

The **Wales Coast Path** (www.walescoastpath.gov.uk), the world's first hiking trail to traverse all of a country's coastline, begins (or ends) beneath the grassy slopes of Chepstow Castle.

The **Wye Valley Walk** (www.wyevalleywalk.org) has one of its trailheads near the castle in Chepstow, while the 177-mile **Offa's Dyke Path** (www.nationaltrail.co.uk) starts just over the river at Sedbury Cliffs. For a taste of both, you can walk upriver to Tintern Abbey on the former, cross the bridge just past the abbey and take the path to Devil's Pulpit, where you can join the latter for the return leg. Total distance: around 13 miles. Ordnance Survey (OS) Explorer map OL14 is recommended. You can cut the walk short at Tintern and return to Chepstow by bus (or stay in Tintern!).

Sleeping & Eating

First Hurdle Guest House GUESTHOUSE $
(☎01291-622189; www.thefirsthurdle.co.uk; 9-10 Upper Church St; r from £55; 📶) One of the best-value bed-and-breakfasts in town is on a pretty street leading along to the castle. There are 12 spick-and-span rooms here, including a cute family room tucked up in the eaves. These guys run an award-winning pizzeria situated next door, too: what's not to love?

Three Tuns PUB $
(☎01291-645797; 32 Bridge St; s/d from £45/65; 📶) This mid-17th-century pub by the castle is Chepstow's best watering hole to grab a pint or take your pick from the pie-heavy pub menu (mains £10.50). With Tintern-based Kingstone Brewery beers, and an artful makeover, with rugs and antique furniture complementing the more rugged features of the ancient building, it's equally conducive to stay in one of the three en-suite guest rooms.

Information

Tourist Information Centre (☎01291-623772; Bridge St; ⊙10am-1.30pm & 2-4pm) One of the most helpful centres in South Wales, with a shop showcasing Welsh produce. Across from the castle.

Getting There & Away

BUS

From Chepstow's **bus station** (Thomas St), frequent X74 and 73 services head to/from Newport (£3.80, 45 minutes to an hour) where many more connections, including to London and Cardiff, await. Up to 10 daily 69 services head to/from Tintern (£2.95, 16 minutes).

TRAIN

There are frequent direct trains to/from Newport (£8, 23 minutes), Gloucester (£10.90, 30 minutes) and Cardiff (£10.60, 40 minutes), but only one direct service per day to Swansea (£29.70, 1¾ hours). Change in Cardiff or Swansea for direct services to Carmarthen, Tenby and Fishguard Harbour.

Lower Wye Valley

The A466 road follows the meandering, steep and tree-cloaked valley of the River Wye from Chepstow to Monmouth, passing through the village of Tintern, strung out around its gorgeous famous abbey as in the late-18th-century heyday of tourism here. This is a beautiful and little-visited pocket of Wales, rendered particularly mysterious when a twilight mist rises from the river and shrouds the illuminated ruins.

Much of this fecund area is now part of the Wye Valley AONB, and the countryside hereabouts is likely to be the highlight of your trip to southeast Wales. Tiny lanes and pathways thread through dense woods to reach serendipitous ancient sites, gastronomic gems and picturesque panoramas.

As with nearby Chepstow, walking is the big activity here after you've eyed the abbey ruins. Tintern is bang on the Wye Valley Walk and just below the Offa's Dyke Path at Devil's Pulpit. Kayaking on the Wye is also rightly popular.

Sights

★Tintern Abbey ABBEY

(Cadw; 0300-025 2239; www.cadw.gov.wales; Tintern; adult/child £5/2.30; 10am-1pm & 2-5pm Wed-Sun Mar-Oct, to 4pm Nov-Feb; P) The haunting riverside ruins of this sprawling monastic complex have inspired poets and artists through the centuries, notably William Wordsworth, who penned 'Lines Composed a Few Miles Above Tintern Abbey' during a 1798 visit, and JMW Turner, who made many paintings and drawings of the site. It was founded in 1131 by the Cistercian order and fell into picturesque ruin after the monks were booted out by Henry VIII in 1536. Tickets must be booked in advance via the website.

Devil's Pulpit VIEWPOINT

(above Tintern; 24hr) This viewpoint high above Tintern Abbey is best combined as part of a 5-mile circular walk from Tintern, and was doubtless an inspiration for the Wordsworth poem 'Lines Composed a Few Miles Above Tintern Abbey', with the hilly forest parting here to allow a majestic peep out and over the Wye floodplain. Extend your leg-stretch by continuing on a section of the Offa's Dyke path, which you can pick up here.

Kingstone Brewery BREWERY

(01291-680111; www.kingstonebrewery.co.uk; NP16 7NX; noon-4pm Mon-Wed, Fri & Sat; P) FREE Kingstone Brewery has something of the maverick about it, making takes on traditional ales and often according to archaic recipes. That would be enough to warrant visiting, but the pretty complex of wood-ensconced wooden buildings, engaging explanations of the brewing process and on-site canoe hire (£45 for a 2½-hour paddle) and bike rental (£24 per day) seal the deal.

Sleeping & Eating

★Hop Garden CABIN $$

(01291-680111; www.thehopgarden.co.uk/glamping; Kingstone Brewery, NP16 7NX; d £115; P) The serene meadows and copses encompassing Kingstone Brewery secrete five creaky glamping retreats, collectively called the Hop Garden: two shepherd's huts and three cabins, all isolated from each other, each sleeping two and abounding with their own fabulous quirks. Escaping the day-to-day is the point, so there's no wi-fi, but each has a wood-burning stove or outside firepit, which is much more fun!

DON'T MISS

RAGLAN CASTLE

The last great medieval castle to be built in Wales, **Raglan** (Cadw; 01291-690228; www.cadw.gov.wales; Castle Rd, Raglan; adult/child £6.50/3.90; 10am-1pm & 2-5pm Wed-Sun Mar-Sep, 11am-4pm Wed-Sun Nov-Feb; P) was designed more as a swaggering declaration of wealth and power than a defensive fortress. A magnificent, sprawling complex built of dusky pink and grey sandstone, it was constructed in the 15th and 16th centuries by Sir William ap Thomas and his son William Herbert, the first earl of Pembroke.

Raglan Castle is on the busy A40, 8 miles southwest of Monmouth and 9 miles southeast of Abergavenny. Buses heading between the two stop at Raglan village, which is a five-minute walk from the castle.

★Whitebrook MODERN BRITISH $$$

(01600-860254; www.thewhitebrook.co.uk; Whitebrook, NP25 4TX; 3-course menu/lunch/dinner £35/55/85, d incl dinner from £330; noon-2pm & 7-9pm Wed-Sun; P) Hidden down green-canopied country lanes in a remote part of the Wye Valley, this wonderful Michelin-starred restaurant-with-rooms is well worth the effort to find. Every plate proceeding from the kitchen is a little work of art, made largely with what can be sourced from within 12 miles and adorned with foraged herbs such as monkwort, nettles, wild garlic and elderflower.

Getting There & Away

Eleven Bus 69 services a day (fewer on Saturday, none on Sunday) stop here on their journey between Chepstow (£2.95, 16 minutes) and Monmouth (£3.95, 30 minutes). You may want your own wheels.

Abergavenny

01873 / POP 12,500

Abergavenny is a classically idiosyncratic Welsh market town, replete with independent businesses and sporting a higgledy-piggledy look that works its workaday charm on you the longer you linger. It has played many roles on history's stage: Roman fort, Norman stronghold and prison for Hitler's deputy – and interesting remnants of that past remain. But, nestled between three shapely peaks – the **Blorenge, Skirrid** (Ysgyryd Fawr) and **Sugar Loaf** (Mynydd Pen-y-Fâl) – it's mainly an excellent base for walkers, with uplifting greenery everywhere around. Hosting a Michelin-starred restaurants on its fringes, as well as Wales' leading annual food festival, it also lures devotees of Welsh produce and cooking.

Sights

★ St Mary's Priory Church CHURCH
(01873-858787; www.stmarys-priory.org; Monk St; 9am-4pm Mon-Sat) FREE Although you wouldn't guess it from the outside, this large stone church has been described as the 'Westminster Abbey of South Wales' because of the remarkable treasury of aristocratic tombs that lies within. It was founded at the same time as the Norman castle (1087) as part of a Benedictine priory, but the present building dates mainly from the 14th century, with 15th- and 19th-century additions and alterations.

Festivals & Events

Abergavenny Food Festival FOOD & DRINK
(www.abergavennyfoodfestival.co.uk; mid-Sep) The most important gastronomic event in Wales is held on the third weekend in September, with demonstrations, debates, competitions, courses, stalls and the odd celebrity. But the real drawcard is that this is an enthusiastically local festival, run by volunteers, and not some big-budget food producer's showcase. At night there's a market and events at the castle.

Sleeping & Eating

Angel Hotel HOTEL $$$
(01873-857121; www.angelabergavenny.com; 15 Cross St; r £135-195, cottages £255-295; P) Abergavenny's top hotel is a fine Georgian building that was once a famous coaching inn. Choose between sleek, sophisticated rooms in the hotel itself, in an adjoining mews, in a Victorian lodge near the castle or in the 17th-century Castle Cottage (sleeping four). There's also a good restaurant and bar, serving modern British food and elaborate afternoon and high teas.

Room prices do increase slightly on weekend nights.

Cwtch Cafe CAFE $
(01873-855466; 58 Cross St; snacks & mains £5-6; 9am-5pm Mon-Sat) Stylish and wonderfully friendly, Cwtch (Welsh for 'hug') entices a scrum of regulars through the doors with its homemade cakes, coffee, and lunchtime dishes such as rarebit, Canadian pancakes (with crispy bacon and maple syrup), quiche and gourmet pasties. There are plenty of gluten-free options, too.

★ Walnut Tree MODERN BRITISH $$$
(01873-852797; www.thewalnuttreeinn.com; Old Ross Rd, Llanddewi Skirrid; mains £28-32, 2-/3-course lunch £30/35; noon-2.30pm & 6-10pm Wed-Sat; P) Established in 1963, the Michelin-starred Walnut Tree serves the cuisine-hopping meat and seafood creations of chef Shaun Hill, with a focus on fresh, local produce. If you're too full to move far after feasting on dishes such as middle white pork loin with glazed cheek and cauliflower, elegant cottage accommodation is available (from £175).

The Walnut Tree is 3 miles northeast of Abergavenny on the B4521.

Information

Tourist Office (0785-499 7541; abergavennytic@yahoo.com; Cross St, by Abergavenny Market; 10am-4pm Mon-Sat) The tourist office was in the process of relocating to new premises next to Abergavenny Market and the Town Hall at the time of research, and also becoming a National Park Centre for the surrounding Brecon Beacons National Park.

Getting There & Away

There are direct trains from Abergavenny's train station to/from Cardiff (£14.70, 45 minutes, hourly), Swansea (£27.20, 1¾ hours, up to 16 daily), Manchester (£65, 2¾ hours, hourly), Tenby (£46, 3¾ hours, up to five daily changing at Carmarthen) and Holyhead (£78.60, 4¾ hours, up to 15 daily changing at Shrewsbury).

Direct services at Abergavenny's bus station (by Swan Meadow) include the X3 to/from Hereford (£5.90, 55 minutes, six daily), the hourly X4 service to/from Cardiff (£8.10, 2¾ hours) and 10 daily X43 services to/from Brecon (£3.90, 40 minutes to one hour).

SOUTH WALES VALLEYS

The valleys fanning north from Cardiff and Newport were once the heart of industrial Wales, playing a part in national (and world) history that can't be overstated. Although the coal, iron and steel industries have withered, the valley names – Rhondda, Cynon,

Rhymney, Ebbw – still evoke a world of tight-knit working-class communities, male-voice choirs and rows of neat terraced houses set amid a scarred, coal-blackened landscape. Today the region is fighting back against a very noticeable and tragic decline by creating a tourism industry celebrating and preserving its industrial heritage – places such as the Big Pit and Blaenavon Ironworks are among Wales' most impressive and historically poignant tourist attractions.

Blaenavon

☎ 01495 / POP 6050

Of all the valley settlements that were decimated by the demise of heavy industry, the one-time coal and iron town of Blaenavon shows the greenest shoots of regrowth, helped in large part by the awarding of Unesco World Heritage status in 2000 to its unique conglomeration of industrial sites. Its proximity to Brecon Beacons National Park and Abergavenny doesn't do it any harm either. Anyone with a passing interest in industrial history (or social history, for that matter) should stop here.

Sights

Blaenavon World Heritage Centre MUSEUM

(☎ 01495-742333; www.visitblaenavon.co.uk; Church Rd; ⏲ 10am-5pm Tue-Sun) FREE Housed in an artfully converted old school, this centre contains a cafe, a tourist office, a gallery, a gift shop and, more importantly, excellent interactive audiovisual displays that explore the industrial heritage of the region. If you're going to explore any of the World Heritage Site, this is the place to start to contextualise it all.

Blaenavon Ironworks HISTORIC SITE

(Cadw; ☎ 01495-792615; www.cadw.gov.wales; North St; adult/child £5.20/3.10; ⏲ 10am-5pm daily Easter-Oct, 11am-4pm Fri-Sun Nov-Easter) When it was completed in 1789, this ironworks was among the most advanced in the world. Today the site is among the best preserved of all its Industrial Revolution contemporaries, with a motion-activated audiovisual display within the hulking remains of one of the blast furnaces. Also on display, but temporarily closed at time of research, are the ironworkers' tiny terraced cottages, furnished as they would have been at different points in history.

WORTH A TRIP

CAERPHILLY CASTLE

The town of **Caerphilly**, centred on a massive, moated masterpiece of a **castle** (Cadw; www.cadw.gov.wales; Castle St; adult/child £8/4.80; ⏲ 10am-1pm & 2-5pm Wed-Sun; 👪) that would be too ostentatiously OTT for most fairy tales, guards the entrance to the Rhymney Valley to the north of Cardiff. Its name is synonymous with a popular variety of mild, slightly crumbly, hard white cheese that was once made in farmhouses all over South Wales.

The easiest way to reach Caerphilly is from Cardiff by train (£4.60, 18 minutes, up to three per hour).

Pontypool & Blaenavon Railway HERITAGE RAILWAY

(☎ 01495-792263; www.bhrailway.co.uk; Furnace Sidings, Garn-Yr-Erw; per 8-person compartment £32) Constructed to haul coal and passengers, this railway has been restored by local volunteers, allowing you to catch a train 3.5 miles from the town centre (Blaenavon High Level Station) to Furnace Sidings (near Big Pit) and then on to Whistle Halt, which at 396m is one of Britain's highest stations. Check online for running days and times, most of which involve restored steam locomotives.

At the time of research, Covid-19 restrictions meant that each separate group needs to book an entire train compartment, seating up to eight people (regardless of their group size).

★ **Big Pit National Coal Museum** MINE

(☎ 0300-111 2333; www.museum.wales/bigpit; car park £3; ⏲ 10am-5pm Tue, Wed, Fri & Sat, guided tours 10am-3.30pm; P 👪) FREE Fascinating Big Pit provides an opportunity to explore a real coal mine and taste what life was like for the miners working here between 1880 to 1980. At the time of research, the biggest attraction, the Real Underground Experience, where tours descend 90m into the mine and explore the tunnels and coalfaces guided by an ex-miner, was closed. Nevertheless, there's plenty going on above ground. You can visit numerous colliery buildings, including the 1939 pithead baths.

TONY BAGGETT/SHUTTERSTOCK ©

1. National Museum Cardiff (p648)
This museum boasts one of the world's most significant impressionist and post-impressionist collections.

2. Blue Lagoon, Porthgain (p678)
This deep, cold pool was formed in a flooded former slate quarry.

3. Tintern Abbey (p661)
Founded in 1131, these sprawling monastic ruins have inspired poets and artists for decades.

4. Big Pit National Coal Museum (p663)
Explore a real coal mine that was in operation from 1880 to 1980.

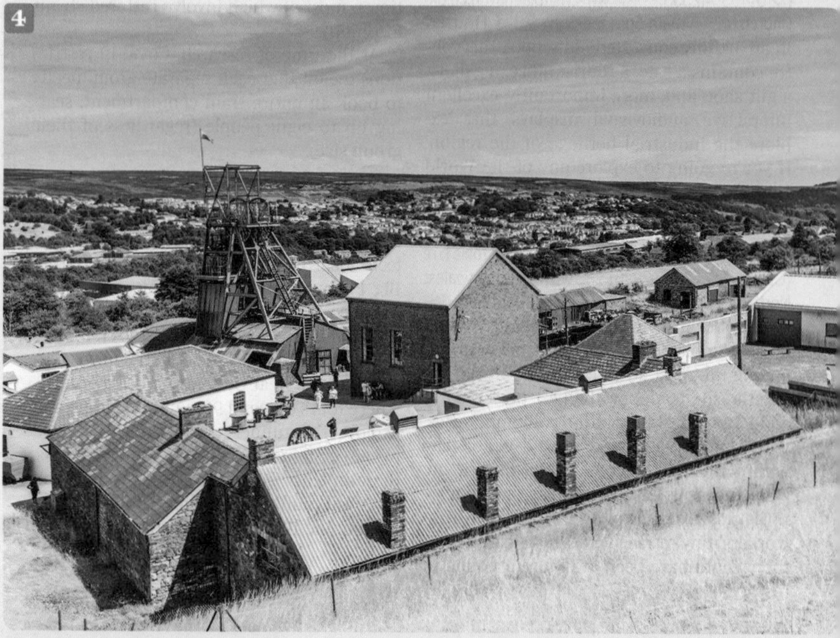

CLAUDIO DIVIZIA/SHUTTERSTOCK ©

Sleeping

Oakfield B&B $$

(☎01495-792829; www.oakfieldbnb.com; 1 Oakfield Tce, Varteg Rd; d £75; P 📶) Paula and Heidi, clued-up owners of this spick-and-span B&B, are a fount of local knowledge. Three well-appointed rooms have a fresh, modern feel. Two have en-suite bathrooms, with the third an interconnected family suite having a bathroom on the landing. At the time of research they were only offering one room (or permitting one household group) at any one time.

Shopping

Blaenavon Cheddar Company CHEESE

(☎01495-793123; www.chunkofcheese.co.uk; 80 Broad St; ⏲10am-3pm Mon-Fri) Showcasing the company's range of award-winning handmade cheese, some of which is matured down in the Big Pit mine shaft, this little store also stocks a range of Welsh speciality ale, chutney, mustard and other local produce.

Getting There & Away

Frequent (one or two hourly) X24 bus services head to/from Newport (£7.70, one hour).

Swansea (Abertawe)

☎01792 / POP 238,000

Swansea's most famous son Dylan Thomas called it an 'ugly, lovely town', which remains a fair description of Wales' second-largest city today. It's in the throes of a regeneration that's slowly transforming some distasteful postwar development into something more worthy of its setting on the glorious 5-mile sandy sweep of Swansea Bay. Already present is a hefty student population that buoys a lively restaurant, nightlife and entertainment scene, and expanding pockets of hipness in suburbs like Sketty and Uplands (which is, conveniently, where all the best B&Bs are located). The main draw for visitors in the city are the many Dylan Thomas–related sights, before making for vibrant suburb the Mumbles, and then the rest of the region.

The city's Welsh name, Abertawe, describes its location at the mouth of the Tawe, where the river empties into the bay.

History

The Normans built a conquest-consolidating castle here in 1106, but Swansea didn't hit its stride until the Industrial Revolution, then developing into an important copper-smelting centre.

By the 20th century, the city's industrial base had declined, worsened by Luftwaffe bombing, which devastated the city centre in 1941. It was rebuilt as a rather uninspired retail development, but recent regeneration, more sensitive to the city's cultural and historical value, is bringing back some aesthetics.

Sights

Dylan Thomas Birthplace HOUSE

(☎01792-472555; www.dylanthomasbirthplace.com; 5 Cwmdonkin Dr, Uplands, SA2 0RA; adult/child £8/6; ⏲10.30am-4.30pm) The bad boy of Welsh poetry was born in this unassuming Uplands house and wrote two-thirds of his poetry here. The house has been lovingly restored and furnished in period style; Dylan's bedroom, preserved as it was in 1934, is tiny. Guides are on hand (bookings advised) but you can also explore solo.

The same people operate excellent tours of Dylan's Swansea stomping grounds (£18 for the Uplands locales) including lovely nearby **Cwmdonkin Park**. You can even stay the night if you're keen (£145 a double for two nights).

Dylan Thomas Centre MUSEUM

(☎01792-463980; www.dylanthomas.com; Somerset Pl; ⏲10am-4.30pm) FREE Housed in the former guildhall, this absorbing museum contains displays on the Swansea-born poet's life and work. It pulls no punches in examining the propensity of Dylan Thomas for puffing up his own myth; he was eventually trapped in the legend of his excessive drinking. Aside from the collection of memorabilia, what really brings his writing to life are recordings of his work performed, part of the centre's permanent, interactive 'Love the Words' exhibition.

Glynn Vivian Art Gallery GALLERY

(☎01792-516900; www.swansea.gov.uk/glynnvivian; Alexandra Rd; ⏲11am-3.30pm Wed-Sun) FREE This elegant Italianate building is once again open to the public following lengthy refurbishment, and with a Covid-19-friendly one-way system whisking you round. There is a prestigious collection of Welsh art here – Richard Wilson, Gwen John, Ceri Richards, Shani Rhys James – along with works by Claude Monet and Lucien Freud and a large ceramics collection. It's probably the best attraction in the city centre proper.

National Waterfront Museum MUSEUM
(☎0300-111 2333; www.museum.wales/swansea; South Dock Marina, Oystermouth Rd; ⏰11am-4pm Thu, Sat & Sun) FREE Housed in a 1901 dockside warehouse with a striking glass and slate extension, this museum's hands-on galleries explore Wales' commercial maritime history and the impacts of industrialisation on its people, using interactive computer screens and audiovisual presentations. There's some fascinating stuff here. A highlight is the Penydarren Steam Locomotive, Richard Trevithick's steam machine that in 1804 chugged from Penydarren to the Merthyr–Cardiff Canal on the world's first railway journey.

Sleeping

Grand Hotel HOTEL $
(☎01792-645898; www.thegrandhotelswansea.co.uk; Ivey Pl, High St; d £55-70) This hotel is conveniently right by the train station, and close to the city centre, which in most cities would be advantageous (but not in Swansea, where the chief appeal lies on its periphery). It's more make-up-smudged old crone than grande dame but clean and with personality. Loud air-con is more noise nuisance than outside traffic.

There are good breakfasts, though, and all told it's an OK one-night base.

Mirador Town House B&B $$
(☎01792-466976; www.themirador.co.uk; 14 Mirador Cres, Uplands, SA2 0QX; s/d from £60/80; 📶) Kooky and kitsch in the extreme, all seven B&B rooms here are fancifully and elaborately themed – Roman, Mediterranean, African, Venetian, Egyptian, Asian and French – with murals on the walls and sometimes the ceilings. The exuberant hosts are enthusiastic cheerleaders for the bars, restaurants and general buzz of the area. Due to reopen in Spring 2021.

Dylan Thomas Birthplace GUESTHOUSE $$$
(☎01792-472555; www.dylanthomasbirthplace.com; 5 Cwmdonkin Dr, Uplands, SA2 0RA; r from £179) Dylan Thomas fans now have the unique opportunity to stay in the house where the poet was born and spent his first 23 years. The house has been diligently maintained in period style, and you'll have the choice of staying in the bedrooms once occupied by Nancy (his sister), DJ and Florrie (his parents), and of course Dylan himself.

Booking a room entails exclusive use of the house, so solo travellers will get it all to themselves! At the time of research there is a two-night minimum stay, although the price given is for one/two people for one night.

Eating & Drinking

★**Square Peg** CAFE $
(☎01792-206593; www.squarepeg.org.uk; 29b Gower Rd, Sketty, SA2 9BX; mains £6-10; ⏰8am-3pm Mon-Sat; 📶✍) With mismatched stools reupholstered in recycled denim and kooky local photography blanketing the walls, this is exactly the hip kind of place you'd expect to deliver seriously good coffee. It doesn't disappoint. But the menu surprises: tasty light breakfasts, salads, soups...and deliciously inventive naans combining the likes of masala yoghurt, Gower bacon and beetroot puree.

Joe's Ice Cream Parlour ICE CREAM $
(☎01792-653880; www.joes-icecream.com; 85 St Helen's Rd; 2 scoops from £3.15; ⏰noon-7pm) For an ice-cream sundae or a cone, locals flock to Joe's, a Swansea institution founded in 1922 by Joe Cascarini, son of immigrants from Italy's Abruzzi mountains. So beloved is this gelato that outlets have sprung up elsewhere across South Wales, including in **the Mumbles** (☎01792-368212; 526 Mumbles Rd; ⏰10.30am-5.30pm Mon, from 10am Tue-Fri, to 6.30pm Sat & Sun).

★**Gigi Gao's Favourite** CHINESE $$
(☎01792-653300; www.favouritechinese.co.uk; 18-23 Anchor Ct; mains £6-20; ⏰noon-10pm; 📶✍) In a new centre-stage waterfront location, this passionately loved Chinese kitchen eschews the batters, all-purpose sauces and replica menus of many Westernised Chinese restaurants to produce food that does justice to China's deep culinary treasures. Homemade organic noodles are served with unapologetically funky Beijing-style sauce, the pork is sweet-braised Hunan style, and the higher-end fish dishes are good too.

Slice MODERN BRITISH $$$
(☎01792-290929; www.sliceswansea.co.uk; 73-75 Eversley Rd, Sketty; 2-/3-course lunch £32/36, 3-/6-course dinner £46/60; ⏰6.15-9.15pm Thu & Sun, 12.30-1.45pm & 6.15-9.15pm Fri & Sat) The

Swansea

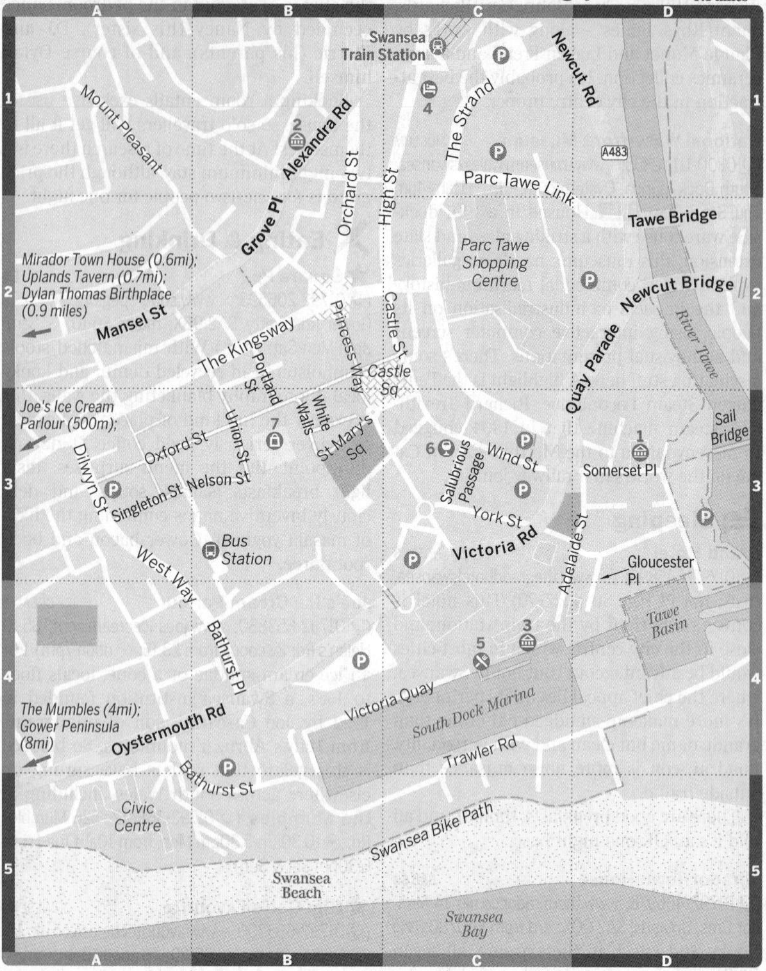

simple decor – wooden floors and furniture, and pale walls – stands in contrast to the elaborate dishes emanating from Slice's kitchen. Its elegantly presented food spans locally sourced meat, fish, cheese and beer, plus homemade bread and home-grown herbs, the foundation of successful adventures such as suckling pig, loin, shoulder and faggot, savoy cabbage, celeriac terrine and caramelised apple puree.

★No Sign Bar WINE BAR
(☎01792-465300; www.nosignwinebar.com; 56 Wind St; ⏲noon-10pm Mon-Sat, to 8pm Sun; 📶) Once frequented by Dylan Thomas (it appears as the Wine Vaults in his story 'The Followers'), the No Sign stands out as the only vaguely traditional bar left on Wind St. Formerly a wine merchant's, it's a haven of dark-wood panelling, old boys in deep conversation, friendly staff and a long, lovely wine list (a dozen by the glass).

Shopping

★Swansea Market MARKET
(www.swanseaindoormarket.co.uk; Oxford St; ⏲8.30am-4.30pm Mon-Sat) There has been a covered market in Swansea since 1652, and

Swansea

Sights

Sleeping

Eating

Drinking & Nightlife

Shopping

at this site since 1830. Rebuilt in 1961 after being bombed in WWII, the current version is a buzzing place to sample local specialities, like Penclawdd cockles, laver bread and Welsh cakes hot from the griddle. However, it's hard to resist stall 58d, Thai Taste (mains £4 to £5).

Information

Morriston Hospital (☎01792-702222; www.sbuhb.nhs.wales; Heol Maes Eglwys, Morriston, SA6 6NL) Has an accident and emergency department; 5 miles north of the centre. Bus 4 from the bus station (35 minutes) heads here regularly.

Getting There & Away

BUS

Swansea's **bus station** (Plymouth St) is at the western edge of the city centre, by Quadrant shopping centre.

National Express (☎0871 781 8181; www.nationalexpress.com) coaches serve bigger, further-away destinations. Services head to/from Tenby (£9.10, 1½ hours, one daily), Cardiff (from £5.50, 1¼ hours, two daily), Bristol (£14, 2¾ to 3½ hours, one daily, sometimes changing in Cardiff) and London (£16 to £23, five hours, two direct daily).

Other direct bus services include the X10 to/from Cardiff (£5, 1¼ hours, every one to two hours), half-hourly X11 services to/from Carmarthen (£5.90, 1¾ hours) and the X13 to/from Llandeilo (£5.90, 1½ hours, five to seven daily).

TRAIN

Swansea's **train station** (High St) is 600m north of Castle Sq along Castle St and High St.

Direct services to/from Swansea include (heading east) Cardiff (£12, one hour, two per hour), Abergavenny (£27, 1¾ hours, up to 11 per day) and London Paddington (£37 to £53, three hours, hourly).

Heading west, you can reach Tenby (£16.80, 1½ hours, three daily) via Carmarthen and Fishguard Harbour (£17.30, two to three daily, 1¾ hours) and, heading north via Llanelli on the Heart of Wales Line, Llandeilo (£8, one hour, two daily), Llandovery and Mid-Wales.

The Mumbles (Y Mwmbwls)

Strung out along the shoreline at the southern end of Swansea Bay, the Mumbles has been Swansea's seaside retreat since 1807, when the Oystermouth Railway, built three years previously for transporting coal, was adapted for human cargo. Closed in 1960, it claims to have been the world's first passenger railway service.

It is today a very fashionable district, with bars and restaurants vying for trade along the promenade, and celebrities such as Hollywood actor and local gal Catherine Zeta-Jones and singer Bonnie Tyler buying homes here.

The origin of the Mumbles' unusual name is uncertain, although one theory is that it's a legacy of French seamen who nicknamed the twin rounded rocks at the tip of the headland *Les Mamelles* – 'the breasts'.

Sights

Going west from Mumbles Head, there are two small bays, Langland Bay and Caswell Bay, which expose hectares of golden sand at low water. Both are popular with families and surfers. About 500m west of Caswell Bay is beautiful **Brandy Cove**, a tiny secluded beach away from the crowds.

★ Clyne Gardens GARDENS

(www.swansea.gov.uk/clyne; Blackpill) **FREE** Spanning 20 hectares, these magnificent gardens are particularly impressive in spring, when the azaleas and rhododendrons are at their most spectacular. Plus there are delicate pieris and enkianthus, bluebell woods, wildflower meadows, a bog garden and even a dogs' graveyard. The entrance is by the Woodman Pub near the junction of Mumbles Rd and Mayals Rd, about halfway between central Swansea and the Mumbles.

Sleeping

Patricks with Rooms HOTEL $$$
(01792-360199; www.patrickswithrooms.com; 638 Mumbles Rd; r £125-185;) Patricks has 16 individually styled bedrooms in bold contemporary colours, with art on the walls, fluffy robes and, in some rooms, roll-top baths and sea views. Some rooms are set back in an annexe. Downstairs are the (excellent) restaurant, in which Patrick cooks (mains £17 to £20), and a bar that practically insists you linger, perhaps with afternoon tea (£17.50).

Eating & Drinking

★ **Môr** SEAFOOD $$
(07932 385217; www.mor-mumbles.co.uk; 620 Mumbles Rd; mains £12-20; 5.30-9pm Tue, 12.30-3.30pm & 5.30-9pm Wed-Sat, 12.30-8pm Sun) Some of the area's scrummiest seafood is proffered at this slick restaurant, such as succulent sea bass with bacon and dashi, although there is also turf beside the surf on the menu. Book in advance. 'Môr' in Welsh simply means sea.

Cakes and Ale WINE BAR
(01792-363828; www.cakesandale.wales; 29 Newton Rd; 10am-10pm Wed-Sat, to 5pm Sun) We confess to gravitating to Cakes and Ale because the sign promised to offer our favourite things: why not, indeed, bridge the gap between cake-stacked cafe and cool evening bar? But it's actually the wine that impresses more than the beer: a discerning old world–new world selection to enjoy with tapas or burgers in friendly, fun-loving environs.

Getting There & Away

Regular 2/2B/2C buses run between Swansea and the Mumbles (£4.30, 30 to 45 minutes). Regular 2C buses run between Oystermouth Sq on Mumbles Rd and Caswell Bay (£2.60, 12 minutes).

Gower Peninsula (Y Gŵyr)

With its broad butterscotch beaches, pounding surf, precipitous clifftop walks and rugged, untamed uplands, the Gower Peninsula feels a million miles from Swansea's urban bustle – yet it's on the doorstep. This 15-mile-long thumb of land stretching west from the Mumbles was designated the UK's first official Area of Outstanding Natural Beauty (AONB) in 1956. You can hike all of the Gower's enchanting seaboard on the Wales Coast Path, and the peninsula has Wales' best surfing outside Pembrokeshire.

The main family beaches, patrolled by lifeguards during summer, are (just west of the Mumbles and easily visitable from there) **Langland Bay** and **Caswell Bay**, along with Port Eynon. The most impressive, and most popular with surfers, is the magnificent 3-mile sweep of Rhossili Bay at the peninsula's far end. Much of the Gower's northern coast is salt marsh, which provides an important habitat for wading birds and wildfowl, not to mention sheep: salt-marsh-grazed lamb is a Gower culinary delicacy.

A **Gower Explorer** (day pass adult/child £7.50/5) is worth purchasing if you're taking two or more bus connections. Buy online (www.firstgroup.com) or on the bus. Buses don't run Sundays.

Getting There & Away

Services are relatively infrequent, but there are buses heading from Swansea to Parkmill, Port Eynon, Rhossili, Reynoldston, Llanmadoc and Llangennith.

Carry coins if you're hoping to park anywhere near a beach.

Oxwich Bay & Parkmill

Oxwich Bay is a windy, 2.5-mile-long curve of sand backed by dunes. Road access and a large car park (per day £6) make it popular with families and water-sports enthusiasts (although there's no lifeguard). Behind the beach lies **Oxwich Nature Reserve**, an area of salt and freshwater marshes, oak and ash woodlands and dunes; it is home to a variety of birdlife.

Some of the Gower's best, most secluded beaches are hereabouts on the stretch between the Mumbles and Oxwich Bay, particularly in the area around the small tourist village of Parkmill.

Sleeping & Eating

★ **Llethryd Barns** B&B $$
(01792-391327; www.llethrydbarns.co.uk; Llethryd; s/d from £80/105; P) Arranged in a horseshoe around a central courtyard, this handsome set of late-Georgian farm buildings has been converted into seven guest suites, each with living area and mezzanine bedroom and all have their own entrances, making them feel utterly private. Breakfasts are indulgent. It's 2 miles north of Parkmill on the B4271.

Parc-le-Breos House HOTEL $$

(☎01792-371636; www.parc-le-breos.co.uk; Parkmill; r £105-150, ste £232; P 📶) Within its own private estate north of the main A4118, Parc-le-Breos offers 16 en-suite rooms in a Gothic Victorian hunting lodge. The majestic lounge, conservatory and dining room have grand fireplaces that crackle into action in winter, and there are great walks nearby, including to **Cathole Rock Cave**. Book ahead for the two-course dinner (£20), served Wednesday to Monday from 6pm to 8pm.

It's a mile (north then west) further down the turning for the Gower Heritage Centre.

Beach House WELSH $$$

(☎01792-390965; www.beachhouseoxwich.co.uk; Oxwich Bay, SA3 1LS; mains £29-34; ⊙noon-2.15pm & 6-8.45pm Wed-Sat, noon-4pm Sun) Wales is famous for having Michelin-starred restaurants in unexpected locations, and of the seven nationwide, this is perhaps the most serendipitous. The Beach House offers wondrous maritime-rich dishes such as pink grapefruit, sea fennel, charred lettuce and laver bread, or octopus with oregano, Kalamata olives and cauliflower, from a photogenic stone building right on the beach.

ℹ Getting There & Away

Nine direct buses head to/from Swansea (£4.60, 36 minutes) and west to Perriswood (for Oxwich, £2.90, 11 minutes) and Rhossili (£4.60, 31 minutes).

Jump off at Scurlage for Port Eynon. It may be quicker to walk from here than wait for the connecting bus.

Port Eynon

☎ 01792 / POP 636

The three-quarter-mile stretch of rock-strewn Blue Flag beach at Port Eynon is the Gower's busiest summer swimming destination. Whatever the time of year, and however fierce the competition for a lunchtime table at the pub or towel space on the beach, it's a thoroughly pleasant little seaside village.

Culver House APARTMENT $$

(☎01792-720300; www.culverhousehotel.co.uk; apt £99-179; 📶) A stone skim from the beach, this renovated 19th-century house offers eight self-contained apartments with all the mod cons, finished in fairly minimalist Scandi style. The upper apartments have balconies, while most of those on the ground floor open onto cute little gardens. Two-night minimum stays are usually required.

OFF THE BEATEN TRACK

THREE CLIFFS BAY

Three Cliffs Bay is named for the pyramid-like, triple-pointed crag pierced by a natural arch that juts out into the water at its eastern point. It's regularly voted one of the most beautiful beaches in Britain, and it's particularly impressive when viewed from the impossibly picturesque ruins of 13th-century Pennard Castle.

The only way to reach the beach is on foot. For the castle view, look for the path across the road and down a bit from Shepherd's Coffee Shop in Parkmill (parking £3). Once you cross the bridge, turn right and then take the next left-hand fork heading up the hill. You'll skirt some houses and Pennard Golf Course before reaching the castle. For a flatter, quicker path, take the right-hand fork instead and follow the stream. Another approach is via the mile-long track along Pennard Cliffs from the National Trust car park in Southgate.

ℹ Getting There & Away

Buses serving Port Eynon are sporadic. For Rhossili (£2.10, 15 minutes) there is one direct bus daily, otherwise take the 119 to Reynoldston (£3.90, 20 minutes, four daily) which continues to Swansea (£4.90, one hour) and change to backtrack with the westbound 118 to Rhossili. You could change at Scurlage, nearest point on the A4118, too, but there's less to do whilst you wait for the next bus.

Change in Reynoldston for buses through Parkmill to Swansea, which run in mornings and evenings only. For Llangennith, take that Reynoldston/Swansea 119 service and jump off at Llanrhidian for one of the two daily services back west to Llangennith.

Easier: come with a car or bike!

Rhossili

☎ 01792 / POP 236

Saving the best for last, the Gower Peninsula ends spectacularly with the 3 miles of golden sand that edges **Rhossili Bay**. Facing nearly due west towards the very bottom of Ireland, this is one of Britain's best and most popular surfing beaches. But be warned: when the surf's up, swimming can be dangerous. At low tide the stark, ghostly ribs of the *Helvetica,* a Norwegian barque wrecked in a storm in 1887, protrude from the middle of the beach.

Rhossili village spreads out along the road approaching the beach for some way and is a pleasant place to eat, drink or spend the night.

Sights

★Worms Head NATURAL FEATURE

The western extremity of the Gower is guarded by this mile-long tentacular promontory, which turns into an island at high tide. Worms Head takes its name from the Old English *wurm*, meaning 'dragon'. Seals bask around its rocks, and the cliffs are thick with razorbills, guillemots, kittiwakes, fulmars and puffins during nesting season (April to July).

There is a five-hour window of opportunity (2½ hours either side of low tide) when you can walk out across a causeway and along the narrow crest of the Outer Head to the furthest point of land. Check the tide tables posted at the **Rhossili Visitor Centre** (☎01792-390707; www.nationaltrust.org.uk/rhosili-and-south-gower-coast; Coastguard Cottages; ⏲11am-5pm daily Mar-Sep, Fri-Sun Oct) carefully. Among those who have spent a cold, nervous night trapped here was the young Dylan Thomas, as he relates in 'Who Do You Wish was with Us?', from *Portrait of the Artist as a Young Dog*. If you do get stuck, do not try to wade or swim back: currents are fierce and the rocks treacherous.

Getting There & Away

The 118/119 to/from Swansea (£4.90, one to 1¼ hours, up to 11 daily) usually runs via Parkmill (£4.50, 30 to 45 minutes).

Reynoldston (£3.90, 20 minutes, up to five daily) is where you will need to change for services to Port Eynon (20 minutes) if you don't want to wait for the one direct connection daily.

Walking the 3 miles along the coast for Llangennith is simpler than bussing there.

Llangennith

☎ 01792 / POP 517

Surfers flock to this pretty village, centred on the 12th-century church of St Cenydd, at the northern end of Rhossili Bay where a good local pub and a large beachside campsite await. There are some unforgettable coastal vistas around here. Llangennith has a local produce market (last Saturday of month, 10am to 1pm April to September).

Activities

PJ's Surf Shop SURFING

(☎01792-386669; www.facebook.com/pjs.s.shop; per day wetsuits £12, surfboards £12-15; ⏲9am-5.30pm Mar-Oct, 10am-5.30pm Mon-Fri Nov-Feb) Run by former surfing champion Peter Jones, this is a very friendly centre of activity for local surfers. Check the Facebook page for current local surfing conditions. In winter it also offers extra protective cold-weather gear (£9 per day).

Sleeping

King's Head HOTEL $$

(☎01792-386212; www.kingsheadgower.co.uk; r £125-155; P 📶 🐾) Up the hill behind (and run by) the pub of the same name, these two stone farm buildings have been simply but stylishly fitted out with modern bathrooms and underfloor heating. As well as the 20 rooms here, there are more in a nearby house. Look online for weekly, five-night and weekend deals that run year-round.

Come down to the picturesque pub for breakfast (included) or to have wholesome meals with a spicy bent towards curries.

Getting There & Away

The 116 service runs once in the morning and once in the evening direct to Swansea (£4.90, 1¼ to 1½ hours). It will head there via Llanrhidian (change for scant connections to the southern Gower) and Pen-clawwd.

For Rhossili, just walk the 3 miles along the beach.

CARMARTHENSHIRE (SIR GAERFYDDIN)

The castle-dotted county of Carmarthenshire enfolds gentle valleys washed by abundant rivers, dense woods and bald yellow hilltops, but most of the action is on and around the wide crescent of Carmarthern Bay (Bae Caerfyrddin), carved up like a crazy jigsaw into wide, winding, sand-flanked estuaries. Caught between attractive neighbours – the Brecon Beacons lie on Carmarthenshire's eastern border whilst Pembrokeshire kicks off to the west – it is often wrongly overlooked. This much calmer and less explored pocket of Wales is predominantly tinted in dazzling

OFF THE BEATEN TRACK

LAUGHARNE

The marooned estuary town of Laugharne is best-known for being where Wales' most famous writer, Dylan Thomas, spent the last four years of his life from 1949 to 1953. The inspiration for Thomas' most famous work, *Under Milk Wood*, was gleaned here, and there are several very worthwhile sights associated with the writer.

Dylan Thomas Boathouse (☎01994-427420; www.dylanthomasboathouse.com; Dylan's Walk; adult/child £4.75/3.75; ⏲2-5pm Fri-Mon) Dylan Thomas, his wife Caitlin and their three children lived in this cliff-clinging house from 1949 to 1953. It's a beautiful setting, looking out over the estuary that Thomas, in his 'Poem in October', described as the 'heron-priested shore'. The parlour has been restored to its 1950s appearance, with a desk that once belonged to Thomas' schoolmaster father. Upstairs are photographs, letters, a video about his life, and his death mask, which once belonged to Richard Burton.

Laugharne Castle (Cadw; ☎01994-427906; www.cadw.gov.wales; cnr King & Wogan Sts; adult/child £3.80/2.20; ⏲10am-1pm & 2-5pm Thu-Mon) Built in the 13th century, picturesque Laugharne Castle was converted into a mansion in the 16th century for John Perrot, thought to be the illegitimate son of Henry VIII. Gazing out over the estuary, it was landscaped with its current lovely lawns in Victorian times.

The adjoining **Castle House** was leased in 1934 by Richard Hughes, author of *A High Wind in Jamaica*. It was Hughes who first invited Dylan Thomas to Laugharne. Thomas stayed with Hughes at Castle House and wrote some of his short-story collection, *Portrait of the Artist as a Young Dog*, in the little gazebo looking over the estuary.

green. It sates those in need of drama-charged castles, glorious landscaped gardens, quietly confident market towns and, importantly for the back of beyond, seriously great cuisine where 'farm to fork' is often a distance no greater than a hedgerow hop.

Getting There & Away

Carmarthen is the main bus hub. National Express (p669) buses stop here with services to/from London (£20, 5¾ hours, one daily). Direct services reach most corners of the county, including Llanarthne, Llandeilo and Llandovery, and onward to Swansea, Tenby, Haverfordwest and Aberystwyth.

The Heart of Wales train line (from Swansea to Shrewsbury) cuts through Carmarthenshire, stopping in Llandeilo and Llandovery.

Llanarthne

☎01558 / POP 760

Tiny Llanarthne is as pleasantly rural and slow-paced as dozens of other Carmarthenshire villages, and would perhaps have remained indistinguishable from the pack if it hadn't been for the National Botanic Garden of Wales opening nearby, along with the presence of probably the county's best place to eat.

Sights

★National Botanic Garden of Wales GARDENS
(☎01558-667149; www.botanicgarden.wales; adult/child £12.65/6.05; ⏲10am-6pm Apr-Oct, to 4pm Nov-Mar; P ♿) Concealed in the rolling Tywi Valley countryside, this lavish complex opened in 2000 and is still maturing. Formerly an aristocratic estate, the garden has a broad range of plant habitats, from lakes and bogs to woodland and heath, with lots of decorative areas and educational exhibits. The centrepiece is the Norman Foster-designed **Great Glasshouse**, a spectacular glass dome sunken into the earth. The garden is 2 miles southwest of Llanarthne village, signposted from the main roads.

Sleeping & Eating

Llwyn Helyg Country House B&B $$$
(☎01558-668778; r £125-145; P 📶) This modern, Georgian-look stone house on the village fringes has three guest bedrooms luxuriously decked out with dark wooden furniture, white Italian marble en suites and spa baths. Audiophiles can make advance requests to use the state-of-the-art 'Listening Room', which has a system that must be heard to be believed.

OFF THE BEATEN TRACK

UPPER TYWI VALLEY

Twisting immediately north from Llandovery, Upper Tywi Valley ia a web of charmingly rural lanes that traces the upper course of the River Tywi up to the valley's highlight, at lofty reservoir **Llyn Brianne**, near the river's source. South Wales' biggest body of water, the reservoir also boasts the UK's highest dam and, with spinach-coloured forest fringing the stark hills above, feels more like Canada than Carmarthenshire.

At the lake, you're on the border between Carmarthenshire and Mid-Wales counties Ceredigion and Powys.

★Wright's Food Emporium CAFE $$
(☎01558-668929; www.wrightsfood.co.uk; Golden Grove Arms, B4300; 2-course meal £22; ⏲noon-3pm Thu-Sun, also 6-8pm Sat; P) Sprawling through the rooms of an old village pub, this hugely popular deli-cafe serves elaborate sandwiches, salads and massive antipasto platters packed full of top-notch local and imported ingredients (with a French bent). Follow up with a craft beer or something from its range of small-estate organic wine, then browse crates of vinyl records and shelves of the area's best produce.

Getting There & Away

Up to two 278/279 buses a day stop here en route between Carmarthen (£2.85, 35 minutes) and Llandeilo (£2.30, 20 to 30 minutes). The 279 stops at the botanic garden.

Llandeilo

☎ 01558 / POP 1800

On a hill encircled by bedazzling green fields and the charmingly meandering River Tywi, Llandeilo is a cute collection of narrow streets lined with grand, vibrant Victorian and Georgian buildings.

Used by many travellers as a springboard for the wilder terrain of Brecon Beacon National Park, it's also within a short drive (or walk, in the case of Dinefwr) of numerous outstanding sights – rolling country estates, castles, enchanting Elizabethan gardens, and more.

Sights

★Dinefwr PARK, HISTORIC BUILDING
(NT, Cadw; ☎01558-824512; www.nationaltrust.org.uk; adult/child £8/4; ⏲grounds 10am-4pm, house 11am-4pm Sat & Sun; P) This idyllic, 324-hectare, beautifully landscaped estate on the edge of Llandeilo incorporates a deer park, an Iron Age fort, pasture, woods, a 12th-century castle and a 17th-century manor with a Victorian Gothic facade. The highlight is the serene parkland, though. There are several marked walks: keep your eyes peeled for fallow deer and one of only a few remaining herds of the very rare White Park cattle, an ancient breed once common in Britain.

★Aberglasney Gardens GARDENS
(☎01558-668998; www.aberglasney.org; Llangathen; adult/child £8.55/free; ⏲10am-6pm late Mar-Oct, 10.30am-4pm Nov-Feb, to 5pm early-late Mar; P) Entering these formal walled gardens feels a bit like wandering into a Jane Austen novel. They date originally from Elizabethan times, evolving continually since then, and contain a unique cloister built solely as a garden decoration. There's also a lake, a 250-year-old yew tunnel, a 'wild' garden in the bluebell woods to the west and various other horticultural havens. In the summer exhibitions and musical events bring further life and gaiety.

Sleeping & Eating

Cawdor HOTEL $$
(☎01558-823500; www.thecawdor.com; Rhosmaen St; r £125-175, apt £225; P) Walking through the broad entrance into the bright-red, quite posh Cawdor, you get some sense of the Georgian house of assembly it once was. The very well appointed rooms, some with beautiful wooden beams, have Egyptian cotton bed linens and marble in the bathrooms.

Downstairs, a snug lounge bar with a roaring fire in winter and a more contemporary courtyard cafe flank a more formal dining room (mains £8.50 to £12.50). Book in advance for food and rooms.

★Ginhaus Deli DELI $
(☎01558-823030; www.ginhaus.co.uk; 1 Market St; mains £8-12; ⏲8am-5pm Mon-Thu, to 10pm Fri & Sat;) Specialising in two of the very finest things in life (gin and cheese), this hip deli-cafe also serves cooked breakfasts, filled baguettes, quiches, tarts, fresh juices

and delicious British food such as smoked haddock with poached egg. Charcuterie and cheese platters are offered too. On Friday and Saturday nights there's pizza from 5pm to 8pm.

Coaltown Coffee Roastery CAFE $
(Foundry Rd, Ammanford; coffee/cakes/pizzas from £3/3/8; ⏲10am-4pm; P 📶) Ammanford, where this understatedly slick outfit is based, was once a flourishing coal-mining town, then once that stopped it was deprived for a long time. With the mantra 'new black gold' (the name given locally to coal back in the day, and here meaning coffee beans), Scott and crew concoct standout java in chic premises that wouldn't look amiss in Brooklyn.

Some wonderful coffee-making contraptions are on-site, where the roasting magic is conducted in a massive old-school Italian roaster. And the pizza is almost as sensational as the coffee. Barista courses too. One of South Wales' best cafes.

Getting There & Away

Eight daily 280/281 services to/from Llandovery (£3.25, 45 minutes) and Carmarthen (£3.60, 45 minutes) are the most frequent buses. Seven daily X13 buses head via Ammanford to Swansea (£5.90, 1½ hours).

Llandeilo is also on the Heart of Wales railway line (Swansea to Shrewsbury). Heading south, direct trains run to/from Swansea (£8, one hour, two daily). Northbound, you can reach Llandovery (£3.90, 20 minutes), Llanwrtyd Wells (£5.60, 45 minutes) and Shrewsbury (£15.40, three hours).

PEMBROKESHIRE

St Davids (Tyddewi)

☎01437 / POP 1841

Capped off by the country's most impressive Norman cathedral, St Davids is officially Britain's smallest city, though it's no bigger than a village. On a fiercely beautiful stretch of the Pembrokeshire coast, this is the birthplace of Wales' patron saint (and his final resting place). And as such it has attracted pilgrims for 1500 years. Back in the Middle Ages, this was a pilgrimage destination to rival Santiago in Spain.

In summer, St Davids becomes a full-on coastal honeypot, attracting hordes of non-religious pilgrims, drawn by the town's laid-back vibe, buoyant food and drink scene, and the excellent hiking, water sports and wildlife-watching right on the doorstep.

WORTH A TRIP

THE COASTAL WAY

Taking the length of Cardigan Bay in its stride, the 180-mile Coastal Way is designed to show off the Welsh coast from its most flattering angles. Part of the Wales Way (three national driving routes), this is a road trip to remember, stitching together some of Britain's most phenomenal coastal scenery, bounded by the Irish Sea to the west and high mountains to the east.

Moving south to north, the route begins in St Davids before diving straight into the Pembrokeshire Coast National Park, ticking off one incredible beach, headland and prehistoric site after the next. From here, it swings north to Ceredigion and Snowdonia before ending in prettily whitewashed Aberdaron on the surf-lashed, wildlife-rich coastline of the Llŷn Peninsula. See www.visitwales.com for more details and inspiration.

Sights & Activities

★ St David's Cathedral CATHEDRAL
(www.stdavidscathedral.org.uk; The Pebbles; ⏲10am-3pm Mon-Sat, 1-4pm Sun) FREE Hidden in a hollow and behind high walls, St David's Cathedral is built on the site of a 6th-century chapel. The valley location was chosen in the vain hope the cathedral would be overlooked by Saxon raiders, but it was ransacked at least seven times. When you pass through the gatehouse and its stone walls come into view, the 12th-century Norman cathedral is astonishingly impressive, its distinctive west front embellished with four pointed towers of purple stone.

St Davids Head AREA
The National Trust tends this heather-wreathed promontory, formed from the oldest rock in Wales and once fortified by the Celts. A magnificent circular 3.5-mile, two-hour hike leads up and over clifftops with staggering views of Whitesands Bay, Ramsey and Skomer Islands and, on clear days, the Wicklow Mountains in Ireland across the water. For prehistory fans, the highlights are **Coetan Arthur**, a burial chamber dating

Pembrokeshire

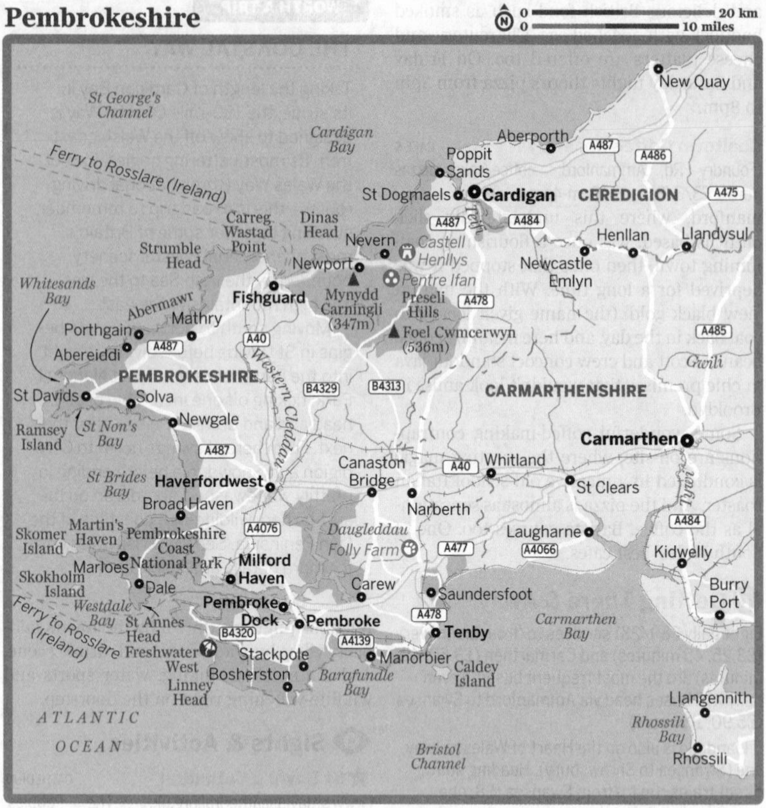

to 3500 BCE, and the neolithic chambered tombs below the rocky fin-shaped peak of **Carn Llidi** (181m).

Ramsey Island BIRD SANCTUARY

Reclining off the coast of St Davids like a sleeping dragon, Ramsey Island (Ynys Dewi) is ringed by dramatic sea cliffs and an offshore armada of rocky islets and reefs. The RSPB reserve is seabird nirvana, famous for its large breeding population of choughs, as well as peregrine falcons, ravens, guillemots, razorbills, fulmars and kittiwakes. The island is also home to one of Britain's largest populations of Atlantic grey seals (and in autumn their adorable pups).

St Non's Bay RUINS

Immediately south of St Davids, this ruggedly beautiful spot is named after St David's mother and traditionally accepted as his birthplace. A path leads to the 13th-century **ruins of St Non's Chapel**. Only the base of the walls remains, along with a stone marked with a cross within a circle that's believed to date from the 7th century. Standing stones in the surrounding field suggest that the chapel may have been built within an ancient pagan stone circle.

Whitesands Bay BEACH

(Porth Mawr) Swimming, surfing and coastal hiking are the big draws at this mile-long sandy beach. At extremely low tide you can see the wreck of a paddle tugboat that ran aground here in 1882, and the fossil remains of a prehistoric forest. If Whitesands is really busy – and it often is – escape the worst of the crowds by walking north along the coastal path for 15 minutes to the gorgeously secluded cliff-rimmed bay at **Porthmelgan**.

TYF Adventure ADVENTURE

(01437-721611; www.tyf.com; 1 High St; half-/full-day activities £70/120; 10.30am-3.30pm Easter-Oct;) Ramp up the adventure along the coast by popping into this one-stop shop, offering everything from coasteering to surfing to sea kayaking, rock climbing, cycle tours and family-friendly rock-pool safaris from its St Davids base.

Sleeping

Ramsey House B&B $$
(01437-720321; www.ramseyhouse.co.uk; Lower Moor; d £90-135; P) Owners Shaun and Suzanne have poured love and creativity into this boutique-style B&B in their duck-egg-blue house on the outskirts of town. The six rooms are all different but feature bold Designer's Guild and Zoffany wallpapers, leather tub chairs, solid oak furniture, goose-down duvets and stylish bathrooms clad in Italian tiles. First-floor rooms afford lovely views of the sea or St David's Cathedral.

★ **Penrhiw** BOUTIQUE HOTEL $$$
(01437-725588; www.penrhiwhotel.com; Pen Rhiw; d £190-240, ste £260; P) Serenely tucked away in grounds with landscaped gardens, wildflower meadows and woodlands, this late-Victorian priory turned boutique hotel is one of St Davids' most fabulous escapes, with its air of understated sophistication, minimalist-chic interiors bearing the imprint of Welsh-born architect Keith Griffiths, and original features from stone arches and stained glass to exquisitely tiled arts and crafts fireplaces.

Twr y Felin HOTEL $$$
(01437-725555; www.twryfelinhotel.com; Caerfai Rd; d £250-290, ste £320-420; P) Pembrokeshire-born architect Keith Griffiths put his stamp on Twr y Felin, using a 19th-century windmill as the impetus for this slickly modern hotel in private landscaped grounds. A collection of specially commissioned, large-scale contemporary art (including works by Welsh street artist Pure Evil) enlivens the monochrome, distinctly minimalist interiors. All rooms are luxurious, but top billing goes to the spectacular three-level circular suite in the tower itself.

Eating

Really Wild Emporium CAFE $
(01437-721755; www.thereallywildemporium.co.uk; 24 High St; cakes £2.50-3, mains £8.50; 10am-4pm) Wild About Pembrokeshire foragers Julia and John have had fun converting a high-ceilinged art-deco building into this fabulous emporium in central St Davids. Exposed brick, reclaimed wood and corrugated iron set an industro-cool scene for dishes peppered with foraged ingredients – from pad thai with wild garlic seeds to insanely delicious seaweed brownies.

> DON'T MISS
>
> **A WALK ON THE WILD SIDE**
>
> Passionate foragers Julia and John, of **Wild About Pembrokeshire** (01437-721035; www.wildaboutpembrokeshire.co.uk; foraging per person from £12; Apr-Oct;), know the shores and hedgerows around St Davids like the backs of their hands. For the inside scoop on edible seaweeds, wild plants and herbs, hook onto one of their informative, sustainably minded foraging walks. These range from beginner's walks to a seashore forage and wild picnic, and family-focused seashore and rock-pool discovery walks.

★ **Grub Kitchen** INTERNATIONAL $$
(07986 698169; www.grubkitchen.co.uk; Lower Harglodd Farm; mains £14.50-17.50; 10.30am-4.30pm Thu-Sun) The grub is excellent at the sustainably minded restaurant at the **Bug Farm** (07966 956357; www.thebugfarm.co.uk; Lower Harglodd Farm; adult/child £7/4.50; 10.30am-4.30pm Thu-Sun;) . With a little help from his entomologist (insect scientist) wife Dr Sarah Beynon, Andy Holcroft rustles up highly original dishes featuring edible insects. Spicy crickets, say, might be the prelude for smoked chipotle cricket and black bean chilli, signature bug burgers with polenta chips, and cricket-cardamom carrot cake.

Blas GASTRONOMY $$$
(01437-725555; www.blasrestaurant.com; Caerfai Rd; mains £22-34, 7-course tasting menu £69) The dark-walled, softly lit, art-slung restaurant at Twr y Felin is deliciously intimate. The chef takes pride in local, seasonal, sustainable sourcing. Homemade sourdough bread piques the appetite for starters like Solva lobster with cucumber, dill and sea vegetables, and mains like lamb rump with hen-of-the-woods mushrooms and black garlic – all big on integral flavours and exquisitely served on slate, wood and bespoke crockery.

Information

Oriel Y Parc Gallery & Visitor Centre
(01437-720392; www.orielyparc.co.uk; High St; 10am-4pm) Oriel y Parc encompasses the National Park tourist office and St Davids'

St Davids

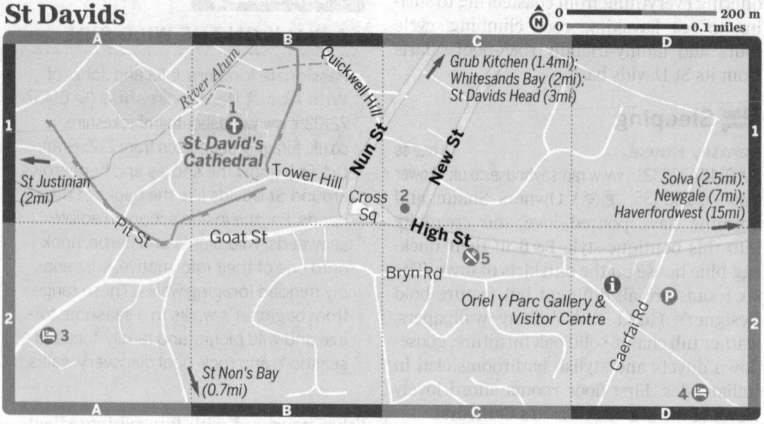

St Davids

Top Sights
1 St David's Cathedral B1

Activities, Courses & Tours
2 TYF Adventure C1
Wild About Pembrokeshire .... (see 5)

Sleeping
3 Ramsey House A2
4 Twr y Felin D2

Eating
Blas .... (see 4)
5 Really Wild Emporium C2

landscape art gallery, showing some terrific exhibitions throughout the year, often with a strong focus on Graham Sutherland and landscape-inspired pieces from the National Museum of Wales. It also has a gift shop and a cafe that stages live music and cultural events throughout the year.

Getting There & Away

Public transport is limited, especially on Sunday and in winter.

The main Pembrokeshire coastal bus services (p686) stopping here are the Strumble and Puffin shuttles. From late July to late September there's also the Celtic Coaster, which circles between St Davids, St Non's Bay, St Justinian and Whitesands.

Up to nine 411 buses per day go to/from Solva (£1.65, 11 minutes), Newgale (£2.50, 21 minutes) and Haverfordwest (£3.40, 43 minutes, 10 daily), while 413 buses run to/from Fishguard (£3.80, 40 minutes, six daily).

Porthgain

01348 / POP 897

For centuries, the tiny harbour of Porthgain consisted of little more than a few sturdy cottages wedged into a rocky cove. From 1851 it began to prosper as the port for shipping out slate quarried just down the coast at Abereiddi, and by 1889 its own deposits of granite and fine clay had put it on the map as a source of building stone and brick until the post-WWI slump burst the bubble.

Today Porthgain is a surprisingly picturesque little port, home to a couple of art galleries, pubs and restaurants, making it an appealing stopover for walks along the Pembrokeshire Coast Path.

Sights & Activities

Blue Lagoon BAY

(Abereiddi) In a flooded former slate quarry, the shockingly turquoise Blue Lagoon is a magnet to brave wild swimmers who don't mind the water being deep and bitterly cold. Slate was quarried at this site on the water's edge in Abereiddi up until 1910 and then transported by tramway to the harbour at Porthgain. After the mining stopped, a channel was blasted through to the sea, creating this brilliant blue-green pool surrounded by a bowl of sheer stone walls.

★**Preseli Venture** ADVENTURE

(01348-837709; www.preseliventure.co.uk; Parc-y-nole Fach, Mathry; coasteering & kayaking

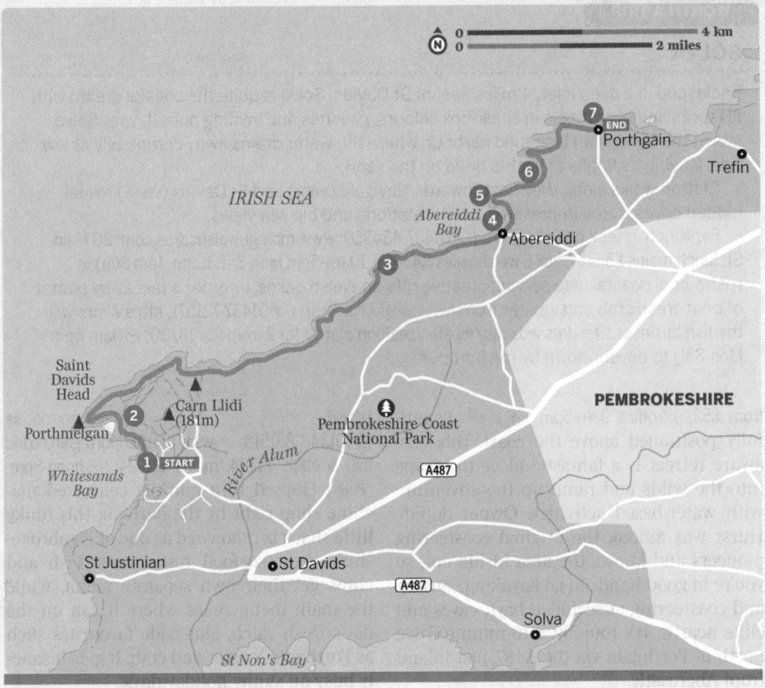

Coastal Walk Whitesands to Porthgain

START WHITESANDS BAY
END PORTHGAIN
LENGTH 10 MILES; FOUR TO SIX HOURS

Covering a beautiful but remote stretch of coast, this rewarding walk takes you over rugged headlands and past dramatic cliffs, pretty coves and flooded quarries. It's a taxing route with several steep descents and ascents, but it's well worth the effort. Bring provisions, as it's a long way between villages.

Start out at busy 1 **Whitesands Bay** (p676) and head west onto wild and rocky St Davids Head. The start of the route is fairly easy, with a good path, wide open views and craggy volcanic outcrops to admire. The only signs of human habitation here are ancient, with the simple 2 **neolithic burial chamber** on the headland predating the surrounding remnants of Celtic forts.

The path soon becomes more rugged, with a rock scramble down to and up from the lovely little cove at 3 **Aberpwll**. Continue on past crumbling cliffs to 4 **Abereiddi**, looking out for seals in the coves, gannets, and possibly porpoises diving for fish out at sea. The beach at Abereiddi is famous for its black sand full of tiny fossils. Ruined quarry buildings and slate workers' cottages flank the path beyond the beach that leads to the 5 **Blue Lagoon** (p678), a deep, turquoise flooded slate quarry. It's now popular with coasteerers and, in early September, cliff divers from all over the world, who compete here, diving 27m into the icy water below.

The 45-minute walk from Abereiddi to Porthgain is one of the best stretches along the entire coast path, following a clifftop plateau past the often deserted 6 **Traeth Llyfn**, an astonishingly lovely beach of fine dark sand, wave-smoothed rocks and looming cliffs. A flight of steep stairs leads down to the golden sand, but beware of strong undercurrents and the tide, which can cut off parts of the beach from the steps.

Continue on for the last descent into the tiny harbour of 7 **Porthgain**, where you can reward yourself with some superb seafood at the Shed or a cold beverage at the welcoming Sloop Inn.

WORTH A TRIP

SOLVA

Enclasped in a deep inlet, 4 miles east of St Davids, Solva is quite the coastal dream with its sprinkling of cottages in chalk-box colours, galleries and inviting pubs. Lower Solva sits at the head of an L-shaped harbour, where the water drains away completely at low tide, leaving its flotilla of yachts tilted on the sand.

Clifftop walks along the coast towards Newgale (east) and St Davids (west) reveal hidden coves, some impressive rock formations and big sea views.

For lunch, check out **MamGu** (☎01437-454369; www.mamguwelshcakes.com; 20 Main St; lunch mains £5.50-7, box 6 welshcakes £4; ⏲9.30am-5pm Mon-Sat, 10am-4pm Sun), a rustic-cool coastal cafe serving creative riffs on Welsh cakes, or order a takeaway platter of boat-fresh crab and lobster from **Mrs Will the Fish** (☎01437-721571; https://mrs-will-the-fish.business.site; dressed crab/lobster/seafood platter for 2 from £5/18/30; ⏲9am-6pm Mon-Sat) to devour down by the harbour.

from £52; ⏲office 9am-5pm; 🚸) 🍃 Beautifully positioned above the coast, this eco-aware retreat is a fantastic place to escape into the wilds and ramp up the adventure with water-based activities. Owner Sophie Hurst was among the original coasteering pioneers and knows the area inside out, so you're in good hands to go kayaking, surfing and coasteering at secluded bays, caves and cliffs nearby. It's roughly a 10-minute drive north of Porthgain via the A487, just inland from Abercastle.

Should you wish to stay the night, there's a low-carbon backpackers' lodge, geodesic dome and camping in a woodland glade.

Sleeping & Eating

Old School Hostel HOSTEL $

(☎07845 625005; https://oldschoolhostel.com; Ffordd-yr-Afon, Trefin; s/d £30/44; 🅿📶) 🍃 Set in a rambling old school building in Trefin, 2 miles east of Porthgain, this is one of the new breed of independent, brightly painted, personally run backpackers. The six rooms have en-suite showers but communal toilets. A great collection of games and a good-quality self-service breakfast are included in the price.

Crug Glâs HOTEL $$$

(☎01348-831302; www.crug-glas.co.uk; Abereiddy Rd; r £150-210; 🅿📶) Set on a big beef and cereal farm that has existed here since at least the 1100s – there's a reference to it in the 12th-century Black Book of St David's – this opulent country house offers rooms decked out with rich fabrics, ornate beds, enormous bathrooms and elegant period grandeur. Five rooms are in the main house, two in converted farm buildings.

Shed SEAFOOD $$

(☎01348-831518; www.theshedporthgain.co.uk; fish & chips £11-14, mains £16-24; ⏲noon-8pm; 📶🚸) Housed in a quirkily converted machine shop right by the harbour, this funky little shack is renowned as one of Pembrokeshire's best seafood restaurants. Fish and chips get their own separate menu, while the main menu relies where it can on the day's fresh catch, alongside favourites such as Porthgain lobster and crab. It gets insanely busy on sunny holiday days.

Sloop Inn PUB FOOD $$

(☎01348-831449; www.sloop.co.uk; mains £12-23; ⏲11am-11pm Mon-Fri, 9.30am-midnight Sat, 9.30am-11pm Sun; 📶🚸) With wooden tables worn smooth by many a bended elbow, timber beams and old photos of Porthgain in its industrial heyday, this nautical-flavoured tavern opened its doors to thirsty seamen back in 1743. The hearty, home-cooked grub will satisfy even the hungriest Coast Path walker, with specials like Pembrokeshire crab salad and beer-battered cod. On summer weekends there's often live music.

Getting There & Away

The only bus heading here is the Strumble Shuttle, one of the Pembrokeshire coastal bus services (p686).

Fishguard (Abergwaun)

☎01348 / POP 3419

Perched on a headland between its modern ferry port and former fishing harbour, Fishguard is often overlooked by travellers on the mad dash to and from Ireland. It doesn't have any standout sights, but it's nevertheless an appealing, culturally vibrant town (which, incidentally, holds the distinction of being the setting for the last foreign invasion of Britain).

Sights & Activities

Strumble Head VIEWPOINT

On wild, lonely, rocky Strumble Head, a lighthouse beams out its signal as high-speed ferries thunder past on their way to Ireland. Jutting into the wave-hammered sea, the headland makes a good vantage point for spotting dolphins, seals, sharks and sunfish; below the parking area is an old coastguard lookout that now serves as a shelter for observing wildlife. It's located 4 miles northwest of Goodwick and the route is well marked.

The Strumble Shuttle (bus 404 between St Davids and Newport) stops here.

Kayak-King KAYAKING

(☎07967 010203; www.kayak-king.com; tours £45; ⏲9.30am-noon & 2-4pm) Twice-daily sea-kayaking tours, tailored to either family groups or adults. Kayak-King is a mobile outfit; its conspicuously painted van can be found in Lower Fishguard Harbour when it's running tours, but it's easier to ring or use the online form to make a booking.

Sleeping

★ **Manor Town House** B&B $$

(☎01348-873260; www.manortownhouse.com; 11 Main St; d £80-160, extra bed £25;) Sea views enthral at this graceful Georgian house, with a garden terrace for gazing across the harbour and Cardigan Bay. With a mix of antiques, upcycled finds and eye-catching fabrics, the spacious rooms have boutiquey flair, tastefully done out in crisp whites, blues and dove greys, with nice touches like Welsh honesty hampers, Noble Isle vegan toiletries and waffle robes.

Eating & Drinking

Gourmet Pig DELI, CAFE $

(☎01348-874404; www.gourmetpig.co.uk; 32 West St; mains £5-7; ⏲9.30am-5.30pm Mon-Fri, to 4.30pm Sat;) Delicious sandwiches, samosas, Iberian-accented deli platters (laden with chorizo, *jamón*, *sobrassada* and manchego), pies and pastries are the main attractions at this relaxed deli-cafe, along with barista-made locally roasted coffee. Grab a window seat and watch Fishguard go about its business.

Ship Inn PUB

(☎01348-874033; 3 Old Newport Rd, Lower Town; ⏲5-11pm Wed-Fri, noon-midnight Sat, noon-10pm Sun) This tremendously snug and convivial little 250-year-old pub has an open fire in winter and walls covered in memorabilia, including photos of Richard Burton filming *Under Milk Wood* outside (the street and nearby quay haven't changed a bit).

Getting There & Away

BOAT

Stena Line (☎08447 707 070; www.stenaline.co.uk; Fishguard Harbour; pedestrian/car & driver from £32.50/95;) has two ferries a day year-round between Rosslare in the south-east of Ireland and Fishguard Harbour.

BUS

Direct services to/from Fishguard include the frequent T5 to Haverfordwest (£3.50, 33 minutes), Newport (£2.50, 15 minutes), Cardigan (£3.85, 37 minutes) and Aberystwyth (£6.10, 2½ hours); the 413 to St Davids (£3.80, 50 minutes, up to six daily); and the useful Pembrokeshire coastal bus services (p686).

TRAIN

There are frequent direct trains between both Fishguard and Goodwick Station and Fishguard Harbour Station (both of which are actually in Goodwick) and destinations including Swansea (£17, 1¾ hours, three daily), Cardiff (£28, 2½ to three hours, two daily), Newport (£33, 3¼ hours, daily) and Manchester (£94, 6¼ hours, daily).

OFF THE BEATEN TRACK

PRESELI HILLS

The only upland area in Pembrokeshire Coast National Park (p684), the Preseli Hills rise to a height of 536m at Foel Cwmcerwyn. They encompass a fascinating prehistoric landscape, scattered with hill forts, standing stones and burial chambers, and are famous as the source of the mysterious bluestones of Stonehenge. The ancient **Golden Road** track, once part of a 5000-year-old trade route between Wessex and Ireland, runs along the crest of the hills, passing prehistoric cairns and the stone circle of Bedd Arthur.

Newport (Trefdraeth)

01239 / POP 1161

As different from the industrial city of Newport near the English border as chalk is to cheese, the Pembrokeshire Newport moves to a deliciously relaxed coastal beat, with a pretty cluster of flower-bedecked cottages huddled beneath a small Norman castle. It sits at the foot of Mynydd Carningli, a large bump on the seaward side of the Preseli Hills, and in recent years it has seriously upped its hospitality game, with restaurants playing up regional sourcing and foraged ingredients, and a peppering of boutiquey guesthouses.

Newport makes a pleasant base for walks along the coastal path or south into the Preseli Hills.

Sights

★ Dinas Island ISLAND

For some of the most ravishing coastscapes in Pembrokeshire, make your way to the rugged headland of Dinas Island between Fishguard and Newport. It's not really an island as it's anchored to the mainland by a neck of land, framed on either side by pretty coves – the sandy strand of Pwllgwaelod to the west, and the rocky inlet of Cwm-yr-Eglwys to the east, where you can see the ruin of 12th-century **St Brynach's Church**, destroyed by the great storm of 1859.

Castell Henllys HISTORIC SITE

(01239-891319; www.castellhenllys.com; Meline; adult/child £5.50/3.50; 10am-5pm Apr-Oct, reduced hours Nov-Mar;) If you've ever wondered what a Celtic village looked, felt and smelt like, rewind time at this Iron Age settlement, 4 miles east of Newport. From 600 BCE and right through the Roman occupation there was a thriving settlement here – now reconstructed on its original foundations. The buildings include three thatched roundhouses, animal pens, a smithy and a grain store, all of which you can enter. There are even Iron Age breeds of pigs and sheep and reconstructions of Celtic gardens.

DON'T MISS

PENTRE IFAN

The largest neolithic dolmen in Wales, **Pentre Ifan** (Cadw; www.cadw.gov.wales; 10am-4pm) is a 5500-year-old neolithic burial chamber set on a remote hillside with superb views across the Preseli Hills and out to sea. The huge, 5m-long capstone, weighing more than 16 tonnes, is delicately poised on three tall, pointed upright stones, made of the same bluestone that was used for the menhirs at Stonehenge. The site is about 3 miles southeast of Newport, signposted off a minor road south of the A487.

Sleeping & Eating

★ Llys Meddyg HOTEL $$

(01239-820008; www.llysmeddyg.com; East St; s £105, d £120-160;) This classily converted Georgian coach house takes contemporary big-city cool and plonks it firmly by the seaside. The rooms ooze boutique flair, with original art gracing the walls, painted wainscotting, locally woven blankets, reclaimed wood furnishings and bright pops of colour. Many bathrooms have free-standing tubs and monsoon showers. Downstairs there's an excellent **restaurant** (mains £15-23; 5-9pm;) and snug bar for pre-dinner cocktails.

Owner Ed takes guests on half-day foraging expeditions with a simple lunch (£70 per person, minimum of two people) on request.

Cnapan B&B $$

(01239-820575; www.cnapan.co.uk; East St; s/d £75/98; Mar-Jan;) This diligently maintained, listed Georgian town house has a flower-filled garden and five light-filled rooms. Renovations have freshened up the decor and left brand-new bathrooms in their wake; ask for room 4 – it's a little bigger than the others. Downstairs was once a restaurant, and restaurant standards carry over into the excellent breakfasts.

Tides Kitchen & Wine Bar BISTRO $

(01239-820777; www.facebook.com/marketstreetnewport; mains lunch £8-12.50, dinner £12-20; 9am-3pm Tue-Sat;) Bare-wood floors, cheek-by-jowl tables, banquette seating and local art dangling on walls create a modern boho-chic feel at Tides. Dig into imaginative takes on local fish and shellfish from Cardigan Bay, plus other well-prepared dishes from Welsh fillet of steak to Black Mountain smoked duck with beetroot crisps. The simpler lunch mains, homemade cakes and sourdough bread are delicious, too.

DON'T MISS

THREE HEAVENLY BEACHES

Southern Pembrokeshire is blessed with some of the country's most seductive beaches. Here are three faves.

Barafundle Bay (♿) Enveloped by dramatic, ragged cliffs and flanked by dunes, this perfect arc of golden sand slides into startlingly turquoise sea. It's a highly scenic walk along the coast path from the Stackpole Estate.

Broad Haven South (♿) Reached on foot via the Bosherston Lily Ponds, this magnificent golden crescent of dune-backed beach looks out to pointed sea stacks like Church Rock, so named because it resembles a submerged church at high tide.

Druidston Haven If you like your beaches wild and wave lashed, this gold-sand bay is the ultimate haven. The geology is spectacular, with caves, rock arches and Ordovician shale cliffs buckled into spectacular faults and folds.

Getting There & Away

Direct services to/from Newport include the frequent T5 to Dinas Cross (£1.65, six minutes), Fishguard (£2.50, 16 minutes), Haverfordwest (£4.15, 52 minutes), Cardigan (£3.45, 23 minutes) and Aberystwyth (£6, 2¼ hours, nine daily). The Pembrokeshire coastal bus services (p686) are also useful, especially in summer.

Saundersfoot

☎01834 / POP 3361

Bright and breezy Saundersfoot has a long, broad curve of beach with a sweet little harbour at one end, built in 1829 for the shipment of coal. Nowadays the only mining activity hereabouts is carried out by the toddlers digging in the golden sand. Well-kept old houses cling to the hilly streets radiating up from the town centre, where there are some interesting shops to peruse.

It makes for a quieter base than neighbouring Tenby, which is only an hour's walk away along the coast path.

Sights

Saundersfoot Beach BEACH

(♿) Bookended by a harbour, this wide, long ribbon of butterscotch sand is at its best at low tide. The gently sloping beach is ideal for families, with water shallow enough for swimming and plenty of space for free play. For more seclusion, follow the coast path around to pretty Coppet Hall Beach, where you can paddle among rock pools and go for a cracking lunch at Coast (p684).

Sleeping

Trevayne Farm CAMPSITE $

(☎01834-813402; www.trevaynefarm.co.uk; Monkstone; sites per tent/camper van £18/28; ⏰Easter-Oct; 🐾) Based on a working 40-hectare permaculture farm, this large clifftop site has beautiful sea views and two separate fields so back-to-basics campers can avoid the looming motorhomes. Perfect, secluded Monkstone Beach feels like the farm's private water frontage, and it's just a mile south of central Saundersfoot via the coast path, or 2 miles by road.

★**St Brides Spa Hotel** HOTEL $$$

(☎01834-812304; www.stbridesspahotel.com; St Brides Hill; r from £190; P📶🏊) Perched on headland with uplifting sea views, this stylishly contemporary spa hotel is one of Wales' finest. Seascapes hang on walls in the light-flooded rooms decked out in breezy blues and whites; the best have terraces overlooking the harbour. The spa is a huge draw, with its hydrotherapy infinity pool, thermal suite and coast-themed treatments ranging from seaweed wraps to lava shell massages.

By night, you can see Saundersfoot twinkle when you dine on high at **Cliff** (☎01834-812304; www.stbridesspahotel.com; St Brides Hill; mains £16-30; ⏰6-9pm; 📶) restaurant.

Eating

Cŵlbox STREET FOOD $

(www.cwlbox.com; Saundersfoot Beach; mains £9-12; ⏰10am-4pm Fri-Sun) The hippest joint on Saundersfoot beach bar none is this converted rice horse trailer, which dishes up terrific street food with a strong seafood slant when the weather permits. Stop by for the likes of crispy halloumi with skin-on fries, bang-bang prawns, popcorn cockle and shredded Tenby lobster with its own riff on mayo.

★Coast MODERN BRITISH $$$

(☎01834-810800; www.coastsaundersfoot.co.uk; Coppet Hall Beach; mains £24-30, tasting menus £35-70; ⊙noon-2.15pm & 6-9pm Wed-Sun;) The sea views are unbeatable at this curving, glass-fronted, sunlit restaurant, dreamily plonked on Coppet Hall Beach. The streamlined design is Scandi-style minimalist, and there's a great terrace for when the weather behaves. Head chef Fred Clapperton plays up locally foraged ingredients and sustainably sourced seafood in ingredient-led menus, delivered with skill and panache.

Getting There & Away

Saundersfoot's request train stop is a mile from the centre of town. Direct services head to/from Swansea (£16.30, 1½ hours, seven daily), Tenby (£3.80, eight minutes, nine daily) and Pembroke (£8.30, 32 minutes, nine daily).

Regular 381 buses head to/from Tenby (£2.50, 18 minutes), Narberth (£3.55, 34 minutes) and Haverfordwest (£5.10, one hour).

Tenby (Dinbych Y Pysgod)

☎01834 / POP 4696

Held high on a headland with magnificent sandy beaches either side, Tenby is the Pembrokeshire of a million postcards, with Georgian houses lavishly painted in pastels gathered around a harbour where fishing boats bob. Tenby's heart is still rimmed by Norman-built walls, funnelling holiday-makers through medieval streets lined with pubs, ice-cream parlours and gift shops.

Without the tackiness of the promenade-and-pier beach towns, it tastefully returns to being a sleepy little place in the low season. In summer it has a more boisterous, boozy, holiday-resort feel.

Sights & Activities

Castle Beach BEACH

() The most central of Tenby's beaches, cliff-backed Castle Beach is a pretty curve of golden sand for a stroll, ice cream or sand-castle building session, with fine views over to St Catherine's Island. It's in the northern crook of the vast South Beach, a 1.5-mile-long swathe of dune-backed sand.

Tenby Boat Trips CRUISE

(☎07980-864509; www.tenbyboattrips.co.uk; Tenby Harbour; ⊙Apr-Oct;) This boat trip operator runs seal safari cruises (adult/child £18/10) around monastic Caldey Island in search of Atlantic grey seals. The Caldey and St Margaret's cruise (adult/child £15/8) takes in impressive cliffs and caverns that are home to thousands of seabirds, including puffins, razorbills, cormorants and gannets. See the website for times and bookings.

Sleeping

Coach B&B $$

(☎01834-842210; www.coachhousetenby.co.uk; 11 Deer Park; d/f from £70/85;) Standing head and shoulders above most B&Bs in Tenby, the Coach extends the warmest of welcomes in a lovingly restored Victorian building. The cosy rooms have plaid throws, plenty of homely touches and pops of bright colour, and a generous breakfast is included.

★Penally Abbey HOTEL $$$

(☎01834-843033; www.penally-abbey.com; Penally; r from £165;) One of Pembrokesh-

PEMBROKESHIRE COAST NATIONAL PARK

Britain's only true coastal national park, the astoundingly beautiful Pembrokeshire Coast National Park, founded in 1952, takes in the full sweep of the coast and its offshore islands, as well as the moorland Preseli Hills in the north. Pembrokeshire's sea cliffs and islands support huge breeding populations of seabirds, while seals, dolphins, porpoises and whales frequently splash around offshore.

Available at visitor centres, the free annual publication and app *Coast to Coast* (online at www.pembrokeshirecoast.wales) give the inside scoop on park attractions, a calendar of events and details of park-organised activities, including guided walks, themed tours, cycling trips, pony treks, island cruises, canoe trips and minibus tours. It's worth getting *Coast to Coast* for the tide tables alone – they're a necessity for many legs of the coast path.

ire's most alluring escapes, this ivy-wreathed fantasy of a Strawberry Gothic country house sits on a hillside amid acres of gardens and woodland, with soul-stirring views across Carmarthen Bay. Rooms blend calm colours and contemporary style with period charm, arched windows, embroidered white bedspreads and espresso machines. Built on the site of an ancient abbey in the village of Penally, it is 2 miles southwest of Tenby along the A4139.

Eating & Drinking

Plantagenet House MODERN BRITISH $$$

(01834-842350; www.plantagenettenby.co.uk; Quay Hill; mains lunch £10-12, dinner £25-28; noon-2.30pm & 6-9pm, reduced hours in winter;) Atmosphere-wise, this place sure has the wow factor, ramping up the romance with cheek-by-jowl tables and candlelight. Tucked down an alley in Tenby's oldest house, parts of which date to the 10th century, it's dominated by an immense 12th-century Flemish chimney hearth. Tenby-caught fish, seafood and local organic beef are seasoned with freshly picked herbs, and the wine list is second to none.

★ **SandBar** BAR

(01834-844068; www.tenbybrewingco.com; The Mews, Upper Frog St; 11am-11pm Tue-Sun) The coolest kid on Tenby's block by a long shot, this retro-hip bar always has a great buzz and mellow sound track. It's the baby of Tenby Brewing Co, so you'll find a cracking assortment of craft beers, including tropical ones like Son of a Beach and Yeah Mango, which pair brilliantly with delicious street food from the Cŵlbox (p683) pop up.

Getting There & Away

BUS

The **bus station** (Upper Park Rd) is next to the tourist office on Upper Park Rd.

Tenby's direct bus connections include two services per day to/from Narberth (£5, 45 minutes), regular 381 buses to/from Saundersfoot (£2.50, 17 minutes), the hourly 349 to/from Manorbier (£3.60, 19 minutes) and Pembroke (£4.30, 48 minutes), and the hourly 381 to/from Haverfordwest (£5.25, 1¼ hours).

National Express (p669) coaches head to/from Swansea (£9.20, 1½ hours, two daily), Cardiff (£19, 3½ hours, one direct daily), Birmingham (£42, six hours, one direct daily) and London (£32, seven hours, one direct daily).

WORTH A TRIP

PEMBROKE CASTLE

This spectacular and forbidding **castle** (01646-681510; www.pembroke-castle.co.uk; Main St; adult/child £7/6; 10am-5pm;) was the home of the earls of Pembroke for over 300 years and the birthplace of Henry VII, the first Tudor king. A fort was established here in 1093 by Arnulph de Montgomery, but most of the present buildings date from the 13th century. It's a great place for both kids and adults to explore – wall walks and passages run from tower to tower, and there are vivid exhibitions detailing the castle's history.

Trains stop in both Pembroke and Pembroke Dock. There are direct services to/from Cardiff (£28.20, 3¼ hours, daily), Swansea (£16.80, 2½ hours, seven daily), Narberth (£9.20, 43 minutes, eight daily) and Tenby (£6, 21 minutes, nine daily).

TRAIN

There are direct trains to/from Pembroke (£6, 22 minutes, nine daily), Narberth (£5.40, 21 minutes, nine daily), Swansea (£16.80, two hours, seven daily) and Cardiff (£28.20, three hours, seven daily).

Narberth (Arberth)

01834 / POP 2489

An arty little hub of independent shops, cafes, restaurants and galleries, Narberth is a south Pembrokeshire market town full of history and charisma. Though light on standout sights (ruined Norman castle aside), it's nevertheless worth visiting for its burgeoning food scene and upbeat vibe, with butchers, delis, antique shops and boutiques lining its pretty pastel-painted streets.

Sights

Narberth Museum MUSEUM

(Amgueddfa Arberth; 01834-860500; www.narberthmuseum.co.uk; Bonded Stores, Church St; adult/child £4.50/1; 10am-5pm Thu-Sat;) Housed in a wonderfully atmospheric restored bonded-stores building, this museum presents a fascinating romp through local history. You can learn about medieval siege warfare and Narberth Castle through models and interactive games, walk historic streets, or listen to Welsh folk stories in the storytelling chair. There are lots of hands-on activities and dress-ups for children, plus a museum shop brimming with local crafts. It doubles as Narberth's tourist office.

Sleeping & Eating

Max & Caroline's GUESTHOUSE $
(☎01834-861835; www.maxandcarolines.com; 2a St James St; s/d/f £55/75/95;) Why bother serving breakfast when you're situated directly above Narberth's best **cafe** (☎01834-862762; 2a St James St; mains £8-10; 9am-5pm Mon-Sat;)? That's the philosophy at this excellent British-and-German-run guesthouse, where the rooms are handsomely decorated with home-style flourishes – pastels, florals and coolly revamped vintage furniture.

★ **Grove of Narberth** HOTEL $$$
(☎01834-860915; www.thegrove-narberth.co.uk; Molleston; r from £170;) Perhaps the escape of your wildest country dreams, the multiple award-winning Grove of Narberth has a pinch of timeless magic and luxury about it from the moment you glide up the drive. Its interiors are a clever warp-and-weft of Georgian elegance, Arts and Crafts flair, contemporary style and Welsh artwork, photography, furniture and pottery. The 11-hectare grounds make for a delightful romp.

Ultracomida SPANISH $$
(☎01834-861491; www.ultracomida.co.uk; 7 High St; tapas £5-9; 10am-6pm Mon-Sat;) The aroma of cured meats, fine cheeses, olives and freshly baked bread hits you as you walk into the buzzy little deli and tapas bar. Stock up on supplies for a gourmet picnic or go for the delicious tapas. Welsh-influenced taste sensations include the likes of Swansea smoked salmon with Galician cream cheese and pickled cucumber.

PEMBROKESHIRE COAST PATH

Straddling the line where Pembrokeshire drops suddenly into the sea, the Pembrokeshire Coast Path is one of the most spectacular long-distance routes in Britain. Established in 1970, it meanders along 186 miles of Britain's most dramatic coastal scenery, running from Amroth to St Dogmaels, taking in vertiginous clifftops and endless beautiful beaches. If you don't have the time or the stamina for the full route, it can easily be split into smaller chunks.

The weather can be quite changeable and mobile-phone coverage is unreliable; come prepared, and bring wet-weather gear and something warm, even in summer. The path has a dedicated website, www.nt.pcnpa.org.uk, that's ideal for planning your trek.

The hiker's best friend, Pembrokeshire's **coastal buses** operate on five main routes three times a day in each direction from May to September. For the remainder of the year, the Puffin Shuttle, Strumble Shuttle and Poppit Rocket operate two services a day on Thursday and Saturday only. For timetables, see www.pembrokeshire.gov.uk or pick up a copy of the national park's *Coast to Coast* magazine.

Best Sections

Dale to Broad Haven (six hours, 15.4 miles) A wonderful walk along dramatic clifftops ending at an impressive beach. Many access points and regular public transport make it good for short circular walks, too.

Whitesands to Porthgain (four to six hours, 10 miles) A beautiful but taxing section worth tackling if your time is limited. It's within easy reach of St Davids and offers the reward of some excellent nosh at the end of your day.

Porthgain to Pwll Deri (four to six hours, 12 miles) An exhilarating section with sheer cliffs, rock buttresses, pinnacles, islets, bays and beaches but some steep ascents and descents in between. Magnificent views of St Davids and Strumble Head.

Newport to St Dogmaels (six to eight hours, 15.5 miles) A tough, roller-coaster section with frequent steep hills but spectacular views of the wild and rugged coast and its numerous rock formations, sheer cliffs and caves.

WORTH A TRIP

MARLOES SANDS & SKOMER

In the southern crook of St Brides Bay, Marloes Sands is deliciously wild, with its mile-long scoop of sand and pebbles, sandstone cliffs and jagged rock formations. At low tide you can go rockpooling and fossil hunting. Sitting on a clifftop just above the beach and right on the coast path, the **Runwayskiln** (☎01646-636545; www.runwayskiln.co.uk; 2-/3-course lunch menu £20/25; ⊙noon-5pm Thu-Sun) lodges in a cluster of lovingly converted farm buildings, with a courtyard for warm-day dining and an imaginative lunch menu playing up farm-to-fork flavours.

Just off the coast is the island of **Skomer** (www.welshwildlife.org; ⊙Apr-Sep). Rimmed by dramatic sea cliffs, this is a real puffin fest of an island, home to 24,000 individual puffins at the last count, as well as the world's largest population of Manx shearwaters (350,000 pairs). Keep a close eye out too for Atlantic grey seals down on the rocks, which are especially plentiful during pupping season (September), and porpoises and dolphins out at sea. **Dale Sailing** (☎01646-603123; www.pembrokeshire-islands.co.uk; ⊙Easter-Sep;) are your best bet for wildlife cruises and rigged-hulled inflatable safaris to the islands. Its offerings include a one-hour cruise around Skomer (adult/child £16/12).

ℹ Getting There & Away

Bus destinations include frequent services to/from Haverfordwest (£4.05, 21 minutes), Carmarthen (£5.35, 37 minutes), Saundersfoot (£3.55, 34 minutes), Tenby (£5, 45 minutes), and twice-daily 430 services to Cardigan (£4.15, one hour).

There are good train connections to/from Newport (£33.30, 2¾ hours, seven daily), Cardiff (£28.20, 2½ hours, seven daily), Swansea (from £16.80, 1½ hours, eight daily), Tenby (£5.40, 20 minutes, nine daily) and Pembroke (£9.20, 48 minutes, eight daily).

AT A GLANCE

POPULATION
Aberystwyth: 13,000

HIGHEST PEAK
Pen-y-Fan (886m)

BEST LUNCH SPOT
International Welsh Rarebit Centre (p701)

BEST OFF-GRID ESCAPE
By the Wye (p693)

BEST FAMILY FUN
Jacob Sheep Trekking (p700)

WHEN TO GO

Mar–May
Wildflowers in bloom, peaceful days spent hiking and mountain biking, good deals on room rates.

Jul & Aug
Swimming, walking and kayaking on the coast, camping under starry night skies, a roster of crazy summer festivals.

Sep–Feb
Forest rambles, quieter mountain climbs, cosy days spent roaming country pubs and bookshops.

Hiking, Pen-y-Fan (p697)
BILLYSTOCK/SHUTTERSTOCK ©

Brecon Beacons & Mid-Wales

Snowdonia has the height edge, but go off-the-beaten track, or *igam-ogam* as the Welsh say, and the Brecon Beacons feel just as wild, with glacier-carved valleys and peaks rising like the prows of great ships. On almost every bend there are nods to the ancient past: ruined castles, Iron Age hill forts, and coaching inns with beams so low you knock your head against them. The outdoors here has serious pulling power, whether seen from a mountain bike, hiking trail or kayaking along a river.

Edging further north, Mid-Wales remains deliciously under the radar. The Cambrian Mountains' heather-misted moors, impenetrable forests and tucked-away valleys are so remote they are nicknamed the 'Desert of Wales'. Where Powys rolls west, Ceredigion's hidden bays and endearingly pretty coastal towns are also largely unsung.

INCLUDES

BRECON BEACONS NATIONAL PARK

Rippling from the English border all the way west to Llandeilo, this 520-sq-mile national park bombards you with lonely, moody beauty. Single-track lanes take you properly off-piste to heather-flecked moors where rowan trees tremble in the breeze and sheep brazenly block roads, and hiking trails lead up through glacier-carved valleys to crest fin-shaped mountains. In between, the ramparts of Iron Age hill forts and the skeletal remains of medieval castles await. While in tiny villages, glorious old coaching inns welcome passers-by – their blazing fires and local ales taking the edge off a bracing, often wet and windy, walk.

Activities

The national park is traversed by hundreds of walking routes: from gentle strolls to strenuous climbs. Walking cards, maps and guides are stocked in tourist offices as well as the National Park Visitor Centre near Libanus.

Likewise, there are many excellent off-road mountain-biking routes, including 14 graded and waymarked trails detailed in guides available from tourist and national-park offices.

Information

The park's main **visitor centre** (☎01874-624437; www.breconbeacons.org; Libanus; ⏰10am-4pm) has details of walks, hiking and biking trails, outdoor activities, wildlife and geology, plus a cafe and souvenir shop. It's located off the A470, 4 miles southwest of Brecon and 15 miles north of Merthyr Tydfil. Any of the buses on the Merthyr Tydfil–Brecon route stop at Libanus village, a 1.25-mile walk away.

Ordnance Survey (OS) Landranger maps 160 and 161 cover most of the park, as do Outdoor Leisure maps 12 and 13. These detailed maps include walking and cycling trails.

Getting There & Away

There are no railway lines through the national park, but trains stop on its periphery in the towns of Abergavenny, Llandeilo, Llangadog and Llandovery.

Most bus services only operate from Monday to Saturday. The most useful routes:

T4 Cardiff, Merthyr Tydfil, Libanus, Brecon, Talgarth, Builth Wells, Llandrindod Wells, Newtown

T6 Brecon, Sennybridge, Deffynog, Dan-yr-Ogof National Showcaves, Swansea

X3 Abergavenny, Llanvihangel Crucorney, Hereford

43/X43 Abergavenny, Crickhowell, Llangattock, Talybont-on-Usk, Llanfrynach, Brecon

Hay-on-Wye (Y Gelli Gandryll)

☎01497 / POP 1598

Straddling the banks of the River Wye, just inside the Welsh border, Hay-on-Wye steals your heart with its location, then sends your soul winging straight to book heaven. This handsome Georgian market town exploded onto the literary scene in the 1970s when Richard Booth, self-proclaimed King of Hay, put it on the map as the centre of the secondhand book trade.

This newfound literary fame was the impetus for the festival of literature and culture founded in 1988, which has grown in stature each year to embrace all aspects of the creative arts. Today the 11-day Hay Festival is a massive draw every May and June, endorsed by former US president Bill Clinton, a high-profile guest in 2001, as 'the Woodstock of the mind'.

Activities

Celtic Canoes CANOEING

(☎07515 905419; www.celticcanoes.co.uk; The Bont, Glasbury; half-/full day £25/35) Half-day excursions take to the Wye waters at Glasbury for a 5-mile paddle to Hay-on-Wye, taking in rapids and river wildlife (kingfishers are often spotted). Full-day trips end over the border in Whitney-on-Wye in England, where you are collected. It can also help organise overnight paddling trips (from £35 per day).

Festivals & Events

★**Hay Festival** LITERATURE

(☎box office 01497-822629; www.hayfestival.com; ticket prices vary; ⏰late May-early Jun) The 11-day Hay Festival is Britain's leading festival of literature and the arts – a kind of bookworms' Glastonbury. Like an iconic music festival, it has the gravity to attract the brightest stars in its corner of the artistic galaxy. Entry to the festival site is free; individual events are ticketed.

HowTheLightGetsIn CULTURAL

(www.howthelightgetsin.org; ticket prices vary; ⏰May) Billed as the word's largest festival of philosophy and music, HowTheLightGetsIn

Brecon Beacons & Mid-Wales Highlights

1 **Cardigan Bay** (p712) Kayaking with dolphins and seals along this rugged stretch of coast.

2 **Black Mountains** (p694) Taking a hair-raising drive through the deliciously off-the-radar Vale of Ewyas.

3 **Hay-on-Wye** (p690) Cracking the spine on a novel in the town that's absolutely besotted with books.

4 **Pen-y-Fan** (p697) Dodging the crowds and marvelling at the views as you surmount the region's peak.

5 **Cambrian Mountains** (p701) Enjoying the sound of silence and starry night skies in these deserted moorlands.

6 **Elan Valley** (p702) Exploring mighty Victorian dams and picking wild berries in this lovely valley.

7 **Aberystwyth** (p708) Experiencing a collision of high culture and student high jinks.

8 **Carreg Cennen** (p699) Gazing up at this dramatically positioned ruined fortress.

Brecon Beacons National Park

0 — 10 km
0 — 5 miles

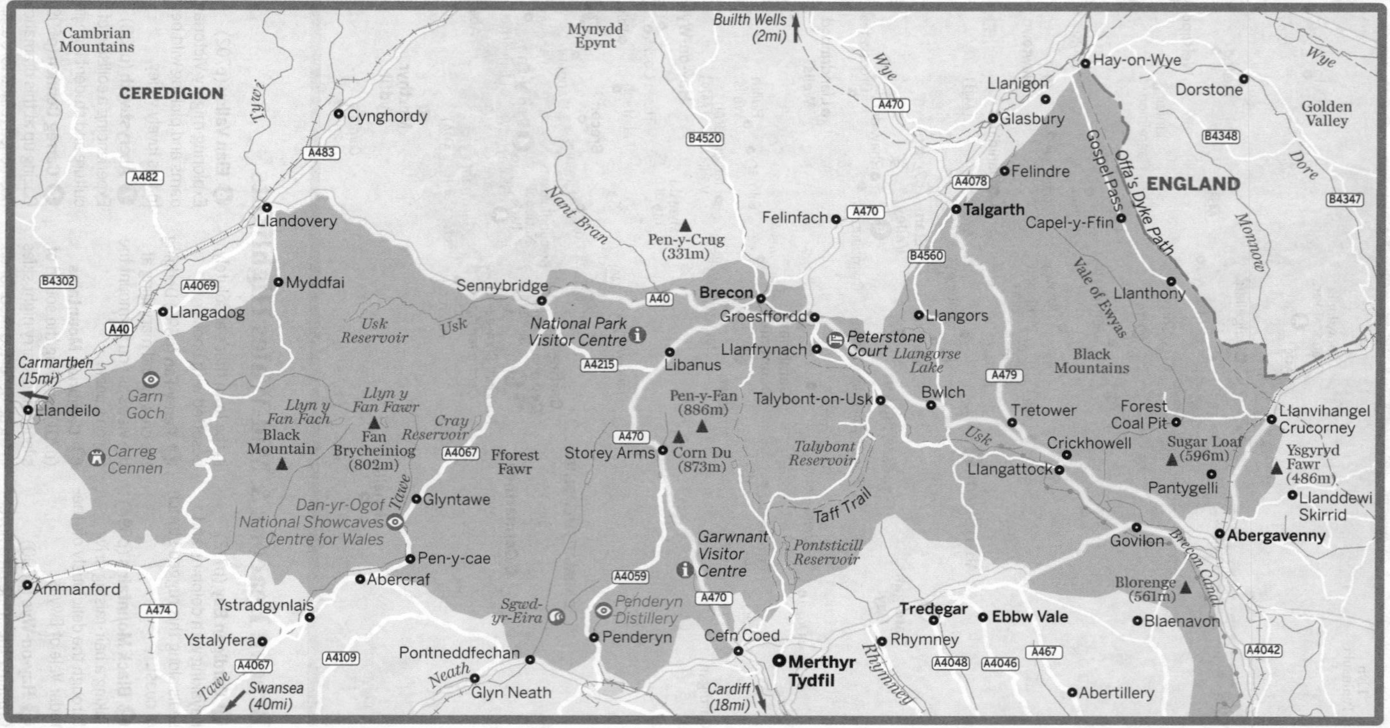

hits Hay each May with a high-profile line-up of music events, debates, readings and talks with world-leading thinkers. Held to coincide with the Hay Festival, it attracts thousands to a site on the banks of the Wye.

Sleeping

Maesyronnen B&B $$
(☎01497-842763; www.maesyronnenbandb.co.uk; Glasbury; s/d £70/95; P 📶) Secluded and relaxed, this 19th-century stone house sits in pretty, rambling gardens with views of the Wye Valley and Black Mountains. Only one of the four rooms is en suite, but all feature antique furnishings and a sense of past generations of peaceful country life. Breakfast features local and homemade produce. Maesyronnen is close to Glasbury, 5 miles from Hay.

★By the Wye B&B $$$
(☎01497-828166; www.bythewye.uk; The Start; safari tents £130-195) Reclining in ancient native woodland on the banks of the River Wye, this eco-minded escape takes glamping to a whole new luxury level. Perched on stilts high in the tree canopy, the safari tents are sublime, with fantasy-like beds handmade from gnarly driftwood and lots of above-and-beyond details, including welcome baskets with local goodies, firepits, decks overlooking the river and binoculars for bird spotting.

The family that runs the place aims to please while protecting the environment – trees and plants on the footpath that follows the river have been carefully labelled, the tents run on solar power, and luggage is transported using – like it! – wheelbarrows.

Eating

Old Electric Shop VEGETARIAN $
(☎01497-821194; www.oldelectric.co.uk; 10 Broad St; light bites £4-8; ⏲10am-4pm Thu-Mon; 📶) Hay's hippest hang-out is this fabulously quirky old curiosity shop of a cafe, crammed with studios selling new and vintage clothing, furniture, crafts and books. There's a nicely chilled boho vibe and a blackboard menu putting creative riffs on vegetarian soups, salads and curries – all made with locally sourced ingredients. The delicious homemade cakes go well with locally roasted coffee and loose-leaf teas.

BEACONS WAY

The 99-mile, eight-day Beacons Way trail wends its way across the national park from Ysgyryd Fawr (Skirrid) near Abergavenny to the village of Bethlehem on the edge of the Black Mountain, knocking off all the highest summits, and immersing you properly in the wilds of the region's sweeping peaks, starkly beautiful moors and glacier-carved valleys.

Needless to say, this is a stretching walk and requires proper walking gear as well as a good Ordnance Survey (OS) map – the moorland sections can be hard to navigate. The route is manageable in eight taxing days, but you may want to take a little longer to make it more enjoyable and less of an endurance test.

Tomatitos Tapas Bar SPANISH $$
(☎01497-820772; www.haytomatitos.co.uk; 38 Lion St; tapas £3-5.50; ⏲noon-9pm Wed-Sat, to 3.30pm Sun; 📶) There's always a good buzz at Tomatitos, which brings together a cosily beamed interior with an España-centric menu. Staples such as tortilla and chorizo in cider aside, daily specials feature guest stars such as roasted *piquillo* peppers stuffed with beef, and even lamb tagine. The food is great, and tastes even better washed down with Spanish wine by the glass.

Old Black Lion PUB FOOD $$
(☎01497-820841; www.oldblacklion.co.uk; 26 Lion St; mains £15-22; ⏲noon-2.30pm & 6.30-9pm Wed-Sat, noon-3.30pm Sun) Walkers, book browsers and the literati all flock to this creaky 17th-century inn, with heavy black beams, and low ceilings keeping things cosy. The food swings global, from Goan-style prawn curry to pan-seared calves liver in red-wine gravy. There are always a couple of vegetarian options.

★Off-Grid Gourmet GASTRONOMY $$$
(☎07538 037770; www.walkers-cottage.co.uk; Walkers Cottage, Locksters Lane; menus £40-50; ⏲www.walkers-cottage.co.uk) If ever there was proof that all you need to knock up a gourmet meal is canvas, sustainable energy, a wood fire and a degree of talent, Hugh Sawyer is it. Setting up camp in a field 3 miles north of Hay-on-Wye, he wows with

expertly crafted menus that are a true off-grid feast of sensational Welsh produce (including lobster in season).

Chapters WELSH $$$
(☎07855 783799; www.chaptershayonwye.co.uk; Lion St; menus £35; ⊙5-9pm Thu-Sat) Atmospherically lodged in the beautifully converted meeting rooms of St Johns Chapel, this intimate yet understated bistro-style restaurant is a real gourmet find. The seasonally changing menu spotlights sustainable regional produce in beautifully presented, ingredient-led dishes such as heritage beetroot with radish and soy, and pork loin with spicy nduja sausage and cider.

☆ Entertainment

Globe at Hay LIVE PERFORMANCE
(☎01497-821762; www.globeathay.org; Newport St; ⊙cafe 11am-11pm Fri & Sat, 10am-4pm Sun, see website for event times; 📶) Run by the Institute of Art and Ideas, the people behind Hay's HowTheLightGetsIn (p690) festival, this converted Methodist chapel wears many hats: cafe (mains £12 to £16), bar, live-music venue, theatre, club and all-round community hub. It's a wonderfully intimate place to catch a gig or listen to a tub-thumping political debate.

Shopping

There are dozens of secondhand and antiquarian bookshops in Hay, with hundreds of thousands of tomes stacked floor-to-ceiling across town. There are also excellent stores selling antiques, local produce, art and historic maps.

★**Richard Booth's Bookshop** BOOKS
(☎01497-820322; www.boothbooks.co.uk; 44 Lion St; ⊙9.30am-5pm Mon-Sat, 11am-5pm Sun) The most famous and still the best, Booth's is a thing of beauty – from the exquisite tiling outside to the immaculately catalogued shelves within (a far cry from the teetering piles of its early years). There's a sizeable Anglo-Welsh literature section, a Wales travel section, a great little cafe (mains £8 to £9) and an art-house cinema.

Eighteen Rabbit ARTS & CRAFTS
(www.eighteenrabbit.co.uk; 2 Lion St; ⊙10am-5.30pm Mon-Sat, 11am-3pm Sun) One of the coolest fair-trade shops you're ever likely to happen upon, Eighteen Rabbit has a terrific array of gifts and crafts from across the globe, from jewellery to ceramics, wooden toys for children to vegan-friendly wallets and bags. You'll also find a good selection of secondhand vinyl and CDs.

Addyman Books BOOKS
(☎01497-821136; www.hay-on-wyebooks.com; 39 Lion St; ⊙10am-5.30pm) A rabbit warren of a shop spread over several levels, with rooms devoted to sci-fi, myths, horror, music and art, among other subjects. Its speciality is rare, out-of-print books.

Murder & Mayhem BOOKS
(☎01497-821613; 5 Lion St; ⊙10am-5.30pm Mon-Sat, to 5pm Sun) Over the road from the parent store, this specialist branch of Addyman Books has a body outline on the floor, monsters on the ceiling and stacks of detective fiction, true crime and horror.

ℹ Information

Tourist Office (☎01497-820144; www.hay-on-wye.co.uk; Chapel Cottage, Oxford Rd; ⊙10am-1pm Mon-Sat) Stocks a map showing all of Hay's bookshops, as well as copious literature and advice on the town and surrounding area.

ℹ Getting There & Away

Bus 39 runs six times a day (except on Sunday) to/from Talgarth (£5.70, 17 minutes), Felinfach (£6.30, 30 minutes), Brecon (£6.80, 37 minutes) and Hereford (£8.10, 57 minutes).

National Cycle Route 42 passes through Hay-on-Wye, heading south to Abergavenny. At nearby Glasbury it also connects with National Cycle Route 8 (Lôn Las Cymru), which heads southwest to Brecon and through Brecon Beacons National Park.

Black Mountains (Y Mynyddoedd Duon)

Puckering up between Abergavenny and Hay-on-Wye, the Black Mountains are untamed and largely uninhabited (if you ignore sheep and red kites, that is). They top out at 811m at the windswept summit of Waun Fach and its graceful sweep of gold-green moorland. Getting lost on single-track lanes is part of the fun: this is remote road-trip country, with drives making their way through forgotten valleys to lookouts with soul-stirring views, walking trails where you'll be accompanied by the skylark's serenade, and medieval ruins that fired the imaginations of the great romantics.

Sights

St Issui's Church CHURCH
(Patrishow) Tucked away on a thickly forested hillside in the **Vale of Ewyas**, this tiny, weathered, 11th-century church is a time capsule of Welsh faith and culture. Inside its wonders reveal themselves: a finely carved wooden rood screen, medieval frescoes of biblical texts, coats of arms and a red-ochre skeleton. The church is usually open and empty. Immediately downhill from the church is the **Holy Well of St Issui**, which is believed to have healing powers and has long been a pilgrimage site.

★**Llanthony Priory** RUINS
(Cadw; www.cadw.gov.wales; 10am-4pm; P) FREE Halfway along the impossibly beautiful Vale of Ewyas lie the wildly romantic ruins of this Augustinian priory, set among pasture and wooded hills by the River Honddu. Perhaps the second most important abbey in Wales when completed in 1230, it was abandoned after Henry VIII dissolved Britain's monasteries in 1538. Running a close second to Tintern for grandeur, Llanthony's setting is even more arresting, and you won't have crowds to fight. JMW Turner was impressed, too: he painted the scene in 1794.

Skirrid MOUNTAIN
(Ysgyryd Fawr) Of the glacially sculpted hills rising above Abergavenny, the Skirrid (486m) is most dramatic. You can trek here from Llanvihangel Crucorney (5.5 miles) or take the B4521 from Abergavenny to the layby at the base of the hill (4 miles). It's a steep climb from here through broadleaf woods thick with ferns. The final climb brings you to the wind-beaten summit, where you'll be rewarded with far-reaching views stretching west to the Brecon Beacons and south to the Severn Estuary.

Sleeping & Eating

★**Llanthony Priory Hotel** HOTEL $$
(01873-890487; www.llanthonyprioryhotel.co.uk; Llanthony; s/d incl breakfast from £75/95; P) Seemingly growing out of the priory ruins and incorporating some of the original medieval buildings, this insanely atmospheric hotel has four-poster beds, stone spiral staircases and rooms squeezed into turrets. Bathrooms are shared and there's no TV or wi-fi. The log-burner-warmed bar in the vaulted undercroft serves simple meals (mains £4.50 to £12) and a solid selection of real ales.

Celyn Farm B&B $$
(01873-890894; www.celynfarm.co.uk; Forest Coal Pit; d £85-95) If you like to get away from all neighbours, you'll love Celyn ('Holy') Farm. Set in 120 hectares of farmland reached by narrow lanes from either Llanvihangel Crucorney or Crickhowell (make sure you print the directions), this remote country house offers four handsome rooms, excellent breakfasts and idyllic views over Sugar Loaf and the Grwyne Fawr River below.

Skirrid Mountain Inn PUB FOOD $
(01873-890258; www.skirridmountaininn.co.uk; Hereford Rd, Llanvihangel Crucorney; mains £8-12; 5.30-11pm Mon, 11am-2.30pm & 5.30-11pm Tue-Fri, 11.30am-11pm Sat, noon-10pm Sun; P) Possibly Wales' oldest and most haunted boozer, the Skirrid Inn's woodsmoke-blackened beams prop up 900 years of history. Lore has it that Shakespeare himself enjoyed a pint here, and the hangman's noose above the stairwell recalls the pub's former life as a courthouse. Downstairs it serves hearty grub (steak pie, leek-and-pork sausages with mash and the like) in front of roaring fires.

Getting There & Away

Bus X3 runs frequently between Abergavenny and Llanvihangel Crucorney (£3.20, 12 minutes) and Hereford (£5.90, 55 minutes).

OFF THE BEATEN TRACK

WALES' HIGHEST ROAD

Pray for clement weather, well-behaved sheep and excellent reversing skills on the sensational **Gospel Pass** drive through the upper reaches of the wild Vale of Ewyas. A single-track lane unspools through harsh but beautiful moorland to climb the 549m Gospel Pass, Wales' highest road. As you crest the pass, views crack open of 677m Hay Bluff to the east and 690m Twmpa (better known as, ahem, Lord Hereford's Knob).

Crickhowell (Crughywel)

01873 / POP 2060

Sitting astride the River Usk, Crickhowell is as pretty as can be, with its neat rows of Georgian houses in chalk-box colours, sloping lanes and wide mountain views all around. Its high street has scooped awards for its old-fashioned flair, with independent shops including a butcher, baker and bookstore. There are fabulous walks in the surrounds, such as the climb up to Crug Hywel Iron Age hill fort.

Sights

Tretower Court & Castle HISTORIC BUILDING
(Cadw; www.cadw.gov.wales; Tretower; adult/child £6.50/3.90; 10am-1pm & 2-5pm Mon-Wed, Sat & Sun) Originally the home of the Vaughan family, Tretower gives you two historic buildings for the price of one: the sturdy circular Norman keep, now roofless and commanding only a sheep-nibbled bailey, and a 15th-century manor house with a fine garden and orchard (now furnished with picnic tables). Together they illustrate the transition from military stronghold to country house that took place in late-medieval times. It's 3 miles northwest of Crickhowell on the A479. Prebook tickets online.

Crug Hywel MOUNTAIN
(Table Mountain) Though not in the same league as its Cape Town cousin, Crickhowell has its very own Table Mountain, 451m Crug Hywel. Rising to the north, the distinctive hump of old red sandstone gave the town its name. The short-but-steep hike to the top is a rite of passage for local ramblers, heading through a wooded dingle and over stile and field to the remains of an Iron Age hill fort. The summit commands tremendous views of the Brecons and Black Mountains.

The tourist office has a leaflet detailing the 4.5-mile, three-hour round-trip route.

> **STARGAZING IN THE BRECON BEACONS**
>
> The Brecon Beacons is just one of a handful of places in the world to be awarded 'Dark-Sky Reserve' status. With almost zero light pollution, this is one of the UK's finest places for stargazing. Meteor showers, nebulae, strings of constellations and the Milky Way twinkle brightly in the night sky when the weather is clear. Among the 10 best spots are Carreg Cennen (p699), Sugar Loaf (p662) and Llanthony Priory (p695).
>
> Visitor centres throughout the park can give you information about stargazing events, or check out www.breconbeacons.org/stargazing.

Festivals & Events

Green Man Festival MUSIC
(www.greenman.net; Glanusk Park; mid-Aug;) This four-day, sustainably minded music festival has a sterling reputation for its mellow, family-friendly vibe and green ethos. It attracts A-list indie acts like Lamb and the Wedding Present, interesting electronic artists and the occasional dead-set rock legend. Tickets include camping on the riverside site 2 miles west of Crickhowell.

Crickhowell Walking Festival SPORTS
(www.crickhowellfestival.com; Mar) Held on the second week in March, this eight-day festival features guided treks, workshops on outdoorsy themes, and music. The thigh-burning highlight is arguably the Table Mountain Challenge, where you walk or run up and down Table Mountain five times in 10 hours. Phew! Book on the website.

Sleeping & Eating

Bear PUB $$
(01873-810408; www.bearhotel.co.uk; Beaufort St; incl breakfast s £99-192, d £123-248; P) If only every village in Wales had a pub like this… Looking back on 600 years of history, the Bear was once an overnight stop on the horse-drawn coach journey from London to West Wales. Now a delightfully old-school gastro pub and hotel, it's full of creaky character, with blackened-oak beams, log fires and cosy nooks.

Old Rectory HERITAGE HOTEL $$
(01873-810373; www.rectoryhotel.co.uk; Llangattock; incl breakfast s £75, d £99-124, ste £139) Reclining peacefully in 7 hectares of grounds and orchards, this 16th-century country abode was once home to the Welsh metaphysical poet Henry Vaughan. You'll find dashes of period charm in the warm-toned, plushly furnished rooms. Overlooking the Black Mountains, the conservatory restaurant (mains £16 to £20) serves the sophisticated likes of maple-glazed pork belly with fondant potato and cider sauce.

★**Gliffaes** HOTEL $$$
(01874-730371; www.gliffaeshotel.com; r incl breakfast £135-290; P) Winging you back

to a more graceful era, Gliffaes is a class act. Set in grounds bristling with rare and exotic trees on the banks of the River Usk, this Italianate Victorian manor has elegant rooms full of period character – the pick of which overlook the gardens and wooded hills beyond. It's about 4 miles northwest of Crickhowell, off the A40.

Book-ish CAFE $
(☎01873-811256; www.book-ish.co.uk/cafe; 18 High St; mains £5-7; ⏰10am-4pm Sun-Fri, to 5pm Sat; ☎👪) Attached to the independent bookshop of your wildest dreams, this cafe has a strong local following. Browse your latest paperback purchase over brunch (with tempting options like smashed avocado on toast and buttermilk pancakes with fruit compote), a ploughman's platter with local Perl Las cheese, ham, pork pie and pickles, or homemade cake with local Black Mountain Roast coffee.

Information

Tourist Office (☎01873-811970; www.visit-crickhowell.co.uk; Beaufort St; ⏰10am-3pm Thu & Sat; 📶) Shares a building with an art gallery and stocks leaflets for local walks.

Getting There & Away

Direct services include 12 daily 43/X43 buses to/from Abergavenny (£2.20, 15 minutes), Llanfrynach (£2.50, 33 minutes) and Brecon (£2.70, 45 minutes). No Sunday services.

Brecon (Aberhonddu)

☎01874 / POP 8250

The call of the mountains is irresistible in Brecon. Sitting astride the convergence of the rushing Rivers Usk and Honddu, this appealing little market town is laced with canals and capped off by an impressive cathedral. The real thrills here, however, are in the national park, hence the reason why hiking boots and backpacks are warmly welcome. If you're looking to combine outdoor adventure with a dash of culture, this is the place.

Sights

Brecon Cathedral CHURCH
(☎01874-623857; www.breconcathedral.org.uk; Cathedral Close; ⏰11am-4pm Mon-Sat, to 3pm Sun) Perched above the River Honddu, Brecon Cathedral was founded in 1093 as part of a Benedictine monastery, though little remains of the original Norman church, except the elaborately carved font. Most of the Gothic structure standing today is early 13th century. Modern additions include its impressive vaulted timber roof. Look out for the stone cresset by the entrance. This rare ancient lighting device contains 30 cups that were once filled with oil and lit to illuminate dark corners or steps.

DON'T MISS

PEN-Y-FAN

No trip to the Brecons is complete without puffing up to Pen-y-Fan (886m), the highest peak. On cloud-free days, views stretch all the way to the Cambrians, Black Mountains and the Bristol Channel. It's popular, so avoid weekends and holidays when the biggest crowds descend. The quickest stomp to the top begins at the Pont ar Daf car park on the A470, 10 miles southwest of Brecon. It's a steep but straightforward ascent to the summit of Corn Du (873m), followed by a short dip and final ascent to Pen-y-Fan (4.5 miles return; allow three hours).

Activities

★**Brecon Beacons Foraging** WALKING
(www.breconbeaconsforaging.com; The Bookhouse, Tregaer Rd; half-day foraging experience from £35; 👪) Get acquainted with wild food on a half-day, child-friendly foraging walk with Adele Nozedar. Bring along a basket or canvas bag and prepare to find a feast of wild ingredients in the surrounding moors, mountains, hedgerows and woodlands. Depending on the season, you can hope to pick everything from wild garlic to young nettles, bilberries and mushrooms.

Dragonfly Cruises BOATING
(☎07831 685222; www.dragonfly-cruises.co.uk; Canal Basin, Canal Rd; adult/child £9/5; ⏰Mar-Oct; 👪) Runs 2½-hour narrowboat cruises on the Monmouthshire and Brecon Canal. There are trips twice daily in July and August, fewer in the cooler months – ring or see the website to enquire.

Biped Cycles CYCLING
(☎01874-622296; www.bipedcycles.co.uk; 10 Ship St; bike hire per day £35; ⏰9am-4pm Mon, Tue & Thu-Sat, to 1pm Wed) Rents mountain and road

Brecon

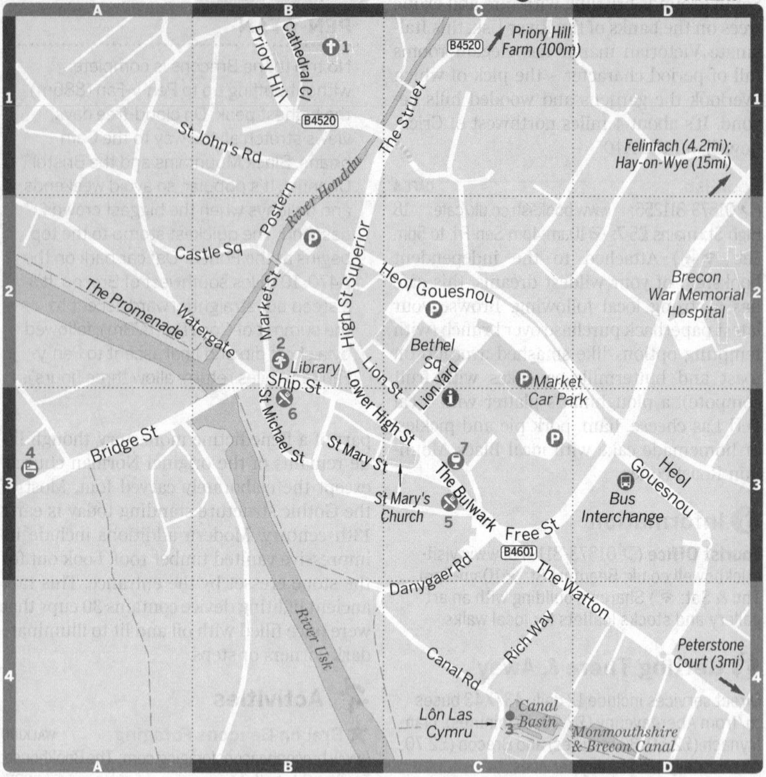

Brecon

Sights
1 Brecon Cathedral B1

Activities, Courses & Tours
2 Biped Cycles B2
3 Dragonfly Cruises C4

Sleeping
4 Coach House A3

Eating
5 Gurkha Corner C3
6 Hours B3

Drinking & Nightlife
7 Brecon Tap C3

bikes, performs repairs and can arrange guided rides. You'll need to leave two forms of ID in the shop.

Festivals & Events

Brecon Fringe Festival MUSIC
(www.breconfringe.co.uk; Aug) Brecon swings to everything from acoustic blues to folk, gypsy and Latin jazz at this high-spirited festival, which brings a wide range of musical styles to pubs and other venues in and around town over four days in August.

Sleeping

Priory Mill Farm CAMPSITE $
(www.priorymillfarm.co.uk; Hay Rd; sites per adult £10; Easter-Sep; P) With a cobbled courtyard, an ancient mill, free-range chickens and a lush camping meadow by the Honddu, this is camping heaven, all just a 10-minute riverside walk from Brecon. Local wood and charcoal are supplied for campfires, plus there's a semi-enclosed shelter for cooking and chatting, and a covered bike locker for riders. Children aged 13 and over only.

Coach House B&B $$
(☎01874-620043; www.coachhousebrecon.com; 12 Orchard St; d £89-150; 📶) This appealing 19th-century coaching inn is well attuned to the needs of walkers, with a drying room for hiking gear, generous breakfasts (including good vegetarian options), and packed lunches should you so wish. The six stylish, modern rooms, decorated in soothing taupes and creams, have ultra-comfy beds and great showers.

Peterstone Court HOTEL $$$
(☎01874-665387; www.peterstone-court.com; Llanhamlach; d £155-235, ste £275; P 📶 ≋) This elegant Georgian manor house on the banks of the Usk offers large rooms brimming with period charm and affording superb views across the valley to the Beacons. The spa is another big draw, with organic beauty treatments, a Moroccan-style relaxation room and a heated outdoor pool. There's also a separate three-bedroom cottage and an excellent restaurant.

Llanhamlach is 3 miles southeast of Brecon, off the A40.

Eating

★Hours CAFE $
(☎01874-622800; www.thehoursbrecon.co.uk; 15 Ship St; mains £5.75-8.25; ⊙11am-4pm Tue-Sat; 📶) You might happily linger for hours in this little dream of an indie bookshop and cafe, lodged in an endearingly wonky olive-green cottage. The cafe takes pride in local sourcing. Besides fair-trade coffee, it does a fine line in lunches and light bites, from homemade soups, quiche and sandwiches to halloumi with roasted veg. The cakes are delicious, too.

Gurkha Corner NEPALI $
(☎01874-610871; 12 Glamorgan St; mains £8-12; ⊙noon-2.30pm & 5.30-11pm Tue-Sun; 🖉) Rustic scenes of the Himalayas brighten the windowless dining room of this friendly Nepalese restaurant. The delicious food dishes – curries, fried rice, lentils and rich veg side dishes – are influenced by, but not identical to, Indian food. The *sisnu* (stinging nettle) curry is a good example.

Drinking & Nightlife

Brecon Tap BAR
(☎01874-622353; www.facebook.com/brecontap; The Bulwark; ⊙noon-8pm Mon-Thu, to 9.30pm Fri & Sat, to 2pm Sun; 📶) Originally crowd-funded into being by the lads at Brecon Brewing, the Tap is a treasure trove of craft beer, traditional cider, estate wines and locally baked meat pies. Occasionally, live music intrudes on the happy hum of locals polishing their favourite bar stools.

Information

Visit Brecon Tourist Office (☎01874-620860; www.visitbrecon.org; 11 Lion Yard; ⊙10am-4pm) Visit Brecon is run by volunteers who are passionate about the town and its surrounds. This handy local visitor information centre is well stocked with information.

Getting There & Away

Direct bus services run to/from Brecon's **bus interchange** (Heol Gouesnou). Services include up to 12 43/X43 buses per day to/from Crickhowell (£3, 30 to 45 minutes) and Abergavenny (£3.90, 45 minutes), up to six T14 buses per day to/from Hay-on-Wye (£7, 37 minutes), and up to eight T4 services per day to/from Llandrindod Wells (£5.30, 55 minutes) and Cardiff (£7.20, 1¾ hours). Smaller routes run no Sunday services.

The Market car park offers short-stay pay-and-display parking. There are long-stay lots on Heol Gouesnou and near the canal basin.

Fforest Fawr & Black Mountain

Narrow single-track lanes, forested hills and moor after sweeping, sheep-nibbled moor lend a thrillingly remote feel to the sparsely inhabited western half of the Brecon Beacons. Rolling across the western fringes of the national park, the Black Mountain (Y Mynydd Du) is a lonely expanse of barren peaks that throws down an irresistible gauntlet to intrepid hikers. Scoured by glaciers, shaped by human action from prehistory through the Romans to today, it's a bleak, wild and utterly captivating place.

Sights

★Carreg Cennen CASTLE
(Cadw; ☎01558-822291; www.cadw.gov.wales; Trapp; adult/child £5.50/3.50; ⊙9.30am-5pm) Dramatically perched atop a steep limestone crag high above the River Cennen are the brooding ruins of Wales' ultimate romantic castle, visible for miles in every direction. Originally a Welsh castle, the current structure dates to Edward I's conquest of Wales

OFF THE BEATEN TRACK

SHEEP TREKKING

With sheep outnumbering people by around three to one, Wales is one seriously wet and woolly land. But one organic farm in particular has raised the baaa (pardon the pun) when it comes to sheep farming. At **Jacob Sheep Trekking** (☎01874-636 797; www.sheeptrekking.co.uk; Aberhyddnant Organic Farm, Crai; £30; ⏲Feb-Sep; 👪), you can actually take a sheep for a walk in the Brecon Beacons National Park.

These are no ordinary sheep – their flock of piebald Jacob, Ouessant (the world's smallest) and Valais Blacknose (the world's shaggiest and quite probably cutest) sheep are very easy-going and, dare we say it, friendly. Bring solid footwear and waterproofs in case conditions are wet and muddy.

If you're not up for trekking, it offers other sheep-related experiences – from lambing sessions to shear a sheep workshops.

in the late 13th century. It was partially dismantled in 1462 during the War of the Roses. On a working farm of the same name, Carreg Cennen is well signposted from the A483 heading south from Llandeilo.

Ystradfellte Waterfalls WATERFALL
(👪) A series of dramatic falls lies between the villages of Pontneddfechan and Ystradfellte, where the Rivers Mellte, Hepste and Pyrddin pass through steep forested gorges. The finest is **Sgwd-yr-Eira** (Waterfall of the Snow), where you can actually walk behind the torrent. At one point the River Mellte disappears into **Porth-yr-Ogof** (Door to the Cave), the biggest cave entrance in Britain (3m high and 20m wide), only to reappear 100m further south.

Llyn-y-Fan Fach LAKE
Out on its lonesome in the Black Mountain range, Llyn-y-Fan Fach is well hidden and worth seeking. Starkly beautiful peaks sweep abruptly down to this steel-blue glacial cirque lake. It is steeped in the legend of the Lady of the Lake. Traipse the 4-mile trail along the sheep-grazed valley, following the river upstream to the lake, ridge and high moors beyond. The views are sensational.

Penderyn Distillery DISTILLERY
(☎01685-810650; www.penderyn.wales; Penderyn; tours adult/child £9.50/4.50; ⏲shop 9am-5pm; P) Wales has carved out its own niche for Brecon Botanicals gin and award-winning single malts thanks to the Penderyn Distillery. What began as a pub chat about whisky back in the 1990s swiftly evolved when Alun Evans bought a copper-pot still. He chose the foothills of the Brecon Beacons for its spring water and produced the first bottle of Welsh whisky in a century in 2004. Stop by the shop or visit the website for details on tours, tastings and more in-depth masterclasses.

Dan-yr-Ogof National Showcaves Centre for Wales CAVE
(☎01639-730284; www.showcaves.co.uk; A4067, Abercraf; adult/child £15.50/12.50; ⏲11am Tue-Thu, 11am & noon Sat & Sun; 👪) The limestone plateau of the southern Fforest Fawr is riddled with some of the largest and most complex cave systems in Britain. Most can only be visited by experienced cavers, but this set of three caves is well lit, spacious and easily accessible, even to children. The complex is just off the A4067, north of Abercraf. Tickets must be prebooked online in advance.

Garn Goch RUINS
FREE You're likely to have the impressive remains of Garn Goch to yourself. One of the largest Iron Age sites in Wales, it comprises a smaller hill fort covering 1.5 hectares, and a much larger one of 11.2 hectares. While what you now see are immense piles of rubble, it's sobering to know that these were once 10m-high ramparts, faced with stone and 5m thick. From the top, jaw-dropping views of Black Mountain country roll to every point of the compass.

Sleeping & Eating

Coed Owen Bunkhouse HOSTEL $
(☎01685-722628, 07508 544044; www.breconbeaconsbunkhouse.co.uk; Cwmtaff; dm/r £30/60; P) On a working sheep farm just south of the Cantref Reservoir, this excellent custom conversion of an old stone barn offers smart six- and 10-bed bunk rooms and two small private rooms. There's an excellent kitchen, a common area, outdoor tables, a boot room and a laundry. At weekends it's usually booked up by groups, but solo travellers shouldn't have trouble midweek.

Mandinam CABIN $$
(☎01550-777368; www.mandinam.com; Llangadog; huts £100 per night; ⏲Easter-Oct; P) This wonderfully remote estate on the park's northwestern fringe offers a bohemian back-to-nature experience in gypsy vans, shepherd's huts and coolly converted wagons, complete with kitchens and wood-fired hot tubs for romantic stargazing. You needn't worry about privacy, as the huts are well spaced within the vast, bucolic property. The kind family that owns the farm has made something very special here. Three-night minimum stay.

Carreg Cennen Tearoom WELSH $
(☎01558-822291; www.carregcennencastle.com; Trap; mains £6-7; ⏲11am-4pm; P) Possibly the best castle tearoom anywhere. The farmer-owner's longhorn beef is on the menu as cottage pie and beef salad, plus it serves warming *cawl* (traditional Welsh stew) and excellent homemade cakes. The location is an impressive converted barn that sits just below the castle (p699).

★**International Welsh Rarebit Centre** CAFE $
(☎01874-636843; High St, Defynnog; rarebits £5.50-7.50; ⏲10am-5pm Wed-Sat;) Dutch owner Roos pulled a rabbit out of a hat when she transformed a dilapidated schoolhouse into this unique cafe, art gallery and cultural hub combination. Served with garden-grown salads and chalked up on a blackboard, the menu is school-dinner fantasy stuff. The delicious rarebits often deviate from the traditional, with the likes of Guinness-laced 'Stout Rarebit', feisty jalapeño and coriander 'Mexican Rarebit' and Caerphilly, leek and chive 'Spring Rarebit'.

Getting There & Away

The only useful bus routes through this region are the 63 between Brecon and Ystradgynlais, which stops at the Dan-yr-Ogof National Showcaves Centre when it's open; and bus T4 between Cardiff and Newtown (via Merthyr Tydfil, Brecon and Llandrindod Wells).

POWYS

Small villages, quiet-but-quirky market towns and an abundance of sheep litter the undulating hills and moorland of predominantly rural Powys, by far Wales' biggest county. Named after an ancient Welsh kingdom, this modern entity was formed in 1974 from the historic counties of Montgomeryshire, Radnorshire and Brecknockshire. Ideal for walking and cycling, Powys isn't just green in a literal sense – Machynlleth has become a focal point for the nation's environmentally friendly aspirations. The red kite – a once-threatened bird, for which the county went to outstanding lengths to save from extinction – is now the very symbol of Powys.

Getting There & Around

BUS

Bus services are the most extensive means of public transport in Powys, with regular connections on major routes, such as those run by Traveline Cymru (www.traveline.cymru), from

WORTH A TRIP

CAMBRIAN MOUNTAINS

The Cambrian Mountains are an empty, starkly beautiful area of uplands running from Snowdonia down to the Brecon Beacons, and covers the majority of Mid-Wales, surrounding the few settlements in the valleys far below. Largely unpopulated, this plateau of yellow-green moorland is the source of both the Rivers Severn and Wye, and laced with lakes, waterfalls and deserted *cwms* (valleys) plus hill farms home to thousands of sheep. Except for around the Elan Valley, which is busier, if you wish to escape there is no more majestic place in Wales in which to hike or bike in solitude. Many tracks criss-cross the area, including the 298-mile **Cambrian Way** that thrusts across Wales from Cardiff to Conwy in the north; a good third of the route is in the Cambrian Mountains themselves. You can discover more about walking some or all of the lonely trail, not every stage of which has lodgings, on www.cambrianway.org.uk - or find more information about the region at www.cambrian-mountains.co.uk.

WORTH A TRIP

ELAN VALLEY

The Elan Valley is filled with beautiful countryside, split by imposing Victorian and Edwardian dams and the lakes they've created. In the late 19th century, dams were built on the River Elan (pronounced 'ellen'), west of Rhayader, mainly to provide a reliable water supply for Birmingham. During WWII, the earliest of the dams was used to perfect the 'bouncing bomb' used in the storied Dambusters raid on targets in Germany's Ruhr Valley. Together their reservoirs now provide over 70 million gallons of water daily for Birmingham and parts of South and Mid-Wales, and generate some 3.9 megawatts of hydroelectric power.

The valley's **visitor centre** (01597-810880; www.elanvalley.org.uk; B4518, Caban-coch Reservoir, LD6 5HP; 9am-5pm Apr-Oct, 10am-4pm Nov-Mar) houses informative exhibits, rents bicycles (adult/child from £26/14 per day), advises on nearby hikes and offers activities such as birdwatching safaris, an autumnal 'Walking Fest' and ranger tours inside Pen y Garreg dam. It's downstream of the lowest dam, 3 miles from Rhayader on the B4518.

Unless you have your own transport, the only route to the Elan Valley is to walk, cycle or take a taxi from Rhayader.

at least Monday to Saturday (Sundays can be sparsely served) and more sporadic services on the minors.

TRAIN

The Heart of Wales Line cuts Powys in two, entering the county near Llanwrtyd Wells and exiting at Knighton. To the north, the Cambrian Line runs from Shrewsbury in England, through Welshpool and Newtown to Machynlleth. Both lines are very scenic, and the most pleasant way to travel in Powys. Tickets and timetables can be found at www.nationalrail.co.uk.

Rhayader (Rhaeadr Gwy)

01597 / POP 2100

Rhayader is a small, fairly uneventful livestock-market and former cattle-droving town. It's elevated to major status because of the lack of anywhere else nearby, and revolves around a central crossroads marked by a war-memorial clock and some rather venerable town houses. Wednesday – market day – sees the most action. What it lacks in urbanity, though, the town compensates for in stunning moorland countryside. The nearby Elan Valley, a series of immense nearby lakes hemmed in by imposing Victorian dams and full of thrilling hiking and biking trails, is the big lure, as is tackling the 136-mile Wye Valley Walk.

Sights & Activities

Gigrin Farm Red Kite Feeding Station BIRDWATCHING

(01597-810243; www.gigrin.co.uk; South St, LD6 5BL; adult/child £7.50/4; 1-5pm Sat-Wed, daily school holidays;) By the 1960s Britain's red kite population had been decimated to near-extinction (there were just 20-odd breeding pairs). Outstanding campaigns by centres like this across Powys, Ceredigion and Carmarthenshire have since brought the bird back to being a common sight in Mid-Wales: one of the greatest-ever UK conservation results. Hundreds of red kites arrive daily at 2pm (3pm British summer time) to gorge on meat scraps.

Clive Powell Mountain Bike Centre MOUNTAIN BIKING

(01597-811343; www.facebook.com/ClivePowellBikes; cnr West & Church Sts; 9am-1pm & 2-5.30pm) This centre is run by a former cycling champion and coach. Hire a mountain/road bike here (£32/24 per day, including helmet and puncture kit; most are new Giant models) or take it easier with an electric bike (£40 per day).

Sleeping & Eating

Camping & Caravanning Club CAMPSITE $

(Wyeside; 01597-810183; www.campingandcaravanningclub.co.uk; Llangurig Rd, LD6 5LB; tent and 2 adults (unpowered site) from £25; Apr-Oct;) A short walk from the centre of

Rhayader, this relaxed, grassy campsite has river views, lots of trees, two shower blocks and a shop.

Lost ARC CAFE $

(☎01597-811226; www.thelostarc.co.uk; Old Drill Hall; breakfasts £5-8, lunches £5-8, pizza £8-10; 10am-4pm Sun, Mon & Thu, to 9pm Fri & Sat;) A breath of fresh air in the Rhayader eating scene, this bright cafe in a stone-built building down by the river off Bridge St tantalises the town with smashed avocado on sourdough, breakfast wraps, Welsh rarebit and weekend wood-fired pizzas – it even has a 'region of the week' street-food special. The venue is an up-and-coming arts centre too.

Triangle Inn PUB FOOD $$

(☎01597-810537; www.triangleinn.co.uk; Cwmdauddwr; mains £8-16; 5-10pm Mon-Sat;) This tiny 16th-century inn, just over the bridge to Cwmdauddwr (the village adjoining Rhayader), is the pick of the local dining choices. A very welcoming place, it serves real ales, including Rev James, and excellent hearty pub classics. If there's no room in the snug interior, there's a pretty outside terrace.

Getting There & Away

Buses stopping here include the X47 to Llandrindod Wells (£2.40, 25 minutes, four to seven daily) and Aberystwyth (1¼ hours, four to seven daily), the X75 to Newtown (£4.35, one hour, two daily), Berriew, on the way to Welshpool (£6.70, two hours, one daily), and Shrewsbury (£9.60, 2¾ hours, one daily).

Llanwrtyd Wells (Llanwrtyd)

☎01591 / POP 850

Llanwrtyd (khlan-*oor*-tid) Wells is an odd little town – placid except during one of its many unconventional festivals, when it's packed to the rafters with crazy contestants and their merrymaking supporters.

Apart from its status as the capital of wacky Wales, Llanwrtyd Wells is encircled by exquisite walking, cycling and horse-riding country, bounded by the Cambrian Mountains to the northwest and Mynydd Epynt to the southeast.

Theophilus Evans, the local vicar, first discovered the healing properties of the Ffynon Droellwyd (Stinking Well) in 1732 when he found it cured his scurvy. The popularity of the waters morphed and Llanwrtyd became a spa town. Nowadays, however, its wells have been capped, and its madcap festivities are its main enticement.

Sleeping & Eating

Lasswade Country House B&B $$

(☎01591-610515; www.lasswadehotel.co.uk; Station Rd; s/d from £70/85;) This excellent country restaurant (with rooms) makes great use of a handsome, three-storey Edwardian house looking over the Irfon Valley towards the Brecon Beacons. Committed to

LLANWRTYD FESTIVALS

While mulling over how to encourage tourism in Llanwrtyd over the dark winter, some citizens started an inspired roll call of unconventionality. There's now something on every month (see www.green-events.co.uk for more details), but these are some of the wackiest events:

World Mountain Bike Chariot Racing Championship (team entry £20; Jan) Specially designed mountain-bike chariots race off; mid-January.

Man vs Horse Marathon (mid-Jun) The first-conceived of Llanwrtyd's wacky races sees two legs take on four; mid-June.

World Bog Snorkelling Championships (adult/child £15/12; bank holiday Aug) Held over the August bank holiday: participants wallow through a bog as quick as they can.

Real Ale Wobble & Ramble (1-day ride £20, 1-/2-day ramble £11/18; Nov) Cyclists and walkers sup pints along a waymarked route; November.

Mari Llwyd (New Year Walk In; New Year's Eve) A celebration of Welsh poetry and the country's deep pagan past; New Year's Eve.

green tourism (it's won multiple awards, sources hydroelectric power and offers electric-vehicle recharging), it's also big on gastronomy: the chef-owner's three-course menu (£36) features Cambrian lamb, Tally goats cheese and other delights.

★**Drovers Rest** WELSH $$
(☎01591-610264; www.food-food-food.co.uk; The Square; 3 courses £35; ⊙noon-2pm & 7.30-9.30pm Wed-Sun; 📶) One of Mid-Wales' best dining venues, this charming restaurant does fantastic things with local produce. Snugly perched by the Irfon, it has a relaxing riverside terrace and a few simple-but-cosy rooms (singles/doubles £45/85, some en suite). The owners also run regular one-day cooking courses (£165 to £195) featuring Welsh cuisine and game. Book ahead.

★**Neuadd Arms Hotel** PUB FOOD $$
(☎01591-610236; www.neuaddarmshotel.co.uk; mains £8.50-14, 3-course meal £18.50; ⊙9am-10pm) At this focal point for Llanwrtyd folks, there's above-average pub food, with delicious curries the standouts, and excellent beers brewed in the stables out back. Bed-and-breakfast rooms (single/double £45/80) are nice enough too. Here, former landlord Gordon Green and his punters cooked up many of the kooky events that put Llanwrtyd Wells on the tourist trail. Full of bygone charm.

Getting There & Away

Bus 48 heads to Builth Wells (£3.80, 25 minutes, up to five per day).

Llanwrtyd is best approached on the Heart of Wales Line (www.heart-of-wales.co.uk), with up to four direct services daily to Swansea (£12.40, two hours) via Llandovery (£.60, 25 minutes) and Llandeilo (£5.60, 45 minutes) and to Shrewsbury (£15.60, 2¼ hours). Buses often replace trains, especially in winter months.

Builth Wells (Llanfair-Ym-Muallt)

☎01982 / POP 2600

Builth (pronounced 'bilth') Wells is perhaps the liveliest of the former spa towns of Mid-Wales, with a bustling, workaday feel – although the only attraction per se is July's mammoth agricultural show, Wales' most important. The town has a pretty location on the River Wye and prominence as a centre of local agriculture, whilst being a handy base for walkers or cyclists tackling the surrounding hill country.

Festivals & Events

Royal Welsh Show FAIR
(www.rwas.co.uk; Llanelwedd; per day adult/child £26/5; ⊙Jul; 👪) Over 200,000 people descend on Builth for four days every July for the Royal Welsh Show (founded in Aberystwyth in 1904) to see everything from gussied-up livestock to lumberjack competitions, falconry and a food hall bursting with farm produce.

Sleeping & Eating

Caer Beris Manor HERITAGE HOTEL $$
(☎01982-552601; www.caerberis.com; A483, LD2 3NP; r £90-150) This 1896 mock-Tudor country manor lies at the end of a long driveway, winding through 7.3 hectares of parkland on the River Irfon. Classic styling, log fires and spacious rooms with swag curtains, heavy fabrics and tasselled lamps await. The oak-panelled Restaurant 1896 dishes up a delightful seasonal menu featuring local produce (mains £13 to £19).

★**Drawing Room** MODERN WELSH $$$
(☎01982-552493; www.the-drawing-room.co.uk; Cwmbach, LD2 3RT; 3 courses £40; ⊙from 7pm, last orders 8.30pm; P📶) Ensconced in a Georgian country house flanked by kitchen gardens, this two-rosette restaurant-with-rooms is one of Mid-Wales' finest. Prime Welsh black beef, Brecon lamb and Cardigan Bay crab feature on the locally sourced menu, while the three gracefully refurbished rooms are well worth considering (from £235, including dinner, bed and breakfast). It's 3 miles north of Builth, off the A470.

Getting There & Away

Bus 48 heads to Llanwrtyd Wells (£3.80, 25 minutes, up to five per day). There are three to four daily T4 services to Llandrindod Wells (£2.30, 20 minutes), Newtown (£6.30, 1¼ hours), Brecon (£3.90, 45 minutes) and Cardiff (£9, 2½ hours), and one X15 per day to Hay-on-Wye (£3.30, 30 minutes) and Hereford (£6.80, 1¼ hours).

Builth is on the Heart of Wales railway line, with two to four daily trains serving Swansea (south) and Shrewsbury (north) but Builth Road station is 2.5 miles outside town, which makes it less convenient.

WORTH A TRIP

WORTH A TRIP: POWIS CASTLE

Surrounded by magnificent gardens, the red-brick **Powis Castle** (NT; ☎01938-551944; www.nationaltrust.org.uk; castle & gardens adult/child £14.20/7.10; ⏱gardens 10am-6pm Apr-Sep, to 4pm Oct-Mar, castle & Clive Museum noon-4pm; P 👪) was originally constructed in the 13th century by Gruffydd ap Gwenwynwyn, prince of Powys, and subsequently enriched by generations of the Herbert and Clive families. The castle's highlight, the **Clive Museum**, houses exquisite treasures brought back from India and the Far East by Clive of India (British conqueror of Bengal at the Battle of Plassey in 1757) and his son Edward, who married the daughter of the first earl of Powys.

The extravagant mural-covered, wood-panelled interior, the mahogany beds, tiger skins and one of Wales' finest collections of paintings proclaim the family's opulence, while the Clive Museum, with its cache of armour, bejewelled weapons, precious stones, textiles, diaries and letters, is testament to a life richly lived in colonial India. You may spot a gold tiger's head encrusted with rubies and diamonds – one of only two to survive from the throne of Tipu Sultan – as well as a Chinese sword with snakeskin scabbard and finely carved ivory chess pieces.

Ridiculous wealth this may be, but it's worth remembering (the museum indeed points this out) that, as with many grand British residences popping up during the colonial era, the Clives looted many of the artefacts for their country pile – in this case during their power seizure and brutal resultant rule in India and Myanmar.

The baroque Italianate gardens are extraordinary, dotted with original lead statues, flowerbeds and ancient yews, with an orangery, formal and wild sections, terraces and orchards.

The castle is just over a mile south of Welshpool, off Berriew Rd, a pretty walk from the centre.

Montgomery

☎01686 / POP 990

Set around a market square lined with handsome stone and brick houses, and overlooked by the ruins of a Norman castle (p706), genteel Montgomery is one of Wales' prettiest small towns, and our favourite base in northeast Powys. An idiosyncratic mixture of Georgian, Victorian and timber-framed houses lines the streets and there are several excellent places to eat.

A mile east of town is one of the best-preserved sections of **Offa's Dyke**, ensuring Montgomery is also a hit with Offa's Dyke Path (p660) hikers.

There are good bus services from here to the nearest train station at Welshpool, on the Cambrian Line between Aberystwyth and Shrewsbury. Here, before making your next connection, you can check out Powys' and perhaps northeast Wales' most impressive fortress, Powis Castle.

Sights

Monty's Brewery Visitor Centre VISITOR CENTRE

(www.montysbrewery.co.uk; Forden Rd) If you have acquired a taste for Welsh craft beer, or want to, make the hop north of the centre to one of the country's most visitor-friendly breweries. The experience encompasses a visitor centre, shop, tasting room and a window onto their developmental brewery (their main brewery cannot be visited, but you can learn about the brewing process here). Walkers will cherish their 'Best Offa' as a beery souvenir: a golden bitter and official beer of the Offa's Dyke Path.

St Nicholas' Church CHURCH

(Church Bank; ⏱9am-dusk) Evocative Norman St Nicholas' Church dates from 1226. Look out for the vaulted ceiling decorated with intricate coloured bosses, a beautifully carved pre-Reformation rood screen, striking mid-19th-century stained-glass windows and the canopied tomb of local landowner Sir Richard Herbert and his wife Magdalen, parents of Elizabethan poet George Herbert.

Montgomery Castle CASTLE
(10am-6pm Apr-Sep, to 4pm Oct-Mar) FREE Rising from the craggy outcrop above the town are the ruins of Montgomery Castle, a 13th-century fortress with its most famous moment occurring in 1267 when, during treaty negotiations here, Henry III granted Llywelyn ap Gruffydd the title of Prince of Wales. Few remains survive today, but the views over the chequerboard countryside are beautiful.

Sleeping & Eating

Dragon Hotel INN $$
(01686-668359; www.dragonhotel.com; Market Sq; r from £63;) Popular with walkers, this extremely noticeable 17th-century half-timbered coaching inn has some 20 en-suite rooms, a common snug (the Den), a pool (yes, really) and a restaurant (mains £13 to £17.50, kitchen open noon to 3pm and 6pm to 8.45pm). The bar is as good a place as any to try ales brewed at Monty's, just down the road.

★**Checkers** FRENCH $
(01686-669822; www.checkerswales.co.uk; Broad St; lunch £5-10; 10am-4pm Tue-Thu, from 9am Fri & Sat;) One of Montgomery's main drawcards is this truly excellent restaurant-with-rooms. With an inquisitive modern-French approach to fresh, locally sourced ingredients, and as a former Michelin-star-holder, it's earned a loyal fan base. It now concocts the likes of Gressingham duck salad with blackberries and smoky beef and chorizo chilli with feta, plus brunches and a few inspired puddings.

Upstairs, this 17th-century coaching inn still welcomes guests. Five quietly stylish rooms (£105 to £125) with extra-comfy beds, two of which are super-king, also sport blissful bathrooms.

Getting There & Away

Up to seven X71/81 buses per day run to Welshpool (18 minutes) and Newtown (23 minutes) – at either of which you can connect to national rail services.

Machynlleth

01654 / POP 2200

Little Machynlleth (ma-*hun*-khleth) is saturated in historical significance: the town was the site where nationalist hero Owain Glyndŵr established the country's first parliament in 1404. But Machynlleth is perhaps better known as the country's green capital – thanks to the Centre for Alternative Technology, 3 miles north, and its proximity to cycle-path-laced forested hills.

Machynlleth is surprisingly cosmopolitan too, with fantastic sleeping and eating options scattered around about.

Sights

★**Centre for Alternative Technology** SCIENCE CENTRE
(CAT; Canolfan y Dechnoleg Amgen; 01654-705950; www.cat.org.uk; Pantperthog, SY20 9AZ; adult/child £6.50/5.50; 10am-5pm;) A small, dedicated band of enthusiasts have spent 40 years practising sustainability at the thought-provoking CAT, set in the Dyfi Unesco Biosphere Reserve, north of Machynlleth. Founded in 1974 (well ahead of its time), it's an education/visitor centre that demonstrates practical solutions for sustainability. Nearly 3 hectares of displays deal with topics such as composting, organic gardening, environmentally friendly construction, renewable energy sources and sewage treatment.

★**MOMA Machynlleth** GALLERY
(01654-703355; http://moma.machynlleth.org.uk; Penrallt St; 10am-4pm Mon-Sat) FREE Housed partly in a former Wesleyan chapel, the Museum of Modern Art exhibits work by contemporary Welsh artists in a permanent collection supplemented by ever-changing temporary exhibitions. The chapel itself has superb acoustics – it's used for concerts, theatre and August's annual celebration of international music, the Machynlleth Festival.

Owain Glyndŵr Centre MUSEUM
(Canolfan Owain Glyndŵr; 01654-702932; www.canolfanglyndwr.org; Maengwyn St; 11am-3pm Jul, Aug & school holidays) FREE Housed in a rare example of a late-medieval Welsh town house, this centre contains an exhibition telling the story of the Welsh hero's fight for independence and starring the Pennal letter, written by Glyndŵr in pursuit of an alliance with the French. It's best to email in advance to book a look round, or ask for the keys at Caffi Alys alongside.

Closed at the time of research.

Sleeping

Wynnstay HOTEL **$$**
(☎01654-702941; www.wynnstay.wales; Maengwyn St; s/d from £65/95; P 📶) This erstwhile Georgian coaching inn (1780) remains the best all-rounder in town, with 22 charming older-style rooms, one with a four-poster bed, and creaky, uneven floors. Downstairs there's a good restaurant (mains £11 to £22), a wine shop with Italian single-estate varietals and, in the courtyard on Friday and Saturday nights between Easter and October, a wood-fired pizzeria (pizzas £10).

★**Living Room Treehouses** CABIN **$$$**
(☎01172-047830; www.living-room.co; Bryn Meurig, SY20 9PZ; 3 days & 2 nights £379; P) Wonderfully designed, these six cosy, rustic-glam tree houses blend organically into an enchanted forest off the A470. You're as close to nature as can be (up a tree!), yet the beds are luxurious, the insulation and wood-burning stoves keep you warm all year, and the seclusion is glorious (all houses are set generously apart). Arrival days are Sunday, Wednesday and Friday.

Eating

Number Twenty One WELSH **$$**
(☎01654-703382; www.numbertwentyone.co.uk; 21 Maengwyn St; mains £11.95-19.95; ⊙noon-10pm Wed-Sun; ✎) Run by a passionate, professional young foodie couple with ambitions exceeding the usual small-town bistro, Number Twenty One has been popular since day one, a status ensured by surprising dishes such as asparagus and sea spinach risotto with focaccia, goats curd and liberal scatterings of fresh-grown garden herbs, or sourdough-encrusted catch of the day. Space is limited: book ahead.

★**Ynyshir Restaurant & Rooms** GASTRONOMY **$$$**
(☎01654-781209; www.ynyshir.co.uk; Eglwysfach, SY20 8TA; set dinner £200; ⊙noon-2pm & 7-9pm Tue-Sat; P 📶) Foraged wild foods, the best local meat and seafood and his own kitchen-garden produce (but mainly meat!) give Gareth Ward of Ynyshir Hall the foundations to concoct some of Wales' most wonderful food. A Michelin-starred restaurant within a luxurious country retreat, Ynyshir offers set, multi-course menus ever-changing in course number, content and composition, and heralding total gastronomic joy.

Getting There & Away

On a bike? Sustrans National Cycling Network Route 8 passes through Machynlleth, heading north to Corris then southeast to Rhayader.

Bus routes include the X28 and T2 to Aberystwyth (£4.25, 40 minutes, at least hourly) and the two-hourly T2 to Dolgellau (£3.55, 30 minutes), Porthmadog (1¾ hours), Caernarfon (2¼ hours) and Bangor (2¾ hours); and up to nine 34 services per day to the Centre for Alternative Technology (£2.25, seven minutes) and Corris (£2.60, 15 minutes).

The bus stops for Newtown (Maengwyn St) and other destinations (Pentrerhedyn St) are either side of the market cross in the centre of town.

By train, Machynlleth directly serves Aberystwyth (£7.20, 35 minutes), Porthmadog (£15.90, two hours), Pwllheli (£18.40, 2½ hours) and Newtown (£10.70, 35 minutes). There are three trains daily to Birmingham (£25, 2½ hours).

CEREDIGION

Bordered by Cardigan Bay on one side and the Cambrian Mountains on the other, Ceredigion (pronounced with a 'dig', not a 'didge') is an ancient Welsh kingdom founded by the 5th-century chieftain Ceredig. The rural communities here escaped the population influxes of the south's coal-mining valleys and the north's slate-mining towns, and, consequently, the Welsh language is stronger here than in any other part of the country except Gwynedd and Anglesey.

The lack of heavy industry also left Ceredigion with some of Britain's cleanest beaches that, with no train access south of Aberystwyth, tend to be pleasantly uncrowded. Adding to the isolation is the massif known as the 'Desert of Wales' – the barren uplands of the Cambrian Mountains. All of this conspires to make Ceredigion's sandy coves, river valleys, quiet towns and wild plateaus as off-the-beaten-track as Wales gets.

Getting There & Away

Aberystwyth is the main rail hub in Ceredigion, linking every two hours with Shrewsbury in England (£22, 1¾ hours) and Pwllheli on the Llŷn Peninsula (£18.50, 3¾ hours) via Machynlleth (£7.20, 33 minutes).

Aberystwyth

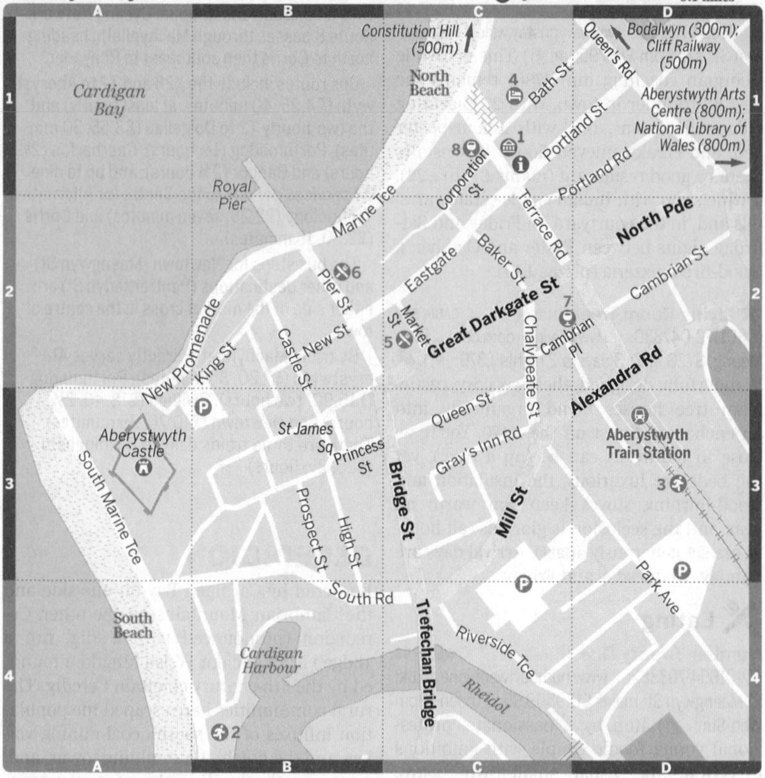

Aberystwyth

Sights
1 Ceredigion Museum C1

Activities, Courses & Tours
2 Rheidol Cycle Trail B4
3 Vale of Rheidol Railway D3

Sleeping
4 Maes-y-Môr C1

Eating
5 Medina C2
6 Ultracomida B2

Drinking & Nightlife
7 Bottle & Barrel C2
8 The Libertine C1

Aberystwyth

01970 / POP 13,000

Spread out along a shingle beach, Aberystwyth is the largest and by far the liveliest town in Mid-Wales. Credit for this is largely due to its sizeable student population, courtesy of Aberystwyth University. During term time the bars and restaurants are buzzing, while in summer the bucket-and-spade brigade enjoys the beach. Meanwhile, the vestiges of a stately seaside resort can be glimpsed in the terrace of grand pastel-hued houses that line the promenade – and the cultural clout the town enjoys is on display for all to see at phenomenal institutions like the National Library of Wales.

Sights

North Beach, with its lovely lengthy sweep of imposing pastel-hued houses and hotels, harks back to the town's Victorian heyday as a fashionable resort – although some buildings have clearly seen better days. When you reach the Constitution Hill end of the 1.5-mile prom, it's customary to kick the white bar, although the locals can't seem to explain the rationale behind this ritual.

The prom pivots around the Old College and Aberystwyth Castle before leading along **South Beach** – a quieter but still attractive seafront. Many locals prefer the stony but emptier **Tanybwlch Beach**, just south of the harbour, where the Rivers Rheidol and Ystwyth meet. **Pen Dinas**, the upland rising behind Tanybwlch, is the site of the important Iron Age hill fort **Dinas Maelor**. The peak is now dominated by a monument to the Duke of Wellington.

National Library of Wales LIBRARY

(Llyfrgell Genedlaethol Cymru; ☎01970-632800; www.llgc.org.uk; Penglais Rd; ⏲9am-6pm Mon-Fri, to 5pm Sat) FREE On a hilltop east of town with a sensational view of Cardigan Bay, the National Library is a cultural powerhouse. Founded in 1916, it holds millions of books in many languages – as a copyright library it has copies of every book published in the UK. Among its 25,000 manuscripts are such gems as the 13th-century *Black Book of Carmarthen* (the oldest existing Welsh text), a text of Chaucer penned by his scribe Adam Pinkhurst, and a 1st edition of *Paradise Lost*.

Another highlight is the Nanteos Cup – one of many candidates across Europe for the Holy Grail. Other galleries display an ever-stimulating set of changing exhibitions (some of which charge fees) featuring the library's collection and Welsh heritage in general. Check the website for the latest opening times.

Ceredigion Museum MUSEUM

(☎01970-633088; www.ceredigionmuseum.wales; Terrace Rd; ⏲10am-5pm Mon-Sat) FREE Ceredigion's county museum inhabits the Coliseum, which opened in 1905 as a theatre, then from 1932 served as a cinema promising 'amusement without vulgarity'. The elegant interior retains its stage, with exhibits from the museum's collection of 60,000-plus artefacts positioned around its three tiers – everything from old chemist furnishings and a replica 1850s cottage to a Bronze Age burial urn and a Roman cooking pot. It was closed at the time of research. Aberystwyth's tourist office (p711) is located here.

Activities

Vale of Rheidol Railway RAIL

(☎01970-625819; www.rheidolrailway.co.uk; Park Ave; return adult/child £26/11; ⏲mid-Feb–Nov; 👪) Due to reopen in March 2021, this scenic narrow-gauge railway is one of Aberystwyth's most popular attractions. Steam locomotives built between 1923 and 1938 have been lovingly restored by volunteers and chug for almost 12 miles up the beautiful wooded valley of the River Rheidol to Devil's Bridge. There's car parking at the Aberystwyth terminus. Timetables vary throughout the year; check the website.

Cliff Railway CABLE CAR

(☎01970-617642; www.aberystwythcliffrailway.co.uk; Cliff Tce; adult/child one way £4.50/3, return £5.50/4; ⏲10am-5pm Apr-Oct, reduced hours Nov-Mar; 👪) If your legs aren't up to the climb of **Constitution Hill** (it's 130m, and you can't drive), catch a lift on the trundling Cliff Railway, the UK's longest electric funicular (and possibly its slowest, too, at a breakneck 4mph). It must have been glacial when first built, in 1896, when it was powered by a water-balance system.

Rheidol Cycle Trail CYCLING

(👪) Sticking mainly to designated cycle paths and quiet country lanes, the 17-mile

CEREDIGION HIGHLIGHTS

Aberaeron

Live it up in this prettily painted beach town with exquisite food and plush seaside accommodation at the **Harbourmaster Hotel** (☎01545-570755; www.harbour-master.com; Pen Cei, SA46 0BT; s/d from £140/150; 📶).

New Quay

Join a dolphin-survey boat trip at informative Cardigan Bay Marine Wildlife Centre (p712).

Tregaron

Venture into the lovely green Ceredigion hinterland and discover a lonely Cistercian ruin at **Strata Florida Abbey** (Abaty Ystrad Fflur; Cadw; ☎01974-831261; www.cadw.gov.wales; Abbey Rd, Pontrhydfendigaid, SY25 6ES; adult/child £4.20/2.50, Nov-late Mar free; ⏲10am-5pm Apr-Oct, to 4pm Nov-Mar).

DON'T MISS

ABERYSTWYTH'S GREAT OUTDOORS

One of the major attractions of Aberystwyth is its proximity to phenomenal countryside. Yes, Snowdonia is only a short drive north, but there are some unforgettable outdoorsy odysseys closer to town. Here, adventurers, is a little appetite-whetter…

Pen Pumlumon Fawr (Plynlimon), mid-Wales' highest point at 752m, is a bald, wind-blasted yellow-green summit that is a fair representation of what the wild Cambrian Mountains offer far more of: lovely, unpeopled moorland panoramas. There are views from the summit cairns up to Snowdonia and the Brecon Beacons on a clear day. Within a couple of miles of here are the sources of the Rivers Wye and Severn (the latter Britain's longest river and marked with more fanfare).

Access is from the remote hamlet of Eisteddfa Gurig, on the border with Powys, 17 miles east of Aber on the A44. Trail signage is non-existent but the track up, once you negotiate the farm buildings by the car park, is distinct. Bring an OS map. The out-and-back route is 5 miles. Bus service 525 (Aberystwyth–Llanidloes) stops at Eisteddfa Gurig five times daily.

Rheidol Cycle Trail climbs from Aberystwyth Harbour to Devil's Bridge through the beautiful Rheidol Valley. Along the way it passes side-routes to sights such as picturesque lake-spotted woodland **Bwlch Nant yr Arian** (☎0300 065 5470; www.naturalresources.wales; Ponterwyd, SY23 3AB; parking 1hr/3hr/day £1.50/3/5; ⊙visitor centre 10am-5pm; P) FREE.

Sleeping

Maes-y-Môr GUESTHOUSE $

(☎01970-639270; www.maesymor.co.uk; 25 Bath St; s without bathroom £45, d with bathroom from £55; P 📶) Above a laundrette you'll find nine clean, bright rooms, basic self-catering equipment and a warm welcome. Bathrooms and kitchen are shared – only the family room has an en-suite bathroom – and there's a locked shed for bicycles.

Bodalwyn B&B $$

(☎07969-298875; www.bodalwyn.co.uk; Queen's Ave; s/d from £49/69; 📶) Simultaneously upmarket and full of home comforts, this handsome Edwardian B&B offers tasteful rooms with sparkling bathrooms and a hearty cooked breakfast (with vegetarian options). Three of the rooms have sea views, but ask for room 3, with the bay window.

★**Nanteos Mansion** HERITAGE HOTEL $$$

(☎01970-600522; www.nanteos.com; Rhydyfelin, SY23 4LU; d & ste from £129; P 📶 🐾) The stately 18th-century residence of the locally prominent Powell family for 180 years, Nanteos is an excellently executed country-house hotel where equal attention is lavished on the rooms (most graced with astounding individual features such as hand-painted wallpaper, ornate chandeliers and silk-lined wardrobes), the restaurant (with one of the best steaks we've ever eaten) and the serene, seemingly endless woodland-dotted estate.

It's located 3 miles southeast of Aber. Take the A487 south, turn off on the B4340 – the access lane is 1km on the left. It's possibly Mid-Wales' finest lodging.

Eating

Medina MIDDLE EASTERN $

(☎01970-358300; www.medina-aberystwyth.co.uk; 10 Market St; meze £6-7, set meals £11, mains £8-12; ⊙9.30am-8.30pm Mon-Fri, to 9.30pm Sat) Hummus, feta and tabbouleh mix it up with Aberystwyth's de facto Middle East at Medina, a large, lively space spread-eagling across the ground floor of the old Talbot Hotel serving the best-value food in town. It's fresh, flavour-packed and there's a shop showcasing more of the same, along with Welsh speciality products.

★**Ultracomida** TAPAS $$

(☎01970-630686; www.ultracomida.co.uk; 31 Pier St; tapas £4-10; ⊙10am-4pm Mon-Sat; 🖉) Aber is lucky to have Ultracomida – an importer, deli and restaurant motivated by a personal love of all things Iberian. Out front is an exceptional collection of Spanish charcuterie, cheese, dry goods and sweetmeats (with nods to France and Wales), while out back is a convivial little dining room serving great tapas and wine without pretension.

★Y Ffarmers
PUB FOOD $$

(☎01974-261275; www.yffarmers.co.uk; Llanfihangel y Creuddyn, SY23 4LA; mains £12-18; ⏲6-10pm Tue-Fri, noon-10pm Sat, noon-3pm Sun) This outstanding whitewashed pub with its cosily contemporary interior is the main reason to visit the pretty hamlet of Llanfihangel y Creuddyn, 7 miles southeast of Aber. Prepare for fantastic Welsh pub food: cockle cakes with laver-bread sauce, guinea fowl with tarragon and shallots, and other delicious creations.

Drinking & Entertainment

Bottle & Barrel
CRAFT BEER

(☎07788 585443; www.bottleandbarrel.cymru; 14 Cambrian Pl; ⏲1-10pm) Mid-Wales' best craft-beer bar serves predominantly Welsh brews – a selection from across the country, from Cardiff's Crafty Devil to Gwynedd's Geipel Brewing – displayed in detail above their bar. There are 30-odd Welsh gins too and the cosy rambling rooms of a Victorian town house to partake in.

The Libertine
COCKTAIL BAR

(☎01970-611331; www.facebook.com/TheLibertineAberystwyth; 54-56 Terrace Rd, SY23 2AJ; ⏲noon-10pm) Going for a suitably louche look – with portraits of Lord Byron and Frida Kahlo above the bar, and tatty rolled-arm leather chairs – this hip cocktail bar shakes up concoctions with names such as Under Milk Wood and 50 Shades of Earl Grey.

Aberystwyth Arts Centre
PERFORMING ARTS

(Canolfan Y Celfyddydau; ☎01970-623232; www.aberystwythartscentre.co.uk; Penglais Rd, SY23 3DE; ⏲box office 10am-8pm Mon-Sat, noon-5.30pm Sun) The largest arts centre in Wales, and part of Aberystwyth University, this cultured complex stages excellent opera, drama, dance and concerts, plus it has an art gallery, a quality bookshop and crafts shop, a bar and a cafe. The cinema shows a great range of cult and foreign-language movies, and there are always workshops to sign up for.

Information

Tourist Office (☎01970-612125; www.discoverceredigion.co.uk; Terrace Rd, SY23 2AQ; ⏲10am-5pm Mon-Sat; 📶) Within Ceredigion Museum, this office stocks pamphlets, maps and books on local history. It was closed at the time of research.

Getting There & Away

BUS

The bus station is next to the train station, on Alexandra Rd.

National Express coaches run a daily service to/from Newtown (£13, 80 minutes), Welshpool (£15, 1¾ hours), Shrewsbury (£15, 2¼ hours), Birmingham (£21, four hours) and London (£29, seven hours).

The T1 service connects Aber with Cardiff once daily Thursday to Sunday (£11, 3½ hours). On other days, change in Carmarthen for Swansea and Cardiff buses. Other Welsh destinations served include Carmarthen (£6.25, 1½ hours, every one to two hours), Dolgellau (£5.60, 1¼ hours, four daily) and Bangor (£6.70, 3¼ hours, three daily).

More locally, buses also run to Ceredigion destinations Tregaron (£3, one hour, up to 10 daily) and all main points down the coast to Cardigan (£5.50, 1¾ hours, hourly) including Aberaeron (£3.80, 40 minutes, hourly).

TRAIN

Aberystwyth is the terminus of the Arriva Trains Wales Cambrian Line, which crosses Mid-Wales to Shrewsbury (£22, 1¾ hours) eight times a day, via Machynlleth (£7.20, 33 minutes) and Welshpool (£16.30, 1½ hours). There are three trains to Birmingham (£34, three hours). Change in Shrewsbury or Birmingham for other destinations UK-wide.

Cardigan (Aberteifi)

☎01239 / POP 4180

Cardigan has the feel of a town waking from its slumber. An important trading port and herring fishery in Elizabethan times, it declined with the coming of the railway and the silting up of the River Teifi in the 19th century. By the late 20th century a shabbiness had encroached, exemplified by the ugly steel buttresses that held up its castle walls.

The new millennium saw the castle restored, buttresses removed and high street rejuvenated. Today's visitors will find a pretty riverside town with an attractive jumble of heritage architecture lining its streets and lanes. However, castle aside, the biggest attraction is still its proximity to the beautiful beaches and walking tracks of North Pembrokeshire and Cardigan Bay.

'Cardigan' is an anglicisation of Ceredigion, the place of Ceredig, but the Welsh name, Aberteifi, refers to its location at the mouth of the River Teifi.

CARDIGAN BAY'S DOLPHINS

Cardigan Bay is home to an amazingly rich variety of marine animals and plants, but the star attraction is Europe's largest pod of bottlenose dolphins (more than 250). With reliable sightings from May to September, there are few places where these sociable creatures are more easily seen in the wild. Along with the dolphins, harbour porpoises, Atlantic grey seals and a variety of birdlife are regularly seen, as well as seasonal visitors such as sunfish, basking sharks and leatherback turtles.

Some of the best places to spot dolphins from the shore are the beaches around New Quay like **New Quay North**, **Little Quay**, **Cwmtydu** and **Llanina**. Also try the beautiful sandy beaches at Mwnt, **Penbryn** (SA44 6QL) and **Aberporth** north of Cardigan.

You can learn more about Cardigan Bay's marine life at the **Cardigan Bay Marine Wildlife Centre** (01545-560032; www.welshwildlife.org; Glanmor Tce, SA45 9PS; 2/4/8hr boat trip from £20/38/65; 9am-5pm Easter-Oct) FREE, in New Quay.

Sights & Activities

Cardigan Castle CASTLE
(Castell Aberteifi; 01239-615131; www.cardigancastle.com; cnr Bridge & Quay Sts; adult/child £6/3; 10am-4pm;) Cardigan Castle holds an important place in Welsh culture, having been the venue for the first competitive National Eisteddfod, held on Christmas Day 1176 under the aegis of Rhys ap Gruffydd, ruler of Deheubarth. Neglected for years, a multimillion-pound refurbishment has once again elevated it into a major centre of regional Welsh culture, with exhibitions on the castle, Cardigan and the Eisteddfod, live performances, festivals, language classes and more taking place within its lovely buildings and courtyard.

Mwnt BEACH
(NT; www.nationaltrust.org.uk; SA43 1QH; parking per day £4) Tucked within an arc of black cliffs, 5 miles north of town, this small stretch of golden sand is one of the region's most picturesque beaches, with a little stream cascading down at one end and frequent visits from dolphins, porpoises and seals. Sitting above it is lonely **Holy Cross Church**, striking for its simplicity and remoteness. Whitewashed, and dwarfed by its windswept setting, this 13th- or 14th-century church is thought to be Ceredigion's oldest.

A Bay to Remember WILDLIFE WATCHING
(01239-623558; www.baytoremember.co.uk; Prince Charles Quay; adult/child from £26/13; Apr-Oct;) Running one- and two-hour trips into Cardigan Bay from St Dogmaels, Gwbert and Poppit Sands, this operation takes groups out in rigid-hulled inflatable boats to spot bottlenose dolphins, harbour porpoises, grey seals and seabirds; its dolphin-sighting rate is 60% on short trips and 90% on longer ones. There's a seasonal booking office at Prince Charles Quay in Cardigan.

Sleeping & Eating

Gwbert Hotel HOTEL $$
(01239-612638; www.gwberthotel.com; Gwbert, SA43 1PP; s/d from £65/85;) With unspoilt views from the cliff-lined inlet through which the Teifi flows into Cardigan Bay, and 21 comfortable, understated en-suite rooms (many better and higher-priced than others), the Gwbert is among Cardigan's most appealing sleeps. There are hearty breakfasts and the Flat Rock bistro, which combines upmarket pub and bistro classics (mains £10 to £17). Located 3 miles north of Cardigan.

★**Fforest Pizzatipi** PIZZA $
(01239-612259; www.pizzatipi.co.uk; Cambrian Quay; pizza £7-9; 4-9pm Thu & Fri, noon-9pm Sat & Sun) Run by four young brothers, this seasonal pop-up venue is the hottest ticket in town on summer nights. Pizzas pumping from two wood-fired ovens, craft beer, music, smartly chosen events and a buzzing atmosphere all set under a candlelit tepee in a hidden riverside courtyard: what more could you ask for? It's open roughly from April to October, weather-dependent.

1176 STEAKHOUSE $$
(01239-562002; www.cardigancastle.com/dining; Cardigan Castle, SA43 1JA; breakfast £5-8, lunch £6-12.50, dinner £12-18; 10am-4pm Sun-Wed, to 9pm Thu-Sat) This glass-and-slate

cafe/steakhouse is an integral part of Cardigan Castle's rebirth. It opens at 8.30am for breakfast when there are guests staying in the castle B&B and has nice lunches, but really comes into its own in its evening incarnation: Holden's Steakhouse. Portions are huge, and served with grilled veggies and potatoes.

Getting There & Away

Direct destinations from the **bus station** (Finch Sq) include hourly T5 services to New Quay (£4.15, 50 minutes), Aberaeron (£4.40, one hour) and Aberystwyth (£5.50, 1¾ hours), and services to Carmarthen (£5.10, 1½ hours, hourly) and Haverfordwest (£5.05, 1¼ hours, five daily).

Hire bikes from **BikeBikeBike.Bike** (01239-621275; www.bikebikebike.bike; 29-30 Pendre; per 3hr/day £17.50/23; 10am-5pm Mon-Sat) for cycling around this prettily countrified region.

AT A GLANCE

POPULATION
Conwy: 117, 203

NUMBER OF MOUNTAIN RANGES
Nine

BEST OFF-THE-BEATEN-TRACK HIKE
Carnedd Loop (p732)

BEST LOCAVORE DINING
Moch a Môr (p750)

BEST ADRENALINE RUSH
Go Below Underground Adventures (p730)

WHEN TO GO

May & Jun
Few crowds, little rain and warm temperatures; the best time to hit the hiking trail.

Jul
Hardcore runners compete in the Snowdon Race, and Llangollen holds its big festivals.

Sep & Oct
Big months for events, with Barmouth's arts and walking festivals, Portmeirion's Festival No 6, and the Gwledd Conwy Feast.

View of Great Orme (p746) from Llandudno Pier

Snowdonia & North Wales

Synonymous with mountains, Snowdonia is densely packed with sky-scraping peaks, post-glacial valleys, and former slate-mining towns turned adventure-tourism hubs celebrating their industrial heritage.

Away from the mighty castles, medieval walled towns and genteel Victorian seaside charms of the coast, slow-paced Llŷn exudes a quiet Celtic spirituality. A pilgrims' destination for many centuries, it rewards slow travel.

Sharing a proud identity with the Llŷn as a staunch enclave of the Cymraeg language and culture, Anglesey offers some of the best dining in Wales, along with rolling pastures, woodlands dotted with ancient burial chambers, and surf-battered wild beaches that draw surfers and other wave-riders.

INCLUDES

NORTH WALES BORDERLANDS

Comprising a chunk of Welsh coast that leads east towards Chester, the Vale of Clwyd, fringed by the Clwydian range, and the broad Dee Valley, the Welsh borderland counties of Denbighshire and Flintshire are hard to pin down. It's well worth pausing here as you make your way towards Snowdonia to peruse the highlights: the stately market town of Ruthin with its handsome medieval buildings, and a splendid aqueduct near Llangollen, a seat of Welsh culture.

Getting There & Away

The main entry points to the region are Wrexham, with trains to Chester (£4.90, 15 minutes, hourly), Birmingham (£27, 1¾ hours, two to three daily) and London (£64, one to two changes, 2½ to four hours); and Llangollen, on the T3 bus route to Wrexham.

Ruthin

01824 / POP 5723

Tucked away in the bucolic Clwyd valley, Ruthin (*rith*-in) has been an important market town since the Middle Ages, and livestock and produce markets still take place weekly. It's also an art hub, with the **Ruthin Craft Centre** (01824-704774; www.ruthincraftcentre.org.uk; Park Rd; 10am-5.30pm; P) FREE showcasing the best of local photography, glasswork, painting and sculpture. The heart of Ruthin is St Peter's Sq, lined with an impressive collection of heritage buildings, including a 1421 half-timbered Old Courthouse (now a bank), and St Peter's Collegiate Church, the oldest parts of which date from 1310.

Sights

Nantclwyd y Dre HISTORIC BUILDING

(01824-706868; www.denbighshire.gov.uk; Castle St; adult/concession £7/6; 11am-5pm Wed-Mon) Dating from 1435, half-timbered Nantclwyd y Dre is thought to be the oldest town house in Wales. It originally belonged to a family of weavers and the rooms have been restored and furnished to reflect the era of each addition, offering windows into the world of the various families that lived in them: a Victorian schoolroom, a Stuart study, Georgian and Jacobean bedchambers. The 13th-century Lord's Garden, behind the house, has also been restored.

A 'bat-cam' lets you peek into the world of the colony of lesser horseshoe bats that resides in the attic – they're the smallest (with bodies about the size of a plum) and rarest bat species in Britain.

Ruthin Gaol HISTORIC BUILDING

(01824-708281; www.denbighshire.gov.uk; 46 Clwyd St; adult/concession £7/6; 11am-5pm Wed-Mon Apr-Sep) This sombre building is the only Pentonville-style Victorian prison in Britain that's open to visitors. A free audio guide allows you to follow the sentence of an imaginary prisoner, 'Will the Poacher', while information panels in the cells fill you in on all the fascinating and grisly details of day-to-day prison life and the daring escapes of John Jones, the 'Welsh Houdini', banged up here in the 1870s. Pentonville-style prisons employed the 'separate system' of isolating and observing inmates.

Sleeping & Eating

Manorhaus BOUTIQUE HOTEL $$

(01824-704830; www.manorhaus.com; 10 Well St; r from £80, ste £120;) This boutique restaurant with rooms offers eight individually styled bedrooms in a stately Georgian town house, each decorated by a different artist. Perks include a spa, library and private cinema, while the superb in-house restaurant (open 6pm to 9pm Tuesday to Saturday; two/three courses £25/30) dishes up the bold flavours of Modern Welsh cuisine for guests and nonguests alike.

Ruthin Castle Hotel HISTORIC HOTEL $$$

(01824-702664; www.ruthincastle.co.uk; Castle St; r/ste from £170/240; P) The forlorn cries of peacocks strutting the gardens of this neo-Gothic mansion are the first hint of the offbeat luxury within. Making use of a Victorian 'castle' constructed amid the ruins of the real thing (built for Edward in 1277), its over-the-top grandeur includes a spa, a wood-panelled library/bar and a medieval banqueting hall that doubles as an atmospheric restaurant.

Leonardo's Deli DELI $

(01824-707161; www.leonardosdeli.co.uk; 4 Well St; sandwiches, wraps & salads £4; 9am-4pm Mon-Sat) Run by a Welsh-German couple, this deli offers an abundance of local cheeses, free-range eggs, preserves, fresh sandwiches, and top-notch pies. Its chicken, leek and laverbread was champion of the 2011

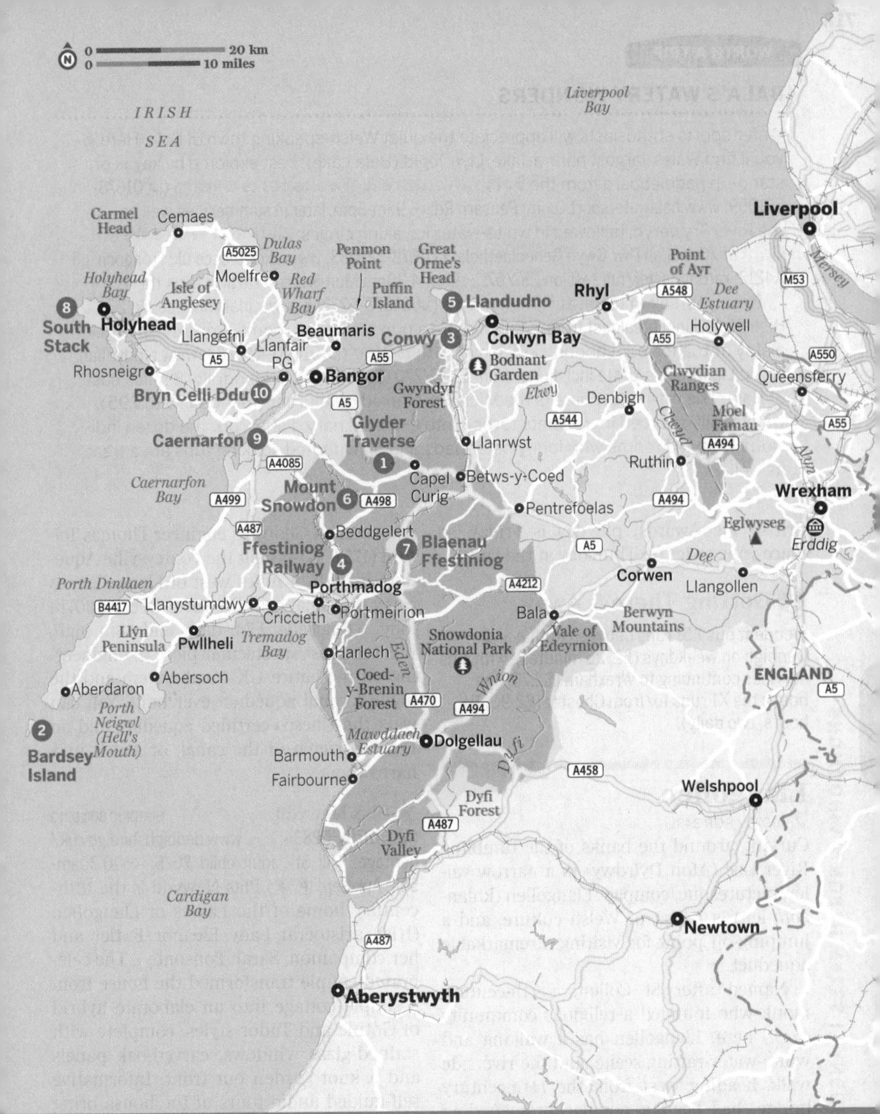

Snowdonia & North Wales Highlights

1. **Glyder Traverse** (p733) Traversing one of Snowdonia's most spectacular panoramas.
2. **Bardsey Island** (p742) Braving the tempestuous boat crossing to mythical Avalon.
3. **Conwy** (p744) Admiring the castle and enjoying medieval Conwy's dining scene.
4. **Ffestiniog Railway** (p738) Riding the most scenic of Welsh heritage railway journeys.
5. **Llandudno** (p746) Exploring mines, the plateau and the town's Victorian pier.
6. **Mount Snowdon** (p735) Conquering the highest peak in Wales, either by foot or by rail.
7. **Blaenau Ffestiniog** (p728) Descending into slate caverns and mining tunnels.
8. **South Stack** (p752) Watching birds wheel above a clifftop lighthouse.
9. **Caernarfon Castle** (p741) Squeezing through wall passages of Edward I's mightiest castle.
10. **Bryn Celli Ddu Burial Chamber** (p751) Marvelling at Anglesey's impressive neolithic crypt.

WORTH A TRIP

BALA'S WATERY WONDERS

Water sports enthusiasts will appreciate the quiet Welsh-speaking town of Bala. Here you'll find Wales' largest natural lake, Llyn Tegid (Bala Lake), best explored by kayak or stand-up paddleboard from the **Bala Adventure & Watersports Centre** (☎01678-521059; www.balawatersports.com; Pensarn Rd; ⏲9am-5pm, later in summer), as well as the River Tryweryn, hallowed in white-water kayaking circles; **National White Water Centre** (Canolfan Dŵr Gwyn Genedlaethol; ☎01678-521083; www.ukrafting.co.uk; Frongoch, off A4212; rafting taster/full session £37/67; ⏲9am-4.30pm Mon-Fri) run rafting trips there.

Base yourself in town, at **Plas-yn-Dre** (☎01678-521256; www.plasyndre.co.uk; 23 High St; s/d incl breakfast from £79/80; 📶) – a pub with snug rooms – or else splurge on a stay at the former shooting lodge of **Tyddyn Llan** (☎01490-440264; www.tyddynllan.co.uk; Llandrillo; s/d/ste incl dinner from £195/270/330; P📶), in Llandrillo, 8 miles east of Bala. The main draw here is the Michelin-starred restaurant (menus £75 to £95), with locally sourced ingredients turned into extraordinary dishes, but the dozen individually styled rooms with four-poster beds and claw-footed soaking tubs are a treat as well.

British Pie Awards; pie day is Friday, so place your order on Thursday at the latest.

Getting There & Away

Frequent bus X51 runs between Ruthin and Denbigh on weekdays (£2, 25 minutes), with nine services continuing to Wrexham (£2.70, one hour); the X1 runs to/from Chester (£2.90, 1¼ hours, two daily).

Llangollen

☎01978 / POP 3491

Curving around the banks of the tumbling River Dee (Afon Dyfrdwy) in a narrow valley, picturesque, compact Llangollen (khlan-*goth*-len) is a seat of Welsh culture, and a jumping-off point for visiting a remarkable aqueduct.

Named after St Collen, a 7th-century monk who founded a religious community *(llan)* here, Llangollen has a walking and white-water-rafting scene, and the riverside walk, heading west from the 14th-century bridge, has been a popular promenading spot since Victorian times. Other boons include a major arts festival and a heritage railway.

Sights

★Pontcysyllte Aqueduct & Canal World Heritage Site CANAL

(☎visitor centre 01978-822912; www.pontcysyllte-aqueduct.co.uk; B5434; guided tours £3; ⏲visitor centre 10am-4pm Easter-Oct, long weekends Nov, Dec & late Feb-Easter) FREE The pre-eminent Georgian engineer Thomas Telford (1757–1834) built the Pontcysyllte Aqueduct in 1805, 4 miles west of Llangollen, to carry the canal over the River Dee. At 307m long, 3.6m wide, 1.7m deep and 38m high, it is the most spectacular piece of engineering on the entire UK canal system and the highest canal aqueduct ever built. You can walk the Unesco-certified aqueduct and an 11-mile stretch of the canal, or sail it in a narrowboat.

★Plas Newydd HISTORIC BUILDING

(☎01978-862834; www.denbighshire.gov.uk/heritage; Hill St; adult/child £6/5; ⏲10.30am-5pm Apr-Sep; P🚻) Plas Newydd is the 18th-century home of the Ladies of Llangollen (Irish aristocrat Lady Eleanor Butler and her companion, Sarah Ponsonby). The celebrated couple transformed the house from a simple cottage into an elaborate hybrid of Gothic and Tudor styles, complete with stained-glass windows, carved-oak panels and a knot garden out front. Informative self-guided audio tours of the house bring the half-dozen dark-wood-panelled rooms to life, including the pared-down attic room of the housekeeper. Access to the gardens is free.

Valle Crucis Abbey RUINS

(Abaty Glyn y Groes; Cadw; www.cadw.gov.wales; A542; adult/concession £3.80/2.20; ⏲10am-5pm Apr-Oct, to 4pm Nov-Mar) The stark ruins of this Cistercian abbey are a 2-mile walk north of Llangollen. Founded in 1201 by Madog ap Gruffydd, ruler of northern

Llangollen

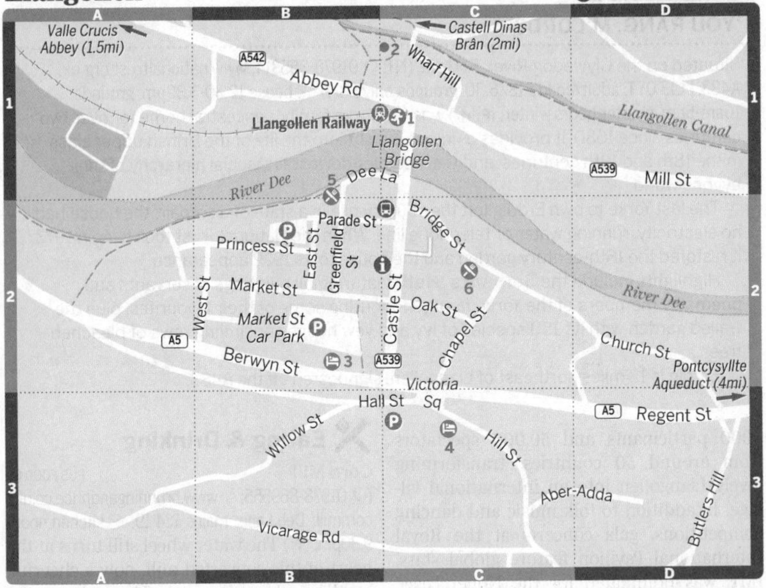

Llangollen

Activities, Courses & Tours
1 Llangollen Railway....C1
2 Welsh Canal Holiday Craft....C1

Sleeping
3 Llangollen Hostel....B2
4 mh Townhaus....C3

Eating
5 Corn Mill....B1
6 Gales Wine Bar....C2

Powys, its largely Gothic form predates its more famous sibling at Tintern (which, on the eve of Valle Crucis' 1537 dissolution, was its only rival as the richest Cistercian abbey in the land). The vaulted chapterhouse, the west wall and the monks' gravestones are intact.

A small interpretive centre brings the monks' daily routines to life.

Activities

Llangollen Railway RAIL
(☎01978-860979; www.llangollen-railway.co.uk; Abbey Rd; adult/child return £16/8.50; ⏱daily mid-Feb–Oct, reduced services rest of year; 👪) This 10-mile jaunt through the Dee Valley via Berwyn (near Horseshoe Falls) and Corwen on the former Ruabon to Barmouth Line, hauled by a steam or diesel engine, is a superb day out for rail fans. There are theme days for children, and Driver Experience Days (£260 to £445) for those wanting to drive a heritage railcar, steam locomotive or diesel locomotive.

Welsh Canal Holiday Craft BOATING
(☎01978-860702; www.horsedrawnboats.co.uk; Llangollen Wharf; ⏱mid-Mar–Oct) Peaceful horse-drawn narrowboats depart on 45-minute trips from Llangollen Wharf every half-hour during the school holidays, and hourly otherwise (adult/child £8/4). Two-hour journeys head to Horseshoe Falls and back, and motorised boats take you up to Pontcysyllte Aqueduct (adult/child £14.50/12, return journey by coach). Self-drive boats are £140/195 per day/weekend. Reservations strongly advised in busy periods.

Festivals & Events

International Musical Eisteddfod PERFORMING ARTS
(☎01978-862000; www.international-eisteddfod.co.uk; ⏱Jul) The International Musical Eisteddfod was established after WWII to promote world harmony. Each July it attracts

DON'T MISS

'YOU RANG, M'LORD?'

Situated on the Clywedog River, **Erddig** (NT; 01978-355314; www.nationaltrust.org.uk; A483, LL13 0YT; adult/child £13/6.30, grounds only £8/5; house 12.30-3.30pm, grounds 10am-5pm, shorter hours winter;) was the Yorke family's ancestral home for over two centuries since 1680. It provides a unique insight into the life of the British upper class in the 18th and 19th centuries, and the 'upstairs-downstairs' social hierarchy of their bygone world.

The last Yorke to own Erddig left the country pile in a state of disrepair: the house had no electricity, running water or telephone line. When the National Trust took over in 1973, it restored the 18th-century garden and the house to its 1922 appearance.

Highlights include the **Servants' Hall**, featuring oil paintings of servants and poems by members of the Yorke family, honouring some of their favourites, plus the walled garden with its 150 species of ivy and yew hedges encircling rows of pleached trees.

Erddig is 12 miles northeast of Llangollen, signposted off the A483.

4000 participants and 50,000 spectators from around 50 countries, transforming lovely Llangollen into an international village. In addition to folk music and dancing competitions, gala concerts at the Royal International Pavilion feature global stars. IME was nominated for the Nobel Peace Prize in 2004.

Sleeping

Llangollen Hostel HOSTEL $
(01978-861773; www.llangollenhostel.co.uk; Isallt, Berwyn St; dm/d/f £20/50/70;) This excellent independent hostel, based in a former family home, has friendly owners and a cared-for feel. It offers various rooms, from private en-suite doubles to a six-bed dorm, as well as an orderly kitchen and a cosy lounge. It actively welcomes cyclists, walkers and canoeists, offering laundry facilities and bike/boat storage. Prices include a self-service cereal-and-toast breakfast.

★**mh Townhaus** B&B $$
(01978-860775; www.manorhaus.com; Hill St; r from £90;) This ultra-stylish boutique guesthouse occupies a multistorey Victorian town house, and comprises nine fairly minimalist rooms in slate greys and whites, a lounge and bar, a library and even a rooftop hot tub. Common spaces double as a gallery for art and installations by local artists, and there's also a semi-detached one-bedroom cottage for self-caterers.

Eating & Drinking

Corn Mill PUB FOOD $$
(01978-869555; www.brunningandprice.co.uk/cornmill; Dee Lane; mains £14-19; kitchen noon-9.30pm;) The water wheel still turns at the heart of this converted mill, now a cheerful, bustling pub and brasserie. The deck over the tumbling Dee is the best spot in town for an unfussy alfresco meal, perhaps braised lamb shoulder or smoked-haddock fishcakes. The bar stays open longer than the kitchen, serving cask ales and other quality local brews.

★**Gales Wine Bar** EUROPEAN $$
(01978-860089; www.gales.wine; 18 Bridge St; mains £6-22; 9am-8.30pm Wed-Sat) Equal parts wine bar and bistro, Gales is something of a Llangollen institution. Perch in the smart bistro area, or the wine garden, and dig into 'simple food done well': haddock and clam stew, gourmet burgers, steak, charcuterie and cheese platters, accompanied by carefully chosen wines from around the globe. Or come for a breakfast brioche and single origin coffee.

The owners – who took a punt in the late 1970s by opening this, the first wine bar in North Wales – also run the wine shop next door. They also own an excellent hotel, with eight of the rooms (from £50) located above the wine bar, all individually styled and retaining period features.

Information

Tourist Office (01978-860828; www.llangollen.org.uk; The Chapel, Castle St;

⌚9.30am-5pm; 📶) This helpful tourist office doubles as an art-and-craft gallery and is well stocked with maps, books and gifts. Download its *Llangollen History Trail* brochure, which details a 9.5km walking circuit taking in Valle Crucis (p718) and Dinas Brân (off Wern Rd).

Getting There & Away

T3 buses head to/from Wrexham (£2, 40 minutes, four to nine daily) and in the other direction to Barmouth (£2.90, two hours) via Bala (£2.20 one hour) and Dolgellau (£2.40, 1½ hours). Buses leave from Parade St. The frequent 5E also serves Wrexham.

Parking is at a premium in Llangollen in summer. If your accommodation doesn't have its own parking, check whether it can provide a pass for the council car parks.

SNOWDONIA NATIONAL PARK (PARC CENEDLAETHOL ERYRI)

For many visitors, Wales is synonymous with Snowdonia – 823 sq miles of mountain ranges, green hills, ancient forests and coastline, bisected by heritage railways. The country's first national park since 1951, dotted with walkers' hub villages, market towns and former slate-mining centres, Snowdonia is a hiker's dream.

While a disproportionate number of people zoom in on the venerable (and very well trodden) Mt Snowdon, Wales' highest peak, those in search of greater challenges and relative solitude need look no further than the Glyder and Carnedd ranges. Some of the most popular attractions are man-made, and combine Snowdonia's slate-mining heritage with adrenaline-packed subterranean assault courses and zip lines above defunct mining pits. And on the coast, classic beachside towns and a formidable castle await you.

Getting There & Away

The main points of entry for Snowdonia are Betws-y-Coed, Bala, Porthmadog and Dolgellau. For the Llŷn Peninsula, it's Pwllheli, and for the North Wales Borderlands, it's Llangollen and Wrexham.

There are two major train lines into the region: the Cambrian/Cambrian Coast Line (for Porthmadog and Pwllheli) and the Conwy Valley (for Betws). The narrow-gauge Welsh Highland and Ffestiniog and Welsh Highland lines run inland from Porthmadog and/or Caernarfon to Blaenau Ffestiniog and Beddgelert.

Major bus routes include the T2 (Aberystwyth to Bangor via Porthmadog and Dolgellau) and T3 (Wrexham, Llangollen, Bala and Dolgellau). Pwllheli is the Llŷn Peninsula bus hub.

Dolgellau

☎01341 / POP 2672

Dolgellau (dol-*geth*-lye) is a charming little market town with Quaker roots, boasting the highest concentration of heritage-listed buildings in Wales. It was a regional centre for Wales' prosperous wool industry in the 18th and early 19th centuries and many of its finest buildings, made of dark, unadorned stone, were built at that time. Local mills failed to keep pace with mass mechanisation, however, and decline set in – preserving the town centre much as it was then.

The region bounced back when the Romantic Revival made Wales' wild landscapes popular with genteel travellers. There was also a minor gold rush in the 1860s. Today Dolgellau is a fine base for fresh-air fiends, as its attractions lie largely outside town.

Sights & Activities

Mawddach Estuary NATURE RESERVE

(www.mawddachestuary.co.uk) The wide, sandy Mawddach Estuary is a striking sight, flanked by woodlands, wetlands and the mountains of southern Snowdonia. There are two Royal Society for the Protection of Birds (RSPB) nature reserves in the valley, both reached on foot or by bike from Dolgellau or Barmouth via the Mawddach Trail (p723). Arthog Bog is 8 miles west of Dolgellau on the access road to Morfa Mawddach station, off the A493, while Coed Garth Gell is 2 miles west, on the A496.

WHEELING ACROSS WALES

Measuring some 250 miles in length, the **Lôn Las Cymru cycle route** (National Cycle Route 8) runs from Cardiff to Holyhead, passing through Dolgellau, Barmouth, Harlech, Criccieth, Porthmadog and Caernarfon en route.

Snowdonia & Llŷn Peninsula

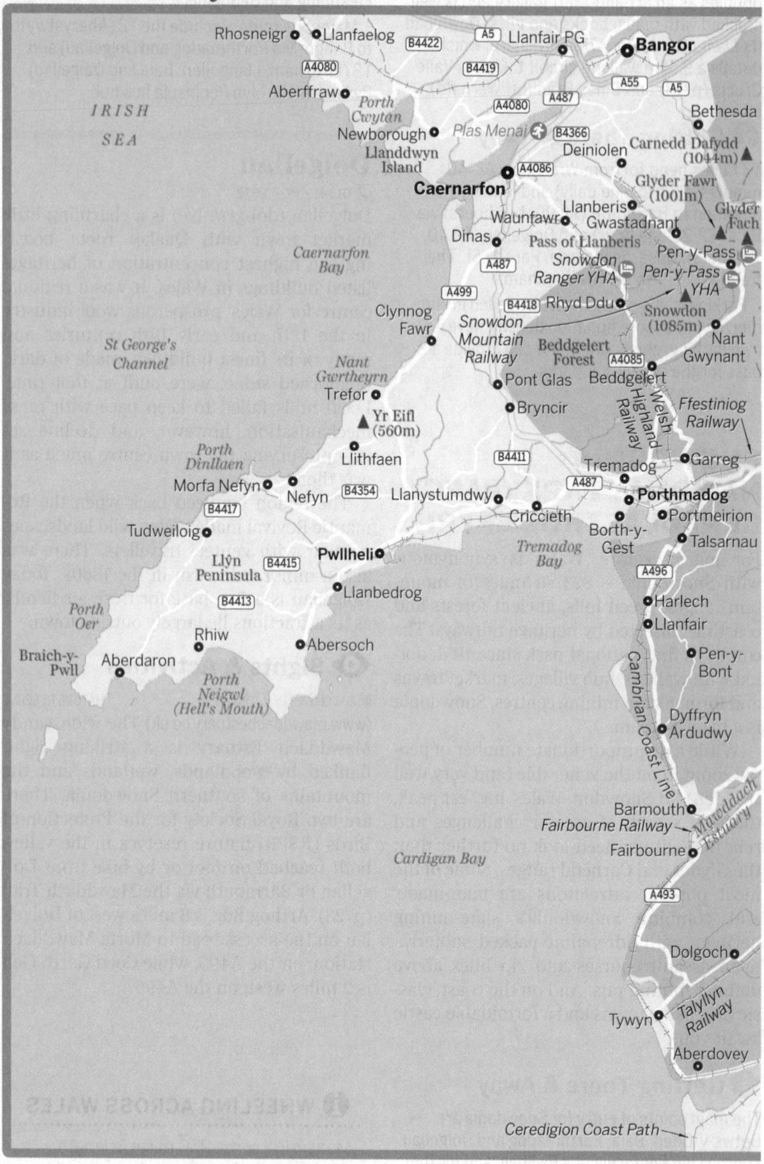

Coed y Brenin Forest Park MOUNTAIN BIKING (☎01341-440747; www.naturalresources.wales/coedybrenin; A470; ⏲9am-5pm Apr-Oct, shorter hours rest of year) **FREE** This woodland park offers some of Wales' best mountain biking. It comprises eight graded routes to suit everyone from beginners to guns. The more challenging trails – such as the Dragon's Back (20 miles; red) and the Beast of Brenin

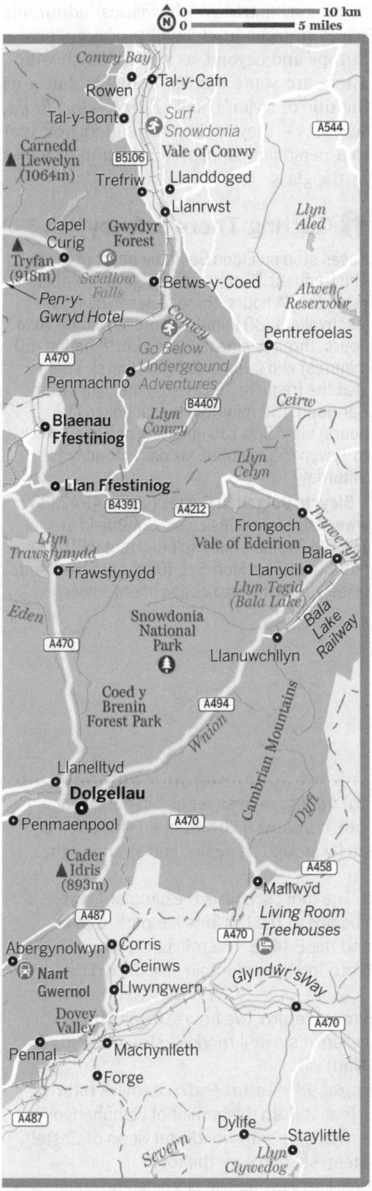

(25 miles; black) – stage major mountain-biking events.

The T2 bus from Bangor to Aberystwyth stops here, 8 miles north of Dolgellau.

Mawddach Trail HIKING

(www.mawddachtrail.co.uk) The 9.5-mile Mawddach Trail is a flat walking and cycling path that follows an old train line through woods and past wetlands on the southern side of the beautiful Mawddach Estuary, before crossing over the train viaduct to Barmouth (where you can catch the bus back). The trail starts in the car park beside the bridge in Dolgellau.

Sleeping

Torrent Walk Campsite CAMPSITE $

(☎01341-422269; www.guesthousessnowdonia.com/en; off A470, Dolgun Uchaf; camping £10, glamping pod £90; P 📶) Run by the working Dolgun Uchaf farm and ideally situated for hiking and other outdoorsy pursuits, this grassy campsite offers tent pitches, caravan spots (May to October) and snug wooden glamping pods – perfect for hobbits or families of three.

It's 1.5 miles northeast of Dolgellau; turn left after the petrol station.

★Tan y Gader B&B $$

(☎01341-421102; www.tanygader.co.uk; Meyrick St; s/d from £80/90; P 📶) There is much to love about this wonderful guesthouse. There are just three rooms, each playfully decorated to reflect a beloved children's classic (Alice, Secret Garden, Narnia); Narnia features a claw-footed tub. There are lots of thoughtful extras, and the owners go the extra mile when it comes to breakfast – a delicious gathering of locally sourced ingredients.

Ffynnon B&B $$$

(☎01341-421774; www.ffynnontownhouse.com; Love Lane; s/d from £100/160; P 📶) With an eye for contemporary design and a super-friendly welcome, this award-winning boutique B&B is homely and stylish. French antiques mix with modern chandeliers, claw-foot tubs and electronic gadgets, and each room has a comfy seating area for admiring the impressive vistas. There's a bar, a library, an outdoor hot tub, and Egyptian cotton and goose down in the bedrooms.

Eating & Drinking

Mawddach Neapolitan Pizza PIZZA $

(Bwyty Mawddach; ☎01341-421752; www.mawddach.com; A496, Llanelltyd; pizza £7-12; ⏲6-9pm Thu, 4-9pm Fri & Sat; P) Occupying a smartly renovated former barn, fine-dining Mawddach has reinvented itself as a stellar 'pizza with a view' establishment, overlooking Cader Idris and the estuary 2 miles west of Dolgellau. The deftly executed wood-fired pizzas are authentic Neapolitan with a Welsh twist, and toppings include nduja sausage from a nearby farm and local Teifi cheese. Just wonderful.

★ Tafarn y Gader TAPAS $$

(☎ 01341-421227; www.facebook.com/dolgellautapas; Smithfield St; tapas £5-11; ⏲ 5-9pm Tue-Sat, 10am-2.30pm Sun; 📝) Kicking Dolgellau's dining scene up a notch, this tapas bar is as ambitious as it is creative. Yes, there are some solid Spanish standards (*patatas bravas*, *serrano* ham croquettes), but then dishes such as crispy rice with seared pigeon and marinated fennel and courgette carpaccio defy expectations, thrilling the taste buds. A convivial atmosphere reigns amid the clinking of wine glasses.

Gwin Dylanwad Wine WINE BAR

(☎ 01341-422870; www.dylanwad.co.uk; Porth Marchnad; snacks £1-5; ⏲ 10am-6pm Mon-Thu, to 8pm Fri & Sat) The eponymous Dylan Rowlands knows his wines. This part-wine-merchant, part-bar showcases admirably select vintages from small producers across Europe and beyond, as well as Welsh wines. There are some nibbles available, but – as the title of Dylan's book, *Rarebit and Rioja*, suggests – they're there as supporting cast to a personally approved selection of wines by the glass.

ℹ Getting There & Away

Buses stop on Eldon Sq in the heart of town. The frequent T2 connects Dolgellau to Aberystwyth (1¼ hours, three to seven daily) via Machynlleth (30 minutes), and to Bangor (two hours, three to nine daily) via Porthmadog (50 minutes) and Caernarfon (1½ hours). There's also the frequent T3 (five to nine daily) from Barmouth (30 minutes) to Llangollen (1½ hours) via Y Bala (35 minutes) and the 28 to Tywyn (55 minutes, six daily Monday to Saturday).

Bicycle Dolgellau Cycles (☎ 01341-423332; www.dolgellaucycles.co.uk; Smithfield St, The Old Furnace; half-/full-day rental £15/20; ⏲ 9.30am-5pm Mon-Sat, 10am-4pm Sun) rents bikes, performs repairs and offers advice.

WORTH A TRIP

CADER IDRIS (CADAIR IDRIS)

The twin-peaked mountain of Cader Idris (893m) may have been named in honour of a mythical giant, a 7thcentury Welsh prince, or both. It's a mystical mountain shrouded in legend; the hounds of the underworld are said to fly around its peaks, and strange light effects are often sighted.

There are three official routes up Cader Idris. The most scenic is the circular **Minffordd Path** (6 miles return, five hours), which begins at the Dôl Idris car park, 6 miles south of Dolgellau at the junction of the A487 and the B4405. The trail takes you up through ancient oak forest, past waterfalls, and around the mountain lake of Llyn Cau, before ascending Pen-y-Gader, the summit.

Less challenging, 'Tŷ Nant' or **Pony Path** (6 miles return, five hours) begins from the Tŷ Nant car park, 3 miles southwest of Dolgellau. It's a well-marked, straightforward route (though you miss out on the scenic Llyn Cau).

The longest route is the 'Tywyn' or **Llanfihangel y Pennant Path** (10 miles return, six to seven hours), a pony track that heads northeast from the hamlet of Llanfihangel y Pennant, joining the Tŷ Nant path at the latter's midpoint, with wonderful views of Castell y Bere and the Mawddach Estuary, and a final steep section near the top.

Whichever route you choose, wear stout shoes, carry protective clothing and check the weather conditions on the Met's website (www.metoffice.gov.uk). The Ordnance Survey (www.ordnancesurvey.co.uk) *OL23* map is handy.

If you're in need of pampering the minute you step off the Minffordd Path, look no further than the **Gwesty Minffordd Hotel** (☎ 01654-761665; www.minffordd.com; Tal-y-llyn, LL36 9AJ; s/d incl breakfast £65/130; 📶). Its individually styled rooms (some with bathtubs) all come with heavy wooden beams and comfy mattresses; the restaurant serves hearty pan-European fare and cooked breakfasts.

Barmouth (Abermaw)

01341 / POP 2221

With a Blue Flag beach and the beautiful Mawddach Estuary on its doorstep, the Victorian resort of Barmouth has been a popular tourist destination since the coming of the railway and the hugely impressive **bridge** across the estuary in 1867. There's a smattering of minor attractions, including the **Last Haul** (The Quay) shipwreck monument and the old **Tŷ Crwn Roundhouse** (www.barsailinst.org.uk/crwn.html; The Quay; 10.30am-5pm) FREE prison for drunken sailors and slatterns, and in summer it's a typical seaside town. Outside of the brash neon of high season it's considerably mellower, allowing space to appreciate its Georgian and Victorian architecture, attractive setting and superb walking trails along the estuary and up **Dinas Oleu** hill.

Sleeping & Eating

Tilman HOTEL $$

(01341-281888; www.facebook.com/thetilmanbarmouth; Church St; r incl breakfast from £110; P) Part watering hole, part hotel, the Tilman succeeds in both categories. The contemporary, blond-wood-panelled bar downstairs is equally good for a coffee or a local brew on tap, and the rooms upstairs are spacious, understated and spotless, with quality furnishings and nice touches, such as Molton Brown toiletries. Cooked breakfast included.

★ **Celtic Cabin Cafe** CAFE $

(07775 331241; www.facebook.com/celticcabinbarmouth; Marine Pde; wraps £5-8; 10am-6pm;) A wonderful addition to Barmouth's dining scene, this beachside cafe/takeaway joint specialises in terrific filled wraps, freshly made and served on the picnic tables with a view of the dunes and the sea. Try wraps with slow-roasted pork shoulder, falafel and hummus or locally caught mackerel and couscous…don't forget to finish with the homemade banana bread!

Bistro Bermo BISTRO $$

(01341-281284; www.bistrobermo.com; 6 Church St; mains £16-23; 6-9pm Tue-Sat, noon-3pm Sun) Discreetly hidden behind an aqua-green shopfront, this intimate restaurant delivers a sophisticated menu chock-full of Welsh farm produce and fresh fish. Featuring dishes such as duck breast with walnut crust and daily seafood specials, the cooking is classical rather than experimental, and generally excellent. There are only half a dozen tables, so book ahead.

> **WORTH A TRIP**
>
> ### TYWYN
>
> Some 19 miles southwest of Dolgellau, at the mouth of the dramatically scenic Talyllyn Valley that leads inland towards the slopes of Cader Idris, the faded resort town of Tywyn is renowned for the narrow-gauge **Talyllyn Railway** (Rheilffordd Talyllyn; 01654-710472; www.talyllyn.co.uk; Wharf Station; compartment per 1-3 people £44, 4-6 people £66; Easter-Oct, varies rest of year), famous as the inspiration for Rev W Awdry's *Thomas the Tank Engine* stories. The **Narrow Gauge Railway Museum** (www.narrowgaugerailwaymuseum.org.uk; Station Rd, Tywyn Wharf; by donation; 10.30am-4.30pm Apr-Sep) is worth a peek too, followed by a meal at **Salt Marsh Kitchen** (01654-711949; www.facebook.com/thesaltmarshkitchen; 9 College Green; mains £12-15; 5-9pm Thu-Sun). To make a day of it, drive there via the dramatically scenic Talyllyn Valley, then make your way back to Dolgellau along the coast, past the Mawddach Estuary.

Getting There & Away

Buses stop on Jubilee Rd, across Beach Rd from the **train station** (Station Rd). Services include the 38/39 to/from Harlech (30 minutes, two to six daily) and Porthmadog (50 minutes, one to four daily), and the T3 to Dolgellau (20 minutes, five to 12 daily), Bala (one hour, five to eight daily) and Llangollen (two hours, five to eight daily).

Barmouth is on the Cambrian Coast Line, with eight direct trains per day to Fairbourne (£3.20, seven minutes), Machynlleth (£10.30, one hour), Harlech (£5.40, 25 minutes), Porthmadog (£8, 50 minutes) and Pwllheli (£13, 80 minutes).

Harlech

01766 / POP 1618

Hilly Harlech is best known for its impressive castle that sits on a promontory overlooking Tremadog Bay, framed by the mountains of Snowdonia to the north. Finished in 1289,

1. Hiking, Snowdonia (p721) **2.** St Ives (p341), Cornwall
3. Castlerigg Stone Circle, Keswick (p593) **4.** Smoo Cave (p924), Durness

2

4

Breathtaking Britain

Britain is best known for the historic capitals of London and Edinburgh, the university towns of Cambridge and Oxford, and the well-preserved Roman remains in Bath. However, beyond the urban sprawl lies another Britain: a landscape of high mountain vistas, dramatic valleys lined with lakes, and – as befitting an island – thousands of miles of spectacular coastline.

Lake District

The Lake District (p578) is home to the highest mountains and largest lakes in England. With summits snow-capped in winter, and spectacular at any time of year, this landscape inspired the poet William Wordsworth, and is a major magnet for hikers today. Since 2017 it's also been a Unesco World Heritage Site.

Snowdonia

Wales is crowned with Snowdonia (p721) – a range of rocky peaks and glacier-hewn valleys stretching across the north of the country. Snowdon itself is accessible by Swiss-style cog railway, while Tryfan and Glyder Fawr offer equally challenging hikes and spectacular views, as well as more chance of solitude.

Cornwall's Coast

In Britain, you're spoilt for choice when it comes to beautiful coastline, but in the far southwest, the coast of Cornwall (p331) is hard to beat, with its stunning combination of sandy beaches, tranquil coves, picture-postcard fishing ports, adrenaline-pumping surf spots and rugged cliffs carved by Atlantic waves.

Scotland's Northwest Coast

The long journey to the far northwest corner of the Scottish Highlands (p923) is repaid with some of the finest scenery anywhere in Britain. In this wild and remote region, the sheer mountainsides drop to the sea, while narrow sea lochs cut deep inland, creating a landscape that is almost other-worldly in its beauty.

Harlech Castle is the southernmost of four fortifications grouped as the 'Castles and Town Walls of King Edward in Gwynedd' Unesco World Heritage Site.

Castle aside, Harlech also has one of the finest beaches in the area, backed by the Morfa Harlech dunes. In summer, the place buzzes with day visitors. Book the sparse accommodation in advance to make the most of the fine hiking in the area.

Sights

★Harlech Castle CASTLE
(Cadw; www.cadw.wales.gov.uk; Castle St; adult/child £6.40/4.30; ⏲10am-1pm & 2-5pm Wed-Sun) Built on a promontory, Harlech Castle was once impregnable, made so by the sea and the moat. Edward I finished this mighty castle in 1289, the southernmost of his 'iron ring' of fortresses designed to keep the Welsh firmly beneath his boot. The grey-sandstone castle's massive twin-towered gatehouse and outer walls are still intact, giving the illusion of impregnability even now. The finest exterior view of the castle (with Snowdon as backdrop) is from a craggy outcrop on Ffordd Isaf.

Sleeping & Eating

★Maelgwyn House B&B $$
(☎01766-780087; www.maelgwynharlech.co.uk; Ffordd Isaf; r £98-135; ⏲Feb-Oct; P 📶) A model B&B in an art-bedecked former boarding school, Maelgwyn has interesting hosts, delicious breakfasts and five elegant rooms (though attic room 5 is rather snug) stocked with DVD players and tea-making facilities (ask for one of the three with sea views – they're definitely worth it). Bridget and Derek can also help arrange birdwatching trips and fungus forays.

Castle Cottage COTTAGE $$
(☎01766-780479; Ffordd Pen Llech; s/d from £75/130; P 📶) Billing itself as a 'restaurant with rooms', this 16th-century cottage has seven spacious bedrooms in a contemporary style, with exposed beams, in-room DVD players and a bowl of fresh fruit for each guest. The award-winning fine-dining restaurant (two-/three-course dinner £39/42) is a great showcase for Welsh produce, featuring local rack of lamb and line-caught sea bass, and other delights.

★As.Is BISTRO $
(☎01766-781208; www.asis-harlech.co.uk; The Square; mains £5-9.50; ⏲5-9pm Mon-Sat) Overlooking the castle, this welcoming bistro features a short and sweet menu of solid, belly- and palate-pleasing food that doesn't bang on about 'taking you on a journey'. Highlights include sourdough pizza and jerk chicken wings, their crisp skin an allspice and chilli kick. The pared-down decor – naked wires, oversized light bulbs and rough timber tables – is equally pleasing.

Castle Bistro BISTRO $$
(☎01766-780416; www.castlebistroharlech.com; Stryd Fawr/High St; mains £12-17; ⏲5.30-10pm Wed-Sun) Beautifully executed comfort food is what you can expect at this justifiably popular bistro. There's the happy marriage of the Welsh lamb shank with the buttery mash and toothsome braised red cabbage, the cod loin risotto, smoky with haddock, and the pork belly with perfect, oven-crisped skin.

Getting There & Away

The Harlech Hoppa bus runs half-hourly during the summer months between Barmouth and Harlech/Porthmadog.

Harlech is on the Cambrian Coast Line, with direct trains to Machynlleth (£13.90, 1½ hours, eight daily) via Barmouth (£5.40, 27 minutes) and Fairbourne (£6.60, 40 minutes), and Pwllheli (£9.20, 47 minutes, eight daily) via Porthmadog (£5.40, 27 minutes). The station is at the base of the rocks below the castle.

Blaenau Ffestiniog

☎01766 / POP 3813

Most of the slate used to roof 19th-century Britain came from the mines of Blaenau Ffestiniog. Even though Blaenau (blay-nye) is in the centre of Snowdonia National Park, the grey mountains of shattered slate that surround the town prevent it from being included in the park, much to the fury of this close-knit community; these mountains, dug out by hand, are part of their heritage.

Although reduced to a single surface mine, the slate industry still dominates Blaenau. Adrenaline junkies pursue subterranean adventures in the abandoned tunnels and caverns, the surrounding landscape attracts mountain bikers, and train buffs retrace slate's past journeys to Porthmadog aboard the historic Ffestiniog Railway.

Sights & Activities

★Llechwedd Slate Caverns MINE
(☎01766-830306; www.llechwedd.co.uk; A470; tours £20; ⊙9.30am-5.30pm; P 👪) Blaenau's main attraction takes you into the depths of a Victorian slate mine. Donning protective gear, you descend the UK's steepest mining cable railway into the 1846, 25-mile network of tunnels and caverns, while 'enhanced-reality technology' brings to life the harsh working conditions of the 19th-century miners – be prepared to duck and scramble around dark tunnels. Knowledgeable guides relate stories of their own connections with the mines, and the softly lit caverns themselves are starkly beautiful.

★Zip World Slate Caverns ADVENTURE SPORTS
(☎01248-601444; www.zipworld.co.uk; off A470, Llechwedd Slate Caverns; ⊙booking office 8am-6.30pm; 👪) If you've ever wanted to practise trampoline tricks in a slate mine (and who hasn't?), then 'Bounce Below' – a 'cathedral-sized' cavern with bouncy nets, walkways, tunnels and slides – is your chance (adult/child one hour £25/20). There are also the caverns themselves, explored via zip wires (including the UK's steepest) through the semi-dark and wobbly rope bridges (£65 for two hours).

The latest attraction is Titan (£30 to £50), Europe's longest zip-line course that has you flying downhill above a disused slate quarry along three tracks – 890m, 630m and 450m – while the world passes you by in a blur at speeds of 70mph. Up to four people can take flight simultaneously.

Antur Stiniog MOUNTAIN BIKING
(☎01766-238007; www.anturstiniog.com; A470, Llechwedd Slate Caverns; 1 uplift £5, day pass from £31; ⊙8am-5pm Thu-Mon Apr-Aug, Thu-Sun Sep-Mar) Opened in 2012, Wales' most ambitious mountain-biking centre has been going from strength to strength. If you don't know the meaning of fear, check out these 14 blue, red and black downhill and free-ride runs down the mountainside near the slate caverns. The double-black jumps and rock sections host international championships.

There's a minibus uplift service (10am to 4.30pm) on-site.

Sleeping & Eating

★Bryn Elltyd Eco Guesthouse GUESTHOUSE $$
(☎01766-831356; www.ecoguesthouse.co.uk; Tanygrisiau; s/d from £60/90; P 📶 🐾) 🌿 Overlooking the Tanygrisiau reservoir, a mile south of Blaenau Ffestiniog, this wonderful guesthouse is 100% carbon-neutral, powered exclusively by renewables, and serving meals on request made from its own produce. Choose between the snug lake-view rooms in the main house or the two turf-roofed, sheep's-wool-insulated doubles in the garden. The location is great for bikers, hikers and canoe enthusiasts.

Caffi Kiki GREEK $
(☎07450-325119; www.kikis-cafe.com; Lakeside Cafe, Tanygrisiau; mains £10; ⊙5.30-8.30pm Fri & Sat; 🖊) Currently operating as a pop-up restaurant from the Lakeside Cafe in Tanygrisiau (its regular home is Newmarket Sq in Blaenau), Kiki's more than delivers on its promise of traditional Greek dishes with a Welsh twist. The moussaka will get you through a siege and the feta-stuffed lamb burger with black-garlic mayo is a thing of beauty and inspiration.

Getting There & Away

Bus services include the hourly (Monday to Saturday) 3/3B to/from Porthmadog (35 minutes), and three or four daily X19 services per day to Betws-y-Coed (30 minutes) and Llandudno (1½ hours).

There are four or five daily trains running along the Conwy Valley Line from Llandudno (£8.70, 1½ hours) via Betws-y-Coed (£5.10, 35 minutes), while the seasonal, steam-powered Ffestiniog Railway (p738) connects Blaenau to Porthmadog.

Betws-y-Coed

☎01690 / POP 1160

Betws-y-Coed (*bet-us-ee-coyd)* sits at the junction of three river valleys (the Llugwy, the Conwy and the Lledr) and on the edge of the Gwydyr Forest. With outdoor-gear shops outnumbering pubs, gentle walking trails leaving right from the centre (and major hikes a short drive away), and guesthouses occupying its slate Victorian buildings, it's the perfect base for exploring Snowdonia.

Betws has been Wales' most popular inland resort since Victorian times, when a

SURF SNOWDONIA

Lying in the lush Conwy Valley, just outside the national park's eastern border, 8 miles north of Betws-y-Coed, is this unexpected slice of Maui: the **Surf Snowdonia** (☎01492-353123; www.adventureparcsnowdonia.com; Conway Rd, Dolgarrog, LL32 8QE; ⏲8am-11pm; 👪) adventure park centred on a vast artificial wave pool. Choose between surfing (adult/child from £40/35) waves of different intensity, based on your ability, lagoon 'crash and splash' sessions (£25 per hour), kayaking, stand-up paddleboarding, walking and more.

There's also a cafe-bar, a restaurant and on-site fixed camping, if you want to dally, while the Electric Wave festival is held on the 'lagoon' shore in late July. Surf Snowdonia is signposted off the A470 from Llandudno Junction to Betws-y-Coed.

group of countryside painters founded an artistic community to record the diversity of the landscape. The arrival of the railway in 1868 cemented its popularity, and today Betws-y-Coed is as busy with families and coach parties as it is with walkers.

Sights

★Fairy Glen WATERFALL
(A470, LL24 0SH; 50p) Reachable via a walking trail signposted off the A470, 2 miles south of Betws-y-Coed, this is a beautiful gorge, hemmed in by mossy rocks and a small waterfall. It's named after the Welsh sprites, the Tylwyth Teg, who allegedly live in these parts, and the pool at the confluence of Afon Lledr and River Conwy is a great swimming spot.

Swallow Falls WATERFALL
(Rhaeadr Ewynnol; A5, LL24 0DW; adult/child £1.50/50p) Betws-y-Coed's main natural tourist draw is 2 miles west of town, alongside the A5 on the River Llugwy. It's a beautiful spot, with the 42m torrent, Wales' highest, weaving through the rocks into a green pool below. Outside seasonal opening hours, bring coins for the turnstile (no change is available).

Gwydyr Forest FOREST
The 28-sq-mile Gwydyr Forest, planted since the 1920s with oak, beech and larch, encircles Betws-y-Coed and is scattered with the remnants of lead and zinc mine workings. Named for a more ancient forest in the same location, it's ideal for a day's walking, though it gets very muddy in wet weather. *Walks Around Betws-y-Coed* (£5), available from the National Park Tourist Office, details several circular forest walks.

Activities

★Go Below Underground Adventures ADVENTURE SPORTS
(☎01690-710108; www.go-below.co.uk; adventures £59-99; ⏲9am-5pm) Head down an old slate mine and try your hand at scrambling along a subterranean via ferrata, zip-lining deep underground above abandoned mining pits, abseiling down shafts and plunging 21m into darkness in underground freefall. There are three experiences of varying intensity and length; caving experience not required.

Meet at Conwy Falls, on the A5, at the turn-off to Penmachno.

Zip World Fforest ADVENTURE SPORTS
(☎01248-601444; www.zipworld.co.uk; A470, LL24 0HX; 3 coaster rides £20, 2hr safari £40; ⏲9am-5pm; 👪) Fun in the Fforest includes the 'Safari', a network of rope ladders and zip lines high in the treetops; the 'Coaster', a child-friendly toboggan ride on rails; and 'Skyride', a 24m, five-person swing that reaches jaw-clenching velocity. The latest addition is 'Plummet', which is exactly what you do, for 30m, dropping through a trapdoor on top of a tower.

Sleeping

Vagabond HOSTEL $
(☎01690-710850; www.thevagabond.co.uk; Craiglan Rd; dm from £22; P 📶 🐾) On the slopes below a forested crag, from which spills its own 'private' waterfall, the Vagabond is Betws' best hostel – and the only one within the town proper. It's a simple set-up, with freshly decorated six- to eight-bed dorms, two family rooms, shared bathrooms and an appealing bar (4.30pm to 11pm), kitchen and common room. Weekends mean pizza night.

Maes-y-Garth B&B $$
(☎01690-710441; www.maes-y-garth.co.uk; A470, Lon Muriau; s/d from £80/90; P 📶) Off the

A470, and accessible from Betws by a footpath (starting behind St Michael's Church) across the river, this top-notch B&B inhabits a 1970s Clough Williams-Ellis–designed 'alpine-style' house. A warm welcome and five quietly stylish guest rooms with gorgeous views await – perhaps the nicest is room 4, which has its own balcony and views of the valley. Two-night minimum.

Tyn-y-Fron B&B **$$$**
(☎01690-710449; www.snowdoniabedandbreakfast.co.uk; A470, Lon Muriau; s/d £170/190; P 📶) This gracious old stone house has five spacious, individually styled rooms; the Valley View super-king room boasts expansive valley views. Friendly owners Barbara and Nigel serve an excellent breakfast, including award-winning sausages and bacon from the local butcher, and are full of advice on local walks. The B&B is off the A470 and accessible from Betws via a footpath.

Eating

★Olif TAPAS **$$**
(☎01690-733942; www.olifbetws.wales; Holyhead Rd; tapas £5-7; ⊙6-8.30pm Tue-Sun, noon-3pm Sat & Sun May-Oct, closed Mon-Wed Nov-Apr) Breakfast first up, burgers for lunch, and tapas and wine in the evening – Olif morphs to please throughout the day. The tapas has a distinctly Welsh flavour, without straying too far into fusion territory (the croquettes are made with Perl Wen cheese and the ham's from Carmarthen), and fun finger foods, like popcorn cockles and cider-cooked mussels, abound.

Upstairs, there's a handful of light and bright boutique rooms, all en suite, with rain showers, and some with deep soaking tubs (rooms from £135).

Tŷ Gwyn Hotel EUROPEAN **$$**
(☎01690-710383; www.tygwynhotel.co.uk; A5; mains £13-18; ⊙noon-2pm & 6-9pm; ✎) This 400-year-old coaching inn with bare stone walls and exposed beams is hands down the town's most characterful restaurant. The menu is creative without trying too hard, the chef does wonderful things with local ingredients to conjure up the likes of slow-braised lamb shoulder and seafood gratin, and the quirky historic building only adds to the appeal.

Information

Snowdonia National Park Tourist Office
(☎01690-710426; www.eryri-npa.gov.uk; Royal Oak Stables; ⊙9.30am-12.30pm & 1.30-4.30pm) More than just a repository of books, maps and local craft, this office is an invaluable source of information about walking trails, mountain conditions and more.

Getting There & Away

Snowdon Sherpa bus service S2 heads 12 times daily to Swallow Falls (seven minutes), Capel Curig (15 minutes), Pen-y-Pass (25 minutes) and Llanberis (35 minutes); all trips are £2. Other buses include 19 to Llandudno (£3.50, 55 minutes, seven daily Monday to Saturday) via Conwy (£3.30, 45 minutes), and to Penmachno (15 minutes, five daily Monday to Saturday), and X19 services to Blaenau Ffestiniog (£2.70, 25 minutes, three daily) and Llandudno (£3.50, one hour, two to three daily).

Bicycle Beics Betws (☎01690-710766; www.bikewales.co.uk; Vicarage Rd; ⊙10am-5pm Mar-Nov, call ahead at other times) rents out both regular and electric mountain bikes.

Betws-y-Coed is on the Conwy Valley Line (www.conwyvalleyrailway.co.uk), with up to five trains daily to Llandudno (£6.30, 50 minutes) and Blaenau Ffestiniog (£5.10, 35 minutes).

Ogwen Valley

Snowdonia's best and most challenging hikes are concentrated in this valley. Hiking trails depart from the shores of Llyn Ogwen, and revolve around the triple-peaked Tryfan and the rugged, spiky Glyderau on the south side of the valley, and the horseshoe formed by the Carneddau range to the north.

To experience the mountains without too much effort, take an hour-long return walk from Idwal Cottage to Cwm Idwal, an amphitheatre-shaped hanging valley sheltering the small and wonderfully scenic glacial lake, **Llyn Idwal** (A5), reflecting the Glyder range.

The best map for Ogwen Valley hikes is the OS 1:25,000 Explorer map *OL17 (Snowdon–Conwy Valley)*.

Sights & Activities

★Tryfan MOUNTAIN
(A5) If Snowdon gets more than its fair share of day trippers, then the menacing-looking, fractured rock spur of Tryfan (918m) draws only experienced mountaineers

and hillwalkers, determined to conquer Snowdonia's most demanding peak. The summit is crowned by two massive boulders, Adam and Eve, and there are three tracks of varying difficulty leading to the top: South Ridge (aka Miners' Track), Heather Terrace and North Ridge. Climbing Tryfan is a serious undertaking, only to be attempted in fine weather.

The easiest way up is the **South Ridge track** (5 miles, five to six hours). It ascends from the Idwal Cottage car park towards Llyn Idwal, then climbs steadily past Llyn Bochlwyd towards Bwlch Tryfan, the saddle between Tryfan's peak and Glyder Fach. You then make your way past the Far Summit Peak and scramble up to the summit. If you're tempted to jump the 1.5m gap between the Adam and Eve boulders (as some do!), consider the consequences of misjudging the distance.

The **Heather Terrace route** (4 miles, four to six hours) climbs up from the Gwern Gof Uchaf farm towards the 'Little Tryfan' rock slab, popular with rock climbers, cutting across Tryfan's east face, and culminating in a col between the Far South peak and the South peak, from where it's a short scramble up a broad, scree-covered slope to the summit.

Starting from a lay-by by Llyn Ogwen, the **North Ridge track** (3 to 4 miles, four to six hours) is the most challenging of the routes, starting as a scree-covered trail and becoming progressively steeper as you climb the ridge. There isn't a single formal path, but thousands of feet have worn a rough trail among the boulders, and if you stick to the middle of the ridge, it's not difficult to follow. We recommend descending via one of the other two routes, though.

★Carnedd Loop HIKING

(A5, Tal-y-Llyn Ogwen Farm) Starting from the Tal-y-Llyn Ogwen farm, just east of Llyn Ogwen, this moderately strenuous 12-mile hike takes in four Carnedd peaks and two glacial lakes, with fantastic views of the Glyder range and Tryfan en route. It's a great mix of gentle ridge walks, plus a couple of challenging scrambles. Park by the trailhead along the A5.

The trail climbs steadily up the Afon Lloer valley before veering west by the Ffynnon Lloer lake, where you perform a short gully scramble up the rock spur. From **Pen-yr Ole Wen** (978m), it's an easy, cairn-marked ridge walk to **Carnedd Dafydd** (1044m), followed by a drop to Bwlch Cyfryd-drum and an ascent to **Carnedd Llewelyn** (1064m), Wales' third-highest peak. Another ridge walk and steep descent are followed by an exposed scramble up **Pen yr Helgi Du** (833m), then descending to the A5 via the gentle ridge of Y Braich.

Getting There & Away

From mid-April to late October, Snowdon Sherpa bus S6 runs twice daily (£2; Saturday and Sunday only) from Bangor to Pen-y-Pass via Llyn Ogwen (25 minutes) and Capel Curig (35 minutes). Own wheels needed the rest of the time.

Llanberis

01298 / POP 1908

Right on the doorstep of Mt Snowdon, Llanberis attracts a steady flow of walkers and climbers, particularly during the warmer months. It's a trekking base like no other, partly because of the Snowdon Mountain Railway, and partly because of its proximity to the most popular trails up the famed peak.

Llanberis originally housed workers from the Dinorwig slate quarry, and hillsides have been left deeply scarred by the mining. While tourism is the cornerstone of life these days, the town hasn't abandoned its industrial roots, and Dinorwig is now part of Europe's biggest pumped-storage power station. Some of the old quarry workshops have been reincarnated as a slate-industry museum, and the narrow-gauge railway that once hauled slate to the coast now transports day trippers along Llyn Padarn.

Sights & Activities

★National Slate Museum MUSEUM

(0300 111 2333; www.museum.wales/slate; off A4086; 10am-4pm Sun, Mon, Wed & Thu; P) FREE At Dinorwig Quarry, much of the slate was carved out of the open mountainside – leaving behind a jagged, sculptural cliff face that's fascinating if not exactly beautiful. This excellent museum, occupying the Victorian workshops beside the lake (Llyn Padarn), features video clips, a huge working water wheel, workers' cottages (progressively furnished in period decor from

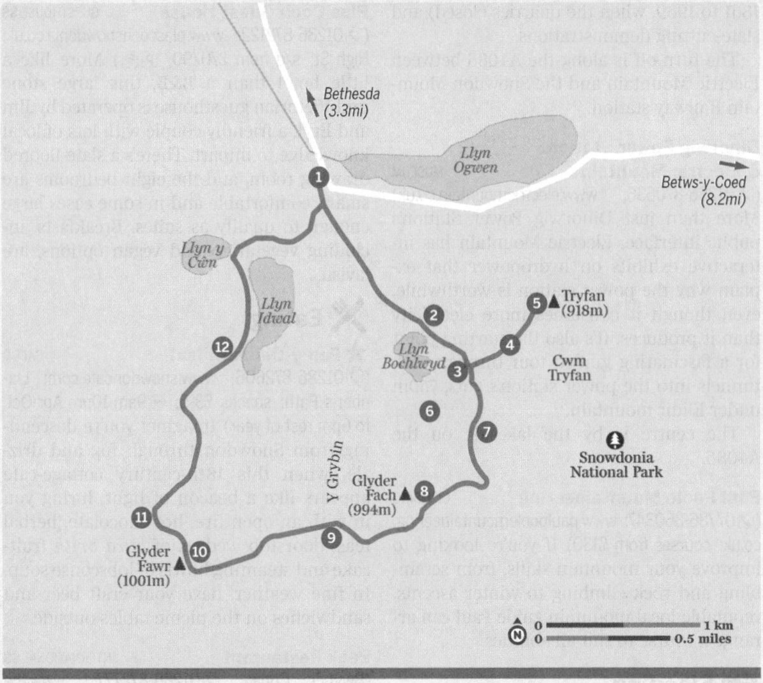

Mountain Walk
The Glyder Traverse

START IDWAL COTTAGE YHA
END IDWAL COTTAGE YHA
LENGTH 6.5 MILES; SIX TO EIGHT HOURS

This rugged hike involves a little scrambling and takes in two of its greatest peaks – Glyder Fach and Glyder Fawr, with an optional scramble up Tryfan peak.

Cross the footbridge from the 1 **Idwal Cottage** (☎0845 371 9744; www.yha.org.uk; A5, Nant Ffrancon, LL57 3LZ; camping £12, dm/tw £25/59; ⏲daily Mar-Oct, Fri & Sat Nov-Feb) car park. At a 2 **fork** in the path, go straight up the Miner's Track that crosses bracken-covered, boggy ground before climbing steeply up Cwm Bochlwyd to sheltered 3 **Llyn Bochlwyd** lake. Ignore the track veering to the right and ascend towards the gap between Tryfan and Glyder Fach. Once you've reached the 4 **ridge**, you have the option of detouring up the 5 **South Ridge of Tryfan**. It's a 30-minute, straightforward scramble up some giant rocks to Tryfan's famous summit (918m) feature – the twin 6 **Adam and Eve rocks**. If it's a windy day, don't climb up and try to jump the 1.5m gap!

Once you've taken in the all-encompassing view of Llyn Ogwen below and the Carnedd mountains opposite, head back to the ridge. Use the ladder crossing and either scramble up the steep shortcut of 7 **Bristly Ridge** or take the 8 **footpath** that cuts across the eastern flank of Glyder Fach. Make a sharp right up towards the jumble of dark rock slabs that mark the 9 **summit of Glyder Fach** (994m), with the famous Cantilever – a slab of rock balanced on two shorter rocks – nearby. It's a straightforward, cairn-marked walk across the bare, rock-strewn plateau to Glyder Fawr (1001m), passing the dramatic black rock spikes of 10 **Castell y Gwynt** (Castle of the Winds). A steep, screen-strewn path zigzags down to 11 **Devil's Kitchen ridge**. Head right along the path between the giant boulders to the shores of 12 **Llyn Idwal**. Skirt the lake from the left for the best views of Cwm Idwal, cross the footbridge, turn left and follow the footpath back to the car park.

1861 to 1969, when the quarries closed) and slate-cutting demonstrations.

The turn-off is along the A4086 between Electric Mountain and the Snowdon Mountain Railway station.

Dinorwig Power Station & Electric Mountain MUSEUM
(☎01286-870636; www.electricmountain.co.uk) More than just Dinorwig Power Station's public interface, Electric Mountain has interactive exhibits on hydropower that explain why the power station is worthwhile, even though it consumes more electricity than it produces. It's also the starting point for a fascinating guided tour through rock tunnels into the power station's guts, 750m under Elidir mountain.

The centre is by the lakeside on the A4086.

Paul Poole Mountaineering CLIMBING
(☎07786-360347; www.paulpoolemountaineering.co.uk; courses from £130) If you're looking to improve your mountain skills, from scrambling and rock climbing to winter ascents, reputable local mountain guide Paul can arrange a course to suit all abilities.

Sleeping

Snowdon Llanberis YHA HOSTEL $
(☎0845 371 9645; www.yha.org.uk; Llwyn Celyn, Ceunant St; dm/tw/tr/pods from £24/69/79/109; reception 8-10am & 5-10pm; P Wi-Fi) Originally a quarry manager's house, this no-frills hostel with spartan six-bed dorms and various configurations of private rooms offers great views from its hillside locale, a self-catering kitchen, a drying room and four-person fixed camping pods. It's about a 10-minute walk above the town, signposted from High St.

★ **Beech Bank** B&B $$
(☎01286-871085; www.beech-bank.co.uk; 2 High St; s/d from £70/80; P Wi-Fi) First impressions of this double-gabled, wrought-iron-trimmed stone house are great, but step inside and it just gets better. A stylish renovation has resulted in beautiful bathrooms and exuberant decor, which matches the gregarious nature of the host. Breakfasts can be packed for early-rising hikers and climbers. Thoughtful touches, such as lending flasks to hikers, are a boon.

Plas Coch Guest House GUESTHOUSE $$
(☎01286-872122; www.plascochsnowdonia.co.uk; High St; s/d from £70/90; P Wi-Fi) More like a little hotel than a B&B, this large stone mid-Victorian guesthouse is operated by Jim and Eryl, a friendly couple with lots of local knowledge to impart. There's a slate-floored drawing room, and the eight bedrooms are smart, comfortable and in some cases large enough to qualify as suites. Breakfasts, including vegetarian and vegan options, are lavish.

Eating

★ **Pen-y-Ceunant Isaf** CAFE $
(☎01286-872606; www.snowdoncafe.com; Llanberis Path; snacks £3-5; 9am-10pm Apr-Oct, to 6pm rest of year) Imagine: you're descending from Snowdon through fog and drizzle, when this 18th-century cottage-cafe appears like a beacon of light, luring you in with an open fire, hot chocolate, herbal teas, doorstop wedges of *bara brith* fruitcake and steaming bowls of lobscouse soup. In fine weather, have your craft beer and sandwiches on the picnic tables outside.

Peak Restaurant INTERNATIONAL $$
(Bwyty'r Copa; ☎01286-872777; www.thepeakrestaurant.co.uk; 86 High St; mains £14-21; 7-10pm Wed-Sat; ✎) A chef-patron who once clattered the pans at the legendary Chez Panisse in California is behind this fine-dining restaurant's popularity and longevity. The open kitchen allows you to see her at work, turning good Welsh produce into internationally inspired dishes such as Anglesey sea bass with lemon butter or Welsh lamb rump with redcurrant jus. Book ahead.

Getting There & Away

Snowdon Sherpa buses stop by Joe Brown's on the High St. S1 heads to Pen-y-Pass (15 minutes, every 30 minutes), while S2 runs roughly hourly via Pen-y-Pass to Capel Curig (20 minutes) and Betws-y-Coed (35 minutes). Other regular buses include the 88 to/from Caernarfon (25 minutes, four to eight daily) and the 85/86 to/from Bangor (50 minutes, four to nine daily).

Bicycle Llanberis Bike Hire (☎07776 051559; www.llanberisbikehire.co.uk; 34 High St; per 3hr/day £18/25; 9am-5pm) rents Genesis Core 30 and Core 20 hardtail mountain bikes, suitable for ascents/descents of Snowdon and can deliver to your lodgings.

The Snowdon Mountain Railway whisks passengers up almost to the summit.

Snowdon (Yr Wyddfa)

No Snowdonia experience is complete without summiting Snowdon (1085m), one of Britain's most awe-inspiring mountains and the highest summit in Wales (and the 61st highest in Britain). 'Yr Wyddfa' in Welsh (pronounced uhr-*with*-vuh, meaning 'the Tomb'), it's the mythical resting place of the giant Rhita Gawr, who demanded King Arthur's beard for his cloak and was killed for his temerity.

On the summit, the granite-clad **Hafod Eryri** (www.snowdonrailway.co.uk; ⏲10.30am-4.30pm May-Oct; 📶) structure houses a cafe and ambient interpretive centre; it's open whenever the train is running. On a clear day the views stretch to Ireland and the Isle of Man over Snowdon's fine jagged ridges, which drop down into sheltered *cwms* (valleys) and deep post-glacial lakes. Thanks to the Snowdon Mountain Railway, the peak is extremely accessible when the winds aren't too high. On fine days, when some of the trails leading to the summit get frustratingly crowded, the only question is: which way up?

Sights & Activities

★Mount Snowdon MOUNTAIN

Summiting Wales' highest mountain (1085m) is neither a cakewalk nor an insurmountable obstacle, and is hugely worth it, in spite of occasional crowds. Seven trails of varying length and difficulty lead to Snowdon's summit, some more scenic than others. That the mountain has a train station and a cafe at its summit does not mean you should underestimate it. No route is completely safe, especially in winter, so sturdy footwear, extra layers, plenty of provisions and a torch are musts.

The longest and most straightforward (read: a bit boring) route to the summit is the **Llanberis Path** (5 miles one way, three hours), a steady ascent that runs beside the train line, with a slightly steeper section once you pass Clogwyn station. This is also the route used by mountain bikes, and graded a black trail.

The two paths starting from Pen-y-Pass require the least amount of ascent but are nevertheless tougher walks. The **Miner's Track** (4 miles one way, three hours) starts off wide and gentle, skirting part of Llyn Llydaw lake, then climbing to Cwm Glaslyn and proceeding steeply up via a series of switchbacks. The **Pyg Track** (3.5 miles one way, 2½ hours) is shorter and steeper, climbing up to the Bwlch y Moch (Pass of Pigs), traversing a ridge above Llyn Llydaw and eventually joining the switchbacks of the Miner's Track.

The classic Snowdon Horseshoe (8 miles return), one of the most spectacular ways to see Snowdon and its glacial lakes, branches off from the Pyg Track to cross the precipitous ridge of **Crib Goch** (the knife-edge traverse, occasionally lethal in windy or wintry conditions, is only recommended for the experienced), with a descent over the peak of Y Lliwedd and a final section down the Miner's Track.

Two tracks start from the Caernarfon–Beddgelert road (A4085): the **Snowdon Ranger Path** (4 miles one way, three hours) is a somewhat dull slog of the shores of Llyn Cwellyn, steep and boggy by turns, that skirts the Clogwyn Du'r Arddu cliffs and connects with the Llanberis Path. The **Rhyd Ddu Path** (4 miles one way, three hours) has two starting points (Rhyl Ddu car park and Pitt's Head Rock) that shortly join up, and a particularly spectacular final section that traverses the Cwm Clogwyn rim and Yr Wyddfa's south ridge.

The most rugged and scenic of the southern routes is the **Watkin Path** (4 miles one way, three hours), involving an ascent of more than 1000m on its southerly approach from Nant Gwynant and finishing with a scramble to Bwlch Ciliau, the saddle between Y Lliwedd and the Snowdon summit.

★Snowdon Mountain Railway RAIL

(☎01286-870223; www.snowdonrailway.co.uk; A4086; adult/child return diesel £29/20, steam £37/27; ⏲9am-5pm mid-Mar–Oct) If you're not physically able to climb a mountain, short on time or just into conserving energy, those industrious Victorians have gifted you an alternative. Opened in 1896, the Snowdon Mountain Railway is the UK's highest – and only – rack-and-pinion railway. Vintage steam and modern diesel locomotives haul carriages from Llanberis up to Snowdon's summit (one hour one way, 2½ hours return).

Sleeping

Snowdon Pen-y-Pass YHA HOSTEL $
(☎0845 371 9534; www.yha.org.uk; A4086; dm/tw/tr/q £26/59/69/79; P) This superbly situated hostel has three of Snowdon's trails at its doorstep. It has a well-equipped kitchen, laundry and drying room; Mallory's Cafe/Bar (named for a past patron who perished on Everest); six-bed dorms and quiet, comfortable rooms, some en suite. Curfew 10.30pm. It's 5.5 miles up the A4086 from Llanberis; the Snowdon Sherpa buses stop here.

Snowdon Ranger YHA HOSTEL $
(☎0845 371 9659; www.yha.org.uk; A4085, Rhyd Ddu; P) On the A4085, 5 miles north of Beddgelert at the trailhead for the Snowdon Ranger Path, this former inn has its own adjoining beach on the shore of Llyn Cwellyn, and is close to the hiking and climbing centres of Llanberis and Beddgelert. The dorms and rooms at this 30-bed hostel are currently only available for exclusive (whole place) hire.

★ **Pen-y-Gwryd** HISTORIC HOTEL $$
(☎01286-870211; www.pyg.co.uk; A4086, Nant Gwynant; r incl breakfast with/without bathroom from £115/95; P 📶 🐾) Eccentric and atmospheric, this creeper-clad Georgian coaching inn was used as a training base by the 1953 Everest team; spot Edmund Hillary's and James (now the late Jan) Morris' signatures on the restaurant ceiling. Traditional rooms are rather spartan, with washbasins; en suites are plusher, some with four-poster beds and claw-footed tubs. The hotel sits at the junction of the A498 and A4086.

Getting There & Away

BUS

Pen-y-Pass is served by Snowdon Sherpa buses. S1 runs from Llanberis twice hourly (15 minutes); a dozen daily S2 buses run from Llanberis to Betws-y-Coed via Pen-y-Pass; S4 serves Caernarfon (one hour, five daily, Monday to Saturday) via Beddgelert, while S97 serves Porthmadog (one hour, seven daily Monday to Saturday) via Tremadog. A Sherpa single/return/day ticket costs £2/3/5).

BICYCLE

Llanberis Bike Hire (p734) can deliver your rental mountain bike up Snowdon for £50, including costs of hire. Bear in mind that bikes are banned from Snowdon's trails between 10am and 5pm from May to September.

CAR

Consider using public transport: car parks can fill up quickly and the Pen-y-Pass car park costs £10 per day.

TRAIN

The Welsh Highland Railway (p738) stops at the trailhead of the Rhyd Ddu Path, and there is a request stop for the Snowdon Ranger Path. Another option is to take the Snowdon Mountain Railway (p735) from Llanberis to the top and walk back down.

Beddgelert

☎01766 / POP 468

Tiny Beddgelert consists of a tight clutch of stone cottages overlooking the River Colwyn and its ivy-covered bridge, upstream from where it meets the River Glaslyn. Named after either a 7th-century saint or the **grave of a mythical hound** (⏲24hr) FREE, an underwhelming local attraction, the village is the starting point for several rewarding hikes, and gets very busy during the warmer months.

Sights & Activities

Sygun Copper Mine MINE
(☎01766-890595; www.syguncoppermine.co.uk; A498; adult/child under 15yr £10/7.50; ⏲9.30am-5pm Apr-Sep, 10am-4pm rest of year; P 🚻) This copper mine dates from Roman times, although extraction was stepped up in the 19th century. Abandoned in 1903, it has since been converted into a family-friendly museum, with a half-hour self-guided underground tour containing dioramas that evoke the life of Victorian miners. You can also try your hand at metal detecting (£2.50) or panning for gold (£2). It's a mile northeast of Beddgelert.

Moel Hebog Ridge HIKING
(off A4085) The ascent of Moel Hebog (783m) is relatively strenuous (8-mile loop, five hours) and includes a scenic ridge walk that encompasses lesser peaks. The trail begins at the Pont Alyn bridge, half a mile northwest of central Beddgelert. Follow the road to Cwm Cloch Isaf Farm, and then the signposted trail up along the northeast ridge of Moel Hebog.

Craflwyn & Dinas Emrys WALKING
(NT; ☎01766-510120; www.nationaltrust.org.uk; A498) A mile northeast of Beddgelert, near Llyn Dinas, National Trust–owned Craflwyn

DON'T MISS

PORTMEIRION

Set on its own tranquil peninsula reaching into the estuary, 2 miles east of Porthmadog, **Portmeirion** (☎01766-770000; www.portmeirion.wales; Minffordd, off High St; adult/concession £13/11; ⏰9.30am-5.30pm; P) is fantastical collection of colourful buildings with a heavy Italian influence, masterminded by Welsh architect Sir Clough Williams-Ellis. Starting in 1925, Sir Clough collected bits and pieces from disintegrating stately mansions and set them alongside his own creations and, with a 'light-opera sort of approach', concocted this seaside utopia. At the age of 90, Sir Clough deemed Portmeirion to be complete – 50 years after he began.

It's really more like a stage set than an actual village and, indeed, it formed the ideally surreal set for cult TV series *The Prisoner*, which was filmed here from 1966 to 1967. It still draws fans of the show during the **PortmeiriCon** (Prisoner Convention; ⏰Apr), held annually in April, and stages the arts, culture and food-fest **Festival No 6** (☎0344-326 4264; www.festivalnumber6.com; tickets from £180; ⏰Sep) in September. The giant plaster-of-Paris Buddha, just off the piazza, featured in the 1958 film *The Inn of the Sixth Happiness*, starring Ingrid Bergman. Architecturally, it's a mishmash: there are Ionic columns topped with Thai figures, and a Jacobean town hall nestles alongside a Mediterranean piazza, but somehow, this flight of imagination comes together.

It's well worth experiencing Portmeirion after the day trippers have left by staying on-site at the **Hotel Portmeirion & Castell Deudraeth** (☎01766-770000; www.portmeirion.wales; r from £184; P ✖). Choose between the over-the-top Hotel Portmeirion in a prime spot by the water, with its individually styled rooms, pool and a terraced bar, or the fancifully Gothic Castell Deudraeth.

Farm is the trailhead for the Dinas Emrys trail. It takes around 30 minutes to walk through fields, alongside a stream, past a waterfall and through woods to the summit. At the top are the remains of 12th-century and Roman-era fortifications and wonderful views over the valley of Nant Gwynant.

Sleeping & Eating

★Plas Tan Y Craig B&B $$

(☎01766-890310; www.plastanygraig.co.uk; Stryd Smith; r £124; 📶) Super central and overlooking the Colwyn, this award-winning, family-run B&B comprises five midsized rooms (twin and king) in cool slate-greys and creams. A generous cooked breakfast is served; other perks include an honesty bar and drying room for your wet gear. Packed meals prepared on request. Minimum of two nights.

Hebog CAFE $$

(☎01766-890400; www.facebook.com/hebogbeddgelert; Fford Caernarfon; mains £16-19; ⏰noon-8pm Thu-Mon; 📶) At the swankier end of Beddgelert's dining options, Hebog is an upmarket cafe serving the likes of braised lamb with samphire and homemade spinach-and-ricotta tortellini with red-pepper pesto. The scenic summer terrace by the babbling Glaslyn fills up quickly on warm days.

Getting There & Away

Snowdon Sherpa buses serve Beddgelert: the S4 (six daily) heads to/from Caernarfon (35 minutes) via Snowdon Ranger (10 minutes) and Rhyd Ddu (six minutes), while the S97 (seven daily) heads to Porthmadog (25 minutes) via Tremadog (18 minutes). No buses on Sundays.

Near the train station, **Beddgelert Bikes** (Beics Beddgelert; ☎01766-890434; www.beddgelertbikes.co.uk; The Bike Barn, High St; per 4/8/24hr from £20/30/35) rents out mountain bikes, e-bikes, children's bikes, tandems and child seats, and can advise on cycling trails in the area.

Beddgelert train station (off High St) is a stop on the historic Welsh Highland Railway (p738), which runs between Caernarfon and Porthmadog from Easter to October, with limited winter service, and stops at the Rhyd Ddu and Snowdon Ranger trailheads.

Porthmadog

☎01766 / POP 2905

Busy Porthmadog (port-*mad*-uk) enjoys an arresting estuarine setting overlooking the

Glaslyn River. It's a convenient gateway both to the Llŷn Peninsula and Snowdonia National Park, and has the fantastical village of Portmeirion on its doorstep.

Porthmadog is also triply-blessed with heritage railways, a legacy of Victorian industry, one of them harking back to the town's past as Wales' busiest slate port. It forms the southern terminus for two of Wales' finest narrow-gauge train journeys and has a third steam-train line connected to a rail-heritage centre.

Sights & Activities

★Ffestiniog Railway RAIL

(Rheilffordd Ffestiniog; ☎01766-516024; www.festrail.co.uk; day ticket £25; ⏰daily Easter-Oct, reduced services rest of year; 👪) The world's oldest surviving narrow-gauge railway, the Ffestiniog wends its way from Porthmadog to the slate-mining town of Blaenau Ffestiniog. Long past its industrial heyday, the railway's 150-year-old steam locomotives and wooden carriages now ferry sightseers through oak woodlands, beneath towering peaks and beside rivers. For an extra £7 each way, you can ride in giant-windowed observation carriages.

★Welsh Highland Railway RAIL

(☎01766-516000; www.festrail.co.uk; return £40 ; ⏰Easter-Oct, limited service winter) Originating in 1923, and departing from Porthmadog Harbour Station, the Welsh Highland Railway is the UK's longest, running for 25 miles to Caernarfon (2½ hours) via Beddgelert (£40 return) and Rhyd Ddu, and skirting the southern slopes of Snowdon. Wonderfully scenic, the track runs through a river estuary and oak woods before steeply climbing some rugged mountainous terrain.

Sleeping

Golden Fleece Inn PUB $

(☎01766-512421; www.goldenfleeceinn.com; Market Sq, Tremadog; s/d from £39/55, ste £114; P📶) Hop flowers hang from the ceiling of this former coaching inn, which offers real ales in a cave-like beer cellar, pub grub, an open fire on cold nights and live acoustic music. The rooms above the pub are snug and simply furnished; however, be prepared for noise. King rooms and king suites with whirlpool baths are in the nearby annex.

★Yr Hen Fecws B&B $$

(☎01766-514625; www.henfecws.com; 16 Lombard St; s/d £80/90; P📶) Probably Porthmadog's nicest digs, 'The Old Bakery' is a stylishly restored stone cottage containing seven en-suite rooms, decorated in shades of grey, with crimson or exposed slate walls and fireplaces. Breakfast is served under the marigold walls and exposed beams of the downstairs bistro where the owner/chef whips up Welsh classics in the evenings (dinner mains £18 to £25).

Eating & Drinking

★Y Sgwâr BISTRO $$$

(☎01766-515451; www.ysgwar-restaurant.co.uk; 12-16 Market Sq, Tremadog; mains £18-28; ⏰5-9pm Mon-Sat, noon-3pm Sun) On the main square in Tremadog, this cosmopolitan Welsh restaurant has the best food in either town. The service is attentive and friendly, and classics such as pork belly with dauphinois potatoes, and slow-roasted lamb shank with garlic mash are presented with flair and enthusiasm. There's great value in the set menus offered between 6pm and 7pm (two/three courses £18.50/23).

Australia PUB

(☎01766-515957; www.facebook.com/australia-porthmadog; 31 High St; ⏰noon-10pm Sun-Thu, to midnight Fri & Sat; 📶) In a prime central location, the pub arm of the Purple Moose brewery proudly showcases its award-winning range of craft beers and real ales, all found on tap here. The brews are complemented by decent pub grub at mealtimes.

Getting There & Away

BUS

Buses stop on High St. Routes include the T2 to/from Bangor (1¼ hours, three to daily) via Caernarfon (50 minutes), and to Aberystwyth (2¼ hours, two to six daily) via Dolgellau (50 minutes, three to nine daily) and Machynlleth (1½ hours, three to seven daily); the frequent (Monday to Saturday only) 3/3B to/from Pwllheli (40 minutes) via Criccieth (15 minutes) and in the other direction to Blaenau Ffestiniog (35 minutes); and up to seven daily (Monday to Saturday) S97 (Snowdon Sherpa) buses serve Beddgelert (15 to 24 minutes).

TRAIN

Cambrian Coast Line trains serve Pwllheli (£5.60, 25 minutes, seven daily) via Criccieth

(£3.20, seven minutes), and Machynlleth (£15.30, two hours, eight daily) via Harlech (£4.40, 23 minutes). The **Ffestiniog & Welsh Highland Railways** (www.festrail.co.uk) runs scenic services to Blaenau Ffestiniog, the Snowdon trailheads and Caernarfon.

LLŶN PENINSULA

Covered in a patchwork of pastureland and heather-covered hills, the green finger of the Llŷn (pronounced 'khleen') juts into the Irish Sea, its westernmost tip as remote as it gets. Welsh is the Llŷn's lingua franca; the peninsula and adjacent island of Anglesey were the last to fall to the Romans and Normans. Welsh culture and the slow pace of life are as much of a draw as the mysticism that shrouds this unique part of Wales: legends of King Arthur abound, and over the centuries the heaviest footfalls have been those of pilgrims bound for Bardsey Island.

The wildlife-rich coastline, remote beaches, Iron Age forts, narrow country lanes and end-of-the-world crags are best explored by bicycle or on foot, via the Llŷn Coastal Path.

Getting There & Away

The Cambrian Coast Line runs as far down the Llŷn as Pwllheli, while buses run from major centres such as Caernarfon, Porthmadog and Pwllheli throughout the peninsula. Between March and October, the **Llŷn Coastal Bus** (01758-721777; www.bwsarfordirllyn.co.uk) runs Thursday to Sunday, ferrying walkers and surfers to some of the peninsula's more remote and beautiful spots.

Criccieth

01766 / POP 1792

An easy-going Victorian seaside town, Criccieth is lined with smart, pastel-coloured town houses. Overlooked by the ruins of a medieval castle on a promontory, it counts two sand-and-stone Blue Flag beaches among its attractions: one a tidy crescent, and the other a far-reaching wild expanse.

Sights

Criccieth Castle CASTLE
(Cadw; www.cadw.gov.wales; Castle St; adult/child £5.10/3.10; 10am-1pm & 2-5pm Wed-Sun) Ruined Criccieth Castle, perched on the seafront's most prominent headland, offers views stretching along the peninsula's southern coast and across Tremadog Bay to Harlech. Constructed by Welsh prince Llywelyn the Great in 1239, it was overrun in 1283 by Edward I's forces and recaptured for the Welsh in 1404 by Owain Glyndŵr, whose troops promptly reduced it to the still-standing gatehouse and some broken walls.

Sleeping & Eating

Caerwylan Hotel HISTORIC HOTEL $$
(01766-522547; www.caerwylan.co.uk; Beach Bank; s/d incl breakfast from £68/115; P) Overlooking Criccieth Beach, this lemon-yellow, rambling Victorian hotel is both well located and wonderfully friendly. Carpeted, snug rooms of various sizes are reached via a maze-like assortment of staircases and corridors, or via the grand lounge. Tonnau, the on-site restaurant, is one of the best in town, serving extravagant breakfasts and superlative Welsh classics.

★**Dylan's** INTERNATIONAL $$
(01766-522773; www.dylansrestaurant.co.uk; Maes y Mor; mains £13-25; noon-9.30pm; P) Making use of Morannedd – a light-filled, 1950s, deco-style beachside pavilion designed by Portmeirion architect Sir Clough Williams-Ellis and once used by Butlin's for afternoon tea dances – Dylan's also has a large alfresco sea-facing terrace. Like its siblings in **Menai Bridge** (01248-716714; St George's Rd; mains £8-25; noon-10pm) and Llandudno, it combines fantastic sea views with a crowd-pleasing, globe-trotting bistro menu spanning pizzas, burgers, curries and seafood.

Getting There & Away

Buses passing along Criccieth's High St include the dozen daily bus 3 (five on Sundays) services to/from Pwllheli (25 minutes), and also to Porthmadog (15 minutes, where you can switch to 3B services to Blaenau Ffestiniog). For services to other parts of the Llŷn, switch buses in Pwllheli.

Cambrian Coast Line service runs eight direct trains each day to Pwllheli (£4, 15 minutes), and to Machynlleth (£17.50, two hours) via Porthmadog (£3.20, nine minutes), Harlech (£6.60, 35 minutes) and Barmouth (£9.60, one hour).

OFF THE BEATEN TRACK

LLŶN COASTAL PATH: THE HIGHLIGHTS

Starting from the Menai Bridge, this 110-mile **coastal path** runs alongside the Menai Strait and Caernarfon Bay, before following the north coast of the Llŷn to the rugged westernmost tip of Mynydd Mawr, passing through seaside villages of the south coast and finishing up in Porthmadog. The walk is typically done in nine days; **Edge of Wales Walk** (01758-760652; www.edgeofwaleswalk.co.uk) can arrange accommodation and baggage transfers.

The most beautiful stretches are found along the north coast – particularly the Trefor to Nefyn section. Some 5 miles southwest of Trefor, reached by a steep, narrow and hairpin bend-y road down towards the sea from Llithfaen, tiny, scenic Nant Gwrtheyrn is home to the **Welsh Language & Heritage Centre** (01758-750334; www.nantgwrtheyrn.org; Nant Gwrtheyrn, Llithfaen; 5-day course incl full board £495; call ahead for times). Even if you don't stay to learn Welsh, it's worth a visit. From the car park above the village you can hike to the **Tre'r Ceiri Hillfort** (24hr) FREE, one of Europe's best-preserved Iron Age forts, with tremendous views of both coasts of the Llŷn.

Four miles southwest, swing by **St Beuno's Church** (07572 776225; www.facebook.com/bromadryn; B4417; hours vary) FREE in tiny Pistyll – one of the main stops along the ancient Bardsey pilgrimage route. Founded by the eponymous 7th-century saint, this tiny stone church retains its original Celtic carved font and a 'leper squint' beside the 11th- century altar that allowed lepers standing outside to watch Mass.

Further west, it's worth detouring to **Porthdinllaen** (parking summer/winter £5/1.50, free to NT members in summer), a hamlet on a tiny thumb of land stretching into the sea from Morfa Nefyn, its main attraction a long, sheltered sandy beach. Beach lovers rejoice: the next leg of the trail, from Porth Colmon to Aberdaron via Mynydd Mawr, passes by **Porthor** (Whistling Sands; NT; www.nationaltrust.org.uk; parking £4), a lovely, remote crescent of sand.

Official Guide: Llŷn Peninsula, of the Wales Coastal Path series, is a good companion.

Abersoch

01758 / POP 705

The former fishing post of Abersoch has reinvented itself as a yachtie magnet, and bona fide seaside resort with excellent dining, as well as a surfing hot spot. Abersoch beach gets particularly busy in summer with sun-seeking families, while Porth Ceiriad and Porth Neigwl attract surfers, particularly in springtime.

Sleeping & Eating

Egryn HOTEL $$

(01758-712332; www.egryn.com; Lôn Sarn Bach, LL53 7EE; s/d/ste from £95/119/220;) With tones as muted as its hosts are ebulliently welcoming, this Edwardian house has eight comfortable, modern rooms with marbled en suites and sea views, plus two spacious family suites. Spa breaks, complete with hydrotherapy and salt saunas, can be organised on request with a nearby spa.

★ **Porth Tocyn** HISTORIC HOTEL $$$

(01758-713303; www.porthtocynhotel.co.uk; Bwlchtocyn, LL53 7BU; s/d incl breakfast from £105/168, cottage £200; mid-Mar–Oct;) Near the south end of Abersoch beach and overlooking Cardigan Bay, this country hotel comprises 17 beautifully appointed rooms, all decked out with luxury fabrics and king-sized beds, and a fine restaurant. Families are welcome, with a dedicated children's play area, but if you're looking for luxurious seclusion and solitary walks, consider renting Bwthyn Bach, a beautifully renovated stone cottage.

At the on-site restaurant, open to nonguests, best bets include dependable classics such as pan-fried sea trout with samphire, moules marinière and lamb rump with colcannon mash (mains £17 to £28). Lighter bites are served at lunchtime.

★ **Dining Room** MODERN WELSH $$$

(01758-740709; www.thediningroomabersoch.co.uk; Stryd Fawr, LL53 7DY; 3-course menu £30; 7pm-midnight Wed-Sat, noon-5pm Sun) At Abersoch's most creative dining space, the menu changes daily, depending on what's fresh and in season. Your plate may be graced by ox cheek in a red-wine and rosemary reduction, wood pigeon with black pudding, or hake, seared on the grill. The desserts are inspired, as are the samphire and blood-orange negroni aperitifs. Book ahead.

Getting There & Away

Bus 18 stops on Stryd Fawr (High St), heading to/from Llanbedrog (£1, seven minutes) and Pwllheli (£1.20, 15 to 20 minutes, seven daily Monday to Saturday). To reach Aberdaron, change to bus route 17 at Llanbedrog.

Aberdaron

01758 / POP 956

Overlooking a pebble beach, the squall-battered fishing hamlet of Aberdaron was traditionally the last resting spot of pilgrims before they made the treacherous crossing to Bardsey Island. The little Gwylan Islands, just offshore, are North Wales' most important puffin-breeding site, while hiking across wild country at the end of the peninsula, with its infinite variety of light, stone and seascape, is an experience that stays with you for a long time.

Sights

★Mynydd Mawr HILL

(NT; www.nationaltrust.org.uk; Lon Uwchmynydd) Some 4km west of Aberdaron, the rugged, ethereally beautiful extremity of the Llŷn Peninsula is where medieval pilgrims set off to reach the holy island of Bardsey; one glimpse of their destination, rising out of the gunmetal-grey sea beyond the surf-pounded rocks, hints at the drama of their final voyage. This hill, overlooking Bardsey Sound, is criss-crossed with walking trails, and while the car park at the top fills with day trippers, come dusk, you have the place to yourself.

Sleeping & Eating

Tŷ Newydd HOTEL $$

(01758-760207; www.gwesty-tynewydd.co.uk; r from £120;) The location is the clincher at this homely hotel. Right on the beach, it has comfortably kitted-out, spacious and light-drenched rooms, the pricier ones with wonderful sea views, plus contemporary touches like iPod docks. The tide comes in right under the terraced pub restaurant (mains £13 to £18), which seems designed with an afternoon G&T in mind.

Y Gegin Fawr WELSH $

(The Big Kitchen; 01758-760359; mains £7-10; 10am-5pm Fri-Wed) With their spiritual needs sorted, Bardsey-bound pilgrims could claim a meal at Y Gegin Fawr, a little thick-walled communal kitchen with tiny windows that sits prettily at the heart of Aberdaron. Dating from 1300, it now serves locally caught crab and lobster, homemade cakes and scones, filled jacket potatoes and the like.

Getting There & Away

Buses calling at Aberdaron include eight 17/17B services per day (Monday to Saturday) to Llanbedrog (£1.50, 30 minutes) and Pwllheli (£1.70, 40 minutes). A weekday 8B service to Pwllheli passes through Aberdaron at 2.30pm and continues on to Porthor/Whistling Sands (£1.30, 15 minutes); in the other direction, it runs to Morfa Nefyn at 12.32pm (£1.45, 23 minutes).

Caernarfon

01286 / POP 9859

Wedged between the Menai Strait and Snowdonia's mountains, Caernarfon's main claim to fame is its magnificent castle, one of Edward I's finest fortress masterpieces. The town's crucial historical importance (a key strategic site since the Roman occupation), its heritage railway, excellent dining scene, and its proximity to Snowdonia's best hiking, as well as the Llŷn Peninsula and Anglesey, all add to its appeal. And the tight grid of narrow streets at the town's core, enclosed within medieval stone walls is an absolute joy to wander.

Sights

★Caernarfon Castle CASTLE

(Cadw; www.cadw.gov.wales; adult/child £5.20/3.10; 10am-1pm & 2-5pm Mon-Wed, Sat & Sun;) Majestic Caernarfon Castle was built by Edward I between 1283 and 1330 as a military stronghold, seat of government and royal palace. Designed by Master James of St George, from Savoy, its brief and scale were extraordinary. Today it remains one of the most complete and impressive castles in Britain – you can walk on and through the interconnected walls and towers gathered around the central green, admiring the

OFF THE BEATEN TRACK

PILGRIMAGE TO THE 'ISLAND OF 20,000 SAINTS'

The mysterious **Bardsey Island** (Ynys Enlli), 2 miles off the tip of the Llŷn, is one of many candidates for the Isle of Avalon – the final resting place of King Arthur. Celtic druids believed the island to be holy, and the obscure St Cadfan founded a monastery here in 516, giving shelter to Celts fleeing the Saxon invaders. Medieval pilgrims followed in their wake.

Modern pilgrims to Bardsey are mostly birders and photographers; during the summer around 17,000 Manx shearwaters nest in burrows here. A colony of Atlantic grey seals lives here year-round, and walking trails bisect the island, leading to the 6th-century **carved stones**, the remains of a 13th-century **abbey tower** and a **lighthouse**.

The only way to reach Bardsey is via boat; **Bardsey Boat Trips** (☎07971 769895; www.bardseyboattrips.com; adult/child £35/25) sails from Porth Meudwy, near Aberdaron, and you can choose between day-tripping or staying for a week at the hostel-like lodgings of the **Bardsey Lodge & Bird Observatory** (☎01626-773908; www.bbfo.org.uk; adult/child per week £210/130; ⏲May-Oct).

defensive capabilities of the multiple gates and portcullises of the **King's Gate**.

Sleeping

Totters HOSTEL $

(☎01286-672963; www.totters.co.uk; 2 High St; dm/d £20/48; 📶) Modern, clean and very welcoming, this excellent independent hostel is Caernarfon's best-value sleep. A 14th-century arch gives a sense of history to the communal kitchen in the basement, and continental breakfast is free. There are small dorms and doubles, an attic en-suite double overlooking the sea, a TV room and library.

★**Victoria House** B&B $$

(☎01286-678263; www.victoriahouse.wales; 13 Church St; s/d from £90/110; @📶) This is pretty much the perfect guesthouse – a delightful, solid Victorian building in Caernarfon's old town, run by exceptionally hospitable and attentive hosts. The four spacious, Victorian-style rooms include thoroughly contemporary touches, such as Chromecast. The Balcony Suite, with a private terrace looking across to Anglesey, is well worth the splurge, and breakfast is a joy.

★**Plas Dinas Country House** B&B $$

(☎01286-830214; www.plasdinas.co.uk; A487, Bontnewydd; cottages/r/ste from £109/119/179; P📶) Until the 1980s, this large 17th-century house belonged to Lord Snowdon's family. The ancestral portraits, the grand drawing room and antique furnishings give off the 'historic home' vibe, and the 10 individually decorated rooms range from snug attic luxury (Butlers) to somewhat austere (Major) to exuberantly grand (Princess Margaret suite with four-poster bed). It's 2 miles south of Caernarfon.

Eating

★**Osteria** TUSCAN $$

(☎01286-238050; 26 Hole in the Wall St; mains £12-15; ⏲6-10pm Thu-Sat; 🖉) Two Tuscan partners opened this excellent addition to Caernarfon's dining scene in a compact building hard up against the city walls. Specialising in classic carpaccios and interesting bruschette (try the gorgonzola with walnuts and honey), they import many of their ingredients and wines from Tuscany and prepare daily specials such as stuffed vegetables and pasta with cod and cherry-tomato ragu.

Black Boy Inn PUB FOOD $$

(☎01286-673604; www.black-boy-inn.com; Northgate St; mains £10-18; ⏲noon-9pm; 📶👪) Retaining many original 16th-century features, this charismatic pub consists of a warren of snug rooms, with low, warped roof beams, open fires and Welsh craft beer on tap. Dishes such as the lobscouse (Caernarfon-style beef-shin stew) highlight local meats and seafood, while such satisfying pub-grub staples as the steak and ale pie will gently ease you into a food coma.

Getting There & Away

BUS

Local services from the **bus station** (Pool Side) include 1R/T2 to Porthmadog (50 minutes, five daily) via Criccieth (45 minutes) and Tremadog (45 minutes); hourly 5C to Llandudno (1½ hours) via Bangor (30 minutes) and Conwy (1¼ hours); 12 to Pwllheli (45 minutes, 10 daily); and 88 to Llanberis (30 minutes, four to eight daily). Snowdon Sherpa bus S4 heads to Beddgelert (30 minutes, seven daily Monday to Saturday) via the Snowdon Ranger (22 minutes) and Rhyd Ddu (24 minutes) trailheads.

BICYCLE

Beics Antur (☎01286-802222; www.anturwaunfawr.org; Porth yr Aur, High St; half-/full-day £12/18; ⏲9.30am-5pm Tue-Sat) hires bikes and can advise on local cycle routes. Information on Gwynedd recreational cycle routes can also be found at www.gwynedd.llyw.cymru.

TRAIN

Caernarfon is the **northern terminus** (Arthur St) of the Welsh Highland Railway, which runs to Porthmadog (£40 return, 2½ hours) via Rhyd Ddu (£24 return, one hour) and Beddgelert (£31 return, 1½ hours) from Easter to October, with limited winter service.

Bangor

☎01248 / POP 18,709

Compared to Snowdonia's smaller towns and villages, Bangor is an artsy metropolis, home to the region's best cultural venues: **Storiel** (☎01248-353368; www.storiel.cymru; Ffordd Gwynedd; ⏲11am-5pm Tue-Sat) FREE and **Pontio** (☎01248-383838, box office 01248-382828; www.pontio.co.uk; Deiniol Rd; ⏲8.30am-11pm Mon-Sat, noon-8pm Sun). Dominated by its university, it's a major North Wales transport hub. The **cathedral** (https://bangorcathedral.churchinwales.org.uk; Glanrafon; ⏲10.30am-4.30pm Mon-Thu, to 1pm Fri & Sat), Victorian **pier** (Garth Rd; adult/child 50/20p; ⏲8am-6pm Mon-Sat, 10am-5pm Sun) and nearby castle aside, there's little to detain visitors.

St Deiniol established a monastery here in the 6th century, which grew up into Bangor's sweet little cathedral. Bangor University, founded in 1884, sits on a ridge above town, its neo-Gothic contours aping those of the cathedral. During term time, over 10,000 students swell the city's population, feeding the region's best nightlife.

Sights

★ **Penrhyn Castle** CASTLE

(NT; www.nationaltrust.org.uk/penrhyn-castle; A5, Llandygai; adult/child £10/5; ⏲castle noon-5pm Mar-early Nov, gardens 10am-4pm year-round; P 👪) Funded by the vast profits from the slate mine of Caribbean sugar-plantation owner and anti-abolitionist Baron Penrhyn, and embellished by his great-great-nephew, this immense 19th-century neo-Norman folly pushes the boundaries of good taste. Flanked by a magnificent Victorian walled garden, the creeper-clad stone walls of the Norman 'fortress' embower the neo-Gothic hall with its darkly extravagant rooms,

DON'T MISS

BODNANT ESTATE

Whether you're a lover of gardens or fine food, Bodnant Estate (www.bodnant-estate.co.uk), 4 miles south of Conwy, should not be missed. While many large country estates fell on hard times in the 20th century, the McLaren family kept hold of theirs. The second Baron Aberconway, a keen horticulturist, donated **Bodnant Garden** (NT; ☎01492-650460; www.nationaltrust.org.uk; Ffordd Bodnant, off A470; adult/child £8/4; ⏲9.30am-3.30pm; 👪) to the National Trust in 1949, although the family continues to maintain it on the trust's behalf. Today it's a thriving seat of horticultural beauty, situated in the Conwy Valley. There's an excellent **delicatessen** (☎01492-651931; www.bodnant-welshfood.co.uk; Furnace Farm, Tal-y-Cafn; ⏲farm shop 9.30am-5pm Mon-Sat, 10am-4pm Sun; P) on-site, showcasing the best of regional produce, as well as a **tea room** (☎01492-651100; www.bodnant-welshfood.co.uk/eat/tea-room; Furnace Farm, Tal-y-Cafn; mains £5-8; ⏲9am-5.30pm Mon-Sat, 10am-4.30pm Sun; P 📶) and the smart **Hayloft Restaurant** (☎01492-651102; www.bodnant-welshfood.co.uk; Bodnant Welsh Food, Furnace Farm, Tal-y-Cafn; mains £15-18; ⏲noon-3pm Sun).

carved ceilings, stained-glass windows, opulent furniture and early flushing toilets.

Penrhyn is 1.5 miles east of Bangor; Llandudno-bound buses stop at the gate.

Eating

★Whistlestop on the Pier CAFE $
(07771 231463; Bangor Pier; mains £3.50-5) Don't let its appearance fool you: this humble kiosk halfway along the pier serves the best homemade scuffins (love child of muffin and scone) for miles around. Locals swear by them. If you're particularly hungry, Terry will feed you some moreish seafood chowder or steamed Menai mussels, with crusty homemade bread for mopping up every last drop.

Getting There & Away

BUS

From the local **bus station** (Garth Rd), services include the 5C to Caernarfon (30 minutes, every 30 minutes); X5 to Conwy (40 minutes, every 30 minutes) and Llandudno (one hour); 4H/42A to Menai Bridge (12 minutes, one to two hourly); X4 to Holyhead, 1¾ hours) via Llangefni (40 minutes); 58 to Beaumaris (30 to 45 minutes, six daily); 85/86 to Llanberis (35 to 50 minutes, six daily); 5C/T2 to Caernarfon (25 to 35 minutes, every 30 minutes); and T2 to Porthmadog (1¼ hours, three daily), Dolgellau (two hours, eight daily), Machynlleth (2½ hours, seven daily) and Aberystwyth (3½ hours, seven daily).

TRAIN

Direct services from the **train station** (Holyhead Rd) head to/from Holyhead (£12, 30 to 45 minutes, 12 daily), Rhosneigr (£6.70, 25 minutes, nine daily), Conwy (£6.80, 18 minutes, 14 daily) and London Euston (£96, 3¼ hours).

Conwy

01492 / POP 4863

Sitting on the Conwy estuary, surrounded by medieval stone walls and founded in the 13th century when the existing Cistercian abbey was relocated by Edward I to make way for the magnificent, World Heritage-listed castle, and accessed via a trio of dramatic bridges from the east, the compact town of Conwy, punches above its weight. Its cluster of lesser historic buildings, an attractive waterfront promenade and an abundance of good restaurants and lodgings encourage you to linger longer.

Sights

★Conwy Castle CASTLE
(Cadw; 01492-592358; www.cadw.wales.gov.uk; Castle Sq; adult/concession £8.80/5.40; 9.30am-5pm Mar-Jun, to 6pm Jul & Aug, shorter hours rest of year; P) Caernarfon is more complete, Harlech more dramatically positioned and Beaumaris more technically perfect, yet out of the four castles that compose the Unesco World Heritage Site, Conwy is the most impressive to gaze upon. Exploring the castle's nooks and crannies makes for a superb living-history visit, but best of all, head to the battlements for panoramic views and an overview of Conwy's majestic complexity. Its historic role – to overawe and dominate the subjugated Welsh – couldn't be clearer.

Town Wall HISTORIC BUILDING
(www.cadw.gov.wales; Rose Hill St) FREE The survival of most of its 1300m-long town wall, built concurrently with the castle, makes Conwy one of the UK's prime medieval sites. The 9m-tall wall, punctuated by 21 horseshoe towers, was erected to protect the English colonists from the Welsh, who were forbidden to live in the town and even the surrounding countryside. You can enter the town wall at Rose Hill St and walk along the battlements; the Porth yr Arden to Porth Uchaf section is particularly picturesque.

Plas Mawr HISTORIC BUILDING
(Cadw; www.cadw.gov.wales; High St; adult/child £6.50/3.90; 9.30am-5pm Easter-Sep, to 4pm Oct) Purchased in 1576 by one of the first Welshmen to live in Conwy – Robert Wynn, merchant and diplomat in the royal courts of Europe – Plas Mawr is arguably Britain's finest surviving Elizabethan town house. The discreet whitewashed exterior hides the vivid interior, with its colourful friezes, heraldic devices bearing the initials of the owner, and superb plasterwork that emphasises the noble Wynn dynasty and the owner's descent from the princes of Gwynedd. An exhibition on 16th-century hygiene will raise eyebrows.

Royal Cambrian Academy GALLERY
(01492-593413; www.rcaconwy.org; Crown Lane; 11am-4pm Thu-Sat) FREE Founded in

Conwy

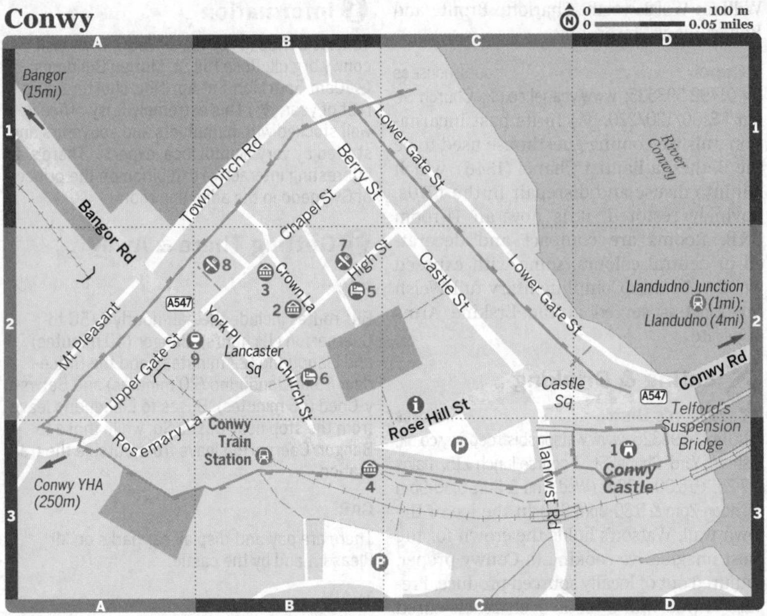

Conwy

Top Sights
1 Conwy Castle ... D3

Sights
2 Plas Mawr ... B2
3 Royal Cambrian Academy ... B2
4 Town Wall ... B3

Sleeping
5 Castle Hotel ... B2
6 Y Capel ... B2

Eating
7 Amelie's ... B2
8 Watson's Bistro ... B2

Drinking & Nightlife
9 Albion ... B2

1881, given the royal imprimatur by Queen Victoria in 1882, and still going strong, the Cambrian runs a full calendar of exhibitions by its members in its twin white-walled galleries, plus visiting shows from the National Museum Wales and elsewhere. Its excellent **Annual Summer Exhibition**, featuring the cream of contemporary fine art in Wales under one roof each August and September, has been a fixture from the academy's early days.

Sleeping

Conwy YHA HOSTEL $
(08453-719732; www.yha.org.uk; Sychnant Pass Rd, Larkhill; dm/d/q £19/59/69; P) Perched on a hill above the town, this former hotel has been converted into a typically utilitarian, minimalist YHA hostel with a fully equipped guest kitchen. Dorms have two or four beds; most of the private rooms have an en-suite bathroom. Head up to the large dining room for awesome mountain and sea views. Wi-fi's in the common areas only.

Castle Hotel HOTEL $$
(01492-582800; www.castlewales.co.uk; High St; s/d/ste from £116/126/183; P) This characterful coaching inn, built on the site of Conwy's vanished Cistercian abbey, has been given a contemporary facelift without sacrificing its history. The bedrooms feature contemporary decor and Bose sound systems, while some boast castle views and free-standing baths, and there's an excellent on-site restaurant. Past guests have included

William Wordsworth, Charlotte Brontë and Robert Louis Stevenson.

Y Capel GUESTHOUSE $$
(☎01492-593535; www.ycapel.co.uk; Church St; s/d/f £100/120/220; 📶) In its past incarnation, this welcoming guesthouse used to be the Bethesda Baptist Chapel (1846), which fell into disuse and disrepair in the 1970s. Lovingly restored, it is now an 11-room B&B. Rooms are compact and decorated in neutral colours, some with exposed wooden beams. Complimentary full Welsh breakfast is served at the Erskine Arms opposite.

Eating & Drinking

★**Watson's Bistro** WELSH $$
(☎01492-596326; www.watsonsbistroconwy.co.uk; Bishop's Yard, Chapel St; 2-course lunch £15, mains £17-25; ⏲5.30-8.30pm Wed, Thu & Sun, 5.30-9pm Fri, noon-2pm & 5.30-9pm Sat) In the lee of the town wall, Watson's holds the crown for the most imaginative cooking in Conwy proper, conjured out of locally sourced produce. Prepare to woo your sweetie over treacle-cured lamb with port and blackberry sauce, or perfectly seared steak with wild mushrooms. Everything is homemade, including the ice cream. An early-bird menu (three courses £25) is served before 6.30pm.

Amelie's FRENCH $$
(☎01492-583142; 10 High St; lunch mains £7-9.50, dinner mains £14-17; ⏲11.30am-2.15pm & 6-9pm Tue-Sat; ✎) Named after the Audrey Tautou film, and as friendly and beguiling as the film's star, this lovely boho bistro serves food that tastes as if it's been prepared by someone who really cares for you. This includes hearty homemade soup and open-faced crayfish sandwiches for lunch, and more substantial dinner mains, such as chicken cassoulet and other international dishes.

★**Albion** PUB
(☎01492-582484; www.albionalehouse.weebly.com; 1-4 Upper Gate St; ⏲noon-11pm Sun-Thu, to midnight Fri & Sat; 📶) Born out of a collaboration between four Welsh craft breweries (Purple Moose, Conwy, Nant and Great Orme), this heritage-listed 1920s boozer is a serious beer-drinker's nirvana. Of the 10 hand pulls, eight are loaded with real ale and two with cider. Winner of multiple Wales and North Wales pub-of-the-year awards, the Albion looks after wine and whisky drinkers, too.

Information

Tourist Office (☎01492-577566; www.visitconwy.org.uk; Rose Hill St, Muriau Buildings; ⏲10am-5pm Mon-Sat Apr-Nov, shorter hours rest of year; 📶) This extremely busy office is well stocked with pamphlets and souvenirs and staffed by very helpful local experts. There's an interesting interactive exhibition on the princes of Gwynedd in the adjoining room.

Getting There & Away

BUS

Bus routes include the half-hourly 5/5C to Caernarfon (1¼ hours), Bangor (40 minutes) and Llandudno (22 minutes), and the thrice-daily 19 to Llandudno (20 minutes) and Betws-y-Coed (45 minutes). Buses to Llandudno leave from the stop near Castle Sq, while those to Bangor/Caernarfon leave from outside the train station.

CAR

There are pay-and-display car parks on Mt Pleasant and by the castle.

TRAIN

From Conwy's **train station** (Rose Hill St) direct services head to/from Holyhead (£17.40, one hour, 11 daily), Rhosneigr (£17.17, 45 minutes), Bangor (£6.80, 20 minutes, 12 daily) and Shrewsbury (£29, two to 2½ hours, six daily).

Llandudno

☎01492 / POP 15,395

When you think of grand Victorian seaside towns of yesteryear, Llandudno, a purpose-built 19th-century resort town, comes to mind. The town is flanked by a sweeping seaside promenade, backed by pastel-coloured hotels and town houses, with holidaymakers strolling past the long, pebbled beach.

Alongside lost-in-time charms of the British seaside (long pier with arcades, Punch and Judy shows), Llandudno's most arresting feature is the near-wilderness of the Great Orme looming above the town, a striking limestone headland offering breathtaking views of Snowdonia and miles of trails.

Sights

★**Great Orme** NATURAL FEATURE
(Y Gogarth) From the top of the vast, windswept limestone plateau known as the Great Orme (Y Gogarth), you get all-encompassing views across the restless Irish Sea, the

Llandudno

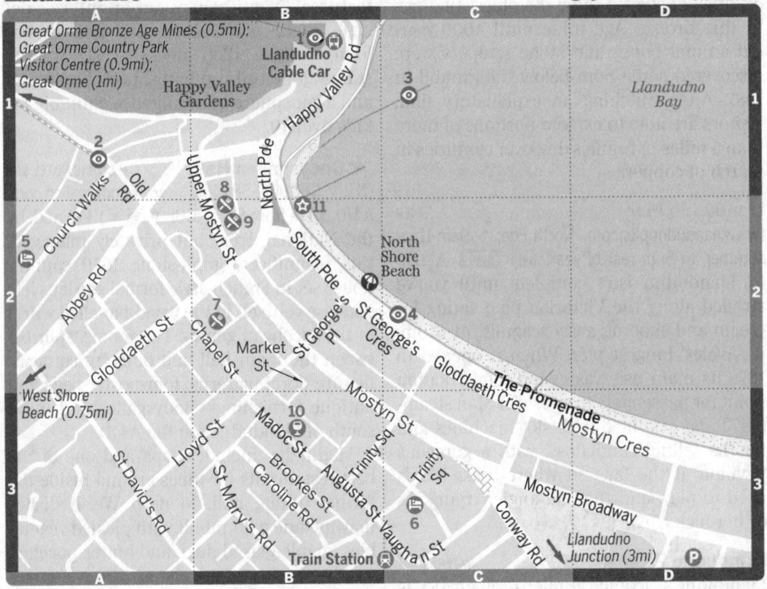

Llandudno

Sights
1 Great Orme Aerial Cable Car.................B1
2 Great Orme Tramway.................A1
3 Llandudno Pier.................C1
4 Llandudno Promenade.................C2

Sleeping
5 Escape B&B.................A2
6 Llandudno Hostel.................C3

Eating
7 Cottage Loaf.................B2
8 Home Cookin'.................B2
9 Johnny Dough's Woodfired Pizza.................B2

Drinking & Nightlife
10 TAPPS Micropub.................B3

Entertainment
11 Professor Codman's Punch & Judy Show.................B2

mountains of the Carneddau range, and Anglesey's shores. Named after an Old Norse word for 'sea serpent', this giant looms over Llandudno. Designated a Site of Special Scientific Interest (SSSI), the headland is home to a cornucopia of flowers, endemic butterflies and seabirds, and is best explored on three waymarked walking trails leading to the summit.

Of the trails, the Haulfre Gardens Trail is the easiest to negotiate. At various points you can find a neolithic burial chamber, a Bronze Age mine, the remains of an Iron Age fort, an ancient church dedicated to Llandudno's namesake, St Tudno, and a herd of around 150 wild Kashmir mountain goats. At the summit there's a cafe, and the Great Orme Country Park Visitor Centre (p749), which has lots of fascinating displays, including a 15-minute video.

Get here by car, on foot, on two wheels or via the **tramway** (☎01492-577877; www.greatormetramway.co.uk; Victoria Station, Church Walks; adult/child return £8.10/5.60; ⊙10am-6pm Easter-Oct) or **cable car** (☎01492-877205; Happy Valley Rd; adult/child return £11/9; ⊙10am-6pm Apr-Oct; P).

Great Orme Bronze Age Mines MINE
(☎01492-870447; www.greatormemines.info; Bishop's Quarry Rd; adult/child £8/5.50; ⊙9.30am-5.30pm mid-Mar–Oct; P) Sitting a short stroll from the Great Orme Tramway's Halfway Station is the largest prehistoric

mine ever discovered. Roman remains were originally believed to be the oldest findings in this Bronze Age mine until 4000-year-old animal bones and stone scrapers were discovered some 60m below the ground in 1987. After watching an explanatory film, visitors are able to explore portions of more than 5 miles of tunnels dug over centuries in search of copper.

Llandudno Pier PIER

(www.llandudnopier.com; North Pde; ⏲9am-11pm summer, to 6pm rest of year; 👪) FREE A trip to Llandudno isn't complete until you've strolled along the Victorian pier, eating ice cream and shooing away seagulls. At 670m, it's Wales' longest pier. When it opened in 1878 its main use was as a disembarkation point for passengers from Isle of Man steamers. Today it's lined with slot machines and booths selling candyfloss, with a gorgeous pavilion at the far end where brass bands used to play, and the odd angler trying his or her luck.

Llandudno Promenade WATERFRONT

Llandudno's iconic 2-mile promenade is one of its distinctive sights. It was here that Queen Victoria herself watched **Professor Codman's Punch & Judy Show** (☎07900-555515; www.punchandjudy.com/codgal.htm; ⏲noon-4pm Sat & Sun year-round, daily school holidays Easter–mid-Sep), performed by the same family since 1860 – let's hope she was amused. Mr Punch's iconic red-and-white-striped tent sits by the entrance to the Victorian pier.

Sleeping

Llandudno Hostel HOSTEL $

(☎01492-877430; www.llandudnohostel.co.uk; 14 Charlton St; dm £25, s/d/f from £39/56/120; P 📶) Staking out the middle ground between hostel and budget B&B, this powder-blue Victorian town house offers tidy rooms, bike storage and a free continental breakfast. It's family run and very family friendly – not the kind of place for booze hounds, but then neither is Llandudno. Kitchen facilities are limited to a microwave and kettle.

★ **Escape B&B** B&B $$

(☎01492-877776; www.escapebandb.co.uk; 48 Church Walks; r from £110; P 📶) 🍃 Escape is the original design B&B in Llandudno, with nine individually styled double bedrooms brimming with boutique-chic ambience and a host of ecofriendly and quirky features. Even if you're not an interior-design geek, you'll love the honesty-bar lounge, Bose iPod docks, DVD library, stand-alone roll-top baths, tasty breakfasts and atmosphere of indulgence. Suitable for kids over 10.

★ **Bodysgallen Hall** HISTORIC HOTEL $$$

(NT; ☎01492-584466; www.bodysgallen.com; A470; r/ste from £275/510; P 📶 🏊) Owned by the National Trust but privately managed, this magnificent pink-stone 1620 country house set in French-style formal gardens lets you lose yourself in the wood-panelled world of the Jacobean gentry. The rooms, split between the main hall and outlying cottages, feature floral patterns, four-poster beds and antique furnishings. Bodysgallen is 3 miles south of Llandudno, on the A470.

Highlights include a spa and one of the best restaurants for miles around inside the formal dining hall. Modern Welsh dishes may include wild rabbit with pickled vegetables, maple-glazed duck and butter-poached sea bass with razor clams (three courses £49). Book ahead and dress nicely.

Eating & Drinking

★ **Cottage Loaf** PUB FOOD $$

(☎01492-870762; www.the-cottageloaf.co.uk; Market St; mains £13-17; ⏲11am-11pm, kitchen noon-9pm; 📶 🐾) Tucked down an alleyway off Mostyn St, this charismatic pub has print-strewn walls, carpeted wooden floors and an atmosphere of genuine bonhomie. On the menu, traditional dishes such as steak-and-Conwy-ale pie mesh with more exotic offerings (try the Goan curry with Conwy mussels), and there are plenty of cask ales and good beers on tap.

Home Cookin' INTERNATIONAL $$

(☎01492-876585; www.homecookin-llandudno.co.uk; 139 Upper Mostyn St; mains £9-16; ⏲10.30am-9.30pm; 🖉) This family-run bistro has won many loyal local fans with, as the name suggests, home cookin' with a flourish. Expect generous platefuls of comfort food, such as smoked haddock and spinach pie, or bangers and mash, at unthreatening prices, prepared with attention to detail and served in stylish surroundings.

Johnny Dough's Woodfired Pizza PIZZA $$

(☎01492-871813; www.johnnydoughs.com; 129 Mostyn St; pizzas £10-11; ⏲noon-9pm; 🖉 👪) There's a lot to love about Johnny's: the inspired combination of superlative wood-fired pizza and the best of regional craft beer, the hit-the-spot cocktails, the cooking classes for kids... Pizza-wise, choose between old-school classics (pepperoni, Hawaiian) and more off-the-wall new-school offerings (Great Orme goats cheese, Peking duck, beetroot pesto) to fill your belly.

TAPPS Micropub CRAFT BEER
(☎01492-870956; www.facebook.com/TAPPS35; 35 Madoc St; ⊙noon-9pm Mon, to 10pm Tue, Wed & Sun, to 11pm Thu-Sat) Their motto is 'No crapp at Tapp' and these guys mean business when it comes to craft beer. Their aim is to support local producers (and select breweries in Cheshire) and you'll find five rotating brews on tap, including the likes of Purple Moose elderflower ale, Crafty Devil coffee milk stout and Brew York 'Rhubarbara Streisand'. Good outdoor seating, too.

Information

Great Orme Country Park Visitor Centre
(☎01492-874151; www.visitconwy.org.uk; Pyllau Rd, Great Orme; ⊙10am-5.30pm Easter-Oct) The visitor centre on the summit of the Great Orme has 3D and interactive displays on the geology, flora and fauna of the area.

Getting There & Away

BUS

Local buses stop at the corner of Mostyn and Gloddaeth Sts. Bus routes include the half-hourly 5/5C to Caernarfon (1½ hours) via Bangor (one hour) and Conwy (22 minutes); and the thrice-daily X19 to Blaenau Ffestiniog (1¼ to 1½ hours) via Betws-y-Coed (50 minutes). Buses run Monday to Saturday.

BICYCLE

Busters Cycles (☎07858 633874; https://family-cyclehire.online; Sunnyvale, Parsons Nose Lane, Kinmel Bay) rents out bicycles, delivered on request to Llandudno and other towns off the A5.

TRAIN

Frequent services head to/from Betws-y-Coed (£6.30, 50 minutes, seven daily), Blaenau Ffestiniog (£8.70, 1½ hours, six daily) and Chester (£19.40, 1¼ hours, five daily); for Holyhead, London Euston, Birmingham New Street and Manchester Piccadilly, change at Llandudno Junction (£2.90, 10 minutes, twice-hourly).

DON'T MISS

ART AT ANGLESEY'S HEART

The linchpin of Anglesey's visual-arts scene, the 'Anglesey Gallery' – or **Oriel Ynys Môn** (☎01248-724444; www.orielmon.org; B5111, Rhosmeirch, Llangefni; ⊙10am-4pm Wed-Sun; P) FREE, as it's properly known – features temporary art exhibitions; a History Gallery exploring the island's past and role in the Roman invasion; licensed cafe Blas Mwy; and children's activity area the Discovery Den. But the main draw is the Oriel Kyffin Williams: exhibits change regularly but always feature some of the gallery's 400-plus works by Sir John 'Kyffin' Williams, a Llangefni boy and prolific artist whose portraits and landscapes provide a unique window into Welsh culture. Find the gallery in Llangefni, 7 miles northeast of Menai Bridge.

ISLE OF ANGLESEY (YNYS MÔN)

At 276 sq miles, the Isle of Anglesey is Wales' largest island. A stronghold of Cymraeg language and culture, it's largely pastoral and mostly flat, compared to neighbouring Snowdonia, with miles of remote coastline, secluded beaches and Wales' greatest concentration of ancient sites. Gastronomy features highly amongst Anglesey's attractions, with some of Wales' most creative dining found here.

Over 85 sq miles of Anglesey – including almost all of its coastline – has been designated an Area of Outstanding Natural Beauty; water sports and hiking the 130-mile Anglesey Coast Path are all key draws. The handsome Georgian town of Beaumaris is Anglesey's most attractive, though Trearddur Bay and Rhosneigr make fine beach bases.

Beaumaris (Biwmares)

POP 1249

Anglesey's most appealing town benefits from a winning combination of a waterfront location on the Menai Strait, with views of Snowdonia's mountains beyond, a formidable castle and handsome Georgian,

DON'T MISS

ANGLESEY'S FOODIE FAVOURITES

Some 4 miles west of Beaumaris, Menai Bridge is home to Anglesey's sole Michelin-starred restaurant, **Sosban & the Old Butchers** (☎01248-208131; www.sosbanandthe oldbutchers.com; Trinity House, 1 High St; 8-course tasting menu £125; ⏱7-11pm Wed-Sat). There's no menu; the husband-and-wife chef team will feed you eight boldly flavoured, contemporary dishes made from fresh North Wales ingredients of the day.

Ten miles southeast of Menai Bridge, off the A4080, **Moch a Môr** (☎01248-440077; www.themarramgrass.com; A4080, Newborough; mains £6.50-13; ⏱8-11am & noon-9pm; P 📶) is the alfresco pop-up incarnation of foodie magnet the Marram Grass. You idle in nooks beneath vine trellises and tuck into dishes made for sharing, from superlative hot dogs and truffle-speckled mac and cheese (with Welsh cheeses) to slow-cooked salt marsh lamb.

Victorian and Edwardian architecture. Some of the houses are extremely old; look for the half-timbered house dating from 1400 on Castle St near the bottom of Church St. Castle aside, it's worth checking out the grim **Beaumaris Gaol** (www.visitanglesey.co.uk; Steeple Lane; adult/child £7/5; ⏱10am-5pm Apr-Oct, to 4pm Mar), the **Old Court House Museum** (Llys Biwmares; www.visitanglesey.co.uk; Castle St; adult/child £4/3; ⏱10.30am-5pm Sat-Thu Apr-Oct), where 'justice' was once dispensed by the English to disadvantaged Welsh, and the ruins of 10th-century Penmon Priory, 4 miles north of Beaumaris. Historical buildings aside, Beaumaris is also the springboard for coastal walks and **Seacoast Safaris** (☎07854 028393; www.seacoastsafaris.co.uk; Alma St, Pier House; ⏱Apr-Oct; 👪) cruises to nearby **Puffin Island** 🍃, a bird sanctuary.

Sights & Activities

★Beaumaris Castle CASTLE
(Cadw; www.cadw.gov.wales; Castle St; adult/child £6.50/3.90; ⏱9.30am-5pm daily Mar-Jun, 10am-1pm & 2-5pm Mon-Wed, Sat & Sun Jul-Oct, shorter hours rest of year) Beyond a water-filled moat, Beaumaris Castle is the last and most technically perfect of the 'iron ring' of fortifications built by Edward I of England to consolidate his subjugation of Wales. Started in 1295, but never completed as fully designed, it enjoys World Heritage status. With its pleasing symmetry, water-filled moat, succession of four concentric 'walls within walls' and stout towers and gatehouse, it was originally connected to the sea from the moat, allowing for efficient delivery of supplies.

Sleeping & Eating

★Bull HISTORIC HOTEL $$
(☎01248-810329; www.bullsheadinn.co.uk; Castle St; d inn/Townhouse from £110/130, ste £166; 📶) These sister properties, the Bull and Townhouse, located across the road from each other, provide quite a contrast. Where the Bull – occupying an ancient coaching inn – is historic and retains original features, such as the heavy wooden beams (we love the suite with roll-top bath), the Townhouse is contemporary, high-tech and design driven. Breakfast is served at the inn.

★Tredici Italian Kitchen ITALIAN $$
(☎01248-811230; www.facebook.com/tredicikitchen; 13 Castle St; mains £14-16; ⏱6-9pm Mon-Wed, noon-9pm Thu, noon-3pm & 6-9pm Fri & Sat) Occupying an intimate 1st-floor dining room above a quality butcher and grocer, Tredici has brought a touch of the Mediterranean to Anglesey. While local produce is used where possible (Halen Môn sea salt perks up the fries, and the mussels are from the Menai Strait), the figs, mozzarella and other pizza toppings and calzone fillings are imported from sunnier climes.

Getting There & Away

Buses stop on Church St. Routes include the dozen 57/58 buses daily (fewer on Sundays) to Menai Bridge (18 minutes) and Bangor (35 to 45 minutes); some 57 and 58 buses continue on to Penmon (10 minutes).

There's a large pay-and-display car park on the waterfront by the castle. There are also free parking spots on the Menai Bridge approach to town, a short walk away.

Holyhead (Caergybi)

01248 / POP 11,864

Unless you're intending to catch a ferry to Ireland, or wish to check out the natural attractions nearby, Anglesey's largest town has little to detain you. However, there are some lovely places to stay and eat at the nearby villages of Trearddur Bay and Rhoscolyn, 2 miles and around 5 miles south, respectively.

Sights

★South Stack Cliffs RSPB Reserve WILDLIFE RESERVE
(01407-762100; www.rspb.org.uk/wales; South Stack Rd; visitor centre 10am-5pm, cafe 10am-3pm;

ANGLESEY'S COASTAL HIGHLIGHTS

Anglesey is a big draw for walkers thanks to the **Isle of Anglesey Coastal Path** (www.angleseycoastalpath.co.uk), a 130-mile coastal walking path with clear, yellow waymarking and spectacular views. Departing from **St Cybi's** (www.holyheadparishchurches.co.uk/st-cybis-church-holyhead; Victoria Rd; hours vary) FREE church in Holyhead, the full trail takes an average of 12 days and passes through a changing landscape of coastal heath, salt marsh, beaches and Wales' largest Area of Outstanding Natural Beauty in its clockwise circumnavigation of the island.

Some of the highlights:

➡ The Holyhead to Porth Swtan section (Day 1) leads you to a tiny smidgeon of a village above a beautiful half-moon bay, with some of the best eating in Anglesey, courtesy of **Wavecrest Cafe** (01407-730650; www.wavecrestcafe.co.uk; Rhyd-wyn; mains £5-10; 10.30am-5pm Thu-Sun, daily summer holidays) and **Lobster Pot** (01407-730241; http://thelobsterpotrestaurant.co.uk; Church Bay; mains £13-25; noon-2.30pm & 4.30-7pm Tue-Sat summer, shorter hours rest of year).

➡ On the Moelfre to Pentraeth stretch (Day 5), it's well worth detouring a little inland, away from the coastal path, to check out the neolithic **Lligwy Burial Chamber** (Siambr Gladdu Lligwy; www.cadw.gov.wales; off A5025; 10am-4pm) FREE and the nearby ruins of the Roman settlement of **Din Lligwy** (Cadw; www.cadw.gov.wales; off A5025; 10am-4pm) FREE.

➡ The Pentraeth to Beaumaris section (Day 6) passes the wide sweep of Red Wharf Bay before detouring to **Penmon Point** (B5109) – Anglesey's easternmost tip – with terrific vistas of Puffin Island (p750) and the Great Orme beyond the gunmetal waters.

➡ En route from Beaumaris to Moel-y-Don (Day 7), don't miss the **Bryn Celli Ddu Burial Chamber** (Cadw; https://cadw.gov.wales/visit/places-to-visit/bryn-celli-ddu-burial-chamber; off A4080; 10am-4pm) FREE, complete with original megalithic carvings, or **Plas Newydd** (NT; 01248-714795; www.nationaltrust.org.uk/plas-newydd-house-and-garden; A4080, Llanfairpwllgwyngyllgogerychwyrndrobwllllantysiliogogogoch; adult/child £12.50/5.80, garden only £8/4; house 11am-4.30pm Mar-early Nov, garden 10.30am-5pm Mar-Oct, 11am-3pm Nov-Feb), the 16th ancestral seat of the marquesses of Anglesey and a Gothic masterpiece.

➡ The Llyn Rhos Ddu to Aberffraw stretch (Day 9) passes through **Newborough Warren** (off A4080, Niwbwrch; seasonal entry £4; P) – dense pine woods that bring you to Abermenai Point, a long, dune-backed, wild beach that borders the 242-hectare woods. Sunsets from the Tŵr Mawr lighthouse on the peninsula here are otherworldly.

➡ On the Abberfraw to Rhosneigr leg (Day 10), **Barclodiad y Gawres** (Cadw; https://cadw.gov.wales/visit/places-to-visit/barclodiad-y-gawres-burial-chamber; off A4080; 10am-4pm) FREE – the largest neolithic tomb in Wales – squats on a headland above gorgeous Trecastle Bay. Inside, it's decorated in spirals and zigzags similar to those found in Ireland's Boyne Valley. Rhosneigr itself is Anglesey's windsurfing and kitesurfing capital.

➡ Arguably the most dramatic walking, from Trearddur to Holyhead (Day 12), is saved for last. Starting from the attractive beach, Trearddur Bay, the walk takes you to the South Stack cliffs and sea-battered lighthouse (p752), before rounding Holyhead mountain.

(P) FREE Two miles west of Holyhead, the sea vents its fury against the vertiginous South Stack Cliffs, an important RSPB reserve where up to 9000 seabirds nest. In May and June, guillemots, razorbills and 15 loved-up puffin couples congregate here, while choughs, fulmars, peregrine falcons and numerous other species may be spotted throughout the year. You can get information, hire binoculars and book guided walks at the visitor centre.

South Stack Lighthouse LIGHTHOUSE
(01407-763900; www.trinityhouse.co.uk; South Stack Rd; adult/child £6/3; 10am-4pm Easter-early Sep) The rocky islet of South Stack (Ynys Lawd) has a gloriously end-of-the-earth feel, with waves crashing around the base of the cliffs and guillemots and razorbills nesting overhead. The trail down to the rickety old bridge anchoring it to Holy Island is not for the faint-hearted, with 400 slippery steps and the promise of a steep return climb. South Stack is 3 miles west of Holyhead along South Stack Rd.

Sleeping & Eating

★Seacroft B&B $$
(01407-860348; www.theseacroft.pub; Ravenspoint Rd, Trearddur Bay; s/d from £67/77; P) There is much to love about this wonderful pub, situated at the southern end of Trearddur Bay's half-moon white-sand beach. Setting aside, there's half a dozen homely rooms upstairs, decked out in soothing neutral shades. Downstairs you can tuck into superlative versions of fish and chips, steak and ale pie and stacked burgers, washed down with award-winning cask ales.

White Eagle GASTROPUB $$
(01407-860267; www.white-eagle.co.uk; Rhoscolyn; mains £12-18; kitchen noon-9pm, bar to 11pm; P) This busy gastropub, with a huge deck and gardens for kids to roam, is *the* place to eat and sample quality beers in this obscure southern corner of Holy Island. The seasonal menu (dry-aged steaks from Pwllheli, mussels from Menai Strait) reflects the pub's relationship with local farmers and producers, the portions are generously pub-sized and the service is friendly.

Getting There & Away

BUS

From the main **bus station** (Summer Hill), destinations include Bangor (route 4R/4B/X4; 1¾ hours, 14 daily Monday to Saturday) via Trearddur (15 minutes) and Menai Bridge (1½ hours); and Cemaes (61; 14 minutes, four daily Monday to Saturday).

FERRY

Two ferry companies, **Irish Ferries** (0818 300 400; www.irishferries.com; foot passenger/motorcycle/car from £33/62/153) and **Stena Line** (08447 707 070; www.stenaline.co.uk; foot passenger/bicycle/car from £33/43/152), offer four daily services to Dublin from the ferry terminal (www.holyheadport.com). Services are sometimes cancelled due to bad weather.

TRAIN

From the **train station** (London Rd), trains head to/from Rhosneigr (£4.40, 10 minutes, 10 daily), Bangor (£9.50, 30 minutes, one to two hourly), Conwy (£15, one to 1¼ hours, 12 daily) and London Euston (£75, 3¾ hours, several daily).

Scotland

EILEAN DONAN CASTLE (P931): NIKIFOROV ALEXANDER/SHUTTERSTOCK ©

Scotland Highlights

1 Orkney (p948) Digging into the islands' beautifully preserved prehistory.

2 Edinburgh (p756) Exploring Scotland's capital, one of the world's most fascinating cities.

3 Loch Lomond (p867) Discovering one of the most scenic parts of Scotland.

4 West Highland Way (p867) Walking the challenging path through some of the country's finest scenery.

5 Ben Nevis (p916) Climbing the highest point in Britain.

6 Glasgow (p800) Enjoying glorious architecture, great nightlife and friendly locals.

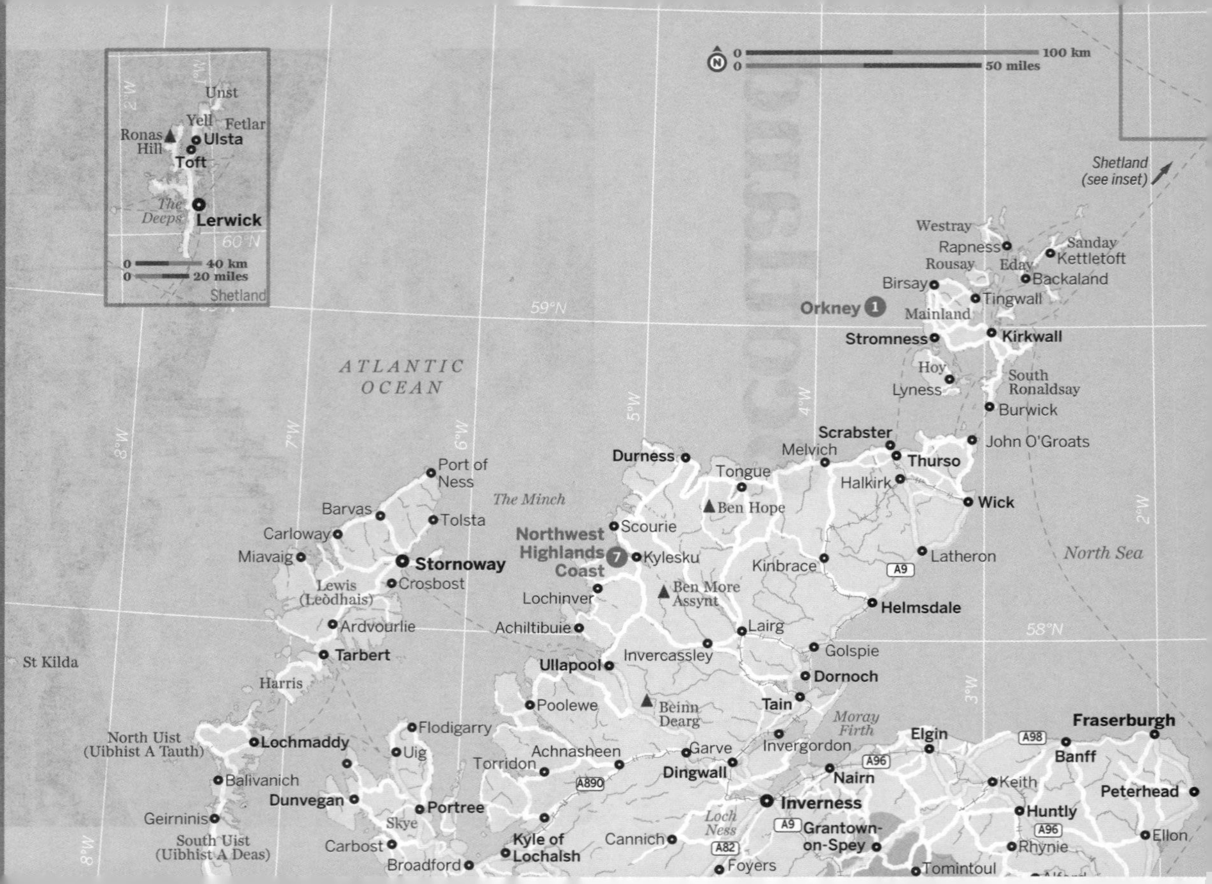

7 Northwest Highlands Coast (p923) Getting permanent jaw-drop from the Highland scenery.

8 Highland Perthshire (p909) Admiring the magnificent forests and lochs.

9 Glen Coe (p913) Uncovering scenic beauty and tragic history.

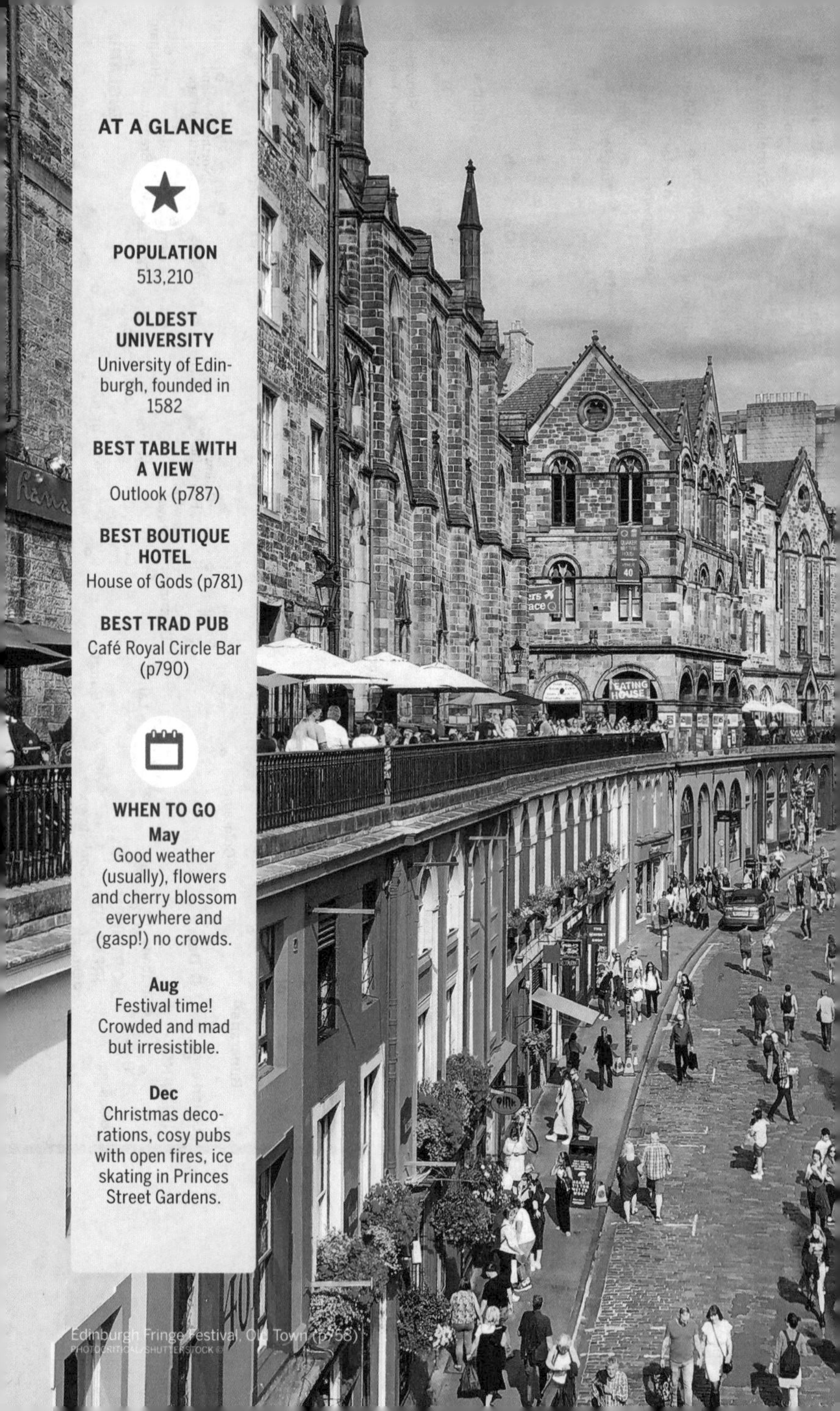

AT A GLANCE

POPULATION
513,210

OLDEST UNIVERSITY
University of Edinburgh, founded in 1582

BEST TABLE WITH A VIEW
Outlook (p787)

BEST BOUTIQUE HOTEL
House of Gods (p781)

BEST TRAD PUB
Café Royal Circle Bar (p790)

WHEN TO GO

May
Good weather (usually), flowers and cherry blossom everywhere and (gasp!) no crowds.

Aug
Festival time! Crowded and mad but irresistible.

Dec
Christmas decorations, cosy pubs with open fires, ice skating in Princes Street Gardens.

Edinburgh Fringe Festival, Old Town (p758)
PHOTOCRITICAL/SHUTTERSTOCK ©

Edinburgh

Edinburgh is a city that begs to be explored. From the vaults and wynds (narrow lanes) that riddle the Old Town to the urban villages of Stockbridge and Cramond, it's filled with quirky, come-hither nooks that tempt you to walk just a little bit further. And every corner turned reveals sudden views and unexpected vistas – green sunlit hills, a glimpse of rustred crags, a blue flash of distant sea.

But there's more to Edinburgh than sightseeing – there are top shops, world-class restaurants and a bacchanalia of bars to enjoy. This is a city of pub crawls and impromptu music sessions, late-night drinking, all-night parties and wandering home through cobbled streets at dawn.

All these superlatives come together at festival time in August, when it seems as if half the world descends on Edinburgh for one enormous party. If you can possibly manage it, join them.

INCLUDES

History

Edinburgh owes its existence to the Castle Rock, the glacier-worn stump of a long-extinct volcano that provided a near-perfect defensive position guarding the coastal route from northeast England into central Scotland.

In the 7th century the Castle Rock was called Dun Eiden (meaning 'Fort on the Hill Slope'). When it was captured by invaders from the kingdom of Northumbria in north-east England in 638, they took the existing Gaelic name 'Eiden' and tacked it onto their own Old English word for fort, 'burh', to create the name Edinburgh.

Originally a purely defensive site, Edinburgh began to expand in the 12th century when King David I held court at the castle and founded the abbey at Holyrood. The royal court came to prefer Edinburgh to Dunfermline and, because parliament followed the king, Edinburgh became Scotland's capital. The city's first effective town wall was constructed around 1450, enclosing the Old Town as far east as Netherbow and south to the Grassmarket. This overcrowded area – by then the most populous town in Scotland – became a medieval Manhattan, forcing its densely packed inhabitants to build upwards instead of outwards, creating tenements five and six storeys high.

The capital played an important role in the Reformation (1560–1690), led by the Calvinist firebrand John Knox. Mary, Queen of Scots held court in the Palace of Holyroodhouse for six brief years, but when her son James VI succeeded to the English throne in 1603 he moved his court to London. The Act of Union in 1707 further reduced Edinburgh's importance.

Nevertheless, cultural and intellectual life flourished during the Scottish Enlightenment (c 1740–1830), and Edinburgh became known as 'a hotbed of genius'. In the second half of the 18th century the New Town was built, and in the 19th century the population quadrupled to 400,000, as suburbs of Victorian tenements spread north and south.

In the 1920s the city's borders expanded again to encompass Leith in the north, Cramond in the west and the Pentland Hills in the south. Following WWII the city's cultural life blossomed, stimulated by the Edinburgh International Festival and its fellow traveller, the Fringe, both held for the first time in 1947 and now recognised as world-class arts festivals.

Edinburgh entered a new era following the 1997 referendum vote in favour of a devolved Scottish parliament, which first convened in 1999 in a controversial modern building at the foot of the Royal Mile. The 2014 independence referendum saw Scots vote to remain part of the United Kingdom.

Sights

Edinburgh's main attractions are concentrated in the city centre – on and around the Old Town's Royal Mile between the castle and Holyrood, and in the New Town. A major exception is the Royal Yacht *Britannia,* which is in the redeveloped docklands district of Leith, 2 miles northeast of the centre.

If you tire of sightseeing, good areas for aimless wandering include the posh suburbs of Stockbridge and Morningside, the pretty riverside village of Cramond and the winding footpaths of Calton Hill and Arthur's Seat.

Old Town

Edinburgh's Old Town is a maze of historic masonry riddled with closes, stairs and wynds leading off the cobbled ravine of the Royal Mile, linking Edinburgh Castle to the Palace of Holyroodhouse. The Old Town tenements support a dwindling city-centre community – many flats have been converted to short-term holiday lets – with the street level crammed with cafes, restaurants, bars, hostels and souvenir shops.

The **Royal Mile** earned its regal nickname in the 16th century when it was used by the king to travel between the castle and the Palace of Holyroodhouse. There are five sections (the Castle Esplanade, Castlehill, Lawnmarket, High St and Canongate), the names of which reflect their historical origins.

★**Edinburgh Castle** CASTLE

(Map p768; ☎0131-225 9846; www.edinburghcastle.scot; Castle Esplanade, EH1 2NG; adult/child £17.50/10.50, audio guide £3.50/1.50; ⏲9.30am-6pm Apr-Sep, to 5pm Oct-Mar, last entry 1hr before closing; 🚌23, 27, 41, 42) Edinburgh Castle has played a pivotal role in Scottish history, both as a royal residence – King Malcolm Canmore (r 1058–93) and Queen Margaret first made their home here in the 11th century – and as a military stronghold. The castle last saw military action in 1745; from then until the 1920s it served as the British army's main base in Scotland. Today it is one

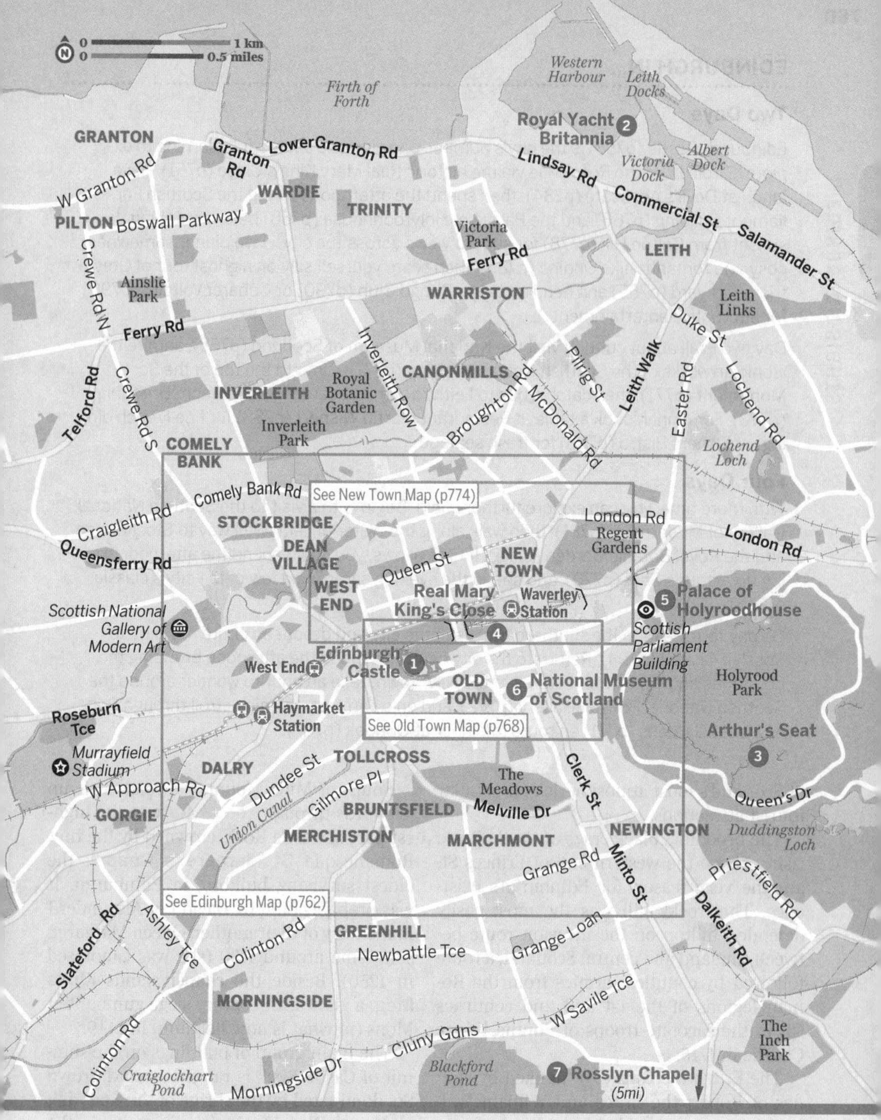

Edinburgh Highlights

1. **Edinburgh Castle** (p758) Admiring city-wide views from Edinburgh's dramatic fortress.
2. **Royal Yacht Britannia** (p773) Stepping on board the Queen's yacht in lively Leith.
3. **Arthur's Seat** (p770) Hiking up an extinct volcano for an unparalleled panorama.
4. **Real Mary King's Close** (p761) Venturing underground to see Edinburgh's hidden secrets.
5. **Palace of Holyroodhouse** (p768) Taking a tour of the city's ostentatious palace.
6. **National Museum of Scotland** (p765) Browsing the collections at Scotland's foremost museum.
7. **Rosslyn Chapel** (p794) Stepping into the real-life inspiration for *The Da Vinci Code*.

EDINBURGH IN...

Two Days

Edinburgh Castle (p758) is the city's number-one sight, so allow a full morning to explore. Stroll down the Royal Mile via the historic Real Mary King's Close (p761). Have lunch at Devil's Advocate (p784), then spend the afternoon touring the Scottish Parliament Building (p766) and the Palace of Holyroodhouse (p768) before watching the sunset from Calton Hill (p778) for superb views across the city. Have dinner somewhere cosy and romantic, like Ondine (p785), then scare yourself silly on a ghost tour of Greyfriars Kirkyard (p765) and head on to the Bongo Club (p790) or Cabaret Voltaire (p790) for alternative entertainment.

Day two is all about culture: visit the National Museum of Scotland (p765), admire the iconic artworks of the Scottish National Gallery (p771), climb to the top of the Scott Monument (p771), then catch a bus to Leith to climb aboard the Royal Yacht Britannia (p773). For dinner, book a table at Restaurant Martin Wishart (p788) for fine French dining, or Fishers Bistro (p788) for fresh seafood.

Four Days

With more time, you can explore further afield. Begin with a visit to the Scottish National Gallery of Modern Art (p781), then walk along the Water of Leith Walkway to Stockbridge and the Royal Botanic Garden (p774). If time allows, you could spend the afternoon hiking up Arthur's Seat (p770), and spend the evening sampling a few of the city's classic pubs (p789).

On day four, head to the southern fringes of the city and devote an entire morning to Rosslyn Chapel (p794). Return to the city centre to spend the afternoon browsing the boutiques and department stores of the New Town. Take an hour to wander around the Scottish National Portrait Gallery (p772), and enjoy an early-evening stroll through Princes Street Gardens (p771) en route to dinner at Outlook (p787).

of Scotland's most atmospheric and popular tourist attractions.

The brooding, black crags of Castle Rock, rising above the western end of Princes St, are the very reason for Edinburgh's existence. This rocky hill was the most easily defended hilltop on the invasion route between England and central Scotland, a route followed by countless armies from the Roman legions of the 1st and 2nd centuries CE to the Jacobite troops of Bonnie Prince Charlie in 1745.

The **Entrance Gateway**, flanked by statues of Robert the Bruce and William Wallace, opens to a cobbled lane that leads up beneath the 16th-century **Portcullis Gate** to the cannons ranged along the Argyle and Mills Mount Batteries. The battlements here have great views over the New Town to the Firth of Forth.

At the far end of Mills Mount Battery is the famous **One O'Clock Gun**, where crowds gather to watch a gleaming WWII 25-pounder fire an ear-splitting time signal at exactly 1pm (every day except Sundays, Christmas Day and Good Friday).

South of Mills Mount, the road curls up leftwards through **Foog's Gate** to the highest part of Castle Rock, crowned by the tiny, Romanesque **St Margaret's Chapel**, the oldest surviving building in Edinburgh. It was probably built by David I or Alexander I in memory of their mother, Queen Margaret, sometime around 1130 (she was canonised in 1250). Beside the chapel stands **Mons Meg**, a giant 15th-century siege gun built at Mons (in what is now Belgium) in 1449.

The main group of buildings on the summit of Castle Rock is ranged around Crown Sq, dominated by the shrine of the **Scottish National War Memorial**. Opposite is the Great Hall, built for James IV (r 1488–1513) as a ceremonial hall and used as a meeting place for the Scottish parliament until 1639. Its most remarkable feature is the original, 16th-century hammer-beam roof.

The **Castle Vaults** beneath the Great Hall (entered via the **Prisons of War Exhibition**) were used variously as storerooms, bakeries and a prison. The vaults have been renovated to resemble 18th- and early 19th-century prisons, where graffiti carved by French and

American prisoners can be seen on the ancient wooden doors.

On the eastern side of the square is the **Royal Palace**, built during the 15th and 16th centuries, where a series of historical tableaux leads to the highlight of the castle: a strongroom housing the **Honours of Scotland** (the Scottish crown jewels), among the oldest surviving crown jewels in Europe. Locked away in a chest following the Act of Union in 1707, the crown (made in 1540 from the gold of Robert the Bruce's 14th-century coronet), sword and sceptre lay forgotten until they were unearthed at the instigation of novelist Sir Walter Scott in 1818. Also on display here is the Stone of Destiny (p772).

Among the neighbouring **Royal Apartments** is the bedchamber where Mary, Queen of Scots, gave birth to her son James VI, who was to unite the crowns of Scotland and England in 1603.

★Real Mary King's Close HISTORIC BUILDING

(Map p768; ☎0131-225 0672; www.realmarykingsclose.com; 2 Warriston's Close, EH1 1PG; adult/child £17.95/11.25; ⌚hours vary, approx 9.30am-9pm Apr-Oct, 10am-5.30pm Nov-Mar; 🚌23, 27, 41, 42) Edinburgh's 18th-century City Chambers were built over the sealed-off remains of Mary King's Close, and the lower levels of this medieval Old Town alley have survived almost unchanged amid the foundations for 250 years. Now open to the public, this spooky, subterranean labyrinth gives a fascinating insight into the everyday life of 17th-century Edinburgh. Costumed characters lead tours through a 16th-century town house and the plague-stricken home of a 17th-century gravedigger. Advance booking is recommended; check hours online.

The scripted tour, complete with ghostly tales and gruesome tableaux, can seem a little naff, milking the scary and scatological aspects of the close's history for all they're worth. But there are also things of genuine interest to see: there's something about the crumbling 17th-century **tenement room** that makes the hair rise on the back of your neck, with tufts of horsehair poking from collapsing lath-and-plaster walls that bear the ghost of a pattern, and the ancient smell of stone and dust thick in your nostrils.

In one of the former bedrooms off the close, a psychic once claimed to have been approached by the ghost of a little girl called Annie. It's hard to tell what's more frightening – the story of the ghostly child, or the bizarre heap of tiny dolls and teddies left by sympathetic visitors.

National War Museum of Scotland MUSEUM

(Map p768; www.nms.ac.uk/national-war-museum; EH1 2NG; incl in Edinburgh Castle entry; ⌚9.45am-5.45pm Apr-Oct, to 4.45pm Nov-Mar; 🚌23, 27, 41, 42) At the western end of Edinburgh Castle (p758), to the left of the castle tearooms, a road leads down to the National War Museum of Scotland, which brings Scotland's military history vividly to life. The exhibits have been personalised by telling the stories of the original owners of the objects on display, making it easier to empathise with the experiences of war than any dry display of dusty weaponry ever could.

Gladstone's Land HISTORIC BUILDING

(NTS; Map p768; ☎0131-226 5856; www.nts.org.uk; 477 Lawnmarket, EH1 2NT; 🚌23, 27, 41, 42) One of Edinburgh's most prominent 17th-century merchants was Thomas Gledstanes, who in 1617 purchased the tenement later known as Gladstone's Land. It contains fine painted ceilings, walls and beams, and some splendid furniture from the 17th and 18th centuries. The building has undergone a major refurbishment, scheduled to reopen by summer 2021 with a traditional ice-cream parlour on street level, exhibitions on the middle floors, and holiday apartments on the upper floors.

Writers' Museum MUSEUM

(Map p768; ☎0131-529 4901; www.edinburghmuseums.org.uk; Lady Stair's Close, EH! 2PA; ⌚10am-5pm; 🚌23, 27, 41, 42) FREE Tucked down a close between the Royal Mile and the Mound you'll find Lady Stair's House (1622), home to this museum that contains manuscripts and memorabilia belonging to three of Scotland's most famous writers: Robert Burns, Sir Walter Scott and Robert Louis Stevenson.

St Giles Cathedral CHURCH

(Map p768; www.stgilescathedral.org.uk; High St, EH1 1RE; ⌚9am-7pm Mon-Fri, to 5pm Sat, 1-5pm Sun Apr-Oct, 9am-5pm Mon-Sat, 1-5pm Sun Nov-Mar; 🚌23, 27, 41, 42) FREE The great grey bulk of St Giles Cathedral dates largely from the 15th century, but much of it was restored in the 19th century. One of the most interesting corners of the kirk is the **Thistle Chapel**, built in 1911 for the Knights of the Most Ancient & Most Noble Order of the Thistle. The elaborately carved Gothic-style stalls

Edinburgh

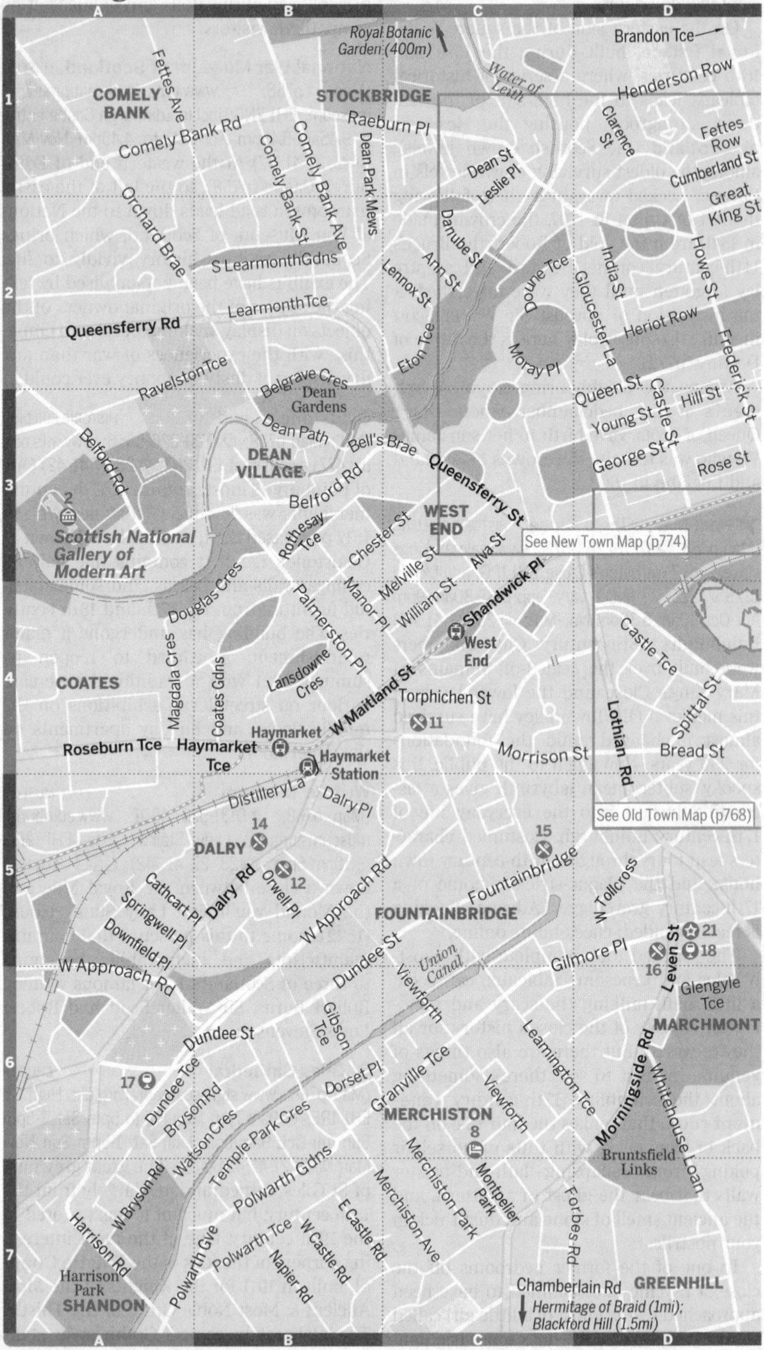

A
B
C
D
1
2
3
4
5
6
7
Royal Botanic Garden (400m)
Brandon Tce
Water of Leith
Henderson Row
COMELY BANK
STOCKBRIDGE
Fettes Ave
Comely Bank Rd
Raeburn Pl
Clarence St
Fettes Row
Cumberland St
Great King St
Comely Bank St
Comely Bank Ave
Dean Park Mews
Dean St
Leslie Pl
Orchard Brae
Danube St
S Learmonth Gdns
Ann St
Lennox St
Doune Tce
Gloucester La
India St
Howe St
Learmonth Tce
Queensferry Rd
Heriot Row
Eton Tce
Moray Pl
Frederick St
Ravelston Tce
Belgrave Cres
Dean Gardens
Queen St
Castle St
Hill St
Young St
Dean Path
Belford Rd
Bell's Brae
DEAN VILLAGE
Queensferry St
George St
Rose St
Belford Rd
2
Scottish National Gallery of Modern Art
Rothesay Tce
Chester St
WEST END
See New Town Map (p774)
Alva St
Melville St
Douglas Cres
Manor Pl
Palmerston Pl
William St
Shandwick Pl
West End
Castle Tce
Magdala Cres
Coates Gdns
Lansdowne Cres
W Maitland St
COATES
Torphichen St
Spittal St
11
Lothian Rd
Haymarket
Roseburn Tce
Haymarket Tce
Haymarket Station
Morrison St
Bread St
Distillery La
Dalry Pl
See Old Town Map (p768)
14
DALRY
15
Fountainbridge
Cathcart Pl
Dalry Rd
Orwell Pl
12
W Approach Rd
W Tollcross
Springwell Pl
FOUNTAINBRIDGE
Downfield Pl
21
Leven St
18
Dundee St
Union Canal
Gilmore Pl
16
W Approach Rd
Viewforth
Glengyle Tce
Gibson Tce
MARCHMONT
Dundee St
Leamington Tce
Morningside Rd
17
Dundee Tce
Dorset Pl
Granville Tce
Bryson Rd
Watson Cres
Temple Park Cres
MERCHISTON
Viewforth
Whitehouse Loan
8
Bruntsfield Links
Polwarth Gdns
Merchiston Park
Montpelier Park
W Bryson Rd
Merchiston Ave
Forbes Rd
Harrison Rd
E Castle Rd
Polwarth Tce
W Castle Rd
Polwarth Gve
Napier Rd
Harrison Park
SHANDON
Chamberlain Rd
GREENHILL
Hermitage of Braid (1mi); Blackford Hill (1.5mi)

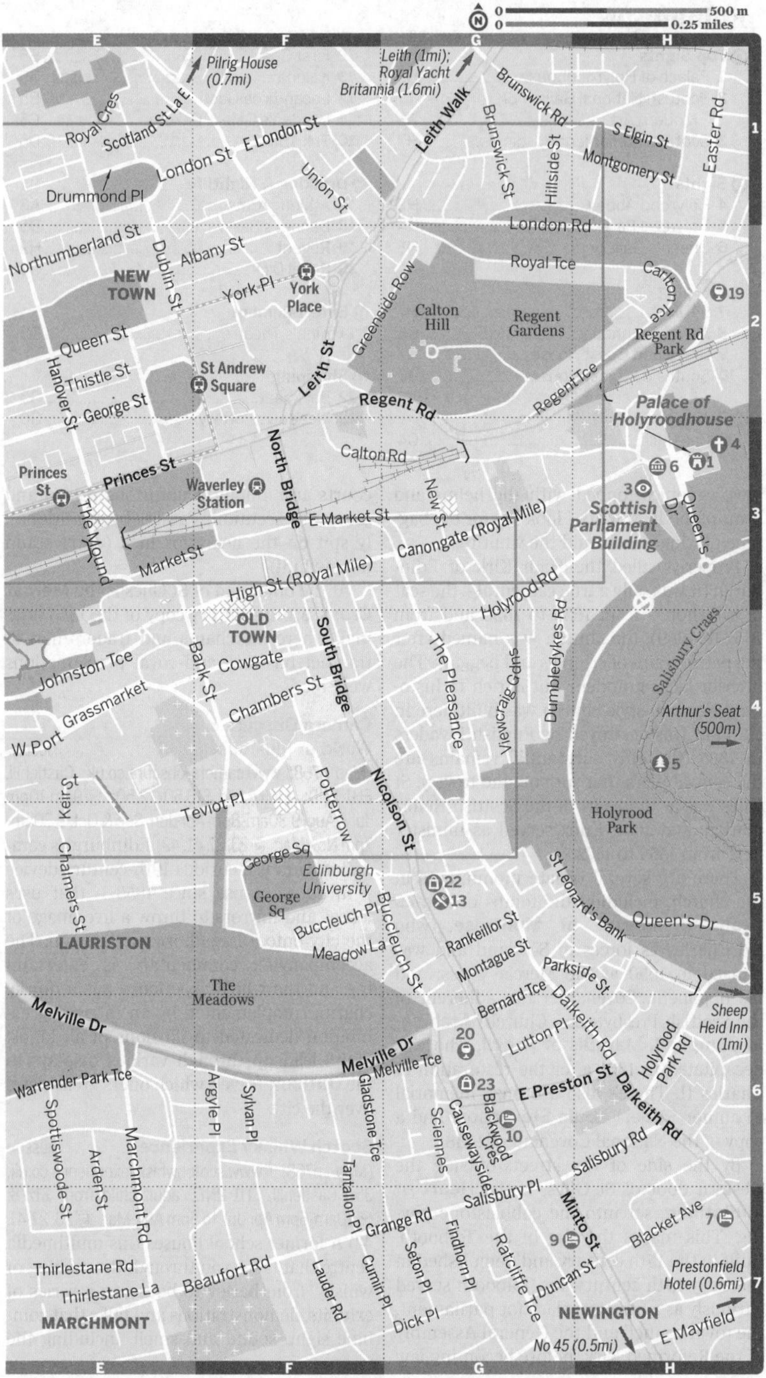

0 500 m
0 0.25 miles
E
F
G
H
1
2
3
4
5
6
7
Pilrig House (0.7mi)
Leith (1mi); Royal Yacht Britannia (1.6mi)
Brunswick Rd
Royal Cres
Scotland St La E
London St
E London St
Leith Walk
Brunswick St
Hillside St
S Elgin St
Montgomery St
Easter Rd
Drummond Pl
Union St
London Rd
Northumberland St
Dublin St
Albany St
Royal Tce
Carlton Tce
NEW TOWN
York Pl
York Place
Greenside Row
Calton Hill
Regent Gardens
Regent Rd Park
Queen St
Hanover St
Thistle St
George St
St Andrew Square
Leith St
Regent Rd
Regent Tce
Palace of Holyroodhouse
Calton Rd
4
6
1
Princes St
Princes St
Waverley Station
North Bridge
New St
3
Scottish Parliament Building
Queen's Dr
The Mound
E Market St
Canongate (Royal Mile)
Market St
High St (Royal Mile)
Holyrood Rd
OLD TOWN
Johnston Tce
Bank St
Cowgate
South Bridge
The Pleasance
Viewcraig Gdns
Dumbiedykes Rd
Salisbury Crags
Grassmarket
Chambers St
Arthur's Seat (500m)
W Port
5
Keir St
Teviot Pl
Potterrow
Nicolson St
Holyrood Park
Chalmers St
George Sq
Edinburgh University
22
13
St Leonard's Bank
George Sq
Buccleuch Pl
Buccleuch St
Rankeillor St
Queen's Dr
LAURISTON
Meadow La
Montague St
Parkside St
The Meadows
Bernard Tce
Dalkeith Rd
Sheep Heid Inn (1mi)
Melville Dr
20
Lutton Pl
Holyrood Park Rd
Melville Dr
Melville Tce
23
E Preston St
Dalkeith Rd
Warrender Park Tce
Argyle Pl
Sylvan Pl
Gladstone Tce
Sciennes
Causewayside
Blackwood Cres
10
Spottiswoode St
Arden St
Marchmont Rd
Salisbury Rd
Tantallon Pl
Salisbury Pl
Minto St
Grange Rd
Findhorn Pl
Blacket Ave
7
Seton Pl
Ratcliffe Tce
9
Thirlestane Rd
Cumin Pl
Lauder Rd
Prestonfield Hotel (0.6mi)
Beaufort Rd
Duncan St
Thirlestane La
Dick Pl
MARCHMONT
NEWINGTON
E Mayfield
No 45 (0.5mi)
19

Edinburgh

Top Sights
1 Palace of Holyroodhouse......H3
2 Scottish National Gallery of Modern Art......A3
3 Scottish Parliament Building......H3

Sights
4 Holyrood Abbey......H3
5 Holyrood Park......H4
6 Queen's Gallery......H3

Sleeping
7 94DR......H7
8 Albyn Townhouse......C6
9 Sherwood Guest House......G7
10 Southside Guest House......G6

Eating
11 Cafe Milk......C4
12 First Coast......B5
13 Kalpna......G5
14 Locanda de Gusti......B5
15 Loudon's Café & Bakery......C5
16 Tuk Tuk......D5

Drinking & Nightlife
17 Athletic Arms......A6
18 Bennet's Bar......D5
19 Regent......H2
20 Royal Dick......G6

Entertainment
21 King's Theatre......D5

Shopping
22 Backbeat......G5
23 Meadows Pottery......G6

have canopies topped with the helms and arms of the 16 knights – look out for the bagpipe-playing angel amid the vaulting.

Properly called the High Kirk of Edinburgh (it was only a true cathedral – the seat of a bishop – from 1633 to 1638 and from 1661 to 1689), the church was named after the patron saint of cripples and beggars. The interior lacks grandeur but is rich in history: a Norman-style church was built here in 1126 but was destroyed by English invaders in 1385 (the only substantial remains are the central piers that support the tower). St Giles was at the heart of the Scottish Reformation, and John Knox served as minister here from 1559 to 1572.

There are several ornate monuments in the church, including the tombs of **James Graham, Marquis of Montrose**, who led Charles I's forces in Scotland and was hanged in 1650 at the Mercat Cross; and his opponent, Covenanter (an adherent of the Scottish Presbyterian Church) **Archibald Campbell, Marquis of Argyll**, who was decapitated in 1661 after the restoration of Charles II. There's also a bronze memorial to author **Robert Louis Stevenson**, and a copy of the National Covenant of 1638.

By the side of the street, outside the western door of St Giles, is the **Heart of Midlothian**, set into the cobblestone paving. This marks the site of the Tolbooth. Built in the 15th century and demolished in the early 19th century, the Tolbooth served variously as a meeting place for parliament, the town council and the General Assembly of the Reformed Kirk, before becoming law courts and, finally, a notorious prison and place of execution. Passers-by traditionally spit on the heart for luck (don't stand downwind!).

At the other end of St Giles is the **Mercat Cross**, a 19th-century copy of the 1365 original, where merchants and traders met to transact business and royal proclamations were read.

Camera Obscura & World of Illusions — MUSEUM

(Map p768; www.camera-obscura.co.uk; Castlehill, EH1 2ND; adult/child £16.50/12.50; 9am-10pm Jul & Aug, 9.30am-8pm Apr-Jun, Sep & Oct, 9.30am-7pm Nov-Mar; 23, 27, 41, 42) Edinburgh's camera obscura is a curious 19th-century device – in constant use since 1853 – that uses lenses and mirrors to throw a live image of the city onto a large horizontal screen. The accompanying commentary is entertaining and the whole experience has a quirky charm, complemented by an intriguing exhibition dedicated to illusions of all kinds. Stairs lead up through various displays to the **Outlook Tower**, which offers great views over the city.

Scotch Whisky Experience — MUSEUM

(Map p768; www.scotchwhiskyexperience.co.uk; 354 Castlehill, EH1 2NE; adult/child from £17/8; 10am-6pm Apr-Jul, to 5pm Aug-Mar; 23, 27, 41, 42) A former school houses this multimedia centre that takes you through the making of whisky, from barley to bottle, in a series of exhibits, demonstrations and talks that combine sight, sound and smell, including the world's largest collection of malt whiskies (3384 bottles!). The pricier tours include extensive whisky tastings and samples of Scottish cuisine. There's also a restaurant (p785) that serves traditional Scottish dishes with, where possible, a dash of whisky thrown in.

Museum of Edinburgh MUSEUM
(Map p768; ☎0131-529 4143; www.edinburghmuseums.org.uk; 142 Canongate, EH8 8DD; ⏲10am-5pm Mon & Thu-Sat, noon-5pm Sun; 🚌300) FREE You can't miss the colourful facade of Huntly House (it featured in Season 3 of the TV series *Outlander*), opposite the Tolbooth clock on the Royal Mile. Built in 1570, it houses a museum covering Edinburgh from prehistory to the present. Exhibits of national importance include an original copy of the National Covenant of 1638, but the big crowd-pleaser is the dog collar and feeding bowl that once belonged to Greyfriars Bobby (p766), the city's most famous canine citizen.

Dunbar's Close Garden GARDENS
(Map p774; Canongate, EH8 8BW; ⏲7am-7.30pm Jun-Aug, to 5.30pm May & Sep, to 4.30pm Apr & Oct, to 3.30pm Nov-Mar; 🚌35) Tucked away at the end of an Old Town close, this walled garden has been laid out in 17th-century style, with gravel paths, neatly trimmed shrubs, herbs, flowers and mature trees. It's a hidden oasis of tranquillity amid the bustle of the Royal Mile.

South of the Royal Mile

★**National Museum of Scotland** MUSEUM
(Map p768; ☎0300 123 6789; www.nms.ac.uk/national-museum-of-scotland; Chambers St, EH1 1JF; ⏲10am-5pm; 👪; 🚌35, 45) FREE Elegant Chambers St is dominated by the long facade of the National Museum of Scotland. Its extensive collections are spread between two buildings: one modern, one Victorian – the golden stone and striking architecture of the new building (1998) make it one of the city's most distinctive landmarks. The museum's five floors trace the history of Scotland from geological beginnings to the present, with many imaginative and stimulating exhibits. Audio guides are available in several languages. Fees apply for special exhibitions.

The modern building connects with the original Victorian museum, dating from 1861, the stolid, grey exterior of which gives way to a beautifully bright and airy, glass-roofed exhibition hall. The old building houses an eclectic collection covering natural history, archaeology, design and fashion, science and technology, and the decorative arts of ancient Egypt, the Islamic world, China, Japan, Korea and the West.

Grassmarket STREET
(Map p768; 🚌2) The site of a cattle market from the 15th century until the start of the 20th century, the Grassmarket has always been a focal point of the Old Town. It was once the city's main place of execution, and over 100 martyred Covenanters are commemorated by a monument at the eastern end, where the gallows used to stand. The notorious murderers Burke and Hare (p780) operated from a now-vanished close off the western end.

Nowadays the broad, open square, lined by tall tenements and dominated by the looming castle, has many lively pubs and restaurants, including the **White Hart Inn** (Map p768; ☎0131-226 2806; www.whitehart-edinburgh.co.uk; 34 Grassmarket, EH1 2JU; ⏲11am-midnight Sun-Thu, to 1am Fri & Sat; 🚌2), which was once patronised by Robert Burns. Claiming to be the city's oldest pub in continuous use (since 1516), it also hosted William Wordsworth in 1803. **Cowgate** – the long, dark ravine leading eastwards from the Grassmarket – was once the road along which cattle were driven from the pastures around Arthur's Seat to the safety of the city walls. Today it is the heart of Edinburgh's nightlife, with around two dozen clubs and bars within five minutes' walk of each other.

Greyfriars Kirkyard CEMETERY
(Map p768; www.greyfriarskirk.com; Candlemaker Row, EH1 2QQ; ⏲24hr; 🚌2, 23, 27, 35, 41, 42, 45) Greyfriars Kirkyard is one of Edinburgh's most evocative cemeteries, a peaceful green oasis dotted with elaborate monuments. Many famous Edinburgh names are buried here, including poet Allan Ramsay (1686–1758); architect William Adam (1689–1748); and William Smellie (1740–95), editor of the first edition of the *Encyclopaedia Britannica*. If you want to experience the graveyard at its scariest – inside a burial vault, in the dark, at night – go on a City of the Dead (p777) guided tour.

A more recent addition to the graveyard's reputation is the idea that it is the resting place of JK Rowling's famous villain

Voldemort. Rowling is said to have been inspired to create the dark lord by the grave of 19th-century gentleman Thomas Riddell, who died in 1806 aged 72.

Greyfriars Bobby Statue MONUMENT

(Map p768; cnr George IV Bridge & Candlemaker Row, EH1 2QQ; 2, 23, 27, 35, 41, 42, 45) Probably the most popular photo opportunity in Edinburgh, the life-size statue of Greyfriars Bobby, a Skye terrier who captured the hearts of the British public in the late 19th century, stands outside Greyfriars Kirkyard (p765). From 1858 to 1872 the wee dog maintained a vigil over the grave of his master, an Edinburgh police officer. The story was immortalised in a novel by Eleanor Atkinson in 1912, and in 1961 was made into a movie by – who else? – Walt Disney.

The statue is always surrounded by crowds of visitors taking photos of themselves posing beside the little dog. Bobby's own grave, marked by a small, pink-granite stone, is just inside the entrance to Greyfriars Kirkyard, behind the monument, and you can see his original collar and bowl in the Museum of Edinburgh (p765).

Holyrood & Arthur's Seat

★Scottish Parliament Building NOTABLE BUILDING

(Map p762; 0131-348 5200; www.parliament.scot; Horse Wynd, EH99 1SP; 9am-6.30pm Tue-Thu, 10am-5pm Mon, Fri & Sat in session, 10am-5pm Tue-Thu in recess; ; 35) FREE The Scottish Parliament Building, designed by Catalan architect Enric Miralles (1955–2000), was opened by the Queen in October 2004. The ground plan of the complex is said to represent a 'flower of democracy rooted in Scottish soil' (best seen looking down from Salisbury Crags). Free, one-hour tours (advance bookings recommended) include visits to the Debating Chamber, a committee room, the Garden Lobby and the office of a member of parliament (MSP).

Miralles believed that a building could be a work of art. However, this weird concrete confection at the foot of Salisbury Crags initially left the good people of Edinburgh scratching their heads in confusion. What does it all mean? The strange forms of the exterior are each symbolic in some way, from the oddly shaped windows on the western wall (inspired by the silhouette of *The Reverend Robert Walker Skating on Duddingston Loch*, one of Scotland's most

Walking Tour Old Town Alleys

START CASTLE ESPLANADE
END COCKBURN ST
LENGTH 1 MILE; ONE TO TWO HOURS

This walk explores the alleys and side streets around the Royal Mile, and involves a bit of climbing up and down steep stairs.

Begin on the 1 **Castle Esplanade**, which provides a grandstand view south over the Grassmarket; the prominent quadrangular building with all the turrets is George Heriot's School. Head towards Castlehill and the start of the Royal Mile.

The 17th-century house on the right is known as 2 **Cannonball House** because of the iron ball lodged in the wall (look between, and slightly below, the two largest windows on the wall facing the castle). The ball was not fired in anger but marks the gravitation height to which water would flow naturally from the city's first piped water supply.

The low, rectangular building across the street (now a touristy tartan-weaving mill) was originally the reservoir that held the Old Town's water supply. On its western wall is the 3 **Witches Well**, where a bronze fountain commemorates around 4000 people (mostly women) who were executed between 1479 and 1722 on suspicion of witchcraft.

Go past the reservoir and turn left down Ramsay Lane. Take a look at 4 **Ramsay Garden** – one of Edinburgh's most desirable addresses – where late-19th-century apartments were built around the octagonal Ramsay Lodge, once home to poet Allan Ramsay. The cobbled street continues around to the right below student residences to the towers of the 5 **New College**, home to Edinburgh University's Faculty of Divinity. Nip into the courtyard to see the statue of John Knox (a firebrand preacher who led the Protestant Reformation in Scotland, and was instrumental in the creation of the Church of Scotland in 1560).

Just past New College, turn right and climb the stairs into Milne's Court, a student residence belonging to Edinburgh University. Exit into Lawnmarket, cross the street (bearing slightly left) and duck

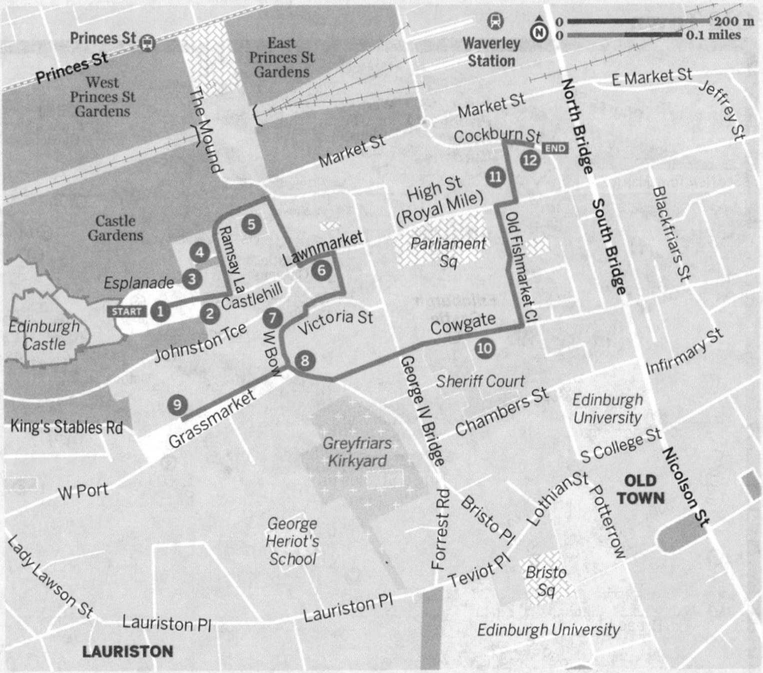

into 6 **Riddell's Court**, a restored Old Town close at No 322–8. You'll find yourself in a small courtyard, but the house in front of you (built in 1590) was originally the edge of the street (the building you just walked under was added in 1726 – look for the date inscribed on the doorway on the right). The arch with the inscription *Vivendo discimus* (We live and learn) leads into the original 16th-century courtyard.

Go back into the street, turn right and right again down Fisher's Close, which leads to the delightful Victoria Tce, strung above the cobbled curve of shop-lined Victoria St. Wander right, enjoying the view – 7 **Maxie's Bistro** (p785), at the far end of the terrace, is a great place to stop for a drink – then descend the stairs at the foot of Upper Bow and continue downhill to the Grassmarket. At the eastern end, outside Maggie Dickson's pub, is the 8 **Covenanters Monument**, which marks the site of the gallows where more than 100 Covenanters were martyred in the 17th century.

If you're feeling peckish, the Grassmarket has several good places to eat and a couple of good pubs – poet Robert Burns once stayed at the 9 **White Hart Inn** (p765). Head east along the gloomy defile of the Cowgate, passing under the arch of George IV Bridge – the buildings to your right are the law courts, while high up to the left you can see the complex of buildings behind Parliament Sq. Past the courts, on the right, is 10 **Tailors Hall** (built 1621, extended 1757), now a hotel and bar but formerly the meeting place of the Companie of Tailzeours (Tailors' Guild).

Turn left and climb steeply up Old Fishmarket Close, a typical cobbled Old Town wynd, and emerge once more onto the Royal Mile. Across the street and slightly downhill is 11 **Anchor Close**, named for a tavern that once stood there. It hosted the Crochallan Fencibles, an 18th-century drinking club that provided its patrons with an agreeable blend of intellectual debate and intoxicating liquor. The club was founded by William Smellie, editor of the 1st edition of the *Encyclopedia Britannica;* Burns was its best-known member.

Go down Anchor Close to finish the walk on 12 **Cockburn St**, one of the city's coolest shopping streets, lined with gift shops and clothing boutiques. The street was cut through Old Town tenements in the 1850s to provide an easy route between Waverley station and the Royal Mile.

Old Town

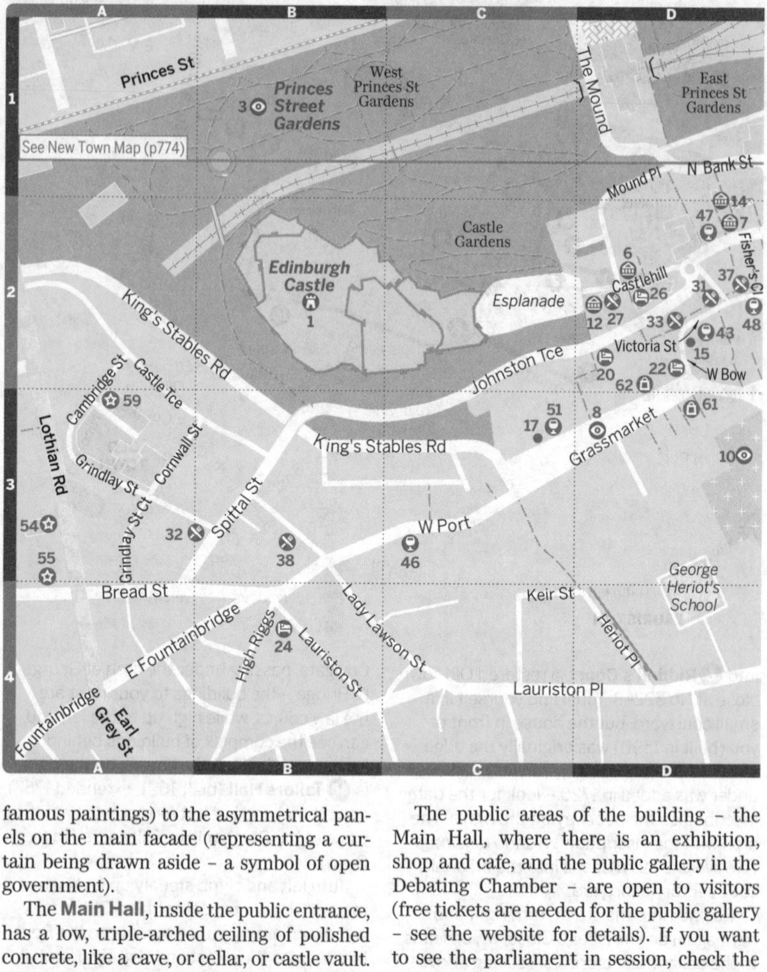

famous paintings) to the asymmetrical panels on the main facade (representing a curtain being drawn aside – a symbol of open government).

The **Main Hall**, inside the public entrance, has a low, triple-arched ceiling of polished concrete, like a cave, or cellar, or castle vault. It is a dimly lit space, the starting point for a metaphorical journey from this relative darkness up to the **Debating Chamber** (sitting directly above the Main Hall), which is, in contrast, a palace of light – the light of democracy. This magnificent chamber is the centrepiece of the parliament, designed not to glorify but to humble the politicians who sit within it. The windows face Calton Hill, allowing parliamentarians to look up to its monuments (reminders of the Scottish Enlightenment), while the massive, pointed oak beams of the roof are suspended by steel threads above the MSPs' heads like so many Damoclean swords.

The public areas of the building – the Main Hall, where there is an exhibition, shop and cafe, and the public gallery in the Debating Chamber – are open to visitors (free tickets are needed for the public gallery – see the website for details). If you want to see the parliament in session, check the website to see when it will be sitting – business days are normally Tuesday to Thursday year-round.

★Palace of Holyroodhouse PALACE

(Map p762; ☎0303 123 7306; www.rct.uk/visit/palace-of-holyroodhouse; Canongate, Royal Mile, EH8 8DX; adult/child incl audio guide £16.50/9.50; ⏱9.30am-6pm, last entry 4.30pm Apr-Oct, to 4.30pm, last entry 3.15pm Nov-Mar; 🚌35) This palace is the royal family's official residence in Scotland but is more famous as the 16th-century home of the ill-fated Mary, Queen of Scots. The highlight of the tour is **Mary's Bedchamber**, home to the unfortunate queen from 1561 to 1567. It was here

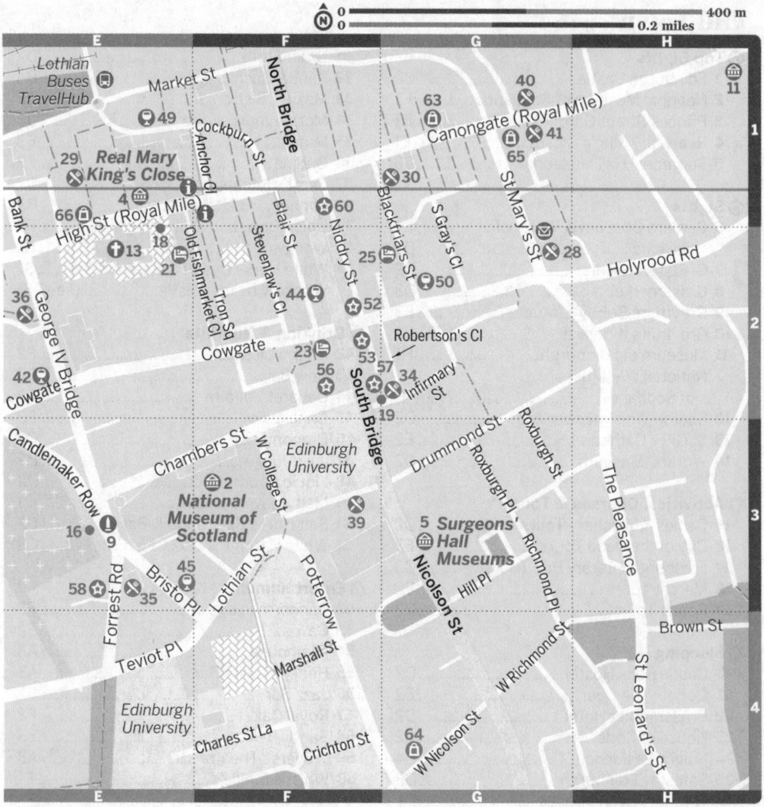

that her jealous second husband, Lord Darnley, restrained the pregnant queen while his henchmen murdered her secretary – and favourite – David Rizzio. A plaque in the neighbouring room marks the spot where Rizzio bled to death.

The palace developed from a guesthouse attached to Holyrood Abbey that was extended by James IV in 1501. The oldest surviving part of the building, the northwestern tower, was built in 1529 as a royal apartment for James V and his wife, Mary of Guise. Mary, Queen of Scots, spent six turbulent years here, during which time she debated with John Knox, married both her second and third husbands, and witnessed Rizzio's murder.

The self-guided audio tour leads you through a series of impressive royal apartments, culminating in the **Great Gallery**. The gallery's 89 portraits of Scottish kings were commissioned by Charles II and supposedly record his unbroken lineage from Scota, the Egyptian pharaoh's daughter who discovered the infant Moses in a reed basket on the banks of the Nile. The tour continues to the oldest part of the palace, which contains Mary's Bedchamber, connected by a secret stairway to her husband's bedroom, and ends with the ruins of Holyrood Abbey.

The palace is closed during royal visits; check the website for dates.

Queen's Gallery GALLERY

(Map p762; www.rct.uk/visit/the-queens-gallery-palace-of-holyroodhouse; Horse Wynd, EH8 8DX; adult/child £7.80/3.90, with Holyroodhouse £21.90/12; ⌚9.30am-6pm, last entry 4.30pm Apr-Oct, to 4.30pm, last entry 3.15pm Nov-Mar; 🚌35) This stunning modern gallery, which occupies the shell of a former church and school, is a showcase for exhibitions of art from the Royal Collections. The exhibitions change every six months or so; for current details, check the website.

Old Town

Top Sights
1 Edinburgh Castle ... B2
2 National Museum of Scotland ... F3
3 Princes Street Gardens ... B1
4 Real Mary King's Close ... E1
5 Surgeons' Hall Museums ... G3

Sights
6 Camera Obscura & World of Illusions ... D2
7 Gladstone's Land ... D2
8 Grassmarket ... D3
9 Greyfriars Bobby Statue ... E3
10 Greyfriars Kirkyard ... D3
11 Museum of Edinburgh ... H1
National War Museum of Scotland ... (see 1)
12 Scotch Whisky Experience ... D2
13 St Giles Cathedral ... E2
14 Writers' Museum ... D2

Activities, Courses & Tours
15 Cadies & Witchery Tours ... D2
16 City of the Dead Tours ... E3
17 Edinburgh Literary Pub Tour ... C3
18 Mercat Tours ... E2
19 Rebus Tours ... G2

Sleeping
20 Castle Rock Hostel ... D2
21 Code – The Court ... E2
22 Grassmarket Hotel ... D2
23 House of Gods ... F2
24 Knight Residence ... B4
25 Safestay Edinburgh ... G2
26 Witchery by the Castle ... D2

Eating
27 Amber ... D2
Cannonball Restaurant ... (see 12)
28 David Bann ... G2
29 Devil's Advocate ... E1
30 Edinburgh Larder ... G1
31 Grain Store ... D2
32 Kanpai Sushi ... B3
33 Maxie's Bistro ... D2
34 Mother India's Cafe ... G2
35 Mums ... E3
36 Ondine ... E2
37 Scott's Kitchen ... D2
38 Timberyard ... B3
39 Union Brew Lab ... F3
40 Wedgwood ... G1
41 White Horse Oyster & Seafood Bar ... G1
Witchery by the Castle ... (see 26)

Drinking & Nightlife
42 Bongo Club ... E2
43 Bow Bar ... D2
44 Cabaret Voltaire ... F2
45 Checkpoint ... E3
46 Dragonfly ... C3
47 Jolly Judge ... D2
48 Liquid Room ... D2
49 Malt Shovel ... E1
50 Salt Horse Beer Shop & Bar ... G2
51 White Hart Inn ... C3

Entertainment
52 Bannerman's ... F2
53 Caves ... F2
54 Filmhouse ... A3
55 Henry's Cellar Bar ... A3
56 Jazz Bar ... F2
57 Royal Oak ... F2
58 Sandy Bell's ... E3
59 Traverse Theatre ... A3
60 Whistle Binkie's ... F1

Shopping
61 Armstrong's ... D3
62 Bill Baber ... D2
63 Geoffrey (Tailor) Inc ... G1
64 Lighthouse ... G4
65 Ragamuffin ... G1
66 Royal Mile Whiskies ... E1

Holyrood Abbey ABBEY

(Map p762; www.historicenvironment.scot; Canongate, EH8 8DX; free with Palace of Holyroodhouse; 9.30am-6pm, last entry 4.30pm Apr-Oct, to 4.30pm, last entry 3.15pm Nov-Mar; 35) David I founded this abbey in the shadow of Salisbury Crags in 1128. It was probably named after a fragment of the True Cross (*rood* is an old Scots word for cross), said to have been brought to Scotland by David's mother, St Margaret. Most of the ruins date from the 12th and 13th centuries, although a doorway in the far-southeastern corner has survived from the original Norman church. Admission is included in the cost of a Palace of Holyroodhouse (p768) ticket.

★ **Arthur's Seat** VIEWPOINT

(Holyrood Park; 35) The rocky peak of Arthur's Seat (251m), carved by ice sheets from the deeply eroded stump of a long-extinct volcano, is a distinctive feature of Edinburgh's skyline. The view from the summit is well worth the walk, extending from the Forth bridges in the west to the distant conical hill of North Berwick Law in the east, with the Ochil Hills and the Highlands on the northwestern horizon. You can hike from Holyrood to the summit in around 45 minutes.

Holyrood Park PARK

(Map p762; 🚌6, 35) In Holyrood Park Edinburgh is blessed with a little bit of wilderness in the heart of the city. The former hunting ground of Scottish monarchs, the park covers 263 hectares of varied landscape, including crags, moorland and loch, and the 251m summit of Arthur's Seat. Holyrood Park can be circumnavigated by car or bike along Queen's Dr.

New Town

Edinburgh's New Town lies north of the Old, on a ridge running parallel to the Royal Mile and separated from it by the valley of Princes Street Gardens. Its regular grid of elegant, Georgian terraces is a complete contrast to the chaotic tangle of tenements and wynds that characterises the Old Town, and is the world's most complete and unspoilt example of Georgian architecture and town planning.

Apart from the streetscape, the main sights are the art galleries and gardens on Princes St, and the Scottish National Portrait Gallery near St Andrew Sq, all within walking distance of each other.

Princes St is one of the world's most spectacular shopping streets. Built up on the north side only, it catches the sun in summer and allows expansive views across Princes Street Gardens to the castle and the crowded skyline of the Old Town.

★**Princes Street Gardens** GARDENS

(Map p768; Princes St; ⏲dawn-dusk; 🚌all Princes St buses, 🚊Princes St) FREE These beautiful gardens lie in a valley that was once occupied by the Nor' Loch (North Loch), a boggy depression that was drained in the early 19th century. At the gate beside the Mound is the **Floral Clock**, a working clock laid out in flowers; it was first created in 1903 and the design changes every year.

In the middle of the western part of the gardens is the **Ross Bandstand** (www.rossbandstand.org), a venue for open-air concerts in summer and at Hogmanay, and the stage for the famous fireworks concert during the Edinburgh International Festival (there are plans to replace the bandstand with a modern pavilion).

The gardens are split in the middle by **the Mound** – around two million cartloads of earth that were dug out from foundations during the construction of the New Town and dumped here to provide a road link across the valley to the Old Town. The road was completed in 1830.

Scott Monument MONUMENT

(Map p774; www.edinburghmuseums.org.uk; East Princes Street Gardens, EH2 2EJ; tours £6; ⏲10am-4pm; 🚌all Princes St buses, 🚊Princes St) The eastern half of Princes Street Gardens is dominated by the massive Gothic spire of the Scott Monument, built by public subscription in memory of novelist Sir Walter Scott after his death in 1832. The exterior is decorated with 64 carvings of characters from his novels; inside you can see an exhibition on Scott's life, and join a tour to climb the 287 steps to the top for a superb view of the city.

Scottish National Gallery GALLERY

(Map p774; ☎0131-624 6200; www.nationalgalleries.org; The Mound, EH2 2EL; ⏲10am-5pm Fri-Wed, to 7pm Thu; 🚌all Princes St buses, 🚊Princes St) FREE Designed by William Playfair, this imposing classical building with its Ionic porticoes dates from 1850. Its octagonal rooms, lit by skylights, have been restored to their original Victorian decor of deep-green carpets and dark-red walls. The gallery houses an important collection of European art from the Renaissance to the post-Impressionism era, with works by Verrocchio (Leonardo da Vinci's teacher), Tintoretto, Titian, Holbein, Rubens, van Dyck, Vermeer, El Greco, Poussin, Rembrandt, Gainsborough, Turner, Constable, Monet, Pissarro, Gauguin and Cézanne.

The upstairs galleries (14 to 18) house portraits by Allan Ramsay and Sir Henry Raeburn, and a clutch of **Impressionist paintings**, including Monet's *Poplars on the River Epto,* Van Gogh's colourful *Orchard In Blossom* and Gauguin's hallucinatory *Vision of the Sermon*. But the painting that really catches your eye is the gorgeous portrait *Lady Agnew of Lochnaw* by John Singer Sargent.

The basement galleries dedicated to **Scottish art** include glowing portraits by Allan Ramsay and Sir Henry Raeburn, rural scenes by Sir David Wilkie and Impressionistic landscapes by William MacTaggart. Look out for Sir George Harvey's hugely entertaining *A Schule Skailin'* (A School Emptying) – a stern *dominie* (teacher) looks on as the boys stampede for the classroom door, one reaching for a confiscated spinning top. Kids will love the fantasy paintings of Sir Joseph Noel Paton in

THE STONE OF DESTINY

On St Andrew's Day 1996 a block of sandstone – 26.5 inches by 16.5 inches by 11 inches in size, with rusted iron hoops at either end – was installed with much pomp and circumstance in Edinburgh Castle. For the previous 700 years it had lain in London, beneath the Coronation Chair in Westminster Abbey. Almost all English, and later British, monarchs from Edward II in 1307 to Elizabeth II in 1953 have parked their backsides firmly over this stone during their coronation ceremony.

The legendary Stone of Destiny – said to have originated in the Holy Land, and on which Scottish kings placed their feet (not their bums; the English got that bit wrong) during their coronation – was stolen from Scone Abbey near Perth by Edward I of England in 1296. It was taken to London and there it remained for seven centuries – except for a brief removal to Gloucester during WWII air raids, and a three-month sojourn in Scotland after it was stolen by Scottish Nationalist students at Christmas in 1950 – as an enduring symbol of Scotland's subjugation by England.

The Stone of Destiny returned to the political limelight in 1996, when the then Scottish Secretary and Conservative Party MP Michael Forsyth arranged for the return of the sandstone block to Scotland. A blatant attempt to boost the flagging popularity of the Conservative Party in Scotland prior to a general election, Forsyth's publicity stunt failed miserably. The Scots said thanks very much for the stone and then, in May 1997, voted every Conservative MP in Scotland into oblivion.

Many people, however, believe Edward I was fobbed off with a shoddy imitation in 1296 and that the true Stone of Destiny remains safely hidden somewhere in Scotland. This is not impossible – some descriptions of the original stone state that it was made of black marble and decorated with elaborate carvings. Interested parties should read *Scotland's Stone of Destiny* by Nick Aitchinson, which details the history and cultural significance of Scotland's most famous lump of rock.

room B5; the incredibly detailed canvases are crammed with hundreds of tiny fairies, goblins and elves.

Recent research has suggested that the iconic 1790s painting of *Reverend Robert Walker Skating on Duddingston Loch*, historically attributed to Sir Henry Raeburn, may in fact be the work of French artist Henri-Pierre Danloux.

Each January the gallery exhibits its **collection of Turner watercolours**, bequeathed by Henry Vaughan in 1900. Antonio Canova's white marble sculpture, **The Three Graces**, is owned jointly with London's Victoria & Albert Museum; when not in London it can be seen in room 10.

There's a charge for some special exhibitions.

Royal Scottish Academy GALLERY

(Map p774; ☎0131-225 6671; www.royalscottishacademy.org; The Mound, EH2 2EL; ⏱10am-5pm Mon-Sat, noon-5pm Sun; 🚌all Princes St buses, 🚊Princes St) **FREE** This Greek Doric temple, with its northern pediment crowned by a seated figure of Queen Victoria, is the home of the Royal Scottish Academy. Designed by William Playfair and built between 1823 and 1836, it was originally called the Royal Institution; the RSA took over the building in 1910. The galleries display a collection of paintings, sculptures and architectural drawings by academy members from 1831 on, and they host temporary exhibitions throughout the year (fees for these vary).

The RSA and the Scottish National Gallery (p771) are linked via an underground mall – the Weston Link – that gives them twice the temporary exhibition space of the Prado in Madrid and three times that of the Royal Academy in London, as well as housing cloakrooms, a lecture theatre and a restaurant.

★Scottish National Portrait Gallery GALLERY

(Map p774; ☎0131-624 6200; www.nationalgalleries.org; 1 Queen St, EH2 1JD; ⏱10am-5pm; 👪; 🚌all York Pl buses, 🚊St Andrew Sq) **FREE** The Venetian Gothic palace of the Scottish National Portrait Gallery is one of the city's top attractions. Its galleries illustrate Scottish history through paintings, photographs and sculptures, putting faces to famous names from Scotland's past and present, from Robert Burns, Mary, Queen of Scots, and Bonnie Prince Charlie to the late Sir Sean Connery, comedian Billy Connolly and poet Jackie Kay. There's an admission fee for special exhibitions.

The gallery's interior is decorated in Arts and Crafts style, and nowhere more splendidly than in the **Great Hall**. Above the Gothic colonnade a processional frieze painted by William Hole in 1898 serves as a 'visual encyclopedia' of famous Scots, shown in chronological order from Calgacus (the chieftain who led the Caledonian tribes into battle against the Romans) to writer and philosopher Thomas Carlyle (1795–1881). The murals on the 1st-floor balcony depict scenes from Scottish history, while the ceiling is painted with the constellations of the night sky.

The gallery's selection of 'trails' leaflets adds a bit of background information while leading you around the various exhibits; the Hidden Histories trail is particularly interesting.

Charlotte Square SQUARE

(Map p774; 19, 36, 37, 41, 47) At the western end of George St is Charlotte Sq, the architectural jewel of the New Town, which was designed by Robert Adam shortly before his death in 1791. The northern side of the square is Adam's masterpiece and one of the finest examples of Georgian architecture anywhere. **Bute House** (Map p774; 6 Charlotte Sq, EH2 4DR), in the centre at No 6, is the official residence of Scotland's first minister.

Georgian House HISTORIC BUILDING

(NTS; Map p774; www.nts.org.uk; 7 Charlotte Sq, EH2 4DR; adult/child £8/6; 10am-5pm Apr-Oct, 11am-4pm Mar & Nov, closed Dec-Feb; 19, 36, 37, 41, 47) The National Trust for Scotland's Georgian House has been beautifully restored and furnished to show how Edinburgh's wealthy elite lived at the end of the 18th century. The walls are decorated with paintings by Allan Ramsay, Sir Henry Raeburn and Sir Joshua Reynolds, and there's a fully equipped 18th-century kitchen complete with china closet and wine cellar.

Leith

Leith has been Edinburgh's seaport since the 14th century, but it fell into decay following WWII. It's now undergoing a steady revival, with old warehouses turned into luxury flats and a lush crop of trendy bars and restaurants sprouting along the waterfront leading to Ocean Terminal, a huge shopping and leisure complex, and the former Royal Yacht *Britannia*.

★Royal Yacht Britannia SHIP

(www.royalyachtbritannia.co.uk; Ocean Terminal, EH6 6JJ; adult/child incl audio guide £17/8.75; 9.30am-6pm Apr-Sep, to 5.30pm Oct, 10am-5pm Nov-Mar, last entry 1½hr before closing; P; 11, 22, 34, 36, 200) The former Royal Yacht *Britannia* was the British royal family's floating holiday home from the time of her launch in 1953 until her decommissioning in 1997, and is now permanently moored in front of Ocean Terminal (p796). The tour, which you take at your own pace with an audio guide (available in 30 languages), lifts the curtain on the everyday lives of the royals, and gives an intriguing insight into the Queen's private tastes. It's best to book online in advance.

Britannia is a monument to 1950s decor, and the accommodation reveals Her Majesty's preference for simple, unfussy surroundings. There was nothing simple or unfussy, however, about the running of the ship. When the Queen travelled, with her went 45 members of the royal household, five tonnes of luggage and a Rolls-Royce that was carefully squeezed into a specially built garage on the deck. The ship's company consisted of an admiral, 20 officers and a 220-strong crew.

The decks (of Burmese teak) were scrubbed daily, but all work near the royal accommodation was carried out in complete silence and had to be finished by 8am. A thermometer was kept in the Queen's bathroom to make sure the water was the correct

ROYAL EDINBURGH TICKET

If you plan to visit the Royal Yacht *Britannia* as well as Edinburgh Castle and the Palace of Holyroodhouse, consider buying a Royal Edinburgh Ticket (www.edinburghtour.com/royal-edinburgh-ticket), which includes admission to all three plus unlimited travel on hop-on, hop-off tour buses among the various attractions.

New Town

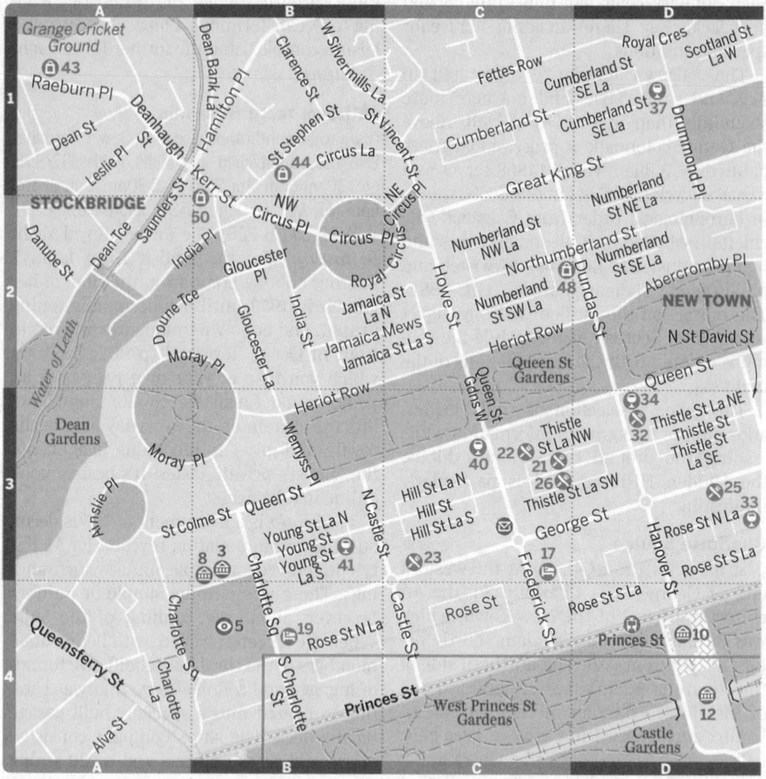

temperature, and when the ship was in harbour one crew member was charged with ensuring that the angle of the gangway never exceeded 12 degrees. Note the mahogany windbreak that was added to the balcony deck in front of the bridge: it was put there to stop wayward breezes from blowing up skirts and inadvertently revealing the royal underwear.

Britannia was joined in 2010 by the 1930s racing yacht *Bloodhound*, which was owned by the Queen in the 1960s. *Bloodhound* is moored alongside *Britannia* (except in July and August, when she is away cruising) as part of an exhibition about the royal family's love of all things nautical.

The Majestic Tour (p778) bus runs from Waverley Bridge to *Britannia* during the ship's opening times.

Greater Edinburgh

★ Royal Botanic Garden GARDENS

(☎0131-248 2909; www.rbge.org.uk; Arboretum Pl, EH3 5LR; ⊙10am-6pm Mar-Sep, to 5pm Feb & Oct, to 4pm Nov-Jan; 8, 23, 27) **FREE** Edinburgh's Royal Botanic Garden is the second-oldest institution of its kind in Britain (after Oxford's), and one of the most respected in the world. Founded near Holyrood in 1670 and moved to its present location in 1823, its 28 beautifully landscaped hectares include splendid **Victorian glasshouses** (admission £7), colourful swathes of rhododendron and azalea, and a world-famous rock garden. There are entrances to the gardens on Inverleith Row (city buses) and Arboretum Pl (Majestic Tour bus only).

The **John Hope Gateway visitor centre** is housed in a striking, environmentally friendly building overlooking the entrance

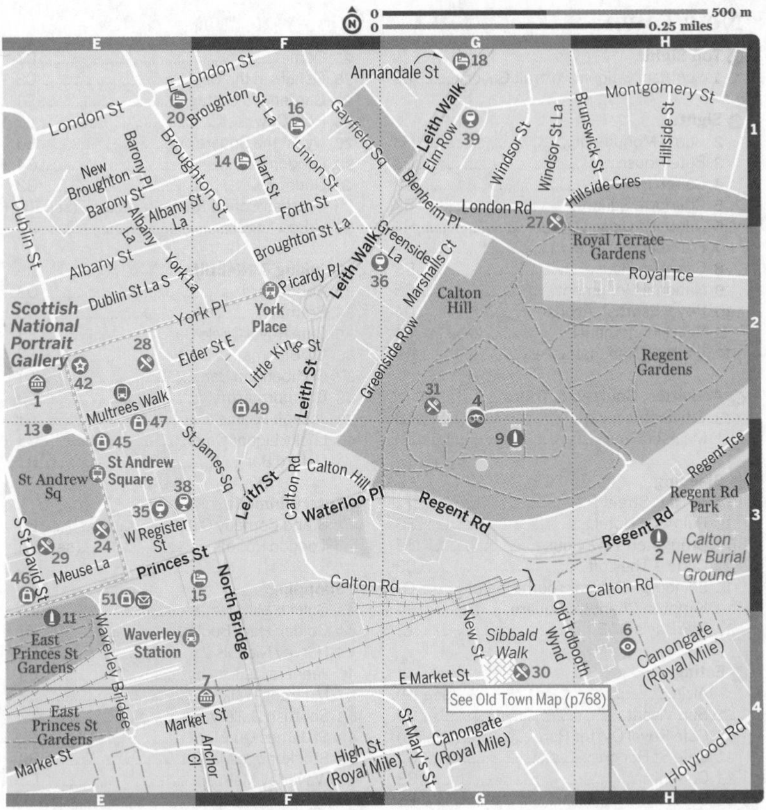

on Arboretum Pl, and has exhibitions on biodiversity, climate change and sustainable development, as well as displays of rare plants from the institution's collection and a specially created biodiversity garden.

Edinburgh Zoo ZOO

(☎0131-334 9171; www.edinburghzoo.org.uk; 134 Corstorphine Rd, EH12 6TS; adult/child £19.95/11.35; ⏰10am-6pm Apr-Sep, to 5pm Oct & Mar, to 4pm Nov-Feb; 👪; 🚌12, 18, 26, 31, 100) Opened in 1913, Edinburgh Zoo is one of the world's leading conservation zoos. Edinburgh's captive breeding programme has helped save many endangered species, including Siberian tigers, pygmy hippos and red pandas. The main attractions are the two **giant pandas**, Tian Tian and Yang Guang, who arrived in December 2011, and the **penguin parade** (the zoo's penguins go for a walk every day at 2.15pm). The zoo is 2.5 miles west of the city centre.

Cramond AREA

(🚌41) With its moored yachts, stately swans and whitewashed houses spilling down the hillside at the mouth of the River Almond, Cramond is the most picturesque corner of Edinburgh. It is also rich in history. The Romans built a fort here in the 2nd century CE, but recent archaeological excavations have revealed evidence of a Bronze Age settlement dating from 8500 BCE, the oldest known settlement site in Scotland. It's 5 miles northwest of the city centre.

Originally a mill village, Cramond has a historic 17th-century church and a 15th-century tower house, as well as some rather unimpressive Roman remains, but most people come to enjoy the walks along the river to the ruined mills and to stroll along the seafront. On the riverside, opposite the cottage on the far bank, is the **Maltings** (www.cramondheritage.org.uk; Riverside, Cramond EH4 6NY; ⏰2-5pm Sat & Sun Apr-Sep, daily during

New Town

Top Sights

1	Scottish National Portrait Gallery	E2

Sights

2	Burns Monument	H3
3	Bute House	B3
4	Calton Hill	G2
5	Charlotte Square	B4
6	Dunbar's Close Garden	H4
7	Fruitmarket Gallery	F4
8	Georgian House	B3
9	National Monument	G3
10	Royal Scottish Academy	D4
11	Scott Monument	E4
12	Scottish National Gallery	D4

Activities, Courses & Tours

13	City Sightseeing	E3
	Majestic Tour	(see 13)

Sleeping

14	14 Hart Street	F1
15	Balmoral Hotel	F3
16	Broughton Townhouse	F1
17	Code – The Loft	C3
18	Edinburgh Central Youth Hostel	G1
19	Kimpton Charlotte Square	B4
20	Ramsay's B&B	E1

Eating

	Aizle	(see 19)
21	Bon Vivant	C3
	Café Royal Oyster Bar	(see 35)
22	Cafe St Honore	C3
23	Contini	C3
24	Dishoom	E3
25	Dome	D3
26	Fishers in the City	C3
27	Gardener's Cottage	G1
28	Holy Cow	E2
29	Ivy on the Square	E3
30	Loudon's	G4
31	Outlook	G2
	Scottish Cafe & Restaurant	(see 10)
32	Urban Angel	D3

Drinking & Nightlife

33	Abbotsford	D3
34	Bramble	D3
35	Café Royal Circle Bar	E3
36	CC Blooms	F2
37	Cumberland Bar	D1
38	Guildford Arms	E3
39	Joseph Pearce's	G1
40	Lucky Liquor Co	C3
41	Oxford Bar	B3

Entertainment

42	Stand Comedy Club	E2
	Voodoo Rooms	(see 35)

Shopping

43	Galerie Mirages	A1
44	Golden Hare Books	B1
45	Harvey Nichols	E3
46	Jenners	E3
47	Multrees Walk	E3
48	Scottish Gallery	C2
49	St James Quarter	F2
50	Stockbridge Market	B2
51	Waverley Mall	E3

Edinburgh Festival; bus 41) FREE, which hosts an interesting exhibition on Cramond's history.

Activities

Edinburgh is lucky to have several good walking areas within the city boundary, including Arthur's Seat (p770), Calton Hill (p778), **Blackford Hill** (Charterhall Rd, EH9 3HR; bus 24, 38, 41), **Hermitage of Braid** (www.facebook.com/friendsofhermitage; bus 5, 11, 15, 16), **Corstorphine Hill** (www.corstorphinehill.org.uk; Clermiston Rd N, EH12 6UR; P; bus 26) and the coast and river at Cramond (p775). The **Pentland Hills** (www.pentlandhills.org) FREE, which rise to over 500m, stretch southwest from the city for over 15 miles, offering excellent high- and low-level walking.

You can follow the **Water of Leith Walkway** (www.waterofleith.org.uk/walkway) from the city centre to Balerno (8 miles), and continue across the Pentlands to Silverburn (6.5 miles) or Carlops (8 miles), and return to Edinburgh by bus. Another good walk is along the **Union Canal towpath**, which begins in Fountainbridge and runs all the way to Falkirk (31 miles). You can return to Edinburgh by bus at Ratho (8.5 miles) or Broxburn (12 miles), or by bus or train from Linlithgow (21 miles).

The **Scottish Rights of Way & Access Society** (0131-558 1222; www.scotways.com) provides information and advice on walking trails and rights of way in Scotland.

Tours

Walking Tours

Edinburgh has a wealth of walking tours that allow you to explore the city by theme, as well as a number of hop-on, hop-off bus tours that run between the city's top sights.

Edinburgh Literary Pub Tour WALKING
(Map p768; www.edinburghliterarypubtour.co.uk; Beehive Inn, Grassmarket, EH1 2JU; adult/student

£16/14; ⏲7.30pm daily May-Sep, limited days Oct-Apr) An enlightening two-hour trawl through Edinburgh's literary history – and its associated howffs (pubs) – in the entertaining company of Messrs Clart and McBrain. One of the city's best walking tours (departing from Beehive Inn).

City of the Dead Tours WALKING
(Map p768; ☎0131-225 9044; www.cityofthedeadtours.com; 26a Candlemaker Row, EH1 2QE; adult/concession £14/10; ⏲9pm Easter-Oct, 8.30pm Tue & Thu-Sat Nov-Easter) This nightly tour of Greyfriars Kirkyard is probably the scariest of Edinburgh's 'ghost' tours. Many people have reported encounters with the Mackenzie Poltergeist, the ghost of a 17th-century judge who persecuted the Covenanters and who now haunts their former prison in a corner of the kirkyard. Not suitable for children under 12.

Invisible (Edinburgh) WALKING
(☎07500-773709; www.invisible-cities.org/cities/edinburgh; per person from £12) This venture trains homeless people as tour guides to explore a different side of the city. Tour themes include Crime & Punishment (including Burke and Hare (p780)) and Powerful Women (from Maggie Dickson to JK Rowling). Must be booked in advance; check the website for times and meeting points.

Cadies & Witchery Tours WALKING
(Map p768; ☎0131-225 6745; www.witcherytours.com; 84 West Bow, EH1 2HH; adult/child £10/7.50; ⏲7pm year-round, plus 9pm Apr-Sep; 🚌2) The becloaked and pasty-faced Adam Lyal (deceased) leads a 'Murder & Mystery' tour of

UNDERGROUND EDINBURGH

As Edinburgh expanded in the late 18th and early 19th centuries, many old tenements were demolished and new bridges were built to link the Old Town to the newly built areas to its north and south. South Bridge (built between 1785 and 1788) and George IV Bridge (built between 1829 and 1834) lead south from the Royal Mile over the deep valley of Cowgate, but so many buildings have been constructed around them that you can hardly tell they're bridges. George IV Bridge has a total of nine arches, but only two are visible; South Bridge has no fewer than 18 hidden arches.

These **subterranean vaults** were originally used as storerooms, workshops and drinking dens. But as Edinburgh's population swelled in the early 19th century with an influx of penniless Highlanders cleared from their lands, and Irish refugees from the potato famine, the dark, dripping chambers were given over to slum accommodation and abandoned to poverty, filth and crime.

The vaults were eventually cleared in the late 19th century, then lay forgotten until 1994, when the **South Bridge vaults** were opened to guided tours. Certain chambers are said to be haunted, and one particular vault was investigated by paranormal researchers in 2001.

Nevertheless, the most ghoulish aspect of Edinburgh's hidden history dates from much earlier – from the plague that struck the city in 1645. Legend has it that the disease-ridden inhabitants of **Mary King's Close** (a lane on the northern side of the Royal Mile, on the site of the City Chambers – you can still see its blocked-off northern end from Cockburn St) were walled up in their houses and left to perish. When the lifeless bodies were eventually cleared from the houses, they were so stiff that workers had to hack off limbs to get them through the small doorways and up the narrow, twisting stairs.

From that day on, the close was said to be haunted by the spirits of the plague victims. The few people who were prepared to live there reported seeing apparitions of severed heads and limbs, and the largely abandoned close fell into ruin. When the Royal Exchange (now the City Chambers) was constructed between 1753 and 1761, it was built over the lower levels of Mary King's Close, which were left intact and sealed off beneath the building.

Interest in the close revived in the 20th century when Edinburgh's city council began to allow occasional guided tours to enter. Visitors have reported many supernatural experiences – the most famous ghost is 'Annie', a little girl whose sad tale has prompted people to leave gifts of dolls in a corner of one of the rooms. In 2003 the close was opened to the public as the Real Mary King's Close (p761).

DON'T MISS

CALTON HILL

Calton Hill (Map p774; 104, 113, 124), which rises dramatically above the eastern end of Princes St, is Edinburgh's acropolis, its summit scattered with grandiose memorials dating mostly from the first half of the 19th century. It is also one of the best viewpoints in Edinburgh, with a panorama that takes in the castle, Holyrood, Arthur's Seat, the Firth of Forth, the New Town and the full length of Princes St. On Regent Rd, on the hill's southern side, is the **Burns Monument** (Map p774; Regent Rd, EH8 8DR; 104, 113, 124) (1830), a Greek-style memorial to poet Robert Burns.

The largest structure on the summit is the **National Monument** (Map p774; Calton Hill; 104, 113, 124), a rather over-ambitious attempt to replicate the Parthenon in Athens, and intended to honour Scotland's dead in the Napoleonic Wars. Construction – paid for by public subscription – began in 1822, but funds ran dry after only 12 columns had been erected. It became known locally as 'Edinburgh's Disgrace'.

The hill is also home to City Observatory, built in 1818 and based on the Temple of the Winds in Athens. Its original function was to provide a precise, astronomical time-keeping service for marine navigators, but it's now a stunning space for contemporary visual art.

the Old Town's darker corners. These tours are famous for their 'jumper-ooters' – costumed actors who 'jump oot' when you least expect it. There's also a 2pm tour of Greyfriars Kirkyard (adult/child £15/12).

Trainspotting Tours WALKING
(www.leithwalks.co.uk; per person £10, minimum charge £20; by arrangement) A tour of locations from Irvine Welsh's notorious 1993 novel *Trainspotting*, and the 1996 film of the book, delivered with wit and enthusiasm. Not suitable for kids.

Rebus Tours WALKING
(Map p768; 0131-553 7473; www.rebustours.com; Royal Oak, Infirmary St, EH1 1LT; per person £20; noon Sat) A two-hour guided tour of the 'hidden Edinburgh' frequented by novelist Ian Rankin's fictional detective, John Rebus. Not recommended for children under 10.

Mercat Tours WALKING
(Map p768; 0131-225 5445; www.mercattours.com; Mercat Cross, EH1 1RF; adult/child £16/11; 10am-9.30pm; 35) Mercat offers a wide range of fascinating history walks and 'Ghosts & Ghouls' tours, but its most famous is Ghostly Underground, a visit to the hidden, haunted subterranean vaults beneath South Bridge. Tours depart from the Mercat Cross.

Boat Tours

3 Bridges Tour BOATING
(www.edinburghtour.com/3-bridges-tour; adult/child £25/12; departs 10am & noon Fri-Sun) This tour begins with a bus trip from St Andrews Sq in Edinburgh to South Queensferry, where you board a boat for a cruise beneath the three bridges that span the Firth of Forth – two road and one rail, dating from 1890 to 2017 – and then go to spot seals at **Inchcolm Island** (HES; www.historicenvironment.scot; KY3 0UA; adult/child £6/3.60; 9.30am-5.30pm Apr-Sep, to 4pm Oct), with the option of going ashore to visit the abbey ruins.

Bus Tours

Open-topped buses leave from the north side of St Andrew Sq, near the east end of Princes St, and offer hop-on, hop-off tours of the main sights, taking in New Town, the Grassmarket and the Royal Mile. They're a good way to get your bearings, although with a bus map and a Day Saver bus ticket you could do much the same thing (but without the commentary).

City Sightseeing (Map p774; www.edinburghtour.com; St Andrew Sq, EH2 1BB; adult/child £16/free; daily year-round except 25 Dec) Bright-red, open-top buses depart every 20 minutes from St Andrew Sq.

Majestic Tour (Map p774; www.edinburghtour.com/majestic-tour; St Andrew Sq, EH2 1BB; adult/child £16/free; daily year-round except 25 Dec) Hop-on, hop-off tour departing every 15 to 20 minutes from St Andrew Sq to the Royal Yacht *Britannia* at Ocean Terminal via the New Town, the Royal Botanic Garden and Newhaven, returning via Leith Walk, Holyrood and the Royal Mile.

Festivals & Events

Edinburgh's Hogmanay NEW YEAR

(☎0131-510 0395; www.edinburghshogmanay.com; street-party tickets £25; ⏲30 Dec-1 Jan) Edinburgh's Hogmanay is the biggest winter festival in Europe, with events including a torchlit procession, a huge street party and the famous 'Loony Dook', a chilly sea-swimming event on New Year's Day. To get into the main party area in the city centre after 8pm on 31 December you'll need a ticket – book well in advance.

Traditionally, the New Year has always been a more important celebration for Scots than Christmas. In towns, cities and villages all over the country, people fill the streets at midnight on 31 December to wish each other a Guid New Year and, yes, to knock back a dram or six to keep the cold at bay.

In 1993 Edinburgh's city council had the excellent idea of spicing up Hogmanay by organising some events, laying on some live music in Princes St and issuing an open invitation to the rest of the world. Most of them turned up, or so it seemed, and had such a good time that they told all their pals and came back again the next year.

Imaginate Festival PERFORMING ARTS

(☎0131-225 8050; www.imaginate.org.uk/festival; late May-early Jun) Britain's biggest festival of performing arts for children, Imaginate is a week-long event suitable for kids aged three to 12. Groups from around the world perform classic tales like *Hansel and Gretel* as well as new material written especially for a young audience.

Royal Highland Show FAIR

(☎0131-335 6200; www.royalhighlandshow.org; Royal Highland Centre, Ingliston EH28 8NB; adult/child £32/free; ⏲late Jun) Scotland's hugely popular national agricultural show is a four-day feast of all things rural, with everything from showjumping and tractor driving to sheep shearing and falconry. Countless pens are filled with coiffed show cattle and pedicured prize ewes. The show is held over a long weekend (Thursday to Sunday).

Edinburgh International Film Festival FILM

(www.edfilmfest.org.uk; ⏲Jun) One of the original Edinburgh Festival trinity, having first been staged in 1947 along with the International Festival (p780) and the Fringe, the two-week June film festival is a major international event, serving as a showcase for new British and European films, and staging the European premieres of one or two Hollywood blockbusters.

Edinburgh Food Festival FOOD & DRINK

(www.edfoodfest.com; George Sq Gdns, EH8 9JZ; ⏲Jul) This four-day festival, based in George Square Gardens, precedes the opening of the Edinburgh Fringe (p779) with a packed programme of talks, cookery demonstrations, tastings, food stalls and entertainment.

Edinburgh International Jazz & Blues Festival MUSIC

(www.edinburghjazzfestival.com; ⏲Jul) Held annually since 1978, the Jazz & Blues Festival pulls in top talent from all over the world. It runs for nine days, beginning on a Friday, a week before the Fringe and Tattoo begin. The first weekend sees a carnival parade on Princes St and an afternoon of free, open-air music in Princes Street Gardens.

Edinburgh Festival Fringe PERFORMING ARTS

(☎0131-226 0026; www.edfringe.com; ⏲Aug) When the first Edinburgh International Festival (p780) was held in 1947, eight theatre companies didn't make it onto the main programme. Undeterred, they grouped together and held their own mini-festival, on the fringe, and an Edinburgh institution was born. Today the Fringe is the biggest festival of the performing arts anywhere in the world.

Edinburgh Military Tattoo CULTURAL

(☎0131-225 1188; www.edintattoo.co.uk; ⏲Aug) The Military Tattoo is a spectacular display of military marching bands, massed pipes and drums, acrobats, cheerleaders and motorcycle display teams, all played out in front of the magnificent backdrop of the floodlit castle. Each show traditionally finishes with a lone piper, dramatically lit, playing a lament on the battlements. Held over the first three weeks of August.

Edinburgh International Festival PERFORMING ARTS

(☎0131-473 2000; www.eif.co.uk; ⏲Aug-Sep) First held in 1947 to mark a return to peace after the ordeal of WWII, the Edinburgh International Festival is festooned with superlatives – the oldest, the biggest, the most famous, the best in the world. The original was a modest affair, but today hundreds of the world's top musicians and performers congregate for three weeks of diverse music, opera, theatre and dance.

Sleeping

Edinburgh offers a wide range of accommodation options, from moderately priced guesthouses set in lovely Victorian villas and Georgian town houses to expensive and stylish boutique hotels. There are also plenty of chain hotels, and a few truly exceptional hotels housed in magnificent historic buildings. At the budget end of the range, there is no shortage of youth hostels and independent backpacker hostels, which often have inexpensive double and twin rooms.

Old Town

★Code – The Court HOSTEL £
(Map p768; ☎0131-510 9380; www.codehostels.com/hostels/the-court; 1a Parliament Sq, EH1 1RF; dm/d from £21/68;) It would be hard to get any closer to the action on the Royal Mile than this hostel housed in a converted Victorian jail, tucked behind St Giles Cathedral. The dorms consist of pod-style bunks with privacy screens, spacious storage with combination locks, and bedside phone-charging points. The atmospheric private rooms occupy former prison cells, while the public areas are bright, modern and appealing.

Safestay Edinburgh HOSTEL £
(Map p768; ☎0131-524 1989; www.safestay.com/edinburgh; 50 Blackfriars St, EH1 1NE; dm £27-37, tw from £70; @; 35) A big, modern hostel with a convivial cafe where you can buy breakfast, and mod cons such as keycard access and charging stations for mobile phones and laptops. Lockers in every room, a huge bar and a central location just off the Royal Mile make this a favourite among the young, party-mad crowd – don't expect a quiet night!

THE RESURRECTION MEN

In 1505 Edinburgh's newly founded Royal College of Surgeons was officially allocated the corpse of one executed criminal per year for the purposes of dissection. But this was not nearly enough to satisfy the curiosity of the city's anatomists, and in the following centuries an illegal trade in dead bodies emerged, which reached its culmination in the early 19th century when the anatomy classes of famous surgeons such as Professor Robert Knox drew audiences of up to 500.

The readiest supply of corpses was to be found in the city's graveyards, especially Greyfriars. Grave robbers – who came to be known as 'resurrection men' – plundered newly buried coffins and sold the cadavers to the anatomists, who turned a blind eye to the source of their research material.

This gruesome trade led to a series of countermeasures, including the mort safe – a metal cage that was placed over a coffin until the corpse had begun to decompose; you can see examples in Greyfriars Kirkyard (p765) and on level five of the National Museum of Scotland (p765). Watchtowers, where a sexton, or relatives of the deceased, would keep watch over new graves, survive in St Cuthbert's and Duddingston kirkyards.

The notorious William Burke and William Hare, who kept a lodging house in Tanner's Close at the western end of the Grassmarket, took the body-snatching business a step further. When an elderly lodger died without paying his rent, Burke and Hare stole his body from the coffin and sold it to Professor Knox. Seeing a lucrative business opportunity, they figured that rather than waiting for someone else to die, they could create their own supply of fresh cadavers by resorting to murder.

Burke and Hare preyed on the poor and weak of Edinburgh's Grassmarket, luring them back to Hare's lodging house, plying them with drink and then suffocating them. Between December 1827 and October 1828, they murdered at least 16 people and sold their bodies to Professor Knox. When the law finally caught up with them, Hare turned king's evidence and testified against Burke.

Burke was hanged outside St Giles Cathedral in January 1829 and, in an ironic twist, his body was given to the anatomy school for public dissection. His death mask, and a pocketbook made from his flayed skin, are still on display in the Surgeons' Hall Museums (p783).

It was as a result of the Burke and Hare case that the *Anatomy Act* 1832 – regulating the supply of cadavers for dissection, and still in force today – was passed.

WORTH A TRIP

SCOTTISH NATIONAL GALLERY OF MODERN ART

Edinburgh's main **modern art gallery** (Map p762; 0131-624 6200; www.nationalgalleries.org; 75 Belford Rd, EH4 3DR; 10am-5pm; 13) FREE is surrounded by landscaped grounds some 500m west of Dean Village. As well as showcasing a stunning collection of paintings by the popular, post-Impressionist Scottish Colourists – in *Reflections, Balloch*, Leslie Hunter pulls off the improbable trick of making Scotland look like the south of France – the gallery is the starting point for a walk along the Water of Leith. Fees apply for some exhibitions.

The main collection, known as Modern One, concentrates on 20th-century art, with various European movements represented by the likes of Matisse, Picasso, Kirchner, Magritte, Miró, Mondrian and Giacometti.

A footpath and stairs at the rear of the gallery lead down to the Water of Leith Walkway, which you can follow along the river for 4 miles to Leith.

Castle Rock Hostel HOSTEL £
(Map p768; 0131-225 9666; www.castlerockedinburgh.com; 15 Johnston Tce, EH1 2PW; dm £15-19, d from £55; @; 2) With its bright, spacious, mixed or female-only dorms, superb views and friendly staff, the 200-bed Castle Rock has lots to like. It has a great location – the only way to get closer to the castle would be to pitch a tent on the esplanade – plus a games room, a reading lounge and big-screen video nights. No under-18s.

★**Witchery by the Castle** B&B £££
(Map p768; 0131-225 5613; www.thewitchery.com; Castlehill, EH1 2NF; ste from £395; P; 23, 27, 41, 42) Set in a 16th-century Old Town house in the shadow of Edinburgh Castle, the Witchery's nine lavish Gothic suites are extravagantly furnished with antiques, oak panelling, tapestries, open fires, four-poster beds and roll-top baths, and supplied with flowers, chocolates and complimentary champagne. It's overwhelmingly popular – you'll have to book several months in advance to be sure of getting a room.

House of Gods BOUTIQUE HOTEL £££
(Map p768; 0131-230 0445; www.houseofgodshotel.com; 233 Cowgate, EH1 1JQ; r from £159;) Forget minimalist – this new hotel in the heart of the Old Town is what might be called 'maximalist'. The over-the-top decor runs to burgundy velvet wall coverings and curtains, faux tiger-skin cushions, gold-tasselled lampshades and marble-lined bathrooms, and the decadence extends to the hotel's cocktail bars, which cultivate an aura of rock-and-roll debauchery.

Grassmarket Hotel HOTEL £££
(Map p768; 0131-220 2299; www.grassmarkethotel.co.uk; 94-96 Grassmarket, EH1 2JR; s/d/tr from £202/215/266; ; 2) An endearingly quirky hotel set in a historic Grassmarket tenement in the heart of the Old Town, this place has bedroom walls plastered with front pages from the *Dandy* (a DC Thomson comic published in Dundee) and coffee stations supplied with iconically Scottish Tunnock's teacakes and Irn-Bru. Some bargain rates are available directly through the website.

New Town

Code – The Loft APARTMENT £
(Map p774; 0131-659 9883; www.codecoliving.com; 50 Rose St N Lane, EH2 2NP; per week pod/tw/apt £99/200/300; ; Princes St) This bold experiment in 'co-living' offers short- to mid-term rental accommodation in innovative sleeping pods that offer more privacy than bunks (up to three people per room, with shared toilet and shower room), and shared kitchen and living areas. There's also a twin/double room and a luxurious double apartment called the Penthouse, complete with kitchenette and roof terrace.

★**14 Hart Street** B&B ££
(Map p774; 07795 203414; www.14hartstreet.co.uk; 14 Hart St, EH1 3RN; r from £95; ; 8) Centrally located and child friendly, 14 Hart Street is steeped in Georgian elegance and old Edinburgh charm. There are three generous bedrooms, all en suite, and a sumptuous dining room where guests can enjoy breakfast at a time of their choosing.

Indulgent extras include whisky decanters and shortbread in every room. There is sometimes a two-night-stay minimum.

Broughton Townhouse GUESTHOUSE ££
(Map p774; 0131-558 9792; www.broughton-hotel.com; 37 Broughton Pl, EH1 3RR; s/d/f from £80/120/150; P; 8) This five-bedroom Georgian guesthouse combines great value with a great location, on a relatively quiet street a few minutes' walk from the restaurants and nightlife of Broughton St and Edinburgh's gay village, and just 10 minutes' walk from Princes St.

Ramsay's B&B B&B ££
(Map p774; 0131-557 5917; www.ramsaysbedandbreakfastedinburgh.com; 25 East London St, EH7 4BN; r from £100; ; 8) The four bright and fresh bedrooms in this tastefully decorated Georgian town house make a great base for exploring the New Town, with the vibrant bar and restaurant scene of Broughton's gay village just around the corner. Breakfasts are freshly prepared, with kippers on the menu as well as the usual options.

★Kimpton Charlotte Square BOUTIQUE HOTEL £££
(Map p774; 0131-240 5500; www.kimptoncharlottesquare.com; 38 Charlotte Sq, EH2 4HQ; r from £340; P; all Princes St buses) Arriving in this modern makeover of a classic Georgian New Town establishment (formerly the Roxburghe Hotel) feels like being welcomed to a country-house party. Service is friendly and attentive without being intrusive, and the atmosphere is informal. In the bedrooms, designer decor meets traditional tweed, and breakfast is served in a lovely glass-roofed garden courtyard.

Balmoral Hotel HOTEL £££
(Map p774; 0131-556 2414; www.roccofortehotels.com/balmoral; 1 Princes St, EH2 2EQ; r from £280; P; all Princes St buses) The sumptuous Balmoral – a prominent landmark at the eastern end of Princes St – offers some of the best accommodation in Edinburgh, including suites with 18th-century decor, marble bathrooms and stunning sunset views of Princes St and the Scott Monument (p771). There's also a spa and gym with a 20m pool in the basement.

Leith

Edinburgh Central Youth Hostel HOSTEL £
(HS; Map p774; 0131-524 2090; www.hostellingscotland.org.uk; 9 Haddington Pl, EH7 4AL; tw from £52; @; all Leith Walk buses) This modern, purpose-built hostel, off Leith Walk about a half-mile north of Waverley train station, is a big, flashy, five-star establishment with its own cafe-bistro as well as a self-catering kitchen, smart and comfortable dorms and private rooms, and mod cons including keycard entry and plasma-screen TVs. Private rooms only during the Covid-19 pandemic.

★Sheridan Guest House B&B ££
(0131-554 4107; www.sheridanedinburgh.com; 1 Bonnington Tce, EH6 4BP; r from £125; P; 11) Flowerpots filled with colourful blooms line the steps of this little haven hidden away north of the New Town. The eight bedrooms (all en suite) blend crisp colours with contemporary furniture, stylish lighting and colourful paintings, which complement the house's clean-cut Georgian lines. The breakfast menu adds omelettes, pancakes with maple syrup, and scrambled eggs with smoked salmon to the usual offerings.

Sandaig Guest House B&B ££
(0131-554 7357; www.sandaigguesthouse.co.uk; 5 East Hermitage Pl, Leith Links, EH6 8AA; d/f from £90/130; ; 21, 25) From the welcoming glass of sherry to the cheerful goodbye wave, the owner of the Sandaig knows a thing or two about hospitality. Numerous details make staying here a pleasure, from the boldly coloured decor to the crisp cotton sheets, big fluffy towels and refreshing power showers, plus a breakfast menu that includes porridge with cream and maple syrup.

★Fingal LUXURY HOTEL £££
(0131-357 5000; www.fingal.co.uk; Alexandra Dock, EH6 7DX; r from £300;) If a tour of the Royal Yacht *Britannia* has whetted your appetite for a life afloat, you can book yourself into this floating hotel housed in a converted lighthouse maintenance vessel. Under the same management as the *Britannia*, the ship has been fitted out to the highest standard, with 14 luxurious cabins and suites that will make you feel like a pampered royal.

OFF THE BEATEN TRACK

SURGEONS' HALL MUSEUMS

Housed in a grand Ionic temple designed by William Playfair in 1832, these three fascinating **museums** (Map p768; ☎0131-527 1711; www.museum.rcsed.ac.uk; Nicolson St, EH8 9DW; adult/child £8/4.50; ⏲10am-5pm; 🚌all South Bridge buses) were originally established as teaching collections. The History of Surgery Museum provides a look at surgery in Scotland from the 15th century to the present day. Highlights include the exhibit on murderers Burke and Hare, which includes Burke's death mask and a pocketbook made from his skin, and a display on Dr Joseph Bell, who was the inspiration for the character of Sherlock Holmes.

The adjacent Dental Collection, with its wince-inducing extraction tools, covers the history of dentistry, while the Pathology Museum houses a gruesome but compelling 19th-century collection of diseased organs and massive tumours pickled in formaldehyde.

★Pilrig House APARTMENT £££
(☎0131-221 1646; www.pilrighouse.com; 30 Pilrig House Close, EH6 5RF; ⏲per week £560-1050; P 📶; 🚌36) Pilrig is a gorgeous 17th-century town house that was once home to Robert Louis Stevenson's grandfather (it gets a mention in his novel *Kidnapped*). Set at the end of a quiet cul-de-sac overlooking a peaceful park, the house offers a luxurious self-catering apartment with fully equipped kitchen and private parking. Seven-night minimum stay, four weeks minimum in August.

South Edinburgh

Sherwood Guest House B&B ££
(Map p762; ☎0131-667 1200; www.sherwood-edinburgh.com; 42 Minto St, EH9 2BR; d/tr from £95/145; P 📶; 🚌all Newington buses) One of the most attractive guesthouses on Minto St's B&B strip, the Sherwood is a refurbished Georgian terrace house decked out with hanging baskets and shrubs. Inside are six en-suite rooms that combine period features with modern fabrics and neutral colours.

No 45 B&B ££
(☎0131-667 3536; www.edinburghbedbreakfast.com; 45 Gilmour Rd; s/d from £80/127; 📶; 🚌all Newington buses) A peaceful setting, a large garden and friendly owners contribute to the appeal of this Victorian terrace house, which overlooks the local bowling green. The decor is a blend of 19th and 20th century, with bold Victorian reds, pine floors and a period fireplace in the lounge, and a 1930s vibe in the three spacious bedrooms. Occasional two-night-stay minimum.

★Southside Guest House B&B £££
(Map p762; ☎0131-466 6573; www.southsideguesthouse.co.uk; 8 Newington Rd, EH9 1QS; s/d from £145/180; 📶; 🚌all Newington buses) Though set in a typical Victorian terrace, the Southside transcends the traditional guesthouse category and feels more like a modern boutique hotel. Its seven stylish rooms, featuring the clever use of bold colours and modern furniture, ooze interior design. Breakfast is an event, with Buck's Fizz (cava mixed with orange juice) on offer to ease any hangovers.

94DR BOUTIQUE HOTEL £££
(Map p762; ☎0131-662 9265; www.94dr.com; 94 Dalkeith Rd, EH16 5AF; r from £130; P; 🚌2, 14, 30, 33) This peaceful and elegant guesthouse is a sensitively restored Victorian town house with six individually designed bedrooms with views towards either Salisbury Crags or the Pentland Hills. Extras include complimentary use of bicycles, a well-equipped honesty bar, seriously impressive breakfasts cooked by the chef-owner, and a lovely conservatory and garden.

Albyn Townhouse B&B £££
(Map p762; ☎07973 146210; www.albyntownhouse.co.uk; 16 Hartington Gardens, EH10 4LD; s/d from £101/154; P 📶; 🚌11, 15, 16, 23, 36, 45) Set in a refurbished Victorian town house tucked away at the end of a quiet cul-de-sac in the fashionable Bruntsfield district, this B&B is a real home-away-from-home. Designer-ish decor doesn't detract from the welcoming atmosphere, and the owners (plus their charming dog) are only too pleased to offer advice on where to go and what to see.

Knight Residence APARTMENT £££
(Map p768; ☎0800 304 7160; www.bymansley.com/the-knight-residence; 12 Lauriston St, EH3 9DJ; 1-/2-/3-bedroom apt from £185/245/295; P 📶; 🚌2) Works by contemporary artists adorn these modern studio and one-, two- and three-bedroom apartments (available by the night; the three-bedroom options sleep up to six), each with fully equipped kitchen and comfortable lounge with cable TV, DVD and stereo. It has a good central location in a quiet street only a few minutes' walk from the Grassmarket.

Eating

Eating out in Edinburgh has changed beyond all recognition since the 1990s. Back then, sophisticated dining meant a visit to the Aberdeen Angus Steak House for a prawn cocktail, steak (well done) and chips, and Black Forest gateau. Today, central Edinburgh has more restaurants per head of population than any other UK city, including a handful of places with Michelin stars.

Old Town

★Mums CAFE £
(Map p768; ☎0131-260 9806; www.monstermashcafe.co.uk; 4a Forrest Rd, EH1 2QN; mains £9-13; ⌚9am-10pm Mon-Sat, 10am-10pm Sun; 📶 👪; 🚌2, 23, 27, 35, 41, 42, 45) 🍃 This nostalgia-fuelled cafe serves up classic British comfort food that wouldn't look out of place on a 1950s menu – bacon and eggs, bangers and mash, shepherd's pie, fish and chips. But there's a twist – the food is all top-quality nosh freshly prepared from local produce. There's also a good selection of bottled craft beers and Scottish-brewed cider.

Scott's Kitchen SCOTTISH, CAFE £
(Map p768; ☎0131-322 6868; www.scottskitchen.co.uk; 4-6 Victoria Tce, EH1 2JL; mains £8-10; ⌚9am-6pm; P 📶; 🚌23, 27, 41, 42) Green tile, brown leather and arched Georgian windows lend an elegant feel to this modern cafe, which combines fine Scottish produce with international favourites. Fill up on a breakfast (served till noon) of eggs Benedict or bacon baps, or linger over a lunch of haggis bonbons, crunchy calamari or a smoked ham and Scottish cheddar sandwich.

Edinburgh Larder CAFE £
(Map p768; ☎0131-556 2350; www.edinburghlarder.co.uk; 15 Blackfriars St, EH1 1NB; mains £9-15; ⌚8am-5pm Mon, Thu & Fri, 8.30am-5pm Sat & Sun; 🖉; 🚌35) This bright and cheerful cafe, handily located just off the Royal Mile, puts the focus on seasonal Scottish produce (a map on the wall highlights their suppliers). Dishes range from brunch favourites such as eggs Benedict, to a Taste of Scotland platter that includes hot and cold smoked salmon, organic cheeses, oatcakes and salad leaves.

★Cannonball Restaurant SCOTTISH ££
(Map p768; ☎0131-225 1550; www.contini.com/cannonball; 356 Castlehill, EH1 2NE; mains £15-30; ⌚noon-3pm & 5.30-10pm Tue-Sat; 📶 👪; 🚌23, 27, 41, 42) The historic Cannonball House next to Edinburgh Castle's esplanade has been transformed into a sophisticated restaurant and whisky bar where the Contini family work their Italian magic on Scottish classics to produce dishes such as haggis balls with marmalade and mustard, and lobster thermidor with macaroni and cheese.

Mother India's Cafe INDIAN ££
(Map p768; ☎0131-524 9801; www.motherindia.co.uk; 3-5 Infirmary St, EH1 1LT; dishes £5-9; ⌚4-9pm Mon & Tue, noon-9pm Wed, Thu & Sun, noon-10pm Fri & Sat; 📶 👪; 🚌all South Bridge buses) A simple concept pioneered in Glasgow has captured hearts and minds – and stomachs – here in Edinburgh: Indian food served in tapas-size portions, so that you can sample a greater variety of deliciously different dishes without busting a gut. It's hugely popular, so book a table to avoid disappointment.

David Bann VEGETARIAN ££
(Map p768; ☎0131-556 5888; www.davidbann.com; 56-58 St Mary's St, EH1 1SX; mains £12-15; ⌚noon-10pm Mon-Fri, 11am-10pm Sat & Sun; 🖉; 🚌35) 🍃 If you want to convince a carnivorous friend that cuisine à la veg can be every bit as tasty and inventive as a meat-muncher's menu, take them to David Bann's stylish restaurant – dishes such as strudel filled with mushroom, rosemary, Isle of Arran cheese and Heather Ale with polenta chips and shallot sauce are guaranteed to win converts.

Devil's Advocate PUB FOOD ££
(Map p768; ☎0131-225 4465; www.devilsadvocateedinburgh.co.uk; 9 Advocates Close, EH1 1ND; mains £15-23; ⌚food served noon-3pm & 5-10pm; 📶; 🚌23, 27, 41, 42) No trip to Edinburgh is complete without exploring the narrow closes (alleys) that lead off the Royal Mile. Lucky you if your explorations lead to this cosy split-level pub-restaurant set in a converted

Victorian pump house, with a menu of top-quality pub grub – the smoked fish and charcuterie platters are irresistible. It gets rammed on weekends, so book ahead.

Maxie's Bistro BISTRO ££
(Map p768; 0131-226 7770; www.maxiesbistro.com; 5b Johnston Tce, EH1 2PW; mains £10-27; noon-11pm; ; 23, 27, 41, 42, 67) This candlelit bistro, with its cushion-lined nooks set amid stone walls and wooden beams, is a pleasant setting for a cosy dinner, but at summer lunchtimes people queue for the tables on the terrace overlooking Victoria St. The food is dependable, ranging from pasta, steak and stir-fries to seafood platters and daily specials. It's best to book, especially in summer.

Amber SCOTTISH ££
(Map p768; 0131-477 8477; www.scotchwhiskyexperience.co.uk/restaurant; 354 Castlehill, EH1 2NE; mains £15-20; 11am-8pm; ; 23, 27, 41, 42) You've got to love a place where the waiter greets you with the words, 'I'll be your whisky adviser for this evening'. Located in the Scotch Whisky Experience (p764), this whisky-themed restaurant manages to avoid the tourist clichés and creates genuinely interesting and flavoursome dishes using top Scottish produce, with a suggested whisky pairing for each dish.

★Grain Store SCOTTISH £££
(Map p768; 0131-225 7635; www.grainstore-restaurant.co.uk; 30 Victoria St, EH1 2JW; mains £24-32; noon-2.30pm & 6-9.45pm Mon-Sat, noon-2.30pm & 6-9.30pm Sun; 2, 23, 27, 41, 42) An atmospheric upstairs dining room on picturesque Victoria St, the Grain Store has a well-earned reputation for serving the finest Scottish produce, perfectly prepared in dishes such as halibut with fried squid and mussel bisque, and roe deer venison with celeriac, beetroot and kale. The two-course lunch for £14 is good value.

★Ondine SEAFOOD £££
(Map p768; 0131-226 1888; www.ondinerestaurant.co.uk; 2 George IV Bridge, EH1 1AD; mains £22-38; noon-9pm Wed-Sat, noon-4pm Sun; ; 23, 27, 41, 42) Ondine is one of Edinburgh's finest seafood restaurants, with a menu based on sustainably sourced fish. Take a seat at the curved Oyster Bar and tuck into oysters with shallot dressing, shellfish bisque, lobster thermidor, a *fruits de mer* platter or just good old haddock and chips (with minted pea puree, just to keep things posh).

White Horse Oyster & Seafood Bar SEAFOOD £££
(Map p768; 0131-629 5300; www.whitehorseoysterbar.co.uk; 266 Canongate, EH8 8AA; seafood platters £48-95; 4-10pm Mon-Fri, noon-10pm Sat & Sun; 35) One of Edinburgh's oldest pubs has been transformed into this intriguing seafood restaurant. The decor is bare stone and wood panelling in shades of slate grey and brown, providing a dark canvas on which white platters of colourful shellfish and crustaceans shine all the more brightly. The menu also includes 'small plates' (£8 to £15), which can be ordered tapas-style.

Wedgwood SCOTTISH £££
(Map p768; 0131-558 8737; www.wedgwoodtherestaurant.co.uk; 267 Canongate, EH8 8BQ; mains £23-30, 2-/3-course lunch £20/25; noon-2pm Fri-Sun & 6-10pm Wed-Sun; ; 35) Fine food without the fuss is the motto at this friendly, unpretentious restaurant. Scottish produce is served with inventive flair in dishes such as fillet of lamb with samphire and mint, or scallops with cauliflower korma, pineapple, and peanut and pistachio dust; the menu includes foraged wild salad leaves collected by the chef. The six-course tasting menu is £55 (vegetarian option £50).

Witchery by the Castle SCOTTISH, FRENCH £££
(Map p768; 0131-225 5613; www.thewitchery.com; Castlehill, EH1 2NF; mains £25-44, 2-course lunch £25; noon-11.30pm; 23, 27, 41, 42) Set in a merchant's town house dating from 1595, the Witchery is a candlelit corner of antique splendour with oak-panelled walls, low ceilings, opulent wall hangings and red-leather upholstery; stairs lead down to a second, even more romantic dining room called the Secret Garden. The menu ranges from oysters to Aberdeen Angus steak and the wine list runs to almost 1000 bins.

Holyrood & Arthur's Seat

★Rhubarb SCOTTISH £££
(0131-225 1333; www.prestonfield.com/dine/rhubarb; Prestonfield, Priestfield Rd, EH16 5UT; mains £23-40; noon-8pm;) Set in the splendid 17th-century **Prestonfield Hotel** (0131-668 3346; www.prestonfield.com; r/ste

from £355/445; P), Rhubarb is a feast for the eyes as well as the taste buds. The over-the-top decor of rich reds set off with black and gold and sensuous surfaces – damask, brocade, marble and gilded leather – are matched by the intense flavours and rich textures of the modern Scottish cuisine. Vegetarian and vegan menus available.

Take your postprandial coffee and brandy upstairs to the sumptuous fireside sofas in the Tapestry and Leather rooms. A two-/three-course lunch menu is available for £27/33.

New Town

Urban Angel CAFE £
(Map p774; 0131-225 6215; www.urban-angel.co.uk; 121 Hanover St, EH2 1DJ; mains £6-11; 8am-5pm Mon-Fri, 9am-5pm Sat & Sun; 23, 27) A wholesome deli that puts the emphasis on fair-trade, organic and locally sourced produce, Urban Angel is also a delightfully informal cafe-bistro that serves all-day brunches (porridge with honey, pancakes, eggs Benedict), mix-and-match salads and a wide range of light, snacky meals.

Holy Cow VEGAN £
(Map p774; 34 Elder St, EH1 3DX; mains £6-12; 10am-10pm;) This hard-to-find cafe is hidden in a New Town basement close to the bus station, but well worth seeking out for its vegan burgers (portobello mushroom, Vietnamese tofu or soya and kidney bean, with chunky fries), and fresh and zingy Mexican salads loaded with chilli, coriander and lime juice.

★Gardener's Cottage SCOTTISH ££
(Map p774; 0131-558 1221; www.thegardenerscottage.co; 1 Royal Tce Gdns, London Rd, EH7 5DX; 2-/3-course lunch £15/19, 6-course dinner £60; noon-2pm & 5-10pm Mon-Fri, 10am-2pm & 5-10pm Sat & Sun; all London Rd buses) This country cottage in the heart of the city, bedecked with flowers and fairy lights, offers one of Edinburgh's most interesting dining experiences – two tiny rooms with communal tables made of salvaged timber, and a set menu based on fresh local produce (most of the vegetables and fruit are from its own organic garden). Bookings essential; brunch served at weekends.

★Aizle SCOTTISH ££
(Map p774; 0131-527 4747; www.aizle.co.uk; Kimpton Charlotte Square Hotel, 38 Charlotte Sq, EH2 4HQ; 6-course dinner £70; 5-9pm Wed-Sun; ; all Princes St buses) If you tend to have trouble deciding what to eat, Aizle (the name is an old Scots word for 'spark' or 'ember') will do the job for you. There's no menu here, just a six-course dinner conjured from a monthly 'harvest' of the finest and freshest local produce (listed on a blackboard), and presented beautifully – art on a plate.

Dishoom INDIAN ££
(Map p774; 0131-202 6406; www.dishoom.com/edinburgh; 3a St Andrew Sq, EH2 2BD; mains £9-15; 8am-10pm Mon-Fri, 9am-10pm Sat & Sun; ; St Andrew Sq) This Edinburgh restaurant was the Dishoom minichain's first opening outside London. Inspired by the Irani cafes of Mumbai, it serves exquisite Indian street food in upmarket surroundings; the breakfasts, including the signature bacon nan, are legendary. Hugely popular – book well ahead, or be prepared to queue for a table. A vegan menu is available.

Café Royal Oyster Bar SEAFOOD ££
(Map p774; 0131-556 1884; www.caferoyaledinburgh.com; 17a W Register St, EH2 2AA; mains £15-23, fillet steak £40; noon-2.30pm & 5.30-9.30pm Mon-Fri, noon-9.30pm Sat & Sun; St Andrew Sq) Pass through the revolving doors on the corner of West Register St and you're transported back to Victorian times – a palace of glinting mahogany, polished brass, marble floors, stained glass, Doulton tiles, gilded cornices and starched table linen so thick it creaks when you fold it. The menu is mostly classic seafood, from oysters on ice to Scottish lobster thermidor.

Ivy on the Square BRITISH ££
(Map p774; 0131-526 4777; www.theivyedinburgh.com; 6 St Andrew Sq, EH2 2BD; mains £15-19; 8am-midnight Mon-Sat, 9am-10.30pm Sun; ; St Andrew Sq) The first Scottish outpost of London's famous celebrity haunt, the Ivy in Covent Garden, this classy but informal brasserie serves up traditional British dishes, from eggs Benedict for brunch through afternoon tea to the Ivy's classic dishes of steak, egg and chips, or shepherd's pie (made with red wine sauce and topped with cheesy mashed potato). A vegan menu is available.

Contini ITALIAN ££
(Map p774; 0131-225 1550; www.contini.com/contini-george-street; 103 George St, EH2 3ES; mains £18-24; 8am-10pm Mon-Fri, 10am-

10.30pm Sat, 11am-8pm Sun; ; all Princes St buses) A palatial Georgian banking hall enlivened by fuchsia-pink banners and lampshades is home to this lively, family-friendly Italian bar and restaurant, where the emphasis is on fresh, authentic ingredients (produce imported weekly from Milan; homemade bread and pasta) and the uncomplicated enjoyment of food.

Dome SCOTTISH ££
(Map p774; 0131-624 8624; www.thedome edinburgh.com; 14 George St, EH2 2PF; mains £16-23, 2-/3-course lunch £20/25; 10am-10pm; ; St Andrew Sq) Housed in the magnificent neoclassical former headquarters of the Commercial Bank, with a lofty glass-domed ceiling, pillared arches and mosaic-tiled floor, the Grill Room at the Dome is one of the city's most impressive dining rooms. The menu is solidly modern Scottish, with great steaks and seafood, or try afternoon tea in the elegant Georgian Tea Room. Reservations strongly recommended.

Bon Vivant BISTRO ££
(Map p774; 0131-225 3275; www.bonvivant edinburgh.co.uk; 55 Thistle St, EH2 1DY; mains £14-19; noon-10pm; ; 23, 27, 42) A firm favourite with New Town foodies, this European bistro-style place offers superb value for this part of the city, with a range of tapas-style 'bites' as well as standard main courses, and a changing menu of seasonal, locally sourced dishes such as sea trout with radish, toasted black onion seeds and parsley sauce.

Fishers in the City SEAFOOD ££
(Map p774; 0131-225 5109; www.fishersbistros.co.uk; 58 Thistle St, EH2 1EN; mains £18-24; noon-10.30pm; ; 24, 29, 42) This more sophisticated city-centre branch of the famous Fishers Bistro (p788) in Leith, with granite-topped tables, a split-level dining area and nautical theme, specialises in superior Scottish seafood – the knowledgeable staff serve up plump and succulent oysters, meltingly sweet scallops, and Atlantic halibut that's been grilled to perfection.

Scottish Cafe & Restaurant SCOTTISH ££
(Map p774; 0131-225 1550; www.contini.com/scottish-cafe-and-restaurant; The Mound, EH2 2EL; mains £9-15; 9am-5pm Mon-Wed, Fri & Sat, to 7pm Thu, 10am-5pm Sun; ; Princes St) This appealing modern restaurant (part of the Scottish National Gallery (p771) complex) has picture windows providing a view along Princes Street Gardens. Try traditional Scottish dishes such as Cullen skink (smoked-haddock soup) and leek-and-potato soup, or seasonal, sustainably sourced produce including smoked salmon and trout, free-range chicken and pork.

★Outlook SCOTTISH £££
(Map p774; 0131-322 1246; www.thelookout edinburgh.co; Calton Hill, EH7 5AA; lunch/dinner from £28/34; noon-9.30pm Tue-Thu, 10am-9.30pm Fri-Sun;) This glass-walled restaurant perched on top of Calton Hill enjoys some of the finest views in the city, and some of the finest food. Run by the same folk as Gardener's Cottage, it has a menu consisting of a tray of seven small dishes (including a vegetarian option) prepared using whatever fresh local produce is in season, plus a choice of sides and wines.

Cafe St Honore FRENCH £££
(Map p774; 0131-226 2211; www.cafesthonore.com; 34 Thistle St Lane NW, EH2 1EA; mains £16-28; noon-2pm & 6-10pm; Princes St) With candlelight glowing against old polished wood and reflected from antique mirrors, this intimate French restaurant is the ideal place for a romantic dinner. Service is discreet, the menu is sumptuous and the wine list is long. You can get a two-/three-course set menu for either lunch or dinner for £23/28.

West End & Dean Village

Cafe Milk CAFE £
(Map p762; 0131-629 6022; www.cafemilk.co.uk; 232 Morrison St, EH3 8EA; mains £6-9; 7.30am-4pm Mon-Fri, 8am-4pm Sat, 8am-3pm Sun; ; Haymarket) This is fast food with a conscience – natural, nutritious, locally sourced and freshly prepared, from organic porridge to courgette, lemon and feta fritters, and North Indian dal with rice or flatbread. Take away, or sit in and soak up the retro vibe amid old Formica tables and battered school benches. There are branches at **Fruitmarket Gallery** (Map p774; www.fruitmarket.co.uk; 45 Market St, EH1 1DF; 11am-6pm; ; all North Bridge buses) FREE and **Edinburgh Sculpture Workshop** (0131-551 4490; www.edinburghsculpture.org; 21 Hawthornvale, EH6 4JT; 9.30am-5pm Mon-Sat; P; 7, 11) FREE.

★Timberyard SCOTTISH ££
(Map p768; 0131-221 1222; www.timberyard.co; 10 Lady Lawson St, EH3 9DS; mains £16-22,

5-course set menu £50; noon-2pm & 5.30-9.30pm Tue-Sat; ; 2, 300) Ancient, worn floorboards, cast-iron pillars, exposed joists, and tables made from slabs of old mahogany create a rustic, retro atmosphere in this slow-food restaurant where the accent is on locally sourced produce from artisan growers and foragers. Typical dishes include honey-glazed monkfish with saffron, samphire and leek, and pigeon with radicchio, chanterelles and sherry.

★Kanpai Sushi JAPANESE ££
(Map p768; 0131-228 1602; www.kanpaisushi.co.uk; 8-10 Grindlay St, EH3 9AS; mains £9-15, sushi per piece £4-10; noon-2.30pm & 5-10.30pm Tue-Sat; all Lothian Rd buses) What is arguably Edinburgh's best sushi restaurant impresses with its minimalist interior, fresh, top-quality fish and elegantly presented dishes – the squid tempura comes in a delicate woven basket, while the sashimi combo is presented as a flower arrangement in an ice-filled stoneware bowl. Bookings recommended.

Leith

Pitt MARKET £
(07534 157477; www.thepitt.co.uk; 125 Pitt St, EH6 4DE; entry £2; noon-8pm Sat, noon-6pm Sun Mar-Dec; 7, 14, 21) A weekly street-food market surrounded by industrial warehouses, the Pitt is a little bit of East London in north Edinburgh. The regularly changing food trucks sell anything from buttermilk-fried chicken burgers to halloumi bao buns to haggis to sweet-potato pierogi (dumplings). Choose a drink from the wine and gin bars, or the Barneys beer truck selling local craft ales.

The vibe is rustic and outdoorsy, with live bands, wooden pallet seating and fire barrels for warming your hands.

★Fishers Bistro SEAFOOD ££
(0131-554 5666; www.fishersbistros.co.uk; 1 The Shore, EH6 6QW; mains £12-26; noon-10.30pm Mon-Sat, 12.30-10.30pm Sun; ; 16, 22, 35, 36) This cosy little restaurant, tucked beneath a 17th-century signal tower, is one of the city's best seafood places. The menu ranges widely in price, from cheaper dishes such as classic fish cakes with lemon-and-chive mayonnaise to more expensive delights such as a whole Fife lobster with garlic-and-herb butter and chips (£45).

★Kitchin SCOTTISH £££
(0131-555 1755; www.thekitchin.com; 78 Commercial Quay, EH6 6LX; 3-course lunch/dinner £39/90; noon-2.30pm & 6-10pm Tue-Sat; ; 16, 22, 35, 36) Fresh, seasonal, locally sourced Scottish produce is the philosophy that's won a Michelin star for this elegant but unpretentious restaurant. The menu moves with the seasons, of course, so expect fresh salads in summer and game in winter, and shellfish dishes such as Orkney scallops baked in the shell with white wine, vermouth and herbs when there's an 'r' in the month.

★Restaurant Martin Wishart FRENCH £££
(0131-553 3557; www.restaurantmartinwishart.co.uk; 54 The Shore, EH6 6RA; 3-course lunch £39, 4-course dinner £75; noon-1.30pm & 7-9pm Wed-Sat; ; 16, 22, 35, 36) In 2001 this restaurant became the first in Edinburgh to win a Michelin star, and it's retained it ever since. The eponymous chef has worked with Albert Roux, Marco Pierre White and Nick Nairn, and brings a modern French approach to the best Scottish produce, from sautéed foie gras and langoustines with braised fennel to a six-course vegetarian tasting menu (£80).

Chop House Leith STEAK £££
(0131-629 1919; www.chophousesteak.co.uk; 102 Constitution St, EH6 6AW; mains £17-30; noon-3pm & 5-10.30pm Mon-Fri, noon-10.30pm Sat & Sun; ; 16, 22, 35, 36) A modern take on the old-fashioned steakhouse, this 'bar and butchery' combines slick designer decor (the ceramic brick tiles are a nod to traditional butcher shops) with a meaty menu of the best Scottish beef, dry-aged for at least 35 days and chargrilled to perfection (chateaubriand for two goes for £80). Sauces include bone-marrow gravy and Argentine chimichurri. Cool cocktails, too.

South Edinburgh

★Union Brew Lab CAFE £
(Map p768; 0131-662 8963; www.brewlabcoffee.co.uk; 6-8 S College St, EH8 9AA; mains £4-6; 9am-5.30pm; ; all South Bridge buses) Students with iPads lolling in armchairs, sipping carefully crafted espressos amid artfully distressed brick and plaster, recycled school-gym flooring, old workshop benches and lab stools...this is coffee-nerd heaven. There's good food, too, with hearty soups

and crusty baguette sandwiches. In summer try the refreshing cold-brew coffee.

Kalpna INDIAN £
(Map p762; ☎0131-667 9890; www.kalpnarestaurant.com; 2-3 St Patrick Sq, EH8 9EZ; mains £8-13; ⏰noon-2pm & 5.30-10.30pm; ; all Newington buses) A long-standing Edinburgh favourite, Kalpna is one of the best Indian restaurants in the country, vegetarian or otherwise. The cuisine is mostly Gujarati, with a smattering of dishes from other parts of India. The all-you-can-eat lunch buffet (£9) is superb value.

Tuk Tuk INDIAN £
(Map p762; ☎0131-228 3322; www.tuktukonline.com; 1 Leven St, EH3 9LH; mains £5-7; ⏰noon-10.30pm Sun-Thu, to 10.45pm Fri & Sat; 11, 15, 16, 23, 36, 45) One of Edinburgh's livelier Indian restaurants, Tuk Tuk serves street-food-style Indian dishes in spacious surroundings with vintage Bollywood posters on the wall. The menu boasts classics such as *channa puri* (curried chickpeas with flatbread) and an excellent signature 'railway station' curry (lamb on the bone, as served on Indian railways). Popular with bigger groups and pre- and post-theatre crowds.

★**First Coast** SCOTTISH ££
(Map p762; ☎0131-313 4404; www.first-coast.co.uk; 97-101 Dalry Rd, EH11 2AB; 2-/3-course dinner £22/26; ⏰noon-2pm & 5-11pm Mon-Sat; ; 2, 3, 4, 25, 33, 44) This popular neighbourhood bistro has a striking main dining area with sea-blue wood panelling and stripped stonework, and a short and simple menu offering hearty comfort food such as maple-syrup- and mustard-glazed ham hock with spinach and nutmeg mash, or cod in banana leaf with lemon, basil, aubergine and shrimp paste. Lunchtime and early evening there's an excellent two-/three-course menu for £14.50/16.

★**Locanda de Gusti** ITALIAN ££
(Map p762; ☎0131-346 8800; www.locandadegusti.com; 102 Dalry Rd, EH11 2DW; mains £14-28; ⏰5.30-10pm Mon-Wed, 12.30-2pm & 5.30-10pm Thu-Sat; ; 2, 3, 4, 25, 33, 44) This bustling family bistro, loud with the buzz of conversation and the clink of glasses and cutlery, is no ordinary Italian but a little corner of Naples, complete with hearty Neapolitan home cooking by friendly head chef Rosario. The food ranges from light and tasty ravioli tossed with butter, sage and nutmeg to delicious platters of grilled seafood.

> LOCAL KNOWLEDGE
>
> **SHEEP HEID INN**
>
> Possibly the oldest inn in Edinburgh (with a licence dating back to 1360), the **Sheep Heid Inn** (www.thesheepheidedinburgh.co.uk; 43-45 The Causeway, EH15 3QA; ⏰11am-11pm Mon-Thu, to midnight Fri & Sat, noon-11pm Sun; ; 42) feels more like an upmarket country pub than an Edinburgh bar. Set in the semirural shadow of Arthur's Seat (p770), it's famous for its 19th-century skittles alley and its lovely little beer garden.

★**Loudon's Café & Bakery** CAFE ££
(Map p762; www.loudons.co.uk; 94b Fountainbridge, EH3 9QA; mains £9-13; ⏰7.30am-5pm Mon-Fri, 8am-5pm Sat & Sun; ; 1, 34, 35, 300) Organic bread and cakes baked on the premises, ethically sourced coffee, daily and weekend newspapers scattered about, even some outdoor tables – what's not to like? The weekend all-day brunch (8am to 4pm) includes eggs Benedict, granola with yoghurt, and vegan vanilla pancakes. A **second branch** (Map p774; ☎0131-556 7734; www.loudons.co.uk/newwaverley; 2 Sibbald Walk, EH8 8FT; mains £9-13; ⏰8am-3pm Mon-Fri, to 4pm Sat & Sun; 35) opened in 2020 at the New Waverley development just off the Royal Mile.

Drinking & Nightlife

Edinburgh has always been a drinkers' city. It has more than 700 pubs – more per square mile than any other UK city – and they are as varied and full of character as the people who drink in them, from Victorian palaces to stylish pre-club bars, and from real-ale howffs (meeting places, often pubs) to cool cocktail lounges.

Old Town

The pubs in the Grassmarket have outdoor tables on sunny summer afternoons, but in the evenings they're favoured by boozed-up packs of party animals, so steer clear if that's not your thing. The Cowgate – the Grassmarket's extension to the east – is Edinburgh's clubland.

★Cabaret Voltaire CLUB

(Map p768; www.thecabaretvoltaire.com; 36-38 Blair St, EH1 1QR; ⏲5pm-3am Tue-Sat, 8pm-1am Sun; 📶; 🚌all South Bridge buses) An atmospheric warren of stone-lined vaults houses this self-consciously 'alternative' club, which eschews huge dance floors and egotistical DJ worship in favour of a 'creative crucible' hosting an eclectic mix of DJs, live acts, comedy, theatre, visual arts and the spoken word. Well worth a look.

★Bow Bar PUB

(Map p768; www.thebowbar.co.uk; 80 West Bow, EH1 2HH; ⏲noon-midnight; 🐾; 🚌2, 23, 27, 41, 42) One of the city's best traditional-style pubs (it's not as old as it looks), serving a range of excellent real ales, Scottish craft gins and a vast selection of malt whiskies, the Bow Bar is often standing-room only on Friday and Saturday evenings.

Bongo Club CLUB

(Map p768; www.thebongoclub.co.uk; 66 Cowgate, EH1 1JR; ⏲11pm-3am Tue & Thu, 7pm-3am Fri-Sun; 📶; 🚌2) Owned by a local arts charity, the weird and wonderful Bongo Club has a long history of hosting everything from wild club nights and local bands to performance art and kids comedy shows.

Salt Horse Beer Shop & Bar BAR

(Map p768; ☎0131-558 8304; www.salthorse.beer; 57-61 Blackfriars St, EH1 1NB; ⏲4pm-midnight Mon-Fri, noon-1am Sat, 12.30pm-midnight Sun; 🚌35) Tucked off the Royal Mile, this independent hybrid combines great beer, food, and a shop next door selling around 400 beers to drink in or take away. Work your way through 12 keg lines of local and imported beers and a small but perfectly formed menu of handmade burgers, Scotch eggs, and cheese and charcuterie platters.

Malt Shovel PUB

(Map p768; ☎0131-225 6843; www.maltshovelinn-edinburgh.co.uk; 11-15 Cockburn St, EH1 1BP; ⏲11am-11pm Mon-Wed, to midnight Thu & Sun, to 1am Fri & Sat; 📶👪; 🚌6) A traditional-looking pub with dark wood and subdued tartanry, the Malt Shovel offers a good range of real ales and more than 40 malt whiskies, and serves excellent pub grub including fish and chips, burgers, and steak-and-ale pies.

Checkpoint BAR

(Map p768; ☎0131-225 9352; www.checkpointedinburgh.com; 3 Bristo Pl, EH1 1EY; ⏲9am-1am; 📶; 🚌2, 47) A friendly cafe, bar and restaurant with a comprehensive menu including breakfasts, bar bites and substantial mains, Checkpoint has gained a reputation as one of the coolest spots in Edinburgh. The utilitarian white-walled space is flooded with light from floor-to-ceiling windows and is vast enough to house, of all things, an old shipping container.

Dragonfly COCKTAIL BAR

(Map p768; ☎0131-228 4543; www.dragonflycocktailbar.com; 52 West Port, EH1 2LD; ⏲4pm-1am; 📶; 🚌2) A superstylish lounge bar with a Raffles of Singapore vibe – it's all crystal chandeliers, polished wood and Asian art – Dragonfly has won rave reviews for both its innovative cocktails and its designer decor. Grab a seat on the neat little mezzanine, from where you can look down on the bar as the Singapore Slings are being slung.

Jolly Judge PUB

(Map p768; www.jollyjudge.co.uk; 7a James Ct, EH1 2PB; ⏲noon-11pm Mon-Thu, to midnight Fri & Sat, 12.30-11pm Sun; 📶; 🚌23, 27, 41, 42) A snug little howff tucked away down a close, the Judge exudes a cosy 17th-century atmosphere (low, timber-beamed painted ceilings) and has the added attraction of a cheering open fire in cold weather. No music or gaming machines, just the buzz of conversation.

Liquid Room CLUB

(Map p768; www.liquidroom.com; 9c Victoria St, EH1 2HE; ⏲live music from 7pm, club nights 10.30pm-3am; 🚌2, 23, 27, 41, 42) Set in a subterranean vault deep beneath Victoria St, the Liquid Room is a superb club venue with a thundering sound system. There are regular club nights every Friday and Saturday, as well as DJs and live bands on other nights. Check the website for upcoming events.

New Town

★Café Royal Circle Bar PUB

(Map p774; ☎0131-556 1884; www.caferoyaledinburgh.com; 17 W Register St, EH2 2AA; ⏲11am-11pm Mon-Wed, to midnight Thu, to 1am Fri & Sat, to 10pm Sun; 📶; 🚉Princes St) The Café Royal is perhaps *the* classic Edinburgh pub; its main claims to fame are its magnificent oval bar and its Doulton tile portraits of famous Victorian inventors. Sit at the bar or claim one of the cosy leather booths beneath the stained-glass windows, and choose from the seven real ales on tap.

Lucky Liquor Co COCKTAIL BAR

(Map p774; ☎0131-226 3976; www.luckyliquorco.com; 39a Queen St, EH2 3NH; ⏰4pm-1am; 🚌24, 29, 42) This tiny, black-and-white bar is all about the number 13: 13 bottles of base spirit are used to create a daily menu of 13 cocktails. The result is a playful list with some unusual flavours, such as tonka-bean liqueur, coconut champagne and salted grapefruit soda (though not necessarily all in the same glass!), served by a fun and friendly crew.

Bramble COCKTAIL BAR

(Map p774; ☎0131-226 6343; www.bramblebar.co.uk; 16a Queen St, EH2 1JE; ⏰4pm-1am; 🚌23, 27) One of those places that easily earns the sobriquet 'best-kept secret', Bramble is an unmarked cellar bar (there's only an inconspicuous brass nameplate beneath a dry-cleaner's shop) where a maze of stone and brick hideaways conceals what is arguably the city's best cocktail venue. No beer taps, no fuss, just expertly mixed drinks.

Cumberland Bar PUB

(Map p774; ☎0131-558 3134; www.cumberlandbar.co.uk; 1-3 Cumberland St, EH3 6RT; ⏰noon-midnight Mon-Wed, to 1am Thu-Sat, 11am-11pm Sun; 📶; 🚌23, 27) Immortalised as the stereotypical New Town pub in Alexander McCall Smith's serialised novel *44 Scotland Street,* the Cumberland has an authentic, traditional wood-brass-and-mirrors look (despite being relatively new) and serves well-looked-after, cask-conditioned ales and a wide range of malt whiskies. There's also a pleasant little beer garden.

Joseph Pearce's PUB

(Map p774; ☎0131-556 4140; www.bodabar.com/joseph-pearces; 23 Elm Row, EH7 4AA; ⏰11am-midnight Sun-Thu, to 1am Fri & Sat; 📶👪; 🚌all Leith Walk buses) This traditional Victorian pub has been remodelled and given a new lease of life by the Swedish owners. It's a real hub of the local community, with good food (very family friendly before 5pm), a relaxed atmosphere, and events like Monday-night Scrabble games and August crayfish parties.

Abbotsford PUB

(Map p774; ☎0131-225 5276; www.theabbotsford.com; 3 Rose St, EH2 2PR; ⏰11am-11pm Mon-Thu, to midnight Fri & Sat, 12.30-11pm Sun; 📶; 🚌all Princes St buses) One of the few pubs in Rose St that has retained its Edwardian splendour, the Abbotsford has long been a hangout for writers, actors, journalists and media people, and has many loyal regulars. Named after Sir Walter Scott's country house, it dates from 1902; the pub's centrepiece is a splendid mahogany island bar. There's a good selection of real ales.

> **LOCAL KNOWLEDGE**
>
> **WHISKY TASTING**
>
> If you don't have time to visit any of Scotland's distilleries, don't fret – the city has some fine places for sampling a wee dram or three.
>
> ➡ Scotch Whisky Experience (p764) Provides a comprehensive overview of Scotland's iconic spirit.
>
> ➡ Bow Bar (p790) Busy Grassmarket-area pub with a huge selection of malt whiskies.
>
> ➡ Malt Shovel (p790) Old-school pub with lots of single malts behind the bar.
>
> ➡ Bennet's Bar (p793) A lovely setting to taste more than 100 malts.
>
> ➡ Cumberland Bar (p791) Good summer choice; enjoy your malt while sitting in the garden.

Guildford Arms PUB

(Map p774; ☎0131-556 4312; www.guildfordarms.com; 1 W Register St, EH2 2AA; ⏰11am-11pm Mon-Thu, to 11.30pm Fri & Sat, 12.30-11pm Sun; 📶; 🚌St Andrew Sq) Located in a side alley off the east end of Princes St, the Guildford is a classic Victorian pub full of polished mahogany, gleaming brass and ornate cornices. The range of real ales is excellent – try to get a table in the unusual upstairs gallery, with a view over the sea of drinkers below.

Oxford Bar PUB

(Map p774; ☎0131-539 7119; 8 Young St, EH2 4JB; ⏰noon-midnight Mon-Thu, 11am-1am Fri & Sat, 12.30-11pm Sun; 📶; 🚌all Princes St buses) The Oxford is that rarest of things: a real pub for real people, with no 'theme', no frills and no pretensions. 'The Ox' has been immortalised by Ian Rankin, author of the Inspector Rebus novels, whose fictional detective is a regular here (as is the author himself). There's occasional live folk music.

Leith

★Roseleaf BAR

(☎0131-476 5268; www.roseleaf.co.uk; 23-24 Sandport Pl, EH6 6EW; ⏰10am-1am; 📶👶; 🚌16, 22, 35, 36) Cute, quaint, and decked out in flowered wallpaper, old furniture and rose-patterned china (cocktails are served in teapots), the Roseleaf could hardly be further from the average Leith bar. The real ales and bottled beers are complemented by a range of speciality teas, coffees and fruit drinks (including rose lemonade), and well-above-average pub grub (served from 10am to 10pm).

Port O'Leith PUB

(☎0131-554 3568; www.facebook.com/ThePortOLeithBar; 58 Constitution St, EH6 6RS; ⏰11am-1am Mon-Sat, noon-1am Sun; 🚌16, 22, 35, 36) This good old-fashioned local boozer has been sympathetically restored – it appeared in the 2013 film *Sunshine on Leith*. Its nautical history is evident in the form of flags and cap bands left behind by visiting sailors (Leith docks are just down the road). Pop in for a pint and you'll probably stay until closing time.

Lioness of Leith BAR

(☎0131-629 0580; www.thelionessofleith.co.uk; 21-25 Duke St, EH6 8HH; ⏰noon-1am Mon-Thu, 11am-1am Fri-Sun; 📶; 🚌21, 34, 35) Duke St was always one of the rougher corners of Leith, but the emergence of pubs like the Lioness is a sure sign of gentrification. Distressed timber and battered leather benches are surrounded by vintage objets trouvés, a pinball machine and a pop-art print of Allen Ginsberg. There are good beers and cocktails, and a tempting menu of gourmet burgers.

Teuchters Landing PUB

(☎0131-554 7427; www.teuchtersbar.co.uk; 1c Dock Pl, EH6 6LU; ⏰10.30am-1am; 📶; 🚌16, 22, 35, 36) A cosy warren of timber-lined nooks and crannies housed in a single-storey red-brick building (once a waiting room for ferries across the Firth of Forth), this real-ale and malt-whisky bar also has tables on a floating terrace in the dock.

LGBT EDINBURGH

Edinburgh has a small – but perfectly formed – gay and lesbian scene, centred on the area around Broughton St (known affectionately as the 'Pink Triangle') at the eastern end of New Town.

Scene Alba (www.scenealba.co.uk) is a monthly magazine covering queer culture in Scotland, with listings of gay-friendly pubs and clubs in Edinburgh and Glasgow.

Useful contacts:

Edinburgh LGBT Centre (www.lgbthealth.org.uk; 4 Duncan Pl, EH6 8HW; ⏰9am-5pm Mon-Fri; 🚌21, 25, 34, 35, 49)

Lothian LGBT Helpline (☎0300 123 2523; www.lgbthealth.org.uk/helpline; ⏰noon-9pm Tue & Wed, 1-6pm Thu & Sun)

Pubs & Clubs

CC Blooms (Map p774; ☎0131-556 9331; www.ccblooms.co.uk; 23 Greenside Pl, EH1 3AA; ⏰11am-3am; 📶; 🚌all Leith Walk buses) The raddled old queen of Edinburgh's 1990s gay scene has been given a shot in the arm, with two floors of deafening dance and disco every night. It can get pretty crowded after 11pm and the drinks can be overpriced, but it's worth a visit – go early, or sample the wild Church of High Kicks cabaret show on Sunday nights.

Regent (Map p762; ☎0131-661 8198; 2 Montrose Tce, EH7 5DL; ⏰noon-1am Mon-Sat, 12.30pm-1am Sun; 🐾; 🚌35) This is a pleasant gay local with a relaxed atmosphere (no loud music) that serves coffee and croissants as well as excellent real ales, including Deuchars IPA and Caledonian 80/-. It's the meeting place for various community groups including Bear Scots (second Saturday of the month) and the Ruby Fruits (first Sunday of the month).

South Edinburgh

★Royal Dick
MICROBREWERY

(Map p762; 0131-560 1572; www.summerhall.co.uk/the-royal-dick; 1 Summerhall, EH9 1PL; 2-10pm; ; 41, 42) The decor at the Royal Dick alludes to its past as the home of Edinburgh University's veterinary school: there are shelves of laboratory glassware and walls covered with animal bones, even an old operating table. But rather than being creepy, it's a warm, welcoming place for a drink, serving artisan ales and craft gins produced by its own microbrewery and distillery.

★Bennet's Bar
PUB

(Map p762; 0131-229 5143; www.kilderkingroup.co.uk/bennets; 8 Leven St, EH3 9DX; 11am-1am; all Tollcross buses) Situated beside the **King's Theatre** (Map p762; 0131-529 6000; www.capitaltheatres.com/kings; 2 Leven St, EH3 9LQ; box office 10am-6pm; all Tollcross buses), Bennet's (established in 1839) has managed to hang on to almost all of its beautiful Victorian fittings, from the stained-glass windows and the ornate mirrors to the wooden gantry and the brass water taps on the bar (for your whisky – there are over 100 from which to choose).

Athletic Arms
PUB

(Diggers; Map p762; 0131-337 3822; www.athleticarms.com; 1-3 Angle Park Tce, EH11 2JX; 11am-1am; ; 1, 34, 35) Nicknamed for the cemetery across the street – gravediggers used to nip in and slake their thirst here – the Diggers dates from 1897. It's still staunchly traditional – the decor has barely changed in 100 years – and is a beacon for real-ale drinkers, serving locally brewed 80-shilling ale. It's packed to the gills with football and rugby fans on match days.

☆ Entertainment

☆ Old Town

★Sandy Bell's
TRADITIONAL MUSIC

(Map p768; 0131-225 2751; 25 Forrest Rd, EH1 2QH; noon-1am Mon-Sat, 12.30pm-midnight Sun; 2, 23, 27, 35, 41, 42, 45) This unassuming pub has been a stalwart of the traditional-music scene since the 1960s (the founder's wife sang with The Corries). There's music every weekday evening at 9pm, and from 2pm Saturday and 4pm Sunday, plus lots of impromptu sessions.

Caves
LIVE MUSIC

(Map p768; www.unusualvenuesedinburgh.com/venues/the-caves-venue-edinburgh; 8-12 Niddry St S, EH1 1NS; 35) A spectacular subterranean venue set in the ancient stone vaults beneath the South Bridge, the Caves stages a series of one-off club nights and live-music gigs, as well as *ceilidh* (traditional music) nights during the Edinburgh Festival. Check the What's On link on the website for upcoming events.

Bannerman's
LIVE MUSIC

(Map p768; www.facebook.com/BannermansBar; 212 Cowgate, EH1 1NQ; noon-1am Mon-Sat, 12.30pm-1am Sun; ; 35) A long-established music venue – it seems like every Edinburgh student for the last four decades spent half their youth here – Bannerman's straggles through a warren of old vaults beneath South Bridge. It pulls in crowds of students, locals and backpackers with live rock, punk and indie bands five or six nights a week.

Jazz Bar
JAZZ, BLUES

(Map p768; www.thejazzbar.co.uk; 1a Chambers St, EH1 1HR; £3-7; 5pm-3am Sun-Fri, 1.30pm-3am Sat; ; 35, 45) This atmospheric cellar bar, with its polished parquet floors, bare stone walls, candlelit tables and stylish steel-framed chairs, is owned and operated by jazz musicians. There's live music every night from 9pm to 3am, and on Saturday from 3pm. As well as jazz, expect bands playing blues, funk, soul and fusion.

Royal Oak
TRADITIONAL MUSIC

(Map p768; 0131-557 2976; www.royal-oak-folk.com; 1 Infirmary St, EH1 1LT; 11.30am-2am Mon-Sat, 12.30pm-2am Sun; all South Bridge buses) This popular folk-music pub is tiny, so get here early (9pm start weekdays, 6pm and 9.30pm sessions on Saturday, 4.30pm and 7pm sessions on Sunday) if you want to be sure of a place. Saturday night in the lounge is open session – bring your own instrument (and/or a good singing voice!).

Whistle Binkie's
LIVE MUSIC

(Map p768; www.whistlebinkies.com; 4-6 South Bridge, EH1 1LL; entry free, except after midnight Fri & Sat; 5pm-3am Sun-Thu, 1pm-3am Fri & Sat; all South Bridge buses) This crowded cellar bar, just off the Royal Mile, has live music most nights till 3am, from rock and blues to folk and jazz. The long-standing open-mic night on Monday is a showcase for new talent.

DON'T MISS

ROSSLYN CHAPEL

Many years may have passed since Dan Brown's novel *The Da Vinci Code* and the subsequent film came out, but floods of visitors still descend on Scotland's most beautiful and enigmatic church – **Rosslyn Chapel** (Collegiate Church of St Matthew; 0131-440 2159; www.rosslynchapel.com; Chapel Loan, Roslin, EH25 9PU; adult/child £9/free; 9.30am-6pm Mon-Sat Jun-Aug, to 5pm Sep-May, noon-4.45pm Sun year-round; P; 37). Built in the mid-15th century for Sir William St Clair, third prince of Orkney, it has an ornately carved interior – at odds with the architectural fashion of its time – that's a monument to the mason's art, rich in symbolic imagery. Hourly talks by qualified guides are included with admission.

The chapel is on the eastern edge of the village of Roslin, 7 miles south of Edinburgh's centre. Lothian Bus 37 to Penicuik Deanburn runs from Edinburgh's West End to Roslin (£1.80, one hour, every 15 minutes). Note that bus 37 to Bush does not go via Roslin – check the bus front and if in doubt ask the driver.

☆ New Town

Voodoo Rooms LIVE MUSIC

(Map p774; 0131-556 7060; www.thevoodoorooms.com; 19a W Register St, EH2 2AA; free-£20; 4pm-1am Mon-Thu, noon-1am Fri-Sun; St Andrew Sq) Decadent decor of black leather, ornate plasterwork and gilt detailing creates a stylish setting for this complex of bars and performance spaces above the Café Royal (p791), hosting everything from classic soul and Motown to blues nights, jam sessions and live local bands.

Stand Comedy Club COMEDY

(Map p774; 0131-558 7272; www.thestand.co.uk; 5 York Pl, EH1 3EB; tickets £3-18; from 7.30pm Mon-Sat, from 12.30pm Sun; St Andrew Sq) The Stand, founded in 1995, is Edinburgh's main independent comedy venue. It's an intimate cabaret bar with performances every night and a free Sunday lunchtime show.

☆ West End & Dean Village

Filmhouse CINEMA

(Map p768; 0131-228 2688; www.filmhousecinema.com; 88 Lothian Rd, EH3 9BZ; tickets £7-11; ; all Lothian Rd buses) The Filmhouse is the main venue for the annual Edinburgh International Film Festival (p779) and screens a full programme of art-house, classic, foreign and second-run films, with lots of themes, retrospectives and 70mm screenings. It has wheelchair access to all three screens.

Henry's Cellar Bar LIVE MUSIC

(Map p768; 0131-629 2992; www.facebook.com/Henryscellarbar; 16 Morrison St, EH3 8BJ; free-£10; 9pm-3am Sun & Tue-Thu, 8pm-3am Mon, 7pm-3am Fri & Sat; all Lothian Rd buses) One of Edinburgh's most eclectic live-music venues, Henry's has something going on most nights of the week, from rock and indie to 'Balkan-inspired folk', and from funk and hip-hop to hardcore, staging both local bands and acts from around the world.

Traverse Theatre THEATRE

(Map p768; 0131-228 1404; www.traverse.co.uk; 10 Cambridge St, EH1 2ED; box office 10am-6pm Mon-Sat, to 7pm show nights; ; all Lothian Rd buses) The Traverse is the main focus for new Scottish writing; it stages an adventurous programme of contemporary drama and dance. The box office is only open on Sunday (from 4pm) when there's a show on.

Shopping

Princes St is Edinburgh's principal shopping street, lined with all the big high-street stores, with many smaller shops along pedestrianised Rose St, and more expensive designer boutiques on George St and Thistle St.

For more offbeat shopping – including fashion, music, crafts, gifts and jewellery – head for the cobbled lanes of Cockburn, Victoria and St Mary's Sts, all near the Royal Mile in the Old Town; William St in the western part of the New Town; and the Stockbridge district, immediately north of the New Town.

There are two big shopping centres in the New Town – **Waverley Mall** (Map p774; 0131-557 3759; www.waverleymall.com; Waverley Bridge, EH1 1BQ; 9am-7pm Mon-Sat, 10am-6pm Sun; all Princes St buses), at the eastern end of Princes St, and the massive new development of St James Quarter (p796) at the top of Leith St.

There's also **Multrees Walk** (Map p774; www.multreeswalk.co.uk; St Andrew Sq, EH1 3DQ; St Andrew Sq), a designer shopping complex with a flagship Harvey Nichols store on the eastern side of St Andrew Sq, and Ocean Terminal (p796), a huge mall in Leith.

Old Town

Armstrong's VINTAGE

(Map p768; 0131-220 5557; www.armstrongsvintage.co.uk; 83 Grassmarket, EH1 2HJ; 10am-5.30pm Mon-Thu, to 6pm Fri & Sat, noon-6pm Sun; 2) Armstrong's is an Edinburgh fashion institution (established in 1840, no less), a quality vintage-clothes emporium offering everything from elegant 1940s dresses to funky 1970s flares. Aside from the retro fashion, it's a great place to hunt for preloved kilts and Harris tweed, or to seek inspiration for that fancy-dress party.

Ragamuffin FASHION & ACCESSORIES

(Map p768; 0131-557 6007; www.facebook.com/ragamuffinclothesandknitwear; 278 Canongate, EH8 8AA; 10am-6pm Mon-Sat, noon-5pm Sun; 35) Quality Scottish knitwear and fabrics, including cashmere from Johnstons of Elgin, Fair Isle sweaters and Harris tweed.

Bill Baber FASHION & ACCESSORIES

(Map p768; 0131-225 3249; www.billbaber.com; 66 Grassmarket, EH1 2JR; 9am-6pm Mon-Sat; 2) This family-run designer-knitwear studio has been in the business for more than 40 years, producing stylish and colourful creations using linen, merino wool, silk and cotton.

Geoffrey (Tailor) Inc FASHION & ACCESSORIES

(Map p768; 0131-557 0256; www.geoffreykilts.co.uk; 57-59 High St, EH1 1SR; 9.30am-6pm Mon-Sat, 10.30am-5.30pm Sun; 35) Geoffrey can fit you out in traditional Highland dress, or run up a kilt in your own clan tartan. The store's offshoot, **21st Century Kilts** (www.21stcenturykilts.com; based at Duntarvie Castle in West Lothian), offers modern fashion kilts in a variety of fabrics.

Royal Mile Whiskies DRINKS

(Map p768; 0131-225 3383; www.royalmilewhiskies.com; 379 High St, EH1 1PW; 10am-6pm; 23, 27, 41, 42) If it's a drap of the cratur ye're after, this place has a selection of single malts in miniature and full-size bottles. There's also a range of blended whiskies, Irish whisky and bourbon, and you can buy online, too.

New Town

Scottish Gallery ARTS & CRAFTS

(Map p774; 0131-558 1200; www.scottish-gallery.co.uk; 16 Dundas St, EH3 6HZ; 10am-6pm Mon-Fri, to 4pm Sat; 23, 27) Home to Edinburgh's leading art dealers Aitken Dott, this private gallery exhibits and sells paintings by contemporary Scottish artists and the masters of the late-19th and early 20th centuries (including the Scottish Colourists). Appointments only on weekdays during the Covid-19 pandemic; walk-ins from 11am to 1pm Saturday.

Jenners DEPARTMENT STORE

(Map p774; 0131-225 2442; www.houseoffraser.co.uk; 48 Princes St, EH2 2YJ; 9.30am-6.30pm Mon-Wed, to 8pm Thu, to 7pm Fri, 9am-7pm Sat, 11am-6pm Sun; Princes St) Founded in 1838, and acquired by House of Fraser in 2005, Jenners is the 'Grand Old Lady' of Scottish department stores. It stocks a wide range of quality goods, both classic and contemporary.

Plans for Jenners to move to new premises in St James Quarter in 2021 have been put on hold because of the Covid-19 pandemic.

Harvey Nichols DEPARTMENT STORE

(Map p774; 0131-524 8388; www.harveynichols.com; 30-34 St Andrew Sq, EH2 2AD; 10am-6pm Mon-Wed, to 8pm Thu, to 7pm Fri & Sat, 11am-6pm Sun; St Andrew Sq) The jewel in the crown of Edinburgh's shopping scene has four floors of designer labels and eye-popping price tags.

St James Quarter MALL

(Map p774; www.stjamesquarter.com; 1 Leith St, EH1 3SS; St Andrew Sq) The former St James Centre has undergone a massive redevelopment, and is scheduled to open in 2021 as a huge shopping centre anchored by John Lewis, alongside new hotels and restaurants.

Stockbridge

★ **Golden Hare Books** BOOKS

(Map p774; 0131-629 1396; www.goldenharebooks.com; 68 St Stephen St, EH3 5AQ; 10am-6pm; 24, 29, 36, 42) Independent bookshops don't get lovelier than this. The Golden Hare – voted UK Independent Bookshop of the Year in 2019 – boasts a top-notch selection of books, an enchanting children's nook, and a small but perfectly formed events programme. A must if you love books, book design and beautiful shops.

Stockbridge Market MARKET

(Map p774; www.stockbridgemarket.com; cnr Kerr & Saunders Sts; ⏰10am-5pm Sun; 🚌24, 29, 36, 42) On Sunday the local community's focus is Stockbridge Market, set in a leafy square next to the bridge that gives the district its name. Wares range from fresh Scottish produce to handmade ceramics, jewellery, soaps and cosmetics. Grab an espresso from Steampunk Coffee, which operates out of a 1970s VW campervan.

Galerie Mirages JEWELLERY

(Map p774; ☎0131-315 2603; www.galeriemirages.com; 46a Raeburn Pl, EH4 1HL; ⏰10am-5.30pm Mon-Sat, noon-4.30pm Sun; 🚌24, 29, 42) An Aladdin's cave packed with jewellery, textiles and handicrafts from all over the world, Mirages is best known for its silver, amber and gemstone jewellery in both culturally traditional and contemporary designs.

Leith

Kinloch Anderson FASHION & ACCESSORIES

(☎0131-555 1390; www.kinlochanderson.com; 4 Dock St, EH6 6EY; ⏰9am-5.30pm Mon-Sat; 🚌16, 22, 35, 36) One of the best tartan shops in Edinburgh, Kinloch Anderson was founded in 1868 and is still family run. It is a supplier of kilts and Highland dress to the royal family.

Ocean Terminal MALL

(☎0131-555 8888; www.oceanterminal.com; Ocean Dr, EH6 6JJ; ⏰10am-8pm Mon-Fri, to 7pm Sat, 11am-6pm Sun; 📶; 🚌11, 22, 34, 36, 200) Anchored by Debenhams department store, Ocean Terminal is home to fashion outlets including New Look, GAP, Schuh, Superdry and White Stuff. The complex also includes access to the former Royal Yacht *Britannia* and a berth for visiting cruise liners.

South Edinburgh

Meadows Pottery CERAMICS

(Map p762; ☎0131-662 4064; www.themeadowspottery.com; 11a Summerhall Pl, EH9 1QE; ⏰10am-5pm Mon-Fri, to 4.30pm Sat; 🚌2, 41, 42) This small shop sells a range of colourful, high-fired oxidised stoneware, both domestic and decorative, all hand thrown on the premises. If you can't find what you want, you can commission custom-made pieces.

Lighthouse BOOKS

(Map p768; ☎0131-662 9112; www.lighthousebookshop.com; 43 W Nicolson St, EH8 9DB; ⏰11am-6pm Mon-Sat, 11.30am-5pm Sun; 🚌41, 42) Lighthouse is a radical independent bookshop that supports both small publishers and local writers. It stocks a wide range of political, gay and feminist literature, as well as non-mainstream fiction and nonfiction.

Backbeat MUSIC

(Map p762; ☎0131-668 2666; 31 E Crosscauseway, EH8 9HE; ⏰10am-5.30pm Mon-Sat; 🚌all Newington buses) If you're hunting for secondhand vinyl from way back, this cramped little shop has a stunning and constantly changing collection of jazz, blues, rock and soul, plus lots of '60s and '70s stuff, though you'll have to take some time to hunt through the clutter.

Information

MEDICAL SERVICES

Edinburgh Royal Infirmary (☎0131-536 1000; www.nhslothian.scot.nhs.uk/GoingToHospital/Locations/RIE; 51 Little France Cres, Old Dalkeith Rd, EH16 4SA; ⏰24hr; 🚌7, 8, 24, 33, 38, 49) Edinburgh's main general hospital; has a 24-hour accident and emergency department.

Western General Hospital (☎0131-537 1000; www.nhslothian.scot.nhs.uk/GoingToHospital/Locations/WGH; Crewe Rd S, EH4 2XU; ⏰8am-9pm; 🚌16, 19, 24, 29, 37, 38 47) For non-life-threatening injuries and ailments, you can attend the Minor Injuries Clinic here without having to make an appointment.

POST

Frederick St Post Office (Map p774; 40 Frederick St, EH2 1EY; ⏰9am-5.30pm Mon & Wed-Fri, 9.30am-5.30pm Tue, 9.30am-12.30pm Sat; 🚌24, 29, 42)

Edinburgh City Post Office (Map p774; upper level, Waverley Mall, Princes St, EH1 1BQ; ⏰10am-5.30pm Mon-Sat; 🚌all Princes St buses)

St Mary's St Post Office (Map p768; 46 St Mary's St, EH1 1SX; ⏰9am-5.30pm Mon-Fri, to 12.30pm Sat; 🚌35)

TOURIST INFORMATION

Edinburgh Tourist Office (Edinburgh iCentre; Map p768; ☎0131-473 3820; www.visitscotland.com/info/services/edinburgh-icentre-p234441; 249 High St, Royal Mile, EH1 1YJ; ⏰10am-4.30pm Mon-Sat, to 4pm Sun Oct-Mar,

QUEENSFERRY & THE FORTH BRIDGES

Queensferry, also known as South Queensferry, is at the narrowest part of the Firth of Forth where ferries have crossed to Fife from the earliest times. The village takes its name from Queen Margaret (1046–93), who gave pilgrims free passage across the firth on their way to St Andrews. Ferries continued to operate until 1964, when the graceful **Forth Road Bridge** was opened; this was followed by a second road bridge, the **Queensferry Crossing** (2017).

Predating the first road bridge by 74 years, the magnificent **Forth Bridge** – only outsiders ever call it the Forth Rail Bridge – was one of the finest engineering achievements of the 19th century. Opened in 1890 as the world's first major steel structure, it has three huge cantilevers spanning 1630m and took 53,000 tonnes of steel, 6.5 million rivets and the lives of 73 men to build.

longer hours Apr-Sep; ; 23, 27, 41, 42) Accommodation-booking service, free city maps, gift shop and bookshop, and sales of tickets for CalMac ferries and CityLink and National Express buses.

Edinburgh Festival Fringe Office (Map p768; 0131-226 0026; www.edfringe.com; 180 High St, EH1 1QS; noon-3pm Mon-Sat mid-Jun–mid-Jul, 10am-6pm daily mid-Jul–1 Aug, 9am-9pm daily Aug; all South Bridge buses) Box office and information centre for Edinburgh Festival Fringe (p779) events.

Edinburgh Festival Guide (www.edinburgh-festivalcity.com) Everything you need to know about Edinburgh's many festivals.

Getting There & Away

AIR

Edinburgh Airport (EDI; 0844 448 8833; www.edinburghairport.com), 8 miles west of the city, has numerous flights to other parts of Scotland and the UK, Ireland and mainland Europe.

BUS

Edinburgh Bus Station (Map p774; St Andrew Sq, EH1 3DX; left-luggage lockers per 12hr £8-12; 4.30am-midnight Sun-Thu, to 12.30am Fri & Sat; St Andrew Sq) is at the northeastern corner of St Andrew Sq, with pedestrian entrances from the square and from Elder St. For timetable information, contact **Traveline** (0871 200 22 33; www.traveline.info).

Scottish Citylink (0871 266 3333; www.citylink.co.uk) buses connect Edinburgh with all of Scotland's cities and major towns. The following are sample one-way fares departing from Edinburgh.

Destination	Fare (£)
Aberdeen	35
Dundee	18.60
Fort William	39
Glasgow	8.50
Inverness	34
Portree	57
Stirling	9.30

It's also worth checking with **Megabus** (0900 1600 900; https://uk.megabus.com) for cheap intercity bus fares (from as little as £5) from Edinburgh to Aberdeen, Dundee, Glasgow, Inverness and Perth.

There are various buses to Edinburgh from London and the rest of the UK.

CAR

Arriving in or leaving Edinburgh by car during the morning and evening rush hours (7.30am to 9.30am and 4.30pm to 6.30pm Monday to Friday) is an experience you can live without. Try to time your journey to avoid these periods.

Major roads leading into and out of Edinburgh:

- M90 north to Perth
- M9 northwest to Stirling
- M8 west to Glasgow
- A7 south to Galashiels
- A68 south to Melrose and Jedburgh
- A1 southeast to Berwick-upon-Tweed

TRAIN

The main rail terminus in Edinburgh is **Waverley train station**, located in the heart of the city. Trains arriving from, and departing for, the west also stop at **Haymarket station**, which is more convenient for the West End.

You can buy tickets, make reservations and get travel information at the **Edinburgh Rail**

Travel Centre (Waverley station, EH1 1BB; ⏲ 5am-midnight Mon-Sat, 7am-midnight Sun; 🚌 all Princes St buses). For fare and timetable information, phone the **National Rail Enquiry Service** (☎ 03457 48 49 50; www.nationalrail.co.uk) or use the journey planner on the website.

If you're travelling as a pair, consider purchasing a **Two Together Railcard** (www.twotogether-railcard.co.uk; per year £30), which offers you one-third off your combined fares on train rides taken throughout Great Britain (outside peak travel times).

ScotRail (☎ 0344 811 0141; www.scotrail.co.uk) operates regular train services from Edinburgh to:

Aberdeen (£37, 2½ hours, hourly)

Dundee (£20, 1¼ hours, hourly)

Glasgow (£15.30, 50 minutes, every 15 minutes)

Inverness (£45, 3½ hours)

ℹ Getting Around

TO/FROM THE AIRPORT

Bus

Lothian Buses' Airlink (www.lothianbuses.co.uk/airport) service 100 runs from South St David St (between Princes St and St Andrew Sq) to the airport (one way/return £4.50/7.50, 30 minutes, every 12 minutes from 4am to midnight) via the West End and Haymarket. Skylink services 200 and 300 run from the airport to Ocean Terminal via north Edinburgh, and to Surgeons' Hall via west Edinburgh, respectively.

Tram

Edinburgh Trams (www.edinburghtrams.com) run from the airport to the city centre (one way/return £6.50/9, 33 minutes, every six to eight minutes from 6.15am to 10.45pm).

Taxi

An airport taxi to the city centre costs around £20 and takes about 20 to 30 minutes.

BUS

Bus timetables, route maps and fare guides are posted at all main bus and tram stops, and you can pick up a copy of the free *Lothian Buses Route Map* from Lothian Buses' **TravelHub** (Map p768; 31 Waverley Bridge, EH1 1BQ; ⏲ 9am-5pm Mon-Sat; 🚌 all Princes St buses).

Adult fares within the city are £1.80; purchase from the bus driver. Children aged under five travel free and those aged five to 15 pay a flat fare of 90p.

On Lothian Buses you must pay the driver the exact fare, but First buses will give change. Lothian Bus drivers also sell a day ticket (£4.50) that gives one day of unlimited travel on Lothian buses and trams (within the City Zone, ie not including the airport); a family day ticket (up to two adults and three children) costs £9.50.

Night-service buses, which run hourly between midnight and 5am, charge a flat fare of £3.

You can also buy a Ridacard (from TravelHub; not available from bus drivers) that gives unlimited travel for one week for £20.

Lost-property enquiries should be made online (www.lothianbuses.com/lost-property).

CAR

Though useful for day trips beyond the city, a car in central Edinburgh is more of a liability than a convenience. There is restricted access on Princes St, George St and Charlotte Sq, many streets are one way, and finding a parking place in the city centre is like striking gold. Queen's Dr around Holyrood Park is closed to motorised traffic on Sunday.

There's no parking on main roads into the city from 7.30am to 6.30pm Monday to Saturday. Also, parking in the city centre can be a nightmare.

On-street parking is controlled by self-service ticket machines from 8.30am to 6.30pm Monday to Saturday, and costs from £2.40 to £4.90 per hour, with a 30-minute to four-hour maximum.

If you break the rules, you'll get a fine, often within minutes of your ticket expiring – Edinburgh's parking wardens are both numerous and notorious. The fine is £60, reduced to £30 if you pay up within 14 days. Cars parked illegally will be clamped or towed away. There are large, long-stay car parks at the Omni Centre, Blackfriars St, Castle Tce, Holyrood Rd and Fountain Park. Motorcycles can be parked free at designated areas in the city centre.

TAXI

Edinburgh's black taxis can be hailed in the street, ordered by phone (extra 80p charge) or picked up at one of the many central ranks. The minimum charge is £3 (£4 at night) for the first 450m, then 25p for every subsequent 168m – a typical 2-mile trip across the city centre will cost around £6 to £7. Tipping is up to you – because of the high fares, local people rarely tip on short journeys, but they occasionally round up to the nearest 50p on longer ones.

Central Taxis (☎ 0131-229 2468; www.taxis-edinburgh.co.uk)

City Cabs (☎ 0131-228 1211; www.citycabs.co.uk)

TRAM

Edinburgh's tram system (www.edinburghtrams.com) consists of one line from Edinburgh Airport to York Pl, at the top of Leith Walk, via Haymarket, the West End and Princes St.

Tickets are integrated with the city's Lothian Buses, costing £1.80 for a single journey within the city boundary, or £6.50 to the airport. Trams run every eight to 10 minutes Monday to Saturday and every 12 to 15 minutes on Sunday, from 5.30am to 11pm.

AT A GLANCE

POPULATION
598,830

TRANSLATION OF GLASGOW'S NAME
'Dear Green Place' in Gaelic

BEST LIVE MUSIC VENUE
King Tut's Wah Wah Hut (p821)

BEST SEAFOOD RESTAURANT
Gamba (p816)

BEST MICROBREWERY
Shilling Brewing Co (p820)

WHEN TO GO

Jun
The perfect time to visit the region's numerous stately homes, with spectacular blooming gardens.

Jul
Summer in Glasgow is a pleasure, with the best weather and locals even cheerier than usual.

Oct
Hit Galloway's forests to see red deer battling it out during rutting season.

Kelvingrove Art Gallery & Museum (p809)
ULMUS MEDIA/SHUTTERSTOCK ©

Glasgow & Southern Scotland

Though wise folk are well aware of its charms, southern Scotland is for many people just something to drive through on the way to the north. Big mistake. But it does mean you'll find plenty of breathing room here in summer.

Proximity to England brought raiding and strife aplenty, but the ruins of many churches now provide some of Scotland's most atmospheric historic sites. The rolling west enjoys extensive forests between bustling market towns, and the hills cascade down to the sandy coastline. But the main draw is undoubtedly Glasgow, Scotland's biggest city, a sassy and welcoming metropolis with excellent museums, restaurants and pubs.

INCLUDES

Glasgow & Southern Scotland Highlights

1 Kelvingrove Art Gallery & Museum (p809) Discovering fine art and natural history in a grand Victorian building.

2 New Lanark (p822) Admiring the radical social reform instituted in a handsome cotton-spinning community.

3 Border Abbeys (p826) Exploring the noble, evocative ruins – Dryburgh is our favourite – and the area's other excellent historic sights.

4 Hermitage Castle (p827) Pondering the violent history on the England-Scottish frontier at this grim castle.

5 Kirkcudbright (p831) Strolling around a charming town blending dignified history and modern creative flair.

6 Robert Burns Birthplace Museum (p831) Getting to know the Scottish Bard behind 'Auld Lang Syne'.

7 Hiking & Cycling (p832) Completing one of the region's breathtaking long-distance routes such as the Southern Upland Way.

8 Culzean Castle (p834) Taking in the architectural genius of an 18th-century castle perched on wild sea cliffs.

GLASGOW

☎0141 / POP 598,830

Glasgow is a good-time city that hides behind a sober facade. Disarmingly blending sophistication and earthiness, Scotland's biggest city has evolved over the last couple of decades to become one of Britain's most intriguing metropolises. Handsomely set along the Clyde River, it's a city with a rich architectural legacy – stately Victorian mansions, grand public buildings and, above all, the sublime designs of Charles Rennie Mackintosh that dot the city – the product of wealth generated from manufacturing and trade.

Apart from its seriously grand architecture, Glasgow is also home to some wonderful museums and galleries, a crackling nightlife and several of Scotland's top restaurants. All in all, it's quite a place – you'll soon find Glasgow's sheer vitality is gloriously infectious.

History

The area where Glasgow now stands was bisected by the Romans in the 2nd century AD when they built the Antonine Wall to protect the fringes of their empire from the Caledonian wildlings beyond.

Glasgow grew around the religious site established in the 6th century by St Kentigern, better known as St Mungo (originally an affectionate nickname). It became an important bishop's seat, but the cathedral that was built here is one of the few remnants of the medieval city. It was swept away by the energies of a new age – the age of capitalism, the Industrial Revolution and the British Empire.

Glasgow's west-coast position led to it becoming an important port for trade with the Americas. In the 18th century much of the tobacco trade between Europe and the USA was routed through Glasgow, providing a great source of wealth. The tobacco barons were responsible for much construction around the city that remains today. Even after the tobacco trade declined in the 19th century, the city continued to prosper as a centre of textile manufacturing, shipbuilding and the coal and steel industries. Many of the city's major buildings and monuments were constructed during the Victorian period, when Glasgow was a byword for mercantile prosperity. The outward appearance, however, was tempered by the dire working conditions in the factories.

In the first half of the 20th century, Glasgow was the centre of Britain's munitions industry, supplying arms and ships for the two world wars, in the second of which the city was carpet-bombed. Post-WWII, the port and heavy industries began to dwindle, and by the early 1970s the city looked doomed. Glasgow became synonymous with unemployment, economic depression and urban violence, centred on high-rise housing schemes such as the infamous Gorbals.

More recently, gentrification and a booming cultural sector have injected style and confidence into the city. Though the standard of living remains low for Britain, and life continues to be tough for many, the ongoing regeneration process gives grounds for optimism. The successful hosting of the 2014 Commonwealth Games highlighted this regeneration to a wide global audience, as has the city's commitment to sustainable urban development. Glasgow is set to host the United Nations Climate Change Conference (COP26) in November 2021 and aims to be Britain's first carbon-neutral city by 2030.

⦿ Sights

⦿ City Centre

Glasgow's city centre changes character as you move from east to west, going from a frenetic blend of services, transport terminals, pubs and shops to the more sedate terraces of thoroughfares such as Bath St, where upmarket offices sit over basements converted into stylish bars. This is where much of the city's quality accommodation is clustered. It is also a studenty zone, with a major nightlife nexus on Sauchiehall St, which runs the length of the neighbourhood.

★City Chambers HISTORIC BUILDING
(Map p806; ☎0141-287 2000; www.glasgow.gov.uk; George Sq; ⏲9am-5pm Mon-Fri) **FREE** The grand seat of local government was built in the 1880s at the high point of Glasgow's wealth. The interior is even more extravagant than the exterior, and the chambers have sometimes been used as a movie location to represent the Kremlin or the Vatican. You can have a look at the opulent ground floor during opening hours. Free guided tours are held at 10.30am and 2.30pm Monday to Friday; it's worth popping in earlier in the day to prebook.

Mackintosh at the Willow HISTORIC BUILDING

(Map p806; ☎0141-204 1903; www.mackintoshatthewillow.com; 217 Sauchiehall St; exhibition adult/child £5.50/4.50; ⏲tearoom noon-5pm, exhibition 10am-4.45pm, last entry 1hr before closing) Opened in 2018, this reconstruction of the original Willow tearoom that Mackintosh designed and furnished in the early 20th century for restaurateur Kate Cranston offers authentic design splendour in its original location. You can admire the architect's distinctive touch in just about every element; he had free rein and even the teaspoons were given his attention. Alongside the tearoom is a visitor centre, with a two-level interactive exhibition about the historical context and Kate Cranston's collaboration with Mackintosh and Margaret Macdonald.

Gallery of Modern Art GALLERY

(GoMA; Map p806; ☎0141-287 3050; www.glasgowmuseums.com; Royal Exchange Sq; ⏲10am-5pm Mon-Wed & Sat, until 8pm Thu, 11am-5pm Fri & Sun) FREE This contemporary art gallery features modern works from local and international artists, housed in a graceful neoclassical building. The original interior is an ornate contrast to the inventive art often on display, though quality varies markedly by exhibition. An effort is made to keep the kids entertained. Usually the horseback statue of the Duke of Wellington outside is cheekily crowned with a traffic cone. The authorities grumble, but it keeps happening and is now an icon.

CHARLES RENNIE MACKINTOSH

Great cities have great artists, designers and architects contributing to their urban environment while expressing their soul and individuality. Charles Rennie Mackintosh's quirky, linear and geometric designs have had an enormous influence on Glasgow. Many of the buildings Mackintosh designed are open to the public, and you'll see his tall, thin, art nouveau typeface repeatedly reproduced.

Born in 1868, Mackintosh studied at the Glasgow School of Art. It was there that he met the influential artist and designer Margaret Macdonald, whom he married; they collaborated on many projects and were major influences on each other's work. Together with her sister Frances and Herbert MacNair, the artist who married her, they formed 'The Four', a pioneering group that developed the Glasgow Style. This contribution to art nouveau incorporated influences from the Arts and Crafts Movement and Japanese design.

In 1896, aged 27, Mackintosh won a competition for his design for the new building of the **Glasgow School of Art** (Map p806; ☎0141-353 4500; www.gsa.ac.uk; 167 Renfrew St), where he had studied. This was his supreme architectural achievement. The first section was opened in 1899 and is considered to be the earliest example of art nouveau in Britain. The second section, opened a decade later, includes some of the earliest art deco. The building demonstrates his skill in combining function and style.

Another of Mackintosh's finest works is Hill House (p867) in Helensburgh. Other buildings around town include the **Daily Record Building** (Map p806; 20 Renfield Lane), **Scotland Street School** (☎0141-287 0500; www.glasgowlife.org.uk; 225 Scotland St; ⏲check online/call ahead) FREE, **Mackintosh Queen's Cross church** (Map p812; ☎0141-946 6600; www.mackintoshchurch.com; 870 Garscube Rd; adult/child £4/free; ⏲11am-4pm Mon-Fri Apr-Oct, Mon, Wed & Fri Nov, Dec, Feb & Mar, closed Jan) and **House for an Art Lover** (☎0141-483 1600; www.houseforanartlover.co.uk; Bellahouston Park, Dumbreck Rd; adult/child £6.50/5; ⏲roughly 10am-4pm Sun-Fri, to noon Sat). At Mackintosh at the Willow, you can see his design concept right down to the smallest level.

Although Mackintosh's genius was quickly recognised in the rest of Europe, he did not receive the same encouragement in Scotland. His architectural career here lasted only until 1914, when he moved to England to concentrate on furniture design. He died in 1928, and it is only since the last decades of the 20th century that Mackintosh's genius has been widely recognised. For more about the man and his work, contact the **Charles Rennie Mackintosh Society** (Map p812; ☎0141-946 6600; www.crmsociety.com; Mackintosh Queen's Cross, 870 Garscube Rd).

Central Glasgow

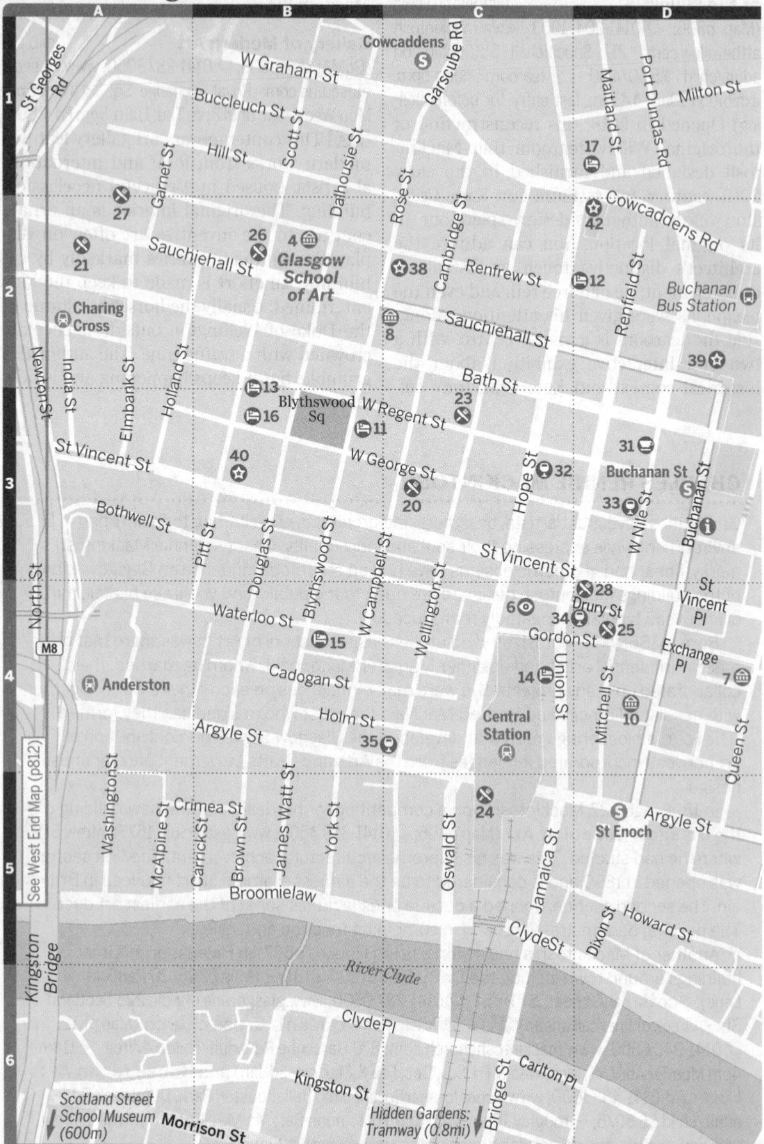

The Lighthouse HISTORIC BUILDING
(Map p806; ☎0141-276 5365; www.thelighthouse.co.uk; 11 Mitchell Lane; ⏲10.30am-5pm Mon-Sat, from noon Sun) FREE Mackintosh's first building, designed in 1893, was a striking new headquarters for the *Glasgow Herald*. Tucked up a narrow lane off Buchanan St, it now serves as Scotland's Centre for Architecture and Design, with fairly technical temporary exhibitions (sometimes admission is payable for these), as well as the Mackintosh Interpretation Centre, a detailed (if slightly

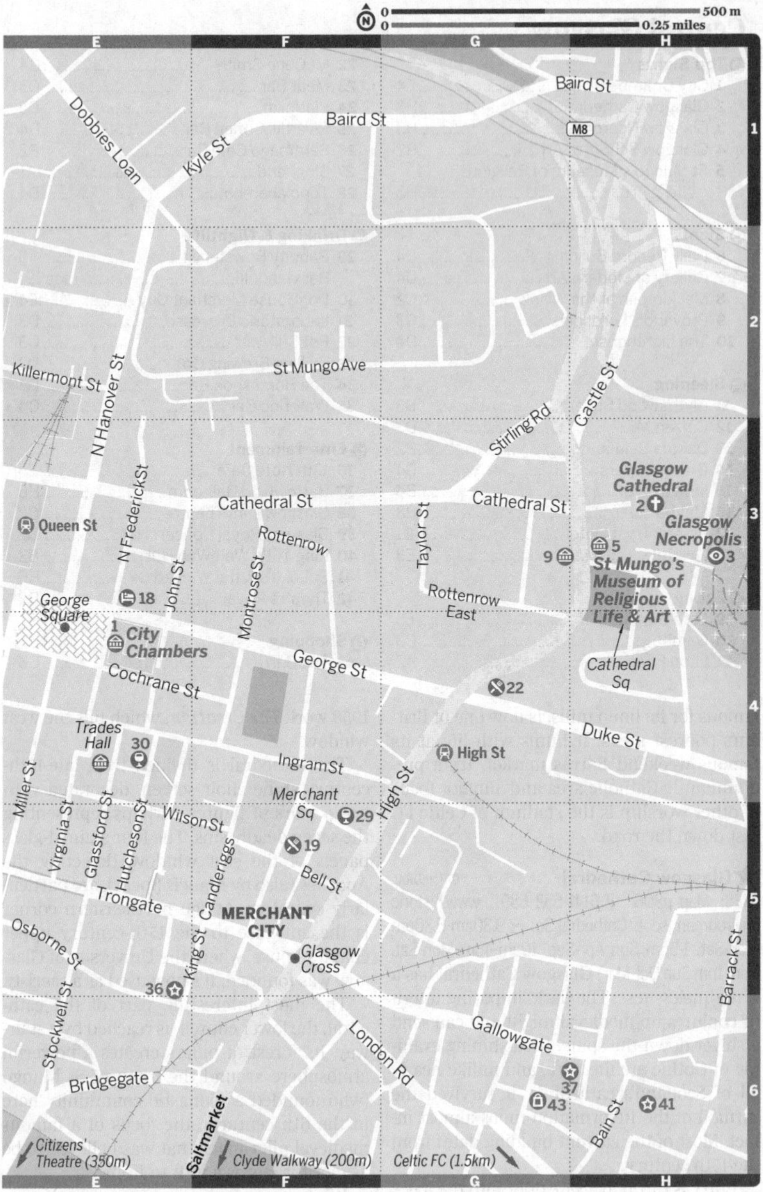

dry) overview of his life and work. On the top floor of the 'lighthouse', drink in great views over the rooftops and spires of the city centre.

Guided tours (adult/child £5/3) are offered on Saturday from 1pm on a first come, first served basis.

East End

The East End includes the oldest part of the city, concentrated around Glasgow Cathedral, and a range of traditional Glasgow districts that are fast becoming hubs of creative activity. One of these, the Calton, once

Central Glasgow

Top Sights
1 City Chambers E4
2 Glasgow Cathedral H3
3 Glasgow Necropolis H3
4 Glasgow School of Art B2
5 St Mungo's Museum of Religious Life & Art H3

Sights
6 Daily Record Building C4
7 Gallery of Modern Art D4
8 Mackintosh at the Willow C2
9 Provand's Lordship G3
10 The Lighthouse D4

Sleeping
11 Blythswood Square B3
12 Citizen M D2
13 Dakota Deluxe B2
14 Grasshoppers C4
15 Indigo B4
16 Malmaison B3
17 Pipers' Tryst Hotel D1
18 Z Hotel E3

Eating
19 Café Gandolfi F5
20 Gamba C3
21 Loon Fung A2
22 McCune Smith G4
23 Meat Bar C3
24 Platform C5
25 Riverhill Coffee Bar D4
26 Saramago Café Bar B2
27 Singl-end A1
28 Topolabamba D4

Drinking & Nightlife
29 Babbity Bowster F5
Bar Gandolfi (see 19)
30 DogHouse Merchant City E4
31 Laboratorio Espresso D3
32 Pot Still C3
33 Shilling Brewing Co D3
34 The Horseshoe Bar D4
35 Waterloo Bar C4

Entertainment
36 13th Note Café E5
37 Barrowland Ballroom H6
38 Glasgow Film Theatre C2
39 Glasgow Royal Concert Hall D2
40 King Tut's Wah Wah Hut B3
41 St Luke's & the Winged Ox H6
42 Theatre Royal D2

Shopping
43 The Barras G6

famous for its linen mills, is now one of Britain's poorest areas; it hums with life at its famous weekend Barras market. It's a predominantly Catholic area and a major focus of other worship is the stadium of Celtic FC just down the road.

★ **Glasgow Cathedral** CATHEDRAL
(HES; Map p806; 0141-552 6891; www.historicenvironment.scot; Cathedral Sq; 9.30am-5.30pm Mon-Sat, 1-5pm Sun Apr-Sep, 10am-4pm Mon-Sat, from 1pm Sun Oct-Mar) Glasgow Cathedral has a rare timelessness. The dark, imposing interior conjures up medieval might and can send a shiver down the spine. It's a shining example of Gothic architecture, and unlike nearly all of Scotland's cathedrals, it survived the turmoil of the Reformation mobs almost intact. Most of the current building dates from the 15th century.

Entry is through a side door into the nave, hung with regimental colours. The wooden roof has been restored many times since its original construction, but some of the timber dates from the 14th century; note the impressive shields. Many of the cathedral's stunning, narrow stained-glass windows are modern – to your left is Francis Spear's 1958 work *The Creation,* which fills the west window.

The cathedral is divided by a late-15th-century stone choir screen, decorated with seven pairs of figures perhaps representing the seven deadly sins. The four stained-glass panels of the east window, depicting the Apostles (also by Francis Spear), are particularly evocative. At the northeastern corner is the entrance to the 15th-century upper chapter house, where the University of Glasgow was founded. It's now used as a sacristy.

The most interesting part of the cathedral, the lower church, is reached by a stairway. Its forest of pillars creates a powerful atmosphere around the tomb of St Mungo (who founded a monastic community here in the 6th century), the focus of a famous medieval pilgrimage that was believed to be as meritorious as a visit to Rome.

While here, don't miss a stroll in the **necropolis** (Map p806; www.glasgownecropolis.org; 7am-4.30pm) FREE.

★ **St Mungo's Museum of Religious Life & Art** MUSEUM
(Map p806; 0141-276 1625; www.glasgowlife.org.uk; 2 Castle St; check online/call ahead) FREE

Set in a reconstruction of the bishop's palace that once stood in the cathedral forecourt, this museum audaciously attempts to capture the world's major religions in an artistic nutshell. A startling achievement, it presents the similarities and differences in how various religions approach common themes such as birth, marriage and death. The attraction is twofold: firstly, impressive art that blurs the lines between religion and culture; and secondly, the opportunity to delve into different faiths, as deeply or shallowly as you wish.

Provand's Lordship HISTORIC BUILDING

(Map p806; ☎0141-276 1625; www.glasgowlife.org.uk; 3 Castle St; ⏲check online/call ahead) FREE Near the cathedral is Provand's Lordship, the oldest house in Glasgow. This rare example of 15th-century domestic Scottish architecture was built in 1471 as a manse. The ceilings and doorways are low, and the rooms are furnished with period furniture and artefacts. Upstairs a room re-creates the living space of an early-16th-century chaplain. The building's biggest draw is its authentic feel, though it's a shame the original wooden floors have had to be covered for protection.

West End

★Kelvingrove Art Gallery & Museum GALLERY

(Map p812; ☎0141-276 9599; www.glasgowmuseums.com; Argyle St; ⏲11am-4pm) FREE A magnificent sandstone building, this grand Victorian cathedral of culture is a fascinating and unusual museum, with a bewildering variety of exhibits. You'll find fine art alongside stuffed animals, and Micronesian shark-tooth swords alongside a Spitfire plane, but it's not mix 'n' match: rooms are carefully and thoughtfully themed, and the collection is of a manageable size. It has an excellent room of Scottish art, a room of fine French impressionist works, and quality Renaissance paintings from Italy and Flanders.

Salvador Dalí's superb *Christ of St John of the Cross* is also here. Best of all, nearly everything, including the paintings, has an easy-reading paragraph of interpretation. You can learn a lot about art here, and it's excellent for children, with plenty to do and displays aimed at a variety of ages. Free hour-long guided tours begin at 11am and 2.30pm. Be here at 1pm to hear the impressive organ being played. Bus 17, among many others, runs here from Renfield St.

Hunterian Museum MUSEUM

(Map p812; ☎0141-330 4221; www.hunterian.gla.ac.uk; University Ave; ⏲10am-5pm Tue-Sat, 11am-4pm Sun) FREE Housed in the glorious sandstone university building, which is in itself reason enough to pay a visit, this quirky museum contains the collection of renowned one-time student William Hunter (1718–83). Hunter was primarily an anatomist and physician, but as one of those wonderfully well-rounded Enlightenment figures, he interested himself in everything the world had to offer.

Pickled organs in glass jars take their place alongside geological phenomena, potsherds gleaned from ancient brochs, dinosaur skeletons and a creepy case of deformed animals. The main halls of the exhibition, with their high vaulted roofs, are magnificent in themselves. Highlights include a display of artefacts from the Antonine Wall and the beautiful 1674 Chinese *Map of the Whole World,* produced for the emperor by a Jesuit at the court.

This collection will perhaps become part of the new museum at Kelvin Hall (p810), but probably not until at least 2025.

Hunterian Art Gallery GALLERY

(Map p812; ☎0141-330 4221; www.hunterian.gla.ac.uk; 82 Hillhead St; ⏲10am-5pm Tue-Sat, 11am-4pm Sun) FREE Across the road from the Hunterian Museum, and part of the same bequest, this art gallery incorporates Mackintosh House as well as a good selection of Dutch Old Masters. A key highlight is a special collection of James McNeill Whistler's limpid prints, drawings and paintings. It also has a good selection of the bold tones of the Scottish Colourists and the Glasgow Boys.

★Mackintosh House HISTORIC BUILDING

(Map p812; ☎0141-330 4221; www.hunterian.gla.ac.uk; 82 Hillhead St; adult/child £6/3; ⏲10am-5pm Tue-Sat, 11am-4pm Sun) Attached to the Hunterian Art Gallery, this is a reconstruction of the home that Charles Rennie Mackintosh shared with his wife, noted designer/artist Margaret Macdonald. It's fair to say that interior decoration was one of their strong points; Mackintosh House is startling even today. The quiet elegance of the hall and dining room on the ground floor give way to a stunning drawing room and bedroom upstairs. Visits are currently self guided.

Botanic Gardens PARK
(Map p812; ☎0141-276 1614; www.glasgowbotanicgardens.com; 730 Great Western Rd; ⏲7am-dusk, glasshouse 10am-6pm summer, to 4.15pm winter) A marvellous thing about walking in here is the way the noise of Great Western Rd suddenly recedes into the background. The wooded gardens follow the bank of the River Kelvin and there are plenty of tropical species to discover. **Kibble Palace**, an impressive Victorian iron and glass structure dating from 1873, is one of the largest glasshouses in Britain; check out the herb garden, too, with its medicinal species.

Kelvin Hall MUSEUM
(Map p812; ☎0141-276 1450; www.glasgowlife.org.uk; 1445 Argyle St; ⏲6.30am-10pm Mon-Fri, 8am-5pm Sat, 8am-8pm Sun) FREE Opened in the 1920s as an exhibition centre, this enormous sandstone palace, renovated and reopened in 2016, is a mixed leisure-and-arts space. In addition to a gym and sports facilities, it hosts the audiovisual archive of the **National Library of Scotland** (Map p812; ☎0845-366 4600; www.nls.uk; ⏲10am-4pm Tue-Sat) FREE and also stores museum collections from the University of Glasgow and Glasgow Museums (available by appointment). The major exhibition halls are being developed and may end up holding the Hunterian collections as well as other city-related exhibits.

Activities

Clyde Walkway WALKING
The Clyde Walkway extends from Glasgow upriver to the Falls of Clyde near New Lanark, some 40 miles away. The Glasgow tourist office has a good leaflet pack detailing different sections of the walk. The 10-mile section through Glasgow has interesting parts, though modern buildings have replaced most of the old shipyards. The loveliest sections are upstream.

Festivals & Events

Celtic Connections MUSIC
(☎0141-353 8000; www.celticconnections.com; ⏲Jan) This two-week music festival focuses on roots music and folk from Scotland and around the world.

Glasgow Film Festival FILM
(www.glasgowfilm.org/glasgow-film-festival; ⏲Feb) Two-week film festival with screenings in various locations across the city.

Glasgow International Comedy Festival COMEDY
(☎0844 873 7353; www.glasgowcomedyfestival.com; ⏲Mar) Two weeks of quality comedy, both home-grown and imported, enlivens stages across the city in March.

Glasgow Jazz Festival MUSIC
(www.jazzfest.co.uk; ⏲Jun) Excellent festival sees big-name international acts come to town, with stages set up in George Sq and Merchant City.

TRNSMT MUSIC
(www.trnsmtfest.com; ⏲Jul) This festival only started in 2017 but has been a huge success, drawing major indie rock acts to Glasgow Green.

Sleeping

City Centre

★**Grasshoppers** HOTEL £££
(Map p806; ☎0141-222 2666; www.grasshoppersglasgow.com; 87 Union St; r £60-125 incl breakfast; ❄📶🐾) Discreetly hidden atop a time-worn railway administration building alongside Central station, this small, well-priced hotel is a modern, upbeat surprise. Rooms are compact (a few are larger) but well appointed, with unusual views over the station roof's glass sea. Numerous touches – friendly staff, interesting art, in-room cafetière, free cupcakes and ice cream, and weeknight suppers – make this one of the centre's homiest choices.

★**Z Hotel** HOTEL ££
(Map p806; ☎0141-212 4550; www.thezhotels.com; 36 North Frederick St; r £55-125; ❄📶) Just off George Sq, the facade of a historic building conceals a stylish contemporary hotel. Chambers are modern but compact – the idea is that you sleep here and socialise in the bar area, especially during the afternoon wine-and-cheese session. Big flatscreens and pleasing showers add comfort to rooms that can be great value if advance booked.

Citizen M HOTEL ££
(Map p806; ☎020-3519 1111; www.citizenm.com; 60 Renfrew St; r £89-199; @📶) This modern chain does away with some normal hotel

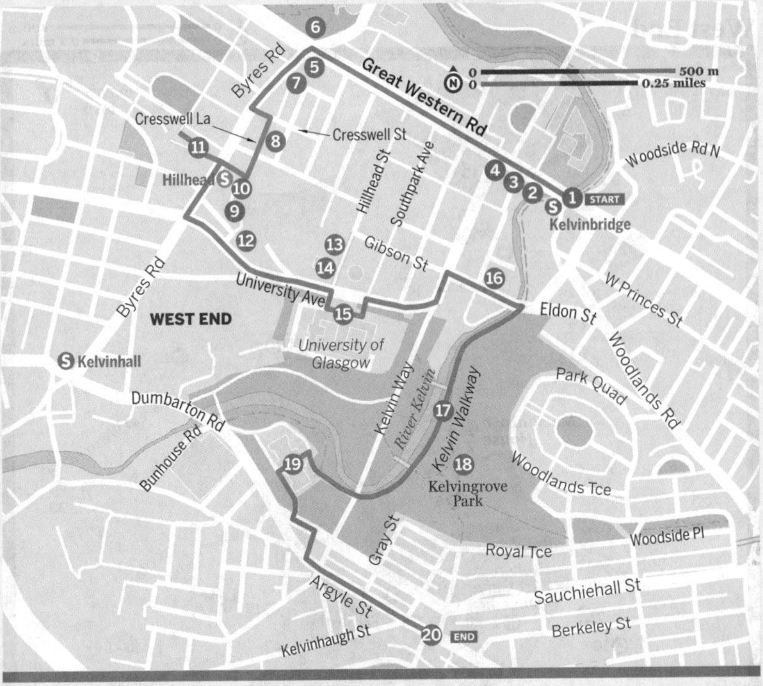

Walking Tour West End

START KELVINBRIDGE SUBWAY STATION
END ARGYLE ST, FINNIESTON
LENGTH 3 MILES; 2 HOURS

From the subway, turn left across 1 **Great Western Bridge (Kelvinbridge)**. It crosses the leafy course of the River Kelvin; note the riverside bar 2 **Inn Deep** (p821) to come back to. Continue along Great Western Rd, stopping for a browse in 3 **Glasgow Vintage Company** (Map p112; ☎0141-338 6633; www.glasgowvintage.com; 453 Great Western Rd; ⏲11am-6pm Mon-Sat, to 5pm Sun) and 4 **Caledonia Books** (Map p112; ☎0141-334 9663; www.caledoniabooks.co.uk; 483 Great Western Rd; ⏲10.30am-6pm Mon-Sat). At the corner of Byres Rd, a former church is now 5 **Oràn Mór** (p821); consider attending its lunchtime theatre session 6 **A Play, a Pie and a Pint** (p821). Across the road stretch the 7 **Botanic Gardens** (p810).

Turn left down Byres Rd; investigate interesting shops on the left. At Cresswell St, turn left then right down Cresswell Lane to check out tiny 8 **De Courcy's Arcade** (Map p112; www.facebook.com/decourcysarcade; Cresswell Lane; ⏲10am-5.30pm Mon-Sat, noon-5pm Sun). Further down is the bar-heavy 9 **Ashton Lane**, where 10 **Ubiquitous Chip** (p817) is still one of Scotland's best places to eat. Turn right to reach Byres Rd again. Cross and examine the quirky shops down 11 **Ruthven Lane**, directly opposite.

Back on Byres Rd, head south, then turn left up University Ave. The ugly 1960s 12 **Boyd Orr tower** is soon replaced by more typical sandstone terraces as you climb the hill. On the left is the 13 **Hunterian Art Gallery** (p809) and 14 **Mackintosh House** (p809); on the right, the University of Glasgow's main building is home to the 15 **Hunterian Museum** (p809).

At the bottom of University Ave, turn left then right onto Gibson St, home to quality lunch stops such as 16 **Stravaigin** (p817). Cross the bridge and turn right into the park, bearing right down to the river and the 17 **Kelvin Walkway**. Follow this for half a mile through lovely 18 **Kelvingrove Park** (Map p112) to reach the 19 **Kelvingrove Art Gallery & Museum** (p809). From here it's a short hop to the Finnieston eating strip on 20 **Argyle St**.

West End

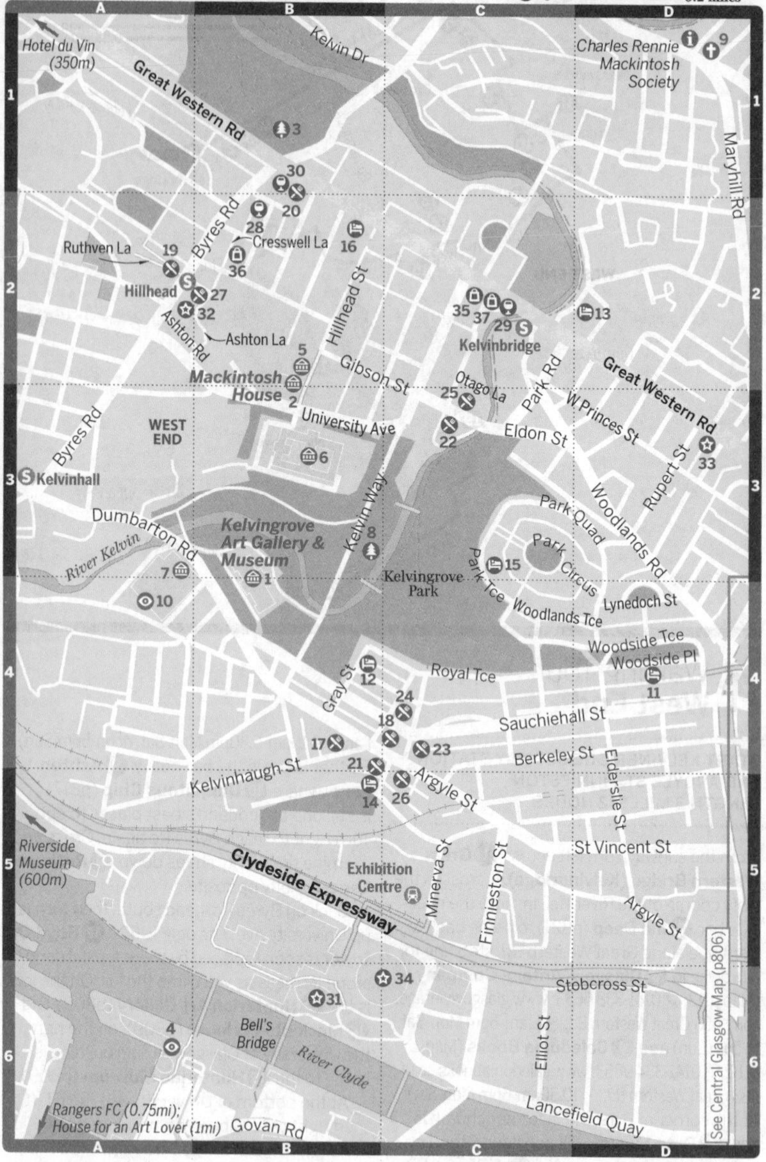

accoutrements in favour of self-check-in terminals and minimalist, plasticky, modern rooms with just two features: a big, comfortable king-sized bed and a decent shower with mood lighting. The idea is that guests make liberal use of the public areas, and why wouldn't you, with upbeat, super-comfortable designer furniture, a 24-hour cafe and iMacs?

Pipers' Tryst Hotel HOTEL ££
(Map p806; ☎0141-353 5551; www.thepipingcentre.co.uk; 30-34 McPhater St; r with/without

West End

Top Sights

Sights

Sleeping

Eating

Drinking & Nightlife

Entertainment

Shopping

breakfast £120/96; 📶) The name is no tartan tourist trap; rather, this cosy hotel with only eight rooms is run by the adjacent bagpiping centre, and profits go towards maintaining it. Cheery staff, great value and a prime city-centre location make this a wise choice. You won't have far to migrate after a night of Celtic music and malts in the snug bar-restaurant.

Indigo HOTEL ££

(Map p806; ☎0141-226 7700; www.hinglasgow.co.uk; 75 Waterloo St; r £100-160; ❄@📶) Once the power station for early trams, this boutique-chain conversion of an elegant building has resulted in a satisfying, surprisingly quiet city-centre option. Rooms have mural-style artwork, great beds and a free minibar (the contents improve as you go up the room grades). Space is good, and bathrooms have rain showerheads. Prices vary; there are usually good online deals.

★Dakota Deluxe HOTEL £££

(Map p806; ☎0141-404 3680; www.dakotahotels.co.uk; 179 West Regent St; r £150-585; ❄📶🐾) Suave and seductive in dark wood and grey tones, Dakota carries a strong design concept, from low-lit basement restaurant to light-filled suites. Rooms are very spacious and feature appealing sitting areas as well as inviting beds. Service is excellent, and the bar area – see how many Jacks you can name – a delight.

Blythswood Square HOTEL £££

(Map p806; ☎0141-248 8888; www.kimptonblythswoodsquare.com; 11 Blythswood Sq; r £195-300; P📶🏊🐾) In a gorgeous Georgian terrace, this elegant five-star offers inner-city luxury, with grey and cerise providing casual soft-toned style throughout. Rooms (recently refurbished) go from standard to penthouse, with corresponding increases in comfort – it's hard to resist the traditional 'classic' rooms with windows onto the delightful square, but at weekends you'll have a quieter sleep in the new wing at the back.

Malmaison HOTEL £££

(Map p806; ☎0141-378 0384; www.malmaison.com; 278 West George St; r £130-250; 📶) This former church is a long-time favourite for its decadent decor and plush lines. Stylish rooms with mood lighting have a dark, brooding tone and opulent furnishings. It's a hedonistic sort of place and can be cheerfully boisterous at weekends. It's best to book online, as it's cheaper and various suite offers can be mighty tempting.

West End

The pleasant terraces of the West End are home to lots of worthwhile places to stay, from a hostel and excellent B&Bs to one of Scotland's plushest urban hotels.

Glasgow SYHA HOSTEL £
(Map p812; 0141-332 3004; www.hostellingscotland.org.uk; 8 Park Tce; dm/s/tw £29/52/69;) Perched on a hill overlooking Kelvingrove Park in a charming town house, this is one of Scotland's best official hostels. Dorms are mostly four to six beds with padlocked lockers, and all have en suite. The common rooms are spacious, plush and good for lounging about in. There's no curfew, it has a good kitchen, and meals are available.

Flower House B&B £
(Map p812; 0141-204 2846; www.theflowerhouse.net; 33 St Vincent Cres; s £40-60, d from £60;) Cosy, old-style B&B in a pretty Victorian terraced house fronted by a riot of creepers and flowers – you can't miss it. Just off the Finnieston strip, its comfortably dignified interior features antiques, curios, striped wallpaper and noble furniture. Bathrooms are exterior but private: they are extraordinary, particularly the 'penny wall'. Hospitality is good humoured and exceptional, with homemade treats for breakfast (£5).

★ **Alamo Guest House** B&B ££
(Map p812; 0141-339 2395; www.alamoguesthouse.com; 46 Gray St; d £100-£169, d without bathroom £59-85;) The Alamo may not sound like a peaceful spot, but that's exactly what this great place is. Opposite Kelvingrove Park, it feels miles from the city's hustle, but several of Glasgow's best museums and restaurants are right at hand. The decor blends antique furnishings and modern design, with excellent bathrooms, and the owners will make you very welcome.

Amadeus Guest House B&B ££
(Map p812; 0141-339 8257; www.amadeusguesthouse.co.uk; 411 North Woodside Rd; s £60-70, s without bathroom £42-45, d £80-100 incl breakfast;) Just off the bustle of Great Western Rd, a minute's walk from the subway but on a quiet street by the riverside pathway, this B&B has compact bright rooms, all distinct, with a cheerful, breezy feel. There's a variety of types, including several singles. It offers excellent value and a genuine welcome. A good continental breakfast is included.

15Glasgow B&B £££
(Map p812; 0141-332 1263; www.15glasgow.com; 15 Woodside Pl; d/ste £150/180;) Glasgow's 19th-century merchants certainly knew how to build a beautiful house, and this 1840s terrace is a sumptuous example. Huge rooms with lofty ceilings have exquisite period detail complemented by attractive modern greys, striking bathrooms and well-chosen quality furniture. Your welcoming host makes everything easy: the in-room breakfast, overlooking the park, is a real treat. They prefer no under-five-year-olds.

Hotel du Vin HOTEL £££
(0141-378 0385; www.hotelduvin.com; 1 Devonshire Gardens; r £169-519;) Traditionally Glasgow's favoured hotel of the rich and famous, and the patriarch of sophistication and comfort. A study in elegance, it's sumptuously decorated and occupies three classical sandstone terrace houses. There's a bewildering array of room types, all different in style and size. The hospitality is old-school courteous, and there's an excellent restaurant on site with a vast wine selection.

Heritage Hotel HOTEL £££
(Map p812; 0141-339 6955; www.theheritagehotel.net; 4 Alfred Tce, Great Western Rd; s/d £70/150 incl breakfast;) A stone's throw from all the West End action, this friendly hotel has an open, airy feel despite the rather dilapidated raised terrace on which it's located. Generally, rooms on the 1st and 2nd floors are a bit more spacious and have a better outlook. The location, parking option and very fair prices mark it out.

Eating

Glasgow is the best place to eat in Scotland, with a stupendous range of restaurants and cafes. The West End is a culinary centre, with Merchant City also boasting a high concentration of quality establishments. Pubs and bars (p820) are often good mealtime options, too.

The excellent *Eating & Drinking Guide,* published by *The List* every second April, covers both Glasgow and Edinburgh.

Central Glasgow

★ **Riverhill Coffee Bar** CAFE £
(Map p806; 0141-204 4762; www.riverhillcoffee.co.uk; 24 Gordon St; breakfast £3-6.50; 7am-5pm Mon-Fri, from 8am Sat, from 10am Sun;) Chain cafes plaster Glasgow's centre, so it's a

WORTH A TRIP

SOUTHSIDE & THE CLYDE

Once a thriving shipbuilding area, the River Clyde sank into dereliction during the post-WWII era but has been subject to extensive rejuvenation. It's an intriguingly multicultural part of Glasgow, and several excellent attractions are dotted across the area.

Glasgow Science Centre (Map p812; ☎0141-420 5000; www.glasgowsciencecentre.org; 50 Pacific Quay; adult/child £12/10, IMAX, Glasgow Tower or Planetarium extra £2.50-3.50; ⏰10am-5pm daily Apr-Oct, to 3pm Wed-Fri, to 5pm Sat & Sun Nov-Mar; 👪) Brings science and technology alive through hundreds of interactive exhibits, an IMAX theatre, a rotating 127m-high observation tower, a planetarium and live science demos. To get here, take bus 89 or 90 from Union St.

Riverside Museum (☎0141-287 2720; www.glasgowmuseums.com; 100 Pointhouse Pl; ⏰11am-4pm; 👪) FREE Designed by the late British-Iraqi architect Zaha Hadid, this transport museum features a fascinating series of cars made in Scotland, plus assorted railway locos, trams, bikes and model Clyde-built ships.

Burrell Collection (☎0141-287 2550; www.glasgowlife.org.uk; Pollok Country Park) FREE This outstanding museum 3 miles out of town houses everything from Chinese porcelain and medieval furniture to paintings by Cézanne. It's closed for refurbishment, and is possibly due to reopen in 2021.

joy to come across this tiny place, which offers great coffee and hot chocolate as well as delicious filled rolls and toasts. Ingredients are sustainably sourced and seriously tasty. It's extremely friendly; you'd come every day if you lived nearby.

★Saramago Café Bar VEGAN £

(Map p806; ☎0141-352 4920; www.cca-glasgow.com; 350 Sauchiehall St; mains £9-12; ⏰10am-10pm Mon-Sat; 📶🌱) In the airy atrium of the Centre for Contemporary Arts, this place does a great line in eclectic vegan fusion food, with a range of top flavour combinations from around the globe. The upstairs bar (open from 4pm Thursday and noon Friday and Saturday) has a great deck on steep Scott St and packs out inside with a friendly, arty crowd enjoying the DJ sets and quality tap beers.

★Singl-end CAFE £

(Map p806; ☎0141-353 1277; www.thesingl-end.co.uk; 265 Renfrew St; dishes £5.50-10; ⏰10am-4pm; 📶🌱) There's something glorious about this long basement cafe with its cheery service and air of brunchy bonhomie. It covers a lot of bases, with good coffee, generous breakfasts and lunches, booze and baking. Dietary requirements are superbly catered for, with fine vegan choices and clear labelling. On a diet? Avert your eyes from the 'eat-me' cornucopia of meringues and pastries by the door.

Platform STREET FOOD £

(Map p806; ☎0345-241 6253; www.platformgla.co.uk; 253 Argyle St; light meals £5-8; ⏰5-11pm Thu, from noon Fri & Sat) This atmospheric series of brick-arched vaults under the railway lines at Central station comes into its own at weekends, when street-food vendors open up stalls and a bar doles out pints to those seeking an escape from the weather. It's family and dog friendly. During the week the cafe is still open.

Café Gandolfi CAFE ££

(Map p806; ☎0141-552 6813; www.cafegandolfi.com; 64 Albion St; mains £12.50-17.50; ⏰8am-11pm Mon-Sat, from 9am Sun; 📶) In Merchant City, this cafe was once part of the old cheese market. It's been pulling in the punters for years and attracts an interesting mix of die-hard Gandolfers, the upwardly mobile and tourists. It covers all bases with excellent breakfasts and coffee, an enticing upstairs **bar** (Map p806; ☎0141-552 4462; ⏰noon-11pm; 📶), and top-notch bistro food, including Scottish and continental options, in an atmospheric, medieval-like setting.

Topolabamba MEXICAN ££

(Map p806; ☎0141-248 9359; www.topolabamba.com; 89 St Vincent St; portions £5-11; ⏰noon-10pm; 📶🌱) Lots of fun and attractively kitted-out in cool Mexican decor – all skulls, figurines and tequila crates – this place brings a real slice of authentic Mexican cuisine to Glasgow, with zingy tacos, tasty tostadas and not a plate of nachos in sight. Portions are tapas-sized, so order a few and share.

Loon Fung CANTONESE ££

(Map p806; ☎0141-332 1240; www.loonfungglasgow.com; 417 Sauchiehall St; mains £11-15; ⏰noon-11pm; 📶) This elegant Cantonese oasis is one of Scotland's most authentic Chinese restaurants; indeed, it's quite a surprise after a traditional dining experience here to emerge to boisterous Sauchiehall St rather than Hong Kong. The dim-sum choices are toothsome, and the seafood – try the sea bass – really excellent.

Meat Bar AMERICAN ££

(Map p806; ☎0141-204 3605; www.themeatbar.co.uk; 142 West Regent St; mains £9-20; ⏰5-10pm Mon-Thu, from 4 pm Fri, from 1pm Sat; 📶) Like a Mafia-film speakeasy where some minor henchman gets whacked, Meat Bar has underworld ambience carried off with style. As the name suggests, it's all about meat: it even makes its way into some of the cocktails. Daily cuts of prime Scottish beef (£25 to £40) accompany a range of American-style slow-smoked meats. Tasty and atmospheric, with interesting beers.

GREEN GLASGOW

Glasgow means 'Dear Green Place' in Gaelic and truly lives up to the name. There are more than 90 parks and gardens, as well as excellent cycling and hiking trails. Now efforts are being made by Glasgow to even become the greenest city in Europe.

Glasgow aims to become Britain's first carbon-neutral city by 2030. City Council, in cooperation with ScottishPower, has made several promises, including the decarbonisation of heating and transport, a mass electric-car-charging scheme, installing LED street lights and expanding the renewable electricity grid.

If successful, Glasgow will beat the Scottish government's target of reaching net-zero carbon emissions by 2045.

With ecofriendly projects and initiatives in place, Glasgow is also primed to host the United Nations Climate Change Conference (COP26) in November 2021. The two-week international summit will be the largest Britain has ever held, with up to 30,000 delegates and heads of state expected to attend.

Gamba SEAFOOD £££

(Map p806; ☎0141-572 0899; www.gamba.co.uk; 225a West George St; mains £21-30; ⏰noon-2.15pm & 5-9.30pm Mon-Fri, noon-9.30pm Sat; 📶) This business-district basement is easily missed but is actually one of the city's premier seafood restaurants. Presentation is elegant, with carefully selected flavours allowing the fish, sustainably sourced from Scotland and beyond, to shine. Service is smart and solicitous. From Thursday to Saturday, there are good lunch and pre-theatre deals (£22/34 for two/three courses).

East End

McCune Smith CAFE £

(Map p806; ☎0141-548 1114; www.mccunesmith.co.uk; 3 Duke St; light meals £4-7.50; ⏰8am-4pm; 📶🌱) This stellar cafe is named after a University of Glasgow graduate who was a noted abolitionist and the first African American to hold a medical degree. The hospitable owners take their coffee seriously and offer scrumptious breakfast and brunch fare, plus delicious sandwiches and soups in a luminous, high-ceilinged interior. They bake their own bread and at least half the menu is vegan.

Southside

Cafe Strange Brew CAFE £

(☎0141-440 7290; www.facebook.com/cafestrangebrew; 1082 Pollokshaws Rd; dishes £5-11; ⏰9am-4pm Mon-Sat, to 3pm Sun) This has such cachet as the Southside's – if not the city's – best cafe that you'll be waiting in line most days. It's worth the enforced contemplation, with generous, vibrant, filling brunchy fare that draws on global influences as well as closer-to-home inspiration. Presentation is a high point; leave room for the sinfully sticky desserts.

West End

78 Bar & Kitchen CAFE £

(Map p812; ☎0141-576 5018; www.the78barandkitchen.com; 10 Kelvinhaugh St; mains £5-10; ⏰food noon-9pm; 📶🌱) More a comfortable lounge than your typical veggie restaurant, this cafe offers cosy couch seating and reassuringly solid wooden tables, as well as an inviting range of ales. The low-priced vegan food includes hearty stews and curries, and there's regular live music in a very welcoming atmosphere.

★Ox & Finch FUSION ££

(Map p812; ☎0141-339 8627; www.oxandfinch.com; 920 Sauchiehall St; small plates £5-14.50; ⏲noon-10pm; 📶✍) This fashionable place could almost sum up the thriving modern Glasgow eating scene, with a faux-pub name, sleek but comfortable contemporary decor and an open kitchen. Grab a cosy booth and be prepared to have your taste buds wowed by innovative, delicious sharing plates. Flavours draw on French and Mediterranean influences but focus on quality Scottish produce, with excellent vegetarian creations on offer.

★Mother India INDIAN ££

(Map p812; ☎0141-221 1663; www.motherindia.co.uk; 28 Westminster Tce, Sauchiehall St; mains £11-16; ⏲5-10pm Thu & Fri, from 1pm Sat & Sun; 📶✍👪) Glasgow curry buffs forever debate the merits of the city's numerous excellent South Asian restaurants; Mother India features in every discussion. It's been a stalwart for years, and the quality and innovation are superb. The three dining areas are all attractive.

Alchemilla MEDITERRANEAN ££

(Map p812; ☎0141-337 6060; www.thisisalchemilla.com; 1126 Argyle St; plates £4-13.50; ⏲5pm-midnight Thu, from noon Fri-Sun) The number of quality eating options opening on the Finnieston strip is phenomenal, and this is a fine example. The casual open-kitchen eatery offers sharing plates with an eastern Mediterranean feel. Interesting ingredients and intriguing textures are key. There are lots of meat-free options and a list of hard-to-find natural wines.

The Finnieston SEAFOOD ££

(Map p812; ☎0141-222 2884; www.thefinniestonbar.com; 1125 Argyle St; plates £7-20; ⏲5-10pm Thu, from noon Fri-Sun; 📶) 🌿 A flagship of this increasingly vibrant strip, this gastropub recalls the area's sailing heritage with a cosily romantic below-decks atmosphere and artfully placed nautical motifs. It's been well thought through, with a short menu of high-quality upmarket pub fare focusing on sustainable Scottish seafood. Excellent G&Ts (slurp one in the little courtyard) and cocktails.

Left Bank BISTRO ££

(Map p812; ☎0141-339 5969; www.theleftbank.co.uk; 33 Gibson St; mains £7-15; ⏲food 9am-10pm Mon-Fri, from 10am Sat & Sun; 📶✍) 🌿 Huge windows fronting the street reveal this outstanding eatery specialising in gastronomic delights and lazy afternoons. Lots of little spaces filled with couches and chunky tables make for intimacy. The wide-ranging menu features delightful creations using seasonal and local produce, with an eclectic variety of influences, including Asian and traditional Scottish fare. Brunch is also a highlight.

Bothy SCOTTISH ££

(Map p812; ☎0845 166 6032; www.bothyglasgow.co.uk; 11 Ruthven Lane; mains £13-23; ⏲5-10pm Wed & Thu, from noon Fri, from 11am Sat & Sun; 📶) This West End player, boasting a combo of modern design and comfy retro furnishings, blows apart the myth that Scottish food is stodgy and uninteresting. The Bothy dishes out traditional home-style fare with a modern twist. It's filling, but leave room for dessert. Smaller lunch plates are a good deal, and there's an attractive outdoor area.

★Stravaigin FUSION £££

(Map p812; ☎0141-334 2665; www.stravaigin.co.uk; 28 Gibson St; breakfast £8-14, restaurant mains £14-25; ⏲9am-10pm; 📶✍) Stravaigin is a serious foodie's delight, with a menu constantly pushing the boundaries of originality and offering creative culinary excellence. With a range of eating spaces across three levels, it's pleasingly casual and easy-going. The entry level also has a buzzing bar with a separate menu. Scottish classics like haggis take their place alongside a range of Asian-influenced and vegetarian dishes.

★Ubiquitous Chip SCOTTISH £££

(Map p812; ☎0141-334 5007; www.ubiquitouschip.co.uk; 12 Ashton Lane; mains £17-26, tasting menu £60; ⏲restaurant 11am-10pm Tue-Sun; 📶) 🌿 The original champion of Scottish produce, Ubiquitous Chip is legendary for its still-unparalleled cuisine and lengthy wine list. Named to poke fun at Scotland's culinary reputation, it offers a French touch but resolutely Scottish ingredients, carefully selected and following sustainable principles. The elegant courtyard space offers some of Glasgow's best dining, while the brasserie above offers a more laid-back vibe.

Cail Bruich SCOTTISH £££

(Map p812; ☎0141-334 6265; www.cailbruich.co.uk; 725 Great Western Rd; 3-course lunch £35,

1

BPERCHA/SHUTTERSTOCK ©

1. Fish and chips **2.** Cornish pasties
3. Roast beef and Yorkshire pudding **4.** Laverbread

3

OBS70/SHUTTERSTOCK ©

Flavours of Britain

Food fans know that Britain has finally shaken off its reputation for bland meals. Wherever you go it's easy to find quality dishes, celebrating tradition – with local ingredients and often with a modern twist.

For many visitors, the culinary day begins in a hotel or B&B with the 'full English breakfast' – also available as the full Welsh, full Scottish, full Yorkshire etc – a plate full of mainly fried meat that might shock, but there's enough fuel here for several hours of energetic sightseeing.

Lunch or dinner is the time to try regional specialities such as haggis or salmon in Scotland, lamb or laver bread in Wales, Cumberland sausage in northern England, Stilton cheese in the Midlands, curry in Birmingham's Balti Triangle or London's Brick Lane, and seafood just about anywhere on the coast.

And if you're feeling peckish in between meals, look out for country cafes serving cream teas: scones, jam and cream, with that other British classic, a hot cup of tea.

BRITISH CLASSICS

Fish and chips Longstanding favourite, best sampled in coastal towns.

Haggis Scottish icon, mainly offal and oatmeal, traditionally served with 'tatties and neeps' (potatoes and turnips).

Sandwich Global snack today, but an English 'invention' from the 18th century.

Laverbread Laver is a type of seaweed, mixed with oatmeal and fried to create this traditional Welsh speciality.

Ploughman's lunch Bread and cheese – pub menu regular, perfect with a pint.

Roast beef & Yorkshire pudding Traditional lunch on Sunday for the English.

Cornish pasty Savoury pastry, a southwest speciality.

dinner £65; ⊙6-10pm Wed, noon-4pm & 6-10pm Thu-Sat;) In an elegant if rather nondescript dining room, the kitchen here turns out some memorable modern Scottish fare. The forage ethos brings surprising, tangy, herbal flavours to plates that are always interesting but never pretentious. Everything from the amuse-bouche to the homemade bread is top-notch – the degustation menu (£60) with optional wine flight (£90) combines the best on offer.

Gannet SCOTTISH £££
(Map p812; 0141-204 2081; www.thegannetgla.com; 1155 Argyle St; menu £50; ⊙6-9.15pm Wed & Thu, noon-2pm & 5.30-9.15pm Fri & Sat, 1-2.30pm & 6-9pm Sun;) In vogue but not starchy, this jewel of the Finnieston strip offers a cosy wood-panelled ambience and gourmet food that excels on presentation and taste without venturing towards cutting-edge. The short, polished daily menu features quality produce sourced mostly from southern Scotland, and the interesting wine list backs it up very well indeed. Solicitous, professional service is another plus.

Drinking & Nightlife

Glaswegians are known to enjoy a beverage or two, and some of Britain's best nightlife is found in the din and sometimes roar of the city's pubs and bars. There are as many different styles of bar as there are punters to guzzle in them. Craft beer, single malt, Scottish gins: it's all here.

Glasgow has a vibrant LGBTQ+ scene, with the gay quarter found in and around the Merchant City (particularly Virginia, Wilson and Glassford Sts). Many straight clubs and bars also have gay and lesbian nights.

Central Glasgow

★**DogHouse Merchant City** BAR
(Map p806; 0141-552 6363; www.brewdog.com; 99 Hutcheson St; ⊙11am-10pm;) Brewdog's zingy beers are matched by its upbeat attitude, so this Merchant City spot was always going to be a fun place. An open kitchen doles out slidery, burgery, smoked-meat fare, while 25 taps run quality craft beer from morning till night.

Shilling Brewing Co MICROBREWERY
(Map p806; 0141-353 1654; www.shillingbrewingcompany.co.uk; 92 West George St; ⊙4-10pm Wed-Fri, from noon Sat & Sun;) Drinking in former banks is a Glasgow thing and this central brewpub offers some of the best of it. The wooden, high-ceilinged space has huge windows out to the city centre and room to spare to try its beers; the almost grapefruity Unicorn IPA is a real palate cleanser. Another couple of dozen taps showcase guest craft brews from around Scotland.

Pot Still PUB
(Map p806; 0141-333 0980; www.thepotstill.co.uk; 154 Hope St; ⊙11am-midnight;) The cheeriest and cosiest of places, the Pot Still has a time-warp feel with its creaky floor and old-style wrought-iron-legged tables. There's a superb whisky selection and knowledgeable staff – constantly up and down ladders to get at bottles – to back it up. Tasty pies (£2 to £4) are on hand for solid sustenance.

Laboratorio Espresso CAFE
(Map p806; 0141-353 1111; www.laboratorioespresso.com; 93 West Nile St; ⊙7.30am-5.30pm Mon-Fri, from 9am Sat, from 11am Sun) A chic space, all concrete and glass, this cafe offers the best coffee we've tried in Glasgow. It's sourced properly, and served in delicious double-shot creations with authentically concentrated espresso; soy milk is available. There are a couple of tables outside even in the coldest weather. Pastries and biscotti are on hand, but it's all about the brew.

Waterloo Bar GAY
(Map p806; 0141-248 7216; www.waterlooglasgow.wixsite.com/home; 306 Argyle St; ⊙noon-11pm Mon-Thu, to midnight Fri & Sat, 12.30-11pm Sun) This traditional pub is Scotland's oldest gay bar. It attracts punters of all ages. It's very friendly and, with a large group of regulars, a good place to meet people away from the scene.

Babbity Bowster PUB
(Map p806; 0141-552 5055; www.babbitybowster.com; 16-18 Blackfriars St; ⊙noon-midnight;) In a quiet corner of Merchant City, this handsome spot is perfect for a tranquil daytime drink, particularly in the adjoining beer garden. Service is attentive, and the smell of sausages may tempt you to lunch; it also offers accommodation. This is one of the city centre's most charming pubs, in one of its noblest buildings. There's a regular folk-music scene.

The Horseshoe Bar PUB
(Map p806; 0141-248 6368; www.thehorseshoebarglasgow.co.uk; 17 Drury St; ⊙10am-10pm) This

legendary city pub and popular meeting place dates from the late 19th century and is largely unchanged. It's a picturesque spot, with the longest continuous bar in the UK, but its main attraction is what's served over it – real ale and good cheer. Upstairs in the lounge is some of the best-value pub food (dishes £4 to £10) in town.

West End

★Inn Deep BAR
(Map p812; ☎0141-264 2777; www.inndeep.com; 445 Great Western Rd; ⏰noon-midnight Mon-Sat, to 11pm Sun) Descend the stairs to find yourself in a fabulous spot on the banks of the Kelvin. It's glorious on a fine day (and Glaswegians set that bar pretty low) to grab a craft beer and spill out onto the riverside path in a happy throng. The vaulted interior spaces under the bridge are also characterful.

Hillhead Bookclub BAR
(Map p812; ☎0141-576 1700; www.hillheadbookclub.co.uk; 17 Vinicombe St; ⏰3-10pm Mon-Thu, from noon Fri, from 10am Sat & Sun; 📶) Atmosphere in spades is the call sign of this easy-going bar. An ornate wooden ceiling overlooks two levels of well-mixed cocktails, seriously cheap drinks, comfort food and numerous intriguing decorative touches. There's even a ping-pong table in a cage.

Òran Mór BAR, CLUB
(Map p812; ☎0141-357 6200; www.oran-mor.co.uk; cnr Byres & Great Western Rds; ⏰9am-2am Mon-Wed, to 3am Thu-Sat, 10am-3am Sun; 📶) Some may be uncomfortable with the thought of drinking in a church. But we say: the Lord giveth. This bar, restaurant, club and theatre venue is a likeable and versatile spot with an attractive interior and a fine whisky selection to replace the holy water. The lunchtime **A Play, a Pie and a Pint** (Map p812; www.playpiepint.com; £12.50-15 incl pie & pint; ⏰1pm Mon-Sat) is an excellent feature.

☆ Entertainment

Glasgow is Scotland's entertainment city, from classical music, fine theatre and ballet to an amazing range of live-music venues. To tap into the scene, check out *The List* (www.list.co.uk), an invaluable free events guide.

For theatre tickets, book directly with the venue. For concerts, a useful booking centre is Tickets Scotland (www.tickets-scotland.com).

☆ Live Music

★King Tut's Wah Wah Hut LIVE MUSIC
(Map p806; ☎0141-221 5279; www.kingtuts.co.uk; 272a St Vincent St; ⏰noon-1am) One of the city's premier live-music pub venues, hosting bands every night of the week. A staple of the local scene, and a real Glasgow highlight.

Hydro CONCERT VENUE
(Map p812; ☎0141-248 3000; www.thessehydro.com; Finnieston Quay; 📶) A spectacular modern building to keep the adjacent **'Armadillo'** (Map p812; ☎0844 395 4000; www.sec.co.uk; Finnieston Quay) company, the Hydro amphitheatre is a phenomenally popular venue for big-name concerts and shows.

Hug & Pint LIVE MUSIC
(Map p812; ☎07429 432713; www.thehugandpint.com; 171 Great Western Rd; ⏰noon-midnight; 📶) With bands almost daily in the downstairs space, this comfortable local is a great destination, which it would be anyway for its excellent atmosphere, highly original Asian-influenced vegan food and colourful interior.

Barrowland Ballroom CONCERT VENUE
(The Barrowlands; Map p806; ☎0141-552 4601; www.barrowland-ballroom.co.uk; 244 Gallowgate) A down-at-heel but exceptional old dance hall above the Barras market, catering for some of the larger acts that visit the city. It's one of Scotland's most atmospheric venues with its sprung floor and authentic character.

13th Note Café LIVE MUSIC
(Map p806; ☎0141-553 1638; www.13thnote.co.uk; 50-60 King St; ⏰noon-9pm Mon-Wed, to midnight Thu-Sat, to 5pm Sun; 📶) Cosy basement venue with small independent bands as well as weekend DJs and regular comedy and theatre performances. At street level the pleasant cafe does decent vegetarian and vegan food (£7 to £10, until 9pm).

St Luke's & the Winged Ox LIVE MUSIC
(Map p806; ☎0141-552 8378; www.stlukesglasgow.com; 17 Bain St; ⏰noon-midnight Mon-Fri, from 11am Sat & Sun; 📶) By the Barras market area, this repurposed church – stained glass and organ still in situ – is a fantastic spot hosting live music every weekend, exhibitions, markets and more. The cosier attached space also does very well just as a pub and serves food all day until 9pm.

WORTH A TRIP

LANARK & NEW LANARK

Below the market town of Lanark, in an attractive gorge by the River Clyde, is the World Heritage Site of **New Lanark** (☎01555-661345; www.newlanark.org; adult/child/family £13/10/40; ⏰10am-5pm Apr-Oct, to 4pm Nov-Mar; 👪). Once Britain's largest cotton-spinning complex, it's better known for the pioneering social experiments of Robert Owen, who managed the mill from 1800. New Lanark is really a memorial to this enlightened capitalist. He provided his workers with housing, a cooperative store, the world's first nursery school, adult-education classes, a sick-pay fund and a social centre he called the New Institute for the Formation of Character.

Admission includes access to a huge working spinning mule, producing woollen yarn, and the historic schoolhouse, which contains an innovative, high-tech journey to New Lanark's past via a 3D hologram of the spirit of Annie McLeod, a 10-year-old mill girl who describes life here in 1820. You can also see a millworker's house, Robert Owen's own home and a 1920s-style village store.

Lanark is 25 miles southeast of Glasgow. Express bus 240X runs hourly Monday to Saturday (£6.50, one hour); trains from Glasgow Central also run to Lanark (£7.30, 55 minutes, every 30 minutes, hourly on Sunday).

It's a pleasant walk to New Lanark, but there's also a half-hourly bus service from the train station (daily).

☆ Cinema

★Glasgow Film Theatre CINEMA
(Map p806; ☎0141-332 6535; www.glasgowfilm.org; 12 Rose St; adult/child £10.90/7.90) This much-loved three-screener off Sauchiehall St shows art-house cinema and classics.

Grosvenor Cinema CINEMA
(Map p812; ☎0845 166 6002; www.grosvenorwestend.co.uk; Ashton Lane) This sweet cinema puts you in the heart of the West End eating and nightlife for post-movie debriefings.

☆ Theatres & Concert Halls

Citizens' Theatre THEATRE
(☎0141-429 0022; www.citz.co.uk; 119 Gorbals St) South of the Clyde, this is one of Scotland's top theatres. It's well worth trying to catch a performance here.

Tramway PERFORMING ARTS
(☎0845 330 3501; www.tramway.org; 25 Albert Dr; ⏰9.30am-8pm Mon-Sat, noon-6pm Sun; 📶) Occupying a former tram depot, this buzzy cultural centre has performance and exhibition spaces as well as a popular cafe. It's a real Southside community hub, with an unusual **garden** (☎0141-433 2722; www.thehiddengardens.org.uk; 25a Albert Dr; ⏰10am-8pm Tue-Sat, noon-6pm Sun Apr-Sep, 10am-4pm Tue-Sat, noon-4pm Sun Oct-Mar) FREE out the back. It attracts cutting-edge theatrical groups, is the home of Scottish Ballet and hosts a varied range of artistic exhibitions. It's very close to Pollokshields East train station.

Theatre Royal CONCERT VENUE
(Map p806; ☎0844 871 7677; www.glasgowtheatreroyal.org.uk; 282 Hope St) Proudly sporting an eye-catching modern facelift, Glasgow's oldest theatre is the home of Scottish Opera.

Glasgow Royal Concert Hall CONCERT VENUE
(Map p806; ☎0141-353 8000; www.glasgowconcerthalls.com; 2 Sauchiehall St; 📶) A feast of classical music is showcased at this concert hall, the modern home of the Royal Scottish National Orchestra. There are also regular pop, folk and jazz performances, typically by big-name solo artists.

☆ Sport

Two Glasgow football clubs – **Rangers** (☎0871 702 1972; www.rangers.co.uk; Ibrox Stadium, 150 Edmiston Dr) and **Celtic** (☎0871 226 1888; www.celticfc.net; Celtic Park, Parkhead) – totally dominate the sporting scene in Scotland, having vastly more resources than other clubs and a long history (and rivalry). This runs along traditionally partisan lines, with Rangers representing Protestant supporters, and Celtic, Catholic. It's worth going to a game; both play in magnificent arenas with great atmosphere. Games between the two (normally four a year) are fiercely contested, but tickets aren't sold to the general public – you'll need to know a season-ticket holder.

Shopping

Boasting the UK's largest retail phalanx outside London, Glasgow is a shopaholic's paradise. The 'Style Mile' around Buchanan and Argyle Sts and Merchant City (particularly upmarket Ingram St) is a fashion hub, while the West End has quirkier, more bohemian shopping options: it's great for vintage clothing. The weekend **Barras market** (Map p806; ☎0141-552 4601; www.theglasgowbarras.com; btwn Gallowgate & London Rd; ⏰10am-5pm Sat & Sun) in the East End is very worthwhile.

Information

INTERNET ACCESS

There's a free wi-fi zone across the city centre. You can get a local SIM card for about £1 and data packages are cheap.

MEDICAL SERVICES

Glasgow Dental Hospital (☎0141-211 9600; www.nhsggc.org.uk; 378 Sauchiehall St)

Glasgow Royal Infirmary (☎0141-211 4000; www.nhsggc.org.uk; 84 Castle St) Medical emergencies and outpatient facilities.

Queen Elizabeth University Hospital (☎0141-201 1100; www.nhsggc.org.uk; 1345 Govan Rd) Modern; south of the river.

TOURIST INFORMATION

Useful websites with tourist information include www.glasgowlife.org.uk, www.peoplemakeglasgow.com and www.list.co.uk, which publishes entertainment listings and restaurant reviews.

Glasgow Tourist Office (Glasgow iCentre; Map p806; ☎0141-566 4083; www.visitscotland.com; 158 Buchanan St; ⏰10am-4pm; 📶) The city's tourist office is in the centre of town.

Getting There & Away

AIR

Glasgow International Airport (GLA; ☎0344-481 5555; www.glasgowairport.com; 📶) Ten miles west of the city, Glasgow International Airport handles domestic traffic and international flights. Facilities include car hire, ATMs and free wi-fi.

Glasgow Prestwick Airport (PIK; ☎0871-223 0700; www.glasgowprestwick.com; 📶) Glasgow Prestwick Airport, 30 miles southwest of Glasgow, is used by Ryanair and some other budget airlines, with many connections to mostly holiday destinations in southern Europe.

BUS

All long-distance buses arrive at and depart from **Buchanan bus station** (Map p806; ☎0141-333 3708; www.spt.co.uk; Killermont St; 📶), which has pricey lockers, ATMs and wi-fi.

Megabus (☎900-160 0900; www.megabus.com) Your first port of call if you're looking for the cheapest fare. Megabus offers very cheap demand-dependent prices on many major bus routes, including to Edinburgh and London.

National Express (☎0871 781 8181; www.nationalexpress.com) Runs daily to several English cities.

Scottish Citylink (☎0871 266 3333; www.citylink.co.uk) Buses to Edinburgh (£8.50, 1¼ hours, every 15 minutes) and most major towns in Scotland.

There are also buses from Buchanan bus station direct to/from Edinburgh Airport (£13, one hour, half-hourly).

TRAIN

As a general rule, **Glasgow Central station** (www.scotrail.co.uk; Gordon St) serves southern Scotland, England and Wales, and **Queen Street station** (www.scotrail.co.uk; George St) serves the north and east (including Edinburgh). Buses run between the two stations every 10 minutes. There are direct trains more than hourly to London Euston station (advance/off peak/any time £31/105.70/191.50); they're much quicker (4½ hours) and more comfortable than the bus.

ScotRail (p798) runs Scottish trains. Destinations include the following:

Aberdeen (£44.30, 2½ to 3½ hours, hourly)

Dundee (£24.60, 1½ hours, hourly)

Edinburgh (£15.30, 50 minutes, every 15 minutes)

Fort William (£32.70, 3¾ hours, three daily)

Inverness (£46, 3½ to four hours, five daily, three on Sunday)

Oban (£26.80, three hours, three to six daily)

Getting Around

TO/FROM THE AIRPORT

Bus 500 runs every half-hour from Glasgow International Airport to Buchanan bus station via Central and Queen Street train stations (single/return £8.50/14, 25 minutes). This is a 24-hour service. You can include a day ticket on the bus network for £4.70, or a one-week ticket for £18.

Another bus, the 77, covers the same route via the West End twice hourly, taking longer.

A taxi costs around £25.

BUS

City bus services, mostly run by **First Glasgow** (☎0345-646 0707; www.firstglasgow.com), are frequent. You can buy tickets when you board buses, but if you don't have a card for contactless payment you'll need exact change. Using the mobile app is recommended (and a little cheaper, too). Short journeys in town cost £1.70 or £2.30; a day ticket (£4.60) is good value and is valid until 1am, when a night network starts. Weekly tickets start at £17. Check route maps online at www.spt.co.uk.

CAR

The most difficult thing about driving in Glasgow is the sometimes-confusing one-way system. For short-term parking (up to two hours), you've got a decent chance of finding something on the street, paying at the meters, which cost up to £4 per hour. Otherwise, multistorey car parks are probably your best bet and are not so expensive. Ask your hotel in advance if it offers parking discounts.

There are numerous car-rental companies; both big names and discount operators have airport offices.

Enterprise (☎0141-221 2124; www.enterprise.co.uk; 40 Oswald St; ⏰8am-6pm Mon-Fri, 9am-4pm Sat, 10am-3pm Sun)

Europcar (☎0371-384 3471; www.europcar.co.uk; 76 Lancefield Quay; ⏰8am-6pm Mon-Fri, to 1pm Sat)

Hertz (☎0141-229 6120; www.hertz.co.uk; Jury's Inn, 80 Jamaica St; ⏰8am-6pm Mon-Fri, to 1pm Sat)

TAXI

There's no shortage of taxis, and if you want to know anything about Glasgow, striking up a conversation with a cabbie is a good place to start. Fares are very reasonable – you can get across the city centre for around £6, and there's no surcharge for calling a taxi. You can pay by credit card with **Glasgow Taxis** (☎0141-429 7070; www.glasgowtaxis.co.uk) if you order by phone; most of its taxis are wheelchair accessible. Download its app to make booking easy.

TRAIN

There's an extensive suburban network of trains in and around Glasgow; tickets should be purchased before travel if the station is staffed, or from the conductor if it isn't.

There's also an underground line, the subway, that serves 15 stations in the city centre, and west and south of the city (single £1.55). The train network connects with the subway at Buchanan Street underground station, next to Queen Street overground station (p823), and St Enoch underground station, near Glasgow Central station (p823). The All Day ticket (£3) gives unlimited travel on the subway for a day, while the Roundabout ticket gives a day's unlimited train and subway travel for £7.40. The subway runs roughly from 6.30am to 11.30pm Monday to Saturday, but annoyingly runs only from 10am to 6pm on Sunday.

BORDERS REGION

The Borders has had a rough history: centuries of war and plunder have left a battle-scarred landscape, exemplified by the magnificent ruins of the Border abbeys. Their wealth was an irresistible magnet during cross-frontier wars, and they were destroyed and rebuilt numerous times. Today these massive stone shells are the region's finest attraction. And don't miss Hermitage Castle: nothing encapsulates the region's turbulent history like this spooky stronghold.

But the Borders region is also genteel. Welcoming villages with ancient traditions pepper the countryside, and grandiose mansions await exploration. It's fine walking and cycling country too, the hills lush with shades of green. Offshore you'll find excellent cold-water diving.

Peebles

POP 8600

With a picturesque main street set on a ridge between the River Tweed and Eddleston Water, Peebles is one of the most handsome of the Border towns. The agreeable atmosphere and good walking options in the rolling, wooded hills hereabouts will entice you to linger.

Sights & Activities

The lovely riverside walk along the Tweed has plenty of grassed areas ideal for a picnic, and there's a children's playground (near the main road bridge).

As well as the activities hub of Glentress, there are further mountain-biking trails at Innerleithen, 7 miles east of Peebles.

★**Traquair House** HISTORIC BUILDING

(☎01896-830323; www.traquair.co.uk; Innerleithen; adult/child/family £10/5/27.50; ⏰11am-5pm daily Easter-Sep, to 4pm daily Oct, to 3pm Sat & Sun Nov) One of Scotland's great country houses, Traquair House has a powerful, ethereal beauty, and exploring it is like time travel. Odd, sloping floors and a musty odour bestow a genuine feel, and parts of the building are believed to have been constructed long before the first official record of its existence in 1107. The massive tower house was gradually expanded but has remained virtually unchanged since the 17th century. Traquair is about 6 miles southeast of Peebles.

Since the 15th century, the house has belonged to various branches of the Stuart family, and the family's unwavering Catholicism and loyalty to the Stuart cause led to famous visitors such as Mary, Queen of Scots and Bonnie Prince Charlie, but also to numerous problems after the deposal of James II of England in 1688. The family's estate, wealth and influence were gradually whittled away as life as a Jacobite became a furtive, clandestine affair.

One of Traquair's most interesting places is the concealed room where priests secretly lived and performed Mass up until 1829, when the Catholic Emancipation Act was finally passed. Other beautiful, time-worn rooms hold fascinating relics, including the cradle used by Mary for her son, James VI of Scotland (who also became James I of England), and fascinating letters from the Jacobite Earls of Traquair and their families, including a particularly moving one written from death row in the Tower of London.

The main gates to the house were locked by one earl in the 18th century until the day a Stuart king reclaimed the throne in London, so meanwhile you'll have to enter by a side gate.

In addition to the house, there's a garden **maze**, a small **brewery** producing the tasty Bear Ale, and a series of **craft workshops**. You can also stay here in one of three opulent B&B rooms (single/double £155/220).

Bus X62 runs from Edinburgh via Peebles to Innerleithen and on to Galashiels.

★7stanes Glentress MOUNTAIN BIKING

(www.7stanesmountainbiking.com) FREE Two miles east of Peebles off the A72, in Glentress forest, this is the busiest of the 7stanes mountain-biking hubs, and also offers osprey viewing and marked walking trails. The **shop** (☎01721-724522; www.tweedvalleybikehire.com; Glentress Forest; hardtail per day £30; ⏲9am-5pm or 6pm) hires rigs and will put you on the right trail for your ability. You can arrange courses with **Dirt School** (☎07545 339938; www.dirtschool.co.uk). These are some of Britain's best biking routes.

Sleeping & Eating

Lindores Guest House B&B ££

(☎01721-729040; www.lindoresgh.co.uk; 60 Old Town; s £55-60, d £75-85; Wi-Fi) Run by an interesting, kind couple, this rather striking house offers commodious, flowery rooms. Both en-suite and shared bathrooms are available, and showers are great. Breakfast features delicious home-baked bread among other goodies. There's secure parking for bikes and motorbikes.

Cringletie House HOTEL £££

(☎01721-725750; www.cringletie.com; Edinburgh Rd/A703; r £180-220; P Wi-Fi pets) Luxury without snobbery is this hotel's hallmark, and more power to it. To call this a house is being coy: it's an elegant baronial mansion, 2 miles north of Peebles, set in lush, wooded grounds. Rooms are plush and feature genteel elegance and linen so soft you could wrap a newborn in it. There's an excellent restaurant on site.

★Coltman's DELI ££

(☎01721-720405; www.coltmans.co.uk; 71 High St; mains £14-17; ⏲10am-5pm Mon-Thu, to 10pm Fri & Sat, to 6pm Sun; Wi-Fi) This main-street deli has numerous temptations, such as excellent cheeses and Italian smallgoods, as well as perhaps Scotland's tastiest sausage roll, with an equally toothsome vegetarian equivalent. Behind the shop, the good-looking dining area serves up confident bistro fare and light snacks with a variety of culinary influences, using top-notch local ingredients. Upstairs is a cosy bar.

Osso BISTRO ££

(☎01721-724477; www.ossorestaurant.com; Innerleithen Rd; share plates £7-13; ⏲11am-9pm Wed-Sat, to 6pm Sun) Osso makes a great stop for a bit of home baking or a sandwich but also for a quality meal based around small and large share plates. There are a number of influences from Asia and the Mediterranean at work here, but also solidly local offerings like slow-cooked lamb. The food is delicious and artfully presented, but the atmosphere is comfortably casual.

Getting There & Away

The bus stop is beside the post office on Eastgate. Bus X62 runs half-hourly (hourly on Sunday) to Edinburgh (£5.90, one hour). In the other direction it heads for Galashiels (£5.90, 1¼ hours), from where you can change to Melrose.

Melrose

POP 2500

Tiny, charming Melrose is a polished village running on the well-greased wheels of tourism. Sitting at the feet of the three heather-covered Eildon Hills, Melrose has a classic market square and one of the great abbey ruins. Just outside town is Abbotsford, the home of Sir Walter Scott, which makes a superb visit.

Sights

★Melrose Abbey RUINS
(HES; ☎01896-822562; www.historicenvironment.scot; adult/child £6/3.60; ⏲9.30am-5.30pm Apr-Sep, 10am-4pm Oct-Mar) Perhaps the most interesting of the Border abbeys, red-sandstone Melrose was repeatedly destroyed by the English in the 14th century. The remaining broken shell is pure Gothic and the ruins are famous for their decorative stonework – look out for the pig gargoyle playing the bagpipes. Though Melrose had a monastery way back in the 7th century, this abbey was founded by David I in 1136 for Cistercian monks, and later rebuilt by Robert the Bruce, whose heart is buried here.

★Abbotsford HISTORIC BUILDING
(☎01896-752043; www.scottsabbotsford.com; visitor centre free, house adult/child £11.50/5; ⏲10am-5pm Apr-Oct, to 4pm Nov-Mar, house closed Dec-Feb) Just outside Melrose, this is where to discover the life and works of Sir Walter Scott, to whom we arguably owe both the modern novel and our mind's-eye view of Scotland. This whimsical, fabulous house where he lived – and which ruined him when his publishers went bust – really brings this 19th-century writer to life. The grounds on the banks of the Tweed are lovely, and Scott drew much inspiration from rambles in the surrounding countryside.

★Dryburgh Abbey RUINS
(HES; ☎01835-822381; www.historicenvironment.scot; adult/child £6/3.60; ⏲9.30am-5.30pm Apr-Sep, 10am-4pm Oct-Mar) This is the most beautiful and complete of the Border abbeys, partly because the neighbouring town of Dryburgh no longer exists (another victim of the wars) and partly because of its lovely site by the Tweed in a sheltered birdsong-filled valley. Dating from about 1150, the abbey belonged to the Premonstratensians, a religious order founded in France, and evokes 12th-century monastic life more successfully than its nearby counterparts. The pink-hued stone ruins are the burial place of Sir Walter Scott.

Sleeping & Eating

★Townhouse BOUTIQUE HOTEL £££
(☎01896-822645; www.thetownhousemelrose.co.uk; Market Sq; s/d/superior d £97/134/151; P 📶) The classy Townhouse exudes warmth and professionalism, and has some of the best rooms in town, tastefully furnished with attention to detail. The superior rooms are enormous, with lavish furnishings and excellent en suites. Standard rooms are a fair bit smaller but they're refurbished and very comfortable. Well worth the price.

Provender SCOTTISH ££
(☎01896-820319; www.provendermelrose.com; West End Lane; mains £15-20; ⏲11am-2.30pm & 6-9pm Mon-Fri, 10am-2.30pm & 6-9pm Sat, 10am-3pm & 6-8pm Sun; ✍) Though a relative newcomer to the local scene, Provender feels very Melrose – classy but comfortable – already. It's a warmly decorated space with attractively low lighting, booth seating and solicitous service. Great seafood creations and other well-executed, appealing fare are complemented by a short but excellent wine list. Weekend brunches are another highlight.

Getting There & Away

The Borders Railway runs from Edinburgh to Tweedbank (£11.30, one hour, half-hourly), which is 1.5 miles from Melrose. Buses run half-hourly from here into Melrose.

For other Borders destinations, you'll most likely need to change in nearby Galashiels, served by regular buses from Edinburgh and elsewhere.

Jedburgh

POP 4000

Attractive Jedburgh, where many old buildings and wynds (narrow alleys) have been intelligently restored, invites exploration by foot. It's centred on the noble skeleton of its ruined abbey.

Sights

★Jedburgh Abbey RUINS
(HES; ☎01835-863925; www.historicenvironment.scot; Abbey Rd; adult/child £6/3.60; ⏲9.30am-5.30pm Apr-Sep, 10am-4pm Oct-Mar; 👪) Dom-

WORTH A TRIP

HERMITAGE CASTLE

The 'guardhouse of the bloodiest valley in Britain', **Hermitage Castle** (HES; ☎01387-376222; www.historicenvironment.scot; B6357; adult/child £6/3.60; ⊙9.30am-5.30pm Apr-Sep) embodies the brutal history of the Scottish Borders. Desolate but proud with its massive squared stone walls, it looks more like a lair for orc-raiding parties than a home for Scottish nobility, and is one of the bleakest and most stirring of Scottish ruins. The castle is about 12 miles south of Hawick.

Strategically crucial, the castle was the scene of many a dark deed and dirty deal with the English invaders, all of which rebounded heavily on the perfidious Scottish lord in question. Here, in 1338, Sir William Douglas imprisoned his enemy Sir Alexander Ramsay and deliberately starved him to death. Ramsay survived for 17 days by eating grain that trickled into his pit (which can still be seen) from the granary above. In 1566 Mary, Queen of Scots famously visited the wounded tenant of the castle, Lord Bothwell, here. Fortified, he recovered to (probably) murder her husband, marry her himself, then abandon her months later and flee into exile.

inating the town skyline, this was the first of the great Border abbeys to be passed into state care, and it shows – audio and visual presentations telling the abbey's story are scattered throughout the carefully preserved ruins (good for the kids). The red-sandstone ruins are roofless but relatively intact, and the ingenuity of the master mason can be seen in some of the rich (if somewhat faded) stone carvings in the nave.

Mary, Queen of Scots' Visitor Centre HISTORIC BUILDING
(Queen St; ⊙9.30am-4.30pm Mon-Sat, 10.30am-4pm Sun early Mar–late Nov) FREE Mary stayed at this beautiful 16th-century tower house in 1566 after her famous ride to visit the injured Earl of Bothwell, her future husband, at Hermitage Castle. The interesting exhibition evokes the sad saga of Mary's life and death. Various objects associated with her, including a lock of her hair, are on display.

Sleeping & Eating

Maplebank B&B £
(☎01835-862051; maplebank3@btinternet.com; 3 Smiths Wynd; s/d £30/50; P 📶 🐾) It's pleasing to come across older-style B&Bs where it feels like you're staying in someone's home. Here, that someone is like your favourite aunt: friendly, chaotic and generous. There's lots of clutter and it's very informal. Rooms are comfortable and large, sharing a good bathroom. Breakfast (including fruit, yoghurts and homemade jams) is brilliant – much better than at most posher places.

Meadhon Guest House B&B ££
(☎01835-862504; www.meadhon.co.uk; 48 Castlegate; s/d/f £61/75/145; 📶) Very close to castle and abbey, this historic house on Jedburgh's main street dates back to 1653 and has lots of character. Bonnie Prince Charlie once stabled his horses here, but the genial Danish owners offer more human comforts, with keypad locks, plush mattresses and impeccable standards. Home-cooked evening meals are available, as are attractive hand-knitted scarves.

Capon Tree SCOTTISH ££
(☎01835-869596; www.thecapontree.com; 61 High St; mains £14-20; ⊙food 6-9pm; 📶) Attractively combining smart and casual, this welcoming bistro and bar does modern Scottish cuisine. Plates are beautifully, though not fussily, presented and ingredients are of high quality. The overall package is appealing, the service good and the ambience romantic.

Information

Jedburgh Tourist Office (☎01835-863170; jedburgh@visitscotland.com; Murray's Green; ⊙9.30am-5pm Mon-Sat, 10am-4pm Sun Apr-Jun, Sep & Oct, 9am-5.30pm Mon-Sat, 10am-4pm Sun Jul & Aug, 10am-4pm Mon-Sat Nov-Mar; 📶) Head tourist office for the Borders region. Very helpful.

Getting There & Away

Jedburgh has good bus connections to Hawick, Melrose and Kelso (all around 25 minutes, roughly hourly, two-hourly on Sunday). For Edinburgh, change in St Boswells or Galashiels.

Kelso

POP 5600

Kelso, a prosperous market town with a broad, cobbled square flanked by Georgian buildings, has a cheery feel and historic appeal. During the day it's a busy little place, but after 8pm you'll have the streets to yourself. The town has a lovely site at the junction of the Tweed and Teviot, and is one of the most enjoyable places in the Borders, particularly popular for fishing.

Sights

Floors Castle HISTORIC BUILDING

(☎01573-223333; www.floorscastle.com; adult/child castle & grounds £11.50/6; ⊙10.30am-5pm daily May-Sep, Sat & Sun Oct) Grandiose Floors Castle is Scotland's largest inhabited mansion, home to the Duke of Roxburghe, and overlooks the Tweed about a mile west of Kelso. Built by William Adam in the 1720s, the original Georgian simplicity was 'improved' in the 1840s with the addition of somewhat OTT battlements and turrets. Inside, view the vivid colours of 17th-century Brussels tapestries in the drawing room and intricate oak carvings in the ornate ballroom. The walled garden is a highlight of the extensive grounds.

Mellerstain House HISTORIC BUILDING

(☎01573-410225; www.mellerstain.com; Gordon; adult/child £11/5.50; ⊙noon-5pm Fri-Mon Easter & May-Sep) Finished in 1778, this is considered to be Scotland's finest Robert Adam–designed mansion. It is huge and famous for its classic elegance, ornate interiors and plaster ceilings; the library in particular is outstanding. The upstairs bedrooms are less attractive, but have a peek at the bizarre puppet-and-doll collection in the gallery.

It's about 6 miles northwest of Kelso, near Gordon. Concerts are held here through the summer months.

Smailholm Tower TOWER

(HES; ☎01573-460365; www.historicenvironment.scot; Sandyknowe Farm, Smailholm; adult/child £6/3.60; ⊙9.30am-5.30pm Apr-Sep) Perched on a rocky knoll above a small lake, this narrow stone tower provides one of the most evocative sights in the Borders and keeps its bloody history alive. Although displays inside are sparse, the view from the top is worth the climb. The tower is 6 miles west of Kelso, a mile south of Smailholm village on the B6397.

Sleeping & Eating

★**Old Priory** B&B ££

(☎01573-223030; www.theoldpriorykelso.com; 33 Woodmarket; s/d £80/90; P 📶) Fantastic rooms here are allied with numerous personal details – genial host Robin turns down the beds at night and makes you feel very welcome. Doubles are top-notch and the family room really excellent. The huge windows flood the rooms with natural light. The wonderful library room (£120) is huge and luxurious, with a super bathroom. Top-class B&B.

★**Cobbles** BISTRO ££

(☎01573-223548; www.cobbleskelso.co.uk; 7 Bowmont St; mains £10-17; ⊙food noon-2.30pm & 5.45-9pm Mon-Fri, noon-9pm Sat, noon-8.30pm Sun; 📶) This inn off the main square is so popular you will need to book a table at weekends. It's cheery, very welcoming and warm, and serves excellent upmarket pub food in generous portions. Pick and mix from bar menu, steaks, kebabs and gourmet options. Leave room for cheese and/or dessert. The bar's own microbrewed ales are excellent. A cracking place.

Getting There & Away

There are regular bus routes to other Borders towns and Berwick-upon-Tweed. For Edinburgh, change at St Boswells.

DUMFRIES & GALLOWAY

Some of southern Scotland's finest attractions lie in the gentle hills and lush valleys of Dumfries and Galloway. It's an ideal destination for families, as there's plenty on offer for the kids. Galloway Forest – with its sublime views, mountain biking and walking trails, red deer, kites and other wildlife – is a highlight, as are the dream-like ruins of Caerlaverock Castle. Adding to the appeal of this enticing region is a string of southern Scotland's most idyllic towns, which are charming when the sun shines. And shine it does. This is the mildest region in Scotland and is warmed by the Gulf Stream, a phenomenon that has allowed the development of some famous gardens.

Dumfries

POP 32,900

Lovely, red-hued sandstone bridges criss-cross the wide, grassy-banked River Nith, which runs through the centre of pleasant Dumfries. Historically the town held a strategic position in the path of vengeful English armies; consequently, though it has existed since Roman times, the oldest standing building dates from the 17th century. Plenty of famous names have passed through: Robert Burns lived here and worked as a tax collector, Peter Pan creator JM Barrie was schooled here and DJ Calvin Harris hails from the town.

Sights

★Burns House MUSEUM

(☎01387-255297; www.dumgal.gov.uk; Burns St; ⊙10am-5pm Mon-Sat, 2-5pm Sun Apr-Sep, 10am-1pm & 2-5pm Tue-Sat Oct-Mar) FREE A place of pilgrimage for Burns enthusiasts. It's here that the poet spent the last years of his life, and there are various possessions of his in glass cases, as well as manuscripts and, entertainingly, letters: make sure you have a read.

Moat Brae MUSEUM

(☎01387-255549; www.peterpanmoatbrae.org; 101 George St; adult/child £6.50/5, garden only £2; ⊙11am-5pm Tue-Sat, 10am-4pm Sun; 👪) Wandering in this house and garden as a child inspired JM Barrie to write *Peter Pan*. This new attraction is a major project; a national centre for children's literacy and a great family visit run with heart-warming enthusiasm. The beautiful house has interactive exhibitions, reading rooms, actors and storytelling activities, while there's a cute shop, cafe and a great garden running down to the river featuring a pirate ship, crocodiles and other favourites from the book.

Check the website for what's on each week.

Robert Burns Centre MUSEUM

(☎01387-264808; www.dgculture.co.uk; Mill Rd; audiovisual presentation £2.30; ⊙10am-5pm Mon-Sat, 2-5pm Sun Apr-Sep, 10am-1pm & 2-5pm Tue-Sat Oct-Mar) FREE A worthwhile Burns exhibition in an old mill on the banks of the River Nith; it tells the story of the poet and Dumfries in the 1790s. The optional audiovisual presentations give more background on Dumfries and explain the exhibition's contents. The centre functions as a cinema in the evenings.

Robert Burns Mausoleum TOMB

(St Michael's Kirk, Brooms Rd) FREE Burns' mausoleum is in the graveyard at **St Michael's Kirk**. It's in the far (eastern) corner from the entrance. There's a grisly account of his reburial on the information panel.

> **WORTH A TRIP**
>
> **PAXTON HOUSE**
>
> **Paxton House** (☎01289-386291; www.paxtonhouse.co.uk; B6461; adult/child £10/4; ⊙10am-5pm Easter-Oct, grounds 10am-sunset; 👪), 6 miles west of Berwick, is beside the River Tweed and surrounded by parkland and gardens. It was built in 1758 by Patrick Home for his intended wife, the daughter of Prussia's Frederick the Great. Unfortunately she stood him up, but it was her loss; designed by the Adam family – brothers John, James and Robert – it's acknowledged as one of Britain's finest 18th-century Palladian houses. Four tours run daily; see the website for limited winter visiting. Bus 32 runs past here every couple of hours from Berwick.

Sleeping

★Ferintosh Guest House B&B ££

(☎01387-252262; www.ferintosh.net; 30 Lovers Walk; s £38-42, d £70-72; 📶🐾) A typically lovely Dumfries sandstone Victorian villa opposite the train station, Ferintosh is a good-humoured place with excellent rooms and a warm welcome. These people have the right attitude towards hospitality, with comfortable plush beds, a free dram on arrival for LP readers, and plenty of good chat on distilleries. The owner's original artwork complements the decor.

Eating & Drinking

Cavens Arms PUB FOOD £

(☎01387-252896; www.cavensarms.com; 20 Buccleuch St; mains £9-15; ⊙food 11am-9pm Tue-Sat, noon-9pm Sun; 📶✍) Engaging staff, 10 real ales on tap and a warm, contented buzz make this a legendary Dumfries pub. Generous portions of typical pub nosh backed by a long list of more adventurous daily specials make it one of the town's most enjoyable places to eat. Gets packed on weekends (but staff will still try to find you a table).

Kings CAFE £

(☎01387-254444; www.kings-online.co.uk; 12 Queensberry St; snacks £3-5; ⏰8am-5.30pm Mon-Sat, noon-4pm Sun; 📶) This buzzy cafe in the centre of town doubles as a bookshop. It does tasty fair-trade coffee, has big windows for observing Dumfries life passing by and serves toothsome sweet things, breakfasts and filled rolls.

Globe Inn PUB

(☎01387-323010; www.globeinndumfries.co.uk; 56 High St; ⏰11am-11pm Tue-Sat) A traditional old nook-and-cranny pub down a narrow wynd off the main pedestrian drag, this was reputedly Burns' favourite watering hole, and scene of one of his numerous seductions. Though Covid had temporarily closed it when we last passed by, locals in the know tell us that new owners have spruced it up and it's looking great, with an interesting menu, Burns memorabilia and some good beers.

Information

Dumfries Tourist Office (☎01387-253862; 64 Whitesands; ⏰9.30am-4.30pm Mon-Sat, 10am-3pm Sun Nov-Mar, 9am-5pm Mon-Sat, 10am-4pm Sun Apr-Oct) By the river. Offers plenty of information on the region, including a leaflet on the Robert Burns trail. You can get a parking disc here to use in the riverside car park opposite.

Getting There & Away

BUS

Buses run via towns along the A75 to Stranraer (£8, 2¼ hours, seven daily Monday to Saturday, three on Sunday), as well as to Castle Douglas and Kirkcudbright. Buses 101 and 102 run to/from Edinburgh (£10.40, 2¾ to three hours, four to seven daily), via Moffat and Biggar.

TRAIN

There are trains between Carlisle and Dumfries (£12.10, 40 minutes, every hour or two), and direct trains between Dumfries and Glasgow (£18.10, 1¾ hours, nine daily Monday to Saturday). Services are reduced on Sundays.

South of Dumfries

The scenic area south of Dumfries, with a picturesque coastline, is well worth exploring. Several excellent sights dot the region; there are also good family-friendly activities.

Sights & Activities

★Caerlaverock Castle CASTLE

(HES; ☎01387-770244; www.historicenvironment.scot; Glencaple; adult/child £6/3.60; ⏰9.30am-5.30pm Apr-Sep, 10am-4pm Oct-Mar) The ruins of Caerlaverock Castle, by Glencaple on a beautiful stretch of the Solway coast, are among the loveliest in Britain. Surrounded by a moat, lawns and stands of trees, the unusual pink-stoned triangular castle looks impregnable, though it fell several times, most famously when it was attacked in 1300 by Edward I: the siege became the subject of an epic poem, 'The Siege of Caerlaverock'.

Caerlaverock Wetland Centre NATURE RESERVE

(☎01387-770200; www.wwt.org.uk/caerlaverock; Eastpark Farm; adult/child £8.27/4.72, free for WWT members; ⏰10am-5pm; 👪) This protects 546 hectares of salt marsh and mudflats, the habitat for numerous birds, including barnacle geese. There are various activities, including badger watching, dawn goose flights and child-focused events. It also has a good bookshop for nature watchers, and a coffee shop that serves organic food.

Sweetheart Abbey RUINS

(HES; ☎01387-850397; www.historicenvironment.scot; adult/child £6/3.60; ⏰9.30am-5.30pm Apr-Sep, 10am-4pm Sat-Wed Oct-Mar) The shattered red-sandstone remnants of this 13th-century Cistercian abbey stand in stark contrast to the manicured lawns surrounding them. The abbey, the last of Scotland's major monasteries to be established, was founded by Devorgilla of Galloway in 1273 in honour of her dead husband, John Balliol. On his death, she had his heart embalmed and carried it with her until she died 22 years later. She and the heart were buried by the altar: hence the name.

7stanes Mabie MOUNTAIN BIKING

(www.7stanesmountainbiking.com; A710) FREE Mabie Forest Park is one of southern Scotland's 7stanes mountain-biking hubs, set among forested hills a couple of miles north of New Abbey. There are nearly 40 miles of trails for all levels; the closest bike hire is in Dumfries. It's very close to the **Mabie Farm Park** (☎01387-259666; www.mabiefarmpark.co.uk; Burnside Farm, Mabie; adult/child £8.50/8; ⏰10am-5pm Apr-Oct, Sat & Sun Mar; 👪), which is handy if you've got kids of different ages.

WORTH A TRIP

ROBERT BURNS

Best remembered for penning the words of 'Auld Lang Syne', Robert Burns (1759–96) is Scotland's most famous poet and a popular hero; his birthday (25 January) is celebrated as Burns Night by Scots around the world.

The pretty, lush village of Alloway (3 miles south of Ayr) should be on the itinerary of every Burns fan – he was born here in 1759. The **Robert Burns Birthplace Museum** (NTS; ☎01292-443700; www.nts.org.uk; Murdoch's Lone; adult/child £10.50/7.50; ⏰10am-5.30pm Apr-Sep, to 5pm Oct-Mar) has collected a solid range of memorabilia, including manuscripts and possessions of the poet, such as the pistols he packed for his work as a taxman. There's plenty of humour that the poet surely would have approved of, and entertaining audio and visual performances will keep the kids amused.

The admission ticket also covers the atmospheric **Burns Birthplace Cottage** (open 11am to 5pm), connected via a walkway to the Birthplace Museum. Born in the little box-bed in this cramped thatched dwelling, the poet spent the first seven years of his life here.

The Burns connection in southern Scotland is milked for all it's worth, and tourist offices have a Burns Heritage Trail leaflet leading you to every place that can claim some link with the bard. Burns fans should have a look at www.robertburns.org.

Getting There & Away

Stagecoach (☎01387-253496; www.stagecoachbus.com) buses run from Dumfries south to Caerlaverock and southeast to Annan via Ruthwell. New Abbey is served regularly from Dumfries.

Kirkcudbright

POP 3400

Kirkcudbright (kirk-*coo*-bree), with its dignified streets of 17th- and 18th-century merchants' houses and appealing harbour, is the ideal base from which to explore the south coast. Look for the nook-and-cranny closes and wynds in the elbow of beautifully restored High St. With its architecture and setting, it's easy to see why Kirkcudbright has been an artist colony since the late 19th century.

Sights

Broughton House GALLERY

(NTS; ☎01557-330437; www.nts.org.uk; 12 High St; adult/child £8/7; ⏰10am-5pm Apr-Oct) Stately 18th-century Broughton House was once home and studio to Glasgow Boy EA Hornel, whose paintings, along with those of several of his contemporaries, grace the interior. Hornel was a great collector of books, and there's an important collection of Robert Burns works. The gallery room is a sumptuous space with wood panelling and a copy of the Parthenon marbles. Behind the house is an exuberant Japanese-inspired garden bristling with life (also opens during winter season; check website for hours).

Kirkcudbright Galleries GALLERY

(☎01557-331276; www.kirkcudbrightgalleries.org.uk; St Mary St; ⏰10am-5pm Tue-Sat) FREE This smart conversion of the town hall into a gallery gives enjoyable context to Kirkcudbright's artistic heritage. The permanent downstairs exhibition tells the story of the artists and designers who came to visit or reside here over the last century and a half, and displays some of their works. Two other galleries host high-quality temporary exhibitions. There's also a pretty cafe. Disabled facilities are excellent.

MacLellan's Castle CASTLE

(HES; ☎01557-331856; www.historicenvironment.scot; Castle St; adult/child £6/3.60; ⏰9.30am-1pm & 2-5.30pm Apr-Sep) Near the harbour is this large, atmospheric ruin built in 1577 by Thomas MacLellan, then provost of Kirkcudbright, as his town residence. Inside, look for the 'lairds' lug', a 16th-century hidey-hole designed for the laird to eavesdrop on his guests.

Sleeping & Eating

★**Selkirk Arms Hotel** HOTEL ££

(☎01557-330402; www.selkirkarmshotel.co.uk; High St; s/d £90/120, compact d £99; P@🛜🐾) What a haven of hospitality this is. Rooms look great, with a stylish purply finish and slate-floored bathrooms. Wood furnishings and views over the back garden give some an extra rustic appeal. There's a good **restaurant** (mains £12-15; noon-2pm & 6-9pm; P) as well as a cute gin and Prosecco bar.

Anchorlee B&B ££
(01557-330197; www.anchorlee.co.uk; 95 St Mary St; s/d £70/82; Easter-Dec; P) This elegant residence on the main road offers great hospitality from cordial hosts. Four lovely rooms offer plenty of space; No 4 is an appealing split-level affair overlooking the garden. Breakfast is excellent.

The Garret BOUTIQUE HOTEL ££
(01557-332040; www.thegarrethotel.co.uk; 116 High St; s/d/f £85/95/105;) With a perfect location on a lovely central street, this handsome Georgian town house has light, spacious rooms decorated in understated style. There's a pleasant cafe-bar with an amazingly large – positively Tardis-like – beer garden. Breakfast is excellent.

★ **Auld Alliance** SCOTTISH, FRENCH ££
(01557-330888; www.auldalliancekirkcudbright.co.uk; 29 St Cuthbert St; mains £14-23; 5.30-8.30pm Thu-Sat, plus Wed & Sun Jul-Oct;) Overlooking the heart of town, this restaurant's cuisine is true to its name, which refers to the historic bond between Scotland and France. Local produce is given a Gallic and Mediterranean twist in a cosy, romantic interior.

Information

Kirkcudbright Tourist Office (Harbour Sq; 10am-4pm) Volunteer-run office with town information.

Getting There & Away

Kirkcudbright is 28 miles southwest of Dumfries. Buses run to Dumfries (£4.70 to £6, 1¼ hours) via (or changing in) Castle Douglas (£2.60, 15 minutes). Change at Ringford or Gatehouse of Fleet for Stranraer.

Galloway Forest Park

South and northwest of the small town of New Galloway is 300-sq-mile Galloway Forest Park, with numerous lochs and great whale-backed mountains covered in heather and pine. The highest point is **Merrick** (843m). The park is criss-crossed by off-road bike routes and some superb signposted walking trails, from gentle strolls to long-distance paths, including the **Southern Upland Way** (01387-273987; www.southernuplandway.gov.uk).

Walkers and cyclists should head for **Glentrool** in the park's west, accessed by the forest road east from Bargrennan off the A714, north of Newton Stewart. Located just over a mile from Bargrennan is the **Glentrool Tourist Office** (0300 067 6800; www.forestryandland.gov.scot; 10.30am-4pm). The road then winds and climbs up to Loch Trool, where there are magnificent views.

The park is very family focused; look out for the booklet of annual events in tourist offices. It's also great for **stargazing**: it's been named a Dark Sky Park by the International Dark-Sky Association (www.darksky.org).

Activities

Galloway Red Deer Range WILDLIFE WATCHING
(0300 067 6900; https://forestryandland.gov.scot/gallowayfp; A712) FREE Observe Britain's largest land-based beast from a hide and viewing area. During rutting season in autumn, it's a bit like watching a bullfight as snorting, charging stags compete for the harem. From April to September there are guided ranger-led visits (adult/child £8/5) to see these impressive beasts.

Nearby, the Wild Goat Range offers the chance to spot the namesake nimble creatures on a hillside.

Raiders' Road SCENIC DRIVE
(www.forestryandland.gov.scot; per vehicle £2; vehicles Apr-Oct;) About a mile west of Clatteringshaws Tourist Office, Raiders' Rd is a 10-mile drive through the forest with various picnic spots, child-friendly activities and short walks marked along the way. Drive slowly as there's plenty of wildlife about. One of the nicest spots is a cascade where you might spot otters. Walkers and cyclists can access the road year-round.

Red Kite Feeding Station BIRDWATCHING
(01644-450202; www.bellymackhillfarm.co.uk; Bellymack Hill Farm, Laurieston; adult/child £5/free; noon-4pm) Just off the B795, this farm has daily feedings of red kites at 2pm. There's a visitor centre (with cafe) here, from where you can observe these beautiful raptors, which congregate from about 1pm. There are often RSPB (Royal Society for the Protection of Birds) volunteers present who can inform you about the birds' lifestyles.

Information

Clatteringshaws Tourist Office (☎0300 067 6800; www.forestryandland.gov.scot; A712; ⏲11am-4pm) On Clatteringshaws Loch's shore, 6 miles west of New Galloway, this is basically a cafe with the odd display panel. From here you can walk to a replica of a Romano-British homestead (0.5 miles), and to Bruce's Stone (1 mile), where Robert the Bruce is said to have rested after defeating the English at the Battle of Rapploch Moss.

Kirroughtree Tourist Office (☎0300 067 6800; www.forestryandland.gov.scot; off A75, Palnure; ⏲11am-4pm) This park tourist office, 3 miles east of Newton Stewart, has a cafe and a nature-watching hide, as well as walking trails from 400m to 4 miles. This is one of the **7stanes mountain-biking hubs** (www.7stanesmountainbiking.com; Kirroughtree Tourist Office), and there's a good **bike shop** (☎01671-401303; www.thebreakpad.com; Kirroughtree Tourist Office; hire bikes from £22/30 per half/full day; ⏲10am-5pm) that does hires and repairs.

Getting There & Away

The scenic 19-mile A712 (Queen's Way) between New Galloway and Newton Stewart slices through the southern section of the park. It's the only road through the park, but no buses run along it. The nearest public-transport point for the western part of this road is Newton Stewart, for the east New Galloway. There's **bike hire** (☎01671-401529; www.facebook.com/KirkcowanCycleRepairs; Victoria Lane; half/full day £20/30, week £120; ⏲10am-4pm Mon-Fri, to 6pm Wed, to 2pm Sat, extended summer hours) available in Newton Stewart.

Stranraer

POP 10,400

The friendly but somewhat ramshackle port of Stranraer has seen its tourist mainstay, the ferry traffic to Northern Ireland, move up the road to Cairnryan. The town's still wondering what to do with itself, but there are good places to stay and lots to explore in the surrounding area.

Sights

Castle Kennedy Gardens GARDENS
(☎01776-702024; www.castlekennedygardens.com; Sheuchan; adult/child £6/2; ⏲10am-5pm Apr-Oct, Sat & Sun Feb & Mar) Three miles east of Stranraer, these magnificent gardens are among Scotland's most renowned. They cover 30 hectares and are set on an isthmus between two lochs and two castles. The landscaping was undertaken in 1730 by the Earl of Stair, who used unoccupied soldiers to do the work. Buses heading east from Stranraer stop at the gate on the main road; it's a pleasant 20-minute stroll from here to the gardens' entrance.

Sleeping & Eating

Ivy House B&B £
(☎01776-704176; www.ivyhouse-ferrylink.co.uk; 3 Ivy Pl; s/d £40/60, s without bathroom £35; 📶) This is a great guesthouse that does Scottish hospitality proud, with excellent facilities, tidy en-suite rooms and a smashing breakfast. Nothing is too much trouble for the genial host, who always has a smile for her guests. Prices are excellent. The room at the back overlooking the churchyard is particularly light and quiet.

★**Thornbank House** B&B ££
(☎01776-706168; www.thornbankhouse.co.uk; Thornbank Rd; r £80-90; P📶🏊🐾) An exceptional place offering extremely comfortable and well-furnished modern rooms (one with a Jacuzzi), Thornbank also offers excellent breakfasts and friendly, casual hospitality. It's already well out of the ordinary before you even consider the large indoor swimming pool and absolutely sensational vista over the bay to Ailsa Craig. One room has an outdoor deck to enjoy the view.

Henrys Bay House SCOTTISH ££
(☎01776-707388; www.henrysbayhouse.co.uk; Cairnryan Rd; mains £13-20; ⏲5-8pm Wed, noon-2pm & 5-8pm Thu-Sat, noon-8pm Sun) Just east of the centre, this is Stranraer's best place to eat, with hearty portions of well-sourced meat and seafood and a welcoming vibe. There's a pleasingly old-fashioned feel to some of the dishes, while others have a more contemporary style. If the weather's fine, the deck overlooking the bay is a great spot to be.

Getting There & Away

Stranraer is 6 miles south of the ferry port of Cairnryan, which is on the eastern side of Loch Ryan. A bus service coinciding with **Stena Line** (☎03447 70 70 70; www.stenaline.co.uk) ferries runs between Stranraer and Cairnryan. Buses running frequently between Stranraer and Ayr also stop in Cairnryan. For a taxi (about £9), call **McLean's Taxis** (☎01776-703343; www.mcleanstaxis.com; 21 North Strand St; ⏲24hr).

DON'T MISS

CULZEAN CASTLE

The Scottish National Trust's flagship property, magnificent **Culzean** (NTS; ☎01655-884455; www.nts.org.uk; Culzean; castle adult/child/family £17/12.65/42; ⏲castle 10.30am-5pm Apr-Oct, last entry 4pm, park 9.30am-sunset year-round; 🅟) (kull-ane) is one of the most impressive of Scotland's stately homes. On approach the castle floats into view like a mirage. It was designed by Robert Adam, the most influential architect of his time, renowned for his meticulous attention to detail and the elegant classical embellishments with which he decorated his ceilings and fireplaces.

The 18th-century mansion is perched dramatically on a clifftop. The beautiful oval staircase is regarded as one of Adam's finest achievements. On the 1st floor, the opulence of the circular saloon contrasts violently with the views of the wild sea below. Lord Cassillis' bedroom is said to be haunted by a lady in green, mourning for a lost baby. Even the bathrooms are palatial: the dressing room beside the state bedroom is equipped with a Victorian state-of-the-art shower.

There's a great kids' play area, which replicates the castle on a smaller scale, as well as a re-creation of a Victorian vinery, an orangery, a deer park and an aviary.

It's even possible to stay in the castle from April to October, and there's a campsite by the gates.

Stagecoach buses running between Ayr and Girvan stop outside the gates, from where it's a 1-mile walk to the castle.

Rhinns of Galloway

The Rhinns (or Rhins) of Galloway is a hammerhead-shaped peninsula west of Stranraer that runs 25 miles from north to south. Its coastal scenery includes rugged cliffs, tiny harbours and sandy beaches. Dairy cattle graze on the greenest grass you've ever seen, and the warm waters of the Gulf Stream give the peninsula the mildest climate in Scotland.

Pretty **Portpatrick**, set around a harbour, is a big drawcard. Further south, sleepy **Port Logan** has an excellent sandy beach and a famous botanical garden. From **Drummore**, a fishing village on the east coast, it's another 5 miles to the spectacular **Mull of Galloway**, Scotland's most southerly point.

Buses from Stranraer cover the peninsula.

Sights

★Mull of Galloway NATURE RESERVE

(www.mull-of-galloway.co.uk) Scotland's southernmost point is a spectacular spot, with windswept green grass and views of Scotland, England, the Isle of Man and Northern Ireland. The lighthouse here was built by Robert Stevenson, grandfather of the writer, in 1826. The Mull of Galloway RSPB nature reserve, home to thousands of seabirds, is also important for its wildflowers. At the entrance to the reserve is a spectacular clifftop cafe (p835). The former homes of the lighthouse keepers are available as accommodation; check out www.lighthouse-holidaycottages.co.uk.

Mull of Galloway Lighthouse LIGHTHOUSE

(www.mull-of-galloway.co.uk; Mull of Galloway; adult/child £3/1, with exhibition £5/1.50; ⏲10am-4pm Sat & Sun Apr-Oct, daily Jul & Aug) You can climb the lighthouse at the Mull of Galloway for views over four different political entities: Northern Ireland, Scotland, England and the Isle of Man. Check the website to coincide your visit with a blast on the newly restored foghorn (outside of seabird nesting season).

Logan Botanic Garden GARDENS

(☎01776-860231; www.rbge.org.uk/logan; Port Logan; adult/child £7/free; ⏲10am-5pm Mar-Oct, to 4pm early Nov) The mild climate in this southwestern part of Scotland is demonstrated at Logan Botanic Garden, a mile north of Port Logan, where an array of subtropical flora includes tree ferns and cabbage palms. The garden is an outpost of the Royal Botanic Garden in Edinburgh. There's a good cafe here.

Sleeping & Eating

Mount Stewart Hotel BOUTIQUE HOTEL ££

(☎01776-810291; www.themountstewarthotel.co.uk; South Cres; d without/with view £110/130; 🅟📶) If you thought the views harbourside were good, stroll up the hill to this hotel and they're even better. You can see Northern Ireland on a good day, or Belfast's lights at night. The rooms have been fitted out in modish urban style with lots of blacks and greys. The outlook from the front rooms is sensational. Downstairs is a bar serving adequate food.

★Corsewall Lighthouse Hotel HOTEL £££
(01776-853220; www.lighthousehotel.co.uk; Kirkcolm; d £140-280; P) It's just you and the cruel sea out here at this fabulously romantic 200-year-old lighthouse. On a sunny day, the water shimmers with light, and you can see Ireland, Kintyre, Arran and Ailsa Craig. But when wind and rain beat in, it's just great to be cosily holed up in the bar-restaurant or snuggling under the covers in your room.

★Knockinaam Lodge HOTEL £££
(01776-810471; www.knockinaamlodge.com; dinner & B&B s £225, d £380-480; P) For a real dose of luxury, head 3 miles south-east of Portpatrick to this former hunting lodge in a dramatic, secluded location with grassy lawns rolling down to a sandy cove. It's where Churchill plotted the endgame of WWII – you can stay in his suite – and it's a very romantic place to get away from it all.

Gallie Craig CAFE £
(01776-840558; www.galliecraig.co.uk; Mull of Galloway; light meals £4-9; 11am-4pm Sat-Wed Feb & Mar, 10am-5pm daily Apr-Oct, 11am-4pm Sat & Sun Nov) Invisible from above, thanks to its turf roof, this clifftop cafe offers spectacular vistas, great cakes and tasty savouries.

AT A GLANCE

POPULATION
2.45 million

MILES OF COASTLINE
3300

BEST AWAY-FROM-IT-ALL HOTEL
Monachyle Mhor (p869)

BEST WALKING TRAIL
Loch Leven Heritage Trail (p851)

BEST CASTLE
Glamis Castle (p859)

WHEN TO GO

May
A magical time to explore before summer crowds arrive, and to enjoy the Perth Arts Festival.

Jul & Aug
Seafood feasts in Fife and fresh raspberries in Blairgowrie.

Oct & Nov
Autumn colours enliven walks in the Perthshire woods around Crieff, Comrie and Blairgowrie.

Glamis Castle (p859)
CLIFF HANDS/SHUTTERSTOCK ©

Stirling & Central Scotland

The Scottish nation's historic roots are deeply embedded in central Scotland. Key battles around Stirling paved the road to independence; dramatic castles adorn the region's hilltops; and Perth, the former capital, is where kings were crowned on the Stone of Destiny.

Arriving from Glasgow or Edinburgh, visitors can get a sense of the country further north as the Lowland scenery ramps up towards Highland splendour. It's here that the landscape's majesty begins to unfold among woodlands, waterfalls, craggy hills and rivers, with silhouettes of soaring peaks on the northern horizon.

Whether in the softly wooded country of Perthshire or along the green Fife coastline, opportunities to enjoy the outdoors abound: walking, cycling and angling are all easy possibilities. The region also has some of the country's best pubs and restaurants.

INCLUDES

Stirling & Central Scotland Highlights

❶ **Stirling Castle** (p840) Admiring the views across ancient independence battlefields from this magnificent castle.

❷ **St Andrews** (p846) Pacing through the historic birthplace of golf to play the famous Old Course.

❸ **Scone Palace** (p856) Strutting with the peacocks at this elegant palace, near where Scottish kings were once crowned.

❹ **East Neuk of Fife** (p851) Feasting on local seafood in picturesque fishing villages.

❺ **V&A Dundee** (p857) Discovering the best of Scottish and international design at this architecturally stunning museum in the heart of Dundee's redeveloped waterfront.

❻ **The Trossachs** (p866) Exploring the lovely lochscapes and accessible walking and cycling trails of this spectacular region.

❼ **Iona** (p881) Journeying through wildlife-rich Mull to reach this holy emerald isle.

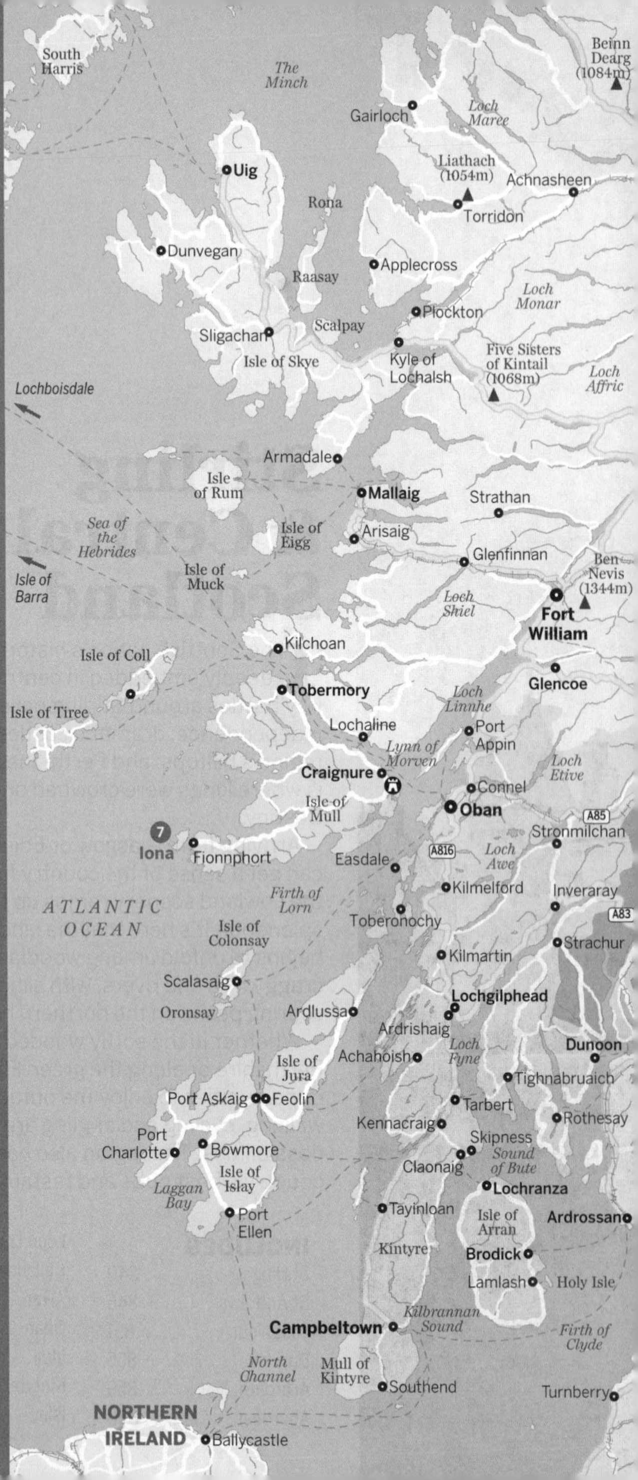

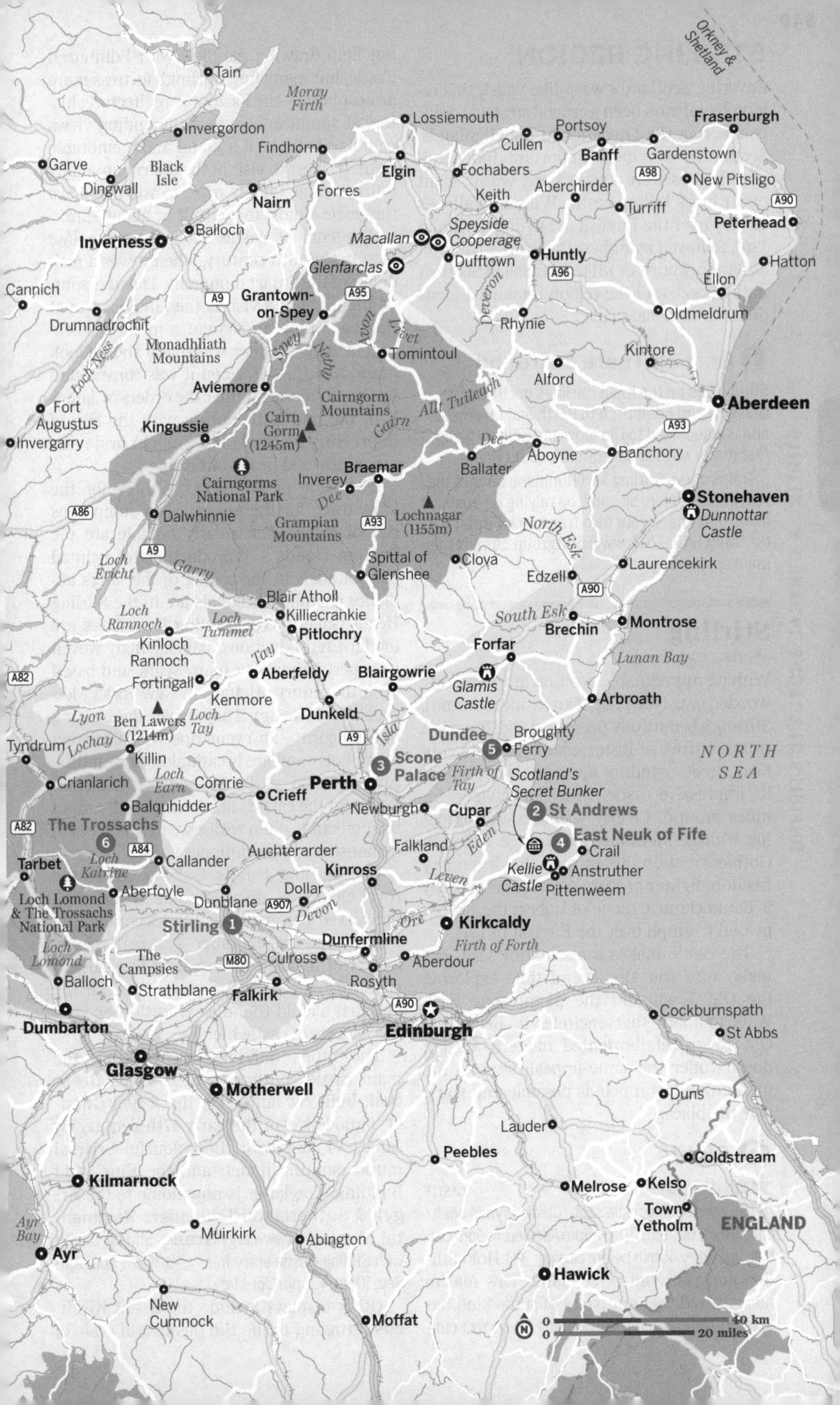

Orkney & Shetland
Tain
Moray Firth
Lossiemouth
Portsoy
Fraserburgh
Invergordon
Cullen
Findhorn
Banff
Gardenstown
Garve
Black Isle
Elgin
Fochabers
A98
New Pitsligo
Dingwall
Forres
Aberchirder
Nairn
Keith
Turriff
A90
Speyside Cooperage
Peterhead
Balloch
Inverness
Macallan
Huntly
Dufftown
Hatton
Glenfarclas
A96
Cannich
Deveron
Ellon
A9
Grantown-on-Spey
A95
Oldmeldrum
Drumnadrochit
Avon
Livet
Rhynie
Spey
Nethy
Monadhliath Mountains
Loch Ness
Tomintoul
Kintore
Alford
Aviemore
Cairngorm Mountains
Allt Tuileach
Fort Augustus
Cairn Gorm (1245m)
Gairn
Aberdeen
Kingussie
A93
Invergarry
Dee
Aboyne
Banchory
Braemar
Ballater
Cairngorms National Park
Inverey
Dee
Stonehaven
Dunnottar Castle
A86
Dalwhinnie
Grampian Mountains
A93
Lochnagar (1155m)
North Esk
A9
Loch Ericht
Garry
Spittal of Glenshee
Clova
Laurencekirk
Edzell
A90
Blair Atholl
Loch Rannoch
Loch Tummel
Killiecrankie
South Esk
Montrose
Brechin
Pitlochry
Kinloch Rannoch
Forfar
Lunan Bay
Tay
A82
Fortingall
Aberfeldy
Blairgowrie
Glamis Castle
Kenmore
Arbroath
Lyon
Ben Lawers (1214m)
Loch Tay
Dunkeld
Isla
A9
Dundee
Broughty Ferry
Tyndrum
Lochay
Killin
5
NORTH SEA
3
Scone Palace
Crianlarich
Loch Earn
Comrie
Perth
Firth of Tay
Scotland's Secret Bunker
Crieff
Balquhidder
Newburgh
Cupar
2
St Andrews
A82
The Trossachs
Edem
4
East Neuk of Fife
6
A84
Auchterarder
Falkland
Crail
Tarbet
Loch Katrine
Callander
Kinross
Kellie Castle
Anstruther
Leven
Pittenweem
Aberfoyle
Dollar
Loch Lomond & The Trossachs National Park
Dunblane
A907
Devon
Stirling
1
Ore
Kirkcaldy
Dunfermline
Loch Lomond
The Campsies
Firth of Forth
M80
Culross
Aberdour
Balloch
Rosyth
Strathblane
Falkirk
A90
Dumbarton
Cockburnspath
Edinburgh
St Abbs
Glasgow
Motherwell
Duns
Lauder
Peebles
Coldstream
Kilmarnock
Melrose
Kelso
Town Yetholm
ENGLAND
Ayr Bay
Muirkirk
Abington
Ayr
Hawick
New Cumnock
Moffat
0
40 km
0
20 miles
N

STIRLING REGION

Covering Scotland's wasp-like waist, this region has always been a crucial strategic point connecting the Lowlands to the Highlands. Scotland's two most important independence battles were fought here, within sight of Stirling's hilltop castle. William Wallace's victory over the English at Stirling Bridge in 1297, followed by Robert the Bruce's triumph at Bannockburn in 1314, established Scottish nationhood, and the region remains a focus of much national pride.

Getting There & Around

Stirling lies on the main rail lines north from Glasgow and Edinburgh to Perth and Inverness, and is also linked to Glasgow and Edinburgh by fast motorways and frequent bus services.

Trains serve Stirling and Dunblane but not the rest of the region, so you'll be relying on buses if you don't have your own transport. **First** (0345 646 0707; www.firstgroup.com) is the main operator.

Stirling

01786 / POP 36,150

With an impregnable position atop a mighty wooded crag (the plug of an extinct volcano), Stirling's beautifully preserved Old Town is a treasure trove of historic buildings and cobbled streets winding up to the ramparts of its impressive castle, which offer views for miles around. Clearly visible is the brooding Wallace Monument, a strange Victorian Gothic creation honouring the legendary freedom fighter of *Braveheart* fame. Nearby is Bannockburn, scene of Robert the Bruce's pivotal triumph over the English in 1314.

The castle makes a fascinating visit, but make sure you also spend time exploring the Old Town and the picturesque Back Walk footpath that encircles it. Below the Old Town, retail-oriented modern Stirling doesn't offer the same appeal; stick to the high ground as much as possible and you'll love the place.

Sights

★**Stirling Castle** CASTLE

(HES; www.stirlingcastle.scot; Castle Wynd; adult/child £16/9.60; 9.30am-6pm Apr-Sep, to 5pm Oct-Mar, last entry 45min before closing; P) Hold Stirling and you control Scotland. This maxim has ensured that a fortress of some kind has existed here since prehistoric times. You cannot help drawing parallels with Edinburgh Castle, but many find Stirling's fortress more atmospheric – the location, architecture, historical significance and commanding views combine to make it a grand and memorable sight. It's best to visit in the afternoon; many tourists come on day trips, so you may have the castle almost to yourself by about 4pm.

The current castle dates from the late 14th to the 16th century, when it was a residence of the Stuart monarchs. The undisputed highlight of a visit is the fabulous **Royal Palace**, which underwent a major restoration in 2011. The idea was that it should look brand new, just as when it was constructed by French masons under the orders of James V in the mid-16th century with the aim of impressing his new (also French) bride and other crowned heads of Europe.

The suite of six rooms – three for the king, three for the queen – is a sumptuous riot of colour. Particularly notable are the **Stirling Heads** – reproductions of painted oak roundels in the ceiling of the king's audience chamber (originals are in the Stirling Heads Gallery). The **Stirling tapestries** are modern reproductions, painstakingly woven by expert hands over many years, and based on 16th-century originals in New York's Metropolitan Museum. They depict the hunting of a unicorn – an event ripe with Christian metaphor – and are breathtakingly beautiful. An exhibition at the far end of the Nether Bailey (at the castle's northern end) describes their creation, often with a weaver on hand to demonstrate the techniques used.

The **Stirling Heads Gallery**, above the royal chambers, displays some of the original carved oak roundels that decorated the king's audience chamber – a real rogue's gallery of royals, courtiers, and biblical and classical figures. In the vaults beneath the palace is a child-friendly **exhibition** on various aspects of castle life.

The other buildings surrounding the main castle courtyard are the vast **Great Hall**, built by James IV; the **Royal Chapel**, remodelled in the early 17th century by James VI and with the colourful original mural painting intact; and the King's Old Building. The latter is now home to the **Argyll & Sutherland Highlanders Regimental Museum** (www.argylls.co.uk; Stirling Castle; with Stirling Castle entry free; 9.30am-5pm Apr-Sep, 10am-4.15pm Oct-Mar).

Other displays include the **Great Kitchens**, bringing to life the bustle and scale of

Stirling

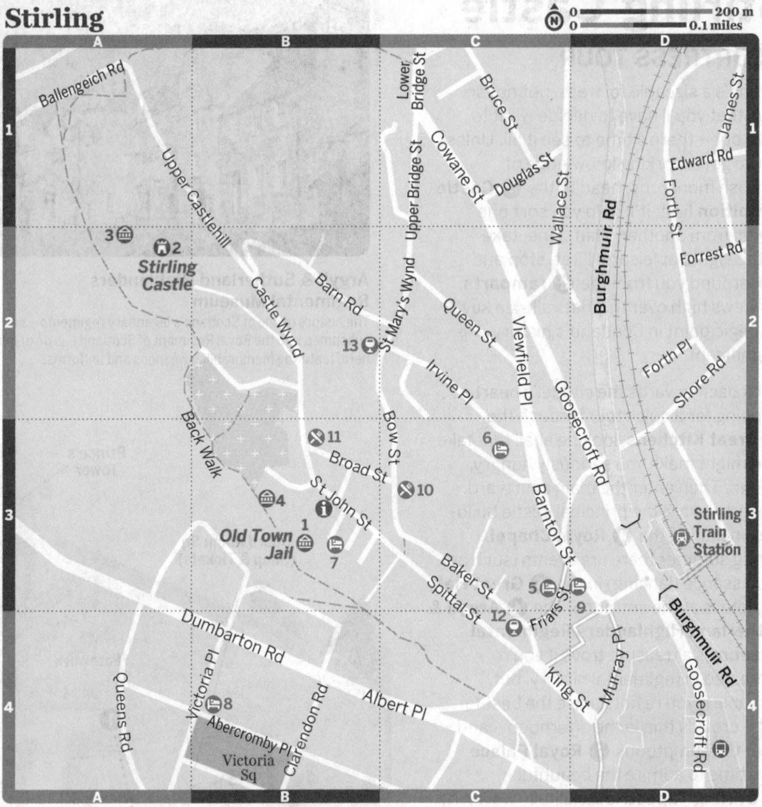

Stirling

Top Sights
1 Old Town Jail B3
2 Stirling Castle A2

Sights
3 Argyll & Sutherland Highlanders Regimental Museum A2
4 Cowane's Hospital B3

Sleeping
5 Friars Wynd C3
6 Munro Guesthouse C3
7 Stirling Youth Hostel B3
8 Victoria Square Guesthouse B4
9 Willy Wallace Backpackers Hostel D3

Eating
Breá .... (see 12)
10 Darnley Coffee House C3
11 Hermann's B3

Drinking & Nightlife
12 Brewdog C4
13 Settle Inn B2

the enterprise of cooking for the king, and, near the entrance, the **Castle Exhibition**, which gives good background information on the Stuart kings and updates on current archaeological investigations. There are magnificent vistas from the ramparts towards the Highlands and the Ochil Hills.

Admission includes an audio guide, and free guided tours leave regularly from near the entrance.

★ Old Town Jail HISTORIC BUILDING
(www.oldtownjail.co.uk; St John St, FK8 1EA; adult/child £8/6; ⊙10.15am-5.15pm mid-Jul–Oct) This impressive Victorian prison building lay

Stirling Castle

A FORTRESS TOUR

Stirling's a sizeable fortress, but not so huge that you'll have to decide what to leave out – there's time to see it all. Unless you've got a working knowledge of Scottish monarchs, head to the 1 **Castle Exhibition** first: it'll help you sort one James from another. That done, take on the sights at leisure. First, stop and look around you from the 2 **ramparts**; the views high over this flat valley, a key strategic point in Scotland's history, are magnificent.

Track back towards the citadel's heart, stopping for a quick tour through the 3 **Great Kitchens**; looking at all that fake food might make you seriously hungry, though. Then enter the main courtyard. Around you are the principal castle buildings, including the 4 **Royal Chapel**. During summer there are events (such as Renaissance dancing) in the 5 **Great Hall**; get details at the entrance. The 6 **Argyll & Sutherland Highlanders Regimental Museum** is a treasure trove if you're interested in regimental history, but missable if you're not. Leave the best for last – crowds thin in the afternoon – and enter the sumptuous 7 **Royal Palace**. Take time to admire the beautiful 8 **Stirling Tapestries**, skillfully woven by hand on-site between 2001 and 2014.

THE WAY UP & DOWN

If you have time, take the atmospheric Back Walk, a peaceful, shady stroll around the Old Town's fortifications and up to the castle's imposing crag-top position. Afterwards, wander down through the Old Town to admire its facades.

FAST FACTS

- Admission is free for Historic Environment Scotland members. If you'll be visiting several Historic Environment Scotland sites a membership will save you plenty.
- Vital Statistics: first constructed before 1110; at least nine sieges; last besieger was Bonnie Prince Charlie (unsuccessful); £12 million spent refurbishing the Royal Palace.

BRIAN JANNSEN / GEFOTOSTOCK ©

Argyll & Sutherland Highlanders Regimental Museum
The history of one of Scotland's legendary regiments – now subsumed into the Royal Regiment of Scotland – is on display here, featuring memorabilia, weapons and uniforms.

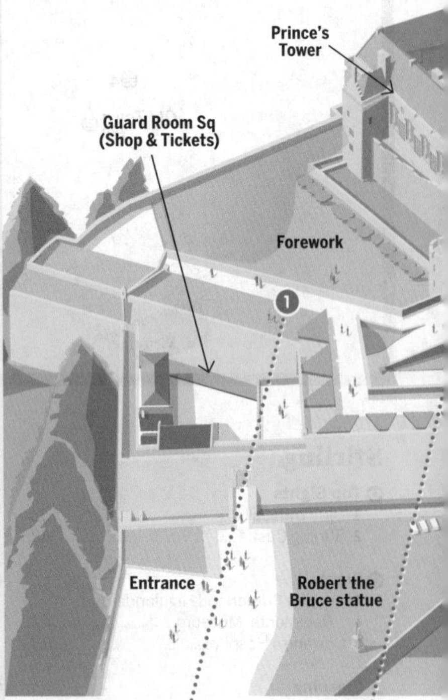

Castle Exhibition
A great overview of the Stuart dynasty here will get your facts straight, and also offers the latest archaeological titbits from the ongoing excavations under the citadel. Analysis of skeletons has revealed surprising amounts of biographical data.

Royal Palace
The impressive highlight of a visit to the castle is this recreation of the royal lodgings originally built by James V. The finely worked ceiling, ornate furniture and sumptuous unicorn tapestries dazzle.

Great Hall & Royal Chapel

Creations of James IV and VI, respectively, these elegant spaces around the central courtyard have been faithfully restored. The vast Great Hall, with its imposing beamed roof, was the largest medieval hall in Scotland.

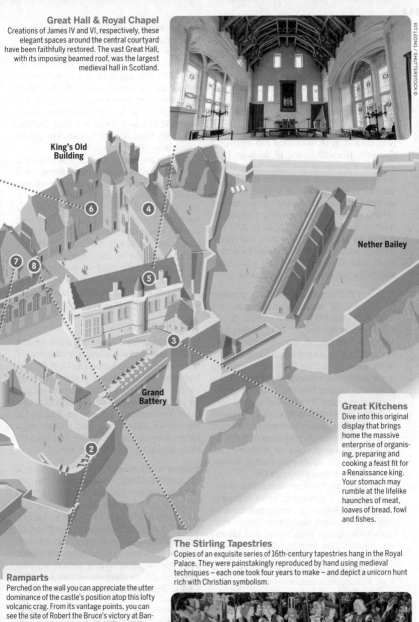

Great Kitchens

Dive into this original display that brings home the massive enterprise of organising, preparing and cooking a feast fit for a Renaissance king. Your stomach may rumble at the lifelike haunches of meat, loaves of bread, fowl and fishes.

The Stirling Tapestries

Copies of an exquisite series of 16th-century tapestries hang in the Royal Palace. They were painstakingly reproduced by hand using medieval techniques – each one took four years to make – and depict a unicorn hunt rich with Christian symbolism.

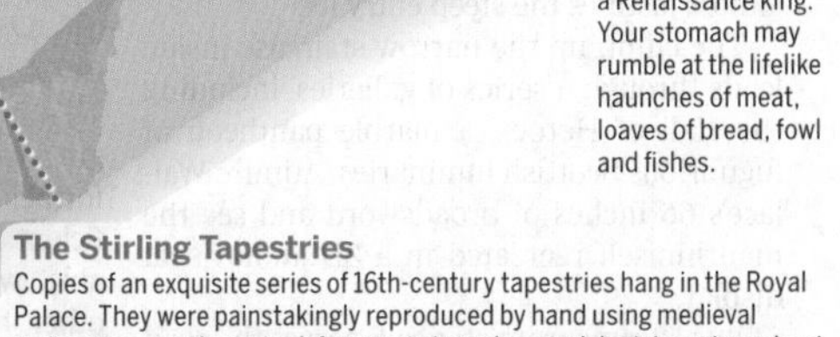

Ramparts

Perched on the wall you can appreciate the utter dominance of the castle's position atop this lofty volcanic crag. From its vantage points, you can see the site of Robert the Bruce's victory at Bannockburn and the monument to William Wallace.

derelict from the 1960s until 2015, when it was reopened as a visitor attraction. Costumed guides lead tours around the former prison cells and up to the top of the observation tower, recounting gruesome tales of prisoners, punishments and executions along with fascinating facts about Stirling's history. Tours depart every 30 minutes.

Cowane's Hospital HISTORIC BUILDING
(www.cowanes.org.uk; 49 John St, FK8 1ED) FREE
Cowane's Hospital is one of Stirling's best-preserved medieval buildings, built in the mid-17th century as a home for elderly pensioners (it later served as a guild hall, and an isolation hospital during an outbreak of cholera in the 1830s). Following a major restoration it opened to the public in 2021 and houses an artists' studio, a cafe, and an exhibition on the building's founder, local merchant John Cowane (1570–1633) – his statue adorns the tower above the main door.

National Wallace Monument MONUMENT
(01786-472140; www.nationalwallacemonument.com; Abbey Craig, FK9 5LF; adult/child £10.75/6.75; 9.30am-5pm Apr-Jun, Sep & Oct, to 6pm Jul & Aug, 10am-4pm Nov-Feb, 10am-5pm Mar; P) Perched high on a crag above the floodplain of the River Forth, this Victorian monument in the shape of a medieval tower is so Gothic it deserves circling bats and croaking ravens. It commemorates William Wallace, the hero of the bid for Scottish independence depicted in the film *Braveheart*. The view from the top over the flat, green gorgeousness of the Forth Valley, including the site of Wallace's 1297 victory over the English at Stirling Bridge, almost justifies the steep entry fee.

The climb up the narrow staircase inside leads through a series of galleries, including the Hall of Heroes, a marble pantheon of lugubrious Scottish luminaries. Admire Wallace's 66 inches of broadsword and see the man himself recreated in a 3D audiovisual display.

Bus 52 runs from stance B across the road from Stirling train station to the visitor centre (£2.80, 10 minutes, every 30 minutes). From July to September, a hop-on, hop-off tourist bus links the bus station, castle and monument (£4.90 per day).

Battle of Bannockburn Experience MUSEUM
(NTS; www.battleofbannockburn.com; Glasgow Rd, FK7 0LJ; battle site free, Experience adult/child £7.50/5.50; 10am-5.30pm Apr-Oct, to 5pm Nov-Mar; P) Robert the Bruce's defeat of the English army on 24 June 1314 at Bannockburn established Scotland as a separate nation. The Battle of Bannockburn Experience uses interactive technology to bring the battle to life. The highlight is a digital projection of the battlefield onto a 3D landscape that shows the movements of infantry and cavalry (entry is by prebooked time slots). Bannockburn is 2 miles south of Stirling; buses run from Stirling bus station (£2.50, 10 minutes, three per hour).

Outside the centre, the 'battlefield' itself is no more than an expanse of neatly trimmed grass, crowned with a circular monument inscribed with a poem by Kathleen Jamie, and a Victorian statue of the victor astride his horse. There has been much debate over exactly where the Battle of Bannockburn took place, but it was definitely somewhere near here on the southern edge of Stirling's urban sprawl. Exploiting the marshy ground around the Bannock Burn, Bruce won a great tactical victory against a much larger and better-equipped force.

Sleeping

Willy Wallace Backpackers Hostel HOSTEL £
(01786-446773; www.willywallacehostel.com; 77 Murray Pl, FK8 1AU; dm/tw from £15/44; @) This highly convenient, central hostel is friendly, roomy and sociable – there's a piano and guitar in the common room. The colourful, spacious dormitories are clean and light, and it has free tea and coffee, a good kitchen and a laissez-faire atmosphere. Other amenities include bicycle hire and laundry service.

Stirling Youth Hostel HOSTEL £
(HS; 01786-473442; www.hostellingscotland.org.uk; St John St, FK8 1EA; dm/tw £18/42; P@) This hostel has an unbeatable location and great facilities. Though its facade is that of a former church, the interior is modern and efficient. The dorms are compact but comfortable, with lockers and en-suite bathrooms; other highlights include a pool table, bike shed and, at busy times, cheap meals on offer. Lack of atmosphere is a possible downside.

★**Friars Wynd** HOTEL ££
(01786-473390; www.friarswynd.co.uk; 17 Friars St, FK8 1HA; r from £89;) Set in a lovingly restored 19th-century town house just a short walk from the train station, Friars Wynd offers eight bedrooms of varying size, many with period features such as Victorian cast-iron fire surrounds or exposed patches of original red-brick walls. The 1st-floor rooms

WORTH A TRIP

DOUNE

Magnificent **Doune Castle** (HES; www.historicenvironment.scot; FK16 6EA; adult/child £6/3.60; ⏲9.30am-5.30pm Apr-Sep, 10am-4pm Oct-Mar; P) is one of the best-preserved medieval fortresses in Scotland, having remained largely unchanged since it was built for the duke of Albany in the 14th century. It has been used as a set for the movie *Monty Python and the Holy Grail* (1975) – the audio guide is narrated by Python member Terry Jones – and the TV series *Outlander* and *Game of Thrones*. Highlights include the cathedral-like Great Hall, and a kitchen fireplace big enough to roast a whole ox.

The castle was a favourite royal hunting lodge, but it was also of great strategic importance because it controlled the route between the Lowlands and Highlands. Mary, Queen of Scots, once stayed here, as did Bonnie Prince Charlie. There are great views from the castle walls, and the lofty gatehouse is very impressive, rising nearly 30m.

are directly above the bar and restaurant, so they can be a little noisy at weekends.

Munro Guesthouse B&B ££
(☎01786-472685; www.munroguesthouse.co.uk; 14 Princes St, FK8 1HQ; s/d from £65/75;) Cosy and cheery, Munro Guesthouse is right in the centre of town but located on a quiet side street. Things are done with a smile, and the smallish rooms are most inviting, particularly the cute attic ones. The breakfast is also better than the norm, with fruit salad on hand. There's easy (pay) parking opposite.

★**Victoria Square Guesthouse** B&B £££
(☎01786-473920; www.victoriasquare.scot; 12 Victoria Sq, FK8 2QZ; s/d from £98/148; P) Though close to the centre of town, Victoria Sq is a quiet oasis of elegant Victorian buildings surrounding a verdant park. This luxury guesthouse's huge rooms, bay windows and period features make it a winner. There are two four-poster rooms (from £161) for romantic getaways, and some bedrooms have views to the castle towering above. No children under 12.

Eating

Darnley Coffee House CAFE £
(☎01786-474468; www.facebook.com/DarnleyCoffeeHouse; 18 Bow St, FK8 1BS; mains £4-6; ⏲10am-4pm;) Just down the hill from Stirling Castle, this is a good pit stop for home baking, soup, vegan food, tea and coffee (no espresso machine, though) during a walk around the Old Town. The cafe is in the vaulted cellars of a 16th-century house where Darnley, the lover and later husband of Mary, Queen of Scots, once stayed.

★**Hermann's** AUSTRIAN, SCOTTISH ££
(☎01786-450632; www.hermanns.co.uk; 58 Broad St, FK8 1EF; mains £14-20, 2-/3-course lunch £13/16; ⏲noon-3pm & 6-10pm;) This elegant Scottish-Austrian restaurant is a reliable and popular choice, with conservative decor oddly offset by magazine-spread skiing photos, but the food doesn't miss a beat and ranges from Scottish favourites such as Cullen skink (smoked haddock soup) or scallops to Austrian schnitzel and spaetzle noodles. Vegetarian options are good, and quality Austrian wines provide an out-of-the-ordinary accompaniment.

Birds & Bees PUB FOOD ££
(☎01786-473663; www.thebirdsandthebees-stirling.com; Easter Cornton Rd, Causewayhead, FK9 5PB; mains £9-12, steaks £16-20; ⏲food served noon-2.30pm & 5-10pm; P) This pub is a bit of a local secret; it's in a converted farm steading hidden away on a back road on the city's northern fringes. There's faux-rustic decor and a crowd-pleasing pub-grub menu that runs from nachos and tempura king prawns to steaks, burgers, chilli con carne and fish and chips. There's outdoor seating and plenty of space for kids to run around.

Breá SCOTTISH ££
(☎01786-446277; www.brea-stirling.co.uk; 5 Baker St, FK8 1BJ; mains £16-27; ⏲noon-9pm Sun-Thu, to 10pm Fri & Sat;) Bringing a bohemian touch to central Stirling, this busy bistro has pared-back contemporary decor and a short menu showcasing carefully sourced Scottish produce, including beef, venison, seafood, haggis and Brewdog beers, as well as gourmet burgers and a vegan menu.

Drinking & Nightlife

Brewdog BAR
(☎01786-440043; www.brewdog.com/bars/uk/stirling; 7 Baker St, FK8 1BJ; ⏲noon-midnight Sun-Thu, to 1am Fri & Sat;) The Stirling outpost of the Brewdog empire has a cool bar, done

out in designer-distressed timber, offering no fewer than 15 taps dispensing craft beers from all over the world, including several from its own famously crowdfunded brewery near Fraserburgh in Aberdeenshire.

Settle Inn PUB
(☎01786-474609; 91 St Mary's Wynd, FK8 1BU; ⏰11am-11pm Mon-Sat, 12.30-11pm Sun; 📶) A warm welcome is guaranteed at Stirling's oldest pub (1733), a spot strong on atmosphere, with its log fire, vaulted back room, low-slung ceilings and Friday-night folk-music sessions. Guest ales, atmospheric nooks where you can settle in for the night, and a blend of local characters make it a classic of its kind.

Information

Stirling Tourist Office (☎01786-475019; www.yourstirling.com; Old Town Jail, St John St, FK8 1EA; ⏰10am-5pm) Accommodation bookings and internet access.

Getting There & Away

BUS

From the **bus station** (Goosecroft Rd), **Citylink** (☎0871 266 3333; www.citylink.co.uk) offers a number of services to/from Stirling, including:

Dundee £15.70, 1¾ hours, hourly
Edinburgh £9.30, 1½ hours, hourly
Glasgow £9.30, 45 minutes, hourly
Perth £9.80, one hour, at least hourly

Some buses continue to Aberdeen, Inverness and Fort William; more frequently a change will be required.

TRAIN

ScotRail (www.scotrail.co.uk) has services to/from a number of destinations, including:

Aberdeen £37, 2¼ hours, hourly weekdays, every two hours Sunday
Dundee £15.90, one hour, hourly weekdays, every two hours Sunday
Edinburgh £9.70, 50 minutes, twice hourly Monday to Saturday, hourly Sunday
Glasgow £10, 40 minutes, twice hourly Monday to Saturday, hourly Sunday
Perth £14.60, 35 minutes, hourly weekdays, every two hours Sunday

FIFE

The Kingdom of Fife (www.visitfife.com), as it calls itself – it was home to Scottish monarchs for 500 years – is a tongue of land protruding between the Firths of Forth and Tay that has managed to maintain an individual Lowland identity quite separate from the rest of the country. Though southern Fife is part of Edinburgh's commuter-belt territory, eastern Fife's rolling green farmland and quaint fishing villages are prime turf for exploration, and the fresh sea air feels like it's doing you a power of good. Fife's biggest attraction, St Andrews, has Scotland's most venerable university and a wealth of historic buildings. It's also, of course, the headquarters of golf and draws professionals and keen amateurs alike to take on the Old Course – the classic links experience.

The **Fife Coastal Path** (www.fifecoastandcountrysidetrust.co.uk) runs for 117 miles, following the entire Fife coastline from Kincardine to Newburgh. It's well waymarked, picturesque and not too rigorous, though winds can buffet. It's easily accessed for shorter sections or day walks, and long stretches of it can also be tackled on a mountain bike.

Getting There & Around

The main bus operator here is Stagecoach East Scotland (www.stagecoachbus.com). The Fife Dayrider ticket (£9.30) gives one day's unlimited travel around Fife on Stagecoach buses.

If you are driving from the Forth bridges to St Andrews, a slower but much more scenic route than the M90/A91 is along the signposted Fife Coastal Tourist Rte.

St Andrews

☎01334 / POP 16,900

For a small town, St Andrews has made a big name for itself: first as a religious centre and place of pilgrimage, then as Scotland's oldest (and Britain's third-oldest) university town. But it is its status as the home of golf that has propelled it to even greater fame, and today's pilgrims mostly arrive with a set of clubs in hand. Nevertheless, it's a lovely place to visit even if you've no interest in the game, with impressive medieval ruins, stately university buildings, beautiful sandy beaches and excellent guesthouses and restaurants.

The Old Course, the world's most famous golf links, has a striking seaside location at the western end of town – it's a thrilling experience to stroll the hallowed turf. Nearby is magnificent West Sands beach, made famous by the film *Chariots of Fire*.

LOCAL KNOWLEDGE

FIFE DISTILLERIES

There are several distilleries around Fife that are well worth a detour, and much less busy than the better-known ones on Speyside. All offer guided tours and tasting experiences.

Lindores Abbey Distillery (01337-842547; www.lindoresabbeydistillery.com; Abbey Rd, Newburgh KY14 6HH; tours per person £12.50; 10am-4pm Apr-Sep, 11am-4pm Oct-Mar; P) Opened in 2017, this distillery stands beside the ruins of Lindores Abbey, the site of the earliest written reference to Scotch whisky, which dates from 1494.

Eden Mill Distillery (01334-834038; www.edenmill.com; Main St, Guardbridge KY16 0US; tours per person £10; 10am-6pm) This brewery-distillery produces beer and whisky but is best known for its range of craft gins made using locally grown botanicals. It's 4 miles northwest of St Andrews, towards Leuchars.

Kingsbarns Distillery (01333-451300; www.kingsbarnsdistillery.com; East Newhall Farm, Kingsbarns KY16 8QE; tours per person from £12; 10am-5pm; P) This distillery in Crail opened in 2015 and uses Fife-grown barley to create a distinctive Lowland whisky.

Sights

St Andrews Cathedral RUINS

(HES; www.historicenvironment.scot; The Pends, KY16 9QL; adult/child £6/3.60; 9.30am-5.30pm Apr-Sep, 10am-4pm Oct-Mar) All that's left of one of Britain's most magnificent medieval buildings are ruined fragments of wall and arch, and a single towering gable, but you can still appreciate the scale and majesty of the edifice from these scant remains. There's also a **museum** with a collection of superb 17th- and 18th-century grave slabs, 9th- and 10th-century Celtic crosses, and the late-8th-century **St Andrews Sarcophagus**, Europe's finest example of early medieval stone carving.

Founded in 1160 and consecrated in 1318, the cathedral stood as the focus of this important pilgrimage centre until 1559, when it was pillaged during the Reformation. The bones of St Andrew himself lie beneath the altar; until the cathedral was built, they had been enshrined in the nearby **Church of St Regulus** (or Rule). All that remains of this church is **St Rule's Tower**, worth the claustrophobic climb for the view across St Andrews. The admission fee only applies for the museum and tower; you can wander freely around the atmospheric ruins.

St Andrews Castle CASTLE

(HES; www.historicenvironment.scot; The Scores, KY16 9AR; adult/child £9/5.40; 9.30am-5.30pm Apr-Sep, 10am-4pm Oct-Mar) The castle is mainly in ruins, but the site itself is evocative and has dramatic coastline views. It was founded around 1200 as a fortified home for the bishop of St Andrews. After the execution of Protestant reformers in 1545, other reformers retaliated by murdering Cardinal Beaton and taking over the castle. They spent almost a year holed up, during which time they and their attackers dug a complex of **siege tunnels**; you can walk (or stoop) along their damp, mossy lengths.

British Golf Museum MUSEUM

(www.britishgolfmuseum.co.uk; Bruce Embankment, KY16 9AB; adult/child £10/free; 9.30am-5pm Mon-Sat, 10am-5pm Sun Apr-Oct, 10am-4pm daily Nov-Mar) This museum provides a comprehensive overview of the history and development of the game and the role of St Andrews in it. The huge collection ranges from the world's oldest set of clubs (late 17th century, used with feather-stuffed golf balls) to modern equipment, trophies and clothing, and there's a large collection of memorabilia from Open winners both male and female, including Tiger Woods' sweat-stained Nike cap.

Festivals & Events

Open Championship SPORTS

(www.theopen.com; Jul) One of international golf's four major championships. The tournament venue changes from year to year, and comes to St Andrews every five years (the 2020 event was postponed due to Covid-19) – the 150th Open will be held here in 2022. Check the website for future venues.

St Andrews Highland Games CULTURAL

(www.standrewshighlandgames.co.uk; adult/child £8/4; Jul) Held on the North Haugh on the last Sunday in July.

Sleeping

St Andrews' accommodation is expensive and often heavily booked, especially in sum-

St Andrews

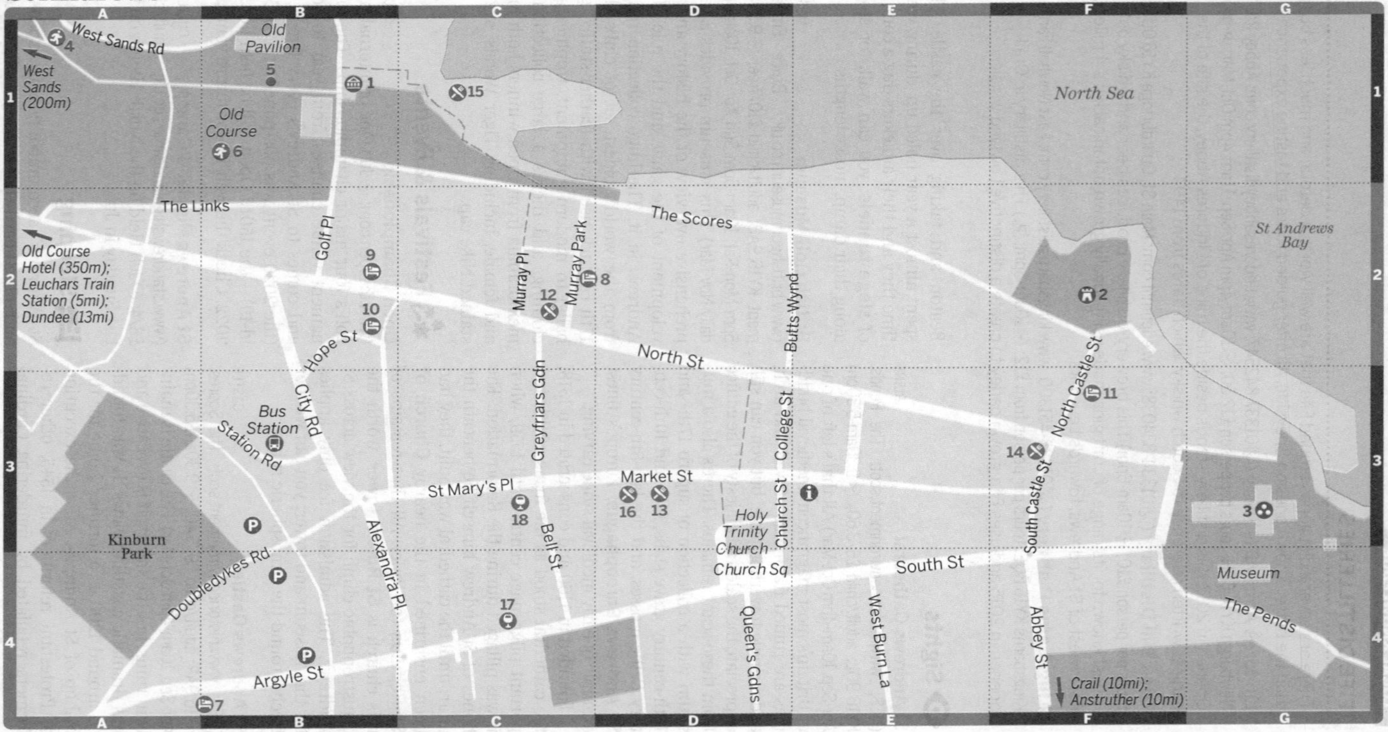
0 200 m
0 0.1 miles
A B C D E F G
1 2 3 4
West Sands Rd
West Sands (200m)
Old Pavilion
Old Course
The Links
Old Course Hotel (350m); Leuchars Train Station (5mi); Dundee (13mi)
Golf Pl
Hope St
City Rd
Bus Station
Station Rd
Kinburn Park
Doubledykes Rd
Argyle St
Alexandra Pl
St Mary's Pl
Murray Pl
Murray Park
Greyfriars Gdn
Bell St
The Scores
North St
Market St
Butts Wynd
College St
Church St
Holy Trinity Church
Church Sq
Queen's Gdns
West Burn La
South St
South Castle St
North Castle St
Abbey St
North Sea
St Andrews Bay
Museum
The Pends
Crail (10mi); Anstruther (10mi)
1 2 3 4 5 6 7 8 9 10 11 12 13 14 15 16 17 18

St Andrews

Sights

Activities, Courses & Tours

Sleeping

Eating

Drinking & Nightlife

mer, at weekends, and during golfing events and university graduations, so reserve well ahead. Almost every house on supercentral Murray Park and Murray Pl is a guesthouse.

Budget accommodation is thin on the ground, but during summer (June to August) three student residences are open to visitors – **Agnes Blackadder Hall** (01334-467000; https://ace.st-andrews.ac.uk/holiday-accommodation; North Haugh, KY16 9XW; s/d from £59/79; Jun-Aug; P@) , **David Russell Hall** (01334-467100; Buchanan Gardens, KY16 9LY; s/d from £59/79; Jun-Aug; P@) and **McIntosh Hall** (01334-467035; Abbotsford Cres, KY16 9HT; s/tw from £52/72; Jun-Aug; P@) . Prices are good value for the standard of accommodation on offer.

Cameron House B&B ££
(01334-472306; www.cameronhouse-sta.co.uk; 11 Murray Park, KY16 9AW; s/d from £65/105;) Beautifully decorated rooms and warm, cheerful hosts make this a real home away from home. The two single rooms share a bathroom. Prices drop £10 per person outside peak season.

St Nicholas Farmhouse B&B ££
(01334-473090; www.stnicholasfarmhouse.com; Albany Park, KY16 8LD; s/d from £75/85;) Tucked away amid leafy modern suburbs just a few paces from the south end of East Sands beach (look out for the inconspicuous gate on Albany Park opposite the brown tourist signpost), this 19th-century farmhouse offers a warm welcome, appealing bedrooms and hearty breakfasts (fun fact for golf fans – Tom Watson once rented the entire house during the Open Championship).

★ **Old Fishergate House** B&B £££
(01334-470874; www.oldfishergatehouse.co.uk; North Castle St; r from £135;) This historic 17th-century town house, furnished with period pieces, is in the oldest part of town, close to the cathedral. The two twin rooms are very spacious and even have their own sitting room. On a scale of one to 10 for quaintness, we'd rate it a 9½. The cracking breakfast menu features pancakes with maple syrup, and smoked-haddock omelette.

★ **34 Argyle St** B&B £££
(07712 863139; www.34argylestreet.com; 34 Argyle St; r from £150;) Set in a fine old stone-built house just west of the town centre, the Argyle has four luxurious, hotel-quality bedrooms with huge modern bathrooms of dark tile, chrome and glass (two of the four have free-standing bath tubs). Little touches like drinks offered on arrival, fresh flowers and sweets add to the atmosphere of hospitality.

Old Course Hotel HOTEL £££
(01334-474371; www.oldcoursehotel.co.uk; Old Station Rd, KY16 9SP; r from £327; P) A byword for golfing luxury, this hotel is right alongside the famous 17th green (Road Hole) on the Old Course (p850) and has huge rooms, excellent service and a raft of facilities, including a spa complex. Fork out the extra £50 or so for a view over the Old Course. You can usually find good deals online.

Five Pilmour Place B&B £££
(01334-478665; www.5pilmourplace.com; 5 Pilmour Pl, KY16 9HZ; s/d from £100/140;) Just around the corner from the Old Course (p850), this luxurious and intimate spot offers stylish, compact rooms with plenty of designer touches. The king-size beds are especially comfortable, and the lounge area is an Edwardian-style retreat of leather armchairs, polished wood and swagged curtains.

Eating

Tailend
FISH & CHIPS £

(www.thetailend.co.uk; 130 Market St, KY16 9PD; takeaway £5-10; noon-9.30pm) Delicious fresh fish sourced from Arbroath, just up the coast, puts this place a class above most chippies; it cooks fries to order and the food's worth the wait. The array of exquisite smoked delicacies at the counter will have you planning a picnic or fighting for a table in the licensed cafe out the back.

Northpoint Cafe
CAFE £

(01334-473997; www.facebook.com/northpointcafe; 24 North St, KY16 9AQ; mains £4-9; 8.30am-5pm Mon-Fri, 9am-5pm Sat, 10am-4pm Sun;) The cafe where Prince William famously met his future wife, Kate Middleton, while they were both students at St Andrews serves good coffee and a broad range of breakfast fare, from porridge topped with banana to toasted bagels, pancake stacks and classic fry-ups. It's a bit too busy for its own good these days, so get in early for lunch, which includes vegan specials.

Mitchell's Deli
DELI, SCOTTISH ££

(01334-441396; www.mitchellsstandrews.co.uk; 110-112 Market St, KY16 2PB; mains £12-16; 8am-10pm Sun-Thu, to 11pm Fri & Sat;) Railway-sleeper floors, cut-down-workbench tables and seats upholstered with recycled tweed jackets lend a utilitarian air to this excellent deli-cafe-restaurant where local produce is king. Brunch (served till 5pm) includes free-range eggs Benedict, and avocado on sourdough toast, while the evening menu runs to fish and chips, mac and cheese, and vegan haggis.

★Haar
SCOTTISH £££

(01334-845750; www.haarrestaurant.com; 127 North St; 5-course tasting menu £60; 4-10pm Wed, noon-10pm Thu-Sun) Chef Dean Banks grew up in Arbroath, of the far side of the Tay estuary from St Andrews, and opened this atmospheric little restaurant after reaching the finals of Masterchef in 2018. Fresh local produce, with an emphasis on seafood, is treated to subtle Asian flavours – Dean's signature dish of lobster served with mirin butter is not to be missed.

★Peat Inn
SCOTTISH £££

(01334-840206; www.thepeatinn.co.uk; KY15 5LH; 3-course lunch/dinner £29/65; 12.30-2pm & 6.30-9pm Tue-Sat; P) This superb Michelin-starred restaurant, backed by a commodious suite of **bedrooms** (s/d from £220/240; P), makes an ideal gourmet break. The chef makes a great effort to source premium-quality Scottish produce and presents it in innovative ways that never feel pretentious or overmodern. The inn is 6 miles from St Andrews; head southwest on the A915, then turn right onto the B940.

ST ANDREWS OLD COURSE

St Andrews Old Course (reception 01334-466666, reservations 01334-466718; www.standrews.com; Golf Pl; green fees £95-195; Mon-Sat) is the oldest and most famous golf course in the world. Golf has been played here since the 15th century – by 1457 it was apparently so popular that James II had to ban it because it was interfering with his troops' archery practice. Although it lies beside the Royal & Ancient Golf Club, the Old Course is a public course.

To play the Old Course, you'll need to book in advance via the website, or by phoning the Reservations Department (or reception, if just one day in advance or on the day). Reservations open on the last Wednesday in August the year before you wish to play. Fewer places than normal may be available in 2021 due to rescheduling of 2020 bookings that were cancelled because of Covid-19.

Unless you've booked months in advance, getting a tee-off time is literally a lottery; enter the ballot at the **caddie office** (01334-466666; West Sands Rd) (or online, or by phoning reception) before 2pm two days before you hope to play (there's no Sunday play). Be warned that applications by ballot are normally heavily oversubscribed, and green fees are £195 from April to October.

A caddie for your round costs £55 plus tip. If you play on a windy day, expect those scores to balloon: Nick Faldo famously stated, 'When it blows here, even the seagulls walk'.

There are **guided walks** (www.standrews.com/walk; per person £12.50; 11am & 2pm daily Apr-Sep) of the Old Course, and you are free to walk over the course on Sunday or follow the footpaths around the edge at any time.

LOCAL KNOWLEDGE

LOCH LEVEN HERITAGE TRAIL

One of the best all-abilities hiking and biking routes in Scotland, this scenic 14-mile **circuit** (www.pkct.org/loch-leven-heritage-trail) of Loch Leven links Kinross Pier, the RSPB Loch Leven nature reserve, and the excellent **Loch Leven's Larder** (01592-841000; www.lochlevenslarder.com; Channel Farm, KY13 9HD; mains £6-11; 9am-5pm; P) farm shop and restaurant. Allow two hours to cycle the trail or five hours to walk it; you can hire bikes and mobility scooters at Kinross Pier. The circuit offers great views of the Lomond Hills, and there's a sandy beach northeast of Kinross.

You can also visit **Lochleven Castle** (HES; www.historicenvironment.scot; Kinross Pier, KY13 8UF; adult/child incl boat ride £9/5.40; 10am-5.15pm Apr-Sep, to 4.15pm Oct, last sailing 1hr before closing; P), an island fortress and prison from the late 14th century, where Mary, Queen of Scots was incarcerated in 1567. The castle is now roofless but basically intact and makes for an atmospheric destination – you cross to the island by boat (included in the admission fee).

The split-level bedrooms look over the garden and fields beyond. Various all-inclusive offers are available.

Seafood Ristorante SEAFOOD £££
(01334-479475; www.theseafoodrestaurant.com; The Scores, KY16 9AB; mains £25-32; noon-9.30pm Wed-Sun) This stylish restaurant occupies a glass-walled room, built out over the sea, with polished wooden floors, crisp white linen, an open kitchen and panoramic views of St Andrews Bay. It offers top-notch seafood and an excellent wine list; an all-day menu offers smaller dishes between lunch and dinner service. There's a two-/three-course set lunch menu (£25/30) available from noon till 2.30pm.

Drinking & Nightlife

St Andrews Brewing Co MICROBREWERY
(www.standrewsbrewingcompany.com; 177 South St, KY16 9EE; 11am-midnight;) Good beer, good food and good company are the order of the day in this friendly, modern brewpub, with 18 beers and ciders on tap (including several of its own brews), more than 170 varieties in bottles, and around 30 craft gins.

Vic BAR
(www.vicstandrews.co.uk; 1 St Mary's Pl, KY16 9UY; 10am-2am;) Warehouse chic meets medieval conviviality in this strikingly restored student favourite. Walls plastered with black-and-white pop culture give way to a handsome, high-ceilinged bar with sociable long tables down the middle and an eclectic assortment of seating. Other spaces include a more romantic bar, a dance floor and a deck for smokers. There are regular events, including weekend club nights.

Information

St Andrews Tourist Office (01334-472021; www.visitscotland.com; 70 Market St, KY16 9NU; 9.15am-6pm Mon-Sat, 10am-5pm Sun Jul & Aug, reduced hours rest of year) Helpful staff with good knowledge of St Andrews and Fife.

Getting There & Away

BUS

All buses leave from the **bus station** (Station Rd). Services include:

Anstruther £4.60, 40 minutes, hourly
Crail £4.60, 25 minutes, hourly
Dundee £5.20, 40 minutes, at least half-hourly
Edinburgh £13, two hours, hourly
Glasgow £13, 2½ hours, hourly

TRAIN

There is no train station in St Andrews itself, but you can take a train from Edinburgh (grab a seat on the right-hand side of the carriage for great sea views) to Leuchars (£15.60, one hour, half-hourly), 5 miles to the northwest. From here, buses leave regularly for St Andrews (£3.30, 10 minutes, every 10 minutes), or a taxi costs around £13.

East Neuk

This charming stretch of coast runs south from St Andrews to the headland at Fife Ness, then as far west as Earlsferry. Neuk is an old Scots word for 'corner', and it's certainly an appealing corner of the country to investigate, with picturesque fishing villages whose distinctive red pantiled roofs and crowstep gables are a legacy of centuries-old trading links with the Low Countries.

The Fife Coastal Path's most scenic stretches are in this area. It's easily visited from St Andrews, or even as a day trip from Edinburgh, but also offers many pleasant places to stay.

Crail

☎01333 / POP 1640

Pretty and peaceful, little Crail has a much-photographed stone-built harbour surrounded by quaint cottages with red-tiled roofs. The village's history is outlined in the Crail Museum, but the main attraction is just wandering the winding streets and hanging out by the harbour. There are views across to the Isle of May.

Cambo Gardens GARDENS

(www.cambogardens.org.uk; Cambo Estate, KY16 8QD; adult/child £6.50/free; 10am-5pm; P) Cambo Estate, 2.5 miles north of Crail, is the country seat of the Erskine family. Its walled garden, with an ornamental stream running through the middle, is famously beautiful in spring and summer, but also in January and February, when its spectacular displays of snowdrops are in flower. There's a visitor centre and cafe, and woodland walks that lead to the Fife Coastal Path, plus kids can feed potatoes to the estate's pigs.

Colstoncraig B&B ££

(☎01333-451013; www.colstoncraigbedandbreakfast.com; West End, KY10 3RH; s/d from £50/75; P) Nothing is too much trouble for the welcoming hosts at this semidetached B&B with a traditional red pantile roof and a view over the houses across the road to the Firth of Forth and the Isle of May. Ask for the ground-floor twin room with a glimpse of the sea from the bay window.

★**Lobster Store** SEAFOOD ££

(☎01333-450476; www.facebook.com/reillyshellfish; 34 Shoregate; mains £6-15; noon-4pm Sat & Sun Easter-Jun, noon-4pm Tue-Sun Jul-Sep) This quaint little shack overlooking Crail harbour serves dressed crab and freshly boiled lobster that has been caught locally. You can have a whole lobster (split) or lobster rolls. This is no-fuss takeaway – there's a single table out the front, but you can find a place to sit and eat your catch anywhere around the harbour.

Getting There & Away

Crail is 10 miles southeast of St Andrews. Stagecoach (www.stagecoachbus.com) bus 95 linking Leven, Anstruther, Crail and St Andrews passes through Crail hourly every day (£4.60, 35 minutes to St Andrews).

Anstruther

☎01333 / POP 3450

Once among Scotland's busiest fishing ports, cheery Anstruther (pronounced *en*-ster by locals) has ridden the tribulations of the declining fishing industry better than some, and now offers a pleasant mixture of bobbing boats, historic streets, and visitors ambling around the harbour grazing on fish and chips or contemplating a boat trip to the Isle of May.

Sights

Scottish Fisheries Museum MUSEUM

(www.scotfishmuseum.org; East Shore; adult/child £9/free; 10am-5.30pm Mon-Sat, 11am-5pm Sun Apr-Sep, 10am-4.30pm Mon-Sat, noon-4.30pm Sun Oct-Mar) This excellent museum covers the history of the Scottish fishing industry in fascinating detail, including plenty of hands-on exhibits for kids. Displays include the **Zulu Gallery**, which houses the huge, partly restored hull of a traditional 19th-century Zulu-class fishing boat, redolent with the scents of tar and timber. Afloat in the harbour outside the museum is the **Reaper**, a fully restored Fifie-class fishing boat built in 1902.

Scotland's Secret Bunker MUSEUM

(www.secretbunker.co.uk; Troywood, KY16 8QH; adult/child £12.95/8.95; 10am-5pm Feb-Nov; P) This fascinating – and chilling – monument to Cold War paranoia was built in the 1950s to serve as one of Britain's regional command centres in the event of a nuclear war. Hidden 30m underground and encased in nearly 5m of reinforced concrete, it houses two levels of austere operations rooms, communication centres, broadcasting studios, weapons stores and dormitories, filled with period artefacts and museum displays. The bunker is 3 miles north of Anstruther, off the B9131 to St Andrews.

Isle of May NATURE RESERVE

(www.nature.scot) The mile-long Isle of May, 6 miles southeast of Anstruther, is a spectacular nature reserve. Between April and July the island's cliffs are packed with breeding kittiwakes, razorbills, guillemots, shags and more than 80,000 puffins. Inland are the remains of the 12th-century St Adrian's Chapel, dedicated to a monk who was murdered on the island by the Danes in 875. Several boats operating out of Anstruther Harbour offer trips to the island.

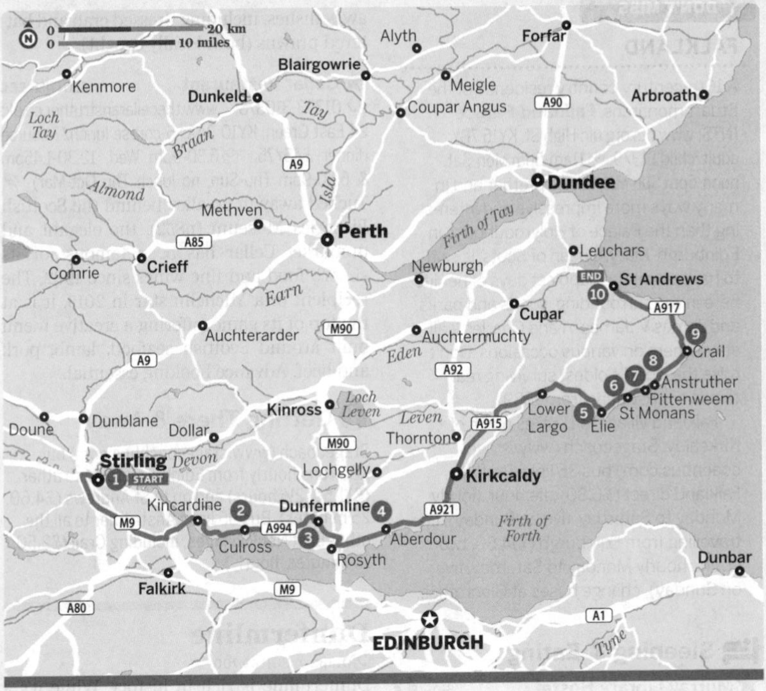

Driving Tour The Fife Coast

START STIRLING
END ST ANDREWS
LENGTH 76 MILES; ONE DAY

This tour links two of the most popular tourist towns in central Scotland via the scenic delights of the Fife coast.

Head south from 1 **Stirling** (p840) on the M9 and at Junction 7 turn east towards Kincardine Bridge. As you approach the bridge, follow signs for Kincardine and Kirkcaldy; then once across the Firth of Forth, follow the Fife Coastal Tourist Rte signposts to the historic village of 2 **Culross** (p855). Spend an hour or so exploring the medieval buildings of Culross before continuing via the A994 to 3 **Dunfermline** (p854), for a look at its fine abbey and palace ruins.

From Dunfermline take the M90 towards the Forth Road Bridge, but leave at Junction 1 (signposted A921 Dalgety Bay) and continue to the attractive seaside village of 4 **Aberdour** for lunch at the Aberdour Hotel. Stay on the A921 as far as Kirkcaldy, then take the faster A915 (signposted St Andrews) as far as Upper Largo, where you'll follow the A917 towards Elie; from here on, you will be following the brown Fife Coastal Tourist Rte signs.

5 **Elie**, with its sandy beaches and coastal footpaths, is a great place to stretch your legs and take in some bracing sea air before driving just a couple of miles further to explore the neighbouring fishing villages of 6 **St Monans** and 7 **Pittenweem**. Just 1 mile beyond Pittenweem, 8 **Anstruther** (p852) deserves a slightly longer stop for a visit to the Scottish Fisheries Museum, a stroll by the harbour and an ice cream. If time allows, you may want to detour inland a couple of miles to visit Kellie Castle or Scotland's Secret Bunker.

The final stop before St Andrews is the pretty fishing village of 9 **Crail** (p852), where the late-afternoon or early-evening light will provide ideal conditions for capturing one of Scotland's most photographed harbours. A brisk hike along the coastal path towards Fife Ness, keeping an eye out for seals and seabirds, will round off the day before you drive the last 10 miles into 10 **St Andrews** (p846).

DON'T MISS

FALKLAND

A 16th-century country residence of the Stuart monarchs, **Falkland Palace** (NTS; www.nts.org.uk; High St, KY15 7BY; adult/child £13/9; 11am-5pm Mon-Sat, noon-5pm Sun Mar-Oct) is prettier and in many ways more impressive and interesting than the Palace of Holyroodhouse in Edinburgh. Mary, Queen of Scots, is said to have spent the happiest days of her life here in the surrounding woods and parks, and James V, James VI and Charles II all stayed here on various occasions. Don't miss the world's oldest surviving real tennis court, dating from 1539.

Falkland village is 11 miles north of Kirkcaldy. Stagecoach (www.stagecoachbus.com) bus 36 links Perth to Falkland direct (£6.80, one hour, hourly Monday to Saturday, five on Sunday). If travelling from Edinburgh (£14.50, two hours, hourly Monday to Saturday, five on Sunday), change buses at Glenrothes.

Sleeping & Eating

★ Murray Library Hostel HOSTEL £

(01333-311123; www.murraylibraryhostel.com; 7 Shore St, KY10 3EA; dm/d from £22/58;) Set in a handsome, red-sandstone waterfront building that once housed the local library, this hostel is beautifully furnished and equipped. There are four- to eight-bed dorms, many with sea views, plus private twins and doubles, a gorgeous modern kitchen and a comfortable lounge.

★ Spindrift B&B ££

(01333-310573; www.thespindrift.co.uk; Pittenweem Rd; s/d/f £80/135/150;) Arriving from the west, there's no need to go further than Anstruther's first house on the left, a redoubt of Scottish cheer and warm hospitality. The rooms are elegant and extremely comfortable – some have views across to Edinburgh, and one is a wood-panelled recreation of a ship's cabin, courtesy of the sea captain who once owned the house.

Anstruther Fish Bar FISH & CHIPS £

(01333-310518; www.anstrutherfishbar.co.uk; 42-44 Shore St, KY10 3AQ; takeaway £6-10; 11.30am-9.30pm Sun-Thu, to 10pm Fri & Sat;) An award-winning chippie famous for its deep-fried haddock and chips, this place also offers classy takes on traditional takeaway dishes, including dressed crab and battered prawns (both locally caught).

★ Cellar Restaurant SCOTTISH £££

(01333-310378; www.thecellaranstruther.co.uk; 24 East Green, KY10 3AA; 5-course lunch/7-course dinner £45/75; 6.30-9pm Wed, 12.30-1.45pm & 6.30-9pm Thu-Sun, no lunch Thu Oct-Mar) Tucked away in an alley behind the Scottish Fisheries Museum (p852), the elegant and upmarket Cellar has been famous for its superb food and fine wines since 1982. The recipient of a Michelin star in 2015, it is at the top of its game, offering a creative menu built around Scottish seafood, lamb, pork and beef. Advance booking essential.

Getting There & Away

Stagecoach (www.stagecoachbus.com) bus X60 runs hourly from Edinburgh to Anstruther (£11.50, 2½ hours) and on to St Andrews (£4.60, 25 minutes). Bus 95 links Anstruther to all the other East Neuk villages, including Crail (£2.50, 15 minutes, hourly).

Dunfermline

01383 / POP 49,700

Dunfermline is rich in history. While it's a large and unlovely town, it's home to the evocative Dunfermline Abbey, its neighbouring palace and the attractive grounds of Pittencrieff Park, the last gifted to the city by local boy made good Andrew Carnegie (1835–1919), of US-steel-industry fame.

Dunfermline Abbey & Palace RUINS

(HES; www.historicenvironment.scot; St Catherine's Wynd, KY12 7PE; adult/child £6/3.60; 9.30am-5.30pm daily Apr-Sep, 10am-4pm Sat-Wed Oct-Mar) Dunfermline Abbey was founded by David I in the 12th century as a Benedictine monastery. The abbey and its neighbouring palace were already favoured by religious royals: Malcolm III married the exiled Saxon princess Margaret here in the 11th century, and both chose to be interred here. More royal burials followed, none more notable than that of Robert the Bruce, whose remains were interred here in 1329.

What remains of the abbey are the ruins of the impressive three-tiered refectory building, and the atmosphere-laden nave of the old church, endowed with geometrically patterned columns and fine Romanesque and Gothic windows. It adjoins the 19th-century **abbey church** (www.dunfermlineabbey.com; St Catherine's Wynd; 10am-4.30pm

Mon-Sat, 2-4.30pm Sun Apr-Oct) FREE where Robert the Bruce lies entombed beneath the ornate pulpit.

Next to the refectory (and included in your abbey admission) is **Dunfermline Palace**. Once the abbey guesthouse, it was converted for James VI, whose son, the ill-fated Charles I, was born here in 1600. Below stretches the leafy, strollable **Pittencrieff Park**.

Andrew Carnegie Birthplace Museum MUSEUM

(☎01383-724302; www.carnegiebirthplace.com; Moodie St, KY12 7PL; ⏲10am-5pm daily Jul & Aug, 10am-5pm Mon-Sat, 1-4pm Sun Mar-Jun, Sep & Oct, reduced hours Nov) FREE The cottage where the great American industrialist and philanthropist Andrew Carnegie was born in 1835 is now a museum. Carnegie emigrated to the US in 1848 and by the late 19th century had become the richest person in the world, but he gave away 90% of his wealth to build libraries, universities and schools all around the world. Dunfermline benefited by his purchase of Pittencrieff Park, beside the palace.

Getting There & Away

There are frequent buses between Dunfermline and Edinburgh (£6.80, 50 minutes), Stirling (£5.60, 1¼ hours) and St Andrews (£12, 1½ hours), plus trains to/from Edinburgh (£6, 35 minutes, half-hourly).

Culross

☎01383 / POP 400

Instantly familiar to fans of the TV series *Outlander,* in which it appears as the fictional village of Cranesmuir, Culross (*koo-ross*) is Scotland's best-preserved example of a 17th-century town. Limewashed white and yellow-ochre houses with red-tiled roofs stand amid a maze of cobbled streets, and the winding Back Causeway to the abbey is lined with whimsical cottages. The National Trust for Scotland (NTS) owns no fewer than 20 of the town's buildings.

As the birthplace of St Mungo, Glasgow's patron saint, Culross was an important religious centre from the 6th century. The burgh developed under local laird Sir George Bruce by extracting coal through ingenious tunnels extending under the seabed. When mining was ended by flooding of the tunnels, the town switched to making linen and shoes.

Sights

Culross Palace HISTORIC SITE

(NTS; www.nts.org.uk; Low Causewayside, KY12 8JH; adult/child £10.50/7.50; ⏲11am-5pm Jul & Aug, to 4pm Apr-Jun, Sep & Oct) More large house than palace, the 17th-century residence of local laird Sir George Bruce features an interior largely unchanged since his time. The decorative wood panelling and painted timber ceilings are of national importance, particularly the allegorical scenes in the Painted Chamber, which survive from the early 1600s. Don't miss the recreation of a 17th-century garden at the back, with gorgeous views from the top terrace.

The Town House (with ticket and information desk downstairs) and the Study, both dating from the early 17th century, can be visited on a 45-minute guided tour of the town (£2 per person, available between 1pm and 3pm).

Getting There & Away

Culross is 16 miles east of Stirling, and 12 miles west of the Forth bridges. Buses run from Dunfermline (£3.30, 30 minutes, hourly) to Culross. Buses from Stirling (£8, 1½ hours, three daily) require a change at Alloa.

DUNDEE & ANGUS

Angus is a fertile farming region stretching north from Dundee – Scotland's fourth-largest city – to the Highland border. It's an attractive area of broad straths (valleys) and low, green hills contrasting with the rich, red-brown soil of freshly ploughed fields. The romantic Angus Glens finger their way into the foothills of the Grampian Mountains, while the scenic coastline ranges from the red-sandstone cliffs of Arbroath to the long, sandy beach of Lunan Bay. This was the Pictish heartland of the 7th and 8th centuries, and many interesting Pictish symbol stones survive here.

Apart from the crowds visiting newly confident Dundee and the coach parties shuffling through Glamis Castle, Angus is a bit of a tourism backwater and a good place to escape the crowds.

Dundee

☎01382 / POP 147,300

London's Trafalgar Sq has Nelson, Edinburgh's Princes St has Sir Walter Scott and Belfast has Queen Victoria outside City

DON'T MISS

SCONE PALACE

'So thanks to all at once and to each one, whom we invite to see us crowned at Scone.' This line from *Macbeth* indicates the importance of **Scone** (01738-552300; www.scone-palace.co.uk; Scone Estate, PH2 6BD; adult/child £20/13, grounds only £9/6; 9.30am-6pm May-Sep, 10am-5pm Apr & Oct, last entry 1hr before closing; P) (pronounced 'skoon') as the coronation place of Scottish monarchs. The original palace of 1580, laying claim to this historic site, was rebuilt in the early 19th century as a Georgian mansion of extreme elegance and luxury. Scone has belonged for centuries to the Murray family, earls of Mansfield, and many of the objects have a fascinating history attached to them (friendly guides are on hand to explain).

Ancient kings were crowned on Moot Hill, now topped by a chapel next to the palace. It's said that the hill was created by bootfuls of earth, brought by nobles attending the coronations as an acknowledgement of the king's rights over their lands, although it's more likely the site of an ancient motte-and-bailey castle. Here in 838 Kenneth MacAlpin became the first king of a united Scotland and brought to Scone the Stone of Destiny, on which Scottish kings were ceremonially invested. In 1296 Edward I of England carted this talisman off to Westminster Abbey, where it remained for 700 years before being returned to Scotland in 1997 (it now sits in Edinburgh Castle, but there are plans afoot to return it to Perth).

Scone Palace is 2 miles north of Perth; from the town centre, cross the bridge, turn left, and bear left along the footway beside the A93 until you reach the gates of the estate. From here, it's another half-mile to the palace (about 45 minutes' walk). Various buses from town stop here; the tourist office can advise.

Hall. Dundee's City Sq, on the other hand, is graced – rather endearingly – by the bronze figure of Desperate Dan. Familiar to generations of British schoolchildren, Dan is one of the best-loved cartoon characters from the comic *Dandy,* published by Dundee firm DC Thomson since 1937.

Dundee enjoys perhaps the finest location of any Scottish city, spreading along the northern shore of the Firth of Tay, and has tourist attractions of national importance in V&A Dundee, Discovery Point and Verdant Works. Add attractive seaside town Broughty Ferry, and the Dundonians themselves – among the friendliest, most welcoming and entertaining people you'll meet – and Dundee is definitely worth a stopover.

The waterfront around Discovery Point has undergone a massive redevelopment, centred on the construction of the architecturally outstanding V&A Dundee museum of design.

History

During the 19th century Dundee grew from its trading-port origins to become a major player in the shipbuilding, whaling, textile and railway engineering industries. Dundonian firms owned and operated most of the jute mills in India (jute is a natural fibre used to make ropes and sacking), and the city's textile industry employed as many as 43,000 people – little wonder Dundee earned the nickname 'Juteopolis'.

Dundee is often called the city of the 'Three Js' – jute, jam and journalism. According to legend, it was a Dundee woman, Janet Keillor, who invented marmalade in the late 18th century; her son founded the city's famous Keillor jam factory. Jute is no longer produced, and when the Keillor factory was taken over in 1988, production was transferred to England. Journalism still thrives, however, led by the family firm of DC Thomson. Best known for children's comics such as the *Beano* and the *Dandy,* and regional newspapers including the *Press and Journal,* Thomson is now the city's largest employer.

In the late 19th and early 20th centuries Dundee was one of the richest cities in the country – there were more millionaires per head of population here than anywhere else in Britain – but the textile and engineering industries declined in the second half of the 20th century, leading to high unemployment and urban decay.

In the 1960s and '70s Dundee's cityscape was scarred by ugly blocks of flats, office buildings and shopping centres linked by unsightly concrete walkways; most visitors passed it by. Since the mid-1990s, however, Dundee has reinvented itself as a tourist destination and a centre for the computer games industry (Grand Theft Auto was invented here), while its waterfront has undergone a major rejuvenation. It also has more university students – one in seven of the population – than any other town in Europe except Heidelberg.

Sights

★V&A Dundee
MUSEUM

(☎01382-411611; www.vam.ac.uk/dundee; 1 Riverside Esplanade, DD1 4EZ; ⊙10am-5pm) FREE The centrepiece of Dundee's revitalised waterfront is this stunning building designed by Japanese architect Kengo Kuma. Opened in late 2018, it houses an outpost of London's Victoria & Albert Museum of art and design. The permanent collections showcase the work of Scottish designers past and present, from famous names such as Charles Rennie Mackintosh to modern creatives such as fashion designer Holly Fulton, while temporary exhibitions celebrate the best of art and design from around the world.

The distinctive horizontal panels on the building's exterior recall the layered ledges of the sea cliffs of Scotland's east coast, while the curved and overhanging corners call to mind the bows and sterns of sailing ships, echoing the shape of the RRS *Discovery* next door. The 1st-floor Tatha Restaurant offers stylish dining with a view across the Firth of Tay.

★Discovery Point
MUSEUM

(www.rrsdiscovery.com; Discovery Quay, DD1 4XA; adult/child £11.50/6.40; ⊙10am-6pm Mon-Sat, 11am-6pm Sun Apr-Oct, to 5pm Nov-Mar; P 👪) The three masts of Captain Robert Falcon Scott's famous polar expedition vessel the RRS *Discovery* provide a historic counterpoint to the modern architecture of the nearby V&A design museum. Exhibitions and audiovisual displays in the neighbouring visitor centre provide a fascinating history of both the ship and Antarctic exploration, but *Discovery* is the star attraction. You can visit the bridge, the galley and the mahogany-panelled officers' wardroom, and poke your nose into the cabins used by Scott and his crew.

The ship was built in Dundee in 1900, with a wooden hull at least half a metre thick to survive the pack ice. It sailed for the Antarctic in 1901 where it spent two winters trapped in the ice. From 1931 it was laid up in London where its condition steadily deteriorated, until it was rescued by the efforts of Peter Scott (Robert's son) and the Maritime Trust, and restored to its 1925 condition. In 1986 the ship was given a berth in its home port of Dundee, where it became a symbol of the city's regeneration.

A joint ticket that gives entry to both Discovery Point and the Verdant Works costs £18.65/10.50/48 per adult/child/family.

★Verdant Works
MUSEUM

(www.verdantworks.com; West Henderson's Wynd, DD1 5BT; adult/child £11.50/6.40; ⊙10am-6pm Mon-Sat, 11am-6pm Sun Apr-Oct, reduced hours Nov-Mar; 👪) One of the finest industrial museums in Europe, the Verdant Works explores the history of Dundee's jute industry. Housed in a restored jute mill, complete with original machinery in working condition, the museum's exhibits follow the raw material from its origins in India through to the manufacture of a wide range of finished products, from sacking to sailcloth to wagon covers for the pioneers of the American West. The museum is 250m west of the city centre.

McManus Galleries
MUSEUM

(www.mcmanus.co.uk; Albert Sq, DD1 1DA; ⊙10am-5pm Mon-Sat, 12.30-4.30pm Sun) FREE Housed in a solid Victorian Gothic building designed by Gilbert Scott in 1867, the McManus Galleries are a city museum on a human scale – you can see everything there is to see in a single visit, without feeling rushed or overwhelmed. The exhibits cover the history of the city from the Iron Age to the present day, including relics of the Tay Bridge Disaster and the Dundee whaling industry.

HMS Unicorn
MUSEUM

(www.frigateunicorn.org; Victoria Dock, DD1 3BP; adult/child £7.25/3.60; ⊙10am-5pm Apr-Oct, 10am-4pm Tue-Sun Nov-Mar) Dundee's second floating tourist attraction – unlike the polished and much-restored RRS *Discovery* – retains the authentic atmosphere of a salty old sailing ship. Built in 1824, the 46-gun *Unicorn* is the oldest British-built ship still afloat – it was mothballed soon after launching and never saw action. Wandering around below deck gives you an excellent impression of what it must have been like for the crew forced to live in such cramped conditions.

Sleeping

Athollbank
B&B £

(☎01382-801118; www.athollbank.com; 19 Thomson St, DD1 4LF; s/d £32/50; 📶🐕) A great-value B&B set on a quiet side street in the city's West End, Athollbank has smart, good-sized bedrooms (none are en suite, though) and is close to local pubs and restaurants.

Dundee Backpackers HOSTEL £
(☎01382-224646; www.hoppo.com/dundeebackpackershostel; 71 High St, DD1 1SD; dm £18, s/tw from £25/45; @ 📶) This hostel is set in a beautifully converted historic building, with a clean, modern kitchen, a pool room and an ideal location right in the city centre. It can get a bit noisy at night, but that's because it's close to pubs and nightlife.

★ **Malmaison** BOUTIQUE HOTEL ££
(☎01382-339715; www.malmaison.com/locations/dundee; 44 Whitehall Cres, DD1 4AY; r from £87; 📶) Housed in a Victorian hotel building, this place has been refurbished in typical Malmaison style with period features such as intricate wrought-iron balustrades complemented by delightfully over-the-top modern decor. The rooms on the south side overlook the redeveloped waterfront and the V&A museum. Room rates are excellent value; check the website for special offers.

Shaftesbury Lodge HOTEL ££
(☎01382-669216; www.shaftesburylodge.co.uk; 1 Hyndford St, DD2 1HQ; s/d from £63/85; 📶) The family-run, 12-room Shaftesbury is set in a Victorian mansion that was built for a jute baron and has many authentic period features, including a fine marble fireplace in the dining room. It's 1.5 miles west of the city centre, just off Perth Rd.

Eating

★ **Bach** CAFE £
(www.the-bach.com; 31 Meadowside, DD1 1DJ; mains £6-13; ⏲9am-5pm; 📶) Easily the best breakfast spot in town (brunch is served all day till 4pm), this place sports a mix of Scottish, New Zealand, Asian and Mexican influences with delightful dishes such as Hebridean eggs (with Stornoway black pudding), homemade Kiwi burgers and bao buns (soft Chinese buns filled with pork belly or tempeh), plus the best flat white in town.

Parlour Cafe CAFE £
(☎01382-203588; 58 West Port, DD1 5ER; mains £6-9; ⏲8am-6pm Mon-Sat, 10am-3pm Sun; 📶) Tiny but terrific, this friendly neighbourhood cafe is bursting with good things to eat including filled tortillas, savoury tarts, Mediterranean-style meze and homemade soup, all freshly prepared using seasonal produce. Great coffee and cakes, too, but be prepared to wait for a table.

★ **Newport** SCOTTISH ££
(☎01382-541449; www.thenewportrestaurant.co.uk; 1 High St, Newport-on-Tay, DD6 8AB; 3-course lunch £32.50, tasting menu £65; ⏲noon-2.30pm Thu-Sat, noon-3pm Sun, 6-9.30pm Wed-Sat; P) The setting is fabulous, with vast windows overlooking the Firth of Tay, and quirky 'recycled' decor. Linger over a lunch that showcases the best of local produce, or opt for the seven-course tasting menu; it has vegetarian and pescatarian options.

Jute Café Bar BISTRO ££
(☎01382-909246; www.jutecafebar.co.uk; 152 Nethergate, DD1 4DY; mains £10-25; ⏲food served noon-9pm; 📶) The industrial-chic cafe-bar in the **Dundee Contemporary Arts centre** (www.dca.org.uk; ⏲10am-6pm Fri-Wed, to 7pm Thu) FREE serves excellent deli sandwiches and burgers, as well as more adventurous Mediterranean-Asian fusion cuisine. Tables spill out into the sunny courtyard in summer.

Information

Dundee Tourist Office (☎01382-527527; www.angusanddundee.co.uk; 16 City Sq, DD1 3BG; ⏲10am-4pm Mon-Sat)

Getting There & Away

AIR

Located 2.5 miles west of the city centre, **Dundee Airport** (www.hial.co.uk/dundee-airport) has scheduled flights to London City (daily except Saturday) and Belfast City (twice weekly). A taxi from the city centre to the airport takes 10 minutes and costs around £6.

BUS

The bus station is northeast of the city centre. Some Aberdeen buses travel via Arbroath, others via Forfar.

Aberdeen £19.40, 1½ hours, hourly
Edinburgh £18.60, 1½ hours, hourly, some change at Perth
Glasgow £18.60, 1¾ hours, hourly
London (Megabus) £45, 11 to 12 hours, daily
Oban £44, 5½ hours, three daily, change at Glasgow
Perth £8.70, 35 minutes, hourly

TRAIN

Trains from Dundee to Aberdeen travel via Arbroath and Stonehaven.

Aberdeen £22, 1¼ hours, twice hourly
Edinburgh £20, 1¼ hours, at least hourly
Glasgow £20, 1½ hours, hourly
Perth £8.80, 20 minutes, hourly

DON'T MISS

GLAMIS CASTLE

Looking every inch the Scottish Baronial castle, with its roofline sprouting a forest of pointed turrets and battlements, **Glamis Castle** (www.glamis-castle.co.uk; DD8 1RU; adult/child £15.50/10; ⏲10am-5.30pm Apr-Oct, last entry 4.30pm; P 👪) claims to be the legendary setting for Shakespeare's *Macbeth*. A royal residence since 1372, it is the family home of the earls of Strathmore and Kinghorne – the Queen Mother (born Elizabeth Bowes-Lyon, 1900–2002) spent her childhood at Glamis (pronounced 'glams') and Princess Margaret (the Queen's sister, 1930–2002) was born here.

The five-storey, L-shaped castle was given to the Lyon family in 1372, but was significantly altered in the 17th century. Inside, the most impressive room is the drawing room, with its vaulted plasterwork ceiling. There's a display of armour and weaponry in the haunted crypt and frescoes in the chapel (also haunted). Duncan's Hall is named for the murdered King Duncan from *Macbeth* (though the scene actually takes place in Macbeth's castle in Inverness). As with Cawdor Castle, the claimed Shakespeare connection is fictitious – the real Macbeth had nothing to do with either castle, and died long before either was built.

You can also look around the royal apartments, including the Queen Mother's bedroom. Hour-long guided tours (included in admission) depart every 15 minutes; the last tour is at 4.30pm.

Glamis Castle is 12 miles north of Dundee, on the way to Kirriemuir.

Arbroath

☎01241 / POP 23,900

Arbroath is an old-fashioned seaside resort and fishing harbour, home of the famous Arbroath smokie (a form of smoked haddock). The humble smokie achieved European Union 'Protected Geographical Indication' status in 2004 – the term 'Arbroath smokie' can only be used legally to describe haddock smoked in the traditional manner within an 8km radius of Arbroath.

Sights & Activities

Arbroath Abbey HISTORIC BUILDING

(HES; www.historicenvironment.scot; Abbey St, DD11 1EG; adult/child £6/3.60; ⏲9.30am-5.30pm Apr-Sep, 10am-4pm Oct-Mar) The picturesque, red-sandstone ruins of Arbroath Abbey, founded in 1178 by King William the Lion, dominate the town of Arbroath. It is thought that Bernard of Linton, the abbot here in the early 14th century, wrote the famous Declaration of Arbroath in 1320, asserting Scotland's right to independence. You can climb part way up one of the towers for a grand view over the ruins.

St Vigeans Museum MUSEUM

(HES; ☎01241-878756; www.historicenvironment.scot; St Vigeans Lane, DD11 4RB; adult/child £6/3.60) About a mile north of Arbroath town centre, this cottage museum houses a superb collection of Pictish and medieval sculptured stones. The museum's masterpiece is the **Drosten Stone**, beautifully carved with animal figures and hunting scenes on one side, and an interlaced Celtic cross on the other (look for the devil perched in the top left corner). Check the website for open days; otherwise phone ahead or ask at Arbroath Abbey to arrange a visit.

Sleeping & Eating

Harbour Nights Guest House B&B ££

(☎01241-434343; www.harbournights.co.uk; 4 The Shore, DD11 1PB; s/d from £55/75; 📶) With a superb location overlooking the harbour, four stylishly decorated bedrooms and a gourmet breakfast menu, Harbour Nights is our favourite place to stay in Arbroath. Rooms 2 and 3, with harbour views, are a bit more expensive (from £80), but well worth asking for when booking.

Townhouse Hotel HOTEL ££

(☎01241-431577; www.townhousehotelarbroath.co.uk; 99 High St, DD11 1DP; r from £70; 📶) The Townhouse, set in a restored Georgian-style building on Arbroath's main street, offers stylishly decorated if smallish rooms in a superb location just a few minutes' walk from Arbroath Abbey.

But'n'Ben Restaurant SCOTTISH ££

(☎01241-877223; www.thebutnben.com; 1 Auchmithie, DD11 5SQ; mains £9-29; ⏲noon-2pm Wed-Mon, 6-9pm Wed-Sat, 4-5.30pm Sun; P 👪) 🌿 Above the harbour in Auchmithie, this cosy cottage restaurant with open fireplace, rustic furniture and sea-themed art serves the best of local seafood – the Arbroath-smokie pancakes are recommended – plus great homemade cakes and desserts, and high teas on Sunday (£19). It's best to book.

Gordon's Restaurant SCOTTISH £££
(☎01241-830364; www.gordonsrestaurant.co.uk; Main St, Inverkeillor; 3-course lunch £39, 4-course dinner £69; ⏲12.30-1.30pm Sun, 7-8.30pm Tue-Sun, closed Sun dinner Oct-Apr) Six miles north of Arbroath, in the tiny and unpromising-looking village of Inverkeillor, lies this intimate and rustic restaurant serving gourmet-quality Scottish cuisine. There are five comfortable **bedrooms** (double £110 to £165) for those who don't want to drive after dinner.

Getting There & Away

BUS

Bus 140 runs from Arbroath to Auchmithie (£1.80, 15 minutes, six daily Monday to Friday, three daily on Saturday and Sunday).

TRAIN

Trains from Dundee to Arbroath (£6.30, 25 minutes, two per hour) continue to Aberdeen (£22, 55 minutes) via Montrose and Stonehaven.

ABERDEENSHIRE

Since medieval times Aberdeenshire and its northwestern neighbour Moray have been the richest and most fertile regions of the Highlands. Aberdeenshire is famed for its Aberdeen Angus beef cattle, its many fine castles and the prosperous 'granite city' of Aberdeen.

North of Aberdeen, the Grampian Mountains fall away to rolling agricultural plains pocked with small, craggy volcanic hills. This fertile Lowland corner of northeastern Scotland is known as Buchan; the old Scots dialect, the Doric, is in everyday use here (if you think the Glaswegian accent is difficult to understand, just try listening in on a conversation in Fraserburgh).

The Buchan coast alternates between rugged cliffs and long, long stretches of sand, dotted with picturesque little fishing villages such as Pennan, where parts of the film *Local Hero* were shot.

Getting There & Around

The main bus routes link Aberdeen to Fraserburgh, Elgin, and Inverness via Huntly. There's a good network of rural bus services, too.

The only railway line runs from Aberdeen to Elgin and Inverness via Huntly and Keith.

Aberdeen

☎01224 / POP 195,000

Aberdeen is northeast Scotland's powerhouse, fuelled by the North Sea petroleum industry. Oil money made the city as expensive as London, with prices charged to match the depth of oil-wealthy pockets, though regular downturns in the industry see prices fall. Happily, most cultural attractions, such as the Maritime Museum and Aberdeen Art Gallery, are free.

Known throughout Scotland as the 'granite city', much of the town was built using silvery-grey granite hewn from the now-abandoned Rubislaw Quarry, at one time the biggest artificial hole in the ground in Europe. On a sunny day the granite lends an attractive glitter to the city, but when low, grey rain clouds scud in off the North Sea it can be hard to tell where the buildings stop and the sky begins.

Royal Deeside is easily accessible to the west, Dunnottar Castle to the south, sandy beaches to the north and whisky country northwest.

Sights & Activities

★**Aberdeen Art Gallery** GALLERY
(☎01224-523700; www.aagm.co.uk; Schoolhill, AB10 1FQ; ⏲10am-5pm Tue-Sat, 2-5pm Sun) FREE Fresh from a major refurbishment, Aberdeen's art gallery eschews the traditional arrangement of its collections by historical period in favour of themes. For example, Gallery 10 (French Impressions) compares and contrasts the works of French Impressionists with contemporary Scottish artists who were inspired by them – William McTaggart, Samuel Peploe, Francis Cadell – while Gallery 16 (Shoreline) looks at the influence of Scotland's coast on landscape artists such as Joan Eardley.

Other highlights include the wide-ranging works of larger-than-life Aberdeenshire artist-adventurer James McBey (1883–1959), and *Gallowgate Lard*, a chilling, ghostly self-portrait by Glaswegian painter Ken Currie (born 1960).

★**Aberdeen Maritime Museum** MUSEUM
(☎01224-337700; www.aagm.co.uk; Shiprow, AB11 5BY; ⏲10am-5pm Mon-Sat, noon-3pm Sun) FREE Overlooking the nautical bustle of Aberdeen harbour is the Maritime Museum, centred on a three-storey replica of a North Sea oil-production platform, which explains all you

ever wanted to know about the petroleum industry. Other galleries, some situated in **Provost Ross's House**, the oldest building in the city and part of the museum, cover the shipbuilding, whaling and fishing industries.

Gordon Highlanders Museum MUSEUM
(www.gordonhighlanders.com; St Lukes, Viewfield Rd, AB15 7XH; adult/child £8/4.50; 10am-4.30pm Tue-Sat Feb-Nov; P) This excellent museum records the history of one of the British Army's most famous fighting units, described by Winston Churchill as 'the finest regiment in the world'. Originally raised in the northeast of Scotland by the 4th Duke of Gordon in 1794, the regiment was amalgamated with the Seaforths and Camerons to form the Highlanders regiment in 1994. The museum is about a mile west of the western end of Union St – take bus 11 or X17 from Union St.

Marischal College HISTORIC BUILDING
(Broad St, AB10 1AB) Marischal College, founded in 1593 by the 5th Earl Marischal, merged with King's College (founded 1495) in 1860 to create the modern University of Aberdeen. The college's huge and impressive facade overlooking Broad St, in perpendicular Gothic style – unusual in having such elaborate masonry hewn from notoriously hard-to-work granite – dates from 1906 and is the world's second-largest granite structure (after El Escorial near Madrid).

Provost Skene's House HISTORIC BUILDING
(01224-641086; www.aagm.co.uk; Guestrow, AB10 1AS) FREE This late-medieval turreted town house was occupied in the 17th century by the provost (Scottish equivalent of a mayor) Sir George Skene. It was also occupied for six weeks by the Duke of Cumberland on his way to Culloden in 1746. The tempera ceiling of the Painted Gallery with its religious symbolism, dating from 1622, is unusual for having survived the depredations of the Reformation. It's a period gem featuring earnest-looking angels, soldiers and St Peter with crowing cockerels.

St Machar's Cathedral CATHEDRAL
(www.stmachar.com; The Chanonry, AB24 1RQ; 9.30am-4.30pm) FREE The 15th-century St Machar's, with its massive twin towers, is a rare example of a fortified cathedral. According to legend, St Machar was ordered to establish a church where the river takes the shape of a bishop's crook, which it does just here. The cathedral is best known for its impressive **heraldic ceiling**, dating from 1520, which has 48 shields of kings, nobles, archbishops and bishops. Sunday services are held at 11am and 6pm.

Sleeping

★Globe Inn B&B ££
(01224-641171; www.the-globe-inn.com; 13-15 North Silver St, AB10 1RJ; r from £63;) This popular pub has seven appealing, comfortable guest bedrooms upstairs, simply but tastefully decorated. There's live music in the pub on weekends so it's not a place for early-to-bed types, but the price versus location factor can't be beaten. There's no dining room, so breakfast is continental, served on a tray in your room. It's cheaper at weekends.

★Dutch Mill Hotel HOTEL ££
(01224-322555; www.dutchmill.co.uk; 7 Queen's Rd, AB15 4NR; s £65-85, d £75-95; P) The grand, granite-hewn, Victorian-era mansions that line Queen's Rd house financial offices, private schools, medical practices and the occasional hotel – this one has nine bedrooms with beautifully understated modern decor, a popular bar and a conservatory restaurant. Rates are cheaper at weekends.

Jays B&B ££
(01224-638295; www.jaysguesthouse.co.uk; 422 King St, AB24 3BR; s/d from £70/100; Mon-Thu; P) Located halfway between the city centre (a 15-minute walk) and Old Aberdeen (a 10-minute walk), this elegantly decorated Edwardian villa is a cosy nest of hospitality, with welcoming owners who seemingly can't do enough to help their guests enjoy their stay. It's popular, so book well in advance (note – open Monday to Thursday nights only).

Jurys Inn HOTEL ££
(01224-381200; www.jurysinns.com; Union Sq, Guild St, AB11 5RG; r from £109;) Conveniently located between the train and bus stations, this business-oriented hotel has stylish, spacious rooms with plenty of space for unpacking suitcases.

Eating

Bonobo Cafe VEGAN £
(www.facebook.com//bonoboaberdeen; 73-75 Skene St, AB10 1QD; mains £5-8; 8am-4pm Tue-Fri, 9am-5pm Sat, 10am-4pm Sun;) Aberdeen has lagged behind a bit in the vegetarian-restaurant stakes, so it was good to see this 100% vegan cafe open in 2017. The menu runs from breakfast (served till noon, and all day on Sunday), of avocado on toast

Aberdeen

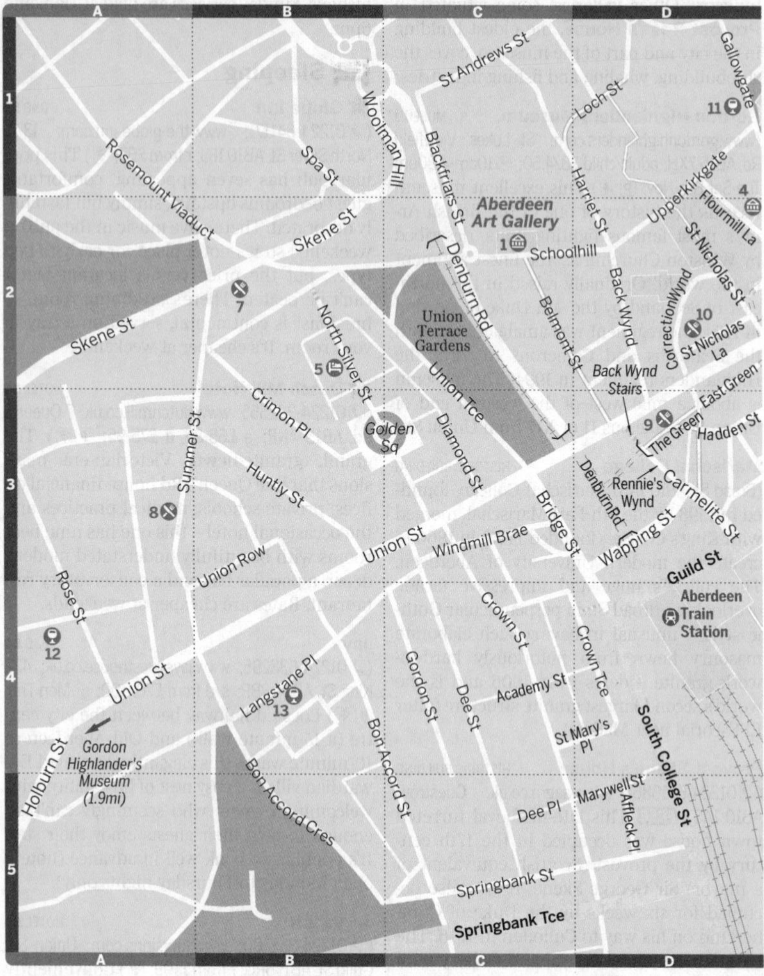

or smoked carrot and cream-cheese bagel, to lunch dishes, such as seitan 'chicken' kebabs.

★Braided Fig INTERNATIONAL ££

(☎01224-620333; www.thebraidedfig.co.uk; 39 Summer St, AB10 1SB; mains £13-18; ⏲food served noon-9pm Mon-Sat, 12.30-8pm Sun;) An actual fig tree, draped in fairy lights, forms the focal point of this delightfully intimate and informal restaurant, its understated decor enlivened with shades of blackberry and avocado. The menu takes local produce and leads it on a journey around the globe, pairing crab cakes with chorizo, roast chicken with satay sauce, and langoustine scampi-style with *petit pois à la française*.

★Café 52 BISTRO ££

(☎01224-590094; www.cafe52.co.uk; 52 The Green, AB11 6PE; mains lunch £7, dinner £12; ⏲noon-midnight Wed-Sat, 6pm-midnight Tue;) This little haven of laid-back industrial chic – a high, narrow space lined with bare stonework, rough plaster and exposed ventilation ducts – serves some of the finest and best-value cuisine in the northeast (slow-cooked beef casserole with roasted root veggies, red wine and garlic), and at incredible prices considering the quality on offer.

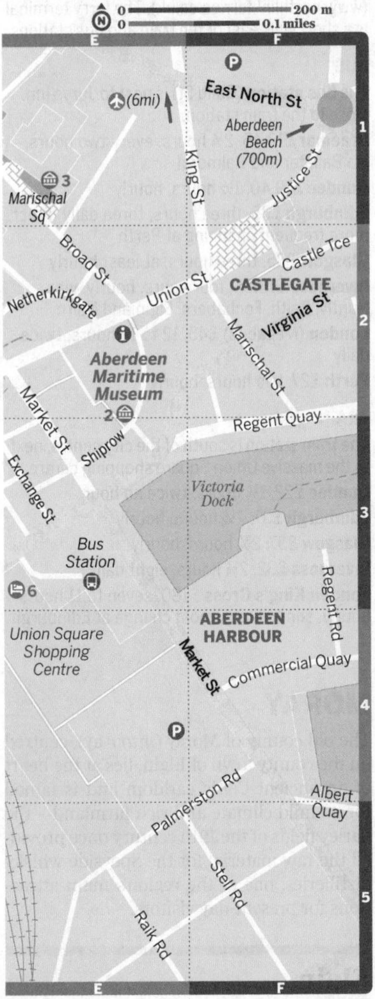

Aberdeen

Top Sights
1 Aberdeen Art Gallery C2
2 Aberdeen Maritime Museum E2

Sights
3 Marischal College E1
4 Provost Skene's House D2

Sleeping
5 Globe Inn B2
6 Jurys Inn E3

Eating
7 Bonobo Cafe B2
8 Braided Fig A3
9 Café 52 .... D3
10 Moonfish Café D2

Drinking & Nightlife
11 BrewDog D1
12 Grape & Grain A4
13 Orchid B4

★Silver Darling SEAFOOD ££
(01224-576229; www.thesilverdarling.co.uk; Pocra Quay, North Pier, AB11 5DQ; mains £15-23, steaks £30-36; noon-2pm & 5.30-9.30pm Mon-Fri, noon-9.30pm Sat, noon-8pm Sun;) The Silver Darling (an old Scottish nickname for herring) is the place for a special meal, housed in a former Customs office at the entrance to Aberdeen harbour with picture windows overlooking the sea. Here you can enjoy fresh Scottish seafood while you watch the porpoises playing in the harbour mouth. Bookings are recommended.

Moonfish Café MODERN SCOTTISH £££
(01224-644166; www.moonfishcafe.co.uk; 9 Correction Wynd, AB10 1HP; 2-/3-course dinner £30/36; noon-2pm & 6-9.30pm Tue-Sat) The menu of this little place hidden on a backstreet concentrates on good-quality Scottish produce but draws its influences from cuisines all around the world, from butter-roasted hake with crab bisque, tomato and olives, to lamb neck fillet with potato gnocchi and pickled mushrooms. Two-course lunches are £17.

Drinking & Nightlife

★Orchid COCKTAIL BAR
(www.orchidaberdeen.com; 51 Langstane Pl, AB11 6EN; 6pm-2am Sun-Thu, 5pm-3am Fri, 6pm-3am Sat) This relaxed and welcoming spot is quietly confident in its wide-ranging knowledge and expertise – two of its bartenders were nominated in the UK Top 100 in 2020. It offers regular gin- and whisky-tasting sessions as well as mixology classes – the house cocktail is the Pink Orchid (vanilla vodka, black raspberry liqueur, cranberry and lime).

BrewDog BAR
(www.brewdog.com/bars/aberdeen; 17 Gallowgate, AB25 1EB; noon-midnight Mon-Thu, to 1am Fri & Sat, 12.30pm-midnight Sun;) The original flagship bar of northeast Scotland's most innovative craft brewery brings a bit of industrial chic to Aberdeen's pub scene along with a vast range of guest beers from around the world.

WORTH A TRIP

DUNNOTTAR CASTLE

A pleasant, 20-minute walk along the clifftops south of Stonehaven harbour leads to the spectacular ruins of **Dunnottar Castle** (01569-766320; www.dunnottarcastle.co.uk; AB39 2TL; adult/child £8/4; 9am-5.30pm Apr-Sep, 10am-4.30pm or dusk Oct-Mar; P), spread out across a grassy promontory 50m above the sea. As dramatic a filmset as any director could wish for, it provided the backdrop for Franco Zeffirelli's *Hamlet* (1990), starring Mel Gibson. The original fortress was built in the 9th century; the keep is the most substantial remnant, but the drawing room (restored in 1926) is more interesting.

Grape & Grain WINE BAR
(01224-633761; www.grapeandgrain.wine; 31 Thistle St, AB10 1UY; 4-11pm Mon-Thu, noon-11pm Fri & Sat, noon-8pm Sun) The decadent decor of deep-blue-green panelling, designer copper light fittings and mirrored walls will entice you to linger in this classy wine bar – there are even wireless phone chargers built into the tabletops. The cellar is stocked with a wide but carefully curated selection of wines, plus craft beers and gins. It also serves tempting platters of Scottish cheeses.

Information

Aberdeen Tourist Office (01224-269180; www.aberdeen-grampian.com; 23 Union St, AB11 5BP; 9am-6.30pm Mon-Sat, 10am-4pm Sun Jul & Aug, 10am-4pm Mon-Sat Sep-Jun;) Handy for general information.

Getting There & Away

AIR

Aberdeen Airport (0344 481 6666; www.aberdeenairport.com; AB21 7DU) is at Dyce, 6 miles northwest of the city centre. There are regular flights to numerous Scottish and UK destinations, including London, Belfast, Orkney and Shetland, and international flights to several European countries.

Stagecoach Jet bus 727 runs regularly from Aberdeen bus station to the airport (single £3.50, 35 minutes). A taxi from the airport to the city centre takes 25 minutes and costs around £15.

BOAT

Car ferries from Aberdeen to Orkney and Shetland are run by **Northlink Ferries** (www.northlinkferries.co.uk). The ferry terminal is a short walk east of the train and bus stations.

BUS

The **bus station** (Guild St) is next to Jurys Inn, close to the train station.

Braemar £12.45, 2¼ hours, every two hours, via Ballater and Balmoral
Dundee £19.40, 1½ hours, hourly
Edinburgh £35, three hours, three daily direct, more frequent changing at Perth
Glasgow £35, three hours, at least hourly
Inverness £13.85, four hours, hourly, via Huntly, Keith, Fochabers, Elgin and Nairn
London (Megabus) £45, 12 to 14 hours, twice daily
Perth £27, two hours, hourly

TRAIN

The train station is south of the city centre, next to the massive Union Square shopping centre.

Dundee £22, 1¼ hours, twice an hour
Edinburgh £37, 2½ hours, hourly
Glasgow £37, 2¾ hours, hourly
Inverness £32, 2¼ hours, eight daily
London King's Cross £180, seven to 11 hours, hourly, some direct, most change at Edinburgh

MORAY

The old county of Moray (*murr*-ay), centred on the county town of Elgin, lies at the heart of an ancient Celtic earldom and is famed for its mild climate and rich farmland – the barley fields of the 19th century once provided the raw material for the Speyside whisky distilleries, one of the region's main attractions for present-day visitors.

Elgin

01343 / POP 23,130

Elgin has been the provincial capital of Moray for over eight centuries and was an important town in medieval times. It's dominated by a hilltop monument to the 5th Duke of Gordon, and the main attractions are its impressive ruined cathedral, where the tombs of the duke's ancestors lie, and its fine museum.

Sights

★Elgin Museum MUSEUM
(www.elginmuseum.org.uk; 1 High St; donations accepted; 10am-5pm Mon-Fri, 11am-4pm Sat Apr-Oct) FREE Scotland's oldest independent

museum is an old-fashioned cabinet of curiosities, a captivating collection artfully displayed in a beautiful, purpose-built Victorian building. Exhibits range from Ecuadorian shrunken heads to Peruvian mummies, and include mysterious Pictish carved stones and internationally important fish and reptile fossils discovered in local rocks.

Elgin Cathedral CATHEDRAL

(HES; www.historicenvironment.scot; King St; adult/child £9/5.40; 9.30am-5.30pm Apr-Sep, 10am-4pm Oct-Mar) Many people think that the ruins of Elgin Cathedral, known as the 'lantern of the north', are the most beautiful and evocative in Scotland; its octagonal chapter house is the finest in the country. Consecrated in 1224, the cathedral was burned down in 1390 by the infamous Wolf of Badenoch, the illegitimate son of Robert II, following his excommunication by the Bishop of Moray.

Sleeping & Eating

Moraydale B&B ££

(01343-546381; www.moraydaleguesthouse.com; 276 High St; s/d/f from £60/80/100; P) The Moraydale is a spacious Victorian mansion filled with period features – check out the stained glass and the cast-iron and tile fireplaces. The bedrooms are all en suite and equipped with modern bathrooms – the three large family rooms are particularly good value.

Southbank Guest House B&B ££

(01343-547132; www.southbankguesthouse.co.uk; 36 Academy St; d/tr from £80/150; P) The family-run, 15-room Southbank is set in a large Georgian town house in a quiet street south of Elgin's centre, just five minutes' walk from the cathedral and other sights. There may be a three-night minimum stay in high season.

★Weavers CAFE £

(www.johnstonsofelgin.com/visit-us/weavers-restaurant; Johnstons of Elgin, Newmill, IV30 4AF; mains £7-15; 10am-4pm; P) The restaurant at Johnstons woollen mill is one of the best places to eat in town, serving breakfast till noon, hot lunches from noon to 3pm (from steak pie to lobster ravioli) and afternoon teas from 2pm.

Batchen Street Coffee CAFE £

(www.facebook.com/batchenstreetcoffee; 33 Batchen St, IV30 1BH; mains £4-7; 8.30am-4pm Mon-Fri, 9.30am-4.30pm Sat;) A great little coffee shop that serves superb espresso (it roasts its

THE SPEYSIDE WHISKY TRAIL

Visiting a distillery can be memorable, but only hardcore malthounds will want to go to more than one or two. Here are the top five whisky sights in the area.

Aberlour (01340-881249; www.aberlour.com; tours from £20; 9.30am-5pm daily Apr-Oct, 10am-4pm Mon-Fri Nov-Mar; P) Has an excellent, detailed tour with a proper tasting session. It's on the main street in Aberlour.

Glenfarclas (01807-500345; www.glenfarclas.com; AB37 9BD; tours £7.50; 10am-5pm Mon-Fri Apr-Sep, also to 4pm Sat Jul-Sep, Mon-Fri Oct-Mar; P) Small, friendly and independent, Glenfarclas is 5 miles south of Aberlour on the Grantown road; the last tour leaves 90 minutes before closing. The in-depth Connoisseur's Tour (Fridays only July to September) is £40.

Glenfiddich (01340-820373; www.glenfiddich.co.uk; entry free, tours from £10; 9.30am-4.30pm; P) It's big and busy, but handiest for Dufftown; foreign-language tours are available. The standard tour (£10) starts with an overblown video, but it's fun and informative. The in-depth half-day Pioneer's Tour (£95) must be prebooked.

Macallan (01340-318000; www.themacallan.com; Easter Elchies, Craigellachie; visitor centre free, distillery tours from £50; 10am-6pm; P) This distillery enjoys a lovely location 1 mile west of Craigellachie and is housed in a spectacular turf-roofed visitor centre made from engineered timber.

Speyside Cooperage (01340-871108; www.speysidecooperage.co.uk; tours from £4; 9am-5pm Mon-Fri, closed Christmas-early Jan; P) Here you can see the fascinating art of barrel-making in action. It's a mile south of Craigellachie on the Dufftown road.

The biannual **Spirit of Speyside** (www.spiritofspeyside.com; early May & early Sep) whisky festival in Dufftown has a number of great events. Both accommodation and events should be booked well ahead.

own beans, and also offers Chemex brews), good-value breakfasts (scrambled eggs on toast), light lunches (soup, quiche) and excellent home baking.

Getting There & Away

BUS

Aberdeen £13.85, 2½ hours, hourly
Banff & Macduff £11.70, 1¾ hours, hourly
Dufftown £6.45, 50 minutes, hourly Monday to Saturday
Inverness £11.55, 1½ hours, hourly

TRAIN

Aberdeen £21, 1½ hours, five daily
Inverness £13.90, 45 minutes, five daily

Dufftown & Aberlour

Rome may be built on seven hills, but Dufftown's built on seven stills, say the locals. Founded in 1817 by James Duff, 4th Earl of Fife, Dufftown is 17 miles south of Elgin and lies at the heart of the Speyside whisky-distilling region. With seven working distilleries nearby, Dufftown has been dubbed Scotland's malt-whisky capital and is host to the biannual **Spirit of Speyside** whisky festival. Ask at the whisky museum about the **Malt Whisky Trail** (www.maltwhiskytrail.com), a self-guided tour around the local distilleries.

Aberlour (www.aboutaberlour.co.uk) – or Charlestown of Aberlour, to give it its full name – is prettier than Dufftown, straggling along the banks of the River Spey. It is famous as the home of Walkers Shortbread, and has the Aberlour Distillery right on the main street. Attractions include salmon fishing on the Spey, nearby Knockando Woolmill and some lovely walks along the Speyside Way.

Getting There & Away

Buses link Elgin to Dufftown (£6.45, 50 minutes) hourly Monday to Saturday, continuing to Huntly and Aberdeen.

On summer weekends you can take a train from Inverness or Aberdeen to Keith (£19, one hour, five daily), and then ride the Keith and Dufftown Railway to Dufftown.

LOCH LOMOND & THE TROSSACHS

The 'bonnie banks' and 'bonnie braes' of Loch Lomond have long been Glasgow's rural retreat – a scenic region of hills, lochs and healthy fresh air within easy reach of Scotland's largest city. The picturesque Trossachs have likewise long been popular for their wild Highland beauty, set so close to the southern population centres.

Together, they are conjoined by the **Loch Lomond & the Trossachs National Park** (☎01389-722600; www.lochlomond-trossachs.org), which extends over a huge area, from Balloch north to Tyndrum and Killin, and from Callander west to the forests of Cowal. The length of Loch Lomond means that access between the western part of the park and the Trossachs is either in the far north of the region via Crianlarich or the far south via Drymen. Walkers and cyclists can link the two more easily via the waterbuses that criss-cross Loch Lomond.

Loch Lomond

Loch Lomond is mainland Britain's largest lake and, after Loch Ness, the most famous of Scotland's lochs. Its proximity to Glasgow (20 miles away) means that the tourist honeypots of Balloch and Luss get pretty crowded in summer. The eastern shore, which is followed by the West Highland Way long-distance footpath, is quieter and offers a better chance to appreciate the loch away from the busy main road along the western shore.

Loch Lomond straddles the Highland border. The southern part is broad and island-studded, fringed by woods and Lowland meadows. However, north of Luss the loch narrows, occupying a deep trench gouged out by glaciers during the Ice Age, with 900m mountains crowding either side.

Activities

The **West Highland Way** (www.westhighlandway.org) runs along the loch's eastern shore, while the **Rob Roy Way** (www.robroyway.com) heads from Drymen to Pitlochry via the Trossachs. The **Three Lochs Way** (www.threelochsway.co.uk) loops west from Balloch through Helensburgh and Arrochar before returning to Loch Lomond at Inveruglas. The **Great Trossachs Path** (www.lochlomond-trossachs.org) links the loch with the Trossachs. There are numerous shorter walks around: get further information from tourist offices.

Rowardennan is the starting point for ascents of **Ben Lomond** (www.nts.org.uk/visit/places/ben-lomond) (974m), a popular and relatively straightforward (if strenuous) climb.

DON'T MISS

HILL HOUSE

Built in 1902 for Glasgow publisher Walter Blackie, **Hill House** (☎01436-673900; www.nts.org.uk; Upper Colquhoun St, Helensburgh; adult/child £12.50/5.50; ⏰10am-5pm Mar-Oct, Thu-Sun only Nov-Feb) is perhaps architect Charles Rennie Mackintosh's finest creation – its timeless elegance still feels chic today. The interiors are stunning, with rose motifs and fabulous furniture. Water soaking through the rendered cement exterior means that you'll find the house enclosed in a giant covering structure. The house also has a beautiful garden. Mackintosh was very protective of his creation: he once chided Mrs Blackie for putting the wrong-coloured flowers in a vase in the hall.

You can stay on the top floor here – check the Holidays section of the NTS website. It's near Upper Helensburgh station, though not all trains stop there. If you're arriving at Helensburgh Central station, it's about a 1-mile uphill walk to Hill House. Buses 302 and 306 can get you close.

The mostly traffic-free **Clyde and Loch Lomond Cycle Way** links Glasgow to Balloch (20 miles), where it joins the **West Loch Lomond Cycle Path**, which continues along the loch shore to Tarbet (10 miles). The park website (www.lochlomond-trossachs.org) details some other local routes.

Cruise Loch Lomond BOATING
(☎01301-702356; www.cruiselochlomond.co.uk; Tarbet; cruises adult/child from £12/7.50; ⏰8.30am-5.30pm late Mar-early Nov) With departures from Tarbet and Luss, this operator runs several cruises, including options exploring loch islands, Rob Roy's cave, the Arklet Falls, or walking a section of the West Highland Way from Inversnaid. The one-hour Northern Highlights cruise is a quick introduction from Tarbet (adult/child £12/7.50), while 90-minute circuits from Luss or Tarbet run at adult/child £15/7.50.

Sleeping & Eating

Rowardennan Youth Hostel HOSTEL £
(Hostelling Scotland; ☎01360-870259; www.hostellingscotland.org.uk; Rowardennan; dm/tw/q £24/54/99; ⏰mid-Mar–mid-Oct; P 📶) Where the road ends on the eastern side of Loch Lomond is this postcard-quality retreat in an elegant ex-hunting lodge, with lawns stretching right down to the water's edge. Whether you're walking the West Highland Way, climbing Ben Lomond or just putting your feet up, it's a great choice, with a huge lounge that has windows overlooking the loch.

Oak Tree Inn INN ££
(☎01360-870357; www.theoaktreeinn.co.uk; Balmaha; s/d £85/110; P 📶) An attractive traditional inn built in slate and timber, this bustling place offers bright, modern bedrooms for pampered hikers, plus super-spacious superior chambers, self-catering cottages and glamping pods with their own deck. The rustic restaurant brings locals, tourists and walkers together and serves generously proportioned pub grub (mains £10 to £14; open noon to 9pm). There's plenty of outdoor seating.

Drover's Inn PUB FOOD ££
(☎01301-704234; www.thedroversinn.co.uk; Inverarnan; bar meals £10-14; ⏰food 11.30am-10pm Mon-Sat, to 9.30pm or 10pm Sun; P 📶) Don't miss this low-ceilinged howff (drinking den), just north of Ardlui, with its smoke-blackened stone, kilted bartenders, and walls adorned with moth-eaten stags' heads and stuffed birds. The convivial bar, where Rob Roy allegedly dropped by for pints, serves hearty hill-walking fuel and hosts live folk music on weekends.

Tourist Information

Balloch Tourist Office (☎01389-753533; www.visitscotland.com; Balloch Rd, Balloch; ⏰9.30am-6pm Jul & Aug, to 5.30pm Jun & Sep, 9.30am-4pm Oct-May) Opposite Balloch train station.

Balmaha National Park Centre (☎01389-722100; www.lochlomond-trossachs.org; Balmaha; ⏰9.30am-4pm Apr-Oct, 9.30am-4pm Sat & Sun Nov-Mar) Has maps showing local walking routes.

Getting There & Around

BUS

Bus 309 runs from Balloch to Drymen (£2.85) and Balmaha (£3.15, 20 minutes, nine to 10 daily), while bus 305 heads to Luss (£3.10, 20 minutes, nine to 10 daily). Bus 207 connects Balloch with Loch Lomond Shores and Alexandria. An **SPT Daytripper ticket** gives a family group unlimited travel for a day on most bus and train services in the Glasgow, Loch Lomond and Helensburgh area. Buy the ticket (£13.10 for one adult and two children, £23.20 for two adults and up to four children) from any train station or Glasgow bus station.

Tarbet and Ardlui are accessible by train and by Citylink buses between Glasgow and north-western destinations.

Local buses also run from Helensburgh to Arrochar (£3.15) via Luss and Tarbet (same price) four times daily Monday to Friday.

BOAT

From mid-March to October a network of boats criss-crosses Loch Lomond, allowing you to explore the loch's hiking and biking trails using public transport. The Loch Lomond Water Bus timetable is available from tourist offices and online (www.lochlomond-trossachs.org).

Callander

POP 3100

Callander, the principal Trossachs town, has been pulling in tourists for over 150 years, and has a laid-back ambience along its main thoroughfare that quickly lulls visitors into lazy pottering. There's an excellent array of accommodation options here, and some intriguing places to eat. Good walking and cycling routes are close at hand.

Sights & Activities

★Hamilton Toy Collection MUSEUM
(01877-330004; www.thehamiltontoycollection.co.uk; 111 Main St; adult/child £3/1; 10.30am-5pm Mon-Sat, noon-5pm Sun Apr-Oct;) A powerhouse of 20th-century juvenile memorabilia, chock-full of dolls houses, puppets and toy soldiers. It's an amazing collection and a guaranteed nostalgia trip. Phone ahead in winter as it opens some weekends.

Bracklinn Falls & Callander Crags WALKING
Impressive Bracklinn Falls are reached by track and footpath from Bracklinn Rd (30 minutes each way from the car park). Also off Bracklinn Rd, a woodland trail leads up to Callander Crags, with great views over the surroundings; a return trip from the car park is about 4 miles.

Wheels Cycling Centre CYCLING
(01877-331100; www.scottish-cycling.com; bike per hour/day/week from £8/20/90; 10am-6pm Mar-Oct) The Trossachs is a lovely area to cycle around. On a cycle route, excellent Wheels Cycling Centre has a wide range of hire bikes. To get here from the centre of Callander, take Bridge St off Main St, turn right onto Invertrossachs Rd and continue for a mile.

TRANSPORT IN THE TROSSACHS

DRT (Demand Responsive Transport; 01786-404040; www.stirling.gov.uk/drt) covers the Trossachs area. It might sound complex, but basically it means for the price of a bus you get a taxi to where you want to go. There are various zones. It's easiest to book online.

Sleeping

★Callander Hostel HOSTEL £
(01877-330141; www.callanderhostel.co.uk; 6 Bridgend; dm/d £20/60; P@) This hostel in a mock-Tudor building has been a major labour of love by a local youth project and is now a top-class facility. Well-furnished dorms (private at the time of research due to Covid-19) offer bunks with individual lights and USB charge ports, while en-suite doubles have super views. Staff are lovely, and it has a spacious common area and share kitchen as well as a cafe and garden.

Abbotsford Lodge HOTEL ££
(01877-330066; www.abbotsfordlodge.com; Stirling Rd; d £95; mid-Feb–early Nov; P) Offering excellent value for stylish contemporary rooms in a handsome Victorian house, this main-road choice has energetic owners who provide first-class hospitality and have a real eye for design. There are fabulous, spacious superiors (£135) as well as cheaper (£75) top-floor rooms – with shared bathroom – that have lovably offbeat under-roof shapes. It caters to cyclists and walkers with bike storage and packed lunches.

Arden House B&B ££
(01877-339405; www.ardenhouse.org.uk; Bracklinn Rd; d £120-130; Mar-Oct; P) This elegant home has a fabulous hillside location with a verdant garden and lovely vistas; it's close to Callander's centre but far from the crowds. The rooms are impeccable, with lots of natural light, and include large upstairs doubles with great views. Welcoming owners, noble architectural features – super bay windows – and a self-catering studio make this a top option. No children.

★Roman Camp Hotel HOTEL £££
(☎01877-330003; www.romancamphotel.co.uk; off Main St; s/d/superior £135/180/290; P 📶 🐾) Callander's best hotel is centrally located but feels rural, set by the river in beautiful grounds. Endearing features include a lounge with blazing fire and a library with a tiny secret chapel. It's an old-fashioned warren of a place with four grades of rooms; standards are certainly luxurious, but superiors are even more appealing, with period furniture, excellent bathrooms, armchairs and fireplace.

Eating

★Callander Meadows SCOTTISH ££
(☎01877-330181; www.callandermeadows.co.uk; 24 Main St; dinner mains £13-19; ⏱10am-2.30pm & 6-8.30pm Thu-Sun year-round, plus Mon May-Sep; 📶) Informal and cosy, this well-loved restaurant in the centre of Callander occupies the front rooms of a Main St house. It's truly excellent; there's a contemporary flair for presentation and unusual flavour combinations, but a solidly British base underpins the cuisine. There's a great beer/coffee garden out the back, where you can also eat. Lighter lunches such as sandwiches are also available.

★Venachar Lochside SCOTTISH ££
(☎01877-330011; www.venachar-lochside.com; Loch Venachar; mains £11-17; ⏱11am-4pm Jan-Nov, plus 5.30-8.30pm Fri & Sat Jun-Sep; 📶 👪) On lovely Loch Venachar, 4.5 miles west of Callander, this cafe-restaurant has a stunning waterside setting and does a nice line in carefully sourced produce (including delicious local trout) prepared in innovative ways. You can also hire boats and tackle to go fishing for trout on the loch.

Mhor Fish SEAFOOD ££
(☎01877-330213; www.mhorfish.net; 75 Main St; mains £9-18; ⏱noon-9pm Tue-Sun, closed Tue Nov–mid-Feb; 📶) 🍃 This simply decorated spot, with Formica tables and a hodgepodge of chairs, sources brilliant sustainable seafood. Browse the fresh catch, then eat it pan-seared in the dining area accompanied by a decent wine selection, or fried and wrapped in paper with chips to take away. It's all great, and calamari and oysters are wonderfully toothsome starters.

Getting There & Away

First (www.firstgroup.com) operates buses from Stirling (£6.30, 45 minutes, hourly Monday to Saturday, every two hours Sunday).

LOCAL KNOWLEDGE

MONACHYLE MHOR

A luxury hideaway with a fantastically peaceful location overlooking two lochs, **Monachyle Mhor** (☎01877-384622; www.monachylemhor.net; Balquhidder; d £195-360; ⏱Feb-Dec; P 📶 🐾) 🍃 is a great fusion of country Scotland and contemporary attitudes to design and food. Rooms are superb and feature quirkily original decor, particularly the fabulous 'feature rooms'. Otherwise, go glamping in a retro wagon or kip in a romantic…ferry waiting room. The restaurant is excellent.

It's an enchanting combination of top-class hospitality with a relaxed rural atmosphere: dogs and kids happily romp on the lawns, and no one looks askance if you come in flushed and muddy after a day's fishing or walking.

It's in Balquhidder, reached via a turn-off on the main road between Callander and Killin.

Kingshouse (☎01877-384768; www.kingshousetravel.com) has buses between Callander and Killin (£5.60, 40 minutes, five to six Monday to Saturday).

For Aberfoyle, use DRT or get off a Stirling-bound bus at Blair Drummond safari park, cross the road and pick up an Aberfoyle-bound bus.

Lochs Katrine & Achray

This rugged area, 7 miles north of Aberfoyle and 10 miles west of Callander, is the heart of the Trossachs. **Loch Katrine Cruises** (☎01877-376315; www.lochkatrine.com; Trossachs Pier, Loch Katrine; 1hr cruise adult £12-14, child £6.50-7.50) run from Trossachs Pier at the eastern tip of beautiful Loch Katrine. One of these is the fabulous centenarian steamship *Sir Walter Scott;* check the website for departures, as it's worth taking a trip on this veteran if possible. Things were a bit disrupted at the time of research while the *Sir Walter Scott* awaited funds for a major repair. Normal service includes various one-hour afternoon sailings, and at 10.30am (plus additional summer departures) there's a trip to Stronachlachar at the other end of the loch. From Stronachlachar (accessible by car via a 12-mile road from Aberfoyle), you can reach Loch Lomond's eastern shore at isolated

Inversnaid. A tarmac path links Trossachs Pier with Stronachlachar, so you can take the boat out and walk/cycle back (14 miles). At Trossachs Pier, **Katrinewheelz** (01877-376366; www.katrinewheelz.co.uk; Trossachs Pier, Loch Katrine; bike hire per half-/full day from £15/20; 9am-5pm Apr-Oct, check for winter hours) hires out good bikes. There's a cafe here and a good one at Stronachlachar.

Killin

POP 800

A fine base for the Trossachs or Perthshire, this lovely village sits at the western end of Loch Tay and has a spread-out, relaxed feel, particularly around the scenic **Falls of Dochart**, which tumble through the centre. On a sunny day people sprawl over the rocks by the bridge, with pint or picnic in hand. Killin offers fine walking around the town, and there are mighty mountains and glens close by.

Sights & Activities

Five miles northeast of Killin, **Ben Lawers** (1214m) rises above Loch Tay. Walking routes abound; one rewarding **circular walk** heads up into the Acharn forest south of town, emerging above the treeline to great views of Loch Tay and Ben Lawers. **Killin Outdoor Centre** (01567-820652; www.killinoutdoor.co.uk; Main St; bike per 24hr £25, kayak/canoe per 2hr £25; 8.45am-5.45pm, hires available roughly Apr-Oct) provides walking advice.

Glen Lochay runs westwards from Killin into the hills of Mamlorn. You can take a **mountain bike** up the glen; the scenery is impressive and the hills aren't too difficult. It's possible, on a nice summer day, to climb over the top of **Ben Challum** (1025m) and descend to Crianlarich, but it's hard work. A potholed road, not maintained and no longer suitable for cars, also connects Glen Lochay with Glen Lyon.

Killin is on the **Lochs & Glens Cycle Way** from Glasgow to Inverness. Hire bikes from helpful Killin Outdoor Centre (which also has canoes and kayaks and, in winter, crampons and snowshoes).

Sleeping & Drinking

Courie Inn INN ££

(01567-831000; www.thecourieinn.com; Main St; d £109-140; P) An excellent all-round choice, Courie Inn has quality, comfortable rooms decorated with restrained modern elegance; they come in a variety of sizes, including a sumptuous suite with views. It artfully blends the traditional and contemporary. A smaller room is a little cheaper (£89). Downstairs, the restaurant does competent food like curries and fish and chips, and there's a cosy bar.

Old Bank B&B ££

(01567-829074; www.theoldbankkillin.co.uk; Manse Rd; s/d £60/85; P) This handsome four-square building with a pretty garden stands proud above the main street in Killin. The hosts are very welcoming and the five rooms are super-comfortable, with contemporary colours, hill views and thoughtful extras.

Falls of Dochart Inn PUB

(01567-820270; www.fallsofdochartinn.co.uk; mains £13-18;) In a prime position overlooking the falls, this pub is a snug, atmospheric space with a roaring fire, real ales and decent food. The outside tables are great spots on a sunny day.

Getting There & Away

Kingshouse (p869) runs five to six buses Monday to Saturday to Callander (£5.60, 40 minutes), where you can change for Stirling. Citylink buses between Edinburgh and Oban/Fort William stop at the main road junction 2½ miles southwest of town.

ARRAN

POP 4600

Enchanting Arran is a jewel in Scotland's scenic crown. The island is a visual feast, and boasts culinary delights, its own brewery and distilleries, and stacks of accommodation options. The variations in Scotland's dramatic landscape can all be experienced on this one island, best explored by pulling on the hiking boots or jumping on a bicycle. Arran offers some challenging walks in the mountainous north, while the island's circular coastal road is very popular with cyclists.

Information

The **tourist office** (01770-303774; www.visitscotland.com; 9am-5pm Mon-Sat Mar-Oct, plus 10am-5pm Sun Apr-Sep, 11am-4pm Mon-Sat Nov-Feb) is in Brodick. The ferry from Ardrossan also has some tourist information. Useful websites include www.visitarran.com.

Getting There & Around

CalMac (☎ 0800 066 5000; www.calmac.co.uk) runs ferries between Ardrossan and Brodick (adult/car £4/15.95, 55 minutes, four to nine daily). From April to late October services also run between Claonaig on the Kintyre peninsula and Lochranza (adult/car £3/9.95, 30 minutes, seven to nine daily). In winter this service runs to Tarbert (1¼ hours) once daily and must be reserved.

Four to seven buses daily go from Brodick pier to Lochranza (£3.25, 45 minutes), and many head the other way to Lamlash (£2.10) and Whiting Bay (£2.85, 30 minutes), then on to Kildonan and Blackwaterfoot. Pick up a timetable from the tourist office.

An Arran Dayrider costs £6.30 from the driver, giving a day's travel. Download a bus timetable from www.spt.co.uk.

Brodick & Around

Most visitors arrive in Brodick, the beating heart of the island of Arran, and congregate along the coastal road to admire the town's long curving bay. On a clear day it's a spectacular vista, with Goatfell looming over the forested shore.

Sights & Activities

Brodick Castle CASTLE
(NTS; ☎ 01770-302202; www.nts.org.uk; castle & park adult/child £13.50/9.50, park only £7/5; castle 11am-4pm Apr-Oct, park 9.30am-sunset year-round) This elegant castle 2 miles north of Brodick evolved from 13th-century origins into a stately home and hunting lodge for the Dukes of Hamilton. The interior is characterised by fabulous 19th-century wooden furniture and an array of horses 'n' hounds paintings. The hunting gallery is wallpapered with deer heads. Helpful guides and good information panels add background.

Isle of Arran Heritage Museum MUSEUM
(☎ 01770-302636; www.arranmuseum.co.uk; Rosaburn; adult/child £5/3; 10.30am-4.30pm Apr-Oct) This museum has a varied collection of historical and ethnographic items, from prehistoric stone tools to farming implements. There's quite a bit to see across several heritage buildings, with good background on the island and its people. Gardens and a cafe round out the experience. It's on the way to the castle from Brodick.

Arran

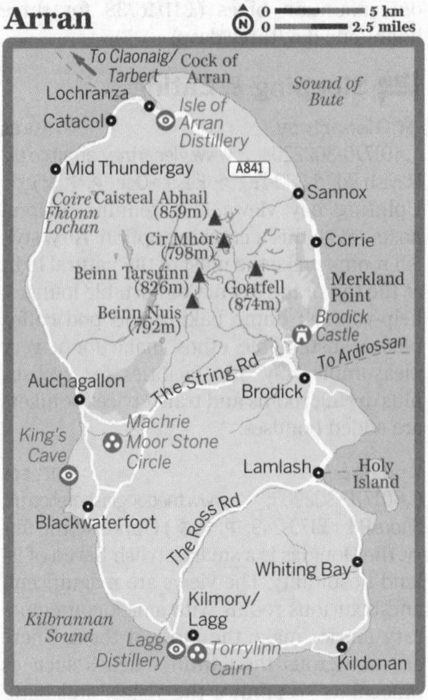

Arran Aromatics WORKSHOP
(☎ 01770-303003; www.arran.com; 9.30am-4.30pm, to 6pm summer;) Near Brodick Castle is this popular shop and visitor centre where you can purchase any number of scented items and watch the production line at work (it operates from Monday to Thursday). It runs child-friendly activities such as soap-making and candle-dipping, too.

★ **Goatfell** HIKING
The walk up and down Goatfell (874m), the island's highest point, is 8 miles return (up to eight hours), with trailheads at Brodick and Brodick Castle among others. In fine weather there are superb views to Ben Lomond and Northern Ireland. It can, however, be very cold and windy up here; take appropriate maps (available at the tourist office), waterproofing and a compass.

Arran Adventure Company OUTDOORS
(☎ 01770-303349; www.auchrannie.co.uk/adventure.html; Auchrannie Rd) Run out of the Auchrannie Resort, this company offers several activities, including gorge walking, archery and mountain biking. Most activities run for about three hours and prices are cheaper for teens/kids. Drop in to see what's available while you're around. It also hires

out mountain bikes (£11/16/38 for three hours/one day/three days).

Sleeping & Eating

★Glenartney B&B ££
(01770-302220; www.glenartney-arran.co.uk; Mayish Rd; d £80-110; Easter-Oct;) Uplifting bay views and genuine, helpful hosts make this a cracking option. Airy, stylish rooms make the most of the natural light at the top of the town. Comfortable lounges, help-yourself home baking and pod coffee plus a sustainable ethos make for a very pleasurable stay. Top facilities for cyclists, plus drying rooms and trail advice for hikers are added bonuses.

Douglas HOTEL £££
(01770-302968; www.thedouglashotel.co.uk; Shore Rd; r £179-249;) Opposite the ferry, the Douglas is a smart, stylish haven of island hospitality. The views are magnificent, and luxurious rooms with smart contemporary fabrics make the most of them. There are numerous thoughtful touches such as binoculars to admire the vistas, and bathrooms are great. The downstairs **bar and bistro** (bistro mains £13-20, bar meals £10-15; bistro 6-9.30pm, bar noon-9.30pm;) are also recommended. Prices drop midweek and in winter.

Brodick Bar & Brasserie BRASSERIE £££
(01770-302169; www.brodickbar.co.uk; Alma Rd; mains £17-28; noon-2.30pm & 5.30-8.30pm Tue-Sat;) A courteous host and excellent service characterise this upmarket Brodick choice. The menu changes seasonally and focuses on local produce, with particularly tasty seafood and game dishes. Portions are small and elegantly presented.

Lamlash

Lamlash, just 3 miles south of Brodick, is in a dazzling setting strung along the beachfront. The bay was used as a safe anchorage by the navy during WWI and WWII.

Sights

Holy Island ISLAND
(www.holyisle.org) Just off Lamlash, this island is owned by the Samye Ling Tibetan Centre and used as a retreat, but day visits are allowed. A tide-dependent **ferry** (07970 771960, 01770-700463; tomin10@btinternet.com; return adult/child £12/6; daily Apr-Oct, by arrangement Tue & Fri Nov-Mar) zips across from Lamlash. No dogs, bikes, alcohol or fires are allowed on the island. A good walk to the top of the hill (314m) takes two or three hours return. You can stay at the **Holy Island Centre for World Peace & Health** (01770-601100; www.holyisle.org; dm/s/d incl full board £32/55/80; Apr-Oct). Prices include full (vegetarian) board.

Sleeping & Eating

Lilybank Guest House B&B ££
(01770-600230; www.lilybank-arran.co.uk; Shore Rd; s/d £65/90; Apr-Sep;) Built in the 17th century, Lilybank retains its heritage but has been refurbished for 21st-century needs. Rooms are clean and comfortable, with one that's good for those with limited mobility. The front rooms have great views over Holy Island. Breakfast includes organic porridge, oak-smoked kippers and other Arran goodies.

★Glenisle Hotel HOTEL £££
(01770-600559; www.glenislehotel.com; Shore Rd; s/d/superior d £110/169/225;) This stylish hotel offers great service and high comfort levels. Rooms are decorated with contemporary fabrics; 'cosy' rooms under the sloping roof are a little cheaper. All feel fresh and include binoculars for scouring the seashore; upgrade to a 'superior' for the best water views. Downstairs is excellent **food** (mains £11-18; noon-8.45pm;) and lovely outdoor seating by the garden.

South Coast

The landscape in the south of Arran is gentler than in the north; the road drops into little wooded valleys, and it's particularly lovely around **Kilmory** and **Lagg**, from where a 10-minute walk will take you to **Torrylinn Cairn**, a chambered tomb over 4000 years old. **Kildonan** has pleasant sandy beaches, a gorgeous water outlook, a hotel, a campsite and an ivy-clad ruined castle.

In genteel **Whiting Bay**, strung out along the water, you'll find small sandy beaches and easy one-hour walks through the forest to the **Giant's Graves** and **Glenashdale Falls** – keep an eye out for golden eagles and other birds of prey.

Sights

Lagg Distillery DISTILLERY
(01770-870565; www.laggwhisky.com; Lagg; tours adult/child £10/free; 10am-5.30pm daily

Apr-Sep, 10am-4pm Tue-Sat Oct-Mar) This new distillery has a spectacular coastal setting and makes an appealing stop along the road around the island. The squat stills produce a modern, robust, peaty whisky that is a good contrast to the more delicate malt from the sibling distillery in Lochranza. Tours run on the hour and tastings are available. A cafe does sandwiches and comfort food like burritos and poutine, while upstairs is a bistro.

Sleeping

★ Sealshore Campsite CAMPSITE £
(☎01770-820320; www.campingarran.com; Kildonan; 1-/2-person tents £9/18, pods for 2 people £40; ⏲Mar-Oct; P 📶 🐾) Living up to its name, this excellent small campsite is right by the sea (and the Kildonan Hotel) and has one of Arran's finest views from its grassy camping area. There are good facilities, including barbecues, power showers and a day room; the breeze keeps the midges away. Camping pods offer a non-tent choice.

Viewbank House B&B ££
(☎01770-700326; www.viewbank-arran.co.uk; Whiting Bay; s £59-65, d £85-99; ⏲Apr-Oct; P 📶 🐾) Appropriately named, this quiet and relaxing place does indeed have tremendous views from its vantage point high above Whiting Bay. Rooms, of which there are a variety with and without bathrooms, are well kept; three have a vista. Owners are very hospitable; check out the Clapton guitar and blues memorabilia in the breakfast room. It's well signposted from the main road.

Lochranza

The village of Lochranza has a stunning location in a small bay on Arran island's north coast. It's characterised by the photogenic 13th-century **Lochranza Castle** (www.historicenvironment.scot; ⏲24hr) FREE, a ruin standing proud on a little promontory. The nearby **Isle of Arran Distillery** (☎01770-830264; www.arranwhisky.com; tours adult/child £10/free; ⏲10am-5pm Mar-Oct, 10.30am-4pm Nov-Feb) produces a light, aromatic single malt. The Lochranza area bristles with red deer, who wander insouciantly into the village to crop the grass.

Sleeping & Eating

★ Lochranza Youth Hostel HOSTEL £
(Hostelling Scotland; ☎01770-830631; www.hostellingscotland.org.uk; dm/s/d/q £23.50/30/60/99; ⏲mid-Mar–Oct, plus Sat & Sun year-round; P @ 📶 🐾) 🍃 An excellent hostel in a charming spot with lovely views. Rooms sport chunky wooden furniture, keycards and lockers. Rainwater toilets, energy-saving heating solutions and a wheelchair-accessible room show thoughtful design, while plush lounging areas, a kitchen you could run a restaurant out of, a laundry, a drying room, red deer in the garden and welcoming management combine for a top option.

Butt Lodge B&B ££
(☎01770-830333; www.buttlodge.co.uk; d £90-100, ste £120-135; ⏲Mar–mid-Oct; P 📶) Down a short potholed road, this Victorian hunting lodge has been adapted to offer contemporary comfort with relaxed style and a genuine welcome. Rooms give perspectives over hills, garden and the rustic village golf course, with its red deer greenkeepers. The Castle suite is a fabulous space with views three ways and a mezzanine seating area. Evening meals are available for guests.

Stags Pavilion BISTRO ££
(☎01770-830600; www.stagspavilion.com; mains £12-20; ⏲5.30-8pm Thu-Tue; 🖉) The best restaurant up this end of Arran island, Stags Pavilion is unassumingly set in the former clubhouse of the rustic Lochranza golf course. There's a strong emphasis on

WORTH A TRIP

KING'S CAVE

Arran is one of several islands that claim the cave where Robert the Bruce had his famous arachnid encounter: the story goes that watching a persistent spider finally manage to swing itself to its goal gave him heart to continue the independence struggle. The seaside grotto known as **King's Cave** can be reached from Blackwaterfoot (6 miles) or on a 3-mile circuit from a car park on the road north of town. Take a torch to spot early Christian carvings and typical Pictish symbols within it.

The walk can easily be extended to **Machrie Moor Stone Circle**, erected around 4000 years ago.

Up the road, hit excellent **Cafe Thyme** (☎01770-840227; www.oldbyre.co.uk; Old Byre Visitor Centre, Machrie; dishes £10-14; ⏲10am-5pm, reduced hours winter; 📶 🖉) for a cuppa or, less predictably, great Turkish pizza.

local seafood, and dishes are created with a marked Italian influence. You'll likely see red deer munching the grass nearby. It's almost always booked out; reserve ahead if possible. BYO booze.

ARGYLL

Oban

POP 8600

Oban, the main gateway to many of the Hebridean islands, is a waterfront town on a delightful bay, with sweeping views to Kerrera and Mull. It's peaceful in winter, but in summer the town centre is jammed with traffic and crowded with holidaymakers and travellers headed for the archipelago. But the setting is still lovely, and Oban's brilliant seafood restaurants are marvellous places to be as the sun sets over the bay. There's a real magic to the location.

Sights

Dunollie Castle CASTLE

(01631-570550; www.dunollie.org; Dunollie Rd; adult/child £6/3; 10am-5pm Mon-Sat, noon-5pm Sun Apr-Oct) A pleasant 1-mile stroll north along the coast road leads to Dunollie Castle, built by the MacDougalls of Lorn in the 13th century and unsuccessfully besieged for a year during the 1715 Jacobite rebellion. It's ruined, but ongoing conservation work is offering increasing access. The nearby 1745 House – seat of Clan MacDougall – is an intriguing museum of local and clan history, and there are pleasant wooded grounds and a cafe. Free tours run twice daily.

Oban Distillery DISTILLERY

(01631-572004; www.malts.com; Stafford St; tours £10; noon or 12.30-4.30pm Dec-Feb, 9.30am-5pm Mar-Jun, Oct & Nov, 9.30am-7.30pm Mon-Fri, 9.30am-5pm Sat & Sun Jul-Sep) This handsome distillery has been in operation since 1794. The standard guided tour leaves regularly (worth booking) and includes a dram, a take-home glass and a taste straight from the cask. Specialist tours (£40) run once on Mondays to Fridays in summer. Even without a tour, it's still worth looking at the small exhibition in the foyer.

McCaig's Tower HISTORIC BUILDING

(cnr Laurel & Duncraggan Rds; 24hr) Crowning the hill above town is this Colosseum-like Victorian folly, commissioned in 1890 by local worthy John Stuart McCaig, with the philanthropic intention of providing work for unemployed stonemasons. To reach it on foot, make the steep climb up Jacob's Ladder (a flight of stairs) from Argyll St; the bay views are worth the effort.

Activities

Hire a bike – try **Oban Cycles** (01631-566033; www.obancyclescotland.com; 87 George St; per day/week £28/150; 10am-5pm Tue-Sat Feb-Dec) – for the local bike rides listed in a leaflet at the tourist office, including a 16-mile route to Seil.

Various operators offer boat trips (adult/child £12/5) to spot seals and other marine wildlife, departing from North Pier.

Oban has lots of outdoor shops and is a good place to get kitted out for the Highlands and island outdoors.

★ **Basking Shark Scotland** WILDLIFE

(07975-723140; www.baskingsharkscotland.co.uk; Mar-Oct) Runs boat trips focused on finding and observing basking sharks – the world's second-largest fish – and other notable marine species. The one-day options (July to September) leave from Coll, synchronised with the ferry from Oban, and cost £195. Multiday trips are available. It also offers diving and wildlife-watching. Book shark trips months in advance.

Sea Kayak Oban KAYAKING

(National Kayak School; 01631-565310; www.seakayakoban.com; Argyll St; 10am-5pm Mon-Fri, 9am-5pm Sat, 10am-4pm Sun, winter hours greatly reduced) Sea Kayak Oban has a well-stocked shop, great route advice and sea-kayaking courses, including an all-inclusive two-day intro for beginners (£195 per person). It also has full equipment rental for experienced paddlers – trolley your kayak from the shop to the ferry (kayaks carried free) to visit the islands. Day trips (£80 to £95) leave regularly in season.

Sleeping

Despite having lots of B&B accommodation, Oban can still fill up quickly in July and August, so try to book ahead. Avoid the substandard, tourist-trap B&Bs south of the roundabout on Dunollie Rd. If you can't find a bed in Oban, consider Connel, 4 miles north.

★ **Backpackers Plus** HOSTEL £

(01631-567189; www.backpackersplus.com; Breadalbane St; dm/s/d £21.50/27/54; @) This is a friendly place in an old church with a good vibe and a large and attractive communal lounge with lots of sofas and armchairs. A buffet breakfast is included, plus there's free tea and coffee, a laundry service and powerful showers. Private rooms are available in adjacent buildings: they are a very good deal.

Oban Backpackers HOSTEL £
(☎01631-562107; www.obanbackpackers.com; Breadalbane St; dm £18.50-20.50; @ Wi-Fi) Simple, colourful, relaxed and casual, this hostel has plenty of atmosphere. Dorms are basic, with high ceilings and plenty of space; prices vary according to size. Top bunks are wall-mounted. There's a sociable downstairs lounge with big windows and zebra-patterned couches, plus a sizeable kitchen. Breakfast is available for £3 and a safe is on hand (no lockers).

Oban Youth Hostel HOSTEL £
(Hostelling Scotland; ☎01631-562025; www.hostellingscotland.org.uk; Corran Esplanade; dm/tw/q £25/69/109; P Wi-Fi) Set in a grand Victorian villa on the Esplanade, 0.75 miles north of Oban's train station, this hostel is modernised to a high standard, with comfy wooden bunks, lockers, good showers and a lounge with great views across Oban Bay. All dorms are en suite; the neighbouring lodge has three- and four-bed rooms. Breakfast is available. Dorm rates drop substantially in low season.

★**Elderslie Guest House** B&B ££
(☎01631-570651; www.obanbandb.com; Soroba Rd; s £55, d £78-92; ⊙Apr–mid-Oct; P Wi-Fi) A B&B can be a difficult balancing act: making things modern without losing cosiness, being friendly and approachable without sacrificing privacy. At this spot a mile south of Oban, the balance is absolutely right, with a variety of commodious rooms with big showers, large towels and lovely outlooks over greenery. Breakfast is great, there's outdoor lounging space and the hosts are excellent.

Old Manse Guest House B&B ££
(☎01631-564886; www.obanguesthouse.co.uk; Dalriach Rd; s/d £80/100; ⊙Mar-Oct; P Wi-Fi) Set on the hillside above town, this Oban B&B commands magnificent views over to Kerrera and Mull. It's run with genuine enthusiasm, and the owners are constantly adding thoughtful new features to the bright, cheerful rooms, such as binoculars, DVDs, poetry, corkscrews and tartan hot-water bottles. There are breakfast menus, with special diets catered for.

Kathmore Guest House B&B ££
(☎01631-562104; www.kathmore.co.uk; Soroba Rd; s £68, d £77-98; P Wi-Fi) A 10-minute stroll from Oban's centre, this warmly welcoming place mixes traditional Highland hospitality and hearty breakfasts with a wee touch of boutique flair in its stylish bedspreads and colourful artwork. It's actually two adjacent houses combined. There's a comfortable lounge and outdoor garden deck where you can enjoy a glass of wine on long summer evenings.

Fàilte B&B ££
(☎01631-570219; www.failtebandb.com; Rockfield Rd; s £55, d £90-100; ⊙Feb-Nov; P Wi-Fi) Solicitous host Thomas knows a thing or two about guest comfort, and the thoughtful extras here (power points, disposable razors, real milk in the mini-fridge) make for a very comfortable stay. Rooms are pleasingly contemporary, with a white-and-blond Scandinavian feel and modern showers. The family's quality artworks decorate the building and breakfast features fresh fruit and homemade breads and jams.

Manor House HOTEL £££
(☎01631-562087; www.manorhouseoban.com; Gallanach Rd; r £174-251; P Wi-Fi pets) Built in 1780 for the Duke of Argyll, the old-fashioned Manor House is Oban's finest hotel. It has small but elegant Georgian-style rooms – the majority with lovely sea views – with antiques and period-style wallpaper, plus a classy restaurant serving Scottish/French cuisine (table d'hôte dinner £42). Rates include access to a local gym and golf course. No under-12s.

Eating

Oban Seafood Hut SEAFOOD £
(☎07881-418565; www.facebook.com/obanseafood.hut.9; Railway Pier; mains £3-14; ⊙10am-6pm mid-Mar–Oct) If you want to savour superb Scottish seafood without the expense of an upmarket restaurant, head for Oban's famous seafood stall – it's the green shack on the quayside near the ferry terminal. Here you can buy fresh and cooked seafood to take away, such as excellent prawn sandwiches, dressed crab and fresh oysters, for a pittance.

Ee-Usk SEAFOOD ££
(☎01631-565666; www.eeusk.com; North Pier; mains £14-24; ⊙noon-3pm & 5.45-9.30pm Apr-Oct, noon-2.30pm & 5.45-9pm Nov-Mar; Wi-Fi) Bright and modern Ee-Usk (how you pronounce *iasg*, Gaelic for fish) occupies a prime pier

location. Floor-to-ceiling windows allow diners on two levels to enjoy sweeping views while sampling local sustainable seafood ranging from fragrant fish cakes to langoustines. A bevy of serving staff make it swift and efficient, and they'll try to give you the best view available.

Waterfront Fishouse Restaurant SEAFOOD ££
(☎01631-563110; www.waterfrontfishouse.co.uk; 1 Railway Pier; mains £15-23; ⊙noon-2pm & 5.30-9pm, extended hours Jun-Aug;) Waterfront is housed on the top floor of a converted seamen's mission, and the stylish, unfussy decor, bathed by the summer evening sun, does little to distract from the seafood freshly landed at the quay just a few metres away. The menu ranges from classic haddock and chips to fresh oysters, scallops and langoustines. It's best to book for dinner.

Coast SCOTTISH ££
(☎01631-569900; www.coastoban.co.uk; 104 George St; mains £17-22; ⊙noon-2pm & 5.30-9pm Mon-Sat, 5.30-9pm Sun Feb-late Dec;) With a stylishly casual contemporary interior, this place in a former bank offers well-integrated plates with a focus on local game and seafood. Dishes are presented with flair but don't stray into pretension; the flavours are trusty and quality combinations that work very well.

Drinking & Nightlife

Aulay's Bar PUB
(☎01631-562596; 8 Airds Cres; ⊙11.30am-midnight;) An authentic Scottish pub, Aulay's is cosy and low-ceilinged, its walls covered with old photographs of Oban ferries and other ships. It pulls in a mixed crowd of locals and visitors with its warm atmosphere and wide range of malt whiskies. There are two sides; the left door leads to a quieter lounge bar.

Oban Inn PUB
(☎01631-567441; www.facebook.com/theobaninn; 1 Stafford St; ⊙11am-1am;) It's a pleasure to drop by this 18th-century pub, with its solid walls, flagstone floor and roof beams in the front bar. It has Fyne Ales on tap, making it a prime spot for a waterfront pint, with a good mix of locals, visitors and yachties.

Information

Oban Tourist Office (☎01631-563122; www.oban.org.uk; 3 North Pier; ⊙10am-5pm Mon-Sat, 11am-3pm Sun Nov-Mar, 9am-5.30pm Mon-Sat, 10am-5pm Sun Apr-Oct) A helpful tourist office on the waterfront.

Getting There & Away

AIR

Hebridean Air Services (☎0845 805 7465; www.hebrideanair.co.uk; Oban Airport, North Connel) Flies from North Connel airfield to the islands of Coll, Tiree, Colonsay and Islay.

BUS

Scottish Citylink (☎0871 266 3333; www.citylink.co.uk) has two to five buses connecting Glasgow (£21.80, three hours) with Oban. Most of these travel via Tarbet and Inveraray; in summer, one goes via Crianlarich. Two buses Monday to Saturday head north to Fort William (£9.40, 1½ hours).

TRAIN

ScotRail trains run to Oban from Glasgow (£26.80, three hours, three to six daily). Change at Crianlarich for Fort William.

FERRY

Oban is a major gateway to the Hebrides. The **CalMac Ferry Terminal** (☎01631-562244; www.calmac.co.uk; Railway Pier) is in the centre, close to the train station, with ferries running from here to Mull, Islay, Colonsay, Coll, Tiree, Barra and Lismore.

Mull

POP 2800

From the rugged ridges of Ben More and the black basalt crags of Burg to the blinding white sand, rose-pink granite and emerald waters that fringe the Ross, Mull can lay claim to some of the finest and most varied scenery in the Inner Hebrides. Noble birds of prey soar over mountain and coast, while the western waters provide good whale watching. Add a lovely waterfront 'capital', an impressive castle, the sacred island of Iona and easy access from Oban, and you can see why it's sometimes impossible to find a spare bed on the island.

Activities & Tours

There's some standout walking on Mull, including the popular climb of **Ben More** and the spectacular **Carsaig Arches Walk**. More information on these and other walks can be obtained from information offices in Oban, Craignure and Tobermory (p878).

Mull's varied landscapes and habitats offer the chance to spot some of Scotland's rarest and most dramatic wildlife, including

Mull, Coll & Tiree

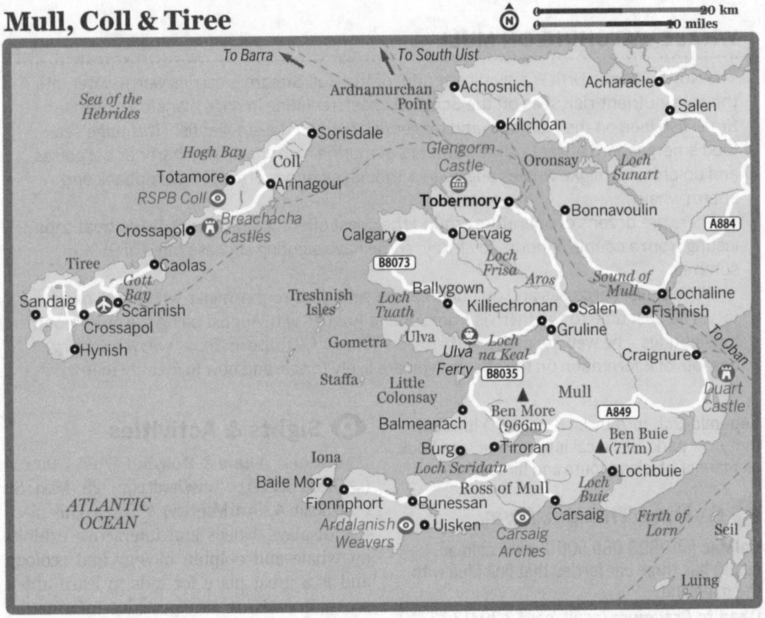

sea eagles, golden eagles, otters, dolphins and whales. Numerous operators offer walking or road trips to see them; email mull@visitscotland.com for a full list.

Mull Eagle Watch BIRDWATCHING
(☎01680-812556; www.mulleaglewatch.com; adult/child £10/5; ⊙Apr-Sep) Britain's largest bird of prey, the white-tailed eagle, or sea eagle, has been successfully reintroduced to Mull, and the island is crowded with birdwatchers raptly observing the raptor. Two-hour tours to observe this bird are held in the mornings and afternoons, and must be booked in advance.

Nature Scotland WILDLIFE
(☎07743 956380; www.naturescotland.com) Enthusiastic, expert guides offer a range of excellent wildlife tours, including afternoon trips that can link to ferries (adult/child £40/30, four hours), evening otter-spotting trips (£50/45, three to four hours), all-day driving/walking trips (£60/50, seven hours) and winter stargazing excursions (£60/50, four hours).

Turus Mara BOATING
(☎01688-400242; www.turusmara.com; ⊙Apr-mid-Oct) Offers trips from Ulva Ferry in central Mull to Staffa and the Treshnish Isles (adult/child £70/35, six hours), with plenty of time ashore on Staffa and Lunga, where you can see seals, puffins, kittiwakes, razorbills and many other species of seabird. There are also trips to Staffa alone (£25/17.50, 3¾ hours) and birdwatching-focused trips (£80/40, eight hours).

Staffa Tours BOATING
(☎07831 885985; www.staffatours.com; ⊙Apr-mid-Oct) Runs boat trips from Fionnphort and Iona to Staffa (adult/child £25/15, 2½ hours), or Staffa plus the Treshnish Isles (also available from Tobermory and Ardnamurchan; £65/35, six hours). Before and after the seabird season, the trip is shorter (£45/25, four hours), not landing on Lunga. There are also connection-plus-tour options leaving from Oban.

ℹ Information

There's a bank with an ATM in Tobermory; otherwise you can get cash back with a purchase from Co-op food stores.

Craignure Tourist Office (☎01680-812377; www.visitscotland.com; Craignure; ⊙9am-5pm Mon, 8.30am-5pm Tue-Sat, 10am-5pm Sun Sep-Jun, 9am-6.15pm Mon, 8.30am-6.15pm Tue-Sat, 10am-4.15pm Sun Jul & Aug) Opposite the ferry slip.

Explore Mull (☎01688-302875; www.isle-of-mull.net; Ledaig; ⊙9am-5pm Easter-Jun &

WHALE WATCHING ON MULL

The North Atlantic Drift – a swirling tendril of the Gulf Stream – carries warm water into the cold, nutrient-rich seas off the Scottish coast, resulting in huge plankton blooms. Small fish feed on the plankton, and bigger fish feed on the smaller fish; this huge seafood smorgasbord attracts large numbers of marine mammals, from harbour porpoises and dolphins to minke whales and even – though sightings are rare – humpback and sperm whales.

There are dozens of operators around the coast offering **whale-watching** boat trips lasting from a couple of hours to all day; some have sighting success rates of 95% in summer.

While seals, porpoises and dolphins can be seen year-round, minke whales are migratory. The best time to see them is from June to August, with August being the peak month for sightings. The website of the **Hebridean Whale & Dolphin Trust** (www.hwdt.org) has lots of information on the species you are likely to see, and how to identify them.

Sep–mid-Oct, to 7pm Jul & Aug;) In Tobermory car park. Has local information, can book all manner of island tours and hires bikes.

Getting There & Away

CalMac (0800 066 5000; www.calmac.co.uk) has three car ferries that link Mull with the mainland:

Oban to Craignure (adult/car £3.70/13.75, 40 minutes, every two hours) The busiest route – bookings are advised if you have a car.

Lochaline to Fishnish (adult/car £2.50/7.35, 15 minutes, at least hourly, except four daily on winter Sundays) On the east coast of Mull.

Tobermory to Kilchoan (adult/car £2.85/8.90, 35 minutes, seven daily Monday to Saturday, five Sunday April to October, three Monday to Saturday November to March) Links to the Ardnamurchan peninsula.

Getting Around

West Coast Motors (01680-812313; www.westcoastmotors.co.uk) connects ferry ports and main villages. Its Discovery Day Pass (adult/child £15/7.50) is available from April to October and grants a day's unlimited bus travel.

The routes useful for visitors are bus 95/495 from Craignure to Tobermory (£12.50 return), bus 96/496 from Craignure to Fionnphort (£17.50 return), and bus 494 from Tobermory to Dervaig and Calgary.

Tobermory

Mull's main town is a very picturesque little fishing and yachting port with brightly painted houses arranged around a sheltered harbour. It's a great base, with good places to eat, inviting pubs and an array of quality accommodation both along the harbourfront and on the hill behind.

Sights & Activities

Hebridean Whale & Dolphin Trust MUSEUM
(01688-302620; www.hwdt.org; 28 Main St; 10.30am-4.30pm Mar-Nov) FREE This place has displays, videos and interactive exhibits on whale and dolphin biology and ecology, and is a great place for kids to learn about sea mammals. It also provides information about volunteering and reporting sightings of whales and dolphins. Opening times are rather variable.

Mull Museum MUSEUM
(01688-301100; www.mullmuseum.org.uk; Main St; 10am-4pm Mon-Sat Easter-Oct) FREE Mull Museum, which records the history of the island, is a good place to go on a rainy day. There are interesting exhibits on crofting, and on the *Tobermory Galleon*, a ship from the Spanish Armada that sank in Tobermory Bay in 1588 and has been the object of treasure seekers ever since. Donations are appreciated in this volunteer-run set-up.

Sea Life Surveys WILDLIFE
(01688-302916; www.sealifesurveys.com; Ledaig; Apr-Oct) Whale-watching trips head from Tobermory harbour to the waters north and west of Mull. The four-hour Wildlife Adventure cruise (adult/child £60/30) is your best chance of seeing a whale. Shorter Ecocruz excursions (adult/child £20/10, 1½ hours) are good for seal-spotting.

Sleeping

Tobermory Youth Hostel HOSTEL £
(Hostelling Scotland; 01688-302481; www.hostellingscotland.org.uk; Main St; dm/tw/q from £18/50/90; Apr-Oct;) This hostel has a great location in a Victorian house right on

the waterfront. It's got an excellent kitchen and spotless if somewhat austere dorms, as well as good triples and quads for families. It books out fast in summer.

★**Sonas House** B&B ££
(☎01688-302304; www.sonashouse.co.uk; Fairways, Erray Rd; s/d £90/130, apt for 2 excl/incl breakfast £100/130; P) Here's a treat: a B&B with a heated, indoor 10m swimming pool! Sonas is a large, modern house (follow signs to the golf course) offering luxury in a beautiful setting with superb Tobermory Bay views. Both rooms are beautifully done out with blond wood and other colours; 'Blue Poppy' has its own balcony. There's also a self-contained studio apartment. Hospitality is faultless.

★**Highland Cottage** BOUTIQUE HOTEL £££
(☎01688-302030; www.highlandcottage.co.uk; Breadalbane St; d £175-190; ⏱Apr–mid-Oct; P) Antique furniture, four-poster beds, embroidered bedspreads, fresh flowers and candlelight lend this small hotel (with only six rooms) an appealingly old-fashioned cottage atmosphere, but with all mod cons, including full-size baths and room service. There's also an excellent restaurant (dinner £49.50), and the personable owners are experts in guest comfort.

Eating & Drinking

Fish & Chip Van FISH & CHIPS £
(☎01688-301109; www.tobermoryfishandchipvan.co.uk; Main St; fish & chips £6-10; ⏱12.30-9pm Mon-Sat Apr & May, 12.30-9pm daily Jun-Sep, 12.30-7pm Mon-Thu, to 8pm Fri & Sat Oct-Mar) If it's takeaway you're after, you can tuck into some of Scotland's best gourmet fish and chips down on the Tobermory waterfront. And where else will you find a chip van selling freshly cooked scallops?

★**Café Fish** SEAFOOD ££
(☎01688-301253; www.thecafefish.com; The Pier; mains £12-26; ⏱noon-3pm & 5.30-11pm mid-Mar–Oct;) Seafood doesn't come much fresher than the stuff served at this warm and welcoming little restaurant overlooking Tobermory harbour. Crustaceans go straight from boat to kitchen to join rich seafood stew, fat scallops, fish pie and catch-of-the-day on the daily-changing menu, where confident use of Asian ingredients adds an extra dimension. Book ahead.

Hebridean Lodge SCOTTISH ££
(☎01688-301207; www.hebrideanlodge.co.uk; Salen Rd, Baliscate; mains £17-22; ⏱6.30-8.30pm Wed-Fri Easter-Dec) Above a gallery and shop, this mezzanine restaurant offers delicious local produce at chunky wooden tables. There's a warm welcome and fine, fresh seafood and lamb, with daily specials complementing the short menu of generous-spirited Scottish cuisine. Book ahead.

★**Mishnish Hotel** PUB
(☎01688-302500; www.themishnish.co.uk; Main St; ⏱11am-1am;) 'The Mish', near the pier on the harbourfront, is a favourite hang-out for visiting yachties and a great place for a pint, with a very convivial atmosphere. Wood-panelled and flag-draped, this is a good old traditional pub where you can listen to live folk music, toast your toes by the open fire or challenge locals to a game of pool.

There are also pub meals and good local seafood available, plus (in summer) Italian upstairs.

North Mull

The road from Tobermory west to Calgary cuts inland, leaving most of Mull's north coast wild and inaccessible. It continues through the settlement of Dervaig to the glorious beach at Calgary. From here onwards you are treated to spectacular coastal views; it's worth doing the route in reverse from Gruline for the best vistas.

Sights

Glengorm Castle GALLERY, PARK
(☎01688-302321; www.glengormcastle.co.uk; Glengorm; ⏱buildings 10am-5pm Easter-Oct) FREE A long, single-track road leads north for 4 miles from Tobermory to majestic Glengorm Castle, with views across the sea to Ardnamurchan, Rum and the Outer Hebrides. The castle outbuildings house a **nature centre** and the excellent **Glengorm Coffee Shop** (light meals £5-10; ⏱10am-5pm Easter-Oct;). The castle, which also has upmarket **B&B acccommodation** (r £160-300; P), is not open to the public, but you're free to explore the beautiful grounds, where several good walks are signposted. Guided nature walks also run from here; check the website for times.

Calgary Beach BEACH
Mull's best (and busiest) silver-sand beach, flanked by cliffs and with views out to Coll

WORTH A TRIP

DUART CASTLE

The ancestral seat of the Maclean clan enjoys a spectacular position on a rocky outcrop overlooking the Sound of Mull. **Duart Castle** (☎01680-812309; www.duartcastle.com; adult/child £8/4; ⏲10.30am-5pm daily May–mid-Oct, 11am-4pm Sun-Thu Apr) was originally built in the 13th century, it was abandoned for 160 years before a 1912 restoration. As well as dungeons, courtyard and battlements with memorable views, there's lots of clan history – none worse than the story of Lachlan Cattanach, who took his wife on an outing to an island in the strait, then left her there to drown when the tide came in.

A bus to the castle meets some of the incoming ferries at Craignure (£13 return including castle entrance), but it's a pretty walk to get here, too.

and Tiree, is about 12 miles west of Tobermory. And yes – this is the place from which Canada's more famous Calgary takes its name.

Calgary Art in Nature GALLERY
(☎01688-400256; www.calgary.co.uk; Calgary; entry by donation; ⏲10am-5pm Mar-Nov) Run with enthusiasm and vision, this place just back from Calgary beach is an excellent art space, and also has great self-catering accommodation. On-site silversmiths and wood sculptors ply their trade in their workshops, while a luminous gallery exhibits high-quality work from local artists. Other pieces dot the woodland ramble on the hill behind. There's also the good **Calgary Farmhouse Tearoom** (light meals £5-9; ⏲10am-5pm Easter-Oct, to 2pm Mon-Fri Nov-Mar; 📶✍) here.

Sleeping

Dervaig Bunkrooms HOSTEL £
(☎07435 656420; www.dervaigbunkrooms.co.uk; Dervaig; dm/q £23/70; ⏲Apr-Oct; P📶) Comfortable bunkhouse accommodation in Dervaig's village hall, with a self-catering kitchen and sitting room. The dorms have good en-suite bathrooms and comfortable bunks.

★ **Calgary Farmhouse** COTTAGE ££
(☎01688-400256; www.calgary.co.uk; Calgary; per week summer apt & cottages £675-1900, per 3 days studios & cabin £180-250; P📶🐾) This brilliant complex near Calgary beach offers a number of fantastic apartments, cottages and houses, beautifully designed and fitted out with timber furniture and wood-burning stoves. The Hayloft is spectacular, with noble oak and local art, while the wood-clad long-hall-like Beach House has luxury and dreamy views. Romantic Kittiwake, a beautiful wooden camping cabin among trees, has bay views and a boat ceiling.

South Mull

The road from Craignure to Fionnphort climbs through wild and desolate scenery before reaching the southwestern part of the island, which consists of a long peninsula called the **Ross of Mull**. The Ross has a spectacular south coast lined with black basalt cliffs that give way further west to white-sand beaches and pink granite crags. The cliffs are highest at Malcolm's Point, near the superb **Carsaig Arches**.

The village of **Bunessan** is home to a cottage museum; a minor road leads south from here to the beautiful white-sand bay of **Uisken**, with views of the Paps of Jura.

At the western end of the Ross, 35 miles from Craignure, is **Fionnphort** (*finn-a-fort*) and the Iona ferry. The coast here is a beautiful blend of pink granite rocks, white sandy beaches and vivid turquoise sea.

Sights

Ardalanish Weavers WORKSHOP
(☎01681-700265; www.ardalanish.com; ⏲10am-5pm Mon-Sat Easter–mid-Oct, 10am-4pm Mon-Fri mid-Oct–Easter) Fleeces from the Hebridean sheep on this farm are woven into fine woollen products using venerable looms, which you can see at work in the old cowshed. Hot drinks and snacks are available at the shop, which sells weaving and farm produce. You can also feed the Highland cattle here. It's on a remote rural back road 2 miles south of Bunessan.

Sleeping

★ **Seaview** B&B ££
(☎01681-700235; www.iona-bed-breakfast-mull.com; Fionnphort; s £65, d £90-110; ⏲mid-Mar–Oct; P📶🐾) Just up from the ferry, Seaview has beautifully decorated bedrooms and a breakfast conservatory with grand views across to Iona. The rooms are compact and charming, with gleaming modern bathrooms. The owners are incredibly helpful and also offer tasty three-course dinners (outside of sum-

mer), often based around local seafood, while breakfasts include locally sourced produce.

Achaban House B&B ££
(☎01681-700205; www.achabanhouse.co.uk; Fionnphort; s/d £49/79; P 📶) This super refurbished rural house has very pleasing contemporary rooms with modern fabrics and a light, uncluttered feel. Some rooms look over the loch below. It's casual and friendly, and the ideal base for visiting Iona with the ferry less than a mile away. Guests have use of an excellent kitchen and a lounge with woodburning stove. Continental breakfasts feature homemade bread.

It's also available as a whole hire. On the same property the owners run an excellent exclusive-use bunkhouse, great value for families and groups. See www.rossofmullbunkrooms.co.uk.

Eating

Creel Seafood Bar SEAFOOD £
(☎07864 605682; Fionnphort; light meals £4-8; ⏰8.30am-7pm Apr-Oct) There's no better way to wait for the Iona ferry than to munch on a crab sandwich or langoustine cocktail from this little seafood shack by the boat ramp. Run by a fishing family, it's got tasty, simply cooked crustaceans and a daily fish special at a sharp price. The seafood platter is a bargain.

★ **Ninth Wave** SCOTTISH £££
(☎01681-700757; www.ninthwaverestaurant.co.uk; Bruach Mhor, Fionnphort; 3-/4-/5-course dinner £50/58/70; ⏰sittings 7-7.30pm Wed-Sun May-Oct) This excellent croft restaurant is owned and operated by a Canadian chef and her lobster fisherman husband. The daily menu makes use of locally landed shellfish and crustaceans, vegetables and salad grown in the garden, and quality meats with a nose-to-tail ethos. It's all served in a stylishly converted bothy. Advance bookings (a couple of weeks at least) are essential. No under-12s.

Iona

POP 200

Like an emerald teardrop off Mull's western shore, enchanting, idyllic Iona, holy island and burial ground of kings, is a magical place that lives up to its lofty reputation. From the moment you embark on the ferry towards its sandy shores and green fields, you'll notice something different about it. To appreciate its charms, spend the night: there are some excellent places to stay. Iona has declared itself a fair-trade island and actively promotes ecotourism.

St Columba sailed from Ireland and landed on Iona in 563, establishing a monastic community with the aim of christianising Scotland. It was here that the *Book of Kells* – the prize attraction of Dublin's Trinity College – is believed to have been transcribed.

Sights & Activities

Past the abbey, look for a footpath on the left signposted **Dun I** (dun-ee). An easy 15-minute walk leads to Iona's highest point, with fantastic 360-degree views, with the hills of Rum and Jura prominent on clear days.

★ **Iona Abbey** HISTORIC BUILDING
(☎01681-700512; www.historicenvironment.scot; adult/child £9/5.40; ⏰9.30am-5.30pm Apr-Sep, 10am-4pm Oct-Mar) Iona's ancient but heavily reconstructed abbey is the spiritual heart of the island. The spectacular **nave**, dominated by Romanesque and early Gothic vaults and columns, is a powerful space; a door on the left leads to the beautiful **cloister**, where medieval grave slabs sit alongside modern religious sculptures. Out the back, the **museum** displays fabulous carved high crosses and other inscribed stones, along with lots of background information. A replica of the intricately carved St John's Cross stands outside the abbey.

Staffa Trips BOATING
(☎01681-700755; www.staffatrips.co.uk; ⏰Apr-mid-Oct) Runs three-hour boat trips to Staffa (adult/child £35/17.50) on the MV *Iolaire*, departing Iona pier at 9.45am and 1.45pm, and from Fionnphort at 10am and 2pm, with one hour ashore on Staffa.

Alternative Boat Hire BOATING
(☎01681-700537; www.boattripsiona.com; ⏰Mon-Thu Apr–mid-Oct) Offers cruises in a traditional wooden sailing boat for fishing, birdwatching, picnicking or just admiring the scenery. Three-hour afternoon trips cost £35/15 per adult/child; on Wednesday there's a full-day cruise (£50/20). Bookings are essential.

Sleeping & Eating

There are B&B options, camping, a hostel and a pair of hotels on the island. It's imperative to book accommodation well ahead in spring and summer. Very little is open in winter apart from the hostel.

★Iona Hostel HOSTEL £

(☎01681-700781; www.ionahostel.co.uk; dm £22, snug or bothy s/d £75/90; P 📶) 🍃 This working ecological croft and environmentally sensitive hostel is one of Scotland's most rewarding and tranquil places to stay. Black Hebridean sheep surround the building, which features pretty, practical and comfy dorms and an excellent kitchen-lounge. There's a fabulous beach nearby, and a hill to climb for views. It's just over a mile from the ferry on Iona, past the abbey.

★Argyll Hotel HOTEL ££

(☎01681-700334; www.argyllhoteliona.co.uk; s £80, d £100-118; ⊙mid-Mar–mid-Oct; 📶🐾) 🍃 This lovable, higgledy-piggledy warren of a hotel has great service and appealing snug rooms (those with sea views cost more – £176 for a double), including good-value family options. The rooms offers simple comfort and relaxation rather than luxury. Most look out to the rear, where a huge organic garden supplies the restaurant. This is a relaxing and amiably run Iona haven.

St Columba Hotel HOTEL ££

(☎01681-700304; www.stcolumba-hotel.co.uk; s £70, d £118-197; ⊙Mar-Oct; 📶) Near the abbey, cosy modernised rooms offer plenty of comfort at this peaceful place, with a good guest lounge adding to the appeal of the sun-dappled restaurant and beer garden that offer sweeping views over fields and down to the water.

Getting There & Away

The ferry from Fionnphort to Iona (£3.50 adult return, five minutes, hourly) runs daily. Cars can only be taken with a permit. There are also various day trips available to Iona from Tobermory and Oban.

Inveraray

POP 600

This historic planned village is all black and white – even logos of high-street chain shops conform. Spectacularly set on the shores of Loch Fyne, Inveraray was built by the Duke of Argyll in Georgian style when he revamped his nearby castle in the 18th century.

Sights

Inveraray Castle CASTLE

(☎01499-302203; www.inveraray-castle.com; adult/child/family £12.50/8/35; ⊙10am-5.45pm Apr-Oct) This visually stunning castle on the north side of town has been the seat of the Dukes of Argyll – chiefs of Clan Campbell – since the 15th century. The 18th-century building, with its fairy-tale turrets and fake battlements, houses an impressive armoury hall, its walls patterned with more than 1000 pole arms, dirks, muskets and Lochaber axes. Entry is slightly cheaper if you book online.

Inveraray Jail MUSEUM

(☎01499-302381; www.inverarayjail.co.uk; Church Sq; adult/child £11.50/6.95; ⊙10am-5pm; 👪) At this entertaining interactive tourist attraction you can sit in on a trial, try out a cell and discover the harsh tortures that were meted out to unfortunate prisoners. The attention to detail – including a life-sized model of an inmate squatting on a 19th-century toilet – is excellent, and actors enliven things during busy periods. Last admission is an hour before closing.

Sleeping & Eating

★George Hotel INN ££

(☎01499-302111; www.thegeorgehotel.co.uk; Main St E; d £100-145; P 📶🐾) The George boasts a magnificent choice of opulent, individual rooms decorated with sumptuous period furniture. Some feature four-poster beds, Victorian roll-top baths and/or private Jacuzzis (superior rooms and suites cost £165 to £225 per double; the library suite is quite a sight). Some rooms are in an annexe opposite and there are also self-catering options.

★Loch Fyne Oyster Bar SEAFOOD ££

(☎01499-600482; www.lochfyne.com; Clachan, Cairndow; mains £15-26; ⊙9am-7pm Mon-Sat, 10am-7pm Sun, to 5pm Nov-Mar, restaurant noon-5pm or 6pm; 📶) 🍃 The success of this cooperative is such that it now lends its name to dozens of restaurants throughout the UK. But the original is still the best, with large, salty, creamy oysters straight out of the lake, and fabulous salmon dishes. The atmosphere and decor is simple, friendly and unpretentious; it also has a shop and deli where you can eat casually.

Samphire SEAFOOD ££

(☎01499-302321; www.samphireseafood.com; 6a Arkland; dinner mains £14-23; ⊙noon-2.30pm & 5-8.45pm Wed-Sun; 📶) 🍃 There's lots to like about this compact restaurant that makes an effort to source sustainable local seafood. It does a delicious seafood stew and you can expect to see lobster, oysters and langoustines from the loch regularly featuring as specials.

Getting There & Away

Scottish Citylink (p876) has buses running from Glasgow to Inveraray (£13.90, 1¾ hours, up to nine daily). Some continue to Campbeltown (£15.10, 2¼ hours), others to Oban (£11.50, 1¼ hours). There are also buses to Dunoon (£4.60, 1¼ hours, three daily Monday to Saturday).

Kilmartin Glen

This magical glen is the focus of one of the biggest concentrations of prehistoric sites in Scotland. Burial cairns, standing stones, stone circles, hill forts and cup-and-ring-marked rocks litter the countryside. Within a 6-mile radius of Kilmartin village there are 25 sites with standing stones and more than 100 rock carvings.

In the 6th century, Irish settlers arrived in this part of Argyll and founded the kingdom of Dál Riata (Dalriada), which eventually united with the Picts in 843 to create the first Scottish kingdom. Their capital was the hill fort of Dunadd, on the plain to the south of Kilmartin.

Sights

Kilmartin House Museum MUSEUM
(01546-510278; www.kilmartin.org; Kilmartin) This museum, in Kilmartin village, is a fascinating interpretive centre that provides a context for the ancient monuments you can go on to explore, alongside displays of artefacts recovered from various sites. A major redevelopment of the museum is underway, and it's due to reopen in 2023. Meanwhile, it's still the best place to head for first, as an outdoors display gives information about all the sites to visit in the surrounding valley. There's a takeaway cafe too.

Dunadd Fort ARCHAEOLOGICAL SITE
(24hr) FREE This atmospheric hill fort, 3.5 miles south of Kilmartin village, was the seat of power of the first kings of Dál Riata, and may have been where the Stone of Destiny was originally located. Atop the hill, a footprint, faint rock carvings of a boar and an ogham inscription may have been used in inauguration ceremonies. The prominent little hill rises straight out of the boggy plain of Moine Mhor Nature Reserve.

Getting There & Away

Bus 423 between Oban and Ardrishaig (three to five Monday to Friday, two on Saturday) stops at Kilmartin (from Oban £6.60, 1¼ hours).

You can walk or cycle along the **Crinan Canal** from Ardrishaig, then turn north at Bellanoch on the minor B8025 road to reach Kilmartin (12 miles one way). It's a lovely journey.

Kintyre

The 40-mile-long Kintyre peninsula is almost an island, with only a narrow isthmus at Tarbert connecting it to Knapdale. During the Norse occupation of the Western Isles, the Scottish king decreed that the Vikings could claim as their own any island they circumnavigated in a longship. So in 1098 the wily Magnus Barefoot stood at the helm while his men dragged their boat across this neck of land, validating his claim to Kintyre.

The coastline is spectacular on both sides, with stirring views of Arran, Islay, Jura and Northern Ireland. On a sunny day the water shimmers beyond the stony shore. Hiking the Kintyre Way is a great means of experiencing the peninsula, which has a couple of cracking golf courses at Machrihanish near Campbeltown.

Getting There & Away

Scottish Citylink (p876) has buses running along the whole length of the peninsula from Glasgow. Campbeltown is also connected by ferry to Ardrossan, Ayrshire in summer. Local buses are run by West Coast Motors (www.westcoastmotors.co.uk).

Tarbert

POP 1100

The attractive fishing village and yachting centre of Tarbert is the gateway to Kintyre, and is most scenic, with buildings strung around its excellent natural harbour. This crossroads for nearby ferry routes is a handy stepping stone to Arran or Islay, but is well worth a stopover on any itinerary.

The picturesque harbour is overlooked by the crumbling, ivy-covered ruins of **Tarbert Castle** (24hr) FREE, rebuilt by Robert the Bruce in the 14th century. You can hike up via a signposted footpath beside **Loch Fyne Gallery** (01880-820390; www.facebook.com/LochFyneGallery; Harbour St; 10am-5pm Mon-Sat, 11am-4pm Sun), which showcases the work of local artists.

Sleeping & Eating

★**Knap Guest House** B&B ££
(01880-820015; www.knapguesthouse.co.uk; Campbeltown Rd; d £90-99;) This cosy upstairs

WORTH A TRIP

MULL OF KINTYRE

A narrow winding road, 15 miles long, leads south from Campbeltown to the **Mull of Kintyre**, passing good sandy beaches near Southend. This remote headland was immortalised in the famous song by Paul McCartney and Wings; the former Beatle owns a farmhouse in the area. From the road's end, a 30-minute steep downhill walk leads to a clifftop lighthouse, with Northern Ireland, only 12 miles away, visible across the channel. Don't leave the road when the frequent mists roll in; it's easy to become disoriented.

spot at the bend in the main road offers faultless hospitality, luxurious furnishings and an attractive blend of Scottish and Far Eastern decor, with wooden elephants especially prominent. The welcome is warm, and there are great harbour views from the breakfast room, where the open kitchen allows you to admire the host at work. Prices drop in low season.

Rooms are plush, with the owner's years in hospitality paying dividends for guests. One is a suite (£135 to £180), which has an excellent, spacious lounge area with vistas.

Moorings B&B ££

(☎01880-820756; www.themooringsbb.co.uk; Pier Rd; s £50-60, d £80-100; P Wi-Fi) Follow the harbour just past Tarbert's centre to this spot, which is beautifully maintained and decorated by one man and his dogs. It has great views over the water, an eclectic menagerie of ceramic and wooden animals plus offbeat artwork; you can't miss it from the street.

★Starfish SEAFOOD ££

(☎01880-820733; www.starfishtarbert.com; Castle St; mains £14-21; ⏰5-8.30pm Tue-Thu, 12.30-2pm & 5-8.30pm Fri & Sat Mar-Oct; Wi-Fi) This attractive, very welcoming restaurant does simple, stylish seafood of brilliant quality. A great variety of specials – anything from classic French fish dishes to Thai curries – are prepared with whatever's fresh off the Tarbert boats that day. There are options for vegetarians and meat eaters, too, and decent cocktails. Closed Sunday and Monday early and late in the season.

Getting There & Away

Tarbert is served by four to five daily coaches with Scottish Citylink (p876), between Campbeltown (£9, one hour) and Glasgow (£18.80, 3¼ hours).

CalMac (☎0800 066 5000; www.calmac.co.uk) operates a car ferry from Tarbert to Portavadie on the Cowal Peninsula (adult/car £2.80/8.65, 25 minutes, six to 12 daily). From late October to March there are also ferries to Lochranza on Arran (adult/car £3/9.95, 1¼ hours, one daily) that must be booked in advance. In summer this leaves from Claonaig near Skipness, 13 miles south.

Ferries to Islay and Colonsay depart from Kennacraig ferry terminal, 5 miles southwest.

Campbeltown

POP 4800

Blue-collar Campbeltown is set around a beautiful harbour. It still suffers from the decline of its fishing and whisky industries and the closure of the nearby air-force base, but is rebounding on the back of golf tourism, increased distillery action and a ferry link to Ayrshire. The spruced-up seafront backed by green hills lends the town a distinctly optimistic air.

Sights & Activities

Springbank DISTILLERY

(☎01586-555468; www.springbank.scot; 85 Longrow; tours from £10; ⏰tours Mon-Sat) There were once no fewer than 32 distilleries around Campbeltown, but most closed in the 1920s. Today this is one of only three still in operation. It is also one of the few around that distills, matures and bottles all its whisky on the one site, making for an interesting tour. It produces a quality malt, one of Scotland's finest. Various premium tours take you deeper into the process.

Davaar Cave CAVE

(⏰24hr) FREE A very unusual sight awaits in this cave on the southern side of Davaar island, at the mouth of Campbeltown Loch. On the wall of the cave is an eerie painting of the Crucifixion by local artist Archibald MacKinnon, dating from 1887. You can walk to the island at low tide: check tide times with the tourist office.

Sleeping & Eating

★Campbeltown Backpackers HOSTEL £

(☎01586-551188; www.campbeltownbackpackers.co.uk; Big Kiln St; dm £22; P Wi-Fi) This beautiful hostel occupies a central former school building: it's great, with a modern kitchen, state-of-the-art wooden bunks and access for people with disabilities. Profits go to maintain the Heritage Centre (opposite) that runs it. Rates are £2 cheaper if you book ahead.

Argyll Hotel INN ££
(01583-421212; www.argyllhotelkintyre.co.uk; A83, Bellochantuy; s £65, d £85-100; P) Right on a fine stretch of beach with a magnificent outlook to Islay and Jura, this traditional inn 10 miles north of Campbeltown on the main road is run with cheery panache. Rooms are cosy and breakfast is a highlight, with creative egg dishes and a wealth of homemade jams, as you gaze over the water.

Drinking

Ardshiel Hotel BAR
(01586-552133; www.ardshiel.co.uk; Kilkerran Rd; noon-11pm Mon-Sat, from 12.30pm Sun;) This friendly hotel has one of Scotland's best whisky bars, the perfect place to learn more about the Campbeltown distilling tradition and to taste the local malts. With over 700 whiskies to choose from, it's not a place for the indecisive.

Getting There & Away

AIR

Loganair (www.loganair.co.uk) flies between Glasgow and Campbeltown's mighty runway at Machrihanish. Depending on the season, there may be other summer connections possible to Islay and Tiree.

BOAT

Kintyre Express (01586-555895; www.kintyreexpress.com; Apr-Sep) operates a small, high-speed passenger ferry from Campbeltown to Ballycastle in Northern Ireland (£50/90 one way/return, 1½ hours, daily May to August, Friday to Sunday April and September). You must book in advance. You can also get to Islay, and charters are available.

CalMac (p871) runs thrice weekly May to September between Ardrossan in Ayrshire and Campbeltown (adult/car £8.30/44.05, 2¾ hours); the Saturday return service stops at Brodick on Arran.

BUS

Scottish Citylink (p876) runs from Campbeltown to Glasgow (£22.90, 4¼ hours, four to five daily) via Tarbert, Inveraray and Loch Lomond. Change at Inveraray for Oban.

Islay

POP 3200

The home of some of the world's greatest and peatiest whiskies, whose names reverberate on the tongue like a pantheon of Celtic deities, Islay (*eye*-lah) is a wonderfully friendly place whose welcoming inhabitants offset its lack of scenic splendour compared to Mull or Skye. The distilleries are well geared up for visits, but even if you're not a fan of single malt, the birdlife, fine seafood, turquoise bays and basking seals are ample reasons to visit. Locals are among Britain's most genial: a wave or cheerio to passers-by is mandatory, and you'll soon find yourself unwinding to relaxing island pace. The only drawback is that the waves of well-heeled whisky tourists have induced many sleeping options to raise prices to eye-watering levels.

The island hosts **Fèis Ìle** (Islay Festival; www.islayfestival.com; late May), a week-long celebration of traditional Scottish music and whisky. Events include *ceilidhs* (evenings of traditional Scottish entertainment), pipe-band performances, distillery tours, barbecues and whisky tastings. The island packs out; book accommodation well in advance.

Getting There & Away

There are two ferry terminals: Port Askaig on the east coast, and Port Ellen in the south. Islay airport lies midway between Port Ellen and Bowmore.

AIR

Loganair (www.loganair.co.uk) flies up to three times daily from Glasgow to Islay, sometimes via Campbeltown, while Hebridean Air Services (p876) operates twice daily on Thursday from Oban to Colonsay and Islay.

BOAT

CalMac (p871) runs ferries from Kennacraig to Port Ellen or Port Askaig (adult/car £6.90/34.30, two hours, three to five daily). On Wednesday and Saturday in summer you can usually travel to Colonsay (adult/car £4.25/17.75, 1¼ hours, day trip possible) and Oban (adult/car £10.05/54.30, four hours).

Book car space on ferries several days in advance.

Getting Around

A bus links Ardbeg, Port Ellen, Bowmore, Port Charlotte, Portnahaven and Port Askaig (Monday to Saturday only). You can get unlimited travel for 24 hours for £10, but fares are low anyway. Pick up a copy of the *Islay & Jura Public*

Islay, Jura & Colonsay

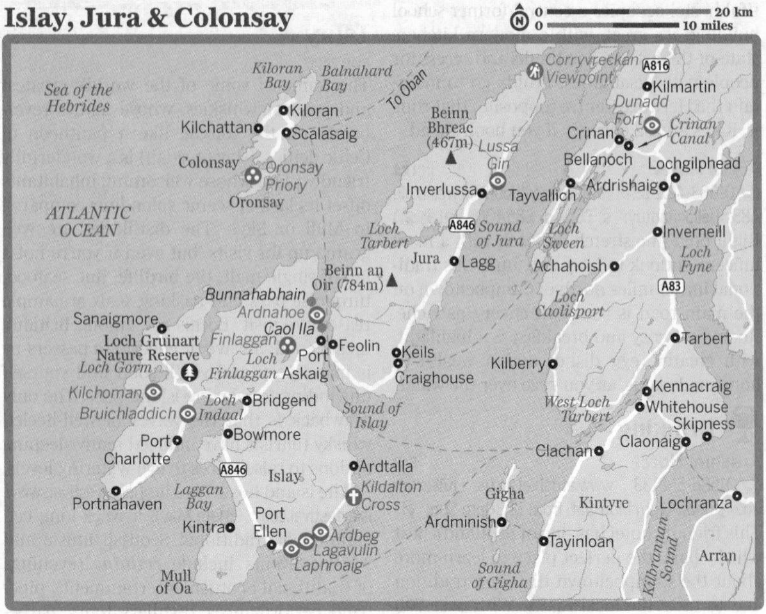

Transport Guide from the Bowmore tourist office or on the ferry on the way over.

There are various places to hire bikes, including **Islay Cycles** (☎07760 196592; www.islaycycles.co.uk; 2 Corrsgeir Pl, Port Ellen; bikes per day/week from £20/70) and **Port Charlotte Bicycle Hire** (☎01496-850488; Main St, Port Charlotte; bike hire 1/3 days £15/35; ⏲9am-6pm).

There are also taxi services on Islay; **Carol's Cabs** (☎07775 782155, 01496-302155; www.carols-cabs.co.uk) is one that can take bikes.

Port Ellen & Around

Port Ellen is Islay's principal entry point. The coast stretching northeast is one of the loveliest parts of the island, where within 3 miles you'll find three of whisky's biggest names: Laphroaig, Lagavulin and Ardbeg.

The kelp-fringed skerries (small rocky islands or reefs) of the **Ardmore Islands**, near Kildalton, are a wildlife haven and home to Europe's second-largest colony of common seals.

Sights

Ardbeg DISTILLERY
(☎01496-302244; www.ardbeg.com; tours from £8; ⏲9.30am-5pm Mon-Fri year-round, plus Sat & Sun Apr-Oct) Ardbeg's iconic peaty whiskies start with their magnificent 10-year-old. The basic tour is good, and it also offers longer tours involving walks, stories and extended tastings. It's 3 miles northeast of Port Ellen; there's a good **cafe** (mains £8-13; ⏲10am-4pm Mon-Fri year-round, plus Sat & Sun Apr-Oct; 📶) for lunch here, too.

Lagavulin DISTILLERY
(☎01496-302749; www.lagavulindistillery.com; tours from £15; ⏲9.15am-5pm daily Mar-Sep, 9.45am-5pm Mon-Sat Oct-Dec, 10.15am-4pm Mon-Sat Jan & Feb) Peaty and powerful whisky is made by Lagavulin, one of the triumvirate of southern distilleries near Port Ellen. The Lagavulin Tasting Experience (£15) is a good option, cutting out much of the distillery mechanics that you might have already seen elsewhere and replacing it with an extended tasting. The Warehouse Tour (£35) is also a lot of fun.

Laphroaig DISTILLERY
(☎01496-302418; www.laphroaig.com; tours from £10; ⏲9.45am-5pm daily Mar-Oct, to 4.30pm daily Nov & Dec, to 4.30pm Mon-Fri Jan & Feb) Laphroaig produces famously peaty whiskies just outside Port Ellen. Of the various premium tastings that it offers, the 'Water to Whisky' tour is recommended – you see the water source, dig peat, have a picnic and try plenty of drams.

Sleeping & Eating

Askernish B&B B&B ££
(☎01496-302536; www.askernishbandb.co.uk; 49 Frederick Cres, Port Ellen; s £70, d £90-110; 📶) Very handy for the Port Ellen ferry slip, this dark-stone Victorian house was once the local medical practice; indeed, one of the rooms is in the former surgery, while another is the waiting room. Rooms are generous, with old-style flowery decor but modern bathroom fittings. The owner Joy takes real interest in her guests and is a delight.

★ **SeaSalt** BISTRO ££
(☎01496-300300; www.seasalt-bistro.co.uk; 57 Frederick Cres, Port Ellen; mains £10-16; ⌚noon-2.30pm & 5-8.45pm) This buzzy modern place represents an unusual combination in Port Ellen: a takeaway doing kebabs, pizzas and bacon rolls, but also a classy bistro. High-backed dining chairs are comfortable for devouring delicious local seafood off a menu of daily specials. The owner and staff are very friendly. It also opens from 10am to noon for coffee and breakfasty fare.

Bowmore

Islay's attractive Georgian capital was built in 1768 to replace the village of Kilarrow, which just had to go – it was spoiling the view from the laird's house. Its centrepieces are the **Bowmore Distillery** (☎01496-810441; www.bowmore.com; School St; tours from £10; ⌚9.30am-6pm Mon-Sat, noon-4pm Sun Mar-Oct, 10am-5pm Mon-Sat Nov-Feb) and distinctive **Round Church** at the top of Main St, built in circular form to ensure that the devil had no corners to hide in. He was last seen in one of the island's distilleries.

Sleeping

★ **Lambeth House** B&B ££
(☎01496-810597; www.lambeth-guesthouse.co.uk; Jamieson St; s/d £75/100; 📶) Cheerily welcoming, and with smart modern rooms with top-notch en-suite bathrooms, this is a sound option in the centre of town. The host is a long-time expert in making guests feel at home, and her breakfasts are reliably good. Rooms vary substantially in size but their prices are the same, so ask for a larger one when booking.

Dha Urlar B&B ££
(☎07967 505991; www.dha-urlar-bed-and-breakfast.co.uk; Cruach; r £120-150; P📶) Just a mile out of Bowmore, this place sits in an elevated position granting spectacular perspectives across moorland to Jura, the Mull of Kintyre and the coast of Ireland. Rooms have lots of space, comfortable beds and modern bathrooms. Breakfast is served from an open kitchen while your hosts helpfully supply you with lots of local information.

Bowmore House B&B £££
(☎01496-810324; www.thebowmorehouse.co.uk; Shore St; s/d from £90/140; P📶) This stately former bank building has plenty of character and super water views. It's a top-level B&B, with coffee machines in the rooms, an honesty minibar with bottles of wine and local ales, and plush king-sized beds. Rooms are spacious, high-ceilinged and light. Further rooms are in adjacent cottages, also available on a self-catering basis.

Harbour Inn BOUTIQUE HOTEL £££
(☎01496-810330; www.bowmore.com/harbour-inn; The Square; s/d from £120/145; 📶) The plush seven-room Harbour Inn, owned by Bowmore Distillery, offers friendly service, a good restaurant, a snug bar and prime location a few steps from the water in Islay's capital. The chambers are well appointed with modern comforts, quality amenities – including whisky soaps and gels – and plush fabrics, though some are on the small side for the price.

Eating & Drinking

Harbour Inn BRITISH ££
(☎01496-810330; www.bowmore.com; The Square; mains £15-24; ⌚noon-2.30pm & 6-9.30pm; 📶) Owned by the Bowmore Distillery, this restaurant at the Harbour Inn is the classiest in town. The conservatory-style dining area offers wonderful sunset views over the water. Islay oysters are a delicious and obvious choice; the rest of the menu could benefit from a little more seasonal and local focus, but is competently prepared and presented.

Peatzeria PIZZA ££
(☎01496-810810; www.peatzeria.com; 22 Shore St; pizzas £9-20; ⌚noon-10pm, closed Mon in winter; 📶) This is one of those names that just had to be. Nice work, punsters! An impressively realised church conversion has created a warmly welcoming Italian restaurant that specialises in toothsome stone-baked pizzas with innovative toppings that include local seafood. The weatherproof conservatory seating area has special views over the bay.

Lochside Hotel PUB
(01496-810244; www.lochsidehotel.co.uk; 20 Shore St; 11am-midnight;) One of Islay's key whisky bars, Lochside Hotel has a fine selection of local malts and a good atmosphere, with locals rubbing shoulders with distillery tourists looking for a taste of a hard-to-find dram. It also does decent bar meals.

Information

Bowmore Tourist Office (01496-305165; www.islayinfo.com; The Square; 10am-5pm Mon-Sat, noon-3pm Sun Mar-May, 9.30am-5.30pm Mon-Sat, noon-3pm Sun Jun-Aug, 10am-5pm Mon-Sat Sep & Oct, 10am-3pm Mon-Fri Nov-Feb) One of the nation's best tourist offices. The staff will bend over backwards to find you accommodation if things look full up.

Port Charlotte & Around

On the opposite shore of Loch Indaal 11 miles from Bowmore is attractive Port Charlotte, a former distillery town that appeals as a base. Museums in town and distilleries close by mean there's plenty to do.

The road ends 6 miles southwest of Port Charlotte at **Portnahaven**, a picturesque fishing village. For seal-spotting, you can't do better; there are frequently dozens of the portly beasts basking in the small harbour.

Sights

★Bruichladdich DISTILLERY
(01496-850190; www.bruichladdich.com; Bruichladdich; tours from £7.50; 9am-6pm Mon-Fri, to 5pm Sat, 10am-4pm Sun Apr-Sep, reduced hours Oct-Mar) A couple of miles from Port Charlotte, Bruichladdich (brook-*lad*-dy) is an infectiously fun distillery to visit and produces a mind-boggling range of bottlings; there's always some new experiment cooking. The standard expression is lightly peated, but Bruichladdich turns out some phenolic monsters under the Port Charlotte and Octomore labels. It also makes a gin here, the Botanist, infused with local herbs. A generous attitude to tastings makes for an uplifting visit.

Kilchoman DISTILLERY
(01496-850011; www.kilchomandistillery.com; Rockfield Farm, Kilchoman; tours from £10; 9.45am-5pm Apr-Oct, closed Sat & Sun Nov-Mar) Likable Kilchoman, set on a farm, is one of Scotland's smallest distilleries. It grows and malts some of its own barley here and does its own bottling by hand. It has a wide variety of attractively packaged expressions: the 100% Islay whiskies are the ones produced from the home-grown barley. The tour is informative and the tasting generous. There's also a good cafe.

Museum of Islay Life MUSEUM
(01496-850358; www.islaymuseum.org; Port Charlotte; adult/child £4/1; 10.30am-4.30pm Mon-Fri Apr-Oct) Islay's long history is lovingly recorded in this museum, housed in the former Free Church. Prize exhibits include an illicit still, 19th-century crofters' furniture, and a set of leather boots once worn by the horse that pulled the lawnmower at Islay House (so it wouldn't leave hoof prints on the lawn!).

Sleeping & Eating

Islay Youth Hostel HOSTEL £
(Hostelling Scotland; 01496-850385; www.hostellingscotland.org.uk; Main St, Port Charlotte; dm/tw/q £23.50/52/97; Apr-Oct;) This clean and modern brick hostel has spotless dorms with washbasins and a large kitchen and living room. It's housed in a former distillery building with views over the loch. The bus stops nearby. Breakfast and heatable dinners are available. Have a crack at Islay Monopoly, one of the board games on hand.

Distillery House B&B ££
(01496-850495; mamak@sky.com; Main St, Port Charlotte; s/d £40/84, tw without bathroom £80;) For genuine islander hospitality at a fair price, head to this homely B&B, on the right as you enter Port Charlotte from the north. Set in part of the former Lochindaal distillery, it's run by a kindly local couple who make their own delicious marmalade and oatcakes. Rooms are well kept and most comfortable. The cute single has sea views. Minimum two-night stay.

Port Charlotte Hotel HOTEL £££
(01496-850360; www.portcharlottehotel.co.uk; Main St, Port Charlotte; s/d/f £180/250/300;) This lovely old Victorian hotel has individually decorated bedrooms – modern but classic in style – with crisp white sheets, good toiletries and sea views. It's a friendly place with a plush lounge, cosy bar and quality restaurant.

Jura

POP 200

Jura lies long, dark and low off the coast like a vast Viking longship, its billowing sail the distinctive triple peaks of the Paps of Jura.

A magnificently wild and lonely island, it's the perfect place to get away from it all – as George Orwell did in 1948. Orwell wrote his masterpiece *Nineteen Eighty-Four* while living at the remote farmhouse of Barnhill in the north of the island.

Jura takes its name from the Old Norse *dyr-a* (deer island) – an apt appellation, as the island supports a population of around 6000 red deer, outnumbering their human cohabitants by about 30 to one.

Sights & Activities

Walking Jura is an adventure. There are few proper footpaths, and off-path exploration often involves rough going through giant bracken, knee-deep bogs and thigh-high tussocks. Hill access may be restricted during the deer-stalking season (July to February); the Jura Hotel can provide details. Look out for adders – the island is infested with them, but they're shy snakes and will move away as you approach.

Isle of Jura Distillery DISTILLERY
(☎01496-820385; www.jurawhisky.com; Craighouse; tours from £5; ⏲10am-5pm Mon-Sat Apr-Oct, to 4pm Mon-Fri Nov-Mar) There aren't a whole lot of indoor attractions on the island of Jura apart from a visit to the Isle of Jura Distillery. The standard tour runs twice a day, while specialist tours (£15 to £25) take you deeper into the production process and should be booked in advance.

Sleeping & Eating

Places to stay are very limited, so book ahead. As well as the Jura Hotel, there's a handful of B&Bs and several self-catering cottages let by the week (see www.juradevelopment.co.uk). One of these is remote Barnhill, where Orwell stayed.

You can camp (£10/15 for two/four people) in the field below the Jura Hotel; there's a toilet and shower block that walkers, yachties and cyclists can also use.

Jura Hotel HOTEL ££
(☎01496-820243; www.jurahotel.co.uk; Craighouse; s £70, d £110-150; P 📶) The heart of Jura's community is this hotel, which is warmly welcoming and efficiently run. Rooms vary in size and shape, but all are renovated and inviting. The premier rooms, which have sea views, are just lovely, with understated elegance and polished modern bathrooms. Eat in the restaurant or the convivial pub.

Ardlussa Estate B&B £££
(☎01496-820323; www.ardlussaestate.com; Ardlussa; d £130; P 📶) This grand shooting lodge in Jura's north offers B&B accommodation in three plush rooms with beautiful vistas. Lavish four-course dinners made with estate produce cost £50 per head. There's also a substantial self-catering wing sleeping up to 10 people.

THE PAPS OF JURA

Climbing the **Paps** is a truly tough hill-walk over ankle-breaking scree requiring good fitness and navigational skills. It's 11 hard miles (allow eight hours). The first peak you reach is Beinn a'Chaolais (734m), the second Beinn an Oir (784m), then Beinn Shiantaidh (755m). Most hikers also climb Corra Bheinn (569m), before joining Evans' Walk to return.

The most popular starting place is by the bridge over the River Corran, 3 miles north of Craighouse. If you succeed in bagging all four hills, reflect on the fact that the record for the annual **Isle of Jura Fell Race** is just three hours; and that includes cresting seven hills!

Getting There & Around

A **car ferry** (☎01496-840681; www.argyll-bute.gov.uk) shuttles between Port Askaig on Islay and Feolin on Jura (adult/car/bicycle £2/8.20/free, five minutes, hourly Monday to Saturday, every two hours Sunday). There is no direct car-ferry connection to the mainland.

From April to September, **Jura Passenger Ferry** (☎07768 450000; www.jurapassengerferry.com; one way £20; ⏲Apr-Sep) runs from Tayvallich on the mainland to Craighouse on Jura (one hour, one or two daily except Wednesday). Booking is recommended (you can do this online).

The island's only **bus service** (☎01436-810200; www.garelochheadcoaches.co.uk) runs between the ferry slip at Feolin and Craighouse (20 minutes, six to seven Monday to Saturday), timed to coincide with ferry arrivals and departures. Some of the runs continue north as far as Inverlussa.

AT A GLANCE

POPULATION
approx 500,000

HIGHEST MOUNTAIN
Ben Nevis (1345m)

BEST MOUNTAIN BIKING
Nevis Range (p916)

BEST FINE DINING
Rocpool (p897)

BEST HIGHLAND GAMES
Braemar Gathering (p909)

WHEN TO GO

Apr & May
Mountain scenery is at its most spectacular, with snow lingering on the higher peaks.

Sep
Ideal for hiking: midges are dying off, but weather is still reasonably good.

Nov–Jan
Great skiing in the Cairngorms; Shetland hosts the Up Helly Aa festival.

Ben Nevis (p916)

Inverness & the Highlands & Islands

Scotland's vast and melancholy soul is here, in an epic landscape with stark beauty that imprints the hearts of those who journey through it. Mist, peat, rock, heather...and long summer evenings that compensate for the occasional days of horizontal rain.

The hills and glens of Highland Perthshire offer a memorable first taste. The region's capital, Inverness, is backed by the craggy Cairngorms, which draw hikers and skiers to their slopes. Further north, ancient stones stand testament to prehistoric builders on the magical islands of Orkney and Shetland.

The most epic mountain scenery is in the northwest Highlands, and it continues into Skye, where the Cuillin Hills tower jaggedly in the setting sun. Beyond, on the Atlantic fringe, the Outer Hebrides offer the nation's most beautiful beaches and a glimpse of traditional island life.

INCLUDES

Inverness & the Highlands & Islands Highlights

1 **Harris** (p943) Admiring the most beautiful beaches in the Western Isles.

2 **Glen Affric** (p897) Hiking among the hills, lochs and forests of this wild and enchanting glen.

3 **Skara Brae** (p954) Shaking your head in astonishment at extraordinary prehistoric perfection.

4 **Rothiemurchus Estate** (p905) Wandering through ancient Caledonian forest in the heart of the Cairngorms.

5 **Cape Wrath** (p925) Taking the trip out to Britain's gloriously remote northwestern shoulder.

6 **Knoydart Peninsula** (p919) Venturing into the country's most remote and rugged wilderness.

7 **Plockton** (p932) Relaxing in a postcard-pretty village with local prawns on the menu.

8 **Glen Coe** (p913) Soaking up the moody but magnificent scenery.

9 **Ben Nevis** (p916) Making it to the summit of the UK's highest mountain.

10 **Hermaness National Nature Reserve** (p966) Capering with puffins at Shetland's birdwatching centre.

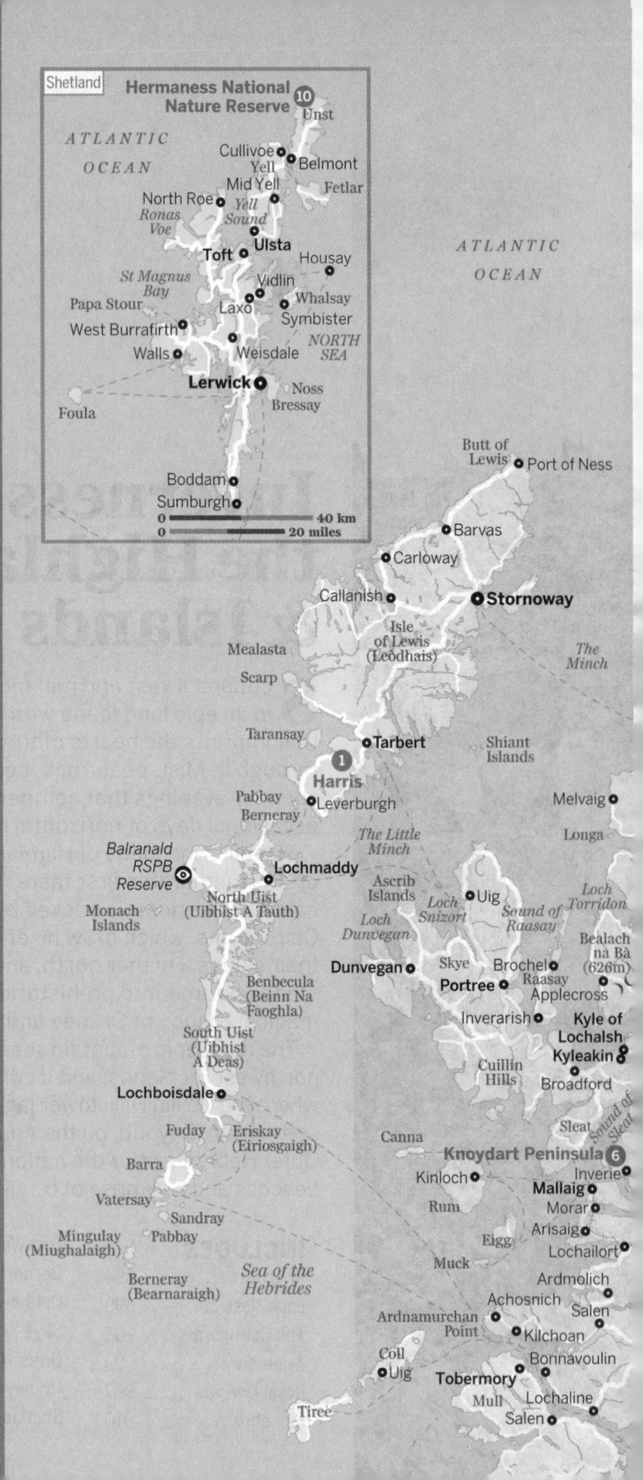

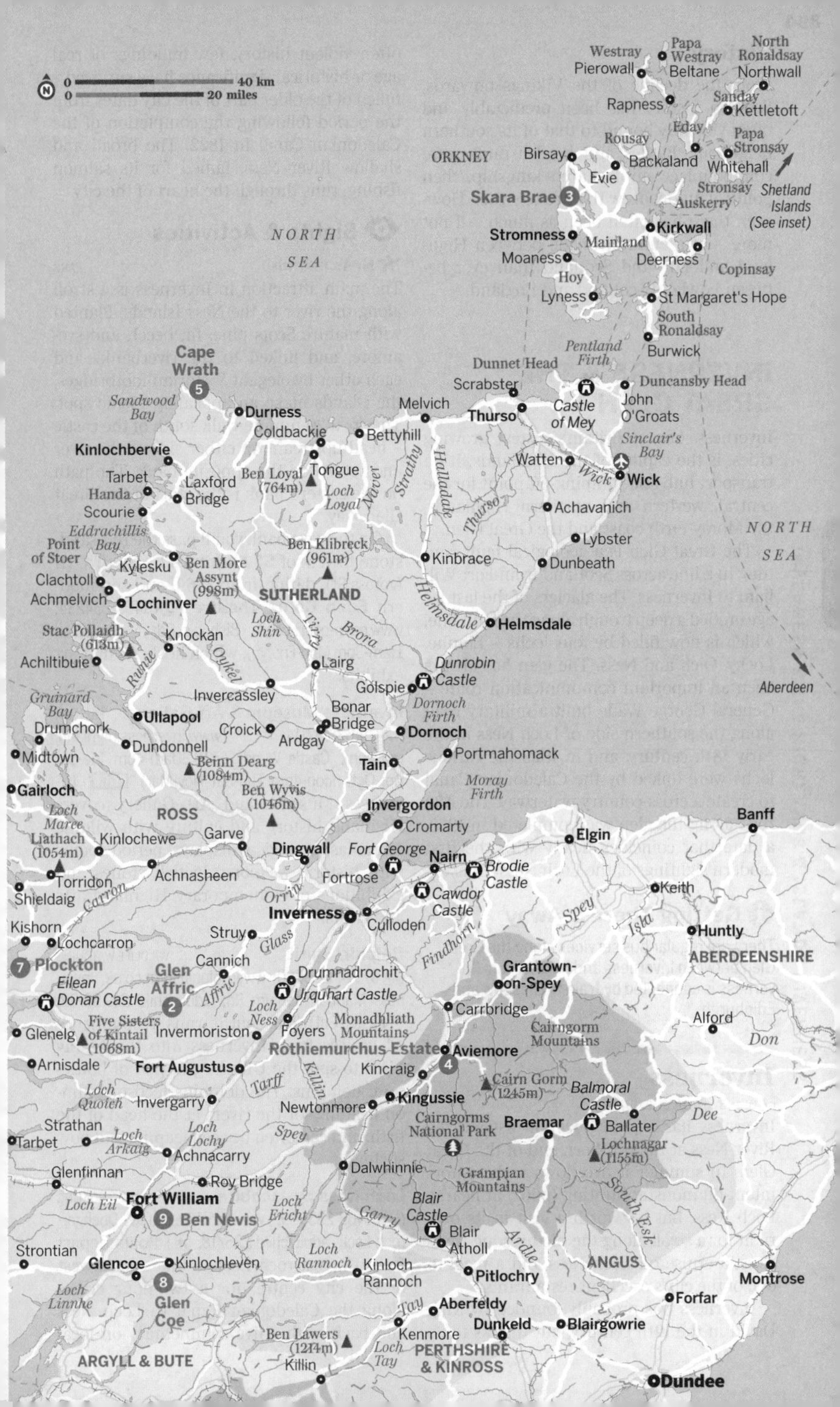
0 40 km
0 20 miles
NORTH SEA
ORKNEY
Westray
Papa Westray
North Ronaldsay
Pierowall
Beltane
Northwall
Rapness
Sanday
Kettletoft
Eday
Rousay
Papa Stronsay
Birsay
Backaland
Whitehall
Evie
Stronsay
Shetland Islands (See inset)
Skara Brae 3
Auskerry
Stromness
Kirkwall
Mainland
Moaness
Deerness
Hoy
Copinsay
Lyness
St Margaret's Hope
South Ronaldsay
Burwick
Pentland Firth
Dunnet Head
Cape Wrath 5
Scrabster
Duncansby Head
Sandwood Bay
Durness
Melvich
Thurso
Castle of Mey
John O'Groats
Coldbackie
Bettyhill
Sinclair's Bay
Kinlochbervie
Tongue
Strathy
Halladale
Watten
Wick
Tarbet
Ben Loyal (764m)
Laxford Bridge
Handa
Loch Loyal
Naver
Thurso
Achavanich
Scourie
Eddrachillis Bay
NORTH SEA
Lybster
Point of Stoer
Ben Klibreck (961m)
Kinbrace
Dunbeath
Kylesku
Ben More Assynt (998m)
Clachtoll
Achmelvich
Lochinver
SUTHERLAND
Helmsdale
Loch Shin
Tirry
Brora
Helmsdale
Stac Pollaidh (613m)
Knockan
Runie
Oykel
Achiltibuie
Lairg
Dunrobin Castle
Golspie
Aberdeen
Gruinard Bay
Invercassley
Dornoch Firth
Ullapool
Bonar Bridge
Drumchork
Croick
Dornoch
Ardgay
Dundonnell
Midtown
Portmahomack
Beinn Dearg (1084m)
Tain
Gairloch
Ben Wyvis (1046m)
Moray Firth
Loch Maree
ROSS
Invergordon
Liathach (1054m)
Kinlochewe
Cromarty
Banff
Garve
Dingwall
Elgin
Fort George
Nairn
Brodie Castle
Torridon
Achnasheen
Fortrose
Shieldaig
Carron
Orrin
Cawdor Castle
Keith
Inverness
Culloden
Spey
Isla
Kishorn
Struy
Glass
Huntly
Lochcarron
Findhorn
ABERDEENSHIRE
7 Plockton
Glen Affric
Cannich
Grantown-on-Spey
Eilean Donan Castle
Affric
Drumnadrochit
Urquhart Castle
2
Loch Ness
Carrbridge
Five Sisters of Kintail (1068m)
Monadhliath Mountains
Alford
Glenelg
Invermoriston
Foyers
Cairngorm Mountains
Don
Rothiemurchus Estate
Aviemore
Arnisdale
Fort Augustus
Killin
4
Kincraig
Cairn Gorm (1245m)
Tarff
Balmoral Castle
Loch Quoich
Invergarry
Newtonmore
Kingussie
Strathan
Loch Lochy
Cairngorms National Park
Braemar
Ballater
Dee
Tarbet
Loch Arkaig
Spey
Achnacarry
Lochnagar (1155m)
Glenfinnan
Dalwhinnie
Grampian Mountains
South Esk
Roy Bridge
Loch Eil
Fort William
Loch Ericht
Blair Castle
9 Ben Nevis
Garry
Blair Atholl
Ardle
Strontian
Loch Rannoch
Glencoe
Kinlochleven
ANGUS
Kinloch Rannoch
Montrose
8
Pitlochry
Loch Linnhe
Glen Coe
Forfar
Tay
Aberfeldy
Dunkeld
Blairgowrie
Ben Lawers (1214m)
Kenmore
ARGYLL & BUTE
Loch Tay
PERTHSHIRE & KINROSS
Killin
Dundee

History

From the decline of the Vikings onwards, Scottish history has been predictably and often violently bound to that of its southern neighbour. Battles and border raids were commonplace until shared kingship, then political union, drew the two together. However, there has often been as much – if not more – of a cultural divide between Highland and Lowland Scotland than ever between Lowland Scotland and England.

INVERNESS & THE GREAT GLEN

Inverness, one of Britain's fastest growing cities, is the capital of the Highlands. It's a transport hub and jumping-off point for the central, western and northern Highlands, the Moray Firth coast and the Great Glen.

The Great Glen is a geological fault running in a line across Scotland from Fort William to Inverness. The glaciers of the last ice age eroded a deep trough along the fault line, which is now filled by four lochs – Linnhe, Lochy, Oich and Ness. The glen has always been an important communication route – General George Wade built a military road along the southern side of Loch Ness in the early 18th century, and in 1822 the various lochs were linked by the Caledonian Canal to create a cross-country waterway. The A82 road along the glen was completed in 1933, a date that coincides neatly with the first modern sightings of the Loch Ness Monster.

Getting There & Away

There are regular bus services along the Great Glen between Inverness and Fort William. Inverness is connected by train to Glasgow and Edinburgh.

Inverness

☎01463 / POP 61,235

Inverness has a great location astride the River Ness at the northern end of the Great Glen. In summer it overflows with visitors intent on monster hunting (p901) at nearby Loch Ness, but it's worth a visit in its own right for a stroll along the picturesque River Ness, a cruise on Loch Ness and a meal in one of the city's excellent restaurants.

Inverness was probably founded by King David in the 12th century, but thanks to its often violent history, few buildings of real age or historical significance have survived – much of the older part of the city dates from the period following the completion of the Caledonian Canal in 1822. The broad and shallow River Ness, famed for its salmon fishing, runs through the heart of the city.

Sights & Activities

★Ness Islands PARK

The main attraction in Inverness is a stroll along the river to the Ness Islands. Planted with mature Scots pine, fir, beech and sycamore, and linked to the riverbanks and each other by elegant Victorian footbridges, the islands make an appealing picnic spot. They're a 20-minute walk south of the castle – head upstream on either side of the river and return on the opposite bank. The path on the eastern bank is the start of the Great Glen Way.

On the west bank you'll pass the red-sandstone towers of **St Andrew's Cathedral** (11 Ardross St), dating from 1869, and the modern **Eden Court Theatre** (☎01463-234234; www.eden-court.co.uk; Bishop's Rd; ⌚box office 11am-3pm Mon-Fri; 📶), which hosts regular art exhibits.

Inverness Museum & Art Gallery MUSEUM

(☎01463-237114; www.inverness.highland.museum; Castle Wynd; ⌚10.30am-4pm Tue-Sat Apr-Oct, noon-4pm Thu-Sat Nov-Mar) FREE Inverness Museum and Art Gallery covers Highland history and culture with wildlife dioramas, geological displays, period rooms with historic weapons, Pictish stones and exhibitions of contemporary Highland arts and crafts.

Dolphin Spirit WILDLIFE WATCHING

(☎07544 800620; www.dolphinspirit.co.uk; Inverness Marina, Stadium Rd; adult/child £19.50/12; ⌚Easter-Oct) This outfit runs recommended cruises from Inverness into the Moray Firth to spot the UK's largest pod of bottlenose dolphins. The dolphins feed on salmon heading for the rivers at the head of the firth, and can often be seen leaping and bow surfing.

Loch Ness by Jacobite BOATING

(☎01463-233999; www.jacobite.co.uk; Dochgarroch Lock; adult/child £25/18; 👪) Boats depart from Dochgarroch Lock, 5 miles southwest of the city centre, for a two-hour cruise along the Caledonian Canal to Loch Ness and back, with a live commentary on local

Inverness

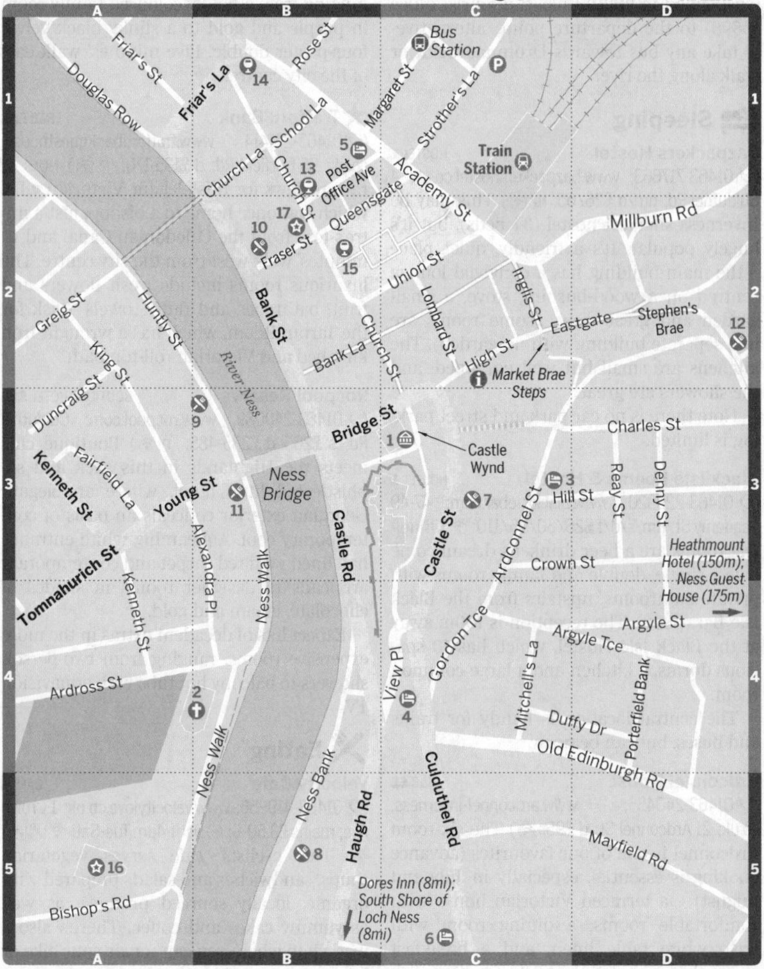

Inverness

Sights
1 Inverness Museum & Art Gallery C3
2 St Andrew's Cathedral B4

Sleeping
3 Ardconnel House C3
4 Bazpackers Hostel C4
5 Black Isle Rooms & Hostel B1
6 Rocpool Reserve C5

Eating
7 Café 1 .... C3
8 Contrast Brasserie B5
9 Kitchen Brasserie B3
10 Mustard Seed B2
11 Rocpool B3
12 Velocity Cafe D2

Drinking & Nightlife
13 Black Isle Bar B1
14 MacGregor's B1
15 Malt Room B2

Entertainment
16 Eden Court Theatre A5
17 Hootananny B2

history and wildlife. A free minibus service (suspended in 2020) links the tourist office (p898) to the departure point; alternatively take any bus towards Drumnadrochit or walk along the river.

Sleeping

Bazpackers Hostel HOSTEL £
(☎01463-717663; www.bazpackershostel.co.uk; 4 Culduthel Rd; dm/d £26/65; @☜) This may be Inverness smallest hostel (34 beds), but it's hugely popular. It's a friendly, quiet place – the main building has a convivial lounge centred on a wood-burning stove, a small garden and great views (some rooms are in a separate building with no garden). The kitchens are small but well equipped, and the showers are great.

Note there is no car park and street parking is limited.

Black Isle Rooms & Hostel HOSTEL £
(☎01463-229920; www.blackislebar.com; 47-49 Academy St; dm/s/d/f £26/60/95/110; ☜) Black Isle rooms are a beer drinker's dream come true – single, double and family rooms with private bathrooms, upstairs from the Black Isle Bar (p898). The reception is 100m away at the Black Isle Hostel, which has 10 spacious dorms, a kitchen and a large common room.

The central location is handy for trains and buses, but can be noisy.

Ardconnel House B&B ££
(☎01463-240455; www.ardconnel-inverness.co.uk; 21 Ardconnel St; d £95; ☜) The six-room Ardconnel is one of our favourites (advance booking is essential, especially in July and August) – a terraced Victorian house with comfortable rooms, a dining room with crisp white table linen, and a breakfast menu that includes Vegemite for homesick Antipodeans.

Ness Guest House B&B ££
(☎01463-559174; www.thenessguesthouse.com; 48 Union Rd; d £72-90; P☜) Friendly owners, neat, well-equipped rooms and a handy location five minutes' walk east of the city centre make the Ness Guest House a good bet. Breakfast is a highlight and features home-baked muffins or cake.

★**Heathmount Hotel** BOUTIQUE HOTEL £££
(☎01463-235877; www.heathmounthotel.com; Kingsmills Rd; d from £170; P☜) Small and friendly, the Heathmount combines a popular local bar and restaurant with eight designer hotel rooms, each one different, ranging from a boldly coloured family room in purple and gold to a slinky black velvet four-poster double. Five minutes' walk east of the city centre.

★**Trafford Bank** B&B £££
(☎01463-241414; www.traffordbankguesthouse.co.uk; 96 Fairfield Rd; d £135-170; P☜) Lots of rave reviews for this elegant Victorian villa, which was once home to a bishop, just a mitre's-toss from the Caledonian Canal and 10 minutes' walk west from the city centre. The luxurious rooms include fresh flowers and fruit, bathrobes and fluffy towels – ask for the Tartan Room, which has a wrought-iron king bed and Victorian roll-top bath.

Rocpool Reserve BOUTIQUE HOTEL £££
(☎01463-240089; www.rocpool.com; Culduthel Rd; s £265, d £285-485; P☜) Boutique chic meets the Highlands in this slick and sophisticated little hotel, where an elegant Georgian exterior conceals an oasis of contemporary cool. A gleaming white entrance hall lined with red carpet and contemporary art leads to designer rooms in shades of chocolate, cream and gold.

Expect lots of decadent extras in the more expensive rooms, ranging from two-person showers to balcony hot tubs with aquavision TV.

Eating

Velocity Cafe CAFE £
(☎01463-419956; www.velocitylove.co.uk; 1 Crown Ave; mains £3.50-6; ⊙9am-4pm Tue-Sat; ☜✍👪) 🍃 This cyclists' cafe serves vegetarian soups, sandwiches and salads prepared with organic, locally sourced produce, as well as yummy cakes and coffee. There's also a workshop where you can repair your bike or book a session with a mechanic.

★**Café 1** BISTRO ££
(☎01463-226200; www.cafe1.net; 75 Castle St; mains lunch £9-11, dinner £12-30; ⊙noon-2.30pm & 5-9.30pm Mon-Fri, 12.30-2.45pm & 5.30-9.30pm Sat; 👪) 🍃 Café 1 is a friendly, appealing bistro with candlelit tables amid elegant blond-wood and wrought-iron decor. There's an international menu based on quality Scottish produce, from Aberdeen Angus steaks to crisp pan-fried sea bass and pappardelle pasta with local wild chanterelles.

Mustard Seed BISTRO ££
(☎01463-220220; www.mustardseedrestaurant.co.uk; 16 Fraser St; mains £14-25; ⊙noon-3pm &

OFF THE BEATEN TRACK

STRATHGLASS & GLEN AFFRIC

The broad valley of Strathglass extends about 18 miles inland from Beauly, and is followed by the A831 to **Cannich** (the only village in the area), where there's a grocery store and a post office.

Glen Affric, one of the most beautiful glens in Scotland, extends deep into the hills beyond Cannich. The upper reaches of the glen are designated as the **Glen Affric National Nature Reserve** (www.nnr.scot), a scenic wonderland of shimmering lochs, rugged mountains and native Scots pines, home to pine martens, otters, red squirrels and golden eagles.

About 4 miles southwest of Cannich is **Dog Falls**, a scenic spot where the River Affric squeezes through a narrow, rocky gorge. A circular walking trail (red waymarks) leads from Dog Falls car park to a footbridge below the falls, returning on the far side of the river (2 miles, allow one hour).

The road continues beyond Dog Falls to a parking area and picnic site at the eastern end of **Loch Affric**, where there are several short walks along the river and the loch shore. The circuit of Loch Affric (10 miles, allow five hours walking, two hours by mountain bike) follows good paths right around the loch and takes you deep into the heart of some very wild scenery.

Stagecoach (p898) bus 17 runs from Inverness to Cannich (£6.10, 50 minutes, five daily Monday to Saturday) and Tomich (£6.10, 1¼ hours) via Drumnadrochit (£3.60, 25 minutes).

5.30-10pm) The menu at this bright and bustling bistro changes weekly, but focuses on Scottish and French cuisine with a modern twist. Grab a table on the upstairs balcony if you can – it's the best outdoor lunch spot in Inverness, with a great view across the river. And a two-course lunch for £12.95 is hard to beat.

On the opposite bank of the river, Mustard Seed's spectacular, glass-fronted sister restaurant **Kitchen Brasserie** (01463-259119; www.kitchenrestaurant.co.uk; 15 Huntly St; mains £11-25; noon-3pm & 5-10pm;) offers a similar menu. Ask for a table upstairs, by the window.

★Rocpool MEDITERRANEAN £££
(01463-717274; www.rocpoolrestaurant.com; 1 Ness Walk; mains £15-30; noon-2.30pm & 5.45-10pm Mon-Sat) Lots of polished wood, crisp white linen and leather booths and banquettes lend a sophisticated nautical air to this relaxed bistro, which offers a Mediterranean-influenced menu that makes the most of quality Scottish produce, especially seafood. The two-course lunch is £18.95.

Contrast Brasserie BRASSERIE £££
(01463-223777; www.glenmoristontownhouse.com; 20 Ness Bank; mains £17-27; noon-2.30pm & 5-9pm Mon-Sat, 1-6.30pm Sun) At the Glenmoriston Town House Hotel, Contrast Brasserie drips designer style, with truly delicious food prepared using fresh Scottish produce. The two-/three-course lunch menu (£14.95/18.95) and three-course pre-theatre menu (£20.95, 5pm to 6.30pm) are good value.

Drinking & Entertainment

★Malt Room BAR
(01463-221888; www.themaltroom.co.uk; 34 Church St; 5pm-1am Sun-Fri, noon-1am Sat) Tucked inside the entrance to the Victorian Market, this cosy little whisky bar is the best place in town for a dram. The carefully curated menu lists a number of themed whisky flights for guided tastings, or customise your own from a selection of more than 200 malts. Whisky cocktails include an excellent Smoky Amaretto Sour made with Lagavulin 16.

MacGregor's BAR
(www.macgregorsbars.com; 113 Academy St; 11am-midnight Mon-Thu, to 1am Fri & Sat, noon-midnight Sun) Decked out in timber and tweed, this bar strikes a distinctly modern chord. There's a huge selection of Scottish craft beers on tap, and even a beer 'set menu' described as 'a journey through the basics of craft beer'. The beer nerdiness extends to the gents' toilets, where urinals and washbasins have been fashioned out of beer kegs.

Black Isle Bar BAR
(www.blackislebrewery.com; 68 Church St; ⏲noon-midnight) Shared wooden tables and a rustic-industrial decor make for a convivial atmosphere at Black Isle Bar, where you'll find 18 beers from the nearby **Black Isle Brewery** (☎01463-811871; Old Allangrange; ⏲10am-5pm Mon-Sat) FREE on tap, along with a selection of ales from other craft breweries, organic wines and wood-fired pizzas (£10 to £14).

Hootananny LIVE MUSIC
(☎01463-233651; www.hootananyinverness.co.uk; 67 Church St; ⏲noon-1am Mon-Thu, to 3am Fri & Sat, 4pm-midnight Sun) Hootananny is the city's best live-music venue, with traditional folk and/or rock sessions nightly, including big-name bands from all over Scotland (and, indeed, the world). The bar is well stocked with a range of beers from the local Black Isle Brewery.

Information

Inverness Tourist Office (☎01463-252401; wwww.visitscotland.com; 36 High St; ⏲9am-5pm;) Accommodation booking service; also sells tickets for tours and cruises.

Getting There & Away

AIR

Inverness Airport (INV; ☎01667-464000; www.invernessairport.co.uk) is at Dalcross, 10 miles east of the city, off the A96 towards Aberdeen. There are scheduled flights to Amsterdam, London, Manchester, Dublin, Orkney, Shetland and the Outer Hebrides, as well as other places in the UK.

Stagecoach (☎01463-233371; www.stagecoachbus.com) bus 11/11A runs from the airport to Inverness bus station (£4.50, 30 minutes, every 30 minutes).

BUS

Services depart from **Inverness bus station** (Margaret St). Most intercity routes are served by **Scottish Citylink** (www.citylink.co.uk) and Stagecoach (p898). Destinations include:

Aberdeen (Stagecoach) £13.85, four hours, hourly
Aviemore £11.50, 45 minutes, eight daily
Edinburgh £34.30, four hours, eight daily
Fort William £11.60, two hours, eight daily
Glasgow £34.30, 3½ to four hours, hourly
Portree £28.10, 3¼ hours, two daily
Thurso (Stagecoach) £21.60, 3½ hours, two daily
Ullapool £14.90, 1½ hours, two daily except Sunday

If you book far enough in advance, **Megabus** (☎0900 1600 900; www.megabus.com) offers fares from as little as £3 for buses from Inverness to Glasgow and Edinburgh, and £32 to London.

TRAIN

The **Caledonian Sleeper** (☎0330 060 0500; www.sleeper.scot) to London (from £120 sharing a two-berth cabin; book well in advance) departs at 8.45pm Monday to Friday, 8.26pm Sunday. Other services:

Aberdeen £31.60, 2¼ hours, 11 daily
Edinburgh £47.40, 3½ hours, eight daily
Glasgow £46, 3½ hours, eight daily
Kyle of Lochalsh £25.60, 2½ hours, four daily Monday to Saturday, two Sunday; one of Britain's great scenic train journeys
London £180, eight hours, one daily direct (others require a change at Edinburgh)
Wick £22.40, 4½ hours, four daily Monday to Saturday, one or two on Sunday; via Thurso

Getting Around

BICYCLE

Ticket to Ride (☎01463-419160; www.tickettoridehighlands.co.uk; Bellfield Park; per day from £30; ⏲9am-5.30pm Apr-Oct) Hires out mountain bikes, road bikes, hybrids and tandems; bikes can be dropped off in Fort William.

BUS

City services and buses to places around Inverness, including Nairn, Forres, the Culloden battlefield, Beauly, Dingwall and Lairg, are operated by Stagecoach. An Inverness Zone 2 Dayrider ticket costs £7 and gives unlimited travel for a day on buses as far afield as Culloden, Fortrose and Drumnadrochit.

TAXI

Inverness Taxis (☎01463-222222; www.inverness-taxis.com) There's a taxi rank outside the train station.

Around Inverness

Culloden Battlefield

The Battle of Culloden in 1746 – the last pitched battle ever fought on British soil – saw the defeat of Bonnie Prince Charlie and the end of the Jacobite dream when 1200 Highlanders were slaughtered by government forces in a 68-minute rout. The Duke of Cumberland, son of the reigning King George II and leader of the Hanoverian army, earned the nickname 'Butcher' for his brutal treatment of the defeated Jacobite forces. The battle sounded the death knell for the old clan system, and the horrors of the Clearances, when tenants were evicted from their lands, soon followed.

The sombre moor where the conflict took place has scarcely changed in the ensuing 260 years. The battlefield has been preserved and enemy lines marked by coloured flags; admission is free.

The impressive **visitor centre** (NTS; www.nts.org.uk/culloden; adult/child £11/9.50; ⏲10am-4pm Wed-Sun; Ⓟ) provides plenty of historical context through film and audio presentations. In 2020 the visitor centre opened with limited hours and an online advance booking system.

Culloden is 6 miles east of Inverness. Bus 2 runs from Eastgate shopping centre in Inverness to Culloden battlefield (£3.15, 30 minutes, hourly except Sunday).

Fort George

One of the finest artillery fortifications in Europe, **Fort George** (HES; ☎01667-462777; www.historicenvironment.scot; adult/child £9/5.40; ⏲10am-4pm; Ⓟ) was established in 1748 in the aftermath of the Battle of Culloden, as a base for George II's army of occupation in the Highlands. By the time of its completion in 1769 it had cost the modern equivalent of around £1 billion. It still functions as a military barracks; public areas have exhibitions on 18th-century soldiery.

The mile-plus walk around the ramparts offers fine views; look out for dolphins in the surrounding waters. Given its size, you'll need at least two hours to do the place justice.

The fort is off the A96, about 11 miles northeast of Inverness; there is no public transport. The fort reopened in September 2020 with reduced opening hours and an online advance booking system.

Cawdor Castle

Cawdor Castle (☎01667-404615; www.cawdorcastle.com; Cawdor; gardens & grounds adult/child £8/4; ⏲10am-5pm May-Sep; Ⓟ), 5 miles southwest of Nairn, was once the seat of the Thane of Cawdor, one of the titles bestowed on Shakespeare's Macbeth. The real Macbeth – an ancient Scottish king – couldn't have lived here though, since he died in 1057, 300 years before the castle was begun. Nevertheless the castle tour gives a fascinating insight into the lives of the Scottish aristocracy.

Even if the castle interior is closed, as it was in 2020, the walled gardens, maze and woodland trails through the grounds are worth a visit, and the courtyard cafe and shop provide a glimpse inside the castle walls.

To get here, take bus 2 from Eastgate shopping centre in Inverness to Cawdor village (50 minutes, hourly except Sunday), from where it's a 1-mile walk to the castle.

Loch Ness

Deep, dark and narrow, Loch Ness stretches for 23 miles between Inverness and Fort Augustus. Its bitterly cold waters have been extensively explored in search of Nessie, the elusive Loch Ness Monster, but most visitors see her only in the form of a cardboard cutout at Drumnadrochit's monster exhibitions. The busy A82 road runs along the northwestern shore, while the more tranquil and picturesque B862 follows the southeastern shore. A complete circuit of the loch is about 70 miles – travel anticlockwise for the better views.

Activities

The 79-mile **Great Glen Way** (www.highland.gov.uk/greatglenway) long-distance walking trail stretches from Inverness to Fort William, where walkers can connect with the **West Highland Way**. The area's newest waymarked trail is the **Loch Ness 360°** (www.lochness360.com), which loops for 80 miles around the circumference of the loch from Inverness. It's possible to mountain bike the Great Glen Way and Loch Ness 360º trails.

The Great Glen can also be cycled on the **Route 78 Caledonia Way** (www.sustrans.org.uk), which runs for 234 miles from Campbeltown to Inverness. You can hire a bike in **Fort William** (☎01397-705555; www.neviscycles.com; cnr Montrose Ave & Locheil Rd, Inverlochy; per day from £35; ⏲9am-5pm) and drop it off in Inverness, and vice versa.

Getting There & Away

Scottish Citylink (www.citylink.co.uk) and Stagecoach buses from Inverness to Fort William (six to eight daily, five on Sunday) run along the shores of Loch Ness; buses headed for Skye turn off at Invermoriston. There are bus stops at Drumnadrochit (to Inverness £3.80, 30 minutes), Urquhart Castle car park (to Inverness £4, 35 minutes) and Fort Augustus (to Inverness £10.80, one hour).

Drumnadrochit

01456 / POP 1100

Seized by Loch Ness Monster madness, its gift shops bulging with Nessie cuddly toys, Drumnadrochit is a hotbed of beastie fever.

Sights & Activities

Urquhart Castle CASTLE

(HES; 01456-450551; www.historicenvironment.scot; adult/child £9.60/5.80; 9.30am-6pm Apr-Oct, to 4.30pm Nov-Mar; P) Commanding a superb location 1.5 miles east of Drumnadrochit, with outstanding views (on a clear day), Urquhart Castle is a popular Nessie-hunting hot spot. The castle was repeatedly sacked and rebuilt (and sacked and rebuilt) over the centuries; in 1692 it was blown up to prevent the Jacobites from using it. The five-storey tower house at the northern point is the most impressive remaining fragment and offers wonderful views across the water. Book tickets at least one day in advance.

The visitor centre includes displays of medieval items discovered in the castle and a video theatre: the film, with a dramatic 'reveal' of the castle at the end, can be downloaded onto your phone using a QR code if the visitor centre is closed. The site also includes a gift shop and cafe.

Loch Ness Centre & Exhibition MUSEUM

(01456-450573; www.lochness.com; adult/child £8.45/4.95; 9.30am-6pm Jul & Aug, to 5pm Easter-Jun, Sep & Oct, 10am-4pm Nov-Easter; P) This Nessie-themed attraction adopts a scientific approach that allows you to weigh the evidence for yourself. Exhibits include original equipment – sonar survey vessels, miniature submarines, cameras and sediment coring tools – used in various monster hunts, plus original photographs and film footage of sightings. You'll find out about hoaxes and optical illusions, as well as learning a lot about the ecology of Loch Ness – is there enough food in the loch to support even one 'monster', let alone a breeding population?

Nessie Hunter CRUISE

(01456-450395; www.lochness-cruises.com; adult/child £16/10; Apr-Oct) One-hour monster-hunting cruises, complete with sonar and underwater cameras. Cruises depart from Drumnadrochit hourly from 10am to 6pm daily, with additional sailings at 9am and 7pm from June to August.

Sleeping

Drumbuie Farm B&B ££

(01456-450634; www.loch-ness-farm.co.uk; d from £75; P) A B&B in a modern house on a working farm surrounded by fields full of sheep and Highland cattle, with views over Urquhart Castle and Loch Ness. Walkers and cyclists are welcome.

★**Loch Ness Inn** INN £££

(01456-450991; www.staylochness.co.uk; Lewiston; inn s/d/f £120/140/170, bunkhouse q £135; P) Loch Ness Inn ticks all the weary traveller's boxes, with comfortable bedrooms (the family suite sleeps two adults and two children), a cosy bar pouring real ales from the local Loch Ness Brewery, and a restaurant (mains £13.50 to £26) serving wholesome fare. It's conveniently located in the quiet hamlet of Lewiston, between Drumnadrochit and Urquhart Castle.

In 2020 a new bunkhouse opened with dorm beds and family rooms as well as a kitchen, drying room and bike storage. Only private rooms (no shared dorms) were available in the summer of 2020.

Drinking & Nightlife

Benleva Hotel MICROBREWERY

(01456-450080; www.benleva.co.uk; Kilmore Rd; noon-midnight Mon-Thu, to 1am Fri, to 12.45am Sat, 12.30-11pm Sun) Set in an 18th-century manse (a spacious house built for the minister of the local church) a half-mile east of the main road, the Benleva is a rough diamond of a pub. The beer is the main event, with a selection of real ales from around the country, including those from its own Hanging Tree Brewery, located in the garden.

Fort Augustus

01320 / POP 620

Fort Augustus, at the junction of four old military roads, was originally a government garrison and the headquarters of General George Wade's road-building operations in the early 18th century. Today it's a neat and picturesque little place bisected by the Caledonian Canal and often overrun by coach-tour crowds in summer.

Sights & Activities

Caledonian Canal CANAL

(www.scottishcanals.co.uk) At Fort Augustus, boats using the Caledonian Canal are raised and lowered 13m by a 'ladder' of five consecutive locks. It's fun to watch, and the

THE NESSIE LEGEND

Highland folklore is filled with tales of strange creatures living in lochs and rivers, notably the kelpie (water horse) that lures unwary travellers to their doom. The use of the term 'monster', however, is a relatively recent phenomenon, its origins lying in an article published in the *Inverness Courier* on 2 May 1933, entitled 'Strange Spectacle on Loch Ness'.

The article recounted the sighting of a disturbance in the loch by Mrs Aldie Mackay and her husband: 'There the creature disported itself, rolling and plunging for fully a minute, its body resembling that of a whale, and the water cascading and churning like a simmering cauldron.'

The story was taken up by the London press and sparked a flurry of sightings that year, including a notorious on-land encounter with London tourists Mr and Mrs Spicer on 22 July 1933, again reported in the *Inverness Courier*: 'It was horrible, an abomination. About 50 yards ahead, we saw an undulating sort of neck, and quickly followed by a large, ponderous body. I estimated the length to be 25ft to 30ft, its colour was dark elephant grey. It crossed the road in a series of jerks, but because of the slope we could not see its limbs. Although I accelerated quickly towards it, it had disappeared into the loch by the time I reached the spot. There was no sign of it in the water. I am a temperate man, but I am willing to take any oath that we saw this Loch Ness beast. I am certain that this creature was of a prehistoric species.'

The London newspapers couldn't resist. In December 1933 the *Daily Mail* sent Marmaduke Wetherell, a film director and big-game hunter, to Loch Ness to track down the beast. Within days he found 'reptilian' footprints in the shoreline mud (soon revealed to have been made with a stuffed hippopotamus foot). Then in April 1934 came the famous long-necked monster photograph taken by the seemingly reputable Harley St surgeon Robert Kenneth Wilson. The press went into overdrive and the rest, as they say, is history.

In 1994, however, Christian Spurling – Wetherell's stepson, by then 90 years old – revealed that the most famous photo of Nessie ever taken was in fact a hoax, perpetrated by his stepfather with Wilson's help. Today, of course, there are those who claim that Spurling's confession is itself a hoax. And, ironically, the researcher who exposed the surgeon's photo as a fake still believes wholeheartedly in the monster's existence.

There have been regular sightings of the monster through the years (see www.lochnesssightings.com), with a peak in 1996–97 (the Hollywood movie *Loch Ness* was released in 1996). Reports have tailed off in recent years, though 2019 saw an uptick in sightings, with the highest number reported since 1983.

Hoax or not, the bizarre mini-industry that has grown up around Loch Ness and its mysterious monster since that eventful summer last century is a spectacle in itself.

neatly landscaped canal banks are a great place to soak up the sun or compare accents with fellow tourists. The **Caledonian Canal Centre** (Ardchattan House, Canalside; ⏲10am-4pm Wed-Sun) FREE, beside the lowest lock, has information on the history of the canal and a cafe.

Cruise Loch Ness BOATING
(☎01320-366277; www.cruiselochness.com; adult/child £15/9; ⏲10am, noon, 2pm & 4pm daily Apr-Nov, fewer sailings Dec-Mar) One-hour cruises on Loch Ness are accompanied by the latest high-tech sonar equipment so you can keep an underwater eye open for Nessie. There are also one-hour evening cruises departing 8pm daily April to August.

Sleeping & Eating

★Morag's Lodge HOSTEL £
(☎01320-366289; www.moragslodge.com; Bunoich Brae; dm/d/f from £25/62/81; P@) This large, well-run hostel is based in a big Victorian house with great views of Fort Augustus' hilly surrounds, and has a convivial bar with an open fire. It's hidden away in the trees up the steep side road just north of the tourist office car park. Breakfast (£5), packed lunches (£5) and dinner (£10) are also available.

★Lovat HOTEL £££
(☎01456-459250; www.thelovat.com; Main Rd; d from £140; P) A boutique-style makeover has transformed this former huntin'-and-shootin' hotel into a luxurious but

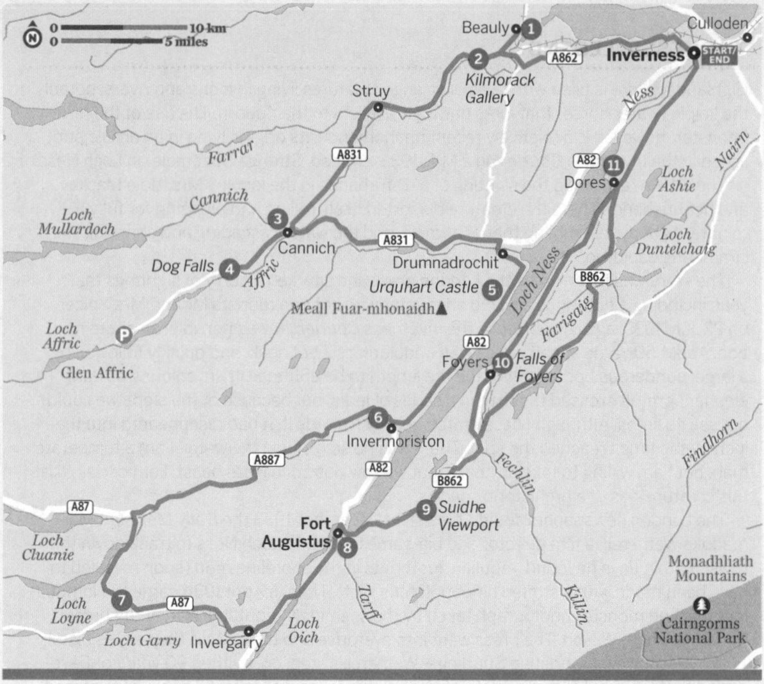

Driving Tour
A Loch Ness Circuit

START INVERNESS
END INVERNESS
LENGTH 130 MILES; SIX TO SEVEN HOURS

Head out of Inverness on the A862 to Beauly and breakfast at **1 Corner on the Square** (01463-783000; www.corneronthesquare.co.uk; 1 High St, Beauly; dishes £2.50-8.50; 8.30am-5pm Mon-Fri, to 8pm Sat, 9am-5pm Sun). Backtrack a mile and turn right on the A831 to Cannich, passing **2 Kilmorack Gallery**, which exhibits contemporary art in a converted church. The scenery gets wilder as you approach **3 Cannich**; turn right and follow the single-track road to the **4 Dog Falls** car park. Stroll along the rushing river, or hike to the viewpoint (about one-hour round trip; 2.5 miles) for a glimpse of remote Glen Affric.

Return to Cannich and turn right on the A831 to Drumnadrochit, then right on the A82 past picturesque **5 Urquhart Castle** (p900) and along the shores of Loch Ness. At **6 Invermoriston**, pause to look at the old bridge, built by Thomas Telford in 1813, then head west on the A887 towards Kyle of Lochalsh; after 16 miles go left on the A87 towards Invergarry. You are now among some of the Highlands' finest mountain scenery; as the road turns east above Loch Garry, stop at the famous **7 viewpoint** (layby on right, signposted Glengarry Viewpoint). Through a quirk of perspective, the lochs to the west appear to form the map outline of Scotland.

At Invergarry, turn left on the A82 to reach **8 Fort Augustus** and a late lunch at the Lock Inn. Take the B862, following the line of General Wade's 18th-century military road, to the **9 Suidhe Viewpoint**. A short (800m) walk up the well-worn path to the summit affords an even better panorama.

Ahead, you can choose the low road via the impressive **10 Falls of Foyers**, or stay on the high road (B862) for more views; both converge on Loch Ness at **11 Dores and the Dores Inn** (01463-751203; www.thedoresinn.co.uk; Dores; mains £10-28; noon-9pm Wed-Sun; P), where you can sip a pint with a view along Loch Ness, and even stay for dinner before returning to Inverness.

eco-conscious retreat set apart from the tourist crush around the canal. The bedrooms are spacious and stylishly furnished, while the lounge is equipped with a log fire, comfy armchairs and grand piano: perfect for a rainy evening.

Its highly acclaimed restaurant, **Station Road** (6.30pm to 8.30pm Tuesday to Saturday, one/three courses £27/42), serves an innovative tasting menu (£65) of beautifully presented plates prepared with home-grown, locally foraged and other seasonal produce; book ahead.

Lock Inn PUB FOOD ££
(01320-366302; www.the-lockinn.co.uk; Canal Side; mains £10-16; kitchen noon-8pm) A superb little pub right on the canal bank, the Lock Inn has a vast range of malt whiskies and a tempting menu of bar meals, which includes Orkney salmon, homemade steak pie and daily seafood specials – the house speciality is beer-battered haddock and chips.

THE CAIRNGORMS

The Cairngorms National Park (www.cairngorms.co.uk) is the largest national park in the UK, more than twice the size of the Lake District. It stretches from Aviemore in the north to the Angus Glens in the south, and from Dalwhinnie in the west to Ballater and Royal Deeside in the east.

The park encompasses the highest landmass in Britain – a broad mountain plateau, riven only by the deep valleys of the Lairig Ghru and Loch Avon, with an average altitude of more than 1000m and including five of the six highest summits in the UK. This wild mountain landscape of granite and heather has a sub-Arctic climate and supports rare alpine tundra vegetation and high-altitude bird species, such as snow bunting, ptarmigan and dotterel.

Getting There & Away

The main A9 Perth–Inverness road and railway line run along the western and northern boundaries of the national park, while the A93 Aberdeen–Braemar road provides the main access to the eastern part. The Angus Glens in the south are reached along minor roads branching out from the small towns of Kirriemuir and Brechin, to the north of Dundee.

The nearest airport (p898) is at Inverness, an hour's drive north of Aviemore.

Aviemore

01479 / POP 3616

The gateway to the Cairngorms, Aviemore is the region's main centre for transport, accommodation, restaurants and shops. It's not the prettiest town in Scotland by a long stretch – the main attractions are in the surrounding area – but when bad weather puts the hills off limits, Aviemore fills up with hikers, cyclists and climbers (plus skiers and snowboarders in winter) cruising the outdoor-equipment shops or recounting their latest adventures in the cafes and bars. Add in tourists and locals, and the eclectic mix makes for a lively little town.

Aviemore is on a loop off the A9 Perth–Inverness road. Almost everything of note is to be found along the main drag, Grampian Rd; the train station and bus stop are towards its southern end.

Cairngorm Mountain lies 10 miles southeast of Aviemore along the B970 (Ski Rd) and its continuation, past Rothiemurchus, Coylumbridge and Glenmore.

Sights & Activities

Craigellachie Nature Reserve NATURE RESERVE
(www.nnr.scot; Grampian Rd) FREE This reserve is a great place for short hikes across steep hillsides covered in natural birch forest where you can spot wildlife such as the peregrine falcons that nest on the crags from April to July. A trail leads west from Aviemore Youth Hostel and passes under the A9 into the reserve.

Strathspey Steam Railway RAIL
(01479-810725; www.strathspeyrailway.co.uk; Station Sq; adult/child return £16.25/8.10) The Strathspey railway runs steam trains on a section of restored line between Aviemore and Broomhill, 10 miles to the northeast, via Boat of Garten. There are four or five trains daily from June to August, and a more limited service in April, May, September, October and December, with the option of afternoon tea, Sunday lunch or a three-course dinner on board.

Sleeping

Aviemore Youth Hostel HOSTEL £
(HS; 01479-810345; www.hostellingscotland.org.uk; 25 Grampian Rd; s/d/tr £40/52/77; P @) Upmarket hostelling in a spacious, well-equipped modern building, five minutes' walk south of the village centre. There are

The Cairngorms

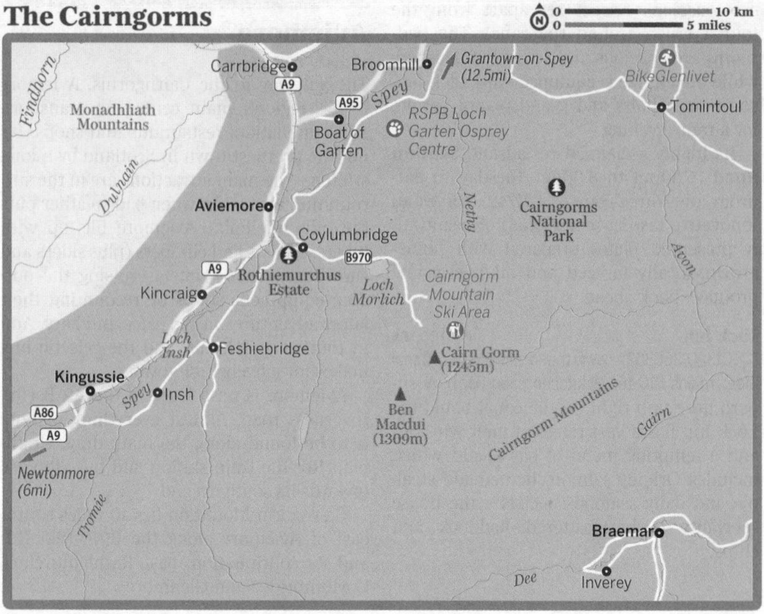

four- and six-bed rooms, and a comfortable lounge with views of the mountains. Bookings for 2021 were for private rooms only (no shared dorms).

Cairngorm Hotel HOTEL ££
(☎01479-810233; www.cairngorm.com; Grampian Rd; s/d £75/110; P 📶) Better known as 'the Cairn', this long-established hotel is set in the fine old granite building with the pointy turret opposite the train station. It's a welcoming place with comfortable rooms and a determinedly Scottish atmosphere, with tartan carpets and stags' antlers. There's live music on weekends, so it can get a bit noisy – not for early-to-bedders.

The restaurant serves traditional Highland comfort food such as fish pie, fillet of venison and haggis, neeps and tatties (£10 to £23).

Ravenscraig Guest House B&B ££
(☎01479-810278; www.ravenscraighouse.co.uk; Grampian Rd; s/d from £65/90; P 📶) Ravenscraig is a large, flower-bedecked Victorian villa with seven spacious and elegantly decorated en suite rooms, plus another six in a modern chalet at the back (one is wheelchair accessible). It serves traditional and veggie breakfasts in an attractive conservatory dining room.

Eating & Drinking

★Route 7 Cafe CAFE £
(☎01479-812433; http://highlandhomecentre.com/route-7-cafe.html; 18 Dalfaber Industrial Estate; mains £6-13; ⊙9am-4.30pm; P 📶 👪) This place, named for the cycle route that passes the door, takes a bit of finding (at the end of the side road that passes Cairngorm Brewery), but is well worth seeking out for its hearty menu of burgers, sandwiches, salads and soups. Cyclists can use the power washer and tools outside.

Rowan Tree SCOTTISH ££
(☎01479-810207; www.rowantreehotel.com; B9152, Loch Alvie; mains £15-28; ⊙6-8.30pm; P 📶 🌶) The menu at this relaxed country hotel ranges from traditional Highland cooking (fillet of beef with homemade haggis; beer-battered haddock and chips) to more innovative dishes (duck dumplings with a cornflake crumb; button mushroom and blue-cheese fricassee), with an emphasis on local seasonal ingredients. It's located in a pretty spot 2 miles south of Aviemore next to Loch Alvie.

Winking Owl PUB
(www.thewinkingowl.co; Grampian Rd; ⊙noon-10pm Wed & Thu, to 11pm Fri & Sat, 12.30-10pm Sun; 📶) Lively local pub that operates under the

wing of the Cairngorm Brewery. It's popular with hikers and climbers, and serves a good range of real ales and malt whiskies. The menu (mains £10 to £14) features burgers, nachos and pizzas.

Information

Aviemore Tourist Office (01479-810930; www.visitaviemore.com; The Mall, Grampian Rd; 10am-4pm Sep-Jun, longer hours Jul & Aug)

Getting There & Around

BICYCLE

Several places in Aviemore, Rothiemurchus Estate and Glenmore have mountain bikes for hire. Easy off-road cycle tracks link Aviemore with Glenmore and Loch Morlich to the east, and Boat of Garten to the north

Bothy Bikes (01479-810111; www.bothybikes.co.uk; 5 Granish Way, Dalfaber; per half-/full-day £20/25; 9am-5pm) Located in northern Aviemore, this place rents out mountain bikes and can also advise on routes and trails. Children's bikes (per day £12), child seats (per day £5) and trailers (per day £10) also available. Booking recommended.

BUS

Buses stop on Grampian Rd opposite the train station; buy tickets at the tourist office. Services include:

Edinburgh £30.40, three to 3½ hours, six daily

Glasgow £30.40, 2¾ hours, six daily

Grantown-on-Spey £4.15, 35 minutes, 10 daily weekdays, two daily weekends

Inverness £11.50, 45 minutes, eight daily

Perth £22.20, 2¼ hours, eight daily

Bus 31 links Aviemore to Cairngorm Mountain car park (£3, 20 minutes, hourly) via Coylumbridge and Glenmore. A Strathspey Dayrider/Megarider ticket (£7.50/18.90) gives one/seven days unlimited bus travel from Aviemore as far as Cairngorm, Carrbridge and Kingussie; buy it from the bus driver.

TRAIN

The train station is on Grampian Rd. Services include the following:

Edinburgh £45, three hours, six daily

Glasgow £45, three hours, six daily

Inverness £3.60, 40 minutes, 12 daily

Around Aviemore

Cairngorm Mountain

Cairn Gorm (1245m), 10 miles southeast of Aviemore, is the sixth-highest summit in the UK and home to the Cairngorm Mountain ski area. In 2018 the Cairngorm Mountain Funicular Railway was closed indefinitely due to structural problems, but the cafe, shop and ranger's station remain open. A number of short, waymarked trails start at the Coire Cas car park, including a mile-long family trail.

Loch Morlich

Six miles east of Aviemore, Loch Morlich is surrounded by some 8 sq miles of pine and spruce forest that make up the Glenmore Forest Park. Its attractions include a sandy beach (at the east end) and a **water sports centre** (01479-861221; www.lochmorlich.com; 9am-5pm Easter-Oct).

Activities

★Glenmore Lodge ADVENTURE SPORTS

(01479-861256; www.glenmorelodge.org.uk; Glenmore; 1-day courses from £90) One of Britain's leading adventure-sports training centres, offering courses in hill walking, rock

DON'T MISS

ROTHIEMURCHUS ESTATE

The **Rothiemurchus Estate** (www.rothiemurchus.net), which extends from the River Spey at Aviemore to the Cairngorm summit plateau, is famous for having one of Scotland's largest remnants of Caledonian forest, the ancient forest of Scots pine that once covered most of the country. The forest is home to a large population of red squirrels, and is one of the last bastions of the capercaillie and the Scottish wildcat.

Activities, including horse riding, mountain biking, fishing, quad and Segway tours, gorge swimming, paddleboarding and clay pigeon shooting, can be booked online or at the **Rothiemurchus Centre** (01479-812345; Ski Rd, Inverdruie; 9.30am-5.30pm; P) FREE, a mile southeast of Aviemore along the B970. The centre sells a map detailing more than 50 miles of footpaths, including the 3-mile trail around **Loch an Eilein**, with its ruined castle and peaceful pine woods.

climbing, ice climbing, canoeing, mountain biking and mountaineering. The centre's comfortable **B&B accommodation** (01479-861256; s/tw £67/88; P) is available to all, even if you're not taking a course, as is the indoor climbing wall and gym.

Cairngorm Reindeer Centre TOURS
(01479-861228; www.cairngormreindeer.co.uk; Glenmore; adult/child £17.50/12.50;) The warden here leads guided walks to see and feed Britain's only herd of reindeer, which are free-ranging but very tame. Walks take place at 11am daily (weather dependent), plus another at 2.30pm from May to September. Book tickets in advance by phone.

Kincraig & Glen Feshie

★ **Highland Wildlife Park** ZOO
(01540-651270; www.highlandwildlifepark.org; Kincraig; adult/child £18.50/12.50; 10am-6pm Jul & Aug, to 5pm Apr-Jun, Sep & Oct, to 4pm Nov-Mar; P) This place features a drive-through safari park as well as animal enclosures, offering the chance to view rarely seen native wildlife, such as wildcats, capercaillies, pine martens, white-tailed sea eagles and red squirrels. It's also home to species that once roamed the Scottish hills but have long since disappeared, including wolf, lynx, wild boar, beaver and European bison.

★ **Old Post Office Cafe** CAFE £
(01540-651779; www.kincraigartcafe.com; The Brae, Kincraig; mains £6-10, pizzas £12-13; 10am-5pm Thu, to 8pm Fri & Sat, 10.30am-5pm Sun; P) This cute little cafe-cum-art-gallery serves top-notch coffee and cake plus comfort food with an Italian touch – focaccia filled with aubergine and hummus or Parma ham and pecorino, for example. Pizzas are available on Friday and Saturday evenings. Tables spill outdoors in summer.

Boat of Garten

Boat of Garten is known as the Osprey Village because these rare and beautiful birds of prey nest nearby at the **Royal Society for the Protection of Birds (RSPB) Loch Garten Osprey Centre** (01479-831694; www.rspb.org.uk/lochgarten; Tulloch; osprey hide adult/child £5/2.50; osprey hide 10am-6pm Apr-Aug). The ospreys migrate here each spring from Africa and nest in a tall pine tree.

Loch Garten lies within the **Abernethy National Nature Reserve** (www.nature.scot), a spectacular tract of ancient Caledonian pine forest, sweeping moorland, wetlands and mountains that extends from the slopes of Ben Macdui to the village of Nethy Bridge.

Boat of Garten is 5 miles northeast of Aviemore. The most interesting way to get here is on the Strathspey Steam Railway (p903) from Aviemore, or you can ride or walk along National Cycle Network Route 7 (allow 30 to 40 minutes by bike, two hours on foot). At Boat of Garten station, **Ride Cairngorm** (01479-831729; www.ridecairngorm.com; Boat of Garten; adult/child per day £20/12; 9am-5pm Tue-Sat) rents mountain bikes and gives advice on local trails.

Kingussie & Newtonmore

The old Speyside towns of Kingussie (kin-*yew*-see) and Newtonmore sit at the foot of the great heather-clad humps known as the Monadhliath Mountains. Newtonmore is best known as the home of the excellent Highland Folk Museum; Kingussie for one of the Highlands' best restaurants.

The road west from Newtonmore to Spean Bridge passes Ardverikie Estate and Loch Laggan.

Sights & Activities

Highland Folk Museum MUSEUM
(01540-673551; www.highlandfolk.com; Kingussie Rd, Newtonmore; 10.30am-4pm Wed-Sun; P) FREE This open-air museum comprises a collection of historical buildings and artefacts revealing many aspects of Highland culture and lifestyle. Laid out like a farming township, it has a community of traditional thatch-roofed cottages, a sawmill, a schoolhouse, a shepherd's bothy (hut) and a rural post office. Actors in period costume give demonstrations of woodcarving, wool-spinning and peat-fire baking. You'll need two to three hours to make the most of a visit. In 2020 advance booking was required.

The thatch-roofed structures of the museum's Baile Gean township were used as a filming location for the TV series *Outlander*.

Laggan Wolftrax MOUNTAIN BIKING
(http://scotland.forestry.gov.uk/visit/laggan-wolftrax; Strathmashie Forest; trails free, parking per day £3; office 10am-5pm;) Ten miles southwest of Newtonmore, on the A86 road towards Spean Bridge, this is one of Scotland's top mountain-biking centres, with five purpose-built, graded trails ranging from

WORTH A TRIP

BALMORAL CASTLE

Built for Queen Victoria in 1855 as a private residence for the royal family, **Balmoral** (☎01339-742534; www.balmoralcastle.com; Crathie; guided tour adult/child £15/6; ⊙10am-5pm Apr-Jul, limited dates Oct-Dec; P) kicked off the revival of the Scottish Baronial style of architecture that characterises so many of Scotland's 19th-century country houses. In 2020 admission was by advance booking only for an hour-long guided tour of the grounds and the castle ballroom. After the tour there's time to further explore the grounds and gardens without a guide.

Inside the castle, only the ballroom, which displays a collection of Landseer paintings and royal silver, is open to the public. Don't expect to see the Queen's private quarters! The main attraction is learning about Highland estate management, rather than royal revelations.

You can buy a booklet that details several waymarked walks within Balmoral Estate – the best is the climb to **Prince Albert's Cairn**, a huge granite pyramid that bears the inscription 'To the beloved memory of Albert the great and good, Prince Consort. Erected by his broken hearted widow Victoria R. 21st August 1862'. The walk to Albert's pyramid is open to the public even when the castle is not, starting from the car park by the A93 at Crathie; directions are available on the castle website.

Balmoral is 8 miles west of Ballater, and can be reached on the Aberdeen–Braemar bus.

family-friendly routes to black-diamond downhills with rock slabs and drop-offs. Has a **bike hire outlet and repairs shop** (☎01528-544751; www.facebook.com/weebikehub; Laggan Wolftrax; adult/child per day £25/18; ⊙10am-5pm Wed-Sun) – advance booking recommended – and a good cafe (open 10am to 5pm April to October).

Sleeping & Eating

Eagleview Guest House B&B ££

(☎01540-673675; www.eagleview-guesthouse.co.uk; Perth Rd, Newtonmore; r £90-105; P 🛜) Welcoming Eagleview is one of the most pleasant places to stay in the area, with beautifully decorated bedrooms and nice little touches such as cafetières (coffee plungers) with real coffee – and fresh milk – on your hospitality tray. Breakfast is bountiful and delicious.

★**Restaurant at the Cross** SCOTTISH £££

(☎01540-661166; www.thecross.co.uk; Tweed Mill Brae, off Ardbroilach Rd, Kingussie; 3-course lunch/dinner £26.50/48.50, tasting menu £57; ⊙noon-2pm & 7-8.30pm; P 🛜) Housed in a converted watermill, the Cross is one of the finest restaurants in the Highlands. The intimate, low-raftered dining room has an open fire and a patio overlooking the stream, and serves a daily changing menu of fresh Scottish produce accompanied by a superb wine list (booking essential).

If you want to stay the night, there are eight stylish rooms (double or twin £130 to £200) to choose from.

Getting There & Away

BUS

Kingussie and Newtonmore are served by Scottish Citylink (p899) and Stagecoach buses. Services include:

Aviemore £3.70, 25 minutes, hourly

Inverness £10.70, 1½ hours, three daily, change at Carrbridge

Perth £17.10, 1¾ hours, one daily

TRAIN

Kingussie and Newtonmore are on the Edinburgh/Glasgow–Inverness railway line. Services include:

Edinburgh £39.80, 2¾ hours, seven daily Monday to Saturday, five Sunday

Inverness £13.60, one hour, 12 daily Monday to Saturday, seven Sunday

Royal Deeside

The upper valley of the River Dee stretches west from Aboyne and Ballater to Braemar, closely paralleled by the A93 road. Made famous by its long association with the monarchy – today's royal family still holidays at Balmoral Castle, built for Queen Victoria in 1855 – the region is often called Royal Deeside.

The River Dee, renowned the world over for its salmon fishing, has its source in the Cairngorm Mountains west of Braemar, the starting point for long walks into the hills. The FishDee website (www.fishdee.co.uk) has all you need to know about fishing on the river.

Ballater

☎ 01339 / POP 1530

The attractive little village of Ballater owes its 18th-century origins to the curative waters of nearby Pannanich Springs (now bottled commercially as Deeside Natural Mineral Water), and its prosperity to nearby Balmoral Castle – note the crests on the shopfronts along the main street proclaiming 'By Royal Appointment'.

After the original station was destroyed by fire in 2015, the **Old Royal Station** (☎ 01339-755306; Station Sq; ⏲ tourist office 10am-3pm) building – newly restored to exactly replicate the one built in 1866 to receive Queen Victoria when she visited Balmoral by train – reopened in 2018. It houses a tourist office, a tearoom and cafe-bistro (www.thecarriage-ballater.co.uk).

Sleeping & Eating

Ballater Hostel HOSTEL £
(☎ 01339-753752; www.ballater-hostel.com; Bridge Sq; r £30-64; 📶) Tucked up a lane near the bridge over the River Dee, this is an attractive hostel with seven en suite rooms, sleeping two to eight. Dorm beds (usually £18.70) were not available in 2020. Rooms have personal lockers and reading lamps, and there's a comfortable lounge with big, soft sofas and a wood-burning stove.

Auld Kirk B&B £££
(☎ 01339-755762; www.theauldkirk.com; Braemar Rd; s/d from £130/140; P 📶 🐾) Here's something a little out of the ordinary – a seven-bedroom B&B and coffee lounge housed in a converted 19th-century church. The interior blends original features with sleek modern decor – the pulpit now serves as the reception desk, while the lounge is bathed in light from leaded Gothic windows.

Rock Salt & Snails CAFE £
(☎ 07834 452583; www.facebook.com/rocksaltandsnailsballater; 2 Bridge St; mains £4-9; ⏲ 10am-5pm Thu-Tue; 📶 👪 🐾) A great little cafe serving excellent coffee and tempting lunch platters featuring locally sourced deli products (cheese, ham, salads etc), including a kids' platter.

Getting There & Away

Bus 201 runs from Aberdeen to Ballater (£12.45, 1¾ hours, hourly Monday to Saturday, six on Sunday) via Crathes Castle, and continues to Braemar (£6.45, 30 minutes) every two hours.

Braemar

☎ 01339 / POP 450

Braemar is a pretty little village with a grand location on a broad plain ringed by mountains where the Dee valley and Glen Clunie meet. In winter this is one of the coldest places in the country – temperatures as low as -27°C have been recorded – and during spells of severe cold, hungry deer wander the streets looking for a bite to eat. Braemar is an excellent base for hill walking, and there's also skiing at nearby Glenshee.

Sights & Activities

Braemar's new **Highland Games Centre** (www.highlandgamescentre.org) is open daily March to December (it was closed in 2020) and contains an exhibition on the Highland Games and a cafe. It's housed in a smart green pavilion at the Princess Royal and Duke of Fife Memorial Park, where the Braemar Gathering is held.

Signs in the village centre give details of a number of waymarked walks along the river and up nearby hills. An easy walk from Braemar is up **Creag Choinnich** (538m; 2-mile round trip), a hill to the east of the village above the A93. For a longer walk (6 miles, about three hours return) and superb views of the Cairngorms, head for the summit of **Morrone** (859m), southwest of Braemar.

Braemar Castle CASTLE
(www.braemarcastle.co.uk; adult/child £10/4; ⏲ 10am-5pm daily Jul & Aug, Wed-Sun Apr-Jun, Sep & Oct; P) Just north of Braemar village, turreted Braemar Castle dates from 1628 and served as a government garrison after the 1745 Jacobite rebellion. In 2007 it was taken over by the local community, which now offers guided tours of the historic castle apartments. The castle interior was closed in 2020, but the grounds were open for walks and picnics.

Festivals & Events

Braemar Gathering SPORTS
(☎01339-755377; www.braemargathering.org; Princess Royal & Duke of Fife Memorial Park; adult/child from £12/2; ⊙Sep) There are Highland Games in many towns and villages throughout the summer, but the best known is the Braemar Gathering, which takes place on the first Saturday in September. It's a major occasion, organised every year since 1817 by the Braemar Royal Highland Society. In 2020 a Virtual Highland Games was held without spectators and broadcast online.

Sleeping

Rucksacks Bunkhouse HOSTEL £
(☎01339-741517; 15 Mar Rd; per person £20; P) This appealing cottage has a comfy dorm and cheaper beds in an alpine-style bothy (shared sleeping platform for 10 people; bring your own sleeping bag). Extras include a drying room (for wet-weather gear), a laundry and even a sauna. The friendly owner is a fount of knowledge about the local area.

In 2020 bookings could be made for individuals, couples and families, but not groups, due to social-distancing measures.

Braemar Lodge Hotel HOTEL £££
(☎01339-741627; www.braemarlodge.co.uk; Glenshee Rd; dm/s/d from £25/85/140, 3-bed cabin per week from £770; P 📶) This Victorian shooting lodge on the southern outskirts of Braemar has bags of character, not least in the wood-panelled Malt Room bar, which is as well stocked with mounted deer heads as it is with single malt whiskies. There's a good restaurant with views of the hills (mains £11 to £35), plus a 12-bed hikers' bunkhouse (book in advance).

The nine self-catering log cabins in the grounds sleep up to six people and are pet friendly.

Getting There & Away

Bus 201 runs from Aberdeen to Braemar (£12.45, 2¼ hours, every two hours Monday to Saturday, five on Sunday). The 50-mile drive from Perth to Braemar is beautiful, but there's no public transport on this route.

HIGHLAND PERTHSHIRE

The Highland border cuts diagonally across Scotland from Dumbarton to Stonehaven, dividing the county of Perthshire into two distinctive regions. Highland Perthshire, spreading north of a line from Comrie to Blairgowrie, is a land of mountains, forest and lochs, with some of the finest scenery in the UK. The ancient city of Dunkeld, on the main A9 road from Perth to Inverness, is the main gateway to the region.

Getting There & Away

Citylink (p899) buses from Edinburgh or Glasgow to Inverness stop at Birnam and Pitlochry. There are regular buses from Perth to most of the towns in the area. Trains running between Perth and Inverness stop at Blair Atholl and Pitlochry.

Dunkeld & Birnam

☎01350 / POP 1280

The Tay runs like a storybook river through the heart of Perthshire's Big Tree Country, where the twin towns of Dunkeld and Birnam are linked by Thomas Telford's graceful bridge of 1808. As well as Dunkeld's ancient cathedral, there's much walking to be done in this area of magnificent forested hills. These same walks were one of the inspirations for Beatrix Potter to create her children's tales.

There's less to see in Birnam, a name made famous by *Macbeth*. There's not much left of Birnam Wood, but a riverside path leads to the **Birnam Oak**, a venerable 500-year-old survivor from Shakespeare's time, its ageing boughs propped up with timber supports. Nearby is the 300-year-old Birnam Sycamore.

Sights & Activities

Dunkeld Cathedral CHURCH
(HS; www.dunkeldcathedral.org.uk; Cathedral St, Dunkeld; ⊙9.30am-5.30pm Apr-Sep, 10am-4pm Oct-Mar) Situated on the grassy banks of the River Tay, Dunkeld Cathedral is one of the most beautifully sited churches in Scotland; don't miss it on a sunny day, when there are few lovelier places to be. Half the cathedral is still in use as a church; the rest is a romantic ruin. It partly dates from the 14th century, having suffered damage during the Reformation and the battle of Dunkeld (Jacobites versus the government) in 1689.

Dunkeld House Grounds GARDENS
(⊙24hr) FREE Waymarked walks lead upstream from Dunkeld Cathedral through the gorgeous grounds of Dunkeld House Hotel,

formerly a seat of the dukes of Atholl. In the 18th and early 19th centuries the 'planting dukes', as they became known, planted more than 27 million conifers on their estates 'for beauty and profit', introducing species such as larch, Douglas fir and sequoia, and sowing the seeds of Scottish forestry.

Loch of the Lowes Wildlife Centre WILDLIFE RESERVE
(☎01350-727337; www.swt.org.uk; adult/child £4.50/free; ⏲10am-5pm Mar-Oct, 10.30am-4pm Fri-Sun Nov-Feb; P) Loch of the Lowes, 2 miles east of Dunkeld off the A923, has a visitor centre devoted to red squirrels and the majestic osprey. There's a birdwatching hide (with binoculars provided), where you can see the birds nesting during breeding season (late April to August), complete with a live video link to the nest. In 2020 advance booking was required.

Hermitage WALKING
(NTS; www.nts.org.uk; parking £3) One of the most popular walks near Dunkeld is the Hermitage, where a well-marked trail follows the River Braan to Ossian's Hall, a quaint folly built by the Duke of Atholl in 1758 overlooking the spectacular Falls of Braan (salmon can be seen leaping here, especially in September and October). It's signposted off the A9 just west of the village.

Sleeping & Eating

★Jessie Mac's HOSTEL £
(☎01350-727324; www.jessiemacs.co.uk; Murthly Tce, Birnam; dm/s/d/f £23/37/61/85;) Set in a Victorian manse complete with baronial turret, Jessie Mac's is a glorious cross between B&B and luxury hostel, with three gorgeous doubles and four shared or family rooms with bunks. Guests make good use of the country-style lounge, sunny dining room and well-equipped kitchen.

Breakfast (£6 to £9) is made with local produce, from organic eggs to Dunkeld smoked salmon.

★Taybank PUB FOOD ££
(☎01350-727340; www.thetaybank.co.uk; Tay Tce, Dunkeld; mains £12-15; ⏲food served noon-9pm; P) Top choice for a sun-kissed pub lunch by the river is the Taybank, a regular meeting place and performance space for folk musicians and a wonderfully welcoming bar. The menu features fresh produce from the kitchen garden in dishes such as cured mackerel with fennel, and wood pigeon with beetroot, blackberries and dukkah.

B&B accommodation is available in two newly renovated Scandi-style rooms (single/double from £120/150).

Getting There & Away

Citylink (p898) buses running between Glasgow/Edinburgh (£19.20, two hours, two or three daily) and Inverness (£22.40, 2½ hours) stop at the Birnam Hotel. Stagecoach (p898) runs hourly buses (seven on Sunday) between Perth and Dunkeld (£2.90, 45 minutes), continuing to Aberfeldy (£3.60, 40 minutes).

Pitlochry

☎01796 / POP 2780

Pitlochry, with the scent of the Highlands already in the air, is a popular stop on the way north. In summer the main street can be a conga line of tour groups, but linger a while and it can still charm – on a quiet spring evening it's a pretty place, with salmon leaping in the Tummel and good things brewing at the Moulin Hotel.

Sights

One of Pitlochry's attractions is its beautiful riverside – the River Tummel is dammed here, and if you're lucky you might see salmon swimming up the **fish ladder** to Loch Faskally above (May to November; best month is October).

Pitlochry Dam Visitor Centre VISITOR CENTRE
(www.pitlochrydam.com; Armoury Rd; ⏲10am-4.30pm; P) FREE Opened in 2017, this architecturally stunning visitor centre is perched above the dam on the River Tummel, and houses an exhibition (closed in 2020) that details the history of hydroelectricity in Scotland, alongside the life cycle of Atlantic salmon (all hydro stations need a fish ladder to allow salmon to migrate upstream past the dams).

The centre's excellent **Salmon Leap Cafe** serves sandwiches, pizzas and cakes (mains £6 to £9), with tables overlooking the river.

Pass of Killiecrankie HISTORIC SITE
(NTS; www.nts.org.uk; parking £3; ⏲24hr; P) FREE The beautiful, rugged Pass of Killiecrankie, 3.5 miles north of Pitlochry, where the River Garry tumbles through a narrow gorge, was the site of the 1689 **Battle of Killiecrankie** that ignited the Jacobite rebellion. The visitor centre (closed

in 2020) has great interactive displays on Jacobite history and local flora and fauna. There are some stunning walks along the wooded gorge, too; keep an eye out for red squirrels.

Explorers Garden GARDENS
(01796-484600; www.explorersgarden.com; Foss Rd; adult/child £4/1; 10am-5pm Apr-Oct; P) This gem of a garden is based around plants brought to Scotland by 18th- and 19th-century Scottish botanists and explorers such as David Douglas (after whom the Douglas fir is named), and celebrates 300 years of collecting and the 'plant hunters' who tracked down these exotic species. It's behind the Pitlochry Festival Theatre, south of the river. The garden was closed in 2020.

Sleeping

Pitlochry Youth Hostel HOSTEL £
(HS; 01796-472308; www.hostellingscotland.org.uk; Knockard Rd; tw/tr/q £44/54/64; Apr-Oct; P@) Great location overlooking the town centre, with a large self-catering kitchen (closed in 2020) and lounge. Popular with families and walkers. In 2020 only private rooms could be booked (no shared dorms).

★ **Craigatin House** B&B ££
(01796-472478; www.craigatinhouse.co.uk; 165 Atholl Rd; d/ste £115/145; P@) Several times more tasteful than the average Scottish B&B, this elegant house and garden is set back from the main road. Chic contemporary fabrics covering expansive beds offer a standard of comfort above and beyond the reasonable price; the rooms in the converted stable block are particularly inviting. A fabulous breakfast and lounge area gives views over the lush garden.

★ **Fonab Castle Hotel** HISTORIC HOTEL £££
(01796-470140; www.fonabcastlehotel.com; Foss Rd; d from £329; P) This Scottish Baronial fantasy in red sandstone was built in 1892 as the country house of Lieutenant Colonel George Sandeman, a scion of the famous port and sherry merchants. Now a luxury hotel and spa, it has a tasteful modern extension with commanding views over Loch Faskally, and a superb restaurant serving the finest Scottish venison, beef and seafood.

Eating

Port-na-Craig Inn BISTRO ££
(01796-472777; www.portnacraig.com; Port-na-Craig; mains £11-15; 11am-8.30pm; P) Across the river from the town centre, this cute little cottage sits in what was once a separate hamlet. Top-quality main meals are prepared with confidence and panache; there are also simpler sandwiches, kids' meals and light lunches. Or you could just sit outdoors by the river with a pint and watch the salmon anglers.

Moulin Hotel PUB FOOD ££
(01796-472196; www.moulinhotel.co.uk; Kirkmichael Rd; mains £11-16; food served noon-9.30pm; P) A mile away from town but a world apart, this atmospheric inn has low ceilings, ageing wood and snug booths. It's a wonderfully romantic spot for a home-brewed ale (there's a microbrewery out back) and some Highland comfort food: try the haggis, neeps and tatties. It's a pleasant uphill stroll from Pitlochry, and an easy roll down afterwards.

★ **Saorsa 1875** VEGAN £££
(01796-475217; www.saorsahotel.com; 2 E Moulin Rd; lunch mains £11-14, 5-course dinner per person £50; noon-3pm & 7.30pm; P) Britain's first vegan hotel can be found in an elegant Victorian building in little Pitlochry. The outstanding five-course dinner menu is served at a communal dining table, where the chef presents each of the dishes made with ingredients such as locally foraged mushrooms. Call in for lunch (banana blossom 'fish', salads, smoothies) in the beautifully styled bar; dinner is by reservation only.

From the drinks list to the cleaning products, everything at Saorsa is carefully sourced to be vegan friendly. Its 11 rooms (doubles £140 to £230) are individually styled with statement wallpaper and upcycled furniture. Yoga classes are held in a yurt in the hotel grounds, which include two acres of woodland.

Entertainment

★ **Pitlochry Festival Theatre** THEATRE
(01796-484626; www.pitlochryfestivaltheatre.com; Port-na-Craig; tickets £17-37) Founded in 1951 (in a tent!), this famous and much-loved theatre is the focus of Highland Perthshire's cultural life. The summer season, from May to mid-October, stages a different production each night of the week except Sunday.

Information

Pitlochry Tourist Office (01796-472215; www.perthshire.co.uk; 22 Atholl Rd; 10am-3pm, longer hours Jul & Aug) Free maps and good information on local walks.

Getting There & Away

BUS

Scottish Citylink (p899) buses run two to five times daily to Inverness (£19.20, 1¾ hours), Perth (£12.30, 50 minutes), Edinburgh (£19.20, two to 2½ hours) and Glasgow (£19.20, 1¾ to two hours).

Megabus (0871 266 3333; www.megabus.com) offers discounted fares to Inverness, Perth, Edinburgh and Glasgow.

Stagecoach (p898) buses run via a change in Ballinluig to Aberfeldy (£3.90, 45 minutes, hourly Monday to Saturday, three Sunday), Dunkeld (£2.70, 40 minutes, hourly Monday to Saturday) and Perth (£4.30, 1¼ hours, hourly Monday to Saturday).

TRAIN

Pitlochry is on the main railway line from Perth (£15.30, 30 minutes, 12 daily Monday to Saturday, seven on Sunday) to Inverness (£24.80, 1¾ hours, same frequency).

Blair Atholl

One of the most popular tourist attractions in Scotland, magnificent **Blair Castle** (01796-481207; www.blair-castle.co.uk; house & gardens adult/child £14/8.50, gardens only £7.70/3.50; 10am-5.30pm Easter-Oct, to 4pm Sat & Sun Nov-Easter; P) – and its surrounding estates – is the seat of the Duke of Atholl, head of the Murray clan. It's an impressive white heap set beneath forested slopes above the River Garry. Thirty rooms are open to the public and they present a wonderful picture of upper-class Highland life from the 16th century on. In 2020 admission to the castle was by prebooked guided tour only.

The original tower was built in 1269, but the castle underwent significant remodelling in the 18th and 19th centuries. Highlights include the 2nd-floor **drawing room** with its ornate Georgian plasterwork and Zoffany portrait of the fourth duke's family, complete with a pet lemur (yes, you read that correctly) called Tommy; and the **tapestry room** draped with 17th-century wall hangings created for Charles I. The **dining room** is sumptuous – check out the nine-pint wine glasses.

In May, the Duke of Atholl visits to review the Atholl Highlanders, Britain's only private army, and attend the **Atholl Gathering and Highland Games**.

Lochs Tummel & Rannoch

The scenic route along Lochs Tummel and Rannoch (www.rannochandtummel.co.uk) is worth doing any way you can – by foot, bicycle or car. Hillsides shrouded with ancient birchwoods and forests of spruce, pine and larch make up the fabulous **Tay Forest Park**, the wooded hills of which roll into the glittering waters of the lochs. A visit in autumn, when the birch leaves are at their finest, is recommended.

Eighteen miles west of Kinloch Rannoch, the road ends at romantic and isolated **Rannoch Station**, which lies on the Glasgow–Fort William railway line. Beyond sprawls the desolate expanse of **Rannoch Moor**, the largest area of moorland in Britain, stretching west for eight barren, bleak and uninhabited miles to the A82 Glasgow–Fort William road. Despite the appearance of desolation, the moor is rich in wildlife. There's an excellent **tearoom** (01882-633247; www.rannochstationtearoom.co.uk; Rannoch Station; mains £3.50-9; 8am-4.30pm Mon-Thu & Sat, 10am-4.30pm Sun; P) on Rannoch Station platform, and the welcoming small **Moor of Rannoch Restaurant & Rooms** (01882-633238; www.moorofrannoch.co.uk; Rannoch Station; s/d incl dinner £248/305; Thu-Mon Feb-Nov; P) alongside. Be aware that Rannoch Station is a dead end, and the nearest service station is at Aberfeldy.

There are three trains daily (two on Sunday) from Rannoch Station north to Fort William (£11.80, one hour) and Mallaig (2½ hours, £26.50), and south to Glasgow (£26.80, 2¾ hours).

Loch Tay

Loch Tay is the heart of the ancient region known as Breadalbane (from the Gaelic Bràghad Albainn, 'the heights of Scotland') – mighty **Ben Lawers** (1214m), looming over the loch, is the highest peak outside the Ben Nevis and Cairngorms regions. Much of the land to the north of Loch Tay falls within the **Ben Lawers National Nature Reserve** (www.nts.org.uk), known for its rare alpine flora.

The main access point for the ascent of Ben Lawers is the car park 1.5 miles north of the A827, on the minor road from Loch Tay to Bridge of Balgie. The climb is 6.5 miles and can take up to five hours (return): pack wet-weather gear, water, food and a map and compass. There's also an easier nature trail here.

Loch Tay is famous for its fishing – salmon, trout and pike are all caught here. **Loch Tay Fish 'n' Trips** (07967 567347; www.lochtayfishntrips.co.uk) can kit you out for a day's fishing with boat, tackle and guide for £130 for two people, or rent you a boat for £65 a day.

The main road from Kenmore to Killin runs along the north shore of Loch Tay. The minor road along the south shore is narrow and twisting (unsuitable for large vehicles), but offers great views of the hills to the north.

★Scottish Crannog Centre MUSEUM
(01887-830583; www.crannog.co.uk; adult/child £10/7; 10am-5.30pm Apr-Oct; P) Less than a mile south of Kenmore, on the banks of Loch Tay, is the fascinating Scottish Crannog Centre, perched on stilts above the loch. Crannogs – effectively artificial islands – were a favoured form of defensive dwelling from the 3rd millennium BCE onwards. This superb recreation (based on studies of Oakbank crannog, one of 18 discovered in Loch Tay) offers a guided tour that includes an impressive demonstration of fire making and Iron Age crafts. Book tours in advance.

WEST HIGHLANDS

This region extends from the bleak blanket-bog of the Moor of Rannoch to the west coast beyond Glen Coe and Fort William, and includes the southern reaches of the Great Glen. The scenery is grand throughout, with high, rocky mountains rising above wild glens. Great expanses of moor alternate with lochs and patches of commercial forest. Fort William, at the inner end of Loch Linnhe, is the only sizeable town in the area.

Since 2007 the region has been promoted as Lochaber Geopark (www.lochabergeopark.org.uk), an area of outstanding geology and scenery.

Getting There & Away

The scenic West Highland railway line from Glasgow to Fort William and Mallaig – the departure point for ferries to the Small Isles, Skye and the Outer Hebrides – runs through the heart of the region, and is an ideal way of travelling between the main centres. A network of local bus services fills in the gaps.

Glen Coe

Scotland's most famous glen is also one of its grandest and – in bad weather – its grimmest. The approach to the glen from the east is guarded by the rocky pyramid of **Buachaille Etive Mor** – the Great Shepherd of Etive – and the lonely Kings House Hotel (p914). After the Battle of Culloden in 1745, the inn was used as a Hanoverian garrison – hence the name.

The A82 road leads over the Pass of Glencoe and into the narrow upper glen. The southern side is dominated by three massive, brooding spurs, known as the **Three Sisters**, while the northern side is enclosed by the continuous steep wall of the knife-edged **Aonach Eagach** ridge, a classic mountaineering challenge. The road threads its way past deep gorges and crashing waterfalls to the more pastoral lower reaches of the glen around Loch Achtriochtan and Glencoe village.

The **Glencoe Visitor Centre** (NTS; 01855-811307; www.nts.org.uk; parking £4; 9.30am-4pm; P) FREE provides comprehensive information on the geological, environmental and cultural history of Glen Coe and tells the story of the Glencoe Massacre in all its gory detail. There's an excellent 3D map of the glen, and a ranger can give advice on local walks. It's 1.5 miles southeast of Glencoe village.

Sleeping & Eating

Glencoe Independent Hostel HOSTEL £
(01855-811906; www.glencoehostel.co.uk; hostel/bunkhouse dm £25/20; P@) This handily located hostel, just 1.5 miles southeast of Glencoe village, is set in an old farmhouse with six- and eight-bed dorms, and a newly renovated bunkhouse with another 16 spaces in communal, alpine-style bunks. There's also a wooden cabin that sleeps up to three (£73 per night).

Kings House Hotel HOTEL £££
(01855-851259; www.kingshousehotel.co.uk; Kingshouse; r £210-290, bunkhouse dm £35; restaurant 6-8.30pm;) A major redevelopment has transformed this remote inn into a luxurious modern hotel, with 57 sleek but cosy rooms sleeping up to four people (two have large balconies with views of the hills) and a large bar and restaurant (mains £10 to £30). A purpose-built wooden chalet houses a 35-bed bunkhouse, with laundry facilities and a drying room.

Clachaig Inn HOTEL £££
(01855-811252; www.clachaig.com; s/d £78/155;) The Clachaig, 2 miles southeast of Glencoe village, has long been a favourite haunt of hill walkers and climbers. As well as comfortable accommodation (opt for a room with a Glen Coe view), there's a lounge bar with snug booths and high refectory tables serving good food (mains £11 to £20) from noon to 9pm.

Glencoe Café CAFE £
(01855-811168; www.glencoecafe.co.uk; Lorn Dr, Glencoe Village; mains £4.50-10; 11am-5pm Fri-Wed May-Oct, to 4pm Nov-Apr;) This friendly cafe is the social hub of Glencoe village, serving breakfast fry-ups (including vegetarian versions) till 11.30am, light lunches based on local produce and the best cappuccino in the glen.

★**Laroch** SCOTTISH ££
(01855-811940; www.thelarochrestaurantandbar.co.uk; Loanfern, Ballachulish; mains £12-22; noon-2.45pm & 6-8.45pm Tue-Sun;) This friendly restaurant and bar in Ballachulish village, 1 mile west of Glencoe village, is highly recommended for its excellent food. Local ingredients are cooked with finesse and burst with flavour: the menu changes regularly but features dishes such as Mallaig halibut with roasted scallops and Loch Leven mussels, and wild mushroom and sweet potato risotto. Book ahead.

Getting There & Away

Scottish Citylink (p899) buses run between Fort William and Glencoe (£13.60, 30 minutes, four to eight daily) and from Glencoe to Glasgow (£24.20, 2¾ hours, four to eight daily). Buses stop at Glencoe village (at the crossroads), Glencoe Visitor Centre and Glencoe Mountain Resort.

Shiel Buses (01397-700700; www.shielbuses.co.uk) route 44 links Glencoe village with Fort William (£4.50, 40 minutes, seven daily Monday to Saturday, four on Sunday) and Kinlochleven (£2.40, 15 minutes).

Fort William

01397 / POP 10,460

Basking on Loch Linnhe's shores amid magnificent mountain scenery, Fort William has one of the most enviable settings in all of Scotland. If it weren't for the busy dual carriageway crammed between the less-than-attractive town centre and the loch, and one of the highest rainfall records in the country, it would be almost idyllic. Even so, the town has carved out a reputation as the 'Outdoor Capital of the UK' (www.outdoorcapital.co.uk), and easy access by rail and bus makes it a good base for exploring the surrounding mountains and glens.

Magical Glen Nevis begins near the northern end of the town and wraps itself around the southern flanks of Ben Nevis (1345m) – Britain's highest mountain and a magnet for hikers and climbers.

Sights

★**Jacobite Steam Train** HERITAGE RAILWAY
(0844 850 4685; www.westcoastrailways.co.uk; day return adult/child from £43/26; mid-May–Oct) The Jacobite Steam Train, hauled by a former LNER K1 or LMS Class 5MT locomotive, travels the scenic two-hour run between Fort William and Mallaig. Classed as one of the great railway journeys of the world, the route crosses the historic Glenfinnan Viaduct, made famous in the *Harry Potter* films – the Jacobite's owners supplied the steam locomotive and rolling stock used in the film.

Trains depart from Fort William train station at 10.15am and (in peak season only) 2.40pm, and return from Mallaig at 2.10pm and 6.40pm. There's a brief stop at Glenfinnan station, and you get 1½ hours in Mallaig (two hours on the afternoon service).

West Highland Museum MUSEUM
(01397-702169; www.westhighlandmuseum.org.uk; Cameron Sq; 10am-2pm Tue-Fri) FREE This small but fascinating museum is packed with all manner of Highland memorabilia. Look out for the secret portrait of Bonnie Prince Charlie – after the Jacobite rebellions, all things Highland were banned, including pictures of the exiled leader, and this tiny painting looks like nothing more than a smear of paint until viewed in a

cylindrical mirror, which reflects a credible likeness of the prince. In 2020 the museum operated with limited opening hours and an advance booking system.

Sleeping

Fort William Backpackers HOSTEL £
(☎01397-700711; www.fortwilliambackpackers.com; Alma Rd; dm/tw £21/50; P@🛜) A 10-minute walk from the bus and train stations, this lively and welcoming hostel is set in a grand Victorian villa, perched on a hillside with great views over Loch Linnhe.

6 Caberfeidh B&B ££
(☎01397-703756; www.6caberfeidh.com; 6 Caberfeidh, Fassifern Rd; d/f £90/120; 🛜) Friendly owners and comfortable accommodation make a great combination; add a good central location and you're all set. Choose from one of two family rooms (one double and one single bed) or a romantic double with four-poster.

★**Grange** B&B £££
(☎01397-705516; www.grangefortwilliam.com; Grange Rd; d £195-225; ⏲closed Sun; P🛜) An exceptional 19th-century villa set in its own landscaped grounds, the Grange is crammed with antiques and warmed by log fires. It has two luxury suites fitted with leather sofas, handcrafted furniture and roll-top baths, one situated in a charming self-contained cottage in the sprawling gardens, all with a view over Loch Linnhe. No children.

Lime Tree HOTEL £££
(☎01397-701806; www.limetreefortwilliam.co.uk; Achintore Rd; d £155-175; P🛜) Much more interesting than your average guesthouse, this former Victorian manse overlooking Loch Linnhe is an 'art gallery with rooms', decorated throughout with the artist-owner's atmospheric Highland landscapes. Foodies rave about the restaurant, and the gallery space – a triumph of sensitive design – stages everything from serious exhibitions (works by David Hockney and Andy Goldsworthy have appeared) to folk concerts.

Eating & Drinking

Wildcat VEGAN £
(www.wildcatcafe.co.uk; 21 High St; mains £4-9; ⏲8am-5.30pm Wed-Sat; 🖉) 🌿 This vegan cafe serves sourdough sandwiches, salads, soups and brunches made with mainly local produce, as well as coffee and cakes. All the ingredients used – nut butters, curry pastes, pesto etc – are made from scratch in the cafe's kitchen. At the back is a small store selling fair-trade, organic snacks and plastic-free produce by weight.

★**Lime Tree** SCOTTISH ££
(☎01397-701806; www.limetreefortwilliam.co.uk; Achintore Rd; mains £19-22.50, set menu £30; ⏲6.30-9.30pm; P🛜) 🌿 The restaurant at this small hotel and art gallery has put the UK's Outdoor Capital on the gastronomic map. The chef turns out delicious dishes built around fresh Scottish produce, such as Loch Fyne oysters, Loch Awe trout and Ardnamurchan venison.

★**Crannog Seafood Restaurant** SEAFOOD ££
(☎01397-705589; www.crannog.net; Town Pier; mains £10-22.50; ⏲noon-9pm) The Crannog wins the prize for the best location in town – perched on the Town Pier, giving window-table diners an uninterrupted view down Loch Linnhe. Informal and unfussy, it specialises in fresh local fish (there are three or four daily fish specials plus the main menu) though there are lamb, venison and vegetarian dishes, too.

At research time Crannog Seafood was operating at **Garrison West** (☎01397-701873; www.garrisonwest.co.uk; 4 Cameron Sq; mains £11-22.50; 🛜👶) while the pier was closed for repairs.

Black Isle Bar BAR
(www.blackislebrewery.com; Gordon Sq; ⏲bar noon-11pm, food noon-9pm; 🛜🐕) In a grand granite building that was once a church, this pub serves craft beers from the Black Isle Brewery (p898) as well as organic wine and local whisky. There are also wood-fired pizzas (£11.50 to £13) with Scottish toppings such as haggis and venison salami.

Getting There & Away

BUS

Scottish Citylink (www.citylink.co.uk) buses link Fort William with other major towns and cities. Services include:

Edinburgh £39.40, 5¼ hours, three daily with a change at Glasgow; via Glencoe and Crianlarich
Glasgow £26.40, three hours, four daily
Inverness £11.60, two hours, six daily
Oban £9.40, 1½ hours, two daily
Portree £34.40, three hours, three daily

Shiel Buses service 500 runs to Mallaig (£6.60, 1½ hours, four daily Monday to Friday, one daily Saturday) via Glenfinnan (£3.50, 30 minutes) and Arisaig (£5.70, one hour).

TRAIN

The spectacular West Highland line runs from Glasgow to Mallaig via Fort William. The overnight **Caledonian Sleeper** (www.sleeper.scot) service connects Fort William and London Euston (from £117 sharing a twin-berth cabin, 13 hours).

There's no direct rail connection between Oban and Fort William – you have to change at Crianlarich, so it's faster to use the bus. Rail services include:

Edinburgh £55.20, five hours; change at Glasgow's Queen St station, three daily, two on Sunday

Glasgow £32.70, 3¾ hours, three daily, two on Sunday

Mallaig £13.80, 1½ hours, four daily, three on Sunday

Around Fort William

Glen Nevis

Scenic Glen Nevis, used as a filming location for *Braveheart* and the *Harry Potter* movies, lies just an hour's walk from Fort William town centre. The **Glen Nevis Tourist Office** (01349-781401; parking £4; 8.30am-4pm, longer hours Jul & Aug) is situated 1.5 miles up the glen, and provides information on hiking, weather forecasts, and specific advice on climbing Ben Nevis.

Sleeping & Eating

★**Glen Nevis Youth Hostel** HOSTEL £
(HS; 01397-702336; www.hostellingscotland.org.uk; tw/q £50/70; P@) A modern, well-equipped hostel located 3 miles from Fort William, right beside one of the starting points for the tourist track up Ben Nevis.

CLIMBING BEN NEVIS

As the highest peak in the British Isles, Ben Nevis (1345m) attracts many would-be ascensionists who would not normally think of climbing a Scottish mountain – a staggering (often literally) 100,000 people reach the summit each year.

Although anyone who is reasonably fit should have no problem climbing Ben Nevis on a fine summer's day, an ascent should not be undertaken lightly; every year people have to be rescued from the mountain. You will need proper walking boots (the path is rough and stony, and there may be snow on the summit), warm clothing, waterproofs, a map and compass, and plenty of food and water. And don't forget to check the weather forecast.

Here are a few facts to mull over before you go racing up the tourist track: the summit plateau is bounded by 700m-high cliffs and has a sub-Arctic climate; at the summit it can snow on any day of the year; the summit is wrapped in cloud nine days out of 10; in thick cloud, visibility at the summit can be 10m or less; and in such conditions the only safe way off the mountain requires careful use of a map and compass to avoid walking over those 700m cliffs.

The tourist track (the easiest route to the top) was originally called the Pony Track. It was built in the 19th century for the pack ponies that carried supplies to a meteorological observatory on the summit (now in ruins), which was in use continuously from 1883 to 1904.

There are three possible starting points for the tourist track ascent: Achintee Farm; the footbridge at Glen Nevis Youth Hostel; and, if you have a car, the car park at Glen Nevis Tourst Office. The path climbs gradually to the shoulder at Lochan Meall an t-Suidhe (known as the Halfway Lochan), then zigzags steeply up beside the Red Burn to the summit plateau. The highest point is marked by a trig point on top of a huge cairn beside the ruins of the old observatory. The plateau is scattered with countless smaller cairns, stones arranged in the shape of people's names and, sadly, a fair bit of litter.

The total distance to the summit and back is 8 miles; allow at least four or five hours to reach the top, and another 2½ to three hours for the descent. Afterwards, as you celebrate in the pub with a pint, consider the fact that the record time for the annual Ben Nevis Hill Race is just under 1½ hours – up and down. Then have another pint.

Breakfasts (£4.50) and packed lunches (£6.50) are available, and the small shop at reception sells local craft beers and snacks. In 2020 only private rooms were available (no shared dorms).

Achintee Farm B&B ££
(01397-702240; www.achinteefarm.com; Achintee; B&B d £115-135, self-catering tw/d from £56/90; B&B May-Oct, self-catering year-round;) This attractive farmhouse offers excellent B&B accommodation and also has a small self-catered apartment attached. It's at the start of the path up Ben Nevis.

★ **Ben Nevis Inn** SCOTTISH ££
(01397-701227; www.ben-nevis-inn.co.uk; Achintee; mains £12-14.50; noon-11pm daily Mar-Oct, Thu-Sun Nov-Feb;) This great barn of a pub serves real ale and tasty bar meals (noon to 9pm), and has a comfy bunkhouse downstairs (£18 to £20 per person). It's at the start of the path from Achintee up Ben Nevis, and only a mile from the end of the West Highland Way.

Getting There & Away

Bus 41 runs from Fort William bus station to Glen Nevis Youth Hostel (£2.20, 15 minutes, two daily Monday to Saturday).

Nevis Range

Six miles to the north of Fort William lies **Nevis Range ski area** (01397-705825; www.nevisrange.co.uk; gondola day ticket adult/child £19.50/11; 9.30am-4pm Thu-Mon), where a gondola gives access to the upper part of Aonach Mor mountain. The facility operates year-round, allowing visitors to access mountain paths and **mountain-biking trails** (www.nevisrange.co.uk/bike; single/multitrip ticket £20.50/33.50; downhill course 10.15am-3.45pm Apr-Oct, forest trails 24hr year-round) outside of the ski season.

Shiel Buses (p914) route 41 runs from Fort William bus station to Nevis Range (£2.70, 25 minutes, four daily Monday to Saturday).

Road to the Isles

The 46-mile A830 road from Fort William to Mallaig is traditionally known as the Road to the Isles, as it leads to the jumping-off point for ferries to the Small Isles and Skye, itself a stepping stone to the Outer Hebrides. This is a region steeped in Jacobite history, having witnessed both the beginning and the end of Bonnie Prince Charlie's doomed attempt to regain the British throne in 1745–46.

The final section of this scenic route, between Arisaig and Mallaig, has been upgraded to a fast straight road; the scenic old road is signposted 'Alternative Coastal Route'.

Between the A830 and the A87 far to the north lie Knoydart and Glenelg – Scotland's 'Empty Quarter'.

Getting There & Away

BOAT

A passenger ferry operated by Western Isles Cruises (p919) links Mallaig to Inverie on the Knoydart Peninsula (25 to 40 minutes) four times daily Monday to Saturday (three on Sunday) from April to October.

CalMac (0800 066 5000; www.calmac.co.uk) operates the passenger-only ferry from Mallaig to the following destinations in the Small Isles:

Canna £11.20 return, two hours, three weekly
Eigg £8.20 return, 1¼ hours, three weekly
Muck £9.50 return, 1½ hours, four weekly
Rum £8.90 return, 1¼ hours, four weekly

There are CalMac car ferry services to Armadale in Skye (car/passenger £9.95/3, 30 minutes, five daily Monday to Saturday, three on Sunday), and Lochboisdale in South Uist (car/passenger £59.05/10.75, 3½ hours, one daily).

BUS

Shiel Buses (p914) service 500 runs between Fort William and Mallaig (£6.60, 1½ hours, four daily Monday to Friday, one daily Saturday and Sunday) via Arisaig (£2.80, 25 minutes) and Glenfinnan (£4.10, 55 minutes).

TRAIN

The West Highland line runs between Fort William and Mallaig (£13.80, 1½ hours, four daily, three on Sunday).

Glenfinnan

01397 / POP 100

Glenfinnan is hallowed ground for fans of Bonnie Prince Charlie; the monument here marks where he raised his Highland army. It's also a place of pilgrimage for steam train enthusiasts and *Harry Potter* fans – the famous railway viaduct features in the Potter films, and is regularly traversed by the Jacobite Steam Train (p914).

Sights & Activities

Glenfinnan Monument MONUMENT

(NTS; www.nts.org.uk; parking £3) This tall column, topped by a statue of a kilted Highlander, was erected in 1815 on the spot where Bonnie Prince Charlie first raised his standard and rallied the Jacobite clans on 19 August 1745, marking the start of his ill-fated campaign, which would end in disaster at Culloden 14 months later. The setting, at the north end of Loch Shiel, is hauntingly beautiful. It's possible to climb the monument on a prebooked tour (adult/child £4/3); check times online.

The **visitor centre** (9.30am-4.30pm; P) FREE here recounts the story of the '45, as the Jacobite rebellion of 1745 is known, when Bonnie Prince Charlie's loyal clansmen marched and fought their way from Glenfinnan south via Edinburgh to Derby, then back north to final defeat at Culloden.

Glenfinnan Station Museum MUSEUM

(www.glenfinnanstationmuseum.co.uk; admission by donation; 9am-5pm Easter-Oct; P) This fascinating little museum records the epic tale of building the West Highland railway line. The famous 21-arch **Glenfinnan viaduct**, just east of the station, was built in 1901, and featured in several *Harry Potter* movies. A pleasant walk of around 1200m east from the station (signposted) leads to a viewpoint for the viaduct and for Loch Shiel.

Loch Shiel Cruises CRUISE

(07801 537617; www.highlandcruises.co.uk; 1hr cruise adult/child £15/7.50; Apr-Sep) Boat trips along Loch Shiel, with the opportunity of spotting golden eagles and other wildlife. There are one- to two-hour cruises offering fabulous views. Twice a week the boat goes the full length of the loch to Acharacle (one way/return £23/35), calling at Polloch and Dalilea, allowing for walks and bike rides using the forestry track on the eastern shore.

The boat departs from a jetty near Glenfinnan House Hotel.

Sleeping

Prince's House Hotel INN £££

(01397-722246; www.glenfinnan.co.uk; s/d from £115/190; P) A delightful old coaching inn dating from 1658, the Prince's House is a great place to pamper yourself – ask for the spacious, tartan-draped Stuart Room (£250), complete with four-poster bed, if you want to stay in the oldest part of the hotel. The relaxed but well-regarded restaurant specialises in Scottish produce; there's also a more casual bistro.

There's no documented evidence that Bonnie Prince Charlie actually stayed here in 1745, but it was the only sizeable house in Glenfinnan at that time, so...

Arisaig & Morar

The 5 miles of coast between the tiny villages of Arisaig and Morar is a fretwork of rocky islets, inlets and gorgeous silver-sand beaches backed by dunes and machair, with stunning sunset views across the sea to the silhouetted peaks of Eigg and Rum. The **Silver Sands of Morar**, as they are known, draw crowds of bucket-and-spade holidaymakers in July and August, when the many campsites scattered along the coast are filled to overflowing.

Activities

Arisaig Marine WILDLIFE WATCHING

(01687-450224; www.arisaig.co.uk; Arisaig Harbour; late Apr-Sep) In summer Arisaig Marine operates wildlife-watching cruises (minke whales, basking sharks, porpoises, dolphins) from Arisaig harbour to Eigg (£18, one hour, six weekly), Rum (£25, 2½ hours, two or three weekly) and Muck (£20, two hours, three weekly). Sailing times allow five hours ashore on Eigg, and two or three hours on Muck or Rum.

There are also twice-weekly three-hour scenic boat trips (£22.50) that return to Arisaig harbour without docking elsewhere. In 2020 there were no boat trips to the Small Isles, which were closed to tourists.

Sleeping & Eating

Old Library Lodge & Restaurant SCOTTISH ££

(01687-450651; www.oldlibrary.co.uk; Arisaig; mains £10.50-17; noon-2pm & 6-8.30pm; P) The Old Library is a charming restaurant with rooms (doubles £120) set in converted 200-year-old stables overlooking the waterfront in Arisaig village. The lunch menu concentrates on soups, burgers and smoked fish or meat platters, while dinner is a more sophisticated affair offering local seafood, beef and lamb.

Mallaig

01687 / POP 810

If you're travelling between Fort William and Skye, you may find yourself staying

OFF THE BEATEN TRACK

KNOYDART PENINSULA

The Knoydart peninsula – a rugged landscape of wild mountains and lonely sea lochs – is the only sizeable area in Britain that remains inaccessible to vehicles, cut off by miles of rough country and the embracing arms of Lochs Nevis and Hourn (Gaelic for the lochs of Heaven and Hell). Walkers come to climb the 1020m peak of **Ladhar Bheinn** (laar-ven), but it's worth visiting just to enjoy the feeling of remoteness.

No road penetrates this wilderness of rugged hills – **Inverie**, its sole village, can only be reached by ferry from Mallaig, or on foot from the remote road's end at Kinloch Hourn (a tough 16-mile hike that affords walk-in bragging rights). A 4WD track leads northwest from Inverie for 7 miles to the outposts of **Doune** and **Airor**, which offer even more remote accommodation options. All accommodation is listed on www.visitknoydart.co.uk.

In Inverie, **Old Forge** (01687-462267; www.theoldforge.co.uk; Inverie; mains £16-24; kitchen 12.30-2.30pm & 5.30-9pm Thu-Tue Mar-Oct;), listed in *Guinness World Records* as Britain's most remote pub, has real ale on tap, including the Belgian owner's own brew, Remoteness. The house special is a seafood platter (£38); all ingredients are sourced within 7 miles of the pub. Opposite the village shop is the **Table** (www.facebook.com/thetableknoydart; Inverie), a wooden shed with a firepit, disco ball and seating area that was set up by the community as a social space.

The **Western Isles Cruises** (01687-462233; www.westernislescruises.co.uk; Mallaig to Knoydart adult/child £11/5.50) passenger ferry links Mallaig to Inverie (25 to 40 minutes) four times daily Monday to Saturday and three on Sunday from April to October. Taking the morning boat gives you up to 10 hours ashore in Knoydart before the return trip (first and last boats of the day should be booked in advance). There's also an afternoon sailing between Inverie and Tarbet on the south side of Loch Nevis, allowing walkers to hike along the northern shore of Loch Morar to Tarbet and return by boat (£10 Inverie–Tarbet–Inverie).

overnight in the bustling fishing and ferry port of Mallaig (*mahl*-ig). Indeed, it makes a good base for a series of day trips by ferry to the Small Isles and Knoydart.

Mallaig has a post office, a bank with an ATM and a co-op supermarket.

Activities

Wildlife Boat Trips CRUISE
(www.westernislescruises.co.uk; Mallaig Harbour; adult/child £13/6.50; 12.45pm & 5pm Apr-Oct;) These one-hour wildlife-spotting trips offer the chance to sight seals, porpoises, dolphins, whales and basking sharks, as well as seabirds. Sailings are timed to fit with the Jacobite Steam Train (p914) and Scotrail services from Fort William.

Sleeping & Eating

Seaview Guest House B&B ££
(01687-462059; www.seaviewguesthousemallaig.com; Main St; s/d £65/90, cottage per week £600;) This comfortable B&B has grand views over the harbour, not only from the upstairs bedrooms but from the breakfast room, too. There's also a cute little cottage next door that offers self-catering accommodation (www.selfcateringmallaig.com; one double and one twin room).

★**Cabin** SEAFOOD ££
(01687-462207; Davies Brae; mains £5.50-18; noon-7.30pm) The lobster, langoustines and calamari served at this fabulous family-run restaurant and takeaway might have been caught that day by your server's father. Local haddock, monkfish and scallops also feature on the menu, served with homemade aioli, salad and chips.

EAST COAST

In both landscape and character, the east coast is where the real barrenness of the Highlands begins to unfold. A gentle splendour and a sense of escapism mark the route along the twisting A9, as it heads north for the last of Scotland's far-flung, mainland population outposts. With only a few exceptions, the tourism frenzy is left behind once the road traverses Cromarty Firth and snakes its way along wild and pristine coastline.

Dornoch

☎01862 / POP 1200

On the northern shore of Dornoch Firth, 2 miles off the A9, this attractive old market town is one of the east coast's most pleasant settlements. Dornoch is best known for its championship golf course, but there's a fine cathedral among other noble buildings. Other historical oddities: the last witch to be executed in Scotland was boiled alive in hot tar here in 1722, and Madonna married Guy Ritchie here in 2000.

Sights & Activities

Dornoch Cathedral CHURCH

(www.dornoch-cathedral.com; St Gilbert St, IV25 3SJ; ⊙9am-7pm or later) FREE Consecrated in the 13th century, beautiful Dornoch Cathedral, one of the Highlands' loveliest churches, is an elegant Gothic edifice with an interior softly illuminated by modern stained-glass windows. The controversial first Duke of Sutherland, whose wife restored the church in the 1830s, lies in a sealed burial vault beneath the chancel.

Royal Dornoch GOLF

(☎01862-810219; www.royaldornoch.com; Golf Rd, IV25 3RW; green fees Apr-Oct £50-195, Nov-Mar £35-105) Royal Dornoch is one of Scotland's most famous links golf courses, described by Tom Watson as 'the most fun I ever had playing golf'. Online booking is straightforward; twilight rates (post 6pm May to July, post 5.30pm August) are the most economical. A golf pass (www.dornochfirthgolf.co.uk) lets you play five local courses at a discount.

Sleeping & Eating

★2 Quail B&B ££

(☎01862-811811; www.2quail.com; Castle St, IV25 3SN; r £90-140; 📶) Intimate and upmarket, 2 Quail offers a warm main-street welcome. Tasteful, spacious bedrooms are full of old-world comfort, with sturdy metal bed frames, plump duvets and plenty of books. The downstairs guest lounge is an absolute delight, with comfy armchairs, open fireplace and an extensive library. It's best to book ahead.

★Links House Hotel HOTEL £££

(☎01862-810279; www.linkshousedornoch.com; Golf Rd, IV25 3LW; r from £225; P📶) Set in a 19th-century manse, this small (15-room) hotel offers an authentic Scottish country-house experience, from the wood-panelled drawing room with its library of vintage angling books, to the whisky-focused cocktail bar and private putting green, plus the first hole of Royal Dornoch just along the road.

Courtroom SCOTTISH ££

(☎01862-810279; www.linkshousedornoch.com/the-courtroom; Castle St, IV25 3SD; mains lunch £8-12, dinner £15-24; ⊙10am-11pm; 📶) Beautifully set in the former town courtroom, which dates from 1849, this is an atmospheric spot for breakfast, lunch or dinner, with a menu that's heavy on Scottish produce enlivened with flourishes of French, Mediterranean and Asian flavours. The modern mural on the wall above the bar celebrates figures from Dornoch's past (and present – see if you can spot Madonna!).

Luigi CAFE ££

(☎01862-810893; www.luigidornoch.com; Castle St, IV25 3SN; lunch £10-13, dinner mains £17-22; ⊙10am-5pm daily, plus 6.45-9pm Fri & Sat Mar-Oct, daily Jul & Aug; 📶) The clean lines of this contemporary Italian-American cafe make a break from the omnipresent heritage and history of the coastline. Ciabattas and salads stuffed with tasty deli ingredients make it a good lunch stop; more elaborate dinners usually include fine seafood choices. The coffee is the best in town.

Getting There & Away

Stagecoach Highland bus X99 runs twice daily from Inverness to Dornoch (£11.40, one hour), continuing north to Wick and Thurso (£17.10, 2½ hours).

CAITHNESS

Once you pass Helmsdale, you are entering Caithness, a place of endless peat bogs and jagged gorse-and-grass-topped sea cliffs hiding tiny fishing harbours. Scotland's top corner was once Viking territory, historically more connected to Orkney and Shetland than the rest of the mainland. It's a mystical, ancient land dotted with old monuments and peopled by folk who are proud of their Norse heritage.

WORTH A TRIP

DUNROBIN CASTLE

Magnificent **Dunrobin Castle** (☎01408-633177; www.dunrobincastle.co.uk; KW10 6SF; adult/child £11/6; ⏱10.30am-4.30pm Apr, May & Oct, 10am-5pm Jun-Sep; P), a mile past Golspie, is the Highlands' largest house. Although it dates to 1275, most of what you see was built in French style between 1845 and 1850. A seat of the dukes of Sutherland, it's richly furnished and offers an intriguing insight into the aristocratic lifestyle. The castle inspires mixed feelings locally; it was once the Sutherland home of the first duke, notorious for his role in some of the cruellest episodes of the Highland Clearances.

In the first half of the 19th century the duke's estate was, at over 6000 sq km, the largest privately owned area of land in Europe. Between 1811 and 1821, he and his family spent most of their time in London, but they were still responsible for the eviction of around 15,000 people from their Sutherland farms to make way for sheep, sometimes burning their homes to prevent them being reoccupied.

The classic fairy-tale castle is adorned with towers and turrets, but only 22 of its 187 rooms are on display, with hunting trophies much to the fore. Beautiful formal gardens, where impressive falconry displays take place two or three times a day, extend down to the sea. In the gardens is a museum with an eclectic mix of archaeological finds, natural-history exhibits, more non-PC animal remains and an excellent collection of Pictish stones.

Getting There & Away

There are trains to both Wick and Thurso. Buses run between towns up the east and along the north coast.

Wick

☎01955 / POP 7100

Wick is worth a visit, particularly for its excellent museum and attractive, spruced-up harbour area, and it has some very good places to stay. More gritty than pretty, however, it's been a little down on its luck since the collapse of the herring industry. It was once the world's largest fishing port for the 'silver darlings', but when the market dropped off after WWII, job losses were huge and the town hasn't ever totally recovered.

Sights

★Wick Heritage Centre MUSEUM

(☎01955-605393; www.wickheritage.org; 20 Bank Row, KW1 5EY; adult/child £4/50p; ⏱10am-5pm Apr-Oct, last entry 3.45pm) Tracking the rise and fall of the herring industry, this great museum displays everything from fishing equipment to complete herring boats. It's absolutely huge inside, and is crammed with memorabilia and extensive displays describing Wick's heyday in the mid-19th century. The Johnston collection is the star exhibit – from 1863 to 1977 three generations of the family photographed everything that happened around Wick, and the 70,000 images constitute an amazing legacy.

Old Pulteney DISTILLERY

(☎01955-602371; www.oldpulteney.com; Huddart St, KW1 5BA; tours £10; ⏱10am-4pm Mon-Fri Oct-Apr, 10am-5pm Mon-Fri, 10am-4pm Sat May-Sep) Though it can no longer claim to be the most northerly whisky distillery on mainland Scotland (that goes to the upstart Wolfburn in Thurso), friendly Pulteney still runs excellent tours twice or more daily (normally at 11am and 2pm), with more expensive visits available for aficionados. Its Stroma whisky liqueur is dangerously more-ish.

Eating

Bord de l'Eau FRENCH ££

(☎01955-604400; 2 Market St, KW1 4AR; mains £17-25; ⏱noon-2pm & 6-9pm Tue-Sat, 6-9pm Sun) This serene, relaxed French restaurant is Wick's best place to eat. It overlooks the river and serves a changing menu of mostly French meat and game classics, backed up by daily fish specials. Starters are great value, and mains include a huge assortment of vegetables. The conservatory dining room with water views is lovely on a sunny evening.

Getting There & Away

BUS

Stagecoach buses run to/from Inverness (£21.60, three hours, twice daily), and from Wick to Thurso (£4.25, 45 minutes, five to eight daily). There's also a connecting service to Gills Bay and John O'Groats (£3.75, 30 minutes, four to five Monday to Saturday) for the car and passenger ferries to Orkney.

TRAIN

Trains service Wick from Inverness (£22.40, 4¼ hours, four daily Monday to Saturday, one on Sunday).

John O'Groats

☎ 01955 / POP 300

Though not actually the northernmost point of the British mainland (that's Dunnet Head), John O'Groats is famous as the end point of the 874-mile trek from Land's End in Cornwall, a popular if arduous route for cyclists and walkers, many of whom raise money for charitable causes. Most of the settlement is taken up by a stylish modern self-catering complex.

Stagecoach runs between John O'Groats and Wick (£3.75, 30 minutes, four to five Monday to Saturday) or Thurso (£4.75, one hour, five to eight Monday to Saturday).

From May to September, a **passenger ferry** (☎ 01955-611353; www.jogferry.co.uk; one way £22, incl bus to Kirkwall £25; ⊙ May-Sep) shuttles across to Burwick in Orkney. Three miles west, a car ferry (p950) runs all year from Gills Bay to St Margaret's Hope in Orkney.

Duncansby Head VIEWPOINT

Two miles east of John O'Groats, Duncansby Head has a small lighthouse and 60m-high cliffs sheltering nesting fulmars. A 15-minute walk through a sheep paddock yields spectacular views of the sea-surrounded monoliths known as Duncansby Stacks.

Mey

The **Castle of Mey** (☎ 01847-851473; www.castleofmey.org.uk; KW14 8XH; adult/child £11.75/6.50; ⊙ 10.20am-5pm May-Sep, last entry 4pm), a big crowd-puller for its Queen Mother connections, is 6 miles west of John O'Groats. The exterior is grand but inside it feels domestic and everything is imbued with the Queen Mum's character. The highlight is the genteel guided tour, with various anecdotes recounted by staff who once worked for her. In the grounds there's a farm zoo, an unusual walled garden that's worth a stroll and lovely views over the Pentland Firth.

The castle normally closes for a couple of weeks at the end of July for royal visits; Prince Charles often comes here in summer. There may also be limited April openings; check the website.

Dunnet Head

Eight miles east of Thurso, a minor road leads to dramatic Dunnet Head, the most northerly point on the British mainland. There are majestic cliffs dropping into the turbulent Pentland Firth, inspiring views of Orkney with basking seals and nesting seabirds below (it's an RSPB reserve), and a lighthouse built by Robert Louis Stevenson's grandad. Two cottages are available for rent (see www.dunnetheadlighthouse.com).

Thurso & Scrabster

☎ 01847 / POP 7600

Britain's most northerly mainland town, Thurso makes a handy overnight stop if you're heading west or across to Orkney. There's a pretty town beach, riverside strolls and a good museum. Ferries for Orkney leave from Scrabster, 2.5 miles away.

Sleeping & Eating

★ **Pennyland House** B&B ££

(☎ 01847-891194; www.pennylandhouse.co.uk; Thurso, KW14 7JU; s £80, d £90-100; P ☜ 🐾) A historic house on the western edge of town, Pennyland is a standout B&B. It offers phenomenal value for this level of accommodation, with huge oak-furnished rooms named after golf courses: we especially loved St Andrews – super-spacious, with a great chessboard-tiled bathroom. Hospitality is enthusiastic and helpful, and there's an inviting breakfast space, garden and terraced area with views across to Hoy.

Two-night minimum stay in summer.

Camfield House B&B ££

(☎ 07711 215823; www.riversideaccommodation.co.uk; Janet St, Thurso, KW14 7EG; r £125-145; P ☜) A Narnia-style portal leads from central Thurso through a gate and you're suddenly in what feels like an opulent rural estate. The garden is sumptuous, and extravagantly features a manicured par-3 golf hole, complete with bunker and water hazard. The interior lacks nothing by comparison, featuring spacious rooms with huge

TVs, quality linen and excellent bathrooms. There's even a full-sized billiard table.

Possible three-night minimum stay.

★ Captain's Galley SEAFOOD £££
(☎01847-894999; www.captainsgalley.co.uk; The Harbour, Scrabster KW14 7UJ; 5-course dinner £55, with wine flight £80; ⏲6.30-9pm Thu-Sat) Classy but friendly Captain's Galley, by the Scrabster ferry, offers a short, seafood-based menu featuring local and sustainably sourced produce prepared in delicious ways that let the natural flavours shine through. The chef picks the best fish off the local boats, and the menu describes exactly which fishing grounds your morsel came from. It's worth scheduling a night in Thurso to eat here.

If you can't get a table, or just want a quick meal while waiting for the Orkney ferry, you can feast on fresh takeaway seafood – haddock, scallops, langoustines, crab and lobster – at the neighbouring **Seafood Bar** (☎07470 004625; www.scrabsterseafoodbar.co.uk; The Harbour, Scrabster KW14 7UJ; mains £9-13, lobster £25; ⏲4.30-6.30pm Tue-Sat).

Getting There & Away

BUS

Stagecoach buses link Thurso/Scrabster with Inverness (£21.60, 3½ hours, twice daily). There are also buses to Wick (£4.25, 45 minutes, five to eight daily), as well as every couple of hours to John O'Groats (£4.75, one hour, five to eight Monday to Saturday).

TRAIN

There are four daily trains (one on Sunday) from Inverness (£22.40, 3¾ hours), with a connecting bus to Scrabster.

NORTH & WEST COAST

Quintessential Highland country such as this, with breathtaking emptiness, a wild, fragile beauty and single-track roads, is a rarity on the modern, crowded, highly urbanised island of Britain. You could get lost up here for weeks – and that still wouldn't be enough time.

Carving its way from Thurso to Kyle of Lochalsh, the north and northwest coastline is a feast of fjord-like sea lochs, forgotten beaches and surging peninsulas. Within the rugged confines, the interior is home to vast, empty spaces, enormous lochs and some of Scotland's shapeliest peaks.

Whether in blazing sunshine or murky greyness, the character of the land is constantly changing – for that window of time in which you can glimpse it, you'll capture an exclusive snapshot of this ancient area in your mind. Stop the car and gaze. This northernmost slab of the Highlands is the stuff of coastal-drive dreams.

Thurso to Durness

It's 80 winding – and utterly spectacular – coastal miles from Thurso to Durness.

Ten miles west of Thurso, the **Dounreay** nuclear power station was the first in the world to supply mains electricity. It's currently being decommissioned; the clean-up is planned to be finished by 2025. Meanwhile it's still a major source of employment for the region.

Beyond, Melvich overlooks a fine beach and there are great views from **Strathy Point** (a 2-mile drive from the coast road, then a 15-minute walk).

MIDGES

Forget Nessie, the Highlands have a real monster: a voracious bloodsucking female fully 3mm long named the Highland midge *(Culicoides impunctatus)*. The bane of campers and as much a symbol of Scotland as the kilt or dram, midges descend in biting clouds, driving sane folk to distraction.

Though normally vegetarian, the female midge needs a dose of blood in order to lay her eggs. And, like it or not, if you're in the Highlands between June and August, you just volunteered as a donor. Midges especially congregate near water, and are most active in the early morning, though squadrons also patrol in the late evening.

Repellents and creams are reasonably effective, though some walkers favour midge veils. Light-coloured clothing also helps. Many pubs and campsites have midge-zappers. Check www.smidgeup.com/midge-forecast for activity levels by area, but don't blame us: we've been eaten alive when the forecast said moderate, too.

Bettyhill is a pretty village that overlooks a magnificent stretch of coastline, and the scenery just improves as you head west through Coldbackie and Tongue, with a succession of gorgeous sea lochs, stunning beaches and striking rock formations backed by imposing hills and mountains.

Sights

Strathnaver Museum MUSEUM
(01641-521418; www.strathnavermuseum.org.uk; Clachan; adult/child £3/free; 10am-5pm Mon-Sat Apr-Oct) Housed in an old church, this museum tells the sad story of the Strathnaver Clearances through posters created by local kids. The museum contains memorabilia of Clan Mackay, various items of crofting equipment and a 'St Kilda mailboat', a small wooden boat-shaped container bearing a letter that was used by St Kildans to send messages to the mainland.

Outside the back door of the church is the **Farr Stone**, a fine carved Pictish cross-slab.

Sleeping & Eating

Cornmill Bunkhouse HOSTEL £
(01641-571219; www.achumore.co.uk; A897; dm £18; P) Cornmill Bunkhouse is a comfortable modern hostel occupying a picturesque old mill on a working croft in the middle of nowhere. It's on the A897, 4 miles south of the coast road.

Bettyhill Hotel INN £££
(01641-521202; www.bettyhillhotel.com; s/d without bathroom £65/95, d with bathroom from £130; Apr-Oct, check for winter opening; P) This former coaching inn has a fabulous position overlooking the sandy beach fringing Torrisdale Bay. The owners have completed a great renovation and the updated bedrooms are bright, with top-grade mattresses. Rooms come in many different types (some have sea or river views) with lots of singles, as well as a two-bedroom holiday cottage. Bar and restaurant meals are available.

★ **Côte du Nord** MODERN SCOTTISH £££
(01641-521773; www.cotedunord.co.uk; The School House, Kirtomy; tasting menu £55, paired wines £35; 7.30pm Wed, Fri & Sat Apr-Sep;) Brilliantly innovative cuisine, wonderfully whimsical presentation and an emphasis on local ingredients are the highlights of the gastronomic tasting menu here. It's an unlikely spot to find such a gourmet experience – the chef is none other than the local GP who forages for wild herbs and flavours in between surgery hours. Top value. It's tiny, so reserve well ahead.

Kirtomy is signposted off the main road about 2.5 miles east of Bettyhill; the restaurant is about a mile down this road.

Durness

01971 / POP 400

Durness (www.durness.org) is wonderfully located, strung out along cliffs rising from a series of pristine beaches. When the sun shines, the effects of blinding white sand, the cry of seabirds and the spring-green-coloured seas combine in a magical way.

Sights & Activities

Walking the sensational sandy coastline is a highlight, as is a visit to **Cape Wrath**. Durness' beautiful beaches include **Rispond** (also known as Ceannabeinne) to the east, **Sango Sands** below town and **Balnakeil** to the west. At Balnakeil, a craft village occupies a one-time early-warning radar station. A northerly beach walk leads to **Faraid Head**, where there are puffins in early summer.

Bikes can be hired from a shed on the square.

Smoo Cave CAVE
FREE A mile east of Durness is a path down to Smoo Cave. From the vast main chamber, you can head through to a smaller flooded cavern where a waterfall sometimes cascades from the roof. There's evidence the cave was inhabited about 6000 years ago. You can take a **tour** (01971-511704; www.smoocavetours.weebly.com; adult/child £6/3; 11am-4pm Apr, May, Sep & Oct, 10am-5pm Jun-Aug) to explore a little further into the interior.

Sleeping & Eating

Lazy Crofter Bunkhouse HOSTEL £
(01971-511202; www.visitdurness.com/bunkhouse; dm from £22;) Durness' best budget accommodation is here, opposite the supermarket. A bothy vibe gives it a very Highland feel, and inviting dorms have lockers and plenty of space. There's also a sociable shared table for meals and board games, and a great wooden deck with sea views, perfect for midge-free evenings.

WORTH A TRIP

CAPE WRATH

Though its name actually comes from the Norse word *hvarf* ('turning point'), there is something daunting and primal about Cape Wrath, the remote northwesternmost point of the British mainland.

The hazardous, stormy seas around the cape led to the building of the lighthouse here by Robert and Alan Stevenson in 1828. The last keepers had left by 1998, when humans were replaced by automation. Three miles to the east are the seabird colonies of Clo Mor, the British mainland's highest vertical sea cliffs (195m).

Part of the moorland here has served for decades as a bombing range. The island of An Garbh-Eilean, 5 miles from the cape, has the misfortune to be around the same size as an aircraft carrier and is regularly ripped up by RAF bombs and missiles. There is no public access when the range is in use; times are displayed at www.visitcapewrath.com.

Getting to Cape Wrath involves taking a **ferry** (☎07719-678729; www.capewrathferry.wordpress.com; return £10, bike £15; ⏲10am-4.30pm May-Sep) – passengers and bikes only – across the Kyle of Durness (10 minutes). It connects with the **Cape Wrath Minibus** (☎07742-670196; www.visitcapewrath.com; return £13; ⏲May-Sep), which runs the very slow and bumpy 11 miles to the cape (50 minutes).

This combination is a friendly but eccentric and sometimes shambolic service with limited capacity, so plan on waiting in high season, and call ahead to make sure the ferry is running. The ferry leaves from 2 miles southwest of Durness, and runs twice or more daily from May to September. If you eschew the minibus, it's a spectacular 11-mile bike ride or hike from boat to cape through bleak scenery.

★**Mackays Rooms** HOTEL £££
(☎01971-511202; www.visitdurness.com; d standard £149, deluxe £169-210; ⏲May-Oct; P📶🐾) You really feel you're at the furthest-flung corner of Scotland here, where the road turns through 90 degrees. But whether heading south or east, you'll go far before you find a better place to stay than this haven of Highland hospitality. With its big beds, soft fabrics and contemporary colours, it's a romantic spot with top-notch service.

There's also a self-contained cabin, which can be rented on a self-catering or B&B basis. With two rooms, it sleeps up to four (from £190 per night).

Smoo Lodge B&B £££
(☎01971-511423; www.smoolodge.co.uk; r from £160; P📶) A sizeable former hunting lodge on ample grounds has been lovingly restored to a very high standard. Bedrooms feature high-quality mattresses and bedding as well as great modern bathrooms. Asian-influenced evening meals are available, and breakfast features an excellent Korean option – a nice change from bacon and eggs. No under-12s.

★**Cocoa Mountain** CAFE £
(☎01971-511233; www.cocoamountain.co.uk; Balnakeil; mains £4-8; ⏲9am-6pm Easter-Oct) 🍃 At the Balnakeil craft village, this upbeat cafe and chocolate maker offers handmade treats, including a chilli, lemongrass and coconut white-chocolate truffle, plus many more unique flavours. Tasty espresso and hot chocolate warm the cockles on those blowy horizontal-drizzle days. It offers light lunches and home-baking too, plus chocolate-making workshops.

ℹ Getting There & Away

A year-round **Far North Bus** (☎07782 110007; www.thedurnessbus.com) service heads to Lairg (£10, 2½ hours, Monday to Friday), where there is a train station. On Saturday minibuses head to Inverness (£14, three hours) and Thurso (£11, 2¼ hours). In summer school holidays, there's also an Ullapool service (£11, 2½ hours). All these services should be prebooked; some have bicycle capacity.

Durness to Ullapool

Perhaps Scotland's most spectacular road, the 69 miles connecting Durness to Ullapool is a smorgasbord of dramatic scenery – almost too much to take in. From Durness you pass through a broad heathered valley with the looming grey bulk of Foinaven and Arkle to the southeast. Heather gives way to a rockier landscape pockmarked with hundreds of lochans (small lochs).

Here you'll find some of the most interesting geology in the UK, including Britain's oldest rock – three-billion-year-old Lewisian gneiss. Next come the magnificent Torridonian sandstone mountains of Assynt and Coigach, including Suilven's distinctive sugarloaf, many-peaked Quinag and pinnacled Stac Pollaidh. The area has been designated as the **Northwest Highlands Geopark** (www.nwhgeopark.com).

Kylesku & Loch Glencoul

Hidden away on the shores of Loch Glencoul, tiny Kylesku served as a ferry crossing on the route north until it was made redundant by elegant Kylesku Bridge in 1984. It's a good base for walks; you can hire bikes, too.

Eas a'Chual Aluinn WATERFALL

Five miles southeast of Kylesku, in wild, remote country, lies 213m-high Eas a'Chual Aluinn, Britain's highest waterfall. You can hike to the top of the falls from a parking area at a sharp bend in the main road 3 miles south of Kylesku; allow five hours for the 6-mile return trip. It can also be seen on **boat trips** (01971-502231; www.kyleskuboattours.com; Kylesku; adult/child £30/20; Apr-Sep) from Kylesku.

★**Kylesku Hotel** SEAFOOD ££

(01971-502231; www.kyleskuhotel.co.uk; Kylesku; mains £15-26; noon-2.30pm & 6-9pm mid-Feb–Apr, Oct & Nov, noon-9pm May-Sep;) In this remote lochside location, it's a real pleasure to gorge yourself on delicious sustainable seafood. Local langoustines grilled on a skewer, squat lobsters and mussels are the specialities at this convivial restaurant, where you have the option of eating outdoors with a view of the sea. There's a good atmosphere of mingling locals and visitors at the bar.

Lochinver & Assynt

With its otherworldly scenery of isolated peaks rising above a sea of crumpled, lochan-spattered gneiss, Assynt epitomises the northwest's wild magnificence. Glaciers have sculpted the hills of Suilven (731m), Canisp (846m), Quinag (808m) and Ben More Assynt (998m) into strange and wonderful silhouettes.

Lochinver is the main settlement, a busy little fishing port that's a popular port of call with its laid-back atmosphere, good facilities and striking scenery. Just north of Lochinver (or if coming from the north, not far south of Kylesku), a 23-mile detour on the narrow B869 rewards with spectacular views and fine beaches. From the lighthouse at Point of Stoer, a one-hour cliff walk leads to the **Old Man of Stoer**, a spectacular sea stack.

Sleeping & Eating

Clachtoll Beach Campsite CAMPSITE £

(01571-855377; www.clachtollbeachcampsite.co.uk; B869, Clachtoll; site incl 1 adult £10-21, per extra adult/child £5/2; Apr–mid-Oct; P) Set among the machair beside a lovely white-sand beach and emerald seas, Clachtoll is a divine coastal camping spot, though somewhat overwhelmed by the adjacent self-catering development. It's 6 miles northwest of Lochinver by road.

Achmelvich Beach Youth Hostel HOSTEL £

(HS; 01571-844480; www.hostellingscotland.org.uk; Achmelvich; dm/tw £22.50/55; Apr-Sep;) Off the B869, this whitewashed cottage is set beside a great beach at the end of a side road. Dorms are simple, and there's a sociable common kitchen and eating area. Heat-up meals are available, as is a basic shop in summer; otherwise, there's a chip van at the adjacent campsite, or you can take the 4-mile walk to Lochinver.

Davar B&B ££

(01571-844501; www.davar-lochinver.co.uk; Baddidarroch, Lochinver; s/d from £85/110; P) Run with a genuine welcome and enthusiasm, this is a beautiful house with a garden and a fabulous outlook across the bay to Suilven and the Assynt mountainscape. The four rooms are well appointed and have plenty of space; it's the ideal base for exploring the region. To find it, turn west at the northern end of Lochinver.

★**Lochinver Larder & Riverside Bistro** BISTRO £

(01571-844356; www.lochinverlarder.com; 3 Main St, Lochinver; pies £5-6, mains £7-13; 10am-7.45pm Mon-Sat, to 5.30pm Sun Apr-Oct, 10am-4pm Mon-Sat Nov-Mar;) An outstanding menu of inventive food made with local produce is on offer here. The bistro turns out delicious seafood dishes in the evening, while the takeaway counter sells tasty pies with a wide range of gourmet fillings (try the venison and cranberry). It also does quality meals to take away and heat up: great for hostellers and campers.

Getting There & Away

Rapsons bus 809 goes from Ullapool to Lochinver (£5.50, one hour, two to four Monday to Saturday).

Ullapool

☎01854 / POP 1500

This pretty harbour town on the shores of Loch Broom, purpose-built as a fishing port in 1788, is the largest settlement in Wester Ross and one of the most alluring spots in the Highlands. It's a wonderful destination in itself, as well as a gateway to the Western Isles. Offering a row of whitewashed cottages arrayed along the loch shore and special views of the loch and its flanking hills, the town has a very distinctive appeal. The harbour served as an emigration point during the Clearances, with thousands of Scots watching Ullapool recede behind as they began the journey to a new continent.

Sights & Activities

Ullapool Museum MUSEUM

(☎01854-612987; www.ullapoolmuseum.co.uk; 7 West Argyle St, IV26 2TY; adult/child £5/free; ⏲11am-4pm Mon, Tue, Thu & Fri, 10am-5pm Sat Apr-Oct) Housed in a converted Telford church, this museum relates the prehistoric, natural and social history of the town and Lochbroom area, with a particular focus on Highland emigration to Nova Scotia and other places. There's also a genealogy section if you want to trace your Scottish roots.

Shearwater Cruises BOATING

(☎01854-612472; www.summerqueen.co.uk; Harbour, IV26 2UH; adult/child £35/30; ⏲Mon-Sat May-Sep) Weather permitting, the catamaran *Shearwater* takes you out to the Summer Isles for a 2¼-hour cruise. They leave twice a day.

Sleeping

Ullapool Youth Hostel HOSTEL £

(HS; ☎01854-612254; www.hostellingscotland.org.uk; Shore St, IV26 2UJ; dm/tw/q £23/59/103; ⏲Apr-Oct; 📶) You've got to hand it to Hostelling Scotland – it's chosen some very sweet locations for its hostels. This one is right in the heart of town on the pretty waterfront; some rooms have harbour views and the busy dining area and little lounge are also good spots for contemplating the water.

★Tamarin Lodge B&B ££

(☎01854-612667; www.tamarinullapool.com; 9 The Braes, IV26 2SZ; s/d from £49/98; P📶🐾) Effortlessly elegant modern architecture in this hilltop house is noteworthy in its own right, but the glorious vistas over the water far below to the hills opposite are unforgettable. All rooms face the view; some have a balcony, and all are spacious, quiet and relaxing, with unexpected features and gadgets. The great lounge and benevolent hosts are a delight.

Follow signs for Braes from the Inverness road.

Waterside House B&B ££

(☎01854-612140; www.waterside.uk.net; 6 West Shore St, IV26 2UR; d from £90; ⏲Apr-Oct; P📶) This typical whitewashed West Highland house is right on the waterfront – so close to the ferry that you can watch it docking from your window. There are three compact but beautifully appointed rooms with excellent modern bathrooms. The location and the friendly welcome are fabulous, and your hosts go the extra mile at breakfast time – delicious. Minimum two-night stay in summer.

★Ceilidh Place HOTEL £££

(☎01854-612103; www.theceilidhplace.com; 14 West Argyle St, IV26 2TY; r £130-180; P📶🐾) This hotel is a celebration of Scottish culture: we're talking literature and traditional music, not tartan and Nessie dolls. Rooms go for character over modernity; instead of TVs they come with a selection of books chosen by Scottish literati, plus eclectic artwork and cosy touches. The sumptuous lounge has sofas, chaises longues and an honesty bar. There's a bookshop here, too.

It's not luxurious but it's one of the Highlands' more unusual and delightful places to stay.

Eating & Drinking

West Coast Delicatessen CAFE £

(☎01854-613450; www.westcoastdeli.co.uk; 5 Argyle St, IV26 2UB; light meals £3-7; ⏲9am-5pm Mon-Sat; 📶) A likeable venue for a coffee or snack, this upbeat modern place has sub rolls, decent coffee and a variety of deli produce, including some very tasty cheeses. It also does a good soup, perfect for chillier Ullapool days.

THE NORTH COAST 500

The drive around Scotland's far northern coastline is one of Europe's finest road trips. Words fail to describe the sheer variety of scenic splendour that unfolds as you cross this empty landscape of desolate moorlands, brooding mountains, fertile coastal meadows and stunning white-sand beaches.

In a clever piece of marketing it's been dubbed the North Coast 500, as the round trip from Inverness is roughly that many miles, though you'll surely clock up a few more if you follow your heart down narrow byroads and seek perfect coastal panoramas.

In our opinion, the scenery is best viewed by travelling anticlockwise, heading north from Inverness up the east coast then turning west across the top of Scotland before returning down the west coast. This way, you'll make the most of the coastal vistas, the light and the awesome backdrop of the Assynt mountains.

Much of the drive is along single-track road, so it's important to pull over to let both oncoming vehicles and faster traffic behind you pass. Though Inverness companies hire out prestige sports cars for the journey, these really aren't roads where you want to open the throttle; a lazy pace with plenty of photo stops makes for the best journey. It's worth taking several days for the drive; in fact you could easily spend a week between Inverness and Ullapool, stopping off for leisurely seafood lunches, tackling some emblematic hills, detouring down valleys to explore the legacy of the Clearances, and daring a dip in the North Sea.

In recent years the North Coast 500 has become something of a victim of its own success. Visitor numbers are well up, which has led to traffic congestion on narrow roads (particularly around Applecross) and shortages of accommodation, so it's well worth booking everything in advance, even campsites.

Seafood Shack SEAFOOD £
(☎07876 142623; www.seafoodshack.co.uk; West Argyle St, IV26 2TY; mains £5-10, half lobster £20; ⊙noon-6pm Apr-late Oct) High-quality fresh seafood is served out of a trailer in this vacant lot by two cheery lasses, Kirsty and Fenella. There's a wide range of tasty fare available, from hand-dived scallops to calamari, mussels, crab, oysters and lobster.

ℹ Getting There & Away

Citylink has buses from Inverness to Ullapool (£14.90, 1½ hours, one to three daily), connecting with the Stornoway ferry.

Two daily **CalMac** (☎0800 066 5000; www.calmac.co.uk) ferries run from Ullapool to Stornoway on Lewis in the Outer Hebrides (adult/car £9.75/53, 2½ hours).

Ullapool to Kyle of Lochalsh

Although it's less than 50 miles as the crow flies from Ullapool to Kyle of Lochalsh, it's more like 150 miles along the circuitous coastal road – but don't let that put you off. It's a delightfully remote region and there are fine views of beaches and bays backed by mountains all the way along.

Twelve miles southeast of Ullapool at Braemore, the A832 doubles back towards the coast as it heads for Gairloch (the A835 continues southeast across the wild, sometimes snowbound, Dirrie More pass to Garve and Inverness). If you're hurrying to Skye, use the A835 and catch up with the A832 further south, near Garve.

Falls of Measach WATERFALL
Just west of the junction of the A835 and A832, 2 miles south of Braemore, a car park gives access to the Falls of Measach, which spill 45m into the spectacularly deep and narrow Corrieshalloch Gorge. You can cross the gorge on a swaying suspension bridge, and walk west for 250m to a viewing platform that juts out dizzyingly above a sheer drop. The thundering falls and misty vapours rising from the gorge are very impressive.

Gairloch & Around

☎01445 / POP 1000

Gairloch is a group of villages (comprising Achtercairn, Strath and Charlestown) around the inner end of a loch of the same name. It's a good base for whale- and dolphin-watching excursions and the surrounding area has beautiful sandy beaches, good trout fishing and birdwatching. Hill walkers also use Gairloch as a base for the Torridon hills and An Teallach.

Sights & Activities

★Inverewe Garden GARDENS
(NTS; ☎01445-712952; www.nts.org.uk; IV22 2LG; adult/concession £13/11.50; ⊙9.30am-6pm Jun-Aug, to 5pm Mar, Apr & Sep, to 5.30pm May, to 4pm Oct, 10am-4pm Nov-Feb) Six miles north of Gairloch, this splendid place is a welcome splash of colour on the otherwise bleak coast. The climate here is warmed by the Gulf Stream, which allowed Osgood MacKenzie to create this exotic woodland garden in 1862. There are free guided tours on weekdays at 1.30pm from March to October. The licensed cafe-restaurant serves great cakes.

Hebridean Whale Cruises WILDLIFE
(☎01445-712458; www.hebridean-whale-cruises.com; Pier Rd, IV21 2BQ; ⊙Apr-Oct) Based at Gairloch's harbour, this set-up runs three trips: a standard 2½-hour whale-watching excursion (£53; from May), a three-hour visit to the seabird-rich Shiant Islands (£57) and a four-hour excursion to further-flung feeding grounds in search of orcas (£84). Other wildlife it's possible to see includes otters, dolphins and seals. Trips are in a zippy rigid inflatable.

Gairloch Marine Wildlife Centre & Cruises WILDLIFE
(☎07751-992666; www.porpoise-gairloch.co.uk; Pier Rd, IV21 2BQ; cruises adult/child £30/25; ⊙10am-4pm Easter-Oct) This small visitor centre has audiovisual and interactive displays, lots of charts, photos and knowledgeable staff. From here, cruises run three times daily (weather permitting) – during the two-hour trips you may see basking sharks, porpoises and minke whales. The crew collects data on water temperature and conditions, and monitors cetacean populations, so you are subsidising important research.

Sleeping & Eating

Gairloch Sands Youth Hostel HOSTEL £
(HS; ☎01445-712219; www.hostellingscotland.org.uk; Carn Dearg, IV21 2DJ; dm/tw/q £22.50/57/99; ⊙Apr-Sep; P 🛜 🐾) Located 2.5 miles west of Gairloch in a stunning coastal position, this hostel is close to beaches and well set up for walkers. Wood-panelled rooms and a large dining room/lounge offer comfort, but the real star is that view...magic!

Rua Reidh Lighthouse LODGE £££
(☎01445-771263; www.stayatalighthouse.co.uk; Melvaig IV21 2EA; r £130-140; ⊙Easter-Oct; P 🐾) Three miles along a narrow private road beyond Melvaig (11 miles north of Gairloch), this simple yet excellent lodge gives a taste of a lighthouse keeper's life. It's a wild, lonely location, great for walking and birdwatching. Breakfast is included and tasty evening meals are available. There's no TV or wi-fi and only a flaky mobile-phone signal. Two-night minimum stay.

There's a separate self-catering apartment that's available year-round.

Shieldaig Lodge HOTEL £££
(☎01445-741333; www.shieldaiglodge.com; Badachro IV21 2AN; s £180, d from £215; P 🛜) This refurbished hunting lodge has a super waterside position on a sizeable estate offering good walking and fishing as well as falconry and archery. It's a cosy place – think drams and a log fire – with a good restaurant, a very well stocked bar and tasteful rooms, the best of which have water views. There's also a snooker table and a lovely library.

Mountain Coffee Company CAFE £
(☎01445-712316; www.facebook.com/mountaincoffee.gairloch; Strath Sq, Strath IV21 2BZ; light meals £4-7; ⊙9am-5.30pm, reduced hours low season) More the sort of place you'd expect to find on the gringo trail in the Andes, this offbeat and cosy (if occasionally brusque) spot is a shrine to mountaineering and travelling. It serves tasty savoury bagels, home baking and sustainably sourced coffees. The conservatory is the place to lap up the sun, while the attached Hillbillies Bookshop is well worth a browse.

There are rather sweet en suite bedrooms available, too.

Information

Gairloch Information Centre (☎01445-712071; www.galeactionforum.co.uk; Achtercairn IV21 2BH; ⊙9.30am-5.30pm Mon-Sat, 10.30am-5pm Sun Jun-Sep, 10am-5.30pm Mon-Sat, 10.30am-4.30pm Sun Oct-May) Community-run information centre in the Gale Centre, on the road through town. Has good walking pamphlets; there's also a cafe.

Getting There & Away

Public transport to Gairloch is very limited. **Westerbus** (☎01445-712255) runs direct to/from Inverness (£11, 2¼ hours) twice weekly (Tuesday and Saturday), but the future of this service was in doubt at time of research.

Loch Maree & Around

Stretching 12 miles between Poolewe and Kinlochewe, Loch Maree is considered one of Scotland's prettiest lochs, with the imposing bulk of Slioch on its northeastern side and Beinn Eighe on the southwestern. Look out for black-throated divers on the lake in summer. At its southern end, tiny Kinlochewe makes a good base for outdoor activities.

Beinn Eighe Mountain Trail WALKING
This waymarked 4-mile loop walk to a plateau and cairn on the side of Beinn Eighe has magnificent views over Loch Maree. It's quite exposed up there, so take some warm clothing. The walk starts from a car park on the A832 about 1.5 miles northwest of the Beinn Eighe Tourist Office.

From the same trailhead there's a shorter 1-mile trail through Scots pine forest.

Torridon

☎01445

The road southwest from Kinlochewe passes through Glen Torridon, amid some of Britain's most beautiful scenery. Carved by ice from massive layers of ancient sandstone that takes its name from the region, the mountains here are steep, shapely and imposing, whether flirting with autumn mists, draped in dazzling winter snows, or reflected in the calm blue waters of Loch Clair on a summer day.

The road reaches the sea at spectacularly sited Torridon village, then continues westwards to lovely Shieldaig, which boasts an attractive main street of whitewashed houses right on the water.

Activities

Torridon Countryside Centre (NTS; ☎01445-791221; www.nts.org.uk/visit/places/torridon; Torridon Village; ⏲10am-5pm Sun-Fri Easter-Sep) offers information on wildlife, geology and walks in the area, and sells walking maps. You can buy food here for a nearby red-deer herd.

Torridon Outdoors ADVENTURE SPORTS
(☎01445-791242; www.thetorridon.com/torridon-outdoors; The Stables; 2 adults half-/full-day £150/250) This activity centre organises sea kayaking, canyoning, mountain biking and climbing, among several other outdoor pursuits. It also rents bikes, including mountain bikes.

Sleeping & Eating

Torridon Youth Hostel HOSTEL £
(HS; ☎01445-791284; www.hostellingscotland.org.uk; Torridon Village; dm/tw £23/59; ⏲daily Mar-Oct, Fri & Sat nights Nov-Feb; P @ 📶 🐾) This spacious modern hostel has enthusiastic, can-do management and sits in a magnificent location, surrounded by spectacular mountains. Roomy dorms and privates (twins have single beds) are allied to a huge kitchen and convivial lounge area, with ales on sale. It's a very popular walking base, with great advice from the in-house mountain-rescue team, so book ahead.

As well as breakfast, there are packed lunches and heat-up dinners on offer.

★**Torridon** HOTEL £££
(☎01445-791242; www.thetorridon.com/stay/hotel; IV22 2EY; r/ste from £350/425; ⏲closed Jan, plus Mon & Tue Feb, Mar, Nov & Dec; P @ 📶 🐾) If you prefer the lap of luxury to the sound of rain beating on your tent, head for this lavish Victorian hunting lodge with a romantic lochside location. Sumptuous contemporary rooms with awe-inspiring views, top bathrooms and a cheery Highland cow atop the counterpane couldn't be more inviting. It's one of Scotland's top country hotels, always luxurious but never pretentious.

Stables INN £££
(☎01445-791242; www.thetorridon.com/stay/the-stables; IV22 2EY; d/f from £155/245; ⏲daily Easter-Oct, Thu-Sun mid-Feb–Easter & Nov, closed Dec–mid-Feb; P 📶 🐾) This convivial but upmarket hikers' hang-out has excellent modern rooms that vary substantially in size and layout. Rooms for groups of up to six (from £285) offer more value than the commodious but overpriced doubles. The sociable bar serves all-day food and there are numerous activities on offer.

Tigh an Eilean HOTEL £££
(☎01520-755251; www.tighaneilean.co.uk; Shieldaig; s/d £80/160; ⏲Feb-Dec; 📶) With a lovely waterfront location in the pretty village of Shieldaig, this is an appealing destination for a relaxing stay, offering old-style rooms that are comfortable rather than luxurious. Loch-view rooms – with gloriously soothing vistas – are allocated on a first-booked basis, so it's worth reserving ahead. Service is very helpful, and there's a cosy lounge with an honesty bar.

Prices drop for stays of three or more nights.

DON'T MISS

EILEAN DONAN CASTLE

Photogenically perched on an island at the entrance to Loch Duich, and elegantly linked to the mainland by a stone-arched bridge, **Eilean Donan Castle** (☎01599-555202; www.eileandonancastle.com; Dornie IV40 8DX; adult/child/family £10/6/29; ⌚10am-6pm Apr-Sep, to 5pm Oct, to 4pm Feb, Nov & Dec, closed Jan; P) is one of Scotland's most evocative castles. Although it looks venerable it's very much a reproduction, having been completed in the 1930s. There's an excellent introductory exhibition, photos of castle scenes from the movie *Highlander*, and a sword used at the Battle of Culloden in 1746. Citylink buses from Fort William and Inverness to Portree stop opposite the castle.

The original 13th-century castle here was bombarded into ruins by government ships in 1719 when Jacobite forces were defeated at the Battle of Glenshiel; it was rebuilt in its present form between 1912 and 1932.

Wee Whistle Stop Cafe CAFE £
(☎01445-791361; www.facebook.com/WeeWhistleStop; Loch Torridon Community Hall; meals £7-15; ⌚9am-6pm Sat-Thu, to 7pm Fri) This is a tempting place to drop by for anything from a coffee to enticing bistro fare – the outdoor terrace has glorious views across Loch Torridon. There are great daily specials and delicious home baking, juices and smoothies. It's very friendly, and used to pumping life back into chilly walkers and cyclists. Opening hours may vary by season; check its Facebook page.

★**Shieldaig Bar & Coastal Kitchen** SEAFOOD ££
(☎01520-755251; www.tighaneilean.co.uk/coastal_kitchen.asp; Shieldaig; mains £13-25; ⌚food noon-2.30pm & 6-8.30pm or 9pm, closed some winter lunchtimes; 📶) This attractive pub has real ales and waterside tables plus a great upstairs dining room with an outdoor deck. There's an emphasis on quality local seafood as well as wood-fired pizzas and bistro-style meat dishes such as steak-frites or sausages and mash. Blackboard specials feature the daily catch – the superb seafood platter costs £32.

Applecross

☎01520 / POP 200

The remote seaside village of Applecross feels like an island retreat due to its isolation and the magnificent views of Raasay and the hills of Skye that set the pulse racing, particularly at sunset. On a clear day it's an unforgettable place. The campsite and pub fill to the brim in school holidays.

Twenty-five winding miles of single-track road lead here from Shieldaig, but more spectacular (accessed from further south on the A896) is the magnificent **Bealach na Bà** (626m; Pass of the Cattle), the third-highest motor road in the UK, and the longest continuous climb (not suitable for caravans or large motorhomes). Originally built in 1822, it climbs steeply and hair-raisingly via hairpin bends perched over sheer drops, with gradients of up to 25%, then plunges dramatically to the village with views of Skye ahead.

Sleeping

Hartfield House HOSTEL £
(☎01520-744333; www.hartfieldhouse.org.uk; Hartfield Rd, IV54 8ND; dm/s/tw/d £27/35/55/70; ⌚Mar-Oct; P📶🐾) This former hunting lodge on the Applecross estate is about a mile off the road in a lovely rural location. With lots of beds across two separate buildings in both dorms and private rooms, plus good common areas, it offers plenty of space and comfort. Walkers and cyclists have decent facilities and a help-yourself continental breakfast is included.

★**Applecross Inn** INN £££
(☎01520-744262; www.applecrossinn.co.uk; Shore St, IV54 8LR; s/d from £100/150; P📶🐾) 🍃 The hub of the spread-out Applecross community, this inn is a great spot to hole up, but you'll need to book ahead. Seven snug bedrooms all have a view of the Skye hills and the sea. It's a magical spot and there's a cracking pub and **restaurant** (mains £12-22; ⌚noon-9pm; 📶) 🍃. It also has some cottage accommodation along the waterfront.

Getting There & Away

There are two buses a week (Wednesday and Saturday) with **Lochcarron Garage** (☎01520-722997; www.lochcarrongarage.co.uk/bus) from Inverness to Applecross (£11.10, 3½ hours) via Shieldaig (ie around the north coast, not over the Bealach na Bà).

Plockton

☎01599 / POP 400

Idyllic little Plockton, with its perfect cottages lining a perfect bay, looks like it was designed as a film set. And it has indeed served as just that – scenes from *The Wicker Man* (1973) were filmed here, and the village became famous as the location for the 1990s TV series *Hamish Macbeth*.

With all this picture-postcard perfection, it's hardly surprising that Plockton is a tourist hot spot, crammed with day trippers and holidaymakers in summer. But there's no denying its appeal, with 'palm trees' (actually hardy New Zealand cabbage palms) lining the waterfront, a thriving small-boat sailing scene and several good places to stay, eat and drink. The big event of the year is the **Plockton Regatta** (https://visitplockton.com/event/plockton-small-boat-regatta; ⏲Jul/Aug).

Activities

Sea Kayak Plockton KAYAKING
(☎01599-544422; www.seakayakplockton.co.uk; 1-day beginner course adult/child £85/65) Sea Kayak Plockton offers everything from beginner lessons and family days out, to multi-day trips around Skye and the Outer Hebrides.

Calum's Seal Trips TOURS
(☎07761-263828; www.calums-sealtrips.com; adult/child £14/6; ⏲Apr-Oct) Wildlife-watching cruises visit a seal colony just outside the harbour. There's excellent commentary and you may even spot otters as well. Trips leave several times daily, and offer your money back if you don't see any seals.

Sleeping & Eating

Plockton Station Bunkhouse HOSTEL £
(☎01599-544235; www.visitplockton.com/stay/bunkhouse; IV52 8TF; dm £18; P 📶) Airily set in the former train station (the new one is opposite), this hostel has cosy four-bed dorms, a garden and kitchen-lounge with plenty of light, and good views over the frenetic comings and goings of the platforms below (OK, that last bit's a lie). The owners also have good-value B&B accommodation (single/double £35/60) next door in the inaccurately named 'Nessun Dorma'.

★**Plockton Hotel** INN £££
(☎01599-544274; www.plocktonhotel.co.uk; 41 Harbour St; s/d £100/150, cottage s/d £65/100; 📶) The Plockton Hotel is one of those classic Highland spots that manages to make everyone happy, whether it's thirst, hunger or weariness that brings people knocking. Assiduously tended rooms are a real delight, with a homely atmosphere and thoughtful touches. Those without a sea view are consoled with more space and a balcony with rock-garden perspectives. The cottage nearby offers simpler comfort.

★**Plockton Shores** SEAFOOD £££
(☎01599-544263; www.facebook.com/TheShoresPlockton; 30 Harbour St, IV52 8TN; restaurant mains £16-35; ⏲cafe 9am-5.30pm Mon-Sat, noon-4pm Sun, restaurant 5-9pm Tue-Sat; 🖉) This restaurant (attached to a shop) has a tempting menu of local seafood, including good-value platters with langoustines, mussels, crab, squat lobster and more, and succulent hand-dived tempura scallops. There's also a very tasty line in venison, steaks and a small selection of good vegetarian dishes that are more than an afterthought. The licensed cafe does home baking and light lunches.

Getting There & Away

Trains running between Kyle of Lochalsh (£3, 15 minutes) and Inverness (£24.50, 2½ hours) stop in Plockton up to four times daily each way.

SKYE

☎01478 / POP 10,000

The Isle of Skye (an t-Eilean Sgiathanach in Gaelic) takes its name from the old Norse *sky-a*, meaning 'cloud island', a Viking reference to the often-mist-enshrouded Cuillin Hills. It's the second-largest of Scotland's islands, a 50-mile-long patchwork of velvet moors, jagged mountains, sparkling lochs and towering sea cliffs.

The stunning scenery is the main attraction, but when the mist closes in there are plenty of castles, crofting museums and cosy pubs and restaurants; there are also dozens of art galleries and craft studios.

Along with Edinburgh and Loch Ness, Skye is one of Scotland's top-three tourist destinations, and as a result can suffer from overcrowding at hotspots such as the Quiraing and the Old Man of Storr. However, it's almost always possible to find peace and quiet in the island's further-flung corners. Come prepared for changeable weather: when it's fine it's very fine indeed, but all too often it isn't.

Skye & Outer Hebrides

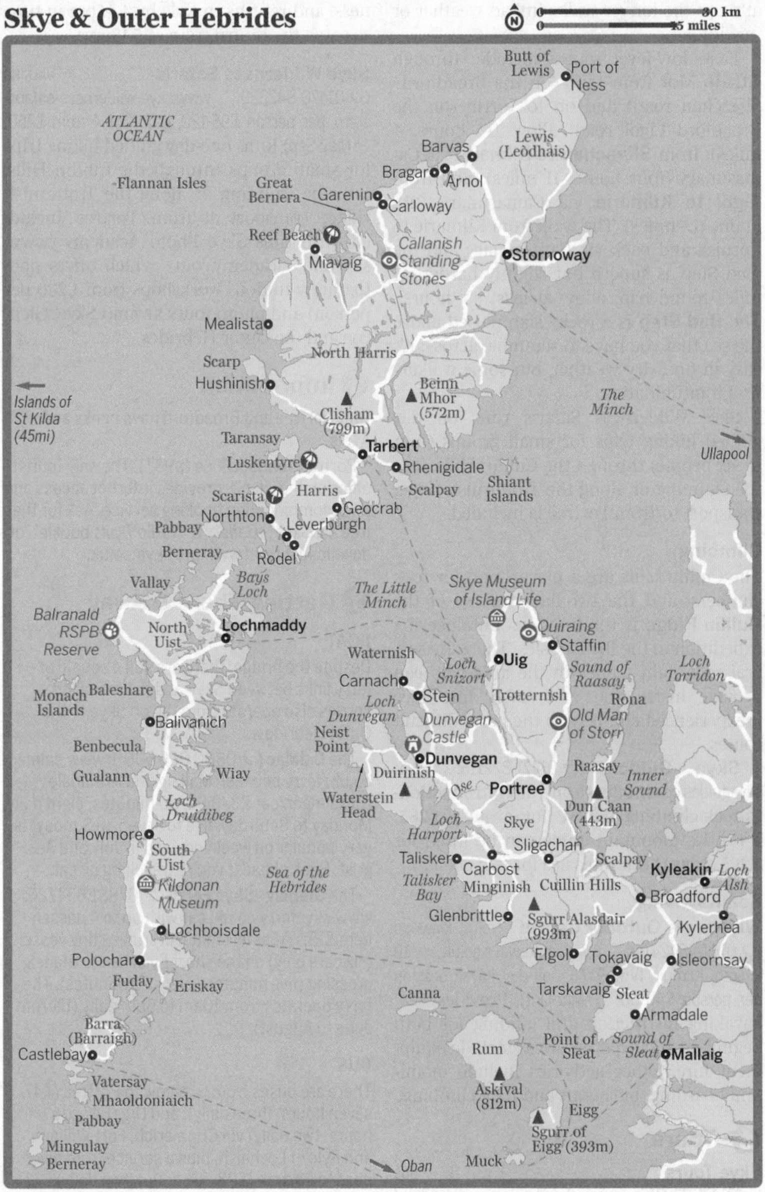

Activities

Walking

Skye offers some of the finest – and in places, the roughest and most difficult – walking in Scotland. There are many detailed guidebooks available, including a series of four walking guides by Charles Rhodes, available from the **Aros Centre** (☎01478-613750; www.aros.co.uk; Viewfield Rd, Portree, IV51 9EU; ⏰9am-5pm; P 🚻) FREE and the tourist office (p937) in Portree. You'll need Ordnance Survey (OS) 1:50,000 maps 23 and 32, or Harvey's 1:25,000 *Superwalker – The Cuillin*. Don't attempt the longer walks in bad weather or in winter.

Easy, low-level routes include: through **Strath Mor** from Luib (on the Broadford–Sligachan road) and on to Torrin (on the Broadford–Elgol road; allow 1½ hours, 4 miles); from **Sligachan to Kilmarie** via Camasunary (four hours, 11 miles); and from **Elgol to Kilmarie** via Camasunary (2½ hours, 6.5 miles). The walk from Kilmarie to Coruisk and back via Camasunary and the 'Bad Step' is superb but slightly harder (11 miles round trip; allow at least six hours). The **Bad Step** is a rocky slab poised above the sea that you have to scramble across; it's easy in fine, dry weather, but some walkers find it intimidating.

Skye Wilderness Safaris runs one-day guided hiking trips for small groups (four to six people) through the Cuillin Hills, into the Quiraing or along the Trotternish ridge; transport to/from Portree is included.

Climbing

The Cuillin Hills are a playground for rock climbers, and the two-day traverse of the **Cuillin Ridge** is the finest mountaineering expedition in the British Isles. There are several mountain guides in the area who can provide instruction and safely introduce inexperienced climbers to the more difficult routes.

Skye Guides (☎01471-822116; www.skyeguides.co.uk) offers a one-day introduction-to-rock-climbing course for around £285; a private mountain guide can be hired for £295 a day (both rates are for two clients).

Sea Kayaking

Whitewave Outdoor Centre KAYAKING
(☎01470-542414; www.white-wave.co.uk; 19 Linicro, Kilmuir, IV51 9YN; half-day kayak session per person £40-50; ⏲Mar-Oct) Provides sea-kayaking instruction and guiding for both beginners and experts; prices include equipment hire. Other activities include mountain boarding, bushcraft and rock climbing.

☞ Tours

Skye Tours BUS
(☎01471-822716; www.skye-tours.co.uk; adult/child £50/40; ⏲Mon-Sat) Five-hour sightseeing tours of Skye in a minibus, taking in the Old Man of Storr (p938), Kilt Rock and Dunvegan Castle (p937). Tours depart from Kyle of Lochalsh train station at 11.30am (connects with the 8.55am train from Inverness, and returns to Kyle by 4.45pm in time to catch the return train at 5.13pm).

Skye Wilderness Safaris WALKING
(☎01470-542229; www.skye-wilderness-safaris.com; per person £95-120, group of 4 from £250; ⏲May-Sep) Runs one-day guided hiking trips for small groups through the Cuillin Hills, into the Quiraing or along the Trotternish ridge; transport to/from Portree included. Also runs Skye Photo Academy (www.skyephotoacademy.com), which offers photography tuition (workshops from £230 per person) and photo tours around Skye, Glencoe and the Outer Hebrides.

ℹ Information

Only Portree and Broadford have banks and ATMs.

Portree Tourist Office (p937), The only tourist office on the island, provides internet access and an accommodation booking service. Ask for the free *Art Skye – Gallery & Studio Trails* booklet, or download it from www.art-skye.co.uk.

ℹ Getting There & Away

BOAT

Despite the bridge, there are still a couple of ferry links between Skye and the mainland. Ferries also operate from Uig on Skye to the Outer Hebrides.

The **CalMac** (☎0800 066 5000; www.calmac.co.uk) ferry between Mallaig and Armadale (passenger/car £3/9.95, 30 minutes, eight daily Monday to Saturday, five to seven on Sunday) is very popular on weekends and in July and August. Book ahead if you're travelling by car.

The **Glenelg–Skye Ferry** (☎07881 634726; www.skyeferry.co.uk; car with up to 4 passengers £15; ⏲Easter–mid-Oct) runs a tiny vessel (six cars only) on the short Kylerhea to Glenelg crossing (five minutes, every 20 minutes). The ferry operates from 10am to 6pm daily (till 7pm June to August).

BUS

There are buses from Glasgow to Portree (£47, seven hours, three daily), and Uig (£47, 7½ hours, two daily) via Crianlarich, Fort William and Kyle of Lochalsh, plus a service from Inverness to Portree (£28, 3¼ hours, two daily).

CAR

The Isle of Skye became permanently tethered to the Scottish mainland when the Skye Bridge opened in 1995. The controversial bridge tolls were abolished in 2004 and the crossing is now free.

Getting Around

BUS

Getting around the island by public transport can be a pain, especially if you want to explore away from the main Kyleakin–Portree–Uig road. Here, as in much of the Highlands, there are fewer buses on Saturday and only a handful of Sunday services.

Stagecoach operates the main bus routes on the island, linking all the main villages and towns. Its Skye Dayrider/Megarider ticket gives unlimited bus travel for one/seven days for £9.50/35.50. For timetable info, call Traveline (☎0871 200 2233).

CAR

Much of the driving on Skye is on single-track roads – remember to use passing places to allow any traffic behind you to overtake. There are petrol stations at Broadford (open 24 hours), Armadale, Portree, Dunvegan and Uig.

TAXI

You can order a taxi or hire a car (arrange for the car to be waiting at Kyle of Lochalsh train station) from **Kyle Taxi Company** (☎01599-534323; www.skyecarhire.co.uk; car hire per day/week from around £45/250).

Armadale

If you cross over the sea to Skye on the ferry from Mallaig you arrive in Armadale, at the southern end of the long, low-lying peninsula known as Sleat (pronounced 'slate'). The landscape of Sleat itself is not exceptional, but it provides a grandstand for ogling the magnificent scenery on either side – take the steep and twisting minor road that loops through Tarskavaig and Tokavaig for stunning views of the Isle of Rum, the Cuillin Hills and Bla Bheinn.

Armadale itself is little more than a grocery store, a post office, a cluster of craft shops and a scattering of houses.

Museum of the Isles MUSEUM
(☎01471-844305; www.armadalecastle.com; adult/child £9/5; 9.30am-5.30pm Apr-Oct, 10am-3pm Mon-Fri Mar & Nov; P) Just along the road from Armadale pier is the part-ruined **Armadale Castle**, former seat of Lord MacDonald of Sleat. The neighbouring museum will tell you all you ever wanted to know about Clan Donald, and also provides an easily digestible history of the Lordship of the Isles. Prize exhibits include rare portraits of clan chiefs, and a wine glass that was once used by Bonnie Prince Charlie. The ticket also gives admission to the lovely castle gardens.

Getting There & Away

From late May to August there are three to five buses a day (three on Sunday) from Armadale to Broadford (£4.25, 30 minutes) and Portree (£7.95, 1¼ hours), timed to meet the arrival of ferries from Mallaig. Outside the summer season, services are less frequent and may not coincide with ferry times.

Broadford (An T-Ath Leathann)

☎01471 / POP 750

The long, straggling village of Broadford is a service centre for the scattered communities of southern Skye. It has a 24-hour petrol station, a bank and a large Co-op supermarket with an ATM.

Sleeping & Eating

Skye Basecamp HOSTEL £
(☎01471-820044; www.skyebasecamp.co.uk; Lime Park, IV49 9AE; dm/q from £20/70; P) Run by the mountaineers at Skye Guides this well-equipped hostel is set in a converted residential house with great views across the sea towards the Crowlin Islands and the Applecross hills. Maps, guidebooks, weather forecasts and walking advice are all to hand.

Skye Picture House B&B ££
(☎01471-822531; www.skyepicturehouse.com; Ard Dorch; s/d from £45/90; P) Perched just a stone's throw above the sea, the setting of this welcoming B&B could hardly be better. Two of the three bedrooms have views across the water to the island of Scalpay, with the chance of spotting an otter. Breakfast is usually a help-yourself buffet, and evening meals may be available (check first, though).

★**Cafe Sia** CAFE ££
(☎01471-822616; www.cafesia.co.uk; Rathad na h-Atha, IV49 9AB; mains £7-17; 10am-9pm;) Serving everything from eggs Benedict and cappuccino to cocktails and seafood specials, this appealing cafe specialises in wood-fired pizzas (also available to take away) and superb artisanal coffee. There's also an outdoor deck with great views of the Red Cuillin. Takeaway coffee from 8am.

Cuillin Hills

The Cuillin Hills are Britain's most spectacular mountain range (the name comes from the Old Norse *kjöllen,* meaning 'keel-shaped'). Though small in stature – Sgurr Alasdair, the highest summit, is only 993m – the peaks are near-alpine in character, with knife-edge ridges, jagged pinnacles, scree-filled gullies and hectares of naked rock. The higher reaches of the Cuillins are off limits except to experienced climbers, but there are plenty of lower-level hiking routes.

One of the best hikes (on a fine day) is the steep climb from Glenbrittle campsite to **Coire Lagan** (6 miles round trip; allow at least three hours). The impressive upper corrie contains a lochan for bathing (for the hardy!), and the surrounding cliffs are a playground for rock climbers – bring your binoculars.

Even more spectacular, but much harder to reach on foot, is **Loch Coruisk** (from the Gaelic Coir'Uisg, the Water Corrie), a remote loch ringed by the highest peaks of the Cuillin. Accessible by **boat trip** (☎01471-866288; www.mistyisleboattrips.co.uk; Elgol Pier, IV49 9BL; adult/child £30/15; ⏲Apr-Oct) from Elgol, or via an arduous 5.5-mile hike from Kilmarie, Coruisk was popularised by Sir Walter Scott in his 1815 poem 'Lord of the Isles'. Crowds of Victorian tourists and landscape artists followed in Scott's footsteps, including JMW Turner, whose watercolours were used to illustrate Scott's works.

There are two main bases for exploring the Cuillin – **Sligachan** to the north (on the Kyle of Lochalsh–Portree bus route), and **Glenbrittle** to the south (no public transport).

Portree (Port Righ)

☎01478 / POP 2320

Portree is Skye's largest and liveliest town. It has a pretty harbour lined with brightly painted houses, and there are great views of the surrounding hills. Its name (from the Gaelic for King's Harbour) commemorates James V, who came here in 1540 to pacify the local clans.

Activities

MV Stardust BOATING

(☎07795-385581; www.skyeboat-trips.co.uk; Portree Harbour; adult/child £20/10) MV *Stardust* offers 1½-hour boat trips around Portree Bay, with the chance to see seals, porpoises and – if you're lucky – white-tailed sea eagles. There are longer two-hour cruises to the Sound of Raasay (adult/child £25/15). You can also arrange fishing trips, or to be dropped off for a hike on the Isle of Raasay and picked up again later.

Sleeping

Portree Youth Hostel HOSTEL £

(HS; ☎01478-612231; www.hostellingscotland.org.uk; Bayfield Rd, IV51 9EW; dm/d from £25/70; P 📶) This HS hostel offers brightly decorated dorms and private rooms, a stylish lounge with views over the bay, and outdoor seating areas. Its location in the town centre just 100m from the bus stop is ideal.

Torvaig Campsite CAMPSITE £

(☎01478-611849; www.portreecampsite.co.uk; Torvaig, IV51 9HU; sites with 2 adults from £23; ⏲Apr-Oct; 📶🐾) An attractive, family-run campsite located 1.5 miles north of Portree, on the road to Staffin.

Ben Tianavaig B&B B&B ££

(☎01478-612152; www.ben-tianavaig.co.uk; 5 Bosville Tce, IV51 9DG; r £110; P 📶) 🍃 A warm welcome awaits from the Irish-Welsh couple who run this appealing B&B bang in the centre of town. All three bedrooms have a view across the harbour to the hill that gives the house its name, and breakfasts include free-range eggs and vegetables grown in the garden. Two-night minimum stay; no credit/debit cards.

Bosville Hotel HOTEL £££

(☎01478-612846; www.bosvillehotel.co.uk; 9-11 Bosville Tce; r from £220; 📶) 🍃 The Bosville brings a little bit of metropolitan style to Portree with its locally made designer fabrics and handcrafted furniture, fluffy bathrobes and bright, spacious bathrooms. It's worth splashing out a bit for the 'premium' rooms, with views over the town and harbour.

Eating

Café Arriba CAFE £

(☎01478-611830; www.cafearriba.co.uk; Quay Brae, IV51 9DB; mains £6-15; ⏲8.30am-4.30pm Thu-Mon Apr-Oct; 🖉) 🍃 Arriba is a funky little cafe, brightly decked out in primary colours and offering delicious flatbread melts (bacon, leek and cheese is a favourite), as well as the best choice of vegetarian grub on the island, ranging from a veggie breakfast fry-up to falafel wraps with hummus and chilli sauce. Also serves excellent coffee.

Dulse & Brose MODERN SCOTTISH ££
(☎01478-612846; www.bosvillehotel.co.uk; Bosville Hotel, 7 Bosville Tce, IV51 9DG; mains £9-17; ⏰noon-3pm & 6-10pm May-Sep, 6-8.15pm Oct-Apr; 📶) This hotel restaurant sports a relaxed atmosphere, an award-winning chef and a menu that makes the most of Skye produce – including lamb, game, seafood, cheese, organic vegetables and berries – and adds a French or Asian twist to traditional dishes.

★**Scorrybreac** MODERN SCOTTISH £££
(☎01478-612069; www.scorrybreac.com; 7 Bosville Tce, IV51 9DG; 4-course dinner £60; ⏰5-9pm Tue-Sat Mar-Oct, limited opening Nov & Dec) Set in the front rooms of what was once a private house, and with just eight tables, Scorrybreac is snug and intimate, offering fine dining without the faff. Chef Calum Munro (son of Donnie Munro, of Gaelic rock band Runrig fame) sources as much produce as possible from Skye, including foraged herbs and mushrooms, and creates the most exquisite concoctions.

Information

Portree Tourist Office (☎01478-612992; www.visitscotland.com/destinations-maps/isle-skye; Bayfield Rd, IV51 9EL; ⏰10am-4pm Mon-Sat year-round, longer hours Jun-Aug; 📶) The only tourist office on the island.

Getting There & Away

The main bus stop is at Somerled Sq. There are four Scottish Citylink buses every day from Kyle of Lochalsh to Portree (£8, one hour), continuing to Uig.

Local buses run from Portree:

Armadale (£7.95, 1¼ hours) Connecting with the ferry to Mallaig late May to August.

Broadford (£6.30, 45 minutes) Two to five daily.

Dunvegan Castle (£5.50, 50 minutes) Three daily Monday to Saturday.

There are also three buses a day on a circular route around Trotternish (in both directions), taking in Flodigarry (£4.75, 40 minutes), Kilmuir (£5.10, 45 minutes) and Uig (£4.20, 30 minutes).

Getting Around

You can hire bikes from **Skye Bike Shack** (☎07826 842160; www.skyebikeshack.com; 6 Carbost, Skeabost Bridge IV51 9PD; bike hire per day from £30; ⏰9am-1pm Tue-Sat) – it's 4 miles west of Portree, on the road towards Dunvegan.

Dunvegan (Dun Bheagain)

Dunvegan, an unremarkable village on the western side of Skye, is famous for its historic namesake castle that has links to Sir Walter Scott and Bonnie Prince Charlie.

Sights

Dunvegan Castle CASTLE
(☎01470-521206; www.dunvegancastle.com; adult/child £14/9; ⏰10am-5.30pm Easter–mid-Oct; P) Skye's most famous historic building, and one of its most popular tourist attractions, Dunvegan Castle is the seat of the chief of Clan MacLeod. In addition to the usual castle stuff – swords, silver and family portraits – there are some interesting artefacts, including the Fairy Flag, a diaphanous silk banner that dates from some time between the 4th and 7th centuries, and Bonnie Prince Charlie's waistcoat and a lock of his hair, donated by Flora MacDonald's granddaughter.

The oldest parts are the 14th-century keep and dungeon, but most of it dates from the 17th to 19th centuries, when it played host to Samuel Johnson, Sir Walter Scott and, most famously, Flora MacDonald. Look out for Rory Mor's Drinking Horn, a beautiful 16th-century vessel of Celtic design that could hold half a gallon of claret. Upholding the family tradition in 1956, John MacLeod – the 29th chief, who died in 2007 – downed the contents in one minute and 57 seconds.

Coral Beaches BEACH
From the end of the minor road beyond Dunvegan Castle entrance, an easy 1-mile walk leads to the Coral Beaches – a pair of blindingly white beaches composed of the bleached exoskeletons of coralline algae known as maerl.

Sleeping & Eating

Eco Bells Glamping CAMPSITE ££
(☎01470-521461; www.facebook.com/skyeecobells; Orbost, Duirinish; cabin/tent per night £92/75; ⏰Apr-Sep; P) Tucked away in a remote corner, on a minor road about 3 miles south of Dunvegan, this place offers accommodation in three cosy cabins and a large bell tent in a rural setting. Each cabin or tent sleeps up to three adults (or two adults and two children) and has beds, heating, a firepit and barbecue. Two-night minimum stay.

DON'T MISS

QUIRAING

Staffin Bay is dominated by the dramatic basalt escarpment of the Quiraing: its impressive land-slipped cliffs and pinnacles constitute one of Skye's most remarkable landscapes. From a parking area at the highest point of the minor road between Staffin and Uig you can walk north to the Quiraing in half an hour.

★Hillstone Lodge B&B £££
(☎01470-511434; www.hillstonelodge.com; 12 Colbost; s/d from £175/195; ⊙Apr-Oct; P 📶) 🌿 You can't help notice the many new houses on Skye that bear the hallmarks of award-winning local architects Rural Design – weathered timber walls and modern materials used with traditional shapes and forms. Hillstone is one of the best, with tasteful modern styling and stunning views across Loch Dunvegan. It's about 1km north of the **Three Chimneys** (☎01470-511258; www.threechimneys.co.uk; Colbost, IV55 8ZT; mains £30-35; ⊙12.15-1.45pm Mon-Sat mid-Mar–Oct, plus Sun Easter-Sep, 6.30-9.15pm daily year-round; P 📶) 🌿, above the pier.

Cafe Lephin CAFE £
(☎01470-511465; www.cafelephin.co.uk; 2 Lephin, Glendale; mains £5-8; ⊙11am-6pm Mon-Sat; 📶 👪 🐾) A mixture of modern and rustic, with touches of tweed and sheepskin, this wee cafe captures the spirit of enterprise that's bringing life back to areas of Skye that were deserted during the Highland Clearances. Great coffee, comfy sofa and a menu that includes haggis panini!

★Loch Bay SEAFOOD £££
(☎01470-592235; www.lochbay-restaurant.co.uk; Stein, Waternish, IV55 8GA; 6-course dinner £95; ⊙12.15-1.45pm Wed-Sun, 6.15-9pm Tue-Sat Apr-early Oct; P) 🌿 This cosy farmhouse kitchen of a place, with terracotta tiles and a wood-burning stove, is one of Skye's most romantic restaurants and was awarded a Michelin star in 2018. The menu includes most things that swim in the sea or live in a shell, but there are non-seafood choices, too. Best to book ahead.

Trotternish

The Trotternish peninsula to the north of Portree has some of Skye's most beautiful – and bizarre – scenery. A loop road allows a circular driving tour of the peninsula from Portree, passing through the village of **Uig**, where the ferry to the Outer Hebrides departs.

Sights

Old Man of Storr NATURAL FEATURE
(P) The 50m-high, pot-bellied pinnacle of crumbling basalt known as the Old Man of Storr is prominent above the road 6 miles north of Portree. Walk up to its foot from the car park at the northern end of Loch Leathan (2-mile round trip). This seemingly unclimbable pinnacle was first scaled in 1955 by English mountaineer Don Whillans, a feat that has been repeated only a handful of times since.

Staffin Dinosaur Museum MUSEUM
(☎01470-562321; www.staffindinosaurmuseum.com; 3 Ellishadder, Staffin, IV51 9JE; adult/child £2/1; ⊙9.30am-5pm; P) In an old stone barn by the roadside, this museum houses an interesting collection of dinosaur footprints, ammonites and other fossils discovered in the local Jurassic sandstones, which have become a focus for dinosaur research in recent years.

Skye Museum of Island Life MUSEUM
(☎01470-552206; www.skyemuseum.co.uk; Kilmuir; adult/child £4/50p; ⊙9.30am-5pm Mon-Sat Easter-late Sep; P) The peat-reek of crofting life in the 18th and 19th centuries is preserved in the thatched cottages, croft houses, barns and farm implements of the Skye Museum of Island Life. Behind the museum is **Kilmuir Cemetery**, where a tall Celtic cross marks the grave of Flora MacDonald – the cross was erected in 1955 to replace the original monument, of which 'every fragment was removed by tourists'.

Fairy Glen AREA
Just south of Uig, a minor road (signposted 'Sheader and Balnaknock') leads a mile or so to the Fairy Glen, a strange and enchanting natural landscape of miniature conical hills, rocky towers, ruined cottages and a tiny roadside lochan.

Sleeping

★Cowshed Boutique Bunkhouse HOSTEL £
(☎07917 536820; www.skyecowshed.co.uk; Uig, IV51 9YD; dm/pod/q £23.50/95/120; P 📶 🐾) This hostel enjoys a glorious setting overlooking Uig Bay, with superb views from its ultra-stylish lounge. The dorms have custom-built wooden bunks that offer comfort and privacy, while the camping pods (sleeping up to four, but more comfortable with two) have heating and en suite shower rooms; there are even mini 'dog pods' for your canine companions.

Shulista Croft CAMPSITE £
(☎01470-552314; www.shulistacroft.co.uk; North Duntulm, Shulista, IV51 9UG; pod per night £95; ⊙Mar-Nov) Set on a working croft amid sheep, lambs and chickens, Shulista has luxury timber camping pods with great views (two-night minimum stay, three in July and August; up to two adults and two kids). Each one is heated and insulated, and has an en suite shower room, basic kitchenette and even a TV.

Flodigarry Hotel HERITAGE HOTEL £££
(☎01470-552203; www.hotelintheskye.co.uk; Flodigarry; r £215-450, ste £640-730; ⊙Easter-Oct; P 📶 🐾) From 1751 to 1759 Flora MacDonald lived in a cottage that is now part of this atmospheric country-house hotel, given a new lease of life by adventurous owners. You can stay in the cottage itself (there are four bedrooms), or in the more spacious rooms and suites in the main hotel. Nonguests are welcome at the stylish bar and restaurant, with great sea views.

Getting There & Away

Two or three daily buses (four on Saturday) follow a circular route (in both directions) from Portree around the Trotternish peninsula, taking in Flodigarry (£4.75, 40 minutes), Kilmuir (£5.60, 45 minutes) and Uig (£4.15, 30 minutes).

Car ferries run from Uig to Tarbert (Harris; car/pedestrian £32/6.50, 1½ hours) and Lochmaddy (North Uist; car/pedestrian £32/6.50, 1¾ hours) in the Outer Hebrides, with one or two crossings a day.

OUTER HEBRIDES

☎01851 / POP 27,670

The Western Isles, or Na h-Eileanan an Iar in Gaelic – also known as the Outer Hebrides – are a 130-mile-long string of islands lying off the northwest coast of Scotland. There are 119 islands in total, of which the five main inhabited islands are Lewis and Harris (two parts of a single island, though often described as if they are separate islands), North Uist, Benbecula, South Uist and Barra. The middle three (often referred to simply as 'the Uists') are connected by road-bearing causeways.

The ferry crossing from Ullapool or Uig to the Western Isles marks an important cultural divide – more than a third of Scotland's registered crofts are in the Outer Hebrides, and no less than 60% of the population are Gaelic speakers.

If your time is limited, head straight for the west coast of Lewis with its prehistoric sites, preserved blackhouses (traditional single-storeyed Scottish houses) and beautiful beaches.

Information

The only tourist office is in Stornoway (p941). See www.visitouterhebrides.co.uk for tourist information.

Getting There & Away

AIR

There are airports at Stornoway (Lewis), Benbecula and Barra.

Loganair (☎0344 800 2855; www.loganair.co.uk) flights operate to Stornoway from Edinburgh, Inverness and Glasgow. There are also flights (weekdays only) between Stornoway and Benbecula.

There are daily Loganair flights from Glasgow to Barra, and from Monday to Saturday to Benbecula. At Barra, the planes land on the hard-sand beach at low tide, so the schedule depends on the tides.

BOAT

Standard one-way fares on **CalMac** (☎0800 066 5000; www.calmac.co.uk) ferries:

Crossing	Duration (hours)	Car (£)	Driver/ Passenger (£)
Ullapool–Stornoway	2¾	52	9.75
Uig–Lochmaddy	1¾	32	6.50
Uig–Tarbert	1½	32	6.50
Oban–Castlebay	4¾	70	15.15
Mallaig–Lochboisdale	3½	59	10.75

There are two or three ferries a day to Stornoway, one or two a day to Tarbert and Lochmaddy, and one a day to Castlebay and Lochboisdale. See the website for ferry timetables.

Advance booking for cars is recommended (essential in July and August); foot and bicycle passengers should have no problems. Bicycles are carried free.

Getting Around

Despite their separate names, Lewis and Harris are actually one island. Berneray, North Uist, Benbecula, South Uist and Eriskay are all linked by road bridges and causeways. There are car ferries between Leverburgh (Harris) and Berneray, and between Eriskay and Castlebay (Barra).

The local council publishes timetables of all bus and ferry services within the Outer Hebrides, which are available at tourist offices. Timetables can also be found online at www.cne-siar.gov.uk.

BICYCLE

Bikes can be hired from **Bike Hebrides** (07775 943355; www.bikehebrides.com; 6 Sand St, HS1 2UE; per day/week £25/100; 9am-5pm Mon-Sat) in Stornoway (Lewis), **Horgabost Bike Hire** (07469 196079; www.facebook.com/horgabostbikehire; Horgabost Campsite, HS3 3HR; per half-/full-day £15/20; 9am-5pm Mon-Sat) in South Harris and Barra Bike Hire (p948) in Castlebay (Barra).

BUS

The bus network covers almost every village on the islands, with around four to six buses a day on all the main routes; however, there are no buses at all on Sunday. You can pick up timetables from Stornoway tourist office, or call Stornoway bus station for information.

CAR

Apart from the fast, two-lane road between Tarbert and Stornoway, most roads are single track. The main hazard is posed by sheep wandering about or sleeping on the road. Petrol stations are far apart (almost all of those on Lewis and Harris are closed on Sunday), and fuel is about 10% more expensive than on the mainland.

There are petrol stations at Stornoway, Barvas, Borve, Uig, Lochs, Ness, Tarbert and Leverburgh on Lewis and Harris; Lochmaddy and Bayhead on North Uist; Balivanich and Creagorry on Benbecula; Howmore, Lochboisdale and Daliburgh on South Uist; and Castlebay on Barra.

Cars can be hired from around £41/202 per day/week from **Car Hire Hebrides** (01851-706500; www.carhire-hebrides.co.uk; Ferry Terminal, Shell St, Stornoway, HS1 2AE), with offices at Stornoway ferry terminal, Stornoway airport and Benbecula airport.

Lewis (Leodhais)

01851 / POP 19,000

The northern part of Lewis is dominated by the desolate expanse of the Black Moor, a vast, undulating peat bog dimpled with glittering lochans, seen clearly from the Stornoway–Barvas road. But Lewis' finest scenery is on the west coast, from Barvas southwest to Mealista, where the rugged landscape of hill, loch and sandy strand is reminiscent of the northwestern Highlands. The Outer Hebrides' most evocative historic sites – Callanish Standing Stones (p942), **Dun Carloway** (Dun Charlabhaigh; P) and Arnol Blackhouse – are also to be found here.

Stornoway (Steornabhagh)

01851 / POP 5715

Stornoway is the bustling 'capital' of the Outer Hebrides and the only real town in the whole archipelago. It's a surprisingly busy little place, with cars and people swamping the centre on weekdays. Though set on a beautiful natural harbour, the town isn't going to win any prizes for beauty or atmosphere, but it's a pleasant enough introduction to this remote corner of the country.

Sights & Activities

Museum nan Eilean MUSEUM
(www.lews-castle.co.uk; Lews Castle, HS2 0XS; 10am-5pm Mon-Wed, Fri & Sat Apr-Sep, 1-4pm Oct-Mar; P) FREE The 'Museum of the Isles' occupies a modern extension built onto the side of Lews Castle. Artefacts, photos and videos celebrate the culture and history of the Outer Hebrides and explore traditional island life. The highlights of the collection are six of the famous Lewis chess pieces (p942), discovered at Uig in west Lewis in 1831. Carved from whale and walrus ivory, they are thought to have been made in Norway more than 800 years ago.

Lews Castle CASTLE
(01851-822750; www.lews-castle.co.uk; HS2 0XS; 8am-5pm; P) FREE The Baronial mansion across the harbour from Stornoway town centre was built in the 1840s for the Matheson family, then owners of Lewis; it was gifted to the community by Lord Leverhulme in 1923. A major redevelopment completed in 2017 saw it converted to luxury

self-catering accommodation, but the grand public rooms on the ground floor are free to visit when not in use. There's also an excellent **cafe** (mains £7-15; ⏲8am-4pm;), one of the few local eateries to open on Sundays.

The beautiful wooded grounds, criss-crossed with walking trails, are open to the public and host the **Hebridean Celtic Festival** (www.hebceltfest.com; ⏲Jul).

Hebridean Adventures WILDLIFE WATCHING
(☎07871 463755; www.hebrideanadventures.co.uk; 22 North Beach, HS1 2XQ; adult/child £120/90; ⏲Apr-Sep) Seven-hour whale-watching trips out of Stornoway harbour in a converted fishing boat with a cosy saloon to shelter from any wild weather (must be prebooked).

Sleeping

★**Heb Hostel** HOSTEL £
(☎01851-709889; www.hebhostel.com; 25 Kenneth St, HS1 2DR; dm/s/d £20/50/55;) The Heb is an easy-going hostel close to the ferry, with comfy wooden bunks, a convivial living room with peat fire and a welcoming owner who can provide all kinds of advice on what to do and where to go. You can also stay in a shepherd's hut in the garden (per night £75, minimum three nights).

29 Kenneth St B&B ££
(☎07917 035295; www.stornowaybedandbreakfast.co.uk; 29 Kenneth St, HS1 2DR; s/d from £65/95;) Nine smartly fitted out bedrooms spread between two houses (the other is across the street at No 32) offer great-value accommodation, just five minutes' walk from the ferry terminal.

Hal o' the Wynd B&B ££
(☎01851-706073; www.halothewynd.com; 2 Newton St, HS1 2RE; s/d from £55/85;) Touches of tartan and Harris tweed lend a traditional air to this welcoming B&B, conveniently located directly opposite the ferry pier. Most rooms have views over the harbour to Lews Castle.

Park Guest House B&B ££
(☎01851-702485; www.the-parkguesthouse.com; 30 James St, HS1 2QN; s/d from £78/98;) A charming Victorian villa with a conservatory and six luxurious rooms (mostly en suite), the Park Guest House is comfortable and central and has the advantage of an excellent restaurant specialising in Scottish seafood, beef and game plus one or two vegetarian dishes (mains £15 to £30). Rooms overlooking the main road can be noisy on weekday mornings.

WORTH A TRIP

ARNOL BLACKHOUSE

One of Scotland's most evocative historic buildings, the **Arnol Blackhouse** (HES; ☎01851-710395; www.historicenvironment.scot; Arnol, HS2 9DB; adult/child £6/3.60; ⏲9.30am-5.30pm Mon-Sat Apr-Sep, 10am-4pm Mon, Tue & Thu-Sat Oct-Mar;) is not so much a museum as a perfectly preserved fragment of a lost world. Built in 1885, this traditional blackhouse – a combined byre (cowshed), barn and home – was inhabited until 1964 and has not been changed since the last inhabitant moved out. The museum is about 3 miles west of Barvas.

Eating

Artizan Cafe CAFE £
(☎01851-706538; www.facebook.com/artizanstornoway; 12-14 Church St, HS1 2DH; mains £4-8; ⏲9.30am-5pm Mon-Sat;) Recycled timber and cool colours mark out this cafe-gallery as one of Stornoway's hip hang-outs, serving great coffee and cake and light lunches (12.30pm to 2.30pm). Turns into a cocktail bar on Saturday nights from 6pm to 11pm.

An Lanntair Cafe Bar BISTRO ££
(https://lanntair.com/cafebar; Kenneth St, HS1 2DS; mains £9-18; ⏲10am-8pm Mon-Sat;) The stylish and family-friendly cafe-bar at the **arts centre** (☎01851-708480; www.lanntair.com; ⏲10am-5pm Tue & Wed, to midnight Thu-Sat, 11am-4pm last Sun of month) FREE serves a broad range of freshly prepared dishes, from tasty bacon rolls at breakfast to burgers, salads and fish and chips for lunch, and char-grilled steaks or local scallops for dinner.

Information

Stornoway Tourist Office (☎01851-703088; www.visitouterhebrides.co.uk; 26 Cromwell St, HS1 2DD; ⏲10am-4pm Apr-Oct, closed Sun Nov-Mar)

Getting There & Away

The **bus station** (☎01851-704327; South Beach) is on the waterfront next to the ferry terminal (left luggage 30p to £1.50 per piece). Bus W10 runs from Stornoway to Tarbert (£4.80,

OFF THE BEATEN TRACK

THE BUTT OF LEWIS

The Butt of Lewis – the extreme northern tip of the Hebrides – is windswept and rugged, with a very imposing lighthouse, pounding surf and large colonies of nesting fulmars on the high cliffs. There's a bleak sense of isolation here, with nothing but the grey Atlantic between you and Canada. The main settlement is **Port of Ness** (Port Nis), which has an attractive harbour. To the west is the sandy beach of **Traigh**, which is popular with surfers.

Just before the turn-off to the Butt at Eoropie (Eoropaidh), you'll find **St Moluag's Church** (Teampull Mholuidh), an austere, barnlike structure believed to date from the 12th century but still used by the Episcopal Church.

one hour, four or five daily Monday to Saturday) and Leverburgh (£6.80, two hours).

The Westside Circular bus W2 runs a circular route from Stornoway through Callanish (£2.70, 30 minutes), Carloway, Garenin and Arnol; the timetable allows you to visit one or two of the sites in a day.

The bus network covers almost every village in the islands, with around four to six buses a day on all the main routes; however, there are no buses at all on Sunday. You can pick up timetables from the tourist offices, or call Stornoway bus station for information.

Callanish (Calanais)

Callanish, on the western side of Lewis, is famous for its prehistoric standing stones. One of the most atmospheric prehistoric sites in the whole of Scotland, its ageless mystery, impressive scale and undeniable beauty leave a lasting impression.

Callanish Standing Stones HISTORIC SITE
(HES; www.historicenvironment.scot; 24hr) FREE The Callanish Standing Stones, 15 miles west of Stornoway on the A858 road, form one of the most complete stone circles in Britain. It is one of the most atmospheric prehistoric sites anywhere. Sited on a wild and secluded promontory overlooking Loch Roag, 13 large stones of beautifully banded gneiss are arranged, as if in worship, around a 4.5m-tall central monolith.

Some 40 smaller stones radiate from the circle in the shape of a cross, with the remains of a chambered tomb at the centre. Dating from 3800 to 5000 years ago, the stones are roughly contemporary with the pyramids of Egypt.

Calanais Visitor Centre MUSEUM
(01851-621422; www.callanishvisitorcentre.co.uk; HS2 9DY; admission free, exhibition £3; 9.30am-8pm Mon-Sat Jun-Aug, 10am-6pm Mon-Sat Apr, May, Sep & Oct, 10am-4pm Tue-Sat Nov-Mar; P) This visitor centre near the Callanish Standing Stones is a tour de force of discreet design. Inside is a small exhibition that speculates on the origins and purpose of the stones, and an excellent **cafe** (mains £4-8; 9.30am-8pm Mon-Sat Jun-Aug, 10am-6pm Mon-Sat Apr, May, Sep & Oct, 10am-4pm Tue-Sat Nov-Mar; P).

Getting There & Away

Bus W2 (Westside Circular) runs from Stornoway to Callanish (£2.70, 30 minutes) twice daily Monday to Saturday, allowing enough time to visit the stones.

Garenin (Na Gearrannan)

The picturesque and fascinating Gearrannan Blackhouse Village is a cluster of nine restored thatch-roofed blackhouses perched above the exposed Atlantic coast. One of the cottages is home to the **Blackhouse Museum** (01851-643416; www.gearrannan.com; HS2 9AL; adult/child £3.60/1.20; 9.30am-5.30pm Mon-Sat Apr-Sep; P), a traditional 1955 blackhouse with displays on the village's history, while another houses a **cafe** (mains £3-6; 9.30am-5.30pm Mon-Sat).

The W2 (Westside Circular) bus runs from Stornoway to Carloway village (£3.40, 45 minutes), a mile from Garenin, twice a day, Monday to Saturday.

Western Lewis

The B8011 road (signposted Uig, on the A858 Stornoway–Callanish road) from Garrynahine to Timsgarry (Timsgearraidh) meanders through scenic wilderness to some of Scotland's most stunning beaches. At **Miavaig**, a loop road detours north through the Bhaltos Estate to the pretty, mile-long white strand of **Reef Beach**; there's a basic but spectacular **campsite** (Cnip; Traigh na Beirigh; tent sites £10; May-Sep) in the machair behind the beach.

From Miavaig, the road continues west through a rocky defile to Timsgarry and the vast, sandy expanse of **Traigh Uige** (Uig Sands). The famous 12th-century **Lewis chess pieces**, made of walrus ivory, were discovered in the sand dunes here in 1831.

The minor road that continues south from Timsgarry to **Mealista** passes a few smaller, but still spectacular, white-sand and boulder beaches on the way to a remote dead end. On a clear day you can see St Kilda on the horizon.

Buses head from Stornoway to Uig (£4.80, one hour, two or three daily); some services continue (by request) to Ardroil and Brenish, a mile or so short of Mealista.

Harris (Na Hearadh)

☎01859 / POP 2000

Harris, to the south of Lewis, is the scenic jewel in the necklace of islands that comprise the Outer Hebrides. It has a spectacular blend of rugged mountains, pristine beaches, flower-speckled machair and barren rocky landscapes. The isthmus at Tarbert splits Harris neatly in two: North Harris is dominated by mountains that rise forbiddingly above the peat moors to the south of Stornoway – Clisham (799m) is the highest point in the whole island chain. South Harris is lower-lying, fringed by beautiful white-sand beaches in the west and a convoluted rocky coastline to the east.

Harris is famous for Harris tweed, a high-quality woollen cloth still hand-woven in islanders' homes. The industry employs around 400 weavers; staff at Tarbert tourist office can tell you about weavers and workshops you can visit.

Getting There & Away

Harris and neighbouring Lewis are actually part of the same island, and Tarbert is linked to Stornoway by a good, fast road (37 miles). Car ferries sail between Tarbert and Uig (on the isle of Skye), and between Leverburgh and Berneray (North Uist).

Tarbert (An Tairbeart)

☎01859 / POP 480

Tarbert is a harbour village with a spectacular location, tucked into the narrow neck of land that links North and South Harris. It is one of the main ferry ports for the Outer Hebrides, and home to the Isle of Harris Distillery.

Village facilities include two petrol stations, a bank, an ATM and two general stores.

Isle of Harris Distillery DISTILLERY

(☎01859-502212; www.harrisdistillery.com; Main St, HS3 3DJ; tours £12; ⏲10am-5pm Mon-Sat; P) This distillery only filled its first batch of whisky barrels in 2017, and its first single malt, called The Hearach (Gaelic for a person from Harris), will not be bottled until the management decides it has reached perfection; meanwhile, it's producing Isle of Harris gin, too. The modern building is very stylish – the lobby feels like a luxury hotel – and 75-minute tours depart two or three times daily (weekdays only) in summer; book in advance. There's a cafe here, too.

Harris Hotel HOTEL £££

(☎01859-502154; www.harrishotel.com; HS3 3DL; s/d from £109/129; P 📶) Run since 1903 by four generations of the Cameron family, the Harris is a 19th-century sporting hotel built in 1865 for visiting anglers and deer stalkers, and retains a pleasantly old-fashioned atmosphere. It has spacious, comfy rooms and a decent restaurant; look out for JM Barrie's initials on the dining-room window (the author of *Peter Pan* visited in the 1920s).

Distillery Canteen CAFE £

(Isle of Harris Distillery, Main St; mains £6-10; ⏲10am-4pm Mon-Sat) The cafe at the Isle of Harris Distillery, with its communal, scrubbed-timber tables and chunky benches, is bright and convivial. The menu is not

LOCAL KNOWLEDGE

HARRIS' GOLDEN EAGLES

Magnificent North Harris is the most mountainous region of the Outer Hebrides. There are few roads here, but many opportunities for climbing, walking and birdwatching. Between the old whaling station and Amhuinnsuidhe Castle, at Miavaig, a parking area and gated track gives hikers access to a **golden eagle observatory**, a 1.3-mile walk north from the road. On Wednesday from April to September, local rangers lead a 3½-hour guided walk (£5 per person) in search of eagles; details from www.north-harris.org.

extensive – a choice of soups, cakes, home-baked bread and platters of cheese or seafood – but the quality of the food, most of it sourced directly from Harris, shines brightly.

Getting There & Away

There are four or five daily buses, Monday to Saturday, from Tarbert to Stornoway (£4.80, one hour) and Leverburgh (£3.20, 50 minutes) via the west-coast road.

Tarbert also has ferry connections to Uig (car/pedestrian £32/6.50, 1½ hours, one or two daily) on Skye.

South Harris

South Harris' west coast has some of the most beautiful beaches in Scotland. The blinding white sands and turquoise waters of Luskentyre and Scarasta would be major holiday resorts if they were transported to somewhere with a warm climate; as it is, they're usually deserted.

The east coast is a complete contrast to the west – a strange, rocky moonscape of naked gneiss pocked with tiny lochans, the bleakness lightened by the occasional splash of green around the few crofting communities. Film buffs will know that the psychedelic sequences depicting an alien landscape in *2001: A Space Odyssey* were shot from an aircraft flying over Harris' east coast.

The narrow, twisting road that winds along this coast is known locally as the **Golden Road** because of the vast amount of money it cost per mile. It was built in the 1930s to link all the tiny communities known as 'The Bays'.

Sights & Activities

★Luskentyre BEACH

(Losgaintir) Luskentyre is one of the biggest and most beautiful beaches in Scotland, famed for its acres of low-tide white sands and turquoise waters. A minor road leads along the northern side of the bay to a parking area beside an ancient graveyard; from here you can walk west along the beach or through the grassy dunes with gorgeous views across the sea to the island of Taransay.

Talla na Mara ARTS CENTRE

(☎01859-503900; www.tallanamara.co.uk; Pairc Niseaboist, HS3 3HR; ⌚9am-5pm Mon-Sat; P) FREE Opened in 2017 as a community enterprise, this beautiful modern building houses several artists' studios and an exhibition space that displays works celebrating the landscapes and culture of Scotland's Western Isles.

Clò Mòr MUSEUM

(☎01859-502040; Old School, Drinishader HS3 3DX; ⌚9am-5.30pm Mon-Sat Mar-Oct; P) FREE The Campbell family has been making Harris tweed for 90 years, and this exhibition (behind the family shop) celebrates the history of the fabric known in Gaelic as *clò mòr* (the 'big cloth'); ask about live demonstrations of tweed weaving on the 70-year-old Hattersley loom. Drinishader is 5 miles south of Tarbert on the east-coast road.

Sea Harris BOATING

(☎01859-502007; www.seaharris.com; Leverburgh Pier, HS5 3UB; per person £220; ⌚Apr-Sep) Operates 10-hour day trips to St Kilda in a fast boat with four to five hours ashore.

Kilda Cruises BOATING

(☎01859-502060; www.kildacruises.co.uk; Leverburgh Pier, HS5 3UB; per person £235) Operates 12-hour day trips to the remote and spectacular island group of St Kilda. Daily from mid-April to mid-September.

Sleeping

Am Bothan HOSTEL £

(☎01859-520251; www.ambothan.com; Ferry Rd, Leverburgh, HS5 3UA; dm £25; P 📶) An attractive, chalet-style hostel, Am Bothan has small, neat dorms and a great porch where you can enjoy morning coffee with views over the bay. The hostel has bike hire and can arrange wildlife-watching boat trips.

Sorrel Cottage B&B ££

(☎01859-520319; www.sorrelcottage.co.uk; 2 Glen, Leverburgh, HS5 3TY; s/d from £70/90; P 📶 🐾) Sorrel Cottage is a pretty crofter's house with beautifully modernised rooms, about 1.5 miles west of the ferry at Leverburgh. Vegetarians and vegans are happily catered for. Bike hire available.

★Borve Lodge Estate COTTAGE £££

(☎01859-550358; www.borvelodge.com; HS3 3HT; Rock House per 4/7 nights £1343/2350; P 📶) This estate on the west side of South Harris has developed some of the most spectacular self-catering accommodation in the Outer Hebrides, including the Rock House, a turf-roofed nook built into the hillside with sweeping views over the sea, and the stunning Broch, a three-storey rock tower based on Iron Age designs (both sleep two people).

OFF THE BEATEN TRACK

ST KILDA

St Kilda is a collection of spectacular sea stacks and cliff-bound islands about 45 miles west of North Uist. The largest island, **Hirta**, measures only 2 miles by 1 mile, with huge cliffs along most of its coastline. Owned by the National Trust for Scotland (NTS), the islands are a Unesco World Heritage Site and are the biggest seabird nesting site in the North Atlantic, home to more than a million birds.

Hirta is the only island on which visitors can land. In addition to watching the birdlife, you can explore the remains of the island's only settlement at **Village Bay**, where there's a ranger's office and small museum, and climb to the summit of Conachair (430m), the island's highest point.

Boat tours to St Kilda are a major undertaking – day trips are at least seven-hour affairs, involving a minimum 2½-hour crossing each way, often in rough seas; all must be booked in advance and are weather-dependent (April to September only).

Tour operators include the following:

Go to St Kilda (07789 914144; www.gotostkilda.co.uk; Stein Jetty; per person £260) Trips depart from Skye.

Kilda Cruises (p944)

Uist Sea Tours (p947)

Sea Harris (p944)

Eating

★Skoon Art Café CAFE £
(01859-530268; www.skoon.com; Geocrab, HS3 3HB; mains £5-9; 10am-4.30pm Tue-Sat Apr-Sep, reduced hours Oct-Mar; P) Set halfway along the Golden Road, this neat little art gallery doubles as an excellent cafe serving delicious homemade soups, sandwiches, cakes and desserts (try the gin-and-tonic cake).

Temple Cafe CAFE £
(07876 340416; www.facebook.com/thetemplecafe; Northton, HS3 3JA; mains £5-12; 10.30am-5pm Tue-Sun Apr-Sep, reduced hours Oct-Mar; P) Set in a cute stone-and-timber 'hobbit house' that was originally a visitor centre, and strewn with cushions covered in Harris tweed, this rustic cafe serves homemade scones, soups, salads and hot lunch specials to a soundtrack of '70s tunes. Evening meals 6.30pm to 8pm Friday to Sunday in summer (must be booked in advance).

An Traigh CAFE ££
(01859-550258; https://antraigh.com; Talla na Mara; mains £8-14; 11am-5pm; P) The cafe-bar in this community centre and art gallery enjoys a stunning location, with views across the sea to the island of Taransay, and an outdoor deck that makes the most of any sunny weather. The menu includes local seafood, plus sandwiches, fish and chips and burgers.

Getting There & Away

A CalMac (p939) car ferry zigzags through the reefs of the Sound of Harris from Leverburgh to Berneray (car/pedestrian £13.90/3.70, one hour, three or four daily Monday to Saturday, two or three Sunday).

North Uist (Uibhist A Tuath)

01876 / POP 1255

North Uist, an island half-drowned by lochs, is famed for its **trout fishing** (www.nuac.co.uk) but also has some magnificent beaches on its north and west coasts. For birdwatchers this is an earthly paradise, with regular sightings of waders and wildfowl ranging from redshank to red-throated diver to red-necked phalarope. The landscape is less wild and mountainous than Harris, but it has a sleepy, subtle appeal.

Little **Lochmaddy** is the first village you hit after arriving on the ferry from Skye. It has a couple of stores, a bank with an ATM, a petrol pump, a post office and a pub.

Sights & Activities

Balranald RSPB Reserve WILDLIFE RESERVE
(www.rspb.org.uk; P) FREE Birdwatchers flock to this RSPB nature reserve, 18 miles west

of Lochmaddy, in the hope of spotting the rare red-necked phalarope or hearing the distinctive call of the corncrake. There's a visitor centre with a resident warden who offers 1½-hour guided walks (£6), departing at 10am Tuesday from May to September.

St Kilda Viewpoint VIEWPOINT

(P) From the westernmost point of the road that runs around North Uist, a minor, drivable track leads for 1.5 miles to the summit of Clettraval hill, where a lookout point with telescope affords superb views west to the distant peaks of St Kilda and the Monach Isles.

Taigh Chearsabhagh ARTS CENTRE, MUSEUM

(☎01870-603970; www.taigh-chearsabhagh.org; Lochmaddy, HS6 5AA; arts centre free, museum £3; ⏲10am-5pm Mon-Sat Apr-Oct, to 4pm Nov-Mar; P) Taigh Chearsabhagh is a museum and arts centre that preserves and displays the history and culture of the Uists, and is also a thriving community centre, post office and meeting place. The centre's cafe (mains £4 to £6, closes at 3pm) dishes up homemade soups, sandwiches and cakes.

Sleeping & Eating

Balranald Campsite CAMPSITE £

(☎01876-510304; www.balranaldhebrideanholidays.com; Balranald Nature Reserve, Hougharry, HS6 5DL; sites £8-10, plus per person £2; wifi) You can bird-watch from your tent at this lovely campsite set on the machair alongside the RSPB's Balranald Nature Reserve (p945), and listen to rare corncrakes calling as the sun goes down beyond the neighbouring white-sand beach. There's also a two-bed timber camping pod looking out over the reserve (per night £50).

★Langass Lodge HOTEL £££

(☎01876-580285; www.langasslodge.co.uk; Locheport, HS6 5HA; s/d from £105/130; P wifi) The delightful Langass Lodge hotel is a former shooting lodge set in splendid isolation overlooking Loch Langais. Refurbished and extended, it now offers a dozen appealing rooms, many with sea views, as well as one of the Hebrides' best **restaurants** (mains £16-25, 3-course dinner £40; ⏲6-8.30pm), noted for its fine seafood and game.

Hamersay House HOTEL £££

(☎01876-500700; www.hamersayhouse.co.uk; Lochmaddy, HS6 5AE; s/d from £110/145; P wifi pets) Hamersay is Lochmaddy's most luxurious accommodation, with nine designer bedrooms, a lounge with leather sofas set around an open fire, and a good restaurant (mains £14 to £21, open 6pm to 8.30pm) with sea views from the terrace.

South Uist (Uibhist A Deas)

☎01878 / POP 1755

South Uist is the second-largest island in the Outer Hebrides and saves its choicest corners for those who explore away from the main north–south road. The low-lying west coast is an almost unbroken stretch of white-sand beach and flower-flecked machair – a waymarked hiking trail, the **Hebridean Way**, follows the coast – while the multitude of inland lochs provide excellent trout fishing (www.southuistfishing.com). The east coast, riven by four large sea lochs, is hilly and remote, with spectacular **Beinn Mhor** (620m) the highest point.

Driving south from Benbecula you cross from the predominantly Protestant northern half of the Outer Hebrides into the mostly Roman Catholic south, a religious transition marked by the granite statue of **Our Lady of the Isles** on the slopes of Rueval and the presence of many roadside shrines.

The ferry port of **Lochboisdale** is the island's largest settlement, with a bank, ATM, grocery store and petrol station.

Sights & Activities

Kildonan Museum MUSEUM

(☎01878-710343; www.kildonanmuseum.co.uk; Kildonan, HS8 5RZ; adult/child £3/free; ⏲10am-5pm Apr-Oct; P) Six miles north of Lochboisdale, Kildonan Museum explores the lives of local crofters through its collection of artefacts, an absorbing exhibition of B&W photography and first-hand accounts of harsh Hebridean conditions. There's also an excellent tearoom (mains £4 to £8, open 11am to 4pm) and craft shop.

Half a mile south of the museum, amid Milton's ruined blackhouses, a cairn marks the site of **Flora MacDonald's birthplace**.

Eriskay ISLAND

There's not much to see on Eriskay, but you'll pass through it on the way to the car ferry that crosses to Ardmhor at the northern end of Barra; Eriskay itself is connected to South Uist by a causeway that was constructed in 2001.

In 1745 Bonnie Prince Charlie first set foot in Scotland on the west coast of Eriskay, on the sandy beach (immediately north of the ferry terminal) still known as **Prince's Strand** (Coilleag a'Phrionnsa).

More recently the SS *Politician* sank just off the island in 1941. The islanders salvaged much of its cargo of around 250,000 bottles of whisky and, after a binge of dramatic proportions, the police intervened and a number of the islanders landed in jail. The story was immortalised by Sir Compton Mackenzie in his comic novel *Whisky Galore*, made into a famous film in 1949 and remade in 2016.

Uist Sea Tours BOATING
(☎07833 690693; www.uistseatours.co.uk; The Pier, Lochboisdale, HS8 5TJ; adult/child from £40/25; ⊙mid-Apr–mid-Sep) This outfit runs two-hour boat trips from Lochboisdale to spot bottlenose dolphins in the Sound of Barra (Monday, Wednesday and Friday evenings), and six-hour trips from Eriskay harbour (adult/child £70/50) to see nesting puffins on the island of Mingulay (Friday). There are also seven-hour day trips to St Kilda (£175/100).

Sleeping

Tobha Mor Crofters' Hostel HOSTEL £
(www.gatliff.org.uk; Howmore HS8 5SH; dm adult/child £16/8, camping per person £10) An atmospheric hostel housed in a restored thatched blackhouse, about 12 miles north of Lochboisdale.

★**Polochar Inn** INN ££
(☎01878-700215; www.polocharinn.com; Polochar, HS8 5TT; s/d from £99/109; P 📶) This 18th-century inn has been transformed into a stylish, welcoming hotel with a stunning location looking out across the sea to Barra. The excellent restaurant and bar menu (mains £11 to £22; booking recommended) includes seafood chowder, venison casserole, local salmon and scallops, and Uist lamb. Polochar is 7 miles southwest of Lochboisdale, on the way to Eriskay.

Lochside Cottage B&B ££
(☎01878-700472; www.lochside-cottage.co.uk; Lochboisdale HS8 5TN; s/d/f £45/70/90; P 📶) Lochside Cottage is a friendly B&B, 1.5 miles west of the ferry, and has rooms with views and a sun lounge barely a fishing-rod's length from its own trout loch. There are also two six-berth caravans in the garden (£180 a week). Alasdair, the owner, is a ghillie who can advise on the local fishing.

Uist Storm Pods CAMPSITE ££
(☎01878-700845; www.uiststormpods.co.uk; Lochboisdale, HS8 5TH; per pod £77; ⊙Mar-Oct; P 🐾) This place has two Scandinavian-style timber camping pods set on a hillside on a working farm. Each has an outdoor deck and barbecue overlooking the sea, a mini-kitchen, fridge and chemical toilet, and can sleep up to four people. The pods are a short walk from the ferry; take the second road on the left, immediately before the RBS bank.

Getting There & Away

Bus W17 runs about four times a day (except Sunday) between Berneray and Eriskay via Lochmaddy, Balivanich and Lochboisdale. The trip from Lochboisdale to Lochmaddy (£5.30) takes 1¾ hours.

CalMac (p939) ferries run between Lochboisdale and Mallaig.

Barra (Barraigh)

☎01871 / POP 1175

With its beautiful beaches, wildflower-clad dunes, rugged little hills and strong sense of community, diminutive Barra – just 14 miles in circumference – is the Outer Hebrides in miniature. For a great view of the island, walk up to the top of **Heaval** (383m), a mile northeast of **Castlebay** (Bagh a'Chaisteil), the largest village.

Sights

Kisimul Castle CASTLE
(HES; ☎01871-810313; www.historicenvironment.scot; Castlebay HS9 5UZ; adult/child incl ferry £6/3.60; ⊙9.30am-5.30pm Apr-Sep) Castlebay takes its name from the island fortress of Kisimul Castle, first built by the MacNeil clan in the 11th century. A short boat trip (weather permitting) takes you out to the island, where you can explore the fortifications and soak up the view from the battlements.

The castle was restored in the 20th century by American architect Robert MacNeil, who became the 45th clan chief. He gifted the castle to Historic Scotland in 2000 for an annual rent of £1 and a bottle of whisky (Talisker single malt, if you're interested).

Traigh Mor BEACH
This vast expanse of firm golden sand (the name means 'Big Strand') serves as Barra's airport (a mile across at low tide, and big enough for three 'runways'), the only beach

airport in the world that handles scheduled flights. Watching the little Twin Otter aircraft come and go is a popular spectator sport. In between flights, locals gather cockles, a local seafood speciality, from the sands.

Sleeping

Dunard Hostel HOSTEL £
(☎01871-810443; www.dunardhostel.co.uk; Castlebay HS9 5XD; dm/tw/pod from £25/55/50; P 📶) Dunard is a friendly, family-run hostel just a five-minute walk from the ferry terminal. There are also two camping pods in the garden, with shared use of hostel facilities. The owners can help to organise sea-kayaking trips.

Tigh na Mara B&B ££
(☎01871-810304; www.tighnamara-barra.co.uk; Castlebay HS9 5XD; s/d from £55/90; ⊙Apr-Oct; P 📶) A lovely cottage B&B with a brilliant location just above the ferry pier, looking out over the bay and Kisimul Castle. Ask for the en suite double bedroom with bay view.

Castlebay Hotel HOTEL £££
(☎01871-810223; www.castlebayhotel.com; Castlebay HS9 5XD; s/d from £79/140; P 📶) The Castlebay Hotel has spacious bedrooms decorated with a subtle tartan motif – it's worth paying a bit extra for a sea view – and there's a comfy lounge and conservatory with grand views across the harbour to the islands south of Barra. The hotel bar is the hub of island social life, with regular sessions of traditional music.

The restaurant specialises in local seafood and game (often rabbit).

Getting There & Away

There are daily flights from Glasgow to Barra airport.

CalMac (p939) ferries link Eriskay with Ardmhor (car/pedestrian £10.85/3.15, 40 minutes, three to five daily) at the northern end of Barra. Ferries also run from Castlebay to Oban.

You can hire bikes from **Barra Bike Hire** (☎07876 402842; www.barrabikehire.co.uk; Buth Bharraigh Community Shop, Castlebay HS9 5XD; per half-/full-day £12/18; ⊙9am-5pm Mon-Sat).

ORKNEY

☎01856 / POP 22,900

There's a magic to Orkney that you begin to feel as soon as the Scottish mainland slips astern. Only a few short miles of ocean separate the chain of islands from Scotland's north coast, but the Pentland Firth is one of Europe's most dangerous waterways, a graveyard of ships that adds an extra mystique to these islands shimmering in the sea mists.

An archipelago of mostly flat, green-topped islands stripped bare of trees and ringed with red sandstone cliffs, its heritage dates back to the Vikings, whose influence is still strong. Famed for ancient standing stones and prehistoric villages, for sublime sandy beaches and spectacular coastal scenery, it's a region whose ports tell of lives shared with the blessings and rough moods of the sea, and a destination where seekers can find melancholy wrecks of warships and the salty clamour of remote seabird colonies.

Tours

Orkney Archaeology Tours TOURS
(www.orkneyarchaeologytours.co.uk) Specialises in all-inclusive multi-day tours focusing on Orkney's ancient sites, with an archaeologist guide. These tours should be booked far ahead (a year or two). Also runs customisable private tours outside of the main season.

See Orkney TOURS
(☎01856-870635; www.see-orkney.co.uk) This mother-and-daughter team runs a variety of different tours of Orkney, including tours focusing on the archaeological sites, local farming culture, and food and drink.

Information

There's an excellent range of tourist information on Orkney, including a useful annual guide, as well as a separate guide to the smaller islands. The Kirkwall Tourist Office (p953) has a good range of info and very helpful staff.

Getting There & Away

AIR

Loganair (☎0141-642 9407; www.loganair.co.uk) flies daily from Kirkwall to Aberdeen, Edinburgh, Glasgow, Inverness and Sumburgh (Shetland). There are summer services to Manchester, Fair Isle and Bergen (Norway).

BOAT

During summer, book car spaces ahead. Peak-season fares are quoted here.

Northlink Ferries (☎0845 6000 449; www.northlinkferries.co.uk) Operates ferries from Scrabster to Stromness (passenger/

Orkney

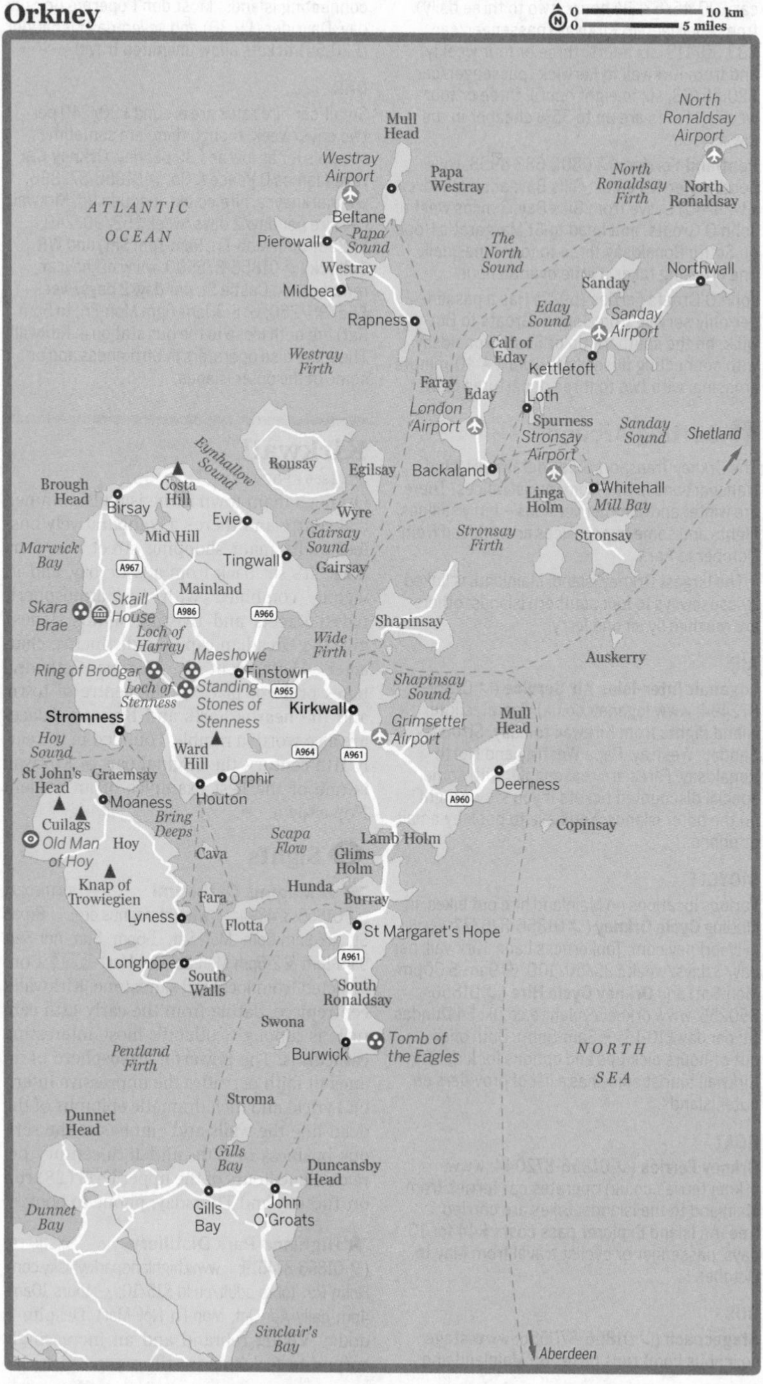
0 10 km
0 5 miles
Mull Head
Westray Airport
Papa Westray
North Ronaldsay Airport
North Ronaldsay Firth
North Ronaldsay
ATLANTIC OCEAN
Beltane
Pierowall
Papa Sound
The North Sound
Westray
Midbea
Northwall
Sanday
Eday Sound
Sanday Airport
Rapness
Westray Firth
Calf of Eday
Kettletoft
Faray
Eday
Loth
London Airport
Spurness
Sanday Sound
Stronsay Airport
Shetland
Eynhallow Sound
Rousay
Egilsay
Backaland
Whitehall
Linga Holm
Mill Bay
Brough Head
Costa Hill
Birsay
Evie
Wyre
Gairsay Sound
Stronsay Firth
Stronsay
Mid Hill
Marwick Bay
A967
Tingwall
Gairsay
Mainland
Skara Brae
Skaill House
A986
A966
Shapinsay
Loch of Harray
Wide Firth
Auskerry
Maeshowe
Ring of Brodgar
Finstown
Loch of Stenness
Standing Stones of Stenness
A965
Shapinsay Sound
Kirkwall
Stromness
Grimsetter Airport
Mull Head
Hoy Sound
Ward Hill
A964
A961
St John's Head
Graemsay
Orphir
Deerness
Houton
Moaness
A960
Cuilags
Bring Deeps
Old Man of Hoy
Hoy
Scapa Flow
Copinsay
Cava
Lamb Holm
Glims Holm
Knap of Trowiegien
Hunda
Fara
Burray
Lyness
Flotta
St Margaret's Hope
A961
Longhope
South Walls
South Ronaldsay
Swona
Tomb of the Eagles
Burwick
Pentland Firth
NORTH SEA
Stroma
Dunnet Head
Gills Bay
Duncansby Head
Gills Bay
John O'Groats
Dunnet Bay
Sinclair's Bay
Aberdeen

car £20.45/63, 1½ hours, two to three daily), from Aberdeen to Kirkwall (passenger/car £33.50/119, six hours, three or four weekly) and from Kirkwall to Lerwick (passenger/car £20.85/88, six to eight hours, three or four weekly). Fares are up to 35% cheaper in the low season.

Pentland Ferries (☎ 0800 688 8998; www.pentlandferries.co.uk; Gills Bay; adult/child/car £17/9/40) Leave from Gills Bay, 3 miles west of John O'Groats, and head to St Margaret's Hope on South Ronaldsay three to four times daily. The crossing takes a little over an hour.

John O'Groats Ferries (p922) Has a passenger-only service from John O'Groats to Burwick, on the southern tip of South Ronaldsay, with connecting buses to Kirkwall. A 40-minute crossing, with two to three departures daily.

Getting Around

The *Orkney Transport Guide* details all island transport and is free from tourist offices. There are winter and summer versions – ferry sailings, flights and some bus services are reduced from October to April.

The largest Orkney island, Mainland, is linked by causeways to four southern islands; others are reached by air and ferry.

AIR

Loganair Inter-Isles Air Service (☎ 01856-872494; www.loganair.co.uk) operates inter-island flights from Kirkwall to Eday, Stronsay, Sanday, Westray, Papa Westray and North Ronaldsay. Fares are reasonable, with some special discounted tickets if you stay a night on the outer islands. You have to book by email or phone.

BICYCLE

Various locations on Mainland hire out bikes, including **Cycle Orkney** (☎ 01856-875777; www.cycleorkney.com; Tankerness Lane, Kirkwall; per day/3 days/week £25/50/100; ⌚ 9am-5.30pm Mon-Sat) and **Orkney Cycle Hire** (☎ 01856-850255; www.orkneycyclehire.co.uk; 54 Dundas St; per day £10-15; ⌚ 8am-5pm). Both offer out-of-hours pick-ups and options for kids. The Kirkwall tourist office has a list of providers on outer islands.

BOAT

Orkney Ferries (☎ 01856-872044; www.orkneyferries.co.uk) operates car ferries from Mainland to the islands. Bikes are carried free. An Island Explorer pass costs £44 for 10 days' passenger or cyclist travel from May to October.

BUS

Stagecoach (☎ 01856-870555; www.stagecoachbus.com) runs buses on Mainland and connecting islands. Most don't operate on Sunday. Dayrider (£9.30) and seven-day Megarider (£20.55) tickets allow unlimited travel.

CAR

Small-car hire rates are around £90/240 per two days/week, though there are sometimes specials for as low as £30 per day. **Orkney Car Hire** (James D Peace & Co; ☎ 01856-872866; www.orkneycarhire.co.uk; Junction Rd, Kirkwall; car hire per day/2 days/week £62/90/240; ⌚ 8am-5pm Mon-Fri, 9am-1pm Sat) and **WR Tullock** (☎ 01856-875500; www.orkneycar-rental.co.uk; Castle St; per day/2 days/week £65/95/260; ⌚ 8.30am-6pm Mon-Fri, to 5pm Sat) are both close to the bus station in Kirkwall. There are also operators in Stromness and on some of the outer islands.

Kirkwall

☎ 01856 / POP 7000

Orkney's main town is the islands' commercial centre and there's a comparatively busy feel to its main shopping street and ferry dock. It's set back from a wide bay, and its vigour, combined with the atmospheric paved streets and twisting wynds (lanes), give the Orcadian capital a distinctive character. Magnificent St Magnus Cathedral takes pride of place in the centre of town, and the nearby Earl's and Bishop's Palaces are also worth a ramble. Founded in the early 11th century, the original part of Kirkwall is one of the best examples of an ancient Norse town.

Sights

★ St Magnus Cathedral CATHEDRAL
(☎ 01856-874894; www.stmagnus.org; Broad St; ⌚ 9am-6pm Mon-Sat, 1-6pm Sun Apr-Sep, 9am-1pm & 2-5pm Mon-Sat Oct-Mar) FREE Constructed from local red sandstone, Kirkwall's centrepiece, dating from the early 12th century, is among Scotland's most interesting cathedrals. The powerful atmosphere of an ancient faith pervades the impressive interior. Lyrical and melodramatic epitaphs of the dead line the walls and emphasise the serious business of 17th- and 18th-century bereavement. Tours of the upper level (£8) run on Tuesday and Thursday; phone to book.

★ Highland Park Distillery DISTILLERY
(☎ 01856-874619; www.highlandparkwhisky.com; Holm Rd; tours adult/child £15/10; ⌚ tours 10am-4pm daily Apr-Oct, Mon-Fri Nov-Mar) Despite a dodgy Viking rebrand and an increasingly corporate feel, this is still a good visit. It's

Kirkwall

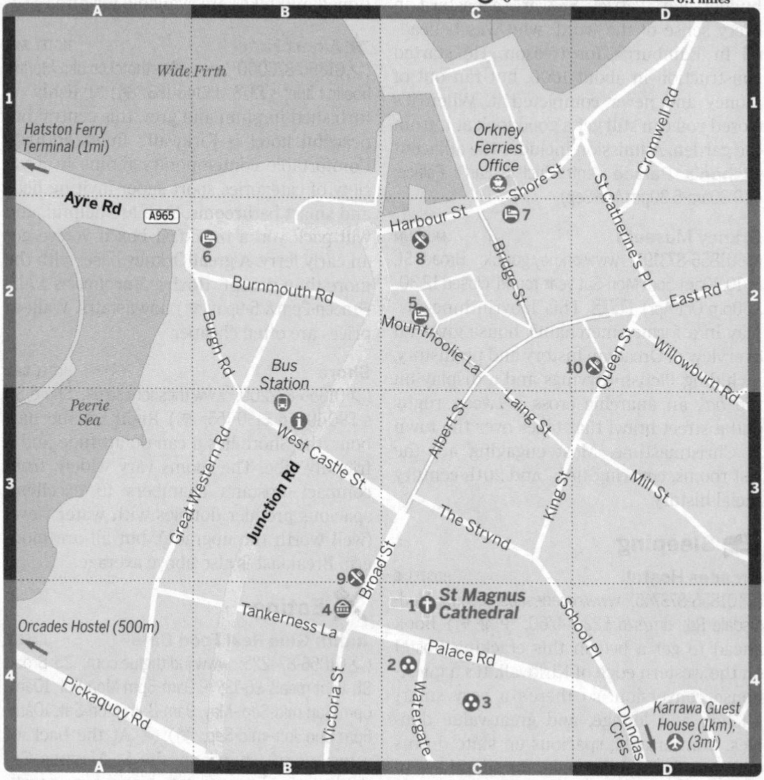

Kirkwall

Top Sights
1 St Magnus Cathedral C4

Sights
2 Bishop's Palace C4
3 Earl's Palace C4
4 Orkney Museum B4

Sleeping
5 Albert Hotel C2
6 Peedie Hostel B2
7 Shore C2

Eating
Bothy Bar .... (see 5)
8 Helgi's C2
9 Judith Glue Real Food Cafe B3
Shore .... (see 7)
10 Storehouse D2

a serious distillery that malts its own barley; see it and the peat kiln used to dry it on the excellent, well-informed, hour-long tour (book ahead). The standard 12-year-old is a soft, balanced malt, great for novices and aficionados alike; the 18-year-old is among the world's finest drams. This and older whiskies can be tasted on more specialised tours (£20 to £100), which you can prearrange.

There's also a shop in the centre of Kirkwall, good for merchandise but not doing tastings at time of research.

Earl's Palace RUINS

(☎01856-871918; www.historicenvironment.scot; Watergate; adult/child £6/3.80; ⏲9.30am-5.30pm Apr-Sep) The intriguing Earl's Palace was once known as the finest example of French Renaissance architecture in Scotland. One room features an interesting history of its builder, Earl Patrick Stewart, a bastard in every sense of the word, who was beheaded in Edinburgh for treason. He started construction in about 1600, but ran out of money and never completed it. When it's closed you can still get a good look at it from the garden. Admission includes the adjacent **Bishop's Palace** (entry incl in Earl's Palace; 9.30am-5.30pm Apr-Sep).

Orkney Museum MUSEUM
(01856-873191; www.orkney.gov.uk; Broad St; 10.30am-5pm Mon-Sat year-round, closed 12.30-1.30pm Oct-Apr) FREE This labyrinthine display in a former merchant's house gives an overview of Orcadian history and prehistory, including Pictish carvings and a display on the *ba'*, an anarchic cross between rugby and a street brawl that takes over the town at Christmastime. Most engaging are the last rooms, covering 19th- and 20th-century social history.

Sleeping

Orcades Hostel HOSTEL £
(01856-873745; www.orcadeshostel.com; Muddisdale Rd; dm/s/d £22/44/60; P @) Book ahead to get a bed in this cracking hostel on the western edge of Kirkwall. It's a guesthouse conversion, so there's a very smart kitchen and lounge, and great-value doubles. Comfortable, spacious en suite dorms with just four bunks make for sound sleeping, and enthusiastic owners give the place spark. There are lockers for valuables at reception.

Peedie Hostel HOSTEL £
(01856-877177; www.stayinkirkwall.co.uk; Ayre Rd; dm/s/tw £22/30/45; P) Nestling into a corner at the end of the Kirkwall waterfront, this marvellously located, recently refurbished hostel set in former fisherfolk's cottages has a cute, tiny downstairs section and a more sizeable upper area. Most of the dorms have just two beds, and there are three separate kitchen areas. It's normally unstaffed but the owner is very helpful.

Karrawa Guest House GUESTHOUSE ££
(01856-871100; www.karrawaguesthouseorkney.co.uk; Inganess Rd; s £70-76, d £90-95; P) In a peaceful location on the southeastern edge of Kirkwall, this enthusiastically run guesthouse offers significant value for well-kept modern double rooms with comfortable mattresses. Breakfast is generously proportioned and bikes are available for hire.

★**Albert Hotel** HOTEL £££
(01856-876000; www.alberthotel.co.uk; Mounthoolie Lane; s £118, d £148-163;) Stylishly refurbished in plum and grey, this central but peaceful hotel is Kirkwall's finest address. Comfortable contemporary rooms in a variety of categories sport super-inviting beds and smart bathrooms. Staff are helpful, and will pack you a breakfast box if you've got an early ferry. A great Orkney base, with the more-than-decent **Bothy Bar** (mains £7-13; noon-2pm & 5-9pm;) downstairs. Walk-in prices are often cheaper.

Shore HOTEL £££
(01856-872200; www.theshore.co.uk; Shore St; s £90-100, d £130-155;) Right on the harbour, the Shore has a can-do attitude and a friendly vibe. The rooms vary widely, from compact upstairs chambers to excellent, spacious premier doubles with water views (well worth the upgrade), but all are modern. Breakfast is also above average.

Eating

Judith Glue Real Food Cafe CAFE £
(01856-874225; www.judithglue.com; 25 Broad St; light meals £6-13; 9am-6pm Mon-Sat, 10am-6pm Sun mid-Sep–May, 9am-8pm Mon-Sat, 10am-6pm Sun Jun–mid-Sep;) At the back of a lively craft shop opposite St Magnus Cathedral, this licensed cafe-bistro serves tasty sandwiches and salads, as well as daily specials and succulent seafood platters. There's a strong emphasis on sustainable and organic ingredients, but put the feel-good factor aside for a moment when fighting for a table at lunchtime. Check Facebook for regular events.

★**Shore** SCOTTISH ££
(01856-872200; www.theshore.co.uk; 6 Shore St; bar meals £9-11, restaurant mains £17-22; food noon-2pm & 6-9pm Mon-Fri, 10am-9pm Sat & Sun, reduced hours winter;) This popular harbourside place is a convivial spot with a helpful attitude. It offers high-standard bar meals and excellent evening meals in the restaurant section, which features local seafood and beautifully prepared meat dishes. Upstairs are some very decent rooms.

Storehouse SCOTTISH ££
(01856-252250; www.thestorehouserestaurantwithrooms.co.uk; Bridge St Wynd; dinner £14-22; 5-9.30pm Tue-Sat;) This transformation

of a listed 19th-century herring warehouse into an Orcadian restaurant is a marvellous success of architecture and design. Much that is great about Orkney – quality produce, craft traditions, literary history – is artfully blended here in the restaurant and eight sumptuous, luxurious, individually designed rooms upstairs (doubles £150 to £190).

Helgi's PUB FOOD ££

(☎01856-879293; www.helgis.co.uk; 14 Harbour St; mains £11-15; ⊙food noon-9pm Mon-Sat, from 12.30pm Sun;) There's a traditional-style cosiness about this place and the decor is comfortable, with contemporary slate floor and quotes from the *Orkneyinga Saga* plastering the walls. It's more find-a-table than jostle-at-the-bar, and serves cheerful, well-priced comfort food in big portions (light bites only between 2pm and 5pm). Take your pint upstairs for quiet harbour contemplation.

★**Foveran** SCOTTISH £££

(☎01856-872389; www.thefoveran.com; St Ola; mains £16-27; ⊙6.30-8.30pm mid-May–mid-Sep, Fri & Sat or by appt mid-Sep–mid-May;) Three miles down the Orphir road, one of Orkney's best dining options is surprisingly affordable for its quality. Tranquilly located, with a cosy eating area overlooking the sea, it shines with its classic Orcadian ingredients – the steak with haggis and whisky sauce is feted, while North Ronaldsay lamb comes in deliciously tender cuts.

Information

Kirkwall Tourist Office (☎01856-872856; www.visitorkney.com; West Castle St; ⊙9am-5pm Mon-Sat Nov-Mar, to 6pm Mon-Sat Apr & Sep-Oct, to 6pm daily May-Aug) Has a good range of Orkney info and helpful staff. Shares a building with the bus station.

Getting There & Away

Kirkwall Airport (☎01856-872421; www.hial.co.uk) is located 2.5 miles southeast of town and is served regularly by bus 4 (15 minutes).

Ferries to Orkney's northern islands depart from the pier in the centre of town. Here, too, is the **Orkney Ferries office** (☎01856-872044; www.orkneyferries.co.uk; Shore St; ⊙7am-5pm Mon-Fri, 7am-noon & 1-3pm Sat) for bookings. Ferries to Shapinsay depart from the next pier to the west.

Ferries to Aberdeen and Shetland use the Hatston Ferry Terminal, 2 miles northwest. Bus X10 heads there to coincide with departures.

Getting Around

All services leave from the **bus station** (West Castle St):

Bus X1 Stromness (£3.35, 30 minutes, hourly Monday to Saturday, seven on Sunday); in the other direction to St Margaret's Hope (£3.15).

Bus 2 Orphir and Houton (£2.20, 20 minutes, four or five daily Monday to Saturday, five on Sunday from mid-June to mid-August).

Bus 6 Evie (£3.65, 40 minutes, three to five daily Monday to Saturday) and Tingwall (Rousay ferry). Runs Sunday in summer to Tingwall only.

East Mainland to South Ronaldsay

After a German U-boat sank battleship HMS *Royal Oak* in 1939, Winston Churchill had causeways of concrete blocks erected across the channels on the eastern side of Scapa Flow, linking Mainland to the islands of Lamb Holm, Glims Holm, Burray and South Ronaldsay. The Churchill Barriers, flanked by rusting wrecks of blockships, now support the main road from Kirkwall to Burwick.

Sights

★**Fossil & Heritage Centre** MUSEUM

(☎01856-731255; www.orkneyfossilcentre.co.uk; adult/child £5.10/3.40; ⊙10am-5pm mid-Apr–Sep) This eclectic museum is a great visit, combining some excellent 360-million-year-old Devonian fish fossils found locally with a well-designed exhibition on the world wars and Churchill Barriers. Upstairs is a selection of household and farming implements. There's a good little gift shop and an enjoyable coffee shop. Coming from Kirkwall, it's on the left half a mile after crossing onto Burray.

★**Tomb of the Eagles** ARCHAEOLOGICAL SITE

(☎01856-831339; www.tomboftheeagles.co.uk; Cleat; adult/child £7.80/3.50; ⊙9.30am-5.30pm Apr-Sep, 10am-noon Mar, 9.30am-12.30pm Oct) Two significant archaeological sites were found here by a farmer on his land. The first is a Bronze Age stone building with a firepit, indoor well and plenty of seating (a communal cooking site, or the original Orkney pub?). Beyond, in a spectacular clifftop position, the neolithic tomb (wheel yourself in prone on a trolley) is an elaborate stone construction that held the remains of up to 340 people who died some five millennia ago.

An excellent personal explanation is given at the **visitor centre**, where you meet a few spooky skulls and can handle some of the artefacts, plus absorb information on the Mesolithic period. It's about a mile's airy walk to the tomb from the centre, which is signposted near Burwick at South Ronaldsay's southern tip.

Italian Chapel CHURCH
(☎01856-781268; Lamb Holm; adult/child £3/free; ⏲9am-6.30pm Jun-Aug, to 5pm May & Sep, 10am-4pm Mon-Sat, to 3pm Sun Apr & Oct, 10am-1pm Nov-Mar) The Italian Chapel is all that remains of a POW camp that housed the Italian soldiers who worked on the Churchill Barriers. They built the chapel in their spare time, using two Nissen huts, scrap metal and their considerable artistic skills. It's quite extraordinary inside and the charming backstory makes it an Orkney highlight. One of the artists returned in 1960 to restore the paintwork.

Shopping

Sheila Fleet Kirk Gallery & Café JEWELLERY
(☎cafe 01856-861758, gallery 01856-861203; www.sheilafleet.com; Tankerness; ⏲10am-5pm Mon-Sat, 11am-5pm Sun) You've normally got the rings sorted out before you walk down the aisle, but not at this audacious conversion of a parish church into a design gallery for Sheila Fleet's shimmering jewellery. It's near the water in Tankerness, 6 miles southeast of Kirkwall beyond the airport, and is a striking sight inside. It's complemented by a lovely conservatory cafe.

The cafe does really tasty breakfasts and lunches (light meals £7 to £12) using local produce. You'd better book a table ahead in summer.

West & North Mainland

This part of Mainland island is sprinkled with outstanding prehistoric monuments: the journey to Orkney is worth it for these alone and they stand proud as some of the world's most important neolithic sites. It would take a day to see all of them – if pushed for time, visit Skara Brae then Maeshowe, but book your visit to the latter in advance.

Bus 8S links Kirkwall and Stromness via a loop past the Ring of Brodgar, Skara Brae (£3.65, 55 minutes) and other prehistoric sights. It runs twice a day, usually every day in summer and two to three times a week in winter.

Sights

★Skara Brae ARCHAEOLOGICAL SITE
(☎01856-841815; www.historicenvironment.scot; Sandwick; adult/child Nov-Mar £7/4.20, Apr-Oct incl Skaill House £8/5; ⏲9.30am-5.30pm Apr-Sep, 10am-4pm Oct-Mar) Idyllically situated by a sandy bay 8 miles north of Stromness, and predating Stonehenge and the pyramids of Giza, extraordinary Skara Brae, one of the world's most evocative prehistoric sites, is northern Europe's best-preserved neolithic village. Even the stone furniture – beds, boxes and dressers – has survived the 5000 years since a community lived and breathed here. It was hidden until 1850, when waves whipped up by a severe storm eroded the sand and grass above the beach, exposing the houses underneath.

There's an excellent interactive exhibit and short video, arming visitors with facts and theory, which will enhance the impact of the site. You then enter a reconstructed house, giving the excavation (which you head to next) more meaning. The official guidebook, available from the visitor centre, includes a good self-guided tour.

In the summer months, your ticket also gets you into adjacent **Skaill House** (☎01856-841501; www.skaillhouse.co.uk; Sandwick; adult/child £5/4 or incl with Skara Brae; ⏲9.30am-5.30pm Apr-Sep, 10am-4pm Oct), a fine 17th-century mansion

Bus 8S runs here sporadically from Stromness and Kirkwall; otherwise a taxi, cycle or hitch from Stromness is the easiest option. Mobility scooters are available at the visitor centre to cut out the walk to the site.

★Maeshowe ARCHAEOLOGICAL SITE
(☎01856-761606; www.historicenvironment.scot; adult/child £9/5.40; ⏲10am-5pm Apr-Sep, to 4pm Oct-Mar, last tour 1hr before close) Constructed about 5000 years ago, Maeshowe is an extraordinary place, a Stone Age tomb built from enormous sandstone blocks, some of which weighed many tonnes and were brought from several miles away. Creeping down the long stone passageway to the central chamber, you feel the indescribable gulf of years that separate us from the architects of this mysterious tomb.

Entry is by 45-minute guided tours (prebooking online is strongly advised) that leave by bus from the visitor centre at nearby Stenness.

Though nothing is known about who and what was interred here, the scope of the project suggests it was a structure of great significance.

In the 12th century, the tomb was broken into by Vikings searching for treasure. A couple of years later, another group sought shelter in the chamber from a three-day blizzard. Waiting out the storm, they carved runic graffiti on the walls. As well as the some-things-never-change 'Olaf was 'ere' and 'Thorni bedded Helga', there are also more intricate carvings, including a particularly fine dragon and a knotted serpent.

Prebook tickets online, as recommended, or buy them at the visitor centre in Stenness, from where the tour buses depart. Guides tend to only show a couple of the Viking inscriptions, but they'll happily show more if asked. Check out the virtual-reality tour in the visitor centre while you wait.

For a few weeks around the winter solstice, the setting sun shafts up the entrance passage and strikes the back wall of the tomb in spooky alignment.

Ring of Brodgar ARCHAEOLOGICAL SITE
(www.historicenvironment.scot; 24hr) FREE A mile northwest of Stenness is this wide circle of standing stones, some over 5m tall. The last of the three Stenness monuments to be built (2500–2000 BCE), it remains a most atmospheric location. Twenty-one of the original 60 stones still stand among the heather. On a grey day, with dark clouds thudding low across the sky, the stones are a spine-tingling sight.

Broch of Gurness ARCHAEOLOGICAL SITE
(www.historicenvironment.scot; Evie; adult/child £6/3.60; 9.30am-5.30pm Apr-Sep) Here's a fine example of the drystone fortified towers that were both a status symbol for powerful farmers and useful protection from raiders some 2200 years ago. The imposing entranceway and sturdy stone walls – originally 10m high – are impressive; inside you can see the hearth and where a mezzanine floor would have fitted. Around the broch are a number of well-preserved outbuildings, including a curious shamrock-shaped house. The visitor centre has some interesting displays on the culture that built these remarkable fortifications.

The broch is on an exposed headland at Aikerness, a 1.5-mile walk northeast from the strung-out village of Evie.

Brough of Birsay ARCHAEOLOGICAL SITE
(www.historicenvironment.scot; adult/child £6/3.60; 9.30am-5.30pm mid-Jun–Sep) At low tide (check tide times at any Historic Environment Scotland site) you can walk out to this windswept island, which is the site of extensive Norse ruins, including a number of longhouses and the 12th-century **St Peter's Church**. There's also a replica of a Pictish stone found here. This is where St Magnus was buried after his murder on Egilsay in 1117, and the island became a pilgrimage place. The attractive lighthouse has fantastic views. Take a picnic, but don't get stranded...

Barnhouse Neolithic Village ARCHAEOLOGICAL SITE
(www.historicenvironment.scot; 24hr) FREE Alongside the Standing Stones of Stenness are the excavated remains of a village thought to have been inhabited by the builders of Maeshowe. Don't skip this: it brings the area to life. The houses are well preserved and similar to Skara Brae with their stone furnishings. One of the buildings was entered by crossing a fireplace: possibly an act of ritual significance.

Standing Stones of Stenness ARCHAEOLOGICAL SITE
(www.historicenvironment.scot; 24hr) FREE Part of this Mainland area's concentration of neolithic monuments, four mighty stones remain of what was once a circle of 12. Recent research suggests they were perhaps erected as long ago as 3300 BCE, and they impose by their sheer size – the tallest measures 5.7m in height. The narrow strip of land they're on, the **Ness of Brodgar**, separates the Harray and Stenness lochs and was the site of a large settlement inhabited throughout the neolithic period (3500–1800 BCE).

Stromness

01856 / POP 1800

This appealing grey-stone port has a narrow, elongated, flagstone-paved main street and tiny alleys leading down to the waterfront between tall houses. It lacks the size of Kirkwall, Orkney's main town, but makes up for that with bucketloads of character, having changed little since its heyday in the 18th century, when it was a busy staging post for ships avoiding the troublesome English Channel during European wars. Stromness is ideally located for trips to Orkney's major prehistoric sites.

Sights

★Stromness Museum MUSEUM
(☎01856-850025; www.stromnessmuseum.co.uk; 52 Alfred St; adult/child £5/1; ⏰10am-5pm Apr-Sep, 10am-5pm Mon-Sat Oct, 11am-3.30pm Mon-Sat Nov-Mar) This superb museum, run with great passion, is full of knick-knacks from maritime and natural-history exhibitions covering whaling, the Hudson's Bay Company and the German fleet sunk after WWI. Recent finds from the jaw-dropping excavations at the Ness of Brodgar are on display and there's always an excellent summer exhibition. You can happily nose around for a couple of hours. Across the street is the house where local poet and novelist George Mackay Brown lived.

Pier Arts Centre GALLERY
(☎01856-850209; www.pierartscentre.com; 30 Victoria St; ⏰10.30am-5pm Thu-Sat year-round, plus Mon Jun-Sep) FREE This gallery has really rejuvenated the Orkney modern-art scene with its sleek lines and upbeat attitude. It's worth a look as much for the architecture as for its high-quality collection of 20th-century British art and changing exhibitions.

Sleeping

Brown's Hostel HOSTEL £
(☎01856-850661; www.brownsorkney.com; 45 Victoria St; s/d from £25/45, d/q with bathroom from £50/90; 📶) On Stromness' main street, this handy, sociable place has cosy private rooms – no dorms, no bunks – at a very good price. There's an inviting common area where you can browse the free internet or swap pasta recipes in the open kitchen. There are good en suite rooms in a house up the street, and an apartment sleeping four.

★Brinkies Guest House B&B ££
(☎01856-851881; yvonneski@btinternet.com; Brownstown Rd; s £65-70, d £80-90; P📶) Just a short walk from the centre of Stromness, but with a lonely, king-of-the-castle position overlooking the town and bay, this exceptional place offers five-star islander hospitality. Compact, modern rooms are handsome, stylish and comfortable, and the public areas are done out attractively in wood, but it's the charming owner's flexibility and can-do attitude that makes this place so special.

Burnside Farm B&B ££
(☎01856-850723; www.burnside-farm.com; North End Rd/A965; s/d £80/100; P📶) On a working dairy farm at Stromness' edge, this place has lovely views over green fields, town and harbour. Rooms are elegant and maintain the style from when the house was built in the late 1940s, with attractive period furnishings. The top-notch bathrooms, however, are sparklingly contemporary. Breakfast comes with views, and the kindly owner couldn't be more welcoming.

Lindisfarne B&B B&B ££
(☎01856-850082; www.stayinstromness.co.uk; off A965; s/d £55/75) Set among green fields with views down over Stromness, Lindisfarne is run by a charming young Orcadian family and makes a great base. It's a modern, spacious home with four commodious bedrooms, common areas for guests and self-catering options. Breakfast is delicious, and a warm welcome from Deborah, Kevin and the kids is guaranteed.

Eating

★Hamnavoe Restaurant SEAFOOD ££
(☎01856-850606, 01856-851226; 35 Graham Pl; mains £15-24; ⏰7-9pm Tue-Sun Jun-Aug) Tucked away off the main street, this Stromness favourite specialises in excellent local seafood in an intimate, cordial atmosphere. There's always something good off the boats, and the chef prides himself on his lobster. Booking is a must. It opens some weekends in low season; it's worth calling ahead to check.

Ferry Inn PUB FOOD ££
(☎01856-850280; www.ferryinn.com; 10 John St; mains £10-19; ⏰food 7am-9pm Apr-Oct; 📶) Every port has its pub, and in Stromness it's the Ferry. Convivial and central, it warms the cockles with folk music, local beers and characters, and eating in a refurbished dining area that offers good local seafood and cheery service.

Getting There & Away

Northlink Ferries (p948) runs services from Stromness to Scrabster on the mainland (passenger/car £20.45/63, 1½ hours, two to three daily).

Bus X1 runs regularly to Kirkwall (£3.35, 30 minutes, hourly Monday to Saturday, seven Sunday), with some going on to St Margaret's Hope (£6.05, 1¼ hours).

Hoy

Orkney's second-largest island, Hoy (meaning 'High Island') got the lion's share of the archipelago's scenic beauty. Shallow turquoise bays lace the east coast and massive sea cliffs guard the west, while peat and moorland cover Orkney's highest hills. Much of the north is a reserve for breeding seabirds. The Scrabster–Stromness ferry gives you a decent perspective of the island's wild good looks.

Lyness was an important naval base during both world wars, when the British Grand Fleet was based in Scapa Flow. The fascinating **Scapa Flow Visitor Centre & Museum** (☎01856-791300; www.orkney.gov.uk; Lyness; ⏲10am-4.30pm Mon-Sat Mar, Apr & Oct, 9am-4.30pm Mon-Sat, 1st to last ferry Sun May-Sep) FREE, located in an old pump house that once fed fuel to the ships, is a must-see for anyone interested in Orkney's military history. It's easily visited, just by the ferry slip at Lyness. The museum was being renovated at time of research and due to reopen in 2021. During renovations there is a temporary exhibition in the Hoy Hotel, half a mile from the Lyness ferry terminal.

Sights

Old Man of Hoy NATURAL FEATURE

Hoy's best-known sight is this 137m-high rock stack jutting from the ocean off the tip of an eroded headland. It's a tough ascent and for experienced climbers only, but the walk to see it is a Hoy highlight, revealing much of the island's most spectacular scenery. You can also spot the Old Man from the Scrabster–Stromness ferry.

The easiest approach to the Old Man is from Rackwick Bay, a 5-mile walk by road from Moaness Pier (in Hoy village on the east coast, where the ferries dock) through the beautiful Rackwick Glen. You'll pass the 5000-year-old **Dwarfie Stane** (Rackwick Glen; ⏲24hr) FREE, the only example of a rock-cut tomb in Scotland. On your return you can take the path via the Glens of Kinnaird and Berriedale Wood, Scotland's most northerly tuft of native forest.

From Rackwick Bay, where there's a hostel, the most popular path climbs steeply westwards then curves northwards, descending gradually to the edge of the cliffs opposite the Old Man of Hoy. Allow seven hours for the return trip from Moaness Pier, or three hours from Rackwick Bay.

Sleeping

Hoy Centre HOSTEL £

(☎office hours 01856-873535, warden 07918 367560; https://orkney.campstead.com; dm/tw £21.90/61.50; P 📶) This clean, bright, modern hostel has an enviable location, around 15 minutes' walk from Moaness Pier, at the base of the rugged Cuilags. Rooms are all en suite and include good-value family options; it also has a spacious kitchen and DVD lounge. It's open year-round: book via the website to avoid an admin fee (private rooms only).

Getting There & Away

Orkney Ferries (p950) runs a passenger/bike ferry (adult £4.55, 30 minutes, two to six daily) between Stromness and Moaness at Hoy's northern end, and a car ferry to Lyness (with one service to/from Longhope) from Houton on Mainland (passenger/car £4.55/14.40, 40 minutes, up to seven daily Monday to Friday, two or three Saturday and Sunday); book cars well in advance. Sunday service is from May to September only.

The Moaness ferry also stops at Graemsay. The Houton service also links to Flotta.

Northern Islands

The group of windswept islands north of Mainland is a haven for birds, rich in archaeological sites and blessed with wonderful white-sand beaches and azure seas. Though some are hillier than others, all offer a broadly similar landscape of flattish green farmland running down to scenic coastline. Some give a real sense of what Orkney was like before the modern world impinged upon island life.

Accessible by reasonably priced ferries or planes, the islands are well worth exploring. Though you can see 'the sights' in a matter of hours, the key is to stay a day or two and relax into the pace of island life.

Note that the 'ay' at the end of island names (from the Old Norse for 'island') is pronounced closer to 'ee'.

Getting There & Away

Orkney Ferries (p950) and Loganair Inter-Isles Air Service (p950) serve these islands. It's possible to make day trips to many of the islands from Kirkwall.

Most islands offer a bus service that meets ferries: you may have to call to book this. The same operator often offers island tours.

Rousay

Just off the north coast of Mainland, hilly Rousay merits exploration for its fine assembly of prehistoric sites, great views and relaxing away-from-it-all ambience. Connected by regular ferry from Tingwall, it makes a great little day trip, but you may well feel a pull to stay longer. A popular option is to hire a bike from **Trumland Farm** (☎01856-821252; trumland@btopenworld.com; dm £17-20, camping £8; P 🐾) near the ferry and take on the 14-mile circuit of the island.

Sights & Activities

★Midhowe Cairn & Broch ARCHAEOLOGICAL SITE
(www.historicenvironment.scot; ⏲24hr) FREE Six miles from the ferry on Rousay, mighty Midhowe Cairn has been dubbed the 'Great Ship of Death'. Built around 3500 BCE and enormous, it's divided into compartments, in which the remains of 25 people were found. Covered by a protective stone building, it's nevertheless memorable. Adjacent Midhowe Broch, the sturdy stone lines of which echo the rocky shoreline's striations, is a muscular Iron Age fortified compound with a mezzanine floor. The sites are on the water, a 10-minute walk downhill from the main road.

Prehistoric Sites ARCHAEOLOGICAL SITE
(www.historicenvironment.scot; ⏲24hr) FREE Rousay's major archaeological sites are clearly labelled from the road ringing the island. Heading west from the ferry, you soon come to **Taversoe Tuick**, an intriguing burial cairn constructed on two levels, with separate entrances – perhaps a joint tomb for different families; a semi-detached solution in posthumous housing. Not far beyond are two other significant cairns: **Blackhammer** then **Knowe of Yarso**, the latter a fair walk up the hill but with majestic views.

Rousay Tours TOURS
(☎01856-821234; www.rousaytours.co.uk; adult/child £38/12) Friendly Patrick offers taxi service and recommended guided tours of the island, including wildlife-spotting (seals and otters), visits to the prehistoric sites and, for a little extra, a tasty packed lunch.

Getting There & Away

A small ferry connects Tingwall on Mainland with Rousay (passenger/bicycle/car £4.55/free/14.40, 30 minutes, up to six daily) and the nearby islands of Egilsay and Wyre.

Westray

If you've time to visit only one of Orkney's Northern Islands, make Westray (www.westraypapawestray.co.uk) the one. The largest of the group, it has rolling farmland, handsome sandy beaches, great coastal walks and several appealing places to stay.

Sights

★Noltland Castle CASTLE
(www.historicenvironment.scot; ⏲9.30am-5.30pm Apr-Sep, 10am-4pm Oct-Mar) FREE A half-mile west of Pierowall stands this sturdy ruined tower house, built in the 16th century by Gilbert Balfour, aide to Mary, Queen of Scots. The castle is super-atmospheric and bristles with shot holes, part of the defences of the deceitful Balfour, who plotted to murder Cardinal Beaton and, after being exiled, the king of Sweden. Like a pantomime villain, he met a sticky end.

At the nearby Links of Noltland, archaeological investigation is regularly unearthing interesting neolithic finds. Most intriguing has been a chamber built over a spring, which was possibly used as a sauna.

Westray Heritage Centre MUSEUM
(☎01857-677414; www.westrayheritage.co.uk; Pierowall; adult/child £3/50p; ⏲11.30am-5pm Mon, 9am-noon & 2-5pm Tue-Sat, 1.30-5pm Sun May-Sep, 2-4pm Wed or by arrangement Oct-Apr) This heritage centre has displays on local history, nature dioramas and archaeological finds, with some famous neolithic carvings (including the 5000-year-old 'Westray Wife'). These small sandstone figurines are the oldest known depictions of the human form so far found in the British Isles.

Noup Head NATURE RESERVE
FREE This bird reserve at Westray's northwestern tip is a dramatic area of sea cliffs, with vast numbers of breeding seabirds from April to July. You can walk here along the clifftops from a car park, passing the impressive chasm of **Ramni Geo**, and return via the lighthouse access road (4 miles).

Sleeping & Eating

★West Manse B&B £
(☎01857-677482; www.westmanse.co.uk; Westside; r per person £25; P 📶 🐾) Be free from timetables at this imposing house with arc-

ing coastal vistas; make your own breakfast when you feel like it. The welcoming hosts have introduced a raft of green solutions for heating, fuel and more. Kids will love this unconventional place, with its play nooks and hobbit house, while art exhibitions, eclectic workshops, venerably comfortable furniture and clean air are drawcards for parents.

Chalmersquoy & the Barn HOSTEL £
(☎01857-677214; www.chalmersquoywestray.co.uk; Pierowall; dm/s/q £25/33/75, B&B s/d £58/80, apt for 4/6 £60/100, tent sites £9-12 plus adult/child £2/1; P 📶) This excellent, intimate, modern hostel is an Orcadian gem. It's heated throughout and has pristine kitchen facilities and an inviting lounge; rooms sleep two or three in comfort. Out front, the lovely owners have top self-catering apartments with great views, and spacious en suite B&B rooms. There's also a campsite and a fabulous byre that hosts atmospheric concerts. A recommended all-round choice.

Pierowall Hotel PUB FOOD £
(☎01857-677472; www.pierowallhotel.co.uk; Pierowall; mains £9-14; ⏰food noon-2pm & 5-8.30pm May-Sep, noon-1.30pm & 6-8pm Oct-Apr; 📶) The heart of the Westray community, this refurbished local pub is famous throughout Orkney for its popular fish and chips – whatever has turned up in the day's catch from the hotel's boats is displayed on the blackboard. There are also some curries, but the sea is the way to go here. It also has rooms.

Getting There & Away

There are daily flights with Loganair (p950) from Kirkwall to Westray (one way £37, 20 minutes).

Orkney Ferries (p950) links Kirkwall with Rapness (passenger/car £8.85/20.90, 1½ hours, daily). A bus to the main town, Pierowall, meets the ferry. You can hire bikes at the Rendall's grocery store in Pierowall (01856-677389 or 07796 538035); it also runs the island's taxi service.

SHETLAND

☎ 01806 / POP 23,000

Close enough to Norway geographically and historically to make nationality an ambiguous concept, Shetland is Britain's most northerly outpost. There's a Scandinavian lilt to the local accent, and streets named King Haakon or St Olaf are reminders that Shetland was under Norse rule until 1469, when it was gifted to Scotland in lieu of the dowry of a Danish princess.

The stirringly bleak setting – it's a Unesco geopark – still feels uniquely Scottish though, with deep, naked glens flanked by steep hills, twinkling, sky-blue lochs and, of course, sheep on the roads.

Despite the famous ponies and woollens, it's no agricultural backwater. Offshore oil makes it quite a busy, comparatively well-heeled place, despite drops in barrel prices. Nevertheless nature still rules the seas and islands, and the birdlife (p964) is spectacular: pack binoculars.

Festivals & Events

Up Helly Aa CULTURAL
(www.uphellyaa.org; ⏰Jan) Shetland's long Viking history has rubbed off in more ways than just street names and square-shouldered locals. Most villages have a fire festival, a continuation of Viking midwinter celebrations of the rebirth of the sun, with the most spectacular happening in Lerwick on the last Tuesday in January.

Shetland Folk Festival MUSIC
(www.shetlandfolkfestival.com; ⏰late Apr or early May) This four-day festival sees local and international folk musicians playing in various venues across Lerwick and beyond.

Information

Lerwick Tourist Office (p964), in the centre of Shetland's main town, has comprehensive information on the islands.

Brochures are also available at Sumburgh Airport. Visit www.shetland.org, an excellent website with good info on accommodation, activities and more.

Getting There & Away

AIR

Sumburgh Airport (☎01950-460905; www.hial.co.uk), 25 miles south of Lerwick, is Shetland's main airport. **Loganair** (☎0141-642907; www.loganair.co.uk) runs daily services to Aberdeen, Kirkwall, Inverness, Edinburgh and Glasgow, and summer services to Manchester and Bergen (Norway).

BOAT

Northlink Ferries (☎0845 600 0449; www.northlinkferries.co.uk; 📶) runs daily overnight car ferries between Aberdeen and Lerwick (high-season passenger/car one way £36/124,

Shetland

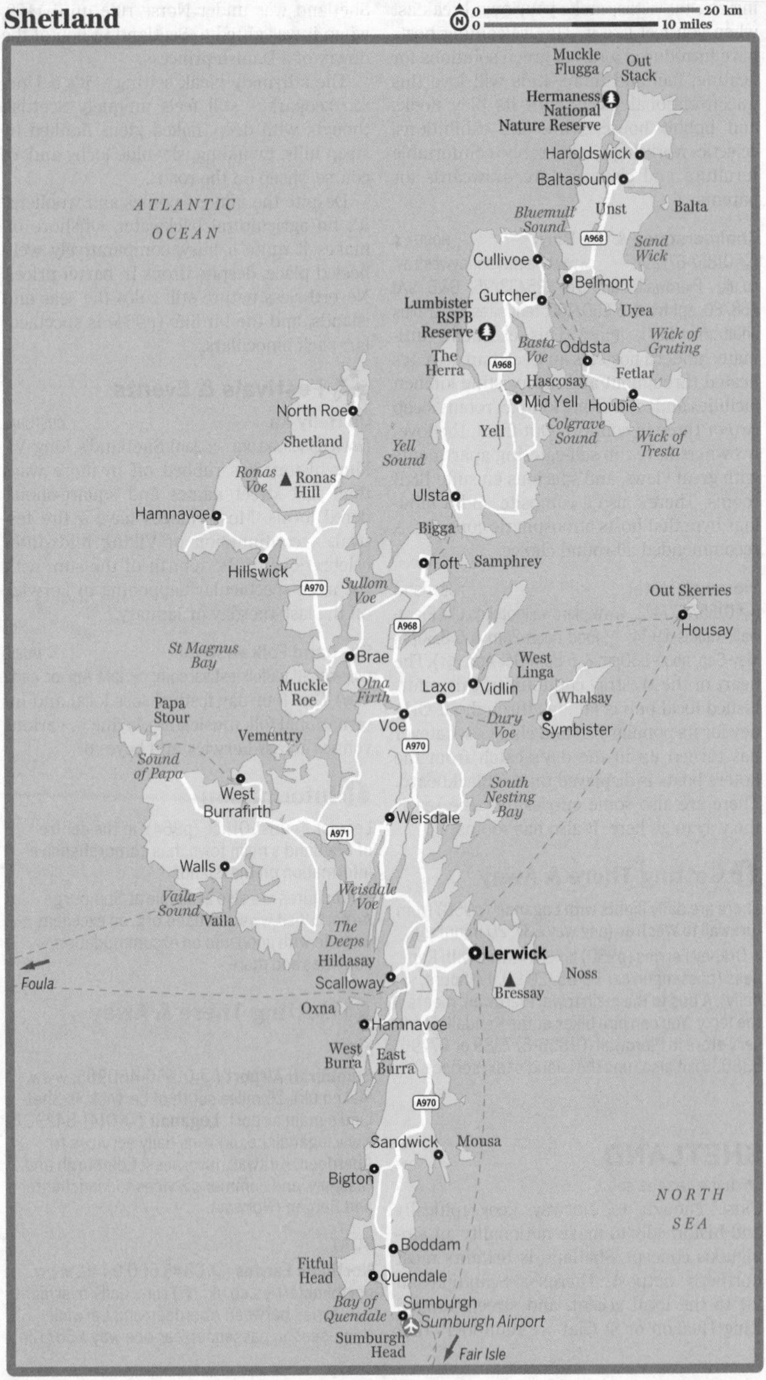
0
20 km
0
10 miles
Muckle
Flugga
Out
Stack
Hermaness
National
Nature Reserve
Haroldswick
Baltasound
Unst
Balta
Bluemull
Sound
A968
Sand
Wick
Cullivoe
Belmont
Gutcher
Uyea
Lumbister
RSPB
Reserve
Basta
Voe
Oddsta
Wick of
Gruting
The
Herra
A968
Fetlar
Hascosay
Mid Yell
Houbie
Yell
Colgrave
Sound
Wick of
Tresta
ATLANTIC
OCEAN
North Roe
Shetland
Yell
Sound
Ronas
Voe
Ronas
Hill
Ulsta
Hamnavoe
Bigga
Hillswick
Toft
Samphrey
A970
Sullom
Voe
Out Skerries
A968
Housay
St Magnus
Bay
Brae
West
Linga
Muckle
Roe
Olna
Firth
Laxo
Vidlin
Whalsay
Papa
Stour
Voe
Dury
Voe
Symbister
Vementry
A970
Sound
of Papa
West
Burrafirth
South
Nesting
Bay
Weisdale
A971
Walls
Weisdale
Voe
Vaila
Sound
Vaila
The
Deeps
Lerwick
Hildasay
Foula
Scalloway
Noss
Bressay
Oxna
Hamnavoe
West
Burra
East
Burra
A970
Sandwick
Mousa
Bigton
NORTH
SEA
Boddam
Fitful
Head
Quendale
Bay of
Quendale
Sumburgh
Sumburgh Airport
Sumburgh
Head
Fair Isle

12 to 15 hours), some stopping at Kirkwall, Orkney. With a basic ticket you can sleep in recliner chairs or the bar area. It's £39.50 for a berth in a shared cabin and from £91 to £150 for a comparatively luxurious double cabin. Sleeping pods (£18) are comfortable, reclinable seats. Ferries have a cafe, bar, paid lounge and cinema on board, plus slow wi-fi.

Getting Around

Public transport within and between the islands of Shetland is managed by **ZetTrans** (www.zettrans.org.uk). Timetable information for all air, bus and ferry services can be obtained at http://travel.shetland.org, from the ZetTrans website and from Lerwick's **Viking Bus Station** (01595-744868; Commercial Rd).

AIR

The **Shetland Inter-Island Air Service** (Airtask; 01595-840246; www.airtask.com) is operated by Airtask from Tingwall airport, 6.5 miles northwest of Lerwick. There are big discounts for under-25s. Flights run to Papa Stour, Foula and Fair Isle.

BOAT

Ferry services run by **Shetland Islands Council** (www.shetland.gov.uk/ferries) link Mainland to other islands from various points.

BUS

An extensive bus network radiates from Lerwick to all corners of Mainland, with connecting services to the islands of Yell, Fetlar and Unst. The schedules aren't generally great for day tripping from Lerwick as they're suited to people coming into the capital for the day.

CAR

Shetland has broad, well-made roads (due to oil money). Car hire is gloriously fuss-free, and vehicles can be delivered to transport terminals. Prices are usually around £40/200 for a day/week.

Bolts Car Hire (01595-693636; www.boltscarhire.co.uk; North Rd; 9am-5.30pm Mon-Fri, to 4pm Sat Apr-Oct, 9am-5.30pm Mon-Fri, to 1pm Sat Nov-Mar) Has an office in Lerwick and by the airport; delivers to Lerwick's ferry terminal.

Grantfield Garage (01595-692709; www.grantfieldgarage.co.uk; Esplanade; 9am-5.30pm Mon-Fri, to 5pm Sat) No longer a garage; this is generally the cheapest.

Star Rent-a-Car (01595-692075; www.starrentacar.co.uk; 22 Commercial Rd; 8am-7pm Mon-Fri, to 6pm Sat, noon-5pm Sun) Opposite Lerwick's Viking Bus Station. Has an office at Sumburgh Airport as well.

Lerwick

01595 / POP 7000

Built on the herring trade and modernised by the oil trade, Lerwick is Shetland's only real town, home to a third of the islands' population. It has a solidly maritime feel, with aquiline oil boats competing for space in the superb natural harbour with the dwindling fishing fleet. Wandering along atmospheric Commercial St is a delight, and the excellent Shetland Museum provides cultural background. Fans of the TV series *Shetland* will easily recognise several buildings around town.

Sights & Activities

★Shetland Museum MUSEUM
(01595-695057; www.shetlandmuseumandarchives.org.uk; Hay's Dock; 10am-5pm Mon-Sat, noon-5pm Sun Apr-Sep, 10am-4pm Tue-Sat Oct-Mar) FREE This museum houses an impressive collection of 5000 years' worth of culture, people and their interaction with this ancient landscape. Comprehensive but never dull, it covers everything from the archipelago's geology to its fishing industry, via local mythology – find out about scary *nyuggles* (ghostly horses), or detect *trows* (fairies). Pictish carvings and replica jewellery are among the finest pieces. The museum also includes a working lighthouse mechanism, a small gallery, a boat-building workshop and an archive for tracing Shetland ancestry.

Clickimin Broch RUINS
(Clickimin Rd; 24hr) FREE This fortified site, just under a mile southwest of Lerwick's town centre, was occupied from the 7th century BCE to the 6th century CE. It's impressively large, and its setting on a tongue of land in a small loch gives it a feeling of being removed from the present day.

Shetland Seabird Tours BIRDWATCHING
(07767 872260; www.shetlandseabirdtours.com; adult/child £45/25; Apr-Oct) With two daily departures, these three-hour cruises head out to watch gannets feeding, observe the raucous seabird colonies of Bressay and Noss, and do a bit of seal-spotting. You can book online.

Sleeping

Woosung B&B £
(01595-693687; www.woosung-bb.com; 43 St Olaf St; d £65, s/d without bathroom £30/60;

Lerwick

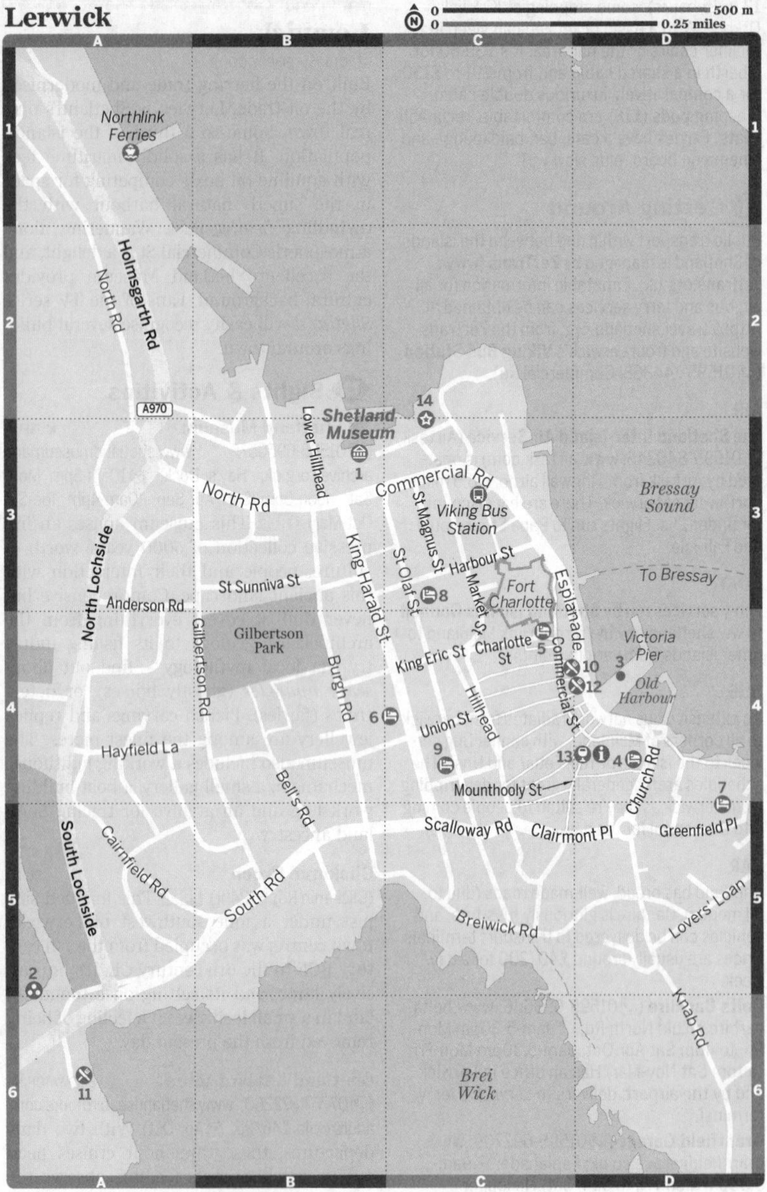

) A budget gem in the heart of Lerwick B&B-land, this place has a wise and welcoming host and comfortable, clean, good-value rooms with fridge and microwave. Two of them share a compact but spotless bathroom. The solid stone house dates from the 19th century, built by a clipper captain who traded tea out of the Chinese port for which it's named.

Lerwick

Top Sights
1 Shetland Museum B3

Sights
2 Clickimin Broch A5

Activities, Courses & Tours
3 Shetland Seabird Tours D4

Sleeping
4 Aald Harbour D4
5 Fort Charlotte Guesthouse C4
6 Islesburgh House Hostel C4
7 Kveldsro House Hotel D5
8 Rockvilla Guest House C3
9 Woosung C4

Eating
10 Dowry C4
11 Fjarå A6
12 Peerie Shop Cafe D4

Drinking & Nightlife
13 The Lounge D4

Entertainment
14 Mareel C3

Islesburgh House Hostel HOSTEL £
(01595-745100; www.shetland.gov.uk; King Harald St; dm/s/tw/q £23/42/48/66; P @ wi-fi) This typically grand Lerwick mansion houses an excellent hostel, with comfortable dorms, a shop, a laundry, a cafe and an industrial kitchen. Electronic keys offer reliable security and no curfew. It's wise to book ahead in summer. If nobody's about, you can check in at the nearby community centre.

★ **Fort Charlotte Guesthouse** B&B ££
(01595-692140; www.fortcharlotte.co.uk; 1 Charlotte St; s/d £50/85; wi-fi) Sheltering under Fort Charlotte's walls, this friendly place offers summery en suite rooms, including great singles. Views down the pedestrian street are on offer in some; sloping ceilings and artful touches add charm to others. It has local salmon for breakfast and a bike shed. Very popular; book ahead.

Aald Harbour B&B ££
(01595-840689; www.aaldharbourbedandbreakfast.com; 7 Church Rd; s/d £60/85; wi-fi) With a handy location just off the pedestrian street, this upbeat spot has four cute rooms decked out in IKEA furniture, with Shetland fabrics and toiletries creating a cosy Nordic fusion. Rooms have fridges, good showers and wi-fi, and there are attractive public areas downstairs. Breakfast includes fresh-fruit and smoked-fish options.

Rockvilla Guest House B&B ££
(01595-695804; www.rockvillaguesthouse.com; 88 St Olaf St; s/d £65/92; wi-fi, pets) Some of Shetland's B&Bs are aimed more at oil workers than visitors, but this is quite the reverse: a relaxing, welcoming spot in a fine house behind a pretty garden. The three rooms are colour themed: Blue is bright, with a front-and-back outlook; Red is sultry, with a sofa in the window; and smaller Green is shyer, under the eaves.

Kveldsro House Hotel HOTEL £££
(01595-692195; www.shetlandhotels.com; Greenfield Pl; s/d £118/145; P wi-fi) Lerwick's best hotel overlooks the harbour and has a quiet but central setting. It's a dignified small setup that will appeal to older visitors or couples. All doubles cost the same, but some are markedly better than others, with four-poster beds or water views. All boast new stylish bathrooms. The bar area is elegant and has fine perspectives.

Eating

Peerie Shop Cafe CAFE £
(01595-692816; www.peerieshop.co.uk; Esplanade; light meals £3-8; 8am-5pm Mon-Sat; wi-fi) If you've been craving proper espresso since leaving the mainland, head to this gem, with art exhibitions, wire-mounted halogens and industrial-gantry chic. Newspapers, scrumptious cakes and sandwiches, hot chocolate that you deserve after that blasting wind outside, and – less often – outdoor seating give everyone a reason to be here.

Dowry CAFE £
(01595-692373; www.thedowry.co.uk; 98 Commercial St; light meals £6-13; 10am-10pm Mon & Thu, 10am-6pm Tue-Wed, 10am-11pm Fri & Sat; vegetarian) A welcome addition to Lerwick's eating scene, pulling in a keen crowd of Shetlanders for its lunches based on solid local produce. Sandwiches with tasty homemade focaccia or brioche, soups, thoughtful vegan choices, craft beer and sharing platters of deli produce mean it's easy to eat well. Booth seating and water views up the back are where it's at.

NATURE WATCHING IN SHETLAND

For birdwatchers, Shetland is paradise – a stopover for migrating Arctic species and host to vast seabird breeding colonies. June is the height of the season.

Every bird has its own name here: rain geese are red-throated divers, bonxies are great skuas, and alamooties are storm petrels. Clownish puffin antics are a highlight. The **Royal Society for the Protection of Birds** (RSPB; www.rspb.org.uk) maintains several reserves, plus there are national nature reserves at **Hermaness**, **Keen of Hamar** and **Noss**. **Foula** and **Fair Isle** also support large seabird populations.

Keep an eye on the sea: sea otters, orcas and other cetaceans are regularly sighted. Latest sightings are logged at useful www.nature-shetland.co.uk.

Shetland Nature Festival (www.shetlandnaturefestival.co.uk; ⏲early Jul) has guided walks, talks, boat trips, open days and workshops.

★**Fjarå** CAFE, BISTRO ££
(☎01595-697388; www.fjaracoffee.com; Sea Rd; mains £8-22; ⏲8am-10pm Tue-Sat ,with food until 8pm, 10am-6pm Sun; 📶) A cute wooden building in a super location, Fjarå is perched above a rocky shore and takes full advantage, with big picture windows looking out over the water and occasionally some basking seals. It does a bit of everything, with breakfasts, sandwiches, salads and bagels, plus beer, cocktails and some excellent dinner offerings, including creative burgers, game and local seafood.

Drinking & Entertainment

The Lounge PUB
(☎01595-692231; 4 Mounthooly St; ⏲11am-1am; 📶) Tucked away behind Lerwick's tourist office, the Lounge features an earthy downstairs bar populated by friendly local characters. The attractive upstairs space features live music several times a week and informal jam sessions at other times. It's well worth checking out.

Mareel ARTS CENTRE
(☎01595-745500; www.mareel.org; Hay's Dock) Modern Mareel is a thriving arts centre with a cinema, concert hall and cafe in a great waterside location.

Information

Lerwick Tourist Office (☎01595-693434; www.shetland.org; cnr Commercial & Mounthooly Sts; ⏲9am-5pm Mon-Sat, 10am-4pm Sun Apr-Sep, 10am-4pm Mon-Sat Oct-Mar) Helpful, with a good range of books and maps.

Getting There & Away

BOAT

Northlink Ferries (p961) from Aberdeen and Kirkwall dock at Holmsgarth Terminal, a 15-minute walk northwest from the town centre.

BUS

From Viking Bus Station (p961), buses service various corners of the archipelago, including regular services to/from Sumburgh Airport.

Sumburgh

With sea cliffs, and grassy headlands jutting into sparkling blue water, Sumburgh is one of the most scenic places on Mainland, with a far greener landscape than the peaty north. It has a handful of excellent attractions clustered near Shetland's major airport.

Sights & Activities

★**Sumburgh Head Visitor Centre** LIGHTHOUSE, MUSEUM
(☎01595-694688; www.sumburghhead.com; adult/child £6/2; ⏲11am-5.30pm Apr-Sep) High on the cliffs at Sumburgh Head, this excellent attraction is set across several buildings. Displays explain about the lighthouse, foghorn and radar station that operated here, and there's a good exhibition on the local marine creatures and birds. You can visit the lighthouse itself on a guided tour for an extra charge.

Jarlshof ARCHAEOLOGICAL SITE
(☎01950-460112; www.historicenvironment.scot; adult/child £6/3.60; ⏲9.30am-5.30pm Apr-Sep, 9.30am-4.30pm Oct-Mar) Old and new collide, with Sumburgh Airport right by this picturesque, instructive archaeological site. Various periods of occupation from 2500 BCE to 1500 BCE can be seen – the complete change upon the Vikings' arrival is obvious, with their rectangular longhouses presenting a marked contrast to the preceding brochs, roundhouses and wheelhouses. Atop the site

is 16th-century Old House, named 'Jarlshof' in a novel by Sir Walter Scott. There's an informative audio tour included with admission.

★Sumburgh Head BIRDWATCHING
(www.rspb.org.uk) At Mainland's southern tip, these spectacular cliffs offer a good chance to get up close to puffins and huge nesting colonies of fulmars, guillemots and razorbills. If you're lucky, you might spot dolphins, minke whales or orcas. Also here is the excellent Sumburgh Head Visitor Centre, in the lighthouse buildings.

Getting There & Away

Bus 6 runs to Sumburgh and Sumburgh Airport from Lerwick (£2.90, one hour, roughly hourly Monday to Friday, nine Saturday, five Sunday).

Eshaness & Hillswick

Eleven miles northwest of Brae the road ends at the red basalt cliffs of Eshaness, site of some of Shetland's most impressive coastal scenery. When the wind subsides there's superb walking and views from the headland lighthouse. On the way, the village of Hillswick is set on a pretty bay.

Sleeping

★Busta House Hotel HOTEL ££
(01806-522506; www.bustahouse.com; Busta; s/d £90/115;) This genteel, characterful hotel near Brae has a long, sad history and inevitable rumours of a (friendly) ghost. Built in the late 18th century (though the oldest part, the sumptuous guest lounge, dates from 1588), it has creaks and quirks and compact, likeable rooms that retain a cosy charm. Sea views and/or a four-poster bed cost a bit more (£125).

★Almara B&B ££
(01806-503261; www.almara.shetland.co.uk; s/d £40/80; Apr-Oct;) Follow the puffin signpost a mile short of Hillswick to find Shetland's finest welcome. With sweeping views over the bay, this house has a great lounge, unusual features in the excellent rooms and bathrooms (including thoughtful extras such as USB chargers), and a good eye on the environment. You'll feel completely at home and appreciated; this is B&B at its best.

St Magnus Bay Hotel HOTEL ££
(01806-503372; www.stmagnusbayhotel.co.uk; Hillswick; s/d £90/120;) This wonderful wooden mansion was built in 1896 and sociable owners have done a cracking job returning it to former glories. Renovated rooms are winningly wood-clad, with modern bathrooms; half boast big windows taking full advantage of the fine water views. The bar serves pub meals complemented by seafood specials: quantities are huge. Breakfast is also a winner; try the delicious smoked haddock.

Getting There & Away

Three buses from Lerwick run to Hillswick (£3.50, 1¼ hours, Monday to Saturday), with a feeder bus on to Eshaness. Two buses run the return route. There are other connections at Brae.

The North Isles

Yell, Unst and Fetlar make up the North Isles of Shetland, which are connected to each other by ferry, as is Yell to Mainland. All are great for nature watching; Unst has the most to offer overall.

Getting There & Away

An integrated bus and ferry connection runs once daily Monday to Saturday from Lerwick to Yell and on to Unst and Fetlar. Smaller local buses serve island destinations off the principal bus route.

If you're going to spend a night on both Yell and Fetlar or Unst, consider visiting Yell on the way back, as the second ferry is free if you are coming from Mainland that same day.

Yell

Yell if you like but nobody will hear; the desolate peat moors here are typical Shetland scenery. The bleak landscape has an appeal, though. Yell is all about colours: the browns and vivid, lush greens of the bogland, grey clouds thudding through the skies, and the steely blue waters of the North Atlantic, which are never far away. The peat makes the ground look cracked and parched, though it's swimming most of the year. Though many folk fire on through to Unst, Yell offers several good hill walks, especially around the Herra peninsula, about halfway up the west coast.

Sleeping

Quam B&B B&B ££

(☎01957-766256; www.quambandbyellshetland.co.uk; Westsandwick; d £80; P 📶) Just off the main road through Yell island, this farm B&B has friendly owners and three good rooms. Breakfast features eggs from the farm, which also has cute ponies that you can meet. Dinners (£15 per person) can be arranged and bikes hired.

Unst

You're fast running out of Scotland once you cross to rugged Unst (www.visit-unst.com). Scotland's most northerly inhabited island is prettier than nearby Yell, with bare, velvety-smooth hills and settlements clinging to waterside locations, fiercely resisting the buffeting winds.

Sights

★Hermaness National Nature Reserve NATURE RESERVE

(www.nnr.scot) At marvellous Hermaness headland, a 4.5-mile round walk takes you to cliffs where gannets, fulmars and guillemots nest, and numerous puffins frolic. You can also see Scotland's most northerly point, the rocks of **Out Stack**, and **Muckle Flugga**, with its lighthouse built by Robert Louis Stevenson's uncle. Duck into the **Hermaness Visitor Centre** (☎01595-711278; ⏲9am-5pm Apr-early Sep) FREE, with its poignant story about one-time resident Albert Ross.

The path to the cliffs is guarded by a squadron of great skuas who nest in the nearby heather, and dive-bomb at will if they feel threatened. They're damn solid birds too, but don't usually make contact.

Unst Bus Shelter LANDMARK

(Bobby's Bus Shelter; www.unstbusshelter.shetland.co.uk; Baltasound) At the turn-off to Littlehamar, just past Baltasound, is Britain's most impressive bus stop. Enterprising locals, tired of waiting in discomfort, decided to do a job on it, bringing in comfortable seats and much more. It now gets decorated to a different theme every year.

Unst Boat Haven MUSEUM

(☎01957-711809; Haroldswick; adult/child £3/free, combined ticket with Unst Heritage Centre £5; ⏲11am-4pm Mon-Sat, 2-4pm Sun May-Sep) This large shed is a boatie's delight, packed with a beautifully cared-for collection of Shetland rowing and sailing boats, all with a backstory. Old photos and maritime artefacts speak of the glory days of Unst fishing. There's a seasonal tearoom out front.

Sleeping

★Gardiesfauld Hostel HOSTEL £

(☎01957-755279; www.facebook.com/gardiesfauldhostel; 2 East Rd, Uyeasound; per adult/child sites £8/4, dm £16/9; ⏲Apr-Sep; P 📶) This spotless hostel has very spacious dorms with lockers, family rooms, a garden, an elegant lounge and a wee conservatory dining area with great bay views. You can camp here, too; there are separate areas for tents and vans. The bus stops right outside. Bring 20p coins for the showers. It will open in winter if you prebook.

Understand Great Britain

History

Britain may be a small country on the edge of Europe, but it has rarely been on the sidelines of history. For nearly 2000 years, this plucky little island nation has been at the centre of global events – from world wars and empires to political landmarks and philosophical breakthroughs. Waves of invaders and immigrants have shaped its history, while a tapestry of kings, queens, princes and pretenders have left it with a rich legacy of castles, cathedrals, sacred sites and battlegrounds just waiting to be explored.

First Arrivals

Around 4000 BCE, as glaciers retreated in the wake of the Ice Age, a group of migrants arrived from Europe. Instead of hunting and moving on, they settled in one place and started farming. Alongside their fields, Britain's Stone Age people used rocks and turf to build massive burial mounds; the remains of many of these can still be seen, including West Kennet Long Barrow in Wiltshire, Pentre Ifan in Pembrokeshire and Maeshowe in Orkney. But the most impressive legacies left by these nascent Britons were the enigmatic stone circles of Callanish, Avebury and Stonehenge.

History Websites

www.royal.uk

www.bbc.co.uk/history

www.englishmonarchs.co.uk

www.victorianweb.org

Iron & Celts

During the Iron Age (from 800 BCE to 100 CE) the population expanded and began to divide into specific tribes. Forests were cleared as more land was used for farming. This led to a patchwork pattern of fields, woods and small villages that still exists today in many parts of rural Britain. As the population grew, territorial defence became an issue, so the Iron Age people left another legacy: the great 'earthwork' castles of southern England, stone forts in northern England and brochs (defensive towers) in Wales and Scotland.

The Celts, a people who originally migrated from Central Europe, had settled across much of Britain by around 500 BCE. A Celtic-British population developed, comprising about 20 tribes, including the Cantiaci (in today's county of Kent), the Iceni (Norfolk), the Brigantes (northern England), the Picts and Caledonii (Scotland), the Ordivices (parts of Wales) and the Scotti (Ireland).

TIMELINE

4000 BCE

Neolithic peoples migrate from continental Europe. They differ significantly from previous arrivals: instead of hunting and moving on, they settle in one place and start farming.

c 500 BCE

The Celts, a group originally from Central Europe, arrive in Britain, and by the middle of the 1st millennium BC have settled across much of the island, absorbing the indigenous people.

43 CE

Emperor Claudius leads the first proper Roman invasion of England. His army wages a ruthless campaign, and the Romans control most of southern England by 50 CE.

You noticed the Latin-sounding names? That's because the tribal tags were first handed out by the next arrivals on Britain's shores…

Enter the Romans

Emperor Claudius led a ruthless campaign to invade Britain, resulting in the Romans controlling pretty much everywhere in southern England by 50 CE. Much of the occupation was straightforward: several Celtic-British tribal kings realised collaboration was more profitable than battle. It wasn't all plain sailing, though, and some locals fought back. The most famous freedom fighter was warrior-queen Boudica, who led an army as far as Londinium, the Roman port on the present site of London.

Settlement by the Romans in Britain lasted almost four centuries. Intermarriage was common between locals and incomers (many from other parts of the empire, including today's Belgium, Spain and Syria), and a Romano-British population evolved, particularly in the towns, while indigenous Celtic-British culture remained in some areas, including parts of Wales, Scotland and Cornwall.

By the late 3rd century CE, as its empire gradually declined, the Roman colony in Britain slowly fizzled out of existence: the end of Roman power in Britain is generally dated at 410 CE.

Christianity was introduced to Britain by the Romans and adopted by the Celts, but the Anglo-Saxons were pagans, and their invasion of Britain forced the Christian religion, along with other aspects of Celtic culture, to the edges of the British Isles – today's Wales, Scotland and Ireland.

The Emergence of England

Britain's post-Roman power vacuum didn't go unnoticed. Angles and Saxons (Teutonic tribes from the lands we now call Germany, Denmark and the Netherlands) advanced across the former Roman turf.

Historians disagree on exactly what happened next. Either the Anglo-Saxons largely replaced or absorbed the Romano-British and Celtic population, or the indigenous tribes simply adopted Anglo-Saxon language and culture. Either way, by the late 6th century much of present-day England was dominated by the Anglo-Saxons and divided into three main kingdoms: Wessex (in today's southern England), Mercia (the Midlands) and Northumbria (northeastern England and southeastern Scotland). Gradually, their language became the lingua franca, developing into Old English (the foundation of modern English): England actually translates as 'land of the Angles'.

It was around this time that a legendary warrior-king by the name of Arthur was supposed to have appeared, along with his fabled Knights of the Round Table. Several historical sources refer to his existence, notably the *Historia Brittonum* (History of the Britons) written in around 828 – although their veracity is disputed by historians. The consensus is that Arthur was probably a Romano-British warrior or chief who fought against the Anglo-Saxon invasion sometime in the late 5th to early 6th centuries.

Probably built around 3000 BCE, Stonehenge has stood on Salisbury Plain for more than 5000 years and is older than the famous Great Pyramids of Egypt.

60

Warrior-queen Boudica leads an army against the Romans, destroys Colchester and gets as far as Londinium. In Wales the Celts, led by their mystic faith healers, the druids, fight a last stand on Anglesey.

122

Rather than conquer wild north British tribes, Emperor Hadrian settles for building a coast-to-coast barricade. For nearly 300 years, Hadrian's Wall marks the northernmost limit of the Roman Empire.

200

The Romans build a defensive wall around the city of London with four main entrance gates, still remembered today by the districts of Aldgate, Ludgate, Newgate and Bishopsgate.

c 410

As the classical world's greatest empire finally declines after centuries of relative peace and prosperity, Roman rule ends in Britain with more of a whimper than a bang.

Celts, Picts & Scotti

On the western fringes of the British Isles, the Celts kept alive their own distinct yet Roman-influenced culture, especially in Wales. Under pressure of invasion both from the Scotti (from today's Ireland) and the Anglo-Saxons, by the 8th century the disparate tribes of Wales had started to band together and sow the seeds of nationhood. They called themselves *cymry* (countrymen); today Cymru is the Welsh word for Wales.

Similar events were happening in the north, where the Picts had become the dominant tribe (in the north and east), and the Scotti had established the kingdom of Dalriada around what is now Argyll. The foundations of a new nation – Scotland – had been lain.

Boudica was queen of the Iceni, a Celtic-British tribe whose territory was invaded by the Romans around AD 60. A year later, she led an army against the Roman settlements of Camulodunum (now Colchester) and Londinium (London), but was eventually defeated at the Battle of Watling Street (in today's Shropshire). A statue of the warrior queen stands at the western end of London's Westminster Bridge.

The Viking Era

In the 9th century, Britain was yet again invaded by a bunch of pesky continentals. This time, it was the Vikings – Nordic people from today's Scandinavia. Tradition has it that Vikings turned up, killed everyone, took everything and left. There's *some* truth in some of that, but in reality many Vikings settled in Britain, and their legacy is especially evident in today's northern England (notably Yorkshire), Orkney and Shetland.

After conquering northern and eastern areas, the Vikings started to expand into central England. Blocking their route were the Anglo-Saxon armies led by Alfred the Great, the king of Wessex and one of English history's best-known characters.

The battles that followed were seminal to the foundation of the nation-state of England, but the fighting didn't all go Alfred's way. For a few months he was on the run, wading through swamps, hiding in peasant hovels and famously burning cakes while distracted by his predicament. It was the stuff of legend, and by 886 Alfred had gathered his strength and pushed the Vikings back to the north.

United England?

Thus England was divided in two: north and east was the Viking 'Danelaw', while south and west was Anglo-Saxon territory. Alfred was hailed as king of the English – the first time the Anglo-Saxons regarded themselves as a truly united people.

Alfred's son and successor was Edward the Elder. After more battles, he gained control of the Danelaw, and thus became the first king to rule the whole of England. His son, Athelstan, took the process a stage further and was specifically crowned King of England in 927. But it was hardly cause for celebration: the Vikings were still around, and later in the 10th century more raids from Scandinavia threatened this fledgling English unity. Over the following decades, control swung from English (King Edgar) to Dane (King Knut) and back to English again (King Edward the

5th century	6th century	7th century	8th century
Teutonic tribes (known today as the Anglo-Saxons) from modern Germany, Denmark and the Netherlands migrate to England and spread across much of the country.	St Augustine is sent to revive Christianity among the southern Anglo-Saxons, along with his colleague St Aidan in the north. St David establishes a place of worship in Pembrokeshire.	Anglo-Saxons from Northumbria colonise southeast Alba (today's southern Scotland) and are met by the Scotti. Against the odds, in 685 Pictish king Bridei defeats the Northumbrians at Nechtansmere in Angus.	King Offa of Mercia orders the construction of a clear border between his kingdom and Wales – a defensive ditch called Offa's Dyke, still visible today.

Confessor). As the country came to the end of the 1st millennium CE, the future was anything but certain.

Highs & Lows in Wales

Meanwhile, as England fought off the Viking threat, Wales was also dealing with the Nordic intruders. Building on the initial cooperation forced upon them by Anglo-Saxon oppression, in the 9th and 10th centuries the small kingdoms of Wales began cooperating, through necessity, to repel the Vikings.

King Rhodri Mawr (who died in 878) defeated a Viking force off the Isle of Anglesey and began the unification process. His grandson Hywel the Good is thought to have been responsible for drawing up a set of laws to bind the disparate Welsh tribes. But just as Wales was becoming a recognisable entity, the fledgling country was faced with more destructive onslaughts than it could handle and in 927 the Welsh kings recognised the Anglo-Saxon King Athelstan as their overlord, in exchange for an anti-Viking alliance.

Great Britain consists of the countries of England, Wales and Scotland. The United Kingdom (UK) is Great Britain plus Northern Ireland. The British Isles is a *geographical* term for the islands that make up the UK and the Republic of Ireland, plus others such as the Channel Islands.

Scotland Becomes a Kingdom

In the 9th century, the king of the Scotti of Dalriada was one Kenneth MacAlpin. His father was a Scot, but his mother was a Pictish princess, so MacAlpin took advantage of the Pictish custom of matrilineal succession to declare himself ruler of both the Scots *and* the Picts, and therefore king of all Alba.

In a surprisingly short time, the Scots gained cultural and political ascendancy. The Picts were absorbed, and their culture disappeared; from the union of Alba and Pictland came the beginnings of a Scottish kingdom.

In the 11th century, Scottish nation-building was further consolidated by King Malcolm III (whose most famous act was the 1057 murder of Macbeth, immortalised by William Shakespeare). With his English queen, Margaret, he founded the Canmore dynasty that would rule Scotland for the next two centuries.

A History of Britain by historian and TV star Simon Schama is a highly accessible set of three books, examining events from 3000 BCE to AD 2000.

1066 & All That

Back in England things were unsettled, as the royal pendulum swung between Saxon and Viking monarchs. When King Edward the Confessor died, the crown passed to Harold, his brother-in-law. That should've settled things, but Edward had a cousin in Normandy (the northern part of today's France) called William, who thought that *he* had a right to the throne of England.

The result was the Battle of Hastings in 1066, the most memorable of dates for anyone who's studied English history – or for anyone who hasn't. William sailed from Normandy with an army of Norman soldiers,

850

Vikings conquer east and northeast England. They establish their capital at Jorvik, modern-day York. The Shetland and Orkney islands become a Viking base for raids of Scotland and northern England.

9th century

Kenneth MacAlpin, the king of the Scotti, declares himself ruler of both the Scots *and* the Picts, thus uniting Scotland north of the Firth of Forth into a single kingdom.

927

Athelstan, grandson of Alfred the Great, son of Edward the Elder, is the first monarch to be specifically crowned King of England, building on his ancestors' success in regaining Viking territory.

1040

Macbeth takes the Scottish throne after defeating Duncan in battle. This, and the fact that he was later killed by Duncan's son Malcolm, are the only parallels with the Shakespeare play.

the Saxons were defeated and Harold was killed (although not, despite popular belief, by an arrow in the eye).

Norman Wisdom

William became king of England, earning the title William the Conqueror. It was no idle nickname – to control the Anglo-Saxons, the Norman invaders wisely built castles across their newly won territory, and by 1086 the Domesday Book provided a census of England's current stock and future potential.

At the top of the feudal system came the monarch, followed by nobles (barons, dukes and bishops), then earls, knights, lords and ladies. At the bottom were peasants or 'serfs'. This strict hierarchy became the basis of a class system that still exists in Britain today.

In the years after the invasion, the French-speaking Normans and the English-speaking Anglo-Saxons kept pretty much to themselves. A strict hierarchy of class developed, known as the feudal system.

Intermarriage was not completely unknown; William's son, Henry I, married a Saxon princess. Nonetheless, such unifying moves stood for nothing after Henry's death: a bitter struggle for succession followed, finally won by Henry II, who took the throne as the first king of the Plantagenet dynasty.

To secure his new kingdom, and keep the Welsh in theirs, William the Conqueror built castles and appointed feudal barons along the border. The Lords Marcher, as they were known, became massively rich and powerful, and the parts of western England along the Welsh border are still called the Marches today.

In Scotland, King Malcolm III and Queen Margaret were more accommodating to Norman ways. Malcolm's successor, David I (1124–53), adopted the Norman feudal system, and granted land to great Norman families. Further north the Highland clans remained inaccessible in their glens, and remained a law unto themselves for another 600 years.

Royal & Holy Squabbling

When the reign of England's Henry I came to an end, the enduring British habit of competition for the throne introduced an equally enduring tendency for bickering between royalty and the church. Things came to a head in 1170 when Henry II had the 'turbulent priest' Thomas Becket murdered in Canterbury Cathedral, where a memorial to Becket can still be seen today.

The Year 1000 by Robert Lacey and Danny Danziger looks long and hard at English life a millennium ago. Apparently it was cold and damp then, too.

Perhaps the next king, Richard I, wanted to make amends for his forebears' unholy sentiments by leading a crusade (a Christian 'holy war') to liberate Jerusalem and the Holy Land from occupation by Muslim 'heathens' under their leader Saladin. The campaign became known as the Third Crusade, and although the Christian armies captured the cities of Acre and Jaffa, they did not take Jerusalem.

Unfortunately, Richard's overseas activities meant he was too busy crusading to bother about governing England and in his absence the

1066
Battle of Hastings – a crucial date in English history. Incumbent King Harold is defeated by an invading Norman army, and England has a new monarch: William the Conqueror.

1085–86
The new Norman rulers establish the Domesday Book census. Within three years they have a snapshot of England's current stock and future potential.

1095
The start of the First Crusade – a campaign of Christian European armies against the Muslim occupation of Jerusalem and the 'Holy Land'. A series of crusades continues until 1272.

1170
Thomas Becket is hacked to death in Canterbury Cathedral on the orders of Henry II.

MAGNA CARTA

In 1215 the barons found King John's erratic rule increasingly hard to swallow and forced him to sign a document called Magna Carta (the Great Charter), limiting the monarch's power for the first time in British history. Although originally intended as a set of handy ground rules, the Magna Carta was a fledgling bill of human rights that eventually led to the creation of parliament – a body to rule the country, independent of the throne. The signing took place at Runnymede, near Windsor, and you can still visit the site today.

country fell into disarray, although his bravery and ruthlessness earned him the sobriquet Richard the Lionheart.

Richard was succeeded by his brother John, but under his harsh rule things got even worse for the general population. According to legend, during this time a nobleman called Robert of Loxley, better known as Robin Hood, hid in Sherwood Forest and engaged in a spot of wealth redistribution.

Among Britain's best-known folk heroes, Robin Hood and his Merry Men were said to have lived in the forests around Nottingham sometimes during the 11th century. Unfortunately, there is no concrete evidence that he actually existed: some historians claim that 'Robin Hood' was merely a catch-all term used at the time for bandits.

Expansionist Edward

Edward I of England (1272–1307) was a skilled ruler and ambitious general. During a busy 35-year reign he was unashamedly expansionist in his outlook, leading campaigns into Wales and Scotland.

Some decades earlier, the Welsh king Llywelyn the Great (d 1240) had attempted to set up a state in Wales, and his grandson Llywelyn the Last was recognised by Henry III as the first Prince (but not King) of Wales. But Edward I had no time for such niceties, and descended on Wales in a bloody invasion that lasted much of the 1270s. In the end, Wales became a dependent principality, owing allegiance to England. There were no more Welsh kings, and Edward made his own son Prince of Wales. Ever since, the British sovereign's eldest son has automatically been given the title. (Most recently, Prince Charles was formally proclaimed Prince of Wales at Caernarfon Castle in 1969, much to the displeasure of Welsh nationalists.)

Edward I then looked north. For 200 years, Scotland had been ruled by the Canmores, but the dynasty effectively ended in 1286 with the death of Alexander III. He was succeeded by his four-year-old granddaughter Margaret ('the Maid of Norway'), who was engaged to the son of Edward I, but she died in 1290 before the wedding could take place.

Scotland on the Rise

There followed a dispute for the Scottish throne between John Balliol and Robert Bruce of Annandale. Arbitration was needed and the nobles asked Edward I, who chose Balliol. Edward then sought to formalise his feudal overlordship and travelled through Scotland, forcing local leaders

1215

King John signs the Magna Carta, limiting the monarch's power for the first time in English history in an early step along the path towards constitutional rule.

13th century

Wales is invaded by English King Edward I, bringing to an end the rule of Welsh leader 'Llywelyn the Last'. Edward builds a ring of castles to suppress further Welsh uprisings.

1296

King Edward I marches on Scotland with an army of 30,000 men and in a brutal invasion captures the castles of Berwick, Edinburgh, Roxburgh and Stirling.

1298–1305

William Wallace is proclaimed Guardian of Scotland in 1298. After Edward's army defeats the Scots at the Battle of Falkirk, Wallace goes into hiding but is betrayed and executed in 1305.

to swear allegiance. In a final blow to Scottish pride, Edward removed the Stone of Destiny, on which the kings of Scotland had been crowned for centuries, and sent it to London.

That was too much. In response, Balliol got in touch with Edward's old enemy, France, and arranged a treaty of cooperation, the start of an anti-English partnership, the 'Auld Alliance', which was to last for many centuries (and to the present day when it comes to rugby or football).

Edward wasn't the sort of bloke to brook opposition, though. In 1296 the English army defeated Balliol, forcing the Scottish barons to accept Edward's rule, and his ruthless retaliation earned him the title 'Hammer of the Scots'. But still the Scottish people refused to lie down; in 1297, at the Battle of Stirling Bridge, the English were defeated by a Scots army under the leadership of William Wallace. Over 700 years later, Wallace is still remembered as a Scottish hero.

The story of William Wallace is told in the Mel Gibson epic *Braveheart*. In devolution debates of the 1990s, the patriotic pride engendered by this movie did more for Scottish nationalism than any politician's speech.

By this time, Robert the Bruce (grandson of Bruce of Annandale) had crowned himself king of Scotland (1290), been beaten in battle, gone on the run and, while hiding in a cave, been famously inspired to renew his efforts by a spider persistently spinning its web. Bruce's army went on to defeat Edward II's superior English forces at the Battle of Bannockburn in 1314, a famous victory that led to the official recognition of Scotland as an independent nation, with Bruce as its king, in 1328.

Bruce's son became David II of Scotland, but he was soon caught up in battles against fellow Scots disaffected by his father and aided by England's Edward III. So when David died in 1371, the Scots quickly crowned Robert Stewart (Robert the Bruce's grandson) as king, marking the start of the House of Stewart.

Houses of York & Lancaster

In 1399 the ineffectual Richard II of England was ousted by a powerful baron called Henry Bolingbroke, who became Henry IV, the first monarch of the House of Lancaster. Less than a year later, his rule was disrupted by a final cry of resistance from the downtrodden Welsh, led by royal descendant Owain Glyndŵr (Owen Glendower). But the rebellion was crushed, Glyndŵr died an outlaw and the Welsh elite were barred from public life for many years.

Henry IV was followed by Henry V, who stirred up the dormant Hundred Years' War and defeated France at the Battle of Agincourt. The patriotic speech penned for him by Shakespeare in *Henry V* ('Cry "God for Harry, England, and St George!"') has ensured his position among the most famous English kings of all time.

When the Hundred Years' War finally ground to a halt in 1453, you'd have thought things would be calm for a while, but no. The English forc-

1314

An army under Robert the Bruce wins against the English at the Battle of Bannockburn – a victory that consolidated Scottish independence for the next 400 years.

1337–1453

England battles France in a long conflict known as the Hundred Years' War. It was actually a series of small conflicts. And it lasted for more than a century, too...

1348

The bubonic plague (called the Black Death) arrives, ultimately killing more than a third of the population. For peasant labourers who survived, an upside was a rise in wages.

1381

Richard II is confronted by the Peasants' Revolt. This attempt by commoners to overthrow the feudal system is brutally suppressed, further injuring an already deeply divided country.

es returning from France threw their energies into a civil war dubbed the Wars of the Roses.

Briefly it went like this: Henry VI of the House of Lancaster (with a red rose emblem) was challenged by Richard, Duke of York (with a white rose emblem). Henry was weak and it was almost a walkover for Richard. But Henry's wife, Margaret of Anjou, was made of sterner stuff and her forces defeated the challenger. It didn't rest there. Richard's son Edward entered the scene with an army, turned the tables and finally drove out Henry. He became King Edward IV, first monarch of the House of York.

Dark Deeds in the Tower

Edward IV hardly had time to catch his breath before Richard Neville, Earl of Warwick, and Margaret of Anjou teamed up in 1471 to force him into exile and bring Henry VI back to the throne. But a year later Edward IV came bouncing back: he killed Warwick, captured Margaret and had Henry snuffed out in the Tower of London.

Although Edward IV's position seemed secure, he ruled for only a decade before being succeeded by his 12-year-old son, Edward V. But the boy-king's reign was even shorter than his dad's. In 1483 he was mysteriously murdered, along with his brother, and once again the Tower of London was the scene of the crime.

With the 'princes in the Tower' dispatched, this left the throne open for their dear old Uncle Richard. Whether he was the princes' killer is still the subject of debate, but his rule as Richard III was short-lived. Despite being given another famous Shakespearean sound bite ('A horse, a horse! My kingdom for a horse!'), few tears were shed in 1485 when he was tumbled from the top job by a nobleman from Wales called Henry Tudor, who became Henry VII.

Shakespeare's *Henry V* (1989) was filmed as a superb epic starring Kenneth Branagh as the eponymous king. Also worth catching is the earlier movie of the same name starring Laurence Olivier, made in 1944 as a patriotic rallying cry.

MARY, QUEEN OF SCOTS

During Elizabeth I's reign, her cousin Mary (the Catholic daughter of Scottish King James V) had become known as Mary, Queen of Scots. She'd spent her childhood in France and had married the French *dauphin* (crown prince), thereby becoming Queen of France as well. Why stop at two? After her husband's death, Mary returned to Scotland, where she claimed the English throne as well, on the grounds that Elizabeth I was illegitimate.

However, Mary's plans failed. She was imprisoned and forced to abdicate in favour of her son (a Protestant, who became James VI of Scotland), but she escaped to England and appealed to Elizabeth for help. This was a bad move; Mary was seen, not surprisingly, as a security risk and imprisoned once again. In an uncharacteristic display of indecision, Elizabeth held Mary under arrest for nearly 19 years before finally ordering her execution. As a prisoner, Mary was frequently moved from house to house, so that today Britain has many stately homes (and even a few pubs) claiming 'Mary, Queen of Scots slept here'.

1400

Welsh nationalist hero Owain Glyndŵr leads the Welsh in rebellion, declaring a parliament in Machynlleth, but his rebellion is short-lived and victory fleeting.

1455–85

The Wars of the Roses – an ongoing conflict between two competing dynasties, the Houses of Lancaster and York. The Yorkists are eventually successful, enabling King Edward IV to gain the throne.

1485

Henry Tudor defeats Richard III at the Battle of Bosworth to become King Henry VII, establishing the Tudor dynasty and ending York–Lancaster rivalry for the throne.

1509–47

The reign of King Henry VIII. The Pope's disapproval of Henry's serial marriage and divorce results in the English Reformation – the founding of the Church of England.

Moves Towards Unity

After the Wars of the Roses, Henry VII's Tudor neutrality was important. He mended fences with his northern neighbours by marrying his daughter to James IV of Scotland, linking the Tudor and Stewart lines. This, however, didn't stop James IV invading England in 1513, only to be killed at the Battle of Flodden. Henry VII married Elizabeth of York (daughter of Edward IV and niece of Richard III), further cementing his claim to the throne.

Matrimony may have been more useful than warfare for Henry VII, but the multiple marriages of his successor, Henry VIII, were a very different story. Not fathering a male heir was his problem, hence the famous six wives, but the Pope's disapproval of divorce and remarriage led to a split with the Roman Catholic Church. Parliament made Henry the head of the Protestant Church of England – the beginning of a pivotal division between Catholics and Protestants that still exists in some areas of Britain.

In 1536 Henry followed this up by 'dissolving' many monasteries in Britain and Ireland, a blatant takeover of their land and wealth rather than a symptom of the struggle between church and state. Nonetheless, the general populace felt little sympathy for the wealthy (and often corrupt) abbeys, and in 1539–40 another monastic land grab swallowed the larger ones as well.

Walks Through Britain's History (published by the Automobile Association) guides you on foot to castles, battlefields and hundreds of other sites with a link to the past. Take the air. Breathe in history!

At the same time, Henry signed the Acts of Union (1536 and 1543), formally uniting England and Wales for the first time. Meanwhile, in Scotland, James IV had been succeeded by James V, who died in 1542. His baby daughter Mary became queen, and Scotland was ruled by regents.

The Elizabethan Age

Henry VIII died in 1547, succeeded by his son Edward VI, then by his daughter Mary I, but their reigns were short. So, unexpectedly, Elizabeth, third in line, came to the throne.

As Elizabeth I, she inherited a nasty mess of religious strife and divided loyalties, but after an uncertain start she gained confidence and turned the country around. Refusing marriage, she borrowed biblical imagery and became known as the Virgin Queen, making her perhaps the first British monarch to create a cult image.

It paid off. Her 45-year reign was a period of boundless optimism, characterised by the naval defeat of the Spanish Armada, the expansion of trade due to the global explorations of seafarers such as Walter Raleigh and Francis Drake, and a cultural flourishing thanks to writers such as William Shakespeare and Christopher Marlowe.

1536–41

Henry VIII orders the Dissolution of the Monasteries, ordering their lands and property to be seized, and forcibly destroying many of England's oldest and most beautiful ecclesiastical institutions.

1560

The Scottish Parliament creates a Protestant Church that is independent of Rome and the monarchy, as a result of the Reformation. The Latin Mass is abolished and the Pope's authority denied.

1588

King Philip of Spain sends a fleet of ships to invade England, known as the Spanish Armada. Francis Drake and the English fleet wreak havoc and the fleet flees or is destroyed.

1603

James VI of Scotland inherits the English throne in the so-called Union of the Crowns, becoming James I of England and James VI of Scotland.

United & Disunited Britain

Elizabeth I died in 1603 without an heir, and was succeeded by her closest relative, James, the safely Protestant son of the executed Mary. Already James VI of Scotland, he became James I of England, the first English monarch of the House of Stuart. Most importantly, James united England, Wales and Scotland into one kingdom for the first time in history.

James' attempts to smooth religious relations were set back by the anti-Catholic outcry that followed the infamous Guy Fawkes Gunpowder Plot, a terrorist attempt to blow up parliament in 1605. The event is still celebrated every 5 November with fireworks, bonfires and burning effigies of Guy himself.

Alongside the Catholic-Protestant rift, the divide between king and parliament continued to smoulder. The power struggle worsened during the reign of the next king, Charles I, and eventually degenerated into the Civil War of 1642–49. The antiroyalist (or 'parliamentarian') forces were led by Oliver Cromwell, a Puritan who preached against the excesses of the monarchy and established Church. His army (known as the Roundheads) was pitched against the king's forces (the Cavaliers) in a conflict that tore Britain, and especially England, apart. The Civil War extended into Scotland where the main struggle was between royalists and radical 'Covenanters', who sought freedom from state interference in church government.

It ended with victory for the Roundheads, with the king executed, the country declared a republic and Cromwell hailed as 'Protector'.

The 1998 film *Elizabeth*, directed by Shekhar Kapur and starring Cate Blanchett, covers the early years of the Virgin Queen's rule, as she graduates from princess to commanding monarch – a time of forbidden love, unwanted suitors, intrigue and death.

The Return of the King

By 1653 Cromwell was finding parliament too restrictive and he assumed dictatorial powers, much to his supporters' dismay. On his death in 1658, he was followed half-heartedly by his son, but in 1660 parliament decided to re-establish the monarchy, as republican alternatives were proving far worse.

Charles II (the exiled son of Charles I) came to the throne, and his rule, known as 'the Restoration', saw scientific and cultural activity bursting forth. Exploration and expansion were also on the agenda. Backed by the army and navy (modernised, ironically, by Cromwell), British colonies stretched down the American coast, while the East India Company set up headquarters in Bombay (now Mumbai), laying foundations for what was to become the British Empire.

The next king, James II/VII, had a harder time. Attempts to ease restrictive laws on Catholics ended with his overthrow and defeat at the Battle of the Boyne by William III, ruler of the Netherlands, better known as William of Orange. William was married to James' own daughter Mary, but it didn't stop him (and her) attacking James.

On the chilly day of his execution, dethroned King Charles I reputedly wore two shirts to avoid shivering and being regarded as a coward.

1642–49
English Civil War between the king's Cavaliers and Oliver Cromwell's Roundheads establishes the Commonwealth of England.

1688
William of Orange and his wife, Mary, daughter of King James II, jointly ascend the throne after William defeats his father-in-law in the Glorious Revolution.

1707
The Act of Union brings England and Scotland under one parliament, one sovereign and one flag.

1745–46
The culmination of the Jacobite uprisings sees Bonnie Prince Charlie land in Scotland, gather an army and march southwards, to be eventually defeated at the Battle of Culloden.

William and Mary came to the throne as King and Queen, each in their own right (Mary had more of a claim, but William would not agree to be a mere consort), and their joint accession in 1688 was known as the Glorious Revolution.

Act of Union

In 1694 Mary died, leaving William as sole monarch. He died a few years later and was succeeded by his sister-in-law Anne (the second daughter of James II). In 1707, during Anne's reign, the Act of Union was passed, bringing an end to the independent Scottish Parliament and linking the countries of England, Wales and Scotland under one parliament (based in London) for the first time. The nation of Great Britain was now established as a single state, with a bigger, more powerful parliament, and a constitutional monarchy with clear limits on the king or queen.

The new-look parliament didn't wait long to flex its muscles. The Act of Union banned any Catholic, or anyone married to a Catholic, from ascending the throne – a rule still in force today. In 1714 Anne died without leaving an heir, marking the end of the Stuart line. The throne was then passed to distant (but still safely Protestant) German relatives: the House of Hanover, better known as the Georgians.

The Jacobite Rebellions

Despite the 1707 Act of Union, anti-English feeling in Scotland refused to disappear. The Jacobite rebellions, most notably those of 1715 and 1745, were attempts to overthrow the Hanoverian monarchy and bring back the Stuarts. Although these are iconic events in Scottish history, in reality there was never much support for the Jacobite cause outside the Highlands: the people of the lowlands were mainly Protestant and feared a return to the Catholicism that the Stuarts represented.

The 1715 rebellion was led by James Edward Stuart (the Old Pretender), the son of the exiled James II of England (James VII of Scotland), but when the attempt failed he fled to France. To impose control on the

WHO'D WANT TO BE KING?

Despite immense power and privilege, the position of monarch (or, perhaps worse, *potential* monarch) probably ranks as one of history's most dangerous occupations. English kings have been killed in battle (Harold), beheaded (Charles I), assassinated (William II), murdered by a wicked uncle (allegedly; Edward V), and bumped off by their queen and her lover (Edward II). Life was just as uncertain for the rulers of Wales and Scotland: some murdered by a wicked uncle (James I of Scotland), others killed in battle (Llywelyn the Last of Wales, and James IV of Scotland, the last British monarch to die on the battlefield).

1775–83
The American War of Independence is the British Empire's first major reversal, a fact not missed by French ruler Napoleon.

1799–1815
In the Napoleonic Wars, Napoleon threatens invasion on a weakened Britain, but his ambitions are curtailed by Nelson and Wellington at the famous battles of Trafalgar (1805) and Waterloo (1815).

1837–1901
During the reign of Queen Victoria the British Empire – 'on which the sun never sets' – expands from Canada through Africa and India to Australia and New Zealand.

1858 & 1860
The first modern national eisteddfods are held in Llangollen and Denbigh – although earlier ones had been organised from the end of the 18th century as part of a Welsh cultural revival.

Highlands, General George Wade was commissioned to build a network of military roads through many previously inaccessible glens.

In 1745 James' son Charles Edward Stuart (Bonnie Prince Charlie, the Young Pretender) landed in Scotland to claim the crown for his father. He was initially successful, moving south into England as far as Derby, but the prince and his Highland army suffered a catastrophic defeat at the Battle of Culloden in 1746; his legendary escape to the western isles is remembered in *The Skye Boat Song*. General Wade is remembered, too, as many of the roads his troops built are still in use today.

The Empire Strikes Out

By the mid-18th century, struggles for the British throne seemed a thing of the past, and the Georgian kings increasingly relied on parliament to govern the country. As part of the process, from 1721 to 1742 a senior parliamentarian called Sir Robert Walpole effectively became Britain's first prime minister.

Meanwhile, the British Empire continued to grow in America, Canada and India. The first claims were made on Australia after Captain James Cook's epic voyage of exploration in 1768.

The empire's first major reversal came when the American colonies won the War of Independence (1775–83). This setback forced Britain to withdraw from the world stage for a while, a gap not missed by French ruler Napoleon. He threatened to invade Britain and hinder the power of the British overseas, before his ambitions were curtailed by naval hero Admiral Nelson and military hero the Duke of Wellington at the famous battles of Trafalgar (1805) and Waterloo (1815).

Captain James Cook's voyage to the southern hemisphere was primarily a scientific expedition. His objectives included monitoring the transit of Venus, an astronomical event that happens only twice every 180 years or so (most recently in 2004 and 2012). 'Discovering' Australia was just a sideline.

The Industrial Age

While the empire expanded abroad, at home Britain became the crucible of the Industrial Revolution. Steam power (patented by James Watt in 1781) and steam trains (launched by George Stephenson in the 1820s) transformed methods of production and transport, and the towns of the English Midlands became the first industrial cities.

From about 1750, much of the Scottish Highlands was emptied of people, as landowners casually expelled entire farms and villages to make way for more profitable sheep, a seminal event in Scotland's history known as the Clearances. Although many of the dispossessed left for the New World, others headed to the burgeoning cotton mills of Lanarkshire and the shipyards of Glasgow.

By the early 19th century, copper, iron and slate were being extracted in the Merthyr Tydfil and Monmouth areas of Wales. The 1860s saw the Rhondda valleys opened up for coal mining, and Wales soon became a major exporter of coal, as well as the world's leading producer of tin plate.

1900

James Keir Hardie (usually known as just Keir Hardie) becomes the first Labour MP, winning a seat in the Welsh mining town of Merthyr Tydfil.

1914

Archduke Franz Ferdinand of Austria is assassinated in today's Bosnian capital of Sarajevo – the final spark in a decade-long crisis that starts the Great War, now called World War I.

1916

The Welsh Liberal MP David Lloyd George becomes the British prime minister in an alliance with the Conservative Party, having built a reputation for championing the poor and needy.

1926

Increasing mistrust of the government, fuelled by soaring unemployment, leads to the General Strike. Millions of workers – train drivers, miners, shipbuilders – down tools and bring the country to a halt.

Across Britain, industrialisation meant people were on the move as never before, leaving the farms and villages their families had occupied for generations. The rapid change from rural to urban society caused great dislocation, and although knowledge of science and medicine also improved alongside industrial advances, for many people the adverse side effects of Britain's economic blossoming were poverty and deprivation.

Age of Empire

Despite the social turmoil of the early 19th century, by the time Queen Victoria took the throne in 1837 Britain's factories dominated world trade and British fleets dominated the oceans. The rest of the 19th century was seen as Britain's Golden Age.

Victoria ruled a proud nation at home and great swaths of territories abroad, from Canada through much of Africa and India to Australia and New Zealand, trumpeted as 'the empire on which the sun never sets'.

The times were optimistic, but it wasn't all tub-thumping jingoism. Prime Minister Disraeli, who rose to office in 1868, and his successor William Gladstone, also introduced social reforms to address the worst excesses of the Industrial Revolution. Education became universal, trade unions were legalised and the right to vote was extended in a series of reform acts, finally being granted to all men over the age of 21 in 1918, and to all women in 1928.

At its height, the British Empire covered 20% of the land area of the earth, which contained a quarter of the world's population.

World War I

When Queen Victoria died in 1901, it seemed Britain's energy fizzled out too. The new king, Edward VII, ushered in the relaxed Edwardian era – and a long period of decline.

Meanwhile, in continental Europe, other states were more active: four restless military powers (Russia, Austria-Hungary, Turkey and Germany) focused their sabre-rattling on the Balkan states, and the assassination of Archduke Ferdinand in Sarajevo in 1914 finally sparked a clash that became the 'Great War' we now call World War I. Soldiers from Britain and Allied countries were drawn into a conflict of horrendous slaughter, most infamously on the killing fields of Flanders and the beaches of Gallipoli.

By the war's weary end in 1918, over a million Britons had died, plus millions more from many other countries, and there was hardly a street or village untouched by death, as the sobering lists of names on war memorials all over Britain still show.

Disillusion & Depression

For the soldiers who did return from WWI, the war had created disillusion and a questioning of the social order. Many supported the ideals of a relatively new political force, the Labour Party, to represent the working class.

1939–45
WWII rages across Europe, and much of Africa and Asia. Britain and the Allies, including America, Russia, Australia, India and New Zealand, eventually defeat the armies of Germany, Japan and Italy.

1946–48
The Labour Party nationalises key industries such as shipyards, coal mines and steel foundries. Britain's 'big four' train companies are combined into British Railways.

1948
Aneurin Bevan, the health minister in the Labour government, launches the National Health Service – the core of Britain as a 'welfare state'.

1952
Princess Elizabeth becomes Queen Elizabeth II when her father, George VI, dies. Her coronation takes place in Westminster Abbey in June 1953.

Meanwhile, the bitter Anglo-Irish War (1919–21) saw most of Ireland achieving full independence from Britain. Six counties in the north remained British, creating a new political entity called the United Kingdom of Great Britain and Northern Ireland. But the decision to partition the island of Ireland was to have long-term repercussions that still dominate political agendas in both the UK and the Republic of Ireland today.

The Labour Party won for the first time in the 1923 election, in coalition with the Liberals. James Ramsay MacDonald was the first Labour prime minister, but by the mid-1920s the right-wing Conservatives were back. The world economy was soon in decline and in the 1930s the Great Depression meant another decade of misery and political upheaval.

One of the finest novels about WWI is *Birdsong* by Sebastian Faulks. Understated, perfectly paced and intensely moving, it tells of passion, fear, waste, incompetent generals and the poor bloody infantry.

World War II

In 1933 Adolf Hitler came to power in Germany and in 1939 Germany invaded Poland, once again drawing Britain into war. The German army swept through Europe and pushed back British forces to the beaches of Dunkirk (northern France) in June 1940. An extraordinary flotilla of rescue vessels turned total disaster into a brave defeat, an event that is still remembered with pride and sadness every year in Britain.

By mid-1940 most of Europe was controlled by Germany. In Russia, Stalin had negotiated a peace agreement. The USA was neutral, leaving Britain virtually isolated. Into this arena came a new prime minister, Winston Churchill.

Between September 1940 and May 1941, the German air force launched the Blitz, a series of (mainly night-time) bombing raids on London and other cities. Despite this, morale in Britain remained strong, thanks partly to Churchill's regular radio broadcasts. In late 1941 the USA entered the war, and the tide began to turn.

By 1944 Germany was in retreat. Russia pushed back from the east, and Britain, the USA and other Allies were again on the beaches of France. The Normandy landings (or D-Day, as they are better remembered) marked the start of the liberation of Europe's western side. By 1945 Hitler was dead and the war was finally over.

D-Day in Figures

Largest military armada in history

More than 5000 ships

Approximately 150,000 Allied troops landed

Campaign time: four days

Swinging & Sliding

Despite victory in WWII, there was an unexpected swing on the political front in 1945. An electorate tired of war and hungry for change tumbled Churchill's Conservatives in favour of the Labour Party.

In 1952 George VI was succeeded by his daughter Elizabeth II and, following the trend set by earlier queens Elizabeth I and Victoria, she has remained on the throne for over six decades, overseeing a period of massive social and economic change.

1955 & 1959

Cardiff is declared the Welsh capital in 1955, and Wales gets its own official flag (the red dragon on a green and white field) in 1959.

1960s

Many of Britain's African and Caribbean colonies achieve independence, and the Swinging Sixties (and a band of mop-tops from Liverpool) turn London into a capital of cool.

1970s

The discovery of oil and gas in the North Sea brings new prosperity to Aberdeen in Scotland and the surrounding area, and also to the Shetland Islands.

1971

Britain adopts the 'decimal' currency (one pound equals 100 pence) and drops the ancient system of one pound equals 20 shillings or 240 pennies.

By the late 1950s, recovery was strong enough for Prime Minister Harold Macmillan to famously remind the British people they had 'never had it so good'. By the time the 1960s had started, grey old Britain was suddenly more fun and lively than it had been for generations. In 1965, Britain's wartime saviour, Sir Winston Churchill, died at the age of 91. He was given a full state funeral, a ceremony usually reserved for the nation's sovereign – one of only a handful of non-royals ever to receive the honour.

Although the 1960s were swinging, the 1970s saw an economic slide thanks to a grim combination of inflation, the oil crisis and international competition. The rest of the decade was marked by strikes, disputes and all-round gloom.

Neither the Conservatives (also known as the Tories), under Edward Heath, nor Labour, under Harold Wilson and Jim Callaghan, proved capable of controlling the strife. The British public had had enough, and in the elections of 1979 the Conservatives won a landslide victory, led by a little-known politician named Margaret Thatcher.

The Thatcher Years

Soon everyone had heard of Margaret Thatcher. Love her or hate her, no one could argue that her methods weren't dramatic. Looking back from a 21st-century vantage point, most commentators agree that by economic measures the Thatcher government's policies were largely successful, but by social measures they were a failure and created a polarised Britain: on one side were the people who gained from the prosperous wave of opportunities in the 'new' industries, while on the other side were those left unemployed and dispossessed by the decline of the 'old' industries such as coal mining and steel production.

WINSTON CHURCHILL

Born in 1874 to an aristocratic family, Winston Churchill is Britain's most famous prime minister. As a young man he joined the British Army and saw action in India and Africa. He was first elected to parliament as a Conservative MP (Member of Parliament) in 1900, and held various ministerial positions through the 1920s.

In 1939 Britain entered WWII, and by 1940 Churchill was prime minister, taking additional responsibility as minister of defence. Hitler had expected an easy victory, but Churchill's extraordinary dedication, not to mention his radio speeches (famously offering nothing but 'blood, toil, tears and sweat' and promising to 'fight on the beaches'), inspired the British people to resist.

Between July and October 1940 the Royal Air Force withstood Germany's aerial raids to win what became known as the Battle of Britain, a major turning point in the war – in Churchill's words of praise for the RAF, 'never was so much owed by so many to so few'. It was an audacious strategy, but it paid off and Churchill was rightly lauded as a national hero.

1979

A Conservative government led by Margaret Thatcher wins the national election, a major milestone of Britain's 20th-century history, ushering in a decade of dramatic political and social change.

1982

Britain is victorious in a war against Argentina over the invasion of the Falkland Islands, leading to a rise in patriotic sentiment.

1990

Mrs Thatcher is ousted as leader and the Conservative Party enters a period of decline but remains in power thanks to inept Labour opposition.

1992

Labour remains divided between traditionalists and modernists. The Conservatives, under their new leader John Major, confound the pundits and unexpectedly win the general election.

Despite, or perhaps thanks to, policies that were frequently described as uncompromising, Margaret Thatcher was, by 1988, the longest-serving British prime minister of the 20th century.

New Labour, New Millennium

Margaret Thatcher was replaced as leader by John Major in 1990 and voters, still regarding Labour with suspicion, gave the Conservatives an unexpected win in the 1992 election. Labour reinvented itself in the succeeding years and in the 1997 election 'New' Labour swept to power under a fresh-faced leader called Tony Blair.

Blair and the Labour Party enjoyed an extended honeymoon period, and the next election (in 2001) was another walkover. The Conservative Party continued to struggle, allowing Labour to win a historic third term in 2005, and a year later Blair became the longest-serving Labour prime minister in British history.

In May 2010 a record 13 years of Labour rule came to an end, and a coalition government (the first in the UK since WWII) was formed between the Conservatives and the Liberal Democrats. It was an experiment that ended disastrously for the Lib Dems at the 2015 general election: they lost 49 seats, and were left with just eight MPs. The same vote left the defeated Labour Party searching for a new identity, and the Conservatives back in sole charge under David Cameron.

The six decades since the end of WWII are neatly covered in *A History of Modern Britain*, a handy overview focusing on political events, by TV presenter and commentator Andrew Marr.

Brexit & Boris

In 2016, partly to appease increasing pressure from the right-wing UK Independence Party (UKIP), run by its contentious and ferociously anti-EU leader Nigel Farage, David Cameron decided to hold a referendum on Britain's membership of the EU. The main parties (Conservative, Labour and Liberal Democrat) advocated remaining, but voters elected to leave 52% to 48% – a seismic shock that shook the nation to its core.

Cameron resigned immediately after the vote, and was succeeded by former home secretary Theresa May, whose premiership was dominated by wrangling over the Brexit issue. In 2017 a rash decision to hold a snap general election resulted in a hung parliament. Unexpectedly, Labour leader Jeremy Corbyn's leftist agenda proved popular with the public – particularly with disillusioned younger voters.

Hamstrung by a hung parliament, the rest of May's premiership was dogged with problems as she struggled to secure a deal with the EU that was acceptable to the right wing of her party, who advocated a 'no deal' exit to trade on World Trade Organisation terms (a highly risky proposition that many experts argued would deliver a hammer blow to the UK economy).

Eventually May was forced from power in 2019, to be replaced by the populist, pro-Brexit ex-London mayor Boris Johnson and his key adviser,

In 2017's *Dunkirk*, British director Christopher Nolan delivered a haunting depiction of the evacuation of British troops from northern France in May 1940. Its stars included Kenneth Branagh, Mark Rylance, Tom Hardy, and pop singer Harry Styles in his first film role.

1997
The general election sees Tony Blair lead 'New' Labour to victory in the polls, with a record-breaking parliamentary majority, ending almost 20 years of Tory rule.

1999
The first National Assembly is elected for Wales, with the members sitting in a new building in Cardiff; Rhodri Morgan becomes First Minister.

1999–2004
Scottish Parliament is convened for the first time on 12 May 1999. Five years later, after plenty of scandal and huge sums of money, a new parliament building is opened at Holyrood in Edinburgh.

2001
Tony Blair and Labour continue to enjoy a honeymoon period, winning the 2001 general election, although their majority is reduced.

BREXIT: WHAT HAPPENED?

On Thursday 23 June 2016, the UK collectively made the most important choice in its modern history – the decision to leave the European Union after more than four decades of membership. In the 2016 referendum, 17.4 million people opted to Leave, versus 16.1m who preferred to Remain – a 52:48% split. It was an astonishingly close result that reflected passionately held opinions on either side – and one which involved its fair share of questionable campaign tactics, political subterfuge and social media shenanigans. The Vote Leave campaign's message to 'Take Back Control' resonated powerfully with the British public – even if they never quite spelled out exactly what that meant. Whether you're an ardent Brexiteer or a sceptical Remoaner, like it or not, the UK voted to leave the EU – the first nation ever to have done so.

In truth, it was a decision decades in the making. After joining the EU in 1973, the UK's relationship was always complicated. While the EU's instincts were towards ever closer integration – especially after the advent of the euro in 1999 – the UK's instincts were nearly always in the opposite direction. The 'Eurosceptics', as they were dubbed, remained a powerful force in parliament, and as successive prime ministers (including Margaret Thatcher, John Major and ultimately David Cameron) found to their cost, the European question was almost impossible to solve to everyone's satisfaction. And as the referendum showed, it wasn't just the UK's political parties that were divided about EU membership – its people were, too.

But while the UK may have voted for Brexit, quite what that means is another question altogether. Does it mean a relatively close relationship with integrated markets and open borders? Or does it mean a clean break in which the UK's laws, standards and trading arrangements diverge wildly from those in the rest of Europe? This is the problem the UK has experienced since 2016: a Yes-No might tell you what most of the nation wants, but it certainly doesn't tell you how to achieve it.

Dominic Cummings – the men who had successfully led the Vote Leave campaign in the European referendum. The following months descended into fierce parliamentary division, as Johnson attempted to force through his hard-line Brexit strategy against the wishes of more moderate MPs (using a variety of arcane strategies, including 'proroguing', or forcibly suspending, parliament).

Finally, to try to seize the agenda, Johnson called an unusual December election in 2019, running on a simple slogan of 'Get Brexit Done'. Unexpectedly, he won a 74-seat majority – the largest since Margaret Thatcher in 1987 – and, even more astonishingly, won many seats in the industrial heartlands of England and Wales, traditionally Labour strongholds. Crushed by his defeat, leader of the Labour Party Jeremy Corbyn resigned, and was replaced by ex-Attorney General, Sir Keir Starmer.

2003
Britain joins America and other countries in the invasion of Iraq, initially with some support from parliament and the public, despite large anti-war street demonstrations in London and other cities.

2007
The Government of Wales Bill heralds the largest transfer of power from Westminster to Cardiff since the founding of the National Assembly.

2010
Labour is narrowly defeated in the general election as the minority Liberal Democrats align with the Conservatives to form the first coalition government in Britain's postwar history.

2016
A referendum is held asking the question 'Should the UK remain a member of the EU or leave the EU?' The result was: 52% Leave, 48% Remain.

Coronavirus

Buoyed by his new majority, Johnson quickly set about enacting his Brexit agenda. The UK formally exited the EU on 31 January 2020, and entered a one-year transition period to try to negotiate the terms of a UK-EU trade deal, with the final deadline on 1 January 2021. Johnson and his colleagues promised economic prosperity whatever the outcome, while others fretted about what a 'no deal' exit might mean for jobs, trade and the economy.

But Johnson's best-laid plans were derailed in early 2020 when the coronavirus pandemic swept across the country. Suffering a huge spike in cases – among the worst in the EU – and fearing the health service would be overwhelmed, Britain entered a six-week period of lockdown, and the government announced a series of unprecedented measures to support the economy through the crisis. Scotland and Wales also decided to follow the national lockdown.

The nation emerged from lockdown in early summer, only to run straight into a second wave again in late 2020. This time Johnson decided on a series of targeted regional lockdowns, a strategy which proved unpopular with local mayors. Faced with stubbornly high infection rates, England entered a second, month-long lockdown in November 2020, while Scotland and Wales increasingly diverged from the UK-wide strategy of early 2020 with their own lockdowns and infection control initiatives.

Meanwhile, the Brexit saga continued to roll on, with negotiations continuing well into late 2020. Eventually, a deal was agreed at the very last minute on Christmas Eve 2020 which finally paved the way for Britain to formally exit the EU just a week later.

Although a damaging 'no deal' exit had been avoided, since the agreement was struck there have been a number of areas where the 'deal' has led to less than satisfactory outcomes - for example for the UK's shellfishing industry, which has found itself unable to export its goods to the EU due to the extra paperwork and customs declarations involved. Similarly, many consumers and small exporters have found themselves facing extra import duties and customs charges due to the fact that the UK is no longer within the EU's single market. But it's not all been negative: the UK's response to procuring and distributing Covid-19 vaccines has been markedly more successful than the lumbering response of the EU, for example, proof (so the Brexiteers claim) of what a good decision leaving the EU was.

In truth, it's still too early to say what the true outcome of Brexit will be - but for now, the main dividend seems to have been plenty of extra bureaucracy, and a whole lot more paperwork.

2017

Conservatives call a snap general election resulting in a hung parliament. Northern Ireland's Democratic Unionist Party (DUP) supports the Conservatives in forming a minority government.

2018

Prince Harry marries Meghan Markle, the first member of the royal family to wed a person of mixed race. New Prime Minister Boris Johnson calls another election and wins an unexpectedly large majority.

2019

In the Covid-19 pandemic, Britain is one of Europe's worst-affected nations, with similar numbers of cases and death rates to France and Spain, but markedly fewer than Germany.

2021

After years of wrangling, Britain formally exits the European Union on 1 January 2021 after 48 years of membership.

The British Table

There's been nothing short of a revolution in British food over the last 20 years. Celebrity chefs, Michelin-starred restaurants, local markets and cool cafes abound these days, and you'll be able to find something good to eat – and drink – no matter where you travel.

Eating in Britain

One of the great joys of eating in Britain is the rich stew of culinary influences that have contributed to modern British dining. Generations of immigrants have all added their own dash of spice to the national palate: Brits are just as likely to name chicken tikka masala, pizza or kung po as their favourite dish these days. Especially in bigger cities, the range of food on offer is huge: Japanese, Vietnamese, Korean, Lebanese, Indian, French and Italian are just a few of the more common cuisines.

Above Full English breakfast

Provenance is an increasingly important issue, as chefs and restaurants look to celebrate their local specialities, support small producers and cut down on food miles. You'll often see menus proudly proclaiming their local credentials, sometimes even going as far as naming individual farmers and growers. The notable exception is the chain restaurants, which still have a long way to go.

Plant-based eating is another rapidly growing trend. Gone are the days when vegetarians would struggle to find a single dish they could eat on a menu; there's generally a good choice these days, and veganism in particular is gaining ground fast.

That being said, there are a couple of British classics that remain evergreen: the fish-and-chip supper and the traditional Sunday roast remain highlights of the week for many Brits.

Britain's most popular restaurant dish is chicken tikka masala, an 'Indian' curry dish created specifically for the British palate and unheard of in India itself.

The Full British

The British day is still punctuated by the three traditional meals of breakfast, lunch and dinner (or supper, as it's sometimes known) – although it has to be said, few people have time for a sit-down lunch, except at weekends.

Breakfast

Many people in Britain make do with toast or a bowl of cereal before dashing to work, but visitors staying in hotels and B&Bs will undoubtedly encounter the 'full English breakfast' – or one of its regional equivalents. This usually consists of bacon, sausages, eggs, tomatoes, mushrooms, baked beans and fried bread. In Scotland the 'full Scottish breakfast' might include tattie scones (potato bread) instead of fried bread. In Wales you may be offered laver bread, which is not a bread at all but seaweed – a tasty speciality often served with oatmeal and bacon on toast. In northern England you may get black pudding (blood sausage). And just in case you thought this insufficient, it's still preceded by cereal, and followed by toast and marmalade or jam.

If you don't feel like eating half a farmyard in the morning, most places offer a lighter alternative or a 'continental breakfast' of croissants, pastries, granola and so on. Sometimes you might come across kippers (smoked herring).

The Scottish dish of haggis is a staple at celebrations like Hogmanay and Burns Night, but it has the most unappetising ingredient list of any British dish (offal minced with oatmeal, suet and spices, wrapped up in a sheep's stomach and boiled). It's traditionally eaten with 'neeps and tatties' (turnips and potatoes).

Lunch

One of the many great inventions that Britain gave the world is the sandwich, often eaten as a midday meal. Slapping a slice of cheese or ham between two bits of bread may seem a simple concept, but no one apparently thought of it until the 18th century, when the Earl of Sandwich (his title comes from the southeast England town of Sandwich that originally got its name from the Viking word for sandy beach) ordered his servants to bring cold meat between bread so he could keep working at his desk, or, as some historians claim, continue playing cards late at night.

Another lunch classic that perhaps epitomises British food more than any other – especially in pubs – is the ploughman's lunch. Basically it's bread and cheese, and although hearty yokels probably did carry such

NO SMOKE, THANK YOU

All restaurants and cafes in Britain are nonsmoking throughout. Virtually all pubs have the same rule, which is why there's often a small crowd of smokers standing on the pavement outside, though some places provide specific outdoor smoking areas. Smoking is permitted in pub gardens, so non-smokers sometimes need to go *inside* to escape the fumes.

food to the fields in days of yore, the meal is actually a modern phenomenon. It was invented in the 1960s by the marketing chief of the national cheesemakers' organisation as a way to boost consumption, neatly cashing in on public nostalgia and fondness for tradition.

The ploughman's is usually served with butter, salad, pickle, pickled onion and dressings. At some pubs you get a selection of cheeses. You'll also find other variations, such as a farmer's lunch (bread and chicken), stockman's lunch (bread and ham), Frenchman's lunch (brie and baguette) and fisherman's lunch (you guessed it, with fish).

For cheese and bread in a different combination, try Welsh rarebit – posh cheese on toast, seasoned and flavoured with butter, milk and sometimes beer. For a takeaway lunch in Scotland, look out for Forfar bridies (pastry turnovers filled with minced beef and onion).

Few British foods are as divisive as Marmite – a strong, tangy spread made from yeast extract, which many people love to spread on buttered toast in the morning. An equal number simply can't stand the stuff – something that Marmite's makers embraced with their 'love it or hate it' ad campaign.

Dinner

While the traditional idea of 'meat and two veg' was an evening staple for many decades, the British have embraced global cuisine with gusto, and you're now just as likely to find a curry, a pizza or a bowl of pasta on the dinner table as you are a serving of chops, chips and peas. The popularity of TV cooking shows and the profusion of celebrity chef cookbooks has helped expand Britain's culinary repertoire exponentially in recent years, and these days most Brits are pretty cosmopolitan in their tastes.

Takeaways ('takeouts' to Americans) are often the dinner choice of many Brits. Curries are particularly popular: most British towns have at least one decent Indian restaurant, and in northern cities especially, the choice can be bewildering (Birmingham even has an entire curry district known as the 'Balti Triangle'). Chinese, Thai and Vietnamese are other possible options – although it's worth noting that the British versions of many ethnic dishes often aren't that close to the originals (Thai food tends not to be nearly as spicy as it is in Thailand, for example, and Chinese food often has a lot more sauce).

One tradition that hasn't changed all that much is the roast dinner, customarily eaten for Sunday lunch. The classic is roast beef (always roast, never 'roasted'), although pork, chicken and lamb are equally popular, and vegetarians/vegans will probably find themselves tucking into some kind of variant on a nut roast. The traditional accompaniments are Yorkshire pudding (portions of crispy baked batter), a selection of vegetables, and lashings of gravy.

And then, of course, there's fish and chips: crispy battered white fish (usually cod or haddock) served with thick-cut chips and ideally eaten somewhere near the seaside. It will be seasoned with salt and vinegar if you wish, and served with a choice of tomato ketchup or brown sauce. The quality varies a lot, so it's worth asking locals to recommend their favourite 'chippie' – they'll usually know the best place nearby to go.

Britain's best-known cheese is cheddar – a strong, nutty hard cheese that's aged for several months and is an essential part of a ploughman's lunch. It gets its name from the village of Cheddar in Somerset; the cheese used to be kept in limestone caves nearby.

Puddings & Desserts

In British English, 'pudding' has two meanings: the course that comes after the main course (ie dessert); and a type of food that might be sweet (such as Bakewell pudding) or savoury (such as Yorkshire pudding).

A classic British dessert is crumble: a fruit base (often apple or rhubarb), stewed and sweetened, then topped with a crunchy mix of flour, butter and more sugar, and served with custard or ice cream.

Scotland's classic pudding is 'clootie dumpling' (a fruit pudding wrapped in a cotton cloth, or *cloot* in Scots dialect, while being steamed). Other sweets include cranachan, whipped cream flavoured with whisky and mixed with toasted oatmeal and raspberries, and Atholl brose, a mixture of cream, whisky and honey, flavoured with oatmeal.

Birmingham balti

Other favourite British puddings include treacle sponge, bread-and-butter pudding and plum pudding, a dome-shaped cake with fruit, nuts and brandy or rum, traditionally eaten at Christmas, when it's called – surprise, surprise – Christmas pudding. This pudding is steamed (rather than baked), cut into slices and served with brandy butter.

While key ingredients of most puddings are self-explanatory, they are perhaps not so obvious for another well-loved favourite: spotted dick. The origin of 'dick' in this context is unclear (it may be a corruption of 'dough' or derived from the German *dicht,* meaning 'thick', or even from 'spotted dog'), but the ingredients are easy: it's just a white suet pudding dotted with blackcurrants. Plus sugar, of course. Most British puddings have loads of butter or loads of sugar, preferably both. Light, subtle and healthy? No chance.

Toad-in-the-hole is a curiously named dish of Yorkshire pudding and sausages cooked together. The sausages are said to resemble a toad peeking from his hole.

Drinking in Britain

The drinks most associated with Britain are tea, beer and whisky. The first two are unlike drinks of the same name found elsewhere in the world, and all three are well worth sampling on your travels around the country.

Tea & Coffee

Britain, famously, is a nation of tea-drinkers – a legacy of its colonial past. Tea has an almost spiritual importance to the British: in times of trouble and stress, putting on the kettle is almost a British reflex (even if most people use a teabag rather than a teapot these days).

The Brits drink their tea hot and always with milk; sugar is optional. Everyone takes their tea differently: some people like it sweet with lots of milk, others bitter with just a dash. A controversial debate still rages over whether the milk should be put in before or after the hot water is added;

if you want to kick off a heated discussion, this is an excellent topic to bring up.

Despite tea's perennial popularity, the Brits are big coffee-drinkers too. On average, Britain consumes 165 million cups a day and the coffee market is worth almost £700 million a year (but with the prices some coffee shops charge, maybe that's not surprising).

In medieval times, labourers often received some of their wages as 'small beer' – a weak ale typically between 0.5% and 2% ABV. Since the ale had been fermented and brewed, it was usually very safe to drink – unlike water, which in pre-sanitation days frequently carried all kinds of diseases and pathogens.

Beer & Cider

British beer typically ranges from dark brown to amber in colour, and is often served at room temperature. Technically it's ale, and known as 'bitter' (or 'heavy' in Scotland). This is to distinguish it from lager – the drink that most of the rest of the world calls 'beer', which is generally yellow and served cold.

Ale that's brewed and served traditionally is called 'real ale' or 'cask ale' to distinguish it from mass-produced brands, and there are many, many regional varieties. But be ready! If you're used to drinking beer elsewhere, a British brew will be a surprise – it's nearly always flat (uncarbonated) and often warm. This is partly to do with Britain's climate, and partly to do with the beer being served by hand pump rather than gas pressure. Most important, though, is the flavour: traditional British beer doesn't need to be chilled or fizzed to make it palatable. Another key feature is that real ale must be properly stored, which usually means a willingness on the part of the pub landlord to put in the effort to ensure the ale tastes as it should.

On hot summer days, you could go for shandy – beer and lemonade mixed in equal quantities. You'll usually need to specify 'lager shandy' or 'bitter shandy'.

The increasing popularity of real ales and a backlash against the big brewing conglomerates has seen a huge rise in the number of craft brewers and microbreweries – in 2020 it was estimated that there were nearly 2000 sprinkled right across Britain, with more than a hundred in London alone.

If beer doesn't tickle your palate, try cider – available in sweet and dry varieties and, increasingly, as craft cider, often with various fruit or herbal flavours added. In western parts of England, notably Herefordshire and the southwestern counties of Devon and Somerset, you could try 'scrumpy', a very strong dry cider traditionally made from local apples. Many pubs serve it straight from the barrel.

THE CORNISH PASTY

A favourite speciality in southwest England is the Cornish pasty. A mix of cooked meat and vegetables wrapped in pastry, it originated as an all-in-one-lunch pack that tin miners carried underground and left on a ledge ready for mealtime. So that pasties weren't mixed up, they were marked with their owner's initials – always at one end, so the miner could eat half and safely leave the rest to snack on later without it mistakenly disappearing into the mouth of a workmate. Before going back to the surface, the miners traditionally left the last few crumbs of the pasty as a gift for the spirits of the mine, known as 'knockers', to ensure a safe shift the next day.

Since 2015, the Cornish pasty has had Protected Geographical Indication status – meaning that by law, only pasties made in Cornwall according to a strict set of guidelines can call themselves Cornish pasties. Beware pale imitations – if you want to taste a proper pasty, to Cornwall you must go.

Other protected UK products include Melton Mowbray pork pie, Newmarket sausage, Stornoway black pudding, Cumberland sausage, Arbroath smokies, Gloucestershire Old Spot pork, Isle of Man lamb and a whole smorgasbord of cheeses (Buxton Blue, Yorkshire Wensleydale and Westcountry farmhouse cheddar cheese, to name a few).

Top Drinking outside a pub, London

Bottom Spotted dick with fresh cream

Tullabardine distillery

Wine

Many visitors are surprised to learn that wine is produced in Britain, and has been since the time of the Romans. Today, more than 400 vineyards produce between three and four million bottles a year – many highly regarded and frequently winning major awards. English sparkling wines have been a particular success story, especially those produced in south-east England where the chalky soil and climatic conditions are similar to those of the Champagne region in France.

The Campaign for Real Ale promotes the understanding of traditional British beer. Look for endorsement stickers on pub windows. For more info, see www.camra.org.uk.

Whisky & Spirits

The spirit most visitors associate with Britain – and especially Scotland – is whisky (note the spelling – it's Irish whiskey that has an 'e'). There's a big difference between single-malt whisky, made purely from malted barley in a single distillery, and blended whisky, made from a blend of cheaper grain whisky and malt whiskies from several distilleries.

A single malt, like a fine wine, somehow captures the terroir or essence of the place where it was made and matured – a combination of the water, the barley, the peat smoke, the oak barrels in which it was aged and (in the case of certain coastal distilleries) the sea air and salt spray. Each distillation varies from the one before, like different vintages from the same vineyard.

To help you find the best ales and a fine pub to drink them in, check out the *Good Beer Guide to Great Britain*, by the Campaign for Real Ale, and the *Good Pub Guide*, by Fiona Stapley.

Gin has taken off in a massive way, too – there's now a huge and growing number of small craft distilleries across Britain, many of which also produce other spirits including vodka, rum and sometimes fruit liqueurs.

Bars & Pubs

In Britain the difference between a bar and a pub is vague, but generally bars are a bit smarter and have a slightly more modern vibe. Drinks are

English craft beers

more expensive, too, unless there's a gallon-of-vodka-and-Red-Bull-for-a-fiver promotion – which there often is.

As well as beer, cider and wine, pubs and bars offer the usual choice of spirits, often served with a 'mixer', producing favourites such as gin and tonic, rum and coke, and vodka and lime. These drinks are served in measures called 'singles' and 'doubles'. A single can be either 25mL or 35mL (depending on the bar) – just over one US fluid ounce. A double is 50mL or 70mL – still disappointingly small when compared with measures in other countries. Note that traditional, old-fashioned village pubs are very unlikely to serve cocktails – although more modern establishments, gastropubs and city bars will have a much better choice.

And while we're serving up warnings, here are two more. First, if you see a pub calling itself a 'free house', it's simply a place that doesn't belong to a brewery or pub company, and thus is 'free' to sell any brand of beer. Unfortunately, it doesn't mean the booze is free of charge.

Second, remember that drinks in British pubs are almost always ordered and paid for at the bar. You can always spot the tourists – they're the ones sitting forlornly at a table hoping to spot a waiter. Pubs that serve food are an exception, however: many, but by no means all, offer table service.

It's not usual to tip pub and bar staff. However, if you're ordering a large round, or the service has been good all evening, you can say to the person behind the bar '...and one for yourself'. They may not have a drink, but they'll add the monetary equivalent to the total you pay and keep it as a tip.

Many towns and cities in England hold farmers markets – a chance for food producers large and small to sell direct to the public. For more info and a database, see www.localfoods.org.uk.

Architecture in Britain

The history of British architecture spans more than four millennia, from the mysterious stone circles of Stonehenge and Callanish to the glittering skyscrapers of modern London. The country's built heritage includes Roman baths and parish churches, mighty castles and magnificent cathedrals, humble cottages and grand stately homes, and exploring it all is one of the great joys of a visit to Britain.

Above London (p68) skyline with Tower Bridge and the Shard

Early Foundations

The oldest surviving structures in Britain are the grass-covered mounds of earth called 'tumuli' or 'barrows', used as burial sites by the country's prehistoric residents. These mounds, measuring anything from a rough hemisphere just 2m high to oval domes around 5m high and 10m long, are dotted across the countryside and are especially common in areas of chalk such as Salisbury Plain and the Wiltshire Downs in southern England.

Perhaps the most famous mound, and certainly the largest and most mysterious, is Silbury Hill near Marlborough. Historians are not sure exactly why this huge conical mound was built – there's no evidence of it actually being used for burials. Theories include the possibility it was used at cultural ceremonies or in the worship of deities in the style of South American pyramids. Whatever its original purpose, it's still awe-inspiring today.

Even more impressive than the giant tumuli are the most prominent legacies of the neolithic era – the iconic stone circles of Stonehenge and Avebury, both in Wiltshire. Again, their original purpose is a mystery, providing fertile ground for hypothesis and speculation. The most recent theories suggest that Stonehenge may have been a place of pilgrimage for the sick, like modern-day Lourdes, though it was also used as a burial ground and a place of ancestor worship.

Bronze Age & Iron Age

After the neolithic era's great stone circles, the Bronze Age architecture we can see today is more domestic in scale. Hut circles from this period can still be seen in parts of Britain, most notably on Dartmoor in Devon and in parts of West Cornwall. The Scottish islands hold many of Europe's best surviving Bronze and Iron Age remains – notably the incredibly well-preserved stone village of Skara Brae in Orkney.

During the Iron Age, the early peoples of Britain began organising themselves into clans or tribes. Their legacy includes forts built to defend territory and protect from rival tribes or other invaders. Most forts consisted of a steep mound of earth behind a large circular or oval ditch; Maiden Castle in Dorset is a prominent example, but there are hundreds more to discover.

The Roman Era

Remains of the Roman Empire are found in many towns and cities (mostly in England and Wales, as the Romans didn't colonise most of what is now Scotland). There are impressive remains in Chester, Exeter and St Albans, as well as in the lavish Roman spa and bath-house complex in Bath. Britain's largest and most impressive Roman relic is the 73-mile-long sweep of Hadrian's Wall, built in the 2nd century as a defensive line stretching from coast to coast across the island. Originally intended to defend the empire's territories in the south from the marauding tribes further north, it became as much a symbol of Roman power as a fortification.

Medieval Masterpieces

In the centuries following the Norman Conquest of 1066, the perfection of the mason's art saw an explosion of architecture in stone, inspired by the two most pressing concerns of the day: religion and defence. Early structures of timber and rubble were replaced with churches, abbeys and

Conservation Organisations

National Trust (www.nationaltrust.org.uk)

National Trust for Scotland (www.nts.org.uk)

English Heritage (www.english-heritage.org.uk)

Cadw (www.cadw.wales.gov.uk)

Historic Environment Scotland (www.historicenvironment.scot)

The Callanish Standing Stones on Scotland's Isle of Lewis, dating from 3800 to 5000 years ago, are even older than those at Stonehenge and Avebury.

HOUSE & HOME

In Britain, it's not all about big houses. Alongside the stately homes, ordinary domestic architecture can still be seen in rural areas. Black-and-white 'half-timbered' houses characterise counties such as Worcestershire, brick-and-flint buildings pepper Suffolk and Sussex, and hardy, centuries-old cottages and farm buildings of slate and local stone are a feature of North Wales. In northern Scotland, the blackhouse is a classic basic dwelling, with walls of dry, unmortared stone packed with earth and a roof of straw and turf.

monasteries built in dressed stone. The round arches, squat towers and chevron decoration of the Norman or Romanesque style (11th to 12th centuries) slowly evolved into the tall pointed arches, ribbed vaults and soaring spires of the Gothic (13th to 16th centuries), a history that can often be seen all in the one church – construction often took a couple of hundred years to complete. Many cathedrals remain modern landmarks, such as Salisbury, Winchester, Canterbury and York.

Stone was also put to good use in the building of elaborate defensive structures. Castles range from the atmospheric ruins of Tintagel and Dunstanburgh, and the sturdy ramparts of Conwy and Beaumaris, to the stunning crag-top fortresses of Stirling and Edinburgh. And then there's the most impressive of them all: the Tower of London, guarding the capital for more than 900 years.

Britain's Best Castles

- *Alnwick*
- *Balmoral*
- *Beaumaris*
- *Caernarfon*
- *Caerphilly*
- *Carlisle*
- *Chepstow*
- *Conwy*
- *Edinburgh*
- *Eilean Donan*
- *Glamis*
- *Harlech*
- *Ludlow*
- *Pembroke*
- *Richmond*
- *Skipton*
- *Stirling*
- *Tintagel*

Stately Homes

The medieval period was tumultuous, but by the start of the 17th century life had become more settled and the nobility had less need for fortifications. While they were excellent for keeping out the riff-raff, castles were often too cold and draughty for comfortable aristocratic living.

Many castles underwent the home improvements of the day, with larger windows, wider staircases and better drainage installed. Others were simply abandoned for a brand-new dwelling next door, as at Hardwick Hall in Derbyshire.

Following the Civil War, the trend away from castles gathered pace, and throughout the 17th century the landed gentry developed a taste for fine 'country houses' designed by famous architects of the day. Many became the stately homes that are a major feature of the British landscape and a major attraction for visitors. Among the most extravagant are Chatsworth House and Blenheim Palace in England, Powis Castle in Wales and Floors Castle in Scotland.

The great stately homes all display the proportion, symmetry and architectural harmony that was in vogue during the 17th and 18th centuries. These styles were later reflected in the fashionable town houses of the Georgian era, most notably in the city of Bath, where the stunning Royal Crescent is the ultimate example of the genre.

Victoriana

Founded by German immigrant Nikolaus Pevsner after WWII, the Pevsner Architectural Guides are the classic travellers' handbooks of British architecture. Around 80 volumes, published between 1951 and the present day, lovingly document the significant buildings of England, Scotland and Wales.

The Victorian era was a time of great building activity. A style called Victorian Gothic (sometimes known as Gothic Revival) developed, imitating the tall, narrow windows and ornamented spires featured in the original Gothic cathedrals. The most famous example is London's Houses of Parliament and the clock tower that everyone knows as Big Ben, which was officially renamed Elizabeth Tower in 2012 to celebrate the Queen's diamond jubilee (although the name doesn't quite seem to have caught on with the general public).

A massive £79.7m restoration program means that Big Ben's noontime bongs (the clock by which most clocks and watches in Britain are set) won't ring out again until at least 2021, although the tower itself should emerge from scaffolding before that.

Other Victorian Gothic highlights in England's capital include the Natural History Museum and St Pancras train station. The style was copied all around the country, especially for civic buildings, with the finest examples including Manchester Town Hall and Glasgow City Chambers.

Industrialisation

Through the late 19th and early 20th centuries, as Britain's cities grew in size and stature, the newly moneyed middle classes built smart town houses in streets and squares. Elsewhere, the first town planners oversaw

Blenheim Palace (p201)

the construction of endless terraces of 'back-to-back' and 'two-up-two-down' houses to accommodate the massive influx of workers required for the country's factories. In South Wales, similar, though often single-storeyed, houses were built for the burgeoning numbers of coal miners. The industrial areas of Scotland saw the construction of tenements, usually three or four storeys high, with a central communal staircase and two dwellings on each floor. In many cases the terraced houses and basic tenements are not especially scenic, but they are perhaps the most enduring mark on the British architectural landscape.

One enduring feature of the British landscape is the boundaries used to divide fields since ancient times. The most common are hedgerows (mostly made of native trees and shrubs such as hazel, ash, blackthorn and alder) and drystone walls (hand-built stone walls, traditionally built without mortar).

Post-war Pains & Pride

WWII bombing damaged many of Britain's cities and the rebuilding that followed showed little regard for the overall appearance of the cities or for the lives of people who lived in them. Rows of terraces were swept away in favour of high-rise tower blocks, while the brutalist architecture of the 1950s and '60s embraced the modern and efficient building materials of steel and concrete.

Perhaps this is why the British are largely conservative in their architectural tastes. They often resent ambitious or experimental designs, especially applied to public buildings or when a building's form appears more important than its function. However, a familiar pattern unfolds: after a few years of resentment, the building is given a nickname, then it gains grudging acceptance, and finally it becomes a source of pride and affection. The British just don't like to be rushed, that's all.

The 21st Century

During the first decade of this century, many areas of Britain placed new importance on having progressive, popular architecture as part of a wider regeneration. Top examples include Manchester's Imperial War

DOMINATING THE LANDSCAPE

If you're travelling through Wales, it won't take you long to notice the country's most striking architectural asset: castles. There are about 600 in all, giving Wales the dubious honour of being Europe's most densely fortified country. Most were built in medieval times, first by William the Conqueror and then by other Anglo-Norman kings, to keep the Welsh in check. In the late 13th century Edward I built spectacular castles at Caernarfon, Harlech, Conwy and Beaumaris, now jointly listed as a Unesco World Heritage Site. Other castles to see include Rhuddlan, Denbigh, Criccieth, Raglan, Pembroke, Kidwelly, Chepstow and Caerphilly. While undeniably great for visitors, the castles are a sore point for patriotic Welsh; the writer Thomas Pennant called them the 'magnificent badge of our subjection'.

Museum North, Birmingham's Bullring shopping centre, Edinburgh's Scottish Parliament Building, the Welsh National Assembly building and the Wales Millennium Centre (both on the Cardiff waterfront), the overlapping arches of Glasgow's Scottish Exhibition and Conference Centre (affectionately called 'the Armadillo') and the Sage concert hall in Gateshead in northeast England.

The most prestigious prize in British architecture is the RIBA Stirling Prize, awarded annually to the UK's best building by the Royal Institute of British Architects (www.architecture.com).

Britain's largest and highest-profile architectural project of recent times was the Olympic Park, the centrepiece of the 2012 Olympic Games. Situated in the London suburb of Stratford, it was renamed the Queen Elizabeth Olympic Park after the games. The main Olympic Stadium – now home to West Ham United Football Club – and other arenas, including the much-admired Velodrome and Aquatics Centre, were built using cutting-edge techniques and are dramatic structures in their own right.

Meanwhile, in the centre of the capital, the Shard – a giant, pointed glass skyscraper – dominates the South Bank; at 306m, it's one of Europe's tallest buildings. On the other side of the River Thames, two more giant skyscrapers were completed in 2014: 20 Fenchurch St (thanks to its shape, nicknamed 'the Walkie-Talkie') and the slanting-walled Leadenhall Building (dubbed, inevitably, 'the Cheese Grater').

Elsewhere around the country – especially the coasts of northern England and Scotland – the most obvious examples of 21st-century architecture are the futuristic wind farms that are appearing offshore. Less obvious, perhaps, but more impactful, are the large-scale housing developments that are currently underway in many areas to try to address Britain's chronic housing shortage. In 2019 more than 170,000 new homes were built – the highest figure in 11 years.

Perhaps the best-known example of 1950/60s brutalist architecture is London's Southbank Centre. A building of its time, it was applauded when finished, then reviled for its ugliness, and is now regarded by Londoners with something close to pride and affection.

The Arts

Britain's contributions to literature, drama, cinema and music are celebrated around the world, thanks in no small part to the dominance of the English language. As you travel around Britain today you can explore artists' childhood homes, movie backdrops and literary settings aplenty – from the birthplace of Shakespeare in Stratford-upon-Avon to the Beatles' Abbey Road. Sadly, coronavirus forced many venues to temporarily close, but hopes are high they'll be able to bounce back once restrictions are lifted.

Literature

Early Writers

Much of Britain's earliest literature survives only in fragments – mainly poems, songs and sagas written in Old English. Many share close similarities with Scandinavian stories, a legacy of the influence of Viking culture on Britain's early history. One of the most important extant works is the epic poem *Beowulf*, a good-versus-evil tale in which the poem's eponymous hero defeats the evil monster Grendel. Consisting of 3182 alliterating lines, it's thought to have been written sometime between 975 and 1025, although the identity of its author is unknown.

Some early literature survives from other parts of Britain. The *Mabinogion* is a collection of folk tales discovered in medieval Welsh manuscripts dating from the 14th century, although not translated into English until the mid-19th century. Drawing on pre-Christian Celtic myths, several of the stories deal with the legendary feats of King Arthur – an evergreen subject.

The first big name in English literature is Geoffrey Chaucer, author of *The Canterbury Tales*. This mammoth collection of fables, stories and morality tales is framed around the stories told by a motley group of pilgrims (the Knight, the Wife of Bath, the Nun's Priest and so on). Varying wildly in style from sober sermon to bawdy farce, it's a rollicking read.

Next on stage: who else but the Bard himself, William Shakespeare, the world's premier playwright and, many would argue, the greatest writer ever to have lived. His canon of plays – comedies, histories and tragedies alike – continues to exert a profound influence on writers, artists and filmmakers the world over (he was also a prolific poet, with his 154 sonnets particularly revered).

The 17th & 18th Centuries

The 17th century saw the publication of John Milton's epic poem *Paradise Lost*, a literary landmark inspired by the tale of Adam and Eve's expulsion from the Garden of Eden. This was followed a few years later by the equally seminal *Pilgrim's Progress* by John Bunyan, an allegorical tale of the everyday struggle to be a good Christian.

More familiar to most are the words of *Auld Lang Syne*, penned by Scotland's national poet Robert Burns, traditionally sung at New Year. His *Address to a Haggis* is also still recited annually on Burns Night, a Scottish celebration held on 25 January (his birthday).

The *Oxford Guide to Literary Britain & Ireland*, edited by Daniel Hahn and Nicholas Robins, gives details of the towns, villages and countryside immortalised by writers, from Chaucer's Canterbury and Austen's Bath to Scott's Highlands.

No comedy captures the British sense of humour better than *Monty Python's Flying Circus*, the surreal, supremely silly sketch show that still inspires legions of fans across the world more than half a century after it first aired.

Another milestone work of this period is Daniel Defoe's *Robinson Crusoe.* On one level it's an adventure story about a man shipwrecked on an island, but it's also a discussion on civilisation, colonialism and faith. It's also been an armchair travellers' favourite since its publication in 1719.

Similarly enduring is *Gulliver's Travels* by the satirist and humorist Jonathan Swift. Often adapted as a harmless children's tale, it is actually a fierce and often biting critique of human nature, commenting on themes of pride, greed, ambition and hubris.

For a taste of surreal humour, try two of Britain's funniest (and most successful) writers: Douglas Adams *(The Hitchhiker's Guide to the Galaxy* plus sequels) and Terry Pratchett (the *Discworld* series).

The Romantic Era

As industrialisation swept Britain in the late 18th and early 19th centuries, a new generation of writers, including William Blake, John Keats, Percy Bysshe Shelley, Lord Byron and Samuel Taylor Coleridge, drew inspiration from human imagination and the natural world (in some cases aided by a dose of laudanum). Known as the 'Romantics', the best known of all was William Wordsworth; his famous line from the poem commonly known as 'Daffodils' – 'I wandered lonely as a cloud' – was inspired by a walk along the shores of Ullswater in the Lake District.

Victoriana

During the reign of Queen Victoria (1837–1901), novels displayed a growing sense of moral conscience and political comment, exemplified by Charles Dickens – arguably the greatest, and certainly the most prolific, British novelist. His books explore many pressing issues of his time: *Oliver Twist* is a tale of child pickpockets surviving in the London slums, while *Hard Times* is a critique of the excesses of capitalism.

The painter, writer, poet and visionary William Blake (1757–1827) mixed fantastical landscapes and mythological scenes with motifs drawn from classical art, religious iconography and legend. For more, see www.blakearchive.org.

Other writers such as George Eliot (or Mary Ann Evans, as she should be known – like many female writers of the period, she adopted a male pseudonym to get her works published) explored social issues against the backdrop of rural England: *Middlemarch* and *Mill on the Floss* are classics.

Many of Thomas Hardy's tales are set in in the county of Wessex, a fictionalised version of the author's Dorset home. In novels like *Tess of the D'Urbervilles* and *Far from the Madding Crowd,* Hardy explored stories of hardship, social change, unrequited love and class, underpinned by a deep love of the English countryside.

The Victorian era also gave Scotland one of its greatest novelists, Sir Walter Scott, who used historical events to tell sprawling tales of life in the mountains and glens of Scotland. *Waverley,* set during the Jacobite rebellion, and *Rob Roy*, a highly fictionalised version of the life of the Scottish outlaw and folk hero, are among his best-known works.

This was also the era of the great detective novel: popular magazines and journals gave a platform for thrilling tales by writers such as Arthur

JANE AUSTEN & THE BRONTËS

The beginning of the 19th century saw the emergence of some of English literature's best-loved female writers: Jane Austen and the Brontë sisters.

Austen's fame stems from her exquisite observations of love, friendship and passion boiling under the buttoned-up surface of middle-class convention. The location most associated with Austen is the city of Bath, where there is a small museum devoted to the writer.

Of the Brontë sisters' prodigious output, Emily Brontë's *Wuthering Heights* is the best known, an epic tale of obsession and revenge, where the dark and moody landscape plays a role as great as any human character. Charlotte Brontë's *Jane Eyre* and Anne Brontë's *The Tenant of Wildfell Hall* are classics of passion and mystery. Visitors still flock to their former home (now the Brontë Parsonage Museum) in the Yorkshire town of Haworth, perched on the Pennine moors that informed their work.

LITERARY LOCATIONS

Bath Grandeur that never tired Jane Austen's heroines.

Canterbury Synonymous with Chaucer's *Canterbury Tales*.

Edinburgh Unesco's first City of Literature, with links to Burns, Scott and Stevenson (and even JK Rowling).

Haworth Home of the Brontë sisters, surrounded by wuthering moors.

Lake District Source of inspiration for William Wordsworth.

Laugharne Dylan Thomas' home.

Stratford-upon-Avon Birthplace of William Shakespeare.

Conan Doyle, whose detective, Sherlock Holmes, continues to inspire adaptations and reimaginings more than a century later.

Modernism to Post-Modernism

Britain – and its literature – changed forever following WWI and the social disruption of the period. This fed into the work of modernist writers like DH Lawrence, whose work set out to challenge accepted conventions. *Sons and Lovers* follows the lives and loves of generations in the English Midlands as the country changes from rural idyll to industrial landscape, while his controversial exploration of sexuality in *Lady Chatterley's Lover* was banned until 1960 because of its 'obscenity'.

The changing nature of British society informed the works of other writers like Evelyn Waugh, whose *Brideshead Revisited* explored moral and social disintegration among the English aristocracy in the 1920s and '30s. Other writers like John Buchan, Daphne du Maurier and Agatha Christie concentrated on popular literature, setting frames and tropes for the mystery, suspense and thriller genres that endure to this day. JRR Tolkien, a bookish Oxford don, also gave the world the ultimate fantasy novel in his three-volume *Lord of the Rings*.

The period was also a powerful one for poetry. Modernist writers such as TS Eliot deconstructed the poetic form to reflect a fractured age, notably in enigmatic poems such as *The Love Song of Alfred J. Prufrock* and *The Wasteland*. Other poets like WH Auden, Stephen Spender and Louis MacNeice used their work for powerful political commentary.

Moat Brae, the absorbing new centre for children's literacy in Dumfries, is set in the house and garden that inspired Peter Pan.

After the trauma of WWII, writers like Graham Greene and George Orwell continued to push the novel into new and experimental areas. In books like *The Heart of the Matter*, *Our Man in Havana* and *The Quiet American*, Greene combined elements of popular genres with philosophical and funny meditations on the human condition, while in seminal books like *1984* and *Animal Farm*, Orwell combined allegory with incisive political commentary (and arguably invented the dystopian novel). The 1940s and '50s were also the heyday of perhaps the most gifted of Welsh poets, Dylan Thomas, whose *Under Milk Wood* (1954) exposed the social tensions of small-town Wales.

The 1970s and '80s saw a rash of new novelists emerge, many of whom continue to dominate the literary landscape. Martin Amis's novels deal with the absurdity and unappealing nature of modern life, such as *London Fields* and *Money*. Ian McEwan made his debut with *The Cement Garden* in 1978, and has since earned critical acclaim for his finely observed studies of the English character in works such as *Atonement* and *On Chesil Beach*. Other important names to emerge during the period include Kazuo Ishiguro, Graham Swift, Salman Rushdie and Julian Barnes.

CHILDREN'S CLASSICS

Britain's greatest literary phenomenon of the 21st century is JK Rowling's *Harry Potter* series, the seven-volume story about a boy wizard's adventures that have entertained millions of children (and many grown-ups too). The magical tales, brought vividly to life in the subsequent movie adaptations, are the latest in a long line of British children's classics. The pedigree stretches back to the works of Lewis Carroll *(Alice's Adventures in Wonderland)*, E Nesbit *(The Railway Children)*, AA Milne *(Winnie-the-Pooh)*, CS Lewis *(The Chronicles of Narnia)* and Roald Dahl *(Charlie and the Chocolate Factory, Matilda)*.

The New Millennium

As the new millennium dawned, Britain's multicultural landscape proved a rich inspiration for contemporary novelists. Hanif Kureishi sowed the seeds with his groundbreaking 1990 novel *The Buddha of Suburbia*, followed by Zadie Smith's acclaimed debut *White Teeth* in 2000, Monica Ali's *Brick Lane* in 2003 and Andrea Levy's *Small Island* in 2004.

The most successful British literary novelist of recent years has been Hilary Mantel, whose bestselling trilogy of Tudor intrigue (*Wolf Hall, Bring Up the Bodies* and *The Mirror and the Light)* became historical blockbusters (the first two instalments also won the Booker Prize).

Meanwhile, 'Tartan Noir' – crime fiction set in Scottish cities – continues to grow. Ian Rankin (known for his Edinburgh-set Inspector Rebus novels) is a master of the genre, as are Val McDermid, Louise Welsh and Christopher Brookmyre.

The British Film Institute (BFI) is dedicated to promoting film and cinema in Britain, and publishes the monthly academic journal *Sight & Sound*. See www.bfi.org.uk and www.screenonline.org.uk for complete coverage of Britain's film and TV industry.

Cinema

British cinema has a long and illustrious history, producing some of the greatest writers, actors, directors and producers ever to have graced the silver screen (even if many of them had to head to Hollywood to find their greatest success). Many major productions are still filmed in British studios and locations – although the domestic industry continues to face a constant struggle for resources.

The Silent Era

Many early directors cut their teeth in the silent film industry. The best-known of these was Alfred Hitchcock, who directed *Blackmail*, one of the first British 'talkies', in 1929, and went on to direct a string of films during the 1930s, before migrating to Hollywood in the early 1940s.

Another early export was Charles Chaplin, who was born in Walworth, London, in 1889, and found early success performing as an actor and comedian in Britain's music halls, before moving to Hollywood and becoming one of the silent era's greatest stars.

In the 1930s, a very young David Lean got his first break editing newsreels at Gaumont Studios.

Wartime to the '50s

During WWII, British films were dominated by patriotic stories designed to raise morale: *Went the Day Well?* (1942), *In Which We Serve* (1942) and *We Dive at Dawn* (1943) are prime examples of the genre. During this period David Lean directed the classic tale of repressed passion, *Brief Encounter* (1945), before graduating to Hollywood epics, including *Lawrence of Arabia* and *Doctor Zhivago*.

Another great film of the 1940s is *How Green Was My Valley*, a tale of everyday life in the coal-mining villages of Wales. Despite its stereotyped characters, absence of Welsh actors, and the fact that it was shot in a Hollywood studio, it's worth seeing for its period flavour.

After the war was over, audiences were in the mood for escape and entertainment. During the late 1940s and early '50s, Ealing Studios produced a number of eccentric British comedies, including *Passport to Pimlico* (1949), *Kind Hearts and Coronets* (1949) and *The Titfield Thunderbolt* (1953).

Other box-office hits included *Hamlet* (1948; the first British film to win an Oscar in the Best Picture category), starring Laurence Olivier, and Carol Reed's *The Third Man* (1949). In a post-war Britain still struggling with rationing and food shortages, tales of heroic derring-do such as *The Dam Busters* (1955) and comedies like *Whisky Galore!* (1949; a remake was filmed in 2016) helped lift the national mood.

The Ladykillers (1955) is a classic Ealing comedy about a band of hapless bank robbers holed up in a London guesthouse, and features Alec Guinness sporting quite possibly the most outrageous set of false teeth ever captured on celluloid.

The '60s & The British New Wave

In the late 1950s and early '60s, 'British New Wave' and 'Free Cinema' explored the gritty realities of life in an intimate, semidocumentary style, with Lindsay Anderson and Tony Richardson crystallising the movement with films such as *This Sporting Life* (1963) and *A Taste of Honey* (1961).

At the other end of the spectrum were the *Carry On* films, packed with bawdy gags and double entendres, and starring a troupe of 'national treasures' including Barbara Windsor, Sid James and Kenneth Williams.

The 1960s saw the birth of another classic British icon: super-spy James Bond, adapted from the Ian Fleming novels and first played by Sean Connery in *Dr No* (1962). Since then over 20 Bond movies have been made, with Bond played by a series of actors from Roger Moore and George Lazenby to Pierce Brosnan and Daniel Craig.

Withnail and I (1987) is one of the great British cult comedies. Directed by Bruce Robinson, it stars Paul McGann and Richard E Grant as a pair of hapless out-of-work actors on a disastrous holiday to the Lake District.

The 1970s & '80s

The '70s were most notable for the emergence of directors such as Mike Leigh and Ken Loach, whose hard-hitting, realist dramas explored stories of everyday life across Britain. Loach's *Kes* (1969) depicted a working-class boy's relationship with a hawk, while Mike Leigh's TV dramas such as *Nuts in May* (1975) and *Abigail's Party* (1977) poked fun at the British class divide. Both directors have continued to work to the present day.

British cinema hit it big again in the early 1980s thanks to David Puttnam's hugely successful *Chariots of Fire* (1981), an Oscar-winning tale of two British athletes at the 1924 Olympics. The same year, Richard Attenborough's lavish *Gandhi* (1982) also bagged eight Academy Awards.

The 1980s were particularly strong for period drama: the British producing duo of Ismail Merchant and James Ivory made epics such as *Heat and Dust* (1983) and *A Room With A View* (1985). The '80s also saw the emergence of a brand-new TV channel, Channel 4, which invested in edgy films such as *My Beautiful Laundrette* (1985).

HAMMER HORROR

The British company Hammer Film Productions produced a string of low-budget horror films in the 1950s and '60s that have now achieved cult status. Early flicks included *The Quatermass Xperiment* (1955) and *The Curse of Frankenstein* (1957). The stars of the latter – Peter Cushing as Dr Frankenstein and Christopher Lee as the Monster – would feature in many of Hammer's best films over the next 20 years, including nine *Dracula* films and six *Frankenstein* sequels.

The studio also launched the careers of several other notable actors (including Oliver Reed, who made his debut in *The Curse of the Werewolf*; 1961) and even spawned its very own spoof, *Carry On Screaming* (1966) – the ultimate British seal of approval. From 1979 the company went into hibernation, but its fortunes revived in 2012 with the release of *The Woman in Black*, starring Harry Potter lead Daniel Radcliffe.

The '90s

In the 1990s, the massively successful *Four Weddings and a Funeral* (1994) introduced Hugh Grant in his trademark role as the likeable, self-deprecating Englishman (an archetype he reprised in subsequent hits *Notting Hill,* 1999, and *Love Actually,* 2003). In a similar feel-good vein, *The Full Monty* (1997), about a troupe of laid-off steel workers turned male strippers, became Britain's most successful film ever (until overtaken by the Harry Potter franchise in 2001).

Grittier films of the 1990s included *Trainspotting* (1996), a hard-hitting film about Edinburgh's drugged-out underworld, which launched the careers of actors Ewan McGregor and Robert Carlyle, while Mike Leigh's *Secrets and Lies* (1996), a Palme d'Or winner at Cannes, told the story of an adopted black woman who seeks out her white mother.

Other films of the decade included gangster movie *Lock, Stock and Two Smoking Barrels* (1998); *Breaking the Waves* (1996), a perfect study of culture clash in 1970s Scotland; and the Oscar-winning Austen adaptation *Sense and Sensibility* (1995) starring English doyennes Emma Thompson and Kate Winslet as the Dashwood sisters, with Hugh Grant as (you guessed it) a likeable and self-deprecating Englishman.

The decade ended with films such as *East Is East* (1999), a beautifully understated study of the clash between first- and second-generation immigrant Pakistanis in Britain, and *Billy Elliott* (2000), about a boy's quest to learn ballet and escape the slag heaps of post-industrial northern England.

Britain's main broadcasters are known for their long-running 'soaps' (soap operas) such as *EastEnders* (BBC), *Emmerdale* and *Coronation Street* (both ITV), which have collectively been running on British screens for well over a century.

The 21st Century

In the early part of the 21st century, literary adaptations provided a rich seam of material. Hits include the blockbuster Harry Potter franchise (based on the books of JK Rowling, and the most financially successful film series of all time) starring Daniel Radcliffe, as well as 2005's *The Constant Gardener* (based on a John Le Carré novel), 2007's *Atonement* (based on Ian McEwan's novel), 2011's *War Horse* (directed by Stephen Spielberg and based on Michael Morpurgo's novel), and 2012's *Anna Karenina,* directed by Joe Wright and starring Keira Knightley. *T2* (2017), the much anticipated sequel to *Trainspotting,* was based on Irvine Welsh's novel *Porno.*

Biopics are also a perennial favourite, with recent highlights including the stories of Queen Elizabeth II (*The Queen,* 2006), Queen Elizabeth I (*Elizabeth: The Golden Age,* 2007), Margaret Thatcher (*The Iron Lady,* 2011), scientist Stephen Hawking (*The Theory of Everything,* 2014) and 19th-century artist JMW Turner (*Mr Turner,* 2014).

British artist-turned-filmmaker Steve McQueen has also found major success with films including *Hunger* (2008), *Shame* (2011) and *12 Years A Slave* (2013), which won the Oscar for Best Picture. Another highly successful theatre and film director is Sam Mendes, who began his career with the Oscar-winning *American Beauty* in 1999, and has since directed a number of high-profile films, most recently *1917* (2019). Arguably the most successful of all is British-born Christopher Nolan, whose mind-bending, genre-twisting stories include *Inception* (2010), *Interstellar* (2014), *Dunkirk* (2017) and *Tenet* (2020).

Comedy is another successful area for British cinema. Building on the success of zombie spoof *Shaun of the Dead* (2004) and cop-movie spoof *Hot Fuzz* (2007), Simon Pegg and Nick Frost returned in alien-invasion spoof *The World's End* (2013), while Paul King produced two brilliant *Paddington* films that scored big at the box office.

Meanwhile, the oldest of British film franchises rolls on, with James Bond played as a tough, toned and occasionally fallible character by

Daniel Craig in *Casino Royale* (2006), *Quantum of Solace* (2008), *Skyfall* (2012) and *Spectre* (2015). Craig completed the 25th instalment in 2019, which he has said will be his last – meaning the search is on for a new Bond. Many commentators speculate that it may go next to an ethnic minority actor or, perhaps, a woman.

Pop & Rock Music

Britain's been putting the world through its musical paces ever since a mop-haired four-piece from Liverpool tuned up their Rickenbackers and became 'more popular than Jesus', to quote John Lennon.

Elvis may have invented rock-and-roll, but it was the Fab Four who transformed it into a global phenomenon, backed by the Rolling Stones, The Who, Cream, The Kinks and the other bands of the 'British Invasion'.

Glam to Punk

Glam rock swaggered in to replace peace and love in the early '70s, with Marc Bolan and David Bowie donning spandex and glittery guitars in a variety of chameleonic guises, succeeded by art-rockers Roxy Music and anthemic popsters Queen and Elton John. Meanwhile Led Zeppelin laid down the blueprint for heavy metal and hard rock, and '60s psychedelia morphed into the spacey noodlings of prog rock, epitomised by Pink Floyd, Genesis and Yes.

By the late '70s the prog bands were looking out of touch in a Britain wracked by rampant unemployment, industrial unrest and the three-day week. Flicking a giant two fingers to the establishment, punk exploded onto the scene in the late '70s, summing up the general air of doom and gloom with nihilistic lyrics and short, sharp, three-chord tunes. The Sex Pistols produced one landmark album (*Never Mind the Bollocks: Here's the Sex Pistols*), a clutch of (mostly banned) singles, and a storm of controversy, ably assisted by other punk pioneers such as The Clash, The Damned, Buzzcocks, and The Stranglers.

While punk burned itself out in a blaze of squealing guitars and ear-splitting feedback, NewWave bands including The Jam and Elvis Costello took up the punk torch, blending spiky tunes and sharp lyrics into a poppier, more radio-friendly sound. Meanwhile, The Specials, The Selecter and baggy-trousered rude boys Madness mixed punk, reggae and ska into 'two-tone' (a nod to the movement's cross-racial ethos).

The '80s

The big money and conspicuous consumption of Thatcherite Britain in the early '80s bled over into the decade's pop scene. Big hair, shiny suits and shoulder pads became the uniform of New Romantics such as Spandau Ballet, Duran Duran, and Culture Club, while the advent of synthesisers and processed beats led to the development of a new electronic sound in the music of Depeche Mode and Human League.

But the glitz and glitter of '80s pop concealed a murky underbelly: bands like The Cure, Bauhaus, and Siouxsie and the Banshees were employing doom-laden lyrics and apocalyptically heavy riffs, while the rock heritage of Led Zeppelin inspired the birth of heavy metal acts such as Iron Maiden, Judas Priest and Black Sabbath.

Meanwhile the arch-priests of miserabilism, The Smiths, fronted by extravagantly quiffed wordsmith Morrissey, summed up the disaffection of mid-'80s England in classic albums such as *The Queen Is Dead* and *Meat Is Murder*.

Dance Music & Britpop

The beats and bleeps of '80s electronica fuelled the burgeoning dance-music scene of the early '90s. Pioneering artists such as New

> The BBC is a public-service broadcaster, financed by an annual licence fee paid by every house in Britain with a TV set (rather than by advertising). This means shows are not interrupted by commercial breaks.

Order (risen from the ashes of Joy Division) and The Orb used synthesised sounds to create the soundtrack for the new ecstasy-fuelled rave culture, centred around famous clubs like Manchester's Haçienda and London's Ministry of Sound. Sub-genres such as trip-hop, drum and bass, jungle, house and big-beat cropped up in other UK cities, with key acts including Massive Attack, Portishead and the Chemical Brothers.

Manchester was also a focus for the burgeoning British 'indie' scene, driven by guitar-based bands such as The Charlatans, The Stone Roses, James, Happy Mondays and Manchester's most famous musical export, Oasis. In the late '90s indie segued into Britpop, a catch-all term covering several bands including Oasis, Pulp, Supergrass and Blur, whose distinctively British music chimed with the country's new sense of optimism following the landslide election of New Labour in 1997 (Noel and Liam Gallagher were even invited for afternoon tea at Number 10).

The Noughties & Beyond

In the new millennium, the British music scene has continued to shapeshift and reinvent itself. R&B, hip-hop and drum and bass fused into grime and dubstep, producing acts like Dizzee Rascal, Tinie Tempah and Stormzy, who have achieved crossover success despite their hard-hitting subject matter. The same spirit infuses bands like Sleaford Mods and the Idles, whose gritty sound and furious lyrics speak to a 21st-century Britain still riven by class, poverty and social divides.

The spirit of alternative and indie lives on in bands like Elbow, Muse, the Arctic Monkeys and a host of other acts, while the all-conquering Radiohead have graduated from cult, indie-tinged albums like *The Bends* and *O.K. Computer* into increasingly experimental and ambient territory.

Folk is another strongpoint, with Laura Marling and Mumford & Sons achieving major success. Another notable name is Michael Kiwanuka, whose third album *Kiwanuka*, a fusion of pop, soul and thoughtful songwriting, won the coveted Mercury Music Prize in 2020.

Pop is still tops, too. Boy bands continue to come and go, most notably One Direction, who clocked up the sales before going the way of all boy bands and splitting up in acrimonious fashion. Several singer-songwriters have proved more enduring – Adele and Ed Sheeran have taken the world by storm (Sheeran alone has sold more than 26 million albums and 100 million singles worldwide).

The works of Henry Moore and Barbara Hepworth can be seen at the Yorkshire Sculpture Park, between Sheffield and Leeds, in northern England. Hepworth is also forever associated with St Ives in Cornwall, while the Hepworth Wakefield gallery is dedicated to her life and work.

Painting & Sculpture

For many centuries, continental Europe – especially Holland, Spain, France and Italy – set the artistic agenda. The first artist with a truly British style and sensibility was arguably William Hogarth, whose riotous canvases exposed the vice and corruption of 18th-century London. His most celebrated work is *A Rake's Progress*, which kick-started a long tradition of British caricatures that can be traced right through to the work of modern-day cartoonists such as Gerald Scarfe and Steve Bell. It's displayed at Sir John Soane's Museum in London.

Portraits & Landscapes

While Hogarth was busy satirising society, other artists were hard at work showing it in its best light. The leading figures of 18th-century British portraiture were Sir Joshua Reynolds, Thomas Gainsborough and George Romney, while George Stubbs is best known for his intricate studies of animals (particularly horses). Works by these artists are displayed at the Tate Britain and the National Gallery in London.

In the 19th century, leading painters favoured the landscape. John Constable's best-known works include *Salisbury Cathedral* and *The Hay Wain*, depicting a mill in Suffolk (and now on show in the National Gallery, London), while JMW Turner was fascinated by the effects of light and colour, with his works becoming almost entirely abstract by the 1840s – vilified at the time but prefiguring the Impressionist movement that was to follow 50 years later.

Fables & Flowers

In the mid- to late 19th century, the Pre-Raphaelite movement harked back to the figurative style of classical Italian and Flemish art, tying in with the prevailing Victorian taste for fables, myths and fairy tales. Key members of the movement included Sir John Everett Millais and William Holman Hunt. Millais' *Ophelia,* showing the damsel picturesquely drowned in a river, is an excellent example of their style, and can be seen at the Tate Britain. However, one of the best collections of Pre-Raphaelite art is in the Birmingham Museum and Art Gallery.

A good friend of the Pre-Raphaelites was William Morris; he saw late-19th-century furniture and interior design as increasingly vulgar, and with Dante Gabriel Rossetti and Edward Burne-Jones founded the Arts and Crafts movement to encourage the revival of a decorative approach to features such as wallpaper, tapestries and windows. Many of his designs are still used today.

North of the border, Charles Rennie Mackintosh, fresh from the Glasgow School of Art, fast became a renowned artist, designer and architect. He is still Scotland's greatest art nouveau exponent, and much of his work remains in Glasgow. He also influenced a group of artists from the 1890s that became known as the Glasgow School (often divided into two groups: the Glasgow Boys and the Glasgow Girls), among them Margaret and Frances MacDonald, James Guthrie and EA Walton. Much of their work can be seen in the Kelvingrove Art Gallery in Glasgow.

Sticks & Stone

In the tumultuous 20th century, art became increasingly experimental, with key painters including Francis Bacon, whose work was influenced by Freudian psychoanalysis, and the Scottish Colourists – Francis Cadell, SJ Peploe, Leslie Hunter and JD Fergusson. Meanwhile, pioneering sculptors such as Henry Moore and Barbara Hepworth experimented with natural forms and new materials.

At around the same time, Welsh artist Gwen John painted introspective portraits of women friends, cats and nuns (and famously became the model and lover of French artist Rodin), while her brother Augustus John became Britain's leading portrait painter, with famous sitters such as Thomas Hardy and George Bernard Shaw. One place to admire the Johns' works is at the Glynn Vivian Art Gallery in Swansea.

Pop Art

The mid-1950s and early '60s saw an explosion of British artists plundering TV, music, advertising and popular culture for inspiration. Leaders of this new 'pop art' movement included David Hockney, who used bold colours and simple lines to depict his dachshunds and swimming pools, and Peter Blake, who designed the collage cover for The Beatles' landmark *Sgt. Pepper's Lonely Hearts Club Band* album.

The '60s also saw the rise of sculptor Anthony Caro, who held his first groundbreaking exhibition at the Whitechapel Art Gallery in 1963. Creating large abstract works in steel and bronze, he remains one of Britain's most influential sculptors.

Britart & Beyond

A new wave of British artists came to the fore in the 1990s. The movement was dubbed, inevitably, 'Britart'; its leading members included

Britain's Best Art Galleries

- *National Gallery (London)*
- *Tate Modern (London)*
- *Turner Contemporary (Margate)*
- *Sage Gateshead (Newcastle)*
- *Scottish National Gallery (Edinburgh)*
- *The Hepworth Wakefield*
- *Walker Art Gallery (Liverpool)*

Around Britain, buildings associated with notable people are marked with a (usually blue) plaque. In early 2012, a plaque was placed at 23 Heddon St in London to commemorate David Bowie's fictional pop character Ziggy Stardust.

Damien Hirst, initially famous (or infamous) for works involving pickled sharks, semi-dissected human figures and a diamond-encrusted skull entitled *For the Love of God*. His pregnant, naked and half-flayed *Verity* towers 20m high beside the harbour mouth at Ilfracombe in Devon.

Another important Britart graduate is Tracey Emin. Once considered an enfant terrible, she incurred the wrath of the tabloids for works such as *My Bed,* a messed-up bedroom scene that sold for £2.2 million in 2014, but is now a respected figure and patron of the Turner Gallery in Margate. Her 20m neon sculpture *I Want My Time With You* was installed at London's St Pancras Station in 2018, and has been interpreted as Emin's comment on the Brexit debate.

The sculptor Anish Kapoor is best known for his large outdoor installations, which often feature curved shapes and reflective materials, such as highly polished steel. You can find one of his major works, *ArcelorMittal Orbit,* in London's Queen Elizabeth Olympic Park.

The most important event in the artistic calendar is the awarding of the Turner Prize (named after JMW Turner), a high-profile (and frequently controversial) annual award for British visual artists. As well as Hirst, winners have included Martin Creed (a room with lights going on and off), Mark Wallinger (a collection of anti-war objects), Rachel Whiteread (a plaster cast of a house) and perhaps the best-known of all, Antony Gormley (the man behind the gigantic *Angel of the North,* which stands beside the busy A1 London–Edinburgh road, where millions of drivers each year can't help but see it). Gormley has a number of other public artworks around the country, including *LOOK II*, a striking new sculpture on Plymouth's waterfront.

A number of high-profile new art museums have opened in recent years, including a new extension to the Tate St Ives, the striking Turner Contemporary in Margate, the sculpture-focused Hepworth Wakefield and Plymouth's The Box, a somewhat controversial addition to the city's streets that's shaped – well, rather like a box.

Jez Butterworth is one of the UK's most successful playwrights. His 2009 state-of-England tale *Jerusalem* was one of the most successful and acclaimed plays in West End history. His 2017 work *The Ferryman*, a moving tale set in IRA-era Northern Ireland, was another smash hit, winning awards and becoming the Royal Court Theatre's fastest-selling play.

Theatre

Theatre in Britain has its roots in medieval morality plays, court jesters and travelling storytellers, but it was during the 1500s when it really took the stage. Most scholars agree that the key milestone in the story is the opening of England's first theatre, called simply The Theatre, in London in 1576. A few years later, two more theatres appeared, the Rose and the Globe, where the plays of writers like Ben Jonson, Kit Marlowe and a certain young bard by the name of William Shakespeare were performed.

WHAT A PANTOMIME!

If any British tradition is guaranteed to bemuse outsiders, it's the pantomime. This over-the-top Christmas spectacle graces stages across the land in December and January, and can trace its roots back to medieval morality plays and the British music hall. The modern incarnation is usually based on a classic fairy tale and features a mix of saucy dialogue, comedy skits, song-and-dance routines and plenty of custard-pie humour, mixed in with topical gags for the grown-ups. Tradition dictates that the leading 'boy' is played by a woman, and the leading lady, or 'dame', is played by a man. B-list celebrities, actors and soap stars famously make a small fortune hamming it up for Christmas panto, and there are always a few staple routines that everyone knows and joins in. The hero (or villain) asks 'Where's that dragon/wizard/pirate/lion?' and the audience shouts back 'He's behind you!' It's cheesy, daft and frequently surreal, but guaranteed to be great fun for the family. Oh, no it isn't! Oh, yes it is! Oh, no it isn't!

WILLIAM SHAKESPEARE

For most visitors to Britain (and for many locals) drama means just one name: Shakespeare. Born in 1564 in the Midlands town of Stratford-upon-Avon, William Shakespeare made his name in London, where most of his plays were performed at the Globe Theatre.

He started writing plays around 1585, and his early theatrical works are grouped together as 'comedies' (like *All's Well that Ends Well*, *The Taming of the Shrew* and *A Midsummer Night's Dream*) and 'histories' (like *Richard III* and *Henry V*). Later, Shakespeare moved into 'tragedies', including *Romeo and Juliet*, *Macbeth*, *Julius Caesar*, *Hamlet* and *King Lear* – complex, deeply philosophical works that continue to encourage debate and dissection more than half a millennium later.

The best place to see the Bard's plays in action is the rebuilt Globe on London's South Bank, a replica of the original which burned down in 1613, and at the theatres of the Royal Shakespeare Company in his hometown of Stratford-upon-Avon.

The debate rages on, however, about precisely how Shakespeare penned his plays. Some academics maintain he was the sole author, while others (including the well-known actor and former director of the RSC, Mark Rylance) maintain that the plays were much more likely to have been written as a collaborative effort – perhaps with other writers, or in collaboration with his troupe of actors, or perhaps both. The truth will probably never be known, but the plays will endure.

British Theatre Today

British theatre continues to be a world leader, especially in London. Other big cities boast their own top-class venues, such as the Birmingham Repertory Theatre, the Bristol Old Vic, the Chichester Festival Theatre, the Playhouse in Nottingham, the New Theatre in Cardiff and the Royal Lyceum in Edinburgh.

For big names, most people head for London's West End, where famous spots include the Shaftesbury, the Adelphi, and the Theatre Royal, Drury Lane. Such venues are mostly the preserve of classic plays, including *The Mousetrap*, the legendary whodunnit and world's longest-running play, showing continuously since 1952.

West End Musicals

As well as drama, the West End means musicals, with a long history of crowd-pullers such as *Cats*, *The Wizard of Oz*, *Les Misérables*, *Sweeney Todd*, *The Phantom of the Opera* and *The Lion King*.

Many of today's shows raid the pop world for material, such as *We Will Rock You*, inspired by the music of Queen, and Abba-based *Mamma Mia!* In 2012, *Matilda*, based on the novel by Roald Dahl, broke records by winning seven Olivier Awards, the most prestigious prize in British theatre, and four US Tony Awards in 2013.

The British Landscape

When it comes to landscapes, Britain is not a place of extremes; there are no Alps or Himalaya here, no Amazon or Sahara. The country may be small, but even a relatively short journey takes you through a surprising mix of scenery. Seeing the change as you travel – subtle in some areas, dramatic in others – is one of this country's great attractions.

Location, Location, Location

Geologically at least, Britain is part of Europe. During the last Ice Age, most of northern Britain and Scotland was covered by vast ice sheets and glaciers, which were responsible for gouging out mountain formations including the Highlands, the Lake District and Snowdonia. At that time, Britain was still connected to Europe by land, with an area (known as Doggerland) stretching out across to the present-day Netherlands, Germany, and Jutland Peninsula. However, when the ice sheets melted, the land was submerged by catastrophic floods, probably around 6500BCE, linking up with the English Channel and turning Britain into an island nation.

Wildlife of Britain by George McGavin et al is subtitled 'the definitive visual guide'. Although too heavy to carry around, this beautiful photographic book is great for pre-trip inspiration or post-trip memories.

Broadly speaking, southern England is a mix of cities, towns and gentle countryside. Eastern England (especially the area called East Anglia) is almost entirely low and flat, while southwest England has wild moors, granite outcrops and rich pastures, plus a rugged coast with sheltered beaches, making it a favourite holiday destination.

In the north of England, farmland is interspersed with towns and cities, but the landscape is noticeably more rugged. A spine of large hills called the Pennines runs from Derbyshire to the Scottish border, and includes the peaty plateau of the Peak District, the wild moors around Haworth (immortalised in Brontë novels), the valleys of the Yorkshire Dales and the starkly beautiful hills of Northumberland. England's highest peak, Scafell Pike (978m), is in the Lake District, a small but spectacular cluster of mountains and lakes in the northwest.

The landscape of Wales is also defined by hills: notably the rounded Black Mountains and Brecon Beacons in the south, and the spiky peaks of Snowdonia in the north, with Snowdon (1085m) the highest Welsh summit. In between lie the wild Cambrian Mountains of central Wales, rolling to the west coast of spectacular cliffs and shimmering river estuaries.

For real mountains, you need to head to Scotland, especially the wild, remote and sparsely populated northwest Highlands – separated from the rest of the country by a diagonal gash in the earth's crust called the Great Glen Fault. Ben Nevis (1345m) is Scotland's – and Britain's – highest summit, but it's one of many dramatic mountains. Offshore, a cluster of archipelagos lie off the coast including the Inner and Outer Hebrides, and the distant chains of Shetland and Orkney.

South of the Scottish Highlands are the relatively flat central Lowlands, home to the bulk of Scotland's population.

National Parks

Back in 1810, English poet and outdoor fan William Wordsworth suggested that the wild landscape of the Lake District in Cumbria, northwest England, should be 'a sort of national property, in which every man has a right'. More than a century later, in 1951, the Lake District did indeed become a national park along with the Peak District, Dartmoor and Snowdonia, followed in later years by the Brecon Beacons, Cairngorms, Exmoor, Loch Lomond and The Trossachs, New Forest, Norfolk and Suffolk Broads, Northumberland, North York Moors, Pembrokeshire Coast, South Downs and Yorkshire Dales. In 2017 the Lake District was also named the UK's newest World Heritage Site by Unesco.

Britain's national parks combined cover over 10% of its area, but the term 'national park' can cause confusion. First, these areas are not state owned: nearly all land in Britain is privately owned, belonging mostly to aristocratic families, private trusts and conservation organisations. Second, they are not areas of wilderness as in many other countries. In Britain's national parks you'll see crop fields in lower areas and grazing sheep on the uplands, as well as roads, railways and villages. Some national parks even contain towns, quarries and factories. It's a reminder of the balance that needs to be struck in this crowded country between protecting the natural environment and catering for the people who live in it.

But don't be put off. Despite these apparent anomalies, Britain's national parks still contain mountains, hills, downs, moors, woods, river valleys and other areas of quiet countryside, all ideal for long walks, easy rambles, cycle rides, sightseeing or just lounging around. To help you get the best from the parks, they all have information centres, and all provide various recreational facilities (trails, car parks, campsites etc) for visitors.

Finally, it's worth noting that there are many beautiful parts of Britain that are *not* national parks (such as central Wales, the North Pennines in England, and many parts of Scotland). These can be just as good for outdoor activities or simply exploring by car or foot, and are often less crowded than the popular national parks.

World Heritage Sites

There are currently 31 Unesco World Heritage Sites in the UK. The first to be established included Stonehenge and Avebury, Ironbridge Gorge, Durham Castle and Cathedral and Studley Royal Park, all of which were listed in 1986. The most recent are Liverpool's Maritime City (2004), the Cornwall and West Devon Mining Heritage Landscape (2006), the Forth Bridge (2015) and the English Lake District (2017).

BRITAIN'S BEST BEACHES

With Europe's longest coastline, Britain has a huge number of beaches, from tiny hidden coves in Cornwall and Pembrokeshire to vast neon-lined strands in resorts such as Brighton and Blackpool. Beaches line the entire southwest peninsula and much of the south coast.

Other great beaches can be found in Suffolk, Norfolk, Lancashire, Yorkshire and Northumberland in England, and pretty much anywhere on the Welsh coast between the Gower Peninsula and Llandudno. Scotland offers even more choice, from the rocky bays of the west coast to the gorgeous white-sand beaches of the Outer Hebrides.

Britain's best resort beaches earn the coveted international Blue Flag (www.blueflag.global) award, meaning sand and water are clean and unpolluted. Other parameters include the presence of lifeguards, litter bins and recycling facilities – meaning some wild beaches may not earn the award, but are still stunning nonetheless.

BRITAIN'S NATIONAL PARKS

NATIONAL PARK	FEATURES	ACTIVITIES	BEST TIME TO VISIT
Brecon Beacons	great green ridgelines, waterfalls; Welsh mountain ponies, otters, red kites, buzzards, peregrine falcons, kingfishers	horse riding, cycling, caving, canoeing, hang-gliding	Mar & Apr (spring lambs on the hills)
Cairngorms	snowy mountains, pine forests; ospreys, pine martens, wildcats, grouse, capercaillies	skiing, climbing, birdwatching, walking	Feb (for the snow)
Dartmoor	rolling hills, rocky outcrops, serene valleys; wild ponies, deer, peregrine falcons	walking, mountain biking, horse riding	May & Jun (wildflowers in bloom)
Exmoor	sweeping moors, craggy sea cliffs; red deer, wild ponies, horned sheep	horse riding, walking	Sep (heather in bloom)
Lake District	majestic fells, rugged mountains, shimmering lakes; red squirrels, osprey, golden eagles	water sports, walking, mountaineering, climbing	Sep & Oct (summer crowds depart, autumn colours abound)
Loch Lomond & The Trossachs	sparkling lochs, brooding mountains; deer, squirrels, badgers, foxes, otters, buzzards	climbing, walking, cycling, canoeing	May (bluebell woods; before the summer rush)
New Forest	woods, heathland; wild ponies, otters, Dartford warblers, southern damselflies	walking, cycling, horse riding	Apr-Sep (lush vegetation)
Norfolk & Suffolk Broads	shallow lakes, rivers, marshlands, water lilies; otters, wildfowl	walking, cycling, boating	Apr & May (birds most active)
North York Moors	heather-clad hills, deep-green valleys; merlins, curlews, golden plovers	walking, mountain biking	Aug & Sep (heather flowering)
Northumberland	wild rolling moors, heather, gorse; red squirrels, black grouse; Hadrian's Wall	walking, cycling, climbing	Apr & May (lambs), Sep (heather flowering)
Peak District	high moors, tranquil dales, limestone caves; badgers, kestrels, grouse	walking, cycling, mountain biking, hang-gliding, climbing	Apr & May (even more lambs)
Pembrokeshire Coast	wave-ravaged shorelines, cliffs, beaches; puffins, fulmars, shearwaters, grey seals, dolphins, porpoises	walking, kayaking, coasteering, mountain biking, horse riding	Apr & May (lambs again)
Snowdonia	major mountain ranges, lakes, estuaries, Snowdon lilies; wild goats, polecats, curlews, choughs, red kites, buzzards	walking, kayaking, climbing, mountain biking, horse riding	May-Sep (better weather)
South Downs	rolling chalky hills, tranquil farmland, sheer white sea cliffs, bastard toadflax; Adonis Blue butterflies, buzzards, red kites, peregrine falcons	walking, mountain biking, cycling, horse riding	any time of year (thanks to mild climate)
Yorkshire Dales	rugged hills, lush valleys, limestone pavements; red squirrels, hares, curlews, lapwings, buzzards	walking, cycling, mountain biking, climbing	Apr & May (you guessed it, lambs)

Wildlife

For a small country, Britain has a very diverse range of plants and animals. Many native species are hidden away, but there are some undoubted gems, from lowland woods carpeted in shimmering bluebells to stately herds of deer on the high moors. Taking the time to have a closer look will enhance your trip enormously, especially if you have the time and inclination to enjoy some walking or cycling through the British landscape.

Farmland

In farmland areas, rabbits are everywhere, but if you're hiking through the countryside be on the lookout for brown hares, an increasingly rare species. They're related to rabbits, but are much larger. Males who battle for territory by boxing on their hind legs in early spring are, of course, as 'mad as a March hare'.

Although hare numbers are on the decline, otters are making a comeback. In southern Britain they inhabit the banks of rivers and lakes, and in Scotland they frequently live on the coast where they are easier to spot. Although their numbers are growing, they are mainly nocturnal, but keep your eyes peeled in the daytime and you might be lucky.

You're much more likely to see a red fox. This classic British mammal was once seen only in the countryside, but these wily beasts adapt well to any situation, so these days you're just as likely to see them scavenging in towns and even in city suburbs.

Elsewhere, another British classic, the badger, is under threat from farmers who believe they transmit bovine tuberculosis to cattle, although conservationists say the case is far from proven.

Herds of 'wild' ponies roam the New Forest, Exmoor and Dartmoor; these animals certainly roam free, but in reality they are privately owned and managed.

Common birds of farmland and similar landscapes (and urban gardens) include the robin, with its instantly recognisable red breast and cheerful whistle; the wren, whose loud trilling song belies its tiny size; and the yellowhammer, with a song that sounds like (if you use your imagination) 'a-little-bit-of-bread-and-no-cheese'. In open fields, the warbling cry of a skylark is another classic, but now threatened, sound of the British outdoors. You're more likely to see a pheasant, a large bird originally introduced from Russia to the nobility's shooting estates, but now considered naturalised.

Between the fields, hedges provide cover for flocks of finches, but these seed-eaters must watch out for sparrowhawks – birds of prey that come from nowhere at tremendous speed. Other predators include barn owls, a wonderful sight as they fly silently along hedgerows listening for the faint rustle of a vole or shrew. In rural Wales or Scotland you will see plenty of buzzards, Britain's most common large raptor.

Woodland

In woodland areas, mammals include the small white-spotted fallow deer and the even smaller roe deer. Woodlands are full of birds too, but you'll hear them more than see them. Listen out for willow warblers (which, as the name suggests, have a warbling song with a descending cadence) and chiffchaffs (once again, the clue's in the name: they make a repetitive 'chiff chaff' noise).

If you hear rustling among the fallen leaves it might be a hedgehog – a cute-looking, spiny-backed insect eater – but it's an increasingly rare sound these days; conservationists say they'll be extinct in Britain by 2025, due to insecticides in farming, increased building in rural areas and hedgehogs' notoriously poor ability to cross roads safely.

In no such danger are grey squirrels, originally introduced from North America. They have proved very adaptable, to the extent that native red squirrels are severely endangered because the greys eat all the food.

WILDLIFE IN YOUR POCKET

Is it a rabbit or a hare? A gull or a tern? Buttercup or cowslip? If you need to know a bit more about Britain's plant and animal kingdoms the following field guides are ideal for entry-level naturalists:

➡ *Complete Guide to British Wildlife* by Paul Sterry is portable and highly recommended, and covers mammals, birds, fish, plants, snakes, insects and even fungi, with brief descriptions and excellent photos.

➡ If feathered friends are enough, the *Complete Guide to British Birds* by Paul Sterry combines clear photos and descriptions, plus when and where each species may be seen.

➡ *Wildlife of the North Atlantic* by world-famous film-maker Tony Soper beautifully covers the animals seen from beach, boat and clifftop in the British Isles and beyond.

➡ The Collins Gem series includes handy little books on wildlife topics such as *Birds, Trees, Fish* and *Wild Flowers*.

Pockets of red squirrels survive in the English Lake District and in many parts of Scotland, especially north of the central Lowlands.

Much larger than squirrels are pine martens, which are seen in some forested regions, especially in Scotland. With beautiful brown coats, they were once hunted for their fur, but are now fully protected.

Britain's most wooded county is Surrey, despite its proximity to London. The soil is too poor for agriculture, so Surrey's trees were spared. But almost half of all Britain's forested areas are in Scotland. The Woodland Trust (www.woodlandtrust.org.uk) campaigns to protect Britain's remaining woodlands.

Mountain & Moorland

On mountains and high moors – including Exmoor, Dartmoor, the Lake District, Northumberland and much of Scotland – the most visible mammal is the red deer. Males of the species grow their famous large antlers between April and July, and shed them again in February.

Also on the high ground, well known and easily recognised birds include the red grouse, which often hides in the heather until almost stepped on then flies away with a loud warning call. On the high peaks of Scotland you may see the grouse's northern cousin, the ptarmigan, dappled brown in summer but white in winter.

Look out, too, for the curlew, with its stately long legs and elegant curved bill. With luck you may see beautifully camouflaged golden plovers, while the spectacular aerial displays of lapwings are impossible to miss.

Other mountain birds include red kites (there have been various successful projects around the country to reintroduce these spectacular fork-tailed raptors). Also in the Scottish mountains, keep an eye peeled for the golden eagle, Britain's second-largest bird of prey, as it glides and soars along ridges.

Would-be twitchers can easily spot majestic red kites in the mountains and moors of the Brecon Beacons, particularly at feeding stations such as Gigrin Farm in Rhayader, Wales.

Rivers & Coasts

If you're near inland water, you have a chance of spotting an osprey; the best places in Britain to see this magnificent bird include Rutland Water in the English Midlands, Bassenthwaite in the Lake District, and the Cairngorms in Scotland. You could also look along the riverbanks for signs of water voles, endearing rodents that were once very common but have been all but wiped out by wild mink (fur farm escapees first introduced from America).

On the coasts of Britain, particularly in Cornwall, Pembrokeshire and northwest Scotland, the dramatic cliffs are a marvellous sight in early summer (around May), when they are home to hundreds of thousands of breeding seabirds. Guillemots, razorbills and kittiwakes, among others, fight for space on impossibly crowded rock ledges. The cliffs become white with droppings and the air is filled with their shrill calls. Even if you're not into birdwatching, this is one of Britain's finest wildlife spectacles.

Another bird to look out for in coastal areas is the comical puffin (especially common in Shetland), with its distinctive rainbow beak and 'nests' burrowed in sandy soil. In total contrast, gannets are one of the largest seabirds and make dramatic dives for fish, often from a great height. The biggest tick in coastal birdwatching, though, is the white-tailed eagle, Britain's largest bird of prey, which can be seen in the west of Scotland, notably on Mull and Skye.

Estuaries and mudflats are feeding grounds for numerous migrant wading birds; easily spotted are black-and-white oystercatchers with their long red bills, as well as the flocks of small ringed plovers that skitter along the sand.

And finally, the sea mammals. There are two species of seal that frequent British waters; the larger grey seal is more often seen than the (misnamed) common (or harbour) seal. Boat trips to see their offshore colonies are available at various points around the coast, and are especially popular when the seal pups are born.

Dolphins, porpoises and minke whales can all be seen off the west coast of Britain, particularly off Scotland, and especially from May to September when viewing conditions are better. Whale-watching trips (also good for seeing other marine wildlife such as basking sharks) are available from harbour towns, especially in Scotland.

Several of Britain's native species are threatened by introduced diseases – most notably the ash, which is facing the ominous prospect of 'ash dieback', caused by a fungus called *Hymenoscyphus fraxineus*. Some experts believe it could wipe out more than 90% of the UK's ash trees, as it has in several other European countries.

Plants

In any part of Britain, the best places to see wildflowers are areas that have escaped large-scale farming. In the chalky downs of southern England and in limestone areas such as the Peak District and Yorkshire Dales, for example, many fields erupt with great profusions of cowslips and primroses in April and May.

Some flowers prefer woodland and, again, the best time for seeing these is April and May. This is because the leaf canopy of the woods is not yet fully developed, allowing sunlight to break through to encourage plants such as bluebells (a beautiful and internationally rare species). Another classic British plant is gorse – you can't miss the swaths of this spiky bush in heath areas, most notably in the New Forest in southern England, and all over Scotland.

In contrast, the blooming season for heather is quite short. On the Scottish mountains, the Pennine moors of northern England, and Dartmoor in the south, the landscape is covered in a riot of purple in August and September.

Britain's natural deciduous trees include oak, ash, beech, birch, hazel and rowan, with seeds and leaves supporting a vast range of insects and birds. The New Forest in southern England and the Forest of Dean on the Wales–England border are good examples of this type of habitat. In some parts of Scotland, most notably Glen Affric, remnants of indigenous Caledonian pine forest can still be seen. As you travel through Britain you're also likely to see non-native conifers, often in vast plantations without any wildlife, although an increasing number of deciduous trees are also planted these days.

Farmer and nature writer John Lewis-Stempel has written a number of fascinating accounts of the British countryside, including *The Running Hare*, *Meadowland: The Private Life of an English Field* and *The Wood*.

Environmental Issues

With Britain's long history, it's not surprising that the country's appearance is almost totally the result of human interaction with the environment. Since the earliest times, people have been chopping down trees and creating fields for crops or animals, but the most dramatic changes in rural areas came in the late 1940s, continuing into the '50s and '60s, when a postwar drive to be self-reliant in food meant new and intensive large-scale farming methods. The result was lowland Britain's ancient patchwork of small meadows becoming a landscape of vast fields, as

RENEWABLE ENERGY IN BRITAIN

Like every nation, Britain is facing up to the pressing need to combat climate change. The UK has committed to reducing greenhouse gas emissions to net zero by 2050 (Scotland has pledged to meet the target by 2045), but critics say this target is not ambitious enough to prevent catastrophic climate change. Ambitious announcements such as the phasing-out of new petrol and diesel cars by 2035, and a recent pledge that all UK homes will receive their energy entirely by wind power by 2030, have raised eyebrows; sceptics claim that behind the rhetoric, there is not enough new investment in green jobs and infrastructure to meet these targets.

Onshore wind farms are a highly controversial topic in the British countryside: some people love them, others loathe them, but they are making an increasingly important contribution to Britain's energy mix. Less contentious is the rapid growth in offshore wind farms, especially around the coasts of northern England and Scotland: the North Sea will soon be home to the largest wind farm in the world, Hornsea 1, a massive development of 174 190m-high turbines that is forecast to generate 1.2GW of electricity – enough for a million homes.

Renewable energy is now responsible for 37% of the UK's electricity. That's progress, considering it was less than 3% just a decade ago – but there's still a long way to go.

walls were demolished, woodlands felled, ponds filled, wetlands drained and, most notably, hedgerows ripped out.

In most cases the hedgerows were lines of dense bushes, shrubs and trees forming a network that stretched across the countryside, protecting fields from erosion, supporting a varied range of flowers, and providing shelter for numerous insects, birds and small mammals. But in the rush to improve farm yields, thousands of miles of hedgerows were destroyed in the postwar decades, and between the mid-1980s and the early 2000s another 25% disappeared.

Up-to-the-minute statistics on the UK's electricity generation are provided by Drax (www.electricinsights.co.uk), one of the nation's largest power stations.

In addition to hedgerow clearance, other farming techniques remain hot environmental issues. Studies have shown that the use of pesticides and intensive irrigation results in rivers running dry or being poisoned by run-off. In 2014 scientists announced that neonicotinoid pesticides – introduced in the 1990s to replace harmful chemicals such as DDT – may actually be even more dangerous, and are implicated in the collapse of the bee population.

Meanwhile, monocropping means vast fields with one type of grass, dubbed 'green deserts' by conservationists as they support no insects, are causing wild bird populations to plummet. This is not a case of wizened old peasants recalling the idyllic days of their forebears; you only have to be over about 40 in Britain to remember a countryside where birds such as skylarks or lapwings were visibly much more numerous.

In fact, a recent report by State of Nature found that one in 10 of the UK's wildlife species is threatened with extinction, and around one-sixth of the nation's animals, birds, fish and plants has been lost since 1970. But it's not all doom and gloom – while populations of many native species such as the hedgehog have crashed, others, such as the otter, have staged an impressive comeback. Another recent returnee is the beaver, once a native resident of England, but trapped out of existence long ago. The animals have now been reintroduced to several locations around England, although the exact sites have been kept secret to ensure their safety.

Sporting Britain

The British are passionate about sport – both as participants and spectators. In most sports (including football and rugby), each of the GB nations fields its own national team for international competitions, and rivalries are fierce. A notable exception is athletics, when the nation comes together to field a GB-wide team – to great success, if the results at the Olympics in 2012 and 2016 are anything to go by.

Football (Soccer)

The Premier League is one of the nation's greatest exports – it's estimated that 3.2 billion people around the world follow its fortunes from week to week. For the hundred years between 1892 and 1992, the top tier of English football was known as the First Division, but it was rebranded as the Premier League to mark its centenary.

Since then, the league has largely been dominated by five clubs: Manchester City, Manchester United, Chelsea, Arsenal and Liverpool, who finally won the title in 2020 – their first title in 30 years, and their first time as Premier League Champions. A notable exception was the 2015–16 season, when little Leicester City defied the odds and became only the second team outside the top five to take a Premier League title (the only other is Blackburn Rovers, who won the title in 1995).

One step down from the Premier League are three other leagues: the Championship, League One and League Two, along with a whole host of smaller and part-time teams.

The Scottish football scene has a similar pattern: the best teams compete in the Scottish Premiership and the rest in the Scottish Football League. The top flight has long been dominated by two Glasgow teams, Celtic and Rangers: Celtic has won every championship since 2012, a record run of nine back-to-back wins. Football is less popular in Wales, where rugby is the national sport.

The football season is the same for all divisions (August to May). Tickets for Premier League matches are like gold dust, but you might have more luck with lower-division games. Try club websites or online agencies such as www.ticketmaster.co.uk and www.myticketmarket.com.

The origin of the term 'soccer', often used outside Britain, is obscure: some sources say it derives from the sport's official name, Association Football, or possibly from 'sock' – a leather foot-cover worn in medieval times to kick around a pig's bladder, the original incarnation of the sport. Now that would be quite a spectacle on a Saturday afternoon.

BRITAIN AT THE OLYMPICS

For many people, the high-water mark of British athletics was the outstanding achievement by Team GB at the 2012 Olympic and Paralympic Games in London, which resulted in a haul of 65 medals (including 29 golds and third place on the medals table behind China and the USA). The British paralympic athletes exceeded even this impressive total by winning 120 medals, and notching up another third place in the medals table behind China and Russia.

At the 2016 Olympics in Rio, Team GB went even better: 27 golds, 23 silvers and 17 bronzes, finishing in second place behind the USA, an achievement equalled by the GB Paralympians (64 golds, 39 silvers, 44 bronzes and another second place overall).

THE FA CUP

The Football Association (FA) held its first interclub knockout tournament in 1871. Fifteen clubs took part, playing for a nice piece of silverware called the FA Cup – then worth about £20.

Nowadays, around 600 clubs compete for this legendary and priceless trophy. It differs from many other competitions in that every team – from the lowest-ranking part-timers to the stars of the Premier League – is in with a chance. The preliminary rounds begin in August, and the FA Cup Final is held the following May at London's Wembley Stadium.

Each of Britain's three nations fields its own national football team at international competitions such as the FIFA World Cup and the European Championship, although it's been a long time indeed since any of them have won anything – famously, the last time England won the World Cup was in 1966, and the nation's hopes have been dashed at nearly every championship since (often as the result of an excruciating penalty shoot-out). At the 2018 World Cup a young, inexperienced England team fared better than expected, reaching the semi-finals before being knocked out by Croatia. Unfortunately, Scotland, Wales and Northern Ireland failed to even qualify.

The women's national teams have a much better record of success, however: the England women's football team took third place in the FIFA Women's World Cup in 2015, and fourth in 2019.

Rugby

A wit once said that football was a gentlemen's game played by hooligans, while rugby was a hooligans' game played by gentlemen. That may be true, but rugby is very popular. Tickets for games cost around £15 to £50 depending on the club's status and fortunes.

There are two versions of the game: rugby union (www.englandrugby.com) is played more in southern England, Wales and Scotland, while rugby league (www.rugby-league.com) is played predominantly in northern England.

Both rugby codes trace their roots back to a football match in 1823 at Rugby School, in Warwickshire. A player called William Webb Ellis, frustrated at the limitations of mere kicking, reputedly picked up the ball and ran with it towards the opponents' goal. True to the British tradition of fair play, rather than Ellis being dismissed from the game, a whole new sport was developed around his tactic, and the Rugby Football Union was formally inaugurated in 1871. Today, the Rugby World Cup is named the Webb Ellis trophy after this enterprising young tearaway.

The highlight of rugby union's international calendar is the annual Six Nations Championship (www.rbs6nations.com), between teams from England, Wales, Scotland, Ireland, France and Italy.

The home nations (especially England) have fared quite well at the four-yearly Rugby Union World Cup: England won the cup in 2003, and lost out to South Africa in the final in 2019. The women's team also has a very respectable record: England's women were runners-up in 2017.

Causing ructions in the cricket world, the fast-paced Twenty20 format emphasises big-batting scores, rather than slow and careful run-building. Traditionalists say it's changing the character of the game, but there's no doubting its popularity – many Twenty20 matches sell out quickly.

Cricket

Cricket is a quintessentially English sport. Dating from the 18th century – although its roots are much older – the sport spread throughout the Commonwealth during Britain's colonial era. Australia, the Caribbean and the Indian subcontinent took to the game with gusto, and today the former colonies delight in giving the old country a good spanking on the cricket pitch.

While many English people follow cricket like a religion, to the uninitiated it's an impenetrable spectacle. Spread over one-day games or five-day test matches, progress seems so *slow* (surely, say the unbelievers, this is the game for which TV highlights were invented) and dominated by arcane terminology such as innings, overs, googlies, out-swingers, leg-byes and silly-mid-offs. At the very least, it's worth trying to understand the scoring system: teams score one run for every successful run between the wickets, four for hitting the ball along the ground to the edge of the pitch (the 'boundary', marked by a rope), and six if the ball reaches the boundary without touching the ground (like a home run in baseball).

One-day games and international tests are played at grounds including Lord's in London, Edgbaston in Birmingham and Headingley in Leeds. Tickets cost from £30 to well over £200. The County Championship pits the best teams from around the country against each other; tickets cost £5 to £25, and only the most crucial games tend to sell out. Details are on the website of the English Cricket Board (www.ecb.co.uk).

The easiest way to watch cricket – and often the most enjoyable – is by stumbling across a local game on a village green as you travel around the country. There's no charge for spectators, and no one will mind if you nip into the pub during a quiet period.

England's men's team has had a good record in recent years, culminating in a nail-biting victory at the 2019 World Cup, when England tied with New Zealand but won thanks to its higher number of boundaries. Even more successful is the England women's cricket team – they won the World Cup in 2009 and 2017.

For the dates and details of major football and cricket matches, horse racing and other sporting fixtures across Britain, a great place to start is the sports pages of www.britevents.com.

Horse Racing

Horse racing in Britain stretches back centuries, and there's a 'race meeting' somewhere pretty much every day. The top event in the calendar is Royal Ascot at Ascot Racecourse in mid-June, where the rich and famous come to see and be seen, and the fashion is almost as important as the nags. Even the Queen turns up to put a fiver each way on Lucky Boy in the 3.15.

Other highlights include the Grand National steeplechase at Aintree in early April and the Derby at Epsom on the first Saturday in June.

Golf

Golf is a popular sport in Britain, with millions taking to the fairways every week. The main tournament for spectators is the Open Championship, often referred to simply as The Open (or the 'British Open' outside

THE ASHES

The historic test cricket series between England and Australia known as the Ashes has been played every other year since 1882, bar a few interruptions during wartime. It is played alternately in England and Australia, with each of the five matches in the series held at a different cricket ground, always in the summer in the host location.

The contest's name dates back to Australia's shock victory in 1882 – a moment that inspired the *Sporting Times* to lament the death of English cricket and its 'ashes' being taken to Australia. Subsequently, the name became associated with a terracotta urn presented the following year to the English captain Ivo Bligh, which supposedly contained the cremated ashes of a stump or bail used in this historic match. Since 1953 this hallowed, 15cm-high relic has resided at the Marylebone Cricket Club (MCC) Museum at Lord's Cricket Ground.

The Ashes is famous for drama, with fortunes ebbing and flowing across the series. In 2015 England won a particularly dramatic 3–2 victory on home turf, before promptly sinking to an ignominious 4–0 whitewash in Australia in 2017–18. Unusually, the 2019 Ashes were a draw, the first time since 1972. The final score was 2–2, but as the holders, Australia retained the urn.

HIGHLAND GAMES

Unique to Scotland are the Highland Games – a contest of traditional sports including caber-tossing (heaving a tree trunk into the air), hammer-throwing and stone-putting. The biggest events are staged at Dunoon, Oban and Braemar. Find out more at the Scottish Highland Games Association website (www.shga.co.uk).

the UK). It's the oldest of professional golf's major championships (dating back to 1860) and the only one held outside the USA. It is usually played over the third weekend in July and the location changes each year, using nine courses around the country – check www.theopen.com for details of past, present and future championships.

The Old Course at St Andrews, often dubbed the 'home of golf', is particularly famous: it was one of the first places the sport was played, all the way back in the early 1400s. Playing here is almost a spiritual experience for golf enthusiasts, but you'll need to plan well ahead to get a game. Thankfully, there are around 2000 private and public golf courses to choose from. Some private clubs admit members or golfers with a handicap certificate, but most welcome visitors. Public golf courses are open to anyone. A round costs around £10 to £30 on public courses, and up to £200 on famous championship courses.

Over 27 tonnes of strawberries and 7000L of cream are consumed during the two weeks of the annual Wimbledon Tennis Championships.

Tennis

Britain's best-known tennis tournament is Wimbledon (officially the All England Championships; www.wimbledon.com), held in June/July every year. Although there's something quintessentially English about the grass courts, polite applause and umpires in straw hats, it's been a long, long time since an Englishman won the championship (the last was Fred Perry in 1936). By far the most successful British player of recent years is Andy Murray, a Scotsman, who won the Wimbledon title in 2013 and 2016.

Demand for seats always far outstrips supply. About 6000 tickets are sold each day (excluding the final four days), but you'll need to be an early riser: dedicated fans start queuing before dawn.

Survival Guide

Directory A-Z

PRACTICALITIES

Newspapers Tabloids include the *Sun*, *Express* and *Mirror*, and *Daily Record* (in Scotland); quality 'broadsheets' include (from right to left, politically) the *Telegraph*, *Times* and *Guardian*.

TV All TV in the UK is digital. The main broadcasters include the BBC, ITV and Channel 4. Satellite and cable TV providers include Sky and Virgin Media.

Radio Main BBC stations and wavelengths are Radio 1 (98–99.6MHz FM), Radio 2 (88–92MHz FM), Radio 3 (90–92.2 MHz FM), Radio 4 (92–94.4MHz FM) and Radio 5 Live (909 or 693 AM). National commercial stations include Virgin Radio (1215Hz MW) and non-highbrow classical specialist Classic FM (100–102MHz FM). All are available on digital.

DVD PAL format (incompatible with NTSC and Secam).

Weights & Measures Britain uses a mix of metric and imperial measures (eg petrol is sold by the litre but beer by the pint; mountain heights are in metres but road distances are in miles).

Smoking Forbidden in all enclosed public places in Britain.

Accessible Travel

The UK is slowly making progress towards making travel easier for travellers with disabilities, but that progress is patchy. All new buildings have wheelchair access lifts, ramps and other facilities, but hotels and B&Bs in historic buildings are often harder to adapt, so you'll have less choice here.

Most modern city buses and trams have low floors for easy access, although some may require a ramp to be physically put out by the driver. Some taxis take wheelchairs, but they are far from the norm.

For long-distance travel, trains are the preferred option. Most intercity trains can be accessed by travellers with accessibility issues, although a ramp may be required depending on the particular train. It's always worth enquiring at the time of booking or prior to travel. When you arrive at the station, ask for assistance from station or train staff who will be happy to oblige. Some stations unfortunately aren't well adapted for disabled travellers, as some still have steps and/or escalators – although there is usually a lift to travel to/from platforms.

A good overview can be found at www.nationalrail.co.uk/stations_destinations/disabled_passengers.aspx. It's worth buying a Disabled Person's Railcard (www.disabledpersons-railcard.co.uk), which costs £20 and gets you 33% off most train fares.

National Express (www.nationalexpress.com) operates wheelchair-friendly coaches on many routes. For details, see the website or ring the dedicated Disabled Passenger Travel Helpline (☎0371 781 8181).

The following are some useful organisations:

BOOK YOUR STAY ONLINE

For more accommodation reviews by Lonely Planet authors, check out http://lonelyplanet.com/hotels/. You'll find independent reviews, as well as recommendations on the best places to stay. Best of all, you can book online.

Disability Rights UK (www.disabilityrightsuk.org) Published titles include a holiday guide. Services include a key for 7000 public disabled toilets across the UK.

Good Access Guide (www.goodaccessguide.co.uk)

Tourism for All (www.tourismforall.org.uk)

Download Lonely Planet's free Accessible Travel guides from https://shop.lonelyplanet.com/products/accessible-travel-online-resources-2017.

Customs Regulations

Travellers arriving in the UK from EU countries don't have to pay tax or duty on goods for personal use, and can bring in as much EU duty-paid alcohol and tobacco as they like. However, if you bring in more than the following, you'll probably be asked some questions:

- 800 cigarettes
- 1kg of tobacco
- 10L of spirits
- 90L of wine
- 110L of beer

Travellers from outside the EU can bring in, duty-free:

- 200 cigarettes *or* 100 cigarillos *or* 50 cigars *or* 250g of tobacco
- 16L of beer
- 4L of non-sparkling wine
- 1L of spirits *or* 2L of fortified wine or sparkling wine
- £390 worth of all other goods, including perfume, gifts and souvenirs

Anything over this limit must be declared to customs officers on arrival. For further details, and for information on reclaiming VAT on items purchased in the UK by non-EU residents, go to www.gov.uk and search for 'Bringing goods into the UK'.

Electricity

Type G
230V/50Hz

Health

Health Insurance

- One of the most unwelcome aspects of Britain leaving the EU is the likely loss of reciprocal healthcare, as provided by the EHIC (European Health Insurance Card). From 1 January 2021, travellers from the EU and all other nations will require private travel insurance to cover medical care.
- Choose your policy carefully: make sure you get a policy that covers you for the worst possible scenarios, including emergency flights home.

Availability & Cost of Health Care

- Chemists (pharmacies) can advise on minor ailments such as sore throats and earaches. In large cities there's always at least one 24-hour chemist.
- For medical advice that is not an emergency you can call the NHS 111 service (phone ☎111).

Vaccinations

- No jabs (vaccinations) are required to travel to Britain. For more information, check with your medical provider in your own country before you travel.

Insurance

- Although everyone receives free emergency treatment, regardless of nationality, travel insurance is still highly recommended. It will usually cover medical treatment, delayed departures, loss or theft of baggage and so on, but every policy is different, so check the small print.
- Cheaper policies often don't include events such as scheduled airline failure, natural disasters and (especially important in the wake of Covid-19) pandemic cover. Do your homework – it's generally worth spending a bit more to get more comprehensive coverage.
- If you're bringing valuable items such as cameras, laptops and tablets, check your policy covers you for theft and damage.

EATING PRICE RANGES

The following price ranges refer to the cost of a main dish.

Category	London	Elsewhere
£	less than £15	less than £12
££	£15–25	£12–22
£££	more than £25	more than £22

➡ Worldwide travel insurance is available at www.lonelyplanet.com/travel-insurance. You can buy, extend and claim online anytime – even if you're already on the road.

Internet Access

➡ 3G and 4G mobile broadband coverage is good in urban areas, but limited or sometimes nonexistent in rural areas. 5G is on its way but is currently not widespread.

➡ EU citizens can currently use their own mobile/cellphone data roaming allowance in the UK for no charge. This may change after Brexit, however, so check before you travel.

➡ Travellers from non-EU countries will usually incur high roaming charges – so buy a local SIM card or stick to wi-fi networks.

➡ Most hotels, B&Bs, hostels, stations, libraries and coffee shops (even some trains and buses) offer wi-fi access.

➡ Internet cafes are now very few and far between. If you're stuck, public libraries often have computers with free internet access.

Legal Matters

➡ Police have the power to detain, for up to six hours, anyone suspected of having committed an offence punishable by imprisonment (including drugs offences). Police have the right to search anyone they suspect of possessing drugs.

➡ Illegal drugs are widely available, especially in clubs. Cannabis possession is a criminal offence; punishment for carrying a small amount may be a warning, a fine or imprisonment. Dealers face much stiffer penalties, as do people caught with other drugs (especially 'Class A' drugs including cocaine, LSD, ecstasy and heroin).

➡ On buses and trains (including the London Underground), people without a valid ticket are fined on the spot (£80, reduced to £40 if you pay within 21 days).

LGBT+ Travellers

Britain is generally a tolerant place. London, Manchester and Brighton have flourishing gay scenes, and in other sizeable cities (even some small towns), you'll find communities not entirely in the closet. That said, you'll still find pockets of homophobic hostility in some areas. Resources include the following:

Diva (www.divamag.co.uk)

Gay Times (www.gaytimes.co.uk)

Switchboard LGBT+ Helpline (www.switchboard.lgbt; ☎0300 330 0630)

Money

ATMs

ATMs (usually called 'cash machines' in Britain) are common in cities and even small towns. Cash withdrawals from some ATMs may be subject to a small charge, but most are free. If you're not from the UK, your home bank will likely charge you for withdrawing money. Watch out for tampered ATMs; a common ruse is to attach a card reader or mini camera.

Credit & Debit Cards

Visa and Mastercard credit and debit cards are widely accepted in Britain. Other credit cards, including Amex, are not so widely accepted. Most businesses will assume your card is 'Chip and PIN' enabled (using a PIN instead of signing). If it isn't, you should be able to sign instead, but some places may not accept your card.

'Contactless' payment, where you wave your card over the reader rather than typing in a PIN, is now very common (you can even use it instead of a ticket on the London Underground). The upper limit for contactless transactions is currently £45.

Currency

The currency of Britain is the pound sterling (£). Paper money ('notes') comes in £5, £10, £20 and £50 denominations. Some shops don't accept £50 notes because fakes circulate.

Other currencies are rarely accepted, except at some gift shops in London, which may take euros, US dollars, yen and other major currencies.

Money Changers

Cities and larger towns have banks and exchange bureaux for changing your money into pounds. Check rates first; some bureaux offer poor rates or levy outrageous commissions. You can also change money at most post offices.

SCOTTISH BANKNOTES

Scottish banks issue their own sterling banknotes. They are interchangeable with Bank of England notes, but you'll sometimes run into problems outside Scotland. They are also harder to exchange once you get outside the UK, though British banks will always exchange them.

Opening Hours

Opening hours may vary throughout the year, especially in rural areas where many places have shorter hours or close completely from October or November to March or April.

Banks 9.30am–4pm or 5pm Monday to Friday; some open 9.30am–1pm Saturday

Pubs and bars Noon–11pm Monday to Saturday (many till midnight or 1am Friday and Saturday, especially in Scotland) and 12.30–11pm Sunday

Restaurants Lunch noon–3pm, dinner 6–9pm or 10pm (or later in cities)

Shops 9am–5.30pm (or to 6pm in cities) Monday to Saturday, and often 11am–5pm Sunday; big-city convenience stores open 24/7

SCHOOL HOLIDAYS

Roads get busy and hotel prices go up during school holidays. Exact dates vary from year to year and region to region, but are roughly as follows:

Easter Holiday Week before and week after Easter

Summer Holiday Third week of July to first week of September in England and Wales, end of June to mid-August in Scotland

Christmas Holiday Mid-December to first week of January

There are also three week-long 'half-term' school holidays – usually late February (or early March), late May and late October. These vary among Scotland, England and Wales.

Museums & Sights

- Large museums and sights usually open daily.
- Some smaller places open Saturday and Sunday but close Monday and/or Tuesday.
- Smaller places open daily in high season but operate weekends only or completely close in low season.

Post

The British postal service is generally efficient and reliable. Information on post office locations and postage rates can be found at www.postoffice.co.uk. Note that the Post Office (which operates actual post offices) and the Royal Mail (which does the deliveries) are now separate businesses.

Public Holidays

Holidays for the whole of Britain:

New Year's Day 1 January (plus 2 January in Scotland)

Easter March/April (Good Friday to Easter Monday inclusive)

May Day First Monday in May

Spring Bank Holiday Last Monday in May

Summer Bank Holiday Last Monday in August

Christmas Day 25 December

Boxing Day 26 December

If a public holiday falls on a weekend, the nearest Monday is usually taken instead. In England and Wales most businesses and banks close on official public holidays (hence the quaint term 'bank holiday'). In Scotland, bank holidays are just for the banks, and many businesses stay open. Many Scottish towns normally have a spring and autumn holiday, but the dates vary.

On public holidays, some small museums and places of interest close, but larger attractions have their busiest times. If a place closes on Sunday, it'll probably be shut on bank holidays as well.

Virtually everything – attractions, shops, banks, offices – closes on Christmas Day, although pubs open at lunchtime. There's usually no public transport on Christmas Day, and a very minimal service on Boxing Day.

Safe Travel

Britain is a remarkably safe country, but crime is not unknown – especially in London and other cities.

- Watch out for pickpockets and hustlers in crowded areas popular with tourists, such as around Westminster Bridge in London.
- When travelling by tube, tram or urban train services at night, choose a carriage containing other people.
- Many town centres can be rowdy on Friday and Saturday nights when the pubs and clubs are emptying.
- Unlicensed minicabs – a driver with a car earning money on the side – operate in large cities, and are worth avoiding unless you know what you're doing.

Telephone

Mobile Phones

The UK uses the GSM 900/1800 network, which covers the rest of Europe, Australia and New Zealand, but isn't compatible with the North American GSM 1900. Most modern mobiles can function on both networks. EU mobile users can currently use their home calls and data package in the UK for no extra charge, although this may change after Brexit.

Roaming charges for non-EU citizens can be prohibitively high, so it's generally worth getting a local number by buying a SIM card (widely available from shops, convenience stores and supermarkets) and sticking it in your phone. Pay-as-you-go SIMs start from £5 including some call credit, and can be 'topped up' with vouchers available from the same locations where you bought the card.

Your phone may be locked to your home network, however, so you'll have to either get it unlocked, or buy a cheap pay-as-you-go phone along with your SIM card (from £10).

Phone Codes

Dialling into the UK Dial your country's international access code, then ☎44 (the UK country code), then the area code (dropping the first 0) followed by the telephone number.

Dialling out of the UK The international access code is ☎00; dial this, then add the code of the country you wish to dial.

Making a reverse-charge (collect) international call Dial ☎155 for the operator. It's an expensive option, but not for the caller.

Area codes in the UK Do not have a standard format or length, eg Edinburgh ☎0131, London ☎020, Ambleside ☎015394.

Directory Assistance A host of agencies offer this service – numbers include ☎118 118, ☎118 500 and ☎118 811 – but fees are extortionate (around £6 for a 45-second call); search online for free at www.thephonebook.bt.com.

Mobile phones Codes usually begin with ☎07.

Free calls Numbers starting with ☎0800 or ☎0808 are free.

National operator ☎100

International operator ☎155

HERITAGE ORGANISATIONS

Many of Britain's castles, stately homes and ancient sites are run by one of two heritage organisations: the National Trust or English Heritage. Membership gets you free admission (usually a good saving) as well as information handbooks, free parking at many sites and other benefits.

National Trust (NT; www.nationaltrust.org.uk) A charity protecting historic buildings and land with scenic importance across England and Wales. Annual membership is £72 (discounts for under-26s and families). For visitors, a Touring Pass (www.nationaltrust.org.uk/features/touring-pass) might be a good idea; it allows free entry to NT properties for one/two weeks (one person £33/38, two people £58/69, family £64/81). The **National Trust for Scotland** (www.nts.org.uk) is a similar organisation in Scotland; annual membership is £61.20.

English Heritage (EH; www.english-heritage.org.uk) A state-funded organisation responsible for numerous historic sites. Annual membership is £63 (couples and seniors get discounts). An Overseas Visitors Pass allows free entry to most sites for nine/16 days for £37/44 (couples £64/74, families £69/79). In Wales and Scotland the equivalent organisations are **Cadw** (www.cadw.wales.gov.uk) and **Historic Environment Scotland** (www.historicenvironment.scot). You can join at the first location you visit. If you join an English heritage organisation, it covers you for Wales and Scotland, and vice versa.

Time

Britain is on GMT/UTC. The clocks go forward one hour for 'summer time' at the end of March, and go back at the end of October. The 24-hour clock is used for transport timetables.

Time Differences

Paris, Berlin, Rome	1hr ahead of Britain
New York	5hr behind
Sydney	9hr ahead Apr-Sep, 10hr Oct, 11hr Nov-Mar
Los Angeles	8hr behind
Mumbai	5½hr ahead Nov-Feb, 4½hr Mar-Oct
Tokyo	9hr ahead Nov-Feb, 8hr Mar-Oct

Toilets

➡ Public toilets in Britain are usually free, but cutbacks in public spending mean that many facilities have been closed down.

➡ Your best bet is to use the toilets in free-to-enter museums; those in railway and bus stations often charge a fee (from 20p to 50p).

➡ Most pubs and restaurants stipulate that their toilets are for customers only.

Tourist Information

Most larger towns and cities in England and Wales have a tourist information centre or visitor information centre (for ease of reference Lonely Planet calls them 'tourist offices'). Staff here are well informed on their local area and can offer lots of advice, along with books, maps, leaflets, bus timetables and other handy information.

Some also offer accommodation booking services.

In more rural areas, and notably in Scotland, many offices have closed down; sometimes you'll find there's just one tourist office in the main town, covering a relatively large region.

Most tourist offices keep regular business hours; in quiet areas they close from October to March, while in popular areas they open daily year-round.

The website of Britain's official tourist board, **Visit Britain** (www.visitbritain.com), is a great planning resource and has links to local sites. There's also usually a corresponding local information website that you can refer to (often a Visit site eg www.visitlondon.com, www.visitcornwall.com, www.visitnortheastengland.com).

Visas

Double-check the latest visa rules before you travel at https://www.gov.uk/check-uk-visa.

➡ If you're a citizen of the EEA (European Economic Area) nations or Switzerland, you currently don't need a visa to enter or work in Britain – but it is no longer possible to enter solely with your identity card. You will need a valid passport for travel that covers the whole of your stay in the UK. In most cases, a stay of maximum 6 months is permitted. In future (probably no earlier than 2025 according to the UK government), it may be necessary to apply for an ETA (electronic travel authorisation) prior to travel, but at present this is not required.

➡ Visa regulations are always subject to change, and immigration restriction is currently big news in Britain, so it's essential to check with your local British embassy, high commission or consulate before leaving home.

➡ Currently, if you're a citizen of Australia, Canada, New Zealand, Japan, Israel, the USA and several other countries, you can stay for up to six months (no visa required), but are not allowed to work.

➡ Nationals of many countries, including South Africa, will need to obtain a visa: for more info, see www.gov.uk/check-uk-visa.

➡ The Youth Mobility Scheme, for Australian, Canadian, Japanese, Hong Kong, Monégasque, New Zealand, South Korean and Taiwanese citizens aged 18 to 30, allows working visits of up to two years, but must be applied for in advance.

➡ Commonwealth citizens with a UK-born parent may be eligible for a Certificate of Entitlement to the Right of Abode, which entitles them to live and work in the UK.

➡ Commonwealth citizens with a UK-born grandparent could qualify for a UK Ancestry Visa, allowing them to work full time for up to five years in the UK.

➡ British immigration authorities have always been tough; you may be required to demonstrate proof of onward travel or an outbound departure date (eg a flight booking home), and possibly evidence that you have sufficient funds to support yourself while in Britain.

Transport

GETTING THERE & AWAY

Most visitors reach Britain by air. As London is a global transport hub, it's easy to fly to Britain from just about anywhere. In recent years, the massive growth of budget 'no-frills' airlines has increased the number of routes – and reduced the fares – between Britain and other countries in Europe.

International trains are much more comfortable and a far more environmentally friendly option. The Channel Tunnel allows direct rail services between Britain, France and Belgium, with onward connections to many other European destinations.

Travel between Britain and mainland Europe by ferry is also easy, either as a pedestrian or by car or coach.

Flights, cars and tours can be booked online at lonelyplanet.com/bookings.

Air

Visitors to the UK arriving by air generally do so at one of London's two largest airports, Heathrow and Gatwick, which have a huge range of international flights to pretty much all corners of the globe. International flights also serve the capital's three other airports (Stansted, Luton and London City) and regional hubs such as Manchester, Bristol and Edinburgh.

Departure tax is included in the price of a ticket.

London Airports

The national carrier is **British Airways** (www.britishairways.com).

The main airports are as follows:

Heathrow (www.heathrowairport.com) Britain's main airport for international flights; often chaotic and crowded. About 15 miles west of central London.

Gatwick (www.gatwickairport.com) Britain's number-two airport, mainly for international flights, 30 miles south of central London.

Stansted (www.stanstedairport.com) About 35 miles north-east of central London, mainly handling charter and budget European flights.

Luton (www.london-luton.co.uk) Some 35 miles north of central London, well known as a holiday-flight airport.

London City (www.londoncityairport.com) A few miles east of central London, specialising in flights to/from European and other UK airports.

Regional Airports

Some planes on European and long-haul routes avoid London and use major regional airports including Manchester and Glasgow. Smaller regional airports such as Southampton, Cardiff and Birmingham are served by flights to and from continental Europe and Ireland.

Land

Bus & Coach

You can easily get between Britain and other European countries via long-distance bus or coach. The international network **Eurolines** (www.eurolines.com) connects a huge number of destinations; you can buy tickets online via one of the national operators.

Services to/from Britain are operated by **National Express** (www.nationalexpress.com). Sample journeys and times to/from London include Amsterdam (12 hours), Barcelona (24 hours), Dublin (12 hours), and Paris (eight hours). If you book early, and

CROSS-BORDER BRITAIN

Travelling between Britain's three nations of England, Scotland and Wales is easy. The bus and train systems are fully integrated and in most cases you won't even know you've crossed the border; passports are not required.

CLIMATE CHANGE & TRAVEL

Every form of transport that relies on carbon-based fuel generates CO_2, the main cause of human-induced climate change. Modern travel is dependent on aeroplanes, which might use less fuel per kilometre per person than most cars but travel much greater distances. The altitude at which aircraft emit gases (including CO_2) and particles also contributes to their climate change impact. Many websites offer 'carbon calculators' that allow people to estimate the carbon emissions generated by their journey and, for those who wish to do so, to offset the impact of the greenhouse gases emitted with contributions to portfolios of climate-friendly initiatives throughout the world. Lonely Planet offsets the carbon footprint of all staff and author travel.

can be flexible with timings (ie travel when few other people want to), you can get some very good deals.

Train

CHANNEL TUNNEL PASSENGER SERVICE

High-speed **Eurostar** (www.eurostar.com) passenger services shuttle at least 10 times daily between London and Paris (2½ hours) or Brussels (two hours). There are three classes: Standard, Standard Premier (which includes wifi and a meal) and Business Premier. Buy tickets from travel agencies, major train stations or the Eurostar website.

The normal one-way fare between London and Paris/Brussels costs around £160; advance booking and off-peak travel gets cheaper fares, as low as £46 one way.

CHANNEL TUNNEL CAR SERVICE

Drivers use **Eurotunnel** (www.eurotunnel.com). At Folkestone in England or Calais in France, you drive onto a train, get carried through the tunnel and drive off at the other end.

Trains run about four times an hour from 6am to 10pm, then hourly through the night. Loading and unloading takes an hour; the journey lasts 35 minutes.

Book in advance online or pay on the spot. Standard one-way fares for a car and passengers start from about £60, but expect to pay substantially more during busy times.

TRAIN & FERRY CONNECTIONS TO EUROPE

As well as Eurostar, many 'normal' trains run between Britain and mainland Europe. You buy one ticket, but get off the train at the port, walk onto a ferry, then get another train on the other side. Routes include Amsterdam–London (via Hook of Holland and Harwich). Travelling between Ireland and Britain, the main train-ferry-train route is Dublin–London, via Dún Laoghaire and Holyhead. Ferries also run between Rosslare and Fishguard or Pembroke (Wales), with train connections on either side.

Sea

Ferry Routes

The main ferry routes between Great Britain and other European countries are as follows:

- Dover–Calais (France)
- Dover–Boulogne (France)
- Newhaven–Dieppe (France)
- Liverpool–Dublin (Ireland)
- Holyhead–Dublin (Ireland)
- Fishguard–Rosslare (Ireland)
- Pembroke Dock–Rosslare (Ireland)
- Newcastle–Amsterdam (Netherlands)
- Harwich–Hook of Holland (Netherlands)
- Hull–Rotterdam (Netherlands)
- Hull–Zeebrugge (Belgium)
- Portsmouth–Santander (Spain)
- Portsmouth–Bilbao (Spain)

Ferry Fares

Most ferry operators offer flexible fares, meaning great bargains at quiet times of day or year. For example, short cross-channel routes such as Dover to Calais or Boulogne can be as low as £50 for a car plus two passengers, although around £75 to £120 is more likely. If you're a foot passenger, or cycling, there's less need to book ahead; fares on short crossings cost about £30 to £50 each way.

Ferry Bookings

Book direct with one of the operators listed here, or use the very handy www.directferries.co.uk – a single site covering all sea-ferry routes, plus **Eurotunnel** (www.eurotunnel.com).

Brittany Ferries (www.brittany-ferries.com)

DFDS Seaways (www.dfdsseaways.co.uk)

Irish Ferries (www.irishferries.com)

P&O Ferries (www.poferries.com)

Stena Line (www.stenaline.com)

GETTING AROUND

Transport in Britain can be expensive compared to continental Europe; bus and rail services are sparse in the more remote parts of the country. For timetables, check out www.traveline.info. Tourist offices can provide maps and information.

Car Useful for travelling at your own pace, or for visiting regions with minimal public transport. Cars can be hired in every town or city.

Train Relatively expensive, with extensive coverage and frequent departures throughout most of the country.

Bus Cheaper and slower than trains, but useful in more remote regions that aren't serviced by rail.

Air

A number of regional airlines operate in Britain, but unless you're travelling a really long way, there's rarely a huge time saving once you factor in travel to/from the airport and waiting for the plane. Short-haul air travel is also hard to defend from an environmental point of view.

The only exception is flying to some of the Scottish islands, when small planes are sometimes the only way to reach them. As always, booking early secures the best fares.

Britain's domestic airline companies include the following:

British Airways (www.britishairways.com)

EasyJet (www.easyjet.com)

Loganair (www.loganair.co.uk)

Ryanair (www.ryanair.com)

Bicycle

Britain is a compact region, and hiring a bike – for an hour or two, or a week or longer – is a great way to really see the country if you've got time to spare.

Bike Hire in London

London is famous for its **Santander Cycles** (☎0343 222 6666; www.tfl.gov.uk/modes/cycling/santander-cycles), known as 'Boris bikes' after the mayor who introduced them to the city. Bikes can be hired on the spot from automatic docking stations. For more information visit the website. Other rental options in the capital are listed at www.lcc.org.uk (under Advice/Bike Shops).

Bike Hire Elsewhere

The **nextbike** (www.nextbike.co.uk) bike-sharing scheme has stations in Exeter, Oxford, Coventry, Glasgow, Stirling and Bath as at the time of research, while tourist towns such as York and Cambridge have plentiful bike-rental options. Bikes can also be hired in national parks and forestry sites now primarily used for leisure activities, such as Kielder Water in Northumberland, Grizedale Forest in the Lake District and the Elan Valley in Mid-Wales. In some areas, disused railway lines are now bike routes, notably the Peak District in Derbyshire. Standard rental rates start at about £10 per day.

Bikes on Trains

Bicycles can be taken free of charge on most local urban trains (although they may not be allowed at peak times when the trains are crowded with commuters) and on shorter trips in rural areas, on a first-come, first-served basis – though there may be space limits.

Bikes can be carried on long-distance train journeys free of charge, but advance booking is required for most services. (Folding bikes can be carried on pretty much any train at any time.) In theory, this shouldn't be too much trouble as most long-distance rail trips are best bought in advance anyway, but you have to go a long way down the path of booking your seat before you start booking your bike – only to find space isn't available.

A final warning: when railways are repaired, cancelled trains are replaced by buses – and they won't take bikes.

The **PlusBike** scheme provides all the information you need for travelling by train with a bike. Leaflets are available at major stations, or downloadable from www.nationalrail.co.uk/118390.aspx.

Boat

There are around 90 inhabited islands off the western and northern coasts of Scotland, which are linked to the mainland by a network of car and passenger ferries. There are two main ferry operators.

Caledonian MacBrayne (CalMac; ☎0800 066 5000; www.calmac.co.uk) Operates car ferry services to the Inner and Outer Hebrides and the islands in the Firth of Clyde.

Northlink Ferries (☎0845 6000 449; www.northlinkferries.co.uk) Operates car ferry services from Aberdeen and Scrabster to the Orkney and Shetland Islands.

Bus & Coach

If you're on a tight budget, long-distance buses (called coaches in Britain) are nearly always the cheapest way to get around, although they're also the slowest – sometimes by a considerable margin. Many towns have separate stations for local buses and long-distance coaches; make sure you go to the right one!

Long-Distance Buses

National Express (www.nationalexpress.com) is the main coach operator, with a wide network and frequent services between main centres. North of the border, services tie in with those of **Scottish Citylink** (www.citylink.co.uk), Scotland's leading coach company. Fares vary: they're cheaper if you book in advance and travel at quieter times, and more expensive if you buy your ticket on the spot and it's Friday afternoon. As a guide, a 200-mile trip (eg London to York) will cost £15 to £25 if you book a few days in advance.

Megabus (www.megabus.com) operates a budget coach service between about 30 destinations around the country. Go at a quiet time, book early and your ticket will be very cheap. Book later, for a busy time and... You get the picture.

Passes & Discounts

National Express offers discount passes to full-time students and under-26s, called Young Persons Coachcards. They cost £12.50 and give you 30% off standard adult fares. Also available are coachcards for people over 60, families, and travellers with disabilities.

Car & Motorcycle

Travelling by car or motorbike around Britain means you can be independent and flexible, and reach remote places. Downsides for drivers include traffic jams, the high price of fuel and high parking costs in cities.

Traffic drives on the left; steering wheels are on the right side of the car. Most rental cars have manual gears (stick shift).

Hire

CAMPERVAN

Hiring a motorhome or camper van (£650 to £1200 a week) is more expensive than hiring a car, but saves on accommodation costs and gives almost unlimited freedom. Sites to check include:

Just Go (www.justgo.uk.com)

Wicked Campers (www.wickedcampers.co.uk)

Wild Horizon (www.wildhorizon.co.uk)

CAR

Compared with many countries (especially the USA), hire rates can be expensive in Britain: the smallest cars start at about £120 per week, and it's around £190 and upwards per week for a medium car. You will require a credit card and a copy of your driving licence; drivers from some countries may also need an IDP (International Drivers' Permit).

Using a rental-broker or comparison site such as **Auto Europe** (www.autoeurope.co.uk), **UK Car Hire** (www.uk-carhire.net) or **Kayak** (www.kayak.com) can also help find bargains, but beware of cheap agencies that often have hidden terms and/or limited mileages. Occasionally, local car hire firms can offer more competitive prices.

Basic third-party insurance is included, which covers liability to other drivers should you have an accident. Standard rental contracts usually have an excess payable in the event of damage to the vehicle, which can be £1000 or more depending on the vehicle you're driving. All car-hire firms will offer you the option of paying extra to waive this excess – but this is usually an expensive option.

Check whether your own car insurance covers you for excess on hire cars, or consider a standalone policy that covers you specifically for the excess (try comparing prices at www.moneymaxim.co.uk). If you damage the car, you will generally have to pay the excess when you return it, and then reclaim it later from your insurance company.

The main players:

Avis (www.avis.co.uk)

Budget (www.budget.co.uk)

Europcar (www.europcar.co.uk)

Sixt (www.sixt.co.uk)

Thrifty (www.thrifty.co.uk)

Motoring Organisations

Motoring organisations in Britain include the **Automobile Association** (www.theaa.com) and the **RAC** (www.rac.co.uk). For both, annual membership starts at around £45, including 24-hour roadside breakdown assistance.

Britannia (www.lv.com/breakdown-cover) offers better value from £30 a year, while a greener alternative is the **Environmental Transport Association** (www.eta.co.uk); it provides breakdown assistance but doesn't campaign for more roads.

Insurance

It's illegal to drive a car or motorbike in Britain without (at least) third-party insurance. This will be included with all rental cars. If you're bringing a car from Europe, you'll need to arrange it.

Parking

Many cities have short-stay and long-stay car parks; the latter are cheaper but may be more out of the way. 'Park & Ride' systems allow you to park on the edge of the city, then ride to the centre on frequent non-stop buses for an all-in-one price.

Yellow lines (single or double) along the edge of the road indicate parking restrictions. Nearby signs will spell out when you can and can't park. In London and other big cities, traffic wardens operate with efficiency; if you park on the yellow lines at the wrong time, your car will be clamped or towed away, and it'll cost you £130 or more to get driving again. In some cities there are also red

TRAVELINE

Traveline (www.traveline.info) is a very useful information service covering bus, coach, taxi and train services nationwide. The website offers access to online timetables, a journey planner, route maps and limited fare information.

TRAVEL FARES

When travelling by long-distance bus, coach or train in Britain, it's important to realise that there's no such thing as a standard fare. Prices vary according to demand and when you buy your ticket. Book long in advance and travel on Tuesday mid-morning and it's cheap. Buy your ticket on the spot late Friday afternoon and it'll be a lot more expensive. Ferries use similar systems.

Lonely Planet sample fares are somewhere in between the very cheapest and most expensive options. The price you pay will almost certainly be different.

To secure the cheapest fares, the two golden rules are: book as early in advance as you can, and be flexible with your travel times (off-peak times are always cheaper).

lines, which mean no stopping at any time.

Also beware of other areas that may be restricted in some other way (eg for local residents or pass-holders only); these can sometimes be tricky to notice, but if you contravene the rules, the results will be the same: a parking ticket, wheel-clamping or towing away.

Roads & Speed Limits

Motorways and main A-roads deliver you quickly from one end of the country to another. Lesser A-roads, B-roads and minor roads are much more scenic – ideal for car or motorcycle touring. You can't travel fast, but you won't care.

Speed limits are usually 30mph (48km/h) in built-up areas, 60mph (96km/h) on main roads and 70mph (112km/h) on motorways and most (but not all) dual carriageways.

Road Rules

A foreign driving licence is valid in Britain for up to 12 months.

Drink-driving is taken very seriously; you're allowed a maximum blood-alcohol level of 80mg/100mL (0.08%) in England and Wales, and 50mg/100mL (0.05%) in Scotland.

Some other important rules:

- drive on the left (!)
- wear fitted seatbelts in cars
- wear helmets on motorcycles
- give way to your right at junctions and roundabouts
- always use the left lane on motorways and dual carriageways unless overtaking (although so many people ignore this rule, you'd think it didn't exist)
- don't use a mobile phone while driving unless it's fully hands-free (another rule frequently flouted)

Hitchhiking

Hitching is not as common as it used to be in Britain: maybe because more people have cars and maybe because few drivers give lifts any more. It's perfectly possible, however, if you don't mind long waits. Nevertheless, hitching is never entirely safe, and we don't recommend it. Travellers who hitch should understand that they are taking a small but potentially serious risk. If you decide to go by thumb, note that it's illegal to hitch on motorways; you must use approach roads or service stations.

However, it's all different in remote rural areas such as Mid-Wales or northwest Scotland, where hitching is a part of getting around – especially if you're a walker heading back to base after a hike on the hills. On some Scottish islands, local drivers may stop and offer a lift without you even asking.

Local Transport

Buses

There are good local bus networks year-round in cities and towns. Buses also run in some rural areas year-round, although timetables are designed to serve schools and businesses, so there aren't many midday and weekend services (and they may stop running during school holidays), or buses may link local villages to a market town on only one day each week.

In tourist areas (especially national parks), there are frequent services from Easter to September. However, it's always worth double-checking at a tourist office before planning your day's activities around a bus that may not actually be running.

If you're taking a few local bus rides in one area, day passes (with names like Day Rover, Wayfarer or Explorer) are cheaper than buying several single tickets. Often they can be bought on your first bus, and may include local rail services. It's always worth asking ticket clerks or bus drivers about your options.

Taxi

Officially there are two sorts of taxi in Britain: those with meters that can be hailed in the street; and minicabs, which are cheaper but can only be called by phone. More recently, in many locations these have been usurped by ride-hailing services like **Uber** (www.uber.com) and **Kabbee** (www.kabbee.com), which now operate in many British cities (including, at the time of writing, London).

In London, most taxis are the famous 'black cabs' (some with advertising livery in other colours), which charge by distance and time: they may be an institution, but be aware that they are also expensive. Depending on the time of day, a 1-mile journey takes five to 10 minutes and costs £7 to £10. Longer journeys are proportionally cheaper. Black cabs also operate in some other large cities around Britain, with rates usually lower than in London.

In London, taxis are best flagged down in the street; a 'for hire' light on the roof indicates availability. In other cities, you can flag down a cab if you see one, but it's usually easier to go to a taxi rank.

In rural areas, taxis need to be called by phone; the best place to find the local taxi's phone number is the local pub. Fares are £3 to £5 per mile.

Traintaxi (www.traintaxi.co.uk) is a portal site for journeys between the train station and your hotel or other final destination.

Train

For long-distance travel around Britain, trains are generally faster and more comfortable than coaches, but can be substantially more expensive – especially if you're used to cheap, subsidised fares in other European countries. In fact, per mile, train travel in Britain is among the most expensive in Europe.

Having said that, trains are usually by far the most convenient way to travel around – and there's a station in most sizeable towns and cities. Services aren't as punctual as they probably should be given the cost, but in general most services tend to run on time.

Train Operators

About 20 different companies operate train services in Britain, while Network Rail operates track and stations (although during the coronavirus crisis, the government was forced to take over a number of railways due to a plummeting in passenger traffic – a state of affairs that was still in effect at the time of writing).

Ticket-buying services are centralised, meaning you normally only need one ticket even if your journey is provided by several operators. The main railcards and passes are also accepted by all train operators.

However, it's worth noting that where more than one train operator services the same route, eg York to Edinburgh, a ticket purchased from one company may not be valid on trains run by another. So if you miss the train you originally booked, you will have to confirm which later services your ticket will be valid for.

Tickets & Reservations

Your first stop should be **National Rail Enquiries** (www.nationalrail.co.uk), the nationwide timetable and fare information service. Its website advertises special offers and has real-time links to station departure boards and downloadable maps of the rail network.

BUYING TICKETS

Once you've found the journey you need on the National Rail Enquiries website, links take you to the relevant train operator to buy the ticket. This can be mailed to you (UK addresses only) or collected at the station on the day of travel from automatic machines. There's usually no booking fee on top of the ticket price.

You can also use a centralised ticketing service to buy your train ticket. These cover all train services in a single site, but they may charge a booking fee on top of every ticket price. The main players include:

QJump (www.qjump.co.uk)

Rail Easy (www.raileasy.co.uk)

Trainline (www.thetrainline.com)

To use operator or centralised ticketing websites, you always have to state a preferred time and day of travel, even if you don't mind when you go, but you can change it as you go through the process, and with a little delving around you can find some real bargains.

You can also buy train tickets on the spot at stations, which is fine for short journeys (under about 50 miles), but discount tickets for longer trips are usually not available and must be bought in advance by phone or online.

One tip that's worth considering is whether splitting your journey may result in a cheaper fare: services like TrainPal (mytrainpal.com) and TrainTickets.com can help you check. Cheap day

LONDON STATIONS

London has several main-line train stations, including Victoria, Paddington, King's Cross, Waterloo, Charing Cross and Liverpool St, positioned in a rough circle around the city's central area (and mostly linked by the Circle Underground line). The stations' proper names are London Victoria, London Paddington, London King's Cross and so on, and this is how you'll see them appear on official timetables, information boards and booking websites – although the British never use the full names in everyday speech.

returns are often not much more expensive than buying single tickets.

COSTS

For longer journeys, on-the-spot fares are always available, but tickets are much, much cheaper if bought in advance, and if you're happy to specify the train on which you travel (which also means you get a reserved seat). The earlier you book, the cheaper it gets – leaving things to the last minute means your ticket is likely to be eye-wateringly expensive. Travelling off-peak (ie outside popular commuter hours) is also cheaper.

One major drawback is that the cheapest fares (eg Advance) are usually nonrefundable, so if you miss your train you'll have to buy a new ticket.

Whichever operator you travel with and wherever you buy tickets, these are the three main fare types:

Anytime Buy anytime, travel anytime – usually the most expensive option.

Off-peak Buy ticket any time, travel off-peak (what is off-peak depends on the journey).

Advance Buy ticket in advance, travel only on specific trains – usually the cheapest option.

For an idea of the (substantial) price differences, a ticket from London to York bought a few days before travel can return the following fares: Advance from around £57.50, Off-Peak from £136.50, and Anytime from £220.50.

Mobile train tickets are gradually becoming more common across the network, but it's a slow process.

ONWARD TRAVEL

If the train doesn't get you all the way to your destination, you can add a **PlusBus** (www.plusbus.info) supplement when making your reservation to validate your train ticket for onward travel by bus. This is more convenient, and usually cheaper, than buying a separate bus ticket.

Train Classes

There are two classes of rail travel: first and standard. First class costs around 50% more than standard fare (up to double at busy periods) and gets you bigger seats, more legroom and usually a more peaceful business-like atmosphere, plus extras such as complimentary drinks and newspapers. At weekends some train operators offer 'upgrades' to first class for an extra £5 to £25 on top of your standard class fare, payable on the spot.

Train Passes

DISCOUNT PASSES

If you're staying in Britain for a while, passes known as **Railcards** (www.railcard.co.uk) are worth considering:

16-25 Railcard For those aged 16 to 25, or full-time UK students.

Two Together Railcard For two specified people travelling together.

Senior Railcard For anyone over 60.

Family & Friends Railcard Covers up to four adults and four children travelling together.

Railcards cost £30 (valid for one year, available from major stations or online) and give a 33% discount on most train fares, except those already heavily discounted. With the Family card, adults get 33% and children get 60% discounts, so the fee is easily recouped in a couple of journeys.

LOCAL & REGIONAL PASSES

Local train passes usually cover rail networks around a city (many include bus travel too). If you're concentrating your travels on southeast England (eg London to Dover, Weymouth, Cambridge or Oxford), a **Network Railcard** (per year £30) covers up to four adults and up to four children travelling together outside peak times.

NATIONAL PASSES

For countrywide travel, **BritRail** (www.britrail.net) passes are available for visitors from overseas. They must be bought in your country of origin (not in Britain) from a specialist travel agency. They're available in seven different versions (eg England only; Scotland only; all of Britain; UK and Ireland) for periods from four to 30 days.

Glossary

almshouse – accommodation for the aged or needy
ap – prefix in a Welsh name meaning 'son of'

bag – originally to 'catch' – a shooting term – now used to mean 'reach the top of' (as in to 'bag a couple of peaks' or *'Munro bagging'*)
bailey – outermost wall of a castle
bar – gate (York, and some other northern cities)
beck – stream (northern England)
bill – the total you need to pay after eating in a restaurant ('check' to Americans)
billion – the British billion is a million million (unlike the American billion – a thousand million)
blackhouse – traditional low-walled stone cottage with thatch or turf roof and earth floors; shared by both humans and cattle and typical of the Outer Hebrides until the early 20th century (Scotland)
bloke – man (colloquial)
Blue Flag – an award given to beaches for their unpolluted sand and water
böd – once a simple trading booth used by fishing communities, today it refers to basic accommodation for walkers etc (used only in Shetland)
bothy – very simple hut or shelter, usually in mountain or wilderness area, used by walkers and hikers
brae – hill (Scotland)
bridleway – track for horse riders that can also be used by walkers and cyclists
broch – ancient defensive tower
burgh – town
burn – stream
bus – local bus; see also *coach*

Cadw – the Welsh historic monuments agency
cairn – pile of stones marking path, junction of paths or the summit of a mountain
CalMac – Caledonian MacBrayne, the main Scottish island ferry operator
canny – good, great, wise (northern England)
castell – castle (Welsh)
ceilidh – (*kay*-lee) a session of traditional music, song and dance; originally Scottish, now more widely used across Britain
Celtic high cross – a large, elaborately carved stone cross decorated with biblical scenes and Celtic interlace designs dating from the 8th to 10th centuries
cheers – goodbye; thanks (colloquial); also a drinking toast
chemist – pharmacist
chine – valley-like fissure leading to the sea (southern England)
chippy – fish-and-chip shop
circus – junction of several city streets, usually circular, and usually with a green or other feature at the centre
Clearances – eviction of Highland farmers from their land by *lairds* wanting to use it for grazing sheep
close – entrance to an alley
coach – long-distance bus
coasteering – adventurous activity that involves making your way around a rocky coastline by climbing, scrambling, jumping or swimming
cob – mixture of mud and straw for building
corrie – circular hollow on a hillside
cot – small bed for a baby ('crib' to Americans)
court – courtyard
craic – lively conversation; pronounced, and sometimes spelt, 'crack'
craig – exposed rock
crannog – an artificial island in a loch built for defensive purposes
croft – smallholding, usually in marginal agricultural area (Scotland); the activity is known as 'smallholding'
Cymraeg – Welsh language (Welsh); also Gymraeg
Cymru – Welsh word for Wales

dene – valley
dirk – dagger
DIY – do-it-yourself, ie home improvements
dram – a measure of whisky
dodgy – suspect, bad, dangerous (colloquial)
dolmen – chambered tomb (Wales)
dough – money (colloquial)
downs – rolling upland, characterised by lack of trees
duvet – quilt replacing sheets and blankets ('doona' to Australians)

EH – English Heritage; state-funded organisation responsible for historic sites

en suite room – hotel room with private attached bathroom (ie shower, basin and toilet)

eisteddfod – literally a gathering or session; festival in which competitions are held in music, poetry, drama and the fine arts; plural eisteddfodau (Welsh)

Evensong – daily evening service (Church of England)

fell race – tough running race through hills or moors

fen – drained or marshy low-lying flat land

firth – estuary

fiver – £5 note (colloquial)

flat – single dwelling in a larger building ('apartment' to Americans)

flip-flops – plastic sandals with a single strap over toes ('thongs' to Australians)

footpath – path through countryside and between houses, not beside a road (that's called a 'pavement')

gate – street (York, and some other northern cities)

graft – work (not corruption, as in American English; colloquial)

grand – 1000 (colloquial)

gutted – very disappointed (colloquial)

guv, guvner – from governor, a respectful term of address for owner or boss; can sometimes be used ironically

hart – deer

HI – Hostelling International (organisation)

hire – rent

Hogmanay – Scottish celebration of New Year's Eve

howff – pub or shelter (Scotland)

HS – Historic Scotland; organisation that manages historic sites in Scotland

inn – pub with accommodation

jumper – woollen item of clothing worn on torso ('sweater' to Americans)

ken – Scottish term for 'understand' or 'know', as in 'do you ken' = 'do you know'

kirk – church (northern England and Scotland)

knowe – burial mound (Scotland)

kyle – strait or channel (Scotland)

laird – estate owner (Scotland)

lass – young woman (northern England and Scotland)

lift – machine for carrying people up and down in large buildings ('elevator' to Americans)

linn – waterfall (Scotland)

loch – lake (Scotland)

lochan – small *loch*

lock – part of a canal or river that can be closed off and the water levels changed to raise or lower boats

lolly – money (colloquial); candy on a stick (possibly frozen)

lorry (s), lorries (pl) – truck

Mabinogion – key source of Welsh folk legends

machair – grass- and wildflower-covered sand dunes

mad – insane (not angry, as in American English)

Marches – borderlands between England and Wales or Scotland

menhir – standing stone

Mercat Cross – a symbol of the trading rights of a market town or village, usually found in the centre of town and usually a focal point for the community

mere – a body of water, usually shallow; technically a lake that has a large surface area relative to its depth

merthyr – burial place of a saint (Welsh)

midge – mosquito-like insect

motorway – major road linking cities (equivalent to 'interstate' or 'freeway')

motte – early Norman fortification consisting of a raised, flattened mound with a keep on top; when attached to a *bailey* it is known as a motte-and-bailey

Munro – hill or mountain 3000ft (914m) or higher, especially in Scotland; those over 2500ft are called Corbetts

Munro bagger – a hill walker who tries to climb all the *Munros* in Scotland

naff – inferior, in poor taste (colloquial)

NCN – National Cycle Network

newydd – new (Welsh)

NNR – National Nature Reserve, managed by the Scottish Natural Heritage (SNH)

NT – National Trust; organisation that protects historic buildings and land with scenic importance in England and Wales

NTS – National Trust for Scotland; organisation dedicated to the preservation of historic sites and the environment in Scotland

oast house – building containing a kiln for drying hops

ogham – ancient Celtic script

oriel – gallery (Welsh)

OS – Ordnance Survey

p – (pronounced pee) pence; ie 2p is 'two p' not 'two pence' or 'tuppence'

pele – fortified house

Picts – early inhabitants of north and east Scotland (from Latin pictus, or 'painted', after their body-paint decorations)

pile – large imposing building (colloquial)

pissed – slang for drunk (not angry)

pissed off – angry (slang)

pitch – playing field

postbus – minibus delivering the mail, also carrying passengers in remote areas

provost – mayor

punter – customer (colloquial)

quid – pound (colloquial)

ramble – short easy walk

reiver – warrior or raider (historic term; northern England)

return ticket – round-trip ticket

RIB – rigid inflatable boat

rood – an old Scots word for a cross

RSPB – Royal Society for the Protection of Birds

RSPCA – Royal Society for the Prevention of Cruelty to Animals

sarsen – boulder, a geological remnant usually found in chalky areas (sometimes used in neolithic constructions, eg Stonehenge and Avebury)

Sassenach – from Gaelic 'Sasannach': anyone who is not a Highlander (including Lowland Scots)

sheila-na-gig – Celtic fertility symbol of a woman with exaggerated genitalia, often carved in stone on churches and castles; rare in England, found mainly in the *Marches*, along the border with Wales

single ticket – one-way ticket

SMC – Scottish Mountaineering Club

SNH – Scottish Natural Heritage, a government organisation directly responsible for safeguarding and improving Scotland's natural heritage

snickelway – narrow alley (York)

snug – usually a small separate room in a pub

sporran – purse worn around waist with the kilt (Scotland)

SSSI – Site of Special Scientific Interest

Sustrans – sustainable transport charity encouraging people to walk, cycle and use public transport; also responsible for instigating and developing the NCN (National Cycle Network)

SYHA – Scottish Youth Hostel Association

tarn – a small lake or pool, usually in mountain areas in England, often in a depression caused by glacial erosion

tenner – £10 note (colloquial)

TIC – Tourist Information Centre

ton – 100 (colloquial)

tor – pointed hill

torch – flashlight

Tory – Conservative (political party)

towpath – path running beside a river or canal, where horses once towed barges

twitcher – obsessive birdwatcher

Tube, the – London's underground railway system (colloquial)

Underground, the – London's underground railway system

wolds – open, rolling countryside

wynd – lane or narrow street (northern England and Scotland)

YHA – Youth Hostels Association

Behind the Scenes

SEND US YOUR FEEDBACK

We love to hear from travellers – your comments keep us on our toes and help make our books better. Our well-travelled team reads every word on what you loved or loathed about this book. Although we cannot reply individually to your submissions, we always guarantee that your feedback goes straight to the appropriate authors, in time for the next edition. Each person who sends us information is thanked in the next edition – the most useful submissions are rewarded with a selection of digital PDF chapters.

Visit **lonelyplanet.com/contact** to submit your updates and suggestions or to ask for help. Our award-winning website also features inspirational travel stories, news and discussions.

Note: We may edit, reproduce and incorporate your comments in Lonely Planet products such as guidebooks, websites and digital products, so let us know if you don't want your comments reproduced or your name acknowledged. For a copy of our privacy policy visit lonelyplanet.com/privacy.

WRITER THANKS

Isabel Albiston

Many thanks to everyone who helped me on my travels through the beautiful Scottish Highlands - your warm welcome, patience with my endless questions and wise advice were greatly appreciated. Thanks to Sandie and my fellow authors, and to my friends and family for your support, especially to Alison and her family for coming to visit me on the road.

Oliver Berry

Thanks to everyone who helped me put this project together in the crazy circumstances of a global pandemic – especially my fellow authors and my commissioning editor Sandie Kestell. On the road, Dan Hinkley, Rebecca Jones, Tom Smith and Hope Delaney deserve a call-out. Back home, thanks to Rosie Hillier, Gracie, Susie Berry and Justin Foulkes. Most of all thanks to all the amazing LP people (especially all the incredible cartos) who started this project but sadly didn't get to see it finished. Best of luck on your next adventures.

Joe Bindloss

I'd like to thank my partner Linda and two boys Benji and Tyler for putting up with me heading off to research at this unsettling time. Thanks to the many helpful staff at tourist offices, bus stations, B&Bs, stately homes and museums who provided local information, and to the pubs and restaurants who were diligent about social distancing to keep everyone safe. Thanks also to everyone who wrote in with tips – it's great to have extra eyes and ears on the ground!

Fionn Davenport

2020 was a tough year for travel – and travel writing. But in the middle of it all, I was reminded more strongly than ever of the salutary effects of exploring other

THIS BOOK

This 14th edition of Lonely Planet's *Great Britain* guidebook was researched and written by Isabel Albiston, Oliver Berry, Joe Bindloss, Fionn Davenport, Belinda Dixon, Peter Dragicevich, Anthony Ham, Damian Harper, Anna Kaminski, Catherine Le Nevez, Andy Symington, Tasmin Waby, Kerry Walker, Luke Waterson, Neil Wilson and Barbara Woolsey. The previous edition was written by Oliver, Fionn, Marc Di Duca, Belinda, Damian, Catherine, Hugh McNaughtan, Lorna Parkes, Andy, Greg Ward and Neil. This guidebook was produced by the following:

Senior Product Editor Sandie Kestell

Cartographer Mark Griffiths

Product Editor Amy Lynch

Book Designer Clara Monitto

Assisting Editors Janet Austin, Andrew Bain, Nigel Chin, Andrea Dobbin, Carly Hall, Kate Kiely, Maja Vatrić, Brana Vladisavljevic

Cover Researcher Fergal Condon

Thanks to Ronan Abayawickrema, Gareth Brown, Gabrielle Stefanos

places. A huge thanks to those who kept me going – Andy Parkinson, Joe Keggin and my editor Sandie Kestell, who made the craziest of times that little bit less crazy. Finally, a big thanks to my wife Laura. We'll never forget this particular update!

Belinda Dixon

To all who showed so many kindnesses while I was on the road, thank you; especially at what was such a challenging time - I hope the storm passes. Sandie and the other LP staff, thank you for keeping the ship on course, and to fellow LP writers a big 'cheers' for keeping spirits up. And countless thanks to Laura and Midge for making me laugh and keeping me sane.

Peter Dragicevich

I flew to Wales for this book just as the shadow of COVID-19 was starting to spread around the globe. Two weeks later, with borders slamming shut and the airlines in disarray, I got on a flight home to New Zealand. My thanks and thoughts are with David Inglis, and all the wonderful travel professionals who have lost their jobs due to this pandemic.

Anthony Ham

I'm very grateful to everyone at Lonely Planet, for the pleasure of working with you on this book and so many more, especially Sandie Kestell and Darren O'Connell.

Damian Harper

Many thanks to everyone who helped and offered tips, including my co-authors, the ever-helpful staff at the Natural History Museum, Amaya Wang, Polly Bussell, Freya Barry, Tania Patel, Norman MacDonald, Penny Aikens, Bill Moran, Hollie and the excellent staff at Japan House, Shannon and James Peake. And big thanks to Tim Harper for his fine suggestions and Emma Harper too.

Anna Kaminski

I'd like to thank Sandie for entrusting me with my favourite part of Wales and everyone else who's helped me along the way. In particular: Mike and Jane in Penmaenmawr, Dolgun Uchaf owners in Dolgellau, Ceri and James in Conwy, Alys and John in Caernarfon, the Caerwylan Hotel staff in Criccieth, the Go Below! folks, Bryn Eltyd Eco Guest House in Blaenau Ffestiniog, Joe Brown staff for trekking advice in Llanberis, and Jan Morris for the memorable meeting in Llanystumdwy.

Catherine Le Nevez

Cheers first and foremost to Julian, and to all of the locals and tourism professionals in the Midlands who provided insights, information and inspiration during this project. Huge thanks too to Sandie Kestell and everyone at LP. As ever, merci encore to my parents, brother, belle-sœur, neveu and nièce.

Andy Symington

I owe many thanks to lots of helpful people along the way who were generous with their time and advice despite the uncertain circumstances of the Covid situation, particularly in tourist offices. I am especially grateful, as ever, to Jenny Neil and Brendan Bolland for their always wonderful hospitality, to Neil Wilson and my other co-authors on this project and to Sandie Kestell and the LP team.

Tasmin Waby

Thank you to Duff Battye for lending me his home in Oxfordshire and his intel on rugby and cycling in England. Cheers to my fellow scribes Oliver Berry, Belinda Dixon, Lauren Keith, Hugh McNaughtan, and Dane Waby for your feedback. To all my co-creators on this guidebook including Sandie Kestell, it's been quite a rollercoaster of a journey this time! And finally to my sometimes companions on the road, Maisie and Willa: you make everything we do magic.

Kerry Walker

Wales is my adopted home and I am deeply indebted to many of its wonderful locals and tourism professionals for making this guide what it is. A special diolch goes to Pat Edgar (Visit Pembrokeshire) and Paula Ellis for their insights and assistance. Big thanks also to my partner (and fellow author) Luke for his support and shared love of Wales, and my beautiful baby daughter, Eira ('Snow') for helping me to see the country through fresh new eyes.

Luke Waterson

A wonderfully array of individuals stepped up to help me this edition: much appreciated given this got researched amidst a global pandemic! Thanks especially to Gemma Simmons and Jane Cook (Cardiff), Angharad and Carey Hill (Swansea) and the guys at the George Borrow Hotel in Ponterwyd: lifesavers and cold beer providers! A big diolch to the other writers too: not least my traveller-truelove Kerry.

Neil Wilson

Thanks to the friendly and helpful tourist office staff all over Scotland; to Morag and Alisdair at Lochside Cottage, Steven Fallon, Keith Jeffrey, Fiona Garven, Derek McCrindle, Brendan Bolland, Jenny Neil, Tom and Christine Duffin, Steve Hall, Elaine Simpson, Duncan and Maja Pepper, Dona Milne and Alastair Short; and, as ever, to Carol Downie. Thanks also to my co-authors, and to Sandie Kestell and the rest of the editorial team at Lonely Planet.

Barbara Woolsey

A heartfelt thanks to all those who supported in this research, and particularly to my wonderful big Scottish family. Special shout-outs to: Clair Woolsey, Remy Woolsey, René Frank, Marlene Dow and Ardelle Kuchinka.

ACKNOWLEDGEMENTS

Climate map data adapted from Peel MC, Finlayson BL & McMahon TA (2007) 'Updated World Map of the Köppen-Geiger Climate Classification', *Hydrology and Earth System Sciences*, 11, 1633–44.

Cover photograph: Little Langdale, Lake District National Park, David C Tomlinson/Getty Images ©

Illustrations: pp94–5, pp630–1 and pp842–3 by Javier Zarracina, pp76–7 by Javier Zarracina and Michael Weldon.

Index

Map Pages **000**
Photo Pages **000**

Map Pages **000**
Photo Pages **000**

Map Pages **000**
Photo Pages **000**

M

Map Pages **000**
Photo Pages **000**

Y

Z

Map Pages **000**
Photo Pages **000**

Tasmin Waby
A London-born writer, Tasmin was raised on the traditional lands of Aboriginal Australians, for which she will always be grateful. As well as reading, writing and editing, she's madly in love with cartography, deserts, and starry skies. When not on assignment she lives on a narrowboat in the UK, raising two hilariously funny school-aged children.

Kerry Walker
Kerry is an award-winning travel writer, photographer and Lonely Planet author, specialising in Central and Southern Europe. Based in Wales, she has authored/co-authored more than a dozen Lonely Planet titles. An adventure addict, she loves mountains, cold places and true wilderness. She tweets @kerrychristiani.

Luke Waterson
Raised in the remote Somerset countryside in Southwest England, Luke quickly became addicted to exploring out-of-the-way places. Completing a Creative Writing degree at the University of East Anglia, he shouldered his backpack and vowed to see as much of the world as possible. Fast-forward a few years and he has travelled the Americas from Alaska to Tierra del Fuego and developed an obsession for Soviet Architecture and Pre-Columbian ruins in equal measure. Luke specialises in writing on South America. His other areas of expertise are the Caribbean, Scandinavia and Eastern Europe.

Neil Wilson
Neil was born in Scotland and has lived there most of his life. Based in Perthshire, he has been a full-time writer since 1988, working on more than 80 guidebooks for various publishers, including the Lonely Planet guides to Scotland, England, Ireland and Prague. An outdoors enthusiast since childhood, Neil is an active hill-walker, mountain-biker, sailor, snowboarder and rock-climber, and a qualified fly-fishing guide and instructor. He has climbed and tramped in four continents, including ascents of Jebel Toubkal in Morocco, Mount Kinabalu in Borneo, the Old Man of Hoy in Scotland's Orkney Islands and the Northwest Face of Half Dome in California's Yosemite Valley.

Barbara Woolsey
Barbara Woolsey was born and raised on the Canadian prairies to a Filipino mother and Irish-Scottish father – and that multicultural upbringing has fuelled a life's passion for storytelling across cultures and borders. Barbara's career started in Bangkok working for Thailand's largest English-language newspaper, then travelling around Asia as a TV host for a Bangkok-based channel. Since then, she's voyaged across five continents and almost 50 countries by plane, train and motorbike. Some highlights: a 3,000-kilometre motorbike journey across India, reporting from wildlife reservations and townships in South Africa, and interviewing gang members in Caracas. In addition to writing for Lonely Planet, Barbara contributes as a journalist to newspapers, magazines, and websites with readerships around the world. She spends most of her time in her adopted home of Berlin, Germany.

Map Legend

Sights
- Beach
- Bird Sanctuary
- Buddhist
- Castle/Palace
- Christian
- Confucian
- Hindu
- Islamic
- Jain
- Jewish
- Monument
- Museum/Gallery/Historic Building
- Ruin
- Shinto
- Sikh
- Taoist
- Winery/Vineyard
- Zoo/Wildlife Sanctuary
- Other Sight

Activities, Courses & Tours
- Bodysurfing
- Diving
- Canoeing/Kayaking
- Course/Tour
- Sento Hot Baths/Onsen
- Skiing
- Snorkelling
- Surfing
- Swimming/Pool
- Walking
- Windsurfing
- Other Activity

Sleeping
- Sleeping
- Camping
- Hut/Shelter

Eating
- Eating

Drinking & Nightlife
- Drinking & Nightlife
- Cafe

Entertainment
- Entertainment

Shopping
- Shopping

Information
- Bank
- Embassy/Consulate
- Hospital/Medical
- Internet
- Police
- Post Office
- Telephone
- Toilet
- Tourist Information
- Other Information

Geographic
- Beach
- Gate
- Hut/Shelter
- Lighthouse
- Lookout
- Mountain/Volcano
- Oasis
- Park
- Pass
- Picnic Area
- Waterfall

Population
- Capital (National)
- Capital (State/Province)
- City/Large Town
- Town/Village

Transport
- Airport
- Border crossing
- Bus
- Cable car/Funicular
- Cycling
- Ferry
- Metro station
- Monorail
- Parking
- Petrol station
- S-Bahn/Subway station
- Taxi
- T-bane/Tunnelbana station
- Train station/Railway
- Tram
- U-Bahn/Underground station
- Other Transport

Routes
- Tollway
- Freeway
- Primary
- Secondary
- Tertiary
- Lane
- Unsealed road
- Road under construction
- Plaza/Mall
- Steps
- Tunnel
- Pedestrian overpass
- Walking Tour
- Walking Tour detour
- Path/Walking Trail

Boundaries
- International
- State/Province
- Disputed
- Regional/Suburb
- Marine Park
- Cliff
- Wall

Hydrography
- River, Creek
- Intermittent River
- Canal
- Water
- Dry/Salt/Intermittent Lake
- Reef

Areas
- Airport/Runway
- Beach/Desert
- Cemetery (Christian)
- Cemetery (Other)
- Glacier
- Mudflat
- Park/Forest
- Sight (Building)
- Sportsground
- Swamp/Mangrove

Note: Not all symbols displayed above appear on the maps in this book

Peter Dragicevich
After a successful career in niche newspaper and magazine publishing, both in his native New Zealand and in Australia, Peter finally gave into Kiwi wanderlust, giving up staff jobs to chase his diverse roots around much of Europe. Over the last 15 years he's written over 100 books for Lonely Planet on an oddly disparate collection of countries, all of which he's come to love. He once again calls Auckland, New Zealand his home – although his current nomadic existence means he's often elsewhere.

Anthony Ham
Anthony is a freelance writer and photographer who specialises in Spain, East and Southern Africa, the Arctic and the Middle East. When he's not writing for Lonely Planet, Anthony writes about and photographs Spain, Africa and the Middle East for newspapers and magazines in Australia, the UK and US.

Damian Harper
With two degrees (one in modern and classical Chinese from SOAS), Damian has been writing for Lonely Planet for over two decades, contributing to titles as diverse as China, Beijing, Shanghai, Vietnam, Thailand, Ireland, London, Mallorca, Malaysia, Singapore & Brunei, Hong Kong, China's Southwest and the UK. A seasoned guidebook writer, Damian has penned articles for numerous newspapers and magazines, including *The Guardian* and *The Daily Telegraph*, and currently makes Surrey, England, his home. A self-taught trumpet novice, his other hobbies include collecting modern first editions, photography and Taekwondo. Follow Damian on Instagram (damian.harper).

Anna Kaminski
Originally from the Soviet Union, Anna grew up in Cambridge, UK. She graduated from the University of Warwick with a degree in Comparative American Studies, a background in the history, culture and literature of the Americas and the Caribbean, and an enduring love of Latin America. Her restless wanderings led her to settle briefly in Oaxaca and Bangkok and her flirtation with criminal law saw her volunteering as a lawyer's assistant in the courts, ghettos and prisons of Kingson, Jamaica. Anna has contributed to almost 30 Lonely Planet titles. When not on the road, Anna calls London home.

Catherine Le Nevez
Catherine's wanderlust kicked in when she roadtripped across Europe from her Parisian base aged four, and she's been hitting the road at every opportunity since, travelling to some 60 countries and completing her Doctorate of Creative Arts in Writing, Masters in Professional Writing, and postgrad qualifications in Editing and Publishing along the way. Over the past decade-and-a-half she's written scores of Lonely Planet guides and articles covering Paris, France, Europe and far beyond. Her work has also appeared in numerous online and print publications. Topping Catherine's list of travel tips is to travel without any expectations.

Andy Symington
Andy has written or worked on over a hundred books and other updates for Lonely Planet (especially in Europe and Latin America) and other publishing companies, and has published articles on numerous subjects for a variety of newspapers, magazines, and websites. He part-owns and operates a rock bar, has written a novel and is currently working on several fiction and non-fiction writing projects. Andy, from Australia, moved to Northern Spain many years ago. When he's not off with a backpack in some far-flung corner of the world, he can probably be found watching the tragically poor local football side or tasting local wines after a long walk in the nearby mountains.

OUR STORY

A beat-up old car, a few dollars in the pocket and a sense of adventure. In 1972 that's all Tony and Maureen Wheeler needed for the trip of a lifetime – across Europe and Asia overland to Australia. It took several months, and at the end – broke but inspired – they sat at their kitchen table writing and stapling together their first travel guide, *Across Asia on the Cheap*. Within a week they'd sold 1500 copies. Lonely Planet was born.

Today, Lonely Planet has offices in Tennessee, Dublin and Beijing, with a network of over 2000 contributors in every corner of the globe. We share Tony's belief that 'a great guidebook should do three things: inform, educate and amuse'.

OUR WRITERS

Isabel Albiston

After 6 years working for the *Daily Telegraph* in London, Isabel left to spend more time on the road. A job as writer for a magazine in Sydney, Australia was followed by a four-month overland trip across Asia and five years living and working in Buenos Aires, Argentina. Isabel started writing for Lonely Planet in 2014 and has contributed to 15 guidebooks. She's currently based in Ireland.

Oliver Berry

Oliver Berry is a writer and photographer from Cornwall. He has worked for Lonely Planet for more than a decade and has worked on more than 30 guidebooks. He is also a regular contributor to many newspapers and magazines, including *Lonely Planet Traveller*. His writing has won several awards, including The Guardian Young Travel Writer of the Year and the *TNT Magazine* People's Choice Award. His latest work is published at www.oliverberry.com.

Joe Bindloss

Joe first got the travel bug on a grand tour of Asia in the early 1990s, and he's been roaming around its temples and paddy-fields ever since on dozens of assignments for Lonely Planet and other publishers, covering everywhere from Myanmar and Thailand to India and Nepal. Joe was Lonely Planet's Destination Editor for the Indian Subcontinent until 2019. See more of his work at www.bindloss.co.uk.

Fionn Davenport

Irish by birth and conviction, Fionn has spent the last two decades focusing on the country of his birth and its nearest neighbour, England, which he has written about extensively for Lonely Planet and others. In between writing gigs he's lived in Paris and New York, where he was an editor, actor, bartender and whatever else paid the rent. He posts his travel shots on instagram - @fionndavenport

Belinda Dixon

Only happy when her feet are suitably sandy, Belinda has been (gleefully) travelling, researching and writing for Lonely Planet since 2006. It's seen her navigating mountain passes and soaking in hot-pots in Iceland's Westfjords, marvelling at Stonehenge at sunrise; scrambling up Italian mountain paths; horse riding across Donegal's golden sands; gazing at Verona's frescoes; and fossil hunting on Dorset's Jurassic Coast. And all in the name of research. Belinda is also a podcaster and adventure writer and helps lead wilderness expeditions. See her blog posts at belindadixon.com.

OVER PAGE MORE WRITERS

Published by Lonely Planet Global Limited
CRN 554153
14th edition – Aug 2021
ISBN 978 1 78701 571 5

10 9 8 7 6 5 4 3 2 1
Printed in Singapore